1996-1997 TEXAS ALMANAC

AND STATE INDUSTRIAL GUIDE

PUBLISHED BY

The Dallas Morning News

ISBN 0-914511-22-X (Hardback)
ISBN 0-914511-21-1 (Paperback)
Library of Congress Card No. 95-69830

Communications Center
P. O. Box 655237
Dallas, TX 75265

Printed in U. S. A.

Distributed by
Andrews and McMeel
A Universal Press Syndicate Company
4900 Main St.
Kansas City, Missouri 64112

1996-1997 TEXAS ALMANAC

Table of Contents

Mary G. Ramos, Editor

Robert Plocheck, Associate Editor

Van Hayes, Cover Artist

Now offering the
Quality and Beauty
of DREXEL
HERITAGE®
HAVERTYS
FURNITURE FOR YOUR HOME
DALLAS — FT. WORTH

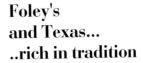

Texas

The Lone Star State

On this and the following page we present a demographic and geographic profile of the second-largest, second-most-populous state in the United States. Look in the index for more detailed information on each subject.

The Government

Capital: Austin
Government: Bicameral Legislature
28th State to enter the Union, Dec. 29, 1845
Present Constitution adopted: 1876
State motto: Friendship (1930)
State symbols: Flower: Bluebonnet (1901); **Bird**: Mockingbird (1927); **Tree:** Pecan (1919); **Song:** "Texas, Our Texas" (1929).
Origin of name: Texas, or Tejas, was the Spanish pronunciation of a Caddo Indian word meaning "friends" or "allies."
Nickname: Texas is called the Lone Star State because of the design of the state flag: a broad vertical blue stripe at left centered by a single white star, with horizontal bars of white (uppermost) and red on the right.

The People

Population (1990 U.S. Census) 16,986,335
Population (July 1993 State Data Center estimate) 18,031,484
Population (July 1994 U.S. Bureau of the Census estimate) 18,378,185
Ethnicity (1990) (categories explained on p. 132):

White 12,775,000
Black 2,022,000
Asian 319,000
American Indian 66,000
Other 1,804,780

Hispanic 4,340,000

Population density (1990) ......64.83 per sq. mi.
Voting-age Pop., 1994 (projected) 13,166,000

On an average day in Texas (in 1993):

The **population** increased by 514.
There were 882 **births**.
There were 368 **deaths**.
There were 486 **marriages**.
There were 265 **divorces**.

Ten largest cities (1993 State Data Center estimates):

Houston (Harris Co.) 1,700,672
Dallas (Dallas Co.) 1,036,309
San Antonio (Bexar Co.) 991,861
El Paso (El Paso Co.) 554,496
Austin (Travis Co.)..................501,637
Fort Worth (Tarrant Co.) 459,085
Arlington (Tarrant Co.)..............277,939
Corpus Christi (Nueces Co.).........266,958
Lubbock (Lubbock Co.)..............193,194
Garland (Dallas Co.) 187,439

Number of counties: 254
Number of incorporated cities:............1,178
Number of cities over 100,000 pop.......... 22
Number of cities over 50,000 pop........... 42
Number of cities over 10,000 pop........... 193

The Natural Environment:

Area (total): .... 266,807 sq. miles (170,756,480 acres)
Land area:.................. 262,017 sq. miles (167,690,880 acres)
Water area: .... 4,790 sq. miles (3,065,600 acres)
Forested area: .... 22.032 million acres
State forests: .... 5 (7,609 acres)
National forests:............. 4 (637,134 acres)
Geographic center: About 15 miles northeast of Brady in northern McCulloch County.
Highest point: Guadalupe Peak (8,749 ft.) in Culberson County in far West Texas.
Lowest point: Gulf of Mexico (sea level).
Normal average annual precipitation range: From 58.3 inches at Orange, on the Gulf Coast, to 8.8 inches at El Paso, in West Texas.
105-year average precipitation.......... 27.21"
Record highest temperature:
Seymour, August 12, 1936............120°F
Record lowest temperature:
Tulia, Feb. 12, 1899..................-23°F
Seminole, Feb. 8, 1933 ....-23°F

Business:

Gross State Product (1990) .... $372 billion
Civilian Labor Force, average 1994 ... 9,384,000
Source: Statistical Abstract of the United States, 1994

Principal products:

Manufactures: Chemicals and allied products, petroleum and coal products, food and kindred products, transportation equipment.

Farm products: Cattle, grain sorghums, cotton lint and seed, wheat, rice, dairy products.

Minerals: Petroleum, natural gas, natural gas liquids.

Finance (as of 12/31/92):
Number of banks 1,091
Total deposits............$148,236,061,000
Number of savings and loan companies:.... 64
Total assets $47,565,516,000

Agriculture (1992):
Number of farms 180,644
Land in farms (acres)........... 130,886,608
Harvested cropland (acres)....... 18,136,653
Pastureland (acres)............ 102,805,890
Woodland (acres) 5,092,616

Texas' Rank Among the United States

Texas' rank among the United States in selected categories are given below. Others categories are covered in other chapters in the book; i.e. Agriculture, Business and Industry, Health and Medicine.

Ten Most Populous States, 1994

Rank	Population est. 1994
1. California	31.4 million
2. Texas	**18.4 million**
3. New York	18.2 million
4. Florida	14.0 million
5. Pennsylvania	12.1 million
6. Illinois	11.8 million
7. Ohio	11.1 million
8. Michigan	9.5 million
9. New Jersey	7.9 million
10. North Carolina	7.1 million
(United States	247.9 million)

Source: U.S. Bureau of the Census

Ten States with Largest Percentage of Foreign-Born, 1990

State	% of Total Population
1. California	21.7
2. New York	15.9
3. Hawaii	14.7
4. Florida	12.9
5. New Jersey	12.5
6. District of Columbia	9.7
7. Massachusetts	9.5
8. Rhode Island	9.5
9. Texas	**9.0**
10. Nevada	8.7
(United States	7.6)

Source: Statistical Abstract of the United States, 1994, Bureau of the Census

States with Highest Birth Rates, 1991

Rank, State	Births per 1,000 Pop.
1. Alaska	20.5
2. Utah	10.4
3. California	10.1
4. Texas	**18.3**
5. Arizona	18.2
6. New Mexico	18.0
7. Hawaii	17.6
8. Nevada	17.2
9. Louisiana	17.0
10. Illinois	16.8
(United States	16.3)

Source: Statistical Abstract of the U.S., 1994, Bureau of the Census

States with Most Vehicles and Drivers, 1992

Rank, State	Vehicles	Lic. Drivers
1. California	22,202	20,111
2. Texas	**12,767**	**11,438**
3. Florida	10,232	10,538
4. New York	9,980	10,360
5. Ohio	9,030	9,169
6. Pennsylvania	8,179	8,019
7. Illinois	7,982	7,411
8. Michigan	7,311	6,481
9. Georgia	5,899	4,600
10. New Jersey	5,591	5,285

Source: Federal Highway Admin., Highway Statistics, annual, and Selected Highway Statistics and Charts, annual.

Miscellaneous Categories

Category	Number	Rank
Gross State Product, 1990	$372 billion	3
Per Capita Personal Income, 1993	$19,189	31
Insured Commercial Banks Closed or Assisted by Federal Government, 1993	10	2
Hazardous Waste Sites, 1993	30	14
Violent Crime Rate per 100,000 Pop.	806	10
Child Abuse Cases Reported, 1992	111,000	4
Social Security Recipients, 1992	13.1% of pop.	45
Public Aid Recipients, 1992	6.3 % of pop.	2
Public School Teachers' Avg. Salaries, 1993	$29,900	34
Public School Enrollment Increase, 1990-93:		
Grades K-8	0.8%	33
Grades 9-12	3.4%	32
Minority College Enrollment, 1992	31.4%	4
Educational Attainment (25 years old or older):		
High School Graduate or higher	72.1	39
Bachelor's degree or higher	20.3	22

Source: Statistical Abstract of the United States, 1994, Bureau of the Census.

Oil and Gas Production

Top States in Crude Petroleum Production, 1992

Rank	Quantity (mil. bbl.)
1. Texas	**651**
2. Alaska	627
3. California	305
4. Louisiana	148
5. Oklahoma	102

Top States in Natural Gas Mktd. Production, 1992

Rank	Quantity (bil. cu. ft.)
1. Texas	**6,146**
2. Louisiana	4,914
3. Oklahoma	2,017
4. New Mexico	1,269
5. Wyoming	843

Source: U.S. Energy Information Admin., Energy Data Reports, Petroleum Supply Annual, Natural Gas Annual & Natural Gas Monthly.

With a central North American location that puts you within 4 hours of any major city in the U.S., Mexico and Canada, it's no surprise that DFW International Airport is the world's second busiest and fastest growing. With more than 2,200 flights daily to nearly 200 worldwide destinations, we're one of the most convenient airports you'll find anywhere. And we offer many unique benefits:
• User-friendly facilities designed with multi-lingual, easy-to-understand signage.
• Passenger Service Agents fluent in 21 languages.
• Quick, efficient customs clearance in three terminals. (We're talking minutes, not hours.)
• Convenient, affordable, one-stop shopping with new food, beverage and retail outlets.
And as if all this were not extraordinary enough—DFW is located in the heart of the Dallas/Fort Worth metroplex, one of the most exciting places on earth with everything from world-class music and art to a world-renowned rodeo. The next time you're shopping for an airport, try DFW - the one airport in the world that has everything in the world, when and where you want it.
DFW
WE'RE CLOSE TO EVERYTHING.
AND FAR FROM ORDINARY.
INTERNATIONAL AIRPORT

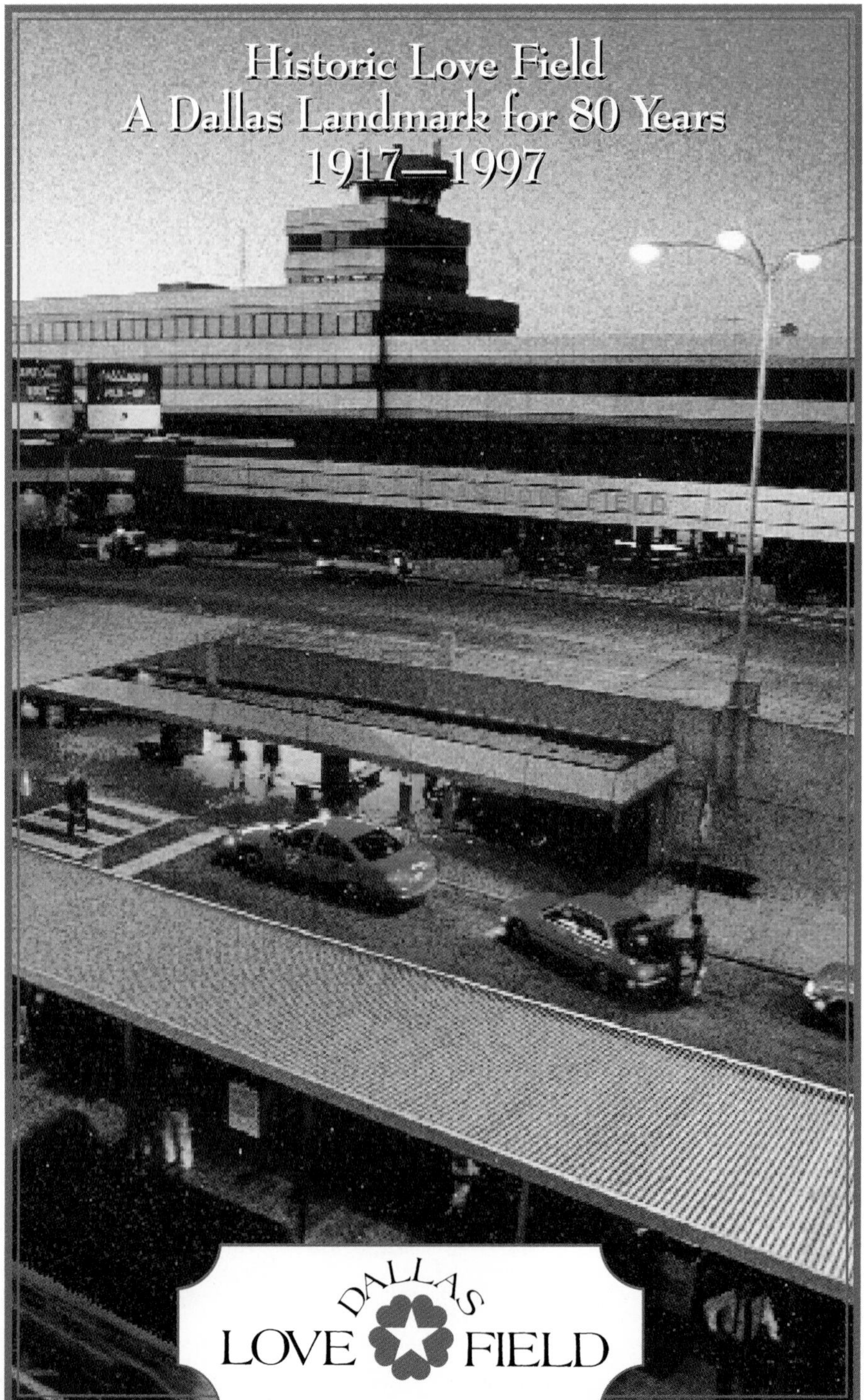
Historic Love Field
A Dallas Landmark for 80 Years
1917—1997
DALLAS
LOVE FIELD

State Flags and Other Symbols

United States, 1845-1861; 1865-Present

Republic, 1836-1845; State, 1845-Present

Spain,
1519-1685
1690-1821

Mexico,
1821-1836

France,
1685-1690

Confederacy,
1861-1865

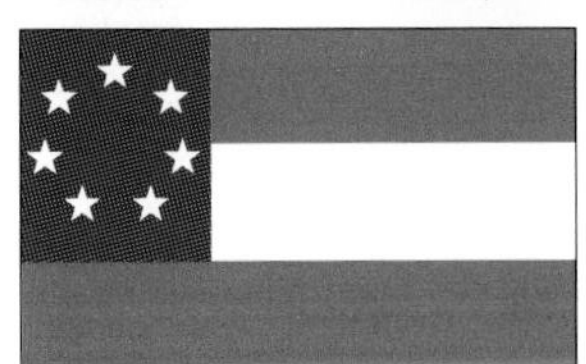

Texas often is called the **Lone Star State** because of its state flag with a single star. This was also the **flag of the Republic of Texas**. The following information about historic Texas flags, the current flag and other Texas symbols may be supplemented by information available from the **Texas State Library**, Austin.

Six Flags of Texas

Six different flags have flown over Texas during eight changes of sovereignty. The accepted sequence of these flags follows:

Spanish — 1519-1685.
French — 1685-1690.
Spanish — 1690-1821.
Mexican — 1821-1836.
Republic of Texas — 1836-1845.
United States — 1845-1861.
Confederate States — 1861-1865.
United States — 1865 to the present.

Evolution of the Lone Star Flag

At the Convention of 1836, at Washington-on-the-Brazos, Lorenzo de Zavala is reported to have designed a flag for the Republic — a blue field with a white star of five points central, with the letters T E X A S between the star points. Probably because of the hasty dispersion of the Convention and loss of part of the Convention notes, nothing further was done with the De Zavala recommendation.

The **first official flag of the Republic,** known as **David G. Burnet's flag,** was adopted on Dec. 10, 1836, as the national standard, "the conformation of which shall be an azure ground with a large golden star central."

The Lone Star Flag

A new national standard was worked out and approved by Mirabeau B. Lamar and was adopted by the Third Congress of the Republic on Jan. 25, 1839. This flag consisted of a blue perpendicular stripe of the width of one-third of the whole length of the flag with a white star of five points in the center thereof, and two horizontal stripes of equal breadth, the upper stripe white, the lower red, of the length of two-thirds of the whole flag. This is the **Lone Star Flag,** which later became the state flag. It is generally accepted that the Texas flag's colors represent the same virtues as they do in the United States flag: Red means courage; white, purity and liberty; and blue, loyalty.

Although generally used, the state flag was not officially described and usage rules adopted until 1933. These rules are from HB 1463, 73rd Legislature (1993).

Flown out-of-doors, the Texas flag should not be displayed earlier than sunrise nor later than sunset unless properly iluminated. It should not be left out in inclement weather unless a weatherproof flag is used. It should be flown with the white stripe uppermost except in case of distress. When the flag is displayed against a wall, the blue field should be at the flag's own right (observer's left). The Texas flag should be displayed on all state memorial days; it should fly at every school on every regular school day.

The Texas flag should be on the marching left in a procession in which the flag of the United States is carried; its staff should be behind the staff of the flag of the United States when the two are displayed with crossed staffs. The Texas flag should be underneath the national flag when the two are flown from the same halyard. When flown from separate, adjacent flagpoles, the United States flag and the Texas flag should be of approximately the same size and on flagpoles of equal length, and the United States flag should be on the flag's own right, i.e., to the observer's left. When the Texas flag is displayed vertically, the blue stripe should be uppermost and the white stripe should be to the flag's right, that is, to the observer's left.

The Texas flag should never be used for any utilitarian or strictly decorative purpose. No advertising should be placed upon the flag or flagstaff, and no picture of the flag should be used in an advertisement. When the Texas flag is in such condition that it is no longer a suitable emblem for display, it should be destroyed, preferably by burning. More information on the use of the state flag can be found in Title 106, Revised Statutes, Article 6139c, "Texas Flag Code."

Pledge to the Texas Flag

A pledge to the Texas flag was adopted by the 43rd Legislature and from 1933 until 1965 that pledge was used. It contained a phrase, "Flag of 1836," which was historically incorrect, as Texas did not have a flag in 1836. On April 3, 1965, Gov. John Connally signed an act of the 59th Legislature officially designating the pledge to the Texas flag as follows:

"Honor the Texas Flag.
I pledge allegiance to thee,
Texas, one and indivisible."

An act of the 71st Legislature in 1989 further stipulated that a person reciting the pledge to the Texas flag shall: (1) face the flag and place the right hand over the heart; (2) remove any hat worn by the person; and (3) recite the pledge with pride and patriotism. The pledge to the Texas flag may be recited at all public and private meetings at which the pledge of allegiance to the United States flag is recited and at historical Texas events and celebrations. The pledge to the Texas flag shall be recited after the pledge of allegiance to the United States flag if both are recited.

Other Symbols

State Motto — The state motto of Texas is **"Friendship."** The word, Texas, or Tejas, was the Spanish pronunciation of a Caddo Indian word meaning "friends" or "allies." (Acts of 1930, fourth called session of the 41st Legislature, p. 105.)

State Tree — The **pecan** is the state tree of Texas. The sentiment that led to its official adoption probably grew out of the request of Gov. James Stephen Hogg that a pecan tree be planted at his grave. (Acts of 1919, 36th Legislature, regular session, p. 155; also Acts of 1927, 40th Legislature, p. 234.)

State Flower — The state flower of Texas is the **bluebonnet,** also called **buffalo clover, wolf flower** and ***el conejo*** (the rabbit). The bluebonnet was adopted as the state flower, on request of the Society of Colonial Dames in Texas, by the 27th Legislature, 1901. (See acts of regular session, p. 232.) The original resolution designated *Lupinus subcarnosus* as the state flower, but a resolution (HCR 44) signed March 8, 1971, by Gov. Preston Smith provided legal status as the state flower of Texas for "*Lupinus Texensis* and any other variety of bluebonnet."

State Bird — The **mockingbird** (*Mimus polyglottos*) is the state bird of Texas, adopted by the Legislature at the request of the Texas Federation of Women's Clubs. (Acts of 1927, 40th Legislature, regular session, p. 486.)

State Song — The state song of Texas is **"Texas, Our Texas."** The music was written by the late William J. Marsh (who died Feb. 1, 1971, in Fort Worth at age 90), and the words by Marsh and Gladys Yoakum Wright, also of Fort Worth. It was adopted as the result of an award offered by the Legislature. (Acts of 1929, first called session, 41st Legislature, p. 286.) The wording has been changed once: Shortly after Alaska became a state in Jan. 1959, the word "Largest" in the third line was changed by Mr. Marsh to "Boldest." The text follows:

Texas Our Texas

Texas, our Texas! All hail the mighty State!
Texas, our Texas! So wonderful, so great!
Boldest and grandest, withstanding every test;
O empire wide and glorious, you stand supremely blest.

Chorus

God bless you, Texas! And keep you brave and strong.
That you may grow in power and worth, throughout the ages long.

Refrain

Texas, O Texas! Your freeborn single star,
Sends out its radiance to nations near and far.
Emblem of freedom! It sets our hearts aglow.
With thoughts of San Jacinto and glorious Alamo.

Texas, dear Texas! From tyrant grip now free,
Shines forth in splendor your star of destiny!
Mother of Heroes! We come your children true.
Proclaiming our allegiance, our faith, our love for you. ☆

Note: For other state symbols and the state seal, see page 446.

Double National Champions — Times Two

Texas is home to two double national sports champions: The Houston Rockets won their second National Basketball Association national championship in Game 4 of the NBA finals on June 14, 1995, in Houston from the Orlando Magic. In 1994, they beat the New York Knicks in the final series for the championship. The Dallas Cowboys won their second national championship in a row — Super Bowl 28 — against the Buffalo Bills by the score of 30 to 13 on January 30, 1994, in the Georgia Dome in Atlanta. In 1993, the Cowboys trounced the Bills 52-17 in the Rose Bowl in Pasadena, Ca., in Super Bowl 27.

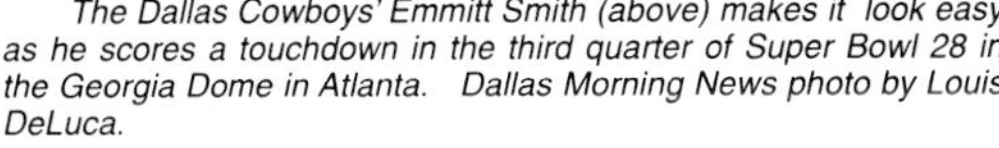
The Dallas Cowboys' Emmitt Smith (above) makes it look easy as he scores a touchdown in the third quarter of Super Bowl 28 in the Georgia Dome in Atlanta. Dallas Morning News photo by Louis DeLuca.

Houston Rockets center Hakeem Olajuwon (right) shoots past Orlando Magic center Shaquille O'Neal during Game 4 of the 1995 NBA finals. AP Photo by Rick Bowmer.

Texas Pro Sports Teams

Below are listed the major pro sports teams in the state. Information includes the team name, where they play, and the address and phone number for obtaining more information on schedules and tickets.

Baseball

Houston Astros
Astrodome
P.O. Box 288, Houston 77001-0288
(713) 799-9600

Texas Rangers
The Ballpark in Arlington
1000 Ballpark Way, Arlington 76011
(817) 273-5222

Basketball

Dallas Mavericks
Reunion Arena*
777 Sports St., Dallas 75207
(214) 748-1808

Houston Rockets
The Summit
10 Greenway Plaza, Houston 77046
(713) 627-3865

San Antonio Spurs
Alamodome
100 Montana St., San Antonio 78203
(210) 554-7700

Football

Dallas Cowboys
Texas Stadium
Cowboys Center, One Cowboys Parkway, Irving 75063
(214) 556-9900

Houston Oilers
Astrodome
6910 Fannin St., Houston 77030
(713) 797-9111

Hockey

Dallas Stars
Reunion Arena*
211 Cowboys Parkway, Irving 75063
(214) 868-2890

**At press time, the Dallas Mavericks and Dallas Stars were negotiating for a different arena.*

Janis Joplin

Buddy Holly

Huddie Ledbetter (Leadbelly)

Texas Music: Its Roots, Its Evolution

by Jay Brakefield

Among the glories of Texas is its music, which is as diverse and vital as the state and its people. Woven into the musical fabric are country, blues, jazz, spirituals, gospel, rock 'n' roll, Tex-Mex, Cajun and the music of Czechs, Germans and other European immigrants.

These forms have not only coexisted, they have evolved and cross-pollinated as Texas has changed, becoming steadily more urban. Texas is the birthplace of Western swing, which incorporates elements of country, blues, pop, big-band jazz and Latin rhythms, and of conjunto, which combines traditional Mexican music with polkas and other European forms. Texas has nurtured zydeco, the music of French-speaking blacks, which has increasingly incorporated elements of rhythm and blues. In Texas, you can catch a performance by Steve Jordan, who has been called the Jimi Hendrix of the button accordion. Or you can walk into a honky-tonk where a cowboy-hatted country band is borrowing a verse from Mississippi Delta bluesman Robert Johnson about a woman who "may be in Ethiopia somewhere."

To many people, Texas music means country, so that seems an appropriate place to begin.

Country music

The white Americans who began to settle in Texas in the 1820s came primarily from elsewhere in the South, bringing with them the religious and secular music they had heard at home. Generally the music they listened to for entertainment and dancing was played on guitars, banjos and fiddles. Even here, the music was hardly a pure Anglo-Saxon strain. The banjo is apparently of African origin, and the fiddle has long had an identification with black as well as white musicians and was widely known as the devil's instrument — apparently because when a fiddle was playing, it was hard to keep still.

Distinctive regional characteristics developed in this transplanted music. Texas fiddlers generally use a relatively slow tempo and long, single-note bow strokes, permitting more variations on the melody. They tend to complement the rhythmic background provided by a guitar and possibly other instruments. Guitarists, too, developed their own style, using swinging rhythms and a greater variety of chords than the traditional I-IV-V progression that is standard in so much folk and dance music, black and white. These instrumental styles laid the groundwork for the Western swing and honky-tonk music of the 20th century.

These early Texas white musicians played primarily for dancing, often in people's homes. On a weekend night, furniture would be cleared out of several rooms for dancing to the music of local players. These were seldom professional musicians, but were usually fellow farmers who played as a sideline for a modest sum. Many also participated in fiddling contests, fierce competitions in which they honed their skills and enhanced their reputations. Often dancers moved to the music of just fiddle and guitar. But sometimes musicians played in larger ensembles called string bands, which included instruments such as mandolin and banjo. In addition, particularly after the Civil War, Texans were exposed to musical entertainment through traveling tent and medicine shows, where they heard comedians (often in blackface) and popular songs of the day. And they heard the music of African-Americans, who sometimes performed for their masters on the plantation and sang to pass the time as they labored, both during and after slavery. Though most worship was segregated, many whites also had some exposure to African-American worship services, with their joyous interaction of preacher and congregation.

Whites and blacks alike throughout the South also had access to itinerant singing masters who taught a shape-note system, which uses symbols rather than standard musical notation, to indicate the pitch of the notes. At least one version, called "sacred harp" singing, is still heard in parts of rural Texas. And the Lone Star State, with its ranches and its cattle drives, had the tradition of cowboy music and dress, which certainly influenced the image of Texas country music and perhaps its sound as well.

Thus by the time the commercial music industry was born in the 1920s, the British folk songs that had formed the basis of early rural white American music had already been cross-fertilized with a wide variety of music, black and white.

Apparently, the first country musicians to record were fiddlers Alexander "Eck" Robertson of Amarillo and Henry Gilliland of Altus, Okla. Robertson, a legendary prize-winning performer, and Gilliland traveled to Virginia in June 1922 to play at a Civil War veterans' reunion. Then, probably on impulse, they went to New York and presented themselves at the Victor recording company — Robertson in a cowboy outfit, Gilliland in a Confederate uniform. They were granted an audition and allowed to record. The standout of the session was Robertson's recording of the dance tune "Sallie Gooden."

Robertson did not record again until 1930, but in 1923, the two men performed two songs on Fort Worth radio station WBAP: "Sallie Gooden" and another song Robertson had recorded, "Arkansas Traveler." In doing so, as Bill Malone points out in "Country Music U.S.A.," Robertson "may have been the first country performer to 'plug' his recordings on a radio broadcast." With another 1923 broadcast, WBAP apparently began the tradition of "barn dance" radio shows that helped to popularize country music in cities throughout the country where Southerners migrated in search of work.

The first true country music star was Jimmie Rodgers, "the singing brakeman." Rodgers was from Mississippi, but lived the last several years of his life in Texas, first in Kerrville, then in San Antonio. His eclectic style, which included elements of jazz, blues and pop as well as his famous "blue yodel," would have a profound influence on later country musicians.

Perhaps the most distinctive strain to emerge from Texas, Western swing, fused the music of the house dances with a number of other styles. Bob Wills, often called the father of Western swing, began as a boy playing for dances in the Panhandle. His father, John Wills, was a fiddler who played for dances and in contests. In fact, his chief rival was none other than "Eck" Robertson. Bob Wills apparently got his famous "Ah-hah" holler from his father, for a disgusted Robertson once remarked after losing a contest to the elder Wills, "He didn't outfiddle me. That damned old man Wills outhollered me," according to Charles R. Townsend's biography of Wills, "San Antonio Rose."

Bob Wills also loved black music and once rode a horse 50 miles to hear the legendary "Empress of the Blues," Bessie Smith. In 1929, Wills moved to Fort Worth, where he performed in blackface with a medicine show and teamed up with guitarist Herman Arnspiger and singer Milton Brown in a group first called the Wills Fiddle Band, then the Aladdin Laddies and the Light Crust Doughboys.

The Doughboys were the creature of W. Lee "Pappy" O'Daniel, a future Texas governor and U.S. senator who was then president and general manager of Burrus Mill in Fort Worth. He used the band to advertise his flour — and not, contrary to many reports, as a vehicle for his political career.

The Doughboys became very popular via their daily radio show on KFJZ in Fort Worth and their appearances at dances. But after a dispute with O'Daniel, Wills left to form his own band, the Texas Playboys, which, ironically, moved its base of operations to Tulsa, Okla.

Brown, too, left and formed his own band, Milton Brown and His Musical Brownies, which remained in Fort Worth and performed regularly at a dance hall on White Settlement Road called the Crystal Springs Dance Pavilion. Brown died young after a 1936 car accident on Fort Worth's Jacksboro Highway. Some scholars believe his role in the formation of Western swing has been slighted, and that the group he put together was really the first Western swing band. It included steel guitarist Bob Dunn, who may have been the first to amplify the instrument and who played in a jazzy style far removed from the "weeping steel" of later tears-in-your-beer country music. Dunn, it is said, made the steel guitar sound like a trombone.

Some of Wills' early recordings feature black-dialect humor straight from his medicine-show days. But his music became increasingly sophisticated, and in his pre-World War II heyday in Tulsa, he fronted a large group that included both fiddles and horns and that could play anything from country dance tunes to big-band jazz. Wills never learned to play the "hot" fiddle style he loved, but hired musicians who could. He was a terrific performer, though, keeping up a constant line of patter ("There's a man after my own heart — with a razor") and inspiring his musicians to innovative solos.

The long career of another Texan is illustrative of the diversity of Texas music. Adolph Hofner, who became a bandleader in the 1930s, actively performed until the '90s. Growing up in the South Texas Czech community of Praha, he spoke Czech before he spoke English, and played a wide-ranging repertoire that included Wills-style Western swing with Czech lyrics, Cajun waltzes and such Tex-Mex staples as "El Rancho Grande."

After World War II, tastes changed, and Wills and other band leaders could no longer afford to carry large orchestras. Wills remained popular until a 1973 stroke ended his career, but his later music was more country, more fiddle-oriented, and he

George Jones

Bob Wills

Ornette Coleman

spent much of his time performing in Las Vegas.

Even before the war, a new wind was blowing through country music, a rougher, amplified sound played by small combos for dancing in urban honky-tonks. This sound was exemplified by the 1941 hit "Walking the Floor Over You" by Ernest Tubb, who had begun his career as a Jimmie Rodgers imitator.

Other Texas musicians had great success with this style, as well, including Corsicana's Lefty Frizzell and Ray Price, who later changed his approach to the pop crooning favored by singers such as Tennessee's Eddy Arnold and fellow Texan Jim Reeves.

Honky-tonk, whose greatest star was Alabama-born Hank Williams, became virtually synonymous with country music through the mid-1950s, when it was knocked from its perch by another form of music that, ironically, it had helped to create: rock 'n' roll. The Nashville-based country music industry responded in the 1960s with music that crossed over into the mainstream and seemed to many like nothing more than country-flavored pop.

Texans Willie Nelson and Waylon Jennings were key players in the 1970s "outlaw country" movement, a fusion of country and rock that rebelled against Nashville's blandness. Nelson moved from Nashville to Austin and helped spawn that city's progressive country sound.

Today, though the airwaves are crowded with the often-indistinguishable music of the latest country hunks, fans continue to support performers such as Nelson, Jennings and East Texan George Jones, whose way with a sad song has gained him a reputation as the greatest country singer around.

In addition, there's a neo-honky-tonk movement that includes such performers as Austin's Junior Brown, inventor of the "guit-steel," a combination of standard and steel guitars. Groups such as Asleep At The Wheel and Alvin Crow and the Pleasant Valley Boys keep traditional Western swing alive. Other bands fuse honky-tonk with punk rock in big-city clubs, proving that country can go anywhere.

Blues, Jazz and Gospel

Some of the Southerners who settled in Texas brought their slaves with them. The singing of African-Americans as they worked long, hot hours on farms and plantations became a part of the larger culture. Black musicians sometimes played for whites, who listened or danced. And the minstrel show, consisting of musical and comedy numbers, became very popular after the Civil War. Both white and black minstrel troupes performed in blackface.

Black music in Texas, as elsewhere, retained some African characteristics, such as the use of polyrhythms, call-and-response patterns of singing and playing and the use of bent or slurred tones known as "blue notes." The field hollers and work songs of slavery were African also in that they were often sung by people working together and reflected a collective effort and consciousness.

But after Emancipation, a new individual consciousness was reflected in the music called the blues, usually played by a lone man accompanying himself on a guitar.

No one really knows where or when the blues began, but it was widespread through the South and much of Texas by the turn of the 20th century. Generally a performer would sing a four-bar line, repeat it, then close the stanza with a rhyming line that often contained an ironic twist. Though this 12-bar form became the most common, eight- and 16-bar blues also existed. Recordings of older musicians from the 1920s provide evidence of what early blues and other late-19th-century forms were like. Henry "Ragtime Texas" Thomas, born in Gladewater about 1875, recorded when he was in his 50s, singing and playing the guitar and a wind instrument called the quills, or panpipes. One of his songs, "Fishing Blues," has been recorded by, among others, the 1960s rock band the Lovin' Spoonful.

Another such songster — one whose repertoire ranged from blues to ballads, dance tunes and religious songs — was Mance Lipscomb. The son of a country fiddler, he was born near Navasota in 1895. After working most of his life as a sharecropper, he was discovered by the folk-music crowd in the 1960s and enjoyed considerable popularity in the last years of his life.

Another significant figure was Huddie Ledbetter. "Leadbelly," as he was popularly known, was born in 1889 on the Louisiana side of Caddo Lake, which lies on the border of northeast Texas and northwest Louisiana. Leadbelly spent much of his life in Texas, in and out of prison.

Through the efforts of Texas folklorists John and Alan Lomax, Leadbelly left a rich legacy of recordings that, like Lipscomb's, cover a wide range of styles. He is best known for popularizing "Good Night, Irene," which, with somewhat sanitized lyrics, has become a pop standard.

After moving to the Dallas area around 1912, Leadbelly found his primary instrument, the 12-string guitar, and learned much about the blues from Blind Lemon Jefferson, who became the first country blues recording star. Born in the farm community of Couchman 70 miles south of Dallas in 1893, the young Jefferson walked the roads around his home, playing for money on the streets and in the cafes and joints of the surrounding towns. He spent time in Mexia, where the local strip of black businesses was known as the Beat, playing both alone and in a string band with other musicians.

Bob Wills, born in 1905, spent the first eight years of his life in nearby Kosse, and it's possible that he heard the young Jefferson and other musicians such as Marlin's Blind Willie Johnson, who played slide guitar and sang in a powerful, gravelly voice in a style called "gospel blues" or "holy blues." Figures such as Johnson demonstrate that church music and the blues were more closely linked than the latter's designation as "the devil's music" would indicate.

Lemon Jefferson married a Mexia woman in 1927, but he also spent a lot of time in Dallas, playing up and down the Central Railroad track in the Deep Ellum section that was the heart of that city's black community life.

Jefferson was certainly not the only such musician in the area. Blind Willie Johnson was in Dallas about the same time and made his first records there. And there were strolling string bands that played a wide repertoire ranging from blues to pop tunes. One such group, the Dallas String Band, included bass player Marco Washington, stepfather of future bluesman Aaron "T-Bone" Walker.

Jefferson attracted the attention of a Paramount record scout, thanks to the efforts of a local record-store and shine-stand owner named R.T. Ashford. From 1926 until 1929, Jefferson made regular trips to Chicago to record and achieved considerably popularity in the "race" market — records marketed exclusively to African-Americans. In addition to blues, he recorded a few spirituals under the name Deacon L.J. Bates.

Blind Lemon Jefferson died in Chicago in December 1929. Apparently he froze to death,

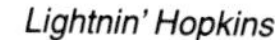
Lightnin' Hopkins

Stevie Ray (l.) and Jimmie Vaughan

Roy Orbison

though the circumstances of his death have never been fully explained. But his brief career exerted considerable influence on many performers who followed. One of his songs, "Matchbox Blues," was recorded years later by both rockabilly star Carl Perkins and the Beatles.

His recording success opened the door to a flood of country blues recordings of a number of artists, including Texans such as "Little Hat" Jones, Alger "Texas" Alexander and J.T. "Funny Papa" Smith. Blind Lemon's dexterous guitar style featured single-string runs and unconventional phrasing — what one musician called "suspended time."

This style was a major influence on T-Bone Walker and other blues players who, starting in the mid-'30s, played the new electric guitar, which allowed the instrument, once consigned to the rhythm section of a large band, to become a solo instrument. Walker's style of playing lead guitar in a call-and-response pattern with an orchestra came to define a whole school of post-World War II blues, though he didn't really achieve star status until he moved to the West Coast in the 1940s.

An earthier strain of blues was exemplified by Sam "Lightnin'" Hopkins of Centerville, who met Jefferson as a child and spent most of his life in Houston, playing an amplified version of the downhome East Texas music he had grown up with.

Texas had a strong tradition of piano blues, too, hard-hitting music with strong elements of ragtime, the music popularized by composers such as Texas-born Scott Joplin. Texas piano blues developed in the rough lumber and turpentine camps of East Texas and in the honky-tonks of Dallas' Deep Ellum and Houston's Third, Fourth and Fifth Wards, in places with names like Mud Alley and The Vamp.

Robert Shaw, a member of the "Santa Fe" group of pianists named for the railroad, survived into old age running a barbecue business and grocery store in Austin, and, like Mance Lipscomb, had a late second career playing for white fans.

Another link to the past was Dallas pianist and singer Alex Moore, who continued to perform up to the time of his death in 1989, at age 89.

Louisiana-born musicians, such as Clarence Garlow and Clifton Chenier, performed extensively in Texas and developed modern zydeco, a lively fusion of Cajun and rhythm and blues. Some scholars trace this development to Frenchtown, a section of Houston's black Fifth Ward.

An urban strain of blues and gospel was recorded beginning in the '50s at nightclub owner Don Robey's Duke and Peacock studios in Houston. Robey recorded such artists as Clarence "Gatemouth" Brown, who plays both guitar and fiddle and mixes blues with country music; smooth-voiced Memphis blues balladeer Bobby "Blue" Bland; and Alabama-born Willie Mae "Big Mama" Thornton, whose recording of "Hound Dog" inspired Elvis Presley.

In jazz, Texas exemplified the swinging, blues-based Southwestern style, very different from the stately polyphony of early New Orleans jazz bands. In the 1920s, black bands such as the Clouds of Joy in Dallas and the Troy Floyd Orchestra in San Antonio performed in white hotels, sweetening their sound somewhat for these audiences.

A rougher music was played for black audiences in places such as Dallas' Tip Top dance hall, which San Antonio band leader Don Albert called the rattiest place he'd ever seen.

It was apparently in the Tip Top in 1925 that Dallas clarinetist and alto sax player Henry "Buster" Smith was hired by the Blue Devils, a top Oklahoma City-based "territory" band, one that played a regular circuit through the South and Midwest. Smith, though little known to the general public, went on to become a significant figure in jazz. Along with other Texas musicians, he became a part of the exciting Kansas City jazz scene of the 1930s. He helped to create Count Basie's theme song, "One O'Clock Jump," and was a strong influence on Charlie Parker, generally regarded as the father of be-bop, the harmonically advanced music that stood jazz on its ear in the 1940s and '50s.

Other major jazz figures from Texas included trombonist Jack Teagarden, born in Vernon, and a whole school of saxophonists called the "Texas Ten-

Left, The Texas Tornados (Flaco Jiménez, Freddy Fender, Augie Meyers and Doug Sahm)

Right, Little Joe Hernández of Little Joe y la Familia

ors" because of their full, distinctive sound, that included Arnett Cobb, Illinois Jacquet and Eddie "Cleanhead" Vinson.

Texas-born musicians played a major role in the development of the electric guitar. In addition to T-Bone Walker, Eddie Durham, who played with Buster Smith in the Blue Devils, and Charlie Christian, of Benny Goodman's band, were among these innovators.

Perhaps the most idiosyncratic and controversial jazz musician to come out of Texas is alto sax player Ornette Coleman, who began in Fort Worth rhythm-and-blues bands and went on to invent a radically new music called free jazz, with his own theory of collective improvisation, called "harmolodics." Such developments indicate the power and complexity beneath the apparently simple music born in slavery.

Tex-Mex

Until the mid-19th century, Mexican Texans, or Tejanos, seem to have danced primarily to music imported from Spain or Mexico, played on violins and various wind instruments, with rhythm provided by guitars and sometimes by a drum. Other European forms gained popularity after being played at the court of Maximilian, who ruled Mexico during the 1860s with the backing of the French army.

The most significant innovation, however, was the introduction of the diatonic button accordion by German and Czech immigrants. Tejano musicians were reported playing this instrument by the 1870s.

Tejanos also listened to the music of *guitarreros*, singing guitarists who performed *corridos*, songs that told stories and carried news, often in cantinas and at social gatherings.

Mexican-Americans in Texas were also entertained by performers such as the Mendoza family of San Antonio, who toured with *variedades* — variety shows staged in tents and theaters. The family sang and performed comedy skits.

One of the Mendoza daughters, Lydia, became the first Tejano recording star when she was recorded in 1934 in a San Antonio hotel room playing her 12-string guitar and singing *Mal Hombre*, whose lyrics she had learned from a bubble-gum wrapper. She became very popular not only in Texas, but throughout Latin America, during her long career, singing folk-based songs that often speak passionately of romantic longings.

For dancing, two basic styles developed: conjunto (literally "ensemble") music and the music of the *orquestas*, or orchestras, outgrowths of earlier string and wind groups.

At first, conjunto was played on two instruments, the button accordion and the *bajo sexto*, a 12-string guitar with bass strings tuned an octave lower than those of the standard six-string instrument. Accordionist Narciso Martínez, born in 1911 in Reynosa, Mexico, across from McAllen, Texas, is regarded as the father of this style, also called *norteño* because its practitioners came from northern Mexico and Texas. In 1935, with *bajo sexto* player Santiago Almeida, Martínez made his first recordings, for the Blue Bird label at the Bluebonnet hotel in San Antonio. Martínez, whose home was near San Benito in the Lower Rio Grande Valley, became known as "*El Huracán del Valle*" — "The Hurricane of the Valley." He was awarded the nation's highest honor for folk musicians in 1983 — a National Heritage Award.

The *tololoche*, or upright bass, was added to the ensemble by accordionist Santiago "El Flaco" (the skinny one) Jiménez of San Antonio. After World War II, drums and vocals were added to the music, which was initially almost exclusively instrumental. The lyrics, like those of country and blues, dealt with heartache and the trials of everyday life, and reflected a consciousness called *lo ranchero* — a longing for a simpler, rural life. The foundation of conjunto is the polka, but these bands also play a variety of other forms, including waltzes, mazurkas and *huapangos*, a fast, rhythmic dance form named for the town near Veracruz where it originated.

The button accordion has a distinctive sound, quite different from that of the more expensive piano accordion. It has from one to three rows of buttons. Like the air holes of a harmonica, each button plays two notes, one pushed, one pulled. In addition, two reeds sound each note, one about a quarter-tone above the other, providing a slight dissonance and the instrument's characteristically sweet sound. And playing two adjacent buttons together almost always produces what guitarist Ry Cooder calls "a pleasant third interval." The first such accordions were relatively primitive models with one row of buttons, but these evolved into a more versatile three-row model.

Conjunto became the music of the working people, those who labored on farms or migrated to the cities, where they often had to support themselves with low-paying jobs. The dance music of the more affluent Mexican-Texans was played by the *orquestas*. The *orquestas* often played the same songs as the conjuntos, but in more complex arrangements for a full band that included wind instruments seldom employed in conjunto. In "The Texas-Mexican Conjunto: History of a Working-Class Music," Manuel Peña writes, "In the hands of such noted leaders as Beto Villa and Balde González, *orquesta* came of age among tejanos beginning in the 1940s. Furthermore, aspiring to be more 'sophisticated,' it turned to both the instrumentation and the repertory of American dance bands of the Glenn Miller-Tommy Dorsey type...."

The coming of the rock 'n' roll era in the '50s further modified these styles. The electric bass replaced the tololoche in conjunto. The *orquestas* employed amplified instruments and incorporated influences from black rhythm and blues to Cuban salsa, creating a new sound exemplified by bands such as Little Joe (Hernández) y La Familia and Sunny Ozuna and the Sunliners. Today's very popular Tejano style employs electronic synthesizers. Its fans are generally contemptuous of conjunto, but Tejano borrows conjunto's polka rhythms, along with any number of other forms, including salsa, country, pop and even rap. Among this music's biggest stars are the groups Mazz, La Mafia and David Lee Garza y Los Musicales and performers Emilio Navaira and, until her death in 1995, the young singer called Selena.

Today, old and new forms coexist in Mexican-American music in Texas. Mariachi bands are popular, though this appears to be a style imported to Texas rather than true Tex-Mex music. Little Joe Hernández and Sunny Ozuna are still musically active. Santiago Jiménez Jr. carries on his father's style of conjunto, while his better-known brother, Leonardo "Flaco" Jiménez, has played with Ry Cooder and other rockers and for several years teamed up with Doug Sahm, Augie Meyers and Freddy Fender in the Texas Tornados, whose repertoire spanned virtually the music of all Texans — black, white and brown.

Rock 'n' roll and beyond

To some extent, in fact, rock 'n' roll is a synthesis of all that went before in popular music, and Texas has played a strong role. Buddy Holly's 1958 appearances in England inspired, among others, the young John Lennon, Paul McCartney and Eric Clapton.

One English rock group, The Hollies, even took name of the Lubbock musician, who called one of his early groups the Western Bop Band.

Southeast Texans Janis Joplin and Johnny Winter and the Vaughan brothers of Dallas, Jimmie and the late Stevie Ray, grew up steeped in the blues. Among Doug Sahm's major influences growing up in San Antonio were Bob Wills, T-Bone Walker and the Tex-Mex music that was all around him.

Texas seems to have spawned the first psychedelic band, Austin's Thirteenth Floor Elevators, as well as Roy Orbison and Joe Ely.

Today, all these forms of music continue to exist and interact, as new immigrant groups add influences. And discoveries are still being made in older forms. In 1994, Dallas folklorist Alan Govenar, through his Documentary Arts foundation, recorded not only Alfred "Snuff" Johnson of Austin playing spirituals and black cowboy blues, but also 95-year-old black songster John T. Samples of Kilgore. Govenar has also recorded Vietnamese musicians playing traditional music, and says younger Vietnamese Texans are already forming rock 'n' roll bands. The possibilities seem limitless. ☆

**Jay Brakefield is a copy editor for* The Dallas Morning News *and co-author with Alan Govenar of "Down on Deep Ellum," a study of the Dallas neighborhood known for its contributions to blues and jazz.*

For Further Reading:

All Music Guide: The best CDs, albums & tapes *ed. by Michael Erlewine; Miller Freeman Books, San Francisco, 1994.*

Finding Her Voice: The Saga of Women in Country Music *by Mary A. Burwack and Robert K. Oermann; Crown Publishers Inc., New York, 1993.*

Lydia Mendoza, A Family Autobiography, *compiled and introduced by Chris Strachwitz, with James Nicolopulos; Arte Publico Press, Houston, 1993.*

Meeting the Blues *by Alan Govenar; Taylor Publishing, Dallas, 1985.*

Milton Brown and the Founding of Western Swing *by Cary Ginell; University of Illinois Press, Urbana, Chicago, London; 1994.*

Nothing But the Blues: the Music and the Musicians, *edited by Lawrence Cohn; Abbeville Press, New York, London, Paris; 1993.*

San Antonio Rose: The Life and Music of Bob Wills *by Charles R. Townsend; University of Illinois Press, Urbana, Chicago, London; 1976.*

Tell me a story, sing me a song: A Texas Chronicle *by William A. Owens; University of Texas Press, Austin, 1983.*

The Texas-Mexican Conjunto: History of a Working Class Music *by Manuel H. Peña; The University of Texas Press, Austin, 1985.*

Texas Rhythm, Texas Rhyme: A Pictorial History of Texas Music *by Larry Willoughby; Texas Monthly Press, Austin, 1984.*

Recordings:

A great deal of historic material is available on major record labels. In addition, two small labels specializing in folk and ethnic music are of particular interest. For information, write:

Arhoolie Records, *10341 San Pablo Ave., El Cerrito, Calif. 94530.*

Documentary Arts Inc., *Box 140244, Dallas 75214.*

Mexia-born Cindy Walker was the first woman inducted into the Nashville Songwriters Hall of Fame.

Women in Texas Music

The music business has been as male-dominated as other aspects of our society. Until recently, women generally could succeed as performers only when they shaped their careers in socially acceptable ways.

But there were always strong, ambitious women who were willing to push the envelope. In some cases, this led to success; in others, to tragedy.

Country

One of the first female performers to challenge male dominance in the country music industry was Texas Ruby, who was billed as the "Sophie Tucker of the Feminine Folk Singers."

Ruby Agnes Owens was born in 1908 in Wise County. Her musical family included niece Laura Lee Owens McBride, who sang with Bob Wills and the Texas Playboys in the '40s.

With her husband, trick fiddler Curly Fox, Texas Ruby was a fixture at the Grand Ole Opry from 1944 to 1948. During that time she also had hit records for Columbia and King. She sang honky-tonk material in a strong, distinctive voice and wrote many of her own songs.

Ruby was a favorite of Texas audiences while she and her husband lived in Houston from 1948 to '62. After returning to Nashville, they recorded a comeback album together in early 1963. A few days later, she died in a fire in their mobile home while her husband was away performing. She apparently passed out while smoking.

Charline Arthur was a classic case of someone born ahead of her time. In the 1950s, "Charline leaped from stage amplifiers, hollered honky-tonk blues, sang lying down on stage, and cavorted wildly to entertain the tough Texas crowds," according to the book, "Finding Her Voice: The Saga of Women in Country Music."

She left Paris, Texas, in 1945, at age 15, with a medicine show. Four years later, she was playing honky-tonks with husband Jack Arthur as her manager and recorded a single, "I've Got the Boogie Blues," for the Bullet label.

Colonel Tom Parker, who later managed Elvis Presley, heard her on a West Texas radio station and, in 1952, brought her to the attention of RCA Records. She toured with the top country stars of the time and appeared on such important programs as "Louisiana Hayride" and Dallas' "Big D Jamboree."

But her relationship with RCA, and particularly with producer Chet Atkins, was stormy, because of her feisty personality and her sometimes racy lyrics. RCA dropped her in 1956, and no other label picked her up; she was reduced to playing small honky-tonks. She managed a comeback in the '70s, but had to give up performing due to crippling arthritis in her hands. She died in her sleep in 1987 at age 58.

Cindy Walker of Mexia achieved success as both singer and songwriter. She broke into show business in 1941 on a trip to Los Angeles with her parents.

Walker remained in LA for 13 years, writing hundreds of songs, many of which became hits for a diverse roster of artists, including "Dream Baby" (Roy Orbison), "You Don't Know Me" (originally recorded by Eddie Arnold, later revived by Ray Charles and Mickey Gilley) and several Bob Wills songs, including "Cherokee Maiden," "Dusty Skies" and "Bubbles in My Beer."

Walker also made "Soundies," the 1940s-filmed predecessors to videos, and appeared in movies with Gene Autry. Her song "When My Blue Moon Turns to Gold Again" was a Top 10 hit in 1944.

Walker quit performing in 1947 to concentrate on songwriting. In 1954, she returned to Mexia, where she continued her writing with the help of her mother, Oree Walker, who played piano on all her daughter's demo tapes. They lived together until Oree Walker's death in 1991.

Cindy Walker was the first woman inducted into the Nashville Songwriters Hall of Fame.

Blues, Gospel and Jazz

"Sippie" Wallace illustrated the connection between blues and gospel, two forms often believed diametrically opposed. Born Beulah Thomas in Houston in 1899, she was playing organ in church by age 7. While living in Chicago in the '20s, she had a string of hit blues records on the OKeh label.

She found not a bit of difference between blues and gospel, she said in the 1985 interview, a year before her death. "I play for a church right now. ... You don't see any place in the Bible that says you'll go to hell if you sing the blues. If you can sing gospel, you can sing the blues. The only thing that

divides the blues from the gospel are the words. Where you say 'Lord' in gospel, in blues you say 'Daddy.' "

Sippie Wallace recorded and performed almost to the end of her long life, sometimes with pop/blues singer Bonnie Raitt, who recorded some of Wallace's delightfully bawdy songs such as "Mighty Tight Woman" and "Women Be Wise."

Katie Webster, too, mixes a number of influences into her sound. The pianist and singer, born in Houston in 1939, explains her style this way in the book, "Meeting the Blues": "I have a little bit of everything in my style. I don't just do blues. I do country and western, gospel. My dad was a minister and my mother was a missionary and classically trained pianist." Though her mother didn't want her playing jazz or blues on the family piano, family friends included rhythm and blues artists Amos Milburn and Little Willie Littlefield. She also listened to jazz singers such as Ella Fitzgerald and Sarah Vaughan, and out of all these influences fashioned her own vital, distinctive style.

Blues artist Sippie Wallace began her public performances in church at an early age. "If you can sing gospel," she said, "you can sing the blues."

In a career that began in the 1950s, Webster performed and recorded with everyone from Houston bluesman Juke Boy Bonner to Otis Redding and James Brown. Today, she's popular with blues audiences, both in this country and in Europe.

Ella Mae Morse had a brief but meteoric career as a ground-breaking big-band singer. Morse was born in Mansfield in 1924. When she was 13, she boldly auditioned with Jimmy Dorsey's band at Dallas' Adolphus Hotel. She and her mother told Dorsey she was 19, and he hired her.

According to the book, "All Music Guide," the teenager was fired when Dorsey learned her true age, and she joined Freddie Slack's band in 1942. Her recording of "Cow Cow Boogie" with Slack's group became Capitol's first gold record. The following year, she began a solo recording career that lasted until her retirement from show business in 1957, when she was 31.

The white singer's recordings often rose higher on the black charts than in the pop category. She mixed jazz, country, pop and R&B, and the beginnings of rock 'n' roll can be heard in such tunes as "Blacksmith Blues," "Milkman, Keep Those Bottles Quiet" and "House of Blue Lights."

Texas-Mexican

The two great solo female performers in Texas-Mexican music were Chelo Silva and Lydia Mendoza, known as "Las Grandes de Tejas" — the two Texas greats. Both enjoyed wide popularity not only in Texas, but throughout Latin America. Their styles were quite different, though both possessed a very soulful quality.

Lydia Mendoza, known as the "Lark of the Border," was born in Houston in 1916. The family moved around a great deal in this country and Mexico when she was young, but by 1927 had settled in San Antonio. The next year, she made her first recordings in that city for the OKeh label as part of her family's traveling musical group. While they were playing in San Antonio's Plaza del Zacate (Haymarket Square), Lydia came to the attention of radio pioneer Manuel J. Cortez and became a local radio success. In 1934 she recorded "Mal Hombre," accompanying herself on 12-string guitar. This record made her the first Texas-Mexican recording star. She performed until suffering a stroke in 1988.

Mendoza performed and recorded with various bands, in a duet with her mother, Leonor, and in a trio with her sisters, Maria and Juanita, who attained popularity on their own as the duet Hermanas Mendoza (the Mendoza Sisters).

Chelo Silva was the undisputed queen of the *bolero*, a form of song in which women, in no uncertain terms and often rather salty language, voice their complaints about the no-good, cheating men in their lives. She should not be confused with a Mexican *ranchera* singer simply known as Chelo, who was popular in the 1970s.

Silva was born in Brownsville in 1922 and began her long career performing at the Continental Club there. She made her first recordings in 1954 for Discos Falcon. During the late 1950s, she was

Lydia Mendoza recorded her first song in 1934, becoming the first Texas-Mexican recording star.

"probably the best-selling female recording artist on either side of the border," according to the liner notes for the Arhoolie album "Tejano Roots: The Women (1946-70)."

Arhoolie founder Chris Strachwitz recalls seeing Chelo Silva perform in San Antonio's Rosedale Park not long before her death in 1988. Though her voice was almost gone and she talked her way through the songs, she held a huge crowd spellbound and inspired her accompanist, accordionist Flaco Jiménez, to new heights of creativity.

The popular duet of Carmen y Laura consisted of sisters Carmen and Laura Hernandez, born in Kingsville in 1921 and 1926, respectively. Carmen married Armando Marroquín, who went into the jukebox business in nearby Alice. After World War II, Marroquín began making his own records, first recording his wife and her sister in the Marroquín kitchen.

A few months later, Marroquín and businessman Paco Betancourt founded Ideal Records and moved the recording operation out of the house. The sisters continued to be the most popular act on the label and toured extensively, often performing with dance bands signed to the label, such as those of Beto Villa and Pedro Bugarín. In their hundreds of records for Ideal, they recorded with a variety of musicians, from orchestras to accordion conjuntos.

Rock 'N' Roll, Etc.

One of Texas' most famous musical performers of either sex was Janis Joplin, born in Port Arthur in 1943. Growing up, she was fascinated by black performers such as blues diva Bessie Smith and the music she heard in the nightclubs in neighboring Louisiana.

Attending the University of Texas at Austin in the early 1960s, Joplin fell in with a crowd of folk musicians who gathered to sing at the gas station/ beer joint of Ken Threadgill, who enjoyed singing Jimmie Rodgers songs. But finding Texas too confining, Joplin moved to San Francisco, where she became a regular performer at such hippie venues as the Fillmore ballroom. Her performance at the 1967 Monterrey Pop Festival made her a national star.

Fame did nothing, however, to ease her personal insecurities, and she worked hard to maintain her tough, hard-living image. She died in 1970 of a drug overdose.

Pianist and singer Marcia Ball originally hails from Louisiana, but has been a fixture on the Austin music scene since the early 1970s, when she led a "progressive country" band called Freda and the Firedogs. She wore cowgirl outfits and sometimes yodeled Patsy Montana songs such as "I Want to Be a Cowboy's Sweetheart."

But Ball found cosmic cowboy music too confining. Her influences range from singers Irma Thomas and Etta James to New Orleans pianist Professor Longhair.

These days, Ball's music is a rollicking, all-but-unclassifiable mixture of any number of influences, from country to blues, rock and zydeco.

Michelle Shocked, too, is tough to classify. Generally she's labeled a folk singer, but she combines her folk with a punk sensibility. Born in 1962 and raised in East Texas, Shocked burst on the scene in 1987 with the album "Texas Campfire Tapes," which was recorded while she was singing offstage at the Kerrville Folk Festival.

Since then, Shocked has gone off in unexpected directions with an album of big-band swing and "Arkansas Traveler," a collection of minstrel-show songs. She became quite involved in the study of this tradition and aroused controversy with her remarks about music and racism at a 1992 Austin music conference. ☆— Jay Brakefield

Photo Credits: History of Texas Music:
Janis Joplin, Texas Tornados: AP Photo
Buddy Holly, Leadbelly, Bob Wills, Ornette Coleman, Lightnin' Hopkins, Little Joe Hernandez: The Dallas Morning News file photo.
George Jones: Pam Berry, The Dallas Morning News.
Vaughan brothers: Evans Caglage, The Dallas Morning News.
Roy Orbison: Paula Nelson, The Dallas Morning News.

Photo Credits: Women in Music:
Cindy Walker: Mary Bufwack and Robert Oermann.
Sippie Wallace: Rod Kennedy, Kerrville Folk Festival.
Lydia Mendoza: The University of Texas Institute of Texan Cultures, San Antonio.

More About Music in Texas:

*A description of **unusual music specialties** offered by Texas colleges and universities can be found on pages 542-543.*

Texas Musicians

Following is a list of Texas musicians grouped by the types of music with which they are associated. Each name is followed by where they were born or the area that had the greatest influence on their music, what their specialty is or was and the decade(s) in which they were musically active, although in many cases, a performer had the greatest impact early in his or her career. Within categories, the names are in chronological order of era of their careers. This is a list of some of the most familiar names; it is not intended to be a complete list. We apologize if we have omitted your favorite performer.

Ragtime:

Scott Joplin; Texarkana; composer, pianist; early 1900s.

Country/Western/Honky-Tonk:

Alexander Campbell (Eck) Robertson; Amarillo; fiddler; 1920s.

Goebel Reeves; Sherman; singer; 1920s.

Vernon Dalhart (born Marion Try Slaughter); Jefferson; singer; 1930s.

Milton Brown (Aladdin Laddies, Light Crust Doughboys, Musical Brownies);Stephenville; band leader; 1930s.

Al Dexter; Troup; singer; 1930s.

Floyd Tillman; Post; singer/songwriter; 1930s-70s.

Ernest Tubb; Crisp; singer; 1930s-40s.

Dale Evans; Uvalde; singer; 1930s-40s.

Gene Autry; Tioga; singer/actor; 1930s-40s.

Woodward Maurice "Tex" Ritter; Panola County; singer/actor; 1930s-40s.

Bob Wills (Aladdin Laddies, Light Crust Doughboys, Texas Playboys); Kosse/Turkey; fiddler/band leader; 1930s-60s.

Henry "Hank" Thompson; Waco; singer/guitarist; 1940s-50s.

William Orville "Lefty" Frizzell; Corsicana; singer; 1940s-50s.

Bill and Joe (born Homer and Walter) Callahan; Dallas (born North Carolina); singers/instrumentalists; 1940s-60s.

Johnny Horton; Tyler; singer/guitarist; 1950s.

Jim Reeves; Panola County; singer; 1950s-61.

Kay Starr; Dallas; singer; 1950s-70s.

Ray Price; Perryville; singer; 1950s-90s.

George Jones; Saratoga; singer; 1950s-90s.

Trini López; Dallas; singer; 1960s.

Carolyn Hester; Waco, Singer; 1960s.

Roger Miller; Fort Worth; singer/songwriter; 1960s, 1980s.

B.J. Thomas; Houston; singer; 1960s-90s.

Jennie C. Riley; Anson; singer; 1960s-90s.

Stephen Stills (Buffalo Springfield; Crosby, Stills, Nash, and Young); Dallas; singer/songwriter; 1960s-90s.

Waylon Jennings; Littlefield; singer; 1960s-90s.

Mac Davis; Lubbock; singer/songwriter; 1970s.

The Gatlin Brothers (Larry, Rudy, Steve); Odessa; singers; 1970s-80s.

John Denver (born John Deutschendorf); grew up in Fort Worth; singer; 1970s-80s.

Freddy Fender (born Baldemar Huerta); San Benito, Corpus Christi; singer; 1970s, 1990s.

Tanya Tucker; Seminole; singer; 1970s-90s.

Steven Fromholz; Austin; singer/songwriter; 1970s-90s.

Michael Murphey; Dallas; songwriter/singer; 1970s-90s.

Kris Kristofferson; Brownsville; singer/songwriter; 1970s-90s.

Willie Nelson; Abbott; singer/songwriter; 1970s-90s.

Johnny Rodríguez; Sabinal; songwriter/ singer; 1970s-90s.

Barbara Mandrell; Houston; singer; 1970s-90s.

Kenny Rogers; Houston; singer; 1970s-90s.

Rodney Crowell; Houston; singer/songwriter; 1980s-90s.

George Strait; San Marcos; singer; 1980s-90s.

Nanci Griffith; Seguin; singer/songwriter; 1980s-90s.

Lyle Lovett; Houston; singer/songwriter; 1980s-90s.

Country & Western Groups:

Texas Ramblers; Prince Albert Hunt; 1920s.

East Texas Serenaders; Daniel Huggins Williams; 1920s-30s.

Aladdin Laddies (see Bob Wills, Milton Brown, Herman Arnspiger).

Light Crust Doughboys (originally Bob Wills, Herman Arnspiger, Milton Brown), 1930s-90s.

Musical Brownies (see Milton Brown).

Texas Playboys (see Bob Wills)

Riders of the Purple Sage; 1940s.

Brazos Valley Boys (see Hank Thompson)

Pleasant Valley Boys; Alvin Crow; 1970s-80s.

Asleep at the Wheel; Ray Benson; 1970s-90s.

Blues/Rhythm and Blues:

Blind Lemon Jefferson; near Wortham; songwriter/ guitarist; 1920s.

Victoria Spivey; Houston; singer/songwriter; 1920s.

Blind Willie Johnson; Marlin; singer/guitarist; 1920s-30s.

Sippie Wallace; Houston; singer; 1920s, 1970s-80s.

"Whistlin'" Alex Moore; Dallas; pianist/singer/whistler; 1920s-80s.

Huddie "Leadbelly" Ledbetter; near Caddo Lake; guitarist/singer; 1930s-40s.

Willie Mae "Big Mama" Thornton; Houston (born Alabama); singer; 1940s-70s.

Aaron "T-Bone" Walker; Linden, Dallas; guitarist/ singer; 1940s-70s.

Sam "Lightnin'" Hopkins; Centerville/Houston; guitarist, composer, singer; 1940s-80s.

Clarence "Gatemouth" Brown; Orange (born Louisiana) ; guitarist/fiddler/singer; 1940s-90s.

Esther Phillips; Galveston; singer; 1950s-70s.

Freddie King; Gilmer; guitarist; 1950s-70s.

King Curtis; Fort Worth; tenor sax; 1950s-60s.

Barbara Lynn; Beaumont; singer; 1950s-90s.

Johnny Copeland; Houston; singer/guitarist; 1950s-90s.

Delbert McClinton; Lubbock, Fort Worth; singer; 1950s-90s.

Albert Collins; Houston; guitarist/singer; 1950s-90s.

Mance Lipscomb; near Navasota and Brazos rivers; singer, guitarist; 1960s-70s.

Jimmie Vaughan; Dallas, Austin; guitarist/singer; 1970s-90s.

Stevie Ray Vaughan; Dallas, Austin; guitarist/singer; 1970s-90.

Angela Strehli; Lubbock, Austin; singer; 1970s-90s.
Lou Ann Barton; Austin; singer; 1970s-90s.
Marcia Ball; Austin; singer/pianist; 1970s-90s.

Jazz:

Keg Johnson; Dallas; trumpet; 1920s-60s.
Budd Johnson; Dallas; tenor sax; 1920s-70s.
Buster Smith; Ellis County, Dallas; alto sax/clarinet/ arranger/band leader; 1920s-80s.
Charlie Christian; Dallas; guitarist; late '30s-early '40s.
Gordon "Tex" Beneke; Fort Worth; tenor sax/conductor of Glenn Miller Orchestra; 1930s-50s.
Weldon Leo (Jack) Teagarden; Vernon; trombonist; 1930s-60s.
Teddy Wilson; Austin; pianist; 1930s-70s.
Gene Ramey; Austin; bass; 1930s-70s.
Buddy Tate; Sherman; tenor sax, clarinet; 1930s-70s.
Eddie "Cleanhead" Vinson; Houston; alto sax/ singer; 1930s-70s.
Arnett Cobb; Houston; tenor sax; 1930s-70s.
Harry James; Beaumont; trumpeter/band leader; 1930s-70s.
Ella Mae Morse; Mansfield; singer; 1940s-50s.
David "Fathead" Newman; Dallas; tenor sax; 1940s-90s.
Dewey Redman; Fort Worth; tenor sax; 1940s-90s.
Ornette Coleman; Fort Worth; alto sax; 1940s-90s.
Tomás Ramírez; South Texas; tenor sax; 1990s.

Rock/Folk:

Buddy Holly; Lubbock; singer/guitarist; 1950s.
Janis Joplin; Port Arthur; singer; 1960s.
Roy Orbison; Wink; singer/guitarist; 1960s, 1980s.
Michael Nesmith (The Monkees); Dallas; singer/ songwriter; 1960s-70s.
William Royce "Boz" Scaggs; Dallas; singer; 1970s.
Christopher Cross; San Antonio, Austin; singer; 1970s-80s.
Steve Miller; Dallas; singer/guitarist; 1970s-90s.
Don Henley (of the Eagles); Linden; singer; 1970s-90s.
ZZ Top (Frank Beard, Dusty Hill, Billy Gibbons); Houston; blues/rock group; 1970s-90s.
Joe "King" Carrasco; Dumas, Austin; guitarist /singer/band leader; 1980s.
Tish Hinojosa; San Antonio; singer/songwriter; 1980s-90s.
Joe Ely; Lubbock, Austin; singer/songwriter; 1980s-90s.

Tex-Mex (Norteño, conjunto) :

Bruno Villarreal; San Benito; accordionist; 1920s-70s.
Narciso Martínez; San Benito (born in Reynosa, Mex.); accordionist/singer; 1930s-70s.
Santiago Jiménez; San Antonio; accordionist/singer; 1930s-60s.
Lydia Mendoza; San Antonio; singer/guitarist; 1930s-80s.
Valerio Longoria; Kenedy; accordionist/singer; 1930s-90s.
Tony de la Rosa; Sarita; accordionist; 1940s-90s.
Chelo Silva; Brownsville; bolero singer; 1950s-80s.
Paulino and Eloy Bernal (brothers); Kingsville; Paulino, accordionist; Eloy, bajo sexto; 1950s-90s.
Flaco Jiménez; San Antonio; accordion; 1960s-90s.
Little Joe Hernandez; Temple, Dallas; singer/band leader; 1960s-90s.
Emilio Navaira; San Antonio; singer; 1990s.
Selena (Quintanilla Perez); Corpus Christi; singer; 1990s.

Uncategorizable:

Kinky Friedman; Austin; singer/songwriter; 1970s.
Michelle Shocked; Gilmer; singer/songwriter; 1980s-90s. ☆

Texas Music Office Supports Industry

The Texas Music Office is authorized by the Texas Legislature to promote the development of the music industry in the state.

The TMO serves as a clearinghouse for Texas music industry information; provides referrals to Texas music businesses, talent and events; serves as liaison between music businesses and government offices and agencies; and publicizes developments within the Texas music industry.

Beginning as the Texas Music Commission in 1985, the TMO became part of the Texas Department of Commerce in 1987. It was transferred to the Governor's Office in January 1990.

The TMO maintains seven computer databases to aid it in its dissemination of information. They are:

- **"The Texas Music Industry"** lists 4,200 Texas music businesses with a full description of each firm's products and services, contact information and more. Categories are commercial music; education; industry services; media; music videos; musical instruments and equipment; record production, distribution and sales; recording services; tour services; and venues;
- **"Texas Music Events"** lists 400 different music-related events around the state;
- **"Texas Talent Register"** lists 730 Texas recording artists;
- **"Texas Radio Stations,"** lists 678 Texas radio stations;
- **"U.S. Record Labels"**;
- **"Classical Texas,"** with detailed information for all classical music organizations in Texas — orchestras, chamber music and choral groups, opera associations, and arts groups that book concerts by touring classical musicians; and
- **"International,"** which lists 400 foreign firms interested in Texas music.

Publications of the TMO, all updated annually, include **"Texas Music Industry Directory"; "Texas Music Events Calendar"; "Texas Music International Tip Sheet"; "Texas Recording and Production Guide,"** listing recording studios, cassette duplicators, CD factories, record producers, pressing plants and state sales tax exemptions; **"Texas Music Education Primer,"** giving detailed information about Texas colleges and universities offering music and music-business courses and a bibliography of music-industry trade books, associations, and books about Texas music; and **"Classical Texas,"** giving information about Texas orchestras, operas and other classical-music organizations. ☆

A Timeline of Texas History

On the following pages is a timeline of history. The major events in Texas history are in the column on the left side of each page, while important happenings in world and United States history are in a parallel column on the right side. Six historians, whose names are given at the end of the list, have reviewed this timeline for the Texas Almanac. We are grateful for their corrections and suggestions.

Texas Events

B.C.

c. 11,000-8000 - First immigrants drift into the area now called Texas.

c. 8000-7000 - Burial from this era is the earliest so far discovered in Texas — a female nicknamed Leann, whose remains have been found at a site in Williamson County north of Austin. The burial of a man and a boy at a site in Bosque County near Waco dates from the same time period. Artifacts found at the Bosque County site indicate participation in an extensive trade network with other tribal groups.

c. 4000 - People in the lower-Pecos River area leave **distinctive forms of art painted on cave walls** and other rock surfaces.

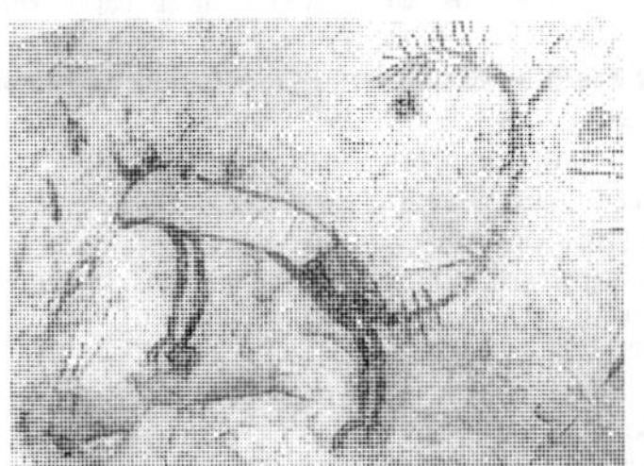

This pictograph in the Fate Bell Shelter can be viewed by visitors to Seminole Canyon State Park near Comstock, Val Verde Co. Photo by Jim Zintgraff, courtesy Texas Archeological Research Laboratory, UT-Austin.

A.D.

800 - 1500 — Farmers/hunters build and occupy what is today called **the Buried City,** stone dwellings located southeast of Perryton in Ochiltree County on

World/National Events

B.C.

c. 40,000 - Cro-Magnon Man enters Europe from Near East.
c. 30,000 - Neanderthal Man disappears.
c. 28,000 - First humans cross into the Americas from Asia.

c. 10,000 - Humans reach southern tip of South America.
c. 8000 - Agriculture develops in Middle East.

c. 7000 - Humans begin to use **metals**.
4236 - First date in **Egyptian** calendar.

3760 - First date in **Jewish** calendar.
3372 - First date in **Mayan** calendar.
2700 - Khufu (Cheops) builds the **Great Pyramid** at Giza in Egypt.
c. 2000 - Village life develops in **Valley of Mexico**.
- Bronze Age in northern Europe.
1860 - Stonehenge built in Britain.
1728 - Hammurabi the Great, writer of Code of Laws, ascends to throne of Babylon.
c. 1450- Height of **Minoan** civilization in Crete.
1420 - Amenhotep III begins **Golden Age of Egypt**.
1250 - Exodus of Israelites from Egypt.
753 - Traditional date of founding of **Rome**.
551 - Birth of **Confucius**, Chinese philosopher.
141 - Jews liberate **Jerusalem**.
55-44 - Rule of **Julius Caesar**.
5 - Jesus born.

A.D.

30 - Crucifixion of Jesus.
43- Roman conquest of Britain.
79 - Pompeii buried under volcanic ash from Vesuvius.
c. 100 - Paper invented in China.
135 - Diaspora, or dispersing of Jews from Palestine, by order of Roman Emperor Hadrian.
180 - Teotihuacán in central Mexico is largest city in the Americas.
370 - Huns invade Europe from Asia.
711 - Moslem conquest of Spain.
756 - Papal states founded in Italy.
800 - Charlemagne crowned emperor.
c. 900-1200 - Toltec empire rules Valley of Mexico.
1066 - Battle of Hastings won by William the Con-

the northern edge of the Panhandle, as well as other sites along the Canadian River.

c. 1400 - The **Caddo Confederacy** establishes a civilization in East Texas based on agriculture.

1519 - Spanish explorer **Alonso Alvarez de Pineda** maps the Texas coastline.

1528 - **Cabeza de Vaca** and crew are shipwrecked near Galveston and begin exploration.

1541 - **Francisco de Coronado** crosses part of West Texas in search of the Seven Cities of Cibola.

Mission San Francisco de la Espada, San Antonio, is still in use as a parish church (see item below). Texas Almanac staff photo.

1681 or 1682 - **First Spanish mission** in what will become Texas is established at Ysleta, near present El Paso.

1685 - French explorer **LaSalle**, looking for the mouth of the Mississippi River, lands in Texas by mistake.

1690 - **San Francisco de los Tejas** mission founded in East Texas near present-day Weches, Houston Co. It was abandoned and closed in 1693.

1716 - Spanish build a **presidio** west of the Neches River, marking the beginning of serious attempts to settle the Texas area.

1718 - **San Antonio de Valero** mission, of which the building known as the Alamo was the chapel, and San José mission are founded in San Antonio.

1731 - **San Francisco de la Espada** mission is founded at San Antonio. Canary Islanders arrive in San Antonio; first formal villa, San Fernando de Béxar, is established.

1758 - Destruction of **Santa Cruz de San Sabá mission** near present-day Menard.

1759 - Spanish defeated by Indian residents of large encampment at **Spanish Fort** in present-day Monqueror.

1215 - **Magna Carta**.

1338-1453 - **Hundred Year's War** between England and France.

1348-1351 - **Black Death** (plague) ravages Europe.

1454 - **Printing with movable type** developed by Johannes Gutenberg in Germany.

1492 - **Christopher Columbus,** on a voyage backed by Spanish sovereigns Ferdinand and Isabella, discovers West Indies.

1498 - **Vasco de Gama** reaches India.

1513 - **Balboa** discovers Pacific Ocean.

1517 - **Martin Luther** presents 95 theses in effort to reform Catholic church.

1519-1521 - **Hernando Cortés** conquers Tenochtitlán, center of Aztec empire, in what is today's Mexico.

1522 - **Magellan**'s expedition completes first circumnavigation of the world.

1533 - **Pizarro** conquers Peru.

1534 - French explorer **Jacques Cartier** lands in the Gulf of St. Lawrence area of Canada.

1541 - **De Soto** discovers Mississippi River.

1558-1603 - **Queen Elizabeth I** rules England.

1588 - **Spanish Armada** defeated.

1607 - English found colony of **Virginia**.

1610 - **Santa Fé** established in present-day New Mexico.

1618 - **Thirty Year's War** begins in Europe.

1619 - **House of Burgesses**, first representative assembly in New World, meets at Jamestown, Va.

- **First blacks** delivered to Virginia by Dutch.

1620 - **Pilgrims** found New Plymouth.

1626 - Dutch found **New Amsterdam** (later New York).

1630-1642 - English settle **Massachusetts**.

1633 - **Connecticut** founded.

1642 - **Montreal** founded by French in Canada.

1649-1660 - **Commonwealth** in England.

1681 - Rene Robert, **Sieur de la Salle** explores Mississippi River.

1692 - **Salem witchcraft trials** held in Massachusetts.

1754 - **French and Indian War** begins in North America.

tague County.

1766 - **Texas' first recorded hurricane** strikes near Galveston.

1813 - **First newspaper** in Texas, *Gaceta de Texas*, is founded by José Alvarez de Toledo in Nacogdoches.

1821 - Spanish government grants permission to **Moses Austin** to settle 300 families in Texas. After his death, son Stephen F. Austin renegotiates the contract in 1822 with newly independent Mexico.

- **Mexico** declares independence from Spain.
- Jane Long gives birth to a daughter, Mary James, thought to be the **first Anglo child** born in Texas.

1822 - Jared E. Groce brings the **first cottonseed** into Texas.

1826 - **Fredonian Rebellion** begins in Nacogdoches.
1830 - **Law of April 6** is passed by Mexican government, stopping legal immigration into Texas from United States except in special cases, and becomes primary factor in growing unrest with Mexican rule.
1832 - First blood of **Texas Revolution** is shed at Battle of Velasco.
1835 - **Gail Borden** begins publishing the newspaper, "Telegraph and Texas Register."

- Oct. 2: **First shots of Texas Revolution** fired at Gonzales.
- **Texas Navy** created.
- **Ben Milam** leads revolutionaries into Béxar to drive out Mexican defenders.

1836 - On March 2, **Texas Declaration of Independence** is adopted at Washington-on-the-Brazos.

- A 13-day **siege of the Alamo** by Mexican troops ends in battle on March 6, in which all remaining defenders are killed.
- On March 27, about 300 Texans prisoners were executed at Goliad by order of Gen. Antonio López de Santa Anna.
- Troops led by Sam Houston defeat the Mexican army led by Santa Anna at **San Jacinto** near Houston on April 21.
- On May 14, Santa Anna and Texas' provisional president David Burnet sign two **Treaties of Velasco**, ending the Texas Revolution.

1837 - **Republic of Texas** is officially recognized by United States, and later by France, England, the Netherlands and Belgium.
1839 - First **homestead exemption act** is passed.
1839-1844 - Five-year **Regulator-Moderator War** in Shelby, Panola and Harrison counties between vigilante bands ends when Pres. Sam Houston orders out

1762-1796 - **Catherine the Great** rules Russia.

1773 - **Boston Tea Party.**
1775-1783 - **American War of Independence.**
1776 - **American Declaration of Independence.**
1783 - **Treaty of Paris** ends American Revolution.
1789 - **Alexander Mackenzie** explores Canadian Northwest.
1789-1792 - **French Revolution.**
1801 - **United Kingdom** created.
1803 - **Louisiana Purchase.**
1804 - **Lewis and Clark** explore northwest United States.
1812 - **War of 1812** begins between U.S. and Britian; ends with Treaty of Ghent in 1814.

1818 - **Zulu Empire** established in South Africa.
1820 - **Missouri Compromise** signed.
1821 - **Peru** gains independence from Spain.

- **Mexico** declares independence from Spain.

1822 - **Brazil** gains independence from Portugal.

1824 - **Mexico** adopts its first written constitution and temporarily becomes a republic.

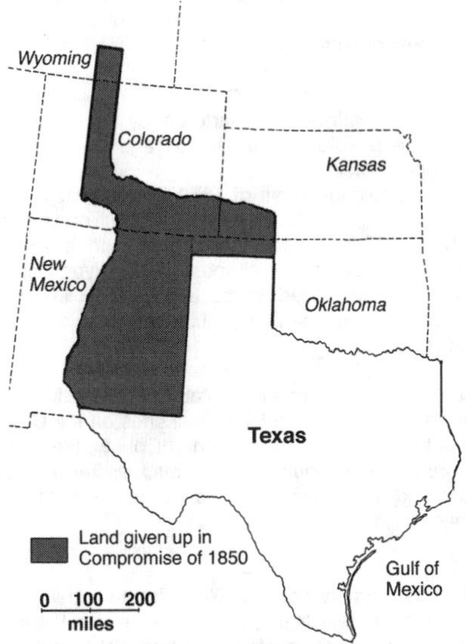

Map of Texas from 1836 to 1850 (see item on next page, left-hand column).

the East Texas militia in August 1844 and forces the two sides to sign a treaty of peace.

1840 - **Council House fight** in San Antonio between Comanches and Texas government during peace negotiations.

- Texas Rangers and volunteer army defeat Comanches at **Battle of Plum Creek** near Lockhart.

1841 - **Santa Fé Expedition**, launched without Texas Congressional authorization by Pres. M.B. Lamar, attempts to establish trade with and solidify Texas' claims to territory around Santa Fé. Members of group are taken prisoner, marched to Mexico City and imprisoned. They are finally released in 1842.

1842 - **German immigration** to Texas, organized by German society, the Adelsverein, leads to founding of New Braunfels, Fredericksburg and other Central Texas communities.

- **Archives War** in December consists of Austin's citizens keeping the state government's official records from being moved to Houston.

- Unauthorized invasion of Mexico by Texas volunteer troops reaches town of **Mier**, where 176 men are captured and imprisoned. After an attemted escape, every tenth one, selected by the drawing of 17 black beans, is executed.

1845 - **Baylor University** founded in February.

- United States admits Texas as 28th state on December 29.

1846 - **Battle of Palo Alto** near Brownsville on May 8, is the first major battle of two-year war with Mexico.

- On May 9, **Battle of Resaca de la Palma**, also near Brownsville, ends with U.S. victory under Gen. Zachary Taylor.

1848 - **Treaty of Guadalupe Hidalgo** ends the War with Mexico; the Rio Grande becomes a permanent international boundary.

1850 - **First railroad** is chartered by the State of Texas - the Buffalo Bayou, Brazos and Colorado. It begins operation in 1853.

- In the **Compromise of 1850**, Texas gives up its claim to land that includes more than half of what is now New Mexico, about a third of Colorado, a corner of Oklahoma and a small portion of Wyoming in exchange for the United States' assumtion of $10 million in debt; Texas keeps its public lands(see map on previous page).

1854 - Two **reservations** are established for Indians in West-Central Texas: one for Comanches on the Clear Fork of the Brazos in Throckmorton County; the other for more sedentary Indian groups, such as Tawakonis, Wacos and Tonkawas, near Fort Belknap in Young County.

1856 - First **camels** arrive in Texas for an experiment using them for the military in the arid American West.

1857 - Southern route of the **Butterfield Overland Mail** crosses Texas on its way between East Coast and West Coast. Route. Discontinued with the outbreak of the Civil War and never resumed.

1859 - Clashes between Juan "Cheno" Cortina and Anglo lawmen lead to series of altercations around Brownsville area. Texas Rangers and federal troops eventually halt the so-called **"Cortina War."**

1846 - **Irish potato famine** at its height.

1846-1848 - **War with Mexico** fought by United States.

1848 - Seneca Falls, New York, is site of **Convention for Women's Rights.**

- Communist Manifesto is produced by Karl Marx and Friedrich Engels.

- **California Gold Rush** begins.

1853-1856 - **David Livingstone** explores Africa.

1854-1856 - **Crimean War**.

1855 - Mexican government under **Benito Juárez** begins period of reform.

1856 - **Gold is discovered** in Fraser River basin in Canada.

1857 - **Dred Scott decision** by U.S. Supreme Court.

1859 - **First commercially productive oil well** is drilled at Titusville, Pa.

- **Indians are moved** by federal government from their reservations in West Texas to Indian Territory.

1860 - South Carolina leads Southern states in seceding from the union to form the **Confederate States of America** the following year.

1861 - **Texas secedes** from Union and joins the Confederate States of America.

1861-1865 - Texas in the **Civil War**.

1861-1865 - **Civil War** in United States.

1862 - Forty-two men thought to be **Union sympathizers are hanged** at various times during October in Gainesville.

- A group of Union loyalists, mostly German immigrants from the area of **Comfort**, try to reach U.S. troops in Mexico. Forty are killed by Confederates, some in August and others in October 1862. Another 28 drown attempting to swim the Rio Grande.

1862 - On May 5, **Cinco de Mayo**, Mexicans defeat French forces at Battle of Puebla.

1863 - In the **Emancipation Proclamation**, U.S. Pres. Abraham Lincoln frees "all slaves in areas that are still in rebellion."

1864 - Kit Carson and his men defeat Kiowas and Comanches in **Battle of Adobe Walls**.

1864 - Maximilian of Austria becomes **emperor of Mexico**.

1865 - **Battle of Palmito Ranch** fought near Brownsville after Civil War over because word of the war's end had not yet reached troops in Texas.

- June 19 - Gen. Gordon Granger arrives at Galveston to announce that slavery has been abolished, an event commemorated today by the festival known as **Juneteenth**.

1865 - **Robert E. Lee surrenders** Confederate troops to U.S. Grant at Appomattox Court House, Va., on April 9.

- President **Lincoln shot April 14; dies April 15.**

- Ratification of the **Thirteenth Amendment** makes abolition of slavery part of the U.S. Constitution.

1866 - **Cattle drives**, which had been sporadic since the 1840s, begin in earnest, mostly to markets and railheads in Midwest.

1866 - Two cavalry regiments and four of infantry composed of **black troops are authorized by Congress**. They are later nicknamed "Buffalo Soldiers."

1867 - United States purchases **Alaska**.

- **Benito Juárez** regains power in Mexico.

1867-1870 - **Congressional (or Military) Reconstruction.**

1869 - **Transcontinental railroad** completed across U.S.

1870 - **Texas readmitted** to Union.

- Edmund J. Davis becomes **first Republican governor** of Texas.

- **Battle of Little Wichita** between Kiowas and Sixth Cavalry on Little Wichita River near Archer City.

1871 - Seven men in a wagon train are **massacred at Salt Creek**, about 20 miles west of Jacksboro, by Kiowas and Comanches led by chiefs Satanta and Big Tree.

1873 - **Black Buffalo Soldiers** are first posted to Texas, serving at virtually every frontier fort in West Texas from the Rio Grande to the Red River and the Panhandle, as well as in other states.

- **Greatest annual rainfall** ever recorded in Texas falls at Clarksville: 109.38 inches.

Lt. Henry Ossian Flipper, the first black graduate of West Point, was stationed in Texas with the Buffalo Soldiers (see items above and left). Photo from U.S. National Archives.

1874 - Inauguration of Democrat government in Texas marks **end of Reconstruction** period.

- Ranald Mackenzie leads his men in the **Battle of Palo Duro Canyon**, south of present-day Amarillo, one of the last major Indian battles in Texas.

1876 - The present **state constitution** is adopted.

- **Texas A&M University** opens.

- **Charles Goodnight** establishes the JA Ranch in Palo Duro Canyon, the first cattle ranch located in northwest Texas.

1876 - **Battle of LIttle Big Horn**.

1876-1880 and 1884-1911 - **Porfirio Díaz** rules Mexico as dictator.

1877 - El Paso **Salt War** is culmination of long dispute caused by Anglos' attempts to take over salt-mining rights at a traditionally Mexican-American salt source.

- **Black laundresses** in Galveston strike for higher wages.

1877 - **Compromise of 1877** ends Reconstruction.

1879 - **Zulu War**.

1881 - **Texas & Pacific Rwy.** reaches Sierra Blanca in

West Texas.

- **Tillotson College** (for blacks) opens in Austin.

1883 - Classes begin at **University of Texas**.

1884 - **Fence-cutting wars** prompt Legislature to pass law making fence-cutting a felony.

1886 - Hurricane destroys port town of **Indianola**.

1888 - The present **state capitol** is dedicated.

- **Jaybird-Woodpecker War** begins in Fort Bend County.

1891 - **Railroad Commission** established by Gov. James Hogg and the Texas Legislature.

1893 - Rebecca Hayes of Galveston forms **Texas Equal Rights Association** to work for woman suffrage.

1894 - Oil discovered at **Corsicana** by workers drilling for water; commercial field opened 1896, beginning Texas' rise as a major oil producer.

1898 - Teddy Roosevelt arrives in San Antonio to recruit **Rough Riders** for the First Volunteer Cavalry to fight in the Spanish-American War in Cuba.

1898-1899 - **Coldest winter** on record statewide.

1899 - One of two **coldest days** on record in Texas: -23 F. at Tulia on Feb. 12.

1900 - Hurricane on Sept. 8 destroys half of **Galveston** and kills 6,000 people, the greatest natural disaster in human terms ever to strike North America.

Galveston after the hurricane of 1900 (see item in left-hand column). Associated Press photo.

1901 - Jan. 10 - Gusher drilled by mining engineer Capt. A.F. Lucas at **Spindletop** near Beaumont catapults Texas into the petroleum age.

- **Bluebonnet** is designated the state flower by the state legislature.

1902 - **Poll tax** becomes requirement for voting.

1905 - **Texas Association of Colored Women's Clubs** organizes.

1910 - Lt. Benjamin D. Foulois makes **first military air flight** in a Wright brothers plane at Fort Sam Houston in San Antonio, the first shaky beginnings of U.S. Air Force.

1912 - Katherine Stinson of San Antonio, becomes **fourth female pilot** to be licensed in the United States.

1916 - **Pancho Villa** and his followers raid villages in Big Bend area.

1917 - **Gov. James Ferguson** is impeached and convicted; he leaves office.

1918 - Texas women win **right to vote** in primary elections.

- Annie Webb Blanton becomes the **first woman elected to a statewide office** when she is elected State Superintendent of Public Instruction.

1919 - Responding to anti-German sentiment, Gov. William P. Hobby **vetoes appropriations for German Dept.** of University of Texas.

- Texans adopt a **prohibition amendment** to the state constitution.

1920 - End of Texas-Mexico **border skirmishes**.

1923 - Women's Joint Legislative Council, informally called the **Petticoat Lobby**, is led by Jane Y. McCal-

1901 - **Australian Commonwealth** established.

1903 - **Pierre and Marie Curie** are awarded Nobel Prize for discovery of the element radium.

1909 - **Henry Ford** begins manufacturing automobiles on an assembly line.

1910 - **Mexican Revolution** begins.

1912 - Ocean liner **Titanic** sinks with loss of more than 1,500 lives.

1914 - United Sattes forces occupy **Vera Cruz.**

1914-1918 - **World War I.**

1917 - **Russian Revolution.**

1917-1918 - U.S. fights in **World War I.**

1920 - **Prohibition** amendment takes effect.

- **19th Amendment** (women's right to vote) ratified.

lum.
1925 - Miriam "Ma" Ferguson becomes **first woman governor,** serving as a figurehead for her husband, former gov. James E. Ferguson.

- Texas Tech University begins classes in Lubbock as Texas Technological College.

1927 - Mockingbird is named state bird by legislature.

1928 - Democratic National Convention is held in Houston in June, the first nominating convention held in a Southern city since 1860.

1929 - League of Latin American Citizens (LULAC) is founded in Corpus Christi.

1930 - The huge **East Texas Oil Field** begins production with the blowing in of the Daisy Bradford well, drilled near Turnertown in Rusk County by wildcatter C.M. (Dad) Joiner.

- Georgetown woman, Jessie Daniel Ames, organizes the **Association of Southern Women for the Prevention of Lynching**.

1931 - Texan **Wiley Post** begins flight around the world.

1932 - Babe Didrikson Zaharias wins three Olympic medals.

1933 - One of **coldest days** on record in Texas: -23 F. at Seminole on Feb. 8.

1936 - One-hundredth anniversary of Texas' independence from Mexico celebrated; **Texas Centennial Exposition** held at Dallas' Fair Park.

- Hottest temperature ever recorded in Texas — at Seymour on Aug. 12: 120 F.

1937 - New London school is destroyed in a natural-gas explosion that kills almost 300 students and teachers.

1938 - Galveston native Douglas Corrigan flies to Ireland, supposedly by mistake, earning him the nickname **"Wrong Way" Corrigan**.

- San Antonio **pecan shellers strike** to protest sweatshop conditions and miniscule wages. The 3-month-long walkout, marked by violence between strikers and police, results in victory for the mostly Latino women workers.

1941-1945 - Texans participate in **World War II** along with rest of nation.

1943 - Race riot in Beaumont put down by National Guard.

1947 - The French-owned S.S. Grandcamp, carrying

1927 - Charles Lindbergh makes the first solo flight across the Atlantic Ocean.

1929 - Oct. 29: Black Tuesday, the stock market crashes, ushering in the **Great Depression**.

1931 - Empire State Building opens in New York.

1932 - Franklin D. Roosevelt is elected president of United States, with Texan **John Nance Garner** as his vice president.

1933 - Prohibition ends.

1934 - Mexican government begins major land reforms.

1936 - King Edward VIII abdicates throne of Great Britain.

San Antonio pecan shellers in 1938 (see item at left). Photo courtesy The Institute of Texan Cultures, San Antonio, San Antonio LIght *Collection.*

1940 - Battle of Britain.

1941 - Bombing of **Pearl Harbor** in Hawaii on Dec. 7 by Japanese pulls United States into World War II.

1944 - Allies invade **Normandy** on June 6 and 7.

1945 - V.E. Day, May 8, marks the end of the war in Europe.

- **Atomic bombs** dropped on Hiroshima and Nagasaki force Japanese to surrender.

- On Sept. 2, war officially ends when Texan, **Adm. Chester Nimitz**, accepts Japanese surrender.

- **United Nations** is formed.

ammonium nitrate, explodes in **Texas City** harbor on April 16, killing almost 600 and injuring 4,000 more. The force creates a 15-foot tidal wave. The concussion of the explosion is felt as far away as Port Arthur, about 75 miles distant (see photo at right).

1948 - Lyndon B. Johnson wins U.S. Senate race by 87 votes, giving him the title "Landslide Lyndon." Winning margin in disputed pirmary is registered in **Ballot Box No. 13** in Jim Wells County.

- **West Texas** becomes a major oil-producing area with drilling of discovery well in Scurry County in November.

1949 - Herman Barnett becomes the **first black student** at The University of Texas Medical Branch in Galveston on Aug. 24.

1950 - U.S. Supreme Court orders **racial integration of University of Texas law school**. Suit had been brought in the name of Heman Marion Sweatt, a Houston post office employee.

1953 - Dwight D. Eisenhower becomes **first Texas-born President** of the United States.

- **Tornado** on May 11 kills 114, injures 597 at Waco; 150 homes, 185 other buildings destroyed.

- **Tidelands Bill**, signed by Pres. Eisenhower on May 22, gives Texas the rights to its offshore oil.

1954 - Women gain **right to serve on juries**.

1956 - The **least annual rainfall** ever recorded in Texas falls at Wink: 1.76 inches.

1958 - Jack Kilby develops idea for **silicon chip** at Texas Instruments, ushering in the semiconductor and electronics age.

1961 - John Tower wins a special election for U.S. Senate and becomes the **first Republican senator** from Texas since Reconstruction.

1962 - NASA opens **Manned Spacecraft Center** offices in leased facilities in Houston.

1963 - Nov. 22, President **John F. Kennedy is assassinated** in Dallas; vice president Lyndon Johnson succeeds to the office, becoming the 36th U.S. president.

1964 - Houston's **Manned Spacecraft Center** moves to new campus-like building complex. Mission Control moves to new facilities in 1965.

1965 - Texas Legislature is reapportioned on the principle of **one man, one vote.**

- San Antonio native Ed White becomes **first American to walk in space.**

1966 - **Poll tax** repealed as a requirement for voting by amendment of the Texas Constitution.

- Barbara Jordan of Houston becomes **first black elected to Texas Senate** since Reconstruction (see related article elsewhere in this edition).

- **Charles Whitman** kills 17 people on Aug. 1, shooting them from the observation deck of the main building tower on the University of Texas campus in Austin.

1969 - Apollo 11 astronaut Neil Armstrong transmits the **first words from the surface of the moon**: "Houston, Tranquility Base here. The Eagle has landed."

1971 - Securities and Exchange Commission investigates illegal manipulation of stock transactions involving Frank Sharp and his Sharpstown State Bank of Houston. **Sharpstown Scandal** results in the conviction of House speaker Gus Mutscher and two associates for consipracy and bribery in 1972.

Texas City, 1947 (See item at left). Dallas Morning News *file photo.*

1950 - Sen. Joseph McCarthy holds hearings investigating **un-American activities.**

1950-1953 - Korean War.

1954 - Racial **segregation of schools ruled unconstitutional** by U.S. Supreme Court.

1958 - First domestic jet airline passenger service begins in U.S.

1961 - Soviet Yuri Gagarin becomes **first human in space.**

- **Berlin Wall** built.

1962 - **Environmental movement** begins in United States with publication of Rachel Carson's Silent Spring.

1964 - **Civil Rights Act** prohibits discrimination in employment and in public accommodations, princially hotels and restaurants.

1965 - United States troops begin massive build-up in **Vietnam.**

1966 - **Medicare** coverage of citizens over 65 years of age begins in United States.

1968 - Soviet troops invade **Czechoslovakia**.

1969 - July 20, **Apollo 11** lands on the moon.

1971 - Voting age lowered from 21 to 18 in U.S. by constitutional amendment.

1978 - William Clements becomes **first Republican governor of Texas** since Reconstruction.

1979 - Several tornadoes on April 10 leave 53 dead in West Texas, including 42 in Wichita Falls and causing $400 million in damages.

1984 - Education reform passes Legislature, including provisions for equalization of financial aid for public education, more stringent teacher certification, and setting academic achievement as a priority, including adoption of a no-pass-no-play rule.

- **National Republican Convention** held in Dallas.

1985 - Federal Home Loan Bank Board suspends deposit insurance for **Texas savings-and-loan companies** applying for state charters.

1988 - Houstonian **George Bush** is elected president of the United States.

- Federal regulators announce **bail-out plans for a large number of Texas thrifts** and begin prosecution of S&L officials after uncovering widespread insider abuse at Texas lending institutions.

1990 - Ann Richards becomes the **first woman governor** of Texas in her own right.

1993 - April 19 - Ending a siege which began on Feb. 28, federal agents storm the compound called Mount Carmel near Waco, where cult leader David Koresh and his followers, called **Branch Davidians**, had reportedly been storing a large cache of assault weapons. The assault and ensuing fire killed 4 agents and 86 Branch Davidians.

- Kay Bailey Hutchison becomes **first woman to serve as U.S. Senator** from Texas. ☆

1973 - Roe vs. Wade decision of Supreme Court ensures freedom of choice in abortion decisions.

- OPEC **oil embargo** leads to long lines of vehicles at gasoline pumps nationwide.

1984 - Canadian Prime Minister Pierre **Trudeau resigns** after serving for 15 years.

1989 - Berlin Wall torn down.

1994 - Jan. 1 - North American Free Trade Agreement (NAFTA), signed into law by Pres. Bill Clinton on Dec. 8, 1993, goes into effect, easing restrictions on trade among Canada, Mexico and the United States. ☆

The editor wishes to thank the following historians for their generous help in reviewing this timeline: ***Robert A. Calvert,*** *Ph.D., Professor of History, Texas A&M University, College Station;* ***Randolph B. Campbell****, Ph.D., Professor of History, The University of North Texas, Denton;* ***Dorothy D. DeMoss****, Ph.D., Professor of History, Texas Woman's University, Denton;* ***Harriett Denise Joseph****, Ph.D., Professor of History, The University of Texas at Brownsville;* ***Milo Kearney****, Ph.D., Professor of History, The University of Texas at Brownsville;* ***David J. Murrah****, Ph.D., Associate Director of Libraries for Special Collections and Director, Southwest Collection, Texas Tech University, Lubbock. Any errors are the editor's own.*

Texas in 1850

The first Texas Almanac, published in 1857, included these items (paraphrased) from the United States census of 1850:

Population: Texas had a population of 212,592, including 154,034 white and 58,558 black. Of those, 137,050 were born in the United States and 16,774 were foreign-born.

Occupations: 7,327 were engaged in manufacturing, commerce and trade; 25,299 in agriculture; 6,194 in non-agricultural labor; 584 in the army; 321 in sea and river navigation; 1,368 in the professions of law, medicine and divinity; 996 in "other pursuits requiring learning"; 677 in the government civil service; and 90 in other occupations.

Agriculture: There were 12,198 plantations, encompassing 643,967 acres of improved land and 10,852,363 acres of unimproved. Cotton was raised on 2,262 plantations; 165 were devoted to sugar.

Newspapers: Five tri-weekly and 29 weekly papers were printed in Texas with an combined circulation of 771,524 copies annually.

Only the ruins of an attempt to rebuild the old fort in 1936 mark the site of historic Real Presidio de San Sabá. The Spanish established the presidio in 1757 as protection for a mission whose purpose was to convert the Apaches to Roman Catholicism. Texas Almanac photo.

Fate of Spanish Mission Changed Face of West Texas

by Mike Kingston

The town of Menard is today a quiet West Texas town with an economy that relies on ranching and oil. But in 1757, four forces converged on the area to play their distinctive roles in history: the Spanish and the French from Europe, the Apaches and the Comanches from the northern regions of what later became the United States.

The drama played out in the bottoms of the San Saba River, and a year later on the banks of the Red River 200 miles away, had its beginnings almost two centuries before, when Spanish military might began cutting a swath across the New World, following its discovery in 1492 by Christopher Columbus. Led by Cortés, Pizarro, Quesada, Valdivia, Mendoza, Cabeza de Vaca and others, Spanish soldiers, mounted and using firearms, overcame the New World inhabitants.

The Spanish at first blush were the most formidable of the forces coming together in 1757 in West Central Texas. Spain's army had once been the best in Europe. In the New World, the natives could not effectively oppose the Spanish, and French forces on the North American continent at this time were no match, either.

Caribs. Aztec. Inca. Maya. Chichimec. Each New World civilization fell to the firepower of Spanish muskets fired from the backs of Spanish horses.

The Indians of the Valley of Mexico were accustomed to the control of a centralized state and were relatively easy for the Spaniards to subjugate. Only occasionally did determined New World Indians, like the Maya of the Yucatan, who were decentralized and lived in city-states, or the Pueblos of New Mexico, temporarily defeat Spanish arms.

Except for the Pueblos, however, the Spaniards enountered Indians with decentralized societies while moving northward from the Aztec empire.

Plains Indians were the most decentralized of all, not even having permanent settlements. Against the Plains Indians of North America, the Spaniards' luck ran out.

Goals of the Europeans in the New World varied. The French traded goods to the Indians for furs and gave them firearms so they could both hunt and defend themselves better. The Spanish goal was to convert Indians and turn them into exploitable copies of themselves. Conflict was inevitable.

Plains Indians Migrate into Texas

Neither the Comanches nor the Apaches were native Texas Indians. At the time of Coronado's expedition of 1540, neither tribe was in the region of today's Texas. Wichitas and Tonkawas migrated south even later. The Caddoes of East Texas, the Karankawas of the Gulf Coast and the Coahuiltecans of the Rio Grande were native.

Apaches, the first great foes of the Spanish in the early 18th century, were originally Athapaskan speakers from the Pacific Northwest. A fierce and warlike people, they migrated into the Rockies and eastward at an undetermined date.

At its peak, the territory of the eastern Apaches ranged from the Dismal River in Nebraska to Central Texas.

Even afoot, the Apaches were potent warriors who preyed on whomever they encountered. But after they acquired the large horse herds left behind by Spanish settlers fleeing the Pueblo Indian revolt in New Mexico in 1680, they became formidable. In a short period, mounted Apaches spread across the

Plains, in the pursuit of plunder and animals. Using horses, they could more easily follow the wandering bison that was the commissary of thousands of Indians. In the process, they made many enemies.

As the Apaches migrated, groups separated along the way. Some, like the Navajos, became sedentary.

Others, like those who finally came to Texas some time in the 17th century, became partly settled. During the summer, these Apaches camped in river bottoms to raise maize and other crops. Originally this group lived between the Red River and the Colorado plains.

Apaches never developed a full horse culture. But the Apaches did use horses to increase their mobility, allowing them to hunt bison more efficiently and to attack unmounted Indians on both the east and west fringes of the Great Plains.

No group, however, adapted to the use of horses more gracefully or completely than the groups within the mountain Shoshones of the far north who became the fearsome Comanches. They found horses to be not just a useful tool, but the answer to their dreams. The horse provided them mobility, honors in war, and respect from those who previously had despised and mistreated them. The horse became the linchpin of their culture.

The Comanches were completely nomadic and relied on bison to provide not only food but also clothing, and other necessities for living. They never camped anywhere for long.

Their raiding range on foot was about 100 miles. On horseback, it increased to 800 miles. Lengthy journeys for a hunt or a raid were common. On hunts, the entire band traveled.

No one knows when the Apaches drew the enmity of the Comanches. But about 1700, the Comanches moved south of the Arkansas River and began driving the Apaches from the plains.

Comanches fought mounted, using firearms or short bows, and occasionally lances.

The sedentary agricultural cycle of the Apaches proved to be their undoing. Comanches roamed the plains during the growing season, attacking and destroying the Apaches' agricultural camps. Since the Apaches were not the horsemen that the Comanches were, they could not effectively pursue and fight back.

For a time, the French sold guns to the Wichitas and the Apaches, among others. The Comanches took the commerce in weapons as a personal affront. In response, they barred the French from crossing the plains, preventing the French from opening trade with the Spanish colonists on the upper Rio Grande valley along what later became the Santa Fe Trail. After the Apaches were routed, the Comanches developed trade with the French, also allowing them to use the Comanche range.

As the Comanches continued their campaign against the Apaches, which lasted several generations, they moved into the Texas Panhandle. As many as 13 bands operated in Texas during historical times. The Panhandle was the most fertile bison range on the Great Plains. For the first time, the Comanches began to defend their hunting area from other tribes.

Spanish Establish East Texas Missions

As early as 1690, when the Spanish had first ventured into the Piney Woods of East Texas, they had earned the enmity of the Apaches. Not only did the Spanish build two missions among the Caddoan tribes of the area, they also aided the Caddoes in battles against the Apaches. Although the Apaches later appeared to cooperate in Spanish efforts to turn them into replicas of Spanish peasants, the Apaches never forgot this early insult. When the San Antonio de Valero mission (now known as the Alamo) was established in 1718, it was time for revenge.

After an Apache raid on San Antonio in 1723, the Spanish sent a punitive expedition against the marauders. Led by Capt. Nicolás Flores y Valdés, the soldiers headed north and located an Apache camp near present-day Brownwood. In an apparent violation of Spanish policy, the soldiers killed 34 warriors and captured many women and children.

Between 1726 and 1731, Apache raids diminished. The Comanches were hammering the Apaches southward, and the temporary lull may have been an Apache attempt to attract missions and the protection they afforded.

Spanish Policy Clarified

A decree outlining Spanish policy was issued by Viceroy Juan de Acuña, Marqués de Casafuerte in 1729. This decree, which bound the frontier for 40 years, forbade attacks on Indians unless attempts to make peace had been tried and had failed. The Spanish military was not to take sides in disagreements between Christianized tribes, and soldiers were not to stir up trouble with mission Indians. And finally, when any group of Indians sued for peace, the Spanish were bound to honor the request.

However, in 1732 the Apaches again began to harass the San Antonio settlement. This led to another military expedition up the San Saba River to within 10 miles of present-day Menard. The expedition was led by the newly appointed governor, Don Juan Antonio Bustillo y Caballos.

Bustillo engaged the Apaches in a four-hour battle Dec. 9, 1732. The 100 Spanish soldiers forced the Apaches to retreat and captured 30 women and children. Historians believe that the battle was on the San Saba River in the vicinity of the site where the San Sabá mission was later established.

Bustillo is credited with discovering the river and naming it El Rio San Sabá de las Nueces, in honor of the abbot, Saint Sabbas, whose feast day it was.

Comanches First Recorded in Texas

The first documented sighting of Comanches in Texas was about 1743, when a group passed near San Antonio. The Spanish had traded with them in New Mexico, however, for many years.

Missions were opened in 1748 on the San Xavier (today's San Gabriel) River, near present-day Rockdale, Milam County. These also were unsuccessful, partly because of constant Apache pressure on them.

However, beginning in the late 1740s, Apaches resumed making overtures to the Spanish government. The Apaches knew that the Spanish were so eager for religious converts that they would protect them from the Comanches, who continued to push the Apaches southward.

Franciscan priests saw in these Apache overtures opportunities for converting the indigenous peoples to Christianity and making them into useful Spanish citizens. The Spanish government soon decided to establish missions in Apache territory.

By the middle of the 18th century, the Comanches had all but driven the Apaches from the plains. The Spanish seemed unaware that the Apaches had lost control of the lower plains.

By this time, the Apaches could not safely hunt on the plains, and many started raiding south of the Rio Grande. The mission of San Juan Bautista, near present-day Eagle Pass on the Mexican side of the river, was a popular gathering place. The mission San Lorenzo, about 50 miles west of San Juan Bautista, was established in 1754 for Apaches. But the Indians burned the buildings and headed north within two years, complaining that the mission was too far from their homelands.

Mounted and armed with French weapons, the Wichitas, Caddoes, Tonkawas, Tawakonis, Kichais and others banded together against the Apaches. These former bully boys had raided into East and Central Texas as Comanche pressure drove them off the plains. Soon the united tribes were joined by their former foes, the Comanches, to present a formidable front to face the Apaches. The goal of these Norteños, as the Spanish called them, was to exterminate the remaining Apaches. Desperate for help, the Apaches absorbed some smaller Texas tribes, such as Coahuiltecan groups and the Jumanos of the Rio Grande area, both of which had once been bitter enemies of the Apaches.

But the Apaches got little help or sympathy from anyone else on the plains — except the Spanish. In 1749 the Spanish and the Apaches solemnized their peace agreement, with a formal ceremony held in San Antonio, in which implements of war, including a live horse, were buried.

Almost immediately, the new relationship caused friction with the Spaniards' other Indian friends. The treaty was condsidered an act of hostility against the Apaches' enemies — the Comanches and their allies, the Norteños. It didn't help, either, when Spanish soldiers gave Apaches protection on their hunting forays onto the plains.

The Apaches' presence around the San Gabriel missions frightened the neophytes, and many of them left. Disease epidemics also hit the San Gabriel location, and a drought dried up water supplies. Capt. Felipe Rábago y Terán, commander of the presidio, was accused of improprieties with the wives of soldiers and neophytes alike. Some of his soldiers were charged with abusing Indians. Rábago's uncle, Pedro, replaced him as commanding officer and finally abandoned the presidio in August of 1755. The missions were moved to the San Antonio River.

While the Spanish government acknowledged that missions in what is now West Central Texas were desirable, it provided no funds to pay for them. Then Pedro Romero de Terreros, one of the wealthiest men in Mexico, offered to finance the first three years of operation of missions created to convert the Apaches. His cousin, Father Alonso Giraldo de Terreros, was to lead the missionary effort.

The first of several expeditions to find a suitable site for the Apache missions in 1753 was led by Lt. Juan Galván. Fray Miguel de Aranda of the mission Concepción in San Antonio helped. After viewing sites on the Pedernales and Llano rivers, they selected a location on the San Saba River near today's Menard. Lt. Galván set up a huge wooden cross on a horseshoe bluff overlooking the river to mark the spot for the presidio, and a religious service was held. Several Apaches were already in the area.

It took four years and two more exploratory expeditions for the Spanish government to confirm Lt. Galván's original decision. Pedro de Rábago y Terán was dispatched to the same area in November 1754. Finally, Col. Diego Ortiz Parrilla, who had been appointed commander of the presidio, and Father Terreros, with soldiers, missionaries, nine families of Tlaxcalan Indians and others arrived on April 17, 1757. Work began immediately on the presidio and mission buildings.

The Spanish didn't seem to realize that the site they had chosen was in Comanche territory, not Apache.

Building of San Sabá Mission and Presidio

Within a short time after arrival on the San Saba River in April 1757, the soldiers completed the presidio stockade, and the friars constructed a mission compound. The mission was formally christened Santa Cruz (Holy Cross) de San Sabá and the presidio, Presidio de San Luis de las Amarillas, in honor of the viceroy of New Spain. (We are spelling the name of the river without an accent, since that is the way it is spelled today, but the correct Spanish spelling of "San Sabá" is used here for the mission.)

The priests wanted to prevent a recurrence of the problems experienced at the San Gabriel missions. They insisted that the mission and the presidio be on

This painting, called "The Destruction of the Mission San Sabá," is considered by art historians to be the oldest painting on canvas about Texas. It was commissioned in 1763 by the prominent Romero de Terreros family of Mexico City to memorialize Father Terreros, who was killed during the attack.

opposite sides of the river and 1.5 leagues apart (about 3.94 miles). This made defense of the mission nearly impossible.

The San Sabá mission was of standard design. Within a wooden compound there was a small church, classrooms, storehouses and workshops. Herds of livestock and horses were established near the compound, and nearby fields were broken and crops planted.

Although the mission was ready to begin operation, no Indians came, much to the frustration of the friars. In June, about 3,000 Apaches camped near the facility, but they did not enter. They planned to go on their annual bison hunt and then campaign against the Norteños.

After that only small groups of Apaches passed the mission, rapidly heading south.

Frustration mounted during the winter of 1757-58 because the Apaches had not kept their word to enter the mission. Three disheartened friars returned to San Antonio; only three missionaries remained.

In February 1758, marauding Indians attacked a supply train bound for the presidio. Late in the month, the same group scattered the presidio's horse herds after taking 59 animals for their own use. Spanish soldiers chased the raiders for eight days, but recovered only one horse. They reported that armed Indians were to been seen all around the area. The presidio went on alert.

By March 15, Col. Parrilla was concerned enough to send a soldier to the mission to urge the friars and their people to come to the presidio. But the missionaries declined. The commander made a personal plea in the afternoon, but the friars were adamant. Eight soldiers were left at the facility, making 35 people in all at the mission. Parrilla also provided lookouts to try to protect the mission from surprise attack. The commander was left with 59 men with which to defend the presidio.

Mission Attacked

Early on the morning of March 16, Juan Leal, a 50-year-old civilian servant for Father Terreros, went to the creek near the mission compound to cut some wood. He was surprised and captured by Indians. But he was recognized as a friend and protected from death by one of the raiders. As far as he could see, there were Indians armed with muskets, swords and lances and painted for war. A few boys riding with the force carried bows and arrows.

The gates of the mission stockade were closed when the mounted horde approached. But there were Tejas, Bidais and Tonkawas among the Indians, and these groups had been at the San Gabriel mission. The soldiers recognized many familiar faces and opened the gates.

Many mounted Indians entered the compound, including a Comanche chief dressed in a red jacket in the style of the French. Father Terreros tried to appease the throng by distributing gifts and tobacco. Other Indians scattered throughout the compound, taking what they wanted from the storehouses. The Spanish did not interfere.

All the mission's horses were rounded up and taken by the Indians, and a chief asked for more. There were no more at the mission, Father Terreros said, but there were horses at the presidio. The chief left with a group of Indians. A short time later, he returned and said the soldiers at the presidio had fired at him. Father Terreros offered to escort the chief back to the fort. But when the priest mounted a horse and started to leave the stockade, he was shot dead.

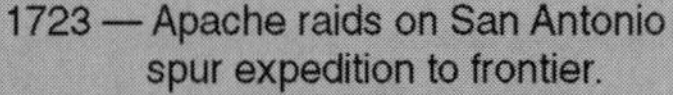

1723 — Apache raids on San Antonio spur expedition to frontier.
1732 — Bustillo's battle with Apaches on San Saba River.
1753 — Mission site selected.
1757 — Spanish and allied Indians build mission, presidio.
1758 — Mission burned. Fathers Terreros, Santiesteban killed.
1759 — Spanish retaliatory force pursues Indians to Red River.
1761 — Presidio rebuilt of stone.
1767 — Inspection tour by Marqués de Rubí.
1772 — Spanish close presidio.

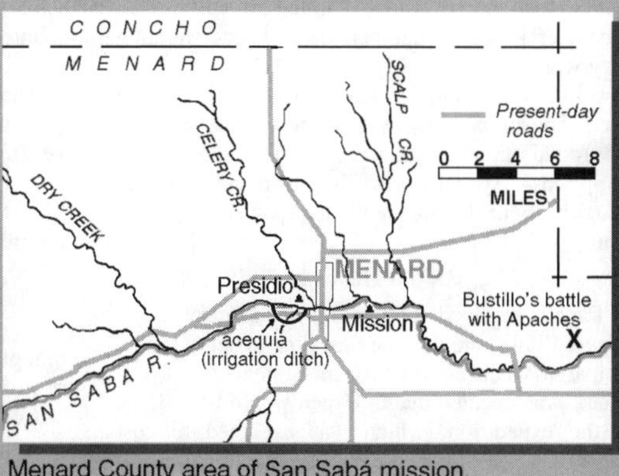

Menard County area of San Sabá mission.

A melee erupted and the Spanish ran for cover. Another priest, Father José de Santiesteban, was probably killed while praying before the altar of the small church. Several other people were wounded. The battle continued most of the day. The small group of Spaniards holed up in building after building, moving as the Indians set each structure on fire. They finally fled into the chapel. Leal, who had escaped from his captors, dragged a small cannon into the building, mounted it on some chests and kept the Indians at bay until the raiders became more interested in looting than in killing Spaniards. All that they could not carry away was destroyed. That night the Norteños held a grand victory celebration that was heard at the presidio.

Early in the battle, a messenger was sent from the mission to the presidio for help. He told of Indians painted for war and carrying French firearms, bullet pouches and powder horns. A scouting party, led by Sgt. Joseph Antonio Flores, was sent to survey the situation from a hill south of the mission. From that vantage point, he saw Indians spread out for miles around the mission. The stockade was overrun. Flores' small party also engaged a band of Indians, suffering three casualties.

After dark 28 defenders of the mission escaped, including several with serious wounds, and reached the safety of the presidio. A scouting party sent to see about the people of the mission also dispatched two soldiers to warn a nearby wagon train of the danger. Spaniards estimated that 1,500 to 2,000 Indians had been involved in the war party. An estimated 17 Indian raiders died during the fighting at the fort and in small skirmishes.

Col. Parrilla had taken many precautions at the presidio. Soldiers scattered around the area on various assignments were called in, and the families of the soldiers were given the protection of the fort.

Patrols sent out on the morning of March 17 found the Indians rapidly retreating to the north.

Visiting the smoldering mission ruins, Parrilla found that two priests and six others had been massacred.

In his reports to his superiors, Col. Parilla absolved himself of any blame for the loss of life. He emphasized that he had tried to get the missionaries to enter the presidio, but that because of the fragmented authority of the operation, he had no standing to order the religious to do anything.

To emphasize the French threat to the province of Texas, Col. Parrilla pointed out that each victim of the raid died of bullet or lance wounds; none was killed by arrows.

The frontier was swept with the reports of the audacious attack by the Plains Indians. Every presidio commander on the frontier was afraid that his installation would be the next one to be attacked by the savage hordes Norteños.

The attack on the San Sabá mission marked the beginning of warfare between Comanches and white settlers — a war that continued for more than a century.

Retaliatory Expedition Planned

Col. Parrilla wanted to mount a punitive expedition against the Norteños immediately. But the Spanish had much to ponder. The attack was the first by such a large body of Indians. They were better armed and fought better than Indians in the past. No doubt there was some French influence in their weapons, clothing and tactics. The makeup of the raiding party, too, was a new development. Comanches, Bidais, Tonkawas and Tejas, who previously had not been enemies, were among the leaders of the raiding party. The Spanish were beginning to understand the magnitude of the consequences of embracing the Apaches.

Spanish colonial bureaucracy moved slowly in the best of times. When questions were raised about the wisdom of an action, the process could grind to a near halt. Compounding the usual slow pace was the fact that no one was sure where the San Saba River project fit into the colonial organization.

While the Spanish pondered their next actions, the Norteños continued to raid. In 1758, they struck a camp near the presidio and killed 50 Apaches. In December 1758, 17 members of an Apache hunting party were killed. In early 1759, 20 Spanish guards were killed near the presidio and 700 horses were taken. The Indians appeared to be reveling in their new-found supremacy over the former scourges of the plains. Apaches also began having second thoughts about the ability of the Spanish to protect them.

Raid a Disaster

Parrilla received approval for a retaliatory raid in August 1758. June was the best time to begin such a campaign because forage for the animals was available. It was decided that 500 men would be ordered on the expedition, which was expected to cost 59,000 pesos. Soldiers were to be drawn from several presidios. Tlaxcalan Indians from Mexico, along with mission Indians, would be used. The viceroy sent Parrilla final approval of his plans in May 1759. More delays followed, but the force finally left San Antonio in August.

Moving north, the group crossed the Concho River near present day Paint Rock and forded the Colorado downstream from today's Ballinger. Then it turned northeast, crossing the Clear Fork of the Brazos near present day Fort Griffin. Near today's Newcastle in Young County, the Spaniards attacked a Tonkawa village, killing 55 Indians and taking 149 prisoners. Plunder from the San Sabá mission was found among the villagers' belongings. This victory made the campaign worthwhile in Col. Parrilla's mind. But the Tonkawas offered information on the location of a large Wichita village on the Red River, still farther to the northeast.

A Tonkawa guide was taken to lead the way. On "Day Seven" (of October) by Parrilla's accounting, the expedition reached the vicinity of the Wichita camp in present-day Montague County. Today the location is known as Spanish Fort, because early Anglo settlers were unaware that the French had been in the area. And they did not believe the Indians could have built the fortifications whose remains they found.

As the Spanish approached the village, a group of Indians ambushed them and then retreated at a run. The Spanish pursued them down a wooded road until they entered a clearing facing a stockaded village. The Indians took cover in the village and closed the gates.

The village was well organized. The Spanish reported seeing herds of horses grazing nearby and corrals near the village. Crops were growing in irrigated fields along the river. Over the village flew a French flag. (Spanish critics have argued that presence of the French flag did not mean Frenchmen were present. The French often gave flags to Indians with whom they traded.)

The Spanish withdrew to regroup. But the Indians in the stockade kept a stream of fire aimed at them, cutting off the road as an escape route. Both mounted Indians and some on foot sallied forth from the fort and engaged the Spanish.

The Apaches and missionary Indians with the Spanish force broke ranks, leaving Spanish flanks open to the attacking Norteños. Sixteen Spaniards died in the action along with three of their Indian allies. Parrilla claimed that 45 enemy Indians died. At dark, the Spanish retreated. At dawn, they began the long trip back to the San Saba.

The experience reaffirmed Parrilla's initial assessment: Great changes were needed in selecting, equipping and training Spain's military on the northern frontier. Nothing was done by the authorities.

Col. Parrilla lost prestige in the expedition against the Norteños. Though he tried to paint the effort as a success because of the victory at the Tonkawa village, no other official embraced his position. The Norteños were not chastised.

After a decade of exile, Capt. Rábago was once again given command of the presidio in 1760.

Presidio Rebuilt of Stone

Apparently anxious to redeem his reputation, Rábago strengthened the fortifications in late 1761 by rebuilding the presidio of stone and renamed it the Real (Royal) Presidio de San Sabá. But much more change was needed than the officer could provide.

New Spain's northern frontier had a serious sag in it around the Great Plains. With the Comanches in control of these plains and their enemies, the Apaches, running amok south of the plains, no short route between San Antonio and the Spanish settlements on the upper Rio Grande existed.

To travel from San Antonio to the capital of the New Mexican colony, the Spaniards were forced to head south through Laredo and on to Saltillo. The route swung west through Durango province to Chihuahua City and then north up the Rio Grande Valley through El Paso to Santa Fe. That was a distance of roughly 990 miles to cover a route of about 500 miles as the crow flies. And none of the route was safe from Indian attacks.

Rábago sent out expeditions in 1761 that explored large sections of western Texas and located the Pecos River. But none ever came close to Santa Fe. An expedition sent south from near Santa Fe to San Sabá presidio a year later had no luck either.

Later Missions

With the zeal of a recent convert, Rábago pursued establishment of missions for the Apaches without prior authorization by the viceroy. In 1762, San Lorenzo de la Santa Cruz mission was opened for the Apaches on the Nueces River, with Nuestra Señora de la Candelaria del Cañon opening nearby a little later. Initially the missions attracted 400 Apaches, but for eight years, they got no support from the crown.

Together the missions were referred to as "El

Cañón." They were located about halfway between San Sabá and San Juan Bautista.

The year 1762 became a watershed year for Spain's northern frontier. In Europe, the Seven Years War ended, with Great Britain prevailing over France. Spain joined the war late on the side of the loser and gave up claims to Florida and other territory for its trouble. France ceded the Louisiana Territory to Spain to keep it out of British hands.

With the long-standing French threat eliminated, Texas became a large buffer zone. Spain turned its attention to keeping English settlers from entering its new territory.

In 1766, an even larger change took place, as Charles III undertook to reorganize the northern frontier of New Spain. The Marqués de Rubí was sent to tour the frontier and to recommend changes. His survey would eventually cover more than 7,000 miles from California on the west to East Texas.

Rubí arrived at the San Sabá presidio in July of 1767 and stayed 10 days. Apparently he was appalled by what he found. Soldiers were short of horses. Only half had pistols. Most of the equipment was shabby and in poor condition. Morale was low; the desertion rate was high.

Rubí noted in a secret report that the presidio cost 40,360 pesos a year to operate and was of no use to the kingdom. He suggested that the improvements be razed and the few settlers around the presidio be shipped to San Antonio. The military manpower could be put to better use on the Rio Grande, he said.

Indians raids had subsided for a few years before Rubí's visit, but after his departure they began again. One raid netted the Indians the presidio's entire herd of cattle. The marauders also kept up raids on supply trains, in an apparent attempt to starve the Spanish out.

Rábago abandoned the fort without authorization at one time in 1768, withdrawing the men to El Cañón, but he was ordered to return. Although still in his 40s, Rábago was in failing health. He began a trip to see the viceroy in 1769, but he died before reaching his destination. Later in the year, Capt. Manuel Antonio de Oca was named commander of the San Sabá presidio.

Little improved under the new commander. In 1770, he, too, apparently abandoned the San Sabá presidio without authorization, again taking the soldiers to El Cañón.

Presidio Closed

King Charles III delivered the coup de grace to the foundering fort, ordering it closed in his decree of reorganization of the frontier in 1772.

Closing the presidio may have been as great a mistake as opening it: As soon at it closed, Indian raids on San Antonio increased alarmingly.

The facilities at San Sabá were never razed as Rubí recommended, and they came in handy with future Indian fighters. Gov. Juan de Ugalde of Coahuila (namesake of Uvalde County despite the difference in spelling) led a successful expedition of Spaniards allied with Comanches, Wichitas and Tonkawas against Apaches in 1789. If such an alliance had been struck 40 years earlier, the face of North America might have been changed.

As it was, the massacre at the mission on the San Saba and the subsequent Spanish defeat at the Red River marked the end to Spain's dreams of conquest and conversion on their northern frontier in the New World. ☆

For Further Reading

The San Sabá Mission: Spanish Pivot in Texas by Robert S. Weddle; The University of Texas Press, Austin, 1964.

Spanish Texas, 1519-1821, by Donald E. Chipman; The University of Texas Press, Austin, 1992.

The Spanish Borderlands Frontier, 1513-1821 by John Francis Bannon; Holt, Rinehart and Winston, Inc., 1963; reprinted by University of New Mexico Press, 1974.

***The author:** Mike Kingston was editor of the Texas Almanac from 1981 until his death in 1994. Kingston had prepared the history of Santa Cruz de San Sabá mission for this edition of the Almanac, and we present it here, edited to include the latest research.*

The Search for Santa Cruz de San Sabá

by Mary G. Ramos, editor of The Texas Almanac

Santa Cruz de San Sabá has been called "the lost mission of Texas." Although its short history, from founding to destruction, has been well documented, its exact location has been unknown until recently.

The 1993 discovery of the mission site in an alfalfa field east of Menard resulted from the latest of several attempts to find it. And the effort was spearheaded by Mark Wolf, a San Antonio architect who is a direct lineal descendant of one of the survivors of the 1758 massacre — Juan Leal. Leal was the civilian servant of Father Terreros who had been captured and spared by the raiders outside the mission walls just before the attack began — the Juan Leal who had set up a cannon to defend the desperate Spanish survivors during their retreat.

The presidio and mission structures built on the San Saba River in 1757 were temporary jacal or wattle-and-daub constructions (daub being a primitive mortar made from mud). Most of the mission was destroyed by fire during the Indian raid in 1758, and time and weather finished off anything that was left. The presidio was rebuilt of stone in 1761; its more permanent construction made its location easier to find.

Of course, the mission would have been more than just a church or chapel building. A mission was a complex of buildings, including small houses and workshops for carpenter, blacksmith and tailor, all enclosed by a log stockade. Often, a mission complex also included a cemetery.

Spanish colonial documents were detailed in many ways, but remained elusive in the description of this mission's site. They did mention that the mission was located one and a half leagues from the presidio site.

Previous Searches Unsuccessful

One of the earliest known searches for the site of Santa Cruz de San Sabá was by a newspaper editor and Texas history enthusiast named John Warren Hunter. Hunter moved to the town then called Menardville in 1884. He published a book in 1905 giving the history of the mission. In a footnote, Hunter referred to the mission's site as being "about three and a half miles below the presently flourishing town of Menardville, and is on what is known as the Hockensmith place..." This would prove to be an important piece of the puzzle, though it was evidently ignored for 90 years by subsequent searchers.

A historical marker commemorating the mission was placed by the state in 1936 about 2 miles east of Menard on Farm-to-Market Road 2092.

In 1956, Robert S. Weddle became owner and editor of the Menard News. When Franciscan priests made a pilgrimage to Menard in 1958 on the 200th anniversary of the massacre, Weddle launched his own research project into the mission's story. From an idea for a tourist pamphlet grew his classic and comprehensive history, "San Sabá Mission, Spanish Pivot in Texas," published in 1964.

In 1967, Kathleen Kirk Gilmore led a team of investigators, involving Southern Methodist University, the State Building Commission, and the office of the State Archeologist, in an investigation of the presidio site and a search for the lost mission. Gilmore figured that a Spanish league was equivalent to 2.63 miles, therefore the mission site should be 3.94 miles from the presidio. Although Gilmore did not find the site, the translations of Spanish documents made during that attempt were helpful to subsequent hunters.

Architect Bruce Johnson's search, on behalf of the Texas Old Missions and Forts Restoration Association in 1984 and 1985, used infrared photography along with field surveys and mechanical testing. Although he was also unsuccessful, his excavations were only about 250 yards from the site.

Perhaps the most intensive search previous to 1993 was made in March 1990 by archaeologists and historians from Texas A&M University using archaeological, historical and geomorphological (the science dealing with the nature and origin of the earth's topographic features) studies. Six hundred acres east of Menard were studied, resulting in 18 possible sites, but none could be definitely identified as Spanish in origin. The geomorphological study revealed a number of former stream channels of the San Saba River.

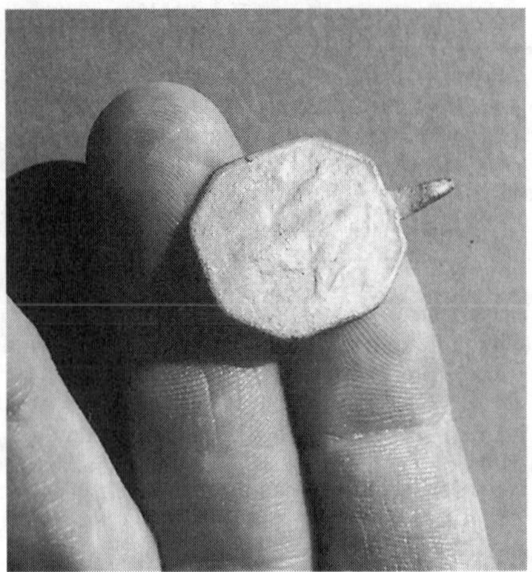

This religious medallion, found in an alfalfa field near Menard in early 1994, is typical of those brought to the New World by Spanish missionaries. They were presented to Indians who agreed to convert to Roman Catholicism. Photo courtesy Grant Hall, Texas Tech University.

Ancestor Search Sparks Investigation

Then came Mark Wolf. In doing research on his family history, Wolf discovered his seven-generation tie to Juan Leal, and he was determined to find the mission site. Wolf launched an exploration in March 1993 involving Kay Hindes, a free-lance archaeologist; Hindes enticed a team of archaeologists from Texas Tech University in Lubbock to join in the hunt.

The search began with aerial reconnaissance using infrared photography. A couple of possible sites were identified. Then Hindes found the reference in John Warren Hunter's 1905 report that the site was located on Hockensmith's property. Through deed records, Hindes traced the ownership of the 43-acre tract from Hockensmith to then-County Judge Otis Lyckman and his wife Dionitia. The site met all the requirements of the Spanish: access to a reliable water source, ample timber for buildings and fuel. It also matched the bits of description of the site that had been gleaned from Spanish documents of the day. The site is also 3.95 miles from the presidio location, a tribute to Kathleen Gilmore's calculations.

First Solid Evidence Found

On a day in September 1993, the researchers drove past the Lyckman's alfalfa field and noticed that it had been recently plowed. Stopping only long enough to gain permission to enter the property, the team members walked over the field, carefully scanning the recently turned dirt. Then Hindes picked up a ceramic fragment, wiped the dirt from it, and realized that its pale green glaze was that of a Spanish olive jar. Triumphantly, she told the others, "This is what we've been looking for."

Further investigation turned up concentrations of burned daub. The clay-rich dirt that had been packed into the cracks in the wooden walls of the mission had hardened like pottery in the heat of the fire when the Indians burned the compound, and chunks of it were lying all over the plowed field.

Test excavations directed by Texas Tech archaeologist Grant Hall in January 1994 went below the surface zone that had been disturbed by modern plowing. The archaeologists identified soil stains left by wooden poles and posts used in building the mission. Metal detectors helped pinpoint more than 400 metal finds, many of them such modern detritus as ring-pull tabs from soft-drink cans or metal ear tags for goats. However, 124 specimens of probably Spanish Colonial origin were also found, among them a wealth of iron nails, hinges, latches and hooks; a copper thimble; religious ornaments; pieces of bridle bit; and numerous lead musket balls. Also found were shards of Majolica, a tin-enameled ceramic; buttons; trade beads; bone; and basalt metate fragments.

Hindes says that one of the most remarkable artifacts is a tiny religious medallion. Although the image on the medallion has not yet been identified, Spanish inventories of the supplies shipped to the San Sabá mission include such medallions, which were given to Indians who agreed to come into the mission for conversion.

Anne Fox, director of the archaeology laboratory at The University of Texas at San Antonio and an authority on Spanish Colonial missions, says that in her mind, there is no doubt that the site is the San Sabá mission site.

Plans for full-scale archaeological dig at the site include stripping the alfalfa field of the layer of dirt that has been disturbed by modern agricultural practices, then investigating the site through painstaking hand excavation. The exact location of each find will be mapped and described, thereby revealing details of life at the mission.

At press time, plans for such a full-scale investigation were on hold awaiting funding. ☆

For Further Reading:

"The Rediscovery of Santa Cruz de San Sabá: A Mission for the Apache in Spanish Texas" by V. Kay Hindes, Mark R. Wolf, Grant D. Hall, and Kathleen Kirk Gilmore; San Saba Regional Survey Report 1, Archaeology Laboratory, Texas Tech University; Texas Historical Foundation, Austin, and Texas Tech University, 1995.

This temperance rally was held in El Campo some time between 1913 and 1919. It was typical of those held in towns all across Texas as women organized to make changes in their lives and the lives of their families. Photo from The Institute of Texan Cultures, San Antonio, courtesy the El Campo Leader-News.

The Road to Women's Rights in Texas

by Mary G. Ramos, editor, Texas Almanac

In the years of Spanish and Mexican colonization, independence and early statehood, many Texans lived in a rough frontier culture in which women plowed fields, planted and harvested crops and roped and branded cattle alongside men. But in legal and social matters, women were still governed by the traditions brought with them mainly from Britain and Europe, including the firmly ingrained idea that husband and wife were one, "and that one is the husband." However, they also brought their Old World respect for education and a desire for cultural enlightenment and diversions.

Women in the United States in the 18th and 19th centuries existed mainly within the circles of their homes. But certain organized activities were considered appropriate to their limited realm of responsibility. Women joined with other women outside the home to establish and support churches, synagogues, kindergartens, schools and libraries.

It was a natural extension of their primary role as protector and nurturer of their families for them also to band together to work for pure-food laws, better sanitation and other public-health matters in the 1800s. They worked to help families less fortunate than theirs in campaigns for legal reform, social welfare, child-labor laws, civil rights and prison reform.

The campaign for passage of the 18th Amendment to the U.S. Constitution — Prohibition — grew out of women's understanding of the link between uncontrolled alcoholism on one hand and domestic violence and poverty on the other. The male alcoholic could sell family property and spend paychecks on feeding his addiction. There was no legal protection for the wife and children.

As the women organized, lobbied and collected signatures on petitions for alcoholic abstinence, which they termed "temperance," they saw that their efforts to gain passage of the prohibition amendment would be enhanced if women could vote on the matter. Even women who considered voting an unwomanly business in general could see the benefit of being able to vote on this one issue.

The Beginnings of the Women's Movement

In the United States, the women's rights movement began in the 1830s and 1840s. At this time, the women settlers of Texas were concerned mainly with simply surviving in a sparsely populated, hazardous frontier environment.

Abolition of slavery was the cause that many American women found important enough that they were willing to push themselves onto the unfamiliar stage of public speaking.

When organizers of an 1840 abolitionists' convention in London refused to seat women delegates from the United States, Elizabeth Cady Stanton and Lucretia Mott made plans to call a women's rights convention in this country. Eight years in the planning, the Seneca Falls Convention, held in Seneca Falls, N.Y., July 19-20, 1848, was the organized beginning of the women's rights movement in the United States. The "Declaration of Sentiments" that was published by the convention paraphrased the U.S. Declaration of Independence: "We hold these truths to be self-evident: that all men *and women* are created equal . . . "

Resolutions called for educational opportunities for women, woman suffrage, changes in oppressive laws and an end to the double standard of behavior.

Press coverage of the convention, and of women's meetings over the next decade, was generally derisive and overwhelmingly negative. A women's rights meeting in New York City in 1853 was described in the New York Herald as an "assemblage of rampant women."

Among the supporters at the Seneca Falls meeting was well-known black abolitionist Frederick Douglass. He and the abolitionist press remained staunch and vocal allies of woman suffrage for the duration of the struggle. After the Seneca Falls convention, he wrote, "in respect to political rights, we hold woman to be justly entitled to all we claim for man . . . There can be no reason in the world for denying to woman the exercise of the elective franchise, or a hand in making and administering the laws of the land. Our doctrine is that 'right is of no sex.' "

From Civil War to 15th Amendment

The women's rights movement virtually stopped during the Civil War. Women during this period provided homefront support services: running hospitals; sewing, knitting and cooking for soldiers; and aiding the families of fighting men. Many women did "men's" work — managing plantations, farms and shops and working in government offices — while the males were serving in the military.

Abolition of slavery was formally added to the U.S. Constitution with ratification of the 13th Amendment on Dec. 18, 1865. It was the first of three amendments intended to assure full civil rights to former slaves.

After the Civil War, some women expected to be given the same freedoms and rights that had been granted to blacks. But many of the so-called freedoms existed only on paper and none of them applied to women. The 14th amendment to the U.S. Constitution, assuring full citizenship rights to all citizens, was finally ratified in July 1868. It specifically referred to voters as males. Black men finally had the right to vote, but not women of any race.

The first national women's rights convention after the war took place in 1866, and gaining the right to vote was the paramount goal. As the movement gathered momentum, opposition became more strident. In November 1866, the New York World managed to offend almost everyone in its description of equal-rights campaigners as "mummified and fossiliated females, void of domestic duties, habits and natural affections; crack-brained, rheumatic, dyspeptic, henpecked men . . . and oily-faced, insolent, gabbling negroes."

Cracks appeared in the heretofore solid front of the women's rights movement in the late 1860s. National movement leaders Elizabeth Cady Stanton and Susan B. Anthony demanded that the organization should not work for equal rights for blacks unless women's rights were granted simultaneously. They also included support of the labor-union movement and economic reform along with a vehement condemnation of capitalism. Frederick Douglass and another male supporter of women's rights, William Lloyd Garrison, advocated throwing all efforts behind passage of the 15th amendment — assuring voting rights for blacks — promising to support a separate amendment later for female suffrage. They believed that including too many other demands in the campaign for the 15th amendment would result in victory for none of them.

The 15th amendment was ratified early in 1870.

Texas Women Organize

As the campaign for woman suffrage was heating up on the national front in the early 1870s, Texas was still recovering from the Civil War and its rancorous aftermath. Texas women began to organize for cultural and educational reasons, much as their counterparts in more northern states had already done.

One of the first woman's clubs in Texas was the Victoria Literary Society. The Pictorial History of Victoria County gives 1873 as the year of the club's founding. It was later renamed the Brontë Club to honor English novelist Charlotte Brontë. The Ladies' Reading Circle of Houston followed in 1884.

Several developments aided the women's attempts to expand their rather narrow worlds:

•The university extension system, which evolved from a study program for English factory workers in 1789, was adopted by several U.S. universities. One of these was The University of Texas, which furnished a series of lectures to several Texas women's clubs.

•The Chautauqua movement began in 1874 in Lake Chautauqua, New York, primarily to train Sunday school teachers. It became a "people's university" in 1878, when it changed its name to the Chautauqua Literary and Scientific Circle, offering a four-year course of home study in history and literature.

•Women's clubs in Fort Worth, Denison and Sherman used materials from the Society to Encourage Studies at Home, founded in Boston in 1873. The society produced outlines for studies in literature, as well as correspondence courses.

The 1870s also saw the establishment among many ethnic groups of benevolent-aid societies to nurse the sick and care for orphans and the elderly.

Organizing to Fight Alcohol

On the national front, some women who couldn't bring themselves to join the women's-rights movement eagerly became members of the National

Women's Christian Temperance Union, which had organized in 1874.

The WCTU was respectable, not controversial. Leaving the sanctuary of the home for the purpose of marching, praying, singing, pouring liquor into gutters and taking axes to whiskey barrels was justified because it was done to protect the home and family.

Many WCTU members felt that too close an alliance with the forces of woman suffrage would threaten support from the church and the general public for their cause. The story is told that at a temperance meeting, one woman asked another why they couldn't have such a large turnout at suffrage meetings. The second woman's reply: "It is easier to see a drunkard than a principle."

But growing numbers of WCTU members saw suffrage as a way to have greater clout in the campaign to eliminate "demon rum." Some suffragists, discouraged by repeated failures to gain the vote on federal and state levels, narrowed their goals: They concentrated their efforts on gaining the right to vote in local elections. In doing so, they picked up more support from WCTU members, since wet-or-dry elections were often on a local-option basis. Delegates to the 1877 WCTU convention adopted a resolution favoring municipal suffrage. By 1890, 19 states had granted women the right to vote in school elections.

The WCTU reluctantly acknowledged in 1881 that temperance legislation was of such importance to the stability of the home that equal franchise was a necessary evil.

Texas entered the WCTU fold with the organization of a chapter in Paris in 1882. It was the first organized political effort of Texas women.

Black women, excluded from the white local WCTU clubs, formed their own chapters.

Suffrage Campaign Heats Up

Meanwhile, suffragists across the nation had made 527 separate attempts to persuade state legislatures or state constitutional conventions to place the question of woman suffrage before the voters. The matter made it to ballots only 17 times. And of those votes, only two were successful before 1900: Colorado in 1893 and Idaho in 1896. State constitutions in Wyoming and Utah contained woman suffrage provisions when those states entered the union in 1890 and 1896, respectively.

Nineteen campaigns were mounted to persuade Congress to approve a suffrage amendment.

Vying for the Vote in Texas

The experience that Texas women gained in speaking out for alcoholic abstinence gave them the confidence to organize for suffrage in 1887. They met with little early success. Rebecca Hayes of Galveston established the first statewide suffrage organization in the Lone Star State in 1893. The group was open to both men and women. Local affiliates were organized in Denison, Taylor and Granger.

Ironically, at this time Texas women were not prohibited from holding most state or county offices. They could not, however, be elected to the legislature or to most municipal offices.

The first woman suffrage amendment introduced in the Texas Legislature was presented to the House of Representatives in the spring of 1895 by A. C. Tompkins of Hempstead. It was referred to the committee on constitutional amendments and was never heard from again. Mrs. Hayes' organization died by 1896.

During the struggle for suffrage, one of the primary opponents was the brewery industry, knowing that many women would vote against alcohol.

From 1890 to 1920 there was a great increase in the number of women's organizations nationwide. Advances in birth control had halved the fertility rate from 1810 to 1900, resulting in smaller families. Machines lightened the burden of housework. Women had more time to further their educations and participate in outside activities by the turn of the century. The Daughters of the American Revolution (1891), the National Council of Jewish Women (1896), the National Association of Colored Women (1896), the National Congress of Mothers, later the PTA (1897), and the YWCA (1906) were established during this period. The numbers of educated women were growing, and professions were opening up to single women.

In 1890, the General Federation of Women's Clubs was formed. It organized member clubs into local, state and national groups. Within 20 years, the organization comprised almost a million members.

Following the national lead, the Woman's Club of Waco hosted a general convention of 18 Texas women's organizations in 1897. They formed the Texas Federation of Literary Clubs. The first program of work adopted by the fledgling federation was the establishment of public libraries across the state. By their meeting the following year, the member chapters had started circulating libraries, traveling libraries and reading rooms in many communities.

Broadening the Goals

By the second convention in 1899, delegates realized that their goals needed to be broader. Changing their emphasis from literature to education and social issues, they dropped "Literary" from the name. They also joined officials of the Patrons of Husbandry (the Texas State Grange), a farmers' organization, in urging the Legislature to establish the State Industrial School for Girls at Denton (several name changes later, it is now Texas Woman's University). In 1903, temperance leader and lobbyist Helen Stoddard of Fort Worth expressed the thinking behind support of a university for women. "A

Texas Women's Impact on Legislation, 1903-1954

Texas women, working together in women's and mothers' clubs, were directly responsible for passing these laws and programs from 1903 to 1954:

1903 — Girls Industrial College (now Texas Woman's University)
1906 — Pure Food Inspection
1907 — Juvenile Court System
1907 — Kindergartens in Public Schools
1909 — Juvenile Training School
1909 — State Library Commission
1910 — Sanitary Drinking Fountains
1913 — Married Women's Property Rights
1915 — Child Labor Laws
1915 — Compulsory School Attendance
1915 — Protection for Working Women
1917 — Aid to Dependent Children
1918 — Free School Textbooks
1919 — County Library Appropriations
1919 — Bureau of Child Hygiene
1921 — Maternal and Infant Health Program
1927 — Stronger School Attendance Law
1932 — Division of Child Welfare
1937 — Department of Public Welfare
1945 — State School for Negro Girls (now Crockett School)
1954 — Jury Service for Women

List reprinted from "Texas Women: A Celebration of History," published by the Texas Foundation for Women's Resources, Austin, 1981. Used by permission of the Foundation for Women's Resources, Austin.

young woman needs more than fitness for the home, since from choice or otherwise she may never have a home of her own. She must be fitted for an independent life . . . thoroughly equipped in some congenial self-supporting commercial business . . . A lack of economic freedom has heretofore made marriage often only a commercial contract."

Opening in 1903, the woman's college suffered, as did many women's colleges of the time, from ambivalence in determining its purpose. Although acknowledging the need for young women to be trained in a practical vocation, college officials tended to emphasize not professions, but the domestic sciences traditionally the realm of wives and mothers. Not until the 1920s and 1930s did the school move toward truly professional training.

The Texas Federation of Women's Clubs continued to support public libraries, but added to their list of goals educational reform, juvenile courts, public kindergartens, marital blood tests, designation of wife and child desertion as a felony, and regulation of adoption.

Rural Organization and Education

In the rural sections of the state, the Grange was the tool that enhanced farm women's educations during the last quarter of the 19th century. The Texas Grange was organized in 1873 in Salado in Central Texas. It was a nonpartisan group whose purposes were to support cooperation in business and to provide opportunity for more social contacts and better education for its members. The bi-monthly Grange meetings, which were attended by entire families, offered speakers on economic and agricultural topics, as well as bringing the members together for social interaction.

Social Reform Movement Expands

Reform became the focus of many women's clubs after 1900: antitrust legislation, woman- and child-labor laws, prohibition, pure food and drug laws, clean streets, weights and measures laws and woman suffrage. Some clubs set up standing committees to monitor labor conditions in their local areas. The goal was not radical upheaval of established economic, political or social institutions, but reform, mainly in areas that directly affected their families' health and safety.

The reform movement soon expanded to embrace prison and government reform, highway safety, conservation and public education improvements. Some clubs retained their original missions of literary and cultural efforts.

Black Women Organize

For the most part, the women's club movement was white and Protestant. Black women had organized in the North as early as the 1830s, primarily establishing antislavery societies. They frequently formed groups centered around church activities. Beginning in the 1890s, black women formed some clubs similar to the white women's organizations — for self-improvement and cultural advancement. But other groups' goals were improvement of racial conditions and overturning the prevailing racial stereotypes, voter registration and tutoring, moving later into the struggle for social reform and civil rights.

In 1895, Josephine St. Pierre Ruffin, a black club leader, urged a federation of black women's clubs in order to "teach an ignorant and suspicious world that our aims and interests are identical with those of all good aspiring women." The following year, the National Association of Colored Women was formed. Goals of the federation included teaching basic household skills and child care to poor black women, establishing missions and securing safe housing and job training for young black women moving to cities. The organization's member clubs also campaigned against lynching.

Mrs. M.E.Y. Moore organized the Texas Association of Colored Women's Clubs in Gainesville in 1905. The group's campaign for a state-financed home for delinquent black girls waspartially successful: The home was approved by the legislature in 1927, but it was not funded until 18 years later.

Women Organize to Protect Children

Women's traditional concerns — children, home and church — were further addressed with the formation of Mother's Clubs, the forerunner of the modern Parent-Teacher Association (PTA). These groups campaigned against exploitation of child labor in fields, mills and kitchens, as well as fighting unsanitary conditions in schools.

The Texas Congress of Mothers, founded in Hillsboro in 1909 by Ella Caruthers Porter, lobbied the legislature for laws protecting children, calling for a juvenile-court system, public kindergartens, compulsory school attendance, a division of child welfare and a bureau of child hygiene.

Hispanic Women Form Assistance Groups

The Mexican-American women of Texas began organizing in Laredo in 1911. Jovita Idar founded *La Liga Femenil Mexicanista* (League of Mexican Women) to support education for poor Mexican-American children. In 1913, when the Mexican Revolution began affecting the Laredo area, she and Leonór Villegas de Magnón founded *La Cruz Blanca* (White Cross) to nurse the wounded. Ms. Idar moved to San Antonio in 1917, where she started a free kindergarten.

Jovita Idar founded La Liga Feminil Mexicanista *in Laredo in 1911. Photo courtesy The Institute of Texan Cultures, San Antonio.*

After World War I and into the Depression years, Mexican-American women in the Hondo area operated a volunteer organization called *La Cruz Azul* (The Blue Cross). They distributed food, money, clothing and household equipment to the poor, ill and unemployed without regard to race, color or creed.

Prohibition Supporters Win

Meanwhile, the fights for prohibition and for woman suffrage continued. Prohibition forces were finally victorious in December 1917, when the 18th Amendment to the U.S. Constitution passed Congress. Ratification came slightly more than a year later, in January 1919.

Suffrage efforts had been mostly on state and local fronts for several years. But in March 1913, national suffrage leaders convened a huge parade of women the day before Woodrow Wilson's inauguration as U.S. president. The march turned into a melee, with troops being called in to restore order. For the first time in 26 years, the suffrage amendment was debated in Congress.

The suffragists continued their more militant tactics, holding parades, rallies and mass demonstrations. The New York Times characterized the campaign as "an advance in the reign of terror."

Texas Suffragists Change Tactics

The first Texas suffrage convention since 1904 was held in San Antonio in April 1913, attended by

Texas Women's Timeline

This list is only a sampler of highlights in the history of Texas Women from the mid-1800s to 1928:

1831 — Mary Austin Holley writes first book in English about Texas.
1850 — Mary Madison files a petition with Texas Legislature to remain a free woman of color.
1872 — Sarah Cockrell builds first iron bridge across Trinity River at Dallas.
1876 — Salado women's literary society starts a circulating library.
1877 — Black laundresses in Galveston strike for higher wages.
1887 — Eleanor Brackenridge of San Antonio becomes first woman bank director in the United States.
1888 — Anna Pennybacker publishes first Texas history textbook.
1893 — Olga Kohlberg and El Paso Woman's Club are responsible for Texas' first public kindergarten.
1897 — Texas Federation of Women's Clubs is organized, making libraries their first priority.
1903 — WCTU leaders spearhead founding of Girls Industrial College of Texas in Denton (now TWU).
1905 — Texas Association of Colored Women's Clubs is founded.
1909 —Ella Caruthers Porter calls first statewide meeting of mother's clubs, later the PTA.
1910 — Hortense Ward, Houston, is first woman admitted to Texas Bar.
1911 — Mexican-American women in Laredo and San Antonio found *La Liga Femenil.* Leonór Villegas de Magnón organizes *La Cruz Blanca* to nurse war refugees from Mexican Revolution.
1912 — Katherine Stinson of San Antonio is fourth female licensed pilot in the United States.
1913 — Hortense Ward authors Married Women's Property Act.
1918 —Women gain right to vote in primary elections. Dr. Annie Webb Blanton is first woman elected to statewide office.
1922 — Edith Wilmans, Dallas, is first woman elected to Texas House of Representatives.
1926 — Margie Neal, Carthage, is first woman elected to Texas Senate.
1928 — Oveta Culp Hobby codifies state's banking laws.

Complied from information in "Texas Women: A Celebration of History," published by the Texas Foundation for Women's Resources, Austin, 1981. Used by permission of the Foundation for Women's Resources, Austin.

Annie W. Blanton, first woman elected to statewide office in Texas. Photo: Institute of Texan Cultures.

Sen. Kay Bailey Hutchison, first female U.S. Senator from Texas. AP Photo.

Carole Keeton Rylander, Texas' first female Railroad Commissioner. Photo courtesy Comm. Rylander.

150 women and a handful of men. Annual conventions were held after 1913. Texas suffrage leaders, among them Jane Y. McCallum of Austin and Minnie Fisher Cunningham of Galveston, stressed the importance of non-confrontational persuasion.

By 1918, Texas suffragist leaders realized that gaining full suffrage was proving to be almost impossible. It required approval by two-thirds of both houses of the Legislature and ratification by a majority of Texas voters. Since Texas was a one-party state at the time, the Democratic Party primary was where the major decisions were made. Primary suffrage could be obtained through a legislative act requiring approval of only a simple majority of the legislators. In a special session of the legislature called by Gov. William P. Hobby in March 1918, the legislature passed the primary suffrage law. Although the registration period for that first primary was a mere 17 days, more than 380,000 women signed up by the deadline.

Even before Texas women could vote in general elections, Annie Webb Blanton became the first woman to win statewide elective office. She was elected the first female State Superintendent of Public Instruction in 1918 after a hard-fought and bitter campaign. She served from 1919 to 1923.

Citizenship At Last

President Wilson had preferred action on woman suffrage by the states, but when he saw that was a futile hope, he began actively to support passage of the 19th Amendment. It passed the House on Jan. 10, 1918; a year and a half later the Senate concurred. Texas was the 9th state to ratify, on June 23, 1919. By Aug. 26, 1920, enough states had ratified the 19th Amendment to make it part of the U.S. Constitution.

Seventy years after the Seneca Falls convention, the American women's struggle for the right to vote was successfully concluded by the addition of these two short sentences to the U.S. Constitution: "The right of citizens of the United States to vote shall not be denied or abridged by the United States or by any State on account of sex. Congress shall have power to enforce this Article by appropriate legislation."

In the years since this watershed event, the participation of women in the political life of the nation has continued to gather momentum. But it has been slow progress. Not until 1954 could women serve on juries in Texas, for example. Although the end of the road to full rights has not yet been reached, women are beginning to hold some of Texas' highest govermental offices. Ann Richards was the first woman to hold the office of governor in her own right, serving from 1991 to 1995. Kay Bailey Hutchison, who became Texas' first female U.S. senator when she won a special election to fill Lloyd Bentsen's unexpired term in 1993, was re-elected to a full term, which she began serving in 1995.

In the November 1994 general election, Carole Keeton Rylander became the first woman elected to the Texas Railroad Commission. In the same election, Sharon Keller was chosen by voters to serve on the Court of Criminal Appeals, becoming the first woman elected to the highest criminal court in the state. Many hundreds of other state and local offices are also occupied by women. ☆

For Further Reading

Crawford, Mary G., "Citizens at Last!" in **The Texas Almanac's Political History of Texas**, pp. 24-33; The Dallas Morning News, Dallas, 1992.

Papachristou, Judith, **Women Together**; Alfred A. Knopf, New York, 1976.

Winegarten, Ruthe, **Finder's Guide to the Texas Women: A Celebration of History Exhibit Archives**; Texas Woman's University Library, Denton, 1984.

Winegarten, Ruthe, **Texas Women: A Pictorial History**; Eakin Press, Austin, 1985.

Environment

Extending from sea level at the Gulf of Mexico to over 8,000 feet in the Guadalupe Mountains of far West Texas and from the semitropical Lower Rio Grande Valley to the High Plains of the Panhandle, Texas has a natural environment best described as "varied." This section discusses the physical features, geology, soils, water, vegetation and wildlife that are found in the Lone Star State.

The Physical State of Texas

Area of Texas

Texas occupies about 7 percent of the total water and land area of the United States. **Second in size** among the states, Texas, according to the 1994 Statistical Abstract of the United States, has a land and water area of 267,277 square miles as compared with Alaska's 615,230 square miles. California, third largest state, has 158,869 square miles. Texas is as large as all of New England, New York, Pennsylvania, Ohio and Illinois combined.

The **state's area** consists of 261,914 square miles of land and 5,363 square miles of water.

The area given here differs from that given by the State Land Office in the chapter on State Government.

Length and Breadth

The **longest straight-line distance** in a general north-south direction is 801 miles from the northwest corner of the Panhandle to the extreme southern tip of Texas on the Rio Grande below Brownsville. The greatest east-west distance is 773 miles from the extreme eastward bend in the Sabine River in Newton County to the extreme western bulge of the Rio Grande just above El Paso. The **geographic center** of Texas is southwest of Mercury in the northern portion of McCulloch County.

Texas' Boundary Lines

The boundary of Texas by segments, including only larger river bends and only the great arc of the coastline, is as follows:

Boundary	Miles
Rio Grande	889.0
Coastline	367.0
Sabine River, Lake and Pass	180.0
*Sabine River to Red River	106.5
Red River	480.0
*East Panhandle line	133.6
*North Panhandle line	167.0
*West Panhandle line	310.2
*Along 32nd parallel	209.0
Total	**2,842.3**

Following the smaller meanderings of the rivers and the tidewater coastline, the following are the boundary measurements:

Rio Grande	1,254
Coastline (tidewater)	624
Sabine River, Lake and Pass	292
Red River	726
*The five unchanged line segments above	926
Total (including segments marked *)	**3,822**

Latitude and Longitude

The extremes of latitude and longitude are as follows: From Latitude 25° 50' N. at the extreme southern turn of the Rio Grande on the south line of Cameron County to Latitude 36° 30' N. along the north line of the Panhandle, and from Longitude 93° 31' W. at the extreme eastern point on the Sabine River on the east line of Newton County to Longitude 106° 38' W. on the extreme westward point on the Rio Grande above El Paso.

Texas' Highs and Lows

The highest point in the state is **Guadalupe Peak** at **8,749 feet** above sea level. Its twin, **El Capitan**, stands at **8,085** feet and also is located in Culberson county near the New Mexico state line. Both are in the Guadalupe Mountains National Park, which includes scenic McKittrick Cañyon. These elevations and the others in this article have been determined by the U. S. Geological Survey, unless otherwise noted.

The highest peaks in Texas and the counties in which they are located are listed in the table below:

The 10 Highest Peaks in Texas

Name, County	Elevation
Guadalupe Peak, Culberson	8,749
Bush Mountain, Culberson	8,631
Shumard Peak, Culberson	8,615
Bartlett Peak, Culberson	8,508
Baldy Peak, Jeff Davis	8,378
Hunter Peak (Pine Top Mtn.), Culberson	8,368
Mount Livermore, Jeff Davis	8,206
El Capitan, Culberson	8,085
Lost Peak, Culberson	7,830
Emory Peak, Brewster	7,825

Fort Davis in Jeff Davis County is the **highest town** of any size in Texas at 5,050 feet, and the county has the **highest average elevation.** The **highest state highway point** also is in the county at **McDonald Observatory** at the end of a tap from State Highway 118 on **Mount Locke.** The observatory stands at 6,781 feet, as determined by the Texas Department of Transportation.

The **highest railway point** is Paisano Pass, 14 miles east of Marfa on the Southern Pacific in Presidio County.

Sea level is the **lowest elevation** determined in Texas, and it can be found in all the coastal counties. No point in the state has been found by the geological survey to be below sea level. ☆

Physical Features

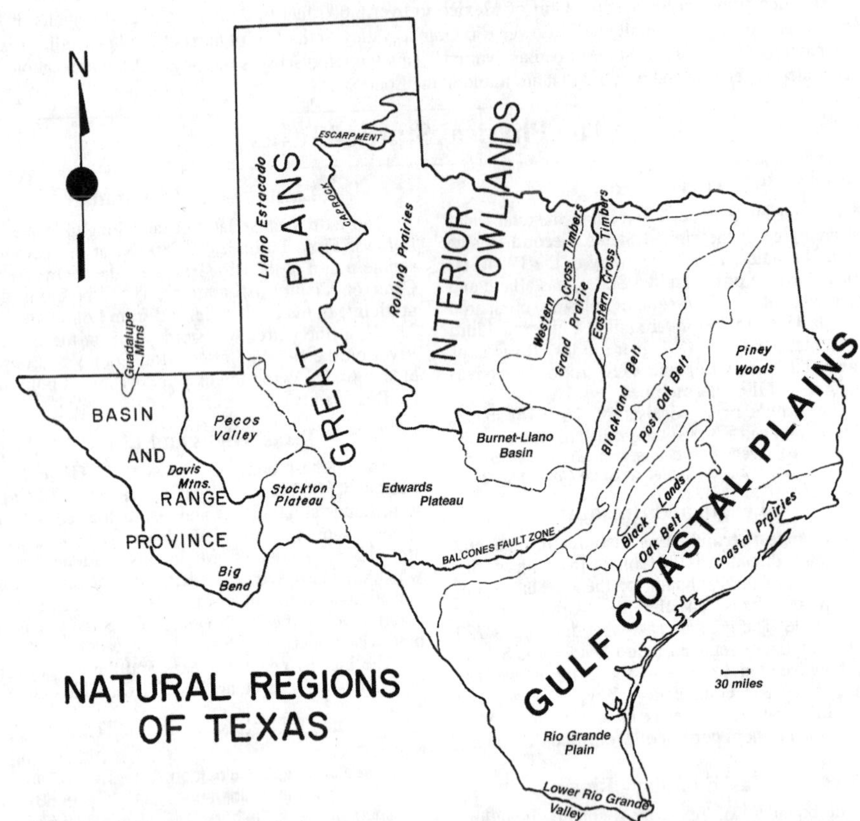

A special thanks to Dr. William M. Holmes, chairman of the Department of Geography at the University of North Texas, for his review of this section.

Physical Regions

The principal physical regions of Texas are usually listed as follows (see also Vegetational Areas and Soils.):

The Gulf Coastal Plains

Texas' Gulf Coastal Plains are the western extension of the coastal plain extending from the Atlantic to beyond the Rio Grande. Its characteristic rolling to hilly surface covered with a heavy growth of pine and hardwoods extends into East Texas. In the increasingly arid west, however, its forests become secondary in nature, consisting largely of post oaks and, farther west, prairies and brushlands.

The interior limit of the Gulf Coastal Plains in Texas is the line of the **Balcones Fault and Escarpment.** This geologic fault or shearing of underground strata extends eastward from a point on the Rio Grande near Del Rio. It extends to the northwestern part of Bexar County where it turns northeastward and extends through Comal, Hays and Travis counties, intersecting the Colorado River immediately above Austin. The fault line is a single, definite geologic feature, accompanied by a line of southward- and eastward-facing hills. The resemblance of the hills to balconies when viewed from the plain below accounts for the Spanish name, *balcones.* North of Waco, features of the fault zone are sufficiently inconspicuous that the interior boundary of the Coastal Plain follows the traditional geologic contact between upper and lower Cretaceous rocks. This contact is along the western edge of the **Eastern Cross Timbers.**

This fault line is usually accepted as the boundary between lowland and upland Texas. Below the fault line the surface is characteristically coastal plains. Above the Balcones Fault the surface is characteristically interior rolling plains.

Pine Belt or "Piney Woods"

The Pine Belt, called the "Piney Woods," extends into Texas from the east 75 to 125 miles. From north to south it extends from the Red River to within about 25 miles of the Gulf Coast. Interspersed among the pines are some hardwood timbers, usually in valleys of rivers and creeks. This area is the source of practically all of Texas' large commercial timber production (see "Forest Resources" in index). It was settled early in Texas' history and is an older farming area of the state. This area's soils and climate are adaptable to production of a variety of fruit and vegetable crops. Cattle raising is widespread, accompanied by the development of pastures planted to improved grasses. Lumber production is the principal industry. There is a large iron-and-steel industry near Daingerfield in Morris County based on nearby iron deposits. Iron deposits are also worked in Rusk and one or two other counties.

A great oil field discovered in Gregg, Rusk and Smith counties in 1931 has done more than anything else to contribute to the economic growth of the area. This area has a variety of clays, lignite and other minerals as potentials for development.

Post Oak Belt

The main Post Oak Belt of Texas is wedged between the Pine Belt on the east, Blacklands on the west, and the Coastal Prairies on the south, covering a considerable area in East Central Texas. Principal industry is diversified farming and livestock raising. Throughout, it is spotty in character, with some insular areas of blackland soil and some that closely resemble those of the Pine Belt. There is a small isolated area of pines in Bastrop County known as the **"Lost Pines."** The Post Oak Belt has lignite, commercial clays and some other minerals.

Blackland Belt

The Blackland Belt stretches from the Rio Grande to the Red River, lying just below the line of the **Balcones Fault**, and varying in width from 15 to 70 miles. It is narrowest below the segment of the Balcones Fault from the Rio Grande to Bexar County and gradually widens as it runs northeast to the Red River. Its rolling prairie, easily turned by the plow, developed rapidly as a farming area until the 1930s and was the principal cotton-producing area of Texas. Now, however, other Texas irrigated, mechanized areas lead in farming. Because of the early growth, the Blackland Belt is still the most thickly populated area in the state and contains within it and along its border more of the state's large and middle-sized cities than any other area. Primarily because of this concentration of population, this belt has the most diversified manufacturing industry of the state.

Coastal Prairies

The Texas Coastal Prairies extend westward along the coast from the Sabine River, reaching inland 30 to 60 miles. Between the Sabine and Galveston Bay, the line of demarcation between the prairies and the Pine Belt forests to the north is very distinct. The Coastal Prairie extends along the Gulf from the Sabine to the Lower Rio Grande Valley. The eastern half is covered with a heavy growth of grass; the western half, which is more arid, is covered with short grass and, in some places, with small timber and brush. The soil is heavy clay. Grass supports the densest cattle population in Texas, and cattle ranching is the principal agricultural industry. Rice is a major crop, grown under irrigation from wells and rivers. Cotton, grain sorghum and truck crops are grown.

Coastal Prairie areas have seen the greatest industrial development in Texas history since World War II. Chief concentration has been from Orange and Beaumont to Houston, and much of the development has been in petrochemicals.

Corpus Christi, in the Coastal Bend, and Brownsville, in the Lower Rio Grande Valley, have seaports and agricultural and industrial sections. Cotton, grain, vegetables and citrus fruits are the principal crops. Cattle production is significant, with the famed King Ranch and other large ranches located here.

Lower Rio Grande Valley

The deep alluvial soils and distinctive economy cause the Lower Rio Grande Valley to be classified as a subregion of the Gulf Coastal Plain. The Lower Valley, as it is called locally, is Texas' greatest citrus-winter vegetable area because of the normal absence of freezing weather and the rich delta soils of the Rio Grande. Despite occasional damaging freezes, as in 1951 and 1961, the Lower Valley ranks high among the nation's fruit-and-truck regions. Much of the acreage is irrigated, although dryland farming also is practiced.

Rio Grande Plain

This may be roughly defined as lying south of San Antonio between the Rio Grande and the Gulf Coast. The Rio Grande Plain shows characteristics of both the Texas Gulf Coastal Plain and the North Mexico Plains because there is similarity of topography, climate and plant life all the way from the Balcones Escarpment in Texas to the Sierra Madre Oriental in Mexico, which runs past Monterrey about 160 miles south of Laredo.

The Rio Grande Plain is partly prairie, but much of it is covered with a dense growth of **prickly pear, cactus, mesquite, dwarf oak, catclaw, guajillo, huisache, blackbrush, cenizo** and other wild shrubs. This country is devoted primarily to raising cattle, sheep and goats. The Texas Angora goat and mohair industry centers in this area and on the **Edwards Plateau,** which borders it on the north. San Antonio and Laredo are its chief commercial centers, with San Antonio dominating trade.

There is some farming, and the **Winter Garden**, centering in Dimmit and Zavala counties north of Laredo, is irrigated from wells and streams to produce vegetables in late winter and early spring. Primarily, however, the central and western part of the Rio Grande Plain is devoted to livestock raising. The rainfall is less than 25 inches annually and the hot summers bring heavy evaporation, so that cultivation without irrigation is limited. Over a large area in the central and western parts of the Rio Grande Plain, the growth of **small oaks, mesquite, prickly pear (Opuntia) cactus** and a variety of wild shrubs is very dense and it is often called the **Brush Country**. It is also referred to as the **chaparral** and the **monte**. (Monte is a Spanish word, one meaning of which is dense brush.)

Interior Lowlands

North Central Plains

The North Central Plains of Texas are a southwestern extension into Texas of the interior lowlands that extend northward to the Canadian border, paralleling the Great Plains to the West. The North Central Plains of Texas extend from the Blackland Belt on the east to the Caprock Escarpment on the west. From north to south they extend from the Red River to the Colorado.

West Texas Rolling Plains

The West Texas Rolling Plains, approximately the western two-thirds of the North Central Plains in Texas, rise from east to west in altitude from about 750 feet to 2,000 feet at the base of the **Caprock Escarpment**. Annual rainfall ranges from about 30 inches on the east to 20 on the west. Temperature varies rather widely between summer's heat and winter's cold.

This area still has a large cattle-raising industry with many of the state's largest ranches. However, there is much level, cultivable land.

Grand Prairie

Near the eastern edge of the North Central Plains is the Grand Prairie, extending south from the Red River in an irregular band through Cooke, Montague, Wise, Denton, Tarrant, Parker, Hood, Johnson, Bosque, Coryell and some adjacent counties. It is a limestone-based area, usually treeless except along the numerous streams, and adapted primarily to livestock raising and staple-crop growing.

Sometimes called the Fort Worth Prairie, it has an agricultural economy and largely rural population, with no large cities except Fort Worth on its eastern boundary.

East and West Cross Timbers

Hanging over the top of the Grand Prairie and dropping down on each side are the East and West Cross Timbers. The two southward-extending bands are connected by a narrow strip along the Red River. The East Cross Timbers extend southward from the Red River through eastern Denton County and along the Dallas-Tarrant County boundary, then through Johnson County to the Brazos River and into Hill County. The much larger West Cross Timbers extend from the Red River south through Clay, Montague, Jack, Wise, Parker, Palo Pinto, Hood, Erath, Eastland, Comanche, Brown and Mills counties to the Colorado River, where they meet the Edwards Plateau. Their soils are adapted to fruit and vegetable crops, which reach considerable commercial production in some areas in Parker, Erath, Eastland and Comanche counties.

Great Plains

The Great Plains which lie to the east of the base of the Rocky Mountains extend into Northwest Texas. This area, which is a vast, flat, high plain covered with thick layers of alluvial material, is known as the **Staked Plains** or the Spanish equivalent, **Llano Estacado**.

Historians differ as to the origin of this name. Some think that it came from the fact that the Coronado expedition, crossing the trackless sea of grass, staked its route so that it would be guided on its return trip. Others think that the "estacado" refers to the palisaded appearance of the Caprock in many places, especially the west-facing escarpment in New Mexico.

The **Caprock Escarpment** is the dividing line between the High Plains and the Lower Rolling Plains of West Texas. Like the Balcones Escarpment, the Caprock Escarpment is a striking physical feature, rising abruptly

200, 500 and in some places almost 1,000 feet above the plains. Unlike the **Balcones Escarpment**, the Caprock was caused by surface erosion. Where rivers issue from the eastern face of the Caprock, there frequently are notable canyons, such as the **Palo Duro Canyon** on the **Prairie Dog Town Fork (main channel) of the Red River** and the breaks along the Canadian as it crosses the Panhandle north of Amarillo.

Along the eastern edge of the Panhandle there is a gradual descent of the earth's surface from high to low plains, but at the Red River the Caprock Escarpment becomes a striking surface feature. It continues as an east-facing wall south through Briscoe, Floyd, Motley, Dickens, Crosby, Garza and Borden counties, gradually decreasing in elevation. South of Borden County the escarpment is less obvious, and the boundary between the High Plains and the Edwards Plateau occurs where the alluvial cover of the High Plains disappears.

Stretching over the largest level plain of its kind in the United States, the **High Plains** rise gradually from about 2,700 feet on the east to more than 4,000 in spots along the New Mexico border.

Chiefly because of climate and the resultant agriculture, subdivisions are called the North Plains and South Plains. The North Plains, from Hale County north, has primarily wheat and grain sorghum farming, but with significant ranching and petroleum developments. Amarillo is the largest city, with Plainview on the south and Borger on the north as important commercial centers. The South Plains, also a leading grain sorghum region, leads Texas in cotton production. Lubbock is the principal city, and Lubbock County is one of the state's largest cotton producers. Irrigation from underground reservoirs, centered around Lubbock and Plainview, waters much of the crop acreage.

Edwards Plateau

Geographers usually consider the Great Plains at the foot of the Rocky Mountains continuing southward from the High Plains of Northwest Texas to the Rio Grande and the Balcones Escarpment. This southern and lower extension of the Great Plains in Texas is known as the Edwards Plateau.

It lies between the Rio Grande and the Colorado River. Its southeastern border is the **Balcones Escarpment** from the Rio Grande at Del Rio eastward to San Antonio and thence to Austin on the Colorado. Its upper boundary is the Pecos River, though the **Stockton Plateau** is geologically and topographically classed with the Edwards Plateau. The Edwards Plateau varies from about 750 feet high at its southern and eastern borders to about 2,700 feet in places. Almost the entire surface is a thin, limestone-based soil covered with a medium to thick growth of **cedar, small oak** and **mesquite** with a varying growth of **prickly pear.** Grass for cattle, weeds for sheep and tree foliage for the browsing goats support three industries — cattle, goat and sheep raising — upon which the area's economy depends. It is the **nation's leading Angora goat and mohair producing region** and one of the nation's leading sheep and wool areas. A few crops are grown.

Toyah Basin

To the northwest of the Edwards and Stockton plateaus is the Toyah Basin, a broad, flat remnant of an old sea floor that occupied the region as recently as Quaternary time. Located in the Pecos River Valley, this region, in relatively recent time, has become important for many agricultural products as a result of irrigation. Additional economic activity is afforded by local oil fields.

The Hill Country

The Hill Country is a popular name for an area of hills and spring-fed streams along the edge of the **Balcones Escarpment**. Notable large springs include **Barton Springs** at Austin, **San Marcos Springs** at San Marcos, **Comal Springs** at New Braunfels, several springs at San Antonio, and a number of others.

The Llano Basin

The Llano Basin lies at the junction of the Colorado and Llano rivers in Burnet and Llano counties. Earlier this was known as the **"Central Mineral Region,"** because of the evidence there of a large number of minerals.

On the Colorado River in this area, a succession of dams impounds two large and five small reservoirs. Uppermost is **Lake Buchanan,** one of the large reservoirs, between Burnet and Llano counties. Below it in the western part of Travis County is **Lake Travis.** Between these two large reservoirs are three smaller ones, **Inks, L. B. Johnson** (formerly Granite Shoals) and **Marble Falls** reservoirs, used primarily for maintaining heads to produce electric power from the overflow from Lake Buchanan. **Lake Austin** is just above the city of Austin. Still another small lake, **Town Lake,** is formed by a low-water dam in Austin.

The recreational area around these lakes is called the **Highland Lakes Country**. This is an interesting area with Precambrian and Paleozoic rocks found on the surface.

Basin and Range Province

The Basin and Range province, with its center in Nevada, surrounds the Colorado Plateau on the west and south and enters far West Texas from southern New Mexico. It consists of broad interior drainage, basins interspersed with scattered fault-block mountain ranges. Although this is the only part of Texas regarded as mountainous, these should not be confused with the Rockies. Of all the independent ranges in West Texas, only the Davis Mountains resemble the Rockies and there is much debate about this.

Texas west of the Edwards Plateau, bounded on the north by New Mexico and on the south by the Rio Grande, is distinctive in its physical and economic conditions. Traversed from north to south by an eastern range of the Rockies, it contains all of **Texas' true mountains** and also is very interesting geologically.

Highest of the Trans-Pecos Mountains is the **Guadalupe Range,** which enters the state from New Mexico. It comes to an abrupt end about 20 miles south of the boundary line, where are situated **Guadalupe Peak**, (8,749 feet, highest in Texas) and **El Capitan** (8,085 feet). El Capitan, because of perspective, appears to the observer on the plain below to be higher than Guadalupe. Lying just west of the Guadalupe range and extending to the **Hueco Mountains** a short distance east of El Paso is the **Diablo Plateau** or basin. It has no drainage outlet to the sea. The runoff from the scant rain that falls on its surface drains into a series of salt lakes that lie just west of the Guadalupe Mountains. These lakes are entirely dry during periods of low rainfall, exposing bottoms of solid salt, and for years they were a source of **commercial salt**.

Davis Mountains

The Davis Mountains are principally in Jeff Davis County. The highest peak, **Mount Livermore**, (8,206 feet) is **one of the highest in Texas;** there are several others more than 7,000 feet high. These mountains intercept the moisture-bearing winds and receive more precipitation than elsewhere in the Trans-Pecos, so they have more vegetation than the other Trans-Pecos mountains. Noteworthy are the **San Solomon Springs** at the northern base of these mountains.

Big Bend

South of the Davis Mountains lies the Big Bend country, so called because it is encompassed on three sides by a great southward swing of the Rio Grande. It is a mountainous country of scant rainfall and sparse population. Its principal mountains, the **Chisos**, rise to 7,825 feet in **Mount Emory**. Along the Rio Grande are the **Santa Elena, Mariscal and Boquillas canyons** with rim elevations of 3,500 to 3,775 feet. They are among the noteworthy canyons of the North American continent. Because of its remarkable topography and plant and animal life, the southern part of this region along the Rio Grande is home to the **Big Bend National Park**, with headquarters in a deep valley in the Chisos Mountains. It is a favorite recreation area.

Upper Rio Grande Valley

The Upper Rio Grande (El Paso) Valley is a narrow strip of irrigated land running down the river from El Paso for a distance of 75 miles or more. In this area are the historic towns and missions of **Ysleta, Socorro and San Elizario, oldest in Texas**. Cotton is the chief product of the valley, much of it long-staple variety. This limited area has a dense urban and rural population, in marked contrast to the territory surrounding it. ☆

For Further Reading

Texas: A Geography, by Terry G. Jordan with John L. Bean Jr. and William M. Holmes; Westview Press, Boulder and London, 1984.

Geology of Texas

This article on the geology of Texas was prepared by the Bureau of Economic Geology at The University of Texas at Austin.

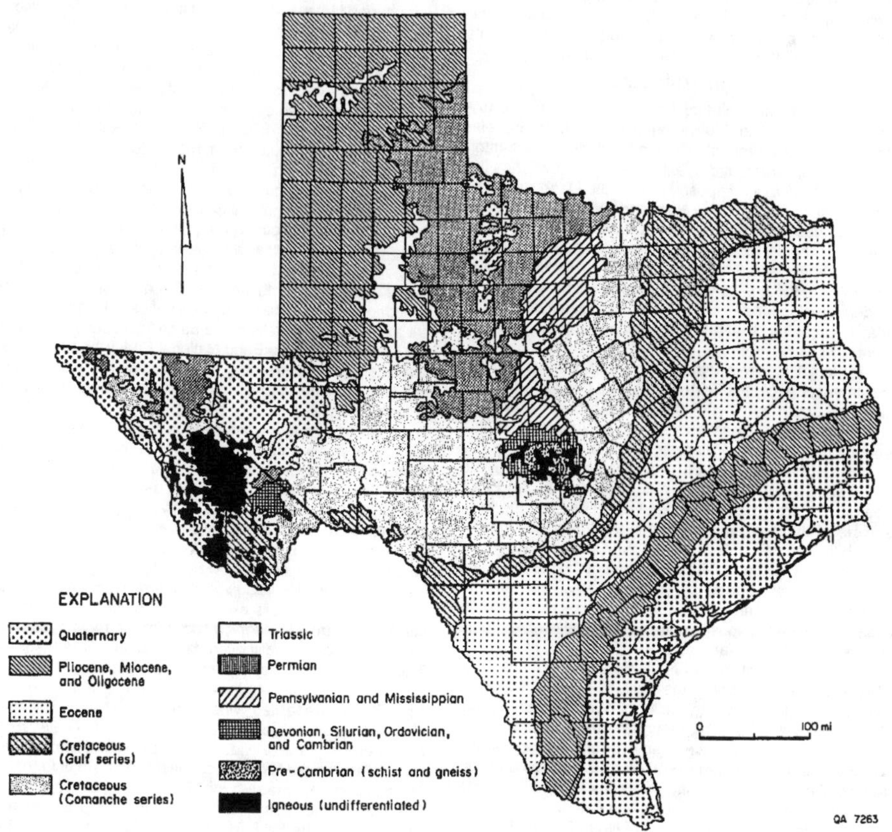

History in the Rocks

Mountains, seas, coastal plains, rocky plateaus, high plains, forests — all this physiographic variety in Texas is controlled by the varied rocks and structures that underlie and crop out in Texas. The fascinating geologic history of Texas is recorded in the rocks — both those exposed at the surface and those penetrated by holes drilled in search of oil and natural gas. The rocks reveal a dynamic, ever-changing earth — ancient mountains, seas, volcanoes, earthquake belts, rivers, hurricanes and winds. Today, the volcanoes and great earthquake belts are no longer active, but rivers and streams, wind and rain, and the slow, inexorable alterations of rocks at or near the surface continue to change the face of Texas. The geologic history of Texas, as documented by the rocks, began more than a billion years ago. Its legacy is the mineral wealth and varied land forms of modern Texas.

Geologic Time Travel

The story preserved in the rocks requires an understanding of the origin of the strata and how they have been deformed. **Stratigraphy** is the study of the composition, sequence and origin of the rocks: what the rocks are made of, how they were formed and the order in which the layers were formed. Structural geology reveals the architecture of the rocks: the locations of the mountains, volcanoes, sedimentary basins and earthquake belts. Above is a map showing where rocks of various geologic ages are visible on the surface of Texas today.

History concerns events through time, but geologic time is such a grandiose concept that most of us find it difficult to comprehend. So, geologists have named the various chapters of earth history.

Precambrian Eon

Precambrian rocks, more than 600 million years old, are exposed at the surface in the Llano Uplift of Central Texas and in scattered outcrops in West Texas, around and north of Van Horn and near El Paso. These rocks, some more than a billion years old, include complexly deformed rocks that were originally formed by cooling from a liquid state as well as rocks that were altered from preexisting rocks.

Precambrian rocks, often called the "basement complex," are thought to form the foundation of continental masses. Precambrian rocks underlie all of Texas. The outcrop in Central Texas is only the exposed part of the Texas Craton, which is primarily buried by younger rocks. (A craton is a stable, almost immovable portion of the earth's crust that forms the nuclear mass of a continent.)

Paleozoic Era

During the early part of the Paleozoic Era (approximately 600 million to 350 million years ago), broad, relatively shallow seas repeatedly inundated the Texas Craton and much of North and West Texas. The evidence for these events is found exposed around the Llano Uplift and in far West Texas near Van Horn and El Paso, and also in the subsurface throughout most of West and North Texas. The evidence includes early Paleozoic rocks — sandstones, shales and limestones, similar to sediments that form in seas today — and the fossils of animals, similar to modern crustaceans — the brachiopods, clams, snails and related organisms that live in modern marine environments.

By late Paleozoic (approximately 350 million to 240 million years ago), the Texas Craton was bordered on the east and south by a long, deep marine basin called the Ouachita Trough. Sediments slowly accumulated in this trough until late in the Paleozoic Era. Plate-tectonic theory postulates that the collision of the North American Plate (upon which the Texas Craton is located) with the European and African-South American plates uplifted the thick sediments that had accumulated in the trough to form the Ouachita Mountains. At that time, the Ouachitas extended across Texas. Today, the Texas portion of the old mountain range is entirely buried by younger rocks, and all that remains at the surface of the once-majestic Ouachita Mountain chain is exposed only in southeastern Oklahoma and southwestern Arkansas.

During the **Pennsylvanian Period**, however, the Ouachita Mountains bordered the eastern margin of shallow inland seas that covered most of West Texas. Rivers flowed westward from the mountains to the sea bringing sediment to form deltas along an ever-changing coastline. The sediments were then reworked by the waves and currents of the inland sea. Today, these fluvial, delta and shallow marine deposits compose the late Paleozoic rocks that crop out and underlie the surface of North Central Texas.

Broad marine shelves divided the West Texas seas into several sub-basins, or deeper areas, that received more sediments than accumulated on the limestone shelves. Limestone reefs rimmed the deeper basins. Today, these reef limestones are important oil reservoirs in West Texas. These seas gradually withdrew from Texas, and by the late **Permian Period,** all that was left in West Texas were shallow basins and wide tidal flats in which salt, gypsum and red muds accumulated in a hot, arid land. Strata deposited during the Permian Period are exposed today along the edge of the Panhandle, as far east as Wichita Falls and south to Concho County, and in the Trans-Pecos.

Mesozoic Era

Approximately 240 million years ago, the major geologic events in Texas shifted from West Texas to East and Southeast Texas. The European and African-South American plates, which had collided with the North American plate to form the Ouachita Mountains, began to separate from North America. A series of faulted basins, or rifts, extending from Mexico to Nova Scotia were formed. These rifted basins received sediments from adjacent uplifts. As Europe and the southern continents continued to drift away from North America, the Texas basins were eventually buried beneath thick deposits of marine salt within the newly formed East Texas and Gulf Coast basins. Jurassic and Cretaceous rocks in East and Southeast Texas document a sequence of broad limestone shelves at the edge of the developing Gulf of Mexico. From time to time, the shelves were buried beneath deltaic sandstones and shales, which built the northwestern margin of the widening Gulf of Mexico to the south and southeast. As the underlying salt was buried more deeply by dense sediments, the salt became unstable and moved toward areas of least pressure. As the salt moved, it arched or pierced overlying sediments forming, in some cases, columns known as "salt domes." In some cases, these salt domes moved to the surface; others remain beneath a sedimentary overburden. This mobile salt formed numerous structures that would later serve to trap oil and natural gas.

By the early **Cretaceous** (approximately 140 million years ago), the shallow Mesozoic seas covered a large part of Texas, eventually extending west to the Trans-Pecos area and north almost to the present-day state boundaries. Today, the limestones deposited in those seas are exposed in the walls of the magnificent canyons of the Rio Grande in the Big Bend National Park area and in the canyons and headwaters of streams that drain the Edwards Plateau, as well as in Central Texas from San Antonio to Dallas.

Animals of many types lived in the shallow Mesozoic seas, tidal pools and coastal swamps. Today these lower Cretaceous rocks are some of the most fossiliferous in the state. Tracks of dinosaurs occur in several localities, and remains of terrestrial, aquatic and flying reptiles have been collected from Cretaceous rocks in many parts of Texas.

During most of the late Cretaceous, much of Texas lay beneath marine waters that were deeper than those of the early Cretaceous seas, except where rivers, deltas and shallow marine shelves existed. River delta and strandline sandstones are the reservoir rocks for the most prolific oil field in Texas. When discovered in 1930, this East Texas oil field contained recoverable reserves estimated at 5.6 billion barrels. The chalky rock that we now call the "Austin Chalk" was deposited when the Texas seas became deeper. Today, the chalk (and other Upper Cretaceous rocks) crops out in a wide band that extends from near Eagle Pass on the Rio Grande, east to San Antonio, north to Dallas and eastward to the Texarkana area. The Austin Chalk and other upper Cretaceous rocks dip southeastward beneath the East Texas and Gulf Coast basins. The late Cretaceous was the time of the last major seaway across Texas, because mountains were forming in the western United States that influenced areas as far away as Texas.

A chain of volcanoes formed beneath the late Cretaceous seas in an area roughly parallel to and south and east of the old, buried Ouachita Mountains. The eruptions of these volcanoes were primarily on the sea floor and great clouds of steam and ash likely accompanied them. Between eruptions, invertebrate marine animals built reefs on the shallow volcanic cones. Pilot Knob, located southeast of Austin, is one of these old volcanoes that is now exposed at the surface.

Cenozoic Era

At the dawn of the Cenozoic Era, approximately 65 million years ago, the northern and northwestern margins of the East Texas Basin were sites of deltas fed by rivers. These streams flowed eastward, draining areas to the north and west. Although there were minor incursions of the seas, the Cenozoic rocks principally document extensive seaward building by broad deltas, marshy lagoons, sandy barrier islands and embayments. Thick vegetation covered the levees and areas between the streams.

Coastal plains were taking shape, under the same processes still at work today.

The Mesozoic marine salt became buried by thick sediments in the coastal plain area. The salt began to form ridges and domes in the Houston and Rio Grande areas. The heavy load of sand, silt and mud deposited by the deltas eventually caused some areas of the coast to subside and form large fault systems, essentially parallel to the coast. Many of these coastal faults moved slowly and probably generated little earthquake activity. However, movement along the Balcones and Luling-Mexia-Talco zones, a complex system of faults along the western and northern edge of the basins, likely generated large earthquakes millions of years ago.

Predecessors of modern animals roamed the Texas Cenozoic coastal plains and woodlands. Bones and teeth of horses, camels, sloths, giant armadillos, mammoths, mastodons, bats, rats, large cats and other modern or extinct mammals have been excavated from coastal plain deposits. Vegetation in the area included varieties of plants and trees both similar and dissimilar to modern ones. Fossil palmwood, the Texas "state stone," is found in sediments of early Cenozoic age.

The Cenozoic Era in Trans-Pecos Texas was entirely different. There, extensive volcanic eruptions formed great calderas and produced copious lava flows. These eruptions ejected great clouds of volcanic ash and rock particles into the air — many times the amount of material ejected by the 1980 eruption of Mount St. Helens. Ash from the eruptions drifted eastward and is found in many of the sand-and-siltstones of the Gulf Coastal Plains. Lava flowed over the older Paleozoic and Mesozoic rocks, and igneous intrusions melted their way upward into the crustal rocks. These volcanic and intrusive igneous rocks are well exposed in the arid areas of the Trans-Pecos today.

In the Texas Panhandle, streams originating in the recently elevated southern Rocky Mountains brought floods of gravel and sand into Texas. As the braided streams crisscrossed the area, they formed great alluvial fans. These fans, which were deposited on the older Paleozoic and Mesozoic rocks, occur from northwestern Texas into Nebraska. Between 1 million and 2 million years ago, the streams of the Texas Panhandle were isolated from their Rocky Mountain source, and the eastern edge of this sheet of alluvial material began to retreat westward, forming the Caprock of the modern High Plains of Texas.

During the latter part of the Cenozoic Era, a great Ice Age descended upon the northern part of the North American continent. For more than 2 million years, there were successive advances and retreats of the thick sheets of glacial ice. Four periods of extensive glaciation were separated by warmer interglacial periods. Although the glaciers never reached as far south as Texas, the state's climate and sea level underwent major changes with each period of glacial advance and retreat. Sea level during times of glacial advance was 300 to 450 feet lower than during the warmer interglacial periods because so much sea water was captured in the ice sheets. The climate was both more humid and cooler than today, and the major Texas rivers carried more water and more sand and gravel to the sea. These deposits underlie the outer 50 miles or more of the Gulf Coastal Plain.

Approximately 3,000 years ago, sea level reached its modern position. The rivers, deltas, lagoons, beaches and barrier islands that we know as coastal Texas have formed since that time.

Mineral Wealth

Oil and natural gas are the most valuable minerals produced in Texas, contributing 23 percent of the oil production and 24 percent of the gas production in the United States in 1993. Oil and gas have been produced from most areas of Texas and from rocks of all geologic eras except the Precambrian. All of the major sedimentary basins of Texas, have produced some oil or gas.

In 1993, the value of nonfuel minerals produced was about $1.4 billion dollars, ranking Texas sixth nationally. Igneous and metamorphic rocks are favorable sites for mineralization and the outcrops of Precambrian rocks provide occurrences of many metals and some rare earths. There is no mining of these at this time.

For a more complete treatment of petroleum, coal and uranium resources, as well as a detailed discussion of nonfuel minerals in Texas, look for "Minerals" in the index. ☆

Soil Conservation and Use

*The following discussion was prepared for the Texas Almanac by the **Natural Resources Conservation Service, U. S. Department of Agriculture, Temple, Texas.** Additional information may be obtained from that source.*

The vast expanse of Texas soils encouraged wasteful use of soil and water throughout much of the state's history. Some 1,100 different soils series are recognized in the state. Settlers were attracted by these rich soils and the abundant water of the eastern half of the region, used them to build an agriculture and agribusiness of vast proportions, then found their abuse had created critical problems.

In the 1930s, interest in soil and water conservation began to mount. In 1935, the Soil Conservation Service, now called the **Natural Resources Conservation Service,** was created in the U. S. Department of Agriculture. In 1939, the **Texas Soil Conservation Law** made it possible for landowners to organize local soil and water conservation districts.

The state as of Aug. 1994, had 213 conservation districts, which manage the conservation functions within the district. A subdivision of state government, each district is governed by a board of five elected landowners. Technical assistance in planning and applying conservation work is provided through the USDA Natural Resources Conservation Service. State funds for districts are administered through the **Texas State Soil and Water Conservation Board.**

The 1987 National Resources Inventory showed that more than twice as much soil is being lost to wind erosion each year than to sheet and rill erosion. It also showed that about 21 percent of all land in Texas is "prime farmland."

Soil Subdivisions

Most authorities divide Texas into 20 major subdivisions that have similar or related soils, vegetation, topography, climate and land uses. These are called **Major Land Resource Areas.** Brief descriptions of these subdivisions follow.

1. Trans-Pecos Soils

The 18.7 million acres of the Trans-Pecos, mostly west of the Pecos River, are diverse plains and valleys intermixed with mountains

Upland soils are **light reddish brown to brown clay loams, clays and sands**, (mostly high in lime) and many areas of shallow soils and rock lands. Main series: **Hoban, Reeves, Reakor, Lajitas and Bissett (lower basins); Brewster, Verhalen, Musquiz (mountains and valleys); Penwell, Wink, Bluepoint (sandy soils); Orla, Holloman (gypsic soils).** Bottomland soils are **dark grayish brown to reddish brown, silt loams to clayey, alluvial soils (some saline)**. Main series: **Harkey, Glendale (Rio Grande); Pecos, Arno (Pecos River).**

Rainfall is sparse, and vegetative cover is as thin and variable as the topography, soils and drainage conditions. In general it is of two types: short grasses and shrubs on the flat soils of the basins and valleys, and a mixture of mid and short grasses and species of **oak, pine, juniper and semiarid plants** and shrubs on the rough and mountainous lands. **Alkali sacaton and other salt-tolerant plants** occur in the basin.

2. High Plains Soils

The High Plains area comprises the vast high plateau of more than 19.4 million acres in Northwestern Texas. It lies in the southern part of the Great Plains province that includes large similar areas in Oklahoma and New Mexico. The flat, nearly level surface of very large areas has few streams of any dissection to cause local relief. However, several major rivers originate in the High Plains or cross the area. The largest is the **Canadian River** which has cut a deep valley across the Panhandle section.

Playas, small intermittent lakes scattered through the area, lie up to 20 feet below the surrounding flat plains. A 1965 survey counted more than 19,000 playas in 44 counties, occupying some 340,000 acres. They receive most of the runoff from rains, but less than 10 percent of this water percolating back to the aquifer.

Soils are **brown to reddish, mostly deep, clay loams, sandy loams and sands**. Free lime is present under many soils at various depths. Main series: **Pullman, Olton, Sherm (hardlands); Amarillo, Portales (mixed lands); Brownfield, Tivoli (sandy lands); Potter** (loamy soils, shallow over caliche). The **Guadalupe, Spur and Bippus** series are the main soils of bottomlands, but are minor in extent.

The soils are moderately productive, and the flat surface encourages irrigation and mechanization. Limited rainfall and constant danger of wind erosion are handicaps; but the region is **Texas' leading producer of three most important crops — cotton, grain sorghums and wheat**.

The native vegetation is of three distinct kinds. In the northern part and on the fine-textured soils south of the Canadian River, the vegetation is short grasses, mainly buffalo with some grama. In the southern part on the sandy loam soils it is largely grama and threeawn. On the deep sands it is mainly little bluestem, sand dropseed, sideoats grama and threeawn grasses. In places these sands support a thick growth of shinoak and sand sage (Artemisia).

3. Rolling Plains Soils

The Rolling Plains comprise an eastern section of the Great Plains in Northwestern Texas. The area lies west of the North Central Prairies and extends from the edge of the Edwards Plateau in Tom Green County northward into Oklahoma. It includes about 21.7 million acres. The **Red Beds** and associated reddish soils led to use of the name **Red Plains** by some.

Upland soils are **pale brown through reddish brown to dark grayish brown sandy loams, clay loams and clays**. Most soils have free lime in the lower part and are saline in places; some are shallow and stony; some are deep sands. Main series: **Miles, Woodward, Springer, Vernon, Tillman (northern two-thirds); Abilene, Rotan, Sagerton, Leeray, Throck, Lueders (southern one-third).**

Bottomland soils include minor areas of **reddish brown, sandy to clayey, alluvial soils**. Main series: **Lincoln, Westola, Colorado, Gageby, Clairemont, Spur, Mangum.**

On the finer-textured soils **curlymesquite, buffalo and grama grasses** are dominant, with some scattered shrubs in places. On the coarser-textured soils the principal grasses are **little bluestem, sideoats grama and threeawn grasses** with **sand sage and shinnery** on areas of deep sand.

4. Rolling Red Prairies Soils

The Rolling Red Prairies occupy about 1 million acres in North Central Texas adjoining Oklahoma. The area is dominantly prairie. The principal soils are of the **Anocon, Bluegrove, Kamay, Kirkland and Stoneburg series.** Bottomland soils are of the **Gaddy, Port, Gowen, Wheatwood and Mangum** series.

Native vegetation is mainly **little bluestem, sideoats, hairy and blue grama, Indiangrass and buffalograss**. The area is mainly used for cattle ranching and growing small grains.

5. North Central Prairie Soils

The North Central Prairies occupy about 7 million acres in Central North Texas. The area lies between the Western Cross Timbers and Rolling Plains and has been referred to as the Reddish Prairie. The area is dominantly prairie, but small wooded areas are intermixed. The principal soils are of the **Truce, Thurber, Bonti and Owens** series. Narrow strips of alluvial soils, mainly of the **Gowen, Clearfork and Westfork** series, occur in the flood plains of local streams. Small areas of other soils similar to those of the West Cross Timbers and Grand Prairie are intermixed. They are best suited for growing small grains and native grasses.

Native vegetation is mainly **little bluestem, sideoats, hairy and blue grama, Indian and buffalo grass.** Scrubby trees and shrubs, mainly **post oak and mesquite**, and **cacti** grow rather thickly in places.

6. Edwards Plateau Soils

The 22.7 million acres of the Edwards Plateau are on an extensive tableland of Southwest Texas. Many of the soils are shallow over limestone, and streams have cut many valleys and canyons. Upland soils are **dark, calcareous clays and clay loams,** mostly gravelly and stony. Some deeper, less stony soils occur on the flat divides. Main series: **Tarrant, Eckrant, Brackett and Tobosa (eastern two-thirds); Ector, Upton, Reagan (western one-third)**. Bottomland soils include minor areas of **dark, calcareous, clayey alluvial soils**. Main series: **Frio, Oakalla and Dev.**

This is principally a ranching region, the center of Texas' and the nation's mohair and wool production. Except where there is limited irrigation, crops are mainly such drought-resistant ones as grain sorghums and grasses. **Grasses, shrubs and scrubby trees** dominate the native vegetation. There are many **cedar brakes**.

7. Central Basin Soils

The Central Basin, also known as the **Llano Basin**, occupies a relatively small area in Central Texas. It includes parts or all of Llano, Mason, Gillespie and adjoining counties. The total area is about 1.6 million acres.

Upland soils are **reddish brown to brown, mostly gravelly and stony, sandy loams shallow over granite, limestone, gneiss and schist; deeper, less stony, sandy loam soils** in the valleys. Main series: **Keese, Ligon, Castell, Katemcy, and Voca.** Bottomland soils are minor areas of **dark gray, alluvial soils**. Main series: **Fieldcreek.**

The native vegetation consists of **grass and small oak and mesquite trees.** On some rocky slopes, **juniper** forms the principal growth. Ranching is the main enterprise, with some farms producing peaches, grain sorghum and wheat.

8. Northern Rio Grande Plain Soils

The Northern Rio Grande Plain comprises about 6.3 million acres in an area of Southern Texas extending from Uvalde to Beeville. The main soils are **deep, reddish brown or dark grayish brown, loamy**, and of the **Clareville, Elmendorf, Floresville, Miguel, Duval and Uvalde** series in the eastern part. Native range is **grassland, thorny brush and cacti**. Most of the area is range grazed by beef cattle. Grain sorghum, cotton, corn, flax and small grain are grown in the eastern part. Irrigated land in the **Winter Garden** area of the western part produces corn, cotton, grain sorghum and truck crops such as spinach, carrots and cabbage.

9. Western Rio Grande Plain Soils

The Western Rio Grande Plain comprises about 5.3 million acres in an area of Southwestern Texas from Del Rio to Rio Grande City. The main upland soils are **clayey, saline** and of the **Catarina, Cotulla, Elindio and Montell** series. The vegetation is **mid and short grasses with low thorny brush and cacti**. Soils along the Rio Grande are mainly the **Laredo, Rio Grande, Lagloria and Zalla** series. Most of the soils along the river are used for growing vegetables and sorghums. The upland soils are used for grazing beef cattle.

10. Central Rio Grande Plain Soils

The Central Rio Grande Plain comprises about 5.9 million acres in an area of Southern Texas from Live Oak to Hidalgo County. The main soils are **Nueces and Sarita series (sandy); Delfina and Delmita (loamy); Randado and Cuevitas series (shallow)**. The vegetation is **tall and mid grasses with scattered trees and shrubs.** Much of the area is used for raising beef cattle. A few areas are used for growing grain sorghum, cotton and small grain.

11. Lower Rio Grande Valley Soils

The Lower Rio Grande Valley comprises about 2.1 million acres in extreme Southern Texas. The main soils are **deep, loamy and clayey**, and of the **Brennan, Hidalgo, Harlingen, Raymondville and Rio Grande** series. Most of the soils are used for growing irrigated vegetables and citrus, along with cotton, grain sorghum and sugar cane. Some areas are in range and used for growing beef cattle.

12. West Cross Timbers Soils

The West Cross Timbers comprises a total of about 2.6 million acres. The area includes the wooded section west of the Grand Prairie and extends from the Red River southward to the north edge of Brown County. Small areas also occur intermixed or interlaced with soils of the western part of the Grand Prairie. The principal series are **Windthorst, Nimrod and Duffau**. Narrow areas of **alluvial soils**, mainly of the **Gowen** series, occur in the flood plains of local streams. Soils of the **Ships, Yahola and Weswood** series occur in the flood plains of the through-flowing rivers.

The native vegetation is mainly **shinnery oak and post oak** trees and a few other hardwoods. The trees are scrubby, of small size and unsuited for most uses other than firewood or fence posts. In places, grasses, including **little bluestem, grama and threeawn**, and scattered **mesquite** trees form a thick ground cover where the oak overstory is thin. Rangeland and pastures are used for grazing beef and dairy cattle. Crops are peanuts, grain sorghum, small grains, peaches, pecans and vegetables.

13. East Cross Timbers Soils

The East Cross Timbers includes a long narrow strip of wooded soils that separates the northern parts of the Blackland Prairie and Grand Prairie. This strip is only a few miles wide and extends from the Red River southward into Hill County and includes a total area of about 1 million acres. The soils are mainly of the **Callisburg, Crosstell, Silstid and Gasil** series.

The native vegetation is mainly **post oak** trees and a few other hardwoods.The trees are scrubby, of small size and unsuited for most uses other than firewood or fence posts. In places, grasses, including **little bluestem, grama and threeawn**, and scattered **mesquite** trees form a thick ground cover where the oak overstory is thin. Rangelands and pastures are used for grazing beef and dairy cattle. Crops are peanuts, grain sorghums, small grains, peaches, pecans and vegetables.

14. Grand Prairie Soils

The Grand Prairie includes the prairie just west of the Blackland Prairie in North Central Texas. It extends south from the Red River to about the Colorado River and comprises about 6.3 million acres.

The principal soils of the Grand Prairie are of the **Eckrant, Slidell and Denton** series. Small areas of soils of the **Crawford, Brackett, Krum and Lewisville** series occur also on the uplands. **Alluvial soils**, mainly of the **Frio and Bosque** series, occur in the flood plains of streams.

The native vegetation is mainly short grasses with some mid and tall grasses on the deeper soils. **Buffalo and grama** grasses, **little bluestem and indiangrass** are the most widespread. In many places, especially on rocky slopes of shallow soils, small **oak and juniper** trees form a thick cover, and scattered **mesquite** trees occur throughout the area. The area is mainly used for growing beef cattle. Some small grain, grain sorghum and corn are grown.

15. Blackland Prairie Soils

An almost treeless area, the Blackland Prairies consist of about 12.6 million acres of East Central Texas extending southwesterly from the Red River to Bexar County. There are smaller, similar areas to the southeast.

The soils of the greater portion of the Blackland Prairie proper are mainly of the **Houston Black, Heiden and Austin** series with smaller areas of **Lewisville, Altoga and Stephen** soils. Bottomland soils are mainly **Tinn and Trinity** clays.

The native vegetation consists of **bunch and short grasses**. The main species are **little and big bluestems, grama, Indian, buffalo and threeawn** grasses. In places, scattered **mesquite** trees, **cacti** and other shrubs form a rather thick cover. Hardwood trees — mainly **elm, hackberry and pecan** — occur in stream bottoms. The main crops are grain sorghum, wheat, cotton, corn and hay. Pastures are used for beef and dairy cattle.

16. Claypan Area Soils

The Claypan Area is a nearly level to gently rolling moderately dissected **woodland savannah to brushy area (Post Oak Belt)** with moderate surface drainage. The area is more than 6.1 million acres.

Upland soils are **sandy loams, commonly thin over gray, mottled or red, firm, clayey subsoils.** Some deep, sandy soils with less clayey subsoils exist. Main series: **Lufkin, Axtell, Tabor (thin-surface claypan soils); Freestone and Padina (thick-surface sandy and loamy soils)**. Bottomlands are **reddish brown to dark gray, to loamy to clayey alluvial soils**. Main series: **Ships, Weswood (Brazos and Colorado Rivers); Kaufman, Trinity, Gladewater, Nahatche** (Trinity River and other smaller streams).

Vegetation consists of scattered stands of **post oak and blackjack oak** with **tall bunchgrasses** in the uplands; **yaupon** and other underbrush prevalent in places. In the bottomlands, **hardwoods** are predominant but **pecans** occur in some areas. The land is woodland and brushy range. A few areas are used for tame pasture and cool-season forage crops.

17. East Texas Timberland Soils

The East Texas Timberlands comprise the forested eastern part of the state, about 16.1 million acres.

The principal soil series are the **Woodtell, Kirvin, Cuthbert, Bowie, Lilbert and Tonkawa** soils in the northern "Redland" section; and **Diboll, Kisatche, Rayburn, Tehran, Doucette, Pinetucky and Shankler** soils in the southern part of the area. Alluvial soils, mainly **Mantachie, Iuka, Severn and Estes** are on flood plains of streams.

The native vegetation is a **pine-hardwood forest**. It is mainly **loblolly pine, shortleaf pine, sweetgum and red oak** trees with an understory of grasses and shrubs. Forestry and pastures are the main uses.

18. Coast Prairie Soils

The Coast Prairie includes the nearly flat strip that is near the Gulf Coast in Southeast Texas in the humid and subhumid zones. It ranges from 30 to 80 miles in width and parallels the coast from the Sabine River in Orange County to Baffin Bay in Kleberg County. Total area of the Coast Prairie is about 8.7 million acres. The principal soils in the eastern portion from about the San Antonio River to the Sabine River are **Lake Charles, Bernard, Edna, Morey and Beaumont** soils near the coast, comprising more than 4 million acres.

The more inland soils in the eastern section are **Hockley, Katy and Crowley** series, comprising nearly 2 million acres. The portions west and south of the San Antonio River are **Victoria, Orelia, Papalote and Clareville** soils, comprising some 2 million acres. Other important soils, which occur in the bottomlands, are **Brazoria, Norwood, Pledger and Kaman**. The nearly level topography and productive soils encourage farming. Rice, grain sorghum, cotton and soybeans are main crops. The native vegetation is **tall prairie grasses**, mainly species of **andropogon, paspalum and panicum**, with a narrow fringe of trees along the streams.

19. Coast Saline Prairies Soils

The Coast Saline Prairies include a narrow strip of wet lowlands adjacent to the coast and the barrier islands that extend from Mexico to Louisiana. The surface is at or only a few feet above sea level and it ranges from 3 to 20 miles wide. The total area is about 3.2 million acres. Important soil series are the **Harris, Tatton, Veston and Galveston** series in the eastern part, and the **Mustang, Aransas, Placedo, Francitas, Barrada and Galveston** in the southern part. Cattle grazing is the chief economic use of the various salt-tolerant **cordgrasses and sedges**. Recreation is popular on the barrier islands of the Texas Coast.

20. Flatwoods Soils

The Flatwoods area includes the flat, rather poorly drained forested area in humid Southeast Texas. Total area is about 2.5 million acres. Most soils have a water table near the surface at least part of the year. Soils are mainly fine **sandy loam with loamy or clayey subsoils**. Important soil series are the **Otanya, Sorter, Splendora, Kirbyville and Evadale.**

The land is mainly used for forest. The typical vegetation is a **pine-hardwood forest** that is **longleaf pine, loblolly pine, sweetgum and various oak species.** ☆

Water Resources

Beginning in September 1993, regulation of the water resources of the state were placed in the jurisdiction of the **Texas Natural Resource Conservation Commission**. In addition, the **Texas Water Development Board** is responsible for the development of Texas water resources and the financing of facilities, such as dams, that are part of that development.

Texas, through its river authorities, municipalities, water districts and state-level agencies, exercises the dominant role in development of municipal and industrial water supplies. Approximately 80 percent of the money invested in the state's water projects has been provided by Texas entities of government.

Ground-water Supplies and Use

Texas has historically relied on its wealth of fresh to slightly saline water that underlies more than 81 percent of the state. Half of the more than 12.4 million acre-feet of water currently being used in Texas is derived from underground sources that occupy nine major and 20 minor aquifers. Approximately 72 percent of the ground water produced is used for irrigating agricultural crops, especially in the Panhandle region. Ground water also supplies about 45 percent of the state's municipal needs.

Major Aquifers (see map on next page):

Ogallala — The Ogallala aquifer extends under 46 counties of the Texas Panhandle and is the southernmost extension of the largest aquifer (High Plains aquifer) in North America. The Ogallala Formation of late Miocene to early Pliocene age consists of heterogeneous sequences of coarse-grained sand and gravel in the lower part grading upward into clay, silt and fine sand. In Texas, the Panhandle is the most extensive region irrigated with ground water. Approximately 95 percent of the water pumped from the Ogallala is used for irrigation. Water-level declines are occurring in part of the aquifer region because of extensive pumping that far exceeds recharge.

Gulf Coast Aquifer — The Gulf Coast aquifer forms an irregularly shaped belt that parallels the Texas coastline and extends through 53 counties from the Rio Grande northeastward to the Louisiana border. The aquifer system is composed of the water-bearing units of the **Catahoula, Oakville, Fleming, Goliad, Willis, Lissie, Bentley, Montgomery** and **Beaumont formations**. This system has been divided into three major water-producing components referred to as the **Chicot, Evangeline**, and **Jasper** aquifers. Municipal uses and irrigation account for about 45 percent each of the total pumpage from the aquifer. Water quality is generally good northeast of the San Antonio River basin, but deteriorates to the southwest. Years of heavy pumpage have caused significant water-level declines in portions of the aquifer. Some of these declines have resulted in compaction of dewatered clays and significant **land-surface subsidence** particularly in the Houston-Galveston area.

Edwards (Balcones Fault Zone) — The Edwards (BFZ) aquifer forms a narrow belt extending through nine counties from a ground-water divide in Kinney County through the San Antonio area northeastward to the Leon River in Bell County. A poorly defined ground-water divide in Hays County hydrologically spearates the aquifer into the San Antonio and Austin regions. Water in the aquifer occurs in fractures, honeycomb zones and solution channels in the Edwards and associated limestone formations of Cretaceous age. More than 50 percent of the pumpage from the aquifer is for municipal use, while irrigation is the principal use in the western segment. San Antonio is one of the largest cities in the world that relies solely on a single ground-water source for its municipal supply. The aquifer also feeds several well-known recreational springs and underlies some of the most environmentally sensitive areas in the state.

Carrizo-Wilcox — Extending from the Rio Grande in South Texas northeastward into Arkansas and Louisiana, the Carrizo-Wilcox aquifer provides water to all or parts of 57 counties. The Wilcox Group and overlying Carrizo Sand of the Claiborne Group form a hydrologically connected system of sand locally interbedded with clay, silt, lignite and gravel. Throughout most of its extent in Texas, the aquifer yields fresh to slightly saline water, which is used primarily for irrigation in the **Winter Garden District** of South Texas and for public supply and industrial use in Central and Northeast Texas. Because of excessive pumping, the water level in the aquifer has been significantly lowered, particularly in the artesian portion of the Winter Garden District of Atascosa, Frio and Zavala counties and in municipal and industrial areas located in Angelina and Smith counties.

Trinity Group — The Trinity aquifer consists of basal Cretaceous-age Trinity Group formations that extend from the Red River in North Texas to the Hill Country of Central Texas. Formations comprising the aquifer include the **Twin Mountains, Glen Rose** and **Paluxy.** Where the Glen Rose thins or is absent, the Twin Mountains and Paluxy formations coalesce to form the **Antlers Formation.** In the southern extent, the Trinity includes the Glen Rose and underlying Travis Peak formations. Water from the Antlers portion of the Trinity is used mainly for irrigation in the outcrop area of North and Central Texas. Elsewhere, water from the Trinity is used primarily for municipal and domestic supply. Extensive development of the Trinity aquifer in the Dallas-Fort Worth and Waco areas has historically resulted in water-level declines of several hundred feet.

Edwards-Trinity (Plateau) — This aquifer underlies the **Edwards Plateau**, extending from the Hill Country of Central Texas westward to the Trans-Pecos region. The aquifer consists of sandstone and limestone formations of theTrinity Group formations and limestones and dolomites of the Edwards and associated limestone formations. Ground-water movement in the aquifer is generally toward the southeast. Near the edge of the plateau, flow is toward the main streams, where the water issues from springs. Irrigation in the northwestern portion of the region accounts for approximately 70 percent of the total aquifer use and has resulted in significant water-level declines in Glasscock and Reagan counties. Elsewhere, the aquifer supplies fresh but hard water for municipal, domestic and livestock use.

Seymour — This aquifer consists of isolated areas of alluvium found in parts of 22 north-central and Panhandle counties in the upper Red River and Brazos River basins. Eastward-flowing streams during the Quaternary Period deposited discontinuous beds of poorly sorted gravel, sand, silt and clay that were later dissected by erosion, resulting in the isolated remnants of the formation. Individual accumulations vary greatly in thickness, but most of the Seymour is less than 100 feet. The lower, more permeable part of the aquifer produces the greatest amount of ground water. Irrigation pumpage accounts for 90 percent of the total use. Water quality generally ranges from fresh to slightly saline. However, the salinity has increased in many heavily pumped areas to the point where the water has become unsuitable for domestic and municipal use. Natural salt pollution in the upper reaches of the Red and Brazos River basins precludes the full utilization of these water resources.

Hueco-Mesilla Bolson — These aquifers are

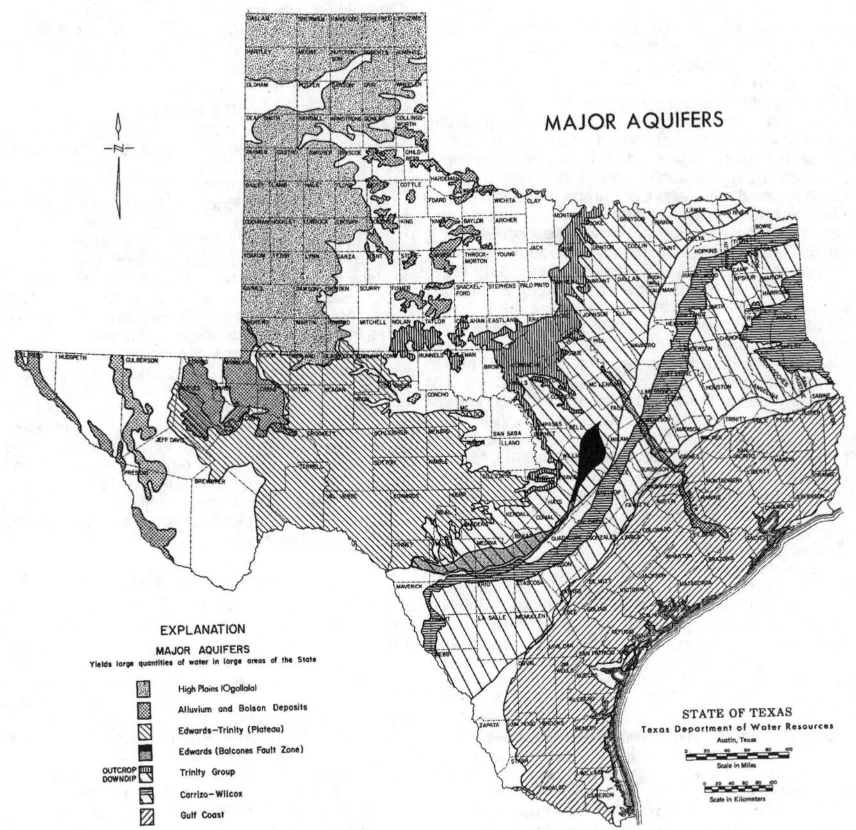

located in El Paso and Hudspeth counties in far western Texas and occur in Quaternary basin-fill deposits that extend northward into New Mexico and westward into Mexico. The Hueco Bolson, located on the eastern side of the Franklin Mountains, consists of up to 9,000 feet of clay, silt, sand and gravel and is the principal source of drinking water for both El Paso and Juarez. Located west of the Franklin Mountains, the Mesilla Bolson reaches up to 2,000 feet in thickness and contains three separate water-producing zones. Ground-water depletion of the Hueco Bolson has become a serious problem. Historical large-scale ground-water withdrawals, especially for the municipal uses of El Paso and Juarez, have caused major water-level declines and significntly changed the direction of flow, causing a deterioration of the chemical quality of the ground water in the aquifer.

Cenozoic Pecos Alluvium — Located in the upper Pecos River Valley of West Texas, this aquifer is the principal source of water for irrigation in Reeves and northwestern Pecos counties and for industrial uses, power supply and municipal use elsewhere. Consisting of up to 1,500 feet of alluvial fill, the aquifer occupies two hydrologically separate basins: the Pecos Trough in the west and the Monument Draw Trough in the east. Water from the aquifer is generally hard and contains dissolved-solids concentrations ranging from less than 300 to more than 5,000 parts per milion. Water-level declines in excess of 200 feet have historically occurred in Reeves and Pecos counties, but have moderated since the mid-1970s with the decrease in irrigation pumpage.

Major Rivers

Some **11,247 named streams** are identified in the **U.S. Geological Survey Geographic Names Information System.** Their combined length is about 80,000 miles, and they drain 263,513 square miles within Texas. **Thirteen major rivers** are described below, starting with the southernmost and moving northward:

Rio Grande

The Pueblo Indians called this river **P'osoge,** "river of great water." In 1582, Antonio de Espejo of Nueva Vizcaya, Mexico, followed the course of the **Río Conchos** to its confluence with a great river, which Espejo named **Río del Norte (River of the North).** The name **Rio Grande** was first given the stream apparently by the explorer **Juan de Oñate,** who arrived on its banks near present-day El Paso in 1598.

Thereafter the names were often consolidated, as **Río Grande del Norte.** (It has its counterpart in the Portuguese Río Grande do Sul in the state of that name in Brazil.) It was shown also on early Spanish maps as **Río San Buenaventura** and **Río Ganapetuan**. In its lower course it early acquired the name

Río Bravo, and it is called by that name today by many Mexicans living in its valley. At times it has also been known as **Río Turbio,** probably because of its muddy appearance during its frequent rises.

Some people erroneously call this watercourse the **Rio Grande River,** but, since "Rio Grande" means "big river," adding "river" to the name is redundant.

From source to mouth, the Rio Grande drops 12,000 feet to sea level as a snow-fed mountain torrent, carver of canyons, desert stream and meandering coastal river. Along its banks and in its valley Indian civilizations developed, and Europeans made some of their first North American settlements.

This river rises in Colorado, flows the north-south length of New Mexico and **forms the boundary of Texas and international U.S.-Mexican boundary for 889 to 1,254 river miles,** depending upon method of measurement. (See **Texas Boundary Line.)** The length of the Rio Grande, as of other rivers, depends on method of measurement and varies yearly as its course changes. Latest **International Boundary and Water Commission** figure is 1,896 miles, which is considerably below the 2,200-mile figure often used. Depending upon methods of measurement, the Rio Grande is the fourth- or fifth-longest North American river, exceeded only by the Missouri-Mississippi, McKenzie-Peace, St. Lawrence and possibly Yukon. Since all of these except the Missouri-Mississippi are partly in Canada, the Rio Grande is the **second-longest river entirely within or bordering the United States.** It is **Texas' longest river.**

The snow-fed flow of the Rio Grande is used for **irrigation** in Colorado below the San Juan Mountains, where the river rises at the Continental Divide. Turning south, it flows through a canyon in northern New Mexico and again irrigates a broad valley of central New Mexico. This is the oldest irrigated area of the United States, where Spanish missionaries encouraged Indian irrigation in the 1600s. Southern New Mexico impounds Rio Grande waters in Elephant Butte Reservoir for irrigation for 150 miles of valley above and below El Paso. Here is the **oldest irrigated area in Texas** and one of the oldest in the United States. Extensive irrigation practically exhausts the water supply. In this valley are situated the **three oldest towns in Texas — Ysleta, Socorro** and **San Elizario.** At the lower end of the El Paso irrigated valley, the upper Rio Grande virtually ends except in seasons of above-normal flow.

It starts as a perennially flowing stream again where the Río Conchos of Mexico flows into it at Presidio-Ojinaga. Through the **Big Bend** the Rio Grande flows through three successive **canyons,** the **Santa Elena,** the **Mariscal** and the **Boquillas**. The Santa Elena has a river bed elevation of 2,145 feet and a canyon rim elevation of 3,661. Corresponding figures for Mariscal are 1,925 and 3,625, and for Boquillas, 1,850 and 3,490. The river here flows around the base of the **Chisos Mountains.** For about 100 miles the river is the southern boundary of **Big Bend National Park.** Below the Big Bend, the Rio Grande gradually emerges from mountains onto the Coastal Plains.

A 191.2-mile strip on the American shore from Big Bend National Park downstream to the Terrell-Val Verde County line, has federal designation as the Rio Grande Wild and Scenic River.

At the confluence of the Rio Grande and the Devils River, the United States and Mexico have built **Amistad Dam**, to impound 3,383,900 acre-feet of water, of which Texas' share is 56.2 percent. **Falcon Reservoir**, also an international project, impounds 2,667,600 acre-feet of water, of which Texas' share in Zapata and Starr counties is 58.6 percent. Where the Rio Grande joins the Gulf of Mexico, has created a fertile delta called the **Lower Rio Grande Valley,** a major vegetable- and fruit-growing area.

The Rio Grande drains over 40,000 square miles of Texas. Principal tributaries flowing from the Texas side of the Rio Grande are the **Pecos** and **Devils** rivers. On the Mexican side are the **Río Conchos**, the **Río Salado** and the **Río San Juan**. About three-fourths of the water running into the Rio Grande below El Paso comes from the Mexican side.

Nueces River

The Nueces River rises in Edwards County and flows 315 miles to Nueces Bay on the Gulf near Corpus Christi. Draining 17,000 square miles, it is a beautiful, **spring-fed stream** flowing through **canyons** until it issues from the **Balcones Escarpment** onto the Coastal Plain in northern Uvalde County. Alonso de León, in 1689, gave it its name. (Nueces, plural of nuez, means nuts in Spanish.) Much earlier, Cabeza de Vaca had referred to a **Río de las Nueces** in this region, probably the same stream. Its original Indian name seems to have been **Chotilapacquen.** Crossing Texas in 1691, Terán de los Rios named the river **San Diego.** The Nueces was the boundary line between the Spanish provinces of Texas and Nuevo Santander. After the Revolution of 1836, both Texas and Mexico claimed the territory between the Nueces and the Rio Grande, a dispute which was settled by the **Treaty of Guadalupe Hidalgo** in 1848, which fixed the international boundary at the Rio Grande. Nueces runoff is about 620,000 acre-feet a year in its lower course. Principal water conservation projects are **Lake Corpus Christi** and **Choke Canyon Reservoir.** Principal tributaries of the Nueces are the **Frio** and the **Atascosa.**

San Antonio River

The San Antonio River has its source in **large springs** within and near the corporate limits of San Antonio. It flows 180 miles across the Coastal Plain to a junction with the **Guadalupe** near the Gulf Coast. Its channel through San Antonio has been developed into a parkway. Its principal tributaries are the **Medina River** and **Cibolo Creek**, both spring-fed streams and this, with its own origin in springs, gives it a remarkably steady flow of clear water.

This stream was first named the **Leon** by Alonso de León in 1689. De Leon was not naming the stream for himself, but called it "lion" because its channel was filled with a rampaging flood.

Because of its limited and rather arid drainage area (4,200 square miles) the average runoff of the San Antonio River is relatively small, about 350,000 acre-feet annually near its mouth, but its flow, because of its springs, is one of the steadiest of Texas rivers.

Guadalupe River

The Guadalupe rises in its north and south prongs in the west-central part of Kerr County. A **spring-fed stream,** it flows eastward through the **Hill Country** until it issues from the **Balcones Escarpment** near New Braunfels. It then meanders across the Coastal Plain to San Antonio Bay. Its total length is about 250 miles, and its drainage area is about 6,000 square miles. Its principal tributaries are the **San Marcos**, another spring-fed stream, which joins it in Gonzales County, the San Antonio, which joins it just above its mouth on San Antonio Bay and the Comal, which joins it at New Braunfels. The **Comal River** has its source in large springs within the city limits of New Braunfels and flows only about 2.5 miles to the Guadalupe. It is the **shortest river in Texas** and also the **shortest river in the United States** carrying an equivalent amount of water.

There has been power development on the Guadalupe near Gonzales and Cuero for many years, and there is now power generation at **Canyon Lake.**

Because of its springs, and its considerable drainage area, the Guadalupe has an annual runoff of more than 1 million acre-feet in its lower course.

The name Guadalupe is derived from **Nuestra**

Señora de Guadalupe, the name given the stream by Alonso de León.

Lavaca River

The Lavaca is considered a primary stream in the Texas Basin because it flows directly into the Gulf, through Lavaca Bay. Without a spring-water source and with only a small watershed, including that of its principal tributary, the **Navidad**, its flow is intermittent. The Spanish called it the Lavaca (cow) River because of the numerous bison they found. It is the principal stream running to the Gulf between the Guadalupe and the Colorado. The principal lake on the **Navidad** is **Lake Texana**. Runoff averages about 600,000 acre-feet yearly into the Gulf.

Colorado River

Measured by length and drainage area, the Colorado is the **largest river wholly in Texas.** (This comparison excludes the Brazos, whose drainage basin extends into New Mexico.) Rising in Dawson County, the Colorado flows about 600 miles to Matagorda Bay on the Gulf. Its drainage area is 39,900 square miles. Its runoff reaches a volume of more than 2 million acre-feet near the Gulf. Its name is a Spanish word meaning **"reddish."** There is evidence that the name, Colorado, was given originally by Spanish explorers to the muddy Brazos, and Spanish mapmakers later transposed the two names. The river flows through a rolling, mostly prairie terrain to the vicinity of San Saba County, where it enters the rugged **Hill Country** and **Burnet-Llano Basin**. It passes through a picturesque series of **canyons** until it issues from the **Balcones Escarpment** at Austin and flows across the Coastal Plain to the Gulf. In this area **the most remarkable series of reservoirs in Texas** has been built. There are two large reservoirs, **Lake Buchanan** in Burnet and Llano counties and **Lake Travis** in Travis County. Between these, in Burnet County, are three smaller reservoirs: **Inks, Johnson** (formerly **Granite Shoals**) and **Marble Falls,** built to aid power production from water running over the Buchanan Lake spillway. Below Lake Travis is the older **Lake Austin**, largely filled with silt, whose dam maintains a head for production of power from waters flowing down from the lakes above. **Town Lake** is in the city of Austin. This area is known as the **Highland Lakes Country.**

As early as the 1820s, Anglo-Americans settled on the banks of the lower Colorado, and in 1839 the **Capital Commission of the Republic of Texas** chose the picturesque area where the river flows from the **Balcones Escarpment** as the site of a new capital of the Republic — now **Austin,** capital of the state. The early colonists encouraged navigation along the lower channel with some success, and boats occasionally ventured as far upstream as Austin. However, a **natural log "raft"** in the channel near the Gulf blocked river traffic. Conservation and utilization of the waters of the Colorado are under jurisdiction of three agencies created by the state Legislature, the **Lower, Central** and **Upper Colorado River Authorities**.

The principal tributaries of the Colorado are the several prongs of the **Concho River** on its upper course, the **Pecan Bayou (farthest west "bayou"** in the United States) and the **Llano, San Saba** and **Pedernales** rivers. All except the Pecan Bayou flow into the Colorado from the **Edwards Plateau** and are spring-fed, perennially flowing. In the numerous mussels found along these streams occasional **pearls** have been found. The Middle Concho was designated on early Spanish maps as **Río de las Perlas.**

Brazos River

The Brazos is the largest river between the Rio Grande and the Red River and is **third in size** of all rivers in Texas. It rises in three upper forks, the **Double Mountain, Salt** and **Clear forks** of the Brazos. The Brazos River proper is considered as beginning where the Double Mountain and Salt Forks flow together in Stonewall County. The Clear Fork joins this main stream in Young County, just above **Possum Kingdom Lake**. The Brazos crosses most of the main physiographic regions of Texas — High Plains, West Texas Lower Rolling Plains, West Cross Timbers, Grand Prairie and Gulf Coastal Plain.

The total length from the source of its longest upper prong, the Double Mountain Fork, to the mouth of the main stream at the Gulf, was reported to be 923.2 miles in a 1970 study by the Army Corps of Engineers. The drainage area is about 42,800 square miles. It flows directly into the Gulf near Freeport. Its annual runoff at places along its lower channel exceeds 5 million acre-feet.

The original name of this river was **Brazos de Dios**, meaning "Arms of God." There are several legends as to why. One is that the Coronado expedition, wandering on the trackless **Llano Estacado,** exhausted its water and was threatened with death from thirst. Arriving at the bank of the river they gave it the name of Brazos de Dios in thankfulness. Another is that a ship exhausted its water supply and its crew was saved when they found the mouth of the Brazos. Still another story is that miners on the San Saba were forced by drouth to seek water near present-day Waco and in gratitude called it Brazos de Dios There is also the theory that the early Spanish cartographers called the river "Arms of God" because of the great spread of its tributaries.

Much early Anglo-American colonization of Texas took place in the Brazos Valley. Along its channel were **San Felipe de Austin,** capital of Austin's colony, **Washington-on-the-Brazos**, where Texans declared independence, and other historic settlements. There was some **navigation of the lower channel** of the Brazos in this period. Near its mouth it intersects the **Gulf Intracoastal Waterway**, which provides connection with the commerce on the Mississippi.

Most of the Brazos Valley lies within the boundaries of the **Brazos River Authority**, which conducts a multipurpose program for development. A large reservoir on the Brazos is **Whitney Lake** (622,800 acre-feet capacity) on the main channel, where it is the boundary line between Hill and Bosque counties. Another large reservoir is **Possum Kingdom Lake** in Palo Pinto, Stephens, Young and Jack counties. **Waco Lake** on the Bosque and **Belton Lake** on the Leon are among the principal reservoirs on its tributaries. In addition to its three upper forks, other chief tributaries are the **Paluxy, Little** and **Navasota** rivers.

San Jacinto River

A short river with a drainage basin of 3,976 square miles and nearly 2 million acre-feet runoff, the San Jacinto runs directly to the Gulf through Galveston Bay. It is formed by the junction of its East and West forks in the northeastern part of Harris County. Its total length, including the East Fork, is about 85 miles. There are two stories of the origin of its name. One is that when early explorers discovered it, its channel was choked with hyacinth (**"jacinto"** is the Spanish word for hyacinth). The other is that it was discovered on Aug. 17, St. Hyacinth's Day. Through the lower course of the San Jacinto and its tributary, **Buffalo Bayou,** runs the **Houston Ship Channel** connecting the Port of Houston with the Gulf. On the shore of the San Jacinto was fought the **Battle of San Jacinto**, April 21, 1836, in which Texas won its independence from Mexico. The **San Jacinto State Park and monument** are there.

Lake Conroe is on the **West Fork**, and **Lake Houston** is located at the junction of the West Fork and the **East Fork**.

Trinity River

The Trinity rises in its East Fork, Elm Fork, West Fork and Clear Fork in Grayson, Montague, Archer and Parker counties, respectively. The main stream begins with the junction of the Elm and West forks at Dallas. Its length is 550 river miles and its drainage area, 17,969 square miles. Because of moderate to heavy rainfall over its drainage area, it has a flow of 5,800,000 acre-feet near its mouth on the Gulf, exceeded only by the Neches, Red and Sabine River basins.

The Trinity derives its name from the Spanish **"Trinidad."** Alonso de León named it **La Santísima Trinidad** (the Most Holy Trinity).

Navigation was developed along its lower course with several riverport towns, such as **Sebastopol** in Trinity County. For many years there has been a basin-wide movement for navigation, conservation and utilization of its water. The **Trinity River Authority** is a state agency and the **Trinity Improvement Association** is a publicly supported nonprofit organization advocating its development.

The Trinity has in its valley **more large cities, greater population and more industrial development** than any other river basin in Texas. On the Lower Coastal Plain there is large use of its waters for **rice irrigation**. Largest reservoir on the Elm Fork is **Lewisville Lake** (formerly **Garza-Little Elm** and **Lake Dallas**). There are four reservoirs above Fort Worth — **Lake Worth, Eagle Mountain** and **Bridgeport** on the West Fork and **Benbrook Lake** on the Clear Fork. **Lavon Lake** in southeast Collin County and **Lake Ray Hubbard** in Collin, Dallas, Kaufman and Rockwall counties are on the East Fork. **Livingston Lake** is in Polk, San Jacinto, Trinity and Walker counties. The three major reservoirs below the Dallas-Fort Worth area are **Cedar Creek Reservoir** and **Richland-Chambers Reservoir**.

Neches River

The Neches is in East Texas, with total length of about 416 miles and drainage area of 10,011 square miles. Abundant rainfall over its entire basin gives it a flow near the Gulf of about 6 million acre-feet a year. The river takes its name from the **Neches Indians** that the early Spanish explorers found living along its banks. Principal tributary of the Neches, and comparable with the Neches in length and flow above their confluence, is the **Angelina River**, so named from **Angelina (Little Angel)**, a Hainai Indian girl who converted to Christianity and played an important role in the early development of this region.

Both the Neches and the Angelina run most of their courses in the **Piney Woods** and there was much settlement along them as early as the 1820s. **Sam Rayburn (McGee Bend) Reservoir**, near Jasper on the Angelina River, was completed and dedicated in 1965.

Reservoirs located on the Neches River include **Lake Palestine** in the upper portion of the basin and **B. A. Steinhagen Lake** located at the junction of the Neches and the Angellina rivers.

Sabine River

The Sabine River is formed by three forks rising in Collin and Hunt counties. From its sources to its mouth on **Sabine Lake**, it flows approximately 360 miles and drains 9,733 square miles. Sabine comes from the **Spanish word for cypress**, as does the name of the **Sabinal River**, which flows into the Frio in Southwest Texas. The Sabine has the largest water discharge (6.8 million acre-feet) at its mouth of any Texas river. Throughout most of Texas history the lower Sabine has been the **eastern Texas boundary line,** though for a while there was doubt as to whether the Sabine or the Arroyo Hondo, east of the Sabine in Louisiana, was the boundary. For a number of years the outlaw-infested **neutral ground** lay between them. There was also a **boundary dispute** in which it was alleged that the Neches was really the Sabine and, therefore, the boundary.

Travelers over the **Camino Real**, or **Old San Antonio Road,** crossed the Sabine at the famous **Gaines Ferry,** and there were famous crossings for the **Atascosito Road** and other travel and trade routes of that day.

Two of Texas' larger man-made reservoirs have been created by dams constructed on the Sabine River. The first of these is **Lake Tawakoni**, in Hunt, Rains and Van Zandt counties, with a capacity of 936,200 acre-feet. **Toledo Bend Reservoir** impounds 4,472,900 acre-feet of water on the Sabine in Newton, Panola, Sabine and Shelby counties. This is a joint project of Texas and Louisiana, through the **Sabine River Authority**.

Red River

The Red River (1,360 miles) is **exceeded in length only by the Rio Grande** among rivers associated with Texas. Its original source is water in Curry County, New Mexico, near the Texas boundary, forming a definite channel as it crosses Deaf Smith County, Texas, in tributaries that flow into **Prairie Dog Town Fork of the Red River.** These waters carve the spectacular **Palo Duro Canyon** of the High Plains before the Red River leaves the **Caprock Escarpment**, flowing eastward.

Where the Red River crosses the 100th meridian, the river becomes the **Texas-Oklahoma boundary** and is soon joined by the Salt Fork to form the main channel. Its length across the Panhandle is about 200 miles and, from the Panhandle east, it is the Texas-Oklahoma boundary line for 440 miles and thereafter the **Texas-Arkansas boundary** for 40 miles before it flows into Arkansas, where it swings south to flow through Louisiana. The Red River is a part of the **Mississippi drainage basin**, and at one time it emptied all of its water into the Mississippi. In recent years, however, part of its water, especially at flood stage, has flowed to the Gulf via the **Atchafalaya**. The Red River takes its name from the red color of the current. This caused every explorer who came to its banks to call it "red" regardless of the language he spoke — **Río Rojo** or **Río Roxo** in Spanish, **Rivìere Rouge** in French and **Red River** in English. The Spanish and French names were often found on maps until the middle of the last century when the English came to be generally accepted. At an early date, the river became the axis for French advance from Louisiana northwestward as far as present-day Montague County. There was consistent **early navigation** of the river from its mouth on the Mississippi to Shreveport, above which navigation was blocked by a **natural log raft**. A number of important gateways into Texas from the North were established along the stream such as **Pecan Point** and **Jonesborough** in Red River County, **Colbert's Ferry** and **Preston** in Grayson County and, later, **Doan's Store Crossing** in Wilbarger County. The river was a menace to the early traveler because of both its variable current and its **quicksands**, which brought disaster to many a trail herd cow as well as ox team and covered wagon.

The largest water conservation project on the Red River is **Texoma Lake**, which is the **largest lake** lying wholly or partly in Texas and the **tenth-largest reservoir (in capacity) in the United States.** Its capacity is 5,382,000 acre feet. Texas' share is 2,722,000.

Red River water's high content of salt and other minerals limits its usefulness along its upper reaches. Ten **salt springs** and tributaries in Texas and Oklahoma contribute most of these minerals.

The uppermost tributary of the Red River in Texas is **Tierra Blanca Creek**, which rises in Curry County, N.M., and flows easterly across Deaf Smith and Randall counties to become the **Prairie Dog Town Fork** a few miles east of Canyon. Other principal tributaries in Texas are the **Pease** and the **Wichita** in North Central Texas and the **Sulphur** in Northeast Texas, which flows into the Red River after it has crossed the boundary line into Arkansas. The last major tributary in Northeast Texas is **Cypress Creek**, which flows into Louisiana before joining with the Red River. Major reservoirs on the Northeast Texas tributaries are **Wright Patman Lake**, **Lake O' the Pines** and **Caddo Lake**. From Oklahoma the principal tributary is the **Washita**. The **Ouachita,** a river with the same pronunciation of its name, though spelled differently, is the principal tributary to its lower course.

Canadian River

The Canadian River heads near **Raton Pass** in northern New Mexico near the Colorado boundary line and flows into Texas on the west line of Oldham County. It crosses the Texas Panhandle into Oklahoma and there flows into the Arkansas. Most of its course across the Panhandle is in a deep gorge. A tributary dips into Texas' northern Panhandle and then flows to a confluence with the main channel in Oklahoma. One of several theories as to how the Canadian got its name is that some early explorers thought it flowed into Canada. **Lake Meredith**, formed by Sanford Dam on the Canadian, provides water for 11 Panhandle cities.

Because of the **deep gorge** and the **quicksand** at many places, the Canadian has been a peculiarly difficult stream to bridge. It is known especially in its lower course in Oklahoma as outstanding among the streams of the country for great amount of quicksand in its channel. ☆

Lakes and Reservoirs

The large increase in the number of reservoirs in Texas during the past half-century has greatly improved water conservation and supplies. As late as 1913, Texas had only eight major reservoirs with a total storage capacity of 376,000 acre-feet. Most of this capacity was in **Medina Lake**, with 254,000 acre-feet capacity, created by a dam completed in May 1913.

By 1920, Texas had 11 major reservoirs with combined storage capacity of 449,710 acre-feet. The state water agency reported 32 reservoirs and 1,284,520 acre-feet capacity in 1930; 47 reservoirs with 5,369,550 acre-feet capacity in 1940; 66 with 9,623,870 acre-feet capacity by 1950; 105 with total capacity of 22,746,200 in 1960; 149 with total capacity of 51,086,200 in 1970; 168 with total capacity of 53,302,400 in 1980.

In January 1995, Texas had **203 major reservoirs** (those with a normal capacity of 5,000 acre-feet or larger) existing or under construction, with a total conservation surface area of 861,381 acres and a conservation storage capacity of 41,822,945 acre-feet.

According to the U.S. Statistical Abstract of 1994, Texas has **4,959 square miles of inland water,** ranking it first in the 48 contiguous states, followed by Minnesota, with 4,780 sq. mi.; Florida, 4,683; and Louisiana, 4,153. There are about **6,736 reservoirs** in Texas with a normal storage capacity of 10 acre-feet or larger.

The following table lists reservoirs in Texas having more than 5,000 acre-feet capacity. With few exceptions, the listed reservoirs are those that were completed by Jan. 1, 1995, and in use. An asterisk (*) indicates those that are under construction.

Conservation storage capacity is used in the table below; the surface area used is that area at conservation elevation only. (Different methods of computing capacity are used; detailed information may be obtained from **Texas Natural Resource Conservation Commission, Austin; U.S. Army Corps of Engineers**; or local sources.) Also, it should be noted that boundary reservoir capacities include water designated for Texas use and non-Texas water.

In the list below, information is given in the following order: (1) Name of lake or reservoir; (2) county or counties in which located; (3) river or creek on which located; (4) location with respect to some city or town; (5) purpose of reservoir; (6) owner of reservoir. Some of these items, when not listed, are not available. For the larger lakes and reservoirs, the dam impounding water to form the lake bears the same name, unless otherwise indicated. Abbreviations in list below are as follows: L., lake; R., river; Co., county; Cr., creek; (C) conservation; (FC) flood control; (R) recreation; (P) power; (M) municipal; (D) domestic; (Ir.) irrigation); (In.) industry; (Mi.) mining including oil production; (FH) fish hatchery; USAE, United States Army Corps of Engineers; WC&ID, Water Control and Improvement District; WID, Water Improvement District; USBR, United States Bureau of Reclamation.

Lakes and Reservoirs	Conservation Service Area (Acres)	Conservation Storage Capacity (Acre-Ft.)
Abilene L. — Taylor Co.; Elm Cr.; 6 mi. NW Tuscola; (M-In.-R); City of Abilene	595	7,900
***Alan Henry Reservoir** — Garza Co.; Double Mountain Fork Brazos River, 10 mi. E Justiceburg; (M-In.-Ir.); City of Lubbock	3,504	115,937
Alcoa L. — Milam Co.; Sandy Cr.; 7 mi. SW Rockdale; (In.-R); Aluminum Co. of America	880	14,750
Amistad Reservoir — Val Verde Co.; Rio Grande, dam between Del Rio and confluence of Rio Grande and Devils River; an international project of the U.S. and Mexico; 12 mi. NWDel Rio; (C-R-Ir.-P-FC); International Boundary and Water Com. (Texas' share of conservation capacity is 56.2 percent.) (Formerly **Diablo R.**)	64,900	3,383,900
Amon G. Carter, L. — Montague Co.; Big Sandy Cr.; 6 mi. S Bowie; (M-In.); City of Bowie	1,540	20,050
Anahuac L. — Chambers Co.; Turtle Bayou; near Anahuac; (Ir.-In.-Mi.); Chambers-Liberty Counties Navigation District	5,300	35,300
Anzalduas Channel Dam — Hidalgo Co.; Rio Grande; 11 mi. upstream from Hidalgo; (Ir.-FC); United States and Mexico	—	8,400
Aquilla L. — Hill Co.; Aquilla Cr.; 10.2 mi. W of Hillsboro; (FC-M-Ir.-In.-R); USAE-razos R. Auth	3,280	52,400
Arlington L. — Tarrant Co.; Village Cr.; 7 mi. W Arlington; (M-In.); City of Arlington	2,275	45,710
Arrowhead, L. — Clay Co.; Little Wichita R.; 13 mi. SE Wichita Falls; (M); City of Wichita Falls	16,200	262,100
Athens, L. — Henderson Co.; 8 mi. E Athens; (M-FC-R); Athens Mun. Water Authority (formerly **Flat Creek Reservoir**)	1,520	32,690
Aubrey R. — (see **Ray Roberts L.**)	—	—
Austin, L. — Travis Co.; Colorado R.; W Austin city limits; (M-In.-P); City of Austin, leased to LCRA (impounded by **Tom Miller Dam**)	1,830	21,000

Ballinger L. — Runnels Co.; Valley Creek; 5 mi. W Ballinger; (M); City of Ballinger (also known as **Moonen Lake**)	—	6,850
Balmorhea, L. — Reeves Co.; Sandia Cr.; 3 mi. SE Balmorhea; (Ir.); Reeves Co. WID No. 1	573	6,350
Bardwell L. — Ellis Co.; Waxahachie Cr.; 3 mi. SE Bardwell; (FC-C-R); USAE	3,570	53,580
Barney M. Davis Cooling Reservoir — Nueces Co.; off-channel storage reservoir of Laguna Madre arm of Gulf; 14 mi. SE Corpus Christi; (In.); Central Power & Light Co.	1,100	6,600
Bastrop, L. — Bastrop Co.; Spicer Cr.; 3 mi. NE Bastrop; (In.); LCRA	906	16,590
Baylor Creek L. — Childress Co.; 10 mi. NW Childress; (M-R); City of Childress	610	9,220
Belton L. — Bell-Coryell counties; Leon R.; 3 mi. N. Belton; (M-FC-In.-Ir.); USAE-Brazos R. Auth.	12,300	457,300
Benbrook L. — Tarrant Co.; Clear Fk. Trinity R.; 10 mi. SW Fort Worth; (FC-R); USAE	3,770	88,200
Big Brown Creek Reservoir — Freestone Co. (see **Fairfield L.**)	—	—
Big Hill Reservoir — Jefferson Co. (see **J. D. Murphree Area Impoundments**)	—	—
Bivins L. — Randall Co.; Palo Duro Cr.; 8 mi. NW Canyon; (M); Amarillo (also known as **Amarillo City Lake**); City of Amarillo	379	5,120
Blackburn Crossing L. — (see **Lake Palestine**)		
Bonham, L. — Fannin Co.; Timber Cr.; 5 mi. NE Bonham; (M); Bonham Mun. Water Auth.	1,020	12,000
Bowie L. — (see **Amon G. Carter, L.**)		
Brady Creek Reservoir — McCulloch Co.; Brady Cr.; 3 mi. W Brady; (M-In.); City of Brady	2,020	29,110
Brandy Branch Reservoir — Harrison Co.; Brandy Br.; 10 mi. SW Marshall; (In.); Southwestern Electric Power Co.	1,240	29,500
Brazoria Reservoir — Brazoria Co.; off-channel reservoir; 1 mi. NE Brazoria; (In.); Dow Chemical Co.	1,865	21,970
Bridgeport, L. — Wise-Jack counties; W. Fk. of Trinity R.; 4 mi. W Bridgeport; (M-In.-FC-R); Tarrant Co. WC&ID Dist. No. 1	13,000	386,420
Brownwood, L. — Brown Co.; Pecan Bayou; 8 mi. N Brownwood; (M-In.-Ir.); Brown Co. WC&ID No. 1	7,300	143,400
Brushy Creek Reservoir — (see **Valley L.**)	—	—
Bryan Utilities L. — Brazos Co.; unnamed stream; 6 mi. NW Bryan; (R-In.); City of Bryan	829	15,227
Buchanan, L. — Burnet-Llano-San Saba counties; Colorado R.; 13 mi. W Burnet; (M-Ir.-Mi-P); LCRA	23,060	955,200
Buffalo Springs L. — Lubbock Co.; Double Mtn.Fk. Brazos R.; 9 mi. SE Lubbock; (M-In.-R); Lubbock Co. WC & ID No. 1; (impounded by **W. G. McMillan Sr. Dam**)	200	4,200
Caddo L. — Harrison-Marion counties, Texas and Caddo Parish, La. An original natural lake, whose surface and capacity were increased by the construction of a dam on Cypress Creek near Mooringsport, La.	25,400	59,800
Calaveras L. — Bexar Co.; Calaveras Cr.; 15 mi. SE San Antonio; (In.); City Public Service Bd. of San Antonio	3,450	61,800
Camp Creek L. — Robertson Co.; 13 mi. E Franklin; (R); Camp Creek Water Co.	750	8,550
Canyon L. — Comal Co.; Guadalupe R.; 12 mi. NW New Braunfels; (M-In.-P-FC); Guadalupe-Blanco R. Authority & USAE	8,240	385,600
Casa Blanca L. — Webb Co.; Chacon Cr.; 3 mi. NE Laredo; (R); Webb County (impounded by **Country Club Dam**)	1,656	20,000
Cedar Bayou Cooling Reservoir — Chambers Co.; Cedar Bayou; 15 mi. SW Anahuac; (In.); Houston Lighting & Power Co.	2,600	20,000
Cedar Creek Reservoir — Henderson-Kaufman counties; Cedar Cr.; 3 mi. NE Trinidad; (also called **Joe B. Hogsett, L.**); (M-R); Tarrant Co. WC&ID No. 1	33,750	679,200
Cedar Creek Reservoir — Fayette Co.; Cedar Cr.; 8.5 mi. E. La Grange; (In.); LCRA	2,420	71,400
Champion Creek Reservoir — Mitchell Co.; 7 mi. S. Colorado City; (M-In.); Texas Electric Service Co.	1,560	41,600
Cherokee L. — Gregg-Rusk counties; Cherokee Bayou; 12 mi. SE Longview; (M-In.-R); Cherokee Water Co.	3,987	46,700
Choke Canyon Reservoir — Live Oak-McMullen counties; Frio R.; 4 mi. W Three Rivers; (M-In.-R-FC); City of Corpus Christi-USBR	26,000	690,400
Cisco, L. — Eastland Co.; Sandy Cr.; 4 mi. N. Cisco; (M); City of Cisco (impounded by **Williamson Dam**)	445	8,800
Cleburne, L. Pat — Johnson Co.; Nolan R.; 4 mi. S. Cleburne; (M); City of Cleburne	1,550	25,300
Clyde, L. — Callahan Co.; N. Prong Pecan Bayou; 6 mi. S. Clyde; (M); City of Clyde and USDA Soil Conservation Service	449	5,748
Coffee Mill L. — Fannin Co.; Coffee Mill Cr.; 12 mi. NW Honey Grove; (R); U.S. Forest Service	650	8,000
Coleman L. — Coleman Co.; Jim Ned Cr.; 14 mi. N. Coleman; (M-In.); City of Coleman	2,000	40,000
Coleto Creek Reservoir — Goliad-Victoria counties; Coleto Cr.; 12 mi. SW Victoria; (In); Guadalupe-Blanco River Auth.	3,100	35,080
Colorado City, L. — Mitchell Co.; Morgan Cr.; 4 mi. SW Colorado City; (M-In.-P); Texas Electric Service Co.	1,612	30,800
Conroe, L. — Montgomery-Walker counties; W. Fk. San Jacinto R.; 7 mi. NW Conroe; (M-In.-Mi.); San Jacinto River Authority, City of Houston and Texas Water Dev. Bd.	20,985	429,900
Cooper L. — Delta-Hopkins counties; Sulphur R.; 3 mi. SE Cooper; (FC-M-R); USAE	19,305	310,000
Corpus Christi, L. — Live Oak-San Patricio-Jim Wells counties; Nueces R.; 4 mi. SW Mathis; (P-M-In.-Ir.-Mi.-R.); Lower Nueces River WSD (impounded by **Wesley E. Seale Dam**)	19,336	269,900
Crook, L. — Lamar Co.; Pine Cr.; 5 Mi. N. Paris; (M); City of Paris	1,226	9,964
Cypress Springs, L. — Franklin Co.; Big Cypress Cr.; 8 mi. SE Mount Vernon; (In-M); Franklin Co. WD and Texas Water Development Board (formerly **Franklin Co. L.**); impounded by **Franklin Co. Dam**)	3,400	66,800
Dallas, L. — (see **Lewisville L.**)	—	—
Dam B Reservoir — (see **Steinhagen L., B.A.**)	—	—

Daniel, L. — Stephens Co.; Gunsolus Cr.; 7 mi. S Breckenridge; (M-In.); City of Breckenridge; (impounded by **Gunsolus Creek Dam**)	924	9,515
Davis L. — Knox Co.; Double Dutchman Cr.; 5 mi. SE Benjamin; (Ir); League Ranch	585	5,395
Decker L.— (see **Walter E. Long L.**)	—	—
DeCordova Bend Reservoir — (see **Granbury Lake**)	—	—
Delta Lake Res. Units 1 and 2 — Hidalgo Co.; Rio Grande (off channel); 4 mi. N. Monte Alto; (Ir.); Hidalgo-Willacy counties WC&ID No. 1 (formerly **Monte Alto Reservoir**)	2,371	25,000
Diablo Reservoir — (see **Amistad Reservoir**)	—	—
Diversion, L. — Archer-Baylor counties; Wichita R.; 14 mi. W Holliday; (M-In.); City of Wichita Falls and Wichita Co. WID No. 2	3,419	40,000
Dunlap, L. — Guadalupe Co.; Guadalupe R.; 9 mi. NW Seguin; (P); Guadalupe-Blanco R. Auth.; (impounded by **TP-1 Dam**)	410	3,550
Eagle L. — Colorado Co.; Colorado R. (off channel); in Eagle Lake; (Ir.); Lakeside Irrigation Co.	1,200	9,600
Eagle Mountain Lake — Tarrant-Wise counties; W. Fk. Trinity R.; 14 mi. NW Fort Worth; (M-In.-Ir.); Tarrant Co. WC&ID No. 1	9,200	190,300
East L. — (see **Victor Braunig Lake**)	—	—
Eddleman L. — (see **Graham Lake**)	—	—
Edinburg L. — (see **Retama Reservoir**)		
Electra City L. — Wilbarger Co.; Camp Cr. and Beaver Cr.; 7 mi. SW Electra; (In.-M); City of Electra	660	8,055
Ellison Creek Reservoir — Morris Co.; Ellison Cr.; 8 mi. S. Daingerfield; (P-In.); Lone Star Steel	1,516	24,700
Fairfield L. — Freestone Co.; Big Brown Cr.; 11 mi. NE Fairfield; (In.); TP&L, Texas Elec. Service Co., DP&L and Industrial Generating Co. (formerly **Big Brown Creek Reservoir**)	2,350	50,600
Falcon Reservoir — Starr-Zapata counties; Rio Grande; (International—U.S.-Mexico); 3 mi. W Falcon Heights; (M-In.-Ir.-FC-P-R); International Boundary and Water Com.; (Texas' share of total conservation capacity is 58.6 per cent)	87,210	2,667,600
Farmers Creek Reservoir — Montague Co.; 8 mi. NE Nocona; (M-In.-Mi.) N Montague County Water Supply District (also known as **Lake Nocona**)	1,470	25,400
Ferrell's Bridge Dam Reservoir — (see **Lake O' the Pines**)	—	—
Flat Creek Reservoir — (see **Athens, Lake**)	—	—
Forest Grove Reservoir — Henderson Co.; Caney Cr.; 7 mi. NW Athens; (In.); Texas Utilities Services, Inc., Agent	1,502	20,038
Forney Reservoir — (see **Ray Hubbard, Lake**)	—	—
Fort Phantom Hill, Lake — Jones Co.; Elm Cr.; 5 mi. S. Nugent; (M-R); City of Abilene	4,246	74,300
Franklin County L. — (see **Cypress Springs, Lake**)	—	—
Galveston County Industrial Water Reservoir — Galveston Co.; off-channel storage Dickinson Bayou; 16 mi. S La Porte; (In.-M.); Galveston Co. Water Auth.	812	7,308
Garza-Little Elm — (see **Lewisville L.**)	—	—
Georgetown, L. — Williamson Co.; N. Fk. San Gabriel R.; 3.5 mi. W Georgetown; (FC-M-In.); USAE (formerly **North Fork L.**)	1,310	37,050
Gibbons Creek Reservoir — Grimes Co.; Gibbons Cr.; 9.5 mi NW Anderson; (In.); Texas Mun. Power Agency	2,490	26,824
Gladewater, L. — Upshur Co.; Glade Cr.; in Gladewater; (M-R); City of Gladewater	800	6,950
Graham L. — Young Co.; Flint and Salt Creeks; 2 mi. NW Graham; (M-In.); City of Graham	2,550	45,000
Granbury L. — Hood-Parker counties; Brazos R.; 8 mi. SE Granbury; (M-In.-Ir.-P); Brazos River Authority (impounded by **DeCordova Bend Dam**)	8,700	151,300
Granger L. — Williamson Co.; San Gabriel R.; 10 mi. NE Taylor; (FC-M-In.); USAE (formerly **Laneport Lake**)	4,400	64,540
Granite Shoals L. — (see **Johnson L., Lyndon B.**)	—	—
Grapevine L. — Tarrant-Denton counties; Denton Cr.; 2 mi. NE Grapevine; (M-FC-In.-R.); USAE	7,380	187,700
Greenbelt L. — Donley Co.; Salt Fk. Red R.; 5 mi. N Clarendon; (M-In.); Greenbelt M&I Water Auth.	1,990	58,200
H-4 Reservoir — Gonzales Co.; Guadalupe R.; 4.5 mi. SE Belmont; (P); Guadalupe-Blanco R. Auth. (also called **Guadalupe Reservoir H-4**)	696	5,200
Halbert, L. — Navarro Co.; Elm Cr.; 4 mi. SE Corsicana; (M-In-R); City of Corsicana	650	7,420
Harris Reservoir — Brazoria Co.; off-channel between Brazos R. and Oyster Cr.; 8 mi. NW Angleton; (In.); Dow Chemical Co.	1,663	12,000
Hawkins, L. — Wood Co.; Little Sandy Cr.; 3 mi. NW Hawkins; (FC-R); Wood County; (impounded by **Wood Co. Dam No. 3**)	776	11,570
Holbrook L. — Wood Co.; Keys Cr.; 4 mi. NW Mineola; (FC-R); Wood County; (impounded by **Wood Co. Dam No. 2**)	653	7,770
Honea Reservoir — (see **Conroe, Lake**)	—	—
Hords Creek L. — Coleman Co.; Hords Cr.; 5 mi. NW Valera; (M-FC); City of Coleman and USAE	510	8,600
Houston County L. — Houston Co.; Little Elkhart Cr.; 10 mi. NW Crockett; (M-In.); Houston Co. WC&ID No. 1	1,282	19,500
Houston, L. — Harris Co.; San Jacinto R.; 4 mi. N Sheldon; (M-In.-Ir.-Mi.-R); City of Houston; (impounded by **Lake Houston Dam**)	12,240	140,500
Hubbard Creek Reservoir — Stephens Co.; 6 mi. NW Breckenridge; (M-In.-Mi.); West Central Texas Mun. Water Authority	15,250	317,800
Imperial Reservoir — Reeves-Pecos counties; Pecos R.; 35 mi. N Fort Stockton; (Ir.); Pecos County WC&ID No. 2	1,530	6,000
Inks L. — Burnet-Llano counties; Colorado R.; 12 mi. W Burnet; (M-Ir.-Mi.-P); Lower Colorado River Authority	803	17,540
Iron Bridge Dam L. — (see **Tawakoni, Lake**)	—	—

Jacksonville, L. — Cherokee Co.; Gum Cr.; 5 mi. SW Jacksonville; (M-R); City of Jacksonville; (impounded by **Buckner Dam**)	1,320	30,500
J. B. Thomas, L. — Scurry-Borden counties; Colorado R.; 16 mi. SW Snyder; (M-In.-R); Colorado River Mun. Water Dist.; (impounded by **Colorado R. Dam**)	7,820	202,300
J. D. Murphree Wildlife Management Area Impoundments — Jefferson Co.; off-channel reservoirs between Big Hill and Taylor Bayous; at Port Acres; (FH-R); Texas Parks & Wildlife Dept. (formerly **Big Hill Reservoir**)	6,881	13,500
Joe B. Hogsett, L. — (see **Cedar Creek Reservoir**)	—	—
Joe Pool Reservoir — Dallas-Tarrant-Ellis counties; Mountain Cr.; 14 mi. SW Dallas; (FC-M-R); USAE-Trinity River Auth. (formerly **Lakeview Lake**)	7,470	176,900
Johnson Creek Reservoir — Marion Co.; 13 mi. NW Jefferson; (In.); Southwestern Electric Co.	650	10,100
Kemp, L. — Baylor Co.; Wichita R.; 6 mi. N Mabelle; (M-P-Ir.); City of Wichita Falls; Wichita Co. WID No. 2	16,540	319,600
Kemp Diversion Dam — (see **Diversion Lake**)	—	—
Kickapoo, L. — Archer Co.; N. Fk. Little Wichita R.; 10 mi. NW Archer City; (M); City of Wichita Falls	6,200	106,000
Kiowa, L. — Cooke Co.; Indian Cr.; 8 mi. SE Gainesville; (R); Lake Kiowa, Inc.	560	7,000
Kirby L. — Taylor Co.; Cedar Cr.; 5 mi. S. Abilene; (M); City of Abilene	740	7,620
Kurth, L. — Angelina Co.; off-channel reservoir; 8 mi. N Lufkin; (In.); Southland Paper Mills, Inc.	770	16,200
Lake Creek L. — McLennan Co.; Manos Cr.; 4 mi. SW Riesel; (In.); Texas P&L Co.	550	8,400
Lake Fork Reservoir — Wood-Rains counties; Lake Fork Cr.; 5 mi. W Quitman; (M-In.); SRA	27,690	635,200
Lake O' the Pines — Marion-Upshur-Harrison-Morris-Camp counties; Cypress Cr.; 9 mi. W Jefferson; (FC-C-R-In.-M); USAE (impounded by **Ferrell's Bridge Dam**)	18,700	252,000
Lakeview L. — (see **Joe Pool Reservoir**)	—	—
Lampasas Reservoir — (see **Stillhouse Hollow Reservoir**)	—	—
Laneport L. — (see **Granger Lake**)	—	—
Lavon L. (Enlargement) — Collin Co.; East Fk. Trinity R.; 2 mi. W Lavon; (M-FC-In.); USAE	21,400	443,800
Leon, Lake — Eastland Co.; Leon R.; 7 mi. S Ranger; (M-In.); Eastland Co. Water Supply Dist.	1,590	26,420
Lewis Creek Reservoir — Montgomery Co.; Lewis Cr.; 10 mi. NW Conroe; (In.); Gulf States Utilities Co.	1,010	16,400
Lewisville L. — Denton Co.; Elm Fk. Trinity R.; 2 mi. NE Lewisville; (M-FC-In.-R); USAE; (also called **Lake Dallas** and **Garza-Little Elm**)	23,280	464,500
Limestone, L. — Leon-Limestone-Robertson counties; Navasota R.; 7 mi. NW Marquez; (M-In.-Ir.); BRA	14,200	225,400
Livingston L. — Polk-San Jacinto-Trinity-Walker counties; Trinity R.; 6 mi. SW Livingston; (M-In.-Ir.); City of Houston and Trinity River Authority	82,600	1,750,000
Loma Alta Lake — Cameron Co.; off-channel Rio Grande; 8 mi. NE Brownsville; (M-In.); Brownsville Navigation Dist.	2,490	26,500
Lone Star Reservoir — (see **Ellison Creek R.**	—	—
***Lost Creek Reservoir** — Jack Co.; Lost Cr.; 4 mi. NE Jacksboro; (M); City of Jacksboro	360	11,960
Lyndon B. Johnson L. — Burnet-Llano counties; (formerly Granite Shoals L.); Colorado R.; 5 mi. SW Marble Falls; (P); LCRA; (impounded by **Alvin Wirtz Dam**)	6,375	138,500
Mackenzie Reservoir — Briscoe Co.; Tule Cr.; 9 mi. NW Silverton; (M); Mackenzie Mun. Water Auth.	910	46,250
Marble Falls L. — Burnet County; Colorado R.; (impounded by Max Starcke Dam); 1.25 mi. SE Marble Falls; (P); LCRA	780	8,760
Martin L. — Rusk-Panola counties; Martin Cr.; 17 mi. NE Henderson; (P); Texas Utilities Service Co., Inc.	5,020	77,620
Max Starcke Dam — (see **Marble Falls Lake**)	—	—
McGee Bend Reservoir — (see **Sam Rayburn Reservoir**)	—	—
McQueeney, L. — Guadalupe Co.; Guadalupe R.; 5 mi. W Seguin; (P); Guadalupe-Blanco R. Authority; (impounded by **Abbott Dam**)	396	5,000
Medina L. — Medina-Bandera counties; Medina R.; 8 mi. W Rio Medina; (Ir.); Bexar-Medina-Atascosa Co. WID No. 1	5,575	254,000
Meredith, L. — Moore-Potter-Hutchinson counties; Canadian R.; 10 mi. NW Borger; (M-In.-FC-R); cooperative project for municipal water supply by Amarillo, Lubbock and other High Plains cities. Canadian R. Municipal Water Authority-USBR; (impounded by **Sanford Dam**)	16,504	821,300
Mexia, L. — Limestone Co.; Navasota R.; 7 mi. SW Mexia; (M-In); Bistone Mun. Water Dist.; (impounded by **Bistone Dam**)	1,200	10,000
Millers Creek Reservoir — Baylor Co.; Millers Cr.; 9 mi. SE Goree; (M); North Central Texas Mun. Water Auth. and Texas Water Development Board	2,350	30,700
Mineral Wells L. — Parker Co.; Rock Cr.; 4 mi. E Mineral Wells; (M); Palo Pinto Co. Mun. WD No. 1	646	6,760
Mitchell County Reservoir — Mitchell Co.; Beals Creek; (Mi.-In.); Colorado River MWD	1,463	27,266
Monte Alto Reservoir — (see **Delta Lake Res. Units 1 and 2**)	—	—
Monticello Reservoir — Titus Co.; Blundell Cr.; 2.5 mi. E. Monticello; (In.); Industrial Generating Co.	2,000	40,100
Moonen L. — Runnels Co. (see **Ballinger L.**)		
Moss L., Hubert H. — Cooke Co.; Fish Cr.; 10 mi. NW Gainesville; (M-In.); City of Gainesville	1,125	23,210
Mountain Creek L. — Dallas Co.; Mountain Cr.; 4 mi. SE Grand Prairie; (In.); Dallas P&L Co.	2,710	22,840
Mud Creek Dam L. — (see **Tyler Lake, East**)	—	—
Murphree, J. D. Area Impoundments — (see **J. D. Murphree**)	—	—

Murvaul L. — Panola Co.; Murvaul Bayou; 10 mi. W Carthage; (M-In.-R); Panola Co. Fresh Water Supply Dist. No. 1	3,820	45,815
Mustang Lake East & **Mustang Lake West** — Brazoria co.; Mustang Bayou; 6 mi. S Alvin; (Ir.-In.-R); Chocolate Bayou Land & Water Co.	—	6,451
Nacogdoches, L. — Nacogdoches Co.; Bayo Loco Cr.; 10 mi. W Nacogdoches; (M); City of Nacogdoches	2,210	41,140
Nasworthy, L. — Tom Green Co.; S Concho R.; 6 mi. SW San Angelo; (M-In.-Ir); City of San Angelo	1,596	12,390
Natural Dam L. — Howard Co.; Sulphur Springs Draw; 8 mi. W Big Spring; (FC); Wilkinson Ranch & Colorado River MWD	—	32,000
Navarro Mills L. — Navarro-Hill counties; Richland Cr.; 16 mi. SW Corsicana; (M-FC); USAE	5,070	60,900
Nocona L. — (see **Farmers Creek Reservoir**)	—	—
North Fk. Buffalo Creek Reservoir — Wichita Co.; 5 mi. NW Iowa Park; (M); Wichita Co. WC&ID No.3	1,500	15,400
North Fork L. — (see **L. Georgetown**)	—	—
North L. — Dallas Co.; S. Fork Grapevine Cr.; 2 mi. SE Coppell; (In.); Dallas P&L Co.	800	17,000
Oak Creek Reservoir — Coke Co.; 5 mi. SE Blackwell; (M-In.); City of Sweetwater	2,375	39,360
O. C. Fisher L. — Tom Green Co.; N. Concho R.; 3 mi. NW San Angelo; (M-FC-C-Ir.-R-In.-Mi); USAE —Upper Colo. Auth. (formerly **San Angelo L.**)	5,440	119,200
O. H. Ivie Reservoir — Coleman-Concho-Runnels counties; 24 mi. SE Ballinger; (M-In.), Colorado R. Mun. Water Dist. (formerly **Stacy Reservoir**)	19,150	554,340
Palestine, L. — Anderson-Cherokee-Henderson-Smith counties; Neches R.; 4 mi. E Frankston; (M-In.-R); Upper Neches R. MWA (impounded by **Blackburn Crossing Dam**)	25,560	411,300
Palmetto Bend Reservoir — (see **Texana, L.**)	—	—
Palo Duro Reservoir — Hansford Co.; Palo Duro Cr.; 12 mi. N Spearman; (M-R); Palo Duro River Auth.	2,410	60,900
Palo Pinto, L. — Palo Pinto Co.; 15 mi. SW Mineral Wells; (M-In.); Palo Pinto Co. Municipal Water Dist. No. 1	2,661	42,200
Panola L. — (see **Murvaul L.**)	—	—
Pat Mayse L. — Lamar Co.; Sanders Cr.; 2 mi. SW Arthur City; (M-In.-FC); USAE	5,993	124,500
Pinkston Reservoir — Shelby Co.; Sandy Cr.; 12.5 mi. SW Center; (M); City of Center; (formerly **Sandy Creek Reservoir**)	523	7,380
Possum Kingdom L. — Palo Pinto-Young-Stephens-Jack counties; Brazos R.; 11 mi. SW Graford; (M-In.-Ir.-Mi.-P-R); Brazos R. Authority; (impounded by **Morris Sheppard Dam**)	17,700	569,380
Proctor L. — Comanche Co.; Leon R.; 9 mi. NE Comanche; (M-In.-Ir.-FC); USAE-Brazos River Authority	4,610	59,300
Quitman, L. — Wood Co.; Dry Cr.; 4 mi. N Quitman; (FC-R); Wood County (impounded by **Wood Co. Dam No.1**)	814	7,440
Randell, L. — Grayson Co.; Shawnee Cr.; 4 mi. NW Denison; (M); City of Denison	311	6,290
Raw Water Lake — Calhoun Co. (See **Cox Lake**)		
Ray Hubbard, L. — Collin-Dallas-Kaufman-Rockwall counties; (formerly **Forney Reservoir**); E. Fk. Trinity R.; 15 mi. E Dallas; (M); City of Dallas	22,745	490,000
Ray Roberts L. — Denton-Cooke-Grayson counties; Elm Fk. Trinity R.; 11 mi. NE Denton; (FC-M-D); City of Denton, Dallas, USAE; (also known as **Aubrey Reservoir**)	29,350	799,600
Recycle Lake — Calhoun Co. (see **Cox Lake**)		
Red Bluff Reservoir — Loving-Reeves counties, Texas; and Eddy Co.; N.M.; Pecos R.; 5 mi. N Orla; (Ir.-P); Red Bluff Water Power Control District	11,700	307,000
Red Draw L. — Howard Co.; Red Draw; 5 mi. E Bi Spring; (Mi.-In.); Colorado River MWD	374	8,538
Resacas — Cameron-Hidalgo-Willacy counties; Rio Grande; these reservoirs are primarily for storage of water during periods of normal or above-normal flow in the river for use when the river's water volume is low. Some of these are old loops and bends in the river that have been isolated by the river's changing its channel. They are known by the Spanish name of resacas. Also a number of reservoirs have been constructed and connected with the main channel of the river by ditches through which the reservoirs are filled either by gravity flow or by pumping. This is reserve irrigation water for use during periods of low flow in the river channel. Most of these reservoirs are near the main channel of the river, but some of them are 20 or 25 miles distant.	—	—
Retama Reservoir — Hidalgo Co.; Off-Channel Rio Grande; 5 mi. N Edinburg; (Ir.); Santa Cruz ID #15; (also known as **Edinburg Lake**)	—	5,000
Richland-Chambers Reservoir — Freestone-Navarro counties; Richland Cr.; 20 mi. SE Corsicana; (M); Tarrant Co. WCID No. 1	44,752	1,135,866
Rita Blanca L. — Hartley Co.; Rita Blanca Cr.; 2 mi. S Dalhart; (R) City of Dalhart	524	12,100
River Crest L. — Red River County; off-channel reservoir; 7 mi. SE Bogata; (In.); Texas P&L	555	7,000
Robert Lee Reservoir — (see **Spence Reservoir**)	—	—
Salt Creek L. — (see **Graham L.**)	—	—
Sam Rayburn Reservoir — Jasper-Angelina-Sabine-Nacogdoches-San Augustine counties; Angelina R.; (formerly **McGee Bend Reservoir**); (FC-P-M-In.-Ir.-R); USAE	114,500	2,876,300
San Angelo L. — (see **O. C. Fisher L.**)	—	—
San Bernard Reservoirs #1, #2, #3 — Brazoria Co.; Off-Channel San Bernard R.; 3 mi. N Sweeney; (In.); Phillips 66 Co.	—	8,610
Sandlin, L. Bob — Titus-Wood-Camp-Franklin counties; Big Cypress Cr.; 5 mi. SW Mount Pleasant; (In.-M-R); Titus Co. FWSD No. 1 (impounded by **Fort Sherman Dam**)	9,460	202,300
Sandow L. — (see **Alcoa Lake**)	—	—
Sandy Creek Reservoir — (see **Pinkston Reservoir**)	—	—
Sanford Reservoir — (see **Meredith, Lake**)	—	—
Santa Rosa L. — Wilbarger Co.; Beaver Cr.; 15 mi. S Vernon; (Mi.); W. T. Waggoner Estate	1,500	11,570
Sheldon Reservoir — Harris Co.; Carpenters Bayou; 2 mi. SW Sheldon; (R-FH); Texas Parks & Wildlife Comm.	1,700	5,420

Reservoir		
Smithers L. — Fort Bend Co.; Dry Creek; 10 mi. SE Richmond; (In.); Houston Lighting & Power Co.	2,480	18,700
Somerville L. — Burleson-Washington counties; Yegua Cr.; 2 mi. S Somerville; (M-In.-Ir.-FC); USAE-Brazos River Authority	11,460	160,100
Southland Paper Mills Reservoir — (see **Kurth, Lake**)	—	—
South Texas Project Reservoir — Matagorda Co.; off-channel Colorado R.; 16 mi. S Bay City; (In.); Houston Lighting & Power	7,000	187,000
Spence Reservoir, E. V. — Coke Co.; Colorado R.; 2 mi. W. Robert Lee; (M-In.-Mi); Colorado R. Mun. Water Dist.; (impounded by **Robert Lee Dam**)	14,950	484,800
Squaw Creek Reservoir — Somervell-Hood counties; Squaw Cr.; 4.5 mi. N Glen Rose; (In.); Texas Utilities Services, Inc.	3,228	151,047
Stacy Reservoir — (see **O. H. Ivie Reservoir**)	—	—
Stamford, L. — Haskell Co.; Paint Cr.; 10 mi. SE Haskell; (M-In.); City of Stamford	4,690	52,700
Steinhagen L., B. A. — (Also called **Town Bluff Reservoir** and **Dam B. Reservoir**); Tyler-Jasper counties; Neches R.; 1/2 mi. N Town Bluff; (FC-R-C); (impounded by **Town Bluff Dam**)	13,700	94,200
Stillhouse Hollow L. — Bell Co.; Lampasas R.; 5 mi. SW Belton; (M-In.-Ir.-FC); USAE-Brazos R. Authority; (sometimes called **Lampasas Reservoir**)	6,430	234,900
Striker Creek Reservoir — Rusk-Cherokee counties; Striker Cr.; 18 mi. SW Henderson; (M -In.); Angelina-Nacogdoches WC&ID No. 1	2,400	26,960
Sulphur Springs L. — Hopkins Co.; White Oak Cr.; 2 mi. N Sulphur Springs; (M); Sulphur Springs WD; (impounded by **Lake Sulphur Springs Dam**; formerly called **White Oak Creek Reservoir**)	1,910	17,710
Swauano Creek Reservoir — (see **Welsh Reservoir**)	—	—
Tawakoni, L. — Rains-Van Zandt-Hunt counties; Sabine R.; 9 mi. NE Wills Point; (M-In.-Ir-R); Sabine River Authority; (impounded by **Iron Bridge Dam**)	36,700	936,200
Terrell City L., New — Kaufman Co.; Muddy Cedar Cr.; 6 mi. E Terrell; (M-R); City of Terrell	830	8,712
Texana, L. — Jackson Co.; Navidad R. and Sandy Cr.; 6.8 mi. SE Edna; (M-Ir); USBR, Lavaca-Navidad R. Auth., Texas Water Dev. Bd.; (formerly **Palmetto Bend Reservoir**)	11,000	157,900
Texarkana L. — (see **Wright Patman Lake**)	—	—
Texoma L. — Grayson-Cooke counties, Texas; Bryan-Marshall-Love counties, Okla.; impounded by **Denison Dam** on Red R. short distance below confluence of Red and Washita Rivers; (P-FC-C-R); USAE	89,000	2,722,000
Thomas L. — (see **J. B. Thomas L.**)	—	—
Toledo Bend Reservoir — Newton-Panola-Sabine-Shelby counties; Sabine R.; 14 mi. NE Burkeville; (M-In.-Ir.-PR); Sabine River Authority (Texas' share of capacity is half amount shown)	181,600	4,472,900
Town Bluff Reservoir — (see **Steinhagen, Lake B. A.**)	—	—
Tradinghouse Creek Reservoir — McLennan Co.; Tradinghouse Cr.; 9 mi. E Waco; (In.); Texas P&L	2,010	35,124
Travis, L. — Travis-Burnet counties; Colorado R.; 13 mi. NW Austin; (M-In.-Ir.-Mi.-P-FC-R); LCRA: (impounded by **Mansfield Dam**)	18,930	1,144,100
Trinidad L. — Henderson Co.; off-channel reservoir Trinity R.; 2 mi. S. Trinidad; (P); Texas P&L Co.	740	7,450
Truscott Brine L. — Knox Co.; Bluff Cr.; 26 mi. NNW Knox City; (Chlorine Control); Red River Auth. of Texas	2,978	107,000
Turtle Bayou Reservoir — (see **Anahuac Lake**)	—	—
Twin Buttes Reservoir — Tom Green Co.; Concho R.; 8 mi. SW San Angelo; (M-In. -FC-Ir.-R.); City of San Angelo-USBR-Tom Green Co. WC&ID No. 1	9,080	177,800
Twin Oaks Reservoir — Robertson Co.; Duck Cr.; 12 mi. N. Franklin; (In); Texas P&L	2,300	30,319
Tyler L. — Smith Co.; Prairie and Mud Crs.; 12 mi. SE Tyler; (M-In); City of Tyler; (impounded by **Whitehouse and Mud Creek dams**)	4,800	73,700
Upper Nueces Reservoir — Zavala Co.; Nueces R.; 6 mi. N Crystal City; (Ir.); Zavala-Dimmit Co. WID No. 1	316	7,590
Valley Acres Reservoir — Hidalgo Co.; off-channel Rio Grande; 7 mi. N Mercedes; (Ir-M-FC); Valley Acres Water Dist.	906	7,840
Valley L. — Fannin-Grayson counties; 2.5 mi. N Savoy; (P); TP&L; (formerly **Brushy Creek Reservoir**)	1,080	16,400
Victor Braunig L. — Bexar Co.; Arroyo Seco; 15 mi. SE San Antonio; (In.); City Public Service Bd. of San Antonio	1,350	26,500
Waco L. — McLennan Co.; Bosque R.; 2 mi. W Waco; (M-FC-C-R); City of Waco-USAE-Brazos River Authority	7,270	151,900
***Wallisville L.** — Liberty-Chambers counties; Trinity R.; 2 mi. S Wallisville; (M-In.-Ir.); USAE	19,700	58,000
Walter E. Long L. — Travis Co.; Decker Cr.; 9 mi. E of capital, Austin; (M-In.-R); City of Austin (formerly **Decker Lake**)	1,269	33,940
Waxahachie L. — Ellis Co.; S Prong Waxahachie Cr.; 4 mi. SE Waxahachie; (M-In); Ellis County WC&ID No. 1; (impounded by **S. Prong Dam**)	690	13,500
Weatherford L. — Parker Co.; Clear Fork Trinity River; 7 mi. E Weatherford; (M-In.); City of Weatherford	1,210	19,470
Welsh Reservoir — Titus Co.; Swauano Cr.; 11 mi. SE Mount Pleasant; (R-In.); Southwestern Electric Power Co.; (formerly **Swauano Creek Reservoir**)	1,365	23,587
White Oak Creek Reservoir — (see **Sulphur Springs Lake**)	—	—
White River L. — Crosby Co.; 16 mi. SE Crosbyton; (M-In.-Mi.); White River Municipal Water Dist.	2,020	44,300
White Rock L. — Dallas Co.; White Rock Cr.; within NE Dallas city limits; (R); City of Dallas	1,119	10,740
Whitney L. — Hill-Bosque-Johnson counties; Brazos R.; 5.5 mi. SW Whitney; (FC-P); USAE	23,560	622,800
Wichita, L. — Wichita Co.; Holliday Cr.; 6 mi. SW Wichita Falls; (M-P-R); City of Wichita Falls	2,200	9,000

Winnsboro, L. — Wood Co.; Big Sandy Cr.; 6 mi. SW Winnsboro; (FC-R); Wood County; (impounded by **Wood Co. Dam No. 4**)	806	8,100
Winters L. — Runnels Co.; Elm Cr.; 4.5 mi. E. Winters; (M); City of Winters	640	8,370
Worth, L. — Tarrant Co.; W. Fk. Trinity R.; in NW Fort Worth; (M); City of Fort Worth	3,560	38,130
Wright Patman L. — Bowie-Cass-Morris-Titus-Red River counties; Sulphur R.; 8 mi. SW Texarkana; (FC-M); USAE; (formerly **Texarkana Lake**)	20,300	142,700

Vegetational Areas

This article was updated for The Texas Almanac by ***Stephan L. Hatch, Curator, S.M. Tracy Herbarium and Professor, Dept. of Rangeland Ecology and Management, Texas A&M University.)***

Difference in amount and frequency of rainfall, in soils and in frost-free days gives Texas a great variety of vegetation. From the forests of East Texas to the deserts of West Texas, from the grassy plains of North Texas to the semi-arid brushlands of South Texas, plant species change continuously.

Sideoats grama, which occurs on more different soils in Texas than any other native grass, was officially designated as the **state grass of Texas** by the Texas Legislature in 1971.

The **10 principal plant life areas** of Texas, starting in the east, are:

1. **Piney Woods.** Most of this area of some 16 million acres ranges from about 50 to 700 feet above sea level and receives 40 to 56 inches of rain yearly. Many rivers, creeks and bayous drain the region. Nearly all of Texas' commercial timber comes from this area. There are three native species of pine, the principal timber: longleaf, shortleaf and loblolly. An introduced species, the **slash pine**, also is widely grown. Hardwoods include **oaks, elm, hickory, magnolia, sweet and black gum, tupelo** and others.

The area is interspersed with **native and improved grasslands.** Cattle are the primary grazing animals. **Deer** and **quail** are abundant in properly managed localities. Primary forage plants, under proper grazing management, include species of the **bluestems, rossettegrass, panicums, paspalums, blackseed needlegrass, Canada and Virginia wildryes, purpletop, broadleaf and spike woodoats, switchcane, lovegrasses, indiangrass** and **legume** species.

Highly disturbed areas have understory and overstory of undesirable woody plants that suppress growth of pine and desirable grasses. The primary forage grasses have been reduced and the grasslands invaded by **threeawns, annual grasses, weeds, broomsedge bluestem, red lovegrass** and shrubby woody species.

2. **Gulf Prairies and Marshes.** The Gulf Prairies and Marshes cover approximately 10 million acres. There are two subunits: (a) The marsh and salt grasses immediately at tidewater, and (b) a little farther inland, a strip of bluestems and tall grasses, with some gramas in the western part. These grasses, except salt and marsh grasses, make excellent grazing. **Oaks, elm** and other hardwoods grow to some extent, especially along streams, and the area has some **post oak** and brushy extensions along its borders. Much of the Gulf Prairies is fertile farmland. The area is well suited for cattle.

Principal grasses of the Gulf Prairies are **tall bunchgrasses,** including **big bluestem, little bluestem, seacoast bluestem, indiangrass, eastern gamagrass, Texas wintergrass, switchgrass** and **gulf cordgrass. Seashore saltgrass** occurs on moist saline sites. Heavy grazing has changed the range vegetation in many cases so that the predominant grasses are the less desirable **broomsedge bluestem, smutgrass, threeawns, tumblegrass** and many other inferior grasses. The other plants that have invaded the productive grasslands include **oak underbrush, Macartney rose, huisache, mesquite, prickly pear, ragweed, bitter sneezeweed, broomweed** and others.

Vegetation of the Gulf Marshes consists primarily of **sedges, bullrush, flat-sedges, beakrush** and other rushes, **smooth cordgrass, marshhay cordgrass, marsh millet** and **maidencane**. The marshes are grazed best during winter.

3. **Post Oak Savannah.** This secondary forest region, also called the **Post Oak Belt**, covers some 7 million acres. It is immediately west of the primary forest region, with less annual rainfall and a little higher elevation. Principal trees are **post oak, blackjack oak** and **elm.** Along streams are growths of **pecans, walnuts** and other kinds of water-demanding trees. The southwestern extension of this belt is often poorly defined, with large areas of prairie.

The upland soils are **sandy and sandy loam**, while the bottomlands are **sandy loams and clays**.

The original vegetation consisted mainly of **little bluestem, big bluestem, indiangrass, switchgrass, purpletop, silver bluestem, Texas wintergrass, spike woodoats, longleaf woodoats, post oak** and **blackjack oak.** The area is still largely native or improved grasslands, with small farms located throughout. Intensive grazing has caused much of this area to degenerate to dense stands of a woody understory of **yaupon, greenbriar** and **oak** brush. **Mesquite** has become a serious problem. Good forage plants have been replaced by such inferior plants as **splitbeard bluestem, red lovegrass, broomsedge bluestem, broomweed, bullnettle** and **western ragweed**.

4. **Blackland Prairies**. This area of about 12 million acres, while called a "prairie," has much timber along the streams, including a variety of **oaks, pecan, elm, horseapple (bois d'arc)** and **mesquite**. In its native state it was largely a grassy plain — the first native grassland in the westward extension of the Southern Forest Region.

Most of this fertile area has been cultivated, and only small acreages of meadowland remain in original vegetation. In heavily grazed pastures, the tall bunchgrass has been replaced by **buffalograss, Texas grama** and other less productive grasses. **Mesquite, lotebush** and other woody plants have invaded the grasslands.

The original grass vegetation includes **big and little bluestem, indiangrass, switchgrass, sideoats grama, hairy grama, tall dropseed, Texas wintergrass** and buffalograss. Nongrass vegetation is largely legumes and composites.

5. **Cross Timbers and Prairies.** Approximately 15 million acres of alternating woodlands, often called the **West Cross Timbers**, and prairies constitute this region. Sharp changes in the vegetational cover are associated with different soils and topography, but the grass composition is rather uniform.

The prairie-type grasses are **big bluestem, little bluestem, indiangrass, switchgrass, Canada wildrye, sideoats grama, hairy grama, tall grama, tall dropseed, Texas wintergrass, blue grama** and **buffalograss**.

On the Cross Timbers soils, the grasses are composed of **big bluestem, little bluestem, hooded windmillgrass, sand lovegrass, indiangrass, switchgrass** and many species of legumes. The woody vegetation includes **shinnery, blackjack, post and live oaks**.

The entire area has been invaded heavily by woody brush plants of **oaks, mesquite, juniper** and other unpalatable plants that furnish little forage for livestock.

6. **South Texas Plains.** South of San Antonio, between the coast and the Rio Grande, are some 21 million acres of subtropical dryland vegetation, consisting of small trees, shrubs, cactus, weeds and grasses. The area is noteworthy for extensive brushlands, known as the **brush country**, or the Spanish equivalents of **chaparral** or **monte**. Principal plants are **mesquite, small live oak, post oak, prickly pear (Opuntia) cactus, catclaw, blackbrush, whitebrush, guajillo, huisache, cenizo** and others which often grow very densely. The original vegetation was mainly perennial warm-season **bunchgrasses** in **post oak, live oak and mesquite savannahs**. Other brush species form dense thickets on the ridges and along streams. Long-continued grazing caused the region to be densely

The gnarled trunks and lacy leaves of mesquite trees are common sights across the southern and western sections of the state. Almanac staff photo.

covered with a mixture of brush. Most of the desirable grasses have persisted under the protection of brush and cacti.

There are distinct differences in the original plant communities on various soils. Dominant grasses on the sandy loam soils are **seacoast bluestem, bristlegrass, paspalum, windmillgrass, chloris, silver bluestem, big sandbur** and **tanglehead**. Dominant grasses on the clay and clay loams are **silver bluestem, Arizona cottontop, buffalograss, common curlymesquite, bristlegrass, pappusgrass, gramas, plains lovegrass, Texas cupgrass, vinemesquite, other panicums and Texas wintergrass**. Low saline areas are characterized by **gulf cordgrass, seashore saltgrass, alkali sacaton and switchgrass**. In the post oak and live oak savannahs, the grasses are mainly **seacoast bluestem, indiangrass, switchgrass, crinkleawn, paspalums and panicums**. Today much of the area has been reseeded to **buffelgrass**.

7. **Edwards Plateau**. These 25 million acres are rolling to mountainous, with woodlands in the eastern part and grassy prairies in the west. There is a good deal of brushy growth in the central and eastern parts. The combination of grasses, weeds and small trees is ideal for **cattle, sheep, goats, deer and wild turkey**.

This limestone-based area is characterized by the large number of **springfed, perennially flowing streams** which originate in its interior and flow across the **Balcones Escarpment**, which bounds it on the south and east. The soils are shallow, ranging from sands to clays and are calcareous in reaction. This area is predominantly rangeland, with cultivation confined to the deeper soils.

In the east-central portion is the well-marked **Central Basin** centering in Mason, Llano and Burnet counties, with a mixture of granitic and sandy soils. The western portion of the area comprises the semi-arid **Stockton Plateau.**

Noteworthy is the growth of **cypress** along the perennially flowing streams. Separated by many miles from cypress growth of the moist Southern Forest Belt, they constitute one of Texas' several **"islands" of vegetation**. These trees grow to stately proportions and, in the past, have been commercialized.

The principal grasses of the clay soils are **cane bluestem, silver bluestem, little bluestem, sideoats grama, hairy grama, indiangrass, common curlymesquite, buffalograss, fall witchgrass, plains lovegrass, wildryes and Texas wintergrass.**

The rocky areas support tall or mid-grasses with an overstory of **live oak, shinnery oak, cedar and mesquite.** The heavy clay soils have a mixture of **tobosagrass, buffalograss, sideoats grama and mesquite.**

Throughout the Edwards Plateau, **live oak, shinnery oak, mesquite and cedar** dominate the woody vegetation. Woody plants have invaded to the degree that they should be controlled before range forage plants can re-establish.

8. **Rolling Plains**. This is a region of approximately 24 million acres of alternating woodlands and prairies. The area is half **mesquite woodland** and half **prairie**. Mesquite trees have steadily invaded and increased in the grasslands for many years, despite constant control efforts.

Soils range from coarse sands along outwash terraces adjacent to streams to tight or compact clays on redbed clays and shales. Rough broken lands on steep slopes are found in the western portion. About two-thirds of the area is rangeland, but cultivation is important in certain localities.

The original vegetation includes **big, little, sand and silver bluestems, Texas wintergrass, indiangrass, switchgrass, sideoats and blue gramas, wildryes, tobosagrass and buffalograss** on the clay soils.

The sandy soils support **tall bunchgrasses, mainly sand bluestem. Sand shinnery oak, sand sagebrush and mesquite** are the dominant woody plants.

Continued heavy grazing causes increase in woody plants, low-value grasses such as **red grama, red lovegrass, tumblegrass, gummy lovegrass, Texas grama, sand dropseed, sandbur, western ragweed, croton** and many other weeds. **Yucca** is a problem plant on certain rangelands.

9. **High Plains**. The High Plains, some 19 million treeless acres, are an extension of the Great Plains to the north. The level nature and porous soils prevent drainage over wide areas. The relatively light rainfall flows into the numerous shallow **"playa" lakes** or sinks into the ground to feed the great **underground aquifer** that is the source of water for the countless wells that irrigate the surface of the plains. A large part of this area is under irrigated farming, but native grassland remains in about one-half of the High Plains.

Blue grama and buffalograss comprise the principal vegetation on the clay and clay loam "hardland" soils. Important grasses on the sandy loam "sandy land" soils are **little bluestem, western wheatgrass, indiangrass, switchgrass and sand reedgrass. Sand shinnery oak, sand sagebrush, mesquite and yucca** are conspicuous invading brushy plants.

10. **Trans-Pecos, Mountains and Basins.** With as little as eight inches of annual rainfall, long hot summers and usually cloudless skies to encourage evaporation, this 18-million-acre area produces only drouth-resistant vegetation without irrigation. Grass is usually short and sparse. The principal growth consists of **lechuguilla, ocotillo, yucca, cenizo** and other arid land plants. In the more arid areas, **yeso, chino and tobosagrass** prevail. There is some **mesquite**. The vegetation includes **creosote-tarbush, desert shrub, grama grassland, yucca and juniper savannahs, pine oak forest and saline flats.**

The mountains are 3,000 to 8,751 feet in elevation and support **piñon pine, juniper** and some **ponderosa pine** and other forest vegetation on a few of the higher slopes.

The grass vegetation, especially on the higher mountain slopes, includes many **southwestern and Rocky Mountain species** not present elsewhere in Texas. On the desert flats, **black grama, burrograss and fluffgrass** are frequent. More productive sites have numerous species of **grama, muhly, Arizona cottontop, dropseed and perennial threeawn grasses**. At the higher elevations, **plains bristlegrass, little bluestem, Texas bluestem, sideoats grama, chino grama, blue grama, piñon ricegrass, wolftail and several species of needlegrass** are frequent.

The common invaders on all depleted ranges are **woody plants, burrograss, fluffgrass, hairy erioneuron, ear muhly, sand muhly, red grama, broom snakeweed, croton, cacti and several poisonous plants.**

Range Uses

More than 100 million acres of Texas are devoted to providing grazing for domestic and wild animals. This is the **largest single use for land in the state.** The **Piney Woods**, primarily valued for timber, also provide significant grazing. More than 80 percent of the acreage is devoted to range in the Edwards Plateau, Cross Timbers and Prairies, South Texas Plains and Trans-Pecos Mountains and Basins. **Range management** seeks to perpetuate plants and methods which yield maximum returns, while controlling or eliminating competitive, undesirable plants. ☆

For Further Reading

Hatch, S. L., K. N. Gandhi and L. E. Brown, ***Checklist of the Vascular Plants of Texas;*** *MP1655, Texas Agricultural Experiment Station, College Station, 1990.*

Texas Forest Resources

This information was provided by Roger Lord, Forest Resource Analyst, Texas Forest Service, The Texas A&M University System, College Station, TX 77843- 2136. Readers needing additional information on forest resources are welcome to contact the author at the above address.

It is a surprise to many people, including life-long Texans, that the state has an abundant and diverse forest resource. Trees cover roughly 13 percent of the state's land area. The 22 million acres of forests and woodlands in Texas is an area larger than the states of Massachusetts, Connecticut, New Hampshire, Rhode Island and Vermont combined. The principal forest and woodlands regions are: the East Texas pine-hardwood region often called the Piney Woods; the Post Oak Belt, which lies immediately west of the pine-hardwood forest; the East and West Cross Timbers areas of North Central Texas; the Cedar Brakes of Central Texas; the mountain forests of West Texas; and the coastal forests of the southern Gulf Coast.

The East Texas Piney Woods

Although Texas contains about 22 million acres of forest and woodlands, detailed forest resource data is available for only the 43-county East Texas timber region. The Piney Woods, which form the western edge of the southern pine region, extend from Bowie and Red River counties in Northeast Texas, to Jefferson, Harris and Waller counties in southeast Texas. This region contains 11.9 million acres of forest and is the most economically important forest area of the state, producing nearly all of the commercial timber. The following discussion summarizes the findings of the most recent Forest Survey of East Texas, conducted in 1992 by the USDA Forest Service Southern Forest Experiment Station.

Timberland Acreage and Ownership

Nearly all (11.8 of 11.9 million acres) of the East Texas forest is classified as "timberland," which is suitable for production of timber products and not reserved as parks or wilderness areas. In contrast to the trends in several other southern states, Texas timberland acreage is on a slight upward track. Acreage in timberland increased by 2 percent between 1986 and 1992. Seventy-four percent of the new timberland acres came from agricultural lands, such as idle farmland and pasture, which was either intentionally planted with trees or naturally reverted to forest.

Sixty-one percent of 11.8 million acres of East Texas timberland is owned by approximately 150,000 farmers, private individuals, families, partnerships and non-wood-using corporations. Thirty-two percent is owned by forest-products companies, and only 7 percent is owned by the government. The following table shows acreage of timberland by ownership:

Ownership Class	Thous. Acres
Non-industrial Private:	
Farmer	1,161.8
Corporate	954.3
Individual	5,106.9
Forest Industry	3,767.4
Public:	
National Forest	576.7
Misc. Federal	91.8
State	68.1
County & Municipal	46.8
Total	**11,773.8**

There are distinct regional differences in ownership patterns. Most forest-industry land is found south of Nacogdoches County, and timberland in some counties, such as Polk and Hardin, is as much as 75 percent owned by the forest-products industry. North of Nacogdoches, the nonindustrial private landowner predominates, and industry owns a much smaller percent of the timberland.

Forest Types

Six major forest types are found in the East Texas Piney Woods. Two pine forest types are most common. The loblolly-shortleaf and longleaf-slash forest types are dominated by the four species of southern yellow pine. In these forests, pine trees make up at least 50 percent of the trees.

Oak-hickory is the second most common forest type. These are upland hardwood forests in which oaks or hickories make up at least 50 percent of the trees, and pine species are less than 25 percent. Oak-pine is a mixed-forest type in which more than 50 percent of the trees are hardwoods, but pines make up 25 to 49 percent of the trees.

Two forest types, oak-gum-cypress and elm-ash-cottonwood, are bottomland types which are commonly found along creeks, river bottoms, swamps and other wet areas. The oak-gum-cypress forests are typically made up of many species including blackgum, sweetgum, oaks and southern cypress. The elm-ash-cottonwood bottomland forests are dominated by those trees but also contain many other species, such as willows, sycamore, and maple. The following table shows the breakdown in acreage by forest type:

Forest Type Group	Thous. Acres
Southern Pine:	
Loblolly-shortleaf	4,063.7
Longleaf-slash	232.9
Oak-pine	2,503.8
Oak-hickory	3,146.9
Bottomland Hardwood:	
Oak-gum-cypress	1,755.8
Elm-ash-cottonwood	71.0
Total	**11,773.8**

Southern pine plantations, established by tree planting and usually managed intensively to maximize timber production, are an increasingly important source of wood fiber. Texas forests include 1.8 million acres of pine plantations, 72 percent of which are on forest-industry-owned land, 22 percent on nonindustrial private, and 6 percent on public land. Plantation acreage increased 48 percent between 1986 and 1992. Genetically superior tree seedlings, produced at industry and Texas Forest Service nurseries, are usually planted to improve survival and growth.

Timber Volume and Number of Trees

Texas timberland contains 12.9 billion cubic feet of timber "growing-stock" volume. This is enough wood fiber to produce 200 billion copies of National Geographic. The inventory of softwood remained steady at 7.9 billion cubic feet, while the hardwood inventory increased nearly 12 percent to 5.1 billion cubic feet, between 1986 and 1992.

There are more trees in East Texas than there are people living on Earth — an estimated 6.9 billion live trees — according to the 1992 survey. This includes 2 billion softwoods, 4.1 billion hardwoods, and .7 billion trees of noncommercial species. The predominant species are loblolly and shortleaf pine; 1.9 billion trees of these two species are found in East Texas.

Timber Growth and Removals

Between 1986 and 1992, an annual average of 691.6 million cubic feet of timber was removed from the inventory either through harvest or land-use changes. Meanwhile, 728.6 million cubic feet were added to the inventory through growth each year, resulting in a net increase in timber inventory in East Texas.

For pine, however, slightly more is being cut than is being grown. An average 530.5 million cubic feet were removed during those years, while 522.9 million feet were added by growth. For hardwoods, 161.1 million feet were removed, while 205.7 million cubic feet were added by growth.

Texas is fortunate in that the rate of pine over-cutting is small compared to most other Southern states. However, if the 1 percent over-harvest of pine were to continue indefinitely, we could eventually run out of timber. Through increased reforestation and improved management, this short-term trend can be reversed before it becomes a long-term problem.

Other Tree Regions

Compared to commercially important East Texas, relatively little data are available for the other tree regions of Texas. However, these areas are environmentally important, with benefits of wildlife habitat, improved water quality, recreation and aesthetics. Following is a brief description of these areas.

- Post Oak Belt: The Post Oak Belt forms a band of wooded savannah mixed with pasture and cropland immediately west of the Piney Woods region. It extends from Lamar and Red River counties southwest as far as Bee and Atascosa counties. Predominant species include post oak, blackjack oak and elm. An interesting area called the "Lost Pines" forms an isolated island of southern-pine forest in Bastrop, Caldwell, Fayette,and Lee counties just a few miles southeast of Austin.
- East and West Cross Timbers: The East and West Cross Timbers cover an area of about 3 million acres in North Central Texas. The term "cross timbers" originated with the early settlers who, in their travels

Total Timber Production and Value by County in Texas, 1993

County	Pine	Hardwood	Total	Stumpage Value	Delivered Value
	Cubic feet			Thousand dollars	
Anderson	9,862,799	2,056,050	11,918,849	$9,686	$14,658
Angelina	31,382,494	3,101,610	34,484,104	28,712	42,890
Bowie	2,945,176	3,934,549	6,879,725	3,086	6,185
Camp	1,134,284	1,317,750	2,452,034	1,178	2,252
Cass	17,088,786	10,580,214	27,669,000	12,433	24,507
Chambers	2,603,261	700,640	3,303,901	3,063	4,454
Cherokee	20,821,020	6,182,655	27,003,675	20,927	32,099
Franklin	282,226	921,713	1,203,939	441	987
Gregg	2,484,153	2,531,194	5,015,347	3,088	5,245
Grimes	4,868,337	314,753	5,183,090	5,082	7,193
Hardin	20,090,911	5,483,676	25,574,587	19,469	30,249
Harris	7,258,556	3,280	7,261,836	7,520	10,467
Harrison	12,578,156	7,120,143	19,698,299	11,760	20,235
Houston	20,092,996	2,985,583	23,078,579	18,288	27,843
Jasper	39,689,248	2,883,019	42,572,267	34,977	52,393
Jefferson	955,168	563,680	1,518,848	867	1,530
Leon	270,199	1,920,719	2,190,918	593	1,642
Liberty	16,686,083	4,186,868	20,872,951	16,694	25,393
Marion	9,301,982	4,722,297	14,024,279	7,706	13,754
Montgomery	25,748,032	2,265,857	28,013,889	21,783	33,322
Morris	2,424,034	1,720,889	4,144,923	2,257	4,068
Nacogdoches	23,375,048	2,871,435	26,246,483	22,668	33,415
Newton	25,248,590	3,676,629	28,925,219	24,311	36,206
Orange	6,983,818	3,432,281	10,416,099	7,246	11,716
Panola	16,753,462	5,198,968	21,952,430	15,238	24,492
Polk	22,484,418	2,563,143	25,047,561	19,792	30,134
Red River	233,429	1,264,965	1,498,394	335	1,051
Rusk	16,991,290	7,123,373	24,114,663	17,253	27,376
Sabine	14,363,280	1,911,005	16,274,285	15,984	22,681
San Augustine	15,831,367	3,106,626	18,937,993	16,939	24,782
San Jacinto	12,334,818	1,839,882	14,174,700	11,081	16,961
Shelby	22,315,653	5,411,700	27,727,353	20,290	31,871
Smith	7,431,941	1,891,180	9,323,121	7,163	11,031
Titus	748,222	1,622,284	2,370,506	713	1,792
Trinity	15,800,410	908,409	16,708,819	14,394	21,260
Tyler	26,887,292	3,271,093	30,158,385	22,751	35,208
Upshur	9,278,131	5,182,355	14,460,486	9,960	16,179
Walker	17,704,259	2,893,200	20,597,459	14,639	23,213
Waller	396,809	76,471	473,280	364	558
Wood	3,739,835	303,275	4,043,110	4,151	5,796
Other Counties	4,664,049	1,681,439	6,345,488	4,173	6,862
Totals	**512,134,022**	**121,726,852**	**633,860,874**	**$479,065**	**$743,949**

from east to west, crossed alternating patches of oak forest and prairies and so affixed the name "cross timbers" to these forests.

• Cedar Brakes: Farther south in the Edwards Plateau region are the cedar brakes, which extend over 3.7 million acres. Cedar, live oak and mesquite dominate these steep slopes and rolling hills. Mesquite is often harvested for cooking wood, knick-knacks and woodworking. Live oak in this region is declining because of the oak wilt disease.

• Mountain Forests: The mountain forests of the Trans-Pecos region of Texas, including Jeff Davis County and the Big Bend, are rugged and picturesque. Several western tree species, including piñon pine, ponderosa pine, southwestern white pine and even Douglas fir are found there, along with aspen and several species of oak.

• Coastal Forests: The coastal forests of the southern Gulf Coast are characterized by a mix of brush and short, scrubby trees. Common species include mesquite, live oak and acacia. Some of these scrub forests are particularly important as migratory bird habitat.

Economic Impact of Timber in Texas

Timber is a major contributor to the state's economy. The forest products industry in Texas manufactures products such as lumber, plywood, oriented-strand board, poles, railroad crossties, wood furniture, pulp, paper and paperboard, and a host of other products from the timber grown in Texas forests. Consider these facts about the Texas forest industry:

• As unbelievable as it may sound, Texas is one of the top producers of forest products in the nation. In 1993, it was the source of 4 percent of lumber, 10 percent of structural panels, and 3 percent of paper and paperboard produced in the U.S.

• In 1993, timber ranked first in East Texas and fifth statewide in the value of agricultural production after beef, cotton, poultry, and milk production. In East Texas, it was the most valuable agricultural commodity. The delivered value of the timber harvest was $744 million.

• In 1991, the forest products industry in Texas produced and sold goods valued at $7.5 billion, 63 percent of which came from the paper sector.

• Forest industry directly employs 61,000 people, ranking first among East Texas manufacturing sectors and ninth statewide.

• Forest industry pays $1.6 billion in wages and salaries each year.

• The total economic impact of the industry in 1991 was $14.6 billion.

The 1993 Timber Harvest

Total Harvest Volume

East Texas set another new timber-harvest record in 1993 as removals of both pine and hardwood continued a steady climb. The total volume removed from the 43-county region was 778.8 million cubic feet, or 28.1 million cubic feet more than in 1992. Included in total removals is the harvest of timber for industrial use and an estimate of the logging residue and other timber removals.

By species group, removals consisted of 591.8 million cubic feet of pine and 187.0 million feet of hardwood. Hardwood removals increased by 7 percent while removals from the softwood inventory were 3 percent over the 1992 mark.

Eighty-one percent of timber removed, including 87 percent of pine and 65 percent of hardwood, was subsequently utilized in the manufacture of wood products. This portion of total removals, called the industrial roundwood harvest, totaled 512.1 and 121.7 million cubic feet for pine and hardwood, respectively. The pine industrial roundwood harvest was up 3 percent, while harvest of hardwood for industrial use climbed by 9 percent between 1992 and 1993. The combined harvest was up 4 percent to 633.9 million cubic feet.

The harvest of sawlogs for production of lumber and ties was 1,308.0 million board feet and comprised 34 percent of the 1993 timber harvest. Timber cut for the production of structural panels (plywood and oriented strand board) and hardwood veneer represented 31 percent of the timber harvest, or 199.0 million cubic feet. The harvest of timber for the manufacture of pulp and paper products totaled 2.7 million cords, representing 35 percent of the total harvest.

Jasper County continued to lead in timber production with a harvest of 42.6 million cubic feet. Other top producing counties included Angelina and Tyler.

Harvest Value

The value of the East Texas timber harvest surged higher in 1993 due to increasing timber prices and higher harvest volumes. The stumpage value of the timber harvest climbed 19 percent to $479.1 million. Pine timber accounted for 95 percent of that total. The value of the timber harvest delivered to the first point of processing (mill or intermediate woodyard) was $743.9 million in 1993, up 23 percent over the previous year's value of $602.5 million.

Primary Forest Products, 1993

Lumber and Ties: Texas sawmills produced 1,416.3 million board feet of lumber and ties in 1993, enough to build 142,000 homes. Production increased 15 percent and was 184.7 million board feet over the mark set in 1992. Production of pine lumber rose nearly 14 percent to 1,244.4 million board feet. This was the fifth consecutive year in which pine-lumber production surpassed the 1 billion board foot mark. Hardwood lumber production increased by 24 percent, to 172.0 million board feet. Part of the increase is attributable to increases in both pine and hardwood tie output.

Texas Lumber Production, 1984-1993

Year	*Lumber Production		Tie Production	
	Pine	Hardwood	Pine	Hardwood
	(thousand board feet)		(thousand pieces)	
1984	898,212	165,460	337	1,001
1985	856,157	175,254	101	926
1986	944,465	176,322	120	772
1987	902,987	163,271	112	587
1988	990,118	154,440	61	604
1989	1,067,458	154,726	31	600
1990	1,007,397	148,581	39	591
1991	1,007,801	146,343	60	575
1992	1,092,738	138,874	13	498
1993	1,244,373	171,976	69	725

*Includes tie volumes.

Structural Panel Products: Production of structural panels at Texas' eight plywood and four oriented strand board mills continued to increase in 1993. Production rose 8 percent to reach 2,754.9 million square feet (3/8-inch basis). Texas accounted for 10 percent of U.S. panel production in 1993.

Texas Structural Panel Production, 1984-1993

Year	Pine (Thd. sq. ft.*)	Year	Pine (Thd. sq. ft.*)
1984......	1,881,071	1989......	2,130,575
1985......	1,985,699	1990......	2,422,151
1986......	2,082,659	1991......	2,203,065
1987......	2,250,279	1992......	2,557,103
1988......	2,343,241	1993......	2,754,949

*3/8-inch basis

Paper Products: Paper production at Texas' seven pulp and paper mills posted a slight decline as the industry suffered nationally from overcapacity and reduced product prices. Production of paper and paperboard totaled 2.8 million tons, off 1 percent from the 1992 mark. Paper production increased 3 percent to 1.2 million tons, while output of paperboard was 1.6 million tons, off 4 percent. Market pulp production was also down. Production declined 34 percent to 218 thousand tons.

Texas Pulpwood Production

Year	Roundwood		Chips & Sawdust		Total Pulpwood Production
	Pine	Hardwood	Pine	Hardwood	
	(Thousand cords)				
1984	1,890	731	1,567	228	4,416
1985	1,901	716	1,591	462	4,670
1986	1,623	715	1,517	570	4,426
1987	1,650	782	1,456	578	4,466
1988	1,695	819	1,562	492	4,568
1989	1,769	935	1,625	518	4,847
1990	1,695	848	1,662	548	4,753
1991	1,835	950	1,632	568	4,985
1992	1,861	1,038	1,769	605	5,273
1993	1,636	1,099	1,782	674	5,191

Future of Texas' Forest Resources

Because of recent reductions of timber harvests from the vast federal forests of the Pacific Northwest brought about by environmental pressures, most analysts believe that the forest-products industry will continue to expand in the South. Demand for wood products continues to grow both domestically and globally. No other region of the United States has as much potential to fill the void left by the decline of timber harvest in the Pacific Northwest.

However, the South's ability to increase its supply of timber will be a limiting factor for long-term industry growth in the region. In Texas, 95 out of every 100 cubic feet of timber grown annually is harvested. The question is, how can we increase timber supplies to ensure that we can continue to meet wood needs in the future without over-harvesting our forests?

Some timberland owners have a good record in reforestation, but others need improvement. The forest-products industry in Texas is doing a credible job in replanting after harvest by maintaining their own tree nurseries, growing and planting 133 million tree seedlings every year. In fact, projections show that timber growth on industry lands may increase by as much as 30 percent as a result of intensive timber-management practices and genetically improved tree seedlings.

Texas' greatest future problem — and opportunity — lies in nonindustrial private forest landowners (NIPF's). These owners are currently replanting only one acre for every nine acres harvested. Thousands of acres in NIPF ownership have been cut-over repeatedly and are not producing the amount of timber they could. Through improved forest management on less productive NIPF forests, and conversion of marginal crop and pastureland to forest, it is estimated that East Texas pine growth could be increased by as much as 40 percent. This would support significant growth of the forest-products industry and provide additional timber income to landowners, while providing environmental benefits such as cleaner air and water, reduced erosion and more wildlife habitat.

Forest Fires

From 1925 through 1994, over 178,000 forest fires were reported and suppressed in East Texas by the Texas Forest Service. In 1994, 996 fires burned 13,045 acres, an average of 13 acres per fire. This was the lightest fire year on record, both in the number and average size of wildfires, attributable in part to higher-than-average rainfall totals for the year. The main causes of wildfires are debris burning (41 percent of the fires in 1994) and arson (40 percent). Other causes include lightning, campfires, smoking, equipment, railroads, children and miscellaneous.

Forest Pests

In the South, southern pine beetles kill more timber annually than forest fires. The Texas Forest Service coordinates all beetle-control activity in Texas, which includes detecting infestations from the air, notifying landowners, and assisting them in controlling the infestations. The most severe outbreak of southern pine beetles known in Texas occurred in 1985 when an estimated 78.7 million cubic feet of timber was killed.

Extensive mortality of oaks in the Hill Country of Central Texas is creating increasing public concern. The vascular wilt disease, "oak wilt," is the major cause of live oak mortality in Central Texas. A suppression project, which offers affected landowners professional assistance and cost sharing is administered by the Texas Forest Service.

Urban Forests

No discussion of Texas' forest resources would be complete without a mention of the "urban and community forests" that are an integral part of Texas cities, towns and villages.

Because an estimated 80 percent of Texans live in cities with more than 100,000 population, urban trees and forests play an important part in the lives of many. Trees mitigate the urban heat island effect through shading and evaporative cooling. They also purify the air by absorbing pollutants, slowing the chemical reactions that produce harmful ozone, and filtering dust. Urban forests reduce stormwater runoff and soil erosion. They also buffer against noise, glare and strong winds, while providing habitat for most of the wildlife city dwellers will ever see. Environmental benefits from a single tree may be worth more than $275 each year. Emotional and psychological benefits of urban trees raise the value even higher. Landscape appraisers may place the value of a healthy, mature shade tree at $8,000 or more. ☆

State Forests

Texas has five state forests, all of which are used primarily for demonstration and research.

The first state forest, now known as the **E.O. Siecke State Forest** in Newton County, was purchased by the state in 1924. It contains 1,722 acres of pine land. An additional 100 acres was obtained by a 99-year lease in 1946.

The **W. Goodrich Jones State Forest**, south of Conroe in Montgomery County, containing 1,725 acres, was purchased in 1926. A 20-acre adjunct was given to the state in 1969.

The **I.D. Fairchild State Forest,** Texas' largest, is located west of Rusk in Cherokee County. This forest was transferred from the state prison system in 1925. An additional 536 acres were added to the original 2,360 acres in 1963 from the Texas State Hospitals and Special Schools, for a total acreage of 2,896.

Th 626-acre **John Henry Kirby State Forest** was donated by the late lumberman, John Henry Kirby, in 1929, and later donors. Revenue from this forest is given to the Association of Former Students of Texas A&M University for student-loan purposes.

The newest state forest, the **Paul N. Masterson Memorial Forest** of 520 acres, was donated in the fall of 1984. Mrs. Leonora O'Neal Masterson of Beaumont donated the land in Jasper County in honor of her husband, an active member of the Texas Forestry Association and a tree farmer. ☆

National Forests and Grasslands in Texas

There are four national forests and all or part of five national grasslands in Texas. These federally owned lands are administered by the **U.S. Department of Agriculture-Forest Service**. These units cover 755,284 acres in parts of 17 Texas counties. Supervision of the East Texas forests and North Texas grasslands is by the Forest Supervisor of the division known as the **National Forests and Grasslands in Texas** (701 N. 1st St., Lufkin 75901; (409) 639-8501). The three **National Grasslands in West Texas** (Black Kettle, McClellan Creek and Rita Blanca) are administered by the Forest Supervisor in Albuquerque, New Mexico, as units of the Cibola National Forest. The forests and grasslands are locally administered by district rangers. The following list gives the name of the forest or grassland, the administrative district(s) for each, the acreage in each county and the total acreage:

Angelina National Forest - Angelina Ranger District (Lufkin) - Angelina County, 58,533 acres; Jasper, 21,011; Nacogdoches, 9,238; San Augustine, 64,392. Total, 153,174.

Davy Crockett National Forest - Neches District (Crockett); Trinity District (Apple Springs) - Houston County, 94,683 acres; Trinity, 67,329. Total, 162,012.

Sabine National Forest - Tenaha District (San Augustine); Yellowpine District (Hemphill) - Jasper County, 64 acres; Newton, 1,781; Sabine, 95,409; San Augustine, 4,317; Shelby, 59,037. Total, 160,608.

Sam Houston National Forest - San Jacinto District (Cleveland); Raven District (New Waverly) -Montgomery County, 47,777 acres; San Jacinto, 60,247; Walker, 53,633. Total, 161,657.

Black Kettle National Grassland - District Ranger in Cheyenne, Okla. - Hemphill County, 576 acres; Roger Mills County, Okla., 31,000 acres. Total, 31,576.

Lyndon B. Johnson and Caddo National Grasslands - District Ranger at Decatur - Fannin County, 17,785 acres; Montague County, 61 acres; Wise, 20,252. Total, 38,098.

McClellan Creek National Grassland - District Ranger at Cheyenne, Okla. - Gray County, 1,449 acres. Total, 1,449.

Rita Blanca National Grassland — District Ranger at Clayton, New Mex. — Dallam County, 78,027 acres; Cimarron County, Okla., 15,736 acres. Total, 93,763.

National Forests

National Forests in Texas were established by invitation of the Texas Legislature by an Act of 1933, authorizing the purchase of lands in Texas for the establishment of national forests. President Franklin D. Roosevelt proclaimed these purchases of national forests on Oct. 15, 1936. The forests are managed for multiple uses, including production and sales of timber and minerals and programs involving recreation, fish and wildlife, soil and water.

Timber Management

More than 521,000 acres of the National Forests in Texas are suitable for timber production. Sales of sawtimber, pulpwood and other forest products are made at regular intervals.

The estimated net growth is over 200 million board feet per year and is valued at $25 million. About one-third of this growth is removed by cutting. The balance is left to grow. By the year 2000, growth is expected to exceed 200 million board feet per year.

National Grasslands

The submarginal Dust Bowl project lands, purchased by the federal government primarily under the Bankhead-Jones Farm Tenant Act (1937), are today well covered with grasses and native shrubs. They are administered for uses including range, watershed, recreation and wildlife.

Grazing Permits

Permits to graze cattle on national forests and national grasslands are granted to the public for an annual fee. Approximately 997 head of cattle are grazed on national forests, and 1,163 head of cattle are grazed on the Caddo-Lyndon B. Johnson National Grasslands annually. On the Rita Blanca NG, 4,000 cattle are grazed each year, most of them in Texas.

Hunting and Fishing

State hunting and fishing laws and regulations apply to all national-forest land. Game-law enforcement is carried out by the Texas Parks and Wildlife Department. The Angelina, Sabine, Neches and San Jacinto rivers, Sam Rayburn and Toledo Bend reservoirs, Lake Conroe and many small streams provide a wide variety of fishing opportunities.

Recreation Facilities

An estimated 3 million people visited the recreational areas in the National Forests and Grasslands in Texas in 1994, primarily for picnicking, swimming, fishing, camping, boating and nature enjoyment. These areas are listed in the Recreation section of the Texas Almanac. ☆

Texas' Endangered and Threatened Species

Strict laws protect species identified as endangered or threatened. It is generally unlawful to take, possess, transport, export, process or sell any of the animal species designated as endangered or threatened without a permit. Commerce in threatened and endangered plants and the collection of listed plant species from public land without a permit is prohibited. The following species of Texas flora and fauna are either endangered or threatened as of Feb. 1, 1995, according to the Texas Parks and Wildlife Department. This list varies slightly from the federal list. Any questions about protected species should be directed to the Resource Protection Division, Texas Department of Parks and Wildlife, 4200 Smith School Road, Austin 78744, or call 1-800-792-1112.

Endangered Species

Animals:

Mammals: Mexican long-nosed **bat**; black and Louisiana black **bears**; **coati**; black-footed **ferret**; **jaguar**; **jaguarundi**; **manatee**; **margay**; **ocelot**; black right, blue, finback and sperm **whales**; Mexican, gray and red **wolves**.

Birds: Whooping **crane**; Eskimo **curlew**; bald **eagle**; American peregrine and northern aplomado **falcons**; brown **pelican**; Attwater's **prairie chicken**; interior least **tern**; black-capped **vireo**; ivory-billed and red-cockaded **woodpeckers**; golden-cheeked **warbler**.

From an estimated 1 million at the turn of the century, the number of Attwater's prairie chickens remaining in the wild in their native Texas coastal-prairie habitat has shrunk to about 65. Captive-breeding programs at Fossil Rim Wildlife Center near Glen Rose and at the Houston Zoological Gardens may save the birds from extinction. Dallas Morning News file photo.

Reptiles: Speckled **racer**; Concho water, Louisiana pine, Northern cat-eyed and smooth green **snakes**; Chihuahuan mud, hawksbill, leatherback, loggerhead and Kemp's ridley **sea turtles**.

Amphibians: White-lipped **frog**; black-spotted **newt**; Blanco blind and Texas blind **salamanders**; Rio Grande lesser **siren**; Houston **toad**.

Fishes: Fountain **darter**; Big Bend, blotched, Clear Creek, Pecos and San Marcos **gambusias**; blackfin **goby**; **paddlefish**; Comanche Springs and Leon Springs **pupfishes**; bluntnose and phantom **shiners**; shovelnose **sturgeon**.

Plants:

Cacti: Black lace, Lloyd's hedgehog, Nellie cory, Sneed pincushion and Tobusch fishhook **cactus**; Davis' green **pitaya**.

Grasses and Grass-like Plants: Little acuja **pondweed**; Texas **wild-rice**.

Orchids: Navasota **ladies'-tresses**.

Trees, Shrubs and Sub-Shrubs: Johnston's **frankenia**; Texas **snowbells**.

Wildflowers White **bladderpod**; Terlingua Creek **catseye**; ashy **dogweed**; Walker's **manioc**; Texas trailing **phlox**; Texas **poppy-mallow**; prairie **dawn**; slender **rush-pea**; large-fruited sand **verbena**.

Threatened Species

Animals:

Mammals: Eastern big-eared, southern yellow and spotted **bats**; Atlantic spotted and rough-toothed **dolphins**; Palo Duro **mouse**; Coues' rice and Texas kangaroo **rats**; dwarf sperm, false killer, Gervais' beaked, goose-beaked, killer, pygmy killer, pygmy sperm and short-finned pilot **whales**.

Birds: Rose-throated **becard**; reddish **egret**; Arctic peregrine **falcon**; common black, northern gray, white-tailed and zone-tailed **hawks**; white-faced **ibis**; American swallow-tailed **kite**; ferruginous pygmy **owl**; tropical **parula**; piping **plover**; Bachman's and Texas Botteri's **sparrows**; wood **stork**; sooty **tern**; northern beardless **tyrannulet**.

Reptiles: Texas **tortoise**; alligator snapping and green **turtles**; reticulated **gecko**; mountain short-horned, reticulate collared and Texas horned **lizards**; timber **rattlesnake**; Big Bend blackhead, black-striped, Brazos water, northern scarlet, indigo, Texas lyre and Texas scarlet **snakes**.

Amphibians: Sheep **frog**; Cascade Caverns, Comal blind and San Marcos **salamanders**; Mexican burrowing **toad**; Mexican **treefrog**.

Fishes: Toothless and widemouth **blindcats**; Rio Grande **chub**; creek **chubsucker**; blackside and Rio Grande **darters**; river **goby**; Devil's River **minnow**; opossum **pipefish**; Conchos and Pecos **pupfishes**; bluehead, Chihuahua and Proserpine **shiners**; Mexican **stoneroller**; blue **sucker**.

Plants:

Cacti: Bunched cory, Chisos hedgehog and Lloyd's mariposa **cactus**.

Trees: Hinckley's **oak**.

Wildflowers: McKittrick **pennyroyal**. ☆

Nature Conservancy Protects Natural Heritage

The Nature Conservancy of Texas (TNCT) is an affiliate of The Nature Conservancy, a national, private, nonprofit organization that uses its resources to preserve unique and significant natural areas. Since 1966, the Texas organization, working closely with government agencies and other private groups, has acquired more than 321,400 acres in 114 projects, ranging from the Trans-Pecos region to the Gulf Coast, from the Edwards Plateau to the Rio Grande Valley.

The Nature Conservancy:

- Identifies areas that should be protected;
- Preserves the land through gift, lease, trade or outright purchase; and
- Manages and maintains some of the preserves itself, while holding others until an appropriate agency can be found to acquire and care for the properties.

Membership in the Nature Conservancy of Texas as of January 1995 was 26,000. ☆

Texas Wildlife

Texas has many native animals and birds, plus species introduced on game preserves.

More than **540 species of birds** — about three fourths of all different species found in the United States — have been identified in Texas.

Some **142 species of animals,** including some that today are extremely rare, are found in Texas; a list of plant and animal species designated as threatened or endangered by federal or state natural resource officials is found elsewhere in this chapter.

Through efforts of the **Texas Parks and Wildlife Department,** several nonprofit organizations, and many individual landowners involved in practicing conservation, our wildlife should be a permanent resource.

A few of the leading native animals of Texas are described here. Information is provided by the **Nongame and Urban Program**, Texas Parks and Wildlife Department.

Mammals

Armadillo — The **nine-banded armadillo** *(Dasypus novemcinctus)* is one of Texas' most interesting mammals. It has migrated north and east and is now common as far north and east as Oklahoma and Mississippi. There has been limited commercialization of the armadillo's shell in the manufacture of curios.

Badger — The **badger** *(Taxidea taxus)* is found throughout West Texas, but in greatly reduced numbers since wholesale eradication of the prairie dog on which the badger preyed. It is a predator, but its pelt is valuable. The range of the badger includes the Texas Panhandle and South Texas, where it is common.

Bat — Thirty-two species of these winged mammals have been found in Texas, more than in any other state in the United States. Of these, 27 species are known residents, though they are seldom seen by the casual observer. The **Mexican free-tailed bat** *(Tadarida brasiliensis)* and the **cave myotis** *(Myotis velifer)* constitute most of the cave-dwelling bats of Southwest and West Texas. They have some economic value for their deposits of nitrogen-rich **guano.** Some commercial guano has been produced from **James River Bat Cave**, Mason County; **Beaver Creek Cavern**, Burnet County; and from large deposits in other caves including **Devil's Sinkhole** in Edwards County, **Blowout Cave** in Blanco County and **Bandera Bat Cave**, Bandera County. The largest oncentration of bats in the world is found at **Bracken Cave** in Comal County. The **big brown bat** *(Eptesicus fuscus),* the **red bat** *(Lasiurus borealis)* and the **evening bat** *(Nycticeius humeralis)* are found in East and Southeast Texas. The evening and big brown bats are forest and woodland dwelling mammals. Most of the rarer species of Texas bats have been found along the Rio Grande and in the Trans-Pecos. Bats can be observed at dusk near a water source, and many species may also be found foraging on insects attracted to street lights. Everywhere bats occur, they are the main predators of night-flying insects, including mosquitoes and many crop pests.

Bear — The **black bear** *(Ursus americanus)* was formerly common throughout most of the state. It is now surviving in the inaccessible river bottoms of eastern Texas and in portions of the Trans-Pecos with potential habitat.

Beaver — Two subspecies of beaver are found in Texas, the **Mexican beaver** *(Castor canadensis mexicanus)* ranging along the Rio Grande and Devils River and the **Texas beaver** *(Castor canadensis texensis)* which has been brought back from the verge of extinction to abundance through restocking.

Bighorn — (See **Sheep**.)

Bison — The largest of native terrestrial wild mammals of North America, the **American bison** *(Bison bison)*, commonly called **buffalo**, is found today on a few ranches and in zoos. Deliberate slaughter of this majestic animal for hides and to eliminate the Plains Indians' main food source reached a peak about 1875, and the bison was almost eradicated by 1885. Estimates of the number of buffalo killed vary, but as many as 200,000 hides were sold in Fort Worth at a single two-day sale. Except for the interest of the late **Col. Charles Goodnight** and a few other foresighted men, the bison might be extinct.

Cat — The **jaguar** *(Felis onca)* is probably now extinct in Texas and, along with the **ocelot, jaguarundi** and **margay,** is listed as rare and endangered by both federal and state wildlife agencies. The **cougar** *(Felis concolor)*, which is also known as **mountain lion, puma, panther** and **Mexican cougar,** is found in many areas of the state, including the broken country of the Edwards Plateau, the Trans-Pecos Mountains and the South Texas brush country. The former panther of the East Texas forest, which was closely related, may be extinct in Texas but still exists in a few areas of Southeastern U.S. The **ocelot** *(Felis pardalis)*, also known as the **leopard cat,** is found usually along the border. The **red-and-gray cat,** or **jaguarundi** *(Felis yagouaroundi Geoffroy)* is found in extreme South Texas. The **margay** *(Felis wiedii)* was reported in 1884 near Eagle Pass. There is currently a margay breeding program underway at a wildlife center near Glen Rose with the goal of eventually reestablishing the small cat in the wild. The **bobcat** *(Felis rufus)* is found over the state in large numbers. The **feral housecat** may have impact on game birds in many parts of Texas.

Chipmunk — The **gray-footed chipmunk** *(Tamias canipes)* is found at high altitudes in the Guadalupe and Sierra Diablo ranges of the Trans-Pecos (see also **Ground Squirrel,** with which it is often confused in public reference).

Coati — The **coati** *(Nasua narica)*, a relative of the raccoon, is occasionally found in southern Texas. It inhabits woodland areas and feeds both on the ground and in trees. The coati, which is on the list of threatened species, is also found occasionally in Big Bend National Park. There is a captive-breeding project for the coati at a wildlife center near Glen Rose in Somervell County.

Coyote — The **coyote** *(Canis latrans)*, great in number, is the most destructive Texas predator of livestock. On the other hand, it is probably the most valuable predator in the balance of nature. It is a protection to crops and range lands by its control of rodents, rabbits, etc. It is found throughout the state, but is most numerous in the brush country of Southwest Texas.

Deer — The **white-tailed deer** *(Odocoileus virginianus)* is an important Texas game animal. Its number in Texas is estimated at 3 million. It thrives best in the wooded and broken areas of the Edwards Plateau and south of San Antonio where it often competes for feed with domestic and exotic animals. Texas Parks and Wildlife Department has had success in **transplanting deer**. In East Texas, the timbered sections of North Central Texas, and even in the thinly populated areas of Northwest Texas, the white-tailed deer population has increased greatly. The **mule deer** *(Odocoileus heminous)* is found principally in the Trans-Pecos and in smaller numbers in the less thickly settled parts of the Staked Plains. It has increased in number in recent years. The little **Del Carmen deer** (white-tailed subspecies) is found in limited numbers in the high valleys of the Chisos Mountains in the Big Bend. The **American elk** *(Cervus canadensis)*, though not the original subspecies found in Texas, has been introduced into the Guadalupe and Davis mountains.

Ferret — The **black-footed ferret** *(Mustela nigripes)* was formerly found widely ranging through the West Texas country of the prairie dog on which it preyed. It is now considered extinct in Texas. It is of the same genus as the weasel and the mink.

Fox — Most common is the **gray fox** *(Urocyon cinereoargenteus)* found in the forested area of East Texas and throughout most of the state where there is cover, notably in the broken parts of the Edwards Plateau and the rough country at the foot of the Staked Plains. The **kit** or **Swift fox** *(Vulpes velox)* is found in the plains country of Northwest Texas. A second species of **kit fox** *(Vulpes macrotis)* is found in the Trans-Pecos and is fairly numerous in some localities. The **red fox** *(Vulpes vulpes)* is not a native but was introduced for sport.

Gopher — Six species of pocket gophers occur in Texas. The **Botta's pocket gopher** *(Thomomys bottae)* is found in West Texas south of the High Plains, notably along the Rio Grande. The **plains pocket gopher** *(Geomys bursarius)* is found in the Panhandle and throughout North Central and East Texas. The **desert pocket gopher** *(Geomys arenarius)* and the **yellow-faced pocket gopher** *(Pappogeomys castanops)* are found in the Trans-Pecos. The **Texas pocket gopher** *(Geomys personatus)* is found in the sandy soils of the lower coastal region.

Ground Squirrel — Five or more species of ground squirrel live in Texas, mostly in the western part of the state. The **rock squirrel** *(Spermophilus variegatus)* is found throughout the Edwards Plateau and Trans-Pecos. The **Mexican ground squirrel** *(Spermophilus mexicanus)* is found in the Mexican border country from Brownsville to the Davis Mountains. The **spotted ground squirrel** *(Spermophilus spilosoma)* is found generally in favorable localities throughout the western half of the state. The **thirteen-lined ground squirrel** *(Spermophilus tridecemlineatus)* is found in the Panhandle and in a narrow strip from Red River to the Gulf between Dallas and Corpus Christi. The **Texas antelope squirrel** *(Ammospermophilus interpres)* is found along the Rio Grande from El Paso to Val Verde County.

Javelina — The **javelina** or **collared peccary** *(Tayassu tajacu)* is found in South and Southwest Texas. It is fairly numerous. Its meat is edible if properly prepared, and there is limited use of its hide for the manufacture of gloves and other leather articles. A scrappy animal, it is the subject of many tall tales.

Mink — The **mink** *(Mustela vison)* is found in East Texas and along the Coastal Belt, usually in forested river bottoms. It yields a considerable fur crop. It is akin to the otter and weasel. **Mink farming,** partly with native and partly with introduced species, is found on a limited scale, usually in East Texas.

Mole — The **mole** *(Scalopus aquaticus)* is found generally throughout the eastern half of the state.

Muskrat — There are three subspecies of muskrat in Texas: the **muskrat** *(Ondatra zibethica rivalicia)*, which is found in Southeast Texas near Beaumont where it is commercially produced on muskrat ranges; the **Pecos River muskrat** *(Ondatra zibethica ripensis)* of Western Texas; and the **Great Plains muskrat** *(Ondatra zibethica cinnamonia)* of the Panhandle region. The muskrat is one of the most valuable of Texas' fur-bearing animals. Production of pelts comes largely from the coastal area near Beaumont.

Nutria — This introduced species *(Myocastor coypus)* is found in Texas, except the Panhandle and extreme western portions. The fur is not highly valued and, since nutria are in competition with muskrats, their spread is discouraged. They are used widely in Texas as a cure-all for ponds choked with vegetation.

Opossum — A **marsupial,** the **Virginia opossum** *(Didelphis virginiana)* is found in nearly all parts of the state. The opossum has economic value for its pelt, and its meat is considered a delicacy by some. It is one of the chief contributors to the Texas fur crop.

Otter — A few **river otter** *(Lutra canadensis)* are found along East Texas rivers and coastal marshes. Although it is a prized fur-bearing animal, there is no evidence that the river otter can be considered either rare or endangered. The species is numerous in Liberty County where biologists have determined that its numbers have increased in recent years. While excess populations of this species, like other forms of wildlife, can be harvested with no danger to the species, loss of habitat through encroaching civilization presents the most formidable threat to its continued existence.

Porcupine — The **yellow-haired porcupine** *(Erethizon dorsatum)* is found in the higher mountain ranges of the Trans-Pecos and in the western Edwards Plateau. It has recently moved into the eastern portion of the Panhandle along the Caprock.

Prairie Dog — Until recent years probably no sight was so universal in West Texas as the **black-tailed prairie dog** *(Cynomys ludovicianus)* and its burrow. Naturalists estimated its population in the hundreds of millions. Its destruction of range grasses, plus its peculiar susceptibility to eradication (usually by the introduction of the fumes of carbon disulphide into its burrow) have caused a great reduction of its numbers over its past range. However, it is making a comeback. Prairie dog towns often covered many acres with thickly spaced burrows or prairie dog holes. It is being propagated in several public zoos, notably in the **prairie dog town in Mackenzie Park** at Lubbock. It has been honored in Texas by the naming of the **Prairie Dog Town Fork** of the Red River, along one segment of which is located the beautiful **Palo Duro Canyon**.

Pronghorn — The **Pronghorn** *(Antilocapra americana)* is primarily a plains animal. It almost became extinct, but a continuous closed season and a sound management program raised its numbers. There have been limited open seasons since 1944. Specifically, these animals inhabit the plains and basin regions of Brewster, Presidio, Jeff Davis, Culberson and Hudspeth counties. They have also sufficiently increased in numbers in the Permian Basin and Panhandle to permit open seasons in recent years.

Rabbit — The **black-tailed jack rabbit** *(Lepus californicus)* is found throughout Texas except in the East Texas forest area. It breeds rapidly, and its long hind legs make it one of the world's faster-running animals. The **Eastern cottontail** *(Sylvilagus floridanus)* is found throughout Texas except in Trans-Pecos region. The **desert cottontail** *(Sylvilagus auduboni)* is found in South and West Texas, usually on the open range. The **swamp rabbit** *(Sylvilagus aquaticus)* is found in East Texas and the coastal area.

Raccoon — The **raccoon** *(Procyon lotor)* is found throughout Texas, especially along streams and in urban settings.

Rats and Mice — There are 40 or 50 species of rats and mice in Texas of varying characteristics, habitats and economic destructiveness. The **Norway rat** *(Rattus norvegicus)* and the **black rat** *(Rattus rattus)* are probably the most common and the most destructive. Some of the species are native, and others, notably the Norway rat, are invaders. The **common house mouse** *(Mus musculis)* is estimated in the hundreds of millions annually. The rare **Guadalupe Mountain vole** *(Microtus mexicanus guadalupensis)* is found only in the Guadalupe Mountains National Park and just over the border into New Mexico.

Ringtail — The **ringtail** *(Bassariscus astutus)* is found generally in wooded areas west of the Trinity and in the broken sections of the Edwards Plateau. It is a valuable fur-bearing mammal.

Sheep — The **barbary,** or **Aoudad, sheep** *(Ammotragus lervia)*, first introduced to the Palo Duro Canyon area in 1957-58, have become firmly established. Barbary sheep have been introduced into many areas of Texas, but are designated as game animals in only eight counties of the Panhandle surrounding Palo Duro Canyon. Efforts are now under way by the Texas Parks and Wildlife Department to establish the **desert bighorn** *(Ovis canadensis)* in range they formerly occupied. Currently 300 bighorns are free-ranging in West Texas.

Shrew — Three species are found in Texas, the **northern short-tailed shrew** *(Blarina brevicauda)*, the **least shrew** *(Cryptotis parva)* and the **desert shrew** *(Notiosorex crawfordi)*. The first-mentioned is rarer, occurring in the Big Thicket. The least shrew is found generally in South Central and East Texas. The **gray shrew** is found in very limited numbers in the semiarid areas of West Texas and along the border.

Skunk — There are six species of skunk in Texas. The **Eastern spotted skunk** *(Spilogale putorius)* is found throughout North Texas. A small skunk, it is often erroneously called civet cat. This skunk also is found in East Texas and the Gulf area. The **Western spotted skunk** *(Spilogale gracilis)* is found in the central, western and southern parts of the state. The **long-tailed,** or **broad-striped skunk** *(Mephitis mephitis)* is found in many parts of the state, usually along streams or in wooded areas. The **hooded skunk** *(Mephitis macroura)* is found in limited numbers in the Trans-Pecos mountains. The Gulf Coast **hog-nosed skunk** *(Conepatus leuconotus)*, found in the Brownsville area, ranges southward into Mexico. The **mountain hog-nosed skunk** *(Conepatus mesoleucus)* is found in sparsely timbered areas of Edwards Plateau, Central Texas, Trans-Pecos.

The armor-plated armadillo was designated the official state small mammal by the 74th Legislature in 1995.

Squirrel — The **fox squirrel** *(Sciurus niger)* is found throughout East, Central and West Central Texas. The **gray,** or **cat, squirrel** *(Sciurus carolinensis)* is found generally in the eastern third of the state. The **flying squirrel** *(Glaucomys volans)* is widely distributed in the Piney Woods and the East Texas Post Oak Belt.

Weasel — The **brindled** or **long-tailed weasel** *(Mustela frenata)*, akin to the mink, is found in the Panhandle-Plains and South Texas.

Wolf — The **red wolf** *(Canis rufus)* was once found over a wide range in Eastern and Central Texas. It is now considered extirpated from the wild, with the only known remnants of the population now in captive propagation. The **gray wolf** *(Canis lupus)* once had a wide range over Central, Southern and Western Texas. It has been reduced almost to extinction. The **red wolf** and **gray wolf** are listed on the federal and state rare and endangered species lists. The few gray wolves which may be encountered in Texas are believed to be occasional individuals crossing over from Mexico.

Reptiles and Arachnids

Most of the more than **100 species and subspecies of snakes** found in Texas are beneficial, as also are other reptiles. There are **16 poisonous species and subspecies**.

Poisonous reptiles include **three species of copperheads** (southern, broad-banded and Trans-Pecos); one kind of **cottonmouth** (western)**; 11 kinds of rattlesnakes** (canebrake, western massasauga, desert massasauga, western pigmy, western diamondback, timber, banded rock, mottled rock, northern blacktailed, Mojave and prairie); and the **Texas coral snake.**

Also noteworthy are the **horned lizard,** also called **horned toad,** which is on the list of **threatened species** (see articles on horned toads on page 99 and on threatened and endangered species on page 90); the **vinegarroon,** a type of whip scorpion; **tarantula,** a hairy spider; and **alligator.** ☆

National Wildlife Refuges

Source: U.S. Fish and Wildlife Service, U.S. Department of the Interior.

Texas has more than 416,000 acres in **18 national wildlife refuges**. Included in this acreage are two conservation easement refuges, Little Sandy and Moody National Wildlife Refuges, where the Fish and Wildlife Service does not have management responsibility. The other 16 refuges may be visited at different times of the year for bird watching and wildlife viewing, and they are listed on the following pages. Write or call before visiting to check on facilities and to be sure the refuge is open to visitors when you plan to go. Addresses and phone numbers are given at the ends of the descriptions of the 16 refuges.

Anahuac: The more than 30,000 acres of this refuge are located along the upper Gulf Coast in Chambers County. **Fresh and saltwater marshes** and miles of beautiful, sweeping **coastal prairie** provide wintering habitat for large flocks of **geese** and other **waterfowl.** The endangered **peregrine falcon** and **bald eagle** also find protection on the refuge; other species include the **alligator, mottled duck, wood stork** and **least tern**. Fishing, bird watching and waterfowl hunting are available. Address: Box 278, Anahuac 77514. (409) 267-3337.

Aransas: This refuge comprises 58,702 acres in three units on the mainland, with additional acreage on Matagorda Island (see below). The main body of the refuge is located midway between Rockport and Port Lavaca seven miles southeast of Austwell on FM 2040. The three mainland units consist of **oak woodlands, fresh and saltwater marshes** and **coastal grasslands**. Besides providing wintering grounds for the endangered **whooping crane,** the refuge is home to many species of waterfowl and other migratory birds. This refuge has reported the largest number of bird species of any refuge in the country. Bird life abounds from fall through May. **White-tailed deer, javelinas, alligators** and many other species of wildlife can be found. Refuge is open daily sunrise to sunset. Interpretive center is open daily except Thanks giving and Christmas. Other facilities include a 40-foot observation tower at the edge of a whooping crane marsh, a paved auto-tour loop and six walking trails. Address: Box 100, Austwell 77950. (512) 286-3559.

Attwater Prairie Chicken: Established in 1972 to preserve habitat for the endangered **Attwater's prairie chicken,** the refuge comprises 7,980 acres of **native prairie,** potholes, sandy knolls and some wooded areas. A 5-mile auto-tour route is available year-round, and 350 acres of marsh are accessible for birding. Refuge open sunrise to sunset. Address: Box 519, Eagle Lake 77434. (409) 234-3021.

Balcones Canyonlands: The **newest national wildlife refuge** in Texas was dedicated in 1992. Located in the **Hill Country** northwest of Austin, it was established to protect the nesting habitat of two endangered birds: **black-capped vireo** and **golden-cheeked warbler.** About 8,000 acres had been purchased by early March 1993. Eventually, the refuge will encompass 41,000 acres of **oak-juniper woodlands** and other habitats. No public facilities are available at this time; viewing must be done from public roadways. Address: 10711 Burnet Rd., #201, Austin 78758. (512) 339-9432.

Big Boggy: This refuge occupies 4,526 acres of **coastal prairie** and **salt marsh** along East Matagorda Bay for the benefit of wintering **waterfowl**, attracting thousands of **ducks and geese** to its ponds and potholes. **The refuge is generally closed,** and visitors are encouraged to visit nearby **San Bernard or Brazoria refuges.** Waterfowl hunting is permitted in season. Address: Box 1088, Angleton 77516. (409) 849-7771.

Brazoria: The 42,338 acres of this refuge, located along the Gulf Coast in Brazoria County, serve as haven for wintering waterfowl and a wide variety of other migratory birds. The refuge also supports many **marsh** and **water birds,** from **roseate spoonbills** and **great blue herons** to **white ibis** and **sandhill cranes**. Brazoria Refuge is within the **Freeport Christmas Bird Count** circle, which frequently achieves the highest number of species seen in a 24-hour period. The first weekend of every month throughout the year, visitors can drive through the refuge to observe coastal wildlife. Fishing is permitted, as well as waterfowl hunting in season; however, access for these activities is by boat only. Address: 1212 North Velasco, #200, Angleton 77516. (409) 849-7771.

Buffalo Lake: Comprising 7,664 acres in Randall County in the Panhandle, this refuge once was a major waterfowl refuge in the **Central Flyway.** Because of changes in rainfall patterns and a decline of undergound water supplies, Buffalo Lake is now dry. Ponds and nearby farmlands provide habitat for waterfowl, and semi-arid grasslands and savannahs provide habitat for numerous birds, reptiles, deer and other mammals. Available activities include picnicking, sightseeing, birding, photography, hiking and camping. Entrance fee. Pheasant hunting allowed by special permit. Address: Box 179, Umbarger 79091. (806) 499-3382.

Hagerman: Hagerman National Wildlife Refuge lies on the Big Mineral arm of Texoma Lake in Grayson County. The 11,320 acres provide a feeding and resting place for migrating **waterfowl.** The refuge includes 3,000 acres of **marsh** and water and 8,000 acres of **farmland, grassland** and **woodlands.** Bird watching and fishing are the most popular activities. Hunting is permitted during limited seasons in designated areas. Address: Rt. 3, Box 123, Sherman 75090-9564. (903) 786-2826.

Laguna Atascosa: Established in 1946 as southernmost waterfowl refuge in the **Central Flyway,** this refuge contains more than 45,000 acres fronting on the **Laguna Madre** in the Lower Rio Grande Valley. Open **lagoons, coastal prairies, salt flats and brushlands** support a wide diversity of wildlife. The United States' largest concentration of **redhead ducks** winters here, along with many other species of **waterfowl** and **shorebirds**. **White-tailed deer, javelina, armadillo** and **Texas tortoise** can be found, along with endangered **ocelot** and **jaguarundi.** Bird watching and nature study are popular, with the abundance of migratory birds in the winter and many **Mexican birds** present year-round. Saltwater fishing is permitted within Adolph Thomae, Jr. County Park. Archery and rifle hunts are held most years for deer and feral hogs. Entrance fee. Address: Box 450, Rio Hondo 78583. (210) 748-3607.

Lower Rio Grande Valley: The U.S. Fish and Wildlife Service is slowly acquiring land in the Lower Rio Grande Valley for a new national refuge, which will encompass some 130,000 acres within Cameron, Hidalgo, Starr and Willacy counties. Area acquired for the refuge will include 11 different habitat types, including **sabal palm forest, tidal flats, coastal brushland, mid-delta thorn forest, woodland potholes and basins, upland thorn scrub, flood forest, barretal, riparian woodland** and **Chihuahuan thorn forest.** At least 100 unique vertebrate species that are listed as endangered, threatened, or which occur at the periphery of their range call the area home. For more information, contact Santa Ana/Lower Rio Grande Valley National Wildlife Refuges, Rt. 2, Box 202A, Alamo 78516. (210) 787-7861.

Matagorda Island: Matagorda Island is jointly owned by the Texas General Land Office and the U.S. Fish and Wildlife Service. The island (30,502 acres of federal lands and 26,166 acres of state lands) is cooperatively managed as the Matagorda Island National Wildlife Refuge and State Natural Area. Texas Parks and Wildlife manages the habitat and wildlife on the island through the Aransas NWR. The island supports a wide variety of migratory birds, some **19 state or federally listed threatened or endangered species,** a large herd of **white-tailed deer, alligators** and other wildlife. Activities include salt-water fishing, hunting (in season), birding, picnicking and historical interpretation. Address: P.O. Box 117, Port O'Connor 77982.

McFaddin: Purchased in 1980, this refuge's 42,955 acres are of great importance to wintering populations of **migratory waterfowl.** The endangered **southern bald eagle** and **peregrine falcon** are rare visitors, but may occasionally be seen during peak fall and spring migrations. One of the densest populations of **alligators** in Texas is found here. Activities on the refuge include wildlife observation, waterfowl hunting, fishing and crabbing. Address: Box 609, Sabine Pass 77655. (409) 971-2909.

Muleshoe: Oldest of national refuges in Texas, Muleshoe provides winter habitat for **waterfowl** and the continent's largest wintering population of **sandhill cranes**. Comprising 5,809 acres in the High Plains of Bailey County, the refuge contains three **playa lakes, marsh areas, caliche outcroppings** and **native grasslands**. Tour roads are available, as well as a **prairie dog town**, nature trail, campground and picnic area. Address: Box 549, Muleshoe 79347. Phone (806)946-3341.

San Bernard: Located on the Gulf of Mexico near Freeport, this refuge's nearly 28,000 acres attract **migrating waterfowl,** including thousands of **snow geese,** which spend the winter on the refuge. Habitats consist of **coastal prairies, salt/mud flats** and saltwater and freshwater ponds and potholes. Visitors may enjoy photography and bird watching; fishing is permitted, as well as waterfowl hunting in season. A special-permit waterfowl hunt is conducted three days per week. Contact refuge office for details. Address: Box 1088, Angleton 77516. (409) 849-7771.

Santa Ana: Established in 1943 and referred to as **"gem of the National Wildlife Refuge System,"** Santa Ana's more than 2,000 acres of **subtropical forest** and **native brushland** are located on the north bank of the Rio Grande in Hidalgo County. Santa Ana attracts birders from across the United States who can view many species of **Mexican birds** as they reach the northern edge of their ranges in South Texas. Also found at Santa Ana are **ocelot** and **jaguarundi,** endangered members of the cat family. Address: Rt. 2, Box 202A, Alamo 78516. (210) 787-3079.

Texas Point: Texas Point's 8,952 acres are located on the Upper Gulf Coast, where they serve a large wintering population of **waterfowl** as well as migratory birds. The endangered **southern bald eagle** and **peregrine falcon** may occasionally be seen during peak fall and spring migrations. **Alligators** are commonly observed during the spring, summer and fall months. Activities include wildlife observation, waterfowl hunting, fishing and crabbing. Access to the refuge is by boat and on foot only. Address: Box 609, Sabine Pass 77655. (409) 971-2909. ☆

Texas Wildlife Management Areas

In addition to the state parks system, the Texas Parks and Wildlife Department administers more than 1.5 million acres of lands for wildlife purposes. These lands, known as Wildlife Management Areas (WMAs), serve a variety of purposes with the common goal of improving the status and the public's enjoyment of the state's wildlife resources.

Some WMAs are used primarily to conduct field research and to demonstrate proper wildlife management practices to land operators in that area. Other areas were acquired primarily to protect unique wildlife species or habitats, and still others were acquired to provide wildlife-oriented public use — hunting, fishing, nature study, wildlife photography and other activities.

Most WMAs, regardless of their primary function, provide some public use. Supervised public hunts are conducted on many of the areas, as well as some state parks, as part of the resource-management program. On other areas, public use is strictly limited to nonconsumptive activities.

Access to WMAs is provided by five types of permits. A $25 to $50 special permit (selection by drawing) is required to participate in hunts where the demand is great. Access for hunting species not so high in demand and that require only a moderate amount of supervision is provided by a permit costing $6 to $12 per day, depending on the species. A $35 annual permit provides access for hunting and other activities on areas where no departmental supervision is required and demand does not exceed the available opportunity.

A $10 annual permit is available on some WMA lands for low-impact activities other than hunting and fishing. In addition, the department has recently initiated "special events" on some WMAs that require the participant to have a Texas Conservation Passport (TCP), a $25 permit that is valid at most state parks. Generally, the special events are tours or outdoor-oriented activities that are conducted by specialists in the wildlife field. For further information, write to Texas Parks and Wildlife, 4200 Smith School Rd., Austin 78744, or call (512) 792-1112.

A brief description of most WMAs is given below:

Candy Cain Abshier WMA (Chambers County) is a 207-acre tract managed primarily for nongame wildlife. Located on Smith Point, approximately 25 miles south of Anahuac, the area is popular with bird watchers during the spring and fall. No public facilities available; commercial facilities are nearby.

Alazan Bayou WMA (Nacogdoches County) was purchased in 1991 and consists of 1,973 acres southwest of Nacogdoches on the north shore of the Angelina River. It was purchased primarily to preserve bottomland hardwoods and is managed for waterfowl habitat enhancement. Public hunting allowed by permit for waterfowl, squirrel, woodcock and archery deer. Camping not permitted; camping and other lodging available in the vicinity.

Atkinson Island WMA (Harris County) consists of 151 acres of wading shorebird habitat adjacent to the Houston Ship Channel. Area is accessible only by boat; there are no public use facilities on the island.

Black Gap WMA (Brewster County) is an area of 106,915 acres on the Rio Grande adjacent to Big Bend National Park. Vegetation is typical of Chihuahuan Desert. Wildlife include desert mule deer, javelina, bobcat, coyotes, scaled quail and other desert species. Hunting allowed by special permit for deer and javelina, annual hunting permit for deer (archery), quail, dove and rabbits. Primitive camping allowed during public hunts at designated campgrounds; other facilities nearby.

Walter Buck WMA (Kimble County) includes 2,123 acres on the South Fork of the Llano River about three miles southwest of Junction. The gently rolling terrain is punctuated by canyons with dense stands of ashe juniper, elm and live oak. Wildlife includes white-tailed deer, feral Spanish goats, axis and sika deer, and wild turkey. No camping or fires; camping permitted at South Llano River State Park; commercial facilities available in Junction.

Chaparral WMA (La Salle and Dimmit counties), comprising 15,200 acres eight miles west of Artesia Wells, is in typical South Texas brush country: thorny brush, or "chaparral," includes mesquite, prickly pear cactus, granjeno, blackbrush and leatherstem. The terrain is flat to gently rolling. Wildlife includes deer, javelina and feral hogs, quail and mourning doves. Western diamondback rattlesnakes are common. Has a driving nature trail and two walking trails. Primitive campground available for hunters; commercial facilities nearby.

Dam B WMA (Jasper and Tyler counties) is located on B. A. Steinhagen Lake. Its 13,445 acres of land and water are generally flat with many sloughs separated by low ridges. Knee-high, waterproof footwear recommended. Trees include oaks and hickories, cedar elm, American hornbeam, black and sweet gums, greenbriers, holly, hawthorn, cypress, tupelo, water elm and buttonbush. Wildlife includes white-tailed deer, gray and fox squirrels, cottontail and swamp rabbits and waterfowl. Access by boat only; airboats are prohibited on the Angelina-Neches Scientific Area of the WMA. Permits are required for camping.

James E. Daughtrey WMA (Live Oak and McMullen counties) is located between Three Rivers and Tilden. Approximately 4,000 acres surrounding Choke Canyon Reservoir are available for public hunting. The rolling terrain is covered with thorny brush dominated by mesquite, blackbrush and cacti. Wildlife includes deer, javelina, turkey, quail, mourning dove, waterfowl and feral hogs. Roads are primitive.

Elephant Mountain WMA (Brewster County) consists of 23,347 acres about 26 miles south of Alpine. Vegetation consists of juniper, piñon, Spanish oak, mesquite, sotol, yucca, lechuguilla and cacti. Wildlife includes deer, pronghorn, javelina, desert bighorn sheep, quail and doves. Primitive camping allowed; water facilities not reliable.

Gus Engeling WMA (Anderson County) comprises 10,941 acres 32 miles southeast of Corsicana. The flat to gently rolling post-oak woodlands, include dense stands of oak-hickory overstory, along with yaupon, greenbrier, dogwood, hawthorn, elm and huckleberry. Wildlife includes numerous deer, feral hogs, squirrels, quail, mourning dove, waterfowl and turkey. Has a driving nature trail and two walking trails.

Granger WMA (Williamson County), three miles southeast of Granger, comprises 11,116 acres of upland grassland with some bottomland hardwoods. Wildlife includes mourning dove, quail, fox squirrel, rabbits, pheasant and migrant waterfowl. Walking nature trail. Only shotguns allowed. No camping on the area; Corps of Engineer campgrounds available at Granger Lake.

Guadalupe Delta WMA (Calhoun County), 6,155 acres of marsh 3.5 miles northeast of Tivoli, is managed primarily for waterfowl and migratory shore birds, alligators and other wetland wildlife.

Gene Howe WMA (Hemphill County) consists of 6,710 acres of rolling sandhills with large natural meadows along the north bank of the Canadian River. Trees and shrubs include sumac, plum, sagebrush, persimmon, cottonwood and buttonbush. Wildlife includes deer, turkey, quail and mourning dove. Four-wheel drive vehicles are recommended.

Keechi Creek WMA (Leon County) consists of 1,500 acres approximately 10 miles south of Oakwood. The terrain is principally bottomland intersected with creek drainages with standing-water sloughs. Vegetation includes willow, water and overcup oaks, elm and sweetgum. Wildlife includes eastern turkey, deer, squirrels, feral hogs and woodland waterfowl. Camping not allowed; commercial facilities nearby.

Kerr WMA (Kerr County), 6,493 acres located on the headwaters of the North Fork of the Guadalupe River 12 miles west of Hunt, has rolling hills, freshwater springs, dense cedar brakes and live oak-shin oak thickets. Wildlife includes Rio Grande turkey, mourning dove, quail, javelina, armadillo, fox, gray squirrels, black-capped vireo and golden-cheeked warbler. Has driving nature trail. No camping or fires; camp at Kerrville-Schreiner State Park; commercial facilities nearby.

Las Palomas WMA (Cameron, Hidalgo, Starr, Willacy and Presidio counties) comprises 24 units, more than 7,689 acres in all, mostly native brush vegetation with some farmland and some wetlands. Managed primarily for white-winged doves. Other wildlife includes black-bellied tree ducks, chachalacas, mourning doves, javelina, scaled quail, mule deer, ocelot and jaguarundi. Camping is permitted on some units; check Parks and Wildlife Department for details.

Lower Neches WMA (Orange County) consists of 7,998 acres of coastal marsh located on Sabine Lake. Wildlife includes wintering waterfowl, migratory shore birds and alligators. Hunting permitted on specified days. A boat-launching ramp is available near the south end of the area; no other public facilities.

Mad Island WMA (Matagorda County), located five miles west of the town of Matagorda, consists of 7,281 acres of marsh. Wildlife includes puddle and diver ducks, sandhill cranes, snow, Canada and white-fronted geese, alligators, mottled duck, raccoon, river otter, mink, armadillo, white-tailed deer, bobcat, gray fox and cottontail, jack and swamp rabbits.

Matador WMA (Cottle County) consists of 28,184 acres located 7 miles north of Paducah. Wildlife includes bobwhite quail, mule deer, turkey and doves. Not generally open for public use except for hunts. Some special events are scheduled throughout the year.

Pat Mayse WMA (Lamar County), located 12 miles northwest of Paris, consists of 8,925 acres of land and water adjacent to Pat Mayse Reservoir. The terrain is primarily upland oak woodlands as well as bottomland hardwoods including post and blackjack oak, pecan, hackberry, cottonwood and Osage orange.

J.D. Murphree WMA (Jefferson County) is approximately 13,360 acres of marsh along the upper Texas coast, divided into three units. Managed primarily for wintering and resident waterfowl and associated wildlife.

Old Tunnel WMA (Kendall County) consists of 10.5 acres of Hill Country habitat and includes an abandoned railroad tunnel, which serves as a summer roost site for bats. Bat-flight tours conducted during summer months. No public-use facilities on the area; facilities available at Comfort.

Peach Point WMA (Brazoria County), five miles west of Freeport, contains 10,312 acres of upland hardwood, upland prairie, fresh and saltwater marshes. Vegetation includes live oak, elm, pecan, Chinese tallow, baccharis, sea ox-eye and shortgrass. Wildlife includes waterfowl, rails, gallinules, mourning doves, quail, squirrel, white-tailed deer, cottontail rabbits, armadillo, feral hogs, alligators and various shore birds. No camping, commercial facilities available nearby.

Playa Lakes WMA (Moore, Castro and Hartley counties) consists of three tracts in the Panhandle totalling 1,660 acres, managed for waterfowl and other wildlife species associated with playa lakes. Hunting permitted only on Taylor Lakes Unit.

Redhead Pond WMA (Nueces County) is a small tract (37 acres) in Flour Bluff acquired as a sanctuary for wintering waterfowl and other birds. Visitors can view large concentrations of birds within short drive of Corpus Christi.

Richland Creek WMA (Freestone County) consists of 13,800 acres 25 miles southwest of Corsicana. Area used primarily for hunting; annual hunting or limited-use permit required for access. Primitive campgrounds available.

Sierra Diablo WMA (Hudspeth and Culberson counties), located in the mountain range of same name, consists of 11,625 acres approximately 32 miles north-northwest of Van Horn. Rough, rugged hills and steep canyons make up most of the area, with an average elevation of 6,200 feet, breaking sharply to desert floor to the east. Has well-established desert mule deer population. Used for bighorn sheep broodstock production. Only primitive camping allowed; nearest commercial facilities are one-and-one-half hours away.

Somerville WMA (Burleson and Lee counties), located 12 miles west southwest of Somerville, comprises 3,180 acres of post, water and blackjack oak, hickory, yaupon, coralberry, American beautyberry, greenbrier and grape. Wildlife includes white-tailed deer, squirrel, rabbit and migrant waterfowl.

Welder Flats Coastal Preserve (Calhoun County) consists of 1,480 acres of submerged coastal wetlands. Numerous species of wading and shore birds use the preserve, with the most distinctive being the whooping crane. ☆

Wildlife Stamps and Prints

Information in the following article was furnished by the ***Texas Parks and Wildlife Dept.****, 4200 Smith School Road, Austin, TX 78744, and* ***Collectors Covey****, Box 57306, Dallas, TX 75207.*

Since 1981, the Texas Parks and Wildlife Department has funded some of its acquisition, development and management of natural areas with the sale of wildlife stamps and matching art prints designed by leading wildlife artists. There are currently four types of state-issued wildlife stamps, as described below. Various other stamps are issued and sold by nonprofit organizations for the benefit of wildlife habitat.

Waterfowl Stamp: Commonly called a **"Duck Stamp,"** the waterfowl stamp has been required of all waterfowl hunters since Fiscal Year 1982. Funds from the sale of waterfowl stamps and prints are used for Texas waterfowl and wetlands conservation. Subjects of waterfowl stamp artwork and artists are: 1981, **mallards**, Larry Hayden; 1982, **pintails,** Ken Carlson; 1983, **American widgeons**, Maynard Reece; 1984, **wood ducks**, David Maass; 1985, **lesser snow geese**, John P. Cowan; 1986, **green-winged teal,** Herb Booth; 1987, **white-fronted geese**, Gary Moss; 1988, **pintails**, John P. Cowan; 1989, **mallards**, David Maass; 1990, **American widgeon**, Robert Bateman; 1991, **wood duck**, Daniel Smith; 1992, **Canada geese**, Larry Hayden; 1993, **blue-winged teal**, Jim Hautman; 1994, **northern shoveler**, Ken Carlson; 1995, **bufflehead**, David Maass.

Saltwater Stamp: Funds from the saltwater stamp, which has been required of all saltwater fishermen since 1986, may be used for coastal fisheries and management. In 1986, the featured fish was the **redfish** as depicted by artist John P. Cowan; in 1987, the **spotted seatrout**, by Al Barnes; 1988, **redfish**, Herb Booth; 1989, **speckled trout**, John P. Cowan; 1990, **redfish**, John Dearman; 1991, **speckled trout**, Al Agnew; 1992, **tarpon**, Mike Stidham; 1993, **king mackerel**, Al Barnes; 1994, **redfish**, Mark Susinno; 1995, **spotted sea trout**, John Dearman.

Nongame and Endangered Species Stamp: The nongame stamp, was offered for the first time in 1985. Funds from sale of the nongame stamps and art prints are used for conservation of nongame and endangered species. The 1985 nongame stamp and art subject was the **whooping crane** by artist Ken Carlson; 1986, **Attwater's prairie chicken** by John P. Cowan; 1987, the **bald eagle** by artist Bob Kuhn; 1988, **kestrels**, Charles Beckendorf; 1989, **ocelot**, Al Agnew; 1990, **Mearn's quail**, Sherrie Russell Meline; 1991, **white-tailed hawk**, Pamela Davis-King; 1992, **yellow-crowned night heron**, Gary Moss; 1993, **reddish egret**, Dee Kelley; 1994, **great horned owl**, Pamela Davis-King; 1995, **roadrunner**, Charles Beckendorf.

1995 Nongame Stamp: Roadrunner. Photo courtesy Collectors Covey.

Anniversary Nongame Stamp Set Offered

The Nongame and Urban Wildlife Program is celebrating the 10th anniversary of the nongame and endangered species stamp. A complete set of nongame stamps from 1985 to present is available for $75 per set. A limited edition collector's set of framed and mounted stamps is available for $300 each. All proceeds from the sale of these items support the Special Nongame and Endangered Species Fund. Call the TP&WD Nongame Program at 1-800-792-1112.

Turkey Stamp: The turkey stamp and print were offered for the first time in 1991. Funds from the sale of turkey stamps and prints are used to help finance the largest eastern turkey restoration program ever attempted, restocking birds on 23 million acres of East Texas habitat. Subject of all the turkey prints and stamps has been the **Rio Grande turkey.** Artists have been: 1991, John Dearman; 1992, Ken Carlson; 1993, Ragan Gennusa; 1994, David Drinkard; 1995, Charles Beckendorf. ☆

Horned Lizards Leave for West, South Texas

In polite society the horny toad is known as the Texas horned lizard.

In the scientific world, the reptile is referred to as *Phrynosoma cornutum*.

But fewer people are referring to the dinosaur-looking creature at all since it began to disappear from Texas backyards over the past few decades.

Forty years ago, the horny toad was generally found across most of the state; the only part of Texas where it was not common was the Piney Woods of East Texas.

After the 1950s, however, its range began to recede to generally west of a line from Fort Worth through Austin and San Antonio to Corpus Christi on the Gulf Coast.

A 1993 study report done by the Texas Parks and Wildlife Department says that no single reason can be given for the decline, but the report concludes that the horned lizards have decreased in numbers and been reduced in range from previous years when they were common as far north as Kansas and as far east as southwestern Missouri.

The lizards are usually from 3 to 5 inches in length. Their color varies from brown to tan to gray depending on the geographic location.

Scientific observation of horned lizards began in this country in the early 1800s with the help — like much research of the period — of Thomas Jefferson.

According to an article for the Catalogue of American Amphibians and Reptiles by Andrew H. Price, who also headed the TPWD study, the American statesman was responsible for procuring the first specimen through explorers Lewis and Clark. Jefferson brought the specimen to the Museum of the Philosophical Society of Philadelphia.

As decade-by-decade scientific observation of horned lizards continued, the species' numbers in the southwestern United States seemed to peak around the 1950s or 1960s. In the last two decades the decline began to be noticed and documented.

The TPWD study of the early 1990s used questionnaires distributed by various means about sightings and also used devices to capture some of the creatures. (The report points out that certain questionnaires that claimed sightings of horny toads in excess of ten inches in length were discounted.)

A sighting study is continuing at Chaparral Wildlife Management Area, about 60 miles north of Laredo, near Cotulla. There TPWD observes the lizards and their habits with the help of convicts from the Texas prison system.

Fire ants (*Solenopsis invicta*) are sometimes cited as a culprit in the ecology of the horned toad.

Hand-size Texas native has diminished in numbers in recent decades. Photo courtesy of Andrew Price, Texas Parks and Wildlife Dept.

There is a correlation in parts of Texas where the fire ants appear and the horned toads disappear. However, there seems to be a decline in the numbers of horned lizards in the Panhandle, where fire ants have not appeared.

If the fire ants are partly responsible for the changes, the survey says, the reason may be the disappearance of the smaller harvester ants (genus *Pogonomyrmex*) when fire ants move into an area. Harvester ants are a food source of the horny toads, as are grasshoppers and beetles.

Other possible threats to horny toads are pet collection, road kill and urbanization. The TPWD study concludes, however, that there is less danger from urbanization than from farming.

The tilling of the earth — plowing — shows up in the survey as suspect number one. It seems the horned lizards hibernate and lay their eggs underground during the winter and summer respectively. Plowing disturbs that process.

Also, the conservation researchers caution that in recent decades pesticides and defoliants have become more common for machine harvesting. So, they say, chemical use cannot be ruled out as also having some possible effect on the decline of the horny toad.

TPWD conservation scientists believe that South and West Texas will continue to have substantial populations of horned lizards. In other parts of the state, such as the coastal prairies southwest of Houston and in the Texas Panhandle, the numbers will probably continue to decline. The area inside the triangle from Dallas to Houston to Austin may have seen the last of the horny toad.

To help preserve the horny toad, the conservation scientists recommend the introduction of vegetation corridors through the more developed and cultivated parts of Texas. They recommend control of fire ants as well. ☆

Fish Hatcheries and Research Facilities

The **Texas Parks and Wildlife Department** (TPWD) operates field stations, fish hatcheries and research facilities to support the conservation and management of fishery resources.

Scheduled tours of hatcheries are available by letter request for groups of 20 or more at no charge. Write to individual hatchery for information.

Inland Fisheries Division

The Inland Fisheries Division of the TPWD operates one research facility, 18 field stations and six fish hatcheries around the state. Most of the facilities are leased from private owners for office space and equipment storage. From these facilities, state fisheries biologists conduct research and management activities on the state's vast and varied freshwater fisheries.

Research Facility

Heart of the Hills — Junction Star Route, Box 62, Ingram, 78025. Fishery management techniques that will enhance the conservation and management of freshwater reservoirs and streams are tested in the laboratory and pond facilities.

Field Offices

The state of Texas is divided into three regions containing 16 management districts. Each district contains a crew of several fisheries biologists and technicians. These personnel are responsible for management activities in all public reservoirs and streams within their district boundaries. Responsibilities include surveying and making recommendations to improve or maintain quality fishing. Consultation by phone or printed material is provided for those waters on private land.

Fish Hatcheries

Dundee — Archer County below the dam on Lake Diversion. Total acreage 141; pond acreage 78. Fishes raised include striped bass, hybrid striped bass, smallmouth and largemouth bass, rainbow trout and yellow perch.

Jasper — Jasper County off State 63. Total acreage 227; pond acreage 64. Fishes raised include largemouth bass, Florida largemouth bass, blue catfish, crappie and bluegill.

Possum Kingdom — Palo Pinto County below Possum Kingdom Reservoir Dam on State 16. Total acreage 103; pond acreage 28.9. Fishes raised are striped bass, hybrid striped bass and rainbow trout.

San Angelo — Tom Green County in the southeast sector of the City of San Angelo. Total area 79 acres; pond acreage 32. Fishes raised include Florida largemouth bass and channel catfish.

A.E. Wood — Hays County south of San Marcos. Total acreage 118; pond acreage 46. The facility produces smallmouth bass, Florida bass, channel catfish, blue catfish, sunfish, paddlefish and rainbow trout.

Tyler — Smith County off State 31. Total acreage 42; pond acreage 15. Fishes produced are largemouth bass, Florida largemouth bass and rainbow trout.

Coastal Fisheries Division

Field Stations

The five field stations and the areas in which they conduct research are: **Corpus Christi** (Nueces County) — Corpus Christi Bay and upper Laguna Madre; **Olmito** (Cameron County) — lower Laguna Madre and Gulf of Mexico; **Palacios** (Calhoun County) — East Matagorda, Matagorda and Lavaca Bay; **Port Arthur** (Jefferson County) — Sabine Lake and Gulf of Mexico; **Port O'Connor** (Calhoun County) — San Antonio Bay and Gulf of Mexico.

Marine Laboratories

Perry R. Bass Marine Fisheries Research Station — Calhoun County off State Hwy. 35 on Wells Point Rd. Experimental marine research and mariculture techniques.

GCCA/CPL Marine Development Center — Nueces County near Corpus Christi. Red drum, common snook and spotted seatrout fry and fingerlings are raised for stocking Texas bays.

Rockport — Aransas County, on Rockport boat basin. Headquarters for field program administrators and personnel assigned to Aransas Bay, Corpus Christi Bay and Gulf of Mexico research programs.

Seabrook — Harris County, on Seabrook waterfront. Headquarters for Coastal Fisheries research on Galveston Bay and Gulf of Mexico and Resource Protection Division chemist and biologist.

Sea Center Texas - Brazoria County near Freeport. Production of red drum, spotted seatrout and other marine species. Large visitor education center. Expected completion in fall 1995.

Saltwater Fishing

The **Coastal Fisheries Division** is responsible for making management recommendations regarding the state's saltwater fishery resources within the bays and estuaries and out to nine nautical miles into the Gulf of Mexico. The coastal fisheries conducted in Texas' 4 million acres of salt water by about 15,000 commercial fishermen and an estimated 1 million recreational fishermen have an economic impact of about $2 billion annually. Landings by saltwater sport-boat fishermen in Texas were more than 1.5 million fish in 1991-92. Commercial landings for 1993 exceeded 89 million pounds. Marine hatcheries produced and stocked into Texas bays nearly 30 million red drum fingerlings in 1993.

Commercial Fisheries

Shrimp made up 83 percent of the pounds landed and 90 percent of the value of all reported commercial marine products during 1993.

Commercial Landings, 1993

Jan. 1 to Dec. 31

Source: Texas Parks and Wildlife Department

Species	Pounds	Value
Finfish		
Drum, Black	841,000	$651,200
Flounder	212,600	328,300
Sheepshead	36,600	14,700
Snapper	1,487,700	2,729,800
Other	2,001,500	2,420 600
Total Finfish	**4,578,400**	**$6,144,600**
Shellfish		
Shrimp (Heads On):		
Brown and Pink	46,968,000	$94,927,700
White	17,235,200	33,173,100
Other	9,574,300	3,105,200
Crabs	8,241,500	3,932,100
Oysters	2,656,300	4,146,300
Other	40,900	25,600
Total Shellfish	**84,716,200**	**$139,310,000**
Grand Total	**89,295,600**	**$145,453,600**

Wild turkeys are popular game birds in the Lone Star State. During the 1993-94 hunting season, 90,000 wild turkeys were harvested by hunters. Texas Almanac file photo.

Freshwater Fishing

During the 1989-90 fiscal year an estimated 2.5 million Texas fishermen spent more than 41 million days fishing on our 1.7 million acres of public impoundments and 80,000 miles of rivers, streams and bayous. These anglers fished for sport and food, avidly seeking such longtime favorites as largemouth bass, crappie, white bass, sunfish and the various species of catfish, as well as introduced species such as smallmouth bass, walleye, striped bass and the striped/white bass hybrid.

Freshwater recreational fishing is big business in Texas. During the fiscal year, these fishermen, both residents and visitors, spent an estimated $4.9 billion on the purchase of goods and services related to recreational fishing.

The increasing number of fishermen is straining some fishery resources. Catch-and-release fishing has emerged on the Texas scene as the conservation theme of fishermen who desire continued quality fishing.

TPWD has continued its programs of stocking fish in public waters to increase fish numbers and species diversity. Among the most successful introductions are: Florida bass, a subspecies of largemouth bass; striped bass; walleyes; smallmouth bass; saltwater red drum; and rainbow trout. ☆

National Fish Hatcheries

The **Fish and Wildlife Service** of the U.S. Department of the Interior operates two national fish hatcheries in Texas:

Inks Dam NFH — (Burnet County) Total acreage 84.7; pond acreage 25. Twenty-eight ponds; produces approximately 800,000 channel catfish and largemouth and striped bass annually. Has visitor facilities. Access is from Highway 29 and Park Road 4. Address: Rt. 2, Burnet 78611. Phone (512) 793-2474. At press time, plans were pending to transfer this facility to the TPWD or close it.

Uvalde NFH — (Uvalde County) Total acreage 100; pond acreage 62. Forty-nine ponds produce approximately 2 million channel catfish and largemouth and striped bass. Has visitor facilities. Access via U.S. 90 west of Uvalde. Address: Box 708, Uvalde 78802. Phone (210) 278-2419.

In addition, the National Biological Service operates the **San Marcos NFH and Technology Cente**r — (Hays County) Total acreage 116 acres; pond acreage four. Fish production is secondary to research. Address: Rt. 1, Box 159-D, San Marcos 78666. Phone (512) 353-0011. ☆

Hunting, Fishing Licenses

A **hunting license** is required of Texas residents and nonresidents of Texas who hunt any bird or animal. Hunting licenses and stamps are valid during the period September 1 through the following August 31 of each year, except lifetime licenses and licenses issued for a specific number of days. A hunting license (except the nonresident special hunting license and nonresident 5-day special hunting license) is valid for taking all legal species of wildlife in Texas including **deer, turkey, javelina, antelope, aoudad (sheep)** and all **small game and migratory game birds**. **Special licenses and tags** are required for taking **alligators**, and a **trapper's license** is required to hunt **furbearing animals.**

All sport fishing licenses and stamps are valid only during the period September 1 through August 31, except lifetime licenses and licenses issued for a specific number of days. In addition to sports hunting and fishing licenses, **hunting/fishing stamps** are required for special hunting/fishing privileges.

Detailed information concerning licenses, stamps, seasons, regulations and related information can be obtained from **Texas Parks and Wildlife Department, 4200 Smith School Road, Austin 78744 (1-800-792-1112 or 512-389-4800).**

The Texas Parks and Wildlife Department reported revenue of $51.5 million from sales of all licenses during fiscal 1994, a $1.7 million increase over fiscal 1993. More than 3 million licenses were sold.

There were 453,000 **white-tailed deer** killed in the 1993-94 hunting season, compared to 469,000 in the 1992-93. The **Wild turkey** harvest was estimated at 90,000. There were 7,200 **mule deer** killed in 1993-94, compared to 6,500 the previous season. The **javelina** harvest was 19,000 in 1993-94 and 21,000 in 1992-93.

The **U.S. Fish and Wildlife Service, Division of Federal Aid**, reports that Texas had the third-largest number of paid hunting license holders in 1994, the last year with complete figures, with 1,072,347, at a gross cost to hunters of $19,238,563. Pennsylvania led the way with 1,149,426 paid hunting license holders; Michigan was second with 1,126,826.

Comparing fishing-licenses issued during 1994 shows Texas second, with 1,810,293, at a gross cost to anglers of $25,624,862. California led with 2,256,403 paid fishing-license holders. ☆

Weather

Unless otherwise noted, the data in the Weather section were prepared for the Texas Almanac by John F. Griffiths and Scott C. Sheridan, Office of the State Climatologist, Texas A&M University, College Station.

Weather Highlights 1993

February 15: In advance of a powerful cold front, thunderstorms producing numerous reports of hail trekked across Northeast Texas from Navarro County to Nacogdoches County. Hail as large as 2.75" in diameter was reported in Henderson (Rusk Co.). Later in the afternoon, another line of severe thunderstorms formed farther south, and hail was reported from McLennan County to Harris County.

March 29: A stationary frontal boundary across the southern reaches of the Panhandle sparked numerous strong to severe thunderstorms, which traveled from western portions of North Texas in the afternoon to North Central Texas by evening. Tornadoes touched down near Truscott (Knox) and Oklaunion (Wilbarger). Hail as large as 3.5" in diameter was reported at Sheppard AFB in Wichita Falls. Numerous other locations received golf-ball size or larger hail. Strong winds were also common, causing, among other things, the overturning of a mobile home in Burkburnett (Wichita).

April 19: Thunderstorms developing late in the afternoon ahead of a cold front in North Central and Northeast Texas moved southeast during the evening, producing three tornadoes in Hunt, San Saba and Rains counties. Several hundred homes were damaged by hailstones in Henderson County.

April 28: The combination of a cold front in North Texas and a dry line passing across the Panhandle initiated an active severe-weather day in the Panhandle and parts of West Texas. Tornadoes were reported in Oldham, Potter and Carson counties. Nearly $1 million in damage was done by thunderstorm winds and hail in Midland-Odessa and nearby Gardendale (Ector).

May 5: A disturbance originating in Mexico moved north and dropped up to 8 inches of rainfall in Bexar County. Three people were killed in San Antonio by floodwaters. Flooding was also reported in Wilson, Atascosa, Guadalupe, Medina, Victoria and Jackson counties.

May 9: Seventeen tornadoes were reported throughout the eastern half of the state. A man in a mobile home was killed, and 62 people were injured by the most powerful of the tornadoes as it passed through the business district of Wylie (Collin), leaving $20 million in damage in its wake. A woman in Dallas was killed by lightning, while wind gusts as high as 84 mph were reported in Galveston County. Flash flooding was also a problem; nearly 7 inches of rain in less than 24 hours led to flooding problems in most of Grayson County.

June 20-22: Tropical Storm Arlene made landfall 45 miles south of Corpus Christi; all of eastern Texas was inundated. Reports of more than 7 inches of precipitation were widespread, leading to the closure of dozens of farm-to-market and county roads. Henderson (Rusk) received 15 inches of rain during these three days.

July and August: From Dallas-Fort Worth south through Central Texas and most of the coastal plain, little to negligible rainfall was received during these two months. Several stations, including College Station, San Antonio and Austin, set new records with more than 50 consecutive days without measurable precipitation. Coupled with the above-normal temperatures for most of the summer, the lack of precipitation caused many crops to be seared throughout the state, and numerous wildfires burned in the Low Rolling Plains and the Edwards Plateau.

September 13: Eleven tornadoes were reported in a line from Denton (Denton) to Bellmead (McLennan), as well as in Breckenridge (Stephens). Six persons were injured, and damage was estimated to be near $20 million. Cleburne was hardest hit, with $8.3 million in damage done to more than 300 structures damaged.

October 17-20: This was a very active period for most of the eastern half of the state. On the 17th, a line of storms traveled from Mills and Hamilton counties in the late afternoon northeast through the Metroplex during the evening hours. Three small tornadoes were reported. However, much damage was done by thunderstorm winds and hail, which was reported to be as large as 4.5 inches in diameter at five different locations. The following day featured a re-forming of the severe weather, slightly farther south and east. A supercell produced five tornadoes within one hour in Kaufman, Rains, Van Zandt and Wood counties; one man was killed. Later in the day, the same mesocyclone produced two more tornadoes in Wood County. On the 19th and 20th, flash flooding was the main problem, from the Oklahoma border down through the Metroplex. Damage was minimal in most areas; however, road closures were quite numerous and extended for many counties.

November 25-26: Behind an Arctic cold front, which had moved through all of North Texas, strong southwest winds aloft produced strong overrunning conditions, which led to sleet and freezing rain being reported across all of the area. Ice and sleet accumulations of up to two inches were reported. Two people were killed in ice-related accidents. Downed power lines left 20,000 homes without electricity some time. Damage was estimated at more than $5 million.

Weather Summary - 1993

Annual mean temperatures for the year 1993 were from 0.5 to 1.0 degrees F below normal in most locations, continuing the trend started in 1992. The only exceptions to this were in the Trans Pecos, where temperatures were above normal, and the Edwards Plateau and Lower Rio Grande Valley, where temperatures were near normal. Precipitation totals for most of the state were within 10 per-

Average Temperatures 1993

	High Plains	Low Plains	North Central	East Texas	Trans-Pecos	Edwards Plateau	South Central	Upper Coast	South Texas	Lower Valley
Jan	35.3	39.1	43.6	46.0	47.3	46.4	51.9	53.7	54.6	59.4
Feb	39.0	43.3	47.7	49.3	49.9	50.8	55.9	56.5	58.9	63.9
Mar	48.0	52.2	54.5	54.4	56.4	57.7	61.4	61.3	65.1	68.0
Apr	56.5	61.1	61.5	60.9	64.8	64.9	66.4	66.0	70.9	73.2
May	66.0	69.2	70.1	70.0	72.3	71.5	72.8	73.2	75.8	77.1
Jun	75.1	79.0	79.7	79.1	80.0	79.9	80.1	80.7	81.9	82.2
Jul	80.0	85.3	85.0	83.7	81.7	83.8	83.9	84.2	85.7	85.2
Aug	77.7	82.9	85.5	84.5	81.4	84.5	85.1	85.0	86.7	85.5
Sep	68.9	72.8	75.9	76.5	73.2	75.3	80.5	80.3	81.6	82.3
Oct	56.8	61.6	63.4	64.3	63.5	65.6	70.6	70.5	73.0	75.2
Nov	42.8	47.2	49.7	50.7	51.3	51.6	56.6	57.6	59.6	64.0
Dec	40.4	45.5	48.4	49.1	47.8	50.6	55.9	55.5	59.2	62.5
Ann	57.2	61.6	63.8	64.0	64.1	65.2	68.4	59.1	71.0	73.2

Precipitation 1993

(Inches)

	High Plains	Low Plains	North Central	East Texas	Trans-Pecos	Edwards Plateau	South Centrall	Upper Coast	South Texas	Lower Valley
Jan	1.21	1.21	2.34	5.19	0.97	1.18	2.53	6.43	1.14	0.79
Feb	0.76	2.10	3.90	3.00	0.38	1.31	3.22	3.41	1.31	1.73
Mar	1.16	1.52	3.20	4.79	0.27	1.54	3.85	6.30	2.17	2.38
Apr	1.15	1.86	3.44	4.40	0.36	1.99	2.91	5.21	1.51	0.92
May	2.08	3.26	3.14	4.72	0.86	2.37	7.88	7.77	4.12	4.25
Jun	2.66	2.41	3.89	8.35	1.08	2.65	7.88	9.10	6.62	8.60
Jul	3.17	1.59	0.04	.28	3.04	1.03	0.15	1.09	0.04	0.04
Aug	2.48	2.06	1.01	2.01	2.00	1.52	0.45	1.98	0.41	0.19
Sep	1.26	1.57	3.83	2.56	1.19	2.82	1.13	1.99	1.86	3.10
Oct	0.93	2.35	6.56	7.00	0.59	1.57	3.66	5.80	1.10	2.47
Nov	0.48	0.48	1.59	3.75	0.13	0.50	1.38	4.42	0.47	1.36
Dec	0.41	1.00	2.12	2.99	0.66	0.83	2.11	3.00	0.86	1.60
Ann	17.8	21.4	35.1	29.0	11.5	19.3	37.2	56.5	21.6	27.4

cent of normal for the entire year. The Trans Pecos and Edwards Plateau, however, were some 10 to 20 percent below normal, and the Upper Coast reported a 20 percent surplus for 1993.

January and February featured above-normal temperatures across most of the state, except in the Panhandle, where both months were 1.5 to 2.0 degrees F below normal. Precipitation for both months was significantly above normal in most places, with values up to 275 percent of normal reported in the Panhandle. Below-normal precipitation was observed in extreme southern Texas in January and the far west and far east corners during February.

The **spring months** brought significantly colder than normal temperatures to all of Texas except the Trans Pecos. Mean temperatures from March to May were consistently 2 to 5 degrees F below normal along the Gulf Coast and in East Texas. The pattern was less consistent for precipitation, however. All areas except the Trans Pecos continued to be wetter than normal during March, with 200 to 350 percent of normal values reported in the eastern and southern parts of Texas. All of Texas returned to near-normal precipitation totals during April, except for a surplus along the Upper Coast.

May and June both brought dry conditions to far west Texas and wetter than normal conditions to the eastern and coastal regions. During June, this excess was largely due to Tropical Storm Arlene, which made landfall on the 20th near Corpus Christi. June 24-hour precipitation records were broken at Shreveport, Midland/Odessa and Del Rio from this storm. Temperatures during June were 1 to 2 degrees F cooler than normal in the south and near normal across the rest of Texas.

During **July**, abnormally hot and dry conditions were observed over the entire eastern half of the state. No measurable rain was reported by 278 stations during the month, including the cities of Austin, Brownsville, College Station, Corpus Christi, Dallas/Fort Worth, San Antonio and Waco. Houston also set a record minimum total precipitation for the month. Incidentally, West Texas was the only wetter-than-normal region during July. Alongside these dry conditions, temperatures averaged up to 2 degrees F above normal for the month.

The above-normal temperatures and dry conditions continued into **August**. Rainfall was in general less sparse, especially toward month's end. Still, the Lower Valley recorded only 8 percent of its normal total, and much of the state received less than half of what is expected.

As summer ended, **September** brought a return to more-normal temperatures, although precipitation stayed below normal statewide. The months of **October and November** were also drier than normal, except in extreme eastern regions, where up to 190 percent of normal was realized. During these months, sharply colder-than-normal temperatures, ranging from 1 to 3 degrees F in October to 2 to over 6 degrees F during November, kept hold of the state. A powerful cold front passing through the state during the last two days of October brought record low temperatures for the entire month to every first-order station except El Paso. The earliest first freeze in station history was recorded in Corpus Christi and Victoria. Snowfall was reported as far south as Corpus Christi, and the earliest measurable snow fell in Abilene, Del Rio and Midland-Odessa.

December saw a reversal of conditions across the state, as all regions were above normal by some 1 to 3.5 degrees F. Precipitation was near normal as the year ended.

1993 Weather Extremes

Lowest Temp.: Stratford, Sherman Co., January 10 ..... -3"F
Highest Temp.: Castolon, Brewster Co., June 26 ..... 113°F
24-hour Precip.: Aransas Wildlife Refuge, Aransas Co., February 10 ..... 10.73"
Monthly Precip.: Longview, Gregg Co., June ..... 17.90"
Least Annual Precip.: Tornillo, El Paso Co. ..... 5.74"
Greatest Annual Precip.: Port Arthur, Jefferson Co. ... 67.12"

Weather Highlights - 1994

January 30: A major snowstorm blanketed the Panhandle and western North Texas this Super Bowl Sunday. At least 4 inches of snow was reported throughout the Panhandle, with totals as high as 15 inches at Silverton (Briscoe). Amarillo's 10.2 inches of snowfall was the largest storm total reported there since 1987.

February 9-10: An Arctic cold front dropped temperatures some 60 degrees in two days across much of the state. It also spurred a severe ice storm across the eastern half of the state, with up to 4 inches of accumulation in some areas. Measurable amounts of ice were received north of a line from Austin to College Station to the northern Houston suburbs.

April 25-26: Three supercell thunderstorms moved across the Dallas-Fort Worth area and most of North Texas on the 25th, producing six tornadoes, which caused over $150 million in damage, as well as widespread hail as large as 4.5 inches in diameter. Hail damage resulted in an additional $50 million loss. Storms redeveloped the following day, with two tornadoes and extensive hail damage again reported. Total damage on the second day was $20 million. On these two days, three people were killed as a result of the tornadoes.

Late June-Early July: A strong high-pressure system led to record heat reported in many West Texas and Panhandle towns. Most reporting stations in the area recorded highs between 110°F and 120°F. Midland-Odessa (116°F), Lubbock (114°F) and El Paso (114°F) were among the stations in more than 40 counties that reported all-time record high temperatures. Wildfires were common from Wichita Falls to El Paso as a result of the extreme heat and dryness. El Paso for the summer of 1994 experienced a record 62 days of triple-digit heat.

October 15-19: Anomalously humid air, even for July, streamed into eastern Texas on the return flow of Pacific Hurricane Rosa's remnants as it crossed the state. A subtropical jet stream and energy ahead of a stalled frontal system combined with this moisture to produce torrential rainfall and record floods. Liberty (Liberty) reported 28.90 inches of rainfall over four days; widespread totals of over 15 inches were recorded north and northwest of Houston.

Average Temperatures 1994

	High Plains	Low Plains	North Central	Eas tTexas	Trans-Pecos	Edwards Plateau	South Central	Upper Coast	South Texas	Lower Valley
Jan	37.7	42.1	44.8	46.0	46.1	48.0	53.4	53.1	56.3	61.2
Feb	38.8	42.7	46.8	48.8	50.2	50.6	55.1	55.3	58.7	62.3
Mar	50.0	55.3	57.9	57.9	58.0	60.1	62.8	62.3	66.3	67.9
Apr	57.0	62.4	64.8	65.8	64.9	66.2	68.8	69.0	72.3	73.8
May	66.1	69.2	70.1	70.3	73.7	72.7	74.3	75.1	77.2	79.2
Jun	80.0	83.3	820	80.7	84.0	83.1	82.3	82.0	84.8	84.3
Jul	79.1	83.6	82.9	81.9	83.7	84.2	85.0	83.9	87.4	85.9
Aug	77.7	82.7	82.6	80.3	81.8	82.9	82.9	81.9	85.1	84.0
Sep	70.2	73.7	74.6	75.0	74.3	75.2	77.2	77.9	79.3	80.1
Oct	60.0	64.9	66.6	66.7	66.1	68.1	71.8	71.9	74.7	76.3
Nov	48.1	53.0	57.0	59.4	56.6	58.2	65.8	66.6	68.1	74.6
Dec	43.1	46.3	48.7	50.4	49.7	51.2	56.5	57.8	60.6	65.0
Ann	59.0	63.3	64.9	65.3	65.8	66.8	69.7	69.8	72.6	74.6

Precipitation 1994

(Inches)

	High Plains	Low Plains	North Central	East Texas	Trans-Pecos	Edwards Plateau	South Central	Upper Coast	South Texas	Lower Valley
Jan	0.54	0.85	1.27	3.31	0.62	1.95	1.26	3.03	1.54	1.86
Feb	0.13	1.03	2.40	4.89	0.28	1.18	1.54	1.64	0.74	0.40
Mar	0.91	0.95	1.78	3.44	0.52	1.69	2.94	2.69	3.15	1.75
Apr	1.68	2.01	2.79	2.60	0.30	1.47	2.87	2.74	1.90	0.82
May	3.35	4.86	7.01	6.56	1.67	3.96	5.61	6.19	2.64	2.58
Jun	1.17	0.60	1.68	2.91	0.70	1.30	2.75	5.50	3.66	3.36
Jul	2.86	1.58	3.69	4.22	1.12	1.68	0.31	1.47	0.92	0.26
Aug	1.80	0.70	1.88	4.05	0.69	0.99	3.68	5.59	1.07	2.36
Sep	1.49	2.58	3.14	2.18	1.18	2.77	3.71	3.15	2.60	3.88
Oct	1.10	2.49	6.53	11.14	0.80	3.22	9.78	13.28	4.17	2.98
Nov	0.88	2.05	4.88	3.36	0.39	2.03	0.88	1.08	0.27	0.50
Dec	0.44	0.85	3.37	7.43	0.56	2.46	4.88	6.06	1.96	2.32
Ann	16.4	20.6	40.4	56.1	8.8	24.7	40.2	52.4	24.6	23.1

The city of Houston was cut off from many other regions of the state, as numerous roads, including I-10, were flooded. Seventeen lives were lost as a result of the flooding. Many rivers reached record levels, including the San Jacinto, which later caught fire due to a pipeline rupture caused by flooding. Damage for the flooding was estimated to be near $700 million; 26 counties were declared disaster areas.

Weather Summary - 1994

An **extremely hot June** and **flooding rains in October** were the main contributors to 1994's being warmer and wetter than normal in most of Texas. Temperatures were above normal throughout every climate region for the first year since 1986; departures ranged from less than 0.5 degrees F in eastern parts, to 0.5 to 1.5 degrees F in the Panhandle and far south, and greater than 2 degrees F in the Trans Pecos. Precipitation totals were 110 percent to 125 percent of normal in the eastern and central parts of the state; drier than normal totals were observed in the Lower Rio Grande Valley, Panhandle and Trans Pecos. Trans Pecos only received 68 percent of the normal annual total.

The warm year began appropriately with a warmer-than-normal **January**, with temperatures 1 to 4 degrees F above normal statewide. Precipitation was below normal across North and South Central Texas, much wetter than normal in the Edwards Plateau, and near normal elsewhere. Significant precipitation occurred across the Panhandle from a major snowstorm at month's end.

During **February**, near-normal temperatures were observed statewide, with the exception of the Panhandle, which was over 2 degrees F below normal, and the Trans Pecos and Lower Valley, both 1 degree F above normal. Precipitation totals were well below normal in all areas except East Texas. This pattern was reversed in **March**, as heavy rainfall during mid-month contributed to regions in southern and western Texas reporting totals from 150 to near 400 percent of normal. Temperatures for the month were consistently around 1 degree F above normal statewide, slightly higher north and west, lower south and east.

April and May were characterized by 1 to 2 degree F cooler-than-normal temperatures in all parts of Texas except the Trans Pecos. Below-normal rainfall was reported in the majority of the state in April; only in the Panhandle were wetter-than-normal conditions experienced. However, the May showers were quite heavy, especially during mid-month in the western half of the state, resulting in all areas of the state, except far southern areas, reporting 120 to 160 percent of normal.

The hottest month of the year in Texas for 1994 was **June**, instead of the usual July. Below-normal rainfall in most of the state, as little as 20 to 50 percent in the northern tier, was coupled with temperatures exceeding normal by from 1 degree F in East Texas to as much as 5 degrees F in the Panhandle and Trans Pecos. Many regions of the state saw a continuation of the well-above-normal temperatures in **July**, generally from 1 to 3 degrees F. Much of the state also continued to be extremely dry as well, parts of southern Texas receiving as little as 15 percent of the normal monthly mean.

August and September featured a fairly consistent thermal pattern of slightly hotter-than-normal conditions in the western half of the state, and slightly below-normal conditions in the eastern half. East Texas, the Upper Coast and South Central Texas reported above-normal rainfall during August; in other areas, with the lack of any tropical systems affecting the state, precipitation during these two months provided only 30 to 80 percent of the normal.

The **main weather event for the state for the year** was the flooding rains which inundated most of eastern Texas during mid-October. As a result, precipitation totaled some 200 to nearly 500 percent of normal at some stations, with all places except the Panhandle and Trans Pecos wetter than normal. Temperatures for the month were near normal in most areas, to around 1.5 degrees F above normal in the southern and western extremes.

The year ended as it began, since **November and December** featured well-above-normal temperatures throughout the state, with departures up to 7 degrees F above normal in the Lower Valley. Precipitation for the two months was generally above normal, the only exception being the southern third of Texas in November, where only around 30 percent of normal was reported.

1994 Weather Extremes

Lowest Temp.: Follett, Lipscomb Co., January 31 .... -6°F
Silverton, Briscoe Co., February 1 ...... -6°F
Highest Temp.: Monahans, Ward Co., June 28 .... 120°F
24-hour Precip: Liberty, Liberty Co., October 18 .... 18.50"
Monthly Precip.: Liberty, Liberty Co., October .... 29.59"
Least Annual Precip.: Marathon, Brewster Co. .... 5.43"
Greastest Annual Precip.: Corrigan, Polk Co. .... 82.82"

Destructive Weather

Source: This list of exceptionally destructive weather in Texas since 1766 was compiled from ESSA-Weather Bureau information.

Sept., 4, 1766: Hurricane. Galveston Bay. A Spanish mission destroyed.

Sept. 12, 1818: Hurricane. Galveston Island. Salt water flowed four feet deep. Only six buildings remained habitable. Of the six vessels and two barges in the harbor, even the two not seriously damaged were reduced to dismasted hulks. **Pirate Jean Lafitte** moved to one hulk so his **Red House** might serve as a hospital.

Aug. 6, 1844: Hurricane. Mouth of Rio Grande. All houses destroyed at the mouth of the river and at **Brazos Santiago,** eight miles north; 70 lives lost.

Sept. 19, 1854: Hurricane. After striking near **Matagorda,** the hurricane moved inland northwestward over **Columbus.** The main impact fell in **Matagorda and Lavaca bays.** Almost all buildings in Matagorda were destroyed. Four lives were lost in the town; more lives were lost on the peninsula.

Oct. 3, 1867: Hurricane. This hurricane moved inland **south of Galveston,** but raked the entire Texas coast **from the Rio Grande to the Sabine. Bagdad and Clarksville,** towns at the mouth of the Rio Grande, were destroyed. Much of Galveston was flooded and property damage there was estimated at $1 million.

Sept. 16, 1875: Hurricane. Struck **Indianola,** Calhoun County. Three-fourths of town swept away; 176 lives lost. Flooding from the bay caused nearly all destruction.

Aug. 13, 1880: Hurricane. Center struck **Matamoros, Mexico; lower Texas coast** affected.

Oct. 12-13, 1880: Hurricane. Brownsville. City nearly destroyed, many lives lost.

Aug. 23-24, 1882: Torrential rains caused **flooding** on the **North and South Concho and Bosque rivers** (South Concho reported 45 feet above normal level), destroying **Benficklen,** then county seat of Tom Green County, leaving only the courthouse and the jail. More than 50 persons were reported drowned in **Tom Green and Erath counties,** with property damage at $200,000 and 10,000 to 15,000 head of livestock lost.

Aug. 19-21, 1886: Hurricane. Indianola. Every house destroyed or damaged. Indianola never rebuilt.

Oct. 12, 1886: Hurricane. Sabine, Jefferson County. Hurricane passed over Sabine. The inundation extended 20 miles inland and nearly every house in the vicinity was moved from its foundation; 150 persons were drowned.

April 28, 1893: Tornado. Cisco, Eastland County; 23 killed, 93 injured; damage $400,000.

May 15, 1896: Tornadoes, Sherman, Grayson County; **Justin,** Denton County; **Gribble Springs,** Cooke County; 76 killed; damage $225,000.

Sept. 12, 1897: Hurricane. Many houses in **Port Arthur** were demolished; 13 killed, damage $150,000.

May 1, 1898: Tornado. Mobeetie, Wheeler County. Four killed, several injured; damage $35,000.

June 27-July 1, 1899: Rainstorm. A storm, centered over the **Brazos River watershed,** precipitated an average of 17 inches over an area of 7,000 square miles. At **Hearne** the gage overflowed at 24 inches, and there was an estimated total rainfall of 30 inches. At **Turnersville,** Coryell County, 33 inches were recorded in three days. This rain caused the **worst Brazos River flood on record.** Between 30 and 35 lives were lost. Property damage was estimated at $9 million.

April 5-8, 1900: Rainstorm. This storm began in two centers, over **Val Verde County** on the Rio Grande, and over **Swisher County** on the High Plains, and converged in the vicinity of **Travis County**, causing disastrous floods in the **Colorado, Brazos and Guadalupe rivers**. McDonald Dam on the Colorado River at Austin crumbled suddenly. A wall of water swept through the city taking at least 23 lives. Damage was estimated at $1,250,000.

Sept. 8-9, 1900: Hurricane. Galveston. The Great Galveston Storm was the **worst natural disaster in U.S. history**. Loss of life at Galveston has been estimated at 6,000 to 8,000, but the exact number has never been definitely ascertained. The island was completely inundated, and not a single structure escaped damage. Most of the loss of life was due to drowning by storm tides that reached 15 feet or more. The anemometer blew away when the wind reached 100 miles per hour at 6:15 p.m. on the 8th. Wind reached an estimated maximum velocity of 120 miles per hour between 7:30 and 8:30 p.m. Property damage has been estimated at $30 to $40 million.

May 18, 1902: Tornado. Goliad. This tornado cut a 250-year-wide path straight through town, turning 150 buildings into rubble. Several churches were destroyed, one of which was holding services; all 40 worshippers were either killed or injured. This tornado killed 114, injured 230 injured, and caused an estimated $200,000 in damages.

April 26, 1906: Tornado. Bellevue, Clay County, demolished; considerable damage done at **Stoneburg**, seven miles east; 17 killed, 20 injured; damage $300,000.

May 6, 1907: Tornado. North of Sulphur Springs, Hopkins County; five killed, 19 injured.

May 13, 1908: Tornado. Linden, Cass County. Four killed, seven injured; damage $75,000.

May 22-25, 1908: Rainstorm; unique because it originated on the Pacific Coast. It moved first into **North Texas** and southern Oklahoma and thence to **Central Texas**, precipitating as much as 10 inches. Heaviest floods were in the upper Trinity basin, but flooding was general as far south as the Nueces. Property damage exceeded $5 million and 11 lives were lost in the Dallas vicinity.

March 23, 1909: Tornado. Slidell, Wise County; 11 killed, 10 injured; damage $30,000.

May 30, 1909: Tornado. Zephyr, Brown County; 28 killed, many injured; damage $90,000.

July 21, 1909: Hurricane. Velasco, Brazoria County. One-half of town destroyed, 41 lives lost; damage $2,000,000.

Dec. 1-5, 1913: Rainstorm. This caused the **second major Brazos River flood**, and caused more deaths than the storm of 1899. It formed over **Central Texas** and spread both southwest and northeast with precipitation of 15 inches at **San Marcos** and 11 inches at **Kaufman**. Floods caused loss of 177 lives and $8,541,000 damage.

April 20-26, 1915: Rainstorm. Originated over Central Texas and spread into North and East Texas with precipitation up to 17 inches, causing floods in **Trinity, Brazos, Colorado, and Guadalupe rivers**. More than 40 lives lost and $2,330,000 damage.

Aug. 16-19, 1915: Hurricane. Galveston. Peak wind gusts of 120 miles recorded at Galveston; tide ranged 9.5 to 14.3 feet above mean sea level in the city, and up to 16.1 feet near the causeway. Business section flooded with 5 to 6 feet of water. At least 275 lives lost, damage $56 million. A new seawall prevented a repetition of the 1900 disaster.

Aug. 18, 1916: Hurricane. Corpus Christi. Maximum wind speed 100 miles per hour. 20 Lives lost; damage $1,600,000.

Jan. 10-12, 1918: Blizzard. This was the most severe since that of February, 1899; it was accompanied by zero degree temperature in **North Texas** and temperatures from 7 to 12 below freezing along the **lower coast**.

April 9, 1919: Tornado. Leonard, Ector and Ravenna in Fannin County; 20 killed, 45 injured; damage $125,000.

April 9, 1919: Tornado. Henderson, Van Zandt, Wood, Camp, and Red River counties, 42 killed, 150 injured; damage $450,000.

May 7, 1919: Windstorms. Starr, Hidalgo, Willacy and Cameron counties. Violent thunderstorms with high winds, hail and rain occurred between **Rio Grande City** and the coast, killing 10 persons. Damage to property and crops was $500,000. Seven were killed at **Mission**.

Sept. 14, 1919: Hurricane. Near **Corpus Christi**. Center moved inland south of Corpus Christi; tides 16 feet above normal in that area and 8.8 feet above normal at **Galveston**. Extreme wind at Corpus Christi measured at 110 miles per hour; 284 lives lost; damage $20,272,000.

April 13, 1921: Tornado. Melissa, Collin County, and **Petty**, Lamar County. Melissa was practically destroyed; 12 killed, 80 injured; damage $500,000.

April 15, 1921: Tornado. Wood, Cass and Bowie counties; 10 killed, 50 injured; damage $85,000.

Sept. 8-10, 1921: Rainstorm. Probably the **greatest rainstorm in Texas history**, it entered Mexico as a hurricane from

Texas Annual Average Precipitation, 1888-1994

Year	Inches	Year	Inches
1888	38.61	**1941	40.94
1889	34.52	1942	30.35
1890	31.52	1943	32.41
1891	27.49	1944	33.38
1892	26.91	1945	29.37
1893	18.66	1946	33.25
1894	25.37	1947	23.73
1895	30.12	1948	20.70
1896	24.94	1949	34.09
1897	24.94	1950	24.98
1898	25.97	1951	20.74
1899	26.34	1952	22.41
1900	38.54	1953	23.64
1901	20.31	1954	18.01
1902	30.83	1955	22.75
1903	30.16	1956	15.52
1904	27.65	1957	37.01
1905	37.89	1958	30.78
1906	28.90	1959	30.33
1907	30.87	1960	31.90
1908	30.10	1961	28.90
1909	21.50	1962	24.32
1910	19.59	1963	19.75
1911	26.47	1964	23.75
1912	23.89	1965	26.82
1913	32.85	1966	26.93
1914	34.66	1967	25.47
1915	29.33	1968	33.20
1916	22.51	1969	29.82
*1917	14.80	1970	23.87
1918	26.28	1971	28.39
1919	41.95	1972	27.06
1920	31.39	1973	35.44
1921	26.19	1974	32.27
1922	29.88	1975	27.30
1923	36.63	1976	30.71
1924	21.36	1977	22.75
1925	23.66	1978	25.87
1926	33.06	1979	31.39
1927	25.41	1980	24.45
1928	26.54	1981	32.69
1929	28.34	1982	26.97
1930	27.12	1983	25.85
1931	27.43	1984	26.19
1932	32.69	1985	30.05
1933	23.11	1986	34.14
1934	23.04	1987	30.56
1935	34.58	1988	21.13
1936	28.57	1989	25.59
1937	25.16	1990	31.77
1938	24.98	1991	37.94
1939	23.24	1992	34.16
1940	32.09	1993	27.60
		1994	29.65

105-year average: 27.21"
*Driest year
** Wettest year
Source: Office of the State Climatologist

the Gulf. Torrential rains fell as the storm moved northeasterly across Texas. **Record floods** occurred in **Bexar, Travis, Williamson, Bell and Milam counties**, killing 215 persons, with property losses over $19 million. Five to nine feet of water stood in downtown **San Antonio**. A total of 23.98 inches was measured at the U.S. Weather Bureau station at **Taylor** during a period of 35 hours, with a 24-hour maximum of 23.11 on September 9-10. The **greatest rainfall recorded in United States history during 18 consecutive hours fell at Thrall**, Williamson County, 36.40 inches fell on Sept. 9.

April 8, 1922: Tornado. Rowena, Runnels County. Seven killed, 52 injured; damage $55,000.

April 8, 1922: Tornado. Oplin, Callahan County. Five killed, 30 injured; damage $15,000.

April 23-28, 1922: Rainstorm. An exceptional storm that entered Texas from the west and moved from the **Panhandle** to **North Central and East Texas**. Rains up to 12.6 inches over Parker, Tarrant, and Dallas counties caused severe floods in the Upper Trinity at **Fort Worth**; 11 lives were lost; damage was estimated at $1 million.

May 4, 1922: Tornado. Austin, Travis County; 12 killed, 50 injured; damage $500,000.

May 14, 1923: Tornado. Howard and Mitchell counties; 23 killed, 100 injured; damage $50,000.

April 12, 1927: Tornado. Edwards, Real and Uvalde counties; 74 killed, 205 injured; damage $1,230,000. Most of damage was in **Rocksprings** where 72 deaths occurred and town was practically destroyed.

May 9, 1927: Tornado. Garland; eleven killed; damage $100,000.

May 9, 1927: Tornado. Nevada, Collin County; **Wolfe City**, Hunt County; and **Tigertown**, Lamar County; 28 killed, over 200 injured; damage $900,000.

Jan. 4, 1929: Tornado. Near **Bay City**, Matagorda County. Five killed, 14 injured.

April 24, 1929: Tornado. Slocum, Anderson County; seven killed, 20 injured; damage $200,000.

May 24-31, 1929: Rainstorm. Beginning over **Caldwell County**, a storm spread over much of **Central and Coastal Texas** with maximum rainfall of 12.9 inches, causing **floods in Colorado, Guadalupe, Brazos, Trinity, Neches and Sabine rivers**. Much damage at from overflow of bayous. Damage estimated at $6 million.

May 6, 1930: Tornado. Bynum, Irene and Mertens in Hill County; **Ennis**, Ellis County; and **Frost**, Navarro County; 41 killed; damage $2,100,000.

May 6, 1930: Tornado. Kenedy and Runge in Karnes County; **Nordheim**, DeWitt County; 36 killed, 34 injured; damage $127,000.

June 30-July 2, 1932: Rainstorm. Torrential rains fell over the upper watersheds of the **Nueces and Guadalupe riv-**

Texas is Tornado Capital

An **average of 123 tornadoes** touch Texas soil each year. The annual total varies considerably, and certain areas are struck more often than others. Tornadoes occur with **greatest frequency** in the Red River Valley.

Tornadoes may occur in any month and at any hour of the day, but they occur with greatest frequency during the late spring and early summer months, and between the hours of 4:00 p.m. and 8:00 p.m. In the period 1951-1993, nearly 62 percent of all Texas tornadoes occurred within the three-month period of April, May and June. Slightly more than one-fourth of the total occurred in May.

Partly because of the state's size, **more tornadoes have been recorded in Texas than in any other state**. Between 1951 and 1993, 5,281 funnel clouds reached the ground, thus becoming tornadoes. In the density of tornadoes, Texas ranks eleventh among the 50 states, with an average of 4.4 tornadoes per 10,000 square miles per year during this period.

The **greatest outbreak of tornadoes on record in Texas** was associated with Hurricane Beulah in September 1967. Within a five-day period, Sept. 19-23, 115 known tornadoes, all in Texas, were spawned by this great hurricane. Sixty-seven occurred on Sept. 20, a **Texas record for a single day**.

In September 1967, Hurricane Beulah produced 124 tornadoes, a **Texas record for a single month**. The **greatest number in Texas in a single year** was 232, also in 1967. The second-highest number in a single year was in 1982, when 203 tornadoes occurred in Texas, 123 of them in May, making it the **worst outbreak of spring tornadoes** in Texas.

The accompanying table, compiled by Environmental Data Service, National Oceanic and Atmospheric Administration, lists tornado occurrences in Texas, by months, for the period 1951-1993.

Number of Tornadoes In Texas, 1951-1993

Source: Office of State Climatologist

Year	Jan.	Feb.	March	April	May	June	July	Aug.	Sept.	Oct.	Nov.	Dec.	Annual
1951	0	0	1	1	5	7	1	0	0	0	0	0	15
1952	0	1	3	4	2	1	0	1	0	0	0	1	13
1953	0	2	2	3	6	2	3	5	0	2	1	6	32
1954	0	3	1	23	21	14	5	1	4	5	0	0	77
1955	0	0	7	15	42	32	1	5	2	0	0	0	104
1956	0	3	5	3	17	5	6	4	2	9	2	0	56
1957	0	1	21	69	33	5	0	3	2	6	5	0	145
1958	2	0	7	12	15	13	10	7	0	0	8	0	74
1959	0	0	8	4	32	14	10	3	4	5	6	0	86
1960	4	1	0	8	29	14	3	4	2	11	1	0	77
1961	0	1	21	15	24	30	9	2	12	0	10	0	124
1962	0	4	12	9	25	56	12	15	7	2	0	1	143
1963	0	0	3	9	19	24	8	4	6	4	5	0	82
1964	0	1	6	22	15	11	9	7	3	1	3	0	78
1965	2	5	3	7	43	24	2	9	4	6	0	3	108
1966	0	4	1	21	22	15	3	8	3	0	0	0	77
1967	0	2	11	17	34	22	10	5	124	2	0	5	232
1968	2	1	3	13	47	21	4	8	5	8	11	16	139
1969	0	1	1	16	65	16	6	7	6	8	1	0	127
1970	1	3	5	23	23	9	5	20	9	20	0	3	121
1971	0	20	10	24	27	33	7	20	7	16	4	23	191
1972	1	0	19	13	43	12	19	13	8	9	7	0	144
1973	14	1	29	25	21	24	4	8	5	3	9	4	147
1974	2	1	8	19	18	26	3	9	6	22	2	0	116
1975	5	2	9	12	50	18	10	3	3	3	1	1	117
1976	1	1	8	53	63	11	16	6	13	4	0	0	176
1977	0	0	3	34	50	4	5	5	12	0	6	4	123
1978	0	0	0	34	65	10	13	6	6	1	2	0	137
1979	1	2	24	33	39	14	12	10	4	15	3	0	157
1980	0	2	7	26	44	21	2	34	10	5	0	2	153
1981	0	7	7	9	71	26	5	20	5	23	3	0	176
1982	0	0	6	27	123	36	4	0	3	0	3	1	203
1983	5	7	24	1	62	35	4	22	5	0	7	14	186
1984	0	13	9	18	19	19	0	4	1	5	2	5	95
1985	0	0	5	41	28	5	3	1	1	3	1	2	90
1986	0	12	4	21	50	24	3	5	4	7	1	0	131
1987	1	1	7	0	54	19	11	3	8	0	16	4	124
1988	0	0	0	11	7	7	6	2	42	4	10	0	89
1989	3	0	5	3	70	63	0	6	3	6	1	0	160
1990	3	3	4	56	62	20	5	2	3	0	0	0	158
1991	20	5	2	39	72	36	1	2	3	8	4	0	192
1992	0	5	13	22	43	66	4	4	4	7	21	0	189
1993	1	4	5	17	39	4	4	0	12	23	8	0	117
Total	68	119	329	832	1639	868	248	303	363	253	164	95	5281

ers, causing destructive floods. Seven persons drowned; property losses exceeded $500,000.

Aug. 13, 1932: Hurricane. Near **Freeport**, Brazoria County. Wind speed at **East Columbia** estimated at 100 miles per hour; 40 lives lost, 200 injured; damage $7,500,000.

March 30, 1933: Tornado. Angelina, Nacogdoches and San Augustine counties; 10 killed, 56 injured; damage $200,000.

April 26, 1933: Tornado. Bowie County near Texarkana. Five killed, 38 injured; damage $14,000.

July 22-25, 1933: Tropical Storm. One of the greatest U.S. storms in area and general rainfall. The storm reached the vicinity of **Freeport** late on July 22 and moved very slowly overland across eastern Texas, July 22-25. The storm center moved into northern Louisiana on the 25th. Rainfall averaged 12.50 inches over an area of about 25,000 square miles. Twenty inches or more fell in a small area of eastern Texas and western Louisiana surrounding Logansport, La. The 4-day total at Logansport was 22.30 inches. Property damage was estimated at $1,114,790.

July 30, 1933: Tornado. Oak Cliff section of Dallas, Dallas County. Five killed, 30 injured; damage $500,000.

Sept. 4-5, 1933: Hurricane. Near **Brownsville.** Center passed inland a short distance north of Brownsville, where an extreme wind of 106 miles per hour was measured before the anemometer blew away. Peak wind gusts were estimated at 120 to 125 miles per hour. 40 known dead, 500 injured; damage $16,903,100. About 90 percent of the citrus crop in the **Lower Rio Grande Valley** was destroyed.

July 25, 1934: Hurricane. Near **Seadrift**, Calhoun County, 19 lives lost, many minor injuries; damage $4.5 million. About 85 percent of damage was in crops.

Sept. 15-18, 1936: Rainstorm. Excessive rains over the **North Concho and Middle Concho rivers** caused a sharp rise in the Concho River, which overflowed **San Angelo**. Much of the business district and 500 homes were flooded. Four persons drowned and property losses estimated at $5 million. Four-day storm rainfall at San Angelo measured 25.19 inches, of which 11.75 inches fell on the 15th.

June 10, 1938: Tornado. Clyde, Callahan County; 14 killed, 9 injured; damage $85,000.

Sept. 23, 1941: Hurricane. Near **Matagorda.** Center moved inland near Matagorda, and passed over **Houston** about midnight. Extremely high tides along coast in the **Matagorda to Galveston** area. Heaviest property and crop losses were in counties from Matagorda County to the Sabine River. Four lives lost. Damage was $6,503,300.

April 28, 1942: Tornado. Crowell, Foard County; 11 killed, 250 injured; damage $1,500,000.

Aug. 30, 1942: Hurricane. Matagorda Bay. Highest wind estimated 115 miles per hour at **Seadrift.** Tide at **Matagorda**, 14.7 feet. Storm moved west-north-westward and finally diminished over the **Edwards Plateau**; eight lives lost, property damage estimated at $11.5 million, and crop damage estimated at $15 million.

May 10, 1943: Tornado. Laird Hill, Rusk County, and **Kilgore**, Gregg County. Four killed, 25 injured; damage $1 million.

July 27, 1943: Hurricane. Near **Galveston**. Center moved inland across **Bolivar Peninsula and Trinity Bay.** A wind gust of 104 miles per hour was recorded at **Texas City**; 19 lives lost; damage estimated at $16,550,000.

Aug. 26-27, 1945: Hurricane. Aransas-San Antonio Bay area. At **Port O'Connor**, the wind reached 105 miles per hour when the cups were torn from the anemometer. Peak gusts of 135 miles per hour were estimated at **Seadrift, Port O'Connor and Port Lavaca**; three killed, 25 injured; damage $20,133,000.

Jan. 4, 1946: Tornado. Near **Lufkin**, Angelina County and

Texas Droughts, 1892-1994

The following table shows the duration (in days) and extent of Texas droughts by climatic division, 1892-1994. For this purpose, droughts are arbitrarily defined as when the division has less than 75 percent of the 1931-1960 average precipitation. The 1931-1960 average precipitation in inches is shown at the bottom of the table for each division. The short table that follows shows the frequency of droughts in each area and the total years of droughts in the area.

Year	High Plains	Low Rolling Plains	North Central	East Texas	Trans-Pecos	Edwards Plateau	South Central	Upper Coast	Southern	Lower Valley
1892	..	...	...	...	68	...	...	73	...	...
1893	..	...	67	70	...	49	56	64	53	59
1894	..	...	...	...	68	...	...	...	...	...
1897	..	...	...	...	...	...	73	...	72	...
1898	..	...	...	...	...	...	...	...	69	51
1901	..	71	70	...	...	60	62	70	44	...
1902	..	...	...	...	...	...	...	...	65	73
1907	..	...	...	...	...	...	...	...	...	65
1909	..	...	72	68	67	74	70	...	...	...
1910	59	59	64	69	43	65	69	74	59	...
1911	..	...	...	...	...	...	...	...	...	70
1916	..	73	...	74	70	...	73	69	...	...
1917	58	50	63	59	44	46	42	50	32	48
1920	..	...	...	...	...	...	...	...	...	71
1921	..	...	...	...	72	...	...	...	...	73
1922	..	...	...	...	68	...	...	...	...	...
1924	..	...	73	73	...	71	...	72	...	...
1925	..	...	72	...	...	...	72	...	...	...
1927	..	...	...	...	...	...	...	74	...	74
1933	72	...	...	...	62	68	...	...	...	...
1934	66	...	...	...	46	69	...	...	...	...
1937	..	...	...	...	...	...	...	...	72	...
1939	..	...	...	...	...	...	69	...	...	72
1943	..	...	72	...	...	...	...	...	...	...
1948	..	...	73	74	62	...	71	67	...	...
1950	..	...	...	...	...	...	68	...	74	64
1951	..	...	...	...	61	53	...	...	...	...
1952	68	66	...	...	73	...	...	...	56	70
1953	69	...	...	...	49	73	...	...	...	...
1954	70	71	68	73	...	50	50	57	71	...
1956	51	57	61	68	44	43	55	62	53	53
1962	..	...	...	...	...	68	...	...	67	65
1963	..	...	63	68	...	65	61	73	...	...
1964	74	...	...	...	69	...	...	...	...	63
1970	65	63	...	...	...	72	...	...	...	...
1988	..	...	...	...	...	67	62	67	68	...
1989	..	...	...	...	...	72	...	...	66	64
1990	..	...	...	...	...	...	...	...	...	73
1994	..	...	...	...	68	...	...	...	...	...

Normal Annual Rainfall by Region

Below is listed the normal annual rainfall in inches for four 10-year periods in the geographical divisions listed in order in which they are listed in the table in the left-hand column. The drought frequency table below is in the same order.

1931-1960 Normal (inches) — 18.51, 22.99, 32.93, 45.96, 12.03, 25.91, 33.24, 46.19, 22.33, 24.27.

1941-1970 Normal (inches) — 18.59, 23.18, 32.94, 45.37, 11.57, 23.94, 33.03, 46.43, 21.95, 23.44.

1951-1980 Normal (inches) — 17.73, 22.80, 32.14, 44.65, 11.65, 23.52, 34.03, 45.93, 22.91, 24.73.

1961-1990 Normal (inches) — 18.88, 23.77, 33.99, 45.67, 13.01, 24.00, 34.49, 47.63, 23.47, 25.31.

Drought Frequency

This table shows the number of years of drought and the number of separate droughts. For example, the High Plains has had 10 drought years, consisting of five 1-year droughts, one 2-year drought and one 3-year drought, for a total of seven droughts.

Years										
1	5	6	8	6	6	8	11	9	10	13
2	1	1	2	2	4	4	2	2	2	2
3	1	...	...	...	1	...	...	...	...	...
Total Droughts	7	7	10	8	11	12	13	11	15	14
Drought Years	10	8	12	10	17	17	15	13	15	17

Nacogdoches, Nacogdoches County; 13 killed, 250 injured; damage $2,050,000.

Jan. 4, 1946: Tornado. Near **Palestine**, Anderson County; 15 killed, 60 injured; damage $500,000.

May 18, 1946: Tornado. Clay, Montague and Denton counties. Four killed, damage $112,000.

April 9, 1947: Tornado. White Deer, Carson County; **Glazier,** Hemphill County; and **Higgins**, Lipscomb County; 68 killed, 201 injured; damage $1,550,000. Glazier completely destroyed. **One of the largest tornadoes on record.** Width of path, 1 miles at Higgins; length of path, 221 miles across portions of Texas, Oklahoma and Kansas. This tornado also struck Woodward, Okla.

May 3, 1948: Tornado. McKinney, Collin County; three killed, 43 injured; $2 million damage.

May 15, 1949: Tornado. Amarillo and vicinity; six killed, 83 injured. Total damage from tornado, wind and hail, $5,310,000. Total destruction over one-block by three-block area in southern part of city; airport and 45 airplanes damaged; 28 railroad boxcars blown off track.

Sept. 8-10, 1952: Rainstorm. Heavy rains over the **Colorado and Guadalupe River watersheds** in southwestern Texas caused major flooding. From 23 to 26 inches fell between **Kerrville, Blanco and Boerne**. Highest stages ever known occurred in the **Pedernales River**; five lives lost, three injured; 17 homes destroyed, 454 damaged. Property loss several million dollars.

March 13, 1953: Tornado. Jud and O'Brien, Haskell County; and **Knox City**, Knox County; 17 killed, 25 injured; damage $600,000.

May 11, 1953: Tornado. Near **San Angelo**, Tom Green County; eleven killed, 159 injured; damage $3,239,000.

May 11, 1953: Tornado. Waco, McLennan County; 114 killed, 597 injured; damage $41,150,000. **One of two most disastrous tornadoes;** 150 homes destroyed, 900 homes damaged; 185 other buildings destroyed; 500 other buildings damaged.

April 2, 1957: Tornado. Dallas, Dallas County; 10 killed, 200 injured; damage $4 million. Moving through Oak Cliff and West Dallas, it damaged 574 buildings, largely homes.

April-May, 1957: Torrential Rains. Excessive flooding occurred throughout the area **east of the Pecos River to the Sabine River** during the last 10 days of April; 17 lives were lost, and several hundred homes were destroyed. During May, more than 4,000 persons were evacuated from unprotected lowlands on the **West Fork of the Trinity above Fort Worth** and along creeks in Fort Worth. Twenty-nine houses at **Christoval** were damaged or destroyed and 83 houses and furnishings at **San Angelo** were damaged. Five persons were drowned in floods in **South Central Texas**.

May 15, 1957: Tornado. Silverton, Briscoe County; 21 killed, 80 injured; damage $500,000.

June 27, 1957: Hurricane Audrey. Center crossed the Gulf coast near the Texas-Louisiana line. **Orange** was in the western portion of the eye between 9 and 10 a.m. In Texas, nine lives were lost, 450 persons injured; property damage was $8 million. Damage was extensive in **Jefferson and Orange counties,** with less in **Chambers and Galveston counties**. Maximum wind reported in Texas, 85 m.p.h. at **Sabine Pass**, with gusts to 100 m.p.h.

Oct. 28, 1960: Rainstorm. Rains of 7-10 inches fell in **South Central Texas**; 11 died from drowning in flash floods. In **Austin** about 300 families were driven from their homes. Damage in Austin was estimated at $2.5 million.

Sept. 8-14, 1961: Hurricane Carla. Port O'Connor; maximum wind gust at **Port Lavaca** estimated at 175 miles per hour. Highest tide was 18.5 feet at Port Lavaca. Most damage was to **coastal counties between Corpus Christi and Port Arthur** and inland **Jackson, Harris and Wharton counties.** In Texas, 34 persons died; seven in a **tornado** that swept across **Galveston Island**; 465 persons were injured. Property and crop damage conservatively estimated at $300 million. The evacuation of an estimated 250,000 persons kept loss of life low. **Hurricane Carla was the largest hurricane of record.**

Sept. 7, 1962: Rainstorm. Fort Worth. Rains fell over the Big Fossil and Denton Creek watersheds ranging up to 11 inches of fall in three hours. Extensive damage from flash flooding occurred in **Richland Hills and Haltom City**.

Sept. 16-20, 1963: Hurricane Cindy. Rains of 15 to 23.5 inches fell in portions of **Jefferson, Newton and Orange counties** when Hurricane Cindy became stationary west of **Port Arthur.** Flooding from the excessive rainfall resulted in total property damage of $11,600,000 and agricultural losses of $500,000.

April 3, 1964: Tornado. Wichita Falls. Seven killed, 111 injured; damage $15 million; 225 homes destroyed, 50 with major damage, and 200 with minor damage. Sixteen other buildings received major damage.

Sept. 21-23, 1964: Rainstorm. Collin, Dallas and Tarrant counties. Rains of more than 12 inches fell during the first eight hours of the 21st. Flash flooding of tributaries of the Trinity River and smaller creeks and streams resulted in two drownings and an estimated $3 million property damage. Flooding of homes occurred in all sections of **McKinney**. In **Fort Worth,** there was considerable damage to residences along Big Fossil and White Rock creeks. Expensive homes in **North Dallas** were heavily damaged.

Jan. 25, 1965: Dust Storm. West Texas. The worst dust storm since February 1956 developed on the **southern High Plains**. Winds, gusting up to 75 miles per hour at **Lubbock**, sent dust billowing to 31,000 feet in the area **from the Texas-New Mexico border eastward to a line from Tulia to Abilene**. Ground visibility was reduced to about 100 yards in many sections. The worst hit was the **Muleshoe, Seminole, Plains, Morton** area on the South Plains. The rain gage at Reese Air Force Base, Lubbock, contained 3 inches of fine sand.

June 2, 1965: Tornado. Hale Center, Hale County. Four killed, 76 injured; damage $8 million.

June 11, 1965: Rainstorm. Sanderson, Terrell County. Torrential rains of up to eight inches in two hours near Sanderson caused a major flash flood that swept through the town. As a result, 26 persons drowned and property losses were estimated at $2,715,000.

April 22-29, 1966: Flooding. Northeast Texas. Twenty to 26 inches of rain fell in portions of Wood, Smith, Morris, Upshur, Gregg, Marion and Harrison counties. Nineteen persons drowned in the rampaging rivers and creeks that swept away bridges, roads and dams, and caused an estimated $12 million damage.

April 28, 1966: Flash flooding. Dallas County. Flash flooding from torrential rains in Dallas County resulted in 14 persons drowned and property losses estimated at $15 million.

Sept. 18-23, 1967: Hurricane Beulah. Near **Brownsville.** The **third largest hurricane of record**, Hurricane Beulah moved inland near the mouth of the Rio Grande on the 20th. Wind gusts of 136 miles per hour were reported during Beulah's passage. Rains 10 to 20 inches over much of the area **south of San Antonio** resulted in record-breaking floods. An unofficial gaging station at **Falfurrias** registered the highest accumulated rainfall, 36 inches. The resultant stream overflow and surface runoff inundated 1.4 million acres. Beulah spawned 115 tornadoes, all in Texas, the **greatest number of tornadoes on record for any hurricane**. Hurricane Beulah caused 13 deaths and 37 injuries, of which five deaths and 34 injuries were attributed to tornadoes. Property losses were estimated at $100 million and crop losses at $50 million.

April 18, 1970: Tornado. Near **Clarendon**, Donley County. Seventeen killed, 42 injured; damage $2,100,000. Fourteen persons were killed at a resort community at Green Belt Reservoir, 7 miles north of Clarendon.

May 11, 1970: Tornado. Lubbock, Lubbock County. Twenty-six killed, 500 injured; damage $135 million. Fifteen square miles, almost one-quarter of the city of Lubbock, suffered damage.

Aug. 3-5, 1970: Hurricane Celia. Corpus Christi. Hurricane Celia was a unique but severe storm. Measured in dollars,

Is It Normal or Average?

Confusion often occurs when climate summaries refer to the "normal" or "average" of a climate variable. The term "normal" indicates calculations based upon data from the most recent 30-year period ending with a year containing a zero for the last digit. Although 1901-1930 was selected as the first International Standard Period for Normals, the 1961-1990 period is the current 30-year "normal."

The "average" refers to calculations based upon the complete period of record. Usually this is from the first complete year on record to the most recent entire year of record. Therefore, the "normal" and "average" values usually differ to some degree.

it was **the costliest in the state's history to that time**. Sustained wind speeds reached 130 miles per hour, but it was great bursts of kinetic energy of short duration that appeared to cause the severe damage. Wind gusts of 161 miles per hour were measured at the **Corpus Christi** National Weather Service Office. At **Aransas Pass**, peak wind gusts were estimated as high as 180 miles per hour, after the wind equipment had been blown away. Celia caused 11 deaths in Texas, at least 466 injuries, and total property and crop damage in Texas estimated at $453,773,000. Hurricane Celia crossed the Texas coastline midway between Corpus Christi and Aransas Pass about 3:30 p.m. CST on Aug. 3. Hardest hit was the metropolitan area of **Corpus Christi**, including **Robstown, Aransas Pass, Port Aransas** and small towns on the north side of Corpus Christi Bay.

Feb. 20-22, 1971: Blizzard. Panhandle. Paralyzing blizzard, worst since March 22-25, 1957, storm transformed Panhandle into one vast snowfield as six to 26 inches of snow were whipped by 40 to 60 miles per hour winds into drifts up to 12 feet high. At **Follett**, three-day snowfall was 26 inches. Three persons killed; property and livestock losses were $3.1 million.

Sept. 9-13, 1971: Hurricane Fern. Coastal Bend. Ten to 26 inches of rain resulted in some of worst flooding since Hurricane Beulah in 1967. Two persons killed; losses were $30,231,000.

May 11-12, 1972: Rainstorm. South Central Texas. Seventeen drowned at **New Braunfels**, one at **McQueeney**. New Braunfels and **Seguin** hardest hit. Property damage $17.5 million.

June 12-13, 1973: Rainstorm. Southeastern Texas. Ten drowned. Over $50 million in property and crop damage. From 10-15 inches of rain recorded.

Nov. 23-24, 1974: Flash Flooding. Central Texas. Over $1 million in property damage. Thirteen people killed, ten in **Travis County.**

Jan. 31-Feb. 1, 1975: Flooding. Nacogdoches County. Widespread heavy rain caused flash flooding here, resulting in three deaths; damage over $5.5 million.

May 23, 1975: Rainstorm. Austin area. Heavy rains, high winds and hail resulted in over $5 million property damage; 40 people injured. Four deaths were caused by drowning.

June 15, 1976: Rainstorm. Harris County. Rains in excess of 13 inches caused damage estimated at near $25 million. Eight deaths were storm-related, including three drownings.

Aug. 1-4, 1978: Heavy Rains, Flooding. Edwards Plateau, Low Rolling Plains. Remnants of **Tropical Storm Amelia** caused some of the worst flooding of this century. As much as 30 inches of rain fell near **Albany** in Shackelford County, where six drownings were reported. **Bandera, Kerr, Kendall and Gillespie counties** were hit hard, as 27 people drowned and the damage total was at least $50 million.

Dec. 30-31, 1978: Ice Storm. North Central Texas. Possibly the **worst ice storm in 30 years** hit Dallas County particularly hard. Damage estimates reached $14 million, and six deaths were storm-related.

April 10, 1979: The worst single tornado in Texas' history hit **Wichita Falls.** Earlier on the same day, **several tornadoes** hit farther west. The destruction in Wichita Falls resulted in 42 dead, 1,740 injured, over 3,000 homes destroyed and damage of approximately $400 million. An estimated 20,000 persons were left homeless by this storm. In all, the tornadoes on April 10 killed 53 people, injured 1,812 and caused over $500 million damages.

May 3, 1979: Thunderstorms. Dallas County was hit by a wave of the most destructive thunderstorms in many years; 37 injuries and $5 million in damages resulted.

July 24-25, 1979: Tropical storm Claudette caused over $750 million in property and crop damages, but fortunately only few injuries. Near **Alvin**, 43 inches of rain fell, a new state record for 24 hours.

Aug. 24, 1979: One of the worst **hailstorms** in **West Texas** in the past 100 years; $200 million in crops, mostly cotton, destroyed.

Meteorological Data

Source: NOAA, Environmental Data Service, Local Climatological Data.

Additional data for these locations are listed in the table of Texas temperature, freeze, growing season, and precipitation records, by counties.

City	Temperature						Precipitation					Relative Humidity		Wind			Sun
	Record High	Month & Year	Record Low	Month & Year	No. Days Max. 90° and Above	No. Days Min. 32° and Below	Maximum in 24 Hours	Month & Year	Snowfall (Mean Annual)	Max. Snowfall in 24 Hours	Month & Year	6:00 a.m., CST	Noon, CST	Speed, MPH (Mean Annual)	Highest MPH	Month & Year	Percent Possible Sunshine
Abilene	110	7-78	-9	1-47	96.6	53.6	6.70	9-61	4.9	7.5	1-73	74	51	12.1	46	9-84	70
Amarillo	108	6-90	-14	2-51	63.8	110.7	6.75	5-51	14.9	13.5	2-71	73	46	13.6	58	9-79	73
Austin	109	‡7-54	-2	1-49	105.0	21.1	7.22	10-60	1.1	7.0	1-44	83	56	9.2	52	9-87	60
Brownsville	106	3-84	16	12-89	117.3	2.2	12.19	9-67	**	0.0	—	89	60	11.5	48	8-80	60
Corpus Christi	104	7-39	13	12-89	101.9	6.6	8.92	8-80	0.1	1.1	2-73	90	62	12.0	55	8-80	62
Dallas-Fort Worth	113	6-80	-1	12-89	96.2	40.9	5.91	10-59	3.2	12.1	1-64	82	56	10.9	73	8-59	64
Del Rio	112	6-88	10	12-89	124.2	17.3	7.60	10-84	0.9	8.6	1-85	79	54	9.9	60	8-70	70
El Paso	114	7-94	-8	1-62	104.0	65.0	2.63	7-68	5.4	16.8	12-87	35	28	8.9	48	2-77	83
Galveston	101	7-32	8	2-99	12.2	3.6	14.35	7-00	0.2	15.4	2-95	83	72	11.0	*100	9-00	62
†Houston	107	8-80	7	12-89	94.2	21.2	10.36	5-89	0.4	2.0	1-73	90	59	7.8	51	8-83	56
Lubbock	114	6-94	-16	1-63	78.6	94.6	5.82	10-83	10.5	16.3	1-83	74	47	12.4	70	3-52	72
Midland-Odessa	116	6-94	-11	2-85	96.2	64.7	5.99	7-61	4.1	6.8	1-74	74	43	11.0	67	2-60	74
Prt. Arthur-Beaumont	107	8-62	12	12-89	81.2	16.3	17.16	9-80	0.4	4.4	2-60	91	64	9.8	55	6-86	58
San Angelo	111	‡7-60	-4	12-89	106.8	53.9	6.25	9-80	3.3	7.4	1-78	78	49	10.4	75	4-69	73
San Antonio	108	8-86	0	1-49	110.8	22.7	7.28	9-73	0.8	13.2	1-85	83	55	9.3	48	7-79	60
Victoria	107	8-62	9	12-89	102.7	12.1	9.30	6-77	0.2	2.1	1-85	89	60	10.0	99	7-63	62
Waco	112	8-69	-5	1-49	108.5	35.2	7.18	5-53	1.5	7.0	1-49	83	57	11.3	69	6-61	63
Wichita Falls	117	6-80	-8	2-85	105.9	68.1	6.22	9-80	6.0	8.1	1-85	82	51	11.7	60	6-54	68
§Shreveport, LA	107	8-62	3	1-62	89.4	37.3	7.17	4-53	1.3	5.6	1-82	87	58	8.4	52	4-75	63

**100 mph recorded at 6:15 p.m. Sept. 8 just before the anemometer blew away. Maximum velocity was estimated to be 120 mph from the northeast between 7:30 p.m. and 8:30 p.m.*

†The official Houston station was moved from near downtown to Intercontinental Airport, located 12 miles north of the old station.

‡ Also recorded on earlier dates, months or years.

§This station is included because it is near the boundary line and its data can be considered representative of the eastern border of Texas.

***Trace, an amount too small to measure.*

How Cold Does It Feel?

Many factors enter into the feeling of coolness or extreme cold, the temperature and wind speed being most important. The following simplified table is based upon more complex "Wind-Chill" indexes available from the National Oceanic and Atmospheric Administration (National Weather Service).

Thermometer readings are listed in the figures across the top of the chart; the wind speeds are shown down the left side. To determine how chilly it really feels, get the proper column for each. Note the figure where they cross.

Thus, a 20-degree temperature with a 20-mile-an-hour wind is equal in chill to 1.8 degrees above zero. A temperature of 10 degrees with a 15 mph wind is equal to 5.3 degrees below.

A 10-mile-an-hour wind sets twigs dancing in the trees. A 25-mile-an-hour wind sets big branches moving, and if the temperature is even cool, it sets teeth chattering.

A chill effect of anything below 25 below zero creates the danger of freezing for persons not properly clothed. *The table below was devised by Dr. Robert G. Steadman, Texas Tech University, and was furnished to the Texas Almanac by the National Oceanic and Atmospheric Administration.*

Windchill Chart

Estimated Wind Speed (MPH)	Actual Thermometer Reading (°F) 50	40	30	20	10	0	—10
	Apparent Temperature (°F)						
Calm	50	40	30	20	10	0	—10
5	48.3	38.0	27.8	17.5	7.1	—3.2	—13.5
10	44.6	33.5	22.5	11.5	0.5	—10.5	—21.4
15	41.3	29.6	18.0	6.3	—5.3	—16.7	—28.1
20	38.5	26.2	14.0	1.8	—10.4	—22.3	—34.2
25	36.1	23.3	10.6	—2.1	—14.8	—27.2	—39.5
30	34.1	20.9	7.8	—5.3	—18.3	—31.0	—43.7
40	30.9	17.1	3.2	—10.6	—24.0	—37.4	—50.7

How Hot Does It Feel?

In the 40-year period from 1936 to 1975, nearly 20,000 people were killed in the United States by the effects ofexcessive heat. The overall effect of excessive heat on the body is known as heat stress. Important factors contributing to heat stress are: (1) air temperature; (2) humidity; (3) air movement; (4) radiant heat from incoming solar radiation (insolation), bright lights, stove or other source; (5) atmospheric pressure; (6) physiological factors which vary among people; (7) physical activity; and (8) clothing.

Of the above factors, temperature and humidity can be controlled by air conditioning. Air movement may be controlled by fans; even a slight breeze is usually effective in reducing heat stress in hot, muggy weather.

However, at very high temperatures (above normal body temperature of about 98.6 F.), winds above 10 miles per hour can increase heat stress in a shaded area by adding more heat to the body, whereas when the body is exposed to direct sunlight the effect of wind is nearly always to reduce heat stress. Radiant heating can be mitigated by shielding or by moving away from the source (for example, seeking shade). Atmospheric pressure is not usually a significant factor. However, at very high elevations, decreased pressure (and therefore decreased air supply) can contribute to heat exhaustion.

General Heat Stress Index

Danger Category	Apparent Temperature (°F)	Heat Syndrome
1. Caution	80°-90°	Fatigue possible with prolonged exposure and physical activity.
2. Extreme Caution	90°-105°	Sunstroke, heat cramps and heat; exhaustion possible with prolonged exposure and physical activity.
3. Danger	105°-130°	Sunstroke, heat cramps or heat exhaustion likely. Heatstroke possible with prolonged exposure and physical activity.
4. Extreme Danger	Greater than 130°	Heatstroke or sunstroke imminent.

Note: Degree of heat stress may vary with age, health and body characteristics.

Heat Discomfort Chart

Actual Thermometer Reading (°F)	Relative Humidity (%) 0	10	20	30	40	50	60	70	80	90	100
	Apparent Temperature (°F)										
70	64.8	65.6	66.4	67.3	68.1	68.8	69.6	70.4	71.1	71.8	72.5
75	70.1	71.2	72.1	73.0	73.7	74.6	75.3	76.1	77.1	78.2	79.2
80	75.6	76.6	77.5	78.4	79.4	80.5	81.7	83.0	84.7	86.4	88.3
85	79.9	81.0	82.2	83.6	85.0	86.7	88.7	91.0	93.7	96.8	100.6
90	84.0	85.5	87.1	89.0	91.2	94.1	97.0	101.0	105.4	110.8	
95	88.0	90.0	92.4	95.3	98.4	102.6	107.4	113.9			
100	91.8	94.6	97.8	101.7	106.6	112.7	120.4				
	Relative Humidity (%) 0	5	10	15	20	25	30	35	40	45	50
105	95.8	97.5	99.4	101.5	103.8	106.4	109.3	112.4	116.5	121.1	126.0
110	99.7	101.9	104.2	107.0	110.3	113.8	118.0	121.8	128.6		
115	103.6	106.4	109.6	113.3	117.6	122.6	128.4				
120	107.4	111.1	115.2	120.1	125.7	132.2					

The table above was devised by Dr. Robert G. Steadman, Texas Tech University, and was furnished to the Texas Almanac by NOAA.

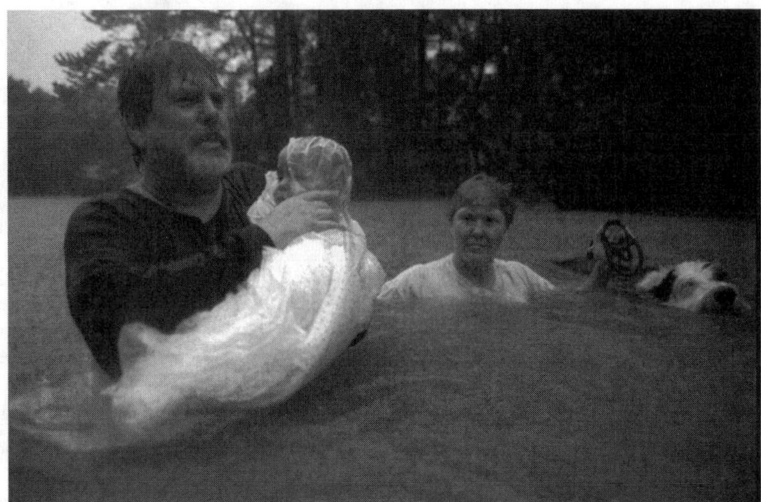

Tannie Shannon, accompanied by his wife Frances and their dog, carries his 11-month-old granddaughter Andrea to safety through swirling floodwaters near Conroe. The child is wrapped in plastic for protection. The severe mid-October 1994 storms brought almost 29 inches of rain to some areas of southeastern Texas in a four-day period; twenty-six counties were declared disaster areas. Photo by David Leeson, The Dallas Morning News.

Sept. 18-20, 1979: Coastal flooding from heavy rain, 18 inches in 24 hours at **Aransas Pass**, and 13 inches at **Rockport**.

Aug. 9-11, 1980: Hurricane Allen hit **South Texas** and left three dead, causing $650 million-$750 million in property and crop damages. Over 250,000 coastal residents had to be evacuated. The worst damage occurred along **Padre Island** and in **Corpus Christi**. Over 20 inches of rain fell in **extreme South Texas**, and 29 tornadoes occurred; one of the worst hurricane-related outbreaks.

Summer 1980: One of the hottest summers in Texas history.

Sept. 5-8, 1980: Hurricane Danielle brought **rain and flooding** to both **Southeast and Central Texas**. Seventeen inches of rain fell at **Port Arthur**, and 25 inches near **Junction**.

May 8, 1981: The **most destructive thunderstorm ever in the United States** occurred in **Tarrant, Dallas and surrounding counties. Hail** damage was estimated at $200 million.

May 24-25, 1981: Severe flooding in **Austin** claimed 13 lives, injured about 100 and caused $40 million in damages. Up to 5.5 inches of rain fell in one hour just west of the city.

Oct. 11-14, 1981: Record rains in North Central Texas caused by the remains of **Pacific Hurricane Norma**. Over 20 inches fell in some locations.

April 2, 1982: A **tornado outbreak in Northeast Texas.** The most severe tornado struck **Paris**; 10 people were killed, 170 injured and 1,000 left homeless. Over $50 million in damages resulted. A total of 7 tornadoes that day left 11 dead and 174 injured.

May 25, 1982: Golf ball-sized **hail** in **Monahans** did $8 million in damages.

May, 1982: Texas recorded **123 tornadoes**, the most ever in May, and one less than the most recorded in any single month in the state. One death and 23 injuries occurred.

Sept. 11, 1982: Tropical Storm Chris. The year's only tropical storm in Texas hit the coast near **Port Arthur** with 55 mph winds. Rainfall was minimal.

Dec. 24, 1982: Rains of up to 15 inches occurred in **Southeast Texas.**

Dec. 1982: Heavy snow. El Paso recorded 18.2 inches of snow, the most in any month there.

Aug. 15-21, 1983: Hurricane Alicia was the first hurricane to make landfall in the continental U.S. in three years (Aug. 18), and **one of the costliest in Texas history** ($3 billion). Alicia caused widespread damage to a large section of **Southeast Texas**, including coastal areas near **Galveston** and the entire **Houston** area. Alicia spawned 22 tornadoes, and highest winds were estimated near 130 mph. In all, 18 people in South Texas were killed and 1,800 injured as a result of the tropical storm.

Jan. 12-13, 1985: A record-breaking snowstorm struck **West and South Central Texas** with up to 15 inches of snow that fell at many locations **between San Antonio and the Rio Grande**. San Antonio recorded 13.2 inches of snow for Jan. 12 (the greatest in a day) and 13.5 inches for the two-day total. **Eagle Pass** reported 14.5 inches of snow.

June 26, 1986: Hurricane Bonnie made landfall between **High Island and Sabine Pass** around 3:45 a.m. The highest wind measured in the area was a gust to 97 m.p.h., which was recorded at the **Sea Rim State Park.** As much as 13 inches of rain fell in **Ace** in southern Polk County. There were several reports of funnel clouds, but no confirmed tornadoes. While the storm caused no major structural damage, there was widespread minor damage. Numerous injuries were reported.

May 22, 1987: A strong, **multiple-vortex tornado** struck the town of **Saragosa** (Reeves Co.), essentially wiping it off the map. Of the town's 183 inhabitants, 30 were killed and 121 were injured. Eight-five percent of the town's structures were completely destroyed, while total damage topped $1.3 million.

Sept. 16-18, 1988: Hurricane Gilbert stuck 125 miles south of **Brownsville**, Cameron County, bringing tides of three to six feet above average, rainfalls of six inches to 10 inches and at least 29 tornadoes. Total damage associated with Gilbert in Texas was estimated at $3 million-$5 million. The only death attributed to the storm was a woman who was killed by a tornado spawned by remnants of Gilbert in the **San Antonio** area.

Dec. 18-31, 1991: Flooding, entire state. The month of December was one of the wettest in Texas since records began in 1888. Rainfall amounts, from the Hill Country into North Central Texas totaled 12 to 16 inches over the four-day period of Dec. 18-21. Eleven people died as a result of the flooding, and more than $50 million dollars in damages were incurred.

June 20-22, 1993: Tropical Storm Arlene made landfall 5 miles south of **Corpus Christi**; all of eastern Texas was inundated by the remains. **Henderson** (Rusk Co.) received 14,83 inches of rain, and widespread areas reported greater than 7 inches. One person was killed; damage, mostly as a result of tidal flooding, was estimated at $22 million.

October 15-19, 1994: Extreme amounts of rainfall, up to 28.90 inches over a 4-day period, fell throughout southeastern part of the state. Seventeen lives were lost, most of them victims of flash flooding. Many rivers reached record flood levels during this period. **Houston** was cut off from many other parts of the state, as numerous roads, including Interstate 10, were under water. Damage was estimated to be near $700 million; 26 counties were declared disaster areas. ☆

Texas Temperature, Freeze, Growing Season and Precipitation Records by Counties

Data in the table below are from the office of the **State Climatologist for Texas**, College Station. Because of the small change in averages, data are revised only at intervals of 10 years. Data below are the latest compilations, as of Jan. 1, 1993. Table shows temperature, freeze, growing season and precipitation for each county in Texas. Data for counties where a National Weather Service Station has not been maintained long enough to establish a reliable mean are interpolated from isoline charts prepared from mean values from stations with long-established records. **Mean maximum temperature for July** is computed from the sum of the daily maxima. **Mean minimum January** is computed from the sum of the daily minima. For stations where precipitation "Length of Record" are designated with an "N," data are based on the 30-year normal period 1961-90. Stations which have a specified precipitation "Length of Record" are based on data mainly from the period 1931-1993.

County and Station	Temperature					Average Freeze Dates				Growing Season	Normal Total Precipitation													
	Length of Record	Mean Max. July	Mean Min. January	Record Highest	Record Lowest	Last in Spring		First in Fall			Length of Record	January	February	March	April	May	June	July	August	September	October	November	December	Annual
	Yr.	F.	F.	F.	F.	Mo.	Day	Mo.	Day	Days	Yr.	In.	In.	In.	In.	In.	In.	In.	In.	In.	In.	In.	In.	In.
Anderson, Palestine	N	94	36	114	—6	Mar.	8	Nov.	27	264	N	3.1	3.2	3.9	3.9	4.8	4.5	2.3	2.3	3.6	4.4	3.9	3.6	43.3
Andrews, Andrews	29	94	29	113	0	Apr.	6	Nov.	5	213	29	0.4	0.5	0.6	0.9	1.6	2.0	2.5	1.9	2.5	1.5	0.6	0.4	15.4
Angelina, Lufkin	N	93	37	108	—2	Mar.	14	Nov.	13	244	N	3.7	2.8	3.2	3.3	4.9	4.2	2.6	2.4	4.0	3.5	3.1	2.3	38.9
Aransas, Rockport	N	91	44	103	9	Feb.	7	Dec.	16	312	N	2.7	2.4	1.4	2.1	4.2	4.7	3.2	3.1	6.2	4.0	2.1	2.7	36.9
Archer, Archer	27	98	29	114	—10	Mar.	31	Nov.	6	220	N	1.0	1.7	2.0	2.6	4.3	3.0	1.7	2.5	4.3	2.9	1.8	1.3	29.3
Armstrong, Claude	28	92	20	108	—7	Apr.	6	Nov.	5	213	N	0.4	0.6	1.1	1.1	3.0	3.7	2.9	3.1	2.4	1.7	0.8	0.4	21.2
Atascosa, Poteet	N	96	38	110	—1	Feb.	25	Dec.	2	282	N	1.4	1.7	1.2	2.5	4.0	3.2	1.8	2.6	3.6	2.9	1.8	1.4	28.0
Austin, Sealy	N	94	39	110	0	Feb.	27	Dec.	5	282	N	3.0	2.9	2.2	2.7	4.8	4.4	2.3	3.2	4.6	3.9	3.6	3.0	40.4
Bailey, Muleshoe	N	92	19	112	—21	Apr.	22	Oct.	20	181	N	0.4	0.5	0.6	0.9	1.9	2.6	2.3	2.9	2.2	1.4	0.8	0.5	16.8
Bandera, Medina*	15	94	31	109	5	Mar.	26	Nov.	16	235	15	1.7	1.8	1.7	3.3	4.5	2.9	2.8	4.7	4.5	3.7	2.3	1.2	35.1
Bastrop, Smithville	N	95	35	111	6	Mar.	7	Nov.	30	268	N	2.6	2.5	2.2	2.9	5.1	3.9	2.2	2.3	4.7	4.0	3.2	2.6	38.3
Baylor, Seymour	N	97	26	116	—14	Apr.	3	Nov.	3	214	N	0.9	1.5	1.6	2.2	4.0	3.4	2.1	2.4	4.1	2.7	1.3	1.2	27.3
Bee, Beeville	N	94	41	109	9	Feb.	22	Dec.	4	285	N	2.0	1.9	1.2	2.3	3.6	3.8	2.8	2.9	4.8	3.1	2.0	1.6	32.1
Bell, Temple	N	95	35	112	—4	Mar.	9	Nov.	24	260	N	1.9	2.7	2.5	2.9	4.6	3.6	2.0	2.3	3.8	3.3	2.9	2.3	34.9
Bexar, San Antonio	N	95	38	108	0	Mar.	6	Nov.	26	265	N	1.7	1.8	1.5	2.5	4.2	3.8	2.2	2.5	3.4	3.2	1.5	1.4	31.0
Blanco, Blanco	N	94	33	109	—6	Mar.	26	Nov.	15	234	N	1.9	2.4	2.2	2.8	4.5	3.8	2.3	2.3	3.9	3.8	2.3	2.0	34.2
Borden, Gail	27	94	31	113	—1	Apr.	6	Nov.	6	214	N	0.5	0.5	0.4	0.5	1.2	2.2	2.7	3.0	3.3	1.5	0.6	0.5	16.9
Bosque, Lake Whitney*	18	97	33	111	—3	Mar.	23	Nov.	21	243	18	1.9	2.4	1.5	4.1	4.4	3.5	1.6	1.5	3.2	2.7	2.8	2.0	31.6
Bowie, Texarkana*	N	93	35	101	—6	Mar.	21	Nov.	11	235	N	3.6	3.3	4.2	5.1	4.4	3.9	3.5	3.2	3.6	2.8	3.9	3.9	45.3
Brazoria, Angleton	N	92	41	105	10	Mar.	5	Nov.	28	268	N	4.5	3.5	3.3	3.2	5.2	6.3	5.2	5.1	7.3	4.0	4.7	4.1	56.4
Brazos, College Station	N	94	39	110	—3	Mar.	1	Nov.	30	274	N	2.7	2.6	2.6	3.4	4.8	3.7	2.3	2.4	4.9	3.8	3.2	2.8	39.1
Brewster, Alpine	N	89	30	106	—2	Apr.	1	Nov.	8	223	N	0.5	0.5	0.4	0.5	1.2	2.2	2.7	2.6	3.3	1.5	0.6	0.5	16.9
Brewster, Chisos Basin	N	85	35	103	—3	Mar.	31	Nov.	9	223	N	0.6	0.6	0.4	0.6	1.6	2.3	3.1	3.6	3.3	1.9	0.6	0.6	19.2
Briscoe, Silverton	29	91	20	109	—9	Apr.	7	Nov.	5	214	N	0.4	0.7	1.1	1.3	2.8	4.2	2.2	3.0	2.7	1.6	0.9	0.5	21.4
Brooks, Falfurrias	N	97	43	110	9	Feb.	10	Dec.	10	303	N	1.3	1.6	0.7	1.3	3.2	3.2	2.2	2.5	4.9	2.7	1.2	1.1	25.9
Brown, Brownwood	N	97	33	111	—6	Mar.	22	Nov.	19	242	N	1.3	1.7	1.9	2.6	3.6	3.4	1.7	2.1	3.2	2.9	1.6	1.4	27.3
Burleson, Somerville*	16	94	37	105	3	Mar.	1	Dec.	1	275	16	2.7	2.5	2.4	3.9	5.1	3.6	2.2	2.4	4.9	3.4	3.1	2.8	39.1
Burnet, Burnet	N	93	32	108	—4	Mar.	29	Nov.	14	230	N	1.7	2.0	2.1	2.7	4.8	3.5	1.9	2.0	3.5	3.5	2.1	1.5	31.2
Caldwell, Luling	N	96	36	110	—3	Feb.	27	Nov.	29	275	N	2.2	2.2	1.9	3.0	4.8	4.4	1.7	2.2	4.4	3.5	3.1	1.9	35.3
Calhoun, Port O'Connor	N	90	46	107	11	Feb.	19	Dec.	16	300	N	3.1	2.7	1.6	1.7	4.0	3.7	3.7	3.3	6.1	4.5	2.7	2.4	39.4
Callahan, Putnam	27	96	32	110	—8	Mar.	28	Nov.	11	228	N	1.4	1.4	1.7	2.0	3.0	3.0	1.8	2.1	3.1	2.9	1.7	1.1	25.2
Cameron, Brownsville	N	93	50	106	16	Feb.	4	Dec.	12	341	N	1.6	1.1	0.5	1.6	2.9	2.7	1.9	2.8	6.0	2.8	1.5	1.3	26.6
Camp, Pittsburg*	N	94	32	109	—3	Mar.	21	Nov.	14	238	N	2.9	3.3	3.8	5.4	4.8	3.4	2.7	2.2	4.0	3.2	4.0	3.5	43.3
Carson, Panhandle	29	93	22	109	—10	Apr.	17	Oct.	25	191	N	0.5	0.8	1.1	1.3	2.6	3.7	2.3	3.1	2.3	1.7	0.9	0.5	20.8
Cass, Linden	22	93	31	103	8	Mar.	19	Nov.	11	237	N	3.3	3.9	4.9	5.0	4.5	4.8	2.9	2.8	3.2	3.6	4.9	4.5	48.3
Castro, Dimmitt	29	91	19	107	—8	Apr.	17	Oct.	25	193	22	0.4	0.6	0.8	0.8	2.3	3.0	2.3	2.8	2.4	1.5	0.7	0.5	18.0

County and Station	Temperature					Average Freeze Dates				Growing Season	Normal Total Precipitation													
	Length of Record	Mean Max. July	Mean Min. January	Record Highest	Record Lowest	Last in Spring		First in Fall			Length of Record	January	February	March	April	May	June	July	August	September	October	November	December	Annual
	Yr.	F.	F.	F.	F.	Mo.	Day	Mo.	Day	Days	Yr.	In.	In.	In.	In.	In.	In.	In.	In.	In.	In.	In.	In.	In.
Chambers, Anahuac	N	92	41	110	8	Mar.	6	Nov.	20	261	N	4.0	2.9	3.0	3.6	4.8	5.8	4.5	4.5	6.2	3.8	4.4	4.2	51.7
Cherokee, Rusk	N	93	35	107	1	Mar.	8	Nov.	21	258	N	3.7	3.5	3.6	4.1	4.0	5.1	4.0	2.9	2.2	4.2	4.2	4.2	46.1
Childress, Childress	N	96	26	117	—7	Apr.	3	Nov.	6	217	N	0.5	0.9	1.2	1.5	3.0	3.0	1.9	2.1	2.8	2.0	1.0	0.7	20.7
Clay, Henrietta	N	97	26	116	—8	Mar.	27	Nov.	14	232	N	1.3	2.0	2.5	3.0	4.3	3.9	1.8	2.6	4.2	3.1	1.7	1.6	31.9
Cochran, Morton	27	91	22	110	—12	Apr.	18	Oct.	24	189	N	0.4	0.6	0.6	0.9	1.8	2.7	2.4	3.3	3.0	1.7	0.7	0.5	18.6
Coke, Robert Lee	28	96	28	111	—2	Mar.	31	Nov.	12	226	N	0.8	1.2	1.1	1.8	3.3	2.8	1.6	2.0	3.7	2.8	1.2	0.9	23.2
Coleman, Coleman	N	96	32	114	—4	Mar.	26	Nov.	16	235	N	1.2	1.5	1.6	2.4	4.1	3.3	2.0	2.5	3.8	2.8	1.6	1.2	28.0
Collin, McKinney	N	95	32	118	—7	Mar.	26	Nov.	11	230	N	2.0	2.8	3.5	3.9	5.8	4.0	2.4	2.4	4.6	3.4	3.1	2.3	40.0
Collingsworth, Wellington	N	97	26	113	—6	Apr.	5	Nov.	3	212	N	0.5	0.8	1.3	1.7	3.4	3.2	2.0	2.1	3.0	2.0	1.0	0.6	21.5
Colorado, Columbus	28	95	37	108	4	Mar.	1	Dec.	6	280	N	3.3	2.8	2.5	3.2	5.5	4.1	2.9	2.9	5.0	3.2	3.6	2.9	41.8
Comal, New Braunfels	N	95	37	110	2	Mar.	12	Nov.	25	261	N	1.9	2.2	1.8	2.6	5.0	4.1	2.0	2.5	4.1	3.5	2.8	2.0	34.3
Comanche, Proctor Reservoir	27	95	30	108	—8	Mar.	27	Nov.	20	238	27	1.6	1.9	2.1	3.1	4.6	3.4	1.7	1.9	3.9	3.0	2.0	1.3	30.4
Concho, Paint Rock	N	98	31	111	—1	Mar.	29	Nov.	12	228	N	1.0	1.3	1.4	1.9	3.4	2.9	1.9	2.1	4.0	2.6	1.3	1.1	24.8
Cooke, Gainesville	N	95	27	112	—7	Mar.	27	Nov.	8	226	N	1.7	2.3	3.3	3.2	4.7	3.5	2.0	2.4	4.5	4.0	2.4	1.8	35.8
Coryell, Gatesville	N	96	33	112	—6	Mar.	25	Nov.	21	241	N	1.8	2.3	2.4	3.1	4.3	3.9	2.1	2.2	3.7	3.1	2.3	1.8	32.9
Cottle, Paducah	N	96	25	118	—7	Apr.	2	Nov.	7	219	N	0.7	1.0	1.2	1.5	3.2	3.4	1.8	2.5	3.1	2.1	1.0	0.8	22.3
Crane, Crane	28	97	31	115	3	Mar.	31	Nov.	11	225	28	0.4	0.6	0.4	0.9	1.7	1.7	1.5	1.9	3.0	1.6	0.7	0.5	14.8
Crockett, Ozona	N	94	30	109	4	Mar.	26	Nov.	14	233	N	0.7	0.9	0.9	1.5	2.3	2.0	1.6	2.1	3.3	2.2	1.0	0.6	19.2
Crosby, Crosbyton	N	93	23	113	—6	Apr.	10	Nov.	2	206	N	0.5	0.9	1.2	1.3	2.9	3.0	2.3	3.1	3.6	2.1	1.0	0.7	22.6
Culberson, Van Horn	N	94	28	112	—7	Apr.	2	Nov.	10	224	N	0.5	0.3	0.2	0.3	0.6	1.4	2.1	2.5	2.7	1.3	0.7	0.6	13.1
Dallam, Dalhart	N	92	19	107	—21	Apr.	23	Oct.	18	178	N	0.4	0.5	0.8	1.1	2.6	2.4	3.1	3.1	1.9	1.0	0.7	0.4	17.9
Dallas, Dallas	N	96	35	113	1	Mar.	23	Nov.	13	235	N	1.8	2.3	3.2	3.9	5.0	3.5	2.4	2.3	3.6	3.9	2.4	1.9	36.1
Dawson, Lamesa	N	95	25	114	—12	Apr.	8	Nov.	6	210	N	0.5	0.6	0.8	1.0	2.3	2.8	2.2	1.9	3.5	1.8	0.7	0.5	16.2
De Witt, Yoakum	N	95	39	110	12	Mar.	3	Nov.	29	270	N	2.4	2.3	2.0	3.3	4.3	4.5	2.9	3.0	4.1	3.2	3.0	2.0	37.0
Deaf Smith, Hereford	N	90	20	108	—17	Apr.	16	Oct.	28	195	N	0.4	0.6	0.8	0.8	1.9	3.0	1.9	3.1	2.1	1.4	0.8	0.4	17.2
Delta, Cooper*	N	94	30	110	—1	Mar.	25	Nov.	13	233	N	2.7	2.9	3.6	4.8	5.0	3.9	2.8	2.2	4.5	3.6	3.3	3.4	42.7
Denton, Denton	N	94	30	113	—3	Mar.	27	Nov.	8	226	N	1.8	2.4	3.0	3.7	5.3	3.3	2.2	2.2	4.8	4.0	2.4	2.1	37.3
Dickens, Dickens*	15	95	26	110	0	Apr.	4	Nov.	7	217	15	0.4	0.6	1.1	1.2	3.3	2.6	2.0	3.3	3.3	1.8	0.7	0.4	20.7
Dimmit, Carrizo Springs	N	99	41	114	10	Feb.	19	Dec.	6	290	N	0.9	1.2	0.8	1.8	3.2	2.6	1.3	2.5	2.9	2.6	1.12	0.9	21.7
Donley, Clarendon	N	94	21	112	—11	Apr.	9	Nov.	1	206	N	0.5	0.8	1.2	1.5	3.1	3.7	2.1	3.3	2.7	1.7	1.0	0.6	22.0
Duval, Freer	28	96	41	109	12	Feb.	16	Dec.	11	298	N	1.3	1.3	1.0	1.7	3.5	3.1	1.6	2.3	4.1	2.8	1.4	0.9	24.8
Eastland, Rising Star	N	94	29	109	—8	Mar.	27	Nov.	11	299	N	1.5	1.7	2.1	2.7	4.2	3.8	2.1	2.1	3.5	3.1	1.7	1.3	29.7
Ector, Penwell	27	95	28	110	0	Apr.	3	Nov.	6	217	27	0.3	0.6	0.5	0.8	1.9	1.6	1.3	1.3	2.5	1.2	0.7	0.5	13.1
Edwards, Carta Valley	27	95	34	109	9	Mar.	16	Nov.	21	250	27	0.7	1.2	0.9	2.0	2.9	2.5	2.5	2.1	3.0	2.4	1.1	0.7	22.0
El Paso, El Paso	N	96	29	114	—8	Mar.	9	Nov.	12	248	N	0.4	0.4	0.3	0.2	0.3	0.7	1.5	1.6	1.7	0.8	0.4	0.6	8.8
Ellis, Waxahachie	N	96	34	114	—4	Mar.	20	Nov.	21	246	N	1.9	2.8	3.1	3.8	5.1	3.1	12.0	2.0	3.9	3.8	2.7	2.4	36.8
Erath, Dublin	N	94	31	110	—7	Mar.	27	Nov.	18	238	N	1.7	2.1	2.3	3.2	4.7	3.4	2.2	2.8	3.6	3.3	2.1	1.6	32.9
Falls, Marlin	N	96	36	112	—7	Mar.	13	Nov.	25	257	N	2.1	2.4	3.0	3.3	5.2	3.5	2.0	2.1	3.6	3.8	3.2	2.5	36.8
Fannin, Bonham	N	94	29	114	—4	Mar.	27	Nov.	10	228	N	2.1	3.1	3.9	3.8	6.1	4.5	3.1	2.3	4.9	4.1	3.4	2.7	44.0
Fayette, Flatonia	N	95	40	110	3	Mar.	2	Nov.	4	277	N	2.5	2.5	2.0	3.0	4.8	4.3	1.9	2.5	5.0	3.2	2.9	2.3	37.1

County and Station	Temperature: Length of Record	Mean Max. July	Mean Min. January	Record Highest	Record Lowest	Average Freeze Dates: Last in Spring		First in Fall		Growing Season	Normal Total Precipitation: Length of Record	January	February	March	April	May	June	July	August	September	October	November	December	Annual
	Yr.	F.	F.	F.	F.	Mo.	Day	Mo.	Day	Days	Yr.	In.	In.	In.	In.	In.	In.	In.	In.	In.	In.	In.	In.	In.
Fisher, Rotan	28	96	30	116	3	Apr.	2	Nov.	6	218	N	0.7	1.1	1.1	1.9	3.8	2.7	2.1	2.6	3.8	2.4	1.2	1.0	24.3
Floyd, Floydada	N	92	22	111	—9	Apr.	7	Nov.	6	213	N	0.4	0.7	1.0	1.2	2.8	3.6	2.2	2.6	3.0	1.7	0.9	0.5	20.5
Foard, Crowell*	N	97	24	114	—7	Apr.	2	Nov.	7	219	N	0.9	1.1	1.3	2.0	4.1	2.5	2.4	1.8	3.1	2.7	1.2	0.8	23.9
Fort Bend, Sugar Land	N	93	41	106	6	Feb.	14	Dec.	7	296	N	3.3	2.8	2.7	2.8	4.6	4.9	3.7	4.1	5.6	3.5	4.0	3.3	45.3
Franklin, Mount Vernon*	18	93	33	105	—1	Mar.	23	Nov.	12	234	18	2.8	3.3	4.3	4.4	4.7	4.1	3.4	2.5	4.9	3.9	3.7	4.8	46.8
Freestone, Fairfield	29	95	36	109	—2	Mar.	11	Nov.	29	263	N	2.5	3.1	3.2	3.7	4.9	3.5	2.0	2.3	4.0	4.1	3.6	3.0	39.8
Frio, Pearsall	N	97	38	111	9	Feb.	23	Dec.	2	291	N	1.2	1.3	1.0	2.2	3.6	3.3	1.6	2.5	3.0	3.1	1.5	1.1	25.4
Gaines, Seminole	N	94	25	114	—9	Apr.	8	Nov.	4	210	N	0.5	0.7	0.7	0.9	2.0	2.6	2.5	2.3	2.5	1.4	0.8	0.6	17.5
Galveston, Galveston	N	87	47	101	8	Jan.	24	Dec.	25	335	N	3.3	2.3	2.2	2.4	3.6	4.4	4.0	4.5	5.9	2.8	3.4	3.5	42.3
Garza, Post	28	94	27	115	—1	Apr.	5	Nov.	7	216	N	0.6	0.8	0.9	1.2	2.7	3.1	2.1	2.8	2.9	2.0	0.9	0.7	20.9
Gillespie, Fredericksburg	N	93	35	109	—5	Apr.	1	Nov.	6	219	N	1.3	1.8	1.4	2.5	4.2	3.6	2.2	2.7	3.6	3.6	1.9	1.3	30.0
Glasscock, Garden City	26	94	25	114	0	Apr.	2	Nov.	10	222	N	0.6	0.7	0.7	1.2	2.2	2.0	2.0	2.0	3.3	1.8	0.8	0.6	18.0
Goliad, Goliad	N	95	43	112	7	Feb.	24	Dec.	6	285	N	2.1	2.1	1.4	2.8	4.1	4.5	3.2	3.4	5.0	3.6	2.3	2.0	36.5
Gonzales, Nixon	N	95	40	113	3	Feb.	28	Dec.	1	276	N	2.2	2.1	1.6	2.9	4.0	3.5	1.9	2.3	4.6	3.2	2.4	1.7	32.4
Gray, Pampa	N	92	21	111	—12	Apr.	15	Oct.	27	195	N	0.5	0.9	1.4	1.3	2.9	3.6	2.4	2.6	2.4	1.5	1.0	0.5	21.0
Grayson, Sherman	N	95	30	110	—2	Mar.	27	Nov.	9	227	N	1.9	2.7	3.4	3.9	5.8	4.2	1.9	2.1	5.1	4.2	3.1	2.0	40.4
Gregg, Longview	N	93	33	110	—7	Mar.	16	Nov.	15	247	N	3.5	3.6	4.1	4.5	5.1	4.4	2.9	2.8	3.9	3.7	4.3	4.3	47.0
Grimes, Anderson*	9	96	40	108	4	Mar.	1	Dec.	4	278	N	3.1	3.3	2.8	4.3	4.3	3.4	2.4	2.8	4.1	3.1	3.4	3.4	40.4
Guadalupe, Seguin*	N	96	40	110	0	Mar.	6	Nov.	28	267	N	1.8	2.5	1.8	3.3	3.4	2.9	1.8	2.1	4.1	3.4	2.1	1.7	31.4
Hale, Plainview	N	92	24	111	—7	Apr.	10	Nov.	6	211	N	0.5	0.7	0.8	1.1	3.0	3.5	2.4	2.3	2.5	1.7	0.8	0.6	19.8
Hall, Memphis	N	96	24	117	—7	Apr.	4.	Nov.	4	213	N	0.5	0.8	1.3	1.7	3.5	3.1	1.7	2.5	2.4	1.6	0.9	0.6	20.5
Hamilton, Hico	N	96	32	111	—11	Mar.	27	Nov.	21	239	N	1.9	2.0	2.4	3.0	4.6	3.2	2.1	2.2	3.4	3.3	2.2	1.5	31.8
Hansford, Spearman	N	95	21	109	—22	Apr.	22	Oct.	25	186	N	0.4	0.7	1.3	1.1	2.9	3.0	2.9	2.4	2.1	1.2	1.0	0.5	19.4
Hardeman, Quanah	N	97	23	119	—15	Mar.	31	Nov.	7	221	N	0.8	1.0	1.5	1.7	3.5	3.2	2.4	2.5	3.6	2.4	1.2	0.9	24.5
Hardin, Evadale	22	93	37	102	12	Mar.	31	Nov.	14	246	N	4.8	3.9	4.0	3.8	5.4	5.8	4.7	4.0	5.3	4.0	4.9	5.1	55.7
Harris, Houston	N	92	43	107	7	Feb.	14	Dec.	11	300	N	3.3	3.0	2.9	3.2	5.2	5.0	3.6	3.5	4.9	4.3	3.8	3.5	46.1
Harrison, Marshall	N	93	32	110	2	Mar.	16	Nov.	17	245	N	3.8	4.0	4.0	4.4	4.9	4.4	3.0	2.5	3.8	3.9	4.3	4.5	47.7
Hartley, Channing*	13	92	21	108	—9	Apr.	22	Oct.	19	180	13	0.4	0.5	0.7	1.2	2.2	1.9	2.4	2.8	1.9	1.2	0.7	0.2	16.1
Haskell, Haskell	N	96	27	115	—6	Mar.	28	Nov.	16	232	N	0.9	1.4	1.4	2.2	3.6	3.0	2.1	2.9	3.7	2.6	1.3	1.1	26.1
Hays, San Marcos	N	95	36	110	—2	Mar.	14	Nov.	23	254	N	2.0	2.3	1.8	2.8	5.0	4.2	2.1	2.3	3.7	3.1	3.1	2.1	34.6
Hemphill, Canadian	N	96	22	112	—14	Apr.	9	Oct.	30	204	N	0.3	0.8	1.3	1.4	3.4	3.1	1.9	2.6	2.6	1.4	0.9	0.5	20.1
Henderson, Athens	N	95	35	110	—2	Mar.	11	Nov.	26	260	N	2.5	3.1	3.6	3.7	5.2	3.6	1.5	1.8	3.8	4.0	3.7	3.3	39.7
Hidalgo, McAllen	N	96	49	106	17	Feb.	7	Dec.	8	327	39	1.4	1.3	0.6	1.3	2.8	2.7	1.7	2.4	4.4	2.6	1.0	1.1	23.4
Hill, Hillsboro	N	95	34	113	—1	Mar.	13	Nov.	18	250	N	1.9	2.6	3.0	3.0	4.8	3.9	2.2	1.9	3.4	3.7	2.5	2.3	35.1
Hockley, Levelland	N	92	22	115	—16	Apr.	15	Oct.	28	196	N	0.4	0.7	0.6	0.9	2.0	2.6	2.5	3.1	3.3	1.7	0.7	0.6	19.3
Hood, Granbury*	28	97	33	110	—6	Mar.	26	Nov.	13	232	28	1.9	2.0	1.7	3.9	4.9	3.4	1.8	1.8	2.9	3.2	2.1	1.5	30.9
Hopkins, Sulphur Springs	N	94	30	110	—4	Mar.	23	Nov.	16	238	N	2.5	3.3	4.1	4.7	5.5	4.1	3.0	2.3	4.4	4.6	4.0	3.5	46.0
Houston, Crockett	N	93	34	110	0	Mar.	6	Nov.	26	265	N	3.5	2.9	3.2	4.1	4.4	3.7	3.0	2.2	4.4	3.9	3.8	3.5	42.4
Howard, Big Spring	N	94	28	114	21	Apr.	4	Nov.	7	217	N	0.6	0.8	0.8	1.3	2.8	2.3	1.7	2.0	3.9	1.6	0.8	0.6	19.2
Hudspeth, Cornudas Ser.	N	95	25	111	—13	Mar.	27	Nov.	11	231	N	0.4	0.3	0.2	0.2	0.5	1.1	1.5	2.2	1.9	0.9	0.4	0.4	10.0
Hunt, Greenville	N	94	29	108	—3	Mar.	21	Nov.	13	237	N	2.2	3.0	3.8	3.9	5.7	3.7	2.7	2.2	4.5	4.1	3.3	2.6	41.6
Hutchinson, Borger	N	93	23	107	—12	Apr.	20	Oct.	24	187	N	0.5	0.9	1.3	1.3	2.8	3.4	2.7	2.9	2.0	1.3	0.8	0.5	20.3

County and Station	Temperature: Length of Record	Temperature: Mean Max. July	Temperature: Mean Min. January	Temperature: Record Highest	Temperature: Record Lowest	Average Freeze Dates: Last in Spring		Average Freeze Dates: First in Fall		Growing Season	Normal Total Precipitation: Length of Record	January	February	March	April	May	June	July	August	September	October	November	December	Annual
	Yr.	F.	F.	F.	F.	Mo.	Day	Mo.	Day	Days	Yr.	In.	In.	In.	In.	In.	In.	In.	In.	In.	In.	In.	In.	In.
Irion, Mertzon	27	95	32	108	4	Mar.	27	Nov.	14	232	N	0.7	1.3	1.0	1.6	3.1	2.3	1.5	2.5	3.1	2.0	1.2	0.9	21.1
Jack, Jacksboro	N	95	29	113	—7	Apr.	1	Nov.	5	218	N	1.3	1.6	2.1	2.8	4.7	2.9	2.5	2.2	3.8	3.2	2.0	1.5	30.7
Jackson, Edna*	8	94	42	105	17	Feb.	19	Dec.	6	290	26	2.2	2.8	1.7	2.8	5.1	4.6	2.2	3.4	5.7	3.9	2.8	2.5	40.9
Jasper, Jasper	22	93	36	106	7	Mar.	18	Nov.	13	230	N	4.4	4.4	4.4	3.7	5.6	5.3	3.8	3.6	4.1	3.6	4.6	5.3	52.7
Jeff Davis, Mount Locke	N	82	30	104	—10	—	—	—	—	—	N	0.5	0.5	0.4	0.5	1.5	2.6	3.9	4.3	3.5	1.7	0.7	0.6	20.8
Jefferson, Port Arthur	N	92	42	107	12	Mar.	11	Nov.	16	250	N	4.8	3.4	3.2	3.5	5.7	5.6	5.4	5.3	6.3	4.3	4.9	4.8	57.2
Jim Hogg, Hebbronville	N	97	42	109	12	Feb.	15	Dec.	15	303	N	1.1	1.3	0.7	1.7	3.4	2.9	1.5	2.0	4.1	1.9	1.2	0.9	22.7
Jim Wells, Alice	N	96	43	111	12	Feb.	18	Dec.	4	289	N	1.3	1.6	0.8	1.6	3.2	3.5	2.5	2.7	5.1	2.7	1.6	1.1	27.8
Johnson, Cleburne	N	97	33	114	—5	Mar.	25	Nov.	14	233	N	1.9	2.2	2.9	3.6	5.4	3.5	2.0	2.1	3.3	3.3	2.1	1.8	34.0
Jones, Anson	N	96	31	114	—12	Mar.	31	Nov.	9.	223	22	1.0	1.4	1.3	2.2	3.4	2.9	2.0	2.6	4.3	2.4	1.3	1.1	25.8
Karnes, Kenedy*	18	97	41	112	7	Feb.	24	Dec.	2	281	18	2.3	2.4	1.1	2.2	4.0	4.2	1.2	3.0	5.3	3.6	2.0	1.8	33.2
Kaufman, Kaufman	N	95	32	112	—3	Mar.	18	Nov.	21	248	N	2.4	3.0	3.2	3.8	5.0	3.1	2.6	1.8	3.8	3.9	3.3	3.0	38.9
Kendall, Boerne	N	93	33	107	—4	Mar.	25	Nov.	11	236	N	1.7	2.1	2.1	3.1	4.1	3.8	2.2	2.9	4.2	3.6	2.7	1.8	34.2
Kenedy, Armstrong*	14	95	45	110	14	Feb.	2	Dec.	18	319	14	1.2	1.7	0.5	1.3	4.4	3.4	2.1	3.2	6.4	2.9	1.3	1.3	29.7
Kent, Jayton	18	96	25	116	—5	Apr.	4	Nov.	6	216	18	0.7	1.0	1.1	1.6	3.0	2.9	1.8	2.7	3.2	2.1	0.9	0.8	21.8
Kerr, Kerrville*	N	94	32	110	—7	Apr.	6	Nov.	6	216	N	1.6	2.2	2.0	3.1	3.8	2.6	1.7	2.1	4.0	3.6	1.6	1.6	29.8
Kimble, Junction	N	96	31	110	—11	Apr.	3	Nov.	3	213	N	1.0	1.6	1.2	2.1	3.6	2.8	1.7	2.5	2.8	2.4	1.2	1.1	23.8
King, Guthrie	27	98	24	119	—10	Apr.	3	Nov.	8	219	N	0.9	1.1	1.1	1.6	3.5	3.1	1.9	2.7	3.7	2.4	1.1	0.7	23.8
Kinney, Brackettville	23	95	36	109	4	Mar.	1	Nov.	26	270	45	0.8	1.3	0.9	2.3	2.6	3.1	1.6	2.0	2.6	2.4	1.2	0.8	21.7
Kleberg, Kingsville	N	95	45	108	10	Feb.	5	Dec.	16	314	N	1.5	1.8	0.9	1.6	3.4	4.0	2.2	2.9	4.3	2.7	1.4	1.0	27.6
Knox, Munday	N	98	28	117	—9	Apr.	3	Nov.	6	217	N	0.9	1.4	1.6	2.1	3.7	3.0	2.0	2.6	3.9	2.8	1.3	1.0	26.2
La Salle, Fowlerton	N	99	38	111	7	Feb.	20	Dec.	6	288	N	1.1	1.1	0.8	1.8	3.2	2.2	1.5	2.4	3.3	3.0	1.2	1.0	22.5
Lamar, Paris	N	94	30	111	—1	Mar.	25	Nov.	14	235	N	2.2	3.2	4.2	4.0	5.9	3.9	3.6	2.7	4.8	4.6	3.9	3.3	46.1
Lamb, Littlefield	N	91	22	112	—14	Apr.	16	Oct.	27	194	N	0.4	0.6	0.6	1.0	2.3	3.3	2.4	2.8	2.5	1.6	0.7	0.5	18.7
Lampasas, Lampasas	N	95	30	111	—12	Apr.	1	Nov.	10	223	N	1.5	2.0	2.1	2.7	4.1	2.9	1.8	2.5	3.1	3.3	2.0	1.7	29.6
Lavaca, Hallettsville	N	95	41	111	5	Mar.	1	Dec.	6	280	N	2.8	2.4	2.2	3.0	5.3	4.4	2.5	2.7	5.1	3.2	3.3	2.4	39.1
Lee, Lexington	28	94	36	104	11	Mar.	1	Nov.	29	273	28	2.2	2.5	2.4	2.9	4.8	3.8	1.7	2.0	4.2	3.8	3.0	2.3	35.6
Leon, Centerville	N	95	34	111	—3	Mar.	6	Dec.	1	270	N	3.1	3.1	3.1	3.9	4.4	3.5	2.5	2.4	4.0	4.1	3.2	3.1	40.5
Liberty, Liberty	N	93	39	107	7	Mar.	3	Nov.	19	261	N	3.8	3.6	3.2	3.5	5.4	6.1	4.5	4.0	5.7	4.5	5.2	4.8	54.1
Limestone, Mexia	N	95	33	110	—5	Mar.	15	Nov.	26	255	N	2.5	3.1	3.4	3.6	4.9	3.5	1.9	2.3	4.7	4.1	3.4	3.2	40.3
Lipscomb, Follett	N	93	20	110	—12	Apr.	10	Oct.	29	202	N	0.5	1.0	1.9	1.7	3.5	3.4	2.3	3.1	2.1	1.4	1.2	0.7	22.8
Live Oak, George West*	N	95	41	109	12	Feb.	20	Dec.	6	289	N	1.7	1.6	0.8	1.9	3.3	2.8	1.5	2.9	4.7	3.1	1.9	1.4	27.6
Llano, Llano	N	96	31	113	—6	Mar.	29	Nov.	13	229	N	1.2	1.8	1.6	2.5	3.8	2.8	1.8	2.4	3.0	2.7	1.8	1.2	26.4
Loving, Mentone*	N	96	28	114	—14	Apr.	3	Nov.	8	222	N	0.3	0.3	0.3	0.2	1.1	0.9	1.8	1.4	1.2	1.0	0.3	0.3	9.1
Lubbock, Lubbock	N	92	25	114	—16	Apr.	9	Nov.	3	208	N	0.4	0.7	0.9	1.0	2.4	2.8	2.4	2.5	2.6	1.9	0,8	0.5	18.7
Lynn, Tahoka	N	92	24	111	—5	Apr.	5	Nov.	6	217	N	0.5	0.8	0.9	1.4	2.7	3.0	2.5	2.2	2.6	1.8	0.8	0.7	19.7
Madison, Madisonville	N	96	38	110	—2	Mar.	5	Dec.	2	272	N	3.0	2.8	3.2	3.5	5.0	3.9	2.3	2.6	4.5	4.1	3.7	3.0	41.6
Marion, Jefferson*	N	94	32	109	—5	Mar.	18	Nov.	9	236	N	3.9	3.5	3.9	5.3	4.6	3.4	3.1	2.5	3.6	2.0	3.8	4.1	44.7
Martin, Lenorah*	N	94	30	109	—8	Apr.	5	Nov.	6	215	N	0.6	0.8	0.8	1.2	2.3	1.6	2.4	1.7	2.7	1.6	0.8	0.6	17.2
Mason, Mason	N	95	31	109	5	Apr.	3	Nov.	6	217	N	1.1	1.6	1.5	2.1	3.7	3.3	1.9	2.6	3.2	3.1	1.6	1.1	26.8
Matagorda, Matagorda	N	91	45	102	9	Feb.	17	Dec.	10	296	N	3.6	2.6	1.9	2.6	4.5	4.8	4.0	3.3	6.9	3.9	3.9	2.7	44.7
Maverick, Eagle Pass	N	98	38	115	10	Feb.	21	Dec.	3	285	N	0.7	0.9	0.7	1.9	3.4	3.0	1.8	2.2	2.8	2.4	1.0	0.8	21.5

County and Station	Temperature					Average Freeze Dates				Growing Season	Normal Total Precipitation													
	Length of Record	Mean Max. July	Mean Min. January	Record Highest	Record Lowest	Last in Spring		First in Fall			Length of Record	January	February	March	April	May	June	July	August	September	October	November	December	Annual
	Yr.	F.	F.	F.	F.	Mo.	Day	Mo.	Day	Days	Yr.	In.	In.	In.	In.	In.	In.	In.	In.	In.	In.	In.	In.	In.
McCulloch, Brady	N	95	30	110	—7	Mar.	31	Nov.	12	226	N	1.1	1.6	1.4	2.1	3.6	2.9	2.3	2.5	3.6	2.4	1.5	1.1	26.1
McLennan, Waco	N	97	34	112	—5	Mar.	16	Nov.	24	253	N	1.7	2.1	2.3	3.2	4.6	3.3	2.0	1.7	3.5	3.4	2.4	1.9	32.0
McMullen, Tilden	N	98	40	109	5	Feb.	19	Dec.	7	291	N	1.3	1.4	0.9	1.8	3.0	2.9	1.7	2.3	3.5	2.0	1.4	1.0	23.4
Medina, Hondo	N	94	37	112	4	Mar.	6	Nov.	24	263	N	1.4	1.7	1.4	2.6	3.8	3.0	1.7	2.7	3.1	3.2	1.5	1.4	27.3
Menard, Menard	28	95	30	109	—2	Mar.	31	Nov.	6	220	N	1.0	1.5	1.9	3.2	2.8	2.1	2.4	3.3	2.5	1.4	1.2	0.9	24.3
Midland, Midland	N	95	29	116	—11	Apr.	3	Nov.	6	218	N	0.5	0.6	0.5	0.7	2.2	1.4	1.6	1.9	3.3	1.3	0.7	0.5	15.2
Milam, Cameron	N	95	38	109	2	Mar.	13	Nov.	24	256	N	2.2	2.6	2.2	3.3	4.7	2.9	1.9	1.7	4.2	3.2	3.0	2.3	34.2
Mills, Goldthwaite	24	95	34	110	—7	Mar.	31	Nov.	16	230	24	1.3	1.8	1.9	2.4	3.7	3.2	1.6	2.1	3.1	3.1	2.0	1.4	27.6
Mitchell, Colorado City*	24	97	30	112	—7	Apr.	4	Nov.	5	217	24	0.6	0.7	0.9	1.9	2.9	2.2	1.7	2.1	3.0	2.1	1.0	0.7	19.8
Montague, Bowie	N	96	31	115	—11	Mar.	27	Nov.	11	229	N	1.4	2.0	2.6	2.9	4.8	3.4	2.0	2.3	4.1	3.7	2.3	1.6	32.9
Montgomery, Conroe	N	94	38	107	3	Mar.	1	Nov.	26	270	N	3.6	3.2	2.9	3.8	5.4	4.5	3.5	3.6	5.0	3.7	4.2	4.0	47.3
Moore, Dumas	N	92	20	109	—18	Apr.	30	Oct.	22	185	N	0.4	0.7	1.0	1.1	2.7	2.8	2.4	2.2	1.9	1.1	0.8	0.4	17.4
Morris, Daingerfield	N	95	35	109	4	Mar.	21	Nov.	12	236	25	2.9	3.5	4.4	4.8	4.7	3.6	2.8	2.4	3.2	3.9	4.5	4.1	44.6
Motley, Matador	N	95	26	116	—5	Apr.	3	Nov.	7	218	N	0.6	0.8	1.1	1.3	2.8	3.4	2.1	2.4	3.0	2.0	1.0	0.7	21.2
Nacogdoches, Nacogdoches*	N	94	36	110	0	Mar.	16	Nov.	12	243	N	4.2	3.9	3.7	4.8	5.5	3.9	3.9	2.5	3.8	3.3	3.8	4.7	47.5
Navarro, Corsicana	N	94	33	113	—5	Mar.	10	Nov.	19	253	N	2.2	2.8	3.1	3.6	5.8	3.1	2.1	1.9	3.4	4.2	2.9	2.9	37.9
Newton, Kirbyville Forest Service*	27	93	40	107	7	Mar.	24	Nov.	9	228	27	4.8	4.3	3.7	4.6	5.3	4.6	5.3	3.7	5.1	3.8	4.7	6.0	56.0
Nolan, Roscoe	N	94	30	113	—11	Apr.	2	Nov.	9	221	N	1.0	1.2	1.3	1.8	2.9	2.9	2.0	2.4	4.3	2.6	1.2	0.9	24.4
Nueces, Corpus Christi	N	93	45	104	13	Feb.	9	Dec.	15	309	N	1.7	2.0	0.9	1.7	3.3	3.4	2.4	3.3	5.5	3.0	1.6	1.3	30.1
Ochiltree, Perryton	26	94	17	110	—8	Apr.	18	Oct.	26	191	N	0.4	0.7	1.3	1.3	3.3	3.3	2.4	2.4	1.8	1.1	1.1	0.5	19.5
Oldham, Vega*	N	91	19	108	—17	Apr.	19	Oct.	21	186	N	0.5	0.6	0.8	1.1	2.4	2.8	2.8	2.5	1.6	1.2	0.7	0.5	17.4
Orange, Orange	27	91	39	104	10	Mar.	16	Nov.	11	240	27	5.2	3.9	3.5	3.4	5.4	5.6	5.6	4.7	6.2	4.3	4.7	5.5	58.3
Palo Pinto, Mineral Wells	N	96	30	114	3	Mar.	31	Nov.	7	221	N	1.6	2.0	2.6	3.2	4.5	3.5	2.2	2.4	3.4	3.5	1.9	1.4	32.2
Panola, Carthage	N	94	33	108	1	Mar.	16	Nov.	11	240	N	4.0	3.7	3.8	4.0	4.9	4.4	3.2	2.7	4.1	3.9	4.7	4.6	48.0
Parker, Weatherford	N	96	28	119	—10	Mar.	29	Nov.	9	225	N	1.6	2.2	2.7	3.3	4.5	3.6	2.3	2.4	3.5	3.3	2.0	1.6	32.9
Parmer, Friona	28	90	21	108	—15	Apr.	20	Oct.	20	183	28	0.5	0.6	0.7	0.8	1.9	2.8	2.1	2.7	2.2	1.3	0.7	0.5	16.8
Pecos, Fort Stockton	N	95	30	117	1	Mar.	31	Nov.	10	224	N	0.5	0.5	0.4	0.7	1.5	1.6	1.3	1.8	2.8	1.6	0.8	0.6	13.9
Polk, Livingston	N	94	35	111	3	Mar.	11	Nov.	16	250	N	4.0	3.4	3.8	3.6	5.5	4.7	3.6	3.1	4.5	3.5	4.3	4.7	48.7
Potter, Amarillo	N	92	21	108	—14	Apr.	17	Oct.	24	190	N	0.5	0.6	1.0	1.0	2.5	3.7	2.6	3.2	2.0	1.4	0.7	0.4	19.6
Presidio, Marfa	N	90	26	106	—2	Mar.	20	Nov.	13	238	22	0.4	0.4	0.3	0.6	1.2	2.1	2.6	2.9	2.9	1.6	0.6	0.5	15.9
Presidio, Presidio	N	102	34	117	4	Mar.	20	Nov.	13	238	N	0.3	0.4	0.2	0.3	0.6	1.7	1.7	1.9	2.0	1.0	0.4	0.5	10.8
Rains, Emory	29	94	31	110	—5	Mar.	21	Nov.	18	242	N	2.6	3.4	3.7	4.1	5.7	3.9	2.5	2.1	3.7	4.2	3.6	3.3	42.9
Randall, Canyon	N	92	23	107	—14	Apr.	15	Oct.	27	195	N	0.4	0.6	0.9	0.9	2.4	3.5	2.2	3.1	2.0	1.6	0.8	0.4	18.9
Reagan, Big Lake	27	94	28	109	1	Mar.	28	Nov.	12	229	27	0.6	0.9	0.9	1.5	2.4	1.8	2.0	1.9	3.2	2.2	1.0	0.8	19.2
Real, Prade Ranch	19	92	29	107	0	Mar.	26	Nov.	17	236	19	1.2	1.5	1.4	2.3	3.3	3.0	2.6	3.1	3.1	3.5	1.7	1.1	25.7
Red River, Clarksville	N	92	28	109	—5	Mar.	23	Nov.	12	234	N	2.3	3.2	4.5	4.3	5.5	3.9	2.9	2.1	3.9	4.5	4.2	3.7	44.9
Reeves, Balmorhea	N	96	29	112	—9	Apr.	2.	Nov.	11	226	N	0.5	0.5	04.	0.6	1.4	1.3	1.8	2.4	3.0	1.3	0.7	0.5	14.3
Reeves, Pecos	N	99	27	118	—9	Apr.	1	Nov.	12	226	N	0.4	0.5	0.4	0.4	1.0	1.2	1.2	1.7	2.1	1.1	0.5	0.5	11.0
Refugio, Refugio	29	94	43	106	8	Feb.	14	Dec.	15	304	N	2.2	2.3	1.3	2.3	4.1	4.4	3.6	3.5	6.7	3.9	2.1	1.7	38.0
Roberts, Miami	N	93	20	111	—15	Apr.	16	Oct.	25	192	N	0.5	1.0	1.6	1.6	3.3	3.4	2.3	2.4	2.4	1.6	1.1	0.5	21.6
Robertson, Franklin	26	95	37	110	—1	Mar.	6	Nov.	29	268	26	2.7	2.8	2.7	3.6	4.5	2.9	2.0	2.4	4.3	4.0	2.9	2.8	37.5
Rockwall, Rockwall*	N	96	33	118	—7	Mar.	23	Nov.	14	236	N	2.1	2.4	3.1	4.7	5.2	3.1	2.4	2.0	3.8	3.3	2.5	2.4	36.9

County and Station	Temperature					Average Freeze Dates				Growing Season	Normal Total Precipitation													
	Length of Record	Mean Max. July	Mean Min. January	Record Highest	Record Lowest	Last in Spring		First in Fall			Length of Record	January	February	March	April	May	June	July	August	September	October	November	December	Annual
	Yr.	F.	F.	F.	F.	Mo.	Day	Mo.	Day	Days	Yr.	In.	In.	In.	In.	In.	In.	In.	In.	In.	In.	In.	In.	In.
Runnels, Ballinger	N	95	30	114	—9	Mar.	30	Nov.	13	228	N	1.0	1.3	1.2	1.9	3.4	2.6	1.5	2.5	3.5	2.3	1.3	1.0	23.3
Rusk, Henderson	N	93	33	108	—1	Mar.	11	Nov.	16	250	N	3.6	3.6	3.8	4.0	5.1	4.3	2.8	2.5	3.6	4.0	4.3	3.9	45.6
Sabine, Hemphill*	6	93	36	104	8	Mar.	21	Nov.	12	236	19	5.2	3.2	5.7	4.8	5.1	4.5	4.0	3.1	3.8	4.5	4.0	4.5	52.5
San Augustine, Broaddus	24	93	35	106	9	Mar.	19	Nov.	12	238	24	4.5	3.9	3.9	3.8	4.8	4.6	3.4	2.9	4.3	3.3	4.3	5.0	48.6
San Jacinto, Coldspring	27	93	36	105	3	Mar.	5	Nov.	21	261	25	3.7	3.3	3.5	3.4	5.5	5.5	3.1	3.1	5.7	3.8	4.1	4.7	48.3
San Patricio, Sinton	N	94	43	107	11	Feb.	14	Dec.	14	303	N	2.0	2.2	1.2	2.1	4.1	3.5	3.4	3.1	6.1	3.8	1.8	1.4	35.0
San Saba, San Saba	27	96	32	112	—1	Apr.	1	Nov.	14	227	N	1.1	1.7	1.8	2.4	3.6	2.8	1.6	2.4	2.8	2.9	2.0	1.2	26.3
Schleicher, Eldorado*	15	93	28	107	3	Mar.	28	Nov.	12	229	N	0.7	0.9	0.7	1.7	2.5	1.9	1.6	2.1	3.1	2.1	1.0	0.6	19.0
Scurry, Snyder	N	93	25	115	—10	Apr.	4	Nov.	4	214	N	0.6	0.8	1.0	1.7	3.2	2.9	2.0	2.5	3.5	2.4	0.9	0.8	22.2
Shackelford, Albany	N	97	31	115	—8	Mar.	30	Nov.	9	224	N	1.2	1.6	1.7	2.6	4.0	3.0	1.9	3.0	3.9	2.8	1.7	1.3	28.6
Shelby, Center	N	94	33	110	0	Mar.	17	Nov.	12	240	N	4.3	4.0	4.1	4.0	5.3	4.4	3.3	3.5	4.5	3.9	4.2	4.7	50.2
Sherman, Stratford	N	92	18	108	—19	Apr.	23	Oct.	22	182	N	0.3	0.5	0.9	1.2	2.7	2.3	2.7	2.5	2.0	0.9	0.7	0.4	17.2
Smith, Tyler*	N	94	33	108	0	Mar.	7	Nov.	21	259	N	3.0	3.3	3.5	4.9	4.9	3.3	2.8	2.5	4.1	3.3	3.8	3.7	43.1
Somervell, Glen Rose	27	98	30	110	—15	Mar.	25	Nov.	16	236	27	1.7	2.1	2.7	3.2	5.3	3.7	2.2	1.8	3.5	3.4	2.0	1.8	33.3
Starr, Rio Grande City	N	99	43	115	10	Feb.	16	Dec.	7	314	N	1.0	1.1	0.5	1.5	2.8	2.5	1.4	2.3	5.2	2.1	1.0	1.0	22.3
Stephens, Breckenridge	N	97	28	111	—7	Apr.	1	Nov.	7	222	N	1.4	1.5	1.8	2.6	3.6	3.0	2.0	1.9	3.6	3.4	1.7	1.3	27.6
Sterling, Sterling City	27	96	29	112	—7	Apr.	1	Nov.	11	224	N	0.8	0.9	0.9	1.4	2.9	2.4	1.6	2.1	3.8	1.7	1.1	0.8	20.3
Stonewall, Aspermont	29	97	27	117	2	Mar.	31	Nov.	10	220	N	0.8	1.1	1.3	1.9	3.2	3.0	1.7	2.3	3.6	2.4	1.3	0.8	23.3
Sutton, Sonora	N	96	30	109	—8	Mar.	26	Nov.	16	235	N	0.8	1.2	1.0	1.9	2.6	2.2	2.1	2.7	3.4	2.7	1.2	0.7	22.4
Swisher, Tulia	N	91	22	110	—10	Apr.	10	Nov.	1	205	N	0.5	0.7	0.9	1.0	2.4	3.9	2.0	2.6	2.5	1.5	0.8	0.6	19.4
Tarrant, Fort Worth*	N	96	35	108	4	Mar.	26	Nov.	11	230	29	2.0	2.2	2.5	3.6	4.6	3.0	1.8	1.7	2.5	2.6	2.5	2.4	31.3
Taylor, Abilene	N	95	31	110	—9	Mar.	31	Nov.	11	225	N	1.0	1.2	1.4	1.9	3.0	2.9	2.1	2.8	3.2	2.5	1.5	1.0	24.4
Terrell, Sanderson	28	92	29	110	2	Mar.	21	Nov.	13	237	N	0.3	0.6	0.4	1.0	1.6	1.8	1.3	1.8	2.7	1.8	0.7	0.5	14.3
Terry, Brownfield	N	93	24	111	—8	Apr.	10	Nov.	2	206	N	0.5	0.7	0.8	0.9	2.7	3.0	2.4	2.4	2.6	1.7	0.7	0.6	19.0
Throckmorton, Throckmorton	N	96	27	114	—11	Mar.	31	Nov.	6	220	N	1.0	1.5	1.6	2.5	3.5	3.1	2.0	2.6	4.2	2.6	1.4	1.3	27.1
Titus, Mount Pleasant	N	94	29	111	—12	Mar.	23	Nov.	12	233	N	2.8	3.7	4.4	4.3	5.1	4.3	3.4	2.4	3.9	4.2	4.5	3.9	46.8
Tom Green, San Angelo	N	96	31	111	—4	Mar.	25	Nov.	15	235	N	0.8	1.1	0.9	1.7	3.0	2.3	1.1	1.9	3.4	2.4	1.1	0.8	20.5
Travis, Austin	N	95	39	109	—2	Mar.	3	Nov.	28	270	N	1.7	2.2	1.9	2.6	4.8	3.7	2.0	2.1	3.3	3.4	2.4	1.9	31.9
Trinity, Groveton	23	94	36	108	1	Mar.	6	Nov.	21	260	23	3.6	3.2	3.6	3.4	4.8	4.5	3.3	3.1	4.1	3.4	3.9	4.1	44.9
Tyler, Warren	N	93	38	106	6	Mar.	17	Nov.	11	241	N	4.5	4.0	3.9	3.9	6.0	5.8	3.8	3.4	4.5	4.0	4.8	5.8	54.3
Upshur, Gilmer	N	93	30	109	—4	Mar.	16	Nov.	16	245	N	2.9	3.7	4.3	4.8	4.6	3.6	2.8	2.3	4.0	3.8	4.4	4.0	45.2
Upton, McCamey	N	95	31	113	—2	Mar.	26	Nov.	12	232	N	0.4	0.6	0.4	0.9	1.7	1.5	1.0	1.6	2.8	2.2	0.7	0.6	14.3
Uvalde, Uvalde	N	96	36	111	6	Mar.	10	Nov.	21	255	N	1.1	1.4	1.1	2.3	3.3	2.8	1.9	2.7	2.8	3.0	1.3	1.1	24.8
Val Verde, Del Rio	N	96	39	112	10	Feb.	12	Dec.	9	300	N	0.6	1.0	0.7	2.0	2.0	2.1	1.9	1.5	2.8	2.2	0.9	0.6	18.2
Van Zandt, Wills Point	N	95	32	113	—2	Mar.	16	Nov.	21	250	N	2.7	3.2	3.6	4.7	5.4	4.2	2.2	1.9	3.9	4.2	3.6	3.3	43.0
Victoria, Victoria	N	94	43	107	9	Feb.	19	Dec.	6	290	N	2.2	2.0	1.6	2.4	4.5	4.9	3.3	3.0	5.6	3.5	2.5	2.0	37.4
Walker, Huntsville	N	94	38	107	2	Mar.	7	Nov.	27	265	N	3.6	3.1	3.1	3.5	5.2	4.2	2.4	3.3	5.0	3.6	4.2	3.8	45.0
Waller, Hempstead*	15	95	38	107	13	Feb.	28	Dec.	4	283	N	2.8	2.9	2.1	3.9	4.7	3.6	2.0	2.4	4.6	4.0	3.2	3.0	38.2
Ward, Monahans	N	96	27	120	—9	Apr.	1	Nov.	10	223	N	0.4	0.6	0.4	0.7	1.8	1.4	1.2	1.4	2.4	1.4	0.6	0.5	12.7
Washington, Brenham	N	96	41	110	1	Mar.	3	Dec.	4	277	N	3.1	2.9	2.8	3.3	5.2	4.3	2.0	2.5	4.8	3.6	3.9	3.2	41.4
Webb, Laredo	27	99	43	110	13	Feb.	7	Dec.	26	322	N	0.8	1.0	0.5	1.6	2.7	3.1	1.4	2.6	3.3	2.5	1.1	0.9	21.4
Wharton, Danevang	N	92	41	108	7	Mar.	5	Nov.	26	266	N	2.8	2.6	2.0	2.5	4.9	4.7	3.6	3.6	5.9	3.9	3.1	2.7	42.3

County and Station	Temperature: Length of Record	Mean Max. July	Mean Min. January	Record Highest	Record Lowest	Average Freeze Dates: Last in Spring		First in Fall		Growing Season	Normal Total Precipitation: Length of Record	January	February	March	April	May	June	July	August	September	October	November	December	Annual
	Yr.	F.	F.	F.	F.	Mo.	Day	Mo.	Day	Days	Yr.	In.	In.	In.	In.	In.	In.	In.	In.	In.	In.	In.	In.	In.
Wheeler, Shamrock	27	95	22	113	—8	Apr.	7	Nov.	1	208	N	0.4	0.8	1.5	1.8	3.5	3.4	2.0	2.5	2.8	1.8	1.0	0.5	22.1
Wichita, Wichita Falls	N	97	28	117	—8	Mar.	27	Nov.	11	229	N	1.0	1.5	2.2	3.0	4.1	3.5	1.7	2.5	3.8	2.7	1.5	1.3	28.9
Wilbarger, Vernon	N	97	25	119	—9	Mar.	31	Nov.	7	221	N	0.9	1.2	1.8	2.3	3.8	2.9	2.0	2.5	3.6	2.6	1.4	0.8	25.7
Willacy, Raymondville	N	96	46	107	14	Feb.	6	Dec.	11	331	N	1.5	1.6	0.8	1.5	3.13	3.3	2.0	3.1	5.8	2.2	1.3	1.2	27.6
Wiliamson, Taylor	N	96	34	112	—5	Mar.	11	Nov.	24	258	N	2.0	2.5	2.3	2.9	4.7	3.6	1.7	2.0	4.2	3.6	2.7	2.1	34.4
Wilson, Floresville	28	96	36	108	7	Feb.	24	Dec.	1	280	N	1.9	1.9	1.2	2.4	3.4	2.9	2.0	2.3	3.6	2.7	2.0	1.6	29.4
Winkler, Wink	N	97	28	117	—14	Apr.	3	Nov.	8	219	N	0.3	0.4	0.4	0.7	1.0	1.9	1.7	1.4	2.3	1.5	0.6	0.4	12.6
Wise, Bridgeport	N	99	30	115	—8	Mar.	31	Nov.	6	220	N	1.5	1.9	2.6	3.1	5.3	3.5	2.3	2.0	3.6	3.3	2.0	1.5	32.6
Wood, Mineola*	14	94	31	107	2	Mar.	17	Nov.	18	246	14	3.1	3.0	4.0	4.7	4.9	3.4	3.0	2.5	4.8	4.3	3.7	3.6	45.0
Yoakum, Plains	N	91	22	111	—12	Apr.	15	Oct.	31	199	N	0.4	0.7	0.6	1.0	2.1	2.4	2.6	2.7	2.6	1.3	0.7	0.7	17.7
Young, Graham	N	96	26	112	—8	Apr.	2	Nov.	4	216	N	1.3	1.6	1.9	2.8	4.5	3.4	2.1	2.3	4.2	3.1	1.9	1.4	30.6
Zapata, Zapata	27	99	43	112	16	Feb.	14	Dec.	15	304	12	0.8	1.1	0.6	1.4	2.4	2.5	1.6	1.7	4.3	1.6	1.0	0.9	19.7
Zavala, Crystal City	N	97	42	109	11	Feb.	24	Dec.	1	280	N	0.9	1.2	0.8	1.8	2.9	2.8	1.6	1.9	2.7	2.5	1.1	0.8	21.0

Extreme Weather Records in Texas

NOAA Environmental Data Service lists the following recorded extremes of weather in Texas:

Temperature

Lowest -Tulia, February 12, 1899 .... -23°F
Seminole, February 8, 1933 .... -23°F
Highest -Seymour, August 12, 1936 .... 120°F
Monahans, June 28, 1994 .... 120°F
Coldest Winter 1898-1899

Rainfall

Wettest year - entire state .... 1941 .... 42.62 in.
Driest year - entire state..... 1917 .... 14.30 in.
Greatest annual - Clarksville .. 1873 .... 109.38 in.
Least annual - Wink .... 1956 ...... 1.76 in.
†Greatest in 24 hours - Thrall, Sept. 9-10 , 1921 .... 38.20 in.

†The greatest 24-hour rainfall ever recorded in Texas at an official observing site occurred at Albany, Shackelford County, on Aug. 4, 1978 - 29.05 inches.

Snowfall

Greatest seasonal - Romero, 1923-1924 .... 65.0 in.
Greatest monthly - Hale Center, Feb. 1956 .... 36.0 in.
Greatest single storm - Hale Center, Feb. 2-5, 1956 .... 33.0 in.
Greatest in 24 Hours - Plainview, Feb. 3-4, 1956 .... 24.0 in.
Maximum depth on ground - Hale Center, Feb. 5, 1956 .... 33.0 in.

Wind Velocity

Highest sustained wind (fastest mile):
*Matagorda, Sept. 11, 1961 .... SE .... 145 mph
*Port Lavaca, Sept. 11, 1961 .... NE .... 145 mph
Highest peak gust (instantaneous velocity):
*Aransas Pass, Aug. 3, 1970 .... SW .... 180 mph
*Robstown, Aug. 3, 1970 (est.) .... WSW .... 180 mph

*These velocities occurred during hurricanes. Theoretically, much higher velocities are possible within the vortex of a tornado, but no measurement with an anemometer has ever been made. The U.S. Weather Bureau's experimental Doppler radar equipment, a device which permits direct measurement of the high speeds in a spinning tornado funnel, received its first big test in the Wichita Falls tornado of April 2, 1958. This was the first tornado tracked by the Doppler radar, and for the first time in history, rotating winds up to 280 mph were clocked.

Calendar For 1996 and 1997

The subsequent calendars were calculated principally from data in the U.S. Naval Observatory's computer program, **MICA for Macintosh, 1990-1999**, and from its publication, **Astronomical Phenomena** for **1996** and **1997**.

Times listed here are **Central Standard Time**, except for the period from 2:00 a.m. on the first Sunday in April until 2:00 a.m. on the last Sunday in October, when **Daylight Saving Time,** which is one hour later than Central Standard Time, is in effect.

All of Texas is in the Central Time Zone except El Paso and Hudspeth counties and the northwest corner of Culberson County, which observe **Mountain Time** (see accompanying map). Mountain Time is one hour earlier than Central Time.

All times are figured for the intersection of 99° 10' west longitude and 31° 23' north latitude, which is about 15 miles northeast of Brady, McCulloch County. This point is the **approximate geographical center of the state.**

To get the time of sunrise or sunset, moonrise or moonset for any point in Texas, apply the following rules: Add four minutes to the time given in this calendar for each degree of longitude that any given place lies west of the 99th meridian, and subtract four minutes for each degree of longitude such place lies east of the 99th meridian.

At times there will be considerable variation for distances north and south of the line of 31° 23' north latitude, but the rule for calculating it would be complicated. The procedure given above will get sufficiently close results.

An accompanying map shows the intersection for which all time is calculated, with some Texas major cities and their longitudes. These make it convenient to calculate time at any given point.

Planetary Configurations and Phenomena

In the center column of the calendar on following pages are given the phenomena and planetary configurations of heavens for 1996 and 1997. Below is an explanation of the signs of the Sun, Moon and planets, and symbols used in the tables:

☉ The Sun	● The Earth	⛢ Uranus
☾ The Moon	♂ Mars	♆ Neptune
☿ Mercury	♃ Jupiter	♇ Pluto
♀ Venus	♄ Saturn	

Aspects

☌ This symbol appearing before the symbols for heavenly bodies means they are "in conjunction," that is, having the same longitude as applies to the sky and appearing near each other.

☍ This symbol means that the two heavenly bodies are in "opposition," or differ by 180 degrees of longi-

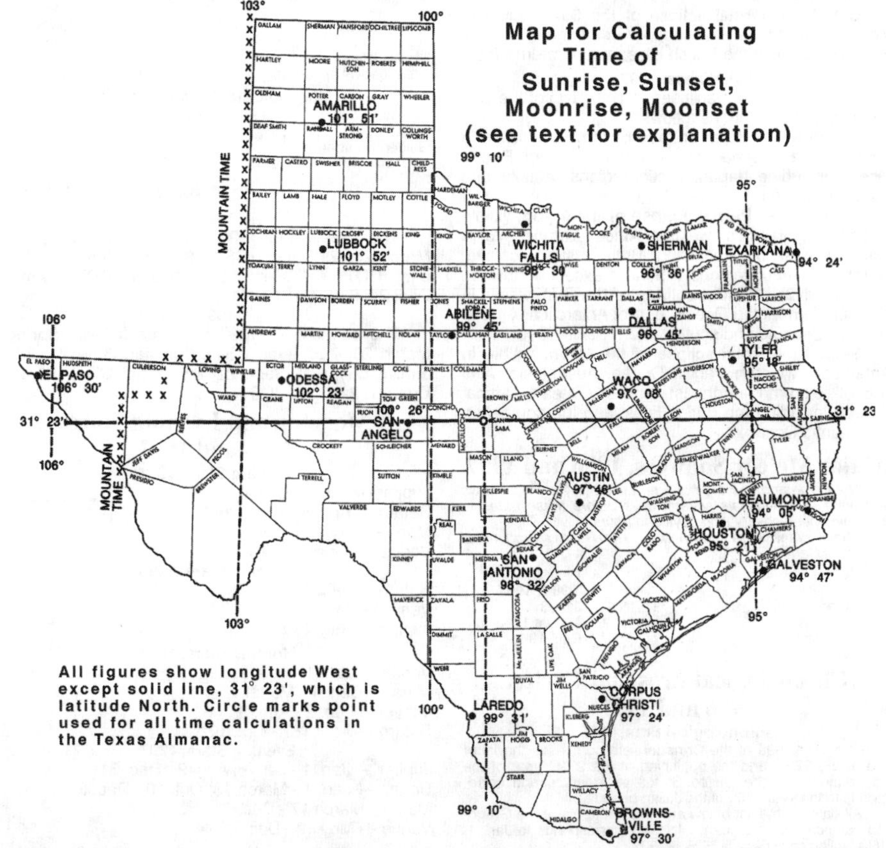

tude.

Common Astronomical Terms

★ **Aphelion** — Point at which a planet's orbit is farthest from the sun.

★ **Perihelion** — Point at which a planet's orbit is nearest the sun.

★ **Apogee** — That point of the moon's orbit farthest from the earth.

★ **Perigee** — That point of the moon's orbit nearest the earth.

★ **Aspect** — Apparent situation of a planet with respect to another body.

Eclipses, 1996 and 1997

Eclipses, 1996

There will be four eclipses during 1996, two of the Sun and two of the Moon, as follows:

April 3-4 — Total eclipse of the Moon, visible in part of Antarctica; western Asia; Africa; Europe, including the British Isles; Iceland; Greenland; South America; West Indies; and the eastern part of North America.

April 17-18 — Partial eclipse of the Sun, visible in New Zealand, part of Antarctica and the southern Pacific Ocean.

Sept. 27 — Total eclipse of the Moon, visible in part of Antarctica; extreme western Asia; Africa; Europe, including the British Isles; Iceland; Greenland; Arctic regions; the Americas except Alaska; and eastern part of the Pacific Ocean.

Oct. 12 — Partial eclipse of the Sun, visible in extreme northeast Canada; Greenland; Iceland; Europe, including the British Isles; and northern Africa.

Eclipses, 1997

There will be four eclipses in 1997, two of the Sun and two of the Moon, as follows:

March 8-9 — Total eclipse of the Sun, visible in eastern part of Asia except south, northern Pacific Ocean including Japan, Arctic regions, Alaska and western Canada.

March 24 — Partial eclipse of the Moon, visible in part of Antarctica; western Africa; Europe except extreme east but including British Isles; Iceland; Greenland; Arctic regions; Americas except northwest.

Sept. 1-2 — Partial eclipse of the Sun, visible in southeastern Indian Ocean, part of Antarctica, Australia, New Zealand and southwestern Pacific Ocean.

Sept. 16 — Total eclipse of the Moon, visible in Antarctica, western Pacific Ocean, Australasia, Asia except extreme northeast, Indian Ocean, Africa, Europe including the British Isles, and the southeastern Atlantic Ocean.

Major Meteor Showers, 1996 and 1997

Note: These dates are not firm. Listen to your local news and weather broadcasts several days before these dates to determine peak observation days and hours.

These dates were furnished by The Royal Astronomical Society of Canada.

Meteor Shower	Peak Day 1996 & 1997
Quadrantids	Jan. 3
Perseids	August 12
Geminids	Dec. 13

Chronological Eras and Cycles, 1996 and 1997

Chronological Eras, 1996

The year 1996 of the **Christian** era comprises the latter part of the 220th and the beginning of the 221st year of the independence of the United States of America, and corresponds to the year 6709 of the Julian period.

All dates in the list below are given in terms of the Gregorian calendar, in which Jan. 14, 1996, corresponds to Jan. 1, 1996, Julian calendar.

Era	Year	Begins
Byzantine	7505	Sept. 14
Jewish (A.M.)*	5757	Sept. 13
Chinese (Ding-chou)	4633	Feb. 19
Roman (A.U.C.)	2749	Jan. 14
Nabonassar	2745	April 24
Japanese	2656	Jan. 1
Grecian (Seleucidae)	2308	Sept. 14 or Oct. 14
Indian (Saka)	1918	March 21
Diocletian	1713	Sept. 11
Islamic (Hegira)*	1417	May 18

**Year begins at sunset.*

Chronological Cycles, 1996

Dominical Letter	GF	Julian Period	6709
Epact	10	Roman Indiction	4
Golden Number or Lunar Cycle	II	Solar Cycle	17

Chronological Eras, 1997

The year 1997 of the **Christian** era comprises the latter part of the 221st and the beginning of the 222nd year of the independence of the United States of America, and corresponds to the year 6710 of the Julian period.

All dates in the list below are given in terms of the Gregorian calendar, in which 1997 January 14 corresponds to 1997 January 1 of the Julian calendar:

Era	Year	Begins
Byzantine	7506	Sept. 14
Jewish (A.M.)*	5758	Oct. 1
Chinese (Ding-chou)	4634	Feb. 7
Roman (A.U.C.)	750	Jan. 14
Nabonassar	2746	April 24
Japanese	2657	Jan. 1
Grecian (Seleucidae)	2309	Sept. 14 or Oct. 14
Indian (Saka)	1919	March 22
Diocletian	1714	Sept. 11
Islamic (Hegira)*	1418	May 8

**Year begins at sunset.*

Chronological Cycles, 1997

Dominical Letter	E	Julian Period	6710
Epact	21	Roman Indiction	5
Golden Number or Lunar Cycle	III	Solar Cycle	I8

The Seasons, 1996 and 1997

1996

The seasons of 1996 begin as follows: **Spring**, March 20, 2:03 a.m. (CST); **Summer**, June 20, 9:24 p.m. (CDT); **Fall**, Sept. 22, 1:00 a.m. (CDT); **Winter**, Dec. 21, 8:06 a.m. (CST).

1997

The seasons of 1997 begin as follows: **Spring**, March 20, 7:55 a.m. (CST); **Summer**, June 21, 3:20 a.m. (CDT); **Fall**, Sept. 22, 6:56 p.m. (CDT); **Winter**, Dec. 21, 2:07 p.m. (CST).

Morning and Evening Stars, 1996 and 1997

Morning Stars, 1996

Jupiter — Jan. 1 - July 4
Saturn — April 4 - Sept. 26
Mars — May 14 - Dec. 31
Venus — June 17 - Dec. 31

Evening Stars, 1996

Saturn — Jan. 1 - Feb. 29; Sept. 26 - Dec. 31
Venus — Jan. 1 - June 4
Jupiter — July 4 - Dec. 31

Morning Stars, 1997

Venus — Jan. 1 - Feb. 21
Mars — Jan. 1 - March 17
Jupiter —Feb. 2 - Aug. 9
Saturn — April 187 - Oct. 10

Evening Stars, 1997

Jupiter — Jan. 1 - Jan. 6; Aug. 9 - Dec. 31
Saturn — Jan. 1 - March 13; Oct. 10 - Dec. 31
Mars — March 17 - Dec. 31
Venus — May 12 - Dec. 31 ☆

Holidays, Anniversaries and Festivals, 1996 and 1997

Bank Holidays — By act of the Sixty-second Legislature, 1971, legally prescribed (compulsory) bank holidays in Texas, in addition to **Sundays**, are **New Year's Day, Washington's Birthday (Presidents' Day), Memorial Day, Independence Day, Labor Day, Columbus Day, Veterans Day, Thanksgiving** and **Christmas**. The 69th Legislature, 1985-1986, established **Martin Luther King's birthday** as an official bank holiday; the 72nd Legislature in 1991 made it an official state holiday and dropped Columbus Day. Should New Year's Day, Independence Day or Christmas fall on Saturday, banks close the preceding Friday. Should any of the three fall on Sunday, banks close the next Monday. At their option, banks may close one day a week besides Sunday, usually Saturday, but on any day selected by individual banks. Prior to this act, permitting a 5-day banking week, bank holidays included all holidays in the list below marked with asterisk (*), double asterisk (**) or dagger (†)

1996

*New Year's Day	Monday, Jan. 1
Epiphany	Saturday, Jan. 6
Sam Rayburn Day	Saturday, Jan. 6
**Confederate Heroes Day	Monday, Jan. 15
*‡‡Martin Luther King's Birthday	Monday, Jan. 15
§§First Day of Ramadan (Tabular)	Monday, Jan. 22
Ash Wednesday	Wednesday, Feb. 21
‡‡Presidents' Day	Wednesday, Feb. 21
†Texas Independence Day	Saturday, March 2
‡Sam Houston Day	Saturday, March 2
‡Texas Flag Day	Saturday, March 2
Primary Election Day (Presidential)	Tuesday, March 12
Palm Sunday	Sunday, March 31
¶First Day of Passover (Pesach)	Thursday, April 4
Good Friday	Friday, April 5
Easter Day	Sunday, April 7
†San Jacinto Day	Sunday, April 21
§Arbor Day	Monday, April 29
Mother's Day	Sunday, May 12
Ascension Day	Thursday, May 16
§§Islamic New Year (Tabular)	Sunday, May 19
Armed Forces Day	Tuesday, May 21
¶First Day of Shavuot (Feast of Weeks)	Friday, May 24
Whit Sunday - Pentecost	Sunday, May 26
‡‡Memorial Day	Monday, May 27
Trinity Sunday	Sunday, June 2
Flag Day (U.S.)	Friday, June 14
†Emancipation Day in Texas	Wednesday, June 19
Father's Day	Sunday, June 9
*Independence Day	Thursday, July 4
†Lyndon B. Johnson's Birthday	Tuesday, Aug. 27
*Labor Day	Monday, Sept. 2
¶First Day of Rosh Hashanah	Saturday, Sept.14
¶Day of Atonement (Yom Kippur)	Monday, Sept. 23
¶First Day of Sukkot	Saturday, Sept. 28
‡‡Columbus Day	Monday, Oct. 14
Halloween	Thursday, Oct. 31
*General Election Day	Tuesday, Nov. 5
*Veterans Day	Monday, Nov. 11
*Thanksgiving Day	Thursday, Nov. 28
¶First Day of Hanukkah	Thursday, Nov. 28
First Sunday in Advent	Sunday, Dec. 1
*Christmas Day	Wednesday, Dec. 25

1997

*New Year's Day	Wednesday, Jan. 1
Epiphany	Monday, Jan. 6
Sam Rayburn Day	Monday, Jan. 6
§§First Day of Ramadan (Tabular)	Friday, Jan. 10
**Confederate Heroes Day	Monday, Jan. 20
*‡‡Martin Luther King's Birthday	Monday, Jan. 20
Inauguration Day	Monday, Jan. 20
Ash Wednesday	Wednesday, Feb. 12
‡‡Presidents' Day	Monday, Feb. 17
†Texas Independence Day	Sunday, March 2
‡Sam Houston Day	Sunday, March 2
‡Texas Flag Day	Sunday, March 2
Palm Sunday	Sunday, March 23
Good Friday	Friday, March 28
Easter Day	Sunday, March 30
†San Jacinto Day	Monday, April 21
¶First Day of Passover (Pesach)	Tuesday, April 22
§Arbor Day	Friday, April 25
Ascension Day	Thursday, May 8
§§Islamic New Year (Tabular)	Friday, May 9
Mother's Day	Sunday, May 11
Armed Forces Day	Saturday, May 17
Whit Sunday - Pentecost	Sunday, May 18
Trinity Sunday	Sunday, May 25
‡‡Memorial Day	Monday, May 26
Father's Day	Sunday, June 8
¶First Day of Shavuot (Feast of Weeks)	Wed., June 11
Flag Day (U.S.)	Saturday, June 14
†Emancipation Day in Texas	Thursday, June 19
*Independence Day	Friday, July 4
†Lyndon B. Johnson's Birthday	Wednesday, Aug. 27
*Labor Day	Monday, Sept. 1
¶First Day of Rosh Hashanah	Thursday, Oct. 2
¶Day of Atonement (Yom Kippur)	Saturday, Oct. 11
‡‡Columbus Day	Monday, Oct. 13
¶First Day of Sukkot	Thursday, Oct. 16
Halloween	Friday, Oct. 31
*Veterans Day	Tuesday, Nov. 11
*Thanksgiving Day	Thursday, Nov. 27
First Sunday in Advent	Sunday, Nov. 30
¶First Day of Hanukkah	Saturday, Dec. 6
*Christmas Day	Thursday, Dec. 25
§§First Day of Ramadan	Wednesday, Dec. 31

In these tables, the Jewish (¶) and Islamic (§§) dates, are tabular dates, which begin at sunset on the previous evening and end at sunset on the date listed above.

** Asterisk designates national holidays that are also state holidays by act of the Texas Legislature.*

†Legal holiday in Texas only.

‡"Special observance days," set aside by Texas Legislature. They are not legal holidays, though two of them fall on March 2, which is otherwise designated as a state legal holiday, except for bank closing.

§A "special observance day" by resolution of the Texas Legislature but also observed by legislative enactment in many other states.

***In 1973, the Texas Legislature made Lyndon B. Johnson's Birthday, Aug. 27, a state holiday and made Jan. 19 Confederate Heroes Day, combining the birthdays of Robert E. Lee (Jan. 19) and Jefferson Davis (June 3).*

††Thanksgiving Day in Texas was designated as the "fourth Thursday in November" by the 55th Legislature, 1957. This made the state Thanksgiving coincide with the national holiday in all years. Prior to that Texas had, beginning with 1939, celebrated separate national and state Thanksgiving Days in all Novembers having five Thursdays. Texas, first by governor's proclamation, and by legislative resolution after 1951, continued to observe the last Thursday, until changed in 1957 to coincide in all years with the national holiday.

‡‡Starting in 1971, these changes were made in official holidays by the U.S. and Texas governments to give employees 3-day holiday weekends: Columbus Day made national holiday and set for second Monday in October; Presidents' Day, combining Washington's and Lincoln's birthdays (Feb. 15 and Feb. 12, respectively), will be observed on third Monday in February; Memorial Day will be observed on last Monday in May (was May 31). The addition of Martin Luther King Jr's. birthday to this list was effective in 1986 (bank holiday only in Texas until 1992, when it became an official state holiday).

Calendar for 1996

Times are **Central Standard Time**, except from April 7 to Oct. 27, during which **Daylight Saving Time** is observed. **Boldface times for moonrise and moonset** indicate p.m. Times are figured for the point **99° 10' West and 31° 23' North,** the approximate center of the state. **See page 119 for explanation of how to get the approximate time at any other Texas point.**

1st Month — January, 1996 — 31 Days

Moon's Phases — Full, Jan. 5, 2:52 p.m.; Last Qtr., Jan. 13, 2:47 p.m.; New, Jan. 20, 6:51 a.m.; First Qtr., Jan. 27, 5:15 a.m.

Day of Year	Day of Month	Day of Week	Planetary Configurations and Phenomena	*Hour of Sunrise	*Hour of Sunset	*Hour of Moonrise	*Hour of Moonset
1	1	Mo.	♂ ☌ ♆	7:09	5:45	**2:54**	3:54
2	2	Tu.	☿ Greatest Elong. E.	7:09	5:45	**3:37**	4:47
3	3	We.		7:09	5:46	**4:23**	5:37
4	4	Th.	● at Perihelion	7:10	5:47	**5:11**	6:26
5	5	Fr.	☾ at Apogee	7:10	5:48	**6:02**	7:11
6	6	Sa.		7:10	5:48	**6:54**	7:53
7	7	Su.	♂ ☍ ♅	7:10	5:49	**7:46**	8:32
8	8	Mo.		7:10	5:50	**8:39**	9:09
9	9	Tu.	☿ Stationary	7:10	5:51	**9:33**	9:45
10	10	We.		7:10	5:52	**10:27**	10:19
11	11	Th.		7:10	5:52	**11:23**	10:53
12	12	Fr.		7:10	5:53	. . .	11:28
13	13	Sa.		7:10	5:54	12:20	**12:05**
14	14	Su.		7:10	5:55	1:19	**12:45**
15	15	Mo.	♆ ☌ ☉	7:10	5:56	2:20	**1:30**
16	16	Tu.		7:10	5:57	3:23	**2:20**
17	17	We.		7:10	5:58	4:27	**3:17**
18	18	Th.	♃ ♂ ☾	7:10	5:59	5:30	**4:20**
19	19	Fr.	☾ at Perigee	7:09	5:59	6:29	**5:27**
20	20	Sa.		7:09	6:00	7:24	**6:36**
21	21	Su.	♅ ☌ ☉	7:09	6:01	8:13	**7:45**
22	22	Mo.		7:09	6:02	8:58	**8:51**
23	23	Tu.	♀ ☌ ☾	7:08	6:03	9:40	**9:55**
24	24	We.		7:08	6:04	10:19	**10:57**
25	25	Th.		7:08	6:05	10:57	**11:56**
26	26	Fr.		7:07	6:06	11:34	. . .
27	27	Sa.		7:07	6:07	**12:13**	12:53
28	28	Su.		7:06	6:08	**12:53**	1:48
29	29	Mo.		7:06	6:09	**1:36**	2:42
30	30	Tu.	☿ Stationary	7:05	6:09	**2:21**	3:33
31	31	We.		7:05	6:10	**3:08**	4:22

2nd Month — February 1996 — 29 Days

Moon's Phases — Full, Feb. 4, 9:59 a.m.; Last Qtr., Feb. 12, 2:38 a.m.; New, Feb. 18, 5:31 p.m.; First Qtr., Feb. 25, 11:53 p.m.

Day of Year	Day of Month	Day of Week	Planetary Configurations and Phenomena	*Hour of Sunrise	*Hour of Sunset	*Hour of Moonrise	*Hour of Moonset
32	1	Th.	☾ at Apogee	7:04	6:11	**3:57**	5:08
33	2	Fr.		7:04	6:12	**4:49**	5:51
34	3	Sa.		7:03	6:13	**5:41**	6:32
35	4	Su.		7:02	6:14	**6:34**	7:10
36	5	Mo.		7:02	6:15	**7:28**	7:46
37	6	Tu.		7:01	6:16	**8:23**	8:21
38	7	We.		7:00	6:17	**9:18**	8:56
39	8	Th.		7:00	6:17	**10:14**	9:31
40	9	Fr.		6:59	6:18	**11:12**	10:07
41	10	Sa.		6:58	6:19	. . .	10:45
42	11	Su.	● through ♄ ring-plane	6:57	6:20	12:11	11:27
43	12	Mo.		6:56	6:21	1:12	**12:13**
44	13	Tu.		6:56	6:22	2:13	**1:05**
45	14	We.		6:55	6:23	3:14	**2:03**
46	15	Th.	♃ ☌ ☾	6:54	6:23	4:13	**3:06**
47	16	Fr.	♆ ☌ ☾	6:53	6:24	5:08	**4:12**
48	17	Sa.	☾ at Perigee	6:52	6:25	5:59	**5:20**
49	18	Su.		6:51	6:26	6:46	**6:27**
50	19	Mo.		6:50	6:27	7:30	**7:33**
51	20	Tu.	♄ ☌ ☾	6:49	6:28	8:11	**8:37**
52	21	We.		6:48	6:28	8:51	**9:40**
53	22	Th.		6:47	6:29	9:30	**10:39**
54	23	Fr.		6:46	6:30	10:09	**11:37**
55	24	Sa.		6:45	6:31	10:50	. . .
56	25	Su.		6:44	6:31	11:32	12:33
57	26	Mo.		6:43	6:32	**12:17**	1:26
58	27	Tu.		6:42	6:57	**1:03**	2:16
59	28	We.		6:41	6:34	**1:52**	3:03
60	29	Th.	☾ at Apogee	6:40	6:34	**2:42**	3:48

*See text before January calendar for explanation.

3rd Month — March 1996 — 31 Days

Moon's Phases — Full, March 5, 3:24 a.m.; Last Qtr., March 12, 11:16 a.m.; New, March 19, 4:46 a.m.; First Qtr., March 26, 7:32 p.m.

Day of Year	Day of Month	Day of Week	Planetary Configurations and Phenomena	*Hour of Sunrise	*Hour of Sunset	*Hour of Moonrise	*Hour of Moonset
61	1	Fr.		6:39	6:35	**3:34**	4:29
62	2	Sa.		6:38	6:36	**4:27**	5:09
63	3	Su.		6:36	6:37	**5:21**	5:46
64	4	Mo.	♂ ☌ ☉	6:35	6:37	**6:16**	6:21
65	5	Tu.		6:34	6:38	**7:12**	6:57
66	6	We.		6:33	6:39	**8:08**	7:32
67	7	Th.	♇ Stationary	6:32	6:40	**9:06**	8:08
68	8	Fr.		6:31	6:40	**10:06**	8:46
69	9	Sa.		6:29	6:41	**11:06**	9:27
70	10	Su.		6:28	6:42	. . .	10:12
71	11	Mo.		6:27	6:42	12:06	11:02
72	12	Tu.		6:26	6:43	1:06	11:56
73	13	We.		6:25	6:44	2:04	**12:55**
74	14	Th.	♃ ☌ ☾	6:23	6:44	2:59	**1:58**
75	15	Fr.	♅ ☌ ☾	6:22	6:45	3:50	**3:02**
76	16	Sa.	☾ at Perigee	6:21	6:46	4:37	**4:08**
77	17	Su.	♄ ☌ ☉	6:20	6:46	5:21	**5:13**
78	18	Mo.		6:18	6:47	6:03	**6:17**
79	19	Tu.		6:17	6:48	6:43	**7:20**
80	20	We.	Spring Begins	6:16	6:48	7:22	**8:22**
81	21	Th.		6:15	6:49	8:02	**9:22**
82	22	Fr.	♂ ☌ ♄; ♀ ☌ ☾	6:13	6:50	8:43	**10:19**
83	23	Sa.	☿ ☌ ♄; ☿ ☌ ♂	6:12	6:50	9:26	**11:15**
84	24	Su.		6:11	6:51	10:10	. . .
85	25	Mo.		6:09	6:52	10:56	12:07
86	26	Tu.		6:08	6:52	11:45	12:56
87	27	We.	☾ at Apogee	6:07	6:53	**12:35**	1:42
88	28	Th.		6:06	6:54	**1:26**	2:25
89	29	Fr.		6:04	6:54	**2:18**	3:05
90	30	Sa.		6:03	6:55	**3:11**	3:43
91	31	Su.	♀ Greatest Elong. E.	6:02	6:56	**4:06**	4:19

4th Month — April, 1996 — 30 Days

Moon's Phases — Full, April 3, 6:08 p.m.; Last Qtr., April 10, 6:37 p.m.; New, April 17, 5:50 p.m.; First Qtr., April 25, 3:42 p.m.

Day of Year	Day of Month	Day of Week	Planetary Configurations and Phenomena	*Hour of Sunrise	*Hour of Sunset	*Hour of Moonrise	*Hour of Moonset
92	1	Mo.		6:00	6:56	**5:01**	4:54
93	2	Tu.		5:59	6:57	**5:58**	5:30
94	3	We.	Total Eclipse ☾	5:58	6:58	**6:56**	6:06
95	4	Th.		5:57	6:58	**7:56**	6:44
96	5	Fr.		5:55	6:59	**8:58**	7:25
97	6	Sa.		5:54	7:00	**10:00**	8:09
98	7	†Su.		6:53	8:00	. . .	9:58
99	8	Mo.		6:52	8:01	12:01	10:52
100	9	Tu.		6:50	8:02	1:00	11:50
101	10	We.	♃ ☌ ☾; ☾ at Perigee	6:49	8:02	1:55	**12:51**
102	11	Th.	♆ ☌ ☾; ♅ ☌ ☾	6:48	8:03	2:47	**1:54**
103	12	Fr.		6:47	8:04	3:34	**2:58**
104	13	Sa.		6:46	8:04	4:18	**4:01**
105	14	Su.		6:44	8:05	4:59	**5:04**
106	15	Mo.		6:43	8:06	5:38	**6:06**
107	16	Tu.		6:42	8:06	6:17	**7:07**
108	17	We.	Partial Eclipse ☉	6:41	8:07	6:56	**8:07**
109	18	Th.		6:40	8:08	7:36	**9:05**
110	19	Fr.	☿ ☌ ☾	6:38	8:08	8:18	**10:02**
111	20	Sa.		6:37	8:09	9:02	**10:57**
112	21	Su.	♀ ☌ ☾	6:36	8:10	9:48	**11:48**
113	22	Mo.		6:35	8:10	10:36	. . .
114	23	Tu.	☿ Greatest Elong. E.	6:34	8:11	11:26	12:36
115	24	We.	☾ at Apogee	6:33	8:12	**12:17**	1:20
116	25	Th.		6:32	8:12	**1:08**	2:01
117	26	Fr.		6:31	8:13	**2:01**	2:40
118	27	Sa.		6:30	8:14	**2:54**	3:16
119	28	Su.		6:29	8:14	**3:49**	3:51
120	29	Mo.	♆ Stationary	6:28	8:15	**4:44**	4:26
121	30	Tu.		6:27	8:16	**5:42**	5:02

†Daylight Saving Time begins at 2:00 a.m.

Calendar for 1996 (Cont'd.)

5th Month **May, 1996** **31 Days**

Moon's Phases — Full, May 3, 6:49 a.m.; Last Qtr., May 10, 12:05 a.m.; New, May 17, 6:47 a.m., First Qtr., May 25, 9:15 a.m.

Day of Year	Day of Month	Day of Week	Planetary Configurations and Phenomena	*Hour of Sunrise	*Hour of Sunset	*Hour of Moon-rise	*Hour of Moon-set
122	1	We.		6:26	8:16	**6:42**	5:39
123	2	Th.		6:25	8:17	**7:43**	6:19
124	3	Fr.		6:24	8:18	**8:46**	7:02
125	4	Sa.	☿ Stationary; ♃ Stationary	6:23	8:19	**9:50**	7:50
126	5	Su.		6:22	8:19	**10:52**	8:44
127	6	Mo.	☾ at Perigee	6:21	8:20	**11:50**	9:42
128	7	Tu.	♃ ☌ ☾	6:20	8:21	. . .	10:43
129	8	We.	♆ ☌ ☾	6:19	8:21	12:44	11:47
130	9	Th.	♅ ☌ ☾	6:18	8:22	1:33	**12:51**
131	10	Fr.		6:17	8:23	2:18	**1:55**
132	11	Sa.		6:17	8:23	2:59	**2:57**
133	12	Su.		6:16	8:24	3:39	**3:58**
134	13	Mo.	♄ ☌ ☾	6:15	8:25	4:17	**4:58**
135	14	Tu.	☿ Inferior; ♂ ☌ ☾	6:14	8:25	4:54	**5:57**
136	15	We.		6:14	8:26	5:33	**6:55**
137	16	Th.		6:13	8:27	6:14	**7:52**
138	17	Fr.		6:12	8:27	6:56	**8:47**
139	18	Sa.		6:12	8:28	7:41	**9:40**
140	19	Su.	♀ ☌ ☾	6:11	8:29	8:28	**10:29**
141	20	Mo.	♀ Stationary	6:10	8:29	9:18	**11:15**
142	21	Tu.		6:10	8:30	10:08	**11:58**
143	22	We.	♇ ☍; ☾ at Apogee	6:09	8:31	11:00	. . .
144	23	Th.		6:09	8:31	11:52	12:37
145	24	Fr.		6:08	8:32	**12:44**	1:14
146	25	Sa.		6:08	8:33	**1:38**	1:49
147	26	Su.		6:07	8:33	**2:32**	2:24
148	27	Mo.	☿ Stationary	6:07	8:34	**3:27**	2:58
149	28	Tu.		6:06	8:34	**4:25**	3:34
150	29	We.		6:06	8:35	**5:25**	4:11
151	30	Th.		6:06	8:36	**6:28**	4:53
152	31	Fr.	☿ ☌ ♂	6:05	8:36	**7:32**	5:38

6th Month **June, 1996** **30 Days**

Moon's Phases — Full, June 1, 3:48 p.m.; Last Qtr., June 8, 6:06 a.m.; New, June 15, 8:37 p.m.; First Qtr., June 24, 12:25 a.m.; Full, June 30, 10:59 p.m.

Day of Year	Day of Month	Day of Week	Planetary Configurations and Phenomena	*Hour of Sunrise	*Hour of Sunset	*Hour of Moon-rise	*Hour of Moon-set
153	1	Sa.		6:05	8:37	**8:36**	6:30
154	2	Su.		6:05	8:37	**9:38**	7:27
155	3	Mo.	☾ at Perigee	6:05	8:38	**10:36**	8:29
156	4	Tu.	♃ ☌ ☾; ♆ ☌ ☾	6:04	8:38	**11:29**	9:34
157	5	We.	♅ ☌ ☾	6:04	8:39	. . .	10:41
158	6	Th.		6:04	8:39	12:17	11:46
159	7	Fr.		6:04	8:40	1:00	**12:50**
160	8	Sa.		6:04	8:40	1:40	**1:52**
161	9	Su.		6:04	8:41	2:19	**2:52**
162	10	Mo.	☿ Greatest Elong W.	6:04	8:41	2:56	**3:51**
163	11	Tu.		6:04	8:41	3:34	**4:49**
164	12	We.		6:04	8:42	4:13	**5:46**
165	13	Th.	☿ ☌ ☾; ♂ ☌ ☾	6:04	8:42	4:54	**6:41**
166	14	Fr.		6:04	8:42	5:38	**7:34**
167	15	Sa.		6:04	8:43	6:24	**8:25**
168	16	Su.		6:04	8:43	7:12	**9:12**
169	17	Mo.		6:04	8:43	8:02	**9:56**
170	18	Tu.		6:04	8:44	8:53	**10:36**
171	19	We.	☾ at Apogee	6:04	8:44	9:45	**11:14**
172	20	Th.	Summer Begins	6:04	8:44	10:37	**11:50**
173	21	Fr.		6:05	8:44	11:30	. . .
174	22	Sa.		6:05	8:45	**12:23**	12:24
175	23	Su.	☿ ☌ ♀	6:05	8:45	**1:17**	12:58
176	24	Mo.		6:05	8:45	**2:12**	1:32
177	25	Tu.		6:06	8:45	**3:09**	2:07
178	26	We.		6:06	8:45	**4:09**	2:46
179	27	Th.		6:06	8:45	**5:11**	3:28
180	28	Fr.		6:07	8:45	**6:15**	4:15
181	29	Sa.	♀ ☌ ♂	6:07	8:45	**7:18**	5:09
182	30	Su.		6:08	8:45	**8:20**	6:09

*See text before January calendar for explanation.

7th Month **July, 1996** **31 Days**

Moon's Phases — Last Qtr., July 7, 1:56 p.m.; New, July 15, 11:16 a.m.; First Qtr., July 23, 2:50 p.m.; Full, July 30, 5:37 a.m.

Day of Year	Day of Month	Day of Week	Planetary Configurations and Phenomena	*Hour of Sunrise	*Hour of Sunset	*Hour of Moon-rise	*Hour of Moon-set
183	1	Mo.	☾ at Perigee; ♃ ☌ ☾	6:08	8:45	**9:17**	7:14
184	2	Tu.	♆ ☌ ☾; ♅ ☌ ☾	6:08	8:45	**10:09**	8:22
185	3	We.		6:09	8:45	**10:56**	9:30
186	4	Th.	♃ ☍	6:09	8:45	**11:39**	10:37
187	5	Fr.	● at Aphelion	6:10	8:45	. . .	11:42
188	6	Sa.		6:10	8:45	12:19	**12:45**
189	7	Su.	♄ ☌ ☾	6:11	8:44	12:58	**1:45**
190	8	Mo.		6:11	8:44	1:36	**2:44**
191	9	Tu.		6:12	8:44	2:15	**3:41**
192	10	We.		6:13	8:44	2:55	**4:37**
193	11	Th.	☿ Superior	6:13	8:43	3:37	**5:30**
194	12	Fr.	♀ ☌ ☾; ♂ ☌ ☾	6:14	8:43	4:22	**6:21**
195	13	Sa.		6:14	8:43	5:09	**7:09**
196	14	Su.		6:15	8:43	5:58	**7:54**
197	15	Mo.		6:16	8:42	6:49	**8:36**
198	16	Tu.	☾ at Apogee	6:16	8:42	7:40	**9:15**
199	17	We.	♀ Greatest Brilliancy	6:17	8:41	8:32	**9:51**
200	18	Th.	♆ ☍	6:17	8:41	9:25	**10:26**
201	19	Fr.	♄ Stationary	6:18	8:40	10:17	**11:00**
202	20	Sa.		6:19	8:40	11:10	**11:33**
203	21	Su.		6:19	8:39	**12:04**	. . .
204	22	Mo.		6:20	8:39	**12:59**	12:07
205	23	Tu.		6:21	8:38	**1:57**	12:44
206	24	We.		6:21	8:38	**2:56**	1:23
207	25	Th.	♅ ☍	6:22	8:37	**3:57**	2:06
208	26	Fr.		6:23	8:36	**4:59**	2:55
209	27	Sa.		6:23	8:36	**6:00**	3:51
210	28	Su.	♃ ☌ ☾	6:24	8:35	**6:59**	4:52
211	29	Mo.	♆ ☌ ☾; ♅ ☌ ☾	6:25	8:34	**7:54**	5:58
212	30	Tu.	☾ at Perigee	6:26	8:34	**8:45**	7:07
213	31	We.		6:26	8:33	**9:31**	8:16

8th Month **August, 1996** **31 Days**

Moon's Phases — Last Qtr., Aug. 6, 12:26 a.m.; New, Aug. 14, 2:35 a.m.; First Qtr., Aug. 21, 10:38 p.m.; Full, Aug. 28, 12:53 p.m.

Day of Year	Day of Month	Day of Week	Planetary Configurations and Phenomena	*Hour of Sunrise	*Hour of Sunset	*Hour of Moon-rise	*Hour of Moon-set
214	1	Th.		6:27	8:32	**10:14**	9:24
215	2	Fr.		6:28	8:31	**10:55**	10:30
216	3	Sa.	♄ ☌ ☾	6:28	8:30	**11:34**	11:33
217	4	Su.		6:29	8:30	. . .	**12:35**
218	5	Mo.		6:30	8:29	12:14	**1:34**
219	6	Tu.		6:30	8:28	12:55	**2:31**
220	7	We.		6:31	8:27	1:37	**3:25**
221	8	Th.		6:32	8:26	2:21	**4:18**
222	9	Fr.	♀ ☌ ☾	6:33	8:25	3:07	**5:07**
223	10	Sa.	♂ ☌ ☾	6:33	8:24	3:55	**5:53**
224	11	Su.		6:34	8:23	4:45	**6:35**
225	12	Mo.	☾ at Apogee	6:35	8:22	5:36	**7:15**
226	13	Tu.	♇ Stationary	6:35	8:21	6:28	**7:53**
227	14	We.		6:36	8:20	7:20	**8:28**
228	15	Th.		6:37	8:19	8:13	**9:02**
229	16	Fr.	☿ ☌ ☾	6:37	8:18	9:06	**9:36**
230	17	Sa.		6:38	8:17	10:00	**10:10**
231	18	Su.		6:39	8:16	10:54	**10:45**
232	19	Mo.	♀ Greatest Elong. W.	6:40	8:15	11:50	**11:23**
233	20	Tu.		6:40	8:14	**12:47**	. . .
234	21	We.	☿ Greatest Elong. E.	6:41	8:13	**1:46**	12:04
235	22	Th.		6:42	8:12	**2:46**	12:49
236	23	Fr.		6:42	8:10	**3:45**	1:40
237	24	Sa.	♃ ☌ ☾	6:43	8:09	**4:43**	2:36
238	25	Su.	♆ ☌ ☾	6:43	8:08	**5:39**	3:38
239	26	Mo.	♅ ☌ ☾	6:44	8:07	**6:31**	4:43
240	27	Tu.	☾ at Perigee	6:45	8:06	**7:19**	5:52
241	28	We.		6:45	8:05	**8:04**	7:00
242	29	Th.		6:46	8:03	**8:47**	8:08
243	30	Fr.	♄ ☌ ☾	6:47	8:02	**9:28**	9:14
244	31	Sa.		6:47	8:01	**10:09**	10:18

Calendar for 1996 (Cont'd.)

9th Month — September, 1996 — 30 Days

Moon's Phases — Last Qtr., Sept. 4, 2:07 p.m.; New, Sept. 12, 6:09 p.m.; First Qtr., Sept. 20, 6:24 a.m.; Full, Sept. 26, 9:52 p.m.

Day of Year	Day of Month	Day of Week	Planetary Configurations and Phenomena	*Hour of Sunrise	*Hour of Sunset	*Hour of Moon-rise	*Hour of Moon-set
245	1	Su.		6:48	8:00	**10:50**	11:20
246	2	Mo.		6:49	7:58	**11:33**	**12:20**
247	3	Tu.	♃ and ☿ Stationary	6:49	7:57	. . .	**1:17**
248	4	We.	♀☌♂	6:50	7:56	12:17	**2:11**
249	5	Th.		6:51	7:55	1:03	**3:02**
250	6	Fr.		6:51	7:53	1:51	**3:49**
251	7	Sa.		6:52	7:52	2:41	**4:33**
252	8	Su.	☾ at Apogee; ♂☌☾	6:52	7:51	3:31	**5:14**
253	9	Mo.		6:53	7:50	4:23	**5:52**
254	10	Tu.		6:54	7:48	5:15	**6:29**
255	11	We.		6:54	7:47	6:08	**7:03**
256	12	Th.		6:55	7:46	7:01	**7:37**
257	13	Fr.		6:55	7:44	7:55	**8:12**
258	14	Sa.		6:56	7:43	8:50	**8:47**
259	15	Su.		6:57	7:42	9:45	**9:24**
260	16	Mo.		6:57	7:41	10:42	**10:04**
261	17	Tu.	☿ Inferior	6:58	7:39	11:40	**10:47**
262	18	We.		6:58	7:38	**12:39**	**11:35**
263	19	Th.		6:59	7:37	**1:37**	. . .
264	20	Fr.		7:00	7:35	**2:34**	12:28
265	21	Sa.	♃☌☾	7:00	7:34	**3:29**	1:26
266	22	Su.	Fall Begins; ♆☌☾	7:01	7:33	**4:20**	2:28
267	23	Mo.		7:02	7:31	**5:09**	3:33
268	24	Tu.	☾ at Perigee	7:02	7:30	**5:54**	4:39
269	25	We.	☿ Stationary	7:03	7:29	**6:37**	5:46
270	26	Th.	♄☍; ♄☌☾	7:03	7:28	**7:19**	6:52
271	27	Fr.	Total Eclipse ☾	7:04	7:26	**8:00**	7:57
272	28	Sa.		7:05	7:25	**8:42**	9:01
273	29	Su.		7:05	7:24	**9:25**	10:03
274	30	Mo.		7:06	7:22	**10:09**	11:03

10th Month — October, 1996 — 31 Days

Moon's Phases — Last Qtr., Oct. 4, 7:06 a.m.; New, Oct. 12, 9:16 a.m.; First Qtr., Oct. 19, 1:10 p.m.; Full, Oct. 26, 9:12 a.m

Day of Year	Day of Month	Day of Week	Planetary Configurations and Phenomena	*Hour of Sunrise	*Hour of Sunset	*Hour of Moon-rise	*Hour of Moon-set
275	1	Tu.		7:06	7:21	**10:56**	**12:00**
276	2	We.		7:07	7:20	**11:44**	**12:53**
277	3	Th.	☿ Greatest Elong. W.	7:08	7:19	. . .	**1:43**
278	4	Fr.		7:08	7:17	12:34	**2:29**
279	5	Sa.		7:09	7:16	1:24	**3:11**
280	6	Su.	♆ Stationary; ☾ at Apogee	7:10	7:15	2:16	**3:50**
281	7	Mo.	♂☌☾	7:10	7:14	3:08	**4:27**
282	8	Tu.	♀☌☾	7:11	7:12	4:00	**5:02**
283	9	We.	♅ Stationary	7:11	7:11	4:53	**5:37**
284	10	Th.		7:12	7:10	5:47	**6:11**
285	11	Fr.		7:13	7:09	6:42	**6:46**
286	12	Sa.	Partial Eclipse ☉	7:13	7:08	7:38	**7:23**
287	13	Su.		7:14	7:07	8:35	**8:03**
288	14	Mo.		7:15	7:05	9:34	**8:46**
289	15	Tu.		7:15	7:04	10:34	**9:33**
290	16	We.		7:16	7:03	11:33	**10:25**
291	17	Th.		7:17	7:02	**12:30**	**11:21**
292	18	Fr.	♃☌☾	7:18	7:01	**1:25**	. . .
293	19	Sa.	♆☌☾; ♅☌☾	7:18	7:00	**2:17**	12:21
294	20	Su.		7:19	6:59	**3:04**	1:23
295	21	Mo.		7:20	6:58	**3:49**	2:27
296	22	Tu.	☾ at Perigee	7:20	6:57	**4:31**	3:32
297	23	We.		7:21	6:56	**5:12**	4:36
298	24	Th.	♄☌☾	7:22	6:55	**5:53**	5:40
299	25	Fr.		7:22	6:54	**6:34**	6:43
300	26	Sa.		7:23	6:53	**7:16**	7:46
301	†27	Su.		6:24	5:52	**7:00**	7:47
302	28	Mo.		6:25	5:51	**7:46**	8:46
303	29	Tu.		6:25	5:50	**8:34**	9:42
304	30	We.		6:26	5:49	**9:24**	10:34
305	31	Th.		6:27	5:48	**10:15**	11:22

*See text before January calendar for explanation.
† Daylight Saving Time ends at 2:00 a.m.

11th Month — November, 1996 — 30 Days

Moon's Phases — Last Qtr., Nov. 3, 1:52 a.m.; New, Nov. 10, 10:17 p.m.; First Qtr., Nov. 17, 7:10 p.m.; Full, Nov. 24, 10:11 p.m.

Day of Year	Day of Month	Day of Week	Planetary Configurations and Phenomena	*Hour of Sunrise	*Hour of Sunset	*Hour of Moon-rise	*Hour of Moon-set
306	1	Fr.	☿ Superior	6:28	5:47	**11:06**	**12:06**
307	2	Sa.		6:28	5:46	**11:58**	**12:47**
308	3	Su.	☾ at Apogee	6:29	5:46	. . .	**1:25**
309	4	Mo.		6:30	5:45	12:51	**2:01**
310	5	Tu.	♀☌☾	6:31	5:44	1:43	**2:35**
311	6	We.		6:32	5:43	2:36	**3:09**
312	7	Th.		6:32	5:43	3:30	**3:43**
313	8	Fr.	♀☌☾	6:33	5:42	4:26	**4:19**
314	9	Sa.		6:34	5:41	5:23	**4:58**
315	10	Su.		6:35	5:41	6:22	**5:40**
316	11	Mo.		6:36	5:40	7:23	**6:27**
317	12	Tu.		6:36	5:39	8:24	**7:18**
318	13	We.		6:37	5:39	9:24	**8:14**
319	14	Th.		6:38	5:38	10:21	**9:14**
320	15	Fr.	♃☌☾; ♆☌☾	6:39	5:38	11:15	**10:17**
321	16	Sa.	☾ at Perigee; ♅☌☾	6:40	5:37	**12:04**	**11:21**
322	17	Su.		6:41	5:37	**12:49**	. . .
323	18	Mo.		6:41	5:36	**1:31**	12:24
324	19	Tu.		6:42	5:36	**2:11**	1:27
325	20	We.	♄☌☾	6:43	5:36	**2:51**	2:30
326	21	Th.		6:44	5:35	**3:30**	3:32
327	22	Fr.		6:45	5:35	**4:10**	4:33
328	23	Sa.		6:45	5:35	**4:53**	5:33
329	24	Su.	♇☌☉	6:46	5:34	**5:37**	6:32
330	25	Mo.		6:47	5:34	**6:24**	7:30
331	26	Tu.		6:48	5:34	**7:14**	8:24
332	27	We.		6:49	5:34	**8:05**	9:14
333	28	Th.		6:49	5:34	**8:56**	10:01
334	29	Fr.		6:50	5:34	**9:49**	10:43
335	30	Sa.		6:51	5:33	**10:41**	11:23

12th Month — December, 1996 — 31 Days

Moon's Phases — Last Qtr., Dec. 2, 11:07 p.m.; New, Dec. 10, 10:58 a.m.; First Qtr., Dec.17, 1:31 a.m.; Full, Dec. 24, 2:41 p.m.

Day of Year	Day of Month	Day of Week	Planetary Configurations and Phenomena	*Hour of Sunrise	*Hour of Sunset	*Hour of Moon-rise	*Hour of Moon-set
336	1	Su.	☾ at Apogee	6:52	5:33	**11:33**	11:59
337	2	Mo.		6:53	5:33	. . .	**12:34**
338	3	Tu.	♂☌☾	6:53	5:33	12:25	**1:07**
339	4	We.	♄ Stationary	6:54	5:33	1:18	**1:41**
340	5	Th.		6:55	5:33	2:12	**2:15**
341	6	Fr.		6:56	5:34	3:08	**2:52**
342	7	Sa.		6:56	5:34	4:06	**3:32**
343	8	Su.	♀☌☾	6:57	5:34	5:06	**4:16**
344	9	Mo.		6:58	5:34	6:07	**5:06**
345	10	Tu.		6:58	5:34	7:09	**6:01**
346	11	We.		6:59	5:34	8:10	**7:01**
347	12	Th.	☾ at Perigee; ♃☌☾	7:00	5:35	9:07	**8:05**
348	13	Fr.	♆☌☾; ♅☌☾	7:00	5:35	10:00	**9:10**
349	14	Sa.		7:01	5:35	10:48	**10:16**
350	15	Su.	☿ Greatest Elong. E.	7:02	5:36	11:32	**11:21**
351	16	Mo.		7:02	5:36	**12:13**	. . .
352	17	Tu.	♄☌☾	7:03	5:36	**12:53**	12:24
353	18	We.		7:04	5:37	**1:31**	1:25
354	19	Th.		7:04	5:37	**2:10**	2:26
355	20	Fr.		7:05	5:38	**2:51**	3:26
356	21	Sa.	Winter Begins	7:05	5:38	**3:34**	4:24
357	22	Su.		7:06	5:39	**4:19**	5:21
358	23	Mo.	☿ Stationary	7:06	5:39	**5:06**	6:16
359	24	Tu.		7:06	5:40	**5:56**	7:07
360	25	We.		7:07	5:40	**6:48**	7:55
361	26	Th.		7:07	5:41	**7:40**	8:40
362	27	Fr.		7:08	5:42	**8:33**	9:21
363	28	Sa.		7:08	5:42	**9:25**	9:58
364	29	Su.	☾ at Apogee	7:08	5:43	**10:17**	10:34
365	30	Mo.		7:09	5:44	**11:09**	11:07
366	31	Tu.		7:09	5:44	. . .	11:40

Calendar for 1997

Times are **Central Standard Time**, except from April 6 to Oct. 26, during which **Daylight Saving Time** is observed. **Boldface times for moonrise and moonset** indicate p.m. Times are figured for the point **99° 10' West and 31° 23' North**, the approximate center of the state. **See page 119 for explanation of how to get the approximate time at any other Texas point.**

1st Month — January, 1997 — 31 Days

Moon's Phases — Last Qtr., Jan. 1, 7:46 p.m.; New, Jan. 8, 10:26 p.m.; First Qtr.,Jan. 15, 2:03 p.m.; Full, Jan. 23, 9:12 a.m.; Last Qtr., Jan. 31, 1:41 p.m.

Day of Year	Day of Month	Day of Week	Planetary Configurations and Phenomena	*Hour of Sunrise	Sunset	Moon-rise	Moon-set
1	1	We.	● at Perihelion	7:09	5:45	12:02	**12:14**
2	2	Th.		7:09	5:46	12:55	**12:48**
3	3	Fr.		7:10	5:47	1:51	**1:25**
4	4	Sa.		7:10	5:47	2:48	**2:06**
5	5	Su.		7:10	5:48	3:47	**2:52**
6	6	Mo.		7:10	5:49	4:49	**3:43**
7	7	Tu.	♀☌☾	7:10	5:50	5:50	**4:41**
8	8	We.		7:10	5:51	6:50	**5:44**
9	9	Th.		7:10	5:51	7:47	**6:51**
10	10	Fr.	☾ at Perigee	7:10	5:52	8:39	**7:59**
11	11	Sa.		7:10	5:53	9:27	**9:07**
12	12	Su.	☿☌♀; ☿ Stationary	7:10	5:54	10:11	**10:13**
13	13	Mo.	♄☌☾	7:10	5:55	10:52	**11:17**
14	14	Tu.		7:10	5:56	11:32	. . .
15	15	We.		7:10	5:57	**12:12**	12:20
16	16	Th.		7:10	5:57	**12:52**	1:20
17	17	Fr.	♆☌☉	7:10	5:58	**1:34**	2:19
18	18	Sa.		7:09	5:59	**2:18**	3:16
19	19	Su.	♃☌☉	7:09	6:00	**3:04**	4:11
20	20	Mo.		7:09	6:01	**3:52**	5:03
21	21	Tu.		7:09	6:02	**4:42**	5:52
22	22	We.		7:08	6:03	**5:34**	6:37
23	23	Th.	☿ Greatest Elong. W.	7:08	6:04	**6:26**	7:19
24	24	Fr.	♅☌☉	7:08	6:05	**7:19**	7:58
25	25	Sa.	☾ at Apogee	7:07	6:06	**8:11**	8:34
26	26	Su.		7:07	6:06	**9:03**	9:09
27	27	Mo.		7:06	6:07	**9:55**	9:42
28	28	Tu.	♂☌☾	7:06	6:08	**10:48**	10:15
29	29	We.		7:05	6:09	**11:41**	10:48
30	30	Th.		7:05	6:10	. . .	11:24
31	31	Fr.		7:04	6:11	12:36	**12:02**

2nd Month — February, 1997 — 28 Days

Moon's Phases — New, Feb. 7, 9:08 a.m.; First Qtr., Feb. 14, 2:58 a.m.; Full, Feb. 22, 4:28 a.m.

Day of Year	Day of Month	Day of Week	Planetary Configurations and Phenomena	*Hour of Sunrise	Sunset	Moon-rise	Moon-set
32	1	Sa.	♀☌♆	7:04	6:12	1:33	**12:43**
33	2	Su.		7:03	6:13	2:31	**1:30**
34	3	Mo.		7:02	6:14	3:31	**2:23**
35	4	Tu.		7:02	6:15	4:30	**3:22**
36	5	We.	♀☌♃; ☿☌☾	7:01	6:15	5:28	**4:26**
37	6	Th.	♆☌☾; ♂ Stationary	7:00	6:16	6:22	**5:33**
38	7	Fr.	☾ at Perigee; ♀☌♅	7:00	6:17	7:13	**6:43**
39	8	Sa.		6:59	6:18	8:01	**7:52**
40	9	Su.		6:58	6:19	8:45	**8:59**
41	10	Mo.	♄☌☾	6:57	6:20	9:28	**10:05**
42	11	Tu.		6:57	6:21	10:09	**11:09**
43	12	We.	☿☌♃	6:56	6:22	10:51	. . .
44	13	Th.		6:55	6:22	11:33	12:10
45	14	Fr.		6:54	6:23	**12:17**	1:10
46	15	Sa.		6:53	6:24	**1:02**	2:06
47	16	Su.	♃☌♅	6:52	6:25	**1:50**	2:59
48	17	Mo.		6:51	6:26	**2:39**	3:49
49	18	Tu.		6:50	6:27	**3:30**	4:35
50	19	We.		6:49	6:27	**4:22**	5:18
51	20	Th.		6:48	6:28	**5:14**	5:58
52	21	Fr.		6:47	6:29	**6:06**	6:35
53	22	Sa.		6:46	6:30	**6:58**	7:10
54	23	Su.		6:45	6:30	**7:50**	7:44
55	24	Mo.	♂☌☾	6:44	6:31	**8:43**	8:17
56	25	Tu.		6:43	6:32	**9:36**	8:50
57	26	We.		6:42	6:33	**10:30**	9:25
58	27	Th.		6:41	6:34	**11:25**	10:02
59	28	Fr.		6:40	6:34	. . .	10:41

*See text before January calendar for explanation.

3rd Month — March, 1997 — 31 Days

Moon's Phases — Last Qtr., March 2, 3:39 a.m.; New, March 8, 7:15 p.m.; First Qtr., March 15, 6:07 p.m.; Full, March 23, 10:46 p.m.; Last Qtr., March 31, 1:39 p.m.

Day of Year	Day of Month	Day of Week	Planetary Configurations and Phenomena	*Hour of Sunrise	Sunset	Moon-rise	Moon-set
60	1	Sa.		6:39	6:35	12:22	11:25
61	2	Su.		6:38	6:36	1:19	**12:13**
62	3	Mo.		6:37	6:37	2:16	**1:07**
63	4	Tu.		6:36	6:37	3:12	**2:06**
64	5	We.	♆☌☾	6:34	6:38	4:07	**3:10**
65	6	Th.	♅☌☾; ♃☌☾	6:33	6:39	4:58	**4:17**
66	7	Fr.		6:32	6:39	5:47	**5:25**
67	8	Sa.	Eclipse ☉; ☾ at Perigee	6:31	6:40	6:33	**6:34**
68	9	Su.		6:30	6:41	7:17	**7:42**
69	10	Mo.	♄☌☾	6:29	6:42	8:00	**8:49**
70	11	Tu.	☿Superior	6:27	6:42	8:43	**9:54**
71	12	We.		6:26	6:43	9:26	**10:56**
72	13	Th.		6:25	6:44	10:11	**11:56**
73	14	Fr.		6:24	6:44	10:57	. . .
74	15	Sa.		6:22	6:45	11:45	12:52
75	16	Su.		6:21	6:46	**12:35**	1:44
76	17	Mo.	♂ ☍	6:20	6:46	**1:25**	2:32
77	18	Tu.		6:19	6:47	**2:17**	3:16
78	19	We.		6:17	6:48	**3:09**	3:57
79	20	Th.	Spring Begins	6:16	6:48	**4:01**	4:35
80	21	Fr.		6:15	6:49	**4:53**	5:11
81	22	Sa.		6:14	6:50	**5:45**	5:45
82	23	Su.	♂☌☾	6:12	6:50	**6:38**	6:18
83	24	Mo.	Eclipse ☾	6:11	6:51	**7:31**	6:52
84	25	Tu.		6:10	6:52	**8:25**	7:26
85	26	We.		6:08	6:52	**9:21**	8:03
86	27	Th.		6:07	6:53	**10:17**	8:41
87	28	Fr.		6:06	6:54	**11:13**	9:23
88	29	Sa.		6:05	6:55	. . .	10:10
89	30	Su.	♄☌☉	6:02	6:56	12:10	11:01
90	31	Mo.		6:39	6:35	1:05	11:57

4th Month — April, 1997 — 30 Days

Moon's Phases — New, April 7, 6:03 a.m.; First Qtr., April 14, 12:01 p.m.; Full, April 22, 3:35 p.m.; Last Qtr., April 29, 9:37 p.m.

Day of Year	Day of Month	Day of Week	Planetary Configurations and Phenomena	*Hour of Sunrise	Sunset	Moon-rise	Moon-set
91	1	Tu.	♆☌☾	6:01	6:56	1:59	**12:56**
92	2	We.	♀ Superior	5:59	6:57	2:49	**2:00**
93	3	Th.	♃☌☾	5:58	6:58	3:37	**3:05**
94	4	Fr.		5:57	6:58	4:23	**4:12**
95	5	Sa.	☾ at Perigee	5:56	6:59	5:06	**5:19**
96	†6	Su.		6:54	7:59	6:49	**7:26**
97	7	Mo.		6:53	8:00	7:32	**8:32**
98	8	Tu.	☿☌☾	6:52	8:01	8:15	**9:37**
99	9	We.		6:51	8:01	9:00	**10:39**
100	10	Th.		6:49	8:02	9:47	**11:39**
101	11	Fr.		6:48	8:03	10:36	. . .
102	12	Sa.		6:47	8:03	11:26	12:34
103	13	Su.		6:46	8:04	**12:17**	1:26
104	14	Mo.		6:45	8:05	**1:10**	2:12
105	15	Tu.		6:43	8:05	**2:02**	2:55
106	16	We.		6:42	8:06	**2:54**	3:34
107	17	Th.	☾ at Apogee	6:41	8:07	**3:46**	4:10
108	18	Fr.		6:40	8:07	**4:38**	4:45
109	19	Sa.	♂☌☾	6:39	8:08	**5:31**	5:19
110	20	Su.		6:38	8:09	**6:24**	5:52
111	21	Mo.		6:36	8:09	**7:18**	6:26
112	22	Tu.		6:35	8:10	**8:14**	7:02
113	23	We.		6:34	8:11	**9:11**	7:40
114	24	Th.		6:33	8:11	**10:08**	8:22
115	25	Fr.	☿ Inferior	6:32	8:12	**11:06**	9:07
116	26	Sa.		6:31	8:13	. . .	9:57
117	27	Su.		6:30	8:14	12:02	10:52
118	28	Mo.		6:29	8:14	12:56	11:50
119	29	Tu.	♂ Stationary; ♆☌☾	6:28	8:15	1:47	**12:51**
120	30	We.	♃☌☾	6:27	8:16	2:34	**1:54**

†Daylight Saving Time begins at 2:00 a.m.

Calendar for 1997 (Cont'd.)

5th Month — May, 1997 — 31 Days

Moon's Phases — New, May 6, 3:48 p.m.; First Qtr., May 14, 5:56 a.m.; Full, May 22, 4:14 a.m., Last Qtr., May 29, 2:52 a.m.

Day of Year	Day of Month	Day of Week	Planetary Configurations and Phenomena	*Hour of Sunrise	Sunset	Moon-rise	Moon-set
121	1	Th.	♆ Stationary	6:26	8:16	3:19	**2:59**
122	2	Fr.		6:25	8:17	4:02	**4:03**
123	3	Sa.	☾ at Perigee	6:24	8:18	4:43	**5:08**
124	4	Su.	♄☌♄; ☿☌☾	6:23	8:18	5:24	**6:13**
125	5	Mo.		6:22	8:19	6:06	**7:18**
126	6	Tu.		6:21	8:20	6:50	**8:21**
127	7	We.	☿ Stationary	6:20	8:20	7:35	**9:23**
128	8	Th.		6:19	8:21	8:24	**10:21**
129	9	Fr.		6:18	8:22	9:14	**11:15**
130	10	Sa.		6:18	8:23	10:06	. . .
131	11	Su.		6:17	8:23	10:59	12:05
132	12	Mo.		6:16	8:24	11:52	12:50
133	13	Tu.	♅ Stationary	6:15	8:25	**12:45**	1:31
134	14	We.		6:15	8:25	**1:38**	2:09
135	15	Th.	☾ at Apogee	6:14	8:26	**2:30**	2:44
136	16	Fr.	♂☌☾	6:13	8:27	**3:22**	3:18
137	17	Sa.		6:12	8:27	**4:15**	3:51
138	18	Su.		6:12	8:28	**5:09**	4:25
139	19	Mo.		6:11	8:29	**6:04**	5:00
140	20	Tu.		6:11	8:29	**7:01**	5:37
141	21	We.		6:10	8:30	**7:59**	6:17
142	22	Th.	☿ Greatest Elong W.	6:09	8:31	**8:57**	7:02
143	23	Fr.		6:09	8:31	**9:55**	7:51
144	24	Sa.		6:08	8:32	**10:51**	8:45
145	25	Su.	♇☍	6:08	8:32	**11:44**	9:43
146	26	Mo.	♆☌☾	6:07	8:33	. . .	10:45
147	27	Tu.	♅☌☾	6:07	8:34	12:34	11:48
148	28	We.	♃☌☾	6:07	8:34	1:19	**12:52**
149	29	Th.	☾ at Perigee	6:06	8:35	2:02	**1:55**
150	30	Fr.		6:06	8:35	2:43	**2:59**
151	31	Sa.	♄☌☾	6:05	8:36	3:23	**4:02**

6th Month — June, 1997 — 30 Days

Moon's Phases — New, June 5, 2:05 a.m.; First Qtr., June 12, 11:53 p.m.; Full, June 20, 2:10 p.m.; Last Qtr., June 27, 7:43 a.m.

Day of Year	Day of Month	Day of Week	Planetary Configurations and Phenomena	*Hour of Sunrise	Sunset	Moon-rise	Moon-set
152	1	Su.		6:05	8:36	4:03	**5:05**
153	2	Mo.		6:05	8:37	4:45	**6:07**
154	3	Tu.	☿☌☾	6:05	8:38	5:28	**7:09**
155	4	We.		6:04	8:38	6:14	**8:08**
156	5	Th.		6:04	8:39	7:03	**9:04**
157	6	Fr.	♀☌☾	6:04	8:39	7:55	**9:56**
158	7	Sa.		6:04	8:40	8:48	**10:44**
159	8	Su.		6:04	8:40	9:41	**11:27**
160	9	Mo.		6:04	8:40	10:35	. . .
161	10	Tu.	♃ Stationary	6:04	8:41	11:28	12:07
162	11	We.		6:04	8:41	**12:21**	12:43
163	12	Th.	☾ at Apogee	6:04	8:42	**1:13**	1:18
164	13	Fr.	♂☌☾	6:04	8:42	**2:05**	1:51
165	14	Sa.		6:04	8:42	**2:58**	2:24
166	15	Su.		6:04	8:43	**3:52**	2:58
167	16	Mo.		6:04	8:43	**4:47**	3:33
168	17	Tu.		6:04	8:43	**5:45**	4:11
169	18	We.		6:04	8:44	**6:43**	4:54
170	19	Th.		6:04	8:44	**7:43**	5:41
171	20	Fr.		6:04	8:44	**8:41**	6:34
172	21	Sa.	Summer Begins	6:05	8:44	**9:37**	7:31
173	22	Su.	♆☌☾	6:05	8:44	**10:29**	8:33
174	23	Mo.	♅☌☾	6:05	8:45	**11:18**	9:38
175	24	Tu.	☾ at Perigee; ♃☌☾	6:05	8:45	. . .	10:43
176	25	We.	☿ Superior	6:06	8:45	12:03	11:48
177	26	Th.		6:06	8:45	12:45	**12:52**
178	27	Fr.		6:06	8:45	1:25	**1:56**
179	28	Sa.	♄☌☾	6:07	8:45	2:05	**2:58**
180	29	Su.		6:07	8:45	2:45	**4:00**
181	30	Mo.		6:07	8:45	3:27	**5:00**

*See text before January calendar for explanation.

7th Month — July, 1997 — 31 Days

Moon's Phases — New, July 4, 1:41 p.m.; First Qtr., July 12, 4:45 p.m.; Full, July 19, 10:21 p.m.; Last Qtr., July 26, 1:30 p.m.

Day of Year	Day of Month	Day of Week	Planetary Configurations and Phenomena	*Hour of Sunrise	Sunset	Moon-rise	Moon-set
182	1	Tu.		6:08	8:45	4:11	**5:59**
183	2	We.		6:08	8:45	4:58	**6:56**
184	3	Th.		6:09	8:45	5:47	**7:49**
185	4	Fr.	● at Aphelion	6:09	8:45	6:39	**8:38**
186	5	Sa.		6:10	8:45	7:32	**9:23**
187	6	Su.	♀☌☾	6:10	8:45	8:26	**10:05**
188	7	Mo.		6:11	8:45	9:19	**10:42**
189	8	Tu.		6:11	8:44	10:12	**11:18**
190	9	We.	☾ at Apogee	6:12	8:44	11:04	**11:51**
191	10	Th.		6:12	8:44	11:56	. . .
192	11	Fr.	♂☌☾	6:13	8:44	**12:48**	12:24
193	12	Sa.		6:14	8:43	**1:41**	12:57
194	13	Su.		6:14	8:43	**2:35**	1:31
195	14	Mo.		6:15	8:43	**3:31**	2:07
196	15	Tu.		6:15	8:42	**4:28**	2:47
197	16	We.		6:16	8:42	**5:26**	3:31
198	17	Th.		6:17	8:41	**6:25**	4:20
199	18	Fr.		6:17	8:41	**7:23**	5:15
200	19	Sa.		6:18	8:40	**8:18**	6:16
201	20	Su.	♅☌☾	6:19	8:40	**9:10**	7:20
202	21	Mo.	♃☌☾; ☾ at Perigee	6:19	8:39	**9:58**	8:27
203	22	Tu.		6:20	8:39	**10:42**	9:35
204	23	We.		6:21	8:38	**11:24**	10:41
205	24	Th.		6:21	8:38	. . .	11:47
206	25	Fr.	♄☌☾	6:22	8:37	12:05	**12:51**
207	26	Sa.		6:23	8:37	12:46	**1:53**
208	27	Su.		6:23	8:36	1:27	**2:54**
209	28	Mo.		6:24	8:35	2:11	**3:54**
210	29	Tu.	♅☍	6:25	8:34	2:56	**4:50**
211	30	We.		6:25	8:34	3:44	**5:44**
212	31	Th.		6:26	8:33	4:34	**6:34**

8th Month — August, 1997 — 31 Days

Moon's Phases — New, Aug. 3, 3:15 a.m.; First Qtr., Aug. 11, 7:43 a.m.; Full, Aug. 18, 5:57 a.m.; Last Qtr., Aug. 24, 9:24 p.m.

Day of Year	Day of Month	Day of Week	Planetary Configurations and Phenomena	*Hour of Sunrise	Sunset	Moon-rise	Moon-set
213	1	Fr.		6:27	8:32	5:26	**7:20**
214	2	Sa.	♄ Stationary	6:28	8:31	6:19	**8:03**
215	3	Su.	☿ Greatest Elong. E.	6:28	8:31	7:12	**8:42**
216	4	Mo.		6:29	8:30	8:05	**9:18**
217	5	Tu.	☿☌☾	6:30	8:29	8:58	**9:52**
218	6	We.	♀☌☾; ☾ at Apogee	6:30	8:28	9:50	**10:25**
219	7	Th.		6:31	8:27	10:42	**10:58**
220	8	Fr.		6:32	8:26	11:34	**11:31**
221	9	Sa.	♃☍◐ ♂☌☾	6:32	8:25	**12:26**	. . .
222	10	Su.		6:33	8:24	**1:20**	12:06
223	11	Mo.		6:34	8:23	**2:15**	12:43
224	12	Tu.		6:35	8:22	**3:12**	1:24
225	13	We.		6:35	8:21	**4:09**	2:09
226	14	Th.		6:36	8:20	**5:06**	3:00
227	15	Fr.		6:37	8:19	**6:02**	3:57
228	16	Sa.	☿Stationary; ♆☌☾	6:37	8:18	**6:55**	4:59
229	17	Su.	♃☌☾	6:38	8:17	**7:46**	6:05
230	18	Mo.		6:39	8:16	**8:33**	7:13
231	19	Tu.	☾ at Perigee	6:39	8:15	**9:18**	8:22
232	20	We.		6:40	8:14	**10:01**	9:30
233	21	Th.		6:41	8:13	**10:43**	10:37
234	22	Fr.		6:41	8:12	**11:25**	11:43
235	23	Sa.		6:42	8:11	. . .	**12:46**
236	24	Su.		6:43	8:10	12:09	**1:47**
237	25	Mo.		6:43	8:08	12:54	**2:45**
238	26	Tu.		6:44	8:07	1:42	**3:40**
239	27	We.		6:45	8:06	2:31	**4:32**
240	28	Th.		6:45	8:05	3:23	**5:19**
241	29	Fr.		6:46	8:04	4:15	**6:02**
242	30	Sa.		6:47	8:02	5:08	**6:42**
243	31	Su.	☿ Inferior	6:47	8:01	6:00	**7:19**

Calendar for 1997 (Cont'd.)

9th Month **September, 1997** **30 Days**

Moon's Phases — New, Sept. 1, 6:53 p.m.; First Qtr., Sept. 9, 8:33 p.m.; Full, Sept. 16, 1:52 p.m.; Last Qtr., Sept. 23, 8:37 a.m.

Day of			Planetary Configurations and Phenomena	*Hour of			
Year	Month	Week		Sunrise	Sunset	Moon-rise	Moon-set
244	1	Mo.	Eclipse ☉	6:48	8:00	6:53	**7:54**
245	2	Tu.	☾ at Apogee	6:48	7:59	7:45	**8:27**
246	3	We.		6:49	7:57	8:37	**9:00**
247	4	Th.		6:50	7:56	9:29	**9:33**
248	5	Fr.	♀☌☾	6:50	7:55	10:21	**10:07**
249	6	Sa.		6:51	7:54	11:14	**10:42**
250	7	Su.	♂☌☾	6:52	7:52	**12:08**	**11:21**
251	8	Mo.		6:52	7:51	**1:03**	. . .
252	9	Tu.	☿ Stationary	6:53	7:50	**1:58**	12:04
253	10	We.		6:53	7:49	**2:53**	12:51
254	11	Th.		6:54	7:47	**3:48**	1:43
255	12	Fr.	♆☌☾	6:55	7:46	**4:41**	2:41
256	13	Sa.	♃☌♄; ♅☌☾	6:55	7:45	**5:32**	3:43
257	14	Su.		6:56	7:43	**6:20**	4:49
258	15	Mo.		6:57	7:42	**7:06**	5:57
259	16	Tu.	Eclipse ☾; ☾ at Perigee	6:57	7:41	**7:50**	7:06
260	17	We.		6:58	7:40	**8:34**	8:15
261	18	Th.	♄☌☾	6:58	7:38	**9:18**	9:23
262	19	Fr.		6:59	7:37	**10:02**	10:30
263	20	Sa.		7:00	7:36	**10:49**	11:34
264	21	Su.		7:00	7:34	**11:37**	**12:36**
265	22	Mo.	Fall Begins	7:01	7:33	. . .	**1:34**
266	23	Tu.		7:01	7:32	12:27	**2:27**
267	24	We.		7:02	7:30	1:18	**3:16**
268	25	Th.		7:03	7:29	2:11	**4:01**
269	26	Fr.		7:03	7:28	3:03	**4:42**
270	27	Sa.		7:04	7:27	3:56	**5:20**
271	28	Su.		7:04	7:25	4:48	**5:55**
272	29	Mo.	☾ at Apogee	7:05	7:24	5:41	**6:29**
273	30	Tu.		7:06	7:23	6:32	**7:02**

10th Month **October, 1997** **31 Days**

Moon's Phases — New, Oct. 1, 11:53 a.m.; First Qtr., Oct. 9, 7:23 a.m.; Full, Oct. 15, 10:47 p.m.; Last Qtr., Oct. 22, 11:50 p.m.; New, Oct. 31, 4:02 a.m.

Day of			Planetary Configurations and Phenomena	*Hour of			
Year	Month	Week		Sunrise	Sunset	Moon-rise	Moon-set
274	1	We.		7:06	7:21	7:24	**7:34**
275	2	Th.		7:07	7:20	8:17	**8:08**
276	3	Fr.		7:08	7:19	9:10	**8:43**
277	4	Sa.		7:08	7:18	10:04	**9:21**
278	5	Su.	♀☌☾	7:09	7:16	10:58	**10:02**
279	6	Mo.	♂☌☾	7:09	7:15	11:53	**10:47**
280	7	Tu.		7:10	7:14	**12:47**	**11:37**
281	8	We.	♃ Stationary	7:11	7:13	**1:41**	. . .
282	9	Th.	♄☍	7:11	7:12	**2:33**	12:31
283	10	Fr.	♆☌☾; ☿☌☾	7:12	7:10	**3:23**	1:29
284	11	Sa.	♃☌☾	7:13	7:09	**4:10**	2:31
285	12	Su.		7:13	7:08	**4:55**	3:36
286	13	Mo.	☿ Superior	7:14	7:07	**5:39**	4:42
287	14	Tu.	☾ at Perigee	7:15	7:06	**6:22**	5:50
288	15	We.	♄☌☾	7:15	7:05	**7:06**	6:58
289	16	Th.		7:16	7:03	**7:50**	8:06
290	17	Fr.		7:17	7:02	**8:37**	9:13
291	18	Sa.		7:17	7:01	**9:26**	10:18
292	19	Su.		7:18	7:00	**10:16**	11:20
293	20	Mo.		7:19	6:59	**11:09**	**12:18**
294	21	Tu.		7:19	6:58	. . .	**1:10**
295	22	We.		7:20	6:57	12:03	**1:58**
296	23	Th.		7:21	6:56	12:56	**2:41**
297	24	Fr.		7:22	6:55	1:50	**3:20**
298	25	Sa.		7:22	6:54	2:43	**3:56**
299	†26	Su.	♀☌♂	6:23	5:53	2:35	**3:30**
300	27	Mo.	☾ at Apogee	6:24	5:52	3:27	**4:03**
301	28	Tu.		6:24	5:51	4:19	**4:36**
302	29	We.		6:25	5:50	5:11	**5:09**
303	30	Th.		6:26	5:49	6:04	**5:44**
304	31	Fr.		6:27	5:48	6:58	**6:21**

*See text before January calendar for explanation.
† Daylight Saving Time ends at 2:00 a.m.

11th Month **November, 1997** **30 Days**

Moon's Phases — First Qtr., Nov. 7, 3:44 p.m.; Full, Nov. 14, 8:13 a.m.; Last Qtr., Nov. 21, 5:59 p.m.; New, Nov. 29, 9:44 a.m.; First Qtr., Nov. 29, 8:15 p.m.

Day of			Planetary Configurations and Phenomena	*Hour of			
Year	Month	Week		Sunrise	Sunset	Moon-rise	Moon-set
305	1	Sa.		6:28	5:48	7:53	**7:01**
306	2	Su.		6:28	5:47	8:49	**7:45**
307	3	Mo.	♂☌☾	6:29	5:46	9:44	**8:33**
308	4	Tu.	♀☌☾	6:30	5:45	10:38	**9:26**
309	5	We.		6:31	5:44	11:30	**10:22**
310	6	Th.	♀ Greatest Elong. E.	6:31	5:44	**12:20**	**11:22**
311	7	Fr.	♃☌☾	6:32	5:43	**1:07**	. . .
312	8	Sa.		6:33	5:42	**1:51**	12:24
313	9	Su.		6:34	5:41	**2:33**	1:27
314	10	Mo.		6:35	5:41	**3:15**	2:32
315	11	Tu.	♄☌☾	6:35	5:40	**3:56**	3:38
316	12	We.	☾ at Perigee	6:36	5:40	**4:39**	4:44
317	13	Th.		6:37	5:39	**5:24**	5:51
318	14	Fr.		6:38	5:38	**6:11**	6:57
319	15	Sa.		6:39	5:38	**7:02**	8:01
320	16	Su.		6:39	5:37	**7:55**	9:02
321	17	Mo.		6:40	5:37	**8:49**	9:59
322	18	Tu.		6:41	5:37	**9:45**	10:50
323	19	We.		6:42	5:36	**10:40**	11:36
324	20	Th.		6:43	5:36	**11:34**	**12:17**
325	21	Fr.		6:44	5:35	. . .	**12:55**
326	22	Sa.		6:44	5:35	12:27	**1:30**
327	23	Su.	☾ at Apogee	6:45	5:35	1:19	**2:03**
328	24	Mo.		6:46	5:34	2:11	**2:36**
329	25	Tu.		6:47	5:34	3:03	**3:09**
330	26	We.		6:48	5:34	3:56	**3:43**
331	27	Th.	♇☌☉	6:48	5:34	4:50	**4:19**
332	28	Fr.	☿ Greatest Elong. E.	6:49	5:34	5:45	**4:58**
333	29	Sa.		6:50	5:34	6:41	**5:41**
334	30	Su.		6:51	5:33	7:37	**6:28**

12th Month **December, 1997** **31 Days**

Moon's Phases — Full, Dec. 6, 7:28 p.m.; Last Qtr., Dec. 14, 11:33 p.m.; New, Dec. 21, 8:24 p.m.; First Qtr., Dec. 28, 1:07 p.m.

Day of			Planetary Configurations and Phenomena	*Hour of			
Year	Month	Week		Sunrise	Sunset	Moon-rise	Moon-set
335	1	Mo.	♀☌☾	6:52	5:33	8:33	**7:21**
336	2	Tu.	♂☌☾	6:52	5:33	9:27	**8:17**
337	3	We.	♀☌☾; ♆☌☾	6:53	5:33	10:18	**9:16**
338	4	Th.	♅☌☾	6:54	5:33	11:07	**10:18**
339	5	Fr.	♃☌☾	6:55	5:33	11:51	**11:20**
340	6	Sa.		6:55	5:34	**12:34**	. . .
341	7	Su.	☿ Stationary; ♀☌♆	6:56	5:34	**1:14**	12:23
342	8	Mo.		6:57	5:34	**1:54**	1:27
343	9	Tu.	♄☌☾; ☾ at Perigee	6:58	5:34	**2:35**	2:31
344	10	We.		6:58	5:34	**3:17**	3:35
345	11	Th.	♀ Greatest Brilliancy	6:59	5:34	**4:02**	4:39
346	12	Fr.		7:00	5:35	**4:49**	5:43
347	13	Sa.		7:00	5:35	**5:40**	6:45
348	14	Su.		7:01	5:35	**6:34**	7:44
349	15	Mo.	♂☌♆	7:02	5:36	**7:30**	8:38
350	16	Tu.		7:02	5:36	**8:26**	9:28
351	17	We.	☿ Inferior; ♄ Stationary	7:03	5:36	**9:21**	10:12
352	18	Th.		7:03	5:37	**10:16**	10:52
353	19	Fr.		7:04	5:37	**11:09**	11:29
354	20	Sa.		7:04	5:38	. . .	**12:03**
355	21	Su.	Winter Begins	7:05	5:38	12:02	**12:36**
356	22	Mo.	♀☌♂	7:05	5:39	12:54	**1:08**
357	23	Tu.		7:06	5:39	1:46	**1:41**
358	24	We.		7:06	5:40	2:39	**2:16**
359	25	Th.	♀ Stationary	7:07	5:40	3:33	**2:53**
360	26	Fr.	♂☌♅	7:07	5:41	4:28	**3:34**
361	27	Sa.	☿ Stationary; ☿☌☾	7:08	5:42	5:25	**4:20**
362	28	Su.		7:08	5:42	6:22	**5:10**
363	29	Mo.		7:08	5:43	7:18	**6:06**
364	30	Tu.		7:09	5:44	8:12	**7:06**
365	31	We.	♆☌☾; ♀☌☾; ♅☌☾	7:09	5:44	9:03	**8:08**

201-Year Calendar, A.D. 1894-2094, Inclusive

Using this calendar, you can find the day of the week for any day of the month and year for the period 1894-2094, inclusive. To find any day of the week, first look in the table of common years or leap years for the year required. Under the months are figures that refer to the corresponding figures at the heads of the columns of days below. For example, To know on what day of the week March 2 fell in the year 1918, find 1918 in the table of years. In a parallel line under March is Fig. 5, which directs you to Col. 5 in the table of days, in which it will be seen that March 2 fell on Saturday.

Common Years, 1894 to 2094											Jan.	Feb.	Mar.	Apr.	May	June	July	Aug.	Sept.	Oct.	Nov.	Dec.
1894	1900	...	...	...	...	...	...	...	...	...	1	4	4	7	2	5	7	3	6	1	4	6
1906	1917	1923	1934	1945	1951	1962	1973	1979	1990	...												
2001	2007	2018	2029	2035	2046	2057	2063	2074	2085	2091												
1895	...	...	...	...	...	...	...	...	...	...	2	5	5	1	3	6	1	4	7	2	5	7
1901	1907	1918	1929	1935	1946	1957	1963	1974	1985	1991												
2002	2013	2019	2030	2041	2047	2058	2069	2075	2086	2097												
1897	...	...	...	...	...	...	...	...	...	...	5	1	1	4	6	2	4	7	3	5	1	3
1909	1915	1926	1937	1943	1954	1965	1971	1982	1993	1999												
2010	2021	2027	2038	2049	2055	2066	2077	2083	2094	2100												
1898	1910	1921	1927	1938	1949	1955	1966	1977	1983	1994	6	2	2	5	7	3	5	1	4	6	2	4
2005	2011	2022	2033	2039	2050	2061	2067	2078	2089	2095												
1899	1905	1911	1922	1933	1939	1950	1961	1967	1978	1989	7	3	3	6	1	4	6	2	5	7	3	5
1995	2006	2017	2023	2034	2045	2051	2062	2073	2079	2090												
1902	1913	1919	1930	1941	1947	1958	1969	1975	1986	1997	3	6	6	2	4	7	2	5	1	3	6	1
2003	2014	2025	2031	2042	2053	2059	2070	2081	2087	2098												
1903	1914	1925	1931	1942	1953	1959	1970	1981	1987	1998	4	7	7	3	5	1	3	6	2	4	7	2
2009	2015	2026	2037	2043	2054	2065	2071	2082	2093	2099												

Leap Years, 1894 to 2094									Jan.	Feb. 29	Mar.	Apr.	May	June	July	Aug.	Sept.	Oct.	Nov.	Dec.
...	...	1920	1948	1976	2004	2032	2060	2088	4	7	1	4	6	2	4	7	3	5	1	3
...	...	1924	1952	1980	2008	2036	2064	2092	2	5	6	2	4	7	2	5	1	3	6	1
...	...	1928	1956	1984	2012	2040	2068	2096	7	3	4	7	2	5	7	3	6	1	4	6
...	1904	1932	1960	1988	2016	2044	2072	...	5	1	2	5	7	3	5	1	4	6	2	4
1896	1908	1936	1964	1992	2020	2048	2076	...	3	6	7	3	5	1	3	6	2	4	7	2
...	1912	1940	1968	1996	2024	2052	2080	...	1	4	5	1	3	6	1	4	7	2	5	7
...	1916	1944	1972	2000	2028	2056	2084	...	6	2	3	6	1	4	6	2	5	7	3	5

1		2		3		4		5		6		7	
Mon.	1	Tues	1	Wed.	1	Thurs.	1	Fri.	1	Sat.	1	SUN.	1
Tues.	2	Wed.	2	Thurs.	2	Fri.	2	Sat.	2	SUN.	2	Mon.	2
Wed.	3	Thurs.	3	Fri.	3	Sat.	3	SUN.	3	Mon.	3	Tues.	3
Thurs.	4	Fri.	4	Sat.	4	SUN.	4	Mon.	4	Tues.	4	Wed.	4
Fri.	5	Sat.	5	SUN.	5	Mon.	5	Tues.	5	Wed.	5	Thurs.	5
Sat.	6	SUN.	6	Mon.	6	Tues.	6	Wed.	6	Thurs.	6	Fri.	6
SUN.	7	Mon.	7	Tues.	7	Wed.	7	Thurs.	7	Fri.	7	Sat.	7
Mon.	8	Tues.	8	Wed.	8	Thurs.	8	Fri.	8	Sat.	8	SUN.	8
Tues.	9	Wed.	9	Thurs.	9	Fri.	9	Sat.	9	SUN.	9	Mon.	9
Wed.	10	Thurs.	10	Fri.	10	Sat.	10	SUN.	10	Mon.	10	Tues.	10
Thurs.	11	Fri.	11	Sat.	11	SUN.	11	Mon.	11	Tues.	11	Wed.	11
Fri.	12	Sat.	12	SUN.	12	Mon.	12	Tues.	12	Wed.	12	Thurs.	12
Sat.	13	SUN.	13	Mon.	13	Tues.	13	Wed.	13	Thurs.	13	Fri.	13
SUN.	14	Mon.	14	Tues.	14	Wed.	14	Thurs.	14	Fri.	14	Sat.	14
Mon.	15	Tues.	15	Wed.	15	Thurs.	15	Fri.	15	Sat.	15	SUN.	15
Tues.	16	Wed.	16	Thurs.	16	Fri.	16	Sat.	16	SUN.	16	Mon.	16
Wed.	17	Thurs.	17	Fri.	17	Sat.	17	SUN.	17	Mon.	17	Tues.	17
Thurs.	18	Fri.	18	Sat.	18	SUN.	18	Mon.	18	Tues.	18	Wed.	18
Fri.	19	Sat.	19	SUN.	19	Mon.	19	Tues.	19	Wed.	19	Thurs.	19
Sat.	20	SUN.	20	Mon.	20	Tues.	20	Wed.	20	Thurs.	20	Fri.	20
SUN.	21	Mon.	21	Tues.	21	Wed.	21	Thurs.	21	Fri.	21	Sat.	21
Mon.	22	Tues.	22	Wed.	22	Thurs.	22	Fri.	22	Sat.	22	SUN.	22
Tues.	23	Wed.	23	Thurs.	23	Fri.	23	Sat.	23	SUN.	23	Mon.	23
Wed.	24	Thurs.	24	Fri.	24	Sat.	24	SUN.	24	Mon.	24	Tues.	24
Thurs.	25	Fri.	25	Sat.	25	SUN.	25	Mon.	25	Tues.	25	Wed.	25
Fri.	26	Sat.	26	SUN.	26	Mon.	26	Tues.	26	Wed.	26	Thurs.	26
Sat.	27	SUN.	27	Mon.	27	Tues.	27	Wed.	27	Thurs.	27	Fri.	27
SUN.	28	Mon.	28	Tues.	28	Wed.	28	Thurs.	28	Fri.	28	Sat.	28
Mon.	29	Tues.	29	Wed.	29	Thurs.	29	Fri.	29	Sat.	29	SUN.	29
Tues.	30	Wed.	30	Thurs.	30	Fri.	30	Sat.	30	SUN.	30	Mon.	30
Wed.	31	Thurs.	31	Fri.	31	Sat.	31	SUN.	31	Mon.	31	Tues.	31

Beginning of the Year

The Athenians began the year in June, the Macedonians in September, the Romans first in March and later in January, the Persians on Aug. 11, and the ancient Mexicans on Feb. 23. The Chinese year, which begins in late January or early February, is similar to the Mohammedan year. Both have 12 months of 29 and 30 days alternating, while in every 19 years, there are seven years that have 13 months. This does not quite fit the planetary movements, hence the Chinese have formed a cycle of 60 years, in which period 22 intercalary months occur

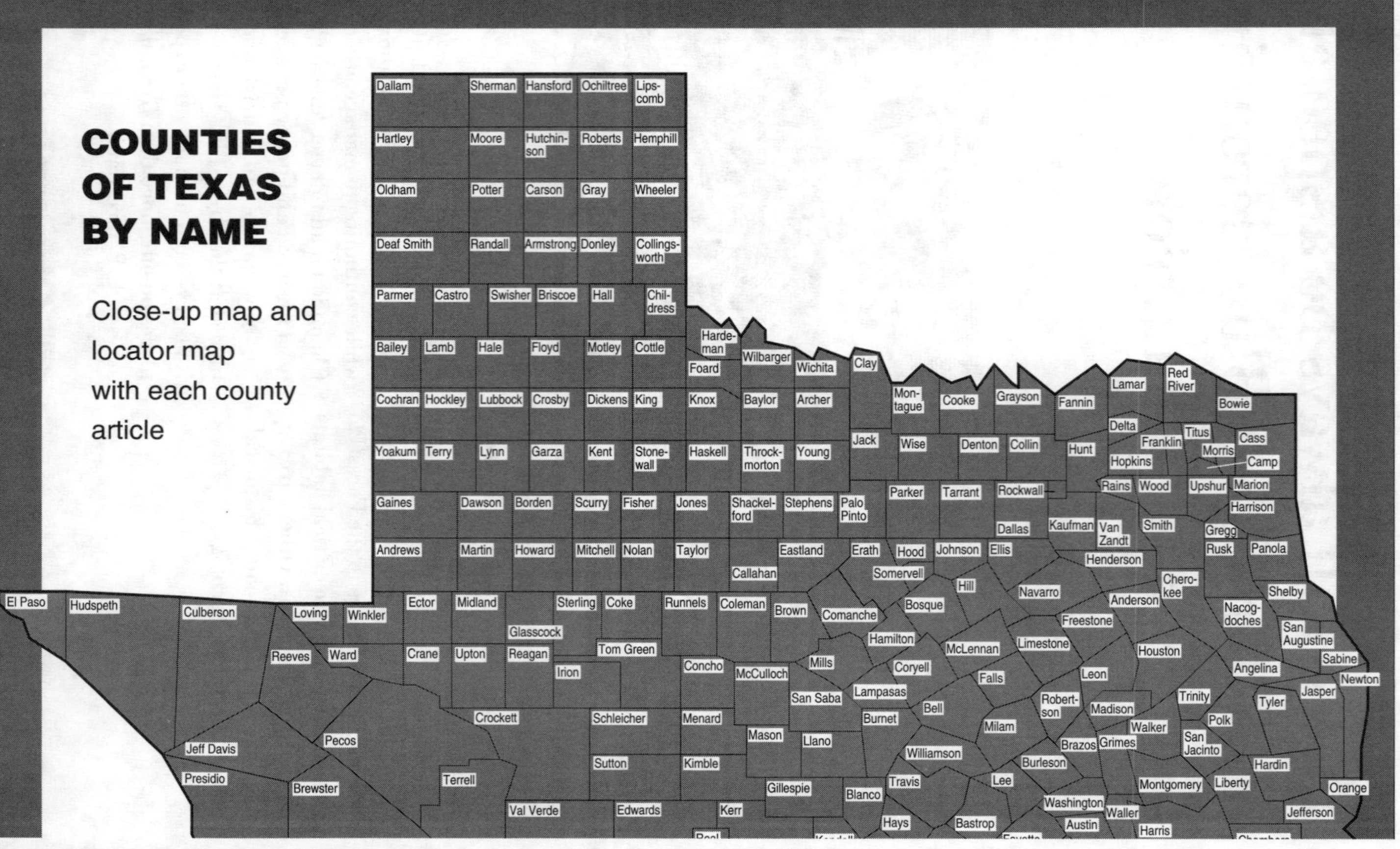
COUNTIES
OF TEXAS
BY NAME
Close-up map and
locator map
with each county
article
Dallam
Sherman
Hansford
Ochiltree
Lips-comb
Hartley
Moore
Hutchin-son
Roberts
Hemphill
Oldham
Potter
Carson
Gray
Wheeler
Deaf Smith
Randall
Armstrong
Donley
Collings-worth
Parmer
Castro
Swisher
Briscoe
Hall
Chil-dress
Bailey
Lamb
Hale
Floyd
Motley
Cottle
Harde-man
Foard
Wilbarger
Wichita
Clay
Cochran
Hockley
Lubbock
Crosby
Dickens
King
Knox
Baylor
Archer
Mon-tague
Cooke
Grayson
Fannin
Lamar
Red River
Bowie
Yoakum
Terry
Lynn
Garza
Kent
Stone-wall
Haskell
Throck-morton
Young
Jack
Wise
Denton
Collin
Hunt
Delta
Franklin
Titus
Cass
Morris
Hopkins
Camp
Gaines
Dawson
Borden
Scurry
Fisher
Jones
Shackel-ford
Stephens
Palo Pinto
Parker
Tarrant
Rockwall
Rains
Wood
Upshur
Marion
Harrison
Dallas
Kaufman
Van Zandt
Smith
Gregg
Andrews
Martin
Howard
Mitchell
Nolan
Taylor
Eastland
Erath
Hood
Johnson
Ellis
Rusk
Panola
Callahan
Somervell
Henderson
Hill
Navarro
Chero-kee
Anderson
Shelby
El Paso
Hudspeth
Culberson
Loving
Winkler
Ector
Midland
Sterling
Coke
Runnels
Coleman
Brown
Comanche
Bosque
Freestone
Nacog-doches
San Augustine
Glasscock
Hamilton
McLennan
Limestone
Houston
Sabine
Reeves
Ward
Crane
Upton
Reagan
Tom Green
Concho
McCulloch
Mills
Coryell
Angelina
Newton
Irion
Falls
Leon
San Saba
Lampasas
Trinity
Jasper
Tyler
Robert-son
Madison
Bell
Crockett
Schleicher
Menard
Burnet
Polk
Walker
Mason
Llano
Milam
Pecos
Jeff Davis
Williamson
Brazos
Grimes
San Jacinto
Sutton
Kimble
Burleson
Hardin
Presidio
Brewster
Terrell
Gillespie
Travis
Lee
Montgomery
Liberty
Orange
Blanco
Washington
Val Verde
Edwards
Kerr
Waller
Jefferson
Hays
Bastrop
Austin
Harris

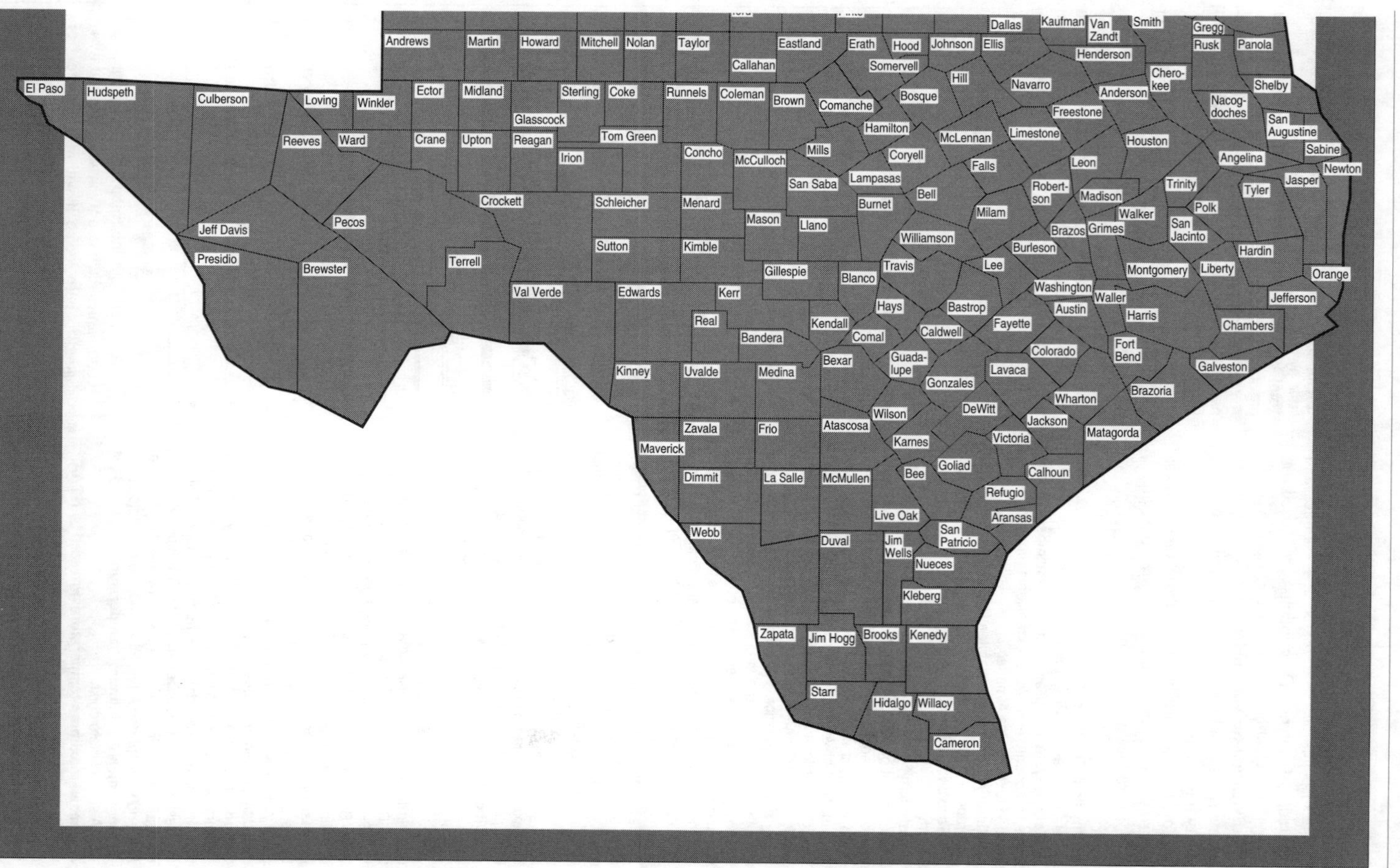
Andrews
Martin
Howard
Mitchell
Nolan
Taylor
Eastland
Erath
Hood
Johnson
Ellis
Dallas
Kaufman
Van Zandt
Smith
Gregg
Rusk
Panola
Callahan
Somervell
Henderson
El Paso
Hudspeth
Culberson
Loving
Winkler
Ector
Midland
Sterling
Coke
Runnels
Coleman
Brown
Comanche
Bosque
Hill
Navarro
Anderson
Chero-kee
Nacog-doches
Shelby
Glasscock
Hamilton
Freestone
San Augustine
Reeves
Ward
Crane
Upton
Reagan
Tom Green
Mills
Coryell
McLennan
Limestone
Houston
Sabine
Irion
Concho
McCulloch
Falls
Leon
Angelina
Newton
San Saba
Lampasas
Robert-son
Madison
Trinity
Tyler
Jasper
Crockett
Schleicher
Menard
Bell
Burnet
Milam
Walker
Polk
Pecos
Mason
Llano
Williamson
Brazos
Grimes
San Jacinto
Jeff Davis
Sutton
Kimble
Burleson
Hardin
Presidio
Terrell
Brewster
Gillespie
Blanco
Travis
Lee
Montgomery
Liberty
Orange
Val Verde
Edwards
Kerr
Washington
Waller
Jefferson
Hays
Bastrop
Austin
Harris
Real
Kendall
Fayette
Chambers
Comal
Caldwell
Bandera
Fort Bend
Galveston
Bexar
Guada-lupe
Colorado
Kinney
Uvalde
Medina
Lavaca
Gonzales
Brazoria
Wharton
DeWitt
Wilson
Jackson
Zavala
Frio
Atascosa
Matagorda
Victoria
Karnes
Maverick
Goliad
Calhoun
Dimmit
La Salle
McMullen
Bee
Refugio
Live Oak
Aransas
San Patricio
Webb
Duval
Jim Wells
Nueces
Kleberg
Zapata
Jim Hogg
Brooks
Kenedy
Starr
Hidalgo
Willacy
Cameron

Geography of Texas Counties

These pages describe Texas' 254 counties and hundreds of towns. Descriptions are based on reports from chambers of commerce, Texas Agricultural Extension Service, federal and state agencies and many other sources. Consult the index for other county information.

County maps are based on those of the Texas Department of Transportation and are copyrighted, 1995, as are the entire contents.

Physical Features: Descriptions are from U.S. Geological Survey and local sources.

Economy: A compilation of local chamber of commerce and county agricultural extension agent information provided to the Texas Almanac.

History: From Texas statutes, Fulmore's History and Geography of Texas as Told in County ical Records Survey and Texas Centennial Commission Report.

Ethnicity, 1990: Based on the U.S. Bureau of the Census count of 1990. In many cases the county percentages will total more than 100, for this reason:

In the forms used by the bureau, residents are asked to classify themselves according to race as "White"; "Black"; "American Indian, Eskimo and Aleut"; "Asian and Pacific Islander"; and "Other."

In another question the bureau asks respondents to mark their ethnic background, such as Mexican, Cuban, Puerto Rican, to be classified by the bureau as "Hispanic". Hispanic people can be of any race, thus their numbers are also included in one of the basic racial categories.

Vital Statistics, 1993: From the Texas Department of Health Annual Report, 1993.

Recreation: From information provided by local chambers of commerce and county agents. Attempts were made to note those activities unique to the area or that point to ethnic or cultural heritage.

Minerals: From agricultural agents.

Agriculture: Condensed from information provided to the Texas Almanac by county agricultural agents in 1995. Principal crops and livestock production are listed.

Cities: The county seat and principal cities are listed as well as some of the other towns in the county.

Sources of Data List

Population: The annual estimate of population from the State Data Center of the Texas Department of Commerce for 1993. The figures are prepared by the Department of Rural Sociology, Texas A&M University. (Also stated in the following line under population is the percentage of increase or decrease from the population reported in 1990 by the U.S. Bureau of the Census.)

Land Area:The total land area in square miles as determined by the census bureau, 1990.

Altitude (ft.): From the U.S. Geological Survey. Not all of the surface of Texas has been precisely surveyed for elevation; in some cases data are from the Texas Railroad Comission or the Texas Department of Transportation.

Rainfall (annual in inches): Provided by the National Oceanic and Atmospheric Administration state climatologist.

January mean minimum temperature: Provided by NOAA state climatologist.

July mean maximum temperature: Provided by NOAA.

Growing season (days): Provided by the NOAA state climatologist.

Civilian labor force: as determined by the Texas Employment Commission for 1994.

Unemployed: The unemployment rate for 1994 as calculated by the Texas Employment Commission.

Total Wages: Based on the quarterly figures for 1994 provided by the Texas Employment Commission.

Average Weekly Wage: Calculated by the Texas Almanac staff from figures provided by the Texas Employment Commission for fourth quarter 1993 through third quarter 1994.

Property Values: The appraised gross market value of real and personal property in each county appraisal district in 1993 as reported to the State Property Tax Board.

Retail Sales: Preliminary figures compiled by the Texas Almanac from quarterly reports for 1994 as reported to the state comptroller. The figures are subject to change in the comptroller's final report.

LEGEND FOR MAPS

Following is explanation of signs and symbols used:

- Principal roads
- Secondary roads
- Local roads
- Divided highways
- o Unincorporated towns
- ◉ Incorporated towns
- ✪ County seat
- ■ or ■ Cities of more than 50,000 population
- (10) Interstate highway numbers
- (59) U.S. highway numbers
- (36) State highway numbers
- [2222] Farm-to-Market roads
- (12) Loop or park road
- [LR] County or local roads
- +-+-+-+ Railroads
- Civilian airport
- Military airport
- State parks
- National park
- ▲ Historic site
- ◆ Other features

Locator maps

A small outline map of Texas counties accompanies each county article. The county is shaded to help locate it within the context of the state. A larger map of Texas with the counties named appears on pages 130 and 131.

Anderson County

Physical Features: Forested, hilly East Texas county, slopes to Trinity and Neches rivers; sandy, clay, black soils; pines, hardwoods.

Economy: Manufacturing, distribution, agribusiness, tourism; hunting and fishing leases; prison units.

History: Settled in 1830s; created from Houston County in 1846; named for K.L. Anderson, last vice president of the Republic of Texas.

Ethnicity, 1990: White, 33,354 (69.5%); Black, 11,143 (23.2%); American Indian, 129 (0.3%); Asian, 125 (0.3%); Other, 3,273 (6.8%). Hispanic, 3,953 (8.2%).

Vital Statistics, 1993: Births, 601; deaths, 411; marriages, 434; divorces, 265.

Recreation: Fishing, hunting, streams, lakes; dogwood trails; historic sites; railroad park; museum. Tourist information at 1890 depot.

Minerals: Oil and gas.

Agriculture: Beef, milk cows, hogs; hay, truck vegetables, grain sorghum, melons, peaches, blackberries; Christmas trees; timber sold.

PALESTINE (18,377) county seat; wholesale meats, auto parts, clothing, metal, wood products; aluminum smelting plant; transportation and agribusiness center; scientific balloon station; library; vocational-technical facilities; hospitals; community college. Other towns include: **Elkhart** (1,116), **Frankston** (1,163), and **Tennessee Colony** (120), site of state prisons.

Population	**49,880**
(Change fm '90)	3.9
Land Area (sq. mi.)	1,070.9
Altitude (ft.)	198-624
Rainfall (in.)	41.7
Jan. mean min.	35
July mean max.	95
Growing season (days)	264
Civ. Labor	19,556
Unemployed	5.5
Total Wages	$316,123,804
Av. Weekly Wage	$395.43
Prop. Value	$1,508,935,137
Retail Sales	$599,576,511

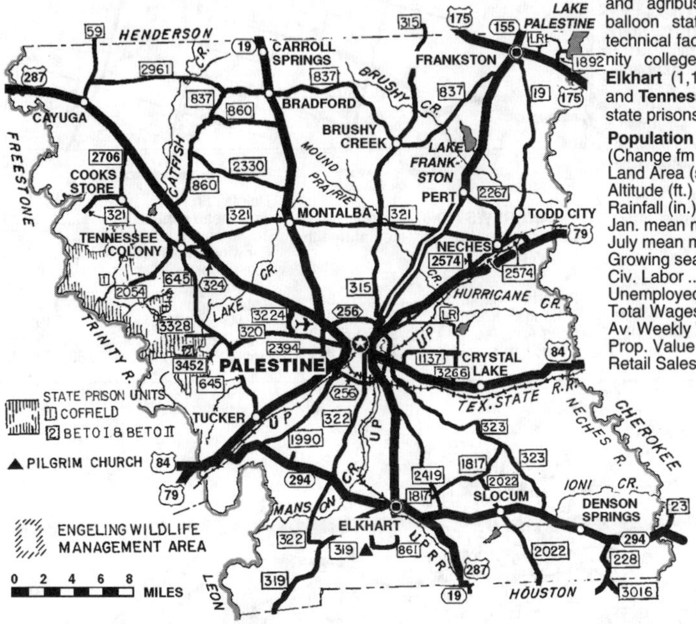

Railroad Abbreviations

ANR	Angelina & Neches River Railroad Co.
ATSF	Atchison, Topeka & Santa Fe Railroad Co.
AUNW	Austin & Northwestern Railroad Company
BN	Burlington Northern Railroad Company
BOP	Border Pacific Railroad Co.
BRG	Brownsville & Rio Grande Int'l Railroad Co.
CHRC	Chaparral Railroad Co., Inc.
CTR	Cen-Tex Rail Link
CYCY	Crystal City Railroad Company
DGNO	Dallas, Garland & Northeastern Railroad
FAPR	Floydada & Plainview Railroad Co.
FWWR	Fort Worth & Western Railroad Company
GCSR	Gulf, Colorado & San Saba RailwayCorp.
GRR	Georgetown Railroad Co.
GVSR	Galveston Railroad, L.P.
HBT	Houston Belt & Terminal Railway Co.
KCS	Kansas City Southern Railway Co., The
KRR	Kiamichi Railroad Company, Inc.
LSR	Lone Star Railroad, Inc.
MCSA	Moscow, Camden & San Augustine RR Co.
PCN	Point Comfort & Northern Railway Company
PNR	Panhandle Northern Railroad Company
PTRA	Port Terminal Railroad Association
PVS	Pecos Valley Southern Railway Co., Inc.
RSS	Rockdale, Sandow & Southern Railroad Co.
RVRR	Rio Valley Railroad
SO	South Orient Railroad Company, LTD
SP	Southern Pacific Lines
SPL	South Plains Lamesa RR. Ltd.
SRN	Sabine River & Northern Railroad Company
SW	Southwestern Railroad
SWGR	Seagraves, Whiteface & Lubbock RR Co.
TCT	Texas City Terminal Railway Co.
TEXC	Texas Central Railroad Company
TM	The Texas Mexican Railway Company
TN	Texas & Northern Railway Co.
TNER	Texas Northeastern Railroad
TNMR	Texas and New Mexico Railroad
TSE	Texas South-Eastern Railroad Company
TXGN	Texas, Gonzales & Northern Railway Co.
TXNW	Texas & North Western Railway Co.
TXOR	Texas and Oklahoma Railroad Company
TXTC	Texas Transportation Company
UP	Union Pacific Railroad Company
WRRC	Western Railroad Co.
WTJR	Wichita, Tillman & Jackson Railway Co.

Andrews County

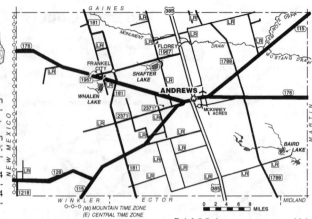

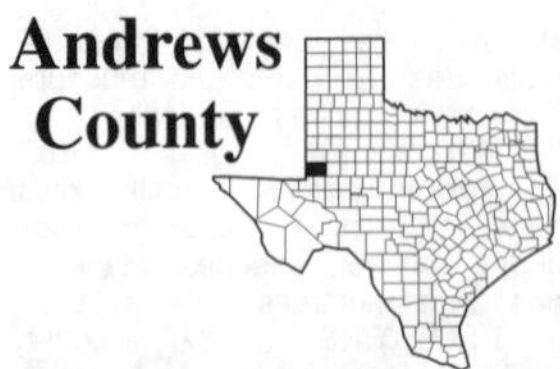

O-O-O (W) MOUNTAIN TIME ZONE (E) CENTRAL TIME ZONE

Physical Features: South Plains, drain to playas; grass, mesquite, shin oak; red clay, sandy soils.

Economy: Oil; agribusiness.

History: Created 1876 from Bexar Territory; organized 1910; named for Texas Revolutionary soldier Richard Andrews.

Ethnicity, 1990: White, 10,834 (75.6%); Black, 274 (1.9%); American Indian, 82 (0.6%); Asian, 154 (1.1%); Other, 2,994 (20.9%). Hispanic, 4,552 (31.7%).

Vital Statistics, 1993: Births, 211; deaths, 109; marriages, 136; divorces, 99.

Recreation: Prairie dog town; museum; camper facilities.

Minerals: Oil and gas.

Agriculture: Cattle; cotton, sorghums contribute; grains, corn, hay raised; significant irrigation.

ANDREWS (10,874) county seat; amphitheatre; hospital, mental health center; parks.

Population	**14,802**
(Change fm '90)	3.2
Land Area (sq. mi.)	1,500.7
Altitude (ft.)	2,297-2,915
Rainfall (in.)	14.1
Jan. mean min.	29
July mean max.	95
Growing season (days)	213
Civ. Labor	6,019
Unemployed	7.0
Total Wages	$116,917,223
Av. Weekly Wage	$495,01
Prop. Value	$2,162,495,506
Retail Sales	$69,973,525

Angelina County

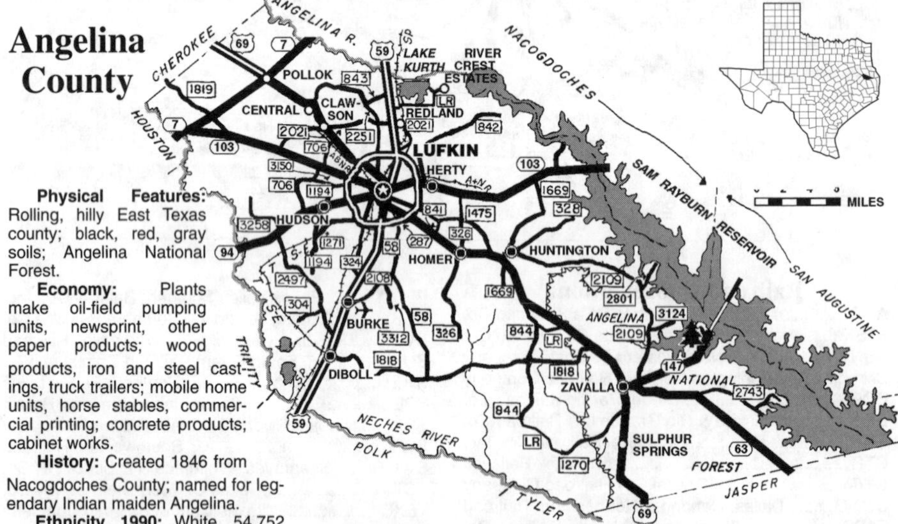

Physical Features: Rolling, hilly East Texas county; black, red, gray soils; Angelina National Forest.

Economy: Plants make oil-field pumping units, newsprint, other paper products; wood products, iron and steel castings, truck trailers; mobile home units, horse stables, commercial printing; concrete products; cabinet works.

History: Created 1846 from Nacogdoches County; named for legendary Indian maiden Angelina.

Ethnicity, 1990: White, 54,752 (78.3%); Black, 10,731 (15.4%); American Indian, 153 (0.2%); Asian, 295 (0.4%); Other, 3,953 (5.7%). Hispanic, 6,072 (8.7%).

Vital Statistics, 1993: Births, 1,131; deaths, 683; marriages, 883; divorces, 497.

Recreation: Sam Rayburn Reservoir; national, state forests, parks; locomotive exhibit; Forest Fest, bike ride in September.

For explanation of sources, abbreviations and symbols, see p. 132.

Minerals: Limited output of natural gas and oil.

Agriculture: Hay/forage, greehouse/landscape; a leading timber-producing county. Beef cattle, poultry, horses, exotic game. Vegetables, peaches marketed.

LUFKIN (31,651) county seat; manufacturing; Angelina College; hospitals; U.S., Texas Forest centers; zoo; Museum of East Texas, civic center.

Other towns include: **Burke** (344); **Diboll** (5,151); **Homer** (200); **Hudson** (2,519); **Huntington** (1,902); **Zavalla** (764).

Population	**73,087**
(Change fm '90)	4.6
Land Area (sq. mi.)	801.6
Altitude (ft.)	139-404
Rainfall (in.)	41.5
Jan. mean min.	38
July mean max.	94
Growing season (days)	244
Civ. Labor	34,406
Unemployed	6.4
Total Wages	$665,164,245
Av. Weekly Wage	$412.59
Prop. Value	$2,159,462,939
Retail Sales	$658,755,601

Aransas County

Population	**18,545**
(Change fm '90)	3.6
Land Area (sq. mi.)	251.9
Altitude (ft.)	sea level-24
Rainfall (in.)	36.9
Jan. mean min.	45
July mean max.	92
Growing season (days)	312
Civ. Labor	8,617
Unemployed	6.7
Total Wages	$77,273,052
Av. Weekly Wage	$336.64
Prop. Value	$833,412,896
Retail Sales	$207,008,779

Physical Features: Coastal plains; sandy loam, coastal clays; bays, inlets; mesquites, oaks.

Economy: Tourism, fishing and shrimping; oil production; refining; shipbuilding, offshore equipment fabricated; carbon plant.

History: Created 1871 from Refugio County; named for Rio Nuestra Señora de Aranzazu, derived from a Spanish palace.

Ethnicity, 1990: White, 15,282 (85.4%); Black, 319 (1.8%); American Indian, 111 (0.6%); Asian, 589 (3.3%); Other, 1,591 (8.9%). Hispanic, 3,588 (20.1%).

Vital Statistics, 1993: Births, 239; deaths, 255; marriages, 320; divorces, 125.

Recreation: Fishing, hunting, tourist facilities; Fulton Mansion; state marine lab; Texas Maritime Museum; bird sanctuaries (a nationally known birding hotspot; Rockport Art Center.

Minerals: Oil and gas, also oyster shell and sand.

Agriculture: Cow-calf operations; major crops are cotton, sorghum, corn; fishing; redfish hatchery.

ROCKPORT (5,271) county seat; fishing; tourist; library; clinics; carbon-black plant; Del Mar College program.

Aransas Pass (7,393); deepwater port on Intracoastal Waterway; oil production, refining; industrial plants; tourism; hospital. **Fulton** (767).

Archer County

Physical Features: North Central county, rolling to hilly, drained by Wichita River forks; black, red loams, sandy soils; mesquites, post oaks.

Economy: Cattle; oil services. Part of Wichita Falls metropolitan area.

History: Created from Fannin Land District, 1858; organized, 1880. Named for Dr. B.T. Archer, Republic commissioner to United States.

Ethnicity, 1990: White, 7,789 (97.7%); Black, 11 (0.1%); American Indian, 36 (0.5%); Asian, 4 (0.1%); Other, 133 (1.7%). Hispanic, 189 (2.4%).

Vital Statistics, 1993: Births, 88; deaths, 66; marriages, 57; divorces, 48.

Recreation: Lakes; quail hunting.

Minerals: Oil and natural gas.

Agriculture: Dairy, beef, stocker cattle operations; wheat, other grains also produced; some irrigation.

ARCHER CITY (1,808) county seat; cattle, oil field service center; hospital, library, museum; book supply center, some manufacturing.

Other towns include: **Holliday** (1,480) Mayfest in spring; **Lakeside City** (927, partly in Wichita County); **Megargel** (248); **Scotland** (507, partly in Clay County); **Windthorst** (269, partly in Clay County); biannual German sausage festival, also in Scotland; and part of **Wichita Falls.**

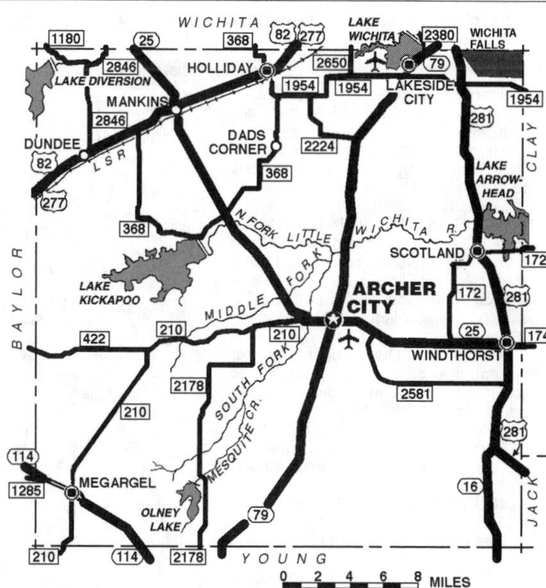

Population	**8,058**
(Change fm '90)	1.1
Land Area (sq. mi.)	909.7
Altitude (ft.)	934-1,286
Rainfall (in.)	27.7
Jan. mean min.	28
July mean max.	98
Growing season (days)	220
Civ. Labor	3,990
Unemployed	4.3
Total Wages	$29,402,454
Av. Weekly Wage	$374.29
Prop. Value	$483,700,949
Retail Sales	$31,228,583

Armstrong County

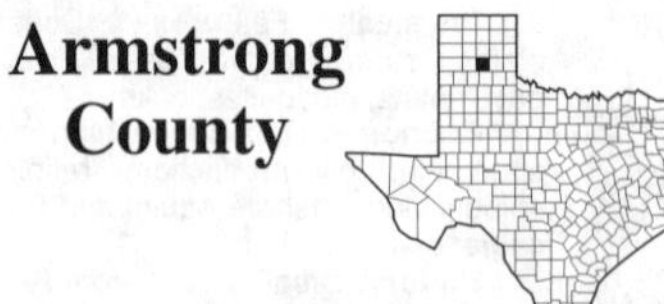

Physical Features: Partly on High Plains, broken by Palo Duro Canyon. Chocolate loam, gray soils.

Economy: Agribusiness, tourism.

History: From Bexar District, 1876; organized 1890; name honors a pioneer family.

Ethnicity, 1990: White, 1,976 (97.8%); Black, 0 (0.0%); American Indian, 10 (0.5%); Asian, 7 (0.3%); Other, 28 (1.4%). Hispanic, 55 (2.7%).

Vital Statistics, 1993: Births, 18; deaths, 24; marriages, 28; divorces, 7.

Recreation: Caprock Roundup in July, state park; Goodnight Ranch Home.

Minerals: Sand, gravel.

Agriculture: Stocker cattle, cow-calf operations; wheat, sorghum, cotton and hay; some irrigation.

CLAUDE (1,213) county seat; farm, ranch supplies; glass company; medical center; nursing home; Caprock Roundup.

Population............................**2,071**
(Change fm '90)..........................2.5

Land Area (sq. mi.)................913.6
Altitude (ft.)..................2,829-8,512
Rainfall (in.)..............................20.6
Jan. mean min...............................19
July mean max...............................92
Growing season (days) 213

Civ. Labor....................................981
Unemployed...................................3.9
Total Wages.....................$6,130,662
Av. Weekly Wage...............$345.17
Prop. Value $146,555,650
Retail Sales.....................$5,026,257

Atascosa County

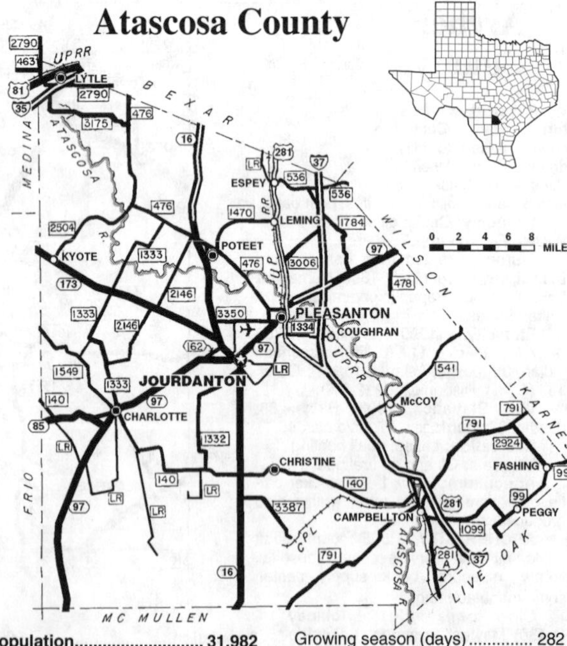

Physical Features: On grassy prairie south of San Antonio, drained by Atascosa River, tributaries; mesquites, other brush.

Economy: Agribusiness, oil-well supplies, services; coal plant; light manufacturing, shipping.

History: Created, organized from Bexar District, 1856. Atascosa means boggy in Spanish.

Ethnicity, 1990: White, 25,019 (81.9%); Black, 143 (0.5%); American Indian, 109 (0.4%); Asian, 65 (0.2%); Other, 5,197 (17.0%). Hispanic, 16,064 (52.6%).

Vital Statistics 1993: Births, 566; deaths, 257; marriages, 248; divorces, 146.

Recreation: Quail, deer hunting; museum; river park; theater group; stock show in January; cowboy homecoming in August, Kactus Kick in May.

Minerals: Oil, gas and lignite.

Agriculture: Beef cattle; peanuts, hay, corn, vegetables, sesame; 25,000 acres irrigated.

JOURDANTON (3,388) county seat; hospital.

Pleasanton (8,100) trading center; hospital.

Other towns include: **Charlotte** (1,635); **Christine** (406); **Lytle** (2,395, partly in Medina, Bexar counties) greenhouse nursery, peanuts processed**Poteet** (3,376) "strawberry capital".

Population...........................**31,982**
(Change fm '90) 4.7
Land Area (sq. mi.)................1,232.2
Altitude (ft.).........................241-725
Rainfall (in.) 27.8
Jan. mean min...............................39
July mean max...............................97

Growing season (days).............282
Civ. Labor 15,093
Unemployed...............................5.0
Total Wages.................$125,468,065
Av. Weekly Wage $348,21
Prop. Value $1,298,583,257
Retail Sales...............$140,780,573

For explanation of sources, abbreviations and symbols, see p. 132.

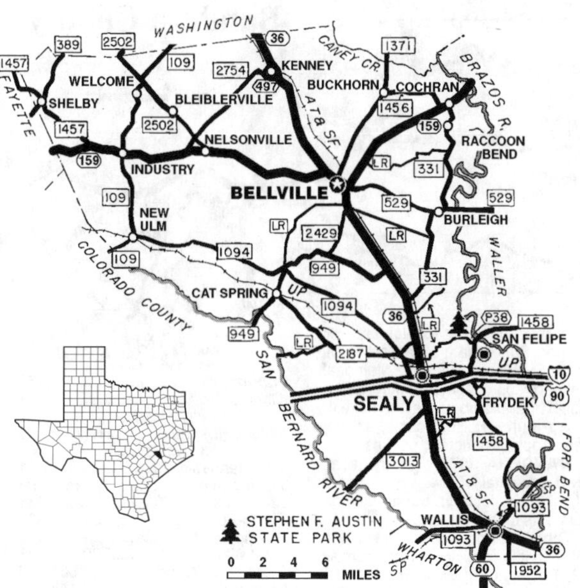

Austin County

Physical Features: Southeast county; level to hilly, drained by San Bernard, Brazos rivers; black prairie to sandy upland soils.

Economy: Agribusiness; steel, other manufacturing, tourism.

History: Birthplace of Anglo-American colonization; named for Stephen F. Austin, father of Texas. County created 1837.

Ethnicity, 1990: White, 16,244 (81.9%); Black, 2,608 (13.2%); American Indian, 46 (0.2%); Asian, 26 (0.1%); Other, 908 (4.6%). Hispanic, 2,073 (10.5%).

Vital Statistics 1993: Marriages, 166; divorces, 100; births, 308; deaths, 265.

Recreation: Fishing, hunting; state park, Pioneer Trail; Country Livin' festival.

Minerals: Oil and natural gas.

Agriculture: Livestock, poultry top cash source; sorghums, small grains, rice, corn, peanuts, cotton.

BELLVILLE (3,484) county seat; varied manufacturing; hospital; oil.

Sealy (4,795) oil-field and military vehicle manufacturing, varied industries.

Other towns include: **Cat Spring** (76); **Frydek** (150); **Industry** (475); **San Felipe** (700) colonial capital of Texas; **Wallis** (1,098).

Population.......................... **20,620**
(Change fm '90).......................... 4.0
Land Area (sq. mi.).................. 652.6
Altitude (ft.)............................ 23-263

Rainfall (in.)............................. 40.4
Jan. mean min. 43
July mean max. 94
Growing season (days)............. 282
Civ. Labor............................. 10,553

Unemployed.............................. 4.5
Total Wages.............. $138,531,591
Av. Weekly Wage.............. $418.01
Prop. Value............ $1,432,625,116
Retail Sales............... $190,517,448

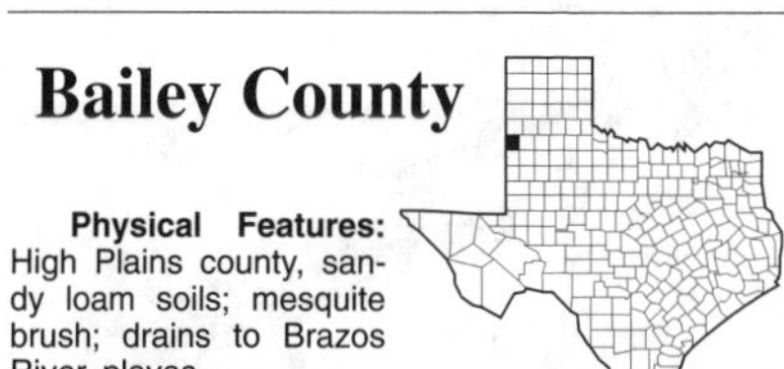

Bailey County

Physical Features: High Plains county, sandy loam soils; mesquite brush; drains to Brazos River, playas.

Economy: Farm supply manufacturing, food-processing plants; muffler manufacturing.

History: Created from Bexar 1876, organized 1917. Named for Alamo hero, Peter J. Bailey.

Ethnicity, 1990: White, 6,537 (92.5%); Black, 124 (1.8%); American Indian, 10 (0.1%); Asian, 12 (0.2%); Other, 381 (5.4%). Hispanic, 2,740 (38.8%).

Vital Statistics, 1993: Births, 115; deaths, 72; marriages, 69; divorces, 35.

Recreation: Muleshoe National Wildlife Refuge; "Old Pete," the national mule memorial; historical building park; museum; motorcycle club rally; pheasant hunting.

Minerals: Insignificant.

Agriculture: Feedlot, stocker cattle, fed sheep operations; cotton, corn, vegetables, wheat for hay; 80,000 acres irrigated.

MULESHOE (4,689) county seat; agribusiness center; feed-corn milling; hospital; livestock show.

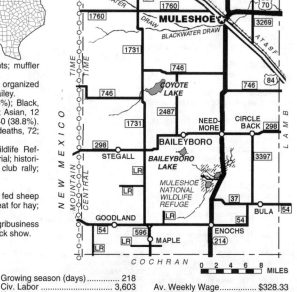

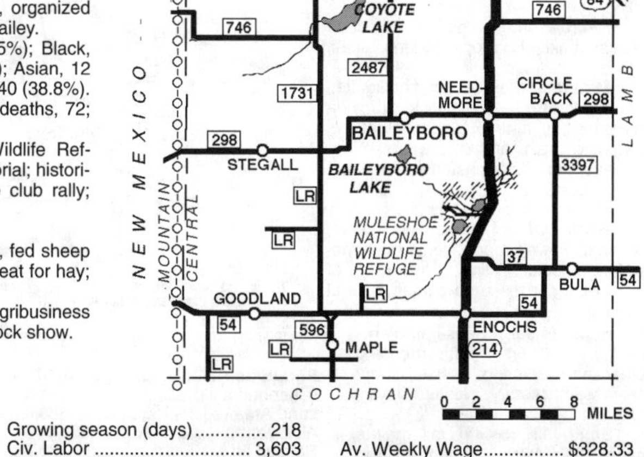

Population............................ **7,285**
(Change fm }90).......................... 3.1
Land Area (sq. mi.) 826.7
Altitude (ft.) 3,790-4,060
Rainfall (in.)............................... 16.1
Jan. mean min. 20
July mean max............................. 91

Growing season (days)............. 218
Civ. Labor 3,603
Unemployed............................. 5,5
Total Wages............... $37,087,807

Av. Weekly Wage............... $328.33
Prop. Value $293,594,930
Retail Sales.............. $53,304,310

Bandera County

Physical Features: Scenic southwestern county of cedar-covered hills on the Edwards Plateau; Medina River; limestone, sandy soils; species of oaks, walnuts, native cherry and Uvalde maple.

Economy: Tourism, hunting, fishing, ranching supplies, marketing, forest products.

History: Created, organized from Bexar, Uvalde counties, 1856; named for Bandera (flag) Mountains.

Ethnicity, 1990: White, 10,027 (94.9%); Black, 23 (0.2%); American Indian, 66 (0.6%); Asian, 26 (0.2%); Other, 420 (4.0%). Hispanic, 1,172 (11.1%).

Vital Statistics, 1993: Births, 122; deaths, 122; marriages, 112; divorces, 62.

Recreation: Resort ranches, RV parks; museum; Lost Maples and Hill Country State Natural Areas; race track; Fun-tier Days on Memorial weekend; apple festival in July, Cajun festival in September; Medina Lake.

Agriculture: Beef cattle, sheep, goats; apple production; pecans.

BANDERA (975) county seat; "cowboy capital of the world"; cedar mill, shingle factory; purse factory; spurs, bits manufactured.

Other towns include: **Medina** (500), apple growing; **Pipe Creek** (66); **Tarpley** (30); **Vanderpool** (20).

Also, the community of **Lakehills** (2,328) on Medina Lake.

Population	**11,288**
(Change fm '90)	6.9
Land Area (sq. mi.)	791.7
Altitude (ft.)	1,175-2,185
Rainfall (in.)	35.1
Jan. mean min.	31
July mean max.	94
Growing season (days)	235
Civ. Labor	6,622
Unemployed	3.4
Total Wages	$30,656,286
Av. Weekly Wage	$317.86
Prop. Value	$916,147,315
Retail Sales	$82,884,236

Bastrop County

Physical Features: Rolling; alluvial, sandy, loam soils; varied timber, Lost Pines; bisected by Colorado River.

Economy: Agribusiness, brick, electronic equipment, other manufacturing; tourism; in Austin metropolitan area.

History: Created 1836; named for Baron de Bastrop, who aided Moses Austin and colonists.

Ethnicity: White, 29,607 (77.4%); Black, 4,512 (11.8%); American Indian, 181 (0.5%); Asian, 129 (0.3%); Other, 3,834 (10.0%). Hispanic, 6,933 (18.1%).

Vital Statistics, 1993: Births, 573; deaths, 355; marriages, 300; divorces, 223.

Recreation: Fishing, hunting; state parks; Lake Bastrop; historic sites; museum; railroad park.

Minerals: Clay, oil, gas and lignite.

Agriculture: Livestock provide most income; emu, ostrich farming; cotton, corn, grain sorghums, wheat; minor irrigation for alfalfa pastures; some forest products.

BASTROP (4,389) county seat; tourism, oil-well supply, some manufacturing; medical clinic; University of Texas cancer research center; federal correctional center.

Elgin (4,992) Sausage plants, brick plants; horse, cattle breeding; other manufacturing; hospital, medical research; library; Western Days in July.

Smithville (3,444) rail maintenance, light manufacturing, environmental science park; hospital, model recycling center; jamboree in April.

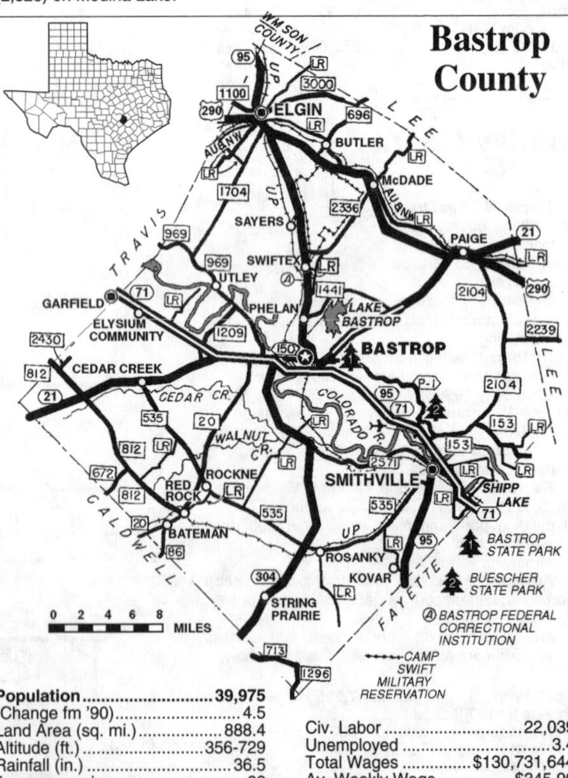

Population	**39,975**
(Change fm '90)	4.5
Land Area (sq. mi.)	888.4
Altitude (ft.)	356-729
Rainfall (in.)	36.5
Jan. mean min.	38
July mean max.	96
Growing season (days)	268
Civ. Labor	22,039
Unemployed	3.4
Total Wages	$130,731,644
Av. Weekly Wage	$345.99
Prop. Value	$1,332,617,279
Retail Sales	$288,005,725

Baylor County

Physical Features: North Central county; level to hilly; drains to Brazos, Wichita rivers; sandy, loam, red soils; grassy, mesquites, cedars.

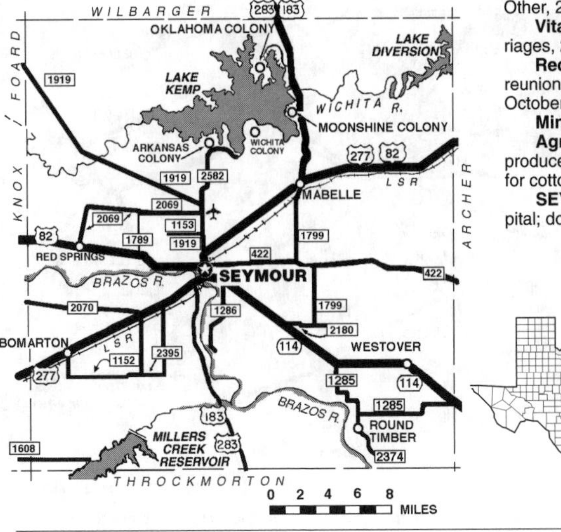

Economy: Agribusiness; oil, gas production; light manufacturing.

History: Created from Fannin County 1858. Named for H.W. Baylor, Texas Ranger surgeon.

Ethnicity, 1990: White, 3,962 (90.4%); Black, 180 (4.1%); American Indian, 9 (0.2%); Asian, 13 (0.3%); Other, 221 (5.0%). Hispanic, 334 (7.6%).

Vital Statistics, 1993: Births, 34; deaths, 77; marriages, 28; divorces, 25.

Recreation: Lakes; park, pavilions; settlers reunion, fish day in spring, autumn leaves festival in October.

Minerals: Oil, gas produced.

Agriculture: Cow-calf operations, stocker cattle produced; wheat, cotton, hay, peanuts; some irrigation for cotton, wheat.

SEYMOUR (3,054) county seat; agribusiness; hospital; dove hunters' breakfast in September.

Population	**4,288**
(Change fm '90)	- 2.2
Land Area (sq. mi.)	870.8
Altitude (ft.)	1,053-1,394
Rainfall (in.)	25.7
Jan. mean min.	26
July mean max.	98
Growing season (days)	275
Civ. Labor	1,868
Unemployed	5.0
Total Wages	$18,162,330
Av. Weekly Wage	$306.20
Prop. Value	$295,238,113
Retail Sales	$20,119,319

Bee County

Physical Features: South Coastal Plain, level to rolling; black clay, sandy, loam soils; brushy.

Economy: Oil supplies, agribusiness; small feedlots; state prison installations.

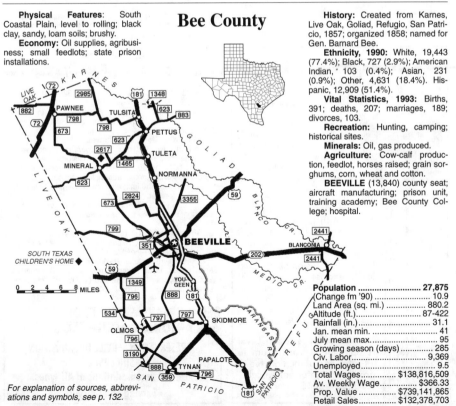

History: Created from Karnes, Live Oak, Goliad, Refugio, San Patricio, 1857; organized 1858; named for Gen. Barnard Bee.

Ethnicity, 1990: White, 19,443 (77.4%); Black, 727 (2.9%); American Indian, 103 (0.4%); Asian, 231 (0.9%); Other, 4,631 (18.4%). Hispanic, 12,909 (51.4%).

Vital Statistics, 1993: Births, 391; deaths, 207; marriages, 189; divorces, 103.

Recreation: Hunting, camping; historical sites.

Minerals: Oil, gas produced.

Agriculture: Cow-calf production, feedlot, horses raised; grain sorghums, corn, wheat and cotton.

BEEVILLE (13,840) county seat; aircraft manufacturing; prison unit, training academy; Bee County College; hospital.

Population	**27,875**
(Change fm '90)	10.9
Land Area (sq. mi.)	880.2
Altitude (ft.)	87-422
Rainfall (in.)	31.1
Jan. mean min.	41
July mean max.	95
Growing season (days)	285
Civ. Labor	9,369
Unemployed	9.5
Total Wages	$138,816,509
Av. Weekly Wage	$366.33
Prop. Value	$739,141,865
Retail Sales	$132,378,703

For explanation of sources, abbreviations and symbols, see p. 132.

Bell County

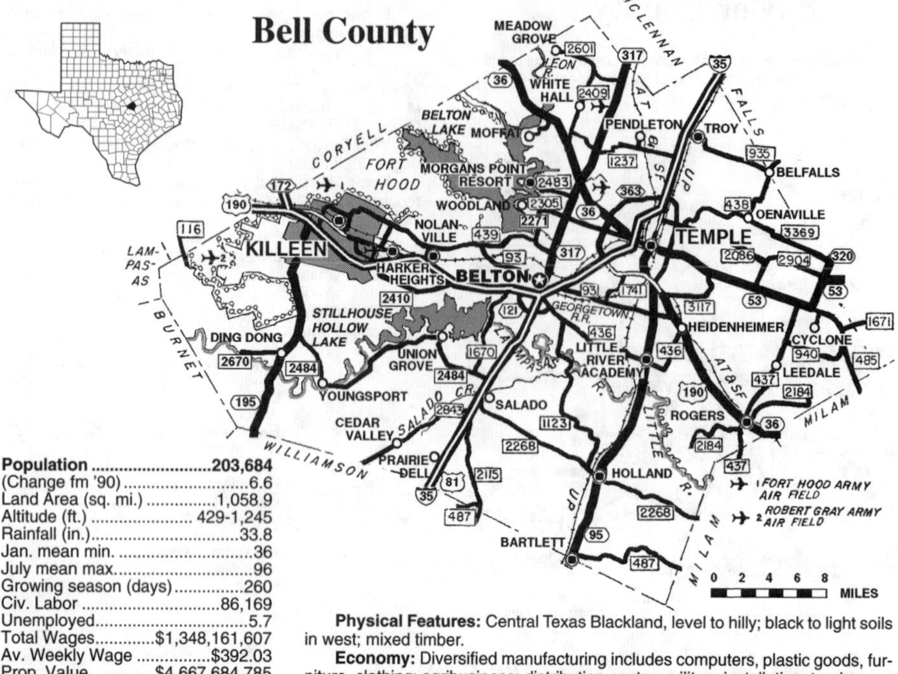

Population	203,684
(Change fm '90)	6.6
Land Area (sq. mi.)	1,058.9
Altitude (ft.)	429-1,245
Rainfall (in.)	33.8
Jan. mean min.	36
July mean max.	96
Growing season (days)	260
Civ. Labor	86,169
Unemployed	5.7
Total Wages	$1,348,161,607
Av. Weekly Wage	$392.03
Prop. Value	$4,667,684,785
Retail Sales	$1,778,976,642

Physical Features: Central Texas Blackland, level to hilly; black to light soils in west; mixed timber.

Economy: Diversified manufacturing includes computers, plastic goods, furniture, clothing; agribusiness; distribution center; military installation; tourism.

History: Created from Milam County in 1850; named for Gov. P.H. Bell.

Ethnicity, 1990: White, 136,066 (71.2%); Black, 36,095 (18.9%); American Indian, 944 (0.5%); Asian, 5,531 (2.9%); Other, 12,452 (6.5%). Hispanic, 24,995 (13.1%).

Vital Statistics, 1993: Births, 4,852; deaths, 1,319; marriages, 3,562; divorces, 2,090.

Recreation: Fishing, hunting; lakes; historic sites; exposition center; Salado gathering of Scottish clans in November.

Minerals: Stone, sand, gravel.

Agriculture: Cattle, turkey operations; corn, wheat, sorghums, hay, soybeans; cedar posts produced.

BELTON (12,900) county seat; University of Mary Hardin-Baylor; manufactures include school, office furniture, roofing felt, athletic equipment; Central Texas State Fair in September.

Killeen (71,031), Fort Hood; colleges; varied manufacturing; convention facilities; medical center, psychiatric center.

Temple (47,251), rail, market, distribution center; diversified industries; exposition center; junior college; medical centers, VA hospital.

Other towns include: **Harker Heights** (14,440); **Holland** (1,197); **Little River-Academy** (1,515); **Nolanville** (2,026); **Rogers** (1,148); **Salado** (1,305) arts, crafts center, new civic center; **Troy** (1,540).

Bexar County

Physical Features: On edge of Balcones Escarpment, Coastal Plain; heavy black to thin limestone soils; spring-fed streams; underground water; mesquite, other brush.

Economy: Government center with large federal payroll, five military bases; tourism second-largest industry; developing high-tech industrial park, research center; education center with 14 colleges.

History: Created 1836 from Spanish municipality named for Duke de Bexar; a colonial capital of Texas.

Ethnicity, 1990: White, 878,736 (74.1%); Black, 84,670 (7.1%); American Indian, 4,265 (0.4%); Asian, 15,429 (1.3%); Other, 202,294 (17.1%). Hispanic, 589,180 (49.7%).

Vital Statistics, 1993: Births, 22,714; deaths, 9,121; marriages, 11,254; divorces, 7,010.

Recreation: Historic sites include the Alamo, other missions; River Walk; Seaworld; El Mercado (market), La Villita; Tower of the Americas; Brackenridge Park; zoo; symphony orchestra; HemisFair Plaza; Fiesta San Antonio; Institute of Texan Cultures; parks, museums; hunting, fishing.

Minerals: Cement, stone, oil, gas, sand and gravel, lime, clays.

Agriculture: Beef, dairy cattle, other livestock; wheat, peanuts, sorghums, vegetables, hay, corn, coommercial nursery stock; some irrigation.

Education: Fourteen colleges including Our Lady of the Lake, St. Mary's University, Trinity University and the University of Texas at San Antonio.

SAN ANTONIO (991,861) county seat; Texas' third largest city; varied manufacturing with emphasis on high-tech industries; other products include construction equipment, concrete and dairy products; industrial warehousing.

Other towns include: **China Grove** (1,099); **Converse** (9,569); **Elmendorf** (668); **Helotes** (1,831); **Kirby** (8,987); **Leon Valley** (9,981); **Live Oak** (10,524); **St. Hedwig** (1,649); **Selma** (629); **Somerset** (1,309); **Universal City** (14,270).

Population	**1,260,287**
(Change fm '90)	6.3
Land Area (sq. mi.)	1,246.9
Altitude (ft.)	486-1,892
Rainfall (in.)	29.1
Jan. mean min.	39
July mean max.	95
Growing season (days)	265
Civ. Labor	623,425
Unemployed	5.0
Total Wages	$11,202,435,979
Av. Weekly Wage	$435.32
Prop. Value	$33,864,741,782
Retail Sales	$11,865,260,086

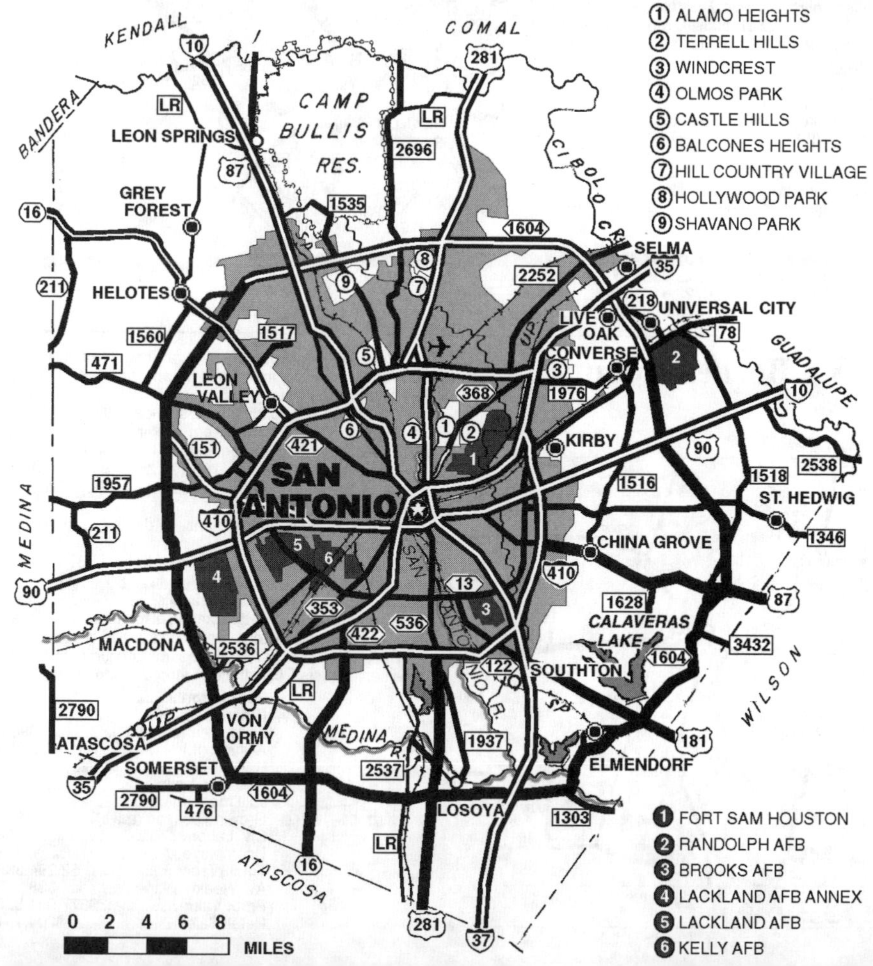

① ALAMO HEIGHTS
② TERRELL HILLS
③ WINDCREST
④ OLMOS PARK
⑤ CASTLE HILLS
⑥ BALCONES HEIGHTS
⑦ HILL COUNTRY VILLAGE
⑧ HOLLYWOOD PARK
⑨ SHAVANO PARK

❶ FORT SAM HOUSTON
❷ RANDOLPH AFB
❸ BROOKS AFB
❹ LACKLAND AFB ANNEX
❺ LACKLAND AFB
❻ KELLY AFB

0 2 4 6 8 MILES

Blanco County

Physical Features: Hill Country county; Blanco, Pedernales rivers; cedars, pecans, other trees.

Economy: Tourism, agribusiness, livestock-trailer manufacturing, ranch supplies, marketing.

History: Created 1858 from Burnet, Comal, Gillespie, Hays counties; named for Blanco (white) River.

Ethnicity, 1990: White, 5,598 (93.7%); Black, 56 (0.9%); American Indian, 17 (0.3%); Asian, 22 (0.4%); Other, 279 (4.7%). Hispanic, 840 (14.1%).

Vital Statistics, 1993: Births, 81; deaths, 67; marriages, 63; divorces, 31.

Recreation: President Lyndon B. Johnson's boyhood home; state parks; hunting, fishing; scenic drives; fiddlefest in June.

Minerals: Insignificant.

Agriculture: Cow-calf operation, some stocker cattle; sheep, goats, turkeys raised, some exotic animal production; vegetables, wheat, coastal hay, peaches, pecans; limited irrigation for hay and other products.

JOHNSON CITY (1,032) county seat; tourism; electric co-op; livestock center.

Blanco (1,368) tourism; ranch supply center; horticultural products; classic car show in May.

Population	**6,486**
(Change fm '90)	8.6
Land Area (sq. mi.)	711.2
Altitude (ft.)	978-1,801
Rainfall (in.)	34.7
Jan. mean min.	33
July mean max.	95
Growing season (days)	234
Civ. Labor	3,264
Unemployed	2.8
Total Wages	$31,736,462
Av. Weekly Wage	$366.27
Prop. Value	$722,610,840
Retail Sales	$29,879,146

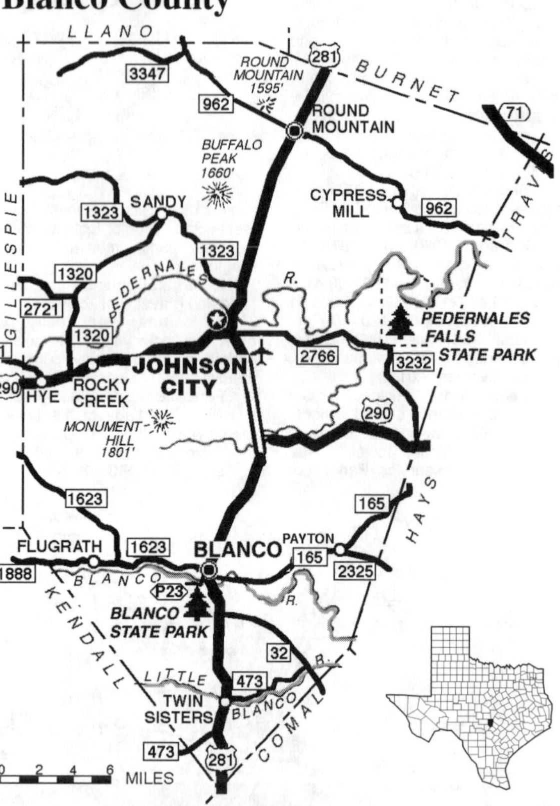

Borden County

Physical Features: West Texas county of rolling surface, broken by Caprock Escarpment; drains to Colorado River; sandy loam, clay soils.

Economy: Oil, agribusiness; service station.

History: Created 1876 from Bexar District, organized 1891; named for Gail Borden, patriot, inventor, editor.

Ethnicity, 1990: White, 769 (96.2%); Black, 2 (0.3%); American Indian, 10 (1.3%); Asian, 0 (0.0%); Other, 18 (2.3%). Hispanic, 120 (15.0%).

Vital Statistics, 1993: Births, 4; deaths, 3; marriages, 10; divorces, 4.

Recreation: Fishing, hunting; Lake J.B. Thomas; museum.

Minerals: Oil, gas, sand, gravel.

Agriculture: Beef cattle, cotton; also, horses, milo, oats, pecans, alfalfa; some irrigation for cotton and soybeans.

GAIL (202) county seat; museum; antique shop, ambulance service; "star" construction atop Gail Mountain.

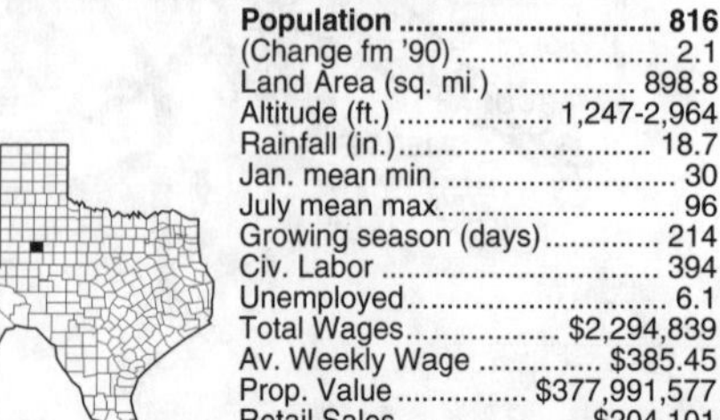

Population	**816**
(Change fm '90)	2.1
Land Area (sq. mi.)	898.8
Altitude (ft.)	1,247-2,964
Rainfall (in.)	18.7
Jan. mean min.	30
July mean max.	96
Growing season (days)	214
Civ. Labor	394
Unemployed	6.1
Total Wages	$2,294,839
Av. Weekly Wage	$385.45
Prop. Value	$377,991,577
Retail Sales	$204,101

Bosque County

Physical Features: North Central county; hilly, broken by Bosque, Brazos rivers; limestone to alluvial soils; cedars, oaks, mesquites.

Economy: Agribusiness, tourism, small industries; tree supplier.

History: Created 1854 from Milam District, McLennan County; named for Bosque (woods) River.

Vital Statistics, 1993: Births, 175; deaths, 251; marriages, 99; divorces, 77.

Ethnicity, 1990: White, 14,173 (93.7%); Black, 319 (2.1%); American Indian, 26 (0.2%); Asian, 41 (0.3%); Other, 566 (3.7%). Hispanic, 1,430 (9.5%).

Recreation: Lake, state park, museum at Clifton, conservatory of fine art; fishing, hunting; scenic routes, Norwegian smorgasbord at Norse in November, Texas Safari Wildlife Park in Clifton.

Minerals: Limestone.

Agriculture: Beef, dairy cattle, and wildlife are major producers; wheat, grain sorghums, hay, oats, corn, pecans, peaches; est. 2,000 acres irrigated for peanuts and Bermuda grass.

MERIDIAN (1,395) county seat; distribution center; varied manufacturing.

Clifton (3,399), trade center; light manufacturing; hospital.

Other towns include: **Cranfills Gap** (287); **Iredell** (349); **Morgan** (485); **Valley Mills** (1,105, partly in McLennan County); **Walnut Springs** (750).

Population	**15,578**
(Change fm '90)	3,0
Land Area (sq. mi.)	989.2
Altitude (ft.)	122-503
Rainfall (in.)	31.6
Jan. mean min.	33
July mean max.	97
Growing season (days)	243
Civ. Labor	6,401
Unemployed	4.9
Total Wages	$54,489,989
Av. Weekly Wage	$339.07
Prop. Value	$861,921,304
Retail Sales	$57,537,804

Bowie County

Physical Features: Forested hills at northeast corner of state; clay, sandy, alluvial soils; drained by Red and Sulphur rivers.

Economy: Manufacturing; agribusiness; government employment; tourism.

History: Created 1840 from Red River County; named for Alamo hero, James Bowie.

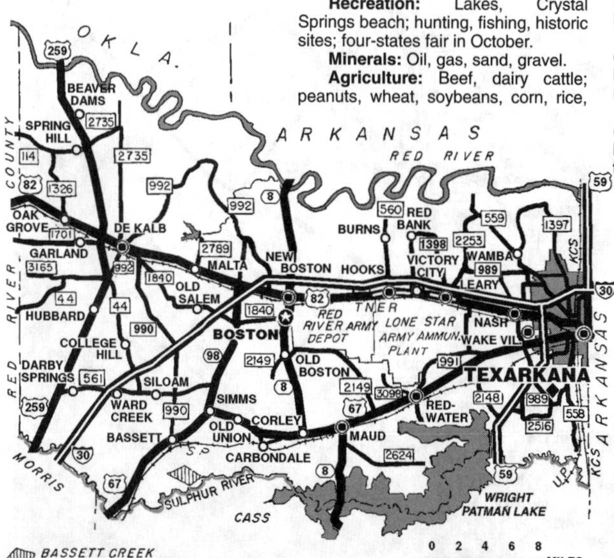

Vital Statistics, 1993: Births, 1,212; deaths, 900; marriages, 757; divorces, 588.

Ethnicity, 1990: White, 62,878 (77.0%); Black, 17,798 (21.8%); American Indian, 412 (0.5%); Asian, 262 (0.3%); Other, 315 (0.4%). Hispanic, 1,334 (1.6%).

Recreation: Lakes, Crystal Springs beach; hunting, fishing, historic sites; four-states fair in October.

Minerals: Oil, gas, sand, gravel.

Agriculture: Beef, dairy cattle; peanuts, wheat, soybeans, corn, rice, milo, blueberries, truck crops; pine timber, hardwoods, pulpwood harvested; some irrigation for rice, peanuts.

BOSTON county seat (but courthouse now located in New Boston).

Texarkana (33,405 in Texas, 22,631 in Arkansas), distribution, manufacturing, regional hospital; tourism; colleges; federal correctional unit; Quadrangle Festival in September, Perot Theatre.

New Boston (5,174) site of courthouse; steel manufactured; agribusiness; paper mill; state prison unit; Pioneer Days in August.

Other towns include: **De Kalb** (1,994); **Hooks** (2,789); **Leary** (420); **Maud** (1,062); **Nash** (2,265); **Redwater** (852); **Wake Village** (5,145).

Population	**84,431**
(Change fm '90)	3.4
Land Area (sq. mi.)	887.9
Altitude (ft.)	225-437
Rainfall (in.)	45.3
Jan. mean min.	35
July mean max.	93
Growing season (days)	235
Civ. Labor	39,881
Unemployed	9.4
Total Wages	$573,390,265
Av. Weekly Wage	$390.49
Prop. Value	$2,176,606,737
Retail Sales	$813,765,559

Brazoria County

Physical Features: Flat Coastal Plain, coastal soils, drained by Brazos and San Bernard rivers.

Economy: Petroleum and chemical industry; fishing; tourism; agribusiness. Part of consolidated Houston metropolitan area.

History: Created 1836 from Municipality of Brazoria; name derived from Brazos River; settled by Stephen F. Austin colonists.

Ethnicity, 1990: White, 154,875 (80.8%); Black, 15,981 (8.3%); American Indian, 812 (0.4%); Asian, 1,961 (1.0%); Other, 18,078 (9.4%). Hispanic, 33,797 (17.6%).

Vital Statistics, 1993: Births, 3,457; deaths, 1,236; marriages, 1,669; divorces, 1,371.

Recreation: Water sports; fishing, hunting; historic sites; state and county parks.

Minerals: Oil, gas, sand gravel.

Agriculture: Rice, hay, greenhouse nurseries, cotton, sorghum, soybeans, corn; beef cattle, hogs, meat goats and ratites; over 32,000 acres of rice irrigated.

ANGLETON (18,763) county seat; banking, distribution center for oil, chemical, agricultural area; fish-processing plant; hospital.

Brazosport is a community of nine cities; chemical complex; deepwater seaport; commercial fishing; tourism; college; hospital; Brazosport cities include **Brazoria (**2,903), **Clute** (9,743), **Freeport** (12,646), **Jones Creek** (2,195), **Lake Jackson** (24,355), **Oyster Creek** (977), **Quintana** (60), **Richwood** (2,847), **Surfside Beach** (681).

Alvin (19,863), rice, chemical processing; Alvin Community College, hospital.

Pearland (22,807, partly in Harris County).

Other towns include: **Bailey's Prairie** (670); **Bonney** (410); **Damon,** (350); **Danbury** (1,614); **Iowa Colony** (743); **Liverpool** (439); **Manvel** (4,259); **Sweeny** (3,480); **West Columbia** (4,872); tortilla factory, chemical companies; San Jacinto Festival.

Population	**203,684**
(Change fm '90)	8.7
Land Area (sq. mi.)	1,386.8
Altitude (ft.)	sea level-146
Rainfall (in.)	52.3
Jan. mean min.	42
July mean max.	92
Growing season (days)	268
Civ. Labor	107,259
Unemployed	7.1
Total Wages	$2,019,658,891
Av. Weekly Wage	$560.32
Prop. Value	$9,747,843,260
Retail Sales	$1,469,178,746

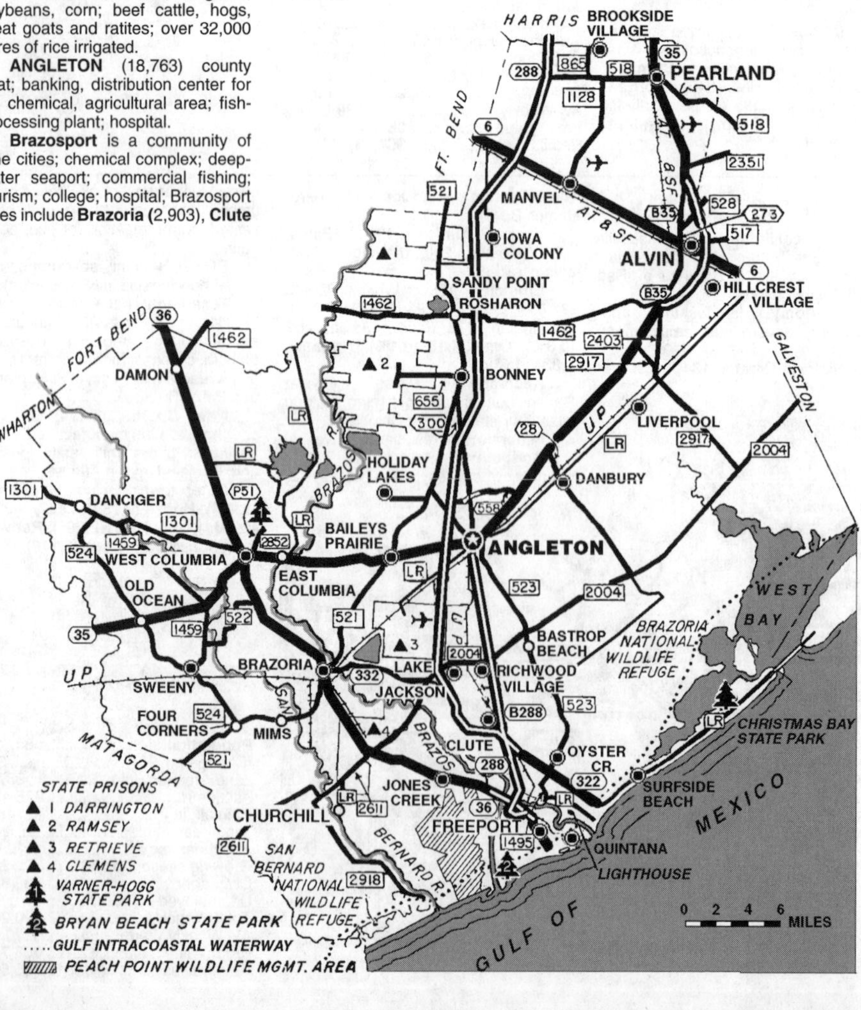

STATE PRISONS
▲ 1 DARRINGTON
▲ 2 RAMSEY
▲ 3 RETRIEVE
▲ 4 CLEMENS
1 VARNER-HOGG STATE PARK
2 BRYAN BEACH STATE PARK
..... GULF INTRACOASTAL WATERWAY
PEACH POINT WILDLIFE MGMT. AREA

0 2 4 6 MILES

Brazos County

Physical Features: South Central county between Brazos, Navasota rivers; rich bottom soils, sandy, clays on rolling uplands; oak trees.

Economy: Texas A&M University is major economic factor; agribusiness; computers, research and development; offshore technology; industrial parks; tourism.

Ethnicity, 1990: White, 94,866 (77.8%); Black, 13,672 (11.2%); American Indian, 274 (0.2%); Asian, 4,313 (3.5%); Other, 8,737 (7.2%). Hispanic, 16,713 (13.7%).

History: Created 1841 from Robertson, Washington counties and named Navasota; renamed for Brazos River in 1842, organized 1843.

Vital Statistics, 1993: Births, 1,951; deaths, 616; marriages, 1,358; divorces, 404.

Recreation: Fishing, hunting; raceway; many events related to Texas A&M activities.

Minerals: Sand and gravel, lignite, gas, oil.

Agriculture: Cattle, eggs; cotton, hay, corn, sorghum.

BRYAN (59,473) county seat; defense electronics, other varied manufacturing; agribusiness center; hospitals, psychiatric facilities; Blinn College system.

College Station (60,012) home of Texas A&M University, varied high-tech manufacturing; research.

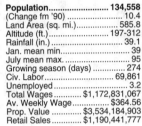

Population	**134,558**
(Change fm '90)	10.4
Land Area (sq. mi.)	585.8
Altitude (ft.)	197-312
Rainfall (in.)	39.1
Jan. mean min.	39
July mean max.	95
Growing season (days)	274
Civ. Labor	69,861
Unemployed	3.2
Total Wages	$1,172,831,067
Av. Weekly Wage	$364.56
Prop. Value	$3,534,184,903
Retail Sales	$1,190,441,777

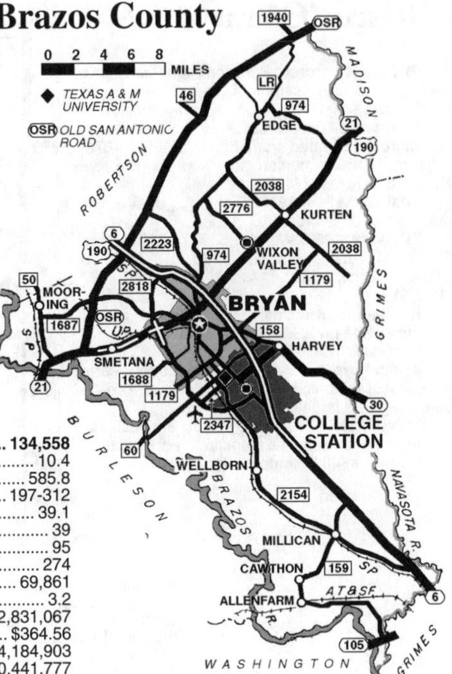

Brewster County

Physical Features: Largest county; area slightly less than that of Connecticut plus Rhode Island; mountains, canyons, distinctive geology, plant life, animals.

Economy: Sul Ross State University; ranching; tourism; retirement developments; hunting leases.

History: Created 1887 from Presidio County; named for Henry P. Brewster, Republic secretary of war.

Ethnicity, 1990: White, 8,300 (95.6%); Black, 85 (1.0%); American Indian, 20 (0.2%); Asian, 52 (0.6%); Other, 224 (2.6%). Hispanic, 3,702 (42.6%).

Vital Statistics, 1993: Births, 114; deaths, 90; marriages, 83; divorces, 29.

Recreation: Big Bend National Park; ghost mining towns; scenic drives; museum; rockhound areas; annual chili cookoff at Terlingua; cavalry post at Lajitas; hunting leases.

Minerals: Fluorspar, bentonite, perlite.

Agriculture: Beef cattle, sheep, goats, horses; pecans, apples; exotic wildlife; other types of fruit.

ALPINE (5,686) county seat; ranch trade center; tourism; Sul Ross State University; hospital; varied manufacturing. Other community, **Marathon** (500) ranching center; burro roping in March.

Population	**8.900**
(Change fm '90)	2.5
Land Area (sq. mi.)	6,193.0
Altitude (ft.)	1,355-7,825
Rainfall (in.)	14.8
Jan. mean min.	32
July mean max.	89
Growing season (days)	223
Civ. Labor	4,736
Unemployed	3.0
Total Wages	$45,727,532
Av. Weekly Wage	$288.16
Prop. Value	$366,024,505
Retail Sales	$71,780,870

Briscoe County

Physical Features: Partly on High Plains, broken by Caprock Escarpment, fork of Red River; sandy, loam soils.

Economy: Agribusiness.

History: Created from Bexar District, 1876, organized 1892; named for Andrew Briscoe, Republic of Texas soldier.

Vital Statistics, 1993: Births, 22; deaths, 33; marriages, 13; divorces, 10.

Ethnicity, 1990: White, 1,559 (79.1%); Black, 68 (3.5%); American Indian, 5 (0.3%); Asian, 0 (0.0%); Other, 339 (17.2%). Hispanic, 367 (18.6%).

Recreation: Hunting, fishing; scenic drives; museum; state park, Mackenzie Reservoir.

Minerals: Insignificant.

Agriculture: Wheat, sorghums, cotton, corn; vegetables, melons; beef cattle, stockers; 60,000 acres of grains irrigated.

SILVERTON (770) county seat; agribusiness center; irrigation supplies manufactured; clinics.

Quitaque (484), trade center.

Population	**1,931**
(Change fm '90)	- 2.0
Land Area (sq. mi.)	900.3
Altitude (ft.)	2,174-3,316
Rainfall (in.)	20.4
Jan. mean min.	19
July mean max.	91
Growing season (days)	214
Civ. Labor	961
Unemployed	4.1
Total Wages	$6,530,325
Av. Weekly Wage	$288.73
Prop. Value	$106,549,637
Retail Sales	$5,624,713

Brooks County

Physical Features: On Rio Grande plain near Gulf; level to rolling; brushy; light to dark sandy loam soils.

Economy: Oil, gas, cattle.

History: Created from Hidalgo, Starr, Zapata counties, 1911. Named for J.A. Brooks, Texas Ranger and legislator.

Ethnicity, 1990: White, 6,748 (82.3%); Black, 3 (0.0%); American Indian, 13 (0.2%); Asian, 10 (0.1%); Other, 1,430 (17.4%). Hispanic, 7,338 (89.4%).

Vital Statistics, 1993: Births, 159; deaths, 77; marriages, 69; divorces, 20.

Recreation: Hunting, fishing; Heritage Museum, Don Pedrito Shrine; Fiestas, May and October.

Minerals: Oil, gas production.

Agriculture: Beef cow-calf operations, stocker, dairy calves; crops include watermelons, grain sorghums, hay, corn.

FALFURRIAS (5,798) county seat; agribusiness; clothing manufacturing; hospital; museum, library.

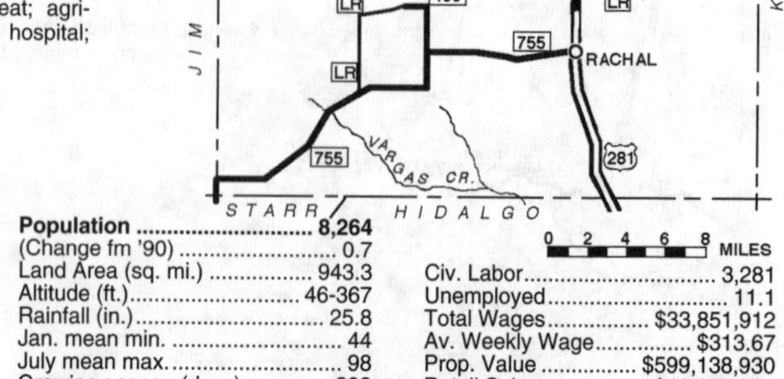

Population	**8,264**
(Change fm '90)	0.7
Land Area (sq. mi.)	943.3
Altitude (ft.)	46-367
Rainfall (in.)	25.8
Jan. mean min.	44
July mean max.	98
Growing season (days)	303
Civ. Labor	3,281
Unemployed	11.1
Total Wages	$33,851,912
Av. Weekly Wage	$313.67
Prop. Value	$599,138,930
Retail Sales	$43,627,369

Brown County

Physical Features: Rolling, hilly; drains to Colorado River; varied soils, timber.

Economy: Agribusinesses, general manufacturing plants, distribution center.

History: Named for frontiersman Henry S. Brown; created 1856 from Comanche, Travis counties.

Ethnicity, 1990: White, 30,267 (88.1%); Black, 1,552 (4.5%); American Indian, 131 (0.4%); Asian, 88 (0.3%); Other, 2,333 (6.8%). Hispanic, 3,799 (11.1%).

Vital Statistics, 1993: Births, 429; deaths, 433; marriages, 413; divorces, 164.

Recreation: State park; museum; fishing, hunting.

Minerals: Oil, gas, paving materials, gravel, clays.

Agriculture: Beef cattle, horses, swine, sheep and goats for mohair; peanuts chief crop, others are hay, wheat oats, pecans, small vegetables; 3,500 acres irrigated for peanuts and hay.

BROWNWOOD (18,641) county seat; retail trade center; varied industries; distribution center; Howard Payne University, MacArthur Academy of Freedom; mental health/mental retardation center; state 4-H Club center; hospitals.

Other towns include: **Bangs** (1,550), **Blanket** (407), **Early** (2,613).

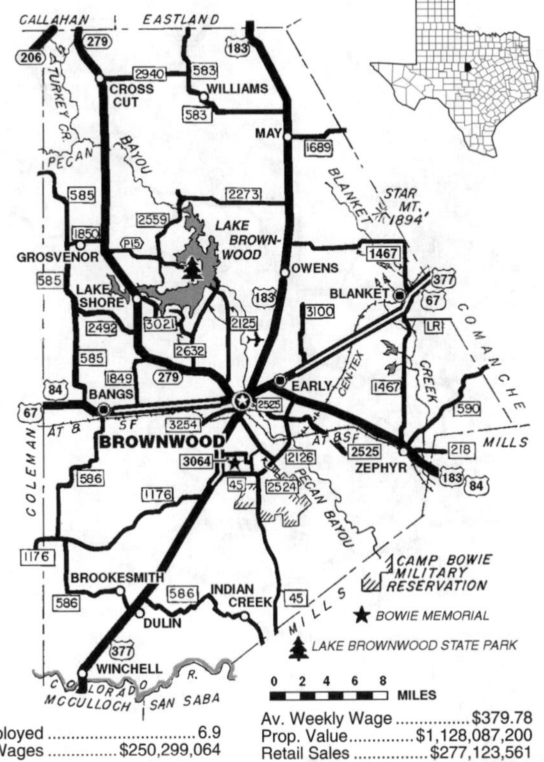

Population	**34,963**
(Change fm '90)	1.7
Land Area (sq. mi.)	943.9
Altitude (ft.)	1,321-1,894
Rainfall (in.)	26.1
Jan. mean min.	31
July mean max.	97
Growing season (days)	242
Civ. Labor	16,353
Unemployed	6.9
Total Wages	$250,299,064
Av. Weekly Wage	$379.78
Prop. Value	$1,128,087,200
Retail Sales	$277,123,561

Burleson County

Physical Features: Rolling to hilly; drains to Brazos, Yegua Creek, Somerville Lake; loam and heavy bottom soils; oaks, other trees.

Economy: Agribusiness, oil and gas; tourism; varied manufacturing, including wire and clothes hangers.

History: Created 1846 from Milam, Washington counties; named for Edward Burleson, a hero of the Texas Revolution.

Ethnicity, 1990: White, 10,173 (74.7%); Black, 2,430 (17.8%); American Indian, 53 (0.4%); Asian, 18 (0.1%); Other, 951 (7.0%). Hispanic, 1,624 (11.9%).

Vital Statistics, 1993: Births, 215; deaths, 173; marriages, 89; divorces, 60.

Recreation: Fishing, hunting; lake recreation; historic sites; Kolache Festival in September.

Minerals: Oil, gas, sand, gravel.

Agriculture: Beef cattle, swine, horses; cotton, corn, wheat major crops, soybeans, grain sorghums, oats also grown; some irrigation.

CALDWELL (3,527) county seat; light manufacturing; oil-field tool and servicing; tourist center; hospital, museum.

Somerville (1,592), tourist, railroad center, some manufacturing.

Other towns include: **Clay** (61), **Snook** (539).

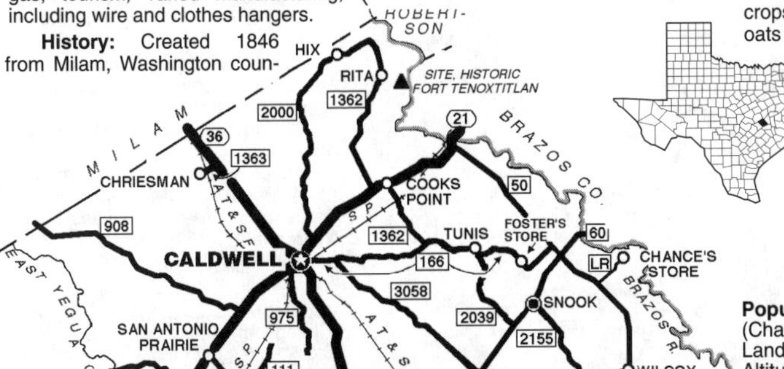

Population	**14,405**
(Change fm '90)	5.7
Land Area (sq. mi.)	665.6
Altitude (ft.)	221-417
Rainfall (in.)	27.8
Jan. mean min.	37
July mean max.	94
Growing season (days)	275
Civ. Labor	7,670
Unemployed	5.0
Total Wages	$64,242,750
Av. Weekly Wage	$376.02
Prop. Value	$972,278,945
Retail Sales	$78,100,225

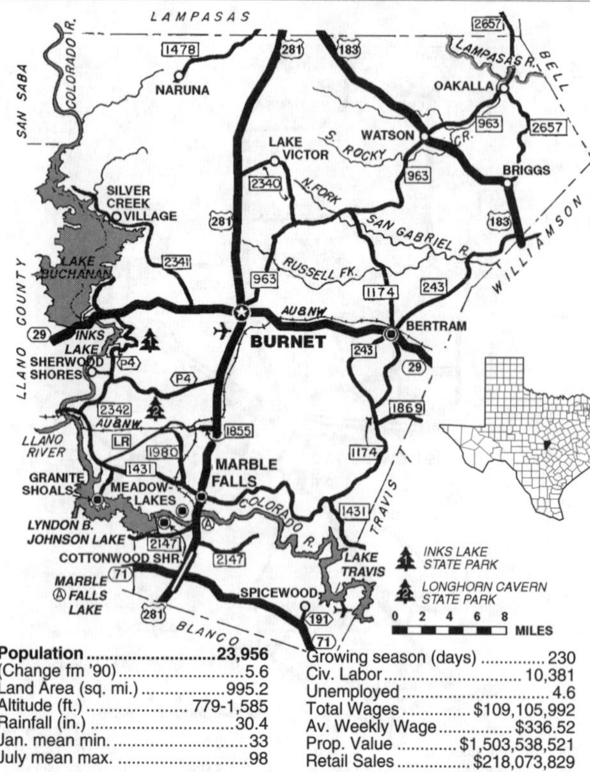

Burnet County

Physical Features: Scenic Hill Country county with lakes; caves; sandy, red, black waxy soils; cedars, other trees.

Economy: Stone processing, manufacturing, agribusinesses, tourism, hunting leases.

History: Created from Bell, Travis, Williamson counties, 1852; named for David G. Burnet, provisional president of the Republic.

Ethnicity, 1990: White, 20,793 (91.7%); Black, 269 (1.2%); American Indian, 109 (0.5%); Asian, 59 (0.3%); Other, 1,447 (6.4%). Hispanic, 2,440 (10.8%).

Vital Statistics, 1993: Births, 310; deaths, 311; marriages, 217; divorces, 128.

Recreation: Water sports on lakes; sites of historic forts; hunting; state parks.

Minerals: Stone, graphite, sand and gravel; granite capital of Texas.

Agriculture: Cattle, sheep, goats; cedar posts, pecans, hay; some grains; 20,000 acres irrigated for pecan, fruit orchards.

BURNET (3,569) county seat; recycling plant, medical center.

Marble Falls (4,266), tourism; ranching; varied manufactured; stone quarry; August drag boat race.

Other towns include: **Bertram** (937); **Cottonwood Shores** (597); **Granite Shoals** (1,478); **Meadowlakes** (597).

Population	**23,956**
(Change fm '90)	5.6
Land Area (sq. mi.)	995.2
Altitude (ft.)	779-1,585
Rainfall (in.)	30.4
Jan. mean min.	33
July mean max.	98
Growing season (days)	230
Civ. Labor	10,381
Unemployed	4.6
Total Wages	$109,105,992
Av. Weekly Wage	$336.52
Prop. Value	$1,503,538,521
Retail Sales	$218,073,829

Caldwell County

Physical Features: Varied soils ranging from black clay to waxy; level, draining to San Marcos River.

Economy: Petroleum, agribusiness, varied manufacturing.

History: Created from Bastrop, Gonzales counties, 1848; named for frontiersman Mathew Caldwell.

Vital Statistics, 1993: Births, 397; deaths, 275; marriages, 175; divorces, 107.

Ethnicity, 1990: White, 18,919 (71.7%); Black, 2,825 (10.7%); American Indian, 65 (0.2%); Asian, 86 (0.3%); Other, 4,497 (17.0%). Hispanic, 9,988 (37.8%).

Recreation: Fishing; state park; Luling Watermelon Thump; Chisholm Trail roundup at Lockhart; museums; nature trails; rodeo.

Minerals: Oil, gas, sand, gravel.

Agriculture: Beef cattle, turkeys, eggs; cotton, grain sorghums, corn, hay.

LOCKHART (9,415) county seat, agribusiness center, tourism; hospital, light manufacturing.

Luling (5,065) oil-industry center; hospital.

Other towns include: **Martindale** (993); **Mustang Ridge** (642, partly in Travis and Bastrop counties), and **Niederwald** (250), **Uhland** (380) partly in Hays County.

Population	**27,125**
(Change fm '90)	2.8
and Area (sq. mi.)	545.7
Altitude (ft.)	388-705
Rainfall (in.)	34.7
Jan. mean min.	37
July mean max.	97
Growing season (days)	275
Civ. Labor	13,717
Unemployed	3.9
Total Wages	$96,630,636
Av. Weekly Wage	$326.31
Prop. Value	$666,676,443
Retail Sales	$141,506,216

Calhoun County

Physical Features: Sandy, broken by bays; partly on Matagorda Island.

Economy: Aluminum manufacturing, plastics plant, marine construction, agribusinesses; petroleum; tourism; fish processing.

History: Created from Jackson, Matagorda, Victoria counties, 1846. Named for John C. Calhoun, U.S. statesman.

Ethnicity, 1990: White, 14,819 (77.8%); Black, 556 (2.9%); American Indian, 35 (0.2%); Asian, 556 (2.9%); Other, 3,087 (16.2%). Hispanic, 6,893 (36.2%);

Vital Statistics, 1993: Births, 389; deaths, 156; marriages, 221; divorces, 133.

Recreation: Beaches, fishing, water sports, duck, goose hunting; historic sites, county park; La Salle Days in April.

Minerals: Oil, gas.

Agriculture: Cotton, grain sorghums, corn, rice; beef cattle, shrimp.

PORT LAVACA (11,656) county seat; commercial seafood operations; offshore drilling operations; tourist center; some manufacturing; convention center; hospital.

Other towns include: **Point Comfort** (1,068), aluminum, plastic plants, deepwater port; **Port O'Connor** (1,187), tourist center; seafood processing; manufacturing; **Seadrift** (1,458).

Population	20,488
(Change fm '90)	7.5
Land Area (sq. mi.)	512.3
Altitude (ft.)	sea level-27
Rainfall (in.)	42.2
Jan. mean min.	44
July mean max.	93
Growing season (days)	300
Civ. Labor	10,042
Unemployed	11.3
Total Wages	$315,039,629
Av. Weekly Wage	$607.56
Prop. Value	$2,842,624,385
Retail Sales	$124,074,259

Callahan County

Physical Features: West Texas county on divide between Brazos, Colorado rivers; level to rolling.

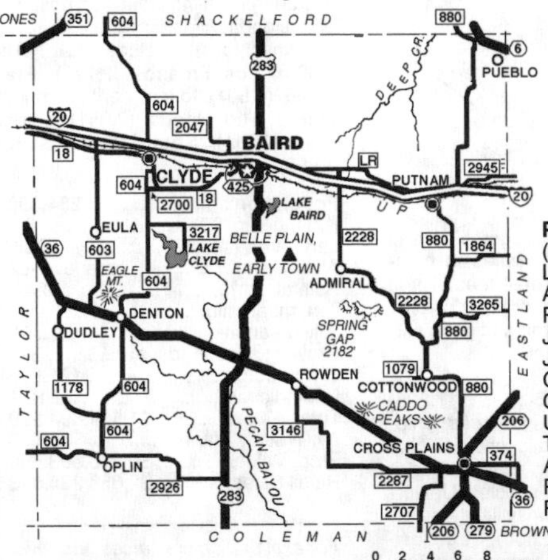

Economy: Agribusiness, oil and gas.

History: Created 1858 from Bexar, Bosque, Travis counties; organized 1877; named for Texas Ranger J.H. Callahan.

Ethnicity, 1990: White, 11,482 (96.8%); Black, 2 (0.0%); American Indian, 44 (0.4%); Asian, 40 (0.3%); Other, 291 (2.5%). Hispanic, 489 (4.1%).

Vital Statistics, 1993: Births, 132; deaths, 134; marriages, 73; divorces, 69.

Recreation: Hunting; museum; lake; old settlers reunion in July.

Minerals: Oil and gas.

Agriculture: Beef cattle; wheat, hay, peanuts, vegetables; sorghums; some irrigation of peanuts and Bermuda.

BAIRD (1,744) county seat; ranching; antique shops; some manufacturing, shipping; hospital.

Clyde (3,024) manufacturing.

Other towns include: **Cross Plains** (1,048), home of creator of Conan the Barbarian; **Putnam** (109).

Population	12,002
(Change fm '90)	1.2
Land Area (sq. mi.)	898.6
Altitude (ft.)	1,604-2,204
Rainfall (in.)	24.5
Jan. mean min.	32
July mean max.	96
Growing season (days)	228
Civ. Labor	5,926
Unemployed	4.6
Total Wages	$28,291,603
Av. Weekly Wage	$325.81
Prop. Value	$554,991,599
Retail Sales	$29,299,523

For explanation of sources, abbreviations and symbols, see p. 132.

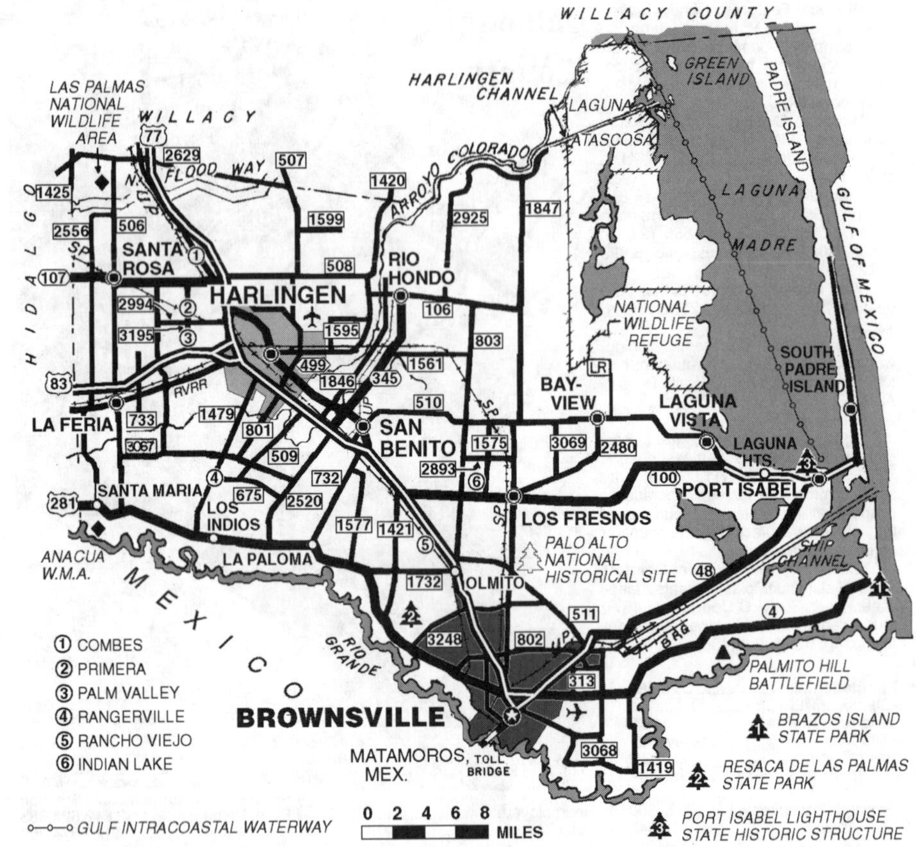

① COMBES
② PRIMERA
③ PALM VALLEY
④ RANGERVILLE
⑤ RANCHO VIEJO
⑥ INDIAN LAKE

GULF INTRACOASTAL WATERWAY

0 2 4 6 8 MILES

BRAZOS ISLAND STATE PARK
RESACA DE LAS PALMAS STATE PARK
PORT ISABEL LIGHTHOUSE STATE HISTORIC STRUCTURE

Cameron County

Physical Features: Southernmost county in rich Rio Grande Valley soils; flat landscape; semitropical climate.

Economy: Agribusiness; tourism; seafood processing; shipping, manufacturing.

History: Created from Nueces County, 1848; named for Capt. Ewen Cameron of Mier Expedition.

Ethnicity, 1990: White, 214,424 (82.4%); Black, 825 (0.3%); American Indian, 413 (0.2%); Asian, 750 (0.3%); Other, 43,708 (16.8%). Hispanic, 212,995 (81.9%).

Vital Statistics, 1993: Births, 7,641; deaths, 1,770; marriages, 3,079; divorces, 969.

Recreation: South Padre Island: Year-round resort; fishing, hunting, water sports; historical sites; gateway to Mexico, state parks; wildlife refuge; recreational vehicle center; Birding Festival in mid-November.

Minerals: Natural gas, oil.

Agriculture: Cotton top crop

with grain sorghums, vegetables, and sugar cane raised; wholesale nursery plants raised; small feedlot and cow-calf operations; 200,000 acres irrigated, mostly cotton and grain sorghums.

BROWNSVILLE (117,326) county seat; varied industries, shipping, college, hospitals, crippled children health center; Gladys Porter Zoo for endangered species; University of Texas at Brownsville.

Harlingen (52,508), agribusiness, tourist center; varied manufacturing; distribution center; college; hospitals; greyhound racing; Valley International Airport.

San Benito (21,780), varied manufacturing, bottling; tourism; hospital; recreation facilities.

Other towns include: **La Feria** (4,934); **Los Fresnos** (2,775); **Port Isabel** (4,801) tourist center, shrimp farming; **Rio Hondo** (2,051); **Santa Rosa** (2,511); **South Padre Island** (1,962).

Population	**284,392**
(Change fm '90)	9.3
Land Area (sq. mi.)	905.5
Altitude (ft.)	sea level-67
Rainfall (in.)	24.5
Jan. mean min.	51
July mean max.	93
Growing season (days)	341
Civ. Labor	121,636
Unemployed	12.1
Total Wages	$1,564,694,979
Av. Weekly Wage	$339.28
Prop. Value	$6,210,503,660
Retail Sales	$2,058,234,643

For explanation of sources, abbreviations and symbols, see p. 132.

Camp County

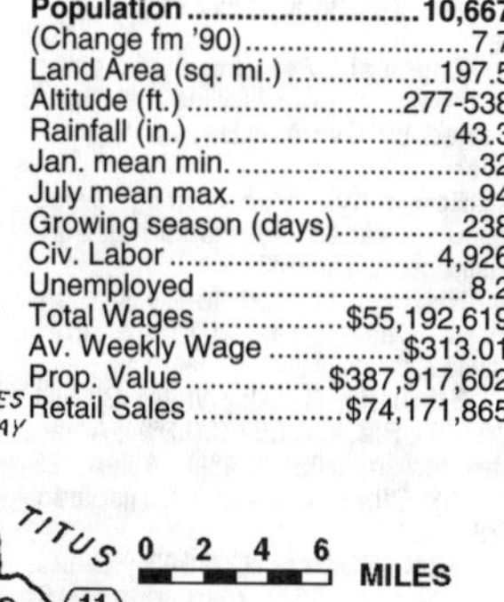

Population	**10,667**
(Change fm '90)	7.7
Land Area (sq. mi.)	197.5
Altitude (ft.)	277-538
Rainfall (in.)	43.3
Jan. mean min.	32
July mean max.	94
Growing season (days)	238
Civ. Labor	4,926
Unemployed	8.2
Total Wages	$55,192,619
Av. Weekly Wage	$313.01
Prop. Value	$387,917,602
Retail Sales	$74,171,865

Physical Features: East Texas county with forested hills; drains to Cypress Creek on north; Lake O' the Pines, Lake Bob Sandlin.

Economy: Agribusiness, chicken processing; timber industries; light manufacturing; retirement center.

History: Third smallest county in Texas; created from Upshur County 1874; named for jurist J.L. Camp.

Ethnicity, 1990: White, 7,130 (72.0%); Black, 2,360 (23.8%); American Indian, 35 (0.4%); Asian, 5 (0.1%); Other, 374 (3.8%). Hispanic, 501 (5.1%).

Vital Statistics, 1993: Births, 198; deaths, 151; marriages, 115; divorces, 40.

Recreation: Water sports, fishing on lakes; Chick Fest in April.

Minerals: Oil, gas, clays, coal.

Agriculture: Beef, dairy cattle; poultry and products important; peaches, hay, blueberries, vegetables; forestry.

PITTSBURG (4,330) county seat; agribusiness; timber; tourism; food processing; light manufacturing; community college; Prayer Tower. **Rocky Mound** (57)

Carson County

Physical Features: In center of Panhandle on level, some broken land; loam soils.

Economy: Agribusinesses, oilfield services.

History: Created from Bexar District, 1876; organized 1888; named for Republic secretary of state S.P. Carson.

Ethnicity, 1990: White, 6,315 (96.0%); Black, 11 (0.2%); American Indian, 44 (0.7%); Asian, 9 (0.1%); Other, 197 (3.0%). Hispanic, 354 (5.4%).

Vital Statistics, 1993: Births, 73; deaths, 53; marriages, 66; divorces, 30.

Recreation: Museum, sausage festivals.

Minerals: Oil, gas production.

Agriculture: Beef cattle; wheat, milo, corn, sunflowers, hay; some irrigation.

PANHANDLE (2,301) county seat; agribusiness, petroleum center; varied manufacturing.

Other towns include: **Groom** (626), **Skellytown** (671), **White Deer** (1,158).

Population	**6,548**
(Change fm '90)	- 0.4
Land Area (sq. mi.)	923.2
Altitude (ft.)	3,204-3,536
Rainfall (in.)	19.7
Jan. mean min.	21
July mean max.	97
Growing season (days)	191
Civ. Labor	3,686
Unemployed	4.3
Total Wages	$164,501,213
Av. Weekly Wage	$674.68
Prop. Value	$649,452,072
Retail Sales	$20,670,087

For explanation of sources, abbreviations and symbols, see p. 132..

Cass County

Physical Features: Forested Northeast county rolling to hilly; drained by Cypress Bayou, Sulphur River.

Economy: Paper mill, wood products, varied manufacturing; agribusinesses, sawmill.

History: Named for U.S. Sen. Lewis Cass; created 1846 from Bowie County.

Ethnicity, 1990: White, 23,651 (78.9%); Black, 6,057 (20.2%); American Indian, 105 (0.4%); Asian, 25 (0.1%); Other, 144 (0.5%). Hispanic, 373 (1.2%).

Vital Statistics, 1993: Births, 391; deaths, 384; marriages, 216; divorces, 172.

Recreation: Fishing, hunting, water sports; state, county parks; lake, wildflower trails.

Minerals: Gas, oil, iron ore.

Agriculture: Timber major revenue; beef cattle; hay; broilers; vegetables.

LINDEN (2,395) county seat; wood-treating plants; timber; oldest courthouse still in use as courthouse; hospital.

Atlanta (6,220), varied manufacturing; timber; cattle; two hospitals.

Other towns include: **Avinger** (495); **Bloomburg** (381); **Domino** (104); **Douglassville** (203); **Hughes Springs** (2,063, partly in Morris County), varied manufacturing, warehousing; **Marietta** (176); **Queen City** (1,882).

Population	**30,653**
(Change fm '90)	2.2
Land Area (sq. mi.)	937.4
Altitude (ft.)	219-486
Rainfall (in.)	46.3
Jan. mean min.	31
July mean max.	93
Growing season (days)	237
Civ. Labor	14,642
Unemployed	9.7
Total Wages	$161,544,521
Av. Weekly Wage	$408.26
Prop. Value	$1,386,746,311
Retail Sales	$164,622,841

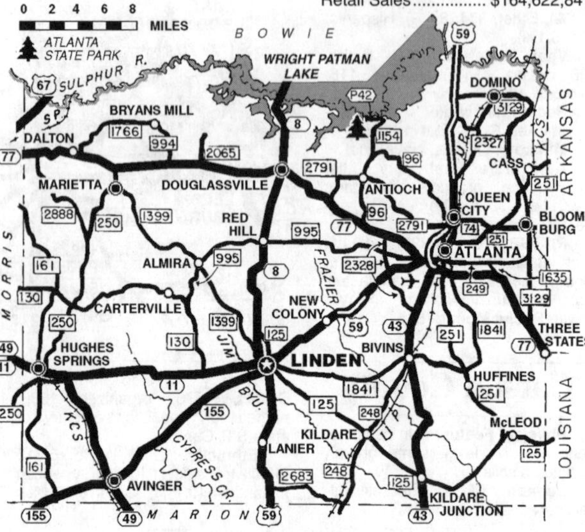

Castro County

Physical Features: Flat northwest county, drains to creeks, draws and playas; underground water.

Economy: Agribusinesses.

History: Created 1876 from Bexar, organized 1891. Named for Henri Castro, Texas colonizer.

Ethnicity, 1990: White, 5,526 (60.9%); Black, 261 (2.9%); American Indian, 10 (0.1%); Asian, 15 (0.2%); Other, 3,258 (35.9%). Hispanic, 4,187 (46.2%).

Vital Statistics, 1993: Births, 164; deaths, 68; marriages, 59; divorces, 28.

Recreation: Pheasant hunting.

Minerals: Not significant.

Agriculture: Fed cattle, stocker cattle; crops include corn, cotton and some wheat.

Population	**9,132**
(Change fm '90)	0.7
Land Area (sq. mi.)	898.4
Altitude (ft.)	3,731-3,942
Rainfall (in.)	16.6
Jan. mean min.	19
July mean max.	91
Growing season (days)	193
Civ. Labor	4,210
Unemployed	5.7
Total Wages	$57,745,942
Av. Weekly Wage	$400.38
Prop. Value	$437,904,041
Retail Sales	$60,402,749

For explanation of sources, abbreviations and symbols, see p. 132.

DIMMITT (4,523) county seat; agribusiness center; library, hospital.

Other towns include: **Hart** (1,295), **Nazareth** (332).

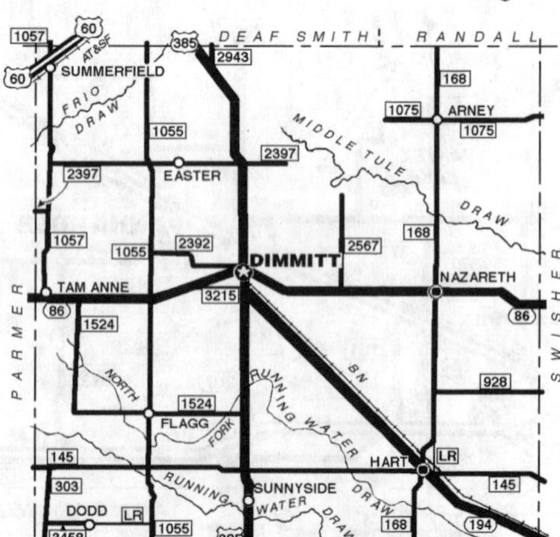

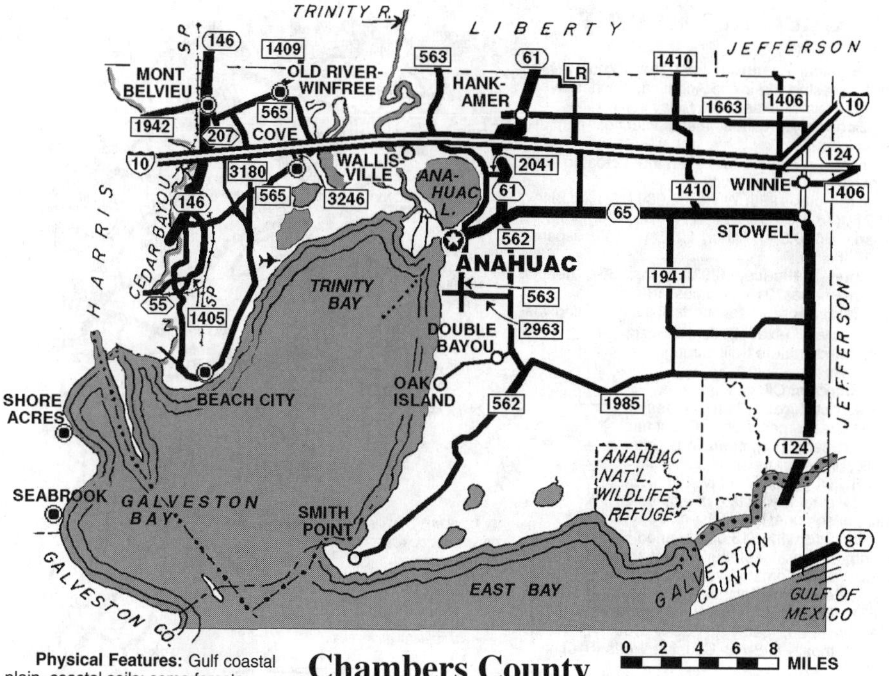

Chambers County

Physical Features: Gulf coastal plain, coastal soils; some forests.

Economy: Petroleum, chemicals, steel plants; agribusinesses; varied manufacturing; fish processing; tourism.

History: Named for Gen. T. J. Chambers, surveyor; created 1858 from Liberty, Jefferson counties.

Ethnicity, 1990: White, 16,725 (83.3%); Black, 2,550 (12.7%); American Indian, 53 (0.3%); Asian, 116 (0.6%); Other, 644 (3.2%). Hispanic, 1,195 (5.9%).

Vital Statistics, 1993: Births, 278; deaths, 137; marriages, 156; divorces, 102.

Recreation: Fishing, hunting; water sports; camping; county parks; wildlife refuge; historic sites; Wallisville Heritage Park; Texas Rice Festival, Texas Gatorfest in September.

Minerals: Oil, gas, salt, clays, sand and gravel.

Agriculture: Rice, soybeans; beef cattle; significant irrigation; timber important.

ANAHUAC (2,064) county seat; canal connects with Houston Ship Channel; agribusiness; hospital.

Winnie (2,360), Fertilizer manufacturing; wholesale greenhouse; medical center; depot museum.

Other towns include: **Cove** (443), **Mont Belvieu** (1,466, partly in Liberty County), **Old River-Winfree** (1,288), **Stowell** (1,562).

Population	**21,709**
(Change fm '90)	8.1
Land Area (sq. mi.)	599.3
Altitude (ft.)	sea level-73
Rainfall (in.)	51.6
Jan. mean min.	41
July mean max.	91
Growing season (days)	261
Civ. Labor	10,439
Unemployed	6.6
Total Wages	$178,150,331
Av. Weekly Wage	$550.04
Prop. Value	$2,741,775,840
Retail Sales	$259,902,893

For explanation of sources, abbreviations and symbols, see p. 132.

"CHAMBERS County: . . . Wallisville, the county seat, on the Trinity River, and about three miles from Turtle Bay, is regarded as a very healthy place. There is here a fine classical school, under the control of J.W. Barrow, a scholar of fine attainments, and a teacher of much experience. There is also at this place a yard for repairing and thoroughly overhauling schooners and steamboats. The old Spanish fort and town of Anahuac is situated near the mouth of the Trinity River in this county. The population of this county is small and much scattered, the voting population not exceeding 140. No oil or coal has yet been discovered in this county. The getting of wood for the Galveston market is the most extensive business, and next to stock-raising."

— *Texas Almanac, 1867*

Cherokee County

Physical Features: East Texas county; hilly, partly forested; drains to Angelina, Neches rivers; many streams, lakes; sandy, clay soils.

Economy: Varied manufacturing; agribusinesses; tourism.

History: Named for Indian tribe; created 1846 from Nacogdoches County.

Ethnicity, 1990: White, 32,039 (78.1%); Black, 6,931 (16.9%); American Indian, 108 (0.3%); Asian, 196 (0.5%); Other, 1,775 (4.3%). Hispanic, 2,697 (6.6%).

Vital Statistics, 1993: Births, 567; deaths, 522; marriages, 315; divorces, 183.

Recreation: Water sports; fishing, hunting; historical sites; Texas State Railroad; state parks; nature trails through forests; lakes.

Minerals: Oil, gas, iron ore.

Agriculture: Plant nurseries, vegetables, peaches, Christmas trees raised; dairy operations, beef cattle; timber production significant.

RUSK (4,500) county seat; agribusiness; tourism, state mental hospital; prison unit; hospital.

Jacksonville (13,053), varied light manufacturing; agribusiness; tourism; retail center; hospital, colleges, Tomato Fest in September.

Other towns include: **Alto** (1,071); **Cuney** (183); **Gallatin** (401); **New Summerfield** (579); **Reklaw** (268, partly in Rusk County); **Troup** (1,814, mostly in Smith County); **Wells** (810).

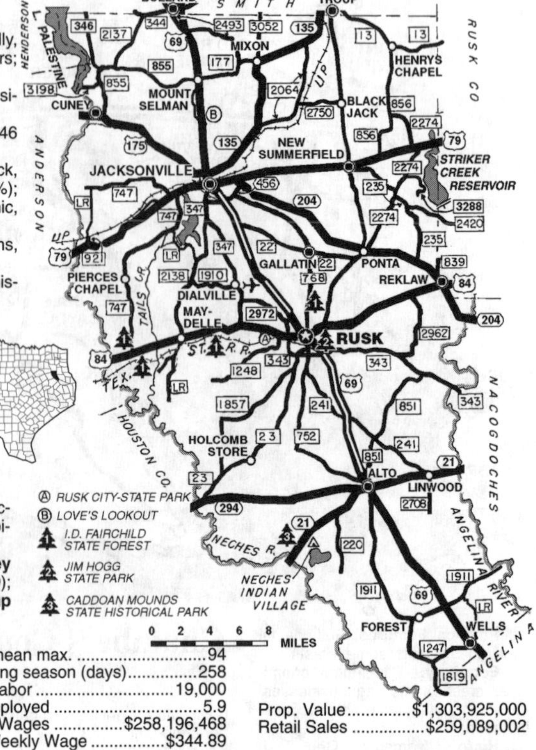

Population	**42,275**	July mean max.	94	Prop. Value	$1,303,925,000
(Change fm '90)	3.0	Growing season (days)	258	Retail Sales	$259,089,002
Land Area (sq. mi.)	1,052.3	Civ. Labor	19,000		
Altitude (ft.)	204-708	Unemployed	5.9		
Rainfall (in.)	44,6	Total Wages	$258,196,468		
Jan. mean min.	35	Av. Weekly Wage	$344.89		

Childress County

Physical Features: Rolling prairie, at corner of Panhandle, draining to fork of Red River; mixed soils.

Economy: Agribusiness; food processing, varied manufacturing.

History: Created 1876 from Bexar, Young districts; organized 1887; named for author of Texas Declaration of Independence, George C. Childress.

Ethnicity, 1990: White, 4,969 (83.5%); Black, 321 (5.4%); American Indian, 26 (0.4%); Asian, 17 (0.3%); Other, 620 (10.4%). Hispanic, 853 (14.3%).

Vital Statistics, 1993: Births, 72; deaths, 108; marriages, 70; divorces, 32.

Recreation: Recreation on lakes and creek, fishing, hunting of turkey, quail and wild hog, some deer; parks; county museum.

Minerals: Small production of oil, gas.

Agriculture: Cotton, wheat, melons, peanuts; cattle, Angora goats, ostriches; some irrigation; some mesquite marketed.

CHILDRESS (5,084) county seat; varied manufacturing, hospital, high school all-star football game; settlers reunion; prison unit.

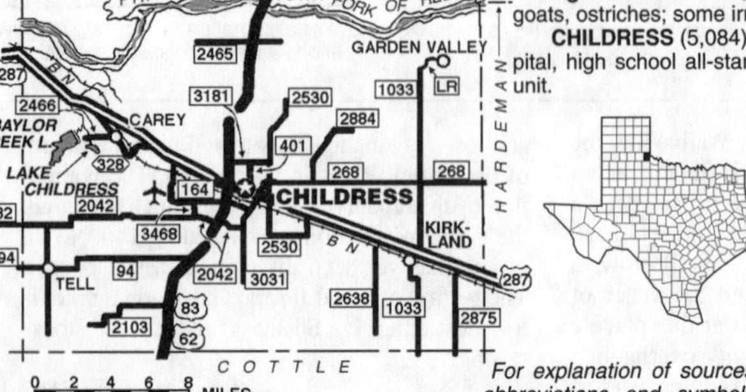

For explanation of sources, abbreviations and symbols, see p. 132.

Population	**6,049**
(Change fm '90)	1.6
Land Area (sq. mi.)	710.3
Altitude (ft.)	1,782-1,934
Rainfall (in.)	19.9
Jan. mean min.	26
July mean max.	96
Growing season (days)	217
Civ. Labor	3,211
Unemployed	4.6
Total Wages	$37,225,273
Av. Weekly Wage	$326.23
Prop. Value	$174,348,806
Retail Sales	$55,091,977

Clay County

Physical Features: Hilly, rolling; north central county drains to Red, Trinity rivers, lake; sandy loam, chocolate soils; mesquites, post oaks.

Economy: Oil; agribusinesses; varied manufacturing.

History: Created from Cooke County, 1857; Indians forced disorganization, 1862; reorganized, 1873; named for Henry Clay, U.S. statesman.

Ethnicity, 1990: White, 9,751 (97.3%); Black, 33 (0.3%); American Indian, 88 (0.9%); Asian, 23 (0.2%); Other, 129 (1.3%). Hispanic, 242 (2.4%).

Vital Statistics, 1993: Births, 93; deaths, 91; marriages, 71; divorces, 42.

Recreation: Fishing, water sports; state park; pioneer reunion.

Minerals: Oil and gas, stone.

Agriculture: Beef and dairy cattle, horses raised; wheat, cotton, pecan, peaches; oaks, cedar, elms sold to nurseries, mesquite cut for firewood.

HENRIETTA (3,016) county seat; agribusiness center; hospital.

Other towns include: **Bellevue** (344), **Byers** (526), **Dean** (306), **Jolly** (203), **Petrolia** (790).

Population	**10,394**
(Change fm '90)	3.7
Land Area (sq. mi.)	1,097.8
Altitude (ft.)	862-1,083
Rainfall (in.)	30.1
Jan. mean min.	27
July mean max.	97
Growing season (days)	232
Civ. Labor	4,647
Unemployed	4.6
Total Wages	$25,922,065
Av. Weekly Wage	$350,08
Prop. Value	$502,684,635
Retail Sales	$45,670,730

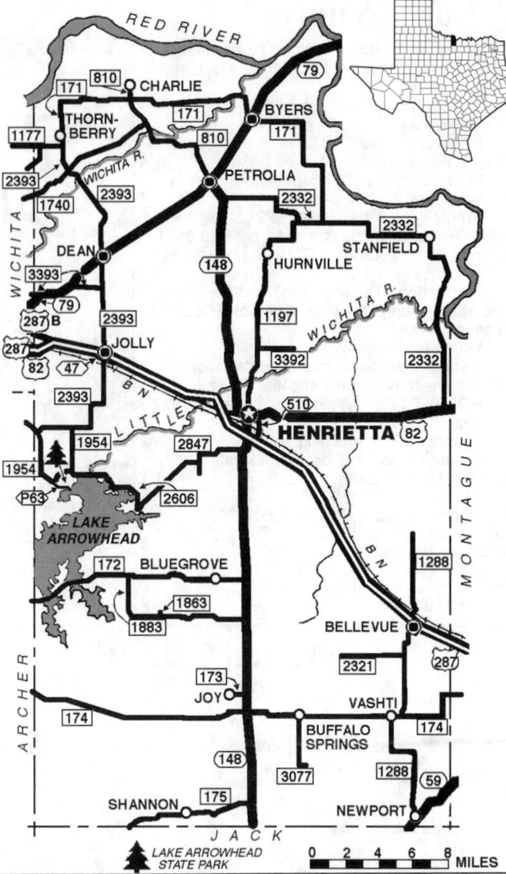

Cochran County

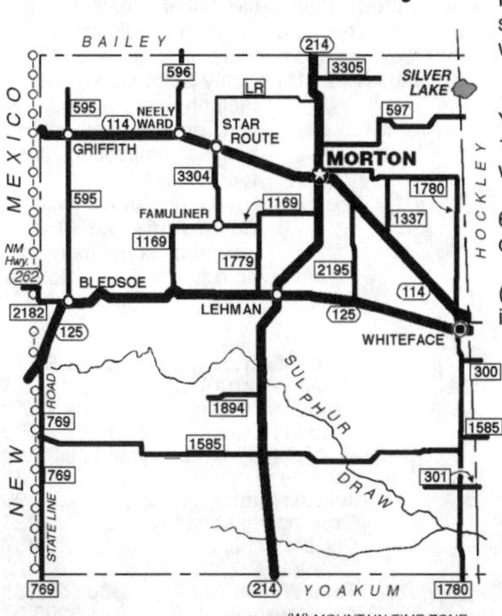

Physical Features: South Plains bordering New Mexico with small lakes (playas); underground water; loam, sandy loam soils.

Economy: Agribusiness, oil.

History: Created from Bexar, Young districts, 1876; organized 1924; named for Robert Cochran, who died in the Alamo.

Vital Statistics, 1993: Births, 65; deaths, 37; marriages, 21; divorces, 18.

Ethnicity 1990: White, 2,997 (68.5%); Black, 234 (5.3%); American Indian, 13 (0.3%); Asian, 1 (0.0%); Other, 1,132 (25.9%). Hispanic, 1,857 (42.4%).

Recreation: Rodeo; last frontier days in July; museum.

Minerals: Oil, gas.

Agriculture: Cotton, grain sorghums, wheat, onions; cattle, extensive cattle feeding; 120,500 acres irrigated for cotton, wheat, grain sorghums.

MORTON (2,586) county seat; oil, farm center, meat packing; light manufacture; hospital.

Other towns include: **Bledsoe** (125), **Whiteface** (499).

For explanation of sources, abbreviations and symbols, see p. 132.

Population	**4,331**
(Change fm '90)	- 1.1
Land Area (sq. mi.)	775.2
Altitude (ft.)	3,687-3,965
Rainfall (in.)	16.6
Jan. temp. min.	22
July temp. max.	91
Growing season (days)	189
Civ. Labor	1,665
Unemployed	8.1
Total Wages	$20,154,439
Av. Weekly Wage	$355.96
Prop. Value	$732,381,170
Retail Sales	$20,327,795

Coke County

Physical Features: West Texas prairie, hills, Colorado River valley; sandy loam, red soils; reservoir.

Economy: Oil-well supplies, agribusinesses, tourism.

History: Created 1889 from Tom Green County; named for Gov. Richard Coke.

Vital Statistics, 1993: Births, 41; deaths, 64; marriages, 27; divorces, 7.

Ethnicity, 1990: White, 3,222 (94.1%); Black, 6 (0.2%); American Indian, 17 (0.5%); Asian, 2 (0.1%); Other, 177 (5.2%). Hispanic, 422 (12.3%).

Recreation: Hunting, fishing; lakes; historic sites, county museum; Ole Coke County Pageant, July 4.

Minerals: Oil, gas.

Agriculture: Cattle, sheep, goats, wool and mohair; wheat, hay; some irrigation for hay.

ROBERT LEE (1,356) county seat; ranching, petroleum center.

Bronte (1,007); ranching, oil.

Other towns include: **Blackwell** (357, mostly in Nolan County),

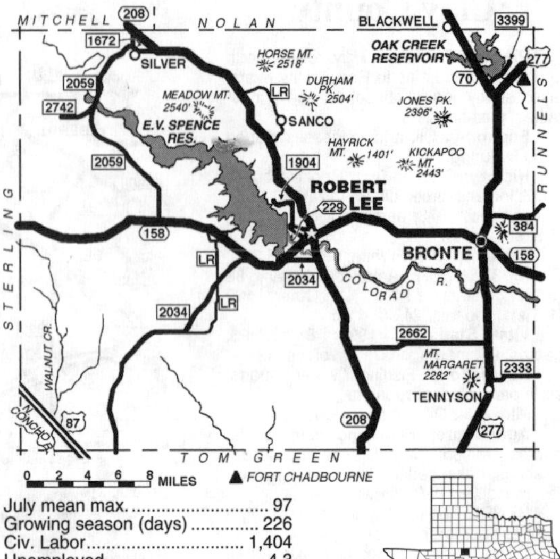

Population	**3,662**
(Change fm '90)	7.0
Land Area (sq. mi.)	898.8
Altitude (ft.)	1,758-2,608
Rainfall (in.)	20.7
Jan. mean min.	28
July mean max.	97
Growing season (days)	226
Civ. Labor	1,404
Unemployed	4.3
Total Wages	$15,615,676
Av. Weekly Wage	$340.96
Prop. Value	$320,890,827
Retail Sales	$26,100,968

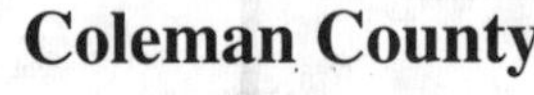

Coleman County

Physical Features: Hilly, rolling; drains to Colorado River, Pecan Bayou; lakes; mesquite, oaks.

Economy: Agribusiness, petroleum, tile, brick plants, other manufacturers.

History: Created 1858 from Brown, Travis counties; organization 1864; named for Houston's aide, R.M. Coleman.

Vital Statistics, 1993: Births, 98; deaths, 155; marriages, 105; divorces, 55.

Ethnicity, 1990: White, 8,995 (92.6%); Black, 246 (2.5%); American Indian, 29 (0.3%); Asian, 7 (0.1%); Other, 433 (4.5%). Hispanic, 1,139 (11.7%).

Recreation: Fishing, hunting; water sports; city park, historic sites; lakes; Santa Anna Peak.

Minerals: Oil, gas, coal, stone, clays.

Agriculture: Beef cattle, sheep, goats, horses, hogs; wheat, cotton, oats, grain sorghums; mesquite for firewood and furniture.

COLEMAN (5,441) county seat; varied manufacturing, aircraft restoration, agribusiness center; hospital, museum, bass tournament.

Other towns include: **Santa Anna** (1,356) agribusiness; some manufacturing; tourism; **Novice** (196).

Population	**9,932**
(Change fm '90)	2.3
Land Area (sq. mi.)	1,272.9
Altitude (ft.)	1,488-2,173
Rainfall (in.)	26.9
Jan. mean min.	32
July mean max.	96
Growing season (days)	226
Civ. Labor	3,857
Unemployed	6.6
Total Wages	$36,552,183
Av. Weekly Wage	$295.02
Prop. Value	$449,079,849
Retail Sales	$52,572,544

For explanation of sources, abbreviations and symbols, see p. 132.

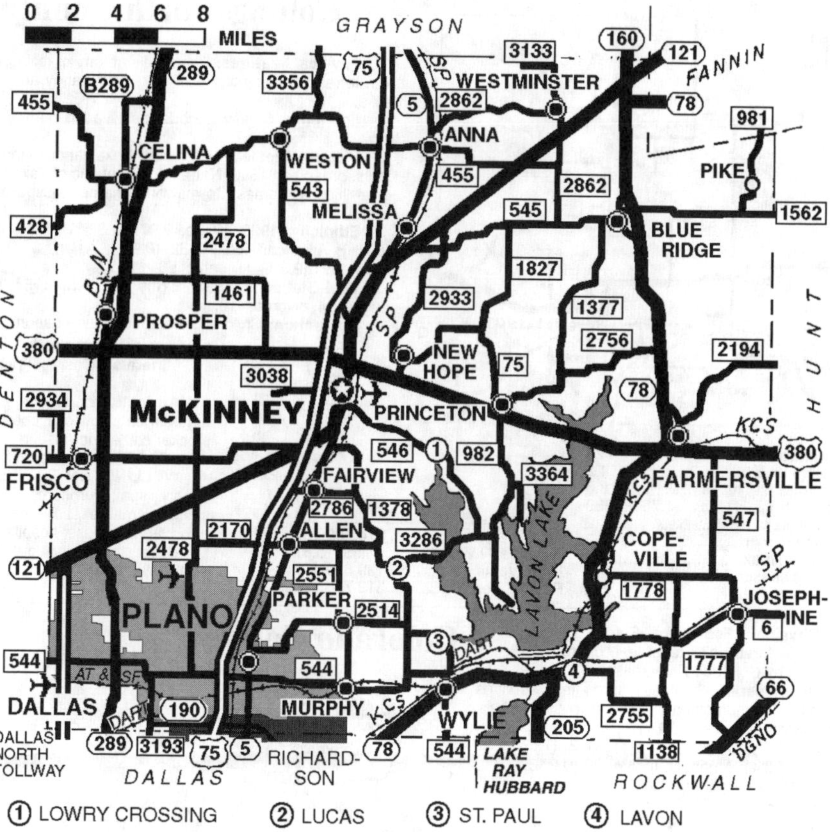

① LOWRY CROSSING ② LUCAS ③ ST. PAUL ④ LAVON

Collin County

Physical Features: North Texas county with heavy, black clay soil; level to rolling; drains to Trinity, Lavon Lake.

Economy: Varied manufacturing plants, agribusinesses, retail and wholesale center; many residents work in Dallas.

History: Created from Fannin County 1846. Named for pioneer settler Collin McKinney.

Vital Statistics, 1993: Births, 5,044; deaths, 1,123; marriages, 3,101; divorces, 1,762.

Ethnicity, 1990: White, 235,290 (89.1%); Black, 10,925 (4.1%); American Indian, 1,112 (0.4%); Asian, 7,480 (2.8%); Other, 9,229 (3.5%). Hispanic, 18,158 (6.9%).

Recreation: Fishing, water sports; historic sites; old homes restoration, tours; natural science museum; hot-air balloon festival.

Minerals: Limited stone production.

Agriculture: Wheat, grain sorghum, corn, hay, cotton; beef cattle, horses and sheep raised.

McKINNEY (25,585) county seat; agribusiness, trade center; varied industry; hospital; museums.

Plano (153,624, partly in Denton County); one of the state's fastest-growing cities; manufacturing; newspaper printing; medical services, research center; community college; commercial and financial center; hospitals.

Other towns include: **Allen** (23,030); **Celina** (1,877); **Fairview** (1,875); **Farmersville** (3,057); **Frisco** (9,780, partly in Denton County) varied manufacturing; community college; **Lucas** (2,586); **Murphy** (1,823); **Parker** (1,347); **Princeton** (2,288); **Prosper** (1,141); **Wylie** (10,884).

Population	**309,670**
(Change fm '90)	17.3
Land Area (sq. mi.)	847.7
Altitude (ft.)	472-753
Rainfall (in.)	36.9
Jan. mean min.	33
July mean max.	96
Growing season (days)	230
Civ. Labor	183,024
Unemployed	4.1
Total Wages	$2,874,632,183
Av. Weekly Wage	$566.95
Prop. Value	$18,615,197,808
Retail Sales	$3,341,126,508

For explanation of sources, abbreviations and symbols, see, p. 132.

Collingsworth County

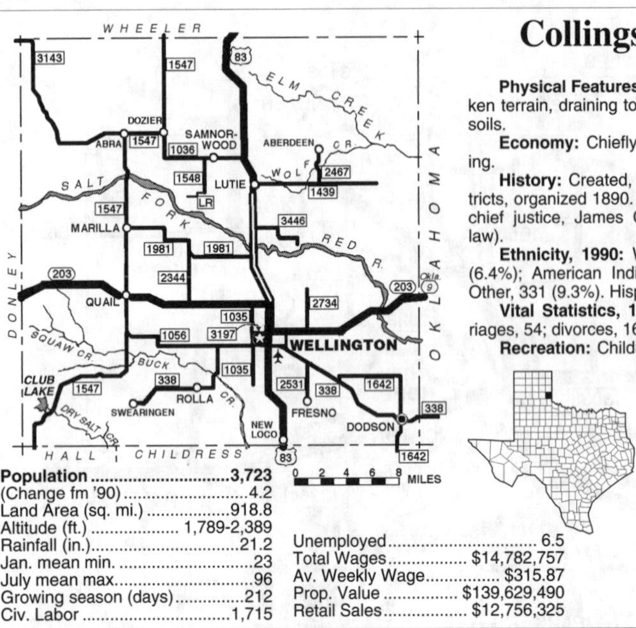

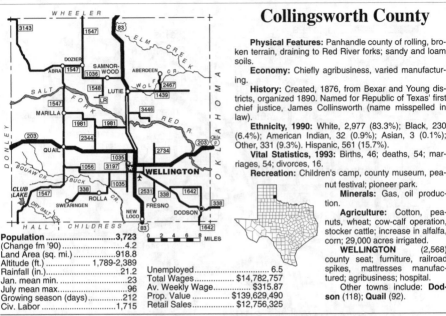

Physical Features: Panhandle county of rolling, broken terrain, draining to Red River forks; sandy and loam soils.

Economy: Chiefly agribusiness, varied manufacturing.

History: Created, 1876, from Bexar and Young districts, organized 1890. Named for Republic of Texas' first chief justice, James Collinsworth (name misspelled in law).

Ethnicity, 1990: White, 2,977 (83.3%); Black, 230 (6.4%); American Indian, 32 (0.9%); Asian, 3 (0.1%); Other, 331 (9.3%). Hispanic, 561 (15.7%).

Vital Statistics, 1993: Births, 46; deaths, 54; marriages, 54; divorces, 16.

Recreation: Children's camp, county museum, peanut festival; pioneer park.

Minerals: Gas, oil production.

Agriculture: Cotton, peanuts, wheat; cow-calf operation, stocker cattle; increase in alfalfa, corn; 29,000 acres irrigated.

WELLINGTON (2,568) county seat; furniture, railroad spikes, mattresses manufactured; agribusiness; hospital.

Other towns include: **Dodson** (118); **Quail** (92).

Population **3,723**
(Change fm '90) 4.2
Land Area (sq. mi.) 918.8
Altitude (ft.) 1,789-2,389
Rainfall (in.) 21.2
Jan. mean min. 23
July mean max. 96
Growing season (days) 212
Civ. Labor 1,715
Unemployed 6.5
Total Wages $14,782,757
Av. Weekly Wage $315.87
Prop. Value $139,629,490
Retail Sales $12,756,325

Colorado County

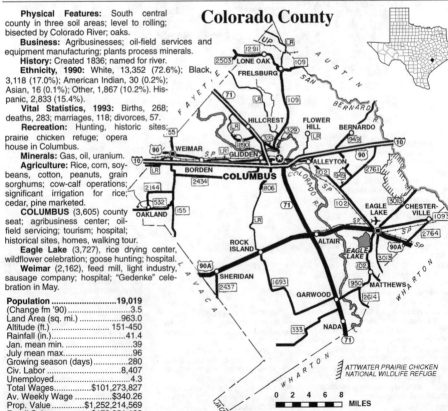

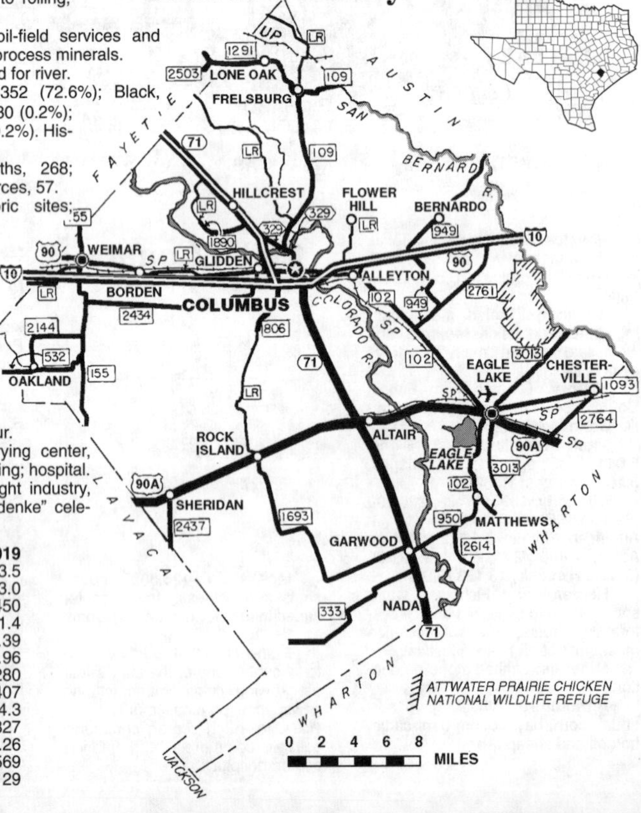

Physical Features: South central county in three soil areas; level to rolling; bisected by Colorado River; oaks.

Business: Agribusinesses; oil-field services and equipment manufacturing; plants process minerals.

History: Created 1836; named for river.

Ethnicity, 1990: White, 13,352 (72.6%); Black, 3,118 (17.0%); American Indian, 30 (0.2%); Asian, 16 (0.1%); Other, 1,867 (10.2%). Hispanic, 2,833 (15.4%).

Vital Statistics, 1993: Births, 268; deaths, 283; marriages, 118; divorces, 57.

Recreation: Hunting, historic sites; prairie chicken refuge; opera house in Columbus.

Minerals: Gas, oil, uranium.

Agriculture: Rice, corn, soybeans, cotton, peanuts, grain sorghums; cow-calf operations; significant irrigation for rice; cedar, pine marketed.

COLUMBUS (3,605) county seat; agribusiness center; oil-field servicing; tourism; hospital; historical sites, homes, walking tour.

Eagle Lake (3,727), rice drying center, wildflower celebration; goose hunting; hospital.

Weimar (2,162), feed mill, light industry, sausage company; hospital; "Gedenke" celebration in May.

Population **19,019**
(Change fm '90) 3.5
Land Area (sq. mi.) 963.0
Altitude (ft.) 151-450
Rainfall (in.) 41.4
Jan. mean min. 39
July mean max. 96
Growing season (days) 280
Civ. Labor 8,407
Unemployed 4.3
Total Wages $101,273,827
Av. Weekly Wage $340.26
Prop. Value $1,252,214,569
Retail Sales $178,351,129

ATTWATER PRAIRIE CHICKEN NATIONAL WILDLIFE REFUGE

0 2 4 6 8 MILES

Comal County

Population	**58,905**
(Change fm '90)	13.6
Land Area (sq. mi.)	561.4
Altitude (ft.)	623-1,473
Rainfall (in.)	33.6
Jan. mean min.	38
July mean max.	96
Growing season (days)	261
Civ. Labor	29,587
Unemployed	4.4
Total Wages	$361,550,561
Av. Weekly Wage	$366.99
Prop. Value	$3,178,162,562
Retail Sales	$3,254,125,738

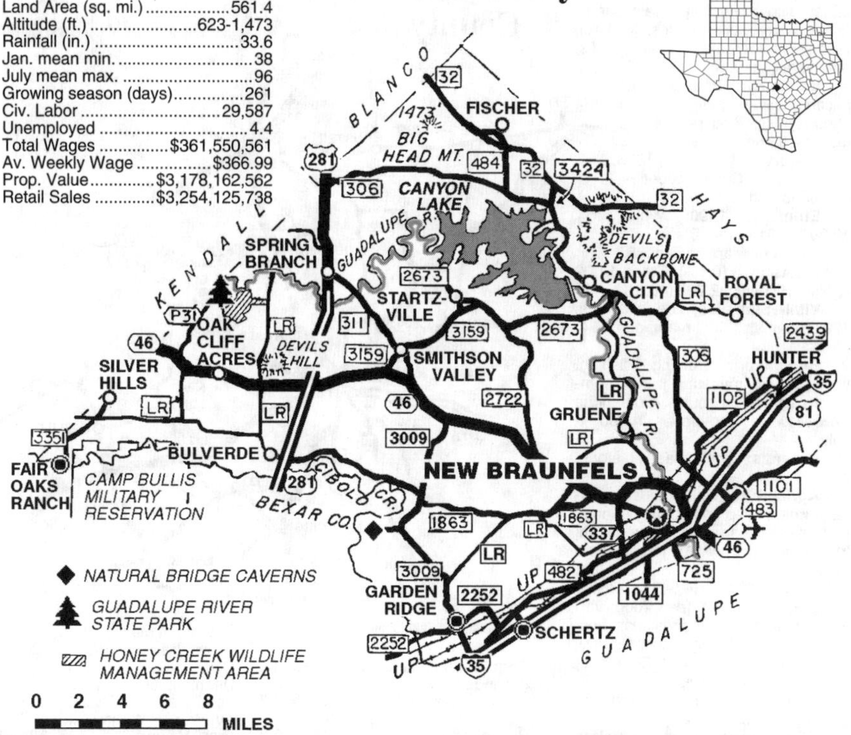

◆ NATURAL BRIDGE CAVERNS

GUADALUPE RIVER STATE PARK

HONEY CREEK WILDLIFE MANAGEMENT AREA

0 2 4 6 8 MILES

Physical Features: Scenic Southwest county of hills. Eighty percent above Balcones Escarpment. Spring-fed streams; 2.5-mile-long Comal River, Guadalupe River; Canyon Lake.

Economy: Varied manufacturing; tourism; county in San Antonio metropolitan area.

History: A pioneer German settlement, created from Bexar, Gonzales, and Travis counties and organized in 1846; named for river, a name for Spanish earthenware or metal pan used for cooking tortillas.

Ethnicity, 1990: White, 46,821 (90.3%); Black, 443 (0.9%); American Indian, 148 (0.3%); Asian, 164 (0.3%); Other, 4,256 (8.2%). Hispanic, 11,864 (22.9%) .

Vital Statistics, 1993: Births, 806; deaths, 580; marriages, 620; divorces, 311.

Recreation: Fishing, hunting; historic sites, Hummel museum; scenic drives; lake facilities; Prince Solms Park, other county parks; Landa Park with 76 species of trees; caverns; river resorts; river tubing; Schlitterbahn water park; Wurstfest in October-November.

Minerals: Stone, lime, sand and gravel.

Agriculture: Beef cattle, calf and stockers; hay, corn, sorghum; some drip irrigation for Christmas trees.

NEW BRAUNFELS (30,402, partly in Guadalupe County) county seat; manufacturing; retail, distribution; one of the most picturesque cities in Texas making it a tourist center; Conservation Plaza; rose garden; hospital; library; center for retarded.

Other towns include: **Garden Ridge** (1,767), and the retirement community area near **Canyon Lake** (11,180).

For explanation of sources, abbreviations and symbols, *see p. 132.*

Comanche County

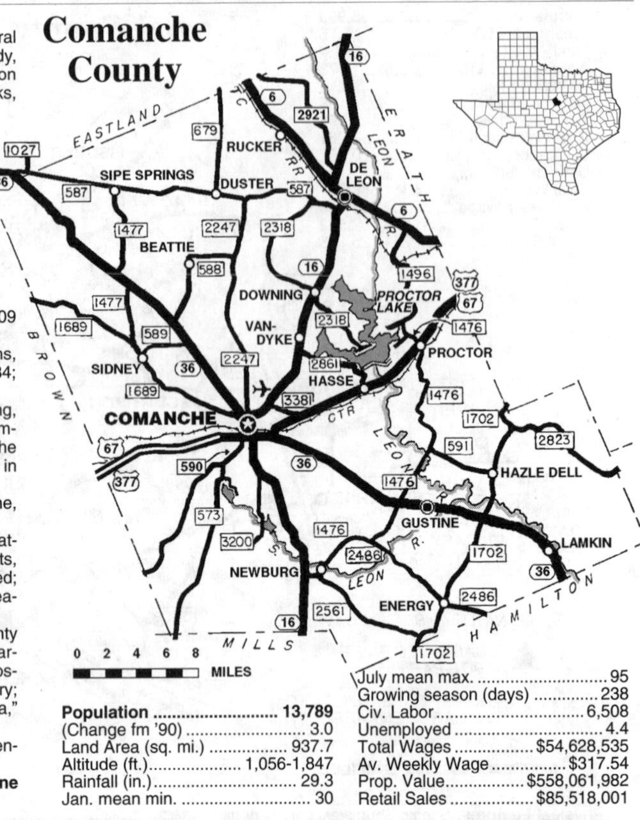

Physical Features: West central county with rolling, hilly terrain; sandy, loam, waxy soils; drains to Leon River, Proctor Lake; pecans, oaks, mesquites, cedars.

Economy: Peanut- and pecan-shelling plants; other agribusiness; food processing; manufacturing.

History: Created 1856 from Bosque, Coryell counties; named for Indian tribe.

Ethnicity, 1990: White, 12,297 (91.9%); Black, 16 (0.1%); American Indian, 51 (0.4%); Asian, 8 (0.1%); Other, 1,009 (7.5%). Hispanic, 2,205 (16.5%).

Vital Statistics, 1993: Births, 139; deaths, 205; marriages, 84; divorces, 66.

Recreation: Hunting, fishing, water sports; museum, parks, community center, museums; Comanche Pow-Wow in September, rodeo in July.

Minerals: Limited gas, oil, stone, clay.

Agriculture: Dairy industry, cattle, swine, sheep and goats; peanuts, hay, pecans, fruit also produced; 38,000 acres irrigated, mostly peanuts.

COMANCHE (4,343) county seat; plants process feed, food; varied manufacturing; agribusiness; hospital; Ranger College branch; library; state's oldest courthouse, "Old Cora," on display on town square.

De Leon (2,292), marketing center for peanuts, pecans.

Other towns include: **Gustine** (458).

Population	**13,789**
(Change fm '90)	3.0
Land Area (sq. mi.)	937.7
Altitude (ft.)	1,056-1,847
Rainfall (in.)	29.3
Jan. mean min.	30
July mean max.	95
Growing season (days)	238
Civ. Labor	6,508
Unemployed	4.4
Total Wages	$54,628,535
Av. Weekly Wage	$317.54
Prop. Value	$558,061,982
Retail Sales	$85,518,001

Concho County

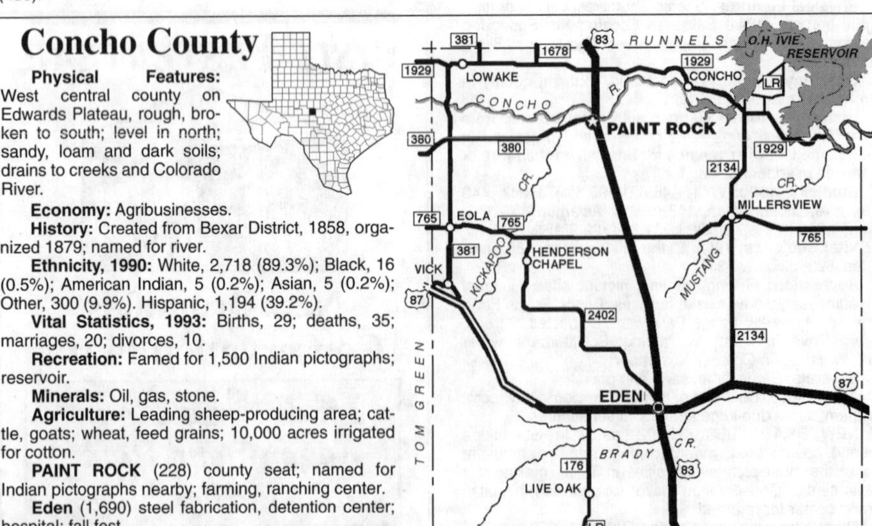

Physical Features: West central county on Edwards Plateau, rough, broken to south; level in north; sandy, loam and dark soils; drains to creeks and Colorado River.

Economy: Agribusinesses.

History: Created from Bexar District, 1858, organized 1879; named for river.

Ethnicity, 1990: White, 2,718 (89.3%); Black, 16 (0.5%); American Indian, 5 (0.2%); Asian, 5 (0.2%); Other, 300 (9.9%). Hispanic, 1,194 (39.2%).

Vital Statistics, 1993: Births, 29; deaths, 35; marriages, 20; divorces, 10.

Recreation: Famed for 1,500 Indian pictographs; reservoir.

Minerals: Oil, gas, stone.

Agriculture: Leading sheep-producing area; cattle, goats; wheat, feed grains; 10,000 acres irrigated for cotton.

PAINT ROCK (228) county seat; named for Indian pictographs nearby; farming, ranching center.

Eden (1,690) steel fabrication, detention center; hospital; fall fest.

Population	**3,211**
(Change fm '90)	5.5
Land Area (sq. mi.)	991.5
Altitude (ft.)	1,631-2,083
Rainfall (in.)	23.9
Jan. mean min.	33
July mean max.	97
Growing season (days)	228
Civ. Labor	1,399
Unemployed	4.2
Total Wages	$11,202,425
Av. Weekly Wage	$321.34
Prop. Value	$353,013,927
Retail Sales	$10,962,048

Cooke County

Physical Features: North central county; drains to Red, Trinity rivers, lakes; sandy, red, loam soils.

Economy: Agribusinesses, oil industries, varied manufacturing.

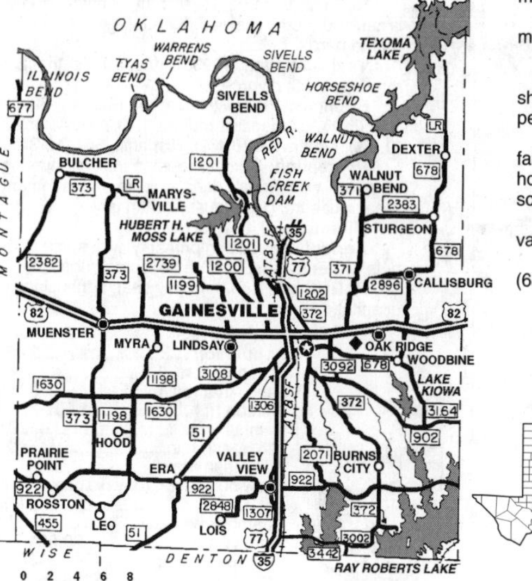

History: Created 1848 from Fannin County; named for Capt. W.G. Cooke of the Texas Revolution.

Ethnicity, 1990: White, 28,375 (92.2%); Black, 1,169 (3.8%); American Indian, 232 (0.8%); Asian, 131 (0.4%); Other, 870 (2.8%). Hispanic, 1,408 (4.6%).

Vital Statistics, 1993: Births, 389; deaths, 338; marriages, 677; divorces, 197.

Recreation: Water sports; hunting, fishing; zoo; museum; park.

Minerals: Oil, gas, sand, gravel.

Agriculture: Beef, dairy operations, horses, swine, sheep; wheat, grain sorghums, oats, corn, soybeans, peanuts, hay; some firewood sold.

GAINESVILLE (14,518) county seat; aircraft, steel fabrication, tourism; agribusiness center; zoo, Victorian homes, walking tours; hospital; community college, state school; Camp Sweeney for diabetic children.

Muenster (1,418), dairy center, food processing, oil, varied manufacturing; hospital, Germanfest.

Other towns include: **Callisburg** (377); **Lindsay** (683); **Oak Ridge** (191); **Valley View** (694).

Population	**31,542**
(Change fm '90)	2.5
Land Area (sq. mi.)	873.7
Altitude (ft.)	636-1,007
Rainfall (in.)	33.0
Jan. mean min.	28
July mean max.	96
Growing season (days)	226
Civ. Labor	15,489
Unemployed	6.0
Total Wages	$188,080,058
Av. Weekly Wage	$367.66
Prop. Value	$1,246,225,333
Retail Sales	$289,881,694

Coryell County

Physical Features: Leon Valley in center, remainder rolling, hilly.

Economy: Fort Hood military business, agribusiness, plastics and other manufacturing.

History: Created from Bell County 1854; named for local pioneer, James Coryell.

Ethnicity, 1990: White, 45,078 (70.2%); Black, 13,592 (21.2%); American Indian, 461 (0.7%); Asian, 1,670 (2.6%); Other, 3,412 (5.3%). Hispanic, 6,243 (9.7%).

Vital Statistics, 1993: Births, 932; deaths, 262; marriages, 256; divorces, 294.

Recreation: state park; hunting; nearby lakes and Leon River. Historic homes; log jail; Shivaree in June.

Population	**65,588**
(Change fm '90)	2.1
Land Area (sq. mi.)	1,051.8
Altitude (ft.)	1,365-1,839
Rainfall (in.)	32.5
Jan. mean min.	34
July mean max.	97
Growing season (days)	241
Civ. Labor	19,811
Unemployed	5.0
Total Wages	$180,436,023
Av. Weekly Wage	$350.72
Prop. Value	$1,048,372,550
Retail Sales	$193,006,730

For explanation of sources, abbreviations and symbols, see p. 132.

Minerals: Small stone, sand and gravel production.

Agriculture: Beef cattle, sheep, goats, turkeys, hogs, horses; hay, grain sorghums, pecans, peaches, grapes; cedar posts; some irrigation.

GATESVILLE (11,874) county seat; varied manufacturing; four prison units; refurbished courthouse; museum; antique shows; branch Central Texas College.

Copperas Cove (24,848), business center for Fort Hood; industrial filters, other manufacturing; hospital; Central Texas College.

Other towns include: **Evant** (453); **Fort Gates** (788); **Oglesby** (463); **South Mountain** (300).

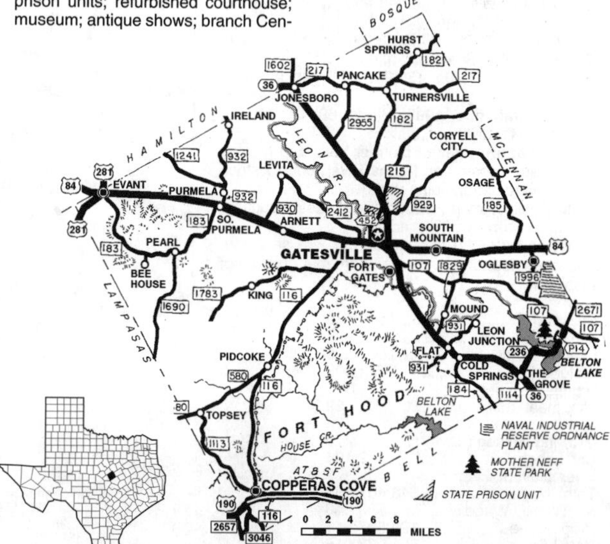

Cottle County

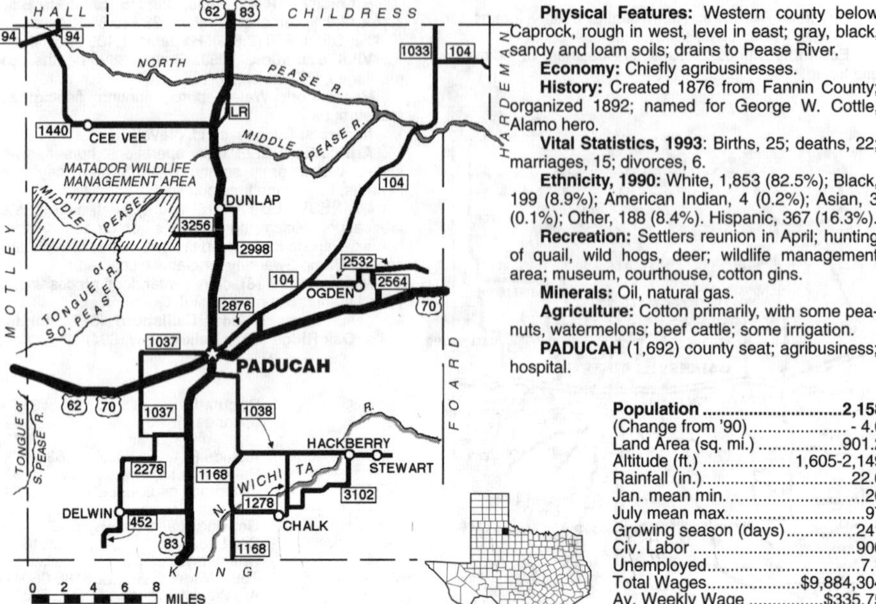

Physical Features: Western county below Caprock, rough in west, level in east; gray, black, sandy and loam soils; drains to Pease River.

Economy: Chiefly agribusinesses.

History: Created 1876 from Fannin County; organized 1892; named for George W. Cottle, Alamo hero.

Vital Statistics, 1993: Births, 25; deaths, 22; marriages, 15; divorces, 6.

Ethnicity, 1990: White, 1,853 (82.5%); Black, 199 (8.9%); American Indian, 4 (0.2%); Asian, 3 (0.1%); Other, 188 (8.4%). Hispanic, 367 (16.3%).

Recreation: Settlers reunion in April; hunting of quail, wild hogs, deer; wildlife management area; museum, courthouse, cotton gins.

Minerals: Oil, natural gas.

Agriculture: Cotton primarily, with some peanuts, watermelons; beef cattle; some irrigation.

PADUCAH (1,692) county seat; agribusiness; hospital.

Population	**2,158**
(Change from '90)	- 4.0
Land Area (sq. mi.)	901.2
Altitude (ft.)	1,605-2,149
Rainfall (in.)	22.0
Jan. mean min.	26
July mean max.	97
Growing season (days)	241
Civ. Labor	900
Unemployed	7.1
Total Wages	$9,884,304
Av. Weekly Wage	$335.75
Prop. Value	$128,867,318
Retail Sales	$10,256,405

Crane County

Physical Features: Rolling prairie, Pecos Valley, some hills; sandy, loam soils; Juan Cordona Lake.

Economy: Oil-based economy.

History: Created from Tom Green County, 1887, organized 1927; named for Baylor University President W. C. Crane.

Ethnicity, 1990: White, 3,097 (66.6%); Black, 130 (2.8%); American Indian, 11 (0.2%); Asian, 10 (0.2%); Other, 1,404 (30.2%). Hispanic, 1,577 (33.9%).

Vital Statistics, 1993: Births, 69; deaths, 33; marriages, 41; divorces, 23.

Recreation: Sites of pioneer trails and historic Horsehead Crossing on Pecos River; county stock show in January; camping park.

Minerals: Among leaders in oil, gas production.

Agriculture: Cattle ranching.

CRANE (3,572) county seat; oil-well servicing, production; foundry; steel, surfboard manufacturing; hospital.

Population	**4,758**
(Change fm '90)	2.3
Land Area (sq. mi.)	785.6
Altitude (ft.)	2,475-2,902
Rainfall (in.)	12.0
Jan. mean min.	29
July mean max.	96
Growing season (days)	225
Civ. Labor	2,196
Unemployed	6.1
Total Wages	$43,407,457
Av. Weekly Wage	$507.48
Prop. Value	$1,198,547,341
Retail Sales	$21,928,016

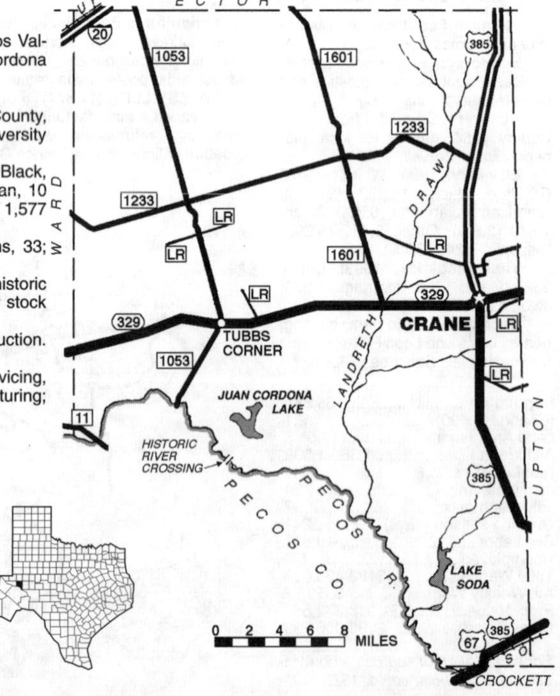

Crockett County

Physical Features: Level to rough, hilly terrain; drains to Pecos River on south; rocky soils.

Economy: Oil, ranching.

History: Created 1875 from Bexar, organized 1891; named for Alamo hero, Davy Crockett.

Ethnicity, 1990: White, 4,018 (98.5%); Black, 39 (1.0%); American Indian, 9 (0.2%); Asian, 4 (0.1%); Other, 8 (0.2%). Hispanic, 2,021 (49.6%).

Vital Statistics, 1993: Births, 71; deaths, 36; marriages, 31; divorces, 11.

Recreation: Hunting; historic sites, state park; county museum; Davy Crockett statue in park.

Minerals: Oil, gas production.

Agriculture: A major sheep, Angora goat producing county; income also from beef cattle.

OZONA (3,326) county seat; trade center for ranching; hunting leases; tourism; hospital.

Population	**4,371**
(Change fm '90)	7.2
Land Area (sq. mi.)	2,807.6
Altitude (ft.)	1,824-3,958
Rainfall (in.)	18.2
Jan. mean min.	31
July mean max.	97
Growing season (days)	233
Civ. Labor	1,860
Unemployed	3.5
Total Wages	$25,045,417
Av. Weekly Wage	$346.99
Prop. Value	$733,423,680
Retail Sales	$23,919,785

Crosby County

Phyical Features: Flat, rich soil above Caprock, broken below; drains into Brazos River forks and playas.

Business: Agribusiness, tourism; food processing, clothes manufacturing, gasohol plant; solar-power plant; drug, alcohol treatment center.

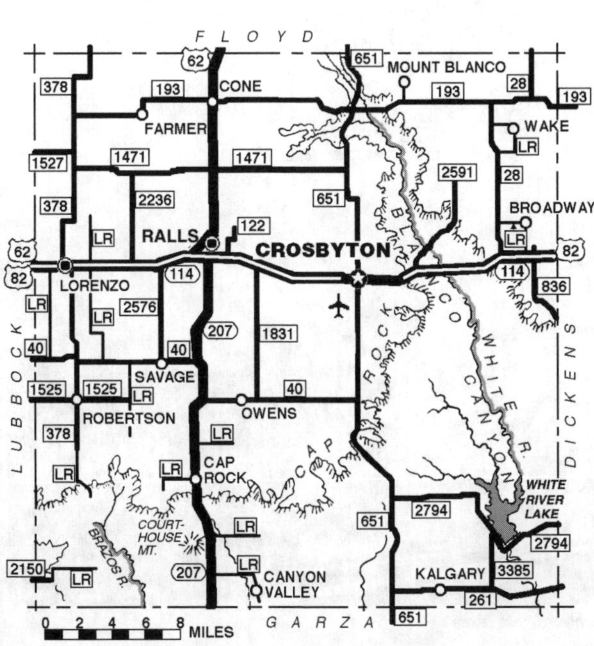

History: Created from Bexar District 1876, organized 1886; named for Texas Land Commissioner Stephen Crosby.

Ethnicity, 1990: White, 5,784 (79.2%); Black, 321 (4.4%); American Indian, 13 (0.2%); Asian, 8 (0.1%); Other, 1,178 (16.1%). Hispanic, 3,111 (42.6%).

Vital Statistics, 1993: Births, 115; deaths, 78; marriages, 49; divorces, 27.

Recreation: Lake; Silver Falls Park; outdoor theater in August.

Minerals: Sand, gravel, oil, gas.

Agriculture: Cotton and beef cattle; also, some grain sorghum and wheat; hogs and sheep; about 145,000 acres irrigated.

CROSBYTON (2,062) county seat; agribusiness center; Pioneer Museum, hospital.

Ralls (2,119), agribusiness, marketing; museum of Indian artifacts; Cotton Boll Fest in September.

Lorenzo (1,246).

Population	**7,308**
(Change fm '90)	0.1
Land Area (sq. mi.)	899.5
Altitude (ft.)	2,369,3,167
Rainfall (in.)	20.5
Jan. mean min.	24
July mean max.	93
Growing season (days)	206
Civ. Labor	3,352
Unemployed	7.6
Total Wages	$34,735,786
Av. Weekly Wage	$324.68
Prop. Value	$283,166,859
Retail Sales	$32,680,360

For explanation of sources, abbreviations and symbols, see p. 132.

Culberson County

Physical Features: Contains Texas' highest mountain; entire county over 3,000 feet in elevation; slopes toward Pecos Valley on east, Diablo Bolson on west; salt lakes; unique vegetation in canyons.

Economy: Agribusiness; tourism; talc mining, processing; oil production.

History: Created from El Paso County 1911, organized 1912; named for D.B. Culberson, Texas congressman.

Vital Statistics, 1993: Births, 57; deaths, 13; marriages, 23; divorces, 7.

Ethnicity, 1990: White, 2,400 (70.4%); Black, 2 (0.1%); American Indian, 16 (0.5%); Asian, 27 (0.8%); Other, 962 (28.2%). Hispanic, 2,419 (71.0%).

Recreation: National park; Guadalupe and El Capitan, twin peaks; scenic canyons and mountains; classic car museum, antique saloon bar; frontier days in June, big buck tournament.

Minerals: Sulfur, talc, marble.

Agriculture: Beef cattle; crops include cotton, vegetables, melons, pecans; 4,000 acres in irrigation.

VAN HORN (2,838) county seat; tourism; ranching; rock crushing; hospital; airport.

Population	**3,335**
(Change fm '90)	- 2.1
Land Area (sq. mi.)	3,812.6
Altitude (ft.)	3,021-8,749
Rainfall (in.)	11.1
Jan. mean min.	30
July mean max.	95
Growing season (days)	224
Civ. Labor	1,307
Unemployed	5.5
Total Wages	$23,665,335
Av. Weekly Wage	$416.65
Prop. Value	$275,915,940
Retail Sales	$34,890,745

For explanation of sources, abbreviations and symbols, see p. 132.

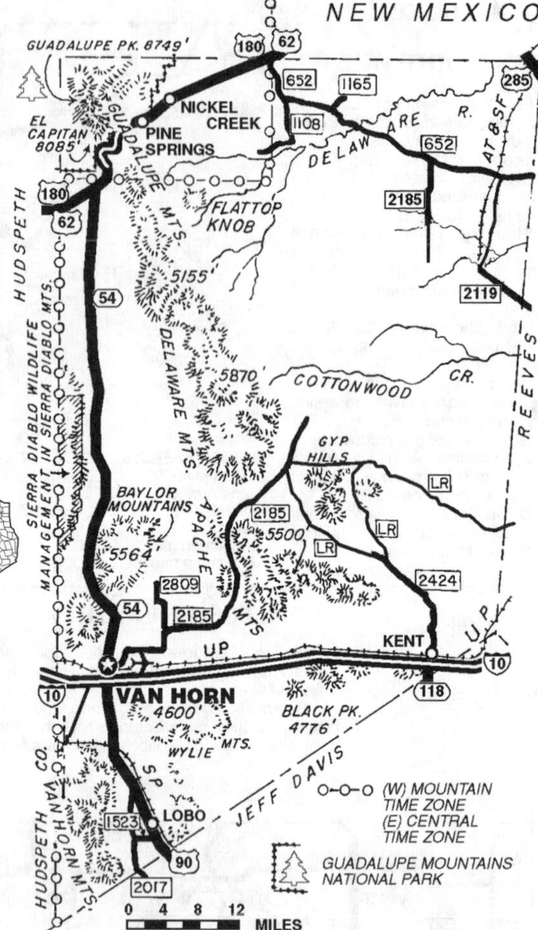

El Capitan in northwestern Culberson County in West Texas.

Dallam County

Physical Features: Prairie, over 3,800-foot elevation, broken by creeks; playas; sandy, loam soils; Rita Blanca National Grassland.

Economy: Agribusinesses, tourism, small manufacturing.

History: Created from Bexar District, 1876, organized 1891. Named for lawyer-editor James W. Dallam.

Ethnicity, 1990: White, 4,600 (84.2%); Black, 112 (2.1%); American Indian, 43 (0.8%); Asian, 14 (0.3%); Other, 692 (12.7%). Hispanic, 1,151 (21.1%).

Vital Statistics, 1993: Births, 96; deaths, 51; marriages, 76; divorces, 38.

Recreation: Interstate Fair in September; XIT Museum; XIT Rodeo and Reunion in August; La Rita Theater in June-August.

Minerals: Not significant.

Agriculture: Beef cattle, feedlots, swine; corn, wheat, grain sorghums, pinto beans, potatoes; substantial irrigation.

DALHART (6,290, partly in Hartley County) county seat; Frank Phillips College branch, agribusiness center for parts of Texas, New Mexico, Oklahoma; railroad; feedlots; some manufacturing; hospital.

Other town, **Texline** (423).

Population	**5,533**
(Change fm '90)	1.3
Land Area (sq. mi.)	1,504.8
Altitude (ft.)	3,869-4,693
Rainfall (in.)	16.5
Jan. mean min.	18
July mean max.	91
Growing season (days)	178
Civ. Labor	3,180
Unemployed	3.3
Total Wages	$44,681,269
Av. Weekly Wage	$353.42
Prop. Value	$392,241,529
Retail Sales	$54,439,676

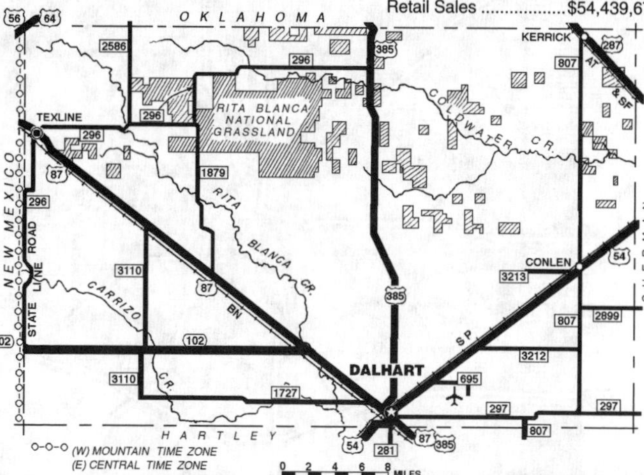

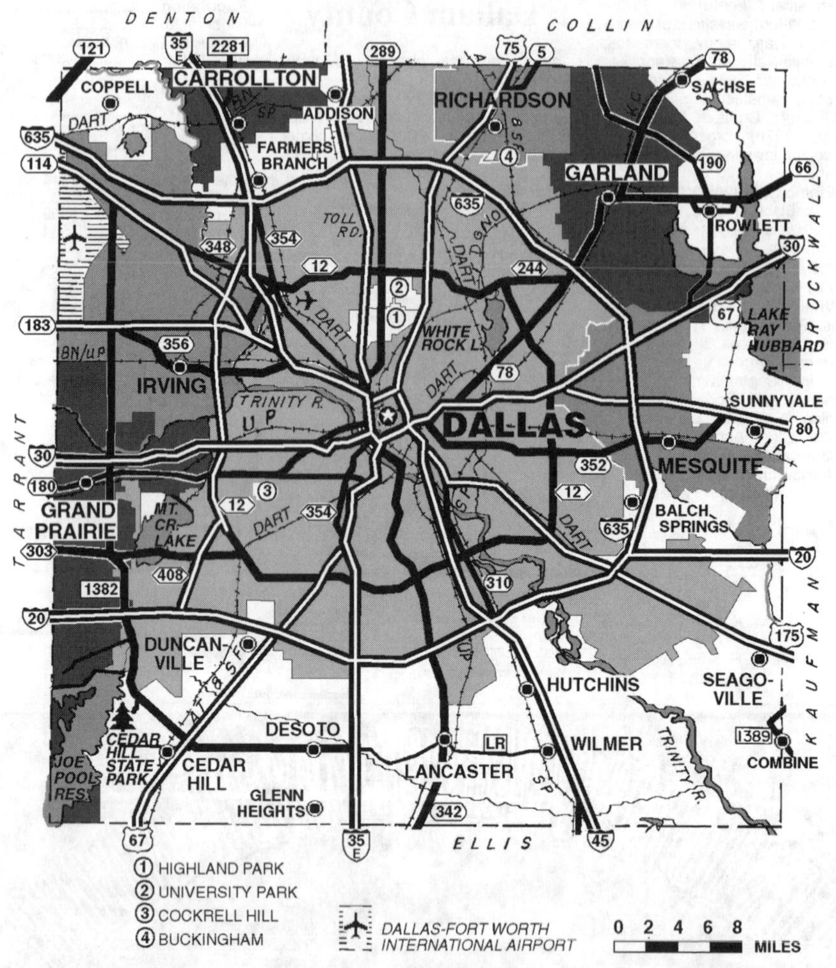
DENTON
COLLIN
TARRANT
ROCKWALL
KAUFMAN
ELLIS
COPPELL
CARROLLTON
ADDISON
RICHARDSON
SACHSE
FARMERS BRANCH
GARLAND
ROWLETT
LAKE RAY HUBBARD
IRVING
WHITE ROCK L.
TRINITY R.
DALLAS
SUNNYVALE
MESQUITE
GRAND PRAIRIE
MT. CR. LAKE
BALCH SPRINGS
DUNCAN-VILLE
HUTCHINS
SEAGO-VILLE
CEDAR HILL STATE PARK
JOE POOL RES.
CEDAR HILL
DESOTO
LANCASTER
WILMER
COMBINE
GLENN HEIGHTS
TOLL RD.
DART
① HIGHLAND PARK
② UNIVERSITY PARK
③ COCKRELL HILL
④ BUCKINGHAM
DALLAS-FORT WORTH INTERNATIONAL AIRPORT
0 2 4 6 8 MILES

CLEMENTS...
"The Source" for antiques and fine reproductions
Why spend valuable time and money elsewhere when you can find it all at Clements? From 18th and 19th century French and English antiques to the finest hand-made reproductions, let Clements be your one source! Clements... the unsurpassed source for quality, selection, service and value!
• 75,000 SQ. FT. SHOWROOM AND WAREHOUSE •
MONTHLY
• ESTATE AUCTIONS •
2ND SATURDAY OF EACH MONTH,
AUCTION TIME - 11:00AM
CALL 564-1520
FOR MORE INFORMATION!
CA
CLEMENTS
ONLY 20 MINUTES EAST OF DALLAS
HWY. 80 AT FM-740
FORNEY, TEXAS
214-564-1520
HOURS: MON-SAT
9AM - 5PM

Dallas County

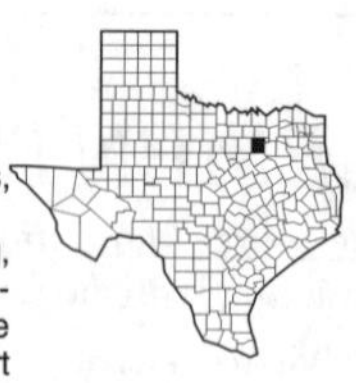

Population 1,938,116
(Change fm '90) 4.6
Land Area (sq. mi.) 879.8
Altitude (ft.) 382-750
Rainfall (in.) 35.9
Jan. mean min. 36
July mean max. 95
Growing season (days) 235
Civ. Labor 1,149,013
Unemployed 5.6
Total Wages $37,309,921,848
Av. Weekly Wage $598.96
Prop. Value $102,312,207,220
Retail Sales............$28,771,909,001

Physical Features: Mostly flat, heavy blackland soils, sandy clays in west; drains to Trinity River.

Economy: A national center for insurance, banking, transportation, electronics manufacturing, data processing, conventions and trade shows; foreign-trade zone located at D/FW International Airport, U.S. Customs port of entry; more than 130 million feet of office space.

History: Created 1846 from Nacogdoches, Robertson counties; named for U.S. Vice President George Mifflin Dallas.

Ethnicity, 1990: White, 1,241,455 (67.0%); Black, 369,597 (19.9%); American Indian, 9,437 (0.5%); Asian, 52,238 (2.8%); Other, 180,083 (9.7%). Hispanic, 315,630 (17.0%).

Vital Statistics, 1993: Births, 36,773; deaths, 13,522; marriages, 17,532; divorces, 11,745.

Recreation: One of the state's top tourist destinations and one of the nation's most popular convention centers.

State Fair, museums, zoo, West End shopping and tourist district, historical sites, including a museum in the old Texas School Book Depository, site of the assassination of President Kennedy.

Other important attractions include the Morton H. Meyerson Symphony Center; performing arts; professional sports; Texas broadcast museum; lakes; theme and amusement parks.

Agriculture: Horticultural crops; corn, wheat, hay; horses, beff cattle, calves, breeder cattle raised.

Education: Southern Methodist University, University of Dallas, Dallas Baptist College, University of Texas at Dallas, University of Texas Southwestern Medical Center and many other education centers.

DALLAS (1,036,309) county seat; second-largest city in Texas and center of state's largest consolidated metropolitan area (4.2 million); D/FW International Airport is world's largest in acreage and one of the world's busiest in emplanements; world headquarters for the U.S. Army and Air Force Exchange Service; Federal Reserve Bank; a leader in fashions and in computer operations; Infomart, a large computer-sales complex; many hotels in downtown area offer adequate accomodations for most conventions (40,000 rooms in greater Dallas area).

Garland (187,439), varied manufacturing; community college branch; hospital; performing arts center.

Irving (166,523), Texas Stadium, home of the Dallas Cowboys; headquarters for the Boy Scouts of America; varied light manufacturing, food processing; distribution center; Northlake College; hospitals.

Other large cities include: **Addison** (10,336) general aviation airport; **Balch Springs** (18,014); **Carrollton** (90,934, partly in Denton, Collin counties), residential community; distribution center; **Cedar Hill** (21,885, partly in Ellis County), Northwood Institute; **Coppell** (19,851) distribution, millwork; varied manufacturing; planned community; **DeSoto** (32,794), residential community, varied light industry; **Duncanville** (36,446); varied manufacturing; residential community; **Farmers Branch** (24,713), distribution center; varied manufacturing; Brookhaven College; hospital; **Grand Prairie** (103,913, partly in Ellis, Tarrant counties), defense industries; distribution center; hospital, Joe Pool Lake; **Highland Park** (9,287); **Hutchins** (2,975), varied manufacturing; **Lancaster** (24,300), industrial, agricultural center; distribution facilities; Cedar Valley College; airport; hospital; **Mesquite** (108,960), residential city with varied industries; hospitals; championship rodeo; Samuel Farm; **Richardson** (80,898), telecommunications, software development; Richland College; hospital; Owens Spring Creek Farm; **Rowlett** (27,899), varied manufacturing; hospital; farmers market; **Sunnyvale** (2,500); **Wilmer** (2,536).

Dawson County

Physical Features: South High Plains county in West Texas, broken on the east; loam and sandy soils.

Economy: Agribusinesses; oil industries; apparel, farm, gin equipment manufacturing.

History: Created from Bexar District, 1876, organized 1905; named for Nicholas M. Dawson, San Jacinto veteran.

Vital Statistics, 1993: Births, 237; deaths, 140; marriages, 127; divorces, 74.

Ethnicity, 1990: White, 9,789 (68.2%); Black, 622 (4.3%); American Indian, 23 (0.2%); Asian, 19 (0.1%); Other, 3,896 (27.2%). Hispanic, 6,120 (42.7%).

Recreation: Parks; museum; campground; May Fun Fest; July 4 celebration.

Minerals: Oil, natural gas.

Agriculture: A major cotton-producing county; also grain sorghums, peanuts; beef cattle, horses, swine raised; 45,000 acres irrigated for cotton.

LAMESA (11,148) county seat; agribusiness; food processing, oil-field services; some manufacturing; computerized cotton-classing office; hospital; campus of Howard College; prison unit.

Other towns include: **Welch** (110); **Los Ybañez** (91). **Ackerly** (265, partly in Martin County).

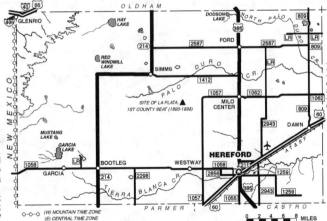

Population	**15,813**
(Change fm '90)	10.2
Land Area (sq. mi.)	902.1
Altitude (ft.)	2,860-3,095
Rainfall (in.)	16.2
Jan. mean min.	25
July mean max.	95
Growing season (days)	210
Civ. Labor	6,292
Unemployed	8.0
Total Wages	$83,893,831
Av. Weekly Wage	$344.39
Prop. Value	$895,257,335
Retail Sales	$100,466,424

Deaf Smith County

Physical Features: Panhandle High Plains county, partly broken; chocolate and sandy loam soils; drains to Palo Duro and Tierra Blanca creeks.

Economy: Sugar refinery; meat packers; offset printing; other varied industries, mostly agribusiness.

History: Created 1876, from Bexar District; organized 1890. Named for famed scout in Texas Revolution, Erastus (Deaf) Smith.

Ethnicity, 1990: White, 14,522 (75.8%); Black, 307 (1.6%); American Indian, 49 (0.3%); Asian, 39 (0.2%); Other, 4,236 (22.1%). Hispanic, 9,356 (48.8%).

Vital Statistics, 1993: Births, 382; deaths, 130; marriages, 173; divorces, 36.

Recreation: Museum, tours; National Cowgirl Hall of Fame.

Minerals: Not significant.

Agriculture: One of leading farm counties; large cattle feedlot operations; crops are sorghums, wheat, oats, barley, beets, corn, cotton, onions, other vegetables, sunflowers; 205,000 acres irrigated.

HEREFORD (14,872) county seat; agribusinesses, food processing; varied manufacturing; hospital.

Population	**19,310**
(Change fm '90)	0.8
Land Area (sq. mi.)	1,497.4
Altitude (ft.)	3,789-4,362
Rainfall (in.)	16.0
Jan. mean min.	21
July mean max.	90
Growing season (days)	195
Civ. Labor	9,332
Unemployed	7.4
Total Wages	$120,629,461
Av. Weekly Wage	$359.35
Prop. Value	$678,883,292
Retail Sales	$135,445,539

Delta County

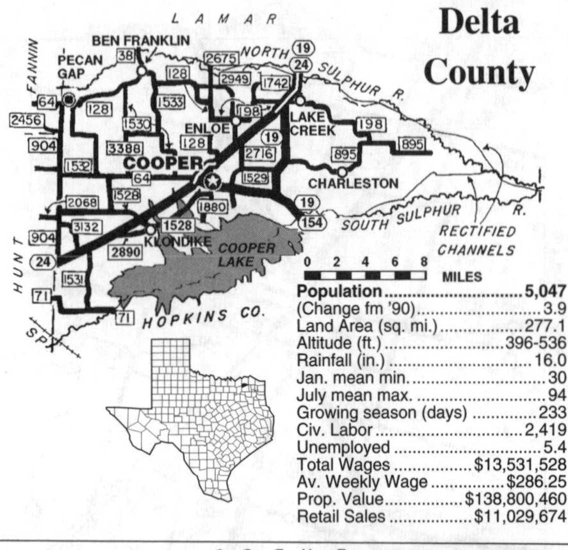

Population	**5,047**
(Change fm '90)	3.9
Land Area (sq. mi.)	277.1
Altitude (ft.)	396-536
Rainfall (in.)	16.0
Jan. mean min.	30
July mean max.	94
Growing season (days)	233
Civ. Labor	2,419
Unemployed	5.4
Total Wages	$13,531,528
Av. Weekly Wage	$286.25
Prop. Value	$138,800,460
Retail Sales	$11,029,674

Physical Features: Northeast county between two forks of Sulphur River; lake; black, sandy loam soils.

Economy: Agribusinesses; tourism; manufacturing.

History: Created from Lamar, Hopkins counties 1870. Greek letter delta origin of name, because of shape of the county.

Ethnicity, 1990: White, 4,388 (90.3%); Black, 404 (8.3%); American Indian, 41 (0.8%); Asian, 7 (0.1%); Other, 17 (0.4%). Hispanic, 67 (1.4%).

Vital Statistics, 1993: Births, 59; deaths, 82; marriages, 41; divorces, 25.

Recreation: Fishing, hunting; lakes, state park; Mayfest.

Minerals: Not significant.

Agriculture: Beef, dairy cattle; crops include hay, wheat, soybeans, cotton, corn, sorghum.

COOPER (2,245) county seat; industrial park, some manufacturing; agribusiness; museum.

Other towns include: **Pecan Gap** (256, partly in Fannin County).

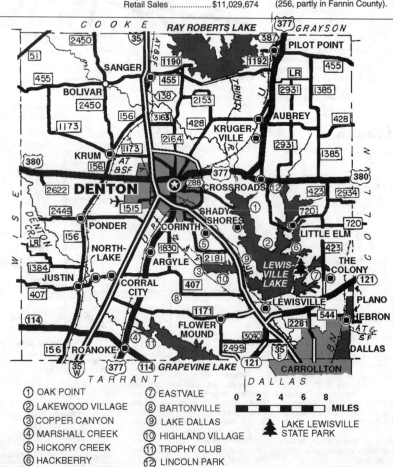

① OAK POINT
② LAKEWOOD VILLAGE
③ COPPER CANYON
④ MARSHALL CREEK
⑤ HICKORY CREEK
⑥ HACKBERRY
⑦ EASTVALE
⑧ BARTONVILLE
⑨ LAKE DALLAS
⑩ HIGHLAND VILLAGE
⑪ TROPHY CLUB
⑫ LINCOLN PARK

0 2 4 6 8 MILES

LAKE LEWISVILLE STATE PARK

Denton County

Physical Features: North Texas county; partly hilly, draining to Trinity River, two lakes; Blackland and Grand Prairie soils and terrain.

Economy: Varied industries; colleges; tourism; part of Dallas-Fort Worth metropolitan area.

History: Created out of Fannin County, 1846; named for John B. Denton, pioneer Protestant minister.

Ethnicity, 1990: White, 241,982 (88.5%); Black, 13,569 (5.0%); American Indian, 1,416 (0.5%); Asian, 6,870 (2.5%); Other, 9,688 (3.5%). Hispanic, 19,013 (7.0%).

Vital Statistics, 1993: Births, 5,049; deaths, 1,233; marriages, 2,598; divorces, 1,684.

Recreation: Water sports on at Lewisville, Grapevine lakes, seven U.S. Corps of Engineers parks; Ray Roberts lake; universities' cultural, athletic activities, including "Texas Women; A Celebration of History'" exhibit at TWU library; State D.A.R. Museum "First Ladies of Texas" collection of gowns and memorabilia; Little Chapel in the Woods, botanical gardens; Denton Jazzfest in September.

Minerals: Limited output oil, sand, gravel, gas, clay.

Education: University of North Texas and Texas Woman's University.

Agriculture: Horses, hen eggs, beef, slaughter cattle; hay and wheat are the top crops; also grown are sorghum, nursery crops and turfgrass; peanuts, turf irrigated.

DENTON (71,702) county seat; University of North Texas, Texas Woman's University, Denton State School (for the retarded); plants manufacture a variety of products; hospitals.

Lewisville (52,908), retail center, electronics and varied industries including missile manufacturing; Lewisville Lake, hospital.

Carrollton (90,934, partly in Dallas, Collin counties).

Other towns include: **The Colony** (24,782), on eastern shore of Lewisville Lake, tourism, IBM offices, chili cook-off in June, Las Vegas Night in April; **Flower Mound** (21,581), real estate centered community, North Central Texas College campus.

Also, **Argyle** (1,803); **Aubrey** (1,238); **Corinth** (4,679); **Double Oak** (1,845); **Hebron** (1,291); **Justin** (1,411); **Krum** (1,835); **Lake Dallas** (4,006), electronics manufacturing; **Little Elm** (1,389); **Pilot Point** (2,767), light manufacturing, agribusinesses, near Lake Ray Roberts, pioneer days in June; **Roanoke** (2,006); **Sanger** (3,831); **Shady Shores** (1,195).

Population	**309,512**
(Change fm '90)	13.2
Land Area (sq. mi.)	888.4
Altitude (ft.)	515-844
Rainfall (in.)	33.5
Jan. mean min.	32
July mean max.	96
Growing season (days)	226
Civ. Labor	188,244
Unemployed	4.2
Total Wages	$1,776,840,049
Av. Weekly Wage	$432.88
Prop. Value	$13,018,683,260
Retail Sales	$2,358,223,977

"DENTON County: . . .Probably no other county in the state has such a variety of productive soils . . . (and) all products grown in the latitude find a congenial soil to bring them to perfection.

". . . There are six modern flouring mills in the county, one of which carried off first honors at the Dallas fair for nine years, at the St. Louis fair four years and at the Paris exposition in competition with the mills of the world for the best soft wheat flour. In each instance Denton County wheat was used, demonstrating conclusively the superior quality of the wheat raised in this county.

". . . Prairie lands vary in price from $25 to $50 per acre, according to location and improvements, and timber land and timber land farms from $10 to $30.

". . . The people of Denton have been very generous in contributing to the establishment and maintenance of schools, and erecting and donating the building to the state for the North Texas Normal College, building the John B. Denton College and paying $30,000 to secure the location here of the State Industrial College for Girls."

— *Texas Almanac, 1904*

For explanation of sources, abbreviations and symbols, see p. 132.

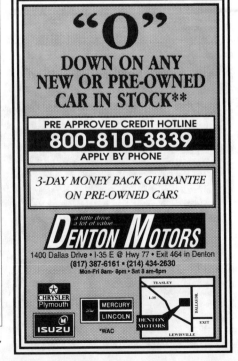

DeWitt County

Physical Features: South central county drained by Guadalupe and tributaries; rolling to level; waxy, loam, sandy soils.

Economy: Wood, furniture plants, textile mill; varied manufacturing; agribusinesses; prison unit.

History: Created from Gonzales, Goliad, Victoria counties 1846; named for Green DeWitt, colonizer.

Ethnicity, 1990: White, 14,356 (76.2%); Black, 2,114 (11.2%); American Indian, 22 (0.1%); Asian, 17 (0.1%); Other, 2,331 (12.4%). Hispanic, 4,567 (24.2%).

Vital Statistics, 1993: Births, 199; deaths, 274; marriages, 110; divorces, 84.

Recreation: Hunting, fishing, historic homes; museum.

Minerals: Oil and natural gas.

Agriculture: Cow-calf operations, poultry, swine, dairy products, ratites (emus, ostriches); corn, sorghum, cotton, hay, pecans.

CUERO (6,839) county seat; agribusiness, varied manufacturing; food processing; hospital, Turkeyfest in October.

Yorktown (2,343), hospital; museum; oil-well servicing.

Other towns include: **Nordheim** (352); **Yoakum** (6,006, mostly in Lavaca County).

Population	**19,479**
(Change fm '90)	3.4
Land Area (sq. mi.)	909.2
Altitude (ft.)	163-462
Rainfall (in.)	36.2
Jan. mean min.	42
July mean max.	96
Growing season (days)	270
Civ. Labor	8,340
Unemployed	5.4
Total Wages	$99,984,113
Av. Weekly Wage	$325.36
Prop. Value	$952,308,653
Retail Sales	$108,975,196

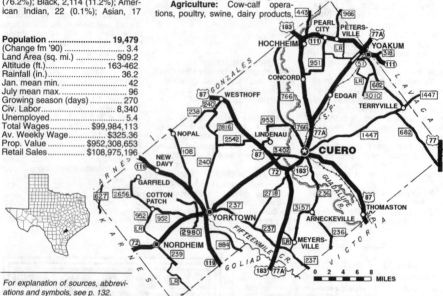

For explanation of sources, abbreviations and symbols, see p. 132.

Javelinas range widely in South and Southwest Texas.

Dickens County

Physical Features: West Texas county; broken land, Caprock in northwest; sandy, chocolate, red soils; drains to Croton, Duck creeks.

Economy: Ranching, farming supplies; hunting leases; prison unit.

History: Created 1876, from Bexar District; organized 1891; named for Alamo hero who is variously listed as James R. Demkins or Dimpkins and J. Dickens.

Ethnicity, 1990: White, 2,193 (85.3%); Black, 113 (4.4%); American Indian, 13 (0.5%); Asian, 1 (0.0%);Other, 251 (9.8%). Hispanic, 479 (18.6%).

Vital Statistics, 1993: Births, 36; deaths, 40; marriages, 26; divorces, 10.

Recreation: Hunting, fishing; Soldiers Mound site.

Minerals: Small oil, gas output.

Agriculture: Beef cattle, cotton; Spanish goats also raised; hay, alfalfa; some irrigation.

DICKENS (340) county seat, market for ranching country.

Spur (1,350), agribusiness and shipping center, homecoming in October; state prison.

Other towns include: **Afton** (100) and **McAdoo** (169).

Population.............................. 2,719
(Change fm '90) 5.8

Land Area (sq. mi.)................. 904.2
Altitude (ft.)................... 1,933-2,991
Rainfall (in.) 20.7
Jan. mean min............................ 26
July mean max. 95

Growing season (days) 217
Civ. Labor................................ 1,039
Unemployed 7.2
Total Wages................ $10,011,747
Av. Weekly Wage............... $338.20
Prop. Value $120,260,908
Retail Sales.................... $8,978,560

Dimmit County

Physical Features: Southwest county; level to rolling; much brush; sandy, loam, red soils; drained by Nueces River.

Economy: Agribusiness; petroleum products; varied manufacturing; tourism.

History: Named for Philip Dimitt of Texas Revolution; law misspelled name; created 1858 from Bexar, Maverick, Uvalde, Webb counties; organized 1880.

Ethnicity, 1990: White, 7,599 (72.8%); Black, 60 (0.6%); American Indian, 16 (0.2%); Asian, 12 (0.1%); Other, 2,746 (26.3%). Hispanic, 8,688 (83.3%).

Vital Statistics, 1993: Births, 206; deaths, 79; marriages, 88; divorces, 10.

Recreation: Hunting, fishing, campsites; winter haven for tourist.

Minerals: Oil, gas production.

Agriculture: Cotton, hay, pecans, vegetables; beef cattle raised; among leading irrigated vegetable-growing counties.

CARRIZO SPRINGS (5,846) county seat; agribusiness center, feedlot, food processing; oil, gas processing; hunting center; hospitals.

Other towns include: **Asherton** (1,643), **Big Wells** (821).

Population............................ 10,787
(Change fm '90)........................... 3.4
Land Area (sq. mi.)............... 1,331.0
Altitude (ft.).......................... 461-591
Rainfall (in.) 21.5
Jan. mean min.............................. 41
July mean max. 100
Growing season (days) 290
Civ. Labor.............................. 3,597
Unemployed 17.0
Total Wages................ $35,405,985
Av. Weekly Wage $300.25
Prop. Value............... $549,685,885
Retail Sales $38,720,916

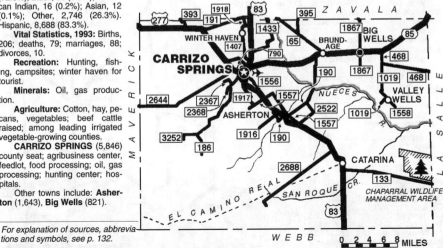

For explanation of sources, abbreviations and symbols, see p. 132.

Donley County

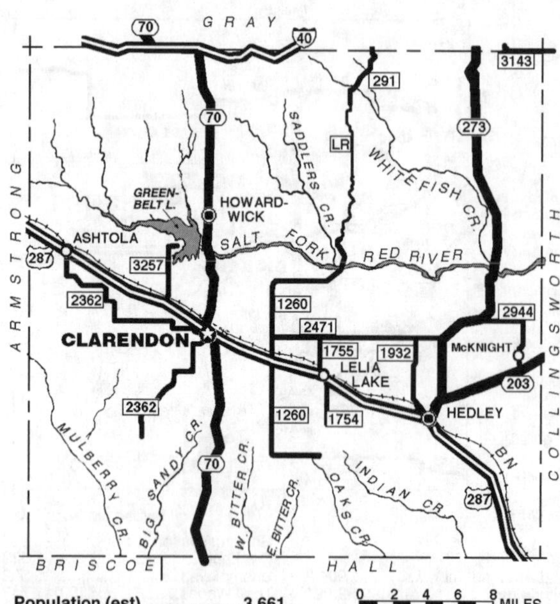

Physical Features: Northwest county bisected by Red River Salt Fork; rolling to level; clay, loam, sandy soils.

Economy: Agribusinesses; distribution; varied manufacturing.

History: Created in 1876, organized 1882, out of Bexar District; named for Texas Supreme Court Justice S.P. Donley.

Ethnicity, 1990: White, 3,522 (95.3%); Black, 127 (3.4%); American Indian, 13 (0.4%); Asian, 2 (0.1%); Other, 32 (0.9%). Hispanic, 139 (3.8%).

Vital Statistics, 1993: Births, 43; deaths, 48; marriages, 39; divorces, 20.

Recreation: Lake, hunting, fishing, camping, water sports; museum.

Minerals: Small amount of natural gas.

Agriculture: Cattle top revenue source; cotton important; some wheat, sorghum; 8,500 acres irrigated; peanuts increasing.

CLARENDON (2,051) county seat; junior college; Saints Roost museum; library; agribusiness, tourism; medical center.

Other towns include: **Hedley** (399), **Howardwick** (210).

Population (est)	**3,661**
(Change fm 90)	- 0.9
Land Area (sq. mi.)	929.8
Altitude (ft.)	2,388-3,213
Rainfall (in.)	21.5
Jan. mean min.	22
July mean max.	95
Growing season (days)	206
Civ. Labor	1,625
Unemployed	4.3
Total Wages	$14,245,669
Av. Weekly Wage	$313.37
Prop. Value	$183,076,002
Retail Sales	$17,591,050

Duval County

Physical Features: Southwestern county; level to hilly, brushy in most areas; varied soils.

Economy: Ranching; petroleum; tourism.

History: Created from Live Oak, Nueces, Starr counties, 1858, organized 1876; named for B.H. Duval, a victim of Goliad massacre.

Ethnicity, 1990: White, 10,183 (78.8%); Black, 12 (0.1%); American Indian, 12 (0.1%); Asian, 17 (0.1%); Other, 2,694 (20.9%). Hispanic, 11,267 (87.2%).

Vital Statistics, 1993: Births, 213; deaths, 119; marriages, 119; divorces, 37.

Recreation: Hunting, tourist crossroads, rattlesnake roundup.

Minerals: Production of oil, gas, salt, uranium, sand and gravel.

Agriculture: Most income from beef cattle; remainder from grains, cotton, vegetables, hay.

SAN DIEGO (4,998, partly in Jim Wells County) county seat; ranching, oil field, tourist center; hospital.

FREER (3,172) center of oil and livestock raising area

Other towns include: **Benavides** (1,811) serves truck farming area.

Population	**12,859**
(Change fm '90)	- 0.5
Land Area (sq. mi.)	1,792.8
Altitude (ft.)	244-783
Rainfall (in.)	24.4
Jan. mean min.	41
July mean max.	97
Growing season (days)	298
Civ. Labor	4,602
Unemployed	12.5
Total Wages	$53,798,182
Av. Weekly Wage	$347.56
Prop. Value	$903,684,678
Retail Sales	$31,035,996

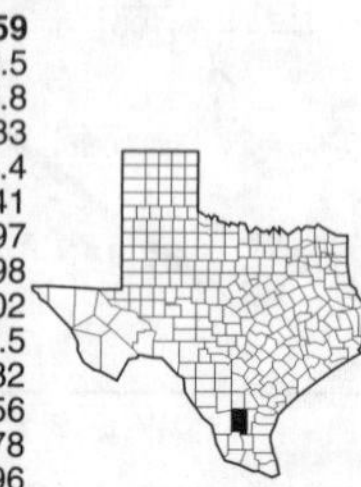

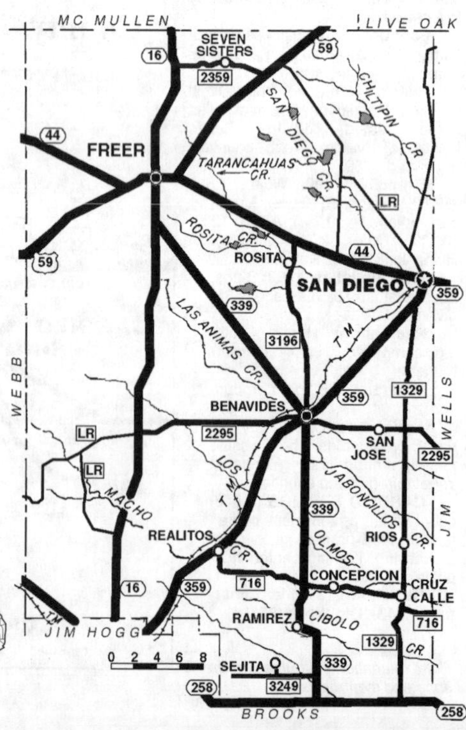

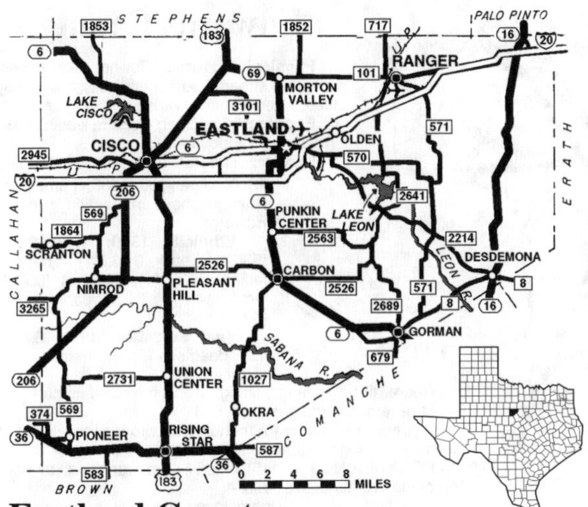

Eastland County

Physical Features: West central county; hilly, rolling; sandy, loam soils; drains to Leon River forks.

Economy: Agribusinesses; education; petroleum industries; varied manufacturing.

History: Created from Bosque, Coryell, Travis counties, 1858, organized 1873; named for W.M. Eastland, Mier Expedition casualty.

Ethnicity, 1990: White, 17,474 (94.5%); Black, 397 (2.1%); American Indian, 52 (0.3%); Asian, 37 (0.2%); Other, 528 (2.9%). Hispanic, 1,404 (7.6%).

Vital Statistics, 1993: Births, 206; deaths, 292; marriages, 154; divorces, 84.

Recreation: Lakes, water sports; fishing, hunting; festivals; historic sites and displays.

Minerals: Production of oil, gas, stone, clays, sand and gravel.

Agriculture: Peanuts; fed beef and dairy cattle, emus, goats; hay; pecans; greenhouse plants; 19,000 acres irrigated, mostly peanuts .

EASTLAND (3,641) county seat; plants make various goods; agribusiness; printing; mental health center; hospital.

Cisco (3,949) agribusiness; plants clothing, windows, molding; Conrad Hilton's first hotel renovated, museum; junior college; hospital; folklife festival; Kendrick Religous Diorama.

Ranger (2,822) oil center, varied manufacturing, junior college, hospital.

Other towns include: **Gorman** (1,337), peanut processing; agribusiness; hospital; **Rising Star** (862), cap manufacturing; **Carbon** (268).

Population	**18,614**
(Change fm '90)	0.7
Land Area (sq. mi.)	926,0
Altitude (ft.)	1,303-1,882
Rainfall (in.)	27.2
Jan. mean min.	30
July mean max.	95
Growing season (days)	299
Civ. Labor	8,173
Unemployed	5.6
Total Wages	$89,140,835
Av. Weekly Wage	$328.07
Prop. Value	$666,751,946
Retail Sales	$126,888,243

Ector County

Physical Features: West Texas county; level to rolling, some sand dunes; meteor crater; desert vegetation.

Business: Center for Permian Basin oil field operations; rubber and plastics.

History: Created from Tom Green County, 1887; organized, 1891; named for jurist M.D. Ector.

Ethnicity, 1990: White, 91,309 (76.8%); Black, 5,557 (4.7%); American Indian, 647 (0.5%); Asian, 662 (0.6%); Other, 20,759 (17.5%). Hispanic, 37,315 (31.4%).

Vital Statistics, 1993: Births, 2,268; deaths, 896; marriages, 1,225; divorces, 853.

Recreation: Globe Theatre replica; presidential museum; art institute; second-largest U.S. meteor crater; antique auto museum; jazz festival in May, oil show in October .

Minerals: More than 2 billion barrels of oil produced since 1926; gas, cement, stone.

Agriculture: Beef cattle, horses are chief producers; pecans, hay raised, also ratites; minor irrigation.

ODESSA (92,257) county seat; oil field services, supplies; petrochemical complex; hosptial; cultural center; Odessa College, University of Texas of Permian Basin; fair and expo in September.

Other towns, **Goldsmith** (302), **Gardendale** (1,870), **West Odessa** (17,051).

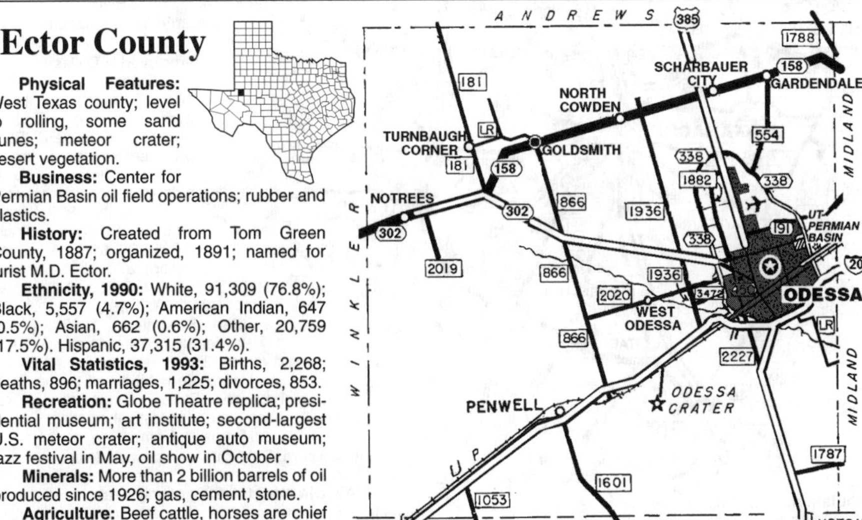

Population	**122,051**
(Change fm '90)	2.6
Land Area (sq. mi.)	901.1
Altitude (ft.)	2,817-8,275
Rainfall (in.)	12.7
Jan. mean min.	28
July mean max.	95
Growing season (days)	217
Civ. Labor	60,889
Unemployed	8.6
Total Wages	$1,036,265,286
Av. Weekly Wage	$440.37
Prop. Value	$4,567,887,576
Retail Sales	$1,168,299,840

For explanation of sources, abbreviations and symbols, see p. 132.

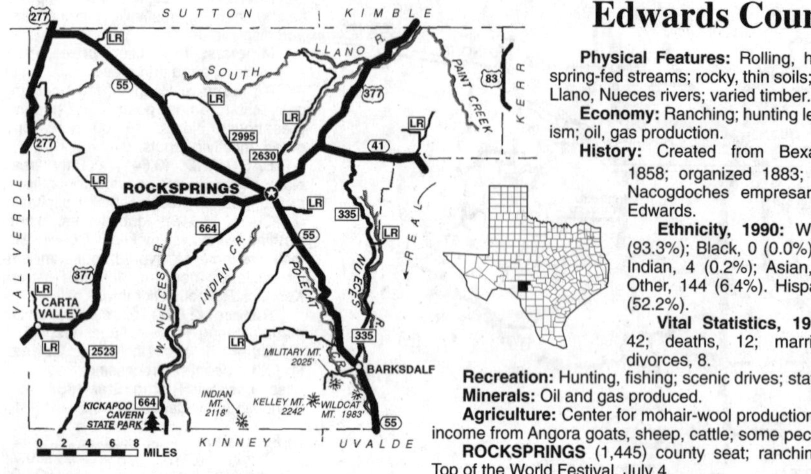

Edwards County

Physical Features: Rolling, hilly; caves; spring-fed streams; rocky, thin soils; drained by Llano, Nueces rivers; varied timber.

Economy: Ranching; hunting leases; tourism; oil, gas production.

History: Created from Bexar District, 1858; organized 1883; named for Nacogdoches empresario Hayden Edwards.

Ethnicity, 1990: White, 2,114 (93.3%); Black, 0 (0.0%); American Indian, 4 (0.2%); Asian, 4 (0.2%); Other, 144 (6.4%). Hispanic, 1,182 (52.2%).

Vital Statistics, 1993: Births, 42; deaths, 12; marriages, 15; divorces, 8.

Recreation: Hunting, fishing; scenic drives; state park.

Minerals: Oil and gas produced.

Agriculture: Center for mohair-wool production; almost all income from Angora goats, sheep, cattle; some pecans.

ROCKSPRINGS (1,445) county seat; ranching, tourism, Top of the World Festival, July 4.

Population	**2,541**
(Change fm '90)	12
Land Area (sq. mi.)	2,119.9
Altitude (ft.)	1,507-2,410
Rainfall (in.)	23.6
Jan. mean min.	35
July mean max.	95
Growing season (days)	250
Civ. Labor	963
Unemployed	7.4
Total Wages	$6,082,762
Av. Weekly Wage	$291.87
Prop. Value	$483,392,912
Retail Sales	$8,863,661

Ellis County

Physical Features: North Texas Blackland soils; level to rolling; Chambers Creek, Trinity River.

Economy: Varied manufacturing; agribusinesses; many residents employed in Dallas.

History: Created 1849, organized 1850, from Navarro County. Named for Richard Ellis, president of Convention of 1836 that declared Texas' independence from Mexico.

Ethnicity, 1990: White, 69,049 (81.1%); Black, 8,525 (10.0%); American Indian, 370 (0.4%); Asian, 214 (0.3%); Other, 7,009 (8.2%). Hispanic, 11,243 (13.2%).

Vital Statistics, 1993: Births, 1,419; deaths, 673; marriages, 935; divorces, 335.

Recreation: Medieval theme Scarborough Faire; Gingerbread Trail homes tour, fall festival; hunting.

Minerals: Cement, oil, gas.

Agriculture: Beef cattle; crops include cotton, corn, wheat, milo.

WAXAHACHIE (19,203) county seat; varied manufacturing; movie production; tourism; hospital; colleges.

Ennis (14,461), agribusiness; manufacturing; bluebonnet trails, National Polka Festival; tourism; hospital.

Midlothian (5,485), trade zone, cement plant, steel manufacturing; other factories; April Mad Hatters parade.

Other towns include: **Bardwell** (404); **Ferris** (2,298); **Garrett** (374); **Italy** (1,790); **Maypearl** (834); **Milford** (782); **Oak Leaf** (1,066); **Ovilla** (2,322); **Palmer** (1,748); **Pecan Hill** (594); **Red Oak** (3,438).

Population	**89,865**
(Change fm '90)	5.5
Land Area (sq. mi.)	939.9
Altitude (ft.)	395-755
Rainfall (in.)	36.3
Jan. mean min.	33
July mean max.	97
Growing season (days)	246
Civ. Labor	47,023
Unemployed	5.5
Total Wages	$589,209,454
Av. Weekly Wage	$444.07
Prop. Value	$3,885,198,373
Retail Sales	$493,829,615

For explanation of sources, abbreviations and symbols see p. 132.

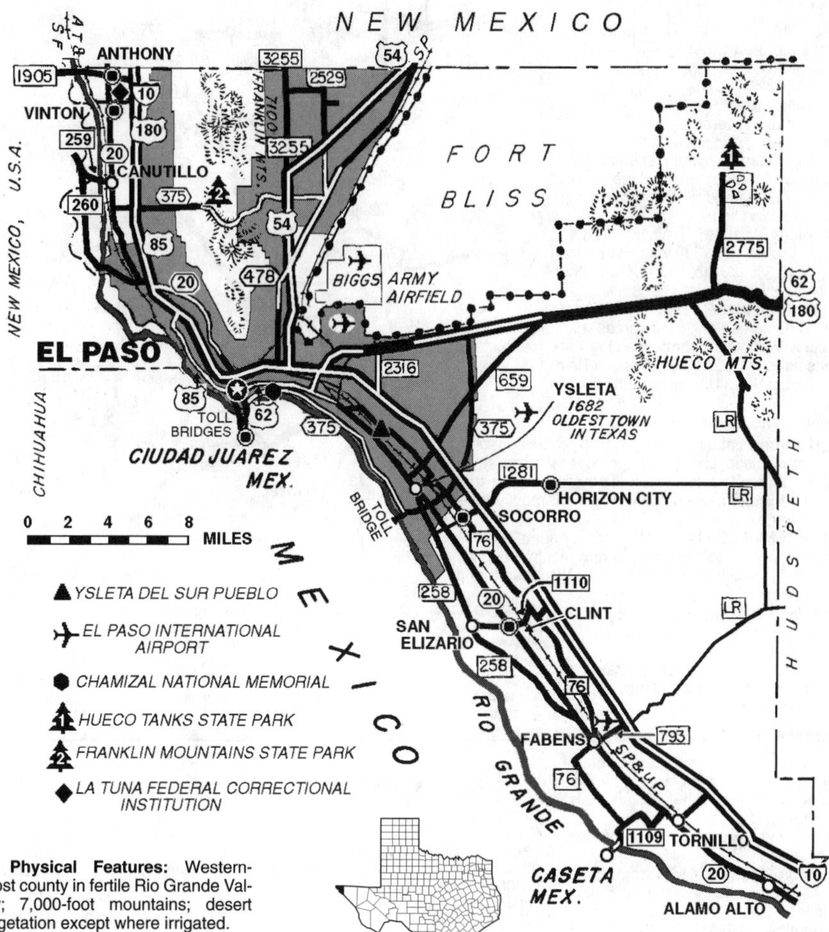

El Paso County

Physical Features: Westernmost county in fertile Rio Grande Valley; 7,000-foot mountains; desert vegetation except where irrigated.

Economy: Government, military is major economic factor; wholesale, retail distribution center; education; tourism; maquiladora plants, varied manufacturers; ore smelting, refining, cotton, food processing.

History: Created from Bexar District, 1849; organized 1850; named for historic northern pass (Paso del Norte), lowest all-weather pass through Rocky Mountains.

Ethnicity, 1990: White, 452,512 (76.5%); Black, 22,110 (3.7%); American Indian, 2,590 (0.4%); Asian, 6,485 (1.1%); Other, 107,913 (18.2%). Hispanic, 411,619 (69.6%).

Vital Statistics, 1993: Births, 15,956; deaths, 3,609; marriages, 7,727; divorces, 2,214.

Recreation: Gateway to Mexico; Chamizal Museum; major tourist center; December Sun Carnival with football game; state parks, missions and other historic sites.

Minerals: Production of cement, stone, sand and gravel.

Agriculture: Dairy and beef cattle; cotton, pecans, onions, forage, peppers also raised; 50,000 acres irrigated, mostly cotton.

EL PASO (554,496) county seat; fourth-largest Texas city, largest U.S. city on Mexican border.

A center for government operations. Federal installations include Fort Bliss, William Beaumont General Hospital, La Tuna correctional institution, and headquarters of the U.S. Army Air Defense Command;

Manufactured products include clothing, electronics, auto equipment, plastics; trade and distribution; refining; processing of ore, oil, food, cotton, and other farm products.

University of Texas at El Paso; UT School of Nursing at El Paso; Texas Tech University Health Science Center; El Paso Community College; 16 hospitals; museums; convention center; theater, symphony orchestra,

Other towns include: **Anthony** (3,491); **Canutillo** (4,625); **Clint** (1,084); **Fabens** (5,702); **San Elizario** (4,476); **Socorro** (25,101); **Sparks** (1,337); **Vinton** (609); **Ysleta**, oldest town in Texas (now within El Paso).

Population	**634,650**
(Change fm '90)	7.3
Land Area (sq. mi.)	1,013.0
Altitude (ft.)	3,582-7,192
Rainfall (in.)	7.8
Jan. mean min.	30
July mean max.	95
Growing season (days)	248
Civ. Labor	282,016
Unemployed	10.0
Total Wages	$4,263,119,332
Av. Weekly Wage	$376.74
Prop. Value	$14,692,788,837
Retail Sales	$5,018,771,434

Erath County

Physical Features: West central county on Rolling Plains; clay loam, sandy soils; drains to Bosque, Paluxy Rivers.

Business: Agricultural, industrial and educational enterprises.

History: Created from Bosque, Coryell counties 1856; named for George B. Erath, Texas Revolution figure.

Ethnicity, 1990: White, 26,413 (94.4%); Black, 195 (0.7%); American Indian, 94 (0.3%); Asian, 115 (0.4%); Other, 1,174 (4.2%). Hispanic, 2,458 (8.8%).

Vital Statistics, 1993: Births, 410; deaths, 275; marriages, 361; divorces, 157.

Recreation: Old courthouse; log cabins; museums; nearby lakes, Bosque River Park; Tarleton State University with fine arts center.

Minerals: Gas, oil.

Agriculture: Leading county in milk production; beef cattle, horses raised; peanuts, the major cash crop, small grains, sorghums; horticulture industry, especially tree growing and greenhouses; some irrigation, mostly peanuts and forage crops.

STEPHENVILLE (14,436) the county seat; Tarleton State University; various manufacturing plants; hospital, clinics, mental health center; Texas A&M Research and Extension Center.

Dublin (3,298), agribusiness center; food processing; St. Patrick's celebration; old Dr Pepper plant.

Other towns include: **Bluff Dale** (123); **Morgan Mill** (206); **Thurber**, former coal-mining town.

Population	**29,272**
(Change fm '90)	4.6
Land Area (sq. mi.)	1,086.4
Altitude (ft.)	943-1,558
Rainfall (in.)	30.1
Jan. mean min.	31
July mean max.	95
Growing season (days)	238
Civ. Labor	15,652
Unemployed	3.7
Total Wages	$199,490,916
Av. Weekly Wage	$336.05
Prop. Value	$1,089,095,912
Retail Sales	$274,161,301

Falls County

Physical Features: East central county on rolling prairie; bisected by Brazos; blackland, red, sandy loam soils; mineral springs.

Economy: Varied manufacturing; agribusinesses.

History: Created 1850 from Limestone, Milam counties; named for Brazos River falls.

Ethnicity, 1990: White, 11,390 (64.3%); Black, 4,810 (27.2%); American Indian, 41 (0.2%); Asian, 21 (0.1%); Other, 1,450 (8.2%). Hispanic, 2,072 (11.7%).

Vital Statistics, 1993: Births, 230; deaths, 236; marriages, 117; divorces, 60.

Recreation: Fishing, camping, mineral baths; Highland Mansion and Falls on the Brazos.

Minerals: Gas, stone, some oil.

Agriculture: Stocker cattle, cow-calf operations, swine, sheep, goats raised; corn, grain sorghums, cotton, soybeans; 5,000 acres, mostly cotton, irrigated.

MARLIN (6,780) county seat; agribusiness, small industries; mineral water and spas; hospital; printing; veterans hospital; tourism; Festival Days in May; prison unit.

Other towns include: **Lott** (838); **Golinda** (354, partly in McLennan County); and **Rosebud** (1,637) feed, fertilizer processing; clothing manufactured.

Population	**18,418**
(Change fm '90)	4.0
Land Area (sq. mi.)	769.1
Altitude (ft.)	314-590
Rainfall (in.)	36.0
Jan. mean min.	36
July mean max.	97
Growing season (days)	257
Civ. Labor	7,269
Unemployed	5.0
Total Wages	$59,167,801
Av. Weekly Wage	$331.83
Prop. Value	$653,772,830
Retail Sales	$68,066,152

For explanation of sources, abbreviations and symbols, see p. 132.

Fannin County

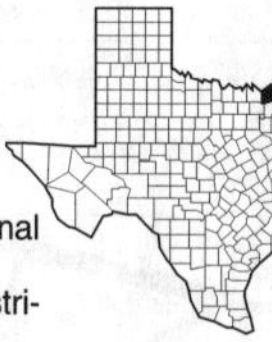

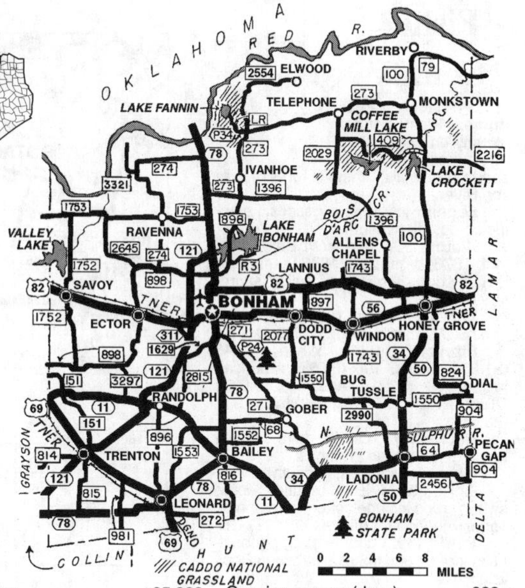

Physical Features: North Texas county of rolling prairie, drained by Red River, Bois d' Arc Creek; mostly blackland soils; national grassland.

Economy: Agribusinesses; distribution, meat packing; tourism.

History: Created from Red River County, 1837, organized, 1838; named for James W. Fannin, a victim of Goliad massacre.

Ethnicity, 1990: White, 22,722 (91.6%); Black, 1,633 (6.6%); American Indian, 182 (0.7%); Asian, 54 (0.2%); Other, 213 (0.9%). Hispanic, 485 (2.0%).

Vital Statistics, 1993: Births, 298; deaths, 408; marriages, 221; divorces, 145.

Recreation: Water activities on lakes; hunting; state park; Ivanhoe Winery; Sam Rayburn home, memorial library.

Minerals: Not significant; some sand produced.

Agriculture: Beef cattle; ratites; goats, sheep hogs; hay, wheat, soybeans, sorghum, corn, turf grass; 2,500 acres irrigated, mainly peanuts.

BONHAM (6,833) county seat; varied manufacturing; hospitals, Veterans Memorial Center; Bois D'Arc Festival in May.

Other towns include: **Bailey** (199); **Dodd City** (378); **Ector** (498); **Honey Grove** (1,695), agribusiness center, varied manufacturing, historic buildings, Davy Crockett Day in October; **Ladonia** (670), restored historical downtown, varied manufacturing; **Leonard** (1,778), varied manufacturing; **Savoy** (929); **Trenton** (667); **Windom** (283);.

Population	**25,382**
Change fm '90	2.3
Land Area (sq. mi.)	891.5
Altitude (ft.)	478-767
Rainfall (in.)	41.6
Jan. mean min.	31
July mean max.	95
Growing season (days)	228
Civ. Labor	11,007
Unemployed	7.1
Total Wages	$101,350,120
Av. Weekly Wage	$351.62
Prop. Value	$820,411,948
Retail Sales	$135,588,566

Fayette County

Physical Features: Southeast county bisected by Colorado River; rolling to level; sandy loam, black waxy soils.

Economy: Agribusinesses; tourism; production of electricity; mineral production; small manufacturing.

History: Created from Bastrop, Colorado counties, 1837; organized, 1838; named for hero of American Revolution, Marquis de Lafayette.

Vital Statistics, 1993: Births, 234; deaths, 246; marriages, 134; divorces, 83.

Ethnicity, 1990: White, 17,323 (86.2%); Black, 1,686 (8.4%); American Indian, 29 (0.1%); Asian, 15 (0.1%); Other, 1,042 (5.2%). Hispanic, 1,702 (8.5%).

Recreation: Monument Hill State Park, Faison Home Museum, brewery, other historic sites including "Painted Churches"; hunting, fishing, lake; German and Czech ethnic foods; Prazska Pout in August.

Minerals: Oil, gas, sand, gravel.

Agriculture: Beef, dairy cows; corn, sorghums, peanuts, hay, pecans, wheat; some firewood sold.

LA GRANGE (4,161) county seat; varied manufacturing; food processing; retail trade center; tourism; power generation; hospital, Spring Fling.

Schulenburg (2,736) varied manufacturing; food processing; Bluebonnet Festival.

Other towns include: **Carmine** (208); **Fayetteville** (308); **Flatonia** (1,373), farm market, Czhilispiel in October; **Round Top** (88) music center and **Winedale**, historic restorations including Winedale Inn.

Population	**21,348**
(Change fm '90)	6.2
Land Area (sq. mi.)	950.1
Altitude (ft.)	245-590
Rainfall (in.)	37
Jan. mean min.	41
July mean max.	95
Growing season (days)	277
Civ. Labor	10,364
Unemployed	3.2
Total Wages	$140,780,909
Av. Weekly Wage	$376.04
Prop. Value	$1,691,947,868
Retail Sales	$209,608,679

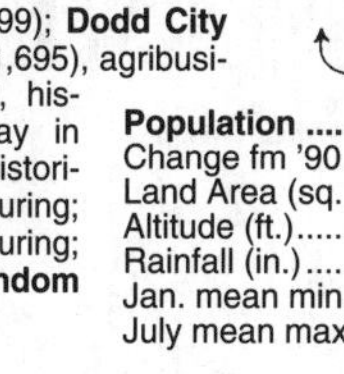

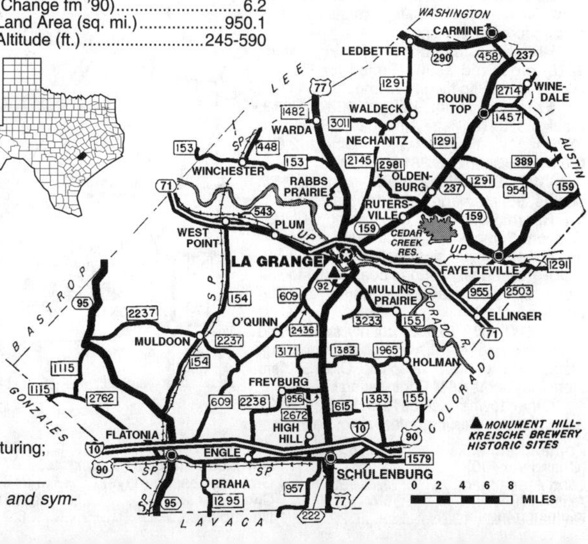

For explanation of sources, abbreviations and symbols, see p. 132.

Fisher County

Physical Features: West central county on rolling prairie; mesquite; red, sandy loam soils; drains to forks of Brazos River.

Economy: Agribusinesses; electric co-op; oil; gypsum.

History: Created from Bexar District, 1876; organized, 1886; named for S.R. Fisher, Republic of Texas secretary of navy.

Vital Statistics, 1993: Births, 55; deaths, 73; marriages, 21; divorces, 6.

Ethnicity, 1990: White, 4,445 (91.8%); Black, 190 (3.9%); American Indian, 19 (0.4%); Asian, 0 (0.0%); Other, 188 (3.9%). Hispanic, 997 (20.6%).

Recreation: Quail, dove, turkey hunting; fair, rodeo in August,

Minerals: Oil, gas, gypsum.

Agriculture: Beef cattle, some swine; crops include cotton, wheat, hay; some irrigation for alfalfa.

ROBY (593) county seat; agribusiness, cotton gin; hospital between Roby and Rotan.

Rotan (1,829), gypsum plant; oil mill; agribusinesses.

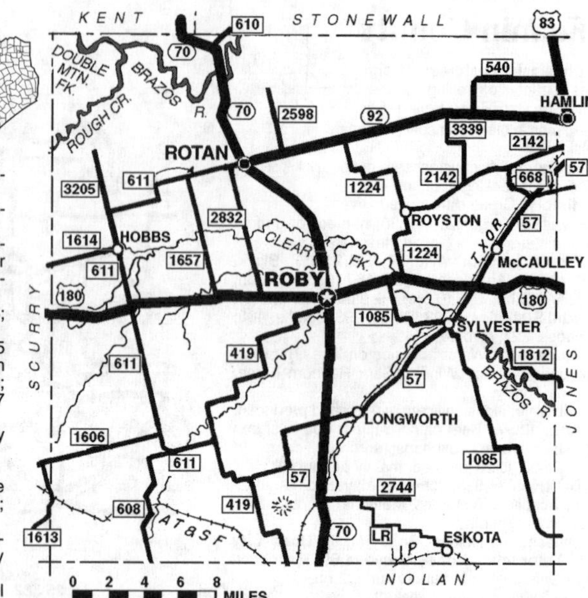

Population **4,655**
(Change fm '90) .... - 3.9
Land Area (sq. mi.) 901.2
Altitude (ft.) 1,723-2,235
Rainfall (in.) 22.5
Jan. mean min. 30
July mean max. 97
Growing season (days) 218
Civ. Labor 1,970
Unemployed 6.4
Total Wages $17,855,912
Av. Weekly Wage $355.61
Prop. Value $331,554,011
Retail Sales $10,743,228

Floyd County

Physical Features: Flat High Plains, broken by Caprock on east, by White River on south; many playas; red, black loam soils.

Economy: Cotton; livestock feedlots; farm machinery and oil-field manufacturing; metal products; printing.

History: Created from Bexar District, 1876; organized 1890. Named for Dolphin Ward Floyd, who died at Alamo.

Ethnicity, 1990: White, 5,523 (65.0%); Black, 320 (3.8%); American Indian, 16 (0.2%); Asian, 15 (0.2%); Other, 2,623 (30.9%). Hispanic, 3,381 (39.8%).

Vital Statistics, 1993: Births, 156; deaths, 95; marriages, 62; divorces, 10.

Recreation: Hunting, fishing; Blanco Canyon; Pumpkin Days; museum.

Minerals: Not significant.

Agriculture: Cotton; beef and stocker cattle; corn, vegetables, sorghum; 260,000 acres irrigated.

FLOYDADA (3,453) county seat; some manufacturing; meat, vegetable processing; distribution center; hospital; Old Settlers Reunion; Texas A&M Engineering Extension.

Other towns include: **Lockney** (2,112), agriculture center; manufacturing; hospital.

Population **8,250**
(Change fm '90) .... - 2.9
Land Area (sq. mi.) 992.3
Altitude (ft.) 2,574-3,316
Rainfall (in.) 22.5
Jan. mean min. 30
July mean max. 97
Growing season (days) 218
Civ. Labor 3,363
Unemployed 6.2
Total Wages $36,282,485
Av. Weekly Wage $308.51
Prop. Value $305,603,487
Retail Sales $40,208,320

Foard County

Physical Features: Northwest county drains to North Wichita, Pease rivers; sandy, loam soils, rolling surface.

Economy: Agribusinesses; clothes manufacturing, oil.

History: Created out of Cottle, Hardeman, King, Knox counties, 1891; named for Maj. Robert L. Foard of Confederate army.

Ethnicity, 1990: White, 1,552 (86.5%); Black, 88 (4.9%); American Indian, 11 (0.6%); Asian, 4 (0.2%); Other, 139 (7.7%). Hispanic, 233 (13.0%).

Vital Statistics, 1993: Births, 30; deaths, 41; marriages, 12; divorces, 6.

Recreation: Three museums.

Minerals: Oil, gas.

Agriculture: Wheat, cotton, hay, alfalfa; cow-calf operations, stockers; irrigation for alfalfa.

CROWELL (1,217) county seat; agriculture center; manufacturing; hospital.

Population	**1,783**
(Change fm '90)	- 0.6
Land Area (sq. mi.)	706.7
Altitude (ft.)	1,300-1,784
Rainfall (in.)	23.9
Jan. mean min.	24
July mean max.	97
Growing season (days)	219
Civ. Labor	1,062
Unemployed	3.8
Total Wages	$7,066,500
Av. Weekly Wage	$260,29
Prop. Value	$116,168,413
Retail Sales	$5,063,178

Fort Bend County

Physical Features: On Gulf Coastal Plain; drained by Brazos, San Bernard rivers; level to rolling; rich alluvial soils.

Economy: Agribusiness, petrochemicals, sulfur, sugar refinery; many residents work in Houston; part of Houston metropolitan area.

History: Named for river bend where some of Austin's colonists settled, among state's more historic counties; created 1837 from Austin County, organized 1838.

Ethnicity, 1990: White, 141,125 (62.6%); Black, 46,593 (20.7%); American Indian, 525 (0.2%); Asian, 14,328 (6.4%); Other, 22,850 (10.1%). Hispanic, 43,892 (19.5%).

Vital Statistics, 1993: Births, 4,183; deaths, 998; marriages, 1,514; divorces, 1,108.

Recreation: Many historic sites, museum, memorials; state park with George Observatory; fishing, waterfowl hunting.

Minerals: Oil, gas, sulphur, salt, clays, sand and gravel.

Agriculture: Cotton, grain sorghum, corn, rice, soybeans; cattle, horses; 29,000 acres irrigated, mostly rice.

RICHMOND (10,984) county seat; foundry, Richmond State School (for mentally retarded).

Rosenberg (23,275), varied industry; annual Czech festival; Wharton County Junior College campus.

Other towns include: **Arcola** (742); **Beasley** (542); **Katy** (9,020, part in Harris, Waller counties); **Kendleton** (574); **Missouri City**, (43,155, partly in Harris County); **Needville** (2,586); **Orchard** (424); **Stafford** (10,326); **Sugar Land** (38,925), sugar refinery, prison unit; **Thompsons** (198).

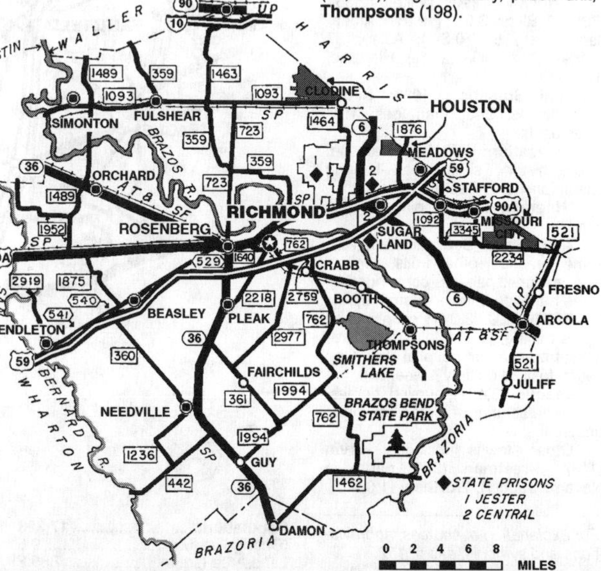

Population	**259,367**
(Change fm '90)	15.1
Land Area (sq. mi.)	875.0
Altitude (ft.)	46-127
Rainfall (in.)	43.9
Jan. mean min.	41
July mean max.	94
Growing season (days)	296
Civ. Labor	139,919
Unemployed	4.6
Total Wages	$1,640,643,317
Av. Weekly Wage	$520.11
Prop. Value	$12,014,691,919
Retail Sales	$1,409,581,270

Franklin County

Physical Features: Small Northeast county with many wooded hills; drained by numerous streams; alluvial to sandy clay soils; two lakes.

Economy: Agribusiness; tourism, retirement center; oil.

History: Created 1875 from Titus County; named for jurist B.C. Franklin.

Ethnicity, 1990: White, 7,139 (91.5%); Black, 349 (4.5%); American Indian, 47 (0.6%); Asian, 18 (0.2%); Other, 249 (3.2%). Hispanic, 357 (4.6%).

Vital Statistics, 1993: Births, 93; deaths, 106; marriages, 69; divorces, 54.

Recreation: Fishing, water sports; Countryfest in October.

Minerals: Oil, gas and lignite.

Agriculture: Among top counties in dairy and broiler production; hay is principal crop; blueberries, peaches, Christmas trees, soybeans sorghum, wheat; beef cattle raised.

MOUNT VERNON (2,306) county seat; tourism; dairy, beef cattle; varied manufacturing; supply center; hospital; airport.

Other towns include: **Winnsboro** (3,093, mostly in Wood County) commercial center.

Population	**8,333**
(Change fm '90)	6.8
Land Area (sq. mi.)	285.6
Altitude (ft.)	377-493
Rainfall (in.)	46.8
Jan. mean min.	33
July mean max.	93
Growing season (days)	234
Civ. Labor	3,671
Unemployed	7.3
Total Wages	$25,425,143
Av. Weekly Wage	$332.70
Prop. Value	$456,861,190
Retail Sales	$38,450,147

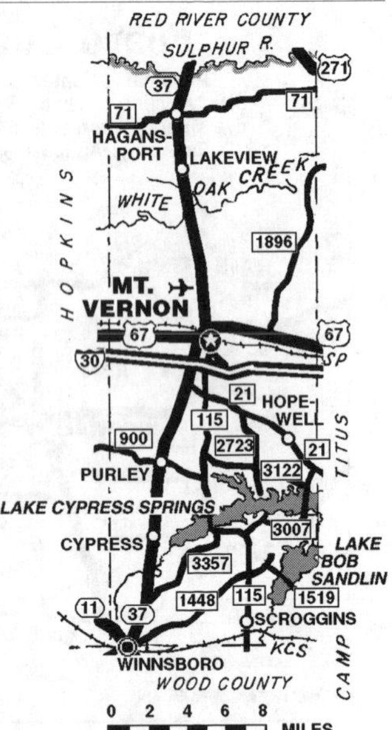

Freestone County

Physical Features: East central county bounded by the Trinity River; rolling Blackland, sandy, loam soils.

Economy: Mining, stone quarry, brick plant; varied manufacturing; agribusinesses; two electricity generating plants.

History: Named for indigenous stone; created 1850 from Limestone County, organized 1851.

Ethnicity, 1990: White, 12,382 (78.3%); Black, 3,013 (19.0%); American Indian, 53 (0.3%); Asian, 37 (0.2%); Other, 333 (2.1%). Hispanic, 619 (3.9%).

Vital Statistics, 1993: Births, 179; deaths, 243; marriages, 101; divorces, 89.

Recreation: Fishing, hunting; lakes; historic sites; coon hunting championship in September.

Minerals: Lignite, oil and gas, sand.

Agriculture: Beef cattle and hay; some peaches, other fruits, vegetables, melons, pecans, corn; hunting; some hardwood, firewood marketed.

FAIRFIELD (3,321) county seat; lignite mining; GTE telephone operations; trade center; hospital, museum; peach festival on July 4 weekend.

Teague (3,457) nursing homes; oil; manufacturing, railroad museum; prison unit.

Other towns include: **Kirvin** (116); **Streetman** (271, partly in Navarro County); **Wortham** (1,034).

For explanation of sources, abbreviations and symbols, see p. 132.

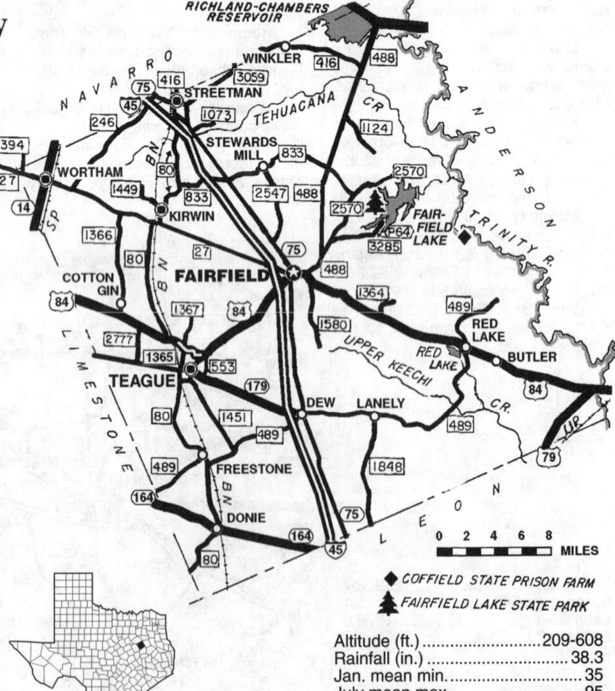

Population	**17,323**
(Change fm '90)	9.5
Land Area (sq. mi.)	885.2
Altitude (ft.)	209-608
Rainfall (in.)	38.3
Jan. mean min.	35
July mean max.	95
Growing season (days)	263
Civ. Labor	7,506
Unemployed	7.0
Total Wages	$87,178,936
Av. Weekly Wage	$431.56
Prop. Value	$1,342,950,586
Retail Sales	$85,414,065

Frio County

Physical Features: South Texas county of rolling terrain with much brush; bisected by Frio River; sandy, red sandy loam soils.

Economy: Agribusinesses; oil-field services.

History: Created 1871 from Atascosa, Bexar, Uvalde counties; named for Frio (cold) River.

Ethnicity, 1990: White, 9,119 (67.7%); Black, 183 (1.4%); American Indian, 23 (0.2%); Asian, 38 (0.3%); Other, 4,109 (30.5%). Hispanic, 9,749 (72.4%).

Vital Statistics, 1993: Births, 270; deaths, 112; marriages, 101; divorces, 30.

Recreation: Hunting; Big Foot Wallace Museum; in Winter Garden area; potato festival.

Minerals: Oil, natural gas, stone.

Agriculture: A leading peanut-producing county; other crops vegetables, grain sorghums, melons, corn, vegetables; cattle, hogs raised.

PEARSALL (7,449) county seat; oil, ranching center; food processing; shipping; old jail museum; hospital.

Dilley (2,362) shipping center for melons, peanuts.

Other towns include: **Bigfoot** (75); **Derby** (50); **Moore** (230).

Population	**14,361**
(Change fm '90)	6.6
Land Area (sq. mi.)	1,133.1
Altitude (ft.)	435-763
Rainfall (in.)	23.9
Jan. mean min.	39
July mean max.	98
Growing season (days)	291
Civ. Labor	6,847
Unemployed	10.7
Total Wages	$68,100,389
Av. Weekly Wage	$319.16
Prop. Value	$627,538,197
Retail Sales	$75,679,517

Gaines County

Physical Features: On South Plains, drains to draws; playas; underground water.

Economy: Oil and gas production, agribusiness.

History: Created from Bexar District, 1876, organized 1905; named for James Gaines, signer of Texas Declaration of Independence.

Ethnicity, 1990: White, 10,378 (73.5%); Black, 334 (2.4%); American Indian, 38 (0.3%); Asian, 15 (0.1%); Other, 3,358 (23.8%). Hispanic, 4,608 (32.6%).

Vital Statistics, 1993: Births, 254; deaths, 92; marriages, 308; divorces, 80.

Recreation: Cedar Lake one of largest alkali lakes on Texas plains; Ag and Oil Day in September.

Minerals: One of leading oil-producing counties; gas.

Agriculture: A leading cotton and peanut producing county; small grains, vegetables raised; cattle, sheep, hogs; substantial irrigation.

SEMINOLE (6,470) county seat; market center; hospital.

Seagraves (2,362), market for three-county area; manufacturing; hospital; state mental health clinic.

Population	**14,252**
(Change fm '90)	0.9
Land Area (sq. mi.)	1,502.4
Altitude (ft.)	241-725
Rainfall (in.)	3,039-3,581
Jan. mean min.	25
July mean max.	95
Growing season (days)	210
Civ. Labor	6,847
Unemployed	4.9
Total Wages	$84,303,220
Av. Weekly Wage	$373.85
Prop. Value	$3,088,057,345
Retail Sales	$88,487,062

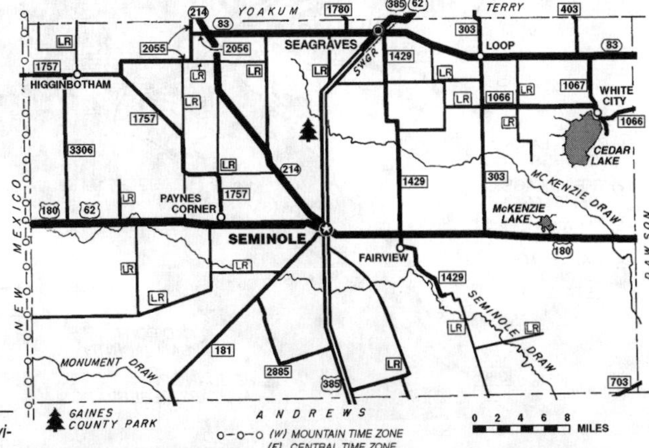

For explanation of sources, abbreviations and symbols, see p. 132.

Galveston County

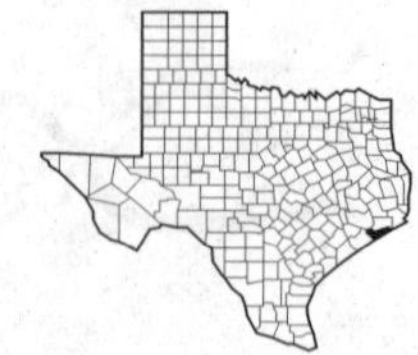

Physical Features: Partly island, partly coastal; flat, artificial drainage; sandy, loam, clay soils; broken by bays.

Economy: Port activities dominate economy; insurance and finance center; petrochemical plants; varied manufacturing; tourism; medical education center; oceanographic research center; ship building; commercial fishing.

History: Created from Brazoria County 1838; organized 1839; named for Spanish governor of Louisiana Count Bernardo de Galvez.

Ethnicity, 1990: White, 164,210 (75.5%); Black, 38,154 (17.6%); American Indian, 752 (0.3%); Asian, 3,569 (1.6%); Other, 10,714 (4.9%). Hispanic, 30,962 (14.2%).

Vital Statistics, 1993: Births, 3,840; deaths, 1,989; marriages, 1,622; divorces, 1,284.

Recreation: One of Texas' most historic cities; popular tourist and convention center; fishing, surfing, boating, sailing and other water sports; state park; Historical District tour in spring includes homes, sites; Mardi Gras celebration; Rosenberg Library; museums, drama "Lone Star" presented in outdoor amphitheater in summer; restored sailing ship, "Elissa," railroad museum; Dickens on the Strand in early December.

For explanation of sources, abbreviations and symbols, see p. 132.

Minerals: Production of oil, gas, clays, sand and gravel.

Agriculture: Rice a major crop; substantial irrigation; cattle, horses also raised; other crops soybeans, grain sorghums, corn; aquaculture.

GALVESTON (62,828) county seat; tourist center; shipyard; other industries; port container facility; University of Texas Medical Branch; National Maritime Research Center; Texas A&M University at Galveston; Galveston College; hospitals.

TEXAS CITY (42,026), refining, petrochemical plants; College of the Mainland; hospitals; Shrimp Boil at end of August.

Other towns include: **Bacliff** (5,714); **Crystal Beach** (387) on Bolivar Peninsula, Fort Travis Seashore Park, shorebird sanctuary; crab festival in May; **Dickinson** (13,035); **Friendswood** (25,788); **Hitchcock** (6,580) residential community, tourism, fishing and shrimping, Good Ole Days in August.

Also, **Kemah** (1,206) fishing; **La Marque** (14,501) refining, greyhound racing, Grill-off in March; **League City** (34,015); **San Leon** (3,651); **Santa Fe** (9,648).

Population	**233,591**
(Change fm '90)	7.4
Land Area (sq. mi.)	398.6
Altitude (ft.)	sea level-23
Rainfall (in.)	40.2
Jan. mean min.	49
July mean max.	87
Growing season (days)	335
Civ. Labor	124,036
Unemployed	8.2
Total Wages	$2,015,971,134
Av. Weekly Wage	$476.31
Prop. Value	$16,066,353,986
Retail Sales	$1,581,986,895

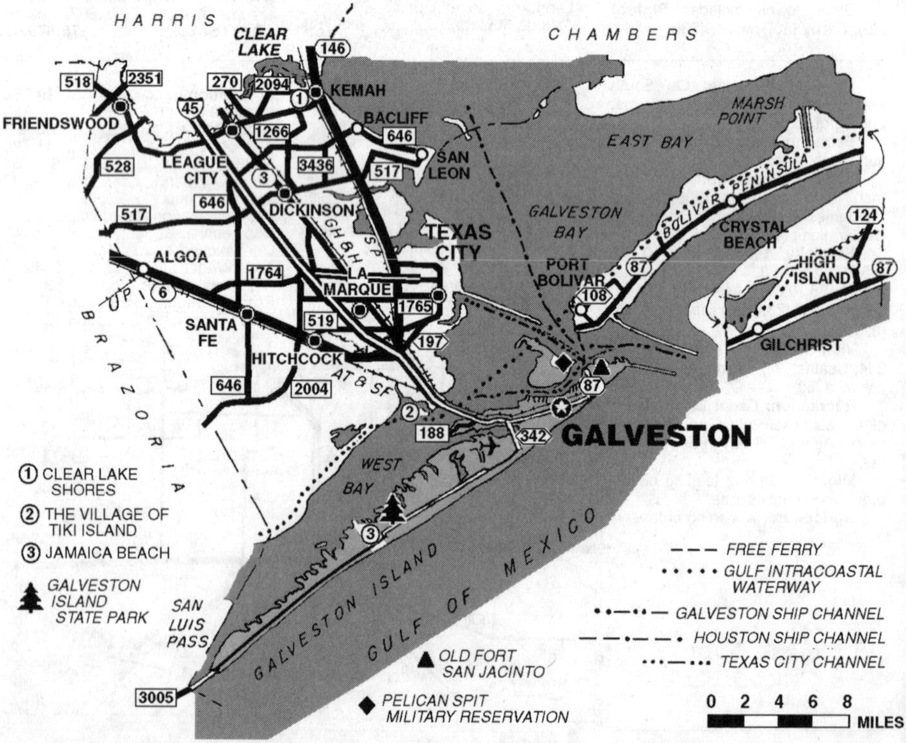

① CLEAR LAKE SHORES
② THE VILLAGE OF TIKI ISLAND
③ JAMAICA BEACH
GALVESTON ISLAND STATE PARK
OLD FORT SAN JACINTO
PELICAN SPIT MILITARY RESERVATION
FREE FERRY
GULF INTRACOASTAL WATERWAY
GALVESTON SHIP CHANNEL
HOUSTON SHIP CHANNEL
TEXAS CITY CHANNEL
0 2 4 6 8 MILES

Garza County

Physical Features: On edge of Caprock; rough, broken land, with playas, gullies, canyons, Brazos River forks; sandy, loam, clay soils.

Economy: Cotton, oil, tourism.

History: Created from Bexar District, 1876; organized 1907; named for early Texas family.

Ethnicity, 1990: White, 4,588 (89.2%); Black, 328 (6.4%); American Indian, 9 (0.2%); Asian, 21 (0.4%); Other, 197 (3.8%). Hispanic, 1,454 (28.3%).

Vital Statistics, 1993: Births, 78; deaths, 69; marriages, 46; divorces, 21.

Recreation: Post Stampede in August, Indian ceremony for crops, March 22; scenic areas; Post-Garza Museum.

Minerals: Oil and gas.

Agriculture: Cotton is major cash crop; hay, eggs, beef, stocker cattle; 4,000 acres irrigated.

POST (3,820) county seat; founded by C.W. Post, cereal manufacturer; oil, agribusiness center; hospital.

Population	**5,298**
(Change fm '90	3.0
Land Area (sq. mi.)	895.6
Altitude (ft.)	2,176-2,986
Rainfall (in.)	19.4
Jan. mean min.	26
July mean max.	94
Growing season (days)	216
Civ. Labor	2,120
Unemployed	7.1
Total Wages	$22,863,040
Av. Weekly Wage	$354.69
Prop. Value	$514,255,190
Retail Sales	$23,760,261

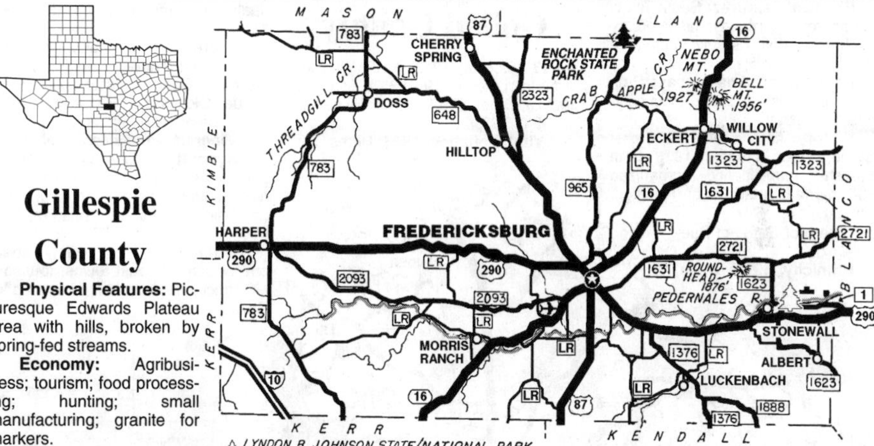

Gillespie County

Physical Features: Picturesque Edwards Plateau area with hills, broken by spring-fed streams.

Economy: Agribusiness; tourism; food processing; hunting; small manufacturing; granite for markers.

History: Created 1848 from Bexar, Travis counties; named for Texas Ranger Capt. R.A. Gillespie; historic German settlement in heart of Comanche country; birthplace of President Lyndon B. Johnson and Fleet Admiral Chester W. Nimitz.

Ethnicity, 1990: White, 16,325 (94.9%); Black, 34 (0.2%); American Indian, 60 (0.3%); Asian, 27 (0.2%); Other, 758 (4.4%). Hispanic, 2,426 (14.1%).

Vital Statistics, 1993: Births, 197; deaths, 238; marriages, 145; divorces, 72.

Recreation: Among leading deer-hunting areas; fishing; numerous historic sites and tourist attractions include LBJ Ranch, Nimitz Hotel; Pioneer Museum Complex, Enchanted Rock.

Minerals: Sand, gravel, granite, gypsum.

Agriculture: Most income from beef cattle, turkeys, sheep and goats; a leading peach-producing county; hay, grain sorghums, oats, wheat also raised.

FREDERICKSBURG (7,745) county seat; varied manufacturing; wine production; food processing; museum; tourist attractions; hospital.

Stonewall (245) agribusiness, tourism, Peach Jamboree in June.

Other towns include: **Harper** (383); **Luckenbach** (25).

Population	**18,653**
(Change fm '90)	8.4
Land Area (sq. mi.)	1,061.1
Altitude (ft.)	1,477-2,244
Rainfall (in.)	28.7
Jan. mean min.	36
July mean max.	95
Growing season (days)	219
Civ. Labor	9,705
Unemployed	2.4
Total Wages	$95,586,954
Av. Weekly Wage	$306.85
Prop. Value	$1,485,654,661
Retail Sales	$173,444,128

For explanation of sources, abbreviations and symbols, see p. 132.

Glasscock County

Physical Features: Western county on rolling plains, broken by small streams; sandy, loam soils.

Economy: Farming, ranching, oil and gas.

History: Created 1887, from Tom Green County; organized, 1893; named for Texas pioneer George W. Glasscock.

Ethnicity, 1990: White, 1,156 (79.9%); Black, 0 (0.0%); American Indian, 2 (0.1%); Asian, 0 (0.0%); Other, 289 (20.0%). Hispanic, 424 (29.3%).

Vital Statistics, 1993: Births, 22; deaths, 7; marriages, 7; divorces, 1.

Recreation: Hunting, St. Lawrence Fall Festival.

Minerals: Production of oil, gas.

Agriculture: Cotton is major crop; grain sorghums; cattle, sheep, swine, Angora goats and milk goats raised; 40,000 acres irrigated, mostly cotton.

GARDEN CITY (300) county seat; serves sparsely settled ranching, oil area.

Population	**1,516**
(Change fm '90)	4.8
Land Area (sq. mi.)	900.8
Altitude (ft.)	2,495-2,727
Rainfall (in.)	15.8
Jan. mean min.	21
July mean max.	93
Growing season (days)	222
Civ. Labor	555
Unemployed	3.0
Total Wages	$5.930,746
Av. Weekly Wage	$350.62
Prop. Value	$406,067,070
Retail Sales	$1,931,803

Goliad County

Physical Features: South Texas county; rolling, brushy; bisected by San Antonio River; sandy, loam, alluvial soils.

Economy: Primarily based on oil; agribusiness; tourism, electricity-generating plant.

History: Among the state's most historic areas; created 1836 from Spanish municipality, organized 1837; name is anagram of (H)idalgo. Birthplace of Gen. Zaragoza, hero of Battle of Puebla (Mexico).

Ethnicity, 1990: White, 4,953 (82.8%); Black, 407 (6.8%); American Indian, 19 (0.3%); Asian, 5 (0.1%); Other, 596 (10.0%). Hispanic, 2,145 (35.9%).

Vital Statistics, 1993: Births, 73; deaths, 66; marriages, 45; divorces, 14.

Recreation: Missions, restored Presidio La Bahia, Fannin Battleground; Gen. Ignacio Zaragoza statue; Old Market House museum; Lake, fishing, hunting, camping.

Minerals: Production of oil, gas.

Agriculture: Beef cattle, stocker operations and fed cattle are top revenue producers; corn, grain sorghums, hay; minor irrigation for pasture, fruit trees.

GOLIAD (2,113) county seat; one of state's oldest towns; tourism; oil; agriculture; hospital; Christmas in Goliad.

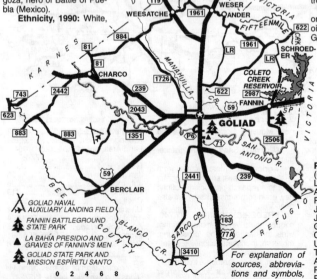

GOLIAD NAVAL AUXILIARY LANDING FIELD
FANNIN BATTLEGROUND STATE PARK
LA BAHÍA PRESIDIO AND GRAVES OF FANNIN'S MEN
GOLIAD STATE PARK AND MISSION ESPÍRITU SANTO

For explanation of sources, abbreviations and symbols, see p. 132.

Population	**6,278**
(Change from '90)	5.0
Land Area (sq. mi.)	853.5
Altitude (ft.)	63-242
Rainfall (in.)	36.8
Jan. mean min.	43
July mean max.	96
Growing season (days)	285
Civ. Labor	2,830
Unemployed	6.6
Total Wages	$20,361,435
Av. Weekly Wage	$328.21
Prop. Value	$699,030,400
Retail Sales	$23,281,604

Gonzales County

Physical Features: South Texas county; rolling, rich bottom soils along Guadalupe River and its tributaries; some sandy areas; many oaks, pecans.

Economy: Agribusinesses.

History: Among first Anglo-American settlements; created 1836, organized 1837; named for Coahuila y Texas Gov. Rafael Gonzales.

Ethnicity, 1990: White, 13,025 (75.7%); Black, 1,716 (10.0%); American Indian, 46 (0.3%); Asian, 23 (0.1%); Other, 2,395 (13.9%). Hispanic, 6,142 (35.7%).

Vital Statistics, 1993: Births, 273; deaths, 232; marriages, 139; divorces, 76.

Recreation: Historic sites, 86 officially recognized homes or historical markers; Pioneer Village Living History Center; state park; museums, Independence Park;.

Minerals: Gas, oil, clay, gravel.

Agriculture: Major poultry county; cow-calf operations important; corn, sorghums.

GONZALES (6,519) county seat; first shot in Texas Revolution fired here; shipping, processing center; manufacturing; hospitals, "Come and Take It" festival.

Other towns include: **Nixon** (1,986, partly in Wilson County) Feather Fest; **Ottine** (90), crippled children's hospital, Gonzales Warm Springs Foundation Hospital; **Smiley** (486) Settlers Set-To; **Waelder** (785) Guacamole Fest.

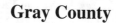

Population	**17,574**
(Change fm '90)	2.1
Land Area (sq. mi.)	1,067.8
Altitude (ft.)	201-504
Rainfall (in.)	32.6
Jan. mean min.	41
July mean max.	97
Growing season (days)	276
Civ. Labor	7,719
Unemployed	4.5
Total Wages	$91,948,552
Av. Weekly Wage	$329,76
Prop. Value	$875,174,130
Retail Sales	$117,905,719

Gray County

Physical Features: Panhandle High Plains, broken by Red River forks, tributaries; sandy loam, waxy soils.

Economy: Petroleum, agriculture, feedlot operations, chemical plant, other manufacturing.

History: Created 1876, from Bexar District; organized, 1902; named for Peter W. Gray, member of first Legislature.

Ethnicity, 1990: White, 21,566 (90.0%); Black, 899 (3.8%); American Indian, 216 (0.9%); Asian, 115 (0.5%); Other, 1,171 (4.9%). Hispanic, 1,895 (7.9%).

Vital Statistics, 1993: Births, 328; deaths, 311; marriages, 217; divorces, 134.

Recreation: Water sports, Lake McClellan National Grassland Park; White Deer Land Museum; barbed-wire museum.

Minerals: Production of oil, gas.

Agriculture: Fed cattle, stocker operations; wheat, grain sorghums, corn, hay and forage raised.

Population	**24,273**
(Change fm '90)	1.3
Land Area (sq. mi.)	928.8
Altitude (ft.)	2,558-3,296
Rainfall (in.)	19.6
Jan. mean min.	22
July mean max.	92
Growing season (days)	195
Civ. Labor	11,222
Unemployed	4.9
Total Wages	$209,031,209
Av. Weekly Wage	$456.15
Prop. Value	$1,121,570,019
Retail Sales	$209,820,860

PAMPA (20,044) county seat; petroleum processing; varied manufacturing; hospital, college.

Other towns include: **Lefors** (695); **McLean** (861) commercial center for southern part of county.

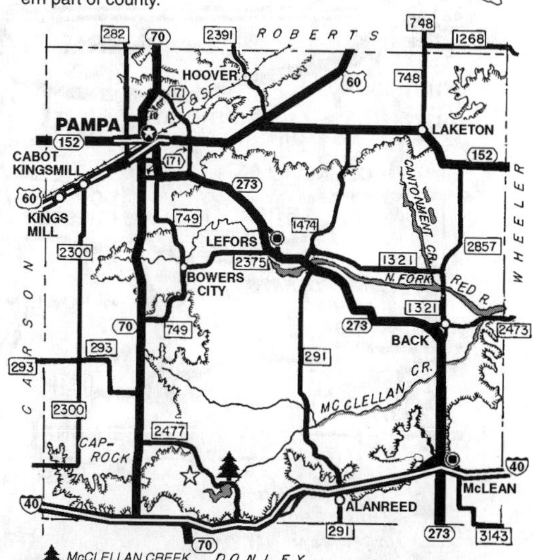

For explanation of sources, abbreviations and symbols, see p. 132.

Grayson County

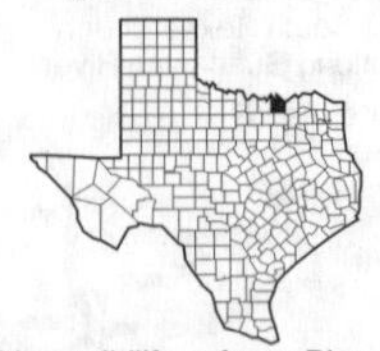

Physical Features: North Texas county; level, some low hills; sandy loam, blackland soils; drains to Red River and tributaries of Trinity River.

Economy: A manufacturing, distribution and trade center for northern Texas and southern Oklahoma; tourism; minerals; agribusiness.

History: Created 1846 from Fannin County; named for Republic Atty. Gen. Peter W. Grayson.

Ethnicity, 1990: White, 85,553 (90.0%); Black, 6,565 (6.9%); American Indian, 1,046 (1.1%); Asian, 412 (0.4%); Other, 1,445 (1.5%). Hispanic, 2,795 (2.9%).

Vital Statistics, 1993: Births, 1,347; deaths, 1,119; marriages, 1,133; divorces, 729.

Recreation: Lakes; fishing; water sports; state park; cultural activities; wildlife refuge; Pioneer Village; antique boat motor museum.

Minerals: Oil, gas and stone.

Agriculture: Most income from cattle; other livestock includes swine, horses; wheat, grain sorghums, corn; some peanuts irrigated.

SHERMAN (32,164) county seat; varied manufacturing; processors, distributors for major companies; Austin College; hospitals.

Denison (21,845), manufacturing; food processing; transportation center; tourism; hospitals.

Grayson County College located between Sherman and Denison.

Other towns include: **Bells** (982); **Collinsville** (1,108); **Gunter** (930); **Howe** (2,226), varied manufacturing, Founders' Day in May; **Pottsboro** (1,308); **Tioga** (637); **Tom Bean** (878); **Whitesboro** (3,301), agribusiness, tourism, Mayfest, Peanut Festival; **Whitewright** (1,722, partly in Fannin County); **Van Alstyne** (2,233), window screen, electronics, saddle, tack manufacturing.

Population	**97,450**
(Change from '90)	2.6
Land Area (sq. mi.)	933.6
Altitude (ft.)	535-867
Rainfall (in.)	38.2
Jan. mean min.	30
July mean max.	95
Growing season (days)	227
Civ. Labor	47,456
Unemployed	6.2
Total Wages	$862,929,210
Av. Weekly Wage	$446.76
Prop. Value	$3,367,219,831
Retail Sales	$890,447,633

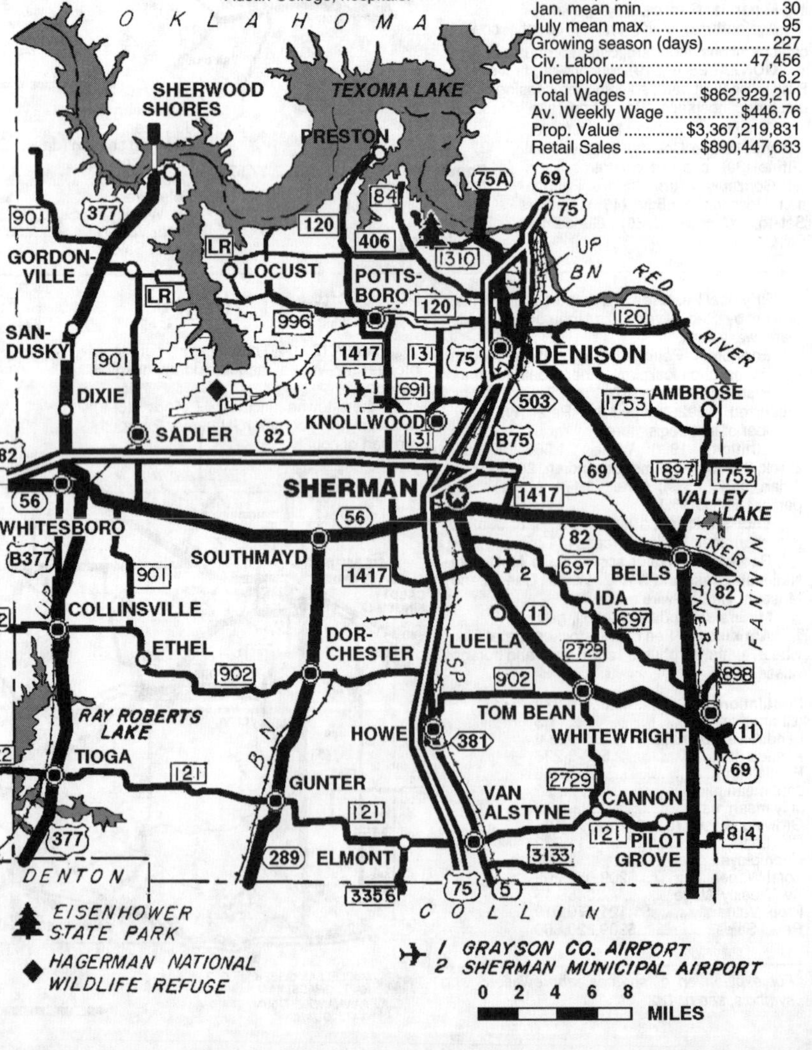

EISENHOWER STATE PARK
HAGERMAN NATIONAL WILDLIFE REFUGE

1 GRAYSON CO. AIRPORT
2 SHERMAN MUNICIPAL AIRPORT

0 2 4 6 8 MILES

Gregg County

Physical Features: A populous, leading petroleum county, heart of the famed East Texas oil field; bisected by the Sabine River; hilly, timbered; with sandy, clay, alluvial soils.

Economy: Oil but with significant other manufacturing; tourism, conventions; agribusinesses and lignite coal production.

History: Created and organized in 1873 from Rusk, Upshur counties; named for Confederate Gen. John Gregg.

Ethnicity, 1990: White, 81,883 (78.0%); Black, 19,937 (19.0%); American Indian, 478 (0.5%); Asian, 491 (0.5%); Other, 2,159 (2.1%). Hispanic, 3,775 (3.6%).

Vital Statistics, 1993: Births, 1,717; deaths, 1,119; marriages, 1,468; divorces, 604.

Recreation: Water activities on lakes; hunting; varied cultural events; the East Texas Oil Museum, Glory Days in Kilgore in May, Depot Fest Art Festival and Loblolly Festival in October.

Minerals: Leading oil-producing county with more than 3 billion barrels produced since 1931; also, sand and gravel and natural gas.

Agriculture: Beef-cattle production, timber, hay; some horses.

LONGVIEW (72,438, partly in Harrison County) county seat; manufacturing, brewery, distribution center; hospitals; LeTourneau University; convention center; balloon race in July.

Kilgore (11,275, partly in Rusk County), oil center; manufacturing; hospital; Kilgore College (junior college); East Texas Treatment Center; Shakespeare festival in summer.

Gladewater (6,184) antique center, gusher days in April, Christmas Tyme in Gusherville on Thanksgiving weekend; airport.

Other towns include: **Easton** (436); **Judson** (650); **Lakeport** (783); **Liberty City** (1,660); **White Oak** (5,358).

Population	**108,172**
(Change fm '90)	3.1
Land Area (sq. mi.)	274.0
Altitude (ft.)	289-436
Rainfall (in.)	46.5
Jan. mean min.	35
July mean max.	94
Growing season (days)	247
Civ. Labor	57,783
Unemployed	8.4
Total Wages	$1,150,705,362
Av. Weekly Wage	$411.44
Prop. Value	$5,667,485,393
Retail Sales	$1,437,095,643

For explanation of sources, abbreviations and symbols, see p. 132.

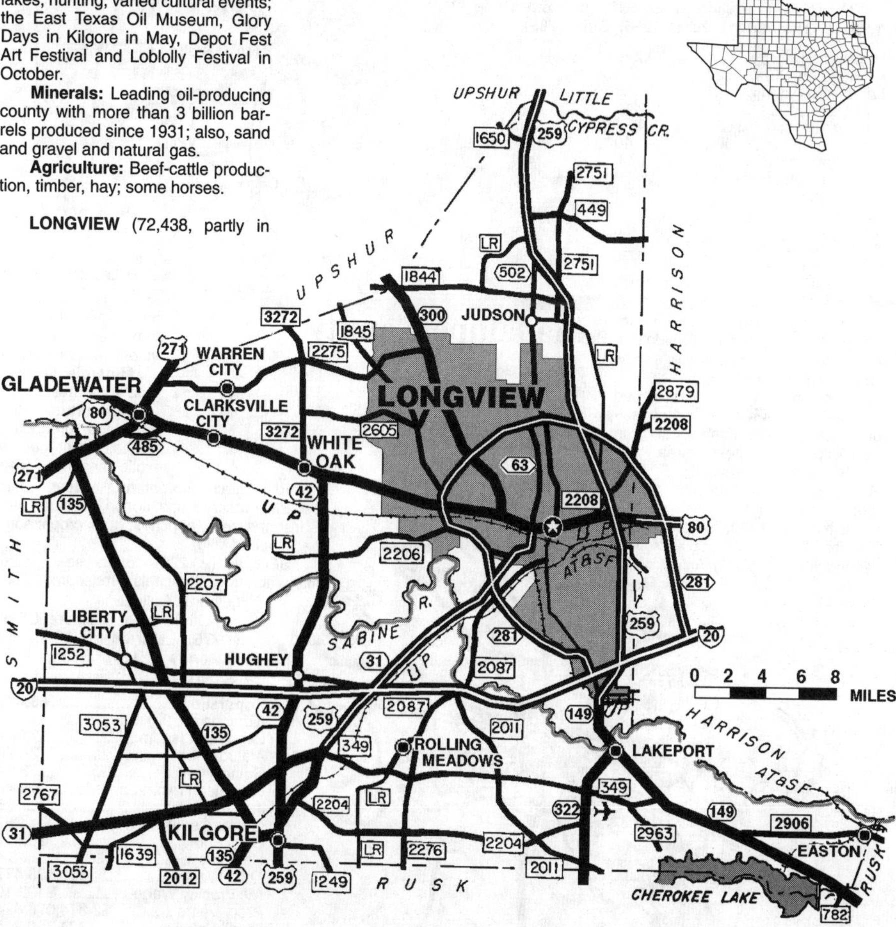

Grimes County

Physical Features: Rich bottom soils along Brazos, Navasota rivers; remainder hilly, partly forested.

Economy: Varied manufacturing; agribusinesses; tourism.

History: Created from Montgomery County 1846; named for Jesse Grimes, who signed Texas Declaration of Independence.

Ethnicity, 1990: White, 12,879 (68.4%); Black, 4,614 (24.5%); American Indian, 52 (0.3%); Asian, 30 (0.2%); Other, 1,253 (6.7%). Hispanic, 2,657 (14.1%).

Vital Statistics, 1993: Births, 274; deaths, 210; marriages, 127; divorces, 88.

Recreation: Hunting, fishing; Gibbons Creek Reservoir; historic sites; fall Renaissance Festival at Plantersville .

Minerals: Lignite coal, oil.

Agriculture: Beef cattle, some dairy cattle; hay, corn, peachaes, pecans; honey sales significant; some timber sold.

ANDERSON (320) county seat; rural center; Fanthorp Inn historical site; Go-Texan weekend.

Navasota (6,659), agribusiness center for parts of three counties; varied manufacturing; food, wood processing; hospital.

Other towns include: **Bedias** (301); **Plantersville** (212); **Todd Mission** (60); **Richards** (296); **Shiro** (205).

Population	**20,240**
(Change fm '90)	7.5
Land Area (sq. mi.)	793.8
Altitude (ft.)	193-415
Rainfall (in.)	40.4
Jan. mean min.	40
July mean max.	96
Growing season (days)	278
Civ. Labor	8,571
Unemployed	4.9
Total Wages	$136,462,908
Av. Weekly Wage	$452.29
Prop. Value	$994,331,713
Retail Sales	$159,537,953

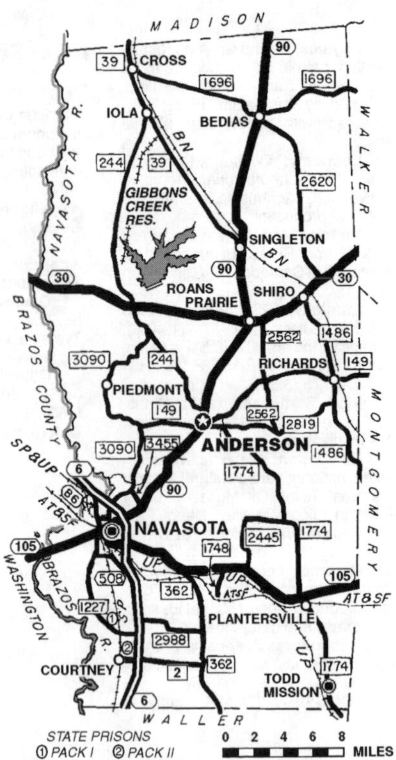

Guadalupe County

Physical Features: South central county bisected by Guadalupe River; level to rolling surface; sandy, loam, blackland soils.

Economy: Agribusiness; varied manufacturing; tourism; many residents work in San Antonio; county in San Antonio metropolitan area.

History: Created 1846 from Bexar, Gonzales counties; named for river.

Ethnicity, 1990: White, 52,948 (81.6%); Black, 3,665 (5.6%); American Indian, 235 (0.4%); Asian, 465 (0.7%); Other, 7,560 (11.7%). Hispanic, 19,246 (29.7%).

Vital Statistics, 1993: Births, 969; deaths, 561; marriages, 514; divorces, 306.

Recreation: Fishing, hunting; historic sites; freedom fiesta in July, historic festival in April.

Minerals: Oil, gas, sand and gravel, clays.

Agriculture: Beef cattle top producers; horses, hogs, poultry, exotic animals, greyhounds; grain sorghums, wheat, corn, pecans, nursery crops, cotton, peanuts, oats, Christmas trees, peaches, truck crops; some pecan wood sold.

SEGUIN (20,228) county seat; varied manufacturing; hospitals, museum; Texas Lutheran College.

Other towns include: **Cibolo** (1,775), **Marion** (1,021), **McQueeney** (2,129), **Selma** (629), **Schertz** (11,973).

Population	**68,426**
(Change fm '90)	5.5
Land Area (sq. mi.)	711.2
Altitude (ft.)	372-726
Rainfall (in.)	31.4
Jan. mean min.	40
July mean max.	96
Growing season (days)	267
Civ. Labor	35,657
Unemployed	3.4
Total Wages	$365,528,477
Av. Weekly Wage	$402.10
Prop. Value	$2,374,076,824
Retail Sales	$324,756,234

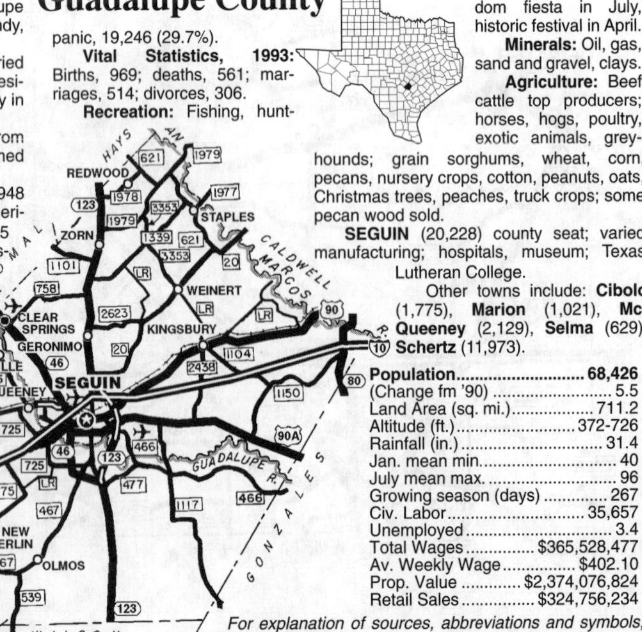

For explanation of sources, abbreviations and symbols, see p. 132.

Hale County

Physical Features: High Plains; fertile sandy, loam soils; many playas; large underground water supply.

Economy: Agribusinesses, food-processing plants; manufacturing.

History: Created from Bexar District, 1876; organized, 1888; named for Lt. J.C. Hale, who died at San Jacinto.

Ethnicity, 1990: White, 23,823 (68.7%); Black, 1,852 (5.3%); American Indian, 148 (0.4%); Asian, 136 (0.4%); Other, 8,712 (25.1%). Hispanic, 14,428 (41.6%).

Vital Statistics, 1993: Births, 636; deaths, 275; marriages, 346; divorces, 191.

Recreation: Llano Estacado Museum.

Minerals: Production of oil, gas.

Agriculture: One of leading farm-producing counties; cotton, major crop; wheat, sorghum, corn also produced; fed cattle, stockers raised; 310,000 acres irrigated, primarily cotton, corn.

PLAINVIEW (22,048) county seat; packing plants, distribution center; food processing, other industries; Wayland Baptist University; hospitals, mental health center; correctional center.

Hale Center (2,094), commercial center.

Other towns include: **Abernathy** (2,735, partly in Lubbock County), **Edmonson** (114), **Petersburg** (1,295), **Seth Ward** (1,485).

Population **35,397**
(Change fm '90) 2.1
Land Area (sq. mi.) 1,004.7

Altitude (ft.) 3,501-3,515
Rainfall (in.) 19.0
Jan. mean min. 23
July mean max. 92
Growing season (days) 211

Civ. Labor 17,071
Unemployed 5.6
Total Wages $254,772,600
Av. Weekly Wage $356.73
Prop. Value $1,320,525,267
Retail Sales $3,346,479,013

Hall County

Physical Features: Rolling to hilly, broken by Red River forks, tributaries; red and black sandy loam.

Economy: Grain, cotton processing; farm, ranch supplies, marketing for large rural area.

History: Created 1876 from Bexar, Young districts; organized 1890; named for Republic of Texas secretary of war W.D.C. Hall.

Ethnicity, 1990: White, 2,908 (74.5%); Black, 303 (7.8%); American Indian, 15 (0.4%); Asian, 7 (0.2%); Other, 672 (17.2%). Hispanic, 727 (18.6%).

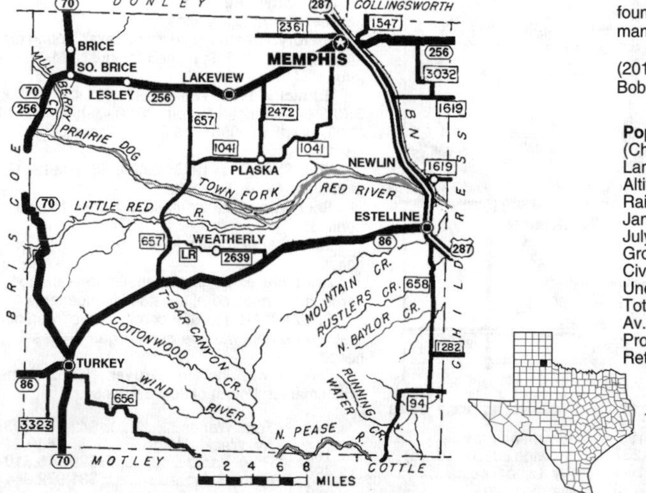

Vital Statistics, 1993: Births, 56; deaths, 61; marriages, 43; divorces, 14.

Recreation: Fishing, hunting; museum.

Minerals: Not significant.

Agriculture: Most income from crops including cotton, peanuts; also beef cattle, hogs; some irrigation.

MEMPHIS (2,516) county seat; foundry; cotton gins; food processing; manufacturing; hospital.

Other towns include: **Estelline** (201), **Lakeview** (215), **Turkey** (546) Bob Wills Day in April.

Population **4,029**
(Change fm '90) 3.2
Land Area (sq. mi.) 903.1
Altitude (ft.) 2,238-3,315
Rainfall (in.) 20.3
Jan. mean min. 25
July mean max. 97
Growing season (days) 213
Civ. Labor 1,941
Unemployed 8.0
Total Wages $13,691,830
Av. Weekly Wage $270.57
Prop. Value $161,391,542
Retail Sales $21,708,170

For explanation of sources, abbreviations and symbols, see p. 132.

Hamilton County

Physical Features: Hilly north central county broken by scenic valleys; loam soils.

History: Created 1842; then re-created, organized 1858, from Bosque, Comanche, Lampasas counties; named for South Carolinian, Gov. James Hamilton, who aided Texas Revolution and Republic.

Economy: Agribusiness; varied manufacturing; hunting leases; tourism; many residents work outside county.

Ethnicity, 1990: White, 7,389 (95.6%); Black, 2 (0.0%); American Indian, 21 (0.3%); Asian, 24 (0.3%); Other, 297 (3.8%). Hispanic, 403 (5.2%).

Vital Statistics, 1993: Births, 95; deaths, 150; marriages, 67; divorces, 59.

Recreation: Deer, quail, duck hunting; dove festival; July arts and crafts show.

Minerals: Limited gas, oil, gravel.

Agriculture: Dairies top revenue sources; beef cattle; wheat, oats, also, hay, sorghums; more land being devoted to pastures.

HAMILTON (2,011) county seat; dairies, hunting, antique shops, historical homes; varied manufacturing; hospital; library.

Hico (1,440) farm center, Old Settlers Reunion in summer.

Other towns include: **Evant** (453) partly in Coryell County .

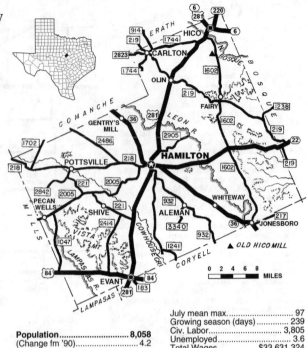

Population **8,058**
(Change fm '90) 4.2
Land Area (sq. mi.) 835.7
Altitude (ft.) 967-1,590
Rainfall (in.) 29.8
Jan. mean min. 33
July mean max. 97
Growing season (days) 239
Civ. Labor 3,805
Unemployed 3.6
Total Wages $33,631,324
Av. Weekly Wage $318.33
Prop. Value $490,168,403
Retail Sales $39,149,055

Hansford County

Physical Features: High Plains, many playas, creeks, draws; sandy, loam, black soils; underground water.

Economy: Agribusinesses; mineral operations.

History: Created 1876, from Bexar, Young districts; organized 1889; named for jurist J.M. Hansford.

Ethnicity, 1990: White, 4,821 (82.4%); Black, 0 (0.0%); American Indian, 23 (0.4%); Asian, 14 (0.2%); Other, 990 (16.9%). Hispanic, 1,174 (20.1%).

Vital Statistics, 1993: Births, 63; deaths, 60; marriages, 52; divorces, 3.

Recreation: Stationmasters House Museum; hunting.

Minerals: Production of gas, oil, stone, helium.

Agriculture: Large cattle-feeding operations; sorghums, wheat, corn; substantial irrigation.

SPEARMAN (3,065) county seat; feedlots; grain marketing, storage center; gas processing; hospital.

Other towns include: **Gruver** (1,120) farm-ranch market; Fourth of July Barbecue.

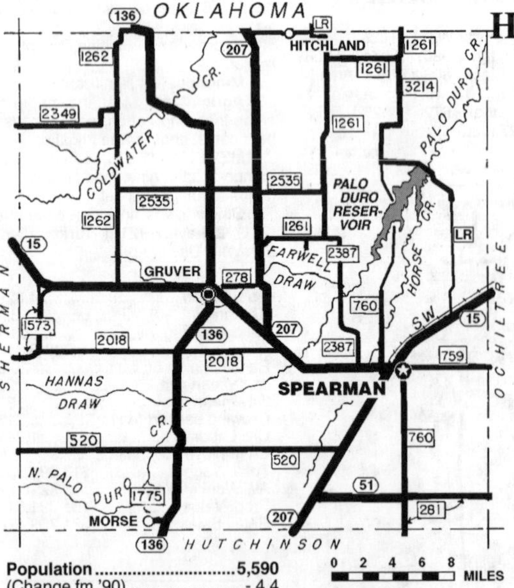

Population **5,590**
(Change fm '90) .... - 4.4
Land Area (sq. mi.) 919.8
Altitude (ft.) 2,986-3,237
Rainfall (in.) 19.2
Jan. mean min. 20
July mean max. 95
Growing season (days) 186
Civ. Labor 2,498
Unemployed 3.4
Total Wages $42,606,603
Av. Weekly Wage $439.64
Prop. Value $699,315,310
Retail Sales $31,972,944

Hardeman County

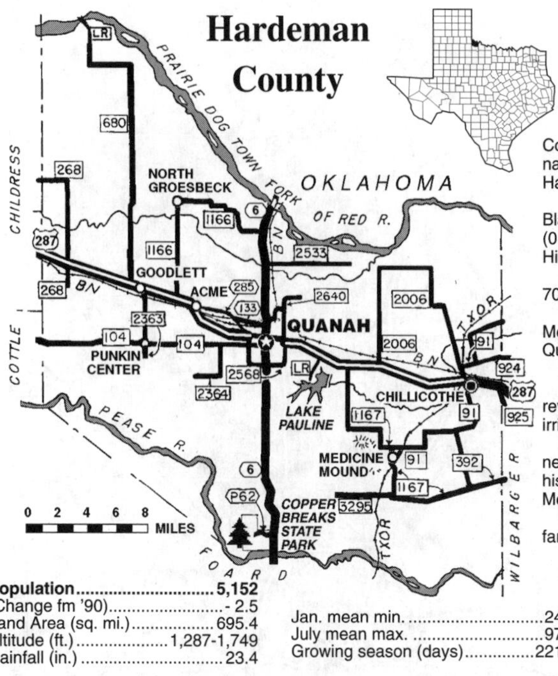

Physical Features: Rolling, broken area on divide between Pease, Red Rivers' forks; sandy loam soils.

Economy: Agribusiness; some manufacturing, tourism.

History: Created 1858 from Fannin County; re-created 1876, organized, 1884; named for pioneer brothers, Bailey and T.J. Hardeman.

Ethnicity, 1990: White, 4,427 (83.8%); Black, 321 (6.1%); American Indian, 26 (0.5%); Asian, 16 (0.3%); Other, 493 (9.3%). Hispanic, 589 (11.1%).

Vital Statistics, 1993: Births, 58; deaths, 70; marriages, 47; divorces, 22.

Recreation: state park; lake activities; Medicine Mound aborigine gathering site; Quanah Parker monument; old railroad depot.

Minerals: Oil, gypsum.

Agriculture: Wheat, cotton, cattle are top revenue producers; pumpkins; some cotton irrigated.

QUANAH (3,325) county seat; agribusinesses; cotton oil mill; manufacturing; hospital; historical sites; Copper Breaks Fun Day on Memorial Day.

Other towns include: **Chillicothe** (795), farm market center.

Population	**5,152**
(Change fm '90)	- 2.5
Land Area (sq. mi.)	695.4
Altitude (ft.)	1,287-1,749
Rainfall (in.)	23.4
Jan. mean min.	24
July mean max.	97
Growing season (days)	221
Civ. Labor	2,006
Unemployed	5.1
Total Wages	$24,628,920
Av. Weekly Wage	$341.58
Prop. Value	$312,827,914
Retail Sales	$19,162,354

Hardin County

Physical Features: Southeast county; timbered; many streams; sandy, loam soils; Big Thicket covers much of area.

History: Created 1858 from Jefferson, Liberty counties. Named for Texas Revolutionary leader William Hardin.

Economy: Paper manufacturing; wood processing; minerals; food processing; county in Beaumont-Port Arthur-Orange metropolitan area.

Ethnicity, 1990: White, 37,485 (90.7%); Black, 3,485 (8.4%); American Indian, 123 (0.3%); Asian, 58 (0.1%); Other, 169 (0.4%). Hispanic, 679 (1.6%).

Vital Statistics, 1993: Births, 628; deaths, 379; marriages, 465; divorces, 327.

Recreation: Big Thicket with rare plant, animal life; national preserve; Red Cloud Water Park; hunting, fishing.

Minerals: Oil, gas, sand, gravel.

Agriculture: Timber provides most income; more than 85 percent of county forested; beef cattle, hogs raised; eggs marketed; forage, fruit and rice; honey sold; minor irrigation.

KOUNTZE (2,271) county seat; sawmill; some manufacturing; tourism; library.

Silsbee (6,680), trade, manufacturing center; oil, gas processing; pine festival; hospital.

Lumberton (7,016) retail center, some tourism.

Other towns include: **Batson** (140); **Saratoga** (1,000) Big Thicket Museum; **Sour Lake** (1,650) oil, lumbering; **Thicket** (306); **Votaw** (160).

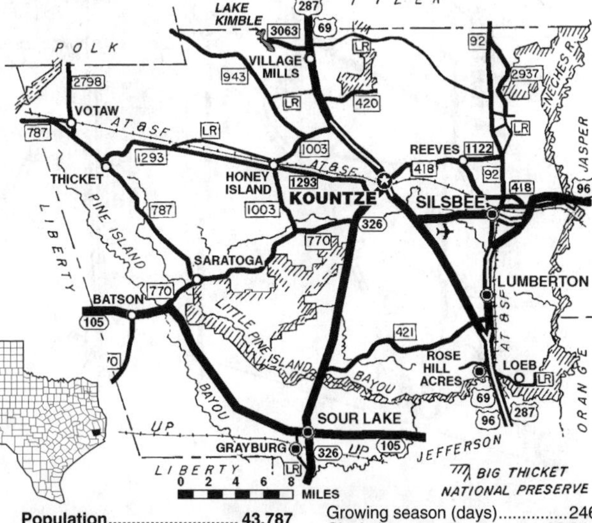

Population	**43,787**
(Change fm '90)	6.0
Land Area (sq. mi.)	894.3
Altitude (ft.)	29-126
Rainfall (in.)	55.4
Jan. mean min.	38
July mean max.	93
Growing season (days)	246
Civ. Labor	20,941
Unemployed	8.4
Total Wages	$156,282,670
Av. Weekly Wage	$352.87
Prop. Value	$1,496,990,838
Retail Sales	$288,689,042

For explanation of sources, abbreviations and symbols, see p. 132.

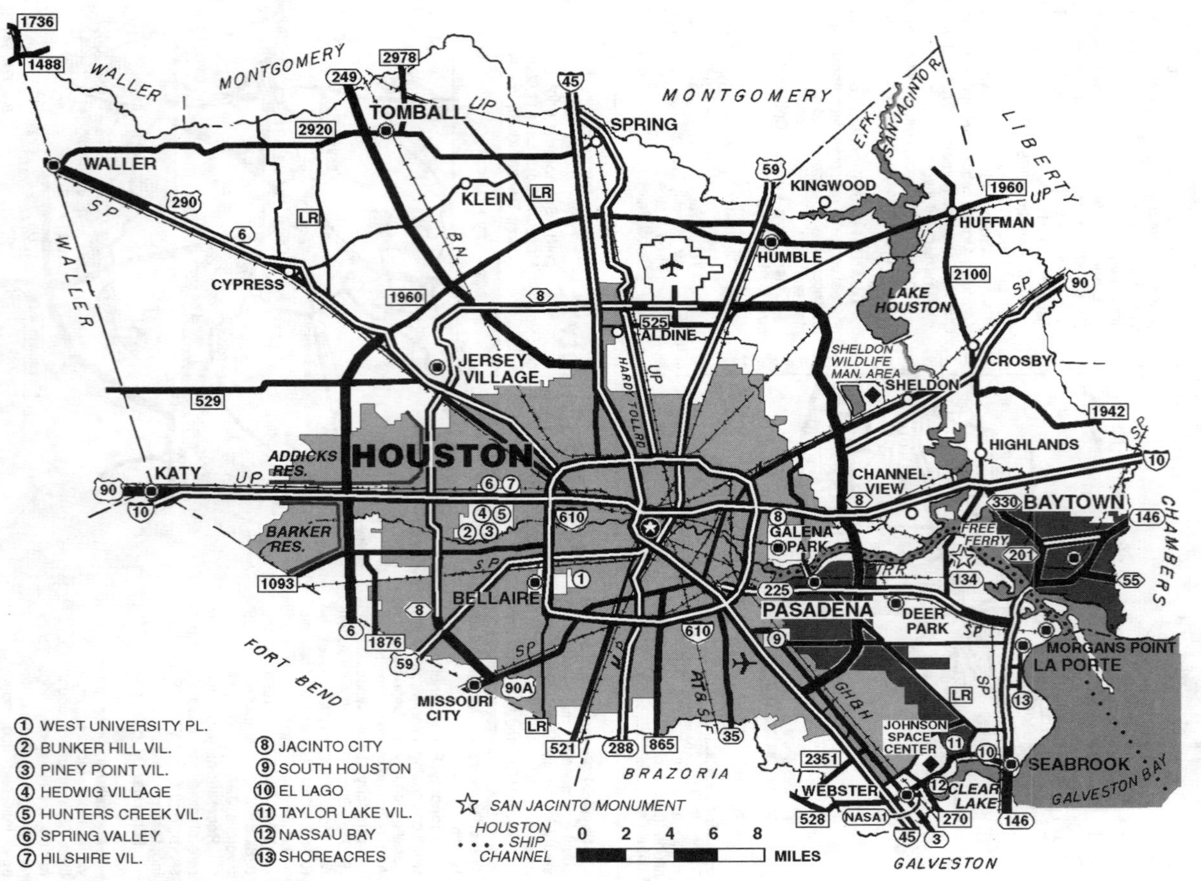

HOUSTON
PASADENA
BAYTOWN
BELLAIRE
MISSOURI CITY
JERSEY VILLAGE
TOMBALL
KLEIN
SPRING
HUMBLE
KINGWOOD
HUFFMAN
LAKE HOUSTON
CROSBY
HIGHLANDS
SHELDON
SHELDON WILDLIFE MAN. AREA
CHANNEL-VIEW
GALENA PARK
DEER PARK
LA PORTE
MORGANS POINT
SEABROOK
CLEAR LAKE
JOHNSON SPACE CENTER
WEBSTER
ALDINE
CYPRESS
WALLER
KATY
ADDICKS RES.
BARKER RES.
FREE FERRY
HARDY TOLLRD
GALVESTON BAY
MONTGOMERY
LIBERTY
CHAMBERS
WALLER
FORT BEND
BRAZORIA
GALVESTON
E. FK. SAN JACINTO R.
① WEST UNIVERSITY PL.
② BUNKER HILL VIL.
③ PINEY POINT VIL.
④ HEDWIG VILLAGE
⑤ HUNTERS CREEK VIL.
⑥ SPRING VALLEY
⑦ HILSHIRE VIL.
⑧ JACINTO CITY
⑨ SOUTH HOUSTON
⑩ EL LAGO
⑪ TAYLOR LAKE VIL.
⑫ NASSAU BAY
⑬ SHOREACRES
SAN JACINTO MONUMENT
HOUSTON SHIP CHANNEL
0 2 4 6 8 MILES

Physical Features: Largest county in eastern half of state; level; typically coastal surface and soils; many bayous, lakes, canals for artificial drainage; partly forested.

History: Created 1836, organized 1837; named for John R. Harris, founder of Harrisburg (now part of Houston) in 1824.

Economy: Highly industrialized county with largest population; more than 55 foreign governments maintain offices in Houston; corporate management center; nation's largest concentration of petrochemical plants; largest U.S wheat-exporting port, among top U.S. ports in the value of foreign trade and total tonnage; petroleum refining, chemicals, food, fabricated metal products, nonelectrical machinery, primary metals, scientific instruments; paper and allied products, printing and publishing; center for energy, space and medical research; center of international business.

Ethnicity, 1990: White, 1,824,137 (64.7%); Black, 541,180 (19.2%); American Indian, 8,044 (0.3%); Asian, 110,848 (3.9%); Other, 333,990 (11.9%). Hispanic, 644,935 (22.9%).

Vital Statistics, 1993: Births, 58,205; deaths, 18,405; marriages, 29,172; divorces, 16,824.

Recreation: Professional football, baseball, basketball, other activities; Jones Hall for the Performing Arts, Nina Vance Alley Theatre, Houston Theatre Center, Music Hall Coliseum, Convention Center, the Summit, a 17,000-seat sports and entertainment center; Astroworld and WaterWorld amusement parks near the Astrodome.

Sam Houston Park, with restored early Houston homes, church, stores; Museum of Fine Arts, Contemporary Arts Museum, Rice Museum; Wortham Theater for performing arts; museum of natural science, planetarium, zoo in Hermann Park; San Jacinto Battleground, Battleship Texas; Johnson Space Center; annual livestock show.

Fishing, boating, other freshwater and saltwater activities.

Minerals: Among leading oil, gas, petrochemical areas; production of petroleum, cement, natural gas, liquids, salt, lime, sulfur, sand and gravel, clays, stone.

Agriculture: Beef cattle, horses, nursery plants and hay are the major revenue sources. Also, some dairies and ratites. Also harvested are rice, vegetables, corn, peanuts; about 14,700 acres irrigated for rice; substantial income from forest products.

Education: Houston is a major center of higher education, with more than 140,000 students enrolled in 28 colleges and universities in the county. Among these are Rice University, the University of Houston, Texas Southern University, University of St. Thomas, Houston Baptist University.

Harris County

Medical schools include University of St. Thomas and Houston Baptist University Schools of Nursing, University of Texas Health Science Center , Baylor College of Medicine, Institute of Religion and Human Development, Texas Chiropractic College, Texas Woman's University-Houston Center.

HOUSTON (1,700,672) county seat; largest Texas city; fourth largest in nation.

Ranks first in manufacture of petroleum equipment, agricultural chemicals, fertilizers, pesticides, oil and gas pipeline transmission; a leading scientific center; ranks high in manufacture of machinery, fabricated metals; a major distribution, shipping center; engineering and research center; food processing and textile mills.

A 67-foot statue of Sam Houston, for whom Texas' largest city is named, was dedicated October 1994. It stands on I-45 south of Huntsville in Walker County. Dallas Morning News photo.

Plants make apparel, lumber and wood products; furniture, paper, chemical, petroleum and coal products; publishing center; one of the nation's largest public school systems; prominent corporate center, with more than 200 firms relocating corporate headquarters, divisions or subsidaries to county since 1970.

Pasadena (127,843), residential city with large industrial area manufacturing petrochemicals and other petroleum-related products; civic center; San Jacinto College, Texas Chiropractic College; four hospitals; historical museum; Strawberry Festival.

Baytown (68,255), refining, petrochemical center; Lee College; hospitals; historical homes;

Bellaire (14,796), residential city with several major office buildings.

The **Clear Lake Area** which includes **El Lago** (3,507); **Nassau Bay** (4,844); **Seabrook** (8,322); **Taylor Lake Village** (3,664), Johnson Space Center, University of Houston-Clear Lake; Bayport Industrial Complex includes Port of Bayport; 12 major marinas; two hospitals; **Webster** (5,376);

Other towns include: **Aldine** (11,751); **Channelview** (27,106); **Crosby** (2,033); **Deer Park** (29,751), ship-channel industries, fall festival; hospital; **Galena Park** (10,746); **Highlands** (7,463); **Humble** (13,711), oil-field equipment manufactured, retail center, hospital; **Jacinto City** (9,680); **Jersey Village** (5,226); **Katy** (9,020, partly in Fort Bend, Waller counties), varied manufacturing, hospital; rice harvest festival in October; **Kingwood** (39,631); **La Porte** (30,127), varied manufacturing; Sylvan Beach Festival in April; Galveston Bay; **Missouri City** (43,155, mostly in Fort Bend County); **South Houston** (15,126); **Spring** (36,493); **Sheldon** (1,876); **Tomball** (7,224) retail center; regional hospital, sports medical center; museum, parks; Go Texan festivities in February.

Population	**3,003,167**
(Change fm '90)	6.6
Land Area (sq. mi.)	1,728.9
Altitude (ft.)	sea level-171
Rainfall (in.)	42.6
Jan. mean min.	46
July mean max.	93
Growing season (days)	300
Civ. Labor	1,667,465
Unemployed	6.6
Total Wages	$45,889,444,890
Av. Weekly Wage	$592.86
Prop. Value	$134,057,527,792
Retail Sales	$32,044,979,155

For explanation of sources, abbreviations and symbols, see p. 132.

Harrison County

Physical Features: East Texas county; hilly, rolling; over half forested; Sabine River; Caddo Lake.

History: Created 1839, from Shelby County; organized, 1842; named for eloquent advocate of Texas Revolution, Jonas Harrison.

Economy: Oil, gas processing; lumbering; pottery, other varied manufacturing.

Ethnicity, 1990: White, 40,387 (70.3%); Black, 16,038 (27.9%); American Indian, 192 (0.3%); Asian, 144 (0.3%); Other, 722 (1.3%). Hispanic, 1,278 (2.2%).

Vital Statistics, 1993: Births, 755; deaths, 601; marriages, 597; divorces, 278.

Recreation: Fishing, other water activities on Caddo and other lakes; hunting; plantation homes, historic sites; Stagecoach Days in May; Old Courthouse Museum; Old World Store; state park, performing arts.

Minerals: Production of oil, gas, coal, clays, sand and gravel.

Agriculture: Cattle, hogs; nursery plants, hay, timber.

MARSHALL (24,471) county seat; petroleum, lumber processing; varied manufacturing; Wonderland of Lights in December; civic center; historic sites; hospital; Wiley College; East Texas Baptist University.

Other towns include: **Hallsville** (2,593), Western Days in October, museum; **Nesbitt** (359); **Scottsville** (294); **Uncertain** (210); **Waskom** (1,866); Also, part of **Longview**.

Population	59,739
(Change fm '90)	3.9
Land Area (sq. mi.)	898.8
Altitude (ft.)	168-417
Rainfall (in.)	46.4
Jan. mean min.	33
July mean max.	94
Growing season (days)	245
Civ. Labor	27,481
Unemployed	9.2
Total Wages	$496,585,564
Av. Weekly Wage	$495.35
Prop. Value	$2,936,975,841
Retail Sales	$312,890,877

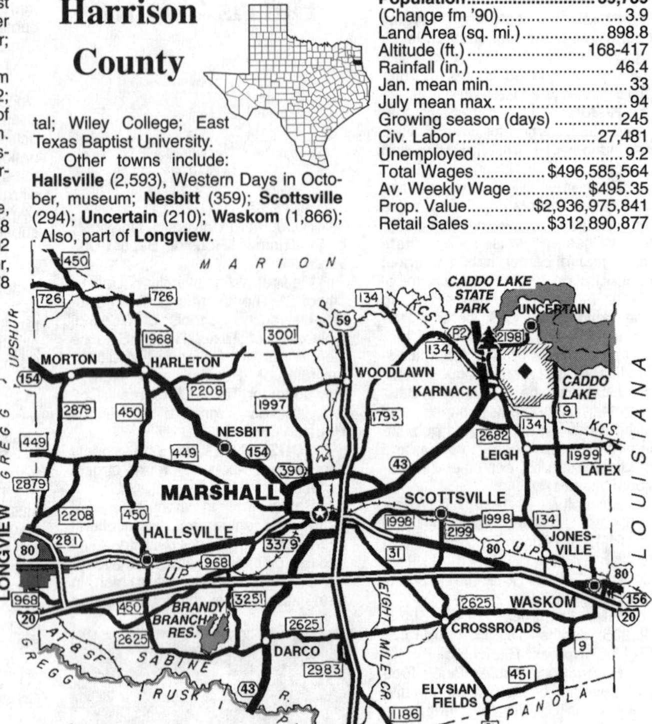

Hartley County

Physical Features: Panhandle High Plains; drains to Canadian River, tributaries; playas; sandy, loam, chocolate soils; lake.

History: Created 1876 from Bexar, Young districts; organized 1891; named for Texas pioneers O.C. and R.K. Hartley.

Economy: Agriculture, gas production; varied manufacturing.

Ethnicity, 1990: White, 3,510 (96.6%); Black, 9 (0.2%); American Indian, 30 (0.8%); Asian, 7 (0.2%); Other, 78 (2.1%). Hispanic, 201 (5.5%).

Vital Statistics, 1993: Births, 43; deaths, 30; marriages, 9; divorces, 14.

Recreation: Rita Blanca Lake activities; ranch museum; local events; XIT Rodeo and Reunion at Dalhart.

Minerals: Natural gas.

Agriculture: Wheat, sorghum, corn; hay; beef cattle; about 120,000 acres irrigated; blue corn, pop corn introduced.

CHANNING (264) county seat.

Dalhart (6,290 mostly in Dallam County), feedlots; feed, meat processing; other industries.

Population	3,561
(Change fm '90)	- 2.0
Land Area (sq. mi.)	1,462,3
Altitude (ft.)	3,439-4,397
Rainfall (in.)	16.1
Jan. mean min.	21
July mean max.	92
Growing season (days)	180
Civ. Labor	2,168
Unemployed	2.2
Total Wages	$11,263,676
Av. Weekly Wage	$341.30
Prop. Value	$297,891,810
Retail Sales	$20,766,507

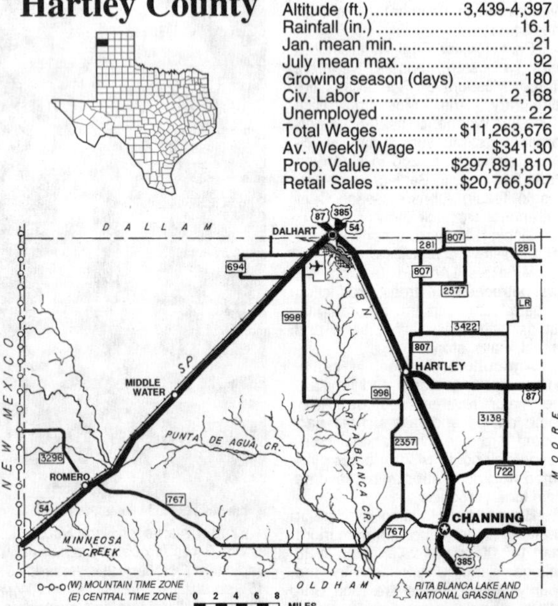

For explanation of sources, abbreviations and symbols, see p. 132.

Haskell County

Physical Features: West central county; rolling; broken areas; drained by Brazos tributaries; lake; sandy loam, gray, black soils.

Economy: Agribusinesses, oil-field operations.

History: Created 1858, from Milam, Fannin counties; re-created 1876; organized 1885; named for Goliad victim C.R. Haskell.

Ethnicity,1990: White, 5,481 (80.4%); Black, 244 (3.6%); American Indian, 17 (0.2%); Asian, 16 (0.2%); Other, 1,062 (15.6%). Hispanic, 1,312 (19.2%).

Vital Statistics, 1993: Births, 60; deaths, 100; marriages, 48; divorces, 33.

Recreation: Lake Stamford activities; bass tournament, arts & crafts show; hunting.

Minerals: Oil and gas.

Agriculture: Most income from cotton, peanuts, grains; beef cattle raised; 27,000 acres irrigated, mostly peanuts, some cotton, wheat.

HASKELL (3,337) county seat; farming center; hospital; city park.

Other towns include: **O'Brien** (158), **Rule** (774), **Rochester** (485), **Weinert** (248). Also, **Stamford** (3,647, mostly in Jones County),

Population	**6,803**
(Change fm '90)	- 0.2
Land Area (sq. mi.)	903.0
Altitude (ft.)	1,416-1,681
Rainfall (in.)	24.1
Jan. mean min.	28
July mean max.	97
Growing season (days)	232
Civ. Labor	3,000
Unemployed	6.0
Total Wages	$27,024,813
Av. Weekly Wage	$306.69
Prop. Value	$376,924,831
Retail Sales	$41,542,999

Hays County

Physical Features: Hilly in west, blackland in east; on edge of Balcones Escarpment.

Economy: Education, tourism, retirement area, some manufacturing; part of Austin metropolitan area.

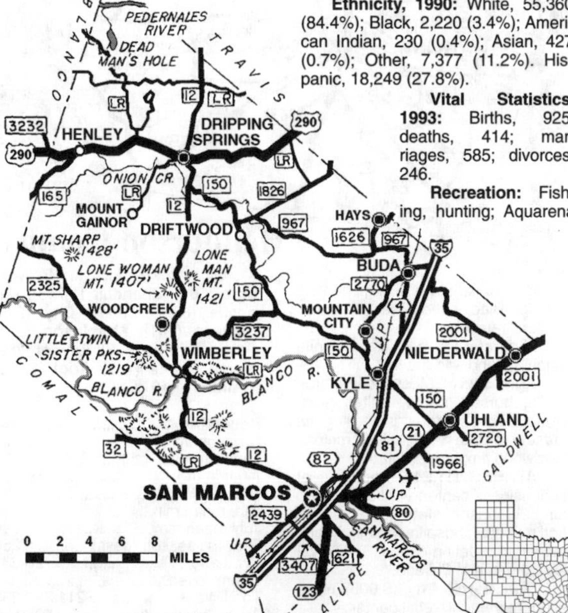

History: Created 1843 from Travis County; named for Capt. Jack Hays, famous Texas Ranger.

Ethnicity, 1990: White, 55,360 (84.4%); Black, 2,220 (3.4%); American Indian, 230 (0.4%); Asian, 427 (0.7%); Other, 7,377 (11.2%). Hispanic, 18,249 (27.8%).

Vital Statistics, 1993: Births, 925; deaths, 414; marriages, 585; divorces, 246.

Recreation: Fishing, hunting; Aquarena Springs; college cultural, athletic events; Cypress Creek and Blanco River resorts, guest ranches.

Minerals: Sand and gravel, cement produced.

Agriculture: Beef cattle, goats, sheep, swine, ratites; some llamas and exotic deer; corn, sorghum, wheat, hay, cotton, and fruit orchards

SAN MARCOS (31,048), county seat; aircraft assemblies, metal stamping; distribution center; 200 stores in two outlet malls; hospital, sports medicine, physical therapy center; Southwest Texas State University, San Marcos Baptist Academy, Gary Job Corps Training Center; Scheib Center for mentally handicapped; Mardi Gras, Cinco de Mayo, Texas Chilympiad in September.

Other towns include: **Buda** (1,871); **Dripping Springs** (1,057); **Hays** (271); **Kyle** (2,321); **Mountain City** (388); **Niederwald** (250, partly in Caldwell County); **Uhland** (308); **Wimberley** (2,537), retirement community, tourism, artists, concert series; **Woodcreek** (946).

Population	**69,428**
(Change fm '90)	5.8
Land Area (sq. mi.)	677.9
Altitude (ft.)	582-1,501
Rainfall (in.)	34.3
Jan. mean min.	36
July mean max.	95
Growing season (days)	254
Civ. Labor	40,539
Unemployed	3.4
Total Wages	$432,271,735
Av. Weekly Wage	$340.89
Prop. Value	$2,790,482,098
Retail Sales	$596,703,846

Hemphill County

Physical Features: Panhandle county; sloping surface, broken by Canadian, Washita rivers; sandy, red, dark soils.

Economy: Petroleum production and refining, livestock production.

History: Created from Bexar, Young districts, 1876; organized 1887; named for Republic of Texas Justice John Hemphill.

Ethnicity, 1990: White, 3,503 (94.2%); Black, 7 (0.2%); American Indian, 22 (0.6%); Asian, 5 (0.1%); Other, 183 (4.9%). Hispanic, 412 (11.1%).

Vital Statistics, 1993: Births, 31; deaths, 38; marriages, 33; divorces, 9.

Recreation: Lake Marvin activities; fall foliage tours; hunting, fishing; Buffalo Wallow Indian Battleground, wildlife management area; 4th of July rodeo.

Minerals: Oil, natural gas.

Agriculture: Fed beef, stocker cattle top revenue sources; crops include wheat, sorghum, hay, improved pastures; some irrigation.

CANADIAN (2,285) county seat; oil, gas production; feedlot; trailer manufacturing.

Population	**3,598**
(Change fm '90)	- 3.3
Land Area (sq. mi.)	909.7
Altitude (ft.)	2,185-2,843
Rainfall (in.)	20.1
Jan. mean min.	22
July mean max.	95
Growing season (days)	204
Civ. Labor	1,829
Unemployed	4.5
Total Wages	$29,880,638
Av. Weekly Wage	$466.45
Prop. Value	$844,057,785
Retail Sales	$20,120,107

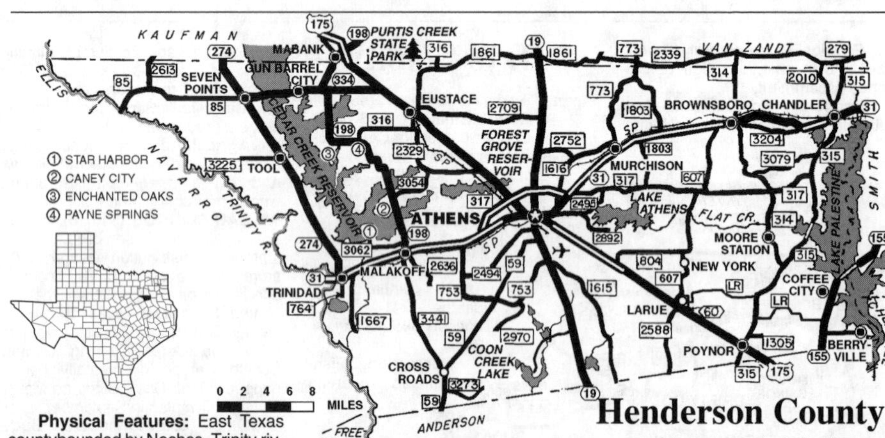

Henderson County

Physical Features: East Texas countybounded by Neches, Trinity rivers; hilly, rolling; one-third forested; sandy, loam, clay soils; commercial timber; Cedar Creek, other lakes.

Economy: Varied manufacturing; agribusinesses; minerals; recreation; tourism.

History: Created 1846 from Nacogdoches, Houston counties and named for Gov. J. Pinckney Henderson.

Ethnicity, 1990: White, 52,216 (89.2%); Black, 4,755 (8.1%); American Indian, 181 (0.3%); Asian, 141 (0.2%); Other, 1,250 (2.1%). Hispanic, 2,368 (4.0%).

Vital Statistics, 1993: Births, 721; deaths, 762; marriages, 537; divorces, 176.

Recreation: Cedar Creek Reservoir, Lake Palestine, and other lakes; Purtis Creek State Park; hunting, fishing; Black-eyed Pea Jamboree, fiddlers' reunion.

Minerals: Oil, gas, clays, lignite, sulphur, sand and gravel.

Agriculture: Most income from cattle, horses, swine, ratites (emu, ostrich, rhea); crops include grain, nursery crops, vegetables, melons; hardwood timber marketed.

ATHENS (11,249) county seat; agribusiness center; varied manufacturing; tourism; state fish hatchery and museum; hospital, mental health/mental retardation center; Trinity Valley Community College.

Gun Barrel City (3,906) recreation, retirement, retail center.

Malakoff (2,140), brick factory, varied industry, Lakefest.

Other towns include: **Brownsboro** (569); **Chandler** (1,748); **Berryville** (830); **Coffee City** (227); **Eustace** (741); **Murchison** (551); **Payne Springs** (663); **Poynor** (252); **Seven Points** (759); **Tool** (1,853); **Trinidad** (1,101).

Population	**61,536**
(Change fm '90)	5.1
Land Area (sq. mi.)	874.3
Altitude (ft.)	256-763
Rainfall (in.)	39.4
Jan. mean min.	36
July mean max.	96
Growing season (days)	260
Civ. Labor	26,633
Unemployed	6.5
Total Wages	$211,395,382
Av. Weekly Wage	$339.96
Prop. Value	$2,596,409,530
Retail Sales	$424,917,799

Hidalgo County

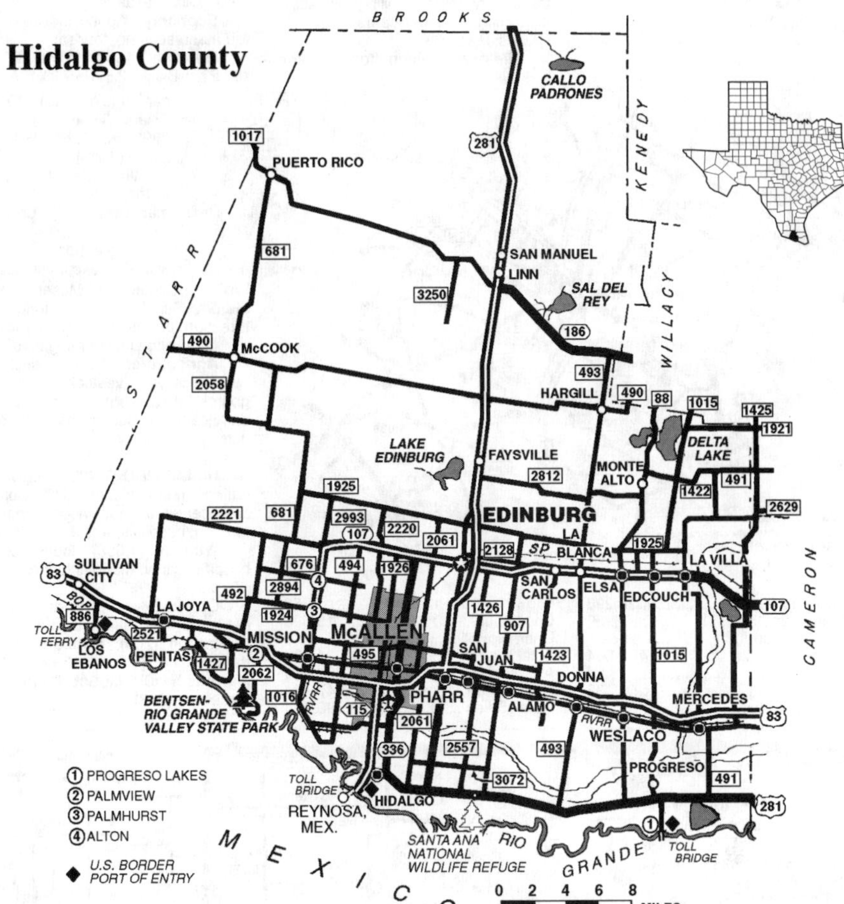

Physical Features: Rich alluvial soils along Rio Grande; sandy, loam soils in north; semitropical vegetation.

History: Settled early by Spaniards; created 1852 from Cameron, Starr counties; named for leader of Mexico's independence movement, Father Miguel Hidalgo y Costillo.

Economy: Food processing, shipping; other agribusinesses; tourism; mineral operations.

Ethnicity, 1990: White, 286,858 (74.8%); Black, 806 (0.2%); American Indian, 668 (0.2%); Asian, 1,088 (0.3%); Other, 94,125 (24.5%). Hispanic, 326,972 (85.2%).

Vital Statistics, 1993: Births, 12,639; deaths, 2,327; marriages, 4,739; divorces, 47.

Recreation: Winter resort, retirement area; fishing, hunting; gateway to Mexico; historical sites; Bentsen-Rio Grande Valley State Park; museums; All-Valley Winter Vegetable Show at Pharr.

Minerals: Oil, gas, stone, sand and gravel.

Agriculture: Ninety percent of farm cash receipts from crops, principally from sugar cane, grain, vegetables, citrus, cotton; livestock includes cattle; 270,000 acres irrigated.

EDINBURG (33,562) county seat; vegetable processing, packing; petroleum operations; clothing; tourism, planetarium; the University of Texas-Pan American; hospital; mental health center; museum; Fiesta Hidalgo in February.

McAllen (91,184) Food processing, packing, shipping; foreign trade zone; agriculture; tourism; varied manufacturing; new air terminal; community college; cancer center.

Mercedes (13,522) "boot capital," citrus, vegetable center; food processing; tourism; recreation vehicle show in January, boat show; Rio Grande Valley livestock show.

Pharr (36,122) agriculture, trading center; trucking; tourism.

Other towns include: **Alamo** (9,285) live steam museum; **Donna** (13,273), citrus center, varied manufacturing; lamb, sheep show; **Elsa** (5,646); **Edcouch** (3,281); **Hidalgo** (4,015); **La Joya** (3,007); **La Villa** (1,577); **Mission** (33,456), Citrus Fiesta; **San Juan** (13,091); **Sullivan City** (2,619); **Weslaco** (24,404) Bicultural Museum; .

Population	**426,940**
(Change fm '90)	11.3
Land Area (sq. mi.)	1,569.0
Altitude (ft.)	28-325
Rainfall (in.)	23.0
Jan. mean min.	48
July mean max.	95
Growing season (days)	327
Civ. Labor	177,583
Unemployed	18.2
Total Wages	$2,105,787,232
Av. Weekly Wage	$332.31
Prop. Value	$8,674,658,092
Retail Sales	$3,487,394,315

For explanation of sources, abbreviation and symbols, see p. 132.

Hill County

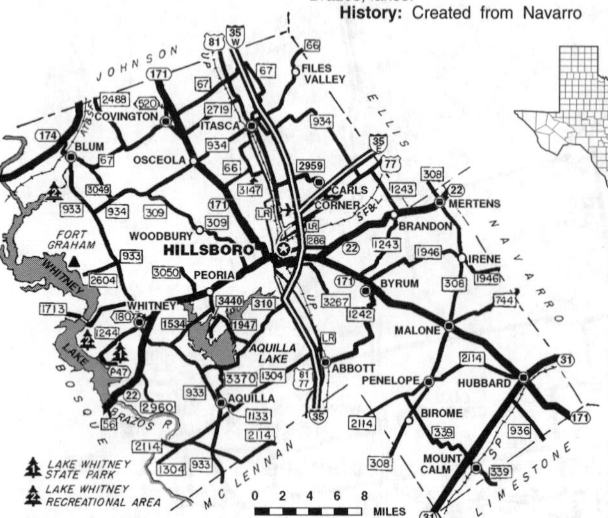

Physical Features: North central county; level to rolling; blackland soils, some sandy loams; drains to Brazos; lakes.

History: Created from Navarro County 1853; named for G.W. Hill, Republic of Texas official.

Economy: Agribusinesses, varied manufacturing, tourism.

Ethnicity, 1990: White, 23,669 (87.2%); Black, 2,520 (9.3%); American Indian, 80 (0.3%); Asian, 38 (0.1%); Other, 839 (3.1%). Hispanic, 2,230 (8.2%).

Vital Statistics, 1993: Births, 340; deaths, 398; marriages, 238; divorces, 135.

Recreation: Lake activities; excursion boat on Whitney; Confederate Museum, Audie Murphy Gun Museum, historic structures; art festival; motorcycle track.

Minerals: Limestone, gas, oil.

Agriculture: Evenly split between crops, livestock; grain sorghums, wheat, corn, cotton, hay; beef, dairy cattle, horses, swine; dairy products; some firewood.

HILLSBORO (7,423) county seat; varied manufacturing; Hill College; retail center; antique shops, depot restoration; hospitals; arts and crafts fair.

Whitney (1,656), tourist center; hospital, varied manufacturing.

Other towns include: **Abbott** (340); **Blum** (394); **Bynum** (203); **Covington** (263); **Hubbard** (1,629); **Itasca** (1,569); **Malone** (333); **Mertens** (110); **Mount Calm** (311); **Penelope** (223).

Population	**28,290**
(Change fm '90)	4.2
Land Area (sq. mi.)	962.4
Altitude (ft.)	481-864
Rainfall (in.)	34.2
Jan. mean min.	33
July mean max.	96
Growing season (days)	250
Civ. Labor	13,528
Unemployed	5.5
Total Wages	$114,024,022
Av. Weekly Wage	$331.14
Prop. Value	$981,447,484
Retail Sales	$263,290,234

Hockley County

Physical Features: West Texas High Plains, numerous playas, drains to Yellow House River, Lake; loam, sandy loam soils.

Economy: Extensive oil, gas production and services; manufacturing; varied agribusiness.

History: Created 1876, from Bexar, Young districts; organized 1921; named for Republic of Texas secretary of war Gen. G.W. Hockley.

Ethnicity, 1990: White, 18,937 (78.3%); Black, 1,023 (4.2%); American Indian, 86 (0.4%); Asian, 33 (0.1%); Other, 4,120 (17.0%). Hispanic, 7,650 (31.6%).

Vital Statistics, 1993: Births, 342; deaths, 188; marriages, 183; divorces, 135.

Recreation: Early Settlers' Day in July, Marigolds Arts, Crafts Festival in November.

Minerals: Oil, gas, stone; one of leading oil counties with more than 1 billion barrels produced.

Agriculture: Cotton, grain sorghums are top crops; cattle, hogs raised; substantial irrigation.

LEVELLAND (14,277) county seat; oil, cotton, cattle center; hospital; South Plains College.

Other towns include: **Anton** (1,266); **Opdyke West** (112); **Smyer** (447); **Sundown** (1,795); **Ropesville** (516).

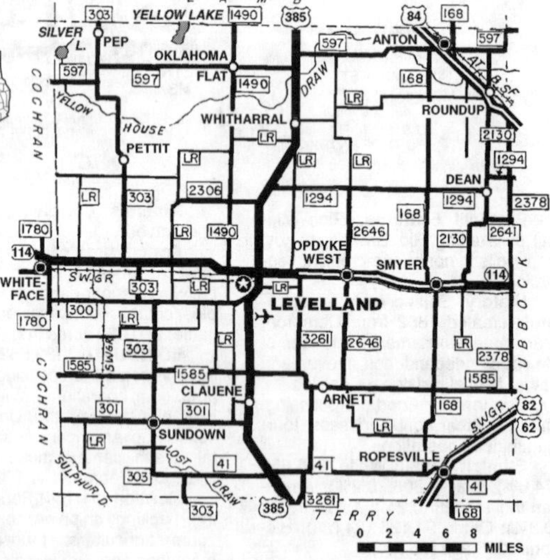

Population	**24,696**
(Change fm '90)	2.1
Land Area (sq. mi.)	908.3
Altitude (ft.)	3,388-3,633
Rainfall (in.)	18.1
Jan. mean min.	23
July mean max.	92
Growing season (days)	196
Civ. Labor	12,128
Unemployed	5.5
Total Wages	$166,892,312
Av. Weekly Wage	$396.30
Prop. Value	$2,804,765,040
Retail Sales	$128,023,452

Hood County

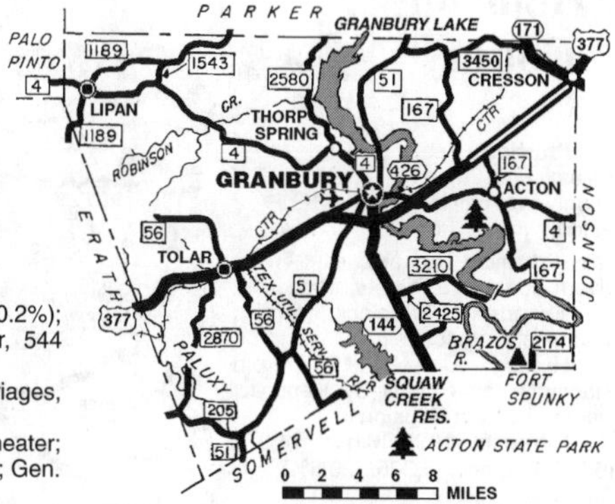

Physical Features: Hilly; broken by Paluxy, Brazos rivers; sandy loam soils.

Economy: Agribusinesses; tourism; nuclear power plant.

History: Created, organized 1866 from Johnson County; named for Confederate Gen. John B. Hood.

Ethnicity, 1990: White, 28,054 (96.8%); Black, 52 (0.2%); American Indian, 154 (0.5%); Asian, 177 (0.6%); Other, 544 (1.9%). Hispanic, 1,353 (4.7%).

Vital Statistics, 1993: Births, 372; deaths, 317; marriages, 300; divorces, 203.

Recreation: Lakes, fishing, scenic areas; summer theater; state park; site of grave of Elizabeth Crockett, wife of Davy; Gen. Granbury's Birthday in March.

Minerals: Oil, gas, stone.

Agriculture: Beef, cow-calf operations, stocker cattle top revenue producers; crops include hay, peanuts, pecans; some irrigation.

GRANBURY (4,458) county seat; agribusiness; tourism; historic downtown area; opera house; hospital; Civil War re-enactment in fall.

Other towns include: **Lipan** (382), **Tolar** (630).

Population	**29,916**
(Change fm '90)	3.2
Land Area (sq. mi.)	421.6
Altitude (ft.)	722-1,230
Rainfall (in.)	30.9
Jan. mean min.	33
July mean max.	97
Growing season (days)	232
Civ. Labor	14,497
Unemployed	7.4
Total Wages	$118,818,508
Av. Weekly Wage	$352.66
Prop. Value	$1,349,613,080
Retail Sales	$213,416,063

Hopkins County

Physical Features: Northeast Texas county of varied timber, including pines; drains north to South Sulphur River; Cooper Lake; light, sandy to heavier black soils.

Economy: Dairies, large milk-processing plants; agribusinesses; varied manufacturing.

History: Created 1846 from Lamar, Nacogdoches counties; named for pioneer Hopkins family.

Ethnicity, 1990: White, 25,381 (88.0%); Black, 2,476 (8.6%); American Indian, 126(0.4%); Asian, 70 (0.2%); Other, 780 (2.7%). Hispanic, 1,407 (4.9%).

Vital Statistics, 1993: Births, 433; deaths, 354; marriages, 321; divorces, 216.

Recreation: Fishing, hunting; lake activities; stew contest in September; dairy museum; dairy festival in June.

Minerals: Oil, gas and lignite.

Agriculture: Leading dairy county in region; also beef cattle production; hay, silage, cotton; broiler industry; some irrigation; firewood and hardwood lumber.

SULPHUR SPRINGS (14,786) county seat; dairy farming center; food processing, distribution; varied manufacturing; tourism; hospital; library, heritage park; music box gallery; civic center.

Other towns include: **Como** (594), **Cumby** (635), **Tira** (263).

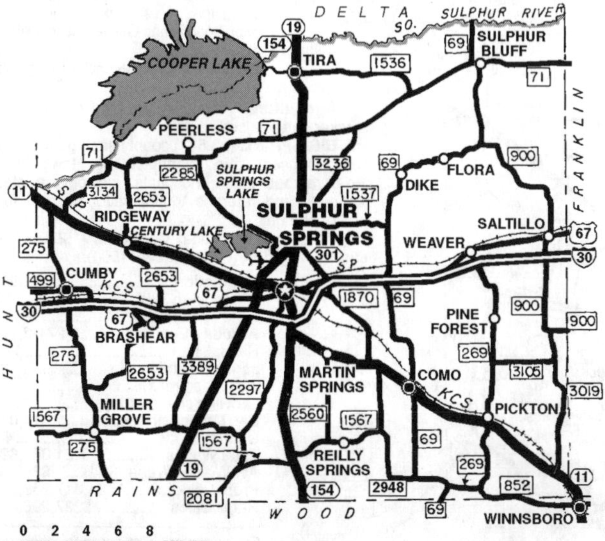

Population	**30,296**
(Change fm '90)	5.1
Land Area (sq. mi.)	784.7
Altitude (ft.)	420-649
Rainfall (in.)	44.2
Jan. mean min.	31
July mean max.	94
Growing season (days)	238
Civ. Labor	16,024
Unemployed	7.0
Total Wages	$196,577,534
Av. Weekly Wage	$376.38
Prop. Value	$1,166,058,205
Retail Sales	$333,599,655

For explanation of sources, abbreviations and symbols, see p. 132.

Houston County

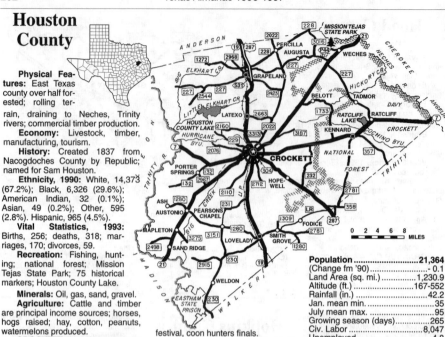

Physical Features: East Texas county over half forested; rolling terrain, draining to Neches, Trinity rivers; commercial timber production.

Economy: Livestock, timber, manufacturing, tourism.

History: Created 1837 from Nacogdoches County by Republic; named for Sam Houston.

Ethnicity, 1990: White, 14,373 (67.2%); Black, 6,326 (29.6%); American Indian, 32 (0.1%); Asian, 49 (0.2%); Other, 595 (2.8%). Hispanic, 965 (4.5%).

Vital Statistics, 1993: Births, 256; deaths, 318; marriages, 170; divorces, 59.

Recreation: Fishing, hunting; national forest; Mission Tejas State Park; 75 historical markers; Houston County Lake.

Minerals: Oil, gas, sand, gravel.

Agriculture: Cattle and timber are principal income sources; horses, hogs raised; hay, cotton, peanuts, watermelons produced.

CROCKETT (6,991) county seat; wood and plastic products; hospital; Crockett State School; fifth oldest town in Texas, historic sites; fiddlers festival, coon hunters finals.

Other towns include: **Grapeland** (1,609); **Kennard** (360); **Latexo** (303); **Lovelady** (609), Lovefest in February.

Population	**21,364**
(Change fm '90)	- 0.1
Land Area (sq. mi.)	1,230.9
Altitude (ft.)	167-552
Rainfall (in.)	42.2
Jan. mean min.	35
July mean max.	95
Growing season (days)	265
Civ. Labor	8,047
Unemployed	4.8
Total Wages	$123,431,483
Av. Weekly Wage	$391.91
Prop. Value	$1,022,311,530
Retail Sales	$110,849,763

Howard County

Physical Features: On edge Llano Estacado; sandy loam soils.

Economy: Oil, gas operations; agribusinesses; varied manufacturing, including clothing.

History: Named for V.E. Howard, legislator; created 1876 from Bexar, Young districts; organized 1882.

Ethnicity, 1990: White, 25,282 (78.2%); Black, 1,225 (3.8%); American Indian, 179 (0.6%); Asian, 162 (0.5%); Other, 5,495 (17.0%). Hispanic, 8,607 (26.6%).

Vital Statistics, 1993: Births, 508; deaths, 350; marriages, 290; divorces, 105.

Recreation: Lakes; state park; campground in Comanche Trail Park; Native Plant Trail; museum; historical sites; West Texas agricultural expo in March; Cranefest in February.

Minerals: Oil, gas, sand, gravel and stone.

Agriculture: Principally dry-land cotton; beef, stocker cattle raised.

BIG SPRING (23,547) county seat; petrochemicals produced; varied manufacturing; Howard College; railroad plaza; hospitals, including a state institution and Veterans Administration hospital; federal prison unit.

Other towns include: **Coahoma** (1,230); **Forsan** (279); **Knott** (685); **Vincent** (500).

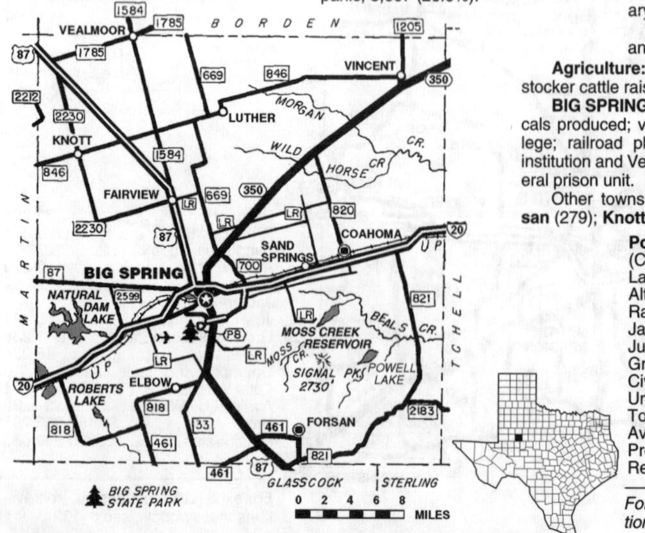

Population	**32,969**
(Change fm '90)	1.9
Land Area (sq. mi.)	902.9
Altitude (ft.)	2,271-2,776
Rainfall (in.)	17.7
Jan. mean min.	30
July mean max.	95
Growing season (days)	217
Civ. Labor	14,033
Unemployed	4.9
Total Wages	$221,084,629
Av. Weekly Wage	$392.39
Prop. Value	$1,317,258,318
Retail Sales	$237,296,496

For explanation of sources, abbreviations and symbols, see p. 132.

Hudspeth County

Physical Features: Plateau, basin terrain, draining to salt lakes; Rio Grande; mostly rocky, alkaline, clay soils and sandy loam soils, except alluvial along Rio Grande; desert, mountain vegetation. Fertile agricultural valleys.

Economy: Agribusiness, mining, tourism, hunting leases.

History: Named for Texas political leader Claude B. Hudspeth; created 1917 from El Paso County.

Ethnicity, 1990: White, 2,345 (80.4%); Black, 15 (0.5%); American Indian, 9 (0.3%); Asian, 2 (0.1%); Other, 544 (18.7%). Hispanic, 1,935 (66.4%).

Vital Statistics, 1993: Births, 70; deaths, 20; marriages, 21; divorces, 3.

Recreation: Scenic drives; fort ruins; hot springs; salt basin; white sands; hunting; part of Guadalupe Mountains National Park, containing unique plant life, canyons.

Minerals: Talc, stone, gypsum.

Agriculture: Most income from cotton, vegetables, hay-alfalfa; beef cattle raised; 35,000 acres irrigated.

SIERRA BLANCA (700) county seat; ranching center; tourist stop on interstate highway; 4th of July fair, livestock show in January.

Dell City (617) feedlots; vegetable packing; gypsum processing; clinic; trade center; airport; some of largest water wells in state.

Population	**2,865**
(Change fm '90)	- 1.7
Land Area (sq. mi.)	4,571.3
Altitude (ft.)	3,492-7,484
Rainfall (in.)	8.0
Jan. mean min.	27
July mean max.	94
Growing season (days)	231
Civ. Labor	1,447
Unemployed	2.5
Total Wages	$9.455,792
Av. Weekly Wage	$262.46
Prop. Value	$276,448,932
Retail Sales	$6,256,787

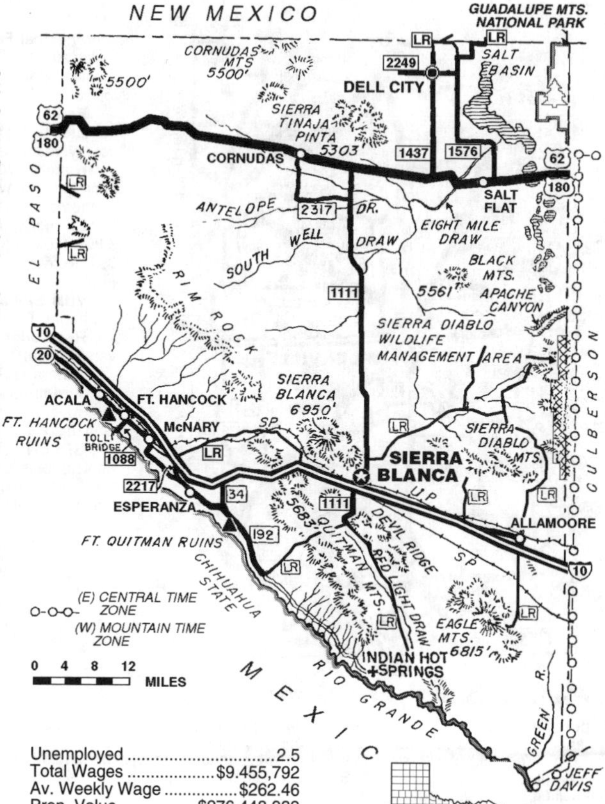

For explanation of sources, abbreviations and symbols, see p. 132.

The basin regions of Hudspeth, Culberson, Jeff Davis, Presidio and Brewster counties are the primary habitats of pronghorns. The animals were almost extinct when a conservation management program was begun in the early part of this century. Its numbers have increased and pronghorns are now also seen in the Permian Basin and the Panhandle. Texas Almanac file photo.

Hunt County

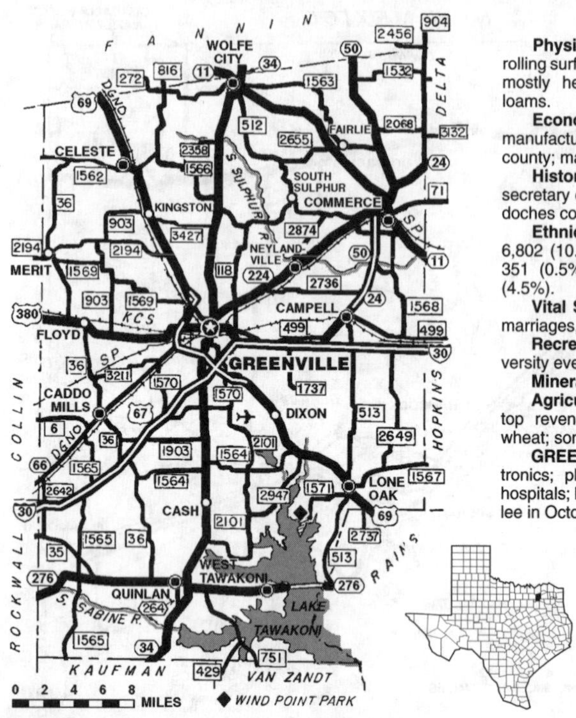

Physical Features: North Texas county; level to rolling surface; Sabine, Sulphur rivers; Lake Tawakoni; mostly heavy Blackland soil, some loam, sandy loams.

Economy: Agribusinesses, education, varied manufacturing; several Fortune 500 companies in county; many residents employed in Dallas area.

History: Named for Memucan Hunt, Republic secretary of navy; created 1846 from Fannin, Nacogdoches counties.

Ethnicity, 1990: White, 55,705 (86.6%); Black, 6,802 (10.6%); American Indian, 266 (0.4%); Asian, 351 (0.5%); Other, 1,219 (1.9%). Hispanic, 2,876 (4.5%).

Vital Statistics, 1993: Births, 875; deaths, 661; marriages, 689; divorces, 441.

Recreation: Lake sports; East Texas State University events; museum; Audie Murphy exhibit.

Minerals: Sand and white rock, gas, oil.

Agriculture: Beef cattle, horses, dairy products top revenue sources; hay, nursery crops, cotton, wheat; some firewood.

GREENVILLE (23,636) county seat; aircraft electronics; plastics distribution; varied manufacturing; hospitals; branch of Paris Junior College; Cotton Jubilee in October.

Commerce (7,036), East Texas State University; varied manufacturing; tourism; Bois d'Arc Bash in September; hospital.

Other towns include: **Caddo Mills** (1,109); **Campbell** (735); **Celeste** (805); **Lone Oak** (557); **Neylandville** (102); **Quinlan** (1,469); **West Tawakoni** (1,015), tourist center, light industry; catfish tournament, Lakefest; **Wolfe City** (1,538).

Population	**66,258**
(Change fm '90)	3.0
Land Area (sq. mi.)	841.2
Altitude (ft.)	688-1,553
Rainfall (in.)	40.4
Jan. mean min.	30
July mean max.	95
Growing season (days)	237
Civ. Labor	34,575
Unemployed	8.1
Total Wages	$532,266,830
Av. Weekly Wage	$431.90
Prop. Value	$1,817,254,612
Retail Sales	$477,190,764

Hutchinson County

Physical Features: Plains, broken by Canadian River and tributaries, Lake Meredith; fertile valleys along streams.

History: Created 1876 from Bexar Territory; organized 1901; named for pioneer jurist Anderson Hutchinson.

Economy: Oil, gas, petrochemicals; agribusiness; varied manufacturing; tourism.

Ethnicity, 1990: White, 22,661 (88.2%); Black, 677 (2.6%); American Indian, 362 (1.4%); Asian, 105 (0.4%); Other, 1,884 (7.3%). Hispanic, 2,509 (9.8%).

Vital Statistics, 1993: Births, 307; deaths, 283; marriages, 266; divorces, 177.

Recreation: Lake activities; fishing, camping; Adobe Walls, historic Indian battle site; fish fry in June.

Minerals: Gas, oil, sand, gravel.

Agriculture: Corn, wheat, grain sorghums; about 45,000 acres irrigated.

STINNETT (2,304) county seat; petroleum refining; farm center.

Borger (16,111), carbon-black production, oil-field servicing; varied manufacturing; retail center; Frank Phillips College; hospital.

Other cities include: **Fritch** (2,587), **Sanford** (237).

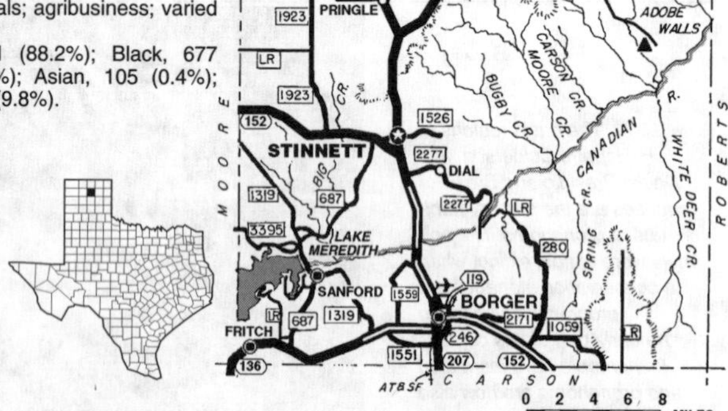

For explanation of sources, abbreviations and symbols, see p. 132.

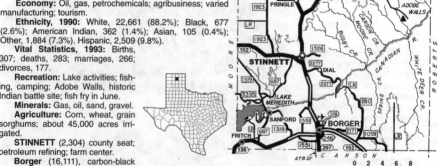

Population	**26,464**
(Change fm '90)	3.0
Land Area (sq. mi.)	887.4
Altitude (ft.)	2,736-3,313
Rainfall (in.)	19.3
Jan. mean min.	24
July mean max.	93
Growing season (days)	187
Civ. Labor	10,565
Unemployed	7.7
Total Wages	$248,295,532
Av. Weekly Wage	$523.60
Prop. Value	$1,549,157,758
Retail Sales	$164,704,947

Irion County

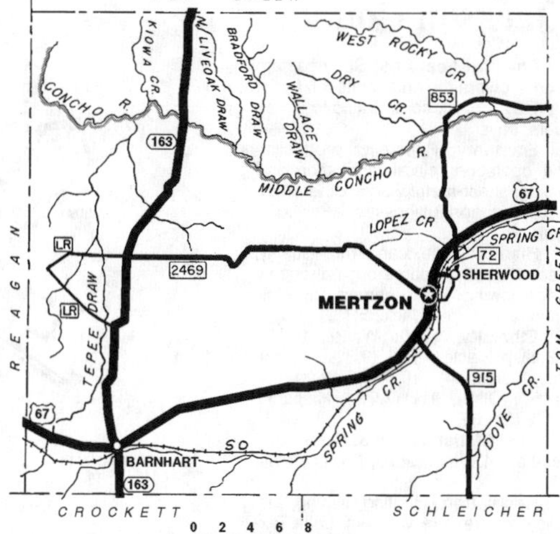

Physical Features: West Texas county with hilly surface, broken by Middle Concho, tributaries; clay, sandy soils.

Economy: Ranching; oil, gas production.

History: Named for Republic leader R.A. Irion; created 1889 from Tom Green County.

Ethnicity, 1990: White, 1,609 (98.8%); Black, 2 (0.1%); American Indian, 1 (0.1%); Asian, 0 (0.0%); Other, 17 (1.0%). Hispanic, 385 (23.6%).

Vital Statistics, 1993: Births 10; deaths, 12; marriages, 14; divorces, 3.

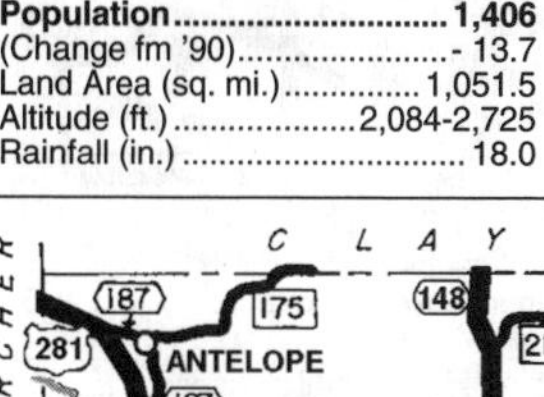

Recreation: Hunting; historic sites, including Dove Creek battlefield and stagecoach stops, old Sherwood courthouse built 1900.

Minerals: Oil, gas.

Agriculture: Angora goats, sheep, cattle; hay, some cotton, milo; some hay irrigated.

MERTZON (631) county seat; farm center; wool warehousing.

Other towns include: **Barnhart**, (135).

Population	**1,406**
(Change fm '90)	- 13.7
Land Area (sq. mi.)	1,051.5
Altitude (ft.)	2,084-2,725
Rainfall (in.)	18.0
Jan. mean min.	30
July mean max.	95
Growing season (days)	232
Civ. Labor	937
Unemployed	3.4
Total Wages	$9,728,336
Av. Weekly Wage	$386.30
Prop. Value	$306,295,920
Retail Sales	$3,161,882

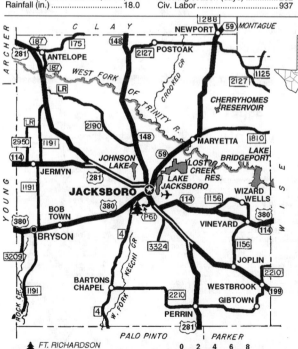

Jack County

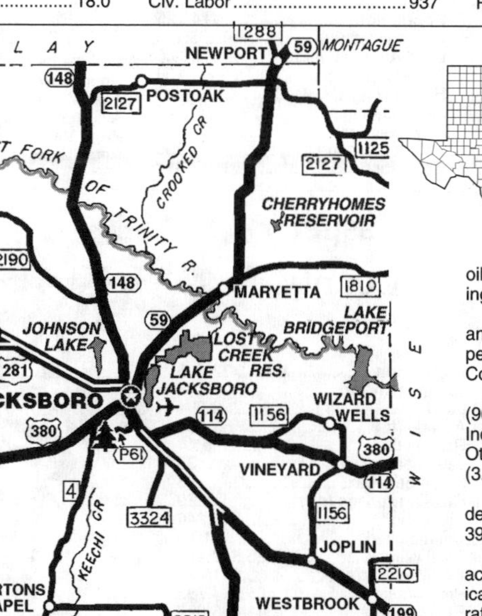

FT. RICHARDSON STATE HISTORICAL PARK

0 2 4 6 8 MILES

Physical Features: Rolling Cross Timbers, broken by West Fork of the Trinity, other streams; sandy, dark brown, loam soils; lakes.

Economy: Petroleum production, oil-field services, livestock, manufacturing, tourism and recreation.

History: Named for brothers, P.C. and W.H. Jack, leaders in Texas' independence effort; created 1856 from Cooke County; organized 1857.

Ethnicity,1990: White, 6,748 (96.7%); Black, 51 (0.7%); American Indian, 18 (0.3%); Asian, 10 (0.1%); Other, 154 (2.2%). Hispanic, 232 (3.3%).

Vital Statistics, 1993: Births, 90; deaths, 88; marriages, 71; divorces, 39.

Recreation: Hunting, fishing; Lake activities; Fort Richardson State Historical Park, museum, other historic sites; rattlesnake hunt.

Minerals: Oil, gas, gravel.

Agriculture: Cow-calf operations provide most income; some horses; hay, wheat, pecans; firewood.

JACKSBORO (3,412) county seat; petroleum production, oil-well servicing; agribusiness; some manufacturing; tourism; hospital; hospice; library; Mesquiteville Festival.

Other towns include: **Bryson** (535), **Perrin** (300).

Population	**7,165**
(Change fm '90)	2.6
Land Area (sq. mi.)	917.4
Altitude (ft.)	976-1,297
Rainfall (in.)	28.0
Jan. mean min.	32
July mean max.	97
Growing season (days)	218
Civ. Labor	3,395
Unemployed	5.0
Total Wages	$33,093,421
Av. Weekly Wage	$394.03
Prop. Value	$589,765,450
Retail Sales	$24,284,741

For explanation of sources, abbreviations and symbols, see p. 132.

Jackson County

Physical Features: Southeastern county of prairie and motts of trees; loam, clay, black soils; drains to creek, rivers, bays.

Economy: Petroleum production and operation; metal fabrication and tooling, sheet-metal works, other manufacturing; agribusinesses; lake recreation.

History: Mexican municipality, created 1835, became original county the following year; named for U.S. President Andrew Jackson.

Ethnicity, 1990: White, 10,857 (83.3%); Black, 1,218 (9.3%); American Indian, 41 (0.3%); Asian, 12 (0.1%); Other, 911 (7.0%). Hispanic, 2,772 (21.3%).

Vital Statistics, 1993: Births, 165; deaths, 147; marriages, 96; divorces, 83.

Recreation: Hunting, fishing; historic sites; Texana Museum; Lake Texana, Brackenridge Plantation campground, state park; county fair, rodeo in October.

Minerals: Oil and natural gas.

Agriculture: Corn, rice, cotton, grain sorghums, soybeans; beef cattle; almost 29,000 acres of rice irrigated.

EDNA (6,190) county seat; oil, gas; tourism; agriculture; varied manufacturing; hospitals.

Other towns include: **Ganado** (1,870), **La Ward** (176), **Vanderbilt** (667) .

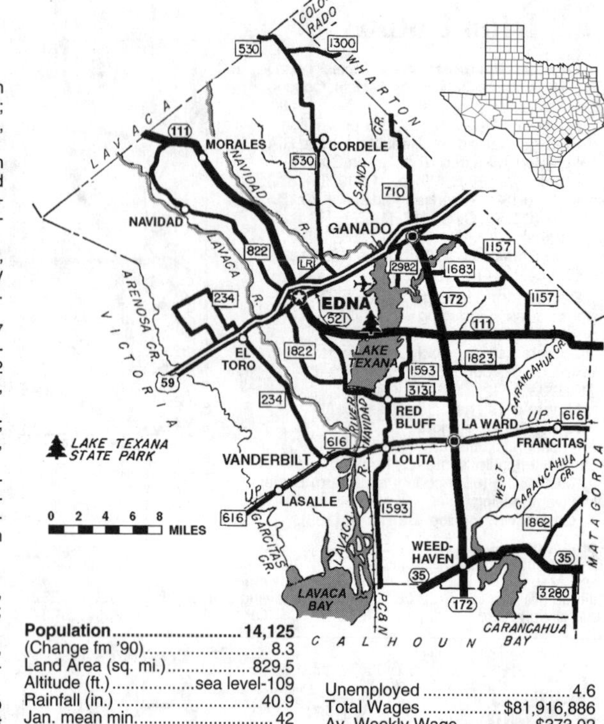

Population	14,125
(Change fm '90)	8.3
Land Area (sq. mi.)	829.5
Altitude (ft.)	sea level-109
Rainfall (in.)	40.9
Jan. mean min.	42
July mean max.	94
Growing season (days)	290
Civ. Labor	7,817
Unemployed	4.6
Total Wages	$81,916,886
Av. Weekly Wage	$373.02
Prop. Value	$775,639,815
Retail Sales	$105,677,142

Jasper County

Physical Features: East Texas county; hilly to level; national forests; lakes; Neches River.

Economy: Timber industries; oil; tourism; fishing; agriculture.

History: Created 1836, organized 1837, from Mexican municipality; named for Sgt. William Jasper of American Revolution.

Ethnicity, 1990: White, 24,750 (79.6%); Black, 5,868 (18.9%); American Indian, 76 (0.2%); Asian, 38 (0.1%); Other, 370 (1.2%). Hispanic, 594 (1.9%).

Vital Statistics, 1993: Births, 472; deaths, 400; marriages, 340; divorces, 199.

Recreation: Lake activities; hunting; state park; azalea trail.

Minerals: Oil, gas produced.

Agriculture: Cattle, hogs, poultry, horses major revenue source; vegetables, fruit, pecans; timber is major income producer.

JASPER (7,586) county seat; wood industries; plywood mill, sawmills; bottled spring water; fall fest.

Other towns include: **Browndell** (213), **Buna** (2,316), **Evadale** (1,611), **Kirbyville** (1,968), **Rayburn Country** (600).

Population	32,556
(Change fm '90)	4.7
Land Area (sq. mi.)	937.4
Altitude (ft.)	68-438
Rainfall (in.)	55.4
Jan. mean min.	38
July mean max.	93
Growing season (days)	229
Civ. Labor	15,246
Unemployed	10.5
Total Wages	$225,532,451
Av. Weekly Wage	$415.21
Prop. Value	$1,465,064,783
Retail Sales	$341,436,027

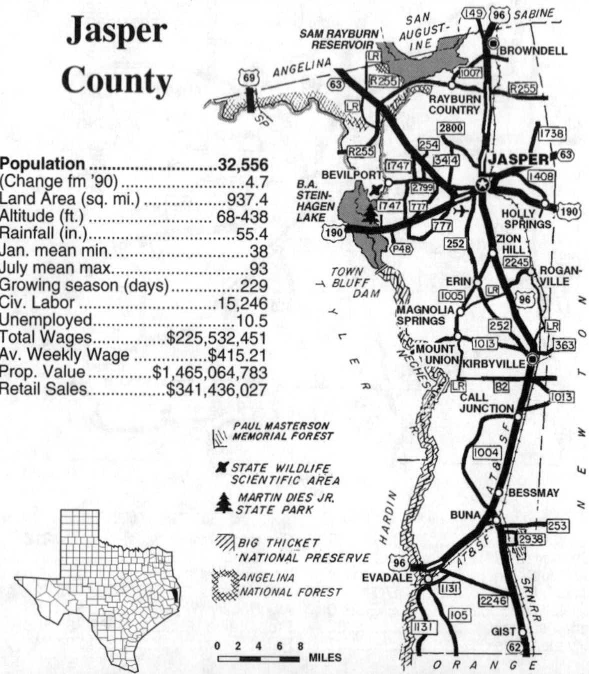

For explanation of sources, abbreviations and symbols, see p. 132.

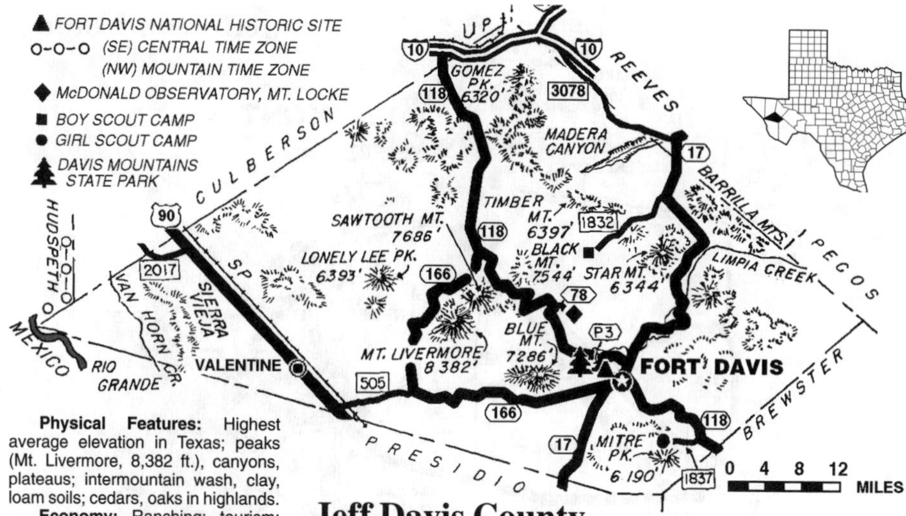

Jeff Davis County

Physical Features: Highest average elevation in Texas; peaks (Mt. Livermore, 8,382 ft.), canyons, plateaus; intermountain wash, clay, loam soils; cedars, oaks in highlands.

Economy: Ranching; tourism; small businesses; government; hunting leases.

History: Named for Jefferson Davis, U.S. war secretary, Confederate president; created 1887 from Presidio County.

Ethnicity, 1990: White, 1,671 (85.9%); Black, 7 (0.4%); American Indian, 12 (0.6%); Asian, 4 (0.2%); Other, 252 (12.9%). Hispanic, 770 (39.6%).

Vital Statistics, 1993: Births, 19; deaths, 14; marriages, 17; divorces, 8.

Recreation: Scenic drives including scenic loop along Limpia Creek, Mt. Livermore, Blue Mountain; hunting; Fort Davis National Historic Site (with Restoration Festival on Labor Day weekend); state park; McDonald Observatory; solar power park.

Minerals: Not significant.

Agriculture: Beef cattle top cash supplier, horses, goats, ratites (ostriches, emus); pecans and apples; greenhouses; hunting leases.

FORT DAVIS (1,212) county seat; ranch center; trade, tourism; government; manufacturing of hats, candles; Harvest Moon fall festival.

Other town, **Valentine** (236).

Population	**1,972**
(Change fm '90)	1.3
Land Area (sq. mi.)	2,264.5
Altitude (ft.)	3,871-8,382
Rainfall (in.)	18.9
Jan. mean min.	32
July mean max.	83
Growing season (days)	226
Civ. Labor	1,039
Unemployed	4.0
Total Wages	$10,006,788
Av. Weekly Wage	$344.11
Prop. Value	$221,581,596
Retail Sales	$13,045,684

Jefferson County

Physical Features: Gulf Coast grassy plain, with timber in northwest; beach sands, sandy loams, black clay soils; drains to Neches River, Gulf of Mexico.

Economy: Petrochemical, other chemical plants; shipbuilding; steel mill; port activity; oil-field supplies.

History: Created 1836 from Mexican municipality; organized 1837; named for U.S. President Thomas Jefferson.

Ethnicity, 1990: White, 154,273 (64.4%); Black, 74,412 (31.1%); American Indian, 578 (0.2%); Asian, 5,145 (2.1%); Other, 4,989 (2.1%). Hispanic,12,629 (5.3%).

Vital Statistics, 1993: Births, 3,828; deaths, 2,427; marriages, 2,698; divorces, 1,487.

Recreation: Beaches, fresh and saltwater fishing; duck, goose hunting; water activities; Dick Dowling Monument and Park; Spindletop site, museums; saltwater lake; wildlife refuges; Lamar University events; historic sites; South Texas Fair.

Minerals: Large producer of oil, gas, sulfur, salt, sand and gravel.

(Map on next page.)

Agriculture: Rice, soybeans; beef cattle; considerable rice irrigated.

BEAUMONT (118,289) county seat; petrochemical production; refining; shipbuilding; port activities; rice milling; Lamar University; hospitals, Main Street on the Neches.

Port Arthur (60,344), oil, chemical activities; shipping; drydock; food processing; tourism.

Other towns include: **Bevil Oaks** (1,474); **China** (1,197); **Fannett** (105); **Groves** (17,177) some manufacturing, hospital, pecan festival; **Hamshire** (350); **Nederland** (17,013) marine manufacturing; tourism, Windmill and French museums; hospital; Tex Ritter memorial and park, heritage festival (city founded by Dutch immigrants in 1898); **Nome** (458); **Port Neches** (13,431) chemical and synthetic rubber industry; varied manufacturing; river-front festival at Christmas.

Population	**249,820**
(Change fm '90)	4.4
Land Area (sq. mi.)	903.5
Altitude (ft.)	sea level-42
Rainfall (in.)	52.8
Jan. mean min.	42
July mean max.	93
Growing season (days)	250
Civ. Labor	119,427
Unemployed	9.2
Total Wages	$2,943,565,760
Av. Weekly Wage	$515.07
Prop. Value	$12,231,200,890
Retail Sales	$2,123,462,038

For explanation of sources, abbreviations and symbols, see p. 132.

Jefferson County

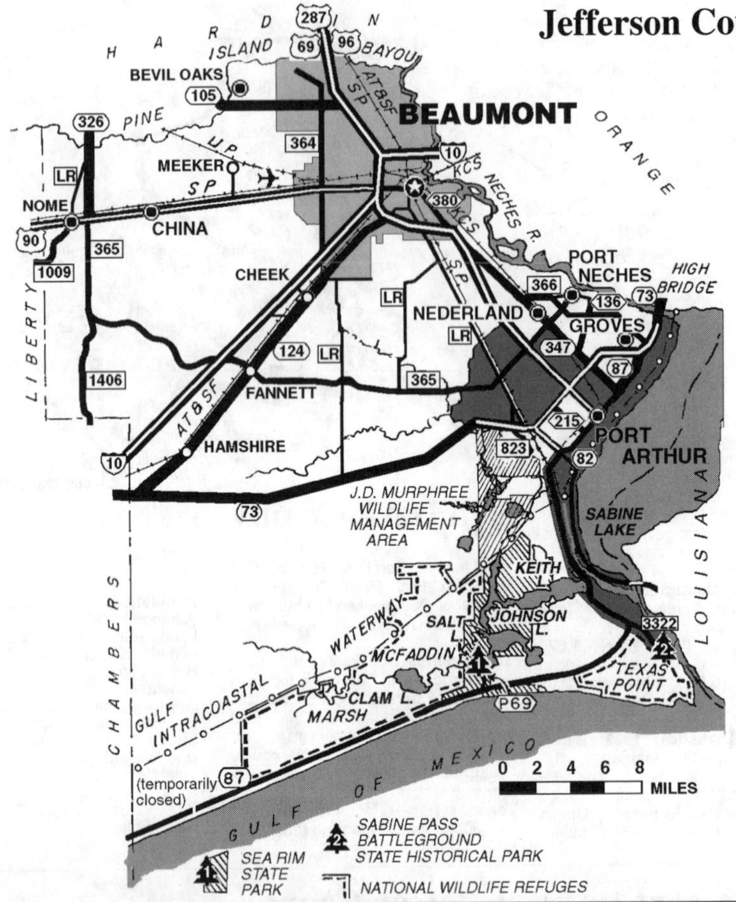

Jim Hogg County

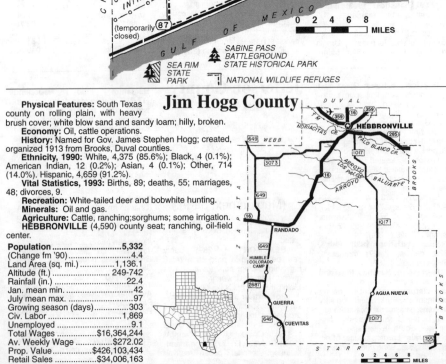

Physical Features: South Texas county on rolling plain, with heavy brush cover; white blow sand and sandy loam; hilly, broken.

Economy: Oil, cattle operations.

History: Named for Gov. James Stephen Hogg; created, organized 1913 from Brooks, Duval counties.

Ethnicity, 1990: White, 4,375 (85.6%); Black, 4 (0.1%); American Indian, 12 (0.2%); Asian, 4 (0.1%); Other, 714 (14.0%). Hispanic, 4,659 (91.2%).

Vital Statistics, 1993: Births, 89; deaths, 55; marriages, 48; divorces, 9.

Recreation: White-tailed deer and bobwhite hunting.

Minerals: Oil and gas.

Agriculture: Cattle, ranching;sorghums; some irrigation.

HEBBRONVILLE (4,590) county seat; ranching, oil-field center.

Population	**5,332**
(Change fm '90)	4.4
Land Area (sq. mi.)	1,136.1
Altitude (ft.)	249-742
Rainfall (in.)	22.4
Jan. mean min.	42
July mean max.	97
Growing season (days)	303
Civ. Labor	1,869
Unemployed	9.1
Total Wages	$16,364,244
Av. Weekly Wage	$272.02
Prop. Value	$426,103,434
Retail Sales	$34,006,163

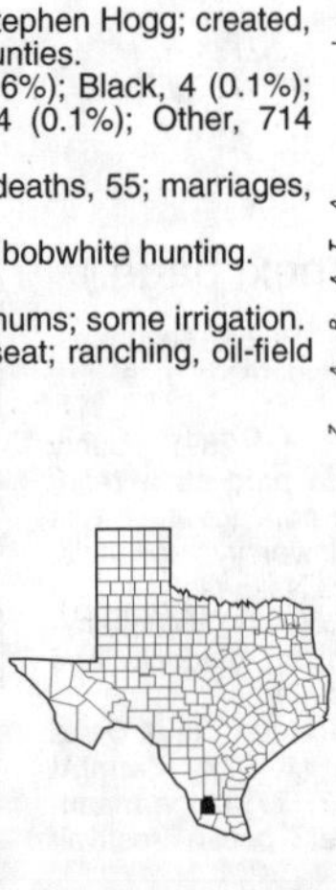

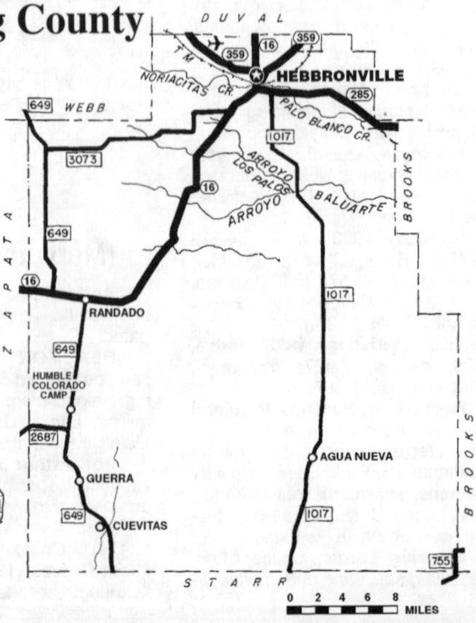

Jim Wells County

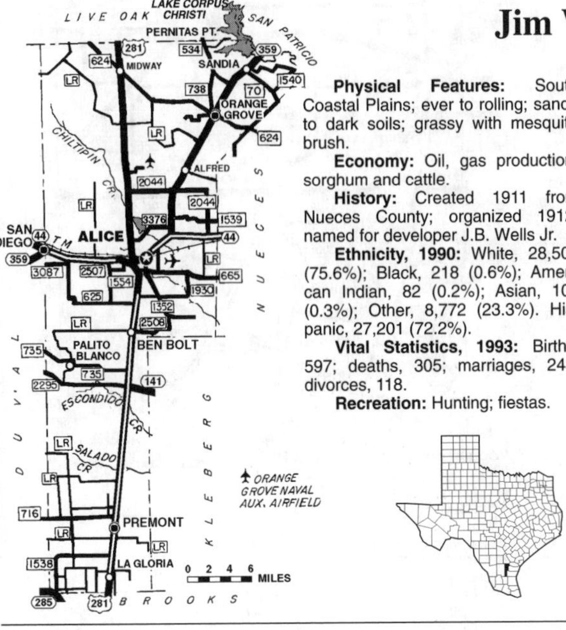

Physical Features: South Coastal Plains; ever to rolling; sandy to dark soils; grassy with mesquite brush.

Economy: Oil, gas production, sorghum and cattle.

History: Created 1911 from Nueces County; organized 1912; named for developer J.B. Wells Jr.

Ethnicity, 1990: White, 28,504 (75.6%); Black, 218 (0.6%); American Indian, 82 (0.2%); Asian, 103 (0.3%); Other, 8,772 (23.3%). Hispanic, 27,201 (72.2%).

Vital Statistics, 1993: Births, 597; deaths, 305; marriages, 243; divorces, 118.

Recreation: Hunting; fiestas.

Minerals: Oil, gas, caliche.

Agriculture: Beef cattle primary income source, dairy cattle, hogs raised; sorghums, cotton, wheat, corn, vegetables; some irrigation for coastal Bermuda, vegetables.

ALICE (19,947) county seat; oilfield service center; agribusinesses; hospital; Fiesta Bandana; Bee County College extension.

Other towns include: **Orange Grove** (1,214), **Premont** (2,792); wildflower tour, youth rodeo; **Sandia** (215). Also part of **San Diego** (4,998).

Population	**38,082**
(Change fm '90)	1.1
Land Area (sq. mi.)	864.6
Altitude (ft.)	62-314
Rainfall (in.)	28.5
Jan. mean min.	43
July mean max.	97
Growing season (days)	289
Civ. Labor	16,151
Unemployed	9.4
Total Wages	$211,334,052
Av. Weekly Wage	$360.24
Prop. Value	$974,402,232
Retail Sales	$254,242,842

Johnson County

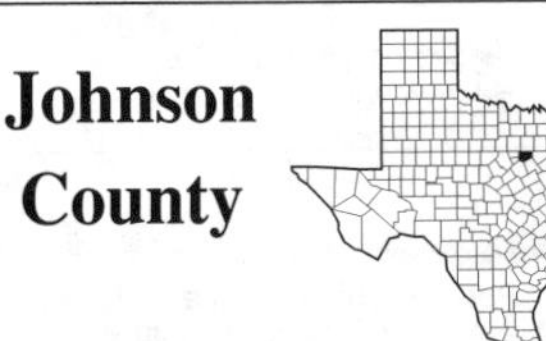

Physical Features: South central county drained by tributaries of Trinity, Brazos rivers; lake; hilly, rolling, many soil types.

Economy: Agribusiness; railroad shops; manufacturing; distribution; lake activities; residents employed in Fort Worth; part of Fort Worth-Arlington metropolitan area.

History: Named for Col. M.T. Johnson of Mexican War, Confederacy; created, organized 1854 out of Ellis, Hill, Navarro counties.

Ethnicity, 1990: White, 90,328 (93.0%); Black, 2,521 (2.6%); American Indian, 419 (0.4%); Asian, 447 (0.5%); Other, 3,450 (3.6%). Hispanic, 7,457 (7.7%).

Vital Statistics, 1993: Births, 1,341; deaths, 843; marriages, 853; divorces, 650.

Recreation: Bird, deer hunting; water activities on Lake Pat Cleburne; state park; museum.

Minerals: Limestone, sand and gravel.

Agriculture: A leading dairy county; 85 percent of annual income from cattle, horses, hogs, and dairy products; crops include hay, silage, sorghum, wheat, corn, cotton; some timber marketed.

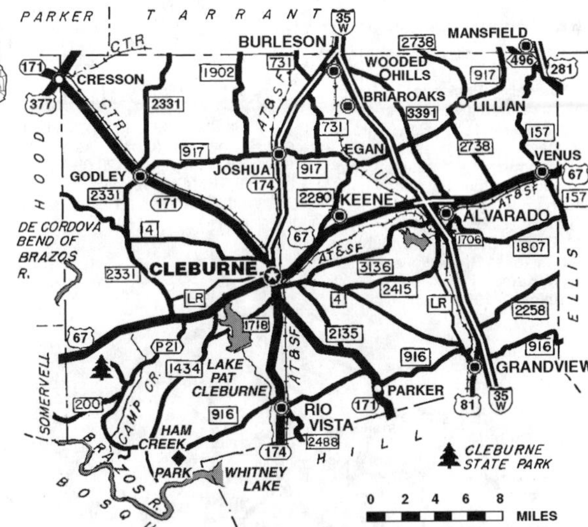

CLEBURNE (22,801) county seat; dairy center; rail-shipping terminal; varied manufacturing; hospital; Layland Museum; Hill College, Cleburne campus.

Burleson (17,457, part in Tarrant County).

Other towns include: **Alvarado** (3,085), County Pioneer Days; **Briaroaks** (577); **Godley** (582); **Grandview** (1,272); **Joshua** (4,008); **Keene** (4,124), Southwestern Adventist College; **Rio Vista** (602), and **Venus** (1,079).

Population	**101,372**
(Change fm '90)	4.3
Land Area (sq. mi.)	729.3
Altitude (ft.)	651-1,065
Rainfall (in.)	32.4
Jan. mean min.	33
July mean max.	98
Growing season (days)	233
Civ. Labor	52,036
Unemployed	5.5
Total Wages	$432,203,368
Av. Weekly Wage	$365.78
Prop. Value	$3,151,008,821
Retail Sales	$578,077,319

Jones County

Physical Features: West Texas Rolling Plains; drained by Brazos River fork, tributaries; Lake Fort Phantom Hill.

Economy: Agribusiness; varied manufacturing.

History: Named for the last president of the Republic, Anson Jones; created 1858 from Bexar, Bosque counties; re-created 1876; organized 1881.

Ethnicity, 1990: White, 13,786 (83.6%); Black, 666 (4.0%); American Indian, 47 (0.3%); Asian, 31 (0.2%); Other, 1,960 (11.9%). Hispanic, 2,786 (16.9%).

Vital Statistics, 1993: Births, 195; deaths, 213; marriages, 110; divorces, 80.

Recreation: Lake activities; Fort Phantom Hill site, museum; Cowboys Christmas Ball; Cowboy Reunion on July 4 weekend; old courthouse, opera house, museum, art show.

Minerals: Oil, gas, sand and gravel, stone.

Agriculture: Cotton, wheat, sesame and peanuts; beef cattle, stockers, calves; some 10,000 acres irrigated for peanuts and hay.

ANSON (2,717) county seat; farming center; boat- trailer factory, Western clothing manufacturing; hospital; historic buildings.

Stamford (3,647) trade center for three counties.

Hamlin (2,687) trade center for farm and oil, gas area; feed mills; historical festival in June.

Other towns include: **Hawley** (631), **Lueders** (375).

Part of **Abilene** extends into the county.

Population	**18,310**
(Change fm '90)	11.0
Land Area (sq. mi.)	931.0
Altitude (ft.)	1,560-1,855
Rainfall (in.)	25.3
Jan. mean min.	31
July mean max.	97
Growing season (days)	223
Civ. Labor	9,039
Unemployed	4.6
Total Wages	$84,972,255
Av. Weekly Wage	$359.88
Prop. Value	$573,496,723
Retail Sales	$119,265,316

Karnes County

Physical Features: Sandy loam, dark clay, alluvial soils in rolling terrain; traversed by San Antonio River; mesquite, oak trees.

Economy: Agribusiness, mineral production, tourism; varied manufacturing.

History: Created 1854 from Bexar, Goliad, San Patricio counties; named for Texas Revolutionary figure Henry W. Karnes.

Ethnicity, 1990: White, 9,548 (76.7%); Black, 362 (2.9%); American Indian, 35 (0.3%); Asian, 14 (0.1%); Other, 2,496 (20.0%). Hispanic, 5,916 (47.5%).

Vital Statistics, 1993: Births, 191; deaths, 150; marriages, 91; divorces, 26.

Recreation: Panna Maria, nation's oldest Polish settlement, founded Dec. 24, 1854; Old Helena restored courthouse, museum; bird hunting; bluebonnet days.

Minerals: Oil, gas, stone; uranium.

Agriculture: Beef cattle, hogs; crops include corn, grain sorghum, wheat, hay, oats.

KARNES CITY (3,035) county seat; agribusiness; tourism; processing center; oil-field servicing; varied manufacturing; hospitals; library.

Kenedy (3,736) farm and oil center.

Other towns include: **Falls City** (520) ranching; sausage making; library; city park on river; **Runge** (1,192) farm center.

Population	**12,604**
(Change fm '90)	1.2
Land Area (sq. mi.)	750.3
Altitude (ft.)	225-525
Rainfall (in.)	33.2
Jan. mean min.	41
July mean max.	97
Growing season (days)	281
Civ. Labor	5,163
Unemployed	5.5
Total Wages	$58,780,824
Av. Weekly Wage	$344.67
Prop. Value	$591,127,510
Retail Sales	$62,284,999

For explanation of sources, abbreviations and symbols, see p. 132.

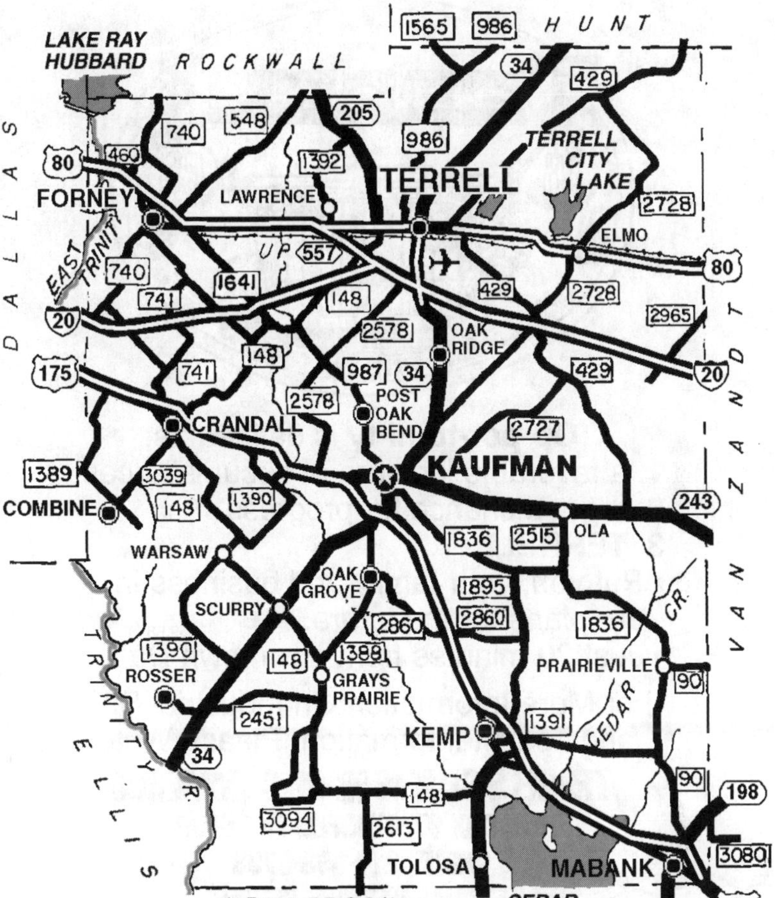

LAKE RAY HUBBARD ROCKWALL HUNT
DALLAS VAN ZANDT
TERRELL CITY LAKE ELMO
FORNEY LAWRENCE TERRELL OAK RIDGE
CRANDALL POST OAK BEND KAUFMAN OLA
COMBINE WARSAW SCURRY OAK GROVE
ROSSER GRAYS PRAIRIE PRAIRIEVILLE KEMP
TOLOSA MABANK
EAST TRINITY R. TRINITY R. CEDAR CR.
ELLIS HENDERSON CEDAR CREEK RES.
0 2 4 6 8 MILES

Kaufman County

Physical Features: North Blackland prairie, draining to Trinity River, Cedar Creek and Lake.

Economy: varied manufacturing; trade center; antique center; part of Dallas metropolitan area.

History: Created from Henderson County and organized, 1848; named for member of Texas and U.S. Congresses D.S. Kaufman.

Ethnicity, 1990: White, 42,810 (82.0%); Black, 7,295 (14.0%); American Indian, 198 (0.4%); Asian, 229 (0.4%); Other, 1,688 (3.2%). Hispanic, 3,340 (6.4%).

Vital Statistics, 1993: Births, 815; deaths, 574; marriages, 445; divorces, 344.

Recreation: Lake activities; Porter Farm near Terrell is site of origin of U.S.-Texas Agricultural Extension program; antique centers near Forney; historic homes at Terrell.

Minerals: Oil, gas, stone.

Agriculture: Beef cattle, horses; hay, wheat, cotton, corn, sorghum; aquaculture; some timber sold.

KAUFMAN (5,917) county seat; varied manufacturing.

Terrell (12,837) agribusiness, varied manufacturing; Terrell State Hospital, Trinity Valley Community College Health-Science Center.

Other towns include: **Crandall** (1,949); **Combine** (1,521, partly in Dallas County); **Forney** (4,355) antiques, light manufacturing, historic homes; **Kemp** (1,287); **Mabank** (1,832, partly in Henderson County) tourism; manufacturing, retail trade; **Oak Grove** (619); **Oak Ridge** (294); **Rosser** (390).

Population	**55,363**
(Change fm '90)	6.0
Land Area (sq. mi.)	786.1
Altitude (ft.)	359-539
Rainfall (in.)	38.2
Jan. mean min.	32
July mean max.	96
Growing season (days)	248
Civ. Labor	27,125
Unemployed	4.9
Total Wages	$293,483,835
Av. Weekly Wage	$382.56
Prop. Value	$2,007,593,362
Retail Sales	$426,219,825

Kendall County

Physical Features: Hill Country, plateau, with springfed streams; caves; scenic drives.

Economy: Agribusiness; some manufacturing.

History: Created from Blanco, Kerr counties 1862; named for pioneer journalist-sheepman and early contributor to Texas Almanac, George W. Kendall.

Ethnicity, 1990: White, 13,682 (93.8%); Black, 58 (0.4%); American Indian, 71 (0.5%); Asian, 38 (0.3%); Other, 740 (5.1%). Hispanic, 2,392 (16.4%).

Vital Statistics, 1993: Births, 270; deaths, 168; marriages, 208; divorces, 84.

Recreation: Hunting, fishing, state park; tourist center; Cascade Caverns; historic sites.

Minerals: Natural gas.

Agriculture: Cattle, sheep, Angora goats raised; some wheat, oats, other grains.

BOERNE (4,697) county seat; livestock center; tourism; antiques; some manufacturing.

Other towns include: **Comfort** (1,593) has state's only Civil War monument honoring Unionists; tourism; **Waring** (76).

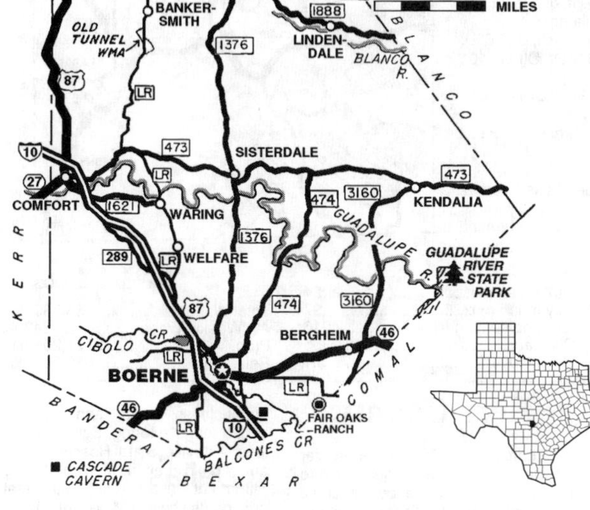

Population	**16,327**
(Change fm '90)	11.9
Land Area (sq. mi.)	662.4
Altitude (ft.)	1,159-2,011
Rainfall (in.)	82.2
Jan. mean min.	35
July mean max.	93
Growing season (days)	236
Civ. Labor	9,755
Unemployed	2.4
Total Wages	$78,443,420
Av. Weekly Wage	$342.78
Prop. Value	$1,302,523,241
Retail Sales	$218,357,704

For explanation of sources, abbreviations and symbols, see p. 132.

Kenedy County

Physical Features: Gulf coastal county; flat, sandy terrain, some loam soils; motts of live oaks.

Economy: Oil, ranching; hunting leases a factor.

History: Among last counties created, organized, 1921, from Cameron, Hidalgo, Willacy counties; named for pioneer steamboat operator and cattleman, Capt. Mifflin Kenedy.

Vital Statistics, 1993: Births, 7; deaths, 7; marriages, 2; divorces, 0.

Ethnicity, 1990: White, 378 (82.2%); Black, 0 (0.0%); American Indian, 0 (0.0%); Asian, 0 (0.0%); Other, 82 (17.8%). Hispanic, 362 (78.7%).

Recreation: Hunting a major enterprise; fishing.

Minerals: Oil, gas.

Agriculture: Cattle, horse production major factors; some watermelons, pasture principal crops.

SARITA (185) county seat; cattle-shipping point; ranch headquarters; gas processing; one of state's least populous counties.

Population	**409**
(Change fm '90)	- 11.1
Land Area (sq. mi.)	1,456,8
Altitude (ft.)	sea level-79
Rainfall (in.)	29.7
Jan. mean min.	45
July mean max.	95
Growing season (days)	31 9
Civ. Labor	233
Unemployed	1.6
Total Wages	$5,169,856
Av. Weekly Wage	$393.07
Prop. Value	$428,951,590
Retail Sales	$512,383

Kent County

Physical Features: West central county of rolling, broken terrain; drains to Salt and Double Mountain forks of Brazos River; sandy, loam soils.

Economy: Agribusinesses, oil-field operations.

History: Created 1876, from Bexar, Young territories; organized 1892. Name honors Andrew Kent, one of 32 volunteers from Gonzales who died at the Alamo.

Ethnicity, 1990: White, 902 (89.3%); Black, 6 (0.6%); American Indian, 1 (0.1%); Asian, 0 (0.0%); Other, 101 (10.0%). Hispanic, 120 (11.9%).

Vital Statistics, 1993: Births, 4; deaths, 12; marriages, 6; divorces, 3.

Recreation: Hunting; scenic croton breaks and salt flat.

Minerals: Oil, gas, sand, gravel.

Agriculture: Cow-calf, stocker operations; cotton, wheat, sorghum.

JAYTON (553) county seat; oil-field services; farming center; fun fest in August.

Other towns include: **Girard** (125).

Population	**924**
(Change fm '90)	- 8.5
Land Area (sq. mi.)	902.3
Altitude (ft.)	1,823-2,830
Rainfall (in.)	20.6
Jan. mean min.	24
July mean max.	97
Growing season (days)	216
Civ. Labor	366
Unemployed	5.1
Total Wages	$3,730,269
Av. Weekly Wage	$343.44
Prop. Value	$777,205,810
Retail Sales	$15,394,008

Kerr County

Physical Features: Picturesque, hills, spring-fed streams; dams, lakes on Guadalupe River.

Economy: Tourism; medical services; retirement area; agribusiness; manufacturing; hunting leases.

History: Created 1856 from Bexar County; named for member of Austin's Colony, James Kerr.

Ethnicity, 1990: White, 32,842 (90.5%); Black, 805 (2.2%); American Indian, 128 (0.4%); Asian, 141 (0.4%); Other, 2,388 (6.6%). Hispanic, 5,994 (16.5%).

Vital Statistics, 1993: Births, 437; deaths, 518; marriages, 366; divorces, 233.

Recreation: Popular area for tourists, hunters, fishermen; private and youth camps; dude ranches; state park; Point theater; camera safari park; wildlife management area; hatchery; Folk Music Festival in Kerrville; experimental aircraft fly-in; Cowboy Artists Museum.

Minerals: Limited sand, gravel.

Agriculture: Cattle, sheep and goats for wool, mohair; crops include apples, hay, pecans; Spanish goats on increase; cedar posts sold.

KERRVILLE (19,134) county seat; tourist center; youth camps; agribusiness; aircraft and parts and varied manufacturing; Schreiner College; Kerrville State Hospital; Veterans Administration Medical Center; retirement center; retail trade; state arts, crafts show in May-June; experimental aircraft fly-in during October.

Other towns include: ; **Hunt** (707) youth camps; **Ingram** (1,493) camps, cabins.

Population	**38,973**
(Change fm '90)	7.4
Land Area (sq. mi.)	1,106.2
Altitude (ft.)	1,524-2,303
Rainfall (in.)	29.8
Jan. mean min.	32
July mean max.	94
Growing season (days)	216
Civ. Labor	16,814
Unemployed	3.9
Total Wages	$214,006,225
Av. Weekly Wage	$341.19
Prop. Value	$1,607,469,259
Retail Sales	$331,916,031

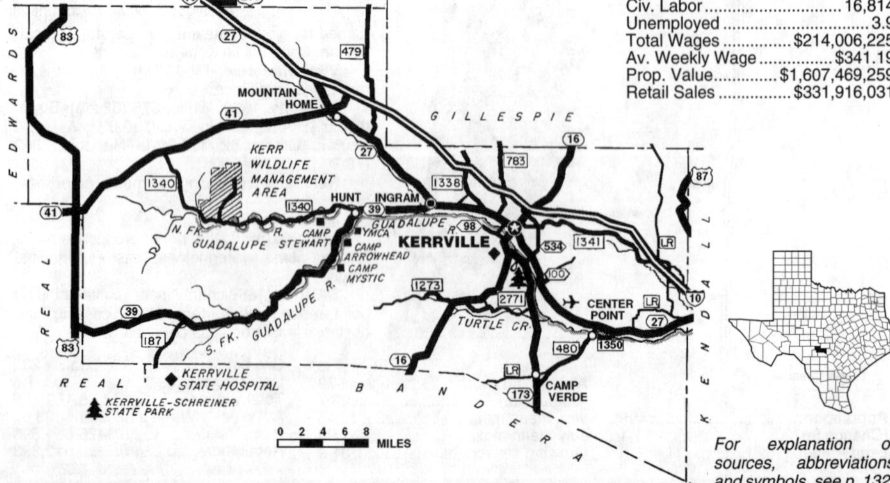

For explanation of sources, abbreviations and symbols, see p. 132.

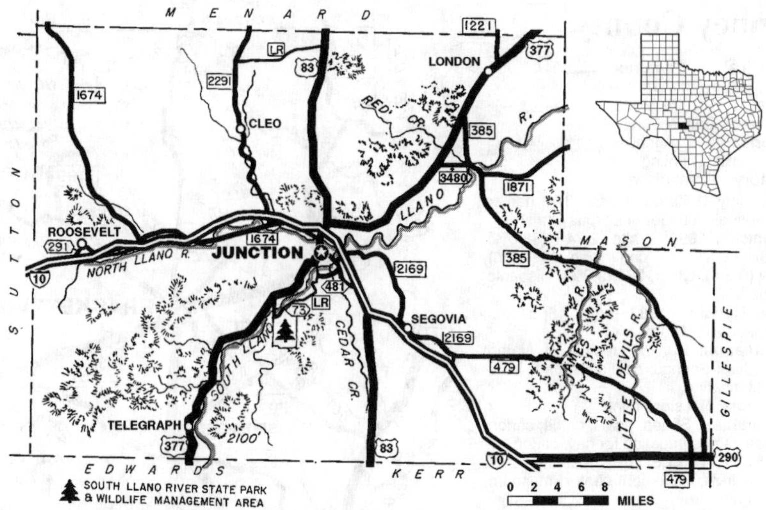

Kimble County

Physical Features: Picturesque southwestern county of broken, rolling plain; drains to Llano River; sandy, gray, chocolate loam soils.

Economy: Livestock production, large goat market, wool, mohair; tourism, hunting, fishing; cedar oil and wood products sold; metal building materials manufactured.

History: Created from Bexar County 1858; organized 1876; named for George C. Kimble, a Gonzales volunteer who died at the Alamo.

Ethnicity,1990: White, 3,654 (88.6%); Black, 2 (0.0%); American Indian, 5 (0.1%); Asian, 10 (0.2%); Other, 451 (10.9%). Hispanic, 772 (18.7%).

Vital Statistics, 1993: Births, 59; deaths, 52; marriages, 40; divorces, 27.

Recreation: Hunting, fishing in spring-fed streams; among leading deer counties; state park; Kimble Kounty Kow Kick on Labor Day.

Minerals: Limited sand, gravel.

Agriculture: Cattle, sheep, Angora and Spanish goats are primary products; pecans raised; some irrigation for forage sorghum, coastal Bermuda; firewood marketed.

JUNCTION (2,771) county seat; goat auction; cedar oil, wood products; two museums; Texas Tech University center; hospital; library; gun and knife show.

Other towns include: **London** (180).

Population	**4,356**
(Change fm '90)	5.7
Land Area (sq. mi.)	1,250.7
Altitude (ft.)	1,783-2,372
Rainfall (in.)	22.5
Jan. mean min.	32
July mean max.	97
Growing season (days)	213
Civ. Labor	2,343
Unemployed	3.9
Total Wages	$21,891,239
Av. Weekly Wage	$298.21
Prop. Value	$441,442,820
Retail Sales	$42,161,433

King County

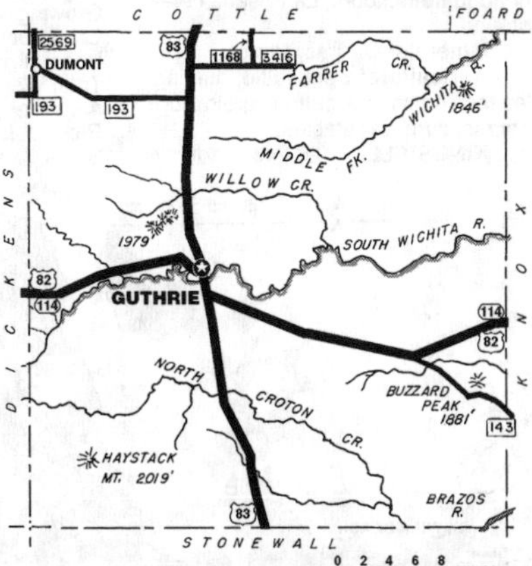

Physical Features: Hilly, broken by Wichita, Brazos tributaries; extensive grassland; dark loam to red soils.

Economy: Minerals, ranching.

History: Created 1876 from Bexar District; organized 1891; named for William P. King, a volunteer from Gonzales who died at the Alamo.

Ethnicity, 1990: White, 317 (89.5%); Black, 0 (0.0%); American Indian, 0 (0.0%); Asian, 0 (0.0%); Other, 37 (10.5%). Hispanic, 53 (15.0%).

Vital Statistics, 1993: Births, 6; deaths, 3; marriages, 3; divorces, 0.

Recreation: Four Sixes, other large ranches, cover most of county.

Minerals: Oil, gas.

Agriculture: Cow-calf, stocker cattle operations, horses; cotton, wheat, sorghum, hay.

GUTHRIE (160) county seat; ranch-supply center; community center complex; museum, library.

Other town: **Dumont** (85).

Population	**390**
(Change fm '90)	10.2
Land Area (sq. mi.)	912.3
Altitude (ft.)	1,739-2,081
Rainfall (in.)	22.5
Jan. mean min.	32
July mean max.	97
Growing season (days)	219
Civ. Labor	173
Unemployed	3.0
Total Wages	$4,646,665
Av. Weekly Wage	$485.39
Prop. Value	$346,494,489
Retail Sales	$850,736

For explanation of sources, abbreviations and symbols, see p. 132.

Kinney County

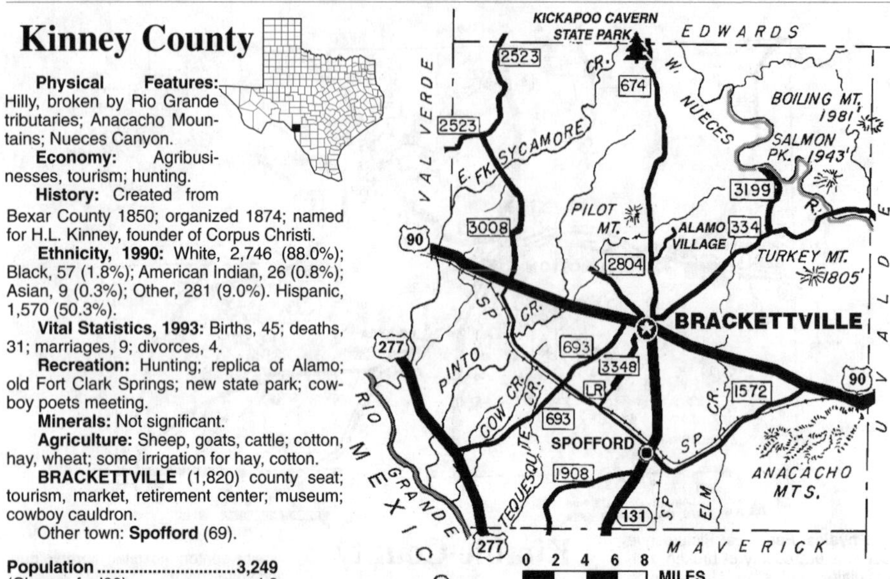

Physical Features: Hilly, broken by Rio Grande tributaries; Anacacho Mountains; Nueces Canyon.

Economy: Agribusinesses, tourism; hunting.

History: Created from Bexar County 1850; organized 1874; named for H.L. Kinney, founder of Corpus Christi.

Ethnicity, 1990: White, 2,746 (88.0%); Black, 57 (1.8%); American Indian, 26 (0.8%); Asian, 9 (0.3%); Other, 281 (9.0%). Hispanic, 1,570 (50.3%).

Vital Statistics, 1993: Births, 45; deaths, 31; marriages, 9; divorces, 4.

Recreation: Hunting; replica of Alamo; old Fort Clark Springs; new state park; cowboy poets meeting.

Minerals: Not significant.

Agriculture: Sheep, goats, cattle; cotton, hay, wheat; some irrigation for hay, cotton.

BRACKETTVILLE (1,820) county seat; tourism, market, retirement center; museum; cowboy cauldron.

Other town: **Spofford** (69).

Population	**3,249**
(Change fm '90)	4.2
Land Area (sq. mi.)	1,363.5
Altitude (ft.)	909-1,981
Rainfall (in.)	21.1
Jan. mean min.	36
July mean max.	96
Growing season (days)	270
Civ. Labor	1,147
Unemployed	7.6
Total Wages	$7,576,535
Av. Weekly Wage	$274.77
Prop. Value	$280,652,026
Retail Sales	$6,488,075

Kleberg County

Physical Features: Coastal plain, broken by bays; sandy, loam, clay soils; tree motts.

Economy: Naval air station; ranch operation; chemicals and plastics; Mexican food products; cotton; Texas A&M University-Kingsville.

History: Created 1913 from Nueces County; named for San Jacinto veteran and rancher, Robert Kleberg.

Ethnicity, 1990: White, 20,650 (68.2%); Black, 998 (3.3%); American Indian, 81 (0.3%); Asian, 414 (1.4%); Other, 8,131 (26.9%). Hispanic, 18,529 (61.2%).

Vital Statistics, 1993: Births, 548; deaths, 186; marriages, 306; divorces, 172.

Recreation: Fishing, water sports, park on Baffin Bay; wildlife sanctuary; winter bird watching; university events, museum; King Ranch headquarters, tours; La Posada celebration.

Minerals: Oil, gas, stone.

Agriculture: Beef cattle; hunting leases; crops are cotton, grain sorghums, corn; vegetables.

KINGSVILLE (26,246) county seat; oil, gas center; agribusiness; tourism; chemical and plastic plant; university, Bee College branch; hospital. Other towns include: **Riviera** (550).

Population	**31,173**
(Change fm '90)	3.0
Land Area (sq. mi.)	871.0
Altitude (ft.)	sea level-151
Rainfall (in.)	27.5
Jan. mean min.	46
July mean max.	95
Growing season (days)	314
Civ. Labor	13,723
Unemployed	7.3
Total Wages	$180,968,387
Av. Weekly Wage	$353.45
Prop. Value	$1,187,797,693
Retail Sales	$179,354,696

KINGSVILLE NAVAL AIR STATION
KING RANCH HQ.
GULF INTRACOASTAL WATERWAY
NATIONAL SEASHORE
0 2 4 6 8 MILES

Knox County

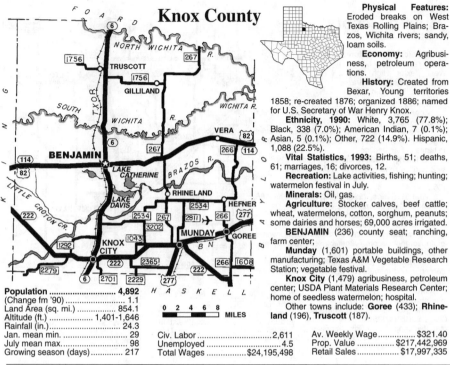

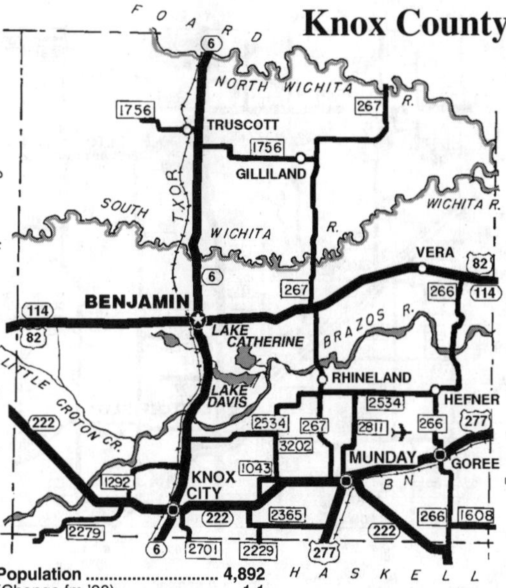

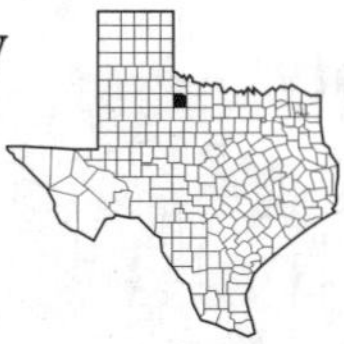

Physical Features: Eroded breaks on West Texas Rolling Plains; Brazos, Wichita rivers; sandy, loam soils.

Economy: Agribusiness, petroleum operations.

History: Created from Bexar, Young territories 1858; re-created 1876; organized 1886; named for U.S. Secretary of War Henry Knox.

Ethnicity, 1990: White, 3,765 (77.8%); Black, 338 (7.0%); American Indian, 7 (0.1%); Asian, 5 (0.1%); Other, 722 (14.9%). Hispanic, 1,088 (22.5%).

Vital Statistics, 1993: Births, 51; deaths, 61; marriages, 16; divorces, 12.

Recreation: Lake activities, fishing; hunting; watermelon festival in July.

Minerals: Oil, gas.

Agriculture: Stocker calves, beef cattle; wheat, watermelons, cotton, sorghum, peanuts; some dairies and horses; 69,000 acres irrigated.

BENJAMIN (236) county seat; ranching, farm center;

Munday (1,601) portable buildings, other manufacturing; Texas A&M Vegetable Research Station; vegetable festival.

Knox City (1,479) agribusiness, petroleum center; USDA Plant Materials Research Center; home of seedless watermelon; hospital.

Other towns include: **Goree** (433); **Rhineland** (196), **Truscott** (187).

Population	**4,892**
(Change fm '90)	1.1
Land Area (sq. mi.)	854.1
Altitude (ft.)	1,401-1,646
Rainfall (in.)	24.3
Jan. mean min.	29
July mean max.	98
Growing season (days)	217
Civ. Labor	2,611
Unemployed	4.5
Total Wages	$24,195,498
Av. Weekly Wage	$321.40
Prop. Value	$217,442,969
Retail Sales	$17,997,335

Lamar County

Physical Features: North Texas county on divide between Red, Sulphur rivers; soils chiefly blackland, except along Red; pines, hardwoods.

Economy: Varied manufacturing; agribusinesses; tourism.

History: Created 1840 from Red River County; organized 1841; named for second president of Republic, Mirabeau B. Lamar.

Ethnicity, 1990: White, 36,814 (83.8%); Black, 6,397 (14.6%); American Indian, 406 (0.9%); Asian, 153 (0.3%); Other, 179 (0.4%). Hispanic, 475 (1.1%).

Vital Statistics, 1993: Births, 618; deaths, 540; marriages, 594; divorces, 345.

Recreation: Lake activities; Gambill goose refuge; hunting, fishing; state park; Sam Bell Maxey Home; State Sen. A.M. Aikin Archives; other museums; fiddlers contest.

Minerals: Negligible.

Agriculture: Beef, dairy cattle, horses; hay, soybeans, wheat, sorghum, corn, cotton; some peanuts irrigated; firewood marketed.

PARIS (25,063) county seat; varied manufacturing; food processing; medical center; junior college.

Other towns include: **Blossom** (1,564), **Deport** (796, partly in Red River County); **Reno** (2,069), **Roxton** (675), **Sun Valley** (66), **Toco** (130).

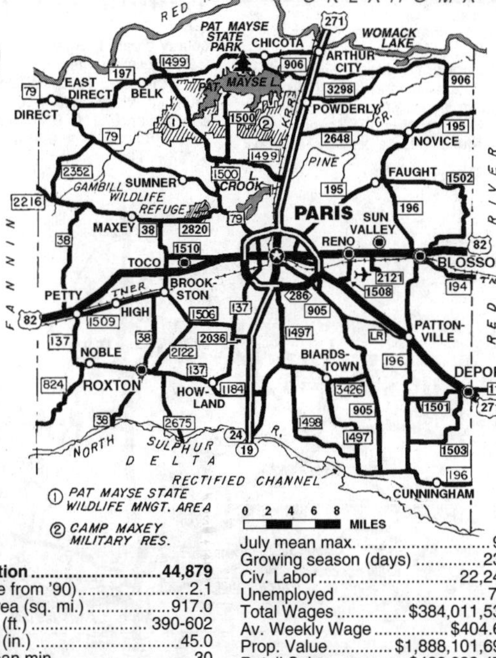

Population	**44,879**
(Change from '90)	2.1
Land Area (sq. mi.)	917.0
Altitude (ft.)	390-602
Rainfall (in.)	45.0
Jan. mean min.	30
July mean max.	94
Growing season (days)	235
Civ. Labor	22,246
Unemployed	7.9
Total Wages	$384,011,530
Av. Weekly Wage	$404.62
Prop. Value	$1,888,101,692
Retail Sales	$432,099,471

For explanation of sources, abbrevations and symbols, see p. 132.

Lamb County

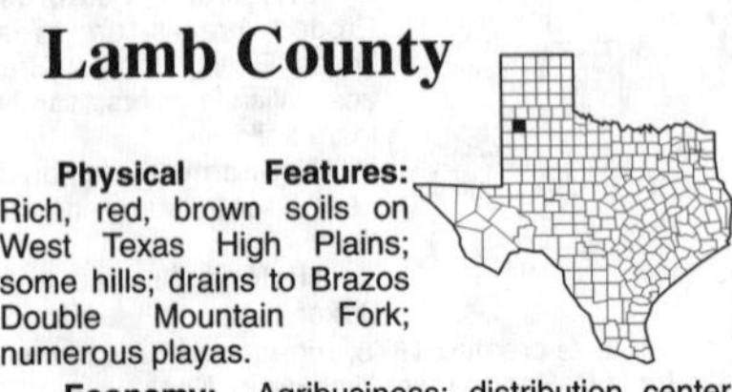

Physical Features: Rich, red, brown soils on West Texas High Plains; some hills; drains to Brazos Double Mountain Fork; numerous playas.

Economy: Agribusiness; distribution center; denim textiles.

History: Created 1876 from Bexar District; organized 1908; named for Lt. G.A. Lamb, who died in battle of San Jacinto.

Ethnicity, 1990: White, 13,036 (86.5%); Black, 822 (5.5%); American Indian, 88 (0.6%); Asian, 25 (0.2%); Other, 1,101 (7.3%). Hispanic, 5,509 (36.6%).

Vital Statistics, 1993: Births, 242; deaths, 185; marriages, 100; divorces, 72.

Recreation: Pioneer celebration in June.

Minerals: Oil, stone, gas.

Agriculture: Fed cattle, sheep; cotton, wheat, grain sorghum, corn, vegetables, soybeans, hay; 385,000 acres irrigated.

LITTLEFIELD (6,518) county seat; agribusiness center; varied manufacturing; hospital; Waylon Jennings celebration on Labor Day.

Olton (2,149) commercial center in northwest part of county.

Other towns include: **Amherst** (754); **Earth** (1,325) farming center; manufacturing; feed lot; supplies; **Springlake** (143); **Sudan** (1,041) farming center, Pioneer Day in June.

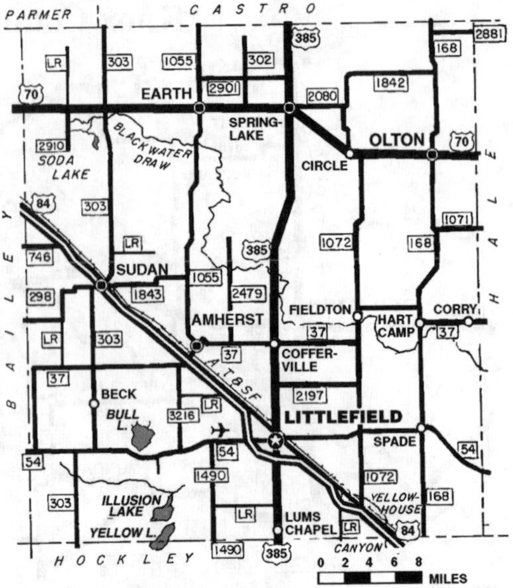

Population	**15,322**
(Change fm '90)	1.7
Land Area (sq. mi.)	1,016.2
Altitude (ft.)	3,486-3,849
Rainfall (in.)	18.6
Jan. mean min.	23
July mean max.	92
Growing season (days)	194
Civ. Labor	6,726
Unemployed	6.4
Total Wages	$79,109,115
Av. Weekly Wage	$363.28
Prop. Value	$1,126,285,687
Retail Sales	$73,288,294

Lampasas County

Physical Features: Central Texas on edge of Hill Country; Colorado, Lampasas rivers; cedars, oaks, pecans.

Economy: Many employed at Fort Hood; several industrial plants; tourism; agribusinesses.

History: Name is Spanish for lilies found beside nearby streams; county created, organized 1856 from Bell, Travis counties.

Ethnicity, 1990: White, 12,164 (90.0%); Black, 268 (2.0%); American Indian, 79 (0.6%); Asian, 136 (1.0%); Other, 874 (6.5%). Hispanic, 1,753 (13.0%).

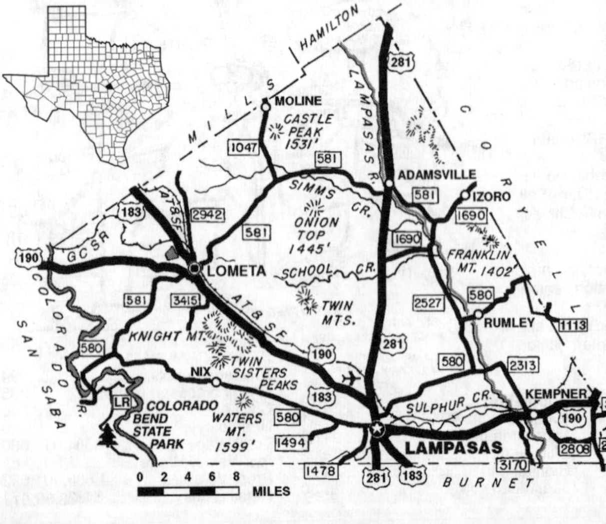

Vital Statistics, 1993: Births, 229; deaths, 162; marriages, 150; divorces, 101.

Recreation: Scenic drives; state park; hunting, fishing in streams.

Minerals: Sand and gravel, building stone.

Agriculture: Beef cattle, Angora goats; hay, wheat, sorghum, oats, pecans.

LAMPASAS (6,617) county seat; ranching, hunting center; varied manufacturing; historic downtown; hospital; Spring Ho in July.

Other towns include: **Adamsville** (28); **Kempner** (420); **Lometa** (681) market and shipping point.

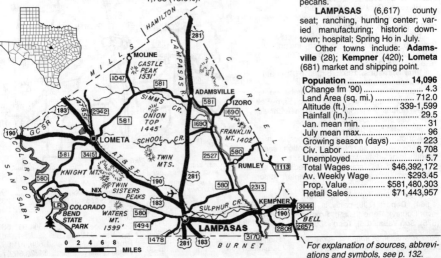

Population	**14,096**
(Change fm '90)	4.3
Land Area (sq. mi.)	712.0
Altitude (ft.)	339-1,599
Rainfall (in.)	29.5
Jan. mean min.	31
July mean max.	96
Growing season (days)	223
Civ. Labor	6,708
Unemployed	5.7
Total Wages	$46,392,172
Av. Weekly Wage	$293.45
Prop. Value	$581,480,303
Retail Sales	$71,443,957

For explanation of sources, abbreviations and symbols, see p. 132.

La Salle County

Physical Features: Southwestern county on brushy plain, broken by Nueces, Frio rivers and their tributaries; chocolate, dark gray, sandy loam soils.

Economy: Agribusiness, hunting leases; tourism.

History: Created from Bexar County 1858; organized 1880; named for Robert Cavalier Sieur de la Salle, French explorer who died in Texas.

Ethnicity, 1990: White, 3,567 (67.9%); Black, 53 (1.0%); American Indian, 9 (0.2%); Asian, 10 (0.2%); Other, 1,615 (30.7%). Hispanic, 4,068 (77.4%).

Vital Statistics, 1993: Births, 83; deaths, 36; marriages, 35; divorces, 3.

Recreation: Nature trails; Cotulla school where Lyndon B. Johnson taught; wildlife management area; deer, bird, javelina hunting; wild hog cookoff in March; fishing.

Minerals: Oil, gas.

Agriculture: Feedlot, stocker and cow-calf operations; crops include peanuts, corn, watermelons, grain sorghum, vegetables; some irrigation.

COTULLA (4,405) county seat; livestock, state prison; hunting center; Brush Country museum. **Encinal** (639).

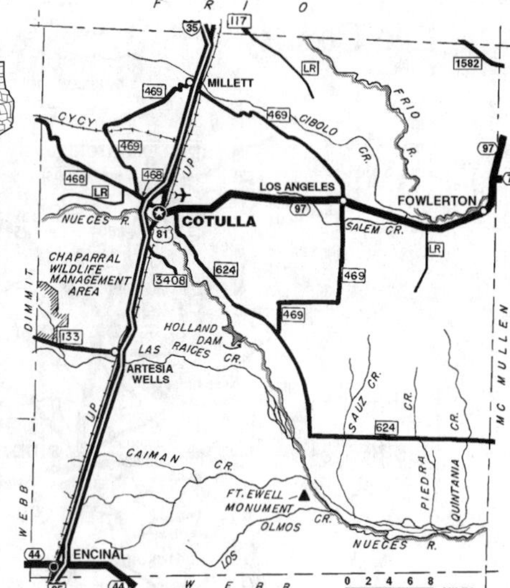

Population............................ **6,028**
(Change fm '90) 14.7
Land Area (sq. mi.).................. 1,488.9
Altitude (ft.)........................... 326-588
Rainfall (in.) 21.6
Jan. mean min.................................. 42
July mean max. 99
Growing season (days) 288
Civ. Labor.................................... 2,653
Unemployed 8.5
Total Wages $17,079,534
Av. Weekly Wage $300.89
Prop. Value.................... $388,841,428
Retail Sales $17,748,867

Lavaca County

Physical Features: Southern Coastal Plains county; north rolling; sandy loam, black waxy soils; drains to Lavaca, Navidad rivers.

Economy: Varied manufacturing; leather goods center; agribusinesses; oil and gas production

History: Name is Spanish word for cow, la vaca, from name of river; created 1846 from Colorado, Jackson, Gonzales, Victoria counties.

Ethnicity, 1990: White, 16,541 (88.5%); Black, 1,342 (7.2%); American Indian, 20 (0.1%); Asian, 14 (0.1%); Other, 773 (4.1%). Hispanic, 1,596 (8.5%);

Vital Statistics, 1993: Births, 227; deaths, 268; marriages, 120; divorces, 76.

Recreation: Deer, other hunting, fishing; wildflower trails, fiddlers frolic; historic sites, churches.

Minerals: Some oil, gas.

Agriculture: Livestock, especially beef cattle, are revenue sources; eggs and poultry; crops include hay, rice, corn, sorghum.

HALLETTSVILLE (1,744) county seat; retail center; varied manufacturing, museum; hospital; domino, "42" tournaments;

Yoakum (6,006, partly in DeWitt County); trading center for two counties; hospital; Land of Leather celebration in February.

Shiner (2,201), brewery, other industry; museum; clinic.

Other towns include: **Moulton** (969) agribusiness; clinic.

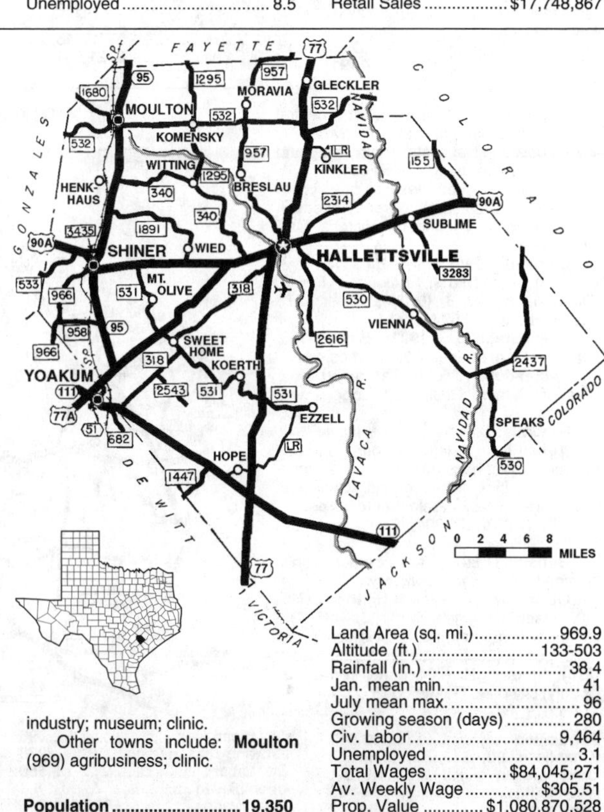

Population........................ **19,350**
(Change fm '90)............................ 3.5
Land Area (sq. mi.)................... 969.9
Altitude (ft.).......................... 133-503
Rainfall (in.) 38.4
Jan. mean min................................ 41
July mean max. 96
Growing season (days) 280
Civ. Labor..................................... 9,464
Unemployed 3.1
Total Wages $84,045,271
Av. Weekly Wage $305.51
Prop. Value $1,080,870,528
Retail Sales $126,892,121

For explanation of sources, abbreviations and symbols, see p. 132.

Lee County

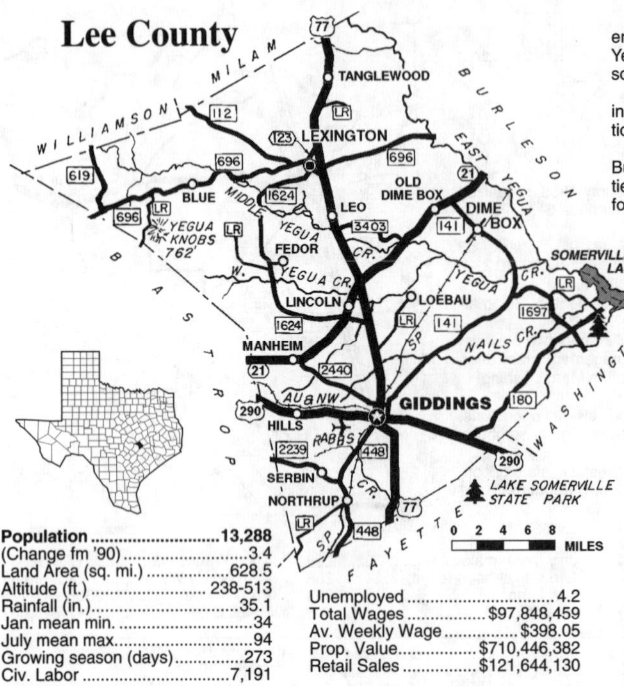

Population **13,288**
(Change fm '90) 3.4
Land Area (sq. mi.) 628.5
Altitude (ft.) 238-513
Rainfall (in.) 35.1
Jan. mean min. 34
July mean max. 94
Growing season (days) 273
Civ. Labor 7,191
Unemployed 4.2
Total Wages $97,848,459
Av. Weekly Wage $398.05
Prop. Value $710,446,382
Retail Sales $121,644,130

Physical Features: Southeastern county; rolling terrain, broken by Yegua and its tributaries; red to black soils, sandy to heavy loams.

Economy: Varied manufacturing; agribusiness; oil and gas operations.

History: Created from Bastrop, Burleson, Fayette, Washington counties and organized in 1874; named for Confederate Gen. Robert E. Lee.

Ethnicity, 1990: White, 10,057 (78.2%); Black, 1,780 (13.8%); American Indian, 14 (0.1%); Asian, 15 (0.1%); Other, 988 (7.7%). Hispanic, 1,410 (11.0%).

Vital Statistics, 1993: Births, 171; deaths, 131; marriages, 103; divorces, 59.

Recreation: Fishing, hunting; state park; pioneer village, Wendish museum and structures; Giddings Geburtstag celebration; historic sites.

Minerals: Oil, gas, lignite.

Agriculture: Beef cattle; meat and milk goats; peanuts and hay are principal crops.

GIDDINGS (4,223) county seat; varied manufacturing, food processing; recycling plant; hospital.

Other towns include: **Dime Box** (313); **Lexington** (991), livestock-marketing center; **Serbin** (90), Wendish museum.

Leon County

Physical Features: East central county; hilly, rolling, almost half covered by timber; drains to Navasota, Trinity rivers and tributaries; sandy, dark, alluvial soils.

Economy: Agribusiness, oil production.

History: Created 1846 from Robertson County; named for founder of Victoria, Martin de Leon.

Ethnicity, 1990: White, 10,730 (84.7%); Black, 1,615 (12.8%); American Indian, 39(0.3%); Asian, 8 (0.1%); Other, 273 (2.2%). Hispanic, 509 (4.0%).

Vital Statistics, 1993: Births, 163; deaths, 177; marriages, 83; divorces, 68.

Recreation: Hilltop Lakes resort area; sites of Camino Real, Fort Boggy; deer hunting.

Minerals: Oil, gas, iron ore, lignite.

Agriculture: A leading county in cow-calf production; hogs raised; hay, watermelons, vegetables, small grains; Christmas trees; forest products sold for cross-ties.

CENTERVILLE (904) county seat; farm center; hunting; tourism; oil, gas; timber.

Buffalo (1,802), farm center; clinic; stampede in September; library.

Other towns include: **Hilltop Lakes** (300) resort, retirement center; **Jewett** (739) electricity-generating plant; civic center, fall frolic; **Leona** (205) candle factory; **Marquez** (278); **Normangee** (704, partly in Madison County) city park; **Oakwood** (577).

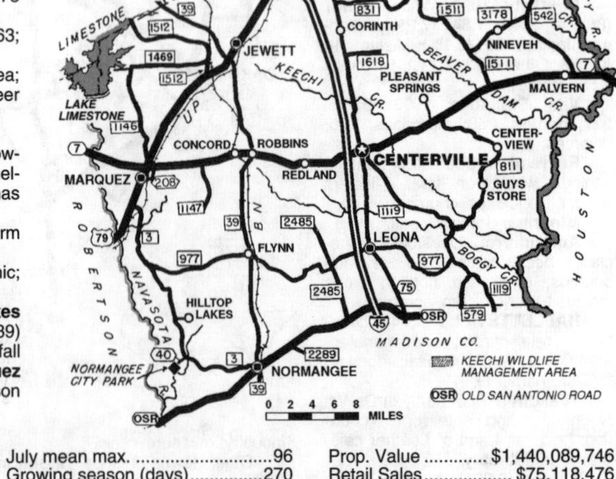

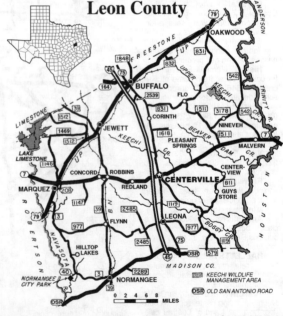

Population **13,342**
(Change fm '90) 5.3
Land Area (sq. mi.) 1,072.1
Altitude (ft.) 190-496
Rainfall (in.) 39.3
Jan. mean min. 35
July mean max. 96
Growing season (days) 270
Civ. Labor 5,550
Unemployed 8.1
Total Wages $88,541,695
Av. Weekly Wage $510.61
Prop. Value $1,440,089,746
Retail Sales $75,118,476

For explanation of sources, abbreviations and symbols, see p. 132.

Liberty County

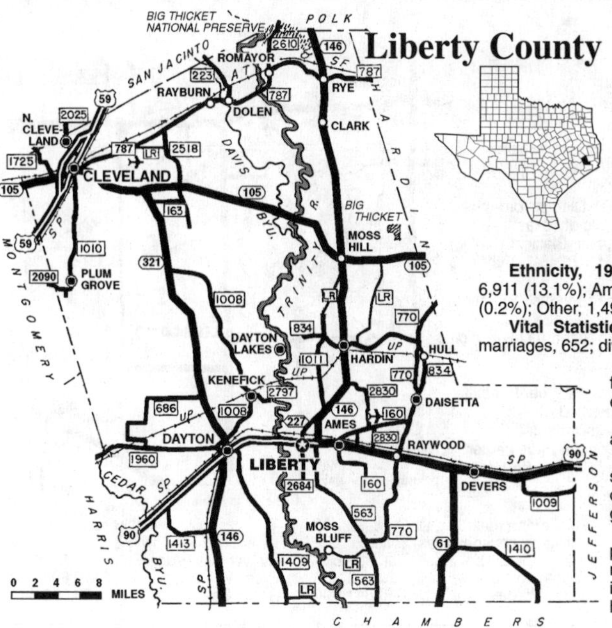

Physical Features: Coastal Plain county east of Houston; 60 percent in pine, hardwood timber; bisected by Trinity River; sandy, loam, black soils; Big Thicket.

Economy: Agribusiness; chemical plants; varied manufacturing; tourism; forest industries; many residents work in Houston; part of Houston metropolitan area.

History: Named for Spanish municipality, Libertad; created 1836, organized 1837.

Ethnicity, 1990: White, 44,014 (83.5%); Black, 6,911 (13.1%); American Indian, 181 (0.3%); Asian, 124 (0.2%); Other, 1,496 (2.8%). Hispanic, 2,880 (5.5%).

Vital Statistics, 1993: Births, 908; deaths, 585; marriages, 652; divorces, 287.

Recreation: Big Thicket; hunting, fishing; historic sites; Trinity Valley exposition; Liberty Opry.

Minerals: Oil, gas, sulphur, sand and gravel.

Agriculture: Rice top crop with soybeans second; sorghums, corn; cow-calf operations; 35,000 acres irrigated for rice; some lumbering.

LIBERTY (8,587) county seat; petroleum-related industry; agribusiness; library; museum; regional historical resource depository; Liberty Bell; hospital; state prisons.

Cleveland (7,455) forest products processed, shipped; tourism; library; museum; hospital.

Dayton (5,411) rice, oil center.

Other towns include: **Ames** (1,102); **Daisetta** (1,011); **Devers** (350); **Hardin** (586); **Hull** (1,800); **Kenefick** (460); **Plum Grove** (537).

Population	**57,351**
(Change fm '90)	8.8
Land Area (sq. mi.)	1,159.8
Altitude (ft.)	23-261
Rainfall (in.)	50.7
Jan. mean min.	40
July mean max.	94
Growing season (days)	261
Civ. Labor	24,883
Unemployed	9.3
Total Wages	$280,391,054
Av. Weekly Wage	$367.42
Prop. Value	$2,029,561,989
Retail Sales	$402,430,716

Limestone County

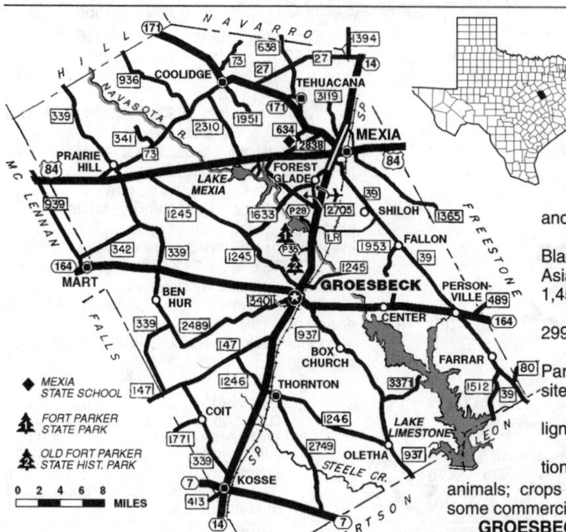

Physical Features: East central county on divide between Brazos and Trinity rivers; borders Blacklands, level to rolling; drained by Navasota and tributaries.

Economy: Varied manufacturing; agribusiness; tourism; mineral operations.

History: Created from Robertson County and organized 1846; named for indigenous rock.

Ethnicity, 1990: White, 15,695 (74.9%); Black, 4,156 (19.8%); American Indian, 41(0.2%); Asian, 50 (0.2%); Other, 1,004 (4.8%). Hispanic, 1,459 (7.0%).

Vital Statistics, 1993: Births, 273; deaths, 299; marriages, 174; divorces, 124.

Recreation: Fishing, lake activities; Fort Parker; Confederate Reunion Grounds; historic sites; museum; hunting; Christmas at the Fort.

Minerals: Oil, gas, sand and gravel, stone, lignite.

Agriculture: Cow-calf, stocker cattle operations; dairies, horses, goats, sheep, some exotic animals; crops include hay, corn, cotton, wheat, peaches; some commercial nursery.

GROESBECK (3,500) county seat; agribusiness; tourism; hunting; mining; prison; power generating; hospital.

Mexia (7,056), agribusiness; grocery distribution; state school; hospital.

Other towns include: **Coolidge** (759); **Kosse** (542); **Tehuacana** (335); **Thornton** (585).

Population	**21,560**
(Change fm '90)	2.9
Land Area (sq. mi.)	908.8
Altitude (ft.)	375-665
Rainfall (in.)	38.3
Jan. mean min.	34
July mean max.	95
Growing season (days)	255
Civ. Labor	9,528
Unemployed	5.7
Total Wages	$132,684,984
Av. Weekly Wage	$374.70
Prop. Value	$1,718,097,025
Retail Sales	$131,824,574

For explanation of sources, abbreviations and symbols, see p. 132.

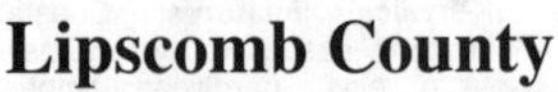

Lipscomb County

Physical Features: High Plain, broken in east; drains to tributaries of Canadian, Wolf Creek; sandy loam, black soils.

Economy: Agribusinesses; oil, gas operations.

History: Created 1876 from Bexar District; organized 1887; named for A.S. Lipscomb, Republic of Texas leader.

Ethnicity, 1990: White, 3,092 (98.4%); Black, 1 (0.0%); American Indian, 34 (1.1%); Asian, 13 (0.4%); Other, 3 (0.1%). Hispanic, 379 (12.1%).

Vital Statistics, 1993: Births, 41; deaths, 29; marriages, 28; divorces, 5.

Recreation: Will Rogers Day; Darrouzett festival; Wolf Creek museum.

Minerals: Oil, natural gas.

Agriculture: Stocker, beef cattle, fed beef; alfalfa, wheat, sorghum, corn; 17,000 acres irrigated.

LIPSCOMB (45) county seat; livestock center.

Booker (1,241, part in Ochiltree County) trade center.

Other towns include: **Darrouzett** (357) **Follett** (453); **Higgins** (484).

Population **3,222**
(Change fm '90) 2.5
Land Area (sq. mi.) 932.1
Altitude (ft.) 2,506-2,834
Rainfall (in.) 21.3
Jan. mean min. 20
July mean max. 93
Growing season (days) 202
Civ. Labor 1,557
Unemployed 2.4
Total Wages $15,841,806
Av. Weekly Wage $374.31
Prop. Value $419,600,730
Retail Sales $9,698,442

Live Oak County

Physical Features: Brushy plains between San Antonio and Corpus Christi, partly broken by Nueces and tributaries; black waxy, gray sandy, other soils.

Economy: Oil, agribusinesses.

History: Named for predominant tree; created, organized 1856 from Nueces, San Patricio counties.

Ethnicity, 1990: White, 8,316 (87.0%); Black, 10 (0.1%); American Indian, 36 (0.4%); Asian, 31 (0.3%); Other, 1,163 (12.2%). Hispanic, 3,324 (34.8%).

Vital Statistics, 1993: Births, 114; deaths, 83; marriages, 64; divorces, 51.

Recreation: Lakes; water activities; state parks; hunting; historic sites.

Minerals: Oil, gas, sand, gravel.

Agriculture: Cow-calf operations; swine produced; corn, grain sorghums, cotton; some irrigation for hay, coastal Bermuda pastures.

GEORGE WEST (2,663) county seat; agribusiness, petroleum refineries.

Three Rivers (1,993) agribusinesses, refineries.

Other towns include: **Oakville** (260); **Whitsett** (360).

Population **9,894**
(Change fm '90) 3.5
Land Area (sq. mi.) 1,036.3
Altitude (ft.) 96-479
Rainfall (in.) 27.6
Jan. mean min. 41
July mean max. 95
Growing season (days) 289
Civ. Labor 5,276
Unemployed 5.2
Total Wages $41,003,640
Av. Weekly Wage $397.44
Prop. Value $880,018,720
Retail Sales $71,332,111

For explanation of sources, abbreviations and symbols, see p. 132.

Llano County

Physical Features: Central county drains to Colorado, Llano rivers; rolling to hilly; Highland lakes.

Economy: Tourism, retirement; ranch trading center; vineyards; granite mined.

History: Name is Spanish for plains; created, organized 1856 from Bexar District, Gillespie County.

Ethnicity, 1990: White, 11,386 (97.9%); Black, 22 (0.2%); American Indian, 39 (0.3%); Asian, 20 (0.2%); Other, 164 (1.4%). Hispanic, 453 (3.9%);

Vital Statistics, 1993: Births, 99; deaths, 224; marriages, 86; divorces, 56.

Recreation: Leading deer-hunting county; fishing; lake activities; major tourist area; Enchanted Rock; bluebonnet festival; hang gliding; fiddle fest in April.

Minerals: Granite, vermiculite, llanite.

Agriculture: Beef cattle; also some swine and sheep raised; hay; peanuts and oats.

LLANO (3,012) county seat; historic district; tourism; hunting center; livestock trading; some manufacturing; hospital; museum.

Kingland (2,835), tourism, retirement community, fishing and water sports; metal fabrication; wood work; library.

Other towns include: **Buchanan Dam** (1,119); **Horseshoe Bay** (1,616, partly in Burnet County); **Sunrise Beach** (523).

Population	**11,998**
(Change fm '90)	3.2
Land Area (sq. mi.)	934.8
Altitude (ft.)	1,038-1,867
Rainfall (in.)	26.6
Jan. mean min.	32
July mean max.	97
Growing season (days)	229
Civ. Labor	4,855
Unemployed	3.8
Total Wages	$54,336,421
Av. Weekly Wage	$341.82
Prop. Value	$1,266,404,949
Retail Sales	$76,571,944

Loving County

Physical Features: Western county of rolling prairies; drains to Pecos River; Red Bluff Reservoir; sandy, loam, clay soils.

Economy: Petroleum operations; some cattle.

History: Last county organized; created 1887 from Tom Green; organized 1931; named for Oliver Loving, trail driver. Loving is Texas' least populous county.

Ethnicity, 1990: White, 93 (86.9%); Black, 0 (0.0%); American Indian, 0 (0.0%); Asian, 0 (0.0%); Other, 14 (13.1%). Hispanic, 14 (13.1%).

Vital Statistics, 1991: Births, 0; deaths, 4; marriages, 1; divorces, 1.

Recreation: N.A.

Minerals: Oil, gas.

Agriculture: Some cattle.

MENTONE (50) county seat; oilfield supply center; only town.

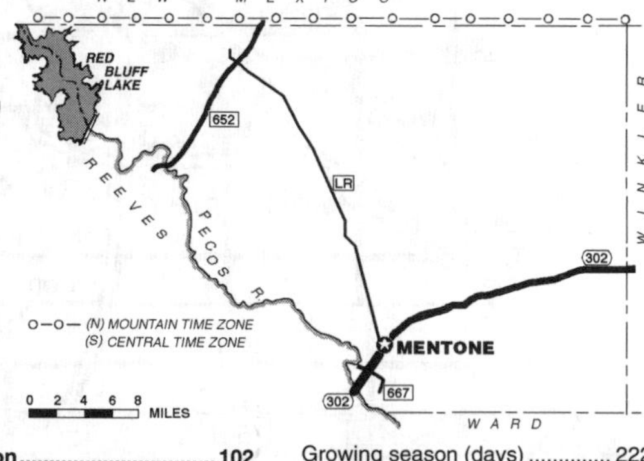

Population	**102**
(Change fm '90)	- 4.7
Land Area (sq. mi.)	673.1
Altitude (ft.)	2,685-3,311
Rainfall (in.)	9.1
Jan. mean min.	28
July mean max.	96
Growing season (days)	222
Civ. Labor	75
Unemployed	9.4
Total Wages	$297.755
Av. Weekly Wage	$365.02
Prop. Value	$165,042,970
Retail Sales	$106,524

Lubbock County

Physical Features: High Plains of West Texas, broken by 1,500 playas, Yellow House River; rich soils with underground water.

Economy: Among world's largest cottonseed processing centers; a leading agribusiness center; cattle feedlots; manufacturing; higher education center; medical center.

History: Named for Col. Tom S. Lubbock, an organizer of Confederate Terry's Rangers; county created 1876 from Bexar District; organized 1891.

Ethnicity, 1990: White, 176,037 (79.1%); Black, 17,154 (7.7%); American Indian, 686 (0.3%); Asian, 2,722 (1.2%); Other, 26,037 (11.7%). Hispanic,51,011 (22.9%).

Vital Statistics, 1993: Births, 3,780; deaths, 1,706; marriages, 2,199; divorces, 1,417.

Recreation: Lubbock Lake State Historical Park and archaeological site; Texas Tech events; civic center, Buddy Holly statue and Walk of Fame, planetarium; Ranching Heritage Center; Panhandle-South Plains Fair; Buffalo Springs Lake.

Minerals: Oil, gas, stone, sand and gravel.

Agriculture: Fed beef, cow-calf operations; also, swine, sheep, poultry; eggs marketed; cotton major crop, others are grain sorghums, wheat, sunflowers, soybeans, hay, vegetables; more than 230,000 acres irrigated, mostly cotton.

Education: Texas Tech University with law and medical schools; Lubbock Christian University, South Plains College; Wayland Baptist University off-campus center.

LUBBOCK (193,194) county seat; center for large agricultural area; manufacturing includes electronics, earth-moving equipment, food containers, fire-protection equipment, clothing, other products; distribution center for South Plains; feedlots; psychiatric hospital; museum; Reese Air Force Base; hospitals, state school for retarded.

Other towns include: **Idalou** (2,126); **New Deal** (580); **Ransom Canyon** (841); **Shallowater** (1,880); **Slaton** (6,223); **Wolfforth** (2,171).

Population	**230,901**
(Change fm '90)	3.7
Land Area (sq. mi.)	899.5
Altitude (ft.)	3,015-3,402
Rainfall (in.)	17.8
Jan. mean min.	24
July mean max.	92
Growing season (days)	208
Civ. Labor	117,927
Unemployed	4.5
Total Wages	$2,087,405,962
Av. Weekly Wage	$403.52
Prop. Value	$6,205,487,310
Retail Sales	$2,577,512,542

For explanation of sources, abbreviations and symbols, see p. 132.

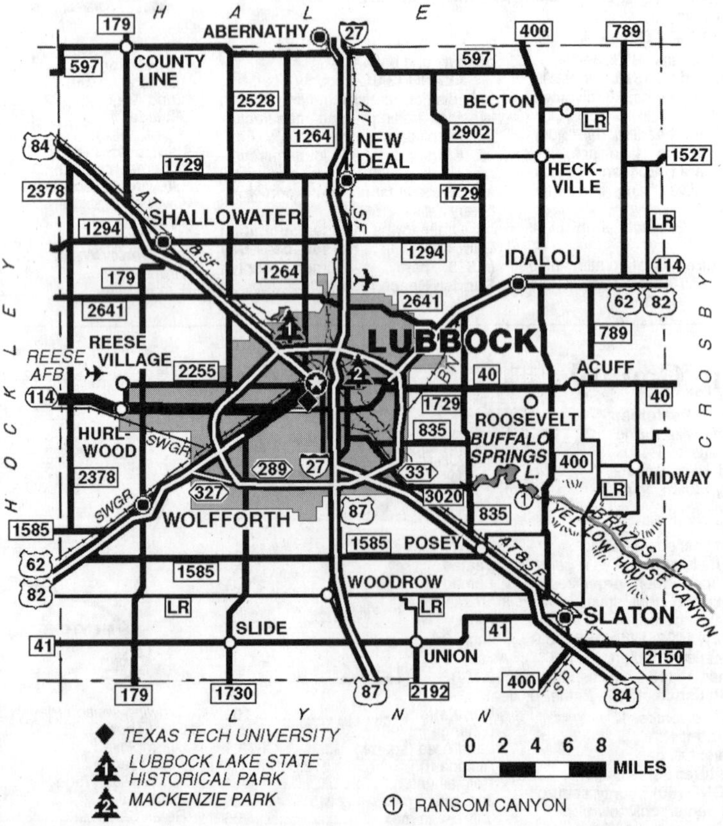

◆ *TEXAS TECH UNIVERSITY*

1 *LUBBOCK LAKE STATE HISTORICAL PARK*

2 *MACKENZIE PARK*

0 2 4 6 8 MILES

① RANSOM CANYON

Lynn County

Physical Features: South High Plains, broken by Caprock Escarpment, playas, draws; sandy loam, black, gray soils.

Economy: Agribusiness.

History: Created 1876 from Bexar District; organized 1903; named for Alamo victim, W. Lynn.

Ethnicity,1990: White, 5,214 (77.2%); Black, 223 (3.3%); American Indian, 22 (0.3%); Asian, 11 (0.2%); Other, 1,288 (19.1%). Hispanic, 2,819 (41.7%).

Vital Statistics, 1993: Births, 101; deaths, 78; marriages, 51; divorces, 18.

Recreation: Pioneer museum in Tahoka; Dan Blocker museum in O'Donnell.

Minerals: Oil, natural gas, stone.

Agriculture: Cotton, grain sorghums, wheat, produce largest income; cattle, sheep, hogs raised; 60,000 acres of cotton irrigated.

TAHOKA (2,792) county seat; agribusiness center; cotton compress; some manufacturing; hospital.

O'Donnell (1,143, partly in Dawson County), commercial center.

Other towns include: **New Home** (186); **Wilson** (598).

Population	**6,7801**
(Change fm '90)	- 0.8
Land Area (sq. mi.)	891.9
Altitude (ft.)	2,881-3,274
Rainfall (in.)	18.3
Jan. mean min.	24
July mean max.	92
Growing season (days)	217
Civ. Labor	2,998
Unemployed	4.9
Total Wages	$27,670,065
Av. Weekly Wage	$366.15
Prop. Value	$348,112,192
Retail Sales	$22,679,612

Madison County

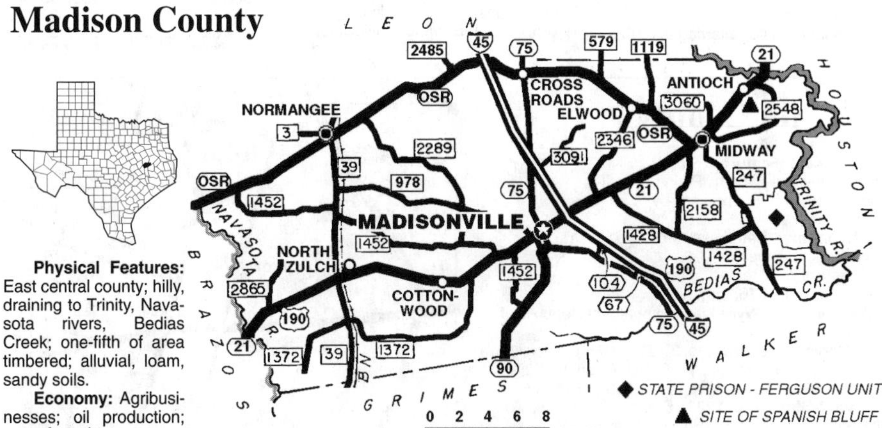

Physical Features: East central county; hilly, draining to Trinity, Navasota rivers, Bedias Creek; one-fifth of area timbered; alluvial, loam, sandy soils.

Economy: Agribusinesses; oil production; manufacturing.

History: Named for U.S. President James Madison; created from Grimes, Leon, Walker counties 1853; organized 1854.

Ethnicity, 1990: White, 7,984 (73.0%); Black, 2,575 (23.6%); American Indian, 67 (0.6%); Asian, 13 (0.1%); Other, 292 (2.7%). Hispanic, 1,178 (10.8%).

Vital Statistics, 1993: Births, 149; deaths, 124; marriages, 83; divorces, 59.

For sources, abbreviations and symbols, see p. 132.

Recreation: Fishing, hunting; Spanish Bluff where survivors of Battle of Medina were executed; other historic sites.

Minerals: Oil, gas, gravel.

Agriculture: Cattle, horses, swine raised; forage for livestock.

MADISONVILLE (3,926) county seat; farm-trade center; varied manufacturing; hospital, library.

Other towns, **Midway** (304); **Normangee** (704, mostly in Leon County).

Population	**11,887**
(Change fm '90)	8.7
Land Area (sq. mi.)	469.6
Altitude (ft.)	213-364
Rainfall (in.)	41.1
Jan. mean min.	39
July mean max.	96
Growing season (days)	272
Civ. Labor	4,247
Unemployed	4.4
Total Wages	$61,567,518
Av. Weekly Wage	$353.16
Prop. Value	$553,086,686
Retail Sales	$60,740,456

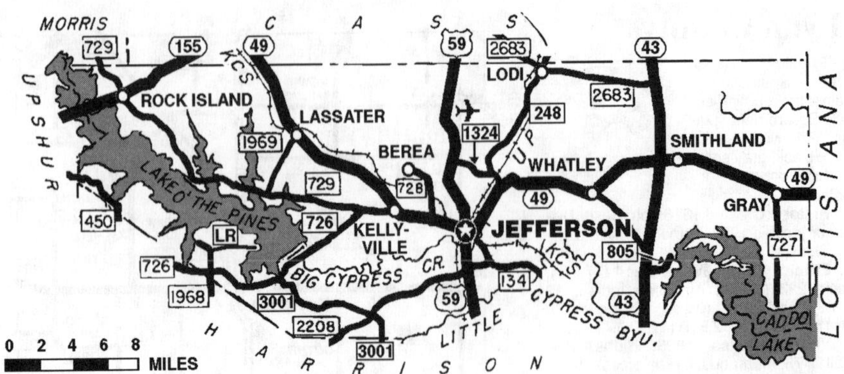

Marion County

Physical Features: Northeastern county; hilly, three-quarters forested with pines, hardwoods; drains to Caddo Lake, Lake O' the Pines, Cypress Bayou.

Economy: Tourism; timber; food processing.

History: Created 1860 from Cass County; named for Gen. Francis Marion of American Revolution.

Ethnicity, 1990: White, 6,792 (68.0%); Black, 3,100 (31.0%); American Indian, 44 (0.4%); Asian, 7 (0.1%); Other, 41 (0.4%). Hispanic, 147 (1.5%).

Vital Statistics, 1993: Births, 119; deaths, 142; marriages, 102; divorces, 72.

Recreation: Lake activities; hunting; Excelsior Hotel; 84 medallions on historic sites including Jay Gould railroad car; museum; Mardi Gras; historical pilgrimage in May, founder's day in October.

Minerals: Oil, gas, clays, lignite, gravel.

Agriculture: Beef cattle, horses, hogs, emus, ostriches also raised; coastal Bermuda major crop, hay; also truck crops grown, landscape horticulture plants, peaches, vegetables, blueberries; some forest products produced.

JEFFERSON (2,378) county seat; tourism; livestock; timber; minerals; museums, library; historical sites.

Population	**10,299**
(Change fm '90)	3.2
Land Area (sq. mi.)	381.2
Altitude (ft.)	168-379
Rainfall (in.)	44.7
Jan. mean min.	32
July mean max.	94
Growing season (days)	236
Civ. Labor	3,985
Unemployed	10.6
Total Wages	$35,148,141
Av. Weekly Wage	$337.86
Prop. Value	$389,599,552
Retail Sales	$35,883,689

Martin County

Physical Features: Western county on South Plains; sandy, loam soils, broken by playas, creeks.

Economy: Petroleum production, agribusiness.

History: Created from Bexar District 1876; organized 1884; named for Wylie Martin, senator of Republic of Texas.

Ethnicity, 1990: White, 3,159 (63.7%); Black, 89 (1.8%); American Indian, 11 (0.2%); Asian, 8 (0.2%); Other, 1,689 (34.1%). Hispanic, 1,960 (39.5%).

Vital Statistics, 1993: Births, 67; deaths, 49; marriages, 61; divorces, 25.

Recreation: Museum, settlers reunion.

Minerals: Oil, gas.

Agriculture: Cotton, hay, sorghum; Beef cattle, sheep, goats, hogs also raised.

STANTON (2,645) county seat; farm, ranch, oil, center; varied manufacturing; electric co-op; hospital, restored convent, other historic buildings; old sorehead days three times a year.

Other towns include: **Ackerly** (246, partly in Dawson County); **Lenorah** (70); **Tarzan** (80).

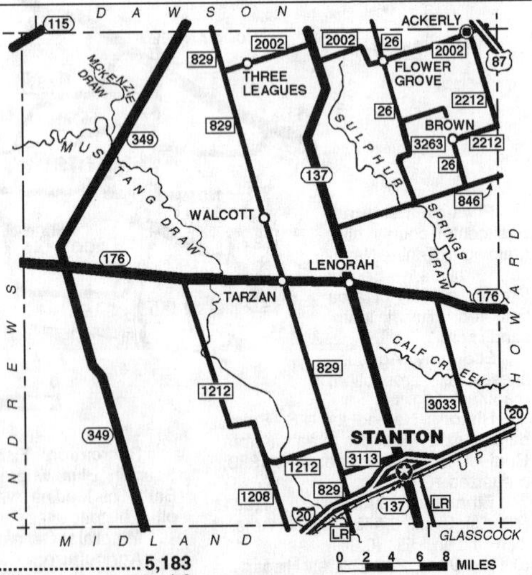

Population	**5,183**
(Change fm '90)	4.6
Land Area (sq. mi.)	914.8
Altitude (ft.)	2,518-2,888
Rainfall (in.)	17.2
Jan. mean min.	30
July mean max.	94
Growing season (days)	215
Civ. Labor	1,977
Unemployed	3.4
Total Wages	$27,055,500
Av. Weekly Wage	$413.09
Prop. Value	$652,903,043
Retail Sales	$31,073,086

For explanation of sources, abbreviations and symbols, see p. 132.

Mason County

Physical Features: Southwestern county; hilly, draining to Llano, San Saba rivers and tributaries; limestone, red soils; varied timber.

Economy: Ranching; hunting; tourism; soft-drink bottling.

History: Created from Bexar, Gillespie counties 1858; named for Mexican War victim U.S. Army Lt. G.T. Mason.

Ethnicity, 1990: White, 3,084 (90.1%); Black, 6 (0.2%); American Indian, 13 (0.4%); Asian, 4 (0.1%); Other, 316 (9.2%). Hispanic, 671 (19.6%).

Vital Statistics, 1993: Births, 30; deaths, 46; marriages, 23; divorces, 17.

Recreation: Outstanding deer, turkey hunting, river fishing; camping; historic homes of stone; restored town; Fort Mason where Robert E. Lee served; pinto bean cookoff; wild game dinner.

Minerals: Topaz, granite.

Agriculture: Cattle, goats, sheep; watermelons; some 7,100 acres of peanuts, hay irrigated.

MASON (1,939) county seat; ranching center; tourism; museum; historical district, homes, rock fences built by German settlers.

Population **3,326**
(Change fm '90) .... - 2.8

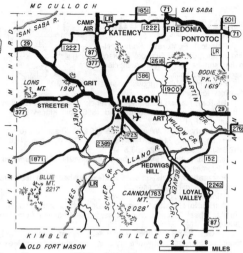

Land Area (sq. mi.) 932.1
Altitude (ft.) 1,258-2,260
Rainfall (in.) 24.8
Jan. mean min. 32
July mean max. 96
Growing season (days) 217

Civ. Labor 1,572
Unemployed 3.6
Total Wages $11,223,288
Av. Weekly Wage $267.44
Prop. Value $436,915,738
Retail Sales $16,382,360

Matagorda County

Physical Features: Gulf Coast county; flat, broken by bays; contains part of Matagorda Island; many different soils; drains to Colorado River, creeks, coast.

Economy: Petroleum operations, petrochemicals, agribusiness; varied manufacturing; tourism significant.

History: An original county, created 1836 from Spanish municipality, named for canebrake; organized 1837; settled by Austin colonists.

Ethnicity, 1990: White, 26,622 (72.1%); Black, 5,106 (13.8%); American Indian, 88 (0.2%); Asian, 842 (2.3%); Other, 4,270 (11.6%). Hispanic, 9,088 (24.6%).

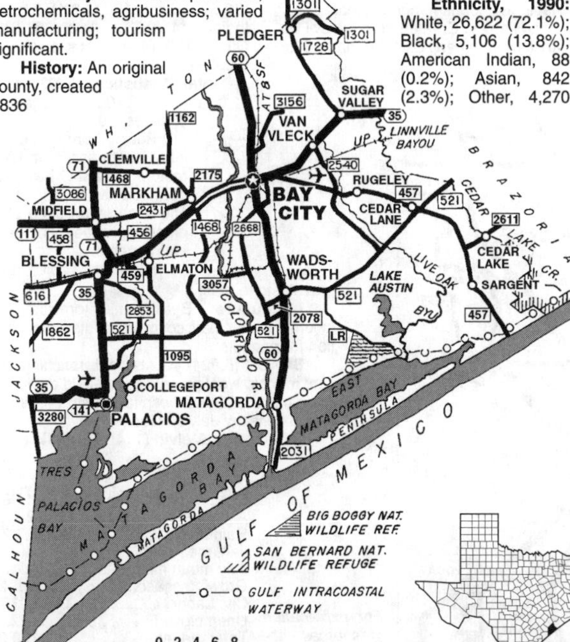

Vital Statistics, 1993: Births, 627; deaths, 324; marriages, 356; divorces, 216.

Recreation: Coastal activities, including fishing, water sports, hunting; historic sites, museums; rice festival; boat show.

Minerals: Gas, oil, salt.

Agriculture: Major rice-growing area, cotton, grains; beef cattle, cow-calf operations; 45,000 acres irrigated for rice, turf.

BAY CITY (18,818) county seat; petrochemicals; oil, gas processing; nuclear power plant; commercial fishing; hospital.

Palacois (4,497) tourism; seafood industry; hospital; Marine Education Center; bayfest; public fishing piers.

Other towns include: **Blessing** (571) historic sites; **Markham** (1,304); **Matagorda** (605); **Pledger** (159); **Van Vleck** (1,674).

Population **38,183**
(Change fm '90) 3.4
Land Area (sq. mi.) 1,114.5
Altitude (ft.) .... sea level-56
Rainfall (in.) 43.2
Jan. mean min. 46
July mean max. 91
Growing season (days) 296
Civ. Labor 17,606
Unemployed 13.5
Total Wages $346,307,214
Av. Weekly Wage $551.24
Prop. Value $4,657,415,776
Retail Sales $229,103,747

For explanation of sources, abbreviations and symbols, see p. 132.

Maverick County

Physical Features: Southwestern county on Rio Grande; broken, rolling surface, with dense brush; clay, sandy, alluvial soils.

Economy: Oil; agribusinesses; feedlots; tourism.

History: Named for Sam A. Maverick, whose name is a synonym for unbranded cattle; created 1856 from Kinney County; organized 1871.

Ethnicity, 1990: White, 23,748 (65.3%); Black, 32 (0.1%); American Indian, 714 (2.0%); Asian, 71 (0.2%); Other, 11,813 (32.5%). Hispanic, 34,024 (93.5%).

Vital Statistics, 1993: Births, 1,164; deaths, 175; marriages, 699; divorces, 105.

Recreation: Tourist gateway to Mexico; white-tailed deer, bird hunting; fishing; historic sites.

Minerals: Oil, gas, sand, gravel.

Agriculture: Cattle feedlots provide most income; oats, sorghums, wheat, pecans, vegetables; some irrigation from Rio Grande.

EAGLE PASS (23,008) county seat; varied manufacturing; tourism center; rail, highway entry point to Piedras Negras, Mex.; hospital.

Population	**39,763**
(Change fm '90)	9.3
Land Area (sq. mi.)	1,280.1
Altitude (ft.)	703-918
Rainfall (in.)	21.0
Jan. mean min.	38
July mean max.	99
Growing season (days)	285
Civ. Labor	16,984
Unemployed	27.0
Total Wages	$136,417,837
Av. Weekly Wage	$299.97
Prop. Value	$829,303,025
Retail Sales	$292,607,489

KINNEY
COAHUILA
QUEMADO
NORMANDY
TOLL BRIDGE
PIEDRAS NEGRAS
EAGLE PASS
EL INDIO
MEXICO
RIO GRANDE
ZAVALA
DIMMIT
WEBB
MULA CR.
ELM CR.
SALADO CR.
PICOSA CR.
SAN AMBROSIA CR.
◆ KICKAPOO INDIAN RESERVATION
0 2 4 6 8 MILES

McCulloch County

Physical Features: Central county; hilly and rolling; drains to Colorado, Brady Creek and Lake, San Saba River; black loams to sandy soils.

Economy: Agribusiness; manufacturing; tourism; hunting leases.

History: Created from Bexar District 1856; organized 1876; named for San Jacinto veteran Gen. Ben McCulloch.

Ethnicity, 1990: White, 7,855 (89.5%); Black, 166 (1.9%); American Indian, 14 (0.2%); Asian, 8 (0.1%); Other, 735 (8.4%). Hispanic, 2,317 (26.4%).

Vital Statistics, 1993: Births, 121; deaths, 140; marriages, 70; divorces, 59.

Recreation: Hunting; lake activities; museum, restored Santa Fe depot, goat cookoff, muzzle-loading rifle association state championship; rodeos; golf, tennis tournaments.

Minerals: Oil, sand, gravel, stone, gas.

Agriculture: Beef cattle provide most income; wheat, hay, cotton, peanuts; some irrigation for peanuts.

BRADY (5,924) county seat; ranching, tourism; mohair, wool processed; oil-field equipment, other manufacturing; hospital; Central Texas College extension; July Jubilee.

Other towns: **Melvin** (174), **Rochelle** (163).

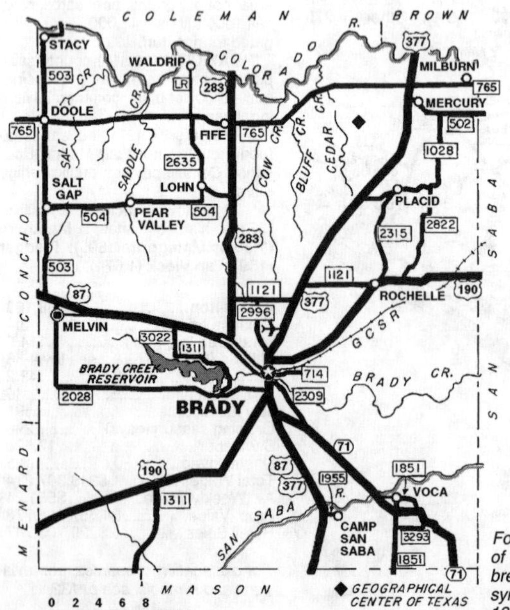

For explanation of sources, abbreviations and symbols, see p. 132.

Population	**8,666**
(Change fm '90)	- 1.3
Land Area (sq. mi.)	1,069.3
Altitude (ft.)	1,442-2,021
Rainfall (in.)	24.7
Jan. mean min.	30
July mean max.	96
Growing season (days)	226
Civ. Labor	3,737
Unemployed	7.2
Total Wages	$41,759,267
Av. Weekly Wage	$327.64
Prop. Value	$474,512,186
Retail Sales	$52,234,610

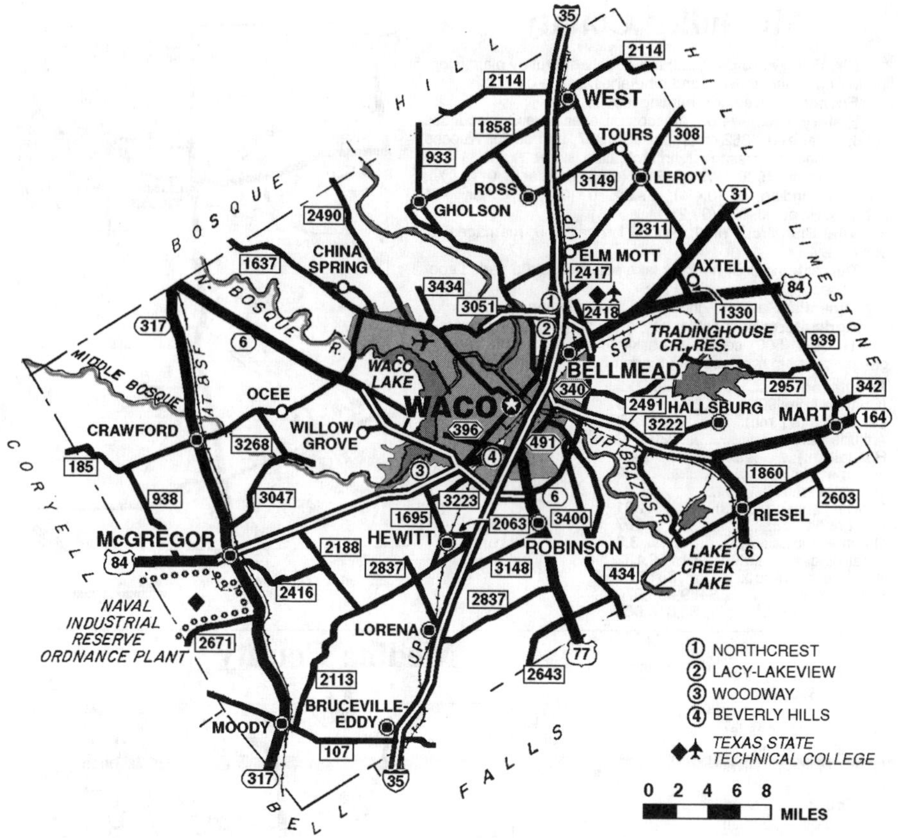

McLennan County

Physical Features: Central Texas county of mostly Blackland prairie, but rolling hills in west; drains to Bosque, Brazos rivers and Lake Waco; heavy, loam, sandy soils.

Economy: A leading distribution, government center for Central Texas; diversified manufacturing; agribusiness; education.

History: Created from Milam County in 1850; named for an original settler, Neil McLennan Sr.

Ethnicity, 1990: White, 146,100 (77.3%); Black, 29,520 (15.6%); American Indian, 563 (0.3%); Asian, 1,384 (0.7%); Other, 11,556 (6.1%). Hispanic, 23,643 (12.5%).

Vital Statistics, 1993: Births, 3,110; deaths, 2,052; marriages, 2,016; divorces, 959.

Recreation: Varied metropolitan activies; Fort Fisher Park with camping facilities; Texas Ranger Hall of Fame; Texas Sports Hall of Fame; Dr Pepper Museum; Cameron Park; Brazos River festival; zoo; historic sites, homes; museums; libraries, art center; symphony; civic theater; Baylor University events; Heart o' Texas Fair.

Minerals: Sand and gravel, stone, clays, oil, gas.

Agriculture: Beef cattle; also dairy cows and turkeys; crops include corn, wheat, hay, grain sorghums, peanuts.

Education: Baylor University; community college; Texas State Technical College.

WACO (107,191) county seat; varied manufacturing; tourism center, conventions; agribusiness; hospitals; Veterans Administration regional office, hospital.

Other towns include: **Bellmead** (8,440); **Bruceville-Eddy** (1,180, partly in Falls County); **Hallsburg** (499); **Hewitt** (9,889), iron works, other manufacturing; hamburger cookoff; **Lorena** (1,342); **Mart** (2,039); **McGregor** (4,792), farming center, some manufacturing; private telephone museum; Frontier Founders Day in Septmeber; **Moody** (1,363); **Riesel** (867); **Robinson** (7,673); **West** (2,719), famous for Czech foods; varied manufacturing; Westfest.

Population	**197,493**
(Change fm '90)	4.4
Land Area (sq. mi.)	1,041.9
Altitude (ft.)	381-734
Rainfall (in.)	31.0
Jan. mean min.	36
July mean max.	97
Growing season (days)	253
Civ. Labor	97,897
Unemployed	5.0
Total Wages	$1,721,940,171
Av. Weekly Wage	$408.72
Prop. Value	$5,132,519,328
Retail Sales	$1,807,988,586

For explanation of sources, abbreviations and symbols, see p. 132.

McMullen County

Physical Features: Southern county of brushy plain, sloping to Frio, Nueces rivers and tributaries; saline clay soils.

Economy: Livestock, hunting leases, hay.

History: Created from Atascosa, Bexar, Live Oak counties 1858; organized 1862, reorganized 1877; named for Nueces River pioneer-empresario John McMullen.

Ethnicity, 1990: White, 713 (87.3%); Black, 0 (0.0%); American Indian, 3 (0.4%); Asian, 0 (0.0%); Other, 101 (12.4%). Hispanic, 320 (39.2%).

Vital Statistics, 1993: Births, 1; deaths, 9; marriages, 6; divorces, 4.

Recreation: Deer hunting; lake activities, state park; Labor Day rodeo.

Minerals: Gas, oil, lignite coal, zeolite-kaline.

Agriculture: Beef cattle; hay, grain sorghum, sunflowers.

TILDEN (500) county seat; kitty-litter production; natural gas processing; ranch center; tourism.

Population	**725**
(Change from '90)	- 11.3
Land Area (sq. mi.)	1,113.0
Altitude (ft.)	230-642
Rainfall (in.)	24.4
Jan. mean min.	39
July mean max.	97
Growing season (days)	291
Civ. Labor	297
Unemployed	3.0
Total Wages	$4,750,132
Av. Weekly Wage	$413.24
Prop. Value	$469,458,670
Retail Sales	$2,018,088

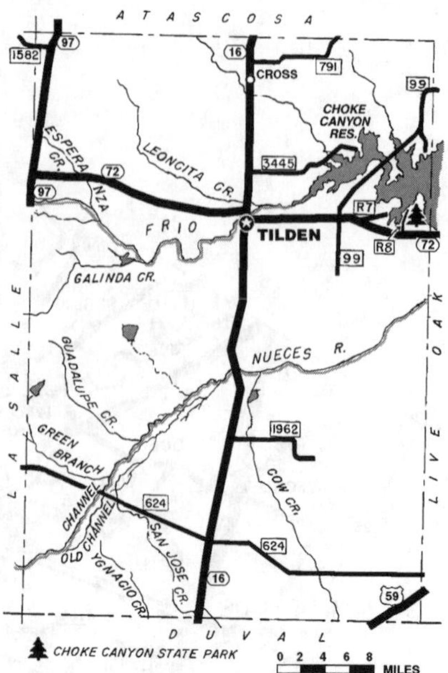

Medina County

Physical Features: Southwestern county with scenic hills in north; south has fertile valleys, rolling surface; Medina River, Lake.

Economy: Agribusinesses; tourism; varied manufacturing.

History: Created 1848 from Bexar; settled by Alsatians led by Henri Castro; named for river, probably for Spanish engineer Pedro Medina.

Ethnicity, 1990: White, 23,608 (86.4%); Black, 92 (0.3%); American Indian, 119 (0.4%); Asian, 68 (0.2%); Other, 3,425 (12.5%). Hispanic, 12,134 (44.4%).

Vital Statistics, 1993: Births, 419; deaths, 257; marriages, 212; divorces, 124.

Recreation: A leading deer area; scenic drives; camping, fishing; historic buildings, museum; market trail days most months.

Minerals: Oil, gas, clay, sand, gravel.

Agriculture: Most income from livestock; crops include grains, peanuts, hay, cotton, vegetables; some irrigation.

HONDO (6,217) county seat; agribusiness; varied manufacturing; hunting leases; Air Force screening center; hospital; prisons.

Castroville (2,380), farm center; food processing; light manufacturing; Landmark Inn; St. Louis Day celebration in August.

Devine (4,344) trade center, shipping for truck crop-livestock.

Other towns include: **D'Hanis** (548); **La Coste** (1,246); **Natalia** (1,254). **Lytle**, which lies partly in Atascosa and Bexar counties, has a population of 2,395.

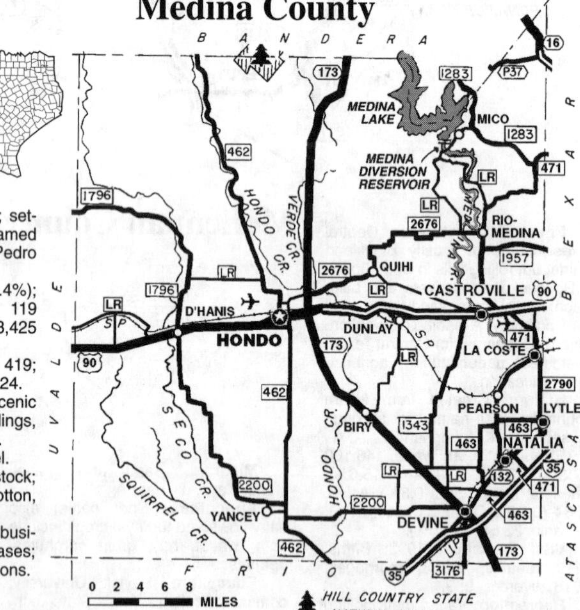

Population	**29,764**
(Change fm '90)	9.0
Land Area (sq. mi.)	1,327.8
Altitude (ft.)	635-1,995
Rainfall (in.)	28.5
Jan. mean min.	39
July mean max.	98
Growing season (days)	263
Civ. Labor	13,124
Unemployed	4.5
Total Wages	$107,890,499
Av. Weekly Wage	$329.37
Prop. Value	$1,360,610,350
Retail Sales	$182,581,272

For explanation of sources, abbreviations and symbols, see. p. 132.

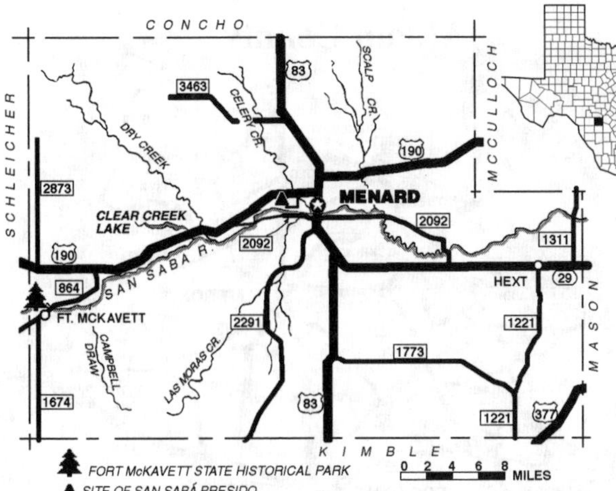

Menard County

Physical Features: West central county of rolling topography, draining to San Saba River and tributaries; limestone soils.

Economy: Agribusiness; tourism; oil, gas production.

History: Created from Bexar County in 1858, organized, 1871; named for Galveston's founder, Michel B. Menard.

Ethnicity, 1990: White, 2,076 (92.2%); Black, 7 (0.3%); American Indian, 5 (0.2%); Asian, 0 (0.0%); Other, 164 (7.3%). Hispanic, 726 (32.2%).

Vital Statistics, 1993: Births, 19; deaths, 29; marriages, 11; divorces, 6.

Recreation: Hunting, fishing; historic sites, including Spanish presidio, mission, state park; museum; Jim Bowie days in June.

Minerals: Oil, gas.

Agriculture: Beef cattle, sheep, goats; crops are pecans, alfalfa, peaches, melons, grapes.

MENARD (1,563) county seat; hunting, ranching center, hospital.

Population	**2,252**
(Change fm '90)	0
Land Area (sq. mi.)	901.9
Altitude (ft.)	1,690-2,346
Rainfall (in.)	22.2
Jan. mean min.	29
July mean max.	95
Growing season (days)	220
Civ. Labor	1,073
Unemployed	3.3
Total Wages	$7,409,504
Av. Weekly Wage	$276.07
Prop. Value	$237,721,960
Retail Sales	$9,046,139

Midland County

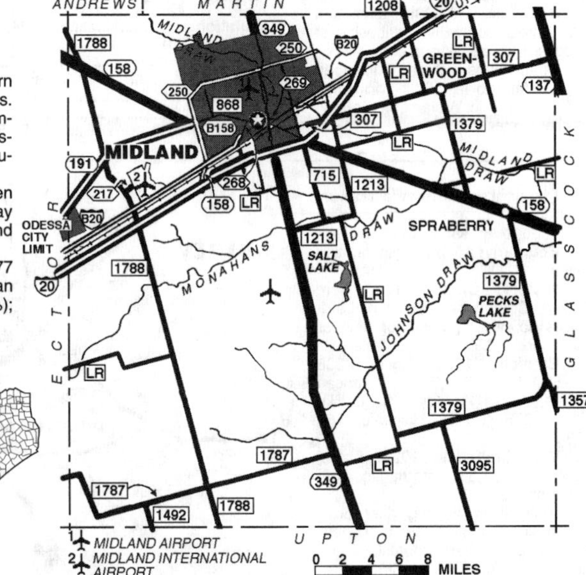

Physical Features: Flat western county, broken by draws; sandy, loam soils.

Economy: Among leading petroleum-producing counties; distribution, administrative center for oil industry; varied manufacturing.

History: Created from Tom Green County 1885; name came from midway location on railroad between El Paso and Fort Worth.

Ethnicity, 1990: White, 86,977 (81.6%); Black, 8,281 (7.8%); American Indian, 414 (0.4%); Asian, 888 (0.8%); Other, 10,051 (9.4%). Hispanic, 22,780 (21.4%).

Vital Statistics, 1993: Births, 1,955; deaths, 727; marriages, 996; divorces, 648.

Recreation: Permian Basin Petroleum Museum, Library, Hall of Fame; Museum of Southwest; Pliska Aviation Museum; Confederate Air Force and Museum; community theater; metropolitan events.

Chihuahua Trail and Emigrant Road were pioneer trails that crossed county.

Minerals: Oil, natural gas.

Agriculture: Horses, beef cattle; cotton top crop, others are alfalfa, pecans; 12,000 acres irrigated.

MIDLAND (92,003) county seat; petroleum, petrochemical center; varied manufacturing; livestock sale center; hospital; cultural activities; Texas League baseball.

Part of **Odessa** city limits extend into Midland County.

Population	**112,855**
(Change fm '90)	5.9
Land Area (sq. mi.)	900.3
Altitude (ft.)	2,613-2,936
Rainfall (in.)	13.7
Jan. mean min.	30
July mean max.	94
Growing season (days)	218
Civ. Labor	58,442
Unemployed	5.7
Total Wages	$1,222,399,810
Av. Weekly Wage	$512.39
Prop. Value	$3,879,275,182
Retail Sales	$1,086,579,698

For explanation of sources, abbreviations and symbols, see p. 132.

Milam County

Physical Features: East central county of partly level Blackland; southeast rolling to Post Oak Belt; Brazos, Little rivers.

Economy: Aluminum manufacturing; other varied manufacturing; lignite mining; agribusiness.

History: Created 1836 from municipality named for Ben Milam, a leader who died at the battle for San Antonio in December 1835; organized 1837.

Ethnicity, 1990: White, 18,603 (81.1%); Black, 2,940 (12.8%); American Indian, 69 (0.3%); Asian, 37 (0.2%); Other, 1,297 (5.7%). Hispanic, 3,456 (15.1%).

Vital Statistics, 1993: Births, 355; deaths, 290; marriages, 172; divorces, 90.

Recreation: Fishing, hunting; historic sites include Fort Sullivan, Indian battlegrounds, mission site; museum in old jail at Cameron.

Minerals: Large lignite deposits; limited oil, natural gas production.

Agriculture: Cattle, poultry, some horses; crops are hay, cotton, corn, sorghum, wheat, oats, melons, peanuts.

CAMERON (5,865) county seat; manufacturing; hospital; library; arts, antique auto fair in October.

Rockdale (5,503) aluminum plant, utility company; agribusiness; hospital; Jubilee Days in June.

Other towns include: **Buckholts** (361); **Milano** (452); **Thorndale** (1,259, partly in Williamson County) market center.

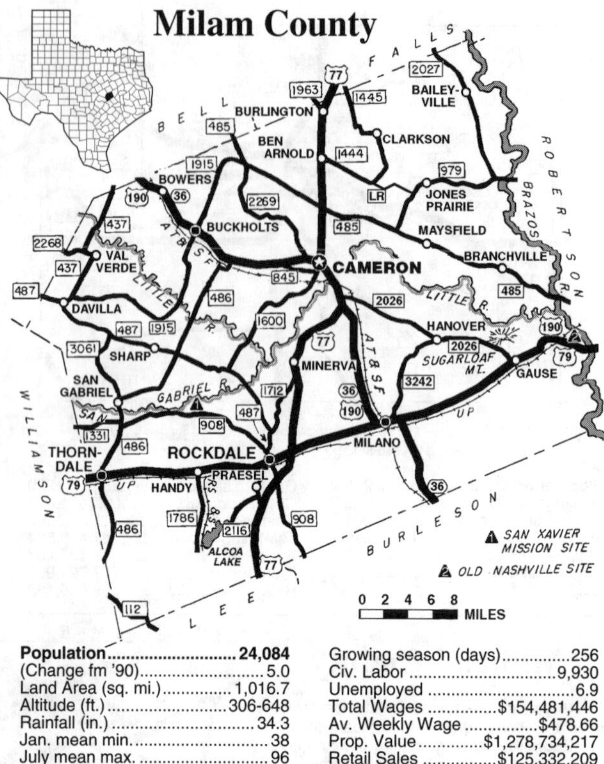

Population	**24,084**
(Change fm '90)	5.0
Land Area (sq. mi.)	1,016.7
Altitude (ft.)	306-648
Rainfall (in.)	34.3
Jan. mean min.	38
July mean max.	96
Growing season (days)	256
Civ. Labor	9,930
Unemployed	6.9
Total Wages	$154,481,446
Av. Weekly Wage	$478.66
Prop. Value	$1,278,734,217
Retail Sales	$125,332,209

Mills County

Physical Features: West central county of hills, plateau draining to Colorado River; sandy, loam soils.

Economy: Agribusiness, hunting leases.

History: Created 1887 from Brown, Comanche, Hamilton, Lampasas counties; named for pioneer jurist John T. Mills.

Ethnicity, 1990: White, 4,238 (93.5%); Black, 10 (0.2%); American Indian, 4 (0.1%); Asian, 1 (0.0%); Other, 278 (6.1%). Hispanic, 484 (10.7%).

Vital Statistics, 1993: Births, 58; deaths, 53; marriages, 36; divorces, 28.

Recreation: Fishing; deer, dove and turkey hunting; historic suspension bridge; fiddlers' contest; rangeland recreation. Site of Comanche-Apache battles.

Minerals: Not significant.

Agriculture: Beef cattle; sheep, goats also raised; hay, small grains, pecans; some irrigation for pecans, Bermuda grass pasture.

GOLDTHWAITE (1,790) county seat; agribusiness, livestock center; light manufacturing; hospital; bike rally, old timers rodeo.

Other towns include: **Mullin** (211); **Priddy** (215).

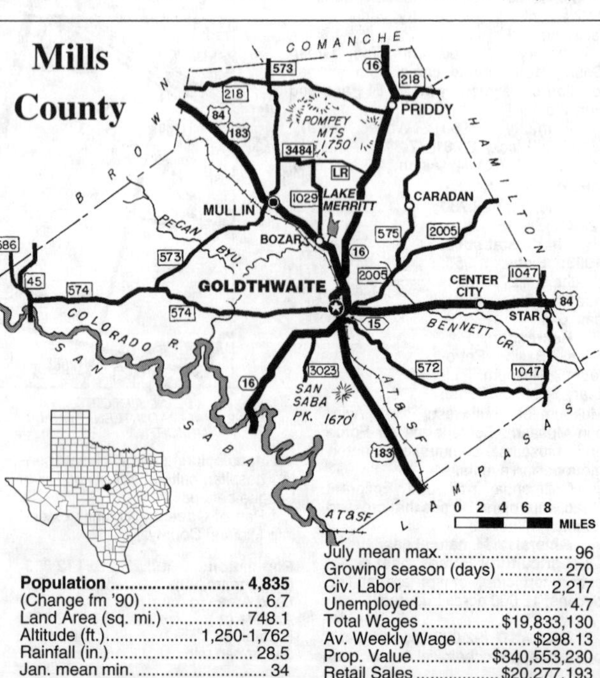

Population	**4,835**
(Change fm '90)	6.7
Land Area (sq. mi.)	748.1
Altitude (ft.)	1,250-1,762
Rainfall (in.)	28.5
Jan. mean min.	34
July mean max.	96
Growing season (days)	270
Civ. Labor	2,217
Unemployed	4.7
Total Wages	$19,833,130
Av. Weekly Wage	$298.13
Prop. Value	$340,553,230
Retail Sales	$20,277,193

Mitchell County

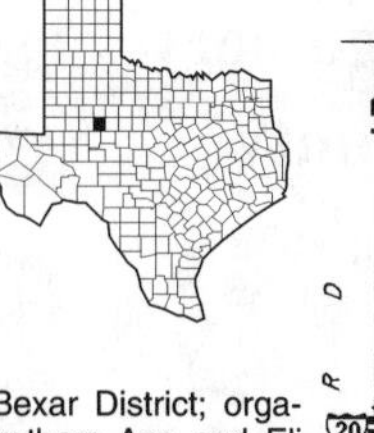

Physical Features: Rolling, draining to Colorado and tributaries; sandy, red, dark soils; Lake Colorado City and Champion Creek Reservoir.

Business: Oil, agribusiness; some manufacturing.

History: Created 1876 from Bexar District; organized 1881; named for pioneer brothers Asa and Eli Mitchell.

Ethnicity, 1990: White, 6,317 (78.8%); Black, 363 (4.5%); American Indian, 14 (0.2%); Asian, 5 (0.1%); Other, 1,317 (16.4%). Hispanic, 2,389 (29.8%).

Vital Statistics, 1993: Births, 105; deaths, 119; marriages, 51; divorces, 52.

Recreation: Lake activities; state park; museum, hunting; railhead arts, crafts show.

Minerals: Oil and natural gas.

Agriculture: Beef cattle top revenue source, sheep raised; cotton principal crop, grains also produced; some irrigation for cotton, alfalfa.

COLORADO CITY (4,643) county seat; varied manufacturing; electric service center; hospital.

Other towns include: **Loraine** (744), **Westbrook** (246).

Population	**7,885**
(Change fm '90)	- 1.6
Land Area (sq. mi.)	910.1
Altitude (ft.)	2,004-2,616
Rainfall (in.)	19.8
Jan. mean min.	30
July mean max.	97
Growing season (days)	217
Civ. Labor	3,390
Unemployed	6.9
Total Wages	$38,284,343
Av. Weekly Wage	$342.34
Prop. Value	$567,135,920
Retail Sales	$40,369,818

Montague County

Physical Features: Rolling, draining to tributaries of Trinity, Red rivers; sandy loams, red, black soils; Farmers Creek Reservoir, Lake Amon G. Carter.

Economy: Agribusinesses; oil production; varied manufacturing.

History: Created from Cooke County 1857, organized 1858; named for pioneer Daniel Montague.

Ethnicity, 1990: White, 16,834 (97.5%); Black, 5 (0.0%); American Indian, 72 (0.4%); Asian, 13 (0.1%); Other, 350 (2.0%). Hispanic, 548 (3.2%).

Vital Statistics, 1993: Births, 213; deaths, 262; marriages, 155; divorces, 97.

Recreation: Lake activities; quail, turkey, deer hunting; scenic drives; museums; historical sites; Chisholm Trail Days, Jim Bowie Days in June; cattleman's roundup.

Minerals: Oil, rock, limestone.

Agriculture: Beef, dairy cattle; crops include wheat, peanuts; watermelons, cantaloupe; some irrigation for peanuts, fruits.

MONTAGUE (400) county seat.

Bowie (5,250) varied manufacturing, livestock, North Central Texas College campus, hospital, library; fall bash; second Monday trade day.

Nocona (3,028) boots, athletic goods manufacturing; hospital.

Other towns include: **Saint Jo** (1,099) farm center; Pioneer Days on Memorial weekend; **Forestburg** (200); **Sunset** (200).

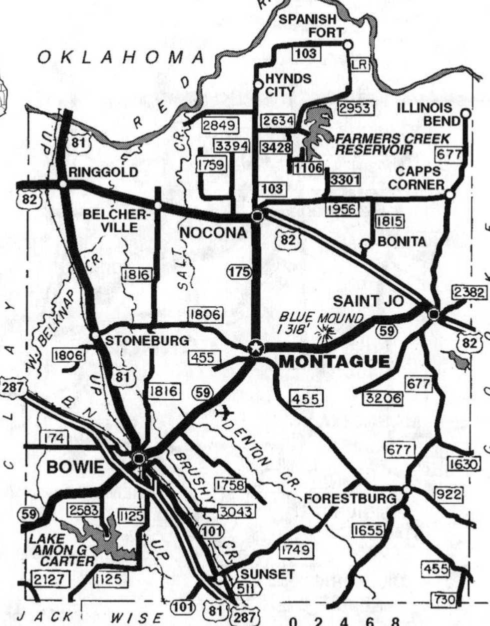

Population	**17,797**
(Change fm '90)	3.0
Land Area (sq. mi.)	930.7
Altitude (ft.)	766-1,318
Rainfall (in.)	32.3
Jan. mean min.	31
July mean max.	97
Growing season (days)	229
Civ. Labor	7,682
Unemployed	6.6
Total Wages	$70,304,115
Av. Weekly Wage	$326.63
Prop. Value	$641,991,770
Retail Sales	$140,721,448

For explanation of sources, abbreviations and symbols, see p. 132.

Montgomery County

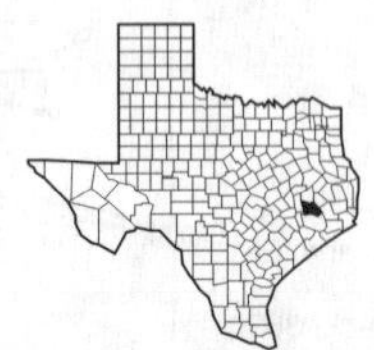

Physical Features: Rolling, three-fourths timbered; Sam Houston National Forest; loam, sandy, alluvial soils.

Economy: Many residents work in Houston; lumber, oil production; part of Houston metropolitan area.

History: Created 1837 from Washington County; named for Richard Montgomery, American Revolution general.

Ethnicity, 1990: White, 166,107 (91.2%); Black, 7,763 (4.3%); American Indian, 687 (0.4%); Asian, 1,232 (0.7%); Other, 6,412 (3.5%). Hispanic, 13,237 (7.3%).

Vital Statistics, 1993: Births, 3,326; deaths, 1,315; marriages, 2,056; divorces, 1,188.

Recreation: Hunting, fishing; Lake Conroe activities; national and state forests; hiking, boating, horseback riding; historic sites.

Minerals: Oil, gas, sand, gravel.

Agriculture: Timber; beef cattle, horses, ratite birds, swine; hay and greenhouse nurseries; also some blueberries and peaches.

CONROE (32,060) county seat; residential community with many people working in Houston; some manufacturing; food processing; hospital.

The Woodlands (33,902) planned community.

Other towns include: **Cut and Shoot** (1,006); **Dobbin** (170); **Magnolia** (1,111); **Montgomery** (406) historic buildings, antique stores; **New Caney** (2,771); **Patton Village** (1,238); **Pinehurst** (3,644); **Porter** (2,146); **Roman Forest** (1,128); **Splendora** (803); **Willis** (3,144); **Woodbranch** (1,424); **Woodloch** (336).

Population	**199,490**
(Change fm '90)	9.5
Land Area (sq. mi.)	1,044.3
Altitude (ft.)	86-380
Rainfall (in.)	46.6
Jan. mean min.	38
July mean max.	95
Growing season (days)	270
Civ. Labor	105,092
Unemployed	5.2
Total Wages	$1,183,907,476
Av. Weekly Wage	$445.47
Prop. Value	$8,187,605,580
Retail Sales	$1,662,946,866

For explanation of sources, abbreviations or symbols, see p. 132.

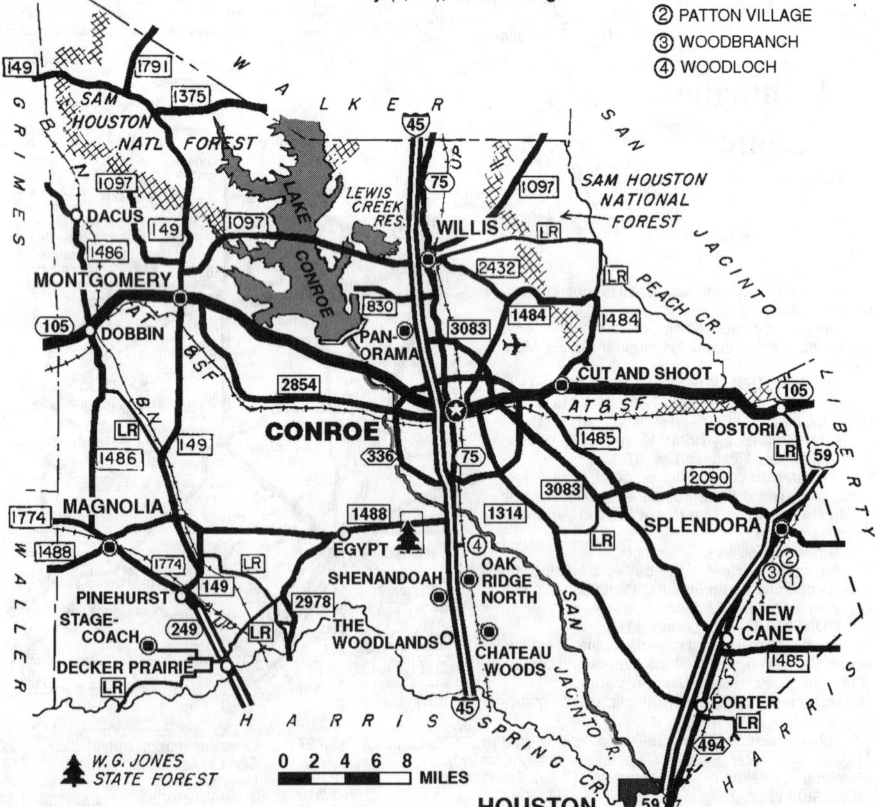

① ROMAN FOREST
② PATTON VILLAGE
③ WOODBRANCH
④ WOODLOCH

Moore County

Physical Features: Northern Panhandle county; flat to rolling, broken by creeks; sandy loams; lake.

Economy: Extensive petroleum operations; major natural gas producing county; varied agribusiness.

History: Created 1876 from Bexar District; organized 1892; named for Republic of Texas navy commander E.W. Moore.

Ethnicity, 1990: White, 12,789 (71.6%); Black, 95 (0.5%); American Indian, 123 (0.7%); Asian, 282 (1.6%); Other, 4,576 (25.6%). Hispanic, 5,693 (31.9%).

Vital Statistics, 1993: Births, 394; deaths, 125; marriages, 199; divorces, 95.

Recreation: Lake Meredith activities; historical museum; arts center; free overnight RV park; dogie days in June.

Minerals: Natural gas, helium and oil.

Agriculture: Fed beef, stocker cattle, cow/calf operations; crops include corn, sorghums, wheat; about 140,000 acres irrigated for wheat, corn, sorghums.

DUMAS (13,477) county seat; tourist, retail trade center; varied agribusiness; hospital, hospice, retirement complex.

Other towns include: **Cactus** (1,717), **Sunray** (1,801).

Population	**18,872**
(Change fm '90)	5.6
Land Area (sq. mi.)	899.7
Altitude (ft.)	3,221-3,770
Rainfall (in.)	18.5
Jan. mean min.	19
July mean max.	92
Growing season (days)	185
Civ. Labor	9,354
Unemployed	4.4
Total Wages	$165,952,501
Av. Weekly Wage	$415.32
Prop. Value	$1,436,393,260
Retail Sales	$115,763,486

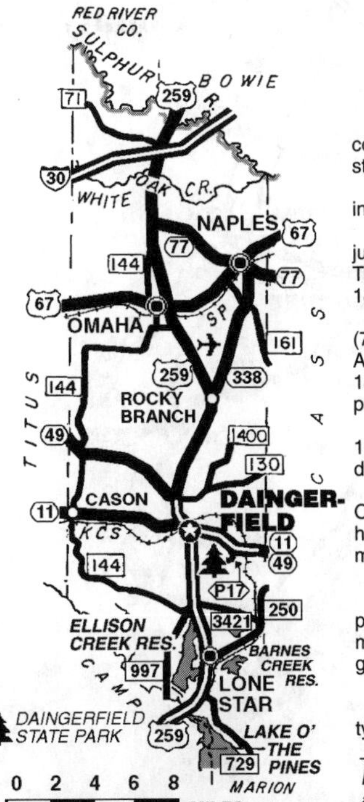

Morris County

Physical Features: East Texas county of forested hills; drains to streams, lakes.

Economy: Varied manufacturing; tourism; livestock, timber.

History: Named for legislator-jurist W.W. Morris; created from Titus County and organized in 1875.

Ethnicity, 1990: White, 9,770 (74.0%); Black, 3,227 (24.4%); American Indian, 70 (0.5%); Asian, 18 (0.1%); Other, 115 (0.9%). Hispanic, 239 (1.8%).

Vital Statistics, 1993: Births, 154; deaths, 188; marriages, 122; divorces, 88.

Recreation: Activities on Lake O' the Pines, small lakes; fishing, hunting; state park; old courthouse museum in Daingerfield.

Minerals: Iron ore.

Agriculture: Beef cattle, broiler production; pine and hardwood marketed; hay, watermelons; new greenhouse development.

DAINGERFIELD (2,653) county seat; varied manufacturing; hospital; library; Northeast Texas Community College; Captain Daingerfield Day in October.

Other towns include: **Lone Star** (1,624) oil-field equipment manufactured; catfish farming; Starfest in September; **Naples** (1,497) trailer manufacturing; livestock; watermelon festival in July; **Omaha** (928).

Population	**13,164**
(Change fm '90)	- 0.3
Land Area (sq. mi.)	254.5
Altitude (ft.)	268-537
Rainfall (in.)	44
Jan. mean min.	35
July mean max.	95
Growing season (days)	236
Civ. Labor	6,007
Unemployed	10.4
Total Wages	$118,456,195
Av. Weekly Wage	$522.55
Prop. Value	$571,096,030
Retail Sales	$46,763,194

For explanation of sources, abbreviations and symbols, see p. 132.

Motley County

Physical Features: Western county just below Caprock; rough terrain, broken by Pease tributaries; sandy to red clay soils.

Economy: Livestock, oil production.

History: Created out of Bexar District 1876; organized 1891; named for Dr. J.W. Mottley, signer of Texas Declaration of Independence (name misspelled in statute).

Ethnicity, 1990: White, 1,362 (88.9%); Black, 68 (4.4%); American Indian, 5 (0.3%); Asian, 4 (0.3%); Other, 93 (6.1%). Hispanic, 136 (8.9%).

Vital Statistics, 1993: Births, 15; deaths, 27; marriages, 11; divorces, 3.

Recreation: Quail, dove, deer hunting; Matador Ranch headquarters; spring-fed pool at Roaring Springs; settlers reunion in August.

Minerals: Oil, gas, sand, gravel.

Agriculture: Beef cattle, cow-calf stocker operations most profitable; cotton, peanuts grown; also some vegetables, watermelons, hay and wheat; some irrigation for peanuts, cotton.

MATADOR (830) county seat; farm trade center.

Other towns include: **Flomot** (171), **Roaring Springs** (270).

Population **1,617**
(Change fm '90) 5.5

Land Area (sq. mi.) 989.4
Altitude (ft.) 1,928-3,034
Rainfall (in.) 20.4
Jan. mean min. 27
July mean max. 96

Growing season (days) 218
Civ. Labor 753
Unemployed 3.9
Total Wages $5,934,352
Av. Weekly Wage $326.25
Prop. Value $102,673,794
Retail Sales $5,041,816

Nacogdoches County

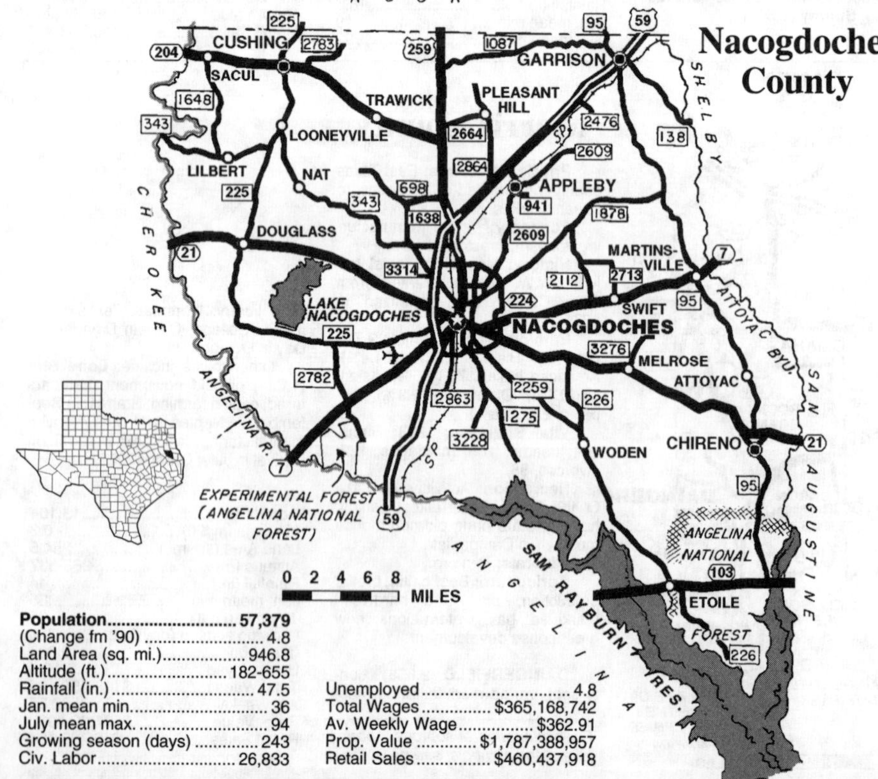

Population **57,379**
(Change fm '90) 4.8
Land Area (sq. mi.) 946.8
Altitude (ft.) 182-655
Rainfall (in.) 47.5
Jan. mean min. 36
July mean max. 94
Growing season (days) 243
Civ. Labor 26,833

Unemployed 4.8
Total Wages $365,168,742
Av. Weekly Wage $362.91
Prop. Value $1,787,388,957
Retail Sales $460,437,918

Nacogdoches County

Physical Features: East Texas county on divide between streams; hilly; two-thirds forested; red, gray, sandy soils; Sam Rayburn Reservoir.

Economy: Agribusiness; manufacturing; education; tourism.

History: One of state's most historic areas. Named for Indian tribe of area. First Europeans were Spanish settlers in mid-1700s. Original county of Republic, created 1836, organized 1837.

Ethnicity, 1990: White, 43,772 (79.9%); Black, 9,020 (16.5%); American Indian, 144 (0.3%); Asian, 311 (0.6%); Other, 1,506 (2.8%). Hispanic, 2,788 (5.1%).

Vital Statistics, 1993: Births, 838; deaths, 494; marriages, 651; divorces,206.

Recreation: Lake, river activities; Stephen F. Austin University events; Angelina National Forest; historic sites major tourist attractions, including Old Stone Fort, pioneer homes, museums, Piney Woods Fair, Heritage Days Festival in June.

Minerals: First Texas oil found here, 1866; gas, oil, clay, stone.

Agriculture: A leading poultry-producing county; extensive dairy operations, beef cattle raised; substantial timber sold.

NACOGDOCHES (32,260) county seat; varied manufacturing; lumber mills, wood products; trade center; hospitals; Stephen F. Austin University.

Other towns include: **Appleby** (499), **Chireno** (456), **Cushing** (631), **Garrison** (1,002).

Navarro County

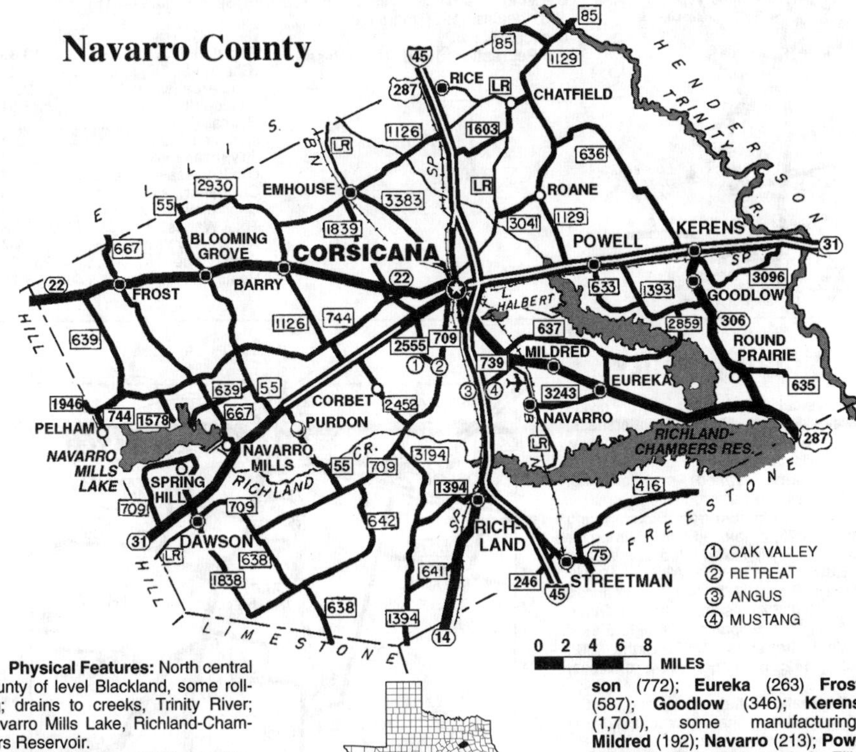

Physical Features: North central county of level Blackland, some rolling; drains to creeks, Trinity River; Navarro Mills Lake, Richland-Chambers Reservoir.

Economy: Diversified manufacturing; agribusinesses; oil-field operations, distribution.

History: Created from Robertson County, organized in 1846; named for Republic of Texas leader Jose Antonio Navarro.

Ethnicity, 1990: White, 30,322 (75.9%); Black, 7,574 (19.0%); American Indian, 127 (0.3%); Asian, 271 (0.7%); Other, 1,632 (4.1%). Hispanic, 2,891 (7.2%).

Vital Statistics, 1993: Births, 555; deaths, 474; marriages, 402; divorces, 271.

Recreation: Lake activities; Pioneer Village; historic buildings; youth exposition, Derrick Days in April.

Minerals: Longest continuous Texas oil flow; more than 200 million barrels produced since 1895; natural gas, sand and gravel also produced.

Agriculture: Beef cattle; hay; also, horses, emus and ostriches raised; crops include cotton, grain sorghums, wheat, herbs, corn.

CORSICANA (23,507) county seat; major distribution center; varied manufacturing; hospital; Navarro College; Texas Youth Commission facility.

Other towns include: **Barry** (184); **Blooming Grove** (844); **Dawson** (772); **Eureka** (263) **Frost** (587); **Goodlow** (346); **Kerens** (1,701), some manufacturing; **Mildred** (192); **Navarro** (213); **Powell** (108); **Rice** (588, partly in Ellis County); **Richland** (276).

Population	**40,917**
(Change fm '90)	2.5
Land Area (sq. mi.)	1,071.2
Altitude (ft.)	293-536
Rainfall (in.)	36.6
Jan. mean min.	34
July mean max.	96
Growing season (days)	253
Civ. Labor	20,337
Unemployed	5.8
Total Wages	$268,760,076
Av. Weekly Wage	$371.55
Prop. Value	$1,471,915,536
Retail Sales	$265,568,412

For explanation of sources, abbreviations and symbols, see p. 132.

Newton County

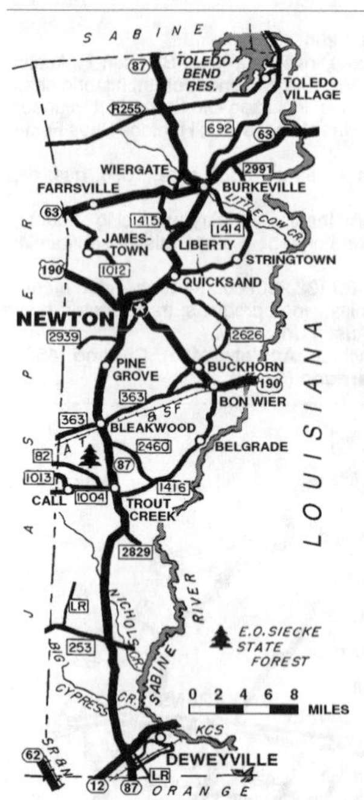

Physical Features: East Texas county of densely forested hills, valleys; spring-fed streams; Toledo Bend Reservoir; Sabine River; mostly sandy soils.

Economy: Forestry, tourism.

History: Created 1846 from Jasper County; named for American Revolutionary soldier John Newton.

Ethnicity, 1990: White, 10,402 (76.7%); Black, 3,039 (22.4%); American Indian, 44 (0.3%); Asian, 11 (0.1%); Other, 73 (0.5%). Hispanic, 153 (1.1%).

Vital Statistics, 1993: Births, 173; deaths, 125; marriages, 116; divorces, 80.

Recreation: Toledo Bend Reservoir; water sports; fishing, hunting; tourism; state forest; Azalea Canyons; spring festival. Belgrade, site of early town.

Minerals: Oil, gas.

Agriculture: Forestry; peaches, vegetables raised.

NEWTON (1,870) county seat; lumber manufacturing; plywood mill; hospital; private prison unit; clinics; tourist center; airport.

Deweyville (1,274) commercial center for forestry, farming area.

Other towns include: **Burkeville** (515); **Wiergate** (461).

Population	**13,834**
(Change fm '90)	2.0
Land Area (sq. mi.)	932.7
Altitude (ft.)	23-510
Rainfall (in.)	56
Jan. mean min.	40
July mean max.	93
Growing season (days)	228
Civ. Labor	6,032
Unemployed	11.3
Total Wages	$41,033,734
Av. Weekly Wage	$369.77
Prop. Value	$740,254,640
Retail Sales	$82,528,150

Nolan County

Physical Features: On divide between Brazos, Colorado watersheds; mostly red sandy loams, some waxy, sandy soils; lakes.

Economy: Varied manufacturing; ranching; oil and gas production.

History: Created from Bexar, Young districts 1876; organized 1881; named for adventurer Philip Nolan killed near Waco.

Ethnicity, 1990: White, 12,942 (78.0%); Black, 775 (4.7%); American Indian, 46 (0.3%); Asian, 18 (0.1%); Other, 2,813 (17.0%). Hispanic, 4,246 (25.6%).

Vital Statistics, 1993: Births, 212; deaths, 192; marriages, 164; divorces, 104.

Recreation: Lakes; hunting; rattlesnake roundup; pioneer museum; national junior rodeo finals in summer.

Minerals: Oil, gas, gypsum, limestone, and gravel.

Agriculture: Beef cattle, sheep, Angora goats, hogs; ratites; cotton is the principal crop, sorghums also raised.

SWEETWATER (11,851) county seat; gypsum plant; varied manufacturing; hospital; Texas State Technical College.

Other towns include: **Blackwell** (357, partly in Coke County), Oak Creek Reservoir; **Roscoe** (1,413).

For explanation of sources, abbreviations and symbols, see p. 132.

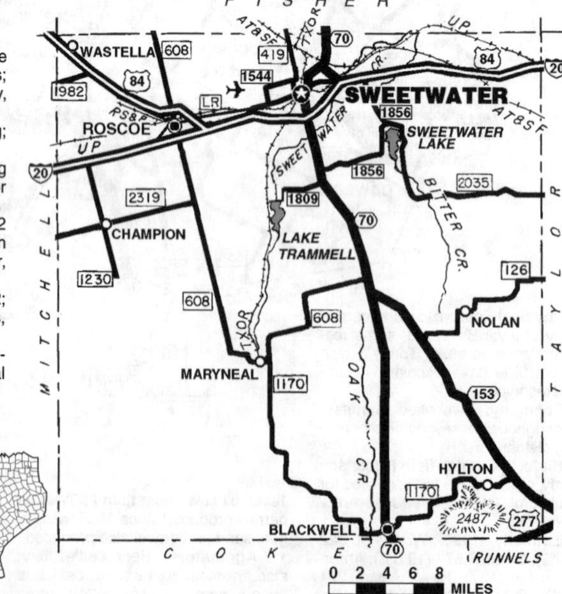

Population	**16,623**
(Change fm '90)	0.2
Land Area (sq. mi.)	912.0
Altitude (ft.)	1,990-2,603
Rainfall (in.)	23.4
Jan. mean min.	30
July mean max.	95
Growing season (days)	221
Civ. Labor	7,559
Unemployed	7.9
Total Wages	$103,221,434
Av. Weekly Wage	$351.44
Prop. Value	$765,076,461
Retail Sales	$101,208,918

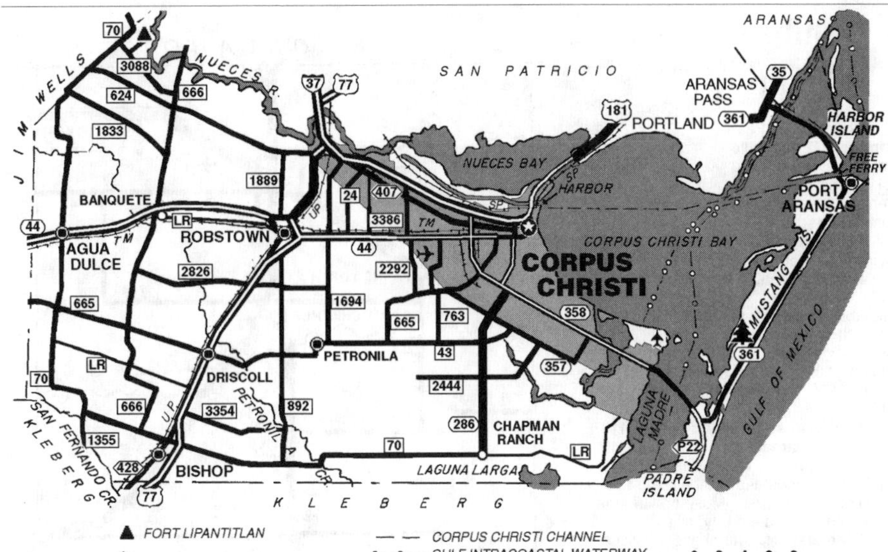

Nueces County

Physical Features: Southern Gulf Coast county; flat, rich soils, broken by bays, Nueces River, Petronila Creek; includes Mustang Island, north tip of Padre Island.

Economy: Diversified economy includes petroleum processing and production; deepwater port facilities; agriculture; tourism, conventions; coastal shipping; manufacturing; military complex.

History: Name is Spanish for nuts; county named for river; created 1846 out of San Patricio County.

Ethnicity, 1990: White, 220,168 (75.6%); Black, 12,691 (4.4%); American Indian, 1,175 (0.4%); Asian, 2,483 (0.9%); Other, 54,628 (18.8%). Hispanic, 152,051 (52.2%).

Vital Statistics, 1993: Births, 5,279; deaths, 2,247; marriages, 2,873; divorces, 1,851.

Recreation: Major resort area; fishing, water sports; Padre Island National Seashore; Mustang Island State Park; Lipantitlan State Historical Park; Art Museum of South Texas, Corpus Christi Museum of Science and History; Texas State Aquarium; various metropolitan events; greyhound race track.

Minerals: Sand and gravel, oil and gas.

Agriculture: A top grain sorghums-producing county; cotton, corn also raised; sunflower seed production introduced. Beef cattle, meat goats and hogs raised.

CORPUS CHRISTI (266,958) county seat; varied manufacturing; petroleum processing; seaport; hospitals; museums; recreation centers; tourist destination; Naval Air Station; Army depot; Texas A&M University-Corpus Christi; Del Mar College; Buccaneer Days; replicas of Columbus' ships on display, U.S.S. Lexington museum.

Other towns include: **Agua Dulce** (811); **Bishop** (3,394), petrochemical, pharmaceutical manufacturing, fall carnival; **Driscoll** (704); **Petronila** (158); **Port Aransas** (2,450) tourism, sea research institute, fishing accomodations, fisheries management, deep sea roundup, birding facility; **Robstown** (13,061) market center for oil, farm area.

Population	**302,479**
(Change fm '90)	3.9
Land Area (sq. mi.)	835.8
Altitude (ft.)	sea level-129
Rainfall (in.)	30.2
Jan. mean min.	46
July mean max.	94
Growing season (days)	309
Civ. Labor	146,883
Unemployed	8.7
Total Wages	$2,822,176,281
Av. Weekly Wage	$445.35
Prop. Value	$11,353,584,147
Retail Sales	$2,779,281,983

For explanation of sources, abbreviations and symbols, see p. 132.

A beach on North Padre Island. Texas Almanac file photo.

Ochiltree County

Physical Features: Panhandle county bordering Oklahoma; level, broken by creeks; deep loam, clay soils.

Economy: Oil; agribusiness, center of large feedlot operations.

History: Created from Bexar District 1876, organized 1889; named for Republic of Texas leader W.B. Ochiltree.

Ethnicity, 1990: White, 8,023 (87.9%); Black, 2 (0.0%); American Indian, 105 (1.2%); Asian, 8 (0.1%); Other, 990 (10.8%). Hispanic, 1,641 (18.0%).

Vital Statistics, 1993: Births, 119; deaths, 80; marriages, 108; divorces, 42.

Recreation: Wolf Creek park; Springfest, Wheatheart of the Nation celebration in August; Museum of the Plains; Indian "Buried City" site.

Minerals: Oil, natural gas, , caliche, sand, gravel.

Agriculture: Beef cattle, hogs; crops include wheat, grain sorghums, corn, hay; 80,000 acres irrigated for most crops.

PERRYTON (7,608) county seat; oil-field services, equipment manufacturing; cattle feeding; grain center; hospital; convention center.

Other towns include: **Farnsworth** (149); **Waka** (145); **Booker** (1,241, mostly in Lipscomb County).

Population	**9,102**
(Change fm '90)	- 0.3
Land Area (sq. mi.)	917.6
Altitude (ft.)	2,642-3,007
Rainfall (in.)	19.6
Jan. mean min.	16
July mean max.	94
Growing season (days)	191
Civ. Labor	4,595
Unemployed	4.5
Total Wages	$73,056,930
Av. Weekly Wage	$413.45
Prop. Value	$520,275,825
Retail Sales	$82,639,012

Oldham County

Physical Features: Northwestern Panhandle county; level, broken by Canadian River and tributaries.

Economy: Ranching center.

History: Created 1876 from Bexar District; organized 1880; named for editor-Confederate senator W.S. Oldham.

Ethnicity, 1990: White, 2,112 (92.7%); Black, 9 (0.4%); American Indian, 29 (1.3%); Asian, 18 (0.8%); Other, 110 (4.8%). Hispanic, 200 (8.8%).

Vital Statistics, 1993: Births, 25; deaths, 18; marriages, 13; divorces, 4.

Recreation: Old Tascosa with Boot Hill Cemetery nearby, pioneer town; County Roundup in August; midway point on old Route 66.

Minerals: Sand and gravel, oil, natural gas, stone.

Agriculture: Beef cattle; crops include wheat, grain sorghums.

VEGA (883) county seat; ranch trade center. Other towns include; **Adrian** (223); **Wildorado** (200). Cal Farley's Boys Ranch.

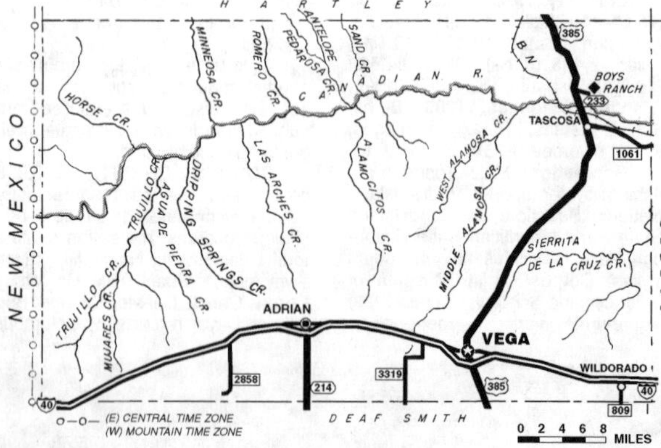

Population	**2,361**
(Change fm '90)	3.6
Land Area (sq. mi.)	1,500.7
Altitude (ft.)	3,238-4,171
Rainfall (in.)	17.4
Jan. mean min.	19
July mean max.	91
Growing season (days)	186
Civ. Labor	1,213
Unemployed	5.3
Total Wages	$14,578,067
Av. Weekly Wage	$336.77
Prop. Value	$167,222,421
Retail Sales	$10,466,677

For explanation of sources, abbrevations and symbols, p. 132.

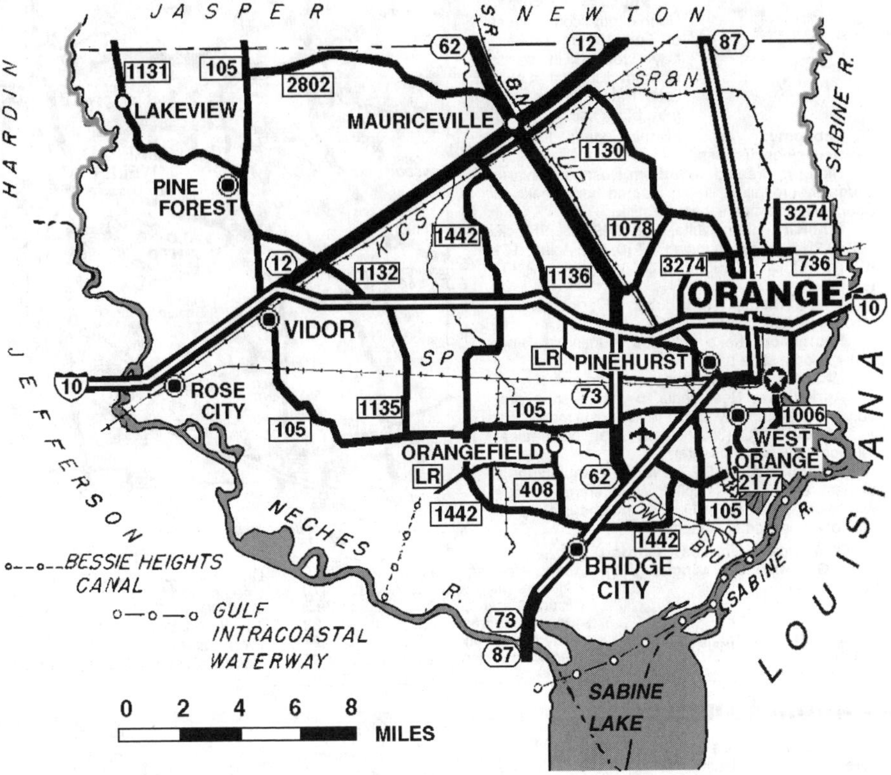

Orange County

Physical Features: In southeastern corner of the state; bounded by Sabine, Neches rivers, Sabine Lake; coastal soils; two-thirds timbered.

Economy: Petrochemicals; shipping; agribusinesses; tourism; lumber processing; county part of Beaumont-Port Arthur metropolitan area.

History: Created from Jefferson County in 1852; named for early orange grove.

Ethnicity, 1990: White, 72,607 (90.2%); Black, 6,768 (8.4%); American Indian, 189 (0.2%); Asian, 484 (0.6%); Other, 461 (0.6%). Hispanic, 1,933 (2.4%).

Vital Statistics, 1993: Births, 1,301; deaths, 722; marriages, 840; divorces, 645.

Recreation: Fishing, hunting; water sports; county park; museums; historical homes; crawfish festivals.

Minerals: Salt, oil, gas, clays, sand and gravel.

Agriculture: Timber, beef cattle, Christmas trees and rice are top revenue sources; honey a significant revenue producer; other agriculture includes vegetable, horses, hogs; hunting leases.

ORANGE (20,102) county seat; seaport; petrochemical plants; varied manufacturing; food, timber processing; shipping; hospital, theater, museums; Lamar University branch; gumbo festival in May.

Other towns include: **Bridge City** (8,490) varied manufacturing; ship repair yard; steel fabrication; fish farming; library; Mayhaw Mania Festival; tallest bridge in South and newer suspension bridge over Neches; stop for Monarch butterfly in fall during its migration to Mexico; **Vidor** (11,636), steel processing; railroad-car refinishing; library; **Mauriceville** (2,210); **Pine Forest** (790); **Pinehurst** (2,759); **Rose City** (630); **West Orange** (4,625).

Population	**85,348**
(Change fm '90)	6.0
Land Area (sq. mi.)	356.4
Altitude (ft.)	sea level-25
Rainfall (in.)	59.2
Jan. mean min.	40
July mean max.	91
Growing season (days)	240
Civ. Labor	41,725
Unemployed	12.2
Total Wages	$610,053,882
Av. Weekly Wage	$502.56
Prop. Value	$3,621,002,620
Retail Sales	$492,649,980

For explanation of sources, abbreviations and symbols, see p. 132.

Palo Pinto County

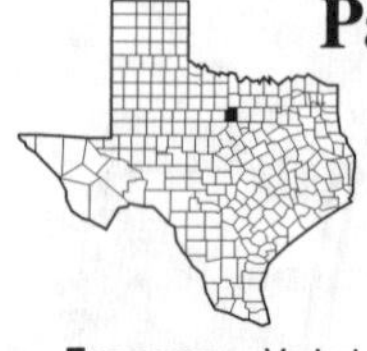

Physical Features: North central county west of Fort Worth; broken, hilly, wooded in parts; Possum Kingdom Lake, Lake Palo Pinto; sandy, gray, black soils.

Economy: Varied manufacturing; tourism; petroleum; agribusiness.

History: Created 1856 from Bosque, Navarro counties; organized 1857; named for creek (in Spanish name means painted stick).

Ethnicity, 1990: White, 22,810 (91.0%); Black, 792 (3.2%); American Indian, 87 (0.3%); Asian, 171 (0.7%); Other, 1,195 (4.8%). Hispanic, 2,301 (9.2%).

Vital Statistics, 1993: Births, 347; deaths, 320; marriages, 242; divorces, 162.

Recreation: Lake activities; hunting, fishing, water sports; state park.

Minerals: Oil, gas, clays, sand and gravel.

Agriculture: Beef cattle, prime revenue producer; wheat and hay; cedar fence posts marketed.

PALO PINTO (350) county seat; old settlers reunion; government center.

Mineral Wells (15,256) varied manufacturing; tourism; agriculture; hospital; Weatherford College extension; Crazy Water Festival in June; state park east of city in Parker County.

Other towns include: **Gordon** (456), **Graford** (566), **Mingus** (219), **Strawn** (691).

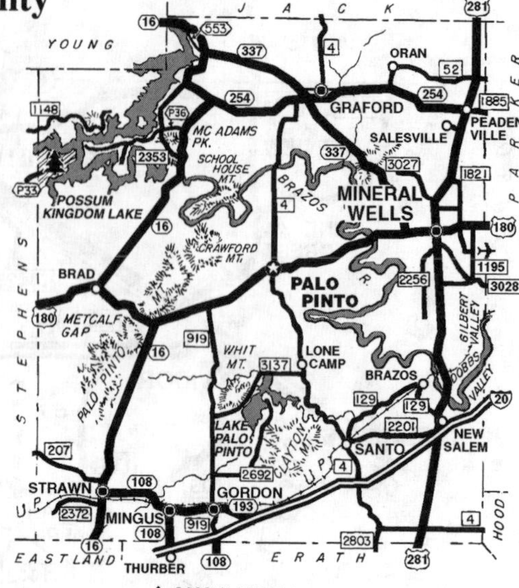

Population 25,711
(Change fm '90) 2.6

Land Area (sq. mi.) 952.9
Altitude (ft.) 782-1,470
Rainfall (in.) 29.3
Jan. mean min. 32
July mean max. 97
Growing season (days) 221

Civ. Labor 12,387
Unemployed 8.6
Total Wages $141,614,513
Av. Weekly Wage $359.27
Prop. Value $984,579,910
Retail Sales $182,262,427

Panola County

Physical Features: East Texas county; sixty percent forested, rolling plain; broken by Sabine, Murvaul Creek and Lake, Toledo Bend Reservoir.

Economy: Agribusinesses; varied manufacturing; forest industries; gas processing; oil-field operation.

History: Name is Indian word for cotton; created from Harrison, Shelby counties 1846.

Vital Statistics, 1993: Births, 273; deaths, 224; marriages, 215; divorces, 137.

Ethnicity, 1990: White, 17,702 (80.3%); Black, 4,057 (18.4%); American Indian, 57 (0.3%); Asian, 23 (0.1%); Other, 196 (0.9%). Hispanic, 477 (2.2%).

Recreation: Lake fishing, other water activities; hunting; scenic drives; Jim Reeves memorial; historic sites, homes; museum.

Minerals: Natural gas, oil, coal.

Agriculture: A leading broiler-producing county; cattle, hogs also raised; timber sales significant.

CARTHAGE (6,724) county seat; petroleum processing; poultry; sawmills; hospital; junior college.

Other towns include: **Beckville** (853), **DeBerry** (191), **Gary** (280). Also, **Tatum** (1,322) mostly in Rusk County).

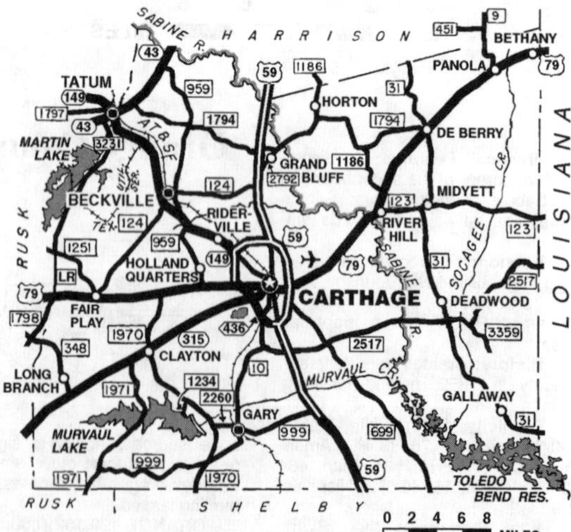

Population **22,653**
(Change fm '90) 2.8
Land Area (sq. mi.) 800.9
Altitude (ft.) 192-481
Rainfall (in.) 46.2
Jan. mean min. 37
July mean max. 95
Growing season (days) 240
Civ. Labor 8,178

Unemployed 10.7
Total Wages $113,768,846
Av. Weekly Wage $362.20
Prop. Value $1,817,539,545
Retail Sales $104,222,276

For explanation of sources, abbreviations and symbols, see p. 132.

Parker County

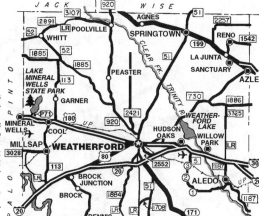

Physical Features: Hilly, broken by Brazos, Trinity tributaries, lakes; varied soils.

Economy: Agribusiness; varied manufacturing; many residents work in Fort Worth; county part of Fort Worth-Arlington metropolitan area.

History: Named for pioneer legislator Isaac Parker; created 1855 from Bosque, Navarro counties.

Ethnicity, 1990: White, 62,267 (96.1%); Black, 589 (0.9%); American Indian, 367 (0.6%); Asian, 231 (0.4%); Other, 1,331 (2.1%). Hispanic, 2,697 (4.2%).

Vital Statistics, 1993: Births, 952; deaths, 540; marriages, 626; divorces, 468.

Recreation: Railroad museum; park; water sports; state park; nature trails; hunting; horse racing at Trinity Meadows; peach festival and frontier days; first Monday trade days monthly.

Minerals: Natural gas, oil, stone, sand and gravel, clays.

Agriculture: Beef cattle, hay, dairies, horses chief income source; horticultural plants, peaches, peanuts, pecans raised; firewood.

WEATHERFORD (15,267) county seat; agribusiness center; varied manufacturing; hospital; Weatherford College.

Other towns include: **Hudson Oaks** (991); **Millsap** (531); **Reno** (2,387); **Sanctuary** (256); **Springtown** (1,788); **Willow Park** (2,442). Also, **Azle** (9,705) mostly in Tarrant County, and part of **Mineral Wells.**

Population	**67,101**
(Change fm '90)	3.6
Land Area (sq. mi.)	903.5
Altitude (ft.)	718-966
Rainfall (in.)	31.1
Jan. mean min.	30
July mean max.	97

Growing season (days)	225
Civ. Labor	34,964
Unemployed	5.5
Total Wages	$256,485,823
Av. Weekly Wage	$365.89
Prop. Value	$2,556,769,716
Retail Sales	$541,116,580

Parmer County

Physical Features: Western High Plains, broken by draws, playas; sandy, clay, loam soils.

Economy: Cattle feeding; grain elevators; meat-packing plant; varied other agribusinesses.

History: Named for Republic figure Martin Parmer; created from Bexar District 1876, organized 1907.

Ethnicity, 1990: White, 8,980 (91.0%); Black, 123 (1.2%); American Indian, 29 (0.3%); Asian, 24 (0.2%); Other, 707 (7.2%). Hispanic, 4,096 (41.5%).

Vital Statistics, 1993: Births, 170; deaths, 91; marriages, 290; divorces, 37.

Recreation: Border Town Days.

Minerals: Not significant.

Agriculture: Among leading counties in total farm income. Beef cattle; crops include corn, grain sorghums, wheat, sugar beets, cotton; soybeans and vegetables also raised; 190,000 acres irrigated.

FARWELL (1,413) county seat; agribusiness center; grain storage; plants make farm equipment.

Friona (3,708) grain elevators, meat packing, feedlots, hospital; Maize Days in September.

Other towns include: **Bovina** (1,656) farm trade center.

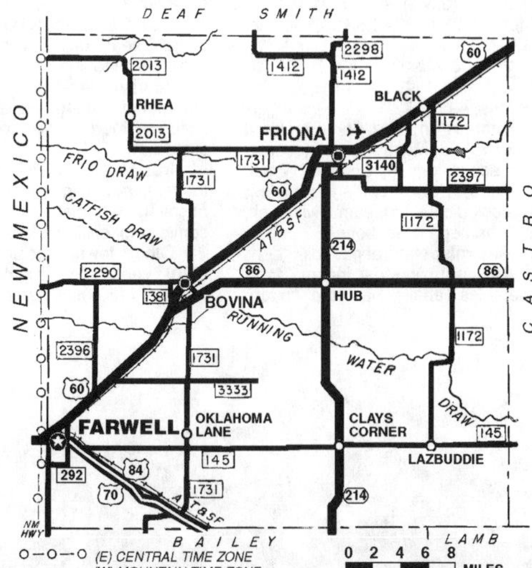

Population	**10,004**
(Change fm '90)	1.4
Land Area (sq. mi.)	881.7
Altitude (ft.)	3,926-4,163
Rainfall (in.)	15.3
Jan. mean min.	21
July mean max.	91

Growing season (days)	183
Civ. Labor	4,388
Unemployed	4.5
Total Wages	$83,747,512
Av. Weekly Wage	$374.07
Prop. Value	$455,700,324
Retail Sales	$39,895,875

For explanation of sources, abbreviations and symbols, see p. 132.

Pecos County

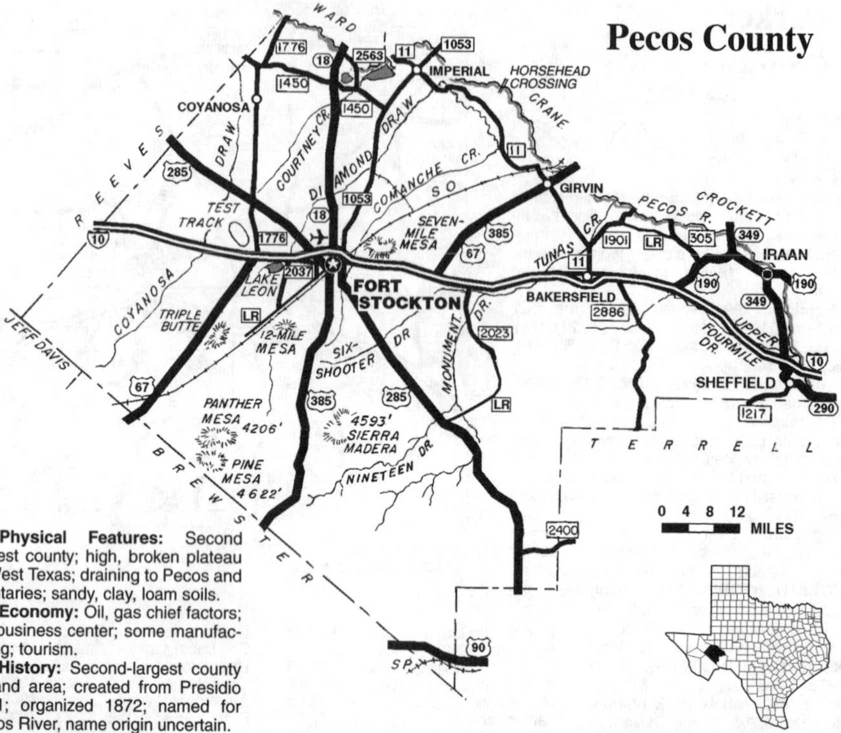

Physical Features: Second largest county; high, broken plateau in West Texas; draining to Pecos and tributaries; sandy, clay, loam soils.

Economy: Oil, gas chief factors; agribusiness center; some manufacturing; tourism.

History: Second-largest county in land area; created from Presidio 1871; organized 1872; named for Pecos River, name origin uncertain.

Ethnicity, 1990: White, 9,449 (64.4%); Black, 62 (0.4%); American Indian, 45 (0.3%); Asian, 31 (0.2%); Other, 5,088 (34.7%). Hispanic, 4,331 (56.8%).

Vital Statistics, 1993: Births, 205; deaths, 123; marriages, 83; divorces, 49.

Recreation: Old Fort Stockton, Annie Riggs Museum, stagecoach stop; scenic drives; Dinosaur Track Roadside Park; cattle-trail sites; archaeological museum with oil, ranch-heritage collections.

Minerals: Natural gas, oil.

Agriculture: Most income from vegetables, alfalfa hay and cotton; beef cattle, sheep, goats raised; other crops include pecans, grapes and sesame; 22,000 acres irrigated.

FORT STOCKTON (9,518) county seat; distribution center for petroleum industry; oil, gas processing; tourism; tire-testing center; varied manufacturing; winery; hospital; historical tours; junior college extension.

Iraan (1,338), oil, gas center, tourism; ranching, meat processing, hospital, birthplace of Alley Oop comic strip, chili, brisket cookoff.

Other towns include: **Imperial** (720) center for irrigated farming; **Sheffield** (600) oil, gas center.

Population	**15,730**
(Change fm '90)	7.2
Land Area (sq. mi.)	4,764.0
Altitude (ft.)	2,168-4,797
Rainfall (in.)	12.2
Jan. mean min.	30
July mean max.	95
Growing season (days)	224
Civ. Labor	6,914
Unemployed	7.5
Total Wages	$94,048,510
Av. Weekly Wage	$377.66
Prop. Value	$3,200,788,422
Retail Sales	$94,755,297

For explanation of sources, abbreviations and symbols, see p. 132.

Mesas of West Texas. Texas Highway Department photo.

Polk County

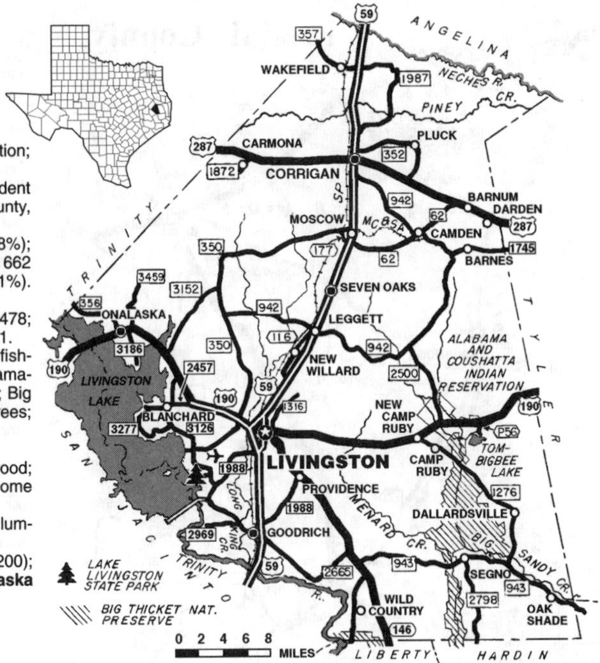

Physical Features: Rolling; densely forested, with Big Thicket, unique plant, animal life; Neches, Trinity rivers, tributaries.

Economy: Timber; lumber production; tourism; oil.

History: Named for U.S. President James K. Polk; created from Liberty County, organized 1846.

Ethnicity, 1990: White, 25,100 (81.8%); Black, 3,896 (12.7%); American Indian, 662 (2.2%); Asian, 78 (0.3%); Other, 951 (3.1%). Hispanic, 1,610 (5.2%).

Vital Statistics, 1993: Births, 478; deaths, 458; marriages, 305; divorces, 91.

Recreation: Lake and state park; fishing, other water activities; hunting; Alabama-Coushatta Indian Reservation, museum; Big Thicket; woodlands trails, champion trees; historic homes.

Minerals: Oil, gas, sand, gravel.

Agriculture: Timber and hardwood; peaches, hay, vegetables raised; income also from beef cattle, horses.

LIVINGSTON (5,585) county seat; lumber, tourism, oil center.

Other towns include: **Camden** (1,200); **Corrigan** (1,833), plywood plant; **Onalaska** (803); **Moscow** (170) historic sites.

Population............................**32,577**
(Change fm '90)............................6.2
Land Area (sq. mi.)..............1,057.3
Altitude (ft.)............................68-404
Rainfall (in.)..................................48.0
Jan. mean min...............................37
July mean max..............................94
Growing season (days).............224
Civ. Labor..............................14,276
Unemployed..................................7.7
Total Wages..............$161,567,273
Av. Weekly Wage....................$368.82
Prop. Value............$1,473,501,511
Retail Sales...............$273,006,957

Potter County

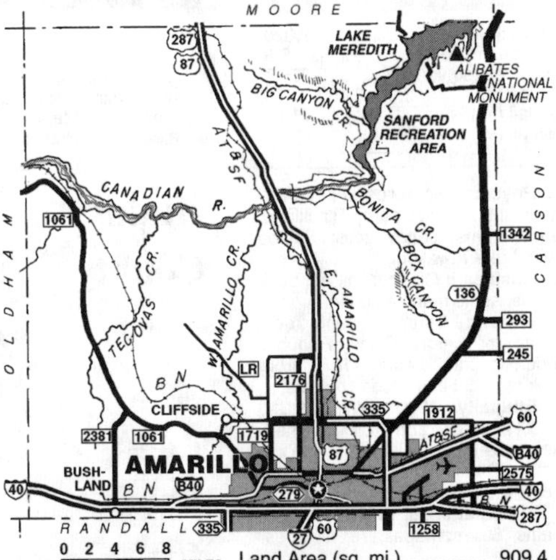

Physical Features: Panhandle county; mostly level, part rolling; broken by Canadian River and tributaries; sandy, sandy loam, chocolate loam, clay soils; Lake Meredith.

Economy: Transportation, distribution hub for large area; feedlot operations; petrochemicals; gas processing; agribusinesses.

History: Named for Robert Potter, Republic leader; created 1876 from Bexar District; organized 1887.

Ethnicity, 1990: White, 73,884 (75.5%); Black, 8,673 (8.9%); American Indian, 901 (0.9%); Asian, 2,570 (2.6%); Other, 11,846 (12.1%). Hispanic, 19,246 (19.7%).

Vital Statistics, 1993: Births, 1,958; deaths, 1,123; marriages, 1,801; divorces, 645.

Recreation: Metropolitan activities, events; lake activities; Alibates Flint Quarries National Monument; hunting, fishing; Tri-State Fair.

Minerals: Natural gas, oil.

Agriculture: Beef cattle; wheat, sorghums, corn, sugar beets are chief crops; 18,000 acres irrigated.

AMARILLO (163,569, part in Randall County) county seat; hub for northern Panhandle oil, ranching; distribution, marketing center; tourism; varied manufacturing; food processing; hospitals; museum; varied cultural, recreational events; Amarillo College, Texas Tech medical, engineering schools; Texas State Technical College branch; Quarter Horse Heritage Center; "Texas" drama, cowboy breakfasts during summer.

Population..........................**101,700**
(Change fm '90)............................3.9
Land Area (sq. mi.)..................909.4
Altitude (ft.)....................3,047-3,824
Rainfall (in.)..................................19.1
Jan. mean min.................................22
July mean max.................................91
Growing season (days)..............190
Civ. Labor................................51,815
Unemployed....................................5.3
Total Wages...............$1,408,573,746
Av. Weekly Wage....................$427.12
Prop. Value...............$3,586,125,502
Retail Sales...............$1,669,654,206

Presidio County

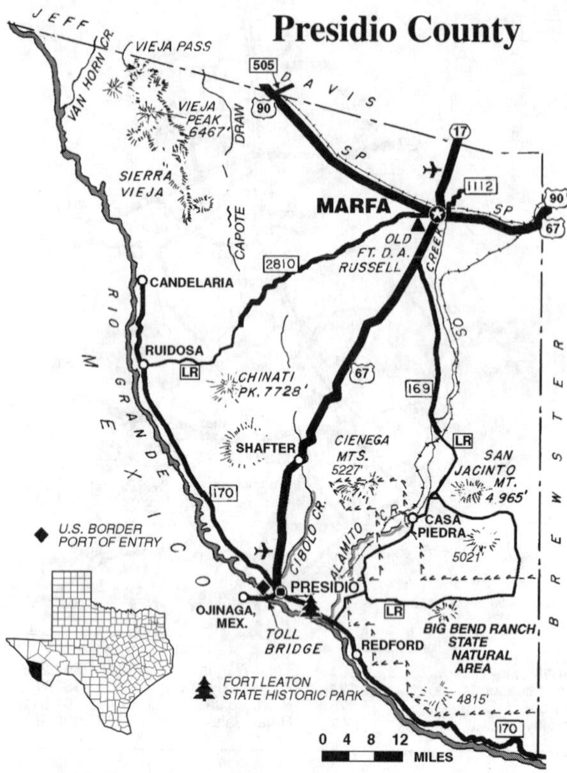

Physical Features: Rugged, some of Texas' tallest mountains; scenic drives; clays, loams, sandy loams on uplands; intermountain wash; timber sparse; Capote Falls, state's highest.

Economy: Ranching; government employment; hunting leases; tourism.

History: Created 1850 from Bexar District; organized 1875; named for Spanish Presidio del Norte (fort of the north).

Ethnicity, 1990: White, 5,624 (84.7%); Black, 6 (0.1%); American Indian, 16 (0.2%); Asian, 16 (0.2%); Other, 975 (14.7%). Hispanic, 5,417 (81.6%).

Vital Statistics, 1993: Births, 136; deaths, 48; marriages, 64; divorces, 12.

Recreation: Mild climate and scenic surroundings; hunting; scenic drives along Rio Grande, in mountains; ghost towns, mysterious Marfa Lights; Fort D.A. Russell; Big Bend Ranch State Natural Area; hot springs.

Minerals: Sand and gravel.

Agriculture: Most income from calf sales, breeder and stocker cattle; horses raised; Top crops include onions, hay, cantaloupes, honeydew melons; 5,500 acres irrigated near Rio Grande.

MARFA (2,515) county seat; ranching supply, Border Patrol sector headquarters; tourist center; gateway to mountainous area; Old Timers Roping in April.

Presidio (3,230), international bridge to Ojinaga, Mex.; gateway to Mexico's West Coast by rail; Fort Leaton State Park ; Onion Festival in May.

Other towns include: **Shafter** (31) old mining town.

Population	**7,020**
(Change fm '90)	5.8
Land Area (sq. mi.)	3,855.7
Altitude (ft.)	2,400-7,730
Rainfall (in.) Marfa	15.9
Rainfall (in.) Presidio	10.8
Jan. mean min. Marfa	26
Jan. mean min. Presidio	34
July mean max. Marfa	90
July mean max. Presidio	102
Growing season (days)	238
Civ. Labor	3,448
Unemployed	34.6
Total Wages	$20,075,306
Av. Weekly Wage	$289.45
Prop. Value	$233,371,464
Retail Sales	$27,347,721

Rains County

Physical Features: Northeastern county; rolling; partly Blackland, sandy loams, sandy soils; Sabine River, Lake Tawakoni.

Business: Oil, tourism, agribusinesses, some manufacturing.

History: County, county seat named for Emory Rains, Republic leader; county created 1870 from Hopkins, Hunt and Wood counties.

Ethnicity, 1990: White, 6,310 (94.0%); Black, 286 (4.3%); American Indian, 29 (0.4%); Asian, 8 (0.1%); Other, 82 (1.2%). Hispanic, 158 (2.4%).

Vital Statistics, 1993: Births, 60; deaths, 69; marriages, 70; divorces, 40.

Recreation: Lake Tawakoni and Lake Fork Reservoir activities.

Minerals: Gas, oil and coal.

Agriculture: Beef, dairy cattle; crops are vegetables, watermelons, sweet potatoes, hay; greenhouses.

EMORY (973) county seat; local trade, tourism; some manufacturing.

Other towns include: **East Tawakoni** (687), **Point** (697).

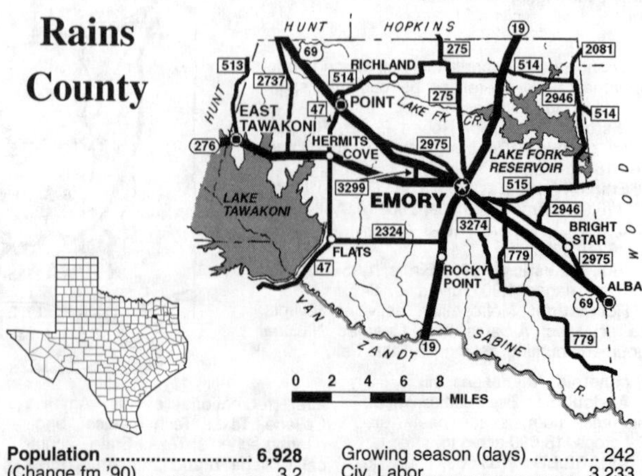

Population	**6,928**
(Change fm '90)	3.2
Land Area (sq. mi.)	232.0
Altitude (ft.)	406-491
Rainfall (in.)	42.2
Jan. mean min.	31
July mean max.	95
Growing season (days)	242
Civ. Labor	3,233
Unemployed	5.5
Total Wages	$18,168,184
Av. Weekly Wage	$335.96
Prop. Value	$303,523,921
Retail Sales	$27,979,506

Randall County

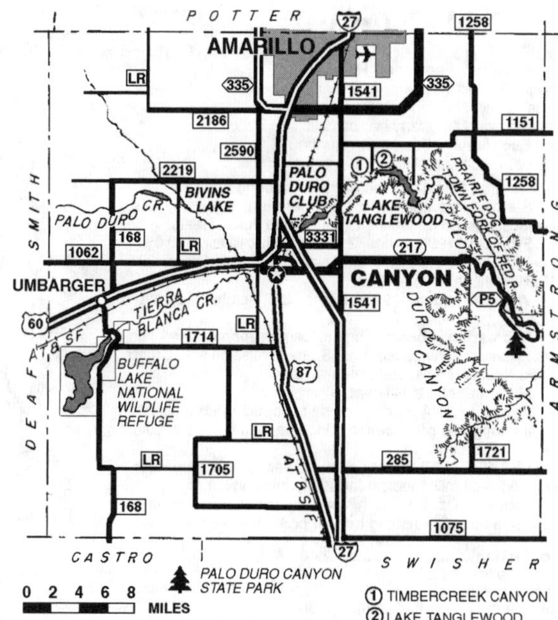

Physical Features: Northwestern county; level, but broken by scenic Palo Duro Canyon, Buffalo Lake; silty clay, loam soils.

Economy: Agribusinesses; education; some manufacturing; tourism; part of Amarillo metropolitan area.

History: Created 1876 from Bexar District; organized 1889; named for Confederate Gen. Horace Randal (name misspelled in statute).

Ethnicity, 1990: White, 84,633 (94.4%); Black, 1,115 (1.2%); American Indian, 454 (0.5%); Asian, 646 (0.7%); Other, 2,825 (3.2%). Hispanic, 6,144 (6.9%).

Vital Statistics, 1993: Births, 1,280; deaths, 598; marriages, 251; divorces, 592.

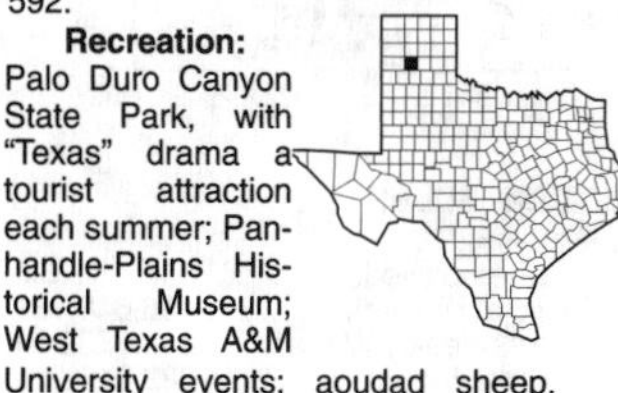

Recreation: Palo Duro Canyon State Park, with "Texas" drama a tourist attraction each summer; Panhandle-Plains Historical Museum; West Texas A&M University events; aoudad sheep, migratory waterfowl hunting in season; Buffalo Lake National Wildlife Refuge.

Minerals: Not significant.

Agriculture: Beef, dairy cattle, horses; wheat, sorghum principal crops; 61,000 acres irrigated.

CANYON (11,918) county seat; West Texas A&M University, a major economic factor; ranching, feedlot, farm center; light manufacturing; gateway to state park; hospital.

Other towns include: **Umbarger** (327). A significant part of **Amarillo** (163,569) lies in the county.

Population **93,821**
(Change fm '90) 4.6
Land Area (sq. mi.) 914.4
Altitude (ft.) 3,158-3,748

Rainfall (in.) 18.4
Jan. mean min. 23
July mean max. 92
Growing season (days) 195
Civ. Labor 55,731
Unemployed 3.0
Total Wages $363,599,684
Av. Weekly Wage $384.21
Prop. Value $2,737,669,603
Retail Sales $609,500,515

Reagan County

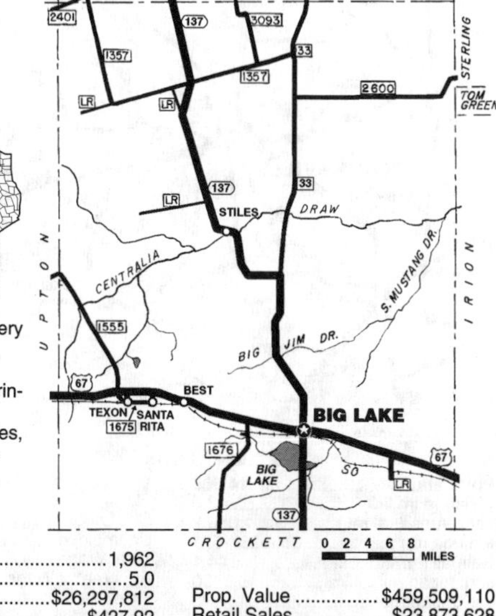

Physical Features: Western county; level to hilly, broken by draws, Big Lake; sandy, loam, clay soils.

Business: Oil production; natural gas; ranching.

History: Named for Sen. John H. Reagan, first chairman, Texas Railroad Commission; county created 1903 from Tom Green County.

Ethnicity, 1990: White, 3,550 (78.6%); Black, 127 (2.8%); American Indian, 7 (0.2%); Asian, 1 (0.0%); Other, 829 (18.4%). Hispanic, 1,941 (43.0%).

Vital Statistics, 1991: Births, 61; deaths, 26; marriages, 25; divorces, 13.

Recreation: Texon reunion; rodeo; site of 1923 discovery well Santa Rita No. 1 on University of Texas land.

Minerals: Gas, oil.

Agriculture: Beef cattle, goats, sheep; cotton, grains principal crops; grapes introduced; substantial irrigated.

BIG LAKE (3,735) county seat; center for oil activities, ranching trade; hospital; Brisket Cook-off in August.

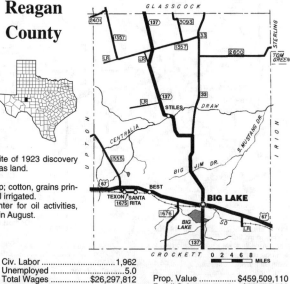

Population **4,623**
(Change fm '90) 2.4
Land Area (sq. mi.) 1,175.4
Altitude (ft.) 2,406-2,953
Rainfall (in.) 19.5
Jan. mean min. 28
July mean max. 94
Growing season (days) 229

Civ. Labor 1,962
Unemployed 5.0
Total Wages $26,297,812
Av. Weekly Wage $427.92

Prop. Value $459,509,110
Retail Sales $23,873,628

Real County

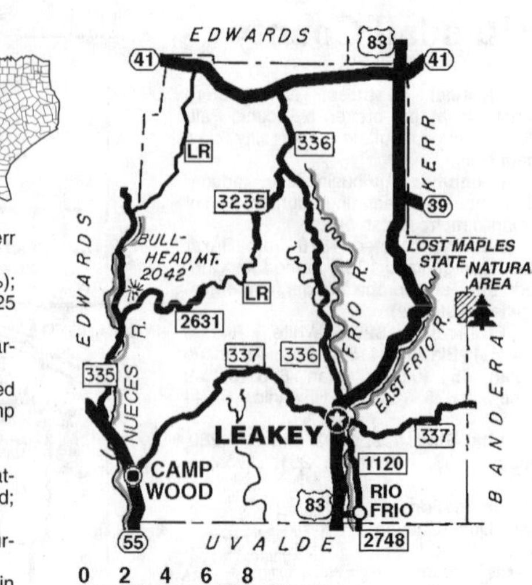

Physical Features: Hill Country, spring-fed streams, scenic canyons; Frio, Nueces rivers; cedars, pecans, walnuts, many live oaks.

Economy: Tourism, hunting leases; ranch supplies; cedar sales; popular area for artists, recreational "second homes."

History: Created 1913 from Bandera, Edwards, Kerr counties; named for legislator-ranchman Julius Real.

Ethnicity, 1990: White, 2,064 (85.6%); Black, 0 (0.0%); American Indian, 23 (1.0%); Asian, 0 (0.0%); Other, 325 (13.5%). Hispanic, 574 (23.8%).

Vital Statistics, 1993: Births, 35; deaths, 52; marriages, 22; divorces, 12.

Recreation: Tourist, hunting center; many deer killed each season; fishing; camping; Spanish mission site, Camp Wood; scenic drives; state natural area.

Minerals: Not significant.

Agriculture: A leading mohair-producing county; cattle, sheep, goats produce most income; some pecans sold; cedar post processed.

LEAKEY (406) county seat; center for ranching, tourism; cedar-oil mill; medical facilities; July Jubilee.

CAMP WOOD (711) historic site; settlers reunion in August; a tourist, ranching hub for parts of three counties.

Population	**2,487**
(Change fm '90)	3.1
Land Area (sq. mi.)	699.9
Altitude (ft.)	1,494-2,381
Rainfall (in.)	25.7
Jan. mean min.	31
July mean max.	92
Growing season (days)	236
Civ. Labor	1,162
Unemployed	6.8
Total Wages	$6,648,182
Av. Weekly Wage	$233.24
Prop. Value	$289,915,555
Retail Sales	$10,368,836

Red River County

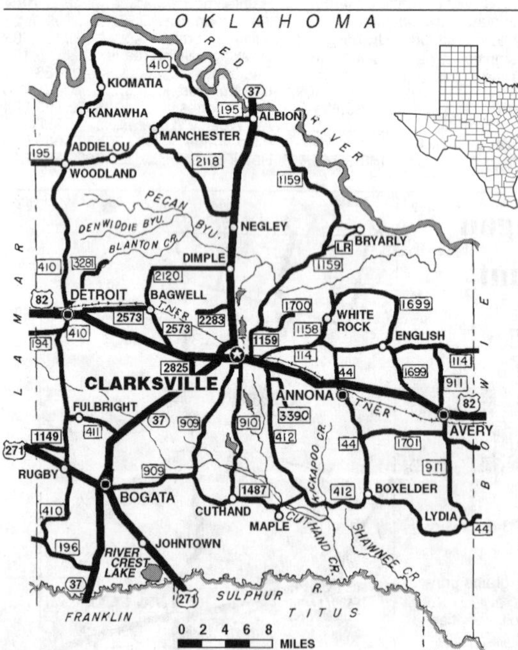

Physical Features: On Red-Sulphur rivers' divide; 39 different soil types; half timbered.

Economy: Agribusinesses; lumbering; manufacturing.

History: One of the oldest counties, settlers were moving in from the United States by the 1810s. Created 1836 as original county of the Republic; organized 1837; named for Red River, its northern boundary.

Ethnicity, 1990: White, 11,203 (78.2%); Black, 2,872 (20.1%); American Indian, 75 (0.5%); Asian, 14 (0.1%); Other, 153 (1.1%). Hispanic, 273 (1.9%).

Vital Statistics, 1993: Births, 186; deaths, 222; marriages, 134; divorces, 80.

Recreation: Historical sites include pioneer homes, birthplace of John Nance Garner; water activities; hunting.

Minerals: Small oil flow, gas.

Agriculture: Beef calves, stocker cattle; soybeans, wheat, cotton and corn are principal crops; timber sales substantial.

CLARKSVILLE (4,396) county seat; varied manufacturing; hospital; library; century-old courthouse; Historical Society bazaar in October.

Other towns include: **Annona** (347); **Avery** (462); **Bogata** (1,415) serves farming area; **Detroit** (756) commercial center in west.

Population	**14,608**
(Change fm '90)	2.0
Land Area (sq. mi.)	1,050.2
Altitude (ft.)	287-525
Rainfall (in.)	44.1
Jan. mean min.	30
July mean max.	93
Growing season (days)	234
Civ. Labor	5,903
Unemployed	8.0
Total Wages	$53,864,241
Av. Weekly Wage	$309.57
Prop. Value	$509,990,941
Retail Sales	$68,429,588

For explanation of sources, abbreviations and symbols, see p. 132.

The Frio River orginates in Real County in the Hill Country. Texas Almanac file photo.

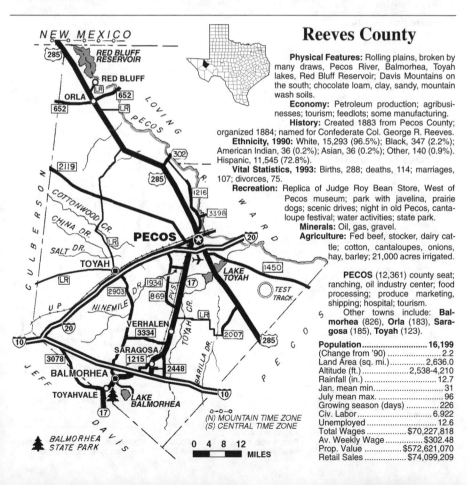

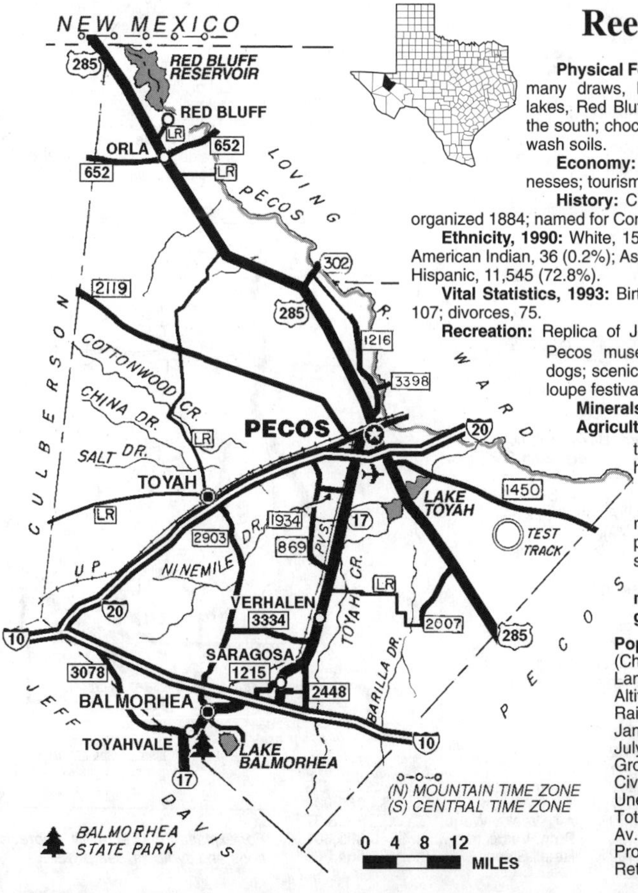

Reeves County

Physical Features: Rolling plains, broken by many draws, Pecos River, Balmorhea, Toyah lakes, Red Bluff Reservoir; Davis Mountains on the south; chocolate loam, clay, sandy, mountain wash soils.

Economy: Petroleum production; agribusinesses; tourism; feedlots; some manufacturing.

History: Created 1883 from Pecos County; organized 1884; named for Confederate Col. George R. Reeves.

Ethnicity, 1990: White, 15,293 (96.5%); Black, 347 (2.2%); American Indian, 36 (0.2%); Asian, 36 (0.2%); Other, 140 (0.9%). Hispanic, 11,545 (72.8%).

Vital Statistics, 1993: Births, 288; deaths, 114; marriages, 107; divorces, 75.

Recreation: Replica of Judge Roy Bean Store, West of Pecos museum; park with javelina, prairie dogs; scenic drives; night in old Pecos, cantaloupe festival; water activities; state park.

Minerals: Oil, gas, gravel.

Agriculture: Fed beef, stocker, dairy cattle; cotton, cantaloupes, onions, hay, barley; 21,000 acres irrigated.

PECOS (12,361) county seat; ranching, oil industry center; food processing; produce marketing, shipping; hospital; tourism.

Other towns include: **Balmorhea** (826), **Orla** (183), **Saragosa** (185), **Toyah** (123).

Population	**16,199**
(Change from '90)	2.2
Land Area (sq. mi.)	2,636.0
Altitude (ft.)	2,538-4,210
Rainfall (in.)	12.7
Jan. mean min.	31
July mean max.	96
Growing season (days)	226
Civ. Labor	6.922
Unemployed	12.6
Total Wages	$70,227,818
Av. Weekly Wage	$302.48
Prop. Value	$572,621,070
Retail Sales	$74,099,209

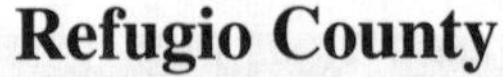

Refugio County

Physical Features: Coastal plain, broken by streams, bays; sandy, loam, black soils; mesquite, oak, huisache motts.

Economy: Petroleum, petrochemical production, agribusinesses, tourism.

History: Mission, for which the county is named, Our Lady of Refuge, was established here in the 1790s. Original county of the Republic created 1836, organized 1837.

Ethnicity, 1990: White, 6,201 (77.7%); Black, 645 (8.1%); American Indian, 25 (0.3%); Asian, 5 (0.1%); Other, 1,100 (13.8%). Hispanic, 3,164 (39.7%).

Vital Statistics, 1993: Births, 103; deaths, 97; marriages, 67; divorces, 34.

Recreation: Water activities; hunting, fishing; historic sites; chili cook-off in August; wildlife refuge, home of the whooping crane.

Minerals: Oil, natural gas.

Agriculture: Cotton, sorghums and corn; beef cattle; hunting leases; soybeans, sunflowers introduced.

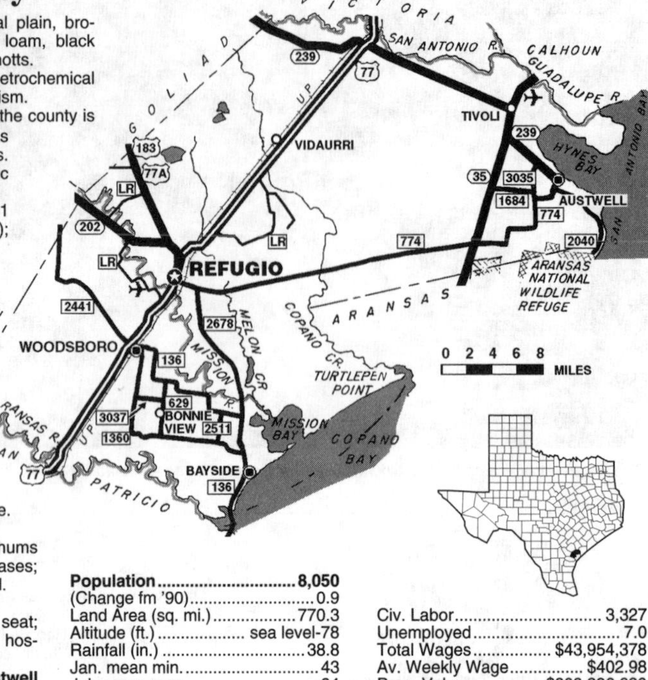

REFUGIO (3,165) county seat; petroleum, agribusiness center; hospital; museum, historic homes.

Other towns include: **Austwell** (198), **Bayside** (426) resorts, **Woodsboro** (1,789) commercial center.

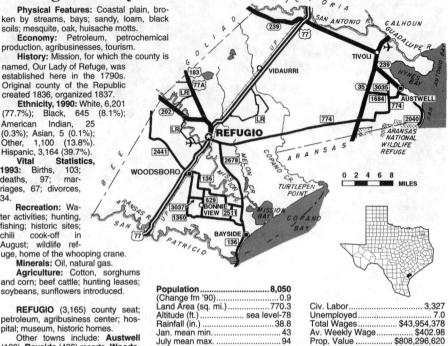

Population	**8,050**
(Change fm '90)	0.9
Land Area (sq. mi.)	770.3
Altitude (ft.)	sea level-78
Rainfall (in.)	38.8
Jan. mean min.	43
July mean max.	94
Growing season (days)	304
Civ. Labor	3,327
Unemployed	7.0
Total Wages	$43,954,378
Av. Weekly Wage	$402.98
Prop. Value	$808,296,620
Retail Sales	$40,452,271

Roberts County

Physical Features: Rolling, broken by Canadian and tributaries; Red Deer Creek; black, sandy loam, alluvial soils.

Economy: Agribusinesses; oil-field operations.

History: Created 1876 from Bexar District; organized 1889; named for Texas leaders John S. Roberts and Gov. O.M. Roberts.

Ethnicity, 1990: White, 1,002 (97.8%); Black, 0 (0.0%); American Indian, 1 (0.1%); Asian, 2 (0.2%); Other, 20 (2.0%). Hispanic, 34 (3.3%).

Vital Statistics, 1993: Births, 7; deaths, 6; marriages, 2; divorces, 3.

Recreation: National cow-calling contest; scenic drives; museum.

Minerals: Production of gas, oil.

Agriculture: Beef cattle top producer; hogs raised; wheat, milo, corn, hay; 9,000 acres irrigated.

MIAMI (570) county seat; ranching, oil center; some manufacturing.

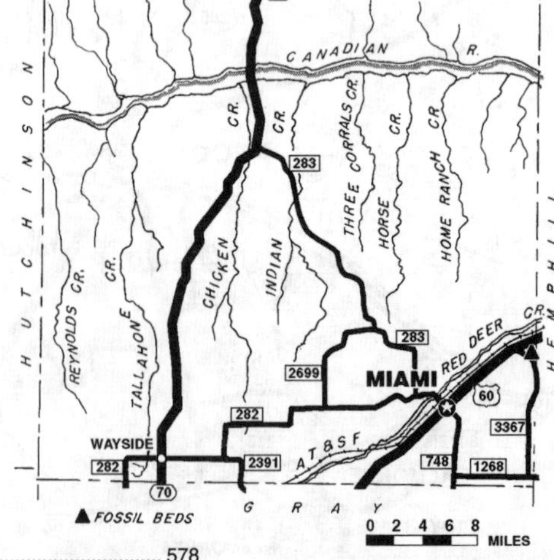

Population	**910**
(Change fm '90)	- 11.2
Land Area (sq. mi.)	924.1
Altitude (ft.)	2,467-3,219
Rainfall (in.)	20.7
Jan. mean min.	19
July mean max.	94
Growing season (days)	192
Civ. Labor	578
Unemployed	5.3
Total Wages	$4,365,904
Av. Weekly Wage	$378.37
Prop. Value	$246,395,801
Retail Sales	$1,864,996

For explanation of sources, abbreviations and symbols, see p. 132.

Robertson County

Physical Features: Rolling in north and east, draining to bottoms along Brazos, Navasota rivers; sandy soils, heavy in bottoms.

Economy: Agribusiness; brick manufacturing; power-generating plant.

History: Among first counties, created 1837, organized 1838, subdivided into many others later; named for pioneer Sterling Clack Robertson.

Ethnicity, 1990: White, 10,047 (64.8%); Black, 4,259 (27.5%); American Indian, 36 (0.2%); Asian, 15 (0.1%); Other, 1,154 (7.4%). Hispanic, 1,904 (12.3%).

Vital Statistics, 1993: Births, 275; deaths, 186; marriages, 81; divorces, 47.

Recreation: Hunting, fishing; historic sites; historic-homes tour; dogwood trails, wildlife preserves.

Minerals: Gas, oil, lignite coal.

Agriculture: Most revenue from beef cattle, cotton and hay; 20,000 acres irrigated, mostly cotton.

FRANKLIN (1,436) county seat; farm-trade center, power plants; old settlers day in July.

Hearne (5,355), some manufacturing; hospital.

Other towns include: **Bremond** (1,182) Polish Days; **Calvert** (1,573) tourism; antiques; tour of homes in April.

Population **16,006**
(Change fm '90) 3.2
Land Area (sq. mi.) 854.6
Altitude (ft.).......................... 277-491
Rainfall (in.) 39.3

Jan. mean min. 37
July mean max. 96
Growing season (days) 268
Civ. Labor.............................. 6,808

Unemployed 6.1
Total Wages $67,804,065
Av. Weekly Wage $382.13
Prop. Value............ $1,493,136,860
Retail Sales $55,100,964

Rockwall County

Physical Features: Rolling prairie, mostly Blackland soil; Lake Ray Hubbard.

Economy: Industrial employment in local plants and in Dallas; in Dallas metropolitan area; tourist and residential development around Lake Ray Hubbard.

History: Texas' smallest county; created 1873 from Kaufman; named for wall-like rock formation.

Ethnicity, 1990: White, 23,991 (93.7%); Black, 855 (3.3%); American Indian, 102 (0.4%); Asian, 164 (0.6%); Other, 492 (1.9%). Hispanic, 1,500 (5.9%).

Vital Statistics, 1993: Births, 479; deaths, 182; marriages, 1,726; divorces, 192.

Recreation: Lake activities; proximity to Dallas; unusual rock outcrop.

Minerals: Not significant.

Agriculture: Most income from cow-calf operations, horses increasing; crops include wheat, grain sorghums, hay; some firewood sold.

ROCKWALL (11,855) county seat; varied manufacturing; hospital; youth fair in April.

Other towns include: **Heath** (2,487); **Fate** (217); **McLendon-Chisholm** (747); **Royse City** (2,490, part in Collin County), varied manufacturing, Funfest in October, North Texas Speedway.

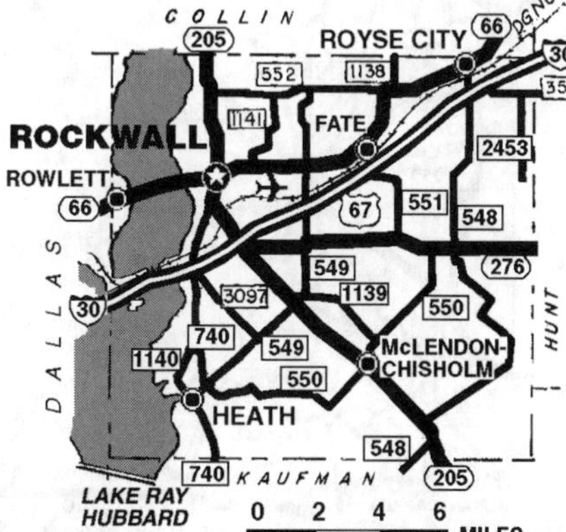

For explanation of sources, abbreviations and symbols, see p. 132.

Population **28,977**
(Change fm '90) 13.2
Land Area (sq. mi.) 128.7
Altitude (ft.) 489-588

Rainfall (in.) 36.9
Jan. mean min. 33
July mean max. 96
Growing season (days)............... 236
Civ. Labor.............................. 16,960
Unemployed 3.5
Total Wages $151,855,272
Av. Weekly Wage $386.25
Prop. Value............ $1,428,976,394
Retail Sales $230,079,063

Runnels County

Physical Features: West central county; level to rolling; bisected by Colorado and tributaries; sandy loam, black waxy soils.

Economy: Agribusiness; oil activity; manufacturing.

History: Named for planter-legislator H.G. Runnels; created 1858 from Bexar, Travis counties; organized 1880.

Ethnicity, 1990: White, 10,438 (92.4%); Black, 183 (1.6%); American Indian, 16 (0.1%); Asian, 16 (0.1%); Other, 641 (5.7%). Hispanic, 2,740 (24.3%).

Vital Statistics, 1993: Births, 160; deaths, 157; marriages, 67; divorces, 40.

Recreation: Deer and turkey hunting; O.H. Ivie Reservoir; fishing; historical markers in county.

Minerals: Oil, gas, sand, gravel.

Agriculture: Beef and stocker cattle, sheep; crops include cotton, sorghums, wheat.

BALLINGER (4,079) county seat; varied manufacturing; oil-field services; meat processing; fertilizer produced; Carnegie Library; hospital; Western Texas College extension; The Cross, 100-ft. tall atop hill south of city; Festival of Ethnic Cultures in April.

Other towns include: **Miles** (842); **Rowena** (466); **Winters** (2,899), manufacturing, museum; hospital.

Population	**11,076**
(Change fm '90)	1.6
Land Area (sq. mi.)	1,054.5
Altitude (ft.)	1,628-2,301
Rainfall (in.)	22.1
Jan. mean min.	30
July mean max.	96
Growing season (days)	228
Civ. Labor	5,306
Unemployed	3.9
Total Wages	$62,864,539
Av. Weekly Wage	$322.30
Prop. Value	$463,722,197
Retail Sales	$63,107,550

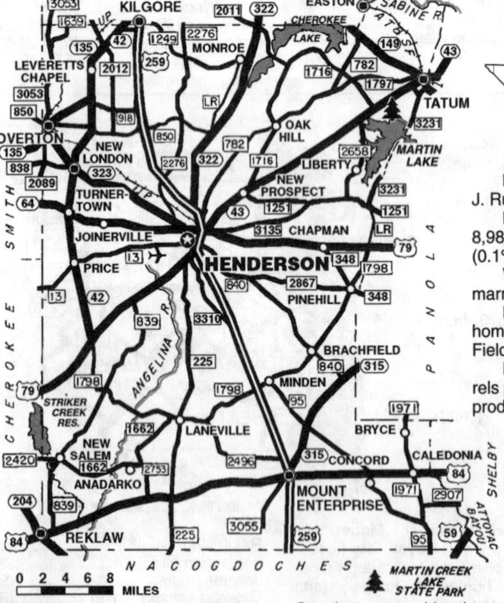

Rusk County

Physical Features: East Texas county on Sabine-Angelina divide; varied deep, sandy soils; over half in pines, hardwoods; lakes.

Economy: Oil, lumbering, agribusiness, tourism.

History: Named for Republic, state leader Thomas J. Rusk; created from Nacogdoches County 1843.

Ethnicity, 1990: White, 33,730 (77.1%); Black, 8,984 (20.5%); American Indian, 150 (0.3%); Asian, 51 (0.1%); Other, 820 (1.9%). Hispanic, 1,736 (4.0%).

Vital Statistics, 1993: Births, 532; deaths, 509; marriages, 334; divorces, 248.

Recreation: Water sports, state park; historic homes, sites; scenic drives; marked site of East Texas Field discovery oil well; syrup festival in November.

Minerals: A leading oil county; over 1.5 billion barrels produced since 1930; natural gas, lignite, clays also produced.

Agriculture: Beef cattle top producer; dairy products, poultry, horses raised; timber income substantial; crops include vegetables, nursery plants, hay and watermelons.

HENDERSON (11,488) county seat; center for agribusiness, oil activities; varied manufacturing; hospital.

Other towns include: **Mount Enterprise** (516); **New London** (991), site of 1937 school explosion that killed 293 students and faculty; **Overton** (2,163, part in Smith County), oil, lumbering center; petroleum processing; A&M research center; blue grass festival in July; prison unit; **Tatum** (1,322, partly in Panola County).

Population	**44,685**
(Change fm '90)	2.2
Land Area (sq. mi.)	923.6
Altitude (ft.)	280-662
Rainfall (in.)	44.7
Jan. mean min.	35
July mean max.	93
Growing season (days)	250
Civ. Labor	20,653
Unemployed	7.4
Total Wages	$265,173,634
Av. Weekly Wage	$450.06
Prop. Value	$2,159,840,980
Retail Sales	$188,514,059

Sabine County

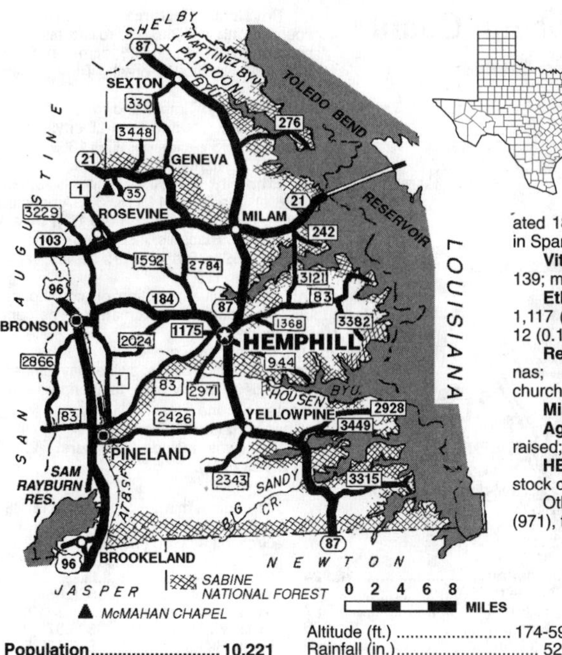

Physical Features: Eighty percent forested; 114,498 acres in national forest; Sabine River, Toledo Bend Reservoir on east; Sam Rayburn Reservoir on southwest.

Economy: Tourism; broilers; timber industries.

History: An original county, created 1836; organized 1837; name means cypress in Spanish.

Vital Statistics, 1993: Births, 122; deaths, 139; marriages, 103; divorces, 31.

Ethnicity, 1990: White, 8,394 (87.6%); Black, 1,117 (11.7%); American Indian, 10 (0.1%); Asian, 12 (0.1%); Other, 53 (0.6%). Hispanic, 111 (1.2%).

Recreation: Lake activities; campsites; marinas; McMahan's Chapel, pioneer Protestant church; Sabine National Forest; hunting.

Minerals: Glauconite.

Agriculture: Beef, poultry; vegetables, fruit raised; significant timber marketing.

HEMPHILL (1,236) county seat; timber, livestock center; tourism.

Other towns include: **Bronson** (261); **Pineland** (971), timber processing.

Population	**10,221**
(Change fm '90)	6.6
Land Area (sq. mi.)	490.2
Altitude (ft.)	174-590
Rainfall (in.)	52.5
Jan. mean min.	36
July mean max.	93
Growing season (days)	236
Civ. Labor	3,687
Unemployed	8.9
Total Wages	$38,834,221
Av. Weekly Wage	$373.02
Prop. Value	$383,645,821
Retail Sales	$45,271,216

San Augustine County

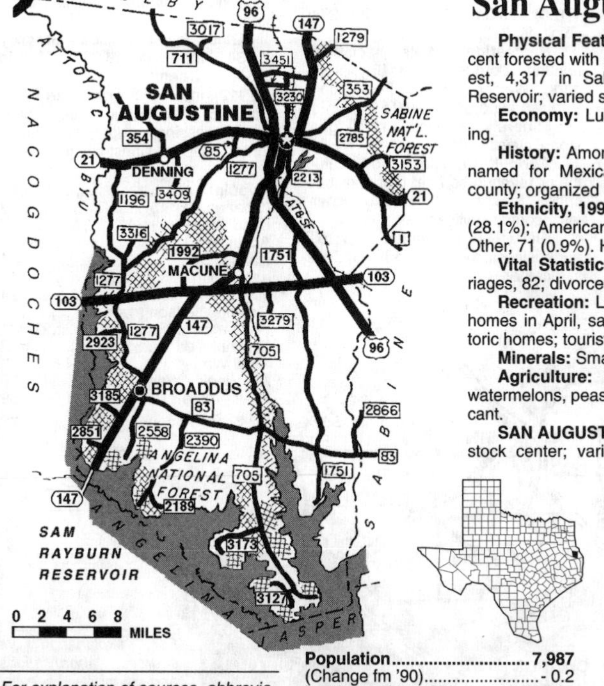

Physical Features: Hilly East Texas county, 80 percent forested with 66,799 acres in Angelina National Forest, 4,317 in Sabine National Forest; Sam Rayburn Reservoir; varied soils, sandy to black alluvial.

Economy: Lumbering; shipping; varied manufacturing.

History: Among most historic counties; created and named for Mexican municipality in 1836; an original county; organized 1837.

Ethnicity, 1990: White, 5,663 (70.8%); Black, 2,244 (28.1%); American Indian, 15 (0.2%); Asian, 6 (0.1%); Other, 71 (0.9%). Hispanic, 138 (1.7%).

Vital Statistics, 1993: Births, 78; deaths, 107; marriages, 82; divorces, 18.

Recreation: Lake activities; pine fest, annual tour of homes in April, sassafras festival in October; many historic homes; tourist facilities in national forests.

Minerals: Small amount of oil.

Agriculture: Broilers, cow-calf operation, horses; watermelons, peas, corn, truck crops; timber sales significant.

SAN AUGUSTINE (2,333) county seat; tourism; livestock center; varied manufacturing; Deep East Texas Electric Cooperative; lumbering; hospital; Tour of Homes.

Other towns include: **Broaddus** (206).

Population	**7,987**
(Change fm '90)	- 0.2
Land Area (sq. mi.)	1,232.2
Altitude (ft.)	156-502
Rainfall (in.)	46.3
Jan. mean min.	35
July mean max.	93
Growing season (days)	238
Civ. Labor	3,077
Unemployed	6.5
Total Wages	$25,402,912
Av. Weekly Wage	$302.36
Prop. Value	$317,930,809
Retail Sales	$39,334,411

For explanation of sources, abbreviations and symbols, see p. 132.

San Jacinto County

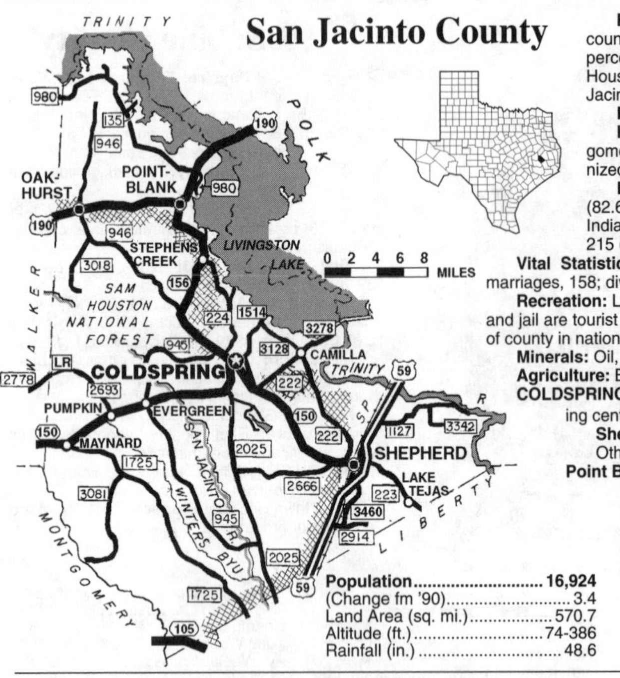

Physical Features: East Texas county north of Houston; rolling hills; 80 percent forested; 58,625 acres in Sam Houston National Forest; Trinity, San Jacinto rivers.

Economy: Timber and oil.

History: Created from Liberty, Montgomery, Polk, Walker counties 1869; organized 1870; named for the battle.

Ethnicity, 1990: White, 13,525 (82.6%); Black, 2,544 (15.5%); American Indian, 74 (0.5%); Asian, 14 (0.1%); Other, 215 (1.3%). Hispanic, 431 (2.6%).

Vital Statistics, 1993: Births, 171; deaths, 174; marriages, 158; divorces, 115.

Recreation: Lake activities; hunting; old courthouse and jail are tourist attractions. Approximately 60 percent of county in national forest.

Minerals: Oil, gas and iron ore.

Agriculture: Beef cattle, horses, swine; hay; timber.

COLDSPRING (549) county seat; lumbering; farming center; historic sites.

Shepherd (1,970) lumbering.

Other towns include: **Oakhurst** (230), **Point Blank** (471).

Population	**16,924**
(Change fm '90)	3.4
Land Area (sq. mi.)	570.7
Altitude (ft.)	74-386
Rainfall (in.)	48.6
Jan. mean min.	36
July mean max.	94
Growing season (days)	261
Civ. Labor	8,060
Unemployed	5.2
Total Wages	$28,684,989
Av. Weekly Wage	$340.75
Prop. Value	$803,373,924
Retail Sales	$38,160,572

San Patricio County

Physical Features: Grassy, coastal prairie draining to Aransas, Nueces rivers, and to bays; sandy loam, clay, black loam soils; lake.

Economy: Oil, petrochemicals; agribusiness; manufacturing; tourism; in Corpus Christi metropolitan area.

History: Settled by Irish families in 1830. Created from and named for Spanish municipality in 1836; organized 1837, reorganized 1847.

Ethnicity, 1990: White, 44,834 (76.3%); Black, 968 (1.6%); American Indian, 219 (0.4%); Asian, 163 (0.3%); Other, 12,565 (21.4%). Hispanic, 29,809 (50.7%).

Vital Statistics, 1993: Births, 1,120; deaths, 480; marriages 274; divorces, 319.

Recreation: Water activities; hunting; Corpus Christi Bay; state park; Welder Wildlife Foundation, Park; shrimporee; birdwatching.

Minerals: Production of oil, gas, stone, clays, caliche.

Agriculture: Beef, fed cattle major revenue source; crops include cotton, grain sorghums, corn; fisheries income significant.

SINTON (5,775) county seat; oil, agribusiness; tourism; Go Texan Days in October.

Aransas Pass (7,393), shrimping, tourist center; offshore oil-well servicing; aluminum, chemical plants; hospitals.

Other towns include: **Gregory** (2,534); **Ingleside** (6,289); **Mathis** (5,566); **Odem** (2,514); **Portland** (13,112), Indian Point pier; **San Patricio** (406); **Taft** (3,506), manufacturing, processing; drug reha-bilitation center, hospital; Christmas parade.

Population	**61,835**
(Change fm '90)	5.3
Land Area (sq. mi.)	691.7
Altitude (ft.)	sea level-137
Rainfall (in.)	34.4
Jan. mean min.	44
July mean max.	94
Growing season (days)	303
Civ. Labor	27,331
Unemployed	10.2
Total Wages	$264,502,786
Av. Weekly Wage	$421.89
Prop. Value	$2,211,503,289
Retail Sales	$292,924,043

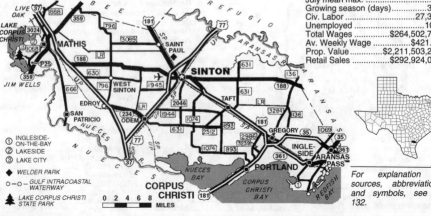

① INGLESIDE-ON-THE-BAY
② LAKESIDE
③ LAKE CITY
◆ WELDER PARK
o–o GULF INTRACOASTAL WATERWAY
▲ LAKE CORPUS CHRISTI STATE PARK

For explanation of sources, abbreviations and symbols, see p. 132.

San Saba County

Physical Features: West central county; hilly, rolling; bisected by San Saba River; Colorado River on east; black, gray sandy loam, alluvial soils.

Economy: Agribusiness; stone processing; tourism; hunting leases.

History: Created from Bexar 1856; named for river.

Ethnicity, 1990: White, 4,944 (91.5%); Black, 14 (0.3%); American Indian, 8 (0.1%); Asian, 1 (0.0%); Other, 434 (8.0%). Hispanic, 998 (18.5%).

Vital Statistics, 1993: Births, 48; deaths, 77; marriages, 30; divorces, 36.

Recreation: Deer hunting; historic sites; log cabin museum, fishing; scenic drives; wildflower trail; Gorman Falls; pecan festival.

Minerals: Limited stone production.

Agriculture: Most income from fed cattle, cow-calf operations, sheep and goats; crops include pecans, wheat, hay, peanuts.

SAN SABA (2,846) county seat; claims title "Pecan Capital of the World"; stone processing; range of manufacturing; state prison unit; hospital, cow camp cookoff.

Other towns include: **Bend** (115); **Cherokee** (175); **Richland Springs** (334).

Population	**5,397**
(Change fm '90)	- 0.1
Land Area (sq. mi.)	1,134.5
Altitude (ft.)	1,110-1,971
Rainfall (in.)	25.9
Jan. mean min.	32
July mean max.	96
Growing season (days)	227
Civ. Labor	2,262
Unemployed	4.5
Total Wages	$31,032,717
Av. Weekly Wage	$391.84
Prop. Value	$435,265,952
Retail Sales	$22,394,331

Schleicher County

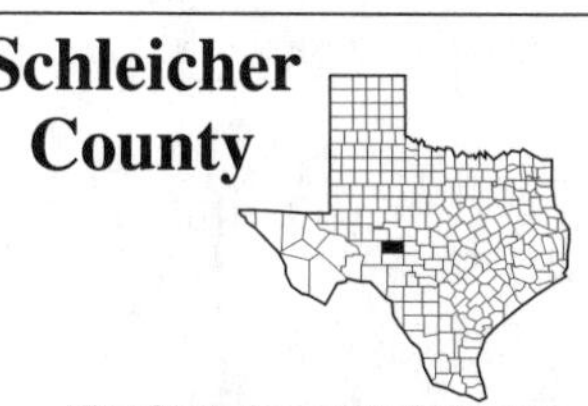

Physical Features: Southwestern county on edge of Edwards Plateau, broken by Devils, Concho, San Saba tributaries; part hilly; black soils.

Economy: Oil and ranching.

History: Named for Gustav Schleicher, founder of German colony; county created from Crockett 1887, organized 1901.

Ethnicity, 1990: White, 2,078 (69.5%); Black, 27 (0.9%); American Indian, 3 (0.1%); Asian, 1 (0.0%); Other, 881 (29.5%). Hispanic, 1,062 (35.5%).

Vital Statistics, 1993: Births, 29; deaths, 25; marriages, 22; divorces, 11.

Recreation: Hunting; livestock show in January, youth, open rodeos; playhouse "Way off Broadway".

Minerals: Oil, natural gas.

Agriculture: Sheep, cattle, Angora and meat goats; crops include cotton, milo, hay, small grain.

ELDORADO (2,005) county seat; center for livestock, woolen mill, mohair marketing; oil activities; medical center.

Population	**3,017**
(Change fm '90)	0.9
Land Area (sq. mi.)	1,310.6
Altitude (ft.)	2,125-2,467
Rainfall (in.)	19.0
Jan. mean min.	28
July mean max.	93
Growing season (days)	229
Civ. Labor	1,354
Unemployed	6.1
Total Wages	$15,688,051
Av. Weekly Wage	$414.93
Prop. Value	$342,528,410
Retail Sales	$7,343,923

For explanation of sources, abbreviations and symbols, see p. 132.

Scurry County

Physical Features: Plains county below Caprock, some hills; drained by Colorado, Brazos tributaries; lake; sandy, loam soils.

Economy: Oil production; agribusinesses; manufacturing; tourism.

History: Created from Bexar 1876; organized 1884; named for Confederate Gen. W.R. Scurry.

Ethnicity, 1990: White, 14,113 (75.7%); Black, 879 (4.7%); American Indian, 62 (0.3%); Asian, 35 (0.2%); Other, 3,545 (19.0%). Hispanic, 4,454 (23.9%).

Vital Statistics, 1993: Births, 249; deaths, 167; marriages, 147; divorces, 92.

Recreation: Lake J.B. Thomas water recreation; Sandstone Canyon Indian pictographs; Towle Memorial Park; museums, community theater, white buffalo days.

Minerals: Leading oil-producing county; also gas, stone.

Agriculture: Beef cattle, hogs, dairy cows and sheep; crops are cotton, hay, grain sorghums, silage, wheat, pecans.

SNYDER (12,441) county seat; oil center; varied manufacturing; Western Texas (Jr.) College; hospital; prison unit: new walking trails along creek in town.

Other towns include: **Hermleigh** (200)

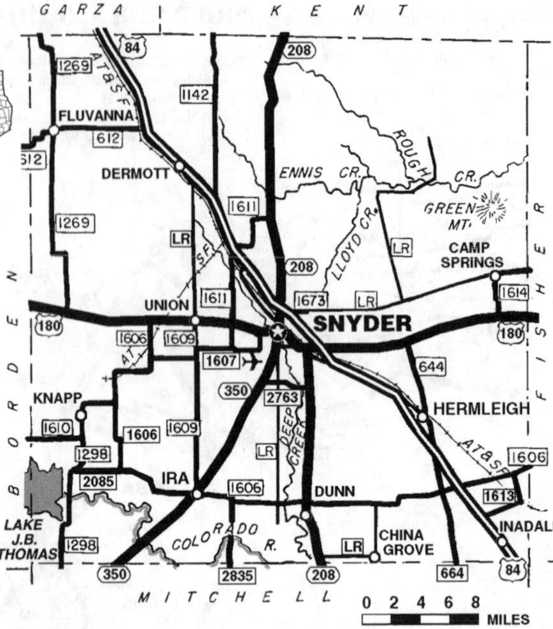

Population	**19,117**
(Change fm '90)	2.6
Land Area (sq. mi.)	902.5
Altitude (ft.)	2,129-2,822
Rainfall (in.)	20.3
Jan. mean min.	26
July mean max.	95
Growing season (days)	214
Civ. Labor	8,140
Unemployed	6.4
Total Wages	$136,917,561
Av. Weekly Wage	$407.76
Prop. Value	$884,208,136
Retail Sales	$111,408,690

Shackelford County

Physical Features: Rolling, hilly, drained by tributaries of Brazos; sandy and chocolate loam soils; lake.

Economy: Oil and ranching; some manufacturing.

History: Created from Bosque County 1858; organized 1874; named for Dr. Jack Shackelford (sometimes referred to as John), Texas Revolutionary hero.

Ethnicity, 1990: White, 3,125 (94.2%); Black, 12 (0.4%); American Indian, 9 (0.3%); Asian, 2 (0.1%); Other, 168 (5.1%). Hispanic, 272 (8.2%).

Vital Statistics, 1993: Births, 40; deaths, 51; marriages, 31; divorces, 8.

Recreation: Fort Griffin State Park, June Fandangle musical production is a major tourist attraction; courthouse historical district; lake activities, hunting.

Minerals: Oil, natural gas.

Agriculture: Beef, stocker cattle, horses, hogs; crops include cotton, wheat; mesquite firewood sold.

ALBANY (2,040) county seat; tourism; oil and agriculture center; quarter-horse breeding, training; hospital; historical district.

Other town: **Moran** (293).

Population	**3,444**
(Change fm '90)	3.9
Land Area (sq. mi.)	914.0
Altitude (ft.)	1,217-1,788
Rainfall (in.)	27.1
Jan. mean min.	29
July mean max.	98
Growing season (days)	224
Civ. Labor	1,607
Unemployed	4.6
Total Wages	$15,849,388
Av. Weekly Wage	$332.51
Prop. Value	$277,989,633
Retail Sales	$11,664,892

Shelby County

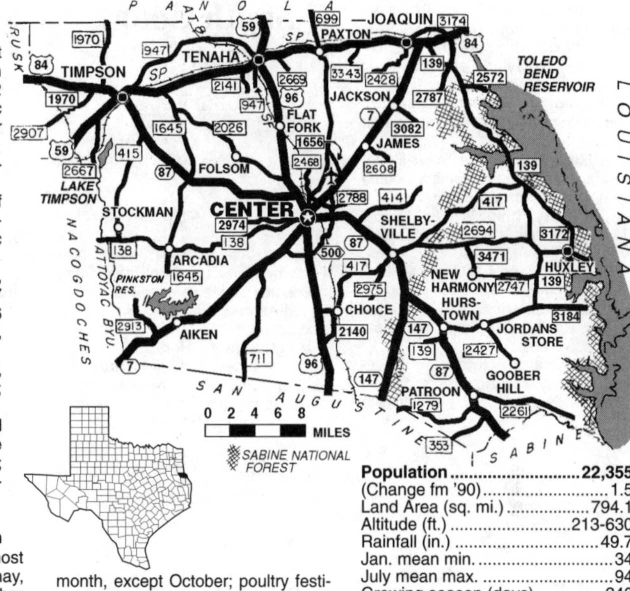

Physical Features: East Texas county; partly hills, much bottomland; well timbered, 67,762 acres in national forest; Attoyac Bayou and Toledo Bend, other streams; sandy, clay, alluvial soils.

Economy: Broiler, egg production; cattle; timber; tourism.

History: Original county of Republic, created 1836; organized 1837; named for Isaac Shelby of American Revolution.

Ethnicity, 1990: White, 17,047 (77.4%); Black, 4,727 (21.5%); American Indian, 36 (0.2%); Asian, 31 (0.1%); Other, 193 (0.9%). Hispanic, 539 (2.4%).

Vital Statistics, 1993: Births, 292; deaths, 333; marriages, 214; divorces, 131.

Recreation: Toledo Bend Reservoir activities; Sabine National Forest; hunting, fishing; camping; historic sites; poultry festival, antique-gun show, wolf hunt.

Minerals: Natural gas, oil.

Agriculture: A leader in broiler and egg production; most income from poultry, beef cattle; hay, vegetables, watermelons; timber sales significant.

CENTER (5,020) county seat; poultry, lumber processing; tourism; hospitals; Shelby College Center; trades day second Saturday of each month, except October; poultry festival; fall fox hunt.

Other towns: **Huxley** (342), **Joaquin** (880), **Tenaha** (1,189), **Timpson** (1,005) timber, poultry, livestock; frontier days in July, chili cookoff in November.

Population	**22,355**
(Change fm '90)	1.5
Land Area (sq. mi.)	794.1
Altitude (ft.)	213-630
Rainfall (in.)	49.7
Jan. mean min.	34
July mean max.	94
Growing season (days)	240
Civ. Labor	9,755
Unemployed	7.6
Total Wages	$115,953,901
Av. Weekly Wage	$334.01
Prop. Value	$697,279,626
Retail Sales	$137,224,841

Sherman County

Physical Features: A northernmost Panhandle county; level, broken by creeks, playas; sandy to dark loam soils; underground water.

Economy: Agribusiness.

History: Named for Texas Gen. Sidney Sherman; county created from Bexar District 1876; organized 1889.

Ethnicity, 1990: White, 2,816 (98.5%); Black, 4 (0.1%); American Indian, 12 (0.4%); Asian, 7 (0.2%); Other, 19 (0.7%). Hispanic, 538 (18.8%).

Vital Statistics, 1993: Births, 31; deaths, 37; marriages, 24; divorces, 7.

Recreation: Depot museum; jamboree in September; pheasant hunting.

Minerals: Natural gas, oil.

Agriculture: Beef and stocker cattle important; wheat, corn, grain sorghum; 130,000 acres irrigated.

STRATFORD (1,741) county seat; agribusiness center; feedlot operations; industrial authority; some manufacturing.

Texhoma (289 in Texas, 746 in Oklahoma), other principal town.

Population	**2,948**
(Change fm '90)	3.1
Land Area (sq. mi.)	923.1
Altitude (ft.)	3,485-3,743
Rainfall (in.)	16.9
Jan. mean min.	18
July mean max.	93
Growing season (days)	182
Civ. Labor	1,357
Unemployed	3.2
Total Wages	$14,554,677
Av. Weekly Wage	$354.63
Prop. Value	$518,596,296
Retail Sales	$12,132,428

Smith County

Physical Features: Populous East Texas county of rolling hills, many timbered; Sabine, Neches, other streams; Tyler, Palestine lakes; alluvial, gray, sandy loam, clay soils.

Economy: Agribusiness; petroleum production; distribution center; tourism; education.

History: Named for Texas Revolutionary Gen. James Smith; county created 1846 from Nacogdoches.

Ethnicity, 1990: White, 113,676 (75.1%); Black, 31,572 (20.9%); American Indian, 520 (0.3%); Asian, 638 (0.4%); Other, 4,903 (3.2%). Hispanic, 8,986 (5.9%).

Vital Statistics, 1993: Births, 2,388; deaths, 1,466; marriages, 1,809; divorces, 955.

Recreation: Activities on Palestine, Tyler lakes and others; famed Rose Garden; Texas Rose Festival in October; Azalea Trail; state park; Goodman Museum; East Texas Fair in September; collegiate events.

Minerals: Oil, gas, clays, sand and gravel, stone.

Agriculture: Horticultural crops and roses; beef cattle important; hay, watermelons, fruits, pecans; timber sales substantial; some sawlogs, pulpwood produced.

TYLER (79,516) county seat; claims title, "Rose Capital of the World"; administrative center for oil production; varied manufacturing; University of Texas at Tyler, Tyler Junior College; Texas College, University of Texas Health Center; hospitals, nursing school.

Other towns include: **Arp** (895) Strawberry Festival in April; **Bullard** (965, part in Cherokee County); **Lindale** (2,558), food processing; county fest, rodeo; **New Chapel Hill** (460); **Noonday** (518); **Troup** (1,814, part in Cherokee County); **Whitehouse** (4,623); **Winona** (518).

Population	**159,652**
(Change fm '90)	5.5
Land Area (sq. mi.)	928.4
Altitude (ft.)	52-631
Rainfall (in.)	43.1
Jan. mean min.	33
July mean max.	94
Growing season (days)	259
Civ. Labor	82,683
Unemployed	5.8
Total Wages	$1,602,902,357
Av. Weekly Wage	$454.22
Prop. Value	$5,743,367,338
Retail Sales	$1,810,686,545

For explanation of sources, abbreviations and symbols, see p. 132.

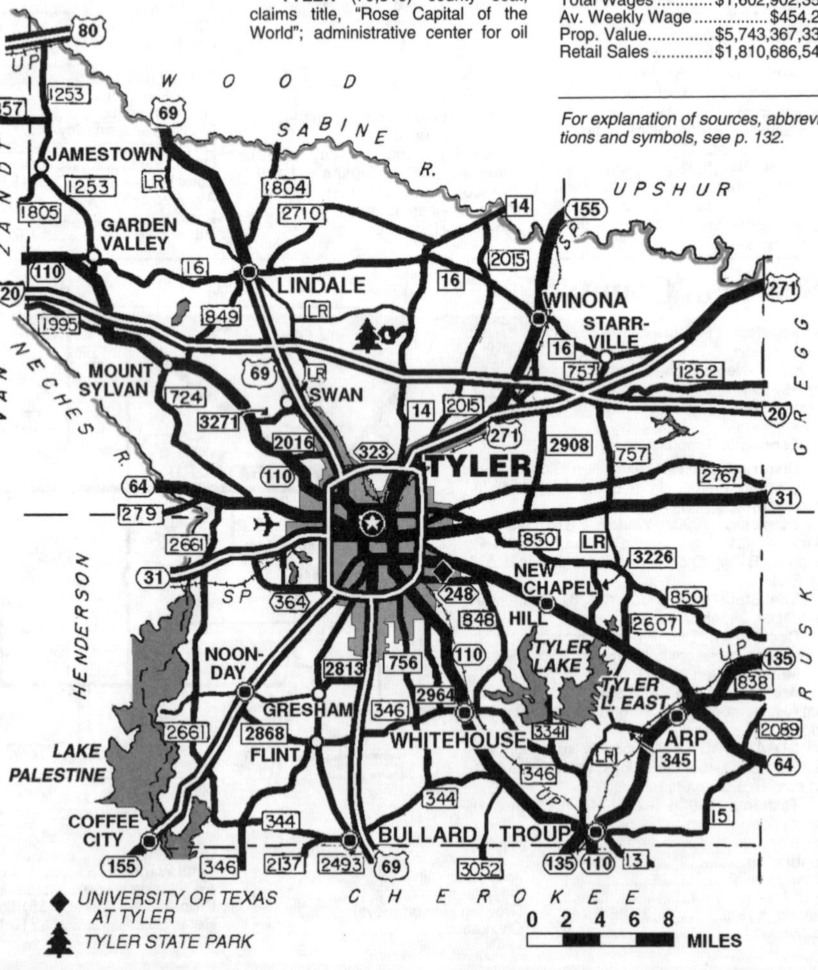

◆ UNIVERSITY OF TEXAS AT TYLER

TYLER STATE PARK

0 2 4 6 8 MILES

Somervell County

Physical Features: Hilly terrain southwest of Fort Worth; Brazos, Paluxy rivers; gray, dark, alluvial soils.

Economy: Nuclear power plant; tourism, agribusiness.

History: Created as Somerville County 1875 from Hood, Bosque; name changed to proper spelling 1876; named for Republic of Texas Gen. Alexander Somervell.

Ethnicity, 1990: White, 4,849 (90.5%); Black, 10 (0.2%); American Indian, 34 (0.6%); Asian, 22 (0.4%); Other, 445 (8.3%). Hispanic, 749 (14.0%).

Vital Statistics, 1993: Births, 68; deaths, 56; marriages, 79; divorces, 39.

Recreation: Fishing, hunting; unique geological formations; state park; Glen Rose Big Rocks Park; Fossil Rim Wildlife Center; nature trails, museum; exposition center; Celtic festival in April; Passion Play at amphitheatre June-October.

Minerals: Sand, gravel, silica.

Agriculture: Beef cattle, dairy products; hay, peanuts, small grains; minor irrigation for peanuts.

GLEN ROSE (2,027) county seat; tourism, farm trade center; hospital, nuclear power plant.

Population	**5,518**
(Change fm '90)	2.9
Land Area (sq. mi.)	187.1
Altitude (ft.)	627-1,013
Rainfall (in.)	32.2
Jan. mean min.	32
July mean max.	98
Growing season (days)	236
Civ. Labor	2,316
Unemployed	12.2
Total Wages	$113,975,201
Av. Weekly Wage	$668.49
Prop. Value	$8,543,013,609
Retail Sales	$25,226,358

Starr County

Physical Features: Rolling, some hills; dense brush; clay, loam, sandy soils, alluvial on Rio Grande; Falcon Reservoir.

Economy: Vegetable packing, shipping, other agribusiness; oil processing; tourism.

History: Named for Dr. J.H. Starr, secretary of treasury of the Republic; county created from Nueces 1848.

Ethnicity, 1990: White, 25,067 (61.9%); Black, 25 (0.1%); American Indian, 31 (0.1%); Asian, 25 (0.1%); Other, 15,370 (37.9%). Hispanic, 39,390 (97.2%).

Vital Statistics, 1993: Births, 1,358; deaths, 215; marriages, 667; divorces, 74.

Recreation: Falcon Reservoir activities; deer, white-wing dove hunting; access to Mexico; historic houses; grotto at Rio Grande City; Roma Fest in November.

Minerals: Oil, gas, sand, gravel.

Agriculture: Vegetables, cotton, sorghum; beef and fed cattle; 18,000 acres irrigated for vegetables.

RIO GRANDE CITY (10,564) county seat; agriculture center; food processing; exports to Mexico; hospital.

Roma-Los Saenz (9,234) agriculture center.

Other towns include: **Escobares** (1,887), **La Casita-Garciasville** (1,311), **La Grulla** (1,566).

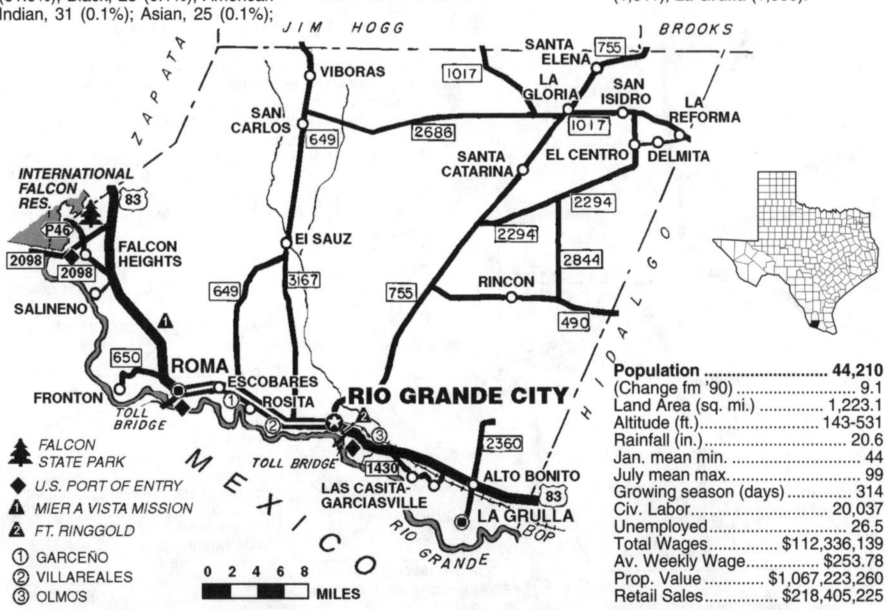

Population	**44,210**
(Change fm '90)	9.1
Land Area (sq. mi.)	1,223.1
Altitude (ft.)	143-531
Rainfall (in.)	20.6
Jan. mean min.	44
July mean max.	99
Growing season (days)	314
Civ. Labor	20,037
Unemployed	26.5
Total Wages	$112,336,139
Av. Weekly Wage	$253.78
Prop. Value	$1,067,223,260
Retail Sales	$218,405,225

Stephens County

Physical Features: West central county; broken, hilly; Hubbard Creek Reservoir, Possum Kingdom, Daniel lakes; Brazos River; loam, sandy soils.

Economy: Oil, agribusinesses, recreation, some manufacturing.

History: Created as Buchanan 1858 from Bosque; renamed 1861 for Confederate Vice President Alexander H. Stephens; organized 1876.

Ethnicity, 1990: White, 8,187 (90.9%); Black, 252 (2.8%); American Indian, 30 (0.3%); Asian, 28 (0.3%); Other, 513 (5.7%). Hispanic, 767 (8.5%).

Vital Statistics, 1993: Births, 107; deaths, 139; marriages, 90; divorces, 44.

Recreation: Lakes activities; hunting; campsites; historical points; Swenson Museum; Sandefer Oil Museum; aviation museum and annual air show; rattlesnake hunt.

Minerals: Oil, natural gas, stone.

Agriculture: Beef cattle, hogs, goats, sheep; wheat, oats, hay, peanuts, grain sorghums, cotton, pecans; firewood, fence posts sold.

BRECKENRIDGE (5,515) county seat; oil and agriculture center; mobil home, aircraft parts manufacturing; petrochemical production; hospital; arts center and library.

Other towns include: **Caddo** (40) gateway to Possum Kingdom State Park.

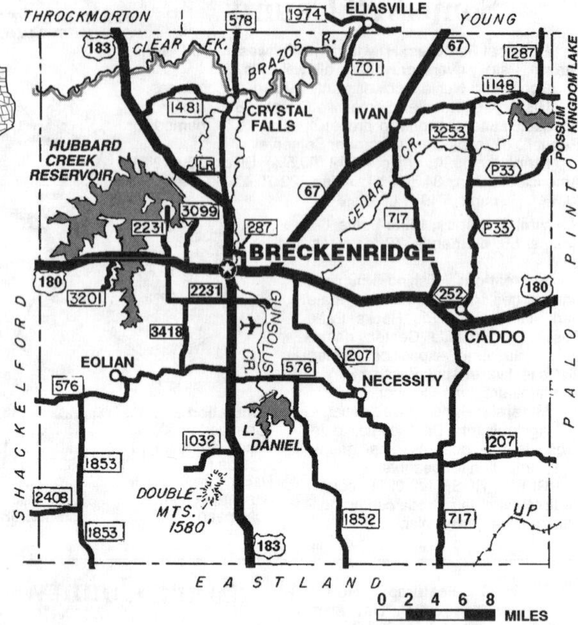

Population	**8,892**
(Change fm '90)	- 1.3
Land Area (sq. mi.)	894.7
Altitude (ft.)	1,127-1,578
Rainfall (in.)	26.4
Jan. mean min.	31
July mean max.	97
Growing season (days)	222
Civ. Labor	3,936
Unemployed	6.2
Total Wages	$46,868,894
Av. Weekly Wage	$344.83
Prop. Value	$584,949,502
Retail Sales	$60,293,000

Sterling County

Physical Features: Central prairie, surrounded by hills, broken by Concho River and tributaries; sandy to black soils.

Economy: Oil and ranching; hunting leases.

History: Named for buffalo hunter W.S. Sterling; created 1891 from Tom Green County.

Ethnicity, 1990: White, 1,244 (86.5%); Black, 0 (0.0%); American Indian, 9 (0.6%); Asian, 0 (0.0%); Other, 185 (12.9%). Hispanic, 366 (25.5%).

Vital Statistics, 1993: Births, 16; deaths, 15; marriages, 17; divorces, 6.

Recreation: Hunting.

Minerals: Oil, natural gas.

Agriculture: Beef cattle and sheep; some wheat raised; about 1,000 acres irrigated.

STERLING CITY (1,054) county seat; farm, ranch trade center; oil-field services; hospital.

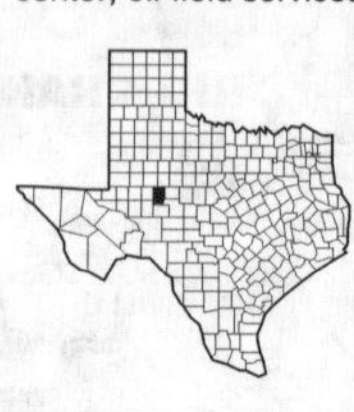

Population	**1,426**
(Change fm '90)	- 0.8
Land Area (sq. mi.)	923.4
Altitude (ft.)	2,167-2,623
Rainfall (in.)	18.6
Jan. mean min.	27
July mean max.	96
Growing season (days)	224
Civ. Labor	782
Unemployed	5.1
Total Wages	$10,281,973
Av. Weekly Wage	$385.35
Prop. Value	$472,215,370
Retail Sales	$7,183,435

For explanation of sources, abbreviations and symbols, see p. 132.

Stonewall County

Physical Features: Western county on rolling plains below Caprock, bisected by Brazos forks; sandy loam, sandy, other soils; some hills.

Economy: Oil, agribusinesses.

History: Named for Confederate Gen. T.J. (Stonewall) Jackson; created from Bexar 1876, organized 1888.

Ethnicity, 1990: White, 1,898 (94.3%); Black, 89 (4.4%); American Indian, 2 (0.1%); Asian, 7 (0.3%); Other, 17 (0.8%). Hispanic, 237 (11.8%).

Vital Statistics, 1993: Births, 19; deaths, 38; marriages, 11; divorces, 14.

Recreation: Deer, quail, feral hog, turkey hunting; rodeo; livestock show.

Minerals: Oil, gas, gypsum.

Agriculture: Beef cattle, goats, swine, sheep; crops include wheat; peanuts, hay and cotton.

ASPERMONT (1,204) county seat; oil field, ranching center; light fabrication; hospital; springfest; livestock show in February.

Other towns include: **Old Glory** (125) farming center; **Peacock** (125); **Swenson** (185).

Population **2,044**
(Change fm '90) 1.5
Land Area (sq. mi.) 918.7
Altitude (ft.) 1,659-1,964
Rainfall (in.) 22.2
Jan. mean min. 27
July mean max. 98
Growing season (days) 220
Civ. Labor 821
Unemployed 5.7
Total Wages $9,588,995
Av. Weekly Wage $316.85
Prop. Value $233,813,610
Retail Sales $8,033,625

Sutton County

Physical Features: Southwestern county; level, broken by tributaries of Devils, Llano rivers; black, red loam soils.

Economy: Oil and gas; agribusinesses; tourism; hunting leases.

History: Created from Crockett 1887; organized 1890; named for Confederate officer Col. John S. Sutton.

Ethnicity, 1990: White, 3,125 (75.6%); Black, 2 (0.0%); American Indian, 16 (0.4%); Asian, 6 (0.1%); Other, 986 (23.8%). Hispanic, 1,866 (45.1%).

Vital Statistics, 1993: Births, 66; deaths, 38; marriages, 29; divorces, 23.

Recreation: Among leading hunting counties; Meirs Museum; Caverns of Sonora; goat cookoff.

Minerals: Oil, natural gas.

Agriculture: Beef cattle, Angora goats, meat goats, fine-wool sheep; wheat raised for grazing, hay; minor irrigation.

SONORA (2,924) county seat; oil field, mohair, wool center; Texas A&M research substation; hospital; wool, mohair show in June.

Population **4,364**
(Change fm '90) 5.5
Land Area (sq. mi.) 1,453.8
Altitude (ft.) 1,942-2,461
Rainfall (in.) 20.7
Jan. mean min. 32
July mean max. 95
Growing season (days) 235
Civ. Labor 2,093
Unemployed 4.7
Total Wages $32,277,573
Av. Weekly Wage $382.97
Prop. Value $618,601,530
Retail Sales $22,629,202

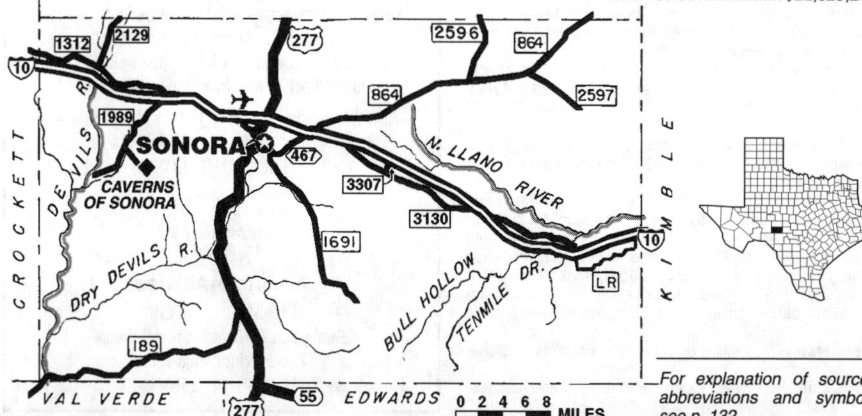

For explanation of sources, abbreviations and symbols, see p. 132.

Swisher County

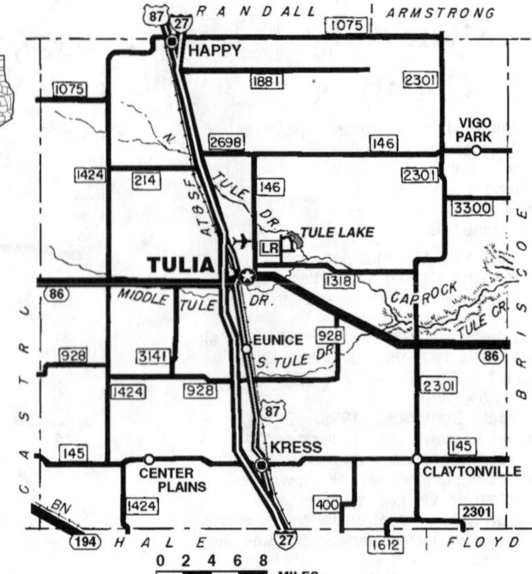

Physical Features: High Plains county; level, broken by Tule Canyon and Creek; playas; large underground water supply; rich soils.

Economy: Feedlots, grain storage, other agribusinesses; varied manufacturing; tourism; prison unit.

History: Named for J.G. Swisher of Texas Revolution; county created from Bexar, Young territories 1876; organized 1890; among last Indian strongholds.

Ethnicity, 1990: White, 5,702 (70.1%); Black, 340 (4.2%); American Indian, 26 (0.3%); Asian, 17 (0.2%); Other, 2,048 (25.2%). Hispanic, 2,496 (30.7%).

Vital Statistics, 1993: Births, 106; deaths, 93; marriages, 42; divorces, 32.

Recreation: Tule Lake activities; museum.

Minerals: Not significant.

Agriculture: A major agricultural county. Cotton, wheat, corn, sorghum raised. Feeder cattle, feed lots. Some 150,000 acres irrigated.

TULIA (5,237) county seat; farming center; varied manufacturing; grain storage; food processing; hospital; library, museum.

Other towns include: **Happy** (615, part in Randall County), **Kress** (734).

Population	**8,620**
(Change fm '90)	6.0
Land Area (sq. mi.)	900.4
Altitude (ft.)	3,354-3,604
Rainfall (in.)	17.5
Jan. mean min.	22
July mean max.	92

Growing season (days)	153
Civ. Labor	4,105
Unemployed	4.7
Total Wages	$41,306,793
Av. Weekly Wage	$318.23
Prop. Value	342,761,617
Retail Sales	$39,380,361

Tarrant County

Physical Features: Part Blackland, level to rolling; drains to Trinity; Worth, Grapevine, Eagle Mountain, Benbrook lakes.

Economy: Diversified; planes, helicopters, foods, mobile homes, electronic equipment, chemicals, plastics among products of more than 1,000 factories; large federal expenditure; D/FW International Airport; economy closely associated with Dallas urban area.

History: Named for Gen. Edward H. Tarrant, who helped drive Indians from area; county created 1849 from Navarro County; organized 1850.

Ethnicity, 1990: White, 917,501 (78.4%); Black, 140,740 (12.0%); American Indian, 5,551 (0.5%); Asian, 29,705 (2.5%); Other, 76,606 (6.5%). Hispanic, 139,879 (12.0%).

Vital Statistics, 1993: Births, 21,772; deaths, 8,318; marriages, 12,062; divorces, 7,930. Fourth most populous Texas county;

Recreation: Scott Theatre; Amon G. Carter Museum; Kimbell Art Museum; Fort Worth Art Museum; Museum of Science and History; Casa Manana; Botanic Gardens; Forest Park Zoo; Log Cabin Village; Six Flags Over Texas at Arlington; Southwestern Exposition, Stock Show; Convention Center; Stockyards Historical District; Texas Rangers major league baseball at Arlington, other athletic events.

Minerals: Production of cement, sand, gravel, stone, gas.

Agriculture: Beef cattle primarily; some dairies;

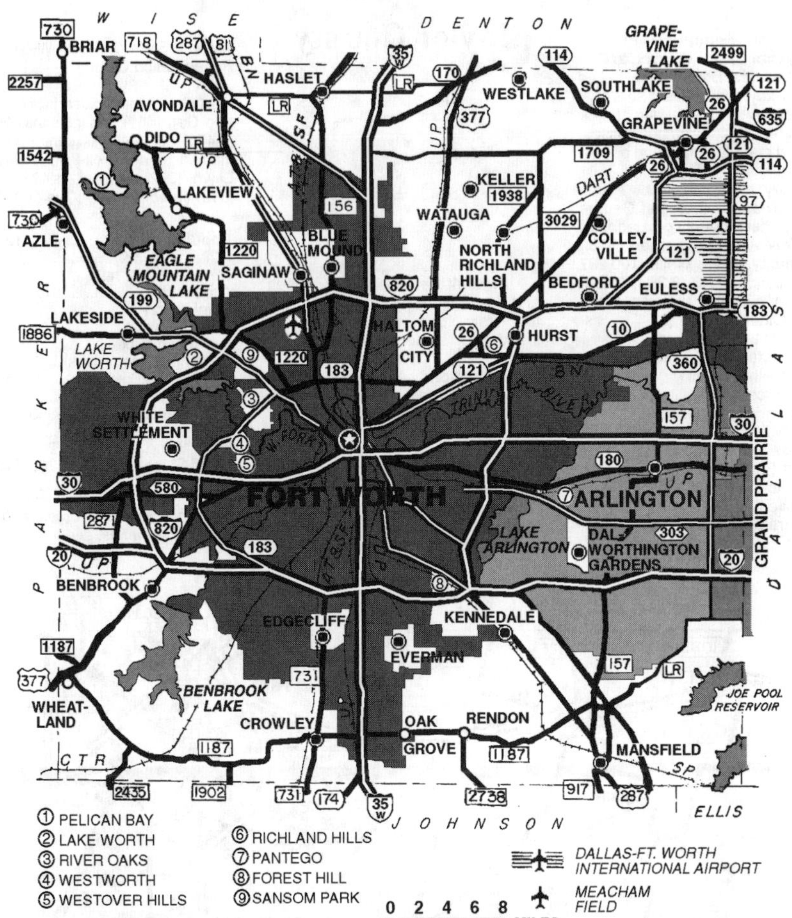

wheat, hay, grain sorghum and corn raised; firewood marketed.

Education: Texas Christian University, University of Texas at Arlington, Texas Wesleyan University, Southwestern Baptist Theological Seminary and several other academic centers including a junior college system (three campuses).

FORT WORTH (459,085) county seat; a major mercantile, commercial and financial center; wholesale trade center for much of West Texas; airplane, helicopter and other plants; a cultural center with renowned art museums; many conventions held in downtown center; agribusiness center for wide area with grain-storage and feed-mill operations; adjacent to D/FW International Airport; hospitals).

ARLINGTON (277,939); industrial and distribution center for automobiles, food products, electronic components, aircraft and parts, rubber and plastic products; medical center, hospitals. A tourist center with Six Flags Over Texas, the Texas Rangers baseball team, numerous restaurants; educational facilities.

Other towns include: **Hurst** (36,484); **Euless** (41,895); **Bedford** (44,791); **North Richland Hills** (47,935); **Azle** (9,705, partly in Parker County), varied industries, Jumpin' Jack Jamboree in October; **Benbrook** (21,186) varied manufacturing; hospitals; **Blue Mound** (2,216); **Colleyville** (15,420) major residential development, some light manufacturing; **Crowley** (7,121, partly in Johnson County), varied manufacturing, hospital; **Dalworthington Gardens** (1,990); **Edgecliff Village** (2866); **Everman** (6,100); **Forest Hill** (11,455).

Also, **Grapevine** (33,718, partly in Denton County), varied manufacturing; near D/FW International Airport; tourist center; **Haltom City** (32,923) light manufacturing, food processing, medical center; **Haslet** (879, partly in Denton County); **Keller** (16,371); **Kennedale** (4,567); **Lakeside** (896); **Mansfield** (17,621, partly in Johnson County), varied manufacturing; hospital; Frontier Days, hometown celebration in fall; **Rendon** (7,950); **Saginaw** (8,683); **Southlake** (8,938) IBM marketing/education center; **Watauga** (21,152); **Westlake** (204, partly in Denton County); **White Settlement** (15,437) near aircraft manufacturing, museum, historical sites; hospital; industrial park.

Part of **Grand Prairie** lies in Tarrant County.

Population	**1,229,066**
(Change fm '90)	5.0
Land Area (sq. mi.)	863.5
Altitude (ft.)	484-864
Rainfall (in.)	31.3
Jan. mean min.	35
July mean max.	96
Growing season (days)	230
Civ. Labor	703,579
Unemployed	5.5
Total Wages	$14,868,200,112
Av. Weekly Wage	$515.85
Prop. Value	$50,649,206,025
Retail Sales	$13,666,609,956

Taylor County

Physical Features: Prairies, with Callahan Divide, draining to Colorado tributaries, Brazos forks; Lakes Abilene, Kirby; mostly loam soils.

Economy: Dyess Air Force Base, feedlots, agribusinesses, diversified manufacturing and education.

History: Named for Alamo heroes Edward, James and George Taylor, brothers; county created from Bexar, Travis 1858; organized 1878.

Ethnicity, 1990: White, 100,237 (83.8%); Black, 7,547 (6.3%); American Indian, 450 (0.4%); Asian, 1,449 (1.2%); Other, 9,972 (8.3%). Hispanic, 17,511 (14.6%).

Vital Statistics, 1993: Births, 1,953; deaths, 1,061; marriages, 1,333; divorces, 867.

Recreation: Abilene State Park; lake activities; Nelson Park Zoo; Texas Cowboy Reunion, West Texas Fair; Fort Phantom Hill; Buffalo Gap historical tour and art festival; rodeo, college events.

Minerals: Oil, natural gas, stone, caliche, clays, sand and gravel.

Agriculture: Beef cattle, sheep and goats; crops include wheat, cotton, grain sorghums, hay; sesame introduced; some 1,000 acres irrigated.

Education: Abilene Christian University, Hardin-Simmons University, McMurry University, Cisco Junior College branch.

ABILENE (110,661, part in Jones County) county seat; distribution center; plants make a variety of products; meat, dairy processing; oil-field service center; medical center; Abilene State School; West Texas Rehabilitation Center.

Other communities include: **Buffalo Gap** (469) historic sites; **Merkel** (2,470) agribusiness center, clothing manufacturing; oil-field services; **Lawn** (362); **Potosi** (1,471); **Trent** (319); **Tuscola** (629); **Tye** (1,109).

Population	**123,920**
(Change fm '90)	3.6
Land Area (sq. mi.)	915.7
Altitude (ft.)	1,672-2,410
Rainfall (in.)	23.3
Jan. mean min.	31
July mean max.	95
Growing season (days)	225
Civ. Labor	58,186
Unemployed	5.4
Total Wages	$955,057,956
Av. Weekly Wage	$389.65
Prop. Value	$3,224,114,674
Retail Sales	$1,266,240,734

For explanation of sources, abbreviations and symbols, see p. 132.

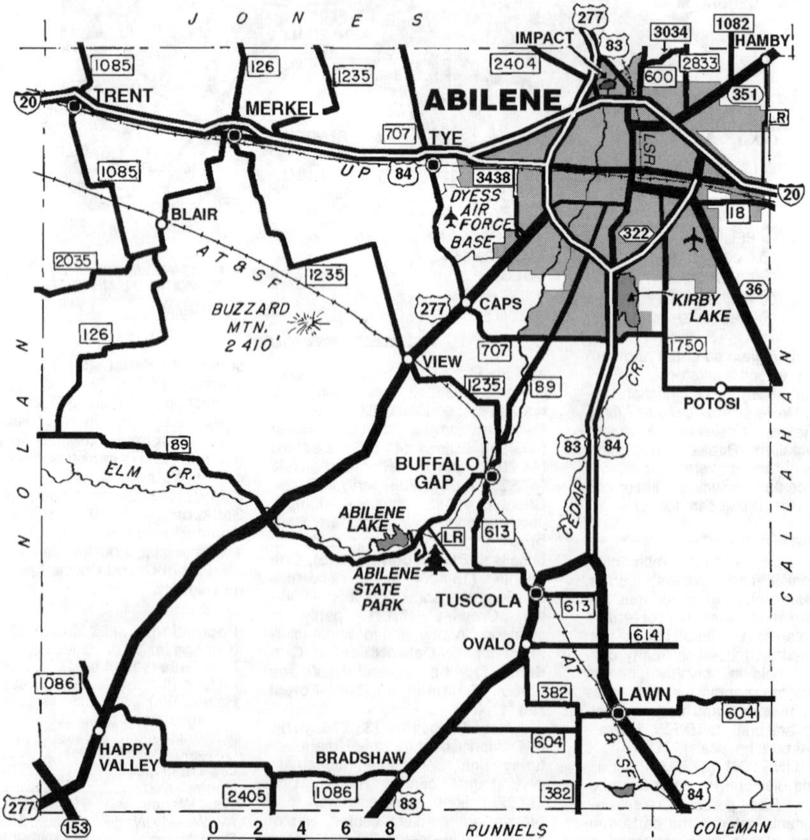

Terrell County

Physical Features: Trans-Pecos southwestern county; semi-mountainous, many canyons; rocky, limestone soils.

Economy: Ranching; some tourism; oil and natural gas exploration.

History: Named for Confederate Gen. A.W. Terrell; county created 1905 from Pecos County.

Ethnicity, 1990: White, 1,189 (84.3%); Black, 1 (0.1%); American Indian, 5 (0.4%); Asian, 2 (0.1%); Other, 213 (15.1%). Hispanic, 751 (53.3%).

Vital Statistics, 1993: Births, 20; deaths, 16; marriages, 18; divorces, 6.

Recreation: Hunting, especially white-tailed, mule deer; lower canyons of Rio Grande accessible by boat; varied wildlife.

Minerals: Gas, oil, limestone.

Agriculture: Sheep, Angora goats, wool, mohair, some beef cattle; alfalfa major crop.

SANDERSON (1,061) county seat; ranching, petroleum operations center; rail terminal. Other town: **Dryden** (13).

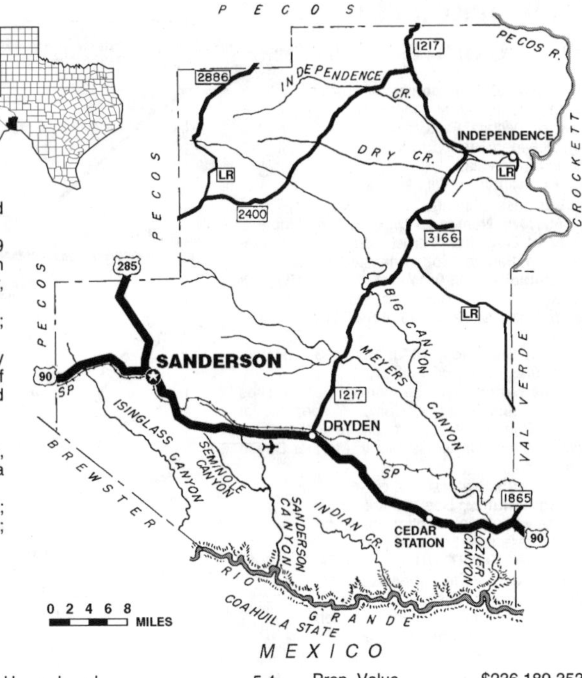

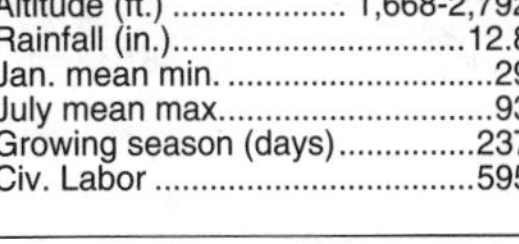

Population	**1,365**
(Change fm '90)	- 3.2
Land Area (sq. mi.)	2,357.9
Altitude (ft.)	1,668-2,792
Rainfall (in.)	12.8
Jan. mean min.	29
July mean max	93
Growing season (days)	237
Civ. Labor	595
Unemployed	5.4
Total Wages	$3,766,324
Av. Weekly Wage	$275.99
Prop. Value	$236,189,353
Retail Sales	$4,094,592

Terry County

Physical Features: Western county on South Plains, broken by draws, playas; sandy, sandy loam, loam soils.

Economy: Petroleum, agribusiness.

History: Named for head of famed Texas Ranger troop, Col. B.F. Terry; county created from Bexar District 1876; organized 1904.

Ethnicity, 1990: White, 10,202 (77.2%); Black, 449 (3.4%); American Indian, 38 (0.3%); Asian, 28 (0.2%); Other, 2,501 (18.9%). Hispanic, 5,194 (39.3%).

Vital Statistics, 1993: Births, 207; deaths, 113; marriages, 132; divorces, 90.

Recreation: Museum; harvest festival in October; all-girl rodeo in April.

Minerals: Oil, natural gas, sodium sulphate.

Agriculture: Cotton is principal crop; some sorghum, wheat, peanuts raised; 143,000 acres irrigated.

BROWNFIELD (9,606) county seat; oil-field services; agribusiness; minerals processed; hospital.

Other towns include: **Meadow** (592), **Wellman** (253).

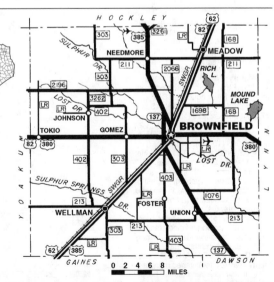

Population	**13,312**
(Change fm '90)	0.7
Land Area (sq. mi.)	889.8
Altitude (ft.)	3,183-3,447
Rainfall (in.)	17.5
Jan. mean min.	24
July mean max.	93
Growing season (days)	206
Civ. Labor	6,065
Unemployed	7.6
Total Wages	$83,404,285
Av. Weekly Wage	$398.04
Prop. Value	$933,734,960
Retail Sales	$95,151,747

For explanation of sources, abbreviations and symbols, see p. 132.

Throckmorton County

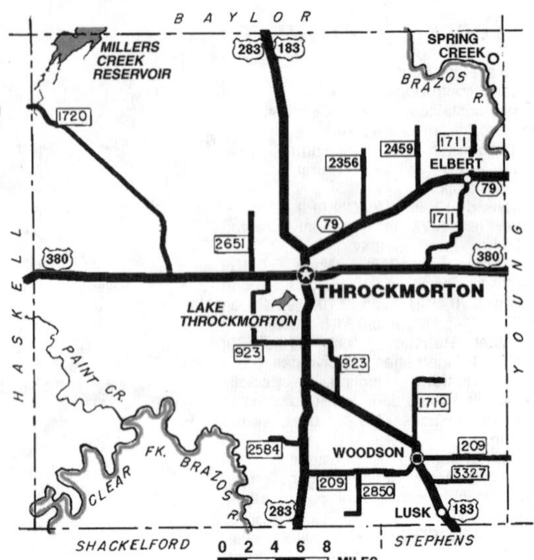

Physical Features: North central county southwest of Wichita Falls; rolling, between Brazos forks; red to black soils.

Economy: Oil and agribusiness; hunting.

History: Named for Dr. W.E. Throckmorton, father of Gov. J.W. Throckmorton; county created from Fannin 1858; organized 1879.

Ethnicity, 1990: White, 1,778 (94.6%); Black, 0 (0.0%); American Indian, 4 (0.2%); Asian, 8 (0.4%); Other, 90 (4.8%). Hispanic, 136 (7.2%).

Vital Statistics, 1993: Births, 30; deaths, 27; marriages, 12; divorces, 6.

Recreation: Hunting, fishing; historic sites include Camp Cooper, Camp Wilson, site of former Comanche reservation; restored ranch home, Miller's Creek Reservoir; Pioneer Day in June.

Minerals: Natural gas, oil.

Agriculture: Beef cattle; crops include wheat, oats, cotton, hay, sorghums; mesquite firewood sold.

THROCKMORTON (1,054) county seat; varied manufacturing; oil-field services; hospital.

Other towns include: **Elbert** (150), **Woodson** (254).

Population	**1,902**
(Change fm '90)	1.2
Land Area (sq. mi.)	912.4
Altitude (ft.)	1,153-1,583
Rainfall (in.)	25.0
Jan. mean min.	28
July mean max.	97
Growing season (days)	220
Civ. Labor	956
Unemployed	5.1
Total Wages	$7,663,212
Av. Weekly Wage	$302.70
Prop. Value	$224,383,360
Retail Sales	$5,714,406

Titus County

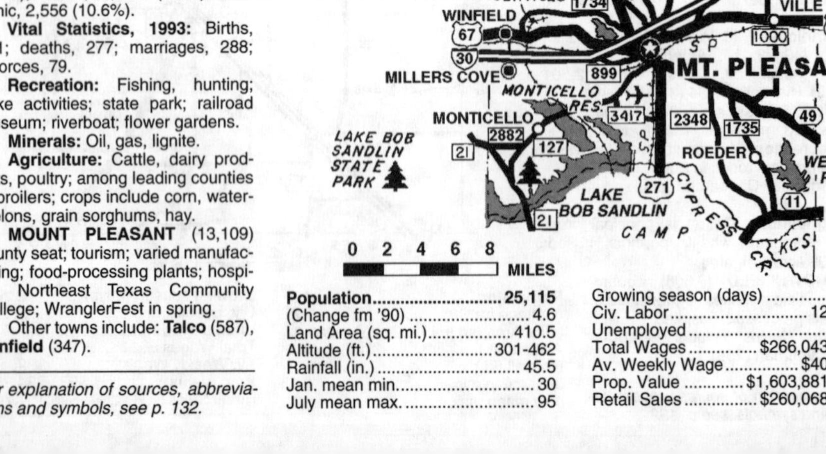

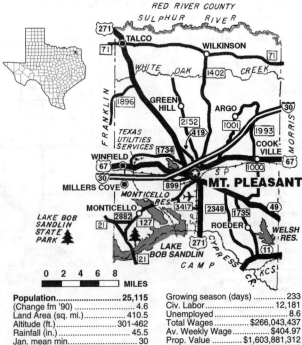

Physical Features: East Texas county; hilly, timbered; drains to Big Cypress Creek, Sulphur River.

Economy: Agribusinesses, varied manufacturing; lignite mining and power generation; tourism.

History: Named for pioneer settler A.J. Titus; county created from Bowie, Red River counties 1846.

Ethnicity, 1990: White, 18,664 (77.7%); Black, 3,229 (13.4%); American Indian, 107 (0.4%); Asian, 27 (0.1%); Other, 1,982 (8.3%). Hispanic, 2,556 (10.6%).

Vital Statistics, 1993: Births, 451; deaths, 277; marriages, 288; divorces, 79.

Recreation: Fishing, hunting; Lake activities; state park; railroad museum; riverboat; flower gardens.

Minerals: Oil, gas, lignite.

Agriculture: Cattle, dairy products, poultry; among leading counties in broilers; crops include corn, watermelons, grain sorghums, hay.

MOUNT PLEASANT (13,109) county seat; tourism; varied manufacturing; food-processing plants; hospital; Northeast Texas Community College; WranglerFest in spring.

Other towns include: **Talco** (587), **Winfield** (347).

Population	**25,115**
(Change fm '90)	4.6
Land Area (sq. mi.)	410.5
Altitude (ft.)	301-462
Rainfall (in.)	45.5
Jan. mean min.	30
July mean max.	95
Growing season (days)	233
Civ. Labor	12,181
Unemployed	8.6
Total Wages	$266,043,437
Av. Weekly Wage	$404.97
Prop. Value	$1,603,881,312
Retail Sales	$260,068,369

For explanation of sources, abbreviations and symbols, see p. 132.

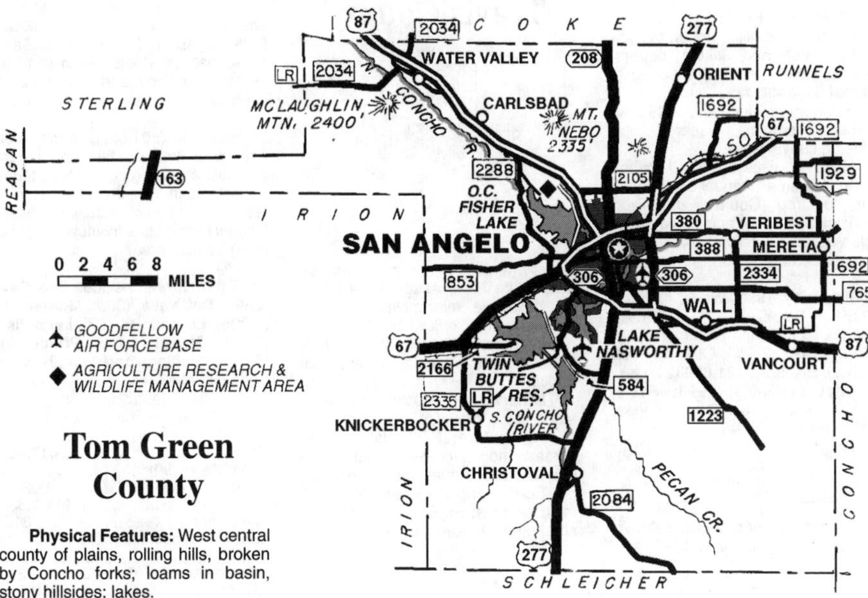

Tom Green County

Physical Features: West central county of plains, rolling hills, broken by Concho forks; loams in basin, stony hillsides; lakes.

Economy: "Sheep and Wool Capital"; varied agribusinesses, manufacturing; trade center for area, education center, medical center.

History: Created from Bexar District 1874, named for Gen. Tom Green of Texas Revolution; organized 1875; 12 other counties created from this original area.

Ethnicity, 1990: White, 79,533 (80.8%); Black, 4,136 (4.2%); American Indian, 373 (0.4%); Asian, 998 (1.0%); Other, 13,418 (13.6%). Hispanic, 25,501 (25.9%).

Vital Statistics, 1993: Births, 1,560; deaths, 943; marriages, 1,205; divorces, 586.

Recreation: Water sports; hunting; Fort Concho Museum; urban, collegiate activities; roping fiesta, June Fiesta del Concho; March rodeo.

Minerals: Oil, natural gas, stone.

Agriculture: A leading producer of wool, mohair. Sheep, goats and beef cattle; crops are cotton, sorghums, small grains, hay; about 30,000 acres irrigated.

SAN ANGELO (87,980) county seat; varied agribusiness; plants make a variety of products including medical devices, denim jeans; distribution center; hospitals; Angelo State University, A&M Extension Center.

Other towns include: **Carlsbad** (100), **Christoval** (216), **Wall** (200).

Population	**102,477**
(Change fm '90)	4.1
Land Area (sq. mi.)	1,522.1
Altitude (ft.)	1,717-2,480
Rainfall (in.)	18.2
Jan. mean min.	32
July mean max.	97
Growing season (days)	235
Civ. Labor	50,082
Unemployed	4.9
Total Wages	$780,502,862
Av. Weekly Wage	$390.03
Prop. Value	$2,905,329,819
Retail Sales	$870,490,654

For explanation of sources, abbreviations and symbols, see p. 132.

"The dryness of this climate is very favorable to sheep-raising, and the sandy nature of the soil is equally so. There is no danger of the foot rot, or other diseases which are caused by the feeding of sheep on land that is soft or muddy.

". . . the profits here on sheep-raising are much larger than on other stock. The business can be counted on as paying fully 50 per cent of the capital invested. This is the estimate made by successful wool-growers in Western Texas.

"The southwestern portion of the state seems to be better adapted to sheep raising than any other part of it; the winters being less rigorous, grass better and natural features of the country present advantages not to be had elsewhere.

". . . There was a manifest increase in our wool exports last year over that of former years, which for several years past has averaged about five millions of pounds.

"We believe the day is not far distant when the revenue of our country, from our wool exports alone, will be exceeded by no other article of commerce, cotton perhaps excepted."

— *Texas Almanac, 1873*

Travis County

Physical Features: Central county of scenic hills, broken by Colorado River and lakes; cedars, pecans, other trees; diverse soils, mineral deposits.

Economy: Education, state government, tourism, research and industry; conventions.

History: Created 1840, when Austin became Republic's capital, from Bastrop County; organized 1843; named for Alamo commander Col. William B. Travis; many other counties created from its original area.

Ethnicity, 1990: White, 422,749 (73.3%); Black, 63,173 (11.0%); American Indian, 2,089 (0.4%); Asian, 16,497 (2.9%); Other, 71,899 (12.5%). Hispanic, 121,689 (21.1%).

Vital Statistics, 1993: Births, 10,625; deaths, 3,467; marriages, 7,012; divorces, 3,448.

Recreation: Colorado River lakes; hunting, fishing; McKinney Falls State Park; Austin Aqua Festival; collegiate, metropolitan, governmental events; official buildings and historic sites; museums; Sixth St. restoration area; scenic drives; city parks.

Minerals: Production of lime, stone, sand, gravel, oil and gas.

Agriculture: Beef, dairy cattle, horses, hogs; crops include sorghums, cotton, small grains, pecans.

Education: University of Texas main campus; St. Edwards's University, Maryhill College, Concordia Lutheran College, Huston-Tillotson College, Austin Community College, Episcopal and Presbyterian seminaries; state schools and institutions for blind, deaf, mental illnesses.

AUSTIN (501,637), county seat and state capital; state and federal payrolls; a leading convention, tourist city; Lyndon B. Johnson Library; research, high-tech industries; hospitals, including state institutions; popular retirement area.

Other towns include: **Bee Cave** (259), **Del Valle** (300), **Jonestown** (1,305), **Lakeway** (4,427), **Lago Vista** (2,328), **Manor** (1,149), **Pflugerville** (6,018), **Rollingwood** (1,459), **West Lake Hills** (2,784).

For explanation of sources, abbreviations and symbols, see p. 132.

Population	**617,489**
(Change fm '90)	7.1
Land Area (sq. mi.)	1,022.1
Altitude (ft.)	444-1,330
Rainfall (in.)	31.5
Jan. mean min.	39
July mean max.	95
Growing season (days)	270
Civ. Labor	408,860
Unemployed	3.9
Total Wages	$10,371,026,416
Av. Weekly Wage	$514.52
Prop. Value	$26,954,285,765
Retail Sales	$7,692,935,514

TEXAS STATE CAPITOL
UNIVERSITY OF TEXAS
McKINNEY FALLS STATE PARK
① BRIARCLIFF
② ROLLINGWOOD
③ SUNSET VALLEY
④ SAN LEANNA
⑤ MUSTANG RIDGE

Trinity County

Physical Features: Heavily forested East Texas county of hills, between Neches and Trinity (Livingston Lake) rivers; rich alluvial soils, sandy upland; 67,910 acres in national forest.

Economy: Forestry, tourism, cattle.

History: Named for river; county created 1850 out of Houston County.

Ethnicity, 1990: White, 9,619 (84.0%); Black, 1,645 (14.4%); American Indian, 24 (0.2%); Asian, 21 (0.2%); Other, 136 (1.2%). Hispanic, 272 (2.4%).

Vital Statistics, 1993: Births, 143; deaths, 155; marriages, 107; divorces, 57.

Recreation: Lake activities; fishing, hiking, hunting; Davy Crockett National Forest; historic sites.

Minerals: Limited oil, gas, lignite, sand and gravel.

Agriculture: Timber sales; other farm income from beef cattle, poultry, hogs; crops include hay, vegetables, peaches, pecans.

GROVETON (1,256) county seat; gateway to national forest recreation areas; lumber center; petroleum processing.

Trinity (2,800), steel fabrication; hospital; forest-industries center; near Livingston Lake.

Other towns include: **Sebastopol** (31) historic town.

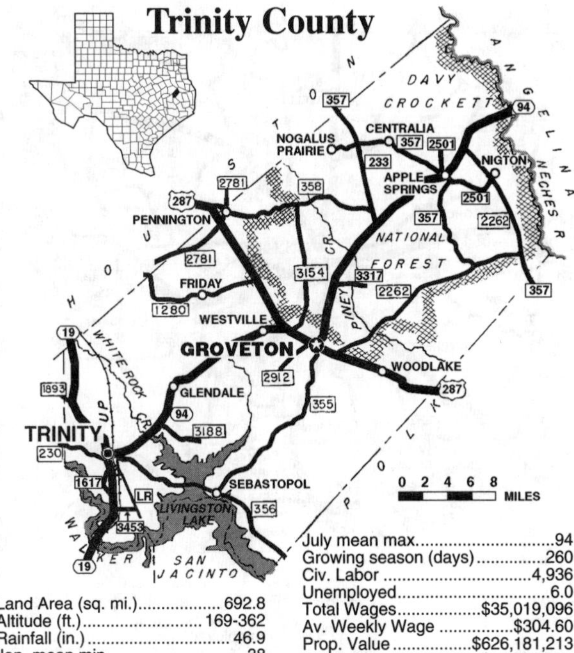

Population	**12,065**
(Change fm '90)	5.4
Land Area (sq. mi.)	692.8
Altitude (ft.)	169-362
Rainfall (in.)	46.9
Jan. mean min.	38
July mean max.	94
Growing season (days)	260
Civ. Labor	4,936
Unemployed	6.0
Total Wages	$35,019,096
Av. Weekly Wage	$304.60
Prop. Value	$626,181,213
Retail Sales	$53,877,795

Tyler County

Physical Features: Hilly East Texas county; densely timbered; drains to Neches, Angelina rivers; B.A. Steinhagen Lake; Big Thicket is unique plant and animal area.

Economy: Lumbering, prison unit, some manufacturing; tourism.

History: Named for U.S. President John Tyler; county created 1846 from Liberty.

Ethnicity, 1990: White, 14,550 (87.4%); Black, 1,994 (12.0%); American Indian, 46 (0.3%); Asian, 12 (0.1%); Other, 44 (0.3%). Hispanic, 177 (1.1%).

Vital Statistics, 1993: Births, 195; deaths, 248; marriages, 156; divorces, 101.

Recreation: Big Thicket National Preserve; Heritage Village; lake activities; Allan Shivers Museum; state forest; historic sites; dogwood festival; rodeo, frontier frolics in September; gospel music fest in June.

Minerals: Oil, natural gas.

Agriculture: Timber sales; beef cattle, hay, hunting leases. Some goats, ostriches and emus.

WOODVILLE (2,873) county seat; lumber, cattle market; varied manufacturing; tourism; hospital; prison unit.

Other towns include: **Chester** (316), **Colmesneil** (618).

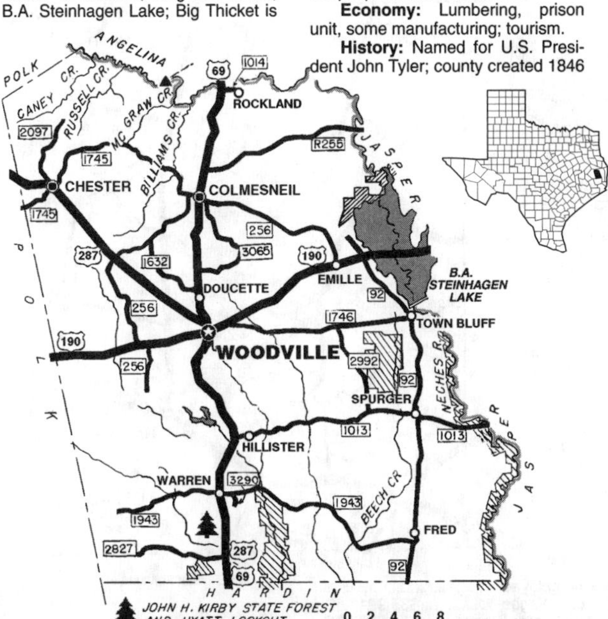

Population	**17,909**
(Change fm '90)	7.6
Land Area (sq. mi.)	922.9
Altitude (ft.)	109-443
Rainfall (in.)	52.0
Jan. mean min.	38
July mean max.	94
Growing season (days)	241
Civ. Labor	6,721
Unemployed	9.2
Total Wages	$62,478,440
Av. Weekly Wage	$322.27
Prop. Value	$863,816,390
Retail Sales	$83,454,357

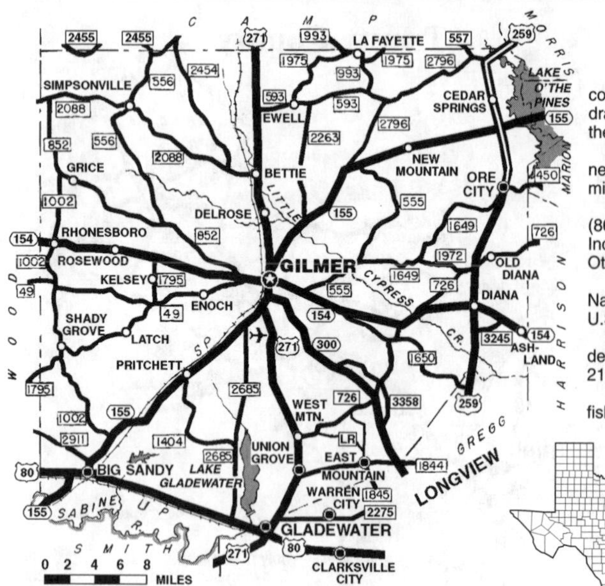

Upshur County

Physical Features: East Texas county; rolling to hilly, over half forested; drains to Sabine, Cypress Creek, Lake O' the Pines, Lake Gladewater.

Economy: Manufacturing, agribusinesses, petroleum products and lumber mill; many residents work at area plants.

Ethnicity, 1990: White, 27,076 (86.3%); Black, 3,881 (12.4%); American Indian, 121 (0.4%); Asian, 29 (0.1%); Other, 263 (0.8%). Hispanic, 641 (2.0%).

History: Created from Harrison, Nacogdoches counties 1846; named for U.S. Secretary of State A.P. Upshur.

Vital Statistics, 1993: Births, 454; deaths, 343; marriages, 273; divorces, 214.

Recreation: Scenic trails; hunting, fishing; rose festival, pecan festival, East Texas Yamboree in October.

Minerals: Oil, gas, sand, gravel.

Agriculture: Beef and dairy cattle, poultry; among leading broiler and dairy producing counties; vegetable crops, hay, peaches raised; timber a major product.

GILMER (5,153) county seat; varied manufacturing; timber, ceramics produced; vegetable processing; medical center; civic center.

Other towns include: **Big Sandy** (1,238); **Diana** (200); **East Mountain** (848); **Ore City** (959); **Union Grove** (286).

Population	**33,092**
(Change fm '90)	5.5
Land Area (sq. mi.)	587.7
Altitude (ft.)	228-685
Rainfall (in.)	45.1
Jan. mean min.	32
July mean max.	94
Growing season (days)	245
Civ. Labor	15,219
Unemployed	5.6
Total Wages	$98,389,107
Av. Weekly Wage	$350.75
Prop. Value	$1,151,140,294
Retail Sales	$165,552,477

Upton County

Physical Features: Western county; north flat, south rolling, hilly; limestone, sandy loam soils, drains to creeks.

Business: Oil, electric power plant, cotton, ranching.

History: Created in 1887 from Tom Green County; organized 1910; name honors brothers John and William Upton, Confederate colonels.

Ethnicity, 1990: White, 3,487 (78.4%); Black, 94 (2.1%); American Indian, 20 (0.4%); Asian, 2 (0.0%); Other, 844 (19.0%). Hispanic, 1,666 (37.5%).

Vital Statistics, 1993: Births, 51; deaths, 41; marriages, 39; divorces, 14.

Recreation: Historic sites, Mendoza Trail Museum; scenic areas; chili cookoff in October, Christmas bazaar.

Minerals: Oil, natural gas.

Agriculture: Cotton, pecans, livestock.

RANKIN (1,005) county seat, oil, ranching.

McCamey (2,487) oil, ranching; hospital; pecan show.

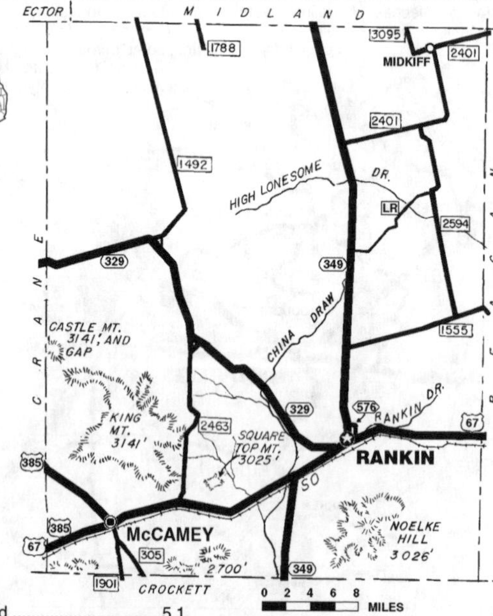

Population	**4,446**
(Change fm '90)	0
Land Area (sq. mi.)	1,241.7
Altitude (ft.)	2,441-3,141
Rainfall (in.)	12.7
Jan. mean min.	31
July mean max.	96
Growing season (days)	232
Civ. Labor	1,925
Unemployed	5.1
Total Wages	$35,991,255
Av. Weekly Wage	$507.06
Prop. Value	$802,199,032
Retail Sales	$13,120,960

For explanation of sources, abbreviations and symbols, see p. 132.

Uvalde County

Physical Features: Edwards Plateau, rolling hills below escarpment; spring-fed Sabinal, Frio, Leona, Nueces rivers; cypress, cedar, other trees; unique maple groves.

Economy: Agribusinesses; light manufacturing; tourism; hunting leases.

History: Created from Bexar 1850; re-created, organized 1856; named for 1778 governor of Coahuila, Juan de Ugalde, with name Anglicized.

Ethnicity, 1990: White, 15,078 (64.6%); Black, 47 (0.2%); American Indian, 49 (0.2%); Asian, 70 (0.3%); Other, 8,096 (34.7%). Hispanic, 14,104 (60.4%).

Vital Statistics, 1993: Births, 463; deaths, 190; marriages, 206; divorces, 114.

Recreation: Deer, turkey hunting area; Garner State Park; water activities on rivers; John Nance Garner Museum; Uvalde Memorial Park; scenic trails; historic sites; recreational homes.

Minerals: Asphalt, stone, sand and gravel.

Agriculture: Beef cattle, goats, sheep; crops include corn, cotton, grain sorghums, hay, wheat; vegetables; substantial irrigation.

UVALDE (15,529) county seat; varied manufacturing; vegetable, wool, mohair processing; junior college; A&M Research Center; hospital.

Other towns include: **Sabinal** (1,634), farm, ranch center; gateway to Frio and Sabinal canyons; tourist, retirement area; **Knippa** (360); **Utopia** (360) resort.

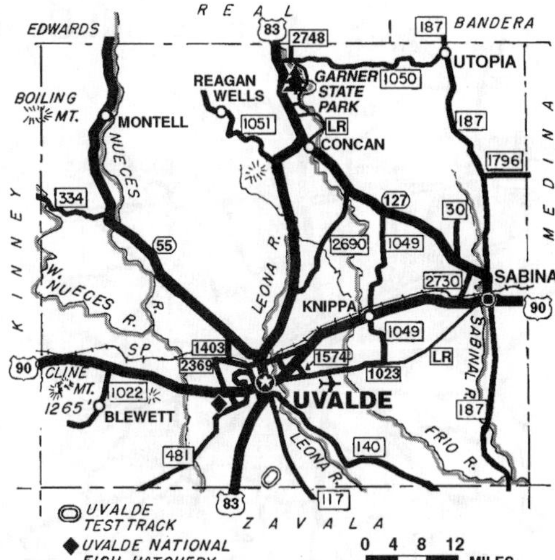

Population	**24,267**
(Change fm '90)	4.0
Land Area (sq. mi.)	1,556.6
Altitude (ft.)	699-1,957
Rainfall (in.)	4.1
Jan. mean min.	37
July mean max.	97
Growing season (days)	255
Civ. Labor	10,459
Unemployed	11.1
Total Wages	$131,046,382
Av. Weekly Wage	$308.55
Prop. Value	$995,383,580
Retail Sales	$180,782,157

Val Verde County

Physical Features: Southwestern county bordering Mexico, rolling, hilly; brushy; Devils, Pecos rivers, Amistad Reservoir; limestone, alluvial soils.

Business: Agribusiness; tourism; area trade center; large military, other federal expenditures.

History: Only county named for Civil War battle; Val Verde means green valley. Created 1885 from Crockett, Kinney, Pecos counties.

Ethnicity, 1990: White, 26,694 (68.9%); Black, 757 (2.0%); American Indian, 126 (0.3%); Asian, 244 (0.6%); Other, 10,900 (28.2%). Hispanic, 27,299 (70.5%).

Vital Statistics, 1993: Births, 942; deaths, 284; marriages, 571; divorces, 171.

Recreation: Gateway to Mexico; deer hunting, fishing; Amistad lake activities; two state parks; Langtry restoration of Judge Roy Bean's saloon; San Felipe Springs.

Minerals: Production sand and gravel, gas, oil.

Agriculture: Sheep, Angora goats, cattle,

DEL RIO (33,271) county seat; tourism and trade with Mexico; varied manufacturing, twin plants; hospital; **Laughlin Air Force Base** (2,819).

Other towns include: **Comstock** (375); **Langtry** (145).

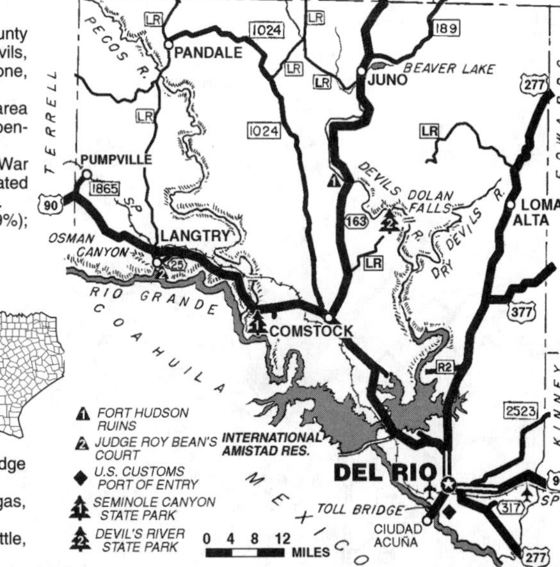

Population	**41,790**
(Change fm '90)	7.9
Land Area (sq. mi.)	3,170.6
Altitude (ft.)	925-2,248
Rainfall (in.)	17.2
Jan. mean min.	38
July mean max.	98
Growing season (days)	300
Civ. Labor	18,230
Unemployed	11.5
Total Wages	$167,567,342
Av. Weekly Wage	$317.25
Prop. Value	$850,923,530
Retail Sales	$277,377,986

Van Zandt County

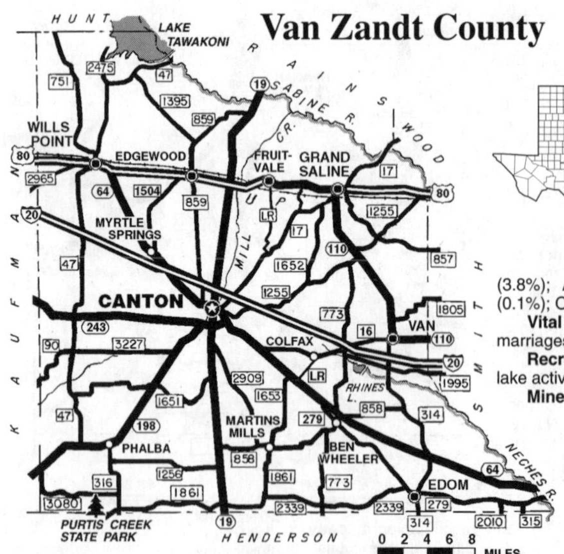

Physical Features: Northeastern county in three soil belts; level to rolling; Sabine, Neches rivers; Lake Tawakoni; partly forested.

Economy: Oil, tourism, agribusinesses, light manufacturing; many commute to jobs in Dallas.

History: Named for Republic leader Isaac Van Zandt; county created from Henderson 1848.

Ethnicity, 1990: White, 35,351 (93.2%); Black, 1,451 (3.8%); American Indian, 155 (0.4%); Asian, 47 (0.1%); Other, 940 (2.5%). Hispanic, 1,515 (4.0%).

Vital Statistics, 1993: Births, 459; deaths, 474; marriages, 325; divorces, 240.

Recreation: Canton First Monday trades days; lake activities; state park; historic sites.

Minerals: Oil, gas, salt, iron ore, clays.

Agriculture: Nursery plants; beef cattle, dairy products; a major hay and sweet potato producer, also vegetables; some timber, firewood sales.

CANTON (3,195) county seat; tourism; agribusiness; hospice; bluegrass festival, motorcycle rally in June.

Wills Point (3,128) livestock market, some manufacturing, clinic.

Other towns include: **Edgewood** (1,380) heritage square; **Edom** (325) fall art fair; **Fruitvale** (356); **Grand Saline** (2,697), salt plant, manufacturing, hospital; salt palace; **Van** (2,000) oil center, medical clinic.

Population	**39,335**
(Change fm '90)	3.7
Land Area (sq. mi.)	848.8
Altitude (ft.)	421-573
Rainfall (in.)	42.4
Jan. mean min.	32
July mean max.	97
Growing season (days)	250
Civ. Labor	18,586
Unemployed	4.9
Total Wages	$125,174,903
Av. Weekly Wage	$340.96
Prop. Value	$1,535,859,846
Retail Sales	$179,432,542

Victoria County

Physical Features: South Central county of rolling prairies, intersected by many streams; sandy loams, clays, alluvial soils.

Economy: Petrochemical plants, oil, manufacturing, agribusiness, tourism.

History: An original county, created 1836 from Mexican municipality named for President Guadalupe Victoria of Mexico.

Ethnicity, 1990: White, 59,251 (79.7%); Black, 4,906 (6.6%); American Indian, 208 (0.3%); Asian, 257 (0.3%); Other, 9,739 (13.1%). Hispanic, 25,372 (34.1%).

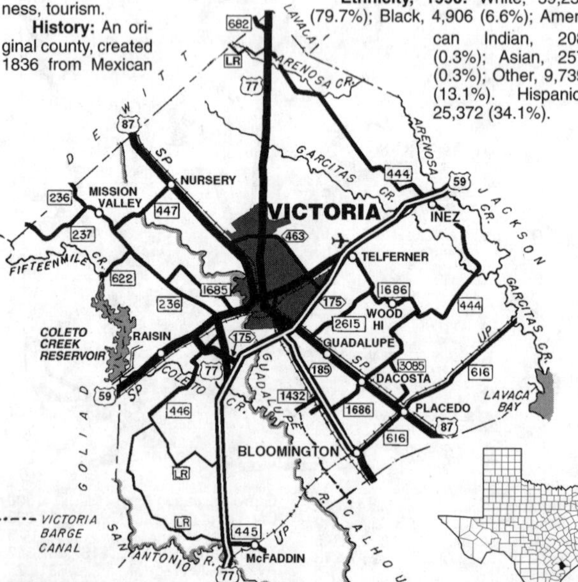

Vital Statistics, 1993: Births, 1,261; deaths, 572; marriages, 732; divorces, 410.

Recreation: Fishing, hunting; saltwater activities; historic homes, sites; riverside park, Coleto Creek Reservoir and park; recreational park; zoo; Czech Heritage Festival in October.

Minerals: Oil, gas, sand, gravel.

Agriculture: Beef cattle provide most income; crops include corn, grain sorghums, cotton, rice, soybeans.

VICTORIA (58,906) county seat; tourism, agribusiness center; on barge canal; petrochemicals; foundry equipment; Victoria College, University of Houston at Victoria; community theater, symphony; hospitals.

Other towns include: **Bloomington** (1,981), **Inez** (1,433).

Population	**78,509**
(Change fm '90)	5.6
Land Area (sq. mi.)	882.5
Altitude (ft.)	38-205
Rainfall (in.)	36.9
Jan. mean min.	43
July mean max.	94
Growing season (days)	290
Civ. Labor	41,995
Unemployed	6.1
Total Wages	$679,654,016
Av. Weekly Wage	$410.49
Prop. Value	$3,108,721,050
Retail Sales	$799,189,362

For explanation of sources, abbreviations and symbols, see p. 132.

Walker County

Physical Features: Southeastern county north of Houston of rolling hills; more than 70 percent forested; national forest; San Jacinto, Trinity rivers.

Economy: State employment in prison system, education; tourism; timber; beef cattle.

History: Created 1846 from Montgomery County; first named for U.S. Secretary of Treasury R.J. Walker; renamed 1863 for Texas Ranger Capt. S.H. Walker.

Ethnicity, 1990: White, 34,946 (68.6%); Black, 12,334 (24.2%); American Indian, 187 (0.4%); Asian, 323 (0.6%); Other, 3,127 (6.1%). Hispanic, 5,493 (10.8%).

Vital Statistics, 1993: Births, 593; deaths, 336; marriages, 463; divorces, 251.

Recreation: Fishing, hunting; lake activities; Sam Houston Museum, homes, grave; prison museum; other historic sites; state park; Sam Houston National Forest; Cinco de Mayo celebration, Sam Houston folk festival in April.

Minerals: Clays, natural gas, oil, sand and gravel, stone.

Agriculture: Timber sales substantial; cattle, exotics; nursery plants, hay, Christmas trees.

HUNTSVILLE (29,907) county seat; Texas Department of Criminal Justice headquarters; Sam Houston State University, museum; varied manufacturing; oil, gas, lignite exploration; hospital.

Other towns include: **New Waverly** (997), **Riverside** (479).

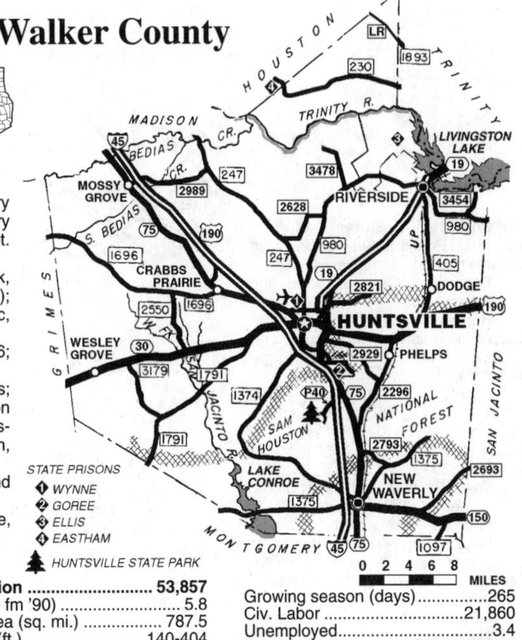

Population	**53,857**
(Change fm '90)	5.8
Land Area (sq. mi.)	787.5
Altitude (ft.)	140-404
Rainfall (in.)	44.2
Jan. mean min.	38
July mean max.	95
Growing season (days)	265
Civ. Labor	21,860
Unemployed	3.4
Total Wages	$386,749,158
Av. Weekly Wage	$385.12
Prop. Value	$1,163,061,560
Retail Sales	$324,047,055

Waller County

Physical Features: Southeastern county near Houston on rolling prairie; drains to Brazos; alluvial soils; about 20 percent forested.

Economy: Oil, agribusiness, manufacturing; education; county part of Houston metropolitan area.

History: Named for Edwin Waller, Republic leader; county created 1873 from Austin, Grimes counties.

Ethnicity, 1990: White, 12,987 (55.5%); Black, 8,796 (37.6%); American Indian, 28 (0.1%); Asian, 69 (0.3%); Other, 1,510 (6.5%). Hispanic, 2,592 (11.1%).

Vital Statistics, 1993: Births, 356; deaths, 205; marriages, 248; divorces, 93.

Recreation: Fishing, hunting; historic sites; museum.

Minerals: Oil, gas, sand, gravel.

Agriculture: Beef cattle, hogs, goats; crops include rice, hay, corn; 10,000 acres irrigated for rice, commercial vegetables and peanuts; some timber marketed.

HEMPSTEAD (3,763) county seat; agribusiness center; varied manufacturing; mental health facility, hospital; watermelon fest.

Prairieview (4,244), home of Prairie View A&M University.

Other towns include: **Brookshire** (3,305), **Pattison** (364), **Pine Island** (564), **Waller** (1,639, partly in Harris County).

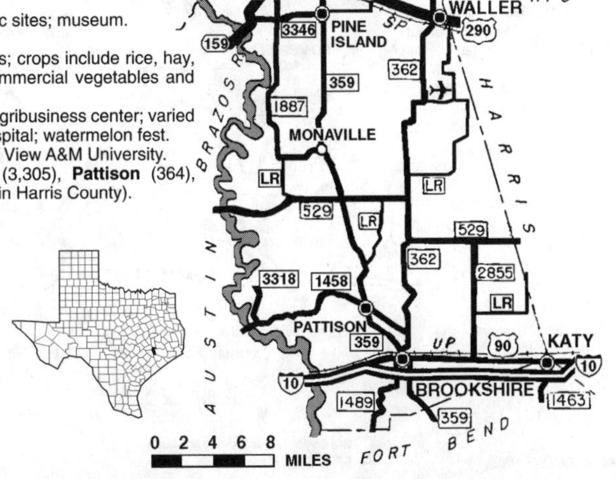

Population	**25,226**
(Change fm '90)	7.8
Land Area (sq. mi.)	513.6
Altitude (ft.)	110-249
Rainfall (in.)	38.2
Jan. mean min.	38
July mean max.	95
Growing season (days)	283
Civ. Labor	10,993
Unemployed	4.6
Total Wages	$157,170,473
Av. Weekly Wage	$389.69
Prop. Value	$5,709,832,281
Retail Sales	$352,622,325

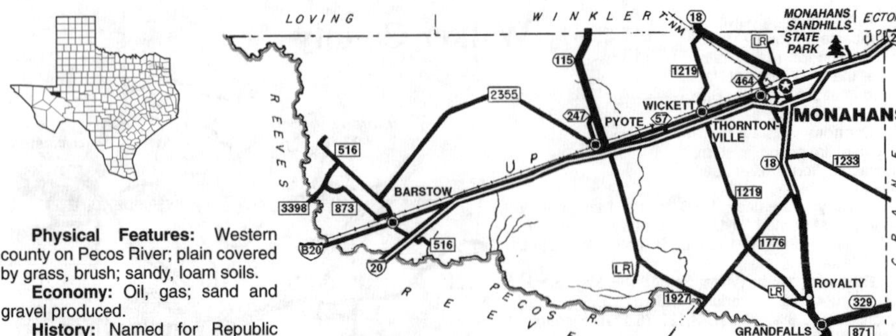

Ward County

Physical Features: Western county on Pecos River; plain covered by grass, brush; sandy, loam soils.

Economy: Oil, gas; sand and gravel produced.

History: Named for Republic leader Thomas W. Ward; county created from Tom Green 1887; organized 1892.

Ethnicity, 1990: White, 9,905 (75.5%); Black, 457 (3.5%); American Indian, 75 (0.6%); Asian, 25 (0.2%); Other, 2,653 (20.2%). Hispanic, 4,830 (36.8%).

Vital Statistics, 1993: Births, 172; deaths, 109; marriages, 79; divorces, 56.

Recreation: Sandhills state park, museum; Pyote Rattlesnake Museum; Million Barrel Museum; county park; freedom fair in July.

Minerals: Oil, gas, sand, gravel.

Agriculture: Beef cattle; horses, hogs and goats also raised; cotton, alfalfa, pecans, hay grown; some irrigation for cotton.

MONAHANS (8,132) county seat; center for oil, agribusiness; gasoline plant; pecan shelling; county hospital, nursing home.

Other towns include: **Barstow** (562); **Grandfalls** (617); **Pyote** (373), West Texas Children's Home; **Thorntonville** (742); **Wickett** (558).

Population	**13,247**
(Change fm '90)	1.0
Land Area (sq. mi.)	8353.5
Altitude (ft.)	2,467-2,799
Rainfall (in.)	12.3
Jan. mean min.	29
July mean max.	96
Growing season (days)	223
Civ. Labor	4,758
Unemployed	8.4
Total Wages	$80,486,226
Av. Weekly Wage	$428.97
Prop. Value	$992,956,582
Retail Sales	$56,238,615

Washington County

Physical Features: Southeastern county in Brazos valley; rolling prairie of sandy loam, alluvial soils.

Business: Agribusinesses, oil, tourism, manufacturing.

History: Named for George Washington; an original county, created 1836, organized 1837.

Ethnicity, 1990: White, 19,782 (75.6%); Black, 5,463 (20.9%); American Indian, 46 (0.2%); Asian, 186 (0.7%); Other, 677 (2.6%). Hispanic, 1,158 (4.4%).

Vital Statistics, 1993: Births, 349; deaths, 301; marriages, 211; divorces, 140.

Recreation: Many historic sites; Washington-on-the-Brazos State Park; Texas Baptist Historical Museum; Star of Republic Museum; Somerville Lake; fishing, hunting; antique rose nursery, spring fling.

Minerals: Oil, gas and stone.

Agriculture: Beef cattle, hogs, horses, dairy products, poultry, ratites; crops chiefly cotton, corn, small grains.

BRENHAM (12,950) county seat; cotton processing; varied manufacturing including ceramics, mattresses, computers; wholesale distribution center; Blinn College, Brenham State School.

Other towns include: **Burton** (318), national landmark cotton gin; **Chappell Hill** (310) historic homes.

Population	**27,914**
(Change fm '90)	6.7
Land Area (sq. mi.)	609.2
Altitude (ft.)	343-460
Rainfall (in.)	39.7
Jan. mean min.	39
July mean max.	96
Growing season (days)	277
Civ. Labor	14,012
Unemployed	3.4
Total Wages	$219,031,592
Av. Weekly Wage	$379.33
Prop. Value	$1,395,817,411
Retail Sales	$214,101,302

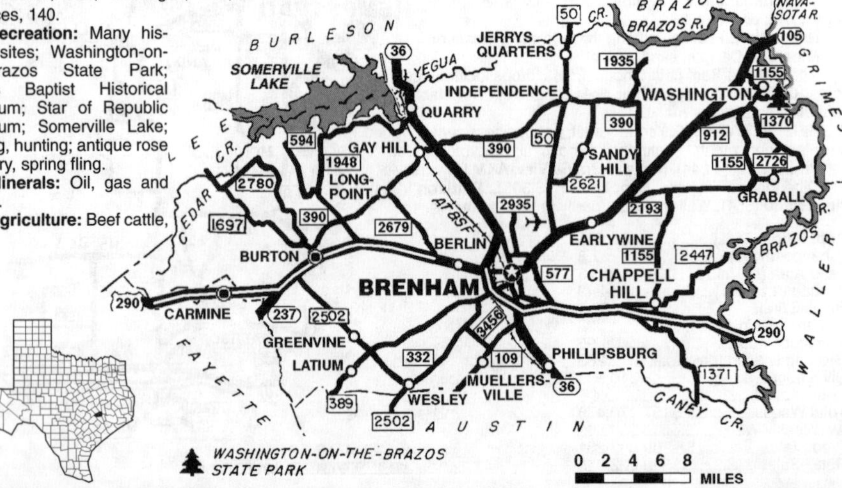

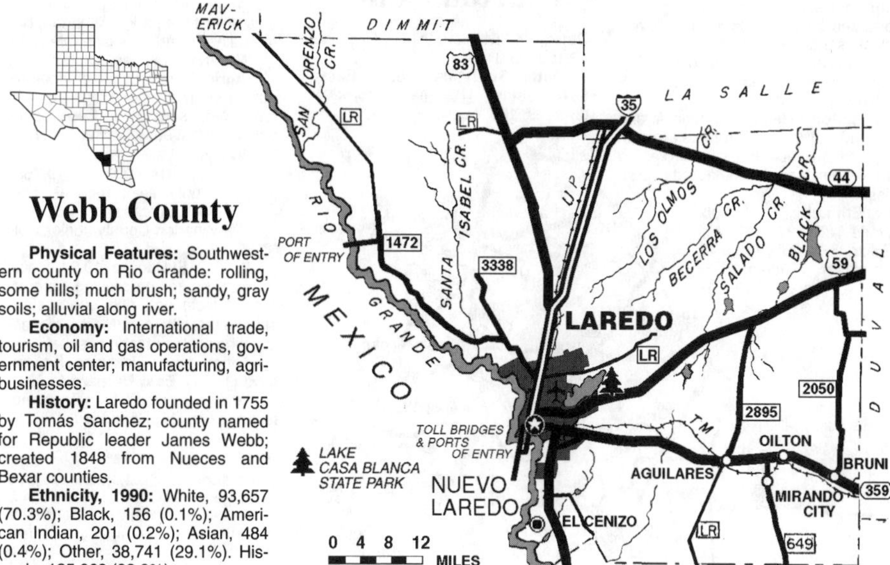

Webb County

Physical Features: Southwestern county on Rio Grande: rolling, some hills; much brush; sandy, gray soils; alluvial along river.

Economy: International trade, tourism, oil and gas operations, government center; manufacturing, agribusinesses.

History: Laredo founded in 1755 by Tomás Sanchez; county named for Republic leader James Webb; created 1848 from Nueces and Bexar counties.

Ethnicity, 1990: White, 93,657 (70.3%); Black, 156 (0.1%); American Indian, 201 (0.2%); Asian, 484 (0.4%); Other, 38,741 (29.1%). Hispanic, 125,069 (93.9%).

Vital Statistics, 1993: Births, 4,745; deaths, 814; marriages, 1,993; divorces, 421.

Recreation: Major tourist gateway to Mexico; top hunting, fishing; Lake Casa Blanca State Park, water recreation; art festival; Washington's Birthday celebration; historic sites; museum; Fort McIntosh.

Minerals: Natural gas, oil, coal, caliche, stone, sand and gravel.

Agriculture: Beef cow-calf operations; some stocker production; vegetables, hay, wheat; about 4,500 acres irrigated; buffelgrass planted to improve pastures; mesquite package wood sales.

LAREDO (140,688) county seat; manufacturing; meat packing; rail, highway gateway to Mexico; junior college, Texas A&M International University; mental health center; hospitals.

Other towns include: **Bruni** (698); **El Cenizo** (1,511); **Mirando City** (559); **Oilton** (458).

For explanation of sources, abbreviations and symbols, see p. 132.

Population	**153,538**
(Change fm '90)	15.2
Land Area (sq. mi.)	3,356.9
Altitude (ft.)	372-899
Rainfall (in.)	20.1
Jan. mean min.	45
July mean max.	99
Growing season (days)	322
Civ. Labor	67,589
Unemployed	9.3
Total Wages	$993,369,177
Av. Weekly Wage	$351.03
Prop. Value	$4,735,644,258
Retail Sales	$1,935,187,782

On the streets of Laredo, the smaller building dates from Spanish times and now is a museum housing a collection of artifacts. The museum sits adjacent to a downtown hotel. Dallas Morning News photo by Kathryn Straach.

Wharton County

Physical Features: Southeastern county near Houston on prairie; bisected by Colorado River; alluvial, black, sandy loam soils.

Economy: Oil, sulphur, other minerals; agribusiness, varied manufacturing.

History: Named for John A. and William H. Wharton, brothers active in the Texas Revolution; county created 1846 from Jackson, Matagorda counties.

Ethnicity, 1990: White, 29,127 (72.9%); Black, 6,308 (15.8%); American Indian, 38 (0.1%); Asian, 131 (0.3%); Other, 4,351 (10.9%). Hispanic, 10,103 (25.3%).

Vital Statistics, 1993: Births, 631; deaths, 419; marriages, 291; divorces, 166.

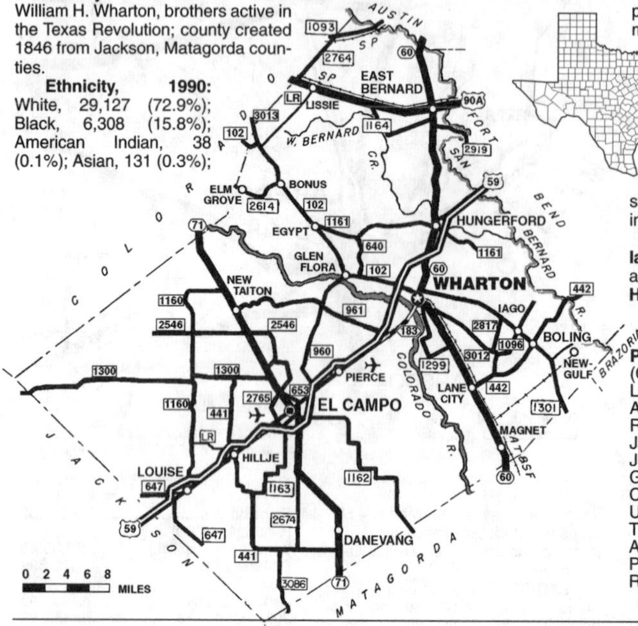

Recreation: Hunting, fishing; big-game, art and historical museums; river-front park in Wharton; historic sites; WhartonFest on Colorado.

Minerals: Oil, gas, sulphur.

Agriculture: Leading rice-producing county; other crops are cotton, corn, sorghums; Beef cattle, poultry; about 90,000 acres irrigated, mostly rice.

WHARTON (9,758) county seat; mineral, produce processing; hospitals; Wharton County Junior College.

El Campo (10,943), aluminum processing, manufacturing, rice processing, storage; plastic, styrofoam processing; wholesale nursery; hospital.

Other towns include: **Boling-Iago** (1,171); **East Bernard** (1,671), agribusiness, varied manufacturing; **Hungerford** (178); **Louise** (310).

Population	**41,618**
(Change fm '90)	4.2
Land Area (sq. mi.)	1,090.2
Altitude (ft.)	71-148
Rainfall (in.)	41.3
Jan. mean min.	44
July mean max.	93
Growing season (days)	266
Civ. Labor	19,166
Unemployed	6.7
Total Wages	$259,118,383
Av. Weekly Wage	$371.75
Prop. Value	$1,878,722,344
Retail Sales	$299,504,975

Wheeler County

Physical Features: Panhandle county adjoining Oklahoma. Plain, on edge of Caprock; Red River, Sweetwater Creek; some canyons; red sandy loam, black clay soils.

Economy: Oil, agribusinesses, tourism.

History: Named for pioneer jurist R.T. Wheeler; county created from Bexar, Young districts 1876; organized 1879.

Ethnicity, 1990: White, 5,424 (92.3%); Black, 154 (2.6%); American Indian, 42 (0.7%); Asian, 23 (0.4%); Other, 236 (4.0%). Hispanic, 378 (6.4%).

Vital Statistics, 1993: Births, 75; deaths, 82; marriages, 105; divorces, 31.

Recreation: Pioneer West museum at Shamrock; historic sites; Old Mobeetie trading post, Fort Elliott; ostrich depot.

Minerals: Oil, natural gas.

Agriculture: Fed beef, cow-calf and stocker cattle, swine, horses, ostriches; crops include wheat, grain sorghums, cotton.

WHEELER (1,407) county seat; agribusiness; petroleum center; tourism; slaughter plant; hospital; library.

Shamrock (2,206) Tourism; agribusiness; hospital; library; St. Patrick's Day event; Octoberfest.

Other towns include: **Allison** (135); **Lela** (135); **Mobeetie** (159).

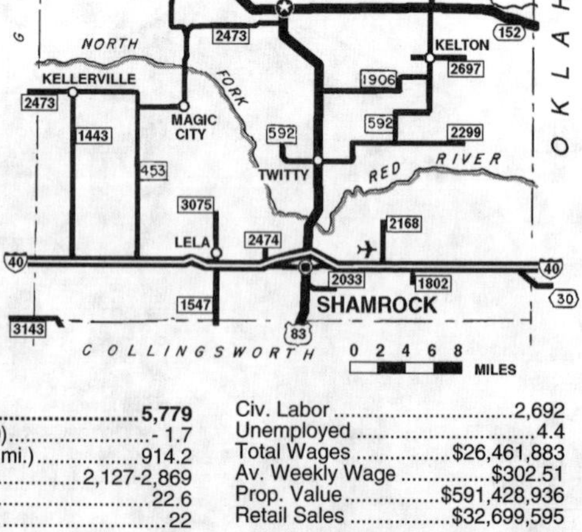

Population	**5,779**
(Change fm '90)	- 1.7
Land Area (sq. mi.)	914.2
Altitude (ft.)	2,127-2,869
Rainfall (in.)	22.6
Jan. mean min.	22
July mean max.	96
Growing season (days)	208
Civ. Labor	2,692
Unemployed	4.4
Total Wages	$26,461,883
Av. Weekly Wage	$302.51
Prop. Value	$591,428,936
Retail Sales	$32,699,595

For explanation of sources, abbreviations and symbols, see p. 132.

Wichita County

Physical Features: North central county in prairie bordering Oklahoma; drained by Red, Wichita rivers; lakes; sandy, loam soils.

Economy: Retail trade center for large area; air base; government, manufacturing, oil, medical services and agribusiness.

History: Named for Indian tribe; county created from Young Territory 1858; organized 1882.

Ethnicity, 1990: White, 102,427 (83.7%); Black, 11,221 (9.2%); American Indian, 903 (0.7%); Asian, 1,851 (1.5%); Other, 5,976 (4.9%). Hispanic, 10,555 (8.6%).

Vital Statistics, 1993: Births, 1,874; deaths, 1,226; marriages, 2,277; divorces, 914.

Recreation: Metropolitan events; museums; historic Kell House; Oil Bowl football game in August; collegiate activities; water sports on lakes.

Minerals: Oil, natural gas, sand, gravel, stone.

Agriculture: Stocker, cow-calf production important; wheat, cotton; 2,500 acres irrigated for cotton and coastal Bermuda.

WICHITA FALLS (98,356) county seat; distribution center for large area in Texas, Oklahoma; varied manufacturing; oil-field services; hospitals; Midwestern State University, vocational-technical training center; Sheppard Air Force Base; Wichita Falls State Hospital; major bicycle race in summer.

Other cities include: **Burkburnett** (11,043) some manufacturing; **Electra** (3,307); **Iowa Park** (6,538) some manufacturing, clinic; **Pleasant Valley** (410).

Population	**126,149**
(Change fm '90)	3.1
Land Area (sq. mi.)	627.6
Altitude (ft.)	954-1,225
Rainfall (in.)	26.7
Jan. mean min.	28
July mean max.	99
Growing season (days)	229
Civ. Labor	59,229
Unemployed	5.6
Total Wages	$1,007,282,643
Av. Weekly Wage	$394.83
Prop. Value	$3,573,568,271
Retail Sales	$1,142,416,826

For explanation of sources, abbreviations and symbols, see p. 132.

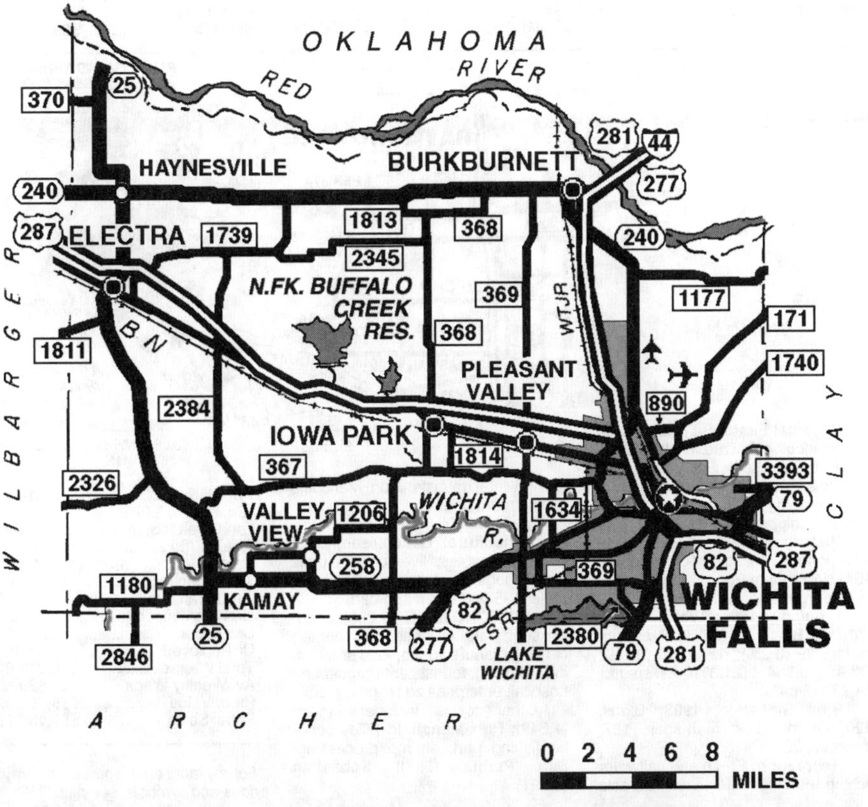

Wilbarger County

Physical Features: Gently rolling prairie draining to Red, Pease rivers, tributaries; sandy, loam, waxy soils; Santa Rosa Lake.

Economy: Agribusinesses, oil.

History: Named for pioneers Josiah and Mathias Wilbarger; created from Bexar District 1858; organized 1881.

Ethnicity, 1990: White, 12,010 (79.4%); Black, 1,349 (8.9%); American Indian, 80 (0.5%); Asian, 82 (0.5%); Other, 1,600 (10.6%). Hispanic, 2,185 (14.5%).

Vital Statistics, 1993: Births, 204; deaths, 213; marriages, 341; divorces, 95.

Recreation: Doan's Crossing, on route of cattle drives; other historic sites; Red River Valley Museum; Santa Rosa roundup in May; hunting, fishing.

Minerals: Oil, natural gas.

Agriculture: Beef calves and hay; also, cotton, wheat, peanuts, watermelons; 25,000 acres irrigated.

VERNON (12,371) county seat; agribusiness, oil-producing center; varied manufacturing; electricity-generating plant; junior college; mental health center, hospital; downtown antiques, crafts mall.

Other towns include: **Harrold** (320); **Lockett** (200) A&M Extension Center; **Oklaunion** (138).

Population **15,607**
(Change fm '90) 3.2
Land Area (sq. mi.) 971.1
Altitude (ft.) 1,099-1,361
Rainfall (in.) 25.3
Jan. mean min. 28
July mean max. 99
Growing season (days) 221
Civ. Labor 7,320
Unemployed 4.5
Total Wages $107,326,586
Av. Weekly Wage $359.87
Prop. Value $882,816,464
Retail Sales $89,953,085

Willacy County

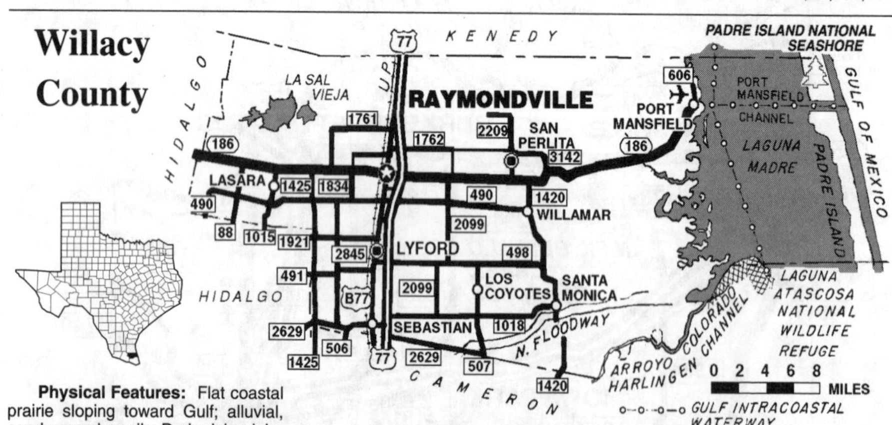

Physical Features: Flat coastal prairie sloping toward Gulf; alluvial, sandy, marshy soils; Padre Island; La Sal Vieja, salt lake; wildlife refuge.

Economy: Oil, agribusinesses; tourism; shipping.

History: Named for Texas legislator John G. Willacy; county created 1911 from Cameron, Hidalgo counties; reorganized 1921.

Ethnicity, 1990: White, 13,820 (78.1%); Black, 79 (0.4%); American Indian, 29 (0.2%); Asian, 13 (0.1%); Other, 3,764 (21.3%). Hispanic, 14,937 (84.4%).

Vital Statistics, 1993: Births, 420; deaths, 122; marriages, 167; divorces, 36.

Recreation: Fresh and saltwater fishing, hunting; mild climate attracts many winter tourists; Port Mansfield fishing tournament.

Minerals: Oil, natural gas.

Agriculture: Cotton, sorghums, corn, vegetables; livestock includes cattle, hogs, horses, Spanish goats raised; 35,000 acres irrigated.

RAYMONDVILLE (9,220) county seat; agribusiness, oil center; clothing manufacturing; food processing, shipping; tourist center; museum; hospital; enterprise zone; prison unit.

Other towns include: **Lyford** (1,849); **Port Mansfield** (731) popular fishing port; shrimp processing; **San Perlita** (562); **Sebastian** (1,691).

Population **18,775**
(Change fm '90) 6.0
Land Area (sq. mi.) 596.7
Altitude (ft.) .... sea level-55
Rainfall (in.) 27.5
Jan. mean min. 47
July mean max. 96
Growing season (days) 331
Civ. Labor 7,278
Unemployed 20.7
Total Wages $56,212,678
Av. Weekly Wage $296.04
Prop. Value $685,799,921
Retail Sales $59,165,794

For explanation of sources, abbreviations and symbols, see p. 132.

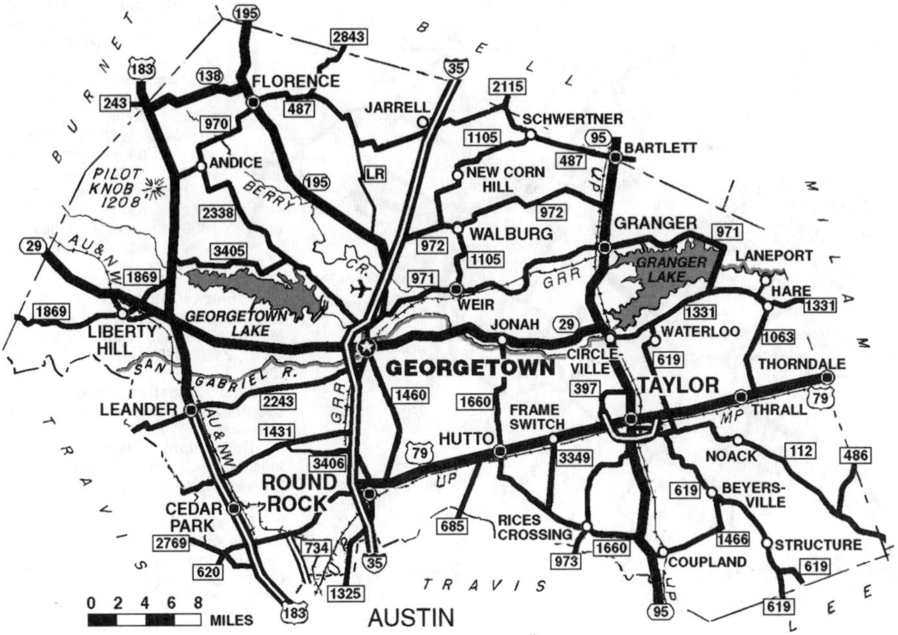

Williamson County

Physical Features: Central county near Austin. Level to rolling; mostly blackland soil, some loam, sand; drained by San Gabriel River and tributaries.

Economy: Agribusinesses, varied manufacturing, education center; the county is part of Austin metropolitan area.

History: Named for Robert M. Williamson, pioneer leader; county created from Milam and organized in 1848.

Ethnicity, 1990: White, 121,914 (87.4%); Black, 6,861 (4.9%); American Indian, 508 (0.4%); Asian, 1,846 (1.3%); Other, 8,422 (6.0%). Hispanic, 20,004 (14.3%).

Vital Statistics, 1993: Births, 2,642; deaths, 842; marriages, 1,203; divorces, 678.

Recreation: Lake recreation; Inner Space Cavern; historic sites; hunting; Gov. Dan Moody Museum at Taylor; San Gabriel Park; old settlers park; walking tours, rattlesnake sacking, barbecue cookoff, frontier days in summer.

Minerals: Building stone, oil, sand and gravel.

Agriculture: Beef cattle are top revenue source; leading crops grown

are sorghum, cotton, corn, wheat.

GEORGETOWN (16,752) county seat; manufacturing, tourism, mining, agriculture; hospital; Southwestern University; Mayfair; Christmas Stroll.

Taylor (11,971), agribusiness, publishing center; varied manufacturing including cottonseed and meat processing; hospital; Temple Junior College extension.

Round Rock (36,924, partly in Travis County), varied manufacturing; tourism and distribution center; hospital; Texas Baptist Children's Home.

Other towns include: **Andice** (25); **Bartlett** (1,509, partly in Bell County), first rural electrification in nation in 1933; clinic; library; **Cedar Park** (6,360); **Coupland** (135); **Florence** (921); **Granger** (1,294); **Hutto** (637).

Jarrell (410); **Leander** (3,634); **Liberty Hill** (300), artisans center; **Thrall** (609): **Walburg** (250); **Weir** (239).

Also, the residential community of **Anderson Mill** (10,347) which extends from Travis County.

Population	**154,669**
(Change fm '90)	10.8
Land Area (sq. mi.)	1,124.3
Altitude (ft.)	454-1,265
Rainfall (in.)	34.2
Jan. mean min.	35
July mean max.	97
Growing season (days)	258
Civ. Labor	97,696
Unemployed	2.3
Total Wages	$794,447,501
Av. Weekly Wage	$399.56
Prop. Value	$7,239,224,940
Retail Sales	$789,004,132

For explanation of sources, abbreviations and symbols, see p. 132.

Wilson County

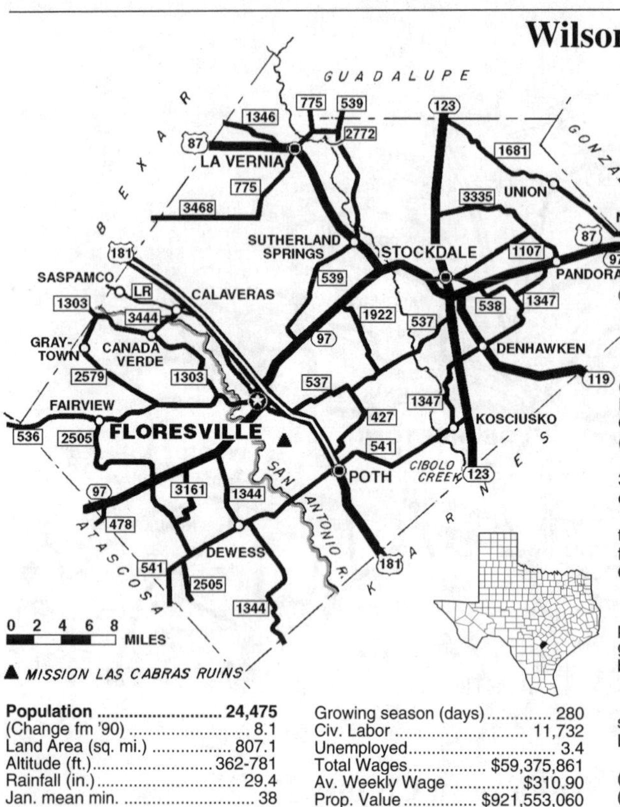

Physical Features: South central county on rolling plains; mostly sandy soils, some heavier; San Antonio River, Cibolo Creek.

Economy: Agribusiness; some residents employed in San Antonio; part of San Antonio metropolitan area.

History: Created from Bexar, Karnes counties 1860; named for James C. Wilson, member of the Mier Expedition.

Ethnicity, 1990: White, 19,652 (86.8%); Black, 242 (1.1%); American Indian, 45 (0.2%); Asian, 22 (0.1%); Other, 2,689 (11.9%). Hispanic, 8,054 (35.6%).

Vital Statistics, 1993: Births, 339; deaths, 206; marriages, 155; divorces, 95.

Recreation: Mission ruins, historic homes; Stockdale watermelon festival; Floresville peanut festival in October.

Minerals: Oil, gas, clays.

Agriculture: Beef cattle, hogs, poultry; crops include peanuts, sorghums, corn, small grains, vegetables, watermelons, fruit.

FLORESVILLE (5,710) county seat; agribusiness center; hospital; Hertiage Days in April.

Other towns include: **La Vernia** (715); **Poth** (1,876); **Stockdale** (1,331), food processing; medical center; recreation facilities.

Population	**24,475**
(Change fm '90)	8.1
Land Area (sq. mi.)	807.1
Altitude (ft.)	362-781
Rainfall (in.)	29.4
Jan. mean min.	38
July mean max.	97
Growing season (days)	280
Civ. Labor	11,732
Unemployed	3.4
Total Wages	$59,375,861
Av. Weekly Wage	$310.90
Prop. Value	$921,553,060
Retail Sales	$87,648,833

Winkler County

Physical Features: Western county adjoining New Mexico on plains, partly sandy hills.

Economy: Oil, natural gas.

History: Named for Confederate Col. C.M. Winkler; county created from Tom Green 1887; organized 1910.

Ethnicity, 1990: White, 6,184 (71.7%); Black, 167 (1.9%); American Indian, 48 (0.6%); Asian, 9 (0.1%); Other, 2,218 (25.7%). Hispanic, 3,172 (36.8%).

Vital Statistics, 1993: Births, 151; deaths, 75; marriages, 69; divorces, 31.

Recreation: Sandhills Park; museum; zoo; wooden oil derrick; Roy Orbison Festival in June at Wink.

Minerals: A leading petroleum-producing county; gas, salt also produced.

Agriculture: Cow-calf production, stocker cattle, horses; no crops.

KERMIT (7,001) county seat, and **Wink** (1,228) are oil-activity centers; hospital.

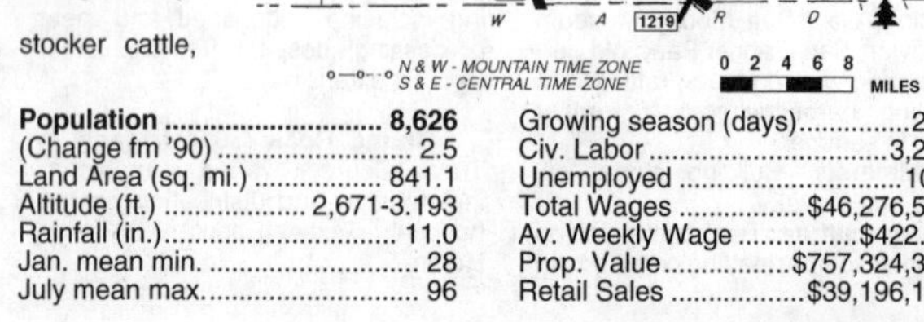

Population	**8,626**
(Change fm '90)	2.5
Land Area (sq. mi.)	841.1
Altitude (ft.)	2,671-3.193
Rainfall (in.)	11.0
Jan. mean min.	28
July mean max.	96
Growing season (days)	219
Civ. Labor	3,264
Unemployed	10.5
Total Wages	$46,276,531
Av. Weekly Wage	$422.72
Prop. Value	$757,324,310
Retail Sales	$39,196,133

For explanation of sources, abbreviations and symbols, see p. 132.

Wise County

Physical Features: North central county of rolling prairie, some oaks; clay, loam, sandy soils; lakes.

Economy: Agribusiness, petroleum, recreation; many residents work in Fort Worth.

History: Created 1856 from Cooke County; named for Virginian, U.S. Sen. Henry A. Wise, who favored annexation of Texas.

Ethnicity, 1990: White, 32,550 (93.9%); Black, 390 (1.1%); American Indian, 210 (0.6%); Asian, 83 (0.2%); Other, 1,446 (4.2%). Hispanic, 2,663 (7.7%).

Vital Statistics, 1993: Births, 437; deaths, 317; marriages, 296; divorces, 258.

Recreation: Lake activities; hunting; exotic deer preserve; historical sites; Lyndon B. Johnson National Grasslands; Chisholm trail days in June, antique auto swap meet; Butterfield stage days; heritage museum, old courthouse.

Minerals: Gas, oil, stone, clays, sand, gravel.

Agriculture: Dairy operations, beef cattle, horses, sheep, ratite birds; a leading dairy county; crops include hay, peanuts, grain sorghums, pecans, wheat and oats.

DECATUR (4,391) county seat; petroleum center; dairying; cattle marketing; some manufacturing; hospital.

Bridgeport (3,695), trade center for lake resort; oil, gas production; time-share housing; artistic community; manufacturing; hospital.

Other towns include: **Alvord** (913), **Aurora** (683), **Boyd** (1,079), **Briar** (4,023, partly in Tarrant, Parker counties), **Chico** (843), **Fairview** (221), **Lake Bridgeport** (349), **Newark** (712), **Rhome** (657).

Population **35,913**
(Change fm '90) 3.6
Land Area (sq. mi.) 904.6

Altitude (ft.) 693-1,180
Rainfall (in.) 28.9
Jan. mean min. 29
July mean max. 100
Growing season (days) 220
Civ. Labor 18,801
Unemployed 4.7
Total Wages $175,965,811
Av. Weekly Wage $412.50
Prop. Value $1,623,417,871
Retail Sales $218.151.214

Wood County

Physical Features: Hilly northeastern county almost half forested; sandy to alluvial soils; drained by Sabine and tributaries; many lakes.

Economy: Oil, natural gas, agribusiness, tourism.

History: Created from Van Zandt County 1850; named for Gov. George T. Wood.

Ethnicity, 1990: White, 26,363 (89.7%); Black, 2,402 (8.2%); American Indian, 109 (0.4%); Asian, 40 (0.1%); Other, 466 (1.6%). Hispanic, 788 (2.7%).

Vital Statistics, 1993: Births, 372; deaths, 418; marriages, 284; divorces, 203.

Recreation: Autumn trails; lake activities; hunting; Gov. Hogg Shrine State Park and museum; historic sites; scenic drives; Mineola May Days; railroad heritage days; autumn trails.

Minerals: A leading petroleum-producing county; natural gas, sand, gravel, clays also produced.

Agriculture: Dairy, beef cattle, horses, broilers, swine; sweet potatoes, truck crops, hay; timber sold.

QUITMAN (1,804) county seat; tourism; food processing; some manufacturing; hospital.

Mineola (4,521), farm, railroad center; food processing; some manufacturing; museum.

Winnsboro (3,093, partly in Franklin County) gas and oil, dairies, tourism; hospital.

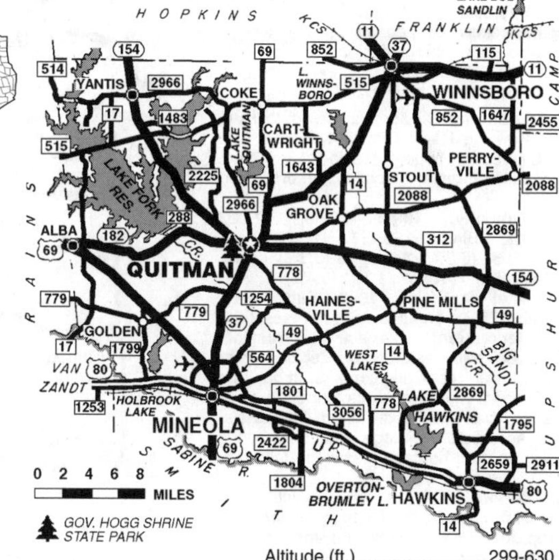

Other towns include: **Alba** (504, partly in Rains County); **Hawkins** (1,441); **Yantis** (232); .

Population **30,789**
(Change fm '90) 4.8
Land Area (sq. mi.) 650.2

Altitude (ft.) 299-630
Rainfall (in.) 45.0
Jan. mean min. 31
July mean max. 94
Growing season (days) 246
Civ. Labor 14,217
Unemployed 6.3
Total Wages $127,537,724
Av. Weekly Wage $334.71
Prop. Value $1,685,006,023
Retail Sales $189,441,196

Yoakum County

Physical Features: Western county is level to rolling; playas, draws; sandy, loam, chocolate soils.

Economy: Oil, agriculture.

History: Named for Henderson Yoakum, pioneer historian; created from Bexar District 1876; organized 1907.

Ethnicity, 1990: White, 6,300 (71.7%); Black, 86 (1.0%); American Indian, 31 (0.4%); Asian, 11 (0.1%); Other, 2,358 (26.8%). Hispanic, 3,217 (36.6%).

Vital Statistics, 1993: Births, 127; deaths, 56; marriages, 100; divorces, 34.

Recreation: Tsa Mo Ga Museum at Plains; settlers reunion in August.

Minerals: Oil, natural gas, salt makes this a leading minerals-producing county.

Agriculture: Grains, cotton, sorghums, wheat, peanuts; beef cattle raised; substantial irrigation.

PLAINS (1,414) county seat; oil, agribusiness center.

Denver City (5,121), center for oil, agriculture activities in two counties; hospital, library.

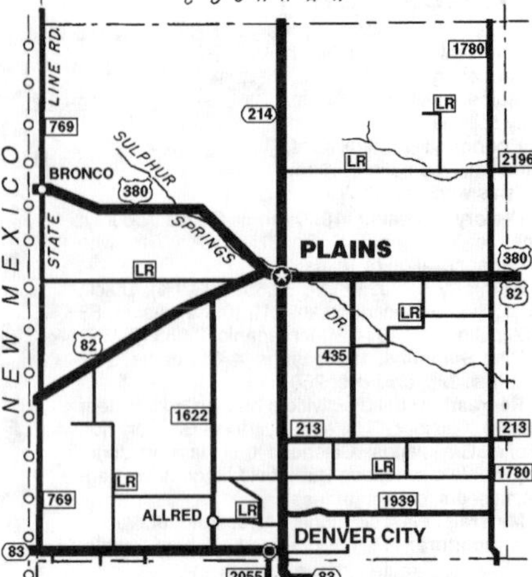

Population **8,705**
(Change fm '90) .... - 0.9
Land Area (sq. mi.) 799.7
Altitude (ft.) 3,490-3,891
Rainfall (in.) 16.2
Jan. mean min. 23
July mean max. 92
Growing season (days) 199
Civ. Labor 3,847
Unemployed 6.0
Total Wages $77,896,947
Av. Weekly Wage $473.69
Prop. Value $2,581,163,800
Retail Sales $49,216,956

Young County

Physical Features: Hilly, broken; drained by Brazos and tributaries; Possum Kingdom Lake, Lake Graham.

Economy: Oil, agribusinesses, tourism.

History: Named for early Texan, Col. W.C. Young; county created 1856 from Bosque, Fannin counties; reorganized 1874.

Ethnicity, 1990: White, 17,023 (93.9%); Black, 268 (1.5%); American Indian, 62 (0.3%); Asian, 49 (0.3%); Other, 724 (4.0%). Hispanic, 1,164 (6.4%).

Vital Statistics, 1993: Births, 227; deaths, 256; marriages, 157; divorces, 96.

Recreation: Lake activities; hunting; Fort Belknap restoration; site of former large Indian reservation; marker at oak tree in Graham where ranchers formed forerunner of Texas and Southwestern Cattle Raisers Association; vintage auto club spring tour; western heritage festiival in fall; one-arm dove hunt at Olney.

Minerals: Oil, gas, sand, gravel.

Agriculture: Beef cattle; wheat chief crop, also hay, cotton, pecans, nursery plants; hunting leases.

GRAHAM (9,014) county seat; agribusiness; manufacturing; oil-well servicing; hospital, mental health clinic; Ranger Junior College extension; Possom Fest in September.

Other towns include: **Olney** (3,473), agribusiness center; some manufacturing; hospital; art in the park in June; **Newcastle** (530).

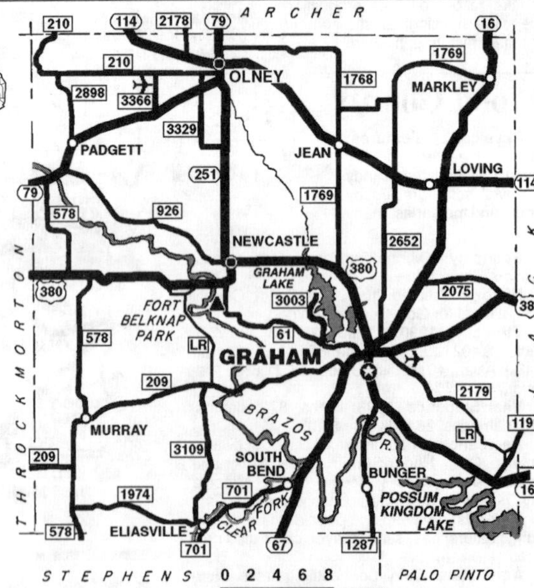

Population **18,153**
(Change fm '90) 0.1
Land Area (sq. mi.) 922.3
Altitude (ft.) 1,038-1,389
Rainfall (in.) 28,0
Jan. mean min. 28
July mean max. 97
Growing season (days) 216
Civ. Labor 8,869
Unemployed 8.4
Total Wages $120,579,231
Av. Weekly Wage $387.02
Prop. Value $738,541,180
Retail Sales $109,007,427

For explanation of sources, abbreviations and syimbols, see p. 132.

Zapata County

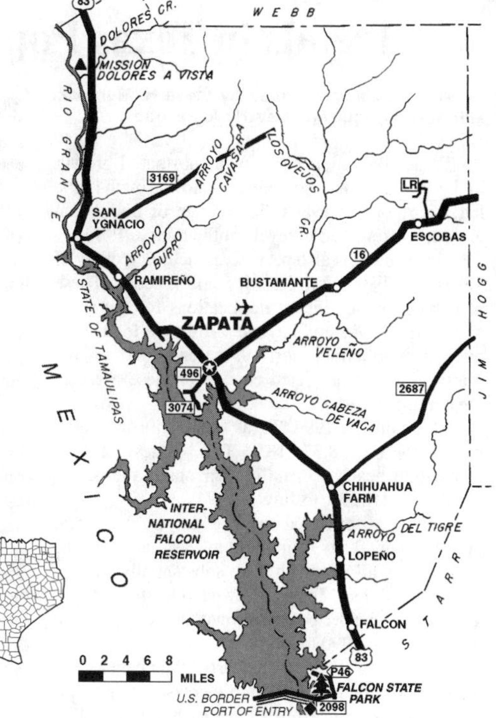

Physical Features: Southern county of rolling, brushy topography; broken by tributaries of Rio Grande; Falcon Reservoir.

Economy: Tourism, oil, ranching, Falcon Reservoir activities.

History: Named for Col. Antonio Zapata, pioneer rancher; county created 1858 from Starr, Webb counties.

Ethnicity, 1990: White, 6,680 (72.0%); Black, 1 (0.0%); American Indian, 9 (0.1%); Asian, 8 (0.1%); Other, 2,581 (27.8%). Hispanic, 7,519 (81.0%).

Vital Statistics, 1993: Births, 217; deaths, 71; marriages, 107; divorces, 2.

Recreation: Lake activities; state park; historic sites; winter tourist center.

Minerals: Natural gas, oil.

Agriculture: Beef cattle; onions, cantaloupes and melons, spinach; some irrigation for vegetables.

ZAPATA (7,523) county seat; tourism, agribusiness, oil center; retirement center; clinic.

Population	**9,958**
(Change fm '90)	7.3
Land Area (sq. mi.)	996.8
Altitude (ft.)	327-562
Rainfall (in.)	19.8
Jan. mean min.	45
July mean max.	99
Growing season (days)	304
Civ. Labor	3,934
Unemployed	14.0
Total Wages	$31,985,517
Av. Weekly Wage	$330.33
Prop. Value	$1,006,402,239
Retail Sales	$33,620,337

Zavala County

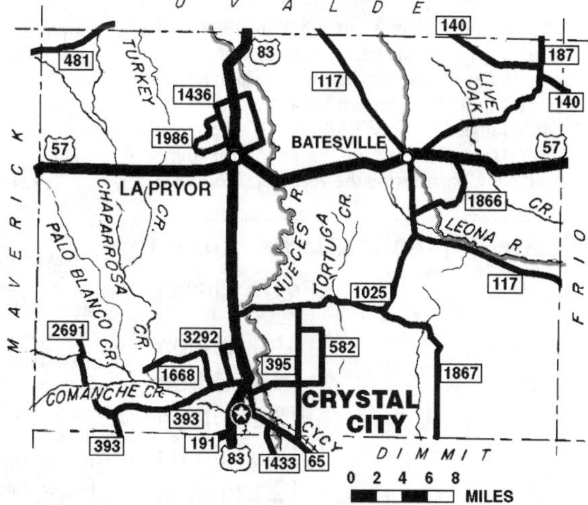

Physical Features: Southwestern county near Mexican border of rolling plains broken by much brush; Nueces, Leona, other streams.

Economy: Agribusinesses, leading county in Winter Garden truck-farming area; oil, gas, hunting.

History: Created from Maverick, Uvalde counties 1858; organized 1884; named for Texas Revolutionary leader Lorenzo de Zavala.

Ethnicity, 1990: White, 6,443 (53.0%); Black, 296 (2.4%); American Indian, 16 (0.1%); Asian, 3 (0.0%); Other, 5,404 (44.4%). Hispanic, 10,875 (89.4%).

Vital Statistics, 1993: Births, 255; deaths, 73; marriages, 95; divorces, 22.

Recreation: Hunting, fishing; annual spinach festival.

Minerals: Oil, natural gas.

Agriculture: Fed cattle; beef, goats, sheep important; cotton, vegetables, corn, pecans, wheat, grain sorghums; about 40,000 acres irrigated; some firewood sold.

CRYSTAL CITY (8,340) county seat; agribusiness; headquarters for Crystal City railroad; food processing; oil-field services; cotton gin; hospital. Home of Popeye statue.

Other towns include: **Batesville** (1,311), **La Pryor** (1,306).

Population	**12,177**
(Change fm '90)	0.1
Land Area (sq. mi.)	1,298.5
Altitude (ft.)	540-956
Rainfall (in.)	21.3
Jan. mean min.	41
July mean max.	98
Growing season (days)	280
Civ. Labor	4,777
Unemployed	23.4
Total Wages	$35,574,207
Av. Weekly Wage	$294.63
Prop. Value	$442,489,176
Retail Sales	$23,689,482

For explanation of sources, abbreviations and symbols, see p. 132.

Trends in Texas Population Growth

This article was written by Steve H. Murdock, Md. Nazrul Hoque and Beverly A. Pecotte

Texas population has shown substantial growth in the 1990s. After showing very slow growth in the latter part of the 1980s, Texas' rate of population growth has returned to levels of the middle 1980s.

This growth is also pervasive, including many of Texas' smallest rural counties and places. These patterns have significant implications for the state, both in the 1990s and beyond. Thus, we focus here on a description of post-1990 trends and on the implications of projected change in these areas in the coming decades.

As of July 1, 1994, Texas' population was estimated to be 18,378,185. This represented an increase of nearly 1.4 million persons in the period from April 1, 1990, to July 1, 1994.

Only California showed a larger numerical increase than Texas from 1990 to 1994, and only 10 other states, all of which have substantially smaller populations than Texas, showed a faster rate of growth than the 8.2 percent growth in the population of Texas from 1990 to 1994.

This rate of growth was nearly 90 percent higher than that for the nation, which increased its population by 4.7 percent from 1990 to 1994, from 248.7 million in 1990 to 260.3 million in 1994.

In the two years from 1992 to 1994, Texas' numerical growth has been the largest of any state, surpassing even that for California, which had more than 31.4 million persons in 1994.

In addition, by July 1, 1994, Texas' population was the second-largest in the nation, having surpassed New York during the year (*see Table 1*).

State Population 1994: Table 1

Rank	Pop. Estimate
1. California	31.4 million
2. Texas	**18.4 million**
3. New York	18.2 million
4. Florida	14.0 million
5. Pennsylvania	12.1 million
6. Illinois	11.8 million
7. Ohio	11.1 million
8. Michigan	9.5 million
9. New Jersey	7.9 million
10. North Carolina	7.1 million

Source: U.S. Bureau of the Census

Texas' rate of growth has increased steadily since the period from 1987 to 1988, when the state's annual rate of growth of only 0.3 percent was the lowest in more than 20 years.

In fact, for each of the last two years for which state-level estimates are available, 1992-93 and 1993-94, Texas' annual rate of growth was 2.0 percent, a rate of growth that if continued would double the population of Texas in 35 years.

By 1994, Texas growth had also come to again show substantial growth as a result of net migration from other states and through immigration from countries other than the United States.

Whereas, Texas' growth during the last few years of the 1980s was due almost entirely to natural increase, with natural increase offsetting net outmigration during several years from 1985 to 1990. From 1990 to 1994, natural increase accounted for about 58 percent of the state's population increase, inmigration from other states for about 20 percent, and immigration from other nations for about 22 percent of the increase in Texas population.

Regional and Metropolitan Patterns

The pervasive nature of Texas population growth and its relative increase compared to the 1980s can be seen by examining patterns of population growth for post-1990 periods for Council of Government (COG) Regions in Texas (*see Table 2*).

These 24 regions represent regional groupings of counties and usually contain at least one metropolitan area as well as counties surrounding that area.

Texas State Data Center county and place estimates are available only for periods through July 1, 1993, so that only 1990 to 1993 patterns of change are examined for substate areas.

The data for Council of Government Regions show that all 24 of these areas increased in population from 1990 to 1993 with four regions (South East Texas, the Panhandle, South Plains, and the Nortex COG) showing increases in population growth in the 1990s after experiencing population decline in the 1980s.

Of the 24 COG regions, 21 were showing higher rates of annual population growth in the 1990s than in the 1980s. In addition, net outmigration reversed to net inmigration for nine regions with only one region (the South Plains region) still showing net outmigration for the 1990 to 1993 period, and 21 of the 24 regions showed higher annualized rates of net migration from 1990 to 1993 than during the 1980s.

Growth was pervasive across the state but there were still substantial differences (*see Table 2*).

South Texas and Lower Rio Grande regions increased their populations by more than 10 percent from 1990 to 1993, and four others (Brazos Valley, Houston-Galveston, Capital Area, and Rio Grande) showed rates of growth exceeding 7 percent.

However, several areas' populations increased by less than 3 percent (the Panhandle, South Plains, West Central Texas, Texoma, and Nortex Regions). Overall, 17 of the State's 24 COG regions showed larger population increases than the 3.7 percent for the nation for 1990 to 1993, and nine regions showed rates of growth equalling or exceeding the 6.1 percent rate of growth for the state as a whole for 1990 to 1993.

Although growing more slowly than some urban areas, many rural areas have shown a turnaround from population decline in the 1980s to population increase in the 1990s. If patterns of population change in the 1990s are examined for metropolitan areas and nonmetropolitan areas, this turnaround is evident. Although metropolitan suburban areas and central-city areas experienced larger population increases than nonmetropolitan areas during the period from 1990 to 1993, the annualized rates of growth for nonmetropolitan areas were larger than those for metropolitan central-city areas and were substantially larger than during the 1980s.

In addition, whereas nonmetropolitan nonadjacent areas showed net outmigration from 1980 to 1990, they showed net inmigration from 1990 to 1993, and nonmetropolitan adjacent areas were showing annual rates of net inmigration that were nearly four times as high in the 1990s as in the 1980s.

When data on individual metropolitan areas are examined, patterns similar to those for regions are evident. The fastest rates of 1990 to 1993 population growth were in Laredo and McAllen-Edinburg-Mission while the slowest growth was in Sherman-Denison and Odessa. (*see metro data, p. 287*).

Growth in Counties

Texas counties have also shown renewed growth during the 1990s. Renewed growth was evident in the fact that while 98 of Texas' 254 counties showed population decline and 136 showed net outmigration during the 1980s, from 1990 to 1993, only 38 showed population decline and only 48 showed net outmigration.

Overall, 119 counties showed a larger percentage increase from 1990 to 1993 than the 3.7 percent increase for the population of the United States as a whole, and 55 showed faster rates of growth than the state's 6.1 percent. The pervasiveness of such growth and the extent of population turnaround in counties is also evident (*See data with each county, pages 133-283*).

While 540 places in Texas (more than 42 percent) showed population decline in the 1980s, from 1990 to 1993, only 87 places (about 7 percent) showed population decline. The patterns of population change among places in Texas in the 1990s are more similar to those of the 1970s, when more than 90 percent of all places in Texas showed population growth, than to the 1980s.

Future Population

Rates of population growth exceeding those for the nation and ones leading to an extensive increase in the state's population are evident when projections from the Texas Population Estimates and Projections Program 1994 are examined.

This program makes several alternative projections of the Texas population, with a middle projec-

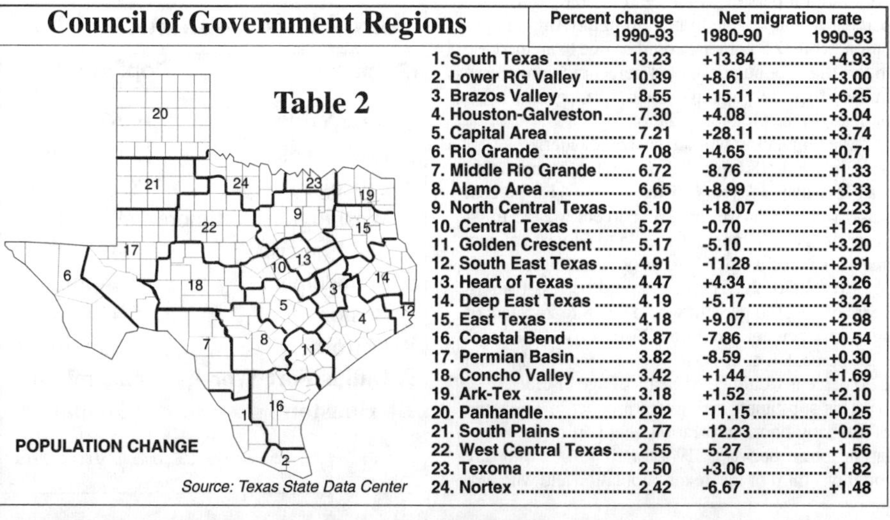

Council of Government Regions

Region	Percent change 1990-93	Net migration rate 1980-90	Net migration rate 1990-93
1. South Texas	13.23	+13.84	+4.93
2. Lower RG Valley	10.39	+8.61	+3.00
3. Brazos Valley	8.55	+15.11	+6.25
4. Houston-Galveston	7.30	+4.08	+3.04
5. Capital Area	7.21	+28.11	+3.74
6. Rio Grande	7.08	+4.65	+0.71
7. Middle Rio Grande	6.72	-8.76	+1.33
8. Alamo Area	6.65	+8.99	+3.33
9. North Central Texas	6.10	+18.07	+2.23
10. Central Texas	5.27	-0.70	+1.26
11. Golden Crescent	5.17	-5.10	+3.20
12. South East Texas	4.91	-11.28	+2.91
13. Heart of Texas	4.47	+4.34	+3.26
14. Deep East Texas	4.19	+5.17	+3.24
15. East Texas	4.18	+9.07	+2.98
16. Coastal Bend	3.87	-7.86	+0.54
17. Permian Basin	3.82	-8.59	+0.30
18. Concho Valley	3.42	+1.44	+1.69
19. Ark-Tex	3.18	+1.52	+2.10
20. Panhandle	2.92	-11.15	+0.25
21. South Plains	2.77	-12.23	-0.25
22. West Central Texas	2.55	-5.27	+1.56
23. Texoma	2.50	+3.06	+1.82
24. Nortex	2.42	-6.67	+1.48

Source: Texas State Data Center

tion scenario being seen as the most likely to occur. The middle projection sees the state population increasing to more than 20.3 million persons by the year 2000 and to 33.8 million by 2030. This suggests an annualized rate of growth of 1.7 percent.

This is slower than the 2.0 percent being experienced at the present time but is substantially faster than the 0.8 percent rate of growth projected for the nation during the same period of time. Texas' population growth is projected to continue to be roughly twice that for the nation.

Texas' population growth will not only be extensive but it will lead to an increasingly diverse population both ethnically and in terms of the age structure of the population.

In these projections, the total population is divided into four mutually exclusive racial/ethnic groups — Anglos (non-Hispanic whites), Blacks (non-Hispanic blacks), Hispanics (from all racial groups) and persons from all Other racial/ethnic groups (persons from all other racial groups who are not of Hispanic origin). These data show that Texas' minority populations are projected to increase substantially faster than Anglo population:

- While the total population would increase by 99 percent from 1990 to 2030, the Anglo population would increase by roughly 20 percent, the Black population would increase by 62 percent, the Hispanic population by nearly 258 percent, and the population in all Other racial/ethnic groups by more than 648 percent.
- As a result of such differentials in growth, Texas' population would be less than 50 percent Anglo by 2010 and would consist of 36.7 percent Anglos, 9.5 percent Blacks, 45.9 percent Hispanics, and 7.9 percent members of Other racial/ethnic groups by 2030.
- Of the total net increase in the population of 16.8 million persons from 1990 to 2030, only 12.5 percent would be due to growth in the Anglo population, while 7.3 percent would be due to an increase in the Black population, 66.4 percent to an increase in the Hispanic population and 13.8 percent to an increase in the Other population.

The population will also become older:

- In 1990, 28.6 percent of the Texas population was less than 18 years of age, while 11.2 percent was 18 to 24 years of age, 33 percent was 25 to 44 years of age, 17.1 percent was 45 to 64 years of age, and 10.1 percent was 65 years of age or older.
- By 2030, 22.7 percent would be less than 18 years of age, 9.0 percent would be 18 to 24 years of age, 27.7 percent would be 25 to 44 years of age, 23.6 percent would be 45 to 64 years of age and 17.0 percent would be 65 years of age or older.

This substantial aging is a product of the aging of the baby-boom generation, that part of the population born between 1946 and 1964, who are roughly a third of the Texas population and who will begin to enter elderly ages after 2010.

This aging will be strongly differentiated among population groups, with minority populations being substantially younger than the Anglo population. For example, in 2030, whereas nearly 24 percent of the Anglo population would be 65 years of age or older, only 14 percent of the Black population and 10 percent of the Hispanic population would be 65 years of age or older.

If recent projections prove to be true, Texas' future population will be substantially larger, older and more ethnically diverse than at any time in Texas' history. Growth and diversity would continue to be key descriptors of Texas.

Summary and Conclusions

In sum, recent data show Texas population to be growing rapidly and show that growth to again be pervasive across nearly all size of areas in Texas.

Although growth is most rapid in Texas' largest urban centers and among areas in Texas that border Mexico, it is occurring in nearly all sizes of areas in all regions of the state in the early 1990s.

The growth of the Texas population is projected to continue at a rate nearly twice as fast as that for the nation and lead to a population that is more mature and more ethnically diverse than at any time in Texas history.

Population change in the state will thus likely continue to produce a growing and ever more diverse Texas. ☆

Dr. Murdock is professor and head of the Department of Rural Sociology at Texas A&M University and chief demographer of the Texas State Data Center. Dr. Hoque is an assistant research scientist in the department, and Ms. Pecotte is a research associate.

U.S. Metro Populations 1992

Rank	Pop. Estimate
1. New York	19.67 million
2. Los Angeles	15.05 million
3. Chicago	8.41 million
4. Washington/Baltimore	6.92 million
5. San Francisco	6.41 million
6. Philadelphia	5.94 million
7. Boston	5.44 million
8. Detroit	5.25 million
9. Dallas/Fort Worth	**4.22 million**
10. Houston	**3.96 million**

Source: U.S. Bureau of the Census

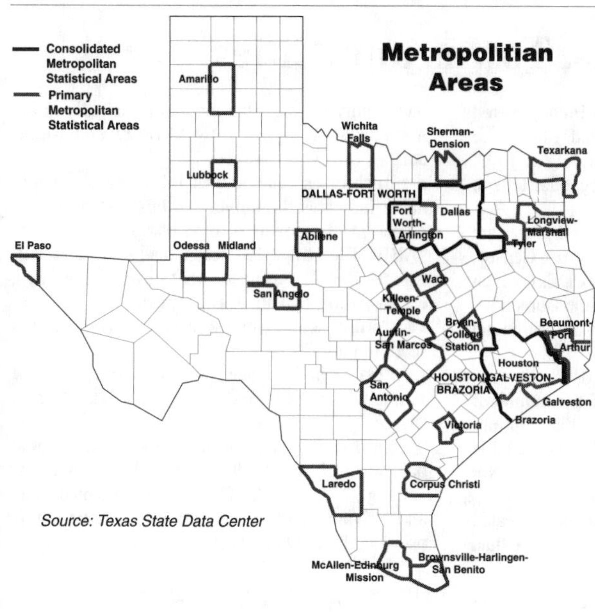

Source: Texas State Data Center

The federal government, effective June 30, 1983, adopted a three-tier system of defining the geographic units it uses to gather statistics in metropolitan areas in the United States.

The **Metropolitan Statistical Areas** (MSA) are free-standing metropolitan areas composed of one or more counties. Primary Metropolitan Statistical Areas (PMSA) are sub-units of a larger classification, the Consolidated Metropolitan Statistical Areas (CMSA).

CMSAs are metropolitan areas with more than one million population and are made up of two or more PMSAs.

Following are the metropolitan areas listed in descending order by population. Population figures are from the Texas **State Data Center** estimates as of July 1, 1993.

Consolidated Metropolitan Statistical Areas (CMSA)	July 1, 1993 Population
Dallas-Fort Worth (Dallas PMSA and Fort Worth-Arlington PMSA)	4,129,042
Houston-Galveston-Brazoria (Houston PMSA, Galveston PMSA and Brazoria PMSA)	3,986,529

Metropolitan Statistical Areas (MSA) and Primary Metropolitan Statistical Areas (PMSA)

Level A — Population 1,000,000 or More:	
1. Houston (Chambers, Fort Bend, Harris, Liberty, Montgomery and Waller counties)	3,544,601
2. Dallas (Collin, Dallas, Denton, Ellis, Henderson, Hunt, Kaufman and Rockwall counties)	2,731,503
3. Fort Worth-Arlington PMSA (Hood, Johnson, Parker and Tarrant counties)	1,397,539
4. San Antonio MSA (Bexar, Comal, Guadalupe and Wilson counties)	1,387,618
Level B — Population 250,000 to 1,000,000	
5. Austin-San Marcos MSA (Bastrop, Caldwell, Hays, Travis and Williamson counties)	841,586
6. El Paso MSA (El Paso County)	634,560
7. McAllen-Edinburg-Mission MSA (Hidalgo County)	426,940
8. Beaumont-Port Arthur MSA (Hardin, Jefferson and Orange counties)	378,955
9. Corpus Christi MSA (Nueces and San Patricio counties)	364,314
10. Brownsville-Harlingen-San Benito MSA (Cameron County)	284,392
11. Killeen-Temple MSA (Bell and Coryell counties)	269,272
Level C — Population 100,000 to 250,000	
12. Galveston-Texas City PMSA (Galveston County)	233,591
13. Lubbock MSA (Lubbock County)	230,901
14. Brazoria PMSA (Brazoria County)	208,337
15. Waco MSA (McLennan County)	197,493
16. Amarillo MSA (Potter and Randall counties)	195,521
17. Longview-Marshall MSA (Gregg, Harrison and Upshur counties)	167,911
18. Tyler MSA (Smith County)	159,652
19. Laredo MSA (Webb County)	153,538
20. Bryan-College Station MSA (Brazos County)	134,558
21. Wichita Falls MSA (Archer and Wichita counties)	126,149
22. Abilene MSA (Taylor County)	123,920
23. Odessa MSA (Ector County)	122,051
24. Texarkana MSA (Bowie County, TX, and Miller County, AR)	120,132
25. Midland MSA (Midland County)	112,855
26. San Angelo MSA (Tom Green County)	102,477
Level D — Population Under 100,000	
27. Sherman-Denison MSA (Grayson County)	97,450
28. Victoria MSA (Victoria County)	78,458

Places, Towns and Cities

Population: Population figures of **incorporated** places and certain Census Designated Places are Texas State Data Center estimates for July 1, 1993. Names of incorporated places are in capital letters, e.g., "ABBOTT."

Population figures of **unincorporated** places are not enumerated by the U. S. Bureau of the Census, except for Census Designated Places (CDPs), which are unincorporated towns selected by the Bureau for enumeration. CDPs are designated in the following list by a double dagger symbol (‡).

The population figure given here for all other unincorporated towns is an estimate of the numberof persons considered locally as living in that community. In some cases, we could not obtain a reliable population estimate; these places show "NA" (Not Available) in place of a population figure.

Location: County in which the town is located immediately follows the name of town. If more than one county is listed, the town is principally in the first-named county, e.g. "AMARILLO, Potter-Randall."

Businesses: The number following the county name indicates the number of business establishments in the town as of Dec. 31, 1992, e.g., "ABBOTT, Hill, 21" means that Abbott in Hill County had 21 businesses that have been given a **credit rating** by Dun & Bradstreet.

County seats: County seats are marked with a section mark (§).

Post Offices: Places with post offices, as of Jan. 1995, are marked with an asterisk (*) e.g., "*Ace."

Banks: Towns with one or more independent banks as of Dec. 31, 1994, are marked with a dagger, e.g., "†ALAMO." This includes national, state and private banking institutions. Information is provided by the Federal Reserve Bank of Dallas.

Town and County	Pop.
A	
A & D Acres, Llano	NA
*ABBOTT, Hill, 21	340
Aberfoyle, Hunt	35
*†ABERNATHY, Hale-Lubbock, 133	2,735
Abex, Navarro	NA
§*†ABILENE, Taylor-Jones, 5,368	110,661
Ables Springs, Kaufman	NA
Abner, Kaufman	NA
‡Abram-Perezville, Hidalgo	4,369
Acala, Hudspeth	25
*Ace, Polk, 1	40
*ACKERLY, Dawson-Martin, 32	265
Acme, Hardeman	14
Acton, Hood	450
Acuff, Lubbock	30
Acworth, Red River	52
Adams, Lamar	NA
Adams Acres, Montgomery	NA
Adams Gardens, Cameron	200
Adams Hill, Bexar	NA
Adams Oaks, Montgomery	NA
Adams Store, Panola	NA
Adamsville, Lampasas	28
Addielou, Red River	31
*†ADDISON, Dallas, 281	10,336
Addran, Hopkins	NA
Adell, Parker	NA
*Adkins, Bexar, 100	241
Admiral, Callahan	18
Adobes, Presidio	NA
*ADRIAN, Oldham, 16	223
Advance, Parker	NA
*Afton, Dickens, 6	100
Afton Park, Montgomery	NA
Agnes, Parker	NA
*AGUA DULCE, Nueces, 25	811
Agua Nueva, Jim Hogg	20
Agua Verde, Travis	NA
Aguilares, Webb	10
*Aiken, Floyd, 4	60
Aiken, Shelby	75
Aikin Grove, Red River	26
Air Country Estates, Williamson	NA
Airport City, Bexar	106
Airville, Bell	10
Alabama-Coushatta Indian Reservation, Polk	478
Alabama Creek, Trinity	20
*†ALAMO, Hidalgo, 222	9,285
Alamo Alto, El Paso	25
Alamo Beach, Calhoun	NA
*ALAMO HEIGHTS, Bexar	7,146
*Alanreed, Gray, 9	60
Alazan, Nacogdoches	NA
*ALBA, Wood-Rains, 66	504
§*†ALBANY, Shackelford, 195	2,040
*Albert, Gillespie, 1	25
Albion, Red River	50
Alderbranch, Anderson	NA
‡Aldine, Harris	11,751
*ALEDO, Parker, 191	1,206
Aleman, Hamilton	60
Alethia, Montgomery	NA
Alexander, Erath	40
Alexanders Store, Shelby	NA
Aley, Henderson	NA
Alfred, Jim Wells	10
Algerita, San Saba, 1	48
Algoa, Galveston	135
§*†ALICE, Jim Wells, 1,110	19,947
Allamoore, Hudspeth	NA
*ALLEN, Collin, 683	23,030
Allendale, Montgomery	NA
Allenfarm, Brazos	30
Allenhurst, Matagorda	NA
Allen's Chapel, Fannin	41
Allen's Point, Fannin	76
*Alleyton, Colorado, 9	165
*Allison, Wheeler, 14	135
Allison, Wise	NA
Allmon, Floyd	NA
Allred, Yoakum	NA
ALMA, Ellis, 1	238
Almeda, Harris	NA
Almira, Cass	NA
Almont, Bowie	NA
§*†ALPINE, Brewster, 385	5,686
Alpine Village, Travis	NA
Alsa, Van Zandt	30
Alsdorf, Ellis	NA
*Altair, Colorado, 14	30
*ALTO, Cherokee, 76	1,071
Alto Bonito, Starr	70
Altoga, Collin	367
*ALTON, Hidalgo	3,160
Alum, Wilson	NA
Alum Creek, Bastrop	NA
*†ALVARADO, Johnson, 269	3,085
*†ALVIN, Brazoria, 1,102	19,863
*ALVORD, Wise, 67	913
§*†AMARILLO, Potter-Randall, 8,322	163,569
Ambia, Lamar	20
Ambrose, Grayson	41
Ames, Coryell	NA
*AMES, Liberty	1,102
Amherst, Lamar	NA
*†AMHERST, Lamb, 35	754
Amity, Comanche	NA
Ammannsville, Fayette	42
Amphion, Atascosa	NA
Amsterdam, Brazoria	NA
Anadarko, Rusk	NA
§*†ANAHUAC, Chambers, 199	2,064
Anchorage, Atascosa	NA
Ander, Goliad	35
§*†ANDERSON, Grimes, 55	370
‡Anderson Mill, Williamson-Travis	10,347
*Andice, Williamson, 8	25
§*†ANDREWS, Andrews, 628	10,874
§*ANGLETON, Brazoria, 888	18,763
ANGUS, Navarro	383
Anhalt, Comal	NA
*†ANNA, Collin, 50	982
Annarose, Live Oak	NA
ANNETTA, Parker	761
ANNETTA NORTH, Parker	272
ANNETTA SOUTH, Parker	459
*ANNONA, Red River, 14	347
§*†ANSON, Jones, 183	2,717
Antelope, Jack, 1	65
*ANTHONY, El Paso, 47	3,491
Anthony, Fannin	10
Anthony Harbor, San Augustine	NA
Antioch, Cass	29
Antioch, Delta	25
Antioch, Madison	20
Antioch, Panola	121
Antioch, Shelby	NA
Antioch, Smith	NA
*†ANTON, Hockley, 53	1,266
Apache Shores, Travis	NA
*APPLEBY, Nacogdoches	499
*Apple Springs, Trinity, 18	149
April Sound, Montgomery	NA
*AQUILLA, Hill, 12	144
Arah, Scurry	NA
*ARANSAS PASS, San Patricio-	

Town and County	Pop.
Aransas-Nueces, 498	7,393
Arbala, Hopkins	41
*Arcadia, Shelby, 32	20
§*†ARCHER CITY, Archer, 114	1,808
ARCOLA, Fort Bend	742
Arden, Irion	1
Argo, Titus	26
*ARGYLE, Denton, 122	1,803
Arkadelphia, Bowie	NA
Arkansas Colony, Baylor	NA
Arlie, Childress	NA
*†ARLINGTON, Tarrant, 11,616	277,939
Armstrong, Bell	22
*Armstrong, Kenedy	20
Arneckeville, DeWitt	50
Arnett, Coryell	NA
Arnett, Hockley	26
Arney, Castro	NA
*†ARP, Smith, 74	895
Arrowhead Lake, Montgomery	NA
Arrowhead Shores, Hood	NA
Arrowhead Village, Comal	NA
Arroyo City, Cameron	NA
*Art, Mason, 1	18
Artesian Lakes Estates, Montgomery	NA
*Artesia Wells, La Salle, 4	30
*Arthur City, Lamar, 12	200
Arvana, Dawson	25
Asa, McLennan	46
Ash, Houston	NA
Ashby, Matagorda	NA
*ASHERTON, Dimmit, 16	1,643
Ashland, Upshur	20
Ashmore, Gaines	25
Ashtola, Donley	20
Ashwood, Matagorda	NA
Asia, Polk	NA
§*†ASPERMONT, Stonewall, 86	1,204
Astro Hills, Comal	NA
*Atascosa, Bexar, 55	300
Ater, Coryell	NA
§*†ATHENS, Henderson, 1,016	11,249
*†ATLANTA, Cass, 477	6,220
Atlas, Lamar	20
Atoy, Cherokee	NA
Attoyac, Nacogdoches	NA
Attoyac Village, Nacogdoches	NA
Atwell, Callahan	NA
*AUBREY, Denton, 182	1,238
Auburn, Ellis	12
Augusta, Houston	20
AURORA, Wise	683
§*†AUSTIN, Travis-Williamson, 31,519	501,637
Austin Lake Estates, Travis	NA
*Austonio, Houston, 3	37
*AUSTWELL, Refugio, 9	198
Authon, Parker	5
*Avalon, Ellis, 13	130
*AVERY, Red River, 32	462
*†AVINGER, Cass, 37	495
*Avoca, Jones, 7	121
*Axtell, McLennan, 28	105
*†AZLE, Tarrant-Parker, 665	9,706
B	
Babyhead, Llano	20
Back, Gray	14
‡*Bacliff, Galveston, 147	5,714
Bagby, Fannin	NA
*Bagwell, Red River, 17	150
*BAILEY, Fannin, 5	199
Baileyboro, Bailey, 1	NA
BAILEY'S PRAIRIE, Brazoria	670
Baileyville, Milam	45
Bainer, Lamb	NA
Bainville, Karnes	NA
§*†BAIRD, Callahan, 95	1,744
Baker, Floyd	NA
Bakersfield, Pecos	30
Balboa Acres, Hidalgo	NA
*BALCH SPRINGS, Dallas	18,014
BALCONES HEIGHTS, Bexar	3,238
Balcones Village, Travis-Williamson	NA
Bald Hill, Angelina	NA
Bald Prairie, Robertson	31
Baldwin, Harrison	NA
§*†BALLINGER, Runnels, 276	4,079
*BALMORHEA, Reeves, 23	826
Balsora, Wise	50
Bammel, Harris	NA
§*†BANDERA, Bandera, 251	975
Bandera Falls, Bandera	NA
*BANGS, Brown, 79	1,550
Bankersmith, Kendall	NA
*Banquete, Nueces, 20	449
Barbarosa, Guadalupe	25
Barclay, Falls	72
*BARDWELL, Ellis, 12	404
*Barker, Harris, 15	160
*Barksdale, Edwards, 16	617
Barnes, Polk	NA
Barnes Switch, Trinity	15
*Barnhart, Irion, 6	135
*Barnum, Polk, 1	29
‡*Barrett, Harris	3,288
*BARRY, Navarro, 7	184
*BARSTOW, Ward, 13	562
*†BARTLETT, Williamson-Bell, 72	1,509
Bartley Woods, Fannin	30
Bartons Chapel, Jack	NA
BARTONVILLE, Denton	1,024
Barwise, Floyd	30
Bascom, Smith	NA
Bassett, Bowie	373
§*†BASTROP, Bastrop, 530	4,389
Bastrop Bayou Acres, Brazoria	NA
Bastrop Beach, Brazoria	NA
Bateman, Bastrop	NA
Batesville, Red River	14
‡*Batesville, Zavala, 28	1,311
*Batson, Hardin, 22	140
Battle, McLennan	NA
Bavarian Hills, Bexar	NA
Baxter, Henderson	20
§*†BAY CITY, Matagorda, 972	18,818
Bay Harbor, Galveston	NA
Baylake, Angelina	NA
Baylor Lake, Childress	27
Bayou Village, Angelina	NA
BAYOU VISTA, Galveston	1,471
*BAYSIDE, Refugio, 7	426
Bayside Terrace, Harris	NA
*†BAYTOWN, Harris-Chambers, 2,550	68,255
*BAYVIEW, Cameron	261
Baywood Estates, Henderson	NA
Bazette, Navarro	30
Beach, Montgomery	NA
BEACH CITY, Chambers	993
Beans, Jasper	NA
Bear Creek, Dallas	1,000
Bear Creek Oaks, Hays	NA
Bear Creek Park, Travis	NA
Bear Creek Ranch, Montgomery	NA
Bear Grass, Leon	NA
*BEASLEY, Fort Bend, 28	542
Beattie, Comanche	50
Beaukiss, Williamson	20
§*†BEAUMONT, Jefferson, 6,199	118,289
Beaumont Place, Harris	NA
Beaux Art Gardens, Jefferson	NA
Beaver Dams, Bowie	NA
*Bebe, Gonzales, 2	52
Beck, Lamb	NA
Becker, Kaufman	NA
*BECKVILLE, Panola, 47	853
Becton, Lubbock	125
*†BEDFORD, Tarrant, 1,843	44,791
*†Bedias, Grimes, 17	301
BEE CAVE, Travis	259
Beechwood, Sabine	NA
*Bee House, Coryell	40
§*†BEEVILLE, Bee, 832	13,840
Behrnville, Williamson	30
Belcherville, Montague	34
Belfalls, Bell	20
Belgrade, Newton	NA
Belk, Lamar	55
*†BELLAIRE, Harris, 899	14,796
Bella Vista, Fort Bend	NA
Bell Branch, Ellis	NA
*BELLEVUE, Clay, 23	344
*BELLMEAD, McLennan, 111	8,440
*†BELLS, Grayson, 51	982
§*†BELLVILLE, Austin, 392	3,484
Belmena, Milam	15
*Belmont, Gonzales, 5	60
Belott, Houston	NA
§*†BELTON, Bell, 710	12,900
Ben-Roy Bay, Smith	NA
*Ben Arnold, Milam	148
*BENAVIDES, Duval, 44	1,811
Ben Bolt, Jim Wells	110
*†BENBROOK, Tarrant	21,186
Benchley, Robertson	110
*Bend, San Saba, 5	115
*Ben Franklin, Delta, 7	75
Ben Hur, Limestone	100
§*BENJAMIN, Knox, 16	236
Bennett, Parker	85
Bennett Estates, Montgomery	NA
Benoit, Runnels	NA
Bentonville, Jim Wells	15
Bentwood Acres, Grayson	NA
*†Ben Wheeler, Van Zandt, 74	400
*Berclair, Goliad, 6	70
Berea, Houston	NA
Berea, Marion	74
*Bergheim, Kendall, 5	22
*Bergstrom Air Force Base, Travis	2,945
Berlin, Washington	NA
Bernard Acres, Brazoria	NA
Bernardo, Colorado	155
Berryhill, Shackelford	NA
Berry's Creek, Williamson	50
BERRYVILLE, Henderson	820
*†BERTRAM, Burnet, 67	937
Bess, Duval	20
*Best, Reagan, 2	25
Bethany, Panola	50
Bethel, Anderson	31
Bethel, Ellis	NA
Bethel, Henderson	NA
Bethel, Runnels	NA
Bethlehem, Upshur	25
Bettie, Upshur	110
Beulah, Limestone	NA
Beverly Hill, Collin	NA
Beverly Hills, Bexar	NA
*BEVERLY HILLS, McLennan	2,122
BEVIL OAKS, Jefferson	1,474
Bevilport, Jasper	NA
Beyersville, Williamson	75
Biardstown, Lamar	75
*Big Bend National Park, Brewster, 7	105
Bigby Corner, Glasscock	NA
Big Creek, Burleson	NA
Big Creek, Franklin	NA
*Bigfoot, Frio, 15	75
*Biggs Field, El Paso	4,226
Big Hill, Limestone	3
§*†BIG LAKE, Reagan, 200	3,735
Big Oaks, Marion	NA
Big Oaks Estates, Montgomery	NA
*†BIG SANDY, Upshur, 113	1,238
§*†BIG SPRING, Howard, 1,212	23,527
Big Square, Castro	NA
Big Thicket, Liberty	NA
Big Thicket Lake Estates, Polk	NA
Big Valley, Mills	35
Big Valley Ranchettes, Coryell	NA
*BIG WELLS, Dimmit, 20	821
Bila Hora, Lavaca	NA
Biloxi, Newton	NA
Birch, Burleson	NA
Birch Creek, Burleson	NA
*Birome, Hill, 1	31
Birthright, Hopkins	40
Biry, Medina	NA
*†BISHOP, Nueces, 133	3,394
Bishop Hills, Potter	250
*Bivins, Cass, 17	105
Bivouac Estates, Kerr	NA
*Black, Parmer	100
Blackfoot, Anderson	33
Black Hill, Atascosa	NA
Black Hills, Navarro	NA

Town and County	Pop.
Black Jack, Cherokee	47
Black Jack, Robertson	NA
Blackjack, Smith	NA
Blackland, Rockwall	49
Black Oak, Hopkins	NA
*BLACKWELL, Nolan-Coke, 17	357
Blair, Shelby	200
Blair, Taylor	25
Blanchard, Polk	50
*†BLANCO, Blanco, 158	1,368
Blanconia, Bee	15
Bland Lake, San Augustine	25
*BLANKET, Brown, 24	407
Blanton, Hill	NA
Bleakwood, Newton	300
*Bledsoe, Cochran, 8	125
*Bleiblerville, Austin, 9	71
*Blessing, Matagorda, 40	571
Blevins, Falls	36
Blewett, Uvalde	25
Block House, Williamson	NA
Blodgett, Titus	NA
*†BLOOMBURG, Cass, 23	381
Bloomdale, Collin	NA
*†BLOOMING GROVE, Navarro, 35	844
‡*Bloomington, Victoria, 18	1,981
*BLOSSOM, Lamar, 44	1,564
Blowout, Blanco	NA
Blue, Lee	50
Blueberry Hill, Montgomery	NA
*Bluegrove, Clay, 5	125
Blue Haven Estates, Hunt	NA
Blue Hills Estates, Travis	NA
Blue Lake Estates, Llano	300
BLUE MOUND, Tarrant	2,216
Blue Mountain, Mason	NA
*BLUE RIDGE, Collin, 32	565
Blue Ridge, Falls	NA
Bluetown, Cameron	40
Bluett, Wise	NA
*Bluff Dale, Erath, 6	123
Bluff Springs, Travis	50
*Bluffton, Llano, 4	75
*BLUM, Hill, 38	394
Bluntzer, Nueces	150
Boardhouse, Blanco	NA
Bobo, Shelby	NA
Bob Town, Jack	NA
Boddie, Grayson	NA
§*BOERNE, Kendall, 656	4,697
*BOGATA, Red River, 66	1,415
Bois d'Arc, Anderson	NA
Bois d'Arc, Rains	10
Bold Springs, Polk	100
Boldtville, Bexar	NA
‡*†Boling-Iago, Wharton, 51	1,171
Bolivar, Denton	40
Bomarton, Baylor	23
*Bonanza, Hill	NA
Bonanza, Hopkins	26
Bonanza Beach, Burnet	NA
Bonanza Beach Estates, Henderson	NA
§*†BONHAM, Fannin, 459	6,833
Bonita, Montague	15
Bonnerville, Freestone	NA
BONNEY, Brazoria	410
Bonnie View, Refugio	25
Bono, Johnson	NA
Bonus, Wharton	42
*Bon Wier, Newton, 18	475
*BOOKER, Lipscomb-Ochiltree, 82	1,241
Boonsville, Wise	52
*Booth, Fort Bend, 25	60
Bootleg, Deaf Smith	NA
Borden, Colorado	NA
*†BORGER, Hutchinson, 902	16,111
Bosqueville, McLennan	72
§*Boston, Bowie, 11	200
Boudreaux Estates, Harris	NA
*BOVINA, Parmer, 58	1,656
Bowers, Polk	NA
Bowers City, Gray	26
*†BOWIE, Montague, 501	5,250
Bowser, San Saba	NA
Box Church, Limestone	45
Boxelder, Red River	258
Boxwood, Upshur	NA
Boyce, Ellis	75
Boyd, Fannin	40
*†BOYD, Wise, 173	1,079
*Boys' Ranch, Oldham, 10	435
Bozar, Mills	NA
Brachfield, Rusk	30
Bracken, Comal	76
§*†BRACKETTVILLE, Kinney, 93	1,820
Brad, Palo Pinto	26
Bradford, Anderson	22
Bradshaw, Taylor	61
§*†BRADY, McCulloch, 385	5,924
Brady, Shelby	NA
Branch, Collin	447
Branchville, Milam	200
*Brandon, Hill, 6	80
Brangus Ranch, Williamson	NA
Branom, Hopkins	NA
*Brashear, Hopkins, 14	280
Braun Station East, Bexar	NA
Braun Station West, Bexar	NA
*BRAZORIA, Brazoria, 246	2,903
Brazos, Palo Pinto	47
Brazos Country, Austin	NA
Brazos Point, Bosque	NA
Brazosport, Brazoria	56,407
Breakaway Park, Williamson	NA
§*†BRECKENRIDGE, Stephens, 651	5,515
*†BREMOND, Robertson, 60	1,182
§*†BRENHAM, Washington, 1,224	12,950
Breslau, Lavaca	65
‡Briar, Tarrant-Wise-Parker	4,023
BRIARCLIFF, Travis	368
BRIAROAKS, Johnson	577
Briarwick, Bexar	NA
Briary, Milam	NA
Brice, Hall	37
*†BRIDGE CITY, Orange, 348	8,490
*†BRIDGEPORT, Wise, 407	3,695
Bridges Chapel, Titus	NA
Brierwood Bay, Henderson	NA
*Briggs, Burnet, 7	92
Bright Star, Rains	75
Brinker, Hopkins	NA
Brinwood Shores, Hunt	NA
*Briscoe, Wheeler, 9	135
Bristol, Ellis	94
Britton, Ellis	30
*BROADDUS, San Augustine, 41	206
Broadway, Crosby	NA
Broadway, Lamar	25
Broadway Junction, Lamar	NA
Brock, Parker	51
Brock Junction, Parker	NA
Brogado, Reeves	122
Bronco, Yoakum	30
*BRONSON, Sabine, 26	276
*†BRONTE, Coke, 39	1,007
*Brookeland, Sabine, 25	220
*Brookesmith, Brown, 7	61
Brook Forest, Montgomery	NA
Brooks, Panola	40
*Brooks Air Force Base, Bexar	720
Brookshier, Runnels	NA
*†BROOKSHIRE, Waller, 190	3,305
BROOKSIDE VILLAGE, Brazoria	1,723
*Brookston, Lamar, 14	70
Broom City, Anderson	NA
Broome, Panola	21
Brown Chapel, Navarro	NA
Brown College, Washington	NA
BROWNDELL, Jasper	213
§*†BROWNFIELD, Terry, 575	9,606
Browning, Smith	25
Brownsboro, Caldwell	NA
*†BROWNSBORO, Henderson, 56	569
§*†BROWNSVILLE, Cameron, 3,648	117,326
§*†BROWNWOOD, Brown, 1,449	18,641
Broyles Chapel, Anderson	NA
*BRUCEVILLE-EDDY, McLennan-Falls, 23	1,180
Brundage, Dimmit	50
*Bruni, Webb, 21	698
Brunswick, Cherokee	50
Brushie Prairie, Navarro	NA
Brushy, Hood	NA
Brushy Bend Park, Williamson	NA
Brushy Creek, Anderson	50
Brushy Creek, Brazos	NA
‡Brushy Creek, Williamson	6,368
Brushy Creek North, Williamson	NA
§*†BRYAN, Brazos, 2,808	59,473
Bryan Beach, Brazoria	NA
Bryans Mill, Cass	71
Bryarly, Red River	5
Bryce, Rusk	NA
Bryden, Moore	NA
*†BRYSON, Jack, 24	535
‡*†Buchanan Dam, Llano, 68	1,119
Buchanan Lake Village, Llano	NA
Buchel, DeWitt	NA
Buck, Polk	NA
Buck Creek, Cottle	69
Buckeye, Matagorda	25
Buck Hills, Montgomery	NA
*†BUCKHOLTS, Milam, 28	361
Buckhorn, Austin	20
Buckhorn, Newton	NA
BUCKINGHAM, Dallas	119
Buckner, Parker	NA
*BUDA, Hays, 247	1,871
Buell Park, Williamson	NA
Buena Vista, Bexar	NA
Buena Vista, Burnet	NA
Buena Vista, Cameron	NA
*†BUFFALO, Leon, 158	1,802
*BUFFALO GAP, Taylor, 25	469
Buffalo Gap, Travis	NA
Buffalo Mop, Limestone	NA
Buffalo Springs, Clay	51
BUFFALO SPRINGS, Lubbock	247
Buford, El Paso	NA
Buford, Mitchell	25
Bugbee Heights, Hutchinson	75
Bug Tussle, Fannin	15
*Bula, Bailey, 4	105
Bulcher, Cooke	NA
*†BULLARD, Smith-Cherokee, 112	965
Bull Run, Newton	NA
*Bulverde, Comal, 68	25
Bulverde Estates, Comal	NA
Bulverde Hills, Comal	NA
‡*Buna, Jasper, 120	2,316
Buncombe, Panola	87
Bunger, Young	26
Bunker Hill, Jasper	NA
Bunker Hill, Lamar	NA
BUNKER HILL VILLAGE, Harris	3,553
Bunns Bluff, Orange	NA
Bunyan, Erath	20
*†BURKBURNETT, Wichita, 405	11,043
BURKE, Angelina	344
*Burkett, Coleman, 9	30
*Burkeville, Newton, 33	515
Burleigh, Austin	69
*†BURLESON, Johnson-Tarrant, 1,164	17,457
*Burlington, Milam, 13	140
§*†BURNET, Burnet, 368	3,569
Burns, Bowie	NA
Burns City, Cooke	61
Burrantown, Houston	NA
Burroughsville, Victoria	NA
Burrow, Hunt	NA
*†BURTON, Washington, 52	318
Busby, Fisher	12
*Bushland, Potter, 16	130
Bushwhacker Peninsula, Henderson	NA
Bustamante, Zapata	25
Busterville, Hockley	NA
Butler, Bastrop	NA
Butler, Freestone	67
*†BYERS, Clay, 16	526
*BYNUM, Hill, 6	203
Byrd, Ellis	15

Town and County	Pop.
Byrds, Brown	NA
Byrdtown, Lamar	NA
C	
C.H. Rouse Estates, Montgomery	NA
Cabot Kingsmill, Gray	62
*CACTUS, Moore, 24	1,717
Caddell Cove, San Augustine	NA
*Caddo, Stephens, 4	40
Caddo Camp, Hunt	NA
Caddo Lake Estates, Marion	NA
*†CADDO MILLS, Hunt, 63	1,109
Cade Chapel, Navarro	NA
Cade Lake, Burleson	NA
Cadiz, Bee	15
Cain City, Gillespie	NA
Calaveras, Wilson	100
§*†CALDWELL, Burleson, 318	3,527
Caledonia, Rusk	NA
Calf Creek, McCulloch	23
Calina, Limestone	NA
*Call, Jasper-Newton, 11	170
*Calliham, McMullen, 6	90
CALLISBURG, Cooke	377
Call Junction, Jasper	50
*CALVERT, Robertson, 54	1,573
Cambridge Shores, Grayson	NA
*Camden, Polk, 5	1,200
Camelot, Travis	NA
§*†CAMERON, Milam, 360	5,865
‡Cameron Park, Cameron	4,206
Camilla, San Jacinto	70
Camp Air, Mason	15
*CAMPBELL, Hunt, 28	735
*Campbellton, Atascosa, 13	275
Camp Creek Lake, Robertson	241
Camp Dale Robertson, Marion	NA
Campo Alto, Hidalgo	NA
Camp Ruby, Polk	35
Camp San Saba, McCulloch	36
Camp Scenic, Kerr	NA
Camp Seale, Polk	NA
Camp Springs, Scurry	10
‡Camp Swift, Bastrop	2,844
Camp Switch, Gregg	70
Campti, Shelby	NA
*Camp Verde, Kerr	41
Camp Willow, Guadalupe	NA
*CAMP WOOD, Real, 40	711
Camp Worth, San Augustine	NA
Canada Verde, Wilson	123
§*†CANADIAN, Hemphill, 277	2,285
Canal City, Galveston	NA
Canary, Leon	NA
Candelaria, Presidio	55
Caney, Matagorda	296
CANEY CITY, Henderson	182
Caney Creek, Henderson	NA
Caney Creek Estates, Matagorda	NA
Caney Creek Estates, Montgomery	NA
Cannon, Grayson	75
Canterbury Estates, Smith	NA
§*†CANTON, Van Zandt, 440	3,195
Cantu, Hidalgo	NA
‡*Canutillo, El Paso, 166	4,625
Canyon, Lubbock	40
§*†CANYON, Randall, 488	11,918
Canyon City, Comal	100
Canyon Corners, Comal	NA
Canyon Creek Estates, Comal	NA
‡*Canyon Lake, Comal	11,180
Canyon Lake Acres, Comal	NA
Canyon Lake Estates, Comal	NA
Canyon Lake Forest, Comal	NA
Canyon Lake Hills, Comal	NA
Canyon Lake Island, Comal	NA
Canyon Lake Shores, Comal	NA
Canyon Lake Village, Comal	NA
Canyon Lake Village West, Comal	NA
Canyon Oak Estates, Comal	NA
Canyon Park Estates, Comal	NA
Canyon Springs, Comal	NA
Canyon Valley, Crosby	NA
Canyon View Acres, Comal	NA
Cape Conroe, Montgomery	NA
Cape Malibu, Montgomery	NA
Cape Tranquility, Henderson	NA
Capitola, Fisher	NA

Town and County	Pop.
Caplen, Galveston	30
Capps Addition, Montgomery	NA
Capps Corner, Montague	NA
Cap Rock, Crosby	NA
Caps, Taylor	100
Cara Blanca, Baylor	NA
Caradan, Mills	20
Carancahua, Jackson	NA
*CARBON, Eastland, 19	268
Carbondale, Bowie	30
Cardinal Hills, Travis	NA
Carey, Childress	60
Carl, Travis	NA
Carlisle, Rusk	161
Carlisle, Trinity	95
Carlos, Grimes	NA
*Carlsbad, Tom Green, 7	100
CARL'S CORNER, Hill	105
Carlson, Travis	61
*Carlton, Hamilton, 10	70
*†CARMINE, Fayette, 33	208
Carmona, Polk	50
Caro, Nacogdoches	113
Carolina, Walker	NA
Carpenter, Wilson	NA
Carpenters Bluff, Grayson	NA
Carriage Hills, Montgomery	NA
Carricitos, Cameron	25
Carrizo Creek Estates, Nacogdoches	NA
§*†CARRIZO SPRINGS, Dimmit, 271	5,846
Carroll, Smith	60
Carroll Springs, Anderson	NA
*CARROLLTON, Denton-Dallas-Collin, 4,214	90,934
Carson, Fannin	22
*Carswell Air Force Base, Tarrant	3,162
*Carta Valley, Edwards	20
Carter Lake, Brazos	NA
Carterville, Cass	25
Carterville, Harrison	NA
§*†CARTHAGE, Panola, 596	6,724
Cartwright, Kaufman	NA
Cartwright, Wood	61
Carver, Leon	NA
Carver Park, Bexar	NA
Casa Piedra, Presidio	21
Casey, El Paso	115
Cash, Hunt	56
*Cason, Morris, 2	173
Cass, Cass	50
Cassie, Burnet	NA
Cassin, Bexar	NA
*Castell, Llano, 4	72
*CASTLE HILLS, Bexar	4,450
Castle Terrace, Burnet	NA
Castlewood Forest, Travis	NA
*†CASTROVILLE, Medina, 173	2,380
*Catarina, Dimmit, 6	45
*Cat Spring, Austin, 20	76
Causeway Beach, Henderson	NA
Cavazos, Cameron	NA
Cave Creek, Gillespie	NA
Caviness, Lamar	80
Cawthon, Brazos	75
Cayote, Bosque	75
*Cayuga, Anderson, 11	56
Cedar Bay, Smith	NA
Cedar Bayou, Harris-Chambers	1,287
Cedar Branch Park, Henderson	NA
Cedar Creek, Anderson	NA
*Cedar Creek, Bastrop, 77	145
Cedar Creek, Waller	NA
Cedar Creek Park, Hill	NA
*CEDAR HILL, Dallas-Ellis, 567	21,886
Cedar Hill, Floyd	NA
Cedar Lake, Matagorda	148
*Cedar Lane, Matagorda, 2	85
Cedar Mills, Grayson	NA
*CEDAR PARK, Williamson-Travis, 441	6,360
Cedar Point, Llano	NA
Cedar Shores Estates, Bosque	170
Cedar Springs, Falls	90
Cedar Springs, Upshur	NA
Cedarvale, Kaufman	NA
Cedar Valley, Bell	4

Town and County	Pop.
Cedar Valley, Travis	70
*Cee Vee, Cottle, 2	71
Cego, Falls	98
Cele, Travis	NA
*†CELESTE, Hunt, 44	805
*†CELINA, Collin, 101	1,877
Celotex, Fisher	NA
Centennial, Coleman	NA
Center, Fisher	NA
Center, Limestone	76
§*†CENTER, Shelby, 503	4,977
Center City, Mills	15
Center Grove, Franklin	NA
Center Grove, Houston	NA
Center Grove, Titus	NA
Center Hill, Houston	NA
Center Line, Burleson	NA
Center Mill, Hood	NA
Center Plains, Swisher	NA
Center Point, Camp	NA
Center Point, Ellis	NA
Centerpoint, Hays	NA
Center Point, Howard	NA
Center Point, Hunt	NA
*Center Point, Kerr, 76	623
Center Point, Panola	NA
Center Point, Upshur	NA
Centerview, Leon	NA
§*CENTERVILLE, Leon, 102	904
Centerville, Trinity	40
Center Vine, Morris	NA
Central, Angelina	105
‡Central Gardens, Jefferson	4,190
Central Heights, Nacogdoches	NA
Central High, Cherokee	NA
*Centralia, Trinity, 1	26
Cestohowa, Karnes	110
Chaille, Grimes	20
*Chalk, Cottle, 2	45
Chalk Bluff Estates, McLennan	NA
Chalk Hill, Rusk	NA
Chalk Mountain, Erath	25
Chambersville, Collin	40
Chambliss, Collin	25
Champion, Nolan	16
Champions, Harris	17,125
Chances Store, Burleson	NA
*†CHANDLER, Henderson, 120	1,748
Chaney, Eastland	35
‡*†Channelview, Harris, 680	27,106
§*CHANNING, Hartley, 22	264
Chaparral Estates, Liberty	NA
Chapel Hill, Smith	NA
Chapman, Rusk	20
Chapman Lakeside, San Augustine	NA
*Chapman Ranch, Nueces, 8	100
Chapparal Park, Hays	NA
Chappel, San Saba	25
*†Chappell Hill, Washington, 46	310
Charco, Goliad	68
Charleston, Delta	120
Charlie, Clay	65
*†CHARLOTTE, Atascosa, 40	1,635
Chase Field Naval Air Stn., Bee	1,221
CHATEAU WOODS, Montgomery	729
*Chatfield, Navarro, 3	40
Chatt, Hill	NA
Cheapside, Gonzales	31
Cheek, Jefferson	62
Cheneyboro, Navarro	NA
*Cherokee, San Saba, 22	175
Cherokee Club Estates, Cherokee	NA
Cherokee Cove, Hunt	NA
Cherokee Hill, Smith	NA
Cherry Spring, Gillespie	75
*CHESTER, Tyler, 15	316
Chesterville, Colorado	NA
*†CHICO, Wise, 95	843
*Chicota, Lamar, 3	125
Chihuahua, Hidalgo	NA
Chihuahua Farm, Zapata	NA
§*†CHILDRESS, Childress, 382	5,084
*†CHILLICOTHE, Hardeman, 52	795
*Chilton, Falls, 24	310
*CHINA, Jefferson, 26	1,197
CHINA GROVE, Bexar	1,099
China Grove, Scurry	15

Town and County	Pop.
*China Spring, McLennan, 73	181
Chinati, Presidio	NA
Chinquapin, Matagorda	NA
*CHIRENO, Nacogdoches, 20	456
Chita, Trinity	75
Choate, Karnes	NA
Chocolate Bayou, Brazoria	60
Choice, Shelby	21
*Chriesman, Burleson	30
*CHRISTINE, Atascosa, 5	406
*Christoval, Tom Green, 25	216
Church Hill, Rusk	15
Churchill Bridge, Brazoria	NA
*CIBOLO, Guadalupe-Bexar, 120	1,775
Cibolo Oaks Landing, Kendall	NA
Cipres, Hidalgo	20
Circle, Cherokee	NA
Circle, Lamb	NA
Circleback, Bailey	10
‡Circle D-KC Estates, Bastrop	1,333
Circleville, Travis	NA
Circleville, Williamson	42
*†CISCO, Eastland, 239	3,949
Cistern, Fayette	75
Citrus City, Hidalgo	NA
Citrus Grove, Matagorda	NA
Clairemont, Kent	15
Clairette, Erath	55
Clara, Wichita	100
Clardy, Lamar	NA
§*†CLARENDON, Donley, 150	2,051
Clareville, Bee	23
Clark, Liberty	NA
Clark, Victoria	NA
Clarkson, Milam	10
§*CLARKSVILLE, Red River, 240	4,396
*CLARKSVILLE CITY, Gregg-Upshur	796
§*†CLAUDE, Armstrong, 93	1,213
Clauene, Hockley	24
Clawson, Angelina	195
*CLAY, Burleson, 1	61
Clays Corner, Parmer	NA
*Clayton, Panola, 10	79
Claytonville, Fisher	21
Claytonville, Swisher	116
Clear Creek, Burnet	NA
Clear Creek, Henderson	NA
Clear Creek Forest, Montgomery	NA
Clear Lake, Collin	50
*CLEAR LAKE SHORES, Galveston	1,231
Clear Springs, Guadalupe	60
Clearview Estates, Henderson	NA
Clearview Point, Henderson	NA
Clearwater, Franklin	NA
Clear Water Bay, Henderson	NA
Clear Water Cove, San Patricio	NA
Clear Water Estates, Comal	NA
§*†CLEBURNE, Johnson, 1,503	22,801
Clegg, Live Oak	25
Clemons, Waller	NA
*Clemville, Matagorda, 2	54
Cleo, Kimble	3
Cleveland, Austin	78
*†CLEVELAND, Liberty, 692	7,455
Cliffside, Potter	206
*CLIFTON, Bosque, 318	3,399
Clifton, Van Zandt	NA
Climax, Collin	40
Cline, Uvalde	10
*CLINT, El Paso, 72	1,084
Clinton, Hunt	NA
*Clodine, Fort Bend	31
Clopton, Franklin	15
Close City, Garza	107
‡Cloverleaf, Harris	19,293
Club Lake, Collingsworth	NA
Club Lakeview, Waller	NA
*†CLUTE, Brazoria, 571	9,743
*†CLYDE, Callahan, 230	3,024
*†COAHOMA, Howard, 53	1,230
Cobb, Archer	NA
Cobbs, Kaufman	NA
Coble, Hockley	NA
Cochran, Austin	116
*COCKRELL HILL, Dallas	4,000
COFFEE CITY, Henderson	227
Coffeeville, Upshur	50
Cofferville, Lamb	NA
Coit, Limestone	NA
Coke, Wood	105
§*†COLDSPRING, San Jacinto, 111	549
Cold Springs, Coryell	NA
Coldwater, Dallam	NA
§*†COLEMAN, Coleman, 366	5,441
Coleman Cove, San Augustine	NA
Colfax, Van Zandt	35
Colita, Polk	NA
College Hill, Bowie	116
College Mound, Kaufman	350
*Collegeport, Matagorda, 2	91
*†COLLEGE STATION, Brazos, 1,546	60,012
*COLLEYVILLE, Tarrant, 523	15,420
*COLLINSVILLE, Grayson, 51	1,108
*†COLMESNEIL, Tyler, 43	618
Cologne, Goliad	85
Colony, Fayette	NA
Colony, Rains	70
Colonys Estates, Medina	NA
Colorado, Jim Hogg	23
§*†COLORADO CITY, Mitchell, 240	4,643
Colorado River Ranchettes, Travis	NA
Colquitt, Kaufman	NA
Coltexo, Gray	5
Coltharp, Houston	NA
Colton, Travis	50
Columbia Lakes, Brazoria	NA
§*†COLUMBUS, Colorado, 351	3,605
Comal, Comal	40
Comal Hills, Comal	NA
§*†COMANCHE, Comanche, 332	4,343
Comanche Cove, Hood	560
Comanche Harbor, Hood	250
Comanche Pass, Travis	NA
Comanche Rancheros, Llano	NA
*COMBES, Cameron, 24	2,297
COMBINE, Kaufman-Dallas	1,521
Cometa, Zavala	NA
‡*†Comfort, Kendall, 162	1,593
*COMMERCE, Hunt, 294	7,036
*COMO, Hopkins, 38	594
Compton, Rusk	NA
*Comstock, Val Verde, 13	375
Comyn, Comanche	27
*Concan, Uvalde, 12	71
*Concepcion, Duval, 5	25
Concho, Concho	NA
Concord, Cherokee	NA
Concord, Hunt	30
Concord, Johnson	NA
*Concord, Leon, 2	28
Concord, Liberty	26
Concord, Madison	50
Concord, Rusk	23
Concordia, Nueces	NA
Concrete, DeWitt	46
*Cone, Crosby, 1	110
Conlen, Dallam	61
Connor, Madison	50
§*†CONROE, Montgomery, 2,821	32,060
Conroe Bay, Montgomery	NA
Content, Bell	25
*CONVERSE, Bexar, 223	9,569
Conway, Carson, 1	50
Cooks Point, Burleson	60
Cooks Store, Anderson	NA
*Cookville, Titus, 24	105
COOL, Parker	233
Cool Crest, Bexar	NA
*†COOLIDGE, Limestone, 41	759
Coon Creek, Bosque	NA
§*†COOPER, Delta, 142	2,245
Cooper, Houston	NA
Copano Village, Aransas	210
Copeland, Montgomery	NA
Copeland, Smith	NA
Copeland Creek, Marion	NA
*Copeville, Collin, 8	106
*†COPPELL, Dallas-Denton, 579	19,851
*†COPPERAS COVE, Coryell-Lampasas, 657	24,848
COPPER CANYON, Denton	1,145
Corbet, Navarro	80
Cordele, Jackson	74
CORINTH, Denton	4,679
Corinth, Jones	25
Corinth, Leon	NA
Corinthian Point, Montgomery	NA
Corley, Bowie	35
Cornersville, Hopkins	NA
Cornett, Cass	30
Corn Hill, Williamson	NA
Cornudas, Hudspeth	NA
§*†CORPUS CHRISTI, Nueces-San Patricio-Kleberg, 10,488	266,958
Corpus Christi NAS, Nueces	500
CORRAL CITY, Denton	49
*†CORRIGAN, Polk, 82	1,823
Corry, Lamb	NA
§*†CORSICANA, Navarro, 1,376	23,507
Coryell City, Coryell	125
*Cost, Gonzales, 8	62
Cotton Center, Fannin	5
*Cotton Center, Hale, 13	205
Cottondale, Wise	NA
Cotton Flat, Midland	NA
Cotton Gin, Freestone	28
Cotton Patch, DeWitt	NA
Cottonwood, Brazos	NA
Cottonwood, Callahan	65
Cottonwood, Erath	23
COTTONWOOD, Kaufman	170
Cottonwood, Madison	40
Cottonwood, McLennan	NA
Cottonwood, Somervell	24
Cottonwood-Concord, Freestone	61
COTTONWOOD SHORES, Burnet	597
§*†COTULLA, La Salle, 167	4,405
Couch, Karnes	NA
Coughran, Atascosa	NA
Council Creek Village, Burnet	NA
Country Colony, Montgomery	NA
Country Estates, Hays	NA
Country Manor Estates, Smith	NA
Country Pines, Montgomery	NA
Country Place, Smith	NA
Country Place Acres, Montgomery	NA
Country Squire Estates, Orange	NA
County Glen, Williamson	NA
County Line, Hale	30
County Line, Lubbock	30
County Line, Rains	40
County Living, Williamson	NA
*†Coupland, Williamson, 18	135
Courtney, Grimes	55
COVE, Chambers	443
Cove Springs, Cherokee	NA
*COVINGTON, Hill, 21	263
Cow Creek, Erath	14
Cox, Upshur	NA
Coxville, Travis	NA
*Coyanosa, Pecos, 10	270
Coy City, Karnes	30
Crabb, Fort Bend	125
Crabbs Prairie, Walker	NA
Craft, Cherokee	21
Crafton, Wise	20
Craig, Rusk	NA
*CRANDALL, Kaufman, 60	1,949
§*†CRANE, Crane, 217	3,572
Cranes Mill, Comal	NA
*†CRANFILLS GAP, Bosque, 28	287
*CRAWFORD, McLennan, 52	652
Creath, Houston	NA
Crecy, Trinity	NA
Creechville, Ellis	NA
*CREEDMOOR, Travis, 2	203
Creekmore Village, Liberty-Polk	NA
Creekwood, Comal	NA
Creekwood Addition, Montgomery	NA
Crenneland, Galveston	NA
Crescent Heights, Henderson	NA

Town and County	Pop.
Crescent Oaks Beach Estates, Denton	NA
*Cresson, Hood-Johnson, 26	208
Crestonia, Duval	NA
Crestwood, Llano	NA
Crestwood, Marion	NA
Crestwood Acres, Bexar	NA
Crestwood Farms, Montgomery	NA
Crete, Trinity	NA
Crews, Runnels	NA
Crims Chapel, Rusk	NA
Cripple Creek Farms, Montgomery	NA
Cripple Creek Farms West, Montgomery	NA
Cripple Creek North, Montgomery	NA
Crisp, Ellis	90
§*†CROCKETT, Houston, 515	6,991
‡*†Crosby, Harris, 449	2,033
§*†CROSBYTON, Crosby, 113	2,062
Cross, Grimes	49
Cross, McMullen	50
Cross Cut, Brown	NA
‡Cross Mountain, Bexar	1,220
*†CROSS PLAINS, Callahan, 95	1,048
Crossroads, Cass	NA
Cross Roads, Comanche	NA
Crossroads, Delta	10
CROSS ROADS, Denton	413
Crossroads, Harrison	NA
Cross Roads, Henderson	135
Crossroads, Hopkins	NA
Crossroads, Jackson	NA
Cross Roads, Milam	35
Cross Roads, Rusk	NA
Cross Timbers, Johnson	245
Croton, Dickens	NA
Crow, Wood	25
§*†CROWELL, Foard, 81	1,217
*†CROWLEY, Tarrant-Johnson, 297	7,121
Crown, Atascosa	NA
Cruz Calle, Duval	NA
Cryer Creek, Navarro	15
*Crystal Beach, Galveston	787
§*†CRYSTAL CITY, Zavala, 208	8,340
Crystal Creek Forest, Montgomery	NA
Crystal Falls, Stephens	10
Crystal Forest, Montgomery	NA
Crystal Lake, Anderson	NA
Crystal Lake Estates, Polk	NA
Crystal Lake Park, Montgomery	NA
Cuadrilla, El Paso	40
Cuba, Johnson	NA
§*CUERO, DeWitt, 400	6,839
Cuevitas, Hidalgo	NA
Cuevitas, Jim Hogg	12
Culebra, Bexar	NA
Culleoka, Collin	NA
Cumberland Estates, Smith	NA
Cumberland Ridge, Smith	NA
*CUMBY, Hopkins, 46	635
Cundiff, Jack	45
*CUNEY, Cherokee, 2	183
*Cunningham, Lamar, 4	110
Currie, Navarro	25
Curtis, Jasper	NA
*CUSHING, Nacogdoches, 39	631
Cusseta, Cass	30
*CUT AND SHOOT, Montgomery	1,006
Cuthand, Red River	116
Cuthbert, Mitchell	NA
Cyclone, Bell	45
Cypress, Franklin	20
*Cypress, Harris, 586	260
Cypress Bend, Montgomery	NA
Cypress Cove, Comal	NA
Cypress Creek, Kerr	200
Cypress Creek Acres, Hays	NA
Cypress Gardens, Comal	NA
*Cypress Mill, Blanco, 8	56
Cyril, Rusk	NA
D	
Dacosta, Victoria	89
Dacus, Montgomery	161
Dads Corner, Archer	NA
Daffan, Travis	NA
§*†DAINGERFIELD, Morris, 197	2,653
*DAISETTA, Liberty, 30	1,011
Dalby Springs, Bowie	141
*Dale, Caldwell, 20	126
§*†DALHART, Dallam-Hartley, 584	6,290
*Dallardsville, Polk, 1	350
§*†DALLAS, Dallas-Collin-Denton-Rockwall, 61,573	1,036,309
Dalton, Cass	NA
DALWORTHINGTON GARDENS, Tarrant	1,990
Dam B (Dogwood Station), Tyler	56
*Damon, Brazoria, 44	375
*DANBURY, Brazoria, 61	1,614
*Danciger, Brazoria, 3	357
*Danevang, Wharton, 6	61
Daniels, Panola	NA
Danville, Collin	NA
Danville, Gregg	NA
Daphne, Franklin	NA
Darby Hill, San Jacinto	NA
Darco, Harrison	85
Darden, Polk	NA
*DARROUZETT, Lipscomb, 25	357
Datura, Limestone	NA
*Davilla, Milam, 3	200
Davis, Atascosa	NA
Davis Hill, Liberty	NA
Davis Prairie, Limestone	NA
Davisville, Angelina	NA
Davy, DeWitt	NA
*Dawn, Deaf Smith, 8	94
*†DAWSON, Navarro, 36	772
*†DAYTON, Liberty, 392	5,411
DAYTON LAKES, Liberty	216
Deadwood, Panola	106
DEAN, Clay	306
Dean, Hockley	18
*Deanville, Burleson, 12	130
*DeBerry, Panola, 24	191
§*†DECATUR, Wise, 485	4,391
Decker Estates, Montgomery	NA
Decker Prairie, Montgomery	NA
Deep Water Point Estates, Collin	NA
Deer Acres, Smith	NA
Deerfield Estates, Brazos	NA
Deer Haven, Llano	NA
Deer Lake Lodge, Montgomery	NA
Deer Meadows, Comal	NA
*†DEER PARK, Harris, 804	29,751
Deer River, Comal	NA
Deer Run, Comal	NA
Deerwood, Montgomery	NA
Deerwood East, Waller	NA
Deerwood Lakes, Waller	NA
Deerwood North, Waller	NA
*†DE KALB, Bowie, 176	1,994
Delaware Bend, Cooke	NA
Delba, Fannin	20
*†DE LEON, Comanche, 188	2,292
Delhi, Caldwell	NA
Delia, Limestone	NA
*DELL CITY, Hudspeth, 44	617
Dellwood, Webb	2,000
Del Mar Heights, Cameron	NA
*Delmita, Starr, 6	99
Delray, Panola	40
§*†DEL RIO, Val Verde, 1,127	33,271
Delrose, Upshur	NA
*Del Valle, Travis, 145	300
Delwin, Cottle	70
Demi-John Island, Brazoria	NA
Denhawken, Wilson	46
*DENISON, Grayson, 1,068	21,845
Denman Crossroads, Van Zandt	NA
Denning, San Augustine	361
*Dennis, Parker, 6	86
Denson Springs, Anderson	NA
Denton, Callahan	NA
§*†DENTON, Denton, 3,131	71,702
Denton, Franklin	NA
*†DENVER CITY, Yoakum, 304	5,121
*DEPORT, Lamar-Red River, 35	796
Derby, Frio	50
*Dermott, Scurry	5
*Desdemona, Eastland, 11	180
Desert, Collin	25
*†DESOTO, Dallas, 1,223	32,794
Dessau, Travis	NA
Detmold, Milam	NA
*†DETROIT, Red River, 47	756
*DEVERS, Liberty, 24	350
Devil's Backbone, Comal	NA
*†DEVINE, Medina, 280	4,344
Dew, Freestone	71
Dewalt, Fort Bend, 1	25
DeWees, Wilson	35
Deweesville, Karnes	NA
‡*Deweyville, Newton, 35	1,274
Dewville, Gonzales	15
Dexter, Cooke	NA
Dextra, Nacogdoches	NA
*†D'Hanis, Medina, 23	548
Dial, Fannin	76
Dial, Hutchinson	20
*Dialville, Cherokee	200
Diamondhead, Montgomery	NA
*Diana, Upshur, 40	200
*†DIBOLL, Angelina, 164	5,151
Dicey, Parker	NA
§*DICKENS, Dickens, 16	340
*†DICKINSON, Galveston, 594	13,035
Dies, Tyler	NA
*Dike, Hopkins, 9	170
*†DILLEY, Frio, 125	2,770
Dilworth, Gonzales	15
Dilworth, Red River	22
*†Dime Box, Lee, 34	313
§*†DIMMITT, Castro, 315	4,523
Dimple, Red River	60
*Dinero, Live Oak, 5	35
Ding Dong, Bell	22
Direct, Lamar	70
Dirgin, Rusk	12
Divide, Hopkins	NA
Divot, Frio	28
Dixie, Grayson	25
Dixie Isle, Henderson	NA
Dixon, Hunt	31
Dixon-Hopewell, Houston	NA
Doak Springs, Lee	NA
Doans, Wilbarger	20
*Dobbin, Montgomery, 7	170
Dobrowolski, Atascosa	10
Dodd, Castro	35
*DODD CITY, Fannin, 13	378
*Dodge, Walker, 8	150
*DODSON, Collingsworth, 7	118
Dodson Prairie, Palo Pinto	NA
Dog Ridge, Bell	125
*Dogwood, Tyler	NA
Dogwood City, Smith	NA
Dogwood Forest, Montgomery	NA
Dogwood Forest, Nacogdoches	NA
Dogwood Point, Sabine	NA
Dolen, Liberty	NA
Dolores, Webb	20
‡Dominion, Bexar	1,294
DOMINO, Cass	104
Donall Estates, Burnet	NA
* Donie, Freestone, 14	206
*DONNA, Hidalgo, 317	13,273
*Doole, McCulloch, 6	74
DORCHESTER, Grayson, 5	151
Dorras, Stonewall	NA
Doss, Cass	NA
*Doss, Gillespie, 7	75
Dot, Falls	21
Dothan, Eastland	20
Dotson, Panola	40
Double Bayou, Chambers	400
Double Diamond Estates, Hutchinson-Moore	175
DOUBLE OAK, Denton	1,845
*Doucette, Tyler, 4	131
*Dougherty, Floyd, 4	100
Dougherty, Rains	75
Douglas, Smith	NA
*Douglass, Nacogdoches, 13	75
*DOUGLASSVILLE, Cass, 13	203
Dove Meadows, Harris	NA
Downing, Comanche	20
Downsville, McLennan	35
Doyle, Limestone	10

Town and County	Pop.
Dozier, Collingsworth, 5	30
Drane, Navarro	16
Draper Addition, Wise	NA
Drasco, Runnels	NA
Draw, Lynn	39
Dreka, Shelby	NA
Dresden, Navarro	25
Dreyer, Gonzales	20
*Driftwood, Hays, 32	21
Driftwood, Henderson	NA
*DRIPPING SPRINGS, Hays, 179	1,057
*DRISCOLL, Nueces, 20	704
Drivers, Nacogdoches	NA
Drumright, Glasscock	NA
*Dryden, Terrell	13
Dubina, Fayette	NA
*†DUBLIN, Erath, 300	3,298
Dudley, Callahan	25
Duffau, Erath, 1	76
Dugger, Guadalupe	10
Dull, La Salle	NA
§*DUMAS, Moore, 698	13,477
*Dumont, King-Dickens, 2	85
Dunbar, Rains	40
*†DUNCANVILLE, Dallas, 1,385	36,446
Dundee, Archer	40
Dunlap, Cottle	30
Dunlap, Travis	80
*Dunlay, Medina, 6	119
*Dunn, Scurry, 2	75
Dunstan, Bastrop	NA
Duplex, Fannin	25
Duran, Mills	NA
Durango, Falls	54
Durham Park, Williamson	NA
Duster, Comanche	NA
Duval, Travis	NA
Dye, Montague	NA
Dyersdale, Harris	NA
*Dyess Air Force Base, Taylor	4,676

E

Town and County	Pop.
Eagle, Chambers	50
*†EAGLE LAKE, Colorado, 210	3,727
‡Eagle Mountain, Tarrant	6,097
§*†EAGLE PASS, Maverick, 1,005	23,008
Eagles Peak, Comal	NA
Eagles Peak Ranch, Comal	NA
Eanes, Travis	NA
*EARLY, Brown	2,613
Earlywine, Washington	NA
*EARTH, Lamb, 68	1,325
East Afton, Dickens	NA
‡*†East Bernard, Wharton, 127	1,671
East Caney, Hopkins	NA
East Columbia, Brazoria	95
East Delta, Delta	50
East Direct, Lamar	NA
Easter, Castro	91
Easterly, Robertson, 1	61
Eastgate, Liberty	NA
East Hamilton, Shelby	NA
§*†EASTLAND, Eastland, 417	3,641
EAST MOUNTAIN, Upshur	848
*EASTON, Gregg-Rusk, 3	436
East Point, Wood	NA
East River, Harris-Montgomery	NA
East Sweden, McCulloch	NA
EAST TAWAKONI, Rains	687
East Tempe, Polk	100
Eastvale, Denton	731
Eastview Terrace, Bexar	NA
East Village, Bexar	NA
Eaton, Robertson	NA
Ebenezer, Camp	55
Ebenezer, Jasper	NA
Echo, Coleman	16
Echo, Orange	25
Echo Forest, Orange	NA
Echols, Limestone	NA
Ecleto, Karnes	22
Eclipse, Jasper	NA
*ECTOR, Fannin, 19	498
*EDCOUCH, Hidalgo, 61	3,281
*Eddy, McLennan-Falls, (See Bruceville-Eddy), 35	NA
*†EDEN, Concho, 67	1,690
Eden, Nacogdoches	NA
Eden Heights, Polk	NA
Edgar, DeWitt	NA
Edge, Brazos	100
EDGECLIFF, Tarrant	2,866
Edgewater, San Augustine	NA
Edgewater Beach, Travis	NA
Edgewater Estates, San Patricio	NA
*†EDGEWOOD, Van Zandt, 82	1,380
Edgeworth, Bell	20
Edhube, Fannin	25
§*†EDINBURG, Hidalgo, 1,164	33,562
*EDMONSON, Hale, 14	114
§*EDNA, Jackson, 350	6,190
Edna Hill, Erath	32
*EDOM, Van Zandt, 5	325
*Edroy, San Patricio, 8	200
Egan, Johnson	21
Egypt, Leon	NA
Egypt, Montgomery	NA
*Egypt, Wharton, 6	26
Elam Springs, Upshur	NA
El Arroyo, Starr	NA
*Elbert, Throckmorton, 9	150
Elbow, Howard	NA
El Camino, Sabine	NA
*†EL CAMPO, Wharton, 851	10,943
El Campo Club, Calhoun	NA
El Carro, Jim Wells	NA
EL CENIZO, Webb	1,511
§*†ELDORADO, Schleicher, 110	2,005
Eldorado Center, Navarro	NA
Eldorado Country, Matagorda	NA
Eldridge, Colorado	NA
*†ELECTRA, Wichita, 216	3,307
Electric City, Hutchinson	350
Elevation, Milam	12
El Gato, Hidalgo	NA
*†ELGIN, Bastrop, 251	4,992
Eli, Hall	30
*Eliasville, Young, 7	116
*El Indio, Maverick, 4	148
Elk, McLennan	NA
*†ELKHART, Anderson, 72	1,116
Elkton, Smith	NA
*EL LAGO, Harris	3,507
*Ellinger, Fayette, 11	200
Elliott, Robertson	NA
Elliott, Wilbarger	50
Ellis, Austin	NA
*Elmaton, Matagorda, 5	165
Elmdale, Taylor	NA
*ELMENDORF, Bexar, 51	668
Elm Grove, Caldwell	NA
Elm Grove, Cherokee	NA
Elm Grove, Fayette	NA
Elm Grove, San Saba	NA
Elm Grove Camp, Guadalupe	110
Elmina, Walker	NA
*Elm Mott, McLennan, 87	190
*Elmo, Kaufman, 9	90
Elmont, Grayson	41
Elm Ridge, Milam	25
Elmtown, Anderson	NA
Elm Valley Park, Bexar	NA
Eloise, Falls	41
El Oso, Karnes	NA
§*†EL PASO, El Paso, 17,508	554,496
El Pinion Estates, San Augustine	NA
Elroy, Travis	125
*†ELSA, Hidalgo, 84	5,646
El Sauz, Starr, 4	85
El Tacalote, Jim Wells	100
Elton, Dickens	NA
El Toro, Jackson	NA
Elwood, Fannin	31
Elwood, Madison	28
Ely, Fannin	15
*Elysian Fields, Harrison, 17	300
Elysium, Bastrop	NA
Emberson, Lamar	80
Emblem, Hopkins	52
Emerald Bay, Smith	NA
*EMHOUSE, Navarro	213
Emille, Tyler	NA
Emmett, Navarro	100
§*†EMORY, Rains, 121	973
‡Encantada-Ranchito El Calaboz, Cameron	1,263
Enchanted Forest, Montgomery	NA
ENCHANTED OAKS, Henderson	313
Enchanted Valley, Burnet	NA
*ENCINAL, La Salle, 15	639
*Encino, Brooks, 16	110
*Energy, Comanche, 1	65
Engle, Fayette	106
English, Red River	92
*Enloe, Delta, 11	113
*†ENNIS, Ellis, 811	14,461
Ennis, Scurry	3
Enoch, Upshur	NA
*Enochs, Bailey, 4	164
Enright, Brazos	NA
Ensign, Ellis	10
Enterprise, Van Zandt	90
*Eola, Concho, 10	218
Eolian, Stephens	9
Equestrian Estates, Brazos	NA
*Era, Cooke, 8	200
Ericksdahl, Jones	75
Erin, Jasper	40
Erlins Green, Comal	NA
Ernies Acres, Brazoria	NA
Erwin, Grimes	NA
‡Escobares, Starr	1,887
Escobas, Zapata, 1	25
Eskota, Fisher	NA
Esperanza, Hudspeth	75
Espey, Atascosa	NA
Esquire Estates, Henderson	NA
Esseville, Live Oak	NA
Estacado, Lubbock	80
*ESTELLINE, Hall, 8	201
Estes, Aransas	50
Ethel, Grayson	25
*Etoile, Nacogdoches, 13	70
Etter, Moore	160
Eubank Acres, Travis	NA
Eula, Callahan	125
*†EULESS, Tarrant, 1,364	41,895
Eulogy, Bosque	45
Eunice, Leon	NA
Eureka, Franklin	NA
EUREKA, Navarro	263
Eureka, Stephens	NA
*EUSTACE, Henderson, 52	741
‡*Evadale, Jasper, 37	1,611
*†EVANT, Coryell-Hamilton, 40	453
Evelena, Dawson	NA
Evergreen, Hamilton	NA
Evergreen, San Jacinto	50
Evergreen Park, Orange	NA
*EVERMAN, Tarrant	6,100
Ewell, Upshur	100
Eylau, Bowie	2,962
Ezzell, Lavaca	55

F

Town and County	Pop.
‡*†Fabens, El Paso, 109	5,702
Fails, Walker	NA
Fairbanks, Harris	1,050
Fairchilds, Fort Bend	150
§*†FAIRFIELD, Freestone, 284	3,321
Fairland, Burnet	NA
Fairlie, Hunt	80
Fairmount, Sabine	NA
Fair Oaks, Freestone	23
Fair Oaks, Limestone	NA
*FAIR OAKS RANCH, Bexar-Comal-Kendall	2,218
Fair Play, Panola	80
Fairview, Angelina	NA
Fairview, Armstrong	NA
Fairview, Brazos	NA
Fairview, Cass	NA
FAIRVIEW, Collin	1,875
Fairview, Comanche	NA
Fairview, Crosby	NA
Fairview, Gaines	NA
Fairview, Hockley	10
Fairview, Hood	NA
Fairview, Howard	85

Town and County	Pop.
Fairview, Rusk	NA
Fairview, Wilson	322
FAIRVIEW, Wise	221
Fairy, Hamilton	31
Falcon, Zapata	50
*Falcon Heights, Starr, 11	361
Falcon Village, Starr	NA
§*†FALFURRIAS, Brooks, 279	5,798
Fallon, Limestone	NA
*†FALLS CITY, Karnes, 49	520
Fambrough, Stephens	NA
Famuliner, Cochran	NA
Fannett, Jefferson	105
*Fannin, Goliad, 10	105
Fargo, Wilbarger	161
Farmers Academy, Titus	NA
*†FARMERS BRANCH, Dallas	24,713
Farmers Valley, Wilbarger	50
*†FARMERSVILLE, Collin, 165	3,057
Farmington, Grayson	20
*Farnsworth, Ochiltree, 10	149
Farr, Ward	NA
Farrar, Limestone	51
Farrsville, Newton	150
§*†FARWELL, Parmer, 93	1,413
Fashing, Atascosa	50
*FATE, Rockwall, 13	327
Faught, Lamar	25
Faulkner (or Pinhook), Lamar	48
Fawil, Newton	NA
Fayburg, Collin	NA
*†FAYETTEVILLE, Fayette, 43	308
Fays Corner, Hidalgo	NA
Faysville, Hidalgo	300
Fedor, Lee	76
*Fentress, Caldwell, 8	85
*FERRIS, Ellis, 104	2,298
Fetzer, Waller	NA
Field Schoolhouse, Erath	12
Field Senate, Jack	NA
Fields Store, Waller	NA
*Fieldton, Lamb, 3	126
*Fife, McCulloch	32
Files Valley, Hill	50
Fincastle, Henderson	NA
Fink, Grayson	25
Finney, Hale	15
‡First Colony, Fort Bend	20,881
*Fischer, Comal, 13	20
Fisk, Coleman	40
Five Notch, Harrison	NA
Five Points, Ellis	NA
Flaccus, Karnes	NA
Flagg, Castro	50
Flamingo Isles, Galveston	NA
Flamingo Lake, Montgomery	NA
*Flat, Coryell, 4	210
Flat Fork, Shelby	NA
*†FLATONIA, Fayette, 118	1,373
Flat Prairie, Trinity	NA
Flats, Rains	100
Flat Top, Stonewall	NA
Flatwoods, Eastland	56
*Flint, Smith, 114	150
Flint Rock Hills, Travis	NA
Flo, Leon	20
*Flomot, Motley, 10	181
Flora, Hopkins	NA
Flora Bluff, Franklin	NA
*†FLORENCE, Williamson, 86	921
§*†FLORESVILLE, Wilson, 306	5,710
Florey, Andrews	25
Flowella, Brooks	NA
Flower Hill, Colorado	NA
*†FLOWER MOUND, Denton, 282	21,581
Floy, Fayette	NA
Floyd, Hunt	220
§*†FLOYDADA, Floyd, 223	3,801
Flugrath, Blanco	NA
*Fluvanna, Scurry, 11	180
Fly Gap, Mason	NA
*Flynn, Leon, 4	81
Foard City, Foard	10
Fodice, Houston	49
*†FOLLETT, Lipscomb, 47	453
Folsom, Shelby	NA
Foncine, Collin	20
Foot, Collin	20
Footes, Gregg	NA
Ford, Deaf Smith	NA
Ford Oaks, Travis	NA
Fords Corner, San Augustine	NA
Fordtran, Victoria	18
*Forest, Cherokee, 1	85
*Forestburg, Montague, 17	200
Forest Chapel, Lamar	NA
Forest Cove, Montgomery	NA
Forest Creek, Bexar	NA
Forest Glade, Bexar	NA
Forest Glade, Limestone	340
Forest Grove, Collin	20
Forest Grove, Milam	60
Forest Heights, Orange	250
Forest Hill, Lamar	NA
FOREST HILL, Tarrant	11,455
Forest Hill, Wood	NA
Forest Hill Estates, Coryell	125
Forest Hills, Montgomery	NA
Forest Lake, Brazos	NA
Forest Lake, Gregg	NA
Forest North Estates, Williamson	NA
Forest Park, Henderson	NA
Forest Springs, Polk	NA
Forest Trail, Montgomery	NA
Forest View North, Comal	NA
*†FORNEY, Kaufman, 247	4,355
*Forreston, Ellis, 3	300
*FORSAN, Howard, 15	279
‡*Fort Bliss, El Paso	14,258
Fort Clark Springs, Kinney	1,070
§*†Fort Davis, Jeff Davis, 69	1,212
FORT GATES, Coryell	788
Fort Griffin, Shackelford	96
*Fort Hancock, Hudspeth, 18	400
‡*†Fort Hood, Bell-Coryell, 110	36,414
*Fort McKavett, Menard, 4	45
Fort Parker, Limestone	2
Fort Parker State Park, Limestone	30
*Fort Sam Houston, Bexar	10,000
Fort Spunky, Hood	15
Fort Stanley Creek, Angelina	NA
§*†FORT STOCKTON, Pecos, 483	9,518
§*†FORT WORTH, Tarrant-Denton, 28,776	459,085
Foster, Fort Bend	NA
Foster, Terry	NA
Foster Creek Estates, Fort Bend	NA
Fostoria, Montgomery	NA
Fouke, Wood	NA
Four Corners, Brazoria	NA
Four Corners, Chambers	NA
Four Corners, Fort Bend	NA
Four Corners, Harris	NA
Four Corners, Montgomery	NA
Four Points, Travis	NA
Four Way, Moore	NA
*Fowlerton, La Salle, 2	100
Fox Chase Farms, Kendall	NA
Fox Hill, Comal	NA
Fox Run, Bexar	NA
Foxwood, Montgomery	NA
Frame Switch, Williamson	20
*Francitas, Jackson	30
Frank, Fannin	3
Frankel City, Andrews	NA
Frankell, Stephens	NA
§*†FRANKLIN, Robertson, 87	1,436
Franklin Center, Scurry	NA
*†FRANKSTON, Anderson, 151	1,163
*Fred, Tyler, 9	239
§*†FREDERICKSBURG, Gillespie, 951	7,745
Fredonia, Gregg	NA
*Fredonia, Mason, 5	50
Freedom, Rains	60
Freeneytown, Rusk	NA
*†FREEPORT, Brazoria, 737	12,646
*†FREER, Duval, 156	3,172
*Freestone, Freestone	35
Freeway Forest, Montgomery	NA
Freeway Oaks Estates, Montgomery	NA
Freheit, Comal	NA
Frelsburg, Colorado	75
Frenstat, Burleson	NA
Fresno, Collingsworth	NA
‡*Fresno, Fort Bend, 56	3,589
Freyburg, Fayette	45
Friday, Trinity	41
Friendly, Van Zandt	NA
Friendship, Dawson	5
Friendship, Lamb	NA
Friendship, Leon	NA
Friendship, Smith	NA
Friendship, Trinity	NA
Friendship, Upshur	NA
Friendship, Williamson	48
Friendship Village, Bowie	200
*FRIENDSWOOD, Galveston-Harris, 1,151	25,788
Frio, Castro	60
*†FRIONA, Parmer, 227	3,708
Frio Town, Frio	38
*FRISCO, Collin-Denton, 297	9,704
*†FRITCH, Hutchinson-Moore, 129	2,505
Frog, Kaufman	NA
Frognot, Collin	NA
Front, Panola	NA
Frontier Lakes, Montgomery	NA
Fronton, Starr	110
*FROST, Navarro, 25	587
Fruitland, Montague	20
*FRUITVALE, Van Zandt, 22	356
Frydek, Austin	150
Fulbright, Red River	150
*FULSHEAR, Fort Bend, 57	652
*FULTON, Aransas, 63	767
Funston, Jones	76
Furrh, Panola	40
G	
Gadston, Lamar	NA
Gafford, Hopkins	NA
§*Gail, Borden, 12	202
§*†GAINESVILLE, Cooke, 1,067	14,518
Galena, Smith	NA
*GALENA PARK, Harris, 193	10,746
Galilee, Smith	NA
Galilee, Walker	NA
*GALLATIN, Cherokee, 5	401
Galle, Guadalupe	80
Galleon Bay, Nueces	NA
Galloway, Panola	71
§*†GALVESTON, Galveston, 2,516	62,828
*†GANADO, Jackson, 118	1,870
Gannon, Fisher	NA
Garceno, Starr	45
Garcia, Deaf Smith	NA
Garcias, Starr	NA
Garciasville, Starr (See La Casita-Garciasville)	
§*Garden City, Glasscock, 140	293
Gardendale, Bexar	NA
‡*Gardendale, Ector, 20	1,131
Gardendale, La Salle	59
†GARDEN RIDGE, Comal	1,767
Garden Valley, Childress	NA
Garden Valley, Smith	150
Garfield, DeWitt	NA
‡Garfield, Travis-Bastrop	1,389
Garland, Bowie	NA
*†GARLAND, Dallas-Collin-Rockwall, 6,357	187,439
Garner, Parker	98
Garner State Park, Uvalde	40
GARRETT, Ellis	374
Garretts Bluff, Lamar	20
*GARRISON, Nacogdoches, 63	1,002
*Garwood, Colorado, 48	975
*GARY, Panola, 29	280
Gas Plant, Terrell	31
Gastonia, Kaufman	30
§*†GATESVILLE, Coryell, 463	11,874
*Gause, Milam, 11	400
Gay Hill, Washington	145
Gayle Estates, Brazoria	NA
*Geneva, Sabine, 1	100
Geneva Estates, Travis	NA

Town and County	Pop.
Geneview, Stonewall	NA
Gentrys Mill, Hamilton	NA
Geola Estates, Llano	NA
George's Creek, Somervell	66
§*†GEORGETOWN, Williamson, 1,131	16,752
§*†GEORGE WEST, Live Oak, 180	2,663
Georgia, Lamar	NA
Germania, Midland	27
Germany, Houston	NA
*Geronimo, Guadalupe, 15	250
Geronimo Forest, Bexar	NA
Geronimo Village, Bexar	NA
Gethsemane, Marion	NA
GHOLSON, McLennan	718
Gibtown, Jack	NA
§*†GIDDINGS, Lee, 447	4,223
Gifco, Ellis	NA
Gilbert, Angelina	NA
*Gilchrist, Galveston, 14	750
Gill, Harrison	NA
*Gillett, Karnes, 8	120
Gilliland, Knox	103
§*†GILMER, Upshur, 492	5,153
Gilpin, Childress	NA
Gilpin, Dickens	NA
Ginger, Rains	96
*Girard, Kent, 6	125
Girlstown USA, Cochran	NA
*Girvin, Pecos, 1	30
Gist, Jasper	NA
Givens, Lamar	135
Glade Branch, Franklin	NA
*†GLADEWATER, Gregg-Upshur, 425	6,184
Gladys, Montague	NA
Glass, Somervell	NA
Glaze City, Gonzales	10
*Glazier, Hemphill	45
Glen Cove, Coleman	40
Glendale, Trinity	78
Glenfawn, Rusk	16
*Glen Flora, Wharton, 9	210
Glenmont Estates, Montgomery	NA
Glen More, Comal	NA
Glenn, Dickens	12
GLENN HEIGHTS, Dallas-Ellis	5,084
Glenn Oaks, Henderson	NA
Glen Oaks, Kerr	NA
Glen Oaks, San Augustine	NA
Glenrio, Deaf Smith	NA
§*†GLEN ROSE, Somervell, 188	2,027
Glenwood, Upshur	NA
*Glidden, Colorado, 4	255
Globe, Lamar	NA
Glory, Lamar	30
*Gober, Fannin, 3	146
*GODLEY, Johnson, 75	582
*Golden, Wood, 13	156
Golden Beach, Llano	NA
Golden Oaks, Williamson	NA
Golden Trails, Montgomery	NA
Goldfinch, Frio	35
*Goldsboro, Coleman, 1	30
*GOLDSMITH, Ector, 26	302
§*†GOLDTHWAITE, Mills, 149	1,790
§*†GOLIAD, Goliad, 138	2,113
GOLINDA, Falls-McLennan	378
Golly, DeWitt	NA
Gomez, Terry	NA
§*†GONZALES, Gonzales, 506	6,519
Goober Hill, Shelby	NA
*Goodfellow Air Force Base, Tom Green	345
Good Hope, Franklin	NA
Goodland, Bailey	25
Goodlett, Hardeman	80
GOODLOW, Navarro	346
Good Neighbor, Hopkins	NA
Goodnight, Armstrong	25
Goodnight, Navarro	NA
*GOODRICH, Polk, 30	252
Goodsprings, Rusk	21
Goodwill, Burleson	NA
Goodwin, San Augustine	NA
*GORDON, Palo Pinto, 27	456
*Gordonville, Grayson, 33	220
*GOREE, Knox, 16	433
*†GORMAN, Eastland, 67	1,337
Goshen, Walker	NA
Gould, Cherokee	NA
*Gouldbusk, Coleman, 4	70
Gourdneck, Panola	30
Graball, Washington	NA
Grace, King	20
Graceton, Upshur	40
*†GRAFORD, Palo Pinto, 81	566
Graham, Garza	183
Graham, Jasper	NA
§*†GRAHAM, Young, 925	9,014
Granada Hills, Travis	NA
§*†GRANBURY, Hood, 1,278	4,458
Grand Bluff, Panola	97
*GRANDFALLS, Ward, 20	617
*†GRAND PRAIRIE, Dallas-Tarrant-Ellis, 3,456	103,913
*GRAND SALINE, Van Zandt, 212	2,697
Grandview, Dawson	NA
Grandview, Gray	13
*†GRANDVIEW, Johnson, 133	1,272
Grandview Beach, Burnet	NA
Grange Hall, Harrison	NA
*†GRANGER, Williamson, 53	1,294
*Grangerland, Montgomery	NA
*GRANITE SHOALS, Burnet	1,478
Granite Shoals Lake Estates, Llano	NA
GRANJENO, Hidalgo	NA
Gran Sabana, Burnet	NA
Gran Sabana, Llano	NA
Grape Creek, Tom Green	NA
*†GRAPELAND, Houston, 107	1,609
Grapetown, Gillespie	NA
*†GRAPEVINE, Tarrant-Dallas-Denton, 1,542	33,718
Grassland, Lynn	61
Grassyville, Bastrop	50
Gray, Marion	NA
Grayback, Wilbarger	25
GRAYBURG, Hardin	287
Gray Rock, Franklin	NA
GRAYS PRAIRIE, Kaufman	316
Graytown, Wilson	64
Great N.W. Emerald Valley, Bexar	NA
Great Oaks, Williamson	NA
Green, Karnes	35
Green Acres, Hunt	NA
Green Acres, Sabine	NA
Green Brier Cove, Henderson	NA
Green Glenn Acres, Medina	NA
Green Hill, Titus	NA
Green Lake, Calhoun	51
Green Pastures, Hays	NA
Greenpond, Hopkins	NA
Greenridge North, Bexar	NA
Greens Creek, Erath	75
Greenshores, Travis	NA
Green Spring Valley, Bexar	NA
Greenview, Hopkins	NA
§*†GREENVILLE, Hunt, 1,326	23,636
Greenvine, Washington	35
Greenway, Bexar	NA
Greenwood, Hopkins	35
Greenwood, Midland	32
Greenwood, Red River	20
*Greenwood, Wise, 6	76
Greenwood Acres, Llano	NA
Greenwood Acres, Orange	NA
Greenwood Forest, Kerr	NA
*GREGORY, San Patricio, 45	2,534
Gresham, Smith, 3	100
*GREY FOREST, Bexar	484
Greystone, Comal	NA
Grice, Upshur	20
Griffin, Cherokee	21
Griffith, Cochran	NA
Griffith Switch, Ellis	10
Grigsby, Shelby	45
Grit, Mason	30
§*†GROESBECK, Limestone, 222	3,500
*†GROOM, Carson, 62	626
Grossville, Mason	NA
*†GROVES, Jefferson, 369	17,177
§*†GROVETON, Trinity, 96	1,125
Grow, King	70
Gruenau, DeWitt	NA
Gruene Oaks, Comal	NA
Grulla, Starr (See La Grulla)	
*†GRUVER, Hansford, 114	1,120
Guadalupe, Victoria	106
Guadalupe Heights, Kerr	NA
Guadalupe Station, Culberson	80
*Guerra, Jim Hogg, 1	75
Guion, Taylor	18
Gulf Dial, Hutchinson	80
Gulf Haven, Galveston	NA
Gum Springs, Cass	NA
Gum Springs, Harrison	NA
*GUN BARREL CITY, Henderson	3,906
Gunsight, Stephens	6
*GUNTER, Grayson, 27	930
Gus, Burleson	NA
*GUSTINE, Comanche, 23	458
§*Guthrie, King, 13	160
*Guy, Fort Bend, 10	60
Guys Store, Leon	NA
H	
Haciendito, Presidio	NA
Hackberry, Cottle	81
HACKBERRY, Denton	217
Hackberry, Edwards	NA
Hackberry, Garza-Lynn	NA
Hackberry, Lavaca	NA
Hagansport, Franklin	40
Hagerville, Houston	NA
Hail, Fannin	30
Hainesville, Wood	74
*†HALE CENTER, Hale, 93	2,094
Halfway, Hale	58
Hall, Marion	NA
Hall, San Saba	NA
§*†HALLETTSVILLE, Lavaca, 352	2,744
Halls Bluff, Houston	NA
HALLSBURG, McLennan	499
Halls Store, Panola	NA
*†HALLSVILLE, Harrison, 100	2,593
Halsted, Fayette	46
*HALTOM CITY, Tarrant	32,923
Hamby, Taylor	100
Hamilton, Franklin	NA
§*†HAMILTON, Hamilton, 306	3,011
*†HAMLIN, Jones-Fisher, 182	2,687
Hammond, Robertson	44
Hamon, Gonzales	15
Hampton, Nacogdoches	NA
*Hamshire, Jefferson, 43	350
Hancock Oak Hills, Comal	NA
*Hankamer, Chambers, 15	189
Hannibal, Erath	NA
Hanover, Milam	27
Hansford, Hansford	NA
*†HAPPY, Swisher-Randall, 54	615
Happy Hill, Johnson	NA
Happy Landing, Shelby	NA
Happy Union, Hale	15
Happy Valley, Taylor	NA
Haralson Lakes, Tyler	NA
Harbin, Erath	21
Harborlight, Sabine	NA
Harbor Point, Henderson	NA
Harborview, Brazoria	NA
Hardin, Coleman	NA
Hardin, Hardin	NA
*HARDIN, Liberty, 25	586
Hardy, Montague	NA
Hare, Williamson	70
*Hargill, Hidalgo, 8	1,349
†HARKER HEIGHTS, Bell	14,440
Harkeyville, San Saba	12
*Harleton, Harrison, 33	260
*†HARLINGEN, Cameron, 2,408	52,208
Harlow, Hunt	NA
Harmon, Lamar	35
Harmon Creek Ridge, Walker	NA
Harmony, Floyd	NA
Harmony, Grimes	12
Harmony, Limestone	NA

Town and County	Pop.
Harmony, Nacogdoches	NA
Harmony Hall, Austin	NA
*Harper, Gillespie, 64	383
Harpersville, Stephens	NA
Harriet, Tom Green	NA
Harris Chapel, Panola	180
Harrison, McLennan	25
*Harrold, Wilbarger, 11	320
*HART, Castro, 92	1,295
Hartburg, Newton	275
Hart Camp, Lamb	NA
*Hartley, Hartley, 30	370
Harvard Switch, Camp	NA
Harvest Acres, Montgomery	NA
Harvey, Brazos	310
Harwell Point, Burnet	NA
*Harwood, Gonzales, 11	112
§*†HASKELL, Haskell, 241	3,337
Haslam, Shelby	101
*HASLET, Tarrant-Denton, 46	879
*Hasse, Comanche, 1	43
Hatchel, Runnels	16
Hatchetville, Hopkins	NA
Havana, Hidalgo	NA
*†HAWKINS, Wood, 115	1,441
*HAWLEY, Jones, 44	631
Hawthorne, Shelby	NA
Hawthorne, Walker	NA
Hawthorn Ridge, Montgomery	NA
Haynesville, Wichita	60
Haynie Flat, Travis-Burnet	NA
HAYS, Hays	271
Hays City, Hays	NA
Hays Country Oaks, Hays	NA
Hazle Dell, Comanche	NA
Hazy Hollow, Montgomery	NA
Headsville, Robertson	NA
*†HEARNE, Robertson, 267	5,355
*HEATH, Rockwall	2,487
Heatherstone, Harris	NA
‡§*†Hebbronville, Jim Hogg, 202	4,590
HEBRON, Denton	1,291
Heckville, Lubbock	NA
*HEDLEY, Donley, 15	399
Hedwigs Hill, Mason	10
HEDWIG VILLAGE, Harris	2,963
Hefner, Knox	76
Hegar, Waller	NA
Heidelberg, Hidalgo	NA
*Heidenheimer, Bell, 6	144
Helena, Karnes	35
Helmic, Trinity	NA
*HELOTES, Bexar, 228	1,831
§*†HEMPHILL, Sabine, 164	1,236
§*†HEMPSTEAD, Waller, 281	3,763
§*†HENDERSON, Rusk, 878	11,488
Henderson Chapel, Concho	NA
Hendricks, Hunt	NA
Henly, Hays	55
§*†HENRIETTA, Clay, 226	3,016
Henry's Chapel, Cherokee	75
§*†HEREFORD, Deaf Smith, 829	14,872
Heritage Farm, Bexar	NA
Heritage Hills, Hays	NA
Heritage Oaks, Hays	NA
Heritage Oaks, Montgomery	NA
Hermits Cove, Rains	40
*Hermleigh, Scurry, 13	200
Herty, Angelina	605
Hester, Navarro	35
*HEWITT, McLennan, 248	9,889
*Hext, Menard, 3	64
HICKORY CREEK, Denton	2,058
Hickory Creek, Fort Bend	NA
Hickory Creek, Houston	NA
Hickory Creek, Hunt	NA
Hickory Forrest, Guadalupe	300
Hickory Hills, Montgomery	NA
Hickory Hills, Sabine	NA
Hickory Hollow, Hunt	NA
Hickory Hollow, San Augustine	NA
Hicksbaugh, Tyler	NA
*†HICO, Hamilton, 108	1,440
*†HIDALGO, Hidalgo, 260	4,015
Hidden Acres, Henderson	NA
Hidden Acres, Williamson	NA
Hidden Forest Estates, Montgomery	NA
Hidden Hill Lakes, Smith	NA
Hidden Hills, Travis	NA
Hidden Hills Harbor, Henderson	NA
Hidden Meadows, Williamson	NA
Hidden Valley, Travis	NA
Hide-A-Way Lake, Smith	NA
Hide-Away Bay, Smith	NA
Hide Away, Brazoria	NA
Hideaway, Comal	NA
Higginbotham, Gaines	210
*HIGGINS, Lipscomb, 35	484
High, Lamar	55
Highbank, Falls	126
High Chaparral, Williamson	NA
High Chapparal, Montgomery	NA
High Gabriel East, Williamson	NA
High Gabriel West, Williamson	NA
High Hill, Fayette	116
*High Island, Galveston, 14	500
Highland, Erath	60
Highland, Smith	NA
Highland Acres, Hunt	NA
Highland Addition, Parker	NA
Highland Bayou, Galveston	1,209
Highland Haven, Burnet	NA
Highland Hollow, Montgomery	NA
HIGHLAND PARK, Dallas	9,287
Highland Park, Nacogdoches	NA
‡*†Highlands, Harris, 287	7,463
*†HIGHLAND VILLAGE, Denton	8,917
High Point, Collin	NA
High Point, Grimes	15
Highsaw, Henderson	NA
Hightower, Liberty	30
Hightown, Polk	NA
Highway 90 Ranch, Medina	NA
Hilda, Mason	NA
Hilger, Fannin	NA
Hill and Dale Acres, Montgomery	NA
Hill Country Ranches, Hays	NA
*HILL COUNTRY VILLAGE, Bexar	1,187
Hillcrest, Colorado	25
HILLCREST VILLAGE, Brazoria	789
*Hillister, Tyler, 9	200
Hillje, Wharton	51
Hills, Lee	20
§*†HILLSBORO, Hill, 590	7,423
Hillside Estates, Henderson	NA
Hills Prairie, Bastrop	35
Hilltop Acres, Bexar	NA
Hilltop Acres, Kaufman	NA
*Hilltop Lakes, Leon	300
HILSHIRE VILLAGE, Harris	764
Hinckley, Lamar	40
Hindes, Atascosa	14
Hines, Johnson	NA
Hinkles Ferry, Brazoria	35
Hippie Ridge (see Draper)., Wise	NA
Hiram, Kaufman	34
*†HITCHCOCK, Galveston, 178	6,580
Hitchland, Hansford	27
Hitson, Fisher	NA
Hix, Burleson	35
Hoard, Wood	NA
Hobbs, Fisher	91
*Hobson, Karnes, 11	135
*Hochheim, DeWitt, 2	70
*Hockley, Harris, 59	300
Hodges, Jones	250
Hogan Acres, Johnson	NA
Hogansville, Rains	200
Hogg, Burleson	NA
Holcomb Store, Cherokee	NA
Holiday Beach, Aransas	1,000
Holiday Estates, Hunt	NA
Holiday Forest, Sabine	NA
Holiday Harbor, Marion	NA
Holiday Hills, Smith	NA
Holiday Hills Estates, Stephens	NA
Holiday Lake Estates, Polk	NA
HOLIDAY LAKES, Brazoria	1,150
Holiday Oaks, Montgomery	NA
Holiday Shores, Brazoria	NA
Holiday Shores, Collin	NA
*†HOLLAND, Bell, 56	1,197
Holland Quarters, Panola	40
*HOLLIDAY, Archer, 89	1,480
Holly, Houston	NA
Holly Acres, Angelina	NA
Holly Beach, Cameron	NA
Holly Grove, Polk	NA
Holly Hills, Polk	NA
Holly Springs, Jasper	50
Holly Terrace, Montgomery	NA
*HOLLYWOOD PARK, Bexar	3,075
Holman, Fayette	116
HOMER, Angelina	360
‡Homestead Meadows, El Paso	5,214
§*†HONDO, Medina, 310	6,217
Honea Forrest Estates, Montgomery	NA
Honey Creek, Comal	NA
*†HONEY GROVE, Fannin, 119	1,695
Honey Island, Hardin	401
Hood, Cooke	75
Hooker Ridge, Rains	250
*HOOKS, Bowie, 110	2,789
Hoop and Holler, Liberty	NA
Hoover, Gray	5
Hoover, Lamar	NA
Hope, Lavaca	45
Hopewell, Franklin	35
Hopewell, Houston	NA
Hopewell, Red River	150
*HORIZON CITY, El Paso	2,650
Hornsby Bend, Travis	20
‡*Horseshoe Bay, Llano-Burnet	1,616
Horseshoe Bay South, Burnet	NA
Horseshoe Bay West, Llano	NA
Horseshoe Bend, Liberty	NA
Horseshoe Falls, Comal	NA
Horseshoe Lake, Smith	NA
Hortense, Polk	25
Horton, Delta	25
Horton, Panola	NA
Hostetter Creek Estates, Montgomery	NA
Houmont Park, Harris	NA
§*†HOUSTON, Harris-Fort Bend-Montgomery, 113,971	1,700,672
Howard, Ellis	26
HOWARDWICK, Donley	210
*†HOWE, Grayson, 83	2,226
Howellville, Harris	36
Howland, Lamar	90
Howth, Waller	65
Hoxie, Williamson	50
Hoyte, Milam	20
Hub, Parmer	NA
Hubbard, Bowie	269
*†HUBBARD, Hill, 92	1,629
Huber, Shelby	NA
Huckabay, Erath	150
Hudd, Scurry	NA
Huddleston, Montague	NA
HUDSON, Angelina	2,519
Hudson Bend, Travis	NA
HUDSON OAKS, Parker	991
Hudsons Chapel, Cherokee	NA
Hudsonville, Fannin	5
Huff, Archer	NA
Huffines, Cass	90
*Huffman, Harris, 181	50
*Hufsmith, Harris	250
*†HUGHES SPRINGS, Cass-Morris, 142	2,063
Hughey, Gregg	NA
*†Hull, Liberty, 34	1,800
Hulon Lakes, Montgomery	NA
*†HUMBLE, Harris, 3,946	13,711
Humble Colorado Camp, Jim Hogg	NA
Humble Government Wells Camp, Duval	NA
Hume, Cherokee	NA
*Hungerford, Wharton, 25	178
*Hunt, Kerr, 49	708
Hunter, Comal	30
Hunter Hills, Comal	NA
Hunter Oaks, Comal	NA
Hunters Creek, Comal	NA
HUNTERS CREEK VILLAGE, Harris	4,366
Hunters Glen, Hays	NA
Hunters Retreat, Montgomery	NA

Town and County	Pop.
*†HUNTINGTON, Angelina, 95	1,902
Huntoon, Ochiltree	21
§*†HUNTSVILLE, Walker, 1,325	29,907
Hurley, Wood	NA
Hurlwood, Lubbock	115
Hurnville, Clay	15
Huron, Hill	NA
*†HURST, Tarrant, 2,129	36,484
Hurstown, Shelby	NA
Hurst Springs, Coryell	NA
*HUTCHINS, Dallas, 134	2,975
*†HUTTO, Williamson, 59	668
HUXLEY, Shelby	352
Huxley Bay, Shelby	NA
*Hye, Blanco, 5	105
Hylton, Nolan	28
Hynds City, Montague	NA
I	
Iago, Wharton	56
Ibex, Shackelford	25
Ida, Grayson	50
*†IDALOU, Lubbock, 90	2,126
Idle Hour Acres, Travis	NA
Ike, Ellis	10
Illinois Bend, Montague	NA
IMPACT, Taylor	24
Impala Point, Henderson	NA
Impala Woods, Polk	NA
*Imperial, Pecos, 25	720
Imperial Valley, Travis	NA
Inadale, Scurry	8
Independence, Washington	140
India, Ellis	12
Indian Creek, Smith	NA
Indian Gap, Hamilton	36
Indian Harbor Estates, Hood	691
Indian Hill, Newton	NA
Indian Hills, Bexar	NA
Indian Hills, Comal	NA
Indian Hills, Llano	NA
INDIAN LAKE, Cameron	407
Indian Lake, Newton	NA
Indian Lodge, Bosque	NA
Indian Mound Estates, Sabine	NA
Indian Oaks, Henderson	NA
Indian Oaks, Waller	NA
Indian Oaks, Williamson	NA
Indianola, Calhoun	NA
Indian Rock, Upshur	NA
Indian Springs, Polk	NA
Indian Woods, Montgomery	NA
Indio, Presidio	NA
*†INDUSTRY, Austin, 40	475
‡*Inez, Victoria, 27	1,433
*INGLESIDE, San Patricio, 189	6,289
INGLESIDE-ON-THE-BAY, San Patricio	NA
*INGRAM, Kerr, 153	1,493
Inks Lake Village, Llano	NA
Inverness Point, Travis	NA
*†Iola, Grimes, 40	331
IOWA COLONY, Brazoria	743
*†IOWA PARK, Wichita, 335	6,538
*Ira, Scurry, 26	250
*†IRAAN, Pecos, 82	1,338
Irby, Haskell	NA
*IREDELL, Bosque, 17	349
Ireland, Coryell	60
*Irene, Hill, 2	160
Irish Meadows, Smith	NA
Ironton, Cherokee	110
*†IRVING, Dallas, 7,986	166,523
Isla, Sabine	29
Island Village, Llano	NA
Israel, Polk	25
*†ITALY, Ellis, 61	1,880
*†ITASCA, Hill, 88	1,569
Ivan, Stephens	15
*Ivanhoe, Fannin, 13	110
Iverson, Hill	NA
*Izoro, Lampasas	31
J	
*†JACINTO CITY, Harris	9,680
§*†JACKSBORO, Jack, 305	3,412
Jackson, Marion	NA
Jackson, Shelby	NA

Town and County	Pop.
Jackson, Van Zandt	NA
*†JACKSONVILLE, Cherokee, 941	13,053
Jacobia, Hunt	60
Jacobs, Rusk	NA
Jakes Colony, Guadalupe	30
JAMAICA BEACH, Galveston	699
James, Shelby	NA
James, Upshur	NA
Jamestown, Newton	70
Jamestown, Smith	75
JA Ranch, Armstrong	20
Jardin, Hunt	22
*†Jarrell, Williamson, 30	410
§*†JASPER, Jasper, 695	7,586
§*†JAYTON, Kent, 41	553
Jean, Young	91
Jeddo, Bastrop	75
§*†JEFFERSON, Marion, 312	2,378
Jenkins, Morris	NA
Jennings, Lamar	NA
Jericho, Shelby	NA
*Jermyn, Jack, 2	75
Jerrys Quarters, Washington	NA
*JERSEY VILLAGE, Harris	5,226
*†JEWETT, Leon, 71	739
Jiba, Kaufman	NA
*†JOAQUIN, Shelby, 39	864
Joe Lee, Bell	2
Johnson, Anderson	NA
Johnson, Terry	NA
§*†JOHNSON CITY, Blanco, 108	1,032
Johnson Creek, Marion	NA
Johnston Store, Nacogdoches	NA
Johnsville, Erath	25
Johntown, Red River	175
Joiner, Fayette	NA
*Joinerville, Rusk, 2	140
Joliet, Caldwell	NA
JOLLY, Clay, 1	208
Jolly Oaks, Williamson	NA
‡Jollyville, Williamson-Travis	16,641
Jonah, Williamson, 1	60
Jones, Van Zandt	NA
*Jonesboro, Coryell-Hamilton, 16	200
JONES CREEK, Brazoria	2,195
Jones Prairie, Milam	35
*JONESTOWN, Travis	1,305
*Jonesville, Harrison, 9	28
Joplin, Jack	NA
Joppa, Burnet	NA
Jordans Store, Shelby	NA
*JOSEPHINE, Collin-Hunt, 8	580
*†JOSHUA, Johnson, 257	4,008
Josselet, Haskell	NA
Josserand, Trinity	NA
Jot-Em-Down, Hunt-Delta	10
§*†JOURDANTON, Atascosa, 173	3,388
Joy, Clay	150
Joyce, Webb	20
Jud, Haskell	40
*Judson, Gregg, 9	650
Jumbo, Castro	NA
Jumbo, Panola	NA
Junction, Coleman	NA
§*†JUNCTION, Kimble, 216	2,771
Juno, Val Verde	10
*Justiceburg, Garza	76
*†JUSTIN, Denton, 134	1,411
K	
Kalgary, Crosby	140
*Kamay, Wichita, 10	642
Kamey, Calhoun	NA
Kanawha, Red River	149
*Karnack, Harrison, 41	775
§*†KARNES CITY, Karnes, 141	3,035
Karon, Live Oak	20
Katemcy, Mason, 3	90
*†KATY, Harris-Waller-Fort Bend, 1,572	9,020
§*†KAUFMAN, Kaufman, 424	5,917
Kaufman Estates, Kaufman	240
*Keechi, Leon	67
*†KEENE, Johnson, 110	4,124
Keeter, Wise	NA
Keith, Grimes	NA

Town and County	Pop.
Keith Lake, Jefferson	NA
*†KELLER, Tarrant, 591	16,371
Kellers Corner, Cameron	NA
*Kellerville, Wheeler	50
Kellogg, Hunt	NA
Kelly, Collin	NA
*Kelly Air Force Base, Bexar	2,363
Kellyville, Marion	NA
Kelsey, Upshur	50
Kelton, Wheeler	75
*Keltys, Angelina	800
*KEMAH, Galveston, 222	1,206
*†KEMP, Kaufman, 222	1,287
Kemper City, Victoria	16
*Kempner, Lampasas, 38	420
Ken Brook Valley, Montgomery	NA
*Kendalia, Kendall, 5	76
*KENDLETON, Fort Bend, 8	574
*†KENEDY, Karnes, 231	3,736
KENEFICK, Liberty	460
*KENNARD, Houston, 23	360
*KENNEDALE, Tarrant, 333	4,576
*Kenney, Austin, 1	200
Kenser, Hunt	NA
Kensing, Delta	35
*Kent, Culberson, 12	60
Kentucky Town, Grayson	NA
*KERENS, Navarro, 72	1,701
§*†KERMIT, Winkler, 311	7,001
*Kerrick, Dallam	60
§*†KERRVILLE, Kerr, 1,687	19,134
Kerrville South, Kerr	6,600
Key, Dawson	20
Key Allegro, Aransas	600
Key Ranch Estates, Henderson	NA
Kiam, Polk	NA
Kicaster, Wilson	100
Kiesling, Tom Green	NA
*Kildare, Cass, 4	49
Kildare Junction, Cass	NA
Kilgore, Goliad	120
*†KILGORE, Gregg-Rusk, 1,037	11,275
*†KILLEEN, Bell, 2,601	71,031
Kimball, Bosque	NA
Kimbro, Travis	50
King, Coryell	25
King Ranch Headquarters, Kleberg	NA
*Kingsbury, Guadalupe, 36	200
Kings Country, Franklin	NA
Kings Cove, Burnet	NA
Kings Highway, Brazos	NA
‡*†Kingsland, Llano, 158	2,835
Kingsland Cove, Burnet	NA
Kingsland Estates, Llano	NA
Kingsland Hills, Burnet	NA
Kingsmill, Gray	65
Kings Point, Bexar	NA
Kingston, Hunt	140
Kings Village, Travis	NA
§*†KINGSVILLE, Kleberg, 1,036	26,246
*Kingsville Naval Air Stn., Kleberg	323
Kingtown, Nacogdoches	NA
‡*†Kingwood, Harris-Montgomery	39,631
Kinkler, Lavaca	75
Kinney Point, Franklin	NA
Kinwood, Harris	NA
Kiomatia, Red River	61
Kiowa Village, Hunt	NA
*KIRBY, Bexar	8,987
Kirby Town, Hardin	NA
*KIRBYVILLE, Jasper, 195	1,968
Kirk, Limestone	NA
*Kirkland, Childress, 1	102
Kirtley, Fayette	43
*KIRVIN, Freestone, 1	116
Kitsee Ridge, Hunt	NA
*Klein, Harris	NA
Klondike, Dawson	20
*Klondike, Delta, 4	135
Klump, Washington	NA
Knapp, Scurry	10
*Knickerbocker, Tom Green	50
Knight, Polk	NA
Knights Forest, Liberty	NA
*Knippa, Uvalde, 28	360

Town and County	Pop.
Knobbs Springs, Lee	20
Knob Hill, Denton	NA
Knolle, Nueces-Jim Wells	NA
Knoll Ridge Acres, Bexar	NA
KNOLLWOOD, Grayson	235
Knollwood, Smith	NA
Knollwood, Travis	NA
*Knott, Howard, 11	685
Knox Acres, Montgomery	NA
*†KNOX CITY, Knox, 101	1,479
Koerth, Lavaca	45
Kohrville, Harris	NA
Kokomo, Eastland	25
Komensky, Lavaca	NA
Kona Kai, Galveston	NA
Koocksville, Mason	NA
Kopernik Shores, Cameron	26
*Kopperl, Bosque, 16	225
Kosciusko, Wilson	390
*†KOSSE, Limestone, 24	542
§*KOUNTZE, Hardin, 159	2,271
Kovar, Bastrop	NA
*†KRESS, Swisher, 75	734
Kreutsberg, Kendall	NA
Kristenstad, Hood	NA
Krohn Ranchettes, Montgomery	NA
KRUGERVILLE, Denton	851
*†KRUM, Denton, 103	1,835
*Kurten, Brazos, 13	150
*KYLE, Hays, 132	2,321
Kyote, Atascosa	25

L

Town and County	Pop.
LaBelle, Jefferson	NA
*La Blanca, Hidalgo, 2	150
La Casa, Stephens	NA
‡*La Casita-Garciasville, Starr, 11	1,311
Laceola, Madison	10
‡*Lackland Air Force Base, Bexar	10,280
*†LA COSTE, Medina, 34	1,246
Lacy, Trinity	24
LACY-LAKEVIEW, McLennan	4,040
*†LADONIA, Fannin, 31	670
LaFayette, Upshur	80
*†LA FERIA, Cameron, 151	4,934
Lagarto, Live Oak	80
La Gloria, Jim Wells	NA
La Gloria, Starr	102
Lago, Cameron	NA
*LAGO VISTA, Travis, 80	2,328
§*†LA GRANGE, Fayette, 480	4,161
*LA GRULLA, Starr, 15	1,566
Laguna, Uvalde	NA
‡Laguna Heights, Cameron	1,844
*Laguna Park, Bosque	550
Laguna Tres Estates, Hood	280
Laguna Vista, Burnet	NA
LAGUNA VISTA, Cameron	1,335
Laguna Vista Estates, Henderson	NA
La Hacienda Estates, Travis	NA
Lahey, Terry	NA
‡La Homa, Hidalgo	1,556
Laird, Montgomery	NA
*Laird Hill, Rusk, 3	405
La Isla, El Paso	29
Lajitas, Brewster	50
*LA JOYA, Hidalgo, 37	3,007
La Junta, Parker	NA
Lake, Wise	NA
Lake Arrowhead, Clay	75
Lake Austin Lodges, Travis	NA
Lake Bonanza, Montgomery	NA
LAKE BRIDGEPORT, Wise	349
‡Lake Brownwood, Brown	1,275
Lake Cisco, Eastland	105
LAKE CITY, San Patricio	484
Lake Conroe Forest, Montgomery	NA
Lake Conroe Heights, Montgomery	NA
Lake Conroe Hills, Montgomery	NA
Lake Conroe Terrace, Montgomery	NA
Lake Conroe West, Montgomery	NA
*Lake Creek, Delta, 5	60
Lake Creek Falls, Montgomery	NA
Lake Crockett Estates, Fannin	5
*†LAKE DALLAS, Denton, 206	4,006
Lake Dunlap, Guadalupe	500
Lake Forest Falls, Montgomery	NA
Lake Forest Lodge, Montgomery	NA
Lake Gardens, Tom Green	NA
Lake Haven, Smith	NA
‡*Lakehills, Bandera	2,328
Lake Hyatt Estates, Tyler	NA
*†LAKE JACKSON, Brazoria, 882	24,355
Lake Jackson Farms, Brazoria	NA
Lake James, Hidalgo	NA
*Lake Kiowa, Cooke	1,200
Lakeland, Montgomery	NA
Lake Lavon Lodges, Collin	NA
Lake Leon, Eastland	75
Lake Livingston Estates, Polk	NA
Lake Lorraine, Montgomery	NA
Lake Louise, Montgomery	NA
Lake Meredith Estates, Hutchinson	262
Lake Mount Pleasant, Montgomery	NA
Lake Nueces, Uvalde	15
Lake Oak, Henderson	NA
Lake Placid, Brazos	NA
Lake Placid, Guadalupe	300
LAKEPORT, Gregg	783
Lake Rayburn Shores, Angelina	NA
Lakeridge Estates, Smith	NA
Lakeridge Heights, Stephens	NA
Lake Rolling Wood, Montgomery	NA
Lake Sam Rayburn Estates, Sabine	NA
Lake Shore, Brown	NA
Lake Shore Estates, Stephens	NA
Lakeshore Estates, Marion	NA
Lakeshore Estates West, Marion	NA
Lakeshore Gardens, San Patricio	NA
Lakeshore Ranch, Travis	NA
LAKESIDE, San Patricio	319
LAKESIDE, Tarrant	896
Lakeside Acres, Bexar	NA
Lakeside Beach, Burnet	NA
LAKESIDE CITY, Archer-Wichita	927
Lakeside Estates, Angelina	NA
Lakeside Estates, Bexar	NA
Lakeside Heights, Llano	NA
Lakeside Village, Bosque	226
Lake Splendora, Montgomery	NA
LAKE TANGLEWOOD, Randall	704
Lake Tejas, San Jacinto	NA
Laketon, Gray	12
Lake Victor, Burnet	215
Lakeview, Floyd	NA
Lakeview, Franklin	NA
*LAKEVIEW, Hall, 12	215
Lakeview, Lynn	NA
Lakeview, Marion	NA
Lakeview, Orange	75
Lakeview, Swisher	NA
Lakeview, Tarrant	NA
Lake View Park, Comal	NA
Lakeview Estates, Johnson	NA
Lakeview Estates, Orange	NA
Lakeview Estates, Wise	NA
Lakeview Heights, Kaufman	240
Lakeview Hills, Travis	NA
Lakeview Manor, Montgomery	NA
Lake Water Wheel, San Jacinto	NA
*LAKEWAY, Travis	4,427
Lake Whitney Estates, Hill	NA
Lake Wildwood, Montgomery	NA
Lakewood, Henderson	NA
Lakewood, San Augustine	NA
Lakewood, Travis	NA
Lakewood Colony, Montgomery	NA
Lakewood Estates, Burnet	NA
Lakewood Estates, Montgomery	NA
Lakewood Estates, Travis	NA
Lakewood Forest, Llano	NA
Lakewood Harbor, Hill	NA
Lakewood Hills, Comal	NA
LAKEWOOD VILLAGE, Denton	187
†LAKE WORTH, Tarrant	4,872
La Leona, Cameron	NA
La Lomita, Hidalgo	NA
Lamar, Aransas	1,600
Lamar, Shelby	NA
*†LA MARQUE, Galveston, 461	14,501
Lamasco, Fannin	32
§*†LAMESA, Dawson, 727	11,148
Lamkin, Comanche	88
§*†LAMPASAS, Lampasas, 499	6,617
Lanark, Cass	NA
*LANCASTER, Dallas, 657	24,300
Landrum Station, Cameron	125
*Lane City, Wharton, 7	111
Laneley, Freestone	27
Laneport, Williamson	60
*Laneville, Rusk, 15	200
Langford Place, Orange	NA
*Langtry, Val Verde, 2	145
Lanham, Hamilton	NA
Lanier, Cass	40
Lannius, Fannin	79
Lansing, Harrison	NA
Lantana, Cameron	NA
La Paloma, Cameron	110
La Parita, Atascosa	NA
*†LA PORTE, Harris, 959	30,127
‡*La Pryor, Zavala, 39	1,306
§*†LAREDO, Webb, 4,315	140,688
La Reforma, Starr	45
Lariat, Parmer	200
Lark, Carson, 3	NA
La Rose, Nueces	20
*Larue, Henderson, 23	160
*LaSalle, Jackson, 4	75
LaSalle Estates, Montgomery	NA
*Lasara, Willacy, 11	100
Las Escobas, Starr	NA
Las Playas, Brazoria	NA
Las Rusias, Cameron	NA
Lassater, Marion	48
Las Yescas, Cameron	NA
Latch, Upshur	50
Latex, Harrison	NA
*LATEXO, Houston, 8	303
La Tina, Cameron	NA
Latium, Washington	30
Lauback, Guadalupe	13
‡*Laughlin Air Force Base, Val Verde	2,819
La Union, Cameron	20
Laurel, Newton	125
Laureles, Cameron	20
Laurel Estates, Hays	NA
Lavada, Franklin	NA
Lavender, Limestone	NA
*†LA VERNIA, Wilson, 103	715
*LA VILLA, Hidalgo, 9	1,577
*LAVON, Collin, 7	352
Lavon Beach Estates, Collin	NA
Lavon Shores Estates, Collin	NA
Law, Brazos	NA
*LA WARD, Jackson, 8	176
*LAWN, Taylor, 22	362
Lawrence, Kaufman	249
Lawsonville, Rusk	NA
Lazare, Cottle-Hardeman	26
*Lazbuddie, Parmer, 19	248
Lazy Acres, Nacogdoches	NA
Lazy Caney Pines, Montgomery	NA
Lazy Forest, Montgomery	NA
Lazy River Resort, Austin	NA
*Leaday, Coleman, 1	55
League, Crosby	NA
*†LEAGUE CITY, Galveston, 924	34,015
Leagueville, Henderson	NA
§*†LEAKEY, Real, 77	406
*LEANDER, Williamson-Travis, 486	3,634
Leander Heights, Williamson	NA
*LEARY, Bowie	420
Lebanon, Collin	50
*Ledbetter, Fayette, 9	76
Leedale, Bell	16
Lees, Glasscock	NA
*Leesburg, Camp, 21	115
Lee Spring, Smith	NA
*Leesville, Gonzales, 7	150
*LEFORS, Gray, 18	695
*Leggett, Polk, 10	375
Legion, Kerr	NA
Lehman, Cochran	NA
Leigh, Harrison	100
Leisure Acres, Coryell	25
Leisure Land, Henderson	NA

Town and County	Pop.
Lela, Wheeler	135
*Lelia Lake, Donley, 4	125
*Leming, Atascosa, 9	250
*Lenorah, Martin, 11	70
Lenz, Karnes	20
Leo, Cooke	80
Leo, Lee	NA
*LEONA, Leon, 8	205
*†LEONARD, Fannin, 86	1,778
Leona Schroder, Nueces	40
Leonidas, Montgomery	NA
*Leon Junction, Coryell	25
Leon Springs, Bexar	137
*LEON VALLEY, Bexar	9,981
*LEROY, McLennan, 15	321
Lesley, Hall	45
§*†LEVELLAND, Hockley, 779	14,277
Leverett's Chapel, Rusk	450
Levi, McLennan	50
Levita, Coryell	70
*LEWISVILLE, Denton-Dallas, 2,918	52,908
*LEXINGTON, Lee, 61	991
Liberty, Coleman	NA
Liberty, Freestone	75
Liberty, Hopkins	NA
§*†LIBERTY, Liberty, 605	8,587
Liberty, Lubbock	10
Liberty, Milam	40
Liberty, Newton	NA
Liberty, Rusk	NA
Liberty Chapel, Johnson	NA
‡Liberty City, Gregg	1,660
Liberty Grove, Collin	NA
Liberty Hill, Houston	NA
Liberty Hill, Milam	25
*Liberty Hill, Williamson, 71	300
Liberty Oaks, Williamson	NA
Lilbert, Nacogdoches	NA
*Lillian, Johnson, 13	105
*Lincoln, Lee, 12	276
LINCOLN PARK, Denton	335
*†LINDALE, Smith, 274	2,558
§*†LINDEN, Cass, 115	2,395
Lindenau, DeWitt	50
Lindendale, Kendall	NA
*LINDSAY, Cooke, 28	683
*Lingleville, Erath, 4	100
*Linn, Hidalgo, 13	450
Linn Flat, Nacogdoches	NA
Linwood, Cherokee	40
*†LIPAN, Hood, 32	382
§*Lipscomb, Lipscomb, 5	45
*Lissie, Wharton, 7	70
Littig, Travis	37
Little Cypress, Orange	1,050
*LITTLE ELM, Denton, 83	1,389
§*†LITTLEFIELD, Lamb, 398	6,518
Little Hope, Wood	NA
Little Midland, Burnet	NA
Little New York, Gonzales	20
Little Ridge Estates, Collin	NA
*LITTLE RIVER-ACADEMY, Bell, 30	1,515
Littleville, Hamilton	NA
Lively, Kaufman	NA
*LIVE OAK, Bexar	10,524
Live Oak, Concho	NA
Live Oak Bend, Matagorda	NA
Live Oak Ranchettes, Williamson	NA
Live Oak Resorts, Hill	NA
Liveoak Estates, Montgomery	NA
*LIVERPOOL, Brazoria, 17	439
§*†LIVINGSTON, Polk, 685	5,585
§*†LLANO, Llano, 289	3,012
Lobo, Culberson	40
Loch Ness Cove, Montgomery	NA
Lochridge, Brazoria	NA
Locker, San Saba	16
Lockett, Wilbarger	200
Lockettville, Hockley	20
§*†LOCKHART, Caldwell, 483	9,415
*†LOCKNEY, Floyd, 107	2,112
Loco, Childress	NA
Locust, Grayson	NA
*Lodi, Marion, 4	164

Town and County	Pop.
Lodwick, Marion	NA
Loeb, Hardin	NA
Loebau, Lee	20
Logan, Panola	40
LOG CABIN, Henderson	516
*Lohn, McCulloch, 10	149
Loire, Wilson	50
Lois, Cooke	60
Lolaville, Collin	NA
*Lolita, Jackson, 19	300
Lollipop, Henderson	NA
Loma, Walker	NA
Loma Alta, McMullen	25
Loma Alta, Val Verde	30
Lomax, Howard	3,554
*†LOMETA, Lampasas, 46	681
*London, Kimble, 5	180
London, Rusk	NA
Londonderry, Harris	NA
Lone Camp, Palo Pinto	32
Lone Cedar, Ellis	18
Lone Elm, Ellis	20
Lone Elm, Kaufman	NA
Lone Grove, Llano	50
Lone Oak, Bexar	NA
Lone Oak, Colorado	NA
Lone Oak, Erath	NA
*†LONE OAK, Hunt, 42	557
Lone Oak Estates, Bexar	NA
Lone Pine, Houston	NA
Lone Star, Cherokee	NA
Lone Star, Floyd	NA
Lone Star, Franklin	NA
Lone Star, Kaufman	NA
Lone Star, Lamar	NA
*†LONE STAR, Morris, 76	1,624
*Long Branch, Panola, 3	181
Long Hollow, Leon	NA
Long Lake, Anderson	NA
Long Lake Estates, Montgomery	NA
*Long Mott, Calhoun, 2	76
Long Mountain, Mason	NA
Longpoint, Washington	80
§*†LONGVIEW, Gregg-Harrison-Upshur, 3,942	72,438
Longworth, Fisher	65
Lonnie, Childress	NA
Loon Bay, Henderson	NA
Looneyville, Nacogdoches	NA
*Loop, Gaines, 24	315
*Lopeno, Zapata, 2	100
‡Lopezville, Hidalgo	3,126
*LORAINE, Mitchell, 28	744
*†LORENA, McLennan, 131	1,342
*†LORENZO, Crosby, 57	1,246
Los Angeles, La Salle	140
Los Barreras, Starr	125
Los Coyotes, Willacy	NA
*Los Ebanos, Hidalgo, 1	100
Los Escondidos, Burnet	NA
*†LOS FRESNOS, Cameron, 131	2,775
*LOS INDIOS, Cameron, 1	206
Losoya, Bexar	322
Lost Creek, Coleman	NA
‡Lost Creek, Travis	4,417
Lost Hollow Creek, Llano	NA
Lost Lakes, Montgomery	NA
Lost Prairie, Limestone	2
Lost River Estates, Williamson	NA
LOS YBANEZ, Dawson	91
*†LOTT, Falls, 48	838
Lotta, Harrison	10
*†Louise, Wharton, 62	310
Lovelace, Hill	NA
*†LOVELADY, Houston, 43	609
*Loving, Young, 13	240
*Lowake, Concho, 3	40
Lowman, Lamar	NA
LOWRY CROSSING, Collin	938
Loyal Valley, Mason	50
Loyola Beach, Kleberg	NA
*Lozano, Cameron, 3	200
§*†LUBBOCK, Lubbock, 9,453	193,194
LUCAS, Collin	2,586
Luckenbach, Gillespie	25

Town and County	Pop.
*LUEDERS, Jones-Shackelford, 18	375
Luella, Grayson	615
§*†LUFKIN, Angelina, 2,279	31,651
*†LULING, Caldwell, 334	5,065
Lull, Hidalgo	NA
*†LUMBERTON, Hardin, 118	7,016
Lumkins, Ellis	20
Lums Chapel, Lamb	NA
Lund, Travis	50
Lusk, Throckmorton	NA
Luther, Howard	335
Lutie, Collingsworth	35
Lux Ranch, Kendall	NA
Lydia, Red River	109
*LYFORD, Willacy, 64	1,849
Lynchburg, Harris	100
Lynn Grove, Grimes	NA
Lynnwood Lakes, Waller	NA
*Lyons, Burleson, 9	360
Lytle Ranch Acres, Medina	NA
*†LYTLE, Atascosa-Medina-Bexar, 110	2,395
Lytton Springs, Caldwell	76

M

Town and County	Pop.
*MABANK, Kaufman-Henderson, 515	1,832
Mabelle, Baylor	6
Mabry, Red River	60
*Macdona, Bexar, 8	297
Macedonia, Harrison	NA
Macey, Brazos	NA
Macon, Franklin	NA
Macune, San Augustine	100
Madero, Hidalgo	NA
§*†MADISONVILLE, Madison, 348	3,926
Madras, Red River	61
Mae, Jim Wells	NA
Magnet, Wharton	42
*MAGNOLIA, Montgomery, 370	1,111
Magnolia, San Jacinto	30
Magnolia Beach, Calhoun	NA
Magnolia Bend, Montgomery	NA
Magnolia Gardens, Harris	NA
Magnolia Hills, Montgomery	NA
Magnolia Lake, Montgomery	NA
Magnolia Oaks, Montgomery	NA
*Magnolia Springs, Jasper, 1	80
Maha, Travis	NA
Mahl, Nacogdoches	NA
Mahomet, Burnet	47
Mahoney, Hopkins	NA
Majors, Franklin	NA
*MALAKOFF, Henderson, 175	2,140
Mallard, Montague	NA
*MALONE, Hill, 28	333
Malta, Bowie	297
Malvern, Leon	NA
Mambrino, Hood	74
*Manchaca, Travis, 140	4,700
Manchester, Red River	185
Mangum, Eastland	15
Mangus Corner, Bexar	NA
Manheim, Lee	40
Mankin, Henderson	NA
Mankins, Archer	45
*MANOR, Travis, 119	1,149
*MANSFIELD, Tarrant-Johnson-Ellis, 846	17,621
*MANVEL, Brazoria, 221	4,259
*Maple, Bailey, 6	130
Maple, Red River	30
Maple Spring, Titus	NA
Mapleton, Houston	NA
*Marathon, Brewster, 34	800
*†MARBLE FALLS, Burnet, 692	4,266
§*†MARFA, Presidio, 140	2,515
Margaret, Foard	51
Marie, Runnels	NA
*MARIETTA, Cass, 18	176
*†MARION, Guadalupe, 77	1,021
Marion Ferry Park, Angelina	NA
‡*Markham, Matagorda, 27	1,304
Mark Heights, Smith	NA
Markley, Young	31
Markout, Kaufman	80

Town and County	Pop.
Marlboro Country, Hays	NA
§*†MARLIN, Falls, 369	6,780
Marlow, Milam	45
*MARQUEZ, Leon, 23	278
Mars, Van Zandt	NA
§*†MARSHALL, Harrison, 1,351	24,471
MARSHALL CREEK, Denton	364
Marshall Ford, Travis	NA
Marshall Northeast, Harrison	1,500
Marston, Polk	25
*†MART, McLennan, 103	2,039
*MARTINDALE, Caldwell, 27	993
Martinez, Bexar	NA
Martin Prairie, Grimes	75
Martins Mills, Van Zandt	125
Martin Springs, Hopkins	115
*Martinsville, Nacogdoches, 2	126
Marvin, Lamar	NA
Maryetta, Jack	7
*Maryneal, Nolan, 4	75
Marys Creek, Baylor	NA
Marysville, Cooke	NA
§*†MASON, Mason, 153	1,939
Mason Lake Estates, Liberty	NA
Massey, Hill	NA
Massey Lake, Anderson	NA
Masters, Throckmorton	NA
*Masterson, Moore, 3	15
§*†MATADOR, Motley, 50	830
*Matagorda, Matagorda, 23	605
*MATHIS, San Patricio, 252	5,566
Matthews, Colorado	NA
Matthey Estate, Bexar	NA
*MAUD, Bowie, 42	1,062
Maudlowe, Refugio	NA
‡*†Mauriceville, Orange, 48	2,210
Maverick, Runnels	31
Maxdale, Bell	4
Maxey, Lamar	55
*Maxwell, Caldwell, 19	185
*May, Brown, 14	285
*Maydelle, Cherokee, 6	250
Mayfield, Hale	NA
Mayfield, Hill	NA
Mayflower, Newton	100
Mayhill, Denton	150
Maynard, San Jacinto	25
*†MAYPEARL, Ellis, 30	834
*Maysfield, Milam, 2	140
*McAdoo, Dickens, 6	169
*†McALLEN, Hidalgo, 4,390	91,184
*†McCAMEY, Upton, 105	2,487
*McCaulley, Fisher, 5	96
McClanahan, Falls	60
McClelland, Shelby	NA
McCollum, Montague	NA
McCook, Hidalgo	91
*McCoy, Atascosa, 11	25
McCoy, Floyd	NA
McCoy, Kaufman	20
McCoy, Panola	NA
McCoy, Red River	175
McCullough, Ellis	NA
*McDade, Bastrop, 15	345
McDade Estates, Montgomery	NA
McDaniels, Brown	NA
*McFaddin, Victoria, 7	320
McGee Landing, Sabine	NA
McGirk, Hamilton	NA
*†McGREGOR, McLennan, 223	4,792
§*†McKINNEY, Collin, 1,272	25,285
McKinney Acres, Andrews	NA
McKnight, Rusk	NA
*†McLEAN, Gray, 49	861
McLENDON-CHISHOLM, Rockwall	747
*McLeod, Cass, 7	50
McMahan, Caldwell	125
McMillan, San Saba	NA
McNair, Harris	2,039
McNary, Hudspeth, 1	250
McNeel, Brazoria	NA
McNeil, Caldwell	NA
*McNeil, Travis, 1	70
‡*McQueeney, Guadalupe, 47	2,129
*MEADOW, Terry, 32	592
Meadowbrook, Montgomery	NA
Meadowbrook, Smith	NA
Meadowcreek, Kaufman	240
Meadow Grove, Bell	10
Meadow Lake, Guadalupe	250
MEADOWLAKES, Burnet	597
Meadowood Acres, Bexar	NA
MEADOWS, Fort Bend	5,418
Meadowview, Hunt	NA
Meadow Village, Bexar	NA
Mecca, Madison	6
Medicine Mound, Hardeman	50
Medill, Lamar	50
*Medina, Bandera, 35	515
Medina Base, Bexar	NA
Medina River West, Medina	NA
Meeker, Jefferson	NA
Meek Estates, Henderson	NA
Meeks, Bell	15
*MEGARGEL, Archer, 23	248
Meldrum, Shelby	NA
*MELISSA, Collin, 41	689
Mellon, Frio	14
Melrose, Nacogdoches	150
*MELVIN, McCulloch, 12	174
§*†MEMPHIS, Hall, 182	2,516
§*†MENARD, Menard, 79	1,563
Mendoza, Caldwell	50
Menlow, Hill	10
§*Mentone, Loving, 8	50
Mentz, Colorado	NA
*†MERCEDES, Hidalgo, 356	13,522
Mercers Gap, Comanche	NA
Mercury, McCulloch	166
*Mereta, Tom Green, 4	75
§*†MERIDIAN, Bosque, 126	1,395
*Merit, Hunt, 12	215
*MERKEL, Taylor, 175	2,470
Merle, Burleson	NA
Merriam, Eastland	14
*MERTENS, Hill, 3	110
§*†MERTZON, Irion, 52	642
Mesa, El Paso	50
Mescalero Park, Randall	NA
*†MESQUITE, Dallas, 3,799	108,960
Mesquite Acres Island, San Patricio	NA
Metcalf Gap, Palo Pinto	NA
*†MEXIA, Limestone, 511	7,056
Mexico, Hunt	NA
*Meyersville, DeWitt, 5	110
§*†MIAMI, Roberts, 46	570
*Mico, Medina, 3	98
Midcity, Lamar	NA
Middle Gabriel Estates, Williamson	NA
Middleton, Leon	26
Middle Water, Hartley	10
Midessa Heights, Midland	NA
*Midfield, Matagorda, 2	70
*Midkiff, Upton, 19	68
Midlake Village, Sabine	NA
§*†MIDLAND, Midland, 6,589	95,003
*†MIDLOTHIAN, Ellis, 456	5,485
Midway, Bell	122
Midway, Bexar	NA
Midway, Dawson	20
Midway, Fannin	7
Midway, Franklin	NA
Midway, Hill	NA
Midway, Howard	NA
Midway, Jim Wells	NA
Midway, Lavaca	NA
Midway, Limestone	NA
*MIDWAY, Madison, 22	304
Midway, Montgomery	NA
Midway, Red River	40
Midway, Scurry	2
Midway, Smith	NA
Midway, Titus	NA
Midway, Upshur	NA
Midway, Van Zandt	31
Midyett, Panola	NA
Mikesta, Live Oak	NA
‡Mila Doce, Hidalgo	2,304
*Milam, Sabine, 13	177
*MILANO, Milam, 21	452
Milburn, McCulloch	NA
MILDRED, Navarro	192
*†MILES, Runnels, 40	842
*†MILFORD, Ellis, 27	782
Mill Creek, Waller	NA
Mill Creek, Washington	40
Mill Creek Forest, Montgomery	NA
Miller Grove, Camp	NA
Miller Grove, Hopkins	115
MILLER'S COVE, Titus	82
*Millersview, Concho, 2	75
Millett, La Salle	90
Millheim, Austin	150
*Millican, Brazos, 9	100
Milligan, Collin	NA
*MILLSAP, Parker, 43	531
Millsville, San Patricio	NA
Milo Center, Deaf Smith	NA
Milton, Lamar	80
Mims, Brazoria	NA
Mims Chapel, Marion	NA
*Minden, Rusk	350
*†MINEOLA, Wood, 405	4,521
*Mineral, Bee, 1	50
*†MINERAL WELLS, Palo Pinto-Parker, 948	15,256
Minerva, Milam, 1	60
Mings Chapel, Upshur	NA
*MINGUS, Palo Pinto, 17	219
Mink Branch Valley, Montgomery	NA
Minter, Lamar	78
*Mirando City, Webb, 11	559
*†MISSION, Hidalgo, 1,035	33,456
‡Mission Bend, Fort Bend	28,032
Mission Hills, Bexar	NA
Mission Valley, Comal	NA
Mission Valley, Victoria	208
*†MISSOURI CITY, Fort Bend-Harris, 838	43,155
Misty Oaks, Bexar	NA
Mitchell, Eastland	46
Mitchell Hill, Tyler	NA
Mixon, Cherokee	50
*†MOBEETIE, Wheeler, 10	159
MOBILE CITY, Rockwall	235
Modern, Jim Wells	NA
Moffat, Bell	150
Moffett, Angelina	NA
Moistown, Cameron	25
Moline, Lampasas	40
§*†MONAHANS, Ward-Winkler, 526	8,132
Monaville, Waller	180
Monkeyville, Hays	NA
Monkstown, Fannin	35
Monroe, Rusk	96
*Monroe City, Chambers, 1	90
Mont, Lavaca	30
Montadale, Williamson	NA
§*Montague, Montague, 25	400
Montague Village, Coryell	1,410
*Montalba, Anderson, 12	110
*MONT BELVIEU, Chambers-Liberty, 122	1,466
*Monte Alto, Hidalgo	1,769
Monte Grande, Cameron	NA
Montell, Uvalde	10
Monte Oaks, Montgomery	NA
Monte Robles Park, Bexar	NA
Montfort, Navarro	NA
*MONTGOMERY, Montgomery, 403	406
Monthalia, Gonzales	65
Monticello, Titus	48
*†MOODY, McLennan, 88	1,363
Moonshine Colony, Baylor	NA
Moore, Brazos	NA
*Moore, Frio, 16	230
Moore Hill, Polk	NA
Moore's Crossing, Travis	25
MOORE STATION, Henderson	278
Mooreville, Falls	91
Mooring, Brazos	80
Morales, Jackson	25
*MORAN, Shackelford, 16	293
Moravia, Lavaca	165
*MORGAN, Bosque, 21	485
Morgan Bluff, Orange	NA

Town and County	Pop.
Morgan Creek, Burnet	NA
*Morgan Mill, Erath, 12	206
MORGAN'S POINT, Harris	390
MORGAN'S POINT RESORT, Bell	1,976
Morrill, Cherokee	NA
Morris Ranch, Gillespie	NA
*Morse, Hansford, 14	150
§*†MORTON, Cochran, 135	2,586
Morton, Harrison	NA
Morton Valley, Eastland	46
*Moscow, Polk, 11	170
Mosheim, Bosque, 2	75
Moss Bluff, Liberty	65
Moss Hill, Liberty	49
Mosswood, Montgomery	NA
Mossy Grove, Walker	NA
Mostyn, Montgomery	NA
*†MOULTON, Lavaca, 63	969
*Mound, Coryell, 3	75
Mound City, Anderson-Houston	NA
MOUNTAIN CITY, Hays	388
Mountain Community, Coryell	300
*Mountain Home, Kerr, 14	96
Mountain Peak, Ellis	20
Mountain Springs, Cooke	100
Mountain Springs, Hill	NA
Mountain Top, Eastland	22
Mountain Valley Estates, Johnson	NA
Mountain View, Smith	NA
Mountain View, Travis	393
Mountain View Estates, Hunt	NA
Mount Bethel, Panola	62
Mount Blanco, Crosby	NA
*†MOUNT CALM, Hill, 15	311
*MOUNT ENTERPRISE, Rusk, 58	516
Mount Gainor, Hays	NA
Mount Haven, Cherokee	NA
Mount Hermon, Shelby	56
Mount Lookout, Comal	NA
Mount Pleasant, Grimes	12
§*†MOUNT PLEASANT, Titus, 942	13,109
Mount Rose, Falls	NA
*Mount Selman, Cherokee	200
Mount Sharp, Hays	NA
*Mount Sylvan, Smith	181
Mount Union, Jasper	NA
§*†MOUNT VERNON, Franklin, 192	2,306
Mount Vernon, Houston	NA
Mouth of Pedernales, Travis	NA
Mozelle, Cochran	NA
Mozelle, Coleman	NA
Mozo, Williamson	NA
Muddig, Hunt	NA
Mudville, Brazos	NA
Muellersville, Washington	40
*†MUENSTER, Cooke, 187	1,418
Mulberry, Fannin	17
Mulberry Cove, Hunt	NA
Mulberry Creek Estates, Taylor	NA
Mulberry Ridge, Angelina	NA
*Muldoon, Fayette, 5	98
§*†MULESHOE, Bailey, 357	4,689
*MULLIN, Mills, 30	211
Mullins Prairie, Fayette	NA
*Mumford, Robertson, 7	170
*†MUNDAY, Knox, 113	1,601
Munger, Limestone	NA
Mungerville, Dawson	NA
Munson, Rockwall	64
*MURCHISON, Henderson, 42	551
*MURPHY, Collin	1,823
Murray, Cameron	NA
Murray, Young	29
Murvaul, Panola	110
Musgrove, Wood	NA
Mustang, Denton	NA
MUSTANG, Navarro	39
Mustang Mott, DeWitt	NA
MUSTANG RIDGE, Caldwell-Travis-Bastrop	642
*Myra, Cooke, 4	70
Myrtle Springs, Van Zandt	131
Mystic Oak, Travis	NA
N	
Nacalina, Nacogdoches	NA
§*†NACOGDOCHES, Nacogdoches, 1,721	32,260
*Nada, Colorado, 15	165
*†NAPLES, Morris, 71	1,497
Naruna, Burnet	45
*NASH, Bowie	2,265
Nash, Ellis, 89	25
NASSAU BAY, Harris	4,844
Nat, Nacogdoches	25
*NATALIA, Medina, 44	1,254
NAVARRO, Navarro	213
Navarro Mills, Navarro	50
*†NAVASOTA, Grimes, 431	6,659
Navidad, Jackson	NA
Navo, Denton	35
*NAZARETH, Castro, 32	332
Necessity, Stephens	10
Nechanitz, Fayette	21
*Neches, Anderson, 11	114
*NEDERLAND, Jefferson, 958	17,013
Needmore, Bailey	98
*†NEEDVILLE, Fort Bend, 188	2,586
Neely Ward, Cochran	NA
Negley, Red River	136
Neinda, Jones	31
Nell, Live Oak	NA
Nelleva, Brazos	NA
Nelson City, Kendall	NA
Nelsonville, Austin	110
Nelta, Hopkins	36
*Nemo, Somervell, 5	56
NESBITT, Harrison	359
Nesbitt, Robertson	NA
Neuville, Shelby	43
*NEVADA, Collin, 17	566
*NEWARK, Wise-Tarrant, 48	712
*New Baden, Robertson, 6	105
NEW BERLIN, Guadalupe	200
Newberry Hollow, Kerr	NA
New Bethel, Jefferson	NA
New Bielau, Colorado	NA
New Birthright, Hopkins	NA
New Blox, Jasper	NA
*†NEW BOSTON, Bowie, 292	5,174
§*†NEW BRAUNFELS, Comal-Guadalupe, 2,313	30,402
New Bremen, Austin	NA
Newburg, Comanche	35
Newby, Leon	40
New Camp Ruby, Polk	NA
*New Caney, Montgomery, 247	2,771
New Caney Heights, Montgomery	NA
*†NEWCASTLE, Young, 21	530
NEW CHAPEL HILL, Smith	460
New Clarkson, Milam	NA
New Colony, Bell	4
New Colony, Cass	NA
New Corn Hill, Williamson	NA
*NEW DEAL, Lubbock, 10	580
*New Diana, Upshur	NA
New Fountain, Medina	NA
*Newgulf, Wharton, 8	963
New Harmony, Shelby	NA
New Harmony, Smith	NA
New Harp, Montague	NA
*NEW HOME, Lynn, 28	186
New Hope, Cherokee	NA
NEW HOPE, Collin	537
New Hope, Franklin	NA
New Hope, Freestone	85
New Hope, Jones	25
New Hope, Rusk	NA
New Hope, San Augustine	NA
New Hope, Smith	NA
New Hope, Wood	NA
Newlin, Hall	31
*NEW LONDON, Rusk, 31	991
New Lynn, Lynn	18
Newman, El Paso	60
New Mesquite, Collin	NA
New Moore, Lynn	NA
New Mountain, Upshur	NA
Newport, Clay-Jack, 2	70
New Prospect, Rusk	NA
New River Lake Estates, Liberty	NA
New Salem, Palo Pinto	NA
New Salem, Rusk	31
Newsome, Camp, 1	100
*NEW SUMMERFIELD, Cherokee, 32	579
New Sweden, Travis	60
Newt, Fannin	2
§*†NEWTON, Newton, 133	1,870
*New Ulm, Austin, 49	650
*†NEW WAVERLY, Walker, 70	997
New Wehdem, Austin	100
New Willard, Polk	160
New York, Henderson	NA
NEYLANDVILLE, Hunt	102
Nickel Creek, Culberson	16
Nickleberry, Cass	NA
Nickleville, Wise	NA
NIEDERWALD, Hays-Caldwell	250
Nigton, Trinity	34
Nimrod, Eastland	85
Nineveh, Leon	101
Nix, Lampasas	NA
*†NIXON, Gonzales-Wilson, 90	1,986
Noack, Williamson	60
Nob Hill, Llano	NA
Nobility, Fannin	21
Noble, Lamar	40
Nockenut, Wilson	10
*NOCONA, Montague, 304	3,028
Nogalus Prairie, Trinity	41
*Nolan, Nolan, 5	131
*NOLANVILLE, Bell, 38	2,026
Nolte, Guadalupe	25
*NOME, Jefferson, 27	458
Noodle, Jones	40
NOONDAY, Smith	518
Nopal, DeWitt	25
*NORDHEIM, DeWitt, 22	352
Norman, Williamson	20
Normandy, Maverick	98
*†NORMANGEE, Leon-Madison, 57	704
*Normanna, Bee, 4	75
Norse, Bosque	110
North Alamo, Hidalgo	NA
North Bancroft Estates, Kendall	NA
North Cedar, Trinity	NA
NORTH CLEVELAND, Liberty	193
Northcliff, Guadalupe	1,800
North Country, Montgomery	NA
North Cowden, Ector	80
NORTHCREST, McLennan	1,799
Northfield, Motley	15
North Groesbeck, Hardeman	NA
North Hopkins, Hopkins	NA
*North Houston, Harris, 1	NA
North Jericho, Shelby	NA
NORTHLAKE, Denton	289
North Lake Estates, Comal	NA
Northlake Estates, Williamson	NA
North Line Oaks, Montgomery	NA
North Oaks, Travis	NA
North Orange Heights, Orange	NA
North Park Estates, Travis	NA
*†NORTH RICHLAND HILLS, Tarrant	47,935
Northrup, Lee	71
North San Antonio Hills, Bexar	NA
‡North San Pedro, Nueces	1,025
North Shore Colony, Travis	NA
North Star, Archer	NA
Northwest Oaks, Burnet	NA
Northwest Woods, Williamson	NA
Northwoods, Comal	NA
North Woods, Montgomery	NA
*North Zulch, Madison, 20	100
*Norton, Runnels, 3	76
Notla, Ochiltree	20
*Notrees, Ector, 3	338
Nottingham Forest, Orange	NA
Nottingham Woods, Houston	NA
*NOVICE, Coleman, 11	196
Novice, Lamar	NA
Noxville, Kimble	3

Town and County	Pop.
Nubia, Taylor	NA
Nugent, Jones	41
Nunelee, Fannin	25
*Nursery, Victoria, 8	106
O	
Oak, Ellis	NA
Oakalla, Burnet	45
Oak Bend, Brazoria	NA
Oak Branch, Ellis	NA
Oak Cliff Acres, Comal	NA
Oak Creek, Bexar	NA
Oak Creek, Comal	NA
Oak Crest Estates, Williamson	NA
Oakdale, Hopkins	NA
Oakdale, Polk	25
Oak Flat, Nacogdoches	NA
Oak Flats, Rusk	NA
Oak Forest, Gonzales	25
Oak Forest, Montgomery	NA
Oak Forest Haven, Hunt	NA
Oak Grove, Bowie	294
Oak Grove, Colorado	NA
Oak Grove, Ellis	10
Oak Grove, Hopkins	NA
OAK GROVE, Kaufman	619
Oak Grove, Wood	74
Oak Harbor, Henderson	NA
Oak Heights, Kerr	NA
Oak Hill, Hood	NA
Oak Hill, Rusk	24
Oakhill Ranches, Bexar	NA
*OAKHURST, San Jacinto, 16	230
Oak Island, Chambers	NA
Oaklake, McLennan	60
Oakland, Brazoria	NA
Oakland, Cherokee	NA
*Oakland, Colorado, 2	80
Oakland, Jack	NA
Oakland, Van Zandt	26
Oak Lane, Montgomery	NA
OAK LEAF, Ellis	1,066
Oak Manor, Brazoria	NA
Oak Meadows Estates, Montgomery	NA
Oak Moss, Bexar	NA
Oak Park, Travis	NA
*OAK POINT, Denton	761
Oak Ridge, Fannin	90
Oak Ridge, Grayson	NA
Oak Ridge, Llano	NA
Oak Ridge, Nacogdoches	NA
Oak Ridge Estates, Marion	NA
OAK RIDGE, Cooke	191
OAK RIDGE, Kaufman	294
OAK RIDGE NORTH, Montgomery	2,623
Oak Shade, Polk	NA
Oaks North, Bexar	NA
Oak Springs, Hill	NA
Oak Terrace, Montgomery	NA
Oak Terrace Estates, Polk	NA
‡Oak Trail Shores, Hood	1,837
OAK VALLEY, Navarro	398
Oak Valley Park, Travis	NA
Oakview, Comal	NA
Oak Village, Bexar	NA
Oak Village North, Comal	NA
*Oakville, Live Oak, 3	260
*†OAKWOOD, Leon, 34	577
Oakwood Acres, Bexar	NA
Oatmeal, Burnet	20
*O'BRIEN, Haskell, 4	158
Oceanshore, Galveston	NA
Ocee, McLennan	35
Ochiltree, Ochiltree	NA
Odds, Limestone	NA
*Odell, Wilbarger, 3	131
*†ODEM, San Patricio, 92	2,514
§*†ODESSA, Ector-Midland, 5,926	92,257
*†O'DONNELL, Lynn-Dawson, 57	1,143
Oenaville, Bell, 2	120
O'Farrell, Cass	20
Ogburn, Wood	NA
*†OGLESBY, Coryell, 15	463
*Oilton, Webb, 7	458
Oklahoma, Montgomery	NA
Oklahoma Flat, Hockley	NA
Oklahoma Lane, Parmer	64
*Oklaunion, Wilbarger, 3	138
Okra, Eastland	20
Ola, Kaufman	50
Old Boston, Bowie	NA
Old Bowling, Leon	20
Old Center, Panola	83
Old Diana, Upshur	NA
Old Dime Box, Lee	200
*Olden, Eastland, 6	110
Oldenburg, Fayette	54
Old Ferry, Travis	NA
*Old Glory, Stonewall, 5	125
Oldham, Tyler	NA
Old Larissa, Cherokee	NA
Old Midway, Leon	NA
*Old Ocean, Brazoria, 18	915
Old River Lake, Liberty	NA
OLD RIVER-WINFREE, Chambers	1,288
Old Sabinetown, Sabine	NA
Old Salem, Bowie	NA
Old Salem, Newton	NA
Old Snake River, Liberty	NA
Old Town Meadows, Williamson	NA
Old Union, Bowie	238
Old Union, Limestone	25
Oletha, Limestone	NA
Olfen, Runnels	NA
Olin, Hamilton	12
Olivia, Calhoun	215
Ollie, Polk	NA
*Olmito, Cameron, 25	200
Olmos, Guadalupe	30
*OLMOS PARK, Bexar	2,291
*†OLNEY, Young, 262	3,473
*OLTON, Lamb, 108	2,149
*OMAHA, Morris, 45	928
Omega, Gregg	NA
Omen, Smith	150
*ONALASKA, Polk, 91	803
One Seventy-Seven Lake Estates, Montgomery	NA
‡Onion Creek, Travis	1,650
Opdyke, Hockley	20
OPDYKE WEST, Hockley	112
Open Air Estates, Smith	NA
Oplin, Callahan	75
O'Quinn, Fayette	25
Oran, Palo Pinto	NA
§*†ORANGE, Orange, 1,418	20,102
Orangedale, Bee	35
*Orangefield, Orange, 23	725
*ORANGE GROVE, Jim Wells, 90	1,214
Orangeville, Fannin	23
*ORCHARD, Fort Bend, 14	424
*†ORE CITY, Upshur, 86	959
Orient, Tom Green	40
*Orla, Reeves, 9	183
Osage, Coryell	30
Oscar, Bell	40
Osceola, Hill	90
Oslo, Hansford	NA
Otey, Brazoria	318
Otis Chalk, Howard	79
*Ottine, Gonzales, 4	90
*Otto, Falls, 3	85
*Ovalo, Taylor, 10	225
*†OVERTON, Rusk-Smith, 151	2,163
*OVILLA, Ellis-Dallas	2,322
Owens, Brown	NA
Owens, Crosby	75
Owensville, Robertson	NA
Owentown, Smith	NA
Owl Creek, Bell	45
OYSTER CREEK, Brazoria	977
‡§*†Ozona, Crockett, 192	3,326
P	
Pacio, Delta	15
Padgett, Young	23
Padre Island, Nueces	NA
§*†PADUCAH, Cottle, 115	1,692
*Paige, Bastrop, 18	275
§*†PAINT ROCK, Concho, 18	228
*†PALACIOS, Matagorda, 227	4,497
Palava, Fisher	12
Paleface Lake Country Est., Travis	NA
§*†PALESTINE, Anderson, 1,277	18,377
Palito Blanco, Jim Wells	35
*†PALMER, Ellis, 61	1,748
Palm Harbor, Aransas	125
PALMHURST, Hidalgo	373
Palm Park, Bexar	NA
PALM VALLEY, Cameron	1,267
PALMVIEW, Hidalgo	2,079
Palo Alto, Nueces	15
Palo Alto Park, Bexar	NA
Paloduro, Armstrong	NA
Palomino Park, Travis	NA
§*Palo Pinto, Palo Pinto, 30	350
*Paluxy, Hood, 1	76
§*†PAMPA, Gray, 1,261	20,044
Pancake, Coryell	NA
Pandale, Val Verde	20
*Pandora, Wilson, 1	125
§*†PANHANDLE, Carson, 141	2,301
*Panna Maria, Karnes, 3	96
*Panola, Panola, 7	296
*PANORAMA, Montgomery	1,733
Panorama Estates, Hunt	NA
Panoramic Hills, Travis	NA
PANTEGO, Tarrant	2,542
Panter Branch, Hood	NA
Pantex, Carson	115
Panther Chapel, Franklin	NA
Papalote, Bee	70
*Paradise, Wise, 49	275
Paradise Bay, Henderson	NA
Paradise Hills, San Augustine	NA
Paradise Manor, Travis	NA
Paradise Point, Llano	NA
§*†PARIS, Lamar, 1,489	25,063
Parita, Bexar	NA
Park, Fayette	22
Park Community, Navarro	160
PARKER, Collin	1,347
Parker, Johnson	21
Parkers Point, Angelina	NA
Parklane, Comal	NA
Parks Camp, Stephens	NA
Park Springs, Wise	NA
Parkview Estates, Guadalupe	500
Parnell, Hall	43
Parsley Hill, Wilbarger	40
Parvin, Denton	44
*†PASADENA, Harris, 3,954	127,843
Paso Real, Willacy	NA
Patillo, Erath	10
Patman Switch, Cass	NA
Patonia, Polk	NA
Patricia, Dawson, 1	60
Patrick, McLennan	NA
Patrole, Reeves	16
Patroon, Shelby	55
*PATTISON, Waller, 12	364
Pattonfield, Upshur	NA
PATTON VILLAGE, Montgomery	1,238
*Pattonville, Lamar, 10	180
Pawelekville, Karnes	105
*Pawnee, Bee, 6	249
Paxton, Shelby	161
Paynes Corner, Gaines	NA
PAYNE SPRINGS, Henderson	663

Town and County	Pop.
Payton Colony, Blanco	NA
Peach Creek, Brazos	NA
Peach Creek Estates, Montgomery	NA
Peach Creek Forest, Montgomery	NA
Peach Creek Oaks, Montgomery	NA
Peacock, Stonewall, 4	125
Peadenville, Palo Pinto	NA
Pearl, Coryell	125
*†PEARLAND, Brazoria-Harris, 1,282	22,807
Pearl City, DeWitt	NA
§*†PEARSALL, Frio, 374	7,449
Pearson, Medina	NA
Pearsons Chapel, Houston	NA
*Pear Valley, McCulloch, 2	37
*Peaster, Parker, 6	80
Pebble Beach, Llano	NA
Pebble Beach-Sunset Acres, Collin	NA
‡Pecan Acres, Wise-Tarrant	1,634
Pecan Creek, Fort Bend	NA
Pecan Creek, Tom Green	NA
*PECAN GAP, Delta-Fannin, 10	256
Pecan Grove, Collin	NA
‡Pecan Grove, Fort Bend	10,799
PECAN HILL, Ellis	594
Pecan Hill, Fort Bend	NA
Pecan Plantation, Hood	990
Pecan Wells, Hamilton	NA
§*†PECOS, Reeves, 518	12,361
Peeltown, Kaufman	NA
Peerless, Hopkins	NA
*Peggy, Atascosa, 3	20
Pelham, Navarro	75
PELICAN BAY, Tarrant	1,276
*Pendleton, Bell, 3	60
Pendleton Harbor, Sabine	NA
*PENELOPE, Hill, 6	223
*PEÑITAS, Hidalgo, 9	1,191
*Pennington, Trinity-Houston, 9	100
*Penwell, Ector, 9	74
Peoria, Hill	81
*Pep, Hockley, 5	50
Percilla, Houston	95
PERNITAS POINT, Live Oak-Jim Wells	179
*Perrin, Jack, 22	300
*Perry, Falls, 4	96
§*†PERRYTON, Ochiltree, 583	7,608
Perryville, Wood	52
Personville, Freestone	NA
Personville, Limestone	NA
Pert, Anderson	35
Peters, Austin	95
*†PETERSBURG, Hale, 51	1,295
Peter's Prairie, Red River	40
Petersville, DeWitt	NA
Petroleum, Jim Hogg	15
*PETROLIA, Clay, 19	790
PETRONILA, Nueces	158
Petteway, Robertson	25
Pettibone, Milam	25
*Pettit, Hockley, 1	26
*Pettus, Bee, 36	400
*Petty, Lamar, 5	100
Petty, Lynn	24
Petty's Chapel, Navarro	25
*PFLUGERVILLE, Travis, 464	6,018
Phalba, Van Zandt	58
*†PHARR, Hidalgo, 988	36,122
Phelan, Bastrop	NA
Phelps, Walker	98
Phillips, Angelina	NA
*Phillips, Hutchinson	1,624
Phillipsburg, Washington	40
Phillips Camp, Hansford	NA
Pickens, Henderson	NA
Pickett, Navarro	NA
Pickney, Polk	NA
*Pickton, Hopkins, 26	90
Pidcoke, Coryell	30
Piedmont, Grimes	46
Piedmont, Upshur	NA
*Pierce, Wharton, 7	49
Pierces Chapel, Cherokee	NA
Pike, Collin	80
Pilgrim, Gonzales	60
Pilgrim Point, Grimes	12
Pilgrim Rest, Rains	72
Pilot Grove, Grayson	75
Pilot Knob, Travis	NA
*†PILOT POINT, Denton, 198	2,767
Pinckney, Polk	NA
Pine, Camp	78
Pine Acres, Montgomery	NA
Pine Branch, Red River	NA
Pine Crest, Montgomery	NA
Pinedale, Walker	NA
Pine Forest, Hopkins	51
Pine Forest, Montgomery	NA
PINE FOREST, Orange	790
Pine Grove, Cherokee	NA
Pine Grove, Harris	NA
Pine Grove, Newton	160
Pinehill, Rusk	49
‡*Pinehurst, Montgomery, 94	3,644
PINEHURST, Orange	2,759
Pine Island, Jefferson	350
PINE ISLAND, Waller	603
Pine Lake, Montgomery	NA
*†PINELAND, Sabine, 44	971
Pine Mills, Wood	2
Pine Park, Sabine	NA
Pine Prairie, Walker	NA
Pine Springs, Culberson	20
Pine Springs, Smith	NA
Pine Trail Shores, Smith	NA
Pineview, Wood	NA
‡Pinewood Estates, Hardin	1,279
Pinewood Estates, Montgomery	NA
Piney, Austin	NA
Piney Creek, Austin	NA
Piney Point, Montgomery	NA
Piney Point, Sabine	NA
PINEY POINT VILLAGE, Harris	3,444
Pinhook (or Faulkner), Lamar	48
Pinwah Pines, Polk	NA
Pioneer, Eastland	40
Pioneer Town, Hays	NA
Pioneer Trails, Montgomery	NA
*Pipe Creek, Bandera, 84	66
Pirates Beach, Galveston	NA
Pirates Cove, Galveston	NA
Pitner Junction, Rusk	NA
§*†PITTSBURG, Camp, 304	4,330
Placation Estates, Sabine	NA
*Placedo, Victoria, 9	515
Placid, McCulloch	32
Plain, Houston	NA
Plains, Borden	NA
§*†PLAINS, Yoakum, 86	1,414
§*†PLAINVIEW, Hale, 1,192	22,048
Plainview, Sabine	NA
Plainview, Scurry	NA
Plank, Hardin	205
*†PLANO, Collin-Denton, 6,588	153,624
*Plantersville, Grimes, 36	212
Plaska, Hall	28
Plateau, Culberson	5
PLEAK, Fort Bend	843
Pleasant Farms, Ector	NA
Pleasant Grove, Bastrop	NA
Pleasant Grove, Bowie	2,312
Pleasant Grove, Falls	35
Pleasant Grove, Hopkins	NA
Pleasant Grove, Limestone	NA
Pleasant Grove, Upshur	NA
Pleasant Grove, Wood	NA
Pleasant Hill, Eastland	15
Pleasant Hill, Franklin	NA
Pleasant Hill, Nacogdoches	NA
Pleasant Hill, Yoakum	NA
Pleasant Oaks, Bexar	NA
Pleasant Oaks, Henderson	NA
*†PLEASANTON, Atascosa, 442	8,100
Pleasant Ridge, Leon	NA
Pleasant Springs, Leon	NA
Pleasant Valley, Blanco	NA
Pleasant Valley, Dallas	NA
Pleasant Valley, Kendall	NA
Pleasant Valley, Lamb	NA
PLEASANT VALLEY, Wichita	410
Pleasant Valley Acres, Montgomery	NA
Pleasant Valley Estates, Comal	NA
Pleasant View Estates, Stephens	NA
Pleasure Point, Angelina	NA
Pleasure Point, Marion	NA
*Pledger, Matagorda, 7	159
Pluck, Polk	NA
*Plum, Fayette, 6	95
Plum Creek, Freestone	NA
Plum Grove, Ellis	NA
PLUM GROVE, Liberty	537
Plum Ridge, Angelina	NA
Pluto, Ellis	NA
Poetry, Kaufman	NA
*POINT, Rains, 36	697
Point Aquarius, Montgomery	NA
*POINTBLANK, San Jacinto, 16	471
*POINT COMFORT, Calhoun, 42	1,068
Point Enterprise, Limestone	200
Point Loma, San Patricio	NA
Point Royal, Henderson	NA
Point Venture, Travis	NA
Polar, Kent	10
*Pollok, Angelina, 30	300
*PONDER, Denton, 37	472
Pond Springs, Williamson	NA
Pone, Rusk	NA
Ponta, Cherokee	50
*Pontotoc, Mason, 7	125
Poole, Rains	50
*Poolville, Parker, 20	230
Porfirio, Willacy	NA
Port-Au-Prince, Brazoria	NA
Port Alto, Calhoun	NA
*PORT ARANSAS, Nueces, 226	2,450
*PORT ARTHUR, Jefferson, 1,772	60,344
*Port Bolivar, Galveston, 82	1,200
Port Brownsville, Cameron	NA
*Porter, Montgomery, 394	2,146
‡Porter Heights, Montgomery	1,663
Porter Springs, Houston	50
Porterville Timbers, Montgomery	NA
*PORT ISABEL, Cameron, 410	4,801
*PORTLAND, San Patricio-Nueces, 440	13,112
§*†PORT LAVACA, Calhoun, 620	11,656
*Port Mansfield, Willacy, 15	731
*†PORT NECHES, Jefferson, 340	13,431
*Port O'Connor, Calhoun, 55	1,184
Port Sullivan, Milam	15
Porvenir, Presidio	NA
Posey, Hopkins	NA
Posey, Lubbock	125
§*†POST, Garza, 273	3,820
Post Oak, Blanco	NA
Postoak, Jack	79
Postoak, Lamar	NA
Post Oak, Lee	NA
Post Oak, Robertson	NA
POST OAK BEND, Kaufman	289
Post Oak Point, Austin	NA
*POTEET, Atascosa, 113	3,376
*POTH, Wilson, 54	1,876
‡Potosi, Taylor	1,471
*†POTTSBORO, Grayson, 162	1,308
*Pottsville, Hamilton, 14	312
*Powderly, Lamar, 42	185
*†POWELL, Navarro, 11	108

Town and County	Pop.
Powell Point, Fort Bend	NA
*POYNOR, Henderson, 5	252
Praesel, Milam	115
Praha, Fayette	25
Prairie Center, Matagorda	NA
Prairie Chapel, McLennan	NA
Prairie Dell, Bell	12
Prairie Grove, Franklin	NA
*Prairie Hill, Limestone, 9	150
Prairie Hill, Washington	NA
*Prairie Lea, Caldwell, 8	100
Prairie Mountain, Llano	NA
Prairie Point, Cooke	30
Prairieview, Hale	NA
*PRAIRIE VIEW, Waller, 46	4,161
Prairieville, Kaufman	50
Preiss Heights, Comal	NA
*†PREMONT, Jim Wells, 115	2,792
*†PRESIDIO, Presidio, 78	3,230
Preston, Grayson	250
*Price, Rusk, 12	275
*Priddy, Mills, 14	215
PRIMERA, Cameron	2,355
Primrose, Van Zandt	24
*†PRINCETON, Collin, 158	2,704
Pringle, Hutchinson	40
Pritchett, Upshur	125
*Proctor, Comanche, 16	220
*PROGRESO, Hidalgo, 35	2,288
PROGRESO LAKES, Hidalgo	181
Progress, Bailey	49
Prospect, Rains	40
*†PROSPER, Collin, 47	1,141
Providence, Floyd	NA
Providence, Polk	NA
Pruitt, Cass	NA
Pruitt, Van Zandt	NA
Pueblo, Callahan	NA
Pueblo, Eastland	46
Pueblo Nuevo, Webb	130
Puerto Rico, Hidalgo	91
Pullman, Potter	31
Pumphrey, Runnels	NA
Pumpkin, San Jacinto	20
Pumpville, Val Verde	21
Punkin Center, Dawson	NA
Punkin Center, Eastland	12
Punkin Center, Hardeman	NA
*Purdon, Navarro, 8	133
Purley, Franklin	81
*Purmela, Coryell, 4	61
Pursley, Navarro	40
Purves, Erath	50
*PUTNAM, Callahan, 11	109
*PYOTE, Ward, 9	373

Q

Town and County	Pop.
*Quail, Collingsworth, 4	92
Quail Creek, San Jacinto	NA
Quail Valley, Williamson	NA
§*†QUANAH, Hardeman, 261	3,325
Quarry, Washington	NA
Quarterway, Hale	12
*QUEEN CITY, Cass, 81	1,882
*Quemado, Maverick, 17	426
Quicksand, Newton	NA
Quihi, Medina	104
*†QUINLAN, Hunt, 168	1,469
*QUINTANA, Brazoria	60
*†QUITAQUE, Briscoe, 27	484
§*†QUITMAN, Wood, 281	1,804

R

Town and County	Pop.
R.O. Ranch Estates, Travis	NA
Rabb, Nueces	20
Rabbit Hollow, Williamson	NA
Rabbs Prairie, Fayette	31
Raccoon Bend, Austin	NA
Rachal, Brooks	36
Radium, Jones	26
Ragtown, Lamar	25
*Rainbow, Somervell, 8	76
Rainbow Hills, Bexar	NA
Raintree Country, Montgomery	NA
Raisin, Victoria	50
Raleigh, Navarro	NA
*†RALLS, Crosby, 81	2,119
Ralph, Randall	NA
Ramireno, Zapata	NA
Ramirez, Duval	40
Ranch Branch, Mason	NA
Ranch Harbor Estates, Hill	NA
Ranchito, Cameron	NA
Ranchland Acres, Midland	NA
Rancho Alegre, Jim Wells	1,950
Rancho de la Parita, Jim Wells	NA
RANCHO VIEJO, Cameron	1,003
Rand, Kaufman	NA
Randado, Jim Hogg	15
*Randolph, Fannin, 6	70
*Randolph Air Force Base, Bexar, 14	3,015
*RANGER, Eastland, 193	2,822
Ranger Country, Williamson	NA
Ranger Estates, Midland	NA
RANGERVILLE, Cameron	306
Rankin, Ellis	12
§*†RANKIN, Upton, 46	1,005
*RANSOM CANYON, Lubbock	841
*Ratcliff, Houston, 3	106
Ratibor, Bell	10
Rattan, Delta	10
*Ravenna, Fannin, 15	186
Ravenwood, Brazos	NA
Ray, Grayson	NA
Rayburn, Liberty	30
*Rayburn Country, Jasper	600
Rayburn Hideaway, Nacogdoches	NA
Rayford Forest, Montgomery	NA
Raylake, Angelina	NA
Rayland, Foard	30
§*†RAYMONDVILLE, Willacy, 342	9,220
Ray Point, Live Oak	75
*Raywood, Liberty, 23	231
Razor, Lamar	15
*Reagan, Falls, 8	200
Reagan Wells, Uvalde	20
Reagor Springs, Ellis	45
*Realitos, Duval, 5	250
Reata Trails, Williamson	NA
Rebecca Creek Park, Comal	NA
Red Bank, Bowie	NA
Red Bluff, Jackson	NA
Red Bluff, Reeves	40
Red Branch, Grayson	NA
Red Branch, Leon	NA
Redbud Acres, Williamson	NA
Red Cut Heights, Bowie	563
Redfield, Nacogdoches	NA
*Redford, Presidio, 1	107
Red Gate, Hidalgo	NA
Red Hill, Cass	20
Red Hill, Limestone	NA
Red Lake, Freestone	NA
Redland, Angelina	NA
Redland, Leon	35
Redland, Van Zandt	NA
Redlawn, Cherokee	NA
Red Lick, Bowie	NA
*†RED OAK, Ellis, 399	3,438
Red Ranger, Bell	12
*Red Rock, Bastrop, 17	100
Red Springs, Baylor, 1	81
Red Springs, Smith	NA
Redtown, Angelina	NA
*REDWATER, Bowie, 20	852
Redwood, Guadalupe	400
Reeds Settlement, Red River	50
Reedville, Caldwell	NA
Reese, Cherokee	75
‡*Reese Air Force Base, Lubbock	1,332
Reese Village, Lubbock	2,600
Reeves, Hardin	NA
Refuge, Houston	NA
§*†REFUGIO, Refugio, 249	3,165
Regency, Mills	25
Rehburg, Washington	NA
Reilly Springs, Hopkins	44
Rek Hill, Fayette	NA
*REKLAW, Cherokee-Rusk, 8	268
Relampago, Hidalgo	NA
Reliance, Brazos	NA
‡Rendon, Tarrant	7,950
*RENO, Lamar	2,069
RENO, Parker	2,387
Reservation, Kerr	NA
Retreat, Grimes	NA
Retreat, Hill	NA
RETREAT, Navarro	343
Retta, Johnson	NA
Reyes, Duval	NA
Reynard, Houston	NA
Rhea, Parmer	98
Rhea Mills, Collin	47
Rhineland, Knox	196
*RHOME, Wise, 62	657
Rhonesboro, Upshur	40
Ricardo, Kleberg	120
*†RICE, Navarro-Ellis, 23	588
Rices Crossing, Williamson	100
*Richards, Grimes, 14	296
*†RICHARDSON, Dallas-Collin, 5,412	80,898
*RICHLAND, Navarro, 9	276
Richland, Rains	100
Richland, Travis	NA
RICHLAND HILLS, Tarrant	8,406
*RICHLAND SPRINGS, San Saba, 18	334
§*RICHMOND, Fort Bend, 754	10,984
†RICHWOOD, Brazoria	2,847
Rico Ranchos, Travis	NA
Riderville, Panola	50
Ridge, Mills	NA
Ridge, Robertson	67
Ridgeheights, Midland	NA
Ridgemar Landing, Williamson	NA
Ridgeway, Hopkins	54
Ridgewood, Midland	NA
Ridings, Fannin	10
*†RIESEL, McLennan, 36	867
Rimwick Forest, Montgomery	NA
Rincon, Starr	NA
*Ringgold, Montague, 9	100
*RIO BRAVO, Webb	3,417
Rio del Sol, Cameron	NA
*Rio Frio, Real, 5	50
‡§*Rio Grande City, Starr, 412	10,564
*RIO HONDO, Cameron, 73	2,051
Rio Llano Ranch, Llano	NA
*Riomedina, Medina, 11	53
Rios, Duval	75
*†RIO VISTA, Johnson, 41	602
*RISING STAR, Eastland, 63	862
Rita, Burleson	50
River, Zavala	NA
River Acres, Tyler	NA
River Bend, Newton	NA
River Bend, Sabine	NA
Riverbend Oaks, Williamson	NA
Riverbrook, Montgomery	NA
Riverby, Fannin	15
River Club Estates, Montgomery	NA
Rivercrest, Travis	NA
River Crest Estates, Angelina	NA
River Hill, Panola	NA
River Hills, Travis	NA
River Meadows, Hays	NA
River Oaks, Brazos	NA
River Oaks, Burnet	NA
River Oaks, Hays	NA
*RIVER OAKS, Tarrant	6,647
River Oaks, Travis	NA

Town and County	Pop.
River Oaks, Williamson	NA
River Oaks Estates, Montgomery	NA
River Plantation, Montgomery	NA
Riverpoint Estates, Comal	NA
River Ridge, Montgomery	NA
Rivers End, Brazoria	NA
*RIVERSIDE, Walker, 17	479
Riverside Estates, Brazoria	NA
River Terrace, Harris	NA
River Trail, Nueces	NA
Riverwood, Montgomery	NA
*Riviera, Kleberg, 51	550
Riviera Beach, Kleberg	NA
Riviera Estates, Polk	NA
Roach, Cass	NA
Roane, Navarro	120
*†ROANOKE, Denton, 388	2,006
*Roans Prairie, Grimes, 5	56
*ROARING SPRINGS, Motley, 14	270
Robbins, Leon	20
§*†ROBERT LEE, Coke, 68	1,356
Robertson, Crosby	35
ROBINSON, McLennan	7,673
Robinson Arms Landing, Reeves	21
*†ROBSTOWN, Nueces, 529	13,061
§*†ROBY, Fisher, 46	593
*Rochelle, McCulloch, 15	163
*†ROCHESTER, Haskell, 29	485
Rock Bluff, Burnet	NA
Rock Creek, McLennan	25
Rock Creek, Somervell	36
*†ROCKDALE, Milam, 346	5,503
Rockett, Ellis	124
Rockford, Lamar	NA
Rock Harbor, Hood	NA
Rockhill, Collin	25
Rock Hill, Franklin	NA
Rock Hill, Wood	21
Rockhouse, Austin	NA
Rock House, Williamson	NA
*Rock Island, Colorado, 6	160
Rock Island, Marion	NA
*Rockland, Tyler	105
Rockne, Bastrop	400
§*ROCKPORT, Aransas, 700	5,271
§*†ROCKSPRINGS, Edwards, 62	1,445
§*†ROCKWALL, Rockwall, 985	11,855
*Rockwood, Coleman, 3	80
Rocky Branch, Morris	135
Rocky Creek, Angelina	NA
Rocky Creek, Blanco	NA
Rocky Hill, Angelina	NA
ROCKY MOUND, Camp	57
Rocky Point, Burnet	NA
Rocky Point, Rains	80
Roddy, Van Zandt	NA
Rodney Calm, Navarro	NA
Roeder, Titus	NA
*Roganville, Jasper	100
*ROGERS, Bell, 47	1,148
Rogers, Taylor	NA
Rogers Hill, McLennan	NA
Rogers Plantation, Brazos	NA
Roland, Collin	NA
Rolling Hills, Hunt	NA
Rolling Hills, Potter	1,000
Rolling Hills, Waller	NA
Rolling Hills Shores, Hood	NA
ROLLING MEADOWS, Gregg	323
Rolling Oaks, Hays	NA
ROLLINGWOOD, Travis	1,459
*†ROMA-Los Saenz, Starr, 171	9,234
ROMAN FOREST, Montgomery	1,128
Roman Hills, Montgomery	NA
*Romayor, Liberty, 6	96
Romero, Hartley	25
Romney, Eastland	12
*Roosevelt, Kimble, 3	98
Roosevelt, Lubbock	3,500
*ROPESVILLE, Hockley, 33	516
Rosalie, Red River	100
*Rosanky, Bastrop, 12	210
Rosborough Springs, Harrison	NA
*†ROSCOE, Nolan, 62	1,413
*†ROSEBUD, Falls, 102	1,637
ROSE CITY, Orange	630
Rose Hill, Harris	NA
Rose Hill, San Jacinto	10
ROSE HILL ACRES, Hardin	521
*†ROSENBERG, Fort Bend, 870	23,275
Rosevine, Sabine	50
Rosewood, Upshur	100
Rosewood Hill, Harris	NA
*Rosharon, Brazoria, 124	435
Rosita, Duval	NA
Rosita, Starr	220
*ROSS, McLennan, 6	209
Ross City, Howard	81
*ROSSER, Kaufman, 5	390
*Rosston, Cooke, 4	110
Rossville, Atascosa	47
*†ROTAN, Fisher, 110	1,829
Rough Creek, San Saba	NA
Round House, Navarro	NA
*†ROUND MOUNTAIN, Blanco, 15	202
Round Mountain, Travis	59
Round Prairie, Navarro	40
Round Prairie, Robertson	NA
*†ROUND ROCK, Williamson-Travis, 1,410	36,924
Round Timber, Baylor	8
*†ROUND TOP, Fayette, 22	88
Round Top, Fisher	NA
Roundup, Hockley	27
Rowden, Callahan	30
*†Rowena, Runnels, 30	466
Rowland, Montague	NA
*ROWLETT, Dallas-Rockwall, 874	27,899
*†ROXTON, Lamar, 19	675
Royal Forest, Comal	NA
Royal Forest, Montgomery	NA
Royal Oaks, Henderson	NA
Royal Oaks, Kerr	NA
Royal Oaks, Llano	NA
Royal Oaks, Montgomery	NA
Royal Oaks, Orange	NA
Royal Oaks, Smith	NA
*Royalty, Ward	196
Royal View, Bexar	NA
Royder, Brazos	NA
*†ROYSE CITY, Rockwall-Collin, 155	2,490
Royston, Fisher	30
Rucker, Comanche	NA
Rucker's Bridge, Lamar	20
Rugby, Red River	24
Ruidosa, Presidio	43
*†RULE, Haskell, 41	774
Rumley, Lampasas	NA
RUNAWAY BAY, Wise	763
*RUNGE, Karnes, 44	1,192
Runn, Hidalgo	NA
Running Water, Hale	NA
Rural Shade, Navarro	30
Rushing, Navarro	NA
Rush Prairie, Navarro	NA
§*†RUSK, Cherokee, 250	4,500
Russell, Leon	27
Russelltown, Cameron	NA
Rustic Acres, Angelina	NA
Rutersville, Fayette	72
Ruth Springs, Henderson	NA
Ryanville, Refugio	NA
*Rye, Liberty, 13	76
S	
Sabanna, Eastland	12
*SABINAL, Uvalde, 68	1,634
Sabine, Gregg	750
Sabine Farms, Harrison	NA
Sabine Sands, Newton	NA
*†SACHSE, Dallas-Collin	6,378
*Sacul, Nacogdoches, 1	170
Saddle and Surrey, Montgomery	NA
*SADLER, Grayson, 12	340
*Sagerton, Haskell, 6	115
*SAGINAW, Tarrant, 103	8,683
Saint Clair Cove, Galveston	NA
Saint Elmo, Freestone	NA
St. Francis, Potter	30
*ST. HEDWIG, Bexar, 33	1,649
Saint Holland, Grimes	50
*†ST. JO, Montague, 63	1,099
Saint John, Harrison	NA
Saint John Colony, Caldwell	NA
Saint Lawrence, Glasscock	NA
ST. PAUL, Collin	486
St. Paul, San Patricio	180
‡*Salado, Bell, 169	1,305
Salem, Cherokee	NA
Salem, Grimes	50
Salem, Newton	85
Salem, Victoria	25
Salesville, Palo Pinto	40
Saline, Menard	58
*Salineno, Starr, 3	155
Salmon Lake, Anderson	20
*Salt Flat, Hudspeth, 5	35
Salt Gap, McCulloch	25
*Saltillo, Hopkins, 8	200
Samaria, Navarro	NA
Sam Houston Lake Estates, Liberty	NA
*Samnorwood, Collingsworth, 3	110
Sample, Gonzales	25
Sanaloma Estates, Williamson	NA
§*†SAN ANGELO, Tom Green, 3,852	87,980
§*†SAN ANTONIO, Bexar, 39,618	991,861
San Antonio Prairie, Burleson	NA
Sanatorium, Tom Green	450
§*†SAN AUGUSTINE, San Augustine, 234	2,333
*†SAN BENITO, Cameron, 582	21,780
San Carlos, Hidalgo	100
San Carlos, Starr	NA
Sanco, Coke	30
SANCTUARY, Parker	256
Sand, Dawson	20
Sandbranch, Dallas	400
‡§*†Sanderson, Terrell, 50	1,061
Sand Flat, Johnson	NA
Sand Flat, Rains	100
Sand Flat, Smith	NA
Sandhill, Floyd	NA
Sand Hill, Upshur	NA
*Sandia, Jim Wells, 45	215
§*†SAN DIEGO, Duval-Jim Wells, 112	4,998
Sand Jack, Newton	NA
Sand Lake, Ellis	NA
Sandlin, Stonewall	NA
Sandoval, Williamson	50
Sand Ridge, Houston	NA
Sand Springs, Howard	903
Sandusky, Grayson	NA
*Sandy, Blanco, 4	25
Sandy, Limestone	5
Sandy Acres, Burnet	NA
Sandy Acres, Midland	NA
Sandy Harbor, Llano	85
Sandy Hill, Washington	50
Sandy Hills, Montgomery	NA
Sandy Point, Brazoria	30
‡*San Elizario, El Paso, 24	4,476
*SAN FELIPE, Austin, 11	700
*SANFORD, Hutchinson, 14	237
Sanford Estates, Hutchinson	70
San Gabriel, Milam	100
San Gabriel Heights, Williamson	NA
San Gabriel River Ranch, Williamson	NA
*†SANGER, Denton, 269	3,831

Town and County	Pop.
San Geronimo, Bexar	NA
*San Isidro, Starr, 10	130
San Jacinto, Walker	NA
San Jose, Duval	15
*†SAN JUAN, Hidalgo, 266	13,091
SAN LEANNA, Travis	361
‡*San Leon, Galveston	3,651
San Manuel, Hidalgo	NA
§*†SAN MARCOS, Hays-Caldwell, 1,529	31,048
San Martin Hills, Medina	NA
SAN PATRICIO, San Patricio	406
San Pedro, Cameron	NA
San Pedro, Zapata	25
*SAN PERLITA, Willacy, 6	562
San Roman, Starr	NA
§*†SAN SABA, San Saba, 240	2,846
SANSOM PARK, Tarrant	3,910
*†SANTA ANNA, Coleman, 59	1,256
Santa Anna, Starr	30
Santa Catarina, Starr	48
*Santa Elena, Starr, 5	64
*†SANTA FE, Galveston, 360	9,648
Santa Margarita, Willacy	NA
*Santa Maria, Cameron, 8	210
Santa Monica, Willacy	NA
Santa Rita, Reagan	NA
*SANTA ROSA, Cameron, 40	2,511
*†Santo, Palo Pinto, 36	312
*San Ygnacio, Zapata, 9	895
San Ysidro, El Paso	400
*Saragosa, Reeves, 3	185
*Saratoga, Hardin, 22	1,000
Sarber, Marion	NA
Sarco, Goliad	40
Sardis, Cass	NA
Sardis, Ellis	NA
Sardis, Fisher	12
*Sargent, Matagorda	76
§*Sarita, Kenedy, 7	185
Saron, Trinity	NA
Saspamco, Wilson	443
*Satin, Falls, 5	138
Satsuma, Harris	NA
Sattler, Comal	30
Saturn, Gonzales	15
Sauney Stand, Washington	NA
Savage, Crosby	NA
*SAVOY, Fannin, 31	929
Sayers, Bexar	NA
Sayersville, Bastrop	NA
Scatter Branch, Hunt	NA
Scenic Brook, Travis	NA
Scenic Brook West, Travis	NA
Scenic Hills, Guadalupe	150
‡Scenic Oaks, Bexar	2,596
Scenic Terrace, Comal	NA
Scharbauer City, Ector	20
Schattel, Frio	130
*†SCHERTZ, Guadalupe-Comal-Bexar, 282	11,973
Schicke Point, Calhoun	NA
Schoolerville, Hamilton	NA
School Hill, Erath	22
Schoolland, Gonzales	NA
Schroeder, Goliad	350
*SCHULENBURG, Fayette, 246	2,736
Schumannsville, Guadalupe	400
Schwab City, Polk	NA
*†Schwertner, Williamson, 6	150
Science Hall, Jasper	NA
‡Scissors, Hidalgo	1,673
*SCOTLAND, Archer-Clay, 12	507
*SCOTTSVILLE, Harrison, 15	294
Scranton, Eastland	40
Scrappin Valley, Newton	NA
*Scroggins, Franklin, 19	125
*Scurry, Kaufman, 33	315
*SEABROOK, Harris-Galveston, 614	8,322
*†SEADRIFT, Calhoun, 38	1,458
*†SEAGOVILLE, Dallas-Kaufman, 424	9,507
*SEAGRAVES, Gaines, 102	2,362
Seale, Robertson	26
*†SEALY, Austin, 403	4,795
Seaton, Bell	60
Seawillow, Caldwell	NA
‡*Sebastian, Willacy, 16	1,691
Sebastopol, Trinity	31
Seco Mines, Maverick	NA
Security, Montgomery	24
Sedalia, Collin	25
Sedwick, Shackelford	NA
*Segno, Polk	80
Segovia, Kimble	25
§*†SEGUIN, Guadalupe, 1,164	20,228
Sejita, Duval	22
Selden, Erath	71
Selfs, Fannin	30
*SELMA, Bexar-Guadalupe-Comal	629
*Selman City, Rusk, 16	271
§*†SEMINOLE, Gaines, 421	6,470
Sempronius, Austin	NA
Senior, Bexar	NA
Sentinel Oaks, Montgomery	NA
Serbin, Lee	90
‡Serenada, Williamson	3,520
Serene Hills, Bexar	NA
‡Seth Ward, Hale	1,485
Settlers Village, Harris	NA
Seven Coves, Montgomery	NA
SEVEN OAKS, Polk	175
Seven Pines, Gregg-Upshur	NA
*†SEVEN POINTS, Henderson-Kaufman	759
Seven Sisters, Duval	60
Seward Junction, Williamson	NA
Sexton, Sabine	27
Sexton City, Rusk	NA
Seymore, Hopkins	NA
§*†SEYMOUR, Baylor, 317	3,054
Seymour Colony, Baylor	NA
Shadow Bay, Montgomery	NA
Shadow Lake Estates, Montgomery	NA
Shadowland Retreat, Montgomery	NA
Shadowood Estates, Smith	NA
Shady Acres, Burnet	NA
Shady Brook Acres, Montgomery	NA
Shady Creek Ranch, Burnet	NA
Shady Dale, Montgomery	NA
Shady Grove, Burnet	NA
Shady Grove, Cherokee	20
Shady Grove, Franklin	NA
Shady Grove, Houston	NA
Shady Grove, Kerr	NA
Shady Grove, Panola	NA
Shady Grove, Smith	NA
Shady Grove, Upshur	NA
Shady Meadow, Montgomery	NA
Shady Oaks, Brazoria	NA
SHADY SHORES, Denton	1,195
Shady Shores, Henderson	NA
Shady Shores, Marion	NA
*Shafter, Presidio	31
*†SHALLOWATER, Lubbock, 69	1,880
*†SHAMROCK, Wheeler, 202	2,206
Shamrock Estates, Collin	NA
Shamrock Shores, Sabine	NA
Shangri La, Burnet	NA
Shankleville, Newton	NA
Shannon, Clay	23
Sharp, Milam	75
*SHAVANO PARK, Bexar	1,968
Shawnee Prairie, Angelina	NA
Shawnee Shores, Hunt	NA
Shawnee Shores, Sabine	NA
Shaws Bend, Colorado	NA
*Sheffield, Pecos, 13	600
Shelby, Austin	175
*Shelbyville, Shelby, 40	215
‡Sheldon, Harris	1,876
Shell Camp, Gregg	225
Shell Shore, Smith	NA
Shelter Cove, Polk	NA
SHENANDOAH, Montgomery	1,857
Shep, Taylor	60
*†SHEPHERD, San Jacinto, 92	1,970
*Sheppard Air Force Base, Wichita	3,825
*Sheridan, Colorado, 18	225
§*†SHERMAN, Grayson, 1,871	32,164
Sherry, Red River	15
Sherwood, Irion	73
Sherwood Forest, Bexar	NA
Sherwood Shores, Bell	600
Sherwood Shores, Burnet	NA
Sherwood Shores, Grayson	NA
Sherwood Shores #3, Burnet	NA
Shields, Coleman	13
Shiloh, Bastrop	NA
Shiloh, Lavaca	NA
Shiloh, Leon	NA
Shiloh, Limestone	110
Shiloh, Williamson	NA
*†SHINER, Lavaca, 144	2,201
Shinnery Lake, Stonewall	NA
Shire, Rusk	200
Shirley, Hopkins	NA
Shirley Creek, Nacogdoches	NA
*Shiro, Grimes, 5	205
Shive, Hamilton	61
*SHOREACRES, Harris-Chambers	1,505
Shore Acres, Hunt	NA
Shore Ridge, Kerr	NA
Short, Shelby	NA
Shovel Mountain, Burnet	NA
*Sidney, Comanche, 14	196
§*†Sierra Blanca, Hudspeth, 33	700
Siesta Shores, Travis	NA
Siesta Verde, Hays	NA
Signal Peak, Culberson	NA
Silas, Shelby	NA
Siloam, Bowie	50
*†SILSBEE, Hardin, 651	6,680
*Silver, Coke, 7	60
Silver City, Fannin	NA
Silver City, Milam	25
Silver City, Montgomery	NA
Silver City, Navarro	NA
Silver City, Red River	25
Silver Creek Village #1, Burnet	NA
Silver Creek Village #2, Burnet	NA
Silver Hills, Comal	NA
Silver Hills, Kendall	NA
Silver Lake, Van Zandt	42
Silver Pines, Smith	NA
§*†SILVERTON, Briscoe, 70	770
Silver Valley, Coleman	20
Simmons, Live Oak	35
Simmons Bottom, Liberty	NA
*Simms, Bowie, 19	240
Simms, Deaf Smith	NA
*SIMONTON, Fort Bend, 30	825
Simpsonville, Matagorda	NA
Simpsonville, Upshur	100
Sims, Brazos	NA
Simsboro, Freestone	NA
Sinclair City, Smith	NA
Singing Sands, Galveston	NA
Singletary Sites, Newton	NA
*Singleton, Grimes	44
§*†SINTON, San Patricio, 335	5,775
Sion, Walker	NA
Sipe Springs, Comanche	75
*Sisterdale, Kendall, 7	63
Sivells Bend, Cooke	100
Six Lakes, Liberty-Polk	NA
Sixmile, Calhoun	NA
Skeeterville, San Saba	NA
*SKELLYTOWN, Carson, 25	671
Skellyville, Travis	NA
*Skidmore, Bee, 29	500
Sky Harbor, Hood	NA
Sky Lakes, Waller	NA
Skyline Acres, Comal	NA
Skyline Acres, Hays	NA
Skyview Acres, Kendall	NA
Slabtown, Lamar	NA
Slate Shoals, Lamar	NA
*†SLATON, Lubbock, 329	6,223
Slaughter Creek Acres, Travis	NA
Slay, Ellis	NA
Slayden, Gonzales	15

Town and County	Pop.
Sleepy Hollow, Hays	NA
Sleepy Hollow, Montgomery	NA
Slide, Lubbock	44
*Slidell, Wise, 6	175
Sloan, San Saba	NA
*Slocum, Anderson, 1	125
Smetana, Brazos	80
*SMILEY, Gonzales, 27	486
Smithfield, Tarrant	1,000
Smith Grove, Houston	NA
*Smithland, Marion	179
Smith Oaks, Grayson	50
Smith Point, Chambers	150
Smiths Bluff, Jefferson	NA
Smithson Valley, Comal	15
*†SMITHVILLE, Bastrop, 225	3,444
Smithwick, Burnet	NA
*SMYER, Hockley, 16	447
Smyrna, Cass	NA
Smyrna, Harrison	NA
Smyrna, Rains	25
*†SNOOK, Burleson, 28	539
Snow Hill, Collin	20
Snow Hill, Upshur	NA
Snuff Ridge, Liberty	NA
Snug Harbor, Brazoria	NA
Snyder, Hale	NA
§*†SNYDER, Scurry, 732	12,441
*SOCORRO, El Paso	25,101
Soldier Mound, Dickens	NA
Solms, Comal	40
*†SOMERSET, Bexar, 47	1,309
*†SOMERVILLE, Burleson, 94	1,592
Sommers Mill, Bell	6
§*†SONORA, Sutton, 233	2,924
Sorghumville, Houston	NA
*†SOUR LAKE, Hardin, 103	1,650
*South Bend, Young, 5	100
South Bosque, McLennan	80
South Brice, Hall	15
South Camp, King	20
Southern Oaks, Montgomery	NA
South Franklin, Franklin	30
South Gale, Grayson	NA
South Groveton, Trinity	175
South Haven, Howard	NA
*SOUTH HOUSTON, Harris, 600	15,126
South Jonestown Hills, Travis	NA
*†SOUTHLAKE, Tarrant-Denton, 281	8,938
*Southland, Garza, 3	168
Southland Plantation, Polk	NA
*SOUTHMAYD, Grayson, 6	707
SOUTH MOUNTAIN, Coryell	300
*†SOUTH PADRE ISLAND, Cameron, 223	1,962
*South Plains, Floyd, 7	25
South Purmela, Coryell	3
Southridge Estates, Guadalupe	100
South San Gabriel Ranches, Williamson	NA
South San Pedro, Nueces	1,912
South Shore, Bell	40
SOUTHSIDE PLACE, Harris	1,486
South Sulphur, Hunt	60
South Texarkana, Bowie	370
Southton, Bexar	113
Sowells Bluff, Fannin	5
*Spade, Lamb, 8	174
Spanish Fort, Montague, 1	50
Spanish Oak Estates, Williamson	NA
Spanish Oak Terrace, Williamson	NA
Spanish Shores, Henderson	NA
Spanish Trail, Hood	400
Sparenberg, Dawson	20
Sparks, Bell	30
‡Sparks, El Paso	1,337
*Speaks, Lavaca, 1	60
§*†SPEARMAN, Hansford, 279	3,065
Specht Store, Bexar	NA
Speegleville, McLennan	111
Spencer, Montague	NA
*Spicewood, Burnet, 88	110
Spicewood Beach, Burnet	NA
Spicewood Springs, Travis	NA
Spider Mountain, Burnet	NA
Spillers Store, Leon	NA
Spillview Estates, Henderson	NA
*SPLENDORA, Montgomery, 100	803
Splendora Estates, Montgomery	NA
Splendora Farms, Montgomery	NA
*SPOFFORD, Kinney, 1	69
Spoke Hills, Hays	NA
Sportsman Village, Marion	NA
Spraberry, Midland	46
‡*Spring, Harris, 3,802	36,493
*Spring Branch, Comal, 70	200
Spring Branch, Smith	NA
Spring Creek, Hutchinson	139
Spring Creek, San Saba	NA
Spring Creek, Throckmorton	NA
Spring Creek Estates, Montgomery	NA
Springdale, Cass	30
Springfield, Anderson	20
Springfield, Jim Wells	NA
Spring Forest, Montgomery	NA
Spring Hill, Bowie	209
†Spring Hill, Guadalupe	400
Spring Hill, Navarro	60
Spring Hill, San Jacinto	NA
Spring Hills, Montgomery	NA
Spring Hills, Sabine	NA
Spring Hills North, Montgomery	NA
*SPRINGLAKE, Lamb, 18	143
Spring Lake Estates, Montgomery	NA
Spring Oaks, Montgomery	NA
Spring Place, Franklin	NA
*SPRINGTOWN, Parker, 213	1,788
†SPRING VALLEY, Harris	3,709
Spring Valley, McLennan	NA
Spring Valley, Travis	NA
Spring Woods, Montgomery	NA
Sprinkle, Travis	NA
*†SPUR, Dickens, 128	1,350
*Spurger, Tyler, 17	472
Stacy, McCulloch	20
Staff, Eastland	65
*STAFFORD, Fort Bend-Harris, 1,362	10,326
Stag Creek, Comanche	50
STAGECOACH, Montgomery	399
Stage Coach Farms, Montgomery	NA
Stage Coach Hills, Bexar	NA
Stage Coach Hills Estates, Bexar	NA
Stairtown, Caldwell	35
Staley, San Jacinto	30
*†STAMFORD, Jones-Haskell, 240	3,647
Stampede, Bell	10
Stamps, Upshur	NA
Stanfield, Clay	25
§*†STANTON, Martin, 130	2,645
*Staples, Guadalupe, 7	75
*Star, Mills, 7	85
STAR HARBOR, Henderson	391
Star Route, Cochran	NA
Starrville, Smith	75
Startzville, Comal	30
State Line, Culberson	18
Steele Hill, Dickens	NA
Steep Creek, San Augustine	NA
Steep Hollow, Brazos	NA
Steiner, Bosque	20
Stephens Creek, San Jacinto	135
§*†STEPHENVILLE, Erath, 1,057	14,436
Sterley, Floyd	10
§*†STERLING CITY, Sterling, 76	1,054
Sterrett, Ellis	28
Stewards Mill, Freestone	22
Stewart, Rusk	NA
Stiles, Reagan	16
Stillwell Crossing, Brewster	3
§*STINNETT, Hutchinson, 95	2,304
Stith, Jones	18
*†STOCKDALE, Wilson, 72	1,331
Stockholm, Hidalgo	50
Stockman, Shelby	52
Stoneburg, Montague	51
Stone City, Brazos	NA
Stone Creek, Harris	NA
Stonegate, Kendall	NA
Stoneham, Grimes	12
Stonehurst, Williamson	NA
Stone Point, Van Zandt	32
Stone Ridge, Smith	NA
*Stonewall, Gillespie, 28	245
Stony, Denton	25
Stout, Wood	86
‡*Stowell, Chambers, 19	1,562
Stranger, Falls	27
§*†STRATFORD, Sherman, 145	1,845
Stratton, DeWitt	25
*STRAWN, Palo Pinto, 36	691
Streeter, Mason	100
*STREETMAN, Freestone-Navarro, 17	271
Strickland Crossing, Sabine	NA
String Prairie, Bastrop	75
Stringtown, Hunt	NA
Stringtown, Newton	NA
Strong, Shelby	NA
Structure, Williamson	60
Stuart Place, Cameron	NA
Stubblefield, Houston	NA
Stubbs, Kaufman	NA
Study Butte, Brewster	120
Styx, Kaufman	NA
*Sublime, Lavaca, 5	75
*†SUDAN, Lamb, 47	1,041
*SUGAR LAND, Fort Bend, 1,851	38,925
Sugar Valley, Matagorda	NA
‡*Sullivan City, Hidalgo, 14	2,619
*Sulphur Bluff, Hopkins, 4	280
Sulphur Springs, Angelina	NA
§*†SULPHUR SPRINGS, Hopkins, 971	14,786
Summerall, Henderson	NA
*Summerfield, Castro, 5	60
Summerfield, Cherokee	25
Summer Hill, Henderson	NA
Summerville, Gonzales	NA
Summit Oaks, Bexar	NA
*Sumner, Lamar, 18	80
*†SUNDOWN, Hockley, 86	1,795
Sunniland, Live Oak	75
Sunnyside, Castro	106
Sunnyside, Waller	120
Sunnyside, Wilson	300
SUNNYVALE, Dallas	2,500
Sun Oil Camp, Starr	100
*†SUNRAY, Moore, 100	1,801
Sunrise, Falls	1,220
*SUNRISE BEACH, Llano	523
*Sunset, Montague, 22	200
Sunset Oaks, Burnet	NA
Sunset Ridge, Montgomery	NA
SUNSET VALLEY, Travis	366
SUN VALLEY, Lamar	66
Sun Valley Village, Comal	NA
Sunview, Marion	NA
SURFSIDE BEACH, Brazoria	681
*Sutherland Springs, Wilson, 17	362
Swamp City, Gregg	8
Swan, Smith	150
Swannerland, Franklin	NA
*SWEENY, Brazoria, 156	3,480
Sweet Farms, Williamson	NA
Sweet Home, Guadalupe	40
*Sweet Home, Lavaca, 10	360
Sweet Home, Lee	NA
Sweet Union, Cherokee	20
§*†SWEETWATER, Nolan, 698	11,851
Swenson, Stonewall	185
Swift, Nacogdoches	125
Swiftex, Bastrop	NA
Swinneytown, Smith	NA
Swiss Alp, Fayette	46
Swiss Village, Burnet	NA
Sylvan, Lamar	68
*Sylvester, Fisher, 5	79

Town and County	Pop.
Sylvester, Trinity	29
T	
Tabor, Brazos	150
Tadmor, Houston	NA
*†TAFT, San Patricio, 184	3,506
‡Taft Southwest, San Patricio	2,199
§*†TAHOKA, Lynn, 126	2,792
Taiton, Wharton	24
*†TALCO, Titus, 38	587
Tall Timbers, Montgomery	NA
Tall Tree, Franklin	NA
*Talpa, Coleman, 8	127
Talty, Kaufman	32
Tam Anne, Castro	NA
Tamina, Montgomery	NA
Tamina Manor, Montgomery	NA
Tanglewilde Farms, Montgomery	NA
Tanglewood, Lee, 1	48
Tanglewood Beach, Kaufman	NA
Tanglewood Forest, San Jacinto	NA
‡Tanglewood Forest, Travis	3,198
Tanglewood Island, Stephens	NA
Tanglewood Manor, Montgomery	NA
Tanglewood Shores, Comal	NA
Tankersley, Tom Green	20
Tapatio Springs, Kendall	NA
Tara, Fort Bend	NA
Tarkington Prairie, Liberty	NA
*Tarpley, Bandera, 6	30
*Tarzan, Martin, 13	80
Tascosa Hills, Potter	90
*†TATUM, Rusk-Panola, 51	1,322
*†TAYLOR, Williamson, 609	11,971
Taylor Lake Estates, Polk	NA
*TAYLOR LAKE VILLAGE, Harris	3,664
Taylorsville, Caldwell	NA
Taylor Town, Lamar	40
Tazewell, Hopkins	NA
*†TEAGUE, Freestone, 206	3,457
Teaselville, Smith	NA
Tecula, Cherokee	NA
*TEHUACANA, Limestone, 11	335
Tejas Village, Hunt	NA
Tejas Village, Marion	NA
*Telegraph, Kimble, 4	3
*Telephone, Fannin, 9	210
*Telferner, Victoria, 12	304
*Telico, Ellis	95
*Tell, Childress, 3	63
*†TEMPLE, Bell, 2,300	47,251
Temple Springs, Jasper	NA
*†TENAHA, Shelby, 53	1,161
Tenmile, Dawson	NA
Tennessee, Shelby	NA
*Tennessee Colony, Anderson, 20	120
*Tennyson, Coke, 1	35
*Terlingua, Brewster, 22	25
Terminal, Midland	421
Terrace, Bexar	NA
Terrace Park, Llano	NA
Terramar Beach, Galveston	NA
*†TERRELL, Kaufman, 775	12,837
*TERRELL HILLS, Bexar	5,040
Terry Chapel, Falls	NA
Terryville, DeWitt	40
*†TEXARKANA (Texas portion only), Bowie, 2,288**	33,405
Including Arkansas Portion (1990 U.S. census count)	54,287
*†TEXAS CITY, Galveston, 1,178	42,026
Texas National, Montgomery	NA
TEXHOMA, Sherman	301
*†TEXLINE, Dallam, 41	423
*Texon, Reagan, 2	35
Thalia, Foard	104
*†THE COLONY, Denton	24,782
Thedford, Smith	65
The Divide, Kerr	250
*The Grove, Coryell	65
The Heights, Brazoria	NA
Thelma, Limestone	NA
The Oaks, Comal	NA
Theon, Williamson	20
Thermo, Hopkins	NA
The Settlement, Hays	NA
The Villages, Smith	NA
The Willows, Burnet	NA
The Woodlands, Brazos	NA
‡*†The Woodlands, Montgomery, 810	33,902
The Woods at Spring Branch, Comal	NA
*Thicket, Hardin, 6	306
Thomas, Upshur	NA
*Thomaston, DeWitt, 3	45
Thompson, Harris	NA
*THOMPSONS, Fort Bend, 8	198
Thompsonville, Gonzales	30
Thompsonville, Jim Hogg	NA
Thornberry, Clay	60
*†THORNDALE, Milam-Williamson, 65	1,259
*THORNTON, Limestone, 28	585
THORNTONVILLE, Ward	742
Thorp Spring, Hood	184
Thousand Oaks, Williamson	NA
*THRALL, Williamson, 22	609
Three Oaks, Wilson	150
Three Points, Travis	NA
*†THREE RIVERS, Live Oak, 141	1,993
Three States, Cass	NA
Three Way, Erath	NA
Thrifty, Brown	NA
§*†THROCKMORTON, Throckmorton, 102	1,054
Thunderbird Shores, Henderson	NA
Thurber, Erath	8
Tidewater Oaks, Matagorda	NA
Tidwell, Hunt	NA
Tidwell Prairie, Robertson	NA
Tigertown, Lamar	NA
TIKI ISLAND VILLAGE, Galveston	639
§*†Tilden, McMullen, 29	500
Tilmon, Caldwell	25
Timber Creek, Bexar	NA
Timber Creek, Smith	NA
TIMBERCREEK CANYON, Randall	316
Timberdale Estates, Smith	NA
Timberhill Village, Hidalgo	NA
Timber Lake, Burnet	NA
Timberlake, Sabine	NA
Timber Lake Acres, Montgomery	NA
Timber Lake Estates, Liberty	NA
Timber Lake Estates, Montgomery	NA
Timber Land, Smith	NA
Timberline Park, Bexar	NA
Timberline West, Williamson	NA
Timber Ridge, Bexar	NA
Timber Ridge, Montgomery	NA
Timberwilde, Brazos	NA
‡Timberwood, Bexar	2,848
Timesville, Leon	NA
*†TIMPSON, Shelby, 83	1,023
Tin Top, Parker	25
*TIOGA, Grayson, 32	637
TIRA, Hopkins	263
*Tivoli, Refugio, 31	540
Tivy, Kerr	NA
Tobacco Patch, Polk	NA
TOCO, Lamar	130
Todd City, Anderson	NA
TODD MISSION, Grimes	60
Tokio, McLennan	NA
*Tokio, Terry, 6	60
*TOLAR, Hood, 39	530
Tolbert, Wilbarger	30
Toledo Beach, Sabine	NA
Toledo Village, Newton	NA
Toledo Village, Sabine	NA
Tolette, Lamar	NA
Tolosa, Kaufman	58
*†TOMBALL, Harris-Montgomery, 973	7,224
*†TOM BEAN, Grayson, 28	878
Tomlinson Hill, Falls	NA
Tonkawa Springs, Williamson	NA
Tonkowon Country, Williamson	NA
TOOL, Henderson	1,853
Topsey, Coryell	20
*Tornillo, El Paso, 19	241
Tours, McLennan	100
*Tow, Llano, 17	305
Towering Pines, Sabine	NA
Tower Lake, Wilson	100
Town Bluff, Tyler	26
Towne West, Fort Bend	NA
Townsend, San Augustine	NA
‡Town West, Fort Bend	7,019
Tow Village, Llano	NA
*TOYAH, Reeves, 5	123
*Toyahvale, Reeves, 4	60
Tradewinds, Henderson	NA
Traildust, Denton	39
Trailwood, Bexar	NA
Travis, Falls	60
Travis Oaks, Travis	NA
Travis Peak, Travis	NA
Trawick, Nacogdoches	100
Treasure Island, Brazoria	NA
Treasure Island, Guadalupe	500
*TRENT, Taylor, 20	319
*†TRENTON, Fannin, 50	667
Tres Palacios Oaks, Matagorda	NA
Tri-Lake Estates, Montgomery	NA
Triangle, Falls	NA
Trickham, Coleman	12
Trimmier, Bell	90
*TRINIDAD, Henderson, 44	1,101
*†TRINITY, Trinity, 212	2,800
Trinity River Lake Estates, Liberty	NA
Triple Peak Ranch Estates, Comal	NA
*TROPHY CLUB, Denton	4,298
*TROUP, Smith-Cherokee, 131	1,814
Trout Creek, Newton	NA
Trout Creek Lodge, Jasper	NA
*†TROY, Bell, 60	1,540
Truby, Jones	26
Trukton, Rusk	NA
Trumbull, Ellis	65
*Truscott, Knox, 7	187
Tubbs Corner, Crane	NA
Tucker, Anderson	304
*Tuleta, Bee, 11	98
§*†TULIA, Swisher, 350	5,127
Tulip, Fannin	10
Tulsita, Bee	25
Tundra, Van Zandt	34
Tunis, Burleson	150
*TURKEY, Hall, 29	546
Turlington, Freestone	27
Turnbaugh Corner, Ector	NA
*Turnersville, Coryell	155
Turnersville, Travis	90
*Turnertown, Rusk	76
Turney, Cherokee	100
Turtle Bayou, Chambers	42
Turtle Cove, Brazoria	NA
Turtle Creek, Montgomery	NA
*†TUSCOLA, Taylor, 53	629
Tuxedo, Jones	42
Twichell, Ochiltree	22
Twin Cedar Retreat, Sabine	NA
Twin Creek, Bexar	NA
Twin Isles, Burnet	NA
Twin Lake Estates, Montgomery	NA
Twin Lake Ranch Estates, Medina	NA
Twin Lakes, Smith	NA
Twin Shores, Montgomery	NA
Twin Sisters, Blanco	78
Twin Valley Terrace, Bexar	NA
*Twitty, Wheeler, 16	60
*TYE, Taylor, 48	1,109
§*†TYLER, Smith, 5,393	79,516
*Tynan, Bee, 10	200
Type, Williamson	40
Tyson, Hill	NA
U	
*UHLAND, Caldwell-Hays	380
*Umbarger, Randall, 11	327
UNCERTAIN, Harrison	210
Union, Brazos	NA
Union, San Augustine	NA
Union, Scurry	20

Town and County	Pop.
Union, Terry	85
Union, Wilson	22
Union Bluff, Hill	NA
Union Center, Eastland	NA
Union Flat, Childress	NA
Union Grove, Bell	4
Union Grove, Erath	12
UNION GROVE, Upshur	286
Union High, Navarro	NA
Union Valley, Hunt	25
Unity, Lamar	NA
*†UNIVERSAL CITY, Bexar, 396	14,270
University Acres, Brazos	NA
†UNIVERSITY PARK, Dallas	22,376
Upper Meyersville, DeWitt	NA
Upshaw, Nacogdoches	NA
Upton, Bastrop	25
Urbana, San Jacinto	10
Utley, Bastrop	30
*Utopia, Uvalde, 39	360
§*†UVALDE, Uvalde, 770	15,529
Uz, Montague	NA
V	
Valdasta, Collin	40
*VALENTINE, Jeff Davis, 4	236
*Valera, Coleman, 5	80
Valley Creek, Fannin	12
Valley Grove, Rusk	NA
Valley Hi, Bexar	NA
*†VALLEY MILLS, Bosque-McLennan, 83	1,105
Valley Ridge, Brazos	NA
*Valley Spring, Llano, 6	50
Valley View, Comal	NA
*VALLEY VIEW, Cooke, 84	694
Valley View, Cottle	20
Valley View, Mitchell	NA
Valley View, Runnels	NA
Valley View, Upshur	NA
Valley View, Wichita	200
Valley View, Williamson	NA
Valleyview Acres, Smith	NA
Valley Wells, Dimmit	25
Valley Wood Acres, Montgomery	NA
Val Verde, Hidalgo	NA
Val Verde, Milam	25
*†VAN, Van Zandt, 125	2,000
*†VAN ALSTYNE, Grayson, 88	2,233
Vance, Real	20
*Vancourt, Tom Green, 6	125
Vandalia, Red River	35
*Vanderbilt, Jackson, 24	667
*Vanderpool, Bandera, 9	20
Vandyke, Comanche	20
§*†VAN HORN, Culberson, 142	2,838
Van Raub, Bexar	NA
Van Sickle, Hunt	NA
‡*Van Vleck, Matagorda, 51	1,674
Vasco, Delta	20
Vashti, Clay	140
Vattman, Kleberg	NA
Vaughan, Hill	70
Veach, San Augustine	NA
*Vealmoor, Howard	179
§*VEGA, Oldham, 69	883
*VENUS, Johnson-Ennis, 53	1,079
*Vera, Knox, 1	276
Verde Mills, Bexar	NA
Verdi, Atascosa	NA
*Verhalen, Reeves	52
*Veribest, Tom Green, 6	40
§*†VERNON, Wilbarger, 760	12,371
Verona, Collin	NA
Vessey, Red River	14
Veterans, Ward	NA
Viboras, Starr	22
Vick, Concho	20
Vicksburg, Montgomery	NA
Victoria, Limestone	25
§*†VICTORIA, Victoria, 3,119	58,906
Victory City, Bowie	NA
Vidaurri, Refugio	85
*†VIDOR, Orange, 757	11,636
Vienna, Lavaca	40

Town and County	Pop.
View, Taylor, 2	75
Viewpoint, Lamar	NA
*Vigo Park, Swisher	31
Villa Cavazos, Cameron	NA
*Village Mills, Hardin, 9	300
Village Oaks, Williamson	NA
Village Shores, Comal	NA
Village West, Travis	NA
Villa Nueva, Cameron	NA
Villareales, Starr	NA
Vincent, Howard, 1	500
Vinegarone, Val Verde	NA
Vineyard, Jack	37
VINTON, El Paso	609
Violet, Nueces	160
Virginia Estates, Montgomery	NA
Vista, Hamilton	NA
Vistula, Houston	NA
Vivian, Foard	NA
*Voca, McCulloch, 3	56
Volente, Travis	NA
Volga, Houston	NA
*Von Ormy, Bexar, 82	264
Von Ormy Heights, Bexar	NA
Vontress, Haskell	NA
*Voss, Coleman, 1	20
*Votaw, Hardin, 2	160
*Voth, Jefferson	NA
Vsetin, Lavaca	NA
Vysehrad, Lavaca	NA
W	
§*†WACO, McLennan, 6,603	107,191
*Wadsworth, Matagorda, 10	152
*WAELDER, Gonzales, 28	785
Wagner, Hunt	NA
*Waka, Ochiltree, 6	145
Wakefield, Polk	NA
*WAKE VILLAGE, Bowie	5,145
*†Walburg, Williamson, 6	250
Walco Hills, Montgomery	NA
Waldeck, Fayette	35
Walden, Montgomery	NA
Waldrip, McCulloch	NA
Walhalla, Fayette	37
Walkers Mill, Harrison	NA
*Wall, Tom Green, 13	200
Wallace, Van Zandt	NA
Wallace Prairie, Grimes	75
*WALLER, Waller-Harris, 201	1,639
Walling, Hill	NA
*†WALLIS, Austin, 56	1,098
*Wallisville, Chambers, 19	377
Walnut Bend, Cooke	100
Walnut Creek, Montgomery	NA
Walnut Forest, Travis	NA
Walnut Grove, Collin	200
Walnut Grove, Kendall	NA
Walnut Grove, Smith	NA
Walnut Hills, Montgomery	NA
Walnut Hills, Potter	60
Walnut Place, Travis	NA
Walnut Ridge, Angelina	NA
*WALNUT SPRINGS, Bosque, 30	750
Walnut Springs, Ellis	NA
Walnut Springs, Montgomery	NA
Walton, Van Zandt	35
Wamba, Bowie	70
Waneta, Houston	NA
Waples, Hood	NA
*Warda, Fayette, 4	67
Wards Creek, Bowie	164
*Waring, Kendall, 6	73
Warlock, Marion	NA
Warner Junction, Grayson	NA
*Warren, Tyler, 34	304
WARREN CITY, Gregg-Upshur	281
*Warrenton, Fayette	50
Warsaw, Kaufman	58
Warwick, Smith	NA
Washburn, Armstrong	104
*Washington, Washington, 22	265
*†WASKOM, Harrison, 124	1,866
Wastella, Nolan	13
*WATAUGA, Tarrant	21,152
Water Front Park, Comal	NA

Town and County	Pop.
Waterloo, Williamson	60
Waterman, Shelby	53
Waters Bluff, Smith	NA
Waters Park, Travis	NA
*Water Valley, Tom Green, 7	120
Waterwood, San Jacinto	NA
Watkins, Van Zandt	NA
Watson, Burnet	NA
Watt, Limestone	NA
Watterson, Bastrop	NA
Watts, Marion	NA
Waverly, San Jacinto	50
§*†WAXAHACHIE, Ellis, 1,173	19,203
Wayne, Cass	NA
*Wayside, Armstrong, 6	40
Wayside, Lynn	NA
Wealthy, Leon	NA
§*†WEATHERFORD, Parker, 1,671	15,267
Weatherly, Hall	20
Weaver, Hopkins	35
Webb, Shelby	NA
Webb, Webb	40
Webberville, Travis	50
Webbville, Coleman	50
*†WEBSTER, Harris, 1,058	5,376
Weches, Houston	26
Weedhaven, Jackson	NA
Weekend Retreats, Montgomery	NA
Weeks Settlement, Newton	NA
Weeping Mary, Cherokee	NA
*Weesatche, Goliad, 7	525
*†WEIMAR, Colorado, 188	2,162
Weinert, Guadalupe	10
*WEINERT, Haskell, 15	248
Weir, Hopkins	NA
*WEIR, Williamson, 7	239
Weiss Bluff, Jasper	NA
*Welch, Dawson, 28	110
Welcome, Austin	150
Weldon, Houston	131
Welfare, Kendall	36
*Wellborn, Brazos, 10	100
Wellborn Oaks, Brazos	NA
§*†WELLINGTON, Collingsworth, 228	2,568
*WELLMAN, Terry, 9	253
*WELLS, Cherokee, 30	810
Wells, Lynn	NA
‡Wells Branch, Travis	7,722
Wells Creek, Anderson	NA
Wellswood, San Augustine	NA
Wentworth, Van Zandt	32
Wesco, Gray	7
Weser, Goliad	50
*†WESLACO, Hidalgo, 927	24,404
Wesley, Washington	60
Wesley Grove, Walker	NA
*†WEST, McLennan, 233	2,719
West Bluff, Orange	NA
Westbrook, Jack	NA
*WESTBROOK, Mitchell, 26	246
*†WEST COLUMBIA, Brazoria, 267	4,872
Westcott, San Jacinto	NA
Western Lake, Parker	NA
West Estates, Williamson	NA
Westfield, Harris	275
West Galveston, Galveston	NA
Westhaven, Comal	NA
*Westhoff, DeWitt, 13	410
WESTLAKE, Tarrant-Denton	204
*WEST LAKE HILLS, Travis	2,784
Westlawn, Orange	NA
West Magnolia Forest, Waller	NA
West Mineola, Wood	NA
*WESTMINSTER, Collin, 3	450
WEST MOUNTAIN, Upshur	445
West Oaks, Travis	NA
‡West Odessa, Ector	17,051
*WESTON, Collin, 3	416
*WEST ORANGE, Orange	4,625
Westover, Baylor	58
WESTOVER HILLS, Tarrant	717
Westphalia, Falls	324

Town and County	Pop.
*West Point, Fayette, 3	205
West Point, Hamilton	NA
West Point, Lynn	NA
Westridge, Smith	NA
Westside, Morris	NA
West Sinton, San Patricio	NA
WEST TAWAKONI, Hunt	1,015
WEST UNIVERSITY PLACE, Harris	13,614
Westville, Trinity	NA
Westway, Deaf Smith	NA
‡Westway, El Paso	2,498
Westwood Estates, Montgomery	NA
WESTWORTH VILLAGE, Tarrant	2,360
*Wetmore, Bexar, 20	NA
Whaley, Bowie	NA
§*†WHARTON, Wharton, 606	9,758
Whatley, Marion	NA
Wheatland, Tarrant	175
§*WHEELER, Wheeler, 106	1,407
Wheeler Springs, Houston	NA
*Wheelock, Robertson, 6	125
Whippoorwill Acres, Williamson	NA
Whispering Oaks, Smith	NA
Whispering Pines, Montgomery	NA
Whispering Winds, Bexar	NA
White City, Gaines	NA
White City, San Augustine	20
White City, Wilbarger	40
White City, Wise	25
*†WHITE DEER, Carson, 62	1,158
White Estates, Hunt	NA
*WHITEFACE, Cochran, 31	499
Whiteflat, Motley	3
White Hall, Bell	45
White Hall, Grimes	NA
White Hall, Jackson	NA
Whitehall, Kaufman	NA
Whitehead, Hunt	NA
*†WHITEHOUSE, Smith, 249	4,623
White Mound, Grayson	NA
*†WHITE OAK, Gregg, 154	5,358
White Oak, Titus	NA
White Oak Junction, Hopkins	NA
White Oak Valley Estates, Montgomery	NA
White River, Crosby	55
White Rock, Hunt	73
White Rock, Red River	85
White Rock, Robertson	80
White Rock, San Augustine	NA
*†WHITESBORO, Grayson, 188	3,301
*WHITE SETTLEMENT, Tarrant	15,437
Whitestone, Motley	5
Whitetail, Williamson	NA
Whiteway, Hamilton	NA
*†WHITEWRIGHT, Grayson-Fannin, 103	1,722
*Whitharral, Hockley, 9	111
Whitman, Washington	25
*†WHITNEY, Hill, 219	1,656
*Whitsett, Live Oak, 8	350
Whitson, Coryell	30
*Whitt, Parker, 3	38
Whitton, Van Zandt	NA
*Whon, Coleman	15
Wichita Colony, Baylor	NA
§*†WICHITA FALLS, Wichita-Archer, 4,924	98,356
Wicker, Brazos	NA
*WICKETT, Ward, 32	558
Wied, Lavaca	65
Wiedeville, Washington	NA
Wieland, Hunt	NA
*Wiergate, Newton, 13	461
Wigginsville, Montgomery	NA
Wilcox, Burleson	40
Wilcox, Gray	5
Wild Country, Polk	NA
Wilderville, Falls	45
Wildhorse, Culberson	35
Wild Hurst, Cherokee	NA
*Wildorado, Oldham, 22	180
‡Wild Peach, Brazoria	2,532
Wild Plum Valley, Williamson	NA

Town and County	Pop.
Wildwood, Bexar	NA
Wild Wood Acres, Montgomery	NA
Wildwood Resort City, Hardin-Tyler	NA
Wilkins, Upshur	NA
Wilkinson, Titus	39
Wilkirk Estates, Henderson	NA
Willamar, Willacy	NA
William Penn, Washington	100
Williams, Hardeman	NA
Williams, Liberty	NA
Williamsburg, Lavaca	NA
Williamson Settlement, Orange	175
*WILLIS, Montgomery, 306	3,144
*Willow City, Gillespie, 4	75
Willow Creek Estates, Hays	NA
Willow Forest, Harris	NA
Willow Grove, McLennan	50
WILLOW PARK, Parker	2,442
Willow Springs, Fayette	NA
Willow Springs, Rains	50
*†WILLS POINT, Van Zandt, 324	3,128
*WILMER, Dallas, 40	2,536
Wilmeth, Runnels	NA
Wilson, Falls	NA
Wilson, Kaufman	NA
*†WILSON, Lynn, 20	598
Wilson Lake, Polk	NA
‡*Wimberley, Hays, 317	2,537
Wimberley Hills, Hays	NA
Winchell, Brown	NA
*Winchester, Fayette, 6	50
*WINDCREST, Bexar	5,789
‡Windemere, Travis	3,476
Windermere Oaks, Burnet	NA
*†WINDOM, Fannin, 15	283
Windsor, McLennan	NA
*†WINDTHORST, Archer-Clay, 59	369
Windwood Estates, Bexar	NA
Winedale, Fayette	NA
*WINFIELD, Titus, 11	347
*†Wingate, Runnels, 17	216
*†WINK, Winkler, 22	1,228
Winkler, Navarro-Freestone	26
‡*†Winnie, Chambers, 221	2,360
*†WINNSBORO, Wood-Franklin, 366	3,093
*WINONA, Smith, 22	518
Winterfield, Hopkins	NA
Winter Haven, Dimmit	112
*†WINTERS, Runnels, 186	2,899
Winter Valley Estates, Liberty	NA
Wise, Van Zandt	29
Witting, Lavaca	90
WIXON VALLEY, Brazos	221
Wizard Wells, Jack	69
*Woden, Nacogdoches, 6	70
Wokaty, Milam	NA
*WOLFE CITY, Hunt, 85	1,538
*†WOLFFORTH, Lubbock, 111	2,171
Womack, Bosque	25
Wonderland Forest, San Jacinto	NA
Woodal Farm, Milam	NA
Woodard Place, Smith	NA
Woodbine, Cooke	246
WOODBRANCH, Montgomery	1,424
Woodbury, Hill	40
Woodcanyon Waters, Henderson	NA
WOODCREEK, Hays	946
Wood Creek, Montgomery	NA
Wooded Hills, Johnson	310
Woodhaven, Montgomery	NA
Wood Hi, Victoria	35
Wood Hollow, Montgomery	NA
Woodlake, Brazos	NA
Woodlake, Grayson	60
*Woodlake, Trinity, 1	301
Woodland, Red River	128
Woodland Estates, Sabine	NA
Woodland Forest Estates, Montgomery	NA
Woodland Hills, Henderson	NA
Woodland Hills, Hill	NA
Woodland Lakes, Montgomery	NA
Woodland Shores, Marion	NA
*Woodlawn, Harrison, 11	370

Town and County	Pop.
Woodlawn, Montgomery	NA
Woodlawn Forest, Bexar	NA
WOODLOCH, Montgomery	336
Woodridge, Orange	1,000
Woodridge Estates, Montgomery	NA
Woodridge Forest, Bexar	NA
Woodridge Park, Bexar	NA
Woodrow, Lubbock	85
Woods, Panola	65
*†WOODSBORO, Refugio, 82	1,789
*WOODSON, Throckmorton, 19	254
Wood Springs, Smith	NA
Woodstock, Bowie	NA
Woodville, Cherokee	NA
§*†WOODVILLE, Tyler, 357	2,873
Woodward, La Salle	20
*WOODWAY, McLennan	9,055
Woody, Dawson	NA
Woody Acres, Montgomery	NA
Woosley, Rains	47
*WORTHAM, Freestone, 56	1,034
Worthing, Lavaca	55
Wright City, Smith	172
*Wrightsboro, Gonzales, 2	76
‡Wyldwood, Bastrop	1,884
*WYLIE, Collin-Rockwall-Dallas, 559	10,646
Wylie, Franklin	NA
Wynne, Van Zandt	175
Y	
*Yancey, Medina, 7	202
*YANTIS, Wood, 45	232
Yard, Anderson	18
Yarrellton, Milam	35
Yaupon Cove, Polk	NA
Yellowpine, Sabine	74
*†YOAKUM, Lavaca-DeWitt, 350	6,006
*†YORKTOWN, DeWitt, 137	2,343
Young, Freestone	27
Youngsport, Bell	40
Yowell, Delta	15
Yowell, Hunt	NA
Ysleta del Sur Pueblo, El Paso	292
Yucote Acres, Collin	NA
Z	
Zabcikville, Bell	38
‡§*†Zapata, Zapata, 199	7,523
*ZAVALLA, Angelina, 39	764
*Zephyr, Brown, 13	198
Zimmerscheidt, Colorado	NA
Zion Grove, Rusk	NA
Zion Hill, Guadalupe	30
Zion Hill, Jasper	NA
Zipperlandville, Falls	NA
Zippville, Guadalupe	98
Zorn, Guadalupe	26
Zuehl, Guadalupe	49
Zunkerville, Karnes	NA

Percentage of population 65 or older by state, 1993

Rank	Percent
41. Maryland	11.1
42. New Mexico	11.0
43. Virginia	11.0
44. Wyoming	10.9
45. California	10.6
46. Texas	**10.2**
47. Georgia	10.1
48. Colorado	10.0
49. Utah	8.9
50. Alaska	4.4
(United States)	(12.7)

Source: U.S. Bureau of the Census

Fine Arts Organizations Across State

The following information on the fine arts in Texas was prepared for the Texas Almanac *by the staff of the Texas Commission on the Arts.*

Culture in Texas, as in any market, is a mixture of activity generated by both the commercial and the nonprofit sectors.

The commercial sector encompasses Texas-based profit-making businesses including commercial recording artists (such as the legendary Willie Nelson), nightclubs, record companies, private galleries, assorted boutiques that carry fine art collectibles and private dance and music halls. In addition, Texas is becoming an important media center, with Texas-based publications, television and film companies gaining national recognition.

Texas also has extensive cultural resources offered by nonprofit organizations that are engaged in charitable, educational and/or humanitarian activities.

The Texas Legislature has authorized six state agencies to administer cultural services and funds for the public good. The agencies, listed below, fall under the auspices of the Texas Legislature's Cultural and Historical Resources Committee.

They are: **State Antiquities Committee**, Box 12276, Austin 78711; **Texas Commission on the Arts**, Box 13406, Capitol Sta., Austin 78711; **Texas Film Commission, the Governor's office**, Box 12428, Austin 78711; **Texas Historical Commission**, Box 12276, Austin 78711; **Texas State Library and Archives Commission**, Box 12927, Austin 78711; and the **State Preservation Board,** Box 13286, Austin 78711.

Although not a state agency, another organization that provides cultural services to the citizens of Texas is the **Texas Committee for the Humanities**, 1604 Nueces, Austin 78701.

The Texas Commission on the Arts was established in 1965 to develop a receptive climate for the arts in Texas, to attract outstanding artists to Texas, to serve as a source of arts information to state government and Texas at large, and to expand and enhance the cultural opportunities for all Texans. The commission accomplishes these goals by providing financial, informational and technical assistance.

The Texas Commission on the Arts provides services and financial assistance to a wide range of non-profit arts organizations. Its clientele includes theaters (professional, civic, children's, ethnic), media (radio, television, film, publications), festivals, music (folk, symphonic, chamber, choral, jazz, opera and new music), visual arts (sculpture, crafts, photography, painting, environmental), dance (modern, ballet, folkloric), schools, presenters of cultural events and services organizations. For more information about the services of the commission, call toll-free (800) 252-9415.

Some of Texas' major nonprofit arts institutions — orchestras, museums, dance companies, theaters and cultural centers — are listed below.

Addison — Addison Centre Theatre, Box 933, (75001).

Amarillo — Amarillo Symphony Orchestra, Box 2552 (79105); Lone Star Ballet, Box 1133 (79178).

Austin — Austin Symphony Orchestra, 1101 Red River (78701); Ballet Austin, 3002 Guadalupe (78705); Laguna Gloria Art Museum, Box 5568 (78763); Paramount Theatre for the Performing Arts, Box 1205 (78767).

Beaumont — Beaumont Art Museum, 1111 9th St. (77702).

Corpus Christi — Art Museum of South Texas, 1902 N. Shoreline Dr. (78401); Corpus Christi Ballet, 5610 Everhart (78469).

Corsicana — Community Playhouse, Box 2224 (75110).

Dallas — Ballet Dallas, 309 S. Pearl (75201); Dallas Opera, 1925 Elm (75201); Dallas Museum of Art, 1717 N. Harwood (75201); Dallas Symphony Orchestra, Box 26207 (75226); Dallas Theatre Center, 3636 Turtle Creek Blvd. (75219); Shakespeare Festival, 3630 Harry Hines (75210); Teatro Dallas, 2204 Commerce (75201); Theatre Three, 2800 Routh (75201).

El Paso — Museum Of Arts, 1211 Montana Ave. (79902); El Paso Symphony Orchestra, Box 180 (79942).

Fort Worth — Amon Carter Museum Of Western Art, Box 2365 (76101); Museum of Modern Art, 1309 Montgomery (76107); Fort Worth Ballet Assn., 6845 Green Oaks Rd. (76116); Fort Worth Opera, 3505 W. Lancaster (76107); Fort Worth Symphony Orchestra, 4401 Trail Lake Dr. (76109); Kimbell Art Museum, Box 9440 (76107); Stage West, Box 2587 (76113); Van Cliburn Foundation, 2525 Ridgmar Blvd. (76116).

Houston — Alley Theatre, 615 Texas (77002); Contemporary Arts Museum, 5216 Montrose Blvd. (77006); Houston Ballet Foundation, Box 130487 (77219); Houston Grand Opera, 510 Preston, #500 (77002); Houston Museum of Fine Arts, Box 6826 (77265); Houston Symphony Orchestra, 615 Louisiana (77002); Texas Opera Theatre, 510 Preston, #440 (77002); Theatre Under the Stars, 4235 San Felipe (77027).

Midland/Odessa — Midland/Odessa Symphony and Chorale, Box 60658 (79711).

Round Top — James Dick Foundation for the Performing Arts, Box 89 (78954).

San Antonio — Carver Cultural Center, 226 N. Hackberry (78202); Guadalupe Cultural Arts Center, 1300 Guadalupe (78207); McNay Art Institute, Box 6069 (78209); San Antonio Art Institute, Box 6069 (78209); San Antonio Museum Association, Box 2601 (78299-2601); San Antonio Performing Arts Assn., 110 Broadway, Ste. 230 (78205); San Antonio Symphony Orchestra, 109 Lexington Ave., Ste. 207 (78205); Southwest Craft Center, 300 Augusta (78205).

The Texas Arts Council, 3939 Bee Caves Rd., Ste. 1A, Austin 78746, promotes, develops and supports local arts agencies. Listed below are the members as of mid-1995.

Abilene — Abilene Cultural Affairs Council, Box 2281 (79604).

Albany — The Old Jail Art Center, Rt. 1, Box 1 (76430).

Amarillo — Amarillo Chamber of Commerce Arts Committee, Box 9480 (79105).

Andrews — Andrews Cultural Affairs Committee, 700 West Broadway (79714).

Arlington — Arlington Arts Council, 505 W. Abram St. (76010).

Athens — Henderson County Arts Council, 500 S. Prairieville (75751).

Austin — Cultural Arts Division — City of Austin, PARD, Box 1088 (78767).

Bastrop — Bastrop Assn. for the Arts, 807 Main (78602).

Bay City — Bay City Cultural Assn., 2922 Ave. I (77414).

Beaumont, Orange and Port Arthur — Southeast

Big Bend — Big Bend Arts Alliance, 505 W. San Antonio, Marfa (79843).

Big Spring — Big Spring Cultural Affairs Council, Box 1427 (79720). West Texas Center for the Arts, Howard College, Box 1810 (79720).

Borger — Magic Plains Arts Council, Box 3101 (79007).

Beckenridge — Breckenridge Fine Arts Center, Box 549 (76424).

Brenham — Arts Council of Washington County, 701 Milroy Dr. (77833).

Brownfield — Brownfield Arts Assn., Box 12 (79316).

Brownwood — Cultural Affairs Commission, 5221 East Baker (76801).

Carrizo Springs — Arts Council of Dimmit County, 412 Pena (78834).

Clear Lake — Alliance for the Arts, Box 580466, Houston (77258).

Clifton — Bosque Co. Conservatory of Fine Arts, Box 373 (76634).

Coleman — Fine Arts League, Box 376 (76834).

College Station — Arts Council of Brazos Valley, 310 University Dr. East (77840).

Columbus — Live Oak Art Center, 1014 Milam (78934).

Conroe — Montgomery County Performing Arts Society, Box 1714 (77305).

Corpus Christi — Municipal Arts Commission, PARD, Box 9277 (78469).

Corsicana — Navarro Council of the Arts, Box 2224 (75151).

Crockett — Piney Woods Fine Arts Assn., Box 1213 (75835).

Cuero — Oscar Scott Memorial Foundation, 203 E. Church (77954).

Cuney — Cuney Cultural Committee, Box 92 (75759).

Dalhart — Dalhart Area Fine Arts Assn., No. 1 Canyon Trail (79022).

Dallas — Office of Cultural Affairs, 1925 Elm, Ste. 500 (75201).

Del Rio — Del Rio Council for the Arts, 120 East Garfield (78840).

Denison — Denison Arts Council, 313 W. Woodward (75020).

Denton — Greater Denton Arts Council, 207 S. Bell (76201).

DeSoto — DeSoto Council of Cultural Arts, Box 1354 (75115).

Dumas — Moore County Arts Assn., 234 West First (79029).

Duncanville — Duncanville Regional Arts Assn., Box 381014 (75138).

Eagle Pass — Arts Council of Eagle Pass, Box 2920 (78853).

El Paso — El Paso Arts Resources Department, City of El Paso, 2 Civic Center Plaza (79901).

Fort Worth — Arts Council of Fort Worth & Tarrant County, 508 Main (76102).

Gainesville — Cooke County Arts Council, Box 194 (76241).

Garland — Garland Center for the Performing Arts, Box 469002 (75046).

Gilmer — Upshur County Arts Council, Box 854 (75644).

Grand Prairie — Grand Prairie Arts Council, Box 531613 (75053).

Harlingen — Harlingen Arts Council, Box 531103 (78553).

Hondo — Art League of Hondo, 1160 26th, (78861).

Houston — Cultural Arts Council of Houston, 1964 W. Gray, Ste. 224 (77019).

Huntsville — Huntsville Arts Commission, 1212 Ave. M (77340).

Ingram — Hill Country Arts Foundation, Box 176 (78025).

Irving — Irving Arts Center, 3333 N. McArthur, Ste. 300 (75062); Irving Cultural Affairs Council, same address.

Kerrville — Guadalupe Arts Alliance, 2213 San Jacinto (78028).

Killeen — Vive les Artes Society, Box 10657 (76547).

Lake Jackson — Brazosport Fine Arts Council, 400 College Dr. (77566).

Lampasas — Keystone Art Alliance, Box 1013 (76550).

Laredo — Laredo Center for the Arts, 500 San Agustin (78040).

Lewisville — Lewisville Cultural Arts Council, Box 416 (75067).

Lubbock — Lubbock Arts Alliance, Inc., 2109 Broadway (79401).

Marble Falls — Highland Lakes Arts Guild, 318 Main (78654).

Marshall — Marshall Regional Arts Council, Box C (75671).

Mesquite — Mesquite Arts Council, 1515 North Galloway (75149).

Midland — Midland Arts Assembly, Box 3494 (79702).

Monahans — Ward County Activities Council, 400 E. 4th (79756).

New Braunfels — Greater New Braunfels Arts Council, Box 311171 (78131).

Odessa — Odessa Cultural Council, Box 7195 (79760).

Pampa — Pampa Fine Arts Assn., Box 818 (79066).

Paris — Paris Area Arts Alliance, 3470 Fargo (75462).

Pasadena — Pasadena Chamber of Commerce Cultural Affairs Committee, 4334 Fairmont Parkway (77504).

Pecos — Pecos Arts Coalition, Box 2399 (79772).

Pittsburg — Pittsburg/Camp County Arts Council, Box 72 (75686).

Plains — Yoakum County Art Assn., Box 605 (79355).

Plainview — Plainview Cultural Council, Box 232 (79073).

Plano — Plano Cultural Arts Council, Box 861011 (75086).

Port Aransas — Port Aransas Council for the Arts, Box 2656 (78373).

Port Lavaca — Calhoun County Arts Council, Box 31 (77979).

Post — Caprock Cultural Assn., Box 37 (79356).

Richardson — Richardson Arts Commission, Box 830309 (75083).

Rockport — Rockport Center for the Arts, 902 Navigation Circle (78382).

San Angelo — San Angelo Cultural Affairs Council, Box 2477 (76902).

San Antonio — City of San Antonio Arts and Cultural Affairs, 222 E. Houston, Ste. 500 (78205).

San Marcos — Performing Arts Assn., Box 651 (78666).

Schulenburg — Backstage Inc. Arts Council, Box 66 (78956).

Seagoville — Seagoville Fine Arts Council, 2403 Seagoville Rd. (75159).

Sherman — Council for the Arts and Humanities, Box 1029 (75091).

Silsbee — Performing and Visual Arts Council, 415 W. Ave. N (77656).

Snyder — Snyder Cultural Affairs Council, Box 1072 (79550).

South Padre Island — Area Funds Foundation, Box 2326 (78597).

Stephenville — Cross Timbers Fine Arts Council, Box 1172 (76401).

Temple — Temple Cultural Activities Center, 3011 N. Third (76501).

Texarkana — Texarkana Regional Arts and Humanities Council Inc., Box 1171 (75504).

The Woodlands — The Woodlands Living Arts Council, Box 7411 (77387).

Tomball — Regional Arts Center, Box 1569 (77377).

Uvalde — Uvalde Arts Council, 104 W. North (78801).

Vernon — Vernon Council of the Arts, Box 222 (76384).

Victoria — Cultural Council of Victoria, Box 1758 (77902).

Waco — Greater Waco Council for the Arts, 3115 Pine, Ste. 202 (76706).

Waxahachie — Waxahachie Arts Council, 311 Olive (75165).

Wimberly — Wimberley Institute of Cultures, Box 167 (78676).

Wichita Falls — Wichita Falls Arts Commission, 607 Tenth (76301). ☆

Texas Institute of Letters Awards

Each year since 1939, the **Texas Institute of Letters** has chosen outstanding books that are either by Texans or about Texas subjects. Awards have been made for fiction, nonfiction, Southwest history, general information, magazine and newspaper journalism, children's books, poetry and book design. The awards for recent years are listed below:

Author: Title

1982

Allen Hannay: *Love & Other Natural Disasters*
Robert A. Caro: *The Path to Power: The Years of Lyndon Johnson*
David J. Weber: *The Mexican Frontier, 1821-1846*
Paul Burka: "The King of the Forest"
Jack Kent: *The Once-Upon-a-Time Dragon*
Ouida Sebestyen: *IOU's*
Roland E. Sodowsky: "Landlady"
Barbara and Fred Whitehead: *Journey to Pleasant Hill*
Naomi Shihab Nye: *Hugging the Jukebox*
Thomas Whitbread: *Whomp and Moonshiver*
Lon Tinkle Award: John Graves

1983

Joe Coomer: *The Decatur Road*
Michael Mewshaw: *Short Circuit*
Lawrence C. Kelly: *The Assault on Assimilation*
Albert Goldbarth: Original Light: New and Selected Poems, 1973-1983
Bryan Woolley: "Where Texas Meets the Sea"
Jack Kent: *Silly Goose*
Tim Zigal: "Curios"
Barbara and Fred Whitehead: *Clem Maverick*
Lon Tinkle Award: William Owens
Special Citation: The Texas Almanac

1984

Max Apple: *Free Agents*
Celia Morris Eckhardt: *Fanny Wright*
John Bloom and Jim Atkinson: *Evidence of Love*
William Roger Louis: *The British Empire in the Middle East, 1945-1951*
Rosemary Catacalos: *Again for the First Time*
Beverly Lowry: "So Far from the Road, So Long Until Morning"
Judith Alter: *Luke and the Van Zandt County War*
Jeff Unger: *Huck at 100*
John Davidson: "The Man Who Dreamed Luckenbach"
Drew Jubera: "To Find a Mockingbird"
George Lenox: *The Other Texas Frontier*
Lon Tinkle Award: Larry McMurtry

1985

Elizabeth W. and Robert A. Fernea: *The Arab World: Personal Encounters*
Larry McMurtry: Lonesome Dove
Darwin Payne: *Owen Wister: Chronicler of the West*
Reginald Gibbons: "Mr. Walsh's Mare"
Paula G. Paul: *Sarah, Sissy Weed and the Ships of the Desert*
C. W. Smith: "Uncle Dad"
Andrew Hudgins: *Saints and Strangers*
Walter McDonald: *Witching on Hardscrabble*
Doug Swanson: Woodrow Wilson High School (Dallas) series
Walter Horton: *Dallas Architecture, 1936-1986*
Lon Tinkle Award: Don Barthelme

Américo Paredes, novelist, folklorist and songwriter, was awarded the 1995 Lon Tinkle Award for lifetime achievement by the Texas Institute of Letters. Larry Murphy photo courtesy The University of Texas at Austin.

1986

William H. and William N. Goetzmann: *The West of the Imagination*
Rosalind Wright: *Veracruz*
Alfred W. Crosby: *Ecological Imperialism: The Biological Expansion of Europe, 900-1900*
Gail Galloway Adams: "Inside Dope"
Edward Hirsch: *Wild Gratitude*
Brenda Bell: "Life After Death"
George Lenox and Omega Clay: *The Panoramic Photography of Eugene O. Goldbeck*
Lon Tinkle Award: Elmer Kelton

1987

Beverly Lowry: *The Perfect Sonya*
Kenneth B. Ragsdale: *The Year America Discovered Texas: Centennial '36*
David Montejano: *Anglos and Mexicans in the Making of Texas 1836-1986*
Walter McDonald: *The Flying Dutchman*
Steve Barthelme: "Zorro"
Mike Cochran: "Texas Fugitives"
Robert Sherrill: "Can Miami Save Itself?"
Ruby C. Tolliver: *Muddy Banks*
Walter Horton: "Texas Wildflower Portraits"
Lon Tinkle Award: A. C. Greene

1988

William Hauptman: *Good Rockin' Tonight*
William Hauptman: "Moon Walking"
Lawrence Wright: *In the New World: Growing Up with America, 1960-1984*
Emily Fourmy Cutrer: *The Art of the Woman: The Life and Work of Elisabet Ney*
William Olsen: *The Hand of God and a Few Bright Flowers*
Evan Moore: "Cult of Terror"
Ronnie Dugger: "Voting by Computer"
David Price: *The Song of Things Begun*
Lon Tinkle Award: C. L. Sonnichsen

1989

James Magnuson: *Ghost Dancing*
Ernestine Sewell Linck and Joyce Gibson Roach: *Eats: A Folk History of Texas Foods*
Randolph B. Campbell: *An Empire for Slavery: The Peculiar Institution in Texas*
Pattiann Rogers: *Splitting and Binding*
James Hoggard: "The Scapegoat"
Lance Bertelsen: "San Pietro and the 'Art' of War"
Ilo Hiller: *Introducing Birds to Young Naturalists*
George Lennox: *Epitaphs for the Living: Words and Images in the Time of AIDS*
Lon Tinkle Award: John Edward Weems

1990

Lionel G. Garcia: *Hardscrub*

Virginia Stem Owens: *If You Do Love Old Men*
Nicolas Kanellos: *A History of Hispanic Theatre in the United States: Origins to 1940*
Daryl Jones: *Someone Going Home Late*
Frances M. Lopez-Morillas: *Behind the Curtains* (trans.)
Rick Bass: "The Legend of the Pig-Eye"
Bryan Woolley: "A Family Nightmare"
Scott McCartney: "S & Ls on Main Street"
Zinita Fowler: *The Last Innocent Summer*
Lon Tinkle Award: Marshall Terry

1991

Sarah Bird: *The Mommy Club*
Max Oelschlaeger: *The Idea of Wilderness*
Robert S. Weddle: *The French Thorn*
Andrew Hudgins: *The Never-Ending*
Lee Merrill Byrd: "Major Six Pockets"
Lawrence Wright: "The Sensual Christian"
Mike Cochran: "Profile of Pinkie Roden"
Charlotte Baker Montgomery: *The Trail North*
W. Thomas Taylor: *Self-Portrait With Birds*
Lon Tinkle Award: Margaret Cousins

1992

Cormac McCarthy: *All the Pretty Horses*
David Weber: *The Spanish Frontier in North America*
Joel Barna: *The See-Through Years: Creation and Destruction in Texas Architecture*
Susan Wood: *Campo Santo*
Christopher Middleton and Letitia Garza-Falcon: *The Andalusian Poems* (trans.)
William Cobb: "The Atmosphere of Venus"
Dudley Althaus: "The New Awakening: Breaking the Chain of Conquest in Latin America"
Dudley Althaus: *Prayers, Death and Angels: A Day in Baidoa*
Sherry Garland: *Song of the Buffalo Boy*
D. J. Stout: *Mojo*
Lon Tinkle Award: Vassar Miller

1993

Dagoberto Gilb: *The Magic of Blood*
Howard Swindle: *Deliberate Indifference*
William H. Goetzmann: *Sam Chamberlain's Mexican War: The San Jacinto Museum Paintings*
Jack Myers: *Blindsided*
Lee Merrill Byrd: *My Sister Disappears*
Dagoberto Gilb: "Nancy Flores"
Elizabeth Franklin: "The Quest of a Projects Kid"
Denise Gamino: "The Lost Children"
W. Thomas Taylor: *Audubon's Great National Work: The Royal Octavo Edition of The Birds of America*
Dee Stuart: *The Astonishing Armadillo*
Lon Tinkle Award: Horton Foote

1994

Reginald Gibbons: *Sweetbitter*
Lawrence Wright: *Remembering Satan*
Ron Tyler: *Prints of the West*
Pattiann Rogers: *Firekeeper*
Donley Watt: *Can You Get THere From Here?*
William J. Cobb: " White Circles"
Mimi Swartz: "Promised Land"
Dr. Bertie Acker: *Iphigenia* (trans.)
Florence George Graves: "The Other Woman"
W. Thomas Taylor: *The War Between the United States and Mexico*
Barbara Elmore: *Breathing Room*
Lon Tinkle Award: Américo Paredes ☆

Public Libraries in Texas

The following information on Texas Public Libraries was furnished by Mark L. Smith of the Library Development Division of the Texas State Library, Austin.

Public libraries provide Texans with access to information and recreational reading materials in traditional print and audio-visual formats, and in electronic formats such, as CD-ROM databases and the Internet, as well.

During 1993, the latest year for which libraries have reported data to the Texas State Library, Texans logged 43,878,232 visits to their local public libraries, checking out a total of 71,523,911 books and other items, the equivalent of 4.54 items for each resident of the state. They also asked 16,168,982 reference questions, both in person and by telephone. Four million persons, mostly children, also attended special programs, such as story hours, puppet shows and summer reading-club activities.

Libraries received only a modest increase in financial support from local governments. Total local library income increased by about 3.2% from 1992 to 1993. Texas public libraries spent $11.15 per capita during 1993, which is significantly lower than the 1992 national average of $18.73 per capita and lower than all but eight other states. The $1.67 spent for books and other library materials per capita in Texas ranked the state 43rd in the nation in materials expenditures. In addition to local sources, the state of Texas spent approximately 31 cents per capita to assist public libraries through 10 cooperative public-library systems statewide.

Current levels of support for public libraries are inadequate to meet the information needs of a growing, better-educated and increasingly industrial state. Of the 499 public libraries in Texas, 29 were unable to meet minimum criteria for accreditation by the Texas State Library. Over 1.2 million Texans are unserved by any library, a figure that continues to grow each year. Approximately 2.3 million Texans are served by libraries with no professionally trained librarians, and nine communities in the state pay their head librarian only a token $1 per year to run the library.

Urban libraries face additional challenges of unserved outlying areas, aging central facilities, growing service demands of new residents, and a pace of demographic change that tends to outstrip the ability of the library's collection and services to meet user needs.

The following table lists all public libraries in Texas as of 1993, along with statistics on two of the most important services provided to citizens: circulation of library materials and reference questions asked. A zero indicates that the information was not available.

Public Libraries by County

Below are listed the numbers of public libraries by county and city in Texas, with the numbers of materials circulated and the numbers of inquiries answered during the year 1993.

County, Number of Libraries / Towns with Libraries	Materials Circulated	Inquiries Answered
Anderson, 2	**119,125**	**16,876**
Frankston	9,981	560
Palestine	109,144	16,316
Andrews, 1	**56,614**	**9,360**
Andrews	56,614	9,360
Angelina, 2	**137,916**	**13,790**
Diboll	41,644	59
Lufkin	96,272	13,191
Aransas, 1	**84,745**	**2,993**
Rockport	84,745	2,993
Archer, 1	**15,500**	**800**
Archer City	15,500	800
Armstrong, 1	**763**	**0**
Claude	763	0
Atascosa, 5	**84,312**	**7,397**
Charlotte	3,285	31
Jourdanton	18,325	1,322
Lytle	18,954	354
Pleasanton	33,827	3,550
Poteet	9,921	2,140
Austin, 3	**111,878**	**3,488**
Bellville	58,283	1,395
Sealy	31,886	1,865
Wallis	21,709	228
Bailey, 1	**42,427**	**2,148**
Muleshoe	42,427	2,148
Bandera, 1	**41,092**	**735**
Bandera	41,092	735
Bastrop, 3	**135,148**	**13,794**
Bastrop	83,941	3,714
Elgin	10,149	2,000
Smithville	41,058	8,080
Baylor, 1	**7,587**	**1,832**
Seymour	7,587	1,832
Bee, 1	**44,314**	**10,038**
Beeville	44,314	10,038
Bell, 6	**561,385**	**64,284**
Bartlett	12,568	1,525
Belton	38,736	2,600
Harker Heights	53,500	7,300
Killeen	140,041	30,897
Temple	310,040	21,942
Salado	6,500	20
Bexar, 4	**3,448,078**	**913,092**
Converse	1,824	500
Leon Valley	64,406	18,420
San Antonio	3,347,472	889,666
Universal City	34,376	4,506
Blanco, 2	**22,858**	**342**
Blanco	13,876	72
Johnson City	8,982	270
Bowie, 4	**252,226**	**24,032**
Hooks	4,040	326
Maud	9,773	526
New Boston	28,605	3,455
Texarkana	209,808	19,725
Brazoria, 1	**1,198,283**	**56,248**
Angleton	1,198,283	56,248
Brazos, 1	**440,552**	**34,085**
Bryan	440,552	34,085
Brewster, 1	**52,123**	**2,711**
Alpine	52,123	2,711
Briscoe, 2	**3,154**	**24**
Silverton	629	0
Quitaque	2,525	24
Brooks, 1	**56,280**	**8,091**
Falfurrias	56,280	8,091
Brown, 1	**87,144**	**3,500**
Brownwood	37,144	3,500
Burleson, 1	**18,741**	**230**
Caldwell	18,741	230
Burnet, 1	**211,635**	**28,109**
Burnet	211,635	28,109
Caldwell, 2	**88,569**	**4,048**
Lockhart	53,174	3,210
Luling	35,295	838
Calhoun, 1	**81,390**	**2,825**
Port Lavaca	81,390	2,825
Callahan, 3	**18,265**	**1,257**
Baird	3,522	190
Clyde	6,712	67
Cross Plains	8,031	1,000
Cameron, 8	**419,503**	**63,573**
Brownsville	113,988	25,350
Harlingen	184,800	22,837
La Feria	23,061	3,738
Laguna Vista	2,556	0
Los Fresnos	24,663	2,500
Port Isabel	14,300	5,600
Rio Hondo	7,556	136
San Benito	48,579	3,412
Camp, 1	**47,490**	**505**
Pittsburg	47,490	505
Carson, 1	**65,377**	**5,439**
Panhandle	65,377	5,439
Cass, 1	**31,998**	**5,204**
Atlanta	31,998	5,204
Castro, 1	**50,827**	**2,478**
Dimmitt	50,827	2,478
Chambers, 1	**137,470**	**7,616**
Anahuac	137,470	7,616
Cherokee, 3	**106,311**	**6,705**
Alto	3,629	203
Jacksonville	87,572	5,942
Rusk	15,110	1,460
Childress, 1	**16,128**	**565**
Childress	16,128	565
Clay, 1	**42,278**	**2,466**
Henrietta	42,278	2,466
Cochran, 1	**6,199**	**370**
Morton	6,199	370
Coke, 1	**5,745**	**100**
Robert Lee	5,745	100
Coleman, 1	**39,509**	**946**
Coleman	39,509	946
Collin, 6	**1,890,019**	**187,952**
Allen	146,583	9,734
Celina	4,384	4,004
Farmersville	22,609	2,366
McKinney	158,012	29,515
Plano	1,510,560	141,312
Wylie	47,871	1,021
Collingsworth, 1	**18,677**	**941**
Wellington	18,677	941
Colorado, 4	**109,205**	**4,089**
Columbus	49,731	1,500
Eagle Lake	31,135	1,470
Sheridan	1,646	30
Weimar	26,693	1,089
Comal, 3	**209,829**	**8,041**
Bulverde	7,671	149
Canyon Lake	25,511	280
New Braunfels	176,647	7,612
Comanche, 2	**29,361**	**6,815**
Comanche	19,021	6,500
DeLeon	10,340	315
Concho, 1	**3,686**	**28**
Eden	3,686	28
Cooke, 2	**165,382**	**18,570**
Gainesville	146,072	18,139
Muenster	19,310	431
Coryell, 2	**165,135**	**6,800**
Copperas Cove	124,160	6,800
Gatesville	40,975	0

County, Number of Libraries Towns with Libraries	Materials Circulated	Inquiries Answered
Cottle, 1	**8,671**	**30**
Paducah	8,671	30
Crane, 1	**26,000**	**3,000**
Crane	26,000	3,000
Crockett, 1	**25,436**	**328**
Ozona	25,436	328
Crosby, 1	**33,071**	**1,889**
Crosbyton	33,071	1,889
Culberson, 1	**7,143**	**686**
Van Horn	7,143	686
Dallam, 2	**25,099**	**1,874**
Dalhart	23,764	1,812
Texline	1,335	62
Dallas, 23	**9,355,491**	**2,553,201**
Balch Springs	41,280	3,678
Carrollton	578,984	58,055
Cedar Hill	80,580	10,709
Cockrell Hill	1,713	50
Coppell	136,730	4,618
Dallas	4,191,263	1,749,923
Highland Park	121,330	912
DeSoto	143,674	20,605
Duncanville	204,253	28,089
Farmers Branch	263,615	55,515
Garland	975,765	156,736
Grand Prairie	330,449	22,938
Hutchins	4,000	200
Irving	996,818	181,159
Lancaster	64,743	7,895
Mesquite	456,687	115,288
Richardson	558,126	131,375
Rowlett	127,137	2,708
Sachse	28,396	0
Seagoville	23,164	172
Sunnyvale	14,653	176
Wilmer	12,131	2,400
Dawson, 1	**160,519**	**13,807**
Lamesa	160,519	13,807
Deaf Smith, 1	**92,172**	**1,002**
Hereford	92,172	1,002
Delta, 1	**13,546**	**1,025**
Cooper	13,546	1,025
Denton, 11	**1,089,273**	**115,618**
Aubrey	11,280	2,400
Denton	567,268	69,533
Flower Mound	75,099	1,756
Justin	7,565	0
Krum	9,329	161
Lake Dallas	34,938	1,022
Lewisville	380,097	25,738
Pilot Point	32,987	529
Roanoke	6,843	720
Sanger	17,569	550
The Colony	87,298	13,209
DeWitt, 3	**73,986**	**5,583**
Cuero	38,215	2,725
Yoakum	21,682	2,338
Yorktown	14,089	520
Dickens, 1	**7,076**	**300**
Spur	7,076	300
Dimmit, 1	**16,789**	**1,505**
Carrizo Springs	16,789	1,505
Donley, 1	**26,393**	**1,187**
Clarendon	26,393	1,187
Eastland, 2	**18,412**	**1,146**
Cisco	6,342	400
Eastland	12,070	746
Ector, 1	**364,566**	**36,989**
Odessa	364,566	36,989
Edwards, 2	**12,953**	**403**
Barksdale	12,000	400
Rocksprings	953	3
El Paso, 2	**1,663,248**	**250,268**
El Paso	1,623,722	249,143
Fabens	39,526	1,125
Ellis, 4	**352,050**	**13,971**
Ennis	88,836	2,473
Ferris	15,932	100
Midlothian	35,713	1,007

County, Number of Libraries Towns with Libraries	Materials Circulated	Inquiries Answered
Waxahachie	211,569	10,391
Erath, 2	**78,430**	**3,946**
Dublin	9,070	46
Stephenville	69,360	3,900
Falls, 1	**14,889**	**1,000**
Marlin	14,889	1,000
Fannin, 3	**81,196**	**6,026**
Bonham	58,076	5,640
Honey Grove	14,601	111
Leonard	8,519	275
Fayette, 3	**67,350**	**2,316**
Flatonia	3,500	30
La Grange	47,981	800
Schulenburg	15,869	1,486
Fisher, 1	**7,721**	**468**
Rotan	7,721	468
Floyd, 1	**14,495**	**1,000**
Floydada	14,495	1,000
Foard, 1	**26,797**	**650**
Crowell	26,797	650
Fort Bend, 1	**1,319,974**	**209,397**
Richmond	1,319,974	209,397
Franklin, 1	**53,548**	**8,400**
Mt. Vernon	53,548	8,400
Freestone, 2	**81,437**	**9,789**
Fairfield	37,045	5,487
Teague	44,392	4,302
Frio, 1	**34,300**	**1,450**
Pearsall	34,300	1,450
Gaines, 1	**49,635**	**2,794**
Seminole	49,635	2,794
Galveston, 8	**1,168,146**	**130,212**
Dickinson	72,586	8,102
Friendswood	187,290	11,100
Galveston	264,233	38,503
Hitchcock	26,098	952
La Marque	36,599	2,364
League City	334,761	45,636
Santa Fe	32,302	568
Texas City	214,277	22,987
Garza, 1	**17,304**	**852**
Post	17,304	852
Gillespie, 1	**89,920**	**7,754**
Fredericksburg	89,920	7,754
Goliad, 1	**24,052**	**850**
Goliad	24,052	850
Gonzales, 2	**3,474**	**2,580**
Smiley	1,324	80
Waelder	3,260	2,500
Gray, 2	**119,796**	**12,868**
McLean	18,870	368
Pampa	100,926	12,500
Grayson, 7	**598,126**	**109,374**
Denison	200,930	26,177
Howe	38,550	49,438
Pottsboro	5,631	388
Sherman	279,242	31,221
Van Alstyne	16,363	129
Whitesboro	36,506	1,671
Whitewright	20,904	350
Gregg, 3	**368,769**	**44,764**
Gladewater	44,944	4,500
Kilgore	65,428	7,500
Longview	258,397	32,764
Grimes, 1	**57,816**	**950**
Navasota	57,816	950
Guadalupe, 3	**227,429**	**24,799**
Marion	28,301	1,432
Schertz	80,216	11,789
Seguin	118,912	11,578
Hale, 4	**101,598**	**9,492**
Abernathy	4,453	335
Hale Center	9,286	57
Petersburg	6,611	100
Plainview	81,248	9,000
Hall, 1	**8,398**	**1,003**
Memphis	8,398	1,003
Hamilton, 1	**22,506**	**179**
Hamilton	22,506	179

County, Number of Libraries Towns with Libraries	Materials Circulated	Inquiries Answered
Hansford, 2	**43,587**	**2,701**
Gruver	3,941	74
Spearman	39,646	2,627
Hardeman, 1	**15,415**	**673**
Quanah	15,415	673
Hardin, 5	**127,832**	**7,487**
Kountze	33,843	2,690
Lumberton	6,262	75
Silsbee	71,193	3,944
Sour Lake	10,534	775
Village Mills	6,000	3
Harris, 6	**12,726,737**	**4,820,682**
Baytown	710,532	32,178
Bellaire	160,301	5,747
Deer Park	140,183	8,423
Houston	6,431,171	4,273,777
Harris County	4,760,763	462,898
Pasadena	532,787	37,659
Harrison, 1	**118,497**	**34,000**
Marshall	118,497	34,000
Haskell, 1	**12,093**	**320**
Haskell	12,093	320
Hays, 5	**273,642**	**33,712**
Buda	17,007	825
Dripping Springs	10,913	1,145
Kyle	8,585	675
San Marcos	220,112	30,909
Wimberley	17,025	158
Hemphill, 1	**45,720**	**2,178**
Canadian	45,720	2,178
Henderson, 2	**137,377**	**12,748**
Athens	105,058	9,536
Malakoff	32,319	3,212
Hidalgo, 9	**1,177,466**	**384,770**
Alamo	26,039	8,088
Donna	30,195	17,605
Edinburg	85,597	11,913
Elsa	52,315	1,613
McAllen	565,868	262,300
Mercedes	67,725	5,730
Mission	106,928	45,695
Pharr	90,052	9,961
Weslaco	152,747	21,865
Hill, 3	**39,738**	**25,000**
Hillsboro	28,712	25,000
Mount Calm	4,059	612
Whitney	6,967	569
Hockley, 1	**67,962**	**2,975**
Levelland	67,962	2,975
Hood, 1	**80,601**	**18,000**
Granbury	80,601	18,000
Hopkins, 1	**46,465**	**3,514**
Sulphur Springs	46,465	3,514
Houston, 1	**29,655**	**0**
Crockett	29,655	0
Howard, 1	**166,042**	**21,341**
Big Spring	166,042	21,341
Hudspeth, 2	**12,114**	**345**
Dell City	11,014	200
Fort Hancock	1,100	145
Hunt, 4	**119,737**	**15,874**
Commerce	21,243	820
Greenville	73,066	13,529
Quinlan	19,401	1,238
Wolfe City	6,027	287
Hutchinson, 1	**90,268**	**6,297**
Borger	90,268	6,297
Irion, 1	**1,300**	**100**
Mertzon	1,300	100
Jack, 1	**37,361**	**425**
Jacksboro	37,361	425
Jackson, 1	**37,501**	**1,431**
Edna	37,501	1,431
Jasper, 3	**129,140**	**7,293**
Buna	29,762	976
Jasper	67,889	1,718
Kirbyville	31,489	4,599
Jeff Davis, 1	**18, 831**	**51**
Fort Davis	18,831	51
Jefferson, 6	**915,695**	**118,200**
Beaumont	349,694	71,381
Groves	65,453	12,076
Jefferson County	91,191	2,364
Nederland	113,683	13,509
Port Arthur	225,286	14,521
Port Neches	70,388	4,349
Jim Hogg, 1	**7,010**	**631**
Hebbronville	7,010	631
Jim Wells, 1	**330,196**	**10,803**
Alice	330,196	10,803
Johnson, 3	**343,487**	**139,106**
Alvarado	14,897	978
Burleson	117,443	21,500
Cleburne	211,147	116,628
Jones, 2	**9,636**	**373**
Anson	4,507	173
Stamford	5,129	200
Karnes, 4	**131,012**	**3,683**
Falls City	24,482	840
Karnes City	42,827	1,953
Kenedy	41,900	306
Runge	21,803	584
Kaufman, 3	**129,903**	**33,899**
Kaufman	40,575	25,629
Mabank	12,649	2,041
Terrell	76,684	6,229
Kendall, 3	**88,426**	**5,472**
Boerne	68,943	3,988
Comfort	16,546	1,449
Kendalia	2,937	35
Kent, 1	**13,632**	**390**
Jayton	13,632	390
Kerr, 1	**222,071**	**25,082**
Kerrville	222,071	25,082
Kimble, 1	**20,926**	**1,368**
Junction	20,189	1,368
King, 1	**1,844**	**250**
Guthrie	1,844	250
Kinney, 1	**36,843**	**2,121**
Brackettville	36,843	2,121
Kleberg, 1	**81,753**	**3,638**
Kingsville	81,753	3,638
Knox, 1	**8,753**	**345**
Munday	3,753	345
La Salle, 1	**15,662**	**375**
Cotulla	15,622	375
Lamar, 1	**190,938**	**39,621**
Paris	190,938	39,621
Lamb, 2	**59,912**	**1,778**
Earth	9,720	315
Littlefield	50,192	1,463
Lampasas, 1	**37,275**	**2,637**
Lampasas	37,275	2,637
Lavaca, 1	**42,348**	**2,231**
Hallettsville	42,348	2,231
Lee, 1	**30,222**	**61**
Giddings	30,222	61
Leon, 1	**2,230**	**35**
Buffalo	2,230	35
Liberty, 3	**167,828**	**13,293**
Cleveland	38,158	6,240
Dayton	41,593	2,476
Liberty	88,077	4,577
Limestone, 2	**58,020**	**8,258**
Groesbeck	29,140	2,642
Mexia	28,880	5,616
Lipscomb, 2	**14,577**	**1,400**
Booker	9,827	300
Higgins	4,750	1,100
Live Oak, 1	**66,934**	**6,977**
George West	66,934	6,977
Llano, 1	**79,787**	**1,100**
Llano	79,787	1,100
Lubbock, 4	**622,160**	**244,062**
Idalou	9,000	900
Lubbock	599,123	242,476
Slaton	11,278	506
Wolfforth	2,759	180

County, Number of Libraries Towns with Libraries	Materials Circulated	Inquiries Answered
Lynn, 1	**6,257**	**600**
Tahoka	6,257	600
Madison, 1	**22,904**	**2,718**
Madisonville	22,904	2,718
Martin, 1	**7,657**	**0**
Stanton	7,657	0
Mason, 1	**13,011**	**620**
Mason	13,011	620
Matagorda, 2	**142,197**	**21,534**
Bay City	103,463	16,334
Palacios	38,734	5,200
Maverick, 2	**38,746**	**72,833**
Eagle Pass	32,195	72,651
Quemado	6,551	182
McCulloch, 1	**58,245**	**1,936**
Brady	58,245	1,936
McLennan, 4	**669,077**	**152,749**
Hewitt	25,889	1,970
McGregor	7,398	22
Waco	606,627	150,231
West	29,163	526
Medina, 3	**54,306**	**5,013**
Castroville	19,590	2,013
Devine	16,917	3,000
Hondo	17,799	0
Menard, 1	**13,333**	**139**
Menard	13,333	139
Midland, 1	**432,729**	**51,386**
Midland	432,729	51,386
Milam, 2	**48,713**	**5,002**
Cameron	19,000	1,379
Rockdale	29,713	3,623
Mitchell, 1	**30,773**	**1,350**
Colorado City	30,773	1,350
Montague, 2	**66,339**	**2,071**
Bowie	54,889	571
Nocona	11,450	1,500
Montgomery, 2	**626,830**	**159,655**
Conroe	577,298	157,495
Splendora	49,532	2,160
Moore, 1	**84,447**	**4,425**
Dumas	84,447	4,425
Morris, 1	**29,528**	**590**
Daingerfield	29,528	590
Motley, 1	**10,845**	**243**
Matador	10,845	243
Nacogdoches, 1	**105,598**	**4,560**
Nacogdoches	105,598	4,560
Navarro, 1	**95,991**	**4,830**
Corsicana	95,991	4,830
Newton, 1	**26,045**	**1,040**
Newton	26,045	1,040
Nolan, 1	**82,268**	**10,051**
Sweetwater	82,268	10,051
Nueces, 2	**1,416,318**	**396,192**
Corpus Christi	1,361,307	394,043
Port Aransas	55,011	2,149
Ochiltree, 1	**89,245**	**2,523**
Perryton	89,245	2,523
Oldham, 1	**4,907**	**50**
Vega	4,907	50
Orange, 3	**303,199**	**17,120**
Bridge City	14,764	1,845
Orange	198,660	13,170
Vidor	89,775	2,105
Palo Pinto, 1	**60,387**	**8,851**
Mineral Wells	60,387	8,851
Panola, 1	**111,098**	**25,726**
Carthage	111,098	25,726
Parker, 2	**339,893**	**19,853**
Aledo	3,120	0
Springtown	4,474	4,863
Weatherford	332,299	14,990
Parmer, 1	**28,494**	**1,037**
Friona	28,494	1,037
Pecos, 3	**149,875**	**20,175**
Fort Stockton	110,003	18,400
Imperial	7,000	150
Iraan	32,872	1,625

County, Number of Libraries Towns with Libraries	Materials Circulated	Inquiries Answered
Polk, 2	**112,494**	**3,654**
Corrigan	34,508	1,657
Livingston	77,986	1,997
Potter, 1	**1,441,379**	**679,306**
Amarillo	1,441,379	679,306
Presidio, 2	**35,322**	**1,582**
Marfa	29,737	1,560
Presidio	5,585	22
Rains, 1	**22,934**	**912**
Emory	22,934	912
Randall, 1	**31,844**	**678**
Amarillo	1,015	75
Canyon	30,829	603
Reagan, 1	**19,267**	**3,000**
Big Lake	19,267	3,000
Real, 1	**6,887**	**1,171**
Leakey	6,887	1,171
Red River, 1	**40,864**	**515**
Clarksville	40,864	515
Refugio, 1	**22,463**	**927**
Refugio	22,463	927
Roberts, 1	**3,773**	**0**
Miami	3,773	0
Robertson, 1	**11,653**	**1,163**
Hearne	11,653	1,163
Rockwall, 1	**88,997**	**11,534**
Rockwall	88,997	11,534
Runnels, 2	**31,467**	**1,612**
Ballinger	25,400	1,008
Winters	6,067	604
Rusk, 1	**158,429**	**59,592**
Henderson	158,429	59,592
Sabine, 1	**28,116**	**343**
Pineland	28,116	343
San Augustine, 1	**30,643**	**2,226**
San Augustine	30,643	2,226
San Jacinto, 2	**38,912**	**1,114**
Coldspring	9,182	0
Shepherd	29,730	1,114
San Patricio, 7	**206,004**	**17,426**
Aransas Pass	28,629	3,851
Ingleside	27,882	2,331
Mathis	9,968	123
Odem	2,748	171
Portland	81,507	2,096
Sinton	24,144	2,932
Taft	31,116	5,922
San Saba, 1	**15,746**	**939**
San Saba	15,746	939
Schleicher, 1	**0**	**490**
Eldorado	0	490
Scurry, 1	**95,895**	**3,612**
Snyder	95,895	3,612
Shackelford, 1	**2,400**	**25**
Albany	2,400	25
Shelby, 1	**16,832**	**770**
Center	16,832	770
Sherman, 1	**9,102**	**579**
Stratford	9,102	579
Smith, 2	**268,262**	**17,217**
Troup	9,469	535
Tyler	243,618	12,654
Whitehouse	15,175	4,028
Somervell, 1	**22,367**	**960**
Glen Rose	22,367	960
Starr, 1	**13,573**	**1,152**
Rio Grande City	13,573	1,152
Stephens, 1	**16,761**	**450**
Breckenridge	16,761	450
Sterling, 1	**5,896**	**0**
Sterling City	5,896	0
Stonewall, 1	**11,813**	**305**
Aspermont	11,813	305
Sutton, 1	**12,053**	**373**
Sonora	12,053	373
Swisher, 1	**29,210**	**1,450**
Tulia	29,210	1,450
Tarrant, 22	**7,681,880**	**1,633,839**
Arlington	1,008,212	190,424

County, Number of Libraries / Towns with Libraries	Materials Circulated	Inquiries Answered
Azle	97,912	5,714
Bedford	402,005	29,358
Blue Mound	3,280	500
Crowley	11,724	1,530
Euless	177,216	16,459
Everman	4,381	518
Forest Hill	11,673	1,902
Fort Worth	3,996,301	1,222,224
Grapevine	441,920	9,746
Haltom City	199,878	3,840
Hurst	310,282	25,380
Keller	107,300	2,000
Kennedale	2,235	1,960
Lake Worth	31,305	3,796
Mansfield	102,642	23,357
North Richland Hills	358,174	50,305
Richland Hills	69,117	11,024
River Oaks	78,610	1,495
Saginaw	66,650	4,001
Watauga	101,468	22,330
White Settlement	99,595	5,976
Taylor, 1	**433,190**	**111,055**
Abilene	433,190	111,055
Terrell, 1	**28,057**	**2,580**
Sanderson	28,057	2,580
Terry, 1	**37,728**	**2,842**
Brownfield	37,728	2,842
Titus, 1	**63,532**	**6,300**
Mt. Pleasant	63,532	6,300
Tom Green, 1	**578,085**	**56,368**
San Angelo	578,085	56,368
Travis, 4	**2,754,363**	**877,513**
Austin	2,620,871	816,429
Del Valle	2,896	900
Jonestown	1,758	24
Lake Travis	18,725	9,200
Pflugerville	24,128	560
Westbank	85,985	50,400
Trinity, 2	**34,421**	**2,571**
Groveton	7,125	135
Trinity	27,296	2,436
Tyler, 1	**185,137**	**50,204**
Woodville	185,137	50,204
Upshur, 1	**53,175**	**11,252**
Gilmer	53,175	11,252
Upton, 2	**58,487**	**7,006**
McCamey	38,647	5,800
Rankin	19,840	1,206
Uvalde, 1	**74,988**	**4,201**
Uvalde	74,988	4,201
Val Verde, 1	**107,286**	**16,634**
Del Rio	107,286	16,634
Van Zandt, 2	**153,794**	**3,050**
Canton	121,555	2,550
Grand Saline	32,239	500
Victoria, 1	**340,466**	**94,208**
Victoria	340,466	94,208
Walker, 2	**71,018**	**72,765**
Huntsville	66,160	72,750
New Waverly	4,858	15
Waller, 1	**59,217**	**5,184**
Hempstead	59,217	5,184
Ward, 1	**119,591**	**2,190**
Monahans	119,591	2,190
Washington, 1	**86,100**	**5,300**
Brenham	86,100	5,300
Webb, 1	**217,372**	**10,775**
Laredo	217,372	10,775
Wharton, 1	**218,015**	**18,876**
Wharton	218,015	18,876
Wheeler, 2	**32,658**	**2,419**
Shamrock	21,500	2,150
Wheeler	11,158	269
Wichita, 4	**384,834**	**42,497**
Burkburnett	32,239	4,729
Electra	36,735	8,100
Iowa Park	46,730	2,800
Wichita Falls	269,130	26,868
Wilbarger, 1	**60,050**	**5,751**
Vernon	60,050	5,751
Willacy, 1	**52,100**	**5,000**
Raymondville	52,100	5,000
Williamson, 6	**543,198**	**31,583**
Cedar Park	85,879	2,080
Florence	6,475	300
Georgetown	159,618	7,500
Leander	8,330	800
Round Rock	252,862	17,703
Taylor	30,034	3,200
Wilson, 1	**47,285**	**7,748**
Floresville	47,285	7,748
Winkler, 1	**56,539**	**5,104**
Kermit	56,539	5,104
Wise, 7	**168,443**	**8,459**
Alvord	15,283	775
Boyd	4,792	242
Bridgeport	49,696	5,669
Chico	11,356	140
Decatur	78,457	1,575
Newark	8,234	58
Rhome	625	0
Wood, 3	**107,293**	**5,787**
Hawkins	16,946	1,085
Quitman	37,036	601
Winnsboro	53,311	4,101
Yoakum, 2	**88,734**	**9,589**
Denver City	63,130	6,000
Plains	25,604	3,589
Young, 2	**239,048**	**14,699**
Graham	180,055	6,020
Olney	58,993	8,679
Zapata, 1	**97,428**	**1,850**
Zapata	97,428	1,850
Zavala, 1	**4,487**	**580**
Crystal City	4,487	580

There were no public libraries reported by the Texas State Library in 1993 in the following counties: Borden, Bosque, Glasscock, Hartley, Loving, Marion, McMullen, Mills and Reeves, although residents of those counties may be served by libraries in adjoining counties. ☆

"In its cultural and social development the transition of Texas of the immediate future should be more marked than its economic and political progress. Not until after the First World War was there sufficient surplus wealth, above that urgently needed for material purposes, to greatly encourage the arts. . .

"So it has been only during recent years that the library, the museum, the art gallery, the theater, the observatory, the lecture forum have begun to spring up and art, music and literature to play a considerable part in the lives of Texans. The severity of the economic depression, followed by the emergencies of the Second World War, has obstructed this development momentarily, but with the return of normal economic conditions the cultural development of Texas will go ahead as never before. The beginning of the second century of Texas' statehood undoubtedly marks also the beginning of a new chapter in the advancement of education and the arts in the state."

— *Texas Almanac, 1945-1946*

Major Film Spending in Texas Continues Rise

Information for the following article was supplied by the Texas Film Commission, a division of the Office of the Governor.

The year 1994 was Texas' best year ever for dollars spent in the state on film and television production. Texas hosted 41 major projects, including feature films, television movies, television miniseries and music videos. Those projects, along with an estimated $40 million spent in making television commercials and corporate films and videos, brought Texas' total production dollars for 1994 to a record high of $191.5 million. The previous record was set in 1994, with 44 major projects, with total budgets of $180.4 million.

Typically, half of a project's budget is spent "on location," so 1994 saw almost $96 million spent in Texas on such diverse goods and services as salaries for locally-hired technicians, actors and extras, location fees, hotel rooms, fuel, hardware, lumber, dry cleaning, security services and many others.

Among 1993's high-profile Texas projects were 29 feature films, including **A Perfect World**, starring Kevin Costner and Clint Eastwood, filmed in the Austin area, and **Bad Girls**, starring Andie McDowell and Drew Barrymore, filmed at the Alamo Village western set near Brackettville.

Among the year's 25 television projects were the hit CBS series, **Walker, Texas Ranger**, starring Chuck Norris, filmed in the Dallas area, and the ABC miniseries **Heaven and Hell: North and South, Book III**. Texas is also the permanent home of the tremendously popular PBS children's series **Barney & Friends**, which is made at the Studios at Las Colinas in Irving.

Highlights from 1994 include the NBC miniseries **A Woman of Independent Means**, starring Sally Field, made entirely in the Houston/Galveston area; the ABC miniseries **Texas Justice**, starring Heather Locklear; and the feature film **The Stars Fell on Henrietta**, starring Robert Duvall, made in Bartlett and near Abilene, and due to be released in late 1995.

Texas remains a popular choice for filmmakers because of its diverse locations; large labor pool of experienced technicians, actors and suppliers; readily available technical equipment; moderate climate; and low costs of doing business. ☆

Below is a table showing the number of major productions shot at least partially in Texas since the Texas Film Commission was established in 1971. Also listed are the gross budgets of those projects.

Year(s)	Number of Projects	Gross Budgets
1971-1979	119	$178,200,000
1980	22	99,500,000
1981	18	55,000,000
1982	13	45,700,000
1983	30	114,400,000
1984	30	89,900,000
1985	27	56,700,000
1986	27	102,100,000
1987	24	66,300,000
1988	24	93,900,000
1989	32	117,100,000
1990	31	42,100,000
1991	44	120,454,000
1992	28	143,207,800
1993	44	180,400,000
1994	41	$191,500,000
Totals	**535**	**$1,696,461,800**

Film Commissions in Texas

In addition to the following film commissions operating in Texas as of summer 1995, many chambers of commerce and convention and visitors' bureaus have employees who specialize in assisting film companies:

Texas Film Commission
Office of Music, Film, Television and Multimedia
Box 13246
Austin 78711
(512) 463-9200
Fax (512) 463-4114

Amarillo Film Office
P.O. Box 9480
Amarillo 79105
(806) 374-1497 or
(806) 692-1338

Austin Film Liaison
P.O. Box 1088
Austin 78767
(512) 499-2404
Fax (512) 499-6385

Brownsville Area Film Commission
P.O. Box 4697
Brownsville 78523
(800) 626-2639
Fax (512) 546-3972

Dallas/Fort Worth Regional Film Commission
P.O. Box 160246
DFW Airport 75261
(214) 621-0400
Fax (214) 912-9016

El Paso Film Commission
1 Civic Center Plaza
El Paso 79901
(800) 351-6024
Fax (915) 532-2963

Houston Film Commission
801 Congress
Houston 77002
(713) 523-5050
(800) 365-7575
Fax (713) 227-6336

Irving Texas Film Commission
1 Dallas Communications Complex
LB 119
6309 N. O'Connor
Irving 75039-3510
(800) 2-IRVING
Fax (214) 869-4609

San Antonio Film Commission
P.O. Box 2277
San Antonio 78298
(800) 447-3372
FAX (210) 270-8782

In San Antonio, the altar for Dia de los Muertos at San Fernando Cathedral, above, includes bread figures representing the dead. Skeletal faces look out from the altar cover. Food and place settings cover a Mexican blanket, and candles in memory of deceased loved ones burn in the background. Photo courtesy of the cathedral.

Mexican Festivals Celebrate Life, Death, Pride in Culture

Texas without Mexicans would not be Texas.

This ethnic group, called Mexican-American, Chicano, Latino, Spanish, Tejano or Hispanic, depending on the political correctness of the time, is so essential to defining Texas culture that sometimes it is impossible to separate "Tex-Mex."

Rodeo, chili, barbecue, ranch, macho, fiesta, tacos: these are words, foods and events that now belong to all Texans.

But three annual events in Texas remain distinctively Mexican: Cinco de Mayo, Fiestas Patrias and Dia de los Muertos.

Although these observances originated in Mexico, the celebrations in Texas are more a statement of cultural roots than any political or patriotic statement.

If there is a common thread, it is a proud acknowledgement of "la raza," the concept of a unique group in history, born out of the discovery of the New World and the mixing of European and native tribal civilizations.

Cinco de Mayo, the Fifth of May, celebrates the rejection of the last attempt of Europeans to rule the Mexican nation. On this day in 1862, forces loyal to President Benito Juarez, an Indian, defeated the French at the Battle of Puebla. The victorious commander, Gen. Ignacio Zaragoza, was born at Goliad in southeast Texas in 1829.

Fiestas Patrias, Sept. 16, Mexican Independence Day (celebrations begin on Sept. 15), are the anniversary of the first move to end European dominance. In 1810 Father Miguel Hidalgo gave his famed grito, or cry, at Dolores for freedom from the Spanish colonial powers.

And, Dia de los Muertos (sometimes called Dias de los Muertos), Day of the Dead, is a counterpart to the All Saints-All Souls observances on the church calendar on Nov. 1 and Nov. 2, but with a special Mexican mix of pre-Columbian pagan homage to ancestors that is combined with Catholic ritual.

Goliad honors its native son, Gen. Zaragoza, and celebrates Cinco de Mayo with an annual fiesta on the weekend closest to Cinco de Mayo. The local Zaragoza Society coordinates the celebration, which includes Mexican food and music.

San Antonio will devote three days in 1996, May 3-5, to the celebration of Cinco de Mayo. In 1997, the dates are May 2-3. Fiestas Patrias will be observed Sept. 13-15 in 1996 and Sept. 12-14 in 1997. Market Square in downtown San Antonio will be the site of the city's planned celebrations. Dia de los Muertos is observed at San Fernando Cathedral each year with an altar of the dead and a processionof photographs of recently deceased civic leaders of the local community.

Alpine schedules an annual Cabrito Cookoff on a weekend for their Cinco de Mayo celebration.

Austin draws crowds in May to the grounds of Fiesta Gardens, where flamenco dancers and Tejano musicians provide entertainment. Fiestas Patrias in September involve more than two dozen concerts held during a six-day festivity. Dia de los Muertos is marked with a special parade down Congress Avenue with low-rider vehicles, skeleton-decorated floats and ceremonial altars. The procession draws as many as 5,000 people each year.

Mexican dress marks Cinco de Mayo in Pike Park, Dallas. Almanac staff photo.

Dallas' Cinco de Mayo celebration usually includes a wreath-laying ceremony at the statue of Gen. Zaragoza in Jaycee Zaragoza Park in West Dallas. Various neighborhoods hold fiestas throughout the city.

Falfurrias holds its annual Cinco de Mayo celebrations each year at Lasater Park.

Fort Stockton has an annual observance the Saturday following the 5th of May.

Fort Worth marks Cinco de Mayo the last weekend of April. In 1996 that will be April 27-28 and in 1997 on April 25-26. The event benefits the Boys & Girls Clubs of Greater Fort Worth.

Freeport celebrates Cinco de Mayo each May, while in September the Fiestas Patrias observance is sponsored by the local chapter of the League of United Latin American Citizens (LULAC).

Grand Prairie in North Texas has a Cinco de Mayo art contest for area children. A parade, usually on the Saturday nearest May 5, starts at 14th and Main and includes the city's school bands, and ballet folklorico groups, as well as speeches and mariachi music.

In Southeast Texas, Fiestas Patrias is celebrated in **Port Arthur** on the second weekend of September. Called the Mexican Fiesta, it provides folkoric entertainment along with Mexican food and music.

Uvalde definitely mixes the two neighboring nations' destiny.

The city opens Cinco de Mayo with the raising of the U.S. flag at the Jardin de los Heros (Garden of the Heros) Park.

The cultural celebrations have been used as a fund raiser by the American Legion for more than 25 years.

FOR FURTHER READING

Carmichael, Elizabeth and Sayer, Chloë, *The Skeleton at the Feast: The Day of the Dead in Mexico*, University of Texas Press, Austin, 1991.

Carrasco, Davíd, *Religions of Mesoamerica*, Harper & Row, New York, 1990.

German Communities Offer Octoberfests After Decades of Keeping Low Profile

After Anglos, Mexican-Americans and African-Americans, the ethnic group with the largest impact on Texas has been the Germans.

By 1930, according to the U.S. Census Bureau, persons born in Germany or whose parents where born there made up a full 36 percent of "foreign white stock" in Texas. The next largest group was from Czechoslovakia at 11.5 percent.

The German-Texan culture started in 1831, when Frederick Ernst acquired land in Austin County near Industry. Within a couple of years his neighbors included other German families, such as the Klebergs, a family later to become associated with the King Ranch in South Texas.

The largest immgration of Germans came in the 1840s when the Adelsverein (The Society for the Protection of German Immigrants in Texas) organized at Biebrich on the Rhine near Mainz. It assisted thousands in coming to Central Texas and establishing such settlements as New Braunfels and Fredericksburg.

The German language was widely used in certain areas, especially Central Texas, and only began to fade from use in the 1970s. Gilbert J. Jordan, a longtime professor of German at Southern Methodist University, says that a kind of German-Texan dialect developed in the state.

Early German festivals in Texas included one grand gathering of singing societies for a "Saengerfest" and "Volkfest" in October 1853. The celebration drew settlers from throughout the state to New Braunfels, the new German center for Texas.

Ancestry groups in selected states

	Leading group	2nd leading group
California	Mexican	German
New York	German	Italian
Hawaii	Japanese	Filipino
Florida	German	Irish
New Jersey	Italian	Irish
D. of C.	Afro-Amer.	German
Mass.	Irish	English
Rhode Is.	Irish	Italian
Texas	**Mexican**	**German**

Source: U.S. Census of Population, Supplementary Reports, Detailed Ancestry Groups for States, 1990.

Octoberfest in Fredericksburg. Photo from the Convention & Visitors Bureau.

German-Texan culture faced its first challenge when many of the recent immigrants took the unpopular stand of siding with the Union cause in the Civil War.

Blending in to an English-speaking culture became especially pronounced when the United States and Germany faced off in the hostilities of World War I.

During that period the German farmers of Brandenburg in North Texas thought it politic to change the name of their community to Old Glory.

Some Texas families even changed names; Schmidts became Smiths.

The German Cemetery in Houston became Washington Cemetery.

The wave of anti-German feeling carried over into the period right after the Great War. In 1919, Gov. William Hobby vetoed appropriations for the German department at The University of Texas at Austin.

Not until the late 1950s and early 1960s did German-Texans again boldly celebrate their heritage with the emergence of annual Octoberfests in various cities and towns of the state.

The customary observance in modern Germany dates from 1810, but that was actually a re-emergence of a centuries-old Munich festival of horse races called the Scarlet Races, named after the prize ribbon.

The tradition was revived for the wedding day of Bavarian King Ludwig I and Baroness Theresa, Oct. 17. The next year, 1811, the races were coupled with an agricultural festival. Eventally, through the fame acquired by increased world tourism, the "Oktoberfest" became synonymous with German culture.

Beer, sausage, waltzes and polka bands are the things that most distinctly flavor the festivals in our state today, although jalapeño peppers and a little barbecue might fill out the Texas menu and ambience.

One of the most popular festivals occurs in **New Braunfels**, which doesn't even call its celebration an Octoberfest but rather the annual Wurstfest. It draws some 100,000 revelers annually. It began in 1961 as a one-weekend event and now runs 10 days beginning on the first Friday before the first Monday in November. In 1996 that will be Nov. 1-10.

In **Fredericksburg**, for the past 15 years, Octoberfest has been observed on the first Saturday of October. It is now a three-day event throughout the weekend, Oct. 4-6 in 1996 and Oct. 3-5 in 1997. Some 10,000 people come to enjoy German food, entertainment and arts and crafts.

For a smaller celebration, there is the **Winedale/Round Top** area of south Central Texas. The Winedale Historical Association puts on an Octoberfest the first weekend of October each year that draws some 500 people. With a more Texas flavor, the German music is mixed with bluegrass and folk to make it a real German-Texan festival.

San Antonio celebrates Octoberfest in the early part of the month with a festival at Beethoven Home.

Fort Worth devotes two weekends for its Oktoberfest held at the FortWorth/Tarrant County Convention Center.

Other cities with Octoberfests include: **Boerne, Violet, Amarillo, Kemah, Galveston, DeKalb, Grand Prairie, Arlington, Cleburne, Wichita Falls** and **Terrell.**

And, **Bryan** observes all of October as German Culture Month. ☆

FOR FURTHER READING

Biesele, Rudolph Leopold, *History of German Settlements in Texas*; German-Texan Heritage Society, San Marcos, 1930.

Jordan, Gilbert J., *German Texana*; Eakin, Burnet, Tex., 1980.

Lich, Glenn and Reeves, Dona, *German Culture in Texas*; Twayne, Boston, 1981.

State Has Religious Diversity

Religion has played an important part in Texas history from pre-Columbian times to the present day. Spanish Catholic missionaries led the initial European contact. The state's earliest inhabitants practiced their own religion, and hundreds of years before the Spanish arrived, proselytizers from the Toltec culture of central Mexico visited the El Paso area.

Even when Texas was a Mexican state and Roman Catholicism was the state religion, Protestant ministers conducted clandestine — and some open — services. In the years immediately preceeding Texas' independence, Mexican officials often looked the other way when Protestants preached, as long as they did not stir up trouble.

Protestantism was spread by circuit preachers sponsored by specific denominations, like the Methodists and Baptists, and by itinerant ministers representing no specific denominations.

Religion played a major role in the social life of the settlers in rural areas. Institutions like camp meetings developed, which attracted people for several days of preaching, praying and singing, accompanied by communal meals.

Often these were the only real social events in thinly populated areas and were popular for both their spiritual and social benefits. The Bloys Camp Meeting, begun in 1890 by Presbyterian minister W.B. Bloys and still held each summer near Fort Davis in West Texas, is a remnant of that period.

Perhaps because of its great size, Texas has more churches than any other state, with almost 17,000. This is almost 2,500 more than second-place California. Texas also has the most members with 5,282,341 *(see chart below.)*

Texas has long been considered a strong link in the Bible Belt that was thought to run westward from North Carolina through Texas.

Dale Jones, a Church of the Nazarene researcher, sees Texas more as a pivot. Mr. Jones believes that Texas stands at the intersection of two swaths of high church-membership areas. One runs from North Carolina into Texas, and the other extends between North Dakota and Texas.

Rural counties still maintain higher church membership and participation than the metropolitan and urban areas.

On the following two pages, the study from which the numbers presented here were taken was published by the Glenmary Research Center, a Catholic agency, of Atlanta, Ga., and the figures have been reprinted here by permission of the center.

The Church of the Nazarene International Headquarters in Kansas City, Mo., collected the data and prepared the information.

The data were compiled from reports from 133 church bodies. The study was sponsored by the Association of Statisticians of American Religious Bodies.

"**Members**" in this study includes only communicant, confirmed members with full membership status.

"**Adherents**" are defined as all members, including regular participants who are not considered as communicant . . . (but) "the baptized."

Roman Catholics are the largest group in Texas with 3.6 million adherents.

The largest Protestant group is the Southern Baptist Convention with 3.3 million adherents.

The Jewish estimate in the study was made by Jewish Federations in local communities.

This study encompasses only Judeo-Christian denominations and religions. With the influx of immigrants from Asia, particularly since the Vietnam War, Eastern religions have flourished in Texas as in the rest of the United States. But such religious groups as Buddhists, Muslims and Hindus were not counted.

Black Baptist churches were included in the study for the first time in 1990, registering 635,179 members, or 4.8 percent of the state total. The specific number of Black Baptist churches was not reported.

A listing follows showing the percentage of the total population of each county that is associated with organized religious groups, i.e. "adherents."

(For more information on the methodology employed in the Glenmary Research Center study, see the report, "Churches and Church Membership in the United States, 1990.")

Texas Leads the Nation in Number of Churches, Members

State	Churches	Members	% Members*	% Adherents*
Texas	16,961	5,282,341	31.10	64.1
California	14,427	2,752,215	9.30	42.3
Pennsylvania	13,284	2,471,624	20.80	61.4
North Carolina	11,331	3,004,855	45.30	60.0
Ohio	11,086	2,278,892	21.01	50.1
New York	10,878	1,974,175	11.07	65.7

** Church membership/adherents as percentage of the 1990 population as counted by the U.S. Bureau of the Census.*
Source: Glenmary Research Center, Atlanta, Ga.

Religious Groups, Members/Adherents, In Texas, 1990

Religious Group	Members	Adherents
Advent Christian Church	172	221
African Methodist Episcopal Zion	1,842	2,191
American Baptist Churches in the USA	10,046	12,905
Apostolic Christian Churches of America	8	13
Assemblies of God	146,688	202,082
Baptist General Conference	218	278
Baptist Missionary Association of America	98,509	125,323
Beachy Amish Mennonite Churches	56	70
Brethren In Christ Church	53	73
Catholic Church	NA	3,574,728
Christ Catholic Church	3	3
Christian & Missionary Alliance, The	1,605	3,082
Christian Church (Disciples of Christ)	74,098	105,495
Christian Churches & Churches of Christ	26,012	33,766
Christian Reformed Church	528	866
Church of Christ, Scientist	NR	NR
Church of God General Conference, Abrahamic Faith	71	93
Church of God (Anderson, Ind.)	4,218	5,854
Church of God (Cleveland, Tenn.)	21,728	27,828
Church of God (Seventh Day) Denver, Col., The	1,243	1,743
Church of God in Christ (Mennonite)	406	522
Church of God of Prophecy	2,251	2,918
Church of Jesus Christ of Latter -Day Saints (Mormon)	NA	111,276
Church of the Brethren	235	302
Church of the Lutheran Brethren of America	36	71
Church of the Lutheran Confession	107	144
Church of the Nazarene	31,163	45,097
Churches of Christ	292,585	380,948
Congregational Christian Churches, National Association of	556	721
Congregational Christian Churches (Not part of any national CCC body)	18	23
Conservative Baptist Association of America	NR	NR
Conservative Congregational Christian Conference	81	104
Cumberland Presbyterian Church	9,177	10,373
Episcopal Church, The	127,315	169,112
Evangelical Free Church of America, The	2,772	5,463
Evangelical Lutheran Church in America	120,004	155,276
Evangelical Lutheran Synod	119	146
Evangelical Bible Churches, Fellowship of (was Ev. Mennonite Bre., Inc.)	18	20
Evangelical Methodist Church	1,154	1,482
Evangelical Presbyterian Church	473	490
Free Lutheran Congregations, The Association of	115	144
Free Methodist Church of North America	549	886
Free Will Baptist, National Association of, Inc.	3,883	4,936
Friends (Quakers)	1,853	2,548
General Conference of Mennonite Brethren Churches	236	329
Greek Orthodox Archdiocese of North and South America	NR	NR
Holy Apostolic Catholic Assyrian Church of the East	70	282
Independent Fundamental Churches of America	NR	NR
International Church of the Foursquare Gospel	3,286	4,278
Interstate & Foreign Landmark Missionary Baptists Association	59	76
Lutheran Church—Missouri Synod, The	99,974	134,280
Mennonite Church	673	1,012
Eastern Pennsylvania Mennonite Church	30	39
Mennonite Church, The General Conference	172	216
North American Baptist Conference	1,262	1,634
Old Order Amish Church	NA	400

Religious Groups, Members/Adherents, In Texas, 1990

Religious Group	Members	Adherents
Open Bible Standard Churches, Inc.	NR	NR
Orthodox Church in America	NR	NR
Pentecostal Church of God	6,477	12,296
Pentecostal Holiness Church, Inc.	4,221	5,517
Christian (Plymouth) Brethren	4,225	6,766
Presbyterian Church (USA)	156,155	200,969
Presbyterian Church in America	4,221	5,445
Primitive Baptists Associations	1,977	2,544
Reformed Church in America	760	1,592
Reformed Episcopal Church	71	115
Romanian Orthodox Episcopate of America	NR	NR
Salvation Army, The	5,257	5,676
Seventh-Day Adventists	31,985	41,470
Seventh Day Baptist General Conference	190	242
Southern Baptist Convention	2,538,245	3,259,395
Syrian Orthodox Church of Antioch (Archdiocese of the USA and Canada)	NA	1,800
Two-Seed-in-the-Spirit Predestinarian Baptists	42	53
Unitarian Universalist Association	4,440	5,843
United Church of Christ	16,321	20,950
United Methodist Church, The	781,389	1,004,318
Wesleyan Church, The	329	892
Wisconsin Evangelical Lutheran Synod	3,117	4,463
Jewish Estimate	NA	107,980
Black Baptists Estimate	635,179	815,771
Independent, Charismatic Churches	NA	127,850
Independent Non-Charismatic Churches	NA	132,292
Statewide Totals	**5,282,341**	**10,896,401**

Source: Glenmary Research Center, Atlanta, Ga.

Religious Population of Texas by County, 1990

Listed below is percentage of residents who are counted as adherents to any group. More than 100 percent results from census undercount or church overcount. The last column names the largest group in the county; abbreviations are explained at end of table.

County	% of total pop.	Largest group
Anderson	54.8	S.BAPT.
Andrews	76.6	S.BAPT.
Angelina	68.3	S.BAPT.
Aransas	43.7	R.C.
Archer	78.0	S.BAPT.
Armstrong	78.0	S.BAPT.
Atascosa	65.3	R.C.
Austin	71.8	R.C.
Bailey	74.7	S.BAPT.
Bandera	49.2	R.C.
Bastrop	46.1	S.BAPT.
Baylor	106.0	S.BAPT.
Bee	64.3	R.C.
Bell	49.7	S.BAPT.
Bexar	64.9	R.C.
Blanco	59.2	S.BAPT.
Borden	26.9	S.BAPT.
Bosque	74.0	S.BAPT.
Bowie	68.3	S.BAPT.
Brazoria	62.0	S.BAPT.
Brazos	49.6	R.C.
Brewster	91.4	R.C.
Briscoe	82.0	S.BAPT.
Brooks	76.7	R.C.
Brown	73.0	S.BAPT.
Burleson	60.2	S.BAPT.
Burnet	57.2	S.BAPT.
Caldwell	52.1	S.BAPT.
Calhoun	98.7	R.C.
Callahan	67.6	S.BAPT.
Cameron	95.5	R.C.
Camp	82.1	S.BAPT.
Carson	93.8	S.BAPT.
Cass	71.0	S.BAPT.
Castro	112.5	R.C.
Chambers	59.4	S.BAPT.
Cherokee	64.7	S.BAPT.
Childress	96.0	S.BAPT.
Clay	76.9	S.BAPT.
Cochran	109.7	S.BAPT.
Coke	84.0	S.BAPT.
Coleman	67.7	S.BAPT.
Collin	45.0	S.BAPT.
Collingsworth	81.4	S.BAPT.
Colorado	103.7	R.C.
Comal	58.6	R.C.
Comanche	63.8	S.BAPT.
Concho	58.5	S.BAPT.
Cooke	68.1	S.BAPT.
Coryell	46.9	S.BAPT.
Cottle	125.1	S.BAPT.
Crane	70.1	S.BAPT.
Crockett	82.7	S.BAPT.
Crosby	75.4	S.BAPT.
Culberson	101.1	R.C.
Dallam	118.7	S.BAPT.
Dallas	60.3	S.BAPT.
Dawson	100.3	S.BAPT.
Deaf Smith	84.4	R.C.
Delta	76.1	S.BAPT.
Denton	37.7	S.BAPT.
DeWitt	80.9	R.C.
Dickens	110.0	S.BAPT.

County	% of total pop.	Largest group
Dimmit	81.0	R.C.
Donley	77.0	S.BAPT.
Duval	75.3	R.C.
Eastland	81.2	S.BAPT.
Ector	64.2	S.BAPT.
Edwards	97.5	R.C.
Ellis	67.3	S.BAPT.
El Paso	82.3	R.C.
Erath	68.0	S.BAPT.
Falls	73.8	S.BAPT.
Fannin	75.7	S.BAPT.
Fayette	91.5	R.C.
Fisher	90.3	S.BAPT.
Floyd	124.3	S.BAPT.
Foard	102.4	S.BAPT.
Fort Bend	44.5	R.C.
Franklin	78.1	S.BAPT.
Freestone	68.1	S.BAPT.
Frio	84.9	R.C.
Gaines	87.2	S.BAPT.
Galveston	51.1	S.BAPT.
Garza	65.7	S.BAPT.
Gillespie	66.9	LUTH.
Glasscock	61.5	R.C.
Goliad	72.2	R.C.
Gonzales	71.4	S.BAPT.
Gray	86.9	S.BAPT.
Grayson	72.3	S.BAPT.
Gregg	83.4	S.BAPT.
Grimes	63.0	S.BAPT.
Guadalupe	48.0	R.C.
Hale	94.4	S.BAPT.
Hall	112.3	S.BAPT.
Hamilton	72.5	S.BAPT.
Hansford	88.0	S.BAPT.
Hardeman	89.3	S.BAPT.
Hardin	69.4	S.BAPT.
Harris	58.3	R.C.
Harrison	61.6	S.BAPT.
Hartley	44.6	METH.
Haskell	109.5	S.BAPT.
Hays	42.7	S.BAPT.
Hemphill	78.5	S.BAPT.
Henderson	48.0	S.BAPT.
Hidalgo	94.1	R.C.
Hill	65.6	S.BAPT.
Hockley	75.6	S.BAPT.
Hood	50.5	S.BAPT.
Hopkins	74.8	S.BAPT.
Houston	68.9	S.BAPT.
Howard	82.3	S.BAPT.
Hudspeth	84.6	R.C.
Hunt	62.6	S.BAPT.
Hutchinson	83.0	S.BAPT.
Irion	74.4	S.BAPT.
Jack	87.2	S.BAPT.
Jackson	72.1	S.BAPT.
Jasper	71.9	S.BAPT.
Jeff Davis	109.0	R.C.
Jefferson	78.5	R.C.
Jim Hogg	90.8	R.C.
Jim Wells	84.5	R.C.
Johnson	57.9	S.BAPT.
Jones	78.9	S.BAPT.
Karnes	91.3	R.C.
Kaufman	63.4	S.BAPT.
Kendall	65.6	R.C.
Kenedy	95.7	R.C.
Kent	95.7	S.BAPT.
Kerr	49.3	S.BAPT.
Kimble	65.5	S.BAPT.
King	68.4	S.BAPT.
Kinney	69.6	R.C.
Kleberg	82.2	R.C.
Knox	110.8	S.BAPT.
Lamar	69.1	S.BAPT.
Lamb	88.0	S.BAPT.
Lampasas	76.6	S.BAPT.
La Salle	110.7	R.C.
Lavaca	85.5	R.C.
Lee	69.3	LUTH.
Leon	70.3	S.BAPT.
Liberty	70.9	S.BAPT.
Limestone	62.1	S.BAPT.
Lipscomb	98.4	S.BAPT.
Live Oak	81.9	R.C.
Llano	62.3	S.BAPT.
Loving	0	0
Lubbock	65.8	S.BAPT.
Lynn	93.3	S.BAPT.
McCulloch	70.0	S.BAPT.
McLennan	73.6	S.BAPT.
McMullen	47.0	S.BAPT.
Madison	62.5	S.BAPT.
Marion	61.3	S.BAPT.
Martin	71.5	S.BAPT.
Mason	70.8	METH.
Matagorda	74.7	R.C.
Maverick	84.5	R.C.
Medina	75.2	R.C.
Menard	94.3	S.BAPT.
Midland	70.0	S.BAPT.
Milam	66.6	S.BAPT.
Mills	82.7	S.BAPT.
Mitchell	78.9	S.BAPT.
Montague	66.8	S.BAPT.
Montgomery	47.9	S.BAPT.
Moore	65.4	S.BAPT.
Morris	69.4	S.BAPT.
Motley	94.3	S.BAPT.
Nacogdoches	52.6	S.BAPT.
Navarro	68.5	S.BAPT.
Newton	47.9	S.BAPT.
Nolan	90.0	S.BAPT.
Nueces	74.6	R.C.
Ochiltree	69.1	S.BAPT.
Oldham	71.6	S.BAPT.
Orange	75.2	S.BAPT.
Palo Pinto	69.3	S.BAPT.
Panola	56.4	S.BAPT.
Parker	54.9	S.BAPT.
Parmer	65.6	S.BAPT.
Pecos	55.1	S.BAPT.
Polk	60.7	S.BAPT.
Potter	100.6	S.BAPT.
Presidio	80.0	R.C.
Rains	59.8	S.BAPT.
Randall	40.8	S.BAPT.
Reagan	70.6	S.BAPT.
Real	78.6	S.BAPT.
Red River	57.4	S.BAPT.
Reeves	127.5	R.C.
Refugio	100.2	R.C.
Roberts	141.6	CHR/CH
Robertson	68.6	S.BAPT.
Rockwall	67.7	Ind. CHA.
Runnels	86.1	S.BAPT.
Rusk	61.0	S.BAPT.
Sabine	49.0	S.BAPT.
San Augustine	58.6	S.BAPT.
San Jacinto	31.7	S.BAPT.
San Patricio	80.7	R.C.
San Saba	81.1	S.BAPT.
Schleicher	75.4	S.BAPT.
Scurry	73.5	S.BAPT.
Shackelford	85.0	S.BAPT.
Shelby	59.2	S.BAPT.
Sherman	80.8	S.BAPT.
Smith	70.2	S.BAPT.
Somervell	57.1	S.BAPT.
Starr	85.6	R.C.
Stephens	77.3	S.BAPT.
Sterling	80.9	S.BAPT.
Stonewall	79.6	S.BAPT.
Sutton	75.0	R.C.
Swisher	99.7	S.BAPT.
Tarrant	56.1	S.BAPT.
Taylor	72.5	S.BAPT.
Terrell	80.3	R.C.
Terry	70.3	S.BAPT.
Throckmorton	128.0	S.BAPT.
Titus	69.8	S.BAPT.
Tom Green	63.2	S.BAPT.
Travis	48.4	R.C.
Trinity	57.7	S.BAPT.
Tyler	74.0	S.BAPT.
Upshur	64.7	S.BAPT.
Upton	108.9	S.BAPT.
Uvalde	72.5	R.C.
Val Verde	35.2	R.C.
Van Zandt	66.8	S.BAPT.
Victoria	83.0	R.C.
Walker	49.5	S.BAPT.
Waller	51.2	S.BAPT.
Ward	133.5	R.C.
Washington	68.7	LUTH.
Webb	80.6	R.C.
Wharton	79.3	R.C.
Wheeler	90.3	S.BAPT.
Wichita	75.8	S.BAPT.
Wilbarger	87.6	S.BAPT.
Willacy	104.7	R.C.
Williamson	46.9	S.BAPT.
Wilson	61.3	R.C.
Winkler	139.6	R.C.
Wise	52.3	S.BAPT
Wood	73.4	S.BAPT.
Yoakum	86.6	S.BAPT.
Young	85.0	S.BAPT.
Zapata	38.5	R.C.
Zavala	83.6	R.C.

S.BAPT. Southern Baptist; R.C., Catholic, METH., Methodist; LUTH., Lutheran; CHR/CH, Church of Christ; Ind. CHA., Independent Charismatic. Source: **"Churches and Church Membership in the United States 1990,"** published by Glenmary Research Center, Atlanta. Reprinted with permission.

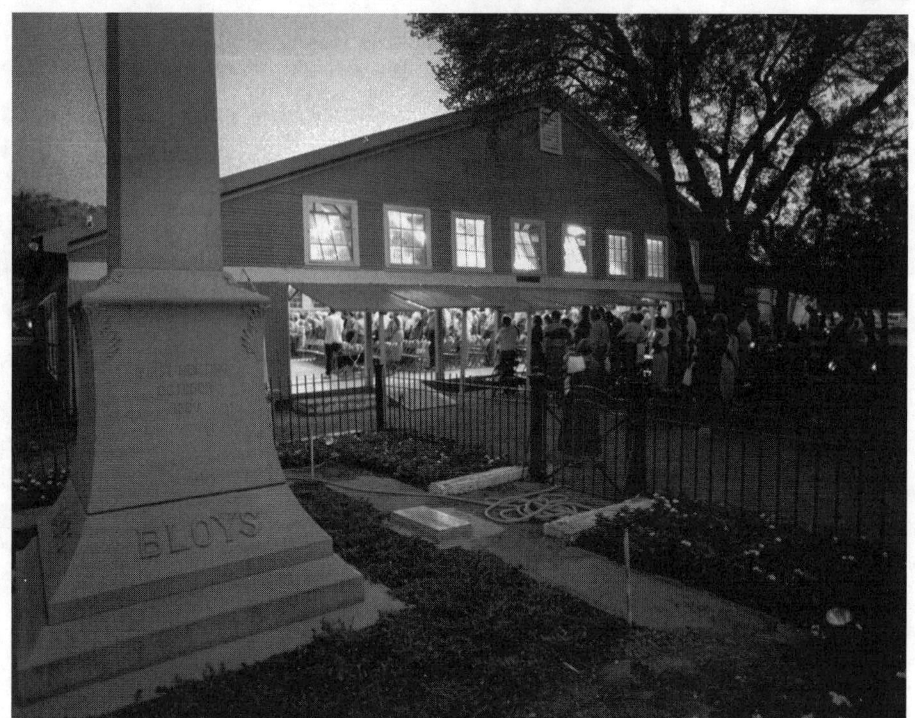

This 1994 Bloys Camp Meeting continued a tradition begun in 1890. The annual religious gathering in the Davis Mountains of West Texas draws hundreds each summer. Dallas Morning News photo by John F. Rhodes.

Some Turn-of-the-Century Women of the Cloth

by Mary G. Ramos, editor, Texas Almanac

The 1880s and 1890s saw women entering the fields of preaching and ministry in various religious denominations in increasing numbers.

Most women who felt a "call" to do Protestant church work answered the call within the narrow context of what was considered proper for a woman to do: They held prayer meetings, raised money to support foreign and domestic missions, participated in ladies-aid activities and organized social events at church.

When the Baptist women of Texas met in 1880 to form a statewide organization, they asked a man to preside, because it was considered improper for a woman to take charge of such an auspicious meeting. From that hesitant beginning, the Baptist women built a formidable organization by the turn of the century.

Some women were not so reluctant to speak up in public, however. Even those who were brought up in the tradition of women keeping silence in church overcame their hesitancy in their eagerness to share their religious beliefs with others.

Some women held joint ministries with their husbands. Others presided over revivals and camp meetings on their own.

Many denominations distinguished between "preachers," who could only preach, but not perform certain rituals, and full-fledged, ordained ministers, who could. During the 19th century, there were many more female preachers than ordained ministers.

Among the women who carried their "call" into the pulpit were these:

Rachel Watkins Dellgren Billings was born in Hiawatha, Kan. in 1861. Ms. Billings received her BS from Lombard University in 1886 and graduated from Ryder Divinity School with a Bachelor of Divinity degree in 1894.

Together with her husband, a Unitarian minister, she served Swedish congregations in the Midwest for a time. After the Dellgrens divorced, she moved to Hico, Tex., and was licensed to preach in January 1898. She served as minister at All Souls Church for a year before she was ordained as a Universalist minister in Jan. 28, 1899. She remarried, moved to Arkansas, and was in charge of a church there from 1904 to 1906.

Eliza J. Rutherford was an ordained minister of the Methodist Protestant church. She received the "call" at a tent revival in Ennis, her hometown, in 1892. She and her husband had a joint ministry.

Mary Lee Cagle was probably one of the most active female preachers and evangelists in Texas. Born Mary Lee Wasson in 1864 in Moulton, Ala., she first felt the pull to do church work at the age of 15.

After she married Rev. R. L. Harris, a Free Methodist minister known as the Texas Cowboy Preacher, at the age of 27, she thought that she could fulfill her "call" by assisting her husband in his work — conducting women's prayer meetings and leading the singing at Harris' meetings.. She knew that she would meet great opposition if she attempted to establish her own ministry.

In 1894, R. L. Harris organized the New Testament Church of Christ in Milan, Tenn., in which women were explicitly given the same right to preach as men.

This new church was one of a growing number of congregations that were part of what is referred to as the holiness movement — an offshoot of traditional Methodism that came to include independent holiness churches and some Church of the Nazarene congregations, as well.

After Harris died in 1894, Mary Lee established her own ministry. While visiting Harris' family in 1895 in Whitney, Tex., Mary Lee organized a congregation in nearby Swedonia.

Then she was asked to organize another about six miles away. This was the beginning of a lifetime of itinerant ministry.

She traveled often between Tennessee and Texas, preaching and founding churches wherever she went.

In Texas, she concentrated her activities in the western counties of Taylor, Jones, Fisher and Nolan.

Since it was unorthodox at the time for women to conduct camp meetings and revivals, Mary Lee found it easier to operate in the frontier atmosphere of West Texas than in the more traditional and established social order of the Old South. Mary Lee was finally ordained in December 1899 in Milan, Tenn.

During one of her meetings in Neinda, Tex., in the spring of 1898, Mary Lee converted Henry Clay Cagle, a local cowboy. They married in August 1900. Henry attended Texas Holiness University in Peniel, near Greenville in Hunt County, to train for their joint ministry.

The university had been established for training Nazarene ministers, but it was also supported by Free Methodists and other holiness advocates.

Before 1908, Mary Lee Cagle had created at least 18 congregations, 11 of which were in Texas: Swedonia, Mount Zion, Roby, Center Point, Nubia, Buffalo Gap, Dora, Truby, Rising Star, Glen Cove and Tahoka. (The Buffalo Gap church building, built in 1901, is preserved today at the Buffalo Gap Historic Village south of Abilene.)

The Cagles bought a house in Buffalo Gap and settled there.

In 1904, the New Testament Church of Christ united with the Independent Holiness Church to become the Holiness Church of Christ. Mary Lee and Henry Cagle continued to work within the new organization.

During her ministry, Mary Lee helped to bring many women into active ministerial roles.

In 1906, of 49 licensed preachers of the united churches, five were women — almost 10 percent of the total. Seven of eight authorized home missionaries were women and six of 12 ordained foreign missionaries were female.

However, after the Holiness Church of Christ merged with two other sects to become the Church of the Nazarene in 1908, the percentage of female preachers gradually diminished. As of January 1989, fewer than one percent of Church of the Nazarene pastors were women.

Mary Lee Cagle preached her last sermon at Rotan in 1954 and died Sept. 27, 1955. Henry Cagle died six years later. ☆

Religious Groups with Most Churches

Southern Baptist Convention	4,285
Churches of Christ	2,215
United Methodist Church	2,186
Catholic Church	1,290
Assemblies of God	1,274
Presbyterian Church USA	579
Baptist Missionary Association	498
Christian Church (Disciples of Christ)	428
Episcopal Church	424
Evangelical Lutheran Church in America	401

Source: Glenmary Research Center, Atlanta, Ga.

Protestant Groups with Most Members

Southern Baptist Convention	2,538,245
United Methodist Church	781,389
Churches of Christ	292,585
Presbyterian Church USA	156,165
Assemblies of God	146,688
Episcopal Church	127,315
Evangelical Lutheran Church in America	120,004
Lutheran Church, Missouri Synod	99,974
Baptist Missionary Association	98,509
Christian Church (Disciples of Christ)	74,098

Source: Glenmary Research Center, Atlanta, Ga.

Texas' Giant New Eye on the Universe

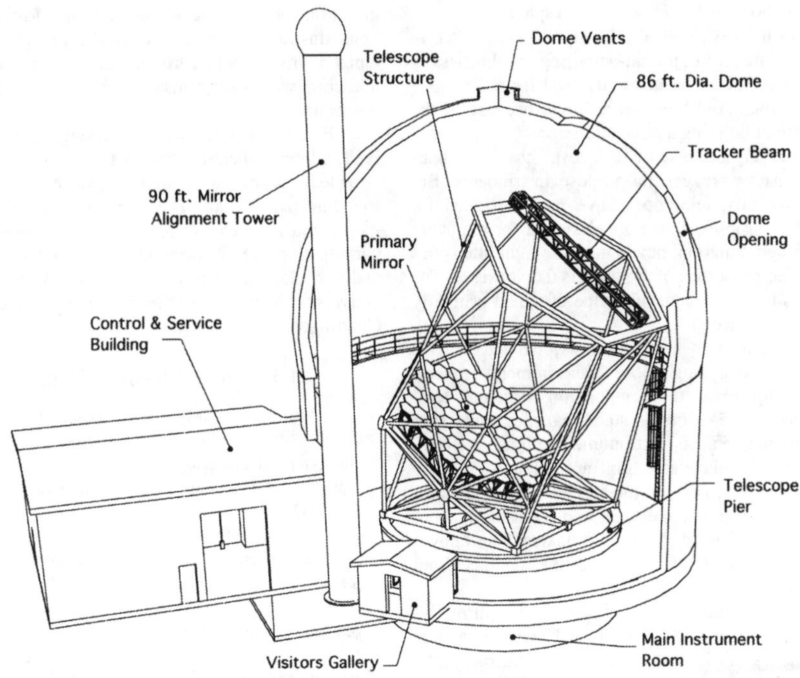

The Hobby-Eberly Telescope under construction in West Texas, is shown in this artist's sketch. The huge astronomical telescope should be fully operational in mid-1997. Drawing used with permission of McDonald Observatory.

One of the world's largest and most powerful astronomical telescopes is taking shape in the Davis Mountains of West Texas. Texas' newest giant eye on the universe is being built on top of Mount Fowlkes in Jeff Davis County, about halfway between El Paso and Big Bend National Park. Mount Fowlkes is adjacent to Mount Locke, home of the main domes of The University of Texas at Austin's McDonald Observatory.

Construction of the William P. Hobby-Robert E. Eberly Telescope (HET) began with a ground-breaking ceremony on March 25, 1994. Hobby is the former lieutenant governor of Texas; Eberly is the donor of Penn State University's contribution to the project. Penn State is UT's major partner in the project. At press time (early summer 1995), "first light" is scheduled for mid-1996. Installation and testing of scientific instruments and support equipment will take about a year, so the HET should be fully operational about a year later.

The HET will join McDonald's five other major telescopes: a 107-inch, completed in 1968; an 82-inch, completed in 1939; a 36-inch, 1956; a 30-inch, 1970; and a 30-inch Laser Ranging System completed in 1981.

McDonald Observatory was established in 1932 with funds willed to The University of Texas by William J. McDonald, a banker from Paris, Texas. The observatory's location offers a very transparent atmosphere and relatively uniform air conditions at its 6,800-foot elevation. About two-thirds of the nights at the site are clear enough to be usable, and there is almost no interference from city lights or smog.

Most of our knowledge of the universe has been obtained from observations of the heavens through telescopes. These instruments have been around since the early 17th century: In 1609, Galileo became the first person known to have used a telescope for astronomical observations. From that simple, hand-held device, telescopes have evolved into precision instruments that weigh hundreds of tons.

Most telescopes are optical in nature. They work by gathering light using either lenses alone or a combination of lenses and mirrors. The more light they can gather, the better they can "see" the individual objects in the universe and the more accurate is the knowledge they derive from that light. Other scopes are radio telescopes, designed to collect and focus radio signals from objects in space.

In the past, optical telescopes were limited in size, and therefore in light-gathering capabilities, by the properties of the materials used for their lenses and mirrors. And there were limits because of the expense of building a large telescope.

Largely because of that cost, most telescopes in the past were general-purpose instruments. But more recently, telescopes have been designed for specific purposes: Some are designed for the study of infrared radiation, others measure light intensities and other properties of the objects they observe. The HET is the first major telescope designed primarily to do spectroscopy.

Spectroscopy measures individual wavelengths of light. Analyzing those measurements reveals information about the composition, structure, temperature and motion of stars, galaxies and other astronomical objects. Astronomers will use the HET to search for planets in orbit around stars, identify and measure activity on the surfaces of stars, monitor activity in some galaxies, and learn more about "dark matter" located within galaxies. The knowledge will enable scientists to refine theories about star formation and evolution.

The primary mirror of the largest currently-operating telescope, the Keck in Hawaii, is almost 400 inches in diameter. The primary mirror of the HET will be slightly larger, but the HET's "mirror" will actually be 91 separate mirrors. Each segment will be hexagonal in shape, about 40 inches across and attached to three small motors. Each trio of motors will move their segment, enabling the operator to maintain the correct overall shape of the mirror. The HET will cost less to build than some other large telescopes because of the segmented mirror, since it is much easier to grind and polish a multitude of small mirrors than it is to precisely grind, polish and transport a giant single mirror.

The HET will be contained in an 86-foot-diameter dome, which will reach 75 feet above ground level. An adjacent 100-foot-high tower will house instruments used to align the 91 mirrors. A temperature-controlled room beneath the 60-ton telescope will contain instruments used in analyzing its findings.

Five universities are cooperating to build the HET, allowing them to share both the costs and the knowledge produced through the giant eye. The two founding partners are The University of Texas at Austin and The Pennsylvania State University. Also participating are California's Stanford University and two German institutions: Ludwig Maximilian University, Munich, and Georg-August University, Goettingen. ☆

McDonald Welcomes Visitors

The W.L. Moody, Jr., Visitors' Information Center offers astronomy exhibits and films along with a gift shop. Open daily 9 a.m. to 5 p.m. except Thanksgiving, Christmas and New Year's Day.

Guided tours of the observatory are available each afternoon. During the summer, a tour is also offered in the morning.

Star Parties are popular at McDonald all year at sunset on Tuesdays, Fridays and Saturdays at the Public Observatory, located just behind the Visitors' Center. Large telescopes are available for viewing celestial objects.

For more information about visiting McDonald Observatory, write or call the Visitor's Information Center, P.O. Box 1337, Fort Davis 79734-1337; (915) 426-3640.

The observatory also publishes a popular-level astronomy magazine, StarDate. The address is StarDate, RLM 15.308, The University of Texas, Austin 78712; (512) 471-5285.

Scientific Balloons Involve Work of Texans

The balloons stand taller than the San Jacinto Monument when they are launched from the NASA facility in Palestine.

And by the time they come down somewhere in West Texas, Texans from as far away as Sulphur Springs in North Texas and Amarillo in the Panhandle will have taken part in the scientific research.

Since 1963, the National Scientific Balloon Facility in East Texas has helped launch more than 1,800 such balloons for research projects from around the world.

The kinds of research involved include cosmic ray studies, infrared astronomy as well as optical and ultra-violet astronomy, gamma and X-ray astromony and atmospheric sciences.

The facility, located a few miles northwest of Palestine on Hwy. 287, is sponsored by the National Aeronautics and Space Administration and has 80 full-time employees. NASA contracts for supervisory administration and for the last five years New Mexico State University's Physical Science Laboratory has had that contract.

The size of balloons launched at Palestine has gone up, so to speak, from an average volume of 2.8

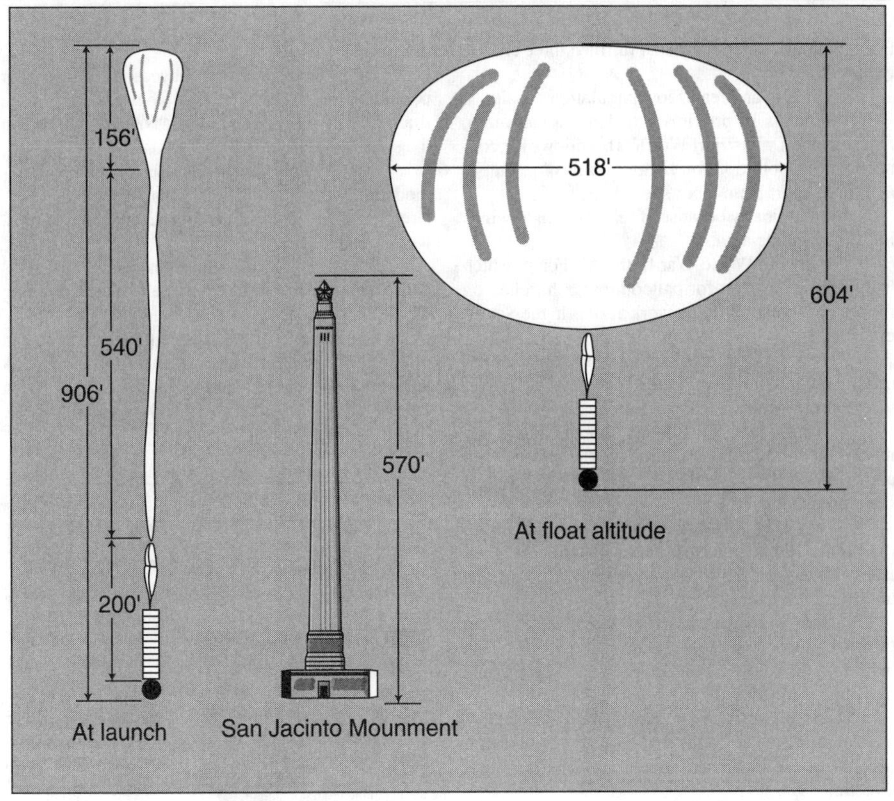

The balloons launched at Palestine are taller than the San Jacinto Monument and fully expand as they rise above the site in East Texas. Texas Almanac graphic.

million cubic feet (MCF) in 1964 to over 40 MFC in recent years.

The increase in size has allowed the payloads to increase from an average of 407 lbs. in 1964 to more than 6,000 lbs. today.

The duties attached to the project include not only the launch, however. Tracking and recovery of the balloon and its payload is also part of the job. That recovery can be as far away as California, but most often is within a 380-mile distance, somewhere in West Texas.

The balloons are assembled at only two manufacturers, one of whom is in Sulphur Springs, where workers handmake the polyethelene plastic "megalifts" by carefully placing tape along the hundreds of seams.

The plastic is "as thin as the covering on your dry cleaning," says Edward Fritsch, supervisor of flight operations.

But by the time the gigantic balloons are finished they weigh about 5,000 lbs. and cost $100,000.

Helium from the gas-processing facility near Amarillo is trucked into Palestine to fill the balloons to about 10 percent capacity at ground level for the launch. As the balloon rises, the gas expands to fill the massive enclosure.

The balloons rise to 150,000 feet above the earth, about four times the usual level of commercial airline flights. There the scientific instruments that make up the payload — often weighing 6,000 lbs.— have as long as 40 hours to sample molecules or rays or magnetic fields, whatever the particular experiment is researching.

Mr. Fritsch says the resident time, or "time at float," provides scientists with a chance of "tasting the atmosphere" as opposed to satellite operations from outer space that are more remote or a rocket launch that would provide only brief time at the higher levels.

Often the balloon experiments complement or clarify the accuracy of observations made from the orbiting satellites.

Palestine was chosen as the location of the national balloon center because it fulfilled three criteria required:

— it is in an area of low population density,

— but is in proximaty to large urban areas, Houston and Dallas/Fort Worth. This allows for connecting transportation for visiting teams of scientists and for support from labor specialists,

— and finally because of relatively light winds in the immediate area.

Following World War II, the Air Force, which had been the catalyst for balloon research, relied on the pool of scientists doing work at sites in the Southern Rockies.

Often the first small launches took place after driving out into the Great Plains to the east of Denver where strong winds became a problem.

Even today in East Texas, thunderstorms can make scheduling difficult, but once the balloons get above the surface weather of the earth things get more predictable.

From May to October the air currents above the highest thunderstorms, about 60,000 feet, flow from east to west. From October to May the currents are from west to east.

There is a time of two or three weeks at the turnaround that has very little directional flow. This period of time is used on occasion for experiments that require longer time in place.

For the last five or six years, the Palestine site has not launched balloons that would drift eastward because of the increased population density in that direction.

For the winter launches, a back-up launch site has been established at Fort Sumner, N.M.

Other launch sites in Canada, Antarctica and Australia are part of the NASA program and each is used for different reasons: Canada because of magnetic field specifications, Antarctica for sun time, and Australia for southern hemisphere requirements.

Still, all the launches are coordinated from Palestine, and about a third of approximately 35 each year occur there.

Once the experiments are completed, the Palestine home base coordinates radio and computer communications to manage the descent. The balloon is detached and a parachute opens on the payload — instrumentation which can be worth $1 million — and the two components, balloon and instruments, begin a return to earth.

An airplane is used to help in the physical recovery. There is a "footprint of uncertainty" that must not include a population center.

This is the "most carefully managed part of the flight," the flight official explains. Vertical control is through release of gas for descent or of glass pellets for ascent. But horizonal drift is at the mercy of the winds.

The chase plane radios to a crane-equipped truck that is within 50 miles of the anticipated landing site.

Often the scenario is played out on the front porch of a West Texas rancher who sees a big white truck driving up the road, with "NASA" marked on the side.

The "typical rancher is usually quite accommodating," the flight official says. "People feel flattered to be involved in an experiment, for the most part."

Sometimes local authorities such as sheriffs' departments are consulted to help in determining whose property needs to be entered.

The finish of the Texas-centered research can provide for some local excitement. And, the NASA operations people acknowledge there have been more than a few reports of UFOs surrounding the flights. — *Robert Plocheck* ☆

Texans in the National Academy of Sciences

Ellen Vitetta was elected to the National Academy of Sciences in 1994 from The University of Texas Southwestern Medical Center at Dallas. Dallas Morning News photo by Juan Garcia.

The National Academy of Sciences is a private organization of scientists and engineers dedicated to the furtherance of science and its use for the general welfare.

Established by congressional acts of incorporation, which were signed by Abraham Lincoln in 1863, the science academy acts as official adviser to the federal government in matters of science or technology.

Election to membership in the Academy is one of the highest honors that can be accorded a U.S. scientist or engineer.

As of May 1, 1995, the total number of active members was 1,733.

In addition, 301 scientists with citizenship outside the United States were nonvoting foreign associates.

In 1948, Karl Folkers of The University of Texas at Austin became the first Texan elected to the academy.

In May 1995, 47 scientists affiliated with Texas institutions when they were elected were full, voting members.

They are listed below, along with the names of their institutions and the years of their elections.

Academy Member	Affiliation*	Yr. Elected
Perry L. Adkisson	A&M	1979
Abram Amsel	UT-Austin	1992
Neal R. Amundon	U of H	1992
Charles J. Arntzen	A&M	1983
Allen J. Bard	UT-Austin	1982
Brian J.L. Berry	UT-Dallas	1975
Norman E. Borlaug	A&M	1968
Michael S. Brown	UTSWMC	1980
C. Thomas Caskey	Baylor Med.	1993
Joseph W. Chamberlain	Rice	1965
C.W. Chu	U of H	1989
F. Albert Cotton	A&M	1967
Gerard H. de Vaucouleurs	UT-Austin	1986
Bryce DeWitt	UT-Austin	1990
Ronald W. Estabrook	UTSWMC	1979
Karl Folkers	UT-Austin	1948
Marye Anne Fox	UT-Austin	1994
David L. Garbers	UTSWMC	1993
Alfred G. Gilman	UTSWMC	1985
Joseph L. Goldstein	UTSWMC	1980
William E. Gordon	Rice	1968
Verne E. Grant	UT-Austin	1968
Norman Hackerman	Welch	1971
A. James Hudspeth	UTSWMC	1991
James L. Kinsey	Rice	1991
Ernst Knobil	UTHSC-Houston	1986
Jay K. Kochi	U of H	1982
John L. Margrave	Rice	1974
S.M. McCann	UTSWMC	1983
Jack Myers	UT-Austin	1975
Bert W. O'Malley	Baylor Med.	1992
Kenneth L. Pike	SIL	1985
Lester J. Reed	UT-Austin	1973
Richard E. Smalley	Rice	1990
Esmond E. Snell	UT-Austin	1955
Richard C. Starr	UT-Austin	1976
Max D. Summers	A&M	1989
Harry L. Swinney	UT-Austin	1992
John T. Tate	UT-Austin	1969
Karen K. Uhlenbeck	UT-Austin	1986
Jonathan W. Uhr	UTSWMC	1984
Roger H. Unger	UTSWMC	1986
Ellen S. Vitetta	UTSWMC	1994
Salih J. Wakil	Baylor Med.	1990
Steven Weinberg	UT-Austin	1972
D. Fred Wendorf	SMU	1987
Jean D. Wilson	UTSWMC	1983

* *A&M - Texas A&M University*
UT-Austin - The University of Texas at Austin
U of H - University of Houston
UT-Dallas - The University of Texas at Dallas
UTSWMC - The University of Texas Southwestern Medical Center at Dallas
Baylor Med. - Baylor College of Medicine
Rice - Rice University
Welch - Robert A. Welch Foundation
UTHSC - Houston - The University of Texas Health Science Center at Houston
SIL - Summer Institute of Linguistics
SMU - Southern Methodist University

In addition to the above full members of the National Academy of Sciences, **D.H.R. Barton** was elected as a Foreign Associate in 1970 from Texas A&M University, and **Cecil H. Green** of Texas Instruments, Inc., was awarded a Public Welfare Medal in 1979. ☆

Source: National Academy of Sciences.

Recent Texas Achievements in Medical Science

by Laura Beil

Dr. Alfred G. Gilman of The University of Texas Southwestern Medical Center at Dallas was in formal attire as he received the Nobel Prize in medicine in 1994. Associated Press photo.

Texas medical researchers came to the attention of the world in 1994, when Alfred G. Gilman of The University of Texas Southwestern Medical Center at Dallas received the Nobel Prize in physiology or medicine.

Dr. Gilman received science's most prestigious honor for discovering molecules that are a key middleman in the process that allows cells to interpret chemical signals from their surroundings.

It was the third time in nine years that researchers at the Dallas medical school have won Nobels, making it one of the few institutions in the world with four active Nobel laureates.

Prizes were awarded to Joseph Goldstein and Michael Brown in 1985 for their research on cholesterol metabolism, and to Johann Deisenhofer in 1988 for determining the three-dimensional structure of a cell membrane protein.

Although Deisenhofer was at the Southwestern Medical Center at the time the Nobel was awarded, the research was done at the Max Planck Institute near Munich, before he came to Texas.

While Dr. Gilman's discoveries haven't yet led to any medical therapies, members of the Nobel Assembly in Stockholm, which awards the prize for physiology or medicine, were convinced that such applications are only a matter of time. Understanding how these molecules work could lead to treatments for diseases as varied as cholera, whooping cough and cancer.

Texas schools

Meanwhile, research generated by other scientists at hospitals and medical schools around the state has already left the test-tube stage.

All eight Texas medical schools conduct scientific exploration, as do some of the state's larger treatment centers, such as Baylor University Medical Center in Dallas, The University of Texas M.D. Anderson Cancer Center in Houston and The University of Texas Health Center at Tyler.

Following is an overview, although by no means a complete listing, of current Texas medical research:

Basic medical research in the 1990s continued drifting more into the field of molecular genetics. Led by the Human Genome Project — the federal government's $3 billion, 15-year effort to catalogue human chromosomes — Texas scientists have isolated genes that cause a host of rare, inherited diseases and have begun using new technology to actually tinker with the basic operating instructions of cells.

Since 1992, researchers at Baylor College of Medicine in Houston, which is not affiliated with either Baylor University in Waco or Baylor University Medical Center in Dallas, found the genes responsible for Fragile X syndrome, spinocerebellar ataxia type 1, Charcot-Marie-Tooth disease, and a genetic defect that causes enlargement of the heart. (Fragile X is the most common cause of inherited mental retardation; Charcot-Marie-Tooth disease results in the wasting of muscles; spinocerebellar ataxia is an inherited, fatal neurological disease.)

Chromosomes

Baylor and UT Southwestern have the only two sites in Texas designated a part of the Human Genome Center, a federally supported center dedicated to studying the 23 human chromosomes. Researchers from UT Southwestern and from Baylor University Medical Center in Dallas in 1993 reported that they had narrowed the location for a gene that may cause a form of psoriasis. The excruciating and mysterious skin disease has seen little medical progress.

Other genetic research doesn't look for molecular defects that can cause disease, but examines the mechanisms that cells use to repair damage that might lead to cancer or cell death. Scientists at The University of Texas Medical Branch at Galveston, for example, identified the importance of two genes that appear responsible for helping to repair the cell damage inflicted by the sun's ultraviolet rays, and discovered how a key enzyme repairs breaks in a cell's genetic material.

The encouragement for finding the genetic basis for disease is that such discoveries will one day enable doctors to correct the underlying flaws that lead to illness, rather than just treat its symptoms. The idea is called gene therapy.

Scientists at Baylor College of Medicine in Houston are part of a team that recently demonstrated that the technique worked in animals as a treatment for a form of hemophilia.

Medical Schools

The following Texas institutions train doctors and other medical personnel. They are listed in alphabetical order. Included is the address, phone number, the average number of students per class and the average number of interns and residents for each school.

Institution	Avg. class size	Avg. # residents
Baylor College of Medicine One Baylor Plaza Houston 77030 (713) 798-4951	160	950
Texas A&M University Health Science Center College of Medicine College Station 77843 (409) 845-3431	48	220
Texas Tech University Health Sciences Center 3601 Fourth Street Lubbock 79430 (806) 743-1000 Satellite campuses: Amarillo 1400 Wallace Boulevard Amarillo 79106 El Paso 4800 Alberta Avenue El Paso 79905 Odessa 800 West Fourth St. Odessa 79763	120	479
University of North Texas Health Science Center at Fort Worth 3500 Camp Bowie Blvd. Fort Worth 76107 (817) 735-2000	108	71
The University of Texas Health Science Center at San Antonio 7703 Floyd Curl Drive San Antonio 78284 (210) 567-7000	200	630
The University of Texas-Houston Medical School 6431 Fannin Houston 77030 (713) 792-4711	200	909
The University of Texas Medical Branch at Galveston 301 University Blvd. Galveston 77555 (409) 772-2618	200	551
The University of Texas Southwestern Medical Center at Dallas 5323 Harry Hines Blvd. Dallas 75235 (214) 648-3111	199	948

In humans, gene therapy may work in ways not even imagined a decade ago. Doctors at M.D. Anderson have permission from the federal government to treat 10 women with ovarian cancer who have not responded to any other treatments. The scientists will remove cells from a patient's bone marrow, and reprogram them on the genetic level to resist normally toxic doses of anti-cancer drugs. The strengthened cells will be able to withstand heavy treatments with a medication called Taxol, which can kill cancer cells but is also extremely damaging to healthy cells as well.

M.D. Anderson scientists are also using gene therapy in patients with advanced lung cancer. In that experiment, doctors will attempt to either turn off genes that can cause cancer or turn on genes that can suppress it.

Genes contain the instructions for making proteins, and some research has looked at the function of specific proteins in the body. For example, scientists at Texas Tech University Health Sciences Center in Lubbock in 1994 announced finding the function of protein that plays a key role in converting cholesterol into steroid hormones. The finding helps further explain how the body makes hormones, and may lead to a treatment for infants who are born with a condition called congenital adrenal hyperplasia, in which their bodies cannot produce steroid hormones.

Cholesterol

Moving beyond the molecular stage, Texas medical centers are the sites of numerous experimental drug studies for a variety of human ills. One of the largest is taking place at the University of North Texas Health Science Center at Fort Worth, which includes the state's only college of osteopathic medicine. Doctors who graduate from the school are D.O.'s instead of M.D.'s, but are licensed to practice medicine just the same.

The Fort Worth medical school is conducting a 5-year study with 2,000 volunteers to examine whether diet alone or diet combined with a cholesterol-lowering drug can prevent heart disease in basically healthy people who have borderline high cholesterol levels.

AIDS

Experimental medications for AIDS are also tested throughout the state, not only in disease epicenters like Dallas and Houston, but also in smaller towns through special programs that increase the availability of promising drugs not yet approved for general use by the federal government.

The state's only federally funded AIDS Clinical Trials Unit is in Galveston, where more than 700 people infected with the virus that causes AIDS have participated in studies of anti-viral drugs and other strategies to bolster the immune system or fight off infections.

Scientists at the school, which is already noted for its infectious-disease research, are also trying to develop a vaccine that could be given after infection with the virus to prevent the full-blown disease from developing.

Dallas researchers in 1992 reported the results of a nationwide study of an AIDS drug that successfully delayed an infection called mycobacterium avium complex, or MAC. The infection can affect many parts of the body, causing fever, fatigue and rapid weight loss because the body loses its ability to absorb nutrients.

A large study to test a new drug that helps keep transplant patients from rejecting their new organs was coordinated in Dallas at Baylor University Medical Center. The study found that the new drug, called FK-506, was better at preventing rejection than the standard drug, cyclosporine. The head of the study was Dr. Goran Klintmalm, the director of the hospital's transplant program who trained under transplant pioneer Thomas Starzl of the University of Pittsburgh.

Public health

Researchers at Texas medical schools also focus on preventing disease as well as treating it, especially in poorer areas of the state, such as inner-city urban areas and along the Texas-Mexico border. Doctors at The University of Texas Health Science Center at San Antonio and Texas Tech University Health Sciences Center, which has a satellite campus in El Paso, are two large providers of medical care along the border. The School of Public Health at the University of Texas-Houston Medical School — which trains students in disease prevention — has a campus in El Paso.

Three Texas medical schools — Texas Tech, Texas A&M and the University of North Texas Health Science Center at Fort Worth — pride themselves in their production of young physicians who choose to provide the most fundamental medical care.

As debate over overhauling the U.S. health care system brought attention to the lack of so-called primary care providers, graduates from those three schools chose basic medical care more often than their counterparts at other schools.

More than half the graduates of Texas A&M choose primary-care specialties, as do three-fourths of the graduates of the osteopathic medical school. Officials from Texas Tech say they encourage students to bring basic care to the state's rural areas. ☆

Laura Beil is the public health writer for The Dallas Morning News.

Persons without health insurance

State rank	Percent of population
1. Texas	**21.9**
2. New Mexico	21.0
3. Louisiana	20.8
4. Oklahoma	19.5
5. Nevada	19.3
5. Mississippi	19.3
7. California	19.0
8. Florida	18.7
9. Arkansas	17.6
10. Alabama	17.3

Source: Statistical Abstract of the United States 1994, U.S. Bureau of the Census.

Health Care in Texas

The following information has been supplied chiefly by the Texas Hospital Association and the Texas Department of Health.

As our population increases and technological advances continue, this field of essential services is greatly expanding in Texas. Houston, Dallas and other Texas cities are internationally known for their medical centers.

However, many small communities of the state have no hospital or access to professional medical care. As our population ages, access to health care becomes a greater concern for many Texans, as evidenced by the coverage of health-care issues in the Texas media.

Hospitals

In 1993, Texas hospitals employed 276,590 full-time equivalent people (FTEs) with a payroll, including benefits of more than $9.5 billion.

These **employees** were reported by the 510 hospitals, with approximately 75,000 **beds**, registered with the American Hospital Association. One of every 12 U.S. hospitals is located in Texas.

The average **length of stay** in the 414 community hospitals was 6.0 days in 1993, compared to 6.8 days in 1975.

The average length of stay in Texas community hospitals was one day less than the U.S. average, and the average cost per admission in Texas was $8,278, which was 1.2 percent less than the U.S. average of $8,385.

Admissions to Texas community hospitals totaled 1,963,869, or 90 percent of the total admissions to all Texas hospitals.

There were 23,909,603 out-patient visits in 1993, of which 17,828,041 or 75 percent were provided by community hospitals.

Psychiatric admissions of 57,802 represented 3 percent of total admissions in 1993.

Of the total 3,949,788 births in U.S. hospitals in 1993, 316,723 were in Texas hospitals.

There were 60,040 Registered Nurse FTEs, 18,308 Licensed Vocational Nurse FTEs, and 4,210 FTE health-care professions trainees working in Texas hospitals in 1993.

Allied Health Training

Hospitals are the leading source of allied health education in Texas.

All allied health personnel are either completely or partially educated in a hospital, clinical, internship or residency program.

Texas continues to experience a need for **rehabilitation workers** in health-care fields. There is still a demand for physical therapists, occupational therapists, respiratory therapists, medical technologists, radiologic technologists and pharmacists.

The **Texas Health Careers Program**, sponsored by the THA Hospital Education and Research Foundation, P.O. Box 15587, Austin, Texas 78761, collects information on nursing, allied health and other medical and dental education programs, and provides free information to anyone interested in a career in the health field.

Death, birth rates continue trends in Texas statistics

Heart disease and cancer remained the major causes of death in 1993, the latest year for which statistics are available from Bureau of Vital Statistics, Texas Department of Health. Heart disease claimed 41,231 victims, and cancer caused 30,989 deaths during the year.

Human Immunodeficiency Virus (HIV), which entered the list of top ten killers in Texas in 1990, totaled 2,551 in 1993.

The remaining top causes of death in Texas were as follows:

- •Cerebrovascular diseases — 8,974
- •Accidents — 6,164
- •Chronic Obstructive Pulmonary Diseases and Allied Conditions — 6,002
- •Diabetes Mellitus — 4,428
- •Pneumonia and Influenza — 3,668
- •Homicide — 2,268
- •Suicide — 2,267

The death rate for the state stood at 7.5 percent per 1,000 estimated population, up from 7.3 percent in 1992. There were 134,417 deaths in Texas in 1993.

While there were a record number of babies born to Texas' mothers in 1993 (321,961), the state's birth rate continued to decline from 18.6 per 1,000 population in 1991 to 17.9.

Infant deaths also declined. The state's infant mortality rate fell to 7.5 per 1,000 births in 1993, an all-time low for the category. However, infant mortality for black mothers stood at 14.6, while the rate for Anglo mothers was 6.3 and for Hispanics 6.8 deaths per 1,000 live births.

Induced terminations of pregnancy (abortions) continued to decline slightly since 1990, with 90,947 in 1993. Abortions were induced in an estimated 21 percent of the state's pregnancies. ☆

Nursing

For nursing professionals, the **Texas Organization of Nurse Executives** and the **Texas Society of Infection Control Practitioners** offer opportunities for continuing education and networking with others in the profession.

They also serve as advocates for nursing and provide representatives to regulatory agency committees, legislative study groups and other related nursing organizations.

These societies are affiliated with the Texas Hospital Association, the principal organization for health-care providers. ☆

State Institutions for MHMR Services

The mission of the Texas Department of Mental Health and Mental Retardation (TXMHMR) is to offer an array of services that respond to the needs of people with mental illness and mental retardation and that enable them to make choices that result in lives of dignity and increased independence.

The agency administers state hospitals for persons with mental illness, state schools for persons with mental retardation, and state centers for persons with mental illness and/or mental retardation. Additionally, TXMHMR contracts with 36 community MHMR centers to provide services. Community MHMR centers are the local mental health authority (MHA) and/or mental retardation authority (MRA) for the counties they serve.

For areas not served by a community MHMR center, the state hospital, state school or state center is the local MHA/MRA. Services are obtained through local MHAs/MRAs.

The mailing address for the TXMHMR central office is P.O. Box 12668, Austin 78711-2668; phone (512) 454-3761.

Information in the list below includes the city where the facility is located, the facility name, the date the facility was established and the name of the executive in charge of the facility.

The number of patients or individuals served for state hospitals and schools is the average daily census for Fiscal Year 1994. The figures for state centers and community MHMR centers are the total numbers of individuals served during Fiscal Year 1994.

During Fiscal Year 1994, a total of 159,586 persons received services from MHMR facilities: 123,964 received mental health services and 38,803 received mental retardation services.

Hospitals for Persons With Mental Illness

Austin State Hospital — Austin; 1857; Harold K. Dudley Jr., superintendent; 324 patients.

Big Spring State Hospital — Big Spring; 1937; Robert von Rosenberg, superintendent; 270 patients.

Kerrville State Hospital — Kerrville; 1950; Gloria P. Olsen,Ph.D., superintendent; 179patients.

Rusk State Hospital — Rusk; 1919; Harold Parrish, superintendent; 394 patients.

San Antonio State Hospital — San Antonio; 1892; Robert C. Arizpe, superintendent; 446 patients.

Terrell State Hospital — Terrell; 1885; Beatrice Butler, superintendent; 333 patients.

Vernon State Hospital — Vernon; 1969; James E. Smith, superintendent; 346 patients.

Waco Center for Youth — Waco; 1979; Stephen Anfinson, superintendent; 65 patients.

Wichita Falls State Hospital — Wichita Falls; 1922; Richard M. Bruner, superintendent; 352 patients.

Schools for Persons with Mental Retardation

Abilene State School — Abilene; 1901; Bill Waddill, superintendent; 662 individuals.

Austin State School — Austin; 1917; James G. Armstrong, Ph. D., superintendent; 445 individuals.

Brenham State School — Brenham; 1974; Stephen L. Fletcher, superintendent; 497 individuals.

Corpus Christi State School — Corpus Christi; 1970; Aurelio Valdez Jr., superintendent; 392 individuals.

Denton State School — Denton; 1960; Pat Jessee, superintendent; 641 individuals.

Fort Worth State School — Closed Aug. 31, 1995.

Lubbock State School — Lubbock; 1969; Lonnie H. Willis, superintendent; 415 individuals.

Lufkin State School — Lufkin; 1962; Sandra Cain, superintendent; 471 individuals.

Mexia State School — Mexia; 1946; William H. Lowry, Ph. D., superintendent; 659 individuals.

Richmond State School — Richmond; 1968; Gerald N. Brunette, M.S., superintendent; 698 individuals.

San Angelo State School — Carlsbad; 1969; R. Allen Williams, superintendent; 372 individuals.

San Antonio State School — San Antonio; 1978; Wilbur Wood, interim superintendent; 305 individuals.

Travis State School — Austin; 1934; Richard L. Smith, Ed. D., superintendent; 293 individuals (scheduled to close Aug. 31, 1997).

State Centers

Amarillo State Center — Amarillo; 1967; Richard D. Browder, director; 907 individuals.

Beaumont State Center — Beaumont; 1968; Gary Hidalgo, director; 833 individuals.

El Paso State Center — El Paso; 1974; Ed Moughon, interim director; 230 individuals.

Laredo State Center — Laredo; 1969; Augustin Sicard, Ph.D., director; 1,408 individuals.

Rio Grande State Center — Harlingen; 1962; Sonia Hernandez, M.S.W., director; 607 individuals.

Community Mental Health and Mental Retardation Centers

(The persons whose names appear in the list below are the executive directors of the centers, unless otherwise specified.)

Abilene — Abilene Regional MHMR Center; 1971; William V. Livingston; 1,572 individuals.

Amarillo — Texas Panhandle Mental Health Authority; 1968; Sanford Skelton; 2,297 individuals.

Austin — Austin-Travis County MHMR Center; 1967; David L. Evans; 8,481 individuals.

Beaumont — Life Resource; 1967; N. Charles Harris; 3,266 individuals.

Brownwood — Central Texas MHMR Center; 1969; Roy A. Cronenberg; 1,859 individuals.

Bryan-College Station — MHMR Authority of Brazos Valley; 1972; Jack Leon Bawcom; 1,601 individuals.

Cleburne — Johnson County MHMR Center; 1985; Joseph P. Mirisciott; 1,413 individuals.

Conroe — Tri-County MHMR Services; 1983; Leon Evans; 2,660 individuals.

Corpus Christi — Nueces County MHMR Community Center; 1970; Wallace E. Whitworth Jr.; 2,404 individuals.

Corsicana — Navarro County MHMR Center; 1979; Julia W. Lang; 699 individuals.

Dallas — Dallas County MHMR Center; 1967; Barry Waller, interim exec. dir.; 9,455 individuals.

Denison — MHMR Services of Texoma; 1974; Carl Kelly; 1,634 individuals.

Denton — Denton County MHMR Center; 1987; Cynthia Sill; 1,572 individuals.

Edinburg — Tropical Texas Center for MHMR; 1967; Marion G. Shirah; 5,373 individuals.

El Paso — Life Management Center; 1968; Michael Nash, Ph.D.; 4,040 individuals.

Fort Worth — Tarrant County MHMR Services; 1969; Jim McDermott, Ph.D.; 9,593 individuals.

Galveston — Gulf Coast Center; 1969; G. Michael Winburn; 2,640 individuals.

Greenville — Hunt County Family Services Center Inc.; 1971; John Brubaker, interim exec. dir.; 1,341 individuals.

Houston — MHMR Authority of Harris County; 1965; Steven Schnee, Ph.D.; 30,041 individuals.

Longview — Sabine Valley Center; 1970; Mack O. Blackwell; 4,641 individuals.

Lubbock — Lubbock Regional MHMR Center; 1969; Gene Menefee; 2,510 individuals.

Lufkin — The Burke Center; 1975; Susan Rushing; 4,020 individuals.

McKinney — Collin County MHMR Center; 1986; Randy Routon, Ph.D.; 1,634 individuals.

Midland/Odessa — Permian Basin Community Centers for MHMR; 1969; Clyde McLean; 2,483 individuals.

Plainview — Central Plains Center for MHMR and Substance Abuse; 1969; Gail Davis; 1,358 individuals.

San Angelo — MHMR Services for the Concho Valley; 1969; James M. Young; 1,460 individuals.

San Antonio — The Center for Health Care Services; 1966; Ruben R. Cardenas; 6,802 individuals.

Stephenville — Pecan Valley MHMR Region; 1977; Theresa B. Mulloy, Ed.D.; 1,961 individuals.

Temple — Central Counties Center for MHMR Services; 1967; Eldon Tietjer; 2,872 individuals.

Texarkana — Northeast Texas MHMR Center; 1974; Joe Bob Hall; 914 individuals.

Tyler — Andrews Center; 1970; Richard DeSanto; 3,327 individuals.

Victoria — Gulf Bend MHMR Center; 1970; Bill Dillard; 1,846 individuals.

Waco — Heart of Texas Region MHMR Center; 1969; Dean Maberry; 2,519 individuals.

Wharton — Riceland Regional Mental Health Authority; 1988; Charlie Boone; 1,454 individuals.

Wichita Falls — Helen Farabee Center; 1969; Henrilu Smith, interim exec. dir.; 2,0623 individuals. ☆

Rate of death from cancer

State rank	per 100,000 population
41. Georgia	175
42. Texas	**168**
43. California	165
44. Idaho	165
45. Colorado	154
46. Wyoming	154
47. New Mexico	152
48. Hawaii	146
49. Utah	112
50. Alaska	88

Source: Statistical Abstract of the United States 1994, U.S. Bureau of the Census, U.S. National Center for Health Statistics>

Belo Is a Texas Pioneer

A. H. Belo Corporation, publisher of *The Dallas Morning News* and the Texas Almanac, has a history parallel to that of Texas itself. Pioneered in 1842 as the one-page Galveston News, Belo has grown to become a leading Southwestern media company, encompassing both newspaper publishing and network-affiliated television broadcasting operations across the country.

The Early Days

A. H. Belo Corporation is the oldest continuously operating business in Texas. Founded by Samuel Bangs, a transplanted publisher from Boston, the company was in the publishing business three years before the Republic of Texas achieved statehood. Bangs sold the business within a year of its founding to Wilbur F. Cherry and Michael Cronican, and Cherry soon acquired sole ownership.

Another Massachusetts emigre, Willard Richardson, became editor of the paper a few years later. He campaigned editorially for annexation, fiscal responsibility and railroads. In 1857, Richardson conceived and founded the Texas Almanac, which he hoped would help attract settlers to the new state. Eight years later, he hired A. H. Belo, for whom the company was eventually named.

A. H. Belo, a former Confederate colonel from North Carolina, joined the company as bookkeeper. He was made a full partner in the growing company after only three months and carved out a new life for himself in the Southwest.

Nine years later, George Bannerman Dealey, a 15-year-old English emigrant, was hired as an office boy. Dealey, like A. H. Belo, was full of enthusiasm and energy. He, too, quickly moved up in the company. Working tirelessly, Dealey made his way from office boy to business manager and then to publisher of *The Dallas Morning News*. It was Dealey who chose the then-small settlement of Dallas as a site for a sister publication. Dealey and several other members of the Galveston News' staff relocated in Dallas, and the company prospered and grew.

The Dallas Morning News

The Dallas Morning News began publication on October 1, 1885, with a circulation of 5,000 subscribers. After being in operation only two months, *The Dallas Morning News* acquired its first competitor, the Dallas Herald (not to be confused with the Dallas Times Herald that closed in December 1991). Rather than compete with each other for subscribers, the two newspapers combined, keeping the name of *The Dallas Morning News*, but dating itself with the volume number of the former Dallas Herald.

In 1906, on the 21st anniversary of *The Dallas Morning News*, Dealey gave a speech that became the motto for the company: "Build The News upon the rock of truth and righteousness. Conduct it always upon the lines of fairness and integrity. Acknowledge the right of the people to get from the newspaper both sides of every important question." Today these words are carved in a three-story-high space above the entrance to *The Dallas Morning News*. The News building, a long-standing dream of Dealey, was completed in 1949, three years after his death.

Belo Was a Radio Broadcasting Pioneer

Belo also was a pioneer in radio in Texas. It began operating a 50-watt radio station, WFAA-AM, on June 26, 1922, which was the first network station in the state. The company sold the last of its radio properties in 1987.

Growth of Publishing Division

While Belo has grown into a multi-faceted media entity, *The Dallas Morning News* remains the flagship of its newspaper business. Growing from that original one-page newspaper in Galveston, *The Dallas Morning News* now has a total circulation of 547,000 daily and more than 820,000 Sunday.

In 1963, Belo expanded its Publishing Division by creating News Texan, Inc., which later formed two subsidiaries, DFW Suburban Newspapers, Inc., and DFW Printing Company, Inc. DFW Suburban Newspapers' eight community newspapers include the Arlington News, Garland News, Grand Prairie News, Irving News, Las Colinas Business News, Metrocrest News, Mid-Cities News and Richardson News. DFW Printing Company publishes these papers as well as USA Today for the Southwest region and other publishing and specialty advertising products.

Television Broadcasting Business

Belo entered the television-broadcasting business in 1950 with the acquisition of its principal station WFAA-TV, Channel 8, the ABC affiliate in Dallas-Fort Worth. The station had begun broadcasting five months earlier as KBTV.

December 1981 marked the beginning of a new era in A. H. Belo Corporation's history. In that month, the company became a publicly held entity, and its common stock is now traded on the New York Stock Exchange.

In 1984, Belo purchased four television stations from Dun & Bradstreet. The company acquired VHF stations KHOU-TV (CBS) in Houston, KXTV (ABC) in Sacramento, Calif., WVEC-TV (ABC) in Hampton-Norfolk, Va., and KOTV (CBS) in Tulsa, Okla. With the acquisitions of WWL-TV (CBS) in New Orleans, La., in June 1994, and KIRO-TV (UPN) in Seattle, Wash., in February 1995, Belo brought the number of network-affiliated television stations it owns to seven. Also part of Belo's Broadcast Division are Belo Productions Inc. and Maxam Entertainment, both based in Dallas.

Officers and Directors

Officers of A. H. Belo Corporation are Robert W. Decherd, chairman of the board, president and chief executive officer; Ward L. Huey Jr., vice chairman of the board and president/Broadcast Division; Michael J. McCarthy, senior vice president, secretary and general counsel; Michael D. Perry, senior vice president and chief financial officer; Harold F. Gaar Jr., vice president of public affairs; Brenda C. Maddox, vice president of corporate taxes; William E. Nolen, vice president/internal audit; Dunia A. Shive, vice president and controller; Marian Spitzberg, vice president and assistant general counsel; and Vicky C. Teherani, vice president and treasurer.

The following are members of A. H. Belo Corporation's board of directors: John W. Bassett Jr.; Judith L.

Craven, M.D., M.P.H.; Robert W. Decherd; Roger A. Enrico; Dealey D. Herndon; Ward L. Huey Jr.; Lester A. Levy; Arturo Madrid, Ph.D.; James M. Moroney Jr.; Burl Osborne; Hugh G. Robinson; William T. Solomon; Thomas B. Walker Jr.; and J. McDonald Williams.

Officers of *The Dallas Morning News* are Burl Osborne, publisher and editor; Jeremy L. Halbreich, president and general manager; Ralph Langer, senior vice president and executive editor; Robert W. Mong Jr., managing editor; Rena Pederson, vice president and editorial page editor; J. William Cox, senior vice president of operations and administration; Richard Starks, senior vice president of sales and marketing; Barry Peckham, senior vice president of circulation; Sergio H. Salinas, vice president of advertising; Barbara van Pelt, vice president of marketing; Reginald K. Brown, vice president of finance; James M. Correu, vice president of production; Grover D. Livingston, vice president of information management; Ellen Silva Wilson, vice president of human resources; and Nancy Barry, vice president of community services.

Officers of Belo's Broadcast Division include James M. Moroney III, who was appointed executive vice president of the television station group in December 1994; Kenneth L. Hatch, senior vice president/Broadcast Division; and Martin Haag Jr., vice president of news/Broadcast Division. Officers of the seven television operating companies are Cathy Creany, president and general manager, WFAA-TV, Dallas-Fort Worth, Tex.; Al Howard, president and general manager, KHOU-TV, Houston, Tex.; Glenn Wright, vice president and general manager, KIRO-TV, Seattle, Wash.; James G. Saunders, president and general manager, KXTV, Sacramento, Calif.; Lee R. Salzberger, president and general manager, WVEC-TV, Hampton-Norfolk, Va.; J. Michael Early, president and general manager, WWL-TV, New Orleans, La.; and Ronald S. Longinotti, vice president and general manager, KOTV, Tulsa, Okla.

Officers of DFW Suburban Newspapers, Inc. are Daniel L. Crowe, president and chief executive officer, and J. Randall Chandler, vice president/operations.

Robert W. Decherd

Robert W. Decherd is a director, chairman of the board, president and chief executive officer of A. H. Belo Corporation. Mr. Decherd has worked for Belo or its principal newspaper subsidiary, *The Dallas Morning News*, since his graduation from Harvard College in 1973.

In addition to his executive role, Mr. Decherd is a major shareholder in the Belo Corporation and is active in a variety of professional and civic activities. He is a past president of the Dallas Society of Professional Journalists and the Freedom of Information Foundation of Texas, Inc. He is presently a director and member of the executive committee of the Newspaper Association of America (NAA) and chairs NAA's Public Policy Committee.

In civic affairs, Mr. Decherd is currently serving as chairman of a $21 million capital and endowment campaign for Paul Quinn College, the only historically black college in North Texas.

He served as president of the board of trustees at St. Mark's School of Texas from 1988-91 and chaired a successful $21 million endowment drive at Southwestern Medical Center in 1989-90. He has been a member of the executive committee of the Dallas Citizens Council and chairman of its Public Planning Policy Committee. Mr. Decherd is also a member of the Dallas Together Forum and a trustee of the Tomás Rivera Center for Policy Studies.

Mr. Decherd graduated cum laude from Harvard, where he was president of The Harvard Crimson. From 1987-91, he co-chaired a $2.5 million national building campaign for The Crimson and later served as vice chairman of The Crimson's graduate board.

Ward L. Huey Jr.

Ward L. Huey Jr., vice chairman of the board and president of the Broadcast Division of A. H. Belo Corporation, has an extensive background of over 30 years in broadcast operations and management.

A graduate of Southern Methodist University in 1960, Mr. Huey initially worked as a copywriter and account executive for Glenn Advertising in Dallas. He joined Belo's WFAA-TV production department that same year, became sales service manager in 1961, and for the next 10 years served in a variety of sales and marketing positions at WFAA-TV, including account executive, regional sales manager and general sales manager.

Mr. Huey was promoted to WFAA-TV station manager in 1972 and elected a vice president in 1973.

In 1975, Mr. Huey was named vice president and general manager of all Belo broadcast properties. He was elected to the board of directors of A. H. Belo Corporation in 1982. In 1987, he was elected vice chairman of the board and president of the broadcast division of A. H. Belo Corporation.

A native of Dallas, Mr. Huey is a past chairman of the ABC Television Affiliates board of governors and past chairman of the Television Operators Caucus board of directors. He currently serves as vice chairman of the board of the Maximum Service Television and has recently completed a four-year term on the board of directors of the Television Bureau of Advertising. His civic activities include past president of the Salesmanship Club of Dallas, the board of trustees of Children's Medical Foundation of Texas, the executive board for Meadows School of the Arts of Southern Methodist University, the State Fair of Texas board, the Cotton Bowl Council and the Dallas Assembly. He has previously served on the boards of the Association of Broadcast Executives of Texas, the Dallas Advertising League and the SMU Alumni Association.

Burl Osborne

Burl Osborne joined *The Dallas Morning News* as executive editor in October 1980 and added the title of vice president in 1981. In 1983, he was named senior vice president and editor; in 1985, he became president and editor. Mr. Osborne was elected to the board of directors in May 1987; he was named publisher of *The Dallas Morning News* in 1991.

Mr. Osborne came to *The News* after 20 years with the Associated Press, where he started as a correspondent and editor-reporter, served in a variety of management positions and became managing editor in 1977.

He holds a bachelor's degree in journalism and mathematics from Marshall University, West Virginia, and a master's degree in business from Long Island University.

He is chairman of the American Press Institute, director and former president of the American Society of Newspaper Editors and was president of the Texas Daily Newspaper Association in 1993. He is chairman of the board of the Foundation for American Communications, among others. He is a member of the Pulitzer Prize Board and the Advisory Council of The University of Texas at Austin, College of Communications Foundation. He is chairman of the board of directors of the Associated Press, and he chairs the Presstime Advisory Committee of the Newspaper Association of America.

James M. Moroney Jr.

James M. Moroney Jr. is the son of the late James M. Moroney and the late Maidie Dealey Moroney. He was born in Dallas, attended Highland Park School and St. John's Military Academy in Delafield, Wis. He graduated from The University of Texas at Austin in 1943. During summer vacations, he worked part-time at radio and television stations WFAA and *The Dallas Morning News*.

During World War II, he entered the U.S. Navy, rising to the rank of lieutenant (jg). He saw much action, including the D-Day landing in Normandy. He was released from active duty in 1946.

Mr. Moroney joined *The News* as a reporter, served as an advertising salesman and worked in the promotion and circulation departments before becoming assistant to the business manager in 1950. He also spent a year at the radio and television stations.

He progressed to assistant treasurer of the corporation and was elected to the board of directors in 1952. In 1955, he was named treasurer, elevated to vice president and treasurer in 1960 and became executive vice president in 1970. In 1973, Mr. Moroney was named president and chief executive officer of Belo Broadcasting Corporation and in 1974 became chairman of the board of that corporation.

In 1980, he was elected president and chief executive officer of *The Dallas Morning News* and president and chief operating officer of A. H. Belo Corporation.

He was promoted to the position of president and chief executive officer of A. H. Belo Corporation January 1983. In April 1984, he was elected to the additional position of chairman of the board. In January 1985 he relinquished the title of president.

Mr. Moroney retired as an active operating officer of A. H. Belo Corporation on Dec. 31, 1986.

John W. Bassett Jr.

John W. Bassett Jr. is a native of Roswell, N.M., where he practices law. After graduating from Roswell High School, he attended Stanford University, where he majored in economics and received a bachelor's degree in 1960.

Following graduation, he was commissioned as a second lieutenant in the Army and entered active duty at Fort Benning, Ga. He served in the Second Infantry Division there and in the Army Reserves, where he was advanced to first lieutenant.

Mr. Bassett attended The University of Texas School of Law and became an associate editor of The Texas Law Review. Upon graduating with honors in June 1964, he was awarded a bachelor of law degree and became a member of the Order of the Coif, a legal honorary organization.

After passing the Texas and New Mexico Bar examinations in 1964, he practiced law in Roswell.

In 1966, Mr. Bassett was selected as a White House Fellow and for a year served as a special assistant to the attorney general of the United States.

In October 1967, Mr. Bassett returned to private practice with the law firm of Atwood, Malone, Mann and Turner, P.A., in Roswell.

Mr. Bassett was elected to the board of directors of A. H. Belo Corporation in 1979. He is a former member of the Board of Education for the State of New Mexico. He is a Rotarian and a member of several boards of directors of local charitable institutions in Roswell.

Judith L. Craven, M.D., M.P.H.

Judith L. Craven is a native of Houston, where she serves as president of the United Way of the Texas Gulf Coast. Dr. Craven holds a bachelor of science degree from Bowling Green University, doctor of medicine from Baylor College of Medicine, and master of public health from The University of Texas School of Public Health. She also completed a program for senior managers in government at the John F. Kennedy School of Government at Harvard University.

Prior to her election as president of the United Way in July 1992, Dr. Craven served nine years as dean of the School of Allied Health Sciences at The University of Texas Health Science Center at Houston, and five years concurrently as vice president of multicultural affairs for The University of Texas Health Science Center.

Previously, she had been chief of Family Health Services and then director of public health for the City of Houston Health Department, and was chief of anesthesia for Riverside General Hospital in Houston.

Dr. Craven was elected to the board of directors of A. H. Belo Corporation in 1992. She has held numerous offices with local, state and national boards and committees, including president of United Way of Texas. She has served on three gubernatorial commissions in Texas. She has received many awards recognizing her achievements, including Outstanding Young Women of America, The NAACP VIP Award for Community Services, and fellowship in the American Leadership Forum. She is the second female and the first African-American to serve as president in the 71-year history of the United Way of the Texas Gulf Coast.

Roger A. Enrico

Roger Enrico is chairman and chief executive officer of PepsiCo Worldwide Restaurants and vice chairman of the board of PepsiCo, Inc. Mr. Enrico has played a major role in PepsiCo's development throughout his 24-year career with the corporation. He was elected to the board of directors of the A.H. Belo Corporation in July 1995.

Prior to his appointment as vice chairman of PepsiCo, Mr. Enrico was chairman and chief executive officer of PepsiCo Worldwide Foods, the corporation's international snack business. Previously he had been chairman and CEO of Frito-Lay, the corporation's domestic snack-food business, president and CEO of PepsiCo Worldwide Beverages and president of Pepsi-Cola USA. He was elected to the PepsiCo board of directors in 1987.

Mr. Enrico grew up in Minnesota. He is a graduate of Babson College with a bachelor's degree in finance, and he holds an honorary doctorate of law from Babson.

He serves on the boards of directors of Dayton Hudson Corporation, The Prudential Insurance Company of America, Inc. and the United Negro College Fund. He is a member of the Babson College Corporation and the executive board of the Dallas Symphony Association.

Dealey D. Herndon

Dealey D. Herndon of Austin was elected to the Board of Directors in 1986. She was born in Dallas and is the daughter of the late H. Ben Decherd and Isabelle Thomason Decherd. She is an honors graduate of Hockaday School and The University of Texas at Austin. She was administrator of Friends of the Governor's Mansion from 1983 to 1984.

Mrs. Herndon has lived in El Paso, Dallas and Austin, where she has been active in civic and non-profit activities for the past eight years. In Dallas, she served on the board of the Dallas County Heritage Society. In Austin, she has been a board member of the Austin Junior League, West Austin Youth Association, the Seton Hospital Development Board and the Pebble Project, a child abuse prevention agency. She served as president of the Austin History Center Association Board. She was treasurer of the St. Andrew's Episcopal School board of trustees and chairman of the Austin High School Excellence Fund.

She is president and a director of the Friends of the Governor's Mansion in Austin, and the executive director of the State Preservation Board of the State of Texas.

Lester A. Levy

Lester A. Levy was born and educated in Dallas. He attended The University of Texas at Austin until early 1943, at which time he entered the Air Force. He received his license to practice law during 1943 while in the service. After an honorable discharge in 1946, he joined his father's company, now known as NCH Corporation, while awaiting a semester change in order to take refresher courses at The University of Texas. His father's untimely death caused him to remain with the company, where he is presently chairman of the board of directors.

Mr. Levy was elected to the board of directors of A. H. Belo Corporation in 1985. He has served on the boards of the University of Dallas, Greenhill School, Baylor College of Dentistry, the Lamplighter School, and was co-founder and director of the Winston School. He has also served as a trustee for Temple Emanu-El, Golden Acres Home for the Aged and Special Care and Career Center (formerly Special Care School for Handicapped Children).

Arturo Madrid, Ph.D.

Dr. Arturo Madrid is the Norine R. and T. Frank Murchison Distinguished Professor of the Humanities at Trinity University. From 1984 to 1993, he served as the founding president of the Tomás Rivera Center for Policy Studies, the nation's first institute for policy studies on Latino issues. In addition to holding academic and administrative appointments at Dartmouth College, The University of California, San Diego, and the University of Minnesota, he has also served as director of the Fund for the Improvement of Post-Secondary Education (FIPSE), U.S. Department of Education and of the Ford Foundation's Graduate Fellowships Program.

Over the past two decades, Dr. Madrid has served on the boards of some of the country's most prominent organizations, including The College Board, the Association for the Advancement of Higher Education, the Council for Basic Education, The Center for Early Adolescence, the National Board for Professional Teaching Standards, the National Center for Education and the Economy, and The National Civic League. Dr. Madrid holds honorary doctorates from New England College and The California State University, Hayward, and is an elected fellow of the Council on Foreign Relations, the nation's premier foreign-policy association, and the National Academy for Public Administration, which honors persons with distinguished records in public administration.

Hugh G. Robinson

Hugh G. Robinson was elected to the board of directors of A. H. Belo Corporation in 1989. He is chief executive officer of The Tetra Group, a construction management firm. For more than five years prior to that, Mr. Robinson was president of Cityplace Development Corporation, a real estate development subsidiary of The Southland Corporation, and vice president of The Southland Corporation.

Mr. Robinson was born in Washington, D.C., and graduated from the U.S. Military Academy, West Point, in 1954. He earned a master's degree in civil engineering from Massachusetts Institute of Technology in 1959, and he holds an honorary doctor of laws degree from Williams College.

He entered the U.S. Army in 1954, following his graduation from West Point, and served until his retirement in 1983 with the rank of major general. He received numerous military awards, including the Distinguished Service Medal. He is a former member of the board of directors of the Federal Reserve Bank of Dallas, and he is currently a member of the boards of directors of Lomas Financial Corporation, Guaranty Federal Savings Bank and TU Electric Company, among others.

William T. Solomon

William T. Solomon is chairman, president and chief executive officer of Austin Industries Inc., which is the largest general contractor in Dallas and one of the five largest contractors in the southern half of the United States. Austin Industries is the only major contractor in its markets that is completely employee-owned.

Born and reared in Dallas, Mr. Solomon holds a civil engineering degree from Southern Methodist University and an M.B.A. from Harvard Graduate School of Business.

Mr. Solomon joined Austin full-time in 1967, becoming president and chief executive officer in 1970. The title of chairman was added in 1987.

Mr. Solomon is a former member of the board of directors of Fidelity Union Life Insurance Company and served on the board of trustees of Southern Methodist University. He is a past chairman of the Dallas Chamber of Commerce and currently serves on the boards of directors of numerous other civic and community organizations. He was elected to the board of directors of A. H. Belo Corporation in 1983.

Thomas B. Walker Jr.

Thomas B. Walker Jr. has been a partner, either general or limited, in Goldman, Sachs & Co., investment bankers, since 1968. He was elected to the board of directors of A. H. Belo Corporation in 1982.

Mr. Walker is a native of Nashville, Tenn. and is a Phi Beta Kappa graduate of Vanderbilt University.

During World War II, he served as a lieutenant in the U.S. Navy operating in the Mediterranean, Atlantic and South Pacific areas.

After the war, Mr. Walker joined the Equitable Securities Corporation and moved to Dallas in 1950. He served as senior vice president and director, Equitable Securities (American Express Company) until 1968.

He is also a member of the boards of directors of NCH Corporation, SYSCO Corporation and Central and Southwest Corporation, and he is a former member of the Kleinwort Benson International Equity Fund board.

J. McDonald Williams

J. McDonald (Don) Williams is a native of Roswell, N.M. He graduated from Abilene Christian University in 1963 and from George Washington University Law School in 1966, both with honors.

He practiced law in Dallas seven years until he joined the Trammell Crow Company in May 1973. He entered the firm as the partner responsible for overseas developments and then was named managing partner in 1977.

Mr. Williams was elected to the board of directors of A. H. Belo Corporation in 1985. He also is a former member of the board of directors of Fidelity Union Life Insurance Company. He currently serves on the boards of Abilene Christian University, George Washington University, Pepperdine University and Southwestern Christian College. ☆

Texas Newspapers, Radio and Television Stations

In the list of print and broadcast media below, frequency of publication of newspapers is indicated after the names by the following codes: (D), daily; (S), semiweekly; (BW), biweekly; (SM), semimonthly; (M), monthly; all others are weeklies. The radio and television stations are those with valid operating licenses as of the dates noted at the end of the list. Not included are those with only construction permits or with applications pending.

Abernathy — Newspaper: Weekly Review.

Abilene — Newspaper: Reporter-News (D). **Radio-AM:** KEAN,1280 Khz; KYYD, 1340; KNTS, 1470; KBBA, 1560. **Radio-FM:** KGNZ, 88.1 MHz; KACU, 89.7; KORQ, 100.7; KEAN, 105.1; KHXS, 106.3; KEYJ, 107.9. **TV:** KRBC-Ch. 9; KTAB-Ch. 32.

Alamo — Radio-FM: KJAV, 104.9 MHz.

Alamo Heights — Radio-AM: KDRY, 1100 Khz.

Albany — Newspaper: News.

Alice — Newspaper: Echo-News (D). **Radio-AM:** KDSI, 1070 Khz. **Radio-FM:** KQNN, 92.1 MHz; KBIC, 102.3.

Allen — Newspaper: American (S).

Alpine — Newspaper: Avalanche. **Radio-AM:** KVLF, 1240 Khz. **Radio-FM:** KALP, 92.7 MHz.

Alvarado — Newspaper: Post.

Alvin — Newspaper: Sun (S). **Radio-AM:** KTEK, 1110 Khz. **Radio-FM:** KACC, 89.7 MHz. **TV:** KHSH-Ch. 67.

Alvord — Newspaper: Gazette.

Amarillo — Newspapers: Globe-News (D); Southwest Stockman. **Radio-AM:** KGNC, 710 Khz; KIXZ, 940; KDJW, 1010; KZIP, 1310; KLCJ, 1360; KPUR, 1440. **Radio-FM:** KJRT, 88.3 MHz; KLMN, 89.1; KACV, 89.9; KYFA, 91.9; KQIZ, 93.1; KBUY, 94.1; KMML, 96.9; KGNC, 97.9; KQAC, 98.7; KFMA, 99.7; KATP, 101.9; KRGN, 103.1; KAEZ, 105.7. **TV:** KACV-Ch. 2; KAMR-Ch. 4; KVII-Ch. 7; KFDA-Ch. 10; KCIT-Ch. 14.

Amherst — Newspaper: Press (SM).

Anahuac — Newspaper: The Progress.

Andrews — Newspaper: Andrews County News (S). **Radio-AM:** KACT, 1360 Khz. **Radio-FM:** KACT, 105.5 MHz.

Angleton — Newspaper: Times (S).

Anson — Newspaper: Western Observer. **Radio-FM:** KKHR, 98.1 MHz.

Aransas Pass — Newspaper: Progress.

Archer City — Newspaper: Archer County News.

Arlington — Newspaper: News (S). **Radio-FM:** KSNN, 94.9 MHz.

Aspermont — Newspaper: Stonewall County Courier.

Athens — Newspaper: Daily Review (D). **Radio-AM:** KLVQ, 1410 Khz.

Atlanta — Newspaper: Citizens Journal (S). **Radio-AM:** KALT, 900 Khz. **Radio-FM:** KPYN, 99.3 MHz.

Austin — Newspapers: American-Statesman (D); Austin Business Journal; Lake Travis View; Texas Observer (BW); Westlake Picayune. **Radio-AM:** KLBJ, 590 Khz; KVET, 1300; KFON, 1490. **Radio-FM:** KAZI, 88.7 MHz; KMFA, 89.5; KUT, 90.5; KLBJ, 93.7; KKMJ, 95.5; KVET, 98.1; KASE, 100.7; KPEZ, 102.3. **TV:** KTBC-Ch. 7; KLRU-Ch. 18; KVUE-Ch. 24; KXAN-Ch. 36; KBVO-Ch. 42.

Azle — Newspaper: News.

Baird — Newspaper: Callahan County Star.

Balch Springs — Radio-AM: KSKY, 660 Khz.

Ballinger — Newspaper: Ledger. **Radio-AM:** KRUN, 1400 Khz. **Radio-FM:** KRUN, 103.1 MHz.

Bandera — Newspaper: Bulletin. **Radio-FM:** KEEP, 98.3 MHz.

Bartlett — Newspaper: Tribune Progress.

Bastrop — Newspaper: Advertiser (S) **Radio-FM:** KGSR, 107.1 MHz.

Bay City — Newspaper: Daily Tribune (D). **Radio-AM:** KIOX, 1270 Khz. **Radio-FM:** KMKS, 102.5 MHz.

Baytown — Newspaper: Sun (D). **Radio-AM:** KWWJ, 1360 Khz. **TV:** KVVV-Ch. 57.

Beaumont — Newspaper: Enterprise (D). **Radio-AM:** KLVI, 560 Khz; KZZB, 990; KZXT, 1380; KAYC, 1450. **Radio-FM:** KTXB, 89.7 MHz; KVLU, 91.3; KQXY, 94.1; KYKR, 95.1; KAYD, 97.5; KXTJ, 107.9. **TV:** KFDM-Ch. 6; KBMT-Ch. 12; KITU-Ch. 34.

Beeville — Newspaper: Bee-Picayune (S). **Radio-AM:** KIBL, 1490 Khz. **Radio-FM:** KYTX, 97.9 MHz; KIBL, 104.9.

Bellville — Newspaper: Times. **Radio-AM:** KFRD, 1090 Khz.

Belton — Newspaper: Journal. **Radio-AM:** KTON, 940 Khz. **Radio-FM:** KOOC, 106.3 MHz. **TV:** KNCT-Ch. 46.

Big Lake — Newspaper: Wildcat. **Radio-AM:** KWGH, 1290 Khz.

Big Sandy — Newspaper: Big Sandy-Hawkins Journal.

Big Spring — Newspaper: Herald (D). **Radio-AM:** KBYG, 1400; KBST, 1490. **Radio-FM:** KBST, 95.3 MHz. **TV:** KWAB-Ch. 4.

Bishop — Radio-FM: KFLZ, 107.1 MHz.

Blanco — Newspaper: Blanco County News.

Bloomington — Radio-FM: KLUB, 106.9 MHz.

Blossom — Newspaper: Times.

Boerne — Newspapers: Hill Country Recorder; Star. **Radio-AM:** KBRN, 1500 Khz.

Bogata — Newspaper: News.

Bonham — Newspaper: Daily Favorite (D). **Radio-AM:** KFYN, 1420 Khz. **Radio-FM:** KFYZ, 98.3 MHz.

Booker — Newspaper: News.

Borger — Newspaper: News-Herald (D). **Radio-AM:** KQTY, 1490 Khz; KBBB, 1600. **Radio-FM:** KQFZ, 104.3 MHz.

Bovina — Newspaper: Blade.
Bowie — Newspaper: News (S). **Radio-AM:** KRJT, 1410 Khz. **Radio-FM:** KRJT, 100.7 Mhz.
Brackettville — Newspaper: Brackett News.
Brady — Newspapers: Herald; Standard. **Radio-AM:** KNEL, 1490 Khz. **Radio-FM:** KNEL, 95.3 MHz.
Breckenridge — Newspaper: American (S). **Radio-AM:** KSTB, 1430 Khz. **Radio-FM:** KROO, 93.5 MHz.
Bremond — Newspaper: Press.
Brenham — Newspaper: Banner-Press (D). **Radio-AM:** KWHI, 1280 Khz. **Radio-FM:** KULF, 94.1 Mhz; KTTX, 106.1.
Bridgeport — Newspaper: Index. **Radio-FM:** KBOC, 96.7 MHz.
Brookshire — Newspapers: Bluebonnet Banner; Times Tribune.
Brownfield — Newspaper: News (S). **Radio-AM:** KKUB, 1300 Khz. **Radio-FM:** KLZK, 103.9 MHz.
Brownsboro — Newspaper: Statesman.
Brownsville — Newspaper: Herald (D). **Radio-AM:** KBOR, 1600 Khz. **Radio-FM:** KBNR, 88.3 MHz; KKPS, 99.5; KTEX, 100.3. **TV:** KVEO-Ch. 23.
Brownwood — Newspaper: Bulletin (D). **Radio-AM:** KXYL, 1240 Khz; KBWD, 1380. **Radio-FM:** KBUB, 90.3 MHz; KPSM, 99.3; KOXE, 101.5; KXYL, 104.1.
Bryan — Newspaper: Bryan-College Station Eagle (D). **Radio-AM:** KTAM, 1240 Khz; KAGC, 1510. **Radio-FM:** KORA, 98.3 MHz; KKYS, 104.7. **TV:** KBTX-Ch. 3.
Buda — Newspaper: Hays County Free Press.
Buffalo — Newspaper: Press.
Buna — Newspaper: Beacon.
Burkburnett — Newspaper: Informer Star. **Radio-FM:** KYYI, 104.7 MHz.
Burleson — Newspaper: Star (S).
Burnet — Newspapers: Bulletin; Citizens Gazette. **Radio-AM:** KHLB, 1340 Khz. **Radio-FM:** KBLK, 92.5 MHz; KHLB, 106.9.
Caldwell — Newspaper: Burleson County Citizen-Tribune.
Calvert — Newspaper: Tribune.
Cameron — Newspaper: Herald. **Radio-AM:** KMIL, 1330 Khz. **Radio-FM:** KHLR, 103.9 MHz.
Canadian — Newspaper: Record. **Radio-FM:** KRBG, 103.1 MHz.
Canton — Newspaper: Herald.
Canyon — Newspaper: News (S). **Radio-AM:** KAKS, 1550 Khz. **Radio-FM:** KWTS, 91.1 MHz; KPUR, 107.1; KAKS, 107.9.
Canyon Lake — Newspaper: Times Guardian.
Carrizo Springs — Newspaper: Javelin. **Radio-AM:** KBEN, 1450 Khz. **Radio-FM:** KCZO, 92.1 MHz.
Carthage — Newspaper: Panola Watchman (S). **Radio-AM:** KGAS, 1590 Khz. **Radio-FM:** KTUX, 98.9 MHz.
Castroville — Newspaper: News Bulletin.
Cedar Hill — Newspaper: Today.
Celina — Newspaper: Record.
Center — Newspaper: Light & Champion (S). **Radio-AM:** KDET, 930 Khz. **Radio-FM:** KDET, 102.3 MHz.
Centerville — Newspaper: News.
Chico — Newspaper: Texan.
Childress — Newspaper: Index (S). **Radio-AM:** KCTX, 1510 Khz. **Radio-FM:** KSRW, 96.1 MHz.
Chillicothe — Newspaper: Valley News.
Cisco — Newspaper: Press (S).
Clarendon — Newspaper: News.
Clarksville — Newspaper: Times. **Radio-AM:** KCAR, 1350 Khz. **Radio-FM:** KGAP, 98.5 HMz.
Claude — Newspaper: News. **Radio-FM**: KARX, 95.7 MHz.
Clear Lake/League City — Newspaper: Citizen (S).
Cleburne — Newspaper: Times-Review (D). **Radio-AM:** KCLE, 1120 Khz.
Cleveland — Newspaper: Advocate. **Radio-FM:** KRTK, 97.1 MHz.
Clifton — Newspaper: Record. **Radio-FM:** KWOW, 103.3 MHz.
Clute — Newspaper: Brazosport Facts (D).
Clyde — Newspaper: Journal.
Cockrell Hill — Radio-AM: KRVA, 1600 Khz.
Coleman — Newspaper: Chronicle & Democrat-Voice (S). **Radio-AM:** KSTA, 1000 Khz. **Radio-FM:** KSTA, 107.1 MHz.
College Station — Newspaper: Battalion (D). **Radio-AM:** WTAW, 1150 Khz. **Radio-FM:** KAMU, 90.9 MHz; KTSR, 92.1. **TV:** KAMU-Ch. 15.
Colleyville — Newspaper: News & Times.
Colorado City — Newspaper: Record (S). **Radio-AM:** KVMC, 1320 Khz. **Radio-FM:** KAUM, 106.3 MHz.
Columbus — Newspapers: Banner Press; Colorado County Citizen. **Radio-FM:** KULM, 98.3 MHz.
Comanche — Newspaper: Chief. **Radio-AM:** KCOM, 1550 Khz.
Comfort — Newspaper: News. **Radio-FM:** KRNH, 95.1 MHz.
Commerce — Newspaper: Journal (S) **Radio-FM:** KETR, 88.9 MHz; KEMM, 92.1.
Conroe — Newspaper: Courier (D). **Radio-AM:** KJOJ, 880 Khz; KSSQ, 1140. **Radio-FM:** KKZR, 106.9 MHz. **TV:** KTFH-Ch. 49.
Cooper — Newspaper: Review.
Coppell — Newspaper: Citizens' Advocate.
Copperas Cove — Newspaper: Leader Press. **Radio-FM:** KOOV, 103.1 MHz.
Corpus Christi — Newspapers: Caller-Times (D); Legal & Business News (D). **Radio-AM:** KCTA, 1030 Khz; KCCT, 1150; KSIX, 1230; KRYS, 1360; KUNO, 1400; KEYS, 1440. **Radio-FM:** KFGG, 88.7 MHz; KEDT, 90.3; KBNJ, 91.7; KMXR, 93.9; KBSO, 94.7; KZFM, 95.5; KLTG, 96.5; KRYS, 99.1. **TV:** KIII-Ch. 3; KRIS-Ch. 6; KZTV-Ch. 10; KEDT-Ch. 16; KORO-Ch. 28.
Corrigan — Newspaper: Times.
Corsicana — Newspaper: Daily Sun (D). **Radio-AM:** KAND, 1340 Khz. **Radio-FM:** KICI, 107.9 MHz.
Cotulla — Radio-FM: KDCY, 97.7 MHz.
Crane — Newspaper: News. **Radio-AM:** KXOI, 810 Khz.
Crockett — Newspaper: Houston County Courier (S). **Radio-AM:** KIVY, 1290 Khz. **Radio-FM:** KIVY, 92.7 MHz; KBHT, 93.5.
Crosbyton — Newspaper: Crosby County News & Chronicle.
Cross Plains — Newspaper: Review.
Crowell — Newspaper: Foard County News.
Crowley — Newspaper: Review.
Crystal City — Newspaper: Zavala County Sentinel. **Radio-FM:** KHER, 94.3 MHz.
Cuero — Newspaper: Record. **Radio-AM:** KQRO, 1600 Khz. **Radio-FM:** KQRO, 97.7 MHz.
Cypress — Radio-AM: KYND, 1520 Khz.
Daingerfield — Newspaper: Bee. **Radio-AM:** KEGG, 1560 Khz. **Radio-FM:** KWSK, 106.9 MHz.
Dalhart — Newspaper: Daily Texan (D). **Radio-AM:** KXIT, 1240 Khz. **Radio-FM:** KXIT, 95.9 MHz.
Dallas — Newspapers: The Dallas Morning News (D); Business Journal; Commercial Record (D); Oak Cliff Tribune; Park Cities News; Park Cities People; Suburban Tribune; Texas Jewish Post; White Rocker. **Radio-AM:** KLIF, 570 Khz; KGGR, 1040; KRLD, 1080; KGBS, 1190; KTCK, 1310; KMRT, 1480. **Radio-FM:** KNON, 89.3 HMz; KERA, 90.1; KCBI, 90.9; KVTT, 91.7; KZPS, 92.5; KRSM, 93.3; KRRW, 97.9; KLUV, 98.7; KJMZ, 100.3; WRR, 101.1; KDMX, 102.9; KKDA, 104.5; KYNG, 105.3. **TV:** KDFW-Ch. 4; WFAA-Ch. 8; KERA-Ch. 13; KDFI-Ch. 27; KDAF-Ch. 33; KXTX-Ch. 39; KDTX-Ch. 58.
Decatur — Newspaper: Wise County Messenger (S).
Deer Park — Newspaper: Progress.
De Kalb — Newspaper: News.
De Leon — Newspaper: Free Press.
Dell City — Newspaper: Hudspeth County Herald.
Del Rio — Newspaper: News-Herald (D). **Radio-AM:** KLKE, 1230 Khz; KWMC, 1490. **Radio-FM:** KDLK, 94.3 MHz; KTDR, 96.3.
Del Valle — Radio-AM: KIXL, 970 Khz.
Denison — Newspaper: Herald (D). **Radio-AM:** KDSX, 950 Khz. **Radio-FM:** KTCY, 104.9 MHz; KDSQ, 101.7.
Denton — Newspaper: Record-Chronicle (D). **Radio-AM:** KICI, 1440 Khz. **Radio-FM:** KNTU, 88.1 MHz; KDZR, 99.1; KHKS, 106.1. **TV:** KDTN-Ch. 2.
Denver City — Newspaper: Press (S).

Deport — Newspaper: Times.
DeSoto — Newspapers: Best Southwest Focus (S); Today.
Detroit — Newspaper: Weekly.
Devine — Newspaper: News. **Radio-FM:** KTXX, 92.1 MHz.
Diboll — Newspaper: Free Press. **Radio-AM:** KAFX, 1260 Khz. **Radio-FM:** KAFX, 95.5 MHz.
Dimmitt — Newspaper: Castro County News. **Radio-AM:** KDHN, 1470 Khz.
Donna — Newspaper: Events-News.
Dripping Springs — Newspaper: Dispatch.
Dublin — Newspaper: Citizen.
Dumas — Newspaper: Moore County News-Press (S). **Radio-AM:** KDDD, 800 Khz. **Radio-FM:** KMRE, 95.3 MHz.
Duncanville — Newspaper: Today.
Eagle Lake — Newspaper: Headlight.
Eagle Pass — Newspapers: News Gram; News-Guide (S). **Radio-AM:** KEPS, 1270 Khz. **Radio-FM:** KINL, 92.7 MHz.
East Bernard — Newspaper: Tribune.
Eastland — Newspaper: Telegram (S). **Radio-AM:** KEAS, 1590 Khz. **Radio-FM:** KVMX, 96.7 MHz; KEAS, 97.7.
Eden — Newspaper: Echo.
Edgewood — Newspaper: Enterprise.
Edinburg — Newspaper: Daily Review (D). **Radio-AM:** KURV, 710 Khz. **Radio-FM:** KOIR, 88.5 MHz; KBFM, 104.1; KVLY, 107.9.
Edna — Newspaper: Jackson County Herald-Tribune. **Radio-AM:** KTMR, 1130 Khz.
El Campo — Newspaper: Leader-News (S). **Radio-AM:** KULP, 1390 Khz. **Radio-FM:** KIOX, 96.9 MHz.
Eldorado — Newspaper: Success.
Electra — Newspaper: Star-News.
Elgin — Newspaper: Courier. **Radio-AM:** KELG, 1440 Khz. **Radio-FM:** KKLB, 92.5 MHz.
El Paso — Newspapers: Herald-Post (D); Times (D). **Radio-AM:** KROD, 600 Khz; KHEY, 690; KAMA, 750; KBNA, 920; KFNA, 1060; KSVE, 1150; KVIV, 1340; KTSM, 1380; KELP, 1590. **Radio-FM:** KTEP, 88.5 MHz; KXCR; 89.5; KVER, 91.1; KOFX, 92.3; KAMZ, 93.1; KINT, 93.9; KSET, 94.7; KLAQ, 95.5; KHEY, 96.3; KBNA, 97.5; KTSM, 99.9; KPRR, 102.1. **TV:** KDBC-Ch. 4; KVIA-Ch. 7; KTSM-Ch. 9; KCOS-Ch. 13; KFOX-Ch. 14; KINT-Ch. 26; KSCE-Ch. 38; KJLF-Ch. 65.
Emory — Newspaper: Rains County Leader.
Ennis — Newspapers: Daily News (D); Ellis County News; The Press.
Everman — Newspaper: Times.
Fabens — Radio-FM: KPAS, 103.1 MHz.
Fairfield — Newspaper: Recorder. **Radio-FM:** KNES, 92.1 MHz.
Falfurrias — Newspaper: Facts. **Radio-AM:** KPSO, 1260 Khz. **Radio-FM:** KPSO, 106.3 MHz.
Farmersville — Newspaper: Times.
Farwell — Newspaper: State Line Tribune. **Radio-AM:** KIJN, 1060 Khz. **Radio-FM:** KIJN, 92.3 MHz; KICA, 98.3.
Ferris — Newspaper: Ellis County Press. **Radio-AM:** KDFT, 540 Khz.
Flatonia — Newspaper: Argus.
Floresville — Newspapers: Chronicle-Journal; Wilson County News. **Radio-FM:** KWCB, 89.7 MHz; KRIO, 94.1.
Flower Mound — Newspaper: FlowerPlex PipeLine.
Floydada — Newspaper: Floyd County Hesperian-Beacon. **Radio-FM:** KFLL, 95.3 MHz.
Follett — Newspaper: The Golden Spread.
Forney — Newspaper: Messenger.
Fort Davis — Newspaper: Jeff Davis County Mountain Dispatch.
Fort Stockton — Newspaper: Pioneer. **Radio-AM:** KFST, 860 Khz. **Radio-FM:** KFST, 94.3 MHz.
Fort Worth — Newspapers: Business Press; Commercial Recorder (D); Star-Telegram (D); Times-Record; Weekly Livestock Reporter. **Radio-AM:** WBAP, 820 Khz; KFJZ, 870; KHVN, 970; KESS, 1270; KAHZ, 1360; KTMO, 1540; KRVA, 1600. **Radio-FM:** KTCU, 88.7 MHz; KLTY, 94.1; KSCS, 96.3; KEGL, 97.1; KPLX, 99.5; KOAI, 107.5; KTXQ, 102.1. **TV:** KXAS-Ch. 5; KTVT-Ch. 11; KTXA-Ch. 21; KFWD-Ch. 52.
Franklin — Newspapers: Advocate; News Weekly.
Frankston — Newspaper: Citizen.
Fredericksburg — Newspaper: Standard/Radio Post. **Radio-AM:** KNAF, 910 Khz. **Radio-FM:** KONO, 101.1 MHz.
Freeport — Radio-AM: KBRZ, 1460 Khz. **Radio-FM:** KJOJ, 103.3 MHz.
Freer — Newspaper: Press. **Radio-FM:** KBRA, 95.9 MHz.
Friendswood — Newspaper: Journal.
Friona — Newspaper: Star.
Frisco — Newspaper: Enterprise.
Fritch — Newspaper: Eagle Press.
Gail — Newspaper: Borden Star.
Gainesville — Newspaper: Register (D). **Radio-AM:** KGAF, 1580 Khz. **Radio-FM:** KDGE, 94.5 MHz.
Galveston — Newspaper: Daily News (D). **Radio-AM:** KHCB, 1400 Khz; KGBC, 1540. **Radio-FM:** KRTX, 104.9 MHz; KQQK, 106.5. **TV:** KLTJ-Ch. 22; KTMD-Ch. 48.
Garland — Newspaper: News (S). **Radio-AM:** KPBC, 770 Khz. **TV:** KUVN-Ch. 23.
Garrison — Newspaper: In the News.
Gatesville — Newspaper: Messenger. **Radio-FM:** KRYL, 98.3 MHz.
Georgetown — Newspapers: Sunday Sun; Williamson County Sun. **Radio-AM:** KWJR, 1530 Khz. **Radio-FM:** KHFI, 96.7 MHz; KNNC, 107.7.
Giddings — Newspaper: Times & News. **Radio-FM:** KOKE, 101.7 MHz.
Gilmer — Newspaper: Mirror (S). **Radio-AM:** KHYM, 1060 Khz. **Radio-FM:** KFRO, 95.3 MHz.
Gladewater — Newspaper: Mirror. **Radio-AM:** KEES, 1430 Khz.
Glen Rose — Newspaper: Reporter. **Radio-FM:** KCLE, 92.1 MHz.
Goldthwaite — Newspaper: Eagle.
Goliad — Newspaper: Texan Express.
Gonzales — Newspaper: Inquirer (S). **Radio-AM:** KCTI, 1450 Khz. **Radio-FM:** KPJN, 106.3 MHz.
Gorman — Newspaper: Progress.
Graham — Newspaper: Leader (S). **Radio-AM:** KSWA, 1330 Khz. **Radio-FM:** KWKQ, 107.1 MHz.
Granbury — Newspaper: Hood County News (S). **Radio-AM:** KPAR, 1420 Khz. **Radio-FM:** KCYT, 106.7 MHz.
Grand Prairie — Newspaper: News (S). **Radio-AM:** KKDA, 730 Khz.
Grand Saline — Newspaper: Sun.
Grandview — Newspaper: Tribune.
Granger — Newspaper: News.
Grapeland — Newspaper: Messenger.
Greenville — Newspaper: Herald-Banner (D). **Radio-AM:** KGVL,1400 Khz. **Radio-FM:** KIKT, 93.5 MHz.
Groesbeck — Newspaper: Journal.
Groom — Newspaper: Groom/McLean News.
Groves — Radio-FM: KTFA, 92.5 MHz.
Groveton — Newspaper: News.
Gun Barrel City — Newspaper: Cedar Creek Pilot (S).
Hale Center — Newspaper: American.
Hallettsville — Newspaper: Tribune-Herald (S). **Radio-AM:** KRJH, 1520 Khz.
Hallsville — Newspaper: Herald.
Hamilton — Newspaper: Herald-News. **Radio-AM:** KCLW, 900 Khz.
Hamlin — Newspaper: Herald. **Radio-FM:** KCDD, 103.7 MHz.
Harker Heights — Radio-FM: KLTX, 105.5 MHz.
Harlingen — Newspaper: Valley Morning Star (D). **Radio-AM:** KGBT, 1530 Khz. **Radio-FM:** KMBH, 88.9 MHz; KFRQ, 94.5; KIWW, 96.1. **TV:** KGBT-Ch. 4; KLUJ-Ch. 44; KMBH-Ch. 60.
Harper — Newspaper: Herald.
Hart — Newspaper: Beat.
Haskell — Newspaper: Free Press. **Radio-FM:** KVRP, 95.5 MHz.
Hearne — Newspaper: Democrat. **Radio-FM:** KHRN, 94.3 MHz.
Hebbronville — Newspapers: Jim Hogg County Enterprise; View.

Hemphill — Newspaper: Sabine County Reporter/Rambler. **Radio-AM:** KAWS, 1240 Khz.
Hempstead — Newspaper: Waller County News-Citizen.
Henderson — Newspaper: Daily News (D). **Radio-AM:** KWRD, 1470 Khz. **Radio-FM:** KGRI, 99.9 MHz.
Henrietta — Newspaper: Clay County Leader.
Hereford — Newspaper: Brand (D). **Radio-AM:** KPAN, 860 Khz. **Radio-FM:** KPAN, 106.3 MHz.
Hico — Newspapers: Community Observer; News Review.
Highland Park — Radio-AM: KDMM, 1150 Khz. **Radio-FM:** KVIL, 103.7 MHz.
Highlands — Newspaper: Star/Crosby Courier.
Hillsboro — Newspaper: Reporter (S). **Radio-AM:** KHBR, 1560 Khz. **Radio-FM:** KBRQ, 102.5 MHz.
Hondo — Newspaper: Anvil Herald. **Radio-AM:** KRME, 1460 Khz.
Honey Grove — Newspaper: Signal-Citizen.
Hooks — Radio-FM: KLLI, 95.9 MHz.
Houston — Newspapers: Business Journal; Chronicle (D); Daily Court Review (D); Forward Times; Informer; Jewish Herald Voice; Post (D); Texas Catholic Herald (BW). **Radio-AM:** KILT, 610 Khz; KTRH, 740; KKBQ, 790; KEYH, 850; KPRC, 950; KLAT, 1010; KENR, 1070; KNUZ, 1230; KXYZ, 1320; KCOH, 1430; KYOK, 1590. **Radio-FM:** KUHF, 88.7 MHz; KPFT, 90.1; KTSU, 90.9; KTRU, 91.7; KKRW, 93.7; KLDE, 94.5; KIKK, 95.7; KHMX, 96.5; KBXX, 97.9; KODA, 99.1; KILT, 100.3; KLOL, 101.1; KMJQ, 102.1; KQUE, 102.9; KRBE, 104.1; KHCB, 105.7. **TV:** KPRC-Ch. 2; KUHT-Ch. 8; KHOU-Ch. 11; KTRK-Ch. 13; KETH-CH. 14; KTXH-Ch. 20; KRIV-Ch. 26; KHTV-Ch. 39.
Howe — Newspaper: Enterprise. **Radio-FM:** KHYI, 95.3 MHz.
Hubbard — Newspaper: City News.
Humble — Radio-AM: KGOL, 1180 Khz. **Radio-FM:** KSBJ, 89.3 MHz.
Huntington — Radio-FM: KAQU, 101.9 MHz.
Huntsville — Newspaper: Item (D).**Radio-AM:** KYLR, 1400 Khz; KSAM, 1490. **Radio-FM:** KSHU, 90.5 MHz; KSAM, 101.7; KVST, 103.7.
Hurst — Newspaper: Mid-Cities News (S).
Hutto — Radio-FM: KIKY, 92.1 MHz.
Idalou — Newspaper: Beacon.
Ingleside — Newspaper: Index.
Iowa Park — Newspaper: Leader.
Iraan — Newspaper: News.
Irving — Newspaper: News (S). **TV:** KHSX-Ch. 49.
Jacksboro — Newspapers: Gazette-News; Jack County Herald.
Jacksonville — Newspaper: Daily Progress (D). **Radio-AM:** KEBE, 1400 Khz. **Radio-FM:** KBJS, 90.3 MHz; KSIZ, 102.3; KOOI, 106.5. **TV:** KETK-Ch. 56.
Jasper — Newspaper: News-Boy. **Radio-AM:** KTXJ, 1350 Khz. **Radio-FM:** KMIA, 100.9 MHz; KWYX, 102.3.
Jefferson — Newspaper: Jimplecute. **Radio-FM:** KJTX, 104.5 MHz.
Jewett — Newspaper: Messenger.
Johnson City — Newspaper: Record-Courier. **Radio-FM:** KFAN, 107.9 MHz.
Joshua — Newspaper: Tribune.
Junction — Newspaper: Eagle. **Radio-AM:** KMBL, 1450 Khz.
Karnes City — Newspaper: Karnes Citation. **Radio-AM:** KAML, 990 Khz.

Katy — Newspaper: Times (S).
Kaufman — Newspaper: Herald.
Keene — Newspaper: Reporter. **Radio-FM:** KJCR; 88.3 MHz.
Kenedy — Newspaper: Advance-Times. **Radio-AM:** KAML, 990 Khz. **Radio-FM:** KTNR, 92.1 MHz.
Kennedale — Newspaper: News.
Kerens — Newspaper: Tribune.
Kermit — Newspaper: Winkler County News. **Radio-AM:** KERB, 600 Khz. **Radio-FM:** KERB, 106.3 MHz.
Kerrville — Newspapers: Daily Times (D); Mountain Sun. **Radio-AM:** KERV, 1230 Khz. **Radio-FM:** KITE, 92.3 MHz; KRVL, 94.3. **TV:** KRRT-Ch. 35.
Kilgore — Newspaper: News Herald (D). **Radio-AM:** KKTX, 1240 Khz. **Radio-FM:** KTPB, 88.7 Mhz; KKTX, 96.1.
Killeen — Newspaper: Daily Herald (D). **Radio-AM:** KRMY, 1050 Khz. **Radio-FM:** KNCT, 91.3 MHz; KIIZ, 92.3; KHHT, 93.3.
Kingsville — Newspaper: Record (S). **Radio-AM:** KINE, 1330 Khz. **Radio-FM:** KTAI, 91.1 MHz; KNGV, 92.7; KWVS, 97.5.
Kirbyville — Newspaper: East Texas Banner.
Knox City — Newspaper: Knox County News.
Kress — Newspaper: Chronicle.
Ladonia — Newspaper: News.
La Feria — Newspaper: News.
La Grange — Newspaper: Fayette County Record (S). **Radio-AM:** KVLG, 1570 Khz. **Radio-FM:** KBUK, 104.9 MHz.
Lake Dallas — Newspaper: Lake Cities Sun. **TV:** KLDT-Ch. 55.
Lake Jackson — Newspaper: Brazorian News. **Radio-FM:** KRQT, 107.5 MHz.
La Marque — Newspaper: Times.
Lamesa — Newspaper: Press Reporter (S). **Radio-AM:** KPET, 690 Khz. **Radio-FM:** KMMX, 100.3 MHz; KIOL, 104.7.
Lampasas — Newspaper: Dispatch Record (S). **Radio-AM:** KCYL, 1450 Khz. **Radio-FM:** KUTZ, 98.9 MHz.
Lancaster — Newspaper: Today.
Laredo — Newspaper: Morning Times (D). **Radio-AM:** KVOZ, 890 Khz; KLAR, 1300; KDOS, 1490. **Radio-FM:** KHOY, 88.1 MHz; KBNL, 89.9; KJBZ, 92.7; KOYE, 94.9; KRRG, 98.1; KZTQ, 106.1. **TV:** KGNS-Ch. 8; KVTV-Ch. 13; KLDO-Ch. 27.
La Vernia — Newspaper: News.
Leakey — Newspaper: Real American.
Leonard — Newspaper: Graphic.
Levelland — Newspaper: Hockley County News-Press (S). **Radio-AM:** KLVT, 1230 Khz. **Radio-FM:** KLVT, 105.5 MHz.
Liberty — Newspaper: Vindicator (S). **Radio-AM:** KPXE, 1050 Khz. **Radio-FM:** KSHN, 99.9 MHz.
Lindale — Newspapers: News; Times.
Linden — Newspaper: Cass County Sun.
Littlefield — Newspaper: Lamb County Leader-News (S). **Radio-AM:** KZZN, 1490 Khz.
Livingston — Newspaper: Polk County Enterprise (S). **Radio-AM:** KETX, 1140 Khz. **Radio-FM:** KETX, 92.3 MHz.
Llano — Newspaper: News. **Radio-FM:** KLKM, 104.7 MHz. **TV:** KXAM-Ch. 14.
Lockhart — Newspaper: Post-Register. **Radio-AM:** KFIT, 1060 Khz.
Longview — Newspaper: News-Journal (D). **Radio-AM:** KARW, 1280 Khz; KFRO, 1370. **Radio-FM:** KYKX, 105.7 MHz. **TV:** KFXK-Ch. 51.
Lorenzo — Newspaper: Examiner. **Radio-FM:** KKCL, 98.1 MHz.
Los Ybanez — Radio-FM: KYMI, 107.9 Mhz.
Lubbock — Newspaper: Avalanche-Journal (D). **Radio-AM:** KRFE, 580 Khz; KFYO, 790; KXTQ, 950; KKAM, 1340; KLFB, 1420; KTLK, 1460; KLLL, 1590. **Radio-FM:** KTXT, 88.1 MHz; KOHM, 89.1; KAMY, 90.1; KYFT, 90.9; KXTQ, 93.7; KFMX, 94.5; KLLL, 96.3; KJBX, 99.5; KONE, 101.1; KZII, 102.5; KEJS, 106.5. **TV:** KTXT-Ch. 5; KCBD-Ch. 11; KLBK-Ch. 13; KAMC-Ch. 28; KJTV- Ch. 34.

Lufkin — Newspaper: Daily News (D). **Radio-AM:** KRBA, 1340 Khz; KSRK, 1420. **Radio-FM:** KLDN, 88.9 Mhz; KSWP, 90.9; KUEZ, 99.3; KYKS, 105.1. **TV:** KTRE-Ch. 9.
Luling — Newspaper: Newsboy & Signal. **Radio-FM:** KFGI, 94.7 MHz.
Lytle — Newspaper: Medina Valley Times. **Radio-FM:** KXPZ, 91.3 MHz.
Mabank — Newspaper: Monitor.
Madisonville — Newspaper: Meteor. **Radio-AM:** KMVL, 1220 Khz. **Radio-FM:** KAGG, 96.1 MHz.
Malakoff — Newspaper: News. **Radio-FM:** KCKL, 95.9 MHz.
Mansfield — Newspaper: News-Mirror (S).
Marble Falls — Newspaper: Highlander.
Marfa — Newspaper: Big Bend Sentinel.
Marion — Radio-AM: KBIB, 1000 Khz.
Marlin — Newspaper: Democrat (S). **Radio-FM:** KEYR, 92.9 MHz.
Marshall — Newspaper: News Messenger (D). **Radio-AM:** KCUL, 1410 Khz; KMHT, 1450. **Radio-FM:** KBWC, 91.1 MHz; KCUL, 92.3; KZEY, 103.9.
Mart — Newspaper: Texan.
Mason — Newspaper: Mason County News.
Matador — Newspaper: Motley County Tribune.
Mathis — Newspaper: News.
McAllen — Newspapers: Monitor (D); News Journal. **Radio-AM:** KRIO, 910 Khz. **Radio-FM:** KHID, 88.1 MHz; KVMV, 96.9; KQXX, 98.5.
McCamey — Newspaper: News.
McGregor — Newspaper: Mirror.
McKinney — Newspaper: Courier-Gazette (D). **Radio-FM:** KRVA, 106.9 MHz.
Memphis — Newspaper: Democrat. **Radio-AM:** KLSR, 1130 Khz. **Radio-FM:** KLSR, 105.3 MHz.
Menard — Newspaper: News.
Mercedes — Newspaper: Enterprise. **Radio-FM:** KTJN, 106.3 MHz.
Meridian — Newspaper: Bosque County News.
Merkel — Newspaper: Mail. **Radio-AM:** KMXO, 1500 Khz. **Radio-FM:** KCWS, 102.7 MHz.
Mesquite — Radio-FM: KEOM, 88.5 MHz.
Mexia — Newspaper: Daily News (D). **Radio-AM:** KRQX, 1590 Khz. **Radio-FM:** KYCX, 104.9 MHz.
Miami — Newspaper: Chief.
Midland — Newspaper: Reporter-Telegram (D). **Radio-AM:** KCRS, 550 Khz; KWEL, 1070; KJBC, 1150; KMND, 1510. **Radio-FM:** KNFM, 92.3 MHz; KBAT, 93.3; KCRS, 103.3; KCHX, 106.7. **TV:** KMID-Ch. 2.
Midlothian — Newspapers: Mirror; Today.
Miles — Newspaper: Messenger.
Mineola — Newspaper: Monitor. **Radio-AM:** KVCI, 1510 Khz. **Radio-FM:** KMOO, 96.7 MHz.
Mineral Wells — Newspaper: Index (D). **Radio-AM:** KJSA, 1140 Khz. **Radio-FM:** KYXS, 95.9 MHz.
Mirando City — Radio-FM: KBDR, 100.5 MHz.
Mission — Newspaper: Progress-Times. **Radio-AM:** KIRT, 1580 Khz. **Radio-FM:** KTJX, 105.5 MHz.
Monahans — Newspaper: News. **Radio-AM:** KLBO, 1330 Khz. **Radio-FM:** KGEE, 99.9 MHz; KCDQ, 102.1.
Moody — Newspaper: Courier.
Morton — Newspaper: Tribune.
Moulton — Newspaper: Eagle.
Mount Pleasant — Newspaper: Daily Tribune (D). **Radio-AM:** KIMP, 960 Khz. **Radio-FM:** KPXI, 100.7 MHz.
Mount Vernon — Newspaper: Optic-Herald.
Muenster — Newspaper: Enterprise. **Radio-FM:** KXGM, 106.5 MHz.
Muleshoe — Newspapers: Bailey County Journal; Journal. **Radio-AM:** KMUL, 1380 Khz. **Radio-FM:** KKCY, 103.1 MHz.
Munday — Newspaper: Courier.
Nacogdoches — Newspaper: Daily Sentinel (D). **Radio-AM:** KSFA, 860 Khz; KEEE, 1230. **Radio-FM:** KSAU, 90.1 MHz; KJCS, 103.3; KTBQ, 107.7. **TV:** KLSB-Ch. 19.
Naples — Newspaper: Monitor.
Navasota — Newspaper: Examiner. **Radio-AM:** KWBC, 1550 Khz. **Radio-FM:** KMBV, 92.5 MHz.
Nederland — Radio-AM: KQHN, 1510 Khz.
Needville — Newspaper: Gulf Coast Tribune.
New Boston — Newspaper: Bowie County Citizens Tribune (S). **Radio-AM:** KNBO, 1530 Khz. **Radio-FM:** KZRB, 103.5 Mhz.
New Braunfels — Newspaper: Herald-Zeitung (D). **Radio-AM:** KGNB, 1420 Khz. **Radio-FM:** KNBT, 92.1 MHz.
Newton — Newspaper: Newton County News.
New Ulm — Newspaper: Enterprise.
Nixon — Newspaper: Cow Country Courier.
Nocona — Newspaper: News.
Normangee — Newspaper: Star.
Odem — Newspaper: Odem-Edroy Times. **Radio-FM:** KKHQ, 98.3 MHz.
Odessa — Newspaper: American (D). **Radio-AM:** KENT, 920 Khz; KOZA, 1230; KOYL, 1310; KRIL, 1410. **Radio-FM:** KENT, 90.5 MHz; KOCV, 91.3; KMRK, 96.1; KQIP, 96.9; KODM, 97.9; KKKK, 99.1. **TV:** KOSA-Ch. 7; KWES -Ch. 9; KPEJ-Ch. 24; KOCV-Ch. 36; KMLM-Ch. 42.
O'Donnell — Newspaper: Index-Press.
Olney — Newspaper: Enterprise.
Olton — Newspaper: Enterprise.
Orange — Newspaper: Leader (D). **Radio-AM:** KOGT, 1600 Khz. **Radio-FM:** KKMY, 104.5 MHz; KIOC, 106.1.
Overton — Newspaper: Press.
Ozona — Newspaper: Stockman. **Radio-FM:** KYXX, 94.3 MHz.
Paducah — Newspaper: Post.
Paint Rock — Newspaper: Concho Herald.
Palacios — Newspaper: Beacon.
Palestine — Newspaper: Herald Press (D). **Radio-AM:** KNET, 1450 Khz. **Radio-FM:** KLIS, 96.7 MHz; KYYK, 98.3.
Pampa — Newspaper: News (D). **Radio-AM:** KGRO, 1230 Khz; KPDN, 1340. **Radio-FM:** KOMX, 100.3 MHz.
Panhandle — Newspaper: Herald.
Paris — Newspaper: News (D). **Radio-AM:** KGDD, 1250 Khz; KPLT, 1490. **Radio-FM:** KOYN, 93.9 MHz; KBUS, 101.9; KPLT, 107.7.
Pasadena — Newspaper: Citizen (D). **Radio-AM:** KIKK, 650 Khz; KLVL, 1480. **Radio-FM:** KFTG, 88.1 MHz; KKBQ, 92.9.
Pearsall — Newspaper: Frio-Nueces Current. **Radio-AM:** KVWG, 1280 Khz. **Radio-FM:** KVWG, 95.3 MHz.
Pecos — Newspaper: Enterprise (D). **Radio-AM:** KIUN, 1400 Khz. **Radio-FM:** KPTX, 98.3 MHz.
Perryton — Newspaper: Herald (S). **Radio-AM:** KEYE, 1400 Khz. **Radio-FM:** KEYE, 95.9 MHz.
Petersburg — Newspaper: Post.
Pflugerville — Newspaper: Pflag.
Pharr — Newspaper: Pharr/San Juan/Alamo Advance News. **Radio-AM:** KVJY, 840 Khz.
Pilot Point — Newspaper: Post-Signal.
Pittsburg — Newspaper: Gazette. **Radio-FM:** KXAL, 103.1 MHz.
Plains — Newspaper: Pride. **Radio-FM:** KPLN, 90.3 MHz.
Plainview — Newspaper: Daily Herald (D). **Radio-AM:** KKYN, 1090 Khz; KVOP, 1400. **Radio-FM:** KWLD, 91.5 MHz; KATX, 97.3; KKYN, 103.9.
Plano — Newspaper: Star Courier (D).
Pleasanton — Newspaper: Express. **Radio-AM:** KBOP, 1380 Khz. **Radio-FM:** KBUC, 98.3 MHz.
Port Aransas — Newspaper: South Jetty.
Port Arthur — Newspaper: News (D). **Radio-AM:** KALO, 1250 Khz; KOLE, 1340. **Radio-FM:** KLTN, 93.3 MHz; KHYS, 98.5. **TV:** KJAC-Ch. 4.
Port Isabel — Newspaper: Port Isabel/South Padre Press (S). **Radio-FM:** KVPA, 101.1 MHz.
Portland — Newspaper: News. **Radio-FM:** KRAD, 105.5 MHz.
Port Lavaca — Newspaper: Wave (S). **Radio-AM:** KGUL, 1560 Khz. **Radio-FM:** KPLV, 93.3 MHz.
Port Neches — Radio-AM: KUHD, 1150 Khz.
Post — Newspaper: Dispatch. **Radio-AM:** KPOS, 1370 Khz. **Radio-FM:** KPOS, 107.3 MHz.
Pottsboro — Newspaper: Press.
Prairie View — Radio-FM: KPVU, 91.3 MHz.
Premont — Radio-FM: KMFM, 104.9 MHz.
Presidio — Newspaper: The International.

Princeton — Newspaper: Herald.
Quanah — Newspaper: Tribune-Chief (S). **Radio-AM:** KVDL, 1150 Khz. **Radio-FM:** KIXC, 100.9 MHz.
Quinlan — Newspaper: Tawakoni News.
Quitaque — Newspaper: Valley Tribune.
Quitman — Newspaper: Wood County Democrat.
Ralls — Radio-AM: KCLR, 1530 Khz.
Ranger — Newspaper: Times (S).
Rankin — Newspaper: News.
Raymondville — Newspaper: Chronicle and Willacy County News. **Radio-AM:** KSOX, 1240 Khz. **Radio-FM:** KSOX, 102.1 MHz.
Red Oak — Newspapers: North Ellis County Chronicle; North Ellis County Weekly Review.
Refugio — Newspaper: County Advantage Press. **Radio-FM:** KZTX, 106.3 MHz.
Richardson — Newspaper: News (S).
Riesel — Newspaper: Rustler.
Rio Grande City — Newspaper: Rio Grande Herald. **Radio-FM:** KCTM, 103.1 MHz.
Rising Star — Newspaper: Rising Star.
Robert Lee — Newspaper: Observer/Enterprise.
Robstown — Newspaper: Nueces County Record-Star. **Radio-AM:** KGLF, 1510 Khz. **Radio-FM:** KLUX, 89.5 MHz; KSAB, 99.9; KMIQ, 105.1.
Rochester — Newspaper: Twin Cities News.
Rockdale — Newspaper: Reporter. **Radio-FM:** KRXT, 98.5 MHz.
Rockport — Newspapers: Herald; Pilot (S). **Radio-FM:** KXCC, 102.3 Mhz.
Rocksprings — Newspaper: Texas Mohair Weekly.
Rockwall — Newspapers: Chronicle; Texas Success (S).
Rollingwood — Radio-AM: KJCE, 1370 Khz.
Roma — Newspaper: South Texas Reporter. **Radio-FM:** KBMI, 97.7 MHz.
Rosebud — Newspaper: News.
Rosenberg — Newspaper: Herald-Coaster (D). **Radio-AM:** KMPQ, 980 Khz. **Radio-FM:** KMPQ, 104.9 Mhz. **TV:** KXLN-Ch. 45.
Rotan — Newspaper: Advance-Star-Record.
Round Rock — Newspaper: Leader (S). **Radio-FM:** KNLE, 88.1 MHz.
Rowena — Newspaper: Press.
Rowlett — Newspaper: Lakeshore Times.
Royse City — Newspaper: News.
Rusk — Newspaper: Cherokeean/Herald. **Radio-AM:** KTLU, 1580 Khz. **Radio-FM:** KWRW, 97.7 Mhz.
Saint Jo — Newspaper: Tribune.
San Angelo — Newspaper: Standard-Times (D). **Radio-AM:** KGKL, 960 Khz; KKSA, 1260; KCRN, 1340. **Radio-FM:** KDCD, 92.9 Mhz; KCRN, 93.9; KIXY, 94.7; KGKL, 97.5; KELI, 98.7; KSJT, 107.5. **TV:** KACB-Ch. 3; KIDY-Ch. 6; KLST-Ch. 8.
San Antonio — Newspapers: Business Journal; Commercial Recorder (D); Express-News (D); North San Antonio Times; Today's Catholic (BW). **Radio-AM:** KTSA, 550 Khz; KSLR, 630; KKYX, 680; KTKR, 760; KONO, 860; KENS, 1160; WOAI, 1200; KZEP, 1250; KXTN, 1310; KCOR, 1350; KCHL, 1480; KEDA, 1540. **Radio-FM:** KPAC, 88.3 MHz; KSTX, 89.1; KSYM, 90.1; KYFS, 90.9; KRTU, 91.7; KROM, 92.9; KSJL, 96.1; KAJA, 97.3; KISS, 99.5; KCYY, 100.3; KQXT, 101.9; KTFM, 102.7; KZEP, 104.5; KXTN, 107.5. **TV:** KMOL-Ch. 4; KENS-Ch. 5; KLRN-Ch. 9; KSAT-Ch. 12; KHCE-Ch. 23; KABB-Ch. 29; KWEX-Ch. 41; KVDA-Ch. 60.
San Augustine — Newspaper: Tribune. **Radio-FM:** KCOT, 92.5 MHz.
San Benito — Newspaper: News (S).
Sanderson — Newspaper: Times.
San Diego — Newspaper: Duval County Picture. **Radio-FM:** KUKA, 105.9 MHz.
Sanger — Newspaper: Courier.
San Juan — Radio-AM: KUBR, 1210 Khz.
San Marcos — Newspaper: Daily Record (D). **Radio-AM:** KUOL, 1470 Khz. **Radio-FM:** KTSW, 89.9 MHz; KEYI, 103.5.
San Saba — Newspaper: News & Star. **Radio-AM:** KBAL, 1410 Khz.
Santa Anna — Newspaper: News.
Santa Fe — Radio-FM: KJIC, 90.5 MHz.
Schulenburg — Newspaper: Sticker.
Seabrook — Radio-FM: KRTS, 92.1 MHz.
Seagoville — Newspaper: Suburbia News.
Seagraves — Newspaper: Gaines County News.
Sealy — Newspaper: News.
Seguin — Newspaper: Gazette-Enterprise (D). **Radio-AM:** KWED, 1580 Khz. **Radio-FM:** KSMG, 105.3 MHz.
Seminole — Newspaper: Sentinel (S). **Radio-AM:** KIKZ, 1250 Khz. **Radio-FM:** KSEM, 106.3 MHz.
Seymour — Newspaper: Baylor County Banner. **Radio-AM:** KSEY, 1230 Khz. **Radio-FM:** KSEY, 94.3 MHz.
Shamrock — Newspaper: Texan.
Shepherd — Newspaper: San Jacinto News-Times.
Sherman — Newspaper: Democrat (D). **Radio-AM:** KXEB, 910 Khz; KJIM, 1500. **Radio-FM:** KIKM, 96.7 MHz; KWSM, 104.1.
Shiner — Newspaper: Gazette.
Silsbee — Newspaper: Bee. **Radio-AM:** KKAS, 1300 Khz. **Radio-FM:** KWDX, 101.7 MHz.
Silverton — Newspaper: Briscoe County News.
Sinton — Newspaper: San Patricio County News. **Radio-AM:** KDAE, 1590 Khz. **Radio-FM:** KNCN, 101.3 MHz; KOUL, 103.7.
Slaton — Newspaper: Slatonite. **Radio-FM:** KJAK, 92.7 MHz.
Smithville — Newspaper: Times.
Snyder — Newspaper: Daily News (D). **Radio-AM:** KSNY, 1450 Khz. **Radio-FM:** KSNY, 101.7 MHz.
Somerset — Radio-AM: KCHG, 810 Khz.
Sonora — Newspaper: Devil's River News. **Radio-AM:** KHOS, 980 Khz. **Radio-FM:** KHOS, 92.1 MHz.
South Padre Island — Radio-FM: KZSP, 95.3 MHz.
Spearman — Newspaper: Hansford County Reporter-Statesman. **Radio-FM:** KRDF, 98.3 MHz.
Springtown — Newspaper: Epigraph. **Radio-FM:** KMQX, 89.1 MHz.
Spur — Newspaper: Texas Spur.
Stamford — Newspaper: American. **Radio-AM:** KVRP, 1400 Khz.
Stephenville — Newspaper: Empire-Tribune (D). **Radio-AM:** KSTV, 1510 Khz. **Radio-FM:** KCUB, 98.3 MHz; KSTV, 105.7.
Sterling City — Newspaper: News-Record.
Stratford — Newspaper: Star.
Sudan — Newspaper: Beacon-News.
Sugar Land — Newspaper: Fort Bend Mirror.
Sulphur Springs — Newspaper: News-Telegram (D). **Radio-AM:** KSST, 1230 Khz. **Radio-FM:** KDXE, 95.9 MHz.
Sweetwater — Newspaper: Reporter (D). **Radio-AM:** KXOX, 1240 Khz. **Radio-FM:** KXOX, 96.7 MHz. **TV:** KTXS-Ch. 12.
Taft — Newspaper: Tribune.
Tahoka — Newspaper: Lynn County News.
Talco — Newspaper: Times.
Tatum — Newspaper: Trammel Trace Tribune.
Taylor — Newspaper: Daily Press (D). **Radio-AM:** KTAE, 1260 Khz.
Teague — Newspaper: Chronicle.
Temple — Newspaper: Telegram (D). **Radio-AM:** KTEM, 1400 Khz. **Radio-FM:** KPLE, 104.3 MHz. **TV:** KCEN-Ch. 6.
Terrell — Newspaper: Tribune (D). **Radio-AM:** KPYK, 1570 Khz. **Radio-FM:** KTLR, 107.1 MHz.
Terrell Hills — Radio-AM: KLUP, 930 Khz. **Radio-FM:** KDIL, 106.7 MHz.
Texarkana — Newspaper: Gazette (D). **Radio-AM:** KCMC, 740 Khz; KTWN, 940; KHSP, 1400. **Radio-FM:** KTXK, 91.5 MHz; KTAL, 98.1; KKYR, 102.5. **TV:** KTAL-Ch. 6.
Texas City — Newspaper: Sun (D). **Radio-AM:** KYST, 920 Khz.
Thorndale — Newspaper: Champion.
Three Rivers — Newspaper: Progress.
Throckmorton — Newspaper: Tribune.
Timpson — Newspaper: Timpson & Tenaha News.
Tomball — Radio-AM: KSEV, 700 Khz.
Trenton — Newspaper: Tribune.

Trinity — Newspaper: Standard.
Tulia — Newspaper: Herald. **Radio-AM:** KTUE, 1260 Khz. **Radio-FM:** KJMX, 104.9 Mhz.
Tuscola — Newspaper: Journal.
Tye — Radio-FM: KBCY, 99.7 MHz.
Tyler — Newspapers: Courier-Times-Telegraph (D); Catholic East Texas (BW). **Radio-AM:** KTBB, 600 Khz; KZEY, 690; KGLD, 1330; KYZS, 1490. **Radio-FM:** KVNE, 89.5 MHz; KGLY, 91.3; KDOK, 92.1; KTYL, 93.1; KNUE, 101.5; KKUS, 104.1. **TV:** KLTV-Ch. 7.
Universal City — Radio-AM: KSAH, 720 Khz.
Uvalde — Newspaper: Leader-News (S). **Radio-AM:** KVOU, 1400 Khz. **Radio-FM:** KUVA, 102.3 MHz; KYUF, 104.9.
Valley Mills — Newspaper: Progress.
Van Alstyne — Newspaper: Leader.
Van Horn — Newspaper: Advocate.
Vega — Newspaper: Enterprise.
Vernon — Newspaper: Daily Record (D). **Radio-AM:** KVWC, 1490 Khz. **Radio-FM:** KVWC, 102.3 MHz.
Victoria — Newspaper: Advocate (D). **Radio-AM:** KAMG, 1340 Khz; KNAL, 1410. **Radio-FM:** KVLT, 92.3 MHz; KVIC, 95.1; KTXN, 98.7; KEPG, 100.9; KIXS, 107.9. **TV:** KVCT-Ch. 19; KAVU-Ch. 25.
Vidor — Newspaper: Vidorian.
Waco — Newspapers: Citizen (S); Tribune-Herald (D). **Radio-AM:** KBBW, 1010; KWTX, 1230 Khz; WACO, 1460; KRZI, 1580. **Radio-FM:** KCKR, 95.5 MHz; KWTX, 97.5; WACO, 99.9; KWBU, 107.1. **TV:** KWTX-Ch. 10; KXXV-Ch. 25; KCTF-Ch. 34; KWKT-Ch. 44.
Wallis — Newspaper: News-Review.
Waskom — Newspaper: Review.
Waxahachie — Newspaper: Daily Light (D). **Radio-AM:** KBEC, 1390 Khz.
Weatherford — Newspapers: Democrat (D); Community News. **Radio-AM:** KZEE, 1220 Khz. **Radio-FM:** KYQX, 89.5 MHz.
Weimar — Newspaper: Mercury.
Wellington — Newspaper: Leader.
Weslaco — Radio-AM: KRGE, 1290 Khz. **TV:** KRGV-Ch. 5.
West — Newspaper: News.
West Lake Hills — Radio-AM: KTXZ, 1560 Khz.
Wharton — Newspaper: Journal-Spectator (S). **Radio-AM:** KANI, 1500 Khz.
Wheeler — Newspaper: Times. **Radio-FM:** KPDR, 90.5 MHz.
White Deer — Newspaper: News.
Whitehouse — Newspaper: Tri County Leader. **Radio-FM:** KISX, 107.3 MHz.
White Oak — Newspaper: Independent.
Whitesboro — Newspaper: News-Record.
Whitewright — Newspaper: Sun.
Whitney — Newspapers: Messenger; Lake Whitney View (M).
Wichita Falls — Newspaper: Times-Record-News (D). **Radio-AM:** KWFT, 620 Khz; KNIN, 990; KLLF, 1290. **Radio-FM:** KMOC, 89.5 MHz; KTEQ, 90.5; KNIN, 92.9; KLUR, 99.9; KQXC, 102.5; KWFS, 103.3; KTLT, 106.3. **TV:** KFDX-Ch. 3; KAUZ-Ch. 6; KJTL-Ch. 18.
Wills Point — Newspapers: Chronicle; Van Zandt News.
Wimberley — Newspaper: View.
Winfield — Radio-FM: KALK, 97.7 MHz.
Winnie — Newspaper: Hometown Press.
Winnsboro — Newspaper: News. **Radio-FM:** KWNS, 104.9 MHz.
Winters — Newspaper: Enterprise.
Wolfe City — Newspaper: Mirror.
Woodville — Newspaper: Tyler County Booster. **Radio-AM:** KVLL, 1490 Khz. **Radio-FM:** KVLL, 94.7 MHz.
Wylie — Newspaper: News.
Yoakum — Newspaper: Herald-Times Four Star Reporter. **Radio-FM:** KYOC, 92.5 MHz.
Yorktown — Newspapers: DeWitt County View; News.
Zapata — Newspapers: Zapata County News. ☆

Sources: Newspapers: 1995 Texas Newspaper Directory, Texas Press Association; Broadcast media: Federal Communications Commission; TV data as of Feb. 25, 1995; FM data as of Jan. 31, 1995; AM data as of March 27, 1995.

Texas Winners of Pulitzer Prizes

Since 1955, Texas journalists and publications have received 19 Pulitzer Prize Awards in Journalism. Joseph Pulitzer, a reporter, editor and publisher, established his namesake system of prizes in 1917. He linked it to the Graduate School of Journalism at Columbia, which he had founded. He hoped that these awards would encourage "public service, public morals, American literature and the advancement of education." It is considered journalism's most prestigious honor. Below are listed these Texas Pulitzer Prize winners:

For Meritorious Public Service

1961 — Amarillo Globe-Times, for exposing a breakdown in local law enforcement, resulting in punitive action that swept lax officials from their posts.

1977 — Lufkin News, for an obituary of a local man who died in Marine training camp, resulting in an investigation leading to reform in recruiting and training practices of the U.S. Marine Corps.

1985 — Fort Worth Star-Telegram (reporter, Mark J. Thompson), for revealing that 250 U.S. servicemen had lost their lives as a result of a design problem in helicopters built by Bell Helicopter.

Local Reporting

(1) General/Spot; (2) Special/Investigative:

1955 — (1) Mrs. Caro Brown, Alice Daily Echo, for her series of news stories dealing with one-man political rule in Duval County.

1955 - (2) Roland Kenneth Towery, Cuero Record, for his series of articles exposing a scandal in the administration of the Veterans' Land Program in Texas.

1963 — (2) Oscar Griffin Jr., Pecos Independent and Enterprise, for his exposure of the Billie Sol Estes scandal.

1965 — (2) Gene Goltz, Houston Post, for his exposé of government corruption in Pasadena, Texas.

1992 — (2) Lorraine Adams and Dan Malone, The Dallas Morning News, for their series on police abuse of authority.

National Reporting

1986 — Craig Flournoy and George Rodrigue, The Dallas Morning News, for their investigation into subsidized housing in East Texas, which uncovered patterns of racial discrimination and segregation in public housing across the United States and led to significant reforms.

International Reporting

1994 — A team of 30 writers, photographers, artists and editors from The Dallas Morning News for a series on violence against women.

Explanatory Journalism

1989 — David Hanners (reporter), William Snyder (photographer) and Karen Blessen (artist), The

Ben Sargent, cartoonist for the Austin American-Statesman was awarded a Pulitzer in 1982. This example, showing former President Nixon after the Watergate scandal broke in the Washington Post, is from his award-winning portfolio. Cartoon used by permission of Ben Sargent and the Austin American-Statesman.

Dallas Morning News, for their special report on the investigation into a 1985 airplane crash.

Photography

1964 — Robert H. Jackson, Dallas Times Herald, for his photograph of the murder of Lee Harvey Oswald by Jack Ruby.

Spot News Photography

1981 — Larry C. Price, Fort Worth Star-Telegram, for photographs from Liberia.

1988 — Scott Shaw, Odessa American, for his photo of Jessica McClure being rescued from a well.

1993 — Ken Geiger and William Snyder, The Dallas Morning News, for their photos of the 1992 Summer Olympics.

Feature Photography

1980 — Erwin H. Hagler, Dallas Times Herald, for a series on the Western cowboy.

1983 — James B. Dickman, Dallas Times Herald, for his photographs of life and death in El Salvador.

1991 — William Snyder, The Dallas Morning News, for his photographs of Romanian orphans.

Cartoons

1982 — Ben Sargent, Austin American-Statesman.

Letters and Music

In addition to journalism, Pulitzers are awarded in several other categories. The following Texans have won Pulitzers in the fields of letters and music:

Drama — 1995, Horton Foote, for *The Young Man from Atlanta.*

Fiction — 1966, Katherine Anne Porter, for *Collected Stories*; **1986, Larry McMurtry** for *Lonesome Dove.*

History — 1967, William H. Goetzmann, for *Exploration and Empire: The Explorer and the Scientist in the Winning of the American West.*

Music, Special Award — 1976, Scott Joplin, posthumously, for his contributions to American music.

If we have failed to recognize any Texas Pulitzer Prize winner, we apologize for the oversight. ☆

Recreation

Information about recreational opportunities in Texas is located throughout the Texas Almanac. Hunting and fishing are discussed in the Wildlife section of the chapter on the Environment; recreation and special events are mentioned for each county in the Counties chapter. The following pages cover the state and national parks and facilities at U.S. Army Corps of Engineers Lakes, as well as some of the myriad festivals and celebrations in individual towns and communities.

Texas' State Parks

Texas' expanding system of state parks attracted 26,018,612 visitors in fiscal 1994. The parks offer contrasting attractions — mountains and canyons, arid deserts and lush forests, spring-fed streams, sandy dunes, saltwater surf and fascinating historic sites.

The state park information below was provided by the **Texas Parks and Wildlife Department** (TPWD). Additional information and brochures on individual parks are available from the Department's Austin headquarters (4200 Smith School Rd., Austin 78744; 1-800-792-1112 or (512) 389-8950).

The TPWD's **Central Reservation Center** can take reservations for almost all parks that accept reservations. Exceptions are Indian Lodge and the Texas State Railroad. Call the center Monday through Friday from 8 a.m. to 6 p.m., except major holidays, at (512) 389-8900. The TDD line is (512) 389-8915.

The **Texas Conservation Passport**, currently costing $25 per year, allows free entrance to state parks that charge an entrance fee, state wildlife management areas open for public use, and state park activities, such as wilderness outings or interpretive tours that require purchase of a Passport. Passport holders also receive discounts on subscriptions to Texas Parks and Wildlife magazine. For further information, contact TPWD at numbers or address above.

For a listing of **trails** in state parks, as well as in state forests and wildlife management areas; national forests, parks and grasslands; and county and city parks, call the TPWD information number listed above. The "Texas Trails" brochure lists the resource, number of trails, total trail miles, types of trails (backpacking, biking, day hiking, horseback, mountain biking and ATV), and other information, arranged by geographic region.

The following information is an overview of what each park has to offer; not all facilities are included in the text below. Refer to the chart on pages 360-362 for a more complete list of available activities and facilities. Road abbreviations used are: IH - interstate highway, US - U.S. Highway, TX - state highway, FM - farm-to-market road, RM - ranch-to-market road, PR - park road.

List of State Parks

Abilene State Park, 19 miles southwest of Abilene on FM 89 in Taylor County consists of 621.4 acres that was deeded by the City of Abilene in 1933. A part of the **official Texas longhorn herd** is located in the park. Large groves of pecan trees shade picnic tables. Activities include camping and hiking; facilities include a swimming pool and screened shelters. In addition to **Lake Abilene, Buffalo Gap,** the original Taylor County seat (1878) and one of the early frontier settlements, is nearby. Buffalo Gap was on the **Western**, or **Dodge City, Trail**, over which pioneer Texas cattlemen drove herds to Kansas.

Acton State Historical Park is a .006-acre cemetery plot where **Davy Crockett's** second wife, Elizabeth, was buried in 1860. It is six miles east of Granbury in Hood County. Day use only.

Adm. Nimitz Museum and Historical Center is 4.5 acres in downtown Fredericksburg first established as a state agency in 1969 by Texas Legislature; transferred to TPWD in 1981. Named for **Adm. Chester W. Nimitz** of World War II fame, it includes the **Pacific War Museum** in the **Nimitz Steamboat Hotel**; the **Japanese Garden of Peace**, donated by the people of Japan; and the **Historic Walk of the Pacific War**, featuring planes, boats, weapons and equipment from World War II. Nearby is **Kerrville State Park**.

Atlanta State Park is 1,475 acres located 11 miles northwest of Atlanta on FM 1154 in Cass County; adjacent to **Wright Patman Dam and Reservoir.** Land acquired from the U.S. Army in 1954 by license to 2004 with option to renew to 2054. Camping and hiking in pine forests or water activities, such as boating, fishing, swimming. Nearby is historic town of **Jefferson.**

Balmorhea State Park is 45.9 acres four miles southwest of Balmorhea on TX 17 between Pecos and Fort Davis in Reeves County. Deeded in 1934-35 by private owners and Reeves Co. Water Imp. Dist. No. 1 and built by the Civilian Conservation Corps (CCC). Swimming pool fed by artesian **San Solomon Springs;** also provides water to **pupfish refuge** in park. Motel rooms available at **San Solomon Springs Courts**. Wildlife includes **deer, javelina, hawks, barn swallows, ground squirrels, roadrunners**. Nearby are city of Pecos, **Fort Davis National Historic Site,** scenic loop drive through **Davis Mountains, Davis Mountains State Park and McDonald Observatory.**

Bastrop State Park is 3,503.7 acres one mile east of Bastrop on TX 71. The park was acquired by deeds from the City of Bastrop and private owners in 1933-35; additional acreage acquired in 1979. Site of famous **"Lost Pines,"** isolated region of loblolly pine and hardwoods. **Swimming pool, cabins**, lodge and seasonal grocery store are among facilities. Fishing in **Lake Bastrop**. Golf course adjacent to park. **State capitol** at Austin 30 miles away; 13-mile drive through forest leads to **Buescher State Park.**

Battleship Texas State Historic Site (see **San Jacinto Battleground State Historic Site and Battleship Texas**)

Bentsen-Rio Grande Valley State Park, a scenic park, is along the Rio Grande west of Mission off FM 2062 in Hidalgo County. The 587 acres of **subtropical resaca woodlands and brushlands** were acquired from private owners in 1944. Park is excellent base from which to tour **Lower Rio Grande Valley** of Texas and adjacent **Mexico;** most attractions within an hour's drive. One hiking trail leads to Rio Grande; another takes you through wilderness. They provide chance to study unique plants, animals and birds of park. Many species of birds unique to southern United States found here, including **Alta Mira oriole, pauraque, groove-billed ani, green jay, Kiskadee flycatcher, red-billed pigeon, elf owl and chachalaca.** Park also one of last natural refuges in Texas for cats such as **ocelot** and **jaguarundi.** Trees include **cedar elm, anaqua, ebony** and **Mexican ash.** Nearby are **Santa Ana National Wildlife Refuge** and **Sabal Palm**

Sanctuary.

Big Bend Ranch State Natural Area, 269,713.9 acres of **Chihuahuan Desert wilderness** in Brewster and Presidio counties, was purchased from private owners in 1988. The purchase more than doubled the size of the state park system, which comprised at that time 220,000 acres. Eastern entrance at Barton Warnock Environmental Education Center just east of Lajitas on TX 170; western entrance is at **Fort Leaton State Historical Park** three miles east of Presidio on FM 170. Texas Conservation Passport is required to visit the part of the park north of TX 170, but not necessary for southern part. The area includes an **extinct volcano,** several **waterfalls,** two **mountain ranges,** at least **11 rare species of plants and animals,** and **90 major archaeological sites**. At this time, there is no development, but there are scheduled **bus tours** to the interior two Saturdays a month. Backpacking, hiking along 30 miles of trails, picnicking, fishing and swimming are allowed. Scenic drive. Part of **state longhorn cattle herd** is in park.

Big Spring State Park is 382 acres located on FM 700 within the city limits of Big Spring in Howard County. Both city and park were named for a natural spring that was replaced by an artificial one. The park was deeded by the city of Big Spring in 1934 and 1935. Drive to top of **Scenic Mountain** provides panoramic view of surrounding country and look at **prairie dog colony**. The "big spring," nearby in a city park, provided watering place for herds of bison, antelope and wild horses. Used extensively also as campsite for early Indians, explorers and settlers.

Blanco State Park is 104.6 acres along the Blanco River on the south side of Blanco, 40 miles north of San Antonio on US 281 in Blanco County. The land was deeded by private owners before the park opened in 1934. Park area was used as campsite by early explorers and settlers. Fishing for **winter rainbow trout, perch, catfish** and **bass**. **LBJ Ranch** and **LBJ State Historical Park, Pedernales Falls** and **Guadalupe River** state parks are nearby.

Bonham State Park is a 261-acre park located two miles southeast of Bonham on TX 78, then two miles southeast on FM 271 in Fannin County. It includes a 65-acre lake, **rolling prairies and woodlands**. The land was acquired in 1933 and 1934 from the city of Bonham; originally constructed by CCC. Swimming beach, camping, playgrounds, lighted fishing pier, boating, boat rentals. **Sam Rayburn Memorial Library** in Bonham. **Sam Rayburn Home** and **Valley Lake** nearby.

Brazoria County Access Point, also known as **San Luis Pass County Park**, is a 16.8-acre park on an island south of Houston. Offers excellent **bird-watching** from the perimeter of a four-and-one-half-acre wetland area near the campsites.

Brazos Bend State Park in Fort Bend County, seven miles west of Rosharon off FM 1462 on FM 762, approximately 28 miles south of Houston. The 4,897-acre park was purchased from private owners in 1976-77. **George Observatory. Observation platform** for spotting and photographing the **270 species of birds and 23 species of mammals** that frequent the park. Interpretive and educational programs every weekend. Backpacking, camping, hiking, biking, fishing.

Bryan Beach State Park is 878 acres of **undeveloped Gulf beach** near Freeport (south on TX 288, then south on FM 523). Has 8,000 feet of Gulf frontage, 5,800 feet of waterway frontage and 7,400 feet of Brazos River frontage. Acquired by purchase in 1973 from private sources. No facilities or supervision provided, but picnicking, fishing, swimming and primitive camping allowed.

Buescher State Park, a scenic area, is 1,016.7 acres just north of Smithville off TX 71 then FM 153 in Bastrop County. Acquired between 1933 and 1936, about one-third deeded by private owner; heirs donated a third; balance from City of Smithville. **El Camino Real (King's Highway)** once ran near park; road connected **San Antonio de Bexar** with **Spanish missions in East Texas** and generally followed present-day TX 21 and **Old San Antonio Road.** Parkland was part of **Stephen F. Austin's colonial grant.** Scenic park road connects with **Bastrop State Park** through **Lost Pines** area.

Caddo Lake State Park, west of Karnack one mile off TX 43 to FM 2198 in Harrison County, consists of 7,090.23 acres (including adjoining wildlife management area) along **Cypress Bayou,** which runs into Caddo Lake. A scenic area, it was acquired from private owners in 1933-37. Nearby Karnack is childhood home of Mrs. Lyndon B. Johnson. Close by is old city of **Jefferson,** famous as commercial center of Northeast Texas during last half of 19th century. Caddo Indian legend attributes formation of Caddo Lake to **earthquake.** Lake originally only natural lake of any size in state; dam added in 1914 for flood control; new dam replaced old one in 1971. **Cypress trees, American lotus** and **lily pads** predominate in lake. **Nutria, beavers, minks, squirrels, armadillos, alligators** and **turtles** abound. Originally constructed by CCC. Activities include camping, hiking, swimming, fishing, boating. Screened shelters, cabins.

Caddoan Mounds State Historical Park in Cherokee County six miles southwest of Alto on TX 21. Total of 93.8 acres acquired in 1975 by condemnation. Open for day visits only, park offers exhibits and interpretive trails through reconstructed **Caddo dwellings and ceremonial areas**, including two temple mounds, a burial mound and a village area of people who lived in region for 500 years beginning about A.D. 800. Nearby are **Jim Hogg State Historical Park, Mission Tejas State Historical Park** and **Texas State Railroad**.

Caprock Canyons State Park, 3.5 miles north of Quitaque off RM 1065 and TX 86 in Briscoe, Floyd and Hall counties, has 15,160.6 acres. Purchased in 1975. Scenic escarpment's **canyons** provided camping areas for **Indians of Folsom culture** more than 10,000 years ago. **Short grasses of High Plains prairie to tall grasses, cottonwood** and **Rocky Mountain juniper** of bottomlands. Wildlife includes **aoudad sheep, coyote, bobcat, porcupine, ringtail, badger** and **ground squirrel**. Activities include scenic drive, camping, hiking, mountain bike riding, rock climbing, horse riding and horse camping.

Cassells-Boykin State Park, 265 acres in Angelina County, seven miles northeast of Zavalla via TX 147 and FM 3123 on **Sam Rayburn Reservoir.** Acquired in October 1982, by lease from the U.S. Army. Water-related activities, primitive camping and picnicking most popular.

Cedar Hill State Park is an urban park located on 1,810.6 acres 10 miles southwest of Dallas via US 67 and FM 1382 on **Joe Pool Reservoir.** Most campsites have electricity and water and are located in wooded areas; reservations recommended. Fishing from two lighted jetties and a perch pond for children. Swimming, boating and picnicking popular. Animals include **bobcats, coyote, fox squirrel, armadillo** and **raccoon.** Vegetation includes **cedar elm, honey locust, mesquite** and **juniper** trees as well as several sections of **tall-grass prairie**. Structures from **19th-century Penn Farm** currently undergoing renovation. Marina nearby with groceries, boat rentals, fishing barge.

Choke Canyon State Park consists of two units, South Shore and Calliham, located on 26,000-acre **Choke Canyon Reservoir**. Park acquired in 1981 in a 50-year agreement among Bureau of Reclamation, City of Corpus Christi and Nueces River Authority. Thickets of **mesquite** and **blackbrush acacia** predominate, supporting populations of **javelina, coyote, skunk** and **alligator**, as well as the **crested caracara**. The 385-acre South Shore Unit is located in Live Oak County four miles west of Tree Rivers on TX 72. The Calliham Unit, containing 1,100 acres, is located in McMullen County 11 miles west of Three Rivers, also on TX 72. Fish in the reservoir include several varieties of **sunfish** and **catfish**, along with **bass, carp, drum** and **gar**. Both units offer camping, picnicking, boating, fishing, lake swimming, and baseball and volleyball areas. The Calliham Unit also has a hiking trail, wildlife educational center, screened shelters, rentable **gym and kitchen, sports complex**, including swimming pool and tennis, volleyball, shuffleboard and basketball courts.

Christmas Bay State Park, located on Follet's Island seven miles northeast of Freeport on San Luis Pass Road, contains 484.8 acres, including 1.5 miles of Gulf frontage and 15,000 feet of water frontage on Christmas and Drum bays. Park, acquired in 1984 by warranty deed and deed of gift, the park preserves **estuarial and coastal marshes** and is home to **migratory and resident waterfowl and shore birds**. Bird watching, swimming, fishing and primitive camping are enjoyed by visitors, but no facilities are provided.

Cleburne State Park is a 528.8-acre park located 10 miles southwest of Cleburne via US 67 and PR 21

"Texas" is a historical musical show presented each summer in Palo Duro Canyon State Park near Amarillo.

in Johnson County with 116-acre spring-fed lake; acquired from the City of Cleburne, Johnson County and private owners in 1935 and 1936. **Oak, elm, mesquite, cedar** and **redbud** cover white rock hills. Bluebonnets in spring. Spring-fed lake. Glen Rose **dinosaur tracks** found on Paluxy River may be seen at nearby **Dinosaur Valley State Park.**

Colorado Bend State Park, a 5,328.3-acre facility, is located 32 miles west of Lampasas in Lampasas and San Saba counties. Access is from Lampasas to Bend on FM 580, then County Road 2578 (access road subject to flooding). Park site was purchased partly in 1986, with balance acquired in 1987; opened in 1988. Public use is primitive at this time. Plans include restoration of parts of it to its natural condition. Rare and endangered species here include **golden-cheeked warblers, black-capped vireos** and **bald eagles**. Primitive camping and river fishing.

Confederate Reunion Grounds State Historical Park, located in Limestone County on the Navasota River, is 77.1 acres in size. Acquired 1983 by deed from Joseph E. Johnston Camp No. 984 CSA. Entrance is 6 miles south of Mexia on TX 14, then 2.5 miles west on FM 2705. **Historic buildings**, two **scenic footbridges** span creek; hiking trail. Day-use only. Nearby are **Fort Parker State Park** and **Old Fort Parker State Historical Park**.

Cooper Lake State Park, comprises 3,026 acres three miles southeast of Cooper in Delta and Hopkins counties. Two units, Doctors Creek and South Sulphur, adjoin 19,300-surface-acre Cooper Lake. Boating is allowed; a boat ramp is provided.

Copano Bay State Fishing Pier, a 5.9-acre park, is located five miles north of Rockport on TX35 in Aransas County. Acquired by transfer of jurisdiction from state highway department in 1967. Picnicking, saltwater fishing, boating and swimming. It is operated by leased concession.

Copper Breaks State Park, 12 miles south of Quanah on TX 6 in Hardeman County, was acquired by purchase from private owner in 1970. Park features rugged scenic beauty on 1,888.7 acres, a 70-acre lake, **grass-covered mesas** and juniper breaks. **Medicine mounds** were important ceremonial sites of Comanche Indians. Nearby **Pease River** was site of 1860 battle in which **Cynthia Ann Parker** was recovered from Comanches. Part of **official Texas longhorn herd** maintained at park. Nature, hiking and equestrian trails; natural and historical exhibits; summer programs, horseback riding.

Daingerfield State Park, off TX 49 and PR 17 southeast of Daingerfield in Morris County, is a 550.9-acre recreational area that includes an 80-surface-acre lake; deeded in 1935 by private owners. This area center of iron industry in Texas; nearby is Lone Star Steel Co. In spring, **dogwood, redbuds** and **wisteria** bloom; in fall, brilliant foliage of **sweetgum, oaks** and **maples** contrast with dark green pines. Campsites, lodge and cabins.

Davis Mountains State Park is 2,677.9 acres in Jeff Davis County, four miles northwest of town of Fort Davis via TX 118 and PR 3. The scenic area, near **Fort Davis,** was deeded 1933-1937 by private owners. **First European, Antonio de Espejo,** came to area in 1583. Extremes of altitude produce both **desert plains grasslands and piñon-juniper-oak woodlands. Montezuma quail**, rare in Texas, visit park. Scenic drives and hiking trails. **Indian Lodge,** built by the Civilian Conservation Corps during the early 1930s, has 39 rooms, a restaurant and a heated swimming pool. Four-mile hiking trail leads to **Fort Davis National Historic Site.** Other nearby points of interest include **McDonald Observatory** and scenic loop through **Davis Mountains. Davis Mountains State Park** located halfway between **Carlsbad Caverns** and **Big Bend National Park.** Nearby are scenic **Limpia, Madera, Musquiz** and **Keesey canyons; Camino del Rio;** ghost town of **Shafter; Capote Falls; Big Bend National Park; Big Bend Ranch State Natural Area; Fort Davis National Historic Site; Monahans Sandhills State Park;** and **Fort Leaton State Historical Park.**

Devil's River State Natural Area comprises 19,988.6 acres in Val Verde County, 22 miles off US. 277, about 45 miles north of Del Rio on graded road. The largest natural area in the State Park system, it is an **ecological and archaeological crossroads**. Ecologically, it is in a **transitional area between the Edwards Plateau, the Trans-Pecos desert and the South Texas brush country**. Archaeological studies suggest occupation and/or use by cultures from both east and west. Camping, hiking and canyon tours are available only to Texas Conservation Passport holders. **Dolan Falls**, owned by The Nature Conservancy of Texas and open only to its members, is nearby.

Dinosaur Valley State Park, located off US 67 just south of Glen Rose in Somervell County, is a 1,274.1-acre scenic park. Land was acquired from private owners in 1969 and 1973. **Dinosaur tracks** in bed of Paluxy River and two full-scale dinosaur models, originally created for New York World's Fair in 1964-65, on display. Part of state **longhorn herd** is in park.

Eisenhower State Park, 457.3 acres five miles northwest of Denison via TX 75A to FM 1310 on the shores of **Lake Texoma** in Grayson County, was acquired by an Army lease in 1954. Named for the **34th U.S. president, Dwight David Eisenhower.** First Anglo settlers came to area in 1835 and 1836; **Fort Johnson** was established in area in 1840; **Colbert's Ferry** established on Red River in 1853 and operated until 1931. Remnants of **tall-grass prairie** exist. Hiking, camping, picnicking, fishing.

Eisenhower Birthplace State Historical Park is 5.99 acres off US 75 in Denison, Grayson County. The property was acquired in 1958 from the Sid Richardson Foundation. Restoration of home of Pres. Dwight David Eisenhower includes furnishings of period and some personal effects of Gen. Eisenhower, including a crank-type telephone with personal greetings from **"Ike."** Guided tour. Town of Denison established on **Butterfield Overland Mail** Route in 1858.

Enchanted Rock State Natural Area is 1,643.5 acres on Big Sandy Creek 17 miles north of Fredericksburg on RM 965 on the line between Gillespie and Llano counties. Acquired in 1978 from The Nature Conservancy of Texas, Enchanted Rock is huge **pink granite boulder** rising 325 feet above ground and covering 640 acres. It is **second-largest batholith** (underground rock formation uncovered by erosion) in the United States. Indians believed **ghost fires** flickered at top and were awed by weird creaking and groaning, which geologists say resulted from rock's heating and expanding by day, cooling and contracting at night. Enchanted Rock is a **National Natural Landmark** and on the **National Register of Historic Places**. Activities include hiking, geological study, technical **rock climbing** and star gazing.

Fairfield Lake State Park is 1,460 acres adjacent to Lake Fairfield, six miles northeast of the city of Fairfield off FM 2570 in Freestone County. It is leased from Texas Utilities. Surrounding, predominantly oak, woods offer sanctuary for many species of birds and wildlife.

Falcon State Park is 572.6 acres located 15 miles north of Roma off US 83 and FM 2098 at southern end of Falcon Reservoir in Starr and Zapata counties. Park leased from International Boundary and Water Commission in 1954. Gently rolling hills covered by **mesquite, huisache, wild olive, ebony, cactus**. Excellent **birding**. Nearby are **Mexico** and **Fort Ringgold** in Rio Grande City; **Bentsen-Rio Grande Valley State Park** is 65 miles away.

Fannin Battleground State Historical Park, 9 miles east of Goliad in Goliad County. The 13.6-acre park was acquired by legislative enactment in 1965. At this site on March 20, 1836, **Col. J. W. Fannin** surrendered to Mexican **Gen. Jose Urrea** after **Battle of Coleto;** 342 massacred and 28 escaped near what is now **Goliad State Historical Park.** Near Fannin site is **Gen. Zaragoza's Birthplace** and partially restored **Mission Nuestra Señora del Espíritu Santo de Zúñiga.** (See also **Goliad State Historical Park** in this list.)

Fanthorp Inn State Historical Park includes a historic cedar-log structure and 1.4 acres in Anderson, county seat of Grimes County; acquired by purchase in 1977 from Edward Buffington and opened to the public in 1987. Inn records report visits from many prominent civic and military leaders, including **Sam Houston, Anson Jones, Ulysses S. Grant** and generals **Robert E. Lee** and **Stonewall Jackson.** Originally built in 1834, it has been restored to its 1850 use a family home and travelers' hotel. Tours available. Call TPWD for stagecoach-ride schedule. No dining or overnight facilities.

Fort Boggy State Historical Park is about five miles south of Centerville in Leon County on the site of an early blockhouse built to provide protection for frontier settlers. Was headquarters in 1840 of the **Boggy and Trinity Rangers.** Open only to Texas Conservation Passport holders. Tours available. For information, contact Lake Fairfield State Park.

Fort Griffin State Historical Park is 506.2 acres 15 miles north of Albany off US 283 in Shackelford County. The state was deeded the land by the county in 1935. Portion of **official state longhorn herd** resides in park. On bluff overlooking townsite of **Fort Griffin** and **Clear Fork of Brazos River** valley are ruins of **Old Fort Griffin,** restored bakery, replicas of enlisted men's huts. Fort constructed in 1867, deactivated 1881; crumbling ruins of various structures still may be seen. Albany annually holds **"Fandangle"** musical show in commemoration of frontier times.

Fort Lancaster State Historical Park, 81.6-acres located about 33 miles west of Ozona on IH 10 then TX 290 and paved access road in Crockett County. Acquired in 1968 by deed from Crockett County; Henry Meadows donated 41 acres in 1975. **Fort Lancaster** established Aug. 20, 1855, to guard San Antonio-El Paso Road and protect movement of supplies and immigrants from Indian hostilities. Site of part of Camel Corps experiment. Fort abandoned March 19, 1861, after Texas seceded from Union. Exhibits on history, natural history and archaeology; nature trail, picnicking. Day use only.

Fort Leaton State Historical Park, four miles east of Presidio in Presidio County on FM 170, was acquired in 1967 from private owners. Consists of 17.5 acres, 5 of which are on site of **pioneer trading post**. In 1848, **Ben Leaton** built fortified adobe trading post known as Fort Leaton near present Presidio. Ben Leaton died in 1851. Guided tours; exhibits trace history, natural history and archaeological history of area. **Big Bend Ranch Natural Area** nearby.

Fort McKavett State Historical Park, 81.94 acres acquired in 1967 and 1968 in part from Fort McKavett Restoration, Inc., and Menard County, is located 17 miles west of Menard off US 190 and RM 864. Originally called **Camp San Saba,** the fort was built by War Department in 1852 to protect frontier settlers and travelers on Upper El Paso Road from Indians. Camp later renamed for **Capt. Henry McKavett,** killed at Battle of Monterrey, Sept. 21, 1846. A **Buffalo Soldier post**. Fort abandoned March 1859; reoccupied April 1, 1868. After **Gen. Ranald S. Mackenzie** subdued Indians, fort no longer needed; abandoned June 30, 1883. Once called by Gen. Wm. T. Sherman, "the prettiest post in Texas." Twenty restored buildings, ruins of many others. Interpretive exhibits. Overnight camping accommodations available in historic structures.

Fort Parker State Park includes 1,458.8 acres, including 735 land acres and 750-acre lake between Mexia and Groesbeck off TX 14 in Limestone County. Named for the former fort located near present park, the site was acquired from private owners and the City of Mexia between 1935 and 1937. Boating, fishing, camping, picnicking. Nearby point of interest is **Old Fort Parker State Historical Park.**

Fort Richardson State Historical Park, located one-half mile south of Jacksboro off US 281 in Jack County, contains 396.1 acres. Acquired in 1968 from City of Jacksboro. Fort founded in summer of 1866, northernmost of line of federal forts established after Civil War for protection from Indians; originally named **Fort Jacksboro**. April 1867 it was abandoned for site 20 miles farther north; on Nov. 19, 1867, made permanent post at Jacksboro and named for **Israel Richardson**, who was fatally wounded at Battle of Antietam. Expeditions sent from Fort Richardson arrested Indians responsible for **Salt Creek Massacre** in 1871 and fought Comanches in **Palo Duro Canyon.** Fort abandoned again in May 1878.

Franklin Mountains State Park, created by an act of the legislature in 1979 to protect the mountain range as a wilderness preserve, comprises 23,867.2 acres in El Paso County. It is the **second-largest state park in Texas** in land area and the **largest urban wilderness park in the nation**. It includes virtually an entire **Chihuahuan Desert mountain range**, with an elevation of 7,192 feet at the summit. Located completely within the city limits of El Paso, the park is habitat for many Chihuahuan Desert plants including **sotol, lechuguilla, ocotillo, cholla** and **barrel cactus**, as well as **mule deer, fox** and an occasional **cougar**. Contains

State park descriptions continue on p. 362.

☆ Texas State Parks ☆

Park/†Type of Park/Special Features	NEAREST TOWN	Day Use Only	Historic Structure	Museum/Exhibit	Restrooms	Showers	Trailer Dump Stn.	††Camping	Screened Shelters	Cabins	Group Facilities	Nature/Hiking Trails	Playground	Picnicking	Boat Ramp	Fishing	Swimming	Water Skiing	Miscellaneous
Abilene SP	BUFFALO GAP				★	★	★	9	★		BG	★	★	★			★		L
Acton SHP (Grave of Davy Crockett's wife)	GRANBURY	★	★																
Admiral Nimitz Museum SHP	FREDERICKSBURG	★	★	★	★							★							A
Atlanta SP	ATLANTA				★	★	★	10			DG	★	★	★	★	☆	☆	☆	
Balmorhea SP (San Solomon Springs Courts)	BALMORHEA				★	★	★	9					★	★			★		I
Bastrop SP	BASTROP				★	★	★	6		★	BG	★	★	★		☆	★		D, F, G
Battleship Texas HS (At San Jacinto Battleground)	HOUSTON	★	★	★															
Bentsen-Rio Grande Valley SP	MISSION				★	★	★	11			BG	★	★	★	★	☆			
Big Bend Ranch SNA (North of Hwy. 170)	PRESIDIO							1			NG	★		★					D, L
Big Bend Ranch SNA (South of Hwy. 170)	PRESIDIO			★				1						★		☆	☆		CT, D
Big Spring SP	BIG SPRING	★		★	★							★	★	★					D
Blanco SP	BLANCO				★	★	★	12	★		DG			★		☆	☆		B
Bonham SP	BONHAM				★	★	★	9			BG		★	★	★	★	☆		B
Brazoria County Access Point ▲	ANGLETON				★	★	★	4					★		★	★			
Brazos Bend SP (George Observatory)	RICHMOND			★	★	★	★	3	★		DG	★	★	★		★			P; T1,2
Bryan Beach SP (Undeveloped Gulf Beach)	FREEPORT							1						☆		☆	☆		
Buescher SP	SMITHVILLE				★	★	★	9	★		BG	★	★	★		☆	☆		
Caddo Lake SP	KARNACK			★	★	★	★	10	★	★	BG	★	★	★	★	★	☆	☆	B
Caddoan Mounds SHP	ALTO	★	★	★	★							★							
Caprock Canyons SP	QUITAQUE			★	★	★	★	6			BG	★	★	★	★	★	☆		B,E, F. P, R, S, T1
Cassells-Boykin SP	ZAVALLA				★		★	5						★	★	☆	☆	☆	
Cedar Hill SP	DALLAS				★	★	★	7			DG		★	★	★	★	★	☆	F
Choke Canyon SP, Calliham Unit	THREE RIVERS				★	★	★	6	★		BG	★	★	★	★	☆	★	☆	
Choke Canyon SP, South Shore Unit	THREE RIVERS				★	★	★	6			DG		★	★	★	☆	☆	☆	
Christmas Bay SP (Undeveloped Gulf Beach)	LA PORTE							1						☆		☆	☆		
Cleburne SP	CLEBURNE				★	★	★	12	★		BG	★	★	★	★	☆	☆		B
Colorado Bend SP (Only 300 Vehicles Allowed)	BEND				★			1				★		☆	★	★	☆		D, P, T1
Confederate Reunion Grounds SHP	MEXIA		★		★			1			BG	★	★	★		☆	☆		
Cooper Lake SP	SULPHUR SPRINGS														★				
Copano Bay SFP▲	ROCKPORT				★										★	★			
Copper Breaks SP	QUANAH			★	★	★	★	6			BG	★	★	★	★	★	☆		L, S
Daingerfield SP	DAINGERFIELD				★	★	★	10		★	BG	★	★	★	★	★	☆		B, F
Davis Mountains SP (Indian Lodge)	FORT DAVIS			★	★	★	★	10			DG	★	★	★					D, I
Devil's River SNA	DEL RIO							1			BG	Use by reservation only							
Dinosaur Valley SP (Dinosaur Footprints)	GLEN ROSE			★	★	★	★	8			DG	★	★	★		☆	☆		L, S, T1
Eisenhower SP (Marina)	DENISON				★	★	★	10	★		BG	★	★	★	★	★	☆	☆	
Eisenhower Birthplace SHP	DENISON	★	★	★	★														
Enchanted Rock SNA	FREDERICKSBURG				★	★		5			DG	★	★	★					P, R
Fairfield Lake SP	FAIRFIELD				★	★	★	6			DG	★	★	★	★	★	☆	☆	P
Falcon SP (Airstrip)	ZAPATA				★	★	★	10	★		BG		★	★	★	☆	☆	☆	
Fannin Battleground SHP	GOLIAD	★		★	★						DG		★	★					
Fanthorp Inn SHP	ANDERSON	★	★	★	★									★					
Fort Boggy SHP	CENTERVILLE	Limited tours by permit only																	
Fort Griffin SHP	ALBANY		★	★	★	★	★	10			BG	★	★	★		☆			L
Fort Lancaster SHP	OZONA	★	★	★	★									☆					
Fort Leaton SHP	PRESIDIO	★	★	★	★									★					
Fort McKavett SHP	FORT McKAVETT	★	★	★	★							★		★					
Fort Parker SP	MEXIA				★	★	★	9	★		BG	★	★	★	★	★	☆		B
Fort Richardson SHP	JACKSBORO		★	★	★	★	★	7			DG	★	★	★		☆			
Franklin Mountains SP	EL PASO	★			★							★		★					
Fulton Mansion HSP	FULTON	★	★	★										★					
Galveston Island SP (Summer Theater)	GALVESTON				★	★	★	3	★		DG	★		★		☆	☆		
Garner SP	CONCAN				★	★	★	9	★	★	BG	★	★	★		☆	☆		M,B,T2
Goliad SHP	GOLIAD		★	★	★	★	★	8	★		DG	★	★	★		☆	★		
Goose Island SP	ROCKPORT				★	★	★	9			BG		★	★	★	★	☆	☆	
Governor Hogg Shrine SHP	QUITMAN	★	★	★	★						DG	★	★	★					
Guadalupe River SP	BOERNE				★	★	★	9			DG	★	★	★		☆	☆		
Hill Country SNA	BANDERA							1			NG	★					☆		S,E,PT1

†Types of Parks: SP - State Park; **SHP** - State Historical Park; **SNA** - State Natural Area; **SFP** - State Fishing Pier.

††Type(s) of Camping: 1-Primitive; **2**-Water Connections; **3**-Water and Electricity; **4**-Water, Electricity, Sewage; **5**-1 & 2; **6**-1, 2 & 3; **7**-1 & 3; **8**-1, 3 &4; **9**-2 & 3; **10**-2, 3 &4; **11**-2 & 4; **12**-3 & 4; **13**-1, 2, 3 & 4.

☆ Texas State Parks ☆

Park/†Type of Park/Special Features	NEAREST TOWN	Day Use Only	Historic Structure	Museum/Exhibit	Restrooms	Showers	Trailer Dump Stn.	††Camping	Screened Shelters	Cabins	Group Facilities	Nature/Hiking Trails	Playground	Picnicking	Boat Ramp	Fishing	Swimming	Water Skiing	Miscellaneous
Honey Creek SNA (Guided Tour Only)	BOERNE	★										★							
Hueco Tanks SHP (Indian Pictographs)	EL PASO				★	★	★	9			DG	★	★	★					R
Huntsville SP	HUNTSVILLE			★	★	★	★	9	★		DG	★	★	★	★	★	☆		B; T1,2
Inks Lake SP	BURNET				★	★	★	6	★		BG	★	★	★	★	★	☆	☆	B,F,G,P
Jim Hogg SHP	RUSK	★	★	★	★							★	★	★					
José Antonio Navarro SHP	SAN ANTONIO	★	★	★	★														
Kerrville-Schreiner SP	KERRVILLE				★	★	★	10	★		BG	★	★	★	★	★	☆		
Kickapoo Cavern SP	BRACKETTVILLE							1			NG	Use by reservation only							
Lake Arrowhead SP	WICHITA FALLS				★	★	★	6			DG		★	★	★	★	☆	☆	S, B
Lake Bob Sandlin SP	MOUNT PLEASANT				★	★	★	8	★		DG	★	★	★	★	★	☆	☆	P
Lake Brownwood SP	BROWNWOOD				★	★	★	10	★	★	BG	★		★	★	★	★	☆	F
Lake Casa Blanca SP	LAREDO				★	★	★	9			DG		★	★	★	★	★	★	
Lake Colorado City SP	COLORADO CITY				★	★	★	9			DG		★	★	★	★	☆	☆	
Lake Corpus Christi SP	MATHIS				★	★	★	10	★		DG		★	★	★	★	☆	☆	B, F
Lake Houston SP	NEW CANEY				★	★		2			BG	★		★					T1
Lake Livingston SP	LIVINGSTON				★	★	★	9	★		DG	★	★	★	★	★	★	☆	F; T1, 2
Lake Mineral Wells SP	MINERAL WELLS				★	★	★	6	★		DG	★	★	★	★	★	☆		E, F, R, P, S, T1
Lake Somerville SP	SOMERVILLE			★	★	★	★	6			BG	★		★	★	★	☆	☆	P, T1
Lake Tawakoni	EUSTACE	Limited tours by permit only																	
Lake Texana SP	EDNA				★	★	★	9			DG		★	★	★	★	☆	☆	
Lake Whitney SP (Airstrip)	WHITNEY				★	★	★	10	★		BG	★		★	★	☆	☆	☆	
Landmark Inn SHP (Hotel Rooms)	CASTROVILLE		★	★	★						DG	★		★		★			I
Lipantitlan SHP	ORANGE GROVE							1						★					
Lockhart SP	LOCKHART				★	★		12			BG		★	★			★		G
Longhorn Cavern SP (Cavern Tours)▲	BURNET	★	★	★	★							★		★					
Lost Maples SNA	VANDERPOOL			★	★	★	★	7				★		★		☆	☆		P
Lubbock Lake Landmark SHP	LUBBOCK	★		★	★						DG	★		★					
Lyndon B. Johnson SHP	STONEWALL	★	★	★	★						DG	★	★	★		☆	★		L, A
Magoffin Home SHP	EL PASO	★	★	★	★														
Martin Creek Lake SP	TATUM				★	★	★	7	★		DG	★	★	★	★	★	☆	☆	P, T1
Martin Dies Jr. SP	JASPER				★	★	★	9	★		BG	★	★	★	★	★	☆	☆	B
Matagorda Island SP (Boat or Air Access Only)	PORT O'CONNOR		★		★			1			NG	★		☆		☆	☆	☆	
Matagorda Peninsula SP (Undeveloped Gulf Beach)	LA PORTE							1						☆		☆	☆		
McKinney Falls SP	AUSTIN		★	★	★	★	★	6	★		NG	★	★	★		☆	☆		T2
Meridian SP	MERIDIAN				★	★	★	8	★		NG	★	★	★	★	☆	☆		
Mission Tejas SHP	WECHES		★		★	★	★	10			NG	★	★	★		☆	☆		
Monahans Sandhills SP	MONAHANS			★	★	★	★	9			DG	★		★					S
Monument Hill/Kreische Brewery SHP	LA GRANGE	★	★	★	★							★	★	★					
Mother Neff SP	MOODY				★	★	★	6			BG	★	★	★		☆			
Mustang Island SP	PORT ARANSAS				★	★	★	7						★		☆	☆		
Old Fort Parker SHP	GROESBECK	★	★	★	★									★					
Palmetto SP	LULING				★	★	★	10			DG	★	★	★		★	☆		
Palo Duro Canyon SP (Summer Drama: "Texas")	CANYON			★	★	★	★	6		★		★	★	★		★			D, L,S,T1
Pedernales Falls SP	JOHNSON CITY				★	★	★	7			NG	★		★		☆	☆		P, S, T1
Port Isabel Lighthouse SHP	PORT ISABEL	★	★																
Port Lavaca SFP▲	PORT LAVACA				★										★	★			
Possum Kingdom SP	CADDO				★	★	★	6		★			★	★	★	★	☆	☆	B, F, L
Purtis Creek SP	EUSTACE				★	★	★	6				★	★	★	★	★	☆		P
Ray Roberts Lake SP	PILOT POINT				★	★	★	9			DG	★	★	★	★	★	☆	☆	P; S; T1,2
Rusk/Palestine SP (Texas State RR Terminals)	RUSK/PALESTINE				★	★	★	10			DG		★	★	★	☆			
Sabine Pass Battleground SHP	PORT ARTHUR	★			★								★	★	☆	☆			
Sam Bell Maxey House SHP	PARIS	★	★	★	★														
San Angelo SP	SAN ANGELO				★			3			DG	★		★	★	☆	☆		T1
San Jacinto Battleground SHP (Battleship Texas)	HOUSTON	★	★	★	★						DG	★		★		☆			

Facilities

▲Facilities not operated by Parks & Wildlife.

★Facilities or services available for activity.

☆Facilities or services not provided.

Miscellaneous Codes

A Auditorium
B Boats for Rent
BG Both Day & Night Group Facilities
CT Chemical Toilets
D Scenic Drive
DG Day Use Group Facilities
E Equestrian Camping
F Groceries (Seasonal)
G Golf
H Horses for Rent
I Hotel-Type Facilities
L Texas Longhorn Herd
M Miniature Golf
NG Overnight Group Facilities
P Camping/Backpacking
R Rock Climbing
S Horseback Areas/Trails
T1 Mountain Bikes
T2 Surfaced Bike Trail

☆ Texas State Parks ☆

Park/†Type of Park/Special Features	NEAREST TOWN	Day Use Only	Historic Structure	Museum/Exhibit	Restrooms	Showers	Trailer Dump Stn.	††Camping	Screened Shelters	Cabins	Group Facilities	Nature/Hiking Trails	Playground	Picnicking	Boat Ramp	Fishing	Swimming	Water Skiing	Miscellaneous
San José Mission SHP▲	SAN ANTONIO	★	★	★	★														
Sea Rim SP	PORT ARTHUR			★	★	★	★	6				★		★	★	☆	☆		
Sebastopol SHP	SEGUIN	★	★	★										★					
Seminole Canyon SHP (Indian Pictographs)	LANGTRY			★	★	★	★	6				★		★					T1
Sheldon Lake SP	HOUSTON	★										★		☆	★	★			
South Llano River SP	JUNCTION		★		★	★	★	6				★		★		☆	☆		P, T1
Starr Mansion SHP	MARSHALL	★	★	★	★														
Stephen F. Austin SHP	SAN FELIPE		★	★	★	★	★	10	★		DG	★	★	★		☆	★		G
Texas State Railroad SHP (Contact Park for Schedule)	PALESTINE/RUSK	★		★	★														
Tips SP▲	THREE RIVERS				★	★		9			DG			★		☆			
Tyler SP	TYLER				★	★	★	12	★		BG	★	★	★	★	★	☆		B, F, T1
Varner-Hogg Plantation SHP (Guided Tours)	WEST COLUMBIA	★	★	★	★							★		★		☆			
Village Creek SP	LUMBERTON				★	★	★	6			BG	★	★	★	★	☆	☆		B, F
Washington-on-the-Brazos SHP (Anson Jones Home)	WASHINGTON	★	★	★	★						DG	★	★	★					A

remnants of one of the few operating **tin mines** in the United States. Pedestrian access for day-use activities such as hiking, nature study and picnicking is permitted. The site is undeveloped, with no facilities or utilities, and vehicular traffic is prohibited.

Fulton Mansion State Historic Structure is 3.5 miles north of Rockport off TX 35 in Aransas County. The 2.3 acre-property was acquired by purchase from private owner in 1976. Three-story wooden structure, built in 1874-1877, was home of **George W. Fulton,** prominent in South Texas for economic and commercial influence; mansion derives significance from its innovative construction and Victorian design. Guided tours Wednesday-Sunday.

Galveston Island State Park, located approximately six miles southwest of Galveston on FM 3005, is a 1,950.01-acre site acquired in 1970 from private owners. Offers camping, nature study and fishing amid **sand dunes and grassland.** Musical productions in **amphitheater** during summer.

Garner State Park is 1,419.8 acres of recreational facilities on US 83 on the Frio River in Uvalde County 10 miles south of Leakey. Named for **John Nance Garner,** U.S. Vice President, 1933-1941, the park was deeded in 1934 by private owners. Camping, hiking, picnicking, river recreation, miniature golf. Cabins available. Nearby is **John Nance "Cactus Jack" Garner Museum** in Uvalde. Nearby also are ruins of historic **Mission Nuestra Señora de la Candelaria del Cañon,** founded in 1749; **Camp Sabinal** (a U.S. Cavalry post and later Texas Ranger camp) established 1856; **Fort Inge,** established 1849.

Goliad State Historical Park is 187.33 acres one mile south of Goliad on US 183 along the San Antonio River in Goliad County. The land was deeded in 1931 by the City and County of Goliad. Nearby are the sites of several battles in the Texas fight for independence from Mexico. The park includes a replica of **Mission Nuestra Señora del Espíritu Santo de Zúñiga,** originally established 1722 and settled at its present site in 1749. Park unit includes **Gen. Zaragoza's Birthplace,** which is located near **Presidio la Bahia.** He was Mexican national hero who led troops against French at historic **Battle of Puebla.** Park property also contains ruins of **Mission Nuestra Señora del Rosario,** established 1754, located four miles west of Goliad on US 59. Other nearby points of historical interest are restored **Presidio Nuestra Señora de Loreto de la Bahía,** established 1722 and settled on site in 1749; it is located short distance south on US 183. Memorial shaft marking common burial site of **Fannin** and victims of **Goliad massacre** (1836) is near **Presidio la Bahía.** Camping, picnicking, historical exhibits, nature trail. (See also **Fannin Battleground State Historical Park,** above.)

Goose Island State Park, 314 acres 10 miles northeast of Rockport on TX 35 and PR 13 on St. Charles and Aransas bays in Aransas County, was deeded by private owners in 1931-1935 plus an additional seven acres donated in the early 1990s by Sun Oil Co. Located here is "Big Tree" estimated to be more than 1,000 years old and listed as the **state champion coastal live oak.** Water activities, picnicking and camping, plus excellent birding. Rare and endangered **whooping cranes** can be viewed during winter just across St. Charles Bay in **Aransas National Wildlife Refuge.**

Gov. Hogg Shrine State Historical Park is a 26.7-acre tract on TX 37 about six blocks south of the Wood County Courthouse in Quitman. Named for **James Stephen Hogg, first native-born governor of Texas,** the park includes a museum housing items which belonged to Hogg. Seventeen acres deeded by the Wood County Old Settlers Reunion Association in 1946; 4.74 acres gift of Miss Ima Hogg in 1970; 3 acres purchased. **Gov. James Stephen Hogg Memorial Shrine** created in 1941. Three museums: Gov. Hogg's wedding held in **Stinson Home; Honeymoon Cottage; Miss Ima Hogg Museum** houses both park headquarters and display of representative history of entire Northeast Texas area.

Guadalupe River State Park comprises 1,938.3 acres on cypress-shaded Guadalupe River in Kendall and Comal counties, 13 miles east of Boerne on TX 46. Acquired by deed from private owners in 1975. Park has four miles of river frontage with several **white-water rapids** and is located in middle of 20-mile stretch of **Guadalupe River** noted for canoeing, tubing. Picnicking, camping, nature study. Trees include **sycamore, elm, basswood, pecan, walnut, persimmon, willow** and **hackberry.** Rare **golden-cheeked warbler** nests here. Animals include **deer, coyotes, gray foxes, bobcats** and **armadillos**. (see also **Honey Creek State Natural Area,** below).

Hill Country State Natural Area (Louise Merrick Unit) in Bandera and Medina counties, nine miles west of Bandera on RM 1077. The 5,369.8-acre site acquired by gift and purchase in 1976. Park is located in typical Texas Hill Country on West Verde Creek and contains several **spring-fed streams.** Primitive and equestrian camping, hiking, horseback riding, all-terrain bicycling.

Honey Creek State Natural Area consists of 2,293.6 acres adjacent to **Guadalupe River State Park** (above). Entrance is in the park. Acquired from The Nature Conservancy of Texas in 1983 with an addition from private individual in 1988. Open Saturdays only for **guided naturalist tours** starting about 9 a.m. Texas Conservation Passport required for all persons 17 and older.

Hueco Tanks State Historical Park, located 32 miles northeast of El Paso in El Paso County on RM 2775 just north of US 62-180, was obtained from the county in 1969, with additional 121 acres purchased in 1970. Featured in this 860.3-acre park are large **natural rock basins** and site of last great Indian battle in county. Apaches, Kiowas, Comanches and earlier Indian tribesmen camped here and left behind **pictographs** telling of their adventures. Tanks served as watering place for **Butterfield Overland Mail Route.** Also in park are **old ranch house** and relocated **ruins of stage station. Rock climbing,** picnicking, camping. Guided tours on weekends. Wildlife includes **gray fox, bobcat, prairie falcons, golden eagles.**

Huntsville State Park is 2,083.2-acre recreational area off IH 45 and PR 40 six miles southeast of Huntsville in Walker County, acquired by deeds from private owners in 1934. Heavily wooded park adjoins **Sam Houston National Forest** and encloses **Lake Raven.** Hiking, biking, pedal boats, canoeing. **Sam Houston State University** located at nearby Huntsville. **Texas Department of Criminal Justice headquarters** also located in Huntsville as well as old homestead of **Sam Houston (Steamboat House)** and his **grave.** Homestead contains personal effects of Houston. Approximately 50 miles away is **Alabama-Coushatta Indian Reservation** in Polk County.

Inks Lake State Park is 1,201.7 acres of recreational facilities along Inks Lake, nine miles west of Burnet on the Colorado River off US 281 or TX 29 on PR 4 in Burnet County. Acquired by deeds from the Lower Colorado River Authority and private owners in 1940. Camping, hiking, fishing, swimming, boating, 9 holes of golf. Nearby are **Longhorn Cavern State Park, LBJ Ranch, LBJ State Historical Park, Pedernales Falls State Park** and **Enchanted Rock State Natural Area. Granite Mountain** and quarry at nearby Marble Falls furnished pink granite for **Texas state capitol. Deer, turkey** and other wildlife abundant. **Buchanan Dam,** largest multi-arch dam in world, located six miles from park.

Jim Hogg State Historical Park is 178.2 acres of East Texas Piney Woods off US 84 and PR 50 two miles northeast of Rusk in Cherokee County. A memorial to the state's **first native-born governor, James Stephen Hogg,** the property was deeded by the city of Rusk in 1941. Scale replica of birthplace houses museum. Family cemetery.

José Antonio Navarro State Historical Park, on .6 acre at corner of S. Laredo and W. Nueva streets in downtown San Antonio, was acquired by donation from San Antonio Conservation Society Foundation in 1975. Has furnished **Navarro House** complex built about 1848, home of the statesman, rancher, Texas patriot.

Kerrville-Schreiner State Park is a 517-acre area three miles southeast of Kerrville off TX 173 and PR 19 along the Guadalupe River in Kerr County. Land deeded by City of Kerrville in 1934. Trees include **redbud, sumac, buckeye, pecan, mesquite.** Near park is site of **Camp Verde,** scene of an experiment involving use of **camels** for transportation; the camp was active from 1855 to 1869. **Bandera Pass,** 12 miles south of Kerrville, noted gap in chain of mountains through which passed camel caravans, wagon trains, Spanish conquistadores, immigrant trains. In nearby **Fredericksburg** is atmosphere of old country of Germany and famous **Nimitz Hotel** (see **Admiral Nimitz Museum Historical Park).**

Kickapoo Cavern State Park is located about 22 miles north of Brackettville on RM 674 on the Kinney/Edwards county line in the southern Edwards Plateau. **Fifteen known caves** in park, two of which are large enough to be significant: **Kickapoo Cavern**, about 1/4 mile in length, has impressive formations, and **Green Cave**, slightly longer, supports a nursery colony of **Brazilian freetail bats** in summer. Tours of Kickapoo and observation of bats available. Birds include rare species such as **black-capped vireo, varied bunting** and **Montezuma quail**. Reptiles and amphibians include **barking frog, mottled rock rattlesnake** and **Texas alligator lizard**. Open only by reservation. Texas Conservation Passport required for all visitors over 17 years of age. Group lodge; primitive camping. Further development pending at press time.

Kreische Brewery State Historical Park (see Monument Hill and Kreische Brewery State Historical Parks)

Lake Arrowhead State Park consists of 524 acres in Clay County, about eight miles south of Wichita Falls on US 281 to FM 1954, then six miles to park. Acquired in 1970 from the City of Wichita Falls. **Lake Arrowhead** is a reservoir on the Little Wichita River and covers approximately 13,500 surface acres with 106 miles of shoreline. The land surrounding the lake is generally semiarid, gently rolling prairie, much of which has been invaded by mesquite in recent decades. Fishing, lake swimming, picnicking, horseback riding area.

Lake Bob Sandlin State Park, on the wooded shoreline of 9,460-acre Lake Bob Sandlin, is located 12 miles southwest of Mount Pleasant off FM 21 in Titus County. Activities in the heavily wooded, 640.8-acre park include picnicking, camping, fishing and boating. **Oak, hickory, dogwood, redbud, maple** and **pine** produce spectacular fall color. Reservoir stocked with **largemouth bass, catfish** and **crappie.**

Lake Brownwood State Park in Brown County is 537.5 acres acquired from Brown County Water Improvement District No. 1 in 1934. Park reached from TX 179 to PR 15, 16 miles northwest of Brownwood on Lake Brownwood near **geographical center of Texas.** Water sports, hiking, camping. Cabins available.

Lake Casa Blanca State Park, located one mile east of Laredo off TX 59 on Lake Casa Blanca Road, was formerly operated by the City of Laredo and Webb County. **Recreation hall** can be reserved. Camping, picnicking, fishing, ball fields, playgrounds, amphitheater, tennis courts and county-operated golf course.

Lake Colorado City State Park, 500 acres leased for 50 years from a utility company. It is located in Mitchell County 11 miles southwest of Colorado City off IH 20 on County Road 2836. Fishing from boats, shore or **covered fishing barge**. Mile of **sandy beaches** for lake swimming plus boating, picnicking, camping and nature study are available.

Lake Corpus Christi State Park, a 288 land-acre park located in San Patricio, Jim Wells and Live Oak counties four miles southwest of Mathis on TX 359 and PR 25, was leased from City of Corpus Christi in 1934. Lake noted for **big blue, channel** and **yellow catfish,** as well as **sunfish, bass** and **crappie**. City of **Corpus Christi** and **Padre Island National Sea-**

shore, Mustang Island State Park, Goliad State Park, Choke Canyon State Park, Aransas National Wildlife Refuge, Goose Island State Park and **Fulton Mansion State Historical Park** are nearby.

Lake Houston State Park is situated at the confluence of Caney Creek and the East Fork of the San Jacinto River. The 4,912.6-acre site, purchased from Champion Paper Company in 198, is northeast of Houston in Harris and Montgomery counties.

Lake Livingston State Park, in Polk County, six miles southwest of Livingston on FM 3126, contains 635.5 acres along Lake Livingston. Acquired by deed from private landowners in 1971. Near ghost town of **Swartwout,** steamboat landing on Trinity River in 1830s and 1840s. Camping, picnicking, swimming pool, fishing, bicycle camping, park store (seasonal).

Lake Mineral Wells State Park, located four miles east of the city of Mineral Wells on US 180 in Parker County, consists of 3,010 acres encompassing Lake Mineral Wells. In 1975, the U.S. Government transferred 1,844 acres of Fort Wolters army post to the State of Texas for use as park. The City of Mineral Wells donated 1,057 land acres and the 646-acre lake to TPWD in 1976. Popular for **rock-climbing/rappelling**. Swimming, fishing, boating, camping; hiking and backpacking trails.

Lake Somerville State Park, northwest of Brenham in Lee and Burleson counties, was leased from the federal government in 1969. **Birch Creek Unit** reached off TX 60 and PR 57. **Nails Creek Unit** accessed from US 290 and FM 180. The 5,220-acre park includes miles of hiking-equestrian-mountain bike trails connecting the two units, with equestrian and primitive camp sites, rest benches, shelters and drinking water. Many species of wild game observed at park; **white-tailed deer, fox, coyote, raccoon, rabbit** and **quail** abundant. Various park areas feature sandy or grassy shallow shorelines for wading or swimming.

Lake Tawakoni State Park consists of 401 acres of mostly upland regrowth and creek bottom post oak woodlands in Hunt County, with 5.2 miles of shoreline on Lake Tawakoni. Leased from Sabine River Authority. Located about 50 miles east of Dallas, accessed from IH 30 on north and IH 20 on south. Water recreation. Limited use pending development.

Lake Texana State Park is 575 acres, six miles east of Edna on TX 111, half-way between Houston and Corpus Christi in Jackson County, with camping, boating, fishing, picnicking facilities. It was acquired by a 50-year lease agreement with the Bureau of Reclamation in 1977. **Oak/pecan woodlands.** Good **birding. Alligators** found in park coves.

Lake Whitney State Park is 955 acres along the east shore of Lake Whitney west of Hillsboro via TX 22 and FM 1244 in Hill County. Acquired in 1954 by a Department of the Army lease, the state has control until 2003. Located on Lake Whitney near ruins of **Towash,** early Texas settlement inundated by Lake Whitney. Towash Village named for chief of Hainai Indians that moved into area in 1835. Park noted for **bluebonnets** in spring.

Landmark Inn State Historical Park, 4.7 acres in Castroville, about 15 miles west of San Antonio, was acquired through donation by Miss Ruth Lawler in 1974. Castroville, settled in the 1840s by Alsatian farmers, is called **Little Alsace of Texas**. Landmark Inn built about 1844 as residence and store for **Caesar Monad,** mayor of Castroville 1851-1864. Special workshops, tours and events held at inn; grounds may be rented for receptions, family reunions and weddings. **Overnight lodging** Wednesday-Sunday nights. No phones; some rooms air-conditioned; continental breakfast served.

Lipantitlan State Historical Park is five acres east of Orange Grove in Nueces County off Texas 359, FM 624 and FM 70. The property was deeded by private owners in 1937. Fort constructed here in 1833 by Mexican government; fort fell to Texas forces in 1835. **Lake Corpus Christi State Park** is nearby.

Lockhart State Park is 263 acres one mile south of Lockhart via FM 20 and PR 10 in Caldwell County. The land was deeded by private owners between 1934 and 1937. Camping, picnicking, swimming pool, **9-hole golf course. Emanuel Episcopal Church** in Lockhart is **one of oldest Protestant churches** in continuous use in Texas. After Comanche raid at Linnville, **Battle of Plum Creek** (1840) was fought in area.

Longhorn Cavern State Park, off US 281 and PR 4 about 6 miles west and 6 miles south of Burnet in Burnet County, is 639 acres dedicated as a natural landmark in 1971. It was acquired in 1932-1937 from private owners. The cave has been used as a shelter since prehistoric times. Among legends about the cave is one that the outlaw **Sam Bass** hid a $2 million cache of stolen money there. Confederates made gunpowder in the cave during the Civil War. **Gen. Robert E. Lee,** while stationed in Texas before the Civil War, is said to have chased some Indians into the cave but lost their trail. **Nature trail; guided tours** of cave. **Inks Lake State Park** and **Lyndon B. Johnson Ranch** located nearby. It is operated by concession agreement.

Lost Maples State Natural Area consists of 2,174.2 scenic acres in Bandera County, four miles north of Vanderpool on RM 187. Acquired by purchase from private owners in 1973. Outstanding example of Edwards Plateau flora and fauna, features isolated stand of uncommon **Uvalde bigtooth maple. Rare golden-cheeked warbler, black-capped vireo** and **green kingfisher** nest and feed in park. Fall foliage can be spectacular. Hiking trails, camping, birdwatching. Wildlife includes **gray fox, mountain lion, Russian boar** and **javelina.**

Lubbock Lake Landmark State Historical Park is a 365.9-acre **archaeological site** and botanical and zoological preserve in **Yellowhouse Draw** on the northwest edge of the city of Lubbock near intersection of Loop 239 and Clovis Road (US 84). The site was leased from the City of Lubbock for 50 years in 1986. Evidence of **human habitation from 12,000 years ago** to the recent past has been uncovered. Only known site in North America containing deposits related to all cultures known to have existed on the Southern Plains. Site is **State Archeological Landmark, National Historic Landmark** and is on the **National Register of Historic Places. Interpretive center,** three interpretive trails, three rest areas, hiking, fishing, swimming. Ongoing excavation can be viewed. Day use only.

Lyndon B. Johnson State Historical Park, off US 290 in Gillespie County 14 miles west of Johnson City near Stonewall, contains 732.8 acres. Acquired in 1967 with private donations. **Home of Lyndon B. Johnson** located north bank of **Pedernales River** across Ranch Road 1 from park; portion of **official Texas longhorn herd** maintained at park. Wildlife exhibit includes **turkey, deer** and **buffalo. Living history demonstrations** at restored **Sauer-Beckmann house.** Reconstruction of **Johnson birthplace,** located east of ranch house at end of PR 49, open to public. Historic structures, amphitheater, swimming pool, tennis courts, baseball field, picnicking. Nearby is family cemetery where former president and relatives are buried. In Johnson City is **boyhood home of President Johnson**. Near outskirts of Johnson City is cluster of stone barns and buildings constructed by his grandfather, Sam Ealy Johnson Sr., and his brother Tom. (See also **National Parks.)**

Magoffin Home State Historical Park, in the City of El Paso, El Paso County; total acreage, 1.5. Purchased jointly by the State of Texas and the City of El Paso in 1976, it is operated by TPWD. The 19-room territorial-style adobe Magoffin Home was built in 1875 by pioneer El Pasoan **Joseph Magoffin**. Furnished with original family artifacts. Open Wednesday-Sunday for guided tours.

Martin Creek Lake State Park, 286 acres, is located 4 miles south of Tatum off TX 43 in Rusk County. It was deeded to the TPWD by the Texas Utilities in 1976. Excellent year-round fishing; water warmed by nearby electric power-generation plant. Camping, picnicking, boating, lake swimming. Old roadbed of **Trammel's Trace,** old Indian trail that became major route for settlers moving to Texas from Arkansas, can be seen. **Hardwood and pine** forest shelters abundant wildlife including **swamp rabbits, gophers, nutria, deer** and numerous species of land birds and waterfowl.

Martin Dies Jr. State Park, until 1965 the **Dam B State Park,** is 705 acres in Jasper and Tyler counties on B. A. Steinhagen Reservoir between Woodville and Jasper via US 190. Land leased from Corps of Engineers in 1964. Located at edge of **Big Thicket.** Plant and animal life varied and abundant. Winter **bald eagle census** conducted at reservoir. In spring, **Dogwood Festival** held at Woodville. Park is approximately 30 miles from **Alabama and Coushatta Indian Reservation.**

Matagorda Island State Park and Wildlife Management Area: Separated from the mainland by San Antonio and Espiritu Santo bays, Matagorda Island is one of the **barrier islands** that border the Gulf and protect the mainland from the great tides and strong wave action of the open ocean. The southwestern tip of the island, consisting of 11,500 acres, is privately-owned. The remainder, extending approximately 24 miles to the northeast, comprises 24,893 acres of state land and 19,000 acres of federal land managed by the TPWD under an agreement reached in 1983. The park occupies abut 7,325 acres of the total. **La Salle** had a camp on the island in 1684; **lighthouse** was constructed in 1852. Nineteen species listed by federal or state government as threatened or endangered found here, including **whooping cranes, peregrine falcons, brown pelicans** and **Ridley sea turtles**. More than **300 species of birds** use island during spring and fall migrations. Access only by boat; passenger **ferry operates from Port O'Connor** on Saturday, Sunday and holidays.

Matagorda Peninsula State Park, 6,322 acres of undeveloped Gulf Beach, is located south of the town of Matagorda on FM 2031. Day use only; **access only by four-wheel-drive vehicles.** Fishing, swimming and picnicking allowed, but no facilities of any kind are provided.

McKinney Falls State Park is 640 acres seven miles southeast of the state capitol in Austin off US 183. Acquired in 1970 by gift from private owners. Named for Thomas F. McKinney, **one of Stephen F. Austin's first 300 colonists**, who built his home here in the mid-1800s on Onion Creek. Ruins of his homestead can be viewed. Hiking, bike and nature trails; amphitheater; picnicking.

Meridian State Park in Bosque County is a 502.4-acre park including a 73-acre lake. The land was acquired from private owners in 1933-1935. **Tonkawa Indians** lived in surrounding area before coming of white man; **Tawakoni Indians** also occupied area prior to 1841. **Texan-Santa Fe expedition** of 1841 passed through Bosque County near present site of park, which is located on Bee Creek in Bosque Valley. **Endangered golden-cheeked warblers** nest here. Camping, picnicking, hiking, lake swimming, bicycling.

Mission Tejas State Historical Park is a 362.4-acre park in Houston County. Situated 12 miles southeast of Alto in Weches via PR 44 in the **Davy Crockett National Forest,** the park was acquired from the Texas Forest Service in 1957 by legislative act. In the park is a replica of the **Mission San Francisco de los Tejas,** which was established in 1690; was first mission in East Texas; abandoned, then re-established 1716; abandoned again 1719; re-established again 1721; abandoned for last time in 1730 and moved to San Antonio. Also in park is restored **Rice Family Log House,** built about 1821. Camping, hiking, fishing, picnicking.

Monahans Sandhills State Park consists of 3,840 acres of sand dunes, some up to 70 feet high, in Ward and Winkler counties five miles northeast of Monahans on IH 20 to PR 41. Land leased by state from private foundation until 2056. Dunes used as meeting place by raiding Indians. Equestrian day-use area. Activities include wildlife observation and **sand-surfing**. **Odessa meteor crater** is nearby, as is **Balmorhea State Park.**

Monument Hill State Historical Park and **Kreische Brewery State Historical Park** are operated as one park unit. Monument Hill consists of 4.4 acres two miles southwest of La Grange on US 77 to Spur Road 92 in Fayette County adjacent to **Kreische Brewery State Historical Park.** The land was acquired in two parcels — monument and tomb area transferred from Board of Control in 1949; the rest from the Archbishop of San Antonio in 1956. The hill, a historical site, bears a memorial shaft dedicated to **Capt. Nicholas Dawson** and his men, who fought at **Salado Creek** in 1842, in Mexican **Gen. Woll's** invasion of Texas, and to the men of the **"black bean lottery"** (1843) of the **Mier Expedition.** Bodies of these heroes were brought to **Monument Hill** for reburial in 1848. Kreische Complex linked to Monument Hill through interpretive trail. **Kreische Brewery State Historical Park** is 36 acres, acquired by purchase from private owners. Contains **Kreische Brewery** and house complex built between 1850-1855 on Colorado River; probably **first commercial brewery** in state. Brewery closed in 1888; now consists of several intact structures surrounded by ruins in various stages of deterioration. Various out-buildings located on site were associated with brewery and family. Interpretive trail around complex and nature trail. Guided tours of brewery on weekends and by special request.

Mother Neff State Park was the **first official state park** in Texas. It originated with six acres designated for park purposes by the will of Mrs. I. E. Neff, mother of **Pat M. Neff,** Governor of Texas from 1921 to 1925. The park, located 6.5 miles west of Moody on TX 236 and PR 14, now contains 259 acres along the Leon River in Coryell County. The additional land was deeded to the state in 1934 by private owners. Heavily wooded. Camping, picnicking, fishing.

Mustang Island State Park, 3,703.6 acres on Gulf of Mexico in Nueces County, 14 miles south of Port Aransas on PR 53, was acquired from private owners in 1972. Mustang Island is a coastal barrier island with a unique and complicated ecosystem, dependent upon the sand dune. The foundation plants of the

More Travel Information

The **Texas Department of Transportation** offers travel information through a toll-free number: **1-800-888-8TEX.** Call this number for:

- The **Texas State Travel Guide** with information about attractions, activities, history and historic sites.
- The official **Texas state highway map.**

dunes are **sea oats, beach panic grass** and **soilbind morning glory.** Beach camping; sun, sand and water activities. Excellent birding, especially during spring and fall migrations. **Padre Island National Seashore** 14 miles south.

Old Fort Parker State Historical Park, a 37.5-acre park between Groesbeck and Mexia off TX 14 in Limestone County, was deeded by private owners in 1933. In the park is a replica of **Fort Parker** stockade, built in 1834 and was site of abduction of **Cynthia Ann Parker** on May 19, 1836, by Comanche and Kiowa Indians. Visitors can explore cabins and blockhouses Wednesday through Sunday. Nearby is **Fort Parker State Park** with recreational facilities (see separate listing).

Palmetto State Park, a scenic park, is 268.6 acres eight miles south of Luling on US 183 and PR 11 along the San Marcos River in Gonzales County. Land deeded in 1934-1937 by private owners and City of Gonzales. Artesian wells produce distinctive, sulfur-laden water. Named for **tropical dwarf palmetto** found there. Diverse plant and animal life. Nearby **Gonzales** and **Ottine** important in early Texas history. Gonzales settled 1825 as center of **Green DeWitt's colonies.** Nearby are **Elks' Hospital** and **Texas Rehabilitation Center.**

Palo Duro Canyon State Park consists of 16,402.1 acres 12 miles east of Canyon on TX 217 and PR 5 in Armstrong and Randall counties. The land was deeded by private owners in 1933 and is the scene of the annual summer production of the drama, **"Texas."** Spectacular **scenic canyon** one million years old exposes rocks spanning about 200 million years of geological time. **Coronado** may have visited canyon in 1541. Canyon officially discovered by **Capt. R. B. Marcy** in 1852. Scene of decisive battle in 1874 between Comanche and Kiowa Indians and U.S. Army troops under **Gen. Ranald Mackenzie.** Also scene of ranching enterprise started by **Charles Goodnight** in 1876. Part of **state longhorn herd** is kept here. Camping, horseback and hiking trails, miniature train ride, horse rentals, park store.

Pedernales Falls State Park, 5,211.7 acres in Blanco County about 14 miles east of Johnson City along Pedernales River. Site was acquired from private owners in 1970. This area typifies **Edwards Plateau** with **live oaks, deer, turkey** and **stone hills.** Camping, picnicking, hiking and nature trails. River recreation in limited area. Falls main scenic attraction.

Port Isabel Lighthouse State Historical Park consists of 0.88 acres in Port Isabel, Cameron County. Acquired by purchase from private owners in 1950, site includes **lighthouse** constructed in 1852; near sites of Civil War battle of **Palmito Ranch** (1865), and Mexican War battles of **Palo Alto** and **Resaca de la Palma**. Lighthouse remodeled 1952 and is still used. Resort facilities available across causeway at **South Padre Island.**

Port Lavaca State Fishing Pier, a 1.8-acre recreational area on Lavaca Bay in Calhoun County, was acquired by transfer of authority from state highway department in 1963. Main attraction is a 3,200-foot fishing pier made from former causeway across the bay. **Port Lavaca City Park** is at base of the pier and offers a boat ramp and picnicking facilities. Operated by City of Port Lavaca.

Possum Kingdom State Park, west of Mineral Wells via US 180 to Caddo then north on PR 33 in Palo Pinto County, is 1,528.7 acres adjacent to **Possum Kingdom Lake,** in **Palo Pinto Mountains** and **Brazos River Valley.** Rugged canyons home to **deer,** other wildlife. Part of **official state longhorn herd** live in park. The area was acquired from the Brazos River Authority in 1940. Camping, picnicking, lake swimming, fishing, boating. Cabins available.

Purtis Creek State Park is located in Henderson and Van Zandt counties three miles north of Eustace on FM 316. Total acreage 1,566, acquired in 1976 from private owners. Fishing for **largemouth bass** on catch-and-release basis only; **catfish and crappie** can be retained. Also camping and picnicking.

Ray Roberts Lake State Park (Isle du Bois Unit), consists of 4,136 acres on the south side of Ray Roberts Lake. The park unit is located on FM 455 between Pilot Point and Sanger in Denton County. Johnson Branch Unit is planned. Fishing, camping, picnicking, swimming.

Rusk/Palestine State Park. Rusk unit located adjacent to **Texas State Railroad Rusk Depot** off US 84, with total acreage of 136. Palestine unit located off US 84 adjacent to **Texas State Railroad Palestine Depot** with 26 acres. Stocked lake, picnicking, camping, tennis courts, playground. **Train rides** in restored passenger cars (see also **Texas State Railroad State Historical Park).**

Sabine Pass Battleground State Historical Park in Jefferson County 1.5 miles south of Sabine Pass on Dowlen Road, contains 56.3 acres acquired by deed from Kountze County Trust in 1971. **Richard W. Dowling,** with small Confederate force, repelled an attempted 1863 invasion of Texas by Union naval gunboats during Civil War. **Monument; World War II ammunition bunkers.** Day use only. Boating, fishing, picnicking. **Sea Rim State Park** nearby.

Sam Bell Maxey House State Historical Park, at the corner of Church and Washington streets in Paris, Lamar County, was donated by City of Paris in 1976. Consists of 1.4 acres with 1868 High Victorian Italianate-style frame house, plus book house and stable. Most of furnishings accumulated by Maxey family. Maxey served in Mexican War and Civil War and was two-term U.S. Senator. House is on the **National Register of Historic Places**. Open for tours.

San Angelo State Park, on **O.C. Fisher Reservoir** adjacent to the city of San Angelo, contains 18,000 acres, including the reservoir, most of which is undeveloped. Management of the property was transferred to TPWD from the U.S. Corps of Engineers in 1995. Access is from US 87 or 67, then FM 2288. Historically, the area gives evidence of **11,000 years of human occupation**. Highly diversified plant and animal life, including **300 species of birds** and 50 species of mammals. Activities include boating, fishing, swimming, hiking, mountain biking, camping, picnicking and wildlife observation. Nearby is **Fort Concho**.

San Jacinto Battleground State Historical Park and **Battleship Texas State Historic Site** are located 22 miles east of downtown Houston off TX 225 East to TX 134 to PR 1836 in east Harris County. The park is 1,005.2 acres with 570-foot-tall monument erected in honor of Texans who defeated Mexican **Gen. Antonio Lopez de Santa Anna** on April 21, 1836, to win Texas' independence from Mexico. The park is original site of Texan's camp acquired in 1883. Subsequent acquisitions made in 1897 and 1899. Park transferred to TPWD in 1965. Park registered as **National Historic Landmark**. Elevator ride to top of monument; museum. Monument known as **tallest masonry structure in the world**. Interpretive trail around battleground. Adjacent to park is the **U.S.S. Texas**, the only survivor of the dreadnought class and the only surviving veteran of two world wars, was donated to people of Texas by U.S. Navy. Ship was moored in the Houston Ship Channel at the **San Jacinto Battleground** on San Jacinto Day, 1948. In Dec. 1988, the ship was dry-docked for refurbishing; it reopened for visitors in July 1990. Restoration is ongoing.

San José Mission is operated as part of **San Anto-**

nio **Missions National Historical Park** (see page 369).

Sea Rim State Park in Jefferson County, 10 miles west of Sabine Pass, off TX 87, contains 15,094.2 acres of marshland with five miles of **Gulf beach** shoreline, acquired from private owners in 1972. It is prime wintering area for **waterfowl.** Abundant wetlands wildlife. Camping, **wildlife observation blinds** in marsh; nature trail; ideal for boating with canoe, kayak, pirogue. **Airboat tours of marsh**, swimming. Habitat of endangered **red wolf, American alligator**, **river otter** and **muskrat**. Near **McFaddin National Wildlife Refuge.**

Sebastopol House State Historical Park at 704 Zorn Street in Seguin, Guadalupe County, was acquired by purchase in 1976 from Seguin Conservation Society; approximately 2.2 acres. Built about 1854 by **Col. Joshua W. Young** of limecrete, concrete made from local gravel and lime, the Greek Revival-style house was restored to its 1870-1880 appearance by the TPWD and opened to the public in 1989. Tours available Wednesday through Sunday.

Seminole Canyon State Historical Park in Val Verde County, nine miles west of Comstock off US 90, contains 2,172 acres; acquired by purchase from private owner in 1973. **Fate Bell Shelter** in canyon contains several important **prehistoric Indian pictograph** sites. Historic interpretive center; guided tours Wednesday through Sunday. Diverse flora and fauna. Hiking, mountain biking, camping.

Sheldon Lake State Park, Harris County on Carpenter's Bayou 20 miles northeast of downtown Houston just north of US 90. Total acreage, 2,503. Acquired by purchase in 1952 from the City of Houston. Facilities include boat ramps, fishing piers and 5.5 miles of levees. Activities include nature study, bird watching of primarily **waterfowl** and **marsh birds,** and fishing.

South Llano River State Park and Wildlife Management Area five miles south of Junction in Kimble County off US 377. The 2,656.9-acre site with 2 miles of river frontage was donated to the TPWD by private owner in 1977. Wooded bottomland along the winding South Llano River is **largest and oldest winter roosting site for the Rio Grande turkey** in Central Texas. Roosting area closed to visitors October-March. Other animals include **wood ducks, javelina, fox, beaver, bobcat, cottontail** and **armadillo.** Camping, picnicking, tubing, swimming and fishing.

Starr Family State Historical Park, 3.1 acres at 407 W. Travis in Marshall, Harrison County. Greek Revival-style mansion, **Maplecroft**, was home to five generations of Starr family, powerful and economically influential Texans. Acquired by gift in 1976. Additional land donated in 1982. Tours Wednesday-Sunday. Special events held during year. Grounds feature **azaleas, camellias, dogwoods, roses, wisteria** and **fruit trees.**

Stephen F. Austin State Historical Park is 667.4 acres along the Brazos River in San Felipe, Austin County, named for the **"Father of Texas."** The area was deeded by the San Felipe de Austin Corporation and the San Felipe Park Association in 1940. Site of township of **San Felipe** was seat of government where conventions of 1832 and 1833 and Consultation of 1835 held. These led to **Texas Declaration of Independence.** San Felipe was home of **Stephen F. Austin** and other famous early Texans; home of **Texas' first Anglo newspaper (the Texas Gazette)** founded in 1829; postal system of Texas originated here; beginning of **Texas Rangers.** Statue of Austin, museum. Wooded. Camping, picnicking, swimming pool, 18-hole golf course.

Texas State Railroad State Historical Park is in Anderson and Cherokee counties between the cities of Palestine and Rusk, adjacent to US 84. Total acreage, 499. Acquired by Legislative Act in 1971. Trains run Thursday-Monday during summer, weekends only spring and fall on 25.5 miles of track. See local Parks and Wildlife office for schedules. The railroad was built by the State of Texas to support the **state-owned iron works** at Rusk. Begun in 1896, the railroad was gradually extended until it reached Palestine in 1909 and established regular rail service between the towns. (See also **Rusk/Palestine State Park.**)

Tips State Park, 31.3 acres of recreational facilities, is on the Frio River in Live Oak County. The park, a mile west of Three Rivers, was deeded by private owners in 1925. Park near site of **first glass factory** in Texas.

Tyler State Park is 985.5 acres two miles north of IH 20 on FM 14 north of Tyler in Smith County. Includes 64-acre lake. The land was deeded by private owners in 1934-1935. Heavily wooded. Camping, hiking, fishing, boating, lake swimming. Nearby Tyler famous as **rose capital of world;** there are located **Tyler Junior College and planetarium, Tyler Rose Garden, Caldwell Children's Zoo** and the **Goodman Museum.** Tyler is home of the **Tyler Rose Festival** each fall. Morton **salt mines** in Grand Saline, 40 miles from park.

Varner-Hogg Plantation State Historical Park is 65.7 acres along Varner Creek east of West Columbia on FM 2852 in Brazoria County. The land originally was owned by Martin Varner, a member of Stephen F. Austin's **"Old Three Hundred"** colony; later was home of Texas governor **James Stephen Hogg**. The property was deeded to the state in 1956 by Miss Ima Hogg, former governor's daughter. **First rum distillery** in Texas established in 1829 by Varner. Mansion tours Wednesday-Sunday.

Village Creek State Park, comprising 943 heavily forested acres, is located in Lumberton, Hardin County, 10 miles north of Beaumont. From US 96, turn east on Dana, south on Village Creek Pkwy., and east on Alma. Acquired in 1979, the park is full of **cypress, water tupelo, river birch, mayhaw and yaupon** trees. Wildlife includes **snapping turtles**, white-tailed deer, possum, spring-peeper and cricket frogs, bullfrogs, armadillos and occasional alligators; the **200 species of birds** found there include wood ducks, egrets and herons. Activities include fishing, camping, canoeing, swimming, hiking and picnicking. Nearby are **Sea Rim** and **Martin Dies Jr. state parks** and **Big Thicket National Preserve**.

Washington-on-the-Brazos State Historical Park consists of 154.144 acres seven miles southwest of Navasota in Washington County on TX 105 and FM 1155. The land was deeded by private owners in 1916 and 1976. The land includes the site of the signing in 1836 of the **Texas Declaration of Independence** from Mexico, as well as the site of the later **signing of the Constitution of the Republic of Texas**. In 1842 and 1845, the land included the **capitol of the Republic**. Barrington, the **home of Anson Jones, last president of the Republic of Texas**, has been restored. **Star of the Republic Museum**.

Future Parks

The following parks were in the planning stages when this edition of the Texas Almanac went to press:

Arroyo Colorado SP, near Rio Hondo; **Davis Hill SP**, Cleveland; **Devil's Sinkhole SNA**, Rocksprings; **Eagle Mountain Lake SP**, Fort Worth; **Elephant Mountain Ranch SP**, Alpine; **Gorman Falls SP**, Bend; **Rancho de las Cabras SHP**, Floresville; and **Resaca de la Palma SP**, Brownsville. ☆

National Parks, Historical Sites, Recreation Areas in Texas

Below are listed the facilities in and the activities that can be enjoyed at the two national parks, a national seashore, a biological preserve, several historic sites, memorials and recreation areas in Texas. They are under supervision of the **U.S. Department of Interior.** In addition, the recreational opportunities in the four national forests in Texas, under the jurisdiction of the **U.S. Department of Agriculture,** are listed at the end of the article.

Alibates Flint Quarries National Monument consists of 1,079 acres in Potter County. For more than 10,000 years, **pre-Columbian Indians** dug agatized limestone from the quarries to make projectile points, knives, scrapers and other tools. The area is presently undeveloped. You may visit the flint quarries on guided walking tours with a park ranger. Tours are at 10:00 a.m. and 2:00 p.m., from Memorial Day to Labor Day. Off-season tours can be arranged by writing to Lake Meredith National Recreation Area, Box 1460, Fritch 79036, or by calling (806) 857-3151.

Amistad National Recreation Area is located on the U.S. side of **Amistad Reservoir**, an international reservoir on the Texas-Mexico border. The recreation area totals 57,292 acres, including 540 miles of shoreline and 43,250 acres of water at normal lake level. Boating, water skiing, fishing, camping and archaeological sites are major attractions. At Panther and Parida caves, accessible only by boat, visitors can see prehistoric pictographs that have been radiocarbon dated to 4,000 years ago. With more than 300 rock art sites in the vicinity, the area is one of the densest concentrations of Archacic rock art in North America. Hunting is allowed in designated areas by permit only. Commercial campgrounds, motels and restaurants are nearby. Full-service marinas are located at Diablo East and Rough Canyon. Open year round.

Big Bend National Park, established in 1944, has spectacular **mountain and desert scenery,** a variety of **unusual geological structures.** Located in the great bend of the Rio Grande, the **international boundary** between United States and Mexico. Park contains 801,163 acres. Numerous campsites are located in park, and the **Chisos Mountain Lodge** has accommodations for approximately 345 guests. Write for reservations to National Park Concessions, Inc., Big Bend National Park, Texas 79834. Park open year round.

Big Thicket National Preserve, established in 1974, consists of 86,000 acres of diverse flora and fauna, often nicknamed the **"biological crossroads of North America."** The preserve has been designated an **"International Biosphere Reserve"** by the United Nations Educational, Scientific and Cultural Organization (UNESCO). The visitor information station, which is handicapped accessible, is located on FM 420, approximately seven miles north of Kountze; phone (409) 261-2337. It is open daily from 9:00 a.m. to 5:00 p.m. Naturalist activities are available by reservation only. Reservations can be made through the station. The eight **hiking trails,** ranging in length from one-half mile to 18 miles, visit a variety of forest communities that demonstrate the diversity of the Big Thicket. Parking and detailed maps are available at the trailheads. The two shortest trails are handicapped accessible. The trails are open year round, but keep in mind that some flooding may occur after heavy rains. Bring drinking water, wear comfortable shoes, and don't forget insect repellent during warm weather. Horses are permitted on the **Big Sandy Horse Trail** only. Pets, off-road vehicles and firearms are not permitted on any trails. Back-country camping and hunting are allowed in certain areas by permit only. Fishing is allowed in accordance with state law. Boating and canoeing are popular on Preserve corridor units. Park headquarters are temporarily located at 3785 Milam, Beaumont 77701; (409) 839-2689.

Chamizal National Memorial, established in 1963 and opened to the public in 1973, consists of 54.9 acres dedicated to the peaceful settlement of a 99-year-old boundary dispute between the United States and Mexico. Located in the south-central part of El Paso, the park is open summer from 10:00 a.m. to 7:00 p.m., winter from 8:00 a.m. to 5:00 p.m., and during performances. It hosts a variety of programs throughout the year, some of which include: the **Border Folk Festival** (first weekend in September); the **Siglo de Oro** ("Spanish Golden Age Presentation") (February-March); the **Zarzuela Festival** (July-August); and the **Sixteenth of September "Grito" Celebration.** Through the promotion of intercultural communication, understanding and harmony, the park's programs commemorate the signing of the **Chamizal Treaty.**

Fort Davis National Historic Site in Jeff Davis County was a key post in the West Texas defense system, guarding immigrants and tradesmen on the San Antonio-El Paso Road. Fort Davis was manned by black troops for many of the years it was active. These troops, called **"Buffalo Soldiers"** because of their curly hair, fought with great distinction in the Indian Wars. **Henry O. Flipper, the first black graduate of West Point,** served at Fort Davis in the early 1880s. The 460-acre historic site is located in the **Davis Mountains,** the second-highest mountain range in the state. The site includes a museum, an auditorium with daily audio-visual programs, restored and refurnished buildings, picnic area and hiking trails. The Friends of Fort Davis NHS Festival is held the Saturday of Labor Day weekend. The site was authorized in 1961 and established in 1963. Lodging is available in the nearby community of Fort Davis. Open year round except Christmas Day.

Guadalupe Mountains National Park, established Sept. 15, 1972, consists of 86,416 acres in Hudspeth and Culberson counties. A mountain mass of Permian limestone, rising abruptly from the surrounding desert, contains one of the most extensive **fossil reefs** on record. Deep **canyons** cut through this exposed fossil reef and provide a rare opportunity for geological study. Special points of interest are **McKittrick Canyon,** a fragile riparian environment, and **Guadalupe Peak,** the highest in Texas. Campground near Pine Springs. Headquarters area has 20 tent sites plus RV parking and is hub for 80 miles of trails. Dog Canyon area located one mile south of Texas-New Mexico state line, at end of NM State Road 137 and County Road 414, contains 18 tent spaces. A comfort station and parking spaces for five self-contained recreational vehicles are also available. Visit the Visitor Center at the headquarters for orientation, free information and natural history exhibits. Also, visit the museum at historic Frijole Ranch. Open year round. Lodging at Van Horn, Texas; White's City or Carlsbad, NM.

Lake Meredith National Recreation Area, about 35 miles northeast of Amarillo, consists of a reservoir behind **Sanford Dam** on the Canadian River, in Moore, Hutchinson and Potter counties. Occupies 44,977 acres; popular for water-based activities. Marine launching ramps, picnic areas, unimproved campsites. Commercial lodging and trailer hookups

Recreational Visits to National Parks in Texas

This information on daily recreational visits to National Parks in Texas was furnished by the **National Park Service**. Because of rounding, totals may not add up.

Name of Facility	1989	1990	1991	1992	1993	1994
Alibates Flint Quarries National Monument	3,831	3,418	3,819	3,419	3,170	3,410
Amistad National Recreation Area	1,321,170	1,527,340	1,217,596	1,560,787	1,529,020	1,592,770
Big Bend National Park	281,750	257,390	298,834	296,899	326,650	333,380
Big Thicket National Preserve	102,180	77,950	64,100	59,701	82,940	139,020
Chamizal National Memorial	200,680	199,000	†	†	257,580	250,670
Fort Davis National Historic Site	555,030	56,550	66,711	78,037	73,430	69,450
Guadalupe Mountains National Park	192,200	192,890	200,398	175,125	201,060	203,520
Lake Meredith National Recreation Area	1,274,910	1,358,790	1,280,021	1,296,962	1,480,990	1,535,460
Lyndon B. Johnson National Historical Park	200,540	193,080	194,220	190,414	184,860	181,570
Padre Island National Seashore	586,260	593,270	973,825	849,873	766,400	915,630
Rio Grande Wild and Scenic River	677	525	628	962	490	690
San Antonio Missions National Historical Park	269,430	313,450	290,519	950,496*	1,230,560	1,504,530
Total Recreational Visits	4,488,658	4,773,653	4,590,671†	5,462,675*†	6,136,850	6,730,100

** In 1992, an electronic method of counting visitors was used at San Antonio Missions National Historical Park for the first time, resulting in an apparent large increase in visitors.*

† We were not able to obtain 1991 and 1992 visitation data for Chamizal National Memorial.

available in nearby towns. Open year round. Headquarters is located at 419 E. Broadway, Fritch 79036; phone (806) 857-3151.

Lyndon B. Johnson National Historical Park includes two separate districts 14 miles apart. The **Johnson City District** comprises the **boyhood home of the 36th President of United States,** and the **Johnson Settlement** where his grandparents resided during the late 1800s. The **LBJ Ranch District** can be visited only by taking the National Park Service bus tour (for a nominal fee) starting at the LBJ State Historical Park, which includes the **LBJ Birthplace,** old school, family cemetery and the Texas White House. Site in Blanco and Gillespie counties was established Dec. 2, 1969, and contains 541 acres. Open year round except Christmas Day. No camping on site; commercial campground, motels in area. Phone (210) 868-7128.

Padre Island National Seashore consists of a 67.5-mile stretch of a barrier island along the Gulf Coast; noted for it wide sand beaches, excellent fishing and abundant bird and marine life. Contains 130,355 acres in Kleberg, Willacy and Kenedy counties. Open year round. One paved campground (fee charged) located north of Malaquite Beach, unpaved (primitive) campground area south on beach. Five miles of the beach are accessible by regular vehicles (including motor homes) and are open to camping. Fifty-five miles of beach are accessible only by 4x4 vehicles. All 55 miles of beach are also open to camping. Commercial lodging available outside boundaries of National Seashore.

Palo Alto Battlefield National Historic Site, Brownsville, preserves the site of the **first major battle in the Mexican-American War.** Fought on May 8, 1836, it is recognized for the innovative use of light or "flying" artillery. Participating in the battle were three future presidents: **General Zachary Taylor and Ulysses S. Grant** on the U.S. side, and **Gen. Mariano Arista** on the Mexican. Historical markers are located at the junction of state highways 1847 and 511. There are no public facilities and no site access at press time. For additional information, write P.O. Drawer 1832, Brownsville 78520, or call (210) 548-2788

Rio Grande Wild and Scenic River is a 191.2-mile strip on the American shore of the Rio Grande in the **Chihuahuan Desert** that protects the river. It begins in Big Bend National Park and continues downstream to the Terrell-Val Verde County line. There are federal facilities in Big Bend National Park only.

San Antonio Missions National Historical Park consists of four Spanish Colonial Missions — **Concepción, San José, San Juan and Espada** — and two of the best-preserved remains of the **Spanish Colonial irrigation system** in the United States represented in the Espada dam and aqueduct. Also in the park is a Spanish Colonial Demonstration farm watered by a revitalized acequia system at Mission San Juan. Acquisition is pending for the site of Las Cabras, the colonial ranch of Mission Espada. All were crucial elements to Spanish settlement on the Texas frontier. When Franciscan attempts to establish a chain of missions in East Texas in the late 1600s failed, the Spanish Crown ordered the missions transferred to the lush valley of the San Antonio River in 1731, where they flourished until secularization was complete in 1824. One of the principal institutions of settlement on Spain's northern frontier, the missions of San Antonio, today part of the National Park System, are physical reminders of a glorious chapter in Spanish Colonial history. The approximately 850-acre park is located in the city of San Antonio. The four missions, which are still in use today as active parishes, are open to the public from 8:00 a.m. to 5:00 p.m., CST and 9:00 a.m. to 6:00 p.m. DST. For more information, write to the park at 2202 Roosevelt Avenue, San Antonio 78210-4919; (210) 229-5701.

Recreation in the National Forests

An estimated 3 million people visited the National Forests in Texas for recreation in 1994. Many of these visitors used established recreation areas primarily for picnicking, swimming, fishing, camping, boating and nature enjoyment. These areas are:

Ratcliff Lake, 25 miles west of Lufkin on Highway 7, includes a 45-acre lake and facilities for picnicking, swimming, boating, fishing, camping. There is also a 250-seat campfire theater. Electrical hookups are available. **Double Lake**, 3 miles south of Coldspring on FM Road 2025, has a 30-acre lake and facilities for picnicking, camping, swimming and fishing. **Stubblefield Lake,** 15 miles west-northwest of New Waverly on the shores of Lake Conroe, has facilities for camping, picnicking and fishing. **Scotts Ridge Boat Ramp**, 8 miles west of Willis, provides a boat ramp and parking lot on Lake Conroe. **Boykin Springs**, 15 miles southeast of Zavalla, has a 6-acre lake and facilities for swimming, picnicking, fishing and camping. **Red Hills Lake,** 4 miles north of Milam on Highway 87, has a 17-acre lake and facilities for fishing, swimming,

Many miles of Gulf of Mexico beaches are included in state and national parks in Texas. Photo courtesy Texas Parks & Wildlife Dept.

camping and picnicking. Electrical hookups are available. **Bouton Lake**, 7 miles southeast of Zavalla off Texas Highway 63, has a 9-acre natural lake with facilities for camping, picnicking and fishing.

Several areas have been built on the shores of **Sam Rayburn Reservoir,** which has 100 miles of national-forest shoreline. These areas provide camping, picnicking, nature enjoyment, boating and fishing. Recreation areas are: **Sandy Creek** on Forest Service Road 333, 25 miles northwest of Jasper; **Harvey Creek,** 10 miles south of Broaddus on FM 2390; and **Townsend,** 7 miles north off FM 1277. **Caney Creek**, 10 miles southeast of Zavalla off FM 2743, has a 500-seat campfire theater in addition to the usual facilities.

The recreational areas at **Toledo Bend Reservoir** are as follows: **Willow Oak Recreation Area**, 14 miles south of Hemphill off State Highway 87, has facilities for picnicking and camping and a boat ramp; **Indian Mounds Recreation Area,** accessible via FM 83 and FM 3382, a total of 15 miles east of Hemphill, has camping facilities and a boat-launch ramp; **Ragtown**, 25 miles southeast of Center and accessible by State Highways 87 and 139, County Highway 3184 and Forest Service Road 132, has facilities for camping and boat launching; **Lakeview**, a primitive campground 12 miles southeast of Hemphill, can be reached via State Highway 87, County Road 2928 and Forest Service Road 120.

Hiking Trails in National Forests

The Lone Star Hiking Trail, approximately 140 miles long, is located on **Sam Houston National Forest** in Montgomery, Walker and San Jacinto counties. Twenty-six miles of the trail in San Jacinto County has been designated as a **national recreation trail.**

The **4Cs National Recreation Trail** is 19 miles long and goes from Ratcliff Recreation Area to the Neches Bluff overlook on **Davy Crockett National Forest**.

The **Saw Mill Trail** is 5 miles long and goes from the old **Aldrich Sawmill** site to Boykin Springs Recreation Area in the **Angelina National Forest**. **Trail Between the Lakes** is 26 miles long from Lakeview Recreation Area on Lake Toledo Bend to Highway 96 near Sam Rayburn Reservoir on the **Sabine National Forest.**

Equestrian Trail

The **Piney Creek Horse Trail,** 50 miles long, is located on the **Davy Crockett National Forest** approximately three miles south of Kennard off F.S. Road 525. There is a 30-unit horse camp at this location, but it does not have drinking water available.

Recreation on the National Grasslands

Lake Davy Crockett Recreation Area, 11 miles north of Honey Grove on FM 100, has a boat-launch ramp and camping sites on a 450-acre lake. **Coffee Mill Lake Recreation Area** has camping and picnic facilities on a 750-acre lake. This area is 4 miles west of Lake Davy Crockett Recreation Area. **Black Creek Lake Picnic Area** is located 8 miles southeast of Alvord. It has camping and picnic facilities and a boat-launch ramp on a 30-acre lake.

Lake McClellan in Gray County and **Lake Marvin**, which is part of the **Black Kettle National Grassland** in Hemphill County, receive over 28,000 recreation visitors annually. These areas provide camping, picnicking, fishing and boating facilities. Concessionaires operate facilities at Lake McClellan, and a nominal fee is charged for use of the areas. At the **Rita Blanca National Grassland**, about 4,500 visitors a year enjoy picnicking and hunting. ☆

Recreational Facilities, Corps of Engineers Lakes 1994

Source: Southwestern Division, Corps of Engineers, Dallas

Reservoir	Swim Areas	Launch Ramps	Picnic Sites	Camp Sites	Rental Units	Visitor Hours, 1994
Addicks*	0	0	721	0	0	5,608,900
Aquilla	0	2	0	0	0	262,200
Bardwell	2	7	49	174	0	1,679,300
Barker*	0	0	25	0	0	2,018,800
Belton	4	21	184	162	0	7,459,700
Benbrook	1	17	133	179	0	3,527,800
Canyon	4	20	124	546	0	7,380,900
Cooper	0	2	0	0	0	377,200
Georgetown	1	3	118	234	0	4,418,500
Granger	2	5	117	146	0	1,504,400
Grapevine	4	17	140	178	0	3,594,300
Hords Creek	1	8	5	150	0	1,762,200
Joe Pool	3	7	315	556	0	9,459,700
Lake O' the Pines	8	34	201	525	0	10,285,700
Lavon	3	22	344	200	0	6,848,600
Lewsville	8	28	331	576	0	10,424,500
Navarro Mills	3	6	16	267	0	3,319,500
O.C. Fisher	0	17	90	61	0	1,856,800
Pat Mayse**	6	11	14	327	0	1,524,000
Proctor	0	6	59	212	0	2,349,800
Ray Roberts	1	6	213	184	0	1,946,500
Sam Rayburn	5	31	31	794	90	16,766,200
Somerville	2	12	272	784	0	15,393,700
Stillhouse Hollow	3	5	98	96	0	2,827,300
Texoma**†	2	26	95	873	123	78,013,400
Town Bluff	2	12	126	355	0	4,842,000
Waco	1	9	95	273	0	4,239,000
Whitney	5	30	46	685	0	7,950,600
Wright Patman	4	22	199	736	4	13,634,500
Totals	79	420	4,563	10,638	455	231,276,000

All above lakes managed by the Fort Worth District, U.S. Army Corps of Engineers, with the following exceptions:
**Managed by Galveston District, USACE.*
***Managed by Tulsa District, USACE.*
†Figures for facilites on Texas side of lake. Visitation is for entire lake.

Fairs, Festivals and Special Events

Fairs, festivals and other special events provide year-round recreation in Texas. Some are of national interest, while many attract visitors from across the state. Most of them are primarily of local and regional interest. In addition to those listed here, the recreational paragraphs in the Counties chapter list numerous events. Information furnished by the event sponsors.

Abilene - West Texas Fair & Rodeo; Sept.; 1700 Hwy. 36 (79602)

Albany - Fort Griffin Fandangle; June; Box 155 (76430)

Alvarado - Pioneers and Old Settlers Reunion; Aug.; Box 577 (76009)

Amarillo - Tri-State Fair; Sept.; Box 31087 (79120)

Arlington - Texas Scottish Festival and Highland Games; June; Box 151943 (76015)

Athens - Black-Eyed Pea Jamboree; July; Box 2600 (75751)

Athens - Old Fiddlers' Reunion; May; Box 1441 (75751)

Austin - Austin Aqua Festival; July-Aug.; 811 Barton Springs Rd., #111 (78704)

Austin - Austin Museum of Art at Laguna Gloria Fiesta; May; c/o Women's Art Guild, P.O. Box 5568 (78763)

Austin - Austin-Travis County Livestock Show; March; Box 9876 (78766)

Bay City - Bay City Rice Festival; Oct.; Box 867 (77404)

Bay City - Matagorda County Fair, Livestock Show & Rodeo; March; Box 1803 (77404-1803)

Beaumont - Neches River Festival; April; 2554 Harrison (77702)

Beaumont - South Texas State Fair; Oct.; Box 3207 (77704)

Bellville - Austin County Fair; Oct.; Box 141 (77418)

Belton - Belton Rodeo and Celebration; July; Box 659 (76513)

Big Spring - Howard County Fair; Sept.; Box 2356 (79720)

Boerne - Kendall County Fair; Sept.; Box 954 (78006)

Brackettville - Western Horse Races and Barbecue; Sept.; Box 528 (78832)

Brenham - Washington County Fair; Sept.; P.O. Box 1257 (77834)

Brownsville - Charro Days Fiesta; Feb.; P.O. Box 3247 (78523)

Buchanan Dam - Highland Lakes Bluebonnet Trail; April; Box Rt. 1, P.O. Box 118 (78609)

Burton - Burton Cotton Gin Festival; April; Box 98 (77835)

Clifton - Norse Smorgasbord; Nov.; Box 104 (76634)

Clute - Great Texas Mosquito Festival; July; Box 997 (77531)

Columbus - Columbus Springtime Festival & Magnolia Homes Tour; May; Box 343 (78934)

Conroe - Montgomery County Fair; March; Box 869 (77305)

Corpus Christi - Bayfest; Sept.-Oct.; Box 1858 (78403-1858)

Corpus Christi - Buccaneer Days; April-May; Box 2664 (78403)

Corpus Christi - Texas Jazz Festival; July; P.O. Box 2664 (78403)

Corsicana - Derrick Days; April; c/o Cindy Llinas, 920 N. Main (75110)

Dalhart - XIT Rodeo & Reunion; Aug.; Box 966 (79022)

Dallas - State Fair of Texas; Sept.-Oct.; Box 150009 (75315)

Decatur - Wise County Old Settlers Reunion; July; Box 203 (76234)

DeLeon - DeLeon Peach & Melon Festival; Aug.; Box 44 (76444)

Denton - North Texas State Fair and Rodeo; Aug.; Box 1695 (76202-1695)

Edna - Jackson County Fair; Sept.-Oct.; Box 457 (77957)

El Paso - Southwestern Intl. Livestock Show & Rodeo; Feb.; Box 10239 (79993)

Ennis - National Polka Festival; May; Box 1237 (75120)

Fairfield - Freestone County Fair; June; Box 196 (75840)

Flatonia - Czhilispiel; Oct.; Box 651 (78941)

Fort Worth - Southwestern Exposition & Livestock Show; Jan.-Feb.; Box 150 (76101)

Fredericksburg - Easter Fires Pageant; Easter; Box 526 (78624)

Fredericksburg - Night in Old Fredericksburg; July; 106 N. Adams (78624)

Fredericksburg - Oktoberfest; Oct.; Box 222 (78624)

Freer - Freer Rattlesnake Roundup; April; Box 717 (78357)

Galveston - Dickens on The Strand; Dec.; 2016 Strand (77550)

Gilmer - East Texas Yamboree; Oct.; Box 854 (75644)

Graham - Wild West Possum Fest; Sept.; Box 299 (76450)

Greenville - Hunt County Fair; Sept.; P.O. Box 1071 (75403)

Groesbeck - Independence Day Celebration; July; Box 326 (76642)

Helotes - Helotes Cornyval; April-May; Box 376 (78023)

Hempstead - Waller County Fair; Oct.; Box 911 (77445)

Hico - Hico Old Settlers Reunion; July; Rt. 3, Box 307 (76457)

Hondo - Medina County Fair; Sept.; Box 4 (78861)

Houston - Harris County Fair; Oct.; One Abercrombie Dr. (77084)

Houston - Houston Livestock Show & Rodeo; Feb.-March; Box 20070 (77225)

Houston - The Houston International Festival; April; 1100 Louisiana, #1275 (77002)

Hughes Springs - Wildflower Trails of Texas; April; Box 805 (75656)

Huntsville - Walker County Fair; March-April; Box 1817 (77342-1817)

Jefferson - Historical Pilgrimage; May; Box 301 (75657)

Johnson City - Blanco County Fair; Aug.; Box 261 (78636)

Kenedy - Bluebonnet Days; April; Box 724 (78119)

Kerrville - Kerr County Fair; Oct.; P.O. Box 842 (78029)

Kerrville - Kerrville Folk Festival; May-June; P.O. Box 1466 (78029-1466)

Kerrville - Texas State Arts & Crafts Fair; May-June; Box 1527 (78029-1527)

La Grange - Fayette County Country Fair; Aug.-Sept.; Box 544 (78945)

Lamesa - Dawson County Fair; Sept.; Box 1268 (79331)

Longview - Gregg County Fair & Expo.; Sept.; Box 1124 (75606)

Lubbock - Panhandle-South Plains Fair; Sept.; Box 208 (79407)

Lufkin - Texas Forest Festival; Sept.; Box 1606 (75901)
Luling - Luling Watermelon Thump; June; Box 710 (78648)
Mercedes - Rio Grande Valley Livestock Show; March; Box 867 (78570)
Mesquite - Mesquite Championship Rodeo; April-Sept.; 1818 Rodeo Dr. (75149)
Mount Pleasant - Titus County Fair; Sept.; Box 1232 (75455)
Nacogdoches - Piney Woods Fair; Oct.; 3615 N.W. Stallings Drv. (75961)
Nederland - Nederland Heritage Festival; March; Box 1176 (77627)
New Braunfels - Comal County Fair; Sept.; Box 310223 (78131-0223)
New Braunfels - Wurstfest; Nov.; Box 310309 (78131-0309)
Odessa - Permian Basin Fair & Exposition; Sept.; Box 4812 (79760)
Palestine - Anderson County Fair; Oct.; P.O. Box 59 (75802)
Palestine - Dogwood Trails Festival; March-April; 1101 East Palestine Ave. (75801)
Paris - Red River Valley Fair; Aug.-Sept.; Box 964 (75461-0964)
Plantersville - Texas Renaissance Festival; Oct.-Nov.; Rt. 2, Box 65 (77363)
Port Lavaca - Calhoun County Fair; Oct.; Box 42 (77979)
Poteet - Poteet Strawberry Festival; April; Box 227 (78065)
Refugio - Refugio County Fair & Rodeo; March; Box 88 (78377)
Rio Grande City - Starr County Fair; March; Box 841 (78582)
Rosenberg - Fort Bend County Fair; Sept.-Oct.; Box 428 (77471)
Salado - Gathering of the Scottish Clans of Texas; Nov.; Central Texas Area Museum, 1 Main St. (76571)
San Angelo - San Angelo Stock Show & Rodeo; March; 200 W. 43rd (76903)
San Antonio - Fiesta San Antonio; April; 122 Herman (78205)
San Antonio - Texas Folklife Festival; Aug.; 801 S. Bowie (78205)
Santa Fe - Galveston County Fair & Rodeo; April; Box 889 (77510)
Seguin - Guadalupe County Fair; Oct.; Box 334 (78155)
Shamrock - St. Patrick's Day Celebration; March; Box 588 (79079)
Stamford - Texas Cowboy Reunion; July; Box 928 (79553)
Sulphur Springs - Hopkins County Fall Festival; Sept.; Box 177 (75483)
Sweetwater - Rattlesnake Roundup; March; Box 416 (79556)
Texarkana - Four States Fair; Sept.; Box 1915 (75502)
Tyler - East Texas State Fair; Sept.; 2112 W. Front (75702)
Tyler - Texas Rose Festival; Oct.; Box 8224 (75711)
Victoria - Victoria Livestock Show; March; Box 2255 (77904)
Waco - Brazos River Festival & Cotton Palace Pageant; April; P.O. Box 8747 (76714-8747)
Waco - Heart O'Texas Fair & Rodeo; Oct.; Box 7581 (76714)
Waxahachie - Gingerbread Trail Tour of Homes; June; Box 706 (75165)
Waxahachie - Scarborough Faire; April-June; Box 538 (75165)
Weatherford - Parker County Peach Festival; July; Box 310 (76086)
Wharton - Wharton County Youth Fair & Exposition; April; Box 266 (77488)
Winnsboro - Autumn Trails Festival; Oct.; 201 W. Broadway (75494)
Woodville - Tyler County Dogwood Festival; March; Box 2151 (75979) ☆

Texas Tourism Facts, 1993

Travel is big business in Texas, according to the Texas Department of Commerce. A study conducted for the agency by D.K. Shifflet & Associates Ltd. during 1993 reported on traveler origins, traveler expenditures, transportation profiles, destination satisfaction ratings and traveler demographics. Below are some of the data from that report.

Length of time spent in Texas was measured in "person-days," one person-day being one person staying in the state for one day. The number of person-days spent by travelers in Texas during 1993 was estimated at 318 million. That included 198 million person-days spent by Texans traveling within the state and 120 milllion person-days spent by non-Texans. This was an increase over 1992 of 7 percent.

Texas received a 6 percent market share of total U.S. person-days, which was estimated at 5.3 billion. This placed Texas third behind California (10.2 percent) and Florida (8.3percent).

Business travel accounted for 33 percent of travel to Texas, while leisure travel accounted for 67 percent..

Only 53 percent of Texas travelers indicated a high level of satisfaction with their destination cities. Florida cities rated high with 62 percent of visitors, while 61 percent of Arizona visitors were highly satisfied with their destination cities.

Texas regions preferred as destinations by non-Texan travelers were North Central (35.3 percent), Gulf Coast (23.8 percent), and South (13.5 percent). These three accounted for 73 percent of non-Texan person-days.

The states generating the largest numbers of non-Texan travelers were Oklahoma (13%), Louisiana (10%), California (9%), Illinois (5%), Michigan (5%), New Mexico (4%), Florida (4%), Missouri (3%) and Arkansas (3%). ☆

Major Crime in Texas Continues to Drop in 1994

After peaking in 1988, the crime rate in Texas declined in the six subsequent years. From 8,019.6 major crimes per 100,000 population in 1988, the rate has steadily decreased to 5,873.1 in 1994.

The crime rate is tabulated on seven major offenses as designated by the Federal Bureau of Investigation as Index Crimes. These seven categories include four violent offenses (murder, rape, robbery and aggravated assault) and three nonviolent crimes (burglary, larceny and auto theft.) In Texas, these figures are collected by the Texas Department of Public Safety and are provided to the FBI.

Although all Texas counties suffered from some major crimes, most of the incidents are confined to the urban areas. In the list of the 10 counties with the highest crime rates (see next page), four are considered urban counties with populations more than 500,000, and six are metro counties with populations between 75,000 and 500,000.

Nonviolent crime rates have been coming down in recent years, while violent crime has increased. In 1992, however, only rape and aggravated assault increased in total incidents while murder, robbery, aggravated assault, burglarly, larceny and auto theft registered declines.

If the current trend continues, another of the state's major problems could be relieved to some extent: the overcrowding of the state prison system and many local jails as well. ☆

Texas Crime History 1975-1994

Year	Murder	Rape	Robbery	Aggravated Assault	Burglary	Larceny	Car Theft	Rate Per 100,000 Population
1975	1,639	3,430	20,076	22,658	203,821	362,665	47,386	5,407.2
1976	1,519	3,666	17,352	21,885	193,208	400,767	43,871	5,464.4
1977	1,705	4,338	19,552	26,714	205,672	383,451	51,018	5,397.1
1978	1,853	4,927	21,395	28,475	209,770	398,923	57,821	5,556.8
1979	2,226	6,028	25,636	33,909	239,263	411,555	72,687	5,911.7
1980	2,389	6,694	29,532	39,251	262,332	450,209	79,032	6,135.7
1981	2,438	6,816	28,516	40,673	275,652	454,210	83,244	6,042.4
1982	2,463	6,814	33,603	45,221	285,757	501,312	87,090	6,297.5
1983	2,238	6,334	29,769	42,195	262,214	503,555	82,522	5,907.1
1984	2,091	7,340	28,537	42,764	266,032	529,469	87,781	6,029.2
1985	2,124	8,367	31,693	47,868	289,913	596,130	99,561	6,570.9
1986	2,255	8,605	40,018	59,002	341,560	664,832	119,095	7,408.2
1987	1,960	8,068	38,049	57,903	355,732	711,739	123,378	7,724.3
1988	2,021	8,122	39,307	60,084	362,099	739,784	134,271	8,019.6
1989	2,029	7,953	37,910	63,978	342,360	741,642	150,974	7,926.8
1990	2,388	8,746	44,316	73,860	314,346	730,926	154,387	7,823.7
1991	2,651	9,265	49,698	84,104	312,719	734,177	163,837	7,818.6
1992	2,240	9,368	44,582	86,067	268,864	689,515	145,039	7,055.1
1993	2,149	9,923	40,464	84,892	233,944	664,738	124,822	1,160,932
1994	2,023	9,101	37,639	81,079	214,698	624,048	110,772	1,079,360

Source: Texas Department of Public Safety, Austin, and the Federal Bureau of Investigation, Washington. Population figures used to determine crime rate per 100,000 population based on U.S. Bureau of Census. The population figure used in determining the crime rate for 1994 in Texas was 18,378,000.

Family Violence Still on the Increase in Texas in 1994

Family violence is defined in the Texas Family Code as an act by a member of a family or household against another member that is intended to result in physical harm, bodily injury, assault or a threat that reasonably places the member in fear of imminent physical harm. In 1994, 166,657 offenders were involved in incidents of family violence against 169,911 victims. Of the offenders whose sex was known, 83 percent were male and 17 percent were female. Of the victims whose sex was known, 79 percent were female and 21 percent were male.

In 63.5 percent of the incidents, the relationship of victim to offender was marital: 32.43 percent of those victims were wives, and 19.1 percent were common-law wives.

Of the remaining offenses, 13.8 percent involved parents against children or children against parents. Other family/household relationships, such as grandparents or grandchildren, siblings, step-siblings, roommates or in-laws were involved in 22.7 percent.

Compared to 1993, the number of reported incidents increased from 155,767 to 163,223, an increase of 4.8 percent. The number of victims increased from 164,975 to 169,911, an increase of 3 percent. But the number of reported offenders decreased from 174,599 to 166,657, a decrease of 4.5 percent. That seems to indicate that fewer offenders are committing more assaults.

Investigation of reports of domestic violence can be hazardous to police officers. During 1994, 755 Texas law officers were assaulted while investigating such reports. ☆

Top 10 County Crime Rates Per 100,000 Population in 1994

1. Potter 13,523
2. Nueces 9,133
3. Lamar 8,264
4. Dallas 8,221
5. Jefferson 8,030
6. Bexar 7,896
7. Gregg 7,793
8. Smith 7,623
9. Wichita 7,529
10. Travis 7,333

Crime Profile of Texas Counties, 1994

County	Agencies	Murder	Rape	Robbery	Assault	Burglary	Larceny	Auto Theft	Total Crimes	*Crime Rate Per 100,000
Anderson	3	3	28	41	220	429	1,149	87	1,957	3,990
Andrews	2	0	3	1	50	87	357	9	507	3,508
Angelina	4	9	31	60	230	635	1,850	141	2,956	3,999
Aransas	2	1	12	4	89	388	571	37	1,102	5,302
Archer	2	1	0	0	15	52	43	4	115	1,448
Armstrong	1	0	0	0	0	26	14	0	45	2,168
Atascosa	5	2	25	6	92	224	363	33	745	2,266
Austin	4	1	1	5	70	94	254	13	438	2,011
Bailey	2	0	3	0	9	37	158	11	218	3,232
Bandera	1	3	2	0	9	104	166	14	298	2,380
Bastrop	4	2	28	14	163	445	750	87	1,489	3,496
Baylor	2	1	2	0	36	28	61	5	133	3,121
Bee	2	0	4	6	99	303	653	44	1,109	4,651
Bell	10	28	177	245	1,014	2,088	6,744	621	10,917	5,066
Bexar	27	214	676	2,956	3,532	18,959	63,880	10,857	101,074	7,896
Blanco	3	1	8	0	6	55	53	1	124	1,756
Borden	1	0	0	0	0	0	2	0	3	391
Bosque	3	2	2	0	22	112	174	16	328	2,029
Bowie	6	4	32	133	343	876	2,648	235	4,271	5,110
Brazoria	17	13	80	78	487	1,356	4,194	453	6,661	3,149
Brazos	4	12	68	122	542	1,306	5,640	378	8,068	6,188
Brewster	3	0	0	0	26	59	109	9	203	2,317
Briscoe	1	0	0	0	1	20	6	1	28	1,548
Brooks	2	0	2	0	2	116	67	4	191	2,311
Brown	4	1	12	17	149	339	1,133	44	1,695	4,806
Burleson	3	2	7	6	109	150	259	17	550	3,747
Burnet	6	1	15	3	62	184	551	42	858	3,381
Caldwell	4	0	10	18	130	326	624	23	1,131	4,030
Calhoun	3	0	7	12	127	258	598	42	1,044	5,117
Callahan	1	0	2	0	5	18	19	4	48	391
Cameron	12	23	54	369	1,243	4,485	11,885	1,396	19,455	6,494
Camp	2	1	3	6	40	128	225	24	427	4,083
Carson	2	0	4	3	18	34	58	10	127	1,933
Cass	2	2	20	15	55	216	361	29	698	2,297
Castro	2	0	2	1	20	52	130	7	212	2,467
Chambers	2	2	10	8	23	122	377	44	586	2,748
Cherokee	5	4	8	18	273	476	820	85	1,684	4,126
Childress	2	0	6	3	24	41	136	5	215	3,373
Clay	1	1	1	1	4	79	143	8	237	2,376
Cochran	1	0	0	1	12	46	84	6	149	3,565
Coke	1	0	0	0	3	31	37	2	73	2,088
Coleman	3	0	1	1	50	100	109	4	265	2,743
Collin	11	4	57	149	882	2,158	7,235	650	11,135	3,414
Collingsworth	1	0	0	0	11	18	22	0	51	1,501
Colorado	4	1	3	5	128	156	353	23	669	3,599
Comal	2	1	32	26	371	699	1,709	124	2,962	4,869
Comanche	3	0	4	2	16	92	149	18	281	2,089
Concho	2	1	0	1	2	18	7	0	29	949
Cooke	2	2	6	9	66	219	623	54	979	3,131
Coryell	3	2	15	12	129	444	1,157	42	1,801	2,512
Cottle	1	0	0	1	3	12	4	4	24	1,162
Crane	2	1	3	0	19	41	107	5	176	3,809
Crockett	1	1	4	0	17	26	75	5	128	3,027
Crosby	1	0	0	2	5	23	19	4	53	728
Culberson	1	0	1	0	9	4	18	0	32	981
Dallam	2	0	0	4	22	27	134	12	199	3,348
Dallas	33	359	1,287	8,280	11,503	28,187	86,721	23,338	159,675	8,221

County	Agencies	Murder	Rape	Robbery	Assault	Burglary	Larceny	Auto Theft	Total Crimes	*Crime Rate Per 100,000
Dawson	2	0	2	3	78	126	389	11	608	4,299
Deaf Smith	2	0	3	7	89	153	652	35	939	4,878
Delta	1	0	0	0	12	39	37	2	90	1,872
Denton	15	5	70	124	613	1,951	7,163	628	10,554	3,297
DeWitt	3	1	4	7	89	130	156	8	395	2,142
Dickens	2	0	1	1	21	25	35	1	84	3,447
Dimmit	1	2	1	2	96	81	238	11	431	4,026
Donley	1	0	0	0	8	9	19	1	37	999
Duval	2	0	3	0	29	104	116	8	260	2,027
Eastland	5	1	2	3	75	120	411	23	635	3,554
Ector	3	11	35	149	495	1,821	5,462	349	8,322	6,759
Edwards	1	0	0	1	20	26	14	7	68	2,318
Ellis	7	4	18	74	298	1,039	2,347	237	4,014	4,370
El Paso	6	54	289	1,162	4,391	4,861	28,611	4,106	43,474	6,539
Erath	4	1	4	6	42	264	748	30	1,095	3,702
Falls	3	1	10	17	127	235	259	44	693	3,882
Fannin	2	0	3	10	36	185	399	32	665	2,651
Fayette	2	2	0	4	37	96	134	2	275	1,317
Fisher	1	0	0	0	0	43	26	2	71	1,598
Floyd	3	0	0	0	9	48	57	5	119	1,447
Foard	1	0	1	0	2	1	2	1	7	428
Fort Bend	9	16	75	268	619	2,253	4,869	601	8,701	3,107
Franklin	1	0	4	3	24	61	100	11	203	2,346
Freestone	3	1	2	2	20	194	191	34	444	2,817
Frio	3	0	1	0	49	117	179	13	359	2,338
Gaines	3	1	7	1	31	56	313	15	424	2,930
Galveston	15	37	165	642	1,687	2,929	9,426	1,607	16,493	7,028
Garza	1	0	4	0	25	34	84	6	153	3,181
Gillespie	2	0	2	1	45	125	316	18	507	2,692
Glasscock	1	0	0	0	0	3	7	2	12	1,051
Goliad	1	0	0	0	0	18	46	0	64	1,053
Gonzales	2	1	5	2	41	129	138	7	323	1,863
Gray	2	0	14	17	73	256	686	34	1,080	4,612
Grayson	6	4	64	91	270	1,098	3,551	237	5,315	5,464
Gregg	5	27	91	235	628	1,890	5,040	645	8,556	7,793
Grimes	2	0	5	13	88	192	357	28	683	3,310
Guadalupe	3	10	21	31	267	627	1,483	143	2,582	3,658
Hale	4	1	5	15	144	309	903	41	1,418	3,975
Hall	2	0	0	0	12	13	16	2	43	1,147
Hamilton	2	0	0	2	16	52	78	3	151	1,990
Hansford	3	0	0	0	6	22	64	6	98	1,814
Hardeman	2	0	0	3	8	25	33	10	79	1,609
Hardin	5	0	14	6	70	306	666	62	1,124	2,463
Harris	38	462	1,736	11,702	16,094	38,417	86,398	32,024	186,833	6,135
Harrison	2	9	26	36	232	716	1,838	155	3,012	5,186
Hartley	1	0	0	0	0	6	11	2	19	508
Haskell	1	0	1	0	1	19	54	3	78	1,194
Hays	4	1	57	41	200	691	1,826	138	2,954	3,980
Hemphill	1	0	0	1	8	4	24	2	39	1,101
Henderson	8	5	24	16	248	739	1,280	97	2,409	3,878
Hidalgo	16	45	105	479	2,105	7,696	17,779	2,528	30,737	6,667
Hill	5	5	18	12	130	369	565	65	1,164	4,135
Hockley	4	0	3	5	30	125	507	26	696	2,845
Hood	2	0	1	5	36	208	629	25	904	2,866
Hopkins	2	2	9	7	231	226	661	63	1,199	4,083
Houston	2	0	7	7	51	125	296	21	507	2,340
Howard	2	1	6	25	96	322	941	47	1,438	4,476
Hudspeth	1	1	0	1	2	10	11	7	32	1,099
Hunt	7	2	41	97	434	1,041	2,382	191	4,188	6,350
Hutchinson	3	0	6	13	61	102	540	31	753	3,028
Irion	1	0	0	0	0	8	16	0	24	1,436
Jack	2	1	0	0	20	66	71	7	165	2,395
Jackson	2	1	4	2	33	92	213	7	352	2,592
Jasper	3	3	2	8	84	158	558	25	838	2,593
Jeff Davis	1	0	0	0	0	0	0	1	1	47
Jefferson	7	32	292	779	1,399	4,536	10,757	1,706	19,501	8,030

County	Agencies	Murder	Rape	Robbery	Assault	Burglary	Larceny	Auto Theft	Total Crimes	*Crime Rate Per 100,000
Jim Hogg	1	0	0	0	7	14	27	1	49	961
Jim Wells	4	6	18	9	147	587	1,108	65	1,940	4,925
Johnson	6	7	41	23	219	803	2,434	193	3,720	3,567
Jones	4	0	2	1	27	113	167	12	322	2,011
Karnes	1	1	0	1	19	59	47	1	128	1,035
Kaufman	5	9	26	49	200	677	1,253	161	2,375	4,076
Kendall	2	0	4	2	33	149	326	12	526	2,846
Kenedy	1	0	0	0	0	1	1	0	2	468
Kent	1	0	0	0	0	2	6	0	8	834
Kerr	3	0	13	11	194	280	973	45	1,516	3,833
Kimble	2	1	2	0	5	11	47	3	69	1,668
King	1	0	0	0	1	4	1	1	7	2,029
Kinney	1	0	0	0	2	17	5	1	25	771
Kleberg	3	1	14	16	148	457	1,069	65	1,770	5,747
Knox	3	0	2	0	23	12	49	3	89	1,922
Lamar	3	1	22	58	666	654	2,171	143	3,715	8,264
Lamb	4	1	2	1	26	92	184	17	323	2,180
Lampasas	2	0	2	1	23	84	338	11	459	3,006
La Salle	1	0	1	0	30	40	33	8	112	2,082
Lavaca	3	1	7	1	31	126	275	10	451	2,426
Lee	3	0	7	5	48	122	225	25	432	3,187
Leon	1	1	0	5	9	49	50	4	118	870
Liberty	4	2	28	20	179	584	1,059	116	1,988	3,426
Limestone	3	0	11	14	112	195	497	35	864	4,131
Lipscomb	1	0	1	0	3	11	21	0	36	1,220
LiveOak	1	2	1	0	22	60	38	10	133	1,308
Llano	2	1	8	2	12	86	149	9	267	2,137
Loving	1	0	0	0	0	1	0	0	1	730
Lubbock	10	26	155	330	1,036	2,834	9,326	922	14,629	6,346
Lynn	2	0	0	0	11	29	88	4	132	1,992
McCulloch	2	0	0	0	25	62	157	10	254	2,995
McLennan	17	31	158	496	1,420	2,543	7,999	1,284	13,931	7,065
McMullen	1	0	0	0	0	1	0	0	1	124
Madison	2	2	2	1	45	87	156	26	319	2,810
Marion	2	7	3	7	69	111	212	14	423	4,201
Martin	2	1	1	0	7	27	51	6	93	1,884
Mason	1	0	1	0	0	8	8	0	17	485
Matagorda	3	0	9	38	188	559	1,628	70	2,492	6,438
Maverick	2	7	7	24	291	827	1,517	94	2,767	6,256
Medina	3	3	8	8	132	334	509	54	1,048	3,442
Menard	1	0	0	0	7	5	10	1	23	986
Midland	3	8	77	93	364	1,275	3,750	237	5,804	5,084
Milam	3	1	7	6	45	166	313	21	559	2,381
Mills	1	0	0	0	2	5	3	0	10	213
Mitchell	2	0	0	5	14	71	153	6	249	3,222
Montague	4	1	5	2	31	133	260	22	454	2,559
Montgomery	6	19	97	138	616	1,962	4,568	633	8,033	3,616
Moore	2	1	6	3	46	99	366	19	540	2,859
Morris	4	2	2	4	59	104	210	22	403	3,049
Motley	1	0	0	0	0	2	6	1	9	653
Nacogdoches	3	3	18	70	277	517	1,626	83	2,594	4,617
Navarro	2	7	27	50	174	480	1,408	93	2,239	5,554
Newton	1	1	3	1	16	54	69	7	151	1,087
Nolan	3	1	9	17	69	152	396	22	666	4,051
Nueces	6	15	191	507	1,817	4,614	19,811	1,439	28,394	9,133
Ochiltree	2	0	3	0	17	46	167	7	240	2,762
Oldham	1	0	0	1	0	6	17	3	27	1,209
Orange	7	2	28	117	251	956	2,757	254	4,365	5,181
Palo Pinto	2	1	19	10	139	283	595	57	1,104	4,399
Panola	2	1	3	10	36	157	308	22	537	2,381
Parker	4	1	53	12	186	539	1,182	98	2,071	2,905
Parmer	2	0	3	1	38	48	110	9	209	2,040
Pecos	2	1	3	2	27	90	332	24	479	3,319
Polk	4	4	7	11	109	397	618	46	1,192	3,197
Potter	5	26	113	240	918	2,248	9,803	571	13,919	13,523
Presidio	2	1	1	2	9	23	16	2	54	727

County	Agencies	Murder	Rape	Robbery	Assault	Burglary	Larceny	Auto Theft	Total Crimes	*Crime Rate Per 100,000
Rains	1	1	1	2	57	60	76	16	213	2,883
Randall	3	0	3	4	53	140	480	36	716	761
Reagan	1	0	5	0	10	15	32	2	64	1,415
Real	1	0	0	0	3	16	10	5	34	1,392
Red River	2	2	2	4	76	158	243	26	511	3,658
Reeves	2	0	1	5	31	102	292	9	440	2,858
Refugio	2	0	0	1	17	49	141	9	217	2,777
Roberts	1	0	0	0	1	6	4	1	12	1,205
Robertson	2	2	1	15	84	200	307	28	637	4,128
Rockwall	4	0	7	6	68	179	508	50	818	2,605
Runnels	3	2	5	1	38	66	147	8	267	2,393
Rusk	4	6	22	30	230	456	1,160	187	2,091	4,728
Sabine	2	1	0	0	13	103	105	12	234	2,310
San Augustine	2	0	0	2	23	51	84	2	162	2,055
San Jacinto	1	1	6	3	24	141	256	23	454	2,436
San Patricio	7	3	12	14	171	672	1,309	62	2,243	3,462
San Saba	1	0	0	1	7	37	75	3	123	2,105
Schleicher	1	0	0	0	0	29	35	3	67	2,246
Scurry	2	0	12	2	38	115	387	13	567	3,115
Shackelford	1	0	0	1	1	13	15	1	31	932
Shelby	2	4	8	14	102	251	392	63	834	3,736
Sherman	2	0	0	1	0	10	20	3	34	1,185
Smith	9	23	161	294	1,029	2,600	7,237	776	12,120	7,623
Somervell	1	0	1	0	9	35	121	7	173	3,029
Starr	2	5	11	20	115	423	572	89	1,235	2,493
Stephens	2	0	0	0	2	61	137	5	205	2,305
Sterling	1	0	3	0	5	4	6	1	19	1,237
Stonewall	1	0	1	0	4	11	17	0	33	1,684
Sutton	2	0	2	0	9	17	137	1	166	3,861
Swisher	2	0	1	2	25	80	159	15	282	3,400
Tarrant	38	165	776	3,432	6,228	15,259	49,991	9,311	85,162	6,774
Taylor	5	6	98	124	537	18	4,109	253	6,475	5,312
Terrell	1	0	0	0	3	2	3	2	10	764
Terry	2	0	8	4	80	78	277	15	462	3,590
Throckmorton	1	0	0	1	3	8	14	1	27	1,488
Titus	2	5	6	15	71	286	747	103	1,233	5,039
Tom Green	4	6	44	49	486	928	3,687	139	5,339	5,273
Travis	12	42	346	1,646	1,813	8,765	30,486	4,304	47,402	7,333
Trinity	2	1	0	6	60	79	172	12	330	2,697
Tyler	2	5	2	3	50	220	163	17	460	2,509
Upshur	4	1	1	12	98	307	330	16	765	2,285
Upton	1	1	3	0	7	25	70	3	109	2,651
Uvalde	3	0	0	5	65	146	318	18	552	2,211
Val Verde	2	4	5	11	123	486	1,470	99	2,198	5,143
Van Zandt	6	3	7	2	55	356	485	58	966	2,376
Victoria	2	7	42	99	565	983	3,376	292	5,364	6,753
Walker	2	1	10	39	184	346	1,146	114	1,840	3,440
Waller	5	2	8	20	74	224	631	64	1,023	3,962
Ward	2	3	6	1	19	75	219	16	339	2,766
Washington	2	4	17	8	144	231	780	38	1,222	4,432
Webb	3	25	7	210	811	1,92	5,532	920	9,447	5,794
Wharton	3	3	24	33	167	480	1,230	63	2,000	5,005
Wheeler	2	0	1	0	13	49	42	4	109	2,000
Wichita	6	9	95	202	727	1,433	6,413	461	9,340	7,529
Wilbarger	2	1	4	10	67	164	226	12	484	3,325
Willacy	2	3	1	3	112	248	296	15	678	3,562
Williamson	9	7	39	62	428	1,033	3,168	298	5,035	2,916
Wilson	3	1	0	0	81	172	257	17	528	2,046
Winkler	2	0	2	2	16	45	91	2	158	1,952
Wise	3	1	10	6	48	252	502	57	876	2,347
Wood	5	3	20	2	104	310	348	36	823	2,580
Yoakum	2	0	1	1	14	26	137	2	181	2,137
Young	3	0	1	1	49	129	357	17	554	3,140
Zapata	1	0	0	1	11	99	91	1	203	1,890
Zavala	2	1	0	1	37	115	174	5	333	2,701

**County population figures used for calculation of crime rate are the U.S. Bureau of the Census estimates for 1994.*

Constitution of Texas

Following is the complete text of the Constitution of Texas. It includes the original document, which was adopted on Feb. 15, 1876, plus the 352 amendments approved through the election of Nov. 2, 1993.

Each amendment is accompanied by a footnote explaining when it was adopted. This text, with footnotes, of the constitution is copyrighted by the A. H. Belo Corporation and may not be reprinted without written permission from the publisher.

Amendment of the Texas Constitution requires a two-thirds favorable vote by both the Texas House of Representatives and the Texas Senate, followed by a majority vote of approval by voters in a statewide election.

Prior to 1973, amendments to the constitution could not be submitted by a special session of the Legislature. But the constitution was amended in 1972 to allow submission of amendments if the special session was opened to the subject by the governor.

Constitutional amendments are not subject to a gubernatorial veto. Once submitted, voters have the final decision on whether to change the constitution as proposed.

The following table lists the total number of amendments submitted to voters by the Texas Legislature and shows the year in which the Legislature approved them for submission to voters; e.g., the Seventieth Legislature in 1987 approved 28 bills proposing amendments to be submitted to voters — 25 in 1987 and three in 1988.

Year	No.	Year	No.	Year	No.
1879	1	1923	2	1965	27
1881	2	1925	4	1967	20
1883	5	1927	8	1969	16
1887	6	1929	7	1971	18
1889	2	1931	9	1973	9
1891	5	1933	12	1975	12
1893	2	1935	13	1977	15
1895	2	1937	7	1978	1
1897	5	1939	4	1979	12
1899	1	1941	5	1981	10
1901	1	1943	3	1982	3
1903	3	1945	8	1983	19
1905	3	1947	9	1985	17
1907	9	1949	10	1986	1
1909	4	1951	7	1987	28
1911	5	1953	11	1989	21
1913	7	1955	9	1990	1
1915	7	1957	12	1991	15
1917	3	1959	4	1993	18
1919	13	1961	14	1995	14
1921	5	1963	7		

Amendments, 1993

The following two amendments (three propositions) were voted on **May 1, 1993:**

SJR 4 — Authorizing the issuance of $750 million in state general obligation bonds or revenue bonds to assist school districts in partially financing facilities. Failed: 1,099,828 against, 869,014 in favor.

SJR 7 — (Part 1) — Providing for redistribution of property taxes levied and collected by school districts to other school districts. Failed: 1,293,224 against, 755,417 in favor. (Part 2) — Exempting school districts from complying with unfunded educational mandates. Failed: 1,007,084 against, 956,056 in favor.

The following 16 amendments were voted on **Nov. 2, 1993:**

HJR 3 — Clearing land titles by relinquishing and releasing any claim of sovereign ownership or title to a fractional interest in the Shelby, Frazier and McCormick League (now located in Fort Bend and Austin counties) arising out of the voiding of a certain interest under a Mexican land grant. Passed: 711,519 in favor, 345,888 against.

HJR 21 — Abolishing the office of county surveyor in Jackson County. Passed: 780,930 in favor, 243,770 against.

HJR 22— Abolishing the office of county surveyor in McLennan County. Passed: 783,693 in favor, 237,034 against.

HJR 23 — Relating to denial of bail to certain persons charged with certain violent or sexual offenses. Passed: 997,890 in favor, 122,547 against.

HJR 37 — Providing for the abolition of the office of county surveyor by election in the affected county. Passed: 925,408 in favor, 150,081 against.

HJR 57 — Repealing the constitutional provision limiting the consideration for which stock and bonds of a corporation may be issued. Passed: 558,487 in favor, 497,299 against.

HJR 86 — Relating to the exemption from ad valorem taxation of real and personal property used for the control of air, water or land pollution. Passed: 626,586 in favor, 475,384 against.

SJR 9 — Authorizing the legislature to provide for the issuance of bonds for the state financing of start-up costs for historically underutilized businesses. Failed: 767,543 against, 332,248 in favor.

SJR 13 — Relating to the amount and expenditure of certain constitutionally dedicated funding for public institutions of higher education. Passed: 610,714 in favor, 438,756 against.

SJR 18 — Authorizing the legislature to prescribe the qualifications of sheriffs. Passed: 646,484 in favor, 449,333 against.

SJR 19 — Modifying the provisions for the redemption of real property sold at a tax sale. Passed: 628,156 in favor, 416,450 against.

SJR 31 — Relating to the duties of trustees of local public pension systems. Passed: 823,370 in favor, 254,094 against.

SJR 34 — Relating to bonds issued to augment the Veterans' Land Fund and the Veterans' Housing Assistance Fund, to fund the Veterans' Housing Assistance Fund II, and to provide financial assistance to veterans of the state. Passed: 579,840 in favor, 514,561 against.

SJR 44 — Relating to the total principal amount of bonds and notes authorized to be issued or sold for the support of the Texas agricultural fund. Failed: 594,889 against, 476,715 in favor.

SJR 45 — Providing for the issuance of up to $1 billion in general obligation bonds for acquiring, constructing, equipping, or repairing corrections institutions and mental health and mental retardation institutions. Passed: 684,001 in favor, 411,694 against.

SJR 49 — Prohibiting a personal income tax without voter approval and dedicating the proceeds of the tax, if enacted, to education and property tax relief. Passed: 775,822 in favor, 343,638 against.

Amendments, 1995

The following 14 amendments were to be voted on **Nov. 7, 1995:**

HJR 31 — Authorizing the exemption from ad valorem taxation of income-producing personal property and mineral interests having a value insufficient to recover the costs of collecting the tax.

HJR 34 — Increasing the amount of general obligation bonds authorized for veterans' housing assistance.

HJR 35 — Authorizing the governing body of a political subdivision to exempt from ad valorem taxation boats and other equipment used in commercial fishing.

HJR 50 — Providing for the issuance of general obligation bonds to finance educational loans to students.

HJR 64 — Exempting from ad valorem taxation the residence homestead of the surviving spouse of an elderly person.

HJR 68 — To raise the limits of exemption from ad valorem taxation of property owned by disabled veterans or by the surviving spouses and surviving minor children of disabled veterans.

HJR 72 — Relating to the ad valorem taxation of open-space land used for wildlife management.

HJR 73 — Reducing the amount of general obligation bonds authorized for undertakings related to the superconducting super collider facility.

HJR 80 — Abolishing the office of constable in Mills, Reagan and Roberts counties.

SJR 1 — Abolishing the office of state treasurer.

SJR 7 — Allowing investment of money from the Texas growth fund in a business without requiring the business to disclose investments in or with South Africa or Namibia.

SJR 36 — Authorizing the legislature to exempt from ad valorem taxation property of certain organizations chartered by the Congress of the Republic of Texas.

SJR 46 — Permitting an encumbrance to be fixed on homestead property for an owelty of partition, including a debt of a spouse resulting from a division or award of a homestead in a divorce proceeding, and for the refinance of a lien against a homestead, including a federal tax lien resulting from the tax debt of the owner.

SJR 51 — Allowing the use of existing bond authority of the farm and ranch finance program to include financial assistance for the expansion, development and diversification of production, processing, marketing and export of Texas agricultural products. ☆

Index to the State Constitution

The following index to the Texas State Constitution includes all amendments voted on through the election of Nov. 2, 1993. In some instances, reference may be to a section that has been deleted from the text of the Constitution as carried here. However, these references are included when it is clear, in the note telling that the section has been deleted, that the reference was once a part of the text.

In some instances, an article number is given after the main heading, indicating that most references to the subject are in that article, and most subheadings will have only section numbers. However, there may also be references to other articles with some subheadings. Example: Under the heading "Courts, Art. V" is a subheading, "Impeachment of judges: XV, Secs. 2, 6, 8."

We trust that this index will be helpful to readers in finding particular sections they are looking for. The Texas Almanac welcomes any suggestions for improving this index or making it more useful to our readers.

Text of Texas Constitution

The following is a complete text of the Constitution of Texas, containing all amendments adopted through Nov. 2, 1993, with explanatory footnotes:

Preamble

Humbly invoking the blessings of Almighty God, the people of the State of Texas do ordain and establish this Constitution.

Article I — Bill of Rights

That the general, great and essential principles of liberty and free government may be recognized and established, we declare:

Sec. 1. **Texas Free and Independent** — Texas is a free and independent State, subject only to the Constitution of the United States, and the maintenance of our free institutions and the perpetuity of the Union depend upon the preservation of the right of local self-government, unimpaired to all the states.

Sec. 2. **All Political Power Is Inherent in the People** — All political power is inherent in the people, and all free governments are founded on their authority, and instituted for their benefit. The faith of the people of Texas stands pledged to the preservation of a republican form of government, and subject to this limitation only, they have at all times the inalienable right to alter, reform or abolish their government in such manner as they may think expedient.

Sec. 3. **All Free Men Have Equal Rights** — All free men, when they form a social compact, have equal rights, and no man, or set of men, is entitled to exclusive separate public emoluments or privileges but in consideration of public services.

Sec. 3-a. Equality under the law shall not be denied or abridged because of sex, race, color, creed or national origin. This amendment is self-operative.

[Note — Sec. 3-a of Art. I was added to set forth civil rights for all. Submitted by 62nd Legislature (1971) and adopted in election Nov. 7, 1972.]

Sec. 4. **There Shall Be No Religious Test for Office** — No religious test shall ever be required as a qualification to any office or public trust in this State; nor shall anyone be excluded from holding office on account of his religious sentiments, provided he acknowledge the existence of a Supreme Being.

Sec. 5. **How Oaths Shall Be Administered** — No person shall be disqualified to give evidence in any of the courts of this State on account of his religious opinions, or for want of any religious belief, but all oaths or affirmations shall be administered in the mode most binding upon the conscience, and shall be taken subject to the pains and penalties of perjury.

Sec. 6. **Freedom in Religious Worship Guaranteed** — All men have a natural and indefeasible right to worship Almighty God according to the dictates of their own consciences. No man shall be compelled to attend, erect or support any place of worship, or to maintain any ministry against his consent. No human authority ought, in any case whatever, to control or interfere with the rights of conscience in matters of religion, and no preference shall ever be given by law to any religious society or mode of worship. But it shall be the duty of the Legislature to pass such laws as may be necessary to protect equally every religious denomination in the peaceable enjoyment of its own mode of public worship.

Sec. 7. **No Appropriation for Sectarian Purposes** — No money shall be appropriated or drawn from the Treasury for the benefit of any sect, or religious society, theological or religious seminary, nor shall property belonging to the State be appropriated for any such purposes.

Sec. 8. **Liberty of Speech and Press Guaranteed; Libel** — Every person shall be at liberty to speak, write or publish his opinions, on any subject, being responsible for the abuse of that privilege; and no law shall ever be passed curtailing the liberty of speech or of the press. In prosecutions for the publication of papers, investigating the conduct of officers or men in public capacity, or when the matter published is proper for public information, the truth thereof may be given in evidence. And in all indictments for libels, the jury shall have the right to determine the law and the facts, under the direction of the court, as in other cases.

Sec. 9. **No Unreasonable Seizures and Searches Allowed** — The people shall be secure in their persons, houses, papers and possessions from all unreasonable seizures or searches, and no warrant to search any place, or to seize any person or thing, shall issue without describing them as near as may be, or without probable cause, supported by oath or affirmation.

Sec. 10. **Rights of Accused Persons in Criminal Prosecutions** — In all criminal prosecutions the accused shall have a speedy public trial by an impartial jury. He shall have the right to demand the nature and cause of the accusation against him, and to have a copy thereof. He shall not be compelled to give evidence against himself and shall have the right of being heard by himself or counsel, or both; shall be confronted by the witnesses against him and shall have compulsory process for obtaining witnesses in his favor, except that when the witness resides out of the State and the offense charged is a violation of any of the antitrust laws of this State, the defendant and the State shall have the right to produce and have the evidence admitted by deposition, under such rules and laws as the Legislature may hereafter provide; and no person shall be held to answer for a criminal offense, unless on an indictment of a grand jury, except in cases in which the punishment is by fine or imprisonment, otherwise than in the penitentiary; in cases of impeachment and in cases arising in the army or navy, or in the militia, when in actual service in time of war or public danger.

[Note — The foregoing section was amended by the addition of the clause relating to depositions of witnesses resident outside of the State in antitrust suits. Submitted by 35th Legislature (1917) and adopted in election on Nov. 5, 1918.]

Sec. 11. **Bail** — All prisoners shall be bailable by sufficient sureties, unless for capital offenses, when the proof is evident; but this provision shall not be so construed as to prevent bail after indictment found upon examination of the evidence, in such manner as may be prescribed by law.

Sec. 11-a. **Multiple Convictions; Denial of Bail** — (a) Any person (1) accused of a felony less than capital in this State, who has been theretofore twice convicted of a felony, the second conviction being subsequent to the first, both in point of time of commission of the offense and conviction therefor, (2) accused of a felony less than capital in this State, committed while on bail for a prior felony for which he has been indicted, (3) accused of a felony less than capital in this State involving the use of a deadly weapon after being convicted of a prior felony, or (4) accused of a violent or sexual offense committed while under the supervision of a criminal justice agency of the State or a political subdivision of the State for a prior felony, after a hearing, and upon evidence substantially showing the guilt of the accused of the offense in (1) or (3) above, of the offense committed while on bail in (2) above, or of the offense in (4) above committed while under the supervision of a criminal justice agency of the State or a political subdivision of the State for a prior felony, may be denied bail pending trial, by a district judge in this State, if said order denying bail pending trial is issued within seven calendar days subsequent to the time of incarceration of the accused; provided, however, that if the accused is not accorded a trial upon the accusation under (1) or (3) above, the accusation and indictment used under (2) above, or the accusation or indictment used under (4) above within sixty (60) days from the time of his incarceration upon the accusation, the order denying bail shall be automatically set aside, unless a continuance is obtained upon the motion or request of the accused; provided, further, that the right of appeal to the Court of Criminal Appeals of this State is expressly accorded the accused for a review of any judgment or order made hereunder, and said appeal shall be given preference by the Court of Criminal Appeals.

(b) In this section:

(1) "Violent offense" means:

(A) murder;

(B) aggravated assault, if the accused used or exhibited a deadly weapon during the commission of the assault;

(C) aggravated kidnapping; or

(D) aggravated robbery.

(2) "Sexual offense" means:

(A) aggravated sexual assault;

(B) sexual assault; or

(C) indecency with a child.

[Note — Sec. 11-a of Art. I was added to permit denial of bail to a person charged with a felony less than capital who has been theretofore twice convicted of a felony. Submitted by 54th Legislature (1955) and adopted in election Nov. 6, 1956. This section was amended to provide for further denial of bail under circumstances (2) and (3) above, and providing for 60-day limit to that person's incarceration without trial; and providing for that person's right of appeal. Submitted by 65th Legislature (1977) and adopted in election Nov. 8, 1977. It was further amended to permit denial of bail to persons charged with certain violent or sexual offenses while under the supervision of a criminal justice agency or a political subdivision of the state for a prior felony; added were definitions of the terms "violent offense" and "sexual offense." Submitted by the 73rd Legislature (1993) and adopted in election Nov. 2, 1993.]

Article I (Cont'd.); Articles II and III

Sec. 12. **The Writ of Habeas Corpus** — The writ of habeas corpus is a writ of right, and shall never be suspended. The Legislature shall enact laws to render the remedy speedy and effectual.

Sec. 13. **Excessive Bail and Fine and Unusual Punishment Prohibited; Courts Open** — Excessive bail shall not be required, nor excessive fines imposed, nor cruel or unusual punishment inflicted. All courts shall be open, and every person for an injury done him in his lands, goods, person or reputation, shall have due course of law.

Sec. 14. **No Person Shall Be Put Twice in Jeopardy** — No person, for the same offense, shall be twice put in jeopardy of life or liberty, nor shall a person be again put upon trial for the same offense after a verdict of not guilty in a court of competent jurisdiction.

Sec. 15. **Right of Trial by Jury** — The right of trial by jury shall remain inviolate. The Legislature shall pass such laws as may be needed to regulate the same, and to maintain its purity and efficiency. Provided, that the Legislature may provide for the temporary commitment, for observation and/or treatment, of mentally ill persons not charged with a criminal offense, for a period of time not to exceed ninety (90) days, by order of the County Court without the necessity of a trial by jury.

[Note — Sec. 15 of Art. I was amended by addition of the last sentence. Submitted by 44th Legislature (1935) and adopted in election Aug. 24, 1935.]

Section 15-a. No person shall be committed as a person of unsound mind except on competent medical or psychiatric testimony. The Legislature may enact all laws necessary to provide for the trial, adjudication of insanity and commitment of persons of unsound mind and to provide for a method of appeal from judgments rendered in such cases. Such laws may provide for a waiver of trial by jury. In cases where the person under inquiry has not been charged with the commission of a criminal offense, by the concurrence of the person under inquiry, or his next of kin, and an attorney ad litem appointed by a judge of either the County or Probate Court of the county where the trial is being held, and shall provide for a method of service of notice of such trial upon the person under inquiry and of his right to demand a trial by jury.

[Note — Sec. 15-a of Art. I was added to require medical or psychiatric testimony for commitment of persons of unsound mind and authorizing Legislature to provide for trial and commitment of such persons and for waiver of trial by jury where the person under inquiry has not been charged with commission of a crime. Submitted by 54th Legislature (1955) and adopted in election Nov. 6, 1956.]

Sec. 16. **There Shall Be No Bill of Attainder or Ex-Post Facto Laws** — No bill of attainder or ex post facto law, retroactive law, or any other law impairing the obligation of contracts shall be made.

Sec. 17. **Privileges and Franchises: Eminent Domain** — No person's property shall be taken, damaged or destroyed for or applied to public use without adequate compensation being made, unless by the consent of such person; and when taken, except for the use of the State, such compensation shall be first made or secured by a deposit of money; and no irrevocable or uncontrollable grant of special privileges or immunities shall be made; but all privileges and franchises granted by the Legislature, or created under its authority, shall be subject to the control thereof.

Sec. 18. **No Imprisonment for Debt** — No person shall ever be imprisoned for debt.

Sec. 19. **Due Course of Law** — No citizen of this State shall be deprived of life, liberty, property, privileges or immunities, or in any manner disfranchised, except by the due course of the law of the land.

Sec. 20. **No Outlawry or Deportations** — No citizen shall be outlawed. No person shall be transported out of the State for any offense committed within the same. This section does not prohibit an agreement with another state providing for the confinement of inmates of this State in the penal or correctional facilities of that state.

[Note — Sec. 20 of Art. I was amended to permit state prisoners to be placed in penal facilities of another state pursuant to an interstate agreement. Submitted by 69th Legislature (1985) and adopted in election Nov. 5, 1985.]

Sec. 21. **Corruption of Blood, Forfeiture; Suicide** — No conviction shall work corruption of blood or forfeiture of estate, and the estates of those who destroy their own lives shall descend or vest as in the case of natural death.

Sec. 22. **Treason** — Treason against the State shall consist only in levying war against it, or adhering to its enemies, giving them aid and comfort; and no person shall be convicted of treason except on the testimony of two witnesses to the same overt act or on confession in open court.

Sec. 23. **Right to Bear Arms** — Every citizen shall have the right to keep and bear arms in the lawful defense of himself or the State; but the Legislature shall have power, by law, to regulate the wearing of arms, with a view to prevent crime.

Sec. 24. **Military Subordinate to Civil Authority** — The military shall at all times be subordinate to the civil authority.

Sec. 25. **Quartering Soldiers** — No soldier shall in time of peace be quartered in the house of any citizen without the consent of the owner, nor in time of war but in a manner prescribed by law.

Sec. 26. **Perpetuities; Monopolies; Primogeniture; Entailments** — Perpetuities and monopolies are contrary to the genius of a free government, and shall never be allowed, nor shall the law of primogeniture or entailments ever be in force in this State.

Sec. 27. **Right of Petition Guaranteed** — The citizens shall have the right, in a peaceable manner, to assemble together for their common good and apply to those invested with the powers of government for redress of grievances or other purposes, by petition, address or remonstrance.

Sec. 28. **Power to Suspend Laws** — No power of suspending laws in this State shall be exercised except by the Legislature.

Sec. 29. **"Bill of Rights" Inviolate** — To guard against transgressions of the high powers being delegated, we declare that everything in this "Bill of Rights" is excepted out of the general powers of government, and shall forever remain inviolate, and all laws contrary thereto, or to the following provisions, shall be void.

Sec. 30. **Rights of Crime Victims** — (a) A crime victim has the following rights:

(1) the right to be treated with fairness and with respect for the victim's dignity and privacy throughout the criminal justice process; and

(2) the right to be reasonably protected from the accused throughout the criminal justice process.

(b) On the request of a crime victim, the crime victim has the following rights:

(1) the right to notification of court proceedings;

(2) the right to be present at all public court proceedings related to the offense, unless the victim is to testify and the court determines that the victim's testimony would be materially affected if the victim hears other testimony at the trial;

(3) the right to confer with a representative of the prosecutor's office;

(4) the right to restitution; and

(5) the right to information about the conviction, sentence, imprisonment, and release of the accused.

(c) The legislature may enact laws to define the term "victim" and to enforce these and other rights of crime victims.

(d) The state, through its prosecuting attorney, has the right to enforce the rights of crime victims.

(e) The legislature may enact laws to provide that a judge, attorney for the state, peace officer, or law enforcement agency is not liable for a failure or inability to provide a right enumerated in this section. The failure or inability of any person to provide a right or service enumerated in this section may not be used by a defendant in a criminal case as a ground for appeal or post-conviction writ of habeas corpus. A victim or guardian or legal representative of a victim has standing to enforce the rights enumerated in this section but does not have standing to participate as a party in a criminal proceeding or to contest the disposition of any charge.

[Note — Sec. 30 of Art. I was added to set forth the rights of crime victims. Submitted by 71st Legislature (1989) and adopted in election Nov. 7, 1989.]

Article II — The Powers of Government

Sec. 1. **Departments of Government to Be Kept Distinct** — The powers of the government of the State of Texas shall be divided into three distinct departments, each of which shall be confined to a separate body of magistracy, to wit: Those which are legislative to one, those which are executive to another, and those which are judicial to another; and no person, or collection of persons, being of one of these departments shall exercise any power properly attached to either of the others, except in the instances herein expressly permitted.

Article III — Legislative Department

Sec. 1. The Legislature: House and Senate — The legislative power of this State shall be vested in a Senate and House of Representatives, which together shall be styled "The Legisla-

Article III (Cont'd.)

lature of the State of Texas."

Sec. 2. **Number of Members Limited** — The Senate shall consist of thirty-one members, and shall never be increased above this number. The House of Representatives shall consist of ninety-three members until the first apportionment after the adoption of this Constitution, when or at any apportionment thereafter the number of Representatives may be increased by the Legislature, upon the ratio of not more than one Representative for every 15,000 inhabitants; provided, the number of Representatives shall never exceed 150.

Sec. 3. **Election of Senators; New Apportionment** — The Senators shall be chosen by the qualified electors for the term of four years; but a new Senate shall be chosen after every apportionment, and the Senators elected after each apportionment shall be divided by lot into two classes. The seats of the Senators of the first class shall be vacated at the expiration of the first two years, and those of the second class at the expiration of four years, so that one half of the Senators shall be chosen biennially thereafter. Senators shall take office following their election, on the day set by law for the convening of the regular session of the Legislature, and shall serve thereafter for the full term of years to which elected and until their successors shall have been elected and qualified.

[Note — Sec. 3 of Art. III was amended to establish the date on which newly elected members of the Senate shall qualify and take office. Submitted by 59th Legislature (1965) and adopted in election Nov. 8, 1966.]

Sec. 4. **Election of Representatives; Term of Office** — The members of the House of Representatives shall be chosen by the qualified electors for the term of two years. Representatives shall take office following their election, on the day set by law for the convening of the regular session of the Legislature, and shall serve thereafter for the full term of years to which elected and until their successors shall have been elected and qualified.

[Note — Sec. 4 of Art. III was amended to provide for the date on which newly elected members of the House of Representatives shall qualify and take office. Submitted by 59th Legislature (1965) and adopted in election Nov. 8, 1966.]

Sec. 5. **Time of Meeting; Method of Procedure** — The Legislature shall meet every two years at such time as may be provided by law and at other times when convened by the Governor. When convened in regular session, the first thirty days thereof shall be devoted to the introduction of bills and resolutions, acting upon emergency appropriations, passing upon the confirmation of the recess appointees of the Governor and such emergency matters as may be submitted by the Governor in special messages to the Legislature; provided, that during the succeeding thirty days of the regular session of the Legislature the various committees of each house shall hold hearings to consider all bills and resolutions and other matters then pending; and such emergency matters as may be submitted by the Governor; provided, further that during the following sixty days the Legislature shall act upon such bills and resolutions as may be then pending and upon such emergency matters as may be submitted by the Governor in special messages to the Legislature; provided, however, either house may otherwise determine its order of business by an affirmative vote of four fifths of its membership.

[Note — Sec. 5 of Art. III was amended to provide for a 120-day session. Submitted, together with amendment of Sec. 24 of Art. III, by 41st Legislature (1929) and adopted in election Nov. 4, 1930.]

Sec. 6. **Qualifications of Senators** — No person shall be a Senator unless he be a citizen of the United States, and, at the time of his election, a qualified elector of this State, and shall have been a resident of this State five years next preceding his election and the last year thereof a resident of the district for which he shall be chosen, and shall have attained the age of twenty-six years.

Sec. 7. **Qualifications of Representatives** — No person shall be a Representative unless he be a citizen of the United States, and, at the time of his election, a qualified elector of this State, and shall have been a resident of this State two years preceding his election, the last year thereof a resident of the district for which he shall be chosen, and shall have attained the age of twenty-one years.

Sec. 8. **Each House to Judge Qualifications of Its Own Members** — Each house shall be the judge of the qualifications and election of its own members; but contested elections shall be determined in such manner as shall be provided by law.

Sec. 9. **President Pro Tem of the Senate; Speaker of the House; Officers** — (a) The Senate shall, at the beginning and close of each session, and at such other times as may be necessary, elect one of its members President pro tempore, who shall perform the duties of the Lieutenant Governor in any case of absence or disability of that officer. If the said office of Lieutenant Governor becomes vacant, the President pro tempore of the Senate shall convene the Committee of the Whole Senate within 30 days after the vacancy occurs. The Committee of the Whole shall elect one of its members to perform the duties of the Lieutenant Governor in addition to his duties as Senator until the next general election. If the Senator so elected ceases to be a Senator before the election of a new Lieutenant Governor, another Senator shall be elected in the same manner to perform the duties of the Lieutenant Governor until the next general election. Until the Committee of the Whole elects one of its members for this purpose, the President pro tempore shall perform the duties of the Lieutenant Governor as provided by this subsection.

(b) The House of Representatives shall, when it first assembles, organize temporarily, and thereupon proceed to the election of a Speaker from its own members.

(c) Each House shall choose its other officers.

[Note — Sec. 9 of Art. III was amended to provide for method of filling a vacancy in the office of Lieutenant Governor. Submitted by 68th Legislature (1983) and approved in an election Nov. 6, 1984.]

Sec. 10. **Quorum** — Two thirds of each house shall constitute a quorum to do business, but a smaller number may adjourn from day to day and compel the attendance of absent members, in such manner and under such penalties as each house may provide.

Sec. 11. **Rules: Power to Punish and Expel** — Each house may determine the rules of its own proceedings, punish members for disorderly conduct, and, with the consent of two thirds, expel a member, but not a second time for the same offense.

Sec. 12. **Journal: Yeas and Nays** — Each house shall keep a journal of its proceedings, and publish the same; and the yeas and nays of the members of either house on any question shall, at the desire of any three members present, be entered on the journals.

Sec. 13. **Vacancies, How Filled** — When vacancies occur in either house, the Governor, or the person exercising the power of the Governor, shall issue writs of election to fill such vacancies; and should the Governor fail to issue a writ of election to fill any such vacancy within twenty days after it occurs, the returning officer of the district in which such vacancy may have happened shall be authorized to order an election for that purpose.

Sec. 14. **Members of Legislature Privileged From Arrest** — Senators and Representatives shall, except in cases of treason, felony or breach of the peace, be privileged from arrest during the session of the Legislature, and in going to or returning from the same, allowing one day for every twenty miles such member may reside from the place at which the Legislature is convened.

Sec. 15. **Each House May Punish Disorderly Conduct** — Each house may punish, by imprisonment, during its sessions, any person not a member for disrespectful or disorderly conduct in its presence, or for obstructing any of its proceedings; provided, such imprisonment shall not, at any one time, exceed forty-eight hours.

Sec. 16. **Sessions to Be Open** — The sessions of each house shall be open, except the Senate when in executive session.

Sec. 17. **Adjournments** — Neither house shall, without the consent of the other, adjourn for more than three days, nor to any other place than that where the Legislature may be sitting.

Sec. 18. **Ineligibility of Members to Certain Offices; Not to Be Interested in Contracts** — No Senator or Representative shall, during the term for which he was elected, be eligible to (1) any civil office of profit under this State which shall have been created, or the emoluments of which may have been increased, during such term, or (2) any office or place, the appointment to which may be made, in whole or in part, by either branch of the Legislature; provided, however, the fact that the term of office of Senators and Representatives does not end precisely on the last day of December but extends a few days into January of the succeeding year shall be considered as de minimis, and the ineligibility herein created shall terminate on the last day in December of the last full calendar year of the term for which he was elected. No member of either House shall vote for any other member for any office whatever, which may be filled by a vote of the Legislature, except in such cases as are in this Constitution provided, nor shall any member of the Legislature be interested, either directly or indirectly, in any contract with the State, or any county thereof, authorized by any law passed during the term for

Article III (Cont'd.)
which he was elected.

[Note — Sec. 18 of Art. III was amended to fix the time during which members of Legislature shall be ineligible to hold other office. Submitted by 60th Legislature (1967) and adopted in election Nov. 5, 1968.]

Sec. 19. **What Officers Ineligible to Membership in Legislature** — No judge of any court, Secretary of State, Attorney General, clerk of any court of record, or any person holding a lucrative office under the United States, or this State, or any foreign government, shall, during the term for which he is elected or appointed, be eligible to the Legislature.

Sec. 20. **Receivers or Disbursers of Public Funds Not Eligible to Membership in the Legislature Until Discharge Received** — No person who at any time may have been a collector of taxes or who may have been otherwise entrusted with public money, shall be eligible to the Legislature, or to any office of profit or trust under the State Government, until he shall have obtained a discharge for the amount of such collections, or for all public moneys with which he may have been entrusted.

Sec. 21. **Freedom in Debate** — No member shall be questioned in any other place for words spoken in debate in either house.

Sec. 22. **Personal Interest in Measure or Bill** — A member who has a personal or private interest in any measure or bill, proposed or pending before the Legislature, shall disclose the fact to the house of which he is a member, and shall not vote thereon.

Sec. 23. **Removal Vacates Office** — If any Senator or Representative remove his residence from the district or county for which he was elected, his office shall thereby become vacant, and the vacancy shall be filled as provided in Sec. 13 of this article.

Sec. 23-a. **John Tarleton Contract Validated** — The Legislature is authorized to appropriate so much money as may be necessary, not to exceed seventy-five thousand ($75,000) dollars, to pay claims incurred by John Tarleton Agricultural College for the construction of a building on the campus of such college pursuant to deficiency authorization by the Governor of Texas on Aug. 31, 1937.

[Note — Sec. 23-a. of Art. III was added to provide for payment of a contractor whose contract had been annulled. Submitted by 49th Legislature (1945) and ratified in election Nov. 5, 1946.]

Sec. 24. **Mileage and Per Diem** — (a) Members of the Legislature shall receive from the Public Treasury a salary of Six Hundred Dollars ($600) per month, unless a greater amount is recommended by the Texas Ethics Commission and approved by the voters of this State in which case each member shall also receive a per diem set by the Texas Ethics Commission for each day during each Regular and Special Session of the Legislature.

(b) No Regular Session shall be of longer duration than one hundred and forty (140) days.

(c) In addition to the per diem the Members of each House shall be entitled to mileage at the same rate as prescribed by law for employees of the State of Texas.

[Note — Sec. 24 of Art. III has been amended five times: (!) Raising the per diem and decreasing the mileage. Submitted with amendment of Sec. 5 of Art. III by 41st Legislature (1929); ratified Nov. 4, 1930. (2) To raise per diem to $25 for first 120 days only. Submitted by 53rd Legislature (1953) and adopted in election Nov. 2, 1954. (3) To fix the salary at $4,800 per year and setting the per diem at $12 per day for first 120 days of regular session and 30 days of each special session. Submitted by 56th Legislature (1959) and adopted in election Nov. 8, 1960. (4) To set salaries of members of Legislature at $600 per month and set per diem of $30 per day during legislative sessions and a mileage allowance at the same rate provided by law for state employees. Submitted by 64th Legislature (1975) and adopted in election April 22, 1975. (5) To authorize the Texas Ethics Commission to recommend salaries of the legislature, subject to approval by the voters, and to allow the commission to set the per diem for the legislature. Submitted by 72nd Legislature (1991) and adopted in election Nov. 5, 1991.]

Sec. 24a. (a). **Texas Ethics Commission** — The Texas Ethics Commission is a state agency consisting of the following eight members:

(1) two members of different political parties appointed by the governor from a list of at least 10 names submitted by the members of the house of representatives from each political party required by law to hold a primary;

(2) two members of different political parties appointed by the governor from a list of at least 10 names submitted by the members of the senate from each political party required by law to hold a primary;

(3) two members of different political parties appointed by the speaker of the house of representatives from a list of at least 10 names submitted by the members of the house from each political party required by law to hold a primary; and

(4) two members of different political parties appointed by the lieutenant governor from a list of at least 10 names submitted by the members of the senate from each political party required by law to hold a primary.

(b) The governor may reject all names on any list submitted under Subsection (a) (1) or (2) of this section and require a new list to be submitted. The members of the commission shall elect annually the chairman of the commission.

(c) With the exception of the initial appointees, commission members serve for four-year terms. Each appointing official will make one initial appointment for a two-year term and one initial appointment for a four-year term. A vacancy on the commission shall be filled for the unexpired portion of the term in the same manner as the original appointment. A member who has served for one term and any part of a second term is not eligible for reappointment.

(d) The commission has the powers and duties provided by law.

(3) The commisison may recommend the salary of the members of the legislature and may recommend that the salary of the speaker of the house of representatives and the lieutenant governor be set at an amount higher than that of other members. The commission shall set the per diem of members of the legislature and the lieutenant governor, and the per diem shall reflect reasonable estimates of costs and may be raised or lowered biennially as necessary to pay those costs, but the per diem may not exceed during a calendar year the amount allowed as of January 1 of that year for federal income tax purposes as a deduction for living expenses incurred in a legislative day by a state legislator in connection with the legislator's business as a legislator, disregarding any exception in federal law for legislators residing near the Capitol.

(f) At each general election for state and county officers following a proposed change in salary, the voters shall approve or disapprove the salary recommended by the commission if the commission recommends a change in salary. If the voters disapprove the salary, the salary continues at the amount paid immediately before disapproval until another amount is recommended by the commission and approved by the voters. If the voters approve the salary, the approved salary takes effect January 1 of the next odd-numbered year.

[Note — Section 24a of Article III was added to establish the Texas Ethics Commission, to authorize the commission to recommend salaries of the legislature and the lieutenant governor and to set the per diem for those officials. Submitted by 72nd Legislature (1991) and adopted in election Nov. 5, 1991.]

Sec. 25. **Senatorial Districts, How Apportioned** — The State shall be divided into senatorial districts of contiguous territory according to the number of qualified electors, as nearly as may be, and each district shall be entitled to elect one Senator; and no single county shall be entitled to more than one Senator.

Sec. 26. **Representative Districts, How Apportioned** — The members of the House of Representatives shall be apportioned among the several counties, according to the number of population in each, as nearly as may be, on a ratio obtained by dividing the population of the State, as ascertained by the most recent United States census, by the number of members of which the House is composed; provided that whenever a single county has sufficient population to be entitled to a Representative, such county shall be formed into a separate representative district, and when two or more counties are required to make up the ratio of representation, such counties shall be contiguous to each other; and when any one county has more than sufficient population to be entitled to one or more Representatives, such Representative or Representatives shall be apportioned to such county, and for any surplus of population it may be joined in a representative district with any other contiguous county or counties.

Sec. 26-a. **Redistricting According to Population** — Provided, however, that no county shall be entitled to or have under any apportionment more than seven (7) Representatives unless the population of such county shall exceed seven hundred thousand (700,000) people as ascertained by the most recent United States census, in which event such county shall be entitled to one additional Representative for each one hundred thousand (100,000) population in excess of seven hundred thousand (700,000) population as shown by the latest United States census; nor shall any district be created which would permit any county to have more than seven (7) Representatives except under the conditions set forth above.

[Note — Sec. 26-a of Art. III was added to limit representation

Article III (Cont'd.)
of counties with large populations. Submitted by 44th Legislature (1935) and adopted in election Nov. 3, 1936.]

Sec. 27. **Election of Members** — Elections for Senators and Representatives shall be general throughout the State, and shall be regulated by law.

Sec. 28. **Reapportionment After Each Census** — The Legislature shall, at its first regular session after the publication of each United States decennial census, apportion the State into senatorial and representative districts, agreeable to the provisions of Sections 25, 26 and 26-a of this Article. In the event the Legislature shall at any such first regular session following the publication of a United States decennial census, fail to make such apportionment, same shall be done by the Legislative Redistricting Board of Texas, which is hereby created, and shall be composed of five (5) members, as follows: The Lieutenant Governor, the Speaker of the House of Representatives, the Attorney General, the Comptroller of Public Accounts and the Commissioner of the General Land Office, a majority of whom shall constitute a quorum. Said board shall assemble in the City of Austin within ninety (90) days after the final adjournment of such regular session. The board shall, within sixty (60) days after assembling, apportion the State into senatorial and representative districts, or into senatorial or representative districts, as the failure of action of such Legislature may make necessary. Such apportionment shall be in writing and signed by three (3) or more of the members of the board duly acknowledged as the act and deed of such board, and when so executed and filed with the Secretary of State, shall have force and effect of law. Such apportionment shall become effective at the next succeeding statewide general election. The Supreme Court of Texas shall have jurisdiction to compel such commission to perform its duties in accordance with the provisions of this section by writ of mandamus or other extraordinary writs conformable to the usages of law. The Legislature shall provide necessary funds for clerical and technical aid and for other expenses incidental to the work of the board, and the Lieutenant Governor and the Speaker of the House of Representatives shall be entitled to receive per diem and travel expense during the board's session in the same manner and amount as they would receive while attending a special session of the Legislature. This amendment shall become effective Jan. 1, 1951.

[Note — The foregoing Section 28 of Art. III was amended to provide for the Legislative Redistricting Board of Texas, this action being taken because of failure of past Legislatures to obey the mandate in the original Sec. 28 to redistrict the state after each decennial census. Submitted by 50th Legislature (1947) and adopted in election Nov. 2, 1948.]

Proceedings

Sec. 29. **Enacting Clause** — The enacting clause of all laws shall be: "Be it enacted by the Legislature of the State of Texas."

Sec. 30. **Laws to Be Passed by Bill: Amendments** — No law shall be passed, except by bill, and no bill shall be so amended in its passage through either house as to change its original purpose.

Sec. 31. **Bills May Originate in Either House and May Be Amended or Rejected by the Other House** — Bills may originate in either house, and when passed by such house may be amended, altered or rejected by the other.

Sec. 32. **Bills to Be Read on Three Several Days: Suspension of Rule** — No bill shall have the force of a law until it has been read on three several days in each house, and free discussion allowed thereon; but in cases of imperative public necessity (which necessity shall be stated in a preamble or in the body of the bill) four fifths of the house in which the bill may be pending may suspend this rule, the yeas and nays being taken on the question of suspension and entered upon the journals.

Sec. 33. **Bills for Raising Revenue** — All bills for raising revenue shall originate in the House of Representatives, but the Senate may amend or reject them as other bills.

Sec. 34. **Bill or Resolution Defeated, Not to Be Considered Again** — After a bill has been considered and defeated by either house of the Legislature, no bill containing the same substance shall be passed into a law during the same session. After a resolution has been acted on and defeated, no resolution containing the same substance shall be considered at the same session.

Sec. 35. **Bills to Contain but One Subject, Which Must Be Expressed in Title** — (a) No bill (except general appropriation bills, which may embrace the various subjects and accounts for and on account of which moneys are appropriated) shall contain more than one subject.

(b) The rules of procedure of each house shall require that the subject of each bill be expressed in its title in a manner that gives the Legislature and the public reasonable notice of that subject. The Legislature is solely responsible for determining compliance with the rule.

(c) A law, including a law enacted before the effective date of this subsection, may not be held void on the basis of an insufficient title.

[Note — The foregoing Sec. 35 of Art. III was amended to require each house to include in its rules of procedure a rule that each bill contain title expressing bill's subject. Submitted by 69th Legislature (1985) and adopted in election Nov. 4, 1986.]

Sec. 36. **Reviving or Amending Laws** — No law shall be revived or amended by reference to its title; but in such case the act revived, or the section or sections amended, shall be re-enacted and published at length.

Sec. 37. **Reference to Committees** — No bill shall be considered unless it has been first referred to a committee and reported thereon, and no bill shall be passed which has not been presented and referred to and reported from a committee at least three days before the final adjournment of the Legislature.

Sec. 38. **Signing Bills** — The presiding officer of each house shall, in the presence of the house over which he presides, sign all bills and joint resolutions passed by the Legislature, after their titles have been publicly read before signing, and the fact of signing shall be entered on the journals.

Sec. 39. **When Laws Take Effect** — No law passed by the Legislature, except the general appropriation act, shall take effect or go into force until ninety days after the adjournment of the session at which it was enacted, unless in case of an emergency, which emergency must be expressed in a preamble or in the body of the act, the Legislature shall, by a vote of two thirds of all the members elected to each house, otherwise direct; said vote to be taken by yeas and nays, and entered upon the journals.

Sec. 40. **Business and Duration of Special Sessions** — When the Legislature shall be convened in special session, there shall be no legislation upon subjects other than those designated in the proclamation of the Governor calling such session, or presented to them by the Governor; and no such session shall be of longer duration than thirty days.

Sec. 41. **Elections: Votes, How Taken** — In all elections by the Senate and House of Representatives, jointly or separately, the vote shall be given viva voce, except in the election of their officers.

[Note — Sec. 42 of Art. III, relating to passage of laws, was deleted by constitutional amendment. Submitted by 61st Legislature (1969) and approved in election Aug. 5, 1969.]

Requirements and Limitations

Sec. 43. **Revision and Publication of Laws** — (a) The Legislature shall provide for revising, digesting and publishing the laws, civil and criminal; provided, that in the adoption of and giving effect to any such digest or revision the Legislature shall not be limited by Secs. 35 and 36 of this article.

(b) In this section, "revision" includes a revision of the statutes on a particular subject and any enactment having the purpose, declared in the enactment, of codifying without substantive change statutes that individually relate to different subjects.

[Note — The foregoing Sec. 43 of Art. III was amended to provide for the continuing revision of state laws. Submitted by 69th Legislature (1985) and adopted in election Nov. 4, 1986.]

Sec. 44. **Compensation of Officers: Payment of Claims** — The Legislature shall provide by law for the compensation of all officers, servants, agents and public contractors, not provided for in this Constitution, but shall not grant extra compensation to any officer, agent, servant or public contractors, after such public service shall have been performed or contract entered into for the performance of the same; nor grant, by appropriation or otherwise, any amount of money out of the Treasury of the State, to any individual, on a claim, real or pretended, when the same shall not have been provided for by pre-existing law; nor employ anyone in the name of the State, unless authorized by pre-existing law.

Sec. 45. **Change of Venue** — The power to change the venue in civil and criminal cases shall be vested in the courts, to be exercised in such manner as shall be provided by law; and the Legislature shall pass laws for that purpose.

[Note — Sec. 46 of Art. III, relating to vagrant laws, was deleted by constitutional amendment in election Aug. 5, 1969.]

Sec. 47. **Lotteries Shall Be Prohibited Except as Authorized or Operated by State; Bingo Games and Charitable Raffles Permitted; Restrictions** — (a) The Legislature shall pass laws prohibiting lotteries and gift enterprises in this State other than those authorized by Subsections (b), (d), and (e) of

Article III (Cont'd.)

this section.

(b) The Legislature by law may authorize and regulate bingo games conducted by a church, synagogue, religious society, volunteer fire department, nonprofit veterans organization, fraternal organization, or nonprofit organization supporting medical research or treatment programs. A law enacted under this subsection must permit the qualified voters of any county, justice precinct, or incorporated city or town to determine from time to time by a majority vote of the qualified voters voting on the question at an election whether bingo games may be held in the county, justice precinct, or city or town. The law must also require that:

(1) all proceeds from the games are spent in Texas for charitable purposes of the organizations;

(2) the games are limited to one location as defined by law on property owned or leased by the church, synagogue, religious society, volunteer fire department, nonprofit veterans organization, fraternal organization, or nonprofit organization supporting medical research or treatment programs; and

(3) the games are conducted, promoted, and administered by members of the church, synagogue, religious society, volunteer fire department, nonprofit veterans organization, fraternal organization, or nonprofit organization supporting medical research or treatment programs.

(c) The law enacted by the Legislature authorizing bingo games must include:

(1) a requirement that the entities conducting the games report quarterly to the Comptroller of Public Accounts about the amount of proceeds that the entities collect from the games and the purposes for which the proceeds are spent; and

(2) criminal or civil penalties to enforce the reporting requirement.

(d) The Legislature by general law may permit charitable raffles conducted by a qualified religious society, qualified volunteer fire department, qualified volunteer emergency medical service, or qualified nonprofit organizations under the terms and conditions imposed by general law.

The law must also require that:

(1) all proceeds from the sale of tickets for the raffle must be spent for the charitable purposes of the organizations; and

(2) the charitable raffle is conducted, promoted, and administered exclusively by members of the qualified religious society, qualified volunteer fire department, qualified volunteer emergency medical service, or qualified nonprofit organization.

(e) The Legislature by general law may authorize the State to operate lotteries and may authorize the State to enter into a contract with one or more legal entities that will operate lotteries on behalf of the State.

[Note — Sec. 47 of Art. III has been amended three times: (1) To authorize bingo games on local option basis if games are conducted by religious society or other charitable society and proceeds are to be spent in Texas for charitable purposes of the organization. Submitted by 66th Legislature (1979) and adopted in election Nov. 4, 1980. (2) Subsection (d) was added to authorize the Legislature to permit and regulate raffles conducted for charitable purposes by certain non-profit organizations. Submitted by 71st Legislature (1989) and adopted in election Nov. 7, 1989. (3) Subsection (a) was amended and Subsection (e) was added to allow for the establishment of a state lottery. Submitted by 72nd Legislature (1991) and adopted in election Nov. 5, 1991.]

[Note — Sec. 48 of Art. III, relating to power to levy taxes, was deleted by constitutional amendment. Submitted by 61st Legislature (1969) and approved in election Aug. 5, 1969.]

[Note — Sec. 48a and Sec. 48b, relating to the Teachers' Retirement Fund and Teachers' Retirement System, respectively, were deleted by constitutional amendment. Submitted by 64th Legislature (975) and approved in election April 22, 1975. See Art. XVI, Sec. 67, which replaces the foregoing sections. (See also note under Art. III, Sec. 51e and Sec. 51f; Art. XVI, Sec. 62 and Sec. 63.)]

Sec. 48-d. **Rural Fire Prevention Districts** — The Legislature shall have the power to provide for the establishment and creation of rural fire-prevention districts and to authorize a tax on the ad valorem property situated in said districts not to exceed three (3¢) cents on the one hundred ($100) dollars valuation for the support thereof; provided that no tax shall be levied in support of said districts until approved by vote of the people residing therein.

[Note — Sec. 48-d of Art. III was added for the stated purpose by the 51st Legislature (1949) and ratified in election Nov. 8, 1949. Section 48-c is missing because it was proposed as an amendment but failed to carry.]

Sec. 48-e. **Jail Districts** — The legislature, by law, may provide for the creation, operation, and financing of jail districts and may authorize each district to issue bonds and other obligations and to levy an ad valorem tax on property located in the district to pay principal of and interest on the bonds and to pay for operation of the district. An ad valorem tax may not be levied and bonds secured by a property tax may not be issued until approved by the qualified electors of the district voting at an election called and held for that purpose.

[Note — Sec. 48-e of Art. III was added to provide for the creation, operation and financing of jail districts. Submitted by the 70th Legislature (1987) and adopted in election Nov. 3, 1987. (See also note after second Sec. 48-e, below.)]

Sec. 48-e. **Emergency Services Districts** — Laws may be enacted to provide for the establishment and creation of special districts to provide emergency services and to authorize the commissioners courts of participating counties to levy a tax on the ad valorem property situated in said districts not to exceed Ten Cents (10¢) on the One Hundred Dollars ($100.00) valuation for the support thereof; provided that no tax shall be levied in support of said districts until approved by a vote of the qualified electors residing therein. Such a district may provide emergency medical services, emergency ambulance services, rural fire prevention and control services, or other emergency services authorized by the Legislature.

[Note — Sec. 48-e of Art. III was added to provide for the creation of emergency medical services districts. Submitted by 70th Legislature (1987) and adopted in election Nov. 3, 1987.]]

[Note — The foregoing two sections of Art. III were both numbered 48-e by 70th Legislature (1987), and they shall remain so designated unless changed by a future Legislature.]

Sec. 49. **Purpose for Which Debts May Be Created** — (a) No debt shall be created by or on behalf of the State, except

(1) to supply casual deficiencies of revenue, not to exceed in the aggregate at any one time two hundred thousand dollars;

(2) to repel invasion, suppress insurrection, or defend the State in war;

(3) as otherwise authorized by this constitution; or

(4) as authorized by Subsections (b) through (f) of this section.

(b) The legislature, by joint resolution approved by at least two-thirds of the members of each house, may from time to time call an election and submit to the eligible voters of this State one or more propositions that, if approved by a majority of those voting on the question, authorize the legislature to create State debt for the purposes and subject to the limitations stated in the applicable proposition. Each election and proposition must conform to the requirements of Subsections (c) and (d) of this section.

(c) The legislature may call an election during any regular session of the legislature or during any special session of the legislature in which the subject of the election is designated in the governor's proclamation for that special session. The election may be held on any date, and notice of the election shall be given for the period and in the manner required for amending this constitution. The election shall be held in each county in the manner provided by law for other statewide elections.

(d) A proposition must clearly describe the amount and purpose for which debt is to be created and must describe the source of payment for the debt. Except as provided by law under Subsection (f) of this section, the amount of debt stated in the proposition may not be exceeded and may not be renewed after the debt has been created unless the right to exceed or renew is stated in the proposition.

(e) The legislature may enact all laws necessary or appropriate to implement the authority granted by a proposition that is approved as provided by Subsection (b) of this section. A law enacted in anticipation of the election is valid if, by its terms, it is subject to the approval of the related proposition.

(f) State debt that is created or issued as provided by Subsection (b) of this section may be refunded in the manner and amount and subject to the conditions provided by law.

(g) State debt that is created or issued as provided by Subsections (b) through (f) of this section and that is approved by the attorney general in accordance with applicable law is incontestable for any reason.

[Note — Article III, Section 49 was amended to authorize the Legislature to submit debt questions to the voters in proposition form. Submitted by 72nd Legislature (1991) and adopted in election Nov. 5, 1991.]

Article III (Cont'd.)

Sec. 49-a. **Limiting Appropriations to Anticipated Revenue; Comptroller's Certification Required; Issuance of Certain General Revenue Bonds Authorized** — It shall be the duty of the Comptroller of Public Accounts in advance of each regular session of the Legislature to prepare and submit to the Governor and to the Legislature upon its convening a statement under oath showing fully the financial condition of the State Treasury at the close of the last fiscal period and an estimate of the probable receipts and disbursements for the then current fiscal year. There shall also be contained in said statement an itemized estimate of the anticipated revenue based on the laws then in effect that will be received by and for the State from all sources showing the fund accounts to be credited during the succeeding biennium and said statement shall contain such other information as may be required by law. Supplemental statements shall be submitted at any special session of the Legislature and at such other times as may be necessary to show probable changes.

From and after Jan. 1, 1945, save in the case of emergency and imperative public necessity and with a four-fifths vote of the total membership of each house, no appropriation in excess of the cash and anticipated revenue of the funds from which such appropriation is to be made shall be valid. From and after Jan. 1, 1945, no bill containing an appropriation shall be considered as passed or be sent to the Governor for consideration until and unless the Comptroller of Public Accounts endorses his certificate thereon showing that the amount appropriated is within the amount estimated to be available in the affected funds. When the Comptroller finds an appropriation bill exceeds the estimated revenue he shall endorse such finding thereon and return to the house in which same originated. Such information shall be immediately made known to both the House of Representatives and the Senate, and the necessary steps shall be taken to bring such appropriation to within the revenue, either by providing additional revenue or reducing the appropriation.

For the purpose of financing the outstanding obligations of the general revenue fund of the State and placing its current accounts on a cash basis the Legislature of the State of Texas is hereby authorized to provide for the issuance, sale and retirement of serial bonds equal in principal to the total outstanding, valid and approved obligations owing by said fund on Sept. 1, 1943, provided such bonds shall not draw interest in excess of 2 per cent per annum and shall mature within twenty years from date.

[Note — Sec. 49-a of Art. III was added to provide for Comptroller's estimates of receipts and disbursements and limit legislative appropriations. Submitted by 47th Legislature (1941) and adopted in election Nov. 3, 1942.]

Sec. 49-b. **Veterans' Land Board: Bonds Authorized for Creation of Veterans' Land Fund; Purchase of Land by State and Sales to Veterans** — By virtue of prior amendments to this Constitution, there has been created a governmental agency of the State of Texas performing governmental duties which has been designated the Veterans' Land Board. Said Board shall continue to function for the purposes specified in all of the prior Constitutional Amendments except as modified herein. Said Board shall be composed of the Commissioner of the General Land Office and two (2) citizens of the State of Texas, one (1) of whom shall be well versed in veterans' affairs and one (1) of whom shall be well versed in finances. One (1) such citizen member shall, with the advice and consent of the Senate, be appointed biennially by the Governor to serve for a term of four (4) years. In the event of the resignation or death of any such citizen member, the Governor shall appoint a replacement to serve for the unexpired portion of the term to which the deceased or resigning member had been appointed. The compensation for said citizen members shall be as is now or may hereafter be fixed by the Legislature; and each shall make bond in such amount as is now or may hereafter be prescribed by the Legislature.

The Commissioner of the General Land Office shall act as Chairman of said Board and shall be the administrator of the Veterans' Land Program under such terms and restrictions as are now or may hereafter be provided by law. In the absence or illness of said Commissioner, the Chief Clerk of the General Land Office shall be the Acting Chairman of said Board with the same duties and powers that said Commissioner would have if present.

The Veterans' Land Board may provide for, issue and sell not to exceed Nine Hundred and Fifty Million Dollars ($950,000,000) in bonds or obligations of the State of Texas for the purpose of creating a fund to be known as the Veterans' Land Fund, Seven Hundred Million Dollars ($700,000,000) of which have heretofore been authorized. Such bonds or obligations shall be sold for not less than par value and accrued interest; shall be issued in such forms, denominations, and upon such terms as are now or may hereafter be provided by law; shall be issued and sold at such times, at such places, and in such installments as may be determined by said Board; and shall bear a rate or rates of interest as may be fixed by said Board but the weighted average annual interest rate, as that phrase is commonly and ordinarily used and understood in the municipal bond market, of all the bonds issued and sold in any installment of any bonds may not exceed the rate specified in Section 65 of this Article. All bonds or obligations issued and sold hereunder shall, after execution by the Board, approval by the Attorney General of Texas, registration by the Comptroller of Public Accounts of the State of Texas, and delivery to the purchaser or purchasers, be incontestable and shall constitute general obligations of the State of Texas under the Constitution of Texas; and all bonds heretofore issued and sold by said Board are hereby in all respects validated and declared to be general obligations of the State of Texas. In order to prevent default in the payment of principal or interest on any such bonds, the Legislature shall appropriate a sufficient amount to pay the same.

In the sale of any such bonds or obligations, a preferential right of purchase shall be given to the administrators of the various Teacher Retirement Funds, the Permanent University Funds, and the Permanent School Funds.

Said Veterans' Land Fund shall consist of any lands heretofore or hereafter purchased by said Board, until the sale price therefor, together with any interest and penalties due, have been received by said Board (although nothing herein shall be construed to prevent said Board from accepting full payment for a portion of any tract), and of the moneys attributable to any bonds heretofore or hereafter issued and sold by said Board which moneys so attributable shall include but shall not be limited to the proceeds from the issuance and sale of such bonds; the moneys received from the sale or resale of any lands, or rights therein, purchased with such proceeds; the moneys received from the sale or resale of any lands, or rights therein, purchased with other moneys attributable to such bonds; the interest and penalties received from the sale or resale of such lands, or rights therein; the bonuses, income, rents, royalties, and any other pecuniary benefit received by said Board from any such lands; sums received by way of indemnity or forfeiture for the failure of any bidder for the purchase of any such bonds to comply with his bid and accept and pay for such bonds or for the failure of any bidder for the purchase of any lands comprising a part of said Fund to comply with his bid and accept and pay for any such lands; and interest received from investments of any such moneys. The principal and interest on the bonds heretofore and hereafter issued by said Board shall be paid out of the moneys of said Fund in comformance with the Constitutional provisions authorizing such bonds; but the moneys of said Fund which are not immediately committed to the payment of principal and interest on such bonds, the purchase of lands as herein provided, or the payment of expenses as herein provided may be invested as authorized by law until such moneys are needed for such purposes.

All moneys comprising a part of said Fund and not expended for the purposes herein provided shall be a part of said Fund until there are sufficient moneys therein to retire fully all of the bonds heretofore or hereafter issued and sold by said Board, at which time all such moneys remaining in said Fund, except such portion thereof as may be necessary to retire all such bonds which portion shall be set aside and retained in said Fund for the purpose of retiring all such bonds, shall be deposited to the credit of the General Revenue Fund to be appropriated to such purposes as may be prescribed by law. All moneys becoming a part of said Fund thereafter shall likewise be deposited to the credit of the General Revenue Fund.

When a Division of said Fund (each Division consisting of the moneys attributable to the bonds issued and sold pursuant to a single Constitutional authorization and the lands purchased therewith) contains sufficient moneys to retire all of the bonds secured by such Division, the moneys thereof, except such portion as may be needed to retire all of the bonds secured by such Division which portion shall be set aside and remain a part of such Division for the purpose of retiring all such bonds, may be used for the purpose of paying the principal and the interest thereon, together with the expenses herein authorized, of any other bonds heretofore or hereafter issued and sold by said Board. Such use shall be a matter for the discretion and direction of said Board; but there may be no such use of any such moneys contrary to the rights of any holder of any of the bonds issued and sold by said Board or violative of any contract to which said Board is a party.

The Veterans' Land Fund shall be used by said Board for the purpose of purchasing lands situated in the State of Texas owned by the United States or any governmental agency thereof, owned by the Texas Prison System or any other government

Article III (Cont'd.)

tal agency of the State of Texas, or owned by any person, firm, or corporation. All lands thus purchased shall be acquired at the lowest price obtainable, to be paid for in cash, and shall be a part of such Fund. Such lands heretofore or hereafter purchased and comprising a part of said Fund are hereby declared to be held for a governmental purpose, although the individual purchasers thereof shall be subject to taxation to the same extent and in the same manner as are purchasers of lands dedicated to the Permanent Free Public School Fund.

The lands of the Veterans' Land Fund shall be sold by said Board in such quantities, on such terms, at such prices, at such rates of interest and under such rules and regulations as are now or may hereafter be provided by law to veterans as they are now or may hereafter be defined by the laws of the State of Texas. The foregoing notwithstanding, any lands in the Veterans' Land Fund which have been first offered for sale to veterans and which have not been sold may be sold or resold to such purchasers, in such quantities, and on such terms, and at such prices and rates of interest, and under such rules and regulations as are now or may hereafter be provided by law.

Said Veterans' Land Fund, to the extent of the moneys attributable to any bonds hereafter issued and sold by said Board may be used by said Board, as is now or may hereafter be provided by law, for the purpose of paying the expenses of surveying, monumenting, road construction, legal fees, recordation fees, advertising and other like costs necessary or incidental to the purchase and sale, or resale, of any lands purchased with any of the moneys attributable to such additional bonds, such expenses to be added to the price of such lands when sold, or resold, by said Board; for the purpose of paying the expenses of issuing, selling, and delivering any such additional bonds; and for the purpose of meeting the expenses of paying the interest or principal due or to become due on any such additional bonds.

All of the moneys attributable to any series of bonds hereafter issued and sold by said Board (a "series of bonds" being all of the bonds issued and sold in a single transaction as a single installment of bonds) may be used for the purchase of lands as herein provided, to be sold as herein provided, for a period ending eight (8) years after the date of sale of such series of bonds; provided, however, that so much of such moneys as may be necessary to pay interest on bonds hereafter issued and sold shall be set aside for that purpose in accordance with the resolution adopted by said Board authorizing the issuance and sale of such series of bonds. After such eight (8) year period, all of such moneys shall be set aside for the retirement of any bonds hereafter issued and sold and to pay interest thereon, together with any expenses as provided herein, in accordance with the resolution or resolutions authorizing the issuance and sale of such additional bonds, until there are sufficient moneys to retire all of the bonds hereafter issued and sold, at which time all such moneys then remaining a part of said Veterans' Land Fund and thereafter becoming a part of said Fund shall be governed as elsewhere provided herein.

This Amendment being intended only to establish a basic framework and not to be a comprehensive treatment of the Veterans' Land Program, there is hereby reposed in the Legislature full power to implement and effectuate the design and objects of this Amendment, including the power to delegate such duties, responsibilities, functions, and authority to the Veterans' Land Board as it believes necessary.

Should the Legislature enact any enabling laws in anticipation of this Amendment, no such law shall be void by reason of its anticipatory nature.

[Note — Sec. 49-b of Art. III has been amended 11 times: (1) To aid war veterans in land purchases. Submitted by 49th Legislature (1945), and ratified in a special election Nov. 7, 1946. (By error, the date was set as Nov. 7 instead of Nov. 5, which was the general election date.) (2) To increase the authorized bond issue from $25,000,000 to $100,000,000 and to make minor changes. Submitted by 52nd Legislature (1951), and ratified in election Nov. 13, 1951. (3) To change membership of the Veterans' Land Board and to raise the total of bonds authorized to $200 million. Submitted by 54th Legislature (1955) and adopted in election Nov. 6, 1956. (4) To fix the rate of interest not to exceed 3 1/2 percent per annum. Submitted by 56th Legislature (1959) and adopted in election Nov. 8, 1960. (5) To provide for offering land in the Veterans' Land Fund to non-veteran purchasers after land has first been offered to veterans. Submitted by 57th Legislature (1961) and adopted in election Nov. 6, 1962. (6) To extend Veterans' Land Program by authorizing sale of bonds to increase Veterans' Land Fund for purchasing land to be sold to Texas veterans who served between Sept. 16, 1940, and date of formal withdrawal of U.S. troops from Vietnam; and providing for additional $200 million in bonds for this program. Submitted by 60th Legislature (1967) and adopted in election Nov. 11, 1967. (7) To provide for additional $100 million in bonds for the Veterans' Land Fund and to make all veterans eligible to participate who served in armed forces after Sept. 16, 1940. Submitted by 63rd Legislature (1973) and adopted in election Nov. 6, 1973. (8) To provide for additional $200 million in bonds for the Veterans' Land Fund and to extend the right to apply to purchase land to unmarried surviving spouses of veterans who meet requirements set out herein. Submitted by 65th Legislature (1977) and adopted in election Nov. 8, 1977. (9) To raise to $950 million the amount of bonds authorized for the Veterans' Land Fund. Submitted by 67th Legislature (1981) and adopted in election Nov. 3, 1981. (10) To define an eligible veteran for purposes of this program. Submitted by 69th Legislature (1985) and adopted in election Nov. 5, 1985. (11) To authorize the Legislature to further clarify the administration of the veterans' housing assistance and land programs and to expand the investment authority of the Veterans' Land Board. Submitted by 72nd Legislature (1991) and adopted in election Nov. 5, 1991.]

Sec. 49-b-1. **Bonds Authorized to Finance Veterans' Land Program and Veterans' Housing Assistance Program** — (a) In addition to the general obligation bonds authorized to be issued and to be sold by the Veterans' Land Board by Sec. 49-b of this article, the Veterans' Land Board may provide for, issue, and sell not to exceed $1.3 billion in bonds of the State of Texas, $800 million of which have heretofore been authorized to provide financing to veterans of the state in recognition of their service to their state and country.

(b) For purposes of this section, "veteran" means a person who satisfies the definition of "veteran" as is now or may hereafter be set forth by the laws of the State of Texas.

(c) The bonds shall be sold for not less than par value and accrued interest; shall be issued in such forms and denominations, upon such terms, at such times and places, and in such installments as may be determined by the board; and, notwithstanding the rate of interest specified by any other provision of this Constitution, shall bear a rate or rates of interest fixed by the board. All bonds issued and sold pursuant to Subsections (a) through (f) of this section shall, after execution by the board, approval by the Attorney General of Texas, registration by the Comptroller of Public Accounts of the State of Texas, and delivery to the purchaser or purchasers, be incontestable and shall constitute general obligations of the state under the Constitution of Texas.

(d) Three hundred million dollars of the state bonds authorized by this section shall be used to augment the Veterans' Land Fund. The Veterans' Land Fund shall be used by the board for the purpose of purchasing lands situated in the State of Texas owned by the United States government or any agency thereof, the State of Texas or any subdivision or agency thereof, or any person, firm, or corporation. The lands shall be sold to veterans in such quantities, on such terms, at such prices, at such rates of interest, and under such rules and regulations as may be authorized by law. The expenses of the board in connection with the issuance of the bonds and the purchase and sale of the lands may be paid from money in the fund. The Veterans' Land Fund shall continue to consist of any lands purchased by the board until the sale price therefor, together with any interest and penalties due, have been received by the board (although nothing herein shall prevent the board from accepting full payment for a portion of any tract) and of the money attributable to any bonds issued and sold by the board for the Veterans' Land Fund, which money so attributable shall include but shall not be limited to the proceeds from the issuance and sale of such bonds; the money received from the sale or resale of any lands, or rights therein, purchased from such proceeds; the money received from the sale or resale of any lands, or rights therein, purchased with other money attributable to such bonds; the interest and penalties received from the sale or resale of such lands, or rights therein; the bonuses, income, rents, royalties, and any other pecuniary benefit received by the board from any such lands; sums received by way of indemnity or forfeiture for the failure of any bidder for the purchase of any such bonds to comply with his bid and accept and pay for such bonds or for the failure of any bidder for the purchase of any lands comprising a part of the fund to comply with his bid and accept and pay for any such lands; and interest received from investments of any such money. The principal of and interest on the general obligation bonds previously authorized by Sec. 49-b of this constitution shall be paid out of the money of the fund in conformance with the constitutional provisions authorizing such bonds. The principal of and interest on the general obligation bonds authorized by this section for the benefit of the Veterans' Land Fund shall be paid out of the money of the fund, but the money of the fund which is not immediately committed to the payment of principal and interest on such bonds, the purchase of lands as herein provided, or the payment of expenses as herein provided may be invested as authorized by law until the money is needed for

Article III (Cont'd.)

such purposes.

(e) The Veterans' Housing Assistance Fund is created, and $1 billion of the state bonds authorized by this section shall be used for the Veterans' Housing Assistance Fund, $500 million of which have heretofore been authorized. Money in the Veterans' Housing Assistance Fund shall be administered by the Veterans' Land Board and shall be used for the purpose of making home mortgage loans to veterans for housing within the State of Texas in such quantities, on such terms, at such rates of interest, and under such rules and regulations as may be authorized by law. The expenses of the board in connection with the issuance of the bonds and the making of the loans may be paid from money in the fund. The Veterans' Housing Assistance Fund shall consist of any interest of the board in all home mortgage loans made to veterans by the board pursuant to a Veterans' Housing Assistance Program which the legislature may establish by appropriate legislation until, with respect to any such home mortgage loan, the principal amount, together with any interest and penalties due, have been received by the board; the money attributable to any bonds issued and sold by theboard to provide money for the fund, which money so attributable shall include but shall not be limited to the proceeds from the issuance and sale of such bonds; income, rents, and any other pecuniary benefit received by the board as a result of making such loans; sums received by way of indemnity or forfeiture for the failure of any bidder for the purchase of any such bonds to comply with his bid and accept and pay for such bonds; and interest received from investments of any such money. The principal of and interest on the general obligation bonds authorized by this section for the benefit of the Veterans' Housing Assistance Fund shall be paid out of the money of the fund, but the money of the fund which is not immediately committed to the payment of principal and interest on such bonds, the making of home mortgage loans as herein provided, or the payment of expenses as herein provided may be invested as authorized by law until the money is needed for such purposes.

(f) To the extent there is not money in either the Veterans' Land Fund or the Veterans' Housing Assistance Fund, as the case may be, available for payment of principal of and interest on the general obligation bonds authorized by this section to provide money for either of the funds, there is hereby appropriated out of the first money coming into the treasury in each fiscal year, not otherwise appropriated by this Constitution, an amount which is sufficient to pay the principal of and interest on such general obligation bonds that mature or become due during that fiscal year.

(g) Receipt of all kinds of the funds determined by the board not to be required for the payment of principal of and interest on the general obligation bonds herein authorized, heretofore authorized, or hereafter authorized by this Constitution to be issued by the board to provide money for either of the funds may be used by the board, to the extent not inconsistent with the proceedings authorizing such bonds, to pay the principal of and interest on general obligation bonds issued to provide money for the other fund, or to pay the principal of and interest on revenue bonds of the board issued for the purposes of providing funds for the purchasing of lands and making the sale thereof to veterans or making home mortgage loans to veterans as provided by this section. The revenue bonds shall be special obligations and payable only from the receipt of the funds and shall not constitute indebtedness of the state or the Veterans' Land Board. The board is authorized to issue such revenue bonds from time to time which shall not exceed an aggregate principal amount that can be fully retired from the receipts of the funds and other revenues pledged to the retirement of the revenue bonds. The revenue bonds shall be issued in such forms and denominations, upon such terms, at such times and places, and in such installments as may be determined by the board; and, notwithstanding the rate of interest specified by any other provision of the Constitution, shall bear a rate or rates of interest fixed by the board.

(h) This Amendment being intended only to establish a basic framework and not to be a comprehensive treatment of the Veterans' Housing Assistance Program and the Veterans' Land Program, there is hereby reposed in the Legislature full power to implement and effectuate the design and objects of this Amendment, including the power to delegate such duties, responsibilities, functions, and authority to the Veterans' Land Board as it believes necessary.

[Note — Sec. 49-b-1 of Art. III was added to provide financial assistance to veterans and to authorize issuance of bonds to finance the Veterans' Land Program and the Veterans' Housing Assistance Program. Submitted by 68th Legislature (1983) and adopted in election Nov. 8, 1983. It was amended to provide $500 million additional bonding authority for the veterans' housing assistance program and changing definition of veterans eligible to participate in veterans' land and housing assistance programs. Submitted by 69th Legislature (1985) and adopted in election Nov. 5, 1985. Subsections (d) and (e) were amended and Subsection (h) was added to further clarify the administration of the veterans' housing assistance and land programs. Submitted by 72nd Legislature (1991) and adopted in election Nov. 5, 1991.]

Sec. 49-b-2. (a) In addition to the general obligation bonds authorized to be issued and to be sold by the Veterans' Land Board by Sections 49-b and 49-b-1 of this article, the Veterans' Land Board may provide for, issue, and sell general obligation bonds of the state in an amount not to exceed $750 million, to provide financing to veterans of the state in recognition of their service to their state and the United States of America.

(b) Two hundred fifty million dollars of the general obligation bonds authorized by this section shall be used to augment the Veterans' Land Fund. Notwithstanding any provision of Section 49-b or 49-b-1 of this article to the contrary, the Veterans' Land Fund shall be used by the Veterans' Land Board to purchase lands situated in the state owned by the United States government, an agency of the United States government, this state, a political subdivision or agency of this state, or a person, firm, or corporation. Lands purchased and comprising a part of the Veterans' Land Fund are declared to be held for a governmental purpose, but the individual purchasers of those lands shall be subject to taxation to the same extent and in the same manner as are purchasers of lands dedicated to the Permanent Free Public School Fund. The lands shall be sold to veterans in quantities, on terms, at prices, and at fixed, variable, floating, or other rates of interest, determined by the Board and in accordance with rules of the Board. Notwithstanding any provisions of this section to the contrary, lands in the Veterans' Land Fund that are offered for sale to veterans and that are not sold may be sold or resold to the purchasers in quantities, on terms, at prices, and at rates of interest determined by the Board and in accordance with rules of the Board. The expenses of the Board in connection with the issuance of the bonds and the purchase and sale of the lands may be paid from money in the Veterans' Land Fund.

(c) The Veterans' Land Fund shall consist of:

(1) lands heretofore or hereafter purchased by the Board;

(2) money attributable to bonds heretofore or hereafter issued and sold by the Board for the fund, including proceeds from the issuance and sale of the bonds;

(3) money received from the sale or resale of lands or rights in lands purchased from those proceeds;

(4) money received from the sale or resale of lands or rights in lands purchased with other money attributable to the bonds;

(5) proceeds derived from the sale or other disposition of the Board's interest in contracts for the sale or resale of lands or rights in lands;

(6) interest and penalties received from the sale or resale of lands or rights in lands;

(7) bonuses, income, rents, royalties, and other pecuniary benefits received by the Board from lands;

(8) money received by way of indemnity or forteiture for the failure of a bidder for the purchase of bonds to comply with the bid and accept and pay for the bonds or for the failure of a bidder for the purchase of lands comprising a part of the Veterans' Land Fund to comply with the bid and accept and pay for the lands;

(9) payments received by the Board under a bond enhancement agreement with respect to the bonds; and

(10) interest received from investments of money in the fund.

(d) The principal of and interest on the general obligation bonds authorized by this section for the benefit of the Veterans' Land Fund, including payments by the Board under a bond enhancement agreement with respect to principal of or interest on the bonds, shall be paid out of the money of the Veterans' Land Fund, but the money in the fund that is not immediately committed to the payment of principal and interest on the bonds, the purchase of lands, or the payment of expenses may be invested as authorized by law until the money is needed for those purposes.

(e) The Veterans' Housing Assistance Fund II is created, and $500 million of the general obligation bonds authorized by this section shall be used for the Veterans' Housing Assistance Fund II. The Veterans' Housing Assistance Fund II is a separate and distinct fund from the Veterans' Housing Assistance Fund established under Section 49-b-1 of this article. Money in the Veterans' Housing Assistance Fund II shall be administered by the Veterans' Land Board and shall be used to make home mortgage loans to veterans for housing within this state in quantities, on terms, and at fixed, variable, floating, or other rates of interest, determined by the Board and in accordance with rules of the Board. The expenses of the Board in connection with the issu-

Article III (Cont'd.)

ance of the bonds and the making of the loans may be paid from money in the Veterans' Housing Assistance Fund II.

(f) The Veterans' Housing Assistance Fund II shall consist of

(1) the Board's interest in home mortgage loans the Board makes to veterans from money in the fund under the Veterans' Housing Assistance Program established by law;

(2) proceeds derived from the sale or other disposition of the Board's interest in home mortgage loans.

(3) money attributable to bonds issued and sold by the Board to provide money for the fund, including the proceeds from the issuance and sale of bonds;

(4) income, rents, and other pecuniary benefits received by the Board as a result of making loans;

(5) money received by way of indemnity or forfeiture for the failure of a bidder for the purchase of bonds to comply with the bid and accept and pay for the bonds;

(6) payments received by the Board under a bond enhancement agreement with respect to the bonds; and

(7) interest received from investments of money.

(g) The principal of and interest on the general obligation bonds authorized by this section for the benefit of the Veterans' Housing Assistance Fund II, including payments by the Board under a bond enhancement agreement with respect to principal of or interest on the bonds, shall be paid out of the money of the Vegterans' Housing Assistance Fund II, but the money in the fund that is not immediately committed to the payment of principal and interest on the bonds, the making of home mortgage loans, or the payment of expenses may be invested as authorized by law until the money is needed for those purposes.

(h) Notwithstanding the provisions of Section 49-b-1 of this article to the contrary, the Veterans' Housing Assistance Fund shall consist of:

(1) the Board's interest in home mortgage loans the Board makes to veterans from the money in the fund under the Veterans' Housing Assistance Program established by law;

(2) proceeds derived from the sale or other disposition of the Board's interest in home mortgage loans;

(3) money attributable to bonds issued and sold by the Board to provide money for the fund, including proceeds from the issuance and sale of bonds;

(4) income, rents, and other pecuniary benefits received by the Board as a result of making loans;

(5) money received by way of indemnity or forfeiture for the failure of a bidder for the purchase of bonds to comply with the bid and accept and pay for the bonds;

(6) payments received by the Board under a bond enhancement agreement with respect to the bonds; and

(7) interest received from investments of money.

(i) The principal of and interest on the general obligation bonds authorized by Section 49-b-1 of this article for the benefit of the Veterans' Housing Assistance Fund, including payments by the Board under a bond enhancement agreement with respect to principal of or interest on the bonds, shall be paid out of money in the Veterans' Housing Assistance Fund.

(j) If there is not enough money in the Veterans' Land Fund, the Veterans' Housing Assistance Fund, or the Veterans' Housing Assistance Fund II, as the case may be, available to pay the principal of and interest on the general obligation bonds authorized by this section or by Section 49-b or 49-b-1 of this article, including money to make payments by the Board under a bond enhancement agreement with respect to principal of or interest on the bonds, there is appropriated out of the first money coming into the treasury in each fiscal year, not otherwise appropriated by this constitution, an amount that is sufficient to pay the principal of and interest on the general obligation bonds that mature or become due during that fiscal year or to make bond enhancement payments with respect to those bonds.

(k) Notwithstanding any provisions of Section 49-b or 49-b-1 of this article to the contrary, receipts of all kinds of the Veterans' Land Fund, the Veterans' Housing Assistance Fund, or the Veterans' Housing Assistance Fund II that the Board determines are not required for the payment of principal of and interest on the general obligation bonds, including payments by the Board under a bond enhancement agreement with respect to principal of or interest on the bonds, authorized by this section or by Section 49-b or 49-b-1 or this article or otherwise authorized by this constitution to be issued by the Board to provide money for the fund, may be used by the Board, to the extent not inconsistent with the proceedings authorizing the bonds to:

(1) make temporary transfers to another of those funds to avoid a temporary cash deficiency in that fund or make a transfer to another of those funds for the purposes of that fund;

(2) pay the principal of and interest on general obligation bonds issued to provide money for another of those funds or make bond enhancement payments with respect to the bonds; or

(3) pay the principal of and interest on revenue bonds of the Board or make bond enhancement payments with respect to the bonds if the bonds are issued to provide funds to purchase lands and sell lands to veterans or make home mortgage loans to veterans.

(l) If the Board determines that assets from the Veterans' Land Fund, the Veterans' Housing Assistance Fund, or the Veterans' Housing Assistance Fund II are not required for the purposes of the fund, the Board may transfer the assets to another of those funds or use the assets to secure revenue bonds issued by the Board under this section.

(m) The revenue bonds shall be special obligations of the Board and payable only from and secured only by receipts of the funds, assets transferred from the funds, and other revenues and assets as determined by the Board and shall not constitute indebtedness of the state or the Veterans' Land Board. The Board may issue revenue bonds from time to time, which bonds may not exceed an aggregate principal amount that the Board determines can be fully retired from the receipts of the funds, the assets transferred from the funds, and other revenues and assets pledged to the retirement of the revenue bonds. The revenue bonds shall be issued and sold in forms and denominations, in the manner, on terms, at times and places, and in installments the Board determines. Notwithstanding the rate of interest specified by any other provision of this constitution, the revenue bonds shall bear a rate or rates of interest the Board determines. A determination made by the Board under this subsection shall be binding and conclusive as to the matter determined.

(n) Notwithstanding any provisions of Section 49-b or 49-b-1 of this article to the contrary, the bonds authorized to be issued and sold by the Veterans' Land Board by this section or by Sections 49-b and 49-b-1 of this article shall be issued and sold in forms and denominations, on terms, at times, in the manner, at places, and in installments the Board determines. The bonds shall bear a rate or rates of interest the Board determines. The bonds shall be incontestable after execution by the Board, approval by the Attorney General of Texas, and delivery to the purchaser or purchasers of the bonds.

(o) This Amendment being intended only to establish a basic framework and not to be a comprehensive treatment of the Veterans' Housing Assistance Program and the Veteran's Land Program, there is hereby reposed in the Legislature full power to implement and effectuate the design and objects of this Amendment, including the power to delegate such duties, responsibilities, functions, and authority to the Veteran's Land Board as it believes necessary.

(p) In this section, "veteran" has the meaning assigned by Section 49-b-1 of this article.

[Note — Sec. 49-b-2 of Art. III was added to authorize issuance of $750 million in general obligation bonds to augment the Veterans' Land Fund and Veterans' Housing Assistance Fund and to fund the Veterans' Housing Assistance Fund II. Submitted by 73rd Legislature (1993) and adopted in election Nov. 2, 1993]

Sec. 49-c. **Texas Water Development Board, Fund; Purpose** — There is hereby created as an agency of the State of Texas the Water Development Board to exercise such powers as necessary under this provision together with such other duties and restrictions as may be prescribed by law. The qualifications, compensation and number of members of said Board shall be determined by law. They shall be appointed by the Governor with the advice and consent of the Senate in the manner and for such terms as may be prescribed by law.

The Texas Water Development Board shall have the authority to provide for, issue and sell general obligation bonds of the State of Texas in an amount not to exceed One Hundred Million Dollars ($100,000,000). The Legislature of Texas, upon two-thirds (2/3) vote of the elected Members of each House, may authorize the Board to issue additional bonds in an amount not exceeding One Hundred Million Dollars ($100,000,000). The bonds authorized herein or permitted to be authorized by the Legislature shall be called "Texas Water Development Bonds," shall be executed in such form, denominations and upon such terms as may be prescribed by law, provided, however, that the bonds shall not bear more than four percent (4%) interest per annum; they may be issued in such installments as the Board finds feasible and practical in accomplishing the purpose set forth herein.

All moneys received from the sale of State bonds shall be deposited in a fund hereby created in the State Treasury to be known as the Texas Water Development Fund to be administered (without further appropriation) by the Texas Water Development Board in such manner as prescribed by law.

Such fund shall be used only for the purpose of aiding or mak-

Article III (Cont'd.)

ing funds available upon such terms and conditions as the Legislature may prescribe, to the various political subdivisions or bodies politic and corporate of the State of Texas including river authorities, conservation and reclamation districts and districts created or organized or authorized to be created or organized under Article XVI, Section 59 or Article III, Section 52, of this Constitution, interstate compact commissions to which the State of Texas is a party and municipal corporations, in the conservation and development of the water resources of this State, including the control, storing and preservation of its storm and flood waters and the waters of its rivers and streams, for all useful and lawful purposes by the acquisition, improvement, extension, or construction of dams, reservoirs and other water storage projects, including any system necessary for the transportation of water from storage to points of treatment and/or distribution, including facilities for transporting water therefrom to wholesale purchasers, or for any one or more of such purposes or methods.

Any or all financial assistance as provided herein shall be repaid with interest upon such terms, conditions and manner of repayment as may be provided by law.

While any of the bonds authorized by this provision or while any of the bonds that may be authorized by the Legislature under this provision, or any interest on any of such bonds, is outstanding and unpaid, there is hereby appropriated out of the first moneys coming into the Treasury in each fiscal year, not otherwise appropriated by this Constitution, an amount which is sufficient to pay the principal and interest on such bonds that mature or become due during such fiscal year, less the amount in the sinking fund at the close of the prior fiscal year.

The Legislature may provide for the investment of moneys available in the Texas Water Development Fund, and the interest and sinking funds established for the payment of bonds issued by the Texas Water Development Board. Income from such investment shall be used for the purposes prescribed by the Legislature. The Legislature may also make appropriations from the General Revenue Fund for paying administrative expenses of the Board.

From the moneys received by the Texas Water Development Board as repayment of principal for financial assistance or as interest thereon, there shall be deposited in the interest and sinking fund for the bonds authorized by this Section sufficient moneys to pay the interest and principal to become due during the ensuing year and sufficient to establish and maintain a reserve in said fund equal to the average annual principal and interest requirements on all outstanding bonds issued under this Section. If any year prior to December 31, 1982 moneys are received in excess of the foregoing requirements then such excess shall be deposited to the Texas Water Development Fund, and may be used for administrative expenses of the Board and for the same purposes and upon the same terms and conditions prescribed for the proceeds derived from the sale of such State bonds. No grant of financial assistance shall be made under the provisions of this Section after December 31, 1982, and all moneys thereafter received as repayment of principal for financial assistance or as interest thereon shall be deposited in the interest and sinking fund for the State bonds; except that such amount as may be required to meet the administrative expenses of the Board may be annually set aside; and provided, that after all State bonds have been fully paid with interest, or after there are on deposit in the interest and sinking fund sufficient moneys to pay all future maturities of principal and interest, additional moneys so received shall be deposited to the General Revenue Fund.

All bonds issued hereunder shall after approval by the Attorney General, registration by the Comptroller of Public Accounts of the State of Texas, and delivery to the purchasers, be incontestable and shall constitute general obligations of the State of Texas under the Constitution of Texas.

[Note — Sec. 49-c of Art. III was added to create the Texas Water Development Board and Fund and to provide for supervision thereof. Submitted by 55th Legislature (1957) and adopted in election Nov. 5, 1957.]

Sec. 49-d. **Development and Conservation of Public Waters** — It is hereby declared to be the policy of the State of Texas to encourage the optimum development of the limited number of feasible sites available for the construction or enlargement of dams and reservoirs for the conservation of the public waters of the state, which waters are held in trust for the use and benefit of the public, and to encourage the optimum regional development of systems built for the filtration, treatment, and transmission of water and wastewater. The proceeds from the sale of the additional bonds authorized hereunder deposited in the Texas Water Development Fund and the proceeds of bonds previously authorized by Art. III, Sec. 49-c of this Constitution, may be used by the Texas Water Development Board, under such provisions as the Legislature may prescribe by general law, including the requirement of a permit for storage or beneficial use, for the additional purposes of acquiring and developing storage facilities, and any system or works necessary for the filtration, treatment and transportation of water or wastewater, or for any one or more of such purposes or methods, whether or not such a system or works is connected with a reservoir in which the state has a financial interest; provided however, the Texas Water Development Fund or any other state fund provided for water development, transmission, transfer or filtration shall not be used to finance any project which contemplates or results in the removal from the basin of origin of any surface water necessary to supply the reasonably foreseeable future water requirements for the next ensuing fifty-year period within the river basin of origin, except on a temporary, interim basis.

Under such provisions as the Legislature may prescribe by general law the Texas Water Development Fund may be used for the conservation and development of water for useful purposes by construction or reconstruction or enlargement of reservoirs constructed or to be constructed or enlarged within the State of Texas or on any stream constituting a boundary of the State of Texas, together with any system or works necessary for the filtration, treatment and/or transportation of water, by any one or more of the following governmental agencies; by the United States of America or any agency, department or instrumentality thereof; by the State of Texas or any agency, department or instrumentality thereof; by political subdivisions or bodies politic and corporate of the state; by interstate compact commissions to which the State of Texas is a party; and by municipal corporations. The Legislature shall provide terms and conditions under which the Texas Water Development Board may sell, transfer or lease, in whole or in part, any reservoir and associated system or works which the Texas Water Development Board has financed in whole or in part.

Under such provisions as the Legislature may prescribe by general law, the Texas Water Development Board may also execute long-term contracts with the United States or any of its agencies for the acquisition and development of storage facilities in reservoirs constructed or to be constructed by the Federal Government. Such contracts when executed shall constitute general obligations of the State of Texas in the same manner and with the same effect as state bonds issued under the authority of the preceding Sec. 49-c of this Constitution, and the provisions in said Sec. 49-c with respect to payment of principal and interest on state bonds issued shall likewise apply with respect to payment of principal and interest required to be paid by such contracts. If storage facilities are acquired for a term of years, such contracts shall contain provisions for renewal that will protect the state's investment.

The aggregate of the bonds authorized hereunder shall not exceed $200,000,000 and shall be in addition to the aggregate of the bonds previously authorized by said Sec. 49-c of Art. III of this Constitution. The Legislature upon two-thirds (2/3) vote of the elected members of each House, may authorize the board to issue all or any portion of such $200,000,000 in additional bonds herein authorized.

The Legislature shall provide terms and conditions for the Texas Water Development Board to sell, transfer or lease, in whole or in part, any acquired facilities or the right to use such facilities at a price not less than the direct cost of the board in acquiring same; and the Legislature may provide terms and conditions for the board to sell any unappropriated public waters of the state that might be stored in such facilities. As a prerequisite to the purchase of such storage or water, the applicant therefor shall have secured a valid permit from the Texas Water Commission or its successor authorizing the acquisition of such storage facilities or the water impounded therein. The money received from any sale, transfer or lease of facilities shall be used to pay principal and interest on state bonds issued or contractual obligations incurred by the Texas Water Development Board, provided that when moneys are sufficient to pay the full amount of indebtedness then outstanding and the full amount of interest to accrue thereon, any further sums received from the sale, transfer or lease of such facilities shall be deposited and used as provided by law. Money received from the sale of water, which shall include standby service, may be used for the operation and maintenance of acquired facilities, and for the payment of principal and interest on debt incurred.

Should the Legislature enact enabling laws in anticipation of the adoption of this amendment, such acts shall not be void by reason of their anticipatory character.

[Note — Sec. 49-d of Art. III was added to authorize the Texas Water Development Board to acquire and develop storage facilities in reservoirs and to dispose of such storage facilities and

Article III (Cont'd.)
water upon such terms as Legislature shall prescribe. Submitted by 57th Legislature (1961) and adopted in election Nov. 6, 1962. It was further amended to provide for optimum development of water reservoirs and investment of the Texas Water Development Fund. Submitted by 59th Legislature (1965) and adopted in election Nov. 8, 1966. It was again amended to encourage optimum regional development of systems built for filtration, treatment and transmission of water and wastewater. Submitted by 69th Legislature (1985) and adopted in election Nov. 5, 1985.]

Sec. 49-d-1. **Water Development Bonds** — (a) The Texas Water Development Board shall upon direction of the Texas Water Quality Board, or any successor agency designated by the Legislature, issue additional Texas Water Development Bonds up to an additional aggregate principal amount of Two Hundred Million Dollars ($200,000,000) to provide grants, loans, or any combination of grants and loans for water quality enhancement purposes as established by the Legislature. The Texas Water Quality Board or any successor agency designated by the Legislature may make such grants and loans to political subdivisions or bodies politic and corporate of the State of Texas, including municipal corporations, river authorities, conservation and reclamation districts, and districts created or organized or authorized to be created or organized under Art. XVI, Sec. 59, or Art. III, Sec. 52, of this Constitution, State agencies, and interstate agencies and compact commissions to which the State of Texas is a party, and upon such terms and conditions as the Legislature may authorize by general law. The bonds shall be issued for such terms, in such denominations, form and installments, and upon such conditions as the Legislature may authorize.

(b) The proceeds from the sale of such bonds shall be deposited in the Texas Water Development Fund to be invested and administered as prescribed by law.

(c) The bonds authorized in this Sec. 49-d-1 and all bonds authorized by Sections 49-c and 49-d of Art. III shall bear interest at not more than 6 percent per annum and mature as the Texas Water Development Board shall prescribe, subject to the limitations as may be imposed by the Legislature.

(d) The Texas Water Development Fund shall be used for the purposes heretofore permitted by, and subject to the limitations in Sections 49-c, 49-d and 49-d-1; provided, however, that the financial assistance may be made pursuant to the provisions of Sections 49-c, 49-d and 49-d-1 subject only to the availability of funds and without regard to the provisions in Sec. 49-c that such financial assistance shall terminate after Dec. 31, 1982.

(e) Texas Water Development Bonds are secured by the general credit of the State and shall after approval by the Attorney General, registration by the Comptroller of Public Accounts of the State of Texas, and delivery to the purchasers, be incontestable and shall constitute general obligations of the State of Texas under the Constitution of Texas.

(f) Should the Legislature enact enabling laws in anticipation of the adoption of this amendment, such acts shall not be void by reason of their anticipatory character.

[Note — Sec. 49-d-1 was added to provide for an additional $100 million for grants and loans for water improvement; also to raise the interest rate on water bonds to 6 percent. Submitted by 62nd Legislature (1971) and adopted in election May 18, 1971. It was amended to increase to $200 million the amount available for water quality enhancement. Submitted by 64th Legislature (1975) and adopted in election Nov. 2, 1976.]

Sec. 49-d-2. (a) The Texas Water Development Board may issue additional Texas Water Development Bonds up to an additional aggregate principal amount of $980 million. Of the additional bonds authorized to be issued, $590 million of those bonds are dedicated for use for the purposes provided by Sec. 49-c and Sec. 49-d of this article with $400 million of those bonds to be used for state participation in the acquisition and development of facilities for the storage, transmission, transportation, and treatment of water and wastewater as authorized by Sec. 49-d of this article. The Legislature may set limits on the extent of state participation in projects in each fiscal year through the General Appropriations Act or other law, and state participation is limited to 50 percent of the funding for any single project. Of the additional bonds authorized, $190 million are dedicated for use for the purposes provided by Sec. 49-d-1 of this article and $200 million are dedicated exclusively for flood control projects and may be made available for any acquisition or construction necessary to achieve structural and nonstructural flood control purposes.

(b) The Texas Water Development Board shall issue the additional bonds authorized by this section for the terms, in the denominations, form, and installments, on the conditions, and subject to the limitations provided by Sec. 49-c, Sec. 49-d, and Sec. 49-d-1 of this article and by laws adopted by the Legislature implementing those sections.

(c) Proceeds from the sale of the bonds authorized by this section shall be deposited in the Texas water development fund to be administered and invested as provided by law.

(d) Financial assistance made available for the purposes provided by this section is subject only to availability of funds. The requirement of Sec. 49-c of this article that financial assistance terminate on Dec. 31, 1982, does not apply to financial assistance made available under this section.

(e) Bonds issued under this section shall bear interest as provided by Sec. 65 of this article.

[Note — Sec. 49-d-2 Art. III was added to authorize issuance of an additional $980 million of Texas Water Development Bonds. Submitted by 69th Legislature (1985) and adopted in election Nov. 5, 1985.]

Sec. 49-d-3. (a) The Legislature by law may create one or more special funds in the state treasury for use for or in aid of water conservation, water development, water quality enhancement, flood control, drainage, subsidence control, recharge, chloride control, agricultural soil and water conservation, desalinization or any combination of those purposes, may make money in a special fund available to cities, counties, special governmental districts and authorities, and other political subdivisions of the state for use for the purposes for which the fund was created by grants, loans, or any other means, and may appropriate money to any of the special funds to carry out the purposes of this section.

(b) Money deposited in a special fund created under this section may not be used to finance or aid any project that contemplates or results in the removal from the basin of origin of any surface water necessary to supply the reasonably foreseeable water requirements for the next ensuing 50-year period within the river basin of origin, except on a temporary, interim basis.

[Note — Sec. 49-d-3 of Art. III was added to create special funds for water conservation, development, quality enhancement, flood control, drainage, subsidence control, recharge, chloride control, agricultural soil and water conservation and desalinization of water. Submitted by 69th Legislature (1985) and adopted in election Nov. 5, 1985.]

Sec. 49-d-4. (a) In addition to other programs authorized by this constitution, the Legislature by law may provide for the creation, administration, and implementation of a bond insurance program to which the state pledges its general credit in an amount not to exceed $250 million to insure the payment in whole or in part of the principal of and interest on bonds or other obligations that are issued by cities, counties, special governmental districts and authorities, and other political subdivisions of the state as defined by law for use for or in aid of water conservation, water development, water quality enhancement, flood control, drainage, recharge, chloride control, desalinization, or any combination of those purposes.

(b) The Legislature by law shall designate the state agency to administer the bond insurance program and may authorize that agency to execute insurance contracts that bind the state to pay the principal of and interest on the bonds if the bonds are in default or the bonds are subject to impending default, subject to the limits provided by this section and by law.

(c) The payment by the state of any insurance commitment made under this section must be made from the first money coming into the state treasury that is not otherwise dedicated by this constitution.

(d) Notwithstanding the total amount of bonds insured under this section, the total amount paid and not recovered by the state under this section, excluding the costs of administration, may not exceed $250 million.

(e) Except on a two-thirds vote of the members elected to each house of the Legislature, the ratio of bonds insured to the total liability of the state must be two to one.

(f) Except on a two-thirds vote of the members elected to each house of the Legislature, the state agency administering the bond insurance program may not authorize bond insurance coverage under the program in any state fiscal year that exceeds a total of $100 million.

(g) Unless authorized to continue by a two-thirds vote of the members elected to each house, this section and the bond insurance program authorized by this section expire on the sixth anniversary of the date on which this section becomes a part of the constitution. However, bond insurance issued before the expiration of this section and the program is not affected by the expiration of this section and the program and remains in effect according to its terms, and the state is required to fulfill all of the terms of that previously issued insurance.

Article III (Cont'd.).

[Note — Sec. 49-d-4 of Art. III was added to authorize a bond insurance program. Submitted by 69th Legislature (1985) and adopted in election Nov. 5, 1985.]

Sec. 49-d-5. For the purpose of any program established or authorized by Sec. 49-c, Sec. 49-d, Sec. 49-d-1, Sec. 49-d-2, or Sec. 49-d-4 of this article, the Legislature by law may extend any benefits to nonprofit water supply corporations that it may extend to a district created or organized under Art. XVI, Sec. 59, of this constitution.

[Note — Sec. 49-d-5 of Art. III was added to clarify the purpose for which Texas Water Development Bonds may be issued. Submitted by 69th Legislature (1985) and adopted in election Nov. 5, 1985.]

Sec. 49-d-6. (a) The Texas Water Development Board may issue additional Texas Water Development Bonds up to an additional aggregate principal amount of $400 million. Of the additional bonds authorized to be issued, $200 million of those bonds shall be used for purposes provided by Section 49-c of this article, $150 million of those bonds shall be used for purposes provided by Section 49-d-1 of this article, and $50 million of those bonds shall be used for flood control as provided by law.

(b) The legislature may require review and approval of the issuance of the bonds, of the use of the bond proceeds, or of the rules adopted by an agency to govern use of the bond proceeds. Notwithstanding any other provision of this constitution, any entity created or directed to conduct this review and approval may include members or appointees of members of the executive, legislative, and judicial departments of state government.

(c) The Texas Water Development Board shall issue the additional bonds authorized by this section for the terms, in the denominations, form, and installments, on the conditions, and subject to the limitations provided by Sections 49-c and 49-d-1 of this article and by laws adopted by the legislature implementing this section.

(d) Subsections (c) through (e) of Section 49-d-2 of this article apply to the bonds authorized by this section.

[Note — Sec. 49-d-6 of Art. III was added to authorize the issuance of an additional $400 million of Texas Water Development Bonds for water supply, water quality, and flood control purposes. Submitted by 70th Legislature (1987) and adopted in election Nov. 3, 1987.]

Sec. 49-d-7. (a) The Texas Water Development Board may issue additional Texas water development bonds up to an additional aggregate principal amount of $500 million. Of the additional bonds authorized to be issued, $250 million of those bonds shall be used for purposes provided by Section 49-c of this article, $200 million of those bonds shall be used for purposes provided by Section 49-d-1 of this article, and $50 million of those bonds shall be used for flood control as provided by law.

(b) The Texas Water Development Board may use the proceeds of Texas water development bonds issued for the purposes provided by Section 49-c of this article for the additional purpose of providing financial assistance, on terms and conditions provided by law, to various political subdivisions and bodies politic and corporate of the state and to nonprofit water supply corporations to provide for acquisition, improvement, extension, or construction of water supply projects that involve the distribution of water to points of delivery to wholesale or retail customers.

(c) The legislature may require review and approval of the issuance of the bond, the use of the bond proceeds, or the rules adopted by an agency to govern use of the bond proceeds. Notwithstanding any other provision of this constitution, any entity created or directed to conduct this review and approval may include members or appointees of members of the executive, legislative, and judicial departments of state government.

(d) Except as specifically provided by Subsection (e) of this section, the Texas Water Development Board shall issue the additional bonds authorized by this section for the terms, in the denominations, form, and installments, on the conditions, and subject to the limitations provided by Sections 49-c and 49-d-1 of this article and by laws adopted by the legislature implementing this section.

(e) The legislature may provide by law for subsidized loans and grants from the proceeds of bonds authorized by this section to provide wholesale and retail water and wastewater facilities to economically distressed areas of the state as defined by law, provided, the principal amount of bonds that may be issued for the purposes under this subsection may not exceed 50 percent of the total amount of bonds authorized by this section. Separate accounts shall be established in the water development fund for administering the proceeds of bonds issued for purposes under this subsection, and an interest and sinking fund separate from and not subject to the limitations of the interest and sinking fund created pursuant to Section 49-c for other Texas water development bonds is established in the State Treasury to be used for paying the principal of and interest on bonds for the purposes of this subsection. While any of the bonds authorized for the purposes of this subsection or any of the interest on those bonds is outstanding and unpaid, there is appropriated out of the first money coming into the State Treasury in each fiscal year, not otherwise appropriated by this constitution, and amount that is sufficient to pay the principal of and interest on those bonds issued for the purposes under this subsection that mature or become due during that fiscal year.

(f) Subsections (c) through (e) of Section 49-d-2 of this article apply to the bonds authorized by this section.

[Note — Sec. 49-d-7 of Art. III was added to authorize the issuance of an additional $500 million of Texas water development bonds for water supply, water quality and flood control purposes. Proposed by 71st Legislature (1989) and adopted in election Nov. 7, 1989. Subsection (e) was amended to increased the amount of bonds for water and wastewater facilities that may be issued for economically distressed areas. Submitted by 72nd Legislature (1991) and adopted in election Nov. 5, 1991.]

Sec. 49-e. **Texas Park Development Bonds** — The Parks and Wildlife Department, or its successor vested with the powers, duties, and authority which deals with the operation, maintenance, and improvement of State Parks, shall have the authority to provide for, issue and sell general obligation bonds of the State of Texas in an amount not to exceed Seventy-Five Million Dollars ($75,000,000). The bonds authorized herein shall be called "Texas Park Development Bond," shall be executed in such form, denominations, and upon such terms as may be prescribed by law, provided, however, that the bonds shall bear a rate or rates of interest as may be fixed by the Parks and Wildlife Department or its successor, but the weighted average annual interest rate, as that phrase is commonly and ordinarily used and understood in the municipal bond market, of all the bonds issued and sold in any installment of any bonds, shall not exceed four and one-half percent (4 1/2%) interest per annum; they may be issued in such installments as said Parks and Wildlife Department, or its said successor, finds feasible and practical in accomplishing the purpose set forth herein.

All moneys received from the sale of said bonds shall be deposited in a fund hereby created with the State Treasurer to be known as the Texas Park Development Fund to be administered (without further appropriation) by the said Parks and Wildlife Department, or its said successor, in such manner as prescribed by law.

Such fund shall be used by said Parks and Wildlife Department, or its said successor, under such provisions as the Legislature may prescribe by general law, for the purposes of acquiring lands from the United States, or any governmental agency thereof, from any governmental agency of the State of Texas, or from any person, firm, or corporation, for State Park Sites and for developing said sites as State Parks.

While any of the bonds authorized by this provision, or any interest on any such bonds, is outstanding and unpaid, there is hereby appropriated out of the first moneys coming into the Treasury in each fiscal year, not otherwise appropriated by this Constitution, an amount which is sufficient to pay the principal and interest on such bonds that mature or become due during such fiscal year, less the amount in the interest and sinking fund at the close of the prior fiscal year, which includes any receipts derived during the prior fiscal year by said Parks and Wildlife Department, or its said successor, from admission charges to State Parks, as the Legislature may prescribe by general law.

The Legislature may provide for the investment of moneys available in the Texas Park Development Fund and the interest and sinking fund established for the payment of bonds issued by said Parks and Wildlife Department, or its said successor. Income from such investment shall be used for the purposes prescribed by the Legislature.

From the moneys received by said Parks and Wildlife Department, or its said successor, from the sale of the bonds issued hereunder, there shall be deposited in the interest and sinking fund for the bonds authorized by this section sufficient moneys to pay the interest to become due during the State fiscal year in which the bonds were issued. After all bonds have been fully paid with interest, or after there are on deposit in the interest and sinking fund sufficient moneys to pay all future maturities of principal and interest, additional moneys received from admission charges to State Parks shall be deposited to the State Parks Fund, or any successor fund which may be established by the

Article III (Cont'd.)

Legislature as a depository for Park revenue earned by said Parks and Wildlife Department, or its said successor.

All bonds issued hereunder shall after approval by the Attorney General, registration by the Comptroller of Public Accounts of the State of Texas, and delivery to the purchasers, be incontestable and shall constitute general obligations of the State of Texas under the Constitution of Texas.

Should the Legislature enact enabling laws in anticipation of the adoption of this amendment, such acts shall not be void by reason of their anticipatory nature.

[Note — Sec. 49-e of Art. III was added to authorize issuance and sale of $75,000,000 in bonds to create the Texas Park Development Fund to acquire lands for State Park sites and to develop State Parks. Submitted by 60th Legislature (1967) and adopted in election Nov. 11, 1967.]

Sec. 49-f. (a) The Legislature by general law may provide for the issuance of general obligation bonds of the state, the proceeds of which shall be used to make loans and provide other financing assistance for the purchase of farm and ranch land.

(b) All money received from the sale of the bonds shall be deposited in a fund created with the state treasurer to be known as the farm and ranch finance program fund. This fund shall be administered by the Veterans' Land Board in the manner prescribed by law.

(c) Sec. 65(b) of this article applies to the payment of interest on the bonds.

(d) The principal amount of bonds outstanding at one time may not exceed $500 million.

(e) While any of the bonds authorized by this section or any interest on those bonds is outstanding and unpaid, there is appropriated out of the first money coming into the treasury in each fiscal year not otherwise appropriated by this constitution an amount that is sufficient to pay the principal and interest on the bonds that mature or become due during the fiscal year less the amount in the interest and sinking fund at the close of the prior fiscal year.

(f) The bonds shall be approved by the attorney general and registered with the comptroller of public accounts. The bonds, when approved and registered, are general obligations of the state and are incontestable.

[Note — Sec. 49-f of Art. III was added to authorize the issuance of general obligation bonds to provide financing for purchase of farm and ranch land. Submitted by 69th Legislature (1985) and adopted in election Nov. 5, 1985.]

Sec. 49-g. **Superconducting Super Collider: Bonds Authorized for Facilities** — (See also second Sec. 49-g below, regarding the economic stabilization fund, and the explanatory note which follows it.) (a) The legislature may authorize (1) the appropriate agency to issue up to $500 million in general obligation bonds and to use the proceeds of the bonds (without further appropriation) to establish a superconducting super collider fund to be used in any manner appropriate to fund undertakings related to a superconducting super collider research facility sponsored or authorized by the United States government, and (2) the appropriate agency to grant land or property, whether or not acquired from proceeds of the bonds, to the United States government for undertakings related to a superconducting super collider research facility. The superconducting super collider fund shall contain a project account, an interest and sinking account and such other accounts as may be authorized by the legislature. The fund shall be composed of the proceeds of the bonds authorized by this section, together with any income from investment of money in the fund, amounts received pursuant to Subsection (b) hereof, and any other amounts authorized to be deposited in the fund by the legislature.

(b) Bonds issued under this section constitute a general obligation of the state. While any of the bonds or interest on the bonds is outstanding and unpaid, there is appropriated out of the first money coming into the treasury in each fiscal year, not otherwise appropriated by this constitution, the amount sufficient to pay the principal of and interest on the bonds that mature or become due during the fiscal year, less any amount in the interest and sinking account at the end of the preceding fiscal year that is pledged to payment of the bonds or interest.

(c) The legislature may require review and approval of the issuance of the bonds, of the use of the bond proceeds, or of the rules adopted by an agency to govern use of the bond proceeds. Notwithstanding any other provision of this constitution, any entity created or directed to conduct this review and approval may include members, or appointees of members, of the executive, legislative, and judicial departments of state government.

(d) Should the legislature enact enabling laws in anticipation of the adoption of this section, such acts shall not be void by reason of their anticipatory character.

[Note — Sec. 49-g of Art. III was added to provide for issuance of bonds relating to a superconducting super collider research facility. Submitted by 70th Legislature (1987) and adopted in election Nov. 3, 1987.]

Sec. 49-g. **Economic Stabilization Fund** — (See also first Sec. 49-g above, regarding the superconducting super collider, and the explanatory note which follows the second Sec. 49-g below.) (a) The economic stabilization fund is established as a special fund in the state treasury.

(b) The comptroller shall, not later than the 90th day of each biennium, transfer to the economic stabilization fund one-half of any unencumbered positive balance of general revenues on the last day of the preceding biennium. If necessary, the comptroller shall reduce the amount transferred in proportion to the other amounts prescribed by this section to prevent the amount in the fund from exceeding the limit in effect for that biennium under Subsection (g) of this section.

(c) Not later than the 90th day of each fiscal year, the comptroller of public accounts shall transfer from general revenue to the economic stabilization fund the amounts prescribed by Subsections (d) and (e) of this section. However, if necessary, the comptroller shall reduce proportionately the amounts transferred to prevent the amount in the fund from exceeding the limit in effect for that biennium under Subsection (g) of this section.

(d) If in the preceding year the state received from oil production taxes a net amount greater than the net amount of oil production taxes received by the state in the fiscal year ending August 31, 1987, the comptroller shall transfer to the economic stabilization fund an amount equal to 75 percent of the difference between those amounts. The comptroller shall retain the remaining 25 percent of the difference as general revenue. In computing the net amount of oil production taxes received, the comptroller may not consider refunds paid as a result of oil overcharge litigation.

(e) If in the preceding year the state received from gas production taxes a net amount greater than the net amount of gas production taxes received by the state in the fiscal year ending August 31, 1987, the comptroller shall transfer to the economic stabilization fund an amount equal to 75 percent of the difference between those amounts. The comptroller shall retain the remaining 25 percent of the difference as general revenue. For the purposes of this subsection, the comptroller shall adjust his computation of revenues to reflect only 12 months of collection.

(f) The legislature may appropriate additional amounts to the economic stabilization fund.

(g) During each fiscal biennium, the amount in the economic stabilization fund may not exceed an amount equal to 10 percent of the total amount, excluding investment income, interest income, and amounts borrowed from special funds, deposited in general revenue during the preceding biennium.

(h) In preparing an estimate of anticipated revenues for a succeeding biennium as required by Article III, Section 49a, of this constitution, the comptroller shall estimate the amount of the transfers that will be made under Subsections (b), (d), and (e) of this section. The comptroller shall deduct that amount from the estimate of anticipated revenues as if the transfers were made on August 31 of that fiscal year.

(i) The state treasurer shall credit to general revenue interest due to the economic stabilization fund that would result in an amount in the economic stabilization fund that exceeds the limit in effect under Subsection (g) of this section.

(j) The comptroller, with the consent of the state treasurer, may transfer money from the economic stabilization fund to general revenue to prevent or eliminate a temporary cash deficiency in general revenue. The comptroller shall return the amount transferred to the economic stabilization fund as soon as practicable, but not later than August 31 of each odd-numbered year. The state treasurer shall allocate the depository interest as if the transfers had not been made. If the comptroller submits a statement to the governor and the legislature under Article III, Section 49a, of this constitution when money from the economic stabilization fund is in general revenue, the comptroller shall state that the transferred money is not available for appropriation from general revenue.

(k) Amounts from the economic stabilization fund may be appropriated during a regular legislative session only for a purpose for which an appropriation from general revenue was made by the preceding legislature and may be appropriated in a special session only for a purpose for which an appropriation from general revenue was made in a preceding legislative session of the same legislature. An appropriation from the economic stabilization fund may be made only if the comptroller certifies that appropriations from general revenue made by the preceding legislature for the current biennium exceed available general

Article III (Cont'd.)

revenues and cash balances for the remainder of that biennium. The amount of an appropriation from the economic stabilization fund may not exceed the difference between the comptroller's estimate of general revenue for the current biennium at the time the comptroller receives for certification the bill making the appropriation and the amount of general revenue appropriations for that biennium previously certified by the comptroller. Appropriations from the economic stabilization fund under this subsection may not extend beyond the last day of the current biennium. An appropriation from the economic stabilization fund must be approved by a three-fifths vote of the members present in each house of the legislature.

(l) If an estimate of anticipated revenues for a succeeding biennium prepared by the comptroller pursuant to Article III, Section 49a, of this constitution is less than the revenues that are estimated at the same time by the comptroller to be available for the current biennium, the legislature may, by a three-fifths vote of the members present in each house, appropriate for the succeeding biennium from the economic stabilization fund an amount not to exceed this difference. Following each fiscal year, the actual amount of revenue shall be computed, and if the estimated difference exceeds the actual difference, the comptroller shall transfer the amount necessary from general revenue to the economic stabilization fund so that the actual difference shall not be exceeded. If all or a portion of the difference in revenue from one biennium to the next results, at least in part, from a change in a tax rate or base adopted by the legislature, the computation of revenue difference shall be adjusted to the amount that would have been available had the rate or base not been changed.

(m) In addition to the appropriation authority provided by Subsections (k) and (l) of this section, the legislature may, by a two-thirds vote of the members present in each house, appropriate amounts from the economic stabilization fund at any time and for any purpose.

(n) Money appropriated from the economic stabilization fund is subject to being withheld or transferred, within any limits provided by statute, by any person or entity authorized to exercise the power granted by Article XVI, Section 69, of this constitution.

(o) In this section, "net" means the amount of money that is equal to the difference between gross collections and refunds before the comptroller allocates the receipts as provided by law.

[Note — Sec. 49-g of Art. III was added to establish the economic stabilization fund. Submitted by 70th Legislature and adopted in election Nov. 8, 1988. Also note that the 70th Legislature submitted two different Section 49-g's for Article III: the first, having to do with the superconducting super collider, approved in election Nov. 3, 1987, and the second, having to do with the economic stabilization fund, approved in election Nov. 8, 1988. They are printed here in the order in which they were adopted.]

Sec. 49-h. (a) The legislature may authorize the issuance of up to $500 million in general obligation bonds and the use of the bond proceeds for acquiring, constructing, or equipping new facilities or for major repair or renovation of existing facilities of corrections institutions, including youth corrections institutions, and mental health and mental retardation institutions. The legislature may require the review and approval of the issuance of the bonds and the projects to be financed by the bond proceeds. Notwithstanding any other provision of this constitution, the issuer of the bonds or any entity created or directed to review and approve projects may include members or appointees of members of the executive, legislative, and judicial departments of state government.

(b) Bonds issued under this section constitute a general obligation of the state. While any of the bonds or interest on the bonds is outstanding and unpaid, there is appropriated out of the first money coming into the treasury in each fiscal year, not otherwise appropriated by this constitution, the amount sufficient to pay the principal of and interest on the bonds that mature or become due during the fiscal year, less any amount in any sinking fund at the end of the preceding fiscal year that is pledged to payment of the bonds or interest.

(c) (1) The legislature may authorize the issuance of up to $400 million in general obligation bonds, in addition to the amount authorized by Subsection (a) of this section, and use the proceeds of the bonds for acquiring, constructing, or equipping new corrections institutions, mental health and mental retardation institutions, youth corrections institutions, and statewide law enforcement facilities and for major repair or renovation of existing facilities of those institutions.

(2) The provisions of Subsection (a) of this section relating to the review and approval of bonds and the provisions of Subsection (b) of this section relating to the status of the bonds as a general obligation of the state and to the manner in which the principal and interest on the bonds are paid apply to bonds authorized under this subsection.

(d) (1) The legislature may authorize the issuance of up to $1.1 billion in general obligation bonds, in addition to the amount authorized by Subsections (a) and (c) of this section, and may use the proceeds of the bonds for acquiring, constructing, or equipping new prisons and substance abuse felony punishment facilities to confine criminals, mental health and mental retardation institutions, and Youth corrections institutions, for major repair or renovation of existing facilities of those institutions, and for the acquisition of, major repair to, or renovation of other facilities for use as state prisons or substance abuse felony punishment facilities. Proceeds of general obligation bonds issued under this subdivision may not be appropriated by any session of the legislature other than the 2nd Called Session of the 72nd Legislature or any subsequent session of the legislature.

(2) The provisions of Subsection (a) of this section relating to the review and approval of bonds and the provisions of Subsection (b) of this section relating to the status of the bonds as a general obligation of the state and to the manner in which the principal and interest on the bonds are paid apply to bonds authorized under this subsection.

(e) (1) The legislature may authorize the issuance of up to $1 billion in general obligation bonds, in addition to the amounts authorized by Subsections (a), (c), and (d) of this section, and use the proceeds of the bonds for acquiring, constructing, or equipping new corrections institutions, including youth corrections institutions, and mental health and mental retardation institutions and for major repair or renovation of existing facilities of those corrections and mental health and mental retardation institutions.

(2) The provisions of Subsection (a) of this section relating to the review and approval of bonds and the provisions of Subsection (b) of this section relating to the status of the bonds as a general obligation of the state and to the manner in which the principal and interest on the bonds are paid apply to bonds authorized under this subsection.

[Note — Sec. 49-h of Art. III was added to provide for issuance of general obligation bonds for construction projects for corrections institutions and mental health and mental retardation institutions. Submitted by 70th Legislature and adopted in election Nov. 3, 1987. Subsection (c) was added to provide for the issuance of general obligation bonds for acquiring, constructing or equipping corrections institutions, youth corrections institutions, statewide law enforcement facilities and mental health and mental retardation institutions. Proposed by 71st Legislature (1989) and adopted in election Nov. 7, 1989. Subsection (d) was added to provide for the funding of new prisons, mental health and mental retardation institutions and youth corrections facilities. Submitted by 72nd Legislature (1991) and adopted in election Nov. 5, 1991. Subsection (e) was added to provide for issuance of general obligation bonds for acquiring, constructing, or equipping corrections institutions and mental health and mental retardation institutions and for repair or renovation of existing facilities. Submitted by 73rd Legislature (1993) and adopted in election Nov. 2, 1993.]

Sec. 49-i. (a) The legislature by law may provide for the issuance of general obligation bonds of the state for the purpose of providing money to establish a Texas agricultural fund in the state treasury to be used without further appropriation in the manner provided by law and for the purpose of providing money to establish a rural microenterprise development fund in the state treasury to be used without further appropriation in the manner provided by law. The Texas agricultural fund shall be used only to provide financial assistance to develop, increase, improve, or expand the production, processing, marketing, or export of crops or products grown or produced primarily in this state by agricultural businesses domiciled in the state. The rural microenterprise development fund shall be used only in furtherance of a program established by the legislature to foster and stimulate the creation and expansion of small businesses in rural areas. The financial assistance offered by both funds may include loan guarantees, insurance, coinsurance, loans, and indirect loans or purchases or acceptances of assignments of loans or other obligations.

(b) The principal amount of bonds outstanding at one time may not exceed $25 million for the Texas agricultural fund and $5 million for the rural microenterprise development fund.

(c) The legislature may establish an interest and sinking account and other accounts within the Texas agricultural fund and within the rural microenterprise development fund. The legislature may provide for the investment of bond proceeds and of the interest and sinking accounts. Income from the investment of money in the funds that is not immediately committed to the payment of the principal of and interest on the bonds or the provi-

Article III (Cont'd.)

sion of financial assistance shall be used to create new employment and business opportunities in the state through the diversification and expansion of agricultural or rural small businesses, as provided by the legislature.

(d) Bonds authorized under this section constitute a general obligation of the state. While any of the bonds or interest on the bonds is outstanding and unpaid, there is appropriated out of the first money coming into the treasury in each fisca l year, not otherwise appropriated by this constitution, the amount sufficient to pay the principal of and interest on the bonds that mature or become due during the fiscal year, less any amounts in the interest and sinking accounts and the close of the preceding fiscal year that are pledged to payment of the bonds of interest.

[Note — Sec. 49-i of Art. III authorizes the Legislature to provide for issuance of bonds and state financing of development and production of Texas products and businesses. Proposed by 71st Legislature (1989) and adopted in election Nov. 7, 1989.]

Sec. 50. **Credit of State Not to Be Pledged** — The Legislature shall have no power to give or to lend or to authorize the giving or lending of the credit of the State in aid of, or to any person, association or corporation, whether municipal or other, or to pledge the credit of the State in any manner whatsoever, for the payment of the liabilities, present or prospective, of any individual, association of individuals, municipal or other corporation whatsoever.

Sec. 50-a. **State Medical Education Board, Fund; Purpose** — The Legislature shall create a State Medical Education Board to be composed of not more than six (6) members whose qualifications, duties and terms of office shall be prescribed by law. The Legislature shall also establish a State Medical Education Fund and make adequate appropriations therefor to be used by the State Medical Education Board to provide grants, loans or scholarships to students desiring to study medicine and agreeing to practice in the rural areas of this State, upon such terms and conditions as shall be prescribed by law. The term "rural areas" as used in this section shall be defined by law.

[Note — Sec. 50-a of Art. III was added to provide scholarships and to set up a State Medical Education Board. Submitted by 52nd Legislature and adopted in election Nov. 4, 1952.]

Sec. 50-b. **Student Loans** — (a) The Legislature may provide that the Coordinating Board, Texas College and University System, or its successor or successors, shall have the authority to provide for, issue and sell general obligation bonds of the State of Texas in an amount not to exceed Eighty-five Million Dollars ($85,000,000). The bonds authorized herein, shall be called "Texas College Student Loan Bonds," shall be executed in such form, denominations and upon such terms as may be prescribed by law, provided, however, that the bonds shall not bear more than four per cent (4%) interest per annum; they may be issued in such installments as the Board finds feasible and practical in accomplishing the purposes of this section.

(b) All moneys received from the sale of such bonds shall be deposited in a fund hereby created in the State Treasury to be known as the Texas Opportunity Plan Fund to be administered by the Coordinating Board, Texas College and University System, or its successor or successors to make loans to students who have been admitted to attend any institution of higher education within the State of Texas, public or private, including Junior Colleges, which are recognized or accredited under terms and conditions prescribed by the Legislature, and to pay interest and principal on such bonds and provide a sinking fund therefor under such conditions as the Legislature may prescribe.

(c) While any of the bonds, or interest on said bonds authorized by this section is outstanding and unpaid, there is hereby appropriated out of the first moneys coming into the Treasury in each fiscal year, not otherwise appropriated by this Constitution, an amount sufficient to pay the principal and interest on such bonds that mature or become due during such fiscal year, less the amount in the sinking fund at the close of the prior fiscal year.

(d) The Legislature may provide for the investment of moneys available in the Texas Opportunity Plan Fund, and the interest and sinking funds established for the payment of bonds issued by the Coordinating Board, Texas College and University System, or its successor or successors. Income from such investment shall be used for the purposes prescribed by the Legislature.

(e) All bonds issued hereunder shall, after approval by the Attorney General, registration by the Comptroller of Public Accounts of the State of Texas, and delivery to the purchasers, be incontestable and shall constitute general obligations of the State of Texas under this Constitution.

(f) Should the Legislature enact enabling laws in anticipation of the adoption of this amendment, such acts shall not be void because of their anticipatory nature.

[Note — Sec. 50-b of Art. III was added to provide a system of student loans at institutions of higher education and to provide for creation of the Texas Opportunity Plan Fund. Submitted by 59th Legislature (1965) and adopted in election Nov. 2, 1965.]

Sec. 50-b-1. (a) The Legislature may provide that the Coordinating Board, Texas College and University System, or its successor or successors, shall have authority to provide for, issue and sell general obligation bonds of the State of Texas in an amount not to exceed Two Hundred Million Dollars ($200,000,000) in addition to those heretofore authorized to be issued pursuant to Sec. 50-b of the Constitution. The bonds authorized herein shall be executed in such form, upon such terms and be in such denomination as may be prescribed by law and shall bear interest, and be issued in such installments as shall be prescribed by the Board provided that the maximum net effective interest rate to be borne by such bonds may be fixed by law.

(b) The moneys received from the sale of such bonds shall be deposited to the credit of the Texas Opportunity Plan Fund created by Sec. 50-b of the Constitution and shall otherwise be handled as provided in Sec. 50-b of the Constitution and the laws enacted pursuant thereto.

(c) The said bonds shall be general obligations of the state and shall be payable in the same manner and from the same sources as bonds heretofore authorized pursuant to Sec. 50-b.

(d) All bonds issued hereunder shall, after approval by the Attorney General, registration by the Comptroller of Public Accounts of the State of Texas, and delivery to the purchasers, be incontestable and shall constitute general obligations of the State of Texas under this Constitution.

(e) Should the Legislature enact enabling laws in anticipation of the adoption of this amendment such acts shall not be void because of their anticipatory nature.

[Note—Sec. 50-b-1 of Art. III was added to provide for additional loans to students at higher educational institutions under the Texas Opportunity Plan. Submitted by 61st Legislature (1969) and adopted in election Aug. 5, 1969.]

Sec. 50-b-2. **Additional Student Loans** — (a) The legislature by general law may authorize the Texas Higher Education Coordinating Board or its successor or successors to provide for, issue, and sell general obligation bonds of the State of Texas in an amount not to exceed $75 million in addition to those bonds issued under Sections 50-b and 50-b-1 of this constitution. Bonds issued under this section shall be issued as college savings bonds as provided by law.

(b) The bonds shall:

(1) be executed in the form, on the terms, and in the denominations as prescribed by law; and

(2) bear interest and be issued in installments as prescribed by the Texas Higher Education Coordinating Board or its successor or successors.

(c) The maximum net effective interest rate to be borne by bonds issued under this section must be set by law.

(d) The proceeds from the sale of bonds issued under this section shall be credited to the Texas opportunity plan fund created by Section 50-b of this constitution and shall be administered as provided by Section 50-b of this constitution and the law enacted under that constitutional provision.

(e) Bonds issued under this section are payable in the same manner and from the same sources as bonds authorized under Section 50-b of this constitution.

(f) Bonds issued under this section, after approval by the attorney general, registration by the comptroller of public accounts, and delivery to the purchasers, are incontestable and are general obligations of the State of Texas under this constitution.

[Note — Sec. 50-b-2 of Art. III was added to provide for the issuance of general obligation bonds as college savings bonds to provide educational loans to students and to encourage the public to save for a college education. Proposed by 71st Legislature (1989) and adopted in election Nov. 7, 1989.]

Sec. 50-b-3. **Additional Student Loans** — (a) The legislature by general law may authorize the Texas Higher Education Coordinating Board or its successor or successors to issue and sell general obligation bonds of the State of Texas in an amount not to exceed $300 million to finance educational loans to students. The bonds are in addition to those bonds issued under Sections 50b, 50b-1, and 50b-2 of Article III of this constitution.

(b) The bonds shall be executed in the form, on the terms and in the denominations, bear interest, and be issued in installments, as prescribed by the Texas Higher Education Coordina-

Article III (Cont'd.)

ting Board or its successor or successors.

(c) The maximum net effective interest rate to be borne by bonds issued under this section must be set by law.

(d) The legislature may provide for the investment of bond proceeds and may establish and provide for the investment of an interest and sinking fund to pay the bonds. Income from the investment shall be used for the purposes prescribed by the legislature.

(e) While any of the bonds issued under this section or interest on the bonds is outstanding and unpaid, there is appropriated out of the first money coming into the treasury in each fiscal year, not otherwise appropriated by this constitution, the amount sufficient to pay the principal of and interest on the bonds that mature or become due during the fiscal year, less any amount in an interest and sinking fund established under this section at the end of the preceding fiscal year that is pledged to the payment of the bonds or interest.

(f) Bonds issued under this section, after approval by the attorney general, registration by the comptroller of public accounts, and delivery to the purchasers, are incontestable.

[Note — Subsection 50b-3 of Article III was added to provide for issuance of general obligation bonds to provide educational loans to students. Submitted by 72nd Legislature (1991) and adopted in election Nov. 5, 1991.]

Sec. 50-c. **Farm and Ranch Loan Security Fund** — (a) The Legislature may provide that the commissioner of agriculture shall have the authority to provide for, issue, and sell general obligation bonds of the State of Texas in an amount not to exceed $10 million. The bonds shall be called "Farm and Ranch Loan Security Bonds" and shall be executed in such form, denominations, and on such terms as may be prescribed by law. The bonds shall bear interest rates fixed by the Legislature of the State of Texas.

(b) All money received from the sale of Farm and Ranch Loan Security Bonds shall be deposited in a fund hereby created with the State Treasurer to be known as the "Farm and Ranch Loan Security Fund." This fund shall be administered without further appropriation by the commissioner of agriculture in the manner prescribed by law.

(c) The Farm and Ranch Loan Security Fund shall be used by the commissioner of agriculture under provisions prescribed by the Legislature for the purpose of guaranteeing loans used for the purchase of farm and ranch real estate, for acquiring real estate mortgages or deeds of trust on lands purchased with guaranteed loans, and to advance to the borrower a percentage of the principal and interest due on those loans; provided that the commissioner shall require at least six percent interest be paid by the borrower on any advance of principal and interest. The Legislature may authorize the commissioner to sell at foreclosure any land acquired in this manner, and proceeds from that sale shall be deposited in the Farm and Ranch Loan Security Fund.

(d) The Legislature may provide for the investment of money available in the Farm and Ranch Loan Security Fund and the interest and sinking fund established for the payment of bonds issued by the commissioner of agriculture. Income from the investment shall be used for purposes prescribed by the Legislature.

(e) While any of the bonds authorized by this section or any interest on those bonds is outstanding and unpaid, there is hereby appropriated out of the first money coming into the treasury in each fiscal year not otherwise appropriated by this constitution an amount that is sufficient to pay the principal and interest on the bonds that mature or become due during the fiscal year less the amount in the interest and sinking fund at the close of the prior fiscal year.

[Note — Sec. 50-c of Art. III was added to provide for the guarantee of loans for purchase of farm and ranch real estate for qualified borrowers by the sale of general obligation bonds of the State of Texas. Submitted by 66th Legislature (1979) and adopted in election Nov. 6, 1979.]

Sec. 50-d. (a) On a two-thirds vote of the members elected to each house of the Legislature, the Texas Water Development Board may issue and sell Texas agricultural water conservation bonds in an amount not to exceed $200 million.

(b) The proceeds from the sale of Texas agricultural water conservation bonds shall be deposited in a fund created in the state treasury to be known as the agricultural water conservation fund.

(c) Texas agricultural water conservation bonds are general obligations of the State of Texas. During the time that Texas agricultural water conservation bonds or any interest on those bonds is outstanding or unpaid, there is appropriated out of the first money coming into the state treasury in each fiscal year, not otherwise appropriated by this constitution, an amount that is sufficient to pay the principal of and interest on those bonds that mature or become due during that fiscal year, less the amount in the sinking fund at the close of the prior fiscal year.

(d) The terms, conditions, provisions, and procedures for issuance and sale and management of proceeds of Texas agricultural water conservation bonds shall be provided by law.

[Note — Sec. 50-d of Art. III was added to authorize issuance and sale of $200 million of Texas agricultural water conservation bonds. Submitted by 69th Legislature (1985) and adopted in election Nov. 5, 1985. Subsection (e) of Sec. 50-d was repealed in order to eliminate certain time limitations relating to the issuance of Texas agricultural water conservation bonds. Repeal proposed by 71st Legislature (1989) and adopted in election Nov. 7, 1989.]

Sec. 50-e. (a) For the purposes of providing surety for the Texas grain warehouse self-insurance fund, the legislature by general law may establish or provide for a guarantee of the fund not to exceed $50 million.

(b) At the beginning of the fiscal year after the fund reaches $5 million, as certified by the comptroller of public accounts, the guarantee of the fund shall cease and this provision shall expire.

(c) Should the legislature enact any enabling laws in anticipation of this amendment, no such law shall be void by reason of its anticipatory nature.

(d) If the provisions of this section conflict with any other provisions of this constitution, the provisions of this section shall prevail.

[Note — Section 50-e was added to establish a self-insurance pool for grain storage facilities. Submitted by 70th Legislature (1987) and adopted in election Nov. 3, 1987.]

Sec. 51. **Tax Levy Authorized for Confederate Soldiers and Sailors and Their Widows** — The Legislature shall have no power to make any grant or authorize the making of any grant of public moneys to any individual, association of individuals, municipal or other corporations whatsoever; provided, however, the Legislature may grant aid to indigent and disabled Confederate soldiers and sailors under such regulations and limitations as may be deemed by the Legislature as expedient, and to their widows in indigent circumstances under such regulations and limitations as may be deemed by the Legislature as expedient; provided that the provisions of this Section shall not be construed so as to prevent the grant of aid in cases of public calamity.

[Note — Sec. 51 of Art. III has been amended nine times (1) Establishing Confederate Home. Submitted by 23rd Legislature (1893) and ratified at election, Nov. 6, 1894, and proclaimed adopted Dec. 21, 1894. (2) Providing for pensions for Confederate veterans from appropriations not to exceed $250,000 annually. Submitted by 25th Legislature (1897), adopted at election, Nov. 1, 1898, and proclaimed Dec. 22, 1898. (3) Raising amount that might be appropriated for Confederate pensions from $250,000 to $500,000 annually. Submitted by 28th Legislature (1903), adopted in election, Nov. 8, 1904, and proclaimed Dec. 29, 1904. (4) Increasing authorized maximum appropriations for Confederate Home from $100,000 to $150,000 annually. Submitted by 31st Legislature (1909), adopted in election, Nov. 8, 1910, and declared adopted Dec. 31, 1910. (5) Authorizing 5¢ ad valorem tax for Confederate pension fund; also omitting "public calamity" clause. Submitted by 32nd Legislature (1911), adopted Nov. 3, 1912, and proclaimed Dec. 30, 1912. (6) Authorizing 7¢ ad valorem tax for Confederate pension fund and reinstating "public calamity" clause. Submitted by 38th Legislature (1923) and adopted Nov. 4, 1924. (7) Eliminating specific restrictions upon grants of aid to Confederate soldiers, sailors and others with respect to date of removal to Texas, etc., and conferring such authority upon the Legislature. Submitted by 40th Legislature (1927); ratified Nov. 6, 1928; proclaimed Feb. 6, 1929. (8) Cutting tax from 7¢ to 2¢ by addition of Sec. 17 of Art. VII, which was deleted by Constitutional amendment in 1982. (9) Further amended to provide for abolition of the 2¢ ad valorem tax for this purpose by Dec. 31, 1976, but making provision for aiding these veterans and their widows. (See also Art. VIII, Sec. 1-e.) Submitted by 60th Legislature (1967) and adopted in election Nov. 5, 1968.]

Sec. 51-a — **Assistance and Medical Care to Needy Aged, Needy Blind, Needy Children and Totally Disabled; Limitation on Expenditures for Same** — The Legislature shall have the power, by General Laws, to provide, subject to limitations herein contained, and such other limitations, restrictions and regulations as may by the Legislature be deemed expedient, for assistance grants to dependent children and the caretakers of

Article III (Cont'd.)

such children, needy persons who are totally and permanently disabled because of a mental or physical handicap, needy aged persons and needy blind persons.

The Legislature may provide by General Law for medical care, rehabilitation and other similar services for needy persons. The Legislature may prescribe such other eligibility requirements for participation in these programs as it deems appropriate and may make appropriations out of state funds for such purposes. The maximum amount paid out of state funds for assistance grants to or on behalf of needy dependent children and their caretakers shall not exceed the amount of Eighty Million Dollars ($80,000,000) during any fiscal year, except that the limit shall be One Hundred Sixty Million Dollars ($160,000,000) for the two years of the 1982-1983 biennium. For the two years of each subsequent biennium, the maximum amount shall not exceed one percent of the state budget. The Legislature by general statute shall provide for the means for determining the state budget amounts, including state and other funds appropriated by the Legislature, to be used in establishing the biennial limit.

Provided further, that if the limitations and restrictions herein contained are found to be in conflict with the provisions of appropriate federal statutes, as they now are or as they may be amended to the extent that federal matching money is not available to the state for these purposes, then and in that event the Legislature is specifically authorized and empowered to prescribe such limitations and restrictions and enact such laws as may be necessary in order that such federal matching money will be available for assistance and/or medical care for or on behalf of needy persons.

Nothing in this section shall be construed to amend, modify or repeal Sec. 31 of Art. XVI of this Constitution; provided further, however, that such medical care, services or assistance shall also include the employment of objective or subjective means, without the use of drugs, for the purpose of ascertaining and measuring the powers of vision of the human eye, and fitting lenses or prisms to correct or remedy any defect or abnormal condition of vision. Nothing herein shall be construed to permit optometrists to treat the eyes for any defect whatsoever in any manner nor to administer nor to prescribe any drug or physical treatment whatsoever, unless such optometrist is a regularly licensed physician or surgeon under the laws of this state.

[Note — Sec. 51-a of Art. III was first submitted by 49th Legislature and adopted in election Aug. 25, 1945. It supplanted four earlier amendments, as follows: An original Sec. 51-a, which provided for issuance of $20,000,000 in state bonds for relief (the so-called **"Bread bonds"**), this amendment having been submitted by 43rd Legislature and adopted Aug. 26, 1933, and also Secs. 51-b, 51-c and 51-d, which originally provided for old-age pensions and other welfare measures, adopted in elections Aug. 24, 1935 and Aug. 23, 1937. Because of this consolidation, the Constitution did skip from Sec. 51-a to Sec. 51-e until a Sec. 51-b was added in election Nov. 2, 1954, and a Subsection 51-a was added in election Nov. 5, 1957. It was further amended to raise the limit from $35 million to $42 million. Submitted by 53rd Legislature (1953) and adopted in election Nov. 2, 1954. It was again amended to raise the limit from $42 million to $47 million and authorizing legislative appropriations to raise the needed money. Submitted by 55th Legislature (1957) and adopted in election Nov. 5, 1957. It was further amended to raise the total amount of assistance to $52 million per year. Submitted by 57th Legislature (1961) and adopted in election Nov. 6, 1962. It was further amended to combine the former Sections 51-a and 51-b-1 of Art. III into one section to be known as Sec. 51-a; further raising the total amount of assistance to $60 million per year and providing that Legislature shall prescribe the residence requirements. Submitted by 58th Legislature (1963) and adopted in election Nov. 9, 1963. It was further amended ito create a new Sec. 51-a, which consolidates the old Sec. 51-a and Subsections 51-a-1 and 51-a-2. The new Sec. 51-a enables the State of Texas to cooperate with the U.S. government in providing assistance and medical care for the needy aged, needy blind, needy children and needy totally disabled; expands age categories of those eligible for blind assistance and of needy children; and extends eligibility for the aged to citizens of the United States or non-citizens who have resided in the United States for 25 years. Submitted by 59th Legislature (1965) and adopted in election Nov. 2, 1965. It was again amended to raise the limit on amount to be expended from $60 million to $80 million a year. It further provided that certain amounts be allocated out of the Omnibus Tax Clearance Fund for aid to permanently and totally disabled, families with dependent children and for old-age assistance. Submitted by 61st Legislature (1969) and adopted in election Aug. 5, 1969. The regular session of the 67th Legislature (1981) submitted an amendment to raise the amount to be expended on Aid for Dependent Children in the 1982-1983 biennium to a maximum of $160 million and, for each subsequent biennium, the maximum amount would not exceed one percent of the state budget. This proposed amendment inadvertently cut out other needy recipients, and SJR 10 of the Called Session of the 67th Legislature (1982) amended the proposed amendment to include other needy recipients in this fund. Adopted in election Nov. 2, 1982.]

Sec. 51-a-1. (a) The legislature by general law may authorize the use of public money to provide to local fire departments and other public fire-fighting organizations:

(1) loans or other financial assistance to purchase fire-fighting equipment and to aid in providing necessary equipment and facilities to comply with federal and state law; and

(2) scholarships and grants to educate and train the members of local fire departments and other public fire-fighting organizations.

(b) A portion of the money used under this section may be used for the administrative costs of the program. The legislature shall provide for the terms and conditions of scholarships, grants, loans, and other financial assistance to be provided under this section.

[Note — Sec. 51-a-1 of Art. III was added to authorize the state to provide scholarships, grants, loans and other financial assistance to local fire departments and other public fire-fighting organizations. Proposed by 71st Legislature (1989) and adopted in election Nov. 7, 1989.]

[Note — Sec. 51-b of Art. III, creating the State Building Commission and the State Building Fund, was eliminated by a constitutional amendment. Proposed by 65th Legislature and adopted in election Nov. 7, 1978.]

Sec. 51-c. **False Imprisonment** — The Legislature may grant aid and compensation to any person who has heretofore paid a fine or served a sentence in prison, or who may hereafter pay a fine or serve a sentence in prison, under the laws of this State for an offense for which he or she is not guilty, under such regulations and limitations as the Legislature may deem expedient.

[Note — Sec. 51-c of Art. III was added to allow the Legislature to grant aid and compensation to persons who have been fined or imprisoned under laws of this state for offenses of which they are not guilty. Submitted by 54th Legislature (1955) and adopted in election Nov. 6, 1956.]

Sec. 51-d. **Assistance to Survivors of Law Enforcement Officers Killed on Duty** — The Legislature shall have the power, by general law, to provide for the payment of assistance by the State of Texas to the surviving spouse, minor children, and surviving dependent parents, brothers, and sisters of officers, employees and agents, including members of organized volunteer fire departments and members of organized police reserve or auxiliary units with authority to make an arrest, of the state or of any city, county, district, or other political subdivision who, because of the hazardous nature of their duties, suffer death in the course of the performance of those official duties. Should the Legislature enact any enabling laws in anticipation of this amendment, no such law shall be void by reason of its anticipatory nature.

[Note — Sec. 51-d was added to provide assistance for survivors of law enforcement officers killed in performance of their duty. Submitted by 59th Legislature (1965), and adopted in election Nov. 8, 1966. It was amended to provide for assistance to survivors of members of volunteer fire departments and organized police reserve, or auxiliary units with authority to make arrests, of political subdivisions of the state. Submitted by 61st Legislature (1969) and adopted in election Aug. 5, 1969. It was again amended to provide compensation for dependent parents, brothers and sisters of officers killed in performing their duties. Submitted by 68th Legislature (1983) and adopted in election Nov. 6, 1984.]

[Note — Sec. 51e and Sec. 51f, relating to City and Town Pension System and Local Pension Plans, respectively, were deleted by a constitutional amendment. Submitted by 64th Legislature (1975) and approved in election April 22, 1975. See Art. XVI, Sec. 67, which replaces the foregoing Sections. (See also note under Art. III, Sec. 48a and Sec. 48b; Art. XVI, Sec. 62 and Sec. 63.)]

Sec. 51-g. **Social Security Coverage for Municipal Employees** — The Legislature shall have the power to pass such laws as may be necessary to enable the State to enter into agreements with the Federal Government to obtain for proprietary employees of its political subdivisions coverage under the old-age and survivors insurance provisions of Title II of the Fed-

Article III (Cont'd.)

eral Social Security Act as amended. The Legislature shall have the power to make appropriations and authorize all obligations necessary to the establishment of such Social Security coverage program.

[Note — Sec. 51-g of Art. III was added to extend Social Security coverage to municipal employees. Submitted by 53rd Legislature (1953) and adopted in election Nov. 2, 1954.]

Sec. 52. **Counties, Cities, Etc., Not Authorized to Grant Money or Become Stockholders; Exceptions** — (a) Except as otherwise provided by this section, the Legislature shall have no power to authorize any county, city, town or other political corporation or subdivision of the State to lend its credit or to grant public money or thing of value in aid of, or to any individual, association or corporation whatsoever, or to become a stockholder in such corporation, association or company. However, this section does not prohibit the use of public funds or credit for the payment of premiums on nonassessable life, health, or accident insurance policies and annuity contracts issued by a mutual insurance company authorized to do business in this State.

[Note — Sec. 52(a) was amended to allow political subdivisions the opportunity to engage in and transact business with authorized mutual insurance companies in same manner as with other insurance companies. Submitted by 69th Legislature (1985) and adopted in election Nov. 4, 1986.]

(b) Under legislative provision any county, any political subdivision of a county, any number of adjoining counties or any political subdivision of the State or any defined district now or hereafter to be described and defined within the State of Texas, and which may or may not include towns, villages or municipal corporations, upon a vote of a two-thirds majority of the resident property taxpayers voting thereon who are qualified electors of such district or territory, to be affected thereby, in addition to all other debts, may issue bonds or otherwise lend its credit in any amount not to exceed one fourth of the assessed valuation of the real property of such district or territory, except that the total bonded indebtedness of any city or town shall never exceed the limits imposed by other provisions of this Constitution, and levy and collect taxes to pay the interest thereon and provide a sinking fund for the redemption thereof, as the Legislature may authorize, and in such manner as it may authorize the same, for the following purposes, to wit:

(1) The improvement of rivers, creeks and streams to prevent overflows and to permit of navigation thereof or irrigation thereof, or in aid of such purposes.

(2) The construction and maintenance of pools, lakes, reservoirs, dams, canals and waterways for the purposes of irrigation, drainage or navigation, or in aid thereof.

(3) The construction, maintenance and operation of macadamized, graveled or paved roads and turnpikes or in aid thereof.

(c) Notwithstanding the provisions of Subsection (b) of this section, bonds may be issued by any county in an amount not to exceed one fourth of the assessed valuation of the real property in the county, for the construction, maintenance, and operation of macadamized, graveled, or paved roads and turnpikes, or in aid thereof, upon a vote of a majority of the resident property taxpayers voting thereon who are qualified electors of the county, and without the necessity of further or amendatory legislation. The county may levy and collect taxes to pay the interest on the bonds as it becomes due and to provide a sinking fund for redemption of the bonds.

(d) Any defined district created under this section that is authorized to issue bonds or otherwise lend its credit for the purposes stated in Subdivisions (1) and (2) of Subsection (b) of this section may engage in fire-fighting activities and may issue bonds or otherwise lend its credit for fire-fighting purposes as provided by law and this constitution.

(e) A county, city, town, or other political corporation or subdivision of the state may invest its funds as authorized by law.

[Note — Sec. 52 of Art. III has been amended four times: (1) To authorize formation of districts for issuance of bonds for leveeing, drainage, irrigation, highway construction and other public improvements. Submitted by 28th Legislature (1903), adopted in election, Nov. 8, 1904, and proclaimed Dec. 29, 1904. (2) To permit any county, on vote of a majority of qualified property taxpaying electors, to issue road bonds in an amount not exceeding one-fourth of assessed valuation of the real property in the county. Submitted by 61st Legislature (1969) and adopted in election Nov. 3, 1970. (3) Subsection (d) was added to authorize certain districts to engage in fire-fighting activities and to issue bonds or otherwise lend their credit for fire-fighting purposes. (See also Subsection (f) of Sec. 59, Art. XVI.) Submitted by 65th Legislature (1977) and adopted in election Nov. 7, 1978. (4) Subsection (e) was added to authorize local governments to invest their funds as authorized by law. (See related amendment at Art. XI, Sec. 3.) Proposed by 71st Legislature (1989) and adopted in election Nov. 7, 1989.]

Sec. 52-a. Notwithstanding any other provision of this constitution, the legislature may provide for the creation of programs and the making of loans and grants of public money, other than money otherwise dedicated by this constitution to use for a different purpose, for the public purposes of development and diversification of the economy of the state, the elimination of unemployment or underemployment in the state, the stimulation of agricultural innovation, the fostering of the growth of enterprises based on agriculture, or the development or expansion of transportation or commerce in the state. Any bonds or other obligations of a county, municipality, or other political subdivision of the state that are issued for the purpose of making loans or grants in connection with a program authorized by the legislature under this section and that are payable from ad valorem taxes must be approved by a vote of the majority of the registered voters of the county, municipality, or political subdivision voting on the issue. An enabling law enacted by the legislature in anticipation of the adoption of this amendment is not void because of its anticipatory character.

[Note — Sec. 52-a of Art. III was added to authorize the Legislature to provide assistance to encourage economic development in the state. Submitted by 70th Legislature (1987) and adopted in election Nov. 3, 1987.]

Sec. 52-b. **Legislature Prohibited to Lend Credit of State in Building or Maintaining Toll Roads and Turnpikes; Exception for Texas Turnpike Authority** — The Legislature shall have no power or authority to in any manner lend the credit of the State or grant any public money to, or assume any indebtedness, present or future, bonded or otherwise, of any individual, person, firm, partnership, association, corporation, public corporation, public agency, or political subdivision of the State, or anyone else, which is now or hereafter authorized to construct, maintain or operate toll roads and turnpikes within this State except that the legislature may authorize the Texas Department of Transportation to expend money, from any source available, for the costs of turnpikes, toll roads, or toll bridges of the Texas Turnpike Authority, or successor agency, provided that any monies expended out of the state highway fund, shall be repaid to the fund from tolls or other turnpike revenue.

[Note — Sec. 52-b of Art. III was added to prohibit Legislature from lending credit of State in building or maintaining toll roads and turnpikes. Submitted by 53rd Legislature (1953) and adopted in election Nov. 2, 1954. It was amended to allow the state to aid turnpikes, toll roads or toll bridges of the Texas Turnpike Authority, provided the money is repaid. Submitted by 72nd Legislature (1991) and adopted in election Nov. 5, 1991.]

Sec. 52-d. **Harris County Road Districts** — Upon the vote of a majority of the resident qualified electors owning rendered taxable property therein so authorizing, a county or road district may collect an annual tax for a period not exceeding five (5) years to create a fund for constructing lasting and permanent roads and bridges or both. No contract involving the expenditure of any of such fund shall be valid unless, when it is made, money shall be on hand in such fund.

At such election, the Commissioners Court shall submit for adoption a road plan and designate the amount of special tax to be levied; the number of years said tax is to be levied; the location, description and character of the roads and bridges; and the estimated cost thereof. The funds raised by such taxes shall not be used for purposes other than those specified in the plan submitted to the voters. Elections may be held from time to time to extend or discontinue said plan or to increase or diminish said tax. The Legislature shall enact laws prescribing the procedure hereunder.

The provisions of this section shall apply only to Harris County and road districts therein.

[Note — Sec. 52-d of Art. III was added to give special local tax powers to Harris County. Proposed by 45th Legislature (1937) and adopted in election Aug. 23, 1937.]

Note that Sec. 52-c has never existed. The 53rd Legislature (1953) submitted an amendment to be numbered 52-b, and same was adopted in election Nov. 2, 1954. Obviously, the designation, "Sec. 52-d," in Senate Joint Resolution No. 16 of the 45th Legislature resulted from confusion of a new section number with the sequence of paragraphs "a, b and c" under section 52 immediately above. Some published texts of the State Constitution give this as "Paragraph d," under Sec. 52, as it might properly have been designated, but SJR No. 16 of the 53rd Leg-

Article III (Cont'd.)

islature definitely gave it as a separate "Sec. 52-d." Sec. 52-b was added in 1954; Sec. 52-a was not added until 1987; and 52-c is still missing.

Sec. 52-e. **Dallas County Road Bonds** — Bonds to be issued by Dallas County under Sec. 52 of Art. III of this Constitution for the construction, maintenance and operation of macadamized, graveled or paved roads and turnpikes, or in aid thereof, may, without the necessity of further or amendatory legislation, be issued upon a vote of a majority of the resident property taxpayers voting thereon who are qualified electors of said county, and bonds heretofore or hereafter issued under Subsections (a) and (b) of said Sec. 52 shall not be included in determining the debt limit prescribed in said Section.

[Note — Sec. 52-e of Art. III was added to allow Dallas County to issue bonds for construction of roads upon majority vote of resident property taxpayers. Submitted by 60th Legislature (1967) and adopted in election Nov. 5, 1968.]

Note — As in the case of Sec. 52-d above, this section might more properly have been designated as paragraph "e" under Sec. 52, but the 60th Legislature designated it as Sec. 52-e. As a result, there are two Sections 52-e, since they also designated the section below, relating to payment of medical expenses for county and precinct officials, as Sec. 52-e.

Sec. 52-e. **Payment of Medical Expenses for County and Precinct Officials** — Each county in the State of Texas is hereby authorized to pay all medical expenses, all doctor bills and all hospital bills for Sheriffs, Deputy Sheriffs, Constables, Deputy Constables and other county and precinct law enforcement officials who are injured in the course of their official duties; providing that while said Sheriff, Deputy Sheriff, Constable, Deputy Constable or other county or precinct law enforcement official is hospitalized or incapacitated that the county shall continue to pay his maximum salary; providing, however, that said payment of salary shall cease on the expiration of the term of office to which such official was elected or appointed. Provided, however, that no provision contained herein shall be construed to amend, modify, repeal or nullify Art. XVI, Sec. 31, of the Constitution of the State of Texas.

[Note — Sec. 52-e of Art. III was added to authorize counties to pay medical bills for county and precinct law enforcement officials who are injured in line of duty; and the county shall continue to pay maximum salary for duration of term to which they were elected or appointed. Submitted by 60th Legislature (1967) and adopted in election Nov. 11, 1967.]

Sec. 52-f. **Private Roads in County** — A county with a population of 5,000 or less, according to the most recent federal census, may construct and maintain private roads if it imposes a reasonable charge for the work. The Legislature by general law may limit this authority. Revenue received from private road work may be used only for the construction, including right-of-way acquisition, or maintenance of public roads.

[Note — Sec. 52-f of Art. III was added to authorize counties with population of 5,000 or less to perform private road work. Submitted by 66th Legislature (1979) and adopted in election Nov. 4, 1980.]

Sec. 53. **No Extra Compensation by Municipal Corporations** — The Legislature shall have no power to grant or to authorize any county or municipal authority to grant any extra compensation, fee or allowance to a public officer, agent, servant or contractor, after service has been rendered or a contract has been entered into and performed in whole or in part; nor pay, nor authorize the payment of any claim created against any county or municipality of the State under any agreement or contract made without authority of law.

Sec. 54. **Liens on Railroads** — The Legislature shall have no power to release or alienate any lien held by the State upon any railroad, or in anywise change the tenor or meaning or pass any act explanatory thereof; but the same shall be enforced in accordance with the original terms upon which it was acquired.

Sec. 55. **Power of Legislature to Release Debt** — The Legislature shall have no power to release or extinguish, or to authorize the releasing or extinguishing, in whole or in part, the indebtedness, liability or obligation of any corporation or individual, to this State or to any county or defined subdivision thereof, or other municipal corporation therein, except delinquent taxes which have been due for a period of at least ten years.

[Note — Sec. 55 of Art. III was amended to add the clause "except delinquent taxes which have been due for a period of at least ten years." Submitted by 42nd Legislature (1931), adopted in election Nov. 8, 1932, and proclaimed Jan. 9, 1933.]

Sec. 56. **Special Laws; Limitations** — The Legislature shall not, except as otherwise provided in this Constitution, pass any local or special law authorizing:

The creation, extension or impairing of liens;

Regulating the affairs of counties, cities, towns, wards or school districts;

Changing the names of persons or places;

Changing the venue in civil or criminal cases;

Authorizing the laying out, opening, altering or maintaining of roads, highways, streets or alleys;

Relating to ferries or bridges, or incorporating ferry or bridge companies, except for the erection of bridges crossing streams which form boundaries between this and any other State;

Vacating roads, town plats, streets or alleys;

Relating to cemeteries, graveyards or public grounds not of the states;

Authorizing the adoption or legitimation of children;

Locating or changing county seats;

Incorporating cities, towns or villages, or changing their charter;

For the opening and conducting of election or fixing or changing the places of voting;

Granting divorces;

Creating offices, or prescribing the powers and duties of officers in counties, cities, towns, election or school districts;

Changing the law of descent or succession;

Regulating the practice or jurisdiction of, or changing the rules of evidence in any judicial proceeding or inquiry before courts, justices of the peace, sheriffs, commissioners, arbitrators or other tribunals, or providing or changing methods for the collection of debts or the enforcing of judgments or prescribing the effect of judicial sales of real estate;

Regulating the fees or extending the powers and duties of aldermen, justices of the peace, magistrates or constables;

Regulating the management of public schools, the building or repairing of schoolhouses, and the raising of money for such purposes;

Fixing the rate of interest;

Affecting the estates of minors or persons under disability;

Remitting fines, penalties and forfeitures and refunding moneys legally paid into the Treasury;

Exempting property from taxation;

Regulating labor, trade, mining and manufacturing;

Declaring any named person of age;

Extending the time for the assessment or collection of taxes, or otherwise relieving any assessor or collector of taxes from the due performance of his official duties or his securities from liability;

Giving effect to informal or invalid wills or deeds;

Summoning or impaneling grand or petit juries;

For limitation of civil or criminal actions;

For incorporating railroads or other works of internal improvements;

And in all other cases where a general law can be made applicable no local or special law shall be enacted; provided, that nothing herein contained shall be construed to prohibit the Legislature from passing special laws for the preservation of the game and fish of this State in certain localities.

Sec. 57. **Notice of Local or Special Laws** — No local or special law shall be passed unless notice of the intention to apply therefor shall have been published in the locality where the matter or thing to be affected may be situated, which notice shall state the substance of the contemplated law, and shall be published at least thirty days prior to the introduction into the Legislature of such bill and in the manner to be provided by law. The evidence of such notice having been published shall be exhibited in the Legislature before such act shall be passed.

Sec. 58. **Sessions to Be Held at Austin, Seat of Government** — The Legislature shall hold its sessions at the City of Austin, which is hereby declared to be the seat of government.

Sec. 59. **Workmen's Compensation for State Employees** — The Legislature shall have power to pass such laws as may be necessary to provide for workmen's compensation insurance for such State employees, as in its judgment is necessary or required; and to provide for the payment of all costs, charges and premiums on such policies of insurance; providing, the state shall never be required to purchase insurance for any employee.

[Note — Sec. 59 of Art. III was added to provide for worker's compensation for state employees. Proposed by 44th Legislature and adopted in election, Nov. 3, 1936.]

Sec. 60. **Workmen's Compensation Insurance for County Employees** — The Legislature shall have the power to pass

Article III (Cont'd.)

such laws as may be necessary to enable all counties and other political subdivisions of this State to provide Workmen's Compensation insurance, including the right to provide its own insurance risk, for all employees of the county or political subdivision as in its judgment is necessary orrequired; and the Legislature shall provide suitable laws for the administration of such insurance in the counties or political subdivisions of this State and for the payment of the costs, charges and premiums on such policies of insurance and the benefits to be paid thereunder.

[Note — Sec. 60 of Art. III was added to provide workmen's compensation insurance for county employees. Submitted by 50th Legislature (1947) and adopted in election Nov. 2, 1948. It was further amended to include all political subdivisions. Submitted by 57th Legislature (1961) and adopted in election Nov. 6, 1962.]

Sec. 61. The Legislature shall have the power to enact laws to enable cities, towns and villages of this state to provide Workmen's Compensation Insurance, including the right to provide their own insurance risk for all employees; and the Legislature shall provide suitable laws for the administration of such insurance in the said municipalities and for payment of the costs, charges, and premiums on policies of insurance and the benefits to be paid thereunder.

[Note — Sec. 61 of Art. III was added to provide workmen's compensation insurance for municipal employees. Submitted by 52nd Legislature and adopted in election Nov. 4, 1952.]

Sec. 61-a. **Salary of Governor, Attorney General, Comptroller of Public Accounts, Treasurer, Commissioner of General Land Office and Secretary of State** — The Legislature shall not fix the salary of the Governor, Attorney General, Comptroller of Public Accounts, the Treasurer, Commissioner of the General Land Office or Secretary of State at a sum less than that fixed for such officials in the Constitution on Jan. 1, 1953.

[Note — Sec. 61-a of Art. III was added to fix the salaries of the aforementioned officials. Submitted by 53rd Legislature (1953) and adopted in election Nov. 2, 1954; as submitted in SJR 5, this amendment was designated merely as "Section 61" duplicating the number of an existing section. To distinguish between the two, it is here designated as "Section 61-a."]

Sec. 62. **Continuity of State and Local Governmental Operations** — (a) The Legislature, in order to insure continuity of state and local governmental operations in periods of emergency resulting from disasters caused by enemy attack, shall have the power and the immediate duty to provide for prompt and temporary succession to the powers and duties of public offices, of whatever nature and whether filled by election or appointment, the incumbents of which may become unavailable for carrying on the powers and duties of such offices. Provided, however, that Article I of the Constitution of Texas, known as the "Bill of Rights" shall not be in any manner affected, amended, impaired, suspended, repealed or suspended hereby.

(b) When such a period of emergency or the immediate threat of enemy attack exists, the Legislature may suspend procedural rules imposed by this Constitution that relate to:

(1) the order of business of the Legislature;

(2) the percentage of each house of the Legislature necessary to constitute a quorum;

(3) the requirement that a bill must be read on three days in each house before it has the force of law; .

(4) the requirement that a bill must be referred to and reported from committee before its consideration; and

(5) the date on which laws passed by the Legislature take effect.

(c) When such a period of emergency or the immediate threat of enemy attack exists, the Governor, after consulting with the Lieutenant Governor and the Speaker of the House of Representatives, may suspend the constitutional requirement that the Legislature hold its sessions in Austin, the seat of government. When this requirement has been suspended, the Governor shall determine a place other than Austin at which the Legislature will hold its sessions during such period of emergency or immediate threat of enemy attack. The Governor shall notify the Lieutenant Governor and the Speaker of the House of Representatives of the place and time at which the Legislature will meet. The Governor may take security precautions, consistent with the state of emergency, in determining the extent to which that information may be released.

(d) To suspend the constitutional rules specified by Subsection (b) of this section, the Governor must issue a proclamation and the House of Representatives and the Senate must concur in the proclamation as provided by this section.

(e) The Governor's proclamation must declare that a period of emergency resulting from disasters caused by enemy attack exists, or that the immediate threat of enemy attack exists, and that suspension of constitutional rules relating to legislative procedure is necessary to assure continuity of state government. The proclamation must specify the period, not to exceed two years, during which the constitutional rules specified by Subsection (b) of this section are suspended.

(f) The House of Representatives and the Senate, by concurrent resolution approved by the majority of the members present, must concur in the Governor's proclamation. A resolution of the House of Representatives and the Senate concurring in the Governor's proclamation suspends the constitutional rules specified by Subsection (b) of this section for the period of time specified by the Governor's proclamation.

(g) The constitutional rules specified by Subsection (b) of this section may not be suspended for more than two years under a single proclamation. A suspension may be renewed, however, if the Governor issues another proclamation as provided by Subsection (e) of this section and the House of Representatives and the Senate, by concurrent resolution, concur in that proclamation.

[Note — Sec. 62 of Art. III was added to provide for temporary succession to powers and duties of public offices in periods of emergency resulting from disaster caused by enemy attack. Submitted by 57th Legislature (1961) and adopted in election Nov. 6, 1962. It was amended to authorize suspension of certain constitutional rules relating to legislative procedure during disasters or during immediate threat of enemy attack. Submitted by 68th Legislature (1983) and adopted in election Nov. 8, 1983.]

Sec. 63. **Consolidation of Governmental Functions in Counties of 1,200,000 or More Inhabitants** — (1) The Legislature may by statute provide for the consolidation of some functions of government of any one or more political subdivisions comprising or located within any county in this state having one million, two hundred thousand (1,200,000) or more inhabitants. Any such statute shall require an election to be held within the political subdivisions affected thereby with approval by a majority of the voters in each of these political subdivisions, under such terms and conditions as the Legislature may require.

(2) The county government, or any political subdivision(s) comprising or located therein, may contract one with another for the performance of governmental functions required or authorized by this Constitution or the laws of this state, under such terms and conditions as the Legislature may prescribe. The term "governmental functions," as it relates to counties, includes all duties, activities and operations of statewide importance in which the county acts for the state, as well as of local importance, whether required or authorized by this Constitution or the laws of this state.

[Note — Sec. 63 of Art. III was added to provide for consolidation of governmental functions between political subdivisions within counties of 1,200,000 or more inhabitants. Submitted by 59th Legislature (1965) and adopted in election Nov. 8, 1966.]

Sec. 64. **Consolidation of Governmental Offices and Functions in Counties** — (a) The Legislature may by special statute provide for consolidation of governmental offices and functions of government of any one or more political subdivisions comprising or located within any county. Any such statute shall require an election to be held within the political subdivisions affected thereby with approval by a majority of the voters in each of these subdivisions, under such terms and conditions as the Legislature may require.

(b) The county government, or any political subdivision(s) comprising or located therein, may contract one with another for the performance of governmental functions required or authorized by this Constitution or the Laws of this State, under such terms and conditions as the Legislature may prescribe. No person acting under a contract made pursuant to this Subsection (b) shall be deemed to hold more than one office of honor, trust or profit or more than one civil office of emolument. The term "governmental functions," as it relates to counties, includes all duties, activities and operations of statewide importance in which the county acts for the State, as well as of local importance, whether required or authorized by this Constitution or the Laws of this State.

[Note — Sec. 64 of Art. III was added to provide for consolidation of governmental functions in El Paso and Tarrant Counties. Submitted by 60th Legislature (1967) and adopted in election Nov. 5, 1968. It was amended to provide for consolidation of governmental functions in any county. Submitted by 61st Legislature (1969) and adopted in election Nov. 3, 1970.]

Article III (Cont'd.); Article IV

Sec. 65. **Interest Rate on State Bonds** — (a) Wherever the Constitution authorizes an agency, instrumentality, or subdivision of the State to issue bonds and specifies the maximum rate of interest which may be paid on such bonds issued pursuant to such constitutional authority, such bonds may bear interest at rates not to exceed a weighted average annual interest rate of 12 percent unless otherwise provided by Subsection (b) of this section. All Constitutional provisions specifically setting rates in conflict with this provision are hereby repealed.

(b) Bonds issued by the Veterans' Land Board after the effective date of this subsection bear interest at a rate or rates determined by the board, but the rate or rates may not exceed a net effective interest rate of 10 percent per year unless otherwise provided by law. A statute that is in effect on the effective date of this subsection and that sets as a maximum interest rate payable on bonds issued by the Veterans' Land Board a rate different from the maximum rate provided by this subsection is ineffective unless reenacted by the Legislature after that date.

[Note — Sec. 65 of Art. III was added to set the interest rate on state bonds not to exceed a weighted average annual interest of 6 percent. Submitted by 62nd Legislature (1971) and adopted in election Nov. 7, 1972. The interest rate was raised to 12 percent in an amendment submitted by a special session of 67th Legislature (1982) and adopted in election Nov. 2, 1982.]

Article IV — Executive Department

Sec. 1. **Officers of Executive Department** — The executive department of the State shall consist of a Governor, who shall be the chief executive officer of the State; a Lieutenant Governor, Secretary of State, Comptroller of Public Accounts, Treasurer, Commissioner of the General Land Office and Attorney General.

Sec. 2. **Election of Executive Officers** — All the above officers of the executive department (except Secretary of State) shall be elected by the qualified voters of the State at the time and places of election for members of the Legislature.

Sec. 3. **Election Results; Ties; Contests** — The returns of every election for said executive officers, until otherwise provided by law, shall be made out, sealed up and transmitted by the returning officers prescribed by law, to the seat of government, directed to the Secretary of State, who shall deliver the same to the Speaker of the House of Representatives as soon as the Speaker shall be chosen, and the said Speaker shall, during the first week of the session of the Legislature, open and publish them in the presence of both houses of the Legislature. The person voted for at said election having the highest number of votes for each of said offices, respectively, and being constitutionally eligible, shall be declared by the Speaker, under sanction of the Legislature, to be elected to said office. But if two or more persons shall have the highest and an equal number of votes for either of said offices, one of them shall be immediately chosen to such office by a joint vote of both houses of the Legislature. Contested elections for either of said offices shall be determined by both houses of the Legislature in joint session.

Sec. 3-a. **Gubernatorial Succession** — If, at the time the Legislature shall canvass the election returns for the offices of Governor and Lieutenant Governor, the person receiving the highest number of votes for the office of Governor, as declared by the Speaker, has died, then the person having the highest number of votes for the office of Lieutenant Governor shall act as Governor until after the next general election. It is further provided that in the event the person with the highest number of votes for the Office of Governor as declared by the Speaker, shall become disabled, or fail to qualify, then the Lieutenant Governor shall act as Governor until a person has qualified for the office of Governor or until after the next general election. Any succession to the governorship not otherwise provided for in this Constitution may be provided for by law; provided, however, that any person succeeding to the office of Governor shall be qualified as otherwise provided in this Constitution, and shall, during the entire term to which he may succeed, be under all the restrictions and inhibitions imposed in this Constitution on the Governor.

[Note — Sec. 3-a was added to provide for gubernatorial succession. Submitted by 50th Legislature (1947) and adopted in election, Nov. 2, 1948.]

Sec. 4. **Governor, When Installed; Term; Qualifications** — The Governor elected at the general election in 1974, and thereafter, shall be installed on the first Tuesday after the organization of the Legislature, or as soon thereafter as practicable, and shall hold his office for the term of four years, or until his successor shall be duly installed. He shall be at least thirty years of age, a citizen of the United States, and shall have resided in this State at least five years immediately preceding his election.

[Note — Sec. 4 of Art. IV was amended to raise the term of office of Governor to four years. Submitted by 62nd Legislature (1971) and adopted in election Nov. 7, 1972.]

Sec. 5. **Governor's Salary and Mansion** — The Governor shall, at stated times, receive as compensation for his service an annual salary in an amount to be fixed by the Legislature, and shall have the use and occupation of the Governor's Mansion, fixtures and furniture.

[Note — Sec. 5 of Art. IV was first amended to raise Governor's salary from $4,000 to $12,000. Submitted by 44th Legislature (1935) and adopted in election Nov. 3, 1936. It was further amended to give Legislature authority to fix salary. Submitted by 53rd Legislature (1953) and adopted in election Nov. 2, 1954.]

Sec. 6. **Governor to Hold No Other Office, Etc.** — During the time he holds the office of Governor he shall not hold any other office, civil, military or corporate; nor shall he practice any profession or receive compensation, reward, fee or the promise thereof for the same; nor receive any salary, reward or compensation or the promise thereof from any person or corporation for any service rendered or performed during the time he is Governor or to be thereafter rendered or performed.

Sec. 7. **Commander in Chief; May Call Out Militia** — He shall be commander in chief of the military forces of the State, except when they are called into actual service of the United States. He shall have power to call forth the militia to execute the laws of the State, to suppress insurrections, repel invasions and protect the frontier from hostile incursions by Indians or other predatory bands.

Sec. 8. **Governor May Convene Legislature** — The Governor may, on extraordinary occasions, convene the Legislature at the seat of government or at a different place in case that should be in possession of the public enemy, or in case of the prevalence of disease threat. His proclamation therefor shall state specifically the purpose for which the Legislature is convened.

Sec. 9. **Governor's Message; to Account for Moneys; Present Estimates, Etc.** — The Governor shall, at the commencement of each session of the Legislature, and at the close of his term of office, give to the Legislature information, by message, of the condition of the State; and he shall recommend to the Legislature such measures as he may deem expedient. He shall account to the Legislature for all public moneys received and paid out by him from any funds subject to his order, with vouchers; and shall accompany his message with a statement of the same. And at the commencement of each regular session he shall present estimates of the amount of money required to be raised by taxation for all purposes.

Sec. 10. **Governor Shall Cause the Laws to Be Executed; Intercourse With Other States** — He shall cause the laws to be faithfully executed and shall conduct, in person, or in such manner as shall be prescribed by law, all intercourse and business of the State with other States and with the United States.

Sec. 11. **Board of Pardons and Paroles: Advisory Authority to Governor in Granting Reprieves, Paroles, Pardons, Etc.** — (a) The Legislature shall by law establish a Board of Pardons and Paroles and shall require it to keep record of its actions and the reasons for its actions. The Legislature shall have authority to enact parole laws and laws that require or permit courts to inform juries about the effect of good conduct time and eligibility for parole or mandatory supervision on the period of incarceration served by a defendant convicted of a criminal offense.

(b) In all criminal cases, except treason and impeachment the Governor shall have power, after conviction, on the written signed recommendation and advice of the Board of Pardons and Paroles, or a majority thereof, to grant reprieves and commutations of punishment and pardons; and under such rules as the Legislature may prescribe, and upon the written recommendation and advice of a majority of the Board of Pardons and Paroles, he shall have the power to remit fines and forfeitures. The Governor shall have the power to grant one reprieve in any capital case for a period not to exceed thirty (30) days; and he shall have the power to revoke conditional pardons. With the advice and consent of the Legislature, he may grant reprieves, commutations of punishment and pardons in cases of treason.

[Note—Sec. 11 of Art. IV was amended to establish the stated procedure for granting pardons and paroles, which was originally vested exclusively in the Governor's office. Submitted by 44th Legislature (1935) and adopted in election Nov. 3, 1936. It was again amended to make the Board of Pardons and Paroles a statutory agency and to give the board power to revoke paroles. Submitted by 68th Legislature (1983) and adopted in election Nov. 8, 1983. It was again amended to authorize jury instructions on good time and eligibility for parole and mandatory supervision. Proposed by 71st Legislature (1989) and adopted in

Article IV (Cont'd.)

election Nov. 7, 1989.]

Sec. 11A. **Suspension of Sentences; Probation** — The courts of the State of Texas having original jurisdiction of criminal actions shall have the power, after conviction, to suspend the imposition or execution of sentence and to place the defendant upon probation and to reimpose such sentence, under such conditions as the Legislature may prescribe.

[Note — Sec. 11A of Art. IV was added to provide for suspended sentences. Submitted by 44th Legislature (1935) and adopted in election Aug. 24, 1935.]

Sec. 11B. (a) The legislature by law may organize and combine into one or more agencies all agencies of the state that:

(1) have authority over the confinement or supervision of persons convicted of criminal offenses;

(2) set standards or distribute state funds to political subdivisions that have authority over the confinement or supervision of persons convicted of criminal offenses; or

(3) gather information about the administration of criminal justice.

(b) The legislature by law may authorize the appointment of members of more than one department of government to serve on the governing body.

[Note — Sec. 11B of Art. IV was added to authorize the legislature to organize and combine various state agencies that perform criminal justice functions. Proposed by 71st Legislature (1989) and adopted in election Nov. 7, 1989.]

Sec. 12. **Governor to Fill Vacancies in State and District Offices** — (a) All vacancies in State or district offices, except members of the Legislature, shall be filled, unless otherwise provided by law, by appointment of the Governor.

(b) An appointment of the Governor made during a session of the Senate shall be with the advice and consent of two thirds of the Senate present.

(c) In accordance with this section, the Senate may give its advice and consent on an appointment of the Governor made during a recess of the Senate. To be confirmed, the appointment must be with the advice and consent of two-thirds of the Senate present. If an appointment of the Governor is made during the recess of the Senate, the Governor shall nominate the appointee, or some other person to fill the vacancy, to the Senate during the first ten days of its next session following the appointment. If the Senate does not confirm a person under this subsection, the Governor shall nominate in accordance with this section the recess appointee or another person to fill the vacancy during the first ten days of each subsequent session of the Senate until a confirmation occurs. If the Governor does not nominate a person to the Senate during the first ten days of a session of the Senate as required by this subsection, the Senate at that session may consider the recess appointee as if the Governor had nominated the appointee.

(d) If the Senate, at any special session, does not take final action to confirm or reject a previously unconfirmed recess appointee or another person nominated to fill the vacancy for which the appointment was made:

(1) the Governor after the session may appoint another person to fill the vacancy; and

(2) the appointee, if otherwise qualified and if not removed as provided by law, is entitled to continue in office until the earlier of the following occurs:

(A) the Senate rejects the appointee at a subsequent session; or

(B) the Governor appoints another person to fill the vacancy under Subdivision (1) of this subsection.

(e) If the Senate, at a regular session, does not take final action to confirm or reject a previously unconfirmed recess appointee or another person nominated to fill the vacancy for which the appointment was made, the appointee or other person, as appropriate, is considered to be rejected by the Senate when the Senate session ends.

(f) If an appointee is rejected, the office shall immediately become vacant, and the Governor shall, without delay, make further nominations until a confirmation takes place. If a person has been rejected by the Senate to fill a vacancy, the Governor may not appoint the person to fill the vacancy or, during the term of the vacancy for which the person was rejected, to fill another vacancy in the same office or on the same board, commission, or other body.

(g) Appointments to vacancies in offices elective by the people shall only continue until the next general election.

(h) The Legislature by general law may limit the term to be served by a person appointed by the Governor to fill a vacancy in a state or district office to a period that ends before the vacant term otherwise expires or, for an elective office, before the next election at which the vacancy is to be filled, if the appointment is made on or after November 1 preceding the general election for the succeeding term of the office of Governor and the Governor is not elected at that election to the succeeding term.

(i) For purposes of this section, the expiration of a term of office or the creation of a new office constitutes a vacancy.

[Note — Sec. 12(a) was changed and Sec. 12(b) was added to Art. IV to limit the authority of a governor to fill vacancies in state and district offices if the governor is not re-elected. Submitted by 70th Legislature (1987) and adopted in election Nov. 3, 1987. It was further amended to clarify the authority of the Senate to consider certain nominees to state and district offices and to provide to filling vacancies in those offices. Submitted by 71st Legislature (1990) and adopted in election Nov. 6, 1990.]

Sec. 13. **Where Governor Shall Reside** — During the session of the Legislature the Governor shall reside where its sessions are held and at all other times at the seat of government, except when, by act of the Legislature, he may be required or authorized to reside elsewhere.

Sec. 14. **Approval of Bills; Veto Bill Not Returned to Become a Law** — Every bill which shall have passed both houses of the Legislature shall be presented to the Governor for his approval. If he approve, he shall sign it, but if he disapprove it, he shall return it with his objections to the house in which it originated, which house shall enter the objections at large upon its journal, and proceed to reconsider it. If, after such reconsideration, two thirds of the members present agree to pass the bill, it shall be sent, with the objections, to the other house, by which likewise it shall be reconsidered, and if approved by two thirds of the members of that house, it shall become a law; but in such cases the votes of both houses shall be determined by yeas and nays; and the names of the members voting for and against the bill shall be entered on the journal of each house, respectively. If any bill shall not be returned by the Governor with his objections within ten days (Sundays excepted) after it shall have been presented to him, the same shall be a law in like manner as if he had signed it, unless the Legislature, by its adjournment, prevent its return, in which case it shall be a law, unless he shall file the same, with his objections, in the office of the Secretary of State and give notice thereof by public proclamation within twenty days after such adjournment. If any bill presented to the Governor contains several items of appropriation he may object to one or more of such items, and approve the other portion of the bill. In such case he shall append to the bill, at the time of signing it, a statement of the items to which he objects, and no item so objected to shall take effect. If the Legislature be in session he shall transmit to the house in which the bill originated a copy of such statement, and the items objected to shall be separately considered. If, on reconsideration, one or more of such items be approved by two thirds of the members present, of each house, the same shall be part of the law, notwithstanding the objections of the Governor. If any such bill containing several items of appropriation not having been presented to the Governor ten days (Sundays excepted) prior to adjournment, be in the hands of the Governor at the time of adjournment, he shall have twenty days from such adjournment within which to file objections to any items thereof and make proclamation of the same, and such item or items shall not take effect.

Sec. 15. **What to Be Presented for Approval** — Every order, resolution or vote to which the concurrence of both houses of the Legislature may be necessary except on questions of adjournment shall be presented to the Governor, and before it shall take effect shall be approved by him; or, being disapproved, shall be repassed by both houses, and all the rules, provisions and limitations shall apply thereto as prescribed in the last preceding section in the case of a bill.

Sec. 16. **Lieutenant Governor; Election; Term; Powers and Duties** — There shall also be a Lieutenant Governor, who shall be chosen at every election for Governor by the same electors, in the same manner, continue in office for the same time and possess the same qualifications. The electors shall distinguish for whom they vote as Governor and for whom as Lieutenant Governor. The Lieutenant Governor shall, by virtue of his office, be President of the Senate and shall have, when in committee of the whole, a right to debate, and vote on all questions; and when the Senate is equally divided, to give the casting vote. In case of the death, resignation, removal from office, inability or refusal of the Governor to serve, or of his impeachment or absence from the State, the Lieutenant Governor shall exercise the powers and authority appertaining to the office of Governor until another be chosen at the periodical election, and be duly qualified; or until the Governor, impeached, absent or disabled, shall be acquitted, return or his disability be removed.

Sec. 17. **Vacancy in Office; Compensation** — (a) If, during

Article IV (Cont'd.); Article V

the vacancy in the office of Governor, the Lieutenant Governor should die, resign, refuse to serve or be removed from office or be unable to serve; or if he shall be impeached or absent from the State, the President of the Senate, for the time being, shall, in like manner, administer the government until he shall be superseded by a Governor or Lieutenant Governor.

(b) The Lieutenant Governor shall, while he acts as President of the Senate, receive for his services the same compensation and mileage which shall be allowed to the members of the Senate, and no more unless the Texas Ethics Commission recommends and the voters approve a higher salary in which case the salary is that amount; and during the time he administers the government, as Governor, he shall receive in like manner the same compensation which the Governor would have received had he been employed in the duties of his office, and no more. An increase in the emoluments of the office of Lieutenant Governor does not make a member of the Legislature ineligible to serve in the office of Lieutenant Governor.

(c) The President, for the time being, of the Senate, shall, during the time he administers the Government, receive in like manner the same compensation, which the Governor would have received had he been employed in the duties of his office.

Note — Section 17 Article IV was amended to authorize the Texas Ethics Commission to recommend the salary for the lieutenant governor, subject to approval by voters. Submitted by 72nd Legislature (1992) and adopted in election Nov. 5, 1991.

Sec. 18. **Succession to Governorship** — The Lieutenant Governor, or President of the Senate, succeeding to the office of Governor shall, during the entire terms to which he may succeed, be under all the restrictions and inhibitions imposed in this Constitution on the Governor.

Sec. 19. **Seal of State; Secretary of State to Keep, Etc.** — There shall be a seal of the State which shall be kept by the Secretary of State and used by him officially under the direction of the Governor. The seal of the State shall be a star of five points, encircled by olive and live oak branches, and the words "The State of Texas."

Sec. 20. **Commissions to Be Signed and Sealed** — All commissions shall be in the name and by the authority of the State of Texas, sealed with the State seal, signed by the Governor, and attested by the Secretary of State.

Sec. 21. **Secretary of State; Term; Duties; Compensation** — There shall be a Secretary of State, who shall be appointed by the Governor, by and with the advice and consent of the Senate, and who shall continue in office during the term of service of the Governor. He shall authenticate the publication of the laws and keep a fair register of all official acts and proceedings of the Governor, and shall, when required, lay the same and all papers, minutes and vouchers relative thereto, before the Legislature or either house thereof, and shall perform such other duties as may be required of him by law. He shall receive for his services an annual salary in an amount to be fixed by the Legislature.

[Note — Sec. 21 of Art. IV was amended to raise the salary of the Secretary of State from $2,000 to $6,000 a year. Submitted by 44th Legislature (1935) and adopted in election Nov. 3, 1936. Further amended to give Legislature authority to fix salary. Submitted by 53rd Legislature (1953) and adopted in election Nov. 2, 1954.]

Sec. 22. **Attorney General; Term; Duties; Residence; Salary** — The Attorney General elected at the general election in 1974, and thereafter, shall hold his office for four years and until his successor is duly qualified. He shall represent the State in all suits and pleas in the Supreme Court of the State in which the state may be a party, and shall especially inquire into the charter rights of all private corporations, and from time to time in the name of the State, take such action in the courts as may be proper and necessary to prevent any private corporation from exercising any power or demanding or collecting any species of taxes, tolls, freight or wharfage not authorized by law. He shall whenever sufficient cause exists, seek a judicial forfeiture of such charters, unless otherwise expressly directed by law, and give legal advice in writing to the Governor and other executive officers, when requested by them, and perform such other duties as may be required by law. He shall reside at the seat of government during his continuance in office. He shall receive for his services an annual salary in an amount to be fixed by the Legislature.

[Note — Sec. 22 of Art. IV was amended to raise the Attorney General's salary from $2,000 to $10,000 a year and to eliminate provisions for fees not to exceed $2,000 a year. Submitted by 44th Legislature (1935) and adopted in election Nov. 3, 1936. Further amended to give Legislature authority to fix salary. Submitted by 53rd Legislature (1953) and adopted in election Nov. 2, 1954. It was again amended to lengthen the term of office from two to four years. Submitted by 62nd Legislature (1971) and adopted in election Nov. 7, 1972.]

Sec. 23. **Comptroller; Treasurer, and Commissioner of the General Land Office; Terms; Salaries; Residence; Fees** — The Comptroller of Public Accounts, the Treasurer and the Commissioner of the General Land Office and any statutory state officer who is elected by the electorate of Texas at large, unless a term of office is otherwise specifically provided in this Constitution, shall each hold office for the term of four years and until his successor is qualified. The four-year term applies to these officers who are elected at the general election in 1974 or thereafter. Each shall receive an annual salary in an amount to be fixed by Legislature; reside at the capital of the State during his continuance in office, and perform such duties as are or may be required by law. They and the Secretary of State shall not receive to their own use any fees, costs or perquisites of office. All fees that may be payable by law for any service performed by any officer specified in this section, or in his office, shall be paid, when received into the State Treasury.

[Note — Sec. 23 of Art. IV was amended to raise salaries of three state officials mentioned from $2,500 each to $6,000 each annually. Submitted by 44th Legislature, and adopted in election Nov. 3, 1936. Further amended to give Legislature authority to fix salary. Submitted by 53rd Legislature (1953) and adopted in election Nov. 2, 1954. It was further amended to raise the term of office of the above-named officials to four years. Submitted by 62nd Legislature (1971) and adopted in election Nov. 7, 1972.]

Sec. 24. **Officers to Account to the Governor; Duty of Governor; False Reports** — An account shall be kept by the officers of the executive department and by all officers and managers of State institutions of all moneys and choses in action received and disbursed or otherwise disposed of by them, severally, from all sources, and for every service performed; and a semi-annual report thereof shall be made to the Governor, under oath. The Governor may, at any time, require information in writing from any and all of said officers or managers upon any subject relating to the duties, conditions, management and expenses of their respective offices and institutions, which information shall be required by the Governor under oath, and the Governor may also inspect their books, accounts, vouchers and public funds; and any officer or manager who, at any time shall willfully make a false report or give false information, shall be guilty of perjury and so adjudged and punished accordingly and removed from office.

Sec. 25. **Laws for Investigation of Breaches of Trust** — The Legislature shall pass efficient laws facilitating the investigation of breaches of trust and duty by all custodians of public funds and providing for their suspensions from office on reasonable cause shown, and for the appointment of temporary incumbents of their offices during such suspensions.

Sec. 26. **Notaries Public** — (a) The Secretary of State shall appoint a convenient number of notaries public for the state who shall perform such duties as now are or may be prescribed by law. The qualifications of notaries public shall be prescribed by law.

(b) The terms of office of notaries public shall not be less than two years nor more than four years as provided by law.

[Note — Sec. 26 of Art. IV was amended to give the Secretary of State the authority, formerly held by the Governor, to appoint notaries public, and to include the stated contents of paragraphs (b) and (c). Submitted by 46th Legislature (1939) and adopted in election Nov. 5, 1940. It was further amended to establish terms of notaries public for not less than two years nor more than four years; deleted old sections (b) and (c) and provided for terms of office for notaries. Submitted by 66th Legislature (1979) and adopted in election Nov. 6, 1979.]

Article V — Judicial Department

Sec. 1. **The Several Courts; Criminal Courts** — The judicial power of this State shall be vested in one Supreme Court, in one Court of Criminal Appeals, in Courts of Appeals, in District Courts, in County Courts, in Commissioners' Courts, in courts of Justices of the Peace and in such other courts as may be provided by law.

The Legislature may establish such other courts as it may deem necessary and prescribe the jurisdiction and organization thereof and may conform the jurisdiction of the district and other inferior courts thereto.

[Note — Sec. 1 of Art. V was amended to provide for "Courts of Civil Appeals" and a "Court of Criminal Appeals" in place of the old "Court of Appeals," making minor changes. Submitted by

Article V (Cont'd.)

22nd Legislature (1891), ratified at election Aug. 11, 1891, and declared adopted Sept. 22, 1891. It was again amended to provide for a Court of Criminal Appeals with nine judges and to permit the court to sit in panels of three judges. (See also note under Sec. 4 below.) Submitted by 65th Legislature (1977) and adopted in election Nov. 8, 1977. It was further amended to change Courts of Civil Appeals to Courts of Appeal. Submitted by 66th Legislature (1979) and adopted in election Nov. 4, 1980.]

Sec. 1-a. **Retirement and Compensation of Judges** — (1) Subject to the further provisions of this section, the Legislature shall provide for the retirement and compensation of justices and judges of the Appellate Courts and District and Criminal District Courts on account of length of service, age and disability, and for their reassignment to active duty where and when needed. The office of every such justice and judge shall become vacant when the incumbent reaches the age of seventy-five (75) years or such earlier age, not less than seventy (70) years, as the Legislature may prescribe; but, in the case of an incumbent whose term of office includes the effective date of this Amendment, this provision shall not prevent him from serving the remainder of said term nor be applicable to him before his period or periods of judicial service shall have reached a total of ten (10) years.

(2) The name of the State Judicial Qualifications Commission is changed to the State Commission on Judicial Conduct. The Commission consists of eleven (11) members, to wit: (i) one (1) Justice of a Court of Appeals; (ii) one (1) District Judge; (iii) two (2) members of the State Bar, who have respectively practiced as such for over ten (10) consecutive years next preceding their selection; (iiii) four (4) citizens, at least thirty (30) years of age, not licensed to practice law nor holding any salaried public office or employment; (v) one (1) Justice of the Peace; (vi) one (1) Judge of a Municipal Court; and, (vii) one (1) Judge of a County Court at Law; provided that no person shall be or remain a member of the Commission, who does not maintain physical residence within this state, or who resides in, or holds a judgeship within or for, the same Supreme Judicial District as another member of the Commission, or who shall have ceased to retain the qualifications above specified for his respective class of membership, except that the Justice of the Peace and the Judges of a Municipal Court and/or a County Court at Law shall be selected at large without regard to whether they reside or hold a judgeship in the same Supreme Judicial District as another member of the Commission. Commissioners of classes (i), (ii), and (vii) above shall be chosen by the Supreme Court with advice and consent of the Senate, those of class (iii) by the Board of Directors of the State Bar under regulations to be prescribed by the Supreme Court with advice and consent of the Senate, those of class (iiii) by appointment of the Governor with advice and consent of the Senate, and the commissioners of classes (v) and (vi) by appointment of the Supreme Court as provided by law, with the advice and consent of the Senate.

(3) The regular term of office of Commissioners shall be six (6) years; but the initial members of each of classes (i), (ii) and (iii) shall respectively be chosen for terms of four (4) and six (6) years, and the initial members of class (iiii) for respective terms of two (2), four (4) and six (6) years. Interim vacancies shall be filled in the same manner as vacancies due to expiration of a full term, but only for the unexpired portion of the term in question. Commissioners may succeed themselves in office only if having served less than three (3) consecutive years.

(4) Commissioners shall receive no compensation for their services as such. The Legislature shall provide for the payment of the necessary expense for the operation of the Commission.

(5) The Commission may hold its meetings, hearings and other proceedings at such times and places as it shall determine but shall meet at Austin at least once each year. It shall annually select one of its members as chairman. A quorum shall consist of six (6) members. Proceedings shall be by majority vote of those present, except that recommendations for retirement, censure, suspension, or removal of any person holding an office named in paragraph A of Subsection (6) of this section shall be by affirmative vote of at least six (6) members.

(6) A. Any justice or judge of the courts established by this Constitution or created by the Legislature as provided in Sec. 1, Art. V, of this Constitution, may, subject to the other provisions hereof, be removed from office for willful or persistent violation of rules promulgated by the Supreme Court of Texas, incompetence in performing the duties of the office, willful violation of the Code of Judicial Conduct, or willful or persistent conduct that is clearly inconsistent with the proper performance of his duties or casts public discredit upon the judiciary or administration of justice. Any person holding such office may be disciplined or censured, in lieu of removal from office, as provided by this section. Any person holding an office specified in this subsection may be suspended from office with or without pay by the Commission immediately on being indicted by a State or Federal grand jury for a felony offense or charged with a misdemeanor involving official misconduct. On the filing of a sworn complaint charging a person holding such office with willful or persistent violation of rules promulgated by the Supreme Court of Texas, incompetence in performing the duties of the office, willful violation of the Code of Judicial Conduct, or willful and persistent conduct that is clearly inconsistent with the proper performance of his duties or casts public discredit on the judiciary or on the administration of justice, the Commission, after giving the person notice and an opportunity to appear and be heard before the Commission, may recommend to the Supreme Court the suspension of such person from office. The Supreme Court, after considering the record of such appearance and the recommendation of the Commission, may suspend the person from office with or without pay, pending final disposition of the charge.

B. Any person holding an office named in paragraph A of this subsection who is eligible for retirement benefits under the laws of this state providing for judicial retirement may be involuntarily retired, and any person holding an office named in that paragraph who is not eligible for retirement benefits under such laws may be removed from office, for disability seriously interfering with the performance of his duties, which is, or is likely to become, permanent in nature.

C. The law relating to the removal, discipline, suspension, or censure of a Justice or Judge of the courts established by this Constitution or created by the Legislature as provided in this Constitution applies to a master or magistrate appointed as provided by law to serve a trial court of this State and to a retired or former Judge who continues as a judicial officer subject to an assignment to sit on a court of this State. Under the law relating to the removal of an active Justice or Judge, the Commission and the review tribunal may prohibit a retired or former Judge from holding judicial office in the future or from sitting on a court of this State by assignment.

(7) The Commission shall keep itself informed as fully as may be of circumstances relating to the misconduct or disability of particular persons holding an office named in paragraph A of Subsection (6) of this section, receive complaints or reports, formal or informal, from any source in this behalf and make such preliminary investigations as it may determine. Its orders for the attendance or testimony of witnesses or for the production of documents at any hearing or investigation shall be enforceable by contempt proceedings in the District Court or by a Master.

(8) After such investigation as it deems necessary, the Commission may in its discretion issue a private or public admonition, warning, reprimand, or requirement that the person obtain additional training or education, or if the Commission determines that the situation merits such action, it may institute formal proceedings and order a formal hearing to be held before it concerning the public censure, removal, or retirement of a person holding an office or position specified in Subsection (6) of this section, or it may in its discretion request the Supreme Court to appoint an active or retired District Judge or Justice of a Court of Appeals, or retired Judge or Justice of the Court of Criminal Appeals or the Supreme Court, as a Master to hear and take evidence in any such matter, and to report thereon to the Commission. The Master shall have all the power of a District Judge in the enforcement of orders pertaining to witnesses, evidence, and procedure. If, after formal hearing, or after considering the record and report of a Master, the Commission finds good cause therefor, it shall issue an order of public censure or it shall recommend to a review tribunal the removal or retirement, as the case may be, of the person in question holding an office or position specified in Subsection (6) of this section and shall thereupon file with the tribunal the entire record before the Commission.

(9) A tribunal to review the Commission's recommendation for the removal or retirement of a person holding an office or position specified in Subsection (6) of this section is composed of seven (7) Justices or Judges of the Courts of Appeals who are selected by lot by the Chief Justice of the Supreme Court. Each Court of Appeals shall designate one of its members for inclusion in the list from which the selection is made. Service on the tribunal shall be considered part of the official duties of a judge, and no additional compensation may be paid for such service. The review tribunal shall review the record of the proceedings on the law and facts and in its discretion may, for good cause shown, permit the introduction of additional evidence. Within 90 days after the date on which the record is filed with the review tribunal, it shall order public censure, retirement or removal, as it finds just and proper, or wholly reject the recommendation. A Justice, Judge, Master, or Magistrate may appeal a decision of the review tribunal to the Supreme Court under the substantial evidence rule. Upon an order for involuntary retirement for disability or an order for removal, the office in question shall become vacant. The review tribunal, in an order for involuntary re-

Article V (Cont'd.)
tirement for disability or an order for removal, may prohibit such person from holding judicial office in the future. The rights of an incumbent so retired to retirement benefits shall be the same as if his retirement had been voluntary.

(10) All papers filed with and proceedings before the Commission or a Master shall be confidential, unless otherwise provided by law, and the filing of papers with, and the giving of testimony before the Commission or a Master shall be privileged, unless otherwise provided by law. However, the Commission may issue a public statement through its executive director or its Chairman at any time during any of its proceedings under this Section when sources other than the Commission cause notoriety concerning a Judge or the Commission itself and the Commission determines that the best interests of a Judge or of the public will be served by issuing the statement.

(11) The Supreme Court shall by rule provide for the procedure before the Commission, Masters, review tribunal, and the Supreme Court. Such rule shall provide the right of discovery of evidence to a Justice, Judge, Master, or Magistrate after formal proceedings are instituted and shall afford to any person holding an office or position specified in Subsection (6) of this section, against whom a proceeding is instituted to cause his retirement or removal, due process of law for the procedure before the Commission, Masters, review tribunal, and the Supreme Court in the same manner that any person whose property rights are in jeopardy in an adjudicatory proceeding is entitled to due process of law, regardless of whether or not the interest of the person holding an office or position specified in Subsection (6) of this section in remaining in active status is considered to be a right or a privilege. Due process shall include the right to notice, counsel, hearing, confrontation of his accusers, and all such other incidents of due process as are ordinarily available in proceedings whether or not misfeasance is charged, upon proof of which a penalty may be imposed.

(12) No person holding an office specified in Subsection (6) of this section shall sit as a member of the Commission in any proceeding involving his own suspension, discipline, censure, retirement or removal.

(13) This Sec. 1-a is alternative to and cumulative of, the methods of removal of persons holding an office named in paragraph A of Subsection (6) of this section provided elsewhere in this Constitution.

(14) The Legislature may promulgate laws in furtherance of this Section that are not inconsistent with its provisions.

[Note — Sec. 1-a was added to provide for retirement and compensation of judges. Submitted by 50th Legislature (1947) and adopted in election, Nov. 2, 1948. It was amended to provide for automatic retirement of district and appellate judges for old age; to create the State Judicial Qualifications Commission and defining its functions; and empowering the Supreme Court to remove district and appellate judges for misconduct and to retire such judges in cases of disability. Submitted by 59th Legislature (1965) and adopted in election Nov. 2, 1965. It was further amended to specifically name those offices under the jurisdiction of the Commission and to broaden the Commission's duties and powers. Submitted by 61st Legislature (1969) and adopted in election Nov. 3, 1970. It was further amended to change the name of the State Judicial Qualifications Commission to the State Commission on Judicial Conduct; raise the number of members of the Commission to 11; set out specific qualifications for membership; and provide for the suspension, censure, removal or involuntary retirement of a justice under certain circumstances. Submitted by 65th Legislature (1977) and adopted in election Nov. 8, 1977. It was again amended to specify ways to discipline active judges, certain retired and former judges, and certain masters and magistrates of courts. Submitted by 68th Legislature (1983) and adopted in election Nov. 6, 1984.]

Sec. 2. **Supreme Court; Quorum; Qualifications; Election; Salary; Vacancy** — The Supreme Court shall consist of the Chief Justice and eight Justices, any five of whom shall constitute a quorum, and the concurrence of five shall be necessary to a decision of a case; provided, that when the business of the court may require, the court may sit in sections as designated by the court to hear argument of causes and to consider applications for writs of error or other preliminary matters. No person shall be eligible to serve in the office of Chief Justice or Justice of the Supreme Court unless the person is licensed to practice law in this state and is, at the time of election, a citizen of the United States and of this State and has attained the age of thirty-five years and has been a practicing lawyer or a lawyer and judge of a court of record together at least ten years. Said Justices shall be elected (three of them each two years) by the qualified voters of the State at a general election; shall hold their offices six years or until their successors are elected and qualified; and shall each receive such compensation as shall be provided by law. In case of a vacancy in the office of the Chief Justice or any Justice of the Supreme Court, the Governor shall fill the vacancy until the next general election for State officers, and at such general election the vacancy for the unexpired term shall be filled by election by the qualified voters of the State. The Justices of the Supreme Court who may be in office at the time this amendment takes effect shall continue in office until the expiration of their terms of office under the present Constitution and until their successors are elected and qualified.

[Note — Sec. 2 of Art. V has been amended three times: (1) To raise salaries and make minor adjustments. Submitted by 22nd Legislature, ratified in election Aug. 11, 1891, and declared adopted Sept. 22, 1891; (2) To raise the number of justices on the Supreme Court from three to nine and make other adjustments. Submitted by 49th Legislature (1945) and adopted in election Aug. 25, 1945; and (3) To change name of Commission of Appeals and qualifications of Supreme Court Justices. Submitted by 66th Legislature (1979) and adopted in election Nov. 4, 1980.]

Sec. 3. **Jurisdiction; Terms of Court** — The Supreme Court shall exercise the judicial power of the state except as otherwise provided in this Constitution. Its jurisdiction shall be co-extensive with the limits of the State and its determinations shall be final except in criminal law matters. Its appellate jurisdiction shall be final and shall extend to all cases except in criminal law matters and as otherwise provided in this Constitution or by law. The Supreme Court and the Justices thereof shall have power to issue writs of habeas corpus, as may be prescribed by law; and under such regulations as may be prescribed by law, the said courts and the Justices thereof may issue the writs of mandamus, procedendo, certiorari and such other writs as may be necessary to enforce its jurisdiction. The Legislature may confer original jurisdiction on the Supreme Court to issue writs of quo warranto and mandamus in such cases as may be specified, except as against the Governor of the State.

The Supreme Court shall also have power, upon affidavit or otherwise as by the court may be determined to ascertain such matters of fact as may be necessary to the proper exercise of its jurisdiction.

The Supreme Court shall appoint a clerk, who shall give bond in such manner as is now or may hereafter be required by law, and he may hold his office for four years and shall be subject to removal by said court for good cause entered of record on the minutes of said court, who shall receive such compensation as the Legislature may provide.

[Note — Sec. 3 of Art. V has been amended three times: (1) To readjust jurisdiction of the Supreme Court to that of the Courts of Civil Appeals that were established by amendment of the same date, and also to consolidate the original Sec. 4, providing for a clerk of the court, with Sec. 3. Submitted by 22nd Legislature (1891), ratified Aug. 11, 1891, and proclaimed Sept. 22, 1891; (2) To eliminate provisions that the Supreme Court "sit from first Monday in October of each year until the last Saturday in June of the next year," by amendment submitted as part of the amendment that added Sec. 3-a. (See note following that section).(3) To redefine the jurisdiction of the Supreme Court. Submitted by 66th Legislature (1979) and adopted in election Nov. 4, 1980.]

Sec. 3-a. **Time of Sitting** — The Supreme Court may sit at any time during the year at the seat of government for the transaction of business and each term thereof shall begin and end with each calendar year.

[Note — Sec. 3-a of Art. V was added to make the time of sitting of the Supreme Court discretionary with that court. It was substituted for a provision formerly incorporated in Sec. 3. (See note following Sec. 3.) Submitted by 41st Legislature (1929), ratified in election Nov. 4, 1930, and proclaimed Dec. 17, 1930.]

Sec. 3-b. **Direct Appeal** — The Legislature shall have the power to provide by law, for an appeal direct to the Supreme Court of this State from an order of any trial court granting or denying an interlocutory or permanent injunction on the grounds of the constitutionality or unconstitutionality of any statute of this State, or on the validity or invalidity of any administrative order issued by any state agency under any statute of this State.

[Note — Sec. 3-b of Art. V was added to provide for direct appeals. Submitted by 46th Legislature (1939) and adopted in election Nov. 5, 1940.]

Sec. 3-c. (a) The supreme court and the court of criminal appeals have jurisdiction to answer questions of state law certified from a federal appellate court.

Article V (Cont'd.)

(b) The supreme court and the court of criminal appeals shall promulgate rules of procedure relating to the review of those questions.

[Note — Sec. 3-c of Art. V was added to grant the Supreme Court and the Court of Criminals Appeals jurisdiction to answer questions of state law certified from a federal appellate court. Submitted by 69th Legislature (1985) and adopted in election Nov. 5, 1985.]

Sec. 4. **Court of Criminal Appeals** — The Court of Criminal Appeals shall consist of eight Judges and one Presiding Judge. The Judges shall have the same qualifications and receive the same salaries as the Associate Justices of the Supreme Court, and the Presiding Judge shall have the same qualifications and receive the same salary as the Chief Justice of the Supreme Court. The Presiding Judge and the Judges shall be elected by the qualified voters of the state at a general election and shall hold their offices for a term of six years. In case of a vacancy in the office of a Judge of the Court of Criminal Appeals, the Governor shall, with the advice and consent of the Senate, fill said vacancy by appointment until the next succeeding general election.

For the purpose of hearing cases, the Court of Criminal Appeals may sit in panels of three Judges, the designation thereof to be under rules established by the court. In a panel of three Judges, two Judges shall constitute a quorum and the concurrence of two Judges shall be necessary for a decision. The Presiding Judge, under rules established by the court, shall convene the court en banc for the transaction of all other business and may convene the court en banc for the purpose of hearing cases. The court must sit en banc during proceedings involving capital punishment and other cases as required by law. When convened en banc, five Judges shall constitute a quorum and the concurrence of five Judges shall be necessary for a decision. The Court of Criminal Appeals may appoint Commissioners in aid of the Court of Criminal Appeals as provided by law.

[Note — Sec. 4 of Art. V superseded, in part, the original Sec. 5, which provided for the former "Court of Appeals." The original Sec. 4 provided for the appointment of Supreme Court clerks, and was absorbed in the amended Sec. 3. Submitted by 22nd Legislature (1891); ratified Aug. 11, 1891, and adopted Sept. 22, 1891. It was further amended to raise number of judges from three to five and define their terms of office. Submitted by 59th Legislature (1965) and adopted in election Nov. 8, 1966. It was again amended to raise the number of judges from five to nine and to provide that the Court of Criminal Appeals may sit in panels of three judges. Submitted by 65th Legislature (1977) and adopted in election Nov. 8, 1977.]

Sec. 5. **Jurisdiction; Power; Terms; Clerk, Etc.** — The Court of Criminal Appeals shall have final appellate jurisdiction coextensive with the limits of the State and its determinations shall be final in all criminal cases of whatever grade, with such exceptions and under such regulations as may be provided in this Constitution or as prescribed by law.

The appeal of all cases in which the death penalty has been assessed shall be to the Court of Criminal Appeals. The appeal of all other criminal cases shall be to the Courts of Appeal as prescribed by law. In addition, the Court of Criminal Appeals may, on its own motion, review a decision of a Court of Appeals in a criminal case as provided by law. Discretionary review by the Court of Criminal Appeals is not a matter of right, but of sound judicial discretion.

Subject to such regulations as may be prescribed by law, the Court of Criminal Appeals and the Judges thereof shall have the power to issue the writ of habeas corpus, and in criminal law matters, the writs of mandamus, procedendo, prohibition, and certiorari. The court and the judges thereof shall have the power to issue such other writs as may be necessary to protect its jurisdiction or enforce its judgments. The court shall have the power upon affidavit or otherwise to ascertain such matters of fact as may be necessary to the exercise of its jurisdiction.

The Court of Criminal Appeals may sit for the transaction of business at any time during the year and each term shall begin and end with each calendar year. The Court of Criminal Appeals shall appoint a clerk of the court who shall give bond in such manner as is now or may hereafter be required by law, and who shall hold his office for a term of four years unless sooner removed by the court for good cause entered of record on the minutes of said court.

The clerk of the Court of Criminal Appeals who may be in office at the time when this amendment takes effect shall continue in office for the term of his appointment.

[Note — Sec. 5 of Art. V superseded primarily the original Sec. 6, which defined jurisdiction, powers, etc. of the old "Court of Appeals." (See also note following Sec. 6 below.) Submitted by 22nd Legislature (1891); ratified at election Aug. 11, 1891, and declared adopted Sept. 22, 1891. It was further amended to redefine jurisdiction, powers and terms of office. Submitted by 59th Legislature (1965) and adopted in election Nov. 8, 1966. (See note following Sec. 4 above.) It was again amended to enlarge the court's jurisdiction and to redefine its term of office. Submitted by 65th Legislature (1977) and adopted in election Nov. 8, 1977. It was again amended to redefine jurisdiction of Courts of Criminal Appeals. Submitted by 66th Legislature (1979) and adopted in election Nov. 4, 1980.]

Sec. 6. **Supreme Judicial Districts; Courts of Civil Appeals; Jurisdiction; Term; Justices; Election; Salary; Clerk** — The state shall be divided into courts of appeals districts, with each district having a Chief Justice, two or more other Justices, and such other officials as may be provided by law. The Justices shall have the qualifications prescribed for Justices of the Supreme Court. The Court of Appeals may sit in sections as authorized by law. The concurrence of a majority of the judges sitting in a section is necessary to decide a case. Said Court of Appeals shall have appellate jurisdiction coextensive with the limits of their respective districts, which shall extend to all cases of which the District Courts or County Courts have original or appellate jurisdiction under such restrictions and regulations as may be prescribed by law. Provided, that the decisions of said courts shall be conclusive on all questions of fact brought before them on appeal or error. Said courts shall have such other jurisdiction, original and appellate, as may be prescribed by law.

Each of said Courts of Appeals shall hold its sessions at a place in its district to be designated by the Legislature and at such time as may be prescribed by law. Said justices shall be elected by the qualified voters of their respective districts at a general election for a term of six years and shall receive for their services the sum provided by law. Each Court of Appeals shall appoint a clerk in the same manner as the clerk of the Supreme Court, which clerk shall receive such compensation as may be fixed by law.

All constitutional and statutory references to the Courts of Civil Appeals shall be construed to mean the Courts of Appeals.

[Note — Sec. 6 of Art. V, establishing the Courts of Civil Appeals, superseded parts of the original Secs. 5 and 6, which provided for the old "Court of Appeals," and defined its jurisdiction, powers, etc. Submitted by 22nd Legislature (1891), ratified in election Aug. 11, 1891, and declared adopted Sept. 22, 1891. It was further amended to increase the number of justices on a Court of Civil Appeals, permitting a Court of Civil Appeals to sit in sections and requiring a concurrence of a majority of justices to decide a case. Submitted by 65th Legislature (1977) and adopted in election Nov. 7, 1978. It was again amended to change the name of the Courts of Civil Appeals to the Courts of Appeal and to redefine the jurisdiction of said courts. Submitted by 66th Legislature (1979) and adopted in election Nov. 4, 1980. It was again amended to redefine the membership and duties of the Courts of Appeals. Submitted by 69th Legislature (1985) and adopted in election Nov. 5, 1985.]

Sec. 7. **Judicial Districts; Judges; Their Qualifications; Residence; Term of Office; Salary; Terms of Court** — The State shall be divided into judicial districts, with each district having one or more Judges as may be provided by law or by this Constitution. Each district judge shall be elected by the qualified voters at a General Election and shall be a citizen of the United States and of this State, who is licensed to practice law in this State and has been a practicing lawyer or a Judge of a Court in this State, or both combined, for four (4) years next preceding his election, who has resided in the district in which he was elected for two (2) years next preceding his election, and who shall reside in his district during his term of office and hold his office for the period of four (4) years, and who shall receive for his services an annual salary to be fixed by the Legislature. The Court shall conduct its proceedings at the county seat of the county in which the case is pending, except as otherwise provided by law. He shall hold the regular terms of his Court at the County Seat of each County in his district in such manner as may be prescribed by law. The Legislature shall have power by General or Special Laws to make such provisions concerning the terms or sessions of each Court as it may deem necessary.

The Legislature shall also provide for the holding of District Court when the Judge thereof is absent, or is from any cause disabled or disqualified from presiding.

[Note — Sec. 7 of Art. V has been amended three times: (1) To eliminate specification that judge must be "twenty-five years of age" and making minor changes. Submitted by 22nd Legislature (1891) and ratified in election Aug. 11, 1891. (2) Providing

Article V (Cont'd.)

that the District Court shall conduct its proceedings in the county seat of the county in which the case is pending "except as otherwise provided by law." Submitted by 51st Legislature (1949) and adopted in election Nov. 8, 1949. (3) Redefining the membership and terms of office of the district courts. Submitted by 69th Legislature (1985) and adopted in election Nov. 5, 1985.]

Sec. 7a. (a) The Judicial Districts Board is created to reapportion the judicial districts authorized by Art. V, Sec. 7, of this constitution.

(b) The membership of the board consists of the Chief Justice of the Texas Supreme Court who serves as chairman, the presiding judge of the Texas Court of Criminal Appeals, the presiding judge of each of the administrative judicial districts of the state, the president of the Texas Judicial Council, and one person who is licensed to practice law in this state appointed by the governor with the advice and consent of the senate for a term of four years. In the event of a vacancy in the appointed membership, the vacancy is filled for the unexpired term in the same manner as the original appointment.

(c) A majority of the total membership of the board constitutes a quorum for the transaction of business. The adoption of a reapportionment order requires a majority vote of the total membership of the board.

(d) The reapportionment powers of the board shall be exercised in the interims between regular sessions of the Legislature, except that a reapportionment may not be ordered by the board during an interim immediately following a regular session of the Legislature in which a valid and subsisting statewide apportionment of judicial districts is enacted by the Legislature. The board has other powers and duties as provided by the Legislature and shall exercise its powers under the policies, rules, standards, and conditions, not inconsistent with this section, that the Legislature provides.

(e) Unless the Legislature enacts a statewide reapportionment of the judicial districts following each federal decennial census, the board shall convene not later than the first Monday of June of the third year following the year in which the federal decennial census is taken to make a statewide reapportionment of the districts. The board shall complete its work on the reapportionment and file its order with the secretary of state not later than Aug. 31 of the same year. If the Judicial Districts Board fails to make a statewide apportionment by that date, the Legislative Redistricting Board established by Art. III, Sec. 28, of this constitution shall make a statewide reapportionment of the judicial districts not later than the 150th day after the final day for the Judicial Districts Board to make the reapportionment.

(f) In addition to the statewide reapportionment, the board may reapportion the judicial districts of the state as the necessity for reapportionment appears by redesignating, in one or more reapportionment orders, the county or counties that comprise the specific judicial districts affected by those reapportionment orders. In modifying any judicial district, no county having a population as large or larger than the population of the judicial district being reapportioned shall be added to the judicial district.

(g) Except as provided by Subsection (i) of this section, this section does not limit the power of the Legislature to reapportion the judicial districts of the state, to increase the number of judicial districts, or to provide for consequent matters on reapportionment. The Legislature may provide for the effect of a reapportionment made by the board on pending cases or the transfer of pending cases, for jurisdiction of a county court where county court jurisdiction has been vested by law in a district court affected by the reapportionment, for terms of the courts upon existing officers and their duties, and for all other matters affected by the reapportionment. The Legislature may delegate any of these powers to the board. The Legislature shall provide for the necessary expenses of the board.

(h) Any judicial reapportionment order adopted by the board must be approved by a record vote of the majority of the membership of both the senate and house of representatives before such order can become effective and binding.

(i) The Legislature, the Judicial Districts Board, or the Legislative Redistricting Board may not redistrict the judicial districts to provide for any judicial district smaller in size than an entire county except as provided by this section. Judicial districts smaller in size than the entire county may be created subsequent to a general election where a majority of the persons voting on the proposition adopt the proposition "to allow the division of ________ County into judicial districts composed of parts of ________ County." No redistricting plan may be proposed or adopted by the Legislature, the Judicial Districts Board, or the Legislative Redistricting Board in anticipation of a future action by the voters of any county.

[Note — Sec. 7a of Art. V was added to create the Judicial Districts Board and to define its membership and duties. Submitted by 69th Legislature (1985) and adopted in election Nov. 5, 1985.]

Sec. 8. **Jurisdiction and Powers of the District Courts** — District Court jurisdiction consists of exclusive, appellate, and original jurisdiction of all actions, proceedings, and remedies, except in cases where exclusive, appellate, or original jurisdiction may be conferred by this Constitution or other law on some other court, tribunal, or administrative body. District Court judges shall have the power to issue writs necessary to enforce their jurisdiction. The District Court shall have appellate jurisdiction and general supervisory control over the County Commissioners' Court with such exceptions and under such regulations as may be prescribed by law.

[Note — Sec. 8 of Art. V was amended to include the words "of contested elections" in the first paragraph and to add the last sentence in the second paragraph. Submitted by 22nd Legislature (1891), ratified in election Aug. 11, 1891, and declared adopted Sept. 22, 1891. It was further amended to give District and County Courts general jurisdiction over probate matters. It further provided that Legislature may increase, diminish or eliminate jurisdiction of District Court or County Court in probate matters and that Legislature may provide that all appeals in such matters be to Courts of Civil Appeals. Submitted by 63rd Legislature (1973) and adopted in election Nov. 6, 1973. It was again amended to define the exact duties of the judges of the district courts. Submitted by 69th Legislature (1985) and adopted in election Nov. 5, 1985.]

Sec. 9. **Clerk of the District Court; Term of Office; How Removed; How Vacancy Is Filled** — There shall be a Clerk for the District Court of each county, who shall be elected by the qualified voters for state and county officers, and who shall hold his office for four years, subject to removal by information, or by indictment of a grand jury and conviction by a petit jury. In case of vacancy the judge of a District Court shall have the power to appoint a Clerk, who shall hold until the office can be filled by election.

[Note — Sec. 9 of Art. V was amended to change the term of office from two to four years. Submitted by 53rd Legislature (1953) and adopted in election Nov. 2, 1954.]

Sec. 10. **Jury Trial; by Whom Fee Is to Be Paid** — In the trial of all cases in the District Courts, the plaintiff or defendant shall, upon application made in open court, have the right of trial by jury; but no jury shall be impaneled in any civil case unless demanded by a party to the case, and a jury fee be paid by the party demanding a jury, for such sum and with such exceptions as may be prescribed by the Legislature.

Sec. 11. **Disqualification of Judges; Special Judges; Exchange of Districts; Vacancies** — No judge shall sit in any case wherein he may be interested, or where either of the parties may be connected with him either by affinity or consanguinity, within such a degree as may be prescribed by law, or when he shall have been counsel in the case. When the Supreme Court, the Court of Criminal Appeals, the Court of Civil Appeals, or any member of either, shall be thus disqualified to hear and determine any case or cases in said court, the same shall be certified to the Governor of the State, who shall immediately commission the requisite number of persons, learned in the law, for the trial and determination of such cause or causes. When a Judge of the District Court is disqualified by any of the causes above stated, the parties may, by consent, appoint a proper person to try said case; or, upon their failing to do so, a competent person may be appointed to try the same in the county where it is pending in such manner as may be prescribed by law.

And the District Judges may exchange districts or hold courts for each other when they may deem it expedient, and shall do so when required by law. This disqualification of Judges of inferior tribunals shall be remedied, and vacancies in their offices filled, as may be prescribed by law.

[Note — Sec. II of Art. V was amended to use correct references to courts as established in amended Secs. 1, 3, 4, 5 and 6. Submitted by 22nd Legislature (1891), ratified at election Aug. 11, 1891, and declared adopted Sept. 22, 1891.]

Sec. 12. **Judges Conservators of Peace; Style of Writs; Prosecution by State** — (a) All judges of courts of this State, by virtue of their office, are conservators of the peace throughout the State.

(b) An indictment is a written instrument presented to a court by a grand jury charging a person with the commission of an offense. An information is a written instrument presented to a court by an attorney for the State charging a person with the commission of an offense. The practice and procedures relating

Article V (Cont'd.)
to the use of indictments and informations, including their contents, amendment, sufficiency, and requisites, are as provided by law. The presentment of an indictment or information to a court invests the court with jurisdiction of the cause.

[Note — Sec. 12 of Art. V was amended to substitute "Courts of the State" for enumeration of kinds of courts contained in original sections and applying to courts before general revision of judiciary in 1891. Submitted by 22nd Legislature (1891), ratified in election Aug. 11, 1891, and declared adopted Sept. 22, 1891. It was further amended to explain the manner in which a person is charged with a criminal offense and certain requirements applicable to state writs and processes. Submitted by 69th Legislature (1985) and adopted in election Nov. 5, 1985.]

Sec. 13. **Jurors, Grand and Petit; Number Required to Return Verdict** — Grand and petit juries in the District Courts shall be composed of twelve men; but nine members of a grand jury shall be a quorum to transact business and present bills. In trials of civil cases and in trials of criminal cases below the grade of felony in the District Courts, nine members of the jury concurring may render a verdict, but when the verdict shall be rendered by less than the whole number, it shall be signed by every member of the jury concurring in it. When, pending the trial of any case, one or more jurors, not exceeding three, may die, or be disabled from sitting, the remainder of the jury shall have the power to render the verdict; provided, that the Legislature may change or modify the rule authorizing less than the whole number of the jury to render a verdict.

[Note — Sec. 14 of Art. V, defining judicial districts and time of holding courts was deleted by constitutional amendment, submitted by 69th Legislature and approved in election Nov. 5, 1985.]

Sec. 15. **County Court; Election; Term of Office of County Judges; Fees** — There shall be established in each county in this State, a County Court, which shall be a court of record; and there shall be elected in each county by the qualified voters a County Judge, who shall be well informed in the law of the state, shall be a conservator of the peace, and shall hold his office for four years and until his successor shall be elected and qualified. He shall receive as compensation for his services such fees and perquisites as may be prescribed by law.

[Note — Sec. 15 of Art. V was amended to change the term of office from two to four years. Submitted by 53rd Legislature (1953) and adopted in election Nov. 2, 1954.]

Sec. 16. **Jurisdiction of County Court; Appeals; Probate Jurisdiction; May Issue Writs; Judge Disqualified, When** — The County Court has jurisdiction as provided by law. The County Judge is the presiding officer of the County Court and has judicial functions as provided by law. County court judges shall have the power to issue writs necessary to enforce their jurisdiction.

County Courts in existence on the effective date of this amendment are continued unless otherwise provided by law. When the Judge of the County Court is disqualified in any case pending in the County Court the parties interested may, by consent, appoint a proper person to try said case, or upon their failing to do so a competent person may be appointed to try the same in the county where it is pending in such manner as may be prescribed by law.

[Note — Sec. 16 of Art. V has been amended four times: (1) To make changes relating to appeals to the county court, relating to disqualification of the judge, and minor changes. Submitted by 22nd Legislature (1891), ratified at election Aug. 11, 1891, and declared adopted Sept. 22, 1891. (2) To extend jurisdiction of Justices of Peace in civil cases. (See also Sec. 19 of Art. V.) Submitted by 65th Legislature (1977) and adopted in election Nov. 7, 1978. (3) To redefine jurisdiction of appellate courts. Submitted by 66th Legislature (1979) and adopted in election Nov. 4, 1980. (4) To define the jurisdiction of the County Judge and his duties. Submitted by 69th Legislature (1985) and adopted in election Nov. 5, 1985.]

[Note — Sec. 16-a of Art. V, providing for probate courts, was deleted by constitutional amendment. Submitted by 69th Legislature (1985) and approved in election Nov. 5, 1985.]

Sec. 17. **Terms of County Court for Criminal Business; Prosecution Commenced by Information; Grand Jury to Inquire Into Misdemeanors; Quashing of Grand Jury Indictments; Jury** — The County Court shall hold terms as provided by law. Prosecutions may be commenced in said court by information filed by the County Attorney, or by affidavit, as may be provided by law. Grand juries empaneled in the District Courts shall inquire into misdemeanors, and all indictments therefor returned into the District Courts shall forthwith be certified to the County Courts, or other inferior courts having jurisdiction to try them, for trial; and if such indictment be quashed in the county, or other inferior court, the person charged shall not be discharged if there is probable cause of guilt, but may be held by such court or magistrate to answer an information or affidavit. A jury in the County Court shall consist of six men; but no jury shall be empaneled to try a civil case, unless demanded by one of the parties, who shall pay such jury fee therefor in advance as may be prescribed by law, unless he makes affidavit that he is unable to pay the same.

[Note — Sec. 17 of Art. V was amended to redefine the terms of office of county judges. Submitted by 69th Legislature (1985) and adopted in election Nov. 5, 1985.]

Sec. 18. **Terms of Justices of the Peace; County Commissioners and Commissioners' Court** — (a) Each county in the state, with a population of 30,000 or more, according to the most recent federal census, from time to time, for the convenience of the people, shall be divided into not less than four and not more than eight precincts. Each county in the State with a population of 18,000 or more but less than 30,000 according to the most recent federal census, from time to time, for the convenience of the people, shall be divided into not less than two and not more than five precincts. Each county in the State with a population of less than 18,000, according to the most recent federal census, from time to time, for the convenience of the people, shall be designated as a single precinct or, if the Commissioners Court determines that the county needs more than one precinct, shall be divided into not more than four precincts. Notwithstanding the population requirements of this subsection, Chambers County, from time to time, for the convenience of the people, shall be divided into not less than two and not more than six precincts. A division or designation under this subsection shall be made by the Commissioners Court provided for by this Constitution. In each such precinct there shall be elected one Justice of the Peace and one Constable, each of whom shall hold his office for four years and until his successor shall be elected and qualified; provided that in a county with a population of less than 150,000, according to the most recent federal census, in any precinct in which there may be a city of 18,000 or more inhabitants, there shall be elected two Justices of the Peace, and in a county with a population of 150,000 or more, according to the most recent federal census, each precinct may contain more than one Justice of the Peace Court.

(b) Each county shall, in the manner provided for justice of the peace and constable precincts, be divided into four Commissioners' precincts in each of which there shall be elected by the qualified voters thereof one County Commissioner, who shall hold his office for four years and until his successor shall be elected and qualified. The County Commissioners so chosen, with the County Judge as presiding officer, shall compose the County Commissioners Court, which shall exercise such powers and jurisdiction over all county business as is conferred by this Constitution and the laws of the state, or as may be hereafter prescribed.

(c) When the boundaries of justice of the peace and constable precincts are changed, each Justice and Constable in office on the effective date of the change, or elected to a term of office beginning on or after the effective date of the change, shall serve in the precinct in which the person resides for the term to which each was elected or appointed, even though the change in boundaries places the person's residence outside the precinct for which he was elected or appointed, abolishes the precinct for which he was elected or appointed, or temporarily results in extra Justices or Constables serving in a precinct. When, as a result of a change of precinct boundaries, a vacancy occurs in the office of Justice of the Peace or Constable, the Commissioners Court shall fill the vacancy by appointment until the next general election.

(d) When the boundaries of commissioners precincts are changed, each commissioner in office on the effective date of the change, or elected to a term of office beginning on or after the effective date of the change, shall serve in the precinct to which each was elected or appointed for the entire term to which each was elected or appointed, even though the change in boundaries places the person's residence outside the precinct for which he was elected or appointed.

[Note — Sec. 18 of Art. V has been amended four times: (1) To change the term of office for Justices of the Peace and Constables from two to four years. Submitted by 53rd Legislature (1953) and adopted in election Nov. 2, 1954. (2) To authorize fewer justice of the peace and constable precincts in counties with populations of less than 30,000 and to provide for continu-

Article V (Cont'd.)
ous service by Justices of Peace, Constables and County Commissioners when precinct boundaries are changed. Submitted by 68th Legislature (1983) and adopted in election Nov. 8, 1983. (3) To allow Chambers County to be divided into two to six precincts. Submitted by 69th Legislature (1985) and adopted in election Nov. 5, 1985. (4) To provide that certain justice precincts may contain more than one justice of the peace court. Submitted by 70th Legislature (1987) and adopted in election Nov. 3, 1987.]

Sec. 19. **Criminal Jurisdiction of Justices of the Peace; Appeals; Justices of the Peace ex-Officio Notaries** — Justice of the peace courts shall have original jurisdiction in criminal matters of misdemeanor cases punishable by fine only, exclusive jurisdiction in civil matters where the amount in controversy is two hundred dollars or less, and such other jurisdiction as may be provided by law. Justices of the peace shall be ex officio notaries public.

[Note — Sec. 19 of Art. V was amended to extend jurisdiction of Justices of Peace and to give them jurisdiction in civil matters involving $200 or less. (See also Sec. 16 of Art. V.) Submitted by 65th Legislature (1977) and adopted in election Nov. 7, 1978. It was again amended to redefine the duties of Justices of the Peace and to make them ex officio notaries public. Submitted by 69th Legislature (1985) and adopted in election Nov. 5, 1985.]

Sec. 20. **County Clerk; Election; Terms; Duties; Vacancies** — There shall be elected for each county, by the qualified voters, a County Clerk, who shall hold his office for four years, who shall be clerk of the County and Commissioners' Courts and recorder of the county, whose duties, perquisites and fees of office shall be prescribed by the Legislature, and a vacancy in whose office shall be filled by the Commissioners' Court until the next general election; provided, that in counties having a population of less than 8,000 persons there may be an election of a single clerk, who shall perform the duties of District and County Clerks.

[Note — Sec. 20 of Art. V was amended to change the term of office from two to four years. Submitted by 53rd Legislature (1953) and adopted in election Nov. 2, 1954.]

Sec. 21. **County and District Attorneys; Duties; Vacancies; Fees** — A County Attorney, for counties in which there is not a resident Criminal District Attorney, shall be elected by the qualified voters of each county, who shall be commissioned by the Governor and hold his office for the term of four years. In case of vacancy the Commissioners' Court of the county shall have power to appoint a County Attorney until the next general election. The County Attorneys shall represent the State in all cases in the District and inferior courts in their respective counties; but if any county shall be included in a district in which there shall be a District Attorney, the respective duties of District Attorneys and County Attorneys shall, in such counties, be regulated by the Legislature. The Legislature may provide for the election of District Attorneys in such districts as may be deemed necessary, and make provisions for the compensation of District Attorneys and County Attorneys. District Attorneys shall hold office for a term of four years, and until their successors have qualified.

[Note — Sec. 21 of Art. V was amended to change the term of office from two to four years; also leaves solely to Legislature provision for annual salary to be paid by State to District and County Attorneys. Submitted by 53rd Legislature (1953) and adopted in election Nov. 2, 1954.]

[Note — Sec. 22 of Art. V, giving Legislature power to change jurisdiction of county courts, was deleted by constitutional amendment. Submitted by 69th Legislature (1985) and adopted in election Nov. 5, 1985.]

Sec. 23. **Sheriff; Term of Office; Vacancy** — There shall be elected by the qualified voters of each county a Sheriff, who shall hold his office for the term of four years, whose duties, qualifications, perquisites, and fees of office shall be prescribed by the Legislature, and vacancies in whose office shall be filled by the Commissioners Court until the next general election.

[Note — Sec. 23 of Art. V was amended to change the term of office from two to four years. Submitted by 53rd Legislature (1953) and adopted in election Nov. 2, 1954. It was further amended to allow the legislature to prescribe the qualifications of sheriffs. Submitted by 73rd Legislature (1993) and adopted in election Nov. 2, 1993.]

Sec. 24. **Certain Officers Removed by District Courts for Drunkenness, Incompetency, Official Misconduct, Etc.** — County Judges, County Attorneys, Clerks of the District and County Courts, Justices of the Peace, Constables and other county officers may be removed by the Judges of the District Courts for incompetency, official misconduct, habitual drunkenness or other causes defined by law, upon the cause therefor being set forth in writing, and the finding of its truth by a jury.

[Note — Sec. 25 of Art. V, giving the Supreme Court power to make rules of procedure, was deleted by constitutional amendment. Submitted by 69th Legislature (1985) and approved in election Nov. 5, 1985.]

Sec. 26. **Limited Right of Appeal by the State in Criminal Cases** — The State is entitled to appeal in criminal cases, as authorized by general law.

[Note — Sec. 26 of Art. V was amended to give the state a limited right to appeal in criminal cases. Submitted by 70th Legislature and adopted in election Nov. 3, 1987.]

Sec. 27. **Transfer of Cases by the Legislature** — The Legislature shall, at its first session provide for the transfer of all business, civil and criminal, pending in District Courts, over which jurisdiction is given by this Constitution to the County Courts or other inferior courts, to such county or inferior courts, and for the trial or disposition of all such causes by such county or other inferior courts.

Sec. 28. **Vacancies in Offices of Judges of Superior Courts to Be Filled by the Governor** — Vacancies in the office of the Judges of the Supreme Court, the Court of Criminal Appeals, the Court of Civil Appeals and District Courts shall be filled by the Governor until the next succeeding general election, and vacancies in the office of County Judge and Justices of the Peace shall be filled by the Commissioners' Court until the next succeeding general election.

[Note — Sec. 28 of Art. V was amended to make names of courts harmonize with names in amended Secs. 1, 3, 4, 5 and 6. Submitted by 22nd Legislature (1891), ratified in election Aug. 11, 1891, and declared adopted Sept. 22, 1891. This section was again amended to provide that appointments to the offices of County Judge and Justice of the Peace should be filled only to the next succeeding general election instead of for the full elected term. Submitted by 55th Legislature (1957) and adopted in election Nov. 4, 1958.]

Sec. 29. **Terms of County Courts; Probate Business; Prosecutions** — The County Court shall hold at least four terms for both civil and criminal business annually, as may be provided by the Legislature, or by the Commissioners' Court of the county under authority of law, and such other terms each year as may be fixed by the Commissioners' Court; provided, the Commissioners' Court of any county having fixed the times and number of terms of the County Court shall not change the same again until the expiration of one year. Said court shall dispose of probate business either in term time or vacation, under such regulations as may beprescribed by law. Prosecutions may be commenced in said courts in such manner as is or may be provided by law, and a jury therein shall consist of six men. Until otherwise provided, the terms of the County Court shall be held on the first Mondays in February, May, August and November, and may remain in session three weeks.

[Note — Sec. 29 of Art. V was added to prescribe county court terms. Submitted by 18th Legislature (1883), ratified in election Aug. 14, 1883, and proclaimed adopted Sept. 25, 1883.]

Sec. 30. **County Judges and Criminal District Attorneys; Terms** — The Judges of all courts of county-wide jurisdiction heretofore or hereafter created by the Legislature of this State, and all Criminal District Attorneys now or hereafter authorized by the laws of this State, shall be elected for a term of four years, and shall serve until their successors have qualified.

[Note — Sec. 30 of Art. V was added to prescribe term of office of county judges and criminal district attorneys. Submitted by 53rd Legislature (1953) and adopted in election Nov. 2, 1954.]

Sec. 31. **Court Administration and Rule-making Authority** — (a) The Supreme Court is responsible for the efficient administration of the judicial branch and shall promulgate rules of administration not inconsistent with the laws of the state as may be necessary for the efficient and uniform administration of justice in the various courts.

(b) The Supreme Court shall promulgate rules of civil procedure for all courts not inconsistent with the laws of the state as may be necessary for the efficient and uniform administration of justice in the various courts.

(c) The Legislature may delegate to the Supreme Court or Court of Criminal Appeals the power to promulgate such other rules as may be prescribed by law or this Constitution, subject

Article V (Cont'd.); Articles VI and VII

to such limitations and procedures as may be provided by law.

[Note — Sec. 31 of Art. V was added to provide for the administration and jurisdiction of constitutional courts. Submitted by 69th Legislature (1985) and adopted in election Nov. 5, 1985.]

Article VI. — Suffrage

Sec. 1. Persons Who Cannot Vote — The following classes of persons shall not be allowed to vote in this State, to wit:

*First: Persons under eighteen (18) years of age.

Second: Idiots and lunatics.

Third: All paupers supported by any county.

Fourth: All persons convicted of any felony, subject to such exceptions as the Legislature may make.

[Note — Sec. 1 of Art. VI has been amended twice: (1) To give privilege of ballot to officers and enlisted men of National Guard, National Guard Reserves, Officers Reserve Corps, Organized Reserves and retired officers and enlisted men of Army, Navy and Marine Corps. Submitted by 42nd Legislature (1931) and adopted in election Nov. 8, 1932. Proclaimed Jan. 9, 1933. (2) To remove restrictions against members of the Armed Forces and to repeal the original Sec. 2-a of Art. VI, which provided for poll tax exemption for war veterans. Submitted by 53rd Legislature (1953) and adopted in election Nov. 2, 1954. (See also note under Sec. 2 and new Sec. 2-a.*) Texas on April 27, 1971, became the 21st state to ratify the 26th Amendment to the U.S. Constitution lowering the voting age to 18 from 21. When Ohio ratified the amendment in July 1971, it was the 38th state to do so, the number required to change the voting age. Since the voting age specified in the U.S. Constitution takes precedence over that in the Texas Constitution, Sec. 2 (below) has not been amended by the Legislature to lower the voting age to 18.]

Sec. 2. **Annual Registration; Absentee Voting** — Every person subject to none of the foregoing disqualifications, who shall have attained the age of *21 years and who shall be a citizen of the United States and who shall have resided in this State one year next preceding an election and the last six months within the district or county in which such person offers to vote, shall be deemed a qualified elector; provided, however, that before offering to vote at an election a voter shall have registered annually, but such requirement for registration shall not be considered a qualification of an elector within the meaning of the term "qualified elector" as used in any other Article of this Constitution in respect to any matter except qualification and eligibility to vote at an election. Any legislation enacted in anticipation of the adoption of this Amendment shall not be invalid because of its anticipatory nature. The Legislature may authorize absentee voting. And this provision of the Constitution shall be self-enacting without the necessity of further legislation.

[Note — Sec. 2 of Art. VI has been amended six times: (1) To provide that declaration of foreigner must be filed at least six months before election to enable him to vote in such election. Submitted by 24th Legislature (1895), ratified in election Nov. 3, 1896, and declared adopted Dec. 18, 1896. (2) To make poll tax receipt the certificate of registration for voting. Submitted by 27th Legislature (1901), ratified in election Nov. 4, 1902, and declared adopted Dec. 26, 1902. (3) To limit suffrage to citizens; allowing husband or wife to pay poll tax for other; authorizing absentee voting. Submitted by 37th Legislature (1921) and ratified in election July 23, 1921. (4) To extend suffrage to members of the Armed Forces of the United States. Submitted by 53rd Legislature (1953) and adopted in election Nov. 2, 1954. (5) To omit the requirement that members of armed services may vote only in county in which they resided at time of entering the service. Submitted by 59th Legislature (1965) and adopted in election Nov. 8, 1966. (6) To repeal the poll tax as a voting requirement and substituting annual registration. Submitted by 59th Legislature (1965) and adopted in election Nov. 8, 1966. (*See also note under Sec. 1 above.)]

Sec. 2-a. **Vote for Electors for President and Vice President and Statewide Offices** — (a) Notwithstanding any other provision of this Constitution, the Legislature may enact laws and provide a method of registration, including the time of such registration, permitting any person who is qualified to vote in this state except for the residence requirements within a county or district, as set forth in Sec. 2 of this article, to vote for (1) electors for president and vice president of the United States and (2) all offices, questions or propositions to be voted on by all electors throughout this state.

(b) Notwithstanding any other provision of this Constitution, the Legislature may enact laws and provide for a method of registration, including the time for such registration, permitting any person (1) who is qualified to vote in this state except for the residence requirements of Sec. 2 of this article, and (2) who shall have resided anywhere within this state at least thirty (30) days next preceding a general election in a presidential election year, and (3) who shall have been a qualified elector in another state immediately prior to his removal to this state or would have been eligible to vote in such other state had he remained there until such election, to vote for electors for president and vice president of the United States in that election.

(c) Notwithstanding any other provision of this Constitution, the Legislature may enact laws and provide for a method of registration, including the time for such registration, permitting absentee voting for electors for president and vice president of the United States in this state by former residents of this state (1) who have removed to another state, and (2) who meet all qualifications, except residence requirements, for voting for electors for president and vice president in this state at the time of the election, but the privileges of suffrage so granted shall be only for such period of time as would permit a former resident of this state to meet the residence requirements for voting in his new state of residence, and in no case for more than twenty-four (24) months.

[Note — Sec. 2-a was added to provide for voting on electors for president and vice president and on all statewide offices. Submitted by 59th Legislature (1965) and adopted in election Nov. 8, 1966.]

Sec. 3. **Electors in Towns and Cities; Only Property Taxpayers to Vote in Certain Instances** — All qualified electors of the State, as herein described, who shall have resided for six months immediately preceding an election within the limits of any city or corporate town, shall have the right to vote for Mayor and all other elective officers; but in all elections to determine expenditure of money or assumption of debt, only those shall be qualified to vote who pay taxes on property in said city or incorporated town; provided, that no poll tax for the payment of debts thus incurred shall be levied upon the persons debarred from voting in relation thereto.

Sec. 3-a. **Only Those Who Have Rendered Property for Taxation May Vote in Bond Elections** — When an election is held by any county, or any number of counties, or any political subdivision of the State, or any political subdivision of a county, or any defined district now or hereafter to be described and defined within the State and which may or may not include towns, villages or municipal corporations, or any city, town or village, for the purpose of issuing bonds or otherwise lending credit, or expending money or assuming any debt, only qualified electors who own taxable property in the State, county, political subdivision, district, city, town or village where such election is held, and who have duly rendered the same for taxation, shall be qualified to vote and all electors shall vote in the election precinct of their residence.

[Note — Sec. 3-a of Art. VI was added to limit voters participating in bond elections to those who have rendered property for taxation. Submitted by 42nd Legislature (1931) and adopted in election Nov. 8, 1932; proclaimed Jan. 9, 1933.]

Sec. 4. **Voter Registration** — In all elections by the people the vote shall be by ballot, and the Legislature shall provide for the numbering of tickets and make such other regulations as may be necessary to detect and punish fraud and preserve the purity of the ballot box; and the Legislature shall provide by law for the registration of all voters.

[Note — Sec. 4 of Art. VI has been amended twice: (1) To provide for the registration of voters in cities of 10,000 or more population. Submitted by 22nd Legislature (1891), ratified in election Aug. 11, 1891, and declared adopted Sept. 22, 1891. (2) To delete this provision for registration of voters in cities of 10,000 or more population. (See also note under Sec. 2, Art. VI.) Submitted by 59th Legislature (1965) and adopted in election Nov. 8, 1966.]

Sec. 5. **Voters Privileged From Arrest** — Voters shall, in all cases except treason, felony or breach of the peace, be privileged from arrest during their attendance at elections and in going to and returning therefrom.

Article VII — Education, The Public Free Schools

Sec. 1. **Public Schools to Be Established** — A general diffusion of knowledge being essential to the preservation of the liberties and rights of the people, it shall be the duty of the Legislature of the State to establish and make suitable provision for the support and maintenance of an efficient system of public free schools.

Sec. 2. **Provisions Governing the Levy and Collection of Taxes for the Support of the Public Free Schools** — All funds, lands and other property heretofore set apart and appro-

Article VII (Cont'd.)

priated for the support of public schools, all the alternate sections of land reserved by the State out of grants heretofore made or that may hereafter be made to railroads or other corporations, of any nature whatsoever, one half of the public domain of the State, and all sums of money that may come to the State from the sale of any portion of the same shall constitute a perpetual public school fund

Sec. 2A. The State of Texas hereby relinquishes and releases any claim of sovereign ownership or title to an undivided one-third interest in and to the lands and minerals within the Shelby, Frazier, and McCormick League (now located in Fort Bend and Austin counties) arising out of the interest in that league originally granted under the Mexican Colonization Law of 1823 to John McCormick on or about July 24, 1824, and subsequently voided by the governing body of Austin's Original Colony on or about December 15, 1830, and title to such interest in the lands and minerals is confirmed to the owners of the remaining interests in such lands and minerals. This section is self-executing.

[Note —Sec. 2A of Art. VII was added to clear certain land titles in Fort Bend and Austin counties. Submitted by 73rd Legislature (1993) and adopted in election Nov. 2, 1993.]

Sec. 3. **School Taxes** — One fourth of the revenue derived from the State occupation taxes and a poll tax of one ($1.00) dollar on every inhabitant of this State, between the ages of 21 and 60 years, shall be set apart annually for the benefit of the public free schools; and in addition thereto, there shall be levied and collected an annual ad valorem State tax of such an amount not to exceed 35¢ on the one hundred ($100.00) dollars valuation, as, with the available school fund arising from all other sources, will be sufficient to maintain and support the public schools of this State for a period of not less than six months in each year, and it shall be the duty of the State Board of Education to set aside a sufficient amount out of the said tax to provide free textbooks for the use of children attending the public free schools of this State; provided, however, that should the limit of taxation herein named be insufficient the deficit may be met by appropriation from the general funds of the State, and the Legislature may also provide for the formation of school districts by general laws, and all such school districts may embrace parts of two or more counties. And the Legislature shall be authorized to pass laws for the assessment and collection of taxes in all said districts and for the management and control of the public school or schools of such districts, whether such districts are composed of territory wholly within a county or in parts of two or more counties. And the Legislature may authorize an additional ad valorem tax to be levied and collected within all school districts heretofore formed or hereafter formed, for the further maintenance of public free schools, and for the erection and equipment of school buildings therein; provided, that a majority of the qualified property taxpaying voters of the district voting at an election to be held for that purpose shall vote such tax not to exceed in any one year $1 on the $100 valuation of the property subject to taxation in such district, but the limitation upon the amount of school district tax herein authorized shall not apply to incorporated cities or towns constituting separate and independent school districts, nor to independent or common school districts created by general or special law.

[Note — Sec. 3 of Art. VII has been amended six times: (1) To authorize a State ad valorem school tax of not more than 20¢, and further to authorize creation by Legislature of school districts for local taxation not to exceed 20¢. Submitted by 18th Legislature (1883), ratified in election Aug. 14, 1883, and declared adopted Sept. 25, 1883. (2) To authorize maximum tax in school districts of 50¢. Submitted by 30th Legislature (1907), ratified in election Nov. 3, 1908, and declared adopted Feb. 2, 1909. (3) To authorize intercounty school districts and authorizing Legislature to pass laws for management and control of districts. Submitted by 31st Legislature (1909), ratified in election Aug. 3, 1909. See note following 3-a below. (4) To increase maximum tax for State school purposes from 20¢ to 35¢ and provide for free textbooks. Submitted by 35th Legislature (1917) and adopted at election of Nov. 5, 1918. (5) To remove 50¢ limit on school district tax. Submitted by 36th Legislature (1919) and adopted in election of Nov. 2, 1920. (6) To eliminate the provision authorizing the Legislature to create districts by special law. Submitted by 39th Legislature (1925) and ratified in election Nov. 2, 1926, and proclaimed Jan. 20, 1927.]

See Sec. 1-e of Art. VIII for provisions to gradually abolish the ad valorem tax as a source for state school support.

[Note — Sec. 3-a of Art. VII, relating to county line districts, validation, bonds and taxation, was deleted by constitutional amendment. Submitted by 61st Legislature (1969) and approved in election Aug. 5, 1969.]

Sec. 3-b. **County School Districts** — No tax for the maintenance of public free schools voted in any independent school district and no tax for the maintenance of a junior college voted by a junior college district, nor any bonds voted in any such district, but unissued, shall be abrogated, canceled or invalidated by change of any kind in the boundaries thereof. After any change in boundaries, the governing body of any such district, without the necessity of an additional election, shall have the power to assess, levy and collect ad valorem taxes on all taxable property within the boundaries of the district as changed, for the purposes of the maintenance of public free schools or the maintenance of a junior college, as the case may be, and the payment of principal of and interest on all bonded indebtedness outstanding against, or attributable, adjusted or allocated to, such district or any territory therein, in the amount, at the rate, or not to exceed the rate, and in the manner authorized in the district prior to the change in its boundaries, and further in accordance with the laws under which all such bonds, respectively, were voted; and such governing body also shall have the power, without the necessity of an additional election, to sell and deliver any unissued bonds voted in the district prior to any such change in boundaries, and to assess, levy and collect ad valorem taxes on all taxable property in the district as changed, for the payment of principal of and interest on such bonds in the manner permitted by the laws under which such bonds were voted. In those instances where the boundaries of any such independent school district are changed by the annexation of, or consolidation with, one or more whole school districts, the taxes to be levied for the purposes hereinabove authorized may be in the amount or at not to exceed the rate theretofore voted in the district having at the time of such change the greatest scholastic population according to the latest scholastic census and only the unissued bonds of such district voted prior to such change, may be subsequently sold and delivered and any voted, but unissued, bonds of other school districts involved in such annexation or consolidation shall not thereafter be issued.

[Note: Sec. 3-b of Art. VII was added to allow independent school districts in Dallas County to work out adjustment of boundaries without abrogating, canceling or invalidating existing tax rates and bonds. Submitted by 57th Legislature (1961) and adopted in election Nov. 6, 1962. It was amended to include school districts in any county of Texas. Submitted by 59th Legislature (1965) and adopted in election Nov. 8, 1966.]

Sec. 4. **Sale of School Lands; No Relief to Purchasers; the Investment of Proceeds** — The lands herein set apart to the public free school fund shall be sold under such regulations, at such times and on such terms as may be prescribed by law; and the Legislature shall not have power to grant any relief to purchasers thereof. The proceeds of such sales must be used to acquire other land for the Public Free School fund as provided by law or the proceeds shall be invested by the comptroller, as may be directed by the Board of Education herein provided for, in the bonds of the United States, the State of Texas, or counties in said State, or in such other securities and under such restrictions as may be prescribed by law; and the State shall be responsible for all investments.

[Note — Sec. 4 of Art. VII was amended to authorize investment of money from sale of State public school lands in securities other than State and U. S. bonds, as was required by the original section, and to make the State responsible for such investments. Submitted by 18th Legislature (1883), ratified in election Aug. 14, 1883, and declared adopted Sept. 25, 1883. It was again amended to authorize proceeds from sale of land dedicated to permanent school fund to be used to acquire other land for that fund. Submitted by 69th Legislature (1985) and adopted in election Nov. 5, 1985.]

Sec. 4A. **Patents Issued for Free Public School Lands** — (a) On application to the School Land Board, a natural person is entitled to receive a patent to land from the commissioner of the General Land Office if:

(1) the land is surveyed public free school fund land, either surveyed or platted according to records of the General Land Office;

(2) the land was not patentable under the law in effect immediately before adoption of this section;

(3) the person acquired the land without knowledge of the title defect out of the State of Texas or Republic of Texas and held the land under color of title, the chain of which dates from at least as early as January 1, 1941; and

(4) the person, in conjunction with his predecessors in interest:

(A) has a recorded deed on file in the respective county court

Article VII (Cont'd.)

house and has claimed the land for a continuous period of at least 50 years as of January 1, 1991; and

(B) for at least 50 years has paid taxes on the land together with all interset and penalties associated with any period of delinquency of the taxes; provided, however, that in the event that public records concerning the tax payments on the land are unavailable for any period within the past 50 years, the tax assessors-collectors of the taxing jurisdictions in which the land is located shall provide the School Land Board with a sworn certificate stating that, to the best of their knowledge, all taxes have been paid for the past 50 years and there are no outstanding taxes nor interest or penalties currently due against the property.

(b) The applicant for the patent must submit to the School Land Board certified copies of his chain of title and a survey of the land for which a patent is sought, if requested to do so by the board. The board shall determine the qualifications of the applicant to receive a patent under this section. On a finding by the board that the applicant meets the requirements of Subsection (a) of this section, the commissioner of the General Land Office shall award the applicant a patent. If the applicant is denied a patent, he may file suit against the board in a district court of the county in which the land is situated within 60 days from the date of the denial of the patent under this section. The trial shall be de novo and not subject to the Administrative Procedure and Texas Register Act (Article 6252-13a, Vernon's Texas Civil Statutes), and the burden of proof is on the applicant.

(c) This section does not apply to beach land, submerged or filled land, or islands and may not be used by an applicant to resolve a boundary dispute. This section does not apply to land that, pursuant to an action filed previous to the date of an application for patent thereon, was found by a court of competent jurisdiction to be state owned or to be land on which the state has given a mineral lease that is in effect on the date of an application for patent thereon. A patent under this section for land within five miles of mineral production shall reserve minerals to the state in the same manner provided by law for reservations of minerals in sales to good faith claimants of unsurveyed school land within five miles of production.

(d) Application for a patent under this section must be filed with the School Land Board before January 1, 1993.

(e) This section is self-executing.

[Note — Sec. 4A of Art. VII, above, replaces the original Sec. 4A, which expired on Jan. 1, 1990. The current Sec. 4A authorizes issuance of patents for certain public free school fund land held in good faith under color of title for at least 50 years as of Jan. 1, 1991. Submitted by 72nd Legislature (1991) and adopted in election Nov. 5, 1991.]

Sec. 5. **Permanent School Fund; Interest; Alienation; Sectarian Schools** — (a) The principal of all bonds and other funds, and the principal arising from the sale of the lands hereinbefore set apart to said school fund, shall be the permanent school fund, and all the interest derivable therefrom and the taxes herein authorized and levied shall be the available school fund. The available school fund shall be applied annually to the support of the public free schools. Except as provided by this section, no law shall ever be enacted appropriating any part of the permanent or available school fund to any other purpose whatever; nor shall the same or any part thereof ever be appropriated to or used for the support of any sectarian school; and the available school fund herein provided shall be distributed to the several counties according to their scholastic population and applied in such manner as may be provided by law.

(b) The Legislature by law may provide for using the permanent school fund and the income from the permanent school fund to guarantee bonds issued by school districts or by the state for the purpose of making loans to or purchasing the bonds of school districts for the purpose of acquisition, construction, or improvement of instructional facilities including all furnishings thereto. If any payment is required to be made by the permanent school fund as a result of its guarantee of bonds issued by the state, an amount equal to this payment shall be immediately paid by the state from the treasury to the permanent school fund. An amount owed by the state to the permanent school fund under this section shall be a general obligation of the state until paid. The amount of bonds authorized hereunder shall not exceed $750 million or a higher amount authorized by a two-thirds record vote of both houses of the legislature. If the proceeds of bonds issued by the state are used to provide a loan to a school district and the district becomes delinquent on the loan payments, the amount of the delinquent payments shall be offset against state aid to which the district is otherwise entitled.

[Note — Sec. 5 (b) of Art. VII was amended to provide for using the permanent school fund and its income to guarantee bonds issued by the state for the purpose of aiding school districts. Proposed by 71st Legislature (1989) and adopted in election Nov. 7 1989.]

(c) The Legislature may appropriate part of the available school fund for administration of the permanent school fund or of a bond guarantee program established under this section.

(d) Notwithstanding any other provision of this constitution, in managing the assets of the permanent school fund, the State Board of Education may acquire, exchange, sell, supervise, manage, or retain, through procedures and subject to restrictions it establishes and in amounts it considers appropriate, any kind of investment, including investments in the Texas growth fund created by Article XVI, Section 70, of this constitution, that persons of ordinary prudence, discretion, and intelligence, exercising the judgment and care under the circumstances then prevailing, acquire or retain for their own account in the management of their affairs, not in regard to speculation but in regard to the permanent disposition of their funds, considering the probable income as well as the probable safety of their capital.

[Note — Sec. 5 of Art. VII has been amended four times: (1) To allow Legislature to add not more than 1 percent annually of the total value of the permanent school fund to the available school fund. Submitted by 22nd Legislature (1891), ratified in election Aug. 11, 1891, and declared adopted Sept. 22, 1891. (2) To delete the provision in (1), above. Submitted by 58th Legislature (1963), and adopted in election Nov. 3, 1964. (3) To authorize use of the permanent school fund to guarantee bonds issued by school districts. Submitted by 68th Legislature (1983) and adopted in election Nov. 8, 1983. (4) To authorize the investment of Permanent School Fund monies in the Texas Growth Fund. Submitted by 70th Legislature (1987) and adopted in election Nov. 8, 1988.]

Sec. 6. **County School Lands; Limitations; Settlers; Proceeds** — All lands heretofore or hereafter granted to the several counties of this State for educational purposes are of right the property of said counties respectively to which they were granted, and title thereto is vested in said counties, and no adverse possession or limitation shall ever be available against the title of any county. Each county may sell or dispose of its lands in whole or in part in manner to be here provided by the Commissioners' Court of the county. Actual settlers residing on said land shall be protected in the prior right of purchasing the same to the extent of their settlement, not to exceed 160 acres, at the price fixed by said court, which price shall not include the value of existing improvements made thereon by such settlers. Said lands, and the proceeds thereof, when sold, shall be held by said counties alone as a trust for the benefit of public schools therein; said proceeds to be invested in bonds of the United States, the State of Texas, or counties in said State, or in such other securities and under such restrictions as may be prescribed by law; and the counties shall be responsible for all investments; the interest thereon and other revenue, except principal, shall be available fund.

[Note — Sec. 6 of Art. VII was amended to authorize the investment of money from sale of county public school lands in securities other than State and U. S. bonds, as was required in the original section, and making counties responsible for such investments. Submitted by 18th Legislature (1883), ratified in election August 14, 1883, and declared adopted Sept. 25, 1883.]

Sec. 6-a. **Taxation of County School Lands** — All agriculture or grazing school land mentioned in Sec. 6 of this article owned by any county shall be subject to taxation except for State purposes to the same extent as lands privately owned.

[Note — Sec. 6-a of Art. VII was added to provide for the taxation of lands mentioned in Sec. 6. Submitted by 39th Legislature (1925), ratified in election Nov. 2, 1926, and proclaimed Jan. 20, 1927.]

Sec. 6-b. Notwithstanding the provisions of Sec. 6, Art. VII, Constitution of the State of Texas, any county, acting through the commissioners court, may reduce the county permanent school fund of that county and may distribute the amount of the reduction to the independent and common school districts of the county on a per scholastic basis to be used solely for the purpose of reducing bonded indebtedness of those districts or for making permanent improvements. The commissioners court shall, however, retain a sufficient amount of the corpus of the county permanent school fund to pay ad valorem taxes on school lands or royalty interests owned at the time of the distribution. Nothing in this Section affects financial aid to any school

Article VII (Cont'd.)

Article VII (Cont'd.)

district by the State.

[Note — Sec. 6-b of Art VII was added to allow a county to reduce its county permanent school fund and distribute the money to independent and common school districts on a per capita basis. Submitted by 62nd Legislature (1971) and adopted in election Nov. 7, 1972.]

[Note — Sec. 7 of Art. VII, relating to separate schools for white and colored, was deleted by constitutional amendment. Submitted by 61st Legislature (1969) and adopted in election Aug. 5, 1969.]

Sec. 8. **Board of Education; Terms and Duties** — The Legislature shall provide by law for a State Board of Education, whose members shall be appointed or elected in such manner and by such authority and shall serve for such terms as the Legislature shall prescribe not to exceed six years. The said board shall perform such duties as may be prescribed by law.

[Note — Sec. 8 of Art. VII was amended to reconstitute the State Board of Education. The original text provided for a Board of Education consisting of Governor, Comptroller and Secretary of State, serving ex officio. Submitted by 40th Legislature (1927); ratified in election Nov. 6, 1928; proclaimed Feb. 6, 1929.]

Asylums

Sec. 9. **Lands of Asylums; Sale** — All lands heretofore granted for the benefit of the lunatic, blind, deaf and dumb, and orphan asylums, together with such donations as may have been or may hereafter be made to either of them, respectively, as indicated in the several grants, are hereby set apart to provide a permanent fund for the support, maintenance and improvement of said asylums. And the Legislature may provide for the sale of the lands and the investment of the proceeds in the manner as provided for the sale and investment of school lands in Sec. 4 of this article.

University

Sec. 10. **University Lands and Funds** — The Legislature shall, as soon as practicable, establish, organize and provide for the maintenance, support and direction of a University of the first class, to be located by a vote of the people of this State and styled "The University of Texas," for the promotion of literature and the arts and sciences, including an agricultural, and mechanical department.

Sec. 11. **University Funds; How Invested** — In order to enable the Legislature to perform the duties set forth in the foregoing section, it is hereby declared all lands and other property heretofore set apart and appropriated for the establishment and maintenance of the University of Texas, together with all the proceeds of sales of the same, heretofore made or hereafter to be made, and all grants, donations and appropriations that may hereafter be made by the State of Texas, or from any other source, except donations limited to specific purposes, shall constitute and become a permanent university fund. And the same as realized and received into the treasury of the State (together with such sums belonging to the fund, as may now be in the treasury) shall be invested in bonds of the United States, the State of Texas, or counties of said State, or in school bonds of municipalities or in bonds of any city of this State or in bonds issued under and by virtue of the Federal Farm Loan Act approved by the President of the United States July 17, 1916, and amendments thereto; and the interest accruing thereon shall be subject to appropriation by the Legislature to accomplish the purpose declared in the foregoing section; provided, that the one tenth of the alternate sections of the lands granted to railroads reserved by the State, which were set apart and appropriated to the establishment of the University of Texas by an act of the Legislature of Feb. 11, 1858, entitled "An act to establish the University of Texas" shall not be included in or constitute a part of, the permanent university fund.

[Note — Sec. 11 of Art. VII has been amended twice: (1) To add a clause giving the Board of Regents of the University of Texas latitude in expending part of the permanent fund for buildings. Submitted by 41st Legislature (1929) and adopted in election Nov. 4, 1930. (2) To eliminate this latitude and to restore the original provisions of the Constitution, which limited investments to bonds of the United States, State or civil subdivisions. This last amendment also added the clause "except donations limited to specific purposes." Submitted by 42nd Legislature (1931), adopted Nov. 8, 1932 and proclaimed Jan. 9, 1933.]

Sec. 11-a. In addition to the bonds enumerated in Section 11 of Article VII of the Constitution of the State of Texas, the Board of Regents of The University of Texas may invest the Permanent University Fund in securities, bonds or other obligations issued, insured, or guaranteed in any manner by the United States Government, or any of its agencies, and in such bonds, debentures, or obligations, and preferred and common stocks issued by corporations, associations, and other institutions as the Board of Regents of The University of Texas System may deem to be proper investments for said funds; provided, however, that not more than one per cent (1%) of said fund shall be invested in the securities of any one (1) corporation, nor shall more than five per cent (5%) of the voting stock of any one corporation be owned; provided, further, that stocks eligible for purchase shall be restricted to stocks of companies incorporated within the United States which have paid dividends for five (5) consecutive years or longer immediately prior to the date of purchase and which, except for bank stocks and insurance stocks, are listed upon an exchange registered with the Securities and Exchange Commission or its successors.

In making each and all of such investments said Board of Regents shall exercise the judgment and care under the circumstances then prevailing which men of ordinary prudence, discretion, and intelligence exercise in the management of their own affairs, not in regard to speculation but in regard to the permanent disposition of their funds, considering the probable income therefrom as well as the probable safety of their capital.

The interest, dividends and other income accruing from the investments of the Permanent University Fund, except the portion thereof which is appropriated by the operation of Sec. 18 of Art. VII for the payment of principal and interest on bonds or notes issued thereunder, shall be subject to appropriation by the Legislature to accomplish the purposes declared in Sec. 10 of Article VII of this Constitution.

This amendment shall be self-enacting, and shall become effective upon its adoption, provided, however, that the Legislature shall provide by law for full disclosure of all details concerning the investments in corporate stocks and bonds and other investments authorized herein.

[Note — Sec.11-a of Art. VII was added to provide for broader investment of the Permanent University Fund in corporate bonds and stocks under certain conditions and limitations. Submitted by 54th Legislature (1955) and adopted in election Nov. 6, 1956. It was further amended to increase the types of securities available for investment to the Permanent University Fund by allowing securities, bonds or other obligations issued, insured or guaranteed in any manner by the federal government. Submitted by 60th Legislature (1967) and adopted in election Nov. 5, 1968.]

Sec. 11-b. Notwithstanding any other provision of this constitution, in managing the assets of the permanent university fund, the Board of Regents of The University of Texas System may acquire, exchange, sell, supervise, manage, or retain, through procedures and subject to restrictions it establishes and in amounts it considers appropriate, any kind of investment, including investments in the Texas growth fund created by Article XVI, Section 70, of this constitution, that persons of ordinary prudence, discretion, and intelligence, exercising the judgment and care under the circumstances then prevailing, acquire or retain for their own account in the management of their affairs, not in regard to speculation but in regard to the permanent disposition of their funds, considering the probable income as well as the probable safety of their capital. This section does not affect the state treasurer's custodial responsibilities for public funds, securities, and other evidences of investment.

[Note — Section 11-b was added to allow the Permanent University Fund to be invested in the Texas Growth Fund. Submitted by 70th Legislature (1987) and adopted in election Nov. 8, 1988.]

Sec. 12. **Lands to Be Sold; No Relief of Purchasers** — The land herein set apart to the university fund shall be sold under such regulations at such times and on such terms as may be provided by law, and the Legislature shall provide for the prompt collection, at maturity, of all debts due on account of university lands heretofore sold, or that may hereafter be sold, and shall in neither event have the power to grant relief to the purchasers.

Sec. 13. **Agricultural and Mechanical College; Appropriations** — The Agricultural and Mechanical College of Texas, established by an act of the Legislature passed April 17, 1871, located in the County of Brazos, is hereby made and constituted a branch of the University of Texas, for instruction in agriculture, the mechanic arts and the natural sciences connected therewith. And the Legislature shall at its next session make an appropriation not to exceed $40,000 for the construction and completion of the buildings and improvements, and for providing the furniture necessary to put said college in immediate and successful operation.

Sec. 14. **Prairie View A&M** — Prairie View A&M University in

Article VII (Cont'd.)
Waller County is an institution of the first class under the direction of the same governing board as Texas A&M University referred to in Article VII, Section 13, of this constitution as the Agricultural and Mechanical College of Texas.

[Note — Sec. 14 of Art. VII was substituted for an earlier Sec. 14 to declare that Prairie View A&M University is an institution of the first class under direction of Texas A&M University governing board. (See also Sections 17 and 18 of Art. VII.) Submitted by 68th Legislature (1983) and adopted in election Nov. 6, 1984.]

Sec. 15. **Land Appropriated for University; How Sold** — In addition to the lands heretofore granted to the University of Texas, there is hereby set apart and appropriated, for the endowment, maintenance and support of said university and its branches, 1,000,000 acres of the unappropriated public domain of the State, to be designated and surveyed as may be provided by law; and said lands shall be sold under the same regulations and the proceeds invested in the same manner as is provided for the sale and investment of the permanent university fund; and the Legislature shall not have the power to grant any relief to the purchasers of said lands.

Sec. 16. **Terms of Office in School Systems** — The Legislature shall fix by law the terms of all offices of the public school system and of the State institutions of higher education, inclusive, and the terms of members of the respective boards, not to exceed six years.

[Note — Sec. 16 of Art. VII is the first of two amendments numbered 16 (See following section and note thereon.). This amendment was added to provide for fixing of terms of office in public school system. Submitted by 40th Legislature (1927); ratified Nov. 6, 1928; proclaimed Feb. 6, 1929.]

Sec. 16 [a.] **Taxation of University Lands** — All land mentioned in Secs. 11, 12 and 15 of Article VII of the Constitution of the State of Texas, now belonging to the University of Texas, shall be subject to the taxation for county purpose to the same extent as lands privately owned; provided, they shall be rendered for taxation upon values fixed by the State Tax Board; and providing, that the State shall remit annually to each of the counties in which said lands are located an amount equal to the tax imposed upon said land for county purposes.

[Note — The foregoing section, which obviously should have been numbered either 16-a or 17, was designated as No. 16 in H.J.R. No. 11 of the 41st Legislature (1929), in which the amendment was submitted. It is customarily printed in legal references as Sec. 16 [a.] This amendment was added to provide for taxation of University of Texas lands. It was ratified in election Nov. 4, 1930; declared adopted Dec. 17, 1930.]

Sec. 17. **Support for Higher Education** — (a) In the fiscal year beginning September 1, 1985, and each fiscal year thereafter, there is hereby appropriated out of the first money coming into the state treasury not otherwise appropriated by the constitution $100 million to be used by eligible agencies and institutions of higher education for the purpose of acquiring land either with or without permanent improvements, constructing and equipping buildings or other permanent improvements, major repair or rehabilitation of buildings or other permanent improvements, acquisition of capital equipment, library books and library materials, and paying for acquiring, constructing, or equipping or for major repair or rehabilitation of buildings, facilities, other permanent improvements, or capital equipment used jointly for educational and general activities and for auxiliary enterprises to the extent of their use for educational and general activities. For the five-year period that begins on September 1, 2000, and for each five-year period that begins after that period, the legislature, during a regular session that is nearest, but preceding, a five-year period, may by two-thirds vote of the membership of each house increase the amount of the constitutional appropriation for the five-year period but may not adjust the appropriation in such a way as to impair any obligation created by the issuance of bonds or notes in accordance with this section.

(b) The funds appropriated under Subsection (a) of this section shall be for the use of the following eligible agencies and institutions of higher education (even though their names may be changed):

(1) East Texas State University including East Texas State University at Texarkana;
(2) Lamar University including Lamar University at Orange and Lamar University at Port Arthur;
(3) Midwestern State University;
(4) University of North Texas;
(5) The University of Texas — Pan American including The University of Texas at Brownsville;
(6) Stephen F. Austin State University;
(7) Texas College of Osteopathic Medicine;
(8) Texas State University System Administration and the following component institutions:
(9) Angelo State University;
(10) Sam Houston State University;
(11) Southwest Texas State University;
(12) Sul Ross State University including Uvalde Study Center;
(13) Texas Southern University;
(14) Texas Tech University;
(15) Texas Tech University Health Sciences Center;
(16) Texas Woman's University;
(17) University of Houston System Administration and the following component institutions:
(18) University of Houston;
(19) University of Houston — Victoria;
(20) University of Houston — Clear Lake;
(21) University of Houston — Downtown;
(22) Texas A&M University — Corpus Christi;
(23) Texas A&M International University;
(24) Texas A&M University — Kingsville;
(25) West Texas A&M University; and
(26) Texas State Technical College System and its campuses, but not its extension centers or programs.

(c) Pursuant to a two-thirds vote of the membership of each house of the legislature, institutions of higher education may be created at a later date by general law, and, when created, such an institution shall be entitled to participate in the funding provided by this section if it is not created as a part of The University of Texas System or The Texas A&M University System. An institution that is entitled to participate in dedicated funding provided by Article VII, Section 18, of this constitution may not be entitled to participate in the funding provided by this section.

(d) In the year 1985 and every 10 years thereafter, the legislature or an agency designated by the legislature no later than August 31 of such year shall allocate by equitable formula the annual appropriations made under Subsection (a) of this section to the governing boards of eligible agencies and institutions of higher education. The legislature shall review, or provide for a review, of the allocation formula at the end of the fifth year of each 10-year allocation period. At that time adjustments may be made in the allocation formula, but no adjustment that will prevent the payment of outstanding bonds and notes, both principal and interest, may be made.

(d-1) Notwithstanding Subsection (d) of this section, the allocation of the annual appropriation to Texas State Technical College System and its campuses may not exceed 2.2 percent of the total appropriation each fiscal year.

(e) Each governing board authorized to participate in the distribution of money under this section is authorized to expend all money distributed to it for any of the purposes enumerated in Subsection (a). In addition, such governing board may issue bonds and notes for the purposes of refunding bonds or notes issued under this section or prior law, acquiring land either with or without permanent improvements, constructing and equipping buildings or other permanent improvements, acquiring capital equipment, library books, and library materials, paying for acquiring, constructing, or equipping or for major repair or rehabilitation of buildings, facilities, other permanent improvements, or capital equipment used jointly for educational and general activities and for auxiliary enterprises to the extent of their use for educational and general activities, and for major repair and rehabilitation of buildings or other permanent improvements, and may pledge up to 50 percent of the money allocated to such governing board pursuant to this section to secure the payment of the principal and interest of such bonds or notes. Proceeds from the issuance of bonds or notes under this subsection shall be maintained in a local depository selected by the governing board issuing the bonds or notes. The bonds and notes issued under this subsection shall be payable solely out of the money appropriated by this section and shall mature serially or otherwise in not more than 10 years from their respective dates. All bonds issued under this section shall be sold only through competitive bidding and are subject to approval by the attorney general. Bonds approved by the attorney general shall be incontestable. The permanent university fund may be invested in the bonds and notes issued under this section.

(f) The funds appropriated by this section may not be used for the purpose of constructing, equipping, repairing, or rehabilitating buildings or other permanent improvements that are to be used only for student housing, intercollegiate athletics, or auxiliary enterprises.

(g) The comptroller of public accounts shall make annual transfers of the funds allocated pursuant to Subsection (d) directly to the governing boards of the eligible institutions.

(h) To assure efficient use of construction funds and the orderly development of physical plants to accommodate the state's

Article VII (Cont'd.)

real need, the legislature may provide for the approval or disapproval of all new construction projects at the eligible agencies and institutions entitled to participate in the funding provided by this section.

(i) The legislature by general law may dedicate portions of the state's revenues to the creation of a dedicated fund ("the higher education fund") for the purposes expressed in Subsection (a) of this section. The legislature shall provide for administration of the fund, which shall be invested in the manner provided for investment of the permanent university fund. The income from the investment of the higher education fund shall be credited to the higher education fund until such time as the fund totals $2 billion. The principal of the higher education fund shall never be expended. At the beginning of the fiscal year after the fund reaches $2 billion, as certified by the comptroller of public accounts, the dedication of general revenue funds provided for in Subsection (a) of this section shall cease. At the beginning of the fiscal year after the fund reaches $2 billion, and each year thereafter, 10 percent of the interest, dividends, and other income accruing from the investments of the higher education fund during the previous fiscal year shall be deposited and become part of the principal of the fund, and out of the remainder of the annual income from the investment of the principal of the fund there shall be appropriated an annual sum sufficient to pay the principal and interest due on the bonds and notes issued under this section and the balance of the income shall be allocated, distributed, and expended as provided for the appropriations made under Subsection (a).

(j) The state systems and institutions of higher education designated in this section may not receive any additional funds from the general revenue of the state for acquiring land with or without permanent improvements, for constructing or equipping buildings or other permanent improvements, or for major repair and rehabilitation of buildings or other permanent improvements except that:

(1) In the case of fire or natural disaster the legislature may appropriate from the general revenue an amount sufficient to replace the uninsured loss of any building or other permanent improvement; and

(2) the legislature, by two-thirds vote of each house, may, in cases of demonstrated need, which need must be clearly expressed in the body of the act, appropriate additional general revenue funds for acquiring land with or without permanent improvements, for constructing or equipping buildings or other permanent improvements, or for major repair and rehabilitation of buildings or other permanent improvements.

This subsection does not apply to legislative appropriations made prior to the adoption of this amendment.

(k) Without the prior approval of the legislature, appropriations under this section may not be expended for acquiring land with or without permanent improvements, or for constructing and equipping buildings or other permanent improvements, for a branch campus or educational center that is not a separate degree-granting institution created by general law.

(l) This section is self-enacting upon the issuance of the governor's proclamation declaring the adoption of the amendment, and the state comptroller of public accounts and the state treasurer shall do all things necessary to effectuate this section. This section does not impair any obligation created by the issuance of any bonds and notes in accordance with prior law, and all outstanding bonds and notes shall be paid in full, both principal and interest, in accordance with their terms. If the provisions of this section conflict with any other provisions of this constitution, then the provisions of this section shall prevail, notwithstanding all such conflicting provisions.

[Note — This Sec. 17 of Art. VII supersedes the old Sec. 17, which provided for a confederate pension fund tax, college building fund tax and reduced the ad valorem ceiling for general purposes. That section was deleted in election Nov. 2, 1982. The above Sec. 17 was added to create from general revenue a special higher education assistance fund for construction and related activities, to restructure the permanent university fund and to increase the number of institutions eligible to benefit from the permanent university fund. (See also Sections 14 and 18 of Art. VII.) Submitted by 68th Legislature (1983) and adopted in election Nov. 6, 1984. Section 17 was amended to adjust the amount and expenditure of certain constitutionally dedicated funds for public institutions of higher education. Submitted by 73rd Legislature (1993) and adopted in election Nov. 2, 1993.]

Sec. 18. **Building Bonds Authorized for the University of Texas and Texas A&M University; Retired From Income From the Permanent University Fund; Etc.** — (a) The Board of Regents of The Texas A&M University System may issue bonds and notes not to exceed a total amount of 10 percent of the cost value of the investments and other assets of the permanent university fund (exclusive of real estate) at the time of the issuance thereof, and may pledge all or any part of its one-third interest in the available university fund to secure the payment of the principal and interest of those bonds and notes, for the purpose of acquiring land either with or without permanent improvements, constructing and equipping buildings or other permanent improvements, major repair and rehabilitation of buildings and other permanent improvements, acquiring capital equipment and library books and library materials, and refunding bonds or notes issued under this Section or prior law, at or for The Texas A&M University System administration and the following component institutions of the system:

(1) Texas A&M University, including its medical college which the legislature may authorize as a separate medical institution; (2) Prairie View A&M University, including its nursing school in Houston; (3) Tarleton State University; (4) Texas A&M University at Galveston; (5) Texas Forest Service; (6) Texas Agricultural Experiment Stations; (7) Texas Agricultural Extension Service; (8) Texas Engineering Experiment Stations; (9) Texas Transportation Institute; and (10) Texas Engineering Extension Service.

(b) The Board of Regents of The University of Texas System may issue bonds and notes not to exceed a total amount of 20 percent of the cost value of investments and other assets of the permanent university fund (exclusive of real estate) at the time of issuance thereof, and may pledge all or any part of its two-thirds interest in the available university fund to secure the payment of the principal and interest of those bonds and notes, for the purpose of acquiring land either with or without permanent improvements, constructing and equipping buildings or other permanent improvements, major repair and rehabilitation of buildings and other permanent improvements, acquiring capital equipment and library books and library materials, and refunding bonds or notes issued under this section or prior law, at or for The University of Texas System administration and the following component institutions of the system:

(1) The University of Texas at Arlington; (2) The University of Texas at Austin; (3) The University of Texas at Dallas; (4) The University of Texas at El Paso; (5) The University of Texas of the Permian Basin; (6) The University of Texas at San Antonio; (7) The University of Texas at Tyler; (8) The University of Texas Health Science Center at Dallas; (9) The University of Texas Medical Branch at Galveston; (10) The University of Texas Health Science Center at Houston; (11) The University of Texas Health Science Center at San Antonio; (12) The University of Texas System Cancer Center; (13) The University of Texas Health Center at Tyler; and (14) The University of Texas Institute of Texan Cultures at San Antonio.

(c) Pursuant to a two-thirds vote of the memberhip of each house of the legislature, institutions of higher education may be created at a later date as a part of The University of Texas System or The Texas A&M University System by general law, and, when created, such an institution shall be entitled to participate in the funding provided by this section for the system in which it is created. An institution that is entitled to participate in dedicated funding provided by Article VII, Section 17, of this constitution may not be entitled to participate in the funding provided by this section.

(d) The proceeds of the bonds or notes issued under Subsection (a) or (b) of this section may not be used for the purpose of constructing, equipping, repairing, or rehabilitating buildings or other permanent improvements that are to be used for student housing, intercollegiate athletics, or auxiliary enterprises.

(e) The available university fund consists of the dividends, interest and other income from the permanent university fund (less administrative expenses) including the net income attributable to the surface of permanent university fund land. Out of one-third of the available university fund, there shall be appropriated an annual sum sufficient to pay the principal and interest due on the bonds and notes issued by the Board of Regents of The Texas A&M University System under this section and prior law, and the remainder of that one-third of the available university fund shall be appropriated to the Board of Regents of The Texas A&M University System which shall have the authority and duty in turn to appropriate an equitable portion of the same for the support and maintenance of The Texas A&M University System administration, Texas A&M University, and Prairie View A&M University. The Board of Regents of The Texas A&M University System, in making just and equitable appropriations to Texas A&M University and Prairie View A&M University, shall exercise its discretion with due regard to such criteria as the board may deem appropriate from year to year, taking into account all amounts appropriated from Subsection (f) of this section. Out of the other two-thirds of the available university fund there shall be appropriated an annual sum sufficient to pay the principal and interest due on the bonds and notes issued by the

Article VII (Cont'd.); Article VIII

Board of Regents of The University of Texas System under this section and prior law, and the remainder of such two-thirds of the available university fund, shall be appropriated for the support and maintenance of The University of Texas at Austin and The University of Texas System administration.

(f) It is provided, however, that, for 10 years beginning upon the adoption of this amendment, before any other allocation is made of The University of Texas System's two-thirds share of the available university fund, remaining after payment of principal and interest on its bonds and notes issued under this section and prior law, $6 million per year shall be appropriated out of that share to the Board of Regents of The Texas A&M University System for said board's use in making appropriations to Prairie View A&M University. This subsection expires and is deleted from this constitution 10 years from the adoption of this amendment.

(g) The bonds and notes issued under this section shall be payable solely out of the available university fund, mature serially or otherwise in not more than 30 years from their respective dates, and, except for refunding bonds, be sold only through competitive bidding. All of these bonds and notes are subject to approval by the attorney general and when so approved are incontestable. The permanent university fund may be invested in these bonds and notes.

(h) To assure efficient use of construction funds and the orderly development of physical plants to accommodate the state's real need, the legislature may provide for the approval or disapproval of all new construction projects at the eligible agencies and institutions entitled to participate in the funding provided by this section except The University of Texas at Austin, Texas A&M University in College Station, and Prairie View A&M University.

(i) The state systems and institutions of higher education designated in this section may not receive any funds from the general revenue of the state for acquiring land with or without permanent improvements, for constructing or equipping buildings or other permanent improvements, or for major repair and rehabilitation of buildings or other permanent improvements except that:

(1) In the case of fire or natural disaster the legislature may appropriate from the general revenue an amount sufficient to replace the uninsured loss of any building or other permanent improvement; and

(2) The legislature, by two-thirds vote of each house, may, in cases of demonstrated need, which need must be clearly expressed in the body of the act, appropriate general revenue funds for acquiring land with or without permanent improvements, for constructing or equipping buildings or other permanent improvements, or for major repair and rehabilitation of buildings or other permanent improvements.

This subsection does not apply to legislative appropriations made prior to the adoption of this amendment.

(j) This section is self-enacting on the issuance of the governor's proclamation declaring the adoption of this amendment, and the state comptroller of public accounts and the state treasurer shall do all things necessary to effectuate this section. This section does not impair any obligation created by the issuance of bonds or notes in accordance with prior law, and all outstanding bonds and notes shall be paid in full, both principal and interest, in accordance with their terms, and the changes herein made in the allocation of the available university fund shall not affect the pledges thereof made in connection with such bonds or notes heretofore issued. If the provisions of this section conflict with any other provision of this constitution, then the provisions of this section shall prevail, notwithstanding any such conflicting provisions.

[Note — Sec. 17 and Sec. 18 of Art. VII were originally added to the Constitution as a single amendment to provide for funding of construction at Texas universities and colleges. Submitted by 50th Legislature (1947) and adopted in election Aug. 23, 1947. It was further amended by 54th Legislature (1956), adopted in election Nov. 6, 1956; and again by 60th Legislature (1967), adopted in election Nov. 8, 1968. Sec. 17 was repealed by 67th Legislature (1981), approved in election Nov. 2, 1982. A new Sec. 17 and Sec. 18 were submitted by 68th Legislature (1983) and adopted in election Nov. 6, 1984. (See also notes under Sec. 14 and Sec. 17.)]

Article VIII — Taxation and Revenue

Sec. 1. **Taxation to Be Equal and Uniform; Occupation and Income Taxes; Exemptions; Limitations Upon Counties, Cities, Etc.** — (a) Taxation shall be equal and uniform.

(b) All real property and tangible personal property in this State, unless exempt as required or permitted by this Constitution, whether owned by natural persons or corporations, other than municipal, shall be taxed in proportion to its value, which shall be ascertained as may be provided by law.

(c) The Legislature may provide for the taxation of intangible property and may also impose occupation taxes, both upon natural persons and upon corporations, other than municipal, doing any business in this State. Subject to the restrictions of Section 24 of this article, it may also tax incomes of both natural persons and corporations other than municipal. Persons engaged in mechanical and agricultural pursuits shall never be required to pay an occupation tax.

[Note — Section 1(c) of Article VIII was amended to add reference to Section 24. Submitted by 73rd Legislature (1993) and adopted in election Nov. 2, 1993.]

(d) The Legislature by general law shall exempt from ad valorem taxation household goods not held or used for production of income and personal effects not held or used for the production of income. The Legislature by general law may exempt from ad valorem taxation: (1) all or part of the personal property homestead of a family or single adult, "personal property homestead" meaning that personal property exempt by law from forced sale for debt; and (2) subject to Subsection (e) of this section, all other tangible personal property, except structures which are personal property and are used or occupied as residential dwellings and except property held or used for the production of income.

(e) the governing body of a political subdivision, other than a county education district, may provide for the taxation of all property exempt under a law adopted under Subdivision (2) of Subsection (d) of this section and not exempt from ad valorem taxation by any other law. In the manner provided by law, the voters of a county education district at an election held for that purpose may provide for the taxation of all property exempt under a law adopted under Subdivision (2) of Subsection (d) of this section and not exempt from ad valorem taxation by any other law.

(f) The occupation tax levied by any county, city or town for any year, on persons or corporations pursuing any profession or business, shall not exceed one half of the tax levied by the State for the same period on such profession or business.

[Note — Sec. 1 of Art. VIII was amended to provide tax relief for residential homesteads and to provide personal property exemptions. (See also Sec. 1-b, and Sec. 23 of Art. VIII.) Submitted by 65th Legislature, (1977) and adopted in election Nov. 7, 1978. It was further amended to provide exemption from ad valorem taxation for certain tangible personal property located in the state. Submitted by 70th Legislature (1987) and adopted in election Nov. 3, 1987. Sec. 1 (b) was amended to authorize the exemption from ad valorem taxation certain personal property temporarily in the state for certain purposes. (See related amendment at Sec. 1-j, Art. VIII.) Submitted by 71st Legislature (1989) and adopted in election Nov. 7, 1989. Subsection (e) was amended to provide for taxation by a county education district. Submitted by 72nd Legislature and adopted in election Aug. 10, 1991.]

Sec. 1-a. **Abolishing Ad Valorem Tax for State's General Fund Purposes; Providing Local Tax Rate, Etc.** — From and after January 1, 1951, no State ad valorem tax shall be levied upon any property within this State for general revenue purposes. From and after January 1, 1951, the several counties of the State are authorized to levy ad valorem taxes upon all property within their respective boundaries for county purposes, except the first three thousand dollars ($3,000) value of residential homesteads of married or unmarried adults, male or female, including those living alone, not to exceed thirty cents (30¢) on each one hundred dollars ($100) valuation, in addition to all other ad valorem taxes authorized by the Constitution of this State, provided the revenue derived therefrom shall be used for construction and maintenance of farm-to-market roads or for flood control, except as herein otherwise provided.

Provided that in those counties or political subdivisions or areas of the State from which tax donations have heretofore been granted, the State Automatic Tax Board shall continue to levy the full amount of the State ad valorem tax for the duration of such donation, or until all legal obligations heretofore authorized by the law granting such donation or donations shall have been fully discharged, whichever shall first occur; provided that if such donation to any such county or political subdivision is for less than the full amount of State ad valorem taxes so levied, the portion of such taxes remaining over and above such donation shall be retained by said county or subdivision.

[Note — Sec. 1-a of Art. VIII was first added and then amended, as follows: (1) Giving homesteads $3,000 exemption from State taxes. Submitted by 42nd Legislature (1931) and adopted in election Nov. 8, 1932. (2) Making more definite the provision for extending the exemption to counties and subdivisions having

Article VIII (Cont'd.)

tax remission as soon as tax remission ceased, whether by expiration of the period designated in the act granting remission or voluntarily by action of local authorities. The original amendment failed to make provision for the latter contingency. Submitted by 43rd Legislature (1933), and adopted in election Aug. 26, 1933. (3) Reducing maximum ad valorem tax for general revenue from 35¢ to 30¢. (4) Abolishing ad valorem tax for state general fund purposes and providing for local taxation as indicated in text of section. (See also Sec. 1-b immediately below and note following.) Submitted by 50th Legislature (1947) and adopted in election Nov. 2, 1948. (5) Extending the $3,000 ad valorem tax exemption to homesteads of unmarried adults. Submitted by 63rd Legislature (1973) and adopted in election Nov. 6, 1973.]

Sec. 1-b. **Homestead Exemption Under State Tax** — (a) Three thousand dollars ($3,000) of the assessed taxable value of all residence homesteads of married or unmarried adults, male or female, including those living alone, shall be exempt from all taxation for all State purposes.

(b) The governing body of any county, city, town, school district, or other political subdivision of the State, other than a county education district, may exempt by its own action not less than Three Thousand Dollars ($3,000) of the market value of residence homesteads of persons, married or unmarried, including those living alone, who are under a disability for purposes of payment of disability insurance benefits under Federal Old-Age, Survivors, and Disability Insurance or its successor or of married or unmarried persons sixty-five (65) years of age or older, including those living alone, from all ad valorem taxes thereafter levied by the political subdivision. As an alternative, upon receipt of a petition signed by twenty percent (20%) of the voters who voted in the last preceding election held by the political subdivision, the governing body of the subdivision shall call an election to determine by majority vote whether an amount not less than Three Thousand Dollars ($3,000) as provided in the petition, of the market value of residence homesteads of disabled persons or of persons sixty-five (65) years of age or over shall be exempt from ad valorem taxes thereafter levied by the political subdivision. In the manner provided by law, the voters of a county education district at an election held for that purpose may exempt an amount not less than Three Thousand Dollars ($3,000), as provided in the petition, of the market value of residence homesteads of disabled persons or of persons sixty-five (65) years of age or over from ad valorem taxes thereafter levied by the county education district. An eligible disabled person who is sixty-five (65) years of age or older may not receive both exemptions from the same political subdivision in the same year but may choose either if the subdivision has adopted both. Where any ad valorem tax has theretofore been pledged for the payment of any debt, the taxing officers of the political subdivision shall have authority to continue to levy and collect the tax against the homestead property at the same rate as the tax so pledged until the debt is discharged, if the cessation of the levy would impair the obligation of the contract by which the debt was created.

An exemption adopted under this subsection based on assessed value is increased, effective January 1, 1979, to an amount that, when converted to market value, provides the same reduction in taxes, except that the market value exemption shall be rounded to the nearest $100.

(c) Five Thousand Dollars ($5,000) of the market value of the residence homestead of a married or unmarried adult, including one living alone, is exempt from ad valorem taxation for general elementary and secondary public school purposes. In addition to this exemption, the Legislature by general law may exempt an amount not to exceed Ten Thousand Dollars ($10,000) of the market value of the residence homestead of a person who is disabled as defined in Subsection (b) of this section and of a person sixty-five (65) years of age or older from ad valorem taxation for general elementary and secondary public school purposes. The Legislature by general law may base the amount of and condition eligibility for the additional exemption authorized by this subsection for disabled persons and for perons sixty-five (65) years of age or older on economic need. An eligible disabled person who is sixty-five (65) years of age or older may not receive both exemptions from a school district but may choose either. An eligible person is entitled to receive both the exemption required by this subsection for all residence homesteads and any exemption adopted pursuant to Subsection (b) of this section, but the Legislature shall provide by general law whether an eligible disabled or elderly person may receive both the additional exemption for the elderly and disabled authorized by this subsection and any exemption for the elderly or disabled adopted pursuant to Subsection (b) of this section. Where ad valorem tax has previously been pledged for the payment of debt, the taxing officers of a school district may continue to levy and collect the tax against the value of homesteads exempted under this subsection until the debt is discharged if the cessation of the levy would impair the obligation of the contract by which the debt was created. The Legislature shall provide for formulas to protect school districts against all or part of the revenue loss incurred by the implementation of Article VIII, Sections 1-b(c), 1-b(d), and 1-d-1, of this constitution. The Legislature by general law may define residence homestead for purposes of this section.

(d) Except as otherwise provided by this subsection, if a person receives the residence homestead exemption prescribed by Subsection (c) of this section for homesteads of persons sixty-five (65) years of age or older, the total amount of ad valorem taxes imposed on that homestead for general elementary and secondary public school purposes may not be increased while it remains the residence homestead of that person or that person's spouse who receives the exemption. If a person sixty-five (65) years of age or older dies in a year in which the person received the exemption, the total amount of ad valorem taxes imposed on the homestead for general elementary and secondary public school purposes may not be increased while it remains the residence homestead of that person's surviving spouse if the spouse is fifty-five (55) years of age or older at the time of the person's death, subject to any exceptions provided by general law. However, taxes otherwise limited by this subsection may be increased to the extent the value of the homestead is increased by improvements other than repairs or improvements made to comply with governmental requirements.

(e) The governing body of a political subdivision, other than a county education district, may exempt from ad valorem taxation a percentage of the market value of the residence homestead of a married or unmarried adult, including one living alone. In the manner provided by law, the voters of a county education district at an election held for that purpose may exempt from ad valorem taxation a percentage of the market value of the residence homestead of a married or unmarried adult, including one living alone. The percentage may not exceed twenty percent. However, the amount of an exemption authorized pursuant to this subsection may not be less than Five Thousand Dollars ($5,000) unless the legislature by general law prescribes other monetary restrictions on the amount of the exemption. An eligible adult is entitled to receive other applicable exemptions provided by law. Where ad valorem tax has previously been pledged for the payment of debt, the governing body of a political subdivision may continue to levy and collect the tax against the value of the homesteads exempted under this subsection until the debt is discharged if the cessation of the levy would impair the obligation of the contract by which the debt was created. The legislature by general law may prescribe procedures for the administration of residence homestead exemptions.

[Note — Sec. 1-b of Art. VIII has been amended six times: (1) To allow county, city, school district or other political subdivision to exempt not less than $3,000 of the assessed value of residence homesteads of persons 65 years and older from all ad valorem taxes levied by the subdivision. Submitted by 62nd Legislature (1971) and adopted in election Nov. 7, 1972. (See also note under 1-c below.) (2) To extend to unmarried persons the $3,000 ad valorem exemption on homesteads. Submitted by 63rd Legislature (1973) and adopted in election Nov. 6, 1973. (See also Art. XVI, Secs. 50, 51 and 52.) (3) To give added tax relief to disabled persons and persons over 65 years of age and to provide for administration of property tax. It also added Subsections (c) and (d). (See also Sec. 1, Sec. 21, and Sec. 23 of Art. VIII.) Submitted by 65th Legislature (1977) and adopted in election Nov. 7, 1978. (4) To add Subsection (e) to authorize political subdivisions to provide property tax relief for owners of residence homesteads and changing certain property tax administrative procedures. (See also Sec. 21, Subsection (c) of Art. VIII.) Submitted by 67th Legislature (1981) and adopted in election Nov. 3, 1981. (5) Subsection (d) of Sec. 1-b of Art. VIII was amended to limit school tax increases on the residence homestead of the surviving spouse of an elderly person. Submitted by 70th Legislature (1987) and adopted in election Nov. 3, 1987. (6) Subsections (b) and (e) were amended to clarify the homestead exemptions allowed to be granted by county education districts. Submitted by 72nd Legislature and adopted in election Aug. 10, 1991.]

Sec. 1-b-1. The references to a county education district in Sections 1 and 1-b of this article neither validate nor invalidate county education districts.

[Note — Sec. 1-b-1 of Article VIII was added to clarify the status of county education districts in reference to this article. Submitted by 72nd Legislature, (1991) and adopted in election Aug. 10, 1992.]]

Sec. 1-c. **Optional Provisions Relating to Sec. 1-a and Sec. 1-b** — Provided, however, the terms of this resolution shall

Article VIII (Cont'd.)

not be effective unless House Joint Resolution No. 24 is adopted by the people and in no event shall this resolution go into effect until January 1, 1951.

[Note — Sec. 1-b and Sec. 1-c of Article VIII were added because of an oversight in writing the text of Sec. 1-a (adopted by joint resolution at an earlier date), which would have abolished the $3,000 homestead exemption under the state school tax on adoption of Sec. 1-a by the people. Submitted by 50th Legislature (1947) and adopted in election Nov. 2, 1948.]

Sec. 1-d. **Taxation of Agricultural Land** — (a) All land owned by natural persons which is designated for agricultural use in accordance with the provisions of this section shall be assessed for all tax purposes on the consideration of only those factors relative to such agricultural use. "Agricultural use" means the raising of livestock or growing of crops, fruit, flowers, and other products of the soil under natural conditions as a business venture for profit, which business is the primary occupation and source of income of the owner.

(b) For each assessment year the owner wishes to qualify his land under provisions of this section as designated for agricultural use he shall file with the local tax assessor a sworn statement in writing describing the use to which the land is devoted.

(c) Upon receipt of the sworn statement in writing the local tax assessor shall determine whether or not such land qualifies for the designation as to agricultural use as defined herein and in the event it so qualifies he shall designate such land as being for agricultural use and assess the land accordingly.

(d) Such local tax assessor may inspect the land and require such evidence of use and source of income as may be necessary or useful in determining whether or not the agricultural use provision of this article applies.

(e) No land may qualify for the designation provided for in this act unless for at least three (3) successive years immediately preceding the assessment date the land has been devoted exclusively for agricultural use, or unless the land has been continuously developed for agriculture during such time.

(f) Each year during which the land is designated for agricultural use, the local tax assessor shall note on his records the valuation which would have been made had the land not qualified for such designation under this section. If designated land is subsequently diverted to a purpose other than that of agricultural use, or is sold, the land shall be subject to an additional tax. The additional tax shall equal the difference between taxes paid or payable, hereunder, and the amount of tax payable for the preceding three years had the land been otherwise assessed. Until paid, there shall be a lien for additional taxes and interest on land assessed under the provisions of this section.

(g) The valuation and assessment of any minerals or subsurface rights to minerals shall not come within the provisions of this section.

[Note — Sec. 1-d of Art. VIII was added to provide that all land designated for agricultural use be assessed only as such. Submitted by 59th Legislature (1965) and adopted in election Nov. 8, 1966.]

Sec. 1-d-1. **Open-Space Land Taxation** — (a) To promote the preservation of open-space land, the legislature shall provide by general law for taxation of open-space land devoted to farm or ranch purposes on the basis of its productive capacity and may provide by general law for taxation of open-space land devoted to timber production on the basis of its productive capacity. The legislature by general law may provide eligibility limitations under this section and may impose sanctions in furtherance of the taxation policy of this section.

(b) If a property owner qualifies his land for designation for agricultural use under Section 1-d of this article, the land is subject to the provisions of Section 1-d for the year in which the designation is effective and is not subject to a law enacted under this Section 1-d-1 in that year.

[Note — Sec. 1-d-1 of Art. VIII was added to promote preservation of open-space land and to provide for taxation of production of timber thereon; also redefines use of open land for agricultural purposes and taxation thereon. Submitted by 65th Legislature (1977) and adopted in election Nov. 7, 1978.]

Sec. 1-e. **Gradual Abolition of Ad Valorem Tax** — (1) No State ad valorem taxes shall be levied upon any property within this State.

(2) All receipts from previously authorized State ad valorem taxes that are collected on or after the effective date of the 1982 amendment to this section shall be deposited to the credit of the general fund of the county collecting the taxes and may be expended for county purposes. Receipts from taxes collected before that date shall be distributed by the Legislature among institutions eligible to receive distributions under prior law. Those receipts and receipts distributed under prior law may be expended for the purposes provided under prior law or for repair and renovation of existing permanent improvements.

[Note — Sec. 1-e of Art. VIII was added to provide for the gradual abolition of the ad valorem tax for all state purposes except those that were listed under Art. VII, Sec. 17 (which was repealed by constitutional amendment in an election Nov. 2, 1982) for certain institutions of higher education and for pension funds for Confederate veterans and their widows, and for Texas Rangers and their widows. Submitted by 60th Legislature (1967) and adopted in election Nov. 5, 1968. Sec. 1-e was amended to abolish the state property tax and to add Subsection (2), which is self-explanatory. Submitted by Called Session of 67th Legislature (1982) and adopted in election Nov. 2, 1982. (See also Art. III, Sec. 51 and Art. XVI, Sec. 66.)]

Sec. 1-f. **Ad Valorem Tax Relief** — The legislature by law may provide for the preservation of cultural, historical, or natural history resources by:

(1) granting exemptions or other relief from state ad valorem taxes on appropriate property so designated in the manner prescribed by law; and

(2) authorizing political subdivisions to grant exemptions or other relief from ad valorem taxes on appropriate property so designated by the political subdivision in the manner prescribed by general law.

[Note — Sec. 1-f of Art. VIII was added to authorize tax relief to preserve certain cultural, historical or natural history resources. Submitted by 65th Legislature (1977) and adopted in election Nov. 8, 1977.]

Sec. 1-g. **Tax Relief to Encourage Development and Improvement of Property** — (a) The legislature by general law may authorize cities, towns, and other taxing units to grant exemptions or other relief from ad valorem taxes on property located in a reinvestment zone for the purpose of encouraging development or redevelopment and improvement of the property.

(b) The Legislature by general law may authorize an incorporated city or town to issue bonds or notes to finance the development or redevelopment of an unproductive, underdeveloped, or blighted area within the city or town and to pledge for repayment of those bonds or notes increases in ad valorem tax revenues imposed on property in the area by the city or town and other political subdivisions.

[Note — Sec. 1-g of Art. VIII was added to encourage development and improvement of certain areas through tax relief. Submitted by 67th Legislature (1981) and adopted in election Nov. 3, 1981.]

Sec. 1-h — **Validation of Assessment Ratio** — Sec. 26.03, Tax Code, is validated as of January 1, 1980.

[Note — Sec. 1-h of Art. VIII was added to give validation date of Sec. 26.03 of the Tax Code. Submitted by Called Session of 67th Legislature (1982) and adopted in election Nov. 2, 1982.]

Sec. 1-i. — The legislature by general law may provide ad valorem tax relief for mobile marine drilling equipment designed for offshore drilling of oil or gas wells that is being stored while not in use in a county bordering on the Gulf of Mexico or on a bay or other body of water immediately adjacent to the Gulf of Mexico.

[Note — Sec. 1-i of Art. VIII was added to provide ad valorem tax relief for certain offshore drilling equipment that is not in use. Submitted by 70th Legislature (1987) and adopted in election Nov. 3, 1987.]

Sec. 1-j. (a) To promote economic development in the State, goods, wares, merchandise, other tangible personal property, and ores, other than oil, natural gas, and other petroleum products, are exempt from ad valorem taxation if:

(1) the property is acquired in or imported into this State to be forwarded outside this State, whether or not the intention to forward the property outside this State is formed or the destination to which the property is forwarded is specified when the property is acquired in or imported into this State:

(2) the property is detained in this State for assembling, storing, manufacturing, processing, or fabricating purposes by the person who acquired or imported the property; and

(3) the property is transported outside of this State not later than 175 days after the date the person acquired or imported the property in this State.

(b) Tangible personal property exempted from taxation in Sub-

Article VIII (Cont'd.)

section (a) of this section is subject to the following:

(1) A county, common, or independent school district, junior college district, or municipality, including a home-rule city, may tax such property otherwise exempt, if the governing body of the county, common, or independent school district, junior college district, or municipality takes official action as provided in this section and in the manner provided by law to provide for the taxation of such property.

(2) Any official action to tax such exempt property must be taken before April 1, 1990. If official action is taken to tax such exempt property before January 1, 1990, such property is taxable effective for the tax year 1990. However, if such official action to tax such exempt property is taken prior to April 1, 1990, but after January 1, 1990, the official action shall not become effective to tax such property until the 1991 tax year.

(3) Any of the above-named political subdivisions shall have the authority to exempt from payment of taxation such property located in such above-named political subdivisions for the taxing year 1989. If a governing body exempts the property from 1989 taxes, the governing body shall waive 1989 taxes already imposed and refund 1989 taxes already paid on such property for that year.

(4) The governing body of a county, common, or independent school district, junior college district, or municipality that acts under Subdivision (2) of Subsection (b) of this section to tax the property otherwise exempt by Subsection (a) of this section may subsequently exempt the property from taxation by rescinding its action to tax the property. The exemption applies to each tax year that begins after the date the action is taken and applies to the tax year in which the action is taken if the governing body so provides. A governing body that rescinds its action to tax the property may not take action to tax such property after the rescission.

(c) For purposes of this section:

(1) tangible personal property shall include aircraft and aircraft parts:

(2) property imported into this State shall include property brought into this State;

(3) property forwarded outside this State shall include property transported outside this State or to be affixed to an aircraft to be transported outside this State; and

(4) property detained in this State for assembling, storing, manufacturing, processing, or fabricating purposes shall include property, aircraft, or aircraft parts brought into this State or acquired in this State and used by the person who acquired the property, aircraft, or aircraft parts in or who brought the property, aircraft, or aircraft parts into this State for the purpose of repair or maintenance of aircraft operated by a certificated air carrier.

[Note — Sec. 1-j of Art. VIII was added to authorize the exemption from ad valorem taxation of certain personal property temporarily in the state for certain purposes. (See related amendment in Sec. 1 (a) of Art. VIII.) Proposed by 71st Legislature (1989) and adopted in election Nov. 7, 1989.]

Sec. 1-k. The legislature by general law may exempt from ad valorem taxation property owned by a nonprofit corporation organized to supply water or provide wastewater service that provides in the bylaws of the corporation that on dissolution of the corporation, the assets of the corporation remaining after discharge of the corporation's indebtedness shall be transferred to an entity that provides a water supply or wastewater service, or both, that is exempt from ad valorem taxation, if the property is reasonably necessary for and used in the acquisition, treatment, storage, transportation, sale, or distribution of water or the provision of wastewater service.

[Note — Sec. 1-k was added to Article VIII to exempt from ad valorem taxation property owned by a non-profit water supply or wastewater service corporation. Submitted by 72nd Legislature (1991) and adopted in election Nov. 5, 1991.]

Sec. 1-l. (a) The legislature by general law may exempt from ad valorem taxation all or part of real and personal property used, constructed, acquired, or installed wholly or partly to meet or exceed rules or regulations adopted by any environmental protection agency of the United States, this state, or a political subdivision of this state for the prevention, monitoring, control, or reduction of air, water, or land pollution.

(b) This section applies to real and personal property used as a facility, device, or method for the control of air, water, or land pollution that would otherwise be taxable for the first time on or after January 1, 1994.

(c) This section does not authorize the exemption from ad valorem taxation of real or personal property that was subject to a tax abatement agreement executed before January 1, 1994.

[Note — Sec. 1-l of Art. VIII was added to authorize the exemption from ad valorem taxation of real and personal property used for the control of air, water, or land pollution. Submitted by 73rd Legislature (1993) and adopted in election Nov. 2, 1993.]

Sec. 2. **Occupation Taxes Equal and Uniform; Exemptions Therefrom** — (a) All occupation taxes shall be equal and uniform upon the same class of subjects within the limits of the authority levying the tax; but the Legislature may, by general laws, exempt from taxation public property used for public purposes; actual places of religious worship, also any property owned by a church or by a strictly religious society for the exclusive use as a dwelling place for the ministry of such church or religious society, and which yields no revenue whatever to such church or religious society; provided that such exemption shall not extend to more property than is reasonably necessary for a dwelling place and in no event more than one acre of land; places of burial not held for private or corporate profit; solar or wind-powered energy devices; all buildings used exclusively and owned by persons or associations of persons for school purposes and the necessary furniture of all schools and property used exclusively and reasonably necessary in conducting any association engaged in promoting the religious, educational and physical development of boys, girls, young men or young women operating under a State or National organization of like character; also, the endowment funds of such institutions of learning and religion not used with a view to profit; and when the same are invested in bonds or mortgages, or in land or other property which has been and shall hereafter be bought in by such institutions under foreclosure sales made to satisfy or protect such bonds or mortgages, that such exemption of such land and property shall continue only for two years after the purchase of the same at such sale by such institutions and no longer, and institutions of purely public charity; and all laws exempting property from taxation other than the property mentioned in this Section shall be null and void.

(b) The Legislature may, by general law, exempt property owned by a disabled veteran or by the surviving spouse and surviving minor children of a disabled veteran. A disabled veteran is a veteran of the armed services of the United States who is classified as disabled by the Veterans Administration or by a successor to that agency; or the military service in which he served. A veteran who is certified as having a disability of less than 10 per cent is not entitled to an exemption. A veteran having a disability rating of not less than 10 per cent nor more than 30 per cent may be granted an exemption from taxation for property valued at up to $1,500. A veteran having a disability rating of more than 30 per cent but not more than 50 per cent may be granted an exemption from taxation for property valued at up to $2,000. A veteran having a disability rating of more than 50 per cent but not more than 70 per cent may be granted an exemption from taxation for property valued at up to $2,500. A veteran who has a disability rating of more than 70 per cent, or a veteran who has a disability rating of not less than 10 per cent and has attained the age of 65, or a disabled veteran whose disability consists of the loss or loss of use of one or more limbs, total blindness in one or both eyes, or paraplegia, may be granted an exemption from taxation for property valued at up to $3,000. The spouse and children of any member of the United States Armed Forces who loses his life while on active duty will be granted an exemption from taxation for property valued at up to $2,500. A deceased disabled veteran's surviving spouse and children may be granted an exemption which in the aggregate is equal to the exemption to which the decedent was entitled at the time he died.

(c) The Legislature by general law may exempt from ad valorem taxation property that is owned by a nonprofit organization composed primarily of members or former members of the armed forces of the United States or its allies and chartered or incorporated by the United States Congress.

[Note — Sec. 2 of Art. VIII has been amended five times: (1) To add clause with reference to endowment fund. Submitted by 29th Legislature (1905); ratified Nov. 6, 1906, and proclaimed adopted Jan. 7, 1907. (2) To permit exemption of ministers' dwellings and certain other property of religious organizations, the original amendment having provided only for exemption for "actual places of worship." Submitted by 40th Legislature (1927); ratified Nov. 6, 1928; proclaimed Feb. 6, 1929. (3) To allow certain tax exemptions to disabled veterans, their surviving spouses and surviving minor children and to survivors of members of the armed forces who lose their lives while on active duty. Submitted by 62nd Legislature (1971) and adopted in election Nov. 7, 1972. (4) To authorize Legislature to exempt from taxation solar- and wind-powered energy devices. Submitted by 65th Legislature (1977) and adopted in election Nov. 7, 1978. (5) To authorize the legislature to exempt from ad valorem

Article VIII (Cont'd.)
taxation certain property of non-profit veterans organizations. Submitted by 71st Legislature (1989) and adopted in election Nov. 7, 1989.]

Sec. 3. **Taxes to Be Collected for Public Purposes Only** — Taxes shall be levied and collected by general laws and for public purposes only.

Sec. 4. **Power to Tax Corporations Not to Be Surrendered** — The power to tax corporations and corporate property shall not be surrendered or suspended by act of the Legislature, by any contract or grant to which the State shall be a party.

Sec. 5. **Railroad Taxes Due Cities and Towns** — All property of railroad companies, of whatever description lying or being within the limits of any city or incorporated town within this State, shall bear its proportionate share of municipal taxation, and if any such property shall not have been heretofore rendered, the authorities of the city or town within which it lies shall have power to require its rendition and collect the usual municipal tax thereon, as on other property lying within said municipality.

Sec. 6. **Appropriations; How Made and for What Period** — No money shall be drawn from the Treasury but in pursuance of specific appropriations made by law; nor shall any appropriation of money be made for a longer term than two years, except by the First Legislature to assemble under this Constitution, which may make the necessary appropriations to carry on the government until the assembling of the Sixteenth Legislature.

Sec. 7. **Special Funds Not to Be Borrowed or Diverted** — The Legislature shall not have power to borrow, or in any manner divert from its purpose any special fund that may, or ought to, come into the Treasury; and shall make it penal for any person or persons to borrow, withhold or in any manner to divert from its purpose, any special fund or any part thereof.

Sec. 7-a. **Net Motor License Fees and Motor Fuel Tax Revenues Restricted, Except One Fourth of Fuel Taxes to Schools, to Highway Improvement, Policing and Administration** — Subject to legislative appropriation, allocation and direction, all net revenues remaining after payment of all refunds allowed by law and expenses of collection derived from motor vehicle registration fees, and all taxes, except gross production and ad valorem taxes, on motor fuels and lubricants used to propel motor vehicles over public roadways, shall be used for the sole purpose of acquiring rights of way, constructing, maintaining, and policing such public roadways and for the administration of such laws as may be prescribed by the Legislature pertaining to the supervision of traffic and safety on such roads; and for the payment of the principal and interest on county and road district bonds or warrants voted or issued prior to January 2, 1939, and declared eligible prior to January 2, 1945, for payment out of the County and Road District Highway Fund under existing law, provided, however, that one fourth (1/4) of such net revenue from the motor fuel tax shall be allocated to the Available School Fund; and, provided, however, that the net revenue derived by counties from motor vehicle registration fees shall never be less than the maximum amounts allowed to be retained by each county and the percentage allowed to be retained by each county under the laws in effect on January 1, 1945. Nothing contained herein shall be construed as authorizing the pledging of the State's credit for any purpose.

[Note — Sec. 7-a of Art. VIII was added to restrict revenues from motor vehicle registration and motor fuel taxes to the of highway improvement, policing and administration. Submitted by 49th Legislature (1945), ratified in election Nov. 5, 1946.]

Sec. 7-b. All revenues received from the federal government as reimbursement for state expenditures of funds that are themselves dedicated for acquiring rights-of-way and constructing, maintaining, and policing public roadways are also constitutionally dedicated and shall be used only for those purposes.

[Note — Sec. 7-b of Art. VIII was added to provide for the dedication of certain funds for highway purposes. Submitted by 70th Legislature (1987) and adopted in election Nov. 8, 1988.]

Sec. 8. **Railroad Property; How Assessed** — All property of railroad companies shall be assessed, and the taxes collected in the several counties in which said property is situated, including so much of the roadbed and fixtures as shall be in each county. The rolling stock may be assessed in gross in the county where the principal office of the company is located, and the county tax paid upon it shall be apportioned as provided by general law in proportion to the distance such road may run through any such county, among the several counties through which the road passes, as part of their tax assets.

[Note — Sec. 8 of Art. VIII was added to allow Legislature to provide by general law for apportionment of value of railroad rolling stock among counties for purposes of property taxation. Submitted by 69th Legislature (1985) and adopted in election Nov. 4, 1986.]

Sec. 9. **Rate of State and Municipal Taxation** — The State tax on property, exclusive of the tax necessary to pay the public debt, and of the taxes provided for the benefit of the public free school, shall never exceed thirty-five cents (35¢) on the One Hundred Dollars ($100) valuation; and no county, city or town shall levy a tax rate in excess of Eighty Cents (80¢) on the One Hundred Dollars ($100) valuation in any one (1) year for general fund, permanent improvement fund, road and bridge fund and jury fund purposes; provided further that at the time the Commissioners Court meets to levy the annual tax rate for each county it shall levy whatever tax rate may be needed for the four (4) constitutional purposes; namely, general fund, permanent improvement fund, road and bridge fund and jury fund so long as the Court does not impair any outstanding bonds or other obligations and so long as the total of the foregoing tax levies does not exceed Eighty Cents (80¢) on the One Hundred Dollars ($100) valuation in any one (1) year. Once the Court has levied the annual tax rate, the same shall remain in force and effect during that taxable year; and the Legislature may also authorize an additional annual ad valorem tax to be levied and collected for the further maintenance of the public roads; provided that a majority of the qualified property tax-paying voters of the county voting at an election to be held for that purpose shall vote such tax, not to exceed fifteen cents (15¢) on the One Hundred Dollars ($100) valuation of the property subject to taxation in such county. Any county may put all tax money collected by the county into one general fund, without regard to the purpose or source of each tax. And the Legislature may pass local laws for the maintenance of the public roads and highways, without the local notice required for special or local laws. This section shall not be construed as a limitation of powers delegated to counties, cities or towns by any other section or sections of this Constitution.

[Note — Sec. 9 of Art. VIII has been amended seven times: (1) To lower State tax rate from 50¢ to 35¢, a separate State school tax having been provided by companion amendment, Sec. 3 of Art. VII. Submitted by 18th Legislature (1883), ratified in election Aug. 14, 1883, and declared adopted Sept. 25, 1883. (2) To authorize Legislature to provide for a 15¢ local road tax. Submitted by 21st Legislature (1889), ratified in election Nov. 3, 1890, and declared adopted Dec. 19, 1890. (3) To authorize 15¢ tax for jurors. Submitted by 29th Legislature (1905), ratified in election Nov. 6, 1906, and declared adopted Jan. 7, 1907. (4) To allow County Commissioners to re-allocate the named county taxes by changing the rates if approved by a majority of the qualified voters, but restricting the period to six years, and restricting total to 80¢ on the $100 valuation. Submitted by 48th Legislature and adopted in election Nov. 7, 1944. (5) To abolish ad valorem tax for State general revenue fund purposes, and making other provisions. (See Sec. 1-a of Art. VIII and note thereon.) Submitted by 50th Legislature (1947) and adopted in election Nov. 2, 1948. (6) To give Commissioners Courts authority to levy taxes for general, permanent improvement, road and bridge and jury fund purposes, so long as total of these tax rates does not exceed 80¢ on the $100 valuation in any one year. Submitted by 54th Legislature (1955) and adopted in election Nov. 6, 1956. (7) To allow counties to put all county taxes into one general fund. Submitted by 60th Legislature (1967) and adopted in election Nov. 11, 1967.]

Sec. 10. **Taxes Not to Be Released Except by Two-Thirds Vote of Each House** — The Legislature shall have no power to release the inhabitants of, or property in, any county, city or town, from the payment of taxes levied for State or county purposes, unless in case of great public calamity in any such county, city or town, when such release may be made by a vote of two-thirds of each house of the Legislature.

Sec. 11. **Where Property Is to Be Assessed** — All property, whether owned by persons or corporations, shall be assessed for taxation and the taxes paid in the county where situated, but the Legislature may by a two-thirds vote authorize the payment of taxes of non-residents of counties to be made at the office of the Comptroller of Public Accounts. And all lands and other property not rendered for taxation by the owner thereof shall be assessed at its fair value by the proper officer.

[Note — Sec. 12 of Art. VIII, relating to unorganized counties, was deleted by constitutional amendment . Submitted by 61st Legislature (1969) and approved in election Aug. 5, 1969.]

Sec. 13. **Tax Sales; Tax Deeds; Redemptions** — (a) Provision shall be made by the Legislature for the sale of a sufficient portion of all lands and other property for the taxes due thereon that have not been paid.

Article VIII (Cont'd.)

(b) The deed of conveyance to the purchaser for all lands and other property thus sold shall be held to vest a good and perfect title in the purchaser thereof, subject only to redemption as provided by this section or impeachment for actual fraud.

(c) The former owner of a residence homestead sold for unpaid taxes and the former owner of land designated for agricultural use sold for unpaid taxes shall within two years from date of filing for record of the Purchaser's Deed have the right to redeem the property on the following basis:

(1) Within the first year of the redemption period, upon the payment of the amount of money paid for the property, including the Tax Deed Recording Fee and all taxes, penalties, interest, and costs paid plus an amount not exceeding 25 percent of the aggregate total; and

(2) Within the last year of the redemption period, upon the payment of the amount of money paid for the property, including the Tax Deed Recording Fee and all taxes, penalties, interest, and costs paid plus an amount not exceeding 50 percent of the aggregate total.

(d) If the property is sold pursuant to a suit to enforce the collection of the unpaid taxes, the Legislature may limit the application of Subsection (c) of this section to property used as a residence homestead when the suit was filed and to land designated for agricultural use when the suit was filed.

(e) The former owner of real property not covered by Subsection (c) of this section sold for unpaid taxes shall within six months from the date of filing for record of the Purchaser's Deed have the right to redeem the property upon the payment of the amount of money paid for the property, including the Tax Deed Recording Fee and all taxes, penalties, interest, and costs paid plus an amount not exceeding 25 percent of the aggregate total.

TEMPORARY PROVISION. (a) This temporary provision applies to the constitutional amendment proposed by S.J.R. No. 19, 73rd Legislature, Regular Session, 1993, and expires January 1, 1997.

(b) The amendment to Article VIII, Section 13, of this constitution takes effect January 1, 1994.

(c) The amendment applies to redemption of real property sold at a tax sale for which the purchaser's deed is filed for record on or after the effective date of this amendment. Redemption of real property sold at a tax sale for which the purchaser's deed is filed for record before the effective date of this amendment is covered by the former law, and the former law is continued in effect for this purpose.

[Note — Sec. 13 of Art. VIII was amended to insert the provisions for redemption given above for the original clause, which provided for "double the amount of money paid for the land" to be paid by the original owner for redemption. Submitted by 42nd Legislature (1931) and adopted in election Nov. 8, 1932. Proclaimed July 26, 1933. It was further amended to modify the provisions for the redemption of real property sold at a tax sale. Submitted by the 73rd Legislature (1993) and adopted in election Nov. 2, 1993.]

Sec. 14. **County Tax Assessor and Collector** — Except as provided in Sec. 16 of this Article, there shall be elected by the qualified electors of each county an Assessor and Collector of Taxes, who shall hold his office for four years and until his successor is elected and qualified; and such Assessor and Collector of Taxes shall perform all the duties with respect to assessing property for the purpose of taxation and of collecting taxes as may be prescribed by the Legislature.

[Note — Sec. 14 of Art. VIII was amended to consolidate offices of Tax Assessor and Tax Collector. (See also Sec. 16.) Submitted by 42nd Legislature (1931), adopted in election Nov. 8, 1932, proclaimed Jan. 9, 1933. It was again amended to change term of office from two to four years. Submitted by 53rd Legislature (1953) and adopted in election Nov. 2, 1954.]

Sec. 15. **Tax Liens and Sales** — The annual assessment made upon landed property shall be a special lien thereon; and all property, both real and personal, belonging to any delinquent taxpayer shall be liable to seizure and sale for the payment of all the taxes and penalties due by such delinquent, and such property may be sold for the payment of the taxes and penalties due by such delinquent, under such regulations as the Legislature may provide.

Sec. 16. **Sheriff to Be County Tax Assessor-Collector in Some Counties** — The Sheriff of each county, in addition to his other duties, shall be the Assessor and Collector of Taxes therefor. But in counties having ten thousand (10,000) or more inhabitants, to be determined by the last preceding census of the United States, an Assessor and Collector of Taxes shall be elected, as provided in Sec. 14 of this Article and shall hold office for four years and until his successor shall be elected and qualified.

[Note — Sec. 16 of Art. VIII was amended to harmonize with section consolidating offices of Assessor and Collector of Taxes. (See also Sec. 14.) Submitted by 42nd Legislature (1931) and adopted in election Nov. 8, 1932; proclaimed Jan. 9, 1933. It was again amended to change term of office from two to four years. Submitted by 53rd Legislature (1953) and adopted in election Nov. 2, 1954.]

Sec. 16-a. **Assessor-Collector of Taxes in Counties of Less Than Ten Thousand** — In any county having a population of less than ten thousand (10,000) inhabitants, as determined by last preceding census of the United States, the Commissioners' Court may submit to the qualified property taxpaying voters of such county at an election the question of adding an Assessor-Collector of Taxes to the list of authorized county officials. If a majority of such voters voting in such election shall approve of adding an Assessor-Collector of Taxes to such list, then such official shall be elected at the next General Election for such Constitutional term of office as is provided for other Tax Assessor-Collectors in this State.

[Note — Sec. 16-a of Art. VIII was added to provide for a Tax Assessor-Collector in counties of less than 10,000 population. Submitted by 53rd Legislature (1953) and adopted in election Nov. 2, 1954.]

Sec. 17. **Power of Legislature as to Taxes** — The specification of the objects and subjects of taxation shall not deprive the Legislature of the power to require other subjects or objects to be taxed, in such manner as may be consistent with the principles of taxation fixed in this Constitution.

Sec. 18. **Equalization of Taxes** — (a) The Legislature shall provide for equalizing, as near as may be, the valuation of all property subject to or rendered for taxation and may also provide for the classification of all lands with reference to their value in the several counties.

(b) A single appraisal within each county of all property subject to ad valorem taxation by the county and all other taxing units located therein shall be provided by general law. The Legislature, by general law, may authorize appraisals outside a county when political subdivisions are situated in more than one county or when two or more counties elect to consolidate appraisal services.

(c) The Legislature, by general law, shall provide for a single board of equalization for each appraisal entity consisting of qualified persons residing within the territory appraised by that entity. Members of the board of equalization may not be elected officials of the county or of the governing body of a taxing unit.

(d) The Legislature shall prescribe by general law the methods, timing and administrative process for implementing the requirements of this section.

[Note — Sec. 18 of Art. VIII was amended to provide for a single appraisal and a single board of equalization within each county for ad valorem tax purposes. Submitted by 66th Legislature (1979) and adopted in election Nov. 4, 1980.]

Sec. 19. **Farm Products in the Hands of the Producer Exempt From All Taxation** — Farm products, livestock, and poultry in the hands of the producer, and family supplies for home and farm use, are exempt from all taxation until otherwise directed by a two-thirds vote of all the members *elect to both houses of the Legislature.

---

*Explanatory Note — Expressed thus in official draft of Constitution.

[Note — Sec. 19 of Art. VIII was added to exempt farm products from taxation. Submitted by 16th Legislature (1879), ratified in election Sept. 2, 1879 and declared adopted Oct. 14, 1879. It was amended to change the wording to include livestock and poultry with farm products as exempt from taxation. Submitted by 67th Legislature (1981) and adopted in election Nov. 3, 1981.]

Sec. 19-a. **Farm Implements Exempt From Taxation** — Implements of husbandry that are used in the production of farm or ranch products are exempt from ad valorem taxation.

[Note — Sec. 19-a of Art. VIII was added to exempt implements of farm husbandry from ad valorem taxation. Submitted by Called Session of 67th Legislature (1982) and adopted in election Nov. 2, 1982.]

Sec. 20. **Limiting Ad Valorem Tax Assessment; Discount for Prompt Payment of Taxes** — No property of any kind in this State shall ever be assessed for ad valorem taxes at a greater value than its fair cash market value nor shall any Board of

Article VIII (Cont'd.)

Equalization of any governmental or political subdivision or taxing district within this State fix the value of any property for tax purposes at more than its fair cash market value; provided, that in order to encourage the prompt payment of taxes, the Legislature shall have the power to provide that the taxpayer shall be allowed by the State and all governmental and political subdivisions and taxing districts of the State a three per cent discount on ad valorem taxes due the State or due any governmental or political subdivision or taxing district of the State if such taxes are paid ninety days before the date when they would otherwise become delinquent; and the taxpayer shall be allowed a two per cent discount on said taxes if paid sixty days before said taxes would become delinquent; and the taxpayer shall be allowed a one per cent discount if said taxes are paid thirty days before they would otherwise become delinquent. This amendment shall be effective Jan. 1, 1939. The Legislature shall pass necessary laws for the proper administration of this Section.

[Note — Sec. 20 of Art. VIII was added (1) to restrict assessed value to true market value, and (2) to provide for stated discounts for prepayment of taxes. Submitted by 45th Legislature (1937) and adopted in election Aug. 23, 1937.]

Sec. 21. **Limitation on Property Taxes** — (a) Subject to any exceptions prescribed by general law, the total amount of property taxes imposed by a political subdivision in any year may not exceed the total amount of property taxes imposed by that subdivision in the preceding year unless the governing body of the subdivision gives notice of its intent to consider an increase in taxes and holds a public hearing on the proposed increase before it increases those total taxes. The legislature shall prescribe by law the form, content, timing, and methods of giving the notice and the rules for the conduct of the hearing.

(b) In calculating the total amount of taxes imposed in the current year for the purposes of Subsection (a) of this section, the taxes on property in territory added to the political subdivision since the preceding year and on new improvements that were not taxable in the preceding year are excluded. In calculating the total amount of taxes imposed in the preceding year for the purposes of Subsection (a) of this section, the taxes imposed on real property that is not taxable by the subdivision in the current year are excluded.

(c) The Legislature by general law shall require that, subject to reasonable exceptions, a property owner be given notice of a revaluation of his property and a reasonable estimate of the amount of taxes that would be imposed on his property if the total amount of property taxes for the subdivision were not increased according to any law enacted pursuant to Subsection (a) of this section. The notice must be given before the procedures required in Subsection (a) are instituted.

[Note — Sec. 21 of Art. VIII was added to limit increases in property revaluation and to prescribe method of giving notice before property revaluated. (See also Sec. 1, Sec. 1-b and Sec. 23 of Art. VIII.) Submitted by 65th Legislature (1977) and adopted in election Nov. 7, 1978. It was further amended to change wording of administrative procedures in notifying property owners. (See also Subsection (e) of Section 1-b of Art. VIII.) Submitted by 67th Legislature (1981) and adopted in election Nov. 3, 1981.]

Sec. 22. **State Tax Revenues** — (a) In no biennium shall the rate of growth of appropriations from state tax revenues not dedicated by this constitution exceed the estimated rate of growth of the state's economy. The Legislature shall provide by general law procedures to implement this subsection.

(b) If the Legislature by adoption of a resolution approved by a record vote of a majority of the members of each house finds that an emergency exists and identifies the nature of the emergency, the Legislature may provide for appropriations in excess of the amount authorized by Subsection (a) of this section. The excess authorized under this subsection may not exceed the amount specified in the resolution.

(c) In no case shall appropriations exceed revenues as provided in Article III, Sec. 49-a, of this constitution. Nothing in this section shall be construed to alter, amend, or repeal Article III, Sec. 49-a, of this constitution.

[Note — Sec. 22 of Art. VIII was added to limit the rate of growth of appropriations from state tax revenues and to provide for emergency spending by state. (See also Sec. 49-a of Art. III.) Submitted by 65th Legislature (1977) and adopted in election Nov. 7, 1978.]

Sec. 23. **No Statewide Real Property Appraisal** — (a) There shall be no statewide appraisal of real property for ad valorem tax purposes; however, this shall not preclude formula distribution of tax revenues to political subdivisions of the state.

(b) Administrative and judicial enforcement of uniform standards and procedures for appraisal of property for ad valorem tax purposes, as prescribed by general law, shall originate in the county where the tax is imposed, except that the Legislature may provide by general law for political subdivisions with boundaries extending outside the county.

[Note — Sec. 23 of Art. VIII was added to prohibit a statewide appraisal of real property for ad valorem tax purposes while allowing local subdivisions to administer tax rate. (See also Sec. 1, Sec. 1-b, Sec. 21 of Art. VIII.) Submitted by 65th Legislature (1977) and adopted in election Nov. 7, 1978.]

Sec. 24. (a) A general law enacted by the legislature that imposes a tax on the net incomes of natural persons, including a person's share of partnership and unincorporated association income, must provide that the portion of the law imposing the tax not take effect until approved by a majority of the registered voters voting in a statewide referendum held on the question of imposing the tax. The referendum must specify the rate of the tax that will apply to taxable income as defined by law.

(b) A general law enacted by the legislature that increases the rate of the tax, or changes the tax, in a manner that results in an increase in the combined income tax liability of all persons subject to the tax may not take effect until approved by a majority of the registered voters voting in a statewide referendum held on the question of increasing the income tax. A determination of whether a bill proposing a change in the tax would increase the combined income tax liability of all persons subject to the tax must be made by comparing the provisions of the proposed change in law with the provisions of the law for the most recent year in which actual tax collections have been made. A referendum held under this subsection must specify the manner in which the proposed law would increase the combined income tax liability of all persons subject to the tax.

(c) Except as provided by Subsection (b) of this section, the legislature may amend or repeal a tax approved by the voters under this section without submitting the amendment or the repeal to the voters as provided by Subsection (a) of this section.

(d) If the legislature repeals a tax approved by the voters under this section, the legislature may reenact the tax without submitting the reenactment to the voters as provided by Subsection (a) of this section only if the effective date of the reenactment of the tax is before the first anniversary of the effective date of the repeal.

(e) The legislature may provide for the taxation of income in a manner which is consistent with federal law.

(f) In the first year in which a tax described by Subsection (a) is imposed and during the first year of any increase in the tax that is subject to Subsection (b) of this section, not less than two-thirds of all net revenues remaining after payment of all refunds allowed by law and expenses of collection from the tax shall be used to reduce the rate of ad valorem maintenance and operation taxes levied for the support of primary and secondary public education. In subsequent years, not less than two-thirds of all net revenues from the tax shall be used to continue such ad valorem tax relief.

(g) The net revenues remaining after the dedication of money from the tax under Subsection (f) of this section shall be used for support of education, subject to legislative appropriation, allocation, and direction.

(h) The maximum rate at which a school district may impose ad valorem maintenance and operation taxes is reduced by an amount equal to one cent per $100 valuation for each one cent per $100 valuation that the school district's ad valorem maintenance and operation tax is reduced by the minimum amount of money dedicated under Subsection (f) of this section, provided that a school district may subsequently increase the maximum ad valorem maintenance and operation tax rate if the increased maximum rate is approved by a majority of the voters of the school district voting at an election called and held for that purpose. The legislature by general law shall provide for the tax relief that is required by Subsection (f) and this subsection.

(i) Subsections (f) and (h) of this section apply to ad valorem maintenance and operation taxes levied by a school district on or after the first January 1 after the date on which a tax on the net incomes of natural persons, including a person's share of partnership and unincorporated association income, begins to apply to that income, except that if the income tax begins to apply on a January 1, Subsections (f) and (h) of this section apply to ad valorem maintenance and operation taxes levied on or after that date.

(j) A provision of this section prevails over a conflicting provision of Article VII, Section 3, of this Constitution to the extent of the conflict.

[Note — Sec. 24 of Article VIII was added to prohibit a personal income tax without voter approval and dedicating the proceeds of such a tax to education and property tax relief. Submitted by 73rd Legislature (1993) and adopted in election Nov. 2, 1993.]

Article IX — Counties

Sec. 1. **Creation and Organization of Counties; Changing of County Lines** — The Legislature shall have power to create counties for the convenience of the people, subject to the following provisions:

First. In the territory of the State exterior to all counties now existing, no new counties shall be created with a less area than 900 square miles in a square form, unless prevented by pre-existing boundary lines. Should the State lines render this impracticable in border counties, the area may be less. The territory referred to may, at any time, in whole or in part, be divided into counties in advance of population and attached for judicial and land surveying purposes to the most convenient organized county or counties.

Second. Within the territory of any county or counties now existing, no new county shall be created with a less area than 700 square miles, nor shall any such county now existing be reduced to a less area than 700 square miles. No new counties shall be created so as to approach nearer than twelve miles of the county seat of any county from which it may, in whole or in part, be taken. Counties of a less area than 900, but of 700 or more square miles, within counties now existing, may be created by a two-thirds vote of each house of the Legislature, taken by yeas and nays, and entered on the journals. Any county now existing may be reduced to an area of not less than 700 square miles by a like two-thirds vote. When any part of a county is stricken off and attached to or created into another county, the part stricken off shall be holden for and obliged to pay its proportion of all the liabilities then existing of the county from which it was taken, in such manner as may be prescribed by law.

Third. No part of any existing county shall be detached from it and attached to another existing county until the proposition for such change shall have been submitted, in such manner as may be provided by law, to a vote of the electors of both counties, and shall have received a majority of those voting on the question in each.

Sec. 1-a. **Regulation of Travel on Gulf Coast Beaches** — The Legislature may authorize the governing body of any county bordering on the Gulf of Mexico or the tidewater limits thereof to regulate and restrict the speed, parking and travel of motor vehicles on beaches available to the public by virtue of public right and the littering of such beaches.

Nothing in this amendment shall increase the rights of any riparian or littoral landowner with regard to beaches available to the public by virtue of public right or submerged lands.

The Legislature may enact any laws not inconsistent with this Section which it may deem necessary to permit said counties to implement, enforce and administer the provisions contained herein.

[Note — Sec. 1-a of Art. IX was added to authorize regulation of travel on Gulf Coast beaches open to the public. Submitted by 57th Legislature (1961) and adopted in election Nov. 6, 1962.]

County Seats

Sec. 2. **How County Seats Are Created and Changed** — The Legislature shall pass laws regulating the manner of removing county seats, but no county seat situated within five miles of the geographical center of the county shall be removed except by a vote of two-thirds of all electors voting on the subject. A majority of such electors, however, voting at such election, may remove a county seat from a point more than five miles from a geographical center of the county to a point within five miles of such center, in either case the center to be determined by a certificate from the Commissioner of the General Land Office.

[Note — Sec. 3 of Art. IX, relating to home rule, was deleted by constitutional amendment. Submitted by 61st Legislature and approved in election Aug. 5, 1969.]

Sec. 4. **County-Wide Hospital Districts** — The Legislature may by law authorize the creation of county-wide Hospital Districts in counties having a population in excess of 190,000 and in Galveston County, with power to issue bonds for the purchase, acquisition, construction, maintenance and operation of any county-owned hospital, or where the hospital system is jointly operated by a county and city within the county, and to provide for the transfer to the county-wide hospital district of the title to any land, buildings or equipment, jointly or separately owned, and for the assumption by the district of any outstanding bonded indebtedness theretofore issued by any county or city for the establishment of hospitals or hospital facilities; to levy a tax not to exceed seventy-five (75¢) cents on the One Hundred ($100.00) Dollars valuation of all taxable property within such district, provided, however, that such district shall be approved at an election held for that purpose, and that only qualified, property taxpaying voters in such county shall vote therein; provided further, that such hospital district shall assume full responsibility for providing medical and hospital care to needy inhabitants of the county, and thereafter such county and cities therein shall not levy any other tax for hospital purposes; and provided further that should such hospital district construct, maintain and support a hospital or hospital system, that the same shall never become a charge against the State of Texas, nor shall any direct appropriation ever be made by the Legislature for the construction, maintenance or improvement of the said hospital or hospitals. Should the Legislature enact enabling laws in anticipation of the adoption of this amendment, such acts shall not be invalid because of their anticipatory character.

[Note — Sec. 4 of Art. IX was added to provide for county-wide hospital districts. Submitted by 53rd Legislature (1953) and adopted in election Nov. 2, 1954.]

Sec. 5 (a). The Legislature may by law authorize the creation of two hospital districts, one to be coextensive with and have the same boundaries as the incorporated City of Amarillo, as such boundaries now exist or as they may hereafter be lawfully extended, and the other to be coextensive with Wichita County.

If such district or districts are created, they may be authorized to levy a tax not to exceed Seventy-five Cents (75¢) on the One Hundred Dollars ($100.00) valuation of taxable property within the district; provided, however no tax may be levied until approved by a majority vote of the participating resident qualified property taxpaying voters who have duly rendered their property for taxation. The maximum rate of tax may be changed at subsequent elections so long as obligations are not impaired, and not to exceed the maximum limit of Seventy-five Cents (75¢) per One Hundred Dollars ($100.00) valuation, and no election shall be required by subsequent changes in the boundaries of the City of Amarillo.

If such tax is authorized, no political subdivision or municipality within or having the same boundaries as the district may levy a tax for medical or hospital care for needy individuals, nor shall they maintain or erect hospital facilities, but the district shall by resolution assume all such responsibilities and shall assume all of the liabilities and obligations (including bonds and warrants) of such subdivisions or municipalities or both. The maximum tax rate submitted shall be sufficient to discharge such obligations, liabilities, and responsibilities, and to maintain and operate the hospital system, and the Legislature may authorize the district to issue tax bonds for the purpose of the purchase, construction, acquisition, repair or renovation of improvements and initially equipping the same, and such bonds shall be payable from said Seventy-five Cents (75¢) tax. The Legislature shall provide for transfer of title to properties to the district.

(b). The Legislature may by law permit the County of Potter (in which the City of Amarillo is partially located) to render financial aid to that district by paying a part of the expenses of operating and maintaining the system and paying a part of the debts of the district (whether assumed or created by the district) and may authorize the levy of a tax not to exceed Ten Cents (10¢) per One Hundred Dollars ($100.00) valuation (in addition to other taxes permitted by this Constitution) upon all property within the county but without the City of Amarillo at the time such levy is made for such purposes. If such tax is authorized, the district shall by resolution assume the responsibilities, obligations, and liabilities of the county in the manner and to the extent hereinabove provided for political subdivisions having boundaries coextensive with the district, and the county shall not thereafter levy taxes (other than herein provided) for hospital purposes nor for providing hospital care for needy individuals of the county.

(c). The Legislature may by law authorize the creation of a hospital district within Jefferson County, the boundaries of which shall include only the area comprising the Jefferson County Drainage District No. 7 and the Port Arthur Independent School District, as such boundaries existed on the first day of January, 1957, with the power to issue bonds for the sole purpose of purchasing a site for, and the construction and initial equipping of, a hospital system, and with the power to levy a tax of not to exceed Seventy-five Cents (75¢) on the One Hundred Dollars ($100) valuation of property therein for the purpose of paying the principal and interest on such bonds.

The creation of such hospital district shall not be final until approved at an election by a majority of the resident property taxpaying voters voting at said election who have duly rendered their property for taxation upon the tax rolls of either said Drainage or said School District, nor shall such bonds be issued or such tax be levied until so approved by such voters.

The district shall not have the power to levy any tax for main-

Article IX (Cont'd.)

tenance or operation of the hospital or facilities, but shall contract with other political subdivisions of the state or private individuals, associations, or corporations for such purposes.

If the district hereinabove authorized is finally created, no other hospital district may be created embracing any part of the territory within its boundaries, but the Legislature by law may authorize the creation of a hospital district incorporating herein the remainder of Jefferson County, having the powers and duties and with the limitations presently provided by Art. IX, Section 4, of the Constitution of Texas, except that such district shall be confirmed at an election wherein the resident qualified property taxpaying voters who have duly rendered their property within such proposed district for taxation on the county rolls, shall be authorized to vote. A majority of those participating in the election voting in favor of the district shall be necessary for its confirmation and for bonds to be issued.

(d). Should the Legislature enact enabling laws in anticipation of adoption of this amendment, such acts shall not be invalid because of their anticipatory character.

[Note — Sec. 5 of Art. IX was added to provide for the creation of special hospital districts and authorizing the levying of taxes for their support. Submitted by 55th Legislature (1957) and adopted in election Nov. 4, 1958.]

(e). The legislature by law may authorize Randall County to render financial assistance to the Amarillo Hospital District by paying part of the district's operating and maintenance expenses and the debts assumed or created by the district and to levy a tax for that purpose in an amount not to exceed seventy-five cents (75¢) on the One Hundred Dollars ($100.00) valuation on all property in Randall County that is not within the boundaries of the City of Amarillo or the South Randall County Hospital District. This tax is in addition to any other tax authorized by this constitution. If the tax is authorized by the legislature and approved by the voters of the area to be taxed, the Amarillo Hospital District shall, by resolution, assume the responsibilities, obligations, and liabilities of Randall County in accordance with Subsection (a) of this section and, except as provided by this subsection, Randall County may not levy taxes or issue bonds for hospital purposes or for providing hospital care for needy inhabitants of the county. Not later than the end of the first tax year during which taxes are levied under this subsection, Randall County shall deposit in the State Treasury to the credit of the state General Revenue Fund $45,000 to reimburse the state for the cost of publishing the resolution required by this subsection.

(f). Notwithstanding the provisions of Article IX of this constitution, if a hospital district was created or authorized under a constitutional provision that includes a description of the district's boundaries or jurisdiction, the legislature by law may authorize the district to change its boundaries or jurisdiction. The change must be approved by a majority of the qualified voters of the district voting at an election called and held for that purpose.

[Note — Subsection (e) of Sec. 5 of Art. IX was added to expand services provided by the Amarillo Hospital District. Submitted by 70th Legislature (1987) and adopted in election Nov. 3, 1987.]

Sec. 6. **Lamar County Hospital District Abolished** — On the effective date of this Amendment, the Lamar County Hospital District is abolished. The Commissioners Court of Lamar County may provide for the transfer or for the disposition of the assets of the Lamar County Hospital District.

[Note — Sec. 6 of Art. IX was added to authorize creation of a hospital district in Lamar County and authorizing the levying of taxes for its support. Submitted by 56th Legislature (1959) and adopted in election Nov. 8, 1960. It was amended to abolish the hospital district. Submitted by 62nd Legislature (1971) and adopted in election Nov. 7, 1972.]

Sec. 7. **Hidalgo County Hospital District; Creation, Tax Rate** — The Legislature may by law authorize the creation of a Hospital District coextensive with Hidalgo County, having the powers and duties and with the limitations presently provided in Art. IX, Sec. 5 (a), of the Constitution of Texas, as it applies to Hidalgo County, except that the maximum rate of tax that the said Hidalgo County Hospital District may be authorized to levy shall be ten cents (10¢) per One Hundred Dollars ($100) valuation of taxable property within the District subject to district taxation.

[Note — Sec. 7 of Art. IX was added to authorize creation of a hospital district in Hidalgo County and authorizing the levying of taxes for its support. Submitted by 56th Legislature (1959) and adopted in election Nov. 8, 1960.]

Sec. 8. **Comanche County Hospital District; Creation, Tax Rate** — The Legislature may by law authorize the creation of a Hospital District to be coextensive with the limits of County Commissioners Precinct No. 4 of Comanche County, Texas.

If such District is created, it may be authorized to levy a tax not to exceed seventy-five cents (75¢) on the One Hundred Dollar ($100) valuation of taxable property within the District; provided, however, no tax may be levied until approved by a majority vote of the participating resident qualified property taxpaying voters who have duly rendered their property for taxation. The maximum rate of tax may be changed at subsequent elections so long as obligations are not impaired, and not to exceed the maximum limit of seventy-five cents (75¢) per One Hundred Dollar ($100) valuation, and no election shall be required by subsequent changes in the boundaries of the Commissioners Precinct No. 4 of Comanche County.

If such tax is authorized, no political subdivision or municipality within or having the same boundaries as the District may levy a tax for medical or hospital care for needy individuals, nor shall they maintain or erect hospital facilities, but the District shall by resolution assume all such responsibilities and shall assume all of the liabilities and obligations (including bonds and warrants) of such subdivisions or municipalities or both. The maximum tax rate submitted shall be sufficient to discharge such obligations, liabilities, and responsibilities and to maintain and operate the hospital system, and the Legislature may authorize the District to issue tax bonds for the purpose of the purchase, construction, acquisition, repair or renovation of improvements and initially equipping the same, and such bonds shall be payable from said seventy-five cents (75¢) tax. The Legislature shall provide for transfer of title to properties to the District.

(b) The Legislature may by law permit the County of Comanche to render financial aid to that District by paying a part of the expenses of operating and maintaining the system and paying a part of the debts of the District (whether assumed or created by the District) and may authorize the levy of a tax not to exceed ten cents (10¢) per One Hundred Dollar ($100) valuation (in addition to other taxes permitted by this Constitution) upon all property within the County but without the County Commissioners Precinct No. 4 of Comanche County at the time such levy is made for such purposes. If such tax is authorized, the District shall by resolution assume the responsibilities, obligations and liabilities of the County in the manner and to the extent hereinabove provided for political subdivisions having boundaries coextensive with the District, and the County shall not hereafter levy taxes (other than herein provided) for hospital purposes nor for providing hospital care for needy individuals of the county.

(c) Should the Legislature enact enabling laws in anticipation of the adoption of this amendment, such Acts shall not be invalid because of their anticipatory character.

[Note — Sec. 8 of Art. IX was added to authorize creation of a hospital district in Comanche County and authorizing the levying of taxes for its support. Submitted by 56th Legislature (1959) and adopted in election Nov. 8, 1960.]

Sec. 9. The Legislature may by general or special law provide for the creation, establishment, maintenance and operation of hospital districts composed of one or more counties or all or any part of one or more counties with power to issue bonds for the purchase, construction, acquisition, repair or renovation of buildings and improvements and equipping same, for hospital purposes; providing for the transfer to the hospital district of the title to any land, buildings, improvements and equipment located wholly within the district which may be jointly or separately owned by any city, town or county, providing that any district so created shall assume full responsibility for providing medical and hospital care for its needy inhabitants and assume the outstanding indebtedness incurred by cities, towns and counties for hospital purposes prior to the creation of the district, if same are located wholly within its boundaries, and a pro rata portion of such indebtedness based upon the then last approved tax assessment rolls of the included cities, towns and counties if less than all the territory thereof is included within the district boundaries; providing that after its creation no other municipality or political subdivision shall have the power to levy taxes or issue bonds or other obligations for hospital purposes or for providing medical care within the boundaries of the district; providing for the levy of annual taxes at a rate not to exceed seventy-five cents (75¢) on the one hundred dollar valuation of all taxable property within such district for the purpose of meeting the requirements of the district's bonds, the indebtedness assumed by it and its maintenance and operating expenses, providing that such district shall not be created or such tax authorized unless approved by a majority of the qualified voters thereof voting at an election called for the purpose; and providing further that

Article IX (Cont'd.)

the support and maintenance of the district's hospital system shall never become a charge against or obligation of the State of Texas nor shall any direct appropriation be made by the Legislature for the construction, maintenance or improvement of any of the facilities of such district.

Provided, however, that no district shall be created by special law except after thirty (30) days' public notice to the district affected, and in no event may the Legislature provide for a district to be created without the affirmative vote of a majority of the qualified voters in the district concerned.

The Legislature may also provide for the dissolution of hospital districts provided that a process is afforded by statute for:

(1) Determining the desire of a majority of the qualified voters within the district to dissolve it;

(2) Disposing of or transferring the assets, if any, of the district; and

(3) Satisfying the debts and bond obligations, if any, of the district, in such manner as to protect the interest of the citizens within the district, including their collective property rights in the assets and property of the district, provided, however, that any grant from federal funds, however dispensed, shall be considered an obligation to be repaid in satisfaction and provided that no election to dissolve shall be held more often than once each year. In such connection, the statute shall provide against disposal or transfer of the assets of the district except for due compensation unless such assets are transferred to another governmental agency, such as a county, embracing such district and using such transferred assets in such a way as to benefit citizens formerly within the district.

[Note — Sec. 9 of Art. IX was added to provide for the creation of special hospital districts and authorizing the levying of taxes for their support. Submitted by 57th Legislature (1961) and adopted in election Nov. 6, 1962. It was further amended to provide method of dissolution of hospital districts. Submitted by 59th Legislature (1965) and adopted in election Nov. 8 1966. It was again amended to authorize the legislature to provide by general or special law for the creation, establishment, maintenance and operation of a hospital district. Submitted by 71st Legislature (1989) and adopted in election Nov. 7, 1989.]

Sec. 9A. The Legislature by law may determine the health care services a hospital district is required to provide, the requirements a resident must meet to qualify for services, and any other relevant provisions necessary to regulate the provision of health care to residents.

[Note — Sec. 9A of Art. IX was added to authorize Legislature to regulate the provision of health care by hospital districts. Submitted by 69th Legislature (1985) and adopted in election Nov. 5, 1985.]

Sec. 9B. The legislature by general or special law may provide for the creation, establishment, maintenance, and operation of hospital districts located wholly in a county with a population of 75,000 or less, according to the most recent federal decennial census, and may authorize the commissioners court to levy a tax on the ad valorem property located in the district for the support and maintenance of the district. A district may not be created or a tax levied unless the creation and tax are approved by a majority of the registered voters who reside in the district. The legislature shall set the maximum tax rate a district may levy. The legislature may provide that the county in which the district is located may issue general obligation bonds for the district and provide other services to the district. The district may provide hospital care, medical care, and other services authorized by the legislature.

[Note — Sec. 9B of Art. XI was added to authorize the legislature to provide for the creation, establishment, maintenance and operation of a hospital district. Submitted by 71st Legislature (1989) and adopted in election Nov. 7, 1989.]

[Note — Sec. 10 of Art. IX is blank.]

Sec. 11. The Legislature may by law authorize the creation of hospital districts in Ochiltree, Castro, Hansford and Hopkins Counties, each district to be coextensive with the limits of such county.

If any such district is created, it may be authorized to levy a tax not to exceed Seventy-five Cents (75¢) on the One Hundred Dollar ($100) valuation of taxable property within the district; provided, however, no tax may be levied until approved by a majority vote of the participating resident qualified property taxpaying voters who have duly rendered their property for taxation. The maximum rate of tax may be changed at subsequent elections so long as obligations are not impaired, and not to exceed the maximum limit of Seventy-five Cents (75¢) per One Hundred Dollar ($100) valuation.

If such tax is authorized, no political subdivision or municipality within or having the same boundaries as the district may levy a tax for medical or hospital care for needy individuals, nor shall they maintain or erect hospital facilities, but the district shall by resolution assume all such responsibilities and shall assume all of the liabilities and obligations (including bonds and warrants) of such subdivisions or municipalities or both. The maximum tax rate submitted shall be sufficient to discharge obligations, liabilities, and responsibilities, and to maintain and operate the hospital system, and the Legislature may authorize the district to issue tax bonds for the purpose of the purchase, construction, acquisition, repair or renovation of improvements and initially equipping the same, and such bonds shall be payable from said Seventy-five Cent (75¢) tax. The Legislature shall provide for transfer of title to properties to the district.

[Note — Sec. 11 of Art. IX was added to provide for the creation of special hospital districts and to authorize the levying of taxes for their support. It is obviously misnumbered, as there is no Sec. 10 of Art. IX. Submitted by 57th Legislature (1961) and adopted in election Nov. 6, 1962.]

Sec. 12. Establishment of Airport Authorities — The Legislature may by law provide for the creation, establishment, maintenance and operation of Airport Authorities composed of one or more counties, with power to issue general obligation bonds, revenue bonds, either or both of them, for the purchase, acquisition by the exercise of the power of eminent domain or otherwise, construction, reconstruction, repair or renovation of any airport or airports, landing fields and runways, airport buildings, hangars, facilities, equipment, fixtures, and any and all property, real or personal, necessary to operate, equip and maintain an airport; shall provide for the option by the governing body of the city or cities whose airport facilities are served by certificated airlines and whose facility or some interest therein, is proposed to be or has been acquired by the authority, to either appoint or elect a board of directors of said authority; if the directors are appointed such appointment shall be made by the County Commissioners Court after consultation with and consent of the governing body or bodies of such city or cities, and if the board of directors is elected they shall be elected by the qualified taxpaying voters of the county which chooses to elect the directors to represent that county, such directors shall serve without compensation for a term fixed by the Legislature not to exceed six (6) years, and shall be selected on the basis of the proportionate population of each county based upon the last preceding federal census, and shall be a resident or residents of such county; provide that no county shall have less than one (1) member on the board of directors; provide for the holding of an election in each county proposing the creation of an authority to be called by the Commissioners Court or Commissioners Courts, as the case may be, upon petition of five percent (5%) of the qualified taxpaying voters within the county or counties, said elections to be held on the same day if more than one county is included, provided that no more than one (1) such election may be called in a county until after the expiration of one (1) year; in the event such an election has failed, and thereafter only upon a petition of ten percent (10%) of the qualified taxpaying voters being presented to the Commissioners Court or Commissioners Courts of the county or counties in which such an election has failed, and in the event that two or more counties vote on the proposition of the creation of an authority therein, the proposition shall not be deemed to carry unless the majority of the qualified taxpaying voters in each county voting thereon vote in favor thereof; provided, however, that an Airport Authority may be created and be composed of the county or counties that vote in favor of its creation if separate propositions are submitted to the voters of each county so that they may vote for a two or more county authority or a single county authority; provide for the appointment by the board of directors of an assessor and collector of taxes in the authority, whether constituted of one or more counties, whose duty it shall be to assess all taxable property, both real and personal, and collect the taxes thereon, based upon the tax rolls approved by the board of directors, the tax to be levied not to exceed seventy-five cents (75¢) per one hundred dollars ($100) assessed valuation of the property, provided, however, that the property of state regulated common carriers required by law to pay a tax upon intangible assets shall not be subject to taxation by the authority, said taxable property shall be assessed on a valuation not to exceed the market value and shall be equal and uniform throughout the authority as is otherwise provided by the Constitution; the Legislature shall authorize the purchase or acquisition by the authority of any existing airport facility publicly owned and financed and served by certificated airlines, in fee or of any interest therein, or to enter into any lease agreement therefor, upon such terms and conditions as may be mutually agreeable to the authority and the owner of such facilities, or authorize the acquisition of same through the exercise of the power of eminent domain, and in the event of such acquisition, if there are any general obligation bonds that the owner of the publicly owned airport facility has outstanding, the same shall be fully assumed by the authority and sufficient taxes levied by the authority to discharge said outstanding indebtedness; and likewise any city or owner that has outstanding revenue bonds where the revenues of the airport have been pledged or said bonds constitute a lien against the airport facilities, the authority shall assume and discharge all the obligations of the city under the ordinances and bond indentures under which said revenue bonds have been issued and sold. Any city which owns airport facilities not serving certificated airlines which are not purchased or acquired or taken over as herein provided by such authority, shall have the power to operate the same under the existing laws or as the same may hereafter be amended. Any such authority when created may be granted the power and authority to promulgate, adopt and enforce appropriate zoning regulations to protect the airport from hazards and obstructions which would interfere with the use of the airport and its facilities for landing and takeoff; an additional county or counties may be added to an existing authority if a petition of five percent (5%) of the qualified taxpaying voters is filed with and an election is called by the Commissioners Court of the county or counties seeking admission to an authority and the vote is favorable, then admission may be granted to such county or counties by the board of directors of the then existing authority upon such terms and conditions as they may agree upon and evidenced by a resolution approved by two-thirds (2/3) of the then existing board of directors, provided, however, the county or counties that may be so added to the then existing authority shall be given representation on the board of directors by adding additional directors in proportion to their population according to the last preceding federal census.

[Note — Sec. 12 was added to provide for the establishment of airport authorities. Submitted by 59th Legislature (1965) and adopted in election Nov. 8, 1966.]

Sec. 13. **Mental Health Services** — Notwithstanding any other section of this article, the Legislature in providing for the creation, establishment, maintenance, and operation of a hospital district, shall not be required to provide that such district shall assume full responsibility for the establishment, maintenance, support, or operation of mental health services or mental retardation services including the operation of any community mental health centers, community mental retardation centers or community health and mental retardation centers which may exist or be thereafter established within the boundaries of such district, nor shall the Legislature be required to provide that such district shall assume full responsibility of public health department units and clinics and related public health activities or services, and the Legislature shall not be required to restrict the power of any municipality or political subdivision to levy taxes or issue bonds or other obligations or to expend public moneys for the establishment, maintenance, support, or operation of mental health services, mental retardation services, public health units or clinics or related public health activities or services or the operation of such community mental health or mental retardation centers within the boundaries of the hospital districts; and unless a statute creating a hospital district shall expressly prohibit participation by any entity other than the hospital district in the establishment, maintenance, or support of mental health services, mental retardation services, public health units or clinics or related public health activities within or partly within the boundaries of any hospital district, any municipality or any other political subdivision or state-supported entity within the hospital district may participate in the establishment, maintenance, and support of mental health services, mental retardation services, public health units and clinics and related public health activities and may levy taxes, issue bonds or other obligations, and expend public moneys for such purposes as provided by law.

[Note — Sec. 13 of Art. IX was added to permit municipalities and other political subdivisions within hospital districts to participate in establishment, maintenance, support or operation of mental health, mental retardation or public health services. Submitted by 60th Legislature (1967) and adopted in election Nov. 11, 1967.]

Article X — Railroads

[Note — All of Art. X relating to railroads, except Sec. 2, was deleted by constitutional amendment. Submitted by 61st Legislature and approved in election Aug. 5, 1969.]

Article [Sec.] 2. **Public Highways; Common Carriers; Duty of the Legislature; Fixing Rates** — Railroads heretofore constructed or which may hereafter be constructed in this State are hereby declared public highways and railroad companies common carriers. The Legislature shall pass laws to regulate railroad freight and passenger tariffs to correct abuses, and prevent unjust discrimination and extortion in the rates of freight and passenger tariffs on the different railroads in this State, and enforce the same by adequate penalties; and to the further accomplishments of these objects and purposes may provide and establish all requisite means and agencies invested with such powers as may be deemed adequate and advisable.

[Note — The foregoing "Article [Sec.] 2" of Art. X was amended by addition of the last clause, which permitted establishment of the Railroad Commission of Texas. Submitted by 21st Legislature (1889), ratified in election Nov. 4, 1890, and declared adopted Dec. 19, 1890.]

*Explanatory Note — The legislative resolution submitting this amendment erroneously used the word, "Article," instead of the usual abbreviation, "Sec." Order used above is according to official draft of the Constitution.

Article XI — Municipal Corporations

Sec. 1. **Counties Are Legal Subdivisions of the State** — The several counties of this State are hereby recognized as legal subdivisions of the State.

Sec. 2. **Public Buildings and Roads** — The construction of jails, courthouses and bridges and the establishment of county poorhouses and farms and the laying out, construction and repairing of county roads shall be provided for by general laws.

Sec. 3. **No County or Municipal Corporation Shall Become a Subscriber to the Capital Stock of Any Private Corporation or Make Any Donation to the Same** — No county, city or other municipal corporation shall hereafter become a subscriber to the capital of any private corporation or association, or make any appropriation or donation to the same, or in anywise loan its credit; but this shall not be construed to in any way affect any obligation heretofore undertaken pursuant to law or to prevent a county, city, or other municipal corporation from investing its funds as authorized by law.

[Note — Sec. 3 of Art. XI was amended to authorize local governments to invest their funds as authorized by law. (See related amendment at Art. III, Sec. 52(e).) Proposed by 71st Legislature (1989) and adopted in election Nov. 7, 1989.]

Sec. 4. **Cities and Towns Having a Population of 5,000 or Less Inhabitants to Be Chartered by General Laws; Dues to Be Collected in Current Money** — Cities and towns having a population of 5,000 or less may be chartered alone by general laws. They may levy, assess and collect such taxes as may be authorized by law, but no tax for any purpose shall ever be lawful for any one year which shall exceed 1 1/2 percent of the taxable property of such city; and all taxes shall be collectible only in current money, and all licenses and occupation taxes levied, and all fines, forfeitures and penalties accruing to said cities and towns shall be collectible only in current money.

[Note — Sec. 4 of Art. XI was amended to provide that towns of 5,000 or less (instead of 10,000 or less, as provided by the original section) may be chartered alone by general law. Submitted by 31st Legislature (1909), ratified in election Aug. 3, 1909, and declared adopted Sept. 24, 1909. It was again amended to authorize a maximum tax rate, in towns of 5,000 or less, of 1 1/2 percent of taxable values in lieu of the originally specified maximum of one fourth of 1 percent. Submitted by 36th Legislature (1919) and adopted in election of Nov. 2, 1920.]

Sec. 5. Cities of More Than 5,000 Inhabitants May by a Majority Vote of the Qualified Voters Adopt Their Own Charter; Limitation as to Taxation and Debt — Cities having more than five thousand (5,000) inhabitants may, by a majority vote of the qualified voters of said city, at an election held for that purpose, adopt or amend their charters. If the number of inhabitants of cities that have adopted or amended their charters under this section is reduced to five thousand (5000) or fewer, the cities still may amend their charters by a majority vote of the qualified voters of said city at an election held for that purpose. The adoption or amendment of charters is subject to such limitations as may be prescribed by the Legislature, and no charter or any ordinance passed under said charter shall contain any provision inconsistent with the Constitution of the State or of the general laws enacted by the Legislature of this State. Said cities may levy, assess and collect such taxes as may be authorized by law or by their charters; but no tax for any purpose shall ever be lawful for any one year, which shall exceed two and one-half percent of the taxable property of such city, and no debt shall ever be created by any city, unless at the same time provision be

Article XI (Cont'd.); Articles XII, XIII, XIV

made to assess and collect annually a sufficient sum to pay the interest thereon and creating a sinking fund of at least two percent thereon. Furthermore, no city charter shall be altered, amended or repealed oftener than every two years.

[Note — Sec. 5 of Art. XI has been amended three times: (1) To authorize towns of more than 5,000 population (instead of more than 10,000, as provided in the original section) to be chartered by special act, and allowing in such cities a maximum tax rate of 2 1/2 percent. Submitted by 31st Legislature (1909), ratified in election Aug. 3, 1909, and proclaimed Sept. 24, 1909. (2) To grant home rule to cities of more than 5,000 population. Submitted by 32nd Legislature (1911), adopted in election Nov. 5, 1912, and proclaimed Dec. 30, 1912. (3) To allow home rule cities with populations of 5,000 or fewer to amend their charters. Submitted by 72nd Legislature (1991) and adopted in election Nov. 5, 1991.]

Sec. 6. **Municipal Taxation** — Counties, cities, and towns are authorized, in such mode as may now or may hereafter be provided by law, to levy, assess and collect the taxes necessary to pay the interest and provide a sinking fund to satisfy any indebtedness heretofore legally made and undertaken; but all such taxes shall be assessed and collected separately from that levied, assessed and collected for current expenses of municipal government and shall, when levied, specify in the act of levying the purpose therefor; and such taxes may be paid in the coupons, bonds or other indebtedness for the payment of which such tax may have been levied.

Sec. 7. **Taxation of Seawalls, Etc.; Restrictions and Limitations; Eminent Domain** — All counties and cities bordering on the coast of the Gulf of Mexico are hereby authorized upon a vote of the majority of the resident property taxpayers voting thereon at an election called for such purpose, to levy and collect such tax for construction of seawalls, breakwaters or sanitary purposes, as may now or may hereafter be authorized by law, and may create a debt for such works and issue bonds in evidence thereof. But no debt for any purpose shall ever be incurred in any manner by any city or county unless provision is made at the time of creating the same, for levying and collecting a sufficient tax to pay the interest thereon and provide at least 2 percent as a sinking fund; and the condemnation of the right of way for the erection of such work shall be fully provided for.

[Note — Sec. 7 of Art. XI was amended to simplify language describing electors' qualifications. Submitted by 42nd Legislature (1931), adopted in election Nov. 8, 1932 and proclaimed Jan. 9, 1933. It was further amended to provide that a majority of resident property taxpayers may vote to issue bonds for construction of seawalls and breakwaters. Submitted by 63rd Legislature (1973) and adopted in election Nov. 6, 1973.]

Sec. 8. **State Aid for Seawalls, Etc.** — The counties and cities on the Gulf Coast being subject to calamitous overflows, and a very large proportion of the general revenue being derived from those otherwise prosperous localities.* The Legislature is specially authorized to aid, by donation of such portion of the public domain as may be deemed proper, and in such mode as may be provided by law, the construction of seawalls or breakwaters, such aid to be proportioned to the extent and value of the works constructed, or to be constructed, in any locality.

*Explanatory Note — The starting of a new sentence at this point follows in the official draft of the Constitution, but it is evident that the foregoing phrase ending with "localities" was meant to modify the following sentence.

Sec. 9. **Public Buildings, Etc.** — The property of counties, cities and towns owned and held only for public purposes, such as public buildings and the sites therefor, fire engines and the furniture thereof, and all property used or intended for extinguishing fires, public grounds and all other property devoted exclusively to the use and benefit of the public, shall be exempt from forced sale and from taxation; provided, nothing herein shall prevent the enforcement of the vendor's lien, the mechanic's or builder's lien, or other liens now existing.

[Note — Sec. 10 of Art. XI, relating to special taxes and school districts, was deleted by constitutional amendment. Submitted by 61st Legislature and approved in election Aug. 5, 1969.]

Sec. 11. **Term of Office for City Officials** — A home rule city may provide by charter or charter amendment, and a city, town or village operating under the general laws may provide by majority vote of the qualified voters voting at an election called for that purpose, for a longer term of office than two (2) years for its officers, either elective or appointive, or both, but not to exceed four (4) years; provided, however, that tenure under Civil Service shall not be affected hereby.

Provided, however, if any of such officers, elective or appointive, shall announce their candidacy, or shall in fact become a candidate, in any general, special or primary election, for any office of profit or trust under the laws of this State or the United States other than the office then held, at any time when the unexpired term of the office then held shall exceed one (1) year, such announcement or such candidacy shall constitute an automatic resignation of the office then held, and the vacancy thereby created shall be filled pursuant to law in the same manner as other vacancies for such office are filled.

A municipality so providing a term exceeding two (2) years but not exceeding four (4) years for any of its non-civil service officers must elect all of the members of its governing body by majority vote of the qualified voters in such municipality, and any vacancy or vacancies occurring on such governing body shall not be filled by appointment but must be filled by majority vote of the qualified voters at a special election called for such purpose within one hundred and twenty (120) days after such vacancy or vacancies occur.

[Note — Sec. 11 of Art. XI was added to provide four-year terms for city officials. Submitted by 55th Legislature (1957) and adopted in election Nov. 4, 1958.]

Sec. 12. **Sanitation Sewer Lines** — The Legislature by general law may authorize a city or town to expend public funds for the relocation or replacement of sanitation sewer laterals or water laterals on private property if the relocation or replacement is done in conjunction with or immediately following the replacement or relocation of sanitation sewer mains or water mains serving the property. The law must authorize the city or town to affix, with the consent of the owner of the private property, a lien on the property for the cost of relocating or replacing the sewer laterals on the property and must provide that the cost shall be assessed against the property with repayment by the property owner to be amortized over a period not to exceed five years at a rate of interest to be set as provided by the law. The lien may not be enforced until after five years have expired since the date the lien was affixed.

[Note — Sec. 12 of Art. XI was added to permit a city or town to expend public funds and levy assessments for relocation or replacement of sanitation sewer laterals on private property. Submitted by 68th Legislature (1983) and adopted in election Nov. 8, 1983. It was again amended to allow Legislature to enact laws permitting a city or town to spend public funds for the relocation or replacement of water laterals on private property. Submitted by 69th Legislature (1985) and adopted in election Nov. 5, 1985.]

Sec. 13. **Classification of Municipal Functions** — (a) Notwithstanding any other provision of this constitution, the legislature may by law define for all purposes those functions of a municipality that are to be considered governmental and those that are proprietary, including reclassifying a function's classification assigned under prior statute or common law.

(b) This section applies to laws enacted by the 70th Legislature, Regular Session, 1987, and to all subsequent regular or special sessions of the legislature.

[Note — Sec. 13, Art. XI was added to define the governmental and proprietary functions of a municipality. Submitted by 70th Legislature (1987) and adopted in election Nov. 3, 1987.]

Article XII — Private Corporations

Sec. 1. **Corporations Created by General Laws** — No private corporation shall be created except by general laws.

Sec. 2. **General Laws to be Enacted** — General laws shall be enacted providing for the creation of private corporations, and shall therein provide fully for the adequate protection of the public and of the individual stockholders.

[Note — Sections 3, 4, 5 and 7 of Art. XII, relating to franchises, and wharfage and freight tolls, were deleted by constitutional amendment. Submitted by 61st Legislature and approved in election Aug. 5, 1969. Section 6 of Art. XII, relating to the limitation on the consideration for which stock and bonds of a corporation may be issued, was repealed by amendment. Submitted by 73rd Legislature (1993) and approved in election Nov. 2, 1993.]

Article XIII — Spanish and Mexican Land Titles

[Note — The entire Art. XIII, relating to Spanish and Mexican Land Titles, was deleted by constitutional amendment. Submitted by 61st Legislature (1969) and approved in election Aug. 5, 1969.]

Articles XIV, XV, XVI

Article XIV — Public Lands and Land Office

Sec. 1. **General Land Office; Grants to Be Registered in; Land Office to Be Self-Sustaining** — There shall be one General Land Office in the State, which shall be at the seat of government, where all land titles which have emanated or may hereafter emanate from the State shall be registered, except those titles the registration of which may be prohibited by this Constitution. It shall be the duty of the Legislature at the earliest practicable time to make the Land Office self-sustaining, and from time to time the Legislature may establish such subordinate offices as may be deemed necessary.

[Note — All of Art. XIV relating to public lands and the Land Office, except Sec. 1, was deleted by constitutional amendment. Submitted by 61st Legislature (1969) and approved in election Aug. 5, 1969.]

Article XV — Impeachment

Sec. 1. **Power of Impeachment Vested in the House of Representatives** — The power of impeachment shall be vested in the House of Representatives.

Sec. 2. **Trial by Senate** — Impeachment of the Governor, Lieutenant Governor, Attorney General, Treasurer, Commissioner of the General Land Office, Comptroller, and the Judges of the Supreme Court, Courts of Appeal and District Courts shall be tried by the Senate.

Sec. 3. **Oath of Senators** — When the Senate is sitting as a court of impeachment, the Senators shall be on oath, or affirmation, impartially to try the party impeached, and no person shall be convicted without the concurrence of two thirds of the Senators present.

Sec. 4. **Judgment; Party Convicted Subject to Indictment Under the Criminal Laws** — Judgment in cases of impeachment shall extend only to removal from office and disqualification from holding any office of honor, trust or profit under this State. A party convicted on impeachment shall also be subject to indictment, trial and punishment, according to law.

Sec. 5. **Officers Suspended During Pending Proceedings** — All officers against whom articles of impeachment may be preferred shall be suspended from the exercise of the duties of their office during the pendency of such impeachment. The Governor may make a provisional appointment to fill the vacancy occasioned by the suspension of an officer until the decision on the impeachment.

Sec. 6. **Removal of District Judges** — Any Judge of the District Courts of the State who is incompetent to discharge the duties of his office, or who shall be guilty of partiality, or oppression, or other official misconduct, or whose habits and conduct are such as to render him unfit to hold such office or who shall negligently fail to perform his duties as Judge, or who shall fail to execute in a reasonable measure the business in his courts, may be removed by the Supreme Court. The Supreme Court shall have original jurisdiction to hear and determine the causes aforesaid when presented in writing, upon the oaths, taken before some Judge of a court of record, of not less than ten lawyers, practicing in the courts held by such Judge, and licensed to practice in the Supreme Court; said presentment to be founded either upon the knowledge of the persons making it or upon the written oaths as to facts of creditable witnesses. The Supreme Court may issue all needful process and prescribe all needful rules to give effect to this section. Causes of this kind shall have precedence and be tried as soon as practicable.

Sec. 7. **Trial and Removal of Other Officers** — The Legislature shall provide by law for the trial and removal from office of all officers of this State, the modes for which have not been provided in this Constitution.

Address

Sec. 8. **Removal of Judges of Supreme Court and Courts of Appeals and of District Courts** — The Judges of the Supreme Court, Courts of Appeals and District Courts shall be removed by the Governor on the address of two thirds of each house of the Legislature, for willful neglect of duty, incompetency, habitual drunkenness, oppression in office, or other reasonable cause which shall not be sufficient ground for impeachment; provided, however that the cause or causes for which such removal shall be required shall be stated at length in such address and entered on the journals of each house; and provided, further, that the cause or causes shall be notified to the Judge so intended to be removed, and he shall be admitted to a hearing in his own defense before any vote for such address shall pass; and in all such cases the vote shall be taken by yeas and nays and entered on the journals of each house, respectively.

Sec. 9. **Removal of Appointed Officials by Governor; Special Session of Senate for This Purpose** — (a) In addition to the other procedures provided by law for removal of public officers, the governor who appoints an officer may remove the officer with the advice and consent of two-thirds of the members of the senate present.

(b) If the Legislature is not in session when the governor desires to remove an officer, the governor shall call a special session of the senate for consideration of the proposed removal. The session may not exceed two days in duration.

[Note — Sec. 9 of Art. XV was added to authorize the governor to remove appointed officers with the advice and consent of the Senate. Submitted by 66th Legislature (1979) and adopted in election Nov. 4, 1980.]

Article XVI — General Provisions

Sec. 1. **Official Oaths** — (a) Members of the Legislature, and all other elected officers, before they enter upon the duties of their offices, shall take the following Oath or Affirmation:

"I, ____________, do solemnly swear (or affirm), that I will faithfully execute the duties of the office of ____________ of the State of Texas, and will to the best of my ability preserve, protect, and defend the Constitution and laws of the United States and of this State, so help me God."

(b) Each member of the Legislature and all other elected officers, before taking the Oath or Affirmation of office prescribed by this section and entering upon the duties of office, shall subscribe to the following statement:

"I, ____________, do solemnly swear (or affirm) that I have not directly or indirectly paid, offered, promised to pay, contributed, or promised to contribute any money or thing of value, or promised any public office or employment for the giving or witholding of a vote at the election at which I was elected so help me God."

The Secretary of State, and all other appointed officers before they enter upon the duties of their offices, shall take the following Oath or Affirmation:

"I, ____________, do solemnly swear (or affirm), that I will faithfully execute the duties of the office of ____________ of the State of Texas, and will to the best of my ability preserve, protect, and defend the Constitution and laws of the United States and of this State so help me God."

(d) The Secretary of State, and all other appointed officers, before taking the Oath or Affirmation of office prescribed by this section and entering upon the duties of office, shall subscribe to the following statement:

"I, ____________, do solemnly swear (or affirm) that I have not directly or indirectly paid, offered, or promised to pay, contributed, or promised to contribute any money, or valuable thing, or promised any public office or employment, as a reward to secure my appointment or confirmation thereof, so help me God."

(e) Members of the Legislature and all other elected officers shall file the signed statement required by Subsection (b) of this section with the Secretary of State before taking the Oath or Affirmation of office prescribed by Subsection (a) of this section.

(f) The Secretary of State and all other appointed officers shall file the signed statement required by Subsection (d) of this section with the Secretary of State before taking the Oath or Affirmation of office prescribed by Subsection (c) of this section.

[Note — Sec. 1 of Art. XVI has been amended three times: (1) To eliminate that part of the oath stating that the incoming official had not fought a duel or sent or accepted a challenge to a duel or acted as a second in a duel. Submitted by 45th Legislature (1937) and adopted in election Nov. 8, 1938. (2) To change the form of the oath of office to include appointive officers of the State. Submitted by 54th Legislature (1955) and adopted in election Nov. 6, 1956. (3) To change the oath of office prescribed for members of the legislature, the secretary of state and other elected and appointed officers. Proposed by 71st Legislature (1989) and adopted in election Nov. 7, 1989.]

Sec. 2. **Right of Suffrage to Be Protected; Criminals Disfranchised** — Laws shall be made to exclude from office, serving on juries, and from the right of suffrage, those who may have been or shall hereafter be convicted of bribery, perjury, forgery or other high crimes. The privilege of free suffrage shall be protected by laws, regulating elections and prohibiting, under adequate penalties, all undue influence therein from power, bribery, tumult, or other improper practice.

[Note — Sections 3 and 4 of Art. XVI, relating to fines and dueling, were deleted by constitutional amendment. Submitted by 61st Legislature and approved in election Aug. 5, 1969.]

Sec. 5. **Bribery in Elections Disqualification for Holding Office** — Every person shall be disqualified from holding any office of profit or trust in this State who shall have been convicted of having given or offered a bribe to procure his election or appointment.

Sec. 6. **Appropriations for Private Purposes Prohibited; Expenditures to Be Published** — (a) No appropriation for pri-

Article XVI (Cont'd.)

vate or individual purposes shall be made, unless authorized by this Constitution. A regular statement, under oath, and an account of the receipts and expenditures of all public money shall be published annually, in such manner as shall be prescribed by law.

(b) State agencies charged with the responsibility of providing services to those who are blind, crippled, or otherwise physically or mentally handicapped may accept money from private or federal sources, designated by the private or federal source as money to be used in and establishing and equipping facilities for assisting those who are blind, crippled, or otherwise physically or mentally handicapped in becoming gainfully employed, in rehabilitating and restoring the handicapped, and in providing other services determined by the state agency to be essential for the better care and treatment of the handicapped. Money accepted under this subsection is state money. State agencies may spend money accepted under this subsection, and no other money, for specific programs and projects to be conducted by local level or other private, nonsectarian associations, groups, and nonprofit organizations, in establishing and equipping facilities for assisting those who are blind, crippled, or otherwise physically or mentally handicapped in becoming gainfully employed, in rehabilitating and restoring the handicapped, and in providing other services determined by the state agency to be essential for the better care or treatment of the handicapped.

The state agencies may deposit money accepted under this subsection either in the state treasury or in other secure depositories. The money may not be expended for any purpose other than the purpose for which it was given. Notwithstanding any other provision of this Constitution, the state agencies may expend money accepted under this subsection without the necessity of an appropriation, unless the Legislature, by law, requires that the money be expended only on appropriation. The Legislature may prohibit state agencies from accepting money under this subsection or may regulate the amount of money accepted, the way the acceptance and expenditure of the money is administered, and the purposes for which the state agencies may expend the money. Money accepted under this subsection for a purpose prohibited by the Legislature shall be returned to the entity that gave the money.

This subsection does not prohibit state agencies authorized to render services to the handicapped from contracting with privately-owned or local facilities for necessary and essential services, subject to such conditions, standards, and procedures as may be prescribed by law.

[Note — Sec. 6 of Art. XVI was amended to authorize public grants to private groups for assistance to the blind, crippled or otherwise physically and mentally handicapped. Submitted by 59th Legislature (1965) and adopted in election Nov. 8, 1966.]

[Note — Sec. 7 of Art. XVI, relating to paper money, was deleted by constitutional amendment. Submitted by 61st Legislature and approved in election Aug. 5, 1969.]

Sec. 8. **Counties May Provide Workhouses, Poorhouses and Farms** — Each county in the State may provide, in such manner as may be prescribed by law, a manual labor poorhouse and farm, for taking care of, managing, employing and supplying the wants of its indigent and poor inhabitants.

Sec. 9. **Absence on Business of the State or United States Shall Not Forfeit a Residence Once Obtained** — Absence on business of the State or of the United States shall not forfeit a residence once obtained, so as to deprive anyone of the right of suffrage, or of being elected or appointed to any office, under the exceptions contained in this Constitution.

Sec. 10. **Deductions From Salaries to be Provided for** — The Legislature shall provide for deductions from the salaries of public officers who may neglect the performance of any duty that may be assigned them by law.

Sec. 11. **Usurious Interest Prohibited** — The Legislature shall have authority to classify loans and lenders, license and regulate lenders, define interest and fix maximum rates of interest; provided, however, in the absence of legislation fixing maximum rates of interest all contracts for a greater rate of interest than ten per centum (10%) per annum shall be deemed usurious; provided, further, that in contracts where no rate of interest is agreed upon, the rate shall not exceed six per centum (6%) per annum. Should any regulatory agency, acting under the provisions of this Section, cancel or refuse to grant any permit under any law passed by the Legislature; then such applicant or holder shall have the right of appeal to the courts and granted a trial de novo as that term is used in appealing from the justice of peace court to the county court.

[Note — Sec. 11 of Art. XVI was amended to set 10 percent and 6 percent as interest rates, in place of original provision for 12 percent and 8 percent. Submitted by 22nd Legislature (1891), ratified in election Aug. 11, 1891, and declared adopted Sept. 22, 1891. It was further amended to grant right of appeal from justice of peace court to county court. Submitted by 56th Legislature (1959) and adopted in election Nov. 8, 1960.]

Sec. 12. **Officers Not Eligible** — No member of Congress, nor person holding or exercising any office of profit or trust under the United States, or either of them, or under any foreign power, shall be eligible as a member of the Legislature or hold or exercise any office of profit or trust under this State.

[Note — Sec. 13 of Art. XVI, relating to arbitration laws, was deleted by constitutional amendment. Submitted by 61st Legislature (1969) and approved in election Aug. 5, 1969.]

Sec. 14. **Residence of Officers** — All civil officers shall reside within the State, and all district or county officers within their districts or counties, and shall keep their offices at such places as may be required by law; and failure to comply with this condition shall vacate the office so held.

Sec. 15. **Community Property of Husband and Wife; Partition Thereof** — All Property, both real and personal, of a spouse owned or claimed before marriage, and that acquired afterward by gift, devise or descent, shall be the separate property of that spouse; and laws shall be passed more clearly defining the rights of the spouses, in relation to separate and community property; provided that persons about to marry and spouses, without the intention to defraud pre-existing creditors, may by written instrument from time to time partition between themselves all or part of their property, then existing or to be acquired, or exchange between themselves the community interest of one spouse or future spouse in any property for the community interest of the other spouse or future spouse in other community property then existing or to be acquired, whereupon the portion or interest set aside to each spouse shall be and constitute a part of the separate property and estate of such spouse or future spouse; spouses may also from time to time, by written instrument, agree between themselves that the income or property from all or part of the separate property then owned or which thereafter might be acquired by only one of them, shall be the separate property of that spouse; if one spouse makes a gift of property to the other that gift is presumed to include all the income or property which might arise from that gift of property; and spouses may agree in writing that all or part of their community property becomes the property of the surviving spouse on the death of a spouse.

[Note — Sec. 15 of Art. XVI was amended to provide for partition of community property of husband and wife. Submitted by 50th Legislature (1947) and adopted in election Nov. 2, 1948. It was further amended to allow spouses to agree that income or property arising from separate property is to be separate property. Submitted by 66th Legislature (1979) and adopted in election Nov. 4, 1980. It was again amended to permit spouses to hold community property with right of survivorship. Submitted by 70th Legislature (1987) and adopted in election Nov. 3, 1987.]

Sec. 16. **Banking Corporations** — (a) The Legislature shall, by general laws, authorize the incorporation of state banks and savings and loan associations and shall provide for a system of state supervision, regulation and control of such bodies which will adequately protect and secure the depositors and creditors thereof.

No state bank shall be chartered until all of the authorized capital stock has been subscribed and paid in full in cash. Except as may be permitted by the Legislature pursuant to subsections (b), (d), and (e) of this Section 16, a state bank shall not be authorized to engage in business at more than one place, which shall be designated in its charter; however, this restriction shall not apply to any other type of financial institution chartered under the laws of this state.

No foreign corporation, other than the national banks of the United States domiciled in this State, shall be permitted to exercise banking or discounting privileges in this State.

(b) If it finds that the convenience of the public will be served thereby, the Legislature may authorize state and national banks to establish and operate unmanned teller machines within the county or city of their domicile. Such machines may perform all banking functions. Banks which are domiciled within a city lying in two or more counties may be permitted to establish and operate unmanned teller machines within both the city and the county of their domicile. The Legislature shall provide that a bank shall have the right to share in the use of these teller machines, not situated at a banking house, which are located within the county or the city of the bank's domicile, on a reasonable, nondiscriminatory basis, consistent with anti-trust laws. Banks may share the use of such machines within the county or city of their

Article XVI (Cont'd.)
domicile with savings and loan associations and credit unions which are domiciled in the same county or city.

(c) A state bank created by virtue of the power granted by this section, notwithstanding any other provision of this section, has the same rights and privileges that are or may be granted to national banks of the United States domiciled in this State.

Should the Legislature enact legislation in anticipation of the adoption of this amendment, such law shall not be invalid because of its anticipatory character.

(d) The Legislature may authorize a state bank or national bank of the United States domiciled in this State to engage in business at more than one place if it does so through the purchase and assumption of certain assets and liabilities of a failed state bank or a failed national bank of the United States domiciled in this State.

(e) The Legislature shall authorize a state bank or national bank of the United States domiciled in this State to establish and operate banking facilities at locations within the county or city of its domicile, subject to limitations the Legislature imposes. The Legislature may permit a bank domiciled within a city located in two or more counties to establish and operate branches within both the city and the county of its domicile, subject to limitations the Legislature imposes.

(f) A bank may not be considered a branch or facility of another bank solely because it is owned or controlled by the same stockholders as the other bank, has common accounting and administrative systems with the other bank, or has a name similar to the other bank's or because of a combination of those factors.

[Note — Sec. 16 of Art. XVI has been amended five times: (1) To eliminate the original provision that "No corporate body shall hereafter be created, renewed or extended with banking or discounting privileges," and making possible the establishment of the present state banking system. Submitted by 28th Legislature (1903), ratified in election Nov. 8, 1904, and declared adopted Dec. 29, 1904. (2) To eliminate a provision, contained in the amendment of 1904, making shareholders of banks liable to the extent of twice the par value of the shares owned. Submitted by 45th Legislature (1937), and adopted in election Aug. 23, 1937. (3) To authorize banks to use unmanned teller machines within the county or city of their domicile on a shared basis. Submitted by 66th Legislature (1979) and adopted in election Nov. 4, 1980. (4) To provide state banks same rights and privileges as national banks. Submitted by 68th Legislature (1983) and adopted in election Nov. 6, 1984. (5) To provide that a bank may offer full service banking at more than one location within the city or county where its principal facility is located, subject to limitations and restrictions provided by law. Submitted by 69th Legislature (1986) and adopted in election Nov. 4, 1986.]

Sec. 17. **Officers to Perform Duties Until Successor Qualified** — All officers within this State shall continue to perform the duties of their offices until their successors shall be duly qualified.

Sec. 18. **Vested Rights** — The rights of property and of action, which have been acquired under the Constitution and the laws of the Republic and State, shall not be divested; nor shall any rights or actions, which have been divested, barred or declared null and void by the Constitution of the Republic and State be reinvested, renewed or reinstated by this Constitution; but the same shall remain precisely in the situation which they were before the adoption of this Constitution, unless otherwise herein provided; and provided, further, that no cause of action heretofore barred shall be revived.

Sec. 19. **Qualifications of Jurors** — The Legislature shall prescribe by law the qualifications of grand and petit jurors; provided that neither the right nor the duty to serve on grand and petit juries shall be denied or abridged by reason of sex. Whenever in the Constitution the term "men" is used in reference to grand or petit juries, such term shall include persons of the female as well as the male sex.

[Note — Sec. 19 of Art. XVI was amended to include women jurors. Submitted by 53rd Legislature (1953) and adopted in election Nov. 2, 1954.]

Sec. 20. **Manufacture and Sale of Intoxicants** — (a) The Legislature shall have the power to enact a Mixed Beverage Law regulating the sale of mixed alcoholic beverages on a local option election basis. The Legislature shall also have the power to regulate the manufacture, sale, possession and transportation of intoxicating liquors, including the power to establish a state monopoly on the sale of distilled liquors.

Should the Legislature enact any enabling laws in anticipation of this amendment, no such law shall be void by reason of its anticipatory nature.

(b) The Legislature shall enact a law or laws whereby the qualified voters of any county, justices precinct or incorporated town or city may, by a majority vote of those voting, determine from time to time whether the sale of intoxicating liquors for beverage purposes shall be prohibited or legalized within the prescribed limits; and such laws shall contain provisions for voting on the sale of intoxicating liquors of various types and various alcoholic content.

(c) In all counties, justices precincts or incorporated towns or cities wherein the sale of intoxicating liquors had been prohibited by local option elections held under the laws of the State of Texas and in force at the time of the taking effect of Section 20, Article XVI of the Constitution of Texas, it shall continue to be unlawful to manufacture, sell, barter or exchange in any such county, justices precinct or incorporated town or city, any spirituous, vinous or malt liquors or medicated bitters capable of producing intoxication or any other intoxicants whatsoever, for beverage purposes, unless and until a majority of the qualified voters in such county or political subdivision thereof voting in an election held for such purposes shall determine such to be lawful; provided that this subsection shall not prohibit the sale of alcoholic beverages containing not more than 3.2 percent alcohol by weight in cities, counties or political subdivisions thereof in which the qualified voters have voted to legalize such sale under the provisions of Chapter 116, Acts of the Regular Session of the Forty-third Legislature.

[Note — Sec. 20 of Art. XVI, which originally provided only for local option elections in "any county, justices precinct, town or city," has been amended five times: (1) To insert a clause in original section "or such subdivision of a county as may be designated by Commissioners' Court of said county," with reference to local option elections. Submitted by 22nd Legislature (1891), ratified in election Aug. 11, 1891, and declared adopted Sept. 22, 1891. (2) To declare state-wide prohibition. Submitted by 36th Legislature (1919), and declared adopted May 24, 1919. (3) To legalize sale of vinous and malt liquors of not more than 3.2 percent alcohol. Submitted by 43rd Legislature (1933), and adopted in election Aug. 26, 1933. (4) To legalize sale of all liquors, as stated in the section printed above. Submitted by 44th Legislature (1935), and adopted in election Aug. 24, 1935. (5) To give Legislature power to enact a Mixed Beverage Law regulating sale of mixed drinks on local option election basis. Submitted by 61st Legislature (1969) and adopted in election Nov. 3, 1970.]

Sec. 21. **Stationery; Public Printing** — All stationery, printing, fuel used in the Legislature and departments of the government other than the judicial department, printing and binding of the laws, journals, and department reports, and all other printing and binding and the repairing and furnishing of the halls and rooms used during meetings of the Legislature and in committees, except proclamations and such products and services as may be done by handicapped individuals employed in nonprofit rehabilitation facilities providing sheltered employment to the handicapped in Texas, shall be performed under contract, to be given to the lowest responsible bidder, below such maximum price and under such regulations as shall be prescribed by law. No member or officer of any department of the government shall in any way have a financial interest in such contracts, and all such contracts or programs involving the state use of the products and services of handicapped individuals shall be subject to such requirements as might be established by the Legislature.

[Note — Sec. 21 of Art. XVI was amended to eliminate reference to the Deaf and Dumb Asylum; to allow certain products and services of handicapped persons to be used by agencies of state government; to require other products and services required for operation of state government be acquired under bids by lowest responsible bidder; and to eliminate requirement that Governor, Secretary of State and Comptroller of Public Accounts be personally involved with such transactions. Submitted by 65th Legislature (1977) and adopted in election Nov. 7, 1978.]

Sec. 22. **Fence Laws** — The Legislature shall have the power to pass such fence laws, applicable to any subdivision of the State or county, as may be needed to meet the wants of the people.

Sec. 23. **Stock Laws** — The Legislature may pass laws for the regulation of livestock and the protection of stock raisers in the stock raising portion of the State, and exempt from the operation of such laws other portions, sections or counties; and shall have power to pass general and special laws for the inspection of cattle, stock and hides, and for the regulation of brands; provided, that any local law thus passed shall be submitted to the freeholders of the section to be affected thereby, and approved by them before it shall go into effect.

Sec. 24. **Roads; Convict Labor** — The Legislature shall

Article XVI (Cont'd.)
make provision for laying out and working public roads, for the building of bridges, and for utilizing fines, forfeitures, and convict labor to all these purposes.

Sec. 25. **Drawbacks and Rebates in Freight Insurance, Transportation, Storage, Etc., Prohibited** — That all drawbacks and rebatement of insurance, freight, transportation, carriage, wharfage, storage, compressing, bailing, repairing, or for any other kind of labor or service of, or to any cotton, grain or any other produce or article of commerce in this State, paid or allowed or contracted for to any common carrier, shipper, merchant, commission merchant, factor, agent or middleman of any kind not the true and absolute owner thereof, are forever prohibited; and it shall be the duty of the Legislature to pass effective laws punishing all persons in this State who pay, receive or contract for or respecting the same.

Sec. 26. **Homicide: Civil Action For** — Every person, corporation or company that may commit a homicide, through willful act or omission or gross neglect, shall be responsible in exemplary damages to the surviving husband, widow, heirs of his or her body, or such of them as there may be, without regard to any criminal proceeding that may or may not be had in relation to the homicide.

Sec. 27. **Vacancies in Offices Filled for Unexpired Term Only** — In all elections to fill vacancies of office in this State, it shall be to fill the unexpired term only.

Sec. 28. **Wages Exempt From Garnishment** — No current wages for personal service shall ever be subject to garnishment, except for the enforcement of court-ordered child support payments.

[Note — Sec. 28 of Art. XVI was amended to provide for additional remedies to enforce court-ordered child support payments. Submitted by 68th Legislature (1983) and adopted in election Nov. 8, 1983.]

[Note — Sec. 29 of Art. XVI, relating to barratry, was deleted by constitutional amendment. Submitted by 61st Legislature (1969) and approved in election Aug. 5, 1969.]

Sec. 30. **Duration of Offices; Term of Railroad Commissioner** — (a) The duration of all offices not fixed by this Constitution shall never exceed two years.

(b) When a Railroad Commission is created by law it shall be composed of three Commissioners, who shall be elected by the people at a general election for state officers, and their term of office shall be six years. Railroad Commissioners first elected after this amendment goes into effect shall hold office as follows: One shall serve two years, and one four years, and one six years; their terms to be decided by lot immediately after they shall have qualified. And one Railroad Commissioner shall be elected every two years thereafter. In case of vacancy in said office the Governor of the State shall fill said vacancy by appointment until the next general election.

(c) The Legislature may provide that members of the governing board of a district or authority created by authority of Art. III, Sec. 52(b) (1) or (2), or Art. XVI, Sec. 59, of this Constitution serve terms not to exceed four years.

(d) The Legislature by general or special law may provide that members of the governing board of a hospital district serve terms not to exceed four years.

[Note — Sec. 30 of Art. XVI was amended to permit six-year terms for the newly created offices of the three-place Railroad Commission of Texas. The original section consisted only of the first clause of the amendment as printed above. Submitted by 23rd Legislature (1893), ratified in election Nov. 6, 1894, and declared adopted Dec. 21, 1894. It was further amended to provide four-year terms for members of governing boards of certain water districts and conservation and reclamation districts. Submitted by 67th Legislature (1981) and adopted in election Nov. 2, 1982. It was again amended by adding Subsection (d) to authorize the members of a hospital district board to serve four-year terms. Proposed by 71st Legislature (1989) and adopted in election Nov. 7, 1989.]

Sec. 30-A. **Board of Regents, Trustees, Managers, Etc.; Term of Office** — The Legislature may provide by law that the members of the Board of Regents of the State University and boards of trustees or managers of the educational, eleemosynary and penal institutions of this State, and such boards as have been or may hereafter be established by law, may hold their respective offices for the term of six (6) years, one third of the members of such boards to be elected or appointed every two years in such manner as the Legislature may determine; vacancies in such offices to be filled as may be provided by law, and the Legislature shall enact suitable laws to give effect to this section.

[Note — Sec. 30-A of Art. XVI was added to give the Legislature authority to provide official terms of more than two years. (See Sec. 30 above and accompanying note.) Submitted by 32nd Legislature (1911), ratified at election Nov. 5, 1912, and declared adopted Dec. 30, 1912.]

Sec. 30-B. **Tenure Under Municipal Civil Service** — Wherever by virtue of statute or charter provisions appointive officers of any municipality are placed under the terms and provisions of Civil Service and rules are set up governing appointment to and removal from such offices, the provisions of Article 16, Section 30, of the Texas Constitution limiting the duration of all offices not fixed by the Constitution to two (2) years shall not apply, but the duration of such offices shall be governed by the provisions of the Civil Service law or charter provisions applicable thereto.

[Note — Sec. 30-B of Art. XVI was added to extend to local officials terms under the Civil Service exemption from the two-year restriction in the first clause of Sec. 30. (See Secs. 30 and 30-a and accompanying notes.) Submitted by 46th Legislature; ratified in election Nov. 5, 1940.]

Sec. 31. **Qualifications of Physicians to Be Prescribed** — The Legislature may pass laws prescribing the qualifications of practitioners of medicine in this State, and to punish persons for malpractice, but no preference shall ever be given by law to any schools of medicine.

[Note — Sec. 32 of Art. XVI, relating to Board of Health and Vital Statistics, was deleted by constitutional amendment. Submitted by 61st Legislature (1969) and approved in election Aug. 5, 1969.]

Sec. 33. **Condition Under Which a Person Can Not Receive Compensation From the State** — The accounting officers in this State shall neither draw nor pay a warrant or check on funds of the State of Texas, whether in the treasury or otherwise, to any person for salary or compensation who holds at the same time more than one civil office of emolument, in violation of Sec. 40.

[Note — Sec. 33 of Art. XVI has been amended four times: (1) To release National Guard of Texas, National Guard Reserve and Officers' Reserve Corps and United States Organized Reserves from the prohibition against holding remunerative office. Submitted by 39th Legislature (1925), adopted in election Nov. 2, 1926 and proclaimed Jan. 20, 1927. (2) To add to those released from the prohibition against holding remunerative office all retired officers and enlisted men of the United States Army, Navy and Marine Corps. Submitted by 42nd Legislature (1931), adopted in election Nov. 8, 1932 and proclaimed Jan. 9, 1933. (3) To allow nonelective state officers and employees to serve in other nonelective offices under this state or the United States until Sept. 1, 1969, and thereafter only if authorized by Legislature, if the offices are of benefit to Texas or are required by state or federal law and there is no conflict of interest; prohibiting elected officers from holding any other office under this state; and adding members of Air National Guard, Air National Guard Reserve, Air Force Reserve and retired members of Air Force to list of persons exempted. Submitted by 60th Legislature (1967) and adopted in election Nov. 11, 1967. (4) To delete the old Sec. 33 of Art. XVI and substitute the Sec. 33 above. (See also note under Sec. 40 of Art. XVI.) Submitted by 62nd Legislature (1971) and adopted in election Nov. 7, 1972.]

[Note — Sections 34, 35, 36 and 38 of Art. XVI, relating to military forts, laborers on public works, payments to schoolteachers, and a Commissioner of Insurance, Statistics and History, were deleted by constitutional amendment. Submitted by 61st Legislature (1969) and approved in election Aug. 5, 1969.]

Sec. 37. **Mechanic's Liens to Be Enforced** — Mechanics, artisans and material men of every class shall have a lien upon the buildings and articles made or repaired by them, for the value of their labor done thereon, or material furnished therefor; and the Legislature shall provide by law for the speedy and efficient enforcement of said liens.

Sec. 39. **Memorials of Texas History** — The Legislature may, from time to time, make appropriations for preserving and perpetuating memorials of the history of Texas, by means of monuments, statues, paintings and documents of historical value.

Sec. 40. **Provision Against Holding More Than One Office; Exceptions** — No person shall hold or exercise at the same time, more than one civil office of emolument, except that of Justice of the Peace, County Commissioner, Notary Public and Postmaster, Officer of the National Guard, the National Guard

Article XVI (Cont'd.)
Reserve, and the Officers Reserve Corps of the United States and enlisted men of the National Guard, the National Guard Reserve, and the Organized Reserves of the United States, and retired officers of the United States Army, Air Force, Navy, Marine Corps, and Coast Guard, and retired warrant officers, and retired enlisted men of the United States Army, Air Force, Navy, Marine Corps, and Coast Guard, and the officers and directors of soil and water conservation districts, unless otherwise specially provided herein. Provided, that nothing in this Constitution shall be construed to prohibit an officer or enlisted man of the National Guard, and the National Guard Reserve, or an officer in the Officers Reserve Corps of the United States, or an enlisted man in the Organized Reserves of the United States, or retired officers of the United States Army, Air Force, Navy, Marine Corps, and Coast Guard, and retired warrant officers, and retired enlisted men of the United States Army, Air Force, Navy, Marine Corps, and Coast Guard, and officers of the State soil and water conservation districts, from holding at the same time any other office or position of honor, trust or profit, under this State or the United States, or from voting at any election, general, special or primary in this State when otherwise qualified. State employees or other individuals who receive all or part of their compensation either directly or indirectly from funds of the State of Texas and who are not State officers, shall not be barred from serving as members of the governing bodies of school districts, cities, towns, or other local governmental districts; provided, however, that such State employees or other individuals shall receive no salary for serving as members of such governing bodies. It is further provided that a non-elective State officer may hold other non-elective offices under the State or the United States, if the other office is of benefit to the State of Texas or is required by the State or Federal law, and there is no conflict with the original office for which he receives salary or compensation. No member of the Legislature of this State may hold any other office or position of profit under this State, or the United States, except as a notary public if qualified by law.

[Note — Sec. 40 of Art. XVI has been amended three times: (1) To release National Guard, National Guard Reserve and Officers' Reserve Corps and United States Organized Reserves from the prohibition against holding remunerative office. Submitted by 39th Legislature (1925), adopted in election Nov. 2, 1926 and proclaimed Jan. 20, 1927. (2) To add to those released from the prohibition against holding remunerative office all retired officers and enlisted men of the United States Army, Navy and Marine Corps. Submitted by 42nd Legislature (1931) and adopted in election Nov. 8, 1932. Proclaimed Jan. 9, 1933. (3) To add to those released from the prohibition against holding remunerative office retired officers or enlisted men of the Air Force and Coast Guard; and officers and directors of soil and water conservation districts, unless otherwise specially prohibited; also certain other state employees who are not officers of the state. Submitted by 62nd Legislature (1971) and adopted in election Nov. 7, 1972.]

Sec. 41. **Bribery of Certain Officials to Be Prohibited** — Any person who shall, directly or indirectly, offer, give or promise any money or thing of value, testimonial, privilege or personal advantage to any executive or judicial officer or member of the Legislature, to influence him in the performance of any of his public or official duties, shall be guilty of bribery and be punished in such manner as shall be provided by law. And any member of the Legislature, or executive or judicial officer, who shall solicit, demand or receive, or consent to receive, directly or indirectly, for himself or for another, from any company, corporation or person any money, appointment, employment testimonial, reward, thing of value or employment, or of personal advantage or promise thereof, for his vote or official influence, or for withholding the same, or with any understanding, expressed or implied, that his vote or official action shall be in any way influenced thereby, or who shall solicit, demand and receive any such money or other advantage, matter or thing aforesaid, for another, as the consideration of his vote or official influence, in consideration of the payment or promise of such money, advantage, matter or thing to another, shall be held guilty of bribery within the meaning of the Constitution, and shall incur the disabilities provided for said offenses, with a forfeiture of the office they may hold, and such other additional punishment as is or shall be provided by law.

[Note — Sec. 42 of Art. XVI, relating to an asylum for inebriates, was deleted by constitutional amendment. Submitted by 61st Legislature (1969) and approved in election Aug. 5, 1969.]

Sec. 43. **Exemption From Public Service** — No man or set of men shall ever be exempted, relieved or discharged from the performance of any public duty or service imposed by general law, by any special law. Exemptions from the performance of such public duty or service shall only be made by general law.

Sec. 44. **County Treasurer and Surveyor** — (a) Except as otherwise provided by this section, the Legislature shall prescribe the duties and provide for the election by the qualified voters of each county in this State, of a County Treasurer and a County Surveyor, who shall have an office at the county seat, and hold their office for four years, and until their successors are qualified; and shall have such compensation as may be provided by law.

(b) The office of County Treasurer in the counties of Tarrant and Bee is abolished and all the powers, duties, and functions of the office in each of these counties are transferred to the County Auditor or to the officer who succeeds to the auditor's functions. The office of County Treasurer in the counties of Bexar and Collin are abolished and all the powers, duties, and functions of the office in each of these counties are transferred to the County Clerk. However, the office of County Treasurer shall be abolished in the counties covered by this subsection only after a local election has been held in each county and the proposition "to abolish the elective office of county treasurer" has passed by a majority of those persons voting in said election.

(c) The office of County Treasurer in the counties of Andrews and Gregg is abolished. In Andrews County, the powers, duties, and functions of the office are transferred to the County Auditor of the county or to the officer who succeeds to the auditor's functions. In Gregg County, the functions of the office are transferred to an elected official or the County Auditor as designated by the Commissioners Court, and the Commissioners Court may from time to time change its designation as it considers appropriate.

(d) The office of County Treasurer in the counties of El Paso and Fayette is abolished. In El Paso County, the Commissioners Court may employ or contract with a qualified person or may designate another county officer to perform any of the functions that would have been performed by the County Treasurer if the office had not been abolished. In Fayette County, the functions of the abolished office are transferred to the County Auditor or to the officer who succeeds to the auditor's functions. However, the office of County Treasurer in El Paso or Fayette County is abolished under this subsection only if, at the statewide election at which the constitutional amendment providing for the abolition of the office in that county is submitted to the voters, a majority of the voters of that county voting on the question at that election favor the amendment.

(e) The office of County Surveyor in the counties of Denton, Randall, Collin, Dallas, El Paso, McLennan, and Henderson is abolished upon the approval of the abolition by a majority of the qualified voters of the respective county voting on the question at an election that the Commissioners Court of the county may call. If the election is called, the Commissioners Court shall order the ballot at the election to be printed to provide for voting for or against the proposition: "Abolishing the office of county surveyor." Each qualified voter of the county is entitled to vote in the election. If the office of County Surveyor is abolished under this subsection, the maps, field notes, and other records in the custody of the County Surveyor are transferred to the County Clerk of the county. After abolition, the Commissioners Court may employ or contract with a qualified person to perform any of the functions that would have been performed by the County Surveyor if the office had not been abolished.

[Note — Subsection (e) of Art. XVI, Sec. 44 was amended to abolish the office of county surveyor in McLennan County. Submitted by 73rd Legislature (1993) and adopted in election Nov. 2, 1993.]

(f) This subsection applies only to the counties of Cass, Ector, Garza, Smith, Bexar, Harris, and Webb. The office of County Surveyor in the county is abolished on January 1, 1990, if at the statewide election at which the addition to the Constitution of this subsection is submitted to the voters, a majority of the voters of that county voting on the question at that election favor the addition of this subsection. If the office of County Surveyor is abolished in a county under this subsection, the powers, duties, and functions of the office are transferred to the county officer or employee designated by the Commissioners Court of the county in which the office is abolished, and the Commissioners Court may from time to time change its designation as it considers appropriate.

[Note — Subsection (f) of Art. XVI, Sec. 44 was added to abolish the office of county surveyor in designated counties. Proposed by 71st Legislature (1989) and adopted in election Nov. 7, 1989. A previous Subsection (f) relating to abolishing the office of county treasurer in Gregg and Fayette counties had expired on Jan. 2, 1988. It had replaced the previous Subsection (f), which expired Jan. 2, 1986.]

(g) The office of County Treasurer in Nueces County is abolished and all powers, duties, and functions of this office are

Article XVI (Cont'd.)

transferred to the County Clerk. However, the office of County Treasurer in Nueces County is abolished under this subsection only if, at the statewide election at which this amendment is submitted to the voters, a majority of the voters of Nueces County voting on the question at that election favor the amendment. The office of County Treasurer of Nueces County is abolished on January 1, 1988, if the conditions of this subsection are met. If that office in Nueces County is not abolished, this subsection expires on January 1, 1988.

(h) (Ed. note: See also second Subsection (h) below and explanation following) The Commissioners Court of a county may call an election to abolish the office of County Surveyor in the county. The office of County Surveyor in the county is abolished if a majority of the voters of the county voting on the question at that election approve the abolition. If an election is called under this subsection, the Commissioners Court shall order the ballot for the election to be printed to provide for voting for or against the proposition: "Abolishing the office of county surveyor of this county." If the office of County Surveyor is abolished under this subsection, the maps, field notes, and other records in the custody of the County Surveyor are transferred to the county officer or employee designated by the Commissioners Court of the county in which the office is abolished, and the Commissioners Court may from time to time change its designation as it considers appropriate

(h) (Ed. note: See also second Subsection (h) above and explanation at end of Note below) The office of County Surveyor in Jackson County is abolished. The powers, duties, and functions of the office are transferred to the county officer or employee designated by the commissioners court, and the commissioners court may change its designation as it considers appropriate.

[Note — Sec. 44 of Art. XVI has been amended eight times: (1) To raise term of office from two to four years. Submitted by 53rd Legislature (1953) and adopted in election Nov. 2, 1954. (2) To abolish the office of county treasurer in Tarrant and Bee counties. Submitted by 67th Legislature (1981) and adopted in election Nov. 2, 1982. (3) To abolish the office of county treasurer in Bexar and Collin counties. Submitted by 68th Legislature (1983) and adopted in election Nov. 6, 1984. (4) To abolish the office of county treasurer in Andrews and El Paso counties; to abolish the office of county surveyor in Collin, Dallas, Denton, El Paso, Henderson and Randall counties. Submitted by 69th Legislature (1985) and adopted in election Nov. 5, 1985. (5) To abolish the office of county treasurer in Gregg, Fayette and Nueces counties. Submitted by 70th Legislature (1987) and adopted in election Nov. 3, 1987. (6) To abolish the office of county surveyor in Cass, Ector, Garza, Smith, Bexar, Harris and Webb counties. Proposed by 71st Legislature (1989) and adopted in election Nov. 7, 1989. (7) and (8) The 73rd Legislature (1993) approved and submitted to the voters two amendments proposing to add Subsection (h) to Art. XVI, Sec. 44. The first given above permits the voters of a county to decide by election to abolish the office of county surveyor in the county. The second listed above abolishes the office of county surveyor in Jackson County. Both were adopted in election Nov. 2, 1993.]

[Note — Sections 45 and 46 of Art. XVI, relating to records of the history of Texas and organization of a militia, were deleted by constitutional amendment. Submitted by 61st Legislature (1969) and approved in election Aug. 5, 1969.]

Sec. 47. **Scruples Against Bearing Arms** — Any person who conscientiously scruples to bear arms shall not be compelled to do so, but shall pay an equivalent for personal service.

Sec. 48. **Laws to Remain in Force** — All laws and parts of laws now in force in the State of Texas which are not repugnant to the Constitution of the United States or to this Constitution shall continue and remain in force as the laws of this State until they expire by their own limitation or shall be amended or repealed by the Legislature.

Sec. 49. **Exemptions From Forced Sales** — The Legislature shall have power, and it shall be its duty, to protect by law from forced sale a certain portion of the personal property of all heads of families, and also of unmarried adults, male and female.

Sec. 50. **Homestead Exemptions; Encumbrances, Pretended Sales** — The homestead of a family, or of a single adult person, shall be, and is hereby protected from forced sale, for the payment of all debts except for the purchase money thereof, or a part of such purchase money, the taxes due thereon, or for work and material used in constructing improvements thereon, and in this last case only when the work and material are contracted for in writing, with the consent of both spouses, in the case of a family homestead, given in the same manner as is required in making a sale and conveyance of the homestead; nor may the owner or claimant of the property claimed as homestead, if married, sell or abandon the homestead without the consent of the other spouse, given in such manner as may be prescribed by law. No mortgage, trust deed, or other lien on the homestead shall ever be valid, except for the purchase money therefor, or improvements made thereon, as hereinbefore provided, whether such mortgage, or trust deed, or other lien, shall have been created by the owner alone, or together with his or her spouse, in case the owner is married. All pretended sales of the homestead involving any condition of defeasance shall be void.

[Note — Sec. 50 of Art. XVI was amended to include single persons under the homestead exemption provision; it further made the wife an equal partner under the homestead provision. Submitted by 63rd Legislature (1973) and adopted in election Nov. 6, 1973.]

Sec. 51. **Homestead Defined** — The homestead, not in a town or city, shall consist of not more than two hundred acres of land, which may be in one or more parcels, with the improvements thereon; the homestead in a city, town or village, shall consist of lot or lots amounting to not more than one acre of land, together with any improvements on the land; provided, that the same shall be used for the purposes of a home, or as a place to exercise the calling or business of the homestead claimant, whether a single adult person, or the head of a family; provided also, that any temporary renting of the homestead shall not change the character of the same, when no other homestead has been acquired.

[Note — Sec. 51 was amended to raise the value of lots, exclusive of improvements, from $5,000 to $10,000 when designated as homesteads. Submitted by 61st Legislature (1969) and adopted in election Nov. 3, 1970. It was further amended to provide that family homesteads may not be abandoned except with consent of both spouses. Submitted by 63rd Legislature (1973) and adopted in election Nov. 6, 1973. It was again amended to replace the limitation on the value of an urban homestead with a limitation based on size. Submitted by 68th Legislature (1983) and adopted in election Nov. 8, 1983.]

Sec. 52. **Descent of Homestead** — On the death of the husband or wife, or both, the homestead shall descend and vest in like manner as other real property of the deceased, and shall be governed by the same laws of descent and distribution, but it shall not be partitioned among the heirs of the deceased during the lifetime of the surviving husband or wife, or so long as the survivor may elect to use or occupy the same as a homestead, or so long as the guardian of the minor children of the deceased may be permitted, under the order of the proper court having jurisdiction, to use and occupy the same.

Sec. 53. **Declaration Validating Process and Writs** — That no inconvenience may arise from the adoption of this Constitution, it is declared that all process and writs of all kinds which have been or may be issued and not returned or executed when this Constitution is adopted shall remain valid, and shall not be in any way affected by the adoption of this Constitution.

[Note — Sections 54 and 55 of Art. XVI, relating to pensions, and the indigent lunatics, were deleted by constitutional amendment. Submitted by 61st Legislature (1969) and approved in election Aug. 5, 1969.]

Sec. 56. **Advertising Texas' Resources** — The Legislature of the State of Texas shall have the power to appropriate money and establish the procedure necessary to expend such money for the purpose of developing information about the historical, natural, agricultural, industrial, educational, marketing, recreational and living resources of Texas, and for the purpose of informing persons and corporations of other states through advertising in periodicals having national circulation, and the dissemination of factual information about the advantages and economic resources offered by the State of Texas; providing, however, that neither the name nor the picture of any living state official shall ever be used in any of said advertising, and providing that the Legislature may require that any sum of money appropriated hereunder shall be matched by an equal sum paid into the State Treasury from private sources before any of said money may be expended.

[Note — Sec. 56 of Art. XVI is substituted for the original Section 56, which prohibited the expenditure of state funds for attracting immigrants. Submitted by 55th Legislature (1957) and adopted in election Nov. 4, 1958.]

[Note — Sections 57, 58 and 60 of Art. XVI, relating to land for state capitol, management of the prison system and the Texas Centennial, were deleted by constitutional amendment. Submitted by 61st Legislature (1969) and approved in election Aug. 5,

Article XVI (Cont'd.)
1969.]

*Sec. 59-a. **Conservation and Development of Natural Resources** — The conservation and development of all the natural resources of this State, including the control, storing, preservation and distribution of its storm and flood waters, the waters of its rivers and streams, for irrigation, power and all other useful purposes, the reclamation and irrigation of its arid, semi-arid and other lands needing irrigation, the reclamation and drainage of its overflowed lands, and other lands needing drainage, the conservation and development of its forests, water and hydro-electric power, the navigation of its inland and coastal waters, and the preservation and conservation of all such natural resources of the State are each and all hereby declared public rights and duties; and the Legislature shall pass all such laws as may be appropriate thereto.

*Note — The resolution submitting this amendment was headed "Sec. 59-a," followed by paragraphs "(b)" and "(c)." Obviously, the first heading should have been "Sec. 59 (a)," the parenthetical (a) referring only to the first paragraph.

(b) There may be created within the State of Texas or the State may be divided into, such number of conservation and reclamation districts as may be determined to be essential to the accomplishment of the purposes of this amendment to the Constitution, which districts shall be governmental agencies and bodies politic and corporate with such powers of government and with the authority to exercise such rights, privileges and functions concerning the subject matter of this amendment as may be conferred by law.

(c) The Legislature shall authorize all such indebtedness as may be necessary to provide all improvements and the maintenance thereof requisite to the achievement of the purposes of this amendment, and all such indebtedness may be evidenced by bonds of such conservation and reclamation districts, to be issued under such regulations as may be prescribed by law and shall, also, authorize the levy and collection within such districts of all such taxes, equitably distributed, as may be necessary for the payment of the interest and the creation of a sinking fund for payment of such bonds; and also for the maintenance of such districts and improvements, and such indebtedness shall be a lien upon the property assessed for the payment thereof; provided, the Legislature shall not authorize the issuance of any bonds or provide for any indebtedness against any reclamation district unless such proposition shall first be submitted to the qualified property taxpaying voters of such district and the proposition adopted.

(d) No law creating a conservation and reclamation district shall be passed unless notice of the intention to introduce such a bill setting forth the general substance of the contemplated law shall have been published at least thirty (30) days and not more than ninety (90) days prior to the introduction thereof in a newspaper or newspapers having general circulation in the county or counties in which said district or any part thereof is or will be located and by delivering a copy of such notice and such bill to the Governor who shall submit such notice and bill to the Texas Water Commission, or its successor, which shall file its recommendation as to such bill with the Governor, Lieutenant Governor and Speaker of the House of Representatives within thirty (30) days from date notice was received by the Texas Water Commission. Such notice and copy of bill shall also be given of the introduction of any bill amending a law creating or governing a particular conservation and reclamation district if such bill (1) adds additional land to the district, (2) alters the taxing authority of the district, (3) alters the authority of the district with respect to the issuance of bonds, or (4) alters the qualifications or terms of office of the members of the governing body of the district.

(e) No law creating a conservation and reclamation district shall be passed unless, at the time notice of the intention to introduce a bill is published as provided in Subsection (d) of this section, a copy of the proposed bill is delivered to the commissioners court of each county in which said district or any part thereof is or will be located and to the governing body of each incorporated city or town in whose jurisdiction said district or any part thereof is or will be located. Each such commissioners court and governing body may file its written consent or opposition to the creation of the proposed district with the governor, lieutenant governor, and speaker of the house of representatives. Each special law creating a conservation and reclamation district shall comply with the provisions of the general laws then in effect relating to consent by political subdivisions to the creation of conservation and reclamation districts and to the inclusion of land within the district.

(f) A conservation and reclamation district created under this section to perform any or all of the purposes of this section may engage in fire-fighting activities and may issue bonds or other indebtedness for fire-fighting purposes as provided by law and this constitution.

[Note — Sec. 59-a, obviously meant to be Sec. 59 (see footnote), was added to establish a conservation policy. Submitted by 35th Legislature (1917), adopted in election of Aug. 21, 1917, and proclaimed Oct. 2, 1917. It has been amended three times: (1) To require notice at both the local and state levels through publication in a newspaper having general circulation in county in which district is to be set up at least 30 days prior to introduction of bill in Legislature. Submitted by 58th Legislature (1963) and adopted in election Nov. 3, 1964. (2) To establish certain requirements relative to enactment of laws creating certain conservation and reclamation districts. Submitted by 63rd Legislature (1973) and adopted in election Nov. 6, 1973. (3) To authorize certain districts to engage in fire-fighting activities and to issue bonds or otherwise lend their credit for fire-fighting purposes. (See also Subsection (d), Sec. 52, Art. III.) Submitted by 65th Legislature (1977) and adopted in election Nov. 7, 1978.]

[Note — See note after Sec. 56 for Sec. 60.]

Sec. 61. **Compensation of District and County Officials** — All district officers in the State of Texas and all county officers in counties having a population of twenty thousand (20,000) or more, according to the then last preceding Federal Census, shall be compensated on a salary basis. In all counties in this State, the Commissioners Courts shall be authorized to determine whether precinct officers shall be compensated on a fee basis or on a salary basis, with the exception that it shall be mandatory upon the Commissioners Courts to compensate all justices of the peace, constables, deputy constables and precinct law enforcement officers on a salary basis beginning January 1, 1973; and in counties having a population of less than twenty thousand (20,000), according to the then last preceding Federal Census, the Commissioners Court shall also have the authority to determine whether county officers shall be compensated on a fee basis or on a salary basis, with the exception that it shall be mandatory upon the Commissioners Courts to compensate all sheriffs, deputy sheriffs, county law enforcement officers, including sheriffs who also perform the duties of assessor and collector of taxes, and their deputies, on a salary basis beginning January 1, 1949.

All fees earned by district, county and precinct officers shall be paid into the county treasury where earned for the account of the proper fund, provided that fees incurred by the State, county and any municipality, or in case where a pauper's oath is filed, shall be paid into the county treasury when collected and provided that where any officer is compensated wholly on a fee basis such fees may be retained by such officer or paid into the treasury of the county as the Commissioners Court may direct. All notaries public, county surveyors and public weighers shall continue to be compensated on a fee basis.

[Note — Sec. 61 of Art. XVI has been amended three times: (1) To put all district and county officials in counties of more than 20,000 population on a salary basis, substituting for fee basis, and making it optional with the Commissioners Courts whether precinct officers in counties of less than 20,000 should be on salary or fee basis and optional with reference to county officers in counties of less than 20,000. Submitted by 44th Legislature (1935), and adopted in election Aug. 24, 1935. (2) To make mandatory a salary basis for constables and precinct enforcement officers in counties of more than 20,000 and making it mandatory, in counties of less than 20,000 population, that all sheriffs, deputy sheriffs and other county enforcement officers, be on salary basis. Submitted by 50th Legislature (1947) and adopted in election Nov. 2, 1948. (3) To include justices of the peace with those to be compensated on salary basis beginning Jan. 1, 1973. Submitted by 62nd Legislature (1971) and adopted in election Nov. 7, 1972.]

[Note — Sec. 62 and Sec. 63 of Art. XVI, pertaining to **Retirement, Disability and Death Compensation Funds** and **Teacher and State Employee Retirement System**, respectively, were repealed by constitutional amendment. Submitted by 64th Legislature (1975) and approved in election April 22, 1975. (See also note under Art. III, Sec. 48-a, 48-b, 51-e and 51-f; also see Sec. 67 of Art. XVI, which replaces the foregoing Sections.)]

Sec. 64. **Inspector of Hides and Animals; Elective District, County and Precinct Offices; Terms of Office** — The office of Inspector of Hides and Animals, the elective district, county and precinct offices which have heretofore had terms of two years, shall hereafter have terms of four years; and the holders of such terms shall serve until their successors are qualified.

Article XVI (Cont'd.)

[Note — Sec. 64 of Art. XVI was added to set term of office for listed officials. Submitted by 53rd Legislature (1953) and adopted in election Nov. 2, 1954.]

Sec. 65. **District and County Officials; Terms of Office** — The following officers elected at the general election in November, 1954, and thereafter, shall serve for the full terms provided in this Constitution.

(a) District Clerks; (b) County Clerks; (c) County Judges; (d) Judges of County Courts-at-Law, County Criminal Courts, County Probate Courts, and County Domestic Relations Courts; (e) County Treasurers; (f) Criminal District Attorneys; (g) County Surveyors; (h) Inspectors of Hides and Animals; (i) County Commissioners for Precincts Two and Four; (j) Justices of the Peace.

Notwithstanding other provisions of this Constitution, the following officers elected at the general election in November, 1954, shall serve only for terms of two years: (a) Sheriffs; (b) Assessors and Collectors of Taxes; (c) District Attorneys; (d) County Attorneys; (e) Public Weighers; (f) County Commissioners for Precincts One and Three; (g) Constables. At subsequent elections, such officers shall be elected for the full terms provided in this Constitution.

In any district, county or precinct where any of the aforementioned offices is of such nature that two or more persons hold such office, with the result that candidates file for "Place No. 1," "Place No. 2," etc., the officers elected at the general election in November, 1954, shall serve for a term of two years if the designation of their office is an uneven number, and for a term of four years, if the designation of their office is an even number. Thereafter, all such officers shall be elected for the term provided in this Constitution.

Provided, however, if any of the officers named herein shall announce their candidacy, or shall in fact become a candidate, in any General, Special or Primary Election, for any office of profit or trust under the laws of this state or the United States other than the office then held, at any time when the unexpired term of the office then held shall exceed one (1) year, such announcement or such candidacy shall constitute an automatic resignation of the office then held, and the vacancy thereby created shall be filled pursuant to law in the same manner as other vacancies for such office are filled.

[Note — Sec. 65 of Art. XVI was added to set the terms of office of the listed officers. Submitted by 53rd Legislature (1953) and adopted in election Nov. 2, 1954. It was further amended to provide that a person must resign his present term of office if same has more than a year to run when he becomes a candidate for another office. Submitted by 55th Legislature (1957) and adopted in election Nov. 4, 1958.]

Sec. 65-A. Notwithstanding Section 65 of this article, the election and term of office of a district attorney serving a judicial district composed entirely of Fort Bend County are governed by the law relating to criminal district attorneys.

[Note — Sec. 65-A of Art. XVI was added relating to the election of a district attorney in Fort Bend County. Proposed by 71st Legislature (1989) and adopted in election Nov. 7, 1989. Subsections (a), (b) and (c), proposed and adopted at the same time, constituted a temporary provision requiring a district attorney serving in a judicial district composed entirely of Fort Bend County to be elected and serve a term in the manner provided by general law for criminal district attorneys. The temporary provision expired Jan. 2, 1990.]

Sec. 66. **Pensions for Texas Rangers** — The Legislature shall have authority to provide for a system of retirement and disability pensions for retiring Texas Rangers who have not been eligible at any time for membership in the Employees Retirement System of Texas as that retirement system was established by Chapter 352, Acts of the Fiftieth Legislature, Regular Session, 1947, and who have had as much as two (2) years service as a Texas Ranger, and to their widows; providing that no pension shall exceed Eighty Dollars ($80) per month to any such Texas Ranger or his widow, provided that such widow was legally married prior to January 1, 1957, to a Texas Ranger qualifying for such pension.

These pensions may be paid only from the special fund created by *Sec. 17, Art. VII for a payment of pensions for services in the Confederate army and navy, frontier organizations, and the militia of the State of Texas, and for widows of such soldiers serving in said armies, navies, organizations or militia.

*Sec. 17, Art. VII was repealed by amendment submitted by 67th Legislature (1981) and adopted in election Nov. 2, 1982, but no provision has been made for deletion of this reference (See Art. VIII, Sec. 1-e.)

[Note — Sec. 66 of Art. XVI was added to provide for retirement pensions for Texas Rangers and their widows. Submitted by 55th Legislature (1957), adopted in election Nov. 4, 1958. (See also Art. VIII, Sec. 1-e.)]

Sec. 67. **State Retirement Systems** — (a) General Provisions. (1) The Legislature may enact general laws establishing systems and programs of retirement and related disability and death benefits for public employees and officers. Financing of benefits must be based on sound actuarial principles. The assets of a system are held in trust for the benefit of members and may not be diverted.

(2) A person may not receive benefits from more than one system for the same service, but the Legislature may provide by law that a person with service covered by more than one system or program is entitled to a fractional benefit from each system or program based on service rendered under each system or program calculated as to amount upon the benefit formula used in that system or program. Transfer of service credit between the Employees Retirement System of Texas and the Teacher Retirement System of Texas also may be authorized by law.

(3) Each statewide benefit system must have a board of trustees to administer the system and to invest the funds of the system in such securities as the board may consider prudent investments. In making investments, a board shall exercise the judgment and care under the circumstances then prevailing that persons of ordinary prudence, discretion, and intelligence exercise in the management of their own affairs, not in regard to speculation, but in regard to the permanent disposition of their funds, considering the probable income therefrom as well as the probable safety of their capital. The Legislature by law may further restrict the investment discretion of a board.

(4) General laws establishing retirement systems and optional retirement programs for public employees and officers in effect at the time of the adoption of this section remain in effect, subject to the general powers of the Legislature established in this subsection.

(b) **State Retirement Systems**. (1) The Legislature shall establish by law a Teacher Retirement System of Texas to provide benefits for persons employed in the public schools, colleges, and universities supported wholly or partly by the state. Other employees may be included under the system by law.

(2) The Legislature shall establish by law an Employees Retirement System of Texas to provide benefits for officers and employees of the state and such state-compensated officers and employees of appellate courts and judicial districts as may be included under the system by law.

(3) The amount contributed by a person participating in the Employees Retirement System of Texas or the Teacher Retirement System of Texas shall be established by the Legislature but may not be less than six percent of current compensation. The amount contributed by the state may not be less than six percent nor more than 10 percent of the aggregate compensation paid to individuals participating in the system. In an emergency, as determined by the governor, the Legislature may appropriate such additional sums as are actuarially determined to be required to fund benefits authorized by law.

(c) **Local Retirement Systems**. (1) The Legislature shall provide by law for:

(A) The creation by any city or county of a system of benefits for its officers and employees;

(B) A statewide system of benefits for the officers and employees of counties or other political subdivisions of the state in which counties or other political subdivisions may voluntarily participate; and

(C) A statewide system of benefits for officers and employees of cities in which cities may voluntarily participate.

(2) Benefits under these systems must be reasonably related to participant tenure and contributions.

(d) **Judicial Retirement System**. (1) Notwithstanding any other provision of this section, the system of retirement, disability, and survivors' benefits heretofore established in the constitution or by law for justices, judges, and commissioners of the appellate courts and judges of the district and criminal district courts is continued in effect. Contributions required and benefits payable are to be as provided by law.

(2) General administration of the Judicial Retirement System of Texas is by the Board of Trustees of the Employees Retirement System of Texas under such regulations as may be provided by law.

(e) Anticipatory Legislation. Legislation enacted in anticipation of this amendment is not void because it is anticipatory.

(f) **Retirement Systems Not Belonging to a Statewide System** —The board of trustees of a system or program that provides retirement and related disability and death benefits for public officers and employees and that does not participate in a statewide public retirement system shall:

Article XVI (Cont'd.)

(1) administer the system or program of benefits;

(2 hold the assets of the system or program for the exclusive purposes of providing benefits to participants and their beneficiaries and defraying reasonable expenses of administering the system or program; and

(3) select legal counsel and an actuary and adopt sound actuarial assumptions to be used by the system or program.

[Note — Sec. 67 of Art. XVI was added to revise and consolidate provisions relating to state and local retirement systems and programs, and providing for a maximum state contribution to state systems of 10% of aggregate compensation paid to individuals. Submitted by 64th Legislature (1975) and adopted in election April 22, 1975. Subsection (f) was added to clarify duties of trustees of local public pension systems. Submitted by 73rd Legislature (1993) and adopted in election Nov. 2, 1993. See also notes under Art. III, Sections 48-a, 48-b, 51-e and 51-f; and Art. XVI, Sections 62 and 63.]

Sec. 68. **Promoting, Marketing Agricultural Products** — The Legislature may provide for the advancement of food and fiber in this state by providing representative associations of agricultural producers with authority to collect such refundable assessments on their product sales as may be approved by referenda of producers. All revenue collected shall be used solely to finance programs of marketing, promotion, research, and education relating to that commodity.

[Note — Sec. 68 of Art. XVI was added to provide for the advancement of food and fiber production and marketing through research, education and promotion, financed by producers of agricultural products. Submitted by 68th Legislature (1983) and adopted in election Nov. 8, 1983.]

Sec. 69. The Legislature may require, by rider in the General Appropriations Act or by separate statute, the prior approval of the expenditure or the emergency transfer of any funds appropriated by the agencies of state government.

[Note — Sec. 69 of Art. XVI was added to protect public funds by authorizing prior approval of expenditure or emergency transfer of state appropriations. Submitted by 69th Legislature (1985) and adopted in election Nov. 5, 1985.]

Sec. 70. **Texas Growth Fund** — (a) In this section:

(1) "Board of trustees" means the board of trustees of the Texas growth fund.

(2) "Fund" means the Texas growth fund.

(3) "Venture capital investment" means an investment in debt, equity, or a combination of debt and equity that possesses the potential for substantial investment returns, and includes investments in new or small businesses, investments in businesses with rapid growth potential, or investments in applied research and organizational activities leading to business formation and opportunities involving new or improved processes or products.

(b) The Texas growth fund is created as a trust fund. Except as otherwise provided by this section, the fund is subject to the general laws of this state governing private sector trusts. The governing boards of the permanent university fund, the permanent school fund, the Teacher Retirement System of Texas, the Employees Retirement System of Texas, and any other pension system created under this constitution or by statute of this state in their sole discretion may make investments in the fund.

(c) The fund is managed by a board of trustees consisting of four public members appointed by the governor and one member from and elected by the membership of each of the following:

(1) the Board of Regents of The University of Texas System;

(2) the Board of Regents of The Texas A&M University System;

(3) the Board of Trustees of the Teacher Retirement System of Texas;

(4) the Board of Trustees of the Employees Retirement System of Texas; and

(5) the State Board of Education.

(d) Each public member of the board must have demonstrated substantial investment expertise. A public member serves for a six-year term expiring February 1 of an odd-numbered year.

(e) A person filling an elected position on the board of trustees ceases to be a member of the board of trustees when the person ceases to be a member of the board the person represents or as otherwise provided by procedures adopted by the board the person represents. The governor shall designate a chairman from among the members of the board of trustees who serves a term of two years expiring February 1 of each odd-numbered year. A member may serve more than one term as chairman.

(f) The board of trustees shall manage the investment of the fund, and may:

(1) employ and retain staff, including a chief executive officer;

(2) analyze and structure investments;

(3) set investment policy of the fund;

(4) take any action necessary for the creation, administration, and protection of the fund;

(5) enter into investment contracts with the participating funds or systems;

(6) adopt rules regarding the operation of the fund;

(7) pay expenses of the fund based on an assessment on investor contributions; and

(8) alternatively, or in combination with its own staff, contract for the management of investments under this section with a private investment management firm or with an investing fund or system electing a member of the board of trustees.

(g) In making investments, including venture capital investments, the board of trustees shall exercise the judgment and care under the circumstances then prevailing that persons of ordinary prudence, discretion, and intelligence exercise in the management of their own affairs, not in regard to speculation but in regard to the permanent disposition of their funds, considering the probable income as well as the probable safety of the capital of the fund. All investments of the fund shall be directly related to the creation, retention, or expansion of employment opportunity and economic growth in Texas. In making venture capital investments, all other material matters being equal, the board of trustees shall invest in technological advances that could be expected to result in the greatest increase in employment opportunity and economic growth in Texas.

(h) The board of trustees shall establish and operate the fund to the extent practical under the generally accepted business procedures relating to a mutual fund and shall value the investments for determining the purchase or sales price of participating shares of investing funds or systems participating in the fund consistent with investment contracts. Evidences of participation in the fund shall be held by the state treasurer in keeping with the custodial responsibilities of that office.

(i) An investing fund or system, without liability at law or in equity to members of the governing board of the fund or system in their personal or official capacities, may cumulatively invest in the Texas growth fund not more than one percent of the book or cost value of the investing fund or system, as determined at the end of each fiscal year.

(j) The board of trustees shall establish criteria for the investment of not more than 10 percent of the fund in venture capital investments. Not more than 25 percent of the funds available for venture capital investments may be used for unilateral investment. Investments of the remainder of the funds available for venture capital investments must be matched at least equally by funds from sources other than the fund, with matching amounts established by the board of trustees. The board of trustees shall also establish criteria for the investment of not less than 50 percent of the fund in equity or debt security, or a combination of equity and debt security, for the initial construction, expansion, or modernization of business or industrial facilities in Texas. The board of trustees may invest in money funds whose underlying investments are consistent and acceptable under the investment policy of the fund.

(k) On a quarterly basis, the amount of income realized on investments under this section shall be distributed to each of the systems and funds investing in the Texas growth fund in proportion to the number of participating shares of each investing system and fund. Capital appreciation becomes a part of the corpus of the Texas growth fund and shall be distributed in accordance with the investment contracts.

(1)The board of trustees shall make arrangements to begin liquidation, phase out investments, and return the principal and capital gains on investments to the investors in the fund not later than the 10th anniversary of the date of the adoption of this section. Except under unusual circumstances where it may be necessary to protect investments previously made, further investments may not be made in or by the fund after the 10th anniversary of the date of the adoption of this section.

(m) At the regular legislative session next preceding the 10th anniversary of the date of adoption of this section, the legislature, by two-thirds vote of each house, may authorize the creation of Texas growth fund II, which shall operate under this section and under the board of trustees created by this section in the same manner as the Texas growth fund. Funds in Texas growth fund II may not be commingled with funds in the Texas growth fund.

(n) The board of trustees may purchase liability insurance for the coverage of the trustees, employees, and agents of the board.

(o) The legislature shall provide by law for the periodic review of the board of trustees in the same manner and at the same intervals as it provides for review of other state agencies, except that the legislature shall provide that the board of trustees is not

Article XVI (Cont'd.); Article XVII

subject to abolishment as part of the review process.

(p) This section expires September 1, 1998, except that if the legislature authorizes the creation of Texas growth fund II as provided by Subsection (m) of this section, this section expires September 1, 2008.

(q) This section is self-executing and takes effect on its adoption by the voters. All state officials named in this section, the state treasurer, and the comptroller of public accounts shall take all necessary actions for the implementation of this section. The legislature shall provide by law for full disclosure of all details concerning investments authorized by this section.

(r) The board of trustees may not invest money from the Texas growth fund in a business unless the business has submitted to the board of trustees an affidavit disclosing whether the business has any direct financial investment in or with South Africa or Namibia.

[Note — Sec. 70 of Article XVI was added to establish the Texas growth fund. Submitted by 70th Legislature (1987) and adopted in election Nov. 8, 1988.]

Sec. 71 (a) The Legislature by law may establish a Texas product development fund to be used without further appropriation solely in furtherance of a program established by the legislature to aid in the development and production of new or improved products in this state. The fund shall contain a program account, an interest and sinking account, and other accounts authorized by the legislature. To carry out the program authorized by this subsection, the legislature may authorize loans, loan guarantees, and equity investments using money in the Texas product development fund and the issuance of up to $25 million of general obligation bonds to provide initial funding of the Texas product development fund. The Texas product development fund is composed of the proceeds of the bonds authorized by this subsection, loan repayments, guarantee fees, royalty receipts, dividend income, and other amounts received by the state from loans, loan guarantees, and equity investments made under this subsection and any other amounts required to be deposited in the Texas product development fund by the legislature.

(b) The legislature by law may establish a Texas small business incubator fund to be used without further appropriation solely in furtherance of a program established by the legislature to foster and stimulate the development of small businesses in the state. The fund shall contain a project account, an interest and sinking account, and other accounts authorized by the legislature. A small business incubator operating under the program is exempt from ad valorem taxation in the same manner as an institution of purely public charity under Article VIII, Section 2, of this constitution. To carry out the program authorized by this subsection, the legislature may authorize loans and grants of money in the Texas small business incubator fund and the issuance of up to $20 million of general obligation bonds to provide initial funding of the Texas small business incubator fund. The Texas small business incubator fund is composed of the proceeds of the bonds authorized by this subsection, loan repayments, and other amounts received by the state for loans or grants made under this subsection and any other amounts required to be deposited in the Texas small business incubator fund by the legislature.

(c) The legislature may require review and approval of the issuance of bonds under this section, of the use of the bond proceeds, or of the rules adopted by an agency to govern use of the bond proceeds. Notwithstanding any other provision of this constitution, any entity created or directed to conduct this review and approval may include members, or appointees of members, of the executive, legislative, and judicial departments of state goverment.

(d) Bonds authorized under this section constitute a general obligation of the state. While any of the bonds or interest on the bonds is outstanding and unpaid, there is appropriated out of the first money coming into the treasury in each fiscal year, not otherwise appropriated by this constitution, the amount sufficient to pay the principal of and interest on the bonds that mature or become due during the fiscal year, less any amount in any interest and sinking account at the end of the preceding fiscal year that is pledged to payment of the bonds or interest.

[Note — Sec. 71 of Art. XVI was added to establish a Texas product development fund to aid in the development and production of new or improved products in this state. Proposed by 71st Legislature (1989) and adopted in election Nov. 7, 1989.]

Article XVII — Mode of Amending the Constitution of This State

Sec. 1. **How the Constitution Is to Be Amended** — The Legislature, at any regular session, or at any special session when the matter is included within the purposes for which the session is convened, may propose amendments revising the Constitution, to be voted upon by the qualified electors for statewide offices and propositions, as defined in the Constitution and statutes of this State. The date of the elections shall be specified by the Legislature. The proposal for submission must be approved by a vote of two-thirds of all the members elected to each House, entered by yeas and nays on the journals.

A brief explanatory statement of the nature of a proposed amendment, together with the date of the election and the wording of the proposition as it is to appear on the ballot, shall be published twice in each newspaper in the State which meets requirements set by the Legislature for the publication of official notices of officers and departments of the state government. The explanatory statement shall be prepared by the Secretary of State and shall be approved by the Attorney General. The Secretary of State shall send a full and complete copy of the proposed amendment or amendments to each county clerk who shall post the same in a public place in the courthouse at least 30 days prior to the election on said amendment. The first notice shall be published not more than 60 days nor less than 50 days before the date of the election, and second notice shall be published on the same day in the succeeding week. The Legislature shall fix the standards for the rate of charge for the publication, which may not be higher than the newspaper's published national rate for advertising per column inch.

The election shall be held in accordance with procedures prescribed by the Legislature, and the returning officer in each county shall make returns to the Secretary of State of the number of legal votes cast at the election for and against each amendment. If it appears from the returns that a majority of the votes cast have been cast in favor of an amendment, it shall become a part of this Constitution, and proclamation thereof shall be made by the Governor.

[Note — Sec. 1 of Art. XVII was amended to revise provisions on time and method of proposing amendments to State Constitution and publishing notice of proposed amendments. Submitted by 62nd Legislature (1971) and adopted in election Nov. 7, 1972.]

Sec. 2. **Rewriting State Constitution** — (a) When the Legislature convenes in regular session in January, 1973, it shall provide by concurrent resolution for the establishment of a constitutional revision commission. The Legislature shall appropriate money to provide an adequate staff, office space, equipment, and supplies for the commission.

(b) The commission shall study the need for constitutional change and shall report its recommendations to the members of the Legislature not later than November 1, 1973.

(c) The members of the Sixty-third Legislature shall be convened as a constitutional convention at noon on the second Tuesday in January, 1974. The Lieutenant Governor shall preside until a chairman of the convention is elected. The convention shall elect other officers it deems necessary, adopt temporary and permanent rules, and publish a journal of its proceedings. A person elected to fill a vacancy in the Sixty-third Legislature before dissolution of the convention becomes a member of the convention on taking office as a member of the Legislature.

(d) Members of the convention shall receive compensation, mileage, per diem as determined by a five-member committee, to be composed of the Governor, Lieutenant Governor, Speaker of the House, Chief Justice of the Supreme Court, and Chief Justice of the Court of Criminal Appeals. This shall not be held in conflict with Art. XVI, Sec. 33 of the Texas Constitution. The convention may provide for the expenses of its members and for the employment of a staff for the convention, and for these purposes may by resolution appropriate money from the general revenue fund of the State Treasury. Warrants shall be drawn pursuant to vouchers signed by the chairman or by a person authorized by him in writing to sign them.

(e) The convention, by resolution adopted on the vote of at least two-thirds of its members, may submit for a vote of the qualified electors of this State a new Constitution which may contain alternative articles or sections, or may submit revisions of the existing Constitution which may contain alternative articles or sections. Each resolution shall specify the date of the election, the form of the ballots, and the method of publicizing the proposals to be voted on. To be adopted, each proposal must receive the favorable vote of the majority of those voting on the proposal. The conduct of the election, the canvassing of the votes, and the reporting of the returns shall be as provided for elections under Sec. 1 of this article.

(f) The convention may be dissolved by resolution adopted on the vote of at least two thirds of its members; but it is automatically dissolved at 11:59 p.m. on May 31, 1974, unless its duration is extended for a period not to exceed 60 days by resolution

Article XVII (Contd.)
adopted on the vote of at least two thirds of its members.

(g) The Bill of Rights of the present Texas Constitution shall be retained in full.

[Note — Sec. 2 of Art. XVII was added to provide for a constitutional convention for the purpose of submitting to the voters a new constitution or revisions of the existing state constitution. Submitted by 62nd Legislature (1971) and adopted in election Nov. 7, 1972.] ☆

State Seal and Other Symbols

The six main flags that have flown over Texas, as well as the major state symbols — state tree, flower, bird and song can be found on pages 11 and 12. The state seal, citizenship designation, motto and other symbols are described below:

State Seal — The design of the obverse (front) of the Great Seal of the State of Texas consists of "a star of five points, encircled by olive and live oak branches, and the words, 'The State of Texas'." (State Constitution, Art. IV, Sec. 19.) This design is a slight modification of the Great Seal of the Republic of Texas, adopted by the Congress of the Republic, Dec. 10, 1836, and readopted with modifications in 1839. An official design for the reverse (back) of the seal was adopted by the 57th Legislature in 1961, but there were discrepancies between the written description and the artistic rendering that was adopted at the same time. To resolve the problems, the 72nd Legislature in 1991 adopted an official design " . . . the design for the reverse side of the Great Seal of Texas shall consist of a shield, the lower half of which is divided into two parts; on the shield's lower left is a depiction of the cannon of the Battle of Gonzales; on the shield's lower right is a depiction of Vince's Bridge; on the upper half of the shield is a depiction of the Alamo; the shield is circled by live oak and olive branches, and the unfurled flags of the Kingdom of France, the Kingdom of Spain, the United Mexican States, the Republic of Texas, the Confederate States of America, and the United States of America; above the shield is emblazoned the motto, "REMEMBER THE ALAMO", and beneath the shield are the words, "TEXAS ONE AND INDIVISIBLE"; over the entire shield, centered between the flags, is a white five-pointed star . . ." Since the description of the design of the reverse of the seal was contained in a concurrent resolution rather than a bill, the design is not a matter of law but can be considered the intent of the Legislature. (CR 159, 72nd Legislature, May 1991).

State Citizenship Designation — The people of Texas usually call themselves **Texans.** However, **Texian** was generally used in the early period of the state's history.

State Motto — The state motto of Texas is **"Friendship."** The word, Texas, or Tejas, was the Spanish pronunciation of a Caddo Indian word meaning "friends" or "allies." (Acts of 1930, fourth called session of the 41st Legislature, p. 105.)

State Air Force — The **Confederate Air Force**, based in Midland at the Midland International Airport, was proclaimed the official air force of the State of Texas by the 71st Legislature in 1989.

State Dish — **Chili** was proclaimed the Texas state dish by the 65th Texas Legislature in 1977.

State Fish — The **Guadalupe bass,** a member of the genus *Micropterus* within the sunfish family, was named the official state fish of Texas by the 71st Legislature in 1989. It is one of a group of fish collectively known as black bass.

State Folk Dance — The **square dance** was designated the official state folk dance by the 72nd Legislature in 1991.

State Fruit — The **Texas red grapefruit** was designated the official state fruit by the 73rd Legislature in 1993.

State Gem — **Texas blue topaz,** the official Texas gem, is found in Llano uplift area, especially west to northwest of Mason. It was designated by the 61st Legislature in 1969.

State Grass — **Sideoats grama** (*Bouteloua curtipendula*), a native grass found on many different soils, was designated by the 62nd Legislature as the state grass of Texas in 1971.

State Seashell — The **lightning whelk** (*Busycon perversum pulleyi*) was adopted as the official state seashell by the 70th Legislature on April 2, 1987. One of the few shells that opens on the left side, the lightning whelk is named for its colored stripes. It is found only on the Gulf Coast.

State Holidays — Texas has five state holidays and several special observance days. The holidays are **Martin Luther King Jr.'s birthday,** third Monday in January; **Texas Independence Day,** March 2; **San Jacinto Day,** April 21; **Emancipation Day,** June 19; and **Lyndon B. Johnson's Birthday,** August 27. (See index for list of Texas holidays and special observances.) ☆

1994 Elections: A Rising Tide of Republicanism

By Carolyn Barta

A rising tide of Republicanism swept Texas in 1994. Like other states in the South, Texas has been trending Republican in national elections for three decades. In this election year, Republicans began achieving parity in state offices.

The 1994 election was one in which voters took out their anger and frustration with government in general and President Bill Clinton in particular by voting against the party in power — a factor that spilled over into state and local races.

While Democrats blamed their losses on national discontent, Republican leaders were predicting that, after 1994, the GOP would become the majority party in Texas by the turn of the century.

With the 1994 election, the top three offices in the state were held by Republicans.

Kay Bailey Hutchison was elected to a full term in the U.S. Senate, joining Sen. Phil Gramm. George W. Bush's win over the popular incumbent governor, Ann Richards, made him only the second Republican governor elected since Reconstruction, following Bill Clements' elections in 1978 and 1986.

Further evidence of partisan realignment was that Republicans possessed almost half of the statewide offices.

The governor's race was a historic one, pitting the 48-year-old son of former President George Bush against Texas' celebrity governor, Ann Richards. And the win was doubly sweet for Bush.

He was able to accomplish what his father never could when Democrats controlled Texas — win a statewide race. The elder Mr. Bush was twice defeated for U.S. senator before he became Vice President and President of the United States.

Mr. Bush, the younger, also settled an old score with Richards, who had gained national prominence with her 1988 Democratic National Convention statement about the GOP nominee: "Poor George. He can't help it. He was born with a silver foot in his mouth."

The Bush-Richards race was predicted to be close — as the colorful Richards said, "tighter than Dick's hatband." But it turned out to be the biggest gubernatorial win in 20 years, with Bush capturing 53.5 percent of the vote over the incumbent in an anti-incumbent year.

Bush obviously benefited from the wave of voter discontent across the nation, which gave Republicans not only control of both houses of Congress but also a majority of governorships for the first time since 1970.

But he also ran an issue-oriented campaign that resonated with voters. His theme was that people should be held accountable for their behavior, and public policy should reflect that principle in all areas

Gov. George W. Bush defeated Ann Richards, the incumbent, in the Nov. 1994 election with 53.5 percent of the vote, the biggest gubernatorial win in 20 years.

— from juvenile justice to welfare and education. He convinced Texans not enough had been done in the Richards administration is such areas as crime and education.

Although Richards had a supportable record in several areas — including strengthening economic development, student test scores and prison time served — she centered her campaign on Bush, personally, at one point calling him a "jerk."

She questioned his credentials since he'd never held public office (an asset, no doubt, in a year of disfavor for professional politicians), attacked his business career, and claimed he never would have been in the race had his name been George Walker instead of George Walker Bush.

Her strategy didn't work, given the national climate and the partisan realignment under way in Texas.

In 1990, Ann Richards' margin of victory had come from crossover Republican women and independent women, embarrassed by the crude jokes and sexist remarks of her Republican opponent Clayton Williams.

With George Bush, a more sophisticated candidate who ran a more careful and disciplined campaign, the Republican women returned home. In addition, Richards suffered from a disintegrating Democratic coalition, even as the Republican party was enjoying an infusion of energy from religious conservatives.

While Bush's win was a stunning victory against a unique Texas personality, other aspects of the '94 election substantiate the claim that political realignment is in progress. These were the important "firsts":

◆ Texas has two Republican senators for the first time this century, with Sen. Phil Gramm and Sen. Kay Bailey Hutchison. Sen. Hutchison, who won a special election in 1993 to fill the unexpired term of Sen. Lloyd Bentsen when he became U.S. Secretary of the Treasury, earned a full term by defeating an able and attractive Democrat, Dallas investment banker Richard Fisher, by the astounding margin of 63 to 38 percent.

◆ Texas has a Republican majority on the State Supreme Court for the first time since Reconstruction.

◆ The Texas Railroad Commission has three Republican commissioners for the first time, as Carole Keeton Rylander, former Austin mayor, and Charles Matthews, former Garland mayor, joined the previously elected Barry Williamson.

◆ The State Board of Education also got its first Republican majority, fueled by members of the Christian Coalition and others seeking a more conservative approach to textbooks and curriculum.

While Democrats still maintain higher numbers of local and county offices across the state, in Dallas and Tarrant counties, and several suburban counties around Dallas and Fort Worth, Republicans controlled all but a handful of local and county offices.

There were Republican sweeps in the judiciary in Dallas County and Harris County, turning several minority judges out of office.

High points for Democrats in the 1994 elections were the strong wins by Lt. Gov. Bob Bullock, who defeated his Republican opponent by a 62-to-38 percent margin, and Comptroller John Sharp, who posted a 56-to-44 percent victory.

The popular Bullock, who campaigned not at all because of health problems, was the ballot's leading vote-getter, amassing more than 2.6 million voters.

However, Republicans increased their numbers in the State Senate, over which Bullock presides, capturing a record 14 seats against the Democrats' 17.

The U.S. Senate race that was expected to be highly competitive in the spring fizzled in the fall. Richard Fisher, a fresh face, turned back two better known Democrats in the primary — U.S. Rep. Mike Andrews of Houston and former attorney general, Jim Mattox, an old-style Democrat with a liberal-labor base.

Fisher, who spoke fluent Spanish on the campaign trail, convinced Democrats he could beat Kay Bailey Hutchison by running as a moderate or "New Democrat." He poured $2 million of his own money into the race, but declined to accept political action committee money, which left him underfinanced in the campaign stretch against the well-funded Hutchison.

Hutchison's win was a dramatic vindication, after she survived indictments for abusing her office while she was state treasurer. In February of the election year, while serving in the Senate, she was acquitted of the charges that she had blamed on a political "witchhunt." Hutchison emerged from the legal arena tougher and stronger and with public sympathy on her side.

In 18 months in office filling the unexpired term of Sen. Bentsen, Hutchison established herself as a solid conservative with leadership potential and a rising star in Washington, as one of the few women senators.

Meanwhile, her aisle-mate Phil Gramm, who was not up for re-election, headed the Republican Senatorial Committee as Republicans took back control of the Senate, thus positioning himself for a run for the Republican nomination for President in 1996.

The year's political review would not be complete without an update on Texas' famous political figure of 1992 — Ross Perot.

In early 1994, Perot announced that his grassroots organization, United We Stand, America, was organized in every congressional district in the nation. It was, however, not a political party, and its impact on the 1994 election was largely undetermined. ☆

Carolyn Barta, author of Perot and his People, *is the former Viewpoints editor of* The Dallas Morning News *and a longtime political analyst.*

Texans Gain Clout in Washington

The 1994 national revolt against the party in power, which put Republicans in control of both houses of Congress for the first time in 40 years, gave Texas more clout on Capitol Hill than the state has enjoyed since the days of Sam Rayburn and Lyndon B. Johnson.

But this time, it's Republican.

Rep. Dick Armey, R-Lewisville, became the first Texas Republican to be elected majority leader and only the third Texan in history to hold the second highest-ranking position in the U.S. House, following Sam Rayburn of Bonham (1937 to 1941) and Jim Wright of Fort Worth (1977 to 1987). Rayburn and Wright both went on to become speaker of the House, the highest leadership job.

In the two years before Republicans won majority status, Armey served as chairman of the House

Republican Conference, the third-ranking minority leadership post, and became known as an aggressive and innovative conservative.

A former economics professor at the University of North Texas, he espoused supply-side economic policies and a simple flat tax to replace the cumbersome income-tax code. He gained national status as a legislative leader with his successful concept to close military bases through an independent commission.

As majority leader, Armey accepted the challenge of trying to pass the Republicans' "Contract with America," a series of reforms and major legislation that Republican candidates promised before the election.

Rep. Dick Armey, R-Lewisville (left), and Tom DeLay, R-Sugar Land (right), led the Texas charge up Capitol HIll after the Nov. 1994 elections. Armey is the first Texas Republican to be elected majority leader, the second highest-ranking position in the U.S. House. DeLay assumed the post of majority whip, third-ranking party post in the House.

Republican control of Congress meant a whole new era of leadership for Texans in Washington. Rep. Tom DeLay of Sugar Land took over the third-ranking party post, House majority whip. Rep. Bill Archer, veteran member from Houston, became chairman of the powerful House Ways and Means Committee.

Also assuming House chairmanships: Larry Combest of Lubbock, Intelligence Committee; Joe Barton of Ennis, oversight and investigations subcommittee of the Goverment Reform Committee; Jack Fields of Houston, telecommunciations subcommittee of the Commerce Committee; and Lamar Smith of San Antonio, immigration subcommittee of the Judiciary Committee.

The anti-incumbent fervor of 1994 unexpectedly took out the longest-serving Texan in Washington, Rep. Jack Brooks, D-Beaumont. Ironically, Brooks was first elected in 1952, the year that Republicans last had control of Congress. Had he won a 22nd term, he would have become the most senior member of Congress.

As dean of the Texas delegation and chairman of the House Judiciary Committee, the cigar-chomping Brooks — a onetime protege of Speaker Rayburn and President Johnson — had become a fixture in the U.S. Congress. It was not a year for fixtures. The Republican party labelled Mr. Brooks the "poster child for term limits."

In an era of change, Mr. Brooks remained a New Deal-Great Society Democrat who worked to bring home the pork for his district.

His efforts to have a police academy funded in his district in the 1994 crime bill produced national outrage, while his support of the bill, which contained a ban on assault weapons, produced opposition at home from the National Rifle Association.

Republican Steve Stockman, an accountant from Friendswood in Galveston County, had twice run unsuccessfully against Brooks on the issue of term limits before winning the Southeast Texas 9th District.

With the defeat of a second Democratic incumbent in the 13th District, Rep. Bill Sarpalius of Amarillo by Amarillo lawyer William M. "Mac" Thornberry, Republicans owned a record 11 seats in the state's 30-member delegation. That number increased to 12 when Rep. Greg Laughlin of West Columbia switched from being Democrat to being Republican in June 1995. Laughlin represents the 14th Congressional District, which stretches from Austin to the Gulf Coast, and was first elected in 1988.

Democrats, however, continue to outnumber Republicans with 18 U.S. House seats largely because of an "incumbents' protection plan" in the last redistricting. After the 1990 census, the Texas Legislature agreed to create districts favorable to all incumbents, thus protecting the Democratic balance.

Two new Democrats won open seats in the 10th and 25th districts, respectively. Lloyd Doggett of Austin, a former state senator and Texas Supreme Court justice, succeeded Rep. J.J. (Jake) Pickle, who retired after 30 years in Congress.

Ken Bentsen of Houston, a nephew of former U.S. Sen. and Treasury Secretary Lloyd Bentsen, succeeded Rep. Michael Andrews, who tried unsuccessfully to move up to the U.S. Senate.

The other new face in the Texas delegation is Sheila Jackson Lee, who succeeded Craig Washington in Houston's 18th District after defeating him in the Democratic primary.

The change in the majority party cost two Texas Democrats their committee chairmanships.

Rep. Henry B. Gonzales of San Antonio was ousted as head of the House Banking Committee and Rep. Kika de la Garza of Mission was forced to give up the chairmanship of the House Agriculture Committee. — *Carolyn Barta* ☆

Governor's Race, General Election, 1994

Below are listed the county-by-county results of the general election held Nov. 8, 1994. The tabulations are the official canvass obtained from the office of the Texas Secretary of State. Republican George W. Bush defeated Democratic incumbent Ann W. Richards and Libertarian Keary Ehlers.

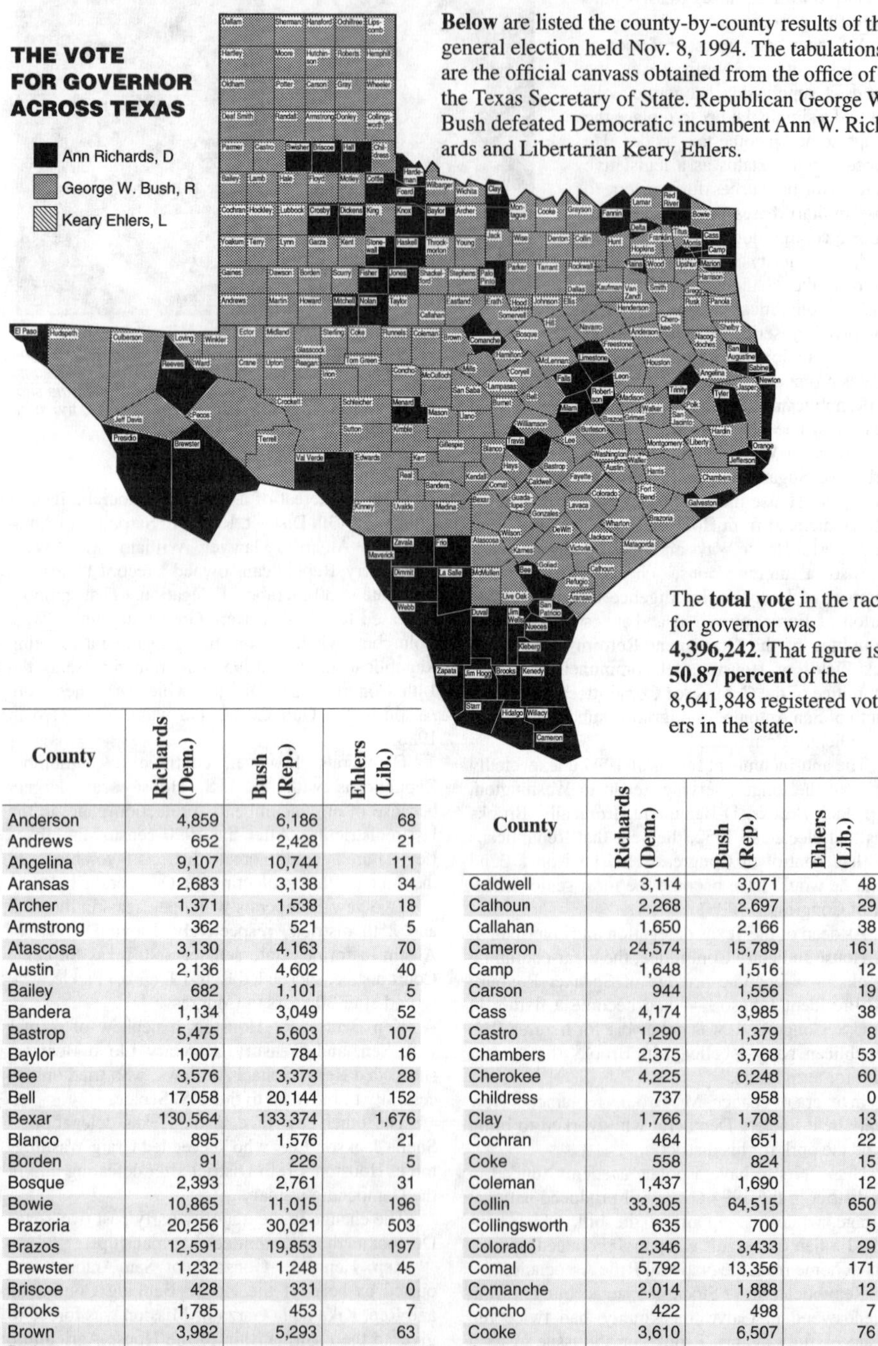

The **total vote** in the race for governor was **4,396,242**. That figure is **50.87 percent** of the 8,641,848 registered voters in the state.

County	Richards (Dem.)	Bush (Rep.)	Ehlers (Lib.)
Anderson	4,859	6,186	68
Andrews	652	2,428	21
Angelina	9,107	10,744	111
Aransas	2,683	3,138	34
Archer	1,371	1,538	18
Armstrong	362	521	5
Atascosa	3,130	4,163	70
Austin	2,136	4,602	40
Bailey	682	1,101	5
Bandera	1,134	3,049	52
Bastrop	5,475	5,603	107
Baylor	1,007	784	16
Bee	3,576	3,373	28
Bell	17,058	20,144	152
Bexar	130,564	133,374	1,676
Blanco	895	1,576	21
Borden	91	226	5
Bosque	2,393	2,761	31
Bowie	10,865	11,015	196
Brazoria	20,256	30,021	503
Brazos	12,591	19,853	197
Brewster	1,232	1,248	45
Briscoe	428	331	0
Brooks	1,785	453	7
Brown	3,982	5,293	63
Burleson	2,099	2,229	37
Burnet	3,608	4,906	67

County	Richards (Dem.)	Bush (Rep.)	Ehlers (Lib.)
Caldwell	3,114	3,071	48
Calhoun	2,268	2,697	29
Callahan	1,650	2,166	38
Cameron	24,574	15,789	161
Camp	1,648	1,516	12
Carson	944	1,556	19
Cass	4,174	3,985	38
Castro	1,290	1,379	8
Chambers	2,375	3,768	53
Cherokee	4,225	6,248	60
Childress	737	958	0
Clay	1,766	1,708	13
Cochran	464	651	22
Coke	558	824	15
Coleman	1,437	1,690	12
Collin	33,305	64,515	650
Collingsworth	635	700	5
Colorado	2,346	3,433	29
Comal	5,792	13,356	171
Comanche	2,014	1,888	12
Concho	422	498	7
Cooke	3,610	6,507	76
Coryell	3,955	4,981	77
Cottle	419	282	9

County	Richards (Dem.)	Bush (Rep.)	Ehlers (Lib.)
Crane	379	1,178	9
Crockett	543	798	8
Crosby	853	788	7
Culberson	214	295	4
Dallam	435	720	11
Dallas	221,266	236,466	2,827
Dawson	1,294	2,365	27
Deaf Smith	1,429	2,538	18
Delta	762	713	7
Denton	31,437	49,740	637
DeWitt	1,821	3,094	33
Dickens	581	454	7
Dimmit	1,772	719	13
Donley	573	871	4
Duval	2,809	595	9
Eastland	2,588	3,264	43
Ector	8,372	16,822	162
Edwards	242	542	9
Ellis	9,987	14,523	140
El Paso	50,560	40,011	938
Erath	3,467	4,423	53
Falls	2,013	1,887	14
Fannin	3,929	3,268	59
Fayette	2,722	4,297	52
Fisher	1,104	547	5
Floyd	1,334	1,558	8
Foard	347	187	2
Fort Bend	27,040	39,763	233
Franklin	1,243	1,389	12
Freestone	2,417	2,569	13
Frio	1,764	1,394	18
Gaines	670	2,061	24
Galveston	32,848	30,716	418
Garza	498	841	9
Gillespie	1,737	5,032	60
Glasscock	83	413	2
Goliad	888	1,202	18
Gonzales	2,001	2,765	23
Gray	2,752	5,550	74
Grayson	12,500	14,650	200
Gregg	11,593	19,357	166
Grimes	1,952	2,560	17
Guadalupe	6,509	11,304	196
Hale	2,879	4,991	42
Hall	655	602	1
Hamilton	1,163	1,464	18
Hansford	437	1,346	11
Hardeman	739	610	10
Hardin	4,723	6,671	98
Harris	290,118	348,507	3,337
Harrison	7.996	8,347	94
Hartley	481	973	11
Haskell	1,309	893	4
Hays	9,916	10,299	179
Hemphill	465	930	8
Henderson	9,007	10,579	130
Hidalgo	39,026	21,676	198
Hill	3,762	4,093	51
Hockley	1,845	3,545	36
Hood	4,987	6,668	88
Hopkins	3,708	4,197	40
Houston	3,028	3,549	55

County	Richards (Dem.)	Bush (Rep.)	Ehlers (Lib.)
Howard	3,279	4,860	51
Hudspeth	219	482	15
Hunt	7,897	10,075	125
Hutchinson	2,816	5,489	48
Irion	214	353	5
Jack	1,157	1,213	20
Jackson	1,392	2,245	7
Jasper	3,741	4,254	92
Jeff Davis	298	422	13
Jefferson	36,346	28,979	512
Jim Hogg	1,096	397	5
Jim Wells	5,436	2,904	24
Johnson	11,958	14,382	218
Jones	2,290	2,165	29
Karnes	1,895	2,429	25
Kaufman	6,639	8,094	141
Kendall	1,585	4,294	44
Kenedy	75	54	0
Kent	182	278	6
Kerr	3,728	9,621	159
Kimble	614	1,054	20
King	40	105	4
Kinney	606	755	6
Kleberg	4,674	3,300	35
Knox	829	619	2
Lamar	5,501	5,958	65
Lamb	1,536	2,125	6
Lampasas	1,678	2,412	26
La Salle	1,031	593	5
Lavaca	2,298	3,408	24
Lee	1,637	2,416	26
Leon	1,789	2,776	26
Liberty	5,893	7,466	117
Limestone	3,463	2,315	28
Lipscomb	447	818	8
Live Oak	1,158	1,887	24
Llano	2,456	3,966	64
Loving	30	67	2
Lubbock	20,827	35,550	287
Lynn	879	983	7
McCulloch	1,161	1,349	11
McLennan	24,818	25,282	272
McMullen	82	309	7
Madison	1,281	1,712	20
Marion	1,911	1,158	23
Martin	344	974	6
Mason	584	941	17
Matagorda	4,206	5,327	69
Maverick	3,650	1,853	44
Medina	3,073	5,189	65
Menard	529	445	10
Midland	7,621	23,346	218
Milam	3,339	2,812	36
Mills	801	858	5
Mitchell	1,155	950	8
Montague	2,530	2,832	50
Montgomery	17,828	40,151	332
Moore	1,340	2,974	31
Morris	2,288	1,628	19
Motley	160	396	3
Nacogdoches	5,433	8,771	79
Navarro	5,218	5,367	71

County	Richards (Dem.)	Bush (Rep.)	Ehlers (Lib.)
Newton	2,101	1,452	35
Nolan	2,061	2,048	37
Nueces	38,399	31,116	376
Ochiltree	654	2,070	16
Oldham	256	451	4
Orange	10,935	10,802	222
Palo Pinto	3,341	3,333	59
Panola	3,207	3,700	53
Parker	8,774	12,275	163
Parmer	794	1,736	7
Pecos	1,558	2,161	29
Polk	5,137	5,678	83
Potter	9,011	11,506	181
Presidio	626	471	15
Rains	1,312	1,287	19
Randall	10,654	20,754	196
Reagan	303	654	3
Real	353	863	9
Red River	2,021	1,965	15
Reeves	2,059	1,242	27
Refugio	1,011	1,181	11
Roberts	138	412	8
Robertson	2,655	1,806	10
Rockwall	3,399	7,114	78
Runnels	1,381	1,914	30
Rusk	4,222	7,434	73
Sabine	1,642	1,625	8
San Augustine	1,426	1,385	15
San Jacinto	2,749	2,796	41
San Patricio	7,049	6,716	74
San Saba	678	906	6
Schleicher	448	569	5
Scurry	1,885	3,180	80
Shackelford	472	738	7
Shelby	2,958	3,639	28
Sherman	327	801	10
Smith	15,489	28,172	233
Somervell	884	1,289	17
Starr	3,247	919	17
Stephens	1,306	1,933	24
Sterling	232	444	10
Stonewall	490	393	6
Sutton	345	632	2
Swisher	1,337	934	6
Tarrant	155,872	180,194	2,139
Taylor	12,600	18,922	235
Terrell	199	207	7
Terry	1,200	1,787	9
Throckmorton	373	396	8
Titus	3,012	3,415	44
Tom Green	10,594	14,642	189
Travis	123,895	85,812	1,642
Trinity	2,497	2,229	33
Tyler	2,549	2,536	37
Upshur	4,469	5,348	96
Upton	310	917	14
Uvalde	2,592	3,876	70
Val Verde	3,472	3,361	53
Van Zandt	5,252	7,374	106
Victoria	6,581	11,397	136
Walker	5,212	6,525	69
Waller	2,975	3,334	33
Ward	1,102	1,979	28
Washington	3,346	6,137	35
Webb	12,475	4,505	76
Wharton	4,160	5,625	52
Wheeler	821	1,298	15
Wichita	15,532	16,008	255
Wilbarger	1,749	2,067	16
Willacy	2,148	1,250	17
Williamson	20,674	28,499	388
Wilson	3,670	4,520	72
Winkler	706	1,375	14
Wise	4,525	5,525	80
Wood	3,772	5,973	70
Yoakum	465	1,600	21
Young	2,624	3,371	36
Zapata	1,934	773	7
Zavala	1,949	539	14
Total	**2,016,928**	**2,350,994**	**28,320**

Source: General Election Returns/County-by-County Totals Report," Jan. 23, 1995, Governor, from the Office of the Texas Secretary of State, Austin.

General Election, 1994

Below are given results of the general election held Nov. 8, 1994, for all statewide races and for contested congressional, state senate, courts of appeals and state board of education races. (*Winners are shaded.*)

U.S. Senator

Richard Fisher (Dem.) . . . 1,639,615
Kay Bailey Hutchison (Rep.) 2,604,218
Pierre Blondeau (Lib.) . . . 36,107
Total vote 4,279,940

Governor

Ann W. Richards (Dem.) . 2,016,928
George W. Bush (Rep.) . . 2,350,994
K. Ehlers (Lib.) 28,320
Total vote 4,396,242

Lieutenant Governor

Bob Bullock (Dem.) 2,629,497
Tex Lezar (Rep.) 1,648,005
Total vote 4,277,502

Attorney General

Dan Morales (Dem.) 2,289,389
Don Wittig (Rep.) 1,850,403
Vicki Flores (Lib.) 123,369
Total vote 4,263,161

Comptroller of Public Accounts

John Sharp (Dem.) 2,318,345
Teresa Doggett (Rep.) . . . 1,860,270
Total vote 4,178,615

State Treasurer

Martha Whitehead (Dem.) 2,085,274
David Hartman (Rep.) . . . 2,060,707
Total vote 4,145,981

Comm. of General Land Office

Garry Mauro (Dem.) 2,089,279
Marta Greytok (Rep.) 1,964,931
David C. Chow (Lib.) 108,230
Total vote 4,162,440

Commissioner of Agriculture

Marvin Gregory (Dem.) . . . 1,479,692
Rick Perry (Rep.) 2,546,287
Clyde L. Garland (Lib.) . . . 85,836
Total vote 4,111,815

Railroad Commissioner

James E. (Jim) Nugent (Dem.) 1,978,759
Charles R. Matthews (Rep.) 2,046,614
Rick Draheim (Lib.) 84,769
Total vote 4,110,142

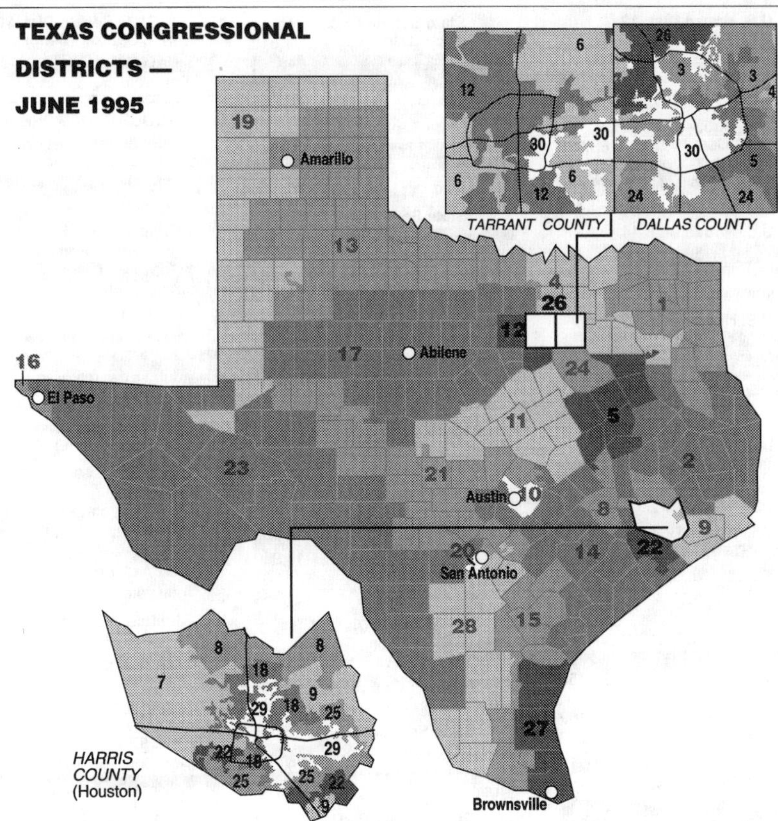

Railroad Commissioner, Unexpired term

Mary Scott Nabers (Dem.)	1,841,349
Carole Keeton Rylander (Rep.)	2,133,752
Buster Crabb (Lib.)	129,380
Total vote	4,104,481

Justice, Supreme Court, Place 1

Raul A. Gonzalez (Dem.)	2,573,534
John B. Hawley (Lib.)	591,252
Total vote	3,164,786

Justice, Supreme Court, Place 2

Alice Oliver Parrott (Dem).	1,791,823
Nathan L. Hecht (Rep.)	2,298,116
Total vote	4,089,939

Justice, Supreme Court, Place 3

Jimmy Carroll (Dem.)	1,747,958
Priscilla Owen (Rep.)	2,294,170
Total vote	4,042,128

Judge, Ct. of Crim. Appeals, Pl. 1

Charles F. Campbell (Dem.)	1,811,399
Steve Mansfield (Rep.)	2,122,407
Total vote	3,933,806

Judge, Ct. of Crim. Appeals, Pl. 2

Betty Marshall (Dem.)	1,792,047
Sharon Keller (Rep.)	2,143,356
Total vote	3,935,403

CONGRESS

U.S. House Dist. 1

Jim Chapman (Dem.)	86,480
Mike Blankenship (Rep.)	63,911
Thomas "Jefferson" Mosser (Ind.)	6,001
Total vote	156,392

U.S. House Dist. 2

Charles Wilson (Dem.)	87,709
Donna Peterson (Rep.)	66,071
Total vote	153,780

U.S. House Dist. 3

Sam Johnson (Rep.)	157,011
Tom Donahue (Lib.)	15,611
Total vote	172,622

U.S. House Dist. 4

Ralph M. Hall (Dem.)	99,303
David L. Bridges (Rep.)	67,267
Steven Rothacker (Lib.)	2,377
Total vote	168,947

U.S. House Dist. 5

John Bryant (Dem.)	61,877
Pete Sessions (Rep.)	58,521
Noel Kopala (Lib.)	876
Regina Arashvand (Ind.)	627
Barbara Morgan (Ind.)	1,715
Total vote	123,616

U.S. House Dist. 6

Terry Jesmore (Dem.)	44,286
Joe Barton (Rep.)	152,038
Bill Baird (Lib.)	4,688
Total vote	201,012

U.S. House Dist. 8

Jack Fields (Rep.)	148,473
Russ Klecka (Ind.)	12,831
Total vote	161,304

U.S. House Dist. 9

Jack Brooks (Dem.)	71,643
Steve Stockman (Rep.)	81,353
Darla K. Beenau (Lib.)	1,656
Bill Felton (Ind.)	2,145
Total vote	156,797

U.S. House Dist. 10

Lloyd Doggett (Dem.)	113,738
Jo Baylor (Rep.)	80,382
Jeff Hill (Lib.)	2,953
Michael L. Brandes (Ind.)	2,579
Jeff Davis (Ind.)	2,334
Total vote	201,986

U.S. House Dist. 11

Chet Edwards (Dem.)	76,667
Jim Broyles (Rep.)	52,876
Total vote	129,543

U.S. House Dist. 12

Candidate	Votes
Pete Geren (Dem.)	96,372
Ernest J. Anderson Jr. (Rep.)	43,959
Total vote	140,331

U.S. House Dist. 13

Candidate	Votes
Bill Sarpalius (Dem.)	63,923
William M. (Mac) Thornberry (Rep.)	79,466
Total vote	143,389

U.S. House Dist. 14

Candidate	Votes
Greg Laughlin (Dem.)	86,175
Jim Deats (Rep.)	68,793
Total vote	154,968

U.S. House Dist. 15

Candidate	Votes
E (Kika) de la Garza (Dem.)	61,527
Tom Haughey (Rep.)	41,119
John C.C. Hamilton (Ind.)	1,720
Total vote	104,366

U.S. House Dist. 16

Candidate	Votes
Ronald Coleman (Dem.)	49,815
Bobby Ortiz (Rep.)	37,409
Total vote	87,224

U.S. House Dist. 17

Candidate	Votes
Charles W. Stenholm (Dem.)	83,497
Phil Boone (Rep.)	72,108
Total vote	155,605

U.S. House Dist. 18

Candidate	Votes
Sheila Jackson Lee(Dem.)	84,790
Jerry Burley (Rep.)	28,153
George M. Hollenbeck (Lib.)	1,169
J. Larry Snellings (Ind.)	1,278
Total vote	115,390

U.S. House Dist. 20

Candidate	Votes
Henry B. Gonzalez (Dem.)	60,114
Carl Bill Colyer (Rep.)	36,035
Total vote	96,149

U.S. House Dist. 21

Candidate	Votes
Lamar Smith (Rep.)	165,595
Kerry L. Lowry (Ind.)	18,480
Total vote	184,075

U.S. House Dist. 22

Candidate	Votes
Scott Douglas Cunningham (Dem.)	38,826
Tom DeLay (Rep.)	120,302
Gregory D. Pepper (Ind.)	4,016
Total vote	163,144

U.S. House Dist. 23

Candidate	Votes
Rolando L. Rios (Dem.)	44,101
Henry Bonilla (Rep.)	73,815
Total vote	117,916

LEGISLATURE

State Senate Dist. 1

Candidate	Votes
George Lavender (Dem.)	55,616
Bill Ratliff (Rep.)	101,207
Total vote	156,823

State Senate Dist. 2

Candidate	Votes
David Cain (Dem.)	61,757
Richard Harvey (Rep.)	60,317
Total vote	122,074

State Senate Dist. 3

Candidate	Votes
Curtis Soileau (Dem.)	76,245
Drew Nixon (Rep.)	83,779
Total vote	160,024

State Senate Dist. 4

Candidate	Votes
Carl A. Parker (Dem.)	71,012
Michael L. Galloway (Rep.)	79,252
Total vote	150,264

State Senate Dist. 5

Candidate	Votes
Jim Turner (Dem.)	82,541
Jerry T. Thornton	64,875
Total vote	147,416

State Senate Dist. 8

Candidate	Votes
Florence Shapiro (Rep.)	156,014
John Wawro (Lib.)	7,642
Paul Bertanzetti (Ind.)	9,247
Total vote	172,903

State Senate Dist. 11

Candidate	Votes
Mike Martin (Dem.)	59,047
Jerry Patterson (Rep.)	73,959
Total vote	133,006

State Senate Dist. 14

Candidate	Votes
Gonzalo Barrientos (Dem.)	135,979
Gary Johnson (Lib.)	27,820
Total vote	163,799

State Senate Dist. 16

Candidate	Votes
John N. Leedom (Rep.)	108,229
Randal Morgan (Lib.)	15,959
Henry Gail Norrid (Wri.)	67
Total vote	124,255

State Senate Dist. 17

Candidate	Votes
Ronnie Ellen Harrison (Dem.)	44,465
J.E. (Buster) Brown (Rep.)	117,727
Total vote	162,192

State Senate Dist. 20

Candidate	Votes
Carlos F. Truan (Dem.)	67,066
Rex Moses (Rep.)	47,686
Total vote	114,752

State Senate Dist. 21

Candidate	Votes
Judith Zaffirini (Dem.)	71,029
Fernando Cantu (Rep.)	32,624
Total vote	103,653

State Senate Dist. 22

Candidate	Votes
Margaret Ross Messina (Dem.)	58,544
David Sibley (Rep.)	83,064
Total vote	141,608

State Senate Dist. 24

Candidate	Votes
Bill Sims (Dem.)	67,536
Hugh D. Shine (Rep.)	59,048
Total vote	126,584

State Senate Dist. 25

Candidate	Votes
Jim Saunders (Dem.)	53,152
Jeff Wentworth (Rep.)	159,729
Total vote	212,881

State Senate Dist. 26

Candidate	Votes
Gregory Luna (Dem.)	55,799
Andrew Longaker (Rep.)	32,375
Total vote	88,174

State Senate Dist. 27

Candidate	Votes
Eddie Lucio Jr. (Dem.)	53,194
Ismael Moran (Rep.)	26,527
Total vote	79,721

State Senate Dist. 28

Candidate	Votes
John T. Montford (Dem.)	78,676
Val Varley (Rep.)	43,854
Total vote	122,530

State Senate Dist. 30

Candidate	Votes
Steven A. Carriker (Dem.)	73,964
Tom Haywood (Rep.)	77,626
Total vote	151,950

COURTS OF APPEALS

Chief Justice, Second Dist.

Candidate	Votes
John Hill (Dem.)	219,233
John Cayce (Rep.)	260,494
Total vote	479,727

Chief Justice, Fourth Dist. unexpired term

Candidate	Votes
Alfonso Chapa (Dem.)	194,026
Rob Kelly (Rep.)	187,467
Total vote	381,493

Chief Justice, Eleventh Dist.

Candidate	Votes
Bud Arnot (Dem.)	55,940
Billy John Edwards (Rep.)	51,013
Total vote	106,953

Justice, First Dist., Pl. 1

Candidate	Votes
Helen Cassidy (Dem.)	363,557
Tim Taft (Rep.)	446,056
Total vote	809,613

Justice, First Dist., Pl. 3

Candidate	Votes
Michol Mary O'Connor (Dem.)	422,763
Mamie Proctor (Rep.)	408,704
Total vote	831,467

Justice, Second Dist., Pl. 5

Candidate	Votes
David Farris (Dem.)	194,692
David Richards (Rep.)	276,308
Total vote	471,000

Justice, Second Dist., Pl. 6

Candidate	Votes
Maryellen Whitlock Hicks (Dem.)	197,275
LeeAnn Campbell Dauphinot (Rep.)	281,491
Total vote	478,766

Justice, Second Dist. Pl. 7 Unexpired Term

Candidate	Votes
Sidney Farrar (Dem.)	191,600
Terrie Livingston ((Rep.)	279,224
Total vote	470,824

Justice, Fourth Dist. Pl. 1

Candidate	Votes
Herman Segovia (Dem.)	168,581
Sarah Duncan (Rep.)	209,886
Total vote	378,467

Justice, Fourth Dist. Pl. 2

Candidate	Votes
Alma L. Lopez (Dem.)	196,229
Jerry Dennard (Rep.)	181,863
Total vote	378,092

Justice, Fourth Dist. Pl. 3

Candidate	Votes
Monroe Spears (Dem.)	188,484
Paul W. Green (Rep.)	193,692
Total vote	382,176

Justice, Fourth Dist. Pl. 4

Candidate	Votes
Catherine Stone (Dem.)	210,379
Diego J. Pena (Rep.)	166,412
Total vote	376,791

Justice, Fourth Dist. Pl. 5

Candidate	Votes
Phil Hardberger (Dem.)	232,739
Dan Diaz (Rep.)	153,713
Total vote	386,452

Justice, Fifth Dist., Pl. 4

Candidate	Votes
Charles McGarry (Dem.)	239,973
Tom James (Rep.)	332,195
Total vote	572,168

1,285,220 sq km

259

im@att.net>
00
owney@ghg.net>
000

stuff, we are sooo eclectic!! Well I will start with dden"things in my house!

at are in Sonlight 6,7,8, and 9th. If you want the
g if your weren't looking for any books
g in the Flow of History) A COMPREHENSIVE
is by Cornerstone Curriculum (David Quine)- This
uotes directly from Mason, Susan Shchafer
s this curriculums' primary focus and intention.
this is the study guide ONLY- not the artwork or
s included for all 3 galleries in this one volume. You
(which was out of our budget) or collect the
bought th

Justice, Fifth Dist., Pl. 6

Barbara Rosenberg (Dem.)	268,080
Joseph A. (Joe) Devany (Rep.)	313,823
Total vote	581,903

Justice, Seventh Dist., Pl.2

H. Bryan Poff Jr. (Dem.)	91,705
Brian Quinn (Rep.)	102,033
Total vote	193,738

Justice, Eighth Dist., Pl. 1

David Wellington Chew (Dem.)	87,979
Julia E. Vaughan (Rep.)	80,375
Total vote	168,354

Justice, Twelfth Dist.

Deborah J. Race (Dem.)	102,651
Roby Hadden (Rep.)	104,909
Total vote	207,560

Justice, Fourteenth Dist., Pl. 1

Bob Moore (Dem.)	368,686
Harvey Hudson (Rep.)	447,486
Total vote	816,172

Justice, Fourteenth Dist., Pl. 2

Ross Sears (Dem.)	357,023
Wanda McKee Fowler (Rep.)	462,500
Total vote	819,523

Justice, Fourteenth Dist., Pl.3

George Ellis (Dem.)	354,124
Richard Edelman (Rep.)	493,492
Total vote	847,616

Justice, Fourteenth Dist., Pl.4

Joe. L. Draughn (Dem.)	392,068
Maurice Amidei (Rep.)	412,672
Total vote	804,740

Justice, Fourteenth Dist., Pl. 5

Ed Cogburn (Dem.)	357,594
John S. Anderson (Rep.)	458,435
Total vote	816,029

Justice, Fourteenth Dist., Pl. 6
Unexpired term

Patrice Barron (Dem.)	345,049
Leslie Ann Brock (Rep.)	472,389
Total vote	817,438

STATE BOARD OF EDUCATION

District 1

Rene Nunez (Dem.)	93,669
Mary Helen Cantu (Rep.)	84,368
Total vote	178,037

District 2

Mary Helen Berlanga (Dem.)	119,464
Juan Vega (Rep.)	81,033
Total vote	200,497

District 8

Mary Knotts Perkins (Dem.)	122,243
Donna Ballard (Rep.)	181,083
Total vote	303,326

1994 Party Primaries

Below are the official returns for contested races only in the Republican and Democratic Party primaries held March 8, 1994. Included are statewide races and selected district races.

Democratic Primary

U.S. Senator

Michael A. Andrews	159,793
Richard Fisher	388,090
Evelyn K. Lantz	63,523
Jim Mattox	416,503
Total Vote	1,027,909

Governor

Gary Espinosa	230,337
Ann W. Richards	806,607
Total Vote	1,036,944

State Treasurer

Martha Whitehead	607,261
Grady Yarborough	310,688
Total Vote	917,949

Railroad Commissioner

Robert Earley	345,603
James E. (Jim) Nugent	572,893
Total Vote	918,496

Railroad Commissioner (unexpired term)

Mary Scott Nabers	519,407
David Young	366,654
Total Vote	886,061

Justice, Supreme Court, Place 1

Raul A. Gonzalez	419,464
Rene Haas	343,015
Bill Yarborough	230,973
Total Vote	993,452

Justice, Supreme Court, Place 2

Alice Oliver Parrott	525,167
Mike Westergren	317,700
Total Vote	842,867

Justice, Supreme Court, Place 3

Jimmy Carroll	446,355
Margaret G. Mirabal	391,071
Total Vote	837,426

Presiding Judge, Court of Criminal Appeals

Charles F. (Charlie) Baird	375,211
Mike McCormick	450,243
Total Vote	825,454

Judge, Court of Criminal Appeals, Place 2

Gene Kelly	189,140
Norman Lanford	119,674
Betty Marshall	271,469
Frances M. (Poppy) Northcutt	157,355
Bennie Ray	73,466
Total Vote	811,104

U.S. HOUSE OF REPRESENTATIVES

District 2

Edgar J. (Bubba) Groce	26,635
Charles Wilson	55,676
Total Vote	82,311

District 4

Doug Dudley	7,250
Ralph M. Hall	27,081
Total Vote	34,331

District 9

Jack Brooks	37,648
Geraldine Sam	15,340
Total Vote	52,988

District 10

Lloyd Doggett	33,682
John Longsworth	7,130
Total Vote	40,812

District 15

E (Kika) de la Garza	40,513
Rigo Martinez	8,998
Eli Ochoa	17,481
Total Vote	66,992

District 16

Ronald Coleman	20,990
Mike Crowley	12,871
Total Vote	33,861

District 18

Sheila Jackson Lee	26,672
Craig A. Washington	15,381
Total Vote	42,053

District 22

Philip Butcher	4,576
Scott Douglas Cunningham	7,978
Total Vote	12,554

District 25

Ken Bentsen	6,778
Beverley Clark	9,614
Paul Colbert	5,914
Joel F. Dejean	266
Carrin Patman	3,373
Total Vote	25,945

District 26

LeEarl Ann Bryant . . . 3,674
Jerry L. Coker . . . 2,464
Total Vote . . . 6,138

District 29

Gene Green . . . 16,934
Ben T. Reyes . . . 13,795
Total Vote . . . 30,729

STATE SENATE

District 1

VaLinda Hathcox . . . 21,743
George Lavender . . . 29,533
Total Vote . . . 51,276

District 6

Yolanda Navarro Flores . . . 4,936
Mario V. Gallegos Jr. . . . 5,990
Roman O. Martinez . . . 9,026
David Thomas McCullough . . . 3,857
Total Vote . . . 23,809

District 27

Eddie Lucio Jr. . . . 33,467
Miguel Wise . . . 13,964
Total Vote . . . 47,431

COURTS OF APPEALS

Chief Justice, Eleventh District

Bud Arnot . . . 23,150
David Stubbeman . . . 12,046
Total Vote . . . 35,196

Justice, First District, Place 1

David Beale . . . 21,034
Gerry Birnberg . . . 23,229
Helen Cassidy . . . 56,665
Jack Lee . . . 33,239
Total Vote . . . 134,167

Justice, Fourth District, Place 1

Pat Priest . . . 49,326
Herman Segovia . . . 49,676
Total Vote . . . 99,002

Justice, Eighth District, Place 1

David Wellington Chew . . . 20,916
Michael R. Gibson . . . 11,846
Luis Cesar Labrado . . . 7,468
Miguel (Mickey) Solis . . . 14,540
Total Vote . . . 54.770

Justice, Eighth District, Place 2

Ann McClure . . . 20,421
Paul McCollum . . . 14,119
Alfonso L. Melendez . . . 21,047
Total Vote . . . 55,587

Justice, Ninth District

Jack Brookshire . . . 36,769
Earl (Smokey) Stover . . . 40,143
Total Vote . . . 76,912

Justice, Twelfth District

Ken Barron . . . 21,416
Daniel Boone Childs . . . 15,717
Deborah J. Race . . . 26,053
Total Vote . . . 63,186

Justice, Thirteenth District, Place 1

Don Allee . . . 48,638
Nelda Vidaurri Rodriguez . . . 63,825
Total Vote . . . 112,463

Justice, Thirteenth District, Place 2

Melchor Chavez . . . 60,209
Tom Matlock . . . 56,613
Total Vote . . . 116,822

Justice, Fourteenth District, Place 1

Henry E. Allee . . . 28,267
Ben G. Levy . . . 45,231
Bob Moore . . . 58,122
Total Vote . . . 131,620

Justice, Fourteenth District, Place 6

Patrice Barron . . . 57,591
Henry L. Burkholder III . . . 30,462
Carl Dudensing . . . 42,539
Total Vote . . . 130,592

STATE BOARD OF EDUCATION

District 13

Robert H. Hester . . . 9,082
Eula Jones . . . 7,053
Rosie Collins Sorrells . . . 9,417
Total Vote . . . 25,552

DEMOCRATIC RUNOFF

Below are listed the results of the Democratic primary runoff election held April 12, 1994.

U.S. Senator

Richard Fisher . . . 400,227
Jim Mattox . . . 346,414
Total Vote . . . 746,641

Justice, Supreme Court, Place 1

Raul A. Gonzalez . . . 393,656
Rene Haas . . . 335,635
Total Vote . . . 729,291

Judge, Court of Criminal Appeals, Place 2

Gene Kelly . . . 252,299
Betty Marshall . . . 378,830
Total Vote . . . 631,129

U.S. Representative, Dist. 25

Ken Bentsen . . . 11,812
Beverley Clark . . . 6,684
Total Vote . . . 18,496

State Senator, Dist. 6

Mario V. Gallegos Jr. . . . 9,613
Roman O. Martinez . . . 7,193
Total Vote . . . 16,806

State Board of Education, Dist. 13

Robert H. Hester . . . 9,586
Rosie Collins Sorrells . . . 16,200
Total Vote . . . 25,786

Courts of Appeals

Justice, First District, Place 1

Helen Cassidy . . . 57,601
Jack Lee . . . 38,743
Total Vote . . . 96,344

Justice, Eighth District, Place 1

David Wellington Chew . . . 25,234
Miguel (Mickey) Solis . . . 17,297
Total Vote . . . 42,531

Justice, Eighth District, Place 2

Ann McClure . . . 22,475
Alfonso L. Melendez . . . 19,980
Total Vote . . . 42,455

Justice, Twelfth District

Ken Barron . . . 25,473
Deborah J. Race . . . 27,221
Total Vote . . . 52,694

Justice, Fourteenth District, Place 1

Ben G. Levy . . . 36,958
Bob Moore . . . 57,911
Total Vote . . . 94,869

Justice, Fourteenth District, Place 6 (unexpired term)

Patrice Barron . . . 49,455
Carl Dudensing . . . 48,196
Total Vote . . . 97,651

Republican Primary

U.S. Senator

James C. Curry . . . 15,625
Roger Henson . . . 14,021
Stephen Hopkins . . . 34,703
Kay Bailey Hutchison . . . 467,975
M. Troy Mata . . . 8,632
Ernest J. Schmidt . . . 8,690
Tom Spink . . . 5,692
Total Vote . . . 555,338

Governor

George W. Bush 520,130
Ray Hollis 37,210
Total Vote 557,340

Attorney General

Antonio O. "Tony" Garza Jr. 87,042
Patricia (Pat) Lykos 145,922
John Marshall 123,618
Don Wittig 141,488
Total Vote 498,070

State Treasurer

David Hartman 336,456
Mike Wolfe 111,261
Total Vote 447,717

Justice, Supreme Court, Place 1

George Busch 187,162
Oliver S. Kitzman 252,010
Total Vote 439,172

Justice, Supreme Court, Place 2

Nathan L. Hecht 277,522
Charles Ben Howell 177,563
Total Vote 455,085

Judge, Court of Criminal Appeals, Place 1

John S. Cossum 132,864
Steve Mansfield 270,980
Total Vote 403,844

Judge, Court of Criminal Appeals, Place 2

Sam Bayless 161,498
Cathy Cochran Herasimchuk 109,897
Sharon Keller 160,266
Total Vote 431,661

U.S. HOUSE OF REPRESENTATIVES

District 1

Mike Blankenship 6,301
Dennis Boerner 3,353
Total Vote 9,654

District 2

Donna Peterson 5,335
John E. Thomas 2,567
Total Vote 7,902

District 3

David Corley 2,063
Sam Johnson 29,546
Dave Schum 1,680
Total Vote 33,289

District 4

David L. Bridges 13,250
Tim McCord 6,534
Total Vote 19,784

District 5

Pete Sessions 5,786
Richard Stokley 4,478
Total Vote 10,264

District 6

Joe Barton 23,063
Jerry Goode 2,707
Total Vote 25,770

District 9

John LeCour 2,468
James C. Milburn 802
Steve Stockman 8,644
Total Vote 11,914

District 10

A. Jo Baylor 7,945
Bryce Goodman 5,747
Herbert Spiro 2,255
Total Vote 15,947

District 13

Wayne Collins 2,147
Flavious Smith 1,714
William M. (Mac) Thornberry 11,568
Total Vote 15,429

District 14

Ed Baker 5,048
Jim Deats 6,880
Total Vote 11,928

District 15

Bonnie Abbott 1,563
Tom Haughey 3,397
Lister H. Reeves Jr. 1,579
Total Vote 6,539

District 16

Dick Bowen 3,069
Rick Ledesma 2,895
Bobby Ortiz 3,055
Total Vote 9,019

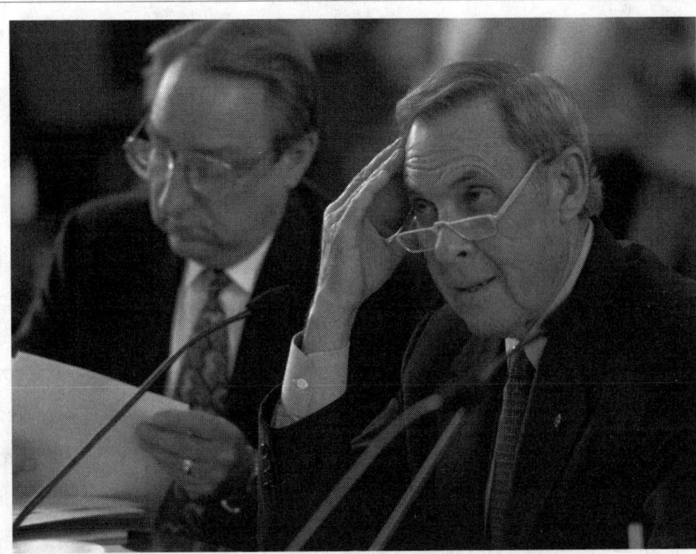

Democratic Lt. Gov. Bob Bullock, at right, was the state's top voter-getter in the 1994 general election despite the Republican tide. He and Speaker of the House Pete Laney, left, preside in the Legislature, which is controlled by the Democrats. The Dallas Morning News photo.

District 17

Phil Boone . . . 10,631
Roy Emerson Falls . . . 1,336
Don Schmidt Jr. . . . 2,977
Total Vote . . . 14,944

District 21

Scott Campbell . . . 10,050
Lamar Smith . . . 44,600
Total Vote . . . 54,650

District 24

Ed Harrison . . . 7,301
Ken Scarborough . . . 3,243
Total Vote . . . 10,544

District 25

Gene Fontenot . . . 8,726
Dolly Madison McKenna . . . 6,866
Total Vote . . . 15,592

STATE SENATE

District 2

Roland Cordobes . . . 3,312
Richard Harvey . . . 7,962
Total Vote . . . 11,274

District 4

Jim Alexander . . . 6,862
Michael L. Galloway . . . 6,932
Total Vote . . . 13,794

District 25

Van Archer . . . 21,341
Jeff Wentworth . . . 32,473
Total Vote . . . 53,814

District 30

Tom Haywood . . . 9,284
Doyle High . . . 4,868
Total Vote . . . 14,152

COURTS OF APPEALS

Justice, First District, Place 1

Tim Taft . . . 57,611
Stephen Touchy . . . 46,000
Total Vote . . . 103,611

Justice, Second District, Place 5

David Richards . . . 29,469
Wayne F. Salvant . . . 9,541
Total Vote . . . 39,010

Justice, Second District, Place 6

LeeAnn Campbell Dauphinot . . . 22,122
Charles Thorn . . . 21,703
Total Vote . . . 43,825

Justice, Fifth District, Place 6

Joseph A. (Joe) Devany . . . 27,830
John Crowder Hendrik . . . 26,455
Total Vote . . . 54,285

Justice, Fourteenth District, Place 2

Wanda McKee Fowler . . . 57,167
Gary A. Hinchman . . . 46,737
Total Vote . . . 103,904

Justice, Fourteenth District, Place 3

Richard Edelman . . . 41,610
Michael Landrum . . . 41,565
Frank Waltermire . . . 16,864
Total Vote . . . 100,039

STATE BOARD OF EDUCATION

District 9

Charles Cadenhead . . . 6,251
Randy Stevenson . . . 17,923
Total Vote . . . 24,174

District 14

Leland Dysart . . . 5,505
Richard Watson . . . 16,171
Total Vote . . . 21,676

REPUBLICAN RUNOFF

Below are listed the results of the Republican primary runoff election held April 12, 1994.

Attorney General

Patricia (Pat) Lykos . . . 91,045
Don Wittig . . . 110,394
Total Vote . . . 201,439

Judge, Court of Criminal Appeals, Place 2

Sam Bayless . . . 78,337
Sharon Keller . . . 105,570
Total Vote . . . 183,907

Justice, 14th Court of Appeals Dist. Place 3

Richard Edelman . . . 31,450
Michael Landrum . . . 30,282
Total Vote . . . 61,732

U.S. Representative, Dist. 10

A. Jo Baylor . . . 5,545
Bryce Goodman . . . 1,669
Total Vote . . . 7,214

U.S. Representative, Dist. 16

Dick Bowen . . . 1,846
Bobby Ortiz . . . 3,402
Total Vote . . . 5,248

Political Party Organizations

Democratic State Executive Committee

Chairman, Bob Slagle, Box 1244, Sherman 75091; **Vice Chair**, Lydia Torres, 2002 Country Club, Midland 79701; **Vice Chairman for Financial Affairs**, Nancy Brannon, 301 E. Scott, Gainesville 76240; **Secretary**, Walter Hinojosa, 7801 Lowdes Dr., Austin 78745; **Treasurer**, Willie Belle Boone, 9211 Dulcimer, Houston 77051; **Counsel**, Harold Hammett, 303 W. 10th St., #300, Fort Worth 76102; **Co-parliamentarians**, Ed Cogburn, 5002 Doliver, Houston 77056, and Frank Thompson, 6937 Payton, Houston 77028. **Office Address:** 815 Brazos, Ste. 200, Austin 78701.

National Committee Members: Al Edwards, Houston; Billie Carr, Houston; Hazel Obey, Austin; Adelfa Callejo, Dallas; Ed Miller, Texarkana; Domingo Garcia, Dallas; Rosa Walker, Austin; K. T. McLeaish, Odessa; William Leo, La Joya; Harold Bob Bennett, Hart.

District — Member and Hometown

1. Lynda Phillips, Gilmer; Leonard Rickwell, Mount Pleasant.
2. Martha Williams, Terrell; Ken Molberg, Dallas.
3. Kathleen Hawkins, Buna; Curt Goetz, San Augustine.
4. Irmalyn Thomas, Beaumont; Guy Jackson, Anahuac.
5. Annie Laura Day, Brookshire; Jim Carter, Huntsville.
6. Pat Gandy, Houston; Frumencio Reyes, Houston.
7. Mary C. Burke, Houston; Stephen Marak, Houston.
8. Linda Ashton-Smith, Plano; Barry Sprouse, Irving.
9. Lisa Payne, Duncanville; Ron Spurlock, Lewisville.
10. Lee Bowden, Arlington; Donald Winters, Fort Worth.
11. Grace Edwards, Friendswood; Daniel Snooks, Houston.
12. Roy Laverne Brooks, Fort Worth; Grover Swift,

Fort Worth.

13. Sue Lovell; Raphus Foley, Houston.

14. Eliza May, Austin; Jeff Heckler, Austin.

15. Roberta Bilsky, Houston; William Rice, Houston.

16. Terri Hodge, Dallas; Jay Newman, Dallas.

17. Alma Nolen, Pearland; Michael Laster, Houston.

18. Diana Rhodes, Nursery; Marion Garcia, Thompsons.

19. Jo McCall, San Antonio;p Gary Woitena, San Antonio.

20. Susan Pizana, Corpus Christi; Martin Garcia, Corpus Christi.

21. Minnie Dora Bunn Haynes, Laredo; Rene A. Trevino, Carrizo Springs.

22. Teresa Smith, Cleburne; John Cullar, Waco.

23. Dorothy Dean, Dallas; Gary Fitzsimmons, Dallas.

24. Aliceanne Wallace, Belton; Eddie Shell, Marble Falls.

25. Cathryn Bell, San Antonio; Raul C. Garcia, San Angelo.

26. Lucinda Rodriguez, San Antonio; Darby Riley, San Antonio.

27. Mary Lou Campbell, South Padre Island; Mike Sinder, McAllen.

28. Betty Condra, Lubbock; Mike Holmes, Odessa.

29. Angie Barajas, El Paso; Jose Raul Kennard, El Paso.

30. Dorthy Wise, Wichita Falls; Calvin Gambill, Seymour.

31. Linda Lowrey, Plains; Milton McNeely, Amarillo.

Young Democrats: Christina Delgadillo, Austin; David Holmes, Austin.

County Chairmen's Association: Ted Lewis, Denton; Maxine Molberg, Fredericksburg.

Republican State Executive Committee

Office Address: 211 E. 7th, #620, Austin 78701. **Chairman,** Tom Pauken, 4403 N. Central Expressway, Dallas 75202; **Vice Chairman,** Mrs. Susan Weddington, 217 Halbart Dr., San Antonio 78213; **Secretary,** Mrs. Barbara Jackson, 1412 North 18th St., Nederland 77627; **Treasurer,** Martha Weisend, 6031 Highplace Circle, Dallas 75240; **General Counsel,** William Elliott, 901 Main St., Ste. 4000, Dallas 75202; **Finance Chairman,** Roy Bailey, 655 Preston Commons East, 8115 Preston, Dallas 75225; **Parliamentarian**, Robert X. Johnson, 11220 Perrin Beitel, San Antonio 78217.

National Committeeman, Ernest Angelo Jr., 410 N. Main, Midland 79701; **National Committeewoman,** Mrs. Penny Butler, 11 E. Briar Hollow Lane, Houston 77056.

District — Member and Hometown

1. Joyce Hugman, Gladewater; Don Kent, Tyler.

2. Shirley McSpedden, Kemp; John T. Tello, Dallas.

3. Linda Newton, Jacksonville; Coleman G. Carter, Livingston.

4. Barbara Jackson, Nederland; Ralph K. Harrison, The Woodlands.

5. Clara L. Sandstedt, College Station; Barnie O. Henderson Jr., Cameron.

6. Ann Makris, Houston; Doug Johnson, Houston.

7. Susan R. Feldtman, Houston; Mark T. Fury, Katy.

8. Donna Blumer, Dallas; Peter Y. Wrench, Dallas.

9. Glenda G. Crenshaw, Lake Dallas; Robert W. Bueker, Dallas.

10. Olivia Eudaly, Fort Worth; Steven M. Weinberg, Grapevine.

11. Lisa Smith, Pasadena; Ben. G. Raimer, Galveston.

12. Mrs. Kerry Lundelius, Fort Worth; James A. Borchert, Fort Worth.

13. Betty Lou Martin, Houston; Al Clements, Houston.

14. Sheri Danzc, Austin; Gregory S. Davidson, Austin.

15. Wilda Lindstrom, Houston; Thomas F.Cottar III, Baytown.

16. Ms. Jodie Laubenberg, Richardson; Larry J. Ward, Dallas.

17. Terese A. Raia, Sugar Land; Timothy J. Turner, Bellaire.

18. Geanie W. Morrison, Victoria; Richard T. Hudgins, Wharton.

19. Mrs. Loyce McCarter, San Antonio; Randy Hurt, Fort Stockton.

20. Karen Bonner, Corpus Christi; Eugene J. Seaman, Corpus Christi.

21. Mrs. Bebe Zuniga, Laredo; Bob Hurley, Pleasanton.

22. Becky Farrar, Hico; Blake Nabors, Glen Rose.

23. Barbara Martin, Dallas; Dr. Jimmy D. Morgan, DFW Airport.

24. Reba Boyd, Abilene; George Dulany, Belton.

25. Rita R. Davis, San Antonio; Randy Staudt, Leander.

26. Nancy McDonald, San Antonio; Gene Ryder, San Antonio.

27. Hazel Moye, McAllen; William A. Faulk Jr., Brownsville.

28. Georgia Lamothe, Monahans; Tim Lambert, Lubbock.

29. Ann Wilbourn, Clint; Roger O'Dell, El Paso.

30. Joseph W. Wolfe, Sherman; Jacque Allen, Wichita Falls.

31. Rick D. Davis Jr., Midland; Bonnie Maynard, Amarillo.

Republican State Party Auxiliaries:

Texas Asian Republican Caucus: Chmn., Elsie Huang, 12625 Memorial Dr. #141, Houston 77024.

Republican National Hispanic Assembly of Texas: Chmn., Dan Fernandez, 2823 Quail Lane, Arlington 76016.

Texas Young Republican Federation: Chmn., Christina A. Melton, 3250 Lincoln Plaza, 500 N. Akard, Dallas 75201.

Black Republican Council of Texas: Chmn., Bill Calhoun, 4200 Montrose, #480, Houston 77006.

College Republicans of Texas: Chmn., Jody Withers, Box 9832, College Station 77842.

Texas Federation of Republican Women: Pres., Marcia W. Saunders, 104 Molala Cove, Lake Kiowa 76240.

Republican Veterans of Texas: Chmn., George R. Leake, 1809 Kensington, Carrollton 75007.

Teen-Age Republicans: James Marchbanks, Box 173, Newark 76071. ☆

Democrat Primary Runoff for U. S. Senate, April 12, 1994

County	R. Fisher	J. Mattox
Anderson	2,900	2,145
Andrews	190	71
Angelina	3,488	2,517
Aransas	526	603
Archer	256	82
Armstrong	80	32
Atascosa	1,587	858
Austin	457	342
Bailey	105	117
Bandera	104	127
Bastrop	1,408	1,496
Baylor	739	415
Bee	922	935
Bell	2,837	1,506
Bexar	14,543	13,606
Blanco	67	67
Borden	50	29
Bosque	1,054	430
Bowie	3,053	2,261
Brazoria	3,072	3,396
Brazos	1,233	998
Brewster	462	551
Briscoe	146	129
Brooks	573	589
Brown	1,640	876
Burleson	775	529
Burnet	1,009	810
Caldwell	779	697
Calhoun	1,192	1,523
Callahan	834	470
Cameron	5,067	3,529
Camp	527	391
Carson	545	442
Cass	1,416	1,278
Castro	408	368
Chambers	931	589
Cherokee	1,657	998
Childress	127	92
Clay	970	405
Cochran	354	410
Coke	194	64
Coleman	1,156	625
Collin	2,621	986
Collingsworth	123	103
Colorado	556	463
Comal	552	729
Comanche	473	250
Concho	464	323
Cooke	1,551	551
Coryell	522	275
Cottle	248	282
Crane	306	197
Crockett	204	186
Crosby	253	294
Culberson	95	109
Dallam	81	56
Dallas	24,983	23,169
Dawson	424	553
Deaf Smith	757	721
Delta	293	125
Denton	1,727	1,280
DeWitt	461	326
Dickens	305	460
Dimmit	1,459	1,333
Donley	74	43
Duval	387	790
Eastland	581	321
Ector	877	1,053
Edwards	103	61
Ellis	1,292	880
El Paso	18,200	12,941
Erath	1,391	628
Falls	770	363
Fannin	1,038	552
Fayette	625	555
Fisher	206	113
Floyd	140	92
Foard	55	52
Fort Bend	1,827	2,574
Franklin	517	225
Freestone	1,800	831
Frio	1,888	1,746
Gaines	317	371
Galveston	7,891	10,641
Garza	87	115
Gillespie	66	118
Glasscock	47	25
Goliad	1,065	868
Gonzales	1,118	671
Gray	203	231
Grayson	2,429	1,123
Gregg	1,896	2,282
Grimes	1,276	919
Guadalupe	970	812
Hale	981	969
Hall	294	276
Hamilton	326	115
Hansford	43	18
Hardeman	281	165
Hardin	1,816	1,825
Harris	30,294	44,047
Harrison	3,427	3,363
Hartley	61	71
Haskell	949	648
Hays	2,164	2,607
Hemphill	43	27
Henderson	3,487	1,770
Hidalgo	21,218	13,479
Hill	971	486
Hockley	199	145
Hood	1,398	664
Hopkins	2,356	993
Houston	1,550	1,069
Howard	1,159	892
Hudspeth	161	173
Hunt	2,599	1,051
Hutchinson	245	257
Irion	361	159
Jack	496	201
Jackson	296	235
Jasper	791	713
Jeff Davis	259	224
Jefferson	4,911	8,339
Jim Hogg	1,007	1,334
Jim Wells	4,003	4,395
Johnson	2,524	1,168
Jones	1,340	807
Karnes	915	521
Kaufman	1,787	937
Kendall	73	99
Kenedy	43	40
Kent	225	251
Kerr	204	319
Kimble	91	52
King	19	21
Kinney	578	376
Kleberg	1,320	1,503
Knox	346	253
Lamar	2,296	1,267
Lamb	240	159
Lampasas	668	331
La Salle	346	399
Lavaca	1,673	1,398
Lee	544	488
Leon	1,275	721
Liberty	2,068	1,935
Limestone	2,269	1,293
Lipscomb	209	126
Live Oak	823	507
Llano	891	966
Loving	27	14
Lubbock	739	1,244
Lynn	420	575
Madison	549	296
Marion	1,031	855
Martin	103	51
Mason	153	95
Matagorda	1,250	1,421
Maverick	711	933
McCulloch	501	221
McLennan	6,458	4,710
McMullen	75	34
Medina	392	222
Menard	135	53
Midland	336	421
Milam	1,200	994
Mills	879	316
Mitchell	306	118
Montague	2,003	717
Montgomery	708	882
Moore	411	342
Morris	1,420	1,471
Motley	45	21
Nacogdoches	1,802	942
Navarro	1,256	534
Newton	318	443
Nolan	487	222
Nueces	15,884	13,851
Ochiltree	43	30
Oldham	102	35
Orange	4,035	4,835
Palo Pinto	1,320	484
Panola	2,803	2,171
Parker	1,483	688
Parmer	120	71
Pecos	246	170
Polk	1,863	1,331
Potter	636	708
Presidio	125	75
Rains	440	189
Randall	454	531
Reagan	47	15
Real	43	45
Red River	1,489	876
Reeves	733	850
Refugio	344	287
Roberts	36	18
Robertson	438	485
Rockwall	437	215
Runnels	807	350
Rusk	1,642	963
Sabine	657	531
San Augustine	560	534
San Jacinto	518	364
San Patricio	2,860	2,714
San Saba	693	376
Schleicher	379	177
Scurry	413	222
Shackelford	215	117
Shelby	1,037	772
Sherman	96	43
Smith	3,167	2,612
Somervell	1,062	432
Starr	1,662	983
Stephens	1,155	498
Sterling	42	23
Stonewall	128	92
Sutton	51	16
Swisher	376	286
Tarrant	14,970	13,618
Taylor	1,848	724
Terrell	31	26
Terry	348	399
Throckmorton	245	98
Titus	1,768	1,230
Tom Green	1,519	622
Travis	13,254	21,064
Trinity	889	699
Tyler	781	781
Upshur	2,725	2,048
Upton	361	288
Uvalde	882	292
Val Verde	774	573
Van Zandt	3,135	1,104
Victoria	811	738
Walker	1,792	1,361
Waller	629	646
Ward	853	615
Washington	377	397
Webb	4,929	2,227
Wharton	2,214	1,766
Wheeler	396	350
Wichita	1,836	831
Wilbarger	699	284
Willacy	2,052	984
Williamson	1,069	1,697
Wilson	391	286
Winkler	778	559
Wise	1,611	721
Wood	1,200	502
Yoakum	263	245
Young	1,344	520
Zapata	504	236
Zavala	653	859
Statewide	400,227	346,414

Source: Official returns from office of Secretary of State, Elections Division.

Elections of U.S. Senators from Texas

Below is given a compilation of past U.S. senatorial elections in Texas insofar as information is available to the Texas Almanac.

1906

Candidate	Votes
J.W. Bailey (unopp.)	283,315

1910
Democratic Primary

Candidate	Votes
C.A. Culberson (unopp.)	359,939

1912
Democratic Primary

Candidate	Votes
Morris Sheppard	178,281
Jacob F. Wolters	142,050
Choice B. Randall	40,349
Matthew Zollner	3,868
Total vote	364,548

1916
1st Democratic Primary

Candidate	Votes
Carles A. Culberson	87,421
Robert L. Henry	37,726
O.B. Colquitt	119,598
S.P. Brooks	78,641
T.M. Campbell	65,721
John Davis	9,924
*G.W. Riddle	335
Total vote	399,366

**Had withdrawn*

2nd Democratic Primary

Candidate	Votes
Charles A. Culberson	163,182
O.B. Colquitt	94,098
Total Vote	257,280

***General Election**

Candidate	Votes
Charles A. Culberson (Dem.)	301,905
Alex W. Atcheson (Rep.)	48,775
E.H. Conibear (Proh.)	2,313
T.A. Hickey (Socialist)	18,616
Total Vote	371,609

**First general election for U.S. senator. Prior to 1916, Legislature appointed senators.*

1918
Democratic Primary

Candidate	Votes
Morris Sheppard (unopp.)	649,876

General Election

Candidate	Votes
Morris Sheppard (Dem.)	155,158
J. Webster Flanagan (Rep.)	22,183
M.A. Smith (Soc.)	1,587
Total vote	178,928

1922
1st Democratic Primary

Candidate	Votes
C.A. Culberson	99,635
Earle B. Mayfield	153,538
Cullen F. Thomas	88,026
James E. Ferguson	127,071
Clarence Ousley	62,451
R.L. Henry	41,567
Sterling P. Strong	1,085
Total vote	573,373

2nd Democratic Primary

Candidate	Votes
Earle B. Mayfield	273,308
James E. Ferguson	228,701
Total vote	502,009

General Election

Candidate	Votes
Earle B. Mayfield (Dem.)	264,260
George E.B. Peddy (Rep.)	130,744
Total vote	395,004

1924
Democratic Primary

Candidate	Votes
Morris Sheppard	440,511
Fred W. Davis	159,663
John F. Maddox	80,070
Total vote	680,244

General Election

Candidate	Votes
Morris Sheppard (Dem.)	579,208
T.M. Kennerly (Rep.)	98,207
Total vote	677,415

1928
1st Democratic Primary

Candidate	Votes
Thomas L. Blanton	126,758
Tom Connally	178,091
Minnie Fisher Cunningham	28,944
Earle B.Mayfield	200,246
Jeff McLemore	9,244
Alvin Owsley	131,755
Total vote	675,038

2nd Democratic Primary

Candidate	Votes
Tom Connally	320,071
Earle B. Mayfield	257,747
Total vote	577,818

General Election

Candidate	Votes
Tom Connally (Dem.)	566,139
T.M. Kennerly (Rep.)	129,910
David Curran (Soc.)	690
John Rust (Communist)	114
Total vote	696,853

1930
Democratic Primary

Candidate	Votes
Morris Sheppard	526,293
C.A. Mitchner	40,130
Robert L. Henry	174,260
Total vote	740,683

Republican Primary (158 counties reporting)

Candidate	Votes
Doran John Haesly	3,645
*Harve H. Haines	2,568
*C.O. Harris	2,784
Total vote	8,997

**No runoff; candidates withdrew.*

General Election

Candidate	Votes
Morris Sheppard (Dem.)	258,929
D.J. Haesly (Rep.)	35,357
Guy. L. Smith (Soc.)	790
W.A. Berry (Com.)	282
Total vote	295,358

1934
Democratic Primary

Candidate	Votes
Joseph W. Bailey	355,963
Tom Connally	567,139
Guy. B. Fisher	41,421
Total vote	964,523

General Election

Candidate	Votes
Tom Connally (Dem.)	439,375
U.S. Goen (Rep.)	12,895
W.B. Starr (Soc.)	1,828
L.C. Keel (Com.)	310
Total vote	454,408

1936
Democratic Primary

Candidate	Votes
Morris Sheppard	616,293
Guy B. Fisher	89,215
Richard C. Bush	37,842
Joseph H. Price	45,919
Joe H. Eagle	136,718
J. Edward Glenn	28,641
Total vote	954,628

General Election

Candidate	Votes
Morris Sheppard (Dem.)	774,975
Carlos G. Watson (Rep.)	59,491
W.B. Starr (Soc.)	958
Gertrude Wilson (Union)	1,836
Total Vote	837,260

1940
Democratic Primary

Candidate	Votes
Tom Connally	923,219
A.P. Belcher	66,962
Guy B. Fisher	98,125
Total vote	1,088,306

General Election

Candidate	Votes
Tom Connally(Dem.)	978,095
George Shannon (Rep.)	59,340
Homer Brooks (Const.)	408
Total vote	1,037,843

1941 Special Election
June 28, 1941
25 Dems., 2 Reps. 1 Ind. and 1 Communist

Candidate	Votes
W. Lee O'Daniel	175,590
Lyndon B. Johnson	174,279
Gerald C. Mann	140,807
Martin Dies	80,653
*Total vote	571,329

**Above candidates only; votes for others not available.*

1942
1st Democratic Primary

Candidate	Votes
James V. Allred	317,501
Dan Moody	178,471
W. Lee O'Daniel	475,541
Floyd E. Ryan	12,213
Total vote	983,726

2nd Democratic Primary

Candidate	Votes
James V. Allred	433,203
W. Lee O'Daniel	451,359
Total vote	884,562

General Election

Candidate	Votes
W.Lee O'Daniel (Dem.)	260,629
Dudley Lawson (Rep.)	12,064
Charles L. Somerville (P.U.P.)	1,934
Total vote	274,627

1946
Democratic Primary

Candidate	Votes
Tom Connally	823,818
Cyclone Davis	74,252
Floyd E. Ryan	85,292
Terrell Sledge	66,947
Laverne Somerville	42,290
Total vote	1,092,599

General Election

Tom Connally (Dem.)	336,931
Murray C. Sells (Rep.)	43,750
Write-in	5
Total vote	380,686

1948

1st Democratic Primary

Otis C. Myers	15,330
F.B. Clark	7,420
Roscoe H. Collier	12,327
Coke R. Stevenson	477,077
Cyclone Davis	10,871
Frank G. Cortez	13,344
Jesse C. Saunders	7,401
George E.B. Peddy	237,195
Lyndon B. Johnson	405,617
Terrell Sledge	6,692
James F. Alford	9,117
Write-in	1
Total vote	1,202,392

2nd Democratic Primary

Lyndon B. Johnson	494,191
Coke R. Stevenson	494,104
Total vote	988,295

General Election

Lyndon B. Johnson (Dem.)	702,985
Jack Porter (Rep.)	349,665
Sam Morris (Proh.)	8,913
Total vote	1,061,563

1952

1st Democratic Primary

Price Daniel	940,770
Lindley Beckworth	285,842
E.W. Napier	70,132
Total vote	1,296,744

General Election

Price Daniel (Dem.)	1,425,007
Price Daniel (Rep.)	469,494
Price Daniel (No Party)	591
Total vote	1,895,192

1954

1st Democratic Primary

Lyndon B. Johnson	883,264
Dudley T. Dougherty	354,188
Total vote	1,237,452

General Election

Lyndon B. Johnson (Dem.)	538,417
Carlos G. Watson (Rep.)	95,033
Fred T. Spangler (Const.)	3,025
Total vote	636,475

1957 Special Election

On April 2. Price Daniel had resigned to run for governorship.

Elmer Adams	2,228
H.J. Antoine Sr.	576
M.T. Banks	2,153
Jacob Bergolofsky	890
Searcy Bracewell	33,384
John C. Burns Sr.	600
*H.Frank Connally Jr.	514
Frank G. Cortez	1,350
*J.Cal Courtney	879
*R.W. (Waire) Currin	646
Martin Dies	290,803
C.O.Foerster Jr.	776
Curtis Ford	767
Ralph W. Hammonds	2,372
James P. Hart	19,739
*Charles W. (Jack) Hill	1,025
Thad Hutcheson	219,591
Walter Scott McNutt	500
Clyde R. Orms	356
John C. White	11,876
J.Perrin Wills	817
Hugh Wilson	851
Ralph W. Yarborough	364,605
Total vote	957,298

**Withdrew, but after ballots printed.*

1958

1st Democratic Primary

William A. Blakley	536,073
Ralph W. Yarborough	760,856
Write-in	4
Total vote	1,296,933

General Election

Ralph W. Yarborough (Dem.)	587,030
Roy Whittenburg (Rep.)	185,926
Bard A. Logan (Const.)	14,172
Total vote	787,128

1960

1st Democratic Primary

Lyndon B. Johnson	1,407,109
Write-in	145
Total vote	1,407,254

General Election

Lyndon B. Johnson (Dem.)	1,306,625
John G. Tower (Rep.)	926,653
Bard A. Logan (Const.)	20,506
Total vote	2,253,784

1961 Special Election

On April 4. Lyndon B. Johnson resigned to assume office of Vice President.

John G. Tower	327,308
William A. Blakley	190,818
Jim Wright	171,328
Will Wilson	121,961
Maury Maverick Jr.	104,992
Henry B. Gonzalez	97,659

The remaining 71 candidates were: Dr. G.H. Allen, 849; Jim W. Amos, 527; Dale Baker, 612; Dr. Mali Jean Rauch Barraco, 434; Tom E. Barton, 395; R.G. Becker, 462; Jacob Bergolofsky, 377; Dr.Ted Bisland, 831; G.E. Blewett,474, Lawrence S. Bosworth Jr., 410; Joyce J. Bradshaw, 352; Chester D. Brooks, 711; W.L. Burlison, 1,695; Ronald J. Byers, 175; Joseph M. Carter, 185; George A. Davisson, 897, Mrs. Winnie K. Derrick, 327, Harry R. Diehl, 293, Harvill O. Eaton, 178; Rev. Jonnie Mae Eckman, 342; Paul F. Eix, 317; Ben H. Faber, 363; Dr. H.E. Fanning, 293, Charles Otto Foerster Jr., 133; Harold Franklin, 196; George N. Gallagher Jr., 985; Richard J. Gay,939; Van T. George Jr., 307; Arthur Glover, 1,528; Delbert E. Grandstaff, 2,959; Curtis E. Hill, 389; Willard Park Holland, 669; John N. Hopkins, 490; Mary Hazel Houston, 726; Ben M. Johnson, 681;Guy Johnson, 748; Morgan H. Johnson, 334; C.B. Kennedy, 770; H. Springer Knoblauch, 186; Hugh O. Lea, 651; V.C. Logan, 314; Frank A. Matera, 599, Brown McCallum, 323; James E. McKee, 762; Steve Nemecek, 1,017; George E. Noyes, 174; Floyd Payne, 227; Cecil D. Perkins, 773; W.H. Posey, 592; George Red, 99; Wesley Roberts, 386; D.T. Sampson, 417; Eristus Sams, 4,490; A. Dale Savage, 400; Carl A. Schrade, 283; Albert Roy Smith, 341; Homer Hyrim Stalarow, 735; Frank Stanford, 240; John B. Sypert, 252; Mrs. Martha Tredway, 1,227; S.S. Vela, 241, Bill Whitten, 350; Hoyt G. Wilson, 2,165; Hugh Wilson, 2,997; Marcos Zertuche, 442; Write-ins, 42.

Total vote	1,058,124

***Runoff Election** held May 27

William A. Blakley	437,874
John G. Tower	448,217
Total vote	886,091

**Change in state law following 1957 special election required runoff.*

1964

1st Democratic Primary

Ralph Yarborough	905,001
Gordon McLendon	672,573
Write-in	23
Total vote	1,577,607

1st Republican Primary

George Bush	62,985
Jack Cox	45,561
Milton V. Davis	6,067
Robert Morris	28,279
Total vote	142,892

2nd Republican Primary

George Bush	49,751
Jack Cox	30,333
Total vote	80,084

General Election

Ralph Yarborough (Dem.)	1,463,958
George Bush (Rep.)	1,134,337
Jack Carswell (Const.)	5,542
Write-in	19
Total vote	2,603,856

1966

1st Democratic Primary

John R. Willoughby	226,598
Waggoner Carr	899,523
Total vote	1,126,121

General Election

Waggoner Carr (Dem.)	643,855
John G. Tower (Rep.)	842,501
Jas. Barker Holland (Const.)	6,778
Total vote	1,493,134

1970

1st Democratic Primary

Lloyd Bentsen	814,316
Ralph Yarborough	726,447
Total vote	1,540,763

Republican Primary

George Bush	96,806
Robert Morris	13,659
Total vote	110,465

General Election

Lloyd Bentsen (Dem.)	1,226,568
George Bush (Rep.)	1,071,234
Other	1,808
Total vote	2,299,610

1972

1st Democratic Primary

Thomas M. Cartlidge	66,240
Barefoot Sanders	787,504
Alfonso Veloz	53,938
Hugh Wilson	125,460
Ralph Yarborough	1,032,606
Total vote	2,065,748

2nd Democratic Primary

Barefoot Sanders	1,008,499
Ralph Yarborough	928,087
Total vote	1,936,586

Republican Primary

John G. Tower (unopp.)	107,648

General Election

Barefoot Sanders (Dem.)	1,511,985
John G. Tower (Rep.)	1,822,877
Flores Amaya (Raza)	63,543
Tom Leonard (Soc.)	14,464
Other	1,034
Total vote	3,413,903

1976

1st Democratic Primary

Lloyd Bentsen	970,983
Leon Dugi	19,870
Phil Gramm	427,597
Hugh Wilson	109,715
Other	1,003
Total vote	1,529,168

Republican Primary

Louis Leman	40,651
Alan Steelman	251,252
Hugh Sweeney	64,404
Total vote	356,307

General Election

Lloyd Bentsen (Dem.)	2,199,956
Alan Steelman (Rep.)	1,636,370
Marjorie P. Gallion (Am.)	17,355
Pedro Vasques (Soc. Worker)	20,549
Total vote	3,874,230

1978

1st Democratic Primary

Joe Christie	701,892
Robert Krueger	853,485
Total vote	1,555,377

Republican Primary

John G. Tower	142,202

General Election

Robert Krueger (Dem.)	1,139,149
John G. Tower (Rep.)	1,151,376
Luis A. Diaz de Leon (Raza Unida)	17,869
Miguel Pendas (Soc. Worker)	4,018
Other	128
Total vote	2,312,540

1982

1st Democratic Primary

Lloyd Bentsen	987,985
Joe Sullivan	276,453
Total vote	1,264,438

Republican Primary

Don I. Richardson	18,616
Jim Collins	152,469
Walter H. Mengden Jr.	91,780
Total vote	262,865

General Election

Jim Collins (Rep.)	1,256,759
Lloyd Bentsen (Dem.)	1,818,223
John E. Ford (Lib.)	23,494
Lineaus H. Lorette (Const.)	4,564
Darryl Anderson (W-I)	39
Other	88
Total vote	3,103,167

1984

1st Democratic Primary

Lloyd Doggett	456,173
Kent Hance	456,446
Robert Krueger	454,886
Harley Schlanger	14,149
Robert Sullivan	34,733
David Young	47,062
Total vote	1,463,449

2nd Democratic Primary

Lloyd Doggett	491,251
Kent Hance	489,906
Total vote	981,157

Republican Primary

Phil Gramm	246,716
Henry Grover	8,388
Robert Mosbacher	26,279
Ron Paul	55,431
Total vote	336,814

General Election

Lloyd Doggett (Dem.)	2,202,557
Phil Gramm (Rep.)	3,111,348
Other	273
Total vote	5,314,178

1988

Democratic Primary

Lloyd Bentsen	1,365,736
Joe Sullivan	244,805
Total vote	1,610,541

1st Republican Primary

Beau Boulter	228,676
Milton E. Fox	138,031
Wes Gilbreath	275,080
Ned Snead	107,560
Total vote	749,347

2nd Republican Primary

Beau Boulter	111,134
Wes Gilbreath	73,573
Total vote	184,707

General Election

Lloyd Bentsen (Dem.)	3,149,806
Beau Boulter (Rep.)	2,129,228
Other	44,572
Total vote	5,323,606

1990

1st Democratic Primary

Hugh Parmer	766,284
Harley Schlanger	249,445
Total vote	1,015,729

1st Republican Primary

Phil Gramm	687,170

General Election

Phil Gram m(Rep.)	2,302,357
Hugh Parmer (Dem.)	1,429,986
Gary Johnson (Lib.)	89,089
Other	725
Total vote	3,822,157

1993 Special Election

On May 1, Lloyd Bentsen resigned to assume post as U.S. Secretary of Treasury.

Kay Bailey Hutchison	593,338
Robert Krueger	593,239
Joe Barton	284,137
Jack Fields	277,560
Richard Fisher	165,560

Others: Billy Brown, 2,187; Louis C. Davis, 1,548; Rick Draheim, 5,677; Rose Floyd, 2,301; Jose Angel Gutierrez, 52,103; Lottie Bolling Hancock, 2,242; Rober Henson, 3,092; Stephen Hopkins, 14,753; Charles Ben Howell, 3,866; Gene Kelly, 11,331; C. (Sonny) Payne, 6,782; Don Richardson, 6,209; Chuck Sibley, 2,406; Thomas D. Spink, 2,281; Herbert Spiro, 4,459; Maco Stewart, 1,260; James Vallaster, 2,124; Clymer Wright, 5,111; Lou Zaeske, 2,191.

Total vote	2,045,757

Runoff Election held June 5

Robert Krueger	574,089
Kay Bailey Hutchison	1,183,766
Total vote	1,757,855

1994

1st Democratic Primary

Michael A. Andrews	159,793
Richard Fisher	388,090
Evelyn K. Lantz	63,523
Jim Mattox	416,503
Total vote	1,027,909

2nd Democratic Primary

Richard Fisher	400,227
Jim Mattox	346,414
Total vote	746,641

1st Republican Primary

James C. Curry	15,625
Roger Henson	14,021
Stephen Hopkins	34,703
Kay Bailey Hutchison	467,975
M. Troy Mata	8,632
Ernest J. Schmidt	8,690
Tom Spink	5,692
Total vote	555,338

General Election

Richard Fisher (Dem.)	1,639,615
Kay Bailey Hutchison (Rep.)	2,604,218
Pierre Blondeau (Lib.)	36,107
Total vote	4,279,940

State Government

State government is divided into executive, legislative and judicial branches under the Texas Constitution adopted in 1876. The chief executive is the Governor, whose term is for 4 years. Other elected state officials with executive responsibilities include the Lieutenant Governor, Attorney General, Comptroller of Public Accounts, Treasurer**, Commissioner of the General Land Office and Commissioner of Agriculture. The terms of those officials are also 4 years. The Secretary of State is appointed by the Governor.

Except for making numerous appointments and calling special sessions of the Legislature, the Governor's powers are limited in comparison with those in most states.

Current state executives and their addresses, phone numbers and salaries for the 1996-97 biennium are:

Governor: George W. Bush
P.O. Box 12428, Austin 78711
(512) 463-2000
$99,122

Attorney General: Dan Morales
P.O. Box 12546, Austin 78711
(512) 463-2100
$79,247

Commissioner of General Land Office: Garry Mauro
1700 N. Congress, Austin 78701
(512) 463-5256
$79,247

State Treasurer: Martha Whitehead**
P.O. Box 12608, Austin 78701
(512) 463-6000
$79,247

Lt. Governor: Bob Bullock
P.O. Box 12068, Austin 78711
(512) 463-0001
For salary, see note* below.

Comptroller of Public Accounts: John Sharp
LBJ State Office Building, Austin 78774
(512) 463-4000
$79,247

Commissioner of Agriculture: Rick Perry
P.O. Box 12847, Austin 78711
(512) 463-7435
$79,247

Secretary of State: Antonio O. "Tony" Garza Jr.
P.O. Box 12697, Austin 78711
(512) 463-5770
$76,966

**Salary of Lt. Gov. is same as a Senator when serving as Pres. of Senate; same as Gov. when serving as Gov.*
***The office of State Treasurer will be abolished if voters approve a constitutional amendment on Nov. 7, 1995.*

Ombudsman Office (Citizens' Advocate): **Citizens' Assistance Hotline: 1-800-843-5789.**
Part of the Governor's office, the Ombudsman Office receives citizens's comments and complaints over the toll-free assistance hotline and passes them to government officials, as well as referring citizens to sources of assistance.

Texas Legislature

The Texas Legislature has **181 members: 31 in the Senate and 150 in the House of Representatives.** Regular sessions convene on the second Tuesday of January in odd-numbered years, but the governor may call special sessions. Article III of the Texas Constitution deals with the legislative branch.

The following lists are of members of the 74th Legislature, which convened on Jan. 10, 1995.

State Senate

Thirty-one members of the State Senate are elected to **four-year, overlapping terms. Salary:** The salary of all members of the Legislature, both Senators and Representatives, is $600 per month and $95 per diem during legislative sessions; mileage allowance at same rate provided by law for state employees. The per diem payment applies during each regular and special session of the Legislature.

Senatorial Districts include one or more whole counties and some counties have more than one Senator.

The **address of Senators** is Texas Senate, P.O. Box 12068, Austin 78711-2068; phone (512) 463-0001; Fax: (512) 463-0039.

President of the Senate is Lt. Gov. Bob Bullock; **President Pro Tempore**, Gonzalo Barrientos (D-Austin); **Secretary of the Senate**, Betty King; **Sergeant-at-Arms**, Carleton Turner.

Texas State Senators

Dist., Name, Party-Hometown; Year Current Term Ends; Occupation.

1. Bill Ratliff, R-Mt. Pleasant; 1999; Consulting Engineer.
2. David Cain, D-Dallas; 1997; Attorney.
3. Drew Nixon, R-Carthage; 1997; CPA, Securities/Insurance Agency.
4. Michael L. Galloway, R-The Woodlands; 1999; Businessman.
5. Jim Turner, D-Crockett; 1999; Attorney.
6. Mario Gallegos, D-Galena Park; 1999; Sr. Fire Capt.
7. Don Henderson, R-Houston; 1997; Attorney/Businessman.
8. Florence Shapiro, R-Plano; 1997; Co. Pres.
9. Jane Nelson, R-Flower Mound; 1997; Businesswoman.
10. Chris Harris, R-Arlington; 1997; Attorney.
11. Jerry Patterson, R-Pasadena; 1999; Employee Benefits Consultant.
12. Mike Moncrief, D-Fort Worth; 1997; Businessman.
13. Rodney Ellis, D-Houston; 1999; Director, Securities Firm, Attorney.
14. Gonzalo Barrientos, D-Austin; 1997; Advertising/Public Relations.
15. John Whitmire, D-Houston; 1997; Attorney/Realtor.
16. John Leedom, R-Dallas; 1999; Company CEO.
17. J. E. "Buster" Brown, R-Lake Jackson; 1999; Attorney.
18. Kenneth Armbrister, D-Victoria; 1999; Businessman.
19. Frank L. Madla Jr., D-San Antonio; 1999; Real Estate, Insurance.
20. Carlos F. Truan, D-Corpus Christi (Dean of the Senate); 1999; Life Insurance.
21. Judith Zaffirini, D-Laredo; 1997; Communications Specialist.
22. David Sibley, R-Waco; 1999; Attorney.

23. Royce West, D-Dallas; 1999; Attorney.
24. Bill Sims, D-Paint Rock; 1997; Rancher, Businessman.
25. Jeff Wentworth, R-San Antonio; 1997; Attorney, Realtor.
26. Gregory Luna, D-San Antonio; 1997; Attorney.
27. Eddie Lucio Jr., D-Brownsville; 1997; Advertising.
28. John T. Montford, D-Lubbock; 1999; Attorney.
29. Peggy Rosson, D-El Paso; 1997; Homemaker.
30. Tom Haywood, R-Wichita Falls; 1999; Businessman.
31. Teel Bivins, R-Amarillo; 1999; Businessman, Cattleman.

House of Representatives

This list shows 150 members of the House of Representatives in the 74th Legislature. They were elected on Nov. 8, 1994, from districts shown below. Members are elected for two-year terms. Representatives and senators receive the same salary; see State Senate. The **address of all Representatives** is House of Representatives, P.O. Box 2910, Austin, 78768-2910; phone (512) 463-3000; Fax: (512) 463-5896.

Speaker: James E. "Pete" Laney (D-Hale Center). **Speaker Pro Tempore**, D.R. "Tom" Uher (D-Bay City). **Chief Clerk**, Cynthia Gerhardt. **Sergeant-at-Arms**, Rod Welsh.

Members of Texas House of Representatives
District, Member, Party-Hometown, Occupation

1. Barry B. Telford, D-DeKalb, Businessman.
2. Tom Ramsay, D-Mount Vernon; Real Estate, Rancher.
3. L.P. "Pete" Patterson, D-Brookston; Farmer, Rancher, Real Estate.
4. Keith Oakley, D-Terrell; Rancher, Businessman.
5. Bob Glaze, D-Gilmer; Chiropractor.
6. Ted Kamel, R-Tyler; Businessman.
7. Jerry Yost, R-Longview; Advertising, Marketing Consultant.
8. Paul Sadler, D-Henderson; Attorney.
9. Jerry Johnson, D-Nacogdoches; Financial Services.
10. Jim Pitts, R-Waxahachie; Attorney.
11. Todd Staples, R-Palestine; Real Estate Appraiser.
12. Clyde H. Alexander, D-Athens; Rancher, Businessman.
13. Dan Kubiak, D-Rockdale; Rancher, Radio, Real Estate.
14. Steve Ogden, R-Bryan; Oil & Gas Producer.
15. Kevin Brady, R-The Woodlands; Chamber of Commerce Executive.
16. Bob Rabuck, R-Conroe; Orthodontist.
17. Billy Clemons, D-Pollok; Transit Director.
18. Allen R. Hightower Jr., D-Huntsville; Manager, Transit Co.
19. Ronald E. Lewis, D-Mauriceville; Insurance, Real Estate.
20. Zeb Zbranek, D-Winnie; Attorney.
21. Mark Stiles, D-Beaumont; Businessman.
22. Albert "Al" Price, D-Beaumont; Retired Pilot.
23. Patricia Gray, D-Galveston; Attorney.
24. Craig Eiland, D-Galveston; Attorney.
25. Jack Harris, R-Pearland; Dentist.
26. Charlie Howard, R-Sugar Land; Realtor/Investor.
27. Huey McCoulskey, D-Richmond; Retired School Administrator.
28. Robert Saunders, D-La Grange; Businessman.
29. D.R. "Tom" Uher, D-Bay City; Attorney.
30. Steve Holzheauser, R-Inez; Rancher.
31. Judy Hawley, D-Portland; Teacher.
32. Todd Hunter, D-Corpus Christi; Attorney.
33. Vilma Luna, D-Corpus Christi; Attorney.
34. Hugo Berlanga, D-Corpus Christi; Businessman.
35. Irma Rangel, D-Kingsville; Attorney.
36. Sergio Muñoz, D-Mission; City A dministrator, Real Estate Development.
37. Rene O. Oliveira, D-Brownsville; Attorney.
38. Jim Solis, D-Harlingen; Attorney.
39. Renato Cuellar, D-Weslaco; Businessman.
40. Eddie de la Garza, D-Edinburg; Attorney.
41. Roberto Gutierrez, D-McAllen; Petroleum Products Distributor.
42. Henry Cuellar, D-Laredo; Attorney, Customs Broker.
43. Tracy King, D-Uvalde; Hearing Aid Specialist.
44. Richard Raymond, D-Benavides; Consultant.
45. Edmund Kuempel, R-Seguin; Salesman.
46. Alec Rhodes, D-Dripping Springs; Businessman.
47. Susan Combs, R-Austin; Rancher.
48. Sherri Greenberg, D-Austin; Public Finance Specialist.
49. Elliott Naishtat, D-Austin; Attorney.
50. Dawna Dukes, D-Austin; Consultant.
51. Glen Maxey, D-Austin; Political Consultant.
52. Mike Krusee, R-Round Rock; Small Business Owner.
53. Harvey Hilderbran, R-Kerrville; Businessman.
54. Layton Black, D-Goldthwaite; Rancher.
55. Dianne Delisi, R-Temple; State Representative.
56. Kip Averitt, R-McGregor; Manufacturing.
57. Barbara Rusling, R-China Spring; Real Estate Broker.
58. Arlene Wohlgemuth, R-Burleson; Flight Instructor.
59. Allen Place, D-Gatesville; Attorney.
60. John R. Cook, D-Breckenridge; Attorney/Rancher.
61. Ric Williamson, R-Weatherford; Entrepreneur.
62. Curtis Seidlits, D-Sherman, Attorney.
63. Mary Denny, R-Aubrey; Businesswoman/Rancher.
64. Jim Horn, R-Denton; Businessman.
65. Burt Solomons, R-Carrollton; Attorney.
66. Brian McCall, R-Plano; Pres., Ins. Agency.
67. Jerry Madden, R-Richardson; Construction.
68. Charles A. Finnell, D-Holliday; Businessman, Attorney.
69. John Hirschi, D-Wichita Falls; Real Estate.
70. David Counts, D-Knox City; Insurance, Real Estate.
71. Bob Hunter, R-Abilene; University Administrator.
72. Robert A. Junell, D-San Angelo; Attorney.
73. Robert R. Turner, D-Voss; Farmer, Rancher.
74. Pete P. Gallego, D-Alpine; Attorney.
75. Gilbert Serna, D-El Paso; Self-Employed.
76. Nancy McDonald, D-El Paso; Registered Nurse.
77. Paul Cruz Moreno, D-El Paso; Attorney.
78. Pat Haggerty, R-El Paso; Real Estate Broker.
79. Joseph Pickett, D-El Paso; Real Estate Broker.
80. Gary Walker, R-Plains; Water Cons. Dist. Mgr.
81. George E. "Buddy" West, R-Odessa; Safety Engineer.
82. Tom Craddick, R-Midland; Businessman.
83. Delwin Jones, R-Lubbock; Farming, Sign Mfr.
84. Robert L. Duncan, R-Lubbock; Attorney.
85. James E. "Pete" Laney, D-Hale Center; Farmer.
86. John T. Smithee, R-Amarillo; Attorney.
87. David Swinford, R-Dumas; Agribusiness.
88. Warren D. Chisum, D-Pampa; Oil & Gas Producer.
89. Homer Dear, D-Fort Worth; School Principal.
90. Doyle Willis, D-Fort Worth; Attorney, Farmer.

91. Bill G. Carter, R-Fort Worth; Insurance Agent.
92. Carolyn Park, R-Euless; State Rep.
93. Toby Goodman, R-Arlington; Attorney.
94. Kent Grusendorf, R-Arlington; Pres., Mfg. Co.
95. Glenn Lewis, D-Fort Worth; Attorney.
96. Kim Brimer, R-Kennedale; Insurance.
97. Anna Mowery, R-Fort Worth; State Rep.
98. Nancy Moffat, R-South Lake; Asst. City Mgr.
99. Kenny Marchant, R-Coppell; Businessman.
100. Samuel W. Hudson III, D-Dallas; Attorney.
101. Elvira Reyna, R-Mesquite; State Rep.
102. Tony Goolsby, R-Dallas; Insurance, Investments.
103. Steve Wolens, D-Dallas; Attorney.
104. Roberto R. Alonzo, D-Dallas; Attorney.
105. Dale Tillery, D-Dallas; Attorney.
106. Ray Allen, R-Grand Prairie; Publishing.
107. Harryette Ehrhardt, D-Dallas; Teacher.
108. John Carona, R-Dallas; Pres. Trans-Cities Cos.
109. Helen Giddings, D-DeSoto; Small Business Owner.
110. Jesse W. Jones, D-Dallas; Educator.
111. Yvonne Davis, D-Dallas; Small Business Owner.
112. Fred Hill, R-Richardson; Businessman.
113. Joe Driver, R-Garland; Insurance.
114. Will Hartnett, R-Dallas; Attorney.
115. Leticia Van de Putte, D-San Antonio; Pharmacist.
116. Leo Alvarado Jr., D-San Antonio; Attorney.
117. John Amos Longoria, D-San Antonio; Attorney.
118. Ciro D. Rodriguez, D-San Antonio; College Professor.
119. Robert Puente, D-San Antonio; Attorney.
120. Karyne Jones Conley, D-San Antonio; College Instructor.
121. Bill Siebert, R-San Antonio; Insurance Marketing.
122. John Shields, R-San Antonio; Attorney.
123. Frank J. Corte, Jr., R-San Antonio; Property Management.
124. Christine Hernandez, D-San Antonio; Education Consultant.
125. Sylvia Romo, D-San Antonio; CPA.
126. Peggy Hamric, R-Houston; Community Activist.
127. Joe Crabb, R-Humble; Minister, Attorney.
128. Fred Bosse, D-Houston; Attorney.
129. Mike Jackson, R-LaPorte; General Contractor.
130. John Culberson, R-Houston; Attorney.
131. Ron Wilson, D-Houston; Attorney.
132. Scott Hochberg, D-Houston; Electronics Consultant.
133. Joe Nixon, R-Houston; Attorney.
134. Kyle Janek, R-Houston; Physician.
135. Gary Elkins, R-Houston; N.A.
136. Beverly Woolley, R-Houston; Business Owner.
137. Debra Danburg, D-Houston; Attorney.
138. Ken Yarbrough, D-Houston; Business Rep.
139. Sylvester Turner, D-Houston; Attorney.
140. Kevin Bailey, D-Houston; Consultant
141. Senfronia Thompson, D-Houston; Attorney.
142. Harold V. Dutton Jr., D-Houston; Attorney.
143.Gerard Torres, D-Houston; State Rep..
144. Robert E. Talton, R-Pasadena; Attorney.
145. Diana Dávila, D-Houston; State Rep.
146. Al Edwards, D-Houston; Real Estate.
147. Garnet F. Coleman, D-Houston; Small Business Owner.
148. Jessica Farrar, D-Houston; Architect Intern.
149. Talmadge Heflin, R-Houston; Businessman, Management Consultant.
150. Paul J. Hilbert, R-Spring; Attorney. ☆

State and Federal Courts

The following lists include U.S. district courts in Texas, state higher courts and administrative judicial districts. The lists were compiled from reports of the Texas Judicial Council, clerks of the courts and other sources.

U.S. District Courts In Texas

Texas is divided into four federal judicial districts, each of which is composed of several divisions. Appeal from all Texas federal district courts is to the **Fifth Circuit Court of Appeals,** New Orleans. Judges are appointed for life and receive a salary of $133,600 annually.

Northern Texas District

District Judges — Chief Judge, Jerry Buchmeyer, Dallas. **Senior Judges:** David O. Belew Jr. and Eldon B. Mahon, Fort Worth; and Halbert O. Woodard, Lubbock. **Judges:** Barefoot Sanders, Dallas; Sam R. Cummings, Lubbock; A. Joe Fish, Sidney A. Fitzwater, Jorge A. Solis, Joe Kendall and Robert B. Maloney, Dallas; and Mary Lou Robinson, Amarillo. **Clerk of District Court:** Nancy Doherty, Dallas. **U.S. Attorney:** Paul Coggins. **U.S. Marshal:** Bruce Beaty, Dallas. Court is in continuous session in each division of the Northern Texas District. Following are the different divisions of the Northern District and the counties in each division:

Dallas Division

Dallas, Ellis, Hunt, Johnson, Kaufman, Navarro and Rockwall. **Magistrates:** William F. Sanderson Jr., John B. Tolle, Jane Jackson and Jeff Kaplan, Dallas.

Fort Worth Division

Comanche, Erath, Hood, Jack, Palo Pinto, Parker, Tarrant and Wise. **Magistrate:** Alex H. McGlinchey, Fort Worth. **Deputy-in-charge:** Pam Murphy.

Amarillo Division

Armstrong, Briscoe, Carson, Castro, Childress, Collingsworth, Dallam, Deaf Smith, Donley, Gray, Hall, Hansford, Hartley, Hemphill, Hutchinson, Lipscomb, Moore, Ochiltree, Oldham, Parmer, Potter, Randall, Roberts, Sherman, Swisher and Wheeler. **Magistrate:** Clinton E. Averitte, Amarillo. **Deputy-in-charge:** Lynn Sherman.

Abilene Division

Callahan, Eastland, Fisher, Haskell, Howard, Jones, Mitchell, Nolan, Shackelford, Stephens, Stonewall, Taylor and Throckmorton. **Magistrate:** Billy W. Boone, Abilene. **Deputy-in-charge:** Marsha Winter.

San Angelo Division

Brown, Coke, Coleman, Concho, Crockett, Glasscock, Irion, Menard, Mills, Reagan, Runnels, Schleicher, Sterling, Sutton and Tom Green. Magistrate: Philip R. Lane, San Angelo. **Deputy-in-charge:** Ann Light.

Wichita Falls Division

Archer, Baylor, Clay, Cottle, Foard, Hardeman, King, Knox, Montague, Wichita, Wilbarger and Young. **Magistrate:** Robert K. Roach, Wichita Falls. **Deputy-in-charge:** Connie Faulkner.

Lubbock Division

Bailey, Borden, Cochran, Crosby, Dawson, Dickens, Floyd, Gaines, Garza, Hale, Hockley, Kent, Lamb, Lubbock, Lynn, Motley, Scurry, Terry and Yoakum. **U.S. District Judge:** Sam R. Cummings, Lubbock. **Magistrate:** J. Q. Warnick Jr., Lubbock. **Deputy-in-charge:** Kristy Weinheimer.

Western Texas District

District Judges — Chief Judge, Harry Lee Hudspeth, El Paso. **Senior Judges:** D. W. Suttle, San Antonio; Lucius D. Bunton III, Midland. **Judges:** Edward C. Prado, H. F. Garcia, Orlando Garcia and Fred Biery, San Antonio; W. Royal Furgeson Jr. and David Briones, El Paso; James R. Nowlin and Sam Sparks, Austin; Walter S. Smith Jr., Waco. **Clerk of District Court:** William G. Putnicki, San Antonio. **Chief Deputy Clerk:** Vacancy. **U.S. Attorney:** James H. DeAtley, San Antonio. **U.S. Marshal:** Jack Dean, San Antonio. Following are the different divisions of the Western District, and the counties in each division.

San Antonio Division

Atascosa, Bandera, Bexar, Comal, Dimmit, Frio, Gonzales, Guadalupe, Karnes, Kendall, Kerr, Medina, Real and Wilson. **Magistrates:** Robert B. O'Connor, John W. Primomo and Nancy Stein Nowak, San Antonio. **Bankruptcy Judges:** Leif M. Clark and Ronald B. King, San Antonio. **Clerk of Bankruptcy Court:** Larry Bick, San Antonio.

Austin Division

Bastrop, Blanco, Burleson, Burnet, Caldwell, Gillespie, Hays, Kimble, Lampasas, Lee, Llano, Mason, McCulloch, San Saba, Travis, Washington and Williamson. **Magistrates:** Alan D. Albright and Stephen H. Capelle, Austin. **Bankruptcy Judges:** Chief, Larry E. Kelly, and Frank P. Monroe. **Deputy-in-charge:** Robert J. Williams.

El Paso Division

El Paso County only. **Magistrates:** Janet Ruesch and Richard P. Mesa, El Paso. **Bankruptcy Judge:** Leif M. Clark, San Antonio. **Deputy-in-charge:** Richard Delgado.

Waco Division

Bell, Bosque, Coryell, Falls, Freestone, Hamilton, Hill, Leon, Limestone, McLennan, Milam, Robertson and Somervell. **Magistrate:** Dennis Green, Waco. **Bankruptcy Judge:** Larry E. Kelly, Austin. **Deputy-in-charge:** Mark G. Borchardt.

Del Rio Division

Edwards, Kinney, Maverick, Terrell, Uvalde, Val Verde and Zavala. **Magistrate:** Durwood Edwards, Del Rio. **Bankruptcy Judge:** Ronald B. King, San Antonio. **Deputy-in-charge:** Kay West.

Pecos Division

Brewster, Culberson, Hudspeth, Jeff Davis, Loving, Pecos, Presidio, Reeves, Ward and Winkler. **Magistrate:** Katherine H. Baker, Pecos. **Bankruptcy Judge:** Ronald B. King, San Antonio. **Deputy-in-charge:** Karen J. White.

Midland-Odessa Division

Andrews, Crane, Ector, Martin, Midland and Upton. Court for the Midland-Odessa Division is held at Midland, but may, at the discretion of the court, be held in Odessa. **Magistrate:** Louis Guirola Jr., Midland. **Bankruptcy Judge:** Ronald B. King, San Antonio. **Deputy-in-charge:** John D. Neil, Midland.

Eastern Texas District

District Judges — Chief Judge, Richard A. Schell, Beaumont. **Judges:** Joe J. Fisher, Thad Heartfield and Howell Cobb, Beaumont; William M. Steger,

John Hannah Jr. and William Wayne Justice, Tyler; Paul N. Brown, Sherman; David J. Folsom, Texarkana. **Clerk of District Court:** David J. Maland, Tyler. **U.S. Attorney:** J. Michael Bradford, Beaumont. **U.S. Marshal:** Norris Batiste, Beaumont. **Chief U.S. Probation Officer:** Wade E. French, Tyler. **Judges in Bankruptcy:** C. Houston Abel, Tyler, and Donald R. Sharp, Beaumont. **Federal Public Defender:** G. Patrtick Black, Tyler. Following are the different divisions of the Eastern District and the counties in each division:

Tyler Division

Anderson, Cherokee, Gregg, Henderson, Panola, Rains, Rusk, Smith, Van Zandt and Wood. **Magistrates:** Henry W. McKee, Tyler, and Judith Guthrie, Tyler. **Chief Deputy:** Jeanne Henderson.

Beaumont Division

Hardin, Jasper, Jefferson, Liberty, Newton, Orange. **Magistrates:** Earl Hines and J. Michael Bradford, Beaumont. **Chief Deputy:** Kelly Gavagan.

Marshall Division

Camp, Cass, Harrison, Marion, Morris, Upshur. **Deputy-in-charge:** Peggy Anderson.

Sherman Division

Collin, Cooke, Denton and Grayson. **Magistrate:** Roger Sanders. **Deputy-in-charge:** Sandra Southerland.

Texarkana Division

Bowie, Franklin and Titus. **Magistrate:** Charles Attaway. **Deputy-in-charge:** Sue Jordan.

Paris Division

Delta, Fannin, Hopkins, Lamar and Red River.

Lufkin Division

Angelina, Houston, Nacogdoches, Polk, Sabine, San Augustine, Shelby, Trinity, Tyler.

Southern Texas District

District Judges — Chief Judge, Norman W. Black, Houston. **Judges:** Kenneth M. Hoyt, Sim Lake, Lynn N. Hughes, David Hittner, John D. Rainey, Melinda Harmon, Vanessa Gilmore, Ewing Werlein Jr. and Lee H. Rosenthal, Houston; Hayden W. Head Jr. and Janis Graham Jack, Corpus Christi; Hugh Gibson and Samuel B. Kent, Galveston; Filemon B. Vela, Brownsville; George P. Kazen, Laredo; Ricardo H. Hinojosa, McAllen. **Clerk of Court:** Michael N. Milby, Houston. **U. S. Attorney:** Gaynelle Griffin Jones, Houston. **U.S. Marshal:** Vacancy, Houston. **Bankruptcy Judges:** Chief, Manuel D. Leal, R. F. Wheless Jr., Letitia Z. Clark, William R. Greendyke and Karen K. Brown, Houston; Richard S. Schmidt, Corpus Christi. Following are the different divisions of the Southern District and the counties in each division:

Houston Division

Austin, Brazos, Colorado, Fayette, Fort Bend, Grimes, Harris, Madison, Montgomery, San Jacinto, Walker, Waller and Wharton. **Magistrates:** Calvin Botley, Frances H. Stacy, Nancy K. Johnson, Marcia A. Crone and Mary Milloy, Houston. **Clerk:** Michael N. Milby.

Brownsville Division

Cameron and Willacy. **Magistrates:** Fidencio Garza Jr. and John Wm. Black, Brownsville. **Deputy-in-charge:** Juan M. Barbosa.

Corpus Christi Division

Aransas, Bee, Brooks, Duval, Jim Wells, Kenedy, Kleberg, Live Oak, Nueces and San Patricio. **Magistrate:** Eduardo E. de Ases, Corpus Christi. **Deputy-in-charge:** Monica Seaman.

Galveston Division

Brazoria, Chambers, Galveston and Matagorda. **Magistrate:** John R. Froeschner. **Deputy-in-charge:** Louise Johnson.

Laredo Division

Jim Hogg, La Salle, McMullen, Webb and Zapata. **Magistrate:** Marcel C. Notzon, Laredo. **Deputy-in-charge:** Rosie Rodriguez.

Victoria Division

Calhoun, DeWitt, Goliad, Jackson, Lavaca, Refugio and Victoria. **Deputy-in-charge:** Maxine Gammon.

McAllen Division

Hidalgo and Starr. **Magistrate:** William M. Mallet and Peter E. Ormsby, McAllen. **Deputy-in-charge:** Ludivina Cervantes.

State Judiciary

The judiciary of the state consists of nine members of the State Supreme Court; nine of the Court of Criminal Appeals; 80 of the Courts of Appeals; 387 of the State District Courts, including 10 Criminal District Courts; 174 of the County Courts at Law; 439 of the County Courts; 885 Justice of the Peace Courts; and 840 Municipal Courts.

State Higher Courts

The state's higher courts are listed below with corrections to **July 1, 1995.** Notations in parentheses indicate dates of expiration of terms of office. Judges of the Supreme Court, Court of Criminal Appeals and Courts of Appeals are elected to 6-year, overlapping terms. District Court judges are elected to 4-year terms.

As of Fiscal Year 1994, the Chief Justice of the Supreme Court and the Presiding Judge of the Court of Criminal Appeals each received $97,470; Justices each received $94,685; Chief Justices of the Courts of Appeals received $90,482; justices received $89,952 from the state. In addition a supplemental amount may be paid by counties, not to exceed $15,000 per year and total salary must be at least $1,000 less than that received by Supreme Court justices. District Court judges received $85,217 from the state, plus supplemental pay from various subdivisions. Their total salary must be $1,000 less than that received by justices of the Court of Appeals in which the district court is located.

Below is given information on only the Supreme Court, Court of Criminal Appeals and Courts of Appeals. The information was furnished by each court as of April 1995. Names of county court judges are given by counties in Table 1 of County and District Officials on pages 519-524. Names of District Court Judges are given by District number on pages 474-476. To get the District numbers of District Courts in a particular county, look on pages 472-474.

Supreme Court

Chief Justice, Thomas R. Phillips (12-31-96). **Justices:** Raul A. Gonzalez (12-31-00); Jack Hightower (12-31-98); Nathan L. Hecht (12-31-00); John Cornyn (12-31-96); Bob Gammage (12-31-96); Craig Enoch (12-31-98); Rose Spector (12-31-98); and Priscilla Owen (12-31-00). **Clerk of Court,** John T. Adams. Location of court, Austin.

Court of Criminal Appeals

Presiding Judge, Michael J. McCormick (12-31-

00). **Judges:** Sam Houston Clinton (12-31-96); Bill M. White (12-31-96); Charles F. Baird (12-31-98); Morris L. Overstreet (12-31-98); Frank Maloney (12-31-96); Lawrence Meyers (12-31-98); Stephen Mansfield (12-31-00; Sharon Keller (12-31-00). **State's Attorney,** Robert Huttash. **Clerk of Court,** Thomas Lowe. Location of court, Austin.

Courts of Appeals

These courts have jurisdiction within their respective supreme judicial districts. A constitutional amendment approved in 1978 raised the number of associate justices for Courts of Appeals where needed. Judges are elected from the district for 6-year terms. Another amendment adopted in 1980 changed the name of the old Courts of Civil Appeals to the Courts of Appeals and changed the jurisdiction of the courts. See Art. V, Sec. 6 of the State Constitution.

First District—*Houston. Chief Justice, Alice Oliver-Parrott (12-31-98). **Justices:** Murry B. Cohen (12-31-00); D. Camille Hutson-Dunn (12-31-96); Margaret G. Mirabal (12-31-96); Adele Hedges (12-31-00); Michol O'Connor (12-31-94); Davie L. Wilson (12-31-98); Eric Andell (12-31-00); Tim G. Taft (12-31-00). **Clerk of court,** Margie Thompson. Counties in the First District: Austin, Brazoria, Brazos, Burleson, Chambers, Colorado, Fort Bend, Galveston, Grimes, Harris, Trinity, Walker, Waller, Washington.

Second District—Fort Worth: Chief Justice, John Cayce (12-31-00). **Justices:** Hal M. Lattimore (12-31-96); Sam Day (12-31-00); Terrie Livingston (12-31-96); Lee Ann Dauphinot (12-31-00); David Richards (12-31-00); and William Brigham (12-31-98). **Clerk of court,** Yvonne Palmer. Counties in Second District: Archer, Clay, Cooke, Denton, Hood, Jack, Montague, Parker, Tarrant, Wichita, Wise, Young.

Third District—Austin: Chief Justice, James L. Carroll (12-31-96). **Justices:** John Powers (12-31-98); Marilyn Aboussie (12-31-00); J. Woodfin Jones (12-31-00); Mack Kidd (12-31-00); and Bea Ann Smith (12-31-00). **Clerk of court,** W. Kenneth Law. Counties in the Third District: Bastrop, Bell, Blanco, Burnet, Caldwell, Coke, Comal, Concho, Fayette, Hays, Irion, Lampasas, Lee, Llano, McCulloch, Milam, Mills, Runnels, San Saba, Schleicher, Sterling, Tom Green, Travis, Williamson.

Fourth District—San Antonio: Chief Justice, Alfonso Chapa (12-31-96). **Justices:** Catherine M. Stone (12-31-00); Tom Rickhoff (12-31-98); Alma Lopez (12-31-00); Paul W. Green (12-31-00); Sarah B. Duncan (12-31-00); and Phil Hardberger (12-31-00). **Clerk of court,** Herb Schaefer. Counties in the Fourth District: Atascosa, Bandera, Bexar, Brooks, Dimmit, Duval, Edwards, Frio, Gillespie, Guadalupe, Jim Hogg, Jim Wells, Karnes, Kendall, Kerr, Kimble, Kinney, La Salle, McMullen, Mason, Maverick, Medina, Menard, Real, Starr, Sutton, Uvalde, Val Verde, Webb, Wilson, Zapata, Zavala.

Fifth District—Dallas: Chief Justice, Linda Thomas (12-31-00). **Justices:** James A. Baker (12-31-00); Sue Lagarde (12-31-00); Mark Whittington (12-31-96); William A. Barber Jr. (12-31-96); Ed Kinkeade (12-31-00); John Ovard (12-31-00); Joseph B. Morris (12-31-00); Frances Maloney (12-31-96); Ron Chapman (12-31-98); Joseph Devany (12-31-00); Tom James (12-31-00); and Carolyn Wright (12-31-98). **Clerk of Court,** Melanie Keeton. Counties in the Fifth District: Collin, Dallas, Grayson, Hunt, Kaufman, Rockwall, Van Zandt.

Sixth District—Texarkana: Chief Justice, William J. Cornelius (12-31-98). **Justices:** Charles M. Bleil (12-31-00) and Ben Z. Grant (12-31-96). **Clerk of court,** Tibby Thomas. Counties in the Sixth District: Bowie, Camp, Cass, Delta, Fannin, Franklin, Gregg, Harrison, Hopkins, Hunt, Lamar, Marion, Morris, Panola, Red River, Rusk, Titus, Upshur, Wood.

Seventh District—Amarillo: Chief Justice, Charles L. Reynolds (12-31-96). **Justices:** Carlton B. Dodson (12-31-98); Brian Quinn (12-31-00) and John T. Boyd (12-31-00). **Clerk of court,** Peggy Culp. Counties in the Seventh District: Armstrong, Bailey, Briscoe, Carson, Castro, Childress, Cochran, Collingsworth, Cottle, Crosby, Dallam, Deaf Smith, Dickens, Donley, Floyd, Foard, Garza, Gray, Hale, Hall, Hansford, Hardeman, Hartley, Hemphill, Hockley, Hutchinson, Kent, King, Lamb, Lipscomb, Lubbock, Lynn, Moore, Motley, Ochiltree, Oldham, Parmer, Potter, Randall, Roberts, Sherman, Swisher, Terry, Wheeler, Wilbarger, Yoakum.

Eighth District—El Paso: Chief Justice, Richard Barajas (12-31-96). **Justices:** Susan J. Larsen (12-31-98); Ann Crawford McClure (12-31-00; and David Wellington Chew (12-31-00). **Clerk of court,** Barbara B. Dorris. Counties in the Eighth District: Andrews, Brewster, Crane, Crockett, Culberson, Ector, El Paso, Gaines, Glasscock, Hudspeth, Jeff Davis, Loving, Martin, Midland, Pecos, Presidio, Reagan, Reeves, Terrell, Upton, Ward, Winkler.

Ninth District—Beaumont: Chief Justice, Ronald L. Walker (12-31-96). **Justices:** Don Burgess (12-31-98) and Earl B. Stover (12-31-00). **Clerk of court,** Carol Anne Flores. Counties in the Ninth District: Angelina, Hardin, Jasper, Jefferson, Liberty, Montgomery, Newton, Orange, Polk, San Jacinto, Tyler.

Tenth District—Waco: Chief Justice, Bob L. Thomas (12-31-00). **Justices:** Bobby L. Cummings (12-31-98) and Bill Vance (12-31-96). **Clerk of court,** Imogene Allen. Counties in the Tenth District: Bosque, Brazos, Coryell, Ellis, Falls, Freestone, Hamilton, Hill, Johnson, Leon, Limestone, McLennan, Madison, Navarro, Robertson, Somervell.

Eleventh District—Eastland: Chief Justice, William G. Arnot (12-31-00). **Justices:** Charles R. Dickenson (12-31-98) and Jim R. Wright (12-31-96). **Clerk of court,** Sherry Williamson. Counties in the Eleventh District: Baylor, Borden, Brown, Callahan, Coleman, Comanche, Dawson, Eastland, Erath, Fisher, Haskell, Howard, Jones, Knox, Mitchell, Nolan, Palo Pinto, Scurry, Shackelford, Stephens, Stonewall, Taylor, Throckmorton.

Twelfth District—Tyler: Chief Justice, Tom B. Ramey Jr. (12-31-96). **Justices:** Charles R. Holcomb (12-31-98) and Roby Hadden (12-31-00). **Clerk of court,** Carolyn Allen. Counties in the Twelfth District: Anderson, Cherokee, Gregg, Henderson, Hopkins, Houston, Kaufman, Nacogdoches, Panola, Rains, Rusk, Sabine, Smith, San Augustine, Shelby, Upshur, Van Zandt.

Thirteenth District—Corpus Christi: Chief Justice, Robert J. Seerden (12-31-00). **Justices:** Linda Reyna Yañez (12-31-98); J. Bonner Dorsey (12-31-96); Federico G. Hinojosa Jr. (12-31-00); Melchor Chavez (12-31-00); and Nelda V. Rodriguez (12-31-00). **Clerk of court,** Cathy Wilborn. Counties in the Thirteenth

District: Aransas, Bee, Calhoun, Cameron, DeWitt, Goliad, Gonzales, Hidalgo, Jackson, Kenedy, Kleberg, Lavaca, Live Oak, Matagorda, Nueces, Refugio, San Patricio, Victoria, Wharton, Willacy.

Fourteenth District—Houston†: Chief Justice, Paul C. Murphy (12-31-96). **Justices:** Norman Lee (12-31-98); Leslie Brock Yates (12-31-98); Maurice Amidei (12-31-00); John S. Anderson (12-31-00); J. Harvey Hudson (12-31-00); Wanda McKee Fowler (12-31-00); Harriet O'Niell (12-31-96); and Richard H. Edelman (12-31-00). **Clerk of court,** Mary Jane Smart. Counties in the Fourteenth District: Austin, Brazoria, Brazos, Burleson, Chambers, Colorado, Fort Bend, Galveston, Grimes, Harris, Trinity, Walker, Waller, Washington.

*The location of the First Court of Appeals was changed from Galveston to Houston by the 55th Legislature, with the provision that all cases originated in Galveston County be tried in that city and with the further provision that any case may, at the discretion of the court, be tried in either city.

†Because of the heavy workload of the Houston area Court of Appeals, the 60th Legislature, in 1967, provided for the establishment of a Fourteenth Appeals Court at Houston.

Administrative Judicial Districts of Texas

There are nine administrative judicial districts in the state for administrative purposes. An active or retired district judge or an active or retired appellate judge with judicial experience in a district court serves as the Presiding Judge upon appointment by the Governor. They receive extra compensation of $5,000 paid by counties in the respective administrative districts.

The Presiding Judge convenes an annual conference of the judges in the administrative district to consult on the state of business in the courts. This conference is empowered to adopt rules for the administration of cases in the district. The Presiding Judge may assign active or retired district judges residing within the administrative district to any of the district courts within the administrative district. The Presiding Judge of one administrative district may request the Presiding Judge of another administrative district to assign a judge from that district to sit in a district court located in the administrative district of the Presiding Judge making the request.

The Chief Justice of the Supreme Court of Texas convenes an annual conference of the nine Presiding Judges to determine the need for assignment of judges and to promote the uniform administration of the assignment of judges. The Chief Justice is empowered to assign judges of one administrative district for service in another whenever such assignments are necessary for the prompt and efficient administration of justice.

First District—Pat McDowell, Dallas: Anderson, Bowie, Camp, Cass, Cherokee, Collin, Dallas, Delta, Ellis, Fannin, Franklin, Grayson, Gregg, Harrison, Henderson, Hopkins, Houston, Hunt, Kaufman, Lamar, Marion, Morris, Nacogdoches, Panola, Rains, Red River, Rockwall, Rusk, Shelby, Smith, Titus, Upshur, Van Zandt and Wood.

Second District—Thomas J. Stovall Jr., Seabrook: Angelina, Bastrop, Brazoria, Brazos, Burleson, Chambers, Fort Bend, Freestone, Galveston, Grimes, Hardin, Harris, Jasper, Jefferson, Lee, Leon, Liberty, Limestone, Madison, Matagorda, Montgomery, Newton, Orange, Polk, Robertson, Sabine, San Augustine, San Jacinto, Trinity, Tyler, Walker, Waller, Washington and Wharton.

Third District—B. B. Schraub, Seguin: Austin, Bell, Blanco, Bosque, Burnet, Caldwell, Colorado, Comal, Comanche, Coryell, Falls, Fayette, Gonzales, Guadalupe, Hamilton, Hays, Hill, Johnson, Lampasas, Lavaca, Llano, McLennan, Mason, Milam, Navarro, San Saba, Somervell, Travis and Williamson.

Fourth District—Olin Bernard Strauss, Jourdanton: Aransas, Atascosa, Bee, Bexar, Calhoun, DeWitt, Dimmit, Frio, Goliad, Jackson, Karnes, LaSalle, Live Oak, Maverick, McMullen, Refugio, San Patricio, Victoria, Webb, Wilson, Zapata and Zavala.

Fifth District—Darrell Hester, Harlingen: Brooks, Cameron, Duval, Hidalgo, Jim Hogg, Jim Wells, Kenedy, Kleberg, Nueces, Starr and Willacy.

Sixth District—Stephen B. Ables, Kerrville: Bandera, Brewster, Crockett, Culberson, Edwards, El Paso, Gillespie, Hudspeth, Jeff Davis, Kendall, Kerr, Kimble, Kinney, Medina, Pecos, Presidio, Reagan, Real, Sutton, Terrell, Upton, Uvalde and Val Verde.

Seventh District—Weldon Kirk, Sweetwater: Andrews, Borden, Brown, Callahan, Coke, Coleman, Concho, Crane, Dawson, Ector, Fisher, Gaines, Garza, Glasscock, Haskell, Howard, Irion, Jones, Kent, Loving, Lynn, McCulloch, Martin, Menard, Midland, Mills, Mitchell, Nolan, Reeves, Runnels, Schleicher, Scurry, Shackelford, Sterling, Stonewall, Taylor, Throckmorton, Tom Green, Ward and Winkler.

Eighth—Clyde R. Ashworth, Fort Worth: Archer, Clay, Cooke, Denton, Eastland, Erath, Hood, Jack, Montague, Palo Pinto, Parker, Stephens, Tarrant, Wichita, Wise and Young.

Ninth—Ray D. Anderson, Brownfield: Armstrong, Bailey, Baylor, Briscoe, Carson, Castro, Childress, Cochran, Collingsworth, Cottle, Crosby, Dallam, Deaf Smith, Dickens, Donley, Floyd, Foard, Gray, Hale, Hall, Hansford, Hardeman, Hartley, Hemphill, Hockley, Hutchinson, King, Knox, Lamb, Lipscomb, Lubbock, Moore, Motley, Ochiltree, Oldham, Parmer, Potter, Randall, Roberts, Sherman, Swisher, Terry, Wheeler, Wilbarger and Yoakum. ☆

Texas Courts by County, 1994

Below are listed the state district court or courts, court of appeals district, administrative judicial district and U.S. judicial district for each county in Texas. For the names of the district court judges, see table by district number on pages 474-476. For the names of other judges, see listing on pages 468-471.

County	State Dist. Court(s)	Court of App'ls Dist.	Adm. Jud. Dist.	U.S. Jud. Dist.
Anderson	3, 87, 349, 369	12	1	E-Tyler
Andrews	109	8	7	W-Mid.-Od.
Angelina	159, 217	9	2	E-Lufkin
Aransas	36, 156, 343	13	4	S-C.Christi
Archer	97	2	8	N-W. Falls
Armstrong	47	7	9	N-Amarillo
Atascosa	81, 218	4	4	W-San Ant.
Austin	155	1, 14	3	S-Houston
Bailey	287	7	9	N-Lubbock
Bandera	216	4	6	W-San Ant.
Bastrop	21, 335	3	2	W-Austin
Baylor	50	11	9	N-W. Falls
Bee	36, 156, 343	13	4	S-C.Christi
Bell	27, 146, 169, 264	3	3	W-Waco
Bexar	37, 45, 57, 73, 131, 144, 150, 166, 175, 186, 187, 224, 225, 226, 227, 285, 288, 289, 290	4	4	W-San Ant.
Blanco	33	3	3	W-Austin
Borden	132	11	7	N-Lubbock
Bosque	220	10	3	W-Waco
Bowie	5, 102, 202	6	1	E-Texark.
Brazoria	23, 149, 239, 300	1, 14	2	S-Galves.
Brazos	85, 272, 361	1, 10, 14	2	S-Houston
Brewster	83	8	6	W-Pecos
Briscoe	110	7	9	N-Amarillo
Brooks	79	4	5	S-C.Christi
Brown	35	11	7	N-San Ang.
Burleson	21, 335	1, 14	2	W-Austin
Burnet	33	3	3	W-Austin
Caldwell	22, 207, 274	3	3	W-Austin
Calhoun	24, 135, 267	13	4	S-Victoria
Callahan	42	11	7	N-Abilene
Cameron	103, 107, 138, 197, 357	13	5	S-Browns-ville
Camp	76, 276	6	1	E-Marshall
Carson	100	7	9	N-Amarillo
Cass	5	6	1	E-Marshall
Castro	64, 242	7	9	N-Amarillo
Chambers	253, 344	1, 14	2	S-Galves.
Cherokee	2, 369	12	1	E-Tyler
Childress	100	7	9	N-Amarillo
Clay	97	2	8	N-W. Falls
Cochran	286	7	9	N-Lubbock
Coke	51	3	7	N-San Ang.
Coleman	42	11	7	N-San Ang.
Collin	199, 219, 296, 366	5	1	E-Sherman
Collingsworth	100	7	9	N-Amarillo
Colorado	25, 2nd 25	1, 14	3	S-Houston
Comal	22, 207, 274	3	3	W-San Ant.
Comanche	220	11	3	N-Ft. Worth
Concho	119, 198	3	7	N-San Ang.
Cooke	235	2	8	E-Sherman
Coryell	52	10	3	W-Waco
Cottle	50	7	9	N-W. Falls
Crane	109	8	7	W-Mid.-Od.
Crockett	112	8	6	N-San Ang.
Crosby	72	7	9	N-Lubbock

County	State Dist. Court(s)	Court of App'ls Dist.	Adm. Jud. Dist.	U.S. Jud. Dist.
Culberson	34, 205, 210	8	6	W-Pecos
Dallam	69	7	9	N-Amarillo
Dallas	14, 44, 68, 95, 101, 116, 134, 160, 162, 191, 192, 193, 194, 195, 203, 204, 254, 255, 256, 265, 282, 283, 291, 292, 298, 301, 302, 303, 304, 305, 330, 363, Cr. 1, Cr. 2, Cr. 3, Cr. 4, Cr. 5	5	1	N-Dallas
Dawson	106	11	7	N-Lubbock
Deaf Smith	222	7	9	N-Amarillo
Delta	8, 62	6	1	E-Paris
Denton	16, 158, 211, 362, 367	2	8	E-Sherman
DeWitt	24, 135, 267	13	4	S-Victoria
Dickens	110	7	9	N-Lubbock
Dimmit	293, 365	4	4	W-San Ant.
Donley	100	7	9	N-Amarillo
Duval	229	4	5	S-C.Christi
Eastland	91	11	8	N-Abilene
Ector	70, 161, 244, 358	8	7	W-Mid.-Od.
Edwards	63	4	6	W-Del Rio
El Paso	34, 41, 65, 120, 168, 171, 205, 210, 243, 327, 346	8	6	W-El Paso
Ellis	40	10	1	N-Dallas
Erath	266	11	8	N-Ft. Worth
Falls	82	10	3	W-Waco
Fannin	6, 336	6	1	E-Paris
Fayette	155	3	3	S-Houston
Fisher	32	11	7	N-Abilene
Floyd	110	7	9	N-Lubbock
Foard	46	7	9	N-W. Falls
Fort Bend	240, 268, 328	1, 14	2	S-Houston
Franklin	8, 62	6	1	E-Texark.
Freestone	77, 87	10	2	W-Waco
Frio	81, 218	4	4	W-San Ant.
Gaines	106	8	7	N-Lubbock
Galveston	10, 56, 122, 212, 306	1, 14	2	S-Galves.
Garza	106	7	7	N-Lubbock
Gillespie	216	4	6	W-Austin
Glasscock	118	8	7	N-San Ang.
Goliad	24, 135, 267	13	4	S-Victoria
Gonzales	25, 2nd 25	13	3	W-San Ant.
Gray	31, 223	7	9	N-Amarillo
Grayson	15, 59, 336	5	1	E-Sherman
Gregg	124, 188, 307	6, 12	1	E-Tyler
Grimes	12, 278	1, 14	2	S-Houston
Guadalupe	25, 2nd 25, 274	4	3	W-San Ant.
Hale	64, 242	7	9	N-Lubbock
Hall	100	7	9	N-Amarillo
Hamilton	220	10	3	W-Waco
Hansford	84	7	9	N-Amarillo
Hardeman	46	7	9	N-W. Falls
Hardin	88, 356	9	2	E-B'mont.

County	State Dist. Court(s)	Court of App'ls Dist.	Adm. Jud. Dist.	U.S. Jud. Dist.
Harris	11, 55, 61, 80, 113, 125, 127, 129, 133, 151, 152, 157, 164, 165, 174, 176, 177, 178, 179, 180, 182, 183, 184, 185, 189, 190, 208, 209, 215, 228, 230, 232, 234, 245, 246, 247, 248, 257, 262, 263, 269, 270, 280, 281, 295, 308, 309, 310, 311, 312, 313, 314, 315, 333, 334, 337, 338, 339, 351	1, 14	2	S-Houston
Harrison	71	6	1	E-Marshall
Hartley	69	7	9	N-Amarillo
Haskell	39	11	7	N-Abilene
Hays	22, 207, 274	3	3	W-Austin
Hemphill	31	7	9	N-Amarillo
Henderson	3, 173	12	1	E-Tyler
Hidalgo	92, 93, 139, 206, 275, 332, 370	13	5	S-McAllen
Hill	66	10	3	W-Waco
Hockley	286	7	9	N-Lubbock
Hood	355	2	8	N-Ft. Worth
Hopkins	8, 62	6, 12	1	E-Paris
Houston	3, 349	12	1	E-Lufkin
Howard	118	11	7	N-Abilene
Hudspeth	34, 205, 210	8	6	W-Pecos
Hunt	196, 354	5, 6	1	N-Dallas
Hutchinson	84, 316	7	9	N-Amarillo
Irion	51	3	7	N-San Ang.
Jack	271	2	8	N-Ft. Worth
Jackson	24, 135, 267	13	4	S-Victoria
Jasper	1, 1A	9	2	E-B'mont.
Jeff Davis	83	8	6	W-Pecos
Jefferson	58, 60, 136, 172, 252, 279, 317, Cr.	9	2	E-B'mont.
Jim Hogg	229	4	5	S-Laredo
Jim Wells	79	4	5	S-C.Christi
Johnson	18, 249	10	3	N-Dallas
Jones	259	11	7	N-Abilene
Karnes	81, 218	4	4	W-San Ant.
Kaufman	86	5, 12	1	N-Dallas
Kendall	216	4	6	W-San Ant.
Kenedy	105	13	5	S-C.Christi
Kent	39	7	7	N-Lubbock
Kerr	198, 216	4	6	W-San Ant.
Kimble	198	4	6	W-Austin
King	50	7	9	N-W. Falls
Kinney	63	4	6	W-Del Rio
Kleberg	105	13	5	S-C.Christi
Knox	50	11	9	N-W. Falls
Lamar	6, 62	6	1	E-Paris
Lamb	154	7	9	N-Lubbock
Lampasas	27	3	3	W-Austin
La Salle	81, 218	4	4	S-Laredo
Lavaca	25, 2nd 25	13	3	S-Victoria
Lee	21, 335	3	2	W-Austin
Leon	12, 87, 278	10	2	W-Waco
Liberty	75, 253	9	2	E-B'mont.
Limestone	77, 87	10	2	W-Waco
Lipscomb	31	7	9	N-Amarillo
Live Oak	36, 156, 343	13	4	S-C.Christi
Llano	33	3	3	W-Austin

County	State Dist. Court(s)	Court of App'ls Dist.	Adm. Jud. Dist.	U.S. Jud. Dist.
Loving	143	8	7	W-Pecos
Lubbock	72, 99, 137, 140, 237, 364	7	9	N-Lubbock
Lynn	106	7	7	N-Lubbock
Madison	12, 278	10	2	S-Houston
Marion	115, 276	6	1	E-Marshall
Martin	118	8	7	W-Mid.-Od.
Mason	33	4	3	W-Austin
Matagorda	23, 130	13	2	S-Galves.
Maverick	293, 365	4	4	W-Del Rio
McCulloch	198	3	7	W-Austin
McLennan	19, 54, 74, 170	10	3	W-Waco
McMullen	36, 156, 343	4	4	S-Laredo
Medina	38	4	6	W-San Ant.
Menard	198	4	7	N-San Ang.
Midland	142, 238, 318	8	7	W-Mid.-Od.
Milam	20	3	3	W-Waco
Mills	35	3	7	N-San Ang.
Mitchell	32	11	7	N-Abilene
Montague	97	2	8	N-W. Falls
Montgomery	9, 2nd 9, 221, 284, 359	9	2	S-Houston
Moore	69	7	9	N-Amarillo
Morris	76, 276	6	1	E-Marshall
Motley	110	7	9	N-Lubbock
Nacogdoches	145	12	1	E-Lufkin
Navarro	13	10	3	N-Dallas
Newton	1, 1A	9	2	E-B'mont.
Nolan	32	11	7	N-Abilene
Nueces	28, 94, 105, 117, 148, 214, 319, 347	13	5	S-C.Christi
Ochiltree	84	7	9	N-Amarillo
Oldham	222	7	9	N-Amarillo
Orange	128, 163, 260	9	2	E-B'mont.
Palo Pinto	29	11	8	N-Ft. Worth
Panola	123	6, 12	1	E-Tyler
Parker	43	2	8	N-Ft. Worth
Parmer	287	7	9	N-Amarillo
Pecos	83, 112	8	6	W-Pecos
Polk	9, 2nd 9, 258	9	2	E-Lufkin
Potter	47, 108, 181, 251, 320	7	9	N-Amarillo
Presidio	83	8	6	W-Pecos
Rains	8, 354	12	1	E-Tyler
Randall	47, 181, 251	7	9	N-Amarillo
Reagan	83, 112	8	6	N-San Ang.
Real	38	4	6	W-San Ant.
Red River	6, 102	6	1	E-Paris
Reeves	143	8	7	W-Pecos
Refugio	24, 135, 267	13	4	S-Victoria
Roberts	31	7	9	N-Amarillo
Robertson	82	10	2	W-Waco
Rockwall	354	5	1	N-Dallas
Runnels	119	3	7	N-San Ang.
Rusk	4	6, 12	1	E-Tyler
Sabine	1, 273	12	2	E-Lufkin
San Augustine	1, 273	12	2	E-Lufkin
San Jacinto	9, 2nd 9, 258	9	2	S-Houston
San Patricio	36, 156, 343	13	4	S-C.Christi
San Saba	33	3	3	W-Austin
Schleicher	51	3	7	N-San Ang.
Scurry	132	11	7	N-Lubbock
Shackelford	259	11	7	N-Abilene
Shelby	123, 273	12	1	E-Lufkin
Sherman	69	7	9	N-Amarillo
Smith	7, 114, 241, 321	12	1	E-Tyler
Somervell	18, 249	10	3	W-Waco
Starr	229	4	5	S-McAllen
Stephens	90	11	8	N-Abilene

County	State Dist. Court(s)	Court of App'ls Dist.	Adm. Jud. Dist.	U.S. Jud. Dist.
Sterling	51	3	7	N-San Ang.
Stonewall	39	11	7	N-Abilene
Sutton	112	4	6	N-San Ang.
Swisher	64, 242	7	9	N-Amarillo
Tarrant	17, 48, 67, 96, 141, 153, 213, 231, 233, 236, 297, 322, 323, 324, 325, 342, 348, 352, 360, 371, 372, Cr. 1, Cr. 2, Cr. 3, Cr. 4	2	8	N-Ft. Worth
Taylor	42, 104, 326, 350	11	7	N-Abilene
Terrell	63	8	6	W-Del Rio
Terry	121	7	9	N-Lubbock
Throckmorton	39	11	7	N-Abilene
Titus	76, 276	6	1	E-Texark.
Tom Green	51, 119, 340	3	7	N-San Ang.
Travis	53, 98, 126, 147, 167, 200, 201, 250, 261, 299, 331, 345, 353	3	3	W-Austin
Trinity	2nd 9, 258	1, 14	2	E-Lufkin
Tyler	1A, 88	9	2	E-Lufkin
Upshur	115	6, 12	1	E-Marshall
Upton	83, 112	8	6	W-Mid.-Od.
Uvalde	38	4	6	W-Del Rio
Val Verde	63	4	6	W-Del Rio
Van Zandt	294	5, 12	1	E-Tyler
Victoria	24, 135, 267, 377	13	4	S-Victoria
Walker	12, 278	1, 14	2	S-Houston
Waller	9, 155	1, 14	2	S-Houston
Ward	143	8	7	W-Pecos
Washington	21, 335	1, 14	2	W-Austin
Webb	49, 111, 341	4	4	S-Laredo
Wharton	23, 329	13	2	S-Houston
Wheeler	31	7	9	N-Amarillo
Wichita	30, 78, 89	2	8	N-W. Falls
Wilbarger	46	7	9	N-W. Falls
Willacy	103, 107, 138, 197, 357	13	5	S-Brownsville
Williamson	26, 277, 368	3	3	W-Austin
Wilson	81, 218	4	4	W-San Ant.
Winkler	109	8	7	W-Pecos
Wise	271	2	8	N-Ft. Worth
Wood	114, 294	6, 12	1	E-Tyler
Yoakum	121	7	9	N-Lubbock
Young	90	2	8	N-W. Falls
Zapata	49	4	4	S-Laredo
Zavala	293, 365	4	4	W-Del Rio

District Judges in Texas, 1995

Below are the names of all district judges in Texas listed in district court order. To determine which judges have jurisdiction in specific counties, refer to the table on pages 472-474.

Court	Judge
1	Joe Bob Golden
1A	Monte D. Lawlis
2	John R. Adamson
3	R.W. Lawrence
4	Donald Rae Ross
5	Jack Carter
6	Webb Biard
7	Louis Gohmert Jr.
8	Lanny R. Ramsay
9	Frederick E. Edwards
2nd 9	John D. Martin
10	David E. Garner
11	Mark Davidson
12	William Lee McAdams
13	Kenneth A. "Buck" Douglas
14	John M. Marshall
15	James Fry
16	John Narsutis
17	Fred W. Davis
18	C. C. "Kit" Cooke
19	Bill Logue
20	Charles E. Lance
21	John L. Placke
22	Charles R. Ramsay
23	Neil Caldwell
24	Joseph P. Kelly
25	Dwight E. Peschel
2nd 25	Gus J. Strauss
26	Billy R. Stubblefield
27	Joe Carroll
28	Robert C. Pate
29	David Cleveland
30	Robert P. Brotherton
31	M. Kent Sims
32	Weldon Kirk
33	Clayton E. Evans
34	William E. Moody
35	Ernest F. Cadenhead Jr.
36	Ronald M. Yeager
37	David Berchelmann Jr.
38	Mickey R. Pennington
39	Charles L. Chapman
40	Gene Knize
41	Mary Anne Bramblett
42	John Wilson Weeks
43	James O. Mullin
44	Candace G. Tyson
45	Carol R. Haberman
46	Tom Neely
47	David Gleason
48	Dixon W. Holman
49	Manuel R. Flores
50	David Wayne Hajek
51	Barbara L. Walther
52	Philip H. Zeigler
53	Mary P. Williams
54	George Allen
55	Kathleen S. Stone
56	I. Allan Lerner
57	Charles A. Gonzalez
58	James W. Mehaffy Jr.
59	Lloyd W. Perkins
60	James G. Sanderson
61	Shearn Smith
62	Jim Noble Thompson
63	George M. Thurmond
64	Jack R. Miller
65	Edward S. Marquez
66	F.B. (Bob) McGregor Jr.
67	George Allen Crowley
68	Gary Hall
69	Ron Enns
70	Jay Gibson
71	Bonnie Leggat
72	Blair Cherry
73	Andy Mireles
74	Alan M. Mayfield
75	J.C. "Zeke" Zbranek
76	Bill D. Moye
77	Horace D. Black Jr.
78	John Keith Nelson
79	Terry A. Canales
80	Scott Link
81	Olin B. Strauss
82	Robert Stem
83	Alex R. Gonzalez
84	William D. (Bill) Smith
85	J.D. Langley
86	Glen M. Ashworth
87	Sam Bill Bournias
88	William D. Beggs
89	Juanita Pavlick
90	C.J. Eden
91	Steven Ray Herod
92	Homer Salinas
93	Fernando Mancias
94	Jack E. Hunter
95	Joe B. Brown
96	Jeff Walker

Court	Judge	Court	Judge	Court	Judge
97	Roger E. Towery	167	Mike Lynch	237	John R. McFall
98	Jeanne Meurer	168	Guadalupe Rivera	238	John Hyde
99	Mackey K. Hancock	169	Oliver Kelley	239	J. Ray Gayle III
100	David M. McCoy	170	Joe N. Johnson	240	Thomas R. Culver III
101	Jay Patterson	171	Peter S. Peca Jr.	241	Kenneth Booker
102	John F. Miller Jr.	172	Donald J. Floyd	242	Marvin F. Marshall
103	Menton Murray Jr.	173	Jack H. Holland	243	David C. Guaderrama
104	Billy John Edwards	174	George H. Godwin	244	Joe Connally
105	J. Manuel Banales	175	Mary R. Roman	245	Annette Galik
106	George H. Hansard	176	James Brian Rains	246	Don Ritter
107	Benjamin Euresti Jr.	177	Miron A. Love	247	Bonnie Crane Hellums
108	Abe Lopez	178	William T. Harmon	248	W.R. Voigt
109	James L. Rex	179	Mike Wilkinson	249	Wayne Bridewell
110	Randy Hollums	180	Debbie Mantooth	250	John K. Dietz
111	Antonio A. Zardenetta	181	Samuel C. Kiser	251	Pat Pirtle
112	M. Brock Jones Jr.	182	Jeannine Barr	252	Leonard J. Giblin Jr.
113	Patricia Hancock	183	Jay W. Burnett	253	W.G. "Dub" Woods Jr.
114	Cynthia S. Kent	184	Jan Krocker	254	Dee Miller
115	Lauren "Laurie" Parish	185	H. Lon Harper	255	Don Koons
116	Frank Andrews	186	Terry McDonald	256	Brenda Garrett Green
117	Robert Blackmon	187	Raymond Angelini	257	Linda Motheral
118	Robert H. Moore III	188	Larry W. Starr	258	Joe Ned Dean
119	John E. Sutton	189	Carolyn Marks Johnson	259	Quay Parker
120	Robert Dinsmoor	190	John Devine	260	Buddie J. Hahn
121	Ray D. Anderson	191	David Brooks	261	Peter M. Lowry
122	Frank Carmona	192	Merrill L. Hartman	262	Doug Shaver
123	Steven M. Dowd	193	Michael J. O'Neill	263	Jim Wallace
124	Alvin G. Khoury	194	Harold Entz	264	Martha Jane (Janie) Trudo
125	Don Wittig	195	John Nelms	265	Keith Dean
126	Joseph H. Hart	196	Joe Leonard	266	Donald R. Jones
127	Sharolyn P. Wood	197	Darrell B. Hester	267	Whayland W. Kilgore
128	Patrick Allen Clark	198	Emil Karl Prohl	268	Brady G. Elliott
129	Greg Wayne Abbott	199	John R. Roach	269	David West
130	Joseph Ann Ottis	200	Paul R. Davis Jr.	270	Richard Hall
131	John D. Gabriel Jr.	201	Suzanne Covington	271	John H. Fostel
132	Ernie B. Armstrong	202	Bill Peek	272	John M. Delaney
133	Lamar McCorkle	203	Lana McDaniel	273	John W. Mitchell
134	Anne Packer	204	Mark Nancarrow	274	Bill Bender
135	Marion M. (Mack) Lewis	205	Kathleen H. Olivares	275	Juan R. Partida
136	Milton Gunn Shuffield	206	Joe B. Evins	276	William R. Porter
137	Cecil G. Puryear	207	Jack Robison	277	John R. Carter
138	Robert Garza	208	Denise Collins	278	Jerry A. Sandel
139	Raul L. Longoria	209	Michael T. McSpadden	279	Robert P. Walker
140	William R. Shaver	210	Sam M. Paxson	280	Tony Lindsay
141	Paul Enlow	211	Dee L. Shipman	281	William F. "Bill" Bell
142	George D. "Jody" Gilles	212	Roy Engelke	282	Tom Price
143	Bob Parks	213	Bob Keith Gill	283	Jack Hampton
144	Susan D. Reed	214	Mike Westergren	284	Olen Undersood
145	Jack Pierce	215	Dwight E. Jefferson	285	Michael Peden
146	Rick Morris	216	Stephen B. Ables	286	Andy Kupper
147	Wil Flowers	217	David V. Wilson	287	Jack D. Young
148	Hilda Tagle	218	Stella Saxon	288	Frank Montalvo
149	Robert "Bob"May	219	Curt B. Henderson	289	Carmen Kelsey
150	Janet Littlejohn	220	James E. Morgan	290	Sharlon MacRae
151	Carolyn C. Garcia	221	Lee G. Alworth	291	Gerry Meier
152	Harvey G. Brown Jr.	222	David Wesley Gulley	292	Michael Keasler
153	Ken C. Curry	223	Lee Waters	293	Rey Perez
154	Felix Klein	224	David Peeples	294	Tommy W. Wallace
155	Dan R. Beck	225	John J. Specia Jr.	295	Tracy E. Christopher
156	Joel B. Johnson	226	Sid L. Harle	296	Verla Sue Holland
157	Michael Schneider	227	Mike M. Machado	297	Everett Young
158	Phillip Vick	228	Ted Poe	298	Adolph Canales
159	Gerald A. Goodwin	229	Ricardo H. Garcia	299	Jon N. Wisser
160	David Godbey	230	Joe Kegans	300	Ogden Bass
161	Tryon D. Lewis	231	Randy Catterton	301	Bob O'Donnell
162	Bill Rhea	232	Mary Lou Keel	302	Frances A. Harris
163	David A. Dunn	233	William W. Harris	303	Richard Johnson
164	Mary K. (Katie) Kennedy	234	Scott A. Brister	304	Harold C. "Hal" Gaither Jr.
165	Elizabeth Ray	235	Jerry W. Woodlock	305	Cheryl Lee Shannon
166	Martha B. Tanner	236	Tom Lowe	306	Susan Baker Olsen

Court	Judge
307	Robin D. Sage
308	Georgia Dempster
309	John D. Montgomery
310	Lisa Millard
311	Bill Henderson
312	James D. Aquier
313	Pat Shelton
314	Mary Craft
315	Kent Ellis
316	John La Grone
317	James M. Farris
318	Dean Rucker
319	Max Bennett
320	Don Emerson
321	Ruth J. Blake
322	Frank Sullivan III
323	Jean Boyd
324	Brian A. Carper
325	Judith Wells
326	Aleta Hacker
327	Philip R. Martinez
328	Tom Stansbury
329	Daniel R. Sklar
330	Theo Bedard
331	Bob Perkins
332	Mario E. Ramirez Jr.
333	Richard P. Bianchi

Court	Judge
334	Russell Lloyd
335	H.R. Towslee
336	Ray Felty Grisham
337	Jim Barr
338	Mary Bacon
339	Caprice Cosper
340	Dick Alcala
341	Elma T.S. Ender
342	Bob McGrath
343	Alonzo "Al" T. Rodriguez
344	Carroll E. Wilborn Jr.
345	Scott McCown
346	Jose J. Baca
347	Joaquin Villarreal III
348	Michael D. Schattman
349	Jerry L. Calhoon
350	Jesse A. Holloway
351	Lupe Salinas
352	Bruce Auld
353	Margaret A. Cooper
354	Richard Bosworth
355	Tom Crum
356	Britton E. Plunk
357	Rogelio (Roy)Valdez
358	Bill McCoy
359	James H. Keeshan
360	V. Sue Koenig

Court	Judge
361	Carolyn L. Ruffino
362	David C. White
363	Faith Johnson
364	Brad Underwood
365	Amado Abascal
366	Nathan E. White Jr.
367	Lee Gabriel
368	Burt Carnes
369	Bascom W. Bentley III
370	Noe Gonzalez
371	James R. Wilson
372	Scott Wisch
377	Robert C. Cheshire
385	Willie B. DuBose

Criminal District Courts

Dallas 1	Janice Warder
Dallas 2	Larry W. Baraka
Dallas 3	Mark Tolle
Dallas 4	John C. Creuzot
Dallas 5	Manny Alvarez
Jefferson	Charles Carver
Tarrant 1	Sharen Wilson
Tarrant 2	Wayne F. Salvant
Tarrant 3	Don Leonard
Tarrant 4	Joe Drago

Source: Texas Judicial System Annual Report for Fiscal Year 1994, by Office of Court Administration, Texas Judicial Council, and the office of the Texas Secretary of State general election returns for 1994

State Agencies

On the following pages is information about several of the many state agencies. The agencies themselves supplied this information to the Texas Almanac.

Texas Department of Commerce

The Texas Department of Commerce is the state's lead economic development agency. Its mission is to create a positive business climate that attracts new companies, promotes Texas as a travel destination and trains today's work force for tomorrow's high-skill, high-wage jobs. It disseminates information on international trade, worker-training incentives, tourism, and other business matters. The department's four main program disivions are:

• The **Business Development Division** assists communities and businesses by marketing Texas as an internationally competitive economic region through business-finance services; foreign offices; community economic-development assistance; research and information; small-business assistance; and Texas Marketplace, an electronic bulletin board and business-referral system.

• The **Work Force Development Division** administers the federally funded **Job Training Partnership Act (JTPA)**. JTPA programs are designed to provide a skilled labor force for Texas employers and to help Texas employees cope with an ever-changing job market. JTPA core programs provide economically disadvantaged youth and adults and dislocated workers basic skills, education, vocational training and job-placement services.

• The **Smart Jobs Fund Program** was enacted in 1993 to assist businesses in upgrading the skills of their workers, potentially enriching the state's economy, and improving a company's profit potential. This program is "employer-driven," allowing businesses to custom-design training programs to meet their specific needs. It serves as an incentive for businesses to expand or to relocate in Texas.

• The **Tourism Division** promotes Texas as a premiere travel destination through advertising, media relations and travel-industry sales programs, targeting both domestic and international markets. The division also assists communities with information, resources, training and community tourism development.

Executive director of the department is Brenda F. Arnett. ☆

The Public Lands of Texas

This History of Texas Public Lands was revised for the Texas Almanac by Commissioner Garry Mauro and the staff of the General Land Office of Texas. It is a summary of a longer history of the Texas public domain in the General Land Office.

The **Texas General Land Office** is one of the oldest governmental entities in the state, dating back to the Republic. The practice of having a commissioner to administer public lands reaches even farther back into Texas history when proprietors of **Spanish and Mexican land grants** "commissioned" representatives to handle land transactions.

Before the American Revolution, proprietors of the colonies along the eastern seaboard established land offices under the supervision of the commissioned representative to sell land and control squatting or trespassing. Later in Texas, when the Mexican government began issuing land grants for colonization, each empresario colony had a land commissioner to issue individual land titles and settle disputes.

The **first General Land Office** was established in the constitution of the Republic of Texas in 1836, and the first Texas Congress enacted the provision into law in 1837. However, President Sam Houston vetoed the act on the grounds that the office would not be able to function properly until the records of the various empresario colonies, Spanish and Mexican land grants, and the appropriate archives could be properly gathered together. But the new Congress was so anxious to settle land questions that it overrode his veto.

The sale of public lands had been temporarily suspended during the War for Texas Independence from Mexico, and there was a great clamor to open up the public lands again. New settlers were arriving every day and the demand for free or cheap land was tremendous.

Because the new Texas government needed to become stable and productive, it sought to attract and keep these settlers. The Texas Congress enacted generous laws offering large tracts of land to just about anyone who wanted them. For example, all heads of households in Texas as of March 2, 1836, were entitled to a league and a labor of land (about 4,605 acres). Single men could claim a third of a league. In the 10 years Texas existed as a Republic, it alloted 41,570,733 acres to encourage settlement, to reward veterans of the War for Independence, to pay the Republic's debts and to finance its operations.

In 1844, as negotiations proceeded for Texas to join the Union, the resulting treaty stipulated that the U.S. would pay $10 million of the Republic's debts and acquire 175 million acres of the public domain. Opponents to statehood in the U.S. Congress felt that Texas' lands were not worth the assumption of the $10 million debt and refused to make the trade. In the final resolution for annexation, Texas was to keep its public domain and the U.S. was to disclaim any responsibility for Texas' debt. **Texas officially came into the Union on Dec. 29, 1845**, keeping both its debt and its public lands.

When the **first state constitution** was drawn up in July, 1845, it provided no major change in the administration of the Texas public domain. All land titles issued under the laws of Spain, Mexico and the Republic of Texas were recognized. The Commissioner of the General Land Office became one of the elected constitutional officials of the state government.

In the early years of statehood, Texas established the precedent of using its vast public domain for public benefit. The first use was to sell or trade off land to eliminate the huge debt remaining from the War for Independence and early years of the Republic. A western area of 67 million acres, now part of New Mexico, Colorado, Oklahoma, Kansas and Wyoming, was transferred to the United States by the Texas Legislature on Nov. 25, 1850. Texas received $10 million in government bonds. The state had shed all its debts by 1855 and still had over 98 million acres of open domain. Texas gave away land for internal improvements, homesteads, veterans grants, capitol construction, and for settlement of boundary disputes. More than 32 million acres were given away to promote railroad construction. And 50 million acres were set aside as an endowment to public schools and colleges.

By 1898, there was very little remaining unappropriated public land in Texas. The homestead policy, which had seen 4.8 million acres of land given away to settlers, was finally abandoned in 1899. The Legislature in 1900 determined that the public schools and the **Permanent School Fund** would receive all unsurveyed land and the few remaining unappropriated public lands. In 1939, all lakes, bays, islands and the submerged areas off the Texas coast accrued to the School Fund.

The end of the vast unappropriated public domain might have signaled the end of the use of public land for the benefit of all Texans. But when **oil was discovered in 1921 on state lands** under lease, this remaining public land became a most valuable economic asset to the state. After selling off 91.4 percent of its surface land without reserving mineral rights, Texas finally had established the right to its subsurface minerals in 1895. The **Relinquishment Act of 1919** gave the surface owners of the land rights to participate in the mineral wealth as "agents" of the state. The economic value of the public lands of Texas in the 20th century thus resulted from the belated development of its mineral ownership.

Today 20.6 million acres are considered to be in the public domain. This includes almost 4 million acres of submerged coastal lands, which are bays, inlets and the area from the Texas shoreline to the three-marine-league line (10.36 miles) in the Gulf of Mexico. In addition, more than one million acres are estimated to make up the state's riverbeds and vacant areas. The **University of Texas System** holds title to 2,109,000 fee acres and other state agencies or special schools hold title to approximately 2 million acres. Texas owns mineral rights alone in approximately 7.5 million covered under the Relinquishment Act, Free Royalty Act and the various sales acts and has outright ownership to approximately 810,000 upland acres, mostly west of the Pecos. Texas has liens on 1.5 million acres of land in the active accounts of the **Veterans Land Board** and another 1.7 million acres of excess land that are not calculated into any category.

Tidelands

Perhaps the most valuable segment of the Texas public domain is its **coastal submerged land.** And for some time, there was serious question about the state's ownership. The Republic of Texas had proclaimed its Gulf boundaries as three marine leagues, recognized by international law as traditional national boundaries. These boundaries were never seriously questioned when Texas joined the Union in 1845, and Texas continued to claim jurisdiction. A congressional resolution in 1930 authorized the U.S. Attorney General to file suit to establish the offshore lands as properties of the federal government.

The legal question was more important to Texas in the 20th century than it would have been upon entering the Union, since offshore oil and gas production had become a source of tremendous income to the state. Gulf of Mexico leases between the three-mile and the three-marine-league limit (the area claimed by the federal government) have brought the state approximately $1.5 billion in revenue since the first oil lease there in 1922. Congress returned the disputed lands to Texas in 1953, and the **Supreme Court finally confirmed Texas' ownership** to the 1,878,394 acres in 1960. (See Tidelands History in 1972-73 Texas Almanac.)

In 1978, the federal government also granted states a "fair and equitable" share of the revenues from offshore federal leases within three miles of the states' outermost boundary. The states did not receive any such revenue until April 1986 when Congress clarified the meaning of "fair and equitable" through additional legislation. Under the 1986 law, coastal states are entitled to 27 percent of all revenues in perpetuity from federal leases within three miles of the state-federal boundary. In addition, Texas received a one-time settlement to cover the 1978 to 1985 period amounting to $426 million in Fiscal Year 1986 and a deferred payment of $134 million over 15 years.

The General Land Office handles leases and revenue accounting on all lands dedicated to the **Permanent School Fund** and on land owned by various state agencies. The **Land Commissioner**, two members of **The University of Texas Board of Regents** and one **Texas A&M University Board of Regents** member make up the **Board for Lease** of lands dedicated to the **Permanent University Fund**. Revenue accounting for income from Permanent University Lands is processed by The University of Texas. Investment income from the fund is divided approximately two-thirds to one-third between The University of Texas and Texas A&M University, respectively. As of Sept. 1, 1992, the **Permanent University Fund** had reached a book value of more than $3.65 billion; the **Permanent School Fund** had a book value of more than $7.9 billion.

All activities on state lands are reviewed for their environmental impact, and restrictions are placed in offshore drilling leases where needed to protect resources.

Veterans Land Program

In 1946, the Legislature created a bond program to aid veterans in purchasing farm land. Up to $1.25 billion in bonding authority has been authorized over the years in a series of constitutional amendments; as of Jan. 1, 1991, more than $1.1 billion of the bonds had been sold to fund loans.

Loans cannot exceed $20,000, and tracts purchased through the program must be at least five acres. To date, more than 106,000 veterans have participated in the land program, purchasing more than 4.5 million acres of land.

Veterans Housing Assistance Program

The 68th Legislature created the Veterans Housing Assistance Program, which also is funded through bond proceeds. Over the years, the people of Texas have passed constitutional amendments authorizing the selling of $1.5 billion in bonds to finance this program. To date, $1.235 billion in bonds have been sold to fund housing loans.

Eligible veterans may borrow up to $45,000 toward the purchase of a home; the balance of the purchase price is financed through private-sector lending institutions. When the low-interest veterans loan is combined with private-sector interest rates, monthly payments are significantly reduced. Since the program began operation in January 1984, more than 33,800 veterans have received housing loans.

Veterans Home Improvement Program

In 1986, the Veterans Land Board implemented the Veterans Home Improvement Program, which is funded through the Veterans Housing Assistance Program. This program allows Texas Veterans to borrow between $4,000 and $25,000 to make substantial home repairs and improvements.

To date, more than 2,500 veterans have received home improvement loans. More than $32 million has been loaned since the program's inception.

All three programs are administered by the **Texas Veterans Land Board**, which is chaired by the Commissioner of the General Land Office. The bonded debt for the programs and all administrative costs are completely financed by the veterans who use the programs; there is no cost to Texas taxpayers. Eligible veterans may participate in each of the three veterans programs once.

Details about the programs may be obtained from the Texas Veterans Land Board by calling toll free 1-800-252-VETS. ☆

Public Lands of Texas

Taken from the records of the **General Land Office of Texas**, the following summary shows the disposition of the **public domain**. The total area given here differs from the U.S. Bureau of the Census figure of 171,096,320 given elsewhere in this volume.

	Acres	Subtotals
Total area to tidewater		172,193,269
Total area to 3-league (10.36-mile) limit		3,997,000
Total		**176,190,269**
Grants to promote citizenship and to induce immigration:		
By governments of Spain and Mexico	26,280,000	
Headrights and bounties	36,876,492	
Colonies—(Peters', Mercer's et al.)	4,494,806	
Homestead donations (pre-emptions)	4,847,136	72,498,434
Donations to veterans:		
San Jacinto veterans—Act of 1879 and 1881	1,169,382	
Confederate veterans—Act of 1881	1,979,852	3,149,234
Sold to pay public debts by Republic	1,329,200	
50¢ sales scrip act of 1879 and $2 sales scrip act of 1887	1,660,936	2,990,136
Internal improvements:		
State Capitol, building of	3,025,000	
Irrigation, drainage, iron works, Kiamasha Road and sundry	4,088,640	7,113,640
To acquire transportation facilities:		
Grants to railroads	32,153,878	32,153,878
For education:		
State University and A&M	2,329,168	
County school purposes	4,229,166	
Eleemosynary institutions	410,600	
Public free school	44,494,162	
Unsold public school land	813,122	52,276,218
Total surveyed land		**170,181,540**
Less conflicts (estimated at one half of 1 percent)		850,908
Net as per original surveys		**169,330,632**
Excess (estimated at approximately 1.1 percent)		1,862,637
River beds and vacancies (estimated)		1,000,000
Submerged coastal areas to three-league limit		3,997,000
Total		**176,190,269**

Department of Human Services

The following information was furnished by the Texas Department of Human Services.

The **Texas Department of Human Services (DHS)**, administers programs that provide financial and medical assistance and social services to those who are eligible. The department's headquarters are in Austin, but its services are available in all 254 Texas counties.

The **Texas Board of Human Services** is responsible for adoption of most policies, rules and regulations of the department. (See State Boards and Commissions for membership.)

Department services are provided through 10 administrative regions, each supervised by a regional administrator. The department's Austin headquarters staff develops program policy and provides support functions, such as legal, personnel, data-processing and fiscal services, that serve all programs.

DHS has two major program divisions: Client Self-support Services and Long-Term Care Services.

• **Client Self-Support Services** — The emphasis in Client Self-support Services (CSS) is on helping build the capacity of families to become and remain self-sufficient. CSS programs include those that provide assistance to meet basic needs, along with support services to promote economic independence.

The **Aid to Families with Dependent Children (AFDC)** program provides temporary financial assistance to needy dependent children and the parents or relatives with whom they live. Financial need must be the result of the absence or disability of a parent or the unemployment of the principal wage-earner parent. The average monthly grant per recipient is $58.

The DHS also determines eligibility for many health-care services through Medicaid. Generally, the people who qualify for Medicaid are those who receive AFDC or other selected categories of low-income families. Among those eligible for health-care services are pregnant women and infants whose family incomes are between 133 percent and 185 percent of the federal poverty level. Children ages 6 and older also can qualify if they were born after Sept. 30, 1983, and their family incomes are below 100 percent of the federal poverty level.

The **Food Stamp program** is a 100 percent federally funded program that provides financial assistance to low-income families to supplement their food-purchasing power and help them to obtain a nutritionally adequate diet. In 1994, DHS began delivering food assistance with a plastic debit card under the Electronic Benefit Transfer (EBT) system. EBT cards should have replaced food-stamp coupons in all Texas counties by the end of 1995.

Employment services help promote the long-term self-sufficiency of AFDC and food-stamp recipients. The **Job Opportunities and Basic Skills (JOBS) program** provides case management, education, vocational training, life-skills training, job preparation and job-search assistance to AFDC-eligible adults and teens. The **Food Stamp Employment and Training program** provides limited case management, job preparation and job-search assistance to food-stamp clients. Support services for clients participating in employment services include child care and allowances for transportation and certain other work- or training-related expenses.

The **Child Care program** uses a mix of funding sources to provide care for children of low-income parents so the parents can work, seek work or receive training that will lead to employment.

Other CSS programs include a 100 percent federally funded **Refugee Resettlement program**. Cash and medical assistance for refugees is limited to their first eight months of residence in the United States.

The **Disaster Assistance program** provides grants to families who are victims of a presidentially declared disaster, such as tornados, floods and hurricanes. Victims are eligible for assistance from this state-administered federal program if they do not have insurance and cannot qualify for low-interest loans from the Small Business Administration.

• **Long-Term Care Services** — The DHS provides assistance to Medicaid-eligible clients who are elderly or disabled in community-based programs or nursing facilities. Clients must meet three eligibility criteria to be certified for nursing facility services: financial need, medical necessity and the preadmission screening and annual resident review. DHS also administers the Community Care Services program to help prevent or delay the long-term institutionalization of eligible individuals through comunity-based services. This program provides in-home services, such as family care, primary home care, electronic monitoring and home-delivered meals. Out-of-home services include day-activity and health services, adult foster-care services and respite services. Residential care is available for those persons who need 24-hour supervision but not daily nursing intervention.

The **DHS Long-Term Care Regulatory** program has responsibility for regulating 1,292 licensed nursing facilities. DHS also licenses personal-care homes, which provide assisted living but not medical care, and adult day health-care facilities.

DHS provides services to more than 3 million Texans each year. Most department services are provided to people with incomes considerably lower than the federal poverty guidelines.

Costs of Services

Costs of most services are shared by the state and federal governments. Expenditures for fiscal year 1994 are as follows:

Family Income Assistance	**$1,332.368,692**
Long-term Care Services	**2,204,838,063**
All other expenditures	**10,845,547**
Grand Total	**$3,548,052,302**

Texas Youth Commission

The following institutions are under the direction of the **Texas Youth Commission,** the agency that administers the juvenile corrections system of the state. The date of founding of each facility is included:

Residential Treatment Center:

Corsicana State Home — Corsicana; 1897; Chester Clay Jr., superintendent; 90 students.

Institutions:

Brownwood State School — Brownwood; 1970; Gaylor Garrison, superintendent; 239 students.

Crockett State School — Crockett; 1947 (as **Brady State School for Colored Girls**; changed to **Crockett State School for Girls**; and in 1975 name changed to present form); Rey Gomez, superintendent; 175 students.

Gainesville State School — Gainesville; 1916; Jerry Day, superintendent; 332 students.

Giddings State School — Giddings; 1972; Sandy Burnam, superintendent; 322 students.

West Texas State School — Pyote; 1966; Johnny B. Williams, superintendent; 212 students.

In addition, almost all youth committed to the **Texas Youth Commission** are processed through either the **Statewide Reception Center** (Brownwood, 1970, Dan Humeniuk, superintendent). Youth committed from the South Texas Region (Alan Steen, regional director) undergo a diagnostic and evaluation process by an assessment team based in the 48-bed **Evins Regional Juvenile Center** in Edinburg (Doris Davila, facility administrator). ☆

Texas Department of Criminal Justice

The Texas Department of Criminal Justice, formed by the Texas Legislature in 1989, is composed of eight divisions. Those most in the public view are:

• The **Institutional Division**, which manages the Department's prisons (more details below).

• The **Pardons and Paroles Division,** which calculates parole release eligibility dates for inmates in the Institutional Division, makes recommendations to grant or deny paroles, and is reponsible for overseeing the reintegration of felons into society after release from prison. In fiscal year 1994, 71,057 adult offenders were under parole or mandatory supervision. A total of 9,963 inmates were released on parole from prison and 9,913 parolees were released from county jails. A total of 21,380 had their paroles revoked.

• The **State Jail Division**, which was established in 1993 to provide community-oriented rehabilitation for property and drug offenders. As of the end of fiscal 1994, 18 state jail division facilities containing 25,000 beds were under construction across the state in or near Beaumont, Houston, Hutchins, Dayton, Atascosita, San Antonio, Georgetown, Jacksboro, Plainview, Bonham, Henderson, Raymondville, El Paso, Gatesville, Colorado City, Edinburg, Dallas and Austin. At press time, all facilities were scheduled to be completed by Dec. 1995.

• The **Community Justice Assistance Division,** which provides punishment, supervision and rehabilitation programs, as well as facilities within the communities, for persons under probation supervision. In fiscal 1994, this division provided services to 214,273 adult felony probationers and 178,644 misdemeanor probationers.

The remaining four divisions are primarily internal in scope: **Administrative Services, Data Services, Engineering** and **Health Services.**

Total monies appropriated to the TDCJ by the Texas Legislature for the 1996-97 biennium amounted to $4.5 billion.

The **Texas Board of Criminal Justice** guides the administration and operation of the department in the areas of policy, planning and budgetary matters. For list of members, see Boards and Commissions list following this article. Mr. Carol S. Vance has served as board chairman since October 1992. The TDCJ executive director is James A. Collins.

Institutional Division of the TDCJ

The Institutional Division of the Texas Department of Criminal Justice operates the state prison system for adult felony offenders (juvenile offenders are under the jurisdiction of a separate state agency, the Texas Youth Commission). The division's headquarters is in Huntsville, with Wayne Scott as director.

The **total number of inmates** on hand at the end of fiscal year 1994 was 75,698. In addition, 2,832 were in private prisons, 8,164 were in transfer facilities, 2,921 were in detention facilities and 2,154 were in substance abuse facilities, for a total of almost 92,000. This population compares with 18,151 on Aug. 31, 1975.

The **agricultural** division provides much of the inmate population's food needs, managing 132,450 acres on 33 units located in 27 counties and employing more than 300 full-time agriculture professionals and 6,000 inmates each year. They operate prison packing plants, cotton gins and feed mills as well as raising crops and tending livestock.

In addition to farming, the division operates 42 factories or plants at 32 prison units. These **industries** utilizing inmate labor produce goods and services for the TDCJ and other tax-supported agencies and political subdivisions. Product categories include automotive repairs and products, textile and leather products, metal and wood products (including license plates), data and graphics services, janitorial products, cardboard containers and concrete products. These industries employed 7,500 inmates during fiscal 1994 and generated sales of more than $94 million.

These enterprises help keep the daily costs per inmate to $45.70. This compares with $41.48 in 1992.

In 1969, an **independent school** (Windham School System) was created within the division to offer education in grades 1-12 and special education leading to a GED, or high school diploma. Participation is mandatory for those who cannot read at the sixth-grade level. Participation is voluntary for those deemed literate but who have less than a high school diploma. In fiscal 1994, more than 60,000 inmates participated in the WSS's programs; 4,399 GED certificates and 10,862 vocational certificates were awarded.

Cooperative programs in **higher education** are being carried out on several units at nearby junior colleges, leading to associate degrees. Four-year and graduate degrees can be earned through cooperating senior colleges and universities. In fiscal 1994, 279 associate degrees, 50 baccalaureate degrees and 14 master's degrees were conferred on inmates. More than 2,000 vocational and extension certificates were also awarded.

Rehabilitative programs are also available in the fields of physiological and psychiatric health care, varied recreational programs, legal services, religious activities, inmate self-help groups, work-release programs, job placement services, pre-release programs and support programs in conjunction with other state agencies.

By the end of fiscal 1994, the Institutional Division was operating units with a combined 93,000 beds. Continued construction was expected to boost the system's capacity to more than 150,000 beds by the end of 1996, which would make the Texas prison system the largest in the nation.

Prison Units

Please note that the town listed is the nearest one to the facility, although the unit may actually be in another county. For instance, the Middleton transfer unit is listed as being near Abilene, which is in Taylor County, but the unit is across the county line in Jones County.

Beto I and II, Tennessee Colony, Anderson County; **Boyd**, Teague, Freestone County; **Briscoe**, Dilley, Frio County; **Central**, Sugar Land, Fort Bend County; **Clemens,** Brazoria, Brazoria County; **Clements,** Amarillo, Potter County; **Coffield,** Tennessee Colony, Anderson County; **Daniel**, Snyder, Scurry County; **Darrington**, Rosharon, Brazoria County; **Diagnostic**, Huntsville, Walker County; **Division Hospital**, Galveston, Galveston County; **Eastham,** Lovelady, Houston County; **Ellis I and II,** Huntsville, Walker County; **Ferguson,** Midway, Madison County; **Gatesville**, Gatesville, Coryell County (Women's Unit); **Goree**, Huntsville, Walker County; **Havens**, Brownwood, Brown County; **Hightower**, Dayton, Liberty County; **Hilltop**, Gatesville, Coryell County; **Hobby**, Marlin, Falls County; **Hughes**, Gatesville, Coryell County; **Huntsville**, Walker County; **Jester I, II, III and IV,** Richmond, Fort Bend County; **Jordan,** Pampa, Gray County; **Lewis**, Woodville, Tyler County; **McConnell**, Beeville, Bee County; **Michael**, Tennessee Colony, Anderson County; **Mountain View**, Gatesville, Coryell County (Women's Unit); **Pack I and II**, Navasota, Grimes County; **Ramsey I, II and III**,

Rosharon, Brazoria County; **Retrieve**, Angleton, Brazoria County; **Robertson**, Abilene, Taylor County; **Sayle**, Breckenridge, Caldwell County; **Skyview,** at Rusk State Hospital, Cherokee County; **Smith**, Lamesa, Dawson County; **Stevenson**, Cuero, DeWitt county; **Stiles,** Beaumont, Jefferson County; **Terrell**, Livingston, Polk County; **T.L. Roach**, Childress, Childress County; **Torres,** Hondo, Medina County; Wallace, Colorado City, Mitchell County; **Wynne**, Huntsville, Walker County.

Transfer Units

Garza East & West, Beeville, Bee county; **Gurney**, Tennessee Colony, Anderson County; **Holliday**, Huntsville, Walker County; **Middleton**, Abilene, Jones County.

State Detention Centers

Cotulla, La Salle County; Diboll, Angelina County; Fort Stockton, Pecos County; Marlin, Falls County; San Saba, San Saba County; and Tulia, Swisher County.

Private Pre-release Centers

The pre-release centers house minimum security inmates who are within two years of their parole eligibility dates. Programs are designed to improve an offender's potential for a successful re-entry into society. Programs include academic and vocational education, counseling services, adult living skills: in Bridgeport, Wise County; Cleveland, Liberty County; Kyle, Hays County; Lockhart, Caldwell County; and Venus, Johnson County. Three additional 500-bed private pre-release centers were under construction during the fiscal year at Diboll, Overton and Venus. ☆

Inmate Profile

Age/Sex/Ethnicity:

Sex:	94% male
Ethnicity:	47% Black
	28% White
	25% Hispanic
Average age:	33 years

Education

Haven't finished high school or passed GED:60%
Average educational level score: 7th grade
Average IQ: 92

Offenses:

Violent offenses were committed by 44 percent of inmates; property offenses by 30 percent; drug offenses by 22 percent.

Sentences/ Length of time served:

Average sentence length:	23 years
Average % of sentence served:	25%
Repeaters:	More than 50%

Death row Inmates, as of June 7, 1995

Ethnicity	Number	Percentage
White:	179	45 %
Black	157	38 %
Hispanic	63	16 %
Other	5	1 %
Total	***404**	

** Includes one federal inmate from Alabama*

Texas State Boards and Commissions

Following is a list of appointees to state boards and commissions, as well as other state officials, revised to July 1, 1995. Information usually includes (1) date of creation of agency; (2) whether the position is elective or appointive; (3) length of term; (4) number of members; (5) names of appointees, their hometowns and the dates of the terminations of their terms. In some instances the dates of expiration of terms have already passed; in such cases, no new appointment had been made by press time, and the official is continuing to fill the position until a successor can be named. Most positions marked "apptv." are appointed by the Governor. Where otherwise, appointing authority is given. Most advisory boards are not listed. Salaries for commissioners and administrators are those for the 1996-97 biennium.

Accountancy, Texas State Board of Public - (1945 with 2-year terms; reorganized 1959 as 9-member board with 6-yr. overlapping terms; number of members increased to 12 in 1979; increased to 15 in 1989); per diem and expenses; 15 members: Cynthia Barnes, Houston (1/31/97); Leopoldo P. Botello Jr., San Antonio (1/31/95); K. Michael Conaway, Midland (1/31/01); Jerry A. Davis, Houston (1/31/01); Nita J. Dodson, Rockwall (1/31/99); Vernon D. Evans, Fort Worth (1/31/97); Carmen C. Garcia, San Antonio (1/31/97); Earl C. Lairson, Houston (1/31/93); Judy J. Lee, Houston (1/31/97); Wanda Lorenz, Dallas (1/31/99); Frank W. Maresh, Houston (1/31/99); Roel (Roy) Martinez, McAllen (1/31/99); Lou Miller, San Antonio (1/31/01); Janet F. Parnell, Canadian (1/31/01); I. Lee Wilson, Rockwall (1/31/97). Exec. Dir., William Treacy, 1033 La Posada Dr., Ste. 340, Austin 78752-3892 ($53,834).

Acupuncture Examiners, Texas State Board of - (1993); apptv.; 6 yrs.; per diem; 9 members: Cheng Ming Chang, San Antonio (1/31/95); William F. Craig, Arlington (1/31/95); Houchi Dung, San Antonio (1/31/95); Gus L. Garcia, Austin (1/31/97); Nancy M. Land, Crockett (1/31/99); Shen Ping Liang, Houston (1/31/99); Lisa Ping-Hui Lin, Austin (1/31/99); Stephen M. Taylor, Fort Worth (1/31/97); Fred Wulf, Center (1/31/97).

Ad Valorem Tax Rate, Board to Calculate the - (1907); ex officio; term in other office; 3 members: Governor, State Comptroller of Public Accounts and State Treasurer.

Adjutant General - (1836 by Republic of Texas; present office established 1905); apptv.: Maj. Gen. Sam C. Turk ($63,431, plus house and utilities), Box 5218, Austin 78763.

Adjutant General - Assistant for Air: Brig. Gen. Lester L. McIntyre, Box 5218, Austin 78763.

Adjutant General - Assistant for Army: Brig. Gen. Wayne D. Marty, Box 5218, Austin 78763.

Administrative Judicial Districts of Texas, Presiding Judges - (Apptv. by Governor); serve terms concurrent with term as District Judge, subject to reappointment if re-elected to bench. No extra compensation. For names of judges, see Administrative Judicial Districts in index.

Aerospace Commission, Texas - (1987; re-established in 1989); apptv.; 6-yr.; 9 members: Wayne Alexander, Bellaire (2/1/97); Joseph P. Allen IV, Houston (2/1/95); Ronald G. Bliss, Houston (2/1/97); Stephanie A. Coleman, San Antonio (2/1/97); Lee L. Kaplan, Houston (2/1/99); Gary Lipe, Fort Worth (2/1/97); David W. Carr, Austin (2/1/95); James R. Royer, Houston (2/1/99); Jack M. Webb, Houston (2/1/93). Amy Kennedy-Reynolds, NASA Liaison; P.O. Box 58574, Houston 77258.

Aging, Texas Board on - (1965 as Governor's Committee on Aging; name changed in 1981 to present form; due to go out of existence 9-1-97 unless continued operation needed); apptv.; 6-yr.; expenses; 9 apptv. members: Nancy S. Bohman, San Antonio (2/1/99); Reginald F. Garrett, Tyler (2/1/95); Elena Bastida Gonzalez, Pharr (2/1/99); J. Kenneth Huff Sr., Whitesboro (2/1/97); Margaret C. Luckie, Wharton (2/1/95); Jan Patterson, Dallas (2/1/95); Evelyn Porter, San Antonio (2/1/91); Dan Roberts, Fort Worth (2/1/99); James W. Roberts, Andrews (2/1/93). Exec. Dir., Mary Sapp ($55,697), Box 12786, Austin 78711.

Agricultural Diversification Board - (1987); 2-yr., expenses; 8 members: 2 ex officio nonvoting (one each apptd. by Speaker and Lt. Gov.); 2 ex officio voting (Commissioner of Agriculture and director of Institute for International Agribusiness Studies at Prairie View A&M Univ.; 4

apptd. by Gov.: Polly Cummings Izoro (1/1/93); Luis Mata, El Paso (1/1/93); Maurice Owens, Hempstead (1/1/93); Joe Bailey Pate Jr., Lubbock (1/1/93). Admin., Jennifer Thompson, Texas Dept. of Agriculture, Box 12847, Austin 78711-2847.

Agricultural Finance Authority, Texas - (1987); expenses; 2-yr.; 6 members: 2 ex officio: Commissioner of Agriculture and director of Institute for International Agribusiness Studies at Prairie View A&M Univ.; 4 apptd. by Governor: Dickie G. Geries, Uvalde (1/1/97); Marvin A. Gregory, Sulphur Springs (1/1/93); R. David Guerrero, Alice (1/1/93); Leodoro Martinez Jr., Cotulla (1/1/93); Brad Rowland, Anson (1/1/95); Mary Esther Webb, Cisco (1/1/91).

Agricultural Resources Protection Authority - (1989); 2-yr., expenses; 9 members: 7 from govt. agencies: Dir., Texas Agricultural Experiment Station; Dean, College of Agricultural Sciences of Texas Tech University; Dean, University of Texas School of Public Health, Houston; Dir. of Environmental Epidemiology at Texas Department of Health; Chief of Groundwater Conservation section, Texas Water Commission; Dir. of Institute for International Agriculture at Prairie View A&M; Commissioner of Agriculture; 2 apptd. by Gov.: Larry Edward Smith, Munday (2/1/95); Max Woodfin, Austin (2/1/95).

Air Control Board, Texas - Abolished effective Sept. 1, 1993. Duties assumed by **Texas Natural Resource Conservation Commission.**

Aircraft Pooling Board, State - (1979); apptv.; 6-yr.; 5 members — 2 ex officio: representative of State Auditor's Office and representative of General Services Commission; 3 apptv. — one by Gov., one by Speaker and one by Lt. Gov. Gov.'s appointee: Joe B. McShane III, Midland (1/31/01). Exec. Dir., Bob DuLaney ($60,500), 4900 Old Manor Road, Austin 78723.

Alcohol and Drug Abuse, Texas Commission on - (1953 as Texas Commission on Alcoholism; name changed and membership increased to 9 in 1986); apptv.; 6-yr.; per diem and expenses; 9 members: Sylvia R. Andrew, San Antonio (6/8/97); Jerry P. Cunningham, Dallas (6/8/95); Fred Dotson, Midland (6/8/99); Dorothy L. Grasty, Arlington (6/8/97); Michael S. Hull, Austin (6/8/97); John McDonald, Palestine (6/8/99); Vernice M. Monroe, Beaumont (6/8/99); Mary Lou Parsons, Odessa (6/8/95); Joe Samuel Ratliff, Houston (6/8/95). Exec. Dir., James Bynum ($72,720), 720 Brazos, #403, Austin 78701.

Alcoholic Beverage Commission, Texas - (1935 as Liquor Control Board; name changed 1970); apptv.; 6-yr; per diem and expenses; administrator apptd. by commission; 3 members: Steven R. Baker, Houston (11/15/95); Martha S. Dickie, Austin (11/15/99); Roy Orr, DeSoto (11/15/97). Admin., Doyne Bailey ($80,761), Box 13127, Austin 78711.

Alzheimer's Disease and Related Disorders, Council on - (1987); 2-yr.; expenses; 17 members: 5 agency heads or their designees: Depts. of Aging, Health, Human Services, Mental Health and Mental Retardation and the Long-Term Care Coordinating Council for the Elderly; plus four apptd. by Lt. Gov.; 4 apptd. by Speaker; 4 apptd. by Gov. as follows: Dr. Bettye Davis-Lewis, Houston (9/1/93); Betty Haisten, Beaumont (9/1/94); Marian Rowe, Tyler (9/1/93); Fredericka G. Younger, San Antonio (9/1/94).

Angelina and Neches River Authority, Board of Directors - (1935 as Sabine-Neches Conservation Dist.; reorganized 1950 and name changed to Neches River Conservation Dist.; changed to present name in 1977); apptv.; expenses; 6-yr.; 9 members: Barbara H. Green, Jacksonville (9/5/97); Harold C. Maxwell, Diboll (9/5/95); Wendel Carl Messec, Henderson (9/5/93); Wylie A. Pirkle III, Larue (9/5/95); C. Wayland Quisenberry, Lufkin (9/5/95); Joe E. Rich Sr., Lufkin (9/5/93); Joyce Swearingen, Nacogdoches (9/5/93); Herman Wright, Jasper (9/5/97). Gen. Mgr., Gary L. Neighbors, Box 387, Lufkin 75902-0387.

Animal Health Commission, Texas - (1893 as Texas Livestock Sanitary Commission; name changed in 1959, membership increased to 9 in 1973; raised to 12 in 1983); apptv.; per diem and expenses; 6-yr.; 12 members: Donald Lee Berend, Wichita Falls (9/6/95); Bradley D. Bouma, El Paso (9/6/99); Jack R. Gardner, Nacogdoches (9/6/97); Joan N. Kelleher, San Antonio (9/6/97); Claude J. Kelley Jr., Fredericksburg (9/6/95); Mike Levi, Spicewood (9/6/95); Ernesto A. Morales, Devine (9/6/99); Allan C. Oltjen, Canyon (9/6/93); Florence Rieck, Roosevelt (9/6/95); Charles R. Sherron, Beaumont (9/6/97); David W. Winters, Del Rio (9/6/97); Richard W. Winters, Brady (9/6/99). Exec. Dir., Terry Beals, DVM ($69,065), Box 12966, Austin 78711-2966.

Antiquities Committee, Texas - (1969 as 7-member board; membership increased to 9 in 1983); apptv.; per diem and expenses; 2-yr., 9 members — 6 ex officio, term in other office: Chmn., Texas Historical Commission; Dir., State Parks and Wildlife Dept.; Commissioner of General Land Office; State Archeologist; State Engineer-Dir., Texas Dept. of Transportation; and Exec. Dir., Texas Dept. of Water Resources. Three apptv. members: James E. Corbin, Nacogdoches (1/31/93); Betty N. Murray, Harlingen (1/31/93); Marion Oettinger Jr., San Antonio (1/31/93). Staff Dir., J. Barto Arnold III, Box 12276, Austin 78711.

Appraiser Licensing and Certification Board, Texas - (1991); 2-yr.; apptd.; per diem on duty; 9 members: Exec. Sec. of Veterans' Land Board and 8 apptees: Gary D. Condra, Lubbock (1/31/91); Lynette T. Fornerette, Houston (1/31/93); Mary Jo Hutton, San Antonio (1/31/93); Robert A. Martin, Grand Prairie (1/31/93); Alvin E. Nelson Jr., Abilene (1/31/93); Gary W. Schur, Munday (1/31/93); Leroy Singleton Sr., Hempstead (1/31/93); Hayden Woodard, Junction (1/31/96). Commissioner, Renil C. Linér, P.O. Box 12188, Austin 78711-2188.

Architectural Examiners, Texas Board of - (1937 as 3-member board; raised to 6 members in 1951; increased to 9 in 1977); apptv.; 6-yr.; per diem and expenses; 9 members: Maricela R. Barr, Austin (1/31/99); Mary Ann Bryan, Houston (1/31/99); Mary French Cable, Sulphur Springs (1/31/99); Thomas D. Carter Jr., El Paso (1/31/97); Paula C. Day, Fort Worth (1/31/01); John Only Greer, Bryan (1/31/01); Norcell D. Haywood, San Antonio (1/31/97); Don W. Kirk, Fort Worth (1/31/97); Cleveland Turner III, Amarillo (1/31/01). Exec. Dir., Cathy Hendricks, ASID/IBD ($53,469), 8213 Shoal Creek Blvd., Ste. 107, Austin 78758.

Arts, Texas Commission on the - (1965 as Texas Fine Arts Commission; name changed to Texas Commission on the Arts and Humanities and membership increased to 18 in 1971; name changed to present form in 1979); apptv.; 6-yr.; expenses; 18 members: Richard Alvarado, El Paso (8/31/95); Dorothy Anne Conn, Beaumont (8/31/95); Timothy J. Crowley, College Station (8/31/97); David R. Durham, Abilene (8/31/99); Ruth Fox, Austin (8/31/95); Carolyn H. Grinstein, Fort Worth (8/31/97); Lisa Hembry, Dallas (8/31/95); William J. Hill, Houston (8/31/95); Nelda S. Lee, Odessa (8/31/99); Joan McGuire Mellard, San Antonio (8/31/99); Lurence D. Miller III, Austin (8/31/97); David Montejano, Austin (8/31/97); Raymond D. Nasher, Dallas (8/31/99); Matilda Robinson, Dallas (8/31/97); Frances Annette Strake, Houston (8/31/93); Marie Swartz, San Antonio (8/31/97); James D. Tittle, Abilene (8/31/95); Jay M. Vogelson, Dallas (8/31/99); Gilberto Zepeda Jr., San Juan (8/31/99). Exec. Dir., John Paul Batiste ($55,287), Box 13406, Austin 78711.

Athletic Trainers, Advisory Board of - (1971 as Texas Board of Athletic Trainers; name changed and membership increased to 6 in 1975); expenses; 6-yr.; 6 members: Miguel Angel Benavides, Pflugerville (1/31/97); Susan Rae Leeper, Watauga (1/31/97); Sanford E. Miller, Nacogdoches (1/31/93); James Glenn Murray, Lubbock (1/31/93); Cynthia Louise Raines, El Paso (1/31/89); Thomas D. Wilson Jr., Houston (1/31/95). Exec. Secretary, Allen Eggert, Texas Dept. of Health, 1100 W. 49th, Austin 78756.

Attorney, State Prosecuting - apptv.: Robert Huttash ($82,209), Box 12405, Austin 78711.

Auditor, State - (1929); apptv. by Legislative Audit Committee, a joint Senate-House committee; 2-yr.: Lawrence F. Alwin, Box 12067, Austin 78711-2067.

Aviation Advisory Committee - (1989 when replaced Aeronautics Commission; present name adopted 1991 on merger into Texas Dept. of Transportation); apptv.; expenses; 6 members, whose terms are at the pleasure of the commission: Dennis A. Blackburn, Kingwood; Oliver K. Kelley, Amarillo; Charles D. Nash Sr., Austin; Stephanie R. Roberts, Tyler; Zena Rucker, Grapevine; Elton Rust, Waring.

Bandera County River Authority - (1971); apptv.; 6-yr.; expenses; 9 members: Phillip F. Becker, Bandera (1/31/91); Jose Manuel Cantu, Pipe Creek (1/31/93); Morgan Keith Cox, Bandera (1/31/91); Tom Denyer, Bandera (1/31/91); J.B. Edwards, Pipe Creek (1/31/95); Paul Garrison Jr., Medina (1/31/93); Don E. Karr, Bandera (1/31/89); Joel K. Leighton, Vanderpool (1/31/95); Craig A. Tips, Bandera (1/31/93). Exec. Dir., P.O. Box 771, Bandera 78003.

Banking Board, State - (1909); 2 ex officio members, term in other office: Commissioner of Banking and State Treasurer; one apptd. by Gov. for 2 years: Patricia Crawford Peale, Lake Kiowa (1/31/97).

Banking Commissioner, State - (1923); apptv. by State Finance Commission; 2-yr.: Catherine Ghiglieri ($97,072), 2601 N. Lamar, Austin 78705 (See also Finance Commission of Texas).

Bar of Texas, State - (1939 as administrative arm of Supreme Court); 30 members elected by membership; 3-yr. terms; expenses paid from dues collected from membership. President, president-elect, vice president and immediate past president serve as ex officio members. Exec. Dir., Antonio Alvarado, Box 12487, Austin 78711.

Barber Examiners, State Board of - (1929 as 3-member board; membership increased in 1975); apptv.; 6-yr.; per diem and expenses; 6 members: Robert Castro, El Paso (1/31/97); Ernest W. Pack Sr., Waco (1/31/01); Hoye D. Tibbets, Grandview (1/31/99); Alan E. Warrick, San Antonio (1/31/99); Janice Elizabeth Wiggins, Kingsland (1/31/97); Charles E. Williams Sr., San Antonio (1/31/01). Exec. Dir., B. Michael Rice ($53,469), 9101 Burnet Rd., Ste. 103, Austin 78758.

Battleship Texas Advisory Board - (1983; superseded Battleship Texas Commission; apptv.; 6-yr.; 9 members: Charles A. Alcorn, Houston (2/1/95); Richard Burton Ballanfant, Houston (2/1/95); Blaine G. Corman, Crosby (2/1/97); Pauline M. Delaney, Houston (2/1/97); Gen. Hugh W. Hardy, Houston (2/1/99); Joshua Hill Sr., Houston (2/1/99); David A. Jones, Houston (2/1/92); Jerry D. Neel, Friendswood (2/1/99); George W. Strake III, Houston (2/1/95). Office Address: 3527 Battleground Rd., LaPorte 77571.

Blind and Severely Disabled Persons, Committee on Purchases of Products of - (1979); apptv.; 2-yr.; 10 members: Karen A. Allison, Lubbock (1/31/93); Pamela J. Daggett, Austin (1/31/95); Sue Evans, Round Rock (1/31/93); Norine W. Jaloway, Seabrook (1/31/93); Patricia K. Martin, Austin (1/31/95); Michael T. Phillips, Austin (1/31/95); Hollis F. Pinyan, Tyler (1/31/93); R. Wayne Sanders, Austin (1/31/95); Leticia M. Turner, Houston (1/31/95); Roger G. Welsch, Austin (1/31/95).

Blind and Visually Impaired, Governing Board of Texas School for the - (1979); apptv.; 6-yr.; expenses; 9 members: Mary G. Behnke, Orange (1/31/97); Anita Bonanno, Houston (1/31/01); Michael David Connolly, Nacogdoches (1/31/01); Roseanna Currey Davidson, Lubbock (1/31/99); Kerry Lee Goodwin, Dallas (1/31/99); Edward F. Guerra, Austin (1/31/97); Gloria Smith, Lufkin (1/31/97); Mary Sue Staples, Fort Worth (1/31/99); Frankie D. Swift, Miles (1/31/01). Exec. Dir., Philip H. Hatlen ($68,000), 1110 W. 45th, Austin 78756.

Blind, Texas Commission for the - (1931 as 6-member State Commission for the Blind; raised to 9 members in 1979; name changed in 1985); apptv.; 6-yr.; expenses; 9 members: Dr. James L. Caldwell, Austin (2/1/95); Carolyn Marie Garrett, Houston (2/1/99); Larry P. Johnson, San Antonio (2/1/97); Ann Masterson, Houston (2/1/95); Dr. Hilda Medrano, McAllen (2/1/97); Olivia Sandoval, San Antonio (2/1/99); Carol Santry, San Angelo (2/1/95); Olivia Chavez Schonberger, El Paso (2/1/99); John M. Turner, Dallas (2/1/97). Exec. Dir., Pat D. Westbrook ($65,166), Box 12866, Austin 78711.

Board of (Note: In most instances, state boards are alphabetized under specific reference word, as **Accountancy, Texas State Board of Public.**)

Brazos River Authority, Board of Directors - (1929 as Brazos River Conservation and Reclamation Dist.; name changed to present form in 1953); apptv.; 6-yr; expenses; 21 members: Deborah H. Bell, Abilene (2/1/01); Ada G. Connor, Mexia (2/1/97); Hulen M. Davis, Prairie View (2/1/99); Patricia S. Eason, Georgetown (2/1/97); Lynn Elliott, Navasota (2/1/01); C.C. "Jack" Farrar, Hico (2/1/01); Ramiro A. Galindo, Bryan (2/1/01); James J. Gibson, Guthrie (2/1/97); Horace R. Grace, Killeen (2/1/99); Everet E. Kennemer III, West Columbia (2/1/99); Lee M. Kidd, Denver City (2/1/99); David F. Lengefeld, Hamilton (2/1/99); Linda Kay Lyle, Plainview (2/1/01); Helen E. Martin, Stephenville (2/1/97); Johnoween Smyth Mathis, Hearne (2/1/99); Karen C. Matkin, Waco (2/1/99); Charles Moser, Brenham (2/1/97); Lyndon Olson Sr., Waco (2/1/97); Ruth Schiermeyer, Lubbock (2/1/01); Judith Vernon, Evant (2/1/01); John M. Wehby, Taylor (2/1/97). Gen. Mgr., Roy A. Roberts, Box 7555, Waco 76714-7555.

Canadian River Compact Commissioner - (1951); apptv.; salary and expenses; (function is to negotiate with other states respecting waters of the Canadian): Xen Harris Oden, Lubbock (12/31/97); Bonnie Pettyjohn. ($10,767).

Cancer Council, Texas - (1985); 6-yr.; 16 members: 1 State Senator; 1 State Representative; Chmn., Board of Health; Chmn., Board of Human Services; 12 apptd: Joseph Switz Bailes, Dallas (2/1/00); Grover L. Bynum Jr., Austin (2/1/96); James D. Dannenbaum, Houston (2/1/96); Karen Hausinkveld, Arlington (2/1/96); C. Stratton Hill Jr., Houston (2/1/00); William C. Levin, Galveston (2/1/96); Arminda Perez, Duncanville (2/1/96); Donald C. Spencer, Austin (2/1/00); Courtney Townsend Jr., Galveston (2/1/98); J. Taylor Wharton, Houston (2/1/98). Exec. Dir., Emily Untermeyer ($57,691), P.O. Box 12097, Austin 78711.

Central Colorado River Authority (See **Colorado River Authority, Central.**)

Chemist, State - (1911); ex officio, indefinite term: George W. Latimer, Box 3160, College Station 77841.

Child Abuse and Neglect Prevention, Council on - (1985); apptv.; 2-yr.; expenses; 9 members: W. B. Howard, Houston (9/1/91); Don T. O'Bannon Jr., Dallas (9/1/93); Ben G. Raimer, Texas City (9/1/95); Michael Atlee Reilly, Arlington (9/1/91); Celia M. Salomons, San Antonio (9/1/95); Mary B. Scruggs, Plano (9/1/91); Emily B. Shelton, Lufkin (9/1/93); Peggy B. Smith, Houston (9/1/95); Roy Edward Turner Jr., Amarillo (9/1/93).

Childhood Intervention Services, Interagency Council on Early - (1981); apptv.; 2-yr.; (5 members; number raised to 9 in 1993): one each apptd. from Dept. of Health, Comm. on Alcohol and Drug Abuse, Dept. of MHMR, Dept. of Human Services, Dept. of Protective and Regulatory Services and Central Education Agency and three apptd. by Gov.: Claudette W. Bryant, Dallas (2/1/95); Karen Douglas, San Antonio (2/1/99); Tammy H. Tiner, College Station (2/1/97). Exec. Dir., Mary Elder ($61,380), 1100 W. 49th, Austin 78756.

Children's Trust Fund of Texas Council - (1985; became independent agency in 1991); apptv., 6-yr; 9 members: J. Randolph Burton, Spring (9/1/99); Thelma Sanders Clardy, DeSoto (9/1/99); Sylvia A. Martinez-Flores, Lubbock (9/1/99); Pauline M. Mouton, Beaumont (9/1/97); Ben G. Raimer, Galveston (9/1/95); Michael Atlee Reilly, Arlington (9/1/97); Celia M. Salomons, San Antonio (9/1/95); Peggy B. Smith, Houston (9/1/95); Connie A. Sonnen, San Antonio (9/1/97). Exec. Dir., Janie D. Fields ($51,840), 8929 Shoal Creek Blvd., #200, Austin 78757-6854.

Chiropractic Examiners, Texas Board of - (1949); apptv.; 6-yr.; expenses; 9 members: Zinetta A. Burney, Houston (8/31/97); Danny Doyle, Fort Worth (8/3/97); Carroll V. Guice, Longview (8/3/97); Toy Brando Halsey, Houston (8/3/99); Sidney E. Isdale, Harker Heights (8/3/99); Nancy Z. Jones, Dallas (8/3/95); William T. Reece, Bay City (8/3/95); Guy L. Watts, Corpus Christi (8/3/99); John H. Wright, Houston (8/3/95). Exec. Dir., Patte B. Kent ($39,140), 333 Guadalupe, Tower III, #825, Austin 78701.

Coastal Water Authority, Board of Directors - (1967 as Coastal Industrial Water Authority, Board of Directors of; name changed in 1985); 7 members — 4 apptd. by mayor of Houston with advice and consent of governing body of Houston; 3 apptd. by Gov.; per diem and expenses; 2-yr.; Gov's. apptees: Buster E. French, Dayton (3/31/92); Johnnie G. Jennings, Baytown (4/1/93); S. Elwood York Jr., Houston (4/1/93). Exec. Dir., Ralph T. Rundle, Citicorp Center, 1200 Smith, Ste. 2260, Houston 77002.

College Opportunity Act Committee - (1989); 6-yr.; 9 members: 6 ex officio: Commissioner, General Land Office; Exec. Admin., Texas Water Development Board; Comptroller; State Treasurer; Exec. Dir., Bond Review

Board; Commissioner of Higher Education. 3 apptd.: Barbara J. Dugas-Patterson, Houston (2/1/97); Linda Perryman, Dallas (2/1/93); W. Ted Shaw, Dallas (2/1/95).

Colorado River Authority, Central, Board of Directors - (1935); apptv.; 6-yr.; per diem on duty; 9 members: Herman B. Cassaday, Talpa (2/1/97); Robert J. Cheaney II, Santa Ana (2/1/93); Thelbert Elkins, Coleman (2/1/97); Zeno Hemphill, Coleman (2/1/95); Jimmie S. Hobbs, Coleman (2/1/97); Clifford L. Horn, Talpa (2/1/93); Cloyce M. Huckabee, Coleman (2/1/95); Ross L. Jones, Coleman (2/1/95); Nicholas J. Knox, Burkett (2/1/93). Operations Mgr., Laneal Maedgen, Box 964, Coleman 76834.

Colorado River Authority, Lower, Board of Directors - (1934 as 9-member board; membership increased in 1951 and 1975); apptv.; 6-yr.; per diem on duty; 15 members: Richard G. Arellano, Llano (2/1/99); Maria Angela F. Beck, La Grange (2/1/97); Theodoral "Teddy" Boehm, Brenham (2/1/97); George Cason, Eagle Lake (2/1/99); I.O. Coleman Jr., Wharton (2/1/99); Frederick L. Henneke, Hunt (2/1/01); Pix D. Howell, Austin (2/1/99); Hilda C. Kroll, Johnson City (2/1/01); Tommy Z. Le Tulle (Mrs.), Bay City (2/1/97); Michael J. Lucksinger, Burnet (2/1/99); Betty Jo Miller, San Saba (2/1/97); Charles Patrick Oles Jr., Austin (2/1/01); E. Peter Pincoffs, Austin (2/1/09); Steve D. Rivers, Bastrop (2/1/09); Clinton Marie Wright, Smithville (2/1/97). Gen. Mgr., Mark Rose, Box 220, Austin 78767.

Colorado River Authority, Upper, Board of Directors - (1935 as 9-member board; reorganized in 1965); apptv.; 6-yr.; per diem and expenses; indefinite number of members: George Ray Alderman, Winters (2/1/95); Victor Wayne Choate, San Angelo (2/1/97); James David Clendennen, Silver (2/1/95); Harry B. Elam, San Angelo (2/1/95); C. Skeete Foster, Sterling City (2/1/99); Patricia P. Ivey, Robert Lee (2/1/97); Sidney J. Long, Robert Lee (2/1/99); Sara T. Ortiz, Colorado City (2/1/97); Carl S. Strain, San Angelo (2/1/93). Gen. Mgr., Robert H. Huckabee, 30 P.O. Box 1482, San Angelo, 76902.

Commerce Policy Board, Texas Department of - (1987, with 6 apptv. members; changed to present configuration in 1991); apptv.; 6-yr.; 9 members: 3 ex officio: Chmn., State Job Training Coordinating Council; Chmn., International Trade Commission; Chmn., Texas-Mexico Authority; 6 apptv. public members, as follows: Vernon E. Faulconer, Tyler (2/1/95); Murphy George, Lufkin (2/1/97); Gerald Grinstein, Fort Worth (2/1/97); Renee Higginbothan-Brooks, Fort Worth (2/1/99); Sonia Perez, McAllen (2/1/99). Exec. Dir., Texas Dept. of Commerce: Brenda Arnett ($79,536), Box 12728, Austin 78711-2728.

Commissioner of (See keyword, as **Agriculture, Commissioner of.**)

Concho River Water and Soil Conservation Authority, Lower - (1939); 6-yr.; 9 members: Leroy Paul Beach, Millersview (2/1/93); Howard E. Loveless, Eden (2/1/93); Billy J. Mikeska, Eola (2/1/93); Eugene R. Rogers, Eden (2/1/97); Benjamin O. Sims, Paint Rock (2/1/97); Alton R. Taylor, Eden (2/1/95); Edwin T. Tickle, Paint Rock (2/1/95); T.E. Wells, Paint Rock (2/1/91); Harvey P. Williams, Eola (2/1/95). Office Address: Rt. 1, Box 4, Paint Rock 76866.

Conservatorship Board, State - (1979); apptv.; expenses; 6-yr.; 3 members: Carolyn Gallagher Austin (2/1/01); Byron Tunnell, Bullard (2/1/97); J. Michael Weiss, Lubbock (2/1/99).

Consumer Credit Commissioner - Leslie Pettijohn (Acting) ($76, 915), 2601 N. Lamar, Austin 78705-4207.

Cosmetology Commission, Texas - (1935 as 3-member State Board of Hairdressers and Cosmetologists; name changed and membership increased to 6 apptv. and one ex officio in 1971); apptv.; per diem and expenses; 6-yr.; apptv. members: Lois Miriam Cohen, Graford (12/31/93); Lucille C. Garcia, San Antonio (12/31/91); Evelyn Aileen Hunter, Dallas (12/31/93); Dianna Gale Mays, Greenville (12/31/91); Nedum C. Muns III, Huntsville (12/31/95); Sergio Shearer, Edinburg (12/31/95). Exec. Dir., Ron Resech ($44,558), P.O. Box 26700, Austin 78755-0700.

Counselors, Texas State Board of Examiners of Professional - (1981); apptv.; 6-yr.; expenses; 9 members: Karen H. Barlow, Fort Worth (2/1/97); Julian L. Biggers Jr., Lubbock (2/1/95); Dr. Burtram B. Butler, Galveston (2/1/97); Graciela Guillen, El Paso (2/1/99); Jane Guzman, Dallas (2/1/95); Alice B. Jones, Houston (2/1/99); James O. Mathis, Huntsville (2/1/97); Anthony P. Picchioni, Grapevine (2/1/99); Norma Lee Walston, Austin (2/1/95). Exec. Sec., Kathy Craft, 1100 W. 49th, Austin 78756-3183.

Court Reporters Certification Board - (1977 as 9-member Texas Reporters Committee; name changed to present form and membership increased to 12 in 1983); apptv. by State Supreme Court; 6-yr.; expenses; 12 members: Ronald C. Bird, San Antonio (12/31/86); Charles Griggs, Sweetwater (12/31/90); Joseph H. Hart, Austin (12/31/88); Linda Hyde, Austin (12/31/86); David B. Jackson, Dallas (12/31/90); John M. Keel, Austin (12/31/88); Judy Kulhanek, Houston (12/31/90); Jack B. Moorhead, Houston (12/31/86); Louise Morse, Austin (12/31/88); Jean Nipper, Austin (12/31/90); Tom Prentice, Austin (12/31/86); Jerry Spence, Big Spring (12/31/88). Exec. Secy., Peg Liedtke ($36,106), Box 113131, Austin 78711-3131.

Credit Union Commission - (1949 as 3-member Credit Union Advisory Commission; name changed and membership increased to 6 in 1969; increased to 9 in 1981); apptv.; 6-yr.; expenses; 9 members: Gilbert E. Andrews, El Paso (2/15/93); Edward L. Ewing, San Antonio (2/15/97); Gerald W. Gurney, Plano (2/15/95); Larry Q. Olivarez, Corpus Christi (2/15/97); William Ruelle Parker, Groves (2/15/95); Jimmy F. Sasser, Edinburg (2/15/93); Terry R. Stapleton, Houston (2/15/97); Donald Greg Storch, Houston (2/15/93); Joe G. Thornton, Texarkana (2/15/95). Commissioner, Robert W. Rogers ($80,661), 914 E. Anderson Lane, Austin 78752-1699.

Crime Stoppers Advisory Council - (1981); apptv.; 2-yr.; 5 members: Elma Barrerra, Houston (9/1/93); Donald R. Geen, Lumberton (9/1/93); Ramona W. Hibbetts, Bryan (9/1/93); Linda Gayle Thompson, Aransas Pass (9/1/93); Leroy J. Wormley Jr., Austin (9/1/93).

Criminal Justice, Texas Board of - (1989: assumed duties of former Texas Board of Corrections and Adult Probation Commission; also oversees Board of Pardons and Paroles Division); apptd; 6-yr.; expenses; 9 members: Joshua W. Allen Sr., Beaumont (2/1/97); Rufus H. Duncan, Lufkin (2/1/97); John David Franz, Hidalgo (2/1/01); Ellen J. Halbert, Austin (2/1/97); Gilberto Hinojosa, Corpus Christi (2/1/99); Allan B. Polunsky, San Antonio (2/1/01); Carol S. Vance, Houston (2/1/99); John R. Ward, Gatesville (2/1/99); Carole S. Young, Dallas (2/1/01). Exec. Dir, Dept. of Criminal Justice: James A. Collins ($120,000), P.O. Box 13084, Austin 78711. (512) 463-9988.

Criminal Justice Policy Council - (1983); all terms at pleasure of appointor; 11 members: 3 ex officio — Gov., Lt. Gov., Speaker; 2 apptd. by Lt. Gov.; 2 apptd. by Speaker; 4 apptd. by Gov. Gov's apptees: Col. James B. Adams, Austin; John Holmes, Houston; D.L. "Sonny" Keesee, Lubbock; Susan D. Reed, San Antonio. Exec. Dir., Tony Fabelo ($60,265), P.O. Box 13332, Austin 78711.

Deaf and Hearing Impaired, Governing Board of the Texas School for the - (1979); 6-yr.; expenses; 9 members: Allan F. Bubeck Jr., Garland (1/31/95); Beatrice M. Burke, Big Spring (1/31/95); Johnelle M. Cortner, Houston (1/31/97); Nancy Ellen Munger, Kyle (1/31/95); Nanci Pagoda-Ciccone, Dallas (1/31/99); Robert E. Parrish, Dallas (1/31/99); Mary Lynch VanManen, Sugar Land (1/31/97); Polly Piercy Walton, Beaumont (1/31/97). Exec. Dir., Marvin B. Sallop ($63,230), Box 3538, Austin 78764.

Deaf and Hearing Impaired, Texas Commission for the - (1971 as 6-member board; membership raised to 9 in 1979); apptv.; 6-yr.; expenses; 9 members: Michelle Bailey, Houston (1/31/95); Paula Bartone-Bonillas, Ingleside (1/31/97); Milburn L. Coleman III, Port Aransas (1/31/95); Larry M. Correu, San Antonio (1/31/99); Donald Howard England, Austin (1/31/95); Delores Elaine Erlandson, Big Spring (1/31/93); Valerie Newell Johnson, Waco (1/31/97); Ruth T. Seeger, Austin (1/31/97); Linda Phillips Thune, Austin (1/31/99). Exec. Dir., David W. Myers ($51,840), Box 12904, Capitol Sta., Austin 78711.

Dental Examiners, State Board of - (1919 as 6-member board; increased to 9 members in 1971; increased to 12 in 1981; increased to 15 in 1991; sunsetted in 1994; reconstituted with 18 members in 1995); appt.; 6-yr.; per diem while on duty; 18 members: Sheryl Ann Beltrane, San Antonio (2/1/99); James L. Bolton, Borger (2/1/97); Jerry T. Burley, Houston (2/1/99); Tammy R. Fisher, Bedford (2/1/01); J. Hadley Hall, Abilene (2/1/99); Cornelius O. Henry, Tyler (2/1/97); James W. Kenedy, Houston (2/1/97);

H. Grant Lappin, Houston (2/1/97); Michael Nogueira, Rancho Viejo (2/1/01); David O. Olson, Bridge City (2/1/01); Miro Arthur Pavelka, Dallas (2/1/99); Felipe Reyna, Lorena (2/1/99); Ronald G. Smith, Lubbock (2/1/01); Kent T. Starr, Waco (2/1/99); Patricia Stuart Blackwell, Midland (2/1/01); Marsha Waugh, El Paso (2/1/97); Gail Wilks, Longview (2/1/97); Joe David Zayas, Rancho Viejo (2/1/01). Exec. Dir., C. Thomas Camp ($54,770), 327 Congress, #500, Austin 78701-4037.

Depository Board, State - (1905); 3 ex officio, term in other office: State Treasurer, Banking Commissioner, Comptroller; one apptd. by Gov. for 2-yr. term: James H. Flinchum, Rockwall (8/22/93). Office Address: P.O. Box 12608, Austin 78711.

Developmental Disabilities, Texas Planning Council for - (1971); apptv.; 6-yr.; 27 members — 8 ex offico: Representatives from Dept. of Mental Health and Mental Retardation, Rehabilitation Commission, Dept. of Health, Dept. of Human Services, Texas Dept. on Aging, Texas Education Agency, Texas Commission for the Blind, Texas Commission for the Deaf; 19 apptv. members: Abel Alonzo, Corpus Christi (2/1/99); David Lee Benson, Houston (2/1/99); Shenikwa Cox, Dallas (2/1/97); Tom Deliganis, San Antonio (2/1/95); Debbie B. Francis, Dallas (2/1/93); Raul Garza Jr., San Benito (2/1/99); Genevieve T. Hearon, Austin (2/1/97); J. Robert Hester Jr., Arlington (2/1/95); Jerijean Houchins, Rusk (2/1/95); Theda N. Hoyt, Cypress (2/1/95); Anita Faye S. Jones, Houston (2/1/97); Barbara G. Loera, Austin (2/1/97); Federico Marquez, El Paso (2/1/97); James McBryde, Abilene (2/1/95); Jan Reimann Newsom, Dallas (2/1/95); Margaret Robinson, Amarillo (2/1/97); Hector Saenz, San Antonio (2/1/97); Billie Sue Sweitzer, Fort Worth (2/1/99); Mildred J. Wait, DeSoto (2/1/95). Exec. Dir., Roger A. Webb, 4900 N. Lamar, Austin 78751.

Diabetes Council, Texas - (1983; with 5 ex officio and 6 public members serving 2-yr. terms; changed in 1987 to 3 ex officio and 8 public members; changed to present configuration in 1991); 4-yr.; 17 members — 5 ex officio; 12 apptv. public members as follows: Mamie L. Abernathy-McKnight, Dallas (2/1/96); Sydney Dale Colvill, Houston (2/1/95); Steve Davidson, Midland (2/1/91); Leonardo de la Garza, El Paso (2/1/94); Charmazel Dudt, Canyon (2/1/95); Elizabeth Diane Limon, San Antonio (2/1/95); Jacqueline S. Martin, Houston (2/1/94); Kathy R. Matney, Plano (2/1/95); Amelie G. Ramirez, San Antonio (2/1/96); Glenda Shelton, Austin (2/1/97); Raymond J. Snokhous, Houston (2/1/95); Sarah E. Villegas, San Antonio (2/1/96). Address: Texas Dept. of Health, 1100 W. 49th, Austin 78756.

Dietitians, Texas State Board of Examiners of - (1983); apptv.; 6-yr.; per diem and expenses: 9 members: Lucille DiDomenico, Arlington (9/1/99); Maxine B. Freeman, Houston (9/1/97); Ethelind S. Gibson, Nacogdoches (9/1/95); Pattye Greer, Nacogdoches (9/1/95); Ada Harden, Austin (9/1/97); Margarette Leggitt Harden, Lubbock (9/1/99); Helen P. O'Reilly, Plano (9/1/99); Cheryl Porter, Midland (9/1/95); Janice M. Walker, Houston (9/1/97). Texas Dept. of Health, 1100 W. 49th, Austin 78756.

Disabilities, Governor's Committee on People with - (1991); 16 members: 4 ex officio: Chmn., TEC; Commissioner, Texas Rehabilitation Comm.; Dir., Texas Commission for the Blind; member, Texas Comm. for the Deaf; 12 members apptd. by Governor serve 2-year terms: James H. Cashion III, Fort Worth (2/1/95); Lena DeLoyce Coleman, Corpus Christi (2/1/95); Rose Aird Minette, Austin (2/1/95); Shirley Ann Pacetti, Houston (2/1/94); Ralph Dean Rouse Jr., Rowlett; Carol Herring Weir, San Antonio (2/1/95); Redge Bolner Westbrook, Austin (2/1/95). Exec. Dir., Virginia Roberts, 4900 N. Lamar, Austin 78751-2613.

East Texas State University, Board of Regents - (1969); apptv.; 6-yr.; 9 members: John R. Armstrong, Bonham (2/15/01); Raymond B. Cameron, Rockwall (2/15/97); Kerry Noble Cammack, Austin (2/15/01); Cynthia A. Gonzalez, Garland (2/15/99); Reuben R. McDaniel III, Duncanville (2/15/97); R. Jay Phillips, Corpus Christi (2/15/01); Eduardo M. Salinas, Lyford (2/15/99); Demetris A. Sampson, Dallas (2/15/97); Nelda Grigsby Strong, Austin (2/15/99). Pres., Dr. Jerry D. Morris, ETSU, Commerce 75429.

Education, Board of Control for Southern Regional - (1969); apptv.; 4-yr.; 5 members: Gov. ex officio, 4 apptd.: Dr. Joann Horton, Houston (6/30/95); Libby Linebarger, Austin (6/30/97); Rene Nuñez, Austin (6/30/98); Carl A. Parker, Austin (6/30/96). Mark E. Musick, Pres., Southern Regional Education Board, 592 10th St. N.W., Atlanta, GA 30318-5790.

Education, Commissioner of - (1866 as Superintendent of Public Instruction; 1949 changed to present name by Gilmer-Aiken Law); apptv. by State Board of Education; 4-yr.: Dr. Michael A. Moses ($156,014) (See also Education, State Board of).

Education, State Board of - (1866; re-created 1928 and re-formed by Gilmer-Aikin Act in 1949 to consist of 21 elective members from districts co-extensive with 21 congressional districts at that time; membership increased to 24 with congressional redistricting in 1971, effective 1973; membership increased to 27 with congressional redistricting in 1981, effective 1983; reorganized by special legislative session as 15-member apptv. board in 1984 to become elective board again in 1988; expenses; 4-yr.; 15 members (numerals before names indicate district numbers): (1) Rene Nuñez, El Paso (1/1/99); (2) Mary Helen Berlanga, Corpus Christi (1/1/99); (3) Esteban Sosa, San Antonio (1/1/97); (4) Dr. Alma A. Allen, Houston (1/1/97); (5) Robert H. Offutt, San Antonio (1/1/97); (6) Jack Christie, Houston (1/1/97); (7) Dr. Carolyn Honea Crawford, Beaumont (1/1/97); (8) Donna Ballard, The Woodlands (1/1/99); (9) Randy Stevenson, Tyler (1/1/99); (10) Will D. Davis, Austin (1/1/97); (11) Diane Patrick, Arlington (1/1/97); (12) Geraldine "Tincy" Miller, Dallas (1/1/97); (13) Rosie Collins Sorrells, Dallas (1/1/99); (14) Richard Watson, Gorman (1/1/99); (15) Monte Hasie, Lubbock (1/1/99). Commissioner of Education, Dr. Michael A. Moses. Office Address: Texas Education Agency, 1701 N. Congress Ave., Austin 78701-1494(see also Education, Commissioner of).

Educational Excellence Committee - (1989); apptv.; 6-yrs.; 15 members: Edward B. Adams, Austin (2/1/93); Brenda F. Arnett, Houston (2/1/93); Patti Clapp, Dallas (2/1/95); Yvonne A. Ewell, Dallas (2/1/97); Irene M. Garcia, Mission (2/1/97); Jacqueline R. Goettsche, Fredericksburg (2/1/97); Nancy Ann Loeffler, San Antonio (2/1/95); Dan Frank Long, Georgetown (2/1/93); Roger C. Minard, Austin (2/1/93); Maxine J. Nance, Atlanta (2/1/97); Bette A. Noble, Victoria (2/1/95); Winston C. Power Jr., Dallas (2/1/95); Donald Reynolds, Goodrich (2/1/93); Glenda Smith, Austin (2/1/91); Larry J. Ward, Richardson (2/1/95).

Edwards Underground Water District - 6-yr. terms, 12 members: Harry Bishop, San Marcos (2/28/93); Jo Ann De Hoyos, San Antonio (2/28/95); Frances D. Emery, San Marcos (2/28/95); Robert C. Hasslocher, San Antonio (2/28/93); Hans R.F. Helland, San Antonio (2/28/97); S. Craig Hollmig, New Braunfels (2/28/97); Kenneth G. Ikels, New Braunfels (2/28/95); Jerri W. Martin, San Marcos (2/28/97); Jack R. Ohlrich, New Braunfels (2/28/93); Carol Patterson, San Antonio (2/28/97); Charles F. Rodriguez, San Antonio (2/28/93); Jesse Zuniga Jr., San Antonio (2/28/95). Gen. Mgr., Russell L. Masters, Box 15830, San Antonio 78212.

Egg Marketing Advisory Board - (1957); apptv.; 6-yr.; 11 members — 2 ex officio: Commissioner of Agriculture is chairman; one apptd. by head of Poultry Science Dept., Texas A&M University; 9 apptv.: Larry J. Berend, Wichita Falls (9/27/97); Gilbert A. Burton, Lufkin (9/27/97); Jack Wilson Evans Jr., Dallas (9/27/93); Kervin E. Jacob, Houston (9/27/97); David M. Jenkins, La Grange (9/27/95); Hobert H. Joe, Houston (9/27/95); Terry A. Legan, Dallas (9/27/95); Ernest A. Mahard, Prosper (9/27/93); James M. (Mike) Robinson, San Antonio (9/27/99). Address: Dept. of Agriculture, Box 12847, Austin 78711.

Election Commission, State - (1973); 9 members, ex officio and apptv. as indicated: Chmn. of Democratic State Executive Committee; Chmn. of Republican State Executive Committee; Chief Justice of Supreme Court; Presiding Judge, Court of Criminal Appeals; 2 persons to be named, one a justice of the Court of Appeals apptd. by Chief Justice of Supreme Court, one a District Judge apptd. by presiding judge of Court of Criminal Appeals; 2 county chairmen, one each from Democratic and Republican parties, named by the parties; Secretary of State.

Emergency Communications, Advisory Commission on State - (1985); expenses; 17 members -- 5 ex offico: exec. directors of Texas Advisory Commission on

Intergovernmental Relations, Depts. of Health, Public Safety, Criminal Justice Policy Council and the major association representing regional planning commissions; 12 public members: 8 apptd. by Gov., 2 by Lt. Gov., 2 by Speaker. Gov's. apptees: Vaughn R. Aldredge, Austin (9/1/93); Arlene R. Aldridge, Laredo (9/1/97); Patrick A. Craven, Buda (9/1/93); William Charles Deere, Dallas (9/1/97); Bradford Eugene Denton, Round Rock (9/1/97); Judge Ron Harris, Plano (9/1/93); Laverne Heath Hogan, Houston (9/1/95); John William Munn, Fort Worth (9/1/93). Exec. Dir., Mary A. Boyd ($66,960), 1101 Capital of Texas Highway S., #B-100, Austin 78746.

Employment Commission, Texas - (See **Workforce Commission, Texas**)

Engineers, State Board of Registration for Professional - (1937 as 6-member board; membership increased to 9 in 1981); apptv.; per diem and expenses; 6-yr.; 9 members: James G. Abbee, Bedford (9/26/95); Linda Yee Chew, El Paso (9/26/97); Earnest F. Gloyna, Austin (9/26/95); Derrell E. Johnson, Southlake (9/26/97); Jose I. Novoa, Dallas (9/26/93); Hubert Oxford III, Beaumont (9/26/99); Roxanne L. Pillar, Fort Worth (9/26/97); C.H. (Herb) Treat, San Antonio (9/26/99); James K. Wilhelm, Houston (9/26/95). Exec. Dir., Charles E. Nemir ($60,516), Drawer 18329, Austin 78760.

Ethics Commission, Texas - (1991); apptd.; 4-yr.; 8 members: 2 apptd. by Speaker, 2 apptd. by Lt. Gov, 4 apptd. by Gov.: John E. Clark, San Antonio (11/19/95); Fran Coppinger, Pearland (11/19/93); James D. Marston, Austin (11/19/95); Isaias Torres, Houston (11/19/93). Exec. Dir., John Steiner ($75,000), Box 12070, Austin 78711-2070.

Evergreen Underground Water Conservation District - (1965); 2-yr.; 5 members — 4 elected: 2 each from Wilson and Atascosa counties; one apptd. by Gov.: William Oren Lamb, Pleasanton (2/1/95).

Family Practice Residency Advisory Committee - (1977); 3-yr.; expenses; 12 members apptv. as follows: one practicing physician apptd. by Texas Osteopathic Medical Assn.; 2 apptd. by Assn. of Directors of Family Practice Training Programs; one apptd. by Texas Medical Assn.; 2 administrators of hospitals apptd. by Texas Hospital Assn.; president, Texas Academy of Family Physicians; and 3 public members apptd. by the Gov., as follows: Tamara J. Cowen Brownsville (8/29/97); Dr. Jack L. Eidson, Weatherford (8/29/93); Judith A. Youngs, Dallas (8/29/95).

Finance Commission, State - (1923 as Banking Commission; reorganized as Finance Commission in 1943 with 9 members; membership increased to 12 in 1983; changed back to 9 members in 1989); apptv.; 6-yr.; per diem and traveling expenses; 9 members: Hubert Bell Jr., Austin (2/1/96); James T. Chambers, Stephenville (2/1/98); Dana H. Cook, Missouri City (2/1/94); Georgina S. Gonzalez, Houston (2/1/98); David M. Laney, Dallas l2/1/96); Katherine B. Reynolds, Austin (2/1/98); Scott B. Smith, Denison (2/1/94); Milton H. Thomas Jr., Dallas (2/1/94); Ruby J. Wimberley, Orange (2/1/96). Banking Commissioner, Catherine Ghiglieri ($97,072), 2601 N. Lamar, Austin 78705, appointee of Finance Commission. (See also Banking Commissioner, State.)

Fire Ant Advisory Board - (1987); apptv.; expenses; 6-yr.; 9 members: 3 ex officio: Commissioner of Agriculture, exec. dir. of Parks and Wildlife Dept., engineer-director of Texas Department of Transportation; 6 apptd. — 2 by Commissioner of Agriculture, 4 apptd. by Gov.: Stanley Carter Haddock, Dallas (1/1/99); Juan D. Nichols, Quitman (1/1/97); Wayne R. Snodgrass, Nassau Bay (1/1/95); Davis Whitehurst Jr., Longview (1/1/99).

Fire Fighters' Pension Commissioner - (1937); apptv.; 2-yr.: Helen Campbell ($45,000), 3910 S. I-35, #235, Austin 78704.

Fire Fighters' Relief and Retirement Fund - (1977); apptv.; expenses; 6-yr.; 9 members: Jennifer S. Armstrong, Mansfield (9/1/99) Robert Barrett, Seminole (9/1/99); Donald A. Eernisse, Alvin (9/1/97); Glenn D. Neutzler, Brenham (9/1/97); Wayne E. Popp, Louise (9/1/93); Robert J. Rice, Canyon (9/1/95); Charles H. Romans, Uvalde (9/1/95); Thomas N. Tourtellotte, Driftwood (9/1/97); Merle D. Wilkins, Kyle (9/1/95). Fire Fighters' Commissioner, Helen L. Campbell, 3901 S. I-35, #235, Austin 78704.

Fire Protection, Texas Commission on - (1991; formed by consolidation of Fire Dept. Emergency Board and Commission on Fire Protection Personnel Standards and Education); apptv.; 6-yrs.; expenses; 12 members: David Abernathy Pittsburg (2/1/01); Chief Juan J. Adame, Corpus Christi (2/1/97); Elizabeth J. Atchley, Lefors (2/1/97); Capt. Marvin G. Dawson, Brownfield (2/1/99); Gerald K. Hood, Fort Worth (2/1/97); Patrick K. Hughes Sr., Keller (2/1/97); Jon M. Hutchens, Houston (2/1/01); Ronnie E. James, Wichita Falls (2/1/99); Gilbert Robinson, Texas City (2/1/99); Capt. Ricardo Saldana, Mission (2/1/99); Kelley Martin Stalder, Parker (2/1/01); Carl Dewayne Wren, Manchaca (2/1/01). Exec. Dir., Michael E. Hines ($68,959), 12675 Research Blvd., Austin 78768.

Food and Fibers Commission, Texas - (1941) as Cotton Research Committee; name changed in 1971 to Natural Fibers and Food Protein Committee; changed to commission in 1975; changed to present name 1989); 4 members are presidents and chancellor of four major universities (Pres., Texas Woman's University, Denton; Pres., Texas Tech University, Lubbock; Chancellor, Texas A&M University System, College Station; Pres., University of Texas at Austin) serving indefinite terms; and one ex officio member who is director of administrative office in Dallas, apptd. to 2-year term: Exec. Dir., Carl Cox ($60,833), 17360 Coit Rd., Dallas 75252.

Funeral Service Commission, Texas - (1903 as State Board of Embalming; 1935 as State Board of Funeral Directors and Embalmers; 1953 as 6-member board; membership increased to 9 in 1979; name changed to present form in 1987); apptv.; per diem and expenses; 6-yr.; 9 members: Russell Wayne Allen, Benbrook (1/31/95); Robert R. Dixon, West Columbia (1/31/97); Martha Fitzwater, San Antonio (1/31/97); Rosa P. Foster, Nacogdoches (1/31/99); Scott Kurth, Cedar Hill (1/31/95); Percy Parsons, Dimmitt (1/31/93); Norberto Salinas Sr., Mission (1/31/97); Lois Villasenor, Austin (1/31/95); Millard F. Zeagler Jr., Lufkin (1/31/99). Exec. Dir., Wayne Butterfield ($42,000), 8100 Cameron Rd., Bldg. B, #550, Austin 78753.

General Services Commission - (1919 as Board of Control; name changed to State Purchasing and General Services Commission in 1979; changed to present form and increased to 6 commissioners in 1991); apptv.; 6-yr.; expenses; 6 members: Ofelia de los Santos, Edinburg (1/31/99); Ramiro Guzman, El Paso (1/31/99); Paul Hobby, Houston (1/31/97); Alphonso Jackson, Dallas (1/31/01); Ronald Kirk, Dallas (1/31/95); Betty McKool, Dallas (1/31/97). Exec. Dir.,John Pouland ($78,000), Box 13047, Austin 78711-3047.

Growth Fund Board of Trustees, Texas - (1988); apptd.; 6-yr.; 9 members — one member from and elected by membership of each of the following: Board of Regents, University of Texas System; Board of Regents, Texas A&M University System; Board of Trustees, Teacher Retirement System; Board of Trustees, Employees Retirement System; State Board of Education; 4 public members apptd. by Gov.: Daphne Ann Brown, Houston (2/1/99); H. Scott Caven, Houston (2/1/99); Matrice Ellis-Kirk, Dallas (2/1/97); C.T. "Carlos" Sharpless, Dallas (2/1/97).

Guadalupe River Authority, Upper - (1939); apptv.; 6-yr.; 9 members: Georgia H. Christley, Kerrville (2/1/99); Robert Lynn Finch, Kerrville (2/1/95); John R. Furman III, Kerrville (2/1/95); Waldean Groff, Kerrville (2/1/97); Mary Virginia Holekamp, Kerrville (2/1/95); Ernest Linares, Kerrville (2/1/99); John R. Mosty, Center Point (2/1/97); Donald C. Oehler, Ingram (2/1/97); Laresa Smith, Kerrville (2/1/99). Gen. Mgr., B. W. Bruns, Box 1278, Kerrville 78029-1278.

Guadalupe-Blanco River Authority - (1935); apptv.; per diem and expenses on duty; 6-yr.; 9 members: William A. Blackwell, Cuero (2/1/95); Marshall Ray Holybee, Bayside (2/1/99); Warren P. Kirksey, Lockhart (2/1/97); Olga Lara, New Braunfels (2/1/99); Catherine Roberts McHaney, Victoria (2/1/97); Jerry Lloyd Moore Jr., San Marcos (2/1/95); Jen F. Ripley, Waelder (2/1/95); Wanda Roberts, Port Lavaca (2/1/99); John C. Taylor, McQueeney (2/1/97). Gen. Mgr., John H. Specht, Box 271, Seguin 78156-0271.

Gulf Coast Waste Disposal Authority - (1969); apptv.; 2-yr.; per diem and expenses on duty; 9 members: 3 apptv. by Gov., 3 by County Commissioners Courts of counties in district, 3 by Municipalities Waste Disposal Councils of counties in district. Gov's. apptees: Roy E. Byerly, Alvin (8/31/96); Jerome J. Pennington, Houston (8/31/95); Oscar G. Weir, Baytown (8/31/92). Gen. Mgr., Richard L. Brown, P.O. Box 58150, Houston 77258-8150.

Gulf States Marine Fisheries Commission - (1949); apptv.; 3-yr.; 3 members — 2 ex officio: exec. dir., Texas Parks & Wildlife Dept.; one member of House; one apptd. by Gov.: Jan J. (Mr.) Harper, Lake Jackson (3/17/96). Exec. Dir., Larry B. Simpson, Box 726, Ocean Springs, MS 30564.

Health, Commissioner of - (1879 as State Health Officer; 1955 changed to Commissioner of Health; 1975 changed to Director, Texas Department of Health Resources; 1977 changed to Commissioner, Texas Department of Health; apptv.; 2-yr.: Dr. David R. Smith ($148,683), 1100 W. 49th, Austin 78756.

Health and Human Services, Commissioner of - (1991); apptd.; 2-yr.; one commissioner: Michael D. McKinney ($156,014), Houston (2/1/97). Box 13247, Austin 78711.

Health Benefits Purchasing Cooperative, Texas, Board of Trustees - (1993); 6-yr., apptd.; expenses; 6 members: Maria E. Crowley, Dallas (2/1/95); Matrice Ellis-Kirk, Dallas (2/1/95); Cappy R. McGarr, Dallas (2/1/99); Joseph F. Phillips, Mission (2/1/99); Marvin L. Ragsdale, Georgetown (2/1/97); Philip Patrick Sun, Missouri City (2/1/97).

Health Care Reimbursement Alternatives, Texas Commission on - (1987); term at pleasure of Gov.; apptd., expenses; 18 members — 4 representatives and 3 public members apptd. by Speaker; 4 senators and 3 public members apptd. by Lt. Gov.; 3 public members and chairman apptd. by Gov.; Gov's apptees: Joel T. Allison, Corpus Christi; Lynda Calcote, Abilene; William P. Daves Jr., Dallas; Carol Carlson Dean, Lakeside City.

Health Coordinating Council, Statewide - (1975); apptv.; 2-yr.; membership decreased from 21 to 15 in 1993: 3 health care professionals, 3 from institutions of higher education, 3 consumer advocates, 6 public members; apptv., as follows: Annabel Barker, Big Spring (8/31/95); Joan Wood Biggerstaff, Plano (8/31/97); Nick U. Curry, Fort worth (8/31/95); Dana S. Fitzsimmons, Houston (8/31/97); Barbara Ann Gonzalez, Alice (8/31/99); John P. Howe III, San Antonio (8/31/97); Ann E. Kitchen, Austin (8/31/99); Man-Ja C. Lee, Little Elm (8/31/99); Linda C. Lopez, San Antonio (8/31/95); Polly L. McFadden, El Paso (8/31/99); Shirley McManigal, Lubbock (8/31/99); Therese Ruffing, Austin (8/31/95); Betty J. Shinn, Nacogdoches (8/31/97); deSaussure M. Treviño, Pharr (8/31/95); Francisco J. Velazquez, San Antonio (8/31/97). Exec. Dir., A. Spires, Texas Dept. of Health, 1100 W. 49th, Austin 78756-3199.

Health, Texas Board of - (1903 as State Board of Health; superseded similar department created in 1891; name changed in 1975 to Texas Board of Health Resources and membership increased to 18; name changed in 1977 to present form); apptv.; per diem and expenses on duty; 6-yr.; 18 members: Ron J. Anderson, Duncanville (2/1/97); Joan W. Biggerstaff, Plano (2/1/95); Dr. Robert E. Bonham, Dallas (2/1/95); Dr. Frank Bryant Jr., San Antonio (2/1/93); Ramiro R. Casso, McAllen (2/1/97); David L. Collins, Missouri City (2/1/97); Dr. Bennett L.G. Harber, Boerne (2/1/95); Larry D. Krupala, Cuero (2/1/93); Dr. Donald M. Peterson, Dallas (2/1/95); Dr. Susan B. Place, Plano (2/1/97); William D. Poteet III, Lubbock (2/1/95); Dr. Milton Lee Risinger, Terrell (2/1/95); Herbert Shore, Dallas (2/1/93); Barbara T. Slover, Fort Worth (2/1/93); Oliver Roy Smith, El Paso (2/1/93); Ruth F. Stewart, San Antonio (2/1/97); Dr. Raleigh R. White IV, Temple (2/1/93); Walter D. Wilkerson Jr., Conroe (2/1/09). Commissioner of Health, David Smith, M.D., 1100 W. 49th, Austin 78756.

Hearing Instruments, State Committee of Examiners in the Fitting and Dispensing of - (1969); apptv.; 6-yr.; expenses; 9 members: Andrew Louis Burns Jr., Texarkana (12/31/95); Joycie L. Burns, Teague (12/31/97); Larry W. Farris, Universal City (12/31/99); Wallace Hamill, Dallas (12/31/95); Austin I. King, Abilene (12/31/95); Thomas C. Lucenay, Hewitt (12/31/97);Andrew Peña, El Paso (12/31/99); Jane W. Porter, Irving (12/31/97); Diane Cecile Shaffer, Beaumont (12/31/97). Exec. Dir., Wanda Stewart, 4800 N. Lamar, Ste. 150, Austin 78756.

Higher Education Coordinating Board, Texas - (1953 as temporary board; 1955 as permanent 15-member Texas Commission on Higher Education; increased to 18 members in 1965; name changed to present form in 1987); apptv.; 6-yr.; expenses; 18 members: Nancy F. Atlas, Houston (8/31/97); Carolyn R. Bacon, Dallas (8/31/93); W. Mike Baggett, Dallas (8/31/95); Herbert L. Butrum, Houston (8/31/95); Frank K. Cahoon, Midland (8/31/93); Hal Daugherty, El Paso (8/31/93); Dr. Carlos D. Godinez, McAllen (8/31/97); Cipriano F. Guerra Jr., San Antonio (8/31/93); Rene Haas, Corpus Christi (8/31/97); Lawrence E. Jenkins, Austin (8/31/95); Janie Strauss McGarr, Dallas (8/31/99); Andrew R. Melontree, Tyler (8/31/97); Martha Miller, Texarkana (8/31/97); Gregory E. Mitchell, Amarillo (8/31/93); Patricia S. Prather, Houston (8/31/95); Ray E. Santos, Lubbock (8/31/97); Charles C. Sprague, Dallas (8/31/95); Mary Beth Williamson, San Antonio (8/31/95). Commissioner of Higher Education, Dr. Kenneth H. Ashworth ($125,106), Box 12788, Austin 78711.

Historical Commission, Texas - (1953); apptv.; expenses; 6-yr.; 18 members: Bruce T. Aiken, Brownsville (2/1/01); Jane Cook Barnhill, Brenham (2/1/01); Jan Felts Bullock, Austin (2/1/99); Shirley W. Caldwell, Albany (2/1/01); George Christian, Austin (2/1/97); T.R. Fehrenbach, San Antonio (2/1/01); Willie Lee Gay, Houston (2/1/97); Mrs. Willie Lee Glass, Tyler (2/1/99); Betty Elliott Hanna, Breckenridge (2/1/99); Thomas E. Kroutter Jr., Port Arthur (2/1/97); F. Lee Lawrence, Tyler (2/1/01); Virginia Long, Kilgore (2/1/99); Archie P. McDonald, Nacogdoches (2/1/97); Carl R. McQueary, Salado (2/1/97); Susan Mead, Dallas (2/1/01); John Liston Nau III, Houston (2/1/99); Rose T. Trevino, Laredo (2/1/99); Dr. Dan Alvin Willis, Fort Worth (2/1/97). Exec. Dir., Curtis Tunnell, Box 12276, Austin 78711 ($63,362).

Historical Records Advisory Board, Texas - (1976); apptv.; 3-yr.; 9 members: Bruce T. Aiken, Brownsville (1/23/96); Felix Almaraz Jr., San Antonio (1/23/95); Diana B. Gonzalez, San Antonio (1/23/97); Chris A. LaPlante, Austin (1/23/91); Elizabeth (Libba); Massey, Dallas (1/23/96); Gleniece A. Robinson, Dallas (1/23/94); Gerald D. Saxon, Arlington (1/23/95); Elizabeth Torrence, Clifton (1/23/95); Eleanor Custis Wright, Austin (1/23/96). State Historical Records Coordinator, Chris LaPlante, State Library, Box 12927, Austin 78711.

Hospital Licensing Advisory Council - (1959); apptd.; 6-yrs.; 9 members: James W. Beard Jr, Missouri City (12/7/99); Susanna E. Bedell, Palestine (12/7/95); David G. Borman, Iowa Park (12/7/93); David C. Bush, Houston (12/7/95); Bob L. Bybee, Canyon (12/7/95); Larry M. Graham, Round Rock (12/7/99); Jane Perez, Hempstead (12/7/97); Ronald D. Stephens, Mexia (12/7/99); Barbara L. Watkins, Dallas (12/7/97). Texas Dept. of Health, 1100 W. 49th, Austin 78756.

Housing and Community Affairs, Board of Texas Dept. of - (1979 as Texas Housing Agency; merged with Department of Community Affairs and name changed in 1991); apptv.; expenses; 6-yr.; 9 members: Donald R. Bethel, Lamesa (1/31/01); Margie Lee Bingham, Houston (1/31/01); Edmund R. Carrera, El Paso (1/31/93); George R. Farish, Houston (1/31/93); Richard C. Hile, Austin (1/31/99); Joseph Kemp, Dallas (1/31/93); Walter Martinez, San Antonio (1/31/97); Paul R. Rodriguez, Mission (1/31/99); Donald W. Sowell, Prairie View (1/31/93). Exec. Dir., Enrique Flores ($90,177), 811 Barton Springs Rd., Ste. 300, Austin 78704.

Human Rights, State Commission on - (1983); apptv.; 6-yr.; expenses; 6 members: Jose E. De Santiago, Houston (9/24/95); L. Maxine Lee, Austin (9/24/97); Rev. Howard Ransom, Port Arthur (9/24/99); Richard A. Solo, Dallas (9/24/97); Frank Thompson Jr., Houston (9/24/95); Laura Zuniga, El Paso (9/24/93). Exec. Dir., William M. Hale ($54,768), Box 13493, Austin 78711.

Human Services, Texas Board of - (1941 as State Board of Public Welfare; name changed to present form in 1985); apptv.; 6-yr.; per diem and expenses; 6 members: Robert Geyer, El Paso (1/20/97); David Herndon, Austin (1/20/01); Anchi H. Ku, Dallas (1/20/99); Yava D. Scott, Missouri City (1/20/97); Carlela K. Vogel, Fort Worth (1/20/99); Carole A. Woodard, Galveston (1/20/01). Commissioner, Burton F. Raiford ($95,000), Box 149030, Austin

78714-9030.

Incentive and Productivity Commission, Texas - (1987 as Productivity and Bonus Commission and Employee Incentive Commission; commissions merged and name changed to present form in 1989); 9 members — 6 state officials (term on commission is term in other office): Gov.; Lt. Gov.; Comptroller; State Treasurer; Administrator, Texas Workforce Comm.; Chmn., Texas Higher Education Coordinating Board; 3 apptd. by gov.: Bill B. Cobb, Wimberley (2/1/96); Hattie Hill-Storks, Carrollton (2/1/95); Jacob (Jake) N. Samuel, Galveston (2/1/95). Exec. Dir., M. Elaine Powell ($42,534), Box 12482, Austin 78711.

Information Resources, Department of - (1981 as Automated Information and Telecommunications Council; name changed in 1990); 6-yr.; expenses; 3 members recommended by Speaker of House, 3 by Lt. Gov.; 3 by Gov.: 9 members: Ken Armbrister, Austin (2/1/97); Elton Bomer, Austin (2/1/99); Jon M. Bradley, Dallas (2/1/95); Jim C. Brunjes, Lubbock (2/1/99); R. Dan Burck, Austin (2/1/97); Robert Junell, Austin (2/1/99); John Keel, Austin (2/1/97); Harry H. Richardson, San Antonio (2/1/95); Jennifer Stamper, Dallas (2/1/01). Exec. Dir., Carolyn Purcell ($80,204), P.O. Box 13564, Austin 78711.

Insurance, Commissioner of - Elton Bomer ($150,000), P.O. Box 149104, Austin 78714.

Insurance, State Board of - Abolished by the 73rd Legislature, eff. Sept. 1, 1994. All members had resigned by Dec. 31, 1993.

International Trade Commission - (1991); apptv.; 6-yr.; 6 members: Robert W. Hsueh, Dallas (2/1/01); Dominic Man-Kit Lam, The Woodlands (2/1/93); Robert B. Reeves, Center (2/1/01); Phillip S. Shinoda, Dallas (2/1/97); Patricia J. Smothers, San Antonio (2/1/93); J. McDonald Williams, Dallas (2/1/97). Dir., J. David Bamberger, San Antonio (2/1/97), c/o Texas Dept. of Commerce.

Interstate Mining Compact Commission - Melvin Hodgkiss, Austin. Exec. Dir.: Gregory Conrad, 459B Carlisle Drv., Herndon, VA 22070.

Interstate Oil and Gas Compact Commission, Texas Rep. - (1935); ex officio or apptv., according to Gov's. choice; per diem and expenses. (Approximately 150 other appointees serve on various committees.) Exec. Dir., Christine Hansen, Box 53127, Oklahoma City, OK 73152.

Interstate Parole Compact Administrator - (1951); apptv.: Knox Fitzpatrick, Dallas.

Jail Standards, Texas Commission on - (1975); apptv.; 6-yr.; expenses; 9 members: Charles E. Chatman, Sherman (1/31/97); Joe Evans, Nacogdoches (1/31/97); Cloyd Onis Hadnot, Hillister (1/31/99); J.D. Johnson, Fort Worth (1/31/99); Patrick O. Keel, Austin (1/31/01); Josephine W. Miller, Sinton (1/31/95); J. David Nelson, Lubbock (1/31/95); Alex F. Perez, Brownsville (1/31/97); Manuel Rivera, El Paso (1/31/99). Exec. Dir., Jack E. Crump ($53,834), Box 12985, Austin 78711.

Judicial Conduct, State Commission on - (1965 as 9-member Judicial Qualifications Commission; name changed in 1977 to present form and membership raised to 11); expenses; 6-yr.; 11 members: 5 apptd. by Supreme Court; 2 apptd. by State Bar; 4 apptd. by Gov. as follows: Lowell Cable, Sulphur Springs (11/19/91); A.H. "Al" Lock, Fort Worth (11/19/95); Roderick M. Nugent Jr., Amarillo (11/19/93); Rosa Walker, Austin (11/19/97). Exec. Dir., Robert C. Flowers, Box 12265, Austin 78711.

Judicial Council, Texas - (1929 as Texas Civil Judicial Council; name changed in 1975); ex officio terms vary; apptv.; 6-yr. terms; expenses; 19 members — 6 ex officio: past Chmn. of House Judiciary Committee, Chief Justice of Texas Supreme Court, Judge of Court of Criminal Appeals, Chmn. of House Judiciary Committee, past Chmn. of Senate Jurisprudence Committee, Chmn. of Senate Jurisprudence Committee; 4 apptd. with ex officio qualifications and 9 apptd. from general public: Ray D. Anderson, (2/1/93); William G. Arnot III, Abilene (2/1/95); Fred V. Barbee Jr., El Campo (6/30/95); Debbie D. Branson, Dallas (6/30/97); Judith K. Guthrie, Tyler (6/30/97); Rae Jackson, Longview (6/30/95); Weldon Kirk, Sweetwater (2/1/95); Ward L. Koehler, El Paso (6/30/93); W.T. McDonald, Bryan (6/30/97); Alan M. Sager, Austin (6/30/93); Blake Tartt, Houston (6/30/93); Nick Taylor, Midland (6/30/95). Exec. Dir., C. Raymond Judice, Box 12066, Austin 78711.

Judicial Districts Board - (1985); 12 ex officio members (term in other office); one apptv. (4 yrs.); ex officio: Chief Justice of Texas Supreme Court; Presiding Judge, Court of Criminal Appeals; Presiding Judge of each of 9 Administrative Judicial Districts; pres. of Texas Judicial Council.

Judicial Districts of Texas, Admin., Presiding Judges of - (See Administrative Judicial Districts, Presiding Judges).

Juvenile Probation Commission, Texas - (1981); apptv.; 6-yr.; expenses; 9 members — 3 judges of District Courts and 6 private citizens: Eric Andell, Bellaire (8/31/97); Victoria H. Baldwin, Austin (8/31/97); Rev. Msgr. Dermot N. Brosnan, San Antonio (8/31/95); Catherine Stayman Evans, Dallas (8/31/95); Raul S. Garcia, San Angelo (8/31/99); W. Clyde Lemon, Houston (8/31/95); Theresa B. Lyons, Fort Worth (8/31/97); Robert Tejeda, San Antonio (8/31/99); Jane A. Wetzel, Dallas (8/31/99). Exec. Dir., Bernard Licarione ($70,000), Box 13547, Austin 78711.

Lamar University System, Board of Regents - (abolished Sept. 1995 upon the transfer of Lamar University System to the Texas State University System).

Land Board, School - (1939); one ex officio (term in other office); 2 apptd. — one by Atty. Gen. and one by Gov. for 2-yr. term; per diem and expenses; ex officio member: Comm. of General Land Office; Gov's. apptee: Richard M. Landsman, San Antonio (8/29/95).

Land Surveying, Texas Board of Professional - (1979); formed from consolidation of membership of Board of Examiners of Licensed Land Surveyors, est. 1977, and State Board of Registration for Public Surveyors, est. 1955); apptv.; 6-yr.; 10 members — Commissioner of General Land Office serving by statute; 3 members of general public, 2 licensed land surveyors, 4 registered public surveyors, as follows: Herman H. Forbes, Round Rock (1/31/95); James Noble Johnson, Austin (1/31/99); Ray Charles Jones, Houston (1/31/97); Paul P. Kwan, Houston (1/31/99); Robert Pounds, El Paso (1/31/97); Robert J. Prejean, New Ulm (1/31/95); Char P. Rothrock, Houston (1/31/97); Andrew L. Sikes, Houston (1/31/93); David A. Vilbig, Dallas (1/31/95). Exec. Dir., Sandy Smith ($36,000), 7701 N. Lamar, #400, Austin 78752.

Lands, Board for Lease of University - (1929 as 3-member board; membership increased to 4 in 1985); ex officio; term in other office; 4 members: Commissioner of General Land Office, 2 members of Board of Regents of University of Texas, 1 member Board of Regents of Texas A&M University.

Lavaca-Navidad River Authority, Board of Directors - (1954 as 7-member Jackson County Flood Control District; reorganized as 9-member board in 1959; name changed to present form in 1969); apptv.; 6-yr.; per diem and expenses; 9 members: Harry Lee Hafernick, Edna (5/1/97); J.B. Housson, Ganado (5/1/97); Joyce H. Jarratt, Edna (5/1/95); Theresa McCaig, Ganado (5/1/97); Carol T. McDonald, Edna (5/1/99); Dennis S. Simons, Edna (5/1/95); Callaway S. Vance, Edna (5/1/99); August E. Westhoff II, Edna (5/1/95); Robert J. Whitworth, Edna (5/1/99). Gen. Mgr., Emmett Gloyna, Box 429, Edna 77957.

Law Enforcement Officer Standards & Education, Comm. on - (1965); expenses; 14 members — 5 ex officio: Atty. Gen., Directory of Public Safety, Commissioner of Education, Exec. Dir. of Governor's Office Criminal Justice Division, and Commissioner of Higher Education; 9 apptv. members: Jamerson J. Berry Jr., Houston (8/30/97); Barbara J. Childress, Hurst (8/30/95); John E. Clark, San Antonio (8/30/93); Louis T. Getterman III, Austin (8/30/93); Carl R. Griffith Jr., Beaumont (8/30/97); Maxine E. Hannifin, Midland (8/30/93); J.C. Mosier, Houston (8/30/95); Adan Munoz Jr., Kingsville (8/30/97); William P. Whitworth, Seguin (8/30/95). Exec. Dir., D.C. Jim Dozier ($53,834), 1033 LaPosada, #175, Austin 78752.

Law Examiners, Board of - Nine attorneys apptd. by Supreme Court biennially for 2-year terms expiring September 30 of odd-numbered years. Compensation set by Supreme Court not to exceed $20,000 per annum. Exec. Dir., Rachel Martin, Box 13486, Austin 78711.

Law Library Board, State - (1971); ex officio; expenses; 3 members: Chief Justice State Supreme

Court, Presiding Judge Court of Criminal Appeals and Atty. General. Dir., Kay Schlueter ($40,026), Box 12367, Austin 78711.

Legislative Budget Board - (1949); 10 members; 6 ex officio members: Lt. Gov.; Speaker of House; Chmn., Senate Finance Comm.; Chmn., Senate State Affairs Comm.; Chmn., House Appropriations Comm.; Chmn., House Ways and Means Comm.; plus 4 other members of Legislature. Director, John Keel, Box 12666, Austin 78711-2666.

Legislative Council, Texas - (1949); 17 ex officio members — 4 senators named by Lt. Gov.; 9 representatives named by Speaker; Chmn., House Administration Committee; Chmn., Senate Administration Committee; Lt. Gov.; and Speaker. Exec. Dir., Robert I. Kelly, Box 12128, Austin 78711.

Legislative Redistricting Board - (1948); 5 ex officio members; term in other office: Lt. Gov., Speaker of House, Atty. Gen., Comptroller and Commissioner of General Land Office.

Librarian, State - (Originally est. in 1839; present office est. 1909); apptv., indefinite term: William D. Gooch ($65,000), Box 12927, Austin 78711.

Library and Archives Commission, Texas State - (1909 as 5-member Library and State Historical Commission; number of members increased to 6 in 1953; name changed to present form in 1979); apptv.; per diem and expenses on duty; 6-yr.; 6 members: Carolyn Armstrong, Kingsville (9/28/95); James H. Banks, Austin (9/28/95); Patrick Heath, Boerne (9/28/99); Marvin A. Rich, Houston (9/28/99); Barbara Silberberg, Dallas (9/28/97); James B. Stewart, Victoria (9/28/97). Dir., William D. Gooch, State Librarian, Box 12927, Austin 78711.

Library, State Legislative Reference - (1909); indefinite term; Director: Sally Reynolds. Box 12488, Austin 78711.

Licensing and Regulation, Texas Commission on - (1989); apptv.; 6-yr.; expenses; 6 members: Arlen D. Bynum, Dallas (2/1/97); Clara Caldwell, Austin (2/1/99); John W. (Wil) Galloway, Beeville (2/1/01); Carmen Mitchell, Dallas (2/1/97); Ronald Lynn Raspberry, Spring (2/1/99); Earl L. Yeakel III, Austin (2/1/95). Exec. Dir., Jack W. Garison ($62,494), P.O. Box 12157, Austin 78711.

Lottery Commission, Texas - (1993); 6-yrs.; apptv.; expenses; 3 members: Richard P. Daly, Austin (2/1/99); Harriet Ellan Miers, Dallas (2/1/01); Anthony J. Sadberry, Cypress (2/1/97). Exec. Dir., Nora Linares ($110,000), Box 16630, Austin 78761-6630.

Lower Colorado River Authority - (See Colorado River Authority, Lower).

Marriage & Family Therapists, Texas State Board of Examiners of - (1991); apptd.; 6 yrs.; per diem and transportation expenses; 9 members: Noe Cavazos, Weslaco (2/1/99); Leslie E. Goolishian, Galveston (2/1/97); Bobbie A. Henderson, Houston (2/1/95); Rev. Jerome McNeil Jr., Dallas (2/1/95); Thomas A. Milholland, Abilene (2/1/97); Harriet H. Roberts, Houston (2/1/99); Lucille M. Romeo, El Paso (2/1/95); David A. Talbot Sr., Commerce (2/1/97). Exec. Dir., Bobby D. Schmidt, Dept. of Health, 1100 W. 49th St., Austin 78756-3183.

Medical District Review Committee: Dist. 1 - (1977); apptv.; 6-hr.; expenses; 20 members — five from each of 4 districts: Jerome L. Armbruster, Pearland (1/15/94); A. David Axelrad, Houston (1/15/00); Robert J. Bacon Sr., Houston (1/15/98); Thomas A. Reiser, Houston (1/15/00). **Dist. 2:** Robert K. Bass, Dallas (1/15/94); Linda Kagy, Mesquite (1/15/94); John L. Sawtelle, Trinidad (1/15/94); Richard C. Wootan, Dallas (1/15/92). **Dist. 3:** Thomas L. Marvelli, Fort Worth (1/15/00); William L. Rector, Wichita Falls (1/15/96); Robert Allan Watson, Fort Worth (1/15/00); Irvin E. Zeitler Jr., San Angelo (1/15/94); Nalin H. Tolia, Odessa (1/15/98). **Dist. 4:** Clyde R. Danks, Austin (1/15/96); Larry Hufford, San Antonio (1/15/00); Julian Gomez III, McAllen (1/15/00); Gladys C. Keene, Laredo (1/15/98); Ann L. Nolen, La Grange (1/15/00).

Medical Examiners, Texas State Board of - (1907 as 12-member board, membership raised to 15 in 1981, raised to 18 in 1993); apptv.; 6-yr.; per diem on duty; 18 members: Penny Angelo, Midland (4/13/01); Carol M. Barger, Dallas (4/13/99); Marianne Beard, Arlington (4/13/97); Carlos Campos, New Braunfels (4/13/99); James Howard Clark Jr., Dallas (4/13/99); William H. Fleming III, Houston (4/13/01); Margaret L. Ford, Houston (4/13/01); Catalina E. Garcia, Dallas (4/13/97); Cynthia "Cindy" Jenkins, Stowell (4/13/97); Thomas D. Kirksey, Austin (4/13/01); John M. Lewis, Houston (4/13/97); Paul G. Meyer, Lubbock (4/13/01); Charles W. Monday Jr., Huntsville (4/13/99); William A. Pollan, Ballinger (4/13/99); Vernon L. Ryan, San Angelo (4/13/01); Ratna Solomon, Dallas (4/13/97); Raymond Russell Thomas, Eagle Lake (4/13/99). Exec. Dir., Bruce Levy ($68,173), Box 149134, Austin 78714-9134.

Medical Physicists, Texas Board of Licensure for Professional - (1991); apptv.; 6-yrs.; 9 members: Ralph Blumhardt, San Antonio (2/1/95); Stewart C. Bushong, Houston (2/1/99); David Lee Goff, San Antonio (2/1/93); Thomas S. Harle, Houston (2/1/97); Paul H. Murphy, Houston (2/1/95); Lester J. Peters, Houston (2/1/97); Wayne A. Wiatgrowski, San Antonio (2/1/95); Ann E. Wright, Houston (2/1/97).

Mental Health and Mental Retardation, Texas Board of - (1965, superseded Board of Texas State Hospitals and Special Schools); apptv.; 6-yr.; per diem and expenses; 9 members: Rodolfc Arredondo Jr., Lubbock (1/31/01); Charles M. Cooper, Dallas (1/31/01); Virginia Eernisse, Alvin (1/31/97); Janelle Smith Jordan, Houston (1/31/99); William A. Lawson, Houston (1/31/97); Rosemary Vivero Neill, El Paso (1/31/99); James I. Perkins, Rusk (1/31/01); Ann K. Utley, Dallas (1/31/97); Edward B. Weyman, Midland (1/31/99). Acting Commissioner of Mental Health and Mental Retardation, Karen F. Hale, Box 12668, Austin 78711-2668 ($95,000, plus house and utilities).

Midwestern State University, Board of Regents - (1959); apptv.; 6-yr.; 9 members: Margaret F. Darden, Dallas (2/25/98); Ervin Garnett, Fort Worth (2/25/98); Milburn E. Nutt, Wichita Falls (2/25/96); Gary H. Shores, Wichita Falls (2/25/96); Joe H. Staley Jr., Dallas (2/25/96); Edward L. Watson, Dallas (2/25/00); Robert G. West, Fort Worth (2/25/98); Harold White Jr., Wichita Falls (2/25/00); Kathryn Anne Yeager, Wichita Falls (2/25/00). Pres., Dr. Louis J. Rodriguez, 3400 Taft, Wichita Falls 76308.

Motor Vehicle Board, Texas Department of Transportation - (1971 as 6-member board; membership increased to 9 in 1979; reduced to 6 in 1987; made division of Texas Dept. of Transportation, name changed to present form and membership increased to 9 in 1992); apptv.; 6-yr.; per diem and expenses; 9 members: Leonard E. Burton, Irving (1/31/93); William W. Collins Jr., Fort Worth (1/31/95); T.J. Connolly, San Antonio (1/31/97); John C. Horton III, Austin (1/31/95); Norman Scott Jones, Dallas (1/31/01); Robyn Elizabeth Ray, Longview (1/31/97); Laurie Brown Watson, Austin (1/31/99); Stephen P. Webb, Austin (1/31/99).

Municipal Retirement System (See Retirement System, Municipal, Board of Trustees).

National Guard Armory Board, Texas - (1935 as 3-member board; reorganized as 6-member board in 1981); 6-yr.; 6 members: Hal Boyd, Big Spring (4/30/97); Lillian Dunlap, San Antonio (4/30/99); William Edgar Murphy, Lubbock (4/30/99); David J. Rist, Dallas (4/30/97); Reynaldo Sanchez, El Paso (4/30/95); Simon Tamez, Weslaco (4/30/95). Exec. Dir., William E. Beaty ($53,469), P.O. Box 5426, Austin 78763.

National Research Laboratory Commission, Texas - (1986); apptv.; expenses; 6-yr.; 9 members: George S. Bayoud Jr., Dallas (2/1/01); J. Fred Bucy, Dallas (2/1/01); G.W. "Bill" Ceverha, Dallas (2/1/01); Charles R. Delgado, Galveston (2/1/99); Peter Flawn, Austin (2/1/97); Gerald Griffin, Houston (2/1/91); Jerome Johnson, Amarillo (2/1/91); Nicholas B. Jordan Jr., Waxahachie (2/1/99); Jack L. Martin, Austin (2/1/93). Exec. Dir., Edward C. Bingler, 2275 N. Highway 77, #100, Waxahachie 75165.

Natural Resource Conservation Commission, Texas - (1913 as State Board of Water Engineers; name changed in 1962 to Texas Water Commission; reorganized and name again changed in 1965 to Water Rights Commission; reorganized and name changed back to Texas Water Commission in 1977 to perform the judicial function for the Texas Dept. of Water Resources; changed to present form Sept. 1, 1993); apptv.; 6-yr.; 3 members full-time at $90,071: John L. Hall, Austin (8/31/97); R.B. (Ralph) Marquez, Texas City (8/31/99); Pam Reed, Austin (8/31/95). Exec. Dir., Wiliam Campbell ($105,000), Box

13087, Austin 78711.

Neches River Municipal Water Authority, Upper - (Est. 1953 as 9-member board; membership changed to 3 in 1959); apptv.; 6-yr.; 3 members: Edward McCoy Jr., Palestine (2/1/97); Cathy Ann Stark, Palestine (2/1/99); Ben L. Swinney, Palestine (2/1/95). Gen. Mgr., Tommy G. Mallory, Drawer 1965, Palestine 75802.

Neches Valley Authority, Lower - (1933); apptv.; per diem and expenses on duty; 6-yr.; 9 members: R.C. Aldrich, Nome (7/28/95); F.M. Archer, Woodville (7/28/97); Clyde L. Cole, Silsbee (7/28/99); Gaylyn L. Cooper, Beaumont (7/28/99); Paul Georgas Jr., Silsbee (7/28/97); Thad Heartfield, Beaumont (7/28/95); Von E. McReynolds, Groves (7/28/97); W.S. Nichols Jr., Woodville (7/28/95); Thomas A. Thomas, Port Arthur (7/28/99). Gen. Mgr. A. T. Hebert Jr., P.O. Box 3464, Beaumont 77704.

Nueces River Authority Board of Directors - (1953 as Nueces River Conservation and Reclamation District; name changed in 1971); apptv.; 6-yr.; per diem and expenses; 21 members: Mary B. Autry, Pipe Creek (2/1/97); Madge E. Belcher, Brackettville (2/1/97); Margaret Bowman, Spofford (2/1/99); Dudley Q. Braly, Beeville (2/1/95); Cleo Bustamante Jr., Carrizo Springs (2/1/97); George A. Finley III, Corpus Christi (2/1/99); Bruce T. Foster, Hondo (2/1/95); Lucinda J. Garcia, Alice (2/1/99); Joseph E. Gardner Jr., Corpus Christi (2/1/95); Susan C. Griffith, Uvalde (2/1/99); Robert D. Johanson, Three Rivers (2/1/97); Edward M. Jones, Ingleside (2/1/97); Daniel Martinez, Corpus Christi (2/1/95); Bob Mullen, Alice (2/1/97); Mary Melissa Ramos, Floresville (2/1/99); Alvaro D. Saenz, Corpus Christi (2/1/95); Celina Solis, San Diego (2/1/95); Patricia H. Sugarek, Skidmore (2/1/99); Paula S. Waddle, Corpus Christi (2/1/95); Robert L. Wagner, Crystal City (2/1/95); Janna Whatley Williams, Odem (2/1/97); Alfredo Zamora Jr., Cotulla (2/1/99). Exec. Dir., Con Mims III, Box 349, Uvalde 78802-0349.

Nurse Examiners, State Board of - (1909 as 6-member board; reorganized and membership increased to 9 in 1981); apptv.; per diem and expenses; 6-yr.; 9 members: Nancy Boston, Temple (1/31/01); Rose Marie Caballero, Corpus Christi (1/31/97); Pat Crowe, Fort Worth (1/31/97); Mary V. Fenton, Galveston (1/31/97); Roselyn Holloway, Lubbock (1/31/99); Kenneth W. Lowrance, Clifton (1/31/01); Doris Price-Nealy, Beaumont (1/31/99); Robert J. Provan, Pflugerville (1/31/99); Iris Snell, Dallas (1/31/01). Exec. Dir., Louise Waddill ($53,469), 9101 Burnet Rd., #104, Austin 78758.

Nurse Examiners, State Board of Vocational - (1951 as 9-member board; membership increased to 12 in 1981); apptv.; 6-yr.; 12 members: Susie Belle Cheney, Pittsburg (9/6/99); Rojelio Cuevas, McAllen (9/6/97); Connie M. Davis, Fort Worth (9/6/95); Albert H. Fairweather, Austin (9/6/97); Melba Lee-Hosey, Houston (9/6/97); Ruth Leopard, San Antonio (9/6/95); Steven H. Levin, Dallas (9/6/99); Betty F. McLemore, Longview (9/6/95); Doris A. Parker, Frankston (9/6/95); Vangie Perez, Needville (9/6/99); Maria Olivia Rivas, Brownsville (9/6/99); Opal M. Robinson, Lubbock (9/6/97); Morris Spector, San Antonio (9/6/97); Rudolph Robert Willmann Jr., San Antonio (9/6/95); Janet Wood-Yanez, Mercedes (9/6/99). Exec. Dir., Marjorie A. Bronk ($46,786), 9101 Burnet Rd., Ste. 105, Austin 78758.

Nursing Facility Administrators, Texas Board of - (1993; assumed duties of abolished Texas Board of Licensure for Nursing Home Administrators); 6-yr., transportation expenses; 2 ex officio, nonvoting members (Tx. Dept. on Aging long-term care ombudsman and Comm. of Human Services or designee); 9 apptd. members: Johnnie Lou Avery, Big Spring (2/1/97); Thomas William Gard, Beaumont (2/1/99); Ramona Kennedy, Flower Mound (2/1/01); Cheryl L. Killian, Arlington (2/1/97); Johnnie Richardson, Houston (2/1/95); Michael O. Sims, Waco (2/1/99); Jack Ray Tinsley, Frisco (2/1/99); Jerry Turner, Hillsboro (2/1/01). Exec. Secy., Bobby D. Schmidt, 1100 W. 49th, Austin 78756.

Occupational Therapy, Texas Advisory Board of - (1983); apptv.; 6-yr.; per diem and expenses; 6 members: Esperanza J. Brattin, McAllen (2/1/97); Frances Derrick, Mesquite (2/1/95); Kikujo Ford, Galveston (2/1/95); M. Judith Lusted, San Antonio (2/1/99); Benny O. McGehee, El Paso (2/1/97); Mary H. Wilson, Austin (2/1/99). Exec. Dir., Linda Vaclavik, 4900 N. Lamar, Austin 78751-2316.

Offenders with Mental Impairments, Texas Council on - (1987); apptv.; expenses; 6-yr.; 27 members: 18 heads of agencies or their designees: Texas Dept. of Criminal Justice, Texas Dept. of MHMR, Board of Pardons and Paroles, Texas Adult Probation Commission, Texas Juvenile Probation Commission, Texas Youth Commission, Texas Rehabilitation Commission, Texas Education Agency, Criminal Justice Policy Council, Mental Health Assn. in Texas, Texas Commission on Alcohol and Drug Abuse, Commission on Law Enforcement Officer Standards and Education, Texas Council of Community MHMR Centers, Commission on Jail Standards, Texas Planning Council for Developmental Disabilities, Texas Assn. for Retarded Citizens, Texas Alliance for the Mentally Ill, and Parent Assn. for the Retarded of Texas; 9 apptd. by Gov. as follows: Michael R. Arambula, San Antonio (2/1/99); C. Anne Bishop, Austin (2/1/95); Dollie Brathwaite, Houston (2/1/99); Betty Hardwick, Baird (2/1/97); Belinda Joy Hill, Houston (2/1/95); Carol A. Oeller, Houston (2/1/99); Mario E. Ramírez, Edinburg (2/1/97); Jeffrey C. Siegel, Dallas (2/1/95); Jodie E. Stavinoha, Richmond (2/1/97).Exec. Dir., Dee Kifowit, 8610 Shoal Creek Blvd., Austin 78757.

Old San Antonio Road Preservation Commission - (1989); term at pleasure of governor; 9 members: 4 representatives of state agencies: Texas Dept. of Transportation, Texas Historical Commission, Parks and Wildlife, Texas Dept. of Commerce (Tourism Div.); 5 at large recommended by Texas Historical Commission and apptd. by Gov.: Dr. Archie P. McDonald, Nacogdoches; Gen. John R. McGiffert, San Antonio; Ingrid B. Morris, Hemphill; Nan Olsen, Bastrop; Rose T. Trevino, Laredo.

Optometry Board, Texas - (1921 as 6-member State Board of Examiners in Optometry; name changed to present form in 1981 and membership increased to 9); apptv.; per diem; 6-yr.; 9 members: Jimmy Bitner, Fredericksburg (1/31/95); Barry J. Davis, Groves (1/31/95); Theresa Karably Giolma, San Antonio (1/31/97); Barry Owen Moores, Sugar Land (1/31/99); Stanley C. Pearle, Dallas (1/31/97); Wesley Edward Pittman, Mexia (1/31/97); Susan B. Place, Plano (1/31/99); Donnya Elle Stephens, Nacogdoches (1/31/99); Elzie Mac Wright, Seminole (1/31/95). Exec. Dir., Lois Ewald ($39,545), 9101 Burnet Rd., Ste. 214, Austin 78758.

Pardons and Paroles Division, Board of - (1893 as Board of Pardon Advisers; changed in 1936 to Board of Pardons and Paroles with 3 members; membership increased to 6 in 1983; made a division of the Texas Department of Criminal Justice and membership increased to 18 in 1990); apptv.; 6-yr.; 18 members: Irma Cauley, Bryan (2/1/97); Bennie L. Elmore, Huntsville (2/1/99); John Escobedo, Huntsville (2/1/99); Gerald L. Garrett, Austin (2/1/01); Donna D. Gilbert, Huntsville (2/1/97); Mae Johnson Jackson, Waco (2/1/97); Daniel Ray Lang, Houston (2/1/01); Mary Leal, Houston (2/1/99); Winona W. Miles, Austin (2/1/97); Thomas W. Moss, Amarillo (2/1/01); Paul Joseph Prejean, Beaumont (2/1/99); Victor Rodriguez, Brownsville (2/1/01); Gilbert Rodriguez, Abilene (2/1/97); Brendolyn Rogers-Gardner, Duncanville (2/1/01); Albert G. Sanchez, Crystal City (2/1/97); Terri Beard Schnorrenberg, Gatesville (2/1/99); Cynthia S. Tauss, League City (2/1/01); W.G. (Billy) Walker, Tyler (2/1/99).

Parks and Wildlife Commission, Texas - (1963 as 3-member board; membership increased to 6 in 1971; increased to 9 in 1983); apptv.; expenses; 6-yr.; 9 members: Lee M. Bass, Fort Worth (2/1/01); Mickey Ruth Burleson, Temple (2/1/99); John Raymond Clymer Jr., Wichita Falls (2/1/99); Ygnacio D. Garza, Brownsville (2/1/97); Richard W. Heath, Dallas (2/1/01); Terese T. Hershey, Houston (2/1/97); Susan Howard, Fair Oaks Ranch (2/1/99); Nolan Ryan, Alvin (2/1/01); Thomas W. Umphrey, Beaumont (2/1/97). Exec. Dir., Andrew S. Sansom ($105,000), 4200 Smith School Rd., Austin 78744.

Pecos River Compact Commissioner - (1942); apptv.; 2-yr.; expenses: Billy Moody, Fort Stockton (1/23/99). 103 W. Callaghan, Fort Stockton 79735 ($20,247).

Pension Boards - For old age, blind and dependent children's assistance, see Human Services, State Board of. For retirement pay to state and municipal employees and teachers, see proper category under Retirement.

Pension Review Board, State - (1979); apptv.; 6-yr.; 9

members — one senator apptd. by Lt. Gov., one representative apptd. by Speaker, 7 apptd. by Gov. as follows: Bruce Cox, Fort Worth (1/31/99); Cheryl L. Dotson, Missouri City (1/31/97); Larry D. Eddington, Garland (1/31/01); Ronald L. Haneberg, Rockwall (1/31/01); Hugh L. Stephens, Dallas (1/31/97); Gilbert F. Vasquez, San Antonio (1/31/97); Paul H. Weyrauch, Marble Falls (3/1/95). Exec. Dir., Rita Horwitz ($47,786), Box 13498, Austin 78711.

Pest Control Board, Texas Structural - (1971 as 7-member board, membership raised to 9 in 1979); apptv.; 6-yr.; expenses; 9 members — 3 ex officio: Commissioner of Agriculture; Commissioner of Health; and head of Entomology Dept., Texas A&M University; 6 apptv. members: Merle M. Carlson, Houston (2/1/95); Charles G. Coyle, Fresno (2/1/99); John M. Gonzalez, Houston (2/1/97); Pat Graves, Abilene (2/1/97); Robert W. Jenkins Sr., Marble Falls (2/1/95); Kathleen St. John, Dallas (2/1/99). Exec. Dir., Benny M. Mathis ($51,493), 9101 Burnet Rd., Ste. 201, Austin 78758.

Pharmacy, State Board of - (1907 as 6-member board; membership increased to 9 in 1981); apptv.; 6-yr.; 9 members: Gilbert P. Acuna, Kingsville (8/31/99); Thomas A. Aday, Plainview (8/31/95); Charlie B. Bethea, Houston (8/31/97); Jeannette H. Coffield, Jasper (8/31/97); David Lee Franklin, Dallas (8/31/95); Susan H. Jacobson, El Paso (8/31/99); Ann Peden, Hondo (8/31/95); Marina P. Sifuentes, Austin (8/31/97); Susan R. Williams, Dallas (8/31/95). Exec. Dir.-Sec., Fred S. Brinkley Jr. ($66,000), 8505 Cross Park Dr., Ste. 110, Austin 78754-4594.

Physical Therapy Examiners, Texas State Board of - (1971); apptv.; 6-yr.; expenses; 9 members: Cecilia G. Akers, San Antonio (1/31/97); Lila C. Cross, Boerne (1/31/95); Julia Hartman, Odessa (1/31/95); Martin Infante, Laredo (1/31/99); Norma L. D. Mancilla, El Paso (1/31/95); Penny Butler Patterson, Tyler (1/31/99); Barbara B. Shell, Houston (1/31/97); Ann L. Walker, Dallas (1/31/97); Theodis Ware, Fort Worth (1/31/99). Admin., John Malina, 3001 South Lamar, #101, Austin 78704.

Plumbing Examiners, State Board of - (1947 as 6-member board; membership increased to 9 in 1981); apptv.; expenses; 6-yr.; 9 members: Stanley J. Briers, Taylor Lake Village (9/5/97); Joe W. Campbell, Houston (9/5/97); Gerald L. Harris, Sugar Land (9/5/93); Phillip A. Lord, Pasadena (9/5/97); Jerry D. Moore, Pollok (9/5/95); Alonzo L. Starkey III, Kerrville (9/5/95); Marcus Torres, Corpus Christi (9/5/99); Michael J. Warren, North Richland Hills (9/5/95); William G. Wheeler, Victoria (9/5/93). Admin., Gilbert Kissling ($61,909), 929 E. 41st, Austin 78751.

Podiatry Examiners, State Board of - (1923 as 6-member State Board of Chiropody Examiners; name changed in 1967; made 9-member board in 1981); apptv.; 6-yr.; expenses; 9 members: Ben Clark Jr., Dallas (7/10/95); Thomas S. Garrison, Webster (7/10/97); Preston Goforth, Temple (7/10/93); Ana Maria Laborde, San Antonio (7/10/97); Eugene R. Scioli, Lubbock (7/10/93); Rick D. Sorrells, Dallas (7/10/95); J. Michael Valenza, Austin (7/10/97); Betty Frances Walker, Odessa (7/10/93); Peter J. Williams, San Antonio (7/10/95). Exec. Dir., D. Branson ($36,000), 3420 Executive Center Dr., #305, Austin 78731.

Polygraph Examiners Board - (1965); apptv.; 6-yr.; 6 members: L.E. Driscoll, Sherman (6/18/9); Michael C. Gougler, Austin (6/18/99); Rob L. Kimmons, Houston (6/18/95); Horacio Ortiz, Corpus Christi (6/18/95); William H. Quimby, Dallas (6/18/97); Antonio V. Suarez-Barrio, Killeen (6/18/97). Exec. Officer, Bryan M. Perot ($31,832), Box 4087, Austin 78773.

Preservation Board, State - (1983); 2-yr.; 7 members — 4 ex officio: Gov., Lt. Gov., Speaker and Architect of Capitol; 3 apptv.: one apptd. by Gov., one senator apptd. by Lt. Gov. and one representative apptd. by Speaker. Gov's. apptee: Joseph F. Pinnelli, Austin (2/1/93). Exec. Dir., Dealey Herndon ($68,958), Box 13286, Austin 78711.

Prison Board, Texas - (See Criminal Justice, Texas Dept. of).

Private Investigators and Private Security Agencies, Board of - (1969); apptv.; expenses; 6-yr.; 8 members — 2 ex officio: Dir., Dept. of Public Safety and Atty. Gen.; 6 apptd. members: James Smith Bowie Houston (1/31/95); Joel K. Glenn, Bedford (1/31/99); Melissa Hirsch, Odessa (1/31/97); Jack Montague, Austin (1/31/93); Robert D. Sanders, Sunnyvale (1/31/97); Jess Ann Thomason, Midland (1/31/95). Exec. Dir., Clema D. Sanders ($44,472), Box 13509, Austin 78711.

Produce Recovery Fund Board - (1977 as 3-member board; membership increased to 6 in 1981); apptv.; expenses; 6-yr.; 6 members — 2 each from commission merchants, general public and producer representatives. Roel Gonzales, Alice (1/31/95); Carmen Jacques, El Paso (1/31/97); Naomi S. Kemp, Wharton (1/31/95); Juan Fermin Leal, Brownsville (1/31/97); Robert G. Neal Sr., Pineland (1/31/99); David Wayne Smith, Hart (1/31/99). Admin., Margaret Alvarez, P.O. Box 12847, Austin 78711.

Protective and Regulatory Services, Board of - (1992); apptv.; 6-yr.; 6 members: Jean P. Beaumont, Bryan (2/1/99); Jon Martin Bradley, Dallas (2/1/01); Maurine Dickey, Dallas (2/1/01); Catherine C. Mosbacher, Houston (2/1/97); Bill H. Sheehan, Dumas (2/1/99); Susan H. Stahl, Dallas (2/1/97). Exec. Dir., Janice M. Caldwell ($84,975), Box 149030, Austin 78714-9030.

Psychologists, Texas Board of Examiners of - (1969 as 6-member board; membership increased to 9 in 1981); apptv.; 6-yr.; per diem and expenses; 9 members: Susan S. Askanase, Houston (10/31/97); Lorraine E. Breckenridge, Houston (10/31/97); Ann M. Enriquez, El Paso (10/31/95); James D. Goldston, Denton (10/31/99); Jane Halebian, Dallas (10/31/99); Kenneth F. Kopel, Houston (1/31/95); Roberta L. Nutt, Flower Mound (10/31/97); Denise Shade, Dallas (10/31/99); Emily G. Sutter, Houston (10/31/95). Exec. Dir., Rebecca Tweedy ($42,716), 9101 Burnet Rd., Ste. 212, Austin 78758.

Public Accountancy, State Board of - (See Accountancy, State Board of Public).

Public Finance Authority, Texas - (1984, assumed duties of Texas Building Authority); apptv.; per diem and expenses; 6-yr.; membership increased from 3 to 6 in 1991: Daniel H. Branch, Dallas (2/1/01); Cheryl D. Creuzot, Houston (2/1/99); Robert B. Davis, Austin (2/1/97); John C. Kerr, San Antonio (2/1/01); Peter Lewis, Dallas (2/1/99); Marc R. Stanley, Dallas (2/1/97). Exec. Dir., Anne L. Schwartz, P.O. Box 12906, Austin 78711.

Public Safety Commission - (1935); apptv.; expenses; 6-yr.; 3 members: James B. Francis Jr., Dallas (12/31/99); Robert B. Holt, Midland (12/31/95); Ronald D. Krist, Houston (12/31/97). Dir. of Texas Dept. of Public Safety, James R. Wilson ($90,000), Box 4087, Austin 78773-0001.

Public Utility Commission - (1975); apptv.; 6-yr., 3 members at $75,748: Robert W. Gee, Houston (9/1/97); Judy W. Walsh, Fair Oaks Ranch (9/1/99); Patrick Henry Wood III, Austin (9/1/95). Exec. Dir., Brenda Jenkins ($74,263), 7800 Shoal Creek Blvd., Austin 78757.

Racing Commission, Texas - (1986); 6-yr.; per diem and expenses; 8 members — 2 ex officio: Chmn. of Public Safety Commission and Comptroller; 6 apptv.: Glenn Blodgett, Guthrie (2/1/95); Anne Dunigan-Wilson, Abilene (2/1/97); Lukin T. Gilliland Jr., San Antonio (2/1/99); A.L. Mangham Jr., Nacogdoches (2/1/95); Deorsey E. McGruder Jr., Dallas (l2/1/99); Patricia H. Pangburn, Southlake (2/1/97). Exec. Secy., David J. Freeman ($68,173), Box 12080, Austin 78711.

Radiation Advisory Board - (1961 as 9-member board, membership increased to 18 in 1981); apptv.; 6-yr.; expenses; 18 members: Fred J. Bonte, Dallas (4/16/91); Doris C. Bryan, Austin (4/16/97); Thomas M. Burnette, Plano (4/16/95); Louis H. Cadena, Del Rio (4/16/97); Dr. James Daniel Cox, Houston (4/16/97); Frances Gonzales, El Paso (4/16/99); Glen Keith King, Houston (4/16/99); Jack S. Krohmer, Georgetown (4/16/93); Jesse W. Locke, Dallas (4/16/95); Donald G. Ludlum, Sweetwater (4/16/97); James C. Martin, Duncanville (4/16/95); James W. Orr, Austin (4/16/91); Jeannette Rogers, Houston (4/16/95); Michael D. Spence, Richardson (4/16/95); Vernie A. Stembridge, Dallas (4/16/93); William R. Underdown Jr., Bruni (4/16/93); Dr. Rodolfo L. Villarreal, Houston (4/16/95); Gregg S. Wilkinson, Santa Fe (4/16/97).

Radioactive Waste Disposal Authority, Texas Low-Level - (1981); apptv.; 6-yr.; expenses; 6 members: William L. Fisher, Austin (2/1/99); Milton J. Guiberteau, Houston (2/1/95); Macario Marquez, Sierra Blanca (2/1/99); David Ojeda Jr., Carrizo Springs (2/1/97); Carmen E. Rodriguez, El Paso (2/1/97); John E. Simek, Bryan (2/1/95). Gen. Mgr., Lawrence R. Jacobi Jr. ($76,384), 7701 N.

Lamar Blvd., Ste. 300, Austin 78752.

Railroad Commission of Texas - (1891); elective; 6-yr.; 3 members, $79,247 each: Charles Matthews, Dallas (1/1/00); Carole Keeton Rylander, Austin (12/31/96); Barry Williamson, Austin (12/31/98). Exec. Dir., Walt Washington, Box 12967, Austin 78711.

Real Estate Commission, Texas - (1949 as 6-member board; membership increased to 9 in 1979); apptv.; per diem and expenses; 6-yr.; 9 members: Rick M. Albers, Austin (1/31/97); Eden Box, Austin (1/31/97); Jay Brummett, Austin (1/31/01); Pete Cantu Sr., Helotes (1/31/99); Christine T. Folmer, El Paso (1/31/01); Mitchell Katine, Houston (1/31/99); Hazel W. Lewis, Arlington (1/31/99); Deanna Mayfield, San Angelo (1/31/01); Weldon E. Traylor Sr., Houston (1/31/97). Admin., William H. Kuntz Jr. ($58,932), Box 12188, Austin 78711.

Real Estate Research Advisory Committee - (1971); apptv.; 6-yr.; 10 members — one ex officio: representative of Texas Real Estate Commission; 9 apptv. members: Michael M. Beal, Bryan (1/31/97); Conrad Bering Jr., Houston (1/31/97); Patsy Bohannan, Midland (1/31/95); Don R. Ellis, Del Rio (1/31/95); Dr. Donald S. Longworth, Lubbock (1/31/97); Andrea Lopes Moore, Houston (1/31/99); John P. Schneider Jr., Austin (1/31/99); Richard S. Seline, Houston (1/31/95); Jack W. Tumlinson, Cameron (1/31/93). Dir., James Christian, Texas A&M, College Station 77843-2115.

Red River Authority, Board of Directors - (1959); apptv.; 6-yr.; per diem and expenses; 9 members: George W. Arrington, Canadian (8/11/95); Eric S. Clifford, Paris (8/11/95); Gerry Daugherty, Denison (8/11/99); Paul F. Engler, Amarillo (8/11/99); Joe L. Johnson Jr., Wichita Falls (8/11/95); Edward L. Lehman Jr., Vernon (8/11/97); Diane Mashburn, Childress (8/11/97); Edna M. Shepherd, Texarkana (8/11/99); Judy Warner, Pampa (8/11/97). Gen. Mgr., Ronald J. Glenn, 520 Hamilton Bldg., Wichita Falls 76301.

Red River Compact Commissioner - (1949); apptv.; 4-yr.; (Function of commissioner is to negotiate with other states respecting waters of the Red.): Lowell Cable, Sulphur Springs (2/1/99); ($24,225).

Redistricting Board, Legislative - (See Legislative Redistricting Board).

Rehabilitation Commission, Texas - (1969); apptv.; expenses; 6-yr.; 6 members: Matthew T. Doyle, Texas City (8/31/99); Dr. Dora L. Gonzalez, San Antonio (8/31/97); Jerry Kane, Corpus Christi (8/31/99); Diane M. Novy, Sugar Land (8/31/97); A. Kent Waldrep Jr., Plano (8/31/95); Ray A. Wilkerson, Austin (8/31/95). Commissioner, Vernon M. Arrell ($84,975), 4900 N. Lamar Blvd., Austin 78751-2316.

Retirement System, Municipal, Board of Trustees - (1947); apptv.; 6-yr.; expenses; 6 members: Kathleen Gunn Buehner, Mansfield (2/1/01); Stephen W. McCullough, Irving (2/1/99); Rick Menchaca, Midland (2/1/01); Isaac Valencia, Corpus Christi (2/1/99); Andres Vega Jr., Brownsville (2/1/97); Charles E. Wilson, Waco (1/31/97). Exec. Dir., Gary W. Anderson, 1200 N. I-35, Austin 78701.

Retirement System of Texas, Employees - (1949); apptv.; 6-yr.; 6 members — one apptd. by Gov., one by Chief Justice of State Supreme Court and one by Speaker; 3 are employee members of the system serving 6-yr. overlapping terms: Pamela A. Carley, Austin (8/31/97); Milton Hixson, Austin (8/31/98); Frank J. Smith, Austin (8/31/99); Byron Tunnell, Austin (8/31/96); J. Michael Weiss, Lubbock (8/31/94); Janice R. Zitleman, Austin (8/31/95). Exec. Dir., Charles D. Travis, Box 13207, Austin 78711-3207.

Retirement System, Teacher - (1937 as 6-member board; membership increased to 9 in 1973); expenses; 6-yr.; 9 members — 2 apptd. by State Board of Education, 3 apptd. by Gov. and 4 TRS members apptd. by Gov. after being nominated by popular ballot of members of the retirement system: Frank W. Camp, Brownfield (8/31/97); George M. Crowson, Houston (8/31/95); Charlsetta W. Finley, El Paso (8/31/97); Sue McGarvey, Hallsville (8/31/95); Ronald G. Steinhart, Dallas (8/31/95); Kathryn S. Stream, Denton (8/31/99); Dana Williams, Corpus Christi (8/31/97); Lee R. Williamson, Wichita Falls (8/31/99); Kneeland Youngblood, Dallas (8/31/99). Exec. Dir., Wayne Blevins, 1000 Red River, Austin 78701.

Retirement System, Texas County and District - (1967); apptv.; 6-yr.; 9 members: Giles W. Dalby, Post (12/31/97); Maxine Darst, Terrell (12/31/99); David U. Flores, Georgetown (12/31/97); Martha Gustavsen, Conroe (12/31/99); Kathy Hynson, Rosenberg (12/31/95); Steve Radack, Houston (12/31/95); Sam D. Seale, Port Lavaca (12/31/99); Nelda Wells Spears, Austin (12/31/97); Bill W. Wallis, Tyler (12/31/95) Dir., Terry Horton, 400 W. 14th, Austin 78701-1688.

Rio Grande Compact Commissioner of Texas - (1929); apptv.; 6-yr.: Jack Hammond, El Paso (6/9/95). Box 1917, El Paso 79950-1917 ($41,195).

Runnels County Water Authority, Board of Directors - (1955); apptv.; 6-yr.; 9 members: Pamela Bauerlein, Ballinger (2/1/97); James D. Condra, Talpa (2/1/95); Dalton E. Crockett, Ballinger (2/1/97); L. Aubrey Faubion Jr., Ballinger (2/1/97); Leon Frerich, Norton (2/1/93); Marvin W. Gerhart, Winters (2/1/95); Werner Harsch, Miles (2/1/93); Elliott J. Kemp, Ballinger (2/1/93); Kenneth H. Slimp, Winters (2/1/95).

Sabine River Authority, Board of Directors - (1949); apptv.; per diem and expenses; 6-yr.; 9 members: Nolton L. Brown, Bridge City (7/6/97); James E. Campbell, Center (7/6/95); Walta Pippen Cooke, Carthage (7/6/99); Jerry G. Forbes, Quinlan (7/6/95); Ottis H. (Bo) Lewis, Pineland (7/6/97); Thomas C. Merritt, Longview (7/6/95); Geraldine J. Nichols, Quitman (7/6/97); Jerry Stallworth, Marshall (7/6/99); Clarence Earl Williams Jr., Orange (7/6/99). Exec. Vice Pres. & Gen. Mgr., Sam F. Collins, Box 579, Orange 77630.

Sabine River Compact Commission - (1953); apptv.; 6-yr.; 5 members — one member and chmn. apptd. by President of United States without a vote; 2 from Texas and 2 from Louisiana. Texas members: David V. Cardner, Orange (7/12/95); Danny Choate, Orange (7/12/98). Box 579, Orange 77630. ($8,487).

San Antonio River Authority - apptv., 6 yr., 12 members: Cecil W. Bain, San Antonio (1/31/97); Roger V. Gary, San Antonio (1/31/99); Paul K. Herder, San Antonio (1/31/97); Truett Hunt, Kenedy (1/31/95); W.W. Lorenz, Stockdale (1/31/95); Mary McCampbell, Goliad (1/31/91); Martha C. McNeel, San Antonio (1/31/95); Jesse Oviedo, San Antonio (1/31/95); R.H. Rmasey Jr., Goliad (1/31/95); H.B. Ruckman III, Karnes City (1/31/97); Nancy Steves, San Antonio (1/31/99); J.C. Turner, Floresville (1/31/97); Otis L. Walker, Goliad (1/31/97). Gen. Mgr., Fred. N. Pfeiffer, P.O. Box 830027, San Antonio 78283-0027.

San Jacinto Historical Advisory Board - (1907 as San Jacinto State Park Commission; changed to San Jacinto Battleground Commission and changed again in 1965 to present name; apptv.; 6-yr.; 5 members — 2 ex officio: Dir., Parks Div., Parks and Wildlife Dept. and pres. of San Jacinto Museum of History Assn.; 3 apptd. by Gov.: Mary C. Burke, Houston (9/1/97); Joel Moore Nash, Bellaire (9/1/95); Frank Calhoun, Houston (9/1/99). Parks Section, Parks and Wildlife Dept., 4200 Smith School Rd., Austin 78744.

San Jacinto River Authority, Board of Directors - (1937); apptv.; expenses while on duty; 6-yr.; 6 members: Henry T. Brooks, Conroe (10/16/99); John H. Choate, Humble (10/16/97); James T. Edmonds, Houston (10/16/99); David L. Mendez, Houston (10/16/97); R. Gary Montgomery, The Woodlands (10/16/95); Walter D. Wilkerson Jr., Conroe (10/16/95). Gen. Mgr., James R. Adams, Box 329, Conroe 77305.

Savings and Loan Commissioner - Apptv. by State Finance Commission: James L. Pledger ($89,116), Box 1089, Austin 78767.

School Land Board - (See Land Board, School).

Securities Board, State - (Est. 1957, the outgrowth of several amendments to the Texas Securities Act, originally passed 1913); act is administered by the Securities Commissioner, who is appointed by the board members; expenses; 6-yr.; 3 members: Nicholas C. Taylor, Midland (1/20/01); Dan R. Waller, Dallas (1/20/99); Thomas D. Warner, Houston (1/20/97). Securities Commissioner, Denise Voigt Crawford ($75,000), Box 13167, Austin 78711-3167.

Seed and Plant Board, State - (1959); apptv.; 2-yr.; 6 members: Aubrey J. Allison, Tulia (10/6/95); Dick L. Auld, Lubbock (10/6/93); Charles Leamons, Giddings (10/6/96); Alfred L. Martin, Hubbard (10/6/96); G.F. "Buz" Poage,

Levelland (10/6/96); Edward C.A. Runge, College Station (10/6/95). Office Address: Texas Dept. of Agriculture, Box 12847, Austin 78711.

Sex Offender Treatment, Interagency Council on - (1983); 12 members — 9 ex officio: one each from Texas Dept. of Criminal Justice, Board of Pardons and Paroles, Texas Adult Probation Commission, Texas Juvenile Probation Commission, Texas Dept. of Mental Health and Mental Retardation, Texas Youth Commission, Sam Houston State University, Texas Dept. of Human Services and one member of Gov's. office administering criminal justice planning; 3 apptv. from general public; 6-yr.; expenses; apptv. members: Collier M. Cole, Dickinson (2/1/97); Walter J. Meyer III, Galveston (2/1/95); Norma W. Reed, El Paso (2/1/93). Exec. Dir., Eliza May ($39,816), P.O. Box 12546, Austin 78711.

Social Work Examiners, Texas State Board of - (1993); apptd.; 6-yr.; per diem and travel expenses; 9 members: Ann Beadel, Brownwood (2/1/95); Ramiro Cabrera, Corpus Christi (2/1/99); Cathy Clancy, Houston (2/1/97); Jennifer Lynn Jorgensen, Fort Worth (2/1/95); Marlene LaRoe, Houston (2/1/99); Roberto A. Mascorro, El Paso (2/1/95); Shonna Lynette Olford, Longview (2/1/97); Sylvia S. Ramirez, Portland (2/1/97); Hoye D. Tibbets, Grandview (2/1/99).

Soil and Water Conservation Board, Texas State - (1939); elected by members of individual districts; 2 yrs.; 5 members: Charles D. Clark, Menard (5/7/96); Harvey Davis, Temple (5/7/95); Albert H. Evans Jr., Henderson (5/5/96); Paul Robertson, Hale Center (5/2/95); C.F. "Dick" Schendel, Goliad (5/7/95). Exec. Dir., Robert G. Buckley ($60,000), P.O. Box 658, Temple 76503.

Speech-Language Pathology and Audiology, State Board of Examiners for - (1983); apptv.; 6-yr.; per diem and expenses; 9 members: John K. Ashby, Abilene (8/31/99); Linda Mora Cano, Corpus Christi (8/31/97); Carol N. Gore, El Paso (8/31/95); Deloris Marie Johnson, Houston (8/31/99); Charles K. Kuratko, Lubbock (8/31/97); Teri Mata-Pistokache, McAllen (8/31/99); Jane D. McConnell, Dallas (8/31/97); Gene R. Powers, Austin (8/31/95); Drew G. Sawyer, Austin (8/31/95). Exec. Secy., Dorothy Cawthon, Texas Dept. of Health, 1100 W. 49th, Austin 78756-3183.

Stephen F. Austin State University, Board of Regents - (1969); apptv.; expenses; 6-yr.; 9 members: Ron Adkison, Henderson (1/31/99); Laurel Ann P. Austin, Jacksonville (1/31/97); Dionne Bagsby, Fort Worth (1/31/97); Richard A. Brookshire, Lufkin (1/31/01); Pattye Greer, Nacogdoches (1/31/01); Retta B. Kelley, Longview (1/31/97); Simon Lynn Montes, Lufkin (1/31/99); Jimmy W. Murphy, Houston (1/31/01); Murray Shaw, Austin (1/31/99). Pres., Dr. William J. Brophy, Box 6078, SFA Sta., Nacogdoches 75962.

Student Loan Corporation, Texas Guaranteed - (1979); 6-yr.; 11-members — one ex officio; Comptroller of Public Accounts; one apptd. by Commissioner of Higher Education and one apptd. by Chmn. of Coordinating Board; 8 apptd. by Gov. as follows: Lee Elliott Brown, Houston (1/31/97); Gary W. Bruner, Arlington (1/31/95); Teofilo Jaime Chahin, Austin (1/31/97); Don E. Cosby, Lubbock (1/31/99); Rene E. Gonzalez, San Antonio (1/31/99); Wright L. Lassiter Jr., Dallas (1/31/95); Jerry Don Miller, Canyon (1/31/99); Alan V. Rash, El Paso (1/31/95); Barbara B. Reagan, Dallas (1/31/97). Pres., Milton G. Wright, Box 201725, Austin 78720.

Sulphur River Basin Authority, Board of Directors - (1985); apptd.; 6-yr.; per diem and expenses; 6 members: David Baucom, Sulphur Springs (2/1/95); Curtis R. Fendley, Paris (2/1/95); John McCool Howison, Bogata (2/1/99); Mike Huddleston, Wake Village (2/1/97); Ivory E. Moore, Commerce (2/1/97); Maxine J. Nanze, Atlanta (2/1/99).

Sunset Advisory Commission - (1977); 10 members: 4 members of House of Representatives, 4 members of Senate, one public member apptd. by Speaker, one public member apptd. by Lt. Gov.; 4-yr.; expenses. Dir., John P. Moore, P.O. Box 13066, Austin 78711.

Tax Board, State - (1905); ex officio; term in other office; no compensation; 3 members: Comptroller, Secretary of State and State Treasurer.

Tax Professional Examiners, Board of - (1977 as Board of Tax Assessor Examiners; name changed to present form 1983); apptv.; expenses; 6-yr.; 6 members: Carol Autry, Amarillo (3/1/01); Darla P. Doss, Crosbyton (3/1/99); Wayne R. Hawkins, Texarkana (3/1/01); Linda D. Jaynes, Plainview (3/1/97); Ciro Trevino, Edinburg (3/1/97); Cora B. Viescas, El Paso (3/1/99). Exec. Dir., Sam Smith ($43,417), 333 Guadalupe, Tower II, #520 Austin 78701-3942.

Teacher Retirement System - (See Retirement System, Teacher).

Texas A&M University System - Board of Regents - (1875); apptv.; 6-yr.; expenses; 9 members: Robert H. Allen, Houston (2/1/01); Alison W. Leland Brisco, Houston (2/1/97); John H. Lindsey, Houston (2/1/99); Frederick Donald McClure, Dallas (2/1/01); T. Michael O'Connor, Victoria (2/1/99); Donald E. Powell, Amarillo (2/1/01); M. Guadalupe Lopez Rangel, Corpus Christi (2/1/99); Mary Nan West, Batesville (2/1/97); Royce W. Wisenbaker, Tyler (2/1/97). Chancellor, Barry B. Thompson, College Station 77843-1123.

Texas Southern University, Board of Regents - (1947); expenses; 6-yr.; 9 members: Joe M. Bailey, Houston (2/1/97); Enos M. Cabell Jr., Missouri City (2/1/01); Rufus Cormier Jr., Houston (2/1/97); Jenard M. Gross, Houston (2/1/97); Anthony D. Lyons, Fort Worth (2/1/99); Gene A. Moore Sr., Houston (2/1/01); Carroll W. Phillips, Houston (2/1/95); Oliver C. Sutton II, San Antonio (2/1/99); Rosie Zamora-Cope, Houston (2/1/99). Pres., Dr. William H. Harris, 3100 Cleburne, Houston 77004.

Texas State Technical College, Board of Regents - (1960 as Board of the Texas State Technical Institute; changed to present name, 1991); apptv.; expenses; 6-yr.; 9 members: Edward B. Adams Sr., Austin (8/31/97); George W. Baur, Houston (8/31/93); Ricardo Gutierrez, Rio Grande City (8/31/95); Jesse S. Harris, Dallas (8/31/93); Odelia M. R. McEachern, Sweetwater (8/31/97); Charles D. Olson, Waco (8/31/99); Gerald D. Phariss, Mesquite (8/31/97); Jere J. Ruff, Longview (8/31/95); Mollie Anna Solomon, Groves (8/31/95). Chancellor, Dr. Cecil L. Groves, TSTC System, Waco 76705.

Texas State University System, Board of Regents - (1911 as Board of Regents of State Teachers Colleges; name changed in 1965 to Board of Regents of State Senior Colleges; changed to present form in 1975); apptv.; per diem and expenses; 6-yr.; 9 members: William L. (Bill) Cunningham, San Marcos (2/1/97); Becky R. Espino, Fort Stockton (2/1/97); Macedonio Villarreal, Sugar Land (2/1/01); Jane Monday, Huntsville (2/1/97); Thomas M. Moeller, Beaumont (2/1/01); Elizabeth T. Nash, San Marcos (2/1/99); Pollyanna A. Stephens, San Angelo (2/1/01); Craig H. Vittitoe, Harlingen (2/1/99); Ray Zapata, Christoval (2/1/99). Chancellor, Lamar G. Urbanovsky, 505 Sam Houston Bldg., Austin 78701.

Texas Tech University, Board of Regents - (1923); apptv.; expenses; 6-yr.; 9 members: J. Robert Brown, El Paso (1/31/01); Dr. Bernard A. Harris Jr., Houston (1/31/99); Patsy W. Martin, Austin (1/31/97); Carl Edward Noe, Dallas (1/31/99); John C. Sims, Lubbock (1/31/97); James E. Sowell, Dallas (1/31/01); Elizabeth (Cissy) Ward, Houston (1/31/97); Edward E. Whitacre Jr., San Antonio (1/31/99); Alan B. White, Lubbock (1/31/01). Pres., Robert Lawless, Box 4039, Lubbock 79409.

Texas Woman's University Board of Regents - (1901); apptv.; expenses; 6-yr.; 9 members: Nan Hutchins Bailey, Flint (2/1/99); Lucy Crow Billingsley, Dallas (2/1/99); Ronald F. Garvey, Dallas (2/1/01); Kay Williams Goodman, Sanger (2/1/01); Richard D. Hayes, Denton (2/1/01); Jayne Lipe, Fort Worth (2/1/97); Diana E. Marshall, Houston (2/1/97); Darlene T. Medrano, Harlingen (2/1/97); Cheryl B. Wattley, Dallas (2/1/99). Pres., Carol D. Surles, Box 23925, TWU Sta., Denton 76204-1925.

Texas-Mexico Authority Advisory Board - (1991); apptd.; 6-yr.; 6 members: Santiago F. Cantu, Austin (2/1/97); Marjorie C. Kastman, Lubbock (2/1/95); Mark Langdale, Dallas (2/1/01); William R. Leo, La Joya (2/1/99); William S. Tilney, El Paso (2/1/97).

Transportation Commission, Texas - (1917 as State Highway Commission; merged with Mass Transportation Commission and name changed to State Board of Highways and Public Transportation in 1975; merged with

Texas Dept. of Aviation and Texas Motor Vehicle Commission and name changed to present form in 1991); apptv.; 6-yr.; ($15,914); 3 members: David Bernsen, Beaumont (2/1/97); David M. Laney, Dallas (2/1/01); Anne Shelmire Wynne, Austin (2/1/99). Exec. Dir., William G. Burnett, P.E. ($105,000), 11th & Brazos, Austin 78701-2483.

Trinity River Authority, Board of Directors - (1955); apptv.; per diem and expenses; 6-yr.; 24 directors — 3 from Tarrant County, 4 from Dallas County, 2 from area-at-large and one each from 15 other districts: Judi Jones Benestante, Coldspring (3/15/99); Anton B. Brucks, Dallas (3/15/97); Jake Caprielian, Crockett (3/15/97); Patricia A. Clapp, Dallas (3/15/01); Horace Perry Flatt, Terrell (3/15/99); Valerie Freeman, Dallas (3/15/01); Michael P. Heiskell, Arlington (3/15/99); William H. Hodges, Huntsville (3/15/01); Mellie R. Howard, Corsicana (3/15/97); Percy Howard Jr., Huntsville (3/15/97); Jo Ann Jenkins, Waxahachie (3/15/99); David B. Jenkins, Stowell (3/15/97); William M. Key, Athens (3/15/01); A. Dawn Knight, Madisonville (3/15/99); Danny K. Kramer, Fort Worth (3/15/97); Maurice L. Locke, Liberty (3/15/01); Carol N. Magee, Dallas (3/15/97); Troy E. Nash, Groveton (3/15/99); James W. Porter, Dallas (3/15/99); H. Gene Reynolds Jr., Fairfield (3/15/01); Constance T. Slocomb, Livingston (3/15/97); Wanda W. Stovall, Fort Worth (3/15/01); Douglas Lee Sumrall, Palestine (3/15/01); F.L. Thompson, Leona (3/15/99). Gen. Mgr., Danny F. Vance, Box 60, Arlington 76004-0060.

Turnpike Authority, Texas - Board of Directors - (1953 as 9-member board; increased to 12 members in 1971; will be incorporated into Texas Dept. of Transportation eff. Sept. 1, 1997); 6-yr.; 12 members — 3 ex officio; 3 members of Texas Transportation Commission; 9 apptv. as follows: Raul A. Besteiro Jr., Brownsville (2/15/97); Tomas Cardenas Jr., El Paso (2/15/99); Michael Y. Chou, Houston (2/15/97); Luther G. Jones Jr., Corpus Christi (2/15/97); Nathelyne A. Kennedy, Sugar Land (2/15/99); William P. Manomes Jr., Dallas (2/15/95); Philip Montgomery, Dallas (2/15/95); Lorraine Perryman, Odessa (2/15/99); Jere W. Thompson Jr., Dallas (2/15/01). Exec. Dir., John Ramming, Box 190369, Dallas 75219.

Uniform State Laws, Commission on - (1941 as 5-member Commissioners to the National Conference on Uniform State Laws; name changed to present form, membership increased to 6 and term of office raised to 6 years in 1977); apptv.; 6-yr.; 6 members: Patrick C. Guillot, Dallas (9/30/94); David Peeples, San Antonio (9/30/98); Marilyn E. Phelan, Lubbock (9/30/98); Rodney W. Satterwhite, Midland (9/30/96); George L. Thompson III, Lubbock (9/30/96); Harry L. Tindall, Houston (9/30/20).

University of Houston, Board of Regents - (1963); apptv.; expenses; 6-yr.; 9 members: Zinetta A. Burney, Houston (8/31/97); Philip J. Carroll, Houston (8/31/99); John T. Cater, Houston (8/31/95); Elizabeth L. Ghrist, Houston (8/31/95); Elyse Lanier, Houston (8/31/97); Vidal G. Martinez, Houston (8/31/95); Wilhelmina R. Morian, Houston (8/31/97); John M. O'Quinn, Houston (8/31/99); Kay Kerr Walker, Victoria (8/31/99). Chancellor, (Vacancy at press time), 1600 Smith, #3400, Houston 77002.

University of North Texas Board of Regents - (1949); apptv.; 6-yr.; expenses; 9 members: William D. Bayless Sr., Denison (5/22/97); Jerry S. Farrington, Dallas (5/22/99); Becky Ann Garth, Temple (5/22/89); Nancy S. Halbreich, Dallas (5/22/97); Joe Kirven, Dallas (5/22/95); E. L. Langley, Irving (5/22/95); Lucille G. Murchison, Dallas (5/22/99); Topsy R. Wright, Grand Prairie (5/22/99). Chancellor, Alfred F. Hurley, Box 13737, Denton 76203-3737.

University of Texas System, Board of Regents - (1881); apptv.; expenses; 6-yr.; 9 members: Linnet F. Deily, Houston (2/1/01); Donald L. Evans, Midland (2/1/01); Thomas O. Hicks, Dallas (2/1/99); Zan Wesley Holmes Jr., Dallas (2/1/97); Lowell H. Lebermann, Austin (2/1/99); Thomas G. Loeffler, San Antonio (2/1/01); Bernard Rapoport, Waco (2/1/97); Martha E. Smiley, Austin (2/1/99); Ellen C. Temple, Lufkin (2/1/97). Chancellor, William H. Cummingham, Box N, University Sta., Austin 78713-7328.

Veterans Commission, Texas - (1927 as Veterans State Service Office; reorganized as Veterans Affairs Commission in 1947 with 5 members; membership increased to 6 in 1981; name changed to present form in 1985); apptv.; 6-yr.; per diem while on duty and expenses; 6 members: Samuel Bier, Austin (12/31/91); Manuel A. Cano, Mercedes (12/31/95); Ralph Lee King, Burkburnett (12/31/97); James S. Novy, San Antonio (12/31/95); Herbert W. Odell, Fort Worth (12/31/99); Patsy L. Palmquist, Devine (12/31/99). Exec. Dir., Douglas K. Brown, Box 12277, Austin 78711 ($60,000).

Veterans Land Board - (Est. 1949 as 3-member ex officio board; reorganized 1956); 4-yr.; per diem and expenses; 3 members: one ex officio: Comm. of General Land Office; 2 apptd.: Mike McKool, Dallas (12/29/94); Jesse D. Martin, Lubbock (12/29/96). Exec. Sec., David Gloier; Stephen F. Austin Bldg., Austin 78701.

Veterinary Medical Examiners, Texas State Board of - (1911; revised 1953; made 9-member board in 1981); apptv.; expenses on duty; 6-yr.; 9 members: James N. Gomez, Brownsville (8/26/97); Robert I. Hughes, Center (8/26/99); Alton F. Hopkins, Dallas (8/26/95); Sharon O. Matthews, Albany (8/26/99); Michael J. McCulloch, Odessa (8/26/99); Joyce G. Schiff, Dallas (8/26/97); Guy Alvin Sheppard, San Angelo (8/26/95); Clark S. Willingham, Dallas (8/26/95); John A. Wood, Lufkin (8/26/97). Exec. Dir., Ron Allen ($48,216), 1946 S. I-35, #306, Austin 78704.

Water Development Board, Texas - (1957; legislative function for the Texas Dept. of Water Resources, 1977); apptv.; per diem and expenses; 6-yr.; 6 members: Elaine Mowinski Barron, El Paso (12/31/99); Noe Fernandez, McAllen (12/31/95); Charles L. Geren, Fort Worth (12/31/99); Charles W. Jenness, Houston (12/31/97); William B. Madden, Dallas (12/31/95); Diane Elaine Umstead, Houston (12/31/97). Exec. Admin., Craig D. Pedersen, Box 13231, Austin 78711 ($63,000).

Workers' Compensation Commission, Texas - (1991); 6-yr.; apptv; expenses; 6 members: Jack E. Abla, Tyler (2/1/01); Ramon Class, Canyon (2/1/97); Royce Faulkner, Austin (2/1/99); O.D. Kenemore, Lake Jackson (2/1/99); Richard F. Reynolds, Austin (2/1/09); Donna Lynn Snyder, Dallas (2/1/97). Exec. Dir., Todd K. Brown ($78,000), 4000 S. I-35, Austin 78704-1287.

Workers' Compensation Insurance Fund Board, Texas - (1991); expenses; 6-yr.; 9 members: Glenn Biggs, San Antonio (2/1/97); Patricia A. (Pat) Crawford, El Paso (2/1/99); Larry K. Durrett, Jacksonville (2/1/99); Irma E. Guzman Flores, San Antonio (2/1/95); Lloyd E. Moss, Cleburne (2/1/97); Ben Munson, Denison (2/1/97); Pat O'Neal, Dallas (2/1/01); Stephen Van Sadler, Cleveland (2/1/93); Martin H. Young Jr., The Woodlands (2/1/01).

Workforce Commission, Texas - (1936 as **Texas Employment Commission**; name changed 1995); apptv.; $84,660; 6-yr.; 3 members: Eddie Cavazos, Corpus Christi (2/1/97); James J. Kaster, Austin (2/1/97); Jackie William St. Clair, Austin (2/1/99). Admin., William Grossenbacher ($82,432), 638 TEC Bldg., 101 E. 15th, Austin 78778.

Youth Commission, Texas - (1949 as 9-member board; reorganized 1957 and again in 1975); 6-yr.; per diem on duty; 6 apptv. members: Gary D. Compton, Amarillo (8/31/95); Pete Harrell, Austin (8/31/97); Marilla B. King, Austin (8/31/95); Leonard E. Lawrence, San Antonio (8/31/97); John W. Odam Jr., Houston (8/31/99); Edna L. Tamayo, Harlingen (8/31/99). Exec. Dir., Steve Robinson, Box 4260, Austin 78765 ($85,000). ☆

— Texas Almanac, 1904

The state government boards filled one page of the Almanac in 1904; that listed the names of all the members and their hometowns. The 21 boards included the Eclectic Medical Examiners, Homeopathic Medical Examiners, the various boards of trustees of the colleges and the Confederate Soldiers' and Sailors' Home in Austin.

State Government Income and Expenditures

Taxes are the state government's primary source of income. Another source was added in May 1992, when the Texas Lottery was inaugurated. Although it produces only about 4 percent of the income of the General Revenue Fund, the Texas Lottery gets more attention than any other revenue producer. On this and the following pages are summaries of state income and expenditures, a brief history of the operations of the Texas Lottery, a summary of the state budget for the 1996-97 biennium and an explanation of major state taxes.

State Revenues by Source and Expenditures by Function

(Amounts in Millions) and Percent of Total

Revenues by Source	1994	%	1993	%	1992	%	1991	%	1990	%
Tax Collections	$18,106	49.3	$17,011	50.3	$15,849	53.5	$14,922	57.0	$13, 633	57.7
Federal Funds	10,552	28.7	9,853	29.2	8,417	28.4	6,964	26.6	5,930	25.1
Licenses, Fees and Permits	3,151	8.6	2,073	6.1	1,863	6.3	1,656	6.3	1,590	6.7
Interest & Other Investment Income	1,697	4.6	2,155	6.4	1,862	6.3	1,714	6.5	1,676	7.1
Land Income	220	0.6	239	0.7	226	0.8	282	1.1	279	1.2
Sales of Goods & Services	141	0.4	128	0.4	41	0.1	123	0.5	138	0.6
Contributions to Employee Benefits	115	0.3	104	0.3	96	0.3	88	0.3	82	0.3
Settlements of Claims	12	0.1	18	0.1	31	0.1	4	0.0	16	0.1
Net Lottery Proceeds	1,586	4.3	1,113	3.3	312	1.0	--	--	--	--
Other Revenues	1,126	3.1	1,101	3.2	951	3.2	438	1.7	278	1.2
Total Net Revenues	$36,707	100	$33,975	100	$29,648	100	$26,190	100	$23,622	100
Expenditures by Function										
General Government	$1,238	3.9	1,372	4.6	1,092	4.2	1,085	4.8	953	4.7
Education	13,416	37.6	12,782	38.3	11,910	40.7	11,084	43.3	10,057	44.4
Employee Benefits	1,618	4.5	1,577	4.8	1,320	4.5	1,278	5.0	1,131	5.0
Health and Human Services	12,005	33.7	11,244	33.7	9,548	32.5	7,015	27.3	5,657	24.9
Public Safety and Corrections	1,938	5.4	1,608	4.8	1,374	4.7	1,193	4.7	1,036	4.6
Transportation	2,726	7.7	2,797	8.4	2,368	8.1	2,496	9.8	2,582	11.4
Natural Resources and Recreational Services	589	1.7	469	1.4	417	1.4	314	1.2	250	1.1
Regulatory Agencies	169	0.5	171	0.5	165	0.6	185	0.7	157	0.7
Debt Service	348	1.0	317	0.9	370	1.3	322	1.3	315	1.4
Capital Outlay	999	2.8	613	1.8	559	1.9	490	1.9	414	1.8
Total Expenditures	$35,638	100	33,389	100	29,290	100	25,603	100	22,680	100

Source: 1994 Comprehensive Annual Financial Report of the Texas State Comptroller's Office, compiled from State of Texas Financial Statements for Fiscal 1990-1994. This table comprises the following funds: General, Special Revenue, Debt Service and Capital Projects. Amounts rounded.

State Tax Collections, 1985-1994

Fiscal Year	State Tax Collections	Resident Population	Per Capita Tax Collections	Taxes as % of Personal Income
1985	$10,721,208,262	16,242,768	660.06	4.9
1986	10,231,670,211	16.512,533	619.63	4.5
1987	10,266,162,781	16,615,360	617.87	4.5
1988	12,364,618,924	16,669,153	741.77	5.1
1989	12,905,940,817	16,795, 968	768.40	5.0
1990	13,632,640,459	†17,025,340	†800.73	4.9
1991	14,922,113,980	†17,314,183	†861.84	5.0
1992	15,848,915,148	†17,641,430	†898.39	5.0
1993	17,010,737,258	†17,984,373	†945,86	5.0
1994	18,105,950,594	*18,325,850	*988.00	*5.0

* *Estimated*
†*Revised*

Tax collection data were compiled from Texas Comptroller of Public Accounts, Annual Financial Report of various years. Population and personal income figures for 1985 to 1993 are from U.S. Dept. of Commerce Bureau of the Census and Bureau of Economic Analysis. 1994 population and personal income are based on Comptroller of Public Accounts estimates.

Texas Lottery

The following was taken from material supplied by the Texas Lottery Commission, P.O.Box 16630, Austin 78761-6630.

The State Lottery Act was passed by the Legislature after many years of discussion in July 1991. The constitutional amendment necessary to approve the lottery, House Joint Resolution 8, was passed in an election on Nov. 5, 1991, by a vote of 1,326,154 to 728,994. The first ticket was purchased by Gov. Ann Richards on May 29, 1992. More than 23 million Lone Star Millions instant tickets were sold the first day alone. By the end of the first week, 102.4 million tickets had been sold.

The lottery began with instant scratch games. Starting on June 18, 1992, three of the four instant games held an additional, weekly grand-prize drawing, which paid the winner $1 million cash. In September 1992, the grand-prize drawings became monthly. These drawings ended in July 1994.

By the end of August 1994, 32 more scratch games had been introduced.

Lotto Texas is perhaps the most ballyhooed game of those offered. Started in Nov. 1992, it requires the player to pick six numbers between 1 and 50, with two drawings held each week. If there is no winner at one drawing, the pot increases for the next. Janie Kallus of Schulenburg won the first jackpot on Nov. 21, 1992: $21.7 million. The largest Lotto Texas jackpot so far was won on March 16, 1994, when five winners shared $77.1 million. As of March 20, 1995, 163 Lotto Texas jackpots had been announced. Of those, one remains unclaimed and one claim was denied. Some jackpots have been split among multiple participants.

A daily (except Sunday) game, Pick 3, was introduced on Oct. 25, 1993, involving selecting a three-digit number.

Combined sales of the Texas Lottery totaled $5.5 billion to the end of fiscal 1994. The amount of that paid into the General Revenue Fund during its first 27 months was $1.681 billion. The Texas Lottery contributes about 3 percent of the total revenue that goes into the General Revenue Fund annually. Annual revenue paid into the fund by the Texas Lottery has been:

Fiscal Year	Revenue
1992	$203 million
1993	$600 million
1994	$869 million
1995 (to 2/15/95)	$445 million

The Texas Lottery was a division of the Comptroller's office until Dec. 1993, when it became a separate agency, the Texas Lottery Commission. In April 1994, the Lottery Commission also assumed regulation and oversight of the state's charitable bingo games.

Nora Linares has managed the lottery since its inception, first as director of the Comptroller's Lottery Division and now as Executive Director of the Texas Lottery Commission.

Texas Lottery Financial Data

Start-up to Aug. 31, 1994

Sales of All Lottery Products	Prizes Won	Cost of Product	Retailer Commissions	Administration	Transferred to General Revenue Fund
$5.5 billion	**$2.78 billion**	**$303 million**	**$260 million**	**$45 million**	**$1.681 billion**

Who Plays the Lottery?

The executive director of the Texas Lottery is required to conduct a biennial demographic survey of lottery players in order to determine the income, age, sex, race, education and frequency of participation of players. The information below is from the survey conducted for the Texas Lottery Commission by the Office of Survey Research of The University of Texas at Austin, College of Communication, in Sept. and Oct. 1994.

A total of 1,710 interviews were completed with adult Texans 18 years of age and older. The margin of error for a sample of 1,710 is approximately plus or minus 2.4 percent.

The percentage of Texans who report purchasing Texas Lottery tickets in the 12 months preceding the survey was 71 percent, an increase since the 1992 study, which found that 64 percent had participated.

Sixty-six percent reported playing Lotto, sometimes called Pick 6, while 57 percent played scratch games and 19 percent played the daily Pick 3 game.

Age: Most lottery players are between 25 and 54 years old. Those playing least frequently are over 65.

Educational Level: Those with less than a high school education were the least likely to play (59 percent), while those with some college were the most likely (76 percent).

Income Level: Seventy-seven percent of Texans making between $20,000 and $49,000 per year played lottery games, 75 percent making $10,000 to $19,000, 73 percent making $50,000 and over, and 60 percent of those making under $10,000 a year play the lottery.

Ethnic Background: The survey found that 71 percent of Anglos play; 73 percent of Hispanics; 68 percent of Blacks; and 69 percent of other ethnic groups.

Sex: Men are more likely to play lottery games than women. Approximately 75 percent of men play; about 68 percent of women. This gender gap is largest for Lotto Texas players, but much less for the other games.

Geography: The largest cities, Houston and Dallas, have the greatest percentage of residents who play: 75 percent and 74 percent respectively. In the 10 Lottery sales regions, the one with the smallest percentage of Lottery players is the Tyler district, with 58 percent. Next lowest is the Lubbock district, with 64. ☆

State Government Budget Summary, 1996-97 Biennium

Source: Legislative Budget Board

Article (Govt. Division)	1996-97 Budget (All funds) (in Millions)
Art. I, General Government	$1,823.7
Art. II, Health and Human Services	26,422.4
Art. III, Education	33,592.9
Art. IV, The Judiciary	257.1
Art. V, Public Safety & Criminal Justice	6,925.6
Art. VI, Natural Resources	1,736.1
Art. VII, Business & Economic Dev.	8,793.1
Art. VIII, Regulatory	416.7
Art. IX, General Provisions	(326.3)
Art. X, The Legislature	221.2
Total	**$79,862.4**

House Bill 1 of the 74th Legislature called for a budget for the operation of state government for the 1996-97 biennium totalling $79.9 billion from all fund sources. This provids for an increase of 6.2 percent, or $4.7 billion, in total state funding.

General revenue-related funding, including funds consolidated with the General Revenue Fund, total $45.1 billion for 1996-97, an increase of 10 percent, or or $4.1 billion, over 1994-95.

Federal funds for the 1996-97 biennium total $23.3 billion.

General revenue-related funds account for 55.2 percent of the 1996-97 budget; general revenue consolidated funds for 1.1 percent, federal funds for 19.3 percent, earned federal funds for 0.1 percent and other funds for 14.3 percent. ☆

Major State Taxes and Rates, 1994

Below are listed the major state taxes, including the percentage of the tax and a description of what is taxed. Following that is a table giving the amount of revenue generated by those taxes during the state's fiscal years of 1993 and 1994.

Source: Annual Cash Report 1994, Volume I, of the Texas Comptroller of Public Accounts.

Sales and Use Tax: 6.25% of retail sale price of tangible personal property and selected services.

Natural and Casinghead Gas Tax: 7.5% of the market value of gas produced in the state.

Oil Production and Regulation Taxes:

- **Production:** 4.6% of the market value of oil produced in the state.
- **Regulation:** 3/16 of one cent on each barrel produced.

Motor Fuels Taxes:

- **Motor Fuels Tax:** 20 cents/gallon of gasoline.
- **Special Fuels Taxes**:
  - **Diesel Fuel:** 20 cents/gallon.
  - **Liquefied Gas:** 15 cents/gallon.

Motor Vehicle Sales and Rental Taxes:

- **Sales:** 6.25% of vehicle sales price, less trade-in.
- **Rental:** 10% of gross rental receipts up to 30 days; 6.25% over 30 days.

Cigarette and Tobacco Products Taxes:

- **Cigarettes:** $20.50 per 1,000 weighing 3 lbs or less (41 cents per pack of 20); $22.60 per 1,000 weighing more than 3 lbs.
- **Cigar and Tobacco products:** based on weight per 1,000 and selling price. Cigars from one cent per 10 cigars to $11 per 1,000 (check with Comptroller's Office for more information).
- **Chewing, snuff, pipe or smoking tobacco:** 35.213% of the manufacturer's list price exclusive of discounts.

Corporate Franchise Tax: Domestic and foreign corporations, banks, savings & loans, and limited liability companies, unless otherwise provided for, pay (1) $2.50 per $1,000 of taxable capital, and (2) the amount by which a tax of 4.5% on earned surplus exceeds the tax on capital, if any.

Alcoholic Beverage Taxes:

- **Beer:** $6/ barrel
- **Liquor:** $2.40/ gallon.
- **Wine:** Alcoholic volume not over 14%: 20.4 cents/gallon. More than 14%: 40.8 cents/gallon.
- **Sparkling wine:** 51.6 cents/gallon.
- **Malt Liquor (Ale):** 19.8 cents/gallon.
- **Mixed Drinks Gross Receipts:** 14% of gross receipts.

Airline/Passenger Train Beverage Tax: 5 cents per serving.

Inheritance Tax: A tax equal to the amount of the federal credit is imposed on the transfer of property at death.

Utility Taxes:

- **Public Utility Gross Receipts:** 1/6 of 1% of gross receipts.
- **Gas, Electric and Water Utility:**
  - Cities 1,000-2,499 pop.: 0.581% of gross receipts.
  - Cities 2,500-9,999 pop.: 1.070%.
  - Cities 10,000 pop. or more: 1.997%.
- **Gas Utility Administration:** 1/2 of 1% of gross income of gas utility.

Hotel and Motel Tax: 6% of consideration paid by occupant.

Other taxes include **insurance company taxes, cement tax, oil and gas well servicing tax, bingo tax, sulphur tax, coin-operated amusement machine tax** and **minor occupation taxes.**

Tax Revenues, 1993, 1994

Below are listed the major taxes and the amounts each contributed to the state in fiscal years 1993 and 1994.

Type of Tax	FY 1993	FY 1994
Sales Tax	$9,122,074,600	$9,810,089,853
Oil Production Tax	492,258,062	361,968,586
Natural Gas Prod. Tax	682,926,381	554,484,493
Motor Fuels Taxes	2,085,523,583	2,170,231,159
Motor Veh. Sales/Rent.*	1,420,655,605	1,616,525,973
Franchise Tax	1,192,811,335	1,260,748,953
Cigarette/Tobacco Taxes	616,836,413	573,336,564
Alcoholic Bev. Taxes	393,248,502	400,483,720
Utility Taxes	227,285,501	263,308,174
Inheritance Tax	142,200,890	152,353,873
Hotel/Motel Tax	135,734,857	145,654,589
Other Taxes**	499,181,529	796,764,657
Totals	**$17,010,737,258**	**$18,105,950,594**

**Includes tax on manufactured housing sales and taxes on interstate motor carriers.*

***Includes taxes listed at the bottom of the preceding text.*

Texas' Chief Governmental Officials

On this and following pages are lists of the principal administrative officials who have served the Republic and State of Texas with dates of their tenures of office. In a few instances there are disputes as to the exact dates of tenures. Dates listed here are those that appear the most authentic.

★ ★ ★ ★ ★ ★ ★

Governors and Presidents

*Spanish Royal Governors

Domingo Terán de los Rios 1691-1692
Gregorio de Salinas Varona 1692-1697
Francisco Cuerbo y Valdéz 1698-1702
Mathías de Aguirre 1703-1705
Martín de Alarcón 1705-1708
Simon Padilla y Córdova 1708-1712
Pedro Fermin de Echevers y Subisa 1712-1714
Juan Valdéz 1714-1716
Martín de Alarcón 1716-1719
Joseph de Azlor, Marqués de San Miguel de Aguayo 1719-1722
Fernando Pérez de Almazan 1722-1727
Melchor de Media Villa y Azcona 1727-1730
Juan Antonio Bustillos y Ceballos 1730-1734
Manuel de Sandoval 1734-1736
Carlos Benites Franquis de Lugo 1736-1737
Prudencio de Orobio y Basterra 1737-1741
Tomás Felipe Wintuisen 1741-1743
Justo Boneo y Morales 1743-1744
Francisco García Larios 1744-1748
Pedro del Barrio Junco y Espriella 1748-1751
Jacinto de Barrios y Jauregui 1751-1759
Angel Martos y Navarrete 1759-1766
Hugo Oconór 1767-1770
Baron de Ripperda 1770-1778
Domingo Cabello 1778-1786
Bernardo Bonavia 1786-1786
Rafael Martínez Pacheco 1787-1788
The office of Governor was ordered suppressed and the province put under a presidial captain for a period in 1788-1789
Manuel Muñoz 1790-1798
José Irigoyen 1798-1800
Juan Bautista de Elguezábal 1800-1805
Antonio Cordero y Bustamante 1805-1810
Juan Bautista Casas 1811-1811
Manuel María de Salcedo 1811-1813
Cristóbal Domínguez 1814-1817
Ignacio Pérez 1817-1817
Manuel Pardo 1817-1817
Antonio Martínez 1817-1822

*Some authorities would include Texas under administrations of several earlier Spanish Governors. The late Dr. C. E. Castañeda, Latin-American librarian of The University of Texas and authority on the history of Texas and the Southwest, would include the following four: Francisco de Garay, 1523-26; Pánfilo de Narváez, 1526-28; Nuño de Guzmán, 1528-30; Hernando de Soto, 1538-43.

Governors Under Mexican Rule

The first two Governors under Mexican rule, Trespalacios and García, were of Texas only as Texas was then constituted. Beginning with Gonzales, 1824, the Governors were for the joint State of Coahuila y Texas.

José Felix Trespalacios 1822-1823
Luciano García 1823-1824
Rafael Gonzáles 1824-1826
Victor Blanco 1826-1827
José María Viesca 1827-1830
Ramón Eca y Músquiz 1830-1831
José María Letona 1831-1832
Ramón Eca y Músquiz 1832-1832
Juan Martín de Veramendi 1832-1833
Juan José de Vidáurri y Villasenor 1833-1834
Juan José Elguezábal 1834-1835
José María Cantú 1835-1835
Agustin M. Viesca 1835-1835
Marciel Borrego 1835-1835
Ramón Eca y Músquiz 1835-1835

Provisional Colonial Governor, Before Independence

Henry Smith (Impeached) 1835
James W. Robinson served as acting Governor just prior to March 2, 1836, after Smith was impeached.

Presidents of the Republic of Texas

David G. Burnet .... Mar. 16, 1836-Oct. 22, 1836
Sam Houston .... Oct. 22, 1836-Dec. 10, 1838
Mirabeau B. Lamar .... Dec. 10, 1838-Dec. 13, 1841
Sam Houston .... Dec. 13, 1841-Dec. 9, 1844
Anson Jones .... Dec. 9, 1844-Feb. 19, 1846

Governors Since Annexation

J. Pinckney Henderson ... Feb. 19, 1846-Dec. 21, 1847
(Albert C. Horton served as acting Governor while Henderson was away in the Mexican War.)
George T. Wood .... Dec. 21, 1847-Dec. 21, 1849
Peter Hansbrough Bell ... Dec. 21, 1849-Nov. 23, 1853
J. W. Henderson .... Nov. 23, 1853-Dec. 21, 1853
Elisha M. Pease .... Dec. 21, 1853-Dec. 21, 1857
Hardin R. Runnels .... Dec. 21, 1857-Dec. 21, 1859
Sam Houston (resigned because of state's secession from the Union) .... Dec. 21, 1859-Mar. 16, 1861
Edward Clark .... Mar. 16, 1861-Nov. 7, 1861
Francis R. Lubbock (resigned to enter Confederate Army) .... Nov. 7, 1861-Nov. 5, 1863
Pendleton Murrah (administration terminated by fall of Confederacy) .... Nov. 5, 1863-June 17, 1865
Fletcher S. Stockdale (Lt. Gov. performed some duties of office on Murrah's departure, but is sometimes included in list of Governors. Hamilton's appointment was for immediate succession as shown by dates.)
Andrew J. Hamilton (Provisional, appointed by President Johnson) ..... June 17, 1865-Aug. 9, 1866
James W. Throckmorton .... Aug. 9, 1866-Aug. 8, 1867
Elisha M. Pease (appointed July 30, 1867, under martial law) .... Aug. 8, 1867-Sept. 30, 1869

Interregnum

Pease resigned and vacated office Sept. 30, 1869; no successor was named until Jan. 8, 1870. Some historians extend Pease's term until Jan. 8, 1870, but in reality Texas was without a head of its civil government from Sept. 30, 1869 until Jan. 8, 1870.

Edmund J. Davis (appointed provisional Governor after being elected) .... Jan. 8, 1870-Jan. 15, 1874
Richard Coke (resigned to enter United States Senate) .... Jan. 15, 1874-Dec. 1, 1876
Richard B. Hubbard .... Dec. 1, 1876-Jan. 21, 1879
Oran M. Roberts .... Jan. 21, 1879-Jan. 16, 1883
John Ireland .... Jan. 16, 1883-Jan. 18, 1887
Lawrence Sullivan Ross .. Jan. 18, 1887-Jan. 20, 1891
James Stephen Hogg ...... Jan. 20, 1891-Jan. 15, 1895
Charles A. Culberson .... Jan. 15, 1895-Jan. 17, 1899
Joseph D. Sayers .... Jan. 17, 1899-Jan. 20, 1903
S. W. T. Lanham .... Jan. 20, 1903-Jan. 15, 1907
Thos. Mitchell Campbell .. Jan. 15, 1907-Jan. 17, 1911
Oscar Branch Colquitt ..... Jan. 17, 1911-Jan. 19, 1915
James E. Ferguson (impeached) .... Jan. 19, 1915-Aug. 25, 1917
William Pettus Hobby ..... Aug. 25, 1917-Jan. 18, 1921
Pat Morris Neff .... Jan. 18, 1921-Jan. 20, 1925
Miriam A. Ferguson .... Jan. 20, 1925-Jan. 17, 1927
Dan Moody .... Jan. 17, 1927-Jan. 20, 1931
Ross S. Sterling .... Jan. 20, 1931-Jan. 17, 1933
Miriam A. Ferguson .... Jan. 17, 1933-Jan. 15, 1935

James V. Allred..............Jan. 15, 1935-Jan. 17, 1939
W. Lee O'Daniel (resigned to enter United States Senate) .... Jan. 17, 1939-Aug. 4, 1941
Coke R. Stevenson .... Aug. 4, 1941-Jan. 21, 1947
Beauford H. Jester .... Jan. 21, 1947-July 11, 1949
Allan Shivers (Lt. Governor succeeded on death of Governor Jester. Elected in 1950 and re-elected in 1952 and 1954) .... July 11, 1949-Jan. 15, 1957
Price Daniel....................Jan. 15, 1957-Jan. 15, 1963
John Connally..................Jan. 15, 1963-Jan. 21, 1969
Preston Smith..................Jan. 21, 1969-Jan. 16, 1973
**Dolph Briscoe ....Jan. 16, 1973-Jan. 16, 1979
William P. Clements.........Jan. 16, 1979-Jan. 18, 1983
Mark White......................Jan. 18, 1983-Jan. 20, 1987
William P. Clements.........Jan. 20, 1987-Jan. 15, 1991
Ann W. Richards.............Jan. 15, 1991-Jan., 17, 1995
George W. Bush .... Jan. 17, 1995 to Present

**Effective in 1975, term of office was raised to 4 years, according to a constitutional amendment approved by Texas voters in 1972. See introduction to State Government chapter in this edition for other state officials whose terms were raised to four years.

★★★★★★★

Vice Presidents and Lieutenant Governors

Vice Presidents of Republic

Date Elected

Lorenzo de Zavala (provisional Vice President.)
Mirabeau B. Lamar..............................Sept. 5, 1836
David G. Burnet.................................. Sept. 3, 1838
Edward Burleson................................. Sept. 6, 1841
Kenneth L. Anderson............................ Sept. 2, 1844

Lieutenant Governors

Albert C. Horton.. 1846-1847
John A. Greer 1847-1851
J. W. Henderson.................................... Aug. 4, 1851
(Served as Governor of Texas from Nov. 23, 1853, to Dec. 21, 1853.)
D. C. Dickson 1853-1855
H. R. Runnels .... Aug. 6, 1855
(Runnels became Governor of Texas in 1857.)
F. R. Lubbock .... Aug. 4, 1857
(Became Governor of Texas during Confederacy.)
Edward Clark....................................... Aug. 1, 1859
(Became Governor of Texas during Confederacy.)
John M. Crockett 1861-1863
Fletcher S. Stockdale 1863-1866
George W. Jones...1866
(Jones was removed by General Sheridan.)
J. W. Flanagan 1869
(Flanagan was appointed U.S. Senator and was never inaugurated as Lt. Gov.)
R. B. Hubbard.. 1873-1876
(Became Governor of Texas in 1876.)
J. D. Sayers... 1878-1880
L. J. Storey.. 1880-1882
Marion Martin 1882-1884
Barnett Gibbs 1884-1886
T. B. Wheeler... 1886-1890
George C. Pendleton.................................. 1890-1892
M. M. Crane.....................Jan. 17, 1893-Jan. 25, 1895
George T. Jester... 1895-1898
J. N. Browning... 1898-1902
George D. Neal 1902-1906
A. B. Davidson... 1906-1912
Will H. Mayes 1912-1914
William Pettus Hobby 1914-1917
(Became Governor of Texas in September 1917.)
W. A. Johnson (succeeded Hobby as Lieutenant Governor, serving his unexpired term and until January, 1920).
Lynch Davidson.. 1920-1922
T. W. Davidson 1922-1924
Barry Miller.. 1924-1931
Edgar E. Witt 1931-1935
Walter Woodul 1935-1939
Coke R. Stevenson...................................... 1939-1941
(Became Governor Aug. 4, 1941.)
John Lee Smith............................ 1943-Jan. 21, 1947
Allan Shivers.................... Jan. 21, 1947-July 11, 1949
(Shivers succeeded to the governorship on death of Governor Beauford H. Jester, July 11, 1949.)
Ben Ramsey 1951-Sept. 18, 1961
(Ben Ramsey resigned to become a member of the State Railroad Commission, Sept. 18, 1961.)
Preston Smith... 1963-1969
Ben Barnes... 1969-1973
William P. Hobby Jr. 1973-1991
Robert D. Bullock.................................1991-Present

★★★★★★★

Secretaries of State

Republic of Texas

Raines Yearbook for Texas, 1901, gives the following record of Secretaries of State during the era of the Republic of Texas:

Under David G. Burnet — Samuel P. Carson, James Collingsworth and W. H. Jack.

Under Sam Houston (first term) — Stephen F. Austin, 1836. J. Pinckney Henderson and Dr. Robert A. Irion, 1837-38.

Under Mirabeau B. Lamar — Bernard Bee appointed Dec. 16, 1838; James Webb appointed Feb. 6, 1839; D. G. Burnet appointed Acting Secretary of State, May 31, 1839; N. Amory appointed Acting Secretary of State, July 23, 1839; D. G. Burnet appointed Acting Secretary of State, Aug. 5, 1839; Abner S. Lipscomb appointed Secretary of State, Jan. 31, 1840, and resigned Jan. 22, 1841; Joseph Waples appointed Acting Secretary of State, Jan. 23, 1841, and served until Feb. 8, 1841; James S. Mayfield appointed Feb. 8, 1841; Joseph Waples appointed April 30, 1841, and served until May 25, 1841; Samuel A. Roberts appointed May 25, 1841, and reappointed Sept. 7, 1841.

Under Sam Houston (second term) — E. Lawrence Stickney, Acting Secretary of State until Anson Jones appointed Dec. 13, 1841. Jones served as Secretary of State throughout this term except during the summer and part of this term of 1842, when Joseph Waples filled the position as Acting Secretary of State.

Under Anson Jones — Ebenezer Allen served from Dec. 10, 1844, until Feb. 5, 1845, when Ashbel Smith became Secretary of State. Allen was again named Acting Secretary of State, March 31, 1845, and later named Secretary of State.

State Secretaries of State

Charles Mariner .... Feb. 20, 1846-May 4, 1846
David G. Burnet ....May 4, 1846-Jan. 1, 1848
Washington D. Miller...........Jan. 1, 1848-Jan. 2, 1850
James Webb..................... Jan. 2, 1850-Nov. 14, 1851
Thomas H. Duval...........Nov. 14, 1851-Dec. 22, 1853
Edward Clark .... Dec. 22, 1853-Dec., 1857
T. S. Anderson .... Dec. 1857-Dec. 27, 1859
E. W. Cave.....................Dec. 27, 1859-Mar. 16, 1861
Bird Holland ....Mar. 16, 1861-Nov., 1861
Charles West ....Nov., 1861-Sept., 1862
Robert J. Townes .... Sept., 1862-May 2, 1865
Charles R. Pryor ....May 2, 1865-Aug., 1865
James H. Bell .... Aug., 1865-Aug., 1866
John A. Green......................... Aug., 1866-Aug., 1867
D. W. C. Phillips..................... Aug., 1867-Jan., 1870
J. P. Newcomb ....Jan. 1, 1870-Jan. 17, 1874
George Clark ....Jan. 17, 1874-Jan. 27, 1874
A. W. DeBerry...................Jan. 27, 1874-Dec. 1, 1876
Isham G. Searcy..............Dec. 1, 1876-Jan. 23, 1879
J. D. Templeton................Jan. 23, 1879-Jan. 22, 1881
T. H. Bowman ....Jan. 22, 1881-Jan. 18, 1883
J. W. Baines.....................Jan. 18, 1883-Jan. 21, 1887
John M. Moore..................Jan. 21, 1887-Jan. 22, 1891
George W. Smith ....Jan. 22, 1891-Jan. 17, 1895

Allison Mayfield ....Jan. 17, 1895-Jan. 5, 1897
J. W. Madden ....Jan. 5, 1897-Jan. 18, 1899
D. H. Hardy.....................Jan. 18, 1899-Jan. 19, 1901
John G. Tod ....Jan. 19, 1901-Jan., 1903
J. R. Curl .... Jan., 1903-April, 1905
O. K. Shannon......................... April, 1905-Jan., 1907
L. T. Dashiel............................ Jan., 1907-Feb., 1908
W. R. Davie .... Feb., 1908-Jan., 1909
W. B. Townsend............................Jan., 1909-Jan., 1911
C. C. McDonald .... Jan., 1911-Dec., 1912
J. T. Bowman .... Dec., 1912-Jan., 1913
John L. Wortham ....Jan., 1913-June, 1913
F. C. Weinert........................... June, 1913-Nov., 1914
D. A. Gregg.............................. Nov., 1914-Jan., 1915
John G. McKay .... Jan., 1915-Dec., 1916
C. J. Bartlett..............................Dec., 1916-Nov., 1917
George F. Howard .... Nov., 1917-Nov., 1920
C. D. Mims............................... Nov., 1920-Jan., 1921
S. L. Staples .... Jan., 1921-Aug., 1924
J. D. Strickland .... Sept., 1924-Jan. 1, 1925
Henry Hutchings...............Jan. 1, 1925-Jan. 20, 1925
Mrs. Emma G. Meharg.........Jan. 20, 1925-Jan., 1927
Mrs. Jane Y. McCallum.............Jan., 1927-Jan., 1933
W. W. Heath ....Jan., 1933-Jan., 1935
Gerald C. Mann .... Jan., 1935-Aug. 31, 1935
R. B. Stanford................Aug. 31, 1935-Aug. 25, 1936
B. P. Matocha .... Aug. 25, 1936-Jan. 18, 1937
Edward Clark.......................Jan. 18, 1937-Jan., 1939
Tom L. Beauchamp ....Jan., 1939-Oct., 1939
M. O. Flowers ....Oct. 26, 1939-Feb. 25, 1941
William J. Lawson............... Feb. 25, 1941-Jan., 1943
Sidney Latham .... Jan., 1943-Feb., 1945
Claude Isbell.............................. Feb., 1945-Jan., 1947
Paul H. Brown ....Jan., 1947-Jan. 19, 1949
Ben Ramsey.................... Jan. 19, 1949-Feb. 9, 1950
John Ben Shepperd.......... Feb. 9, 1950-April 30, 1952
Jack Ross........................ April 30, 1952-Jan. 9, 1953
Howard A. Carney .... Jan. 9, 1953-Apr. 30, 1954
C. E. Fulgham .... May 1, 1954-Feb. 15, 1955
Al Muldrow..................... Feb. 16, 1955-Nov. 1, 1955
Tom Reavley................... Nov. 1, 1955-Jan. 16, 1957
Zollie Steakley ....Jan. 16, 1957-Jan. 2, 1962
P. Frank Lake ....Jan. 2, 1962-Jan. 15, 1963
Crawford C. Martin ....Jan. 15, 1963-March 12, 1966
John L. Hill...................March 12, 1966-Jan. 22, 1968
Roy Barrera....................March 7, 1968-Jan. 23, 1969
Martin Dies Jr. .... Jan. 23, 1969-Sept. 1, 1971
Robert D. (Bob) Bullock..... Sept. 1, 1971-Jan. 2, 1973
V. Larry Teaver Jr...............Jan. 2, 1973-Jan. 19, 1973
Mark W. White Jr. ....Jan. 19, 1973-Oct. 27,1977
Steven C. Oaks ....Oct. 27, 1977-Jan. 16, 1979
George W. Strake Jr. ....Jan. 16, 1979-Oct. 6, 1981
David A. Dean ....Oct. 22, 1981-Jan. 18, 1983
John Fainter .... Jan. 18, 1983-July 31, 1984
Myra A. McDaniel .... Sept. 6, 1984-Jan. 26, 1987
Jack Rains.....................Jan. 26, 1987-June 15, 1989
George Bayoud Jr. ....June 19, 1989-Jan. 15, 1991
John Hannah Jr. ....Jan. 17, 1991-March 11, 1994
Ronald Kirk...................April 4, 1994 to Jan. 17, 1995
Antonio O. "Tony" Garza Jr... Jan. 18, 1995 to Present

★★★★★★★

Attorneys General

Of the Republic

David Thomas and
Peter W. Grayson ....Mar. 2-Oct. 22, 1836
J. Pinckney Henderson, Peter W. Grayson,
John Birdsall, A. S. Thurston 1836-1838
J. C. Watrous....................... Dec., 1838-June 1, 1840
Joseph Webb and F. A. Morris 1840-1841
George W. Terrell, Ebenezer Allen 1841-1844
Ebenezer Allen 1844-1846

*Of the State

Volney E. Howard............Feb. 21, 1846-May 7, 1846
John W. Harris....................May 7, 1846-Oct. 31, 1849
Henry P. Brewster...........Oct. 31, 1849-Jan. 15, 1850
A. J. Hamilton.................. Jan. 15, 1850-Aug. 5, 1850
Ebenezer Allen .... Aug. 5, 1850-Aug. 2, 1852
Thomas J. Jennings .... Aug. 2, 1852-Aug. 4, 1856
James Willie .... Aug. 4, 1856-Aug. 2, 1858
Malcolm D. Graham........... Aug. 2, 1858-Aug. 6, 1860
George M. Flournoy..........Aug. 6, 1860-Jan. 15, 1862
N. G. Shelley ....Feb. 3, 1862-Aug. 1, 1864
B. E. Tarver.......................Aug. 1, 1864-Dec. 11, 1865
Wm. Alexander .... Dec. 11, 1865-June 25, 1866
W. M. Walton ....June 25, 1866-Aug. 27, 1867
Wm. Alexander ....Aug. 27, 1867-Nov. 5, 1867
Ezekiel B. Turner ....Nov. 5, 1867-July 11, 1870
Wm. Alexander .... July 11, 1870-Jan. 27, 1874
George Clark ....Jan. 27, 1874-Apr. 25, 1876
H. H. Boone ....Apr. 25, 1876-Nov. 5, 1878
George McCormick............Nov. 5, 1878-Nov. 2, 1880
J. H. McLeary ....Nov. 2, 1880-Nov. 7, 1882
John D. Templeton.............Nov. 7, 1882-Nov. 2, 1886
James S. Hogg ....Nov. 2, 1886-Nov. 4, 1890
C. A. Culberson ....Nov. 4, 1890-Nov. 6, 1894
M. M. Crane ....Nov. 6, 1894-Nov. 8, 1898
Thomas S. Smith ....Nov. 8, 1898-Mar. 15,1901
C. K. Bell .... Mar. 20, 1901-Jan., 1904
R. V. Davidson ....Jan., 1904-Dec. 31, 1909
Jewel P. Lightfoot............. Jan. 1, 1910-Aug. 31, 1912
James D. Walthall............. Sept. 1, 1912-Jan. 1, 1913
B. F. Looney..........................Jan. 1, 1913-Jan., 1919
C. M. Cureton ....Jan., 1919-Dec., 1921
W. A. Keeling ....Dec., 1921-Jan., 1925
Dan Moody ....Jan., 1925-Jan., 1927
Claude Pollard ....Jan., 1927-Sept., 1929
R. L. Bobbitt (Apptd.) .... Sept., 1929-Jan., 1931
James V. Allred ....Jan., 1931-Jan., 1935
William McCraw ....Jan., 1935-Jan., 1939
Gerald C. Mann (resigned) ....Jan., 1939-Jan., 1944
Grover Sellers.............................Jan., 1944-Jan., 1947
Price Daniel ....Jan., 1947-Jan., 1953
John Ben Shepperd................Jan., 1953-Jan. 1, 1957
Will Wilson ....Jan. 1, 1957-Jan. 15, 1963
Waggoner Carr ....Jan. 15, 1963-Jan. 1, 1967
Crawford C. Martin ....Jan. 1, 1967-Dec. 29, 1972
John Hill.............................Jan. 1, 1973-Jan. 16, 1979
Mark White ....Jan. 16, 1979 to Jan. 18, 1983
Jim Mattox ....Jan. 18, 1983 to Jan. 15, 1991
Dan Morales ....Jan. 15, 1991 to Present

*The first few Attorneys General held office by appointment of the Governor. The office was made elective in 1850 by constitutional amendment and Ebenezer Allen was the first elected Attorney General.

★★★★★★★

Treasurers

Of the Republic

Asa Brigham 1838-1840
James W. Simmons.................................... 1840-1841
Asa Brigham 1841-1844
Moses Johnson 1844-1846

Of the State

James H. Raymond ....Feb. 24, 1846-Aug. 2, 1858
†C. H. Randolph ....Aug. 2, 1858-June, 1865
†Samuel Harris..................Oct. 2, 1865-June 25, 1866
W. M. Royston ....June 25, 1866-Sept. 1, 1867
John Y. Allen ....Sept. 1, 1867-Jan., 1869
*George W. Honey.........................Jan., 1869-Jan., 1874
*B. Graham(short term) ....beginning May 27, 1872
A. J. Dorn...Jan., 1874-Jan., 1879
F. R. Lubbock.....................................Jan., 1879-Jan., 1891
W. B. Wortham....................................Jan., 1891-Jan., 1899
John W. Robbins ....Jan., 1899-Jan., 1907
Sam Sparks ....Jan., 1907-Jan., 1912
J. M. Edwards.....................................Jan., 1912-Jan., 1919
John W. Baker ....Jan., 1919-Jan., 1921
G. N. Holton ....July, 1921-Nov. 21, 1921
C. V. Terrell ....Nov. 21, 1921-Aug. 15, 1924
S. L. Staples ....Aug. 16, 1924-Jan. 15, 1925
W. Gregory Hatcher...........Jan. 16, 1925-Jan. 1, 1931
Charley Lockhart ....Jan. 1, 1931-Oct. 25, 1941

Jesse James .... Oct. 25, 1941-Sept. 29, 1977
Warren G. Harding .... Oct. 7, 1977-Jan. 3, 1983
Ann Richards...................... Jan. 3, 1983- Jan. 2, 1991
Kay Bailey Hutchison .... Jan. 2, 1991 to June 1993
Martha Whitehead..................... June 1993 to Present

*Honey was removed from office for a short period in 1872 and B. Graham served in his place.

†Randolph fled to Mexico upon collapse of Confederacy. No exact date is available for his departure from office or for Harris' succession to the post. It is believed Harris took office Oct. 2, 1865.

★★★★★★★

Railroad Commission of Texas

John H. Reagan................. June 10, 1891-Jan. 20, 1903.
L. L. Foster...................... June 10, 1891-April 30, 1895.
W. P. McLean.................... June 10, 1891-Nov. 20, 1894.
L. J. Storey (succeeding McLean), Nov. 21, 1894-Mar. 28,1909.
N. A. Stedman (succeeding Foster), May 1, 1895-Jan. 4, 1897.
Allison Mayfield (succeeding Stedman), Jan. 5, 1897-Jan. 23, 1923.
O. B. Colquitt (succeeding Reagan), Jan. 21, 1903-Jan. 17, 1911.
William D. Williams (succeeding Storey), April 28, 1909-Oct. 1, 1916.
John L. Wortham (succeeding Colquitt), Jan. 21, 1911-Jan. 1, 1913.
Earle B. Mayfield (succeeding Wortham), Jan. 2, 1913-March 1, 1923.
Charles H. Hurdleston (succeeding Williams), Oct. 10, 1916-Dec. 31, 1918.
Clarence E. Gilmore (succeeding Hurdleston), Jan. 1, 1919-Jan. 1, 1929.
N. A. Nabors (succeeding A. Mayfield), March 1, 1923-Jan. 18, 1925.
William M. W. Splawn (succeeding E.B. Mayfield), March 1, 1923-Aug. 1, 1924.
C. V. Terrell (succeeding Splawn), Aug. 15, 1924-Jan. 1, 1939.
Lon A. Smith (succeeding Nabors), Jan. 29, 1925-Jan. 1, 1941.
Pat M. Neff (succeeding Gilmore), Jan. 1, 1929-Jan. 1, 1933.
Ernest O. Thompson (succeeding Neff), Jan. 1, 1933-Jan. 8, 1965.
G. A. (Jerry) Sadler (succeeding Terrell), Jan. 1, 1939-Jan. 1, 1943.
Olin Culberson (succeeding Smith), Jan. 1, 1941-June 22, 1961.
Beauford Jester (succeeding Sadler), Jan. 1, 1943-Jan. 21, 1947.
William J. Murray Jr. (succeeding Jester), Jan. 21, 1947-Apr. 10, 1963.
Ben Ramsey (succeeding Culberson), Sept. 18, 1961-Dec. 31, 1976.
Jim C. Langdon (succeeding Murray), May 28, 1963-ec. 31, 1977.
Byron Tunnell (succeeding Thompson), Jan. 11, 1965-Sept. 15, 1973.
Mack Wallace (succeeding Tunnell), Sept. 18, 1973-Sept. 22, 1987.
Jon Newton (succeeding Ramsey), Jan. 10, 1977-Jan. 4, 1979.
John H. Poerner (succeeding Langdon), Jan. 2, 1978-Jan. 1, 1981.
James E. (Jim) Nugent (succeeding Newton), Jan. 4, 1979-Jan. 3, 1995
Buddy Temple (succeeding Poerner), Jan. 2, 1981-March 2, 1986.
Clark Jobe (succeeding Temple), March 3, 1986-Jan. 5, 1987.
John Sharp (succeeding Jobe), Jan. 6, 1987-Jan. 2, 1991.
Kent Hance (succeeding Wallace), Sept. 23, 1987-Jan. 2, 1991.
*Robert Krueger (succeeding Hance), Jan. 3, 1991-Jan. 22, 1993.
Lena Guerrero (succeeding Sharp), Jan. 23, 1991-Sept. 25, 1992.
James Wallace (succeeding Guerrero), Oct. 2, 1992-Jan. 4, 1993.
Barry Williamson (succeeding Wallace), Jan. 5, 1993-Present.
Mary Scott Nabers (succeeding Krueger), Feb. 9, 1993-Dec. 9, 1994.
Carole Keeton Rylander (succeeding Nabers), Dec. 10, 1994-Present
Charles Matthews (succeeding Nugent), Jan. 3, 1995-Present

** Robert Krueger resigned when Gov. Ann Richards appointed him interim U.S. Senator on the resignation of Sen. Lloyd Bentsen.*

★★★★★★★

Comptroller of Public Accounts

Of the Republic

John H. Money .... Dec. 30, 1835-Jan. 17, 1836
H. C. Hudson.................. Jan. 17, 1836-Oct. 22, 1836
E. M. Pease.......................... June, 1837-Dec., 1837
F. R. Lubbock .... Dec., 1837-Jan., 1839
Jas. W. Simmons .... Jan. 15, 1839-Sept. 30, 1840
Jas. B. Shaw ....Sept. 30, 1840-Dec. 24, 1841
F. R. Lubbock .... Dec. 24, 1841-Jan. 1, 1842
Jas. B. Shaw .... Jan. 1, 1842-Jan. 1, 1846

Of the State

Jas. B. Shaw ....Feb. 24, 1846-Aug. 2, 1858
Clement R. Johns..............Aug. 2, 1858-Aug. 1, 1864
Willis L. Robards .... Aug. 1, 1864-Oct. 12, 1865
Albert H. Latimer ....Oct. 12, 1865-Mar. 27, 1866
Robert H. Taylor ....Mar. 27, 1866-June 25, 1866
Willis L. Robards .... June 25, 1866-Aug. 27, 1867
Morgan C. Hamilton .... Aug. 27, 1867-Jan. 8, 1870
A. Bledsoe......................... Jan. 8, 1870-Jan. 20, 1874
Stephen H. Darden ....Jan. 20, 1974-Nov. 2, 1880
W. M. Brown.......................Nov. 2, 1880-Jan. 16, 1883
W. J. Swain ....Jan. 16, 1883-Jan. 18, 1887
John D. McCall...............Jan. 18, 1887-Jan. 15, 1895
R. W. Finley.....................Jan. 15, 1895-Jan. 15, 1901
R. M. Love...........................Jan. 15, 1901-Jan., 1903
J. W. Stephen............................ Jan., 1903-Jan., 1911
W. P. Lane ....Jan., 1911-Jan., 1915
H. B. Terrell...............................Jan., 1915-Jan., 1920
M. L. Wiginton ....Jan., 1920-Jan., 1921
Lon A. Smith...............................Jan., 1921-Jan., 1925
S. H. Terrell...............................Jan., 1925-Jan., 1931
Geo. H. Sheppard .... Jan., 1931-Jan. 17, 1949
Robert S. Calvert..................Jan. 17, 1949-Jan., 1975
Robert D. (Bob) Bullock ....Jan., 1975-Jan. 3, 1991
John Sharp............................ Jan. 3, 1991 to Present

★★★★★★★

U.S. Senators from Texas

U.S. Senators were selected by the legislatures of the states until the U.S. Constitution was amended in 1913 to require popular elections. In Texas, the first senator chosen by the voters in a general election was Charles A. Culberson in 1916. Because of political pressures, however, the rules of the Democratic Party of Texas were changed in 1904 to require that all candidates for office stand before voters in the primary. Consequently, Texas' senators faced voters in 1906, 1910 and 1912 before the U.S. Constitution was changed.

Following is the succession of Texas representatives in the United States Senate since the annexation of Texas to the Union in 1845:

Houston Succession

Sam Houston .... Feb. 21, 1846-Mar. 4, 1859
John Hemphill .... Mar. 4, 1859-July 11, 1861

Louis T. Wigfall and W. S. Oldham took their seats in the Confederate Senate, Nov. 16, 1861, and served until the Confederacy collapsed. After that event, the State Legislature on Aug. 21, 1866, elected David G. Burnet and Oran M. Roberts to the United States Senate, anticipating immediate readmission to the Union, but they were not allowed to take their seats.

†Morgan C. Hamilton .... Feb. 22, 1870-Mar. 3, 1877
Richard Coke .... Mar. 4, 1877-Mar. 3, 1895

Horace Chilton.................. Mar. 3, 1895-Mar. 3, 1901
Joseph W. Bailey................Mar. 3, 1901-Jan. 8, 1913
Rienzi Melville Johnston..... Jan. 8, 1913-Feb. 3, 1913
‡Morris Sheppard (died)....Feb. 13, 1913-Apr. 9, 1941
Andrew J. Houston ....June 2-26, 1941
W. Lee O'Daniel................ Aug. 4, 1941-Jan. 3, 1949
Lyndon B. Johnson...........Jan. 3, 1949-Jan. 20, 1961
William A. Blakley..........Jan. 20, 1961-June 15, 1961
†John G. Tower ....June 15, 1961-Jan. 21, 1985
†Phil Gramm .... Jan. 21, 1985-Present

Rusk Succession

Thomas J. Rusk (died) .....Feb 21, 1846-July 29, 1857
J. Pinckney Henderson (died) .... Nov. 9, 1857-June 4, 1858
Matthias Ward (appointed interim).......................Sept. 29, 1858-Dec. 5, 1859
Louis T. Wigfall ....Dec. 5, 1859-March 23, 1861

Succession was broken by the expulsion of Texas Senators following secession of Texas from Union. See note above under "Houston Succession" on Louis T. Wigfall and W. S. Oldham and Burnet and Roberts.

†James W. Flanagan........ Feb. 22, 1870-Mar. 3, 1875
Samuel B. Maxey .... Mar. 3, 1875-Mar. 3, 1887
John H. Reagan (resigned).......Mar. 3, 1887-June 10, 1891
Horace Chilton (filled vacancy on appointment)................ Dec. 7, 1891-Mar. 30,1892
Roger Q. Mills................... Mar. 30, 1892-Mar. 3, 1899
‡Charles A. Culberson .... Mar. 3, 1899-Mar. 4, 1923
Earle B. Mayfield .... Mar. 4, 1923-Mar. 4, 1929
Tom Connally......................Mar. 4, 1929-Jan. 3, 1953
Price Daniel.......................Jan. 3, 1953-Jan. 15, 1957
William A. Blakley .... Jan. 15. 1957-Apr. 27, 1957
Ralph W. Yarborough ...... Apr. 27, 1957-Jan. 12, 1971
§Lloyd Bentsen................Jan. 12, 1971-Jan. 20, 1993
Robert Krueger...............Jan. 20, 1993-June 14, 1993
†Kay Bailey Hutchison .... June 14, 1993-Present

† Republican members

‡ First election to U.S. Senate held in 1916. Prior to that time, senators were appointed by the Legislature.

§ Resigned from Senate when appointed U.S. Secretary of Treasury by Pres. Bill Clinton.

★★★★★★★

Commissioners of the General Land Office

For the Republic

John P. Borden ....Aug. 23, 1837-Dec. 12, 1840
H. W. Raglin .... Dec. 12, 1840-Jan. 4, 1841
*Thomas William Ward......Jan. 4, 1841-Mar. 20, 1848

For the State

George W. Smyth ....Mar. 20, 1848-Aug. 4, 1851
Stephen Crosby................. Aug. 4, 1851-Mar. 1, 1858
Francis M. White .... Mar. 1, 1858-Mar. 1, 1862
Stephen Crosby................Mar. 1, 1862-Sept. 1, 1865
Francis M. White ....Sept. 1, 1865-Aug. 7, 1866
Stephen Crosby...............Aug. 7, 1866-Aug. 27, 1867
Joseph Spence.............. Aug. 27, 1867-Jan. 19, 1870
Jacob Kuechler..............Jan. 19, 1870-Jan. 20, 1874
J. J. Groos ....Jan. 20, 1874-June 15, 1878
W. C. Walsh.....................July 30, 1878, Jan. 10, 1887
R. M. Hall.........................Jan. 10, 1887-Jan. 16, 1891
W. L. McGaughey............Jan. 16, 1891-Jan. 26, 1895
A. J. Baker........................Jan. 26, 1895-Jan. 16, 1899
George W. Finger.............Jan. 16, 1899-May 4, 1899
Charles Rogan ....May 11, 1899-Jan. 10, 1903
John J. Terrell..................Jan. 10, 1903-Jan. 11, 1909
J. T. Robison......................... Jan, 1909-Sept. 11, 1929
J. H. Walker........................ Sept. 11, 1929-Jan., 1937
William H. McDonald ....Jan, 1937-Jan., 1939
Bascom Giles ....Jan., 1939-Jan. 5, 1955
J. Earl Rudder .... Jan. 5, 1955-Feb. 1, 1958
Bill Allcorn........................... Feb. 1, 1958-Jan. 1, 1961
Jerry Sadler ....Jan. 1, 1961-Jan. 1, 1971
Bob Armstrong.......................Jan. 1, 1971-Jan. 1, 1983
Garry Mauro .... Jan. 1, 1983-Present

*Part of term after annexation.

★★★★★★★

Administrators of Public Education

Superintendents of Public Instruction

Pryor Lea ....Nov. 10, 1866-Sept. 12, 1867
Edwin M. Wheelock ....Sept. 12, 1867-May 6, 1871
Jacob C. DeGress ....May 6, 1871-Jan. 20, 1874
O. H. Hollingsworth...........Jan. 20, 1874-May 6, 1884
B. M. Baker.........................May 6, 1884-Jan. 18, 1887
O. H. Cooper ....Jan 18, 1887-Sept. 1, 1890
H. C. Pritchett .... Sept. 1, 1890-Sept. 15, 1891
J. M. Carlisle..................Sept. 15, 1891-Jan. 10, 1899
J. S. Kendall ....Jan. 10, 1899-July 2, 1901
Arthur Lefevre.....................July 2, 1901-Jan. 12, 1905
R. B. Cousins.....................Jan. 12, 1905-Jan. 1, 1910
F. M. Bralley ....Jan. 1, 1910-Sept. 1, 1913
W. F. Doughty ....Sept. 1, 1913-Jan. 1, 1919
Annie Webb Blanton..........Jan. 1, 1919-Jan. 16, 1923
S. M. N. Marrs ....Jan. 16, 1923-April 28, 1932
C. N. Shaver .... April 28, 1932-Oct. 1, 1932
L. W. Rogers.......................Oct. 1, 1932-Jan. 16, 1933
L. A. Woods ....Jan. 16, 1933-*1951

State Commissioner of Education

J. W. Edgar.....................May 31, 1951-June 30, 1974
Marlin L. Brockette............ July 1, 1974-Sept. 1, 1979
Alton O. Bowen................Sept. 1, 1979-June 1, 1981
Raymon Bynum ....June 1, 1981-Oct. 31, 1984
W. N. Kirby.......................April 13, 1985-July 1, 1991
Lionel R. Meno ....July 1, 1991-March 1, 1995
Michael A. Moses ....March 9, 1995-Present

*The office of State Superintendent of Public Instruction was abolished by the Gilmer-Aikin act of 1949 and the office of Commissioner of Education created, appointed by a new State Board of Education elected by the people.

★★★★★★★

Speaker of the Texas House

The Speaker of the Texas House of Representatives is the presiding officer of the lower chamber of the State Legislature. The official is elected at the beginning of each regular session by a vote of the members of the House.

Speaker, Residence	Year Elected	Legislature
William E. Crump, Bellville	1846	1st
William H. Bourland, Paris	1846	1st
James W. Henderson, Houston	1847	2nd
Charles G. Keenan, Huntsville	1849	3rd
David C. Dickson, Anderson	1851	4th
Hardin R. Runnels, Boston	1853	5th
Hamilton P. Bee, Laredo	1855	6th
William S. Taylor, Larissa	1857	7th
Matt F. Locke, Lafayette	1858	7th
Marion DeKalb Taylor, Jefferson	1859	8th
Constantine W. Buckley, Richmond	1861	9th
Nicholas H. Darnell, Dallas	1861	9th
Constantine W. Buckley, Richmond	1863	9th
Marion DeKalb Taylor, Jefferson	1863	10th
Nathaniel M. Burford, Dallas	1866	11th
Ira H. Evans, Corpus Christi	1870	12th
William H. Sinclair, Galveston	1871	12th
Marion DeKalb Taylor, Jefferson	1873	13th
Guy M. Bryan, Galveston	1874	14th
Thomas R. Bonner, Tyler	1876	15th
John H. Cochran, Dallas	1879	16th
George R. Reeves, Pottsboro	1881	17th
Charles R. Gibson, Waxahachie	1883	18th
Lafayette L. Foster, Groesbeck	1885	19th
George C. Pendleton, Belton	1887	20th
Frank P. Alexander, Greenville	1889	21st
Robert T. Milner, Henderson	1891	22nd
John H. Cochran, Dallas	1893	23rd
Thomas Slater Smith, Hillsboro	1895	24th
L. Travis Dashiell, Jewett	1897	25th
J. S. Sherrill, Greenville	1899	26th
Robert E. Prince, Corsicana	1901	27th
Pat M. Neff, Waco	1903	28th
Francis W. Seabury, Rio Grande City	1905	29th
Thomas B. Love, Lancaster	1907	30th

Name	Year	Legislature
Austin M. Kennedy, Waco	1909	31st
John W. Marshall, Whitesboro	1909	31st
Sam Rayburn, Bonham	1911	32nd
Chester H. Terrell, San Antonio	1913	33rd
John W. Woods, Rotan	1915	34th
Franklin O. Fuller, Coldspring	1917	35th
R. Ewing Thomason, El Paso	1919	36th
Charles G. Thomas, Lewisville	1921	37th
Richard E. Seagler, Palestine	1923	38th
Lee Satterwhite, Amarillo	1925	39th
Robert L. Bobbitt, Laredo	1927	40th
W. S. Barron, Bryan	1929	41st
Fred H. Minor, Denton	1931	42nd
Coke R. Stevenson, Junction	1933	43rd
"	1935	44th
Robert W. Calvert, Hillsboro	1937	45th
R. Emmett Morse, Houston	1939	46th
Homer L. Leonard, McAllen	1941	47th
Price Daniel, Liberty	1943	48th
Claud H. Gilmer, Rocksprings	1945	49th
William O. Reed, Dallas	1947	50th
Durwood Manford, Smiley	1949	51st
Reuben Senterfitt, San Saba	1951	52nd
"	1953	53rd
Jim T. Lindsey, Texarkana	1955	54th
Waggoner Carr, Lubbock	1957	55th
"	1959	56th
James A. Turman, Gober	1961	57th
Byron M. Tunnell, Tyler	1963	58th
Ben Barnes, DeLeon	1965	59th
"	1967	60th
Gus F. Mutscher, Brenham	1969	61st
"	1971	62nd
Rayford Price, Palestine	1972	62nd
Price Daniel Jr., Liberty	1973	63rd
Bill Clayton, Springlake	1975	64th
"	1977	65th
"	1979	66th
"	1981	67th
Gibson D. Lewis, Fort Worth	1983	68th
"	1985	69th
"	1987	70th
"	1989	71st
"	1991	72nd
James M. (Pete) Laney, Hale Center	1993	73rd
"	1995	74th

★★★★★★★

Chief Justice of the Supreme Court

Republic of Texas

James Collinsworth .... Dec. 16, 1836-July 23, 1838
John Birdsall .... Nov. 19-Dec. 12, 1838
Thomas J. Rusk .... Dec. 12, 1838-Dec. 5, 1840
John Hemphill .... Dec. 5, 1840-Dec. 29, 1845

Under the Constitutions of 1845 and 1861

John Hemphill .... Mar. 2, 1846-Oct. 10, 1858
Royall T. Wheeler .... Oct. 11, 1858-April 1864
Oran M. Roberts .... Nov. 1, 1864-June 30, 1866

Under the Constitution of 1866 (Presidential Reconstruction)

*George F. Moore .... Aug. 16, 1866-Sept. 10, 1867

*Removed under Congressional Reconstruction by military authorities who appointed members of the next court.

Under the Constitution of 1866 (Congressional Reconstruction)

Amos Morrill .... Sept. 10, 1867-July 5, 1870

Under the Constitution of 1869

Lemuel D. Evans .... July 5, 1870-Aug. 31, 1873
Wesley Ogden .... Aug. 31, 1873-Jan. 29, 1874
Oran M. Roberts .... Jan. 29, 1874-Apr. 18, 1876

Under the Constitution of 1876

Oran M. Roberts .... Apr. 18, 1876-Oct. 1, 1878
George F. Moore .... Nov. 5, 1878-Nov. 1, 1881
Robert S. Gould .... Nov. 1, 1881-Dec. 23, 1882
Asa H. Willie .... Dec. 23, 1882-Mar. 3, 1888
John W. Stayton .... Mar. 3, 1888-July 5, 1894
Reuben R. Gaines .... July 10, 1894-Jan. 5, 1911
Thomas J. Brown .... Jan. 7, 1911-May 26, 1915
Nelson Phillips .... June 1, 1915-Nov. 16, 1921
C. M. Cureton .... Dec. 2, 1921-Apr. 8, 1940
W. F. Moore .... Apr. 17, 1940-Jan. 1, 1941
James P. Alexander .... Jan. 1, 1941-Jan. 1, 1948
J. E. Hickman .... Jan. 5, 1948-Jan. 3, 1961
Robert W. Calvert .... Jan. 3, 1961-Oct. 4, 1972
Joe R. Greenhill .... Oct. 4, 1972-Oct. 25, 1982
Jack Pope .... Nov. 23, 1982-Jan. 5, 1985
John L. Hill Jr. .... Jan. 5, 1985-Jan. 4, 1988
Thomas R. Phillips .... Jan. 4, 1988-Present

Presiding Judges, Court of Appeals (1876-1891) and Court of Criminal Appeals (1891-Present)

Mat D. Ector .... May 6, 1876-Oct. 29, 1879
John P. White .... Nov. 9, 1879-Apr. 26, 1892
James M. Hurt .... May 4, 1892-Dec. 31, 1898
W. L. Davidson .... Jan. 2, 1899-June 27, 1913
A. C. Prendergast .... June 27, 1913-Dec. 31, 1916
W. L. Davidson .... Jan. 1, 1917-Jan. 25, 1921
Wright C. Morrow .... Feb. 8, 1921-Oct. 16, 1939
Frank Lee Hawkins .... Oct. 16, 1939-Jan. 2, 1951
Harry N. Graves .... Jan. 2, 1951-Dec. 31, 1954
W. A. Morrison .... Jan. 1, 1955-Jan. 2, 1961
Kenneth K. Woodley .... Jan. 3, 1961-Jan. 4, 1965
W. T. McDonald .... Jan. 4, 1965-June 25, 1966
W. A. Morrison .... June 25, 1966-Jan. 1, 1967
Kenneth K. Woodley .... Jan. 1, 1967-Jan. 1, 1971
John F. Onion Jr. .... Jan. 1, 1971-Jan. 1, 1989
Michael J. McCormick .... Jan. 1, 1989-Present

First Ladies of Texas

Martha Evans Gindratt Wood	1847-49
†Bell Administration	1849-53
Lucadia Christiana Niles Pease	1853-57; 1867-69
‡Runnels Administration	1857-59
Margaret Moffette Lea Houston	1859-61
Martha Evans Clark	1861
Adele Barron Lubbock	1861-63
Susie Ellen Taylor Murrah	1863-65
Mary Jane Bowen Hamilton	1865-66
Annie Rattan Throckmorton	1866-67
Ann Elizabeth Britton Davis	1870-74
Mary Home Coke	1874-76
Janie Roberts Hubbard	1876-79
Frances Wickliff Edwards Roberts	1879-83
Anne Maria Penn Ireland	1883-87
Elizabeth Dorothy Tinsley Ross	1887-91
Sarah Stinson Hogg	1891-95
Sally Harrison Culberson	1895-99
Orlene Walton Sayers	1899-1903
Sarah Beona Meng Lanham	1903-07
Fannie Brunner Campbell	1907-11
Alice Fuller Murrell Colquitt	1911-15
§Miriam A. Wallace Ferguson	1915-17
Willie Cooper Hobby	1917-21
Myrtle Mainer Neff	1921-25
Mildred Paxton Moody	1927-31
Maud Gage Sterling	1931-33
Jo Betsy Miller Allred	1935-39
Merle Estella Butcher O'Daniel	1939-41
**Fay Wright Stevenson	1941-42
**Edith Will Scott Stevenson	1942-46
Mabel Buchanan Jester	1946-49
Marialice Shary Shivers	1949-57
Jean Houston Baldwin Daniel	1957-63
Idanell Brill Connally	1963-69
Ima Mae Smith	1969-73
Betty Jane Slaughter Briscoe	1973-79
Rita Crocker Bass Clements	1979-83
Linda Gale Thompson White	1983-87
Rita Crocker Bass Clements	1987-91
Laura Welch Bush	1995-Present

†Gov. Peter Hansbrough Bell was not married while in office.

‡Gov. Hardin R. Runnels never married.

§Also Mistress of the Mansion during her own terms as Governor: 1925-27 and 1933-35.

***Mrs. Coke R. (Fay Wright) Stevenson, the governor's mother, died in the Governor's Mansion Jan. 3, 1942.* ☆

Local Governments

Texas has **254 counties**, a number which has not changed since 1931 when Loving County was organized. Loving had a population of 107 in the 1990 U.S. Census Bureau count, compared with 164 in 1970 and its peak of 285 in 1940. It is the **least-populous county** in Texas. In contrast, Harris County has **the most residents** in Texas, with a population in 1990 of 2,818,199.

Counties range in area from Rockwall's 148.6 square miles to the 6,193.1 square miles in Brewster, which is equal to the combined area of the states of Connecticut and Rhode Island.

The Texas Constitution makes a county a legal subdivision of the state. Each county has a **commissioners court**. It consists of four commissioners, each elected from a commissioner's precinct, and a county judge elected from the entire county. In smaller counties, the county judge retains judicial responsibilities in probate and insanity cases. For names of county and district officials, see tables on pages 516-530.

Eleven hundred and seventy-nine **incorporated Texas municipalities** range in size from 24 residents to Houston's 1,700,672 in the 1993 population estimate by the State Data Center. More than 80 percent of the state's population lives in cities and towns meeting the U.S. Bureau of the Census definition of urban areas.

Texas had **298 municipalities with more than 5,000 population** in the 1990 U.S. census. Under law, these cities may adopt their own charters by a majority vote. Cities of less than 5,000 may be chartered only under the general law. There were **284 home-rule cities** on June 1, 1995, most of them cities with over 5,000 residents. Some of these cities now show fewer than 5,000 residents, because population has declined since they adopted their home-rule charters. A list of home-rule cities follows the list of mayors and city managers in this volume. ☆

Mayors and City Managers of Texas Cities

The list below was compiled from questionnaires sent out immediately after the municipal elections in May 1995. Included is the name of each city's mayor, as well as the name of the city manager, city administrator, city coordinator or other managing executive of munipalities having that form of government.

An asterisk (*) before the city name indicates that the Almanac received no response to the questionnaire and that the information on city officials is from the most recent information available to us from unofficial sources.

Abbott .... Robert L. Tufts
City Mgr., Harry Frank Holland
Abernathy .... Shane Cunningham
City Mgr., Frank D. Russell
*Abilene .... Gary D. McCaleb
City Mgr., Roy McDaniel
Ackerly .... Jimmie L. Schuelke
Addison .... Richard N. Beckert
City Mgr., Ronald N. Whitehead
Adrian .... Jeff Fairchild
Agua Dulce .... Carl Vajdos
Alamo .... Rudolfo "Rudy" Villarreal
City Mgr., James Pliska
*Alamo Heights (6116 Broadway, San Antonio 78209 .... Wm. D. Balthrope
City Admin., Susan Hennessy
Alba .... James Reid
Albany .... Jack Bryant
Aledo .... Robert A. Lewis
Alice .... Octavio Figueroa Jr
City Mgr., Roel G. Valadez
Allen .... Joe Farmer
City Mgr., Jon McCarty
*Alma (Rt. 1, Box 109, Ennis 75119) .... Don Keilers
*Alpine .... Paul Weyerts
City Mgr., Jerry Carvajal
Alto .... H.C. Williams
Alton (P.O. Drawer 9004, Mission 78572) .... Salvador Vela
City Mgr., Israel Sagredo
Alvarado .... Jay Tidwell
*Alvin .... Elmer Dezso
*Alvord .... Edwin Strange
Amarillo .... Kel Seliger
City Mgr., John Q. Ward
Ames .... John White
Amherst .... George Thompson
*Anahuac .... Lloyd Dobbs
Andrews .... Greg Sweeney
City Mgr., Len L. Wilson
Angleton .... Roy Gardner
City Mgr., Ruth Hertel
*Angus (Rt. 3, Box 3060, Corsicana 75110) .... Eben D. Stover
Anna .... Ronald Ferguson
Annetta (Box 191, Aledo 76008) .... Bruce Moore
Annetta North (P.O. Box 262, Aledo 76008) .... Edward K. Hensley
Annetta South (P.O. Box 61, Aledo 76008) .... Doug Koldin
Annona .... George H. English Sr.
Anson .... E.M. Spraberry
City Mgr., Tex Middlebrook
Anthony .... Art Franco
Anton .... Mary E. Grace
City Mgr., Larry G. Conkin
*Appleby (Rt. 10, Box 5186, Nacogdoches 75961) .... N. F. Burt
*Aquilla .... Carol Finley
Aransas Pass .... Billy St. Clair
City Mgr., Rick Ewaniszyk
*Archer City .... Max . Wood Sr.
City Mgr., L. B. Boren Jr.
*Arcola .... Linda de Leon
Argyle .... Yvonne A. Jenkins
*Arlington .... Richard Greene
City Mgr., George C. Campbell
Arp .... Vernon L. Bedair
*Asherton .... Sam Galvan Jr.
*Aspermont .... P. C. Carr
*Athens .... C.R. Stonier
City Mgr., Donald R. Manning
Atlanta .... Peyton Childs
Aubrey .... Gene King
Aurora (P.O. Box 558, Rhome 76078) .... Owen J. Landers
Austin .... Bruce Todd
City Mgr., Jesús Garza
*Austwell .... P.J. Martínez
Avery .... Jack Williams
Avinger .... David P. Simpson
Azle .... Shirley Bradley
City Mgr., Harry H. Dulin Jr.
Bailey .... Jewel A. Mims (Mr.)
Bailey's Prairie (Box 71, Angleton 77516) .... Jo Mapel
Baird .... Steve Bowen
*Balch Springs .... David Haas
City Mgr., Angie Warner
Balcones Heights (123 Altgelt, San Antonio 78201) .... Lucille M. Wohlfarth
City Admin., Roy L. Miller
Ballinger .... Rudolf Hoffman
City Mgr., Judy Miller
Balmorhea .... Norman Roman
City Mgr., Freddie Schrier
*Bandera .... Robert Skinner
Bangs .... C.B. Alexander
*Bardwell .... Richard Burgess
Barry .... John W. Braly
*Barstow .... Abram Flores
Bartlett .... Jim Franz
Bartonville (1941 E. Jeter Road, Argyle 76226) .... Fritz Range
*Bastrop .... David Lock
City Mgr., Michael M. Talbot
Bay City .... Charles Martinez Jr.
*Bayou Vista (2929 Hwy. 6, #100, Hitchcock 77563) .... Billie Moore
Bayside .... Timothy Delaney
*Baytown .... Pete C. Alfaro
City Mgr., Bobby Rountree
Bayview (Rt. 3, Box 19-A, Los Fresnos 78566) .... Robert E. Middleton Jr.
Beach City .... James E. Standridge
Beasley .... Wilbert Preuss
Beaumont .... David W. Moore
City Mgr., Ray A. Riley
*Beckville .... Thomas R. Adams
Bedford .... R.D. Hurt
City Mgr., Linda M. Barton
Bee Cave (13225 Hwy. 71-W, Austin 78738) .... Gene Butler
City Mgr., John Figer
Beeville .... John P. Ybañez
City Mgr., Ford Patton
Bellaire .... Harold L. Penn
Acting City Mgr., Christopher J. Brady
*Bellevue .... Wallace Horton
Bellmead (3015 Bellmead Dr., Waco 76705) .... Ruth M. Haines
City Mgr., S.G. Radcliffe
*Bells .... Jeff S. Thackerson
Bellville .... James A. Bishop
City Mgr., Lloyd B. Drake
Belton .... Charley Powell
City Mgr., Jeff Holberg
Benavides .... Cynthia Oliveira
*Benbrook (P.O. Box 26569, Fort

Worth 76126)...................Jerry Dunn
City Mgr., Ken Neystel
Benjamin............ Bobby Frank Hudson
City Mgr., Ronnie White
Berryville (P.O. Box 908, Frankston 75763)............... John T. McElvany
Bertram.................................B.J. Goble
*Beverly Hills (3418 Memorial Dr., Waco 76711)...............Betty Gibbs
Bevil Oaks (7390 Sweetgum Rd., Beaumont 77713)............ Don Smith
*Big Lake ....H. F. Ritchie
Big Sandy .... R.L. "Buzz" Long
Big Spring ....Tim Blackshear
City Mgr., Gary Fuqua
*Big Wells.............Margarita Rodriguez
*Bishop .... Janie Shafer
Blackwell......................... Ronnie Harris
Blanco............................. Ryan Trimble
*Blanket .... Bobby Thomas
*Bloomburg ............................E.M. Davis
Blooming Grove ....Boyd Bryant
Blossom .... Orville Allen
Blue Mound (201 Blue Mound Rd., Fort Worth 76131)........Jim Watkins
Blue Ridge .... John Worley
Blum...............................Bernilla F. Gunn
Boerne ....Patrick Heath
City Mgr., Ron Bowman
Bogata .... Mildred F. Eudy
*Bonham ....Bob McCraw
City Mgr., Jim Stiff
*Bonney (19007 Mottesheard Rd., Rosharon 77583)..Mary M. Coleman
Booker .... Dennis Cochran
City Mgr., Lois J. Sheets
Borger ....Judy Flanders
City Mgr., Alyn Rogers
Bovina..................................Gene Hutto
Bowie .... Bert Cunningham
City Mgr., James Cantwell
Boyd................................. Steve Cotter
Brackettville ....Carmen M. Berlanga
City Mgr., David G. Luna
Brady ....H. L. Gober Jr.
City Mgr., Dennis Smith
*Brazoria .... W. V. James
City Mgr., Kenneth Timmermann
Breckenridge................Bruce W. Curry
City Mgr., Gary G. Ernest
Bremond .... Ricky Swick
Brenham ....Robert Appel Jr.
City Mgr., Kent R. Van Eman
Briarcliff (HCO 1, Box 24, Spicewood 78669)...............V.E. McDaniel
*Briaroaks (Rt. 5, Box 963, Burleson 76028) .... Alan W. Myers
Bridge City ....John Dubose
Bridgeport ....William E. Huddleston
Broaddus .... Billie Faye Sanders
Bronte .... Martin Lee
Brookshire.......................... Clyde Allen
Brookside Village (Rt. 3, Box 3440, Pearland 77581). Natividad Martinez
*Browndell (P.O. Box 430, Brookeland 75931) .... Erma L. Garrett
Brownfield .... Graham Swain
City Mgr., R.C. Fletcher
*Brownsboro ...................W.E. McLean
Brownsville................. Henry González
City Mgr., Andres Vega
Brownwood .... Bert Massey
City Mgr., Gary Butts
Bruceville-Eddy .... Gene McBride
Bryan .... Lonnie Stabler
City Mgr., Michael Conduff
Bryson........................ Willard Schlittler
Buckholts .... Gwen Hauk
Buckingham (P.O. Box 831452, Richardson 75083)....... Clifford Mongold
Buda .... W.G. White
Buffalo........................... Byron M. Ryder

*Buffalo Gap.................. Charles Peugh
Buffalo Springs (Rt. 10, Box 500, Lubbock 79404) ...... W.B. McMillan
Bullard..................................S.R. McCugh
Bunker Hill Village (11977 Memorial, Houston 77024)George Stubblefield III
City Admin., Ruthie Sager
Burkburnett .... Pat Norriss (Mrs.)
City Mgr., Gary B. Bean
Burke (Rt. 1, Box 3151, Diboll 75941) ....................................J.L. Bell
Burleson........................... Rick Roper
City Mgr., H. Kay Godbey
*Burnet...................Howard R. Benton
City Mgr., Johnny Sartain
Burton .... Marsha Marland
*Byers .... W.A. Landrum
Bynum............................. Jerry Hooker
Cactus......................Leon W. Graham
City Mgr., Darrel Read
Caddo Mills .... Joan Bentley
City Mgr., Romey Tilley
Caldwell .... Bernard E. Rychlik
City Mgr., William L. Broaddus
Callisburg (Rt. 2, Gainesville 76240)..................Bobby McDaniel
Calvert........................... Cooper Wiese
Cameron .... James E. Lafferty
City Admin., Lanny C. French
Campbell...................Weldon R. Wallace
Camp Wood..................... Austin Dean
*Canadian .... Micah Lewis
City Mgr., Dean Looper
Caney City .... Joe Barron
Canton .... Jack Etheridge
City Mgr., Johnny M. Mallory
*Canyon .... Lois Rice
City Mgr., Glen Metcalf
Carbon .... Kenneth Halford
Carl's Corner................ Carl Cornelius
Carmine .... Barney A. Eilers
Carrizo Springs ......Jesús D. Rodriguez
City Mgr., Richard Cantu
Carrollton .... Gary W. Blanscet
City Mgr., Daniel A. Johnson
Carthage .... Carson C. Joines
City Mgr., Charles Thomas
Castle Hills (6915 West Ave., San Antonio 78213).. Felicitas K. Meyer
City Mgr., David R. Seyfarth
Castroville .... Dwight Green
City Mgr., James Fisher
*Cedar Hill..................... Chris L. Rose
City Mgr., Gregory Vick
*Cedar Park .... Dorthey Duckett
City Mgr., Daron K. Butler
Celeste.......................Frank Patterson
*Celina ....John W. Shaw Sr.
City Admin., R. Mike Daugherty
Center ....John D. Windham
City Mgr., (Vacancy)
Centerville ...... William A. (Billy) Walters
Chandler .... Winston Reagan
Channing.......................Ethel Hunnicutt
Charlotte ....Mark T. Wilson
Chester ....Bryan Davis
Chico ....Nobie Tucker
Childress .... Pat Y. Steed
City Mgr., David Galligan
Chillicothe .... E.A. Kennedy Jr.
*China .... Marquita Foster
China Grove............. Mac S. Morris Jr.
*Chireno.....................Joanna Johnson
City Mgr., Alton Holt
*Christine .... Alvie H. Smith
*Cibolo .... Sam Bauder
City Admin., Charles Balcar
Cisco .... Joe Wheatley
City Mgr., Michael Moore
Clarendon ....Steve Smith
Clarksville.............. James Mark Lewis
City Mgr., Wayne Dial

*Clarksville City (Box 1209, Gladewater 75647) .... H.E. Griffin
City Mgr., Billy F. Silvertooth Jr.
Claude............................ Leon G. James
Clear Lake Shores (931 Cedar Road, Kemah 77565) .... Gary Groover
*Cleburne .... Katherine P. Raines
City Mgr., Joel Victory
Cleveland ....Lloyd Meadows
City Mgr.,Hector A. Forestier
Clifton .... Truman Blum
*Clint.................... G. Michael Goodwin
Clute.................................. Jerry Adkins
City Mgr., Barbara Hester
Clyde...................................Merv Warrick
City Admin., Robert J. Bradshaw
Coahoma................................ Bill Read
Cockrell Hill (4125 W. Clarendon, Dallas 75211) ..... Tony Hinojosa Jr.
Coffee City (Box 716, Frankston 75763).................... Wayne Phillips
City Mgr., Jan McGully
Coldspring.................John Benestante
*Coleman .... Woodrow J. Maddox
City Mgr., David S. Sooter
College Station............. Larry J. Ringer
City Mgr., George K. "Skip" Noe
Colleyville .... Ed Baker
City Mgr., C. Robert Stripling
Collinsville ....Wayne McCorkle
Colmesneil .... Jackie Brown
Colorado City .... James G. Baum
City Mgr., Steve Shutt
*Columbus................Dwain K. Dungen
City Mgr., John Brasher
Comanche....................Jimmie Warren
Combes.......... Silvestre (Silver) Garcia
City Mgr., Alicia Duran
*Combine (P.O. Box 231, Seagoville 75159)...........Charles Stringer
Commerce.................... John R. Sands
City Mgr., Roger McKinney
Como................................... Don Collins
Conroe ....Carter Moore
City Mgr., Craig Lonon
Converse ....Earl Lynn Garrison
City Mgr., Sam Hughes
*Cool (R. Rte, Box 150, Weatherford 76086)..............Jim Heineman
Coolidge................ Bobby Lee Jacobs
Cooper .... Richard C. Huie
Coppell ....Tom J. Morton
City Mgr., Jim Witt
Copperas Cove .... J.A. Darossett
City Mgr., Mark P. Sowa
Copper Canyon .... Tom Rogers
Corinth (2003 S. Corinth, Denton 76205)........... Shirley Spellerberg
City Admin., Richard H. Huckaby
*Corpus Christi .... Mary Rhodes
City Mgr., Juan Garza
Corral City (14003 Corral City Dr., Argyle 76226)........James E. Draper
Corrigan ...... Robert R. "Bobby" Smiley
City Mgr., Bradley K. Johnson
Corsicana ....Wilson Griffin
City Mgr., Jim D. Dunaway
Cottonwood Shores (3915 Cottonwood Drive, Marble Falls 78654) .... Kathy Griffith
*Cotulla...........................Joe R. Lozano
*Cove ....Carl Crowder
Covington .... Annabell Stone
*Crandall ....Terry Joe Hedrich
Crane ....Terry L. Schul
City Admin., Bill Sanders
Cranfills Gap .... Marc Johnson
*Crawford .... Neal Plemons
Creedmoor .... Robert Wilhite
Crockett.............................Bill Holcomb
City Mgr., Ann McNabb
*Crosbyton .... Lance Morris

Cross Plains .... Gene Dillard
*Cross Roads (P.O. Box 412, Aubrey 76227) .... John Findley
*Cross Timber (Box 2042, Burleson 776028 .... Alf Lamb
Crowell .... Robert Kincaid
Crowley .... Nancy Behrens
City Mgr., Jay Singleton
Crystal City . Severita Lara de la Fuente
Cuero .... Michael Thamm
City Mgr., John M. Trayhan
Cumby .... LaVerne Battle
*Cuney .... Hildred Lee Barnes
Cushing .... James W. Dawson
Cut and Shoot (Box 7364, Conroe 77303) .... W. Mark Patterson
Daingerfield .... William L. Thorne
City Mgr., Margie Hargrove
Daisetta .... Marvin Murray
Dalhart .... Gene Rahll
City Mgr., Greg Duggan
Dallas .... Ronald Kirk
City Mgr., John Ware
*Dalworthington Gardens (2600 Roosevelt, Arlington 76016) .... Al Taub
Danbury .... Ken Walters
Darrouzett .... Cindy Durfey
City Mgr., Terry Howard
Dawson .... Bobby Nesmith
*Dayton .... Guy L. Harris
City Mgr., Clarence Cowart
*Dayton Lakes (P.O. Box 1566, Day ton 77535) .... Talmadge Powell
Dean (Rt. 5, Box 516, Wichita Falls 76031) .... Steve Sicking
Decatur .... Bobby Wilson
Deer Park .... Jimmy Burke
City Mgr., Ron V. Crabtree
De Kalb .... Billy M. Willis
De Leon .... Charles Chupp
City Coord., Fred Turner
Dell City .... Bill Williams
Del Rio .... Alfredo Gutierrez Jr.
City Mgr., Gus H. Pappas
Denison .... Wayne Cabaniss
City Mgr., Larry Cruise
Denton .... Bob Castelberry
City Mgr., Lloyd Harrell
*Denver City .... Royce Hemmeline
City Mgr., Ray Hohstadt
Deport .... Charles Foster
DeSoto .... Richard Rozier
City Mgr., Ron Holifield
Detroit .... Hazel Rundles
*Devers .... R.B. Evans
Devine .... Linda L. Gunn
City Admin., Erik T. Dahler
Diboll .... James P. Simms
City Mgr., Vernon Cupit
Dickens .... R.L. (Bob) Porter
Dickinson .... John W. Mitchiner
Dilley .... Mary Ann Obregon
City Mgr., Catarino Delgado
Dimmitt .... Wayne Collins
City Mgr., Reeford Burrous
Dodd City .... Jackie Lackey
Dodson .... H.M. Red Riddle
Domino .... Frank Propps
Donna .... Hilda R. Adame
City Mgr., Robert Diaz de Leon
Dorchester (Box 838, Howe 75059) .... Alice F. Stewart
Double Oak .... Richard Cook
Douglassville .... Douglass B. Heath
Dripping Springs .... Terry W. Garnett
Driscoll .... Helen Rose
Dublin .... Keith Nichols
City Mgr., David Johnson
*Dumas .... M. Brent Futrell
City Mgr., Larry A. Smith
*Duncanville .... Ed Purcell

City Mgr., Dan Savage
Eagle Lake .... Robert L. Cook III
City Mgr., Ronald Holland
Eagle Pass .... Raul Treviño Jr.
City Mgr., John Ruiz Jr.
Early .... Earl Rhea
City Mgr., Ken Thomas
Earth .... R. R. Daniel Jr.
Eastland .... C.W. Hoffmann Jr.
City Mgr., Paul N. Catoe
East Mountain (Rt. 1, Box 500, Gilmer 75644) .... Marion White
Easton .... Leroy Mitchellt
East Tawakoni .... James R. Thomas
*Ector .... Steve Grant
*Edcouch .... Tom Rocchio
City Admin., John Montalvo
Eden .... Thomas F. Kelso
Edgecliff .... Bill Sherman
Edgewood .... Finis Skinner Jr.
Edinburg .... Joe Ochoa
City Mgr., John R. Milford
*Edmonson .... Don Ketchum
Edna .... Joe D. Hermes
City Mgr., Nicholas Caruso
Edom (Rt. 1, Box 512, Brownsboro 75756) .... Mary Scott
El Campo .... Paul Soechting
City Mgr., Terry Roberts
*El Cenizo (P.O. Box 6180, Laredo 78042) .... Guadalupe de Leon
Eldorado .... John Nikolauk
Electra .... Jim Bentley
City Mgr., David Vestal
Elgin .... Eric W. Carlson
City Mgr., Jack A. Harzke
*Elkhart .... Jimmy Parker
City Admin., Sue Harris
El Lago .... Roger E. Nylin
Elmendorf .... Mary Jane Nunez
El Paso .... Larry Francis
City Admin., Ken Beasley
*Elsa .... Greg Madrigal
City Mgr., Juan Cedillo
*Emhouse .... Harold Clemens
Emory .... Rubye McKeown
Enchanted Oaks (Box 517, Mabank 75147) .... Blair Whitelaw
*Encinal .... Roy Salinas
Ennis .... Bill Lewis
City Mgr., Steve Howerton
*Estelline .... T.H. Seay
Euless .... Mary Lib Saleh
City Mgr., Tom Hart
Eureka .... Barney Thomas
*Eustace .... Doug Caison
Evant .... Randall Rigney
Everman .... Cathey Thurston
City Mgr., David Hunnicutt
Fairfield .... Luke Ward Jr.
City Admin., Ted Mayo
Fair Oaks Ranch .... E.L. Gaubatz
Fairview (Collin Co.) (Box 551, McKinney 75069) .... David N. Link
Fairview (Wise Co.) (Rt. 1, Box 34, Rhome 76078) .... Paulette Layfield
Falfurrias ... Ernesto "Pepe" Williams Jr.
City Mgr., Aurora C. Rodriguez
Falls City .... Stanley Kolodzie
Farmers Branch .... Dave Blair
City Mgr., Richard L. Escalante
*Farmersville .... George C. Crump
City Mgr., Randall E. Holly
Farwell .... Jimmie Mace
Fate .... Gerry Boren
Fayetteville .... William Graeter
*Ferris .... Jimmy Birdwell
*Flatonia .... Dan Bowling
City Mgr., William P. Cornelius Jr.
*Florence .... Lee Roy Knauth
*Floresville .... Raymond M. Ramirez
City Admin., Gary Pelech

Galveston, where the elegant Moody Mansion is open to the public as a house museum, pioneered the commission form of city government.

Flower Mound .... Larry Lipscomb
City Mgr., Van James
Floydada .... Hulon Carthel
City Mgr., Gary Brown
*Follett .... Betty Redelsperger
City Mgr., Rober. Williamson
*Forest Hill (6800 Forest Hill Dr., Fort Worth 76140) .... Donald Walker
City Mgr., Edward Badgett
Forney .... Don T. Cates
City Mgr., James McConnell
Forsan .... Johnny Sherman
*Fort Gates (Rt. 5, Box 371, Gatesville 76528) .... Gail Ussery
Fort Stockton .... Joe Shuster
City Mgr., Jesse Garcia
Fort Worth .... Kay Granger
City Mgr., Bob Terrell
*Franklin .... Charles Ellison
*Frankston .... James Gouger
Fredericksburg ..... Linda K. Langerhans
City Mgr., Gary Neffendorf
Freeport .... James A. Barnett Jr.
City Mgr., Gary Stone
Freer .... Malloy A. Hamilton
Friendswood .... Evelyn B. Newman
City Mgr., Ronald E. Cox
Friona .... Clarence Monroe
City Mgr., Paula Wilson
Frisco .... Robert M. Warren
City Mgr., George Purefoy
Fritch .... John Stevens
City Mgr., Deck Shaver
*Frost .... J. O. Williams
Fruitvale .... Bea Whisenhunt
*Fulshear .... Viola Randall
Fulton .... Leslie Cole Sr.
Gainesville .... Jim J. Hatcher
City Mgr., Alan Mueller
*Galena Park .... James B. Havard
Gallatin .... Johnnie B. Grimes
Galveston .... Barbara K. Crews
City Mgr., Douglas W. Matthews
Ganado .... Dana J. Parks
Garden Ridge .... Jay P. Millikin
Garland .... James B. Ratliff
City Mgr., Jeffrey B. Muzzy
Garrett .... David Clemmons
Garrison .... Marion H. Stoddard
*Gary .... Ruth Ann Simpson
Gatesville .... Wyllis H. Ament
City Mgr., Bob Stevens
Georgetown .... Leo Wood
City Mgr., Bob Hart
George West .... August Caron Jr.
City Mgr., Terri Garza

*Gholson (Rt. 5, Box 495, Waco 76705)............... Howard T. Sexton
Giddings............... Lavonne D. Morrow
City Mgr., James E. Dover
Gilmer .... Everett Dean
City Mgr., R. Timothy Gump
Gladewater .... Jackie D. Wood
City Mgr., Sharon G. Johnson
*Glenn Heights (1938 S. Hampton, DeSoto 75115)...... Michael Burgett
City Mgr., Earl Keaton
Glen Rose .... Bobbie Glidewell
Godley .... Sam F. Owens
Goldsmith............... Bennie V. Cope
*Goldthwaite .... Richard Poss
City Mgr., Dale Allen
Goliad .... Buddy Zavesky
City Admin., Jayne Hoff
*Golinda (Rt. 2, Box 629, Lorena 76655)............... Ennis Degrate Jr.
Gonzales............... Jack L. Finch
City Mgr., E.T. Gibson
Goodlow (Box 248, Kerens 75144)............... Willie Washington
Goodrich .... Shirley Murphy
Gordon .... David A. Johnson
Goree .... Jimmy Harlan
City Mgr., Glenda Decker
Gorman .... Jack Simpson
Graford............... Vernon Bridges
*Graham .... Jerrye Milam
City Mgr., Larry M. Fields
Granbury............... David Southern
City Mgr., Bob Brockman
Grandfalls .... Mary Everett
Grand Prairie .... Charles England
City Mgr., Gary Gwyn
Grand Saline............... Larry W. Martin Sr.
City Mgr., Sam E. Beeler Sr.
Grandview............... Larry Moore
Granger............... Perry Denny Pickett
Granite Shoals .... Herman Williams
Granjeno (Rt. 4, Box 491, Mission 78572)............... NA
Grapeland .... Dick Bridges
Grapevine .... William D. Tate
City Mgr., Trent Petty
*Grayburg (P.O. Box 23, Sour Lake 77659)............... J.W. Floyd
*Grays Prairie (Rt. 2, Box 38, Scurry 75158) .... Jim Todd
Greenville............... Sue Ann Harting
City Mgr., Ed Thatcher
Gregory .... Luis Galvan
Grey Forest (18502 Scenic Loop Rd., Helotes 78023) ... Jack Nottingham
Groesbeck .... Jim Longbotham
Groom .... Greg Lamb
Groves .... Sylvester Moore
City Mgr., A. R. Kimler
Groveton .... Arvalee Dial
Gruver............... Archie Nelson
City Mgr., A. J. Ratliff
Gun Barrel City .... Joe Agnes
Gunter............... Billy Gravley
Gustine .... Roger Oliver
*Hackberry (P.O. Box 945, Little Elm 75068)............... Lawrence R. Nielsen
*Hale Center .... Bob Stroud
Hallettsville............... Warren Grindeland
City Admin., David J. Drury Jr.
Hallsburg (Rt. 7, Box 428, Waco 76705)............... Margie N. Wilbanks
Hallsville............... T. Bynum Hatley
Haltom City .... Gary W. Larson
City Mgr., William E. Eisen
Hamilton............... Joe M. Crane
City Mgr., Bill Funderburk
Hamlin............... Melvin J. Scott
Happy .... R.N. McDonald
Hardin .... Doug Tinkle Jr.
Harker Heights............... Stewart Meyer
City Mgr., Steve Carpenter
Harlingen............... H. Wm. Card Jr.
City Mgr., A. Brent Branham
*Hart............... Tony Leibel
Haskell .... Ken Lane
City Mgr., Sam Watson
Haslet............... I.J. Frazier
Hawkins .... W. C. Maynard
*Hawley............... Don Tatum
*Hays (P.O. Box 1285, Buda 78610)............... Bill Couch
Hearne .... Ruben Gomez
City Mgr., Floyd T. Hafley
Heath .... Chris Cuny
*Hebron (Rt. 2, Box 184, Carrollton 75010)............... Stanley Dozier
Hedley............... Shauna Monroe
Hedwig Village (955 Piney Point Rd., Houston 77024) .. Robert I. Goehrs
Helotes............... Charles A. McAfee
City Admin., L.J. Cott
*Hemphill............... Robert Hamilton
Hempstead............... Herbert L. Johnson
City Mgr., James A. Vines
Henderson .... Chester E. Johnson
City Mgr., Earl Heath
Henrietta .... W.L. Hill
City Mgr., Joe Pence
Hereford......... Robert "Bob" Josserand
City Mgr., Chester R. Nolen
*Hewitt............... Pike Anderson
City Mgr., Dennis Woodard
Hickory Creek (Box 453, Lake Dallas 75065)........ Marvourene Matthews
*Hico .... Melton Murff
Hidalgo............... John David Franz
Higgins .... Hilton Menser
*Highland Park (4700 Drexel, Dallas 75205)......... Wade C. Smith
City Mgr., L.A. Patterson
Highland Village (948 Highland Village, Lewisville 75067)............... (Vacancy)
City Mgr., Bo McDaniel
Hill Country Village (116 Aspen, San Antonio 78232) ... Edward R. McNabb
City Admin., Jack Flesher
Hillcrest Village (Box 1172, Alvin .77512)............... Bruce King
Hillsboro .... Henry Moore
City Mgr., Gene Cravens
Hilshire Village (P.O. Box 55233, Houston 77255) .. Steven Tacconelly
Hitchcock .... Harry W. Robinson
Holiday Lakes (Rt. 4, Box 747, Angleton 77515) .... Norman C. Schroeder
Holland............... Alan Johnson
Holliday .... Grady Graves
Hollywood Park (2 Mecca Dr., San Antonio 78232)..... Ralph S. Hoggatt
*Homer (Rt. 2, Box 319N, Lufkin 75901)............... Nita Noel
Hondo .... James E. Barden
City Mgr., Scott Wall
Honey Grove..... Maquestia J. Johnson
Hooks............... Michael W. Babb
Horizon City (14999 Darrington, El Paso 79927).... Lillard S. Thompson
Houston............... Robert C. Lanier
Howardwick (Box 1410, Clarendon 79226) .... Joe Riggins
Howe............... Ray Bledsoe
City Admin., Ray Houston
Hubbard .... Steven Weatherby
Hudson (Rt. 8, Box 4065, Lufkin 75904)............... M.B. Baker
Hudson Oaks ...... Forrest G. Thompson
City Admin., Mary Jane Holybee
Hughes Springs .... Reba N. Simpson
City Mgr., George Fite
Humble............... Wilson Archer
City Mgr., James P. Baker
Hunters Creek Village (#1 Hunters Creek Pl., Houston 77024)............... Jack W. Howeth
Huntington............... Dean McMullen
Huntsville............... William B. Green
City Mgr., Gene Pipes
Hurst............... Bill Souder
City Mgr., Jim D. Starr
Hutchins .... Carroll W. Merlick
Hutto............... Michael E. Yuhr
Huxley (Rt. 1, Box 1410, Shelbyville 75973)............... Larry Vaughn
Idalou .... Mike Mauldin
Impact (Box 3116, Abilene 79604)............... Dallas Perkins
*Indian Lake (62 So. Aztec Cove, Los Fresnos 78566) .... Joe Rymer
Industry .... Alan W. Kuehn
*Ingleside .... Chuck Rittiman
City Mgr., Steve Fitzgibbons
Ingleside on the Bay............ Al Robbins
Ingram .... Harold Wunsch
Iowa Colony (12003 County Road 65, Rosharon 77583) .... Maurice Bright
Iowa Park .... Wayne House
City Mgr., Mike Price
Iraan............... D. Randy Peterson
Iredell .... A. D. Woody Jr.
Irving .... Morris H. Parrish
City Mgr., Steve McCullough
Italy............... John Goodman
City Admin., Lyall Kirton
Itasca............... J.D. Lawson
City Admin., Mel Coker
Jacinto City (10301 Market St. Rd., Houston 77029) .... David Gongre
City Mgr., Joann Griggs
Jacksboro............... Jerry Craft
City Mgr., LeRoy Lane
Jacksonville............... Larry K. Durrett
City Mgr., Jim Anderson
Jamaica Beach (Box 5264, Galveston 77554) .... Kenneth R. Dennis
City Admin., Sharon Turnley
Jasper .... Frank Lindsey Jr.
City Mgr., Kerry Lacy
Jayton............... Travis R. Smith
Jefferson .... Charles C. Haggard Jr.
Jersey Village (16501 Jersey Dr., Houston 77040) ... Stephen Schneider
City Mgr., R. Dale Brown
Jewett............... Herman Hammond
Joaquin............... Steve Hughes
Johnson City .... Kermit A. Roeder
*Jones Creek (Rt. 1, 7207 SFA Rd., Freeport 77541) ..... Wayne Dubose
City Mgr., Tamie Schmidt
Jonestown............... Sam Billings
City Admin., Cindy Lent
Josephine............... Richard Murray
Joshua............... James W. McFarland
City Mgr., (Vacancy)
*Jourdanton............... Paul W. Wilson
City Mgr., Roy Underwood
Junction........ William Keaton Blackburn
City Admin., Jack L. Smith
*Justin .... Virgil Eaves
Karnes City............... Don Tymrak
City Admin., David Carrothers
Katy............... M.H. "Hank" Schmidt Jr.
Kaufman............... Jess M. Murrell
City Mgr., Bob Woodard
Keene............... Gary Heinrich
Keller .... Ron Lee
City Mgr., Bob Salinas
Kemah............... Richard A. Diehl
Kemp............... James Stroman Jr.
City Mgr., Gary McDaniel
Kendleton............... Eddie Maxwell
Kenedy .... R.C. Franklin
Kenefick (Rt. 5, Box 525-A, Dayton 77535) .... Jerry L. Gore Sr.

Kennard .... Bill Thomas
Kennedale............................ Bill Abbott
Kerens .... Ottis Ray Spurlock
Kermit .... Ted Westmoreland
City Mgr., Wayne Reynolds
Kerrville................. Charels P. Johnson
City Mgr., Glenn D. Brown
Kilgore.................................Bill Wilson
City Mgr., Ronald H. Stephens
Killeen .... Raul G. Villaronga
City Mgr.,Talmadge N. Buie
Kingsville...................... Douglas Hicks
City Mgr., Carlos E. Lerma
Kirby (112 Baumann, San Antonio 78219)....................... Pryor Smithr
City Mgr., Ricardo T. Cortes
Kirbyville .... Jerry Nobles
City Mgr., Tommy Neal
*Kirvin .... Billie Walthall
*Knollwood (100 Collins Dr., Sherman 75090)...................Richard Roelke
Knox City ....Tommie "Bud" Reynolds
City Mgr., Joseph R. Rice
Kosse .... W. C. Graeber
*Kountze .... Charles Bilal
Kress............................... Louise Kirk
Krugerville (#8 Carrigan Center, Aubrey 76227) .... Harry Richards
Krum .... Jan Farris
Kyle............................ Merle D. Wilkins
*La Coste .... Eugene Sherrer
City Admin., Larry Joe Capps
Lacy-Lakeview (501 E. Craven, Waco 76705).... Charles W. Doherty
Ladonia ....Leon Hurse
La Feria.......................Paul F. Beechner
City Mgr., Sunny K. Philip
Lago Vista....................Russell L. Allen
City Mgr., Dennis Jones
*La Grange .... Don Chovanec
City Mgr., Shawn Raborn
*La Grulla (City Hall, Grulla 78548).........................Rene Martínez
Laguna Vista .... Hap Fairhart
*La Joya ....Rodolfo Farias
City Admin., Oscar Cuellar Jr.
Lake Bridgeport (Rt. 2, Box 244F, Bridgeport 76426) ...Jeanita VanDerLee
Lake City (Box 177, Mathis 78368).............. George W. Watkins
Lake Dallas ....Jerry McCutcheon
*Lake Jackson .... Doris Williams
City Mgr., William P. Yenne
Lakeport (P.O. Box 7728, Longview 75607)........................ Ricky Shelton
Lakeside (Box 787, Mathis 78368)................James M. Thomas
Lakeside (9830 Confederate Park, Fort Worth 76108) . Raymond E. Beck
City Mgr., William F. Mohr
*Lakeside City (Box 4287, Wichita Falls 76308).............................. Bill Baker
*Lake Tanglewood (Rt. 8, Box 35-15, Amarillo 79118) .... M.L. Ott
Lakeview .... Russell Payne
Lakeway (104 Cross Creek, Austin 78734)......................... Jack O'Neill
City Mgr., Dave Benson
*Lakewood Village (100 Highridge Dr., Little Elm 75068) .... Brian Refoy
Lake Worth (6720 Telephone Rd., Fort Worth 76135)..... Walter Bowen
City Mgr., Mark Todd
La Marque................. Pete W. Rygaard
City Mgr., Nick J. Finan
Lamesa .... Mike Tyler
City Mgr., Paul Feazelle
Lampasas .... Jack Calvert
City Mgr., Kim R. Foutz
Lancaster .... Margie Waldrop
City Mgr., Steven Norwood
La Porte ....Norman L. Malone
City Mgr., Robert T. Herrera
*Laredo .... Saul N. Ramirez Jr.
City Mgr., Peter Vargas
*Latexo .... Billie Jo Bennett
La Vernia.................Charles R. Malloy
La Villa .... Carlos Perez
City Mgr., Antonio Barco
*Lavon ....John K. Smith
La Ward..................Tillman M. Hunt Sr.
Lawn ....Johnny B. Hudson
*League City .... Joe L. Lamb
City Admin., Paul Nutting
Leakey .... J. H. Chisum
Leander................ Kenneth O. Craven
City Mgr., Brenda D. Wilson
*Leary (Rt. 5, Box 435, Texarkana 75501)............. Donald McGonigal
Lefors .... J.W. Franks
*Leona...........................Travis J. Oden
*Leonard .... Robert Damesworth
City Admin., Darvin Nolen
Leon Valley (6400 El Verde, San Antonio 78238) .... Marcus Semmelmann
City Mgr., Henry Brummett
Leroy .... Tim Harrington
Levelland..............Raymond O. Dennis
City Mgr., Malhon G. Ingham
Lewisville................. Bobbie J. Mitchell
City Mgr., Charles R. Owens
Lexington ....Louis Knipstein
Liberty .... Paul J. Henryr
City Mgr., Norman W. Dykes
*Lincoln Park (Rt. 1, Box 701, Aubrey 76227)........................ Roger Pock
Lindale ....Bobby McClenny
City Mgr., Owen Scott
Linden .... Marvin W. Kelly
*Lindsay ....Robert Walterscheid
Lipan .... James Reece
Little Elm ....Jim Pelley
Littlefield........................Ray G. Keeling
City Mgr., Marty Mangum
*Little River-Academy (Box 521, Little River 76554) .... Ronnie W. White
Live Oak (8001 Shin Oak Dr., San Antonio 78233) .... Ray Hildebrand
City Mgr., Douglas G. Faseler
*Liverpool .... Allan F. Moore
Livingston.............. Ben R. Ogletree Jr.
City Mgr., Sam Gordon
*Llano...............................Jeffrey Hopf
Lockhart .... M. Louis Cisneros
City Mgr., Joe Michie
*Lockney ....Kenneth R. Wofford
Log Cabin................ Aubrey L. Monroe
*Lometa...........................Charles Kelly
Lone Oak .... Elmer Dean Jr.
*Lone Star................ James W. Smith
*Longview ........................I.J. Patterson
City Mgr., Isaac Turner
*Loraine..........Catarino G. Martínez Jr.
Lorena............................William E. Boyd
Lorenzo .... Tommy D. Fondren
City Mgr., Roger Cypert
*Los Fresnos................Manuel Abrego
City Mgr., Don R. Badeaux
Los Indios.........Diamantina O. Bennett
*Los Ybanez (HCR 7, Box 52, Lamesa 79331) .....Mary A. Ybanez
Lott .... Bob Collier
*Lovelady .... Ronald G. LaRue
*Lowry Crossing (1405 S. Bridgefarmer, McKinney 75069) ......John Kenwell
Lubbock .... David R. Langston
City Mgr., Bob Cass
Lucas ....Bruce Hopewell
*Lueders............... Robert Wingrove Jr.
Lufkin ....Louis A. Bronaugh
City Mgr., C.G. Maclin
Luling ....John A. Moore
City Mgr.,Randy G. Thomas
Lumberton.................Jerry Williamson
Lyford ....Frank Quintanilla
Lytle.............................. Horace Fincher
Mabank .... Larry Teague
Madisonville .... Leroy Stanton
City Mgr., Curtis McLemore
Magnolia..........................John Bramlett
*Malakoff .... James Anders
City Admin., John Lott
Malone .... Ray Watson
Manor ....Luis Suarez
Mansfield...................... Duane Murray
City Mgr., Clayton Chandler
Manvel.............................Merl Bradley
*Marble Falls .... Griff Morris
City Mgr., Vida Nelson (Acting)
Marfa ..........................C.M. "Fritz" Kahl
*Marietta........Danny Wilson (Pro Tem)
Marion .... Glenn Hild
*Marlin .... Tom Black
City Mgr., Sue Philley
Marquez .... James Kenneth Clary
Marshall.....................Audrey D. Kariel
City Mgr., Tony N. Williams
Marshall Creek (P.O. Box 1080, Roanoke 76262)......... Bobby Ward
Mart ....Paul S. Thronburg
City Mgr., David E. White
Martindale .... Robby D. Powell
Mason .... R. Clinton Schulze
Matador .... Gary L. Lancaster
*Mathis ....Eva F. Medrano
Maud ....Edward M. Holley
Maypearl .... David K. Evans
McAllen ....Othal E. Brand Sr.
City Mgr., Mike R. Perez
McCamey .... Jimmy L. McClure
McGregor .... Felix A. Morris
City Mgr., Bill Dake
McKinney .... John E. Gay
City Mgr., Donald E. Paschal Jr.
*McLean .... Sam A. Haynes
McLendon-Chisholm (1248 SH 205, Rockall 75087) .. Michael D. Donegan
Meadow.................................Dale Wylie
Meadowlakes (271 Deer Lick, Marble Falls 78654) Donald E. Reed
Meadows (1 Troyan Dr., Stafford 77477) .... Jim McDonald
Megargel ....Danny Falls
*Melissa..................Buck Weatherby
Melvin .... Mattie Lou Davis
Memphis......................... Homer Tucker
Menard .... Max E. Hooten
City Mgr., James F. Cannon
*Mercedes ....Miguel Castillo Jr.
City Mgr., Alan Kamasaki
Meridian .... Billy Kibler
*Merkel .... J.T. Naron
City Mgr., Robert Harris
Mertens .... Linda Maples
Mertzon .... Patsy Kahlig
Mesquite............................ Cathye Ray
City Mgr., James A. Prugel Jr.
Mexia......................... Eugene Forsythe
City Mgr., Jim White
*Miami ....Gene Hodges
Midland...................... Robert E. Burns
City Mgr., Fred Michael McGregor
Midlothian................... Maurice Osborn
City Mgr., Robert Powers
Midway ....Patrick H. Wakefield
Milano........................ James T. Hartley
*Mildred (Rt. 6, Corsicana 75110) .... Rebecca Hall
*Miles ....Warner Harsch
Milford .... Bobby. Cooper
*Miller's Cove (Rt. 3, Box 3, Mt. Pleasant 75455) .... Wayne Miller
Millsap ....Julia Dinda-Weston
Mineola.................. Celia Scott Boswell
Mineral Wells.......... Myron M. Crawford
City Mgr., Lance Howerton

Mingus .... Robert Bearden
Mission .... Ricardo A. Perez
Missouri City .... Allen Owen
City Mgr., James Thurmond
Mobeetie .... Dale Corcoran
Mobile City (824 Lilac Lane, Rockwall 75087) .... Billie M. Easley
*Monahans .... David B. Cutbirth
City Mgr., David Mills
*Mont Belvieu .... H.J. (Joe) Dutton
Montgomery .... John A. Butler
*Moody .... MMike Alton
City Admin., Charleen Dowell
*Moore Station (Rt. 1, Box 133, Larue 75770) .... Arthur Earl
Moran .... Marvin Kays
Morgan.... Harold E. Vandiver*Morgan's Point (P.O. Box 839, La Porte 77571) .... Russel Applebe
City Admin., David A. Paulissen
Morgan's Point Resort (8 Morgan's Point Blvd, Belton 76513) . E.W. Berry
City Mgr., Donald Gee
Morton .... Ray Lewis
City Mgr., Brad Stafford
Moulton .... Minnie Lee Fisbeck
*Mountain City (116 Cedar, Buda 78610) .... Beth Smith
Mount Calm .... Mackey McCaghren
Mount Enterprise .... Danny Garcia
Mount Pleasant .... Bill Chambers
City Mgr., Richard E. Chaffin
Mount Vernon .... Mike Edwards
City Mgr., Eddie G. Turner
Muenster .... Henry Weinzapfel
City Mgr., Chris Yosten
Muleshoe .... Robert Montgomery
City Mgr., Dave Marr Jr.
*Mullin .... A. R. Whisenhunt
Munday .... Richard Albus
City Mgr., Jim Slayton
*Murchison .... David Williams
Murphy (205 N. Murphy Rd., Plano 75094) .... Greg Singleton
Mustang (P.O. Box 325, Corsicana 75151) .... Archie Glenn Albritton
*Mustang Ridge (112800 U.S. 138 So., Buda 78610) .... Billie Morrison
Nacogdoches .... James E. Raney
City Mgr., Gordon C. Pierce
Naples .... Ellen Robinson
Nash .... Bennie Duck
*Nassau Bay (1800 NASA Rd. One, Houston 77058) ... Donald Johnson
City Mgr., David K. Stall
*Natalia .... Gloria G. Vasquez
Navarro (P.O. Box 7502, Corsicana 75110) .... Yvonne Capehart
Navasota .... Wm. A. Miller Jr.
City Mgr., Harold Underwood
Nazareth .... Ralph Brockman
Nederland .... Carl N. "Cropo" LeBlanc
City Mgr., André Wimer
Needville .... Kermit Blezinger
*Nesbitt (Rt. 5, Box 88, Marshall 75670) .... Roy A. Nesbitt
*Nevada .... Giles Caldwell
Newark .... Bill Malone
New Berlin (Rt. 1, Box 215-A, La Vernia 78121) ... Freddie Friederick
New Boston .... Hubert C. May
New Braunfels .... Paul E. Fraser Jr.
City Mgr., Mike Shands
Newcastle .... Earline Swarts
*New Chapel Hill (Rt. 25, Box 834, Tyler 75707) .... J. T. Pinkerton
New Deal .... William L. Bigham
New Home .... J.A. Evans
New Hope (Box 562, McKinney 75070) .... Johnny Hamm
*New London .... Charlie McConnico
New Summerfield .... Janette Murphy
Newton .... Charles Glover
City Admin., Donnie Meek
New Waverly .... Dan Underwood
Neylandville (General Delivery, Greenville 75401) .... Lois K. Callagan
Niederwald (13851 Camino Real, Kyle 78640) .... Shirley Whisenant
Nixon .... Collie L. Murray
City Mgr., John (Pete) Byrd
*Nocona .... John Gibbs
City Mgr., Melvin Adams
Nolanville .... Robert Lyall
Nome .... David R. Studdert
Noonday (P.O. Box 6425, Tyler 75711) .... Bennie H. Smith
Nordheim .... Roy L. McMillan
*Normangee .... Mike Moss
North Cleveland (Box 1266, Cleveland 77327) .... Woodrow Squier
*Northcrest (613 N. Lacy Dr., Waco 76705) .... A. Hinojosa
Northlake (P.O. Box 729, Justin 76247) .... James Morton
*North Richland Hills (Box 820609, Fort Worth 76180) ...... Tommy Brown
City Mgr., Rodger Line
*Novice .... Don Poe
*Oak Grove (P.O. Box 309, Kaufman 75142) .... Don Moore
*Oakhurst .... Mary D. Rosier
*Oak Leaf .... A.L. Curry
Oak Point (P.O. Box 818, Little Elm 75068) .... Harold Bowden
*Oak Ridge (Rt. 3, Box 325, #27, Gainesville 76240) . Shannon Wimmer
Oak Ridge (Rt. 1, Box 228, Terrell 75160) .... Hue Arredondo
Oak Ridge North (27326 Robinson, Conroe 77385) .... Gary A. Louie
City Mgr., Paul Mendes
Oak Valley (P.O. Box 2193, Corsicana 75151) .... Jake Jacobs
Oakwood .... Dorothy Bell
O'Brien .... Charlene Brothers
*Odem .... Jessie Rodriguez Sr.
Odessa .... Lorraine Perryman
City Mgr., Jerry S. McGuire
O'Donnell .... Thomas Woolam
Oglesby .... Kenneth Goodwin
*Old River-Winfree (Box 1169, Mont Belvieu 77580) ...... Frank J. Landry
Olmos Park (119 W. El Prado, San Antonio 78212) .. Gerald Z. Dubinski Sr.
City Mgr., Byron E. Hollinger
Olney .... Marc Wipperman
City Admin., Jack R. Northrup
Olton .... Mike Foskey
City Mgr., Layton Covington
Omaha .... D.D. Tuck
Onalaska .... Jeanne Ann Smith Byrd
Opdyke West (P.O. Box 1179, Levelland 79336) .... Wayne Riggins
Orange .... Dan Cochran
City Mgr., Charles W. Pinto
Orange Grove .... T.L. Thomas
City Admin., Perry R. Young
Orchard .... Eugene L. Demny
*Ore City .... Robert Cook II
Overton .... Robert Raney
City Mgr., Raymond Litton
Ovilla .... Leo A. Wrobel
Oyster Creek .... Richard D. Merriman
Paducah .... C.D. Dickens
Paint Rock .... Paul Thorpe
Palacios .... George D. Holst
City Admin., Charles R. Winfield
*Palestine .... Jackson Hanks
City Mgr., Andy McCuistion
Palmer .... Wallace Hughey
*Palmhurst (Rt. 2, Box 80, Mission 78572) .... Elton L. Key
Palm Valley (Rt. 4, Harlingen 78552) .... John Puhl
*Palmview (Rt. 10, Box 598-B, Mission 78572) .... Jose R. Pena
City Mgr., Carlos Blanco
Pampa .... Robert L. Neslage
City Mgr., Bob Eskridge
*Panhandle .... Les McNeill
City Mgr., Thomas J. Blazek
Panorama (98 Hiwon Dr., Conroe 77304) .... Larry A. Albritton
Pantego .... Susan Abercrombie
City Mgr., Larry W. Smith
Paris .... Eric S. Clifford
City Mgr., Michael E. Malone
Parker .... Jack Albritton
City Admin., Betty McMenamy
Pasadena .... Johnny Isbell
Pattison .... Linda A. Mladenka
*Patton Village (P.O. Box 437, Splendora 77372) .... Cecil White
Payne Springs .... Dick Henderson
Pearland .... (Election pending 8/95)
City Mgr., Paul Grohman
Pearsall .... Victor Vinton
City Mgr., Daniel Carbajal Jr.
Pecan Gap .... Don Woodall
Pecan Hill (P.O. Box 443, Red Oak 75154) .... Linda White
Pecos .... Dot Stafford
City Mgr., Harry Nagel
Pelican Bay (1300 Pelican Circle, Azle 76020) .... Billy W. Heaton
*Penelope .... Robert E. Tobola
Peñitas .... Servando Ramirez
*Pernitas Point (HCR-1, Box 1440, Sandia 78383) .... Dorothy Keetch
*Perryton .... David Hale
City Mgr., David Landis
Petersburg .... Jim Fox
City Mgr., Jesse J. Nave
Petrolia .... Ardell Watson
Petronila (Rt. 3, Box 317, Robstown 78380) .... William J. Ordner
Pflugerville .... Haywood L. Ware
City Mgr., Truitt Gilbreath
Pharr .... Victor Garcia
City Mgr., Pete Sepulveda Jr.
Pilot Point .... Allen Groff
Pine Forest (Box 1004, Vidor 776700) .... William G. Elliott
Pinehurst (3640 Mockingbird, Orange 77630) .... L.E. Buker
City Mgr., Curtis Jeanis
Pineland .... John O. Booker
Piney Point Village (7745 San Felipe, #101, Houston 77063) Joe Stockdale
Pittsburg .... D. H. Abernathy
City Mgr., Ned C. Muse
Plains .... T. J. Miller
City Admin., David Brunson
Plainview .... Lloyd C. Woods
City Mgr., James P. Jeffers
Plano .... James N. Muns
City Mgr., Thomas H. Muehlenbeck
Pleak (5809 Pleak Rd., Richmond 77469) .... William Poncik
Pleasanton .... Bob Hurley
City Mgr., Larry Pippin
Pleasant Valley (3870 Bus. 287, Iowa Park 76367) .... Raymond Haynes
*Plum Grove (Rt. 5, Box 322-G, Cleveland 77327) .... Noble Enloe
Point .... Raymond Clifton
Point Blank .... Lillian Bratton
Point Comfort .... Pam Lambden
Ponder .... Wayne Futch
Port Aransas .... James H. Sherrill
City Mgr., Tommy M. Brooks
Port Arthur .... Robert T. Morgan Jr.
City Mgr., (Vacancy)
*Port Isabel .... Calvin Byrd
City Mgr., Manuel Hinojosa

Portland .... Billy G. Webb
City Mgr., Rick Conner
*Port Lavaca ....Tiney Browning
City Mgr., C.J. Webster
Port Neches .... Gary C. Graham Sr.
City Mgr., James L. Harrington
Post............................. Jim Jackson
City Mgr., Ricky Hanna
Post Oak Bend (Rt. 2, Box 357, Kaufman 75142) .... Bret L. Shafer
*Poteet .... Alfred Catala
Poth .... Gene Maeckel
Pottsboro ....David P. Gibson
*Powell.........................Royce Bancroft
*Poynor ....Dannie Smith
Prairie View......................Ron Leverett
City Mgr., Hazel Gilliard
*Premont......................... Luis S. Saenz
Presidio............................Locho Nichols
City Mgr., Arturo J. Ochoa
Primera .... José J. Ramirez
*Princeton ....Bill Caldwell
*Progreso .... Ofelia Garcia
Progreso Lakes (Box 511, Progreso 78579)............. Beverly M. Meyers
Prosper .... Don Brown
*Putnam ....Winford Fry
*Pyote ....Jerry McGee
*Quanah................... Weldon Dickerson
City Admin., Joel M. Epps
Queen City .... James McCormack
*Quinlan .... Lois Cagle
City Admin., Chris Hadjison
Quintana (814 N. Lamar, Freeport 77541)....................Debbie Alongis
Quitaque ....James M. Davidson
City Admin., Robert Patrick
*Quitman .... Jerry Edwards
Ralls ....David A. Prewitt
Rancho Viejo (3461 Carmen, Brownsville 78520) ....Bob Cummins
*Ranger.................. Ronnie Ainsworth
*Rangerville (Rt. 4, Box 77, San Benito 78586) ....Wayne Halbert
Rankin.......... Cora Gaynelle McFadden
Ransom Canyon .... Lee Kitchens
Raymondville ....C. M. Crowell
City Mgr., José L. López
Red Oak..................... Dennis R. Brown
City Mgr., Ken Pfeifer
Redwater .... James B. Stokes
Refugio .... Roger Fancher
*Reklaw....................... Harlan Crawford
*Reno (Lamar Co.) (165 Bybee St., Paris 75460) .... Pat Bailey
City Admin., Sue Ross
Reno (Parker Co.) (Rt. 4, Box 270, Azle 76020)................... L.L. Bailey
*Retreat (Rt. 3, Box 2050, Corsicana 75110).................. Betty Carpenter
*Rhome ....Karl R. Little
Rice...............................Roger A. Wear
Richardson..................... Gary A. Slagel
City Mgr., Bill Keffler
Richland ....Guy Lansford
Richland Hills (3200 Diana Dr., Fort Worth 76118) .... C.F. Kelley
City Mgr., Stephen Hughes
Richland Springs......Dale McKinnerney
Richmond.................. Hilmar G. Moore
City Mgr., R. Glen Gilmore
Richwood .... James M. Vera
*Riesel ....Mike Posey
*Rio Bravo (1419 Centeno Lane, Laredo 78043) .... Raul Aguero
Rio Grande City ....Basilio Villarreal
City Admin., José A. Escamilla
Rio Hondo .... Alejandro Chavez Jr.
Rio Vista...........................Sam Bigham
Rising Star .... Jerrell Bible
City Mgr., Philip Donaldson
*River Oaks (4900 River Oaks Blvd, Fort Worth 76114). James M. Walker
Riverside....................Randell L. Vincent
Roanoke.................Jewell (Joe) Grace
*Roaring Springs .... Joe Thacker
City Mgr., Frances Walters
Robert Lee .... John Q. Conley
City Supt., James Royall
Robinson (111 W. Lyndale, Waco 76706).................... Diane Rendon
*Robstown.................. Hector Gallegos
Roby................................. Cecil J. King
City Mgr., Jimmy C. Price
*Rochester .... Rod Townsend
Rockdale .... Bill T. Avrett
City Mgr., Sue Foster
Rockport..............................Ray O'Brien
City Mgr., M.H. Gildon
Rocksprings .... Mary C. Simone
Rockwall................. George R. Hatfield
City Mgr., Julie Couch
*Rocky Mound (Box 795, Pittsburg 75686)............................ Noble Smith
City Mgr., Vince E. Henry
*Rogers.............................Billy Ray Crow
*Rolling Meadows (105 McKinnon Dr., Kilgore 75662) .. E. N. Roberson
*Rollingwood (403 Nixon Dr., Austin 78746).........Courtland L. Logue Jr.
Roma .... Fernando Peña
City Mgr., Rogelio Salinas
*Roman Forest (Box 397, New Caney 77357)..................Kenneth Corder
*Ropesville .... Byron Mitchell
Roscoe..................John C. Brasuell Jr.
City Mgr., Kevin Tate
Rosebud............. Ernestine Hill-Warren
City Mgr., Wanda Fischer
*Rose City (370 Rose City Dr., Vidor 77662)........... Ruth Vee Dubuisson
*Rose Hill Acres (Box 8285, Lumberton 77711) .... Rayedene Graves
Rosenberg .... Dorothy W. Ryan
City Mgr., Jeff D. Braun
*Ross .... Jim Jaska
*Rosser .... Albert Davis
Rotan .... Jerry Marshall
City Mgr., Harold Sanders
Round Mountain.......... Emmet B. Seals
Round Rock .... Charles Culpepper
City Mgr., Robert L. Bennett Jr.
*Round Top .... Dave Nagel
Rowlett .... Mark C. Enoch
City Mgr., Mike Gibson
Roxton.............................Luther Smith
Royse City................................ Paul Fisk
City Admin., Tommie McBrayer
Rule................. Malcolm Herttenberger
Runaway Bay.....................Clay N. Dent
City Mgr., Mike Evans
Runge .... Dorothy Reasonover
Rusk.................. Emmett H. Whitehead
City Mgr., Brenda Williams
Sabinal .... Reynaldo Rodriguez
*Sachse........................... Larry Holden
City Mgr., Lloyd Henderson
*Sadler ....Janice R. Bullard
Saginaw .... Monte Nichols
City Mgr., Pat Moffatt
St. Hedwig .... Albert (Dutch)Strzelczyk
Saint Jo .... J. C. Donnell
Saint Paul .............................J.H. Treece
*San Angelo .... Dick Funk
City Mgr., Stephen Brown
San Antonio...........William E. Thornton
City Mgr., Alex Biseno
San Augustine................Gertrude Lane
City Mgr., Alton Shaw
*San Benito .... Charles F. Weekley
City Mgr., Richard Torres
Sanctuary (2017 Dorothy Lane, Azle 76020).................. Donald A. Raab
*San Diego...........Alfredo E. Cardenas
City Mgr., José H. Jiménez
San Felipe .... Diana Boring
Sanford.................. Billy Dean Reeves
Sanger................................Nel Armstrong
City Admin., John Hamilton
San Juan .... Arturo Guajardo
City Mgr., Jorge A. Arcaute
San Leanna (Box 1107, Manchaca 78652) ....James E. Payne
*San Marcos.........................Kathy Morris
City Mgr., Larry Gilley
San Patricio (Rt. 2, Box 45, Mathis 78368) .... Lonnie Glasscock III
*San Perlita .... Oscar de Luna
San Saba .... Marcus D. Amthor
City Mgr., Joe Ragsdale
*Sansom Park (5500 Buchanan, Fort Worth 76114)........Merle Easterling
Santa Anna....................... Danny Kellar
City Mgr., Tommy Jackson
*Santa Fe.............. George Willoughby
City Mgr., Vince Di Piazza
Santa Rosa .... Ruben Ochoa Jr.
Savoy .... Clete Stogsdill
Schertz ....Hal Baldwin
City Mgr., Kerry R. Sweatt
Schulenburg .... Leo Kopecky
City Mgr., Ronald Brossmann
*Scotland....................... Robert W. Krahl
*Scottsville.................... Jack Verhalen
*Seabrook .... Larry King
City Mgr., Ronald J. Wicker
Seadrift...............................Mark Daniel
Seagoville.................... Lonnie Hopkins
City Mgr., Odis Lacey
*Seagraves..............Patrick L. McAdoo
Sealy ....Betty Reinbeck
City Mgr., Roger Carlisle
Seguin .... Ed Gotthardt
City Mgr., Jack Hamlett
Selma .... Harold Friesenhahn
Seminole .... Wayne Mixon
City Mgr., Tommy Phillips
Seven Oaks (Rt. 1, Box 833, Livingston 77351)......... Viola Jones
Seven Points .... Marian Hill
Seymour..................................Dick Wirz
Shady Shores (Box 362, Lake Dallas 75065) .... Olive Stephens
Shallowater .... Moe Dozier
Shamrock ........................R.L. Roberts
City Mgr., Johnny Rhodes
Shavano Park (99 Saddletree Rd., San Antonio 78231) .... John Horner
Shenandoah (801 Maplewood, Spring 77381) ....Robert A. Knight
City Admin., Diane Price
Shepherd.......................Frances Shank
Sherman........................ Julie Ellis Starr
City Mgr., Jim Andrews
Shiner .... Arthur T. Ward
Shoreacres (601 Shoreacres Blvd., La Porte 77571) .... Wayne Gamble
Silsbee .... Helen Larsh
City Mgr., Cliff Bowden Jr.
Silverton .... John Bowman
Simonton ....Maurice Berkman
*Sinton...................... José A. Gutierrez
City Mgr., Ron Garrison
*Skellytown......................... Max Owens
Slaton .... Don Kendrick
City Mgr., Mitch Grant
Smiley ....Donald R. Janicek
Smithville................... Vernon Richards
City Mgr., Gerald Decker
*Smyer ....Foy E. Thompson Jr.
Snook .... David Kovar
Snyder .... David Holt
City Mgr., John W. Gayle
Socorro.......................... Rogelio Lozoya
Somerset .... Paul G. Cuellar
Somerville .... Don L. Strickland

City Admin., Lloyd A. Behm
Sonora ....Margaret Cascadden
City Mgr., Kelly Carta
Sour Lake .... Jack Bennett
City Mgr.,(Vacancy)
South Houston ....Don Gaylor
Southlake........................ Gary Fickes
City Mgr., Curtis E. Hawk
Southmayd...........................Billy Kerr
*South Mountain (Rt. 2, Box 298 A, Gatesville 76528) ...... Billy Mayhew
South Padre Island ....Peggy Trahan
City Mgr., James Chisholm
*Southside Place (6309 Edloe, Houston 77005) ..... Ben M. Hurst III
City Mgr., Seth M. Young
Spearman ....Burl Buchanan
City Mgr., Kelvin Knauf
Splendora ....Grace Myers
*Spofford......................... J. B. Herndon
Springlake.................. P.A. Washington
Springtown.................. Thomas Gentry
City Mgr., Scott Albert
Spring Valley (1025 Campbell Rd., Houston 77055) ....Louise T. Richman
Spur .... Glenn T. Williams
Stafford .... Leonard Scarcella
Stagecoach (Box 364, Tomball 77377)...............Daniel K. Donnelly
Stamford ....Louis E. Johnson
City Mgr., Ken Roberson
Stanton ....Lester Baker
City Mgr., Danny Fryar
Star Harbor (P.O. Drawer 949, Malakoff 75148) ......Jack Ferguson
Stephenville ....Lavinia Lohrmann
City Mgr., Don Davis
*Sterling City ....Ross Foster
*Stinnett ................J.F. (Buck) Formby
City Admin., Charlie M. Boyd
Stockdale ....Hubert Tomerlin
City Mgr., Carl Lambeck
*Stratford................ Kenneth Forthman
City Mgr., E.R. Bell
Strawn......................Paul L. Stepen II
Streetman ....Arnold Lewis
Sudan .... Glen D. Cardwell
Sugar Land ....Lee Duggan
City Mgr., David E. Neeley
*Sulphur Springs.... Aubrey Washington
City Mgr., Olen Petty
Sundown..............................V.R. Childress
City Mgr., Dorothy F. Dominguez
Sunnyvale .... Jim Wade
City Mgr., Bob Ewalt
*Sunray ....Dow Brewer
City Mgr., Greg Smith
Sunrise Beach Village.........................
.............................Delores M. Smith
Sunset Valley (2 Lone Oak Trail, Austin 78745)........ Michael Francis
*Sun Valley (Rt. 2, Paris 75460)................Maria Z. Wagnon
Surfside Beach (1304 Monument Dr., Freeport 77541) .... Jack Gibson
Sweeny ....Larry G. Piper
City Mgr., Exa Mae Keller
Sweetwater .... Jay Lawrence
City Mgr., David Maddox
*Taft......................................J.D. Mayo
City Mgr., Mike Rhea
*Tahoka .... Jim Solomon
City Mgr., Barry Pittman
Talco .......................K.M. (Mike) Sloan
Tatum .... Walter N. Mullins Jr.
Taylor ....Donald Hill
City Mgr., Kenneth A. Taylor
Taylor Lake Village (1202 Kirby, Seabrook 77586)....James E. Cumming
Teague ....Jerrell Sartor
City Mgr., J.D. Teague
Tehuacana .... Edward Bounds Trotter
*Temple .... J.W. Perry
City Mgr., David R. Taylor
Tenaha .... George N. Bowers
Terrell .... Don L. Lindsey
City Mgr., Blaine R. Hinds
*Terrell Hills (5100 N. New Braunfels, San Antonio 78209)........................
..........................Barbara B. Christian
City Mgr., Cal D. Johnson
*Texarkana ....John Jarvis
City Mgr., George Shackleford
Texas City ....Charles T. Doyle
Texhoma .... Garland K. Dahl
Texline...........................Doug Antwiler
City Mgr., Bernard Eads
The Colony................Wm. W. Manning
City Mgr., Johnny P. Smith
Thompsons .................G.W. Longserre
Thorndale..................Garry L. Williams
Thornton..........................Wayne Mills
Thorntonville (2414 W. 2nd, Monahans 79756) ....Donald W. McKenzie
*Thrall.................................James Dvorak
Three Rivers .... Louise Shumate
City Admin., M.R. Forehand
*Throckmorton .... John O. Kunkel
Timbercreek Canyon (Rt. 7, Box 4-5, Amarillo 79118) ....Ed Tunnicliff
Timpson .... F.M. Foshee
Tioga .... Bobby Gray
*Tira (Rt. 7, Box 240, Sulphur Springs 75482).......... Coy O. Vicars
Toco (2103 Chestnut, Brookston 75421).............Hugh D. Thompson
*Todd Mission (Rt. 2, Box 650, Plantersville 77363) ..George Coulam
Tolar .... Terry Johnson
Tomball.........................H.G. Harrington
City Mgr., Warren Driver
Tom Bean.............................. Ralph Hall
Tool (Rt. 6, Box 843, Kemp 75143)......................... A.J. Phillips
Toyah ....Charlotte H. Waight
Trent.......................................Jim Wallis
Trenton.........................Richard P. Agan
Trinidad .... Jim Carter
Trinity .... Lyle Stubbs
Trophy Club.............................. Jim Carter
City Mgr., Donna Welsh
Troup.............................. Steve Patterson
City Mgr., Jyl Moose
Troy................ Thomas R. Vanderveer
Tulia .... John C. Emmitt
City Mgr., Bryan Easum
Turkey .... George Colvin
City Mgr., Jerry Landry
Tuscola..........................JC. Phariss Jr.
Tye .... James E. Dean
*Tyler...................... Smith Reynolds Jr.
City Mgr., Ernest Clark
*Uhland .... Dan Sorrels
Uncertain...........................Betty Hines
*Union Grove (Box 1326, Gladewater 75647)............. Randy Lee Simcox
Universal City .... James T. Carroll
City Mgr., Gene Thorpe
University Park (P.O. Box 8005, Dallas 75205).............F.B. Pete Goldman
City Mgr., Bob Livingston
Uvalde............................ George Horner
City Mgr., H.G. (Bert) Lumbreras
*Valentine .... Jesús Calderon
Valley Mills ....Howard Hillin
Valley View............................ Cecil Neu
*Van .... E.L. Raulston
Van Alstyne .... Teddie Ann Salmon
*Van Horn....................... Okey D. Lucas
Vega.......................... Mark J. Groneman
*Venus............................. James A. Flatt
City Mgr., John Daniel
Vernon........................ Jack H. McGann
City Mgr., Paul T. Hawkins
Victoria .... Gary Middleton
City Mgr., Denny L. Arnold
Vidor........................ Lamech N. Wright
City Mgr., Dan Graves
Village of Tiki Island ..... Charles Everts
*Vinton (436 Vinton Rd., Canutillo 79835) .... Samuel Monrreal
*Waco..................J. Robert Sheehy Sr.
City Mgr., Jim Holgersson
Waelder ....Roy Tovar
Wake Village .... Mike Huddleston
Waller .... Danny Marburger
Wallis....................... Tony I. Salazar Jr.
*Walnut Springs.................. Doris Fenn
Warren City (2004 George Richey, Gladewater 75647) H.L. Hearnsberger
Waskom .... Chris C. Miller
Watauga......................Hector F. Garcia
City Mgr., Lee Maness
*Waxahachie .... Mackey Morgan
City Mgr., Bob Sokoll
Weatherford .... Sherry Watson
City Mgr., Kenneth Reneau
Webster........ Fred Stratman (Pro Tem)
City Mgr., James A. (Jim) McFellin
Weimar............................ Bennie Kosler
City Mgr., Francis E. Parks
*Weinert ....Leonard Mahan
Weir.............................. Mervin Walker
Wellington ....Gary Brewer
City Mgr., Jon Sessions
Wellman .... Lynn Hudson Sr.
Wells .... William M. Bailey
*Weslaco ....Eugene A. Braught
City Mgr., Wai-Lin Lam
West ....Russell Willsey
Westbrook ....J. L. Rees
West Columbia .... Robert R. Dixon
City Mgr., Max Pitts
Westlake (3 Village Cr. #207, Roanoke 76262)......... Scott Bradley
West Lake Hills (911 Westlake Dr., Austin 78746).............Tom H. Taylor
City Mgr., Daniel E. Sowada
Westminster ....Richard J. Davis
*Weston................... Kenneth Cowan
West Orange (2700 Austin Ave., Orange 77630) .....Roy C. McDonald
Westover Hills (5824 Merrymount, Ft. Worth 76107).......Earle A. Shields Jr.
City Mgr., B.J. Tuttleton
West Tawakoni (Rt. 1, Box 354, Quinlan 75474)....... Donald Retzlaft
City Admin., Kevin Burke
West University Place (3800 University Blvd., Houston 77005) .... Bill Watson
City Mgr., Mike Tanner
Westworth Village (311 Burton Hill Rd., Ft. Worth 76114) ..Raymond L. Landy
Wharton................Dennis M. Voulgaris
City Mgr., Andres Garza Jr.
Wheeler............................Wanda Herd
*White Deer.........................Tom Stamp
Whiteface .... Mack Ashmore
City Mgr., Syd Albus
Whitehouse .... Mary Elizabeth Pike
City Mgr., Thom Smyser
*White Oak .... Rob Thompson
City Mgr., Ralph J. Weaver
Whitesboro .... Alfred C. Miller
City Mgr., Joe N. West
White Settlement...... James M. Herring
City Mgr., Stuart A. Bach
Whitewright .... Joe Cureton
*Whitney............................ Billy Peacock
Wichita Falls................ Michael L. Lam
City Mgr., James Berzina
Wickett .... Harold Ferguson
Willis......................Ruth Castleschouldt
Willow Park .... William J. Clemens
City Admin., C. Guy Natale

Wills Point .... Bobby Mitchell
City Mgr., C.C. Girdley
*Wilmer .... Billy Widkliffe
Wilson .... Jackie Bishop
Windcrest (8601 Midcrown, San Antonio 78239) .... Joe D. Cochran
Windom .... Bill Roberts
*Windthorst .... Donald J. Frerich
*Winfield.............. James K. Norramore
*Wink .... Edith A. Jones
Winnsboro....................... Jerry Hopper
Winona.................... Carl W. Granberry
Winters...................... Dawson McGuffin
City Mgr., Aref Hassan
Wixon Valley (P.O. Box 105, Kurten 77862) .... Ruby Andrews
Wolfe City................ Ronald H. Wensel
*Wolfforth .... Glen Rasberry
City Admin., Frankie Pittman
Woodbranch (P.O. Box 804, New Caney 77357) .... Dorothy N. Quinn
Woodcreek (P.O. Box 1570, Wimberley 78676) ....Jeannine C. Pool
Woodloch (P.O. Box 1379,Conroe 77385) .... Diane L. Lincoln
Woodsboro.................. Janie M. Daniel
*Woodson .... Bobby Mathiews
Woodville.......................... Billy W. Rose
City Mgr., Donald W. Shaw
*Woodway (P.O. Box 20937, Waco 76702-0937) .... Donald J. Baker
City Mgr., Mark McDaniel
Wortham.............................. F.B. Covert
Wylie .... Jim Swartz
City Mgr., (Vacancy)
Yantis .... Colleen Nolen
*Yoakum .... M. W. Harbus Jr.
City Mgr., William H. Lewis
Yorktown........................ Eugene Czaja
*Zavalla .... Opal C. Gant

Home-Rule Cities

The 284 home-rule cities of Texas are listed below, as reported by the cities themselves May 1995. No response was received from those marked by an asterisk (*).

City	Present Form of Government	Present Form Adopted	First Charter
*Abilene	Council-Mgr.	1981	1911
Addison	Council-Mgr.	1993	1978
Alamo	Council-Mgr.	1992	1979
*Alamo Heights	Mayor-Aldermen	1954	1954
Alice	Council-Mgr.	1981	1949
Allen	Council-Mgr.	1995	1979
*Alpine	Council-Mgr.	1993	1993
*Alvin	Council-Mgr.	1990	1963
Amarillo	Commission-Mgr.	1913	1913
Andrews	Council-Mgr.	1959	1959
Angleton	Council-Mgr.	1991	1967
Anson	Council-Mgr.	1939	1939
Aransas Pass	Mayor-Council	1986	1979
*Arlington	Council-Mgr.	1990	1920
*Athens	Council-Mgr.	1956	1956
Atlanta	Mayor-Council	1992	1968
Austin	Council-Mgr.	1994	1919
Azle	Council-Mgr.	1990	1971
Ballinger	Mayor-Council	1993	1963
Bay City	Mayor-Council	1991	1989
*Baytown	Council-Mgr.	1948	1948
Beaumont	Council-Mgr.	1986	1947
Bedford	Mayor-Mgr.	1977	1966
Beeville	Council-Mgr.	1974	1953
Bellaire	Council-Mgr.	1987	1947
Bellmead	Council-Mgr.	1962	1954
Belton	Council-Mgr.	1990	1951
*Benbrook	Council-Mgr.	1990	1983
Big Spring	Council-Mgr.	1992	1926
*Bonham	Commission-Mgr.	1947	1914
Borger	Council-Mgr.	1988	1930
Bowie	Mayor-Council	1984	1984
Brady	Council-Mgr.	1993	1982
Breckenridge	Commission-Mgr.	1988	1954
Brenham	Council-Mgr.	1976	1920
Bridge City	Council-Mgr.	1993	1974
Brownfield	Council-Mgr.	1954	1954
Brownsville	Commission-Mgr.	1915	1915
Brownwood	Council-Mgr.	1980	1955
Bryan	Council-Mgr.	1994	1941
Burkburnett	Council-Mgr.	1967	1923
Burleson	Council-Mgr.	1982	1969
Cameron	Mayor-Council	1980	1956
*Canyon	Commission-Mgr.	1959	1959
Carrollton	Council-Mgr.	1992	1963
Carthage	Commission-Mgr.	1949	1949
*Cedar Hill	Council-Mgr.	1975	1975
*Cedar Park	Council-Mgr.	1987	1987
Center	Council-Mgr.	1984	1984
Childress	Council-Mgr.	1917	1917
Cisco	Council-Mgr.	1974	1919
Cleburne	Council-Mgr.	1950	1914
Cleveland	Council-Mgr.	1993	1981
Clute	Council-Mgr.	1993	1976
*Coleman	Council-Mgr.	1950	1950
College Station	Council-Mgr.	1992	1952
Colleyville	Council-Mgr.	1992	1977
Colorado City	Council-Mgr.	1983	1948
Commerce	Council-Mgr.	1954	1954
Conroe	Mayor-Council	1992	1965
Converse	Council-Mgr.	1984	1981
Coppell	Council-Mgr.	1991	1986
Copperas Cove	Council-Mgr.	1979	1979
*Corpus Christi	Council-Mgr.	1993	1926
Corsicana	Commission-Mgr.	1990	1917
Crockett	Council-Mgr.	1964	1964
Crystal City	Council-Mgr.	1986	1958
Cuero	Council-Mgr.	1993	1944
Daingerfield	Council-Mgr.	1980	1980
Dalhart	Council-Mgr.	1979	1960
Dallas	Council-Mgr.	1907	1889
*Dayton	Council-Mgr.	1992	1976
Deer Park	Council-Mgr.	1981	1960
De Leon	Mayor-Council	1994	1919
Del Rio	Council-Mgr.	1968	1967
Denison	Council-Mgr.	1984	1975
Denton	Council-Mgr.	NA	1959
*Denver City	Council-Mgr.	1985	1985
DeSoto	Council-Mgr.	1995	1969
Dickinson	Mayor-Council	1987	1987
Dimmitt	Council-Mgr.	1989	1989
Donna	Council-Mgr.	1981	1957
*Dumas	Commission-Mgr.	1991	1965
*Duncanville	Council-Mgr.	1984	1962
Eagle Pass	Council-Mgr.	1964	1964
Eastland	Commission-Mgr.	1923	1919
Edinburg	Council-Mgr.	1949	1919
Edna	Council-Mgr.	1984	1966
El Campo	Council-Mgr.	1993	1954
Electra	Mayor-Council	1988	1917
Elgin	Council-Mgr.	1993	1985
El Paso	Mayor-Council	1907	1873
Ennis	Commission-Mgr.	1981	1913
Euless	Council-Mgr.	1995	1962
Everman	Council-Mgr.	1986	1986
Farmers Branch	Council-Mgr.	1989	1956
Flower Mound	Council-Mgr.	1989	1981
*Forest Hill	Council-Mgr.	1976	1976
Fort Worth	Council-Mgr.	1985	1924
Fredericksburg	Council-Mgr.	1991	1991
Freeport	Council-Mgr.	1994	1969
Friendswood	Council-Mgr.	1993	1971
Frisco	Council-Mgr.	1987	1987
Gainesville	Council-Mgr.	1994	1933
*Galena Park	Mayor-Council	1975	1946
Galveston	Council-Mgr.	1991	1982
Garland	Council-Mgr.	1994	1951
Gatesville	Council-Mgr.	1968	1968

City	Present Form of Government	Present Form Adopted	First Charter
Georgetown	Council-Mgr.	1969	1969
George West	Mayor-Council	1980	1980
Giddings	Council-Mgr.	1984	1982
Gladewater	Council-Mgr.	1985	1955
*Glenn Heights	Council-Mgr.	1987	1987
Gonzales	Council-Mgr.	1957	1957
Gorman	Mayor-Commission	1922	1920
Graham	Council-Mgr.	1928	1928
Granbury	Council-Mgr.	1989	1989
Grand Prairie	Council-Mgr.	1987	1948
Grapevine	Council-Mgr.	1992	1965
Greenville	Council-Mgr.	1992	1952
Groves	Council-Mgr.	1977	1953
Haltom City	Council-Mgr.	1989	1955
Harker Heights	Council-Mgr.	1991	1971
*Harlingen	Commission-Mgr.	1987	1927
Hearne	Council-Mgr.	1964	1964
Henderson	Council-Mgr.	1947	1947
Hereford	Commission-Mgr.	1952	1952
*Hewitt	Council-Mgr.	1982	1982
Hidalgo	Council-Mgr.	1995	1995
*Highland Park	Council-Mgr.	1974	1974
Highland Village	Council-Mgr.	1990	1986
Hillsboro	Council-Mgr.	1981	1950
Hitchcock	Mayor-Council	1960	1960
Houston	Mayor-Council	1994	1905
Humble	Mayor-Council	1991	1970
Huntsville	Council-Mgr.	1992	1968
Hurst	Council-Mgr.	1992	1956
*Ingleside	Council-Mgr.	1979	1979
Irving	Council-Mgr.	1989	1952
Jacinto City	Council-Mgr.	1987	1981
Jacksonville	Council-Mgr.	1954	1931
Jasper	Council-Mgr.	1964	1964
Jersey Village	Council-Mgr.	1993	1986
Katy	Aldermen-Admin.	1993	1981
Kaufman	Council-Mgr.	1988	1987
Keller	Council-Mgr.	1985	1982
Kermit	Council-Mgr.	1989	1989
Kerrville	Council-Mgr.	1942	1942
Kilgore	Commission-Mgr.	1960	1960
Killeen	Council-Mgr.	1994	1948
Kingsville	Commission-Mgr.	1986	1913
Kirby	Council-Mgr.	1994	1988
La Feria	Commission-Mgr.	1989	1914
*La Grange	Council-Mgr.	1983	1983
*Lake Jackson	Council-Mgr.	1992	1958
Lakeway	Council-Mgr.	1994	1990
Lake Worth	Mayor-Council	1965	1965
La Marque	Council-Mgr.	1985	1953
Lamesa	Council-Mgr.	1972	1945
Lampasas	Council-Mgr.	1986	1986
Lancaster	Council-Mgr.	1974	1956
La Porte	Council-Mgr.	1980	1980
Laredo	Council-Mgr.	1982	1921
League City	Mayor-Council	1962	1962
Levelland	Mayor-Council	1992	1949
Lewisville	Council-Mgr.	1992	1963
Liberty	Council-Mgr.	1958	1958
Littlefield	Council-Mgr.	1995	1959
Live Oak	Council-Mgr.	1990	1976
Lockhart	Council-Mgr.	1990	1973
*Longview	Council-Mgr.	1979	1943
Lubbock	Council-Mgr.	1988	1917
Lufkin	Commission-Mgr.	1994	1919
Luling	Council-Mgr.	1977	1977
Mansfield	Council-Mgr.	1975	1975
*Marble Falls	Council-Mgr.	1986	1986
*Marlin	Council-Mgr.	1977	1915
Marshall	Council-Mgr.	1958	1909
McAllen	Commission-Mgr.	1980	1927
McGregor	Council-Mgr.	1989	1979
McKinney	Council-Mgr.	1988	1959

City	Present Form of Government	Present Form Adopted	First Charter
*Mercedes	Commission-Mgr.	1973	1971
Mesquite	Council-Mgr.	1987	1953
Mexia	Commission-Mgr.	1924	1924
Midland	Council-Mgr.	1940	1940
Midlothian	Council-Mgr.	1980	1980
Mineral Wells	Council-Mgr.	1966	1966
Mission	Council-Mgr.	1987	1961
Missouri City	Council-Mgr.	1992	1974
*Monahans	Council-Mgr.	1954	1954
Mount Pleasant	Council-Mgr.	1948	1948
Muleshoe	Council-Mgr.	1960	1960
Nacogdoches	Commission-Mgr.	1988	1929
*Nassau Bay	Council-Mgr.	1989	1973
Navasota	Council-Mgr.	1947	1927
Nederland	Council-Mgr.	1977	1955
New Braunfels	Council-Mgr.	1995	1964
*No. Richland Hills	Council-Mgr.	1989	1963
Odessa	Council-Mgr.	1991	1945
Olney	Mayor-Council	1979	1979
Orange	Council-Mgr.	1986	1960
*Palestine	Council-Mgr.	1983	1871
Pampa	Commission-Mgr.	1982	1927
Paris	Council-Mgr.	1948	1948
Pasadena	Mayor-Council	1992	1943
Pearland	Council-Mgr.	1994	1971
Pearsall	Council-Mgr.	1994	1994
Pecos	Council-Mgr.	1985	1983
Pharr	Commission-Mgr.	1982	1949
Plainview	Council-Mgr.	1920	1907
Plano	Council-Mgr.	1993	1961
Pleasanton	Council-Mgr.	1995	1982
Port Aransas	Council-Mgr.	1995	1978
Port Arthur	Council-Mgr.	1992	1930
*Port Isabel	Commission-Mgr.	1985	1985
Portland	Council-Mgr.	1987	1967
*Port Lavaca	Mayor-Council	1972	1956
Port Neches	Council-Mgr.	1980	1955
*Quanah	Council-Mgr.	1919	1919
*Ranger	Mayor-Council	1919	1919
Raymondville	Commission-Mgr.	1955	1955
Richardson	Council-Mgr.	1989	1954
Richland Hills	Council-Mgr.	1995	1986
*River Oaks	Mayor-Council	1949	1949
*Robstown	Mayor-Council	1948	1948
Rockdale	Council-Mgr.	1978	1978
Rockport	Council-Mgr.	1994	1983
Rockwall	Council-Mgr.	1993	1985
Rosenberg	Council-Mgr.	1986	1956
Round Rock	Council-Mgr.	1986	1977
Rowlett	Council-Mgr.	1991	1979
Rusk	Council-Mgr.	1987	1987
*Sachse	Council-Mgr.	1988	1986
Saginaw	Council-Mgr.	1988	1988
*San Angelo	Council-Mgr.	1915	1915
*San Antonio	Council-Mgr.	1951	1914
*San Benito	Council-Mgr.	1969	1969
San Juan	Council-Mgr.	1975	1975
*San Marcos	Council-Mgr.	1992	1970
*Santa Fe	Council-Mgr.	1978	1978
Schertz	Council-Mgr.	1994	1974
*Seabrook	Council-Mgr.	1979	1979
Seagoville	Council-Mgr.	1991	1969
Seguin	Council-Mgr.	1993	1971
Seminole	Council-Mgr.	1995	1991
Sherman	Council-Mgr.	1993	1915
Silsbee	Council-Mgr.	1985	1937
Sinton	Council-Mgr.	1966	1966
Slaton	Mayor-Council	1978	1929
Snyder	Council-Mgr.	1989	1952
Southlake	Council-Mgr.	1995	1987
Stamford	Council-Mgr.	1918	1918
Stephenville	Council-Mgr.	1961	1961
Sugar Land	Council-Mgr.	1990	1979

City	Present Form of Government	Present Form Adopted	First Charter
*Sulphur Springs	Council-Mgr.	1983	1947
Sweetwater	Commission-Mgr.	1956	1927
Taylor	Commission-Mgr.	1988	1914
Temple	Council-Mgr.	1990	1922
Terrell	Council-Mgr.	1973	1913
*Terrell Hills	Council-Mgr.	1992	1957
*Texarkana	Council-Mgr.	1969	1943
Texas City	Mayor-Commission	1946	1946
The Colony	Council-Mgr.	1986	1979
Tomball	Council-Mgr.	1995	1987
Tulia	Council-Mgr.	1972	1972
*Tyler	Council-Mgr.	1937	1937
Universal City	Council-Mgr.	1989	1972
University Park	Council-Mgr.	1989	1924
Uvalde	Council-Mgr.	1951	1934
Vernon	Commission-Mgr.	1962	1921
Victoria	Council-Mgr.	1994	1957
Vidor	Mayor-Council	1969	1969
*Waco	Council-Mgr.	1958	1913
Watauga	Mayor-Council	1994	1980
*Waxahachie	Council-Mgr.	1971	1971
Weatherford	Mayor-Council	1983	1918
*Weslaco	Council-Mgr.	1927	1927
West Orange	Mayor-Aldermen	1954	1954
W. University Place	Council-Mgr.	1983	1983
White Settlement	Council-Mgr.	1991	1954
Wichita Falls	Council-Mgr.	1953	1953
*Woodway	Council-Mgr.	1973	1973
Wylie	Council-Mgr.	1992	1985
*Yoakum	Council-Mgr.	1915	1915

Is It One Word or Two?

These Texas county and city names are often misspelled. Some that are two words are spelled as one, and vice versa. The spellings below were verified by the county clerk or city secretary of the county or town:

Counties

DeWitt
La Salle

Cities

De Kalb
De Leon
DeSoto
La Coste
La Grange
La Marque
La Porte
LaSalle
La Vernia
La Ward
Sugar Land

Texas Main Street Project

To encourage Texas cities to rehabilitate and reuse existing historic buildings, the Texas Historical Commission established the Texas Main Street Project in 1981.

The project is primarily a technical assistance program. Each year, several towns, or neighborhoods within large cities, are designated Main Street cities.

Each designated city/neighborhood hires a Main Street manager to coordinate its project. The Texas Main Street Project office provides architectural-design assistance, as well as supervision for the Main Street manager.

Since 1986, when San Marcos joined the Main Street Project, $16 million in private-sector money has been invested in their downtown area. One side of the renovated historic courthouse square is shown above.

Each city receives a three-day visit by a team of professional consultants, who provide immediate and long-term suggestions for the community's revitalization. Other state agencies, including the Texas Department of Commerce, the Texas Department of Housing and Community Affairs and the Governor's Office, provide additional assistance.

Cities that are not officially designated, but that wish to begin a revitalization program on their own following Main Street guidelines, are called self-initiated cities.

Following is a list of Texas Main Street cities/neighborhoods as of spring 1995, grouped by year of designation. An asterisk before the name denotes a city no longer active in the program. Self-initiated cities are listed last.

1981: *Eagle Pass, Hillsboro, *Navasota, Plainview, *Seguin. **1982:** *Gainesville, Georgetown, *Kingsville, *Marshall, *McKinney. **1983:** *Brenham, *Harlingen, Lufkin, *Stamford, *Waxahachie. **1984:** *Belton, *Brownwood, *Ennis, *Goliad, *Paris. **1985:** Corsicana, *Cuero, *Lampasas, *Mineral Wells, *Sweetwater. **1986:** *Greenville, *Palestine, *Pampa, Pittsburg, San Marcos. **1987:** *Kilgore, Post, *Terrell, Weatherford, *Wharton. **1988:** *Center, *Daingerfield, Gonzales, *Henderson, Longview, *Temple. **1989:** Denison, Fort Stockton, Mineola, Sulphur Springs, Yoakum. **1990:** Athens, Denton, El Campo, Elgin, Jasper, Tyler. **1991:** *Abilene, Angleton, Glen Rose, Jefferson Avenue/Dallas, Market Square/Houston, New Braunfels, Odessa. **1992:** Bay City, Cleburne, McGregor, Mission, Mount Vernon. **1993:** Dallas City Center, Littlefield, Mount Pleasant, Sherman, Van Alstyne. **1994:** Decatur, Graham, Lancaster, Marlin, Sonora and Martin Luther King Boulevard/Dallas. **1995:** Alpine, Bonham, Clifton, Kerrville and Rusk, plus Irving's commercial district.

Self-initiated cities for 1995 include Duncanville, Olton, Royse City and Whitesboro. ☆

County Tax Appraisers

The following list of Chief Appraisers for Texas counties was furnished by the ***State Property Tax Division of the State Comptroller's office.*** *It includes the mailing address for each appraiser and is current to March 1, 1995.*

Anderson—R. Cliff Wooten, Box 279, Palestine 75802
Andrews—Mickey Green, 600 N. Main, Andrews 79714
Angelina—Charles Stone, Box 2357, Lufkin 75902
Aransas—Jad Smith, 601 S. Church, Rockport 78382
Archer—Edward H. Trigg III, Box 1141, Archer City 76351
Armstrong—Ron Patterson, Drawer 835, Claude 79019
Atascosa—Vernon A. Warren, Box 139, Poteet 78065
Austin—Glen Whitehead, 5 E. Main, Bellville 77418
Bailey—Kaye Elliott, 104 E. Ave. C, Muleshoe 79347
Bandera—P. H. Coates IV, Box 1119, Bandera 78003
Bastrop—Dana Ripley, Drawer 578, Bastrop 78602
Baylor—Grady Hicks, 101 S. Washington, Seymour 76380
Bee—Blaine Luthringer, Box 1262, Beeville 78104
Bell—Mike Watson, Box 390, Belton 76513
Bexar—Walter Stoneham, Box 830248, San Antonio 78283
Blanco—Ms. Hollis Boatright, Box 338, Johnson City 78636
Borden—Royale D. Lewis, Box 298, Gail 79738
Bosque—F. Janice Henry, Box 393, Meridian 76665
Bowie—Wayne Hawkins, Box 6527, Texarkana 75505
Brazoria—Jack Simmons, 500 N. Chenango, Angleton 77515
Brazos—Gerald L. Winn, 1673 Briarcrest Dr., #A-101, Bryan 77802
Brewster—Jerry Ratcliff, Box 1231, Alpine 79831
Briscoe—Carlye Fleming, Box 728, Silverton 79257
Brooks—Humberto Rivera, Drawer A, Falfurrias 78355
Brown—Doran E. Lemke, 403 Fisk, Brownwood 76801
Burleson—Elizabeth Plagens, Box 1000, Caldwell 77836
Burnet—Stan Hemphill, Drawer E, Burnet 78611
Caldwell—Russell Sanders, Box 59, Lockhart 78644
Calhoun—Andrew J. Hahn, Box 48, Port Lavaca 77979
Callahan—Rodney Lewallen, Box 806, Baird 79504
Cameron—mike Amezquita, Box 1010, San Benito 78586
Camp—Vaudene Bennett, Box 739, Pittsburg 75686
Carson—Donita Herber, Box 970, Panhandle 79068
Cass—Janelle Clements, Box 1150, Linden 75563
Castro—Jerry Heller, 204 S.E. 3rd (Rear), Dimmitt 79027
Chambers—Michael Fregia, Box 1520, Anahuac 77514
Cherokee—Sid R. Danner, Box 494, Rusk 75785
Childress—Nadine Parr, Box 13, Childress 79201
Clay—A. G. Reis, 101 E. Omega, Henrietta 76365
Cochran—H. Loy Kern, 109 S.E. 1st, Morton 79346
Coke—Patsy N. Dunn, Box 2, Robert Lee 76945
Coleman—Bill N. Jones, Box 914, Coleman 76834
Collin—Jimmie Honea, 1024 S. Greenville, #120, Allen 75002
Collingsworth—Ann Wauer, Courthouse 1st Floor, Rm. 4, Wellington 79095
Colorado—William Youens Jr., Box 10, Columbus 78934
Comal—Lynn Rodgers, Box 311222, New Braunfels 78131
Comanche—Clay Fowler, Box 6, Comanche 76442
Concho—Eugene Dillard, Box 68, Paint Rock 76866
Cooke—Robert Lewis, 200 W. California, Gainesville 76240
Coryell—Darrell Lisenbe, Box 142, Gatesville 76528
Cottle—Rue Young, Box 459, Paducah 79248
Crane—Peggy Dickson, 511 West 8th, Crane 79731
Crockett—W. Tom Stokes, Drawer H, Ozona 76943
Crosby—Darla Doss, Box 479, Crosbyton 79322
Culberson—Sally Carrasco, Box 550, Van Horn 79855
Dallam—Huie V. Stanley, Box 592, Dalhart 79022
Dallas—Foy Mitchell Jr., 2949 N. Stemmons Frwy., Dallas 75247
Dawson—Tom Anderson, Box 797, Lamesa 79331
Deaf Smith—Fred Fox, Box 2298, Hereford 79045
Delta—Toyce Phillips, Box 47, Cooper 75432
Denton—Joe Rogers, Box 2816, Denton 76201
DeWitt—John Haliburton, Box 4, Cuero 77954
Dickens—Jerrie Ballard, Box 119, Dickens 79229
Dimmit—Rufino Lozano, 402 N. 7th, Carrizo Springs 78834
Donley—Paula Lowrie, Box 1220, Clarendon 79226
Duval—Ernesto Molina Jr., Box 809, San Diego 78384
Eastland—Steve Thomas, Box 914, Eastland 76448
Ector—James Goodwin, 1301 E. 8th, Odessa 79761
Edwards—Teresa Sweeten, Box 378, Rocksprings 78880
Ellis—Richard Rhodes, Box 878, Waxahachie 75165
El Paso—Cora Viescas, 1720 Murchison, El Paso 79902
Erath—Jerry Lee, Box 94, Stephenville 76401
Falls—Joyce Collier, Drawer 430, Marlin 76661
Fannin—Carrol Garrison, 920 N. Center, Bonham 75418
Fayette—Kathleen Stewart, Box 836, La Grange 78945
Fisher—Betty Mize, Box 516, Roby 79543
Floyd—Sheila Faulkenberry, Box 249, Floydada 79236
Foard—Jo Ann Vecera, Box 419, Crowell 79227
Fort Bend—Gene Brewer, 12946 Dairy Ashford Rd., #100, Sugar Land 77478
Franklin—Edward Morrow, Box 720, Mount Vernon 75457
Freestone—Sherrill Minze, Box 675, Fairfield 75840
Frio—Irma Gonzalez, Box 1129, Pearsall 78061
Gaines—Betty Caudle, Box 490, Seminole 79360
Galveston—Ken Wright, Box 3647, Texas City 77592
Garza—Billie Windham, Drawer F, Post 79356
Gillespie—Olan Tisdale, Box 429, Fredericksburg 78624
Glasscock—Royce Pruit, Box 89, Garden City 79739
Goliad—E. J. Bammert, Box 34, Goliad 77963
Gonzales—Glenda Strackbein, Box 867, Gonzales 78629
Gray—W. Pat Bagley, Box 836, Pampa 79066
Grayson—Robert Tollison, 205 N. Travis, Sherman 75090
Gregg—Bill Carroll, Box 6700, Longview 75608
Grimes—Bill Sullivan, Box 489, Anderson 77830
Guadalupe—Pat Fox, 3000 N. Austin, Seguin 78155
Hale—Linda Jaynes, Box 29, Plainview 79073
Hall—Jack Scott, 721 Robertson, Memphis 79245
Hamilton—Doyle Roberts, 119 E. Henry, Hamilton 76531
Hansford—Alice Peddy, Box 519, Spearman 79081
Hardeman—Twila Butler, Box 388, Quanah 79252
Hardin—Edwin Barry, Box 670, Kountze 77625
Harris—Jim Robinson, Box 920975, Houston 77292
Harrison—David Whitmire, Box 818, Marshall 75671
Hartley—Donna Bryant, Box 405, Hartley 79044
Haskell—Jamie Weaver, Box 467, Haskell 79521
Hays—William Cassidy, 21001 N. IH-35, Kyle 78640
Hemphill—James McCarley, Box 65, Canadian 79014
Henderson—Bill Jackson (Interim), Box 430, Athens 75751
Hidalgo—Daniel Boone, Box 632, Pharr 78577
Hill—Shirley Holub, Box 416, Hillsboro 76645
Hockley—Nick Williams, Box 1090, Levelland 79336
Hood—Harold Chestnut, Box 819, Granbury 76048
Hopkins—William Sherman, 109 College St., Sulphur Springs 75483
Houston—Kathryn Keith, Box 112, Crockett 75835
Howard—Keith Toomire, Box 1151, Big Spring 79721
Hudspeth—John Ferrell, Box 429, Sierra Blanca 79851
Hunt—Mildred Colmpton, Box 1339, Greenville 75403
Hutchinson—George Nies, Box 5065, Borger 79008
Irion—Frances Grice, Box 980, Mertzon 76941
Jack—Gary Zeitler, Box 958, Jacksboro 76058
Jackson—James Surratt, 112 E. Main, Edna 77957
Jasper—David Luther, Box 1300, Jasper 75951
Jeff Davis—John Ferrell, Box 373, Fort Davis 79734
Jefferson—Roland Bieber, Box 1470, Groves 77619
Jim Hogg—Lowson Bolton, Box 459, Hebbronville 78361
Jim Wells—Sidney Vela, Box 607, Alice 78333
Johnson—Don Gilmore, 109 N. Main, Cleburne 76031
Jones—Susan Holloway, Box 348, Anson 79501
Karnes—Oscar Caballero, 120 W. Calvert, Karnes City 78118
Kaufman—Jackie Self, Box 819, Kaufman 75142
Kendall—Mick Mikulenka, Box 788, Boerne 78006
Kenedy—Clyde Hamilton Jr., Box 705, Bastrop 78602
Kent—Garth Gregory, Box 68, Jayton 79528
Kerr—David Oehler, Box 1885, Kerrville 78029
Kimble—Paul Bierschwale, Box 307, Junction 76849
King—Sandy Burkett, Box 117, Guthrie 79236
Kinney—Marcus Tidwell, Box 1377, Brackettville 78832
Kleberg—Tina Loera, Box 1027, Kingsville 78364
Knox—Stanton Brown, Box 47, Benjamin 79505
Lamar—Joe Welch, Box 400, Paris 75461
Lamb—Vaughn McKee, Box 950, Littlefield 79339
Lampasas—Tom Watson, Box 175, Lampasas 76550

Lipscomb—Jerry Reynolds, Box 128, Darrouzett 79024
Live Oak—Robert Dirks, Box MM, George West 78022
Llano—Bill Stewart, Box 608, Llano 78643
Loving—J. W. Busby, Box 351, Mentone 79754
Lubbock—Dave Kimbrough, Box 10542, Lubbock 79408
Lynn—Dovie Miller, Box 789, Tahoka 79373
Madison—Dan Singletary, Box 1328, Madisonville 77864
Marion—Brenda Keith, Box 690, Jefferson 75657
Martin—Delbert Dickinson, Box 1349, Stanton 79782
Mason—Deborah Geistweidt, Drawer 1119, Mason 76856
Matagorda—Vince Maloney, Box 179, Bay City 77404
Maverick—Victor Perry, Box 2628, Eagle Pass 78853
McCulloch—Orlando Rubio, 104 N. College, Brady 76825
McLennan—Charles Gauer, Box 2297, Waco 76703
McMullen—Donald Haynes, Box 38, Tilden 78072
Medina—James Garcia, 1410 Ave. K, Hondo 78861
Menard—Margaret Cannon, Box 1058, Menard 76859
Midland—Ron Stegall, Box 908002, Midland 79708
Milam—Patricia Moraw, Box 769, Cameron 76520
Mills—Cynthia Partin, Box 565, Goldthwaite 76844
Mitchell—Clarence Burt, Box 358, Colorado City 79512
Montague—Wanda Russell, Box 121, Montague 76251
Montgomery—Jimmy Foreman, Box 2233, Conroe 77305
Moore—Joyce Cearley, Box 717, Dumas 79029
Morris—Rhonda Hall, Box 563, Daingerfield 75638
Motley—Brenda Osborn, Box 779, Matador 79244
Nacogdoches—Gary Woods, 216 W. Hospital, Nacogdoches 75961
Navarro—Harry Hudson, Box 3118, Corsicana 75151
Newton—Margie Herrin, Drawer X, Newton 75966
Nolan—Ms. Pat Davis, Box 1256, Sweetwater 79556
Nueces—George Moff, 201 N. Chaparral, Corpus Christi 78401
Ochiltree—Terry Symons, 825 S. Main, #100, Perryton 79070
Oldham—Jen Carter, Drawer 310, Vega 79092
Orange—Ms. Pat Sanderson, Box 457, Orange 77630
Palo Pinto—Carol Holmes, Box 250, Palo Pinto 76484
Panola—John Pepper, 2 Ball Park Rd., Carthage 75633
Parker—Larry Hammonds, 118 W. Columbia, Weatherford 76086
Parmer—Ron Proctor, Box 56, Bovina 79009
Pecos—John Oglesby, Box 237, Fort Stockton 79735
Polk—Clyde Arrendell, 312 N. Washington, Livingston 77351
Potter—Jim Childers, Box 7190, Amarillo 79114
Presidio—Irma Salgado, Box 879, Marfa 79843
Rains—Loudele Dowdy, Box 70, Emory 75440
Randall—Jim Childers, Box 7190, Amarillo 79114
Reagan—Byron Bitner, Box8, Big Lake 76932
Real—Ruth Sanderlin, Box 158, Leakey 78873
Red River—Betty Parker, Box 461, Clarksville 75426
Reeves—Carol King Markham, Box 1229, Pecos 79772
Refugio—Bettye Kret, Box 156, Refugio 78377
Roberts—Carol Billingsley, Box 476, Miami 79059
Robertson—Dan Brewer, Box 998, Franklin 77856
Rockwall—Ray Helm, 106 N. San Jacinto, Rockwall 75087
Runnels—Gene Stewart, Box 524, Ballinger 76821
Rusk—Melvin Cooper, Box 7, Henderson 75653
Sabine—Jim Nethery, Box 137, Hemphill 75948
San Augustine—Jamie Doherty, 122 N. Harrison, San Augustine 75972
San Jacinto—Mac Ridley, Box 1170, Coldspring 77331
San Patricio—Kathryn Vermillion, Box 938, Sinton 78387
San Saba—Dave Davenport, 423 E. Wallace, San Saba 76877
Schleicher—Ray Ballew, Box 936, Eldorado 76936
Scurry—L. R. Peveler, 2612 College Ave., Snyder 79549
Shackelford—Bruce Bailey, Box 565, Albany 76430
Shelby—Harold Robertson, 5907 Loop 500, Center 75935
Sherman—Teresa Edmond, Box 239, Stratford 79084
Smith—Michael Barnett, 245 South S.E. Loop 323, Tyler 75702
Somervell—Sandra Montgomery, Box 747, Glen Rose 76043
Starr—José Jaime Treviño, Box 137, Rio Grande City 78582
Stephens—Troy Sloan, Box 351, Breckenridge 76424
Sterling—Linda Low, Box 28, Sterling City 76951
Stonewall—Stacey Meador, Box 308, Aspermont 79502
Sutton—Rex Ann Friess, 300 E. Oak, Sonora 76950
Swisher—Rose Lee Powell, Box 8, Tulia 79088
Tarrant—John Marshall, 2315 Gravel Rd., Fort Worth 76118
Taylor—Richard Petree, Box 1800, Abilene 79604
Terrell—Blain Chriesman, Box 747, Sanderson 79848
Terry—Ronny Burran, Box 426, Brownfield 79316
Throckmorton—Ruby Dunlap, Box 788, Throckmorton 76483
Titus—Lois McKibben, Box 528, Mount Pleasant 75456
Tom Green—Elvin Field, Box 3307, San Angelo 76902
Travis—Art Cory, Box 149012, Austin 78714
Trinity—Allen McKinley, Box 950, Groveton 75845
Tyler—Travis Chalmers, Drawer 9, Woodville 75979
Upshur—Louise Stracener, Box 280, Gilmer 75644
Upton—Jo Beth Wright, Box 1110, McCamey 79752
Uvalde—Brownie Jones, 209 N. High, Uvalde 78801
Val Verde—Buster Vernor, Box 1059, Del Rio 78841
Van Zandt—Ron Groom, Box 926, Canton 75103
Victoria—Marvin Hahn, 1611 E. North, Victoria 77901
Walker—Grover Cook, Box 1798, Huntsville 77342
Waller—David Piwonka, Box 159, Katy 77492
Ward—Arlice Wittie, Box 905, Monahans 79756
Washington—Charles Gaskamp, Box 681, Brenham 77834
Webb—Leta Schlinke, Box 719, Laredo 78042
Wharton—Larry Holub, Box 1068, Wharton 77488
Wheeler—Larry Schoenhals, Box 1200, Wheeler 79096
Wichita—Lanier Wilson, Box 5172, Wichita Falls 76307
Wilbarger—Doyle Graham, Box 1519, Vernon 76384
Willacy—Augustin Colchado, Rt. 2, Box 256, Raymondville 78580
Williamson—Donna Moff, Box 1120, Georgetown 78627
Wilson—Louis Wall, Box 849, Floresville 78114
Winkler—Helen Oldham, Box 1219, Kermit 79745
Wise—Mickey Hand, 206 S. State, Decatur 76234
Wood—Carson Wages, Box 951, Quitman 75783
Yoakum—Saundra Stephens, Box 748, Plains 79355
Young—Pat Butler, Box 337, Graham 76450
Zapata—Rosalva Dominguez, Box 2315, Zapata 78076
Zavala—Richard Diaz, 323 W. Zavala, Crystal City 78839 ☆

Wet-Dry Counties

When approved in local-option elections in "wet" precincts of counties, sale of **liquor by the drink** is permitted in Texas. This resulted from adoption of an amendment to the Texas Constitution in 1970 and subsequent legislation, followed by local-option elections. This amendment marked the first time in 50 years that the sale of liquor by the drink was legal in Texas.

The list below shows the wet-or-dry status of counties in Texas as of Aug 31, 1994. A dagger (†) indicates counties in which the sale of mixed beverages is legal in all or part of the county (96). An asterisk (*) indicates counties wholly wet (37). All others are dry in part (79).

Counties in Which Distilled Spirits Are Legal (185): Anderson, †*Aransas, Archer, Atascosa, †*Austin, †Bandera, *Bastrop, †*Bee, †Bell, †*Bexar, †Blanco, Bosque, †Brazoria, †*Brazos, †*Brewster, Brooks, Brown, Burleson, †Burnet, †Calhoun, Callahan, †*Cameron, †Camp, Carson, Cass, Castro, Chambers, Childress, Clay, Coleman, Collin, †*Colorado, †*Comal, Comanche, Cooke, Coryell, Crane, *Crockett, *Culberson, Dallam, †Dallas, †Dawson, Deaf Smith, †Denton, †DeWitt, Dickens, †Dimmit, †Donley, †*Duval, Eastland, †Ector, Edwards, Ellis, †*El Paso, †Falls, Fannin, Fayette, †*Fort Bend, †Frio, †Galveston, Garza, †Gillespie, †Goliad, Gonzales, Gray, Grayson, Gregg, †Grimes, †Guadalupe, Hall, Hamilton, Hardin, †Harris, Harrison, Haskell, †Hays, †Henderson, †*Hidalgo, †Hill, †Hockley, Hood, †Howard, †*Hudspeth, Hunt, Hutchinson, Jack, †Jackson, †Jasper, Jeff Davis, †Jefferson, †*Jim

Hogg, †Jim Wells, *Karnes, Kaufman, †*Kendall, Kenedy, †Kerr, Kimble, King, †*Kinney, †Kleberg, †Lamar, Lampasas, †La Salle, †Lavaca, †Lee, Leon, Liberty, Lipscomb, Live Oak, †Llano, †*Loving, †Lubbock, Marion, †Matagorda, †Maverick, †McCulloch, †McLennan, †Medina, Menard, †Midland, Milam, Mills, Mitchell, Montague, †Montgomery, †*Moore, Nacogdoches, †Navarro, Newton, Nolan, †Nueces.

Also, †Orange, Palo Pinto, Parker, Pecos, †Polk, †Potter, †*Presidio, Rains, †Randall, *Reagan, Red River, †Reeves, Refugio, Robertson, †Rockwall, Runnels, San Augustine, San Jacinto, †San Patricio, San Saba, *Schleicher, Shackelford, Shelby, †*Starr, Stonewall, †*Sutton, †Tarrant, †Taylor, *Terrell, †Titus, †Tom Green, †*Travis, *Trinity, Upshur, *Upton, Uvalde, †Val Verde, †Victoria, †Walker, †Waller, Ward, †*Washington, †*Webb, †Wharton, †Wichita, Wilbarger, †Willacy, †Williamson, †*Wilson, *Winkler, Young, †*Zapata, †Zavala.

Counties in Which Only 4 Percent Beer Is Legal (11): Baylor, Caldwell, Cherokee, Concho, Hartley, Irion, Mason, McMullen, Oldham, Sabine, Stephens.

Counties in Which 14 Percent or Less Alcoholic Beverages Are Legal (5): Glasscock, Johnson, Limestone, Somervell, Wise.

Counties Wholly Dry (53): Andrews, Angelina, Armstrong, Bailey, Borden, Bowie, Briscoe, Cochran, Coke, Collingsworth, Cottle, Crosby, Delta, Erath, Fisher, Floyd, Foard, Franklin, Freestone, Gaines, Hale, Hansford, Hardeman, Hemphill, Hopkins, Houston, Jones, Kent, Knox, Lamb, Lynn, Madison, Martin, Morris, Motley, Ochiltree, Panola, Parmer, Real, Roberts, Rusk, Scurry, Sherman, Smith, Sterling, Swisher, Terry, Throckmorton, Tyler, Van Zandt, Wheeler, Wood, Yoakum. ☆

Regional Councils of Government

The concept of regional planning and cooperation, fostered by enabling legislation in 1965, has spread across Texas since organization of the **North Central Texas Council of Governments** in 1966.

Regional councils are responsible for making studies and plans to guide the unified development of their areas, eliminating duplication and promoting economic and efficient cooperative area development. They make recommendations to member governments and may assist in implementing the plans.

The Texas Association of Regional Councils, Jim Ray, Executive Director, is at 508 W. 12th, Austin 78701; (512) 478-4715. Financing is provided by the local governments, the state and the federal government. A list of the **24 regional councils**, the **counties served** and the **executive director** as of February 1995, follows (A map of regional councils can be found on page 285.):

Alamo Area Council of Governments: Counties — Atascosa, Bandera, Bexar, Comal, Frio, Gillespie, Guadalupe, Karnes, Kendall, Kerr, Medina and Wilson. Al J. Notzon III, 118 Broadway, Ste. 400, San Antonio 78205.

Ark-Tex Council of Governments: Bowie, Cass, Delta, Franklin, Hopkins, Lamar, Morris, Red River and Titus. James C. Fisher Jr., Box 5307, Texarkana, Texas 75505.

Brazos Valley Development Council: Brazos, Burleson, Grimes, Leon, Madison, Robertson and Washington. Tom Wilkinson Jr., Box 4128, Bryan 77805-4128.

Capitol Area Planning Council: Bastrop, Blanco, Burnet, Caldwell, Fayette, Hays, Lee, Llano, Travis and Williamson. Richard G. Bean, 2520 South IH 35 South, Suite 100, Austin 78704.

Central Texas Council of Governments: Bell, Coryell, Hamilton, Lampasas, Milam, Mills and San Saba. A. C. Johnson, Box 729, Belton 76513.

Coastal Bend Council of Governments: Aransas, Bee, Brooks, Duval, Jim Wells, Kenedy, Kleberg, Live Oak, McMullen, Nueces, Refugio and San Patricio. John P. Buckner, Box 9909, Corpus Christi 78469.

Concho Valley Council of Governments: Coke, Concho, Crockett, Irion, Kimble, Mason, McCulloch, Menard, Reagan, Schleicher, Sterling, Sutton and Tom Green. Robert R. Weaver, Box 60050, San Angelo 76906.

Deep East Texas Council of Governments: Angelina, Houston, Jasper, Nacogdoches, Newton, Polk, Sabine, San Augustine, San Jacinto, Shelby, Trinity and Tyler. Walter Diggles, 274 E. Lamar, Jasper 75951.

East Texas Council of Governments: Anderson, Camp, Cherokee, Gregg, Harrison, Henderson, Marion, Panola, Rains, Rusk, Smith, Upshur, Van Zandt and Wood. Glynn J. Knight, 3800 Stone Rd., Kilgore 75662.

Golden Crescent Regional Planning Commission: Calhoun, De Witt, Goliad, Gonzales, Jackson, Lavaca and Victoria. Patrick J. Kennedy, Box 2028, Victoria 77902.

Heart of Texas Council of Governments: Bosque, Falls, Freestone, Hill, Limestone and McLennan. Leon Wilhite, 320 Franklin Ave., Waco 76701-2297.

Houston-Galveston Area Council: Austin, Brazoria, Chambers, Colorado, Fort Bend, Galveston, Harris, Liberty, Matagorda, Montgomery, Walker, Waller and Wharton. Jack Steele, Box 22777, Houston 77227.

Lower Rio Grande Valley Development Council: Cameron, Hidalgo and Willacy. Ken Jones, 4900 N. 23rd, McAllen 78504.

Middle Rio Grande Development Council: Dimmit, Edwards, Kinney, La Salle, Maverick, Real, Uvalde, Val Verde and Zavala. Paul Edwards, Box 1199, Carrizo Springs 78834-7199.

Nortex Regional Planning Commission: Archer, Baylor, Clay, Cottle, Foard, Hardeman, Jack, Montague, Wichita, Wilbarger and Young. Dennis Wilde, Box 5144, Wichita Falls 76307.

North Central Texas Council of Governments: Collin, Dallas, Denton, Ellis, Erath, Hood, Hunt, Johnson, Kaufman, Navarro, Palo Pinto, Parker, Rockwall, Somervell, Tarrant and Wise. R. Michael Eastland, P.O. Drawer 5888, Arlington 76005-5888.

Panhandle Regional Planning Commission: Armstrong, Briscoe, Carson, Castro, Childress, Collingsworth, Dallam, Deaf Smith, Donley, Gray, Hall, Hansford, Hartley, Hemphill, Hutchinson, Lipscomb, Moore, Ochiltree, Oldham, Parmer, Potter, Randall, Roberts, Sherman, Swisher and Wheeler. Gary Pitner, Box 9257, Amarillo 79105-9257.

Permian Basin Regional Planning Commission: Andrews, Borden, Crane, Dawson, Ector, Gaines, Glasscock, Howard, Loving, Martin, Midland, Pecos, Reeves, Terrell, Upton, Ward and Winkler. Ernie Crawford, Box 60669, Midland 79711-0660.

Rio Grande Council of Governments: Brewster, Culberson, El Paso, Hudspeth, Jeff Davis and Presidio. Justin K. Ormsby, 123 Pioneer Plaza, Ste. 210, El Paso 79901.

South East Texas Regional Planning Commission: Hardin, Jefferson and Orange. Don Kelly, P.O. Drawer 1387, Nederland 77627.

South Plains Association of Governments: Bailey, Cochran, Crosby, Dickens, Floyd, Garza, Hale, Hockley, King, Lamb, Lubbock, Lynn, Motley, Terry and Yoakum. Jerry D. Casstevens, Box 3730, Freedom Sta., Lubbock 79452.

South Texas Development Council: Jim Hogg, Starr, Webb and Zapata. Amando Garza Jr., Box 2187, Laredo 78044-2187.

Texoma Regional Planning Commission: Cooke, Fannin and Grayson. Frances Pelley, 10000 Grayson Dr., Denison 75020.

West Central Texas Council of Governments: Brown, Callahan, Coleman, Comanche, Eastland, Fisher, Haskell, Jones, Kent, Knox, Mitchell, Nolan, Runnels, Scurry, Shackelford, Stephens, Stonewall, Taylor and Throckmorton. Brad Helbert, Box 3195, Abilene 79604. ☆

Texas County and District Officials — Table No. 1

County Seats, County Judges, County Clerks, County Attorneys, County Treasurers, Tax Assessors-Collectors and Sheriffs.

See Table No. 2 on pages following this table for District Clerks, District Attorneys and County Commissioners. The officials listed here are elected by popular vote.

County	County Seat	County Judge	County Clerk	County Attorney	County Treasurer	Assessor-Collector	Sheriff
Anderson	Palestine	*Jack W. Rogers	Lena Smith		Sharon Peterson	Connie Rose	Mickey Hubert
Anrews	Andrews	Gary W. Gaston	F. Wm. Hoermann	Dennis Cadra	Office abolished 11-5-85.	Royce Underwood	Wayne Farmer
Angelina	Lufkin	†Joe Berry	JoAnn Chastain	Ed Jones	Joann Denby	Bill Shanklin	Michael P. Lawrence
Aransas	Rockport	Agnes A. "Tony" Harden	Peggy L. Friebele	James L. Anderson Jr.	Marvine Wix	Allena Jones	David L. Petrusaitis
Archer	Archer City	Paul O. Wylie Jr.	Jane Ham	R.B. "Burke" Morris	Betty Tarno	Teresa Martin	P. L. Pippin Jr.
Armstrong	Claude	Hugh Reed	Kathy Byrd		Ray C. Minkley	Ronald Patterson	Carmella Jones
Atascosa	Jourdanton	Deborah Herber	Laquita Hayden	R. Thomas Franklin	Gloria P. Smith	Barbara Schorsch	Tommy Williams
Austin	Bellville	‡Carolyn Bilski	Carrie Gregor		Betty Krueger	Harlan Schrader	Vernon Brzozowski
Bailey	Muleshoe	Marilyn Cox	Billie R. Downing	Michael Paul Crosnoe	Dorothy Turner	Kathleen Hayes	Jerry N. Hicks
Bandera	Bandera	Roger Raser	Bernice Bates	K. H. Schneider	Kay Welch	Jean Stevens	James MacMillan
Bastrop	Bastrop	§Peggy Walicek	Shirley Wilhelm		Doris Oldfield	Barbara Brinkmeyer	Fred W. Hoskins
Baylor	Seymour	Robin Randal Smajstrla	Doris S. Rushing	Lee Price Fernon	Mary Benge	Grady Hicks	Jerry Barton
Bee	Beeville	Jay Kimbrough	Julia V. Torres	José Luis Aliseda Jr.	Office abolished 11-2-82.	Andrea Gibbud	Robert L. Horn
Bell	Belton	¶John Garth	Vada Sutton	Rick Miller	Charles Jones	Betty Willingham	Dan Smith
Bexar	San Antonio	**Cyndi Taylor Krier	Gerry Rickhoff		Office abolished 11-6-84.	Rudy A. Garza	Ralph Lopez
Blanco	Johnson City	George E. Byars Jr.	Dorothy Uecker	Dean Myane	Doris Cage	Hollis Boatright	Harry Carpenter
Borden	Gail	Van L. York	Joyce Herridge		Kenneth P. Bennett	Royale Lewis	Royale Lewis
Bosque	Meridian	B.J. Conrad	Patsy Owen Mize	B. J. Shepherd	Randy Pullin	Denise E. Wallace	Tim S. Gage
Bowie	Boston	James M.Carlow	Marylene Megason		Pansy Baird	Aleatha Lyle Hanna	Mary Choate
Brazoria	Angleton	††John Willy	Dolly Bailey		Sharon L. Reynolds	Ray M. Cornett	E. J. "Joe" King
Brazos	Bryan	‡‡Al Jones	Mary Ann Ward	Jim Kuboviak	Kay Hamilton	Gerald L. Winn	Bobby A. Riggs
Brewster	Alpine	Val Clark Beard	Berta Rios Martinez	Shane Ann Green	Hortencia Ramos	Jerry Ratcliff	Jack McDaniel
Briscoe	Silverton	Jimmy Burson	Bess McWilliams	Sharon Sutton Pigg	Janice S. Hill	Betty Ann Stephens	Richard C. Roehr
Brooks	Falfurrias	Joe B. Garcia	Ruben Castellano	David T. Garcia	Gilberto Vela	Ruben M. Longoria	Ruben M. Longoria
Brown	Brownwood	E. Ray West III	Margaret Woods		Carmeleta Smith	Coline Nabers	William B. Donahoo
Burleson	Caldwell	Paul J. Batista	Evelyn M. Henry	Joseph J. Skrivanek III	Beth Andrews Bills	Sandra Faust	Thomas E. Barber
Burnet	Burnet	Martin McLean	Janet Parker	Ross Lavin	Katy Gilmore	Sheri Frazier	Joe Pollock
Caldwell	Lockhart	§§Rebecca M. Hawener	Nina S. Sells		Amelia G. Rizzuto	Mary Smith	Mike Bading
Calhoun	Port Lavaca	¶¶Howard G. Hartzog	Marlene Paul		Sharron Marek	Annette Baker	Kenneth D. Bowden
Callahan	Baird	Bill Johnson	Darlene Walker	Allen Wright	Dora Hounshell	Bun Barry	Eddie G. Curtis
Cameron	Brownsville	***Gilberto Hinojosa	Joe G. Rivera	Doug Wright	Eddie A. Gonzalez	Tony Yzaguirre	Alex F. Perez
Camp	Pittsburg	Preston Combest	Elaine Young	Michael Lantrip	LaJuana Leftwich	Brenda Irby	Charles Elwonger
Carson	Panhandle	Jay Robert Roselius	Barbara S. White	Ed Hinshaw	Jeannie Cunningham	Roslyn Watson	Loren Brand
Cass	Linden	Tommy E. Kessler	Wilma O'Rand	Joe Lovelace	Jo Ellen Whatley	Bobbie Derrick	Paul Boone
Castro	Dimmitt	Irene Miller	Joyce Thomas		Oleta Raper	Billy Hackleman	C. D. Fitzgearld
Chambers	Anahuac	Oscar Nelson	Norma W. Rowland	Charles Brack	Carren Sparks	Irene Clore	Phil Burkhalter
Cherokee	Rusk	†††Harry Tilley	Fairy Upshaw	Robert (Bob) McNatt	Duann Norton	Linda Beard	James Campbell
Childress	Childress	Dean Decker	Nancy Garrison	Derrill Nippert Jr.	Liz Kitchens	Juanell Halford	Reece Bowen
Clay	Henrietta	Kenneth Liggett	Kay Hutchison	Eddy Atkins	Sue Sims Brock	Linda Overstreet	Paul Bevering
Cochran	Morton	Robert J. Yeary	Rita Tyson	J. C. Adams Jr.	Jean Abbe	Betty Akin	Royce Fred
Coke	Robert Lee	Jackie Walker	Ettie Hubbard	Chris A. Wyatt	Phelan Wrinkle	D. Kristeen Roe	Marshall Wayne Millican

Anderson County Court at Law**: J. Christopher Kolstad. **†Angelina County Courts at Law**: No. 1, Joe Martin; No. 2, Holly Perkins-Meyers. **‡Austin County Court at Law:** Gladys M. Oakley. **§Bastrop County Court at Law:** Benton Eskew. **¶ Bell County Courts at Law:** No. 1, Edward Johnson; No. 2, John Barina. * Bexar County Courts at Law:** No. 1, Anthony J. Ferro; No. 2, Paul H. Canales; No. 3, Shay Gebhardt; No. 4, Sarah E. Garrahan; No. 5, Timothy F. Johnson; No. 6, Ray Adams; No. 7, Bill C. White; No. 8, Karen Crouch; No. 9, Bonnie Reed. **County Probate Courts:** No. 1, Polly J. Spencer; No. 2, Sandee Bryan Marion. **††Brazoria County Courts at Law:** No. 1, Jerri Mills; No. 2, Garvin Germany; No. 3, James Blackstock. **‡‡Brazos County Courts at Law:** No. 1, Steve Smith; No. 2, Sarah Ryan. **§§Caldwell County Court at Law:** Edward L. Jarrett. **¶¶Calhoun County Court at Law:** Michael M. Fricke. *****Cameron County Courts at Law:** No. 1, Everardo Garcia; No. 2, Migdalia Lopez. **†††Cherokee County Court at Law:** A. LeRue Dixon

County	County Seat	County Judge	County Clerk	County Attorney	County Treasurer	Assessor-Collector	Sheriff
Coleman	Coleman	Sherill Radsdale	Joann Hale	Joe D. LeMay	Kay LeMay	Billie Baker	Wade Turner
Collin	McKinney	*Ron Harris	Helen Starnes		Office abolished 11-5-85.	Kenneth L. Maun	Terry G. Box
Collingsworth	Wellington	Jim Forrester	Karen Coleman	Charles W. Darter	Yvonne Brewer	Rose Mary Throne	Dale Tarver
Colorado	Columbus	Vince Slominski	Darlene Hayek	John Moore	Joyce M. Stancik	Mary Jane Poenitzsch	Bill Esterling
Comal	New Braunfels	†Carter Casteel	Joy Streater	Nathan Rheinlander	R. A. Bartholomew	Gloria K. Clennan	Jack Bremer
Comanche	Comanche	John M. Weaver	Betty Conway	C. H. McCall	Billy Ruth Rust	Gay Horton	Billy J. Works
Concho	Paint Rock	Allen Amos	Margaret T. Taylor	William Campbell	Dorothy Kirkpatrick	William J. Fiveash	William J. Fiveash
Cooke	Gainesville	Paul F. Hesse	Evelyn Walterscheid	D. August Boto	Janet Johnson	Joyce Zwinggi	Joe Y. Nichols
Coryell	Gatesville	‡John Hull	Barbara Simpson	Edwin E. Powell Jr.	Donna Medford	Joan Blanchard	Gerald Kitchens
Cottle	Paducah	Billy J. Gilbert	Beckey J. Tucker	John H. Richards	Atha Prater	Rue Young	Frank Taylor
Crane	Crane	Arlen White	Maxine Willis	Gene Clack	Gayla Phillips	Diana Earp	Tommy L. Jones
Crockett	Ozona	Jeffrey K. Sutton	Debbi Puckett	Orlando DeHoyos	Burl Myers	Tom Stokes	Jim Wilson
Crosby	Crosbyton	Jerry Robertson	Floyd McGinnes	Tom J. Brian	Joyce M. Whitehead	Buran House	Lavoice "Red" Riley
Culberson	Van Horn	John Conoly	Linda McDonald	Stephen L. Mitchell	Norma Hernandez	Amalia Hernandez	Placido Nuñez
Dallam	Dalhart	David D. Field	LuAnn Taylor	Greg Oelke	Jiggs Payne	Patricia Radford	E. H. Little
Dallas	Dallas	§Lee Jackson	Earl Bullock		Bill Melton	David Childs	Jim Bowles
Dawson	Lamesa	Charles C. Arthur	Gloria Vera	Steven B. Payson	Gene DeFee	Diane Hogg	J. Terry Brown
Deaf Smith	Hereford	Tom Simons	David Ruland		Nan Rogers	Margaret del Toro	Joe C. Brown Jr.
Delta	Cooper	John I. Hickman	Patsy P. Barton	Frank D. Moore	Glynanna Stockton	Dawn Curtis	Bill Allen
Denton	Denton	¶Jeff Moseley	Tim Hodges		Claudia Mulkey	Mary Horn	Weldon Lucas
DeWitt	Cuero	Ben E. Prause	Ann Drehr	Raymond H. Reese	Peggy Ledbetter	Susie Dreyer	David G. Dodge
Dickens	Dickens	Woodie McArthur Jr.	Yvonne "Tookie" Cash	Robert Heald (pro tem)	Druline Rape	Jerrie Ballard	Ken Brendle
Dimmit	Carrizo Springs	Charles D. Johnson	Mario Zuvia Garcia	James B. Davis	Elisa G. Duran	Esther Zuvia Perez	Candido R. DeAnda Jr.
Donley	Clarendon	W. R. Christal	Fay Vargas	Kyle Allen	Wanda Smith	Wilma Lindley	Jimmy Thompson
Duval	San Diego	Edmundo Garcia Jr.	Oscar Garcia Jr.	José Ramón Falcón	Daniel S. Lopez	Zaragosa Gutierrez III	Santiago Barrera Jr.
Eastland	Eastland	Scott Bailey	Joann Johnson		Ruth Pugliese Hart	Nancy Trout	Ronnie B. White
Ector	Odessa	**Jim T. Jordan	Barbara Bedford	Tracey Bright	Carolyn Bowen	Lea Taylor	Bob Brookshire
Edwards	Rocksprings	Neville G. Smart Jr.	Dorothy R. Hatley	Allen Ray Moody	Lupe Sifuentes-Enriquez	Teresa Sweeten	Warren B. Guthrie
Ellis	Waxahachie	††Al Cornelius	Cindy Polley	Joe F. Grubbs	Mark Price	Carol Calvert	John Gage
El Paso	El Paso	‡‡Charles Mattox	Hector Enriquez Jr.	José Rodriguez	Office abolished 1-1-86.	James Hicks	Leo Samaniego
Erath	Stephenville	§§Tab Thompson	Nelda Crockett	Elizabeth E. Barber	Donna Kelley	Jennifer Schlicke	David O. Coffee
Falls	Marlin	Robert D. Cunningham	Bryant L. Hinson		Marilyn Ejems	Gwen Atkins	Larry Pamplin
Fannin	Bonham	Jimmy L. Doyle	Margaret Gilbert	James S. Moss	Florence Keahey	Earlene Wix	Talmage Moore
Fayette	La Grange	Edward F. Janecka	Carolyn Kubos Roberts	John W. Wied	Office abolished 11-3-87.	Carol Johnson	Rick Vandel
Fisher	Roby	Marshal Bennett	Bettie Rivers	Rudy V. Hamric	Martha Williamson	Betty Mize	Gene Pack
Floyd	Floydada	William D. Hardin	Margaret Collier		Mary Shurbet	Penny Golightly	Charles Overstreet
Foard	Crowell	Charlie Bell	Sherry Weatherred	Daryl Halencak	Esther Kajs	Bobby D. Bond	Bobby D. Bond
Fort Bend	Richmond	¶¶Michael D. Rozell	Dianne Wilson	Ben W. "Bud" Childers	Kathy Hynson	Marsha P. Gaines	R. George Molina
Franklin	Mount Vernon	A. Wayne Foster	Wanda Johnson	Walt Sears Jr.	Angie Penny	Marjorie Jaggers	Charles "Chuck" White
Freestone	Fairfield	Joel E. Lane	Mary Lynn White	J. Keith Meredith	Patricia Robinson	Carolyn Varley	J. R. Sessions Jr.
Frio	Pearsall	Carlos A. Garcia	Gloria Cubriel	James W. Smith Jr.	Mary Hornbostel	Ysabela C. Peña	Carl H. Burris
Gaines	Seminole	Max Townsend	Pat Lacy	Sterling Harmon	Linda Clark	Edith Renfroe	Jon Key

***Collin County Courts at Law:** No. 1, Weldon Copeland; No. 2, Jerry Lewis; No. 3, John O'Keefe Barry. **†Comal County Court at Law:** Fred Clark. **‡Coryell County Court at Law:** Susan Stephens. **§Dallas County Courts at Law:** No. 1, David W. Evans; No. 2, Martin Richter; No. 3, Victoria Welcome; No. 4, Bruce Woody; No. 5, Charles Stokes. **County Criminal Courts:** No. 1, Henry Wade Jr.; No. 2, Jim Pruitt; No. 3, Mike Schwille; No. 4, Ralph Taite; No. 5, Tom Fuller; No. 6, Phil Barker; No. 7, Elizabeth Crowder; No. 8, Vic Cunningham; No. 9, Molly Francis; No. 10, Marshall W. Gandy. **County Probate Courts:** No. 1, Nikki DeShazo; No. 2, Robert E. Price; No. 3, Joe H. Loving. **County Criminal Courts of Appeals:** No. 1, Kenneth Vaughan; No. 2, Lynn Burson. **¶Denton County Courts at Law:** No. 1, Darlene Whitten; No. 2, Virgil Vahlenkamp; No. 3, Don Windle. ****Ector County Courts at Law:** No. 1, Jim (J. A.) Bobo; No. 2, Mark D. Owens. **††Ellis County Court at Law:** Al Scoggins. **‡‡El Paso County Courts at Law:** No. 1, Ricardo Herrera; No. 2, John L. Fashing; No. 3, Javier Alvarez; No. 4, Kitty Schild; No. 5, Herbert Cooper. **County Probate Court:** Max Higgs. **Domestic Relations/Juvenile Court:** Phil Martinez. **§§Erath County Court at Law:** E. Bart McDougal. **¶¶Fort Bend County Courts at Law:** No. 1, Larry Wagenbach; No. 2, Walter S. McMeans.

County	County Seat	County Judge	County Clerk	County Attorney	County Treasurer	Assessor-Collector	Sheriff
Galveston	Galveston	*James D. Yarbrough	Patricia Ritchie	Harvey Bazaman	Gerald Burks	Charles E. Wilson	Joe Max Taylor
Garza	Post	Giles W. Dalby	Sonny Gossett	Preston L. Poole Jr.	Ruth Ann Young	Laura Hataway	Kennith Ratke
Gillespie	Fredericksburg	Mark Stroeher	Doris Lange	Gerald W. Schmidt	Jeanie Bel Crenwelge	Leola Brodbeck	Milton E. Jung
Glasscock	Garden City	Wilburn E. Bednar	Betty Pate	Rick Hamby	Alan Dierschke	Royce Pruit	Royce Pruit
Goliad	Goliad	Steven G. Paulsgrove	Gail M. Turley	Brenda J. Heinold	La Nell Ressman	Neva Thigpen	J. K. McMahan
Gonzales	Gonzales	Henry H. Vollentine	Sonny Sievers	Robert B. Scheske	Marie Scoggins	Norma Jean DuBose	D. J. Brzozowski
Gray	Pampa	Richard D. Peet	Wanda Carter	Todd Alvey	Scott B. Hahn	Sammie Morris	Randy Stubblefield
Grayson	Sherman	†Horace Groff	Sara Jackson	Robert T. Jarvis	Virginia Hughes	John W. Ramsey	L. E. "Jack" Driscoll
Gregg	Longview	‡Mickey D. Smith	Laurie Woloszyn		Office abolished 1-1-88.	Bobby Crawford	Bobby Weaver
Grimes	Anderson	Ira E. (Bud) Haynie	David Pasket	Joe S. Falco Jr.	Phillis Allen	Claude Jolly Jr.	Bill Foster
Guadalupe	Seguin	§James E. Sagebiel	Lizzie M. Lorenz	Bob Covington	Larry Jones	Betty Boyd	Melvin L. Harborth
Hale	Plainview	Bill Hollars	Diane Williams		Evelyn Carroll	Kemp Hinch	Charles Tue
Hall	Memphis	Kenneth E. Dale	Raye Bailey	John M. Deaver II	Marion Bownds	Pat Floyd	Garvin Speed
Hamilton	Hamilton	Charles Garrett	Virginia Lovell	Thomas E. White	Karen S. Tyson	Ray Horner	Randy Murphree
Hansford	Spearman	Jim D. Brown	Kim V. Vera	John L. Hutchison	Norma Jean Mackie	Helen Dry	R. L. McFarlin Jr.
Hardeman	Quanah	K. D. McNabb	Judy Cokendolpher	Stanley K. Watson	Van R. White Jr.	Betty Lay	Randy L. Akers
Hardin	Kountze	Tom Mayfield	Dee Hatton	David Sheffield	Eddie Doggett	Billy Bruce Caraway	H. R. "Mike" Holzapfel
Harris	Houston	¶Robert Eckels	Beverly B. Kaufman		Don Sumners	Carl S. Smith	Johnny Klevenhagen
Harrison	Marshall	**Rodney Gilstrap	Martha Dieste		Jamie Noland	Marie F. Noland	Bob Green
Hartley	Channing	Ronnie Gordon	Diane Thompson	William A. Cunningham	Betty Edwards	John E. Williams Jr.	John E. Williams Jr.
Haskell	Haskell	B. O. Roberson	Rhonda Moeller	L. W. (Bill) Jones III	Willie Faye Tidrow	Bobbye Collins	Johnny Mills
Hays	San Marcos	††Eddy A. Etheredge	Ronnie Dannelley		Michele Tuttle	Luanne Caraway	Paul Logan Hastings
Hemphill	Canadian	Bob Gober	Davene Hendershot	Charles Kessie	Claudette Hand	Gladene Woodside	Billy V. Bowen
Henderson	Athens	‡‡Tommy G. Smith	Gwen Moffeit	Lawrence E. Heffington	Carolyn Herrington	Milburn Chaney	H. B. Alfred
Hidalgo	Edinburg	§§J. Edgar Ruiz	José Eloy Pulido		Norma Garcia	Ciro Treviño	Enrique Escalon
Hill	Hillsboro	Tommy J. Walker	Ruth Pelham	Mark F. Pratt	Jewel Burton	Thomas J. Davis	Brent Button
Hockley	Levelland	Larry D. Sprowls	Mary K. Walker	J. M. "Pat" Phelan	Jo Beth Hittson	Christy Clevenger	Leroy Schulle
Hood	Granbury	Don Cleveland	Anjanette Ables	Vincent J. Messina	Peggy Moreno	Sandra Tidwell	Rodney Jeanis
Hopkins	Sulphur Springs	¶¶Joe B. Minter	Mary Attlesey	Robert Newsom	Betty Moore	Jo Ruth Hodge	Billy G. Dirks
Houston	Crockett	***R.C. von Doenhoff	Nancy Huff	John E. Bobbitt	Dianne Rhone	Joan Lucas	Jimbo Rains
Howard	Big Spring	Ben Lockhart	Margaret Ray	Hardy L. Wilkerson	Bonnie Franklin	Kathy A. Sayles	A. N. Standard
Hudspeth	Sierra Blanca	James Peace	Patricia Bramblett	Tom Chellis	Pilar R. West	Kay Scarbrough	Arcadio Ramirez
Hunt	Greenville	†††Joe Bobbitt	Jim Hamilton	Peter Morgan	Louise Walker	Joyce Barrow	Bobby Young
Hutchinson	Stinnett	David M. Willard	Carol Ann Herbst	Michael D. Milner	Kathy Sargent	Mary Henderson	Lon Blackmon
Irion	Mertzon	Sidney Mabry	Reba Criner	Coleta Stewart	Betty Dennis	Joyce Gray	Jimmy Martin
Jack	Jacksboro	Mitchell G. Davenport	Patsy Ramzy	Michael G. Mask	Floyd Easter	Sarah Pruit	Robert B. Perry Jr.
Jackson	Edna	Harrison Stafford II	Martha Knapp		Marcell Maresh Jr.	LaVerne Ellison	Kelly Janica
Jasper	Jasper	Joe Folk	Evelyn Stott	Guy James Gray	Mary Jane Hancock	Robert C. Pace Jr.	Roscoe Davis
Jeff Davis	Fort Davis	Peggy Robertson	Sue Blackley	Glen Halsell	Geen Parrott	Harvey Adams	Harvey Adams
Jefferson	Beaumont	‡‡‡R. P. LeBlanc Jr.	Lolita Ramos	Tom Maness	Linda P. Robinson	Nicholas V. Lampson	Carl R. Griffith Jr.
Jim Hogg	Hebbronville	Horacio S. Ramirez	Gloria Diana Rodriguez	Richard R. Gonzales	Linda Jo G. Soliz	Marina Vasquez	Gilberto Ybañez

***Galveston County Courts at Law:** No. 1, Mary Nell Crapitto; No. 2, C.G. Dibrell III; **County Probate Court:** Jerome Jones. **†Grayson County Courts at Law:** No. 1, Donald L. Jarvis; No. 2, Kenneth D. Daniel. **‡Gregg County Court at Law:** John Sharp; **Domestic Relations Court**, Robin D. Sage. **§Guadalupe County Court at Law:** Linda Z. Jones. **¶Harris County Courts at Law:** No. 1, Ed Landry; No. 2, Tom Sullivan; No. 3, Carolyn D. Hobson; No. 4, Charles Coussons. **County Criminal Courts at Law:** No. 1, Bill Ragan; No. 2, Michael Peters; No. 3, Donald Wayne Jackson; No. 4, James E. Anderson; No. 5, Hannah Chow; No. 6, J.R. Musslewhite; No. 7, Shelly P. Hancock; No. 8, Neel Richardson; No. 9, Alfred G. Leal; No. 10, Sherman P. Ross; No. 11, David Mendoza Jr.; No. 12, Joseph T. Terracina; No. 13, Mark Atkinson; No. 14, James Barkley. **County Probate Courts:** No. 1, John Hutchison III; No. 2, Mike Wood; No. 3, Jim Edward Scanlan; No. 4, William C. McCulloch. ****Harrison County Court at Law:** Max A. Sandlin, Jr. **††Hays County Courts** at Law: No. 1, Howard S. Warner II; No. 2, Linda A. Rodriguez. **‡‡Henderson County Court at Law:** D. Matt Livingston. **§§Hidalgo County Courts at Law:** No. 1, Rodolfo Delgado; No. 2, G. Jaime Garza; No. 3, Richard H. Garcia; No. 4, Leticia Hinojosa. **¶¶Hopkins County Court at Law:** Chad Cable. *****Houston County Court at Law:** Lynn E. Markham. **†††Hunt County Court at Law:** Steve Shipp. **‡‡‡Jefferson County Courts at Law:** No. 1, Alfred Gerson; No. 2, Harold P. Plessala; No. 3, John Paul Davis.

County	County Seat	County Judge	County Clerk	County Attorney	County Treasurer	Assessor-Collector	Sheriff
Jim Wells	Alice	L. Arnoldo Saenz	Arnoldo Gonzalez	Jesusa Sanchez-Vera	Pearlie Jo Valadez	Antonio "Cone" Lozano	Oscar Lopez
Johnson	Cleburne	*Roger Harmon	Curtis H. Douglas	Bill Moore	Barbara Robinson-Cole	W. E. "Ed" Carroll	Martin L. Griffith
Jones	Anson	Brad Rowland	Margaret Jones	Dwade R. King	Irene Hudson	Tom Isbell	Mike Middleton
Karnes	Karnes City	Alfred Pawelek	Elizabeth Swize	John Wilson Berry	Charlene Blaschke	Phillis Pawelek	Terry W. Schmidt
Kaufman	Kaufman	†Maxine Darst	Crissy Gann		Linda Spencer	Donna Sprague	Robert Harris
Kendall	Boerne	James W. (Bill) Gooden	Darlene Herrin	Pamela K. McKay	Barbara J. Schwope	Betty J. Asher	Lee H. D'Spain Jr.
Kenedy	Sarita	J. A. Garcia Jr.	Barbara B. Turcotte	Roy C. Turcotte	John W. Turcotte	Lynwood G. Weiss	Rafael M. Cuellar Jr.
Kent	Jayton	Tommy Stanaland	Cornelia Cheyne	Howard Freemyer	Linda McCurry	Larry Doyle Rider	Larry Doyle Rider
Kerr	Kerrville	‡Robert A. Denson	Patricia Dye	David Motley	Barbara Nemec	Paula Rector	Frances A. Kaiser
Kimble	Junction	Wilbur R. Dunk	Elaine Carpenter	Callan Graham	Sheila D'Spain	Mike Chapman	Mike Chapman
King	Guthrie	Kerry Havins	Tavia Vinson	Bobby Burnett	Mary Lee Hurt	Sadie Mote	Jim Waller
Kinney	Brackettville	Tommy Seargeant	Dora Elia Sandoval	Tully Shahan	Janis Floyd	Martha Peña-Hooten	Norman H. Hooten
Kleberg	Kingsville	§Pete de la Garza	Sam D. Deanda	Delma Rios	Elaine Maca	Juanita R. Lara	Winston R. Kelly
Knox	Benjamin	David N. Perdue	Danny Speck	Bobby D. Burnett	Judie Whitten	Stanton Brown	Michael Carlson
Lamar	Paris	Deane A. Loughmiller	Kathy Lou Poole	Tom Wells	Latricia Miller	Peggy Noble	B. J. McCoy
Lamb	Littlefield	Wayne Whiteaker	Bill Johnson	Mark Yarbrough	Janice B. Wells	Linda G. Charlton	Jerry Collins
Lampasas	Lampasas	Tommy Honeycutt	Connie Hartmann	Larry W. Allison	Leona Hurst	Glenda Henderson	Gordon Morris
La Salle	Cotulla	Jimmy P. Patterson	Nora Mae Tyler	Edward Hargrove	Joel Rodriguez Jr.	Elida A. Linares	Darwin D. Avant
Lavaca	Hallettsville	Charles J. Rother	Henry J. Sitka	James W. Carr	Thomas M. Grahmann	Margaret M. Kallus	Robert E. Wurm
Lee	Giddings	E. W. Kraus	Carol Dismukes	Steven W. Keng	Rose Fritsche	Virginia Jackson	Joe G. Goodson
Leon	Centerville	Donald "Gene" Douget	Margaret Wells	Gary Joe Taylor	William D. Lemons	Louise Wilson	Royce G. Wilson
Liberty	Liberty	¶Lloyd Kirkham	Wanda Barker	A. J. Hartel III	Winn Skidmore	Mark McClelland	O. J. Stewart
Limestone	Groesbeck	Elenor Holmes	Sue Lown	Don Cantrell	Imogene Archibald	Barbara Rader	Dennis Walker
Lipscomb	Lipscomb	Willis V. Smith	Coeta Sperry	Randy M. Phillips	Pat Wyatt	Ellen Garis	Calvin J. Babitzke
Live Oak	George West	Jim Huff	Mildred James	W. L. "Bill" Hardwick	Violet Person	Larry R. Busby	Larry R. Busby
Llano	Llano	J.P. Dodgen	Bette Sue Hoy	Cheryll Mabray	Ma'Joyce Swope	Anna Henderson	Nathan Garrett
Loving	Mentone	Donald C. Creager	Juanita Busby		Jaime Jones	Richard Putnam	Richard Putnam
Lubbock	Lubbock	**Don McBeath	Ann Davidson		Connie H. Nicholson	Stephen P. Watt	D. L. "Sonny" Keesee
Lynn	Tahoka	J. F. Brandon	Ima Robinson	Jimmy B. Wright	Janet Porterfield	Sherry Pearce	Dennis (Jake) Diggs
Madison	Madisonville	Cecil N. Neely	Joyce M. Coleman	David Hammit	Judy Weathers	Judy Nickerson	Travis Neeley
Marion	Jefferson	Gene S. Terry	Clairece Ford	James P. Finstrom	Dorothy T. Whatley	Mary Alice Biggs	Eugene Tefteller
Martin	Stanton	Bob Deavenport	Susie Hull	James L. McGilvray	H.D. Howard	Kathy Hull	Mike Welling
Mason	Mason	Tommy Reardon	Beatrice Langehennig	Harold R. Schmidt	Polly McMillan	Don K. Grote	Don K. Grote
Matagorda	Bay City	Loy E. Sneary	Sarah Vaughn	Melissa Abshier	Suzanne S. Kucera	William B. Wiginton	Keith Kilgore
Maverick	Eagle Pass	Rocky Escobedo	Linda Sumpter	Ernest G. Mireles	Manuel Reyes Jr.	Esteban Luna	Salvador Rios
McCulloch	Brady	Randy Young	Rose Marie Luttrell	Jim Oglesby	Donna Robinett	Deena G. Moore	Dwain Hendsley
McLennan	Waco	††Jim Lewis	J.A. "Andy" Harwell		Bill Helton	A. F. "Buddy" Skeen	Jack Harwell
McMullen	Tilden	Elaine Franklin	Nell Hodgin		Donald Haynes Jr.	Mary K. Edwards	W. I. "Tito" Potts
Medina	Hondo	‡‡David F. Montgomery	Anna Van De Walle	Maida Modgling	Rita L. Moos	Loraine Neuman	Wesley Scott
Menard	Menard	Tim Childers	Elsie Maserang	Ben Neel	Robert Bean	Madelon Highsmith	Bruce Hough
Midland	Midland	§§Jeff Norwood	Rosenelle Cherry	Mark Dettman	Carol Baker	Kathy Reeves	Gary Painter
Milam	Cameron	Roger Hashem	La Verne Soefje	Hollis C. Lewis Jr.	Grover C. "Pete" York Jr.	Porter C. Young Jr.	Leroy Broadus
Mills	Goldthwaite	Randy Wright	Beulah L. Roberts	Tommy M. Adams	Patsy Miller	Beverly Baker	Glenn Carr
Mitchell	Colorado City	Ray Mayo	Debby Carlock	Mark Piland	Ann Hallmark	Clarence C. "Mike" Burt	Patrick Toombs
Montague	Montague	Cleve E. Steed	Gayle Edwards	Jeb McNew	James M. Johnson	Christine P. Brock	Kevin L. Benton

***Johnson County Courts at Law:** No. 1, Tommy Altaras; No. 2, William Anderson. **†Kaufman County Court at Law:** Joe M. Parnell. **‡Kerr County Court at Law:** Spencer W. Brown. **§Kleberg County Court at Law:** Martin J. Chiuminatto Jr. **¶Liberty County Court at Law:** Chap B. Cain III. ****Lubbock County Courts at Law:** No. 1, WilliamC. Dodson; No. 2,G. Thomas Cannon; No. 3, Paula Lanehart. **††McLennan County Courts at Law:** No. 1, David Hodges; No. 2, Mike Gassaway. **‡‡Medina County Court at Law:** Watt Murrah. **§§Midland County Courts at Law:** No. 1, Al Walvoord; No. 2, Marvin Moore.

County	County Seat	County Judge	County Clerk	County Attorney	County Treasurer	Assessor-Collector	Sheriff
Montgomery	Conroe	*Alan B.Sadler	Mark Turnbull	Frank Bass	Martha Gustavsen	J. R. Moore Jr.	Guy Williams
Moore	Dumas	†Billie Faye Schumacher	Rhonnie C. Mayer	Rayford A. Ratliff	Phyllis Holmes	Jane Hendrix	H.T. "Ted" Montgomery
Morris	Daingerfield	Vanoy Boozer	Doris McNatt	Richard Townsend	Peggy Campbell	Jerry L. Chambliss	Charles R. Blackburn
Motley	Matador	Laverna M. Price	Lucretia Campbell		Joe E. Campbell	Elaine Hart	James B. "Jim" Meador
Nacogdoches	Nacogdoches	‡Ocie L. Westmoreland	Carol Wilson	Bryan H. Davis	Kay Watkins	Patsy Cates	Joe Evans
Navarro	Corsicana	James Bagnall	James F. Doolen		Joe Graves	Peggy Blackwell Moore	Leslie Cotten
Newton	Newton	Lon M. Sharver	Mary Cobb	Ed Tracy	Ruth Dickerson	Bea Westbrook	Wayne Powell
Nolan	Sweetwater	§Jack Aycock	Elsie Pierce	Lisa L. Peterson	Gayle Biggerstaff	Betty Bryant	Jim Blackley
Nueces	Corpus Christi	¶Richard M. Borchard	Ernest M. Briones	Carl Lewis	Office abolished 11-3-87.	Ronnie Canales	J. P. Luby
Ochiltree	Perryton	Kenneth R. Donahue	Jane Hammerbeck	Bruce Roberson	Ginger Hays	Helen Bates	Joe Hataway
Oldham	Vega	Don R. Allred	Martha Thompson	Donald L. Davis	Shirley Galbraith	Cynthia Artho	David T. Medlin
Orange	Orange	**Carl Thibodeaux	Karen Jo Vance	John Kimbrough	Vergie Moreland	Rosemary Slaton	Huel Fontenot
Palo Pinto	Palo Pinto	Harold M. Couch	Bobbie Smith	Phil Garrett	Tanya Fallin	Max Wheeler	Larry Watson
Panola	Carthage	††John Cardray	Sue Grafton		Gloria Portman	Lurline Wilson	Jack Ellett
Parker	Weatherford	‡‡Ben Long	Jeane Brunson	Patrick J. Fleming	Jim Thorp	Marjorie King	Ben Whiteman
Parmer	Farwell	Bonnie Clayton	Bonnie Warren	Charles Aycock	Anne G. Norton	Doris Herington	Rex Williams
Pecos	Fort Stockton	Fredie Capers	Judy Deerfield	Steve Spurgin	Barry McCallister	Kaye Creech	Bruce Wilson
Polk	Livingston	§§John P. Thompson	Barbara Middleton		Cheryl Henry	Marion A. "Bid" Smith	Billy Ray Nelson
Potter	Amarillo	¶¶Arthur Ware	Sue Daniel	Sonja Letson	Juny Messer	L. R. "Bob" Roberts	Jimmy Don Boydston
Presidio	Presidio	Jake Brisbin Jr.	Ramona Lara	Teresa Todd	Mario S. Rivera	Sandra S. Serrano	Abelardo Gonzalez
Rains	Emory	Diana Fleming	Mary Sheppard	L. M. Braziel	Teresa Northcutt	Richard Wilson	Richard Wilson
Randall	Canyon	***Ted Wood	LeRoy Hutton		Geneva Bagwell	Carol Autry	Harold Hooks
Reagan	Big Lake	Mike Elkins	Billie Havis	J. Russell Ash	Nancy L. Ratliff	Venitta Terral	Efrain Gonzales
Real	Leakey	G. W. Twilligear Jr.	Rosemary Brice	John A. Daniel	Kathy Brooks	Donna Brice	James Brice
Red River	Clarksville	L. D. Williamson	Mary Hausler	Jack O. Herrington	Beverly White	Leslie Nix	Bob Edrington
Reeves	Pecos	†††Jimmy B. Galindo	Dianne O. Florez	Bill Weinacht	Linda Clark	Elfida Zuniga	Arnulfo "Andy" Gomez
Refugio	Refugio	Charles S. Stone	Janelle Morgan	Robert P. McGuill	Betty Greebon	Veronica Rocha	Jim Hodges
Roberts	Miami	Vernon H. Cook	Donna L. Goodman	Richard J. Roach	Billie J. Lunsford	Susie Billingsley	Billy Britton
Robertson	Franklin	Billy Lee Stellbauer	Mary B. Reagan	John C. Paschall	Jacqueline Vann	Charlene Bush	Lee Scott Hurley
Rockwall	Rockwall	William B. Lofland	Paulette Burks		Scott Self	Kathryn Feldpausch	Jacques I. Kiere
Runnels	Ballinger	Michael B. Murchison	Linda Bruchmiller	John W. McGregor	Margarette Smith	Robin Burgess	William A. Baird
Rusk	Henderson	‡‡‡Sandra Hodges	Frank Hudson	Kyle Freeman	Nora Rousseau	Matt B. Johnson	Cecil R. West
Sabine	Hemphill	John L. Hyden	Janice McDaniel	Dwight P. McDaniel	Ollie Faye Sparks	Tammy Reeves	W. G. Bradberry
San Augustine	San Augustine	Curt Goetz	Geraldine Smith	Michael T. Adams	Carol W. Vaughn	Deborah Kay Woods	Charles Bryan
San Jacinto	Coldspring	Robert E. "Bob" Smith	Joyce Hogue		Charlene Everitt	Vernon Lilley	Lacy Rogers
San Patricio	Sinton	§§§Josephine W. Miller	Dottie Maley	David Aken	Judy Burr	Thelma Kelley	Leroy Moody
San Saba	San Saba	Harlen Barker	Kim Wells	David M. Williams	Gayla Hawkins	John Benner	John Benner
Schleicher	Eldorado	Johnny F. Griffin	Peggy Williams	Thomas Giovannitti	Karen Henderson	Dorothy M. Evans	Richard L. Harris
Scurry	Snyder	Ricky Fritz	Frances Billingsley	LeLand Greene	Charlie Bell	Rona Sikes	Keith Collier
Shackelford	Albany	Ross Montgomery	Frances Wheeler	Gary M. Brown (pro tem)	Sherry Enloe	Larry V. Bonner	Larry V. Bonner
Shelby	Center	Floyd A. Watson	Peaches Conway	Gary W. Rholes	Lamerle Davis	Janie Ruth Graves	Carl Shofner
Sherman	Stratford	¶¶¶W. C. Fesler	M. L. Albert	Jack Q. Barton	Linda R. Keener	Valerie McAlister	Jack Haile
Smith	Tyler	****Larry Craig	Mary Morris		Joyce Woodward- Smith	Kay M. Smith	J. B. Smith
Somervell	Glen Rose	Dale McPherson	Lovella Williams	Ronald Hankins	Vicki Crisp	Janet Boren	Mac Yocham

***Montgomery County Courts at Law**: No. 1, Suzanne Stovall; No. 2, Jerry Winfree; No. 3, Mason Martin. **†Moore County Cou**rt at Law: Delwin McGee. **‡Nacogdoches County Court at Law:** J. Jack Yarbrough. **§Nolan County Court at Law:** Glen Harrison. **¶Nueces County Courts at Law:** No. 1, Robert J. Vargas; No. 2, Hector de Peña Jr.; No. 3, Marisela Saldaña; No. 4, James E. Klager. ****Orange County Court at Law:** Michael W. Shuff. **††Panola County Court at Law:** Crawford Parker Jr. **‡‡Parker County Court at Law:** Graham Quisenberry. **§§Polk County Court at Law:** Stephen Phillips. **¶¶Potter County Courts at Law:** No. 1, W. F. "Corky" Roberts; No. 2, Richard P. Dambold. *****Randall County Court at Law:** Darrell R. Carey. **†††Reeves County Court at Law**: Lee S. Green. **‡‡‡Rusk County Court at Law:** Darrell Hyatt. **§§§San Patricio County Court at Law:** Michael E. Welborn. **¶¶¶Sherman County Court at Law:** Dewin McQuee. ******Smith County Courts at Law:** No. 1, Diane DeVasto; No. 2, Randall Lee Rogers.

County	County Seat	County Judge	County Clerk	County Attorney	County Treasurer	Assessor-Collector	Sheriff
Starr	Rio Grande City	*José M. Martinez Jr.	Omar J. Garza	Romero Molina	David Porras	Maria Ofelia Saenz	Eugenio Falcón Jr.
Stephens	Breckenridge	Gary Fuller	Helen Haddock	Gary D. Trammel	Nancy Clary	Allena Dover	James D. Reeves
Sterling	Sterling City	Robert L. Browne	Diane A. Haar	Robert Herring	Beth Kilpatrick	Lloyd Brown	Lloyd Brown
Stonewall	Aspermont	Bobby F. McGough	Betty L. Smith	Norman Arnett	Linda Messick	Joyce Y. McNutt	Bill Mullen
Sutton	Sonora	Carla Garner	Bobbie Smith	David W. Wallace	Joyce H. Chalk	Peggy W. Sharp	W. W. "Bill" Webster
Swisher	Tulia	Harold Keeter	Brenda Hudson	J. Michael Criswell	Lanelle Dovel	Shirley Whitehead	Larry P. Stewart
Tarrant	Fort Worth	†Tom Vandergriff	Suzanne Henderson		Office abolished 4-2-83.	June Garrison	David Williams
Taylor	Abilene	‡Lee Hamilton	Janice Lyons		Anna Moore	Lavena Cheek	Jack Dieken
Terrell	Sanderson	Dudley Harrison	Martha Allen	Marsha Monroe	Sherry Hall	Y. E. "Chel" Duarte	Y. E. "Chel" Duarte
Terry	Brownfield	Douglas Ryburn	Ann Willis	G. Dwayne Pruitt	Bobbye Jo McClure	Redelle Cox	Jerry Johnson
Throckmorton	Throckmorton	Joe Ed Thompson	Cathey Mitchell	R. David Helton	Brenda Rankin	Greg Dunlap	Greg Dunlap
Titus	Mt. Pleasant	Danny Pat Crooks	Sherry Jo Mars	Timothy Taylor	Cynthia Agan	June Roach	John A. Moss
Tom Green	San Angelo	§Michael D. Brown	Judith Hawkins	Tom Goff	Donna Long	Evelyn Vordick	Ule E. (Pete) Skains
Travis	Austin	¶Bill Aleshire	Dana DeBeauvoir	Ken Oden	Dolores Ortega-Carter	Nelda Wells Spears	Terry Keel
Trinity	Groveton	Mark Evans	Elaine I. Lockhart	Joe Warner Bell	Frances Worsham	Charlene Carr	Daryll Brent Phillips
Tyler	Woodville	Jerome P. Owens Jr.	Donece Gregory		Tina Bump	Sandra H. Crittenden	Gary Hennigan
Upshur	Gilmer	Charles L. Still	Rex A. Shaw		Myra Harris	Michael L. Smith	R. D. "Buck" Cross
Upton	Rankin	Vikki Bradley	Phyllis Stephens	Roy L. Scott	Nancy Poage	Dan W. Brown	Dan W. Brown
Uvalde	Uvalde	William R. Mitchell	Lucille C. Hutcherson	Jerry Evans	Joni Deorsam	Margarita Del Toro	Beaumont Watkins
Val Verde	Del Rio	**Ray Kirkpatrick	Maria Elena Cardenas	Ana Markowski Smith	Morris L. Taylor	Wayne H. Hyde	James R. Koog
Van Zandt	Canton	Richard Lawrence	Elizabeth Everitt	Leslie Poynter Dixon	Shirley Morgan	Joyce Fugate	Pat Jordan
Victoria	Victoria	††Helen R. Walker	Val D. Huvar		Cathy Bailey	Rena Scherer	Michael Ratcliff
Walker	Huntsville	‡‡Charles H. Wagamon	James D. Patton		Barbara T. McGilberry	Robert Massey	Dale Myers
Waller	Hempstead	§§Freddie R. Zach	Cheryl Peters		Susan Winfree	Ellen C. Shelburne	Randy Smith
Ward	Monahans	Sam G. Massey	Pat V. Finley	Kevin D. Acker	Nell Berry	Dolores Hannah Fine	Ben Keele
Washington	Brenham	¶¶Dorothy Morgan	Beth A. Rothermel	Craig P. Lesser	Norman Draehn	Rita Jezierski	J. W. Jankowski
Webb	Laredo	***Mercurio Martínez Jr.	Henry Flores	Ana Cavazos Ramirez	William N. Hall Jr.	Patricia Ann Barrera	Juan Garza
Wharton	Wharton	Lawrence E. Naiser	Sandra K. Sanders	Dayle B. Aulds	Gus Wessels Jr.	Patrick Kubala	Jess Howell
Wheeler	Wheeler	Wendell Morgan	Margaret Dorman	Steven R. Emmert	Jerrie Moore	Jerry Dan Hefley	Jimmy Adams
Wichita	Wichita Falls	†††Nick Gipson	Vernon Cannon		Marsha Watson	Monette Pemberton	Thomas J. Callahan
Wilbarger	Vernon	Gary Streit	Frances McGee	Paul Scott	Janice King	Joan Bourland	David Quisenberry
Willacy	Raymondville	Simon Salinas	Terry Flores	Gustavo Ch. Garza	Dolores Duron	LaQuita Garza	Larry G. Spence
Williamson	Georgetown	‡‡‡John C. Doerfler	Elaine Bizzell	Eugene Taylor	Vivian Wood	Dorothy E. Jones	Ed Richards
Wilson	Floresville	Martha B. Schnabel	Eva S. Martinez	Jerry P. Heltzel	Carolyn Orth	Anna D. Gonzales	Joe D. Tackitt Jr.
Winkler	Kermit	Bonnie Leck	Sonja Fullen	Thomas A. Cameron	Dawn McLennan	Patti Franks	Robert L. Roberts Jr.
Wise	Decatur	§§§L. B. McDonald	Sherry Parker	Stephen L. Hale	Emma Ray	Tommie Farris	Phil Ryan
Wood	Quitman	Lee E. Williams	Brenda Taylor		June Robinson	Fred Morrow	Bill Skinner
Yoakum	Plains	Dallas Brewer	Ruby Bruton		Toni Jones	Wanda Smith	Jimmie Rice
Young	Graham	Ken Andrews	Shirley Choate	Stephen E. Bristow	Wanda Primrose	Tim Moreland	Carey W. Pettus
Zapata	Zapata	Norma Villarreal-Ramirez	Consuelo R. Villarreal	Arturo A. Figueroa Jr.	Alejandro R. Ramirez	Rosalva Dominguez	Sigifredo Gonzalez Jr.
Zavala	Crystal City	Pablo Avila	Teresa P. Flores	Joe Taylor	Susie Perez	Martha P. Cruz	José Serna

***Starr County Court at Law:** Alex W. Gabert. **†Tarrant County Courts at Law:** No. 1, R. Brent Keis; No. 2, Steve Wallace; No. 3, Vincent G. Sprinkle. **County Criminal Courts at Law:** No. 1, Sherry Hill; No. 2, Michael D. Mitchell; No. 3, Billy D. Mills; No. 4, Wallace Bowman; No. 6, Rufus J. Adcock; No. 7, Howard M. Fender; No. 8, Daryl Coffee; No. 9, Brent A. Carr; No. 10, Pete Gilfeather. **County Crtiminal Court of Appeals:** Mamie Bush Johnson. **Probate Courts:** No. 1, Steve M. King; No. 2, Patrick Ferchill. **‡Taylor County Courts at Law:** No. 1, Jack Grant; No. 2, Barbara Rollins. **Domestic Relations Court:** Aleta Hacker. **§Tom Green County Court at Law:** R. L. Blann. **¶Travis County Courts at Law:** No. 1, J. David Phillips; No. 2, Orlinda Naranjo; No. 3, David Crain; No. 4 (Probate), Guy Herman; No. 5, Wilfred Aguilar; No. 6, David Puryear; No. 7, Brenda P. Kennedy. ****Val Verde County Court at Law:** James M. Simmonds. **††Victoria County Courts at Law:** No. 1, Laura A. Weiser; No. 2, Juan Velasquez. **‡‡Walker County Court at Law:** Barbara Hale. **§§Waller County Court at Law:** June Jackson. **¶¶Washington County Court at Law:** Matthew Reue. *****Webb County Courts at Law:** No. 1, Raul Vasquez; No. 2, Jesús Garza. **†††Wichita County Courts at Law:** No. 1, Jim Hogan; No. 2, Tom Bacus. **‡‡‡Williamson County Courts at Law**: No. 1, Kevin Henderson; No. 2, Robert "Skip" Morse. **§§§Wise County Court at Law:** Melton D. Cude.

Texas County and District Officials — Table No. 2

District Clerks, District Attorneys and County Commissioners

See Table No. 1 on preceding pages for County Seats, County Judges, County Clerks, County Attorneys, County Treasurers, Tax Assessors-Collectors and Sheriffs.

County	District Clerk	District Attorney*	Comm. Precinct 1	Comm. Precinct 2	Comm. Precinct 3	Comm. Precinct 4
Anderson	Maxine Barnette	Jeff Herrington	Joe Chaffin	Arthur Sherrod	T. L. Beard	J. T. Davis
Andrews	Imogene Tate	Dennis Cadra	Bill Chesney	John Hogue	Jerry McPherson	Willard Snow
Angelina	Jimmie Robinson	Clyde Herrington	I.D. Henderson	Clayton C. Richardson	Jim Risinger	James Stanley
Aransas	Bobbie Rogers	George P. Morrill II	Oscar Piña	Ray Longino	Elliott McConnell	Larry Barnebey
Archer	Jane Ham	Tim Cole	Richard Shelley	James R. Wolf	Ben Buerger	D. W. Stone
Armstrong	Kathy Byrd	Danny Hill	Rex A. Bagwell	Thomas G. Fulgham	Tim Bagwell	C. M. Bryant
Atascosa	Jerome T. Brite	Lynn Ellison	Tommy Shearrer	Alfred Korus	Freddie Ogden	Weldon P. Cude
Austin	Lorri Coody	Travis J. Koehn	Stanley Jackson	Mark C. Wittner	James Bubba Duke	J. Royce Burger
Bailey	Nelda Merriott	Johnny Actkinson	Floyd "Butch" Vandiver	C. E. Grant Jr.	Joey R. Kindle	Bennie Claunch
Bandera	Bernice Bates	E. Bruce Curry	Bennie Barker	Dan C. Alanis III	Ralph Chancy	N. P. Thompson
Bastrop	LaNelle Hibbs	Charles Penick	Johnny Sanders	Charles McKeown	G. L. Hanna	Lee Dildy
Baylor	Doris Rushing	Bill Neal	Don Matus	Jackie Brown	Wes Hollar	Billy Joe Carlock
Bee	Sandra Clark	George P. Morrill II	Victor G. Salazar	Susan Stasny	Jimmy Martinez	Curtis H. Roberts
Bell	Sheila Norman	Arthur C. Eads	Richard Cortese	Tim Brown	John Thomas	Royce Matkin
Bexar	David J. Garcia	Steven C. Hilbig	Robert Tejeda	Paul Elizondo	Walter Bielstein	Mike Novak
Blanco	Dorothy Uecker	Sam Oatman	Dorsey L. Smith	Robert Riddell	Robert A. Mauck	Paul Granberg
Borden	Joyce Herridge	Ernie B. Armstrong	Frank Currey	Larry D. Smith	Vernon Wolf	Hurston Lemons Jr.
Bosque	Sandra L. Woosley	Andy J. McMullen	Rick Kelley	David H. Jones	Calvin Rueter	Carl Smith Jr.
Bowie	Billy Fox	Bobby Lockhart	Jack Stone	John Addington	Dale Barrett	Paul Fannin
Brazoria	Jerry Deere	Jerome Aldrich	Ronnie Broaddus	James Clawson	Billy Joe Plaster	Jack Patterson
Brazos	Marc Hamlin	Bill Turner	Gary Norton	Sandie Walker	Randy Sims	Carey Cauley
Brewster	Jo Ann Salgado	Albert G. Valadez	Asa "Cookie" Stone	J.W. "Red" Pattillo	Emilio Salmon	Abelardo Leyva
Briscoe	Bess McWilliams	Becky McPherson	Aaron E. Younger	J. L. Chandler	L. B. Garvin Jr.	Gary Weaks
Brooks	Pete Martinez	Joe Frank Garza	Elma Huerta	Ramon Navarro	José G. Garcia	Salvador Gonzalez
Brown	Jan Brown	G. Lee Haney	Steve Adams	Wayne Worley	Richard Gist	Vernon Moore
Burleson	Doris H. Brewer	Charles J. Sebesta Jr.	Frank W. Kristof	Don L. Groce	W. J. Stracener	Bobby E. Schoppe
Burnet	Modena Curington	Sam Oatman	James Holbrook	Carroll McCoy	Kenny Baker	Craig Seward
Caldwell	Emma Jean Schulle	Charles Kimbrough	Morris Alexander	Charles Bullock	Ronnie Duesterheft	Joe Ivan Roland
Calhoun	Pamela Martin	John D. Whitlow	Leroy Belk	Stanley Mikula	Helen J. Smith	Kenneth W. Finster
Callahan	Cubelle Harris	Allen Wright	Harold Hicks	Bryan Farmer	Tommy Holland	Charlie Grider
Cameron	Aurora de la Garza	Luis S. Saenz	Lucino Rosenbaum	Carlos H. Cascos	James R. Matz	Hector Peña
Camp	Doloria Bradshaw	Charles C. Bailey	Jack Efurd	Larry Shelton	O. C. Taylor	Curtis Wall
Carson	Barbara S. White	Randall C. Sims	Mike Britten	C. F. Smith	Jerry Strawn	Kevin Howell
Cass	Becky Wilbanks	Randall Lee	Taylor Duncan	H.B. (Barry) Frost	Lupton Willis	Freddie Tyson
Castro	Joyce Thomas	Jerry Matthews	Newlon Rowland	Larry Gonzales	W.A. (Bay) Baldridge	Vincent Guggemos
Chambers	R. B. Scherer	Mike Little	Mark Huddleston	Sidney Desormeaux Jr.	Jimmy Sylvia	Paul Lott
Cherokee	Marlys Mason	James (Jim) Cromwell	E. R. (Bob) Gregg	Alton J. Hicks	F. E. Hassell	Billy McCutcheon
Childress	Nancy Garrison	Randall C. Sims	David Hill	Dan Imhof	Lyall Foster	Mike Wilson
Clay	Dan Slagle	Tim Cole	G. E. Liggett	Harlan Hicks	Wilson Scaling	Brice Jackson
Cochran	Rita Tyson	Gary Goff	Billy D. Carter	Joe Bob Allen	A.W. Coffman	Jimmy Mullinax

County	District Clerk	District Attorney*	Comm. Precinct 1	Comm. Precinct 2	Comm. Precinct 3	Comm. Precinct 4
Coke	Ettie Hubbard	Charlotte Harris	Paul Burns	Billy Joe Luckett	Tim Millican	James A. Tidwell
Coleman	Louise Thompson	Ross L. Jones	Willard Allen	Billy McCrary	Vernon Slate	Alan Davis
Collin	Hannah Kunkle	Tom O'Connell	Phyllis Cole	Jerry Hoagland	John D. Witherspoon	Jack Hatchell
Collingsworth	Karen Coleman	Randall C. Sims	Glen Taylor	Zeb Roberson	Joe Tipton	Dudley Coleman
Colorado	Harvey Vornsand	W. C. Kirkendall	Richard Charles Seifert	Johnnie Elstner	Jerome Wicke	Leon Spanihel
Comal	Margaret Herbrich	Bill M. Reimer	J. L. Evans	Danny Scheel	Christina Zamora	Moe Schwab
Comanche	LaNell S. Williams	Andy J. McMullen	Gary Loudermilk	Dwight Biggs	Mark Pinson	Clyde Brinson
Concho	Margaret T. Taylor	Stephen H. Smith (119th) Ronald L. Sutton (198th)	Larry Kiesling	John Hruska	Alvin Beyer	John B. Williams
Cooke	Patricia A. Payne	Janelle M. Haverkamp	Murrell F. Harrison	Richard Brown	Jerry Lewis	Virgil Hess
Coryell	Carolyn Pollard	Sandy Gatley	John W. Carlton	Don Thompson	Hiram Davidson	Kyle Pruitt
Cottle	Beckey J. Tucker	Bill Neal	Paul Whitener	John Shavor	Manuel Cruz Jr.	D.N. Gregory Jr.
Crane	Maxine Willis	Michael Fostel	Larry Harbin	John D. Daniell	Ellis Lane	Weldon J. McCutchen Jr.
Crockett	Debbi Puckett	J. W. Johnson Jr.	Frank Tambunga	Fred Deaton	Freddie Nicks	Rudy Martínez
Crosby	Billie Jo Freeman	Tom J. Brian	Nelton Chote	William M. Odom	Herschel Bird	James A. Boydstun
Culberson	Linda McDonald	Jaime Esparza	Cornelio Garibay	Joel Sanchez	John Jones	Lupe Escajeda
Dallam	LuAnn Taylor	Barry Blackwell	Bob Sheets	Oscar Przilas	Don Bowers	Eulan Sheets
Dallas	Bill Long	John Vance	Jim Jackson	Mike Cantrell	John Wiley Price	Kenneth Mayfield
Dawson	Carolyn Turner	Ricky B. Smith	Delmar Moore	Bill Meares	Troy Howard	Guy Kinnison
Deaf Smith	Lola Faye Veazey	Roland Saul	Tony Castillo	Lupe Chavez	Troy Don Moore	Johnny Latham
Delta	Patsy P. Barton	Frank L. Long	C. D. (Mickey) Goforth	David Max Moody	Ardell Allison	Ted Carrington
Denton	Tracy Kunkel	Bruce Isaacks	Kirk Wilson	Sandy Jacobs	Scott Armey	Don Hill
DeWitt	Tabeth Ruschhaupt	Wiley L. Cheatham	Wallace W. Beck	Billy E. Moore	Gilbert Pargmann	Alfred Rangnow
Dickens	Yvonne "Tookie" Cash	Becky McPherson	Scrub Hawley	Billy George Drennan	Doc Edwards	Duane "Slim" Durham
Dimmit	Agustin G. Martínez Jr.	Roberto Serna	Larry Speer	Joaquin Salgado	Oscar Alvarado	Rodrigo Jaime
Donley	Fay Vargas	Randall C. Sims	Steve Reynolds	C. W. Cornell	Ronny Hill	William R. Chamberlain
Duval	Richard M. Barton	Heriberto Silva	Alejo C. Garcia	Rene M. Perez	Nestor Garza Jr.	Gilberto Uribe Jr.
Eastland	Bill Miears	Mike Siebert	Ken Lyerla	Calvin Ainsworth	L. T. Owen	Reggie Pittman
Ector	Jackie Sue Barnes	John W. Smith	Jack Crider	Mike Patton	Tom Todd	Bob Bryant
Edwards	Dorothy R. Hatley	Thomas F. Lee	Nicholas Gallegos	L.A. Field Sr.	Ivan H. Smart	Robert Perez
Ellis	Billie Fuller	Joe F. Grubbs	James Harper	Jerry Holland	Connie Doyle	Ron Brown
El Paso	Edie Rubalcaba	Jaime Esparza	Charles C. Hooten	Carlos Aguilar	Rogelio Sanchez	Dan Haggerty
Erath	Thomas Pack	John Terrill	C. H. Adams	Don Stone	Douglas Eberhart	Tommy Shelton
Falls	Larry R. Hoelscher	Thomas B. Sehon	Roy F. Jund	Bishop W. Williams	Tony Lynn Hoelscher	James Phillips
Fannin	Tommie Eaton		Jerry L. Jenkins	Lloyd Flanagan	Kurt Fogelberg II	Pat Hilliard
Fayette	Virginia Wied	John W. Wied	Lawrence Adamcik	Ronnie Stork	Wilbert L. Gross	Tom Muras
Fisher	Bettie Hargrove	Frank W. Conard II	Charles Meek	Billy Henderson	Jay Hendon	Gene Terry
Floyd	Barbara Edwards	Becky McPherson	Connie D. Bearden	Leonard Gilroy	George Taylor	Jon Jones
Foard	Sherry Weatherred	Dan Mike Bird	T. R. Cates	Johnny Urquizo	Larry Wright	Edward Crosby
Fort Bend	Glory Hopkins	John Healey	R. L. "Bud" O'Shieles	Grady Prestage	Alton Pressley	Bob Lutts
Franklin	Wanda Johnson	Frank Long	Jearl Cooper	Bobby R. Elbert	Deryl W. Carr	Charles Davis
Freestone	Janet Chappell		Tommy J. Robinson	W. R. McSwane	Stanley Gregory	John B. Massey
Frio	Ramona B. Rodriguez	Lynn Ellison	Mario Siller	Jesse M. Lindsey III	Pedro T. Espinosa	Humberto Berrones
Gaines	Virginia Stewart	Ricky B. Smith	Robert Wood	Joe Rowlett	Ray Garrett	Charlie Lopez

County	District Clerk	District Attorney*	Comm. Precinct 1	Comm. Precinct 2	Comm. Precinct 3	Comm. Precinct 4
Galveston	Evelyn Wells Robinson	Michael J. Guarino II	Eddie Barr	Eddie Janek	Wayne Johnson III	Ed Stuart
Garza	Sonny Gossett	Ricky Smith	Lee Norman	Mason McClellan	John Valdez	Royce Josey
Gillespie	Barbara Meyer	E. Bruce Curry	Dayton E. Weidenfeller	William A. Roeder	James J. Knopp	Eldon Ray Feller
Glasscock	Betty Pate	Rick Hamby	Jimmy Strube	J. E. Wooten	Hugh Schafer	Michael Hoch
Goliad	Gail M. Turley	Wiley L. Cheatham	Tony Garcia	Jerry Rodriguez	Louis Fromme Jr.	W. Wayne Key
Gonzales	Patricia Heinemeyer	William Kirkendall	E. R. Breitschopf	Truman DuPree	David Kuntschik	Welly Gibson
Gray	Yvonne Moler	John Mann	Joe Wheeley	Jim Greene	Gerald L. Wright	James Hefley
Grayson	Cyndi Mathis-Spencer	Robert T. Jarvis	Douglas Walker	Johnnie McCraw Jr.	Carol Ann Shea	Gene Short
Gregg	Ruby Cooper	David Brabham	Charles Davis	Darryl Primo	David McBride	James Johnson
Grimes	Wayne Rucker	Tuck Moody McLain	L. M. (Perk) Gressett	Thomas Kitkoski	Zac H. Falkenbury	Marcus Mallard
Guadalupe	James Behrendt	W. C. Kirkendall	Edward A. Springs	Casareo Guadarrama III	James M. Brannon	Wyatt L. "Butch" Kunde
Hale	Anna Ruth Evans	Terry McEachern	Nina Jo Morris	Mario Martinez	Roy Borchardt	Benny Cantwell
Hall	Raye Bailey	Randall C. Sims	Larry Don Maddox	Joe Neal Berry	Buddy C. Logsdon	U. F. Coker Jr.
Hamilton	LaJuan Mizell	Andy J. McMullen	Bill Snell	Ora Dell Tyson	James Akard	Loyd Crownover
Hansford	Kim V. Vera	Stephen F. Cross	Worley J. Smith	Joe T. Venneman	Kent Guthrie	Danny Henson
Hardeman	Judy Cokendolpher	Dan Mike Bird	Charles McSpadden	James Rine	Charles Taylor	Van D. Foster
Hardin	Vicki Johnson	R. F. "Bo" Horka	Bob Burgess	John Golden	W. P. "Bill" Fregia	John D. Brown
Harris	Charles Bacarisse	John B. Holmes Jr.	El Franco Lee	Jim Fonteno	Steve Radack	Jerry Eversole
Harrison	Betty Cawood	Rick Berry	James D. Mooney	Charles Bennett	Mike Adkisson	Jeffrey Thompson
Hartley	Diane Thompson	Barry Blackwell	Don McWhirter	Ron Sherman	James Yoder	R.B. Reynolds
Haskell	Carolyn Reynolds	John Fouts	Billy Wayne Hester	Ronnie Chapman	J. R. (Ray) Perry	C. A. (Bud) Turnbow
Hays	W. H. Moore	Marcos Hernandez Jr.	Pete Rodriguez	Jefferson W. Barton	Craig D. Payne	Russ G. Molenaar
Hemphill	Davene Hendershot	John Mann	Joe Schaef	Ed Culver	John Ramp	Lee Young
Henderson	Betty Ramsey	Donna Little Bennett	Walter Jackson	Harold Hammer	Cleburn Shavor	Jerry West
Hidalgo	Pauline Gonzalez	Rene Guerra	Samuel Sanchez	Lalo Arcaute	Juan Rosel	Guadalupe Garces
Hill	Charlotte Barr	Dan V. Dent	M. L. (Bud) Raulston	Kenneth Reid	Bobbie Brustrom	John W. Erwin
Hockley	Wynelle Donnell	Gary Goff	Sam Langford	El Lea Hensley	J. R. Stanley	Billy W. Thetford
Hood	Tonna Trumble	Richard Hattox	John Robert Anderson	Cliff Moody	David Cleveland	Kennith Umphress
Hopkins	Patricia Dorner	Frank Long	William a. Sparks	H. W. Halcomb	Don Patterson	Calvin Prince
Houston	Pam Pugh Crouch	Cindy Garner	George "Buzzy" Bush	Gene Musick	Burtis Wooten	Billy Ray Duren
Howard	Glenda Brasel	Rick Hamby	Emma Puga Brown	Jerry Kilgore	W. B. "Bill" Crooker	John M. "Sonny" Choate
Hudspeth	Patricia Bramblett	Jaime Esparza	Wayne R. West	Lester Ray Talley	Jim Ed Miller	Larry Brewton
Hunt	Ann Prince	F. Duncan Thomas	Johnnie Lyon	Ralph Green	Jim Hart	Allen Martin
Hutchinson	Sharron Orr	Stephen F. Cross	R. D. Cornelison	J. C. Berry	Litch Sparks Jr.	John E. Bayless
Irion	Reba Criner	Charlotte Harris	Mike Dolan	O. K. Wolfenbarger	Steve Elkins	Barbara Searcy
Jack	Lelia Vene Cozart	Barry Green	Lewis Kirk	Jerry M. Adams	James L. Cozart	Milton R. Pruitt
Jackson	Dolores Gabrysch	Robert E. Bell	Miller Rutledge	Erwin Skalicky	Priscilla Hurta	W. O. Walker
Jasper	Nell Powers	Guy James Gray	Edgar W. Lewis	Cecil "Buddy" Ellis	James E. Smith	Corbit Whitehead
Jeff Davis	Sue Blackley	Albert Valadez	Billy C. Cotton	Joe Dominguez	Billie Weston	Bill Gearhart
Jefferson	John S. Appleman	Tom Maness	Jimmie P. Cokinos	Mark L. Domingue	Waymon D. Hallmark	Edward C. Moore
Jim Hogg	Gloria Diana Rodriguez	Heriberto Silva	José Zuñiga III	Oscar O. Gonzalez	Alberto Benavides Jr.	Ruben Rodriguez
Jim Wells	Olga Villarreal	Joe Frank Garza	Zenaida "Sandy" Sanchez	C. L. "Tommy" Cornelius	J. B. "Red" Freiley	Javier Garcia
Johnson	Jeaniv Johnson	Dale Hanna	R. C. McFall	Ron Harmon	Bobby Estes	Troy Thompson
Jones	Nona Carter	Jack Willingham	James Clawson	Mike Polk	Vonay Davis	Steve Lollar

County	District Clerk	District Attorney*	Comm. Precinct 1	Comm. Precinct 2	Comm. Precinct 3	Comm. Precinct 4
Karnes	Patricia Brysch	Lynn Ellison	Darrel Blaschke	Carl E. Beam	Juan Martinez	Gus Osburn
Kaufman	Sandra Featherston	Louis W. Conradt Jr.	Pete Hammock	Rod Kinkaid	Ivan Johnson	Jerry Brewer
Kendall	Shirley R. Stehling	E. Bruce Curry	Charles Goodman	L.M. Holman	Sue Whitworth	Victor King
Kenedy	Barbara B. Turcotte	Carlos Valdez	Leonard May	Louis E. Turcotte Jr.	Tobin Armstrong	Gus A. Puente
Kent	Cornelia Cheyne	John Fouts	Bob E. Hamilton	Don Long	Michael W. Owen	Don Trammel
Kerr	Linda Uecker	Ronald L. Sutton (198th) E. Bruce Curry (216th)	Ray Lehman	T. H. "Butch" Lackey	Glenn K. Holekamp	Bruce Oehler
Kimble	Elaine Carpenter	Ronald L. Sutton	Ray Jacoby	Ilee Simon	Russell Fleming	Victor Herbst
King	Tavia Vinson	Bill Neal	Jordan Rogers	Sam Fulton	Bob Tidmore	Darwood Marshall
Kinney	Dora Elia Sandoval	Thomas F. Lee	Freddie Frerich	Joe Montalvo	Cordelia Mendeke	Paul O'Rourke
Kleberg	Martha Soliz	Carlos Valdez	David Rosse	Tony R. Barbour	Allen M. May	Romeo Lomas
Knox	Danny Speck	Bill Neal	Leonard L. Phipps	Jerry Parker	Phillip F. Homer	Johnny Birkenfeld
Lamar	Marvin Ann Patterson		Troy L. Owens	Carl L. Steffey	J. E. "Gene" Buster	Alan R. Weatherford
Lamb	Teresa McGaa	Mark Yarbrough	Willie Gene Green	Thurman Lewis	Emil Macha	Leonard Pierce
Lampasas	Terri Cox	Larry Allison	Robert L. Vincent Jr.	Edd Barefoot	Travis Herring	Tommy Harkey
La Salle	Nora Mae Tyler	Lynn Ellison	Raymond A. Landrum Jr.	Roberto F. Aldaco	Arcenio A. Garcia	Carlos B. Gonzalez
Lavaca	Calvin J. Albrecht	W. C. Kirkendall	Johnny Jahn Jr.	Eddie Vrana	Daniel Peters	Glen Blundell
Lee	Adeline Melcher	Steven Keng	Maurice Pitts Jr.	Otto Becker Jr.	O. B. "Butch" Johnson	Larry Wachsmann
Leon	Gloria McCarty	Tuck Moody McLain	Joseph P. Sullivan	F. G. (Bubba) Lipsey	Jim Miles	Burel Biddle
Liberty	Joy K. McManus	Michael Little	Harry D. Hylton	Lee Groce	Melvin Hunt	Bobby Payne
Limestone	Mary D. Budde	Don Cantrell	John Barnett Lown	Billy Waldrop	G. Z. Stone	Curtis Fountain
Lipscomb	Coeta Sperry	John A. Mann	John W. Floyd	F.R. Loesch	Marvin V. Born	John D. Fritzlen
Live Oak	Ellen Jane McCarley	George P. Morrill II	J.J. Houdmann	Hilbert Kopplin	Jimmy Strause	Emilio Garza
Llano	Debbie Honig	Sam Oatman	Randy Leifeste	Keith Faulkner	Cecil Mings	Marc Miller
Loving	Juanita Busby	John Stickels	Harlan Hopper	Joe R. Renteria	Skeet L. Jones	Royce Creager
Lubbock	Jean Anne Stratton	William C. "Bill" Sowder	Kenny Maines	James Kitten	Gilbert Flores	Gary Schwantz
Lynn	Sandra Laws	Ricky B. Smith	Jacky Henry	T. A. Stone	Sandra Cox	J. T. Miller
Madison	Joyce Batson	Tuck Moody McLain	Reed Reynolds	Walton Reynolds	Ford Hooper	Bob Grisham
Marion	Janie McCay	James P. Finstrom	R. M. (Ric) Blevins	T. W. (Sam) Smith	Don Kranz	C. W. (Charlie) Treadwell
Martin	Susie Hull	Rick Hamby	James N. Biggs	Homer Henson	Eldon A. Welch	C.W. Turner
Mason	Beatrice Langehennig	Sam Oatman	Carl Martin	T. J. Webster	Drew Tallent	Billy Kothmann
Matagorda	Becky Denn	Steven E. Reis	Michael J. Pruett	George W. Deshotels	F. P. "Sonny" Brhlik	E. R. Vacek
Maverick	Diamantina Treviño	Roberto Serna	Johnny E. Martinez	Guillermo Mancha	Enrique Ibarra	Roberto Ruiz
McCulloch	Mackye Johnson	Ronald Sutton	Joe H. Johnson	Jackie Behrens	Gary Doyal	Jerry Tedder
McLennan	Joe Johnson	John Segrest	Wayne Davis	Lester Gibson	Fred Binner	Ray Meadows
McMullen	Nell Hodgin	George P. Morrill II	Asa M. Farrer Jr.	Rodney Swaim Jr.	Herman Smith	Maximo G. Quintanilla Jr.
Medina	Jean Marty	Anton E. (Tony) Hackebeil	Jim E. Jenkins	Stanley Keller Jr.	Enrique G. Santos	Kelly Carroll
Menard	Elsie Maserang	Ronald Sutton	Franklin Gainer	Richard Cordes	Ray McGuffin	Donald Kothmann
Midland	Vivian Wood	Al Schorre	Henry Goulet	Guy McCrary	Louisa Valencia	James Brezina
Milam	Leola L. Komar	Hollis C. Lewis Jr.	V. W. Hauk	Troy Mode	C. Dale Jaecks	Burke Bauerschlag
Mills	Beulah L. Roberts	G. Lee Haney	Joe Karnes	Carroll Bunting	Lee Roy Schwartz	Hawley B. Jernigan
Mitchell	Sharon Hammond	Frank Conard II	Edward B. Roach	Carl Guelker	Buddy Hertenberger	Billy H. Preston
Montague	Condell Lowrie	Tim Cole	Jon A. Kernek	Jerry Clement	Glen Seay	Tommie Sappington
Montgomery	Peggy Stevens	Dan Rice	Mike Meador	Malcolm Purvis	Ed Chance	Jim Simmons

County	District Clerk	District Attorney*	Comm. Precinct 1	Comm. Precinct 2	Comm. Precinct 3	Comm. Precinct 4
Moore	June Mills	Barry A. Blackwell	Jerrie Howe	Louis Dubuque	Keith Christie	Lynn Cartrite
Morris	Welton Walker	Richard Townsend	Coy L. Roney	Dearl Quarles	Forrest A. Clair	Bob Scaff
Motley	Lucretia Campbell	Beckey McPherson	John M. Russell	Donald Hughes	Franklin Jameson	J. N. Fletcher
Nacogdoches	Shelby Solomon	Tim James	C. W. "Joe" Corley	Norman Henderson	Fred Nelson	George Self
Navarro	Marilyn Greer	Patrick C. Batchelor	Betty Armstrong	Olin Nickelberry	Jerry Blackmon	Paul Slaughter
Newton	Abbie N. Stark	Charles Mitchell	Weldon R. Wilkinson	Anderson White	Melton G. Jarrell	Ricky Odom
Nolan	Vera Holloman	Frank Conard II	Edsel Bankhead	Harold Ware	Tommy White	Dalton Owens
Nueces	Oscar Soliz	Carlos Valdez	Frank L. Schwing Jr.	David Berlanga Sr.	Oscar O. Ortiz	Joe McComb
Ochiltree	Shawn Rogers		Jack Kile	Tom O'Dell	Cliff McGarraugh	Larry Hardy
Oldham	Martha Thompson	Don Davis	Kirk Montgomery	Donnie Knox	Roger Morris III	Grady Skaggs
Orange	Stella Winter		Ron Sigler	C.J. Huckaby	Donald Cole	Bill E. Harland
Palo Pinto	Helen Slemmons	Jerry Ray	David Lee	Robert Murray	George Nowak	Earnest Pechacek
Panola	Sandra King	Danny Buck Davidson	Herbert T. Koonce	Forrest (Buddy) Harris	Edwin (Dick) Haynes	Jimmy E. Davis
Parker	Lana Tibbitts	Amy Adams	Waymon Wright	Mack Dobbs	Coy Carter	Rena Peden
Parmer	Sandra Warren	Johnny Actkinson	Johnny G. Mars	Thomas Ware	Robert White	Raymond McGehee
Pecos	Janice Stockburger	Albert Valadez(83rd) J.W. Johnson Jr. (112th)	Gregg McKenzie	Tony Villarreal	Neal Sconiers	Paul Valenzuela
Polk	Nell Lowe	John S. Holleman	B. E. "Slim" Speights	Bobby Smith	James J. "Buddy" Purvis	R. R. "Dick" Hubert
Potter	Cindy Groomer	Danny E. Hill	Cliff Roberts	Manuel Perez Villasenor	Strick Watkins	Will C. Thirlkill
Presidio	Ramona Lara	Albert Valadez	Felipe Cordero	Juan José Muñiz	Jaime Rodriguez	Jack W. Brunson
Rains	Mary Sheppard	J. Frank Long	Jimmy Roberts	William Potts	Gary Bishop	Rayford Briggs
Randall	LaQuitta Polvadore	James Farren	John Currie Jr.	Jan Reid	George (Skip) Huskey	John M. Dodson
Reagan	Billie Havis	Albert Valadez (83rd) J. W. Johnson Jr. (112th)	Jim O'Bryan	Michael Fisher	Bill Schneemann	Thomas Strube
Real	Rosemary Brice	Anton E. (Tony) Hackebeil	W. B. Sansom Jr.	Kenneth B. Shackelford	Castulo San Miguel	Milburn Wooldridge
Red River	Clara Gaddis		Tommie Corbell	Ronnie James	Elmer Caton	Alton D. Peek
Reeves	Juana Jaquez	John W. Stickels	Lupe Garcia	W. J. Bang	Herman Tarin	Bernardo Martínez
Refugio	Ruby Garcia	Wiley Cheatham	James Pfeil	Ronald K. Hicks	James Henry	Richard Martinez
Roberts	Donna L. Goodman	John Mann	William H. Clark	Ken Gill	Don W. Morrison	James F. Duvall Jr.
Robertson	Cornelia A. Starkey	John C. Paschall	Tommy C. Singleton	Bobby R. Madden	Joe Smith	Marie Abraham
Rockwall	Marty Beaty	Galen Ray Sumrow	Dosville Peoples	Dale Troutt	Joe Florey	Trey Chaney
Runnels	Loretta Michalewicz	Stephen H. Smith	Skipper Wheeless	Keith Collom	James Thurman Self	Richard W. Strube
Rusk	Linda J. Smith	Kyle Freeman	Talmadge Mercer	Harold Kuykendall	Dan Cates	Kimble Harris
Sabine	Tanya Walker	Charles Mitchell	Keith C. Clark	S. Lynn Smith	Charles W. Ellison	Will Smith Sr.
San Augustine	Jean Steptoe	Charles R. Mitchell	Tommy Hunter	Edward Wilson	Joey Lee Holloway	Bill T. Langford
San Jacinto	Marilyn Nettles		Norman Street	Weaver Stripling	Thomas Bonds	Will Copeland Jr.
San Patricio	Patricia Norton	George P. Morrill II	Nina Treviño	Fred P. Nardini	Pedro G. Rodriguez	Gordon Porter
San Saba	Kim Wells	Sam Oatman	Roger Crockett	Hollis Lord	Wayland Perry	Jackie Brister
Schleicher	Peggy Williams	Charlotte Harris	Johnny F. Mayo Jr.	Kerry Joy	Jerry Jones	Ross Whitten
Scurry	Elois Pruitt	Ernie Armstrong	Ralph Trevey	Roy L. Idom	C. D. Gray Jr.	Jerry Gannaway
Shackelford	Frances Wheeler	Jack Willingham	James Tabor	R. P. Mitchell	Jimmy T. Brooks	James Waddington
Shelby	Marsha Singletary	John R. Smith	Charles Williams	O. K. (Buddy) Hagler	Spencer Hamilton	Wilfred Harris
Sherman	M. L. Albert	Barry E. Blackwell	Wayne Cummings	Wayland Brown	David Hass	Tommy Asher
Smith	R. Brad Burger		Bill Wallis	Gus Ramirez	Derrell Cooper	Andrew R. Melontree
Somervell	Lovella Williams	Dale Hanna	Larry Hulsey	Foy Edwards	Randy Whitworth	Jim Gartrell

County	District Clerk	District Attorney*	Comm. Precinct 1	Comm. Precinct 2	Comm. Precinct 3	Comm. Precinct 4
Starr	Juan Erasmo Saenz	Heriberto Silva	José María Alvarez	Adrian Gonzalez	Eloy Garza	Abel Gonzalez
Stephens	Shirley Parker	John Neal	Jerry Toland	D. C. "Button" Sikes	Ozell Devenport	Carter Fore
Sterling	Diane A. Haar	Charlotte Harris	Billy Joe Blair	Eddie Michulka	Patsy Bynum	Melvin Foster
Stonewall	Betty L. Smith	John Fouts	Carl W. Willingham	Pat Cumbie	Billy Kirk Meador	Dickey Parker
Sutton	Bobbie Smith	J. W. Johnson Jr.	Miguel "Mike" Villanueva	John Wade	Bill Keel	Belia Castaneda
Swisher	Brenda Hudson	Terry McEachern	Lloyd Rahlfs	A. G. House	B. F. "Smitty" Smith	W. C. Weatherred
Tarrant	Tom Wilder	Tim Curry	Dionne Bagsby	Marti VanRavenswaay	Bob Hampton	J. D. Johnson
Taylor	JoAnn Lackey	James Eidson	Jack Turner	Don Dudley	Stan Egger	Neil Fry
Terrell	Martha Allen	Thomas F. Lee	Thelma Calzada	Santiago Flores	Henry Petty	Hudson Kerr
Terry	Frances Hyman		Earl J. Brown Jr.	Bill Keesee	Don Robertson	John Franks
Throckmorton	Cathey Mitchell	John Fouts	Doyle Wells	John Jones	Carlton Sullivan	George Seedig
Titus	Bobby LaPrade	Charles Bailey	Mike Price	Mike Fields	J. W. Terrell Jr.	Thomas E. Hockaday
Tom Green	Sue Bramhall	Charlotte Harris (51st) Stephen H. Smith (119th)	Gary Acevedo	Karl Bookter	Delbert Caffey	Tim Weatherby
Travis	Amalia Rodriguez-Mendoza	Ronald Earle	Sam Biscoe	Karen Sonleitner	Valarie Bristol	Margaret Gomez
Trinity	Cheryl Cartwright	Joe Lynn Price	Lynn Reynolds	Dean Price	Cecil Webb	Wayne Odom
Tyler	Patricia (Pat) Brown	James A. Clark	Maxie Riley	Arthur M. (Pete) Barnes	Jerry Mahan	Henry Earl Sawyer
Upshur	Horace A. Ray	Tim Cone	Gaddis Lindsey	Tommy L. Stanley	David G. Loyd	Charles K. Thompson
Upton	Phyllis Stephens	Albert G. Valadez (83rd) J. W. Johnson Jr. (112th)	Morris E. (Mac) McKenzie	Tommy Owens	W.E. (Willie) Martínez	Leon Patrick
Uvalde	Lydia Steele	Anton E. (Tony) Hackebeil	Randy Scheide	Gilbert Torres	Ed Jones	Jesse R. Moreno
Val Verde	Martha Germany	Tom Lee	Gary Leonard	Arturo Gallegos	John M. Cody	John F. Qualia
Van Zandt	Nancy Young	Leslie Poynter Dixon	O. D. Hazel	Cary Hilliard	Leonard M. Morris	Loy D. Hutchins
Victoria	Mary Elizabeth Jimenez	George J. Filley III	Frank J. Targac	Jerry Nobles	John J. Hammack	Rex L. Easley
Walker	Betty Tackett	David P. Weeks	B. J. Gaines	Robert Autery	James "Buddy" Reynolds	Joe Malak Jr.
Waller	Beverly A. Kluna	Sherry Lynn Robinson	Delmar Barry	Frank Pokluda	Frank Jackson	Eddie Neuman
Ward	Jo Ann Roark	John W. Stickels	Ben Villalobos	Bill Welch	Larry Hunt	Don Creech
Washington	Blondean Kuecker	Charles Sebesta Jr.	David M. Simpson	Robert Mikeska	Gilbert Janner	Paul Pipes
Webb	Manuel Gutierrez	Joe Rubio	Jorge O. de la Garza	Roque Vela	Rick Reyes	David Cortez
Wharton	Evelyn Kramer	Steven E. Reis	Carl W. Nichols	D. C. "Chris" King	Merrill T. Adamcik	Catherine Drapela
Wheeler	Sherri Jones	John Mann	Kenneth Childress	Tommy Puryear	Hubert C. Moore	Boyd Hiltbrunner
Wichita	Dorsey Trapp	Barry L. Macha	Woodrow W. Gossom Jr.	Weldon Nix	Gordon Griffith	Harold White
Wilbarger	Wilda Byers	Dan Mike Bird	John Milner	Freddie Streit	Glen Turner	Lenville Morris
Willacy	Santiago Fonseca	Gustavo Ch. Garza	Israel Tamez	Gene McGee	Alfredo S. Serrato	Pete Garcia
Williamson	Bonnie Wolbrueck	Ken Anderson	Mike Heiligenstein	Gregory Boatright	David Hays	Jerry Mehevec
Wilson	Shirley Polasek	Lynn Ellison	Roger Lopez	Albert Pruski	Mark A. Johnson	Wayne Stroud
Winkler	Virginia Healy	Michael L. Fostel	Tommy R. Smith	James A. Winn	Stephen R. Brown	Benito Davila
Wise	Lawana Snider	Barry Green	Kyle E. Stephens	James A. Hubbard	Kenneth E. Steel	L. Paul Wood
Wood	Jo Anna Nelson	Marcus D. Taylor	Glenn Bevill	Kenneth Wilson	Roger Pace	Roger Tinney
Yoakum	Mae Barnett	Richard Clark	John Avara	R. W. Thurston	Jim Barron	Macky McWhirter
Young	George C. Birdwell	John Neal	Duane Downey	John C. Bullock	R. L. Spivey	John L. Hawkins
Zapata	Consuelo R. Villarreal	José Rubio	José Luis Flores	Angel Garza	Adolfo Gonzalez Jr.	Amaro Bustamante
Zavala	Rosa Elva Mata	Roberto Serna	Jesús Vasquez	Miguel (Mike) Acosta	Pilo Vasquez	Matthew McHazlett Jr.

If more than one District Attorney is listed for a county, the district court number is noted in parentheses after each attorney's name. If no District Attorney is listed, the County Attorney, whose name can be found in Table No. 1, assumes the duties of that office.

Texans in Congress

Texas is allocated 30 members in the U.S. House of Representatives and two in the U.S. Senate. The term of office for members of the House is two years; the terms of all members will expire on Jan. 1, 1997. Senators serve six-year terms. Phil Gramm's term will end in 1997 and Kay Bailey Hutchison's will end in 2001.

Addresses and phone numbers of the lawmakers' Washington and district offices are given below, as well as the committees on which they serve. Washington **zip codes** are **20515** for members of the House and **20510** for senators. The telephone **area code** for Washington is **202**. See map of congressional districts on p. 453.

U.S. Senate

GRAMM, Phil, R-College Station; Washington Office: 370 RSOB, Washington, D.C. 20510; (202) 224-2934, Fax 228-2856.

Texas Offices: 22 E. Van Buren, Suite 404 **Harlingen** 78550, (512) 423-6118; 712 Main, Suite 2400, **Houston** 77002, (713) 229-2766; 112 Federal Building, 1205 Texas Ave., **Lubbock** 79401, (806) 743-7533; 2323 Bryan, Suite 1500, **Dallas** 75201, (214) 767-3000; 310 N. Mesa, **El Paso** 79901, (915) 534-6896; 102 N. College, Suite 201, **Tyler** 75710, (214) 593-0902; 402 E. Ramsey Rd., **San Antonio** 78216, (512) 366-9494. **Committees**: Budget, Appropriations, Banking.

HUTCHISON, Kay Bailey, R-Dallas; Washington Office: 703 HSOB, Washington, D.C. 20510; (202) 224-5922, Fax 224-0776.

Texas Offices: 961 Federal Bldg., 300 E. 8th St., **Austin** 78703, (512) 482-5834; 10440 N. Central Expy., Suite 1160, **Dallas** 75231, (214) 361-3500; 1919 Smith St., Suite 800, **Houston** 77002, (713) 653-3456. **Committees**: Armed Services, Commerce, Select Intelligence, Small Business.

U.S. House of Representatives

ARCHER, Bill, R-Houston, District 7; Washington Office: 1236 LHOB; (202) 225-2571, Fax 225-4381; **District Office:** 10000 Memorial Dr., Suite 620, Houston 77024, (713) 682-8828. **Committees:** Ways and Means (chairman).

ARMEY, Richard, R-Lewisville, District 26; Washington Office: 301 CHOB; (202) 225-7772, Fax 225-7614; **District Office:** 9901 Valley Ranch Parkway East, Suite 3050, Irving 75063, (214) 556-2500. **House Majority Leader**.

BARTON, Joe, R-Ennis, District 6; Washington Office: 2264 RHOB; (202) 225-2002. Fax 225-3052; **District Offices**: 3509 Hulen, No. 110, Fort Worth 76107, (817) 543-1000; 303 West Knox, Suite 101, Ennis 75119, (817) 543-1000; 2019 E. Lamar Blvd., Suite 100, Arlington 76006, (817) 543-1000. **Committees:** Commerce, Science.

BENTSEN, Ken, D-Houston, District 25; Washington Office: 128 CHOB; (202) 225-7508, Fax 225-2947. **Committees**: Banking and Financial Services, Small Business.

BONILLA, Henry, R-San Antonio, District 23; Washington Office: 1427 LHOB; (202) 225-4511, Fax 225-2237; **District Offices**: 11120 Wurzbach, No. 330, San Antonio 78230, (210) 697-9055; 1300 Matamoros St., Suite 113B, Laredo 78040, (210) 726-4682; 111 E. Broadway, Suite 101, Del Rio 78840, (210) 774-6547; 4400 N. Big Spring, Suite 211, Midland 79705, (915) 686-8833. **Committee:** Appropriations.

BRYANT, John, D-Dallas, District 5; Washington Office: 2330 CHOB; (202) 225-2231, Fax 225-0327; **District Office:** 8035 East R. L. Thornton Freeway, No. 518, Dallas 75228, (214) 767-6554. **Committees**: Commerce, Judiciary.

CHAPMAN, Jim, D-Sulphur Springs, District 1; Washington Office: 2417 RHOB; (202) 225-3035, Fax 225-7265; **District Offices:** P.O. Box 538, Sulphur Springs, 75842, (903) 885-8682, Fax (903) 885-2976. **Committee:** Appropriations.

COLEMAN, Ron, D-El Paso, District 16; Washington Office: 440 CHOB; (202) 225-4831, Fax 225-4825, **District Office:** Federal Building, Suite 723-700 East San Antonio St., El Paso 79901, (915) 534-6200. **Committees**: Appropriations, Select Intelligence.

COMBEST, Larry, R-Lubbock, District 19; Washington Office: 1511 LHOB; (202) 225-4005, Fax (202) 225-9615; **District Office:** 1205 Texas Avenue, Room 613, Lubbock, 79401, (806) 763-1611. **Committees:** Select Intelligence (chairman), Agriculture.

De la GARZA, E. (Kika), D-Mission, District 15; Washington Office: 1401 LHOB; (202) 225-2531, Fax 225-2534; **District Office:** 1418 Beech St., Suite 135, McAllen 78501. **Committee**: Agriculture (ranking minority member).

DeLAY, Tom, R-Sugar Land, District 22; Washington Office: 203 CHOB; (202) 225-5951, Fax 225-5241; **District Office:** 12603 Southwest Freeway, Suite 285, Stafford 77477, (713) 240-3700. **House Majority Whip. Committee**: Appropriations.

DOGGETT, Lloyd, D-Austin, District 10; Washington Office: 126 CHOB; (202) 225-4865, Fax 225-3073; **District Office:** 673 Federal Bldg, Austin 78701, (512) 482-5921. **Committees**: Budget, Science.

EDWARDS, Chet, D-Waco, District 11; Washington Office: 328 CHOB; (202) 225-6105, Fax 225-0350. **District Office:** 710 Clifton-Robinson Tower, 700 S. University Parks Dr., Waco 76706; (817) 752-9600, Fax 752-7769. **Committees:** National Security, Veterans' Affairs.

FIELDS, Jack, R-Humble, District 8; Washington Office: 2228 RHOB; (202) 225-4901, Fax 225-2772; **District Offices**: 300 West Davis, Suite 507, Conroe 77301, (409) 756-8044; 111 East University Dr., Suite 216, College Station 77840, (409) 846-6068; 9810 FM 1960 Bypass West, Suite 165, Humble 77338, (713) 540-8000. **Committee**: Commerce.

FROST, Martin, D-Dallas, District 24; Washington Office, 2459 RHOB; (202) 225-3605, Fax 225-4951; **District Offices**, 400 South Zang, Suite 1319, Dallas 75208, (214) 948-3401; 3020 S.E. Loop 820, Fort Worth 76140, (817) 293-9231. **Committee**: Rules.

GEREN, Pete, D-Fort Worth, District 12; Washington Office: 2448 RHOB; (202) 225-5071, Fax 225-2786; **District Office**, 1600 West 7th St., No. 740, Fort Worth 76102, (817) 338-0909. **Committees**: National Security, Science.

GONZALEZ, Henry B., D-San-Antonio, District 20; Washington Office: 2413 RHOB; (202) 225-3236,

1994 Medal of Freedom Honors Former Member of Congress

Barbara Jordan. Dallas Morning News photo.

Barbara Jordan, former member of Congress from Houston, was awarded the nation's highest civilian honor in 1994 with a Medal of Freedom from President Bill Clinton.

Ms. Jordan, a professor at the Lyndon B. Johnson School of Public Affairs at The University of Texas at Austin, was recognized for her "dramatically articulated and enduring standard of morality in American politics. Guided by an unshakable faith in the Constitution, she insists that it is the sacred duty of those who hold power to govern ethically and to preserve the rule of law," according to the citation on her medal.

Ms. Jordan's public career began in 1966 when she became the first black woman elected to the Texas Senate. In her six years in Austin she proposed and helped pass bills establishing the Texas Fair Employment Practices Commission and expansion of minimum wage provisions to cover domestics, farm laborers and laundry workers.

In 1972, she was elected to the U.S. House of Representatives, where she received national renown serving on the Judiciary Committee during the Watergate scandal.

In 1978, she decided not to seek re-election to Congress because of frustration with the slowness of government. "After six years I had wearied of the little chips that I could put on a woodpile," she said.

Ms. Jordan returned to Texas as a full professor at UT-Austin, teaching political values and ethics.

Barbara Jordan was born Feb. 21, 1936, in the largest black ghetto in Houston. Her father, Ben, was a Baptist preacher and warehouse laborer. Her mother, Arlyne, was known for her church speaking, as well.

The future Democratic member of Congress graduated from Wheatley High School and attended Texas Southern University in Houston. She received her law degree from Boston University in 1959 and returned to Houston to practice law. She made two unsuccessful runs for the Texas Legislature in 1962 and 1964 before winning the state Senate race in 1966.

Ms. Jordan was among nine persons honored by President Clinton in 1994. Others included Cesar Chavez (posthumously), labor leader Lane Kirkland, Sargent Shriver, UNICEF director James Grant, civil servant Arthur Flemming, civil rights leader Dorothy Height, cartoonist Herbert Block and House Republican leader Bob Michel of Illinois.

The Medal of Freedom was established in 1945 by President Harry Truman.

Other Texans who have received the honor include Dr. Michael DeBakey, Lady Bird Johnson and J. Frank Dobie.

Also, several astronauts and NASA officials serving in Houston have received the award, as well as national figures who have spent part of their professional lives in Texas, including writer James Michener, now associated with UT-Austin, and artist Georgia O'Keeffe, who was attracted to the openness of the Southwest while teaching in public schools in the Panhandle. ☆

Fax 225-1915; **District Office**: 124-B Federal Building, 727 East Durango, San Antonio 78206, (210) 229-6199. **Committee**: Banking and Financial Services (**ranking minority member**).

GREEN, Gene, D-Houston, District 29; Washington Office: 1024 LHOB; (202) 225-1688, Fax 225-9903; **District Office**: 5502 Lawndale, Houston 77023, (713) 923-9961. **Committees**: Economic and Educational Opportunities, Government Reform and Oversight.

HALL, Ralph M., D-Rockwall, District 4; Washington Office: 2236 RHOB; (202) 225-6673, Fax, (202) 225-3332; **District Office**: 104 N. San Jacinto, 119 Federal Building, Rockwall 75087, (214) 771-9118. **Committees**: Commerce, Science.

JOHNSON, Eddie Bernice, D-Dallas, District 30; Washington Office: 1123 LHOB; (202) 225-8885, Fax 226-1477; **District Office**: 2515 McKinney Ave., No. 1565, Dallas 75201, (214) 922-8885. **Committees**: Science, Transportation and Infrastructure.

JOHNSON, Sam, R-Plano, District 3; Washington Office: 1030 LHOB; (202) 225-4201, Fax 225-

1485; **District Office**: Glen Lake Tower, No. 610, 9400 North Central Expressway, Dallas 75231, (214) 739-0182, Fax 423-2841. **Committees**: Economic and Educational Opportunities, Ways and Means.

LAUGHLIN, Greg, R-West Columbia, District 14; Washington Office: 442 CHOB; (202) 225-2831, Fax 225-1108; **District Offices**: 312 South Main St., Victoria 77901, (512) 576-1231, Fax 576-0381; 111 North 10th St., West Columbia 77486, (409) 345-1414; 102 North LBJ, Hays County Courthouse Annex, San Marcos 78666, (512) 396-1400. **Committees**: Select Intelligence, Transportation and Infrastructure.

LEE, Sheila Jackson, D-Houston, District 18; Washington Office: 152 LHOB; (202) 225-3816, Fax 225-3317; **District Office**: 1919 Smith St., No. 1180, Houston 77002, (713) 655-0050. **Committees**: Judiciary, Science.

ORTIZ, Solomon P., D-Corpus Christi, District 27; Washington Office: 2136 RHOB; (202) 225-7742, Fax 226-1134; **District Offices**: 3649 Leopard, Suite 510, Corpus Christi 78408, (512) 883-5868; 3505 Boca Chica Blvd., Brownsville 78521, (512) 541-1242. **Committees**: National Security, Natural Resources.

SMITH, Lamar S., R-San Antonio, District 21; Washington Office: 2443 RHOB; (202) 225-4236, Fax 225-8628; **District Offices**: 1100 NE Loop 410, Suite 640, San Antonio 78216, (210) 821-5024; 201 West Wall St., Suite 104, Midland 79701, (915) 687-5232; 33 East Twohig, Suite 302, San Angelo 76903, (915) 653-3971; 1006 Junction Highway, Kerrville 78028, (512) 895-1414; 221 East Main, Suite 318, Round Rock 78664, (915) 653-3971. **Committees**: Budget, Judiciary.

STENHOLM, Charles, D-Stamford, District 17, Washington Office, 1211 LHOB; (202) 225-6605, Fax 225-2234; **District Office**: P. O. Box 1237, Stamford 79553, (915) 773-3623. **Committees**, Agriculture, Budget.

STOCKMAN, Steve, R-Webster, District 9; Washington Office: 417 CHOB; (202) 225-6565, Fax 225-3483; **District Offices**: 201 Federal Bldg. Beaumont 77701, (409) 839-2508; 216 U.S. Post Office and Courthouse, Galveston 77550, (409) 766-3608. **Committees**: Science, Veterans' Affairs.

TEJEDA, Frank, D-San Antonio, District 28; Washington Office, 323 CHOB; (202) 225-1640, Fax 225-1641; **District Office:** 1313 Southeast Military Drive, No. 115, San Antonio 78214, (210) 924-7383, Fax 927-6222. **Committees**: National Security, Veterans' Affairs.

THORNBERRY, William M. (Mac), R-Clarendon, District 13; Washington Office: 1535 LHOB; (202) 225-3706, Fax 225-3486; **District Offices**: 724 S. Polk, No. 400, Amarillo 79101, (806) 371-8844; and 811 6th St., No. 130, Wichita Falls 76301, (817) 767-0541. **Committees**: National Security, Natural Resources.

WILSON, Charles, D-Lufkin, District 2; Washington Office: 2256 RHOB; (202) 225-2401, Fax 225-1764; **District Office**: 701 North 1st St., Room 201, Lufkin 75901, (409) 637-1770, Fax 632-8588. **Committee:** Appropriations. ☆

Major Military Installations

Below are listed the major military installations in Texas. Data are taken from "Guide to Military Installations in the U.S.," Nov. 1994. The base closings or re-arrangements under consideration in mid-1995 may alter the list: some bases may be closed altogether; others may be assigned alternate roles; some units may be reassigned ; and numbers of personnel may change.

U.S. Army

Fort Bliss

Location: Northeast El Paso.

Address: Fort Bliss, Texas 79916-0058

Main phone number: (915) 568-2121

Population: 19,000 active-duty; 24,000 family members; 8,000 civilians.

Major units: Army Air Defense Artillery Center and School; Army Sergeants Major Academy; 11th Air Defense Artillery Brigade; 3rd Armored Cavalry Regiment; 6th Air Defense Artillery Brigade; 1st Combined Arms Support Battalion; 7th Ranger Training Battalion.

Fort Hood

Location: In Killeen.

Address: Fort Hood, Texas 76544-5066

Main phone number: (817) 287-1110

Population: 45,113 active-duty; 76,323 family members; 6,586 civilians.

Major units: 1st Cavalry Div.; 2nd Armored Div.; 13th Corps Support Command; 3rd Signal Brigade; 6th Cavalry Brigade; 89th Military Police Brigade; 504th Military Intelligence Brigade; Combat Aviation Training Brigade, Third Personnel Group; 13th Finance Group; 3rd Air Support Group; Test and Experimentation Command.

Fort Sam Houston

Location: In San Antonio.

Address: Fort Sam Houston, Texas 78234-5000

Main phone number: (210) 221-1211

Population: 17,358 active-duty; 33,729 family members; 1,151 Guard; 20,078 Reserve; 7,863 civilians.

Major units: U.S. Army Garrison; 5th U.S. Army; Health Services Command; Army Medical Dept. Center and School; Brooke Army Medical Center; Army Medical Command Provisional.

U.S. Air Force

Brooks Air Force Base

Location: In San Antonio.

Address: Brooks AFB, Texas 78235-5304

Main phone number: (210) 536-1110

Population: 1,620 active-duty; 2,175 family members; 54 Guard; 31 Reserve; 1,560 civilians.

Major units: Headquarters, Human Systems Center; Air Force School of Aerospace Medicine; Armstrong Laboratory; Human Systems Program Office; Air Force Center for Environmental Excellence; U.S. Army Medical Research Detachment.

Dyess AFB

Location: On west side of Abilene.

Address: Dyess AFB, Texas 79607-1960

Main phone number: (915) 696-0212

Population: 4,928 active-duty; 7,304 family members; 508 civilians.

Major units: 7th Wing (Air Combat Command); 9th Bomb Squadron; 337th Bomb Squadron; 39th Airlift Squadron; 40th Airlift Squadron.

Goodfellow AFB

Location: On southwest side of San Angelo.

Address: Goodfellow AFB, San Angelo, Texas 76908-5000

Main phone number: (915) 654-3231

Population: 1,816 active-duty; about 3,000 family members; 1,213 students; 469 civilians.

Major units: 17th Training Group; 17th Support Group; 17th Medical Group; 344th Military Intelligence Battalion; Naval Technical Training Center Detachment; Marine Corps Detachment; 8th Space Warning Squadron of nearby Eldorado AFS.

Kelly AFB

Location: Five miles southwest of San Antonio.

Address: Kelly AFB, Texas 78241-5842

Main phone number: (210) 925-1110

Population: 5,078 active-duty; 1,704 family members; 1,000 Guard; 3,867 Reserve; 15,966 civilians.

Major units: San Antonio Air Logistics Center; Headquarters, Air Intelligence Agency; 651st Air Base Group; 433rd Airlift Wing-Reserve; 149th Airlift Wing (Texas Air National Guard).

Lackland AFB

Location: Eight miles southwest of San Antonio.

Address: Lackland AFB, Texas 78236-5110

Main phone number: (210) 671-1110

Population: 5,774 active-duty; 7,273 active-duty students; 1,947 family members; 4,066 civilians.

Major units: 37th Training Wing, host to 37th Training Group, 737th Training Group; Defense Language Institute English Language Center, Inter-American Air Forces Academy; 59th Medical Wing-Wilford Hall Medical Center.

Laughlin AFB

Location: Six miles east of Del Rio.

Address: Laughlin AFB, Texas 78843-5000

Main phone number: (210) 298-3511

Population: 1,277 active-duty; 1,367 family members; 1,738 civilians.

Major units: 47th Flying Training Wing.

Randolph AFB

Location: In Universal City, about 13 miles northeast of San Antonio.

Address: Randolph AFB, Texas 78150-4562

Population: 5,638 active-duty; 11,053 family members; 4,581 civilians.

Major units: Headquarters, Air Education and Training Command; Air Force Military Personnel Center; Headquarters, 19th Air Force; 12th Flying Training Wing; U.S. Air Force Recruiting Service.

Reese AFB:

Location: 10 miles west of Lubbock.

Address: Reese AFB, Texas 79489-6301

Main phone number: (806) 885-4511

Population: 1,440 active-duty; 1,535 family members; 401 civilians.

Major units: 64th Flying Training Wing; 64th Medical Group; 64th Support Group; 64th Operations Group.

Sheppard AFB

Location: Five miles north of Wichita Falls.

Address: Sheppard AFB, Texas 76311-2943

Main phone number: (817) 676-2511

Population: 9,850 active-duty; 6,215 family members; 2,153 civilians.

Major units: 82nd Training Wing; 82nd Training Group; 782nd Training Group; 82nd Logistics Group; 82nd Medical Group; 82nd Support Group; 982nd Training Group; 882nd Training Group; 80th Flying Training Wing.

U.S. Navy

Corpus Christi Naval Air Station

Location: 12 miles east of Corpus Christi.

Address: NAS Corpus Christi, 11001 D St., #143, Corpus Christi 78419-5021

Main phone number: (512) 939-2383

Population: 1,534 active-duty; 4,800 family members; 5,000 civilians.

Major units: Headquarters, Naval Air Training Command; Training Air Wing 4; Commander of Mine Warfare Command; Coast Guard Air Group; Corpus Christi Army Depot.

Dallas NAS

Location: 10 miles west of downtown Dallas.

Address: Naval Air Station, Dallas, Texas 75211-9501

Main phone number: (214) 266-6111

Population: 1,835 active-duty; 3,500 family members; 5,988 Reserve; 1,498 civilians.

Major units: Fighter Squadron 201, Marine Air Group 41; 14th Marines; Fleet Support Squadron 59; Army Reserve; Coast Guard Reserve; Texas Air Guard.

(**Dallas NAS is scheduled to move** to Carswell Field Joint Reserve Base near Fort Worth in early summer 1996. Details were pending at press time.)

Ingleside NAS

Location: In Ingleside.

Address: 1455 Ticonderoga Rd., #W123, Ingleside 78362-5001

Main phone number: (512) 776-4200.

Population: 2,200 active-duty; 4,500 family members; 150 civilians.

Major units: Mine Countermeasures Groups 1, 2, and 3; Shore Intermediate Maintenance Activity; 14 mine countermeasures ships. An additional six coastal mine hunters may be added when homeport program is completed.

Kingsville NAS:

Location: In Kingsville.

Address: NAS Kingsville, Texas 78363-5000

Main phone number: (512) 595-6136

Population: 900 active-duty; 1,260 civilians.

Major units: Naval Auxiliary Landing Field Orange Grove; Squadrons: VT-21, VT-22; Training Air Wing 2; McMullen Target Range, Escondido Ranch. ☆

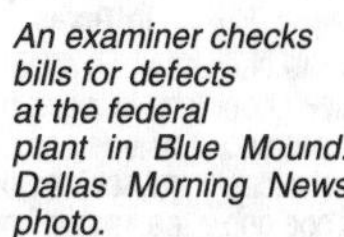

An examiner checks bills for defects at the federal plant in Blue Mound. Dallas Morning News photo.

The Money Factory Outside Fort Worth

There is $7 billion under a big pyramid near Blue Mound, Texas.

Digging to it will not work though, because the cash is stashed in a large vault with walls so thick that when they were built in 1990 there was no concrete to be had in all of Dallas-Fort Worth for the following three days, or so the story goes.

The bills, mostly $20s, $10s, $5s and $1s, are at the only money factory outside Washington, D.C.

The glass pyramid, a motif taken from the greenback, is atop the entrance to the U.S. Bureau of Engraving and Printing's Western Currency Facility. The gray and white building on the prairie northwest of Fort Worth feels and looks as crisp as a new dollar bill and it smells like money.

Ten printing presses produce around 3 million notes a year, which is one-third the volume of the D.C. plant. Plans are for this second U.S. plant to do about one-half the volume of the main D.C. plant.

You'll recognize the notes produced in Texas by the letters "FW" on the face of the bills in the lower right-hand corner. Some 450 employees work three shifts a day — including national holidays — to keep up with the demand for the cash, even in the age of the credit card. The Western plant, a legacy of the years when Fort Worth's congressman Jim Wright was Speaker of the House, printed its first notes in January 1991.

One-dollar bills last about 18 months in circulation before constant handling requires replacement. Ninety-five percent of the notes printed each year are used to replace worn notes. Destruction of the old notes is done by the 12 Federal Reserve Banks.

Flat sheets of paper composed of 25 percent linen and 75 percent cotton are used in the two-stage printing: black ink in five presses for the face and green ink in the other five presses for the backs.

All the paper comes from one paper plant and has red and blue fibers distributed throughout as one defense against counterfeiting. Recently a line of small vertical printing has been added. It says, for example on $20 bills, "USA TWENTY."

After printing, examiners — people, not machines — eye-ball the sheets quickly for the slightest defects before serial numbers are stamped on the bills and the sheets are sliced into 32 notes. The notes are wrapped in bricks of 4,000 each and placed on skids.

One skid of $1 notes would be $640,000. These skids are shipped to Federal Reserve and other banks throughout the country. It is the Federal Reserve Banks who place the orders for new currency that is transported by security contractors such as Wells Fargo and others. Officials at the plant say that in order to be ready, on occasion they print ahead of orders and the skids of currency are stored in the cool vault. That's the $7 billion.

Security is important, of course, for the money plant: 60 to 70 employees are federal police. A corridor of barbed-wire-topped dual fences surrounds the huge building, and spikes in the road threaten to slash car tires if you go in the wrong direction.

Not that outsiders are unwelcome. Group tours of the plant can be arranged through the public affairs office at the Blue Mound plant. — *Robert Plocheck* ☆

U.S. Tax Collections in Texas

Source: ***Internal Revenue Service***

*Fiscal Year	Individual Income and Employment Taxes	Corporation Income Taxes	Estate Taxes	Gift Taxes	Excise Taxes	Total U.S. Taxes Collected in Texas
1994	$63,916,496,000	$9,698,069,000	$624,354,000	$347,900,000	$9,528,449,000	$84,086,676,000
1993	59,962,756,000	7,211,968,000	618,469,000	111,896,000	7,552,247,000	75,457,335,000
1992	57,367,765,000	6,338,621,000	598,918,000	121,164,000	7,558,642,000	71,985,109,000
1991	55,520,001,000	8,761,621,000	588,298,000	87,739,000	6,647,312,000	71,604,791,000
1990	52,795,489,000	6,983,762,000	521,811,000	196,003,000	5,694,006,000	66,191,071,000
1989	50,855,904,000	8,675,006,000	458,106,000	96,699,000	5,766,594,000	66,052,309,000
1988	45,080,428,000	6,058,172,000	444,349,000	39,137,000	5,957,085,000	57,579,171,000
1987	43,165,241 ,000	4,124,164,000	443,947,000	27,342,000	3,908,826,000	51,669,519,000
1986	44,090,929,000	4,808,703,000	493,405,000	35,355,000	4,169,857,000	53,598,248,000
1985	44,090,929,000	4,808,703,000	493,405,000	35,355,000	4,169,857,000	53,598,248,000
1984	41,497,114,000	5,637,148,000	528,106,000	41,560,000	6,058,110,000	53,762,038,000
1983	37,416,203,000	4,750,079,000	494,431,000	19,844,000	5,553,491,000	48,234,047,000

Federal Funds to Texas by County, 1994

The first figure represents total **direct expenditures to the county** for fiscal year 1994 in millions of dollars. The second figure is that part of the total that went directly to individuals, primarily in **retirement and disability benefits** such as Social Security. *For a more complete explanation, see end of chart.

County	Total	To indiv.
Texas	**$79.8 bil**	**$41.7 bil**
Anderson	181.0 mil	121.6 mil
Andrews	38.1 mil	30.0 mil
Angelina	265.9 mil	195.1 mil
Aransas	68.3 mil	61.1 mil
Archer	38.9 mil	32.6 mil
Armstrong	10.3 mil	6.1 mil
Atascosa	100.9 mil	72.0 mil
Austin	94.6 mil	55.9 mil
Bailey	38.1 mil	19.1 mil
Bandera	60.5 mil	37.9 mil
Bastrop	139.0 mil	97.2 mil
Baylor	27.8 mil	19.6 mil
Bee	99.6 mil	66.4 mil
Bell	1,895.8 mil	548.6 mil
Bexar	7,399.1 mil	3,539.3 mil
Blanco	39.6 mil	33.7 mil
Borden	4.2 mil	0.9 mil
Bosque	67.6 mil	56.6 mil
Bowie	558.4 mil	271.0 mil
Brazoria	442.2 mil	340.6 mil
Brazos	427.2 mil	197.5 mil
Brewster	36.2 mil	23.6 mil
Briscoe	19.3 mil	11.0 mil
Brooks	44.0 mil	22.3 mil
Brown	144.2 mil	113.5 mil
Burleson	63.9 mil	46.4 mil
Burnet	103.6 mil	88.2 mil
Caldwell	91.2 mil	65.8 mil
Calhoun	59.3 mil	42.9 mil
Callahan	49.5 mil	37.4 mil
Cameron	969.6 mil	558.2 mil
Camp	48.0 mil	34.9 mil
Carson	55.8 mil	16.3 mil
Cass	136.2 mil	97.0 mil
Castro	$38.9 mil	$17.1 mil
Chambers	53.5 mil	36.0 mil
Cherokee	170.1 mil	125.8 mil
Childress	39.5 mil	25.5 mil
Clay	32.1 mil	25.3 mil
Cochran	28.6 mil	10.8 mil
Coke	16.7 mil	12.9 mil
Coleman	55.6 mil	40.0 mil
Collin	537.8 mil	334.0 mil
Collingsworth	23.2 mil	12.6 mil
Colorado	90.9 mil	63.0 mil
Comal	252.5 mil	220.6 mil
Comanche	65.8 mil	48.0 mil
Concho	21.6 mil	11.1 mil
Cooke	104.8 mil	89.5 mil
Coryell	161.2 mil	117.6 mil
Cottle	18.1 mil	10.6 mil
Crane	8.8 mil	7.5 mil
Crockett	17.8 mil	8.9 mil
Crosby	42.1 mil	22.7 mil
Culberson	9.0 mil	5.0 mil
Dallam	34.3 mil	21.7 mil
Dallas	7,930.7 mil	3,685.6 mil
Dawson	77.1 mil	38.1 mil
D. Smith	69.3 mil	39.3 mil
Delta	27.4 mil	19.0 mil
Denton	741.5 mil	322.0 mil
DeWitt	80.0 mil	58.2 mil
Dickens	20.4 mil	13.5 mil
Dimmit	45.1 mil	23.9 mil
Donley	21.2 mil	15.0 mil
Duval	68.4 mil	38.7 mil
Eastland	92.6 mil	74.6 mil
Ector	309.6 mil	249.5 mil
Edwards	13.3 mil	5.4 mil
Ellis	$549.0 mil	$180.6 mil
El Paso	2,751.9 mil	1,352.6 mil
Erath	96.0 mil	78.0 mil
Falls	96.2 mil	58.0 mil
Fannin	144.1 mil	95.1 mil
Fayette	93.4 mil	71.6 mil
Fisher	32.5 mil	15.2 mil
Floyd	54.0 mil	24.2 mil
Foard	14.8 mil	7.8 mil
Fort Bend	312.5 mil	224.6 mil
Franklin	29.3 mil	22.9 mil
Freestone	62.7 mil	48.0 mil
Frio	53.9 mil	32.2 mil
Gaines	61.5 mil	24.7 mil
Galveston	932.2 mil	553.2 mil
Garza	26.1 mil	14.0 mil
Gillespie	78.1 mil	65.0 mil
Glasscock	8.8 mil	1.5 mil
Goliad	22.9 mil	15.9 mil
Gonzales	88.0 mil	59.0 mil
Gray	97.2 mil	80.6 mil
Grayson	383.0 mil	315.2 mil
Gregg	387.1 mil	306.5 mil
Grimes	74.5 mil	54.0 mil
Guadalupe	220.5 mil	173.3 mil
Hale	149.8 mil	91.5 mil
Hall	29.6 mil	15.3 mil
Hamilton	39.6 mil	31.8 mil
Hansford	24.2 mil	13.2 mil
Hardeman	33.9 mil	22.1 mil
Hardin	134.8 mil	112.1 mil
Harris	10,736.8 mil	5,042.4 mil
Harrison	229.3 mil	142.4 mil
Hartley	9.6 mil	2.9 mil
Haskell	44.1 mil	24.7 mil

County	Total	To indiv.
Hays	$204.1 mil	$125.6 mil
Hemphill	10.1 mil	7.5 mil
Henderson	181.5 mil	145.4 mil
Hidalgo	1,342.1 mil	759.9 mil
Hill	133.8 mil	102.9 mil
Hockley	91.8 mil	54.8 mil
Hood	108.8 mil	98.6 mil
Hopkins	108.5 mil	79.7 mil
Houston	104.9 mil	73.5 mil
Howard	163.5 mil	97.7 mil
Hudspeth	10.0 mil	4.4 mil
Hunt	565.2 mil	181.4 mil
Hutchinson	78.2 mil	66.2 mil
Irion	6.4 mil	4.0 mil
Jack	28.4 mil	21.5 mil
Jackson	62.1 mil	38.4 mil
Jasper	164.1 mil	104.0 mil
Jeff Davis	7.0 mil	5.1 mil
Jefferson	1,197.2 mil	740.0 mil
Jim Hogg	26.2 mil	13.6 mil
Jim Wells	149.8 mil	97.4 mil
Johnson	277.5 mil	228.6 mil
Jones	88.4 mil	55.5 mil
Karnes	64.7 mil	40.0 mil
Kaufman	226.4 mil	190.0 mil
Kendall	68.5 mil	61.7 mil
Kenedy	1.1 mil	0.7 mil
Kent	6.9 mil	3.5 mil
Kerr	203.6 mil	162.5 mil
Kimble	23.0 mil	13.7 mil
King	2.3 mil	0.5 mil
Kinney	21.4 mil	12.7 mil
Kleberg	298.0 mil	101.9 mil
Knox	32.6 mil	19.3 mil
Lamar	208.3 mil	145.1 mil
Lamb	82.1 mil	48.0 mil
Lampasas	65.7 mil	55.1 mil
La Salle	29.4 mil	14.1 mil
Lavaca	96.0 mil	72.7 mil
Lee	39.3 mil	30.4 mil
Leon	75.1 mil	55.1 mil
Liberty	201.6 mil	148.6 mil
Limestone	92.3 mil	66.8 mil
Lipscomb	13.2 mil	8.0 mil
Live Oak	107.1 mil	21.4 mil
Llano	69.8 mil	64.1 mil
Loving	0.5 mil	0.3 mil
Lubbock	820.6 mil	522.8 mil
Lynn	41.7 mil	18.7 mil
Madison	36.3 mil	27.9 mil

County	Total	To indiv.
Marion	$47.6 mil	$31.4 mil
Martin	26.4 mil	9.2 mil
Mason	17.8 mil	13.3 mil
Matagorda	142.1 mil	89.8 mil
Maverick	142.1 mil	77.5 mil
McCulloch	44.0 mil	32.2 mil
McLennan	979.1 mil	534.3 mil
McMullen	2.5 mil	1.7 mil
Medina	100.4 mil	76.0 mil
Menard	13.9 mil	9.3 mil
Midland	261.9 mil	197.3 mil
Milam	108.6 mil	73.6 mil
Mills	29.2 mil	16.8 mil
Mitchell	45.0 mil	28.3 mil
Montague	78.7 mil	63.0 mil
Montgomery	444.2 mil	364.7 mil
Moore	46.8 mil	30.4 mil
Morris	62.2 mil	48.9 mil
Motley	11.9 mil	6.8 mil
Nacogdoches	196.8 mil	144.8 mil
Navarro	169.4 mil	122.3 mil
Newton	50.2 mil	35.3 mil
Nolan	71.7 mil	51.6 mil
Nueces	1,528.2 mil	720.9 mil
Ochiltree	28.5 mil	17.6 mil
Oldham	9.6 mil	5.1 mil
Orange	265.0 mil	205.1 mil
Palo Pinto	107.0 mil	77.6 mil
Panola	87.0 mil	60.6 mil
Parker	167.3 mil	143.0 mil
Parmer	63.8 mil	18.2 mil
Pecos	40.1 mil	25.9 mil
Polk	171.1 mil	143.2 mil
Potter	800.2 mil	385.2 mil
Presidio	31.9 mil	16.5 mil
Rains	22.8 mil	17.6 mil
Randall	91.9 mil	74.0 mil
Reagan	10.1 mil	5.6 mil
Real	14.5 mil	10.6 mil
Red River	88.5 mil	55.2 mil
Reeves	49.8 mil	29.6 mil
Refugio	34.1 mil	24.2 mil
Roberts	4.6 mil	2.3 mil
Robertson	78.7 mil	51.8 mil
Rockwall	49.5 mil	42.6 mil
Runnels	60.3 mil	40.6 mil
Rusk	145.0 mil	109.6 mil
Sabine	57.5 mil	46.8 mil
S. Augustine	43.1 mil	30.1 mil
S. Jacinto	55.9 mil	43.1 mil

County	Total	To indiv.
S. Patricio	$286.9 mil	$146.1 mil
San Saba	32.8 mil	20.8 mil
Schleicher	17.2 mil	7.3 mil
Scurry	65.2 mil	47.2 mil
Shackelford	14.2 mil	11.8 mil
Shelby	115.7 mil	79.4 mil
Sherman	15.9 mil	5.5 mil
Smith	573.5 mil	409.2 mil
Somervell	14.7 mil	11.7 mil
Starr	140.6 mil	68.0 mil
Stephens	34.7 mil	28.6 mil
Sterling	4.6 mil	2.6 mil
Stonewall	12.4 mil	7.7 mil
Sutton	15.3 mil	8.3 mil
Swisher	46.5 mil	22.9 mil
Tarrant	6,008.7 mil	2,322.0 mil
Taylor	660.7 mil	319.5 mil
Terrell	$8.6 mil	$4.1 mil
Terry	68.7 mil	35.1 mil
Throckmorton	11.4 mil	8.5 mil
Titus	93.3 mil	72.1 mil
Tom Green	443.6 mil	269.0 mil
Travis	4,644.6 mil	1,180.1 mil
Trinity	61.5 mil	47.9 mil
Tyler	76.2 mil	62.1 mil
Upshur	114.0 mil	93.0 mil
Upton	12.1 mil	8.1 mil
Uvalde	98.4 mil	61.0 mil
Val Verde	259.7 mil	92.4 mil
Van Zandt	140.2 mil	119.0 mil
Victoria	236.9 mil	175.7 mil
Walker	141.0 mil	109.1 mil
Waller	81.9 mil	55.4 mil
Ward	39.3 mil	31.0 mil
Washington	105.4 mil	78.8 mil
Webb	546.8 mil	246.3 mil
Wharton	158.2 mil	101.6 mil
Wheeler	33.9 mil	23.2 mil
Wichita	800.9 mil	368.4 mil
Wilbarger	71.4 mil	51.1 mil
Willacy	73.6 mil	34.2 mil
Williamson	285.9 mil	222.2 mil
Wilson	71.4 mil	52.8 mil
Winkler	25.7 mil	22.0 mil
Wise	95.4 mil	73.5 mil
Wood	139.3 mil	113.7 mil
Yoakum	29.8 mil	15.2 mil
Young	74.8 mil	60.4 mil
Zapata	35.3 mil	23.8 mil
Zavala	47.8 mil	25.3 mil

*__Total__ federal government expenditures include the **categories:** grants, salaries and wages (Postal Service, Dept. of Defense, etc.), procurement, direct payments for individuals, other direct payments, direct loans, insured loans and insurance.

Retirement and disability programs include Federal employee retirement and disability benefits, Social Security payments of all types, selected Veterans Administration programs and military retirees.

Direct payments for individuals also includes earned income tax credit payments, Higher Education Act Insured Loans interest subsidies and federal housing assistance programs.

Source: *Consolidated Federal Funds Report, Fiscal Year 1994, U.S. Department of Commerce, Bureau of the Census.*

Public Schools

Source: Texas Education Agency

Public school enrollment in Texas reached a peak of 3,677,171 in 1994-95, according to the **Texas Education Agency**. Enrollment in 1993-94 was 3,688,262.

The **seven largest districts** (listed in descending order by average daily attendance), Houston, Dallas, Fort Worth, Austin, El Paso, San Antonio and Northside (Bexar Co.).

Texas has **two types of school districts**, independent and common, each administering local affairs through a board of trustees. Independent school districts deal directly with Texas Education Agency; common districts are supervised by elected county school superintendents and county trustees. In 1994, the last year for which figures are available, there were six common districts and 1,051 independent districts.

History of Public Education

Public education was one of the primary goals of the early settlers of Texas, who listed the failure to provide education as one of their grievances in the **Texas Declaration of Independence** from Mexico.

As early as 1838, **President Mirabeau B. Lamar's** message to the Republic of Texas Congress advocated setting aside public domain for public schools. His interest caused him to be called the **"Father of Education in Texas."** In 1839 Congress designated three leagues of land to support public schools for each Texas county and 50 leagues for a state university. In 1840 each county was allocated one more league of land.

The Republic, however, did not establish a public school system or a university. The 1845 State Constitution advocated public education, instructing the Legislature to designate at least 10 percent of the tax revenue for schools. Further delay occurred until **Gov. Elisha M. Pease**, on Jan. 31, 1854, signed the bill setting up the **Texas public school system.**

The public school system was made possible by setting aside $2 million out of $10 million Texas received for relinquishing its claim to land to the north and west of its present boundaries in the Compromise of 1850.

During 1854, legislation provided for state apportionment of funds based upon an annual census and required railroads that were granted land to survey alternate sections to be set aside for public school financing. The **first school census** that year showed 65,463 scholastics; state fund apportionment was 62¢ per student.

When adopted in 1876, the present Texas Constitution provided: "All funds, lands and other property heretofore set apart and appropriated for the support of public schools; all the alternate sections of land reserved by the state of grants heretofore made or that may hereafter be made to railroads, or other corporations, of any nature whatsoever; one half of the public domain of the state, and all sums of money that may come to the state from the sale of any portion of the same shall constitute a **perpetual public school fund**."

Over 52 million acres of the Texas **public domain** were allotted for school purposes. (See table, **Public Lands of Texas**, in chapter on **State Government**.)

The Constitution also provided for one-fourth of occupation taxes and a poll tax of one dollar for school support, and made provisions for local taxation. No provision was made for direct ad valorem taxation for maintenance of an **available school fund**, but a maximum 20¢ state ad valorem school tax was adopted in 1883, and raised to 35¢ in connection with provision of **free textbooks** in the amendment of 1918.

In 1949, the **Gilmer-Aikin Laws** reorganized the state system of public schools by making sweeping changes in administration and financing. All schools below college level were, prior to 1984, headed by the **State Board of Education**, whose members were elected from congressional districts as set in 1981. Under the **educational reforms of 1984**, a new 15-member board was appointed by the governor to replace the existing 27-member elected panel. This board appoints a **State Commissioner of Education** who is executive head of the **Texas Education Agency**, which administers the public school system. Under the law, TEA consists of (1) the State Board of Education, (2) the State Commissioner of Education, (3) the State Department of Education and (4) the State Board of Vocational Education. The personnel of the State Board of Education and the State Board of Vocational Education are the same, the members of the State Board of Education serving ex officio as members of the State Board of Vocational Education when considering matters relating to vocational education.

The **School Tax Assessment Practices Board** was created during a special session of the 65th Legislature (1977) to determine, on a statewide basis, the property wealth of school districts. The board was also charged with upgrading professional standards for appraising and assessing school district property taxes.

The 66th Legislature (1979), among other education-related actions, required the establishment of countywide appraisal districts.

School Reform

Members of the 68th Legislature passed a historic education-reform bill in the summer of 1984. House Bill 72 came in response to growing concern over deteriorating literacy in America's schoolchildren over two decades, a deterioration reflected in Texas test scores.

The school-reform bill was formulated by a Select Committee headed by Dallas computer magnate Ross Perot and appointed by Gov. Mark White following failures by the Legislature — and resistance from the voters — to support teacher pay raises or additional public-school funding without education reform.

The resulting legislation raised teacher salaries, but tied those raises to teacher performance. It also introduced more stringent teacher certification and initiated competency testing for teachers.

Academic achievement was set as a priority in public education with stricter attendance rules, adoption of a **no-pass, no-play rule** prohibiting students who

Enrollment

(Refined Average Daily Attendance)

Year	Enrollment	Year	Enrollment
1994-95	3,677,171	1989-90	3,151,659
1993-94	3,608,262	1988-89	3,098,092
1992-93	3,541,769	1987-88	3,057,147
1991-92	3,173,143	1986-87	3,039,416
1990-91	3,073,966	1985-86	2,933,081

High School Graduates*

Source: Texas Education Agency

Year	Graduates	Year	Graduates
1992-93	160,546	1987-88	171,436
1991-92	176,209	1986-87	168,430
1990-91	185,013	1985-86	161,150
1989-90	172,480	1984-85	159,343
1988-89	176,951	1983-84	161,580

1993-94 and 1994-95 data not available at press time.

were failing courses from participating in sports and other extracurricular activities for a six-week period, and national norm testing through the grades to assure parents of individual schools' performance through a common frame of reference.

The 74th Legislature passed what is called the **Public Schools Reform Act of 1995**. Broadly, it limits state control of public schools by limiting the Texas Education Agency to recommending and reporting on educational goals; granting, modifying and revoking campus charters; managing the permanent, foundation and available school funds; setting standards for graduation and curriculum; administering an accountability system; recommending educator appraisal and counselor evaluation instruments; and developing plans for special, bilingual, compensatory, gifted and talented, vocational, and technology education.

Each school district may choose to operate as either an independent school district subject to general law requirements of the Education Code; a special-purpose district, such as Boys Home Ranch, that now have special status; or a home-rule district with a charter approved by the district's voters that must comply with graduation requirements, accountability, no-pass, no-play, federal law and court orders, compulsory attendance, pre-kindergarten, bilingual education, and information-reporting requirements; teacher certification and a few other basic matters.

Local boards do not manage, but oversee the management of school districts.

Charter schools may be granted by school districts free of all local board instructional rules and policies, subject only to pre-kindergarten, bilingual education and graduation requirements, no pass-no play, reporting requirements and accountability.

Graduation from high school requires proficiency in a foundation curriculum including English language arts, mathematics, science and social studies and an enrichment curriculum of other languages, fine arts, and health, physical, career and technology education.

No pass-no play now requires only a three-week suspension for failing a course grade, during which time the student can continue to practice, but not participate in competition.

High-school graduation requires passing either current exit-level TAAS (Texas Assessment of Academic Skills) exams or end-of-course exams in algebra and English and biology or history.

A teacher may remove a disruptive student from class and, subject to review by a campus committee, veto the student's return to class. The district must provide alternative education for students removed from class. A student must be placed in alternative education for assault, selling drugs or alcohol, substance abuse or public lewdness. A student must be expelled and referred to the appropriate court for serious offenses, such as murder or aggravated assault.

Texas School Personnel, Salaries

Year/ Personnel Type	Personnel (Full-Time Equivalent)*	Average Base Salaries†
1992-93 All Personnel	**421,124**	**$23,687**
Teachers	219,492	28,397
Support Staff*	28,028	35,286
Administrators	14,658	47,848
Total Professional	262,178	30,221
Educational Aides	36,940	10,880
Auxiliary Staff	122,006	13,525
1993-94 All Personnel	**433,078**	**$24,196**
Teachers	224,995	29,118
Support Staff*	28,487	36,325
Administrators	14,906	48,954
Total Professional	268,389	30,985
Educational Aides	39,037	11,041
Auxiliary Staff	125,652	13,783

**Support staff includes supervisors, counselors, educational diagnosticians, librarians, nurses/physicians, therapists and psychologists.*

†Supplements for non-teaching duties and career-ladder supplements are not included in this figure.

Permanent School Fund

Year	Total Investment Fund*	Total Income Earned by P.S.F.
1854	$2,000,000.00	. . .
1880	3,542,126.00	. . .
1900	9,102,872.75	783,142.08
1910	16,752,406.93	1,970,526.52
1920	25,698,281.74	2,888,555.44
1930	38,718,106.35	2,769,547.05
1940	68,299,081.91	3,331,874.12
1950	161,179,979.24	3,985,973.60
1960	425,821,600.53	12,594,000.28
1970	842,217,721.05	34,762,955.32
1980	2,464,579,397.00	163,000,000.00
1985	5,095,802,979.00	417,080,383.00
1988	6,493,070,622.00	572,665,253.00
1989	6,873,610,771.00	614,786,823.00
1990	7,328,172,096.00	674,634,994.00
1991	10,227,777,535.00	661,744,804.00
1992	10,944,944,872.00	704,993,826.00
1993	11,822,465,497.00	714,021,754.00
1994	11,330,590,652.00	716,972,115.00

**Includes cash — bonds at par and stocks at book value.*

Scholastic Population, Apportionment, 1854-1994

The Texas public school system was established and the permanent fund set up by the Fifth Legislature, Jan. 31, 1854. The first apportionment by the state to public schools was for the school year 1854-55.
Source: ***Texas Education Agency***

Years	Amount of P.S.F. Distributed to Schools	No. of Students	Per Capita
1854-55	. . .	65,463	$0.62
1880-81	$679,317	266,439	3.00
1900-01	3,002,820	706,546	4.25
1910-11	5,931,287	949,006	6.25
1920-21	18,431,716	1,271,157	14.50
1930-31	27,342,473	1,562,427	17.50
1940-41	34,580,475	1,536,910	22.50
1950-51	93,996,600	1,566,610	60.00
1960-61	164,188,461	2,249,157	73.00
1970-71	287,159,758	2,800,500	119.45
1980-81	3,042,476	*	397.00
1985-86	807,680,617	*	280.00
1988-89	882,999,623	*	295.00
1989-90	917,608,395	*	303.00
1990-91	700,276,846	*	227.69
1991-92	739,200,044	*	240.19
1992-93	739,494,967	*	232.94
1993-94	737,677,545	*	227.83

**See enrollment figures for these years in separate table.*

Texas Higher Education

This article was prepared by the staff of the Texas Higher Education Coordinating Board.

The $79.9 billion 1996-97 state budget approved by the 74th Legislature included $9.3 billion for higher education, a 4.3 percent increase in all funds appropriations over the previous biennium. General-revenue appropriations were increased by 7.3 percent to $6.3 billion.

Tuition and Fees Increase

Legislation increased **undergraduate tuition** and allowed for increases in **fees** to university students. For the first time, schools will be able to retain the increased tuition revenue at the schools instead of having their budgets' general-revenue funds reduced in an amount equal to the tuition increase.

For residents of Texas, the undergraduate tuition increase will continue to be implemented in annual increments of $2 per semester credit hour, topping out at $40 per hour in the 2000-2001 academic year. In addition to increases in some institutional-specific fees at some universities, the Legislature authorized university boards of regents to increase general-use fees to the level of tuition rates. The University of Texas System, the Texas A&M University System, and Texas Tech University are prohibited from using the increased general-use fees generated at one institution to meet the obligations of another institution in the system, but other systems do not have the same restriction.

Changes were made in the way **nonresident tuition rates** at Texas public universities are calculated. Beginning in fall 1995, they will be set at the average of the nonresident undergraduate tuition charged to a Texas resident attending a public university in the five most populous states other than Texas.

Scholarship for 3-year High School Grads

Texas students who complete high school within 36 months will receive a **$1,000 college scholarship**.

Prepaid College Tuition Program

The Legislature established the **Prepaid Higher Education Tuition Program** to enable parents and others to save money towards a child's post-secondary education. The cost of the contract will vary depending on which type of institution is chosen — two-year junior college, four-year public university or four-year private college or university. The program will be administered by the Comptroller's Office, which will determine the amount of money to be paid into the fund each year by each purchaser to cover the estimated tuition and fees.

Student Loan Program

The Legislature took steps to continue the state's Hinson-Hazlewood College **Student Loan Program**

The University of Texas formally opened in September 1883 with a ceremony in the unfinished west wing of the original main building (right). Classes were held in the temporary state capitol at the corner of Congress and Eleventh Street until the building was finished in December. Photo courtesy American History Center, University of Texas at Austin.

by authorizing the Texas Higher Education Coordinating Board to issue an additional $300 million in state general obligation bonds to provide money for loans through this program, subject to approval of a constitutional amendment by Texas voters in November 1995. In 1994, the program provided more than $90 million in loans to nearly 20,000 Texas students.

Health-Education Programs

The 74th Legislature provided $18 million to enhance **health-education programs** in the border region of the state, including expanding residency programs in primary-care specialties, enhancing existing clinical sites and recruiting faculty and staff, concentrating on the Lower Rio Grande Valley and Middle Rio Grande Valley. Other plans call for pilot programs to provide indigent health care and training family practice physicians in an urgan area, a rural area and in the border region. They must provide services to an economically depressed or medically underserved area of the state.

Exemptions to TASP Testing

The 74th Legislature established several new **exemptions from the Texas Academic Skills Program** (TASP). The TASP was created by the 70th Legislature to assess the basic reading, writing and mathematics skills of entering college students and to provide remedial education for those who score low on TASP tests. These exemptions include a student permanently enrolled in an independent or out-of-state institution of higher education who enrolls on a temporary basis in a Texas public institution; a student who has previously been granted a degree; a student enrolled in a certificate program of one year or less in length; and a person 55 years of age or older who is not seeking a certificate or a degree.

Changes in State Higher-Education Entities

Changes approved by the 74th Legislature, effective September 1995, include:

• Abolishing the **Lamar University System** and transferring the four instructional entities to the **Texas State University System**;

• Transferring the two instructional entities of the **East Texas State University System** to the **Texas A&M University System**;

• Merging the **Baylor College of Dentistry** with the **Texas A&M University System**;

• Transferring **Texas State Technical College-Amarillo** operations and facilities to **Amarillo Community College**; and

• Changing the name **Sul Ross University Uvalde Study Center** to **Sul Ross State Rio Grande College**.

Enrollment

Enrollment in Texas' public and independent colleges and universities in fall 1994 was 923,197, an increase of 1,694 students from the previous fall.

Enrollment at the 35 public universities decreased by 848 students from the presious year, to 406,466. Twenty-one public universities reported combined net increases of 4,044 students, while 14 reported a combined net decrease of 4,892 students.

The state's 50 public community-college districts reported fall 1994 enrollments totaling 400,323 students, an increase of 175 students over fall 1993. The Texas State Technical College System's four campuses reported an enrollment of 7,732 students, an increase of 498.

Enrollments at 38 independent senior colleges and universities increased to 92,029, up 1,459 students. The state's two independent junior colleges reported decreases totaling 59 students, reducing their enrollments to 619 students in fall 1994.

Public medical, dental, nursing and allied health schools reported enrollment increases of 452 students over fall 1993, or 14,421. Independent medical, dental and health-related institutions increased to 1,607 students, up by 17 for fall 1994. Veterinary medicine programs reported 484 students. ☆

At South Plains College in Levelland, instructor Chris Vandertuin (left) demonstrates repair techniques to students Danny Dolinger and Bill Chapin (center and right). The West Texas college is one of only a few in the nation offering a certificate program in fretted and stringed instrument repair. Photo courtesy South Plains College.

Texas Universities Offer Unusual Music Specialties

Music courses have long been offered in universities and colleges throughout Texas. The traditional music-school curriculum includes training in solo instruments and voice, the training of music teachers, and performance opportunities, both individually and with orchestras, bands, choruses and small ensembles.

Music as business

Today, approximately 86 programs in 84 Texas institutions of higher learning are preparing students to perform or to teach music. But many Texas universities and colleges — acknowledging that music today is not only an art, it is also a business — provide course work in all facets of the music industry. Business-side specialties cover business management, artist management, concert promotion, entertainment law, and merchandising and selling techniques. Technical studies include sound enhancement and recording technology, as well as computer science relating to musical composition and sound effects.

Students have numerous opportunities to perform in traditional orchestras, marching bands, concert bands, chamber-music groups, opera workshops and choirs. More surprising are the jazz combos and choirs, plus pop, rock, mariachi, steel-drum, ragtime, country-Western and bluegrass performing groups.

Perhaps the **most unusual music specialties** at Texas universities and colleges are these four:

Jazz at one o'clock

Jazz rocks the rafters at the **University of North Texas**' College of Music in Denton. In 1947, UNT became the first university in the United States to offer a degree program in jazz, and this American musical idiom has been a staple at UNT ever since. Today, UNT offers bachelor and master of music degrees in jazz studies. Performing opportunities include nine lab bands and other small ensembles, plus the UNT Jazz Singers.

UNT's One O'Clock Lab Band has received national and international acclaim for many years. The One O'Clock, named for its regular rehearsal time, comprises the school's 20 best jazz musicians selected by auditions each semester. This student band shared billing with jazz legends Duke Ellington and Stan Getz at the White House in 1967; appeared as the official big band at the Montreux International Jazz Festival in Switzerland in 1970; and has been enthusiastically received on tours to Germany, Portugal, Mexico and the former Soviet Union. Since 1967, the One O'clock has performed at such prestigious jazz festivals as Pori (Finland), North Sea, Montreux and Antibes (France) in 1982, Australia in 1986, Mexico in 1990, and Canada and the Pacific Northwest in 1991. It has recorded 30 albums, two of which were nominated for the National Academy of Recording Arts and Sciences'

Grammy award. The One O'Clock was the first student band so honored.

From its hesitant beginnings in a degree program in dance band under Gene Hall in 1947, the jazz program at UNT has grown under the leadership of Leon Breeden (1959-1981) and Neil Slater (1981-present). The band continues to tour extensively.

The UNT Music Department's reputation for excellence also extends to its more traditional music specialties.

Guitars and banjos

Country and bluegrass music styles are the specialty at **South Plains College** in Levelland. South Plains is one of only a handful of institutions in the nation offering an associate degree in commercial music. It is the only one in Texas that specializes in country and bluegrass music styles.

South Plains's program began in 1975, offering traditional styles of country, Western swing and bluegrass music. The course work now includes rock-and-roll, rhythm and blues, and contemporary Christian. The program is designed to train not only performers, but also songwriters, promoters, vocal and instrumental arrangers, publishers, booking agents and teachers.

Paramount among the performing opportunities at South Plains is Country Caravan, a traveling country-music variety show. For 17 summers, this troupe of about a dozen student performers, plus support staff, has been entertaining audiences throughout Texas and Eastern New Mexico, with occasional forays into Florida and Kansas.

South Plains also offers two-year associate degree programs in performing arts technology, sound technology, and string and fretted-instrument repair.

Recording the stars

Southwest Texas State University in San Marcos is the only university in the southwestern United States to offer a baccalaureate degree in **sound recording technology.** STSU students participate regularly in commercial recording sessions. The centerpiece of Southwest Texas' sound-recording program is the Fire Station, a multipurpose recording facility and television/film sound stage housed in a renovated fire house.

Equipment includes both analog and digital 24-track recorders with a 36-channel automated console. The list of clients who have used the Fire Station for their recording sessions includes Joe Ely, Timbuk 3, Tish Hinojosa, Ian Moore, the late Stevie Ray Vaughan, Omar and the Howlers, Asleep at the Wheel, Freddy Fender, the Fabulous Thunderbirds, Fats Domino, Jerry Jeff Walker, Lou Ann Barton and the Air Force Concert Band.

Merging music and computers

Southern Methodist University meshes music and electronics to offer a unique **dual-degree program combining a Bachelor of Arts in Music with either a Bachelor of Arts or a Bachelor of Science in Computer Science.** The four-and-a-half-year program was designed for students who want to make music their careers but are concerned about possible lack of job opportunities. The program also fills the needs of students who choose computer science as their primary field but don't want to sacrifice their musical talents.

Computers are vital to the recording process, and they are also being used increasingly in the composition of nontraditional forms of music. Central to the dual-degree program is the Meadows Electronic Music Studio, with an eight-track recording system and a full range of Musical Instrument Digital Interface (MIDI) equipment for synthesis, sampling, scoring and digital recording. Composers using computers are not limited by the range of notes produced by traditional musical instruments. They create music by synthesizing a vast number of sounds by measuring and controlling amplitude, frequency and spectral content.

A composer using a traditional piano at the Meadows facility no longer has to use pen and paper to record the composition. A computer-assisted keyboard automatically identifies and transcribes the sounds into musical notation as the composer is playing.

Other nontraditional music specialties

Other nontraditional, primarily business-oriented, music programs at Texas institutions are:

• **Austin Community College** offers a two-year program leading to an Associate in Applied Science in Commercial Music Management. Students augment their classroom education with hands-on experience in the lively Austin music industry.

• **The Art Institute of Houston and the Art Institute of Dallas** both offer courses with a strong concentration on music and video management, promotion and merchandising, leading to an associate degree.

• **The Houston Community College System** Northwest College offers both a two-year associate degree and a one-year certificate in Recording Technology.

• **Cedar Valley College** of the Dallas County Community College District offers an Associate in Commercial Music.

• **The University of Texas at San Antonio, Division of Music,** offers a Combination Music/Business degree, which includes the placement of students into music-business internships.

• **The University of Texas at San Antonio Institute for Music Research** promotes research in the areas of music psychology and technology primarily through computer services (available via Internet), conferences, research projects and publications. ☆ —*Mary G. Ramos*

*(Note: See also **History of Texas Music**, pages 23-36.)*

Brief History of Higher Education in Texas

While there were earlier efforts toward higher education, the first permanent institutions established were church-supported schools: **Rutersville University**, established in 1840 by Methodist minister Martin Ruter in Fayette County, predecessor of **Southwestern University**, Georgetown, established in 1843; Baylor University, now at Waco, but established in 1845 at Independence, Washington County, by the Texas Union Baptist Association; and **Austin College**, now at Sherman, but founded in 1849 at Huntsville by the Brazos Presbytery of the Old School Presbyterian Church.

Other historic Texas schools of collegiate rank included: **Larissa College**, 1848, at Larissa, Cherokee County; **McKenzie College**, 1841, Clarksville; **Chappell Hill Male and Female Institute**, 1850, Chappell Hill; **Soule University**, 1855, Chappell Hill; **Johnson Institute**, 1852, Driftwood, Hays County; **Nacogdoches University**, 1845, Nacogdoches; **Salado College**, 1859, Salado, Bell County. **Add-Ran College**, established at Thorp Spring, Hood County, in 1873, was the predecessor of present **Texas Christian University**, Fort Worth.

Texas A&M and University of Texas

The **Agricultural and Mechanical College of Texas** (now Texas A&M University), authorized by the Legislature in 1871, opened its doors in 1876 to become the **first publicly supported institution of higher education**. In 1881, Texans established the **University of Texas** in Austin, with a **medical branch in Galveston.** The Austin institution opened Sept. 15, 1883, the Galveston school in 1891.

First College for Women

In 1901, the 27th Legislature established the **Girls Industrial College**, which began classes at its campus in Denton in 1903. A campaign to establish a state industrial college for women was led by the State Grange and Patrons of Husbandry. A bill was signed into law on April 6, 1901, creating the college. It was charged with a dual mission, which continues to guide the university today — to provide a liberal education and to prepare young women with a specialized education "for the practical industries of the age." In 1905 the name of the college was changed to the **College of Industrial Arts**; in 1934, it was changed to **Texas State College for Women**. Since 1957 the name of the institution, which is now the largest university principally for women in the United States, has been the **Texas Woman's University.**

Historic, Primarily Black Colleges

A number of Texas schools were established primarily for blacks, although collegiate racial integration is now complete in the state. The black-oriented institutions include state-supported **Prairie View A&M University** (originally established as **Prairie View State Normal School** for the training of black schoolteachers), Prairie View; **Texas Southern University**, Houston; and privately supported **Huston-Tillotson College**, Austin; **Jarvis Christian College**, Hawkins; **Wiley College**, Marshall; **Paul Quinn College**, originally located in Waco, now in Dallas; and **Texas College**, Tyler. Predominantly black colleges that are important in the history of higher education in Texas, but that have ceased operations, include **Bishop College**, established in Marshall in 1881, then moved to Dallas; **Mary Allen College**, established in Crockett in 1886; and **Butler College**, originally named the **Texas Baptist Academy**, in 1905 in Tyler. ☆

Universities and Colleges

Source: Texas Higher Education Coordinating Board and institutions. In some cases, dates of establishment differ from those given in the preceding discussion because schools use the date when authorization was given, rather than actual date of first classwork. For explanation of type of institution and other symbols, see notes at end of table.

Name of Institution; Location; (Type* - Ownership, if private sectarian institution); Date of Founding; President (unless otherwise noted)	Number in Faculty†	Enrollment: Fall Term 1994	Enrollment: Summer Session 1994	Enrollment: Extension or Continuing Ed.
Abilene Christian University—Abilene; (3 - Church of Christ); 1906 (as **Childers Classical Institute;** became **Abilene Christian College** by 1914; became university in 1976); Dr. Royce Money	234	4,207	1,064	0
ALAMO COMMUNITY COLLEGE DISTRICT (9) — Robert Ramsay, Chancellor				
Palo Alto College—San Antonio; (7); 1985; Dr. Joel E. Vela	98	7,570	3,544	732
‡St. Philip's College—San Antonio; (7); 1898; Dr. Stephen R. Mitchell	200	5,700	2,000	3,000
San Antonio College—San Antonio; (7); 1925; Dr. Ruth Burgos-Sasscer	930	20,729	12,550	2,581
Alvin Community College—Alvin; (7); 1949; Dr. A. Rodney Allbright	233	3,881	3,379	1,361
Amarillo College—Amarillo; (7); 1929 (In Sept. 1995, opertions and facilities of Texas State Technical College-Amarillo merged into Amarillo College; number given are pre-merger); Dr. Luther "Bud" Joyner	827	6,791	3,477	9,314
Amber University—Garland; (3); 1971; Dr. Douglas W. Warner	45	1,500	1,400	NA
Angelina College—Lufkin; (7); 1968; Dr. Larry Phillips	84	3,862	0	12,427
Angelo State University—San Angelo (See **Texas State University System**)				
Arlington Baptist College—Arlington; (3 - Baptist); 1939 (as **Bible Baptist Seminary**; changed to present name in 1965); Dr. David Bryant	23	210	48	20
Austin College—Sherman; (3 - Presbyterian USA); 1849; Dr. Oscar C. Page	§85	1,178	175	363
Austin Community College—Austin; (7); 1972; Dr. Bill Segura	1,797	25,276	20,678	7,481

Name of Institution; Location; (Type* - Ownership, if private sectarian institution); Date of Founding; President (unless otherwise noted)	Number in Faculty†	Enrollment: Fall Term 1994	Enrollment: Summer Session 1994	Enrollment: Extension or Continuing Ed.
Austin Presbyterian Theological Seminary—Austin; Presbyterian; 3-yr; 1902 (successor to **Austin School of Theology**, est. 1884); Dr. Jack L. Stotts	26	327	171	293
Baptist Missionary Association Theological Seminary—Jacksonville; Baptist Missionary, 3-yr.; 1955; Dr. Philip R. Bryan	14	75	16	NA
Baylor College of Dentistry—Transferred to **Texas A&M** system (which see) Sept. 1995				
Baylor College of Medicine—Houston; (5 - Baptist until 1969); 1903 (Dallas; moved to Houston, 1943); Dr. William T. Butler	3,774	1,126	NA	NA
Baylor University—Waco; (3 - Baptist); 1845 (at Independence; merged with **Waco University** in 1887 and moved to Waco); Dr. Herbert H. Reynolds	599	12,240	4,937	633
Bee County College—Beeville; (7); 1966; Dr. Norman E. Wallace	§125	2,633	2,420	401
Blinn College—Brenham; (7); 1883 (as academy; junior college, 1927); Dr. Donald Voelter	368	9,018	8,461	9,018
Brazosport College—Lake Jackson; (7); 1967; Dr. John Grable	157	3,189	2,274	1,822
Brookhaven College—Farmers Branch (See **Dallas County Community College District**)				
Cedar Valley College—Lancaster (See **Dallas County Community College District**)				
Central Texas College—Killeen; (7); 1965; Dr. James R. Anderson, Chancellor	‡‡‡	‡‡‡	‡‡‡	‡‡‡
Cisco Junior College—Cisco; (7); 1909 (as private institution; became state school in 1939); Dr. Roger C. Schustereit	140	2,639	1,410	173
Clarendon College—Clarendon; (7); 1898 (as church school; became state school in 1927); Dr. Jerry D. Stockton	60	900	450	250
College of the Mainland—Texas City; (7); 1967; Larry L. Stanley	430	4,013	3,014	4,500
Collin County Community College—McKinney; (7); 1985; Dr. John H. Anthony	¶532	9,865	6,826	3,199
Concordia Lutheran College—Austin; (3 - Mo. Lutheran); 1926; Dr. David Zersen	65	707	NA	NA
Cooke County College—Gainesville (See **North Central Texas College**)	85	4,150	1,600	3,500
Corpus Christi State University—(See **Texas A&M University-Corpus Christi** listing under **Texas A&M University System**)				
Dallas Baptist University—Dallas; (3 - Southern Baptist).; 1898 (as **Decatur Baptist College**; moved to Dallas and name changed in 1965); Dr. Gary Cook	179	2,989	1,966	NA
Dallas Christian College—Dallas; (3 - Christian); 1950; Dr. Keith Ray	9	94	NA	NA
DALLAS COUNTY COMMUNITY COLLEGE DISTRICT (9) —J. William Wenrich, Chancellor				
Brookhaven College—Farmers Branch; (7); 1978; Dr. Walter Bumphus	500	7,585	8,300	9,000
Cedar Valley College—Lancaster; (7); 1977; Dr. Carol J. Spencer	60	2,884	1,588	3,100
‡Eastfield College—Mesquite; (7); 1970; Dr. Roberto Aguero	‡505	10,088	9,554	5,028
El Centro College—Dallas; (7); 1966; Dr. Wright L. Lassiter Jr.	547	4,852	2,813	3,000
Mountain View College—Dallas; (7); 1970; Dr. Monique Amerman	300	6,113	4,500	2,948
‡North Lake College—Irving; (7); 1977; Dr. James F. Horton Jr.	65	6,835	4,040	4,406
Richland College—Dallas; (7); 1972; Dr. Stephen K. Mittelstet	640	12,010	10,459	9,534
Dallas Theological Seminary—Dallas; private, graduate; 1924; Dr. Charles R. Swindoll	75	1,349	752	198
Del Mar College—Corpus Christi; (7); 1935; Dr. Terry L. Dicianna	500	11,000	6,000	12,000
Eastfield College—Mesquite (See **Dallas County Community College District**)				
East Texas Baptist University—Marshall; (3 - Baptist); 1913 (as **College of Marshall**; changed to **East Texas Baptist College** in 1944; became university in 1984); Dr. Bob E. Riley	102	1,333	505	80
East Texas State University and **East Texas State University at Texarkana** were transferred to **Texas A&M University System** (which see) effective Sept. 1995.				
El Centro College—Dallas (See **Dallas County Community College District**)				
El Paso Community College District—El Paso; (7); 1969; three campuses: **Rio Grande, TransMountain** and **Valle Verde**; Dr. Adriana D. Barrera	1,041	**22,264	8,499	10,205
Episcopal Theological Seminary of the Southwest—Austin; Episcopal; Graduate-level; 1952; Very Rev. Durstan R. McDonald, Dean	12	65	35	NA
Frank Phillips College—Borger; (7); 1948; Dr. William A. Griffin	26	1,167	NA	500
Galveston College—Galveston; (7); 1967; Dr. Marc Nigliazzo	56	2,477	1,330	4,000
Grayson County College—Denison; (7); 1963; Dr. Jim M. Williams	§97	††3,400	††1,200	††3,000
Hardin-Simmons University—Abilene; (3 - Southern Baptist); 1891 (as **Simmons College**; changed to **Simmons University** in 1925; changed to present name in 1934); Dr. Lanny Hall	161	2,133	1,019	217
Hill College—Hillsboro; (7); 1923 (as **Hillsboro Junior College**; name changed in 1962); Dr. William R. Auvenshine	40	2,500	400	NA
Houston Baptist University—Houston; (3 - Baptist); 1960; Dr. E. D. Hodo	102	2,131	1,387	NA

Name of Institution; Location; (Type* - Ownership, if private sectarian institution); Date of Founding; President (unless otherwise noted)	Number in Faculty†	Enrollment		
		Fall Term 1994	Summer Session 1994	Extension or Continuing Ed.
‡‡HOUSTON COMMUNITY COLLEGE SYSTEM—Houston; (9); 1971; **Dr. Charles A. Green, Chancellor**	2,352	42,757	25,210	11,860
System consists of following colleges (president): **Central College** (James P. Engle); **College Without Walls** (Baltazar Acevedo Jr.); **Northeast College** (Elaine P. Adams); **Northwest College** (Judith Winn); **Southeast College** (Sylvia Ramos); **Southwest College** (Sue Cox).				
Howard County Junior College District—Big Spring; (7); 1945; includes **Howard College** and **Southwest Collegiate Institute for the Deaf**; Dr. Cheryl T. Sparks	84	§§2,359	1,378	NA
Howard Payne University—Brownwood; (3 - Baptist); 1889; Dr. Don Newbury	89	1,486	467	100
Huston-Tillotson College—Austin; (3 - Methodist/Church of Christ); 1875 (**Tillotson College**, 1875, **Samuel Huston College**, 1876; merged 1952); Dr. Joseph T. McMillan Jr.	49	612	184	NA
Incarnate Word College—San Antonio; (3 - Catholic); 1881; Dr. Louis Agnese Jr.	205	2,852	NA	NA
International Bible College—San Antonio; private, 4-yr.; 1944; David B. Coote	15	170	NA	NA
Jacksonville College—Jacksonville; (8 - Missionary Baptist.; 1899; Dr. Edwin Crank	25	320	85	50
Jarvis Christian College—Hawkins; (3); 1912; Dr. Sebetha Jenkins	34	486	NA	NA
Kilgore College—Kilgore; (7); 1935; Dr. J. Frank Thornton	§173	4,351	2,258	3,964
LAMAR UNIVERSITY SYSTEM - Abolished effective Sept. 1995 and its four entities transferred to **Texas State University System** (which see).				
Laredo Community College—Laredo; (7); 1946; Dr. Ramón H. Dovalina	§170	7,193	4,206	2,500
LeTourneau University—Longview; (3); 1946 (as **LeTourneau Technical Institute**; became 4-yr. college in 1961); Dr. Alvin O. Austin	138	2,047	258	30
Lee College—Baytown; (7); 1934; Dr. Jackson N. Sasser	326	5,628	4,011	2,703
Lon Morris College—Jacksonville; (8 - Methodist); 1854 (as **Danville Academy**; changed in 1873 to **Alexander Inst.**; present name, 1923); Dr. Clifford M. Lee	40	325	NA	50
Lubbock Christian University—Lubbock; (3 - Church of Christ); 1957; Dr. L. Ken Jones	104	1,174	592	NA
McLennan Community College—Waco; (7); 1965; Dr. Dennis Michaelis	406	5,547	5,458	2,148
McMurry University—Abilene; (3 - Methodist); 1923; Dr. Robert E. Shimp	132	1,384	682	NA
‡Midland College—Midland; (7); 1972; Dr. David E. Daniel	200	4,000	1,900	5,000
Midwestern State University—Wichita Falls; (2); 1922; Dr. Louis J. Rodriguez	177	5,827	3,768	2,194
Mountain View College—Dallas (See **Dallas County Community College District**)				
Navarro College—Corsicana; (7); 1946; Dr. Gerald E. Burson	189	3,216	1,590	1,149
North Central Texas College—Gainesville; (7); 1924 (as Gainesville Jr. College; Cooke County College, eff. 1960; present name, 1994); Dr. Ronnie Glasscock	257	4,254	21,021	1,201
Northeast Texas Community College—Mount Pleasant; (7); 1984; Dr. Mike Bruner	46	2,291	1,000	646
‡‡NORTH HARRIS MONTGOMERY COMMUNITY COLLEGE DISTRICT (9)— John Pickelman, Chancellor	315	19,000	NA	30,000
Includes these colleges, location (president): **Kingwood College**, Kingwood (Stephen Head); **Montgomery College**, Conroe (William D. Law); **North Harris College**, Houston (Sanford Shugart); **Tomball College**, Tomball (Roy Lazenby)				
North Lake College—Irving (See **Dallas County Community College District**)				
Northwood Institute—Cedar Hill; private; 1966; Donald B. Tallman, Provost	46	756	420	NA
Oblate School of Theology—San Antonio; Rom. Catholic, 4-yr.; 1903 (formerly **DeMazenod Scholasticate**); Rev. Patrick Guidon, O.M.I.	24	138	50	444
Odessa College—Odessa; (7); 1946; Dr. Vance W. Gipson	233	4,529	2,479	¶¶282,817
Our Lady of the Lake University of San Antonio—San Antonio; (3 - Catholic); 1895 (as academy for girls; senior college, 1911; university, in 1975); Sister Elizabeth Anne Sueltenfuss	205	3,338	NA	NA
Palo Alto College—San Antonio (See **Alamo Community College District**)				
Panola College—Carthage; (7); 1947 (as **Panola Junior College**; name changed, 1988); Dr. William F. Edmonson	52	1,650	1,577	186
Paris Junior College—Paris; (7); 1924; Bobby R. Walters	76	2,653	1,612	9,669
Paul Quinn College—Dallas; (3); 1872 (in Waco; Dallas, 1990); Dr. Lee E. Monroe	43	667	NA	NA
Prairie View A&M University—Prairie View (See **Texas A&M University System**)				
Ranger College—Ranger; (7); 1926; Dr. Joe Mills	122	829	590	65
Rice University (William Marsh)—Houston; (3); chartered 1891, opened 1912 (as **Rice Institute**; name changed in 1960); Dr. S. Malcolm Gillis	782	4,073	300	2,525
Richland College—Dallas (See **Dallas County Community College District**)				
St. Edward's University—Austin; (3 - Roman Catholic); 1885; Dr. Patricia A. Hayes	222	3,129	843	NA
St. Mary's University of San Antonio—San Antonio; (3 - Catholic); 1852; Rev. John Moder, S.M., Ph.D.	312	4,166	2,215	150

Name of Institution; Location; (Type* - Ownership, if private sectarian institution); Date of Founding; President (unless otherwise noted)	Number in Faculty†	Enrollment		
		Fall Term 1994	Summer Session 1994	Extension or Continuing Ed.
St. Philip's College—San Antonio (See **Alamo Community College District**)				
Sam Houston State University—Huntsville (See **Texas State University System**)				
San Antonio College—San Antonio (See **Alamo Community College District**)				
SAN JACINTO COLLEGE DISTRICT (9) —Dr. Dr. J.B. Whiteley, Interim Chancellor				
‡Central Campus—Pasadena; (7); 1961; Dr. Monte Blue.	532	10,264	6,285	3,353
San Jacinto College North—Houston; (7); 1974; Dr. Edwin E. Lehr	188	3,912	650	NA
San Jacinto College South—Houston; (7); 1979; Dr. Parker Williams.	200	5,157	3,025	1,354
Schreiner College—Kerrville; (3 - Presbyterian); 1923; Dr. Sam M. Junkin	74	584	102	NA
South Plains College—Levelland; (7); 1957; Dr. Gary D. McDaniel	339	5,866	2,695	853
South Texas College of Law—Houston; private, 3-yr.; 1923; Dean Frank Read).	56	‡1,200	692	‡2,364
South Texas Community College—McAllen; (7); NA; Dr. Shirley A. Reed	†200	††2,500	NA	NA
Southern Methodist University—Dallas; (3 - Methodist); 1911; Dr. R. Gerald Turner	‡648	9,014	3,652	***3,131
Southwest Collegiate Institute for the Deaf — Big Spring (See **Howard County Junior College District**)				
Southwest Texas Junior College—Uvalde; (7); 1946; Dr. Billy Word	69	3,139	1,381	392
Southwest Texas State University—San Marcos (see **Texas State University System**)				
Southwestern Adventist College—Keene; (3 - Seventh-Day Adventist); 1893 (as **Keene Industrial Academy**; became **Southwestern Junior College**; changed to **Southwestern Union College** in 1963); Dr. Marvin Anderson	75	978	293	201
Southwestern Assemblies of God College—Waxahachie; (3 - Assemblies of God); 1927 (in Enid, Okla., as **Southwestern Bible School**; moved to Fort Worth and merged with **South Central Bible Institute** in 1941; moved to Waxahachie as **Southwestern Bible Institute** in 1943; present name since 1963); Dr. Delmer R. Guynes	35	1,007	222	247
Southwestern Baptist Theological Seminary—Fort Worth; Southern Baptist, 4-yr.; 1908; Dr. Ken Hemphill.	190	2,903	1,255	152
Southwestern Christian College—Terrell; (3 - Church of Christ); 1948 (as **Southern Bible Institute** in Fort Worth; moved to Terrell and changed name to present form in 1950); Dr. Jack Evans	20	200	NA	NA
Southwestern University—Georgetown; (3 - Methodist); 1840 (**Southwestern University** was a merger of **Rutersville** (1840), **Wesleyan** (1846) and **McKenzie** (1841) colleges and **Soule University** (1855). First named **Texas University**; chartered under present name in 1875); Dr. Roy B. Shilling Jr.	105	1,238	NA	NA
Southwest Texas State University — San Marcos (See **Texas State University System**)				
Stephen F. Austin State University—Nacogdoches; (2); 1921; Dr. Dan Angel	683	12,206	6,398	5,825
Sul Ross State University—Alpine (See **Texas State University System**)				
Sul Ross State University Uvalde Study Center—Uvalde (See **Texas State University System**)				
Tarleton State University—Stephenville (See **Texas A&M University System**)				
Tarrant County Junior College District—Fort Worth; (7); 1965; three campuses: **Northeast, Northwest** and **South**; C.A. Roberson, Chancellor	953	26,253	16,128	66,513
Temple Junior College—Temple; (7); 1926; Dr. Marvin R. Felder	80	2,563	1,224	2,364
Texarkana College—Texarkana; (7); 1927; Dr. Carl Nelson	207	3,924	1,550	450
Texas A&I University—Kingsville (See **Texas A&M University-Kingsville** listing under **Texas A&M University System**)				
TEXAS A&M UNIVERSITY SYSTEM (1) —Dr. Barry B. Thompson, Chancellor				
Baylor College of Dentistry—Dallas; (5); 1905 (transferred to **Texas A&M** system 1995); Dr. Dominick P. DePaola	239	471	245	966
East Texas State University—Commerce; (2); 1889 (as **East Texas Normal College**; renamed **East Texas State Teachers College** in 1923; "Teachers" dropped, 1957; university status conferred, 1965; transferred to Texas A&M system 1995); numbers include **ETSUMetroplex Commuter Facility** in Mesquite); Dr. Jerry D. Morris	383	7,952	6,794	333
East Texas State University at Texarkana—Texarkana; (2 - upper-level); 1971 (transferred to Texas A&M system 1995); Dr. Stephen Hensley	29	1,210	NA	NA
Prairie View A&M University—Prairie View; (2); 1876 (as **Alta Vista Agricultural College**; name changed to **Prairie View State Normal School** in 1879; called **Prairie View University** by 1947, when it was changed to **Prairie View Agricultural and Mechanical College** as a branch of **Texas A&M University System;** present name since 1973); Dr. Charles A. Hines	319	5,849	2,221	NA

Name of Institution; Location; (Type* - Ownership, if private sectarian institution); Date of Founding; President (unless otherwise noted)	Number in Faculty†	Enrollment		
		Fall Term 1994	Summer Session 1994	Extension or Continuing Ed.
Tarleton State University—Stephenville; (2); 1899 (as **John Tarleton College**; taken over by state in 1917 as **John Tarleton Agricultural College**; changed 1949 to **Tarleton State College**; present name since 1973); Dr. Dennis McCabe	§231	6,463	2,631	450
Texas A&M International University-Laredo; (2); 1970 (as **Laredo State University**; name changed to present form 1993); Dr. Leo Sayavedra	99	1,964	2,085	NA
Texas A&M University—College Station; (2); 1876 (as **Agricultural and Mechanical College of Texas**; present name since 1963; includes **College of Veterinary Medicine** and **College of Medicine** at College Station); Dr. Ray M. Bowen	3,287	43,256	17,885	3,940
Texas A&M University-Corpus Christi —Corpus Christi; (2); 1973 (as upper-level **Corpus Christi State University**; changed to present name in 1993; became four-year in 1994); Dr. Robert R. Furgason	270	5,152	NA	NA
Texas A&M University at Galveston—Galveston; (2); 1962 (as **Texas Maritime Academy**; changed to **Moody College of Marine Sciences and Maritime Resources** and became 4-yr. college in 1971; changed to present name); Dr. David J. Schmidly, CEO and Campus Dean	95	1,350	400	1,000
Texas A&M University-Kingsville—Kingsville; (2); 1925 (as **South Texas Teachers College**; name changed to **Texas College of Arts and Industries** in 1929, to **Texas A&I University** in 1967; made part of **Univ. of South Texas System** in 1977; entered A&M system in 1993); Dr. Manuel L. Ibañez	370	6,548	3,398	652
West Texas A&M University—Canyon; (2); 1910 (as **West Texas State Normal College**; became **West Texas State Teachers College** in 1923; in 1949 became **West Texas State College**; changed to **West Texas State University** in 1949; name changed to present form in 1993); Dr. Russell C. Long, Interim	344	6,633	4,183	1,916
Texas Baptist Institute and Seminary—Henderson; (3 - Calvary Baptist); 1948; Dr. Ray O. Brooks	15	58	53	12
Texas Christian University—Fort Worth; (3 - Disciples of Christ); 1873 (as **Add-Ran College** at Thorp Spring; name changed to **Add-Ran Christian University** 1890; moved to Waco 1895; present name since 1902; moved to Fort Worth 1910); Dr. William E. Tucker, Chancellor	600	6,481	2,181	225
Texas College—Tyler; (3 - C.M.E.); 1894; Dr. Haywood L. Strickland	37	251	NA	NA
Texas College of Osteopathic Medicine—Fort Worth (See **University of North Texas Health Science Center at Fort Worth**)	152	416	NA	NA
Texas Lutheran College—Seguin; (3 - Lutheran); 1891; Dr. Jon N. Moline	89	1,301	490	57
‡**Texas Southern University**—Houston; (2); 1926 (as **Houston Colored Junior College**; upper level added and name changed to **Houston College for Negroes** in mid-1930s; became **Texas State University for Negroes** in 1947; present name since 1951); Dr. Joann Horton	‡514	9,441	1.903	NA
Texas Southmost College—Brownsville (see **The University of Texas at Brownsville** under **University of Texas System** listing)				
TEXAS STATE TECHNICAL COLLEGE SYSTEM—Dr. Cecil Groves, Chancellor				
Texas State Technical College-Amarillo—Amarillo; (7); 1970 (Operations and facilities moved to Amarillo Community College eff. Sept. 1995); Dr. Ron DeSpain, Campus President	82	591	500	1,456
Texas State Technical College-Harlingen—Harlingen; (7); 1967; Dr. J. Gilbert Leal, Campus President	200	3,000	2,116	NA
Texas State Technical College - East Texas Center at Marshall—Marshall; (7); Jack L. Foreman, Campus Dean	34	266	167	NA
Texas State Technical College-Sweetwater—Sweetwater; (7); 1901; Dr. Clay G. Johnson, Campus President	71	866	NA	14,211
Texas State Technical College- Waco—Waco; (7); 1965 (as **James Connally Technical Inst.**; name changed in 1969); Dr. Cecil Groves, Interim Campus President	250	3,200	3,200	NA
TEXAS STATE UNIVERSITY SYSTEM (1)—Dr. Lamar G. Urbanovsky, Chancellor				
Angelo State University—San Angelo; (2); 1928; Dr. E. James Hindman	204	6,276	4,344	575
Lamar University - Beaumont—Beaumont; (2); 1923 (as **South Park Junior College**; name changed to **Lamar College**, 1932; name changed to **Lamar State College of Technology** in 1951; to present name in 1971; transferred from Lamar University System, Sept. 1995); Dr. Rex Cottle	433	8,693	4,977	894
Lamar University - Orange—Orange; (7); 1969 (transferred from Lamar University System, Sept. 1995); Dr. J. Michael Shahan, Interim	80	1,473	778	NA
Lamar University - Port Arthur—Port Arthur; (7); 1909 (as **Port Arthur College**; became part of **Lamar University** in 1975; became part of TSU system, Sept. 1995); Dr. W. Sam Monroe	115	2,038	1,436	376
Lamar University Institute of Technology—Beaumont; (7); (became part of TSU system, Sept. 1995); Dr. Robert D. Krienke	110	2,600	400	800

Name of Institution; Location; (Type* - Ownership, if private sectarian institution); Date of Founding; President (unless otherwise noted)	Number in Faculty†	Enrollment		
		Fall Term 1994	Summer Session 1994	Extension or Continuing Ed.
Sam Houston State University—Huntsville; (2); 1879; Dr. Martin J. Anisman	500	12,906	9,129	Unavail.
Southwest Texas State University—San Marcos; (2); 1903 (as **Southwest Texas Normal School**; changed1918 to **Southwest Texas State Normal College**, in 1923 to **Southwest Texas State Teachers College**, in 1959 to **Southwest Texas State College**, and in 1969 to present form); Dr. Jerome H. Supple	900	20,896	15,980	1,579
Sul Ross State Rio Grande College—Uvalde; (2 - upper-level); 1973 (name changed from **Sul Ross State University, Uvalde Center 1995);** Dr. Frank W. Abbott, Dean	§35	726	616	NA
Sul Ross State University—Alpine; (2); 1917 (as **Sul Ross State Normal College**; changed to **Sul Ross State Teachers College** in 1923; to **Sul Ross State College** in 1949; present name since 1969); Dr. R. Vic Morgan	93	3,145	1,798	NA
Texas Tech University—Lubbock; (2); 1923 (as **Texas Technological College**; present name since 1969); Dr. Robert W. Lawless	1,581	24,083	9,196	32,000
Texas Tech University Health Sciences Center—Lubbock; (4); 1972; Dr. Robert W. Lawless	610	1,276	753	5,503
Texas Wesleyan University—Fort Worth; (3 - United Methodist); 1891 (as college; present name since 1989); Dr. Jake B. Schrum	§109	2,632	1,200	NA
Texas Woman's University—Denton; (2); 1901 (as **College of Industrial Arts**; name changed to **Texas State College for Women**, 1934; present name since 1957); Dr.Carol D. Surles	††500	10,090	5,600	NA
Trinity University—San Antonio; (3 - Presbyterian); 1869 (at Tehuacana; moved to Waxahachie, 1902; to San Antonio, 1942); Dr. Ronald K. Calgaard	224	2,479	305	NA
Trinity Valley Community College—Athens; also campus at Terrell; (7); 1946 (originally **Henderson County Junior College**); Dr. Ronald C. Baugh	120	4,774	2,799	75
Tyler Junior College—Tyler; (7); 1926; Dr. William R. Crowe, Interim President	453	7,981	2,486	NA
University of Central Texas—Killeen; (3); 1973 (originally **American Technological University;** name changed, 1989); Dr. Jack Fuller	43	858	663	NA
University of Dallas—Irving; (3 - Catholic); 1956; Dr. Robert A. Sasseen	160	4,048	NA	20
UNIVERSITY OF HOUSTON SYSTEM (1) — (Vacancy), Chancellor				
University of Houston—Houston; (2); 1927; (Vacancy)	1,892	31,298	NA	NA
University of Houston-Clear Lake—Houston; (2 - upper level and grad.); 1974; Dr. Glenn A. Goerke	392	7,229	4,172	400
University of Houston-Downtown—Houston; (2); 1948 (as **South Texas College**; became part of **University of Houston** in 1974) ; Dr. Max Castillo	367	7,715	3,042	1,300
University of Houston-Victoria—Victoria; (2 - upper-level); 1973; (Vacancy)	85	1,616	NA	NA
University of Mary Hardin-Baylor—Belton; (3 - Southern Baptist); 1845; Dr. Jerry G. Bawcom	155	2,244	767	NA
University of North Texas—Denton; (2); 1890 (as **North Texas Normal College**; name changed in 1923 to **North Texas State Teachers College**; in 1949 to **North Texas State College**; became a university in 1961; present name since 1988); Dr. Alfred F. Hurley, Chancellor	1,048	25,605	21,266	1,016
University of North Texas Health Science Center at Fort Worth—Fort Worth; (4);1966 (as private college; came under direction of **North Texas State University** in 1975; name changed to present form in 1993); Dr. David M. Richards	170	508	NA	NA
University of St. Thomas—Houston; (3); 1947; Dr. Joseph M. McFadden	192	2,298	1,066	NA
UNIVERSITY OF TEXAS SYSTEM (1) —William Cunningham, Chancellor				
University of Texas at Arlington, The—Arlington; (2); 1895 (as **Arlington College**; in 1917, became state institution, renamed **Grubbs Vocational College**; 1923 became **North Texas Agricultural and Mechanical College**; 1949, became **Arlington State College**; 1967, present name); Dr. Robert E. Witt, Interim President	876	23,280	15,350	5,573
University of Texas at Austin, The—Austin; (2); 1883; Dr. Robert M. Berdahl	5,418	47,957	19,353	†††45,925
University of Texas at Brownsville, The (2 - upper-level); 1973 (as branch of **Pan American College**; changed to **The University of Texas-Pan American - Brownsville**; present name since Sept. 1991) and **Texas Southmost College** (7); 1926 (as **Brownsville Junior College**; name changed in 1949) — Brownsville; Dr.Juliet V. Garcia, UT-Brownsville; Michael Putegnat, TSC Exec. Dir.	359	7,475	5,738	2,044
University of Texas at Dallas, The—Richardson; (2); 1961 (as **Graduate Research Center of the Southwest**; changed to **Southwest Center for Advanced Studies** in 1967; joined U.T. System and present name adopted in 1969; full undergraduate program since 1975); Dr. Franklyn G. Jenifer	402	8,487	5,104	3,500
University of Texas at El Paso, The—El Paso; (2); 1913 (as **Texas College of Mines and Metallurgy;** changed to **Texas Western College of U.T.** in 1949; present name since 1967); Dr. Diana S. Natalicio	¶808	17,188	8,217	4,796

Name of Institution; Location; (Type* - Ownership, if private sectarian institution); Date of Founding; President (unless otherwise noted)	Number in Faculty†	Enrollment		
		Fall Term 1994	Summer Session 1994	Extension or Continuing Ed.
University of Texas-Pan American, The—Edinburg; (2); 1927 (as **Edinburg Junior College;** changed to **Pan American College** and made 4-yr. institution, 1952; became **Pan American University** in 1971; present name since 1991); Dr. Miguel A. Nevárez	587	13,750	7,561	1,202
University of Texas of the Permian Basin, The—Odessa; (2); 1969 (as 2-yr. upper- level institution; expanded to 4-yr., Sept. 1991); Dr. Charles A. Sorber	117	2,315	1,100	57
University of Texas at San Antonio—San Antonio; (2); 1969; Dr. Samuel Kirkpatrick	798	17,577	8,306	NA
University of Texas at Tyler—Tyler; (2 - upper-level); 1971 (as **Tyler State College;** became **Texas Eastern University** in 1975; joined **U.T. System** in 1979); Dr. George F. Hamm	266	3,986	2,734	NA
UNIVERSITY OF TEXAS-HOUSTON HEALTH SCIENCE CENTER (4) —Dr. M. David Low	1,122	3,290	NA	NA
Established 1972; consists of following divisions (year of founding): **Dental Branch** (1905); **Graduate School of Biomedical Sciences** (1963); **Medical School** (1970); **School of Allied Health Sciences** (1973); **School of Nursing** (1972); **School of Public Health** (1967); **Division of Continuing Education** (1958).				
UNIVERSITY OF TEXAS HEALTH SCIENCE CENTER AT SAN ANTONIO (4) —Dr. John P. Howe III	1,254	2,790	NA	NA
Established 1968; consists of following divisions (year of founding): **Dental School** (1970); **Graduate School of Biomedical Sciences** (1970); **Health Science Center** (1972); **Medical School** (1959 as **South Texas Medical School of University of Texas;** 1966 name changed to present form); **School of Allied Health Sciences** (1976); **School of Nursing** (1969).				
UNIVERSITY OF TEXAS MEDICAL BRANCH AT GALVESTON (4) —Dr. Thomas N. James	984	2,877	2,814	495
Established 1891; consists of following divisions (year of founding): **Graduate School of Biomedical Sciences** (1952); **Medical School** (1891); **School of Allied Health Sciences** (1968); **School of Nursing** (1890).				
UNIVERSITY OF TEXAS SOUTHWESTERN MEDICAL CENTER AT DALLAS (4) — Dr. Kern Wildenthal	1,102	3,091	NA	4,421
Established 1943 (as private institution; became **Southwestern Medical College** of UT 1948; in 1967 became **UT Southwestern Medical School at Dallas**; made part of **UT Health Science Center at Dallas** in 1972; name changed again to present form); consists of following divisions (year of founding): **Graduate School of Biomedical Sciences** (1947); **School of Allied Health Sciences** (1968); **Southwestern Medical School** (1943).				
Vernon Regional Junior College—Vernon; (7); 1970; Dr. R. Wade Kirk	109	1,872	1,101	3,078
Victoria College, The —Victoria; (7); 1925; Dr. Jimmy Goodson	108	3,667	1,750	350
Wayland Baptist University—Plainview; (3 -Southern Baptist); 1910; Dr. Wallace Davis	61	3,438	487	331
Weatherford College—Weatherford; (7); 1869 (as branch of **Southwestern University**; 1922, became denominational junior college; became municipal junior college, 1949); Dr. Jim Boyd	160	2,600	800	900
Western Texas College—Snyder; (7); 1969; Dr. Harry Krenek	68	1,212	673	591
Wharton County Junior College—Wharton; (7); 1946; Dr. Frank R. Vivelo	212	3,394	2,352	1,179
Wiley College—Marshall; (3 - Methodist); 1873; Dr. Lamore J. Carter	35	589	152	NA

***Type:** (1) Public University System
(2) Public University
(3) Independent Senior College or University
(4) Public Medical School or Health Science Center
(5) Independent Medical or Dental School
(6) Public Technical College System
(7) Public Community College
(8) Independent Junior College
(9) Public Community College System

† Faculty includes professors, associate professors, instructors and tutors, unless otherwise noted.
‡ No reply received to questionnaire. Information repeated from 1994-95 Texas Almanac.
§ Full-time faculty only.
¶ Does not include tutors.
** Includes students enrolled for the second summer "mini-mester."
†† Approximate count.
‡‡ Includes faculty and enrollment at all branches or divisions.
§§ Includes students enrolled in extension and continuing-education courses, fall semester of 1994.
¶¶ Count given in "contact hours" rather than students.
*** Students counted separately for each course enrolled in; duplicate counts inevitable.
††† Number is for 1993-94 school year; semester system does not apply to continuing-education or extension courses.
‡‡‡ Information not supplied.
NA - Not applicable

Texas Economy is Building

The Texas economy turned in another strong year in fiscal 1994. When measured by the number of new jobs created, the state had its best economic year since 1990, and the second best in ten years

Overall employment growth, at 3.3 percent, lies midway between the booming 1970s and the weaker 1980s. For the fifth straight year, the state's employment growth rate exceeded that of the United States, and once again, Texas added more jobs during the year than any other state.

Gross State Product, 1990

Rank	billions of dollars
1. California	$ 745
2. New York	467
3. Texas	**372**
4. Illinois	272
5. Pennsylvania	245
6. Florida	245
7. Ohio	222
8. New Jersey	208
9. Michigan	188
10. Massachusetts	154

Source: U.S. Bureau of Economic Analysis, Survey of Current Business, Dec. 1993.

Fastest Job Growth in Construction

The fastest-growing major industry in Texas during the fiscal year was construction, which has not ranked first in the rate of job growth since 1976. The state added 24,200 jobs, for a nearly 7 percent increase over the end of fiscal 1993.

The combination of a strong state economy, increased net in-migration and relatively low mortgage rates at the beginning of the fiscal year particularly fueled single-family home construction. During the year, construction began on a total of 95,000 new homes and apartments in the state, the highest number since 1986.

Petroleum Employment Declines

Relatively low oil and gas prices, declining production, and the continuing shift of drilling activity overseas resulted in another weak year for the state's oil-and-gas sector.

The industry closed the year with under 161,500 employees, its lowest level since fiscal 1976, and only half the industry's peak in early 1982. By the end of the year, industry employment was down 3.1 percent, or a total of 5,200 jobs.

Oil and gas continues to decline in importance in the state economy, now making up only 11 percent of the state's gross product.

Manufacturing Underlies Growth

A strong manufacturing sector underlies much of the current strength of the Texas economy. During fiscal 1994, the manufacturing sector continued to expand, with statewide employment rising by 1.2 percent, or a total of 12,200 jobs.

Several factors, including an internationally-competitive manufacturing sector, growing Sunbelt markets, relatively low Texas business costs, and the rebound in state home-building activity, account for the strong growth of many of the state's key manufacturing industries.

Construction-related manufacturing has fueled much of the growth in the production of durable goods during the year.

By the end of the year, employment in furniture and fixtures increased by nearly 10 percent, while employment in lumber and wood products and stone, clay and glass products increased by 9 percent and 6 percent, respectively.

Altogether, these three rapidly-growing industries contributed a total of 6,500 jobs to the Texas economy in fiscal 1994.

Other durable-goods industries that grew by more than 3 percent during the year included fabricated metals, computers and electronics, adding a combined total of 9,800 new jobs. In total, despite the loss of 5,000 aerospace jobs, durables manufacturing added a total of 11,200 new jobs to the Texas economy in fiscal 1994.

Because of ongoing defense cuts, state aerospace manufacturing has lost more than 27,000 jobs since the end of fiscal 1989.

In the production of nondurable goods, no single industry accounted for more than 1,000 new jobs in fiscal 1994. The biggest gainers were miscellaneous plastics manufacturing, which grew by 4.3 percent, or 700 jobs, and apparel manufacturing, particularly in El Paso, which gained 800 jobs.

During the year, jobs in petrochemicals declined by 0.2 percent, while petroleum refining employment fell by almost 1 percent. All together, employment in nondurables industries increased by a total of just over 1,000 during the year.

Transportation Trucking Along

Transportation, communications, and public utilities (TPU) continued to generate new jobs in fiscal 1994. By the end of the year, TPU employment was up by 12,000, or 2.7 percent. Trucking, with a 7 percent increase in employment, due largely to the state's strong manufacturing sector, accounted for most of this growth.

On the other hand, both railroad transportation and utilities lost jobs during the year. Despite recent layoffs by many commercial carriers nationwide, statewide air transportation gained a total of 800 jobs, a 1 percent gain, during the year. The communications industry, burgeoned by rapid growth of high-tech communications, gained 2,500 jobs.

Finance, Trade Strongest in Nearly a Decade

In response to relatively low interest rates and the rebound in the state's construction sector, finance, insurance and real estate added more jobs to the economy in fiscal 1994 than in any year since 1985.

After six years of declining employment, the industry added 8,500 jobs in fiscal 1993 and another 9,200 jobs in 1994. Most of the growth was in insurance, with employment up by 3.6 percent, and real estate, with a 2.5 percent increase in employment.

Strong Retail Sales

With overall retail sales up about 9 percent statewide, wholesale and retail trade employment increased by 68,300 jobs, or 3.8 percent. Fiscal 1994 was the best year for the state's trade sector since 1984.

Strong employment and wage gains, combined with significant gains in consumer confidence, fueled the growth of statewide retail employment in fiscal 1994. During the year, wholesale trade also showed strong gains, due to the growth in retailing and the state's strong manufacturing sector.

Services Still Generate Most New Jobs

The Texas service industry — composed of health, business, private educational, engineering, consulting and personal services — continued to lead all sectors in terms of new jobs in fiscal year 1994. Texas services employment surpassed 2 million at the end of fiscal 1994, comprising one-fourth of all employed Texans.

The services industry added 90,000 jobs, for an employment gain of 4.7 percent, during the fiscal year. All subcategories of services added jobs in fiscal year 1994: Employment in business and engineering services increased by 38,000 jobs, health services gained a total of almost 25,000 new jobs, and employment in miscellaneous other services, mainly amusements, hotels and private educational services, increased by 27,000.

Shopping centers, 1993

Rank	Number
1. California	5,221
2. Florida	3,044
3. Texas	**2,790**
4. Illinois	1,917
5. New York	1,564
6. Ohio	1,539
7. Pennsylvania	1,493
8. Georgia	1,397
9. North Carolina	1,386
10. Virginia	1,138

Source: Statistical Abstract of the United States 1994; International Council of Shopping Centers in Shopping Centers Today, April 1994, (copyright-Blackburn Marketing Services (U.S.), Inc.).

Government Employment Grows

Texas government employment grew by nearly 36,000 jobs, or 2.5 percent, over the year. Until recently, court-ordered improvements in the state's educational and prisons systems caused the growth of government employment to exceed the overall state average.

In fiscal 1994, however, government employment grew slower than the over-all statewide employment for the first time in nine years. During the year, employment in state government increased by 2.1 percent, while local-government employment increased by 3.7 percent. Federal-government employment in Texas, however, fell by 1.7 percent in fiscal 1994 due to fiscal restraint in Washington.

Major Cities in Review

The **Austin-San Marcos** metro area (including Bastrop, Caldwell, Hays, Travis and Williamson counties) has grown at an impressive rate over the past year despite the closing of Bergstrom Air Force Base and downsizing at IBM and Lockheed. The Austin-San Marcos MSA added 21,400 jobs during fiscal 1994, a 4.7 percent increase from 455,900 in September 1993 to 477,300 in August 1994.

Employment growth in the metro area is distributed over most sectors of the local economy, with increases in trade (+6,200), government (+6,200), construction (+3,200), services (+1,300), manufacturing (+3,100) and finance, insurance and real estate (FIRE) (+1,000). In August 1994, the unemployment rate in the capital city and surrounding areas fell to 3.8 percent, from 4.4 percent in September 1993.

In fiscal 1994, the construction sector boasted a 17.8 percent increase in jobs to 21,200 in August 1994. Sparked by increased activity in local real estate markets, employment in FIRE increased 3.9 percent rising to 26,900.

Together, the services and trade sectors account for about half of the metro area's total employment. Providing 123,500 jobs, the services sector increased a more modest 1.1 percent, while the trade sector exhibited a 6.6 percent increase over the year, employing 99,700 in August 1994.

Contributing to the employment growth in the

manufacturing sector is the increased concentration of high-tech manufacturers like Motorola, IBM, Advanced Micro Devices, Dell and Texas Instruments in the area.

Manufacturing employment increased 5.2 percent to 62,300 over the past year.

Government employment remains a cornerstone of the local economy, accounting for 127,600 jobs, a 5.1 percent increase, with growth in local government. Government employment in the area is concentrated in education services.

Austin has been highlighted by Fortune and Money magazines for its relaxing yet competitive atmosphere. Austin ranked as the fifth-best city for doing business, one of the top ten cities for "knowledge" workers and the seventeenth-best place to live. The University of Texas and high-tech companies enhance Austin's competitive business climate, while its lakes and hills provide an enjoyable atmosphere.

The **Dallas** MSA (made up of Collin, Dallas, Denton, Ellis, Henderson, Hunt, Kaufman and Rockwall counties) experienced impressive employment growth during fiscal 1994. During the period, employment grew by 5.0 percent or 73,500 jobs to stand at 1,552,700, an all-time high. In addition, Dallas' unemployment rate fell to 5.5 percent in August 1994, down from 5.8 percent in September 1993.

More than a quarter of all new jobs created in Texas over the past year have been in the Dallas MSA.

This growth, a result of increased consumer confidence, a strong national economy and a growing service sector in the Dallas area, iindicates that Dallas is taking advantage of its diverse economy.

The service industry, Dallas' largest employment sector, with more than 28 percent of total employment, grew by 23,600 jobs, or 5.7 percent, in the past year. The construction sector posted gains as employment growth, coupled with increased housing and apartment demand, ignited Dallas' construction market. From September 1993 to August 1994, construction employment rose 11.6 percent or 6,300 jobs to 60,800.

The banking industry has made an impressive recovery from its demise during the late 1980s. Finance, insurance and real-estate employment increased 4.9 percent or 6,200 jobs during fiscal 1994 to 132,100. Trade-sector employment grew to 391,400 adding 20,700 jobs for a 5.6 percent increase, and government added 8,500 jobs to stand at 194,700.

Manufacturing, which represents 14 percent of total Dallas employment, is still experiencing modest employment gains as major oil companies continue to downsize operations. Employment in the manufacturing sector rose to 221,600, gaining 600 jobs in the past year, while the transportation industry increased by 7,200 jobs or 8.2 percent.

Dallas has fought through the economic downturns and emerged with a diverse economy that more closely follows national trends. With worldwide attention focusing on Dallas as a result of the World Cup and NAFTA, Dallas is poised to reap even further employment gains.

In the seven months since the passage of the North American Free Trade Agreement (NAFTA) in January 1994, several sectors of **El Paso**'s economy are showing the preliminary effects of the free trade agreement.

During fiscal 1994, El Paso's employment rose by 2,200, or 1.0 percent to 226,800. The University of Texas-El Paso and Fort Bliss provided the area with economic stability helped by slight increases in manufacturing and retail-trade employment. While the government and manufacturing sectors continued to be the foundation of the El Paso economy, the construction and services sectors recorded impressive growth during the fiscal year.

Government employment in El Paso was virtually unchanged between September 1993 and August 1994. Continued population growth and rising public-school enrollments, however, will increase the demand for government services.

Moreover, rising trade with Mexico, due to reduced trade barriers, and the establishment of a U.S. Environmental Protection Agency satellite office (as part of the Border Environment Cooperation Commission) will create additional government jobs in the areas of international trade and environmental protection.

During fiscal 1994, manufacturing employment rose slightly increasing by 200, or 0.4 percent. El Paso's apparel industry has stabilized — still at record levels — after almost a decade of impressive employment growth. While apparel and copper production remain local manufacturing mainstays, electronics, auto parts and plastics continue to gain importance. The El Paso plastics industry is an international endeavor involving the manufacturing of components in El Paso and assembling the components into finished goods by the maquiladora plants in Juarez.

Fueled by a growing population, the passage of NAFTA, an improving economy and low interest rates, new-home construction and retail and commercial development proceeded at a record pace during the fiscal year. Construction employment experienced strong growth and reached one of its highest levels since the late-1980s, rising by 700, or 8.4 percent, to 9,000 workers.

The services sector experienced the largest employment increase of the last year, adding 1,400 workers between September 1993 and August 1994. At 49,500 jobs, employment in this major component of El Paso's economy rose 2.9 percent over last year.

City officials project NAFTA will continue to increase El Paso's role as a distribution hub for the United States. This heightened role as a trade center will promote further economic growth in El Paso.

The **Fort Worth-Arlington** MSA (comprising Tarrant, Parker, Hood and Johnson counties) posted healthy increases in employment figures during fiscal 1994. Fort Worth, after more than two years of declining employment, is showing signs of consistent employment growth.

During the past year, employment jumped by 17,200 jobs, a 2.8 percent increase, the highest employment growth since 1990. While the manufacturing sector continues to feel the negative effects of defense cutbacks, gains have been felt in other sectors.

In August 1994, employment in the Fort Worth metropolitan area totaled 632,500, an impressive increase over September 1993's employment total of 615,300. Fort Worth's service sector led all other industries in employment growth. Growing by 6.1 percent, this sector added 9,600 of the 17,200 total new jobs in the area. The trade industry grew by 3,800 jobs, or 2.4 percent, to total 160,100.

Construction saw an increase of 3,300 jobs, up a booming 13.6 percent from September 1993. The manufacturing sector lost 1,600 jobs from September 1993 to August 1994.

After employing more than 120,000 in the mid-1980s, Fort Worth's manufacturing employment fell to an early-1992 level of 99,900. Continued defense cuts and airline restructuring has kept manufacturing employment flat, rising to only 101,000 in August 1994.

All of Fort Worth's other industries exhibited strong gains during the fiscal year. The area's finance, insurance and real estate sector grew by 3.5 percent, or 1,000 jobs, as the construction and banking industries continued their recovery.

The transportation and public utilities sector added 800 jobs, while the government sector added 500 jobs in the Fort Worth-Arlington MSA.

Fort Worth's increasing prominence and its commitment to a diversified economy that is less dependent on the defense industry should push employment even higher as the nation's economy continues to grow.

Rebounding from recent economic downturns, the **Houston** metropolitan area (consisting of Chambers, Fort Bend, Harris, Liberty, Montgomery and Waller counties) experienced slow growth during the fiscal year, rising from 1.66 million in September 1993 to 1.69 million in August 1994, a 1.8 percent increase.

Job increases were concentrated in services (+10,800), construction (+8,100), trade (+6,600), government (+3,700) and transportation and public utilities (+2,100). The manufacturing sector posted an employment decrease, losing 1,500 jobs. Unemployment in the metro area stood at 6.7 percent in August 1994, down from 7.0 percent in September 1993.

*City officials project that NAFTA will continue to increase **El Paso**'s role as a distribution hub for the U.S.*

*(**Houston**'s) transportation and public-utilities sector employs 114,800, and is anticipated to increase with NAFTA.*

Houston's mining sector remained relatively stable over the past year, providing 65,100 jobs. Houston remains home to many oil and gas extraction and production companies like Exxon, Shell and Lyondell Petrochemical. Downsizing continues in many parts of the industry as Halliburton Energy Services and Marathon Oil both announced restructuring plans.

The manufacturing sector has yet to recover from past economic woes, falling to 177,800 jobs, down 0.8 percent. The construction sector posted a 7.7 percent increase in jobs, rising to 113,800 in August 1994, but sparked only minimal growth in the finance, insurance and real estate sector, increasing 1.0 percent, or 1,000 jobs, to 98,300.

The service and trade sectors comprise the largest percentages of total employment, 30.0 percent and 23.5 percent respectively. Service-sector employment rose to 490,500 over the year, a 2.3 percent increase. Employment in wholesale and retail trade experienced a 1.7 percent increase to reach 398,000 in August.

Government currently employs 235,500, concentrated in education and city services, and accounts for 13.9 percent of total employment. The transportation and public-utilities sector employs 114,800, and is anticipated to increase with NAFTA.

Last year, Houston was cited by Fortune magazine as one of the top 10 cities for "knowledge" workers and the seventh-best city for doing business.

Houston is recognized for its abundance of world-class academic and governmental research centers, namely NASA's Johnson Space Center, the Houston Advanced Research Center and the Texas Medical Center. Furthermore, Money ranked Rice

University as the nation's second-best education bargain, based on costs and academic quality.

Employment in the **San Antonio** metro area (composed of Bexar, Comal, Guadalupe and Wilson counties) experienced impressive growth during fiscal 1994. Total employment, more than half a million strong at 588,400, grew 2.4 percent adding 13,900 jobs. Growth in the metro area occurred as the finance, insurance and real estate sector rebounded, residential construction boomed and tourism sparked increased employment in the services sector.

Services comprise the largest industrial sector in San Antonio, employing 168,200. The sector grew 1.5 percent during the fiscal year, adding 2,500 jobs. Health services at the South Texas Health Science Center and modern facilities at metro-area hospitals bring in patients from South Texas and Mexico.

Attractions drawing from San Antonio's rich history and cultural diversity, including the Alamo, the River Walk and Mission Trail, lure both national and international tourists. In addition, new attractions at the metro area's two theme parks — Monster Mash at SeaWorld and the Boardwalk at Fiesta Texas — increased the number of tourists during the 1994 summer season.

During fiscal 1994, the finance, insurance and real estate sector added 1,800 jobs, growing 4.5 percent, while construction added 1,500 jobs and grew 6.0 percent. Low interest rates and corporate relocations spurred home sales. Southwestern Bell's relocation is lauded as a major cause of the increase in upscale home building and sales.

The choice of San Antonio as the future site of the North American Development Bank will increase the metro area's credibility as an international financial center.

Transportation, communications and public utilities added 800 jobs, growing 3.0 percent. In addition to Southwestern Bell's move from St. Louis, the planned expansion of West Telecommunications should help keep up this pace.

Moreover, the transportation industry will grow as NAFTA increases trade between the United States and Mexico.

Manufacturing added 1,100 jobs, growing a respectable 2.4 percent. Manufacturing companies employ 47,800 in the metro area.

The trade sector — retail and wholesale trade — is the second largest in San Antonio, employing 147,200. Trade added 5,700 jobs, growing 4.0 percent. Several new stores, including Target and a K-Mart Superstore, opened in the metro area during the year.

Government is the third-largest employment sector in San Antonio, accounting for 127,500 jobs. Government grew a sluggish 0.3 percent during the year, adding 400 jobs.

Although San Antonio has a large military presence, national downsizing in the Department of Defense is affecting employment. Growth in government is centered in local government, primarily in public safety and at area schools. ☆

Non-Agricultural Employment

Employment in Texas increased to 7,820,800 in Jan. 1995 up from 7,498,900 in Jan. 1994.

The following table shows the Texas Employmnent Commission estimates of the nonagricultural labor force in Texas for Jan. 1994 and 1995, together with the change in the number employed.

(in thousands)

Industry	(Jan.) 1995	1994	%Chng.
MANUFACTURING	1015.8	988.6	27.2
Durable Goods	575.8	558.7	17.1
Lumber & Wood Products	40.0	36.6	3.4
Logging Camps, Sawmills, Planing Mills	8.1	7.7	0.4
Furniture & Fixtures	17.7	17.4	0.3
Stone, Clay & Glass Products	39.2	37.2	2.0
Concrete, Gypsum & Plaster - Prod.	17.8	16.5	1.3
Primary Metal Industries	30.8	29.3	1.5
Fabricated Metal Industries	91.2	84.8	6.4
Fabr. Structural Metal Prod.	45.7	41.6	4.1
Industrial Machinery & Equipment	120.1	115.5	4.6
Oil & Gas Field Machinery	23.2	23.8	-0.6
Electronic & Other Electrical Equipment	109.2	13.1	6.1
Transportation Equipment	70.4	76.6	-6.2
Aircraft & Parts	42.5	48.9	-6.4

Industry	1995	1994	Chng.
Instruments & Related Products	38.0	40.1	-2.1
Misc. Manufacturing Industries	19.2	18.1	1.1
Non-Durable Goods	440.0	429.9	10.1
Food & Kindred Products	96.0	93.2	2.8
Meat Products	30.9	29.6	1.3
Dairy Products	5.4	5.1	0.3
Bakery Products	11.0	10.2	0.8
Malt Beverages	2.6	2.7	-0.1
Textile Mill Products	3.6	3.7	-0.1
Apparel & Other Finished Textile Prod.	64.7	64.0	0.7
Paper & Allied Products	28.9	27.8	1.1
Printing & Publishing	75.2	72.9	2.3
Newspapers, periodicals, Books, Misc.	34.5	34.3	0.2
Chemicals & Allied Products	83.9	84.4	-0.5
Petroleum & Coal Products	29.5	29.2	0.3
Petroleum Refining	26.3	26.1	0.2
Rubber & Misc. Plastic Prod.	49.2	46.0	3.2
Leather & Leather Products	8.9	8.5	0.4
TOTAL NON-MANUFACTURING			
Mining	158.5	165.1	-6.6
Oil & Gas Extraction	150.4	157.0	-6.6
Construction	393.0	355.0	38.0
Transportation & Public Utilities	466.1	445.4	20.7
Railroad Transportation	19.3	17.9	1.4
Transportation by Air	81.9	79.9	2.0
Communications	95.6	91.8	3.8

Industry	(Jan.) 1995	1994	Chng.
Electric, Gas & Sanitary Services	74.6	75.1	-0.5
Electric Services	33.9	34.8	-0.9
Gas Production & Distribution	26.5	26.6	-0.1
Wholesale & Retail Trade	1,889.4	1,817.9	71.5
Wholesale Trade	452.8	438.1	14.7
Retail Trade	1,436.6	1,379.8	56.8
Building Materials & Garden Supplies	46.7	44.0	2.7
General Mercha. Stores	203.0	189.8	13.2
Food Stores	248.8	245.9	2.9
Automotive Dealers & Service Stations	147.9	140.9	7.0
Apparel & Accessory Stores	83.7	83.3	0.4
Eating & Dining Places	492.1	470.2	21.9
Other Retail Trade	214.4	205.7	8.7
Finance, Insurance & Real Estate	445.3	432.5	12.8
Depository Insts., incl. Banks	115.7	112.9	2.8
Insurance Carriers, Agents & Brokers	150.5	145.1	5.4
Other Finance, Insurance & Real Estate	179.1	174.5	4.6
Services	2,014.5	1,903.0	111.5
Hotels & Other Lodging Places	77.1	78.4	-1.3
Personal Services	88.6	85.2	3.4
Business Services	459.4	410.8	48.6
Auto Repair Services	68.3	65.6	2.7
Misc. Repair Services	24.3	24.2	0.1
Amusement, including Motion Pictures	90.9	83.0	7.9
Health Services	584.3	554.1	30.2
Educational Services	88.8	88.1	0.7
Engineering & Mgmt Services	172.4	167.5	4.9
Other Services & Misc.	240.7	227.2	13.5
Total Government	1,438.2	1,391.4	46.8
Federal Government	190.7	192.2	-1.5
State Government	314.5	301.0	13.5
Local Government	933.0	898.2	34.8

Average Hours and Earnings

The following table shows the average weekly hours and earnings for selected industries for 1994. Figures are provided by the Texas Employment Commission in cooperation with the U. S. Bureau of Labor Statistics.

Industry	Earnings	Hours	Wage
MANUFACTURING	$480.13	43.1	$11.14
Durable Goods	471.75	43.6	10.82
Lumber & Wood Products	349.24	43.6	8.01
Logging Camps, Saw Mills, Planing Mills	386.91	42.8	9.04
Furniture & Fixtures	334.90	42.5	7.88
Household, Office & Public Bldg	320.85	41.4	7.75
Concrete, Gypsum & Plaster	430.91	44.7	9.64
Primary Metals Industries	421.44	48.0	8.78
Blast Furnace & Basic Steel	697.66	44.1	15.82
Iron & Steel Foundries	482.08	46.0	10.48
Primary Non-Ferrous Mtls.	706.13	42.9	16.46
Fabricated Metal Products	464.14	44.5	10.43
Fabricated Structural Metal	421.60	44.1	9.56
Ordnance & Accessories	628.66	43.0	14.62
Misc. Fab. Metal Products	479.17	43.8	10.94
Industrial Machinery and Equipment	475.52	44.4	10.71
Oil & Gas Field Machinery	559.67	46.6	12.01
Special Industry Machinery	523.53	44.9	11.66
Refrigeration & Service Mach.	463.05	44.1	10.50
Electronic & Other Electrical Equipment	473.61	42.4	11.17
Communications Equipment	451.97	43.5	10.39
Transportation Equipment	667.25	43.3	15.41
Motor Vehicles & Equipment	631.23	44.8	14.09
Aircraft & Parts	765.29	41.3	18.53
Instruments & Related Prodcts	452.35	41.5	10.90
Misc. Manufacturing	309.10	40.3	7.67
Non-Durable Goods	489.30	42.4	11.54
Food & Kindred Products	386.40	42.0	9.20
Meat Products	334.20	44.5	7.51
Dairy Products	434.50	43.8	9.92
Preserved Fruits, Veg.	376.58	38.0	9.91
Grain Mill Products	440.34	42.3	10.41
Bakery Products	488.31	41.0	11.91
Malt Beverages	891.11	43.3	20.58
Textile Mill Products	396.06	42.0	9.43
Apparel & Textile Prod.	258.23	38.6	6.69
Men's & Boy's Suits, Coats	264.50	38.5	6.87
Women's & Miss (Clothing)	265.69	38.9	6.83
Paper & Allied Products	567.16	44.0	12.89
Paperboard Containers & Boxes	458.76	43.9	10.45
Printing & Publishing	466.46	41.5	11.24
Newspapers, Periodicals & Books	413.01	39.0	10.59
Chemicals & Allied Products	780.53	44.5	17.54
Industrial Inorg. & Org.	865.49	45.6	18.98
Petroleum & Coal Products	877.89	46.4	18.92
Petroleum Refining	919.71	46.9	19.61
Rubber & Misc. Plastics	430.15	44.3	9.71
Leather & Leather Products	270.36	39.7	6.81
NON-MANUFACTURING			
Mining	642.78	42.4	15.16
Metal & Bit Coal & Non-Metallic Minerals	643.84	48.3	13.33
Oil & Gas Extraction	646.50	42.2	15.32
Crude Petroleum, Nat. Gas.	817.44	39.3	20.80
Oil & Gas Field Services	520.97	44.3	11.76
Commun. & Public Util.	602.94	41.1	14.67
Communications	608.59	40.9	14.88
Telephone Communications	670.25	42.8	15.66
Radio & TV Broadcast	463.47	34.9	13.28
Electric, Gas & Sanitary Ser.	593.48	41.3	14.37
Trade	263.38	32.8	8.03
Wholesale Trade	459.20	40.0	11.48
Wholesale Trade, Durable Goods	493.28	40.7	12.12
Motor Vehicle Parts	418.26	39.2	10.67
Lumber & Other Construction	401.58	41.4	9.70
Professional & Commercial	659.75	40.5	16.29
Metals & Minerals	472.14	43.0	10.98
Electrical Goods	483.89	40.8	11.86
Hardware, Plumbing & Heating	407.84	40.3	10.12
Machinery, Equipment	500.58	41.2	12.15
Wholesale Trade, Non-Dur.	406.89	38.9	10.46
Paper & Paper Products	394.57	37.4	10.55
Drugs, Proprietaries	553.44	38.3	14.45
Groceries & Related Products	431.72	39.9	10.82
Farm-Product Raw Material	227.55	31.3	7.27
Chemicals & Allied Products	589.11	41.9	14.06
Petroleum & Petroleum Prod.	357.79	41.7	8.58
Beer, Wine & Distilled Bev.	412.54	38.7	10.66
Misc. Non-Durable Goods	321.00	37.5	8.56
Retail Trade	208.21	30.8	6.76
Building Materials & Garden Supplies	288.35	37.4	7.71
Lumber & Other Build. Mat.	308.89	39.1	7.90
General Merchandise Stores	212.21	31.3	6.78
Department Stores	217.09	31.6	6.87
Food Stores	231.74	33.2	6.98
Grocery Stores	234.02	33.1	7.07
Automotive Dealers & Serv.	341.07	36.4	9.37
New & Used Car Dealers	402.14	35.4	11.36
Apparel & Accessory Stores	176.47	28.1	6.28
Furniture & Home Furnishings Equip	339.31	31.8	10.67
Furniture & HomeFurnishing	334.80	32.6	10.27
Eating & Drinking	131.00	26.9	4.87
Misc. Retail	242.63	32.7	7.42
Depository Instns.	318.82	36.8	8.65
Commercial Banks	300.49	36.6	8.21
Natl Comm. Banks	304.34	36.8	8.27

Construction Industry

Contract awards for construction in 1994 totaled $4,369,199,988. Although the number of contracts stayed strong, dollar value was considerably lower than the record volume of 1993: $5,394,342,718, as shown in the Analysis of Awards tables below. Another table shows the approved Texas construction for 1995. These data were compiled by editors of **Texas Contractor** from official sources.

Comparison of Construction Awards by Years, 1956-1994

Source: Texas Contractor

Year	Total Awards
1994	$4,396,199,988
1993	5,394,342,718
1992	4,747,666,912
1991	3,926,799,801
1990	3,922,781,630
1989	4,176,355,929
1988	3,562,336,666
1987	4,607,051,270
1986	4,636,310,266
1985	4,806,998,065
1984	3,424,721,025
1983	4,074,910,947
1982	3,453,784,388
1981	3,700,112,809
1980	3,543,117,615
1979	3,353,243,234
1978	2,684,743,190
1977	2,270,788,842
1976	1,966,553,804
1975	1,737,036,682
1974	2,396,488,520
1973	1,926,778,365
1972	1,650,897,233
1971	1,751,331,262
1970	1,458,708,492
1969	1,477,125,397
1968	1,363,629,304
1967	1,316,872,998
1966	1,421,312,029
1965	1,254,638,051
1964	1,351,656,302
1963	1,154,624,634
1962	1,132,607,006
1961	988,848,239
1960	1,047,943,630
1959	1,122,290,957
1958	1,142,138,674
1957	1,164,240,546
1956	1,220,831,984

Approved Texas Construction, 1995

The following is a recapitulation of all approved Texas construction for 1995. The data were compiled by the editors of **Texas Contractor** from official sources.

Federal:	
General Services Administration	$32,000,000
Federal Aviation Administration	95,000,000
Veterans Administration	40,000,000
NASA	30,230,000
Department of Defense	161,899,000
Rural Electrification Administration	90,000,000
U.S. Department of Agriculture	150,000,000
Soil Conservation Service	5,300,000
Federal Highway Administration	1,256,061,831
U S. Department of Energy	15,000,000
Total Federal	**$1,676,500,831**
State:	
Texas Dept. of Transportation	$1,818,948,633
State Agencies	349,567,753
State Colleges and Universities	213,796,690
Total State	**$2,382,313,076**
Water Projects:	
Corps of Engineers	$98,521,000
River Authorities	250,000,000
Total Water Projects	**$348,521,000**
Cities:	
Schools, Colleges	$178,808,000
Streets, Bridges	339,448,456
Waterworks, Sewers	735,433,252
Apartments, Residences	1,436,356,725
Commercial	1,429,809,000
City Buildings	252,498,000
Total Cities	**$4,372,353,433**
Counties:	
New Roads-County Funds	$14,890,000
Road Maintenance	167,587,384
Machinery Purchases	81,683,846
County Buildings	66,502,368
Miscellaneous	5,850,000
Total Counties	**$336,483,598**
Grand Total 1995 Approved Construction	**$9,116,171,938**

Analysis of Awards

The following table analyzes and classifies awards in Texas for the year 1994, as compared with 1993, as reported by **Texas Contractor**.

Category	1994		1993	
	No.	Amount	No.	Amount
Engineering Awards	1,717	$2,141,519,093	1,697	$2,788,612,080
Non-Residential Awards	1,072	2,254,680,895	1,107	2,605,730,638
Total	**2,789**	**$4,396,199,988**	**2,804**	**$5,394,342,718**

ENGINEERING AWARDS

Type of Project	1994		1993	
	No.	Amount	No.	Amount
Highways, Streets, Airports	1,221	$1,673,277,464	1,111	$2,045,651,102
Waterworks, Sewers, etc.	426	418,209,205	428	472,031,351
Irrigation, Drainage, etc.	58	48,074,586	84	117,263,271
Misc.	12	1,957,838	74	153,666,356
Total	**1,717**	**$2,141,519,093**	**1,697**	**$2,788,612,080**

NON-RESIDENTIAL CONSTRUCTION AWARDS

Type of Project	1994		1993	
	No.	Amount	No.	Amount
Educational Bldgs	285	$635,958,369	300	$897,414,057
Churches, Theaters, etc.	23	38,593,077	34	17,761,555
Hospitals, Hotels, Motels	66	270,179,135	85	343,914,462
Public Bldgs	396	1,084,865,896	337	1,119,689,055
Commercial/ Industrial	300	224,887,273	349	226,738,740
Misc.	2	197,145	2	212,769
Total	**1,072**	**$2,254,680,895**	**1,107**	**$2,605,730,638**

Savings Institutions

The state savings bank charter was approved by the Legislature in 1993 and the first state savings bank in Texas was chartered in January 1994. Savings banks have existed for many years primarily in the Northeast and, in fact, is one of the oldest types of financial-institution charters in the country. Savings banks operate similarly to savings and loans associations in that they are housing-oriented lenders.

Under federal law a state savings bank is categorized as a commercial bank and not a thrift. Therefore savings-bank information is also reported with state and national-bank information.

Texas Savings Banks

Year	No. Assn./Banks	Thousands of Dollars						
		Total Assets	*Mortgage Loans	†Cash	†Investment Securities	Savings Capital	FHLB Advances and other Borrowed Money	‡Net Worth
Dec. 31, 1994	8	$6,347,505	$2,825,012	$3,139,573		$3,227,886	$2,628,847	$352,363

Texas Savings and Loan Associations

Year	No. Assn./Banks	Total Assets	*Mortgage Loans	†Cash	†Investment Securities	Savings Capital	FHLB Advances and other Borrowed Money	‡Net Worth
Dec. 31, 1994	50	$50,014,102	$24,148,760	$6,790,416	...	$29,394,433	$15,973,056	$3,447,110
Dec. 31, 1993	62	$42,983,595	$14,784,215	$10,769,889	...	$25,503,656	$13,356,018	$2,968,840
Dec. 31, 1992	64	$47,565,516	$14,137,191	$14,527,573	...	$33,299,278	$10,490,144	$2,917,881
Dec. 31, 1991	80	53,500,091	15,417,895	11,422,071	...	41,985,117	8,189,800	2,257,329
Dec. 31, 1990§	131	72,041,456	27,475,664	20,569,770	...	56,994,387	17,738,041	-$4,566,656
Conservatorship	51	14,952,402	6,397,466	2,188,820	...	16,581,525	4,304,033	-6,637,882
Privately Owned	80	57,089,054	21,078,198	18,380,950	...	40,412,862	13,434,008	2,071,226
Dec. 31, 1989§	196	90,606,100	37,793,043	21,218,130	...	70,823,464	27,158,238	-9,356,209
Conservatorship	81	22,159,752	11,793,445	2,605,080	...	25,381,494	7,103,657	-10,866,213
Privately Owned	115	68,446,348	25,999,598	18,613,050	...	45,441,970	20,054,581	1,510,004
Dec. 31, 1988	204	110,499,276	50,920,006	26,181,917	...	83,950,314	28,381,573	-4,088,355
Dec. 31, 1987	279	99,613,666	56,884,564	12,559,154	...	85,324,796	19,235,506	-6,677,338
Dec. 31, 1986	281	96,919,775	61,489,463	9,989,918	...	80,429,758	14,528,311	109,807
Dec. 31, 1985	273	91,798,890	60,866,666	10,426,464	...	72,806,067	13,194,147	3,903,611
Dec. 31, 1984	273	77,544,202	45,859,408	10,424,113	...	61,943,815	10,984,467	2,938,044
Dec. 31, 1983	273	56,684,508	36,243,290	6,678,808	...	46,224,429	6,317,947	2,386,551
Dec. 31, 1982	288	42,505,924	28,539,378	4,713,742	...	34,526,483	5,168,343	1,631,139
Dec. 31, 1981	311	38,343,703	30,013,805	3,294,327	...	30,075,258	4,846,153	1,493,795
Dec. 31, 1980	318	34,954,129	27,717,383	3,066,791	...	28,439,210	3,187,638	1,711,201
Dec. 31, 1979	310	31,280,006	25,238,483	2,512,797	...	25,197,598	2,969,838	1,640,049
Dec. 31, 1978	318	27,933,526	22,830,872	142,721	$1,876,882	22,848,519	2,251,631	1,444,607
Dec. 31, 1977	328	24,186,338	19,765,901	154,027	1,579,440	19,994,347	1,515,045	1,235,096
Dec. 31, 1976	316	19,921,694	16,096,166	196,790	1,344,827	16,908,949	949,231	1,044,611
Dec. 31, 1975	303	16,540,181	13,367,569	167,385	1,000,095	13,876,780	919,404	914,502
Dec. 31, 1974	295	13,944,524	11,452,013	117,097	806,302	11,510,259	1,038,386	834,892
Dec. 31, 1973	288	12,629,928	10,361,847	126,106	795,989	10,483,113	740,725	763,618
Dec. 31, 1972	278	10,914,627	8,919,007	155,901	841,904	9,249,305	459,019	678,086
Dec. 31, 1971	272	9,112,590	7,481,751	140,552	670,622	7,647,906	458,152	589,077
Dec. 31, 1970	271	7,706,639	6,450,730	122,420	509,482	6,335,582	559,953	531,733
Dec. 31, 1969	270	7,055,949	5,998,172	105,604	391,175	5,894,398	473,066	487,308
Dec. 31, 1968	267	6,601,846	5,556,617	131,440	415,958	5,712,331	287,588	429,087
Dec. 31, 1967	268	6,156,108	5,149,689	194,684	359,443	5,402,575	218,569	390,508
Dec. 31, 1966	268	5,693,908	4,816,505	190,820	280,927	4,898,223	331,694	361,697
Dec. 31, 1965	267	5,351,064	4,534,073	228,994	230,628	4,631,999	286,497	333,948
Dec. 31, 1964	262	4,797,085	4,071,044	208,083	218,993	4,145,085	266,242	296,444
Dec. 31, 1963	256	4,192,188	3,517,676	208,698	201,724	3,591,951	257,426	259,169
Dec. 31, 1962	248	3,533,209	2,960,182	173,343	180,192	3,049,144	185,476	230,920
Dec. 31, 1961	240	2,990,527	2,472,648	146,710	183,116	2,647,906	74,762	193,579
Dec. 31, 1960	233	2,508,872	2,083,066	110,028	157,154	2,238,080	48,834	166,927

* Beginning in 1982, net of loans in process.

† Beginning in 1979, cash and investment securities data combined.

‡ Net worth includes permanent stock and paid-in surplus general reserves, surplus and undivided profits.

§ In 1989 and 1990, the Office of Thrift Supervision, U.S. Department of the Treasury, separated data on savings and loans (thrifts) into two categories: those under the supervision of the Office of Thrift Supervision (Conservatorship Thrifts) and those still under private management (Privately Owned).

*Details in the table above were supplied by the Dallas District of the Office of Thrift Supervision of the U.S. Department of the Treasury and **the Texas Savings and Loan Department**.*

Leading Commercial Banks Ranked by Deposits

Source: Federal Reserve Bank of Dallas, Dec. 31, 1994

Abbreviations used in this table: Bk-Bank; St-State; NB-National Bank; B&TC-Bank and Trust Company

Rank	Name and Location of Bank	Total Deposits
1.	Nationsbank Tx NA, Dallas	$22,541,022
2.	Texas Commerce Bk NA, Houston	15,796,537
3.	Bank One Texas NA, Dallas	14,658,360
4.	Bank America Tx NA, Irving	7,513,224
5.	First Interstate Bk Tx NA, Houston	5,383,252
6.	Frost NB, San Antonio	3,012,533
7.	Comerica Bk-Tx, Dallas	2,622,980
8.	Compass Bk-Houston, Houston	1,810,291
9.	International Bk of Cmrc, Laredo	1,703,337
10.	Victoria B&TC, Victoria	1,463,645
11.	Laredo NB, Laredo	1,328,381
12.	State NB, El Paso	952,270
13.	Compass Bk, Dallas	945,932
14.	Norwest Bk Tx, Lubbock	895,892
15.	Prime Bk, Channelview	813,940
16.	Boatmens First NB, Amarillo	738,751
17.	Central B&TC, Fort Worth	726,440
18.	Amarillo NB, Amarillo	711,175
19.	Mercantile Bk NA, Brownsville	679,424
20.	Broadway NB, San Antonio	626,286
21.	American St Bk, Lubbock	534,928
22.	Plains NB, Lubbock	499,521
23.	Southwest Bk Tx NA, Houston	489,836
24.	Texas St Bk, McAllen	481,506
25.	Sunwest Bk, El Paso	449,270
26.	First NB, Abilene	441,739
27.	Overton B&T NA, Fort Worth	418,058
28.	Southside St Bk, Tyler	385,376
29.	First St Bk Tx, Denton	380,270
30.	Charter NB-Houston, Houston	355,997
31.	Bank of N. Tx NA, Hurst	347,915
32.	First St B&TC, Mission	345,692
33.	American NB, Terrell	341,351
34.	First American Bk, Bryan	335,038
35.	First Victoria NB, Victoria	334,728
36.	Sterling Bk, Houston	327,219
37.	First St Bk, Austin	318,851
38.	North Dallas B&TC, Dallas	316,787
39.	American Bk of Tx, Sherman	298,179
40.	Texarkana NB, Texarkana	292,967
41.	Citizens NB, Henderson	285,927
42.	Post Oak Bk, Houston	263,692
43.	Community Bk, Beaumont	251,089
44.	Texas Bk, Weatherford	249,901
45.	Midland NB, Midland	248,511
46.	First B&TC, Groves	244,735
47.	Parker Square Bk NA, Wichita Falls	244,135
48,	Plano B&TC, Plano	244,002
49.	BankTexas NA, Houston	242,145
50.	Union NB Tx, Laredo	241,105
51.	Norwest Bk Tx Waco NA, Waco	233,855
52.	Jefferson St Bk, San Antonio	232,541
53.	Citizens B&TC, Baytown	229,226
54.	First NB, Temple	227,567
55.	Merchants Bk, Houston	227,120
56.	Groos Bk Na, San Antonio	225,839
57.	Longview B&TC, Longview	224,879
58.	Sulphur Springs St Bk, Sulphur Springs	216,747
59.	Fredonia St Bk, Nacogdoches	215,175
60.	Tyler B&TC, Tyler	210,488
61.	Firstbank, Los Fresnos	208,684
62.	First Bk, Katy	206,834
63.	First Prosperity Bk, El Campo	206,768
64.	Riverway Bk, Houston	205,981
65.	Tanglewood Bk NA, Houston	203,781
66.	First NB, Grapevine	199,384
67.	Moody NB, Galveston	197,761
68.	Metrobank NA, Houston	197,135
69.	Park NB, Houston	195,997
70.	First St Bk, Uvalde	195,422
71.	Charter NB-Colonial, Houston	193,800
72.	Citizens Bk, Kilgore	193,395
73.	International Bk of Commerce, Brownsville	191,431
74.	Klein Bk, Harris County	190,767
75.	First NB of Park Cities, Dallas	190,343
76.	Security St B&TC Fredericksburg	190,150
77.	First NB, Marshall	189,190
78.	First NB, Kerrville	186,933
79.	Citizens NB of Tx, Houston	185,989
80.	First NB South Tx, San Antonio	185,700
81.	First St Bk, Athens	185,223
82.	Kelly Field NB, San Antonio	183,508
83.	First St Bk, Rio Vista	182,967
84.	University St Bk, Houston	182,351
85.	Harrisburg Bk Houston Tx, Houston	181,732
86.	Bank of the West, El Paso	181,555
87.	Heritage Bank, Wharton	181,248
88.	First NB, Big Spring	180,020
89.	Texas Comm. Bk-San Angelo, San Angelo	178,453
90.	Queststar Bk NA, Houston	178,065
91.	First Bk of Tx, Tomball	175,707
92.	American NB, Corpus Christi	175,360
93.	First NB, Athens	174,628
94.	First NB, Killeen	173,034
95.	Central NB, Waco	172,888
96.	Texas NB, Waco	171,159
97.	Texas Capital Bk NA Houston	164,319
98.	First NB, Edinburg	164,197
99.	Citizens 1st Bk, Rusk	161,559
100.	First NB, Bryan	160,288
101.	Harlingen NB, Harlingen	160,172
102.	Provident Bk, Dallas	159,121
103.	Citizen St Bk Corpus Christi, Corpus Chr	157,647
104.	Lamesa NB, Lamesa	157,188
105.	Texas NB, Midland	156,711
106.	Guaranty Bk, Mount Pleasant	156,163
107.	National Bk, Gatesville	155,919
108.	First NB, Bowie	153,608
109.	American Bk of Commerce, Wolfforth	151,116
110.	Bayshore NB, La Porte	150,449
111.	Northern TR Bk Tx NA, Dallas	149,511
112.	First United Bk, Dimmitt	147,564
113.	Texas Gulf Bk NA, Freeport	144,563
114.	Liberty NB, Paris	143,907
115.	Hale County St Bk, Plainview	142,972
116.	Equitable Bk, Dallas	142,682
117.	Longview NB, Longview	142,126
118.	Lubbock NB, Lubbock	142,108
119.	Kleberg First NB, Kingsville	141,955
120.	Alice Bk Tx, Alice	141,594
121.	American Bk, Houston	138,915
122.	Firstbank, Texarkana	137,794
123.	First B&TC East Tx, Diboll	137,481
124.	First NB in Pampa, Pampa	137,318
125.	Security St Bk, Abilene	136,021
126.	1st Bk, Coppell	133,730
127.	American NB, Wichita Falls	132,961
128.	Liberty NB, Austin	132,921
129.	Security NB, San Antonio	132,785
130.	NBC Bk-Eagle Pass NA, Eagle Pass	132,672
131.	Kilgore First NB, Kilgore	132,220
132.	First NB, Jasper	132,196
133.	Bank of the West, San Angelo	132,006
134.	South Tx NB, Laredo	131,747
135.	Bank of Houston, Houston	131,532
136.	First NB Albany/Breckenridge, Albany	130,266
137.	San Benito B&TC, San Benito	129,528
138.	Seguin St B&TC, Seguin	129,283
139.	Norwest Bk Tx Plainview NA, Plainview	127,775
140.	Bank of San Antonio, San Antonio	126,844
141.	United States NB of Galveston, Galveston	126,696
142.	First St Bk, Livingston	125,632
143.	Southwest Bk, Fort Worth	125,240
144.	National Commerce Bk, Houston	124,902
145.	First St B&TC, Carthage	124,194
146.	First NB, Gilmer	123,813
147.	Community Bk, Waco	122,784
148.	Silsbee St Bk, Silsbee	122,748
149.	First NB, Granbury	122,708
150.	Inwood NB, Dallas	122,020

Total Domestic Deposits and Assets of All Insured Commercial Banks in Texas by County

Source: Federal Reserve Bank of Dallas as of Dec. 31, 1994

(in thousands of Dollars)

County	No. of Banks	Total Deposits	Total Assets
Anderson	5	$326,717	$372,146
Andrews	3	89,442	98,558
Angelina	4	408,440	456,104
Archer	2	48,256	48,628
Armstrong	1	17,453	19,042
Atascosa	4	153,852	173,929
Austin	5	300,179	338,370
Bailey	2	100,685	111,871
Bandera	2	65,964	75,935
Bastrop	4	215,984	242,233
Baylor	2	54,832	61,189
Bee	3	178,073	200,982
Bell	10	812,574	903,357
Bexar	17	5,203,822	6,129,079
Blanco	3	95,656	105,317
Bosque	3	96,539	107,436
Bowie	5	695,668	798,466
Brazoria	10	633,845	715,409
Brazos	3	545,590	603,357
Brewster	1	62018	67,838
Briscoe	2	43,039	49,580
Brooks	2	54,939	66,413
Brown	2	166,066	181,333
Burleson	4	189,087	208,285
Burnet	3	141,597	158,700
Caldwell	3	133,912	149,578
Calhoun	2	97,425	111,487
Callahan	3	135,298	148,928
Cameron	10	1,584,508	1,770,208
Camp	2	176,413	199,857
Carson	3	107,3437	117,207
Cass	5	221,878	244,762
Castro	1	147,564	160,525
Chambers	4	121,896	145,343
Cherokee	4	328,039	392,398
Childress	1	38,690	41,566
Clay	2	79,194	89,584
Cochran	1	44,142	48,444
Coke	2	45,484	51,174
Coleman	3	101,135	114,530
Collin	8	508,219	552,321
Collingsworth	2	75,604	83,212
Colorado	4	239,663	290,339
Comal	2	51,133	56,409
Comanche	3	141,284	157,959
Concho	2	31,289	35,141
Cooke	4	282,865	317,668
Coryell	5	294,059	328,753
Cottle	1	30,484	38,244
Crane	1	19,586	21,115
Crockett	2	123,917	139,487
Crosby	3	72,810	80,433
Culberson	1	13,983	17,020
Dallam	3	155,403	178,956
Dallas	58	51,889,262	74,679,419
Dawson	2	257,435	281,715
Deaf Smith	2	152,794	171,862
Delta	3	44,914	50,654
Denton	10	674,500	741,687
DeWitt	2	140,810	158,709
Dickens	1	21,231	23,559
Dimmit	1	19,065	20,983
Donley	2	59,220	65,539
Duval	2	64,316	70,043
Eastland	3	96,145	110,477
Ector	4	296,128	355,156
Edwards	1	26,347	34,128
Ellis	10	443,005	489,681
El Paso	7	1,901,457	2,175,392
Erath	4	168,006	185,063
Falls	1	15,200	16,399
Fannin	5	156,985	172,287
Fayette	7	266,714	300,558
Fisher	2	74,474	86,575
Floyd	2	126,586	139,943
Foard	1	19,031	21,036
Fort Bend	4	211,729	242,120
Franklin	2	71,490	84,689
Freestone	2	63,636	69,573
Frio	2	146,486	185,775
Gaines	2	104,427	1112,227
Galveston	13	1,062,498	1,187,647
Garza	1	40,829	46,072
Gillespie	2	224,584	248,031
Goliad	1	28,594	31,405
Gonzales	3	78,489	86,657
Gray	4	233,012	276,179
Grayson	7	507,419	545,537
Gregg	10	988,155	1,095,295
Grimes	5	150,741	165,269
Guadalupe	4	274,018	819,250
Hale	5	340,474	364,290
Hall	2	58,141	63,488
Hamilton	2	44,187	47,659
Hansford	3	119,431	141,992
Hardeman	3	76,762	83,512
Hardin	3	178,327	193,700
Harris	77	31,542,707	37,417,947
Harrison	5	314,010	352,426
Haskell	4	99,709	111,606
Hays	1	106,777	114,794
Hemphill	2	87,711	99,424
Henderson	5	484,075	536,895
Hidalgo	15	1,685,539	1,885,963
Hill	5	195,623	222,556
Hockley	3	78,723	85,146
Hood	4	290,218	319,425
Hopkins	4	393,281	434,002
Houston	6	194,044	213,980
Howard	4	345,278	399,526
Hudspeth	1	11,025	11,881
Hunt	5	169,029	186,053
Hutchinson	3	94,459	102,671
Irion	1	73,029	82,302
Jack	3	110,956	121,899
Jackson	1	31,995	34,517
Jasper	2	220,359	241,644
Jeff Davis	1	13,240	14,688
Jefferson	4	664,080	732,277
Jim Hogg	2	79,747	92,078
Jim Wells	4	227,990	266,149
Johnson	9	553,829	612,680
Jones	2	100,873	118,779
Karnes	3	115,112	127,016

County	No. of Banks	Total Deposits	Total Assets
Kaufman	5	489,445	533,538
Kendall	1	38,415	42,598
Kent	1	8,618	9,482
Kerr	1	186,933	204,018
Kimble	2	41,594	47,856
Kinney	1	11,983	12,963
Kleberg	2	171,349	194,421
Knox	2	58,271	66,151
Lamar	5	346,035	414,957
Lamb	4	91,533	101,704
Lampasas	2	99,389	110,305
La Salle	1	21,455	24,107
Lavaca	3	175,532	197,681
Lee	3	107,046	120,202
Leon	4	96,729	110,013
Liberty	6	284,915	319,090
Limestone	5	137,969	153,476
Lipscomb	1	24,753	28,421
Live Oak	2	91,206	106,936
Llano	4	179,935	203,624
Lubbock	11	2,515,995	3,129,610
Lynn	3	106,035	122,296
McCulloch	2	84,948	97,801
McLennan	15	1,121,740	1,264,710
McMullen	1	21,425	24,265
Madison	2	118,609	132,258
Marion	2	46,622	53,281
Martin	2	50,775	60,061
Mason	2	48,999	53,906
Matagorda	2	154,519	187,626
Maverick	2	251,207	274,353
Medina	7	188,418	207,973
Menard	2	27,812	34,309
Midland	4	563,177	627,859
Milam	5	295,415	342,175
Mills	2	111,004	121,420
Mitchell	2	78,406	88,467
Montague	3	178,537	199,452
Montgomery	3	251,161	274,719
Moore	1	50,847	55,875
Morris	3	102,284	110,250
Motley	1	9,156	10,090
Nacogdoches	4	463,884	512,096
Navarro	6	203,719	227,469
Newton	1	67,214	73,793
Nolan	2	115,295	128,245
Nueces	9	742,028	859,531
Ochiltree	2	146,679	170,555
Orange	4	171,489	187,192
Palo Pinto	4	143,341	158,155
Panola	3	189,346	257,823
Parker	4	444,637	520,964
Parmer	2	127,877	149,246
Pecos	3	127,231	140,167
Polk	4	314,146	349,332
Potter	4	1,584,199	2,059,397
Presidio	2	44,540	50,443
Rains	1	42,627	46,408
Randall	1	60,451	67,517
Reagan	1	20,788	23,143
Real	1	18,885	20,818
Red River	1	14,288	15,806
Reeves	2	104,142	118,824
Refugio	2	73,467	89,171
Roberts	1	11,686	12,857
Robertson	3	147,803	168,203
Rockwall	3	91,113	99,611
Runnels	5	79,130	86,710

County	No. of Banks	Total Deposits	Total Assets
Rusk	4	417,102	461,189
Sabine	2	94,930	105,958
San Augustine	1	47,796	52,621
San Jacinto	2	37,247	40,437
San Patricio	3	108,938	125,166
San Saba	1	32,873	38,335
Schleicher	1	29,484	34,340
Scurry	2	169,101	190,182
Shackelford	1	130,266	148,949
Shelby	4	157,181	174,773
Sherman	1	50,071	59,112
Smith	8	845,154	946,156
Somervell	1	22,296	25,021
Starr	1	58,917	66,7815
Stephens	1	56,432	63,478
Sterling	1	28,077	33,829
Stonewall	1	24,695	32,593
Sutton	2	58,548	65,453
Swisher	3	110,343	123,407
Tarrant	31	3,101,657	3,557,174
Taylor	5	739,235	817,475
Terrell	1	16,258	17,690
Terry	1	98,960	111,938
Throckmorton	2	43,449	47,447
Titus	3	193,840	212,343
Tom Green	5	555,800	617,931
Travis	8	896,278	1,000,976
Trinity	3	68,421	75,809
Tyler	2	88,437	95,565
Upshur	4	263,500	306,963
Upton	2	73,898	79,819
Uvalde	2	215,933	255,934
Val Verde	2	190,496	208,571
Van Zandt	7	189,076	206,864
Victoria	3	1,854,027	2,198,602
Walker	3	176,273	191,853
Waller	2	60,749	67,297
Ward	2	97,796	113,150
Washington	4	180,065	196,436
Webb	7	3,589,144	4,353,549
Wharton	7	687,487	760,447
Wheeler	3	56,443	62,217
Wichita	7	627,012	696,277
Wilbarger	3	206,342	243,211
Willacy	2	140,482	154,884
Williamson	12	440,498	496,103
Wilson	3	181,437	198,743
Winkler	2	57,668	69,174
Wise	4	291,659	317,572
Wood	6	255,758	291,414
Yoakum	3	73,643	81,783
Young	4	199,788	232,410
Zapata	2	107,648	125,709
Zavala	1	32,978	35,676
Statewide Total	**980**	**149,425,485**	**187,614,698**

No banks were reported in eight counties: Aransas, Borden, Glasscock, Hartley, Kenedy, King, Loving and Oldham.

Texas Bank Resources and Deposits—1905-1994

On Dec. 31, 1994, Texas had a total of 983 national and state banks with total deposits of $153,403,984,000 and total resources of $188,144,234,000.

Source: **Federal Reserve Bank of Dallas.**

Date	National Banks			State Banks			Combined Total		
	No. Banks	Total Resources (add 000)	Deposits (add 000)	No. Banks	Total Resources (add 000)	Deposits (add 000)	No. Banks	Total Resources (add 000)	Deposits (add 000)
Sept. 30, 1905	440	$189,484	$101,285	29	$4,341	$2,213	469	$193,825	$103,498
Oct. 31, 1906	483	221,574	116,331	136	19,322	13,585	619	240,896	129,916
Dec. 3, 1907	521	261,724	141,803	309	34,734	20,478	830	296,458	162,281
Nov. 27, 1908	535	243,240	115,843	340	40,981	27,014	875	284,221	142,857
Dec. 31, 1909	523	273,473	139,024	515	72,947	51,472	1,038	346,420	190,496
Nov. 10, 1910	516	293,245	145,249	621	88,103	59,766	1,137	381,348	205,015
Dec. 5, 1911	513	313,685	156,083	688	98,814	63,708	1,201	412,499	219,791
Nov. 26, 1912	515	352,796	179,736	744	138,856	101,258	1,259	491,652	280,994
Oct. 21, 1913	517	359,732	183,623	832	151,620	101,081	1,349	511,352	284,704
Dec. 31, 1914	533	377,516	216,953	849	129,053	73,965	1,382	506,569	290,648
Dec. 31, 1915	534	418,094	273,509	831	149,773	101,483	1,365	567,867	374,992
Dec. 27, 1916	530	567,809	430,302	836	206,396	160,416	1,366	774,205	590,718
Dec. 31, 1917	539	679,316	531,066	874	268,382	215,906	1,413	947,698	746,972
Dec. 31, 1918	543	631,978	431,612	884	259,881	191,500	1,427	891,859	623,112
Dec. 31, 1919	552	965,855	777,942	948	405,130	336,018	1,500	1,370,985	1,113,960
Dec. 29, 1920	556	780,246	564,135	1,031	391,127	280,429	1,587	1,171,373	844,564
Dec. 31, 1921	551	691,087	501,493	1,004	334,907	237,848	1,555	1,025,994	739,341
Dec. 29, 1922	557	823,254	634,408	970	338,693	262,478	1,527	1,161,947	896,886
Sept. 14, 1923	569	860,173	648,954	950	376,775	306,372	1,519	1,236,948	955,326
Dec. 31, 1924	572	999,981	820,676	933	391,040	322,392	1,505	1,391,021	1,143,068
Dec. 31, 1925	656	1,020,124	832,425	834	336,966	268,586	1,490	1,357,090	1,101,011
Dec. 31, 1926	656	1,020,113	820,778	782	290,554	228,741	1,438	1,310,667	1,049,519
Dec. 31, 1927	643	1,134,595	938,129	748	328,574	267,559	1,391	1,463,168	1,205,688
Dec. 31, 1928	632	1,230,469	1,017,168	713	334,870	276,875	1,345	1,565,339	1,294,043
Dec. 31, 1929	609	1,124,369	897,538	699	332,534	264,013	1,308	1,456,903	1,161,551
Dec. 31, 1930	560	1,028,420	826,723	655	299,012	231,909	1,215	1,327,432	1,058,632
Dec. 31, 1931	508	865,910	677,307	594	235,681	172,806	1,102	1,101,591	850,113
Dec. 31, 1932	483	822,857	625,586	540	208,142	148,070	1,023	1,030,999	773,653
Dec. 30, 1933	445	900,810	733,810	489	185,476	132,389	934	1,086,286	866,199
Dec. 31, 1934	456	1,063,453	892,264	460	197,969	148,333	916	1,261,422	1,040,597
Dec. 31, 1935	454	1,145,488	1,099,172	442	205,729	162,926	896	1,351,217	1,172,098
June 30, 1936	456	1,192,845	1,054,284	426	228,877	169,652	882	1,421,722	1,223,936
Dec. 31, 1937	453	1,343,076	1,194,463	415	217,355	177,514	868	1,560,431	1,371,977
Sept. 28, 1938	449	1,359,719	1,206,882	406	217,944	170,286	855	1,577,663	1,377,168
Dec. 31, 1939	445	1,565,108	1,409,821	395	235,467	201,620	840	1,800,575	1,611,441
Dec. 31, 1940	446	1,695,662	1,534,702	393	227,866	179,027	839	1,923,528	1,713,729
Dec. 31, 1941	444	1,975,022	1,805,773	391	312,861	269,505	835	2,287,883	2,075,278
Dec. 31, 1942	439	2,696,768	2,525,299	391	417,058	353,109	830	3,113,826	2,878,408
Dec. 31, 1943	439	3,281,853	3,099,964	391	574,463	536,327	830	3,856,316	3,636,291
Dec. 31, 1944	436	4,092,473	3,891,999	398	780,910	738,779	834	4,873,383	4,630,778
Dec. 31, 1945	434	5,166,434	4,934,773	409	998,355	952,258	843	6,164,789	5,887,031
Dec. 31, 1946	434	4,883,558	4,609,538	418	1,019,369	964,938	852	5,902,927	5,574,476
Dec. 31, 1947	437	5,334,309	5,039,963	436	1,149,887	1,087,347	873	6,484,196	6,127,310
Dec. 31, 1948	437	5,507,823	5,191,334	444	1,208,884	1,137,259	881	6,716,707	6,328,593
Dec. 31, 1949	440	5,797,407	5,454,118	446	1,283,139	1,203,244	886	7,080,546	6,657,362
Dec. 31, 1950	442	6,467,275	6,076,006	449	1,427,680	1,338,540	891	7,894,955	7,414,546
Dec. 31, 1951	443	6,951,836	6,501,307	453	1,571,823	1,473,569	896	8,523,659	7,974,876
Dec. 31, 1952	444	7,388,030	6,882,623	457	1,742,270	1,631,757	901	9,130,300	8,514,380
Dec. 31, 1953	443	7,751,667	7,211,162	460	1,813,034	1,696,297	903	9,564,701	8,907,459
Dec. 31, 1954	441	8,295,686	7,698,690	465	1,981,483	1,851,724	906	10,277,169	9,550,414
Dec. 31, 1955	446	8,640,239	7,983,681	472	2,087,066	1,941,706	918	10,727,305	9,925,387
Dec. 31, 1956	452	8,986,456	8,241,159	480	2,231,497	2,067,927	932	11,217,953	10,309,086
Dec. 31, 1957	457	8,975,321	8,170,271	486	2,349,935	2,169,898	943	11,325,256	10,340,169
Dec. 31, 1958	458	9,887,737	9,049,580	499	2,662,270	2,449,474	957	12,550,007	11,499,054
Dec. 31, 1959	466	10,011,949	9,033,495	511	2,813,006	2,581,404	977	12,824,955	11,614,899
Dec. 31, 1960	468	10,520,690	9,560,668	532	2,997,609	2,735,726	1,000	13,518,299	12,296,394
Dec. 30, 1961	473	11,466,767	10,426,812	538	3,297,588	3,009,499	1,011	14,764,355	13,436,311
Dec. 28, 1962	486	12,070,803	10,712,253	551	3,646,404	3,307,714	1,037	15,717,207	14,019,967
Dec. 30, 1963	519	12,682,674	11,193,194	570	4,021,033	3,637,559	1,089	16,703,707	14,830,753
Dec. 31, 1964	539	14,015,957	12,539,142	581	4,495,074	4,099,543	1,120	18,511,031	16,638,685
Dec. 31, 1965	545	14,944,319	13,315,367	585	4,966,947	4,530,675	1,130	19,911,266	17,846,042
Dec. 31, 1966	546	15,647,346	13,864,727	591	5,332,385	4,859,906	1,137	20,979,731	18,724,633

Date	National Banks			State Banks			Combined Total		
	No. Banks	Total Resources (add 000)	Deposits (add 000)	No. Banks	Total Resources (add 000)	Deposits (add 000)	No. Banks	Total Resources (add 000)	Deposits (add 000)
Dec. 31, 1967	542	17,201,752	15,253,496	597	6,112,900	5,574,735	1,139	23,314,652	20,828,231
Dec. 31, 1968	535	19,395,045	16,963,003	609	7,107,310	6,489,357	1,144	26,502,355	23,452,360
Dec. 31, 1969	529	19,937,396	16,687,720	637	7,931,966	7,069,822	1,166	27,869,362	23,757,542
Dec. 31, 1970	530	22,087,890	18,384,922	653	8,907,039	7,958,133	1,183	30,994,929	26,343,055
Dec. 31, 1971	530	25,137,269	20,820,519	677	10,273,200	9,179,451	1,207	35,410,469	29,999,970
Dec. 31, 1972	538	29,106,654	23,892,660	700	12,101,749	10,804,827	1,238	41,208,403	34,697,487
Dec. 31, 1973	550	32,791,219	26,156,659	716	14,092,134	12,417,693	1,266	46,883,353	38,574,352
Dec. 31, 1974	569	35,079,218	28,772,284	744	15,654,983	13,758,147	1,313	50,734,201	42,530,431
Dec. 31, 1975	584	39,138,322	31,631,199	752	17,740,669	15,650,933	1,336	56,878,991	47,282,132
Dec. 31, 1976	596	43,534,570	35,164,285	761	19,846,695	17,835,078	1,357	63,381,265	52,999,363
Dec. 31, 1977	604	49,091,503	39,828,475	773	22,668,498	20,447,012	1,377	71,760,001	60,275,487
Dec. 31,1978	609	56,489,274	44,749,491	786	25,987,616	23,190,869	1,395	82,476,890	67,940,360
Dec. 31,1979	615	65,190,891	50,754,782	807	30,408,232	26,975,854	1,422	95,599,123	77,730,636
Dec. 31,1980	641	75,540,334	58,378,669	825	35,186,113	31,055,648	1,466	110,726,447	89,434,317
Dec. 31, 1981	694	91,811,510	68,750,678	829	42,071,043	36,611,555	1,523	133,882,553	105,362,233
Dec. 31, 1982	758	104,580,333	78,424,478	841	48,336,463	41,940,277	1,599	152,916,796	120,364,755
Dec. 31, 1983	880	126,914,841	98,104,893	848	55,008,329	47,653,797	1,728	181,923,170	145,758,690
Dec. 31, 1984	999	137,565,365	105,862,656	855	60,361,504	52,855,584	1,854	197,926,869	158,718,240
Dec. 31, 1985	1,058	144,674,908	111,903,178	878	64,349,869	56,392,634	1,936	209,024,777	168,295,812
Dec. 31, 1986	1,077	141,397,037	106,973,189	895	65,989,944	57,739,091	1,972	207,386,981	164,712,280
Dec. 31, 1987	953	135,690,678	103,930,262	812	54,361,514	47,283,855	1,765	190,052,192	151,214,117
Dec. 31, 1988	802	130,310,243	106,740,461	690	40,791,310	36,655,253	1,492	171,101,553	143,395,714
Dec. 31, 1989	687	133,163,016	104,091,836	626	40,893,848	36,652,675	1,313	174,056,864	140,744,511
Dec. 31, 1990	605	125,808,263	103,573,445	578	45,021,304	40,116,662	1,183	170,829,567	143,690,107
Dec. 31, 1991	579	123,022,3148	106,153,441	546	46,279,752	41,315,420	1,125	169,302,066	147,468,861
Dec. 31, 1992	562	135,507,244	112,468,203	529	40,088,963	35,767,858	1,091	175,596,207	148,236,061
Dec. 31, 1993	502	139,409,250	111,993,205	510	44,566,815	39,190,373	1,012	183,976,065	151,183,578
Dec. 31, 1994	481	140,374,540	111,881,041	502	47,769,694	41,522,943	983	188,144,234	153,403,984

Texas State Banks

Consolidated Statement, Foreign and Domestic Offices, as of Dec. 31, 1994

Source: ***Federal Reserve Bank of Dallas***

Number of Banks		**502**
(All figures in thousand dollars)		
Assets		
Cash and due from banks:		
Non-interest-bearing balances and currency and coin		2,689,687
Interest-bearing balances		324,607
Securities		19,986,636
Federal funds sold		1,906,141
Securities purchased under agreement to resell		27,495
Loans and lease financing receivables:		
Loans and leases, net of unearned income	21,155,288	
Less: allowance for loan and lease losses	359,492	
Less: allocated transfer risk reserve	0	
Loans and leases, net	20,795,802	
Assets held in trading accounts		271
Premises and fixed assets		963,930
Other real estate owned		148,027
Investments in unconsolidated subsidiaries and associated companies		1,627
Customers liability on acceptances outstanding		1,781
Intangible assets		158,465
Other assets		765,223
Total Assets		**47,769,694**
Liabilities		
Deposits:		
In domestic offices		41,522,943
Non-interest-bearing	9,024,843	
Interest-bearing	32,498,101	
In foreign offices, edge & agreement subsidiaries & IBF's		
Non-interest-bearing		
Interest-bearing		
Federal funds purchased		932,021
Securities sold under agreements to repurchase		597,685
Demand notes issued to the U.S. Treasury		123,779
Other borrowed money		243,810
Mortgage indebtedness and obligations under capitalized leases		8,496
Banks' liability on acceptances executed and outstanding		1,781
Notes and debentures subordinated to deposits		2,500
Other liabilities		276,323
Total Liabilities		**43,709,338**
Equity Capital		
Limited-life preferred stock		0
Perpetual preferred stock		6,162
Common stock		528,258
Surplus (exclude all surplus related to preferred stock)		1,883,317
Undivided profits and capital reserves		1,842,550
Less: Net unrealized loss on marketable equity securities		(199,931)
Cumulative foreign currency translation adjustments		
Total Equity Capital		**4,060,356**
Total liabilities, limited-life preferred stock and equity capital		**47,769,694**

Texas National Banks

Consolidated Statement, Foreign and Domestic Offices, as of Dec. 31, 1994

*Source: **Federal Reserve Bank of Dallas***

Number of Banks		**481**
(All figures in thousand dollars)		
Assets		
Cash and due from banks:		
Non-interest-bearing balances and currency and coin		10,142,433
Interest-bearing balances		1,223,056
Securities		37,784,185
Federal funds sold		6,095,424
Securities purchased under agreement to resell		356,053
Loans and lease financing receivables:		
Loans and leases, net of unearned income	78,653,541	
Less: allowance for loan and lease losses	1,108,717	
Less: allocated transfer risk reserve	0	
Loans and leases, net		77,544,824
Assets held in trading accounts		100,417
Premises and fixed assets		2,453,774
Other real estate owned		209,802
Investments in unconsolidated subsidiaries and associated companies		43,092
Customers liability on acceptances outstanding		208,110
Intangible assets		1,395,406
Other assets		2,817,964
Total Assets		**140,374,540**
Liabilities		
Deposits:		
In domestic offices		107,902,542
Non-interest-bearing	27,132,919	
Interest-bearing	80,769,623	
In foreign offices, edge & agreement subsidiaries & IBF's		3,978,499
Non-interest-bearing	225	
Interest-bearing	3,978,274	
Federal funds purchased		9,708,941
Securities sold under agreement to repurchase		1,855,387
Demand notes issued to the U.S. Treasury		966,902
Other borrowed money		2,989,562
Mortgage indebtedness and obligations under capitalized leases		46,213
Banks' liability on acceptances executed and outstanding		208,110
Notes and debentures subordinated to deposits		650,381
Other liabilities		1,282,766
Total Liabilities		**129,589,304**
Equity Capital		
Perpetual preferred stock		16,323
Common stock		2,128,930
Surplus		5,755,074
Undivided profits and capital reserves		3,229,674
Less: Net unrealized loss on marketable equity securities		(344,763)
Cumulative foreign currency translation adjustments		0
Total Equity Capital		**10,785,236**
Total liabilities, limited preferred stock and equity capital		**140,374,540**

Economic data

There are **additional data** on each county's total wages, average weekly wage, civilian labor force, unemployment and retail trade and other economic factors on pages 132-283.

Insurance in Texas

The **State Board of Insurance** reported that on Aug. 31, 1994, there were **2,626** firms licensed to handle insurance business in Texas, including **773** Texas firms and **1,853** out-of-state companies.

Annual premium income of firms operating in Texas caused Dallas and some other cities to rank among the nation's major insurance centers.

The former **Robertson Law**, enacted in 1907 and repealed in 1963, encouraged the establishment of many Texas insurance firms.

It required life insurance companies operating in the state to invest in Texas three-fourths of all reserves held for payment of policies written in the state.

Many out-of-state firms withdrew from Texas. Later many companies re-entered Texas and the law was liberalized and then repealed.

The State Board of Insurance administers legislation relating to the insurance business. This agency was established in 1957, following discovery of irregularities in some firms.

It succeeded two previous regulatory groups, established in 1913 and changed in 1927.

The governor appoints the three-member board, which, in turn, appoints the **State Commissioner of Insurance**.

The commissioner serves as chief administrator of the agency and has other powers with which to regulate the insurance industry. In 1991, the legislature moved to revise the operation of the commission.

Companies in Texas

The following table shows the number and kinds of insurance companies licensed in Texas on Aug. 31, 1994:

Type of Insurance	Texas	Out-of-State	Total
Stock Life	182	629	811
Mutual Life	2	82	84
Stipulated Premium Life	59	...	59
Non-profit Life	...	1	1
Stock Fire	1	7	8
Stock Fire and Casualty	111	638	749
Mutual Fire and Casualty	7	64	71
Stock Casualty	6	71	77
Mexican Casualty	...	9	9
Lloyds	77	...	77
Reciprocal Exchanges	13	14	27
Fraternal Benefit Societies	11	28	39
Titles	6	17	23
Non-profit Legal Services	1	...	1
Health Maintenance	32	1	33
Risk Retention Groups	1	...	1
Multiple Employers Welfare Arrang.	1	1	2
Joint Underwriting Associations	...	6	6
Third Party Administrators	162	283	445
Continuing Care Retirement Communities	16	2	18
Total	688	1,853	2,541
Statewide Mutual Assessment	1	0	1
Local Mutual Aid Associations	17	0	17
Burial Associations	7	0	7
Exempt Associations	13	0	13
Non-profit Hospital Service	2	0	2
County Mutual Fire	23	0	23
Farm Mutual Fire	22	0	22
Total	85		85
Grand Total	**773**	**1,853**	**2,626**

Foreign Trade A Major Target for Texas

Since its days as an independent republic, Texas has attracted attention from foreign countries. With a gross state product larger than many nations in the world, the state is an attractive trading partner.

As the world economy further embraces that of the United States and Texas, channels of communications between nations become more important.

In 1857, the Texas Almanac reported that 17 foreign consuls and commercial agents from 16 countries were in Texas.

Among the countries represented were France, Great Britian, Mexico, Prussia, Switzerland, Uruguay, Austria and the Netherlands. All but three lived in Galveston. (The others lived in Indianola and Brownsville).

As the world economy of the 21st century develops, the State of Texas Department of Commerce keeps private businesses informed about the possibilities in foreign trade. Through the Office of International Marketing, the state provides basic and advanced export counseling; distributes leads for trade and matches foreign needs with producers in Texas; and displays the state's wares at overseas trade shows and promotional events organized by the Office of International Marketing.

The office is divided into three groups: one for Mexico; another for Europe; and a third for Asia-Pacific-Canada.

Information on the services provided can be obtained by writing the Office of International Marketing, P. O. Box 12047, Austin 78711. The street address is 410 East 5th St., Austin. The telephone number is 512-472-5059 and the Fax number is 512-320-9424.

Foreign Consulates in Texas

In the list below, the following abbreviations appear in parentheses after the name of the city: (CG) Consulate General; (C) Consulate; (VC) Vice Consulate. The letter "H" before the designation indicates honorary status. Compiled from "Foreign Consular Offices in the United States," U.S. Dept. of State, Sept. 1994.

Albania: Houston (HC); 7400 Fannin St., Ste. 1200, 77054. (713) 790-1341.

Argentina: Houston (CG); 1990 S. Post Oak Rd., Ste. 770, 77056. (713) 871-8935.

Australia: Houston (CG); 1990 S. Post Oak Rd., Ste. 800, 77056. (713) 629-9131.

Austria: Houston (HCG); 7887 Katy Frwy., Ste. 200, 77024. (713) 688-1226.

Belgium: Dallas (HC); 8350 N. Central Expy., Ste. 2000, 75206. (214) 750-2554.

Houston (HCG); 2929 Allen Pkwy., Ste. 2222, 77019. (713) 224-8000.

San Antonio (HC); 105 S. St. Mary's St., #2115, 78205. (210) 225-1951.

Belize: Houston (HC); 7101 Breen, 77086. (713) 999-4484.

Bolivia: Houston (HCG); 8811 Westheimer, Ste. 206, 77063. (713) 780-8001.

Botswana: Houston (HC); 4615 Post Oak Pl., Ste. 104, 77027. (713) 622-1900.

Brazil: Houston (C); 1700 W. Loop S., Ste. 1450, 77027. (713) 961-3063.

Cameroon: Houston (HC); 2711 Weslayan, 77027. (713) 499-3502.

Canada: Dallas (CG); 750 N. St. Paul, Ste. 1700, 75201. (214) 922-9806.

Chile: Houston (CG):1360 Post Oak Blvd., Ste. 2330, 77056; (713) 621-5853.

Dallas (HC); 3500 Oak Lawn, Apt. 200, 75219-4343. (214) 528-2731.

China: Houston (CG); 3417 Montrose, 77006. (713) 524-0780.

Colombia: Houston (CG); 2990 Richmond St., Ste. 544, 77098; (713) 527-8919.

Costa Rica: Austin (C); 1730 E. Oltorf, Unit 320, 78741. (512) 445-0023.

Houston (CG); 3000 Wilcrest, Ste. 145, 77042. (713) 266-0484.

San Antonio (CG); 7500 Callaghan Rd., Unit 350, 78229. (210) 340-8499.

Cyprus: Houston (HC); 320 S. 66th St. 77011. (713) 928-2264.

Denmark: Corpus Christi (HC); 22 Townhouse Lane (P.O. Box 4585), 78408. (512) 991-3112.

Dallas (HC); 3200 Trammell Crow Center, 2001 Ross Ave., 75201. (214) 979-6200.

Houston (HC); 5 Post Oak Park, Ste. 2180, 77027. (713) 622-9018.

Dominican Republic: Houston (C); 3300 S. Gessner, Ste. 113, 77024. (713) 467-4372.

Dallas (HC); 12127 Ridgelake Dr., 75218. (214) 341-3250.

El Paso (HC); 67977 Granero Dr., 79912.

Ecuador: Houston (CG); 4200 Westheimer, Ste. 218, 77027. (713) 622-1787.

Egypt: Houston (CG); 3 Post Oak Central, 1990 Post Oak Blvd., Ste. 2180, 77056. (713) 961-4915.

El Salvador: Dallas (CG); 1555 W. Mockingbird Lane, Ste. 216, 75235.

Houston (CG); 6655 Hillcroft, Ste. 1002, 77081. (713) 270-6239.

Finland: Houston (HC); 2190 North Loop W., Ste. 410, 77018. (713) 680-2727.

France: Houston (CG); 2777 Allen Pkwy., Ste. 650, 77019. (713) 528-2181. **Trade Commission:** 6857 San Felipe, Ste. 1600, 77056. (713) 266-6595.

Austin (HC); 2300 Interfirst Tower, Ste. 976, 78701. (512) 480-5605.

Dallas (HC); Poston Bldg., 750 N. St. Paul, Ste. 670, 75201. (214) 855-5495.

San Antonio (HC); Route 1, 78109. Box 229. (210) 659-3101.

Germany: Houston (CG); 1330 Post Oak Blvd., Ste. 1850, 77056. (713) 627-7770.

Corpus Christi (HC); 5440 Old Brownsville Rd., 78469. (512) 289-2416.

Dallas (HC); 5580 Peterson Lane, Ste. 150, 75240. (214) 239-0788.
San Antonio (HC); 1500 Alamo Bldg., 105 S. St. Mary's St., 78205. (210) 224-4455.
Greece: Houston (CG); Cigna Tower, 13670 Post Oak Blvd., Ste. 2480, 77056.
Guatemala: Houston (CG); 10200 Richmond Ave., Ste. 270, 77042. (713) 953-9531.
San Antonio (HC); 4840 Whirlwind, 78217.
Haiti: Houston (HC); 3535 Sage Rd., 77027.
Honduras: Houston (CG); 4151 Southwest Fwy., Ste. 700, 77027. (713) 622-4572.
Hungary: Houston (HC); 50 Briar Hollow Lane., 77027.
Iceland: Dallas (HC); 3890 W. Northwest Hwy., Ste. 304 , 75220. (214) 699-5417.
Houston (HC); 2348 W. Settler's Way, The Woodlands, 77380.
Indonesia: Houston (CG); 10900 Richmond Ave., 77042.
Ireland: Houston (HC); 1900 W. Loop S., Suite 850, 77027.
Israel: Houston (CG); Weslayan Tower, 24 Greenway Pz., Ste. 1500, 77046. (713) 627-3780.
Italy: Houston (CG); 1300 Post Oak Blvd., Ste. 660, 77056. (713) 850-7520.
Dallas (HVC); 6255 W. Northwest Hwy., Apt. 304, 75225.
Japan: Houston (CG);1000 Louisiana, Ste. 5300, 77002. (713) 652-2977.
Dallas (HCG); 1601 Elm St., 40th Floor, 75201.
Jordan: Houston (HC); 723 Main St., Ste. 408 (P.O. Box 3727), 77002. (713) 224-2911.
Korea: Houston (CG); 1990 Post Oak Blvd., Ste. 1250, 77056. (713) 961-0186.
Dallas (HC); 13111 N. Central Expy., 75243. (214) 454-1112.
Lesotho: Austin (HC); 7400 Valburn Dr., 78731.
Liberia: Houston (HCG); 3300 S. Gessner, 77063.
Luxembourg: Dallas (HC); 2001 Bryan Tower, Ste. 3600 75201. (214) 746-7200.
Malta: Houston (HCG); 654 N. Belt E., Ste. 400, 77060. (713) 999-1812.
Mexico: Austin (C); Littlefield Bldg., 200 E. 6th St., Ste. 200, 78701.
Brownsville (C); 724 E. Elizabeth (P.O. Box 1711), 78520. (210) 542-4431.
Corpus Christi (C); 800 N. Shoreline, Ste. 410, 78401.
Dallas (CG); 1349 Empire Central, Ste. 100, 75247. (214) 522-9740.
Del Rio (C); 300 East Losoya, 78840. (210) 775-2352.
Eagle Pass (C); 140 Adams St., 78852. (210) 773-9255.
El Paso (CG); 910 E. San Antonio St., 79901. (915) 533-3644.
Fort Worth (HC); 1 Commerce Plaza, 76102. (817) 335-5691.
Houston (CG); 3015 Richmond Ave., Ste. 100, 77064. (713) 524-3400. **Tourism Office:** 2707 N. Loop, Ste. 450, 77008. **Consulate Annex:** 9 Greenway Pz., Ste. 3110, 77046.
Laredo (C); 1612 Farragut St., 78040. (210) 723-6369.
McAllen (C); 1418 Beach St., Ste. 102, 78501. (210) 686-0243.
Midland (C); 511 W. Ohio St., Ste. 121, 79701.
San Antonio (CG); 127 Navarro St., 78205. (210) 227-9145. **Commercial Affairs Office**: 1100 NW Loop 410, St.e 754, 78213.
Monaco: Dallas (HC); 4700 St. Johns Dr., 75205. (214) 521-1058.
Morocco: Houston (HC); 5555 Del Monte, No. 2405, 77056. (713) 963-9110.
Netherlands: Houston (CG); 2200 Post Oak Blvd., Ste. 610, 77056. (713) 622-8000.
Nicaragua: Houston (CG); 6300 Hillcroft, Ste. 470, 77081. (713) 272-9628.
Norway: Houston (CG); 2777 Allen Parkway, 77019. (713) 521-2900.
Dallas (HC); L.B. 24, 7502 Greenville Ave., Ste. 500, 75231. (214) 368-3110.
Galveston (HC); 2201 Market St., Ste. 1000, 77550. (409) 762-9792.
Panama: Houston (CG); Weslayan Tower, 24 Greenway Plaza, Ste. 1705, 77046. (713) 493-5997.
Paraguay: Houston (HC); 14770 Cindywood, 77079.
Peru: Houston (CG); 5847 San Felipe Ave., Ste. 1481, 77056. (713) 781-5000.
San Antonio (HC); 28055 Ruffian Drive., 78006.
Philippines: Houston (CG); Texas Commerce Bank Bldg., 5177 Richmond Ave., Ste. 1100, 77056. (713) 524-0234.
Portugal: Houston (HC); 601 Jefferson Ave., Ste. 2200, 77002.
Saint Kitts/Nevis: Dallas (HC); 6336 Greenville Ave., 75206.
Saudi Arabia: Houston (CG); 5718 Westheimer, Ste. 1500, 77057. (713) 785-5577.
Spain: Houston (CG); 1800 Bering Dr., Ste. 660, 77057. (713) 783-6200.
Dallas (HC); 3141 Hood St., 75219. (214) 520-1717.
El Paso (HC); 3816 Mattox, 79925. (915) 592-5252.
San Antonio (HC); 8350 Delphian, 78148.
Sweden: Houston (HCG); 5123 Bellaire Blvd., 77401, (713) 295-5747.
Dallas: (HC); 5956 Sherry Lane, Ste. 1616, 75225;
(214) 363-0800.
Switzerland: Houston (CG); 1000 Louisiana, Ste. 5670, 77002. (713) 650-0000.
Syria: Houston (HCG); 6330 W. Loop S. 870. 77401. (713) 668-1928.
Thailand: Dallas (HCG); 1717 Main St., Ste. 4100, 75201.
El Paso (HCG); 4401 N. Mesa, Ste. 200, 79902. (915) 533-9511.
Tunisia: Houston (HC); 1010 Milam St., 77252 (P.O. Box 2511). (713) 757-8969.
Turkey: Houston (CG); 1990 Post Oak Central, 77056. (713) 622-5849.
United Kingdom: Houston (CG); 1000 Louisiana St., Ste. 1900, 77002. (713) 659-6270.
Dallas (C); 813 Stemmons Tower W., 2730 Stemmons Frwy., 75207. (214) 637-3600.
Venezuela : Houston (CG); 2700 S. Post Oak Blvd., Ste. 1500, 77056. (713) 961-5141.

Multinationals in Texas Market

There are approximately 1,950 foreign companies operating in the state according to the Texas Department of Commerce.

There are also 425 Texas companies with operations abroad.

Houston and Dallas-Fort Worth account for the bulk of the international business, with 1,023 foreign companies in the Houston metropolitan area and the Dallas-Fort Worth area home to 596 foreign companies.

The Austin-San Antonio corridor has 125, leaving 207 affiliates of foreign companies around the rest of the state. Those companies range from French wine interests in Fort Stockton to a German chemical firm in Pampa and a Taiwanese shrimp-farm operation in the Lower Rio Grande Valley.

Most Texas firms operating abroad are also associated with the state's two major metropolitan areas. More than 300 of the 425 Texas companies working in other countries have headquarters in Dallas-Fort Worth or Houston. Those Texas businesses include endeavors as varied as oil and engineering firms working in Singapore to law firms operating in Russia.

Where Texas Firms Operate
(most operate in more than one nation)

United Kingdom	191
Canada	126
Mexico	104
Singapore	94
Australia	72

Texas counties with more than 10 foreign firms

County	No. of affiliates
Harris	970
Dallas	480
Tarrant	90
Bexar	65
Travis	55
El Paso	39
Fort Bend	26
Jefferson	17
Collin	16
Montgomery	15
Nueces	13

Origin of Foreign Firms in Texas

Japan	409
United Kingdom	257
France	249
Germany	181
Canada	127

The Texas Department of Commerce estimates that Texas is home to about 1 percent of the world's parent companies and 1 percent of the world's foreign subsidiaries based on United Nation's tallies.

The state agency cautions that the state government does not require reports from multinational companies and that companies are merged, relocated and traded frequently. But the agency directory that supplied these numbers is the most accurate information yet available.

Source: Texas Directory of Multinational Companies, Oct. 1994.

Utilities in Texas

Because of its large size, population and economic activity, Texas ranks high among the states in the scope of its utilities. It was one of the first states to utilize the telegraph and telephone extensively. A history of telephones in Texas appeared in the 1972-73 Texas Almanac, and other editions record much of the development of utilities. The following information was prepared through the cooperation of utility firms and their trade associations.

Telephones

Texas had 9,482,234 telephone lines in service on Dec. 31, 1992, served by 58 local-exchange companies. In addition to local service, those companies also provide approximately one-third of the intrastate long distance service in Texas. AT&T and some 154 other competitive carriers provide most of the intrastate and all of the interstate long distance service enjoyed by Texans. SBC Communications Inc. (formerly Southwestern Bell Corporation) has its headquarters in San Antonio. It serves Arkansas, Kansas, Missouri and Oklahoma. SBC became a separate entity Jan. 1, 1984, the date of divestiture of the Bell System, and is no longer associated with AT&T.

The largest subsidiary of the corporation is Southwestern Bell Telphone Company, which provides local telephone access service to about 13.6 million customers in five states, including Texas. Other SBC companies in Texas include SWB Mobile Systems, SWB Telecommunications, SWB Yellow Pages and SWB Messaging.

Southwestern Bell Telephone of Texas was created in 1992, with headquarters in Dallas.

Southwestern Bell Telephone of Texas serves more than 7.5 million customers in 530 Texas communities. This includes approximately 77 percent of the state's total telephone customers. SBC employs 29,988 people statewide.

Southwestern Bell handles more than 95 million local calls, and provides access for an additional 6 million direct-

Telephones in Texas

The following tabel refers to access lines.

City	1994	1992
Abilene	64,625	60,849
Amarillo	107,078	99,426
Arlington	128,143	119,639
Austin (Metro)	526,434	463,099
Bay City	12,758	12,434
Beaumont	71,920	69,851
Brownsville-Harlingen	90,733	81,228
Cleburne	21,409	20,002
Corpus Christi (Metro)	147,532	138,126
Corsicana	14,431	13,825
Dallas	1,149,379	1,103,104
El Paso	274,209	252,513
Fort Worth	553,600	534,163
Galveston	38,267	37,610
Greenville	15,568	14,883
Houston	1,746,992	1,654,790
Laredo	65,342	56,761
Longview	59,036	55,724
Lubbock	131,305	122,842
McAllen-Edinburg	74,585	68,891
McKinney	19,672	16,117
Midland	70,739	62,042
Mineral Wells	9,244	8,880
Odessa	62,447	59,277
Paris	20,974	19,803
Port Arthur	33,276	33,105
San Antonio Metro	689,409	639,988
Temple	32,064	29,536
Texas City	15,951	15,278
Tyler	70,530	66,209
Vernon	6,906	6,686
Victoria	39,627	36,766
Waco	103,414	97,404
Wichita Falls	58,119	54,990

dialed long distance calls each day. The company serves Texas with more than 100 million conductor miles of copper and515,653 miles of fiber cable.

By the end of 1992, the Texas telephone industry had made a total in-service investment of more than $19 billion. The industry's 33,000 employees are paid wages of $1.2 billion annually. Telephone companies in Texas paid state and local taxes of $1.6 billion in 1992 and federal income taxes of $670 million.

Major independent telephone companies in Texas and their total access lines as of Dec. 31, 1992, were: GTE Central, with 1,473,961 lines; Central Telephone Co. of Texas (Centel), with 145,970 lines; United Telephone Co. of Texas, with 117,324 lines; and Lufkin-Conroe Telephone Exchange, with 70,932. Because telephone customers can now own the wiring within their premises, as well as all the equipment inside, the industry no longer counts total telephones they serve. Access lines reflect the number of connections the companies provide, and does not equate to number of customers.

The 58 independent telephone companies in Texas include 24 telephone cooperatives, subscriber-owned systems making up 40 percent of the companies in the state. While the Bell System companies serve approximately 78 percent of all Texans, the independent companies serve more than half of the state's 250,000 square miles of certified service territory.

Gas Utilities

Approximately 274 investor-owned gas companies in Texas are classified as gas utilities and come under the regulatory jurisdiction of the Texas Railroad Commission. Approximately 161 of these companies reported gas operating revenue of $6 billion in 1993, with operating expenses of $6 billion.

In 1993, fixed investment for distribution facilities in Texas was $2 billion and for transmission facilities, $5 billion. Investment in Texas plants in service totaled $8.27 billion. There were 36 investor-owned and 85 municipally owned distribution systems in operation in 1993 serving 1,017 Texas cities.

The eight largest distribution systems — six private and two municipal — served 96 percent of all residential customers. In 1993, there were approximately 3.3 million residential customers, 281,593 small commercial and industrial users, 299 large industrial customers and 10,577 other gas-utility customers. The breakdown of distribution sales to these customers was: 63 Mcf (thousand cubic feet) per residential customer, 550 Mcf per commercial customer, 172,866 Mcf per industrial customer and 2,651 Mcf for customers in the "other" category. Distribution sales amounted to 373.9 billion cubic feet in 1993.

In addition to industrial sales made by distribution companies, transmission companies reported pipeline-to-industry sales of 1.4 trillion cubic feet and revenue from these sales of $3.2 billion.

In 1993, the average annual residential gas bill in the United States was $568. The average annual bill in Texas for the same year was $391, up $36 from the previous year. The State of Texas collected $5 million in gas-utility taxes from gas utilities in fiscal year 1994.

There were 47,245 producing gas wells in the state at the end of 1993, up 947 from the previous year. New gas-well completions during 1993 numbered 1,827, up 264 from 1992.

Texas had a total of 134,888 miles of natural-gas pipelines in operation in 1993, including 16,123 miles of field and gathering lines, 44,084 miles of transmission lines and 74,681 miles of distribution lines.

Estimated proved gas reserves in the state amounted to 34.71 trillion cubic feet in 1993. Gross production of natural gas, including casinghead gas, in 1992 was 6.7 trillion cubic feet. At year end in 1992, 22 underground storage reservoirs in the state contained 297.29 billion cubic feet of gas.

Electric Cooperatives

The following information was furnished by the Texas Electric Cooperatives.

Electric cooperatives are nonprofit, consumer-owned utilities providing electric service primarily in rural areas.

They were organized in the 1930s and 1940s when investor-owned utilities neglected or refused to serve farms and rural communities.

By the end of 1994, there were 74 electric-distribution cooperatives serving over 1.2 million meters in all but nine of the 254 counties in Texas.

There are also 11 generation and transmission cooperatives (G&Ts) that are owned by local distribution cooperatives. Three of the G&Ts generate power while the others represent their member distribution systems in wholesale power supply arrangements The systems operate more than 263,000 miles of line with an average density of fewer than 5 meters per mile of line.

The distribution systems and G&Ts employ more than 5,500 persons. ☆

Texans Move by Land, Sea, Air

Texas is a leader among the states in a number of transportation indicators, including total road and street mileage, total railroad mileage and total number of airports. Texas ranks second behind California in motor-vehicle registrations and in number of general-aviation aircraft.

The Texas transportation system includes more than 220,000 miles of municipal and rural highways, more than 13,000 miles of **railroad line**, approximately 1,600 **landing facilities** and 13 major **Gulf Coast ports**. Texans own and operate almost 15 million motor vehicles and about 21,000 aircraft.

The transportation industry is a major employer in Texas. Texas Employment Commission statistics indicate that transportation employs more than 300,000 Texans.

The largest group, 108,637, is employed in trucking and warehousing. Railroads employ 11,400, air transportation 77,492 and water transportation 16,030.

The largest state government agency involved in transportation, the **Texas Department of Transportation**, is responsible for highways, motor vehicles and aviation. The **Railroad Commission** has intrastate authority over railroad safety, truck lines, buses and pipelines.

Vehicles, Highway Miles, Construction, Maintenance, 1994

The following mileage, maintenance and construction figures refer only to roads that are maintained by the state: Interstates, U.S. highways, state highways, farm-to-market and ranch-to-market roads and some loops around urban areas. Not included are city-maintained or county-maintained streets and roads.

County	Vehicles Registered	*Lane Miles of Highway	Miles Driven Per Day	Maintenance Expenditure	Construction Expenditure	Vehicles Reg. Fees	County Net Receipts	State Net Receipts
Anderson	35,499	942	945,359	$5,195,132	$8,284,567	$1,951,810	$733,728	$1,218,082
Andrews	12,987	540	382,547	1,081,872	1,297,177	702,112	368,622	333,490
Angelina	67,207	911	1,591,599	3,923,972	10,671,711	3,961,310	1,079,587	2,881,723
Aransas	13,760	161	321,926	976,918	7,499,325	742,294	400,936	341,358
Archer	8,438	524	304,136	1,540,987	1,931,577	435,432	341,025	94,407
Armstrong	2,478	372	244,714	902,123	13,956	132,259	130,828	1,431
Atascosa	22,562	1,010	892,232	4,044,678	48,171	1,314,735	653,053	661,682
Austin	20,483	607	864,249	1,773,191	630,937	1,349,855	671,456	678,399
Bailey	6,272	473	166,725	851,021	100,749	395,7491	352,401	43,348
Bandera	11,005	393	224,579	1,261,724	1,034	655,586	519,949	135,637
Bastrop	32,661	776	1,036,017	2,870,797	3,066,422	2,039,573	920,695	1,118,878
Baylor	4,957	434	154,627	1,889,663	628,777	283,803	252,365	31,438
Bee	17,555	639	504,673	1,421,850	663,711	1,202,334	605,934	414,400
Bell	159,659	1,383	3,571,962	4,717,527	13,168,641	9,721,139	3,181,102	6,540,037
Bexar	922,896	2,937	16,424,849	16,924,011	109,343,345	56,722,692	16,064,949	40,657,743
Blanco	6,699	451	302,292	1,291,515	841,788	430,209	324,764	105,445
Borden	941	344	50,062	1,108,750	0	47,274	46,884	390
Bosque	15,118	695	381,859	1,409,757	322,792	873,164	551,784	321,380
Bowie	75,682	1,157	2,142,686	4,210,047	8,519,287	4,357,190	1,569,623	2,787,567
Brazoria	179,374	1,175	3,350,125	6,808,389	26,874,582	9,882,425	2,422,660	7,459,765
Brazos	87,416	762	1,664,802	3,281,375	19,718,755	5,139,198	1,683,294	3,455,904
Brewster	6,318	588	166,238	2,306,706	6,793,099	348,598	302,824	45,774
Briscoe	2,149	328	55,565	719,200	275,282	116,698	115,145	1,553
Brooks	4,956	264	347,386	780,246	1,637,993	246,579	195,154	51,425
Brown	33,022	742	583,615	3,512,321	4,470,777	1,731,273	704,855	1,026,418
Burleson	13,962	517	547,461	3,093,132	454,074	761,018	476,479	234,539
Burnet	25,071	793	657,347	1,723,740	3,079,409	1,430,167	609,874	820,293
Caldwell	18,710	602	558,549	1,744,336	3,101,128	1,124,152	605,743	518,409
Calhoun	16,808	382	428,476	1,174,864	1,528,337	906,554	417,879	488,675
Callahan	13,582	743	666,572	1,925,328	8,060,651	722,488	510,070	212,418
Cameron	150,916	1,504	3,311,901	6,903,122	18,792,014	8,666,721	2,049,367	6,617,354
Camp	10,655	267	211,441	465,039	493,726	705,165	397,559	307,606
Carson	6,314	776	567,563	2,223,118	131,929	352,161	318,825	33,336
Cass	26,797	974	796,555	3,604,749	1,313,905	1,342,392	609,807	732,585
Castro	7,890	529	220,564	1,787,172	35,264	527,815	428,326	99,489
Chambers	21,708	700	1,453,769	2,380,794	10,050,765	1,222,050	538,569	683,481
Cherokee	33,087	1,113	940,759	3,785,386	842,572	2,082,573	900,170	1,182,403
Childress	5,962	477	271,820	1,284,868	3,816,429	305,674	292,664	13,010
Clay	8,812	789	563,974	2,411,403	1,490,030	546,935	452,834	94,101
Cochran	3,624	470	96,438	816,133	2,107,597	193,718	191,407	2,311
Coke	4,400	357	154,568	1,279,537	0	222,198	19,042	3,156
Coleman	10,000	738	270,606	2,485,998	3,456,356	538,404	450,449	87,955
Collin	256,367	1,244	3,329,939	8,186,443	55,504,809	16,329,653	5,002,690	11,326,963
Collingsworth	3,410	445	89,667	1,004,566	639,808	188,986	186,134	2,852
Colorado	18,605	761	1,056,668	2,381,942	840,083	1,166,843	614,532	552,311
Comal	55,569	604	1,693,741	3,078,447	9,006,548	3,467,431	1,191,918	2,275,513

County	Vehicles Registered	*Lane Miles of Highway	Miles Driven Per Day	Maintenance Expenditure	Construction Expenditure	Vehicles Reg. Fees	County Net Receipts	State Net Receipts
Comanche	13,104	726	380,346	$2,325,772	$501,829	$733,558	$519,141	$214,417
Concho	2,954	422	188,866	1,017,390	49,097	148,817	146,619	2,198
Cooke	28,495	842	896,756	3,426,732	2,784,104	1,698,023	777,659	920,364
Coryell	32,900	682	682,151	1,742,300	4,616,330	1,923,922	847,088	1,076,834
Cottle	2,082	391	75,403	895,965	971,071	102,333	100,680	1,653
Crane	5,724	319	166,895	1,078,816	133,411	430,595	283,996	146,599
Crockett	3,919	782	320,949	1,256,010	4,629,011	199,213	196,839	2,374
Crosby	6,299	569	173,965	1,354,619	0	319,909	301,046	18,863
Culberson	2,237	744	435,209	2,245,526	969,411	115,698	114,385	1,313
Dallam	5,245	603	275,769	1,389,234	134,137	339,024	307,609	31,415
Dallas	1,540,368	2,902	27,087,880	23,673,158	145,747,335	99,309,074	28,727,910	70,581,164
Dawson	11,992	710	323,892	1,578,814	285,876	745,244	527,929	217,315
Deaf Smith	16,377	601	306,706	1,805,960	218,493	1,194,622	611,915	582,707
Delta	4,930	342	137,149	812,358	598,257	254,854	238,450	16,404
Denton	234,181	1,238	4,814,521	7,509,531	32,297,887	14,622,250	4,194,541	10,427,709
DeWitt	15,184	641	363,683	1,758,560	1,488,885	878,360	586,719	291,641
Dickens	2,607	460	96,013	1,308,831	737,166	118,297	116,697	1,600
Dimmit	6,266	504	251,178	1,206,579	1,052,136	375,311	308,543	66,768
Donley	3,707	455	359,189	2,048,968	956,020	180,385	177,832	2,553
Duval	8,211	630	366,329	2,105,851	1,097,018	474,081	386,361	87,720
Eastland	17,866	1,025	877,893	3,066,254	3,037,432	996,615	534,945	461,670
Ector	107,527	927	1,326,616	3,697,082	9,210,809	6,537,744	1,689,110	4,848,634
Edwards	2,067	500	63,271	1,117,059	47,747	114,995	113,456	1,539
Ellis	82,940	1,422	2,644,313	6,820,197	29,777, 312	5,222,515	1,559,577	3,662,938
El Paso	341,773	1,429	6,516,256	5,758,252	35,667,496	20,917,953	5,732,228	15,185,725
Erath	26,725	784	752,514	2,760,346	3,992,577	1,420,746	634,212	786,534
Falls	12,854	706	485,879	2,236,590	125,819	680,236	505,872	174,364
Fannin	23,120	906	489,176	2,597,001	3,973,820	1,386,319	700,559	685,760
Fayette	20,815	981	1,016,683	2,809,882	6,005,354	1,164,124	565,203	598,921
Fisher	4,443	553	144,931	1,488,098	185,395	256,960	253,687	3,273
Floyd	8,132	668	168,560	1,072,529	1,068,465	481,841	417,048	64,793
Foard	1,587	299	59,105	1,335,101	0	86,239	85,044	1,195
Fort Bend	181,243	942	3,420,005	3,996,005	42,930,515	11,317,547	3,226,860	8,090,687
Franklin	7,071	334	329,335	1,975,561	96,519	358,750	283,995	74,755
Freestone	14,607	822	970,332	2,585,107	2,813,127	770,859	523,312	247,547
Frio	9,202	758	603,258	1,951,168	996,984	576,048	451,249	124,799
Gaines	11,817	668	381,650	1,355,220	82	644,484	404,322	240,162
Galveston	174,158	956	3,650,090	4,834,111	19,806,582	10,444,045	3,147,873	7,296,172
Garza	4,704	460	290,891	887,454	2,381,815	261,022	233,614	27,408
Gillespie	18,230	703	444,862	1,553,908	272,279	1,048,908	625,274	423,634
Glasscock	2,446	274	152,628	605,221	125,769	178,633	162,091	16,542
Goliad	5,504	500	253,455	1,262,303	596,004	262,358	256,429	5,929
Gonzales	15,450	876	819,461	1,688,755	6,666,664	868,474	511,630	356,844
Gray	25,373	770	504,116	2,779,129	6,772,937	1,312,813	521,323	791,490
Grayson	88,268	1,173	1,952,383	4,815,269	7,777,124	5,289,195	1,828,417	3,460,778
Gregg	110,688	741	1,992,897	3,317,401	7,497,890	7,227,695	2,287,702	4,939,993
Grimes	15,750	610	525,712	3,703,777	2,428,017	930,353	615,447	314,906
Guadalupe	58,259	912	1,668,098	2,649,532	8,900,297	3,682,543	1,353,309	2,329,234
Hale	28,552	1,054	643,745	3,814,107	912,609	1,792,608	778,639	1,013,969
Hall	3,431	449	172,722	949,024	4,089,065	184,167	181,588	2,579
Hamilton	7,905	575	239,199	1,704,871	491,869	499,147	390,905	58,242
Hansford	6,713	509	104,585	1,857,229	2,479,956	388,319	344,710	43,069
Hardeman	4,574	466	260,026	2,372,519	2,071,923	283,345	279,698	3,647
Hardin	40,984	531	1,019,687	1,775,195	9,668,307	2,297,612	1,028,522	1,269,090
Harris	2,252,675	4,045	37,112,860	29,794,536	389,122,593	142,458,494	40,697,699	101,760,795
Harrison	48,438	1,154	1,699,604	3,321,744	13,718,120	2,808,322	1,087,753	1,720,569
Hartley	4,780	508	228,861	1,137,759	1,663,767	309,825	279,549	30,276
Haskell	7,506	646	194,852	1,726,152	1,535,365	379,183	354,629	24,556
Hays	53,904	634	1,936,765	2,673,069	10,650,229	3,062,171	1,151,936	1,910,235
Hemphill	4,309	384	99,998	1,033,060	386,515	246,461	241,277	5,184
Henderson	61,117	933	1,228,705	2,526,927	3,459,001	3,288,624	1,167,342	2,121,282
Hidalgo	228,431	1,902	4,974,381	25,754,560	9,088,940	14,296,976	3,288,957	11,008,019
Hill	26,909	1,086	1,420,155	1,338,170	3,798,812	1,513,761	756,212	757,549
Hockley	21,651	750	484,975	1,667,278	27,870	1,290,710	573,082	717,628
Hood	33,761	375	647,903	1,263,931	95,219	1,682,637	734,698	947,939
Hopkins	31,703	952	1,110,174	2,641,664	4,358,200	1,992,981	903,303	1,089,678
Houston	18,207	835	482,382	2,205,893	2,080,048	965,050	541,579	423,471
Howard	28,337	837	729,827	3,682,559	3,689,897	1,670,272	751,281	918,991
Hudspeth	2,091	817	784,671	2,332,819	664,568	100,825	99,627	1,198
Hunt	61,347	1,279	1,746,193	4,825,225	7,006,014	3,139,549	970,905	2,168,655
Hutchinson	29,366	475	325,992	1,171,770	3,714,299	1,723,056	677,431	1,045,625
Irion	2,063	247	86,328	699,996	0	128,171	126,862	1,309
Jack	7,510	571	259,786	1,706,075	4,882,340	480,353	382,784	97,569
Jackson	12,994	636	621,770	1,909,492	2,145,360	704,658	490,311	214,347
Jasper	31,101	682	929,237	2,478,800	14,007,281	1,678,196	706,522	971,674

County	Vehicles Registered	*Lane Miles of Highway	Miles Driven Per Day	Maintenance Expenditure	Construction Expenditure	Vehicles Reg. Fees	County Net Receipts	State Net Receipts
Jeff Davis	2,160	469	131,461	$985,849	$4,997,664	$126,252	$122,276	$13,976
Jefferson	200,299	992	3,834,011	5,371,164	24,779,141	11,226,191	2,784,056	8,442,135
Jim Hogg	3,318	288	103,425	670,477	7,531	197,926	162,404	35,522
Jim Wells	26,686	633	794,659	2,529,208	4,358,995	1,676,199	656,610	1,019,589
Johnson	94,155	881	1,786,283	5,212,662	17,187,557	5,147,596	1,762,987	3,384,609
Jones	14,948	978	419,925	2,906,498	1,622,332	941,342	593,418	347,924
Karnes	9,972	691	293,388	2,008,861	264,370	521,810	419,505	102,305
Kaufman	50,669	1,191	2,373,757	4,075,743	2,151,697	2,820,605	1,124,329	1,696,276
Kendall	20,793	443	503,690	1,005,148	43,807	1,247,193	747,108	500,085
Kenedy	372	187	309,322	618,404	0	16,658	16,488	170
Kent	1,570	326	48,042	807,572	87,812	66,254	65,475	779
Kerr	35,128	702	753,400	2,251,851	400,730	1,959,884	817,605	1,142,279
Kimble	4,883	687	346,292	1,349,890	1,247,973	242,627	227,198	15,429
King	556	199	62,017	322,245	283,398	44,075	43,810	265
Kinney	2,392	407	134,330	1,486,650	446,555	128,683	119,344	9,339
Kleberg	21,257	363	552,864	1,215,525	4,585,934	1,275,079	589,799	685,280
Knox	4,343	434	125,858	1,277,093	2,395,931	258,796	249,899	8,897
Lamar	43,522	991	906,366	4,259,304	4,453,312	2,412,984	972,764	1,440,220
Lamb	14,106	809	364,893	1,794,773	1,891,329	731,324	484,883	246,441
Lampasas	12,887	476	300,611	1,538,849	553,589	675,883	495,195	180,688
LaSalle	2,958	648	365,570	1,701,653	533,589	178,381	175,885	2,496
Lavaca	19,549	639	402,639	1,899,507	1,280,340	1,118,463	623,968	494,495
Lee	13,570	514	458,874	1,778,643	3,712,262	846,623	383,023	315,139
Leon	12,836	834	877,000	3,709,444	3,559,371	698,162	505,928	192,234
Liberty	47,770	805	1,361,921	4,607,117	3,712,262	3,203,280	1,123,409	2,079,871
Limestone	18,802	769	531,298	2,343,312	1,874,814	851,359	455,745	395,614
Lipscomb	3,617	447	57,310	1,395,278	156,393	240,436	237,704	2,732
Live Oak	10,050	947	824,912	2,655,476	7,681,400	566,290	456,186	110,734
Llano	13,744	498	295,278	995,675	2,031,094	725,826	501,704	224,122
Loving	293	67	12,343	88,890	0	17,162	17,041	121
Lubbock	190,998	1,627	2,474,994	6,435,094	4,034,387	10,902,256	3,122,499	7,779,757
Lynn	6,347	708	229,317	2,202,696	70,821	318,873	304,785	14,088
Madison	9,178	569	598,739	1,705,409	459,801	475,413	372,930	102,483
Marion	7,997	316	250,675	1,060,422	172,293	429,123	361,462	67,661
Martin	5,550	572	299,393	1,936,283	1,048,212	348,847	320,223	28,624
Mason	3,743	416	123,475	870,517	1,585,230	174,804	172,664	2,140
Matagorda	30,733	681	708,802	2,327,842	3,260,269	1,510,257	509,852	1,000,405
Maverick	18,493	447	412,031	1,286,670	298,255	1,165,962	522,871	643,091
McCulloch	8,639	608	223,667	1,638,074	155,387	456,652	385,591	71,061
McLennan	158,273	1,593	3,847,524	4,850,137	10,446,601	10,469,840	2,636,366	7,833,474
McMullen	1,513	317	93,316	817,366	2,426,267	124,400	123,732	668
Medina	16,805	727	715,125	2,826,880	3,607,061	1,474,500	704,537	769,963
Menard	4,555	346	100,176	786,468	5,015	845,498	252,435	593,063
Midland	98,978	930	1,370,498	3,891,937	6,869,949	6,034,196	1,742,326	4,291,870
Milam	20,562	685	621,162	1,831,127	3,687,497	1,036,514	537,171	499,343
Mills	5,117	424	173,494	1,348,149	711,849	269,966	265,907	4,059
Mitchell	6,959	657	438,053	2,036,770	279,612	339,749	309,878	29,871
Montague	18,819	825	509,200	3,389,544	5,539,574	1,081,280	624,591	456,689
Montgomery	178,961	1,038	4,167,036	8,349,554	66,574,292	10,948,820	3,488,852	7,459,968
Moore	16,718	469	374,896	1,560,446	121,162	1,081,999	509,803	572,196
Morris	13,952	357	365,202	944,294	815,025	911,769	448,117	463,652
Motley	1,632	331	62,184	689,739	1,695,715	81,595	80,288	1,307
Nacogdoches	42,516	908	1,277,497	3,581,479	4,784,232	2,505,983	1,043,044	1,462,939
Navarro	34,844	1,154	1,354,555	3,811,760	5,976,710	1,981,909	843,793	1,138,116
Newton	10,731	547	350,667	2,765,532	2,525,463	510,487	407,018	103,469
Nolan	13,547	690	649,394	2,489,531	2,458,152	819,302	559,194	260,108
Nueces	222,195	1,356	4,018,038	7,042,435	23,136,794	13,676,695	4,165,135	9,511,560
Ochiltree	9,709	428	165,069	855,674	114,881	635,749	496,432	139,317
Oldham	2,240	462	507,845	766,014	1,405,474	134,798	133,466	1,332
Orange	71,063	576	1,982,056	2,892,275	5,189,983	4,002,492	1,341,138	2,661,345
Palo Pinto	25,552	829	710,159	3,076,584	1,801,403	1,765,673	711,479	1,054,194
Panola	21,270	746	749,353	2,844,150	10,553,690	1,044,650	462,227	582,423
Parker	69,954	855	1,829,651	3,353,812	6,724,108	3,775,968	1,386,608	2,389,360
Parmer	9,353	539	314,047	1,110,138	10,272,358	597,552	481,136	116,416
Pecos	12,193	1,658	685,471	3,593,498	1,150,828	621,237	399,195	222,042
Polk	32,227	833	1,202,862	3,870,138	4,833,216	2,061,719	866,128	1,195,591
Potter	90,418	860	1,877,618	4,327,941	10,116,133	5,813,993	1,979,595	3,834,398
Presidio	4,789	545	132,085	2,123,379	3,831,755	248,042	244,834	3,208
Rains	7,435	270	198,120	506,841	24,458	358,958	285,241	73,717
Randall	87,083	878	878,258	2,632,536	2,219,270	5,279,400	1,801,692	3,477,708
Reagan	3,698	320	118,181	739,950	2,943,300	212,446	206,626	5,820
Real	2,640	297	66,592	1,142,482	147,334	143,417	141,554	1,863
Red River	12,446	748	361,997	3,082,613	878,484	661,371	517,579	143,792
Reeves	9,794	1,170	571,369	3,530,855	1,492,306	525,719	423,218	102,501
Refugio	6,935	464	514,901	2,130,327	38,118	406,910	315,534	91,376

County	Vehicles Registered	*Lane Miles of Highway	Miles Driven Per Day	Maintenance Expenditure	Construction Expenditure	Vehicles Reg. Fees	County Net Receipts	State Net Receipts
Roberts	1,316	241	54,429	$657,896	$12,311	$61,411	$60,630	$781
Robertson	12,355	625	479,615	2,112,942	1,992,244	627,700	471,408	156,292
Rockwall	27,900	317	861,549	1,845,741	11,576,660	1,721,641	616,279	1,105,362
Runnels	11,508	735	289,809	1,633,782	877,432	677,146	506,536	170,610
Rusk	36,428	1,143	1,006,534	3,673,573	2,557,702	2,167,863	865,589	1,302,274
Sabine	9,240	454	241,519	1,204,433	1,776,841	487,559	398,723	88,836
San Augustine	7,331	516	231,867	2,061,635	3,640,422	439,976	390,723	49,253
San Jacinto	14,208	506	526,106	1,603,471	1,630,329	769,472	469,039	300,433
San Patricio	46,377	880	1,357,225	3,597,967	16,527,829	2,519,317	844,881	1,674,436
San Saba	5,638	427	129,416	1,272,340	1,491,575	323,781	319,391	4,390
Schleicher	3,190	362	105,571	753,884	272,521	146,533	144,974	1,559
Scurry	17,333	660	466,477	2,272,186	922,145	1,052,740	546,336	506,404
Shackelford	3,786	353	131,524	1,156,697	8,184	207,079	203,552	3,527
Shelby	22,798	857	602,054	2,715,124	1,424,001	1,675,301	793,848	881,453
Sherman	3,347	429	202,967	1,195,726	221,919	201,845	199,184	2,661
Smith	142,680	1,500	3,498,081	8,755,725	6,083,847	8,755,725	2,776,119	5,979,606
Somervell	5,466	184	181,542	1,037,326	1,467	264,707	194,155	70,552
Starr	21,028	463	619,302	1,707,895	4,471,257	1,354,639	672,189	682,450
Stephens	8,878	553	205,983	1,751,570	3,197,389	503,719	403,631	100,088
Sterling	1,694	240	139,405	652,714	217,769	78,100	77,191	909
Stonewall	2,398	329	87,095	1,774,581	283,943	151,092	149,789	1,303
Sutton	5,273	592	325,102	1,408,864	256,852	330,663	239,720	90,943
Swisher	7,383	808	302,557	2,263,325	34,094	432,937	382,314	50,623
Tarrant	1,028,413	2,780	18,910,439	18,074,675	102,195,530	61,949,059	17,355,943	44,593,116
Taylor	107,332	1,151	1,727,233	4,334,546	6,823,853	6,763,201	2,196,672	4,566,529
Terrell	1,308	343	65,694	785,433	1,368,954	62,521	61,686	835
Terry	13,236	631	339,580	1,991,586	70,507	780,807	535,436	245,371
Throckmorton	3,080	341	72,048	1,402,886	42,203	105,448	104,237	1,211
Titus	22,561	540	759,014	2,105,533	2,152,647	1,209,803	625,812	583,991
Tom Green	86,585	948	1,035,750	2,834,838	4,184,635	5,083,155	1,759,717	3,323,438
Travis	496,407	1,562	9,199,573	9,641,179	108,228,254	30,339,425	9,434,983	20,904,442
Trinity	11,551	429	282,558	1,219,305	1,390,150	633,536	425,270	208,266
Tyler	15,846	510	457,519	3,048,932	341,228	812,110	501,967	310,143
Upshur	28,458	744	684,914	1,869,024	494,306	1,412,958	616,982	795,976
Upton	3,456	388	136,055	1,303,016	8,916	186,668	184,494	2,174
Uvalde	18,277	719	524,953	1,738,463	1,566,625	1,240,861	597,808	643,053
Val Verde	29,181	665	360,167	2,528,130	3,579,594	1,582,415	612,599	969,816
Van Zandt	41,673	1,153	1,437,484	4,269,849	10,723,551	2,249,399	948,363	1,031,036
Victoria	68,026	716	1,356,279	3,775,814	3,859,283	3,768,326	1,153,971	2,614,355
Walker	31,356	783	1,473,002	2,936,481	7,254,532	1,917,106	852,142	1,064,964
Waller	27,307	550	1,002,028	2,359,036	24,553,351	1,630,567	1,103,004	527,563
Ward	11,391	672	464,008	2,450,246	29,669	625,123	387,424	237,699
Washington	25,412	627	713,242	3,036,192	6,037,000	1,652,626	769,761	882,865
Webb	80,209	898	1,401,404	2,853,430	15,700,161	6,245,197	1,673,216	4,571,981
Wharton	35,136	883	1,205,886	3,010,486	2,202,641	2,071,561	730,239	1,341,322
Wheeler	6,005	670	413,936	2,156,358	3,191,974	271,862	268,013	3,849
Wichita	107,732	1,059	1,655,086	3,631,486	7,156,052	5,912,491	1,578,185	4,334,306
Wilbarger	13,552	723	503,617	1,735,313	6,717,733	705,795	498,312	207,483
Willacy	11,363	478	314,731	1,527,574	42,900	684,584	474,794	209,790
Williamson	132,172	1,398	3,085,859	6,000,953	19,377,962	8,149,033	2,567,368	5,581,665
Wilson	20,151	724	513,852	2,161,308	1,848,288	1,108,496	617,445	491,051
Winkler	7,371	295	139,126	552,617	38,753	440,703	331,766	108,937
Wise	45,570	841	1,335,922	4,017,516	9,430,857	2,793,418	1,001,412	1,792,006
Wood	32,533	890	619,992	2,757,235	1,526,584	1,647,617	652,997	994,620
Yoakum	8,723	427	198,020	1,053,449	269,710	572,339	424,814	147,525
Young	20,308	711	333,270	2,299,079	1,064,606	1,169,152	625,555	543,597
Zapata	6,118	250	265,146	941,057	1,729,706	346,798	252,088	94,710
Zavala	5,567	556	221,219	1,210,201	78,941	351,987	278,357	73,630
State Collections						606,629,455		606,629,455
Exempt Reg.	527,000							
Special Veh.	229,060							
Totals	14,237,283	183,304	307,576,524	703,033,794	1,977,243,657	864,657,577	296,015,388	568,547,869

* A lane mile of highway is one highway lane for one mile; i.e., one mile of four-lane highway equals four lane miles.

Please note: Some columns may not balance because of rounding.

Source: Texas Department of Transportation.

Motor Vehicle Accidents, Losses

Year	No. Killed	†No. Injured	Accidents by Kinds: No. Fatal	†No. Involving Injury	†No. Non-Injury	†Total	‡Vehicle Miles Traveled: *Number	Deaths per 100 million Miles	§Economic Loss
1960	2,254	127,980	1,842	71,100	239,300	312,242	46,352,734,855	4.9	$350,022,500
1965	3,028	186,062	2,460	103,368	365,160	470,988	*52,163,239,027	5.8	498,087,000
1966	3,406	208,310	2,784	115,728	406,460	524,972	55,260,849,798	6.2	557,414,000
1967	3,367	205,308	2,778	114,060	768,430	885,268	58,123,603,943	5.8	793,094,000
1968	3,481	216,972	2,902	120,540	816,830	940,272	62,794,494,339	5.5	836,802,000
1969	3,551	223,000	2,913	124,000	850,000	976,913	67,742,000,000	5.2	955,300,000
1970	3,560	223,000	2,965	124,000	886,000	1,012,965	‡68,031,000,000	5.2	1,042,200,000
1971	3,594	224,000	2,993	124,000	890,000	1,016,993	70,709,000,000	5.1	1,045,000,000
1972	3,688	128,158	3,099	83,607	346,292	432,998	76,690,000,000	4.8	1,035,000,000
1973	3,692	132,635	3,074	87,631	373,521	464,226	80,615,000,000	4.6	1,035,000,000
1974	3,046	123,611	2,626	83,341	348,227	434,194	78,290,000,000	3.9	1,095,000,000
1975	3,429	138,962	2,945	92,510	373,141	468,596	84,575,000,000	4.1	1,440,000,000
1976	3,230	145,282	2,780	96,348	380,075	479,203	91,279,000,000	3.5	1,485,000,000
1977	3,698	161,635	3,230	106,923	393,848	504,001	96,998,000,000	3.8	1,960,000,000
1978	¶3,980	178,228	3,468	117,998	**304,830	**426,296	102,624,000,000	3.9	2,430,000,000
1979	4,229	184,550	3,685	122,793	322,336	448,814	101,909,000,000	4.1	2,580,000,000
1980	4,424	185,964	3,863	123,577	305,500	432,940	103,255,000,000	4.3	3,010,000,000
1981	4,701	206,196	4,137	136,396	317,484	458,017	111,036,000,000	4.2	3,430,000,000
1982	4,271	204,666	3,752	135,859	312,159	451,770	††124,910,000,000	3.4	3,375,000,000
1983	3,823	208,157	‡‡3,328	137,695	302,876	443,899	129,309,000,000	3.0	3,440,000,000
1984	3,913	220,720	3,466	145,543	293,285	442,294	137,280,000,000	2.9	3,795,000,000
1985	3,682	231,009	3,270	151,657	300,531	452,188	143,500,000,000	2.6	3,755,000,000
1986	3,568	234,120	3,121	154,514	298,079	452,593	150,474,000,000	2.4	3,782,000,000
1987	3,261	226,895	2,881	146,913	246,175	395,969	151,221,000,000	2.2	3,913,000,000
1988	3,395	238,845	3,004	152,004	237,703	392,711	152,819,000,000	2.2	4,515,000,000
1989	3,361	243,030	2,926	153,356	233,967	390,249	159,679,000,000	2.1	4,873,000,000
1990	3,243	262,576	2,882	162,424	216,140	381,446	163,103,000,000	2.0	4,994,000,000
1991	3,079	263,430	2,690	161,470	207,288	371,448	162,780,000,000	1.9	5,604,000,000
1992	3,057	282,025	2,690	170,513	209,152	382,355	162,769,000,000	1.9	6,725,000,000
1993	3,037	298,891	2,690	178,194	209,533	390,417	167,988,000,000	1.8	11,784,000,000

**Vehicle miles traveled since 1964 were estimated on the basis of new data furnished by U.S. Bureau of Public Roads through National Safety Council. Vehicle miles and deaths per 100 million vehicle miles after 1964 cannot, therefore, be compared with previous years.*

†In August 1967, amended estimating formula received from National Safety Council. Starting with 1972, actual reported injuries are listed rather than estimates.

‡Vehicle miles traveled estimated by Texas Highway Department starting with 1970. Method of calculation varies from that used for prior years. Vehicle miles and deaths per 100,000,000 vehicle miles for 1969 and before cannot be compared to subsequent years.

§Economic loss formula last changed 1984.

¶Change in counting fatalities. Counted when injury results in death within 90 days of vehicle accident in which the injury occurred.

***Total accidents and non-injury accidents for 1978 and after cannot be compared with years prior to 1978 due to changes in reporting laws.*

††Method of calculating vehicle miles traveled revised for 1982 by the Texas State Department of Highways and Public Transportation. Vehicle miles and deaths per 100,000,000 miles cannot be compared to prior years.

‡‡Change in counting fatalities. Counted when injury results in death within 30 days of vehicle accident in which the injury occurred.

Source: Analysis Section, Accident Records Bureau of the ***Texas Department of Public Safety****, Austin.*

Vehicles and Drivers, 1992

Source: Federal Highway Admin.

Rank	Autos, trucks, buses	(Drivers licenses)
1. California	22,202,000	20,111,000
2. Texas	**12,767,000**	**11,438,000**
3. Florida	10,232,000	10,538,000
4. New York	9,980,000	10,360,000
5. Ohio	9,030,000	9,169,000
6. Pennsylvania	8,179,000	8,019,000
7. Illinois	7,982,000	7,411,000
8. Michigan	7,311,000	6,481,000
9. Georgia	5,899,000	4,600,000
10. New Jersey	5,591,000	5,285,000

One of the last of the steam engines to operate over the Burlington line stops beside one of the big diesels in the Union Terminal, Fort Worth, around 1950. Texas Almanac file photo.

The Development of Texas Railroads: Republic of Texas to Present

The following condensed history of railroading in Texas was written for the 1956-57 edition of the Texas Almanac by the late Arthur L. Carnahan, Chief Statistician of the Railroad Commission of Texas. It has been revised and brought up to date for the 1996-97 Texas Almanac by Edward Kasparik, manager, Rail Projects, Texas Railroad Commission.

Transportation was a problem facing Texas from the beginning of its economic development. The state had great resources for the production of freight tonnage, yet had no navigable rivers of consequence. Early Texas leaders were quick to appreciate this problem and, as early as the days of the Republic, there was great enthusiasm for railroad construction.

The Republic and the State of Texas both subsidized railroad building by land grants totaling 32,153,878 acres. There were also some local subsidies aimed at obtaining rail connections. Because of the instability of the Republic, the Civil War and Reconstruction, however, railroad building was slow until the 1870s, when a boom began. Construction continued with alternating rapid and slow developments until a peak of 17,078.29 miles was reached in 1932. Line abandonments have now reduced total mileage to less than 12,000 miles.

Earliest Texas Railroad Projects

Within six years after steam-powered railroads began operating in the United States, the Republic of Texas made a first gesture toward building one. But not until seven years after Texas had become one of the United States was this accomplished.

During its lifetime, the Republic issued four railroad charters, none of which resulted in a working railroad. The first charter, issued by the Republic on Dec. 16, 1836, was the first railroad charter west of the Mississippi. The Texas Railroad, Navigation and Banking Company (TRRN&B) was authorized to construct a continuous transport route from the Rio Grande to the Sabine River, using a combination of railroad and canal. Its incorporators included two senators of the Republic, four representatives, a founder of the city of Houston, a merchant-banker and Stephen F. Austin, the "Father of Texas," all men of the highest integrity. The charter passed the House almost without debate, passed the Senate without a recorded vote, and was signed by Texas President Sam Houston two days later.

Then unpopularity caught up with it. A letter from one congressman to another became public, boasting privileges in the charter "beyond arithmetical calculation." Newspaper opposition developed, a candidate was elected to Congress on his pledge to get rid of the company, and, as a final stroke, the prospective sale in the United States of $1,025,000 in company stock was blocked by the financial panic of May 1837. When this stock was offered in Houston, only $86,000 in Texas paper money was raised.

The provisions of the TRRN&B charter were not unusual or irregular. Free transportation of soldiers and war munitions was required, as was a tax of 2 percent on the net profit. The company was given the right to purchase private land by eminent domain and to take possession of public lands to a depth of a half mile on either side of the right of way.

Construction was to begin after the bank went into operation, and to establish the bank a bonus of $25,000 in gold or silver was required to be paid to the Republic within 18 months. This limitation would end June 16, 1838, and when the bonus was proffered on June 5 in Texas paper money, it was refused by the Treasurer of the Republic, with the support of the attorney general.

Thus the charter was violated, and the first effort to build a railroad in Texas ended. Public opinion was troubled by the pitiful outcome, and fervor was dampened by the continued financial depression in the United States. But hope for a railroad did not die.

Galveston, Harrisburg and Houston Compete

The Republic issued its second railroad charter on May 24, 1838, to the Brazos and Galveston Railroad Company, to connect Galveston with the rich agricultural lands of the Brazos River valley by means of railroads, roads and later, through charter amendments, by canals. Bank privileges were prohibited. A 150-foot right of way was granted across public domain at the minimum land price. Rates were limited to 2 cents per hundredweight-mile; soldiers and war munitions would be carried free; the charter would forfeit upon failure to build 10 miles within four years.

The financing for the Brazos and Galveston Railroad was never accomplished, but it stimulated action in the rival town of Houston, now itself a seaport through navigation via Buffalo Bayou. To its citizens, including some promoters of the defunct TRRN&B, the Republic issued its third railroad charter Jan. 26, 1839, in the name of the Houston and Brazos Rail Road Company. Its provisions resembled those of the B&G RR Co., but without canals; allowed a 300-foot right of way at no cost; set no freight rates or free army transportation; permitted tolls after 10 miles of turnpike were finished; required work to start within 18 months and be finished within seven years; and called for a down payment of $5 per share for capital stock, and a stockholders' meeting to elect officers after 1,000 shares were sold.

The stockholders' meeting was held on Dec. 29, 1839. Directors and officers were elected, a 10-mile contract was let on May 6, 1840, and advertisements for laborers were published. On July 25 elaborate ground-breaking ceremonies were held, with a parade of Masons Odd-Fellows, the Milam Guards and the citizenry. No evidence, however, has ever been found of any actual construction. The abandonment of the project has been attributed to the threat of a Mexican invasion.

Andrew Briscoe's Project

The fourth charter issued by the Republic was based on a realistic foundation. Andrew Briscoe of Harrisburg was a signer of the Texas Declaration of Independence and a veteran of the War of Independence. In 1836, the Congress of the Republic appointed him chief justice of the town of Harrisburg. This town was a strong business rival of its close neighbor, Houston, to the northwest and Galveston, 50 miles south. Ships navigating up Buffalo Bayou reached Harrisburg before the town of Houston, and Briscoe planned to go after the Brazos River valley trade in competition with both of his larger neighbors. He used the unincorporated name of Harrisburg & Brazos Railroad, and on Feb. 28, 1840, signed a contract for 3,000 hardwood cross ties, and for grading the roadbed.

To carry forward his plan, Briscoe advertised the sale of town lots for the benefit of the railroad, and for 50 black men to work on the grading. His ultimate plan was to build to the Pacific Ocean by way of El Paso, financing the work by town-lot sales along the route.

The Republic issued its fifth railroad charter on Jan. 9, 1841, to incorporate Briscoe's project as the Harrisburg Railroad and Trading Company (the word "trading" presumably to allow for the sale of town lots).

Similar to its two predecessors, it provided for a railroad from the head of navigation on Buffalo Bayou at Harrisburg to the Brazos River valley. Imported engines and supplies for the railroad were to be duty-free. It was given no right of way, freight rates and capital-stock sales were unregulated, and railroad transportation was authorized. Construction was required to begin within 18 months, and 30 miles of track were to be completed within five years. The issuing of exchange bills or promissory notes for general circulation was prohibited.

About two miles of grading were completed, but a deadly stagnation of business because of Mexican threats, accentuated by the two-day and four-day occupations of San Antonio by the Mexican army in September 1842, and the financial depression in the United States, forced work to stop. Grading was not resumed until after Texas had entered the Union. Although Briscoe did not live to see the outcome, his project was eventually carried through after the Civil War much as he planned — down to the transcontinental extension to California.

First Railroad to Operate in Texas

Texas' first operating railroad was the successor to Andrew Briscoe's project. Gen. Sidney Sherman, veteran of the Texas War of Independence, associated himself with Briscoe, bought his 1,272 unsold town lots and 3,617 adjoining acres on March 30, 1847. Sherman then took the idea of a railroad to Boston, Mass., his earlier home, and secured financial support. On Oct. 31, 1847, he entered into an agreement that was incorporated in Massachusetts as the Harrisburg City Company.

The Texas Legislature issued a charter to the Buffalo Bayou, Brazos and Colorado Railway Company on Feb. 11, 1850, to implement the project developed in Boston. The same legislative act also authorized the City of Houston to build a branch railway to connect with the BBB&C. No provision was made for the use of public domain land. Passenger fares were limited to 5 cents per mile, freight rates to 50 cents per hundredweight for every 100 miles, and the price for carrying the mails was to be regulated by the state.

By amendment on Jan. 29, 1853, the Legislature granted the BBB&C eight sections of land for every mile of railroad completed, the first railroad land grant in Texas. Grading began in June 1851 at Harrisburg. A locomotive, the "General Sherman," arrived in Galveston by ship in November 1852, and 20 miles of track were completed and in operation to Stafford's Point by Aug. 22, 1853. This is the pioneer railroad of Texas. The BBB&C reached the Brazos River at Richmond in December 1855, and on to Alleyton, 80 miles from Harrisburg and only a few miles short of the Colorado River at Columbus, in April 1861.

Houston and Texas Central

The Galveston & Red River, begun in 1853, was Texas' second railroad. Originally promoted by Galveston men, it was taken over by Houston interests and the named changed on Sept. 1, 1856, to Houston and Texas Central Railway Company. Before the outbreak of the war, 80 miles had been completed northward from Houston to Millican, near the Brazos River.

Washington County's Railroad

Another railroad, the Washington County Rail Road Company, chartered Feb. 2, 1856, later made a part of the H&TC, was built by Washington County farmers and merchants from Hempstead to Brenham (21 miles) in 1859-1861.

San Antonio Project

The coastal railroad projects threatened the trade of inland San Antonio. That city's citizens, led by S. A. Maverick, secured a charter on Sept. 5, 1850, for the San Antonio and Mexican Gulf Railroad to run from Port Lavaca or any other point on the Gulf to San Antonio. Twenty-eight miles were completed to Victoria early in 1861, but the line was practically destroyed in December 1862, by Confederate Gen. John B. Magruder to prevent the federal army, then threatening the coast near Port Lavaca, from using it. It was rebuilt by the U.S. Army in 1865-66 and was sold in 1870 to satisfy a claim of the United States government for this expense.

Galveston Reacts

Galveston, concerned over Houston's aggressive railroad activity, secured a charter for the Galveston, Houston and Henderson Railroad Company on Feb. 7, 1853. Islanders began laying track in 1856, from Virginia Point on the mainland to the outskirts of Houston, and building a bridge across the bay into the island city for a total length of 48 miles by 1866.

Sugar Bowl Rail

None of these Houston and Galveston projects helped the planters of Brazoria County, then the richest in the state, nor Matagorda, Colorado and Wharton counties, collectively known as the "sugar bowl." They decided to build their own railroad from Columbia to Houston, the Houston Tap & Brazoria, chartered on Sept. 1, 1856, and completed by Dec. 1, 1859. The charter provided for a line extending to the Rio Grande; 50 miles to East Columbia were in service when the war broke out. The HT&B embraced the Houston Tap Railroad, built in 1857 by a bond issue voted by Houston, to connect that city with the BBB&C at Pierce Junction. A year after completion it was sold to the planters at a $42,000 profit.

"Defense" Road

The Sabine & Galveston Bay Railroad & Lumber Company was chartered Sept. 1, 1856, but no work had been done up to 1859 and probably none would have been done then but for a resolution adopted on Sept. 1 of that year by the Louisiana legislature. Addressed to the Legislature of Texas, the resolution called attention to the project, stressing its strategic importance in the event of civil war then impending, and authorized the road to build from the Sabine River eastward to the Mississippi River under the name of the Texas and New Orleans Railroad Company, Louisiana division. The Texas Legislature approved the plan. The company had no trouble raising funds and the road was completed from Houston to Orange, 106 miles, by Jan. 1, 1861, but only 45 miles were ready in Louisiana. The gap was not filled until after the war.

Coast Road

The next road built along the coast before the war was the Eastern Texas Railroad. Sabine Pass in those days was a thriving port. Beaumont was also becoming a city. Since 1852 both had been trying to get a railroad to extend northward from the Gulf through the East Texas Piney Woods to the Red River. Finally on Jan. 21, 1858, this road was chartered. By 1861, 25 miles of track was built between the two cities. Another 25 miles were graded north from Beaumont, but never operated. Dick Dowling used the iron rails to erect a fort at Sabine Pass, which enabled his little band of 41 Confederates to withstand bombardment and to disperse a strong federal fleet with heavy loss in September 1863.

Early North Texas Roads

The other two railroads constructed before the Civil War were in North Texas, which by the 1850s had attracted many immigrants. Jefferson and Clarksville, the largest communities, were the centers of heavy freighting by wagon and river shipping. This section clamored for railroads and wanted to be on the route of the Southern Transcontinental Road, which all Texas then thought would be built through the state.

Two roads were projected as parts of the plan. The first was the Texas Western, chartered Feb. 16, 1852. It built 20 miles of railroad from the head of navigation on Caddo Lake towards Marshall. In 1856, the Legislature renewed the charter and changed the name to the Southern Pacific Railroad. (This has no connection with the present Southern Pacific Lines.) A little more line was built (totaling 27.5 miles operated) and 25 more miles graded when the war broke out. Gen. Magruder took up about 15 miles of the rails and relaid track toward Shreveport, using it for transporting war materials. The other road was the Memphis, El Paso & Pacific, chartered Feb. 7, 1853, to build across the state. Before the war began they had graded 57 miles but had only six miles in operation from Caddo Lake to Jefferson.

Indianola Railroad

The Indianola Railroad was chartered Jan. 21, 1858, to build 15 miles to connect the then-thriving port city of Indianola with the SA&MG. The grading was done and ties on hand, but they were destroyed in 1862 to prevent the federal military forces then threatening the coast from using them. The road was finally completed in 1871, but Indianola was heavily damaged by a hurricane in 1875 and destroyed by another in 1886. The city was abandoned, and track was taken up.

By 1861, 10 Railroads and 500 Miles of Track

At the outbreak of the Civil War in 1861, there were 10 railroads operating on almost 500 miles of track in Texas. Virtually all were focused on Houston, which was the rail center of Texas.

When the war ended in 1865, all 10 railroads were bankrupt, with roadbed and equipment sadly deteriorated. It would be several years before most were able to begin rebuilding or any new ones were undertaken. One exception — the Houston & Texas Central — resumed construction in 1867, reaching Dallas in 1872 (the first railroad to do so) and Denison in 1873.

Railroad Boom Begins in the 1870s

By 1870, however, it looked as if Texas were in for an era of railroad building. Money and confidence were plentiful. The BBB&C, reorganized as the Galveston, Harrisburg & San Antonio, was preparing for extension westward towards the Alamo City. The GH&SA finally rolled into San Antonio to great fanfare and celebration on February 16, 1877.

The Texas & Pacific Railway was on its way to El Paso, the H&TC was pushing northward, and the International & Great Northern was about to begin construction. These lines and others did build more than 5,000 miles during the 1870s and early 1880s. Then construction practically ceased for several reasons. One was the legislated reduction in passenger fares from 5 cents to 3 cents per mile; another was the repeal of the land grant act, both in 1882.

There were many roads under construction that had been financed in part by grants of lands. There was, however, no alternative for the state but to repeal the land grant act, because it had already issued certificates calling for about 8 million acres more state lands than there were state lands left to dispense.

Beginning of Railroad Regulation

Still another deterrent to railroad building was the rising tide of feeling over the abuses by the railroad managements and the resulting demand for more effective regulation. In the second railroad charter, for the Brazos & Galveston in 1838, the Republic had reserved the right to fix rates. All of the later charters fixed maximum rates for freight and passengers. In 1853, the state passed a comprehensive law regulating railroads, the first of its kind in the United States, although Texas at that time still had no operating railroad. A later supplement was adopted, but it did not deal with rates. Prior to the war, there were no complaints about rail rates because even the maximum, when charged, was so much less than the cost of "freighting" by wagon.

After the Civil War, the roads were criticized for allegedly excessive and discriminatory rates and other abuses, but they were powerful enough to prevent any punitive laws or stricter rate regulation. The Grange, which in 1872 had over 40,000 members in Texas, forced a constitutional convention in 1875 which required the Legislature to pass laws "to correct abuses and prevent unjust discriminations and extortion in rates of freight and passenger tariffs and to enforce all such laws by adequate penalties."

Establishment of Railroad Commission

One leader calling for regulation was Attorney General James Stephen Hogg. Railroad regulation

Amtrak Passengers On/Off at Texas Stations, 1988-1994

City	1994	1993	1992	1991	1990	1989	1988
Alpine	2,746	2,873	2,312	1,718	1,754	2,008	1,720
Austin	13,211	20,290	19,633	22,795	18,913	11,973	15,621
Beaumont	2,362	2,671	2,945	3,026	3,677	4,058	5,010
Cleburne	859	1,865	2,350	2,845	3,579	1,939	2,302
College Station-Bryan	4,287	10,603	10,687	10,582	8,370	7,090	—
Corsicana	889	1,985	2,110	2,141	2,380	3,143	—
Dallas	46,139	74,680	69,062	76,695	64,350	54,982	33,035
Del Rio	1,444	1,245	1,122	1,136	1,235	1,745	1,598
El Paso	22,099	22,193	19,300	18,591	19,676	22,656	26,516
Fort Worth	12,577	21,773	22,607	23,926	23,623	14,049	15,565
Hearne	289	374	—	—	—	—	—
Houston	35,274	50,332	48,480	55,297	47,514	45,370	22,151
Longview	7,556	11,429	10,426	11,431	9,519	7,069	6,759
Marshall	4,870	7,985	8,389	8,349	6,901	4,537	4,203
McGregor	1,692	3,203	2,670	3,202	3,099	1,955	2,308
San Antonio	38,839	51,730	46,217	48,667	43,186	22,691	31,272
San Marcos	1,264	2,067	1,805	2,541	2,211	1,621	2,652
Sanderson	365	313	297	380	413	952	665
Taylor	1,617	3,317	3,214	4,596	4,626	3,723	4,732
Temple	4,033	8,155	6,994	7,478	7,495	5,191	5,958
Texarkana	5,843	8,334	—	—	—	—	—
Totals	208,255	307,417	280,620	305,396	272,521	216,752	182,067

Source: Texas Railroad Commission, 1995.

was an active issue in state politics during these years, and it was the leading issue in 1890 when Hogg was elected governor on a platform calling for a constitutional amendment to authorize the creation of a Railroad Commission. The amendment was approved by the people and the commission was created April 3, 1891. The Texas Railroad Commission was patterned after the Interstate Commerce Act of 1887. U.S. Senator John H. Reagan, who had long been an advocate of both state and interstate commissions and had been involved in framing both plans, resigned his seat in the Senate to accept the chairmanship, which he held until his death on March 6, 1905. At first, commissioners were appointed by the governor, but by constitutional amendment in 1894, the three commissioners were made elective.

After 1890, slow but steady railroad building continued at the rate of 300 or 400 miles a year until World War I. After 1914 there was little new construction until 1925, when the Santa Fe, Rock Island and Fort Worth & Denver railroads began building into the South Plains, as did the Southern Pacific into the Lower Rio Grande Valley.

The Texas Almanac of 1931 contains an interesting article with a detailed map of then new, as well as anticipated, railroad lines. At that time, just before the Depression had fully set in in the Lone Star State, Texas ranked first among the states in track mileage, and continued to lead in new construction. Between 1925 and 1932, more than 1,000 miles of main-line rail were laid, predominantly on the high South Plains of the Panhandle where the new lines battled for grain, cattle and oil. Santa Fe completed the famous "Orient" route between the Midwest and Mexico by closing the United States' remaining gap between Alpine and Presidio. Southern Pacific provided a long-awaited extension into the Lower Rio Grande Valley, where fruit and vegetable growers welcomed the competitive service.

Ultimately, even this state's robust economy fell victim — and with it, new construction of all types, but especially railroads. The 1932 total of 17,078 main-line miles would later prove to be the state's all-time peak. The extent of steel rails would forever decline as many small railroads and branch lines were formally abandoned after petitions to the U.S. Interstate Commerce Commission had been approved. By 1941, when the United States entered World War II, the railroads of Texas had retrenched and more than a few small communities had lost all rail service. Highways and motor vehicles were increasingly the mode of choice.

World War II and the Postwar Years

Pearl Harbor changed everything. In retrospect, World War II was the rail industry's shining moment. Texas was blessed with lots of space, good weather, and deep-water ports. The result was an influx of new military bases, war-production factories, and record traffic of nearly 166 million tons of freight moved on Texas railroads during 1944.

Post-war prosperity was initially shared by the railroad industry as steam locomotives gave way to more efficient diesels and worn-out passenger trains were replaced with new "streamliners" named Eagle, Sunset or Chief. Large rail-served industrial districts were built in Dallas, Arlington and Houston. In the late 1950s, however, freight tonnage was at the same level as in 1944, and passenger traffic had fallen to less than 10 percent of wartime highs. Mileage continued to decline and railroad employment in the state was reduced by 10,000. The only main-line construction was Santa Fe's 50-mile-long entry into Dallas from Denton.

Problem years in the 1960s and 1970s

The 1960s and 1970s were difficult decades for the rail industry of the United States. Texas carriers reflected the pressures of a transportation system increasingly oriented to trucks and autos on interstate highways. But the state's railroads fared better than their counterparts in the Midwest or Northeast of the United States. Heavy, bulk commodities such as grain, chemicals, crushed rock and coal, moving to and from larger but fewer rail-served business locations, became characteristic. Track maintenance standards often declined in short-sighted attempts to minimize operating costs during a time of very low rates of return on invested capital. Total track length fell by 1,878 miles from 1960 to 1979 as Texas line abandonments increased. The industry sought increased operating efficiencies by merging into larger companies: In 1976, the historic Texas & Pacific Railway was merged into the Missouri Pacific Railroad.

The few remaining passenger trains in 1971 were absorbed into the National Railroad Passenger Corporation, better known as "Amtrak." Amtrak instituted only three routes serving 20 Texas communities as part of a sparse national network.

Railroading in the 1980s and 1990s

Observers of Texas railroading during the decades of the 1980s and early 1990s witnessed the disappearance by merger of the well-known Missouri-Kansas-Texas Railroad, the sale of the Southern Pacific railroad, some additional Amtrak passenger service, the promise — but not the reality — of new high-speed passenger trains, the sale of much urban freight trackage, further declines in track mileage, many line abandonments, and the creation of numerous new "short-line" railroads. Passage of the federal Staggers Act in 1980 essentially removed most economic regulation of the industry by government at both the federal and state levels. The Staggers Act was a precursor to major (some would say revolutionary) change in the railroad's ability to compete with trucks and pipelines.

"Katy" Railroad Merged into the Union Pacific

In November 1986 the Union Pacific Railroad system applied to the U.S. Interstate Commerce Commission (ICC) for approval to acquire by merger the Missouri-Kansas-Texas Railroad (the M-K-T or Katy). In May 1988, the ICC handed down a favorable decision. The famous Katy, a well-known institution in Texas since 1880, disappeared into the huge Union Pacific.

Southern Pacific and Cotton Belt Railroads Sold

A proposed merger of the Southern Pacific and the Santa Fe (Atchison, Topeka & Santa Fe Railway) was rejected by the ICC in June 1987. In 1988, the large but financially troubled Southern Pacific plus subsidiary St. Louis Southwestern Railway (known as the "Cotton Belt"), were sold to Rio Grande Industries, parent company of Colorado-based Denver and Rio Grande Western Railroad.

Improved Amtrak Passenger Service

Amtrak's "Texas Eagle" between Chicago, St. Louis and San Antonio (via Dallas/Fort Worth and Austin) became a daily operation in June 1990. At the same time, Amtrak re-established service (also daily) into Houston from Dallas and Chicago by running a Texas Eagle connection between Dallas and Houston over Southern Pacific tracks. Unfortunately, budgetary pressures have since returned both Eagles to tri-weekly only scheduling. The "Sunset Limited" continues tri-weekly runs between Florida and California by way of Houston, San Antonio, Del Rio and El Paso.

Non-Amtrak passenger developments have included weekend rail service between Houston and Galveston and the initiation of a dinner train between San Antonio and Hondo. By summer 1994, both trains had stopped running. A steam-powered excursion train from Cedar Park (near Austin) to Burnet is in seasonal, weekend operation as is the Texas State Railroad from Palestine to Rusk. Others are being planned.

High-Speed Trains

Far removed from the likes of Amtrak and dinner trains was the Texas TGV, a proposed high-speed (200 mph max) passenger train. This sleek train was to be constructed and operated by a consortium of United States, French and Canadian companies over a new, double-tracked, electrified rail line between Dallas and Houston and between Dallas, Austin and San Antonio. Texas TGV planned to use an improved version of the French "TGV Atlantique" train, holder of the world speed record of 320 mph. The Texas TGV high-speed rail consortium possessed a 50-year franchise from the State of Texas and was responsible for financing, constructing, operatin, and maintaining the estimated $8.4 billion system, using private sources of funding. No state-appropriated funds were permitted. After failing to meet a required initial commitment of $170 million by December 1993, Texas TGV agreed in 1994 that the franchise was terminated.

Urban Rail Transit

Other passenger rail developments under way in Texas include urban rail transit systems in Dallas (and perhaps Houston and Austin) using former rail-freight right-of-way. Over the past several years, Dallas Area Rapid Transit (DART) has purchased from Union Pacific, Santa Fe, and Southern Pacific much of the rail network in the greater Dallas area.

DART is transforming these routes into a modern light-rail system and will continue to provide local shippers located on some lines with freight service at night.

Short-Line Railroads

Many line sales or leases have been made during the 1980s and 1990s to companies starting new short-line railroads. These spin-offs of light-density branch lines by large Class 1 carriers have become alternatives to the abandonment of otherwise economically marginal rail properties. The resulting Class 3 carriers often provide a lower-cost operation that better meets the needs of shippers and communities.

The newest Class 3 short-line railroads in Texas include: Cen-Tex Rail Link from Fort Worth to Brownwood (ex-Santa Fe trackage); Dallas, Garland & Northeastern Railroad (ex-MKT trackage) from Garland to Trenton; Fort Worth and Western Railroad (formerly Burlington Northern) within the Fort Worth area; Gulf, Colorado & San Saba Railway between Lometa and Brady (ex-Santa Fe); Panhandle Northern Railroad from Panhandle to Borger (ex-Santa Fe); Rio Valley Switching Company from Harlingen to Mission (ex-MoPac); South Orient Railroad between Brownwood and Presidio (ex-Santa Fe); South Plains Lamesa Railroad Company (ex-Santa Fe) from Slayton to Lamesa; Seagraves, Whiteface and Lubbock Railroad (ex-Santa Fe) from Lubbock to Seagraves; Southern Switching Company (ex-BN) from Wichita Falls to Abilene; Texas & Oklahoma Railroad between Chillicothe and Maryneal (ex-Santa Fe); Texas Northeastern (ex-MoPac) from Texarkana to Sherman; Texas, Gonzales & Northern Railway between Harwood and Gonzales (ex-SP); and the Wichita, Tillman and Jackson (ex-MKT) from Wichita Falls to Altus, Okla.

Abandonments Continue; Tonnage is Up

Abandonments have continued occurring in the 1990s on the weakest branches of Class I carriers - especially Southern Pacific — even as the better branch lines have been transformed into independent short-line railroads. Total track mileage continues falling, but Texas easily retains first place among all states. The reduced network of track in Texas is actually carrying ever increasing freight tonnage. During 1993 and first half of 1994, the rail industry nationwide experienced what some characterize as a renaissance. Especially notable increases in carloadings are evident in Texas traffic with Mexico and in intermodal movements of containers over long distances on railroad flatcars. A few, not many, rail corridors are showing signs of constrained capacity, and improvements must be made in signaling or additional trackage. ☆

Railroads Changed the Face of Texas

When railroads spanned the Lone Star State, they hastened the end of cattle drives, as they brought the railheads close to the ranches where the cattle were raised.

With their speedy delivery of produce and reasonable freight rates, the railroads changed agriculture from self-contained subsistence farming to a major industry. But they did more than bring easy and inexpensive access to swift transportation to the Texas countryside. They profoundly changed the face of the state.

In the eastern part of the United States, railroad tracks were laid from one population center to the next. But in the sparsely settled Texas of the 1870s and 1880s, it was too expensive to zigzag across the landscape from one tiny settlement to another. The Texas & Pacific made a beeline westward across the plains; the Houston and Texas Central sprouted northward at the same time. And many smaller railroads operated in their own districts, serving as feeders to the major lines.

As railroad construction crews hammered their way across the vast stretches of sparsely populated miles, towns sprouted in their wakes.

Some towns developed from the seeds of temporary railroad camps. When the crews moved on down the line, businesses that had sprung up to serve the workers often stayed in place, serving the settlers that inevitably followed the trains.

Many small towns that were bypassed by the gleaming rails dried up and disappeared within a few years.

To prevent premature death, some bypassed towns pulled up and moved to the rail line.

Some existing towns, whose residents felt blessed by the arrival of the railroad, changed their names to honor railroad officials. Sometimes local residents who helped lure railroads through towns by donating land for right of way or for depot sites were rewarded by the renaming of the town for them.

Belle Plain in Callahan County is one of the towns that died. Belle Plain boasted a number of businesses and a college with a three-story main building when it was voted the county seat in 1877. Then the T&P laid its tracks about six miles north of Belle Plain in 1881. Some of the town's businesses moved to the rails, and soon enough people had collected in that spot to form the town of Baird. When enough of Belle Plain's residents had abandoned it, the county's residents voted to move the county seat to Baird. The county jail in Belle Plain was dismantled stone-by-stone and rebuilt in Baird. Belle Plain withered, and the college finally closed in 1892. Ruins of some of the buildings on private ranchland are all that is left of the once-thriving village.

Another community abandoned by its citizens because the railroad bypassed it was Queen's Peak in Montague County. The railroad came through the area about four miles south of Queen's Peak in 1882, when the town already had seven stores, a livery stable, a hotel, a school, a church and plans for building a health resort. The town of Bowie was established on the railroad, and most Queen's Peak citizens bailed out for Bowie soon after.

Belgrade in southeastern Newton County, a thriving river port on the Sabine River established in 1840, was almost made the county seat in the mid-1850s. But when the railroad bypassed it, shifting the population, Belgrade declined and is today only a tiny community.

Sweetwater, on the other hand, moved and survived. In 1877, Billie Knight opened a store in a dugout on the banks of Sweetwater Creek to sell supplies to bison hunters. By March 1879, there was a settlement with a post office, and in 1881, the growing town became the temporary county seat of Nolan County. When the T&P laid its tracks two miles to the northwest in 1882, the citizens picked up Sweetwater and moved it to the railroad.

The small town of Celina in Collin County is another that saved itself by moving. Celina was named in 1881 by its first postmaster for his home in Tennessee. In 1902, the St. Louis and San Francisco Railroad bypassed Celina about one mile north; Celina saved itself by moving to the tracks.

One town not only moved, it also changed its name because of the railroad. The town of Booker was originally in Oklahoma, and its name was La Kemp. When the Panhandle and Santa Fe Railroad arrived in the area in 1919, the town moved to the tracks, which were across the state line and changed its name to Booker, to honor B.F. Booker, a civil engineer with the railroad company. Booker is now on the border between Lipscomb and Ochiltree counties in Texas

As the Texas & Pacific Railway headed for the West Coast, laying track at the rate of about a mile a day, it established construction camps every 30 to 60 miles. The list of railroad-spawned towns along the route of the T&P in West Texas includes Gordon, Eastland, Abilene, Colorado City, Big Spring, Midland, Odessa, Monahans and Pecos.

Towns also sprouted along the routes of the smaller railroads. A couple of them are Wells and Lott.

Wells, in southern Cherokee County, about 16 miles north of Lufkin, was established when the Kansas and Gulf Short Line Railroad Co. laid tracks through the area. It was named for Maj. E. H. Wells, a railroad engineer.

Lott, named for Uriah Lott, president of the San Antonio and Aransas Pass Railway, was established in 1890 on a tract of land purchased by the Texas Townsite Co. of Waco to furnish right of way for the railroad. Lott is in Falls County, about 27 miles south of Waco on U.S. 77 and State Highway 320.

Buckholts in Milam County was established in 1881 when the Gulf, Colorado and Santa Fe arrived. John A. Buckholts donated the right of way and a townsite of 113 acres; he was honored in the naming of the town.

The present-day town of Moore in northeastern Frio County, about 40 miles southwest of San Antonio, was originally named Moore Hollow when it was settled in 1873. When the International and Great Northern Railroad (I&GN) arrived in 1880, the town's name was changed to Moore's Station. Today, with the railroad gone, the name is just "Moore."

These examples were repeated many times over: The railroads spread their network of tracks across the Lone Star State, and as they went, the face of Texas changed. The locations and names of towns — even their very existence — was forever altered by the coming of the shining rails. ☆

Statistical History of Railroad Operation in Texas, 1891-1993

The table below shows development and trends of railroad line operations, freight tonnage, operating revenues and expenses in Texas since the Railroad Commission's first report.

Year	Average Miles Operated Including Trackage Rights	Tons Revenue Freight	Railway Operating Revenues	Railway Operating Expenses	Operating Ratio	*Net Revenue From Railway Operations	Amounts per mile operated: Freight Revenue	Amounts per mile operated: Passenger Revenue	Amounts per mile operated: Net From Operations	Freight Revenue Per Ton Mile
1993	10,430	283,533,150	$2,265,753,000	$1,793,032,000	80.93	$472,721,000	$201,524.00	. . .	$39,667.00	$.0260
1992	10,522	270,172,326	2,213,517,000	1,786,709,000	87.60	426,808,000	188,872.00	. . .	30,633.00	.0276
1991	11,396	262,484,463	2,110,479,000	1,886,405,000	89.40	223,975,000	162,630.00	. . .	8,700.00	.0260
1990	11,541	253,778,285	2,061,579,000	1,709,369,000	89.00	352,210,000	161,178.00	. . .	22,984.00	.0270
1989	12,225	265,583,737	2,098,829,000	1,801,451,000	89.30	297,378,000	157,927.00	. . .	22,547.00	.0270

Year	Average Miles Operated Including Trackage Rights	Tons Revenue Freight	Railway Operating Revenues	Railway Operating Expenses	Operating Ratio	*Net Revenue From Railway Operations	Amounts per mile operated: Freight Revenue	Amounts per mile operated: Passenger Revenue	Amounts per mile operated: Net From Operations	Freight Revenue Per Ton Mile
1988	12,337	315,073,199	2,111,522,843	1,678,802,000	82.90	415,169,412	143,882.00	. . .	23,999.00	.0270
1987	12,683	299,473,842	1,908,188,000	1,528,948,000	82.70	379,334,000	141.430.00	. . .	27,820.00	.0250
1986	12,774	207,679,132	1,827,330,000	1,736,580,000	96.90	90,750,000	134,532.00	. . .	7,834.00	.0298
1985	12,860	217,096,477	2,026,001,000	1,713,245,620	83.90	312,755,380	148,040.00	. . .	26,816.00	.0300
†1980	13,075	268,445,039	2,064,108,000	1,761,650,000	85.34	304,742,000	151,918.00	. . .	23,310.00	.0268
1975	14,717	230,120,781	1,073,029,254	792,786,773	73.88	280,242,481	69,982.79	. . .	19,042.09	.0196
1970	14,683	211,069,076	655,638,834	504,146,691	76.89	151,492,143	42,245.42	170.71	10,317.52	.0134
1965	15,214	181,553,163	502,191,485	380,412,080	75.75	121,779,405	29,754.73	605.40	8,004.43	.0118
1960	15,445	149,360,161	438,531,081	347,353,628	79.21	91,177,453	26,149.41	937.69	5,903.36	.0121
1955	16,151	166,742,660	450,865,455	341,963,345	75.85	108,902,110	24,482.83	1,085.84	6,742.75	.0134
1950	16,296	155,970,914	420,864,968	310,731,697	73.83	210,133,271	22,021.66	1,366.76	6,758.30	.0132
1945	16,376	159,795,571	390,672,459	263,883,854	67.54	126,788,605	17,635.26	4,370.32	7,742.36	.0102
1940	17,057	69,107,695	144,124,269	110,626,057	76.76	33,498,212	7,028.74	944.72	1,963.85	.0106
1935	17,296	61,452,202	117,611,146	93,681,088	79.65	23,930,058	5,579.27	802.07	1,383.58	.0112
1930	17,569	88,942,552	204,371,667	152,169,952	74.46	52,201,715	9,557.06	1,739.55	2,971.24	.0123
1925	16,647	90,338,397	227,252,064	169,382,692	74.54	57,869,372	10,653.42	2,673.33	3,476.36	.0142
1920	16,383	77,803,926	235,353,895	234,718,643	99.73	635,252	9,714.47	4,291.77	38.77	.0139
1915	16,294	54,354,684	107,414,011	85,900,985	79.97	21,513,026	4,504.81	1,809.82	1,320.29	.0100
1910	14,339	47,084,828	94,731,430	72,524,020	76.56	22,207,410	4,601.92	1,981.27	1,548.72	.0103
1905	11,671	30,653,070	68,145,132	52,411,748	76.91	15,733,384	4,044.88	1,493.65	1,348.12	.0108
1900	9,971	22,380,607	47,062,868	35,626,922	75.70	11,435,946	3,537.81	1,106.78	1,167.98	.0096
1895	9,354	15,591,262	39,387,869	28,864,994	73.28	10,522,875	3,159.04	984.73	1,124.98	.0130
1891	8,719	10,944,195	35,666,498	28,762,836	80.64	6,903,662	2,956.58	1,081.59	791.83	.0146

*Net revenue before interest and taxes.
†No data available for Rock Island in 1979 and 1980.
Beginning in 1978, data no longer reported for Class II and III carriers.

Aviation in Texas

In 1945 the Texas Aeronautics Commission (TAC) was created by the Legislature to assist in the development of aeronautics within the state, and to encourage the establishment of airports and air navigational facilities. The commission's first annual report stated that Texas had 592 designated airports and 7,756 civilian aircraft.

On September 1, 1991, when the Texas Department of Transportation (TxDOT) was created the aviation agency became the Division of Aviation within the Department.

TxDOT Aviation Division reports that in 1994 Texas airports with scheduled passenger service enplaned more than 56 million passengers; and scheduled carriers served 29 Texas airports in 26 cities. This was an increase of almost 3 million passengers or 5.0 percent over 1993 figures.

According to Federal Aviation Administration data, **Texas leads the United States in aircraft departures** and ranks second after California in passengers enplaned by scheduled air carriers.

The Texas general-aviation fleet (all aircraft except military and commercial airlines) consisted of 20,508 registered aircraft as of December 31, 1993.

The proportion of the general-aviation fleet consisting of single-engine airplanes, planes associated with personal or pleasure flying, is decreasing, while the proportion of multi-engine airplanes, planes associated with business and executive transportation, is increasing.

Business continues to increase its use of general-aviation aircraft. Texas has 7.6 percent of the nation's registered aircraft, including 9 percent of the turbine-powered aircraft. The state's 50,194 active pilots represent 7.7 percent of the nation's pilots.

Over 91 percent of the state's population lived within 50 miles of an airport with scheduled air passenger service. Dallas/Forth Worth International, Dallas Love Field, Houston Intercontinental, and Houston's William P. Hobby together accounted for 82 percent of these enplanements.

Texas leads the nation in the number of landing facilities — 1,703 as of December 1992, followed by California with 920. These include 1,295 airports, 400 heliports and 8 stolports.

One of the goals of TxDOT is to develop a statewide system of airports that will provide adequate air access to the population and economic centers. The 307 airports identified by TxDOT in the Texas Aeronautical Facilities Plan are needed to meet the forecast aviation demand for the state and to maximize access by aircraft to the state's population, business activity, and agricultural production and mineral production value.

Of these 307 sites, 27 are commercial-service airports, 24 are reliever airports, 66 are transport airports, 128 are general-utility airports, and 63 are basic-utility airports.

The commercial-service airports provide scheduled passenger service.

The reliever airports provide alternative landing facilities in metropolitan are-as separate from the commercial-service airports and, together with the transport airports provide access for business and executive turbine-powered aircraft.

The general and basic-utility airports provide access for single- and multi-engined, piston-powered

Top Airports in Texas — 1993

DOT Certificated Air Carriers

Source: FAA

City	Aircraft Departures Performed	Percent of Total	Enplaned Passengers	Percent of Total
Dallas-Fort Worth	402,669	52	27,853,401	55
Houston	177,425	23	12,758,326	25
San Antonio	40,393	5	2,757,274	5
Austin	34,916	5	2,268,486	4
El Paso	29,870	4	1,771,047	4
Lubbock	11,307	1	588,130	1
Midland/Odessa	10,063	1	533,093	1
Corpus Christi	8,678	1	531,197	1
Brownsville-Harlingen-San Benito	8,200	1	454,419	1
Amarillo	6,454	1	423,600	1
Totals	**769,797**		**50,594,658**	

Airline Markets: Leading Domestic Routes, 1992

Rank, Route	Passengers
1. New York to-from Los Angeles	2.90 million
2. NY to-from Boston	2.35 million
3. NY to-from Chicago	2.33 million
4. NY to-from Washington	2.28 million
5. LA to-from San Francisco	2.15 million
6. NY to-from Miami	2.14 million
7. Dallas/Fort Worth to-from Houston	**2.09 million**
8. Honolulu to-from Maui	2.04 million
9. NY to-from San Francisco	2.01 million
10. NY to-from Orlando	1.73 million
. . . 24. NY to-from Dallas/Fort Worth	**1.03 million**

Source: Air Transport Assoc. of America, Washington, D.C., Air Transport 1993.

aircraft to smaller communities.

TxDOT plans improvement projects at approximately 256 general-aviation airports. In carrying out these responsibilities, TxDOT channels Airport Improvement Program (AIP) funds provided by the Federal Aviation Administration (FAA) for all general-aviation airports in Texas.

TxDOT's Aviation Facilities Development Program oversees research, assists with engineering and provides financial assistance through state grants and loans to public bodies for constructing, enlarging or repairing airports.

To administer the Aviation Facilities Development Program, the 73rd Legislature appropriated $8.5 million for the 1994-1995 biennium.

TxDOT's Aeronautical Services and Information Section provides training programs and safety information to individuals and groups who are involved or interested in aviation. ☆

Top States, 1993

DOT Certificated Air Carriers

Source: FAA

State	Aircraft Departures	Passenger Enplanements
Texas	**769,797**	**50,594,658**
California	709,104	56,729,242
Illinois	469,251	32,943,206
Florida	434,919	35,312,992
New York	353,960	23,067,095
Georgia	292,581	23,104,609

Passengers by Airport 1994

Source: Quarterly Aviation Activity Report, Texas Department of Transportation, Division of Aviation

This table shows passenger enplanements at Texas communities from reports filed by airport operators.

City	Enplanements
Abilene	74,121
Amarillo	433,442
Austin	2,549,651
Beaumont-Port Arthur	111,074
Brownwood	2,039
College Station	87,494
Corpus Christi	534,793
Dallas-Fort Worth Intl.	26,226,728
Dallas Love Field	3,412,858
El Paso	1,879,205
Harlingen	505,689
Houston Intercont.	11,323,220
Houston Hobby	4,079,553
Houston Ellington	982,217
Killeen	55,805
Laredo	101,211
Longview	37,520
Lubbock	611,495
McAllen	338,785
Midland	564,654
San Angelo	52,218
San Antonio	1,824,662
Sugar Land	20,008
Temple	4,272
Texarkana	45,976
Tyler	81,422
Victoria	20,448
Waco	52,862
Wichita Falls	62,160
Total	**56,075,582**

Texas Enplaned Traffic—1993

DOT Certificated Carriers

Source: FAA

This table shows airline traffic at Texas cities during calendar year 1993, as reported by the Federal Aviation Administration.

City	Aircraft Departures	Enplaned Passengers	Air Mail Tons	Cargo Tons
Scheduled and Non-scheduled Service				
Amarillo	6,454	423,600	681.81	264.02
Austin	34,916	2,268,486	4,159.90	19,425.50
Brownsville-Harlingen-San Benito	8,678	531,197	3.75	11,350.59
Corpus Christi	8,200	454,419	592.50	313.42
Dallas-Fort Worth	402,669	27,853,401	105,510.27	196,421.97
El Paso	29,870	1,771,047	2,166.14	13,254.39
Houston	177,425	12,758,326	23,601.42	87,080.79
Lubbock	11,307	588,130	455.48	7,703.67
Midland- Odessa	10,063	533,093	400.17	695.30
Mission-McAllen-Edinburg	3,476	40,457	5.38	344.25
San Antonio	40,393	2,757,274	9,720.02	18,438.93
Totals	769,797	50,594,658	148,048.45	363,652.71

Air Traffic History

Source: FAA

Airline passenger traffic enplaned in Texas by scheduled certificated carriers.

Year	Domestic	International	Total
1957	2,699,393	109,165	2,808,558
1973	11,954,536	276,325	12,230,861
1974	12,934,999	274,569	13,209,568
1975	12,918,790	264,248	13,182,957
1976	14,218,189	267,151	14,485,340
1977	15,595,237	275,910	15,871,147
1978	17,805,693	435,336	18,241,029
1979	20,966,571	580,223	21,546,794
1980	24,693,080	610,134	25,303,214
1981	26,853,393	596,087	27,449,480
1982	29,031,114	510,674	29,541,788
1983	30,291,548	561,749	30,853,297
1984	34,524,502	606,259	35,130,762
1985	38,152,612	760,415	38,913,027
1986	39,127,357	830,035	39,957,392
1987	40,391,079	1,102,146	41,493,225
1988	41,328,616	1,327,355	42,655,971
1989	43,848,662	1,499,295	45,348,326
1990	46,435,641	†	46,435,641
1991	45,825,027	†	45,825,027
1992	48,869,034	†	48,869,034
1993	50,594,658	†	50,594,658

*Fiscal year July 1 through June 30; all others are calendar years.

†Prior to 1990, data were reported as either domestic or international. Beginning with the 1991 Airport Activity Statistics report, domestic and international enplanement and departure numbers are combined.

Foreign and Domestic Commerce Through Major Texas Ports

Data in table below represent receipts and shipments for only the 13 major Texas ports in 1993. Total receipts and shipments for these 13 ports amounted to 345,236,254 tons. Total receipts and shipments for all Texas ports in 1993 was 361,017,695 tons.
Source: U.S. Army Corps of Engineers

(All figures in short tons)

Port	Total	Foreign		Domestic				
				Coastwise		Internal		Local
		Imports	Exports	Receipts	Shipments	Receipts	Shipments	
Sabine Pass	393,547	0	0	0	0	141,989	251,558	0
Orange	579,062	8	19,733	452,558	106,923	0	0	0
Beaumont	25,409,757	8,207,459	3,678,910	369,349	1,582,840	4,617,747	6,497,072	456,380
Port Arthur	38,326,902	28,044,238	4,416,130	95,995	595,961	1,908,578	3,080,074	185,925
Houston	141,476,979	51,466,146	25,701,648	3,295,158	10,562,761	21,560,504	16,005,218	12,905,544
Texas City	53,652,781	33,908,578	2,306,836	208,514	4,112,487	6,139,398	6,680,351	296,617
Galveston	9,755,324	1,428,360	4,518,723	344,506	1,300,107	1,506,535	649,502	7,591
Freeport	14,024,604	7,404,082	1,243,189	614,070	477,736	2,170,204	1,891,841	223,482
Corpus Christi	58,408,549	27,914,637	6,989,884	329,845	9,528,745	3,201,202	7,777,417	2,666,819
Port Isabel	239,370	154,025	85,345	0	0	154,025	85,345	0
Brownsville	1,734,526	330,166	66,884	0	56,619	1,188,217	53,010	9,073
Port Aransas (Harbor Island)	1,231,072	1,156,210	0	0	0	47,122	27,740	0
Port Mansfield	3,781	0	0	0	0	3,781	0	0
Grand Total	345,236,254	159,993,909	49,027,282	5,709,995	28,324,179	42,639,302	42,999,128	16,751,431

Tonnage Handled by Texas Ports, 1986-1993

Source: Corps of Engineers, U.S. Army

Table below gives consolidated tonnage handled by ports. All figures are in short tons (2,000 lbs.).

Ports	1993	1992	1991	1990	1989	1988	1987	1986
Brownsville	1,734,526	1,594,222	1,610,295	1,371,606	1,360,964	1,237,027	1,234,039	1,212,743
Port Isabel	239,370	234,401	247,455	269,174	263,335	318,466	298,789	291,713
Corpus Christi	58,408,549	58,678,726	56,973,650	60,165,497	58,440,714	56,310,445	51,239,602	48,053,926
Freeport	14,024,604	14,952,599	15,665,993	14,526,096	15,176,018	15,137,891	13,980,280	13,370,117
Galveston	9,755,324	12,317,599	10,858,221	9,619,891	11,837,611	12,354,709	8,684,216	7,987,857
Houston	141,476,979	137,663,612	131,513,521	126,177,627	125,583,156	124,886,883	112,546,187	101,659,064
Texas City	53,652,781	43,104,101	43,289,659	48,052,157	41,272,401	42,746,698	37,233,420	35,479,909
Sabine	393,547	418,927	499,817	631,157	726,141	1,248,308	722,151	385,202
Port Arthur	38,326,902	33,525,819	29,835,115	30,680,942	31,127,913	23,801,409	20,615,945	18,879,546
Beaumont	25,409,757	22,701,500	22,383,039	26,728,664	31,668,257	31,947,319	29,758,759	27,453,660
Orange	579,062	552,504	849,307	709,940	727,454	657,627	771,673	661,570
Port Lavaca	5,892,656	5,899,832	6,266,244	6,097,107	4,715,349	5,061,695	4,995,099	4,858,515
Anahuac	0	0	0	0	21,399	3,033	2,850	48,662
Moss Bluff	0	0	0	0	294,125	0	0	0
Channel to Liberty	0	2,800	20,987	0	4,791	4,433	0	0
Double Bayou	0	240	0	0	0	2,850	14,445	14,145
Cedar Bayou	349,680	302,824	217,692	219,206	308,807	275,458	247,093	275,900
Colorado River	536,811	505,198	577,379	476,300	618,147	682,328	693,885	571,818
Sweeny	718,118	684,274	477,370	534,406	529,648	480,519	360,272	324,528
Palacios	0	0	0	0	0	0	0	0
Dickinson	423,368	449,336	532,184	555,523	475,275	722,645	420,062	330,172
Aransas Pass	25,226	13,398	16,851	169,020	1,893	84,325	14,445	821
Port Mansfield	3,781	2,657	120	102	88	3,909	11,949	3,883
Harlingen	898,132	786,994	795,305	764,577	728,954	753,937	718,645	668,733
Channel to Victoria	3,937,400	4,265,228	3,407,884	3,740,374	3,142,614	3,562,336	3,655,454	3,078,476
Chocolate Byu.	3,715,107	3,343,072	3,469,030	3,462,762	3,278,422	3,526,758	2,750,380	2,874,357
Johnsons Bayou	515,957	567,298	596,247	715,917	765,454	839,594	0	0
Rockport	0	0	0	643,563	0	2,336	0	0
Clear Creek	66	0	0	0	0	0	0	0
Other Ports	0	0	0	0	0	0	614,273	388,265
TOTAL	361,017,695	390,567,161	330,103,365	335,311,608	330,068,930	326,652,938	291,583,913	268,873,582

Oil & Gas Exploration in Texas

Source: Texas Railroad Commission

Year(s)	Wells Completed	Oil Wells	Gas Wells	Stratigraphic & Core Tests	Service Wells	Dry Holes	Percent Dry
1889-1900*	97	71	2			24	24.7
1901-1910*	692	462	9			221	32.0
1911-1920*	2,451	1,682	66			703	28.7
1921-1930*	6,352	3,745	306			2,301	36.2
1931-1940*	9,915	7,404	288	...	...	2,224	22.9
1941-1950*	9,147	5,767	457	...	44	2,901	32.5
1951-1960*	18,439	10,838	814	...	155	6,632	36.0
1961-1970*	11,595	5,798	1,115	367	393	4,121	35.8
1971	7,728	3,880	810	8	449	2,581	33.4
1972	8,088	3,963	943	8	414	2,760	34.1
1973	8,494	3,686	1,475	34	362	2,937	34.6
1974	9,808	4,402	1,843	19	260	3,284	33.5
1975	12,483	6,074	2,135	36	361	3,877	31.1
1976	12,740	5,779	2,443	45	285	4,188	32.9
1977	14,759	6,533	3,064	37	443	4,682	31.7
1978	15,037	6,086	3,292	26	415	5,218	34.7
1979	16,149	6,765	3,609	35	515	5,225	32.4
1980	19,253	9,668	3,684	10	546	5,345	27.8
1981	23,940	13,052	3,807	2	368	6,711	28.0
1982	26,849	13,851	4,345	4	692	7,957	29.6
1983	24,616	13,102	3,317	...	652	7,545	30.6
1984	26,134	14,591	3,242	17	678	7,606	29.1
1985	18,882	11,206	2,215	...	666	5,461	28.9
1986	11,425	6,141	1,326	2	345	3,958	34.6
1987	10,797	5,504	1,589	...	365	3,704	34.3
1988	9,106	6,441	2,665	...	...	3,155	...
1989	8,590	4,003	1,758	...	528	2,380	...
1990	9,821	4,704	1,925	...	525	2,744	27.5
1991	9,848	5,051	1,786		543	2,515	25.5
1992	8,065	4,154	1,615		409	1,930	23.9
1993	8,277	3,724	2,220		365	2,028	24.5
1994	7,571	3,058	2,527		287	1,784	23.6

*Annual Averages.

A History of Oil in Texas

Oil and natural gas are the most valuable minerals produced in Texas, contributing 23 percent of the oil production and 24 percent of the gas production in the United States in 1993.

Oil and gas have been produced from most areas of Texas and from rocks of all geologic eras except the Precambrian.

All of the major sedimentary basins of Texas, have produced some oil or gas.

The well-known Permian Basin of West Texas has yielded large quantities of oil since 1921. It is an area of considerable promise for future production as well.

Although large quantities of petroleum have been produced from rocks of Permian age, production in the area also occurs from older Paleozoic rocks. Production from rocks of Paleozoic age occurs primarily from North Central Texas westward to New Mexico and southwestward to the Rio Grande, but there is also significant Paleozoic production in North Texas in Tarrant, Grayson and Cooke counties.

Mesozoic rocks are the primary hydrocarbon reservoirs of the East Texas Basin and the area south and east of the Balcones Fault Zone. Cenozoic sandstones are the main reservoirs along the Gulf Coast and offshore state waters.

Coal and lignite occur in rocks of Pennsylvanian, Cretaceous and Tertiary ages. Coal was produced in Texas from about 1850 to the 1940s, when petroleum became the common fuel.

Significant production of coal did not resume until the mid-1970s. Most of the pre-1940 production was **bituminous coal** from North Central Texas, an area near Eagle Pass or from near Laredo.

North Central Texas production was from Pennsylvanian rocks. Thurber, Newcastle and Bridgeport all had viable coal industries in the early 1900s. As early as 1850, soldiers from Fort Duncan near Eagle Pass are reported to have mined coal from the Cretaceous rocks.

Commercial mining of coal from Eocene rocks near Laredo began in 1881. In addition to the commercial mining, small amounts of coal occurring in the Trans-Pecos were used to roast the ore in mercury mining districts in the Big Bend.

Small amounts of "brown coal" or **lignite** have been produced throughout the history of the state. It was mined by many early settlers for family and small industry use. It was also used to generate "coal gas" or "producer gas" for Texas cities around the turn of the century.

Today, Texas ranks sixth nationally in coal production, and lignite accounts for most of this. Almost all of the lignite is consumed by mine-mouth electrical generating plants. Approximately 20 percent of the electricity generated in the state in 1990 was from plants fired by Texas lignite.

Uranium occurs in several widely separated Texas localities, but production has been limited to the Cenozoic sandstones along the coastal plains of south-central Texas, roughly from Karnes County southwest to Webb County.

The surface mines, active from 1959 to the mid-1970s, have largely been abandoned and reclaimed, and production today is all from in-situ leaching. This requires the injection of a leaching fluid into the uranium-bearing strata, reaction of the fluid with the uranium ore and return of the fluid to the surface for stripping of the uranium. The fluid is then re-used.

Indians found oil seeping from the soils of Texas long before the first Europeans arrived. They told explorers that the fluid had medicinal values. The first record of Europeans using crude oil, however, was the caulking of boats in 1543 by survivors of the **DeSoto expedition** near Sabine Pass.

Melrose, in Nacogdoches County, was the site in 1866 of the **first drilled well to produce oil** in Texas. The driller was **Lyne T. Barret** (whose name has been spelled several ways by historians). Barret used an auger, fastened to a pipe and rotated by a cogwheel driven by a steam engine — a basic principle of rotary drilling that has been used since, although with much improvement.

In 1867 **Amory (Emory) Starr** and **Peyton F. Edwards** brought in a well at **Oil Springs,** in the same area. Other wells followed and **Nacogdoches County** was the site of Texas' **first commercial oil field, pipeline and effort to refine crude.** Several thousand barrels of oil were produced there during these years.

Other oil was found in crudely dug wells in Texas, principally in Bexar County, in the latter years of the 19th century. But it was not until June 9, 1894, that Texas had a **major discovery**. This occurred in the drilling of a water well for the City of Corsicana. Oil caused that well to be abandoned, but a company formed in 1895 drilled several producing wells.

The first well-equipped refinery in Texas was built, and this plant usually is called the state's **first refinery,** despite the earlier effort at Nacogdoches. Discovery of the **Powell Field** near Corsicana followed in 1900.

Spindletop, 1901

Jan. 10, 1901, is the most famous date in Texas petroleum history. This is the date that the great gusher erupted in the oil well being drilled at **Spindletop,** near Beaumont, by a mining engineer, **Capt. A. F. Lucas.** Thousands of barrels of oil flowed before the well could be capped. This was the **first salt dome oil discovery**.

It created a sensation throughout the world, and encouraged exploration and drilling in Texas that has continued since.

Texas oil production increased from 836,039 barrels in 1900 to 4,393,658 in 1901; and in 1902 Spindletop alone produced 17,421,000 barrels, or 94 percent of the state's production. Prices dropped to 3c a barrel, an all-time low.

A water-well drilling outfit on the W. T. Waggoner Ranch in Wichita County hit oil, bringing in the **Electra Field** in 1911. In 1917, came the discovery of the **Ranger Field** in Eastland County. The **Burkburnett Field** in Wichita County was discovered in 1919.

Oil discoveries brought a short era of swindling with oil stock promotion and selling on a nationwide scale. It ended after a series of trials in a federal court.

The **Mexia Field** in Limestone County was discovered in 1920, and the **second Powell Field** in Navarro County in 1924.

Another great area opened in 1921 with discovery of oil in the **Panhandle,** a field which developed rapidly with sensational oil and gas discoveries in Hutchinson and contiguous counties and the booming of **Borger.**

The **Luling Field** was opened in 1922 and 1925 saw the comeback of Spindletop with a production larger than that of the original field. Other fields opened in this period included **Big Lake**, 1923; **Wortham**, 1924-25 and **Yates**, 1926.

In 1925 **Howard County** was opened for production. **Winkler** in West Texas and **Raccoon Bend**, Austin County, were opened in 1927. **Sugar Land** was the most important Texas oil development in 1928.

The **Darst Creek Field** was opened in 1929. In the same year, new records of productive sand thickness were set for the industry at **Van**, Van Zandt County. **Pettus** was another contribution of 1929 in Bee County.

East Texas Field

The **East Texas field**, biggest of them all, was discovered near Turnertown and Joinerville, Rusk County, by veteran wildcatter **C. M. (Dad) Joiner,** in October 1930. The success of this well — drilled on land condemned many times by geologists of the major companies — was followed by the biggest leasing campaign in history. The field soon was extended to Kilgore, Longview and northward. The East Texas field brought overproduction and a rapid sinking of the price. Private attempts were made to prorate production, but without much success.

On Aug. 17, 1931, **Gov. Ross S. Sterling** ordered the National Guard into the field, which he placed under **martial law.** This drastic action was taken after the **Texas Railroad Commission** had been enjoined from enforcing production restrictions. After the complete shutdown, the Texas Legislature enacted legal **proration,** the system of regulation still utilized.

The most significant subsequent oil discoveries in Texas were those in **West Texas**, following a discovery well in Scurry County, Nov. 21, 1948, and later major developments in that region. Many of the leading Texas counties in minerals value are in that section.

Major Fields

Texas fields with estimated ultimate recovery of 100 million barrels of oil or more are in the following list, which gives the name of the field, county and discovery date.

Data furnished by the **Oil and Gas Journal.**

Panhandle, Carson-Collingsworth-Gray-Hutchinson-Moore-Potter-Wheeler, 1910; **Thompson** (all fields), Fort Bend, 1921; **Howard-Glasscock,** Howard, 1925; **Iatan East,** Howard, 1926; **Yates,** Pecos, 1926; **Waddell,** Crane, 1927; **Van,** Van Zandt, 1929; **Ward Estes North,** Ward, 1929; **Cowden North,** Ector, 1930; **East Texas,** Gregg-Rusk, 1930; **Sand Hills,** Crane, 1930; **Conroe,** Montgomery, 1931; **Tom O'Connor**, Refugio, 1931; **Cowden South,** Ector, 1932; **Greta** (all fields), Refugio, 1933; **Tomball,** Harris, 1933; **Means** (all fields), **Andrews-Gaines**, 1934; **Anahuac**, Chambers, 1935; **Goldsmith** (all fields), Ector, 1935; **Hastings**, Brazoria, 1935; **Magnet Withers** (all fields), Wharton, 1936; **Seminole** (all fields), Gaines, 1936; **Webster**, Harris, 1936; **Jordan**, Crane-Ector, 1937; **Slaughter**, Cochran, 1937; **Wasson** (all fields), Gaines, 1937; **Dune**, Crane, 1938; **West Ranch**, Jackson, 1938; **Keystone**, Winkler, 1939; **Diamond M**, Scurry, 1940; **Hawkins**, Wood, 1940; **Fullerton** (all fields), Andrews, 1941; **McElroy**, Crane, 1941; **Oyster Bayou**, Chambers, 1941; **Welch**, Dawson, 1941; **Quitman** (all fields), Wood, 1942; **Anton-Irish**, Hale, 1944; **TXL** (all fields), Ector, 1944; **Block 31**, Crane, 1945; **Levelland**, Cochran-Hockley, 1945; **Midland Farms** (all fields), Andrews; 1945; **Andector**, Ector, 1946; **Dollarhide**, Andrews, 1947; **Kelly-Snyder**, Scurry, 1948; **Cogdell Area**, Scurry, 1949; **Prentice**, Yoakum, 1950; **Salt Creek**, Kent, 1950; **Spraberry Trend**, Glasscock-Midland, 1952; **Lake Pasture**, Refugio, 1953; **Neches**, Anderson-Cherokee, 1953; **Fairway**, Anderson-Henderson, 1960; **Giddings**, Lee-Fayette-Burleson, 1971.

Crude Oil and Condensate Production to Jan. 1, 1995

County	Year of Discovery	Production in Barrels* 1993	Production in Barrels* 1994	Total Production to Jan. 1, 1995
Anderson	1929	1,429,525	1,44,0405	288,800,485
Andrews	1930	33,532,772	32,606,975	2,508,051,974
Angelina	1936	4,816	5,030	447,012
Aransas	1936	902,034	876,367	80,911,371
Archer	1911	2,588,693	2,353,872	478,502,673
Atascosa	1917	921,167	830,024	142,550,085
Austin	1915	633,667	503,021	111,144,067
Bastrop	1913	840,573	295,663	14,679,246
Baylor	1924	243,401	277,085	56,274,013
Bee	1930	634,304	604,090	101,776,101
Bell	1980	0	0	446
Bexar	1889	353,409	296,722	34,078,563
Borden	1949	4,696,172	4,547,647	358,953,203
Bowie	1944	308,633	288,138	4,236,768
Brazoria	1902	3,776,775	3,537,054	1,241,690,510
Brazos	1942	10,426,281	8,431,926	107,987,382
Brewster	1969	0	0	56
Briscoe	1982	0	0	3,554
Brooks	1936	848,785	1,065,846	157,121,909
Brown	1917	279,045	228,786	51,736,684
Burleson	1938	8,669,457	8,189,028	147,495,363
Caldwell	1922	1,439,841	1,256,400	271,951,406
Calhoun	1935	1,124,020	1,098,715	97,120,642
Callahan	1923	750,624	802,066	82,599,420
Cameron	1944	3,569	3,244	445,773
Camp	1940	463,394	435,238	24,668,515
Carson	1921	656,002	586,116	175,497,639
Cass	1935	878,067	786,662	108,920,251
Chambers	1916	2,532,883	2,290,145	889,460,665
Cherokee	1926	587,990	532,674	67,229,013
Childress	1961	4,567	5,370	1,371,695
Clay	1902	1,434,181	1,411,082	194,120,737
Cochran	1936	6,526,407	6,053,642	454,785,360
Coke	1942	1,214,783	1,226,422	214,251,612
Coleman	1902	597,910	506,046	91,029,721
Collin	1963	0	0	53,000
Collingsworth	1936	7,586	7,573	1,200,904
Colorado	1932	683,274	691,147	34,430,814
Comanche	1918	19,486	14,468	5,848,395
Concho	1940	1,859,285	1,292,715	17,175,696
Cooke	1926	2,465,496	2,168,429	370,331,216
Coryell	1964	0	0	1,100
Cottle	1955	86,693	94,835	3,668,855
Crane	1926	16,620,227	15,860,944	1,619,345,836
Crockett	1925	4,066,083	3,860,918	826,879,347
Crosby	1955	766,216	644,751	17,010,061
Culberson	1953	404,298	324,977	23,187,337
Dallas	1986	0	0	231
Dawson	1937	5,875,107	6,011,187	319,199,701
Delta	1984	0	0	64,058
Denton	1937	13,784	15,782	3,402,838
DeWitt	1930	505,948	462,868	63,503,354
Dickens	1953	420,364	502,563	7,479,508
Dimmit	1943	1,678,386	1,262,391	97,476,157
Duval	1905	3,102,237	2,602,566	568,918,337
Eastland	1917	734,241	679,619	152,438,234
Ector	1926	31,746,732	29,617,208	2,857,143,216
Edwards	1946	4,702	3,175	435,650
Ellis	1953	5,681	5,547	817,082
Erath	1917	12,132	10,000	2,032,519
Falls	1937	12,013	11,352	794,000
Fannin	1980	0	0	13,281
Fayette	1943	15,011,019	11,566,157	108,548,847
Fisher	1928	1,683,599	1,528,873	237,814,282
Floyd	1952	3,476	2,950	138,091
Foard	1929	294,439	321,699	22,123,261
Fort Bend	1919	3,103,235	2,778,951	660,123,988
Franklin	1936	953,394	678,308	171,489,825

County	Year of Discovery	Production in Barrels*		Total Production to Jan. 1, 1995
		1993	1994	
Freestone	1916	388,100	350,300	42,160,563
Frio	1934	5,148,763	2,957,557	135,635,742
Gaines	1936	39,671,463	38,456,817	1,833,164,853
Galveston	1922	1,554,185	1,446,929	435,525,643
Garza	1926	6,856,824	6,721,872	278,576,527
Glasscock	1925	5,378,667	5,685,075	212,488,583
Goliad	1930	622,888	477,368	76,145,426
Gonzales	1902	1,460,164	937,684	38,375,134
Gray	1925	2,524,368	2,410,841	652,829,995
Grayson	1930	1,987,638	1,846,869	239,569,586
Gregg	1931	26,020,059	24,313,658	3,186,004,389
Grimes	1952	353,829	1,914,318	9,018,860
Guadalupe	1922	1,251,017	1,264,775	192,749,745
Hale	1946	1,456,279	1,218,291	152,506,200
Hamilton	1938	1,667	2,477	137,312
Hansford	1937	376,196	407,883	36,472,184
Hardeman	1944	2,604,740	2,433,667	58,401,924
Hardin	1893	2,103,993	1,855,440	420,120,426
Harris	1905	4,768,440	4,311,431	1,343,595,167
Harrison	1928	1,322,139	1,147,718	79,772,812
Hartley	1937	323,163	307,432	4,090,631
Haskell	1929	1,011,696	846,285	110,482,358
Hays	1956	5	19	296
Hemphill	1955	691,605	579,023	31,072,032
Henderson	1934	1,841,567	1,906,532	164,088,996
Hidalgo	1934	3,258,766	2,998,588	73,787,786
Hill	1949	2,844	2,363	65,175
Hockley	1937	28,406,339	27,085,205	1,395,252,846
Hood	1958	4,568	2,416	99,468
Hopkins	1936	747,065	659,200	85,371,444
Houston	1934	678,289	703,720	48,376,810
Howard	1925	9,574,226	9,447,869	733,710,522
Hunt	1942	50,772	30,324	1,982,969
Hutchinson	1923	1,705,092	1,651,250	517,665,628
Irion	1928	2,990,458	2,786,115	79,436,877
Jack	1923	1,505,586	1,311,717	193,943,789
Jackson	1934	2,445,688	2,097,729	666,397,417
Jasper	1928	961,270	1,546,204	24,766,672
Jeff Davis	1980	0	0	20,866
Jefferson	1901	3,017,436	2,687,381	509,062,731
Jim Hogg	1922	488,550	415,864	108,282,517
Jim Wells	1933	553,967	457,108	459,492,231
Johnson	1962	0	0	194,000
Jones	1926	1,043,153	1,080,458	211,303,952
Karnes	1930	614,595	506,659	104,265,081
Kaufman	1948	182,554	147,869	23,668,189
Kenedy	1947	599,780	505,946	33,997,946
Kent	1946	8,221,015	10,719,473	487,650,569
Kerr	1982	1,623	2,242	69,772
Kimble	1939	977	879	91,320
King	1943	5,773,081	4,817,835	145,144,059
Kinney	1960	0	0	402
Kleberg	1926	896,366	881,572	328,907,374
Knox	1946	631,817	490,541	58,601,121
Lamb	1945	398,892	414,714	29,632,709
Lampasas	1985	0	0	111
La Salle	1940	929,366	680,806	24,493,033
Lavaca	1941	509,812	768,319	24,232,256
Lee	1939	5,772,633	7,584,874	105,873,408

Crude Petroleum Production, 1992

Rank.	Quantity (mil. bbl.)
1. Texas	651
2. Alaska	627
3. California	305
4. Louisiana	148
5. Oklahoma	102

Source: U.S. Energy Information Administration, Energy Data Reports, Petroleum Supply Annual, Natural Gas Annual, and Natural Gas Monthly.

County	Year of Discovery	Production in Barrels*		Total Production to Jan. 1, 1995
		1993	1994	
Leon	1936	3,453,969	2,642,755	50,380,689
Liberty	1905	2,590,990	2,475,125	506,287,877
Limestone	1920	288,367	344,848	117,233,063
Lipscomb	1956	1,122,868	1,036,345	53,417,425
Live Oak	1931	1,354,556	1,438,403	53,417,425
Llano	1978	0	0	647
Loving	1925	1,658,441	1,504,672	96,989,380
Lubbock	1941	2,214,645	2,078,265	50,947,426
Lynn	1950	368,152	291,631	16,785,079
Madison	1946	642,246	580,433	26,960,240
Marion	1910	311,799	315,192	53,316,844
Martin	1945	6,966,007	6,678,673	256,525,454
Matagorda	1904	1,120,462	1,033,685	266,035,372
Maverick	1929	1,087,299	1,022,454	41,439,654
McCulloch	1938	31,188	135,822	360,611
McLennan	1902	3,559	2,442	319,033
McMullen	1919	2,223,591	1,916,697	88,814,024
Medina	1901	145,746	130,990	9,780,807
Menard	1941	112,076	93,202	6,156,698
Midland	1945	10,744,107	11,702,148	497,260,853
Milam	1921	267,959	247,615	12,695,664
Mills	1982	0	0	28,122
Mitchell	1920	3,959,874	3,773,903	193,302,182
Montague	1924	1,893,343	1,781,848	275,179,436
Montgomery	1931	1,991,795	1,791,573	759,923,535
Moore	1936	551,654	453,155	26,445,837
Motley	1957	134,209	145,531	10,175,365
Nacogdoches	1866	55,041	46,653	3,077,687
Navarro	1895	578,021	431,680	214,888,814
Newton	1937	2,034,048	3,012,977	51,728,898
Nolan	1939	1,918,646	1,960,718	179,821,062
Nueces	1930	1,962,430	1,826,866	547,086,424
Ochiltree	1951	1,263,500	1,243,487	146,998,900
Oldham	1957	270,373	218,373	12,685,670
Orange	1913	3,211,227	2,813,264	142,867,476
Palo Pinto	1902	296,842	374,500	19,136,126
Panola	1917	1,862,745	1,774,807	71,670,700
Parker	1942	22,666	20,245	2,732,729
Parmer	1963	0	0	144,000

Top Counties in Oil Production

Rank	bbls since discovery
1. Gregg	3,186,004,389
2. Ector	2,857,143,216
3. Andrews	2,508,051,974
4. Scurry	1,948,359,365
5. Gaines	1,833,164,853
6. Rusk	1,790,730,250
7. Yoakum	1,789,512,441
8. Crane	1,619,345,836
9. Pecos	1,595,504,226
10. Hockley	1,395,252,846
11. Harris	1,343,595,167
12. Refugio	1,273,409,931
13. Brazoria	1,241,890,610
14. Wood	1,136,715,723
15. Winkler	1,027,881,137

County	Year of Discovery	Production in Barrels*		Total Production to Jan. 1, 1995
		1993	1994	
Pecos	1926	21,268,165	22,154,417	1,595,504,226
Polk	1930	1,076,942	1,320,904	101,173,508
Potter	1925	299,658	282,567	7,430,624
Presidio	1980	0	0	1,873
Rains	1955	3	0	148,766
Reagan	1923	5,513,171	5,247,411	445,131,288
Red River	1951	241,169	318,296	3,315,765
Reeves	1939	1,218,799	1,153,235	69,455,133
Refugio	1928	6,840,902	6,080,900	1,273,409,931
Roberts	1945	482,504	491,300	42,115,139
Robertson	1944	209,626	744,670	3,065,939
Runnels	1927	954,803	989,744	140,078,119
Rusk	1930	5,908,046	5,387,378	1,790,730,250
Sabine	1981	657,948	683,003	3,075,067
San Augustine	1947	44,051	924,503	986,569
San Jacinto	1940	287,014	301,668	23,250,123
San Patricio	1930	1,303,937	1,270,454	474,481,378
San Saba	1982	0	0	32,362
Schleicher	1937	699,913	622,561	82,130,716
Scurry	1923	10,087,846	88,827,252	1,948,359,365
Shackelford	1910	1,452,611	1,514,026	171,249,778
Shelby	1917	78,348	43,455	1,944,196
Sherman	1938	422,150	350,838	7,108,338
Smith	1931	2,375,735	2,130,025	248,832,967
Somervell	1978	0	0	119
Starr	1929	1,585,543	1,488,135	272,533,932
Stephens	1916	4,833,889	4,600,755	306,627,502
Sterling	1947	2,661,751	2,170,531	75,100,697
Stonewall	1938	3,585,946	3,128,228	243,331,357
Sutton	1948	218,559	125,438	6,873,024
Swisher	1981	0	0	6
Tarrant	1969	36	17	53
Taylor	1929	9,990,821	856,425	136,895,050
Terrell	1952	72,984	147,776	3,888,058
Terry	1940	5,880,258	6,041,416	388,694,035
Throckmorton	1924	1,735,414	1,670,218	207,103,896
Titus	1936	1,053,821	688,744	205,440,829
Tom Green	1940	1,832,060	1,480,786	85,572,246
Travis	1934	3,722	2,943	722,499
Trinity	1946	59,202	48,862	437,197
Tyler	1937	675,101	613,128	35,966,690
Upshur	1931	743,520	743,444	279,757,782
Upton	1925	12,197,645	12,463,430	725525451
Uvalde	1950	0	0	1,814
Val Verde	1935	397	898	118,926
Van Zandt	1929	2,303,166	2,195,903	532,603,736
Victoria	1931	1,458,892	1,324,603	242,997,390
Walker	1934	9,773	9,223	424,203
Waller	1934	70,292	72,779	19,798,307
Ward	1928	6,799,278	6,159,332	697,416,599
Washington	1915	1,501,419	1,523,273	23,583,370
Webb	1921	3,270,076	2,716,447	139,088,478
Wharton	1925	2,962,174	2,664,138	316,142,933
Wheeler	1921	887,920	807,715	94,242,077
Wichita	1910	3,495,225	3,359,055	801,988,650
Wilbarger	1915	907,755	865,900	256,061,607
Willacy	1936	881,803	765,308	107,002,023
Williamson	1915	12,903	11,951	9,438,538
Wilson	1941	1,397,444	1,013,496	43,861,657
Winkler	1926	4,853,056	4,722,955	1,027,881,137
Wise	1942	1,121,002	1,143,386	92,355,019
Wood	1941	9,564,874	8,709,300	1,136,715,723
Yoakum	1936	30,759,807	30,627,561	1,789,512,441
Young	1917	2,481,462	2,294,299	291,182,616
Zapata	1919	338,805	328,635	44,472,314
Zavala	1937	2,702,855	1,524,902	41,142,789

*Total includes condensate production.
Source: Railroad Commission, 1992 production report.

Natural Gas Production, 1992

Rank	Quantity (bil. cu. ft.)
1. Texas	**6,146**
2. Louisiana	4,914
3. Oklahoma	2,017
4. New Mexico	1,269
5. Wyoming	843

Source: U.S. Energy Information Administration, Energy Data Reports, Petroleum Supply Annual, Natural Gas Annual, and Natural Gas Monthly.

Receipts By Texas From Tidelands

Source: General Land Office

The following table shows receipts from tidelands in the Gulf of Mexico by the Texas General Land Office to Aug. 31, 1993. It does not include revenue from bays and other submerged area owned by Texas.

From	To	Total	Bonus	Rental	Royalty	Lease*
6-09-1922	9-28-1945	$924,363.81	$814,055.70	$61,973.75	$48,334.36	...
9-29-1945	6-23-1947	296,400.30	272,700.00	7,680.00	16,020.30	...
6-24-1947	6-05-1950	7,695,552.22	7,231,755.48	377,355.00	86,441.74	...
6-06-1950	5-22-1953	55,095.04	—	9,176.00	45,919.04	...
5-23-1953	6-30-1958	54,264,553.11	49,788,639.03	3,852,726.98	623,187.10	...
7-01-1958	8-31-1959	771,064.75	—	143,857.00	627,207.75	...
9-01-1959	8-31-1960	983,335.32	257,900.00	98,226.00	627,209.32	...
9-01-1960	8-31-1961	3,890,800.15	3,228,639.51	68,578.00	593,582.64	...
9-01-1961	8-31-1962	1,121,925.09	297,129.88	127,105.00	697,690.21	...
9-01-1962	8-31-1963	3,575,888.64	2,617,057.14	177,174.91	781,656.59	...
9-01-1963	8-31-1964	3,656,236.75	2,435,244.36	525,315.00	695,677.39	...
9-01-1964	8-31-1965	54,654,576.96	53,114,943.63	755,050.12	784,583.21	...
9-01-1965	8-31-1966	22,148,825.44	18,223,357.84	3,163,475.00	761,992.60	...
9-01-1966	8-31-1967	8,469,680.86	3,641,414.96	3,711,092.65	1,117,173.25	...
9-01-1967	8-31-1968	6,305,851.00	1,251,852.50	2,683,732.50	2,370,266.00	...
9-01-1968	8-31-1969	6,372,268.28	1,838,118.33	1,491,592.50	3,042,557.45	...
9-01-1969	8-31-1970	10,311,030.48	5,994,666.32	618,362.50	3,698,001.66	...
9-01-1970	8-31-1971	9,969,629.17	4,326,120.11	726,294.15	4,917,214.91	...
9-01-1971	8-31-1972	7,558,327.21	1,360,212.64	963,367.60	5,234,746.97	...
9-01-1972	8-31-1973	9,267,975.68	3,701,737.30	920,121.60	4,646,116.78	...
9-01-1973	8-31-1974	41,717,670.04	32,981,619.28	1,065,516.60	7,670,534.16	...
9-01-1974	8-31-1975	27,321,536.62	5,319,762.85	2,935,295.60	19,066,478.17	...
9-01-1975	8-31-1976	38,747,074.09	6,197,853.00	3,222,535.84	29,326,685.25	...
9-01-1976	8-31-1977	84,196,228.27	41,343,114.81	2,404,988.80	40,448,124.66	...
9-01-1977	8-31-1978	118,266,812.05	49,807,750.45	4,775,509.92	63,683,551.68	...
9-01-1978	8-31-1979	100,410,268.68	34,578,340.94	7,318,748.40	58,513,179.34	...
9-01-1979	8-31-1980	200,263,803.03	34,733,270.02	10,293,153.80	155,237,379.21	...
9-01-1980	8-31-1981	219,126,876.54	37,467,196.97	13,100,484.25	168,559,195.32	...
9-01-1981	8-31-1982	250,824,581.69	27,529,516.33	14,214,478.97	209,080,586.39	...
9-01-1982	8-31-1983	165,197,734.83	10,180,696.40	12,007,476.70	143,009,561.73	...
9-01-1983	8-31-1984	152,755,934.29	32,864,122.19	8,573,996.87	111,317,815.23	...
9-01-1984	8-31-1985	140,568,090.79	32,650,127.75	6,837,603.70	101,073,959.34	...
9-01-1985	8-31-1986	†88,736,086.55	6,365,426.23	4,241,892.75	78,289,592.27	$427,606,859.83
9-01-1986	8-31-1987	†50,812,221.85	4,186,561.63	1,933,752.50	44,691,907.22	9,254,349.70
9-01-1987	8-31-1988	†44,080,535.71	14,195,274.28	1,817,058.90	28,068,202.53	12,794,533.51
9-01-1988	8-31-1989	†49,447,445.51	12,995,892.74	1,290,984.37	35,160,568.40	12,345,934.53
9-01-1989	8-31-1990	†49,315,436.47	7,708,449.54	1,289,849.87	40,331,537.06	19,371,915.04
9-01-1990	8-31-1991	†75,027,931.45	3,791,832.77	1,212,497.67	70,023,601.01	15,724,712.14
9-01-1991	8-31-1992	†32,483,840.29	4,450,850.00	1,256,798,94	26,776,191.35	18,101,896.37
9-01-1992	8-31-1993	†39,152,269.26	3,394,230.00	904,359.58	34,853,679.68	21,135,443.34
Total		†$2,180,914,582.47	$563,137,432.91	$121,179,240.29	$34,853,679.68	$21,135,443.34
Recapitulation:						
Inside three-mile line		$385,142,070.41	$135,303,640.41	$33,375,158.31	$216;,463,271.69	0
Between three-mile line and three marine-league line		$1,792,947,146.48	$425,181,708.11	$87,630,800.79	$1,280,134,637.58	0
Outside three marine-league line		$2,825,365.58	$2,652,084.39	$173,281.19	0	$536,335,644.46

Totals including revenue in "Lease" column:

Total mineral leases: $2,65,962,514.33

Total outside 3-marine league limit: $518,025,566.70

*Revenue from continental shelf settlement with federal government under Public Law 99-272 (for fuller explanation, see article, "History of Texas Public Land" in Politics and Government section).

†Does not include amounts in "Lease" column.

Nonfuel Mineral Production and Value, 1992, 1993 and 1994

Source: U.S. Dept. of the Interior, Bureau of Mines (Production measured by mine shipments, sales or marketable production, including consumption by producer.)

Mineral	1992		1993		1994*	
	Production	Value (add 000)	Production	Value (add 000)	Production	Value (add 000)
Cement:						
Masonry (thous. metric tons).....	**	**	245	$18,365	316	$23,700
Portland (thous. metric tons).....	6,840	$308,749	8,127	397,600	7,820	383,000
††Clays (thous. metric tons)......	2,237	12,610	2,183	17,441	2,260	21,200
Gemstones................	†	3,834	†	400	†	**
Gypsum (thous. metric tons)......	1,624	9,920	1,756	10,088	1,920	11,100
Helium, crude (million cu. meters)	**	**	6	5,385	6	5,940
Lime (thous. metric tons).........	1,337	83,359	1,604	103,274	1,280	82,100
Salt (thous. metric tons)..........	7,985	76,125	8,253	76,054	7,960	76,000
Sand and gravel:						
Construction (thous. metric tons)	41,404	166,362	47,100	*195,000	42,000	176,400
Industrial (thous. metric tons)....	1,392	26,501	1,433	28,558	**	**
Stone:						
Crushed (thous. metric tons).....	*64,682	*253,100	70,772	279,245	*75,800	*315,000
Dimension (thous. metric tons)...	**	**	**	**	*46,500	*7,900
Sulfur (Frasch) (thous. metric tons)	1,495	**	1,164	**	**	**
Talc and pyrophyllite (metric tons)	235,919	5,720	235,857	5,662	262,000	5,630
‡Combined value.............	...	357,458	...	311,041	...	301,000
Total Texas Values...........	...	**$ 1,303,738**	...	**$ 1,448,113**	...	**‡‡$1,410,00**

**Estimated. † Not available.*
*‡Includes clays (ball, bentonite, fuller's earth, kaolin), fluorspar (1993-94), helium (grade A), iron ore, magnesium compounds, magnesium metal, sodium sulfate (natural) and values indicated by symbol **.*
***Data withheld to avoid disclosing proprietary data; value included with "Combined value."*
††Excludes certain clays; kind and value included in "Combined value."
‡‡Data do not add to total shown because of independent rounding.

Nonpetroleum Minerals

The nonpetroleum minerals that occur in Texas constitute a long list. Some are currently mined; some may have a potential for future development; some are minor occurrences only. Although overshadowed by the petroleum, natural gas and natural gas liquids that are produced in the state, many of the nonpetroleum minerals are, nonetheless, important to the economy. In 1993, they were valued at approximately $1.4 billion. Texas is annually **among the nation's leading states in value of nonpetroleum mineral production.** In 1993, **Texas ranked sixth nationally** in total mineral output.

The **Bureau of Economic Geology**, which functions as the state geological survey of Texas, revised the following information about nonpetroleum minerals for this edition of the Texas Almanac. Publications of the bureau, on file in many libraries, contain more detailed information. Among the items available are a map, "Mineral Resources of Texas," showing locations of resource access of many nonpetroleum minerals, and a computer-generated list of Texas nonpetroleum mineral producers.

A catalog of Bureau publications is also available free on request from the Bureau Publications Sales, University Station, Box X, Austin, TX 78713-7508; 512-471-7144.

Texas' nonpetroleum minerals are as follows:

ALUMINUM — No aluminum ores are mined in Texas, but three Texas plants process aluminum materials in one or more ways. Plants in San Patricio and Calhoun counties produce **aluminum oxide (alumina)** from imported raw ore **(bauxite)**, and a plant in Milam County reduces the oxide to aluminum.

ASBESTOS — Small occurrences of amphibole-type asbestos have been found in the state. In West Texas, **richterite**, a white, long-fibered amphibole, is associated with some of the **talc deposits** northwest of **Allamoore** in Hudspeth County. Another type, **tremolite**, has been found in the **Llano Uplift** of Central Texas where it is associated with **serpentinite** in eastern Gillespie and western Blanco County. No asbestos is mined in Texas.

ASPHALT (Native) — Asphalt-bearing Cretaceous limestones crop out in Burnet, Kinney, Pecos, Reeves, Uvalde and other counties. The most significant deposit is in southwestern Uvalde County where asphalt occurs naturally in the pore spaces of the Anacacho Limestone. The material is quarried and used extensively as **road-paving material**. Asphalt-bearing sandstones occur in Anderson, Angelina, Cooke, Jasper, Maverick, Montague, Nacogdoches, Uvalde, Zavala and other counties.

BARITE — Deposits of a heavy, nonmetallic mineral, barite (barium sulphate), have been found in many localities, including Baylor, Brown, Brewster, Culberson, Gillespie, Howard, Hudspeth, Jeff Davis, Kinney, Llano, Live Oak, Taylor, Val Verde and Webb counties. During the 1960s, there was small, intermittent production in the **Seven Heart Gap** area of the **Apache Mountains** in Culberson County, where barite was mined from open pits. Most of the deposits are known to be relatively small, but the Webb County deposit has not been evaluated. Grinding plants, which prepare barite mined outside of Texas for use chiefly as a **weighting agent** in well-drilling muds and as a **filler**, are located in Brownsville, Corpus Christi, El Paso, Galena Park, Galveston, and Houston.

BASALT (TRAP ROCK) — Masses of basalt — a hard, dark-colored, fine-grained igneous rock — crop out in Kinney, Travis, Uvalde and several other counties along the **Balcones Fault Zone**, and also in the Trans-Pecos area of West Texas. Basalt is quarried near Knippa in Uvalde County for use as **road-building material, railroad ballast and other aggregate.**

BENTONITE (see **CLAYS**).

BERYLLIUM — Occurrences of beryllium minerals at several Trans-Pecos localities have been recognized for several years. Evaluation and development of a beryllium prospect near **Sierra Blanca** in Hudspeth County, a portion of which is on state-owned land, is now underway. **Behoite** and other beryllium minerals are associated with **fluorspar** at this site.

BRINE (see also **SALT, SODIUM SULPHATE**) — Many wells in Texas produce brine by solution mining of subsurface salt deposits, mostly in West Texas counties such as Andrews, Crane, Ector, Loving, Midland, Pecos, Reeves, Ward and others. These wells in the Permian Basin dissolve salt from the **Salado Formation,** an enormous salt deposit that extends in the subsurface from north of the Big Bend northward to Kansas, has an east-west width of 150 to 200 miles, and may have several hundred feet of net salt thickness. The majority of the brine is used in the **petroleum industry**, but it also is used in **water softening, the chemical industry** and other uses. Three Gulf Coast counties, Fort Bend, Duval and Jefferson, have brine stations that produce from **salt domes**.

BUILDING STONE (DIMENSION STONE) — **Granite** and **limestone** currently are quarried for use as dimension stone. The granite quarries are located in Burnet, Gillespie, Llano and Mason counties; the limestone quarries are in Shackelford and

Williamson counties. Past production of limestone for use as dimension stone has been reported in Burnet, Gillespie, Jones, Tarrant, Travis and several other counties. There has also been production of **sandstone** in various counties for use as dimension stone.

CEMENT MATERIALS — Cement is currently manufactured at 13 plants in Bexar, Comal, Dallas, Ector, Ellis, Hays, McLennan, Nolan, and Potter counties. Many of these plants utilize Cretaceous limestones and shales or clays as raw materials for the cement. On the Texas High Plains, a cement plant near Amarillo uses impure **caliche** as the chief raw material. **Iron oxide**, also a constituent of cement, is available from the iron ore deposits of East Texas and from smelter slag. **Gypsum**, added to the cement as a retarder, is found chiefly in North Central Texas, Central Texas and the Trans-Pecos area.

CHROMIUM — Chromite-bearing rock has been found in several small deposits around the margin of the Coal Creek **serpentinite** mass in northeastern Gillespie County and northwestern Blanco County. Exploration has not revealed significant deposits.

CLAYS — Texas has an abundance and variety of ceramic and non-ceramic clays and is one of the country's leading producers of clay products.

Almost any kind of clay, ranging from common clay used to make ordinary brick and tile to clays suitable for manufacture of specialty whitewares, can be used for ceramic purposes. **Fire clay** suitable for use as **refractories** occurs chiefly in East and North Central Texas; **ball clay**, a high-quality plastic ceramic clay, is found locally in East Texas.

Ceramic clay suitable for quality structural clay products such as **structural building brick, paving brick and drain tile** is especially abundant in East and North Central Texas. Common clay suitable for use in the manufacture of cement and ordinary brick is found in most counties of the state. Many of the Texas clays will expand or bloat upon rapid firing and are suitable for the manufacture of lightweight aggregate, which is used mainly in concrete blocks and highway surfacing.

Nonceramic clays are utilized without firing. They are used primarily as **bleaching and adsorbent clays, fillers, coaters, additives, bonding clays, drilling muds, catalysts** and potentially as sources of alumina. Most of the nonceramic clays in Texas are **bentonites and fuller's earth**. These occur extensively in the Coastal Plain and locally in the High Plains and Big Bend areas. **Kaolin clays** in parts of East Texas are potential sources of such nonceramic products as **paper coaters and fillers, rubber fillers and drilling agents**. Relatively high in alumina, these clays also are a potential source of metallic aluminum.

COAL (see also LIGNITE) — **Bituminous coal**, which occurs in North Central, South and West Texas, was a significant energy source in Texas prior to the large-scale development of oil and gas. During the period from 1895 to 1943, Texas mines produced more than 25 million tons of coal. The mines were inactive for many years, but the renewed interest in coal as a major energy source prompted a revaluation of Texas' coal deposits. In the late 1970s, bituminous coal production resumed in the state on a limited scale when mines were opened in Coleman, Erath and Webb counties.

Much of the state's bituminous coal occurs in North Central Texas. Deposits are found there in Pennsylvanian rocks within a large area that includes Coleman, Eastland, Erath, Jack, McCulloch, Montague, Palo Pinto, Parker, Throckmorton, Wise, Young and other counties. Before the general availability of oil and gas, underground coal mines near **Thurber, Bridgeport, Newcastle, Strawn** and other points annually produced significant coal tonnages. Preliminary evaluations indicate substantial amounts of coal may remain in the North Central Texas area. The coal seams there are generally no more than 30 inches thick and are commonly covered by well-consolidated overburden. Ash and sulphur content are high. Beginning in 1979, two bituminous coal mine operations in North Central Texas — one in southern Coleman County and one in northwestern Erath County — produced coal to be used as fuel by the cement industry. Neither mine is currently operating.

In South Texas, bituminous coal occurs in the Eagle Pass district of Maverick County, and bituminous **cannel coal** is present in the **Santo Tomas district** of Webb County. The Eagle Pass area was a leading coal-producing district in Texas during the late 1800s and early 1900s. The bituminous coal in that area, which occurs in the Upper Cretaceous Olmos Formation, has a high ash content and a moderate moisture and sulfur content. According to reports, Maverick County coal beds range from four to seven feet thick.

The **cannel coals** of western Webb County occur near the Rio Grande in middle Eocene strata. They were mined for more than 50 years and used primarily as a boiler fuel. Mining ceased from 1939 until 1978, when a surface mine was opened 30 miles northwest of Laredo to produce cannel coal for use as fuel in the cement industry and for export. An additional mine has since been opened in that county. Tests show that the coals of the Webb County Santo Tomas district have a high hydrogen content and yield significant amounts of gas and oil when distilled. They also have a high sulfur content. A potential use might be as a source of various petrochemical products.

Coal deposits in the Trans-Pecos country of West Texas include those in the Cretaceous rocks of the Terlingua area of Brewster County, the Eagle Spring area of Hudspeth County and the **San Carlos** area of Presidio County. The coal deposits in these areas are believed to have relatively little potential for development as a fuel. They have been sold in the past as a soil amendment (see **LEONARDITE**).

COPPER — Copper minerals have been found in the **Trans-Pecos** area of West Texas, in the **Llano Uplift** area of Central Texas and in redbed deposits of North Texas. No copper has been mined in Texas during recent years, and the total copper produced in the state has been relatively small. Past attempts to mine the North Texas and Llano Uplift copper deposits resulted in small shipments, but practically all the copper production in the state has been from the **Van Horn-Allamoore** district of Culberson and Hudspeth Counties in the Trans-Pecos area. Chief output was from the **Hazel copper-silver mine** of Culberson County that yielded over 1 million pounds of copper during 1891-1947. Copper ores and concentrates from outside of Texas are processed at **smelters** in El Paso and Amarillo.

CRUSHED STONE — Texas is among the leading states in the production of crushed stone. Most production consists of **limestone**; other kinds of crushed stone produced in the state include **basalt (trap rock), dolomite, granite, marble, rhyolite, sandstone and serpentinite**. Large tonnages of crushed stone are used as **aggregate** in concrete, as **road material** and in the manufacture of cement and lime. Some is used as **riprap, terrazzo, roofing chips, filter material, fillers** and for other purposes.

DIATOMITE (DIATOMACEOUS EARTH) — Diatomite is a very lightweight siliceous material consisting of the remains of microscopic aquatic plants (diatoms). It is used chiefly as a **filter and filler**; other uses are for **thermal insulation**, as an **abrasive**, as an **insecticide carrier** and as a **lightweight aggregate**, and for other purposes. The diatomite was deposited in shallow fresh-water lakes that were present in the High Plains during portions of the Pliocene and Pleistocene epochs. Deposits have been found in Armstrong, Crosby, Dickens, Ector, Hartley and Lamb counties. No diatomite is mined in Texas.

DOLOMITE ROCK — Dolomite rock, which consists largely of the mineral dolomite (calcium-magnesium carbonate), commonly is associated with limestone in Texas. Areas in which dolomite rock occurs include Central Texas, the Callahan Divide and parts of the Edwards Plateau, High Plains and West Texas. Some of the principal deposits of dolomite rock are found in Bell, Brown, Burnet, Comanche, Edwards, El Paso, Gillespie, Lampasas, Mills, Nolan, Taylor and Williamson counties. Dolomite rock can be used as crushed stone (although much of Texas dolomite is soft and not a good aggregate material), in the manufacture of lime and as a source of **magnesium**.

FELDSPAR — Large crystals and crystal fragments of feldspar minerals occur in the Precambrian pegmatite rocks that crop out in the **Llano Uplift** area of Central Texas — including Blanco, Burnet, Gillespie, Llano and Mason counties — and in the **Van Horn area** of Culberson and Hudspeth Counties in West Texas. Feldspar has been mined in Llano County for use as **roofing granules** and as a **ceramic material**, but is not currently mined anywhere within the state.

FLUORSPAR — The mineral fluorite (calcium fluoride), which is known commercially as fluorspar, occurs in both Central and West Texas. In Central Texas, the deposits that have been found in Burnet, Gillespie and Mason counties are not considered adequate to sustain mining operations. In West Texas, deposits have been found in Brewster, El Paso, Hudspeth, Jeff Davis and Presidio counties. Fluorspar has been mined in the **Christmas Mountains** of Brewster County and processed in Marathon. Former West Texas mining activity in the **Eagle Mountains** district of Hudspeth County resulted in the production of approximately 15,000 short tons of fluorspar during the peak years of 1942-1950. No production has been reported in Hudspeth County since that period. Imported fluorspar is processed in Brownsville, Eagle Pass, El Paso and Houston. Fluorspar is used in the **steel, chemical, aluminum, magnesium, ceramics and glass industries** and for various other purposes.

FULLER'S EARTH (see **CLAY**).

GOLD — No major deposits of gold are known in Texas. Small amounts have been found in the **Llano Uplift** region of Central Texas and in West Texas; minor occurrences have been reported on the **Edwards Plateau** and the **Gulf Coastal Plain** of Texas. Nearly all of the gold produced in the state came as a by-product of silver and lead mining at **Presidio mine**, near **Shafter**, in Presidio County. Additional small quantities were produced as a by-product of copper mining in Culberson County and from residual soils developed from gold-bearing quartz stringers in metamorphic rocks in Llano County. No gold mining has been reported in Texas since 1952. Total **gold production** in the state, 1889-1952, amounted to more than 8,419 troy ounces according to U.S. Bureau of Mines figures. Most of the production — at least 73 percent and probably more — came from the Presidio mine.

GRANITE — Granites in shades of red and gray and related intrusive igneous rocks occur in the **Llano Uplift** of Central Texas and in the **Trans-Pecos** country of West Texas. Deposits are found in Blanco, Brewster, Burnet, El Paso, Gillespie, Hudspeth, Llano, McCulloch, Mason, Presidio and other counties. Quarries in Burnet, Gillespie, Llano and Mason counties produce Precambrian granite for a variety of uses as **dimension stone and crushed stone.**

GRAPHITE — Graphite, a soft, dark-gray mineral, is a form of very high-grade carbon. It occurs in Precambrian schist rocks of the **Llano Uplift** of Central Texas, notably in Burnet and Llano counties. Crystalline-flake graphite ore formerly was mined from open pits in the **Clear Creek area** of western Burnet County and processed at a plant near the mine. The mill now occasionally grinds imported material. Uses of natural crystalline graphite are **refractories, steel production, pencil leads, lubricants, foundry facings and crucibles** and for other purposes.

GRINDING PEBBLES (ABRASIVE STONES) — Flint pebbles, suitable for use in **tube-mill grinding**, are found in the **Gulf Coastal Plain** where they occur in gravel deposits along rivers and in upland areas. Grinding pebbles are produced from **Frio River terrace** deposits near the McMullen-Live Oak county line, but the area is now part of the Choke Canyon Reservoir area.

GYPSUM — Gypsum is widely distributed in Texas. Chief deposits are bedded gypsum in the area east of the **High Plains**, in the **Trans-Pecos** country and in **Central Texas**. It also occurs in **salt-dome caprocks** of the Gulf Coast. The massive, granular variety known as rock gypsum is the kind most commonly used by industry. Other varieties include **alabaster, satin spar and selenite.**

Gypsum is one of the important industrial minerals in Texas. Bedded gypsum is produced from surface mines in Culberson, Fisher, Gillespie, Hardeman, Hudspeth, Kimble, Nolan and Stonewall counties. Gypsum was formerly mined at **Gyp Hill salt dome** in Brooks County and at **Hockley salt dome** in Harris County. Most of the gypsum is calcined and used in the manufacture of **gypsum wallboard, plaster, joint compounds** and other construction products. Crude gypsum is used chiefly as a **retarder in portland cement** and as a **soil conditioner.**

HELIUM — Texas is a leading producer of this very light, non-flammable, chemically inert gas. Helium is extracted from natural gas of the **Panhandle area** at the **U.S. Bureau of Mines Exell plant** near Masterson in Moore County and at two privately owned plants in Moore and Hansford counties. As a conservation measure, the Bureau of Mines injects the helium that is not sold when the gas is produced into the **Cliffside gas field** near Amarillo for storage. Helium is used in **cryogenics, welding, pressurizing and purging, leak detection, synthetic breathing mixtures** and for other purposes.

IRON — Iron oxide **(limonite, goethite and hematite)** and **iron carbonate (siderite)** deposits occur widely in East Texas, notably in Cass, Cherokee, Marion and Morris counties, and also in Anderson, Camp, Harrison, Henderson, Nacogdoches, Smith, Upshur and other counties. **Magnetite (magnetic, black iron oxide)** occurs in Central Texas, including a deposit at **Iron Mountain** in Llano County. Hematite occurs in the **Trans-Pecos** area and in the **Llano Uplift** of Central Texas. The extensive deposits of **glauconite** (a complex silicate containing iron) that occur in East Texas and the hematitic and goethitic Cambrian sandstone that crops out in the northwestern Llano Uplift region are potential sources of low-grade iron ore.

Limonite and other East Texas iron ores are mined from open pits in Cherokee and Henderson counties for use in the preparation of **portland cement**, as a **weighting agent in well-drilling fluids**, as an **animal feed supplement** and for other purposes. East Texas iron ores also were mined in the past for use in the iron-steel industry.

KAOLIN (see **CLAY**).

LEAD AND ZINC — The lead mineral **galena (lead sulphide)** commonly is associated with zinc and silver. It formerly was produced as a by-product of West Texas silver mining, chiefly from the **Presidio mine at Shafter** in Presidio County, although lesser amounts were obtained at several other mines and prospects. Deposits of galena also are known to occur in Blanco, Brewster, Burnet, Gillespie and Hudspeth counties.

Zinc, primarily from the mineral **sphalerite (zinc sulphide)**, was produced chiefly from the **Bonanza** and **Alice Ray** mines in the **Quitman Mountains** of Hudspeth County. In addition, small production was reported from several other areas, including the **Chinati** and **Montezuma mines** of Presidio County and the **Buck Prospect** in the **Apache Mountains** of Culberson County. Zinc mineralization also occurs in association with the lead deposits in Cambrian rocks of Central Texas.

LEONARDITE — Deposits of weathered (oxidized) low-Btu value bituminous coals, generally referred to as "leonardite," occur in Brewster County. The name leonardite is used for a mixture of chemical compounds that is high in humic acids. In the past, material from these deposits was sold as **soil conditioner**. Other uses of leonardite include **modification of viscosity of drill fluids and as sorbants in water-treatment.**

LIGHTWEIGHT AGGREGATE (see **CLAY, DIATOMITE, PERLITE, VERMICULITE**).

LIGNITE — Lignite, a low-rank coal, is found in belts of Tertiary Eocene strata that extend across the Texas Gulf Coastal Plain from the Rio Grande in South Texas to the Arkansas and Louisiana borders in East Texas. The largest resources and best grades (approximately 6,500 BTU/pound) of lignite occur in the Wilcox Group of strata north of the Colorado River in East and Central Texas.

The near-surface lignite resources, occurring at depths of less than 200 feet in seams of three feet or thicker, are estimated at 23 billion short tons. **Recoverable reserves of strippable lignite** — those that can be economically mined under current conditions of price and technology — are estimated to be 9 billion to 11 billion short tons.

Additional lignite resources of the Texas Gulf Coastal Plain occur as deep-basin deposits. Deep-basin resources, those that occur at depths of 200 to 2,000 feet in seams of five feet or thicker, are comparable in magnitude to near-surface resources. The deep-basin lignites are a potential energy resource that conceivably could be utilized by *in situ* (in place) recovery methods such as underground gasification.

As with bituminous coal, lignite production was significant prior to the general availability of oil and gas. Remnants of old underground mines are common throughout the area of lignite occurrence. Large reserves of strippable lignite have again attracted the attention of energy suppliers, and Texas is now the nation's **6th leading producer of coal**, 99 percent of it lignite. Eleven large strip mines are now producing lignite that is burned for **mine-mouth electric-power generation**, and additional mines are planned. One of the currently operating mines is located in Milam County, where part of the electric power is used for **alumina reduction**. Other mines are in Atascosa, Bastrop, Freestone, Grimes, Harrison, Limestone, Rusk, Panola, Titus and Hopkins counties, where the electricity generated supplies municipal, domestic and industrial needs. Another Harrison County strip mine produces lignite that is used to make **activated carbon.**

LIME MATERIAL — **Limestones**, which are abundant in some areas of Texas, are heated to produce lime (calcium oxide) at a number of plants in the state. High-magnesium limestone and dolomite are used to prepare lime at a plant in Burnet County. Other lime plants are located in Bexar, Bosque, Comal, Hill, Johnson and Travis counties. Lime production captive to the kiln's operator occurs in several Texas counties. Lime is used in **soil stabilization, water purification, paper and pulp manufacture, metallurgy, sugar refining, agriculture, construction, removal of sulfur from stack gases** and for many other purposes.

LIMESTONE (see also **BUILDING STONE**) — Texas is one of the nation's leading producers of limestone, which is quarried in more than 60 counties. Limestone occurs in nearly all areas of the state with the exception of most of the Gulf Coastal Plain and High Plains. Although some of the limestone is quarried for use as **dimension stone**, most of the output is crushed for uses such as **bulk building materials (crushed stone, road base, concrete aggregate), chemical raw materials, fillers or extenders, lime and portland cement raw materials, agricultural limestone and removal of sulfur from stack gases.**

MAGNESITE — Small deposits of magnesite (natural magnesium carbonate) have been found in Precambrian rocks in Llano and Mason counties of Central Texas. At one time there was small-scale mining of magnesite in the area; some of the material was used as **agricultural stone** and as **terrazzo chips**. Magnesite also can be calcined to form **magnesia**, which is used in **metallurgical furnace refractories** and other products.

MAGNESIUM — On the Texas Gulf Coast in Brazoria County, magnesium chloride is **extracted from sea water** at a plant in Freeport and used to produce **magnesium compounds and magnesium metal**. During World War II, high-magnesium Ellenburger dolomite rock from Burnet County was used as magnesium ore at a plant near Austin.

MANGANESE — Deposits of manganese minerals, such as **braunite, hollandite and pyrolusite**, have been found in several areas, including Jeff Davis, Llano, Mason, Presidio and Val Verde counties. Known deposits are not large. Small shipments have been made from Jeff Davis, Mason and Val Verde counties, but no manganese mining has been reported in Texas since 1954.

MARBLE — Metamorphic and sedimentary marbles suitable for **monument and building stone** are found in the **Llano Uplift** and nearby areas of Central Texas and the **Trans-Pecos** area of West Texas. Gray, white, black, greenish black, light green, brown and cream-colored marbles occur in Central Texas in Burnet, Gillespie, Llano and Mason counties. West Texas metamorphic marbles include the bluish-white and the black marbles found southwest of Alpine in Brewster County and the white marble from **Marble Canyon** north of Van Horn in Culberson County. Marble can be used as **dimension stone, terrazzo and roofing aggregate** and for other purposes.

MERCURY (QUICKSILVER) — Mercury minerals, chiefly **cinnabar**, occur in the **Terlingua district** and nearby districts of southern Brewster and southeastern Presidio counties. Mining began there about 1894, and from 1905 to 1935, Texas was one of the nation's leading producers of quicksilver. Following World War II, a sharp drop in demand and price, along with depletion of developed ore reserves, caused abandonment of all the Texas mercury mines.

With a rise in the price, sporadic mining took place between 1951-1960. In 1965, when the price of mercury moved to a record high, renewed interest in the Texas mercury districts resulted in the reopening of several mines and the discovery of new ore reserves. By April 1972, however, the price had declined and the mines have reported no production since 1973.

MICA — Large crystals of flexible, transparent mica minerals in igneous pegmatite rocks and mica flakes in metamorphic schist rocks are found in the **Llano area** of Central Texas and the **Van Horn area** of West Texas. Most Central Texas deposits do not meet specifications for sheet mica, and although several attempts have been made to produce West Texas sheet mica in Culberson and Hudspeth counties, sustained production has not been achieved. A mica quarry operated for a short time in the early 1980s in the Van Horn Mountains of Culberson and Hudspeth counties to mine mica schist for use as an **additive in rotary drilling fluids**.

MOLYBDENUM — Small occurrences of molybdenite have been found in Burnet and Llano counties, and **wulfenite**, another molybdenum mineral, has been noted in rocks in the **Quitman Mountains** of Hudspeth County. Molybdenum minerals also occur at **Cave Peak** north of Van Horn in Culberson County, in the **Altuda Mountain area** of northwestern Brewster County and in association with uranium ores of the Gulf Coastal Plain.

PEAT — This spongy organic substance forms in bogs from plant remains. It has been found in the **Gulf Coastal Plain** in several localities including Gonzales, Guadalupe, Lee, Milam, Polk and San Jacinto counties. There has been intermittent, small-scale production of some of the peat for use as a **soil conditioner**.

PERLITE — Perlite, a glassy igneous rock, expands to a lightweight, porous mass when heated. It can be used as a **lightweight aggregate, filter aid, horticultural aggregate** and for other purposes. Perlite occurs in Presidio County, where it has been mined in the **Pinto Canyon area** north of the **Chinati Mountains**. No perlite is currently mined in Texas, but perlite mined outside of Texas is expanded at plants in Bexar, Dallas, El Paso, Guadalupe, Harris and Nolan counties.

PHOSPHATE — Rock phosphate is present in Paleozoic rocks in several areas of Brewster and Presidio counties in West Texas and in Central Texas, but the known deposits are not large. In Northeast Texas, sedimentary rock phosphate occurs in thin conglomeratic lenses in Upper Cretaceous and Tertiary rock units; possibly some of these low-grade phosphorites could be processed on a small scale for local use as a **fertilizer**. Imported phosphate rock is processed at a plant in Brownsville.

POTASH — The potassium mineral **polyhalite** is widely distributed in the subsurface Permian Basin of West Texas and has been found in many wells in that area. During 1927-1931, the federal government drilled a series of potash-test wells in Crane, Crockett, Ector, Glasscock, Loving, Reagan, Upton and Winkler counties. In addition to polyhalite, which was found in all of the counties, these wells revealed the presence of the potassium minerals **carnallite and sylvite** in Loving County and carnallite in Winkler County. The known Texas potash deposits are not as rich as those in the New Mexico portion of the Permian Basin and have not been developed.

PUMICITE (VOLCANIC ASH) — Deposits of volcanic ash occur in Brazos, Fayette, Gonzales, Karnes, Polk, Starr and other counties of the Texas Coastal Plain. Deposits also have been found in the Trans-Pecos area, High Plains and in several counties east of the High Plains. Volcanic ash is used to prepare **pozzolan cement, cleansing and scouring compounds and soaps and sweeping compounds**; as a **carrier for insecticides**, and for other purposes. It has been mined in Dickens, Lynn, Scurry, Starr and other counties.

QUICKSILVER (see **MERCURY**).

RARE-EARTH ELEMENTS AND METALS — The term, "rare-earth elements," is commonly applied to elements of the **lanthanide** group (atomic numbers 57 through 71) plus **yttrium**. Yttrium, atomic number 39 and not a member of the lanthanide group, is included as a rare-earth element because it has similar properties to members of that group and usually occurs in nature with them. The metals **thorium and scandium** are sometimes termed "rare metals" because their occurence is often associated with the rare-earth elements.

The majority of rare-earth elements are consumed as **catalysts** in petroleum cracking and other chemical industries. Rare earths are widely used in the **glass industry for tableware, specialty glasses, optics and fiber optics**. Cerium oxide has growing use as a **polishing compound** for glass, gem stones, cathode-ray tube faceplates, and other polishing. Rare earths are alloyed with various metals to produce materials used in the **aeronautic, space and electronics** industries. Addition of rare-earth elements may improve resistance to metal fatigue at high temperatures, reduce potential for corrosion, and selectively increase conductivity and magnetism of the metal.

Various members of this group, including **thorium**, have anomalous concentrations in the **rhyolitic and related igneous rocks** of the **Quitman Mountains** and the **Sierra Blanca area** of Trans-Pecos.

SALT (SODIUM CHLORIDE) (see also **BRINES**) — Salt resources of Texas are virtually inexhaustible. Enormous deposits occur in the subsurface **Permian Basin** of West Texas and in the **salt domes of the Gulf Coastal Plain**. Salt also is found in the alkali **playa lakes** of the High Plains, the **alkali flats or salt lakes in the Salt Basin** of Culberson and Hudspeth counties and along some of the bays and lagoons of the South Texas **Gulf Coast**.

Texas is one of the leading salt-producing states. **Rock salt** is obtained from underground mines in **salt domes at Grand Saline** in Van Zandt County. Approximately one-third of the salt produced in the state is from rock salt; most of the salt is produced by solution mining as brines from wells drilled into the underground salt deposits.

SAND, INDUSTRIAL — Sands used for special purposes, due to **high silica content** or to unique physical properties, command higher prices than common sand. Industrial sands in Texas occur mainly in the **Central Gulf Coastal Plain** and in **North Central Texas**. They include **abrasive, blast, chemical, engine, filtration, foundry, glass, hydraulic-fracturing (propant), molding and pottery sands**. Recent production of industrial sands has been from Atascosa, Colorado, Hardin, Harris, Liberty, Limestone, McCulloch, Newton, Smith, Somervell and Upshur counties.

SAND AND GRAVEL (CONSTRUCTION) — Sand and gravel are among the most extensively utilized resources in Texas. Principal occurrence is along the major streams and in stream terraces. Sand and gravel are important **bulk construction materials, used as railroad ballast, base materials** and for other purposes.

SANDSTONE — Sandstones of a variety of colors and textures are widely distributed in a number of geologic formations in Texas. Some of the sandstones have been quarried for use as **dimension stone** in El Paso, Parker, Terrell, Ward and other counties. **Crushed sandstone** is produced in Freestone, Gaines, Jasper, McMullen, Motley and other counties for use as **road-building material, terrazzo stone and aggregate**.

SERPENTINITE — Several masses of serpentinite, which formed from the alteration of basic igneous rocks, are associated with other Precambrian metamorphic rocks of the **Llano Uplift**. The largest deposit is the **Coal Creek serpentinite mass** in northern Blanco and Gillespie counties from which **terrazzo chips** have been produced. Other deposits are present in Gillespie and Llano counties. (The features that are associated with surface and subsurface Cretaceous rocks in several counties in or near the **Balcones Fault Zone** and that are commonly known as **"serpentine plugs"** are not serpentine at all, but are altered igneous volcanic necks and pipes and mounds of altered volcanic ash — **palagonite** — that accumulated around the former **submarine volcanic pipes.**)

SHELL — Oyster shells and other shells in shallow coastal waters and in deposits along the **Texas Gulf Coast** have been produced in the past chiefly by dredging. They were used to a limited extent as raw material in the **manufacture of cement, as concrete aggregate and road base**, and for other purposes. No shell has been produced in Texas since 1981.

SILVER — During the period 1885-1952, the production of silver in Texas, as reported by the U.S. Bureau of Mines, totaled about **33 million troy ounces**. For about 70 years, silver was the most consistently produced metal in Texas, although always in moderate quantities. All of the production came from the **Trans-Pecos country** of West Texas, where the silver was mined in Brewster County (**Altuda Mountain**), Culberson and Hudspeth counties (**Van Horn Mountains and Van Horn-Allamoore district**), Hudspeth County (**Quitman Mountains and Eagle Mountains**) and Presidio County (**Chinati Mountains area, Loma Plata mine and Shafter district**).

Chief producer was the **Presidio mine in the Shafter district**, which began operations in the late 1800s, and, through September 1942, produced more than 30 million ounces of silver — more than 92 percent of Texas' total silver production. Water in the lower mine levels, lean ores and low price of silver resulted in the closing of the mine in 1942. Another important silver producer was the **Hazel copper-silver mine** in the **Van Horn-Allamoore district** in Culberson County, which accounted for more than 2 million ounces.

An increase in the price of silver in the late 1970s stimulated prospecting for new reserves, and exploration began near the old **Presidio mine**, near the old **Plata Verde mine** in the Van Horn Mountains district, at the **Bonanza mine** in the **Quitman Mountains** district and at the old **Hazel mine**. A decline in the price of silver in the early 1980s, however, resulted in reduction of exploration and mine development in the region. There is no current exploration in these areas.

SOAPSTONE (see **TALC AND SOAPSTONE**).

SODIUM SULFATE (SALT CAKE) — Sodium sulfate minerals occur in salt beds and brines of the alkali **playa lakes** of the High Plains in West Texas. In some lakes, the sodium sulfate minerals are present in deposits a few feet beneath the lakebeds. Sodium sulfate also is found in underground brines in the Permian Basin. Current production is from brines and dry salt beds at alkali lakes in Gaines and Terry counties. Past production was reported in Lynn and Ward counties. Sodium sulfate is used chiefly by the **detergent and paper and pulp industries**. Other uses are in the **preparation of glass and other products**.

STONE (see **BUILDING STONE** and **CRUSHED STONE**).

STRONTIUM — Deposits of the mineral **celestite (strontium sulfate)** have been found in a number of places, including localities in Brown, Coke, Comanche, Fisher, Lampasas, Mills, Nolan, Real, Taylor, Travis and Williamson counties. Most of the occurrences are very minor, and no strontium is currently produced in the state.

SULFUR — Texas is **one of the world's principal sulfur-producing areas**. The sulfur is mined from deposits of native sulfur, and it is extracted from sour (sulfur-bearing) natural gas and petroleum. **Recovered sulfur** is a growing industry and accounted for approximately 60 percent of all 1987 sulfur production in the United States, but only approximately 40 percent of Texas production. Native sulfur is found in large deposits in the caprock of some of the **salt domes** along the Texas Gulf Coast and in some of the surface and subsurface Permian strata of West Texas, notably in Culberson and Pecos counties.

Native sulfur obtained from the underground deposits is known as **Frasch sulfur**, so-called because of Herman Frasch, the chemist who devised the method of drilling wells into the deposits, melting the sulfur with superheated water and forcing the molten sulfur to the surface. Most of the production now goes to the users in molten form.

Frasch sulfur is produced from only one Gulf Coast salt dome in Wharton County and from West Texas underground Permian strata in Culberson County. Operations at several Gulf Coast domes have been closed in recent years. During the 1940s, acidic sulfur earth was produced in the **Rustler Springs district** in Culberson County for use as a **fertilizer and soil conditioner.** Sulfur is recovered from sour natural gas and petroleum at plants in numerous Texas counties.

Sulfur is used in the preparation of **fertilizers and organic and inorganic chemicals, in petroleum refining** and for many other purposes.

TALC AND SOAPSTONE — Deposits of talc are found in the Precambrian metamorphic rocks of the **Allamoore area** of eastern Hudspeth and western Culberson counties. Soapstone, containing talc, occurs in the Precambrian metamorphic rocks of the **Llano Uplift** area, notably in Blanco, Gillespie and Llano counties. Current production is from surface mines in the **Allamoore area**. Talc is used in **ceramic, roofing, paint, paper, plastic, synthetic rubber** and other products.

TIN — Tin minerals have been found in El Paso and Mason counties. Small quantities were produced during the early 1900s in the Franklin Mountains north of El Paso. **Cassiterite (tin dioxide)** occurrences in Mason County are believed to be very minor. The **only tin smelter in the United States**, built at **Texas City** by the federal government during World War II and later sold to a private company, processes tin concentrates from ores mined outside of Texas, tin residues and secondary tin-bearing materials.

TITANIUM — The titanium mineral **rutile** has been found in small amounts at the **Mueller prospect** in Jeff Davis County. Another titanium mineral, **ilmenite**, occurs in sandstones in Burleson, Fayette, Lee, Starr and several other counties. Deposits that would be considered commercial under present conditions have not been found.

TRAP ROCK (see **BASALT**).

TUNGSTEN — The tungsten mineral **scheelite** has been found in small deposits in Gillespie and Llano counties and in the **Quitman Mountains** in Hudspeth County. Small deposits of other tungsten minerals have been prospected in the **Cave Peak area** north of Van Horn in Culberson County.

URANIUM — Uranium deposits were discovered in the **Texas Coastal Plain** in 1954 when abnormal radioactivity was detected in the Karnes County area. A number of uranium deposits have since been discovered within a belt of strata extending more than 250 miles from the middle Coastal Plain southwestward to the Rio Grande.

Various uranium minerals also have been found in other areas of Texas, including the **Trans-Pecos**, the **Llano Uplift** and the **High Plains**. With the exception of small shipments from the High Plains during the 1950s, all the uranium production in Texas has been from the Coastal Plain. Uranium has been obtained from surface mines extending from northern Live Oak County, southeastern Atascosa County, across northern Karnes County and into southern Gonzales County.

All mines are now reclaimed. All current uranium production is by **in-situ leaching**, brought to the surface through wells, and stripped from the solution at several Coastal Plain recovery operations. Decreased demand and price of uranium since 1980 has brought a sharp decline in operations in Texas.

VERMICULITE — Vermiculite, a mica-like mineral that expands when heated, occurs in Burnet, Gillespie, Llano, Mason and other counties in the **Llano region**. It has been produced at a surface mine in Llano County. Vermiculite, mined outside of Texas, is exfoliated (expanded) at plants in Dallas, Houston and San Antonio. Exfoliated vermiculite is used for **lightweight concrete aggregate, horticulture, insulation** and other purposes.

VOLCANIC ASH (see **PUMICITE**).

ZEOLITES — The zeolite minerals **clinoptilolite** and **analcime** occur in Tertiary lavas and tuffs in Brewster, Jeff Davis and Presidio counties, in West Texas. Clinoptilolite also is found associated with Tertiary tuffs in the southern Texas Coastal Plain, including deposits in Karnes, McMullen and Webb counties, and currently is produced in McMullen County. Zeolites, sometimes called **"molecular sieves,"** can be used in **ion-exchange processes to reduce pollution**, as a catalyst in **oil cracking**, in obtaining **high-purity oxygen and nitrogen** from air, in **water purification** and for many other purposes.

ZINC (see **LEAD AND ZINC**). ☆

Agriculture

Agribusiness, the combined phases of food and fiber production, processing, transporting and marketing, is a leading Texas industry. Most of the following discussion is devoted to the phase of production on farms and ranches.

Information was provided by Agricultural Extension Service specialists, the Texas Agricultural Statistics Service, the U.S. Department of Agriculture, and U.S. Department of Commerce. It was coordinated by Dr. Carl G. Anderson, Extension Marketing Economist, Texas A&M University. All references are to Texas unless otherwise specified.

Agriculture is one of the most important industries in Texas. Many businesses, financial institutions and individuals are involved in providing supplies, credit and services to farmers and ranchers and in processing and marketing agricultural commodities.

Including all its agribusiness phases, agriculture added about $42 billion in 1994 to the economic activity of the state. The estimated value of farm assets in Texas — the land, buildings, livestock, machinery, crops, inventory on farms, household goods, and farm financial assets — totaled approximately $76 billion at the beginning of 1994, down $12 billion from the beginning of 1992.

Texas agriculture is a strong industry. Receipts from farm and ranch marketings in 1994 were estimated at $12.8 billion. In 1984, this figure stood at $9.7 billion.

The potential for further growth is great. With increasing demand for food and fiber throughout the world, and the importance of agricultural exports to this nation's trade balance, agriculture in Texas is destined to play a very important role in the future.

Major efforts of research and educational programs by the Texas A&M University System and other institutions are directed toward developing the state's agricultural industry to its fullest potential. The goal is to capitalize on natural advantages that agriculture has in Texas because of the relatively warm climate, productive soils and availability of excellent export and transportation facilities.

The number and the nature of farms have changed over time. The number of farms in Texas has decreased from 418,000 in 1940 to 185,000 in 1994 with an average size of 708 acres. Average value per farm of all farm assets, including land and buildings, has increased from $20,100 in 1950 to $331,200 in 1993.

Mechanization of farming continues as new and larger machines replace manpower. Even though machinery price tags are high, machine power is much cheaper than manpower. Tractors, mechanical harvesters and numerous cropping machines have virtually eliminated menial tasks that were traditional to farming.

Balance Sheet of Texas Farms and Ranches Jan. 1, 1985-Dec. 31, 1993

Table below shows the financial status of Texas farms and ranches as of Jan. 1 of the years 1985-93.

Item	1985	1986	‡1987	1988	1989	1990	††1991	1992	§1993
ASSETS:									
Physical Assets:									
Real estate	80,439	73,101	73,264	68,467	58,853	57,673	55,355	55,719	57,204
Non-real estate:									
Livestock and poultry	4,729	4,761	6,621	7,514	7,929	8,570	8,343	8,983	8,986
Machinery and motor vehicles	5,461	5,384	5,330	5,437	5,411	5,503	5,590	5,554	5,675
*Crops stored on and off farms	652	721	810	794	841	562	598	618	531
Purchased Inputs	85	136	349	317	222	134	111	157	147
†Household equipment and furnishings	1,804	1,861	3,347	3,482	—	—	—	—	—
Financial assets:									
‡Investments in co-ops	1,356	1,538	—	—	—	—	—	—	—
‡Other financial	2,777	3,286	—	—	—	—	—	—	—
‡Financial	—	—	5,104	5,121	2,746	2,929	3,136	3,406	3,788
Total Assets	**97,303**	**90,789**	**94,824**	**91,131**	**76,003**	**75,371**	**73,133**	**74,437**	**76,331**
LIABILITIES:									
**Real estate debt	6,486	6,071	5,678	5,143	4,560	4,604	4,589	4,489	4,521
***Non-real estate debt:									
****Excluding CCC loans	6,545	5,878	5,763	5,576	5,104	4,876	5,059	4,811	5,153
Total Liabilities	**13,031**	**11,949**	**11,441**	**10,718**	**9,663**	**9,479**	**9,648**	**9,300**	**9,674**
Owners' equities	84,271	78,840	83,383	80,412	66,339	65,892	63,485	65,137	66,657
TOTAL CLAIMS	**97,303**	**90,789**	**94,824**	**91,131**	**76,003**	**75,371**	**73,133**	**74,437**	**76,331**

**All crops held on farms including value above loan rates for crops held under CCC.*

***Includes CCC storage and drying facilities loans.*

****Includes debt owed to institutional lender and to noninstitutional or miscellaneous lenders.*

*****Nonrecourse CCC loans secured by crops owned by farmers. These crops are included as assets in this balance sheet.*

†As of 1993, Household equipment and furnishings not reported.

‡As of 1987, Investments in Co-ops and Other Financial reported as Financial.

§Preliminary.

*Source: **"Economic Indicators of the Farm Sector: State Financial Summary 1985,"** USDA, ERS, January 1987, p.229.; 1988, 1989, 1991, 1993, p. 136 (including operator households).*

Revolutionary agricultural chemicals have appeared, along with improved plants and animals and methods of handling them. Hazards of farming and ranching were reduced by better use of weather information, machinery and other improvements; but rising costs, labor availability, and high energy costs have added to concerns of farmers and ranchers.

Among the major changes in Texas agriculture since World War II are these:

- Farms have become fewer, larger, specialized, and much more expensive to own and operate, but far more productive.
- Irrigation is more important in crop production.
- Crops and livestock have made major changes in production areas, as in the concentration of cotton on the High Plains and livestock increases in Central and Eastern Texas.
- Pest- and disease-control methods have greatly improved. Herbicides are relied upon for weed control.
- Ranchers and farmers are better educated and informed, more science- and business-oriented.
- Feedlot finishing, commercial broiler production, artificial insemination, improved pastures and brush control, reduced feed requirements and other changes have greatly increased livestock and poultry efficiency. Biotechnology and genetic engineering promise new breakthroughs in reaching even higher levels of productivity. Horticultural plant and nursery businesses have expanded. Improved wildlife management has increased deer, turkey and other wildlife populations.
- Cooperation among farmers in marketing, promotion and other endeavors has increased.
- Agricultural producers have become increasingly dependent on outside sources for such supplies as feeds, chemicals, credit and other essentials.

*Realized Gross Income and Net Income from Farming, Texas, 1960-1993

Year	**Realized Gross Farm Income	Farm Production Expenses	Net Change In Farm Inventories	***Total Net Farm Income	***Total Net Income Per Farm
	— Million Dollars —				Dollars
1960	2,547.0	1,751.5	43.2	838.7	3,396.0
1970	4,026.5	3,232.5	106.8	900.8	4,249.0
1980	§9,611.4	9,081.1	-542.5	530.4	2,806.3
1981	11,545.7	9,564.7	699.9	1,981.0	10,481.5
1982	11,372.7	9,581.5	-124.3	1,791.2	9,527.7
1983	11,129.2	9,387.9	-590.7	1,741.4	9,312.3
1984	12,058.8	9,762.8	168.8	2,296.0	11,835.0
1985	11,272.7	9,226.3	-9.0	2,046.4	10,658.3
1986	10,282.0	9,459.5	-349.0	1,012.3	5,327.9
1987	11,155.6	9,945.5	-563.2	2.328.1	12,383.5
1988	12,133.0	10,363.9	-62.1	2,280.6	12,195.7
1989	12,873.3	10,658.7	-637.6	2,214.6	11,906.0
1990	14,356.0	11,366.0	311.9	2,990.0	15,904.0
1991	14,336.9	11,344.6	69.1	2,992.4	16,175.0
1992	14,181.4	10,982.0	299.0	3,199.5	17,484.0
1993	15,724.7	11,626.7	310.7	4,098.0	22,151.0

**Details for items may not add to totals because of rounding. Series revised, September, 1981.*

***Cash receipts from farm marketings, government payments, value of home consumption and gross rental value of farm dwellings.*

****Farm income of farm operators.*

§Starting in 1977, farms with production of $1,000 or more used to figure income.

Source: "Economic Indicators of the Farm Sector, State Financial Summary, 1985," 1987," 1989,: 1993"; USDA/ERS; "Texas Agricultural Cash Receipts and Price Statistics," USDA/NASS/Agricultural Statistician, Texas Agricultural Statistics Service, Bulletin 252, Nov. 1994.

Agribusiness

Many Texas farmers and ranchers have become specialized, producing only specific crops and livestock. They rely on outside suppliers of production needs and services. On the output side, they need assemblers, processors and distributors.

The proportion of Texans whose livelihood is linked to agriculture has changed dramatically. In 1940, about 23 percent were agricultural producers, and about 17 percent were suppliers or were engaged in assembly, processing and distribution of agricultural products. The agribusiness alignment in 1994 was less than 2 percent on farms and ranches, with about 17 percent of the labor force providing production or marketing supplies and services and retailing food and fiber products. In 1991, just over 1 million people were employed in agribusiness with over $14.5 billion in wages. The impact of production agriculture on the economy of Texas is about $42 billion annually.

Cash Receipts

Farm and ranch cash receipts in 1993 totaled $12.617 billion. With estimates of $1,421 billion for government payments, $682.1 million of noncash income and $694.1 million of other farm income included, realized gross farm income totaled $15.414 billion. With farm production expenses of $11.323 billion, net income totaled $4.098 billion. The value of inventory adjustment was $310.7 million.

Farm and Ranch Assets

Farm and ranch assets totaled $76.3 billion on Jan. 1, 1994. This was up from the 1992 level of $74.4 billion. Value of real estate increased almost 3 percent to $57.2 billion. Liabilities totaled $9.7 billion, up slightly from $9.3 billion in 1992.

Percent of Income From Products

Livestock and livestock products accounted for 66.1 percent of the $12.6 billion cash receipts from farm marketings in 1993 with the remaining 33.9 percent from crops. Receipts from livestock have trended up largely because of reduced crop acreage associated with farm programs and low prices. However, these relationships change because of variations in commodity prices and volume of marketings.

Cattle, hogs and sheep accounted for 51.6 percent of total cash receipts received by Texas farmers and ranchers in 1993, mostly from cattle and calf sales. Dairy products made up 6.2 percent of receipts, poultry and eggs 6.4 percent, and miscellaneous livestock 1.9 percent.

Cotton accounted for 10.6 percent of total receipts, feed crops 7.7 percent, food grains 3.3 percent, vegetables 2.8 percent, greenhouse/nursery products 5.6 percent, oil crops 1.6 percent, fruits and nuts .5 percent, and other crops 1.8 percent.

Texas' Rank Among States

Measured by cash receipts for farm and ranch marketings, Texas ranked second overall in 1993. California ranked first and Iowa third.

Texas normally leads all other states in numbers of farms and ranches, farm and ranch land, cattle slaughtered, cattle on feed, calf births, sheep and lambs slaughtered, goats, cash receipts from livestock marketings, cattle and calves, beef cows, sheep and lambs, wool production, mohair production and exports of lard and tallow. The state also usually leads in production of cotton and grain sorghum.

Texas Agricultural Exports

The value of Texas' share of agricultural exports in fiscal year 1994 was $2.955 billion. Cotton accounted for $736.8 million of the exports; feed grains, $372.0 million; wheat and flour, $170.7 million; rice, $85.8 million; fats, oils and greases, $75.0 million; cottonseed products, $40.2 million; hides and skins, $218.6 million; meats and meat products, $585.1 million; fruits, $35.7 million; peanuts, $35.6 million; soybeans, $11.7 million; vegetables, $36.8 million; poultry products, $87.2 million; dairy products, $23.3 million; and miscellaneous other products, $432.4 million.

Texas' 1994 exports of $2.955 billion of agricultural products compares with $2.464 billion in 1993 and $2.649 billion in 1992.

Hunting

The management of wildlife as an economic enterprise through leasing for hunting makes a significant contribution to the economies of many counties. The income from hunting leases for farmers and ranchers in 1994 was estimated at $185 million.

The demand for hunting opportunities is growing, while the land capable of producing huntable wildlife is decreasing. As a result, farmers and ranchers are placing more emphasis on wildlife management to help meet the market for hunting leases.

Irrigation

Texas farmers irrigate approximately 6 million acres of land. Although some irrigation is practiced in nearly every county of the state, about 60 percent of Texas' total irrigated acreage is on the High Plains. Other concentrated areas of irrigation are the Gulf Coast rice-producing areas, the Lower Rio Grande Valley, the Winter Garden district of South Texas, the Trans-Pecos area of West Texas and the peanut-producing area in North Central Texas centered around Erath, Eastland and Comanche counties. Sprinkler irrigation is used on about 34 percent of the total irrigated acreage with surface irrigation methods — primarily furrow, border and contour check methods — being used on the rest.

Drip, or trickle, irrigation has attracted much attention in recent years for use on tree crops such as citrus, pecans, avocados, peaches and apples, or for irrigating vegetables under plastic mulch. It is also used on much of the grape acreage in Texas vineyards. The use of drip irrigation is increasing, with present acreage estimated to be 75,000 acres.

Approximately 70 percent of the state's irrigation water is pumped from wells. Surface water sources supply the remainder. Declining groundwater levels in several of the major aquifers is a serious problem. As the water level declines, well yields decrease and pumping costs increase. Decreasing groundwater supplies and higher fuel prices have contributed to the decrease in irrigated acreage.

The value of crop production from irrigated acreage is 50 to 60 percent of the total value of all crop production, although only about 30 percent of the state's total harvested cropland acreage is irrigated.

Cash Receipts from Farm Marketings 1940-1993

Year	Crops	Livestock and Livestock Production	Total Crops and Livestock	*Government Payments	Total Crops, Livestock and Payments
	— 1,000 dollars —				
1940	261,949	253,422	515,371	82,416	597,787
1950	1,215,538	882,253	2,097,791	24,934	2,122,725
1960	1,258,286	983,189	2,241,475	72,531	2,314,006
1970	1,264,766	1,956,991	3,221,757	543,156	3,764,913
1980	3,925,092	5,185,067	9,110,159	231,840	9,341,999
1981	4,371,497	5,448,215	9,819,712	321,365	10,141,077
1982	4,206,582	5,421,060	9,627,642	643,598	10,271,240
1983	3,654,911	5,521,428	9,176,339	1,129,855	10,306,194
1984	3,754,843	5,900,842	9,655,685	782,441	10,438,126
1985	3,814,575	5,447,863	9,262,438	848,079	10,110,517
1986	3,100,048	5,512,607	8,612,655	978,393	9,591,048
1987	3,042,544	6,089,748	9,132,292	1,441,175	10,573,467
1988	3,714,902	6,628,558	10,343,460	1,155,332	11,498,792
1989	4,059,369	6,860,870	10,920,239	1,248,713	12,168,952
1990	4,065,209	7,750,906	11,816,115	974,702	12,790,817
1991	4,335,318	7,880,901	12,216,219	777,925	12,994,144
1992	3,936,886	7,524,215	11,461,101	1,162,039	12,623,101
1993	4,274,683	8,342,222	12,616,905	1,420,830	14,037,705

**Includes Payment-in-kind (PIK) of $661 million.*
Source: "1985 Texas Agricultural Cash Receipts, Prices Received and Paid by Farmers," Texas Agricultural Statistical Service, USDA, Bulletin 239, August 1986, page 3; Nov. 1994, p. 3. "Economic Indicators of the Farm Sector, State Financial Summary, 1989," USDA, ERS, Feb. 1991, page 54; March 1993, pp. 124-126; Jan. 1995.

Texas Export Shares of Agricultural Commodities, 1991-1994

Commodity*	1991	1992	1993	1994	1994 % of U.S. Total
	— million dollars —				
Rice	118.2	113.4	100.5	85.8	9.7
Cotton.	844.2	584.8	313.9	736.8	31.9
Fats, Oils & Greases	59.6	68.7	73.2	75.0	14.1
Hides & Skins. . .	214.9	197.8	191.4	218.6	15.2
Meats other than Poultry. . .	477.5	540.4	527.2	585.1	14.6
Feed Grains	265.2	408.7	353.4	372.0	6.3
Poultry Products	54.4	61.5	66.2	87.2	5.1
Fruits	14.9	16.5	32.8	35.7	1.2
Vegetables	17.2	20.0	39.7	36.8	1.1
Wheat & Flour . .	116.0	177.2	223.4	170.7	4.0
Soybeans	12.2	16.0	35.9	11.7	0.2
Cottonseed & Prod.	24.7	30.4	20.9	40.2	33.9
Peanuts	28.2	43.9	41.6	35.6	16.2
Tree Nuts	13.3	10.4	18.2	8.4	0.8
Dairy Products . .	8.4	18.7	25.5	23.3	3.3
†All Other	281.4	340.9	400.5	432.4	5.7
TOTAL.	2,550.3	2,649.3	2,464.3	2,955.3	6.8

Totals may not add because of rounding.
† Mainly confectionary, nursery and greenhouse, essential oils, sunflower seed oil, beverages, and other miscellaneous animal and vegetable products.
**Commodity and related preparations.*
*Source: **Foreign Agricultural Trade of the United States**, various issues, March/April, 1994 and 1995.*

The percentage of total crop production from irrigated lands varies from year to year, depending primarily on the amount of rainfall received. In good rainfall years, the proportion of irrigated crop production to total crop production is somewhat less. However, in years of below-average rainfall, the percentage of the total crop production that comes from irrigated lands increases. Irrigation enables Texas farmers to produce a dependable supply of food and fiber products without total dependence upon natural rainfall.

Principal Crops

In most recent years, the value of crop production in Texas is less than half of the total value of the state's agricultural output. Cash receipts from farm sales of crops are reduced somewhat because some grain and roughage is fed to livestock on farms where they were produced and also because of the farm program for crops.

Receipts from all Texas crops totaled $4.3 billion in 1992; $3.9 billion in 1992; and $4.3 billion in 1991.

Cotton, sorghum grain and corn account for a large part of total crop receipts. In 1993, cotton contributed about 31.4 percent of the crop total; corn, 12.1 percent; sorghum grain 10 percent; and wheat 7.7 percent. Hay, vegetables, rice, cottonseed, peanuts and soybeans are other important cash crops.

Value of Texas Cotton and Cottonseed, 1900-1994

Crop Year	Cotton Production (Bales)	Cotton Value	Cottonseed Production (Tons)	Cottonseed Value
	(All Figures in Thousands)			
1900	3,438	$157,306	1,531	$20,898
1910	3,047	210,260	1,356	31,050
1920	4,345	376,080	1,934	41,350
1930	4,037	194,080	1,798	40,820
1940	3,234	162,140	1,318	31,852
1950	2,946	574,689	1,232	111,989
1960	4,346	612,224	1,821	75,207
1970	3,191	314,913	1,242	68,310
*1980	3,320	1,091,616	1,361	161,959
1981	5,645	1,259,964	2,438	207,230
1982	2,700	664,848	1,122	90,882
1983	2,380	677,443	1,002	162,324
1984	3,680	927,360	1,563	157,863
1985	3,910	968,429	1,634	102,156
1986	2,535	560,945	1,053	82,118
1987	4,635	1,325,981	1,915	157,971
1988	5,215	1,291,651	2,131	238,672
1989	2,870	812,784	1,189	141,491
1990	4,965	1,506,182	1,943	225,388
1991	4,710	1,211,789	1,903	134,162
1992	3,265	769,495	1,346	145,368
1993	5,095	1,308,396	2,147	255,493
1994	4,915	1,639,644	2,111	213,211

**Beginning in 1971, the basis for cotton prices was changed from 500-pound gross weight to 480-pound net weight bale. To compute comparable prices for previous years, multiply price times 1.04167.*

Source: "Texas Agricultural Facts," May 19, 1995, and "1993 Texas Crop Statistics," Texas Agricultural Statistics Service, Austin for recent statistics.

This table was compiled by Texas Cottonseed Crushers from their historical records and reports of the U.S.Department of Commerce and U.S. Department of Agriculture.

Cotton

Cotton has been a major crop in Texas for more than a century. Since 1880, Texas has led all states in cotton production in most years; today, the annual Texas cotton harvest amounts to approximately a fourth of total production in the United States. The annual cotton crop has averaged 4.2 million bales since 1984.

Total value of upland and pima lint cotton produced in Texas in 1994 was $1.61 billion. Cottonseed value in 1994 was $209,916,000, making the total value of the Texas crop around $1.82 billion.

Upland cotton was harvested from 5.15 million acres in 1994 and American-Pima from 27,000 acres, for a total of 5.177 million acres. Cotton acreage harvested in 1993 totaled 5.08 million. Production amounted to 5.05 million bales in 1994 and 5.14 million in 1993. Counties leading in production of upland cotton in 1993 include Gaines, Lubbock, Hale, Terry and Hockley.

Cotton is the raw material for processing operations at gins, oil mills, compresses, and a small number of textile mills in Texas. Less than 10 percent of the raw cotton is processed within the state.

Cotton in Texas is machine harvested. Growers in the 1993-94 season used stripper harvesters to gather 71 percent of the crop and spindle pickers to harvest the remaining 29 percent. Field storage of harvested seed cotton is gaining in popularity as gins decline in number. In 1993-94, 85 percent of the cotton was ginned from modules and 15 percent from trailers. Much of the Texas crop is exported; Japan, South Korea and Mexico are major buyers.

The state's major cotton-producing areas are tied together by an electronic marketing system — a computer network that links producers through terminals that are usually located at gins to a relatively large number of buyers. The network provides farmers with a centralized market that allows many sellers and buyers to trade with each other on a regular basis.

The first high-volume, instrument cotton-classing office in the nation was opened at Lamesa, Dawson County, in 1980.

Cotton Ginning

In 1994, 4,845,700 running bales of cotton were processed at Texas' 404 active gins. This compares with 4,996,900 bales in 1993 and 3,037,350 in 1992. Gaines County's 13 active gins topped the list with 332,850 bales, down slightly from 1993's 347,350 bales. Hale County's 18 gins processed 327,100 bales in 1994.

Active gins were reported in 97 Texas counties in 1994. Topping the list was Hale County with 18, followed by Lubbock with 17 and Gaines and Lamb with 13 each. Floyd, Hidalgo and Lynn reported 12 each; Dawson and Hockley each had 11. Counties reporting 10 gins were San Patricio and Terry; nine each, Cameron, Jones and Martin; eight each, Crosby, Haskell, Nueces, Tom Green and Willacy; seven each, Bailey, Castro, Fort Bend, Parmer and Runnels; six each, El Paso, Wharton and Williamson; five each, Collingsworth, Hall, Hill, Howard, Knox, Swisher, Wilbarger and Yoakum; four, Robertson; three each, Brazoria,

Brazos, Briscoe, Collin, Ellis, Fisher, Garza, Milam, Mitchell, Scurry and Zavala; two each Baylor, Childress, Cochran, Concho, Cottle, Dickens, Falls, Glasscock, Hardeman, Hunt, Kleberg, Lamar, Medina, Motley, Navarro, Reeves, Taylor and Throckmorton. Those counties reporting one active gin in 1994 were Borden, Burleson, Caldwell, Calhoun, Clay, Coleman, Deaf Smith, Delta, Denton, Donley, Fannin, Foard, Houston, Jackson, Kaufman, Kent, McCulloch, McLennan, Matagorda, Midland, Nolan, Pecos, Refugio, Schleicher, Starr, Travis, Upton, Uvalde, Walker, Wheeler, Wichita and Young.

Grain Sorghum

Grain sorghum in 1993 ranked third in dollar value among crops. Much of the grain is exported, as well as being used in livestock and poultry feed.

Production of grain sorghum in 1994 was 85,904,000 hundredweight (cwt). With an average price of $3.93 per cwt., the total value reached $337,480,000. In 1993, 2.75 million acres of grain sorghum were harvested, yielding an average of 3,192 pounds per acre for a total production of 87,780,000 cwt. It was valued at $4.18 per cwt, for a total value of $366,795,000. In 1992, 4.5 million acres were harvested with an average of 3,472 pounds per acre, or 156,240,000 cwt. At a price of $3.61 per cwt., the total value was $563,580,000.

Although grown to some extent in all counties where crops are important, the largest concentrations are in the High Plains, Rolling Plains, Blackland Prairie, Coastal Bend and Lower Rio Grande Valley areas. Counties leading in production in 1993 were Nueces, Hidalgo, Willacy, San Patricio, Cameron and Williamson.

Research to develop high-yielding hybrids resistant to diseases and insect damage continues.

Rice

Rice, which is grown in about 20 counties on the Coastal Prairie of Texas, ranked third in value among Texas crops for many years. Recently, however, cotton, grain sorghum, wheat, corn, peanuts and hay have outranked rice.

Farms are highly mechanized, producing rice through irrigation and using airplanes for much of the planting, fertilizing and application of insecticides and herbicides.

Texas farmers grow long- and medium-grain rice only. The Texas rice industry, which has grown from 110 acres in 1850 to a high of 642,000 acres in 1954, has been marked by significant yield increases and improved varieties. Record production was in 1981, with 27,239,000 hundredweights harvested. Highest yield was 6,250 pounds per acre in 1986.

Several different types of rice-milling procedures are in use today. The simplest and oldest method produces a product known as regular milled white rice, the most prevalent on the market today.

During this process, rice grains are cleaned to remove chaff, dust and foreign seed, then husks are

Cash Receipts for Commodities, 1991-1993

Commodity	1991	1992	1993
	— Value in $1,000 —		
All Commodities:	$12,216,219	$11,461,101	$12,616,905
Livestock and products	7,880,901	7,524,215	8,342,222
Crops, Fruits and others	4,335,318	3,936,886	4,274,683
Livestock and products:			
Cattle and calves	6,115,818	5,644,620	6,353,371
Milk	683,260	760,213	780,710
Broilers	508,939	553,784	608,700
Eggs	203,038	181,755	202,541
Hogs	95,156	75,505	88,270
Sheep and lambs	64,461	74,495	62,097
Mohair	19,388	12,354	11,197
Wool	13,861	16,896	11,050
Honey	5,897	5,525	4,563
Farm Chickens	2,285	1,330	2,179
Catfish	2,555	2,386	1,576
†Other Livestock	166,243	195,352	215,968
Crops:			
Cotton lint	1,505,831	827,012	1,136,596
Corn	422,261	465,373	519,031
Sorghum, grain	413,197	465,995	437,998
Wheat	230,934	367,504	329,550
Cottonseed	128,105	124,490	207,659
Peanuts	191,100	182,960	156,250
Hay	127,870	121,825	113,801
Onions	72,619	64,921	90,306
Rice	152,323	153,279	90,042
Watermelons	72,038	29,304	42,336
Cabbage	$31,460	$31,536	$37,191
Soybeans	25,496	59,187	35,224
Sugar cane	27,750	33,731	34,731
Cantaloupes	65,828	24,123	31,738
Potatoes	28,690	30,839	30,433
Sugar beets	20,600	28,911	28,359
Peppers, Green	21,870	28,277	19,488
Sweet potatoes	10,791	10,560	14,449
Cucumbers	15,783	18,522	14,296
Celery	7,409	5,363	12,463
Spinach	5,832	11,693	11,428
Carrots	14,331	11,744	11,163
Beans, Dry	5,387	6,339	9,089
Honeydew melons	20,215	12,096	8,944
Oats	4,995	6,028	7,345
Broccoli	6,251	8,259	4,067
Corn, sweet	1,568	1,118	1,350
Tomatoes	2,075	2,191	1,105
Cauliflower	564	515	905
Lettuce	1,680	862	880
Rye	379	569	738
Barley	578	525	532
††Other crops	67,488	73,226	65,702
Fruits and Nuts			
Pecans	66,000	87,300	48,000
Grapefruit	963	3,304	9,786
Oranges	285	1,709	2,572
Peaches	8,772	7,696	8,136
Other Farm Income:			
Greenhouse and nursery	556,000	628,000	701,000

†Includes milkfat, turkey eggs, bees, equine, goats, goat milk and other poultry and livestock.
††Miscellaneous vegetables, field crops, fruits and nuts.
Includes only sales from farms but excluded in cash receipts for all farm commodities.

*Source: **"Economic Indicators of the Farm Sector, State Financial Summary, 1989,"** USDA, ERS, Feb. 1991, pp. 118-119; "Economic Indicators of the Farm Sector, State Financial Summary, 1991," USDA, ERS, March 1993, pp. 124-125; "Texas Agricultural Cash Receipts and Price Statistics, 1993," USDA/NASS/Texas Agricultural Statistics Service, Bulletin 252, Nov. 1994.*

removed from the grains. At this point, the product is called brown rice — the whole unpolished grain of rice with only the outer hull and a small amount of bran removed. It is sometimes sold without further treatment other than grading. It has a delightful nutlike flavor and a slightly chewy texture.

When additional layers of the bran are removed, in a number of steps using several types of machines, the rice becomes white in color and begins to appear as it is normally recognized at retail level. At this point, the product is ready for classification as to size. Rice is more valuable if the grains are not broken. In many cases, additional vitamins are added to the grains to produce what is called "enriched rice."

Another process may be used in rice milling to produce a product called parboiled rice. In this process, the rice is subjected to a combination of steam and pressure prior to the time it is milled in the manner described above. This process gelatinizes the starch in the grain, the treatment aiding in the retention of much of the natural vitamin and mineral content. After cooking, parboiled rice tends to be fluffy, more separate, and plump.

Still another type is precooked rice, which is actually milled rice that, after milling, has been cooked. Then the moisture is removed through dehydration. Precooked rice requires a minimum of preparation time since it needs merely to have the moisture restored.

The United States produces only a small part of the world's total rice, but it is one of the leading exporters. American rice is popular abroad and is exported to more than 100 foreign countries.

Rice production in 1994 totaled 21,252,000 cwt. from 354,000 harvested acres. The crop value total was $138,138,000. Rice production was 16,095,000 cwt. in 1993 on 298,000 acres. Total value was $122,322,000. Rice production was 20,357,000 cwt. in 1992 on 351,000 harvested acres. Value of the 1992 crop was $125,603,000.

Wheat

Wheat for grain is one of the state's most valuable cash crops. In 1994, wheat was exceeded in value by cotton, corn, hay, grain sorghum and fresh vegetables. Wheat pastures also provide considerable winter forage for cattle, which is reflected in value of livestock produced.

Texas wheat production totaled 75,400,000 bushels in 1994, as yield averaged only 26 bushels per acre. Planted acreage totaled 6 million, and 2,900,000 acres were harvested. With an average price of $3.20 per bushel, the 1994 wheat value totaled $241,280,000. In 1993, Texas wheat growers planted 6,100,000 acres and harvested 3,700,000 acres. The yield was 32 bushels per acre for a total production of 118,400,000 bushels. At a price of $2.86 per bushel, total value was $338,624,000.

Texas wheat growers planted 6,100,000 acres in 1992 and harvested grain from 3,700,000 acres. The yield was 32 bushels per acre, for a total production of 118,400,000 bushels with a value of $337,440,000.

Leading wheat-producing counties, based on 1993 production, are Hansford, Ochiltree, Moore, Deaf Smith, Dallam and Sherman. The leading counties, based on acreage planted in 1993 were Ochiltree, Hansford, Swisher, Dallam and Deaf Smith.

Wheat was first grown commercially in Texas near Sherman about 1833. The acreage expanded greatly in North Central Texas after 1850 because of rapid settlement of the state and introduction of the well-adapted Mediterranean strain of wheat. A major family flour industry developed in the Fort Worth/Dallas/Sherman area between 1875 and 1900. Now, around half of the state's acreage is planted on the High Plains and about a third of this is irrigated. Most of the Texas wheat acreage is of the hard red winter class. Because of the development of varieties with improved disease resistance and the use of wheat for winter pasture, there has been a sizable expansion of acreage in Central and South Texas.

Most wheat harvested for grain is used in some phase of the milling industry. The better-quality hard red winter wheat is used to produce commercial bakery flour. Lower grades and soft red winter varieties are used in family flours. By-products of milled wheat are used for feed.

Corn

Interest in corn production throughout the state has increased since the 1970s. Once the principal grain crop, corn acreage declined as plantings of grain sorghum increased. Only 500,000 acres were harvested annually until the mid-1970s, when new hybrids

Top Twenty Counties in Net Cash Return* to Farms, 1992

1. Deaf Smith	$52.7 million
2. Dallam	$50.4 million
3. Hartley	$50.1 million
4. Parmer	$40.0 million
5. Sherman	$35.5 million
6. Moore	$34.6 million
7. Erath	$30.0 million
8. Hidalgo	$29.3 million
9. Hansford	$29.0 million
10. Gaines	$29.0 million
11. Cherokee	$28.5 million
12. Hopkins	$27.3 million
13. Gonzales	$25.5 million
14. Swisher	$24.7 million
15. Comanche	$23.5 million
16. Wharton	$21.3 million
17. Ochiltree	$18.4 million
18. Starr	$17.2 million
19. Hockley	$16.9 million
20. Nacogdoches	$16.6 million

**Net cash return from agricultural sales, government payments, other farm-related income, direct sales, and Commodity Credit Corporation loans.*

Source: 1992 Census of Agriculture (AC92-A-43), Volume 1, Texas, U.S. Dept. of Commerce, Economics and Statistics Admin., Bureau of the Census.

became available.

Harvested acreage was 2,040,000 in 1994; 1,850,000 in 1993; and 1,620,000 in 1992. Yields for the corresponding years (1992-1994) were 125, 115, and 117 bushels per acre, respectively.

Most of the acreage and yield increase has occurred in Central and South Texas. In 1994, corn has ranked second in value among the state's crops. It was valued at $608,634,000 in 1994; $555,278,000 in 1993; and $488,025,000 in 1992. The grain is largely used for livestock feed; it is also important in manufacturing food products.

The leading counties in production for 1993 were Palmer, Castro, Dallam, Hale and Hartley.

Rye

Rye is grown mainly on the Northern and Southern High Plains, the Northern Low Plains, Cross Timbers, Blacklands and East Texas areas. Minor acreages are seeded in South Central Texas, the Edwards Plateau and the Upper Coast. Rye is grown primarily as a cover crop and for grazing during the fall, winter and early spring.

Rye production in 1994 totaled 435,000 bushels valued at $1,414,000. Of the 120,000 acres planted, 15,000 were harvested, yielding an average of 29 bushels per acre. In 1993, 11,000 of the 130,000 acres planted were harvested, with an average yield per acre of 33 bushels. Value of production for the 363,000 bushels was $1,009,000. In 1992, 120,000 acres were planted to rye with 14,000 acres harvested, averaging 20 bushels per acre. The crop value was estimated at $784,000 or $2.80 per bushel.

Leading rye-producing counties based on 1993 production value were Dawson, Gaines, Collingsworth, Wheeler and Montague.

Oats

Oats are grown extensively in Texas for winter pasture, hay, silage and greenchop feeding, and some acreage is harvested for grain.

Of the 650,000 acres planted to oats in 1994, 130,000 acres were harvested, with an average yield of 40 bushels per acre. Production totaled 5,200,000 bushels with a value of $9,620,000. In 1993, 800,000 acres were planted, from which 140,000 acres were harvested, with an average yield of 53bushels per acre. Total 1993 production was 7,420,000 bushels. Average price per bushel was $1.59; the total production value was $11,798,000.

Texas farmers planted 700,000 acres of oats in 1992. They harvested 130,000 acres, averaging 44 bushels per acre for a total production of 5,720,000 bushels. At an average price of $1.66 per bushel, the estimated value was $9,495,000. Most of the acreage was used for grazing.

Almost all oat grain produced in Texas is utilized as feed for livestock within the state. A small acreage is grown exclusively for planting seed.

Leading oat grain-producing counties in 1993 were Hamilton, Coryell, McLennan, Gillespie and Cooke.

Barley

Texas barley acreage and production falls far below that of wheat and oats. In 1994, barley was harvested from 8,000 of the 17,000 acres planted. Production totaled 264,000 bushels and was valued at $700,000. In 1993, farmers harvested 7,000 of the 20,000 acres planted to barley. Yields averaged 44 bushels per acre for total production of 308,000 bushels. Value of production was $770,000 at an average price of $2.50 per bushel. In 1992, farmers planted 20,000 acres and harvested 6,000 acres, which averaged 45 bushels per acre for a total production of 270,000 bushels. With price averaging $2.30 per bushel, the estimated value totaled $621,000.

Leading barley-producing counties in 1993 were Gillespie, Parmer, Moore and Hamilton.

Sugar Beets

Sugar beets have been grown on a commercial scale in Texas since 1964, when the first beet-sugar factory was built by Holly Sugar Company in Hereford. The leading counties in production in 1993 were Castro, Deaf Smith, Parmer, Swisher and Hale.

Sugar-beet production in 1994 totaled 497,000 tons from 24,500 harvested acres. In 1993, 40,300 acres were planted and 39,200 were harvested. Average yield was 21 tons per acre and total production was 823,000. In 1992, 40,100 acres were planted with 39,900 harvested. The yield averaged 21 tons per acre for total production of 838,000 tons.

Sugar Cane

Sugar cane is grown from seed cane planted in late summer or fall. It is harvested 12 months later and

Changing Rank of Texas Crops by Acres Harvested 1959-1992

1959

Sorghum	6.72 million acres
Cotton	6.13 million acres
Wheat	3.03 million acres
Hay	1.44 million acres
Corn	1.34 million acres

1987

Cotton	4.35 million acres
Wheat	3.65 million acres
Hay	3.25 million acres
Sorghum	2.67 million acres
Corn	1.23 million acres

1992

Sorghum	3.98 million acres
Wheat	3.73 million acres
Cotton	3.62 million acres
Hay	3.60 million acres
Corn	1.55 million acres

Source: 1992 Census of Agriculture (AC92-A-43), Volume 1, Texas, U.S. Dept. of Commerce, Economics and Statistics Admin., Bureau of the Census.

milled to produce raw sugar and molasses. Raw sugar requires additional refining before it can be offered to consumers.

The sugar-cane grinding mill operated at Santa Rosa, Cameron County, is considered one of the most modern mills in the United States. Texas' sugar cane-producing counties are Hidalgo, Cameron and Willacy.

Sugar-cane production in 1994 totaled 1,327,000 tons from 43,800 harvested acres. In 1993, 44,400 acres were harvested for total production of 1,439,000 tons valued at $37,126,000. The yield was 32.4 tons per acre. In 1992, 39,300 acres were harvested, from which 1,328,000 tons of sugar cane were milled. The yield average 33.8 tons per acre. The price averaged $25.40 per ton, for a total value of $33,731,000.

Hay, Silage and Other Forage Crops

A large proportion of Texas' agricultural land is devoted to forage-crop production. This acreage produces forage and provides the total feed requirements for most of the state's large domestic livestock population, as well as game animals.

Approximately 80 million acres of native rangeland, which are primarily in the western half of Texas, provide grazing for beef cattle, sheep, goats, horses and game animals. An additional 20 million acres are devoted to introducing forage species. Of this total, approximately 16 million acres are established to introduce improved perennial grasses and legumes and are harvested by grazing animals. The average annual acreage of crops grown for hay, silage and other forms of machine-harvested forage is close to 4 million, with an estimated value in excess of $600 million.

Hay, principally annual and perennial grasses and alfalfa, accounts for a large amount of this production, with some corn and sorghum silage being produced. Production in 1994 totaled 8,455,000 tons from 3,590,000 acres. Value of hay was $524,360,000. In 1993, 7,506,000 tons of hay were produced with a value of $455,112,000. In 1992, 9,800,000 tons of hay were produced with a value of $553,675,000.

Grass hay production is widely distributed, with some leading counties being Hopkins, Kaufman, Anderson, Leon, Henderson and Van Zandt.

Alfalfa hay production in 1994 totaled 405,000 tons, with 90,000 acres harvested. At a value of $122 per ton, total value was $49,410,000. In 1993, 366,000 tons of alfalfa hay were harvested from 85,000 acres. Value was $40,992,000. Alfalfa hay was harvested from 110,000 acres in 1992, averaging 5 tons per acre for total production of 550,000 tons valued at $54,175,000.

An additional sizable acreage of annual forage crops, such as sudan and millet, is grazed, as well as much of the small-grain acreage. Alfalfa, sweet corn, vetch, arrowleaf clover, grasses and other forage plants also provide income as seed crops.

Peanuts

Peanuts are grown on approximately 300,000 acres in Texas, well over half of it on irrigated land. Texas ranked second nationally in production of peanuts in 1993. Among Texas crops, peanuts rank about seventh in value.

Until 1973, essentially all of Texas' peanut acreage was planted to the Spanish-type, which was favored because of its earlier maturity and better drought tolerance than other types. The Spanish variety also is preferred for some uses because of its distinctive flavor. The Florunner variety, a runner market type, is now planted on a sizable proportion of the acreage where soil moisture is favorable. The variety is later maturing but better yielding than Spanish varieties under good growing conditions. Florunner peanuts have acceptable quality to compete with the Spanish variety in most products.

In 1994, peanut production totaled 616 million pounds from 280,000 harvested acres. At 28.5 cents per pound, value was estimated at $175,560,000. In 1993, peanut production amounted to 550,175,000 pounds from 305,000 acres planted and 295,000 harvested. With an average yield of 1,865 pounds per acre and average price of 29.6 cents per pound, the value was estimated at $162,852,000. Production in 1992 amounted to 680,150,000 pounds of peanuts from 308,000 acres planted and 305,000 acres harvested, or an average of 2,230 pounds per harvested acre valued at 26.9 cents per pound for a $182,960,000 value.

Leading counties in peanut production in 1993 included Gaines, Comanche, Atascosa, Haskell, Frio and Eastland.

Soybeans

Soybean production is largely in the Upper Coast, irrigated High Plains and Red River Valley of Northeast Texas. Soybeans are adapted to the same general soil and climate conditions as corn, cotton or grain sorghum, provided that moisture, disease and insects are not limiting factors. The major counties in soybean production in 1993 were Lamar, Victoria, Hale, Liberty, Falls and Fannin.

In low-rainfall areas, yields have been too low or inconsistent on dry land for profitable production. Soybeans' moisture needs in late summer minimize economic crop possibilities in the Blacklands and Rolling Plains. In the Blacklands, cotton root rot is a serious problem. Limited moisture at critical growth stages may prevent economical yields, even in high-rainfall areas of Northeast Texas and the Coastal Prairie.

Because of day-length sensitivity, soybeans should be planted in Texas during the long days of May and June to obtain sufficient vegetative growth for optimum yields. Varieties planted during this period usually cease vegetative development and initiate reproductive processes during the hot, usually dry months of July and August. When moisture is insufficient during the blooming and fruiting period, yields are drastically reduced. In most areas of the state, July and August rainfall is insufficient to permit economical dryland production. The risk of dryland soybean production in the Coastal Prairie and Northeast Texas is considerably less when compared to other dryland areas because moisture is available more often during the critical fruiting period.

The 1994 soybean crop totaled 7,140,000 bushels valued at $37,842,000. Of the 220,000 acres planted, 210,000 were harvested, with an average yield of 34 bushels per acre. In 1993, the soybean crop averaged only 19 bushels per acre from 205,000 acres harvested. Total production of 3,895,000 bushels was valued at $21,851,000. In 1992, the crop averaged 33 bushels per acre from 390,000 acres harvested. Total production of 12,870,000 bushels was valued at $65,251,000, or $5.07 per bushel. Soybeans were planted on acreage that had been planted to cotton but was lost to adverse weather.

Sunflowers

Sunflowers are one of the most important annual oilseed crops in the world. The cultivated types, which are thought to be descendants of the common wild sunflower native to Texas, have been successfully grown in several countries, including Russia, Argentina, Romania, Bulgaria, Uruguay, Western Canada and portions of the northern United States. Extensive trial plantings conducted in the Cotton Belt states since 1968 showed sunflowers have considerable potential as an oilseed crop in much of this area, including Texas. This crop exhibits good cold and drought tolerance, is adapted to a wide range of soil and climate conditions, and tolerates higher levels of hail, wind, and sand abrasion than other crops normally grown in the state.

In 1994, sunflower production totaled 36,300,000 pounds, harvested from 33,000 acres. With an average price of $10.70 per pound, the crop was valued at $3,839,000. In 1993, 29,000 of the 33,000 acres planted to sunflowers were harvested with an average yield of 1,117 pounds per acre. Total production of 32,400,000 pounds was valued at $4,033,000.

In 1992, all 45,000 acres planted to sunflowers were harvested, yielding 1,396 pounds per acre for a total yield of 62,820,000 pounds valued at $7,108,000. The leading counties in production in 1993 were Floyd, Hale, Deaf Smith, Hidalgo and Cochran.

Reasons for growing sunflowers include the need for an additional cash crop with low water and plant nutrient requirements, the development of sunflower hybrids, and interest by food processors in Texas sunflower oil, which has a high oleic acid content. Commercial users have found many advantages in this high oleic oil, including excellent cooking stability, particularly for use as a deep-frying medium for fried snack products.

Sunflower meal is a high-quality protein source free of nutritional toxins that can be included in rations for swine, poultry and ruminants. The hulls constitute a source of roughage that can also be included in livestock rations.

Flaxseed

Earliest flax planting was at Victoria in 1900. Since the first planting, Texas flax acreage has fluctuated depending on market, winterkill and drought. Flax acreage has dropped in recent years, and estimates were discontinued in 1980.

Horticultural Specialty Crops

Production of horticulture specialty crops continues to rise as transportation costs on long-distance hauling increases. This has resulted in a marked increase in the production of container-grown plants within the state. This increase is noted especially in the production of bedding plants, foliage plants, sod and the woody landscape plants.

Plant-rental services — providing plants and maintaining them in office buildings, shopping malls, public buildings and homes for a fee — have become a multimillion dollar business. The response has been good, as evidenced by the growth of companies providing these services.

The interest in plants for interior landscapes is confined to no specific age group. Retail nurseries and florist shops report that people of all ages are buying plants — customers range from the elderly in retirement homes to high school and college students in dormitory rooms and apartments.

Extension specialists estimated cash receipts from horticultural specialty crops in Texas to be around $720 million in 1994. Texans are creating colorful and green surroundings by improving their landscape plantings.

Truck Crops

Some market vegetables are produced in almost all Texas counties, but most of the commercial crop comes from about 200 counties. Hidalgo County is the leading county in vegetable acres harvested, followed by Starr and Cameron counties. Other leading producing counties are Frio, Uvalde, Duval, Webb, Hale and Zavala.

Texas is one of the five leading states in the produc-

Texas Fruit-Vegetable Shipments

1992-1994

Amounts are shown in units of 1,000 hundredweight for rail (RL) and truck (TR).

Commodity	1992		1993		1994	
	RL	TR	RL	TR	RL	TR
Beets		45		64		87
Broccoli		107		124		96
Cabbage		2,691		3,353		2,837
Cantaloupes		1,660		1,322		1,368
Carrots	6	340	9	307	20	382
Cauliflower		18		9		6
Celery		678		711		548
Chinese Cabbage				3		
Cucumbers		324		108		155
Eggplant				1		2
Endive				1		
Escarole				1		
Grapefruit		362		1,461	1	2,927
Grapefruit, Export				36		65
Greens		196		175		190
Honeydews		614		573	1	667
Lettuce, Romaine				2		
Limes						10
Misc. Herbs		32		61		17
Misc. Oriental Vegetables				3		
Onions, dry	6	2,566	1	3,883	2	4,540
Onions, green		3		13		12
Oranges		163		407		768
Parsley		53		71		48
Peppers, bell		461		395		321
Peppers, other		24		16		7
Potatoes, table	59	1,201	120	1,519	238	1,453
Potatoes, chipper		152		115		87
Spinach		203	1	258		185
Squash		5		1		5
Tomatoes				32		24
Turnips-Rutabagas		5		3		15
Watermelons		3,295	*8	3,780	†5	4,267
TOTALS	**71**	**15,198**	***139**	**18,808**	**†267**	**21,089**

Note: Export data are not complete and should not be interpreted as representing total exports.

*Includes 8 piggyback loads of watermelons.

†Includes 5 piggyback loads of watermelons.

tion of fresh market vegetables. Nationally, in 1994, Texas ranked third in harvested acreage and value of fresh-market vegetables, behind only California and Florida. Texas had 7.1 percent of the harvested acreage, 6.8 percent of the production, and 4.9 percent of the value of fresh-market vegetables produced. Texas ranked first in the production of spinach for processing. Onions were the No. 1 cash crop, with watermelons second. Other vegetables leading in value of production usually are carrots, cantaloupes, cabbage and Irish potatoes.

In 1994, production of 27,937,000 cwt. was valued at $315,217,000 from 160,800 acres harvested. In 1993, Texas growers harvested principal vegetable crops valued at $330,687,000 from 144,800 acres. Texas growers harvested commercial vegetable crops valued at $296,418,000 from 149,800 acres in 1992.

See chart at the bottom of this page for production of individual truck crops for 1992, 1993 and 1994.

Fruits and Nuts

Texas produces a wide variety of fruit. The pecan is the only commercial nut crop in the state. Native to most of the state's river valleys, the **pecan** is the **state tree**. Citrus is produced in the three southernmost counties in the Lower Rio Grande Valley. Production continued to increase in the 1993-94 season after the severe freeze in 1989. Some new orchards have been planted. Peaches are the next most important Texas fruit crop; there is also considerable interest in growing apples.

Citrus

Prior to the 1989 freeze, Texas ranked with Florida, California and Arizona as a leading state in citrus production. Most of Texas' production is in Cameron, Hidalgo and Willacy counties of the Lower Rio Grande Valley. Following the freeze, grapefruit production in 1993-94 recovered to 3 million boxes at $5.08 per box for a total of $15,238,000.

Production in 1992-93 was 1,875,000 boxes at $6.86 per box for a total of $12,856,000. Production of oranges in 1993-94 was 550,000 boxes at $9.60 per box for a total of $5,280,000. Production in 1992-93 reached 510,000 boxes at $8.15, for a value of $4,156,100.

Peaches

Primary production areas are East Texas, the Hill Country and the West Cross Timbers, with some pro-

Texas Truck Crops 1992, 1993, 1994

Crop	1992			1993			1994		
	Acres Harvested (add 000)	Production (thousand cwt.)	Value (add 000)	Acres Harvested (add 000)	Production (thousand cwt.)	Value (add 000)	Acres Harvested (add 000)	Production (thousand cwt.)	Value (add 000)
Onions	17	NA	$64,921	17.1	NA	$90,306	19.9	5,541	$64,813
Carrots	6.8	NA	11,744	7.5	NA	13,718	8.7	1,714	12,839
Irish Potatoes	11.8	NA	31,698	12.8	2,935	31,380	13.0	2,900	35,315
Cataloupes	11.0	NA	24,123	13.4	2,144	37,306	13.1	2,358	52,348
Honeydews	4.8	NA	12,096	5.2	832	17,888	NA	900	14,760
Cabbage	7.7	NA	31,536	9.7	3,395	46,851	11.2	4,144	30,666
Cauliflower	.8	NA	515	NA	75	905	.9	97	1,880
Broccoli	4.4	NA	8,259	3.3	158	4,067	3.7	229	4,281
Watermelons	44.0	NA	29,304	50.0	NA	50,400	52.0	7,800	60,060
Tomatoes	3.3	NA	2,191	3.7	NA	1,105	3.3	83	1,793
Bell Peppers	4.3	NA	28,277	5.0	NA	23,200	4.6	644	29,753
Lettuce	.5	NA	862	.3	53	530	*	*	*
Sweet Potatoes	5.5	NA	10,395	6.0	NA	18,180	5.4	NA	10,822
Spinach†	3.4	NA	6,688	2.8	NA	5,376	2.3	115	2,829
Cucumbers	2.3	NA	4,444	1.9	NA	2,736	2.2	242	3,630
Sweet Corn	1.5	NA	1,118	3.5	NA	3,150	3.2	114	1,555
Vegetables for Processing‡	20.6	NA	22,884	19.3	NA	20,686	29.9	NA	27,094

**Estimates of lettuce crop were discontinued in 1994.*
†Grown primarily in Winter Garden area of South Texas.
‡ Includes cucumbers, snap beans, tomatoes and spinach.
Source: Texas A&M University Agricultural Extension Service, College Station.

duction in South and West Texas. Production varies substantially because of adverse weather conditions. Low-chilling varieties for early marketings are being grown in Atascosa, Frio, Webb, Karnes and Duval counties.

The Texas peach crop totaled 14,900,000 pounds in 1994 for a value of $5,811,000 or 39 cents per pound. In 1993, 22,600,000 pounds were produced, valued at $8,136,000 or 36 cents per pound. The 1992 crop totaled 20,800,000 pounds and was valued at $7,696,000.

The demand for high-quality Texas peaches greatly exceeds the supply. The state ranked 10th nationally in peach production in 1993. Leading Texas counties in production are Gillespie, Parker, Montague, Comanche, Limestone and Eastland.

Apples

Small acreages of apples, usually marketed within the state, are grown in a number of counties, the leading ones being Montague and Gillespie. Other counties that produce apples include Callahan, Collingsworth, Clay, Cass, Donley, Eastland, Hudspeth, Jeff Davis, Lampasas, Parker, San Saba and Young. The crop is harvested and marketed from July to October.

A considerable number of apple trees have been planted in the Hill Country. Most of the trees are new varieties of Red and Golden Delicious types on semi-dwarfing rootstocks. Trees are established in high-density plantings of 100 to 200 trees per acre. Most of the apples are sold at roadside stands or go to nearby markets.

Pears

Well adapted for home and small orchard production, the pear is not commercially significant in Texas. Comanche, Parker, Lampasas, Cooke, McCulloch and Eastland counties lead in trees. Usually the fruit goes for home consumption or to nearby markets.

Apricots

Not a commercial crop, apricots are grown chiefly in Comanche, Denton, Wilbarger, Parker and Collingsworth counties. Others reporting apricots include: Martin, Clay, Young, Lampasas, Gillespie, Anderson, Erath, Wichita and Eastland counties.

Plums

Plum production is scattered over a wide area of the state, with the heaviest production in East and Central Texas. The leading counties in production are Smith, Gillespie and Knox. Most of the production goes to nearby markets or to processors.

Blackberries

Smith County is a blackberry center, with the Tyler-Lindale area having processed the crop since 1890. Other counties with blackberry acreage include Wood, Van Zandt and Henderson. The Brazos blackberry is grown as a local market or "pick-your-own" fruit in many sections of the state. Dewberries grow wild in Central and East Texas and are gathered for home use and local sale in May and June.

Strawberries

Atascosa County is the leading commercial area, although strawberries are grown for local markets in Wood, Van Zandt and Smith Counties in East Texas. The most concentrated production occurs in the Poteet area below San Antonio.

Avocados

Avocados grow on a small acreage in the Lower Rio Grande Valley. Interest in this crop is increasing, and production is expected to expand. Lulu is the principal variety.

Pecans

The pecan is native to more than 150 counties and is grown commercially in some 30 additional counties. The pecan is also widely used as a dual-purpose yard tree.

Commercial plantings of pecans have greatly accelerated in Central and West Texas, and many new orchards are irrigated. Trickle-irrigation systems are popular. The development and use of the new USDA pecan varieties have greatly helped to increase quality and yields.

In 1994, pecan production totaled 40 million pounds and was valued at $50,500,000, or $1.26 per pound. In 1993, 75,000,000 pounds were produced. Total value was estimated at $48,000,000, averaging 64 cents per pound. The 1992 crop totaled 62 million pounds valued at $87,420,000 or $1.41 per pound. In 1991, the crop totaled 60 million pounds valued at $66 million or $1.10 per pound.

Nationally, Texas ranked second, behind Georgia, in pecan production in 1993. Leading Texas counties in pecan production are Hood, El Paso, Pecos, San Saba, Mills, Comanche, Wharton and Gonzales.

Forest Products

The 1993 harvest of timber from East Texas' 11.8 million acres of timberland was valued at $744 million (measured as the value delivered to the first point of processing). An estimated 53 percent of the timber harvest came from nonindustrial private lands, 41 percent came from forest-industry lands and the remaining 6 percent form public lands. The volume harvested totaled 778.7 million cubic feet, including 591.8 million cubic feet of pine and 187 million cubic feet of hardwood.

The stumpage value of the 1993 harvest, which is the value of the timber before cutting, was $479.1 million. Based on the proportions of harvest listed above, nonindustrial private landowners received approximately $254 million in timber income in 1993.

In addition to these timber products, Texas' forests produce other benefits as well. More than 400,000 Christmas trees, grown primarily in East Texas, but found throughout the state, were sold in the Texas market.

In Central Texas, some timber is harvested for fuel, lumber, veneer, crossties, posts and cedar oil. The forests of Texas provide a multitude of additional benefits, such as wildlife habitat, watershed protection, livestock grazing and opportunities for outdoor recreation. Minor products include pine straw, edible berries and nuts, wild honey and decorative plants such as mistletoe.

For more information on forests products, refer to the section titled, "Texas Forest Resources" in the Environment section of the Almanac.

Livestock and Their Products

Livestock and their products usually account for about two-thirds of the agricultural cash receipts in Texas. The state ranks first nationally in all cattle, beef cattle, cattle on feed, sheep and lambs, wool, goats and mohair.

Meat animals normally account for around 80 percent of total cash receipts from marketings of livestock and their products. Sales of livestock and products in 1993 totaled $8.342 billion, up from $7.524 billion in 1992.

Cattle dominate livestock production in Texas, contributing more than 70 percent of cash receipts from livestock and products each year. The Jan. 1, 1995 inventory of all cattle and calves in Texas totaled 15,100,000 head, valued at $8.532 billion.

On Jan. 1, 1995, the sheep and lamb inventory stood at 1.7 million head, compared with 1,895,000 head in 1994. Sheep and lambs numbered 3,214,000 on Jan. 1, 1973, down from a high of 10,829,000 in 1943. Sheep and lamb production fell from 148,295,000 pounds in 1973 to 90 million pounds in 1994. Wool production decreased from 26,352,000 pounds, valued at $23,190,000 in 1973, to 14,840,000 pounds valued at $15,582,000 in 1994. Production was 17 million pounds in 1993, valued at $11,050,000. The price of wool per pound was 88 cents in 1973, 65 cents in 1993, and $1.05 in 1994.

Lamb prices averaged $64.80 per cwt. in 1994, $64.90 per cwt. in 1993, and $62 per cwt. in 1992. The average value per head of sheep stock was $59 in 1995, $56 in 1994 and $58 in 1993.

Mohair production in Texas has dropped from a 1965 high of 31,584,000 pounds to 11,680,000 pounds in 1994. Production was valued at $30,602,000, or $2.62 per pound. In 1993, production was 13,490,000 pounds valued at $11,197,000, or 83 cents per pound. Mohair production in 1992 was 14,200,000 pounds valued at $12,354,000 or 87 cents per pound.

Beef Cattle

Raising beef cattle is the most extensive agricultural operation in Texas. In 1993, 50.4 percent of total cash receipts from farm and ranch marketings — $6,353,371 of $12,616,905 — came from cattle and calves, compared with $5,644,620 of $11,461,101 in 1992 (49.3 percent) and $6,115,818 of $12,216,219 in 1991 (50.1 percent). The next leading commodity is cotton.

Nearly all of the 254 counties in Texas derive more revenue from cattle than from any other agricultural commodity, and those that don't usually rank cattle second in importance.

Within the boundaries of Texas are 14 percent of all the cattle in the United States, as are 16 percent of the beef breeding cows and 13 percent of the calf crop.

The number of all cattle in Texas on Jan. 1, 1995, totaled 15,100,000, compared with 14,800,000 on January 1, 1994; and 14,100,000 in 1993.

Calves born on Texas farms and ranches in 1994 totaled 5,750,000, compared with 5,350,000 in 1993; and 5,150,000 in 1992.

Sale of cattle and calves at approximately 159 livestock auctions inspected by Texas Animal Health Commission totaled 5,825,000 head in 1994; 6,048,000 in 1993; and 5,611,000 in 1992. The number of cattle and calves shipped into Texas totaled 2,960,901 head in 1994; 3,439,653 head in 1993; and 3,168,536 head in 1992.

Livestock Industries

A large portion of Texas livestock is sold through local auction markets. In 1993, 159 livestock auctions were reported by the Texas Animal Health Commission. Auctions sold 5,825,000 head of cattle and calves, 238,000 hogs and 1,834,000 sheep and lambs in 1994. This compared with 6,048,000 cattle and calves, 292,000 hogs and 1,656,000 sheep and lambs in 1993. Figures for 1992 were 5,611,000 cattle and calves, 329,000 hogs and 1,416,000 sheep and goats.

During 1994, the commission reported 1,705,266 cattle and calves shipped from Texas to other states and 2,960,901shipped in, compared with 1,940,558 shipped out and 3,439,653 shipped in during 1993; 1,948,022 shipped out and 3,168,536 shipped in during 1992. (Figures exclude cattle shipped direct to slaughter where no health certificates are required.)

During 1994, Texas shipped out 1,021,719 sheep and lambs and shipped in 98,694, compared with 1,039,337 shipped out and 113,210 shipped in during 1993; 1,024,000 shipped out in 1992 and 169,000 shipped in.

Feedlot fattening of livestock, mainly cattle, is a major industry in Texas. Annual fed cattle marketings

Texas Cattle Marketed, 1965-1993
by Size of Feedlot

Year	Feedlot Capacity (head)						
	Under 1,000	1,000 1,999	2000-3,999	4,000-7,999	8,000-15,999	16,000-& Over	Total
	Cattle Marketed — 1,000 head —						
1965	104	108	205	324	107	246	1,094
1970	98	53	112	281	727	1,867	3,138
1975	50	22	51	134	485	2,325	3,067
1976	60	33	62	170	583	3,039	3,947
1977	146	22	38	206	604	3,211	4,227
1978	80	20	50	242	697	3,826	4,915
1979	54	19	46	227	556	3,543	4,445
1980	51	18	47	226	533	3,285	4,160
1981	50	20	50	220	510	3,110	3,960
1982	55	20	60	210	540	3,190	4,075
1983	100	20	80	130	490	3,580	4,400
1984	60	20	180	150	540	4,140	5,090
1985	70	10	20	170	620	4,140	5,030
1986	90	10	40	180	550	4,390	5,260
1987	90	20	35	170	625	4,375	5,255
1988	30	15	35	185	650	4,120	5,035
1989	40	15	40	165	675	3,810	4,745
1990	35	24	56	180	605	3,940	4,840
1991	35	25	45	225	500	4,250	5,080
1992	50	10	25	140	505	4,065	4,795
1993	30	20	70	160	640	4,370	5,290

Number of feedlots with 1,000 head or more capacity is number of lots operating any time during the year. Number under 1,000 head capacity and total number of all feedlots is number at end of year.

*Source: **"1985 Agricultural Facts,"** Texas Agricultural Statistics Service, April 20, 1989. Numbers for 1986-1992, "1993 Texas Livestock Statistics," Bulletin 252, August 1994.*

totaled 5,290,000 in 1993. Texas lots marketed 4,795,000 head of grain-fed cattle in 1992. In recent years, more cattle have been fed in Texas than any other state in the nation.

During 1993, there were 138 feedlots in Texas with capacity of 1,000 animals or more. This compared with 152 in 1992, 170 in 1991, and 152 in 1990.

Federally-inspected slaughter plants in Texas numbered 43 in 1994. This compared with 46 in 1993 and 50 in 1992. In 1993, the number of cattle slaughtered in Texas totaled 5,996,000 cattle; 169,000 hogs; and 22,000 calves. This compared with 5,585,000 cattle; 164,000 hogs; and 30,000 calves in 1992; and 5,513,000 cattle; 27,000 calves; 132,000 hogs in 1991.

Feeding of cattle in commercial feedlots is a major economic development that has stimulated the establishment and expansion of beef slaughtering plants. Most of this development is in the Panhandle-Plains area of Northwest Texas. This area alone accounts for more than 70 percent of the cattle fed in the state.

Feedlots with capacities of 1,000 head or more accounted for more than 99 percent of the cattle fed in Texas. Feedlot marketings represented about 23 percent of total U.S. fed cattle marketings. Large amounts of capital are required for feedlot operations. This has forced many lots to become custom feeding facilities.

Feedlots are concentrated on the High Plains largely because of extensive supplies of sorghum and other feed. Beef breeding herds have increased most in East Texas, where grazing is abundant.

Dairying

Ninety-five percent of the state's dairy industry is located east of a line from Wichita Falls to Brownwood, to San Antonio to Corpus Christi.

Leading counties in milk production are Erath, Hopkins, Comanche and Johnson, which combined, produce almost 45 percent of the milk in the state. Erath produces more than 20 percent of the total.

All the milk sold by Texas dairy farmers is marketed under the terms of Federal Marketing Orders. Most

Texas Livestock Numbers and Values

Class of Livestock	Numbers of Animals				Farm Value					
					Value per Head			Total Value		
	1992	1993	1994 (Preliminary	% Change	1992	1993	1994	1992	1993	1994
	Thousands				Dollars			Thousand Dollars		
All Cattle	13,400	14,800	15,100	102	$600	$615	$595	$8,040,000	$8,671,500	$8,806,000
*Beef Cows	5,365	5,800	6,200	107	NA	NA	NA	NA	NA	NA
*Milk Cows	385	400	400	100	NA	NA	NA	NA	NA	NA
†Hogs	540	500	NA	—	68	83	50	34,680	41,500	28,750
†All Sheep	2,140	1,940	1,710	88	52	58	56	111,280	118,320	106,120
†Goats	2,000	1,960	1,960	100	42	43	38	84,000	84,280	74,480
†Chickens	18,550	19,600	19,300	98	2.10	2.20	2.20	38,955	43,120	42,460
Total Value	—	—	—	—	—	—	—	**$8,631,640**	**$8,430,955**	**$8,994,780**

**Included in "All Cattle."*

†Figures are as of January 1. Turkey figures not released to avoid disclosing individual operations.

NA = Not Available.

Source: "Texas Agricultural Facts," Texas Agricultural Statistical Service, Feb. 24, 1995; "1993 Texas Livestock Statistics," August 1994.

Texas dairymen are members of one of four marketing cooperatives. Associated Milk Producers, Inc., is the largest, representing the majority of the state's producers.

Texas dairy farmers received an average price for milk of $13.40 per hundred pounds in 1994, $13.90 in 1993, and $13.70 in 1992. A total of 6.2 billion pounds of milk was sold to plants and dealers in 1994, bringing in cash receipts from milk to dairy farmers of $834,150,000. This compared with 5.87 billion pounds sold in 1993 that brought in $786,030,000 in cash receipts. In 1992, Texas dairymen sold 5.549 billion pounds of milk, which brought in cash receipts of $760,213,000.

The annual average number of milk cows in Texas was 400,000 head during 1994. This compared with 390,000 head during 1993 and 376,000 during 1992. Average production per cow in the state has increased steadily over the past several decades. The average production per cow in 1994 was 15,660 pounds. Milk per cow in 1993 was 115,600 pounds. In 1992, milk per cow was 14,867 pounds. Total milk production in Texas was 5.59 billion pounds in 1992; 5.418 bilion pounds in 1991.

There were 4,200 operations reporting milk cows in Texas in 1994. In 1993, 5,000 operations reported milk cows. In 1992, 5,300 operations reported milk cows in Texas.

Dairy Manufacturing

The major dairy products manufactured in Texas include condensed, evaporated and dry milk, creamery butter and cheese. However, data on these operations are not available because of the small number of manufacturing plants producing these products.

Frozen Desserts

Production of frozen desserts in Texas totaled 119,045,000 gallons in 1994. The 1993 production was 105,957,000 gallons and 117,730,000 in 1992. Ice cream production in Texas in 1994 amounted to 47,711,000 gallons, compared to 44,430,000 in 1993 and 56,031,000 in 1992. Ice cream mix produced in Texas in 1994 amounted to 27,038,000 gallons; 24,836,000 in 1993; and 30,470,000 in 1992. Ice milk production in Texas in 1994 amounted to 25,095,000 gallons; 20,651,000 in 1993 and 20,603,000 in 1992. Milk sherbet production in 1994 totaled 1,885,000 gallons. This compared with 1993 milk sherbet production of 1,888,000 gallons and 1992 production of 2,268,000 gallons.

Swine

Texas had 500,000 head of swine on hand on Dec. 1, 1994 — only 9 percent of the U.S. swine herd. Swine producers in the state usually produce about one-fifth of the pork consumed by the state's population, or about 780,000 head marketed annually.

Although the number of farms producing hogs has steadily decreased, the size of production units has increased substantially. There is favorable potential for increased production.

In 1993, 830,000 head of hogs were marketed in Texas, producing 214,080,000 pounds of pork valued at $89,464,000, or $39.90 per 100 pounds. Comparable figures for 1992 were 762,000 head marketed, and 213,604,000 pounds of pork produced with a value of $76,433,000, or $36.40 per 100 pounds. In 1991, 810,000 head were marketed, and produced 207,023,000 pounds of pork valued at $97,398,000, or $45.10 per 100 pounds.

Goats and Mohair

Goats in Texas numbered 1,950,000 on Jan. 1, 1995. This compares with 1,960,000 at the beginning

Hog Production 1960-1993

Year	Production (1,000 Pounds)	Avg. Market Wt. (Pounds)	Avg. Price Per Cwt. (Dollars)	Gross Income (1,000 Dollars)
1960	288,844	228	14.70	44,634
1970	385,502	241	22.50	75,288
1980	315,827	259	35.90	111,700
1981	264,693	256	41.70	121,054
1982	205,656	256	49.60	112,726
1983	209,621	256	45.20	95,343
1984	189,620	262	45.50	95,657
1985	168,950	266	43.40	72,512
1986	176,660	269	47.30	82,855
1987	216,834	NA	50.60	103,983
1988	236,658	NA	41.30	100,029
1989	224,229	NA	39.90	93,178
1990	196,225	NA	48.20	92,222
1991	207,023	NA	45.10	97,398
1992	213,604	NA	36.40	76,433
1993	214,080	NA	39.90	89.464

*Source: **"1985 Texas Livestock, Dairy and Poultry Statistics,"** USDA, Bulletin 235, June 1986, pp. 32, 46; "Texas Livestock Statistics"; USDA, "Meat Animals - Prod., Dips., & Income," 1993; "1993 'Texas Livestock Statistics," Bulletin 252, Texas Agricultural Statistics Service, August 1994.*

Angora Goats and Mohair 1900-1994

Year	Goats		Mohair	
	*Number	Farm Value	Production (lbs)	Value
1900	627,333	$923,777	961,328	$267,864
1910	1,135,000	2,514,000	1,998,000	468,000
1920	1,753,000	9,967,000	6,786,000	1,816,000
1930	2,965,000	14,528,000	14,800,000	4,995,000
1940	3,300,000	10,560,000	18,250,000	9,308,000
1950	2,295,000	13,082,000	12,643,000	9,735,000
1960	3,339,000	29,383,000	23,750,000	21,375,000
1970	2,572,000	19,033,000	17,985,000	7,032,000
1980	1,400,000	64,400,000	8,800,000	30,800,000
1981	1,380,000	53,130,000	10,100,000	35,350,000
1982	1,410,000	57,810,000	10,000,000	25,500,000
1983	1,420,000	53,250,000	10,600,000	42,930,000
1984	1,450,000	82,215,000	10,600,000	48,160,000
1985	1,590,000	76,797,000	13,300,000	45,885,000
1986	1,770,000	70,977,000	16,000,000	40,160,000
1987	1,780,000	82,592,000	16,200,000	42,606,000
1988	1,800,000	108,180,000	15,400,000	29,876,000
1989	1,850,000	100,270,000	15,400,000	24,794,000
†1990	1,900,000	93,100,000	14,500,000	13,775,000
1991	1,830,000	73,200,000	14,800,000	19,388,000
1992	2,000,000	84,000,000	14,200,000	12,354,000
1993	1,960,000	84,280,000	13,490,000	11,197,000
1994	1,960,000	74,480,000	11,680,000	30,602,000

**Goat number includes all goats, not just Angora goats.*

Source: "1985 Texas Livestock, Dairy and Poultry Statistics," USDA Bulletin 235, June 1986, p. 25. "Texas Agricultural Facts," Crop and Livestock Reporting Service, various years; "1993 Texas Livestock Statistics," Texas Agricultural Statistics Service, Bulletin 252, August 1994.

of 1994 and 1,960,000 at the beginning of 1993. They had a value of $85,800,000 or $44.00 per head in 1995; $74,480,000 or $38.00 per head in 1994; and $84,280,000 or $43.00 per head in 1993.

The goat herd largely consists of Angora goats for mohair production. Angora goats totaled 1,230,000 in 1995, 1,490,000 in 1994, and 1,560,000 in 1993. Spanish goats and others numbered 720,000 in 1995, 470,000 in 1994, and 400,000 in 1993.

Mohair production during 1994 totaled 11,680,000 pounds. This compares with 13,490,000 in 1993 and 14,200,000 in 1992. Average price per pound in 1994 was $2.62 from 1,600,000 goats clipped for a total value of $30,602,000. In 1993, producers received 83 cents per pound from 1,900,000 goats clipped for a total value of $11,197,000. In 1992, producers received 87 cents per pound from 2 million goats clipped for a total value of $12,354,000.

Nearly half of the world's mohair and 92 percent of the U.S. clip are produced in Texas. The leading Texas counties in Angora goats are Edwards, Val Verde, Sutton, Crockett, Uvalde, Terrell, Kimble, Mason, Mills and Kinney.

Sheep and Wool

Sheep and lambs in Texas numbered 1,700,000 head on Jan. 1, 1995, down from 1,895,000 in 1994; and 2,220,000 in 1993. All sheep were valued at $100,300,000 or $59 per head on Jan. 1, 1995, compared with $106,120,000 or $56 per head in 1994 and $118,320,000 or $58 per head in 1993.

Breeding ewes one year old and over numbered 1,100,000 in 1995; 1,180,000 in 1994; and 1,400,000 in 1993. Replacement lambs totaled 195,000 head in 1995; 295,000 in 1994. Sheep operations in Texas were estimated to be 7,600 in 1995, 7,800 in 1994 and 8,000 in 1993.

Texas wool production in 1994 was 14,840,000 pounds from 2,120,000 sheep. Value totaled $15,582,000 or $1.05 per pound. This compared with 17 million pounds of wool valued at $11,050,000 or 65 cents per pound in 1993; and 17,600,000 pounds from 2,450,000 sheep valued at $16,896,000 or 96 cents per pound in 1992.

Most sheep in Texas are concentrated in the Edwards Plateau area of West Central Texas and nearby counties. The 10 leading counties are Val Verde, Crockett, Tom Green, Concho, Schleicher, Menard, Pecos, Gillespie, Kinney and Castro.

Sheep production is largely dual purpose, for both wool and lamb production.

San Angelo long has been the largest sheep and wool market in the nation and the center for wool and mohair warehouses, scouring plants and slaughterhouses.

Texas Sheep and Wool Production, 1850-1994

Year	Sheep		Wool	
	*Number	Value	Production (lbs)	Value
1850	100,530	N A	131,917	N A
1860	753,363	N A	1,493,363	N A
1870	1,223,000	$2,079,000	N A	N A
1880	6,024,000	12,048,000	N A	N A
1890	4,752,000	7,128,000	N A	N A
1900	2,416,000	4,590,000	9,630,000	N A
1910	1,909,000	5,536,000	8,943,000	$1,699,170
1920	3,360,000	33,600,000	22,813,000	5,019,000
1930	6,304,000	44,758,000	48,262,000	10,135,000
1940	10,069,000	49,413,000	79,900,000	23,171,000
1950	6,756,000	103,877,000	51,480,000	32,947,000
1960	5,938,000	85,801,000	51,980,000	21,832,000
1970	3,708,000	73,602,000	30,784,000	11,082,000
1980	2,400,000	138,000,000	18,300,000	17,751,000
1981	2,360,000	116,820,000	20,500,000	24,600,000
1982	2,400,000	100,800,000	19,300,000	16,212,000
1983	2,225,000	86,775,000	18,600,000	15,438,000
1984	1,970,000	76,830,000	17,500,000	16,100,000
1985	1,930,000	110,975,000	16,200,000	13,284,000
1986	1,850,000	107,300,000	16,400,000	13,284,000
1987	2,050,000	133,250,000	16,400,000	19,844,000
1988	2,040,000	155,040,000	18,200,000	35,854,000
1989	1,870,000	133,445,000	18,000,000	27,180,000
1990	2,090,000	133,760,000	17,400,000	19,662,000
1991	2,000,000	108,000,000	16,700,000	13,861,000
1992	2,140,000	111,280,000	17,600,000	16,896,000
1993	2,220,000	118,320,000	17,000,000	11,050,000
1994	1,895,000	106,120,000	14,840,000	15,582,000

**Number given here represents all sheep on farms as of Jan. 1; number clipped will vary because of spring and fall clipping.*

*Source: **"1985 Texas Livestock, Dairy and Poultry Statistics,"** USDA Bulletin 235, June 1986, pp. 24-25. **"Texas Agricultural Facts,"** Crop and Livestock Reporting Service, various years; "1993 Texas Livestock Statistics," Texas Agricultural Statistics Service, Bulletin 252, August 1994.*

Horses

Nationally, Texas ranks as one of the leading states in horse numbers and is the headquarters for many national horse organizations. The largest single-breed registry in America, the American Quarter Horse Association, has its headquarters in Amarillo. The National Cutting Horse Association and the American Paint Horse Association are both located in Fort Worth. In addition to these national associations, Texas also has active state associations that include Palominos, Arabians, Thoroughbreds, Appaloosa, and Ponies.

Horses are still used to support the state's giant beef cattle and sheep industries. However, the largest horse numbers within the state can be found near urban and suburban areas. Residential subdivisions have been developed within the state to provide facilities for urban and suburban horse owners.

Poultry and Eggs

Poultry and eggs annually contribute about 6 percent to the average yearly cash receipts of Texas farmers. In 1993, Texas ranked 6th among the states in broilers produced, 7th in eggs produced and 7th in hens.

In 1993, cash receipts to Texas producers from the production of poultry and eggs totaled $897,788,000. This compares with $816,621,000 in 1992 and $787,903,000 in 1991.

Gross income from eggs was $202,541,000 in 1993. This compares with $181,755,000 in 1992 and $203,038,000 in 1991. Eggs produced in 1994 totaled 3.86 billion, compared with 3.57 billion in 1993 and 3.46 billion in 1992. The average price received per dozen in 1993 was 68.1 cents, compared with 63 cents in 1992 and 72.6 cents in 1991. Leading egg-producing counties are Camp, Brazos, Fayette, Lavaca, Gonzales, Lubbock, Collin, Shelby, Garza and Angelina.

Broiler production in 1993 totaled 360,700,000 birds, compared with 359,600,000 in 1992 and 340,200,000 in 1991. Value of production totaled $608,700,000 in 1993, $553,784,000 in 1992, and $508,939,000 in 1991. Price per pound averaged 37.5 cents in 1993, 35 cents in 1992, and 34 cents in 1991. Leading broiler-producing counties are Camp, Cass, Gonzales, Nacogdoches, Panola, Rusk, Shelby, Titus, Bowie and Wood. ☆

The Introduction of Cattle and Horses into Texas

by Mary G. Ramos, editor, Texas Almanac

The great cattle industry of the Lone Star State, the industry that is synonymous with Texas in many minds, began with the arrival of the Spanish in the New World.

The Spanish conquered the Caribbean archipelago following Christopher Columbus' voyages of discovery in the 15th century. They moved onto the mainlands of what are now Central and South America, then proceeded northward into Mexico. As the Spanish expanded their colonial empire, they spread their open-range ranching system — as well as their culture, religion, laws and language — over the conquered territories. The ranches they set up in the Caribbean, principally Cuba, helped support their exploratory expeditions into the frontiers of New Spain.

In Mexico, the Spanish established ranches on large, private estates. As the Spanish moved their settlements north from Mexico into the area that would become Texas, the cattle industry came within the purview of the mission-presidio system of the frontier. The missionaries and soldiers brought with them herds of cattle, mules, sheep and goats. The mission herds were sometimes augmented by feral cattle already in the region. These wild cattle were descendants of those brought by Spanish explorers, beginning in the 16th century, to supply transportation and food for their troops. As the explorers left the area, some of the cattle escaped or were turned loose.

East Texas Missions Established

The earliest documented European settlement in what is today East Texas was the Mission San Francisco de los Tejas, established in 1690 on the Neches River northeast of present Crockett, Houston County. The East Texas mission included 200 head of cattle brought by the missionaries for breeding purposes and for food. A second mission was started nearby, but the triple scourges of disease, famine and flood forced the missionaries to retreat to Mexico in late 1693. By this time, the original mission cattle had disappeared, and the wild descendants of this and other mission herds formed the nucleus of domestic herds in civilian settlements that were established later.

Because of French incursions into East Texas, the Spanish re-established missions in the area in 1716. And with the return of the missions came the establishment of the first permanent ranching institutions in Texas. The Spanish missionaries and soldiers founded five missions and their accompanying presidios in East Texas, bringing in "seed" cattle from Coahuila, Mexico.

The second permanent ranching establishment was associated with the San Antonio de Valero mission and the San Antonio de Bexar presidio on the San Antonio River in 1718 in present-day San Antonio. From these beginnings, ranching spread throughout Central and South Texas as the mission network expanded.

Spanish Use Ranches in Missionary Efforts

The missionaries intended to "civilize" and convert American Indians, turning them into European-style productive laborers. The ranch was to be a tool for conquering the Texas frontier, as it had been in other parts of New Spain. The Spanish plan called for mission ranches to provide meat for the Indians to eliminate their desire to chase the bison, deer and other game that made up their usual diet. The Indians already possessed skills that could be easily adapted to ranch work: hunting, chasing and herding. The church also offset some mission expenses by selling ranch products, such as hides, wool and tallow.

The Spanish had made this plan work among some of the civilized tribes of Mexico and Peru. They even had limited success with the more settled East Texas Caddoes. But their attempts to turn the fierce and nomadic Apache and Comanche warriors of the Texas plains into farmers were not as successful. (See story of San Sabá mission in History section.)

Ranching Begun in San Antonio Area

The civilian settlement of San Fernando de Béxar extended ranching past the frontier institutions. When immigrants from the Canary Islands founded San Fernando around the nucleus of the missions and presidio at San Antonio in 1731, they worked cattle on the fringe of the settlement. Ranches were soon to be found from San Antonio to the La Bahía mission and presidio near present-day Goliad in South Texas.

The Spanish cattle had low-swinging heads with wide horns, as well as narrow sides and long legs. They had no dairy or draft uses, but produced hides, tallow and stringy beef. They were tough and strong and readily reverted to the wild when turned loose. The Spanish cattle were at home on the arid and semiarid lands of West Texas, which was similar in climate and physiography to their native Spanish countryside.

Spanish Ranching Techniques Used Today

The Spanish ranching system, with everyone's cattle mingling on the open range as they grazed, necessitated round-ups to separate the cattle prior to slaughtering or selling. All the cattle that shared a range were rounded up at least once a year, and cowhands from the ranches involved separated the cattle

A cowboy sports adaptations of Spanish ranching gear: broad-brimmed hat to protect his eyes from the sun; lariat, to help in managing the cattle; and chaps, to protect his legs from thorny brush. Almanac file photo.

into individual herds. Each ranch was responsible for culling its herd and for marking its calves with the ranch's distinctive identifying symbols.

The Spanish use of branding and ear-clipping for identification, a necessary component of the open-range system, was also used by the Texans. The Spanish method of brand registration was also adopted to assure that each ranch's brand remained distinctive and unique, much as an automobile has a state-registered number on a license plate for identification today.

Other Spanish ranching techniques translated easily to the Texas plains, as well. One was the use of mounted herdsmen. The French and English colonists in the eastern United States sometimes worked cattle and sheep on foot, often aided by trained dogs. East of the Appalachians, where the land holdings were small, these methods were usable. But the sparse vegetation of the plains required ranchers to run their cattle on much larger pieces of land. The long distances on the plains and the wild nature of the Spanish cattle required cowhands to have the agility and greater range provided by horses. Along with the use of horses came Spanish riding equipment, including the Western saddle, with curved cantle, long stirrups and a high pommel, which served as a roping post.

Because of the sharp climatic changes in Spain, Spanish ranchers moved their herds to different grazing lands seasonally. They also drove their herds to market, a technique echoed in the 19th-century cattle drives from Texas to markets and railheads mainly in the American Midwest.

Spanish Equipment Adapted for American Southwest

Perhaps the most visible evidence of Spanish influence on Western American ranching is the specialized clothing and equipment of the modern cowhand: wide-brimmed hat, boots, spurs and the leather leg coverings called chaps that protect legs from brambles and thorns. The lasso or lariat, with which the cowboy ropes cattle during roundups and rodeos, and the rodeo itself, evolved from Spanish ranching practices.

Vocabulary borrowed from the Spanish ranchers includes lasso (*lazo*) or lariat (*la reata*), rodeo, sombrero, mustangs (borrowed from the Spanish *mesteños*, meaning unbranded cattle) and chaps (*chaparejos*).

The *Mesta*, a Spanish quasi-governmental organization, was established to enforce livestock laws. It served as a pattern for today's ranchers' organizations, such as the Texas and Southwestern Cattle Raisers' Association.

Spanish cattle ranching spread northward from Texas into the American West and became the only Spanish frontier institution to survive intact into modern times. It left a legacy of equipment, cattle-handling techniques, legal codes, stockmen's association, vocabulary and folklore to enrich Texas culture. ☆

State Civic Organizations

Listed below are privately supported civic, commericial and other nonprofit Texas organizations. Listing is alphabetical by the keyword in the title; i.e. Texas Egg Council is found under "Egg."

AFL-CIO, Texas — Box 12727, Austin 78711.

Advertising & Magazine Publishing, Texas Council of — 1104 West Ave. #101, Austin 78701.

Agricultural Organizations

Agricultural Cooperative Council, Texas — Box 9527, Austin 78766.

Agricultural Workers of Texas, Professional — Agricultural Services & Development Dept., Tarleton State University, Stephenville 76402.

Airport Executives, Assn. of Texas — 1821 Rutherford Lane, #400, Austin 78756-5128.

Allergy and Immunology Society, Texas — 401 W. 15th St., Austin 78701

American Legion, Dept. of Texas — Box 789, Austin 78767.

Anesthesiologists, Texas Society of — 401 W. 15th, #990, Austin 78701.

Apartment Assn., Texas — 606 W. 12th, Austin 78701.

Archaeological Organizations

Archeological Society, The Texas, Center for Archeological Research, UTSA, San Antonio 78249-0658.

Archeological Assn., Southern Texas — Box 791032, San Antonio 78279.

Archeological Society, Central Texas — 4229 Mitchell Rd., Waco 76710.

Archeological Society, El Paso — Box 4345, El Paso 79914.

Archeological Society, Houston — Box 6751, Houston 77265.

Archeological Society, Midland — Box 4224, Midland 79704.

Archaeology, Institute of Nautical — Drawer HG, College Station 77841-5137.

Architects, American Inst. (Dallas Chapter) — 2811 McKinney, LB 104, Dallas 75204.

Arts, Texans for the — 6757 Arapaho Rd., #711-278, Dallas 75248.

Assessing Officers, Texas Assn. of — 7600 Burnet Rd., #520, Austin 78757.

Association Executives, Texas Society of — 2550 S. I-35, #200, Austin 78704.

Austin College Alumni Assn. — 900 N. Grand Ave., Ste. 6G, Box 1177, Sherman 75090-4440.

Automobile Dealers Assn., Texas — Box 1028, Austin 78767-1028.

Automotive Service Association — Box 929, Bedford 76095-0929.

Automotive Parts & Services Assn. — 505 E. Huntland Dr., #490, Austin 78752-3714.

Bankers Assn., Texas — 203 W. Tenth, Austin 78701-2388.

Bankers Assn. of Texas, Independent — 408 W. 14th, Austin 78701.

Bank Counsel, Texas Assn. of — 203 W. Tenth, Austin 78701.

Baptist General Convention of Texas — 333 N. Washington, Dallas 75246.

Bar of Texas, State — Box 12487, Austin 78711.

Baylor Alumni Assn. — Box 97116, Waco 76798.

Big Bend Natural History Assn. — Box 68, Big Bend National Park 79834.

Blueberry Growers Assn., Texas — Box 891, Georgetown 78627.

B'nai B'rith Women (Southwest Region) — 8323 Southest Freeway, #385, Houston 77074.

Boating Trades Assn. of Texas — 3811 Turtle Creek Blvd., #950, Dallas 75219.

Book Publishers of Texas — 3404 S. Ravinia, Dallas 75233.

Bowling Proprietors' Assn. of America — Box 5802, Arlington 76015.

Brahman Breeders Assn., American — 1313 La Concha Ln., Houston 77054.

Brangus Assn., American Red — 3995 E. Highway 290, Dripping Springs 78620.

Brangus Breeders Assn., Texas — Box 690750, San Antonio 78269-0750.

Broadcasters, Texas Assn. of — 1907 N. Lamar, #300, Austin 78705.

Building Officials Assn. of Texas — 1601 Rio Grande, #440, Austin 78701.

Business & Chamber of Commerce, Texas Assn. of — Box 2989, Austin 78760-2989.

Business, Natl. Federation of Independent — 815 Brazos, #900, Austin 78701.

Cancer Society, American (Texas Div., Inc.) — Box 149054, Austin 78714.

Cattle Raisers Assn., Inc., Texas and Southwestern — 1301 W. Seventh, Fort Worth 76102.

Chambers of Commerce Managers and Secretaries Association/East Texas — Box 1582, Kilgore 75662.

Chili Appreciation Society International — 1516 Prairie Dr., El Paso 79925-2543

Churches, Texas Conference of — 6633 E. Highway 290, #200, Austin 78723.

Circulation Management Assn., Texas — 685 John B. Sias Memorial Pkwy., Fort Worth 76134.

Citrus and Vegetable Assn., Texas — 901 Business Park Dr. #500, Mission 78572.

City Attorneys Assn., Texas — 1821 Rutherford Lane, #400, Austin 78754.

City Planners Assn. of Texas — 1821 Rutherford Lane, #400, Austin 78754.

Communication Assn., International — Box 9589, Austin 78766.

Contractors Assns. of Texas, Mechanical — 1033 La Posada Dr., #220, Austin 78752-3880.

Contractors, Texas Council of Painting and Decorating — 1601 Rio Grande, #440, Austin 78701.

Contractors, Assn. of Drilled Shaft — Box 280379, Dallas 75228.

Contractors of Texas, Hwy., Heavy Util. & Indus. — Box 2185, Austin 78768.

Contractors Assn. of Texas, Roofing — 1033 La Posada Dr., #220, Austin 78752.

Convention and Visitor Bureaus, Texas Assn. of — Box 1264, Fredericksburg 78624.

Corrections Assn., Texas — 1033 La Posada Dr., #220, Austin 78752-3880.

Cotton Organizations

Cotton Growers Co-operative Assn., Texas — Box 391, Taylor 76574.

Cotton Growers, Inc., Plains — 4510 Englewood, Lubbock 79414.

Cotton Growers Assn., Rolling Plains — Box 1108, Stamford 79553.

Counseling Assn., Texas — 316 W. 12th, #402, Austin 78701.

Counties, Texas Assn. of — 1204 San Antonio St., Austin 78768.

Credit Union League and Affiliates, Texas — Box 655147, LBJ Freeway, Dallas 75265-5147.

Dancing, Texas Assn. of Teachers of — 2200 Cabaniss Lane, Weatherford 76088.

Daughters Associations

Daughters of American Colonists, Texas Soc. of — 4104 Saranac Dr., Dallas 75220-1949.

Daughters of Colonial Wars, Texas Society — 6408 Dovenshire Terrace, Fort Worth 76132.

Daughters of the Republic of Texas — 501 E. Anderson Lane, Austin 78752.

Daughters of 1812, Texas Society, United States — 704 N. Lamar Dr., Euless 76039-7415.

Diabetes Assn., Inc., American (Texas Affiliate) — 9430 Research, II-300, Austin 78759.

Diabetes and Endocrine Assn., Texas — 2401 S. 31st St., Temple 76508.

Dietetic Assn., Texas — 1033 La Posada Dr., #220, Austin 78752.

Donkey and Mule Society, Inc., American — 2901 N. Elm, Denton 76201.

Dulcimer Society, Lone Star State — 1114 Vine, Denton 76201.

Earth Scientists, Society of Indepen. Professional — 4925 Greenville, #170, Dallas 75206-4008.

East Texas Tourism Association — Box 1592, Longview 75606.

Educational Secretaries Assn., Texas — Box 1565, Austin 78767.

Egg Council, Texas — Box 9589, Austin 78766

Electric Cooperatives, Inc., Texas — Box 9589, Austin 78766-9589.

Electronics Assn., Inc., Texas — 2708 W. Berry, #7, Fort Worth 76109.

Engineers Council of Texas, Consulting — 400 W.15th, #820, Austin 78701.

Engineers, Texas Society of Professional — Box 2145, Austin 78768.

Faculty Assn., Texas — 316 W. 12th, Austin 78701.

Fair Assn., East Texas — 2112 W. Front, Tyler 75702.

Fair of Texas, State — Box 150009, Dallas 75315.

Fairs and Expositions, Texas Assn. of — Box 577, Santa Rosa 78593.

Family & Consumer Sciences, Tex. Assn. of — Box 831, Hurst 76053.

Farm Bureau, Texas — Box 2689, Waco 76702-2689.

Farm and Ranch Club, East Texas — 2112 W. Front, Tyler 75702.

FFA, Texas Assn. of — Box 13064, Austin 78729.

Fashion Assn., Inc., American — Box 586454, #5442, Dallas 75258.

Finance Officers Assn. of Texas, Government — 1821 Rutherford Lane, #400, Austin 78754-5128.

Fire Chiefs Assn., Texas — 1821 Rutherford Lane, #400, Austin 78754-5128.

Folklore Society, Texas — Box 13007, SFA Station, Nacogdoches 75962-3007.

Food Processors Assn., Texas — Box 341, College Station 77841.

Forage and Grassland Council, Texas — Box 891, Georgetown 78627.

Foresters, Texas Society of American — Box 150555, Lufkin 75915.

Forestry Assn., Texas — Box 1488, Lufkin 75902.

Fruit Growers Assn., Texas — 4348 Carter Creek, #101, Bryan 77802.

Furnishings and Design Assn., International — Box 580045, Dallas 75258.

Gas Assn., Southern — 3030 LBJ Frwy., #1300, Dallas 75234.

Genealogical Institute of Texas — Box 832856, Richardson 75083-2856.

Genealogical Society, Texas State — Rt. 4, Box 56, Sulphur Springs 75482.

German-American Heritage Society — Box 684171, Austin 78768.

Goat Breeders Assn., American Angora — Box 195, Rocksprings 78880.

Grange, Texas State — HC-13, Box 6A, Fredericksburg 78624.

Grocers Assn., D-FW — 3001 LBJ Fwy, #133, Dallas 75234-7756.

Healthcare Environmental Service, Texas Soc. — Box 15587, Austin 78761.

Healthcare Financial Administration, Texas Assn. for — Box 15587, Austin 78761.

Health, Physical Education, Recreation and Dance, Texas Assn. — 6800 La Calma, #100, Austin 78752.

Heart Assn., American, Texas Affiliate — Box 15186, Austin 78761.

Highway 67 Assn., U.S. — Box 701, Cleburne 76033-0701.

Historical Organizations

Historic Accommodations of Texas — 231 W. Main, Fredericksburg 78624.

Historical Society, Texas Baptist — Box 22000, Fort Worth 76122-2490.

Historical Society, Texas Catholic — Texas Catholic Conference, 3001 S. Congress, Austin 78704.

Historical Assn., East Texas — Box 6223, SFA Station, Nacogdoches 75962.

Historical Foundation, Texas — Box 50314, Austin 77863.

Historical Society, Texas Jewish — Box 10193, Austin 78766-0193.

Historical Society, Texas United Methodist — Bridwell Library, SMU, Dallas 75275-0476.

History Assn., Texas Oral — BU Box 97271, Baylor U., Waco 76798.

Historical Society, Panhandle Plains — Box 967, W.T. Station, Canyon 79016.

Historical Society, Permian — 4901 E. University, Odessa 79762-0001.

Historical Assn., Texas State — 2/306 Sid Richardson Hall, Austin 78712.

Historical Assn., West Texas — Box 152, HSU, Abilene 79698.

Home Economics Assn., Texas — Box 831, Hurst 76053.

Home Furnishings International Association — Box 581207, Dallas 75258.

Horse Organizations

Horse Club, Texas Appaloosa — Box 557, Cedar Hill 75104.

Horse Assn., National Cutting — 4704 Hwy. 377 S, Fort Worth 76116-8805.

Horse Assn., American Quarter — 1600 Quarter Horse Drive, Amarillo 79104.

Horticultural Society, Texas State — 4348 Carter Creek, #101, Bryan 77802.

Hospital Assn., Texas — Box 15587, Austin 78761.

Hospital Auxiliaries, Texas Assn. of — Box 15587, Austin 78761.

Hospital Trustees, Texas — Box 15587, Austin 78761-5587.

Insurance Advisory Assn., Texas — Box 15, Austin 78767.

Insurance Agents, Texas Assn. of — Box 684488, Austin 78767.

(Insurance) General Agents and Managers Assn., Southwest — 1920 S. IH-35, Austin 78704.

Insurance Information Service, Inc., Southwest — 8705 Shoal Creek Blvd., # 212, Austin 78757.

Interior Designers, Texas Chapter of American Soc. — 1909-C Hi Line Drive, Dallas 75207.

Jewelers Assn., Inc., Texas — 504 W. 12th Austin, 78701.

Keep Texas Beautiful, Inc. — Box 2251, Austin 78768.

Knights of the Order of San Jacinto — 5942 Abrams Rd., #222, Dallas 75231.

Lawyers Assn., Texas Young — Box 12487, Austin 78711.

Letters, Texas Institute of — Box 9032, Wichita Falls 76308.

Libertarian Party of Texas — Box 56426, Houston 77256.

Library Directors Assn., Texas Municipal — 1821 Rutherford Lane, #400, Austin 78754-5128.

Life Underwriters, Texas Assn. of — 1920 S. IH-35, Austin 78704.

Llama Assn., South Central — Box 163654, Austin 78716.

Lung Assn. of Texas, American — Box 26460, Austin 78755-0460.

Lupus Foundation of America, Inc., North Texas Chapter — 2997 LBJ Frwy., #108-N, Dallas 75234.

Manufactured Housing Assn., Texas — Box 14428, Austin 78761-4428.

Medical Organizations

Medical Assn., Texas — 401 W. 15th, Austin 78701.

Medical Assn. Alliance, Texas — 401 W. 15th, Austin 78701.

Medicine, Texas Society of Internal — 401 W. 15th, Austin 78701-1680.

Mental Health Assn. in Texas — 8401 Shoal Creek Blvd., Austin 78757.

Motorcycle Dealers Assn., Texas — 1601 Rio Grande, #440, Austin 78701.

Municipal Organizations

Municipal Advisory Council of Texas — Box 2177, Austin 78768-2177.

Municipal Clerks Assn., Texas — Chilton Hall, Room 263, Denton 76203.

Municipal Information Officers, Texas Assn. of — 1821 Rutherford Lane, #400, Austin 78754.

Municipal League, Texas — 1821 Rutherford Lane, #400, Austin 78754.

Municipal Parks and Recreation Assn., Texas — 1821 Rutherford Lane, #400, Austin 78754-4128.

Municipal Tax Administrators, Texas Assn. of — 1821 Rutherford Lane #400, Austin 78754.

Music Schools, Texas Assn. of — 1281 Canterbury, Abilene 79698.

National Guard Assn. of Texas — Box 10045, Austin 78766-1045.

Nature Conservancy of Texas, The — Box 1440, San Antonio 78295-1440.

Neurological Society, Texas — 401 W. 15 St. Austin 78701.

New England Women, Nat'l Soc. of, Texas Colony 121 — 9835 Elmcrest, Dallas 75238-1831.

Newspaper Assn., Texas Daily — 98 San Jacinto Blvd., #1250, Austin 78701.

Nurse Executives, Texas Organization of — Box 15587, Austin 78761.

Nurserymen, Texas Assn. of — 7730 S. IH-35, Austin 78745-6698.

Nursing, Texas League for — Box 530147, Austin 78753.

Obstetricians and Gynecologists, Texas Assn. of — 401 W. 15th, Austin 78701.

Oil & Gas Assn., Texas Mid-Continent — 1115 San Jacinto Blvd., #275, Austin 78701-1980.

Oil and Gas Assn., North Texas — 726 Scott #801, Wichita Falls 76301.

Ophthalmological Assn., Texas — 401 W. 15th, #681, Austin 78701-1680.

Optometric Assn., Texas — 1503 South IH-35, Austin 78741-2502.

Orthopaedic Assn., Texas — 401 W. 15th St., #680, Austin 78701.

Pain Society, Texas — 401 W. 15th St., Austin 78701.

Paper & Sanitary Supply Assn., Southwest — Box 140046, Austin 78714-0046.

Parents and Teachers, Texas Congress of — 408 W. 11th, Austin 78701.

Peanut Growers' Assn., Southwest — Box 338, Gorman 76454.

Pecan Growers Assn., Texas — 4348 Carter-Creek, #101, Bryan 77802.

Pediatric Society, Texas — 401 W. 15th, #682, Austin 78701.

Personnel Consultants, Texas Assn. of — Box 100927, San Antonio 78201.

Petroleum Engineers, Society of — Box 833836, Richardson 75083-3836.

Pharmaceutical Assn., Texas — P.O. Box 14709, Austin 78761.

Philosophical Society of Texas — SRH 2/306, U.T. Station, Austin 78712.

Physical Therapy Assn., Texas — 400 W. 15th, #805, Austin 78701.

Plastic Surgeons, Texas Society of — 401 W. 15th, Austin 78701.

Poetry Society of Texas — 4244 Skillman, Dallas

75206.

Police Assn., Texas — Box 4247, Austin 78765.

Poultry Organizations

Broiler Council, Texas — Box 9589, Austin 78766.

Poultry Assn., Texas Allied — Box 9589, Austin 78766.

Poultry Federation, Texas — Box 9589, Austin 78766.

Poultry Improvement Assn., Texas — Box 9589, Austin 78766.

Prairies Assn. of Texas, Native — 301 Nature Center Dr., Austin 78746.

Press Organizations

Press Assn., Texas — 718 W. 5th, Austin 78701.

Press Assn., Texas High School — Abilene Christian University, Abilene, 79699.

Press Assn., West Texas — 2502 Ivanhoe, Abilene 79605-6216.

Prevent Blindness (Dallas Branch), Tex. Society to — 3610 Fairmount St., Dallas 75219.

Producers & Royalty Owners Assn., Texas Independent — 515 Congress, #1910, Austin 78701.

Property Tax Professionals, Texas Assn. of — 1033 La Posada Dr., #220, Austin 78752.

Public Employees Assn., Texas — Box 12217, Austin 78711.

Radiological Society, Texas — 401 W. 15th, Austin 78701-1680.

Ranching Heritage Association — Box 43201, Lubbock 79409.

Range Management, Texas Section of Society for — Box 918, Sonora 76950.

Realtors, Texas Association of — Box 2246, Austin, 78768.

Recreational Vehicle Assn., Texas — 3355 Bee Cave Rd., #104, Austin 78746.

Research League, Texas — Box 12456, Austin 78711-2456.

Retailers Assn., Texas — 504 W. 12th Austin, 78701.

Roads/Transportation Assn., Texas — 1122 Colorado, #305, Austin 78701.

Santa Gertrudis Breeders International — Box 1257, Kingsville 78364.

Savings and Community Bankers Assn., Texas — 910 Congress, 2nd Floor, Austin 78701.

School Boards, Texas Assn. of — Box 400, Austin 78767-0400.

Sheep Breeders Assn., American Rambouillet — 2709 Sherwood Way, San Angelo 76901.

Sheriffs' Assn. of Texas, Inc. — Box 448, Austin 78765.

Shrine Assn., Texas — 2202 Avondale, Wichita Falls 76307.

Sign Manufacturers Assn., Texas — 729 Grapevine Hwy., #339, Hurst 76054.

Skeet Shooters Assn., Texas — Box 830530, Richardson 75083-0530.

Social Workers, Texas Chapter of the Natl Assn. of — 810 W. 11th, Austin 78701.

Socialist Party of Texas — Box 2640, Austin 78768-2640.

Sons Organizations

Sons of the American Revolution (Texas Society) — 922 Oak Lane, New Braunfels 78130.

Sons of Confederate Veterans (Texas Division) — Box 619, Hillsboro 76645.

Sons of Hermann in the State of Texas, Grand Lodge of — Box 1941, San Antonio 78297.

Sons of the Republic of Texas — 5942 Abrams Road, #222, Dallas 75231.

Sons of the Revolution in the State of Texas — 3207 Top Hill Rd., San Antonio 78209.

Soybean Assn., Texas — RR 7, Box 999, Beaumont 77713.

Sportsmen Conservationists of Texas — 807 Brazos, #311, Austin 78701.

Surgeons, American College of (North Texas Chapter) — UTSMC, Div. of Vascular Surgery, Dallas 75235-9031.

Taxpayers, Inc., Texas Assn. of — 400 W. 15th, #400, Austin 78701.

TCU Alumni Assn. — Box 32921, Fort Worth 76129.

Teachers Organizations (See also **Faculty**)

Teachers, Texas Classroom — Box 1489, Austin 78767.

Teachers, Texas Association of College — 9513 Burnet Road, #206, Austin 78758.

Teachers, Texas Federation of — 300 South IH-35, #175, Austin 78704.

Teachers, Texas Junior College — 901 MoPac So., Bldg. 1, #410, Austin 78746-5747.

Teachers Assn., Texas State — 316 W. 12th, Austin 78701.

Telephone Pioneers of America, Texas Pride — (Chap. 22), One Bell Plaza, Room 315, Dallas 75202.

Texas Rangers Assn., Former — P.O. Box 6354, San Antonio 78202.

Thoracic Society, Texas, Medical Section of American Lung Assn. — Box 26460, Austin 78755-0460.

Trailer Manufacturers, Nat'l Assn. of — 1033 La Posada Dr., #220, Austin 78752-3830.

Transplantation Society, Texas — 401 W. 15th, Austin 78701-1680.

Turkey Federation, Texas — Box 9589, Austin 78766.

United Way of Texas — 505 E. Huntland Dr., #455, Austin 78731.

University Presidents & Chancellors, Council of Public — 2609 Coatbridge, Austin 78745-3423.

Veterans of Foreign Wars of U.S. (Dept. of Texas) — 8503 N. IH-35, Austin 78753.

Veterinary Medical Assn., Texas — 6633 Hwy. 290 E, #201, Austin 78723-1157.

War of 1812 in State of Texas, General Society of the — 5009 Ascot Parkway, Temple 76502.

Wars in Texas, Society of Colonial — 922 Oak Lane, New Braunfels 78130-6069.

Water Conservation Assn., Texas — 922 E. 9th, #206, Austin 78701.

Wheat Producers Assn., Texas — 2201 Civic Circle, #803, Amarillo 79109.

Wholesale Distributors, Texas Assn. of — 7320 N. MoPac Expy., #209, Austin 78731.

Women Voters of Texas, League of — 1212 Guadalupe, #107, Austin 78701-1800.

Women's Clubs, Texas Federation of — 2312 San Gabriel, Austin 78705.

Writers Assn., Texas Outdoor — 1415 Northridge, Austin 78723. ☆

Texas Pronunciation Guide

Texas' rich cultural diversity is reflected no where better than in the names of places. Standard pronunciation is used in many cases, but purely colloquial pronunciation often is used, too.

In the late 1940s, George Mitchel Stokes, a graduate student at Baylor University, developed a list of pronunciations of 2,300 place names across the state.

Stokes earned his doctorate and eventually served as director of the speech division in the Communications Studies Department at Baylor University. He retired in 1983.

In the following list based on Stokes longer list, pronunciation is by respelling and diacritical marking. Respelling is employed as follows: "ah" as in the exclamation, ah, or the "o" in tot; "ee" as in meet; "oo" as in moot; "yoo" as in use; "ow" as in cow; "oi" as in oil; "uh" as in mud.

Note that ah, uh and the apostrophe(') are used for varying degrees of neutral vowel sounds, the apostrophe being used where the vowel is barely sounded. Diacritical markings are used as follows: bāle, băd, lĕt, rīse, rĭll, ōak, brōōd, fŏŏt.

A

Abernathy—Ă ber nă thĭ
Abilene—ĂB uh leen
Acala—uh KĀ luh
Ackerly—ĂK er lĭ
Acme—ĂK mĭ
Acton—ĂK t'n
Acuff—Ā kuhf
Addicks—Ă dĭks
Addielou—ă dĭ LŌŌ
Addison—A di s'n
Adrian—Ā drĭ uhn
Agua Dulce—ah wuh DŌŌL sĭ
Agua Nueva—ah wuh nyōō Ā vuh
Aiken—Ā kĭn
Alamo—ĂL uh mō
Alamo Heights—ăl uh mō HĪTS
Alanreed—ĂL uhn reed
Alba—ĂL buh
Albany—AWL buh nĭ
Aledo—uh LEE dō
Alexander—ĕl ĭg ZĂN der
Alief—Ā leef
Allenfarm—ălĭn FAHRM
Alleyton—Ă lĭ t'n
Allison—ĂL uh s'n
Alma—AHL muh
Altair—awl TĂR
Alta Loma—ăl tuh LŌ muh
Alto—ĂL tō
Altoga—ăl TŌ guh
Alvarado—ăl vuh RĀ dō
Alvord—ĂL vord
Amarillo—ăm uh RĬL ō
Amherst—AM herst
Ammannsville—ĂM 'nz vĭl
Anahuac—ĂN uh wăk
Anderson—ĂN der s'n
Andice—ĂN dīs
Angelina—ăn juh LEE nuh
Angleton—ĂNG g'l t'n
Anna—ĂN uh
Annona—ă NŌ nuh
Anson—ĂN s'n
Anton—ĂNT n
Appleby—Ă p'l bi
Aquilla—uh KWĬL uh
Aransas—uh RĂN zuhs
Aransas Pass—uh răn zuhs PĂS
Arbala—ahr BĀ luh
Arcadia—ahr KĀ dĭ uh
Arcola—ahr KŌ luh
Argo—AHR gō
Argyle—ahr GĪL
Arneckeville—AHR nĭ kĭ vĭl
Arnett—AHR nĭt
Arp—ahrp
Asherton—ĂSH er t'n
Aspermont—ĂS per mahnt
Atascosa—ăt uhs KŌ suh
Attoyac—AT uh yăk
Aubrey—AW brĭ
Augusta—aw GUHS tuh
Austin—AWS t'n
Austonio—aws TŌ nĭ ŏ
Austwell—AWS wĕl
Avalon—ĂV uhl n
Avery—Ā vuh rĭ
Avinger—Ă vĭn jer
Avoca—uh VŌ kuh
Axtell—ĂKS t'l
Azle—Ā z'l

B

Baileyboro—BĀ lĭ ber ruh
Baird—bărd
Ballinger—BĂL ĭn jer
Balmorhea—băl muh RĀ
Bandera—băn DĔR uh
Banquete—băn KĔ tĭ
Barclay—BAHRK lĭ
Barksdale—BAHRKS dāl
Barnhart—BAHRN hahrt
Barnum—BAHR n'm
Barstow—BAHRS tō
Bastrop—BĂS trahp
Batson—BĂT s'n
Baxter—BĂKS ter
Baylor—BĀ ler
Beasley—BEEZ lĭ
Beaukiss—bō KĬS
Beaumont—BŌ mahnt
Bebe—bāb
Beckville—BĔK v'l
Becton—BĔK t'n
Bedias—BEE dīs
Beeville—BEE vĭl
Belcherville—BĔL cher vĭl
Bellaire—bĕl ĂR
Bellevue—BĔL vyōō
Bellmead—bĕl MEED
Bellville—BĔL vĭl
Belton—BĔL t'n
Ben Arnold—bĕn AHR n'ld
Benavides—bĕn uh VEE d's
Benbrook—BĬN brŏŏk
Benchley—BĔNCH lĭ
Bentonville—BĔNT n vĭl
Berclair—ber KLĂR
Bertram—BERT r'm
Bessmay—bĕs MĀ
Bettie—BĔT ĭ
Bexar—BĀ ăr
Beyersville—BĪRZ vĭl
Biardstown—BĂRDZ t'n
Bigfoot—BĬG fŏŏt
Big Sandy—bĭg SĂN dĭ
Birome—bī RŌM
Birthright—BERTH rīt
Bivins—BĬ vĭnz
Blair—blăr
Blanchard—BLĂN cherd
Blanco—BLĂNG kō
Bleakwood—BLEEK wŏŏd
Bledsoe—BLĔD sō
Blewett—BLŌŌ ĭt
Bluffton—BLUHF t'n
Blum—bluhm
Boerne—BER nĭ
Bogata—buh GŌ duh
Boling—BŌL ĭng
Bolivar—BAH lĭ ver
Bomarton—BŌ mer t'n
Bonham—BAH n'm
Bonita—bō NEE tuh
Bonney—BAH nĭ
Bonus—BŌ n's
Bon Wier—bahn WEER
Boonsville—BŌŌNZ vĭl
Borger—BŌR ger
Bosque—BAHS kĭ
Bovina—bō VEE nuh
Bowie—BŌŌ Ĭ
Boyce—bawis
Boyd—boid
Brachfield—BRĂCH feeld
Bracken—BRĂ kĭn
Brackettville—BRĂ kĭt vĭl
Brandon—BRĂN d'n
Brashear—bruh SHĬR
Brazoria—bruh ZŌ rĭ uh
Brazos—BRĂZ uhs
Breckenridge—BRĔK uhn rĭj
Bremond—bree MAHND
Brenham—BRĔ n'm
Brewster—BRŌŌ ster
Brice—brīs
Briscoe—BRĬS kō
Britton—BRĬT n

Broaddus—BRAW d's
Brock—brahk
Bronte—brahnt
Brookeland—BRO͝OK l'nd
Brookesmith—BRO͝OK smith
Brookshire—BRO͝OK sher
Brookston—BRO͝OKS t'n
Browndel—brown DĔL
Brownsboro—BROWNZ buh ruh
Brownsville—BROWNZ vĭl
Bruceville—BRO͝OS v'l
Brundage—BRUHN dĭj
Bruni—BRO͝O nĭ
Bryarly—BRĪ er lĭ
Bryson—BRĪ s'n
Buchanan Dam—buhk hăn uhn DĂM
Buckholts—BUHK hōlts
Buckhorn—BUHK hawrn
Buda—BYO͝O duh
Buena Vista—bwā nuh VEES tuh
Bula—BYO͝O luh
Bullard—BO͝OL erd
Bulverde—bo͝ol VER dĭ
Buna—BYO͝O nuh
Burkburnett—berk ber NET
Burkett—BER kĭt
Burkeville—BERK vĭl
Burleson—BER luh s'n
Burlington—BER lĭng t'n
Burnet—BER nĕt
Burton—BERT n
Bushland—BO͝OSH l'nd
Bustamante—buhs tuh MAHN tĭ
Butler—BUHT ler
Byers—BĪ erz
Bynum—BĪ n'm
Byrd—berd

C

Cactus—KĂK t's
Caddo Mills—kă dō MĬLZ
Calallen—kăl ĂL ĭn
Calaveras—kăl uh VĔR's
Caldwell—KAHL wĕl
Calhoun—kăl HO͝ON
Calliham—KĂL uh hăm
Callisburg—KĂ lĭs berg
Call Junction—kawl JUHNGK sh'n
Calvert—KĂL vert
Camden—KĂM dĭn
Cameron—KĂM uh r'n
Camilla—kuh MEEL yuh
Campbellton—KĂM uhl t'n
Canadian—kuh NĀ dĭ uhn
Candelaria—kăn duh LĔ rĭ uh
Canton—KĂNT n
Canyon—KĂN y'n
Caplen—KĂP lĭn
Caradan—KĂR uh dăn
Carbon—KAHR b'n
Carey—KĀ rĭ
Carlisle—KAHR līl
Carlsbad—KAHR uhlz bad
Carlton—KAHR uhl t'n
Carmine—kahr MEEN
Carmona—kahr MŌ nuh
Caro—KAH rō
Carrizo Springs—kuh ree zuh SPRĬNGZ
Carrollton—KĂR 'l t'n
Carthage—KAHR thĭj
Cason—KĀ s'n
Cass—kăs
Castell—kăs TĔL
Castro—KĂS trō
Castroville—KĂS tro vĭl
Catarina—kăt uh REE nuh
Caviness—KĂ vĭ nĕs
Cayuga—kā YO͝O guh
Cedar Bayou—see der BĪ ō
Cee Vee—see VEE
Celeste—suh LĔST
Celina—suh LĪ nuh
Centerville—sĕn ter vĭl
Centralia—sĕn TRĀL yuh
Channelview—chăn uhl VYO͝O
Channing—CHĂN ĭng
Chappell Hill—chă p'l HĬL
Charco—CHAHR kō
Charleston—CHAHR uhls t'n
Charlie—CHAHR lĭ
Charlotte—SHAHR l't
Chatfield—CHĂT feeld
Cheapside—CHEEP sīd
Cherokee—CHĔR uh kee
Chester—CHĔS ter
Chico—CHEE kō
Chicota—chĭ KŌ tuh
Childress—CHĬL drĕs
Chillicothe—chĭl ĭ KAH thĭ
Chilton—CHĬL t'n
China—CHĪ nuh
China Spring—chī nuh SPRĬNG
Chireno—sh' REE nō
Chisholm—CHĬZ uhm
Chita—CHEE tuh
Chocolate Bayou—chah kuh lĭt BĪ ō
Chriesman—KRĬS m'n
Christine—krĭs TEEN
Christoval—krĭs TŌ v'l
Cibolo—SEE bō lō
Cisco—SĬS kō
Cistern—SĬS tern
Clairemont—KLĂR mahnt
Clairette—klăr ĭ ĔT
Clarendon—KLĂR ĭn d'n
Clareville—KLĂR vĭl
Clarksville—KLAHRKS vĭl
Clarkwood—KLAHRK wo͝od
Claude—klawd
Clawson—KLAW s'n
Clayton—KLĀT n
Cleburne—KLEE bern
Clemville—KLĔM vĭl
Cleveland—KLEEV l'nd
Clifton—KLĬF t'n
Cline—klīn
Clint—klĭnt
Clodine—klaw DEEN
Clute—klo͝ot
Clyde—klīd
Coahoma—kuh HŌ muh
Cockrell Hill—kahk ruhl HĬL
Coldspring—KŌLD sprĭng
Coleman—KŌL m'n
Colfax—KAHL făks
Collegeport—kah lĭj PŌRT
Collin—KAH lĭn
Collingsworth—KAH lĭnz werth
Collinsville—KAH lĭnz vĭl
Colmesneil—KŌL m's neel
Colorado—kahl uh RAH dō
Colorado City—kah luh rā duh SĬT ĭ
Columbus—kuh LUHM b's
Comal—KŌ măl
Comanche—kuh MĂN chĭ
Combes—kōmz
Como—KŌ mō
Comstock—KAHM stahk
Concan—KAHN kăn
Concepcion—kuhn sep sĭ ŌN
Concho—KAHN chō
Concord—KAHN kawrd
Concrete—kahn KREET
Conlen—KAHN lĭn
Conroe—KAHN rō
Converse—KAHN vers
Conway—KAHN wā
Cooke—ko͝ok
Cookville—KO͝OK vĭl
Coolidge—KO͝O lĭj
Cooper—KO͝O per
Copeville—KŌP v'l
Coppell—kuh PĔL
Copperas Cove—kahp ruhs KŌV
Corbett—KAWR bĭt
Cordele—kawr DĔL
Corinth—KAH rĭnth
Corley—KAWR lĭ
Corpus Christi—kawr p's KRĬS tĭ
Corrigan—KAWR uh g'n
Corsicana—kawr sĭ KĂN uh
Coryell—kō rĭ ĔL
Cottle—KAH t'l
Cotulla—kuh TO͝O luh
Coupland—KŌP l'n
Courtney—KŌRT nĭ
Covington—KUHV ĭng t'n
Coy City—koi SĬT ĭ
Craft—krăft
Crafton—KRĂF t'n
Crandall—KRĂN d'l
Cranfills Gap—krăn f'lz GĂP
Crawford—KRAW ferd
Creedmore—KREED mōr
Cresson—KRĔ s'n
Crisp—krĭsp
Crockett—KRAH kĭt
Crosby—KRAWZ bĭ
Crosbyton—KRAWZ bĭ t'n
Crowell—KRŌ uhl
Crowley—KROW li
Cuero—KWĔR o
Culberson—KUHL ber s'n
Cumby—KUHM bĭ
Cuney—KYO͝O nĭ
Cunningham—KUHN ĭng hăm
Currie—KER rĭ
Cushing—KO͝O shĭng
Cuthand—KUHT hănd
Cyclone—SĪ klōn

Cypress—SĪ prĕs

D
Dabney—DĂB nĭ
Dacosta—duh KAHS tuh
Dacus—DĂ k's
Daingerfield—DĀN jer feeld
Daisetta—dā ZĔT uh
Dalby Springs—dĂl bĭ SPRĬNGZ
Dale—dāl
Dalhart—DĂL hahrt
Dallam—DĂL uhm
Dallas—DĂ luhs
Damon—DĀ m'n
Danbury—DĂN bĕrĭ
Danciger—DĂN sĭ ger
Danevang—DĂN uh văng
Darrouzett—dăr uh ZĔT
Davilla—duh VĬL uh
Dayton—DĀT n
Deaf Smith—dĕf SMĬTH or dēēf Smĭth
Deanville—DEEN vĭl
De Berry—duh BĔ rĭ
Decatur—dee KĀT er
De Kalb—dĭ KĂB
De Leon—da lee AHN
Del Rio—dĕl REE o
Delta—DĔL tuh
Delvalle—dĕl VĂ lĭ
Delwin—DĔL wĭn
Denhawken—DĬN haw kĭn
Denison—DĔN uh s'n
Denning—DĔN ĭng
Dennis—DĔ nĭs
Denton—DĔNT n
Deport—dĭ PŌRT
Derby—DER bĭ
Desdemona—dĕz dĭ MŌ nuh
DeSoto—dĭ SŌ tuh
Detroit—dee TROIT
Devers—DĔ vers
Devine—duh VĪN
Dew—dyōō
Deweyville—DYŌŌ ĭ vĭl
DeWitt—dĭ WĬT
Dewville—DYŌŌ vĭl
Dexter—DĔKS ter
D'Hanis—duh HĂ nĭs
Dialville—DĪ uhl vil
Diboll—DĪ bawl
Dickens—DĬK ĭnz
Dickinson—DĬK ĭn s'n
Dike—dĭk
Dilley—DĬL i
Dilworth—DĬL werth
Dimebox—dīm BAHKS
Dimmit—DĬM ĭt
Dinero—dĭ NĔ rō
Direct—duh RĔKT
Dixon—DĬK s'n
Dobbin—DAH bĭn
Dobrowolski—dah bruh WAHL skĭ
Dodd City—dahd SĬT ĭ
Donie—DŌ nĭ
Donley—DAHN lĭ
Donna—dah nuh
Doole—DOO lĭ
Dorchester—dawr CHĔS ter
Doss—daws
Doucette—DŌŌ sĕt
Dougherty—DAHR tĭ
Douglass—DUHG l's
Douglassville—DUHG lĭs vĭl
Downing—DOWN ĭng
Downsville—DOWNZ vĭl
Dozier—DŌ zher
Driscoll—DRĬS k'l
Dryden—DRĪD n
Dublin—DUHB lĭn
Duffau—DUHF ō
Dumas—DŌŌ m's
Dumont—DYŌŌ mahnt
Dundee—DUHN dĭ
Dunlap—DUHN lăp
Dunlay—DUHN lĭ
Dunn—duhn
Durango—duh RĂNG go
Duval—DŌŌ vawl

E
East Bernard—eest ber NAHRD
Easterly—EES ter lĭ
Eastland—EEST l'nd
Easton—EES t'n
Ector—ĔK ter
Edcouch—ĕd KOWCH
Eddy—E di
Edgewood—ĔJ wŏŏd
Edinburg—ĔD n berg
Edmonson—ĔD m'n s'n
Edna—ED nuh
Edom—EE d'm
Edroy—ĔD roi
Edwards—ĔD werdz
Egan—EE g'n
Egypt—EE juhpt
Elbert—ĔL bert
El Campo—ĕl KĂM pō
Eldorado—ĕl duh RĀ duh
Electra—ĭ LĔK truh
Elgin—ĔL gĭn
Eliasville—ee LĪ uhs vĭl
El Indio—ĕl ĬN dĭ ō
Elkhart—ĔLK hahrt
Ellinger—ĔL ĭn jer
Elliott—ĔL ĭ 't
Ellis—ĔL uhs
Elmendorf—ĔLM 'n dawrf
Elm Mott—ĕl MAHT
Elmo—ĔL mō
Eloise—ĔL o eez
El Paso—ĕl PĂS ō
Elsa—ĔL suh
Elysian Fields—uh lee zh'n FEELDZ
Emhouse—ĔM hows
Emory—ĔM uh rĭ
Encinal—ĕn suh NAHL
Encino—ĕn SEE nō
Engle—ĔN g'l
Enloe—ĔN lō
Ennis—ĔN ĭs
Enochs—EE nuhks
Eola—ee Ō luh
Era—EE ruh
Erath—EE răth
Esperanza—ĕs per RĂN zuh
Estelline—ĔS tuh leen
Etoile—ĭ TOIL
Etter—ĔT er
Eula—YŌŌ luh
Euless—YŌŌ lis
Eureka—yōō REE kuh
Eustace—YŌŌS t's
Evadale—EE vuh dāl
Evant—EE vănt
Evergreen—Ĕ ver green
Everman—Ĕ ver m'n

F
Fabens—FĀ b'nz
Fairbanks—FĂR bangks
Fairfield—FĂR feeld
Fairlie—FĂR lee
Fairview—FĂR vyōō
Falfurrias—făl FYŌŌ rĭ uhs
Fannett—fă NĔT
Fannin—FĂN ĭn
Fargo—FAHR gō
Farnsworth—FAHRNZ werth
Farrar—FĂR uh
Farrsville—FAHRZ vĭl
Farwell—FAHR w'l
Fashing—FĂ shĭng
Fayette—fā ĔT
Fayetteville—FĀ uht vĭl
Fentress—FĔN trĭs
Ferris—FĔR ĭs
Fieldton—FEEL t'n
Fife—fīf
Fisher—FĬSH er
Fischer—fĭ sher
Fisk—fĭsk
Flagg—flăg
Flatonia—flă TŌN yuh
Flomot—FLŌ maht
Florence—FLAH ruhns
Floresville—FLŌRZ vil
Florey—FLŌ ri
Floyd—floid
Floydada—floi DĀ duh
Fluvanna—flōō VĂN uh
Flynn—flĭn
Foard—fōrd
Foard City—fōrd SĬT ĭ
Fodice—FŌ dĭs
Follett—fah LĔT
Fordtran—fōrd TRĂN
Forestburg—FAW rĕst berg
Forney—FAWR nĭ
Forreston—FAW rĕs t'n
Forsan—FŌR săn
Fort Bend—fōrt BĔND
Fort Chadbourne—fōrt CHĂD bern
Fort Davis—fōrt DĀ vĭs
Fort Griffin—fōrt GRĬF ĭn
Fort Hancock—fōrt HĂN kahk
Fort McKavett—fōrt muh KĂ vet
Fort Stockton—fōrt STAHK t'n
Fort Worth—fōrt WERTH
Fowlerton—FOW ler t'n

Francitas—frăn SEE t's
Franklin—FRĂNGK lĭn
Frankston—FRĂNGS t'n
Fredericksburg—FRĔD er rĭks berg
Fredonia—free DŌN yuh
Freeport—FREE pōrt
Freer—FREE er
Freestone—FREE stōn
Frelsburg—FRĔLZ berg
Fresno—FRĔZ nō
Friendswood—FRĔNZ wŏŏd
Frio—FREE ō
Friona—free O nuh
Frisco—FRĬS ko
Fritch—frĭch
Fruitland—FRŎŎT lănd
Fruitvale—FRŎŎT vāl
Frydek—FRĪ dĕk
Fulbright—FŎŎL brīt
Fulshear—FUHL sher
Fulton—FŎŎL t'n

G

Gail—gāl
Gaines—gānz
Gainesville—GĀNZ vuhl
Galena Park—guh lee nuh PAHRK
Gallatin—GĂL uh t'n
Galveston—GĂL vĕs t'n
Ganado—guh NĀ dō
Garceno—gahr SĀ nō
Garciasville—gahr SEE uhs vĭl
Garner—GAHR ner
Garrett—GĂR ĭt
Garrison—GĂ rĭ s'n
Garwood—GAHR wŏŏd
Gary—GĔ rĭ
Garza—GAHR zuh
Gause—gawz
Geneva—juh NEE vuh
Geronimo—juh RAH nĭ mō
Giddings—GĬD ĭngz
Gillespie—guh LĔS pĭ
Gillett—juh LĔT
Gilliland—GĬL ĭ l'nd
Gilmer—GĬL mer
Ginger—JĬN jer
Girard—juh RAHRD
Girvin—GER vĭn
Gladewater—GLĀD wah ter
Glasscock—GLĂS kahk
Glazier—GLĀ zher
Glenfawn—glĕn FAWN
Glen Flora—glĕn FLŌ ruh
Glenn—glĕn
Glidden—GLĬD n
Gober—GŌ ber
Godley—GAHD lĭ
Goldfinch—GŌLD fĭnch
Goldsboro—GŌLZ buh ruh
Goldthwaite—GŌLTH wāt
Goliad—GŌ lĭ ăd
Golindo—gō LĬN duh
Gonzales—guhn ZAH l's
Goodland—GŎŎD l'n
Goodlett—GŎŎD lĕt
Goodnight—GŎŎD nīt
Goodrich—GŎŎD rĭch
Gordon—GAWRD n
Gordonville—GAWRD n vĭl
Goree—GŌ ree
Gorman—GAWR m'n
Gouldbusk—GŌŌLD buhsk
Graford—GRĀ ferd
Graham—GRĀ 'm
Granbury—GRĂN bĕ rĭ
Grandfalls—grănd FAWLZ
Grand Saline—grăn suh LEEN
Grandview—GRĂN vyōō
Granger—GRĀN jer
Grapeland—GRĀP l'nd
Grapevine—GRĀP vīn
Grassland—GRĂS l'nd
Grassyville—GRĂ sĭ vĭl
Grayburg—GRĀ berg
Grayson—GRA s'n
Greenville—GREEN v'l
Greenwood—GREEN wŏŏd
Gregg—grĕg
Gregory—GRĔG uh rĭ
Grimes—grīmz
Groesbeck—GRŌZ bĕk
Groveton—GRŌV t'n
Gruene—green
Grulla—GRŎŎL yuh
Gruver—GRŌŌ ver
Guadalupe—gwah duh LŌŌ pĭ
Guerra—GWĔ ruh
Gunter—GUHN ter
Gustine—GUHS teen
Guthrie—GUHTH rĭ
Guy—gī

H

Hagansport—HĀ gĭnz pōrt
Hainesville—HĀNZ v'l
Hall—hawl
Hallettsville—HĂL ĕts vĭl
Hallsville—HAWLZ vĭl
Hamilton—HĂM uhl t'n
Hamlin—HĂM lĭn
Hammond—HĂM 'nd
Hamon—HĂ m'n
Hamshire—HĂM sher
Handley—HĂND lĭ
Hankamer—HĂN kăm er
Hansford—HĂNZ ferd
Hardeman—HAHR duh m'n
Hardin—HAHRD n
Hare—hăr
Hargill—HAHR gĭl
Harleton—HAHR uhl t'n
Harlingen—HAHR lĭn juhn
Harper—HAHR per
Harrold—HĂR 'ld
Hartburg—HAHRT berg
Hartley—HAHRT lĭ
Harwood—HAHR wŏŏd
Haskell—HĂS k'l
Haslam—HĂZ l'm
Haslet—HĂS lĕt
Hasse—HĂ sĭ
Hatchell—HĂ ch'l
Hawkins—HAW kĭnz
Hawley—HAW lĭ
Hays—hāz
Hearne—hern
Heath—heeth
Hebbronville—HĔB r'n vĭl
Hebron—HEE br'n
Hedley—HĔD lĭ
Heidenheimer—HĪD n hīmer
Helena—HĔL uh nuh
Helotes—hĕl Ō tĭs
Hemphill—HĔMP hĭl
Hempstead—HĔM stĕd
Henderson—HĔN der s'n
Henly—HĔN lĭ
Henrietta—hĕn rĭ Ĕ tuh
Hereford—HER ferd
Hermleigh—HER muh lee
Hewitt—HYŎŎ ĭt
Hicks—hĭks
Hico—HĪ kō
Hidalgo—hĭ DĂL gō
Higgins—HĬ gĭnz
High—hī
Highbank—HĪ băngk
High Island—hī Ī l'nd
Highlands—HĪ l'ndz
Hightower—HĪ tow er
Hill—hĭl
Hillister—HĬL ĭs ter
Hillsboro—HĬLZ buh ruh
Hindes—hīndz
Hiram—HĪ r'm
Hitchcock—HĬCH kahk
Hitchland—HĬCH l'nd
Hobson—HAHB s'n
Hochheim—HŌ hīm
Hockley—HAHK lĭ
Holland—HAHL 'nd
Holliday—HAH luh dā
Hondo—HAHN dō
Honey Grove—HUHN ĭ grōv
Honey Island—huhn ĭ Ī l'nd
Honey Springs—huhn ĭ SPRĬNGZ
Hood—hŏŏd
Hooks—hŏŏks
Hopkins—HAHP kĭnz
Houston—HYŎŎS t'n or YŎŎS t'n
Howard—HOW erd
Howe—how
Howland—HOW l'nd
Hubbard—HUH berd
Huckabay—HUHK uh bĭ
Hudspeth—HUHD sp'th
Huffman—HUHF m'n
Hufsmith—HUHF smĭth
Hughes Springs—hyōōz SPRĬNGZ
Hull—huhl
Humble—HUHM b'l
Hungerford—HUHNG ger ferd
Hunter—HUHNT er
Huntington—HUHNT ĭng t'n
Huntsville—HUHNTS v'l
Hurlwood—HERL wŏŏd
Hutchins—HUH chĭnz
Hutchinson—HUH chĭn s'n
Hutto—HUH tō
Hye—hī

Hylton—HĬL t'n

I
Iago—ī Ā gō
Idalou—Ī duh lo͞o
Imperial—ĭm PĬR ĭ uhl
Inadale—Ī nuh dāl
Inez—ī NĔZ
Ingleside—ĬNG g'l sīd
Ingram—ĬNG gr'm
Iola—ī Ō luh
Iowa Park—ī uh wuh PAHRK
Ira—Ī ruh
Iraan—ī ruh ĂN
Iredell—Ī ruh dĕl
Ireland—Ī rĭ l'nd
Irene—ī REEN
Irion—ĪR i uhn
Ironton—ĪRN t'n
Irving—ER vĭng
Italy—ĬT uh lĭ
Itasca—ī TĂS kuh
Ivan—Ī v'n
Ivanhoe—Ī v'n hō

J
Jacksboro—JĂKS buh ruh
Jacksonville—JĂK s'n vĭl
Jamestown—JĀMZ town
Jardin—JAHRD n
Jarrell—JĂR uhl
Jasper—JĂS per
Jayton—JĀT n
Jeddo—JĔ dō
Jeff Davis—jĕf DA vĭs
Jericho—JĔ rĭ kō
Jermyn—JER m'n
Jewett—JO͞O ĭt
Jiba—HEE buh
Jim Hogg—jĭm HAWG
Joaquin—waw KEEN
Johnson City—jahn s'n SĬT ĭ
Johntown—JAHN town
Johnsville—JAHNZ vĭl
Joinerville—JOI ner vĭl
Jolly—JAH lĭ
Jollyville—JAH lĭ vĭl
Jonah—JŌ nuh
Jonesboro—JŌNZ buh ruh
Jonesville—JŌNZ vĭl
Josephine—JŌ suh feen
Joshua—JAH sh' wa
Jourdanton—JERD n t'n
Juliff—JO͞O lĭf
Junction—JUHNGK sh'n
Juno—JO͞O nō
Justiceburg—JUHS tĭs berg
Justin—JUHS tĭn

K
Kalgary—KĂL gĕ rĭ
Kamay—KĀ ĭm ā
Kanawha—KAHN uh wah
Karnack—KAHR năk
Karnes—kahrnz
Karnes City—kahrnz SĬT ĭ
Katemcy—kuh TĔM sĭ
Katy—KĀ tĭ
Kaufman—KAWF m'n
Keechi—KEE chī
Keene—keen
Kellerville—KĔL er vĭl
Kemah—KEE muh
Kempner—KĔMP ner
Kendalia—kĕn DĀL yuh
Kenedy—KĔN uh dĭ
Kennard—kuh NAHRD
Kennedale—KĔN uh dāl
Kerens—KER 'nz
Kermit—KER mit
Kerr—ker
Kerrville—KER vĭl
Kildare—KĬL dăr
Kilgore—KĬL gōr
Killeen—kuh LEEN
Kimble—KĬM b'l
Kingsbury—KĬNGZ bĕ rĭ
Kingsland—KĬNGZ l'nd
Kingsmill—kĭngz MĬL
Kingston—KĬNGZ t'n
Kingsville—KĬNGZ vĭl
Kinney—KĬN ĭ
Kirby—KER bĭ
Kirbyville—KER bĭ vĭl
Kirkland—KERK l'nd
Kirvin—KER vĭn
Kleberg—KLĀ berg
Kleberg (Dallas County)—KLEE berg
Klondike—KLAHN dīk
Knickerbocker—NĬK uh bah ker
Knippa—kuh NĬP uh
Knott—naht
Knox—nahks
Knox City—nahks SĬT ĭ
Kosciusko—kuh SHO͞OS kō
Kosse—KAH sĭ
Kountze—ko͞ontz
Kress—kres
Krum—kruhm
Kurten—KER t'n
Kyle—kīl

L
La Blanca—lah BLAHN kuh
Lacoste—luh KAWST
Ladonia—luh DŌN yuh
LaFayette—lah fī ĔT
Laferia—luh FĔ rĭ uh
Lagarto—luh GAHR tō
La Gloria—lah GLŌ rĭ uh
La Grange—luh GRĀNJ
Laguna—luh GO͞O nuh
Laird Hill—lărd HĬL
La Joya—luh HŌ yuh
Laketon—LĀK t'n
Lake Victor—lāk VĬK ter
Lakeview—LĀK vyo͞o
Lamar—luh MAHR
Lamarque—luh MAHRK
Lamasco—luh MĂS kō
Lamesa—luh MEE suh
Lamkin—LĂM kĭn
Lampasas—lăm PĂ s's
Lancaster—LĂNG k's ter
Laneville—LĀN vĭl
Langtry—LĂNG trĭ
Lanier—luh NĬR
La Paloma—lah puh LŌ muh
La Porte—luh PŌRT
La Pryor—luh PRĪ er
Laredo—luh RĀ dō
Lariat—LĂ ri uht
La Rue—luh RO͞O
LaSalle—luh SĂL
Lasara—luh SĔ ruh
Lassater—LĂ sĭ ter
Latexo—luh TĔKS ō
Lavaca—luh VĂ kuh
La Vernia—luh VER nĭ uh
La Villa—lah VĬL uh
Lavon—luh VAHN
La Ward—luh WAWRD
Lawn—lawn
Lawrence—LAH r'ns
Lazbuddie—LĂZ buh dĭ
League City—leeg SĬT ĭ
Leakey—LĀ kĭ
Leander—lee ĂN der
Leary—LĬ er ĭ
Ledbetter—LĔD bĕt er
Leesburg—LEEZ berg
Leesville—LEEZ vĭl
Lefors—lĭ FŌRZ
Leggett—LĔ gĭt
Leigh—lee
Lela—LEE luh
Lelia Lake—leel yuh LĀK
Leming—LĔ mĭng
Lenorah—lĕ NŌ ruh
Leo—LEE ō
Leon—lee AHN
Leona—lee Ō nuh
Leonard—LĔN erd
Leon Springs—lee ahn SPRĬNGZ
Leroy—LEE roi
Levelland—LĔ v'l lănd
Levita—luh VĪ tuh
Lewisville—LO͞O ĭs vĭl
Lexington—LĔKS ĭng t'n
Lillian—LĬL yuhn
Lincoln—LĬNG k'n
Lindale—LĬN dāl
Linden—LĬN d'n
Lindenau—lĭn duh NOW
Lindsay—LĬN zĭ
Lingleville—LĬNG g'l vĭl
Linn—lĭn
Lipan—lī PĂN
Lipscomb—LĬPS k'm
Lissie—LĬ sĭ
Littlefield—LĬT uhl feeld
Liverpool—LĬ ver po͞ol
Livingston—LĬV ĭngz t'n
Llano—LĂ nō
Locker—LAH ker
Lockett—LAH kĭt
Lockhart—LAHK hahrt
Lockney—LAHK nĭ
Lodi—LŌ dī
Lohn—lahn

Lolita—lō LEE tuh
Loma Alto—lō muh ĂL tō
Lometa—lō MEE tuh
London—LUHN d'n
Long Mott—lawng MAHT
Longview—LAWNG vyōō
Longworth—LAWNG werth
Loop—lōōp
Lopeno—lō PEE nō
Loraine—lō RĀN
Lorena—lō REE nuh
Los Angeles—laws AN juh l's
Los Ebanos—lōs ĔB uh nōs
Los Fresnos—lōs FRĔZ nōs
Los Indios—lōs ĬN dĭ ōs
Losoya—luh SAW yuh
Lott—laht
Louise—LŎŎ eez
Lovelady—LUHV lā dĭ
Loving—LUH vĭng
Lubbock—LUH b'k
Lueders—LŎŎ derz
Luella—lōō ĔL uh
Lufkin—LUHF kĭn
Luling—LŎŎ lĭng
Lund—luhnd
Lutie—LŎŎ tĭ
Lyford—LĪ ferd
Lynn—lĭn
Lyons—LĪ 'nz
Lytton Springs—lĭt n SPRĬNGZ

M

Mabank—MĀ băngk
Macune—muh KŎŎN
Madisonville—MĂ duh s'n vĭl
Magnolia—măg NŌL yuh
Malakoff—MĂL uh kawf
Malone—muh LŌN
Malta—MAWL tuh
Manchaca—MĂN shăk
Manchester—MĂN chĕs ter
Manheim—MĂN hīm
Mankins—MĂN kĭnz
Manor—MĀ ner
Mansfield—MĂNZ feeld
Manvel—MĂN v'l
Marathon—MĂR uh th'n
Marble Falls—mahr b'l FAWLZ
Marfa—MAHR fuh
Marietta—mĕ rĭ Ĕ tuh
Marion—MĔ rĭ uhn
Markham—MAHR k'm
Marlin—MAHR lĭn
Marquez—mahr KĀ
Marshall—MAHR sh'l
Martin—MAHRT n
Martinsville—MAHRT nz vĭl
Maryneal—mā rĭ NEEL
Marysville—MĀ rĭz vĭl
Matador—MĂT uh dōr
Matagorda—măt uh GAWR duh
Mathis—MĂ thĭs
Maud—mawd
Mauriceville—maw REES vĭl
Maverick—MĂV rĭk
Maxey—MĂKS ĭ
Maxwell—MĂKS w'l
Maydell—MĀ dĕl
Maypearl—mā PERL
Maysfield—MĀZ feeld
McAdoo—MĂK uh dōō
McAllen—măk ĂL ĭn
McCamey—muh KĀ mĭ
McCaulley—muh KAW lĭ
McCoy—muh KOI
McCulloch—muh KUH luhk
McFaddin—măk FĂD n
McGregor—muh GRĔ ger
McKinney—muh KĬN ĭ
McLean—muh KLĀN
McLennan—muhk LĔN uhn
McLeod—măk LOWD
McMahan—măk MĂN
McMullen—măk MUHL ĭn
McNary—măk NĂ rĭ
McNeil—măk NEEL
McQueeney—muh KWEE nĭ
Medill—mĕ DĬL
Medina—muh DEE nuh
Megargel—muh GAHR g'l
Melissa—muh LĬS uh
Melrose—MĔL rōz
Melvin—MĔL vĭn
Menard—muh NAHRD
Mendoza—mĕn DŌ zuh
Mentone—mĕn TON
Mercedes—mer SĀ deez
Mercury—MER kyuh ri
Mereta—muh RĔT uh
Meridian—muh RĬ dĭ uhn
Merkel—MER k'l
Mertens—mer TĔNZ
Mertzon—MERTS n
Mesquite—muhs KEET
Mexia—muh HĀ uh
Meyersville—MĪRZ vĭl
Miami—mī ĂM ĭ
Mico—MEE kō
Middleton—MĬD uhl t'n
Midfields—MĬD feeldz
Midland—MĬD l'nd
Midlothian—mĭd LŌ thĭ n
Milam—MĪ l'm
Milano—mĭ LĂ nō
Mildred—MĬL drĕd
Milford—MĬL ferd
Millett—MĬL ĭt
Millheim—MĬL hīm
Millican—MĬL uh kuhn
Millsap—MĬL săp
Minden—MĬN d'n
Mineola—mĭn ĭ Ō luh
Minerva—mĭ NER vuh
Mingus—MĬNG guhs
Minter—MĬNT er
Mirando City—mĭ răn duh SĬT ĭ
Mission—MĬSH uhn
Missouri City—muh zōōr uh SĬT ĭ
Mobeetie—mō BEE tĭ
Moline—mō LEEN
Monahans—MAH nuh hănz
Monaville—MŌ nuh vĭl
Monkstown—MUHNGKS town
Monroe—MAHN rō
Monroe City—mahn rō SĬT ĭ
Montague—mahn TĀG
Montalba—mahnt ĂL buh
Mont Belvieu—mahnt BĔL vyōō
Montell—mahn TĔL
Montgomery—mahnt GUHM er ĭ
Monthalia—mahn THĀL yuh
Moody—MŎŎ dĭ
Moore—mor
Morales—muh RAH lĕs
Moran—mō RĂN
Morgan—MAWR g'n
Morgan Mill—mawr g'n MĬL
Morton—MAWRT n
Moscow—MAHS kow
Mosheim—MŌ shīm
Moss Bluff—maws BLUHF
Motley—MAHT lĭ
Moulton—MŌL t'n
Mount Calm—mownt KAHM
Mount Selman—mownt SĔL m'n
Mount Sylvan—mownt SĬL v'n
Muenster—MYŎŎNS ter
Muldoon—muhl DŎŎN
Muleshoe—MYŎŎL shōō
Mullin—MUHL ĭn
Mumford—MUHM ferd
Munday—MUHN dĭ
Murchison—MER kuh s'n
Murphy—MER fĭ
Mykawa—mĭ KAH wuh
Myra—MĪ ruh
Myrtle Springs—mert l SPRĬNGZ

N

Nacogdoches—năk uh DŌ chĭs
Nada—NĀ duh
Naples—NĀ p'lz
Natalia—nuh TĂL yuh
Navarro—nuh VĂ rō
Navasota—năv uh SŌ tuh
Nazareth—NĂZ uh r'th
Neches—NĀ chĭs
Nederland—NEE der l'nd
Needville—NEED vĭl
Nelsonville—NĔL s'n vĭl
Neuville—NYŎŎ v'l
Nevada—nuh VĀ duh
Newark—NŎŎ erk
New Baden—nyōō BĀD n
New Berlin—nyōō BER lin
New Braunfels—nyōō BROWN fĕlz
Newby—NYŎŎ bĭ
New Caney—nyōō KĀ nĭ
Newcastle—NYŎŎ kăs uhl
New Gulf—nyōō GUHLF
New Hope—nyōō HŌP
Newlin—NYŎŎ lĭn
Newman—NYŎŎ m'n
Newport—NYŎŎ pōrt
New Salem—nyōō SĀ l'm
Newsome—NYŎŎ s'm
New Summerfield—nyōō SUHM er feeld
Newton—NYŎŎT n
New Ulm—nyōō UHLM

New Waverly—nyōō WĀ ver lĭ
New Willard—nyōō WĬL erd
Nimrod—NĬM rahd
Nineveh—NĬN uh vuh
Nocona—nō KŌ nuh
Nolanville—NŌ l'n vĭl
Nopal—NŌ păl
Nordheim—NAWRD hīm
Normandy—NAWR m'n dĭ
Normangee—NAWR m'n jee
Normanna—nawr MĂN uh
Northrup—NAWR thr'p
North Zulch—nawrth ZŎŎLCH
Novice—NAH vĭs
Nueces—nyōō Ā sĭs
Nugent—NYŎŎ j'nt
Nursery—NER suh rĭ

O

Oakalla—ō KĂL uh
Oakhurst—ŌK herst
Oakland—ŌK l'nd
Oakville—ŌK vĭl
O'Brien—ō BRĪ uhn
Ochiltree—AH k'l tree
Odell—ō DĔL
Odem—Ō d'm
Odessa—ō DĔS uh
O'Donnell—ō DAH n'l
Oenaville—ō EEN uh v'l
Oglesby—Ō g'lz bĭ
Oilton—OIL t'n
Oklaunion—ōk luh YŎŎN y'n
Olden—ŌL d'n
Oldenburg—ŌL dĭn berg
Oldham—ŌL d'm
Old Glory—ōld GLŌ rĭ
Olivia—ō LĬV ĭ uh
Olmito—awl MEE tuh
Olmos Park—ahl m's PAHRK
Olney—AHL ni
Olton—ŌL t'n
Omaha—Ō muh haw
Omen—Ō mĭn
Onalaska—uhn uh LĂS kuh
Oplin—AHP lĭn
Orange—AHR ĭnj
Orangefield—AHR ĭnj feeld
Orange Grove—AHR ĭnj GRŌV
Orchard—AWR cherd
Ore City—ōr SĬT ĭ
Osceola—ō sĭ Ō luh
Otey—Ō tĭ
Otis Chalk—ō tĭs CHAWLK
Ottine—ah TEEN
Otto—AH tō
Ovalo—ō VĂL uh
Overton—Ō ver t'n
Owens—Ō ĭnz
Ozona—ō ZŌ nuh

P

Paducah—puh DYŎŎ kuh
Paige—pāj
Palacios—puh LĂ sh's
Palestine—PAL uhs teen
Palito Blanco—p' lee to BLAHNG kō
Palmer—PAH mer
Palo Pinto—pă lō PĬN tō
Paluxy—puh LUHK sĭ
Pampa—PĂM puh
Pandora—păn DŌR uh
Panhandle—PĂN hăn d'l
Panna Maria—păn uh muh REE uh
Papalote—pah puh LŌ tĭ
Paradise—PĂR uh dīs
Paris—PĂ rĭs
Parmer—PAH mer
Parnell—pahr NĔL
Pasadena—păs uh DEE nuh
Patricia—puh TRĬ shuh
Patroon—puh TRŎŎN
Pattison—PĂT uh s'n
Pattonville—PĂT n vĭl
Pawnee—paw NEE
Paxton—PĂKS t'n
Pearl—perl
Pearland—PĂR lănd
Pearsall—PEER sawl
Peaster—PEES ter
Pecan Gap—pĭ kahn GAP
Pecos—PĀ k's
Penelope—puh NĔL uh pĭ
Penitas—puh NEE t's
Pennington—PĔN ĭng t'n
Penwell—PĬN wĕl
Peoria—pee Ō rĭ uh
Percilla—per SĬL uh
Perrin—PĔR ĭn
Perryton—PĔ rĭ t'n
Petersburg—PEET erz berg
Petrolia—puh TRŌL yuh
Petteway—PĔT uh wā
Pettit—PĔT ĭt
Pettus—PĔT uhs
Petty—PĔT ĭ
Pflugerville—FLŎŎ ger vĭl
Pharr—fahr
Phelps—fĕlps
Pickton—PĬK t'n
Pidcoke—PĬD kŏk
Piedmont—PEED mahnt
Pierce—PĪ ers
Pilot Point—pī l't POINT
Pineland—PĪN land
Pioneer—pī uh NĬR
Pipecreek—pīp KREEK
Pittsburg—PĬTS berg
Placedo—PLĂS ĭ dō
Placid—PLĂ sĭd
Plano—PLĀ nō
Plantersville—PLĂN terz vĭl
Plaska—PLĂS kuh
Plateau—plă TŌ
Pleasant Grove—plĕ z'nt GRŌV
Pleasanton—PLĔZ uhn t'n
Pledger—PLĔ jer
Pointblank—pint BLĂNGK
Polk—pōlk
Pollock—PAHL uhk
Ponder—PAHN der
Ponta—pahn TĀ
Pontotoc—PAHNT uh tahk
Poolville—PŎŎL vĭl
Port Aransas—pōrt uh RĂN zuhs
Port Arthur—pōrt AHR ther
Port Bolivar—pōrt BAH lĭ ver
Porter Springs—pōr ter SPRĬNGZ
Port Isabel—pōrt ĬZ uh bĕl
Portland—PŌRT l'nd
Port Lavaca—pōrt luh VĂ kuh
Port Neches—pōrt NĀ chĭs
Port O'Connor—pōrt ō KAH ner
Posey—PŌ zĭ
Postoak—PŌST ōk
Poteet—pō TEET
Poth—pōth
Potosi—puh TŌ sĭ
Potter—PAHT er
Pottsboro—PAHTS buh ruh
Pottsville—PAHTS vĭl
Powderly—POW der li
Powell—POW w'l
Poynor—POI ner
Prairie Lea—prĕr ĭ LEE
Prairieville—PRĔR ĭ vĭl
Premont—PREE mahnt
Presidio—pruh SĬ dĭ ō
Priddy—PRĬ dĭ
Primera—pree MĔ ruh
Princeton—PRĬNS t'n
Pritchett—PRĬ chĭt
Proctor—PRAHK ter
Progreso—prō GRĔ sō
Prosper—PRAHS per
Purdon—PERD n
Purley—PER lĭ
Purmela—per MEE luh
Putnam—PUHT n'm
Pyote—PĪ ōt

Q

Quail—kwāl
Quanah—KWAH nuh
Quemado—kuh MAH dō
Quihi—KWEE hee
Quinlan—KWĬN l'n
Quintana—kwĭn TAH nuh
Quitaque—KĬT uh kwa
Quitman—KWĬT m'n

R

Ralls—rahlz
Randall—RĂN d'l
Randolph—RĂN dahlf
Rangerville—RĀN jer vĭl
Rankin—RĂNG kĭn
Ratcliff—RĂT klĭf
Ravenna—rĭ VĔN uh
Rayburn—RĀ bern
Raymondville—RĀ m'nd vĭl
Raywood—RĀ wŏŏd
Reagan—RĀ g'n
Real—REE awl
Realitos—ree uh LEE t's
Redford—RĔD ferd
Reeves—reevz
Refugio—rĕ FYŎŎ rĭ ō
Reilly Springs—rī lĭ SPRĬNGZ
Reklaw—RĔK law
Reno—REE nō

Rhineland—RĪN l'nd
Rhome—rōm
Rhonesboro—RŌNZ buh ruh
Ricardo—rĭ KAHR dō
Richards—RĬCH erdz
Richardson—RĬCH erd s'n
Richland—RĬCH l'nd
Richland Springs—rĭch l'nd SPRĬNGZ
Richmond—RĬCH m'nd
Ridge—rĭj
Ridgeway—RĬJ wā
Riesel—REE s'l
Ringgold—RĬNG gōld
Rio Frio—ree ō FREE ō
Rio Grande City—ree ō grahn dĭ SĬT ĭ
Rio Hondo—ree ō HAHN dō
Riomedina—ree ō muh DEE nuh
Rios—REE ōs
Rio Vista—ree ō VĬS tuh or rye ō VĬS tuh
Riverside—RĬ ver sīd
Riviera—ruh VĬR uh
Roane—rōn
Roanoke—RŌN ōk
Roans Prairie—rōnz PRĔR Ĭ
Robertson—RAH bert s'n
Robinson—RAH bĭn s'n
Robstown—RAHBZ town
Roby—RŌ bĭ
Rochelle—rō SHĔL
Rochester—RAH chĕs ter
Rockdale—RAHK dāl
Rockland—RAHK l'nd
Rockport—rahk PŌRT
Rocksprings—rahk SPRĬNGZ
Rockwall—rahk WAWL
Rockwood—RAHK wŏŏd
Roganville—RŌ g'n vĭl
Roma—RŌ muh
Romayor—rō MĀ er
Roosevelt—RŌŌ suh v'lt
Ropesville—RŌPS vĭl
Rosanky—rō ZĂNG kĭ
Roscoe—RAHS kō
Rosebud—RŌZ b'd
Rosenberg—RŌZ n berg
Rosenthal—RŌZ uhn thawl
Rosewood—RŌZ wŏŏd
Rosharon—rō SHĔ r'n
Rosita—rō SEE tuh
Ross—raws
Rosser—RAW ser
Rosston—RAWS t'n
Rossville—RAWS vĭl
Roswell—RAHZ w'l
Rotan—rō TĂN
Rowena—rō EE nuh
Rowlett—ROW lĭt
Roxton—RAHKS t'n
Royalty—ROI uhl tĭ
Royse City—roi SĬT ĭ
Royston—ROIS t'n
Rugby—RUHG bĭ
Ruidosa—ree uh DŌ suh
Runge—RUHNG ĭ
Runnels—RUHN 'lz
Rusk—ruhsk
Rutersville—RŌŌ ter vĭl

S

Sabinal—SĂB uh năl
Sabine—suh BEEN
Sabine Pass—suh been PĂS
Sabinetown—suh been TOWN
Sachse—SĂK sĭ
Sacul—SĂ k'l
Sadler—SĂD ler
Sagerton—SĀ ger t'n
Saginaw—SĂ guh naw
Saint Jo—sănt JŌ
Saint Paul—sănt PAWL
Salado—suh LĀ dō
Salesville—SĀLZ vĭl
Salineno—suh LEEN yō
Salmon—SĂL m'n
Saltillo—săl TĬL ō
Samfordyce—săm FŌR dis
Samnorwood—săm NAWR wŏŏd
San Angelo—săn ĂN juh lō
San Antonio—săn ăn TŌ nĭ ō
Sanatorium—săn uh TŌ rĭ uhm
San Augustine—săn AW g's teen
San Benito—săn buh NEE tuh
Sanderson—SĂN der s'n
Sandia—săn DEE uh
San Diego—săn dĭ Ā gō
Sandy Point—săn dĭ POINT
San Felipe—săn fuh LEEP
Sanford—SĂN ferd
San Gabriel—săn GĀ brĭ uhl
Sanger—SĂNG er
San Jacinto—săn juh SĬN tuh
San Juan—săn WAHN
San Marcos—săn MAHR k's
San Patricio—săn puh TRĬSH ĭ ō
San Perlita—săn per LEE tuh
San Saba—săn SĂ buh
Santa Anna—săn tuh ĂN uh
Santa Elena—săn tuh LEE nuh
Santa Maria—săn tuh muh REE uh
Santa Rosa—săn tuh RŌ suh
Santo—SĂN tō
San Ygnacio—săn ĭg NAH sĭ ō
Saragosa—sĕ ruh GŌ suh
Saratoga—sĕ ruh TŌ guh
Sargent—SAHR juhnt
Sarita—suh REE tuh
Saspamco—suh SPĂM kō
Satin—SĂT n
Savoy—suh VOI
Schattel—SHĂT uhl
Schertz—sherts
Schleicher—SHLĪ ker
Schroeder—SHRĀ der
Schulenburg—SHŌŌ lĭn berg
Schwertner—SWERT ner
Scotland—SKAHT l'nd
Scottsville—SKAHTS vĭl
Scranton—SKRĂNT n
Scurry—SKUH rĭ
Scyene—sĭ EEN
Seabrook—SEE brŏŏk
Seadrift—SEE drĭft
Seagoville—SEE gō vĭl
Seagraves—SEE grāvz
Seale—seel
Sealy—SEE lĭ
Sebastian—suh BĂS tĭ 'n
Security—sĭ KYŌŌR ĭ tĭ
Segno—SĔG nō
Segovia—sĭ GŌ vĭ uh
Seguin—sĭ GEEN
Selfs—sĕlfs
Selma—SĔL muh
Seminole—SĔM uh nōl
Seymour—SEE mōr
Shackelford—SHĂK uhl ferd
Shafter—SHĂF ter
Shallowater—SHĂL uh wah ter
Shannon—SHĂN uhn
Sheffield—SHĔ feeld
Shelbyville—SHĔL bĭ vĭl
Sheldon—SHĔL d'n
Shepherd—SHĔ perd
Sherwood—SHER wood
Shiner—SHĪ ner
Shiro—SHĪ rō
Shive—shīv
Sidney—SĬD nĭ
Sierra Blanca—sĭer ruh BLĂNG kuh
Siloam—suh LŌM
Silsbee—SĬLZ bĭ
Silverton—SĬL ver t'n
Simonton—SĪ m'n t'n
Singleton—SĬNG g'l t'n
Sinton—SĬNT n
Sipe Springs—SEEP sprĭngz
Sivells Bend—sĭ v'lz BĔND
Skellytown—SKĔ lĭ town
Skidmore—SKĬD mōr
Slaton—SLĀT n
Slayden—SLĀD n
Slidell—slĭ DĔL
Slocum—SLŌ k'm
Smiley—SMĪ lĭ
Smithson Valley—smĭth s'n VĂ lĭ
Smithville—SMĬTH vĭl
Smyer—SMĪ er
Snook—snŏŏk
Snyder—SNĪ der
Somerset—SUH mer sĕt
Somervell—SUH mer vĕl
Somerville—SUH mer vĭl
Sonora—suh NŌ ruh
South Bosque—sowth BAHS kĭ
South Houston—sowth HYŌŌS t'n
Southmayd—sowth MĀD
Sparenberg—SPĂR ĭn berg
Spearman—SPĬR m'n
Splendora—splĕn DŌ ruh
Spofford—SPAH ferd
Spring Lake—sprĭng LĀK
Spur—sper
Spurger—SPER ger
Stacy—STĀ sĭ
Stafford—STĂ ferd
Stamford—STĂM ferd
Stanton—STĂNT n
Staples—STĀ p'lz
Starr—stahr

Stephens—STEE vĕnz
Stephenville—STEEV n vĭl
Sterley—STER lĭ
Stiles—stīlz
Stinnett—stĭ NĔT
Stockdale—STAHK dāl
Stoneburg—STŌN berg
Stoneham—STŌN uhm
Stonewall—STŌN wawl
Stout—stowt
Stowell—STO w'l
Stranger—STRĀN jer
Stratford—STRĂT ferd
Strawn—strawn
Streeter—STREET er
Streetman—STREET m'n
Study Butte—styōō dĭ BYŌŌT
Sublime—s'b LĪM
Sudan—SŌŌ dăn
Sugar Land—SHŌŌ ger lănd
Sullivan City—suh luh v'n SĬT ĭ
Sulphur Bluff—suhl fer BLUHF
Sulphur Springs—suhl fer SPRĬNGZ
Summerfield—SUHM er feeld
Sumner—SUHM ner
Suniland—SUH nĭ lănd
Sutherland Springs—suh ther l'nd SPRĬNGZ
Sutton—SUHT n
Sweeny—SWEE nĭ
Sweethome—sweet HŌM
Sweetwater—SWEET wah ter
Swenson—SWĔN s'n
Swisher—SWĬ sher
Sylvester— sil VES ter

T

Tahoka—tuh HŌ kuh
Talco—TĂL kō
Talpa—TĂL puh
Tanglewood—TĂNG g'l wŏŏd
Tankersley—TĂNG kers lĭ
Tarrant—TAR uhnt
Tarzan—TAHR z'n
Tascosa—tăs KŌ suh
Tatum—TĀ t'm
Tavener—TĂV uh ner
Taylor—TĀ ler
Teague—teeg
Tehuacana—tuh WAW kuh nuh
Telephone—TĔL uh fōn
Telferner—TĔLF ner
Tenaha—TĔN uh haw
Tennyson—TĔN uh s'n
Terlingua—TER lĭng guh
Terrell—TĔR uhl
Terrell Hills—ter uhl HILZ
Texarkana—tĕks ahr KĂN uh
Texas City—tĕks ĕz SĬT ĭ
Texhoma—tĕks Ō muh
Texline—TĔKS līn
Texon—tĕks AHN
Thalia—THĀL yuh
Thicket—THĬ kĭt
Thomaston—TAHM uhs t'n
Thompsons—TAHMP s'nz
Thorndale—THAWRN dāl
Thornton—THAWRN t'n
Thorp Spring—thawrp SPRING
Thrall—thrawl
Throckmorton—THRAHK mawrt n
Thurber—THER ber
Tilden—TĬL d'n
Timpson—TĬM s'n
Tioga—tī Ō guh
Titus—TĪT uhs
Tivoli—tī VŌ luh
Tokio—TŌ kĭ ō
Tolar—TŌ ler
Tolbert—TAHL bert
Tolosa—tuh LŌ suh
Tomball—TAHM bawl
Tool—tōōl
Topsey—TAHP sī
Tornillo—tawr NEE yō
Tow—tow
Toyah—TOI yuh
Toyahvale—TOI yuh vāl
Trawick—TRĀ wĭk
Travis—TRĂ vĭs
Trent—trĕnt
Trenton—TRĔNT n
Trickham—TRĬK uhm
Trinidad—TRĬN uh dăd
Trinity—TRĬN ĭ tĭ
Troup—trōōp
Troy—TRAW ĭ
Truby—TRŌŌ bĭ
Trumbull—TRUHM b'l
Truscott—TRUHS k't
Tucker—TUHK er
Tuleta—tōō LEE tuh
Tulia—TŌŌL yuh
Tulsita—tuhl SEE tuh
Tundra—TUHN druh
Tunis—TŌŌ nĭs
Turlington—TER lĭng t'n
Turnersville—TER nerz vĭl
Turnertown—TER ner town
Turney—TER nĭ
Tuscola—tuhs KŌ luh
Tuxedo—TUHKS ĭ dō
Twitty—TWĬ tĭ
Tye—tī
Tyler—TĪ ler
Tynan—TĪ nuhn

U

Uhland—YŌŌ l'nd
Umbarger—UHM bahr ger
Upshur—UHP sher
Upton—UHP t'n
Urbana—er BĀ nuh
Utley—YŌŌT lĭ
Utopia—yōō TŌ pĭ uh
Uvalde—yōō VĂL dĭ

V

Valdasta—văl DĂS tuh
Valentine—VĂL uhn tīn
Valera—vuh LĪ ruh
Valleyview—vă lĭ VYŌŌ
Van Alstyne—văn AWLZ teen
Vancourt—VĂN kōrt
Vanderbilt—VĂN der bĭlt
Vanderpool—VĂN der pōōl
Van Vleck—văn VLĔK
Van Zandt—văn ZĂNT
Vashti—VĂSH tī
Vaughan—vawn
Vega—VĀ guh
Velasco—vuh LĂS kō
Venus—VEE n's
Vera—VĪ ruh
Veribest—VĔR ĭ bĕst
Vernon—VER n'n
Vickery—VĬK er ĭ
Victoria—vĭk TŌ rĭ uh
Vidor—VĪ der
Vienna—vee ĔN uh
View—vyōō
Vincent—VĬN s'nt
Vinegarone—vĭn er guh RŌN
Vineyard—VĬN yerd
Violet—VĪ ō lĕt
Voca—VŌ kuh
Von Ormy—vahn AHR mĭ
Voss—vaws
Votaw—VŌ taw

W

Waco—WĀ kō
Wadsworth—WAHDZ werth
Waelder—WĔL der
Waka—WAH kuh
Walberg—WAWL berg
Waldeck—WAWL dĕk
Walker—WAWL ker
Wall—wawl
Waller—WAW ler
Wallis—WAH lĭs
Wallisville—WAH lĭs vĭl
Walnut Springs—wawl n't SPRĬNGZ
Walton—WAWL t'n
Warda—WAWR duh
Ward—wawrd
Waring—WĂR ĭng
Warren—WAW rĭn
Warrenton—WAW rĭn t'n
Washburn—WAHSH bern
Washington—WAHSH ĭng t'n
Waskom—WAHS k'm
Wastella—wahs TĔL uh
Watauga—wuh TAW guh
Water Valley—wah ter VĂ lĭ
Waxahachie—wawks uh HĂ chĭ
Wayland—WĀ l'nd
Weatherford—WĔ ther ferd
Webberville—WĔ ber vĭl
Webster—WĔBS ter
Weches—WEE chĭz
Weesatche—WEE săch
Weimar—WĪ mer
Weinert—WĪ nert
Weir—weer
Welch—wĕlch
Weldon—WĔL d'n
Wellborn—WĔL bern
Wellington—WĔL ĭng t'n

Wellman—WĔL m'n
Weser—WEE zer
Weslaco—WĔS luh kō
Westbrook—WĔST broŏk
Westfield—WĔST feeld
Westhoff—WĔS tawf
Westminster—
wĕst MĬN ster
Weston—WĔS t'n
Westover—WĔS tō ver
Westphalia—wĕst FĀL yuh
Wetmore—WĔT mōr
Wharton—HWAWRT n
Wheeler—HWEE ler
Wheelock—HWEE lahk
Whiteface—HWĪT hows
Whiteflat—hwīt FLĂT
Whitesboro—HWĪTS buh ruh
Whitewright—HWĪT rīt
Whitharral—HWĬT hăr uhl
Whitney—HWĬT nĭ
Whitsett—HWĬT sĭt
Whitson—HWĬT s'n
Whitt—hwĭt
Whon—hwahn
Wichita—WĬCH ĭ taw
Wichita Falls—
wĭch ĭ taw FAWLZ
Wickett—WĬ kĭt
Wiergate—WEER gāt
Wilbarger—WĬL bahr ger
Wildorado—wĭl duh RĀ dō
Willacy—WĬL uh sĭ
Williamson—WĬL yuhm s'n
Willis—WĬ lĭs
Wilmer—WĬL mer
Wimberley—WĬM ber lĭ
Winchester—WĬN ches ter
Windom—WĬN d'm
Windthorst—WĬN thr'st
Winfield—WĬN feeld
Wingate—WĬN gāt
Winkler—WĬNGK ler
Winnie—WĬ nĭ
Winnsboro—WĬNZ buh ruh
Winona—wī NŌ nuh
Winterhaven—WĬN ter hā v'n
Wizard Wells—wĭ zerd WĔLZ
Woden—WŌD n
Wolfe City—woŏlf SĬT ĭ
Wolfforth—WOŎL forth
Woodbine—WOŎD bīn
Woodlake—woŏd LĀK
Woodland—WOŎD l'nd
Woodlawn—woŏd LAWN
Woodrow—WOŎD rō
Woodsboro—WOŎDZ buh ruh
Woodson—WOŎD s'n
Woodville—WOŎD v'l
Wortham—WERTH uhm
Wright City—rīt SĬT ĭ
Wrightsboro—RĪTS buh ruh
Wylie—WĪ lĭ

Y

Yancey—YĂN sĭ
Yantis—YĂN tĭs
Yoakum—YŌ k'm
Yorktown—YAWRK town
Youngsport—YUHNGZ pōrt
Ysleta—ĭs LĔT uh

Z

Zapata—zuh PAH tuh
Zavalla—zuh VĂL uh
Zephyr—ZĔF er
Zuehl—ZEE uhl

Obituaries 1994-1995

Alkek, Albert B., 85; oilman who helped establish the Texas Medical Center in Houston; in San Antonio, March 1995.

Bock, George "Pete," 86; longtime Dallas conservative and business leader; in Dallas, Feb. 8, 1995.

Butler, Eugene, 100; longtime crusading editor of *Progressive Farmer,* known by many as "Mr. Texas Agriculture;" in Dallas, June 5, 1995.

Calvert, Robert W., 89; former chief justice of the Texas Supreme Court and former Texas House speaker; in Waco, Oct. 6, 1994.

Clark, R. Lee, 87; longtime chief administrator of the University of Texas M.D. Anderson Cancer Center in Houston; in Houston, May 3, 1994.

Cliburn, Rildia Bee, 97; mother of classical pianist Van Cliburn; in Fort Worth, Aug. 3, 1994.

Coburn, Herbert D., 74; inventor whose discoveries led to nine Texas Instruments patents; in Dallas, Aug. 29, 1994.

Cravotta, Charles D., 84; a 1930s national and international boxing titlist, longtime member of the U.S. Olympic boxing committee; in Dallas, July 21, 1995.

Crouch, Doug, 72; Tarrant County district attorney in 1950s and 1960s, hired first black and female prosecutors, former legislator; in Granbury, July 4, 1995.

Cuellar, Frank X. Sr., 91; founder of the El Chico restaurant chain; in Dallas, April 2, 1995.

Dealey, Joe. M., 75; former president and publisher of *The Dallas Morning News*; in Dallas, April 7, 1995.

Devall, Charles, 86; veteran newspaper publisher; in Kilgore, Jan. 28, 1995.

Dowdy, John V., 83; represented East Texas in Congress for more than two decades; in Athens, April 12, 1995.

Duff, Katharyn, 80; longtime columnist for the *Abilene Reporter-News*; July 14, 1995.

Estes, Carroll Cox, 87; writer of mystery novels, business woman and teacher at Mary Baldwin College in Virginia and at East Texas State University; in Dallas, May 21, 1995.

Fisher, Ovie Clark, 91; served 32 years as a member of Congress from west-central Texas; in Junction, Dec. 9, 1994.

Galloway, C.A. (Cleophus Anthony), 90; Dallas' first black city council member; in Dallas, June 10, 1995.

Gatti, John, 76; former mayor of San Antonio (1971-73) and city council member; Oct. 25, 1994.

Gee, Thomas G., 69; federal judge retired from 18 years on the U.S. 5th Circuit Court of Appeals in New Orleans; in Houston, Oct. 25,1994.

George, Zelma, 90; trained soprano and leading researcher of African-American music; born in Hearne; in Cleveland, Ohio, July 3, 1994.

Goff, Frances E., 78; retired director of the M.D. Anderson Cancer Center in Houston and former Army Air Force top aide; in Houston, Sept. 15, 1994.

Goldberg, Irving L., 88; served almost three decades on 5th U.S. Circuit Court of Appeals, adviser to Lyndon Johnson; in Dallas, Feb. 11, 1995.

Graves, L.C., 76; Dallas police officer who wrested Jack Ruby's revolver from him at Oswald shooting, in Kaufman, Feb. 11, 1995.

Haas, R.E. "Buster," 70; assistant managing editor of *The Dallas Morning News* for 32 years; in Dallas, March 26, 1995.

Hernández, Onesimo, 69; Dallas surgeon revered as the godfather of Hispanic politics in the city, in Dallas, Sept. 28, 1994.

Highsmith, Patricia, 74; crime writer, native of Fort Worth; in Locarno, Switzerland, Feb. 4, 1995.

Hogue, Alexandre, 96; an acclaimed painter of the Southwest, one of the core members of the Depression-era group known as the Dallas Nine; in Tulsa, July 22, 1994.

Hooks, Ralph Sr., 75; business, civic leader and former mayor of Abilene; in Abilene, Feb. 8, 1995.

Horgan, Paul, 91; one of the foremost writers of the Southwest, Pulitzer Prize winner and honoree of the Texas Institute of Letters; in Middletown, Conn., March 8, 1995.

Hultgreen, Kara S., 29; Navy's first woman combat pilot, in a training accident off the coast of Southern California, Oct. 25, 1994; graduate of Alamo Heights High School in San Antonio.

Jackson, Ruth, 91; First woman orthopedic surgeon in United States; in Dallas, Aug. 28, 1994.

Jenkins, M.T. "Pepper," 77; pioneer anesthesiologist at Parkland Memorial Hospital in Dallas; treated President Kennedy, Oswald and later Jack Ruby; in Dallas, Nov. 21, 1994.

Johnson, Bob, 66; parliamentarian of the Texas Senate since 1991 and House parliamentarian for 15 years; in Temple, March 27, 1995.

Jones, John T., 76; chief executive of the *Houston Chronicle* for 16 years; in Houston, April 21, 1994.

Kingston, Mike, 56; journalist, editor of the Texas Almanac since 1981, in Dallas, Feb. 13, 1994.

Laws, Clarence A., 87; leader of the NAACP, "Mr. Civil Rights" to a generation of Dallas blacks; in Dallas, March 15, 1995.

Lockett, Clodovia, 81; nationally recognized educator, longtime University of Dallas science professor, Catholic nun; in Magnolia, Miss., July 18, 1994.

Mahoney, Don, 74; former rodeo performer who appeared on Houston television stations for 27 years; in Houston, Dec. 28, 1994.

Mata, Eduardo, 52; former Dallas Symphony conductor; in a plane crash in Cuernavaca, Mexico, Jan. 4, 1995.

Mays, Avery, 83; epitome of the Dallas business and civic leader of the 1950s and '60s, led renovation of State Fair Music Hall; in Dallas, Oct. 2, 1994.

McCain, Claude Jr., 63; first black administrator at Dallas' Parkland Hospital; in Dallas, March 12, 1995.

McCall, Abner, 80; led Baylor University from 1961-81; in Waco, June 11, 1995.

Miller, Chris, 68; served in Legislature 1973-78, was a leader for equal rights for women; in Fort Worth, March 12, 1995.

Moczygemba, Henry, 80; well-known priest of the Archdiocese of San Antonio and descendant of the founders of Panna Maria, first U.S. Polish settlement; March 2, 1995.

Montalvo, Jose Luis, 47; known as the "black hat poet"; in San Antonio, Aug. 14, 1994.

Overcash, Reece A. Jr., 68; Dallas business and civic leader; in Dallas, Jan. 17, 1995.

Penick, Harvey, 90; legendary golf instructor at the University of Texas and Austin Country Club; in Austin, April 2, 1995.

Phinney, Louise Snow, 91; early female lawyer in Texas who was first woman to serve as chief clerk for a state legislature; in Dallas, Aug. 24, 1994.

Powell, Robert, 45; paraplegic and vice president of the National Right to Life Committee; in Galveston, June 14, 1995.

Pye, A. Kenneth, 62; president of Southern Methodist University in Dallas since 1987; in Lake City, Colo., July 11, 1994.

Ratliff, David W., 82; a West Texas legislator for more than 21 years; in Stamford, March 21, 1995.

Rolark, Calvin, 67; founder of the United Black Fund of America, native of Texarkana; in Washington, D.C., Oct. 23, 1994.

Ryburn, Frank, 80; directed trust which funded Nobel-winning research on cholesterol at UT Medical Center in Dallas; in Dallas, June 5, 1994.

Sanchez, Henry Jr., 63; served in Legislature from South Texas 1967-74; on South Padre Island, Feb. 25, 1995.

San Pedro, Enrique, 68; bishop of Catholic Diocese of Brownsville since 1991; in Miami Beach, Fla., July 17, 1994.

Selena (Selena Quintanilla Perez), 23; leading Tejano music performer; shot in Corpus Christi, March 31, 1995.

Slater, Norvell, 87; radio broadcaster whose Sunday morning show of hymns aired for 41 years in Dallas; in Dallas, April 18, 1995.

Spence, Ralph, 76; leading East Texas oilman; in Houston, June 24, 1995.

Stennis, Hampton, 76; assistant makeup editor at the *Dallas Times Herald* for 19 years, in Dallas, March 24, 1995.

Thomas, Lera, 92; first Texas woman elected to Congress in 1966 to fill out the term of her husband Albert Thomas; in Nacogdoches, July 24, 1993.

Tobolowsky, Hermine Dalkowitz, 74; Dallas lawyer widely regarded as the mother of the Texas Equal Rights Amendment; in Dallas, July 25, 1995.

Umlauf, Charles J., 83, sculptor and professor of art at the University of Texas in Austin from 1941-81; in Austin, Nov. 19, 1994.

Vincent, Lloyd D., 70; president of Angelo State University in San Angelo since 1967; in Alpine, Aug. 5, 1994.

Watson, Willard, 73; one of the region's leading folk artists; in Dallas, June 12, 1995.

Wheeler, Nina Daniels, 60; civil rights crusader and Democratic party activist; in Dallas, July 10, 1995.

White, John C., 70; longtime Texas agriculture commissioner and Democratic party leader; in Washington, D.C., Jan. 20, 1995.

Williams, Mack, 77; founding president of the Press Club of Fort Worth and publisher of the *Fort Worth News-Tribune*; in Fort Worth, March 12, 1995.

Willis, Phillip, 76; captured first World War II prisoner after Pearl Harbor attack, served in Legislature; in Dallas, Jan. 27, 1995.

Witherspoon, Joseph, 78; professor emeritus of law at the University of Texas in Austin and one of the founders of Texas Right to Life Committee; June 21, 1995.

Young, Albert, 82; sculptor who carved the "Texas Heros" on the Hall of State at Fair Park in Dallas; in Dallas, July 13, 1994.

Zale, Morris Bernard "MB," 93; Russian immigrant who built the world's largest retail jewelry chain; in Dallas, March 8, 1995.

Advertisers' Index

General Index

C

For towns not listed in the index, see complete list of towns and communities, pp. 288-311.

For towns not listed in the index, see complete list of towns and communities, pp. 288-311.

For towns not listed in the index, see complete list of towns and communities, pp. 288-311.

For towns not listed in the index, see complete list of towns and communities, pp. 288-311.

G

For towns not listed in the index, see complete list of towns and communities, pp. 288-311.

For towns not listed in the index, see complete list of towns and communities, pp. 288-311.

For towns not listed in the index, see complete list of towns and communities, pp. 288-311.

For towns not listed in the index, see complete list of towns and communities, pp. 288-311.

For towns not listed in the index, see complete list of towns and communities, pp. 288-311.

For towns not listed in the index, see complete list of towns and communities, pp. 288-311.

For towns not listed in the index, see complete list of towns and communities, pp. 288-311.

N

For towns not listed in the index, see complete list of towns and communities, pp. 288-311.

For towns not listed in the index, see complete list of towns and communities, pp. 288-311.

For towns not listed in the index, see complete list of towns and communities, pp. 288-311.

For towns not listed in the index, see complete list of towns and communities, pp. 288-311.

For towns not listed in the index, see complete list of towns and communities, pp. 288-311.

For towns not listed in the index, see complete list of towns and communities, pp. 288-311.

For towns not listed in the index, see complete list of towns and communities, pp. 288-311.

For towns not listed in the index, see complete list of towns and communities, pp. 288-311.

For towns not listed in the index, see complete list of towns and communities, pp. 288-311.

For towns not listed in the index, see complete list of towns and communities, pp. 288-311.

For towns not listed in the index, see complete list of towns and communities, pp. 288-311.

For towns not listed in the index, see complete list of towns and communities, pp. 288-311.

For towns not listed in the index, see complete list of towns and communities, pp. 288-311.